Current Law
STATUTES
1995

VOLUME FOUR

AUSTRALIA
The Law Book Company
Brisbane • Sydney • Melbourne • Perth

CANADA
Carswell
Ottawa • Toronto • Calgary • Montreal • Vancouver

Agents:
Steimatzky's Agency Ltd., Tel Aviv;
N. M. Tripathi (Private) Ltd., Bombay;
Eastern Law House (Private) Ltd., Calcutta;
M.P.P. House, Bangalore;
Universal Book Traders, Delhi;
Aditya Books, Delhi;
MacMillan Shuppan KK, Tokyo;
Pakistan Law House, Karachi

Current Law

STATUTES

1995

VOLUME FOUR

SWEET & MAXWELL EDITORIAL TEAM
SARAH ANDREWS
MELANIE BHAGAT
ALA KUZMICKI
SOPHIE LOWE
CERI PICKERING

W. GREEN EDITORIAL TEAM
CHARLOTTE HALL
PETER NICHOLSON

LONDON
SWEET & MAXWELL

EDINBURGH
W. GREEN

1996

Published by
SWEET & MAXWELL LIMITED
of 100 Avenue Road, London NW3 3PF,
and W. GREEN LIMITED
of Alva Street, Edinburgh,
Typeset by MFK Information Services Limited, Hitchin, Herts.
and printed in Great Britain
by The Bath Press,
Somerset

ISBN This Volume only : 0 421 54790 1
As a set : 0 421 54800 2

CONTENTS

CHRONOLOGICAL TABLE

VOLUME FOUR

Public General Acts

c.47. Northern Ireland (Remission of Sentences) Act 1995
48. Charities (Amendment) Act 1995
49. Town and Country Planning (Costs of Inquiries etc.) Act 1995
Professor Malcolm Grant, Head of Department of Land Economy, University of Cambridge
50. Disability Discrimination Act 1995
Gareth Thomas, LL.B., B.C.L., Senior Lecturer in Law, University of East Anglia
51. Medical (Professional Peformance) Act 1995
Anthony Barton, Solicitor and Medical Practitioner
52. Mental Health (Patients in the Community) Act 1995
Richard Jones, M.A., Solicitor and Hilary Patrick, Solicitor, Legal Adviser, the Scottish Association for Mental Health
53. Criminal Injuries Compensation Act 1995
Professor David Miers, LL.M. D.Jur; Director, Centre for Professional Legal Studies, Cardiff Law School
54. Consolidated Fund (No. 2) Act 1995

Private Acts

c.i. British Waterways Act 1995
ii. Letchworth Garden City Heritage Foundation Act 1995
iii. Malvern Hills Act 1995
iv. Bell's Bridge Order Confirmation Act 1995
v. Sheffield Assay Office Act 1995
vi. Birmingham Assay Office Act 1995
vii. Loch Leven and Lochaber Water Power Order Confirmation Act 1995
viii. Accommodation Level Crossing Act 1995

CHRONOLOGICAL TABLE

VOLUMES 1–4

VOLUME 1

c.1. European Communities (Finance) Act 1995
2. Consolidated Fund Act 1995
3. South Africa Act 1995
4. Finance Act 1995
5. Building Societies (Joint Account Holders) Act 1995
6. Civil Evidence (Family Mediation) (Scotland) Act 1995
7. Requirements of Writing (Scotland) Act 1995
8. Agricultural Tenancies Act 1995
9. Commonwealth Development Corporation 1995
10. Home Energy Conservation Act 1995
11. Proceeds of Crime Act 1995
12. Carers (Recognition and Services) Act 1995
13. Road Traffic (New Drivers) Act 1995
14. Land Registers (Scotland) Act 1995
15. Activity Centres (Young Persons' Safety) Act 1995
16. Prisoners (Return to Custody) Act 1995
17. Health Authorities Act 1995
18. Jobseekers Act 1995
19. Appropriation Act 1995
20. Criminal Justice (Scotland) Act 1995

VOLUME 2

21. Merchant Shipping Act 1995
22. Shipping and Trading Interests (Protection) Act 1995
23. Goods Vehicles (Licensing of Operators) Act 1995
24. Crown Agents Act 1995
25. Environment Act 1995
26. Pensions Act 1995

VOLUME 3

27. Geneva Conventions (Amendment) Act 1995
28. Sale of Goods (Amendment) Act 1995
29. Insurance Companies (Reserves) Act 1995
30. Landlord and Tenant (Covenants) Act 1995
31. National Health Service (Amendment) Act 1995
32. Olympic Symbol etc. (Protection) Act 1995
33. Licensing (Sunday Hours) Act 1995
34. Child Support Act 1995
35. Criminal Appeal Act 1995
36. Children (Scotland) Act 1995
37. Atomic Energy Authority Act 1995
38. Civil Evidence Act 1995

39. Criminal Law (Consolidation) (Scotland) Act 1995
40. Criminal Procedure (Consequential Provisions) (Scotland) Act 1995
41. Law Reform (Succession) Act 1995
42. Private International Law (Miscellaneous Provisions) Act 1995
43. Proceeds of Crime (Scotland) Act 1995
44. Statute Law (Repeals) Act 1995
45. Gas Act 1995
46. Criminal Procedure (Scotland) Act 1995

VOLUME 4

47. Northern Ireland (Remission of Sentences) Act 1995
48. Charities (Amendment) Act 1995
49. Town and Country Planning (Costs of Inquiries etc.) Act 1995
50. Disability Discrimination Act 1995
51. Medical (Professional Performance) Act 1995
52. Mental Health (Patients in the Community) Act 1995
53. Criminal Injuries Compensation Act 1995
54. Consolidated Fund (No. 2) Act 1995

Private Acts

*c.*i. British Waterways Act 1995
ii. Letchworth Garden City Heritage Foundation Act 1995
iii. Malvern Hills Act 1995
iv. Bell's Bridge Order Confirmation Act 1995
v. Sheffield Assay Office Act 1995
vi. Birmingham Assay Office Act 1995
vii. Loch Leven and Lochaber Water Power Order Confirmation Act 1995
viii. Accommodation Level Crossing Act 1995
ix. Queen Mary and Westfield College Act 1995
x. London Local Authorities Act 1995
xi. Church of Scotland (Property and Endowments) Amendment Order Confirmation Act 1995

Church Measures

1. Team and Group Ministries Measure 1995
2. Church of England (Miscellaneous Provisions) Measure 1995

Commencement Orders

1. Commencement Diary 1995
2. Commencement Orders 1995 C.1–79

Numerical Table of Statutory Instruments

Listing of all Instruments released for 1995

Alphabetical Table of Statutes

Listing of all Public Acts passed, 1700–1995

Legislation Citator 1995

Statutory Instrument Citator 1995

Index 1995

ALPHABETICAL INDEX OF SHORT TITLES

PUBLIC GENERAL ACTS 1995

(References are to chapter numbers of 1995)

ALPHABETICAL INDEX OF SHORT TITLES

PRIVATE ACTS 1995

(References are to chapter numbers of 1995)

NORTHERN IRELAND (REMISSION OF SENTENCES) ACT 1995

(1995 c. 47)

An Act to provide for the release on licence of persons serving sentences to which section 14 of the Northern Ireland (Emergency Provisions) Act 1991 applies; and for connected purposes. [8th November 1995]

Parliamentary Debates

Hansard, H.C. Vol. 264, col. 1155; Vol. 265, col. 21. H.L. Vol. 566, cols. 1405, 1507.

Introduction

This Act, *inter alia*, allows for the release on licence of prisoners serving sentences and subject to restricted remission by virtue of s.14 of the Northern Ireland (Emergency Provisions) Act 1991 (c. 24). The Secretary of State may revoke the licence where it appears that the person's continued liberty would present a risk to the safety of others or that he is likely to commit further offences.

Release on licence of persons subject to restricted remission

1.—(1) This section applies to persons serving sentences to which section 14 of the Northern Ireland (Emergency Provisions) Act 1991 applies (restricted remission for persons sentenced for scheduled offences).

(2) A person to whom this section applies shall be released on licence for the period (or, where that period has partly elapsed, for the remainder of the period) during which, by reason only of section 14, he is prevented from being discharged in pursuance of prison rules.

(3) The Secretary of State may revoke a person's licence under this section if it appears to him that the person's continued liberty would present a risk to the safety of others or that he is likely to commit further offences; and a person whose licence is revoked shall be detained in pursuance of his sentence and, if at large, be deemed to be unlawfully at large.

(4) If a person's licence is revoked—

(a) he may make representations in writing to the Secretary of State about the revocation, and

(b) he shall as soon as is practicable be informed of the reasons for the revocation and of his right to make representations.

(5) If a person's licence is revoked the Secretary of State may again release him on licence under this section at any time during the period mentioned in subsection (2).

(6) Section 15 of the Northern Ireland (Emergency Provisions) Act 1991 and Part II of the Treatment of Offenders (Northern Ireland) Order 1976 (conviction within certain period after discharge from prison, etc.) shall apply in relation to a person released on licence under this section as if he had been discharged in pursuance of prison rules.

Commencement

2. This Act shall come into force on such day as the Secretary of State may by order made by statutory instrument appoint.

Suspension and revival of section 1

3.—(1) The Secretary of State may make orders suspending, or later reviving, the operation of section 1.

(2) An order suspending the operation of section 1 shall not apply in relation to a person who is on licence when the order comes into force.

(3) Where an order revives the operation of section 1, subsection (2) of that section shall not apply in relation to a person who is detained pursuant to revocation under subsection (3).

Suspension and revival orders: supplementary

4.—(1) An order under section 3 shall be made by statutory instrument.

(2) Subject to subsection (3), no order under section 3 shall be made unless a draft of the order has been approved by resolution of each House of Parliament.

(3) An order suspending the operation of section 1 may be made without a draft having been approved if it appears necessary to the Secretary of State by reason of urgency, in which case the order—

(a) shall include a declaration to that effect;
(b) shall be laid before Parliament after being made; and
(c) shall cease to have effect at the end of the period of forty days (computed in accordance with section 7(1) of the Statutory Instruments Act 1946) after the day on which it was made unless a resolution has been passed by each House approving it.

(4) Where an order suspending the operation of section 1 ceases to have effect by virtue of subsection (3)(c) above, the detention of a person while the order was in force shall not be treated as unlawful by reason only of the order's ceasing to have effect.

Short title and extent

5.—(1) This Act may be cited as the Northern Ireland (Remission of Sentences) Act 1995.

(2) This Act extends to Northern Ireland only.

INDEX

References are to sections

CHARITIES (AMENDMENT) ACT 1995

(1995 c. 48)

An Act to make provision for the treatment of two or more charities as a single charity for all or any of the purposes of the Charities Act 1993.

[8th November 1995]

PARLIAMENTARY DEBATES

Hansard, H.C. Vol. 254, col. 636; Vol. 263, col. 1282. H.L. Vol. 566, cols. 70, 732, 1283, 1541.

INTRODUCTION

This Act, which only extends to England and Wales, makes provision for two or more charities sharing the same charity trustees to be treated as a single charity for the purposes of the Charities Act 1993.

Treatment of charities with same charity trustees as single charity

1. In section 96 of the Charities Act 1993 (meaning of "charity" etc.), the following subsection shall be inserted after subsection (5)—

"(6) The Commissioners may direct that for all or any of the purposes of this Act two or more charities having the same charity trustees shall be treated as a single charity."

Short title and extent

2.—(1) This Act may be cited as the Charities (Amendment) Act 1995.

(2) This Act extends only to England and Wales.

INDEX

References are to sections

TOWN AND COUNTRY PLANNING (COSTS OF INQUIRIES ETC.) ACT 1995*

(1995 c. 49)

ARRANGEMENT OF SECTIONS

SECT.

An Act to make provision authorising or requiring certain local authorities with functions under the enactments relating to Town and Country Planning to make to, or to persons appointed by, certain Ministers of the Crown, or to persons appointed by those authorities, payments in respect of the administrative cost of, or otherwise connected with, certain local inquiries or other hearings, examinations in public, or the consideration of certain objections, under those enactments; to validate the imposition by such Ministers on those authorities of requirements to make such payments, and the making by those authorities of such payments, whether before or after the passing of this Act; to make provision with respect to the remuneration and allowances payable to persons appointed to hold such local inquiries or other proceedings; and for connected purposes.

[8th November 1995]

PARLIAMENTARY DEBATES

Hansard, H.C. Vol. 252, col. 292; Vol. 262, col. 213. H.L. Vol. 565, cols. 317, 970; Vol. 566, cols. 829, 1292, 1541.

INTRODUCTION AND GENERAL NOTE

This short Act has an interesting and instructive background. Its sole purpose is to render lawful a practice in which the Government and local planning authorities have engaged for the past 25 years. Hence it has both prospective and retrospective effect.

The Act authorises the Secretary of State to recover from local planning authorities the costs borne by him in relation to the appointment of inspectors to hold public local inquiries into objections into local plans, unitary development plans and simplified planning zone schemes, and for examinations-in-public of structure plans. This, indeed, has been the Secretary of State's practice since 1970, when the first local plan inquiry was held under what was then the Town and Country Planning Act 1968 (c. 72). The duty of causing an inquiry to be held into unresolved objections lay with the local planning authority, and it seems to have been generally assumed that they should also bear the cost.

However, the practice was challenged in 1992 by Birmingham City Council, first as to the amount charged them by the Planning Inspectorate Agency, and then, more fundamentally, as to the entire practice in light of the decision by the House of Lords in *R. v. Richmond-upon-Thames London Borough Council, ex. p. McCarthy & Stone (Developments)* [1992] 2 A.C. 48. It was held in that case that there was no power for a public body to levy a charge for its services, in the absence of an express or implied statutory power. In particular, the statutory power under the Local Government Act 1972 (c. 70), s.111 to do anything which is calculated to facilitate, or

*Annotations by Professor Malcolm Grant, Head of Department of Land Economy, University of Cambridge.

which is conducive or incidental to the discharge of any of their functions, did not allow a local planning authority to charge for giving planning advice, which they were under no legal obligation to furnish, to prospective applicants for planning permission.

The Government in due course accepted that validating legislation would be necessary. Thereupon, receipts collected in 1993–94 of £1.4 million were paid into a special suspense account pending the enactment of this legislation, and no further sums were collected. As a result, a further £2.6 million was then owing to the Department for that year, and another £3 million for 1994–95. Authorities were advised to make full budgetary provision for these payments in the event of this legislation being enacted. Additionally, some £3 million was repaid to some authorities who demanded their repayment. Hence s.2(11) now allows the Secretary of State to require them to be paid back to him, with interest.

The Retrospective Provisions

The Act also seeks to validate, with retrospective effect, all payments of this nature made in past years. The relevant provision, s.2, deems the Minister to be taken at all times to have had the requisite powers to charge the sums he did charge.

Commencement

The Act came into effect on the day of Royal Assent (November 8, 1995), but in relation to its applicability there are three relevant periods:

(1) where the appointment of any person to hold, or participate in holding, a qualifying inquiry took place after the commencement date the new s.303A (for Scotland, the amendments to s.11) applies in full, and the powers to recover costs extend to the expenses of all appointed persons for that inquiry, and also to any costs in relation to that inquiry arising before the commencement date (s.303A(11)).

(2) for the period between the commencement date and the coming into force of regulations under s.303A(5) prescribing a standard daily amount (see the General Note to s.1 below), the recoverable amount is the amount determined by the Secretary of State and notified to the local planning authority (subs. (2)). Similar provision is made in respect of persons appointed for an examination in public, and remunerated direct by the local planning authority, by subss. (3), (4) and (5).

(3) for qualifying inquiries held, or to which all persons were appointed, prior to the commencement date: provision is made by s.2 (s.4 for Scotland) for retrospective validation of the Secretary of State's practice of recovering costs in accordance with a prescribed standard daily amount. Where any sums previously paid to the Secretary of State by a local planning authority have since been repaid, he may require them to be paid back to him with interest (s.2(13)).

Extent

By virtue of s.5(3)–(6), ss.1 and 2 extend to England only and ss.3 and 4 extend to Scotland only. The Act does not extend to Northern Ireland.

Costs of holding certain inquiries etc.

1.—(1) In the Town and Country Planning Act 1990 (in this Act referred to as "the 1990 Act") after section 303 (fees for planning applications etc) there shall be inserted—

"**Responsibility of local planning authorities for costs of holding certain inquiries etc.**

303A.—(1) This section applies in any case where, at any time after its coming into force, the Secretary of State appoints any person to hold, or as one of the persons who are to hold, a qualifying inquiry, within the meaning of this section, that is to say—

(a) to hold a local inquiry or other hearing under section 16 or 42 or under paragraph 8(1)(a) of Schedule 7;

(b) to consider objections under paragraph 8(1)(b) of that Schedule; or

(c) to conduct an examination in public under section 35B(1);

and the references in paragraphs (a) to (c) above to the enactments there mentioned include references to those enactments as from time to time amended, extended or applied by or under any other enactment whether before or after the coming into force of this section.

(2) The Secretary of State may require the whole or any part of the costs borne by him in relation to the qualifying inquiry to be paid by the local planning authority causing the qualifying inquiry to be held.

(3) The Secretary of State may cause the amount of any such costs to be certified; and any amount so certified and required by him to be paid by a local planning authority shall be recoverable from that authority as a civil debt.

(4) What may be recovered under this section by the Secretary of State is the entire administrative cost of, or incidental to, the qualifying inquiry, so far as borne by him, including, in particular, such reasonable amount or element as he may determine in respect of the general staff costs and overheads of his department.

(5) For the purposes of subsection (4), the Secretary of State may by regulations prescribe a standard daily amount in relation to any description of qualifying inquiry and any description of person appointed to hold it, or appointed as one of the persons who are to hold it; and where, in relation to a qualifying inquiry of that description, a person of that description is or has been so appointed, what may be recovered in respect of that qualifying inquiry by virtue of the appointment of that person (in addition to what may be recovered by virtue of the appointment of any other person) is—

(a) the prescribed standard amount from time to time applicable in the case of that qualifying inquiry and that person in respect of each day, or an appropriate proportion of that amount in respect of a part of a day, on which that person is engaged in the holding of, or is otherwise engaged on work connected with, the qualifying inquiry;

(b) any costs actually incurred on travelling or subsistence allowances payable to that person in connection with the qualifying inquiry;

(c) any costs attributable to the appointment of an assessor to assist that person (or, in a case where that person is appointed as one of the persons who are to hold the qualifying inquiry, an appropriate proportion of any costs attributable to the appointment of an assessor to assist those persons); and

(d) any other costs attributable to the appointment of that person.

(6) The cost of, or incidental to, a qualifying inquiry which does not take place may be recovered by the Secretary of State from the local planning authority from which it would have been recoverable, had the qualifying inquiry taken place, to the same extent, and in the same way, as the cost of, or incidental to, a qualifying inquiry which does take place.

(7) In the application of subsections (2) to (6) in relation to an examination in public under section 35B(1), there shall be left out of account any person—

(a) who is appointed to conduct, or is appointed as one of the persons who are to conduct, the examination; and

(b) whose remuneration, and travelling or subsistence allowances (if any), in respect of that appointment are (whether by agreement or arrangement or otherwise) to be paid to him by the local planning authority causing the examination to be held.

(8) The Secretary of State may by regulations prescribe a standard daily amount in relation to any description of person who is appointed to conduct, or is appointed as one of the persons who are to conduct, an

examination in public under section 35B(1) and whose remuneration, and travelling or subsistence allowances (if any), in respect of that appointment are to be paid as mentioned in subsection (7)(b); and where—

(a) a standard daily amount is so prescribed in relation to any description of person,

(b) a person of that description is or has been appointed to conduct, or is or has been appointed as one of the persons who are to conduct, such an examination, and

(c) the remuneration, and travelling or subsistence allowances (if any), of that person in respect of that appointment are to be paid as mentioned in subsection (7)(b),

the amount of the remuneration so payable to that person by the local planning authority in question in respect of the appointment shall be the prescribed standard amount from time to time applicable in the case of that person in respect of each day, or an appropriate proportion of that amount in respect of a part of a day, on which that person is engaged in the conduct of, or is otherwise engaged on work connected with, that examination (whether that examination does or does not take place).

(9) The Secretary of State may also by regulations under subsection (8) prescribe, in relation to any description of person, the rates or amounts of any travelling or subsistence allowances payable as mentioned in subsection (7)(b) by a local planning authority causing an examination in public under section 35B(1) to be held to a person of that description appointed to conduct, or appointed as one of the persons who are to conduct, the examination.

(10) In this section—

(a) any reference to costs borne by the Secretary of State includes a reference to costs which, apart from this section, would fall, or would have fallen, to be borne by him; and

(b) any reference to any remuneration or allowance being paid or payable to a person includes a reference to its being paid or payable for him.

(11) This section applies in relation to costs arising before, as well as costs arising after, its coming into force."

(2) As respects costs borne by the Secretary of State in respect of a qualifying inquiry, within the meaning of section 303A of the 1990 Act, which arise or arose before the coming into force of the first regulations made by virtue of subsection (5) of that section, that section shall have effect with the following modifications, that is to say—

(a) in subsection (5)—

(i) for the words "may by regulations prescribe" there shall be substituted the words "may determine"; and

(ii) after the words "is or has been so appointed" there shall be inserted the words "and that standard daily amount has been notified to the local planning authority causing the qualifying inquiry to be held"; and

(b) in paragraph (a) of that subsection, for the words "the prescribed standard amount" there shall be substituted the words "the standard amount, determined and notified as mentioned above,".

(3) As respects the remuneration, and travelling or subsistence allowances (if any), payable by a local planning authority to a person falling within subsection (7) of section 303A of the 1990 Act in respect of any day before the coming into force of the first regulations under subsection (8) of that section, that section shall have effect with the following modifications, that is to say—

(a) in subsection (8), for the words "may by regulations prescribe" there shall be substituted the words "may determine";

(b) in paragraph (a) of that subsection, for the word "prescribed" there shall be substituted the word "determined";

(c) after paragraph (c) of that subsection there shall be inserted the words "and

(d) that standard daily amount has been notified to the local planning authority causing the examination to be held,";

(d) in the words following that paragraph, for the words "the prescribed standard amount" there shall be substituted the words "the standard amount, determined and notified as mentioned above,";

(e) in subsection (9), for the words "may also by regulations under subsection (8) prescribe" there shall be substituted the words "may also determine"; and

(f) after that subsection there shall be inserted—

"(9A) Where any such rate or amount as is mentioned in subsection (9)—

(a) is so determined in relation to any description of person, and

(b) has been notified to a local planning authority causing an examination in public under section 35B(1) to be held,

the rate or amount of any travelling or subsistence allowances payable by that local planning authority as mentioned in subsection (7)(b) to a person of that description in respect of his appointment as mentioned in subsection (9) shall be the rate or amount, so determined and notified, from time to time applicable in the case of that person."

(4) In section 303A of the 1990 Act as it has effect by virtue of subsection (2) or (3) above, any reference to a determination or notification of a rate or amount—

(a) is a reference to a determination or notification of the rate or amount in question, whether before or after the passing of this Act, and

(b) includes (as respects determination) a reference to such a determination made before the passing of this Act with the approval of the Treasury, whether given as mentioned in section 2(15) below or otherwise.

(5) In section 35B of the 1990 Act (examinations in public in connection with structure plans) after subsection (7) there shall be added—

"(8) Without prejudice to section 303A(8) and (9), regulations may make provision with respect to the remuneration and allowances of any person or persons appointed by the Secretary of State to conduct an examination in public under this section."

DEFINITIONS

"the 1990 Act": subs. (1); s.5(1).
"qualifying inquiry": s.303A(1).

GENERAL NOTE

Introduction

The purpose of this section is to authorise the Secretary of State to charge local planning authorities for the whole or part of his costs of holding certain planning inquiries under the Town and Country Planning Act 1990 (c. 8). It specifies the inquiries to which the charging regime is to apply, and authorises the Secretary of State to make regulations prescribing a standard daily amount which is to be recoverable.

The section achieves its objectives by inserting (by subs. (1)) a new s.303A into the Town and Country Planning Act 1990; and by making (by subss. (2) to (5)) consequential provision in respect of qualifying inquiries held between the date of Royal Assent (November 8, 1995) and the making of the regulations under the new s.303A(8) specifying the standard daily amount.

Qualifying inquiries

The power to charge applies only to the following inquiries (s.303A(1)):

(1) local inquiries or hearings for considering objections to unitary development plans, under s.16 of the 1990 Act, or objections to a local plan under s.42 of that Act, or objections to a proposed simplified planning zone scheme, under Sched. 7, para. 8(1)(a);

(2) an inquiry into objections to a proposed simplified planning zone scheme where the local planning authority have required them to be so considered under Sched. 7, para. 8(1)(b) of the 1990 Act;
(3) an examination in public of proposals for the alteration or replacement of a stucture plan, under s.35B(1) of the 1990 Act.

The recoverable amount: the standard daily amount

The sum recoverable by the Secretary of State is the entire administrative cost of, or incidental to, the qualifying inquiry, and actually incurred by him, and including an overhead element, in respect of the general staff costs and overheads of his department (s.303A(4)). The Secretary of State's intention is not to seek to recover his departmental headquarters' costs, but to include nothing more than a component representing the hypothecated cost to the Planning Inspectorate Agency of that Agency's staff and administrative costs of holding development plan inquiries.

For the purposes of calculation he is empowered to prescribe by regulations, a standard daily amount which can be calculated by reference to: (1) the description of qualifying inquiry; and (2) the description of persons appointed in respect of it. A model for this approach is the Fees for Inquiries (Standard Daily Amount) Regulations 1994 (S.I. 1994 No. 642), which prescribes the daily amount chargeable in cases where the Secretary of State is entitled, under the Housing and Planning Act 1986 (c. 63), s.42(1), to recover his costs in relation to public local inquiries under the Local Government Act 1972 (c. 70), s.250(4); the Road Traffic Regulation Act 1984 (c. 27), s.129(1)(d); the Water Resources Act 1991 (c. 57), s.214(5) and the Land Drainage Act 1991 (c. 59), s.69(5).

The Town and Country Planning (Costs of Inquiries etc.) (Standard Daily Amount) Regulations 1996 (S.I. 1996 No. 24) were made under this section, with effect from February 6, 1996 and prescribe a standard daily amount of £340.

The days for which charges may be made include not only the days of the actual hearing, but any day (or part) on which that person is engaged on work connected with the inquiry. Actual travel costs, the costs of any assessor, and any other actual costs to the department are charged in addition to the standard daily amount (s.303A(5)(b), (c) and (d)).

In the case of an examination in public, costs which are remunerated direct by the local planning authority are excluded from these provisions (s.303(7)), and are instead the subject of a different standard daily amount prescribed by regulations under s.303A(8).

Service agreements

During parliamentary debates on the Bill, Opposition Members argued that present arrangements for development plan inquiries forced local planning authorities to use a service that was being offered by only one agency—the Planning Inspectorate—for a function which they were statutorily required to undertake. They maintained that the level of service required from the Inspectorate should be formally specified, together with some means of redress. The Government resisted all attempts to legislate for this, or for the introduction of a contractual relationship between local authorities and the Inspectorate, on the ground that many of the factors that influenced the practical operation of development plan inquiries, such as the number of objections, were outside the Inspectorate's control. Nonetheless, there had been consultation between the local authority associations, the Planning Inspectorate and the Department of the Environment about a draft informal service level agreement.

The Planning Inspectorate announced on December 12, 1995, that it was introducing, immediately, service agreements for development plan inquiries, which would offer local planning authorities improved opportunities to budget more accurately for the cost of inquiries. The Inspectorate believes that the agreements should improve the efficiency and effectiveness of the local plan inquiry process generally. The agreements will cover the planned date of delivery of the Inspector's report and the estimated cost of his or her services; they will confirm the duty of the local planning authority to appoint a programme officer in good time, and to provide the necessary documentation quickly; and the Inspectorate and the local planning authority will undertake to use their best endeavours to achieve the targets set out for them in the agreement.

Validation, with retrospective effect, of certain requirements to pay, and certain payments made, in connection with past appointments

2.—(1) This section applies in any case where, at any time before the passing of this Act, the Minister appointed any person to hold, or as one of the persons who are or were to hold, a qualifying inquiry, within the meaning of this section, that is to say—

(a) to hold a local inquiry or other hearing under—

(i) section 8 of the Town and Country Planning Act 1968;
(ii) section 13 of the Town and Country Planning Act 1971;
(iii) paragraph 6 of Schedule 1 to the Local Government Act 1985;
(iv) section 16 or 42 of the 1990 Act;
(v) paragraph 9 of Part II of Schedule 2 to that Act; or
(vi) paragraph 8(1)(a) of Schedule 7 to that Act;

(b) to consider objections under paragraph 8(1)(b) of Schedule 7 to the 1990 Act; or

(c) to conduct an examination in public under section 35B(1) of the 1990 Act;

and the references in paragraphs (a) to (c) above to the enactments there mentioned are references to those enactments as originally enacted, and include references to those enactments as from time to time amended, extended or applied by or under any other enactment, whether before or after the passing of this Act.

(2) The Minister shall have, and shall be taken at all times to have had, power to require the whole or any part of the costs borne by him in relation to the qualifying inquiry to be paid by the local planning authority causing the qualifying inquiry to be held; and any amount so required by him to be paid by a local planning authority shall be, and shall be taken at all times after the making of the requirement to have been, recoverable from that authority as a civil debt.

(3) What may be recovered under this section by the Minister is, and shall be taken at all times to have been, the entire administrative cost of, or incidental to, the qualifying inquiry, so far as borne by him, including, in particular, such reasonable amount or element as he may determine, or may have determined, in respect of the general staff costs and overheads of his department.

(4) For the purposes of subsection (3) above, the Minister shall have, and shall be taken at all times to have had, power to determine a standard daily amount in relation to any description of qualifying inquiry and any description of person appointed to hold it, or appointed as one of the persons who are or were to hold it; and where—

(a) a standard daily amount is or was so determined in relation to any description of qualifying inquiry and any description of person appointed to hold it or appointed as one of the persons who are or were to hold it,

(b) a person of that description was so appointed in relation to a qualifying inquiry of that description, and

(c) that standard daily amount has or had been notified to the local planning authority causing the qualifying inquiry to be held,

what may be recovered in respect of that qualifying inquiry by virtue of the appointment of that person (in addition to what may be recovered by virtue of the appointment of any other person) shall be, and shall be taken at all times to have been, the amounts specified in subsection (5) below.

(5) For the purposes of subsection (4) above, the amounts in question are—

(a) the standard amount, determined and notified as mentioned in that subsection, from time to time applicable in the case of the qualifying inquiry in question and the person in question in respect of each day, or an appropriate proportion of that amount in respect of a part of a day, on which that person is or was engaged in the holding of, or is or was otherwise engaged on work connected with, the qualifying inquiry;

(b) any costs actually incurred on travelling or subsistence allowances which are or were payable to that person in connection with the qualifying inquiry;

(c) any costs attributable to the appointment of an assessor to assist that person (or, in a case where that person was appointed as one of the persons who are or were to hold the qualifying inquiry, an appropriate proportion of any costs attributable to the appointment of an assessor to assist those persons); and

(d) any other costs attributable to the appointment of that person.

(6) If no such standard daily amount as is mentioned in subsection (4) above is or was applicable in relation to—

(a) the qualifying inquiry in question, or

(b) the person appointed to hold it, or appointed as one of the persons who are or were to hold it,

the amount that may be recovered shall be, and shall be taken at all times to have been, such sum as the Minister considers or considered reasonable in all the circumstances of the case, and may, without prejudice to the generality of subsection (3) above, include elements (whether separately identified or not) in respect of any item specified in paragraph (b), (c) or (d) of subsection (5) above.

(7) The cost of, or incidental to, a qualifying inquiry which did not, or does not, take place shall be, and shall be taken at all times to have been, recoverable by the Minister from the local planning authority from which it would have been recoverable, had the qualifying inquiry taken place, to the same extent, and in the same way, as the cost of, or incidental to, a qualifying inquiry which did, or does, take place.

(8) In the application of subsections (2) to (7) above in relation to an examination in public under section 35B(1) of the 1990 Act, there shall be left out of account any person—

(a) who was appointed to conduct, or was appointed as one of the persons who are or were to conduct, the examination; and

(b) whose remuneration, and travelling or subsistence allowances (if any), in respect of that appointment are or were (whether by agreement or arrangement or otherwise) to be paid to him by the local planning authority causing the examination to be held.

(9) The Minister shall have, and shall be taken at all times to have had, power to determine a standard daily amount in relation to any description of person who was appointed to conduct, or was appointed as one of the persons who are or were to conduct, an examination in public under section 35B(1) of the 1990 Act and whose remuneration, and travelling or subsistence allowances (if any), in respect of that appointment are or were to be paid as mentioned in subsection (8)(b) above; and where—

(a) a standard daily amount is or was so determined in relation to any description of person;

(b) a person of that description was appointed to conduct, or was appointed as one of the persons who are or were to conduct, such an examination,

(c) the remuneration, and travelling or subsistence allowances (if any), of that person in respect of that appointment are or were to be paid as mentioned in subsection (8)(b) above, and

(d) that standard daily amount has or had been notified to the local planning authority causing the examination in public to be conducted,

the amount of the remuneration so payable to that person by the local planning authority in question in respect of the appointment shall be, and shall be taken at all times to have been, the standard amount so determined and notified, from time to time applicable in the case of that person in respect of each day, or an appropriate proportion of that amount in respect of a part of a day, on which that person is or was engaged in the conduct of, or is or was otherwise engaged on work connected with, the examination in public concerned (whether that examination did or did not, or does or does not, take place).

(10) The Minister shall have, and shall be taken at all times to have had, power to determine, in relation to any description of person, the rates or amounts of any travelling or subsistence allowances payable as mentioned in subsection (8)(b) above by a local planning authority causing an examination in public under section 35B(1) of the 1990 Act to be held to any person of that description falling within subsection (8) above and appointed as mentioned in subsection (1) above to conduct, or as one of the persons who are or were to conduct, the examination.

(11) Where any such rate or amount as is mentioned in subsection (10) above—

(a) is or was so determined in relation to any description of person, and
(b) has or had been notified to a local planning authority causing an examination in public under section 35B(1) of the 1990 Act to be held,

the rate or amount of any travelling or subsistence allowances payable by that local planning authority as mentioned in subsection (8)(b) above to a person of that description in respect of his appointment as mentioned in subsection (10) above shall be, and shall be taken at all times to have been, the rate or amount, so determined and notified, from time to time applicable in the case of that person.

(12) Without prejudice to the generality of section 111 of the Local Government Act 1972 (subsidiary powers of local authorities), a local planning authority shall have, and shall be taken at all times to have had, power to make payments to the Minister on account of any actual or contingent liability under or by virtue of this section, whether or not the Minister has or had, before the making of the payment in question, required the whole or any part of the costs in question to be paid to him by the authority.

(13) Where any sums paid to the Minister by a local planning authority in respect of the whole or any part of the costs borne by him in relation to a qualifying inquiry have, before the passing of this Act, been repaid to a local planning authority, with or without interest,—

(a) the Minister may require those sums, together with any interest so paid, to be paid back to him by the local planning authority; and
(b) any amount so required to be paid back shall be recoverable by the Minister from the local planning authority as a civil debt.

(14) Where both this section and section 303A of the 1990 Act apply in relation to the same qualifying inquiry, the same costs, or the same part of any costs, shall not be recoverable both under this section and under that section; but the Minister may make any such apportionment as he considers appropriate for the purpose of securing that the costs in question may be recovered by him either under the one section or the other or partly under the one section and partly under the other.

(15) Any reference in subsection (4), (9) or (10) above to the Minister having determined, or having had power to determine, any rate or amount includes, as respects any time before the passing of this Acts a reference to his having done so, or having had power to do so, with the approval of the Treasury; and the Treasury shall be taken at any such time to have had power to give the Minister their general approval for the making of such determinations of any class or description which was specified by them for the purpose.

(16) In this section—

(a) any reference to costs borne by the Minister includes a reference to costs which, apart from this section, would fall, or would have fallen, to be borne by him; and
(b) any reference to any remuneration or allowance being paid or payable to a person includes a reference to its being paid or payable for him.

(17) In this section—

"local planning authority" includes, as respects any time before the passing of this Act, any body which was, at that time, a local planning authority within the meaning of the enactments relating to Town and Country Planning, as in force at that time in England and Wales;

"the Minister" means the Secretary of State, except that in relation to section 8 of the Town and Country Planning Act 1968 it means the Secretary of State or the Minister of Housing and Local Government.

DEFINITIONS

"costs borne by Minister": subs. (16).
"local planning authority": subs. (17).
"Minister": subs. (17).
"qualifying inquiry": subs. (1).
"standard daily amount": subs. (4).
"the 1990 Act": s.5(1).

GENERAL NOTE

Purpose of section

This section seeks to authorise retrospectively the practice of the Secretary of State and of local planning authorities since 1970 of, respectively, charging and paying for the administrative costs of running inquiries relating to development plans and to simplified planning zone schemes. The provisions are necessarily highly technical, because of the need to ensure that all possibilities are adequately covered. The content of the section closely follows that of s.1.

The Government was persuaded that, exceptionally, retrospection was justified, for two main reasons. First, that the section imposed no new burdens on local planning authorities, but simply validated payments made by authorities in good faith, and for which provision had been made in the annual local authority finance settlements. Secondly, a wish to retain parity between those authorities who had already held, and those who were yet to hold, development plan inquiries (per Viscount Ullswater, Minister of State, Department of the Environment, *Hansard*, H.L. Vol. 565, col. 971; July 3, 1995).

The qualifying inquiry

The section applies to "qualifying inquiries", which includes only:

(1) local inquiries or hearings for considering objections to unitary development plans, under s.16 of the 1990 Act (or its predecessor, the Local Government Act 1985 (c. 51), Sched. 1, para. 6);
(2) local inquiries or hearings for considering objections to a local plan under s.42 of the 1990 Act (or its predecessor, s.13 of the Town and Country Planning Act 1971 (c. 78));
(3) an examination in public of proposals for the alteration or replacement of a structure plan, under s.35B(1) of the 1990 Act;
(4) local inquiries or hearings into objections to a proposed simplifed planning zone scheme, under the 1990 Act, Sched. 7, para. 8(1)(a);
(5) an inquiry into objections to a proposed simplified planning zone scheme where the local planning authority have required them to be so considered, under the 1990 Act, Sched. 7, para. 8(1)(b) of the 1990 Act;

Power of local planning authority to make required payment

Subsection (12) confers power retrospectively on local planning authorities, without prejudice to the Local Government Act 1972, s.111, to make the requisite payments. Section 111 enables local authorities to do anything which is calculated to facilitate, or which is conducive or incidental to, the discharge of any of their functions, and this might be thought to have encompassed the payment to the Secretary of State of the costs of holding a planning inquiry or examination in public. However the House of Lords in *R. v. Richmond-upon-Thames London Borough Council, ex p. McCarthy & Stone (Developments)* [1992] 2 A.C. 48 (see also *Hazell v. Hammersmith and Fulham London Borough Council* [1992] 2 A.C. 1 and *Allsop v. North Tyneside Metropolitan Borough Council* 90 L.G.R. 462) had construed this section narrowly, and in a manner which cast doubt on the legal capacity of local authorities to make such payments, hence the reinforcement provided by subs. (12).

Power of recovery of money repaid by Secretary of State

When doubts about the lawfulness of the Government's past practice arose, the Government repaid some £3 million to local authorities who demanded repayment. Subsection (11) now allows the Secretary of State to require those sums to be paid back to him, with interest.

Costs of holding certain Scottish inquiries etc.

3.—(1) The Town and Country Planning (Scotland) Act 1972 (in this Act referred to as "the 1972 Act") shall be amended as follows.

(2) In section 11 (inquiries etc. with respect to local plans)—

(a) after subsection (1) there shall be inserted—

"(1A) The planning authority shall—

(a) where a person appointed under or by virtue of this section is in the public service of the Crown, pay the Secretary of State; and

(b) in any other case, pay the person so appointed,

a sum, determined in accordance with regulations under subsection (1B) below, in respect of the performance by the person so appointed of his functions in relation to the inquiry or hearing (whether or not it takes place).

(1B) Regulations made by the Secretary of State may make provision with respect to the determination of the sum referred to in subsection (1A) above and may in particular prescribe, in relation to any class of person appointed under or by virtue of this section, a standard daily amount applicable in respect of each day on which a person of that class is engaged in holding, or in work connected with, the inquiry or hearing.

(1C) Without prejudice to the generality of subsection (1B) above, the Secretary of State may, in prescribing by virtue of that subsection a standard daily amount for any class of person—

(a) where the persons of that class are in the public service of the Crown, have regard to the general staff costs and overheads of his department; and

(b) in any other case, have regard to the general administrative costs incurred by persons of that class in connection with the performance by them of their functions in relation to such inquiries and hearings."; and

(b) in subsection (2)(b), the words "remuneration and" shall be omitted.

(3) In paragraph 7 of Schedule 6A (inquiries etc. with respect to simplified planning zones)—

(a) after sub-paragraph (3) there shall be inserted—

"(3A) The planning authority shall—

(a) where a person appointed under or by virtue of this paragraph is in the public service of the Crown, pay the Secretary of State; and

(b) in any other case, pay the person so appointed,

a sum, determined in accordance with regulations under sub-paragraph (3B) below, in respect of the performance by the person so appointed of his functions in relation to the inquiry or hearing (whether or not it takes place).

(3B) Regulations made by the Secretary of State may make provision with respect to the determination of the sum referred to in sub-paragraph (3A) above and may in particular prescribe, in relation to any class of person appointed under or by virtue of this paragraph, a standard daily amount applicable in respect of each day on which a person of that class is engaged in holding, or in work connected with, the inquiry or hearing.

(3C) Without prejudice to the generality of sub-paragraph (3B) above, the Secretary of State may, in prescribing by virtue of that sub-paragraph a standard daily amount for any class of person—

(a) where the persons of that class are in the public service of the Crown, have regard to the general staff costs and overheads of his department; and

(b) in any other case, have regard to the general administrative costs incurred by persons of that class in connection with the performance by them of their functions in relation to such inquiries and hearings."; and

(b) in sub-paragraph (4)(c), the words "remuneration and" shall be omitted.

(4) The amendments made by subsections (2) and (3) above shall have effect in relation to the performance of functions in relation to inquiries or hearings before as well as after the passing of this Act.

(5) Until the coming into force of the first regulations under section 11(1B) of, or as the case may be paragraph 7(3B) of Schedule 6A to, the 1972 Act—

(a) the Secretary of State—

(i) may, subject to subsection (6) below, determine, in relation to any class of person appointed under or by virtue of that section or, as the case may be, that paragraph, the standard daily amount applicable in respect of each day on which a person of that class is engaged in holding, or in work connected with, the inquiry or hearing; and

(ii) shall notify the applicable standard daily amount to the planning authority causing the inquiry or hearing to be held; and

(b) the sum payable by the planning authority under section 11(1A) or, as the case may be, paragraph 7(3A) shall be determined by reference to the applicable standard daily amount determined under paragraph (a)(i) above.

(6) In determining under subsection (5)(a)(i) above the standard daily amount for any class of person, the Secretary of State may—

(a) where the persons of that class are in the public service of the Crown, have regard to the general staff costs and overheads of his department; and

(b) in any other case, have regard to the general administrative costs incurred by persons of that class in connection with the performance by them of their functions in relation to such inquiries and hearings.

DEFINITIONS

"the 1972 Act": s.5(1).

GENERAL NOTE

This section makes parallel provision for Scotland to that made by s.1 for England and Wales. The position of payments by local planning authorities in Scotland has not been tested in the courts, nor had any pressed for repayment of sums already paid to the Secretary of State for Scotland. Nevertheless, this section ensures that there should be no doubt for the future. It proceeds by inserting new subss. (1A), (1B) and (1C) in the Town and Country Planning (Scotland) Act 1972 (c. 52), s.11 (inquiries with respect to local plans), requiring the planning authority to pay a sum in respect of the performance by the person appointed, in relation to an inquiry or hearing under that section, and authorises the Secretary of State for Scotland to make regulations specifying a standard daily amount.

Subsection (3) makes parallel provision for inquiries and hearings with relation to simplified planning zones, and both sets of amendments apply to the performance of functions in relation to inquiries and hearings before, as well as after, the passing of this Act. Full retrospective application of the Scottish provisions is achieved by s.4.

Retrospective validation of payments etc. in connection with certain past Scottish inquiries and hearings

4.—(1) As respects any inquiry or other hearing under section 8 of the Town and Country Planning (Scotland) Act 1969 or section 11 of the 1972 Act held before the passing of this Act—

(a) the Secretary of State shall be taken always to have had power to determine, in relation to any class of person appointed under or by virtue of the provision in question, the standard daily amount applicable in respect of each day on which a person of that class is engaged in holding, or in work connected with, the inquiry or hearing, and in so determining, to have regard—

(i) where the persons of that class are in the public service of the Crown, to the general staff costs and overheads of his department; and

(ii) in any other case, to the general administrative costs incurred by persons of that class in connection with the performance by them of their functions in relation to such inquiries and hearings; and

(b) the planning authority shall be taken always to have been under an obligation to pay to—

(i) the Secretary of State, where the person appointed under or by virtue of the provision in question was in the public service of the Crown; and

(ii) in any other case, the person so appointed,

a sum, determined by reference to the applicable standard daily amount, in respect of the performance by the person so appointed of his functions in relation to the inquiry or hearing (whether or not it took place).

(2) Where any sums paid to the Secretary of State by a planning authority in respect of the performance by a person appointed as mentioned in subsection (1) above of his functions in relation to an inquiry or hearing referred to in that subsection have, before the passing of this Act, been repaid to the authority, with or without interest, the authority shall, if the Secretary of State so requires, pay those sums, together with any interest so paid, to him.

(3) Where both this section and, as the case may be, section 8 of the Town and Country Planning (Scotland) Act 1969 or section 11 of the 1972 Act apply in relation to the same inquiry or hearing, the Secretary of State may make such apportionment as he considers appropriate for the purpose of securing payment by the planning authority under this section or that section, or partly under this section and partly under that section.

DEFINITIONS

"the 1972 Act": s.5(1).

GENERAL NOTE

This section applies retrospectively the provisions of s.3 relating to charges made by the Secretary of State for Scotland for inquiries and other hearings held under the Town and Country Planning (Scotland) Act 1969 (c. 30), s.8 and its successor, the Town and Country Planning (Scotland) Act 1972 (c. 52), s.11.

Short title, interpretation, financial provision, and extent

5.—(1) This Act may be cited as the Town and Country Planning (Costs of Inquiries etc.) Act 1995.

(2) In this Act—

"the 1972 Act" means the Town and Country Planning (Scotland) Act 1972;

"the 1990 Act" means the Town and Country Planning Act 1990;

"Minister of the Crown" has the same meaning as in the Ministers of the Crown Act 1975.

(3) There shall be paid out of money provided by Parliament—

(a) any administrative expenses incurred by a Minister of the Crown in consequence of this Act; and

(b) any increase attributable to this Act in the sums payable out of money so provided under any other Act;

and any sums received by a Minister of the Crown under or by virtue of this Act shall be paid into the Consolidated Fund.

(4) Sections 1 and 2 above extend to England and Wales only.

(5) Sections 3 and 4 above extend to Scotland only.

(6) This Act does not extend to Northern Ireland.

INDEX

References are to sections

DISABILITY DISCRIMINATION ACT 1995*

(1995 c. 50)

* Annotations by Gareth Thomas, LL.B., B.C.L., Senior Lecturer in Law, University of East Anglia.

PART VII

SUPPLEMENTAL

PART VIII

MISCELLANEOUS

SCHEDULES:

An Act to make it unlawful to discriminate against disabled persons in connection with employment, the provision of goods, facilities and services or the disposal or management of premises; to make provision about the employment of disabled persons; and to establish a National Disability Council. [8th November 1995]

PARLIAMENTARY DEBATES

Hansard, H.C. Vol. 253, col. 147; Vol. 257, cols. 697, 840. H.L. Vol. 564, cols. 800, 830, 1182, 1640, 1723, 1895, 1975; Vol. 565, cols. 608, 686, 1839; Vol. 566, cols. 114, 168, 205, 386, 434, 969.

INTRODUCTION AND GENERAL NOTE

The Disability Discrimination Act 1995 (c. 50) is the first piece of legislation in the U.K. to tackle discrimination against disabled people. It outlaws discrimination against disabled people in relation to employment, the provision of goods, facilities and services, and the sale and letting of property; it requires schools, colleges, universities and local education authorities to provide fuller information concerning their arrangements and facilities for disabled people; and it allows the Government to issue regulations setting minimum standards for the accessibility of land-based public transport for disabled people. It also establishes the National Disability Council and the Northern Ireland Disability Council to advise the Government on discrimination against disabled people. The Act, a Government-sponsored measure, was the culmination of a lengthy period of intense pressure for anti-discrimination legislation by disability rights campaigners, during which no fewer than 14 abortive Private Members' Bills were introduced. Until recently, the Government had consistently argued that discrimination against disabled people was a matter best tackled by education and persuasion, rather than by legislative means. However, in the aftermath of the furore surrounding the "talking-out" of the Civil Rights (Disabled

Persons) Bill in 1994, the Government published a Consultation Document on *Government Measures to Tackle Discrimination Against Disabled People* (July 1994), which invited views on the enactment of statutory anti-discrimination rights for disabled people. The Disability Discrimination Bill was published in early 1995, at the same time as the White Paper, *Ending discrimination against disabled people*, Cm. 2729.

As originally published, the Disability Discrimination Bill fell some way short of meeting the aspirations of disabled rights campaigners. The principal areas of concern were: the scope of the definition of disability in s.1, and in particular the exclusion of those with a history or reputation of disability, and those with a genetic predisposition to a disability; the exclusion of small firms from the employment provisions in Pt. II; the ability of employers and service providers to justify discrimination against disabled people in certain circumstances; the exclusion of education and transport from the right of access to goods and services under Pt. III; and the absence of a Commission with powers to investigate complaints of discrimination, to provide assistance to individuals in enforcing their rights, and to take enforcement action on its own account. The Bill was heavily amended during its passage through Parliament, more than doubling in length from 32 to 80 pages, and a number of these concerns were addressed in the process; for example, the definition of disability was extended to cover those with a history of disability, and measures were introduced in the areas of employment and transport, although falling some way short of the right not to be discriminated against advocated by many campaigners. Notwithstanding these amendments, the Disability Discrimination Act still fails to meet the aspirations of many disabled rights campaigners for comprehensive civil rights legislation, and is therefore unlikely to represent the last word of Parliament in this area.

A noteable feature of the Act is the extent to which it allows for the issue of regulations, Guidance and Codes of Practice to expand upon and clarify a number of its most fundamental aspects, for example, the definition of disability, and the duty of employers and service providers to make reasonable adjustments.

Part I of the Act defines disability as a physical or mental impairment which has, or has had, a substantial and long-term adverse effect on a person's ability to carry out normal day-to-day activities. This definition is supplemented by Scheds. 1 and 2, which allow for regulations to be made clarifying the definition, and s.3, which empowers the Secretary of State to issue guidance about the matters to be taken into account in determining whether an impairment has the necessary substantial or long-term adverse effect.

Part II makes it unlawful for an employer who has 20 or more employees to discriminate against a disabled employee or job applicant in relation to employment by treating that person less favourably, for a reason which relates to his or her disability, than the employer treats or would treat others. Unlike the legislation prohibiting discrimination on grounds of sex or race however, discrimination by an employer against a disabled person may be justified if the reason for it is both material to the circumstances of the particular case and substantial. There is no specific prohibition on indirect discrimination, but the Act places a duty on employers to make reasonable adjustments to working practices and the physical environment where these would place a disabled job applicant or employee at a substantial disadvantage in comparison with people who are not disabled. An unjustified failure to make a reasonable adjustment will amount to unlawful discrimination. Where an employer leases premises, the Act provides that the landlord must not unreasonably withhold consent to alterations which the employer needs to make in order to comply with the duty to make reasonable adjustments. Enforcement is by complaint to an industrial tribunal, and the remedies available are similar to those which apply in cases of sex and race discrimination, *i.e.* a declaration of rights, compensation and a recommendation that the employer take steps to remove or reduce the effect of the discrimination on the complainant. The Act does not set a maximum award of compensation. This part of the Act also outlaws discrimination in trade organisations and against contract workers.

Part III makes it unlawful for a service provider (*i.e.* a provider of goods, facilities or services) to discriminate against a disabled person by treating that person less favourably, for a reason which relates to his or her disability, than he treats or would treat others. It also places a duty on service providers to make reasonable adjustments in relation to the provision of services to disabled people. So, a service provider must take reasonable steps (i) to change any practice, policy or procedure which makes it impossible or unreasonably difficult for a disabled person to make use of a service which is provided to other members of the public, (ii) to remove or alter any physical barrier which makes it impossible or unreasonably difficult for a disabled person to make use of such a service, or to provide some alternative means of making the service accessible and (iii) to provide auxiliary aids or services which would make it easier for disabled people to use their services. As in the case of employment, discrimination by a service provider may be justified in certain circumstances, for example, where the treatment is necessary in order to ensure that health and safety is not endangered, or to enable the service provider to continue providing the service to other members of the public. The Government has indicated its intention to use its powers under the Act to set a financial limit on the duty to make adjustments. The provisions in Pt. III apply to all goods, facilities and services, with the exception of education and transport vehicles. Part III also makes it unlawful to discriminate against a disabled person in connection with the sale, letting and management of premises, for example, by refusing to sell or rent property to a disabled person, or by offering the property on worse terms than would be offered to anyone else. Enforcement under Pt. III is by way of complaint in the county court, and the remedies available are those available in the High Court. As with employment, there is no upper limit on compensation, although there is a power to set an upper limit on the damages which may be awarded for injury to feelings.

Part IV concerns education. As originally published, the Bill did not apply to education. The Government were however persuaded during the passage of the Bill through Parliament to strengthen the provisions of the Education Acts of 1993 (c. 35) and 1994 (c. 30) and the Further and Higher Education Act 1992 (c. 13) relating to the provision of information by schools, colleges, universities and local education authorities on arrangements and facilities for disabled pupils and students.

Part V contains a series of provisions empowering the Secretary of State for Transport to issue regulations setting a timetable for the achievement of a fully accessible public transport system by introducing minimum access standards for buses, trains, taxis and other public service vehicles. As originally published, the Bill was heavily criticised for making no provision for access to public transport. Indeed, during the debates on the Bill it was pointed out that, as a consequence of the exclusion of transport vehicles from the provisions on access to goods and services in Pt. III, a disabled person would have a right of access to a railway station, but no right to get onto a train. The Government were persuaded to use the opportunity presented by the Bill to set minimum access standards for taxis, public service vehicles and rail vehicles, with a timetable for implementation. The new requirements are likely to apply only to new vehicles, and do not extend to travel by air or sea.

Part VI provides for the establishment of a National Disability Council ("NDC") to advise the Government on general issues relating to discrimination against disabled people. The NDC also has a duty to draw up codes of practice at the request of the Secretary of State. Unlike the Equal Opportunities Commission and the Commission for Racial Equality, the NDC is not empowered to investigate complaints, to provide assistance to individuals in enforcing their rights before the courts and tribunals, or to take strategic enforcement action of its own accord. Nor will it have responsibility for advising the Government on employment matters, the giving of advice in that area remaining for the time being the preserve of the National Advisory Council on Employment of People with Disabilities. Separate provision is made in Sched. 8 for a Northern Ireland Disability Council.

Parts VII and VIII contain supplemental and miscellaneous provisions. In particular, s. 61 repeals the provisions of the Disabled Persons (Employment) Act 1944 (c. 10) relating to the register of disabled persons, the quota system which obliges employers with more than 20 employees to employ a three per cent quota of registered disabled persons, and the designated employment scheme whereby certain types of employment are reserved for disabled employees.

The Government's intention is that the Act will be implemented in a number of stages. At the time of writing the likely timing for commencement of various parts of the Act was as follows:
—the education provisions—from July 1996;
—protection in the field of employment—around the end of 1996;
—protection from being refused goods, facilities and services—around the end of 1996;
—the duty of service providers to make adjustments to practices, policies or procedures—1998;
—the duty of service providers to provide auxiliary aids and services—2000;
—the duty of service providers to remove physical barriers—2005.

ABBREVIATIONS

ACAS	:	Advisory, Conciliation and Arbitration Service.
A.D.A.	:	Americans with Disabilities Act 1990.
CEPDs	:	Committees for the Employment of People with Disabilities.
CORAD	:	Committee on Restrictions Against Disabled People.
CRE	:	Commission for Racial Equality.
DIAL	:	Disability Information and Advice Line Service.
DPTAC	:	Disabled Persons Transport Advisory Committee.
E.A.T.	:	Employment Appeal Tribunal.
EOC	:	Equal Opportunities Commission.
E.P.(C.)A. 1978	:	Employment Protection (Consolidation) Act 1978 (c.44).
NACEDP	:	National Advisory Council on Employment of People with Disabilities.
NDC	:	National Disability Council.
PACTs	:	Employment Service's Placing, Assessment and Counselling Teams.
PSVs	:	public service vehicles.
RADAR	:	Royal Association for Disability and Rehabilitation.
R.N.I.D.	:	Royal National Institute for the Deaf.
R.R.A.	:	Race Relations Act 1976 (c. 74).
S.D.A.	:	Sex Discrimination Act 1975 (c. 65).
T.U.L.R.A.	:	Trade Union and Labour Relations (Consolidation) Act 1992 (c. 51).
1847 Act	:	Town Police Clauses Act 1847.
1869 Act	:	Metropolitan Public Carriage Act 1869.

PART I

DISABILITY

Meaning of "disability" and "disabled person"

1.—(1) Subject to the provisions of Schedule 1, a person has a disability for the purposes of this Act if he has a physical or mental impairment which has a substantial and long-term adverse effect on his ability to carry out normal day-to-day activities.

(2) In this Act "disabled person" means a person who has a disability.

GENERAL NOTE

At the heart of the Act is the definition of "disability" in subs. (1). This definition proved to be a major source of controversy during the Act's passage through Parliament. It is based on a predominantly medical model of disability, in that it defines disability in terms of impairments and their effect on a person's ability to carry out "normal day-to-day activities". In contrast, the social model of disability favoured by many commentators views disability as a social construct whereby disabled people are handicapped by the organisation and structure of the society in which they live and work. This was acknowledged in the report of the Committee on Restrictions against Disabled People (CORAD, 1982), which stated:

> "There is no direct relationship between the degree of disability and the degree of handicap; adverse social and environmental factors can place the mildly disabled at a severe disadvantage and an enabling environment can reduce any disadvantage experienced by a severely disabled individual .... The frustrating experience of almost all disabled people is that not only are they often restricted by their own physical limitations, but they have imposed on them additional restrictions by the structure of the society in which they live." (paras. 2.2 and 2.3).

The definition adopted for the purposes of the Act was however defended by the Government as a "commonsense" definition based on the general perception of the population as to the meaning of disability. In the words of the Minister for Social Security and Disabled People, William Hague, the definition of disability;

> "... must fit a generally acceptable perception of what disability means to employers, to service providers, to disabled people and to the nation at large. It must also give as much certainty as possible to courts and tribunals .... Our definition would not be credible if it did not include every commonly accepted form of the term 'disability'. But the definition—and, consequently, the law—would not be credible if it embraced people who were not fairly or generally recognised as disabled." (*Hansard*, H.C., Standing Committee E, col. 73).

One important consequence of the adoption of this "commonsense" approach is that the definition does not include certain categories of people who might well be considered "disabled" in a broader sense of the word. In particular, the definition does not extend to people who are mistakenly believed to be disabled (for example, a person with a slight speech impediment who is mistakenly assumed to be mentally handicapped), or who may become disabled in the future (for example, a person who has a latent condition or is pre-symptomatic). The Government was however persuaded during the Act's passage through Parliament to extend the definition to cover those who have in the past had a disability, but who are no longer disabled: see the note to s.2.

The definition in this section has been described as a framework definition, with the detailed interpretation left to the schedules. Schedule 1 in particular contains extensive powers for the Government to make regulations: "... to clarify and confirm the definition in the future, rather than leaving wide areas of vague legislation to be interpreted by courts differently at different times." (Minister for Social Security and Disabled People, *Hansard*, H.C., Standing Committee E, col. 73). The Minister emphasised that it was "most important ... to have adequate powers to ensure that the detail can be re-examined in the light of experience and changes in medical knowledge. A once-and-for-all definition would be inadequate. Parliament needs to have the regulatory powers to enable it to be specific and to keep up to date with future medical developments." (*ibid.* col. 74).

In addition, s.3 gives the Secretary of State wide powers to issue guidance in relation to the definition, which must be taken into account by courts and tribunals where relevant.

The definition of "disability" may be broken down into the following six elements:

Physical or mental impairment. These key concepts are not defined by the Act, although Sched. 1, para. 1(1) provides that "mental impairment" includes an impairment resulting from or consisting of a mental illness only if the illness is a "clinically well-recognised illness". The Secretary of State is empowered to issue regulations providing for conditions of a prescribed description to be treated as or as not amounting to impairments, as the case may be (Sched. 1, para. 1(2)).

Attempts to include in the definition an express reference to sensory impairments were resisted, on the grounds that its inclusion would not add to the legal or medical meaning: "sensory disorders are always either physical or mental, and the word sensory, therefore, does not represent a genuinely separate category ... The terms physical and mental are intended to be seen in their widest sense and should comprehensively cover all forms of impairment." (Minister for Social Security and Disabled People, *Hansard*, H.C., Standing Committee E, col. 71). In an attempt to put the matter beyond doubt, the Minister added: "... the Government have drafted the Bill so that it will cover sensory impairments. Anyone reading the record of our proceedings will be left in no doubt whatever that that was the intention of the Committee and the Government" (*ibid.* col. 72).

The requirement that mental illness be 'clinically well-recognised' in order to fall within the definition is further evidence of the medical model underlying the definition, and is designed to avoid "the possibility of claims based on obscure conditions unrecognised by reputable clinicians, which courts and tribunals would find extremely difficult to assess" (*ibid.* col. 104). The Minister indicated that a mental illness would be regarded as 'clinically well-recognised' if there is "a reasonably substantial body of practitioners who accept that a condition exists" (*ibid.* col. 100), and suggested that such illnesses "would include ... schizophrenia, manic depression, and severe and extended depressive psychoses." (*ibid.* col. 104). However, the Minister added: "We are clear ... that it is no function of the [Act] to cover moods or mild eccentricities and to say that they constitute a disability." (*ibid.* col. 104). The Minister also indicated that the Government intends to use its power to issue regulations in order to exclude certain psychopathic or anti-social disorders and addictions from the coverage of the Act (*ibid.* col. 105). Examples of the sorts of conditions which it intends to exclude are kleptomania, pyromania, paedophilia and personality disorders including psychopathic disorders (*ibid.* col. 109).

Long-term and substantial adverse effect. The protection of the Act is restricted to people with impairments which have a "substantial and long-term adverse effect" on their ability to carry out normal day-to-day activities. The intention is to exclude those with minor or trivial conditions, or conditions which, although disabling, are only temporary (for example, short-term illness). The Government considered that "... the law would begin to seem ridiculous if we did not ensure that it related to people who have a long-term impairment.... We must have a sense of time and of the long-term nature of disability" (Minister for Social Security and Disabled People, *Hansard*, H.C., Standing Committee E, col. 77). Ministers were however careful to acknowledge that it is the effect of the impairment which is important, not the severity of the impairment itself: "The [Act] covers disabilities which have a substantial and long-term or recurring effect on the ability to carry out normal day-to-day activities. Such effects may well be, and frequently will be, caused by disabilities which are not severe. The focus is thus on the effects and not on the disability itself." (Minister of State, *Hansard*, H.L., Vol. 564, col. 1650).

Schedule 1, para. 2(1) provides that the effect of an impairment will be deemed to be a long-term effect, if (a) it has lasted at least 12 months, (b) it is likely to last for at least 12 months, or (c) it is likely to last for the rest of the life of the person affected (the latter designed to cover a person suffering from a terminal illness who is unlikely to live for 12 months, who might otherwise fall outwith the Act's protection). A person suffering from a condition which is intermittent or sporadic (for example, conditions such as epilepsy or multiple sclerosis) may be covered by Sched. 1, para. 2(2), which provides that an impairment which stops having a substantial adverse effect on a person's ability to carry out normal day-to-day activities will be treated as continuing to have that effect, however long the intervening period of good health, where the disabling effects of the impairment are likely to recur. Again, there are regulation-making powers which enable the Government to prescribe circumstances in which the likelihood of an effect recurring is to be disregarded (para. 2(3)), or the effects are to be treated as being, or as not being, long-term effects (para. 2(4)). The Government has indicated that it intends to use these powers to exclude conditions "in which the effects may recur and be substantial for a brief time, but for the overwhelming majority of someone's life they would be non-existent or virtually so.... Severe hay fever is one example." (Minister for Social Security and Disabled People, *Hansard*, H.C., Standing Committee E, col. 113).

'Substantial' is not defined by the Act. Schedule 1, para. 3 does however provide that severe disfigurement will be treated as having a substantial adverse effect on a person's ability to carry out normal day-to-day activities, although once again regulations may provide for circumstances in which a severe disfigurement is not to be treated as having that effect. The Government has indicated that it intends to use this power to exclude those with deliberately acquired disfigurements, such as tattoos or body piercing (*ibid.* col. 111).

Normal day-to-day activities. The definition of disability revolves around the ability of a person to carry out normal day-to-day activities, yet it is a truism that what is normal for one person may not be normal for another. This phrase is intended to refer to the activities of an ordinary, average person rather than those of a person with specialised skills or abilities, for example, a mountaineer or a concert-pianist; "... we say 'normal day-to-day activities' to avoid people thinking that it covers ability to participate in some specialised sport or activity that most of us would not be capable of anyway and would not regard as part of normal day-to-day life." (Minister for Social Security and Disabled People, *Hansard*, H.C., Standing Committee E, col. 120.) Schedule 1, para. 4, lists the categories of activity which are to be treated as normal day-to-day activities for the purposes of the definition, namely, mobility; manual dexterity; physical co-ordination; continence; ability to lift, carry or otherwise move everyday objects; speech, hearing or eyesight; memory or ability to concentrate, learn or understand; or the perception of the risk of physical danger. The list is intended to be exhaustive (Minister of State, *Hansard*, H.L., Vol. 564, col. 1671), although it may be added to by regulations. Regulations may also provide for circumstances in which an impairment will be deemed to affect a person's ability to carry out normal day-to-day activities, and vice versa.

Effect of medical or other treatment. Specific provision is made in Sched. 1, para. 6, for cases where measures are being taken to treat or correct an impairment, for example, through medical treatment or the use of a prosthesis or other aid. An obvious example would be a potentially disabling condition such as epilepsy or diabetes which is controlled by medication. In such cases the impairment will be deemed to have a substantial adverse effect on a person's ability to carry out normal day-to-day activities, if it would be likely to have such an effect were it not for the medical treatment or corrective measures. In other words, the effect of the impairment must be considered without taking account of any medical treatment or other intervention which is being used to treat or correct it. This does not however extend to those with impaired sight where the impairment is correctable by spectacles or contact lenses or by some other prescribed method, whether or not those aids are in fact used. This exception reflects the fact that the correction of impaired sight by spectacles and contact lenses is usually so effective that "people who wear spectacles or contact lenses would not generally think of themselves as disabled." (Minister for Social Security and Disabled People, *Hansard*, H.C., Standing Committee E, col. 122). The Secretary of State may issue regulations making a similar exception in relation to other impairments:

"For example, at the moment, people wearing hearing aids will be covered by the definition because hearing aids usually provide only a partial correction of a disability. Those people are still usually, and should be, seen as disabled. But if at some future date, as a result of improved technology, hearing aids became as completely effective as spectacles or contact lenses are today, it might be appropriate to exclude people in that situation from the general definition of disability." (*ibid.* col. 122).

The Minister did however add: "There is no group that I intend to exclude in the immediately foreseeable future." (*ibid.* col. 122).

Persons deemed to be disabled. Schedule 1, para. 7 provides for a range of circumstances in which persons may be deemed to be disabled. In particular, para. 7(1) provides that a person who was registered as disabled under the Disabled Persons (Employment) Act 1944 on January 12, 1995, and who is still registered as disabled on the date when para. 7 comes into force, will be deemed to be a disabled person for an initial period of three years from that date; a certificate of registration issued under s.6 of the 1944 Act will be conclusive evidence of the matters certified therein (para. 7(3)), and a document purporting to be a certificate of registration will be deemed to be genuine and to have been validly issued unless proved to the contrary (para. 7(4)). In addition, there is a general power whereby prescribed descriptions of person may be deemed by regulation to be disabled for the purposes of the Act (para. 7(5)). In both cases, circumstances may be prescribed in which a person who has been deemed to be disabled under these provisions should no longer be deemed to be disabled (para. 7(6)).

Progressive conditions. One of the most controversial aspects of the definition of disability concerns its application to progressive conditions such as cancer, Parkinson's disease and multiple sclerosis. The problem here is that a considerable period of time may elapse between the diagnosis of a person as suffering from a progressive condition, and the point in time when that condition can be said to have a substantial adverse effect on that person's ability to carry out normal day-to-day activities—indeed, the condition may never reach that stage—yet the person may well face discrimination as a result of the medical prognosis long before that stage. It may also be very difficult in practice to define the point in time at which someone with a progressive condition becomes 'disabled' within the s.1 definition. The solution adopted is that where a person has a progressive condition which has resulted in an impairment which has *some* effect, but not necessarily a substantial effect, on his ability to carry out normal day-to-day activities, that person will be deemed to fall within the definition of a disabled person if the likely prognosis is that the condition will result in his having an impairment which has a substantial adverse effect on his ability to carry out normal day-to-day activities. Schedule 1, para. 8(1), gives cancer, multiple sclerosis, muscular dystrophy and infection by the human immunodeficiency virus (HIV) as examples of progressive conditions, and para. 8(2) empowers the Secretary of State to make regulations deeming other conditions to be or not to be progressive. The inclusion of HIV as an example of a progressive condition was a result of concerted pressure during the passage of the Bill.

Crucially, the protection for those suffering from progressive conditions only arises from the point in time when a condition becomes symptomatic, in the sense that it begins to have an effect on a person's ability to carry out normal day-to-day activities. The protection does not apply while a potentially disabling condition, although diagnosed, remains latent. It could be argued that if it is right that a person should be protected from discrimination once he or she begins to show symptoms of a potentially disabling condition, there is an equally strong case for protecting a person from discrimination before he or she begins to show any such symptoms. As matters stand, however, the Act permits discrimination against a person who has been diagnosed as suffering from or at risk of a progressive condition, as long as that person remains pre-symptomatic. This places a person at risk of a potentially disabling condition at a significant disadvantage compared with someone who has already developed such a condition, and could be said to provide a positive incentive to discriminate before such a person manifests any symptoms of the condition. This issue is likely to become increasingly significant as more sophisticated and reliable diagnostic techniques become available, and in particular with the development of tests for a genetic predisposition to conditions such as Huntingdon's chorea, Alzheimer's disease and certain forms of cancer. According to the Minister,

"... except in a few well-publicised cases, genetic tests are not as yet a useful indicator of future actual disability. Their inclusion would open up the [Act] to large numbers of people who are clearly not, and may never become, disabled ... we cannot wander into a situation whereby, for some reason or another, potentially the entire population could claim protection under the [Act]." (*Hansard*, H.C., Vol. 257, col. 887).

On the other hand, as Baroness Jay observed in the House of Lords:

"The paradox which is possible in the present situation is that where genetic counselling, genetic testing and identifying genetic markers is potentially one of the most exciting and liberating developments in medical science at the end of the 20th century, if it becomes the case that people feel that identifying those markers in their own personal situation will lead to discrimination, they will be less likely to take advantage of those extraordinary scientific advances which may help their own condition and in which medical science may be able to help future generations of children" (*Hansard*, H.L., Vol. 564, col. 1713).

Past disabilities

2.—(1) The provisions of this Part and Parts II and III apply in relation to a person who has had a disability as they apply in relation to a person who has that disability.

(2) Those provisions are subject to the modifications made by Schedule 2.

(3) Any regulations or order made under this Act may include provision with respect to persons who have had a disability.

(4) In any proceedings under Part II or Part III of this Act, the question whether a person had a disability at a particular time ("the relevant time") shall be determined, for the purposes of this section, as if the provisions of, or made under, this Act in force when the act complained of was done had been in force at the relevant time.

(5) The relevant time may be a time before the passing of this Act.

GENERAL NOTE

This section was added to the Bill in the House of Lords following sustained Opposition pressure. It extends the s.1 definition, for the purposes of Pts. I, II and III of the Act, to cover those who have had a disability but who are no longer disabled. Initially, the Government took the view that the protection of the Act should only apply to those who are "commonly accepted as being disabled", and should not therefore extend to those who have been disabled in the past. However, the Government was persuaded that the exclusion of those who have had a disability from the Act's coverage might allow discrimination against, for example, those with a history of mental illness who have made a full recovery, but who continue to suffer discrimination on account of their previous illness. As the Minister stated in introducing the amendment:

"It has become increasingly clear that people who have had a disability, although they may be no longer disabled as such, share with people who are currently disabled a need for protection against discrimination in relation to their disability.... It is clearly a very important part of the whole process of recovery that someone who has been disabled is able not only to participate fully in employment and social activities but to feel confident in doing so.... In addition, we have been persuaded that it is not always possible to tell when a person has fully recovered from a disability and when the condition is no longer likely to recur. The inclusion of people in the [Act] who have had a disability removes the need for individuals, businesses, courts and tribunals to have to deal with this grey area." (*Hansard*, H.L., Vol. 564, col. 1655).

Subs. (2)

Note that in order to fall within the extended definition, the past disability must have had a long-term effect, in the sense that it must have lasted for at least 12 months: see Sched. 2, para. 5.

Subs. (4)

This makes clear that if a person alleges discrimination in respect of a past disability, the question of whether that person had a disability will be decided by reference to the definition of disability in force at the time of the alleged act of discrimination: "This makes clear that the Bill will cover people who have recovered before the Bill has passed and it will also ensure consistency of treatment between people who are currently disabled and those who have recovered from the same treatment." (Minister of State, *Hansard*, H.L., Vol. 564, col. 1656).

Guidance

3.—(1) The Secretary of State may issue guidance about the matters to be taken into account in determining—

(a) whether an impairment has a substantial adverse effect on a person's ability to carry out normal day-to-day activities; or

(b) whether such an impairment has a long-term effect.

(2) The guidance may, among other things, give examples of—

(a) effects which it would be reasonable, in relation to particular activities, to regard for purposes of this Act as substantial adverse effects;

(b) effects which it would not be reasonable, in relation to particular activities, to regard for such purposes as substantial adverse effects;

(c) substantial adverse effects which it would be reasonable to regard, for such purposes, as long-term;

(d) substantial adverse effects which it would not be reasonable to regard, for such purposes, as long-term.

(3) A tribunal or court determining, for any purpose of this Act, whether an impairment has a substantial and long-term adverse effect on a person's ability to carry out normal day-to-day activities, shall take into account any guidance which appears to it to be relevant.

(4) In preparing a draft of any guidance, the Secretary of State shall consult such persons as he considers appropriate.

(5) Where the Secretary of State proposes to issue any guidance, he shall publish a draft of it, consider any representations that are made to him about the draft and, if he thinks it appropriate, modify his proposals in the light of any of those representations.

(6) If the Secretary of State decides to proceed with any proposed guidance, he shall lay a draft of it before each House of Parliament.

(7) If, within the 40-day period, either House resolves not to approve the draft, the Secretary of State shall take no further steps in relation to the proposed guidance.

(8) If no such resolution is made within the 40-day period, the Secretary of State shall issue the guidance in the form of his draft.

(9) The guidance shall come into force on such date as the Secretary of State may appoint by order.

(10) Subsection (7) does not prevent a new draft of the proposed guidance from being laid before Parliament.

(11) The Secretary of State may—

(a) from time to time revise the whole or part of any guidance and re-issue it;

(b) by order revoke any guidance.

(12) In this section—

"40-day period", in relation to the draft of any proposed guidance, means—

(a) if the draft is laid before one House on a day later than the day on which it is laid before the other House, the period of 40 days beginning with the later of the two days, and

(b) in any other case, the period of 40 days beginning with the day on which the draft is laid before each House,

no account being taken of any period during which Parliament is dissolved or prorogued or during which both Houses are adjourned for more than 4 days; and

"guidance" means guidance issued by the Secretary of State under this section and includes guidance which has been revised and re-issued.

GENERAL NOTE

This section gives the Secretary of State wide powers to issue guidance in relation to the definition of disability. Any such guidance must be taken into account by a court or tribunal where it appears to it to be relevant (subs. (3)). Subsections (4) to (12) lay down the detailed procedures for the issue, revision and revocation of guidance under this section, which is subject to the negative resolution procedure.

PART II

EMPLOYMENT

Discrimination by employers

Discrimination against applicants and employees

4.—(1) It is unlawful for an employer to discriminate against a disabled person—

(a) in the arrangements which he makes for the purpose of determining to whom he should offer employment;

(b) in the terms on which he offers that person employment; or

(c) by refusing to offer, or deliberately not offering, him employment.

(2) It is unlawful for an employer to discriminate against a disabled person whom he employs—

(a) in the terms of employment which he affords him;

(b) in the opportunities which he affords him for promotion, a transfer, training or receiving any other benefit;

(c) by refusing to afford him, or deliberately not affording him, any such opportunity; or

(d) by dismissing him, or subjecting him to any other detriment.

(3) Subsection (2) does not apply to benefits of any description if the employer is concerned with the provision (whether or not for payment) of benefits of that description to the public, or to a section of the public which includes the employee in question, unless—

(a) that provision differs in a material respect from the provision of the benefits by the employer to his employees; or

(b) the provision of the benefits to the employee in question is regulated by his contract of employment; or

(c) the benefits relate to training.

(4) In this Part "benefits" includes facilities and services.

(5) In the case of act which constitutes discrimination by virtue of section 55, this section also applies to discrimination against a person who is not disabled.

(6) This section applies only in relation to employment at an establishment in Great Britain.

GENERAL NOTE

This section makes it unlawful for an employer to discriminate against a disabled person (including a person who has had a disability: see s.2) in relation to employment. It is intended to be comprehensive in its coverage. It prohibits discrimination in all aspects of employment, including recruitment, terms of employment, promotion, training and dismissal, and is "intended to cover ... the use of standards, criteria, administrative methods, work practices or procedures that adversely affect a disabled person." (Parliamentary Under-Secretary of State, *Hansard*, H.C., Standing Committee E, col. 142). The wording closely follows that of the legislation outlawing discrimination in the employment field on grounds of sex and race (see the Sex Discrimination Act 1975 (c. 74), s.6, and the Race Relations Act 1976 (c. 65), s.4), and decisions on the interpretation of those provisions are likely to be in point here also.

The right not to be discriminated against covers employees and applicants for employment, including contract workers (see the note to s.12), apprentices, and self-employed people who contract personally to do any work (s.68(1)), but the protection only applies in relation to employment at an establishment in Great Britain (see below). There are specific exclusions in s.64 covering the armed forces, prison officers, firefighters and certain other occupations, and police officers also fall outside the scope of the Act's provisions, but the most significant limitation on the scope of the protection is undoubtedly the exclusion of employers with fewer than 20 employees (see the note to s.7). Curiously, while the Act covers partnerships in their capacity as employers, it does not prohibit discrimination for reasons relating to disability against partners or prospective partners themselves. This contrasts with the sex and race discrimination legislation, which expressly prohibits discrimination against partners or prospective partners, albeit only for firms consisting of six or more partners in the case of discrimination on racial grounds (S.D.A., s.11; R.R.A., s.10). The Minister's explanation for the difference of approach in this context is not wholly convincing: "Since partners put their own resources into a firm, it is not clear how the question of the cost of adjustment should be dealt with, and in particular to what extent it would be reasonable for the disabled person to seek a contribution from the other partner or partners to meet the cost of the necessary adjustments." (*Hansard*, H.L., Vol. 564, col. 1782).

Employment at an establishment in Great Britain. This is to be construed in accordance with s.68(2) to (5).

Arrangements. According to the Minister, "The broad term 'arrangements' has deliberately been used [in s.4(1)(a) and s.6(1)] to cover anything done by or for an employer as part of his recruitment process or in making available opportunities in employment. It would not only include work practices and procedures, so far as such practices or procedures have any bearing on determining who is offered employment or to whom such opportunities are made available; it would go wider than that." (*Hansard*, H.C., Standing Committee E, col. 142).

There are specific provisions in s.11 relating to discriminatory job advertisements. If an advertisement indicates, or might reasonably be taken to indicate, that the employer might discriminate against a disabled applicant, then that advertisement will give rise to a presumption of discrimination. For such a presumption to arise, the disabled person must have applied for and been refused the employment in question, and must have presented a complaint to a tribunal under s.8 of the Act. Where these conditions are satisfied, the tribunal will presume that the employer's reason for not offering the employment to the complainant was related to his disability, unless the employer is able to prove to the contrary. See the note to s.11.

The Act contains no measures expressly dealing with medical examinations, despite evidence that pre-employment health screening is one of the most common ways in which disabled job applicants are discriminated against, by being screened out at an early stage in the selection process. At the Committee stage in the House of Commons, the Opposition tabled an amendment which would have made it unlawful for an employer, in advance of making an offer of employment, to require candidates to undergo a medical examination or to ask questions about the nature or severity of an applicant's disability, except in order to ascertain the applicant's ability to perform job related functions, or to conduct equal opportunities monitoring. The amendment was however rejected by the Government: "In general, employers should be free to use whatever recruitment procedures best meet their needs and to conduct medical examinations of employees where that seems appropriate." (Parliamentary Under-Secretary of State, *Hansard*, H.C., Standing Committee E, col. 151). In the Minister's view, forbidding medical examinations in all but the circumstances contemplated by the proposed amendment could have worked to the detriment of disabled applicants and employees: "For example, a prospective employer would not be able to ask questions about whether an applicant needed special arrangements to attend an interview, or about his ability to use ancillary facilities such as car parks and rest rooms. Perhaps more seriously, in some industries, an employer could not operate compulsory medical examinations for employees doing work involving a health risk." (*ibid.* col. 152). The Minister expressed sympathy "with the intention of avoiding the institution of a spurious system of medical examination intentionally designed to discriminate", but considered that the Act "deals with that possibility in other ways." (*ibid.* col. 160). Even in the absence of any specific restriction on pre-employment medical screening, an employer who insists on a medical check for a disabled applicant but not for other, non-disabled applicants might still be held to have discriminated unlawfully against the disabled applicant, as such a requirement would almost certainly be held to constitute less favourable treatment of that person for a reason relating to his or her disability; however, such treatment would only constitute unlawful discrimination if the employer could not show that his insistence on the medical check was justified, within the meaning of s.5(3): see the note to s.5 below.

Meaning of "discrimination"

5.—(1) For the purposes of this Part, an employer discriminates against a disabled person if—

(a) for a reason which relates to the disabled person's disability, he treats him less favourably than he treats or would treat others to whom that reason does not or would not apply; and

(b) he cannot show that the treatment in question is justified.

(2) For the purposes of this Part, an employer also discriminates against a disabled person if—

(a) he fails to comply with a section 6 duty imposed on him in relation to the disabled person; and

(b) he cannot show that his failure to comply with that duty is justified.

(3) Subject to subsection (5), for the purposes of subsection (1) treatment is justified if, but only if, the reason for it is both material to the circumstances of the particular case and substantial.

(4) For the purposes of subsection (2), failure to comply with a section 6 duty is justified if, but only if, the reason for the failure is both material to the circumstances of the particular case and substantial.

(5) If, in a case falling within subsection (1), the employer is under a section 6 duty in relation to the disabled person but fails without justification to comply with that duty, his treatment of that person cannot be justified under subsection (3) unless it would have been justified even if he had complied with the section 6 duty.

(6) Regulations may make provision, for purposes of this section, as to circumstances in which—

(a) treatment is to be taken to be justified;

(b) failure to comply with a section 6 duty is to be taken to be justified;

(c) treatment is to be taken not to be justified;

(d) failure to comply with a section 6 duty is to be taken not to be justified.

(7) Regulations under subsection (6) may, in particular—

(a) make provision by reference to the cost of affording any benefit; and

(b) in relation to benefits under occupational pension schemes, make provision with a view to enabling uniform rates of contributions to be maintained.

GENERAL NOTE

The definition of discrimination contained in this section differs in several important respects from that contained in the sex and race discrimination legislation. It retains the familiar concept of direct discrimination which is used in the Sex Discrimination Act 1975 and the Race Relations Act 1976, by providing that an employer discriminates against a disabled person if, for a reason which relates to that person's disability, he treats him less favourably than he treats or would treat others to whom that reason does not apply. However, in sharp contrast with direct discrimination on the grounds of sex or race, under these provisions less favourable treatment of a disabled person may be justified in certain circumstances. This difference reflects the fact that while a person's sex or race will rarely have a bearing on their ability to do a job, a person's disability may well have. Less favourable treatment of a disabled person is justified if the reason for it "is both material to the circumstances of the particular case and substantial" (subs. (3)).

The second major difference is that unlike the S.D.A. and the R.R.A., this definition does not expressly prohibit indirect discrimination (*i.e.* the application of a requirement or condition which has a disproportionate impact on a particular group or class). It does however provide, in subs. (2), that an employer discriminates against a disabled person if he fails to comply with the duty imposed on him under s.6 to make reasonable adjustments in relation to the disabled person (again, subject to a defence if the employer can show that the failure to comply with that duty is justified), and the Government has claimed that this provides effective protection against indirect discrimination:

> "The right has been formulated to leave few, if any, of the ways in which disability can indirectly disadvantage a person outside the scope of the right. The intention is that any situation where an employer imposes a condition or requirement which might exclude a disabled person will be covered by the basic right and the duty on employers to make a reasonable adjustment." (White Paper, *Ending discrimination against disabled people*, Cm. 2729, 1995, para. 3.8).

Subs. (1)

Others to whom that reason does not or would not apply. The appropriate comparison for these purposes is with the treatment of a person to whom the reason for the less favourable treatment does not (or would not) apply, and not with the treatment of a person who does not have the disability in question. To use the example of an employee with arthritis who is refused employment because he or she cannot type, the appropriate comparison is with the treatment of a person to whom that reason does not apply (*i.e.* a person who is able to type), and not with a person who is unable to type because he or she has never learned to do so:

"... if the employer is rejecting people who cannot type, he will be treating more favourably those who can. The person with arthritis who did not get the job can show that he or she was treated less favourably than the person with typing abilities who did. The employer may well be able to justify that treatment—for example, if a disabled person was not adequately able to do the job, even taking account of any reasonable adjustment. But at least the disabled person would have to be given the consideration due under the [Act]." (Minister of State, *Hansard*, H.L. Vol. 566, col. 120).

If the comparison were with a person who is not disabled, the employer might have been able to argue that he was not treating the disabled applicant less favourably than a person without that disability, because he was treating all those who cannot type in the same way; the result would have been that the disabled applicant would have had no ground for complaint, even though the employment was refused for a reason which related to that person's disability.

Subss. (3) and (4)

Material to the circumstances of the particular case and substantial. Less favourable treatment of a disabled person is justified if the reason for it is both material to the circumstances of the particular case and substantial. This phrase was substituted for the original, more detailed version of the justification defence at a late stage in the Parliamentary proceedings. The earlier version focused on the employer's reasonable opinion as to the suitability of the disabled person for the employment in question, and was heavily criticised for its subjective approach (a similar approach is however retained for the purposes of Pt. III: see the note to s.20). Although not open to criticism on that particular ground, the present version offers precious little guidance as to the scope of the defence, although matters may become clearer if and when regulations are made under subs. (6) providing for circumstances in which an employer's actions are to be deemed to be, or not to be, justified. To be "material", a reason has to be related to the individual circumstances of the case in question, rather than, for example, being based on ill-informed assumptions about the effects of disability; and in the context of the duty to make adjustments, the Government has indicated that "substantial" is intended to exclude minor or trivial matters: see the note to s.6(1).

Subs. (5)

Where an employer has discriminated against a disabled person by treating that person less favourably for a reason relating to his or her disability, and has also failed without justification to comply with his duty under s.6 to make reasonable adjustments in relation to that person, the employer's treatment of that person cannot be justified under subs. (3), unless it would have been justified even if he had complied with his duty to make reasonable adjustments.

Subs. (7)

The power to make regulations under subs. (6) deeming less favourable treatment, or a failure to comply with a s.6 duty, to be justified in certain circumstances, includes the power to stipulate that discrimination may be justified by reference to the cost of affording a benefit, and, in relation to benefits under occupational pension schemes, to make provision enabling uniform rates of contributions to be maintained. These provisions form part of a series of measures in the Act designed to address the specific issue of discrimination in relation to occupational pension benefits (see the notes to s.6(11) and s.17). They reflect the Government's view that employers should in appropriate circumstances be allowed to justify less favourable treatment of disabled people on account of the increased risks and extra costs of providing such benefits:

"Where a disabled applicant [to an occupational pension scheme] has a pre-existing medical condition which is likely to increase the risk of ill-health retirement or death in service it is important that employers should be able to take just as much account of that as they would if the person were not disabled." (Minister of State, *Hansard*, H.L., Vol. 566, col. 995).

However, since it would clearly run counter to the whole philosophy of the legislation if the less favourable treatment of a disabled person could be justified on the basis of assumptions about that person's health and life expectancy which were ill-founded, the Government has been at pains to stress that any such assumptions must be based on sound evidence if they are to play a part in the calculation of risk in relation to disabled people:

"... employers will want to ensure that their decisions are based on sound evidence; for example, actuarial or medical evidence. Many disabled people have disabilities which do not affect their life expectancy or likelihood of ill-health retirement and these [provisions] will make sure they can no longer be unfairly denied access to an employer's pension scheme." (Minister of State, *ibid.* col. 995).

During the Bill's passage through the House of Lords, the Minister, rejecting an opposition amendment which sought to disapply the power to deem less favourable treatment in relation to occupational pension schemes to be justified, suggested that there might be two types of case in which occupational benefits for a disabled person might justifiably be less than those for a non-disabled person:

"The first is that pensions are almost always linked to pay. If there is a justifiable difference in pay received by the two workers—perhaps, for example, because the disability means that the disabled person has to work fewer hours—it must be right that the pension can also reflect that difference ... The second reason is that the disability might create actuarial risks which the employer or the pension fund should not have to take. For example, depending on the circumstances, we believe that an employer who takes on an employee who is terminally ill can be justified in refusing such a person cover under any scheme he operates for death-in-service benefits. The removal of any justification in the case of these benefits and payments would place quite unwarranted burdens on employers." (Minister of State, *Hansard*, H.L., Vol. 566, cols. 169 and 170).

The Government intends to consult on the use of the regulation-making powers, and in particular on what kind of additional cost might justify less favourable treatment of a disabled person; in moving the amendments at Third Reading in the House of Lords, the Minister declared his wish to "put on the record the fact that we have absolutely no intention legislating for what might be trivial costs." (*ibid.* col. 1000).

Duty of employer to make adjustments

6.—(1) Where—

(a) any arrangements made by or on behalf of an employer, or

(b) any physical feature of premises occupied by the employer,

place the disabled person concerned at a substantial disadvantage in comparison with persons who are not disabled, it is the duty of the employer to take such steps as it is reasonable, in all the circumstances of the case, for him to have to take in order to prevent the arrangements or feature having that effect.

(2) Subsection (1)(a) applies only in relation to—

(a) arrangements for determining to whom employment should be offered;

(b) any term, condition or arrangements on which employment, promotion, a transfer, training or any other benefit is offered or afforded.

(3) The following are examples of steps which an employer may have to take in relation to a disabled person in order to comply with subsection (1)—

(a) making adjustments to premises;

(b) allocating some of the disabled person's duties to another person;

(c) transferring him to fill an existing vacancy;

(d) altering his working hours;

(e) assigning him to a different place of work;

(f) allowing him to be absent during working hours for rehabilitation, assessment or treatment;

(g) giving him, or arranging for him to be given, training;

(h) acquiring or modifying equipment;

(i) modifying instructions or reference manuals;

(j) modifying procedures for testing or assessment;

(k) providing a reader or interpreter;

(l) providing supervision.

(4) In determining whether it is reasonable for an employer to have to take a particular step in order to comply with subsection (1) regard shall be had, in particular, to—

(a) the extent to which taking the step would prevent the effect in question;

(b) the extent to which it is practicable for the employer to take the step;

(c) the financial and other costs which would be incurred by the employer in taking the step and the extent to which taking it would disrupt any of his activities;

(d) the extent of the employer's financial and other resources;

(e) the availability to the employer of financial or other assistance with respect to taking the step.

This subsection is subject to any provision of regulations made under subsection (8).

(5) In this section, "the disabled person concerned" means—

(a) in the case of arrangements for determining to whom employment should be offered, any disabled person who is, or has notified the employer that he may be, an applicant for that employment;

(b) in any other case, a disabled person who is—

(i) an applicant for the employment concerned; or

(ii) an employee of the employer concerned.

(6) Nothing in this section imposes any duty on an employer in relation to a disabled person if the employer does not know, and could not reasonably be expected to know—

(a) in the case of an applicant or potential applicant, that the disabled person concerned is, or may be, an applicant for the employment; or

(b) in any case, that that person has a disability and is likely to be affected in the way mentioned in subsection (1).

(7) Subject to the provisions of this section, nothing in this Part is to be taken to require an employer to treat a disabled person more favourably than he treats or would treat others.

(8) Regulations may make provision, for the purposes of subsection (1)—

(a) as to circumstances in which arrangements are, or a physical feature is, to be taken to have the effect mentioned in that subsection;

(b) as to circumstances in which arrangements are not, or a physical feature is not, to be taken to have that effect;

(c) as to circumstances in which it is reasonable for an employer to have to take steps of a prescribed description;

(d) as to steps which it is always reasonable for an employer to have to take;

(e) as to circumstances in which it is not reasonable for an employer to have to take steps of a prescribed description;

(f) as to steps which it is never reasonable for an employer to have to take;

(g) as to things which are to be treated as physical features;

(h) as to things which are not to be treated as such features.

(9) Regulations made under subsection (8)(c), (d), (e) or (f) may, in particular, make provision by reference to the cost of taking the steps concerned.

(10) Regulations may make provision adding to the duty imposed on employers by this section, including provision of a kind which may be made under subsection (8).

(11) This section does not apply in relation to any benefit under an occupational pension scheme or any other benefit payable in money or money's worth under a scheme or arrangement for the benefit of employees in respect of—

(a) termination of service;

(b) retirement, old age or death;

(c) accident, injury, sickness or invalidity; or

(d) any other prescribed matter.

(12) This section imposes duties only for the purpose of determining whether an employer has discriminated against a disabled person; and accordingly a breach of any such duty is not actionable as such.

GENERAL NOTE

This section contains the all-important provisions which set out the duty of an employer to make reasonable adjustments to his or her employment arrangements and premises in order to help a disabled person overcome the practical effects of a disability. The duty exists where any arrangements made by or on behalf of the employer, or any physical feature of premises occupied by the employer, place a disabled person at a "substantial disadvantage" in comparison with people who are not disabled. The duty does not however arise in the abstract: employers are not required to adapt their working arrangements or their premises "in anticipation of possibly having a disabled applicant or employee at some point in the future." (White Paper, *Ending discrimination against disabled people*, Cm. 2729, 1995, para. 3.7). Rather, the duty only arises in respect of a disabled person who is an employee of the employer concerned, or who has applied (or notified the employer that he may apply) for the employment in question (subs. (5)). In the case of applicants (including potential applicants) for employment, the employer is not under a duty to make adjustments if he does not know, and could not reasonably be expected to know, that the disabled person concerned is or may be an applicant for the employment (subs. (6)(b)). In general, a disabled person is protected from unlawful discrimination whether or not the employer knows of that person's disability (see the note to s.5); however, the duty to make adjustments does not arise unless the employer knows, or could reasonably be expected to know, that the person has a disability which is likely to place him or her at a substantial disadvantage in comparison with persons who are not disabled (subs. (6)(a)).

The duty of adjustment, as expressed in subs. (1), requires the employer to take any steps which it is reasonable for him or her to have to take in order to overcome any substantial disadvantage to a disabled applicant or employee caused by the employer's employment arrangements or premises. This may involve the employer in taking one step, or perhaps a combination of steps, in order to comply with this duty. Subsection (3) gives a number of examples of steps, one or more of which might be appropriate in particular circumstances, while subs. (4) lists a number of factors encompassing issues of practicability, cost and effectiveness which must be considered in determining whether it is reasonable for an employer to have to take a particular step or combination of steps. They are:

(a) *the extent to which taking the step would prevent the effect in question*. It might not be reasonable to require an employer to take a step which involves little benefit to the disabled employee.

(b) *the extent to which it is practicable for the employer to take the step*. During the Bill's passage through Parliament, the Minister of State commented: "it might not be reasonable for an employer needing an employee urgently to have to wait for an adjustment to be made to allow a disabled person to be employed. That is more likely to be the case with smaller employers but could apply to larger ones." (*Hansard*, H.C., Vol. 566, col. 185).

(c) *the financial and other costs which would be incurred by the employer in taking the step and the extent to which taking it would disrupt any of his activities*. Many adjustments will involve little or no cost to the employer (see below). "[I]t would not normally be reasonable for an employer to spend fewer resources on retaining a disabled person than on recruiting a replacement." (*ibid*. col. 185).

(d) *the extent of the employer's financial and other resources*. "Although the size of a business is not necessarily an indication of the resources available, it is more reasonable for an employer with considerable resources to make an adjustment with a significant cost than for an employer with few resources." (*ibid*. col. 185).

(e) *the availability to the employer of financial or other assistance with respect to taking the step*. "A step is not unreasonable if the availability of help from an outside organisation or from the disabled person would compensate for the factors that would have made it unreasonable. For example, it might be unreasonable on grounds of costs for a particular employer to provide a laptop computer with a Braille keyboard. However, if a suitable one could be loaned or borrowed when needed, for example under the Access to Work scheme, or if the individual has a suitable one he could provide, then the employer could not successfully claim that provision of the laptop was unreasonable because of the cost." (*ibid*. col. 185).

Subsection (8) contains a number of powers to make regulations relating to the duty of reasonable adjustment. Regulations may provide, for example, for circumstances in which arrangements or physical features must be deemed to place, or not to place, a disabled person at a substantial disadvantage, and may prescribe steps which are or are not reasonable for an employer to have to take in specific circumstances, and steps which it is always or never reasonable for an employer to have to take. There is a specific provision in subs. (9) which allows the issue of reasonableness to be determined by reference to the cost of taking the steps concerned. The Government indicated during the passage of the Bill that it has no immediate intention of using this power to put a financial ceiling on the concept of reasonable adjustment in employment cases, preferring to leave the issue of the extent of reasonable cost to the judgment of industrial tribunals on general principles (including those set out in subs. (4)), in conjunction with the guidance in the forthcoming Code of Practice:

"We believe that the concept of 'reasonable' will ensure that employers are not faced with an undue cost burden in making adjustments, but wish nonetheless to have regulation-making powers available in case that should prove not to be the case ... The Government have made clear from the outset that, while there is no upper financial limit to the duty on the employer to make a reasonable adjustment, should the need arise, Ministers would be prepared to consider setting a financial cap." (Minister of State, *Hansard*, H.L., Vol. 564, cols. 1761, 1768).

A financial limit is however planned for the provisions relating to goods, facilities and services in Pt. III (see the note to s.21).

It seems that the Government took the decision not to impose a financial ceiling on adjustments in employment cases in the light of evidence that in most cases adjustments will have a nil or minimal cost. The Compliance Cost Assessment for the Act assumes an average cost of £200 per disabled employee for the 10 per cent of cases where a disabled employee is likely to require an adjustment. In those relatively few cases where the cost of an adjustment would be much higher, the question of whether an employer should be required to make that adjustment will be decided in accordance with the general test of reasonableness, taking into account the extent of the employer's resources, the availability of outside financial assistance, etc. The experience of the United States under the Americans with Disabilities Act 1990 suggests that in most cases the necessary adaptations can be made at modest cost. The Minister reported during the debates on the Bill that in 43 per cent of cases under the A.D.A., reasonable accommodation by the employer cost nothing, merely involving the moving of furniture or the introduction of different working hours. A survey by the Job Accommodation Network in 1987 revealed that the average cost of adjustments made by employers in the United States amounted to only $200, while 68 per cent of adjustments cost less than $500; in only 5 per cent of cases did the cost exceed $5,000 (*Evaluation Survey*, President's Commission on Employment of People with Disabilities, Washington, D.C., 1987).

A failure on the part of an employer to comply with the duty to make reasonable adjustments in relation to a disabled person will itself be an act of unlawful discrimination under s.4, unless the employer can show that his failure to comply with that duty is justified, in the sense that the reason for the failure is both material to the circumstances of the particular case and substantial (see the note to s.5). Where an employer has discriminated against a disabled person by treating that person less favourably for a reason relating to his or her disability, and has also failed without justification to comply with his duty to make reasonable adjustments in relation to that person, the employer's treatment of that person cannot be justified under s.5(3), unless it would have been justified even if he had complied with his duty to make reasonable adjustments under this section: see s.5(5).

It is now widely accepted that disability is a social construct, in that disabled people are handicapped not so much by their impairments as by the organisation and structure of the society in which they live and work. This was acknowledged in the report of the Committee on Restrictions against Disabled People (CORAD, 1982), which stated:

"There is no direct relationship between the degree of disability and the degree of handicap; adverse social and environmental factors can place the mildly disabled at a severe disadvantage and an enabling environment can reduce any disadvantage experienced by a severely disabled individual ... the frustrating experience of almost all disabled people is that not only are they often restricted by their own physical limitations, but they have imposed on them additional restrictions by the structure of the society in which they live." (paras. 2.2 and 2.3).

The duty to make reasonable adjustments in this section is a recognition of the fact that, while "the majority of disabled people who want to work need no, or only very modest help ... some disabled people need practical help to enable them to get a job." (White Paper, *Ending discrimination against disabled people*, Cm. 2729, 1995, para. 3.5).

Subs. (1)

Arrangements made by or on behalf of an employer. The term "arrangements", as defined in subs. (2), applies only in relation to arrangements for determining who should be offered employment, and to any term, condition or arrangements on which employment, promotion, transfer, training or any other benefit is offered or afforded. According to the Minister; "The broad term 'arrangements' has deliberately been used [in s.4(1)(a) and subs. (1)] to cover anything done by or for an employer as part of his recruitment process or in making available opportunities in employment. It would not only include work practices and procedures, so far as such practices or procedures have any bearing on determining who is offered employment or to whom such opportunities are made available; it would go wider than that." (*Hansard*, H.C., Standing Committee E, col. 142). Examples of arrangements which might place a disabled person at a disadvantage include: working times which are inconvenient because of the needs of carers or the difficulty of negotiating rush-hour crowds; instructions which are difficult to understand for a person with a learning disability; or, where the employer has car parking facilities, not allocating a parking space to a disabled employee who finds it very difficult to use public transport. There is a power in subs. (8) to make regulations as to the circumstances in which arrangements are or are not to be taken to place a disabled person at a substantial disadvantage.

Premises occupied by the employer. The duty of employers to make reasonable adjustments to premises where some physical feature of those premises causes substantial disadvantage to a disabled person applies only in relation to premises which are occupied by the employer:

> "employers are not under a duty to make reasonable adjustments in respect of, for example, features of the disabled person's private house. It would also not apply to some other employer's premises in the case, say, of a travelling salesman or to the disabled person's home in the case of a homeworker." (Minister of State, *Hansard,* H.L., Vol. 566, col. 184).

Examples of physical features of premises which might place a disabled person at a disadvantage include: doors that are too narrow for someone using a wheelchair; taps that someone with arthritis cannot turn; or lighting too dim for someone with restricted vision.

The duty of an employer to make reasonable adjustments to premises may present problems where the employer occupies premises under a lease, the terms of which prevent or restrict the occupier from making alterations to the premises. In those circumstances, the terms of the lease are overridden by s.16 of the Act, which entitles the occupier to alter the premises, with the written consent of the landlord, in order to comply with a duty to make adjustments under this section. See the note to s.16.

Part M of the Building Regulations 1988 (revised in 1991) contains mandatory requirements for new non-domestic buildings (including substantial extensions) relating to the provision of access and facilities for disabled people. In the Bill as originally published, the duty to make adjustments did not apply to a physical feature of a building or extension erected in compliance with any requirement of the Building Regulations relating to disabled people. That exemption was subsequently dropped from the Bill at Report stage in the House of Commons (*Hansard*, H.C., Vol. 257, col. 891), but the Government is considering making regulations under subs. (8)(e) to similar effect. The effect would be that where a building or extension was constructed in accordance with Building Regulations relating to disabled people, the duty to make adjustments would not apply to any aspect of a feature specifically covered by those regulations (*e.g.* the width of a door), as long as that feature continued to meet the requirements which were in force when the building or extension was constructed (an important *caveat* in view of the fact that Pt. M contains no mechanism for continuing control over buildings). The exemption would not apply to other aspects of physical features which were not covered by Building Regulations. The Government is contemplating the introduction of a similar exemption for buildings or extensions constructed in accordance with a requirement of the British Standard on "Access for the disabled to buildings" (BS5810).

Substantial disadvantage. The duty to make adjustments only arises where the employer's arrangements or premises place a disabled person at a "substantial disadvantage" in comparison with people who are not disabled. In Committee, the Minister indicated that the use of the term "substantial" is intended to exclude minor and trivial disadvantage:

> "To a lawyer, the word 'substantial' literally means of substance. It does not necessarily mean the large, grand, highly significant object that a layman might imagine. . . . The word 'substantial' is included to remove the possibility of the most minor things being brought into play." (Parliamentary Under-Secretary of State, *Hansard*, H.C., Standing Committee E, col. 196).

Subs. (3)

Other examples of steps which it might be reasonable for an employer to take are: providing signers, hearing aid-compatible telephones or minicom facilities, or allocating a dedicated parking space.

Subs. (11)

This subsection disapplies the duty of reasonable adjustment in relation to benefits under occupational pension schemes and certain other similar benefits, and should be read together with the provisions in s.5(7) which allow less favourable treatment of disabled employees in certain circumstances: see the note to s.5 above. The case for excluding the duty was explained in the following terms:

> "Where a disabled person has been lawfully refused access to part of an occupational pension scheme—for example, based on a reasonable belief that his health condition presents an unreasonable risk—the employer will not have to consider ways in which his overall remuneration package can be brought up to the level enjoyed by other employees; for example, by increasing his salary." (Minister of State, *Hansard*, H.L., Vol. 566, col. 1001).

So, for example, if regulations were to be made under s.5(7)(b) enabling employers to maintain uniform rates of contribution in relation to occupational pension schemes, so that a disabled person could be required to pay the same rate of contributions as other employees although not eligible for some of the benefits of the scheme, an employer would not be required to make a reasonable adjustment to overcome the disadvantage to the disabled employee.

Exemption for small businesses

7.—(1) Nothing in this Part applies in relation to an employer who has fewer than 20 employees.

(2) The Secretary of State may by order amend subsection (1) by substituting a different number (not greater than 20) for the number for the time being specified there.

(3) In this section—

"anniversary" means the anniversary of the coming into force of this section; and

"review" means a review of the effect of this section.

(4) Before making any order under subsection (2), the Secretary of State shall conduct a review.

(5) Unless he has already begun or completed a review under subsection (4), the Secretary of State shall begin to conduct a review immediately after the fourth anniversary.

(6) Any review shall be completed within nine months.

(7) In conducting any review, the Secretary of State shall consult—

(a) such organisations representing the interests of employers as he considers appropriate; and

(b) such organisations representing the interests of disabled persons in employment or seeking employment as he considers appropriate.

(8) If, on completing a review, the Secretary of State decides to make an order under subsection (2), he shall make such an order to come into force not later than one year after the commencement of the review.

(9) If, on completing a review, the Secretary of State decides not to make such an order, he shall not later than one year after the commencement of the review lay before Parliament a report—

(a) summarising the results of the review; and

(b) giving the reasons for his decision.

(10) Any report made by the Secretary of State under subsection (9) shall include a summary of the views expressed to him in his consultations.

General Note

The exemption of small businesses (*i.e.* employers with fewer than 20 employees) from the employment provisions of the Act is one of its most controversial measures. The effect of the exemption is to exclude 96 per cent of employers from the duty not to discriminate against disabled persons, and while Government statistics indicate that 83 per cent of employees will be covered by the Act (Parliamentary Under-Secretary of State, *Hansard*, H.C., Standing Committee E, col. 248), if one includes self-employed workers (who come within the scope of the protection where they contract personally to do any work: s.68(1)), the coverage falls to 65 per cent (Prescott-Clarke, *Employment and Handicap*, 1990, SCPR, London). There is a similar exemption in the Disabled Persons (Employment) Act 1944 (c. 10), in that the provisions in s.9 of that Act requiring employers to employ a 3 per cent quota of registered disabled employees only apply to those employing 20 or more employees (s.9 and the associated provisions are prospectively repealed by s.62(7), from a date to be announced). The Government has indicated that 20 was chosen as the appropriate figure for the cut-off because that is the figure which applies under the 1944 Act (Parliamentary Under-Secretary of State, *Hansard*, H.C., Standing Committee E, col. 246). In the context of the 1944 Act, an exemption for small employers was perhaps inevitable, because statistically it is difficult to apply a 3 per cent quota to small firms (in a firm of 17 employees or less, 3 per cent rounded to the nearest whole number is zero). Such technical considerations do not apply where legislation is based on a principle of non-discrimination rather than on the enforcement of a quota. The main reason for the exemption of small employers from the new provisions is a desire on the part of the Government to reduce the administrative and cost burdens on small employers.

The Government has not sought to justify the small business exemption on the grounds of compliance cost alone. It would have been difficult to do so, given the evidence that in most cases, the necessary adjustments will have a nil or minimal cost (see the note to s.6). The Government's own Compliance Cost Assessment for the Act assumes an average cost of £200 per disabled employee for the 10 per cent of cases where a disabled employee is likely to require an adjustment. In some cases the cost of an adjustment may of course be much higher, but it can be argued that the interests of small businesses are adequately protected, without the need for a blanket exemption, by the fact that employers are only required to make *reasonable* adjustments, taking into account the extent of the employer's resources, the availability of outside financial assistance, etc. The Government also has the power to place a financial limit on adjustments, but significantly it decided not to impose any such cap in employment cases (unlike in cases involving the supply of goods and services) because it was not persuaded that a financial limit was necessary in view of the likely cost burden on employers.

During the passage of the Bill through Parliament, the Government placed greater emphasis on the administrative burden of complying with the legislation:

> "the Government have no desire that small businesses should discriminate against disabled people or any other group of people . . . but we want it recognised that small firms are subject to many constraints, not least that they cannot be expected to have the personnel resources—the range of abilities, knowledge, competence and time—to allow them to concern themselves with the minutiae of legislation. That is why . . . we maintain the view that businesses with fewer than 20 employees should be exempted from the legislation." (Parliamentary Under-Secretary of State, *Hansard*, H.C., Standing Committee E, col. 248).

This argument was anticipated in the White Paper, *Ending discrimination against disabled people*, which stated that the proposed exemption for small employers ". . . reflects the Government's recognition that it may be more difficult and burdensome for smaller firms without specialist personnel to get to grips with the new right and obtain the advice they need in particular cases." (Cm. 2729, 1995, para. 3.10). There is however, no exemption from the complex provisions of Pt. III of the Act for small suppliers of goods and services (*e.g.* the proverbial corner shop), even though an argument based on administrative burdens would seem to apply with equal if not greater force in that context. Neither is there any exemption for small employers from the sex and race discrimination legislation, or from the health and safety legislation. The Minister's claim that the comparison with the S.D.A. and the R.R.A. is misleading because "they are much more simple, straightforward pieces of legislation, and are much easier for a small business man to grasp than the implications of [this Act]" (*Hansard*, H.C., Vol. 257, col. 730) may well ring hollow with employers who have had to grapple with, for example, equal value claims under the Equal Pay Act 1970 (c. 41).

The Secretary of State has the power to change the threshold of 20 employees, but only to a lower number (subs. (2)), and he must conduct a review of the effect of the exemption before making any changes (subs. (4)). The exemption must in any event be reviewed after the employment provisions of the Act have been in force for four years (subs. (5)), unless it has been reviewed earlier, and the results of the review must be reported to Parliament a year after that (subs. (9)). Given that the Government's explanation for the exemption relies in part at least on the difficulty for small employers in getting to grips with the new provisions, it may not be unduly optimistic to expect that the current threshold of 20 will be reduced as the Act's provisions become more familiar: "It is unrealistic to expect [the small-scale employer] to know what might or might not be reasonable, to take advice or follow case law as it develops, *especially in the early years of an Act's implementation.*" (Parliamentary Under-Secretary of State, *Hansard*, H.C., Vol. 257, col. 728, emphasis added).

Subs. (1)

An employer who has fewer than 20 employees. In calculating the number of employees, any apprentices and self-employed workers who contract personally to do any work must be included (s.68(1)). The threshold applies to the number of employees which the employer has. Unlike the small employer threshold which applies in some other areas of employment law (*e.g.* under ss.146(4B) and s.56A of the Employment Protection (Consolidation) Act 1978 (c. 44)), employees who are employed by associated employers are not to be included in the calculation. The Minister confirmed during debates on the Bill that, for these purposes, "Each individual company within a group is a separate employer." (Minister of State, *Hansard*, H.L., Vol. 564, col. 1917).

Although not expressly spelt out in the Act, it seems that the relevant date for determining whether or not the exemption applies is the date on which the discriminatory act complained of took place (Parliamentary Under-Secretary of State, *Hansard*, H.C., Standing Committee E, col. 227). A small firm which expands above the threshold will therefore have to fulfil the obligations imposed by the Act (including the duty to make reasonable adjustments) from that point in time onwards, unless and until the number of employees falls below the threshold once again. Difficult problems are likely to arise in the case of firms with fluctuating workforces where the number of employees oscillates above and below the threshold, or where a seasonal influx of casual workers takes a small firm over the threshold for a limited period. If the exemption ceases to apply, the protection against disability discrimination applies to all employees, not just to those who are newly employed: "Once the firm [has] expanded to 20 employees or more, it would have to fulfil the obligations that we propose. That would include reassessing a previous series of acts in the light of the new obligations and ceasing any form of discrimination." (Parliamentary Under-Secretary of State, *Hansard*, H.C., Standing Committee E, col. 249). However, that protection will be lost if the number falls below the threshold again, along with the entitlement to any adjustments made by the employer, unless the employee had a contractual entitlement to the adjustment. It is unclear whether, in a case where an employer's workforce fluctuates above and below the threshold, a tribunal will be able to take that fact into account in determining whether it would be reasonable to require the employer to make an adjustment.

Enforcement etc.

Enforcement, remedies and procedure

8.—(1) A complaint by any person that another person—

(a) has discriminated against him in a way which is unlawful under this Part, or

(b) is, by virtue of section 57 or 58, to be treated as having discriminated against him in such a way,

may be presented to an industrial tribunal.

(2) Where an industrial tribunal finds that a complaint presented to it under this section is well-founded, it shall take such of the following steps as it considers just and equitable—

(a) making a declaration as to the rights of the complainant and the respondent in relation to the matters to which the complaint relates;

(b) ordering the respondent to pay compensation to the complainant;

(c) recommending that the respondent take, within a specified period, action appearing to the tribunal to be reasonable, in all the circumstances of the case, for the purpose of obviating or reducing the adverse effect on the complainant of any matter to which the complaint relates.

(3) Where a tribunal orders compensation under subsection (2)(b), the amount of the compensation shall be calculated by applying the principles applicable to the calculation of damages in claims in tort or (in Scotland) in reparation for breach of statutory duty.

(4) For the avoidance of doubt it is hereby declared that compensation in respect of discrimination in a way which is unlawful under this Part may include compensation for injury to feelings whether or not it includes compensation under any other head.

(5) If the respondent to a complaint fails, without reasonable justification, to comply with a recommendation made by an industrial tribunal under subsection (2)(c) the tribunal may, if it thinks it just and equitable to do so—

(a) increase the amount of compensation required to be paid to the complainant in respect of the complaint, where an order was made under subsection (2)(b); or

(b) make an order under subsection (2)(b).

(6) Regulations may make provision—

(a) for enabling a tribunal, where an amount of compensation falls to be awarded under subsection (2)(b), to include in the award interest on that amount; and

(b) specifying, for cases where a tribunal decides that an award is to include an amount in respect of interest, the manner in which and the periods and rate by reference to which the interest is to be determined.

(7) Regulations may modify the operation of any order made under paragraph 6A of Schedule 9 to the Employment Protection (Consolidation) Act 1978 (power to make provision as to interest on sums payable in pursuance of

industrial tribunal decisions) to the extent that it relates to an award of compensation under subsection (2)(b).

(8) Part I of Schedule 3 makes further provision about the enforcement of this Part and about procedure.

GENERAL NOTE

As with complaints of discrimination on grounds of sex and race, complaints of unlawful disability discrimination under Pt. II must be made to an industrial tribunal. The detailed procedures, and the remedies available, are similar to those which apply in complaints under the Sex Discrimination Act 1975 and the Race Relations Act 1976. There are however some important differences; in particular, the Act makes no provision for the enforcement of the employment provisions, or for the assistance of individual complainants, by a body equivalent to the Equal Opportunities Commission or the Commission for Racial Equality. The National Disability Council established under Pt. VI is only empowered to advise the Government on general issues relating to discrimination against disabled people. It has no power to investigate complaints of discrimination, to provide assistance to individuals in enforcing their rights before the courts and tribunals, or to take strategic enforcement action of its own accord (see the note to s.50). Predictably, this has been a major source of criticism of the Act's provisions. There is however provision, as in claims of sex and race discrimination, for the Secretary of State to issue a questionnaire which a potential complainant may serve on the employer to help him or her decide whether to make a complaint, and if so, to formulate and present the case in the most effective manner: see the note to s.56. The employer's replies to these questions will be admissible in evidence in any subsequent tribunal proceedings, and a tribunal may draw adverse inferences from a failure to reply, or a reply which is evasive or equivocal. Special provision is also made for the application of reporting restrictions where evidence of a personal nature is likely to be heard by the tribunal hearing the complaint: see the notes to ss.62 and 63. There is an appeal to the Employment Appeal Tribunal on a point of law from the decision of an industrial tribunal under this Act: Sched. 6, para. 2, amending the E.P.(C.)A. 1978, s.136(1).

Subs. (1)

Presented to an industrial tribunal. Complaints under Pt. II must be presented to an industrial tribunal before the end of the period of three months beginning when the act complained of was done (Sched. 3, para. 3(1)), although the tribunal may consider a complaint which is out of time "if, in all the circumstances of the case, it considers that it is just and equitable to do so" (*ibid.* para. 3(2)). This discretionary power of the tribunal to extend the time-limit is more flexible than the escape clause normally used in employment protection legislation (*e.g.* in complaints of unfair dismissal under the E.P.(C.)A. 1978, s.67), which focuses on whether it was "reasonably practicable" for the complaint to be brought in time. Where the act of discrimination is attributable to a contract term, the discriminatory act will be treated as extending throughout the duration of the contract; an act "extending over a period" (see below) will be treated as done at the end of that period; and a deliberate omission will be treated as done when the person decided upon it (Sched. 3, para. 3(3)). A person will be taken to have decided upon an omission when he or she does an act inconsistent with doing the omitted act, or, if no such inconsistent act has been done, at the expiry of the period within which he or she might reasonably have been expected to do the omitted act, if it was to be done (*ibid.* para. 3(4)).

These provisions mirror those in the S.D.A., s.76, and the R.R.A., s.68, and decisions on the interpretation of those provisions are likely to be in point here also. In cases under the S.D.A. and R.R.A., the following points, *inter alia*, have emerged:

(i) the question of whether it is just and equitable to extend the three-month time limit has been held to be a question of fact for the tribunal (*Foster v. South Glamorgan Health Authority* [1988] I.R.L.R. 277), and the decision of the tribunal on this point is likely to be difficult to challenge on appeal (*Hutchinson v. Westward Television* [1977] I.R.L.R. 69).

(ii) the discovery of facts indicating possible discrimination after the expiry of the three-month time-limit may be a good reason to allow an application out of time: see for example, *Clarke v. Hampshire Electro-Plating Co.* [1991] I.R.L.R. 490; *Berry v. Ravensbourne National Health Service Trust* [1993] I.C.R. 871.

(iii) in cases involving dismissal, the time-limit runs from the date on which the complainant actually finds himself or herself out of a job, and not (as in unfair dismissal complaints) from the effective date of termination: see *Lupetti v. Wrens Old House* [1984] I.C.R. 348, a case under the R.R.A., which was applied in the context of the S.D.A. in *Gloucester Working Men's Club & Institute v. James* [1986] I.C.R. 603; see also *Adekeye v. Post Office* [1993] I.R.L.R. 324, where the time limit was held to run from the rejection of an internal appeal, rather than from the date of the dismissal.

(iv) the rule concerning acts "extending over a period" has been held to apply only to a *continuing* act of discrimination, and not to a situation where a *single* act or event of discrimination has continuing *consequences*. So, for example, in *Amies v. Inner London Education Authority* [1977] I.C.R. 308, a case under the S.D.A., s.76(6)(b), the E.A.T. rejected the complainant's argument that the employer's failure to appoint her to a particular post was a continuing act of discrimination; in contrast, in *Calder v. James Findlay Corporation (Note)* [1989] I.R.L.R. 55, the employer's refusal to allow the complainant access to a mortgage subsidy scheme was held by the E.A.T. to be a continuing discrimination against her, so that she was entitled to bring her complaint more than three months after the refusal. These cases were approved by the House of Lords in *Barclays Bank v. Kapur* [1991] I.R.L.R. 136, a case under the R.R.A., s. 68(7)(c), in which the employer's refusal to recognise the complainant's previous service for pensions purposes was held to be a continuing act of discrimination. That decision was followed in *Littlewoods Organisation v. Traynor* [1993] I.R.L.R. 154, where the employer's failure to take promised remedial action in relation to a complaint of discrimination was held to constitute a continuing act of discrimination, but was distinguished in *Sougrin v. Haringey Health Authority* [1991] I.R.L.R. 447, affirmed [1992] I.R.L.R. 416 where the employer's decision on grading was held to be a single event, not a continuing act of discrimination. See also *Owusu v. London Fire & Civil Defence Authority* [1995] I.R.L.R. 574.

(v) in *Swithland Motors v. Clarke* [1994] I.C.R. 231, a case under the S.D.A., s.76(6)(c), involving an alleged deliberate omission to offer employment, the E.A.T. held that "decided" means "decided at a time and in circumstances when [the person] was in a position to implement that decision."

Subss. (2)–(5)

The remedies available for an act of unlawful discrimination are similar to those which apply under S.D.A., s.65, and R.R.A., s.56: the tribunal may make a declaration as to the rights of the parties, order the respondent to pay the complainant compensation, and/or recommend that the respondent take, within a specified period, action which appears to the tribunal to be reasonable, in all the circumstances, for the purpose of obviating or reducing the adverse effect of the unlawful conduct on the complainant.

Compensation. There is no upper limit on the compensation which may be awarded in a complaint under this section, in line with the equivalent provisions under the S.D.A. and the R.R.A., where the upper limits were removed by the Sex Discrimination and Equal Pay (Remedies) Regulations 1993 (S.I. 1993 No. 2798), and the Race Relations (Remedies) Act 1994 (c. 10), respectively. As in cases under the S.D.A. and R.R.A., compensation is to be assessed by applying the principles applicable to the calculation of damages in tort or, in Scotland, reparation for breach of statutory duty (subs. (3)), and may include compensation for injury to feelings (subs. (4)). Amounts awarded for injury to feelings in cases under the S.D.A. and R.R.A. have traditionally tended to be low, although in *Noone v. North West Thames Regional Health Authority* [1988] I.R.L.R. 195, the Court of Appeal awarded £3,000 under that head in a case of unlawful race discrimination where it considered that the injury to feelings was severe. More recently, in *Sharifi v. Strathclyde Regional Council* [1992] I.R.L.R. 259, the E.A.T. indicated that £500 was "at or near the minimum" for an award of damages for injury to feelings in race discrimination cases, and in *Ministry of Defence v. Sullivan* [1994] I.C.R. 193, the E.A.T. said that there would be an award for injury to feelings in most sex discrimination cases, and approved an award of £750. For detailed guidance from the Court of Appeal on the assessment of compensation in cases under the R.R.A., see *Alexander v. Home Office* [1988] I.R.L.R. 190; I.C.R. 685.

In some earlier Court of Appeal decisions in cases under the S.D.A. and the R.R.A., it was assumed that exemplary damages could be awarded in sex and race discrimination cases (see for example, *Alexander v. Home Office* (above), and *Bradford City Metropolitan Council v. Arora* [1989] I.C.R. 719). However, in *Deane v. Ealing London Borough Council* [1993] I.R.L.R. 209, the E.A.T. held that a tribunal has no power to make an award of exemplary damages under the R.R.A., following the decision of the Court of Appeal in *Gibbons v. South Western Water Services* [1993] 1 All E.R. 609 that exemplary damages may only be awarded for torts recognised as existing before the decision of the House of Lords in *Rookes v. Barnard* [1964] A.C. 1129. For a similar ruling with respect to exemplary damages under the S.D.A., see *Ministry of Defence v. Meredith* [1995] I.R.L.R. 539. It follows that exemplary damages may not be awarded under this section. The E.A.T. in *Deane* upheld an award of aggravated damages under the R.R.A., and in *Meredith* the E.A.T. confirmed that aggravated damages may also be awarded under the S.D.A.

Action appearing to the tribunal to be reasonable. The tribunal is also empowered to recommend that the respondent takes certain specified remedial action. This discretion is not unfettered, as the recommendation must be for the purpose of remedying the matter to which the complaint relates. In *Noone v. North West Thames Regional Health Authority (No 2)* [1988] I.R.L.R. 550, the Court of Appeal held, under the similar provisions of the R.R.A., that a tribunal had no power to recommend that an applicant who had not been promoted because of unlawful discrimination should be appointed to the next available vacancy, or be given preferential treatment in the selection procedure; indeed, any such response on the part of the employer might constitute an act of unlawful positive discrimination (see for example, *British Gas v. Sharma* [1991] I.R.L.R. 101). Curiously, whereas under the S.D.A. and R.R.A. the tribunal may recommend that the respondent take "action appearing to the tribunal to be *practicable*", this section refers to "action appearing to the tribunal to be *reasonable*"; unfortunately it is not clear whether the difference in wording is intended to be of any significance. If the respondent fails without reasonable justification to comply with a recommendation, the tribunal may increase the amount of compensation already awarded, or may make such an award, if it thinks it is just and equitable to do so (subs. (5)).

Subs. (8)

Schedule 3, para. 1 makes provision for conciliation through ACAS, as with complaints under the S.D.A. and the R.R.A.; para. 2 provides that the remedies available for an infringement of Pt. II are (with the exception of judicial review) exclusively those provided by this section; para. 3 makes provision for time-limits (see the note to subs. (1)); and para. 4 concerns certification by Ministers: see the note to s.59.

Validity of certain agreements

9.—(1) Any term in a contract of employment or other agreement is void so far as it purports to—

(a) require a person to do anything which would contravene any provision of, or made under, this Part;
(b) exclude or limit the operation of any provision of this Part; or
(c) prevent any person from presenting a complaint to an industrial tribunal under this Part.

(2) Paragraphs (b) and (c) of subsection (1) do not apply to an agreement not to institute proceedings under section 8(1), or to an agreement not to continue such proceedings, if—

(a) a conciliation officer has acted under paragraph 1 of Schedule 3 in relation to the matter; or
(b) the conditions set out in subsection (3) are satisfied.

(3) The conditions are that—

(a) the complainant must have received independent legal advice from a qualified lawyer as to the terms and effect of the proposed agreement (and in particular its effect on his ability to pursue his complaint before an industrial tribunal);
(b) when the adviser gave the advice there must have been in force a policy of insurance covering the risk of a claim by the complainant in respect of loss arising in consequence of the advice; and
(c) the agreement must be in writing, relate to the particular complaint, identify the adviser and state that the conditions are satisfied.

(4) In this section—

"independent", in relation to legal advice to the complainant, means that it is given by a lawyer who is not acting for the other party or for a person who is connected with that other party; and

"qualified lawyer" means—

(a) as respects proceedings in England and Wales, a barrister (whether in practice as such or employed to give legal advice) or a solicitor of the Supreme Court who holds a practising certificate; and

(b) as respects proceedings in Scotland, an advocate (whether in practice as such or employed to give legal advice) or a solicitor who holds a practising certificate.

(5) For the purposes of subsection (4), any two persons are to be treated as connected if—

(a) one is a company of which the other (directly or indirectly) has control, or
(b) both are companies of which a third person (directly or indirectly) has control.

General Note

This section places restrictions on contracting out of the Act's provisions. It renders void any term in a contract of employment or other agreement if it, (a) requires a person to contravene this Part of the Act; (b) attempts to exclude or limit the operation of this Part of the Act; or (c) attempts to prevent a person from presenting a complaint to an industrial tribunal under this Part of the Act. Exception is however made in the case of an agreement not to institute or continue proceedings, where that agreement has been reached with the assistance of an ACAS conciliation officer, or where the parties have made a valid compromise contract.

The requirements for a valid compromise contract are set out in subs. (3); they mirror the corresponding provisions introduced into the S.D.A. and the R.R.A. by the Trade Union Reform and Employment Rights Act 1993 (c. 19), s.39 and Sched. 6. The principal requirements are that the complainant must have received independent legal advice from a qualified lawyer as to the terms and effect of the proposed agreement, and its effect on his ability to pursue his complaint before a tribunal; the adviser must be covered by appropriate insurance at the time when the advice is given; and the agreement must be in writing, relate to the particular complaint, identify the adviser and state that these conditions are satisfied.

Charities and support for particular groups of persons

10.—(1) Nothing in this Part—
(a) affects any charitable instrument which provides for conferring benefits on one or more categories of person determined by reference to any physical or mental capacity; or
(b) makes unlawful any act done by a charity or recognised body in pursuance of any of its charitable purposes, so far as those purposes are connected with persons so determined.

(2) Nothing in this Part prevents—
(a) a person who provides supported employment from treating members of a particular group of disabled persons more favourably than other persons in providing such employment; or
(b) the Secretary of State from agreeing to arrangements for the provision of supported employment which will, or may, have that effect.

(3) In this section—
"charitable instrument" means an enactment or other instrument (whenever taking effect) so far as it relates to charitable purposes;
"charity" has the same meaning as in the Charities Act 1993;
"recognised body" means a body which is a recognised body for the purposes of Part I of the Law Reform (Miscellaneous Provisions) (Scotland) Act 1990; and
"supported employment" means facilities provided, or in respect of which payments are made, under section 15 of the Disabled Persons (Employment) Act 1944.

(4) In the application of this section to England and Wales, "charitable purposes" means purposes which are exclusively charitable according to the law of England and Wales.

(5) In the application of this section to Scotland, "charitable purposes" shall be construed in the same way as if it were contained in the Income Tax Acts.

General Note

This section contains specific exemptions from Pt. II for charities and for the providers of supported employment. Subsection (1) is designed to enable charities which confer benefits on particular categories of disabled people in pursuance of their charitable purposes, to continue to do so without fear of infringing the provisions of Pt. II. It means, for example, that an organisation like the Royal National Institute for the Deaf will continue to be able to employ people with hearing impairments in preference to people with other kinds of disability "because of their experience or the techniques they have learned in coping with their specific impairment. They may also wish to encourage the employment of people with such disabilities by setting a personal example of doing so themselves." (Minister of State, *Hansard*, H.L., Vol. 564, col. 1932).

Subsection (2) provides an exemption for the providers of supported employment who treat members of a particular group of disabled persons more favourably that other persons in providing such employment. The supported employment programme was set up under the Disabled Persons (Employment) Act 1944, s.15 to provide employment opportunities for severely disabled people who would otherwise be unlikely to obtain employment because of the nature or severity of their disability. The provisions in the 1944 Act on supported employment are to continue, notwithstanding the repeal of much of that Act: see the note to s.61.

Charity. The exemption is not restricted to registered charities.

Advertisements suggesting that employers will discriminate against disabled persons

11.—(1) This section applies where—

(a) a disabled person has applied for employment with an employer;

(b) the employer has refused to offer, or has deliberately not offered, him the employment;

(c) the disabled person has presented a complaint under section 8 against the employer;

(d) the employer has advertised the employment (whether before or after the disabled person applied for it); and

(e) the advertisement indicated, or might reasonably be understood to have indicated, that any application for the advertised employment would, or might, be determined to any extent by reference to—

(i) the successful applicant not having any disability or any category of disability which includes the disabled person's disability; or

(ii) the employer's reluctance to take any action of a kind mentioned in section 6.

(2) The tribunal hearing the complaint shall assume, unless the contrary is shown, that the employer's reason for refusing to offer, or deliberately not offering, the employment to the complainant was related to the complainant's disability.

(3) In this section "advertisement" includes every form of advertisement or notice, whether to the public or not.

General Note

This section tackles the difficult issue of discriminatory job advertisements. It provides that where a job advertisement suggests (or might reasonably be taken to suggest) that the employer might discriminate against disabled applicants, then in any complaint by a disabled person under s.8 of the Act, the tribunal must assume, unless the contrary is shown, that the employer's reason for not offering the employment to the complainant was related to his or her disability. This assumption applies where the job advertisement indicated (or might be understood to have indicated) that the outcome of any application for the job would, or might be determined to any extent, by reference to the successful applicant not having any disability, or the kind of disability which the complainant has, or to the employer's reluctance to make a reasonable adjustment. The complainant must have sought and been refused the employment to which the advertisement relates, but it does not matter whether the employment was advertised before or after the complainant applied for it. It can be seen that the only significance of a discriminatory job advertisement under this section is that it gives rise to an assumption of discrimination in a complaint under s.8. As such a complaint may not be brought against an employer with fewer than 20 employees, it follows that there is nothing in this section which prevents a small employer from placing an advertisement which clearly demonstrates an intention to discriminate against disabled applicants.

The approach to discriminatory advertisements in this section differs significantly from that taken in the sex and race discrimination legislation, under which it is unlawful to publish or cause to be published an advertisement which indicates or might reasonably be understood as indicating an intention to commit an unlawful act of discrimination (S.D.A., s.38; R.R.A., s.29). Enforcement under those Acts is placed in the hands of the Equal Opportunities Commission and the Commission for Racial Equality, which may seek a declaration or, if the defendant appears likely to commit further unlawful acts, an injunction, or alternatively may serve a non-discrimination notice on the defendant. One obvious explanation for the difference in approach lies in the lack of a suitable body to bring enforcement proceedings in this context, the role of the National Disability Council being confined to the giving of advice to Ministers: see the note to s.50.

The approach of this section more closely resembles that of the Trade Union and Labour Relations (Consolidation) Act 1992 (c. 52), s.137, to job advertisements which discriminate on grounds of union membership. There are however some important differences: first, a job advertisement is only caught by the T.U.L.R.A. provisions where it indicates (or might reasonably be understood as indicating) that a particular job "is open only to a person who is, or is not, a union member"; in contrast, the provisions in this section apply where the advertisement indicates (or might reasonably be understood as indicating) that an application "would or might be determined to any extent by reference to" the applicant not having a disability, etc. Secondly, under the T.U.L.R.A. provisions, a person who does not satisfy the condition regarding union membership and who applies unsuccessfully for the job is conclusively presumed to have been refused it unlawfully, regardless of any other reason there may have been for the employer's decision not to appoint that person, whereas under this section the employer has the opportunity of rebutting the presumption by showing that the reason the employment was not offered to the complainant was not related to his or her disability. Furthermore, even if the employer fails to rebut the presumption, he may be able to show that the refusal of employment is justified within the meaning of s.5.

A major source of controversy in this area is the mentioning of health requirements in job advertisements. The Government's view is that a blanket ban on mentioning health requirements in job advertisements would be inappropriate, because there might be legitimate reasons why an employer would wish to mention such requirements in an advertisement, for example, where they are relevant to the job (Minister of State, *Hansard*, H.L., Vol. 566, col. 176). "What is important is to cover the problem of employers trying to dissuade disabled people from applying for jobs that they might be able to do..." (Minister of State, *Hansard*, H.L., Vol. 564, col. 1935). However, the Minister also emphasised that, while employers should be able to advise potential applicants of the genuine physical and mental requirements of a specific job, "employers will be well advised to consider the duty of reasonable adjustment in identifying health requirements which might be overcome by such an adjustment." (Minister of State, *Hansard*, H.L., Vol. 566, col. 176).

Subs. (3)

Advertisement. The same definition is also applied for the purposes of T.U.L.R.A., s.137: see T.U.L.R.A., s.143(1). The definition is a broad one, encompassing every form of advertisement or notice, whether public or not. It is certainly wide enough to cover notices on company notice-boards and in internal newsletters, as well as advertisements in the press.

Discrimination by other persons

Discrimination against contract workers

12.—(1) It is unlawful for a principal, in relation to contract work, to discriminate against a disabled person—

(a) in the terms on which he allows him to do that work;

(b) by not allowing him to do it or continue to do it;

(c) in the way he affords him access to any benefits or by refusing or deliberately omitting to afford him access to them; or

(d) by subjecting him to any other detriment.

(2) Subsection (1) does not apply to benefits of any description if the principal is concerned with the provision (whether or not for payment) of benefits of that description to the public, or to a section of the public which includes the contract worker in question, unless that provision differs in a material respect from the provision of the benefits by the principal to contract workers.

(3) The provisions of this Part (other than subsections (1) to (3) of section 4) apply to any principal, in relation to contract work, as if he were, or would be, the employer of the contract worker and as if any contract worker supplied to do work for him were an employee of his.

(4) In the case of an act which constitutes discrimination by virtue of section 55, this section also applies to discrimination against a person who is not disabled.

(5) This section applies only in relation to contract work done at an establishment in Great Britain (the provisions of section 68 about the meaning of "employment at an establishment in Great Britain" applying for the purposes of this subsection with the appropriate modifications).

(6) In this section—

"principal" means a person ("A") who makes work available for doing by individuals who are employed by another person who supplies them under a contract made with A;

"contract work" means work so made available; and

"contract worker" means any individual who is supplied to the principal under such a contract.

GENERAL NOTE

In common with the sex and race discrimination legislation, this section extends the prohibition on discrimination against disabled persons to the hirer of contract labour, by placing hirers under a duty of non-discrimination similar to the duty imposed on employers by s.4 of the Act. The provisions apply where workers ("contract workers") are supplied under contract by their employer to a third party hirer (the "principal") who makes "contract work" available for them. Subsection (1) provides that it is unlawful for a principal, in relation to contract work, to discriminate against a disabled person (a) in the terms on which he allows that person to do contract work, (b) by not allowing that person to do or to continue to do contract work, (c) in the way in which that person is given access to any benefits, or by refusing or deliberately omitting to give him access to those benefits (unless benefits of that description are also provided by the principal to the public at large within subs. (2)) or (d) by subjecting that person to any other detriment. In all other respects, the provisions of Pt. II (for example, in relation to the definition of discrimination, the duty to make reasonable adjustments and the defence of justification) apply to the hirer of a contract worker as if that person were the employer of that worker (subs. (3)). However, the duty of a principal to make reasonable adjustments for a contract worker is bound to reflect the fact that the relationship between principal and contract worker is not the same as the relationship between employer and employee: "Clearly what would be reasonable in the case of the hirer would depend on the hirer's circumstances and this would necessarily take account of the often much more limited relationship between the hirer and worker. For example, there might be very few types of adjustment a principal could reasonably be required to make for people hired for only a couple of weeks or for people whom the employer needed at very short notice." (Minister of State, *Hansard*, H.L., Vol. 566, col. 222).

There is of course a potential overlap where the duty to make reasonable adjustments is imposed on both the principal and the employment business which is the contract worker's employer. It seems that the principal's duty of reasonable adjustment "would include the hirer co-operating as far as was reasonable with adjustments made by the employment business" (*ibid.* col. 222), and the Government has indicated that it intends to make regulations to provide in detail for the allocation of the duty to make reasonable adjustments between the two organisations. Although not expressly stated in the Act, it would appear that the small business exemption applies to a hirer of contract labour under this section as it applies to an employer, by virtue of subs. (3); "The provisions of this Part . . . apply to any Principal . . . as if he were, or would be, the employer of the contract worker. . .". This gives rise to a confusing variety of permutations: circumstances may arise where the contract worker's employer is exempt from the Act's provisions because he has fewer than 20 employees, but the hirer is not, and vice versa; alternatively both parties, or neither party, may be exempt, depending on the numbers employed or hired (as the case may be) by each of them at the relevant time. To make matters worse, the position as regards exemption may change from day to day, as the numbers employed or hired by the parties changes. It is to be hoped that the regulations will clarify exactly where the duty to make reasonable adjustments lies in such cases.

For the equivalent provisions in relation to sex and race discrimination, see the S.D.A., s.9, and the R.R.A., s.7.

Who supplies them under a contract. Under the equivalent provisions in the S.D.A., s.9, the E.A.T. has held that there must be an undertaking by the supplier to supply the workers in question to the principal: *Rice v. Fon-a-Car* [1980] I.C.R. 133.

Discrimination by trade organisations

13.—(1) It is unlawful for a trade organisation to discriminate against a disabled person—

(a) in the terms on which it is prepared to admit him to membership of the organisation; or

(b) by refusing to accept, or deliberately not accepting, his application for membership.

(2) It is unlawful for a trade organisation, in the case of a disabled person who is a member of the organisation, to discriminate against him—

(a) in the way it affords him access to any benefits or by refusing or deliberately omitting to afford him access to them;

(b) by depriving him of membership, or varying the terms on which he is a member; or

(c) by subjecting him to any other detriment.

(3) In the case of an act which constitutes discrimination by virtue of section 55, this section also applies to discrimination against a person who is not disabled.

(4) In this section "trade organisation" means an organisation of workers, an organisation of employers or any other organisation whose members carry on a particular profession or trade for the purposes of which the organisation exists.

General Note

Trade organisations are covered by s.4 of the Act in their relationship with their employees or prospective employees; in line with the legislation which prohibits discrimination on grounds of sex and race, this section prohibits discrimination by trade organisations against disabled members or prospective members. As defined in subs. (4), "trade organisation" means an organisation of workers (such as a trade union), an organisation of employers (such as an employers' association), or any other organisation whose members carry on a particular profession or trade for the purposes of which the organisation exists (for example, a professional association such as the Institute of Personnel and Development). It is unlawful for any such organisation to discriminate against a disabled person in relation to the terms on which it is prepared to admit that person into membership, or by refusing to accept or deliberately not accepting that person's application for membership (subs. (1)). It is also unlawful for a trade organisation to discriminate against a disabled member in relation to that person's access to any benefits, or by depriving that person of membership or varying the terms of his membership, or by subjecting that person to any other detriment (subs. (2)). "Discrimination" in relation to trade organisations is defined in s.14 in the same terms as discrimination in relation to employers under s.5, and s.15 places trade organisations under a duty to make reasonable adjustments similar to that which applies to employers under s.6. As with the provisions relating to employers, less favourable treatment of a disabled person by a trade organisation may be justified in certain circumstances: "For example, in the case of a trade union delegation to inaccessible premises not controlled by the union it might be necessary to leave out a wheelchair user" (Minister of State, *Hansard*, H.L., Vol. 566, col. 225). The duty to make reasonable adjustments might, for example, require a trade union "to ensure that, where it is reasonable, visually impaired members could get union literature in braille and members with hearing impairments could have signers at meetings" (*ibid.* col. 225).

For the equivalent provisions in relation to sex and race discrimination, see the S.D.A., s.12, and the R.R.A., s.11.

Trade; business. As defined in s.68(1), "profession" includes any vocation or occupation, and "trade" includes any business.

Meaning of "discrimination" in relation to trade organisations

14.—(1) For the purposes of this Part, a trade organisation discriminates against a disabled person if—

(a) for a reason which relates to the disabled person's disability, it treats him less favourably than it treats or would treat others to whom that reason does not or would not apply; and

(b) it cannot show that the treatment in question is justified.

(2) For the purposes of this Part, a trade organisation also discriminates against a disabled person if—

(a) it fails to comply with a section 15 duty imposed on it in relation to the disabled person; and

(b) it cannot show that its failure to comply with that duty is justified.

(3) Subject to subsection (5), for the purposes of subsection (1) treatment is justified if, but only if, the reason for it is both material to the circumstances of the particular case and substantial.

(4) For the purposes of subsection (2), failure to comply with a section 15 duty is justified if, but only if, the reason for the failure is both material to the circumstances of the particular case and substantial.

(5) If, in a case falling within subsection (1), the trade organisation is under a section 15 duty in relation to the disabled person concerned but fails without justification to comply with that duty, its treatment of that person cannot be justified under subsection (3) unless the treatment would have been justified even if the organisation had complied with the section 15 duty.

(6) Regulations may make provision, for purposes of this section, as to circumstances in which—

(a) treatment is to be taken to be justified;

(b) failure to comply with a section 15 duty is to be taken to be justified;

(c) treatment is to be taken not to be justified;

(d) failure to comply with a section 15 duty is to be taken not to be justified.

General Note

The definition of discrimination in relation to trade organisations in this section is substantially the same as that which applies to employers under s.5: see the note to that section. As to discrimination by trade organisations generally, see the note to s.13.

Appeal against refusal of exemption certificate

15.—(1) Where—

(a) any arrangements made by or on behalf of a trade organisation, or

(b) any physical feature of premises occupied by the organisation,

place the disabled person concerned at a substantial disadvantage in comparison with persons who are not disabled, it is the duty of the organisation to take such steps as it is reasonable, in all the circumstances of the case, for it to have to take in order to prevent the arrangements or feature having that effect.

(2) Subsection (1)(a) applies only in relation to—

(a) arrangements for determining who should become or remain a member of the organisation;

(b) any term, condition or arrangements on which membership or any benefit is offered or afforded.

(3) In determining whether it is reasonable for a trade organisation to have to take a particular step in order to comply with subsection (1), regard shall be had, in particular, to—

(a) the extent to which taking the step would prevent the effect in question;

(b) the extent to which it is practicable for the organisation to take the step;

(c) the financial and other costs which would be incurred by the organisation in taking the step and the extent to which taking it would disrupt any of its activities;

(d) the extent of the organisation's financial and other resources;

(e) the availability to the organisation of financial or other assistance with respect to taking the step.

This subsection is subject to any provision of regulations made under subsection (7).

(4) In this section "the disabled person concerned" means—

(a) in the case of arrangements for determining to whom membership should be offered, any disabled person who is, or has notified the organisation that he may be, an applicant for membership;

(b) in any other case, a disabled person who is—

(i) an applicant for membership; or

(ii) a member of the organisation.

(5) Nothing in this section imposes any duty on an organisation in relation to a disabled person if the organisation does not know, and could not reasonably be expected to know that the disabled person concerned—

(a) is, or may be, an applicant for membership; or

(b) has a disability and is likely to be affected in the way mentioned in subsection (1).

(6) Subject to the provisions of this section, nothing in this Part is to be taken to require a trade organisation to treat a disabled person more favourably than it treats or would treat others.

(7) Regulations may make provision for the purposes of subsection (1) as to any of the matters mentioned in paragraphs (a) to (h) of section 6(8) (the references in those paragraphs to an employer being read for these purposes as references to a trade organisation).

(8) Subsection (9) of section 6 applies in relation to such regulations as it applies in relation to regulations made under section 6(8).

(9) Regulations may make provision adding to the duty imposed on trade organisations by this section, including provision of a kind which may be made under subsection (7).

(10) This section imposes duties only for the purpose of determining whether a trade organisation has discriminated against a disabled person; and accordingly a breach of any such duty is not actionable as such.

General Note

This section places trade organisations under a duty to make reasonable adjustments to their arrangements and premises to prevent disabled people from being placed at a substantial disadvantage in comparison with people who are not disabled. The duty of trade organisations to make adjustments under this section is substantially the same as the duty placed on employers under s.6: see the note to that section. Unlike s.6, however, this section does not contain a list of examples of steps which a trade organisation may have to take in relation to a disabled person in order to comply with the duty to make adjustments. As to discrimination by trade organisations generally, see the note to s.13.

Premises occupied under leases

Alterations to premises occupied under leases

16.—(1) This section applies where—

(a) an employer or trade organisation ("the occupier") occupies premises under a lease;

(b) but for this section, the occupier would not be entitled to make a particular alteration to the premises; and

(c) the alteration is one which the occupier proposes to make in order to comply with a section 6 duty or section 15 duty.

(2) Except to the extent to which it expressly so provides, the lease shall have effect by virtue of this subsection as if it provided—

(a) for the occupier to be entitled to make the alteration with the written consent of the lessor;

(b) for the occupier to have to make a written application to the lessor for consent if he wishes to make the alteration;

(c) if such an application is made, for the lessor not to withhold his consent unreasonably; and
(d) for the lessor to be entitled to make his consent subject to reasonable conditions.

(3) In this section—
"lease" includes a tenancy, sub-lease or sub-tenancy and an agreement for a lease, tenancy, sub-lease or sub-tenancy; and
"sub-lease" and "sub-tenancy" have such meaning as may be prescribed.

(4) If the terms and conditions of a lease—
(a) impose conditions which are to apply if the occupier alters the premises, or
(b) entitle the lessor to impose conditions when consenting to the occupier's altering the premises,

the occupier is to be treated for the purposes of subsection (1) as not being entitled to make the alteration.

(5) Part I of Schedule 4 supplements the provisions of this section.

General Note

The duty of an employer or trade organisation to make reasonable adjustments for the benefit of disabled people under ss.6 and 15 of the Act may necessitate the alteration of premises, but this could present problems for employers and organisations who occupy premises under a lease, where the terms of the lease prevent or restrict them from making alterations to those premises. This section, which was added to the Bill at Third Reading in the House of Lords, overrides the terms of the lease in such circumstances by entitling the occupier, with the written consent of the landlord, to alter the premises to comply with a s.6 or s.15 duty. The occupier must apply in writing to the landlord seeking his consent for the alterations, and the landlord must not withhold that consent unreasonably, although the consent may be made subject to reasonable conditions (subs. (2)). An occupier of premises who fails to apply to the landlord for consent to make the alterations will not be able to claim that he was prevented by the terms of the lease from making a reasonable adjustment to the premises (Sched. 4, para. 1). In a complaint under s.8, the complainant or the occupier may ask the tribunal to join the landlord as a party to the proceedings, and if the tribunal finds that the landlord has unreasonably refused consent to the alterations, or has imposed unreasonable conditions, it may do one or more of the following: make a declaration; make an order authorising the occupier to make the alterations specified in the order (subject to any specified conditions); or order the landlord to pay compensation to the complainant. Any such order may be instead of or in addition to an order made against the occupier under s.8(2), although if the tribunal orders the landlord to pay compensation, it cannot order the occupier to do so (Sched. 4, para. 2).

According to the Government: "This approach [will] ensure that the lease will not operate to frustrate the duty of adjustment. It also has the advantage of protecting the landlord where he has a legitimate objection to allowing an alteration to premises." (Minister of State, *Hansard*, H.L., Vol. 566, col. 1016).

The Secretary of State may make regulations specifying circumstances in which it would or would not be reasonable for a landlord to withhold his consent to adjustments, and whether a condition imposed by the landlord is to be taken to be reasonable or unreasonable (Sched. 4, para. 3). "Obviously, if the building was listed and there were concerns about making alterations, it would be perfectly reasonable to refuse consent on those grounds." (Minister of State, *ibid.* col. 1018). Regulations may also make provision for cases where premises are occupied under a sub-lease or sub-tenancy (*ibid.* para. 4).

Occupational pension schemes and insurance services

Occupational pension schemes

17.—(1) Every occupational pension scheme shall be taken to include a provision ("a non-discrimination rule")—
(a) relating to the terms on which—
(i) persons become members of the scheme; and
(ii) members of the scheme are treated; and
(b) requiring the trustees or managers of the scheme to refrain from any act or omission which, if done in relation to a person by an employer,

would amount to unlawful discrimination against that person for the purposes of this Part.

(2) The other provisions of the scheme are to have effect subject to the non-discrimination rule.

(3) Without prejudice to section 67, regulations under this Part may—

(a) with respect to trustees or managers of occupational pension schemes make different provision from that made with respect to employers; or

(b) make provision modifying the application to such trustees or managers of any regulations made under this Part, or of any provisions of this Part so far as they apply to employers.

(4) In determining, for the purposes of this section, whether an act or omission would amount to unlawful discrimination if done by an employer, any provision made under subsection (3) shall be applied as if it applied in relation to the notional employer.

GENERAL NOTE

Entitlement to occupational pension benefits under the contract of employment is covered by s.4(2) of the Act, which prohibits discrimination by an employer against a disabled person in the terms of employment and in the opportunities for receiving any other benefit (subject to certain modifications in ss.5(7) and 6(11) which take account of the particular problems raised by occupational pension benefits in this context: see the notes to ss.5 and 6). This section extends those principles to the trustees and managers of occupational pension schemes, by implying into every such scheme a "non-discrimination rule". The effect of this rule is that any discrimination by the trustees or managers of an occupational pension scheme in relation to the terms on which people become members of the scheme, or the way in which members of the scheme are treated, will be treated as a breach of the rules of the scheme (subs. (1)). For these purposes, an act or omission by the trustees or managers will be contrary to the rules of the scheme if it would amount to unlawful discrimination under this Part of the Act if done by an employer, although regulations made under subs. (3) may make provision for trustees and managers which is different from that made for employers. Unlike the provisions prohibiting unlawful discrimination by employers, a complaint of unlawful discrimination against the trustees or managers of an occupational pension scheme does not lie to an industrial tribunal. Rather, a disabled person who is affected by an infringement of the non-discrimination rule "will be able to seek redress through the dispute resolution mechanisms which already exist for pensions (sic) schemes." (Minister of State, *Hansard*, H.L., Vol. 566, col. 994).

Occupational pension scheme. This has the same meaning as in the Pension Schemes Act 1993 (c. 48).

Insurance services

18.—(1) This section applies where a provider of insurance services ("the insurer") enters into arrangements with an employer under which the employer's employees, or a class of his employees—

(a) receive insurance services provided by the insurer; or

(b) are given an opportunity to receive such services.

(2) The insurer is to be taken, for the purposes of this Part, to discriminate unlawfully against a disabled person who is a relevant employee if he acts in relation to that employee in a way which would be unlawful discrimination for the purposes of Part III if—

(a) he were providing the service in question to members of the public; and

(b) the employee was provided with, or was trying to secure the provision of, that service as a member of the public.

(3) In this section—

"insurance services" means services of a prescribed description for the provision of benefits in respect of—

(a) termination of service;

(b) retirement, old age or death;

(c) accident, injury, sickness or invalidity; or

(d) any other prescribed matter; and

"relevant employee" means—

(a) in the case of an arrangement which applies to employees of the employer in question, an employee of his;

(b) in the case of an arrangement which applies to a class of employees of the employer, an employee who is in that class.

(4) For the purposes of the definition of "relevant employee" in subsection (3), "employee", in relation to an employer, includes a person who has applied for, or is contemplating applying for, employment by that employer or (as the case may be) employment by him in the class in question.

General Note

This section provides for the situation where an employer enters into arrangements with an insurance company for insurance services (for example, private health insurance) to be received by the employer's employees. It provides that the insurer will be taken to have discriminated unlawfully against a disabled employee if it treats that person in a way which would be unlawful discrimination under Pt. III if it were providing the service in question to the employee as a member of the public: "That means that refusal to insure a disabled employee, or levying a higher premium, will be unlawful unless it is justified; for example, where there are reasonable grounds for supposing that the disabled person represents a higher risk than normal." (Minister of State, *Hansard*, H.L., Vol. 566, col. 995). "Insurance services", as defined in subs. (3), include the provision of benefits in respect of termination of service, retirement, old age, death, accident, injury, sickness, invalidity or any other matter that may be prescribed by regulations. A complaint of an infringement of this section lies to an industrial tribunal under s.8.

Part III

Discrimination in Other Areas

Goods, facilities and services

Discrimination in relation to goods, facilities and services

19.—(1) It is unlawful for a provider of services to discriminate against a disabled person—

(a) in refusing to provide, or deliberately not providing, to the disabled person any service which he provides, or is prepared to provide, to members of the public;

(b) in failing to comply with any duty imposed on him by section 21 in circumstances in which the effect of that failure is to make it impossible or unreasonably difficult for the disabled person to make use of any such service;

(c) in the standard of service which he provides to the disabled person or the manner in which he provides it to him; or

(d) in the terms on which he provides a service to the disabled person.

(2) For the purposes of this section and sections 20 and 21—

(a) the provision of services includes the provision of any goods or facilities;

(b) a person is "a provider of services" if he is concerned with the provision, in the United Kingdom, of services to the public or to a section of the public; and

(c) it is irrelevant whether a service is provided on payment or without payment.

(3) The following are examples of services to which this section and sections 20 and 21 apply—

(a) access to and use of any place which members of the public are permitted to enter;

(b) access to and use of means of communication;
(c) access to and use of information services;
(d) accommodation in a hotel, boarding house or other similar establishment;
(e) facilities by way of banking or insurance or for grants, loans, credit or finance;
(f) facilities for entertainment, recreation or refreshment;
(g) facilities provided by employment agencies or under section 2 of the Employment and Training Act 1973;
(h) the services of any profession or trade, or any local or other public authority.

(4) In the case of an act which constitutes discrimination by virtue of section 55, this section also applies to discrimination against a person who is not disabled.

(5) Except in such circumstances as may be prescribed, this section and sections 20 and 21 do not apply to—
(a) education which is funded, or secured, by a relevant body or provided at—
(i) an establishment which is funded by such a body or by a Minister of the Crown; or
(ii) any other establishment which is a school as defined in section 14(5) of the Further and Higher Education Act 1992 or section 135 (1) of the Education (Scotland) Act 1980;
(b) any service so far as it consists of the use of any means of transport; or
(c) such other services as may be prescribed.

(6) In subsection (5) "relevant body" means—
(a) a local education authority in England and Wales;
(b) an education authority in Scotland;
(c) the Funding Agency for Schools;
(d) the Schools Funding Council for Wales;
(e) the Further Education Funding Council for England;
(f) the Further Education Funding Council for Wales;
(g) the Higher Education Funding Council for England;
(h) the Scottish Higher Education Funding Council;
(i) the Higher Education Funding Council for Wales;
(j) the Teacher Training Agency;
(k) a voluntary organisation; or
(l) a body of a prescribed kind.

GENERAL NOTE

This section introduces a right of access for disabled people, by making it unlawful for a service provider to discriminate against a disabled person in the provision of goods, facilities or services. The right is "a universal, all-embracing right of non-discrimination against disabled people ... applicable to all providers of goods, facilities and services to the general public, with the specific exclusions of transport and education" (Minister for Social Security and Disabled People, *Hansard*, H.C., Standing Committee E, col. 290). The new right of access "will not only prohibit discriminatory behaviour but also require positive action which is reasonable and readily achievable to overcome the physical and communication barriers that impede disabled people's access" (White Paper, *Ending discrimination against disabled people*, Cm. 2729, 1995, para. 4.4).

The new right imposes four main duties on service providers. First, it makes it unlawful for a service provider to discriminate against a disabled person by refusing to provide goods, facilities or services which he provides to other members of the public, or by providing them on different terms or to a different standard. So, for example, it might be unlawful for a supermarket owner to refuse to serve someone whose disability means that they shop slowly, or for a restaurant owner to insist that a person with a facial disfigurement sits out of sight of other customers, or for a travel agent to ask a disabled person for a bigger deposit when they are booking a holiday (*A Brief Guide to the Disability Discrimination Act*, DL40, p.6). Secondly, it places a duty on a service provider to take reasonable steps to change any practice, policy or procedure which makes it impossible or unreasonably difficult for disabled people to make use of a service which he provides to other members of the public. Thirdly, it places a duty on a service provider to take reasonable steps to remove or alter any physical barrier which makes it impossible or unreasonably difficult for disabled people to make use of such a service, or to provide some alternative means of making the service accessible to a disabled person. Fourthly, it places a duty on a service provider to take reasonable steps to provide auxiliary aids or services (*e.g.* information on tape or in braille) which would make it easier for disabled people to use their services.

Subsection (1) makes it unlawful for a service provider to discriminate against a disabled person by failing to comply with any of the above duties. The duty to make reasonable adjustments to practices, policies and procedures, to remove to physical barriers and to provide auxiliary aids, is contained in s.21 (see the notes to that section). A similar duty is placed on employers under Pt. II, although in that context the duty arises where a disabled person is put at a "substantial disadvantage" by the employer's arrangements or premises. Surprisingly, the Act does not contain any express prohibition on discriminatory advertisements for goods, facilities and services to mirror the provisions in s.11 outlawing discriminatory job advertisements. This contrasts with the corresponding provisions in the sex and race discrimination legislation, which apply both to advertisements for employment and for goods and services. The Government were not persuaded that there was a problem which needed to be addressed in this area, and suggested that any discriminatory advertisement for goods and services would be covered by the s.21 duty to make adjustments:

> "[Section 21] puts a duty on service providers to change any policy, practice or procedure which makes it impossible or unreasonably difficult for a disabled person to make use of their services. Given the need to adjust such policies, it seems most unlikely that a trader, determined to evade this requirement, would advertise his or her failure to comply with the law." (Minister of State, *Hansard*, H.L., Vol. 565, col. 676).

Discrimination is defined for the purposes of this section in s.20. As with the provisions relating to employment, the definition is in two parts: a service provider discriminates against a disabled person (a) if he treats that person less favourably, for a reason which relates to his or her disability or (b) if he fails to comply with a duty to make reasonable adjustments. In both cases, the discriminatory conduct may be justified, but the justification defence which applies here differs significantly from that which applies in the case of employment, and it has been argued that the grounds upon which discriminatory conduct may be justified (danger to health and safety, lack of informed consent, preserving the service for other members of the public, etc.) are so wide and subjective as to render the right not to be discriminated against almost worthless.

That *caveat* aside, these provisions are very broad in their scope. They apply to the provision of any service (including the provision of goods and facilities) by a person concerned with the provision in the U.K. of such services to the public or a section of the public, whether or not for payment (subs. (2)). The breadth of coverage is illustrated by the list of examples in subs. (3) which, with the exception of heads (b) and (c), corresponds to the lists contained in the equivalent provisions in the Sex Discrimination Act 1975 and the Race Relations Act 1976; heads (b) and (c) were added to reflect the importance of communication and information services to disabled people, although the list is not exhaustive (Minister for Social Security and Disabled People, *Hansard*, H.C., Standing Committee E, col. 291). Unlike the sex and race discrimination legislation, there are specific exclusions in subs. (5) for educational establishments and transport vehicles, despite vigorous Opposition attempts to include those areas in this Part of the Act. The Government were however persuaded to make some important concessions in those areas: see Pts. IV and V.

At the time of writing, the implementation date for the duties contained in this Part of the Act had yet to be announced. The Government has however made it clear that the duties are to be phased in over a number of years, with the right not to be refused service coming into force first, towards the end of 1996, and the duties relating to auxiliary aids and the removal of physical barriers being brought into force over a longer period of up to ten years, to allow service providers enough time to prepare for and make the necessary changes (Minister of State, *Hansard*, H.L., Vol. 564, cols. 803, 1696).

Subs. (1)

Provider of services. This is defined in subs. (2)(b) as a person concerned with the provision, in the U.K., of "services to the public or to a section of the public". For the interpretation of this phrase in the context of discrimination in the provision of goods, facilities and services on grounds of race, see *Charter v. Race Relations Board* [1973] A.C. 868 (a case under the R.R.A. 1968, s.2, the forerunner of the provisions now contained in the R.R.A., s.20), where it was held that the provisions did not apply to situations of a purely private character; see also *Dockers' Labour Club and Institute v. Race Relations Board* [1976] A.C. 285. It follows that this section does not apply to the provision of services to their members by trade unions and other similar organisations; separate provision for discrimination by trade organisations is made in s.13: see the note to that section.

The provision of services includes the provision of any goods or facilities (subs. (2)(a)). Manufacturers and designers who supply their services directly to the public will be covered by this section as service providers, but the Government has made clear that the Act is not intended to cover the design and manufacture of products: "It is one thing to give an individual a legal right of access to goods and services as the [Act] does; but it is quite another to give him a right to products of a certain type or design." (Minister of State, *Hansard*, H.L., Vol. 566, col. 241; and see *ibid*. Vol. 564, col. 1768). "This is the case even where the product could be regarded as "information"; for example, newspapers, books and television programmes. There will therefore be no requirement for those items to be made available in an accessible format." (*ibid*. Vol. 566, col. 251). Nor does the Act require manufacturers to provide information on products (operating instructions, etc.) in accessible formats (*ibid*.).

Although not specifically mentioned in subs. (3), "services" is intended to include legal services provided to members of the public by courts, tribunals, solicitors, the Legal Aid Board and other agencies of the criminal justice system (Minister of State, *Hansard*, H.L., Vol. 566, col. 260). Service as a juror is not covered by Pt. III, since that cannot be construed as a service being provided to members of the public (*ibid*. col. 261); the position of witnesses is however less clear: "The fact that witnesses are classed as users of the court services (*i.e.* for the purposes of the National Survey of Court Users) does not mean that they are receiving a service within the meaning of the [Act]." (*ibid*. col. 262). The Government has also confirmed that "services" includes all medical and health care services (Minister of State, *Hansard*, H.L., Vol. 564, col. 1952).

Refusing to provide, or deliberately not providing. For the interpretation of the phrase "refusing or deliberately omitting to provide" as it appears in the equivalent provisions outlawing discrimination in the provision of goods, facilities and services in the S.D.A., s.29, see *Gill v. El Vino Co.* [1983] Q.B. 425.

Meaning of "discrimination"

20.—(1) For the purposes of section 19, a provider of services discriminates against a disabled person if—

(a) for a reason which relates to the disabled person's disability, he treats him less favourably than he treats or would treat others to whom that reason does not or would not apply; and
(b) he cannot show that the treatment in question is justified.

(2) For the purposes of section 19, a provider of services also discriminates against a disabled person if—

(a) he fails to comply with a section 21 duty imposed on him in relation to the disabled person; and
(b) he cannot show that his failure to comply with that duty is justified.

(3) For the purposes of this section, treatment is justified only if—

(a) in the opinion of the provider of services, one or more of the conditions mentioned in subsection (4) are satisfied; and
(b) it is reasonable, in all the circumstances of the case, for him to hold that opinion.

(4) The conditions are that—

(a) in any case, the treatment is necessary in order not to endanger the health or safety of any person (which may include that of the disabled person);
(b) in any case, the disabled person is incapable of entering into an enforceable agreement, or of giving an informed consent, and for that reason the treatment is reasonable in that case;
(c) in a case falling within section 19(1)(a), the treatment is necessary because the provider of services would otherwise be unable to provide the service to members of the public;
(d) in a case falling within section 19(1)(c) or (d), the treatment is necessary in order for the provider of services to be able to provide the service to the disabled person or to other members of the public;
(e) in a case falling within section 19(1)(d), the difference in the terms on which the service is provided to the disabled person and those on

which it is provided to other members of the public reflects the greater cost to the provider of services in providing the service to the disabled person.

(5) Any increase in the cost of providing a service to a disabled person which results from compliance by a provider of services with a section 21 duty shall be disregarded for the purposes of subsection (4)(e).

(6) Regulations may make provision, for purposes of this section, as to circumstances in which—

(a) it is reasonable for a provider of services to hold the opinion mentioned in subsection (3)(a);
(b) it is not reasonable for a provider of services to hold that opinion.

(7) Regulations may make provision for subsection (4)(b) not to apply in prescribed circumstances where—

(a) a person is acting for a disabled person under a power of attorney;
(b) functions conferred by or under Part VII of the Mental Health Act 1983 are exercisable in relation to a disabled person's property or affairs; or
(c) powers are exercisable in Scotland in relation to a disabled person's property or affairs in consequence of the appointment of a curator bonis, tutor or judicial factor.

(8) Regulations may make provision, for purposes of this section, as to circumstances (other than those mentioned in subsection (4)) in which treatment is to be taken to be justified.

(9) In subsections (3), (4) and (8) "treatment" includes failure to comply with a section 21 duty.

GENERAL NOTE

The definition of discrimination which is used for the purposes of the right of access to goods, facilities and services is similar to that which applies in employment cases under Pt. II (see the note to s.5). It adopts the same two-fold approach, by providing that a service provider discriminates against a disabled person if (a) he treats that person less favourably than he treats or would treat others, for a reason which relates to that person's disability or (b) he fails to comply with a duty imposed on him under s.21 to make reasonable adjustments in relation to the provision of services to disabled persons. As in the employment provisions, the Act departs from the approach which is normally taken in anti-discrimination legislation by allowing a service provider to argue that the less favourable treatment, or the failure to make adjustments, is justified. However, while the justification defence in employment cases takes an objective approach, focusing on whether the reason for the employer's conduct "is both material to the circumstances of the particular case and substantial" (see s.5(3)), in this context a more detailed and more subjective test of justification is used, which turns on the service provider's reasonable opinion as to whether certain conditions are satisfied (subs. (3)). A similar test was originally intended for the employment provisions, but in a late amendment to s.5 that test was substituted by the "material and substantial" test, after concern was expressed that the original version was too complex and allowed too much discretion to employers. The explanation for the difference in approach was explained in the following terms: "Service providers often have to take very quick and perhaps less informed decisions when serving someone. So an opinion-based approach remains appropriate." (Minister of State, *Hansard*, H.L., Vol. 566, col. 119).

By subs. (3), discriminatory treatment of a disabled person may be justified if, in the reasonable opinion of the service provider, one or more of the following conditions set out in subs. (4) are satisfied:

(a) the treatment is necessary in order not to endanger health and safety. It is not unlawful for a service provider to refuse to provide a service, or to do so on different terms, if the health and safety of the disabled person or of other people would be put in danger: "An example of this could be if a swimming instructor, taking an adult beginners class, has to focus most of his attention on a disabled person and cannot cover the programme for each class. Other members of the class might be put at risk." (Minister of State, *Hansard*, H.L., Vol. 566, col. 1025).
(b) the treatment is reasonable because the disabled person is incapable of entering into an enforceable agreement or of giving an informed consent. Concern has been expressed by organisations such as MIND and Mencap that the subjective nature of this test might

enable it to be used as a general justification for refusing to serve people with mental impairments, reinforcing the widespread misunderstanding which exists in society about the ability of mentally ill people and people with learning difficulties to manage their own affairs. The Government has indicated that this justification is intended to be narrow in its scope, and is not intended to be used as a loophole to allow people to refuse to serve disabled persons:

"It will not be reasonable for service providers to cite this justification when the purchase of a product or service would not normally be the subject of a written agreement. For example, it cannot be used in relation to buying groceries in a supermarket. The subsection will apply only to major purchases—a motor car perhaps—or credit agreements, and it is meant to apply only in a few cases." (Minister for Social Security and Disabled People, *Hansard*, H.C., Standing Committee E, col. 350; see also *Hansard*, H.C., Vol. 257, col. 893).

Regulations may be made under subs. (4) disapplying this justification for discrimination where someone is acting on behalf of a disabled person under a power of attorney, or where a person's property or affairs are under the management of the Court of Protection under Pt. VII of the Mental Health Act 1983 (c. 20).

(c) it is necessary to refuse to serve a disabled person because otherwise the service provider would be unable to provide that service to other customers. This defence has been described as "the strictest test of all. It applies only in circumstances in which, if a service provider were to serve a particular disabled person, he would not be able to continue to provide his service at all. That is our intention. . . . the use of the word necessary would be a tough test, with a meaning akin to essential. That is intended to be its legal meaning." (Minister for Social Security and Disabled People, *Hansard*, H.C., Standing Committee E, col. 354). The defence would not apply where providing the service to a disabled person would merely delay or disrupt the provision of the service to other customers (*ibid*. col. 355).

(d) it is necessary to provide the service to a disabled person on different terms or to a different standard in order to be able to provide that service to that person or to other customers.

(e) where a service is provided to a disabled person on different terms, the difference in those terms reflects the greater cost to the service provider in providing that service to a disabled person. On the face of it, this seems to give a service provider the right to surcharge disabled customers for providing, for example, information in an accessible format, or otherwise making their services more accessible. However, subs. (5) makes it clear that any increase in the cost of providing a service to a disabled person which results from compliance with a duty under s.21 to make that service more accessible may not be passed on to the disabled customer under this head. The Government has confirmed that subs. (4)(e) is not intended to "give businesses the opportunity to load opportunity costs on to a disabled person or allow service providers to charge more to a disabled person where they have to make their services more accessible to suit his or her disability . . . It is certainly not our intention that, for example, a large organisation which had to produce information in an alternative format for some of its disabled customers should be able to charge them more for it." (Minister of State, *Hansard*, H.L., Vol. 564, col. 2009). The defence is therefore much narrower in scope than it might initially seem to be, covering those who provide specialised goods or services for disabled people:

"I have in mind a shoemaker who is asked by a disabled person to make a shoe to an unusual pattern or using an unusual fabric. The task might take the shoemaker longer than usual and require a special order for equipment and materials. That would amount to a different, more specialised service than he would usually provide, and it is reasonable that he should be able to charge more." (Minister for Social Security and Disabled People, *Hansard*, H.C., Standing Committee E, col. 357).

Regulations may specify circumstances in which it is or is not reasonable for a service provider to believe that one or more of these conditions are satisfied (subs. (6)), and may also provide for other circumstances in which discriminatory treatment by service providers will be deemed to be justified (subs. (8)). The Government has indicated that it intends to make regulations permitting insurance companies to charge higher premiums to disabled customers "to the extent that the extra charge is based on actuarial data or other good reasons." (White Paper, *Ending discrimination against disabled people*, Cm. 2729, 1995, para. 4.4), while at the same time declaring its intention of eliminating unfair discrimination in insurance:

"we have been convinced that disabled people, when they seek insurance cover, sometimes face unfair discrimination, whether in the form of a loaded premium or a refusal to provide cover at all. We want to ensure that the treatment of disabled customers is based on a reasonable assessment of risk rather than on any prejudicial assumptions of the insurer." (Minister of State, *Hansard*, H.L., Vol. 564, col. 2013).

In common with employment provisions in Pt. II, the definition of discrimination in this section does not expressly prohibit indirect discrimination (*i.e.* the application of a requirement or condition which has a disproportionate impact on a particular group or class). As in that context, however, the Government's view is that the duty to make reasonable adjustments will protect disabled people against indirect discrimination in the provision of goods, facilities and services:

"Indirect discrimination typically occurs where a practice or condition of access has a disproportionately adverse effect, often unintended, on a particular section of society. Because disabled people constitute a very diverse group, a general prohibition of indirect discrimination against them could have unforeseen consequences which were unfairly burdensome for businesses. Nonetheless, the Government accepts that there may be particular practices, indirectly denying disabled people access to goods and services, which should be prevented. Banning animals, for example, has a disproportionate effect on those blind people who rely on guide dogs. The Government will therefore require practical modifications to such practices [*i.e.* under s.21] so that disabled people are not unjustifiably denied access." (White Paper, *Ending discrimination against disabled people*, Cm. 2729, 1995, para. 4.5).

Subs. (1)
Others to whom that reason does not or would not apply. See the note to s.5(1).

Duty of providers of services to make adjustments

21.—(1) Where a provider of services has a practice, policy or procedure which makes it impossible or unreasonably difficult for disabled persons to make use of a service which he provides, or is prepared to provide, to other members of the public, it is his duty to take such steps as it is reasonable, in all the circumstances of the case, for him to have to take in order to change that practice, policy or procedure so that it no longer has that effect.

(2) Where a physical feature (for example, one arising from the design or construction of a building or the approach or access to premises) makes it impossible or unreasonably difficult for disabled persons to make use of such a sentence, it is the duty of the provider of that service to take such steps as it is reasonable, in all the circumstances of the case, for him to have to take in order to—

(a) remove the feature;
(b) alter it so that it no longer has that effect;
(c) provide a reasonable means of avoiding the feature; or
(d) provide a reasonable alternative method of making the service in question available to disabled persons.

(3) Regulations may prescribe—

(a) matters which are to be taken into account in determining whether any provision of a kind mentioned in subsection (2)(c) or (d) is reasonable; and
(b) categories of providers of services to whom subsection (2) does not apply.

(4) Where an auxiliary aid or service (for example, the provision of information on audio tape or of a sign language interpreter) would—

(a) enable disabled persons to make use of a service which a provider of services provides, or is prepared to provide, to members of the public, or
(b) facilitate the use by disabled persons of such a service,

it is the duty of the provider of that service to take such steps as it is reasonable, in all the circumstances of the case, for him to have to take in order to provide that auxiliary aid or service.

(5) Regulations may make provision, for the purposes of this section—

(a) as to circumstances in which it is reasonable for a provider of services to have to take steps of a prescribed description;

(b) as to circumstances in which it is not reasonable for a provider of services to have to take steps of a prescribed description;
(c) as to what is to be included within the meaning of "practice, policy or procedure";
(d) as to what is not to be included within the meaning of that expression;
(e) as to things which are to be treated as physical features;
(f) as to things which are not to be treated as such features;
(g) as to things which are to be treated as auxiliary aids or services;
(h) as to things which are not to be treated as auxiliary aids or services.

(6) Nothing in this section requires a provider of services to take any steps which would fundamentally alter the nature of the service in question or the nature of his trade, profession or business.

(7) Nothing in this section requires a provider of services to take any steps which would cause him to incur expenditure exceeding the prescribed maximum.

(8) Regulations under subsection (7) may provide for the prescribed maximum to be calculated by reference to—
(a) aggregate amounts of expenditure incurred in relation to different cases;
(b) prescribed periods;
(c) services of a prescribed description;
(d) premises of a prescribed description; or
(e) such other criteria as may be prescribed.

(9) Regulations may provide, for the purposes of subsection (7), for expenditure incurred by one provider of services to be treated as incurred by another.

(10) This section imposes duties only for the purpose of determining whether a provider of services has discriminated against a disabled person; and accordingly a breach of any such duty is not actionable as such.

General Note

This section places a duty on service providers to make reasonable adjustments to overcome any barriers that make it impossible or unreasonably difficult for disabled people to gain access to goods, facilities and services. A similar duty is placed on employers under Pt. II of the Act, although in that context the duty arises where a disabled person is put at a "substantial disadvantage" by the employer's arrangements or premises: see the note to s.6.

The duty to make adjustments is in three parts. First, subs. (1) provides that a service provider has a duty to take reasonable steps to change any practice, policy or procedure which makes it impossible or unreasonably difficult for disabled people to make use of a service which he provides to other members of the public, so that it no longer has that effect. For example, it would be unlawful for a restaurant which does not allow animals to refuse admission to a disabled person with a guide dog. The Government has insisted that service providers "will not be able to get away with treating disabled people without the same dignity and respect as any other customer. If, for example, a cafe proprietor does have to change a 'no dogs' rule it will not be good enough for him to suggest that he is happy to see the animal tied up outside with a bowl of water!" (Minister of State, *Hansard*, H.L., Vol. 566, col. 266). Regulations made under subs. (5) may define what is or is not to count as a "practice, policy or procedure" for these purposes.

Secondly, subs. (2) provides that a service provider has a duty to take reasonable steps to remove or alter any physical feature (for example, a physical barrier) which makes it impossible or unreasonably difficult for disabled people to make use of a service which he provides to other members of the public, or to provide a reasonable method of avoiding the feature or of making the service available to disabled people in some other way. For example, a supplier of goods might be required to widen entrance doors, remove steps or install a lift to make its premises accessible to people in wheelchairs; alternatively, it might be reasonable to provide an illustrated catalogue and order form, or to arrange for items to be brought down to the disabled person. The Government has conceded that this may result in a wheelchair user having less choice than other customers, and therefore receiving a lower standard of service: "The requirement . . . is to provide access to a service as close as it is reasonably possible to get to the standard normally offered." (Minister of State, *Hansard*, H.L., Vol. 566, col. 267). Provided the Act's requirements are satisfied, it is for service providers themselves to decide how best their services can be made accessible to disabled people. The Government rejected an Opposition amendment which sought to provide that the use of an alternative means of providing a service should be allowed only as a last resort when physical alterations were unreasonably difficult:

"the legislation has been deliberately drafted in a way that ensures that sensible, low-cost accessibility solutions are encouraged wherever possible, so long as they are reasonable. The amendment could impose much unnecessary cost on businesses in situations where to contemplate expensive building work which might be considered reasonable in its own right would be to fly in the face of common sense if, as a prior option, a work-around solution could not be considered as well." (Minister of State, *Hansard*, H.L., Vol. 564, col. 2022).

The Minister did however concede that in some situations (*e.g.* restaurants, theatres and art galleries) physical alterations to premises would be the only reasonable solution "because physical access to premises is a fundamental attribute of the service... It would clearly not be reasonable for the proprietor of a cafe to suggest that a take-away meal was a suitable alternative to making an adjustment to the layout or construction of his premises which would allow disabled people to enter." (*ibid*). The Minister also confirmed that the means of entrance must also be reasonable in such cases: "It would not be reasonable ... to expect a wheelchair user to have to negotiate the rubbish bins and general detritus of a back alley to be let into a restaurant via the kitchens..." (*ibid.* col. 2023).

Any physical alterations remain subject to the control of the planning and highway authorities, by virtue of the provisions in s.59 which provide that obligations under the Act are subordinate to other enactments. Concern has been expressed over the possible impact which the duty to make physical alterations might have on historic buildings, and the need to balance the reasonable expectations of disabled people as regards access with the desire to preserve the fabric of such buildings. In the White Paper, *Ending discrimination against disabled people* (Cm. 2729, 1995, at para. 4.10), the Government indicated that it was considering an exemption from the new right for listed buildings where the alterations would damage the essential character for which the building is protected. The Government has since concluded that any such exemption is unnecessary, since s.59 will prevent a service provider having to act without listed building consent in order to comply with the Act: "So if, for example, listed building consent to replace a medieval archway with a pair of sliding doors was refused, the service provider who then declined to install the new doorway could not be held to have discriminated against a disabled person for whom the building remained consequently inaccessible." (Minister of State, *Hansard*, H.L., Vol. 564, col. 2023). Physical adjustments for which listed building consent would be granted would however have to be considered.

The duty of a service provider to make reasonable adjustments to physical features may present problems where the premises are occupied under a lease, the terms of which prevent or restrict the occupier from making alterations to the premises. In those circumstances, the terms of the lease are overridden by s.27 of the Act, which entitles the occupier to alter the premises, with the written consent of the landlord, in order to comply with a duty to make adjustments under this section. See the note to s.27.

Part M of the Building Regulations 1988 (revised in 1991) contains mandatory requirements for new non-domestic buildings and substantial extensions concerning the provision of access and facilities for disabled people. In the Bill as originally published, there was a specific exemption from the duty to make physical adjustments for buildings and extensions erected in compliance with any requirement of the Building Regulations relating to disabled people:

"The Government takes the view that service providers should be able to rely on Part M of the building regulations as representing a bona fide national standard of accessibility for disabled people... It is only natural justice that a service provider who sets up in a new building which complies with building regulations should be entitled to believe that his premises have been certified as accessible." (Minister of State, *Hansard*, H.L., Vol. 564, col. 2026).

That exemption was dropped from the Bill at Committee stage in the House of Lords: "We now recognise that the subsection as drafted is something of a blunt instrument and that the problem needs to be tackled in a rather more sophisticated way." (Minister of State, *Hansard*, H.L., Vol. 564, col. 2026). The Government has indicated that it intends to make regulations under subs. (5) addressing the issue. For the Government's proposals in relation to the Building Regulations and the duty to make adjustments under Pt. II of the Act, see the note to s.6.

Thirdly, subs. (4) provides that a service provider has a duty to take reasonable steps to provide auxiliary aids or services which would enable disabled people to make use of their services, or make it easier for them to do so. For example, a service provider might be expected to provide information on tape or in braille for visually impaired customers, an induction loop for people with hearing aids, or a handrail for those who have difficulty walking up stairs.

"The extent to which a provider must provide auxiliary aids depends on the goods, facilities and services available. For example, a catalogue company that offers a telephone ordering service could reasonably be expected to provide a minicom service for deaf people, but a local butcher's shop that does not offer anyone a telephone ordering service could not reasonably be expected to provide minicom." (Minister for Social Security and Disabled People, *Hansard*, H.C., Standing Committee E, col. 292).

Regulations made under subs. (5) may provide that certain things are or are not to be treated as "auxiliary aids or services" for these purposes.

It is unlawful for a service provider to discriminate against a disabled person by failing to comply with any of these duties where the effect of that failure is to make it "impossible or unreasonably difficult" for the disabled person to make use of the service in question (s.19(1)(b)), unless the service provider can show that his failure to comply with the duty is justified within the meaning of s.20 (see the note to that section). The Government has denied that this test of discrimination is insufficiently tough on service providers:

"[I]n this context, the term 'service' includes the concept of service as far as possible to the same standard as that received by other people. There is no question of service providers being able to get away with providing access to a lower standard than normal *unless there are inescapable reasons*." (Minister of State, *Hansard*, H.L., Vol. 566, col. 266, emphasis added).

However, this assurance sits uneasily with the views of the Minister, quoted above, on the desirability of encouraging low-cost accessibility solutions, which suggests that the choice of access solution may be driven primarily by considerations of cost rather than standard of service. Ultimately, the extent of the duty on service providers will turn upon how the phrase "impossible or unreasonably difficult" is interpreted by the courts, and on whether, in each individual case, the court considers that the service provider has taken "such steps as it is reasonable, in all the circumstances of the case, for him to have to take" to enable a disabled person to make use of the service in question.

There are two further limitations on the scope of the duty to make adjustments imposed by this section. First, subs. (6) provides that a service provider is not required to take any steps which would fundamentally alter the nature of the service in question or the nature of his trade, business or profession. For example, the owner of a night club would not be expected to raise lighting levels for visually-impaired people; and a trainer of champion athletes would still be entitled to exclude the majority of the population from his classes (White Paper, *Ending discrimination against disabled people*, Cm. 2729, 1995, para. 4.4). Secondly, subs. (7) provides that a service provider is not required to take any steps which would cause him to incur expenditure over a prescribed maximum amount. At the time of writing, the Government had yet to announce what the limit on the expenditure on adjustments would be. Subsection (8) allows the maximum to be calculated according to aggregate amounts of expenditure on adjustments, the period over which the expenditure is made, the type of service and premises, and other as yet unspecified criteria, while subs. (9) allows expenditure incurred by one service provider to be treated as incurred by another. Regulations may also be made under subss. (3) and (5), fleshing out the details of the duty to make adjustments. In particular, subs. (3)(b) allows certain prescribed categories of service provider to be exempted from the duty to remove physical barriers.

Premises

Discrimination in relation to premises

22.—(1) It is unlawful for a person with power to dispose of any premises to discriminate against a disabled person—

(a) in the terms on which he offers to dispose of those premises to the disabled person;

(b) by refusing to dispose of those premises to the disabled person; or

(c) in his treatment of the disabled person in relation to any list of persons in need of premises of that description.

(2) Subsection (1) does not apply to a person who owns an estate or interest in the premises and wholly occupies them unless, for the purpose of disposing of the premises, he—

(a) uses the services of an estate agent, or

(b) publishes an advertisement or causes an advertisement to be published.

(3) It is unlawful for a person managing any premises to discriminate against a disabled person occupying those premises—

(a) in the way he permits the disabled person to make use of any benefits or facilities;
(b) by refusing or deliberately omitting to permit the disabled person to make use of any benefits or facilities; or
(c) by evicting the disabled person, or subjecting him to any other detriment.

(4) It is unlawful for any person whose licence or consent is required for the disposal of any premises comprised in, or (in Scotland) the subject of, a tenancy to discriminate against a disabled person by withholding his licence or consent for the disposal of the premises to the disabled person.

(5) Subsection (4) applies to tenancies created before as well as after the passing of this Act.

(6) In this section—

"advertisement" includes every form of advertisement or notice, whether to the public or not;

"dispose", in relation to premises, includes granting a right to occupy the premises, and, in relation to premises comprised in, or (in Scotland) the subject of, a tenancy, includes—
(a) assigning the tenancy, and
(b) sub-letting or parting with possession of the premises or any part of the premises;
and "disposal" shall be construed accordingly;

"estate agent" means a person who, by way of profession or trade, provides services for the purpose of finding premises for persons seeking to acquire them or assisting in the disposal of premises; and

"tenancy" means a tenancy created—
(a) by a lease or sub-lease,
(b) by an agreement for a lease or sub-lease,
(c) by a tenancy agreement, or
(d) in pursuance of any enactment.

(7) In the case of an act which constitutes discrimination by virtue of section 55, this section also applies to discrimination against a person who is not disabled.

(8) This section applies only in relation to premises in the United Kingdom.

General Note

This section makes it unlawful for a person with the power to dispose of premises to discriminate against a disabled person in the sale, letting and management of those premises, for example, by refusing to sell or rent property to a disabled person, by offering the property on worse terms than would be offered to anyone else, or by preventing a disabled tenant from using any benefits or facilities. It mirrors the corresponding provisions in the Sex Discrimination Act 1975, s.30, and the Race Relations Act 1976, s.21, and, in common with those provisions, is subject to an exemption in the case of small dwellings (see s.23). Discrimination is defined for these purposes in broadly similar terms to those which apply in the case of goods, facilities and services (see s.24), but with the important difference that, in this context, there is no duty on a person selling, renting or managing property to make adjustments to the property to make it accessible to a disabled person.

Exemption for small dwellings

23.—(1) Where the conditions mentioned in subsection (2) are satisfied, subsection (1), (3) or (as the case may be) (4) of section 22 does not apply.

(2) The conditions are that—
(a) the relevant occupier resides, and intends to continue to reside, on the premises;
(b) the relevant occupier shares accommodation on the premises with persons who reside on the premises and are not members of his household;

(c) the shared accommodation is not storage accommodation or a means of access; and
(d) the premises are small premises.

(3) For the purposes of this section, premises are "small premises" if they fall within subsection (4) or (5).

(4) Premises fall within this subsection if—
(a) only the relevant occupier and members of his household reside in the accommodation occupied by him;
(b) the premises comprise, in addition to the accommodation occupied by the relevant occupier, residential accommodation for at least one other household;
(c) the residential accommodation for each other household is let, or available for letting, on a separate tenancy or similar agreement; and
(d) there are not normally more than two such other households.

(5) Premises fall within this subsection if there is not normally residential accommodation on the premises for more than six persons in addition to the relevant occupier and any members of his household.

(6) For the purposes of this section "the relevant occupier" means—
(a) in a case falling within section 22(1), the person with power to dispose of the premises, or a near relative of his;
(b) in a case falling within section 22(4), the person whose licence or consent is required for the disposal of the premises, or a near relative of his.

(7) For the purposes of this section—
"near relative" means a person's spouse, partner, parent, child, grandparent, grandchild, or brother or sister (whether of full or half blood or by affinity); and
"partner" means the other member of a couple consisting of a man and a woman who are not married to each other but are living together as husband and wife.

GENERAL NOTE

This section contains an exemption for small dwellings similar to that found in the Sex Discrimination Act 1975, s.32, and the Race Relations Act 1976, s.22.

Meaning of "discrimination"

24.—(1) For the purposes of section 22, a person ("A") discriminates against a disabled person if—
(a) for a reason which relates to the disabled person's disability, he treats him less favourably than he treats or would treat others to whom that reason does not or would not apply; and
(b) he cannot show that the treatment in question is justified.

(2) For the purposes of this section, treatment is justified only if—
(a) in A's opinion, one or more of the conditions mentioned in subsection (3) are satisfied; and
(b) it is reasonable, in all the circumstances of the case, for him to hold that opinion.

(3) The conditions are that—
(a) in any case, the treatment is necessary in order not to endanger the health or safety of any person (which may include that of the disabled person);
(b) in any case, the disabled person is incapable of entering into an enforceable agreement, or of giving an informed consent, and for that reason the treatment is reasonable in that case;
(c) in a case falling within section 22(3)(a), the treatment is necessary in order for the disabled person or the occupiers of other premises forming part of the building to make use of the benefit or facility;

(d) in a case falling within section 22(3)(b), the treatment is necessary in order for the occupiers of other premises forming part of the building to make use of the benefit or facility.

(4) Regulations may make provision, for purposes of this section, as to circumstances in which—

(a) it is reasonable for a person to hold the opinion mentioned in subsection 2(a);

(b) it is not reasonable for a person to hold that opinion.

(5) Regulations may make provision, for purposes of this section, as to circumstances (other than those mentioned in subsection (3)) in which treatment is to be taken to be justified.

General Note

Discrimination is defined for the purposes of s.22 in broadly similar terms to those which apply in the case of access to goods, facilities and services (see s.20), save that in this context there is no duty to make reasonable adjustments to the property. Less favourable treatment of a disabled person may be justified if the person renting or selling property believes that one or more of the conditions in subs. (3) is satisfied, and it is reasonable for him to hold that opinion. So, for example, by virtue of subs. (3)(a), it may be justifiable for a landlord to refuse to let a flat to a disabled person if that person is unable to negotiate the stairs in safety or use the fire escape in an emergency.

Enforcement, etc.

Enforcement, remedies and procedure

25.—(1) A claim by any person that another person—

(a) has discriminated against him in a way which is unlawful under this Part; or

(b) is by virtue of section 57 or 58 to be treated as having discriminated against him in such a way,

may be made the subject of civil proceedings in the same way as any other claim in tort or (in Scotland) in reparation for breach of statutory duty.

(2) For the avoidance of doubt it is hereby declared that damages in respect of discrimination in a way which is unlawful under this Part may include compensation for injury to feelings whether or not they include compensation under any other head.

(3) Proceedings in England and Wales shall be brought only in a county court.

(4) Proceedings in Scotland shall be brought only in a sheriff court.

(5) The remedies available in such proceedings are those which are available in the High Court or (as the case may be) the Court of Session.

(6) Part II of Schedule 3 makes further provision about the enforcement of this Part and about procedure.

General Note

Claims of unlawful discrimination under this Part of the Act must be brought in a county court (or, in Scotland, a sheriff court), and the remedies available are those available in the High Court (or, in Scotland, the Court of Session). The court may award damages, which may include compensation for injury to feelings (subs. (2)). There is no limit on the amount of damages which may be awarded for financial loss under this section. There is however a power in Sched. 3, para. 7 to set an upper limit on the damages available for injury to feelings. This contrasts with the employment provisions in Pt. II, and with the position under the Sex Discrimination Act 1975 and the Race Relations Act 1976, where there is no upper limit on the damages which may be awarded for injury to feelings, or indeed for any other head of recoverable loss. The Government has indicated that it intends to set the limit "close to or at the level which applies at any time to claims which fall to be considered by the small claims court" (Minister of State, *Hansard*, H.L., Vol. 565, col. 735). The upper limit for the small claims procedure is currently set at £3,000:

> "We want to ensure that as many cases as possible can be resolved without recourse to the court system. However, where that becomes inevitable, we want the system for redress to be as informal and easy to use as possible.... we wish to set the limit on the amount payable for

injured feelings so as to help ensure that the vast majority of cases can be dealt with under the small claims procedure, with its advantages of cheap and informal resolution." (Minister of State, *Hansard*, H.L., Vol. 566, col. 1065).

At the present time, legal aid is not available for claims under £1,000. The National Disability Council established under Pt. VI of the Act has no power to investigate complaints of discrimination in the provision of goods, facilities and services, or to assist individuals in enforcing their rights before the courts (see the note to s.50). However, provision is made in s.28 for the establishment by the Government of an advisory service "to provide free advice to help disabled people and businesses to resolve individual disputes arising from the right of access ... without recourse to legal action." (White Paper, *Ending discrimination against disabled people*, Cm. 2729, 1995, para. 4.8).

As to compensation for injury to feelings and the award of exemplary damages in sex and race discrimination cases, see the note to s.8.

Subs. (6)

Schedule 3, para. 5 provides that the remedies available for an infringement of Pt. III are (with the exception of judicial review) exclusively those provided by this section; para. 6 makes provision for time limits (see below); para. 7 allows an upper limit to be placed on damages for injury to feelings (see the General Note to this section); and para. 8 concerns certification by Ministers (see the note to s.59).

Period within which proceedings must be brought. Proceedings in respect of a claim under Pt. III must be instituted before the end of the period of six months beginning when the act complained of was done (Sched. 3, para. 6(1)), although that period may be extended for a further two months where an adviser appointed by the Secretary of State under s.28 is approached before the end of the initial six-month period in relation to actual or prospective proceedings under this section (*ibid.* para. 6(2)). A court may consider a claim which is out of time "if, in all the circumstances of the case, it considers that it is just and equitable to do so" (*ibid.* para. 6(3)). Where a discriminatory act is attributable to a contract term, that act will be treated as extending throughout the duration of the contract; an act extending over a period will be treated as done at the end of that period; and a deliberate omission will be treated as done when the person decided upon it (Sched. 3, para. 6(4)). A person will be taken to have decided upon an omission when he or she does an act inconsistent with doing the omitted act, or, if no such inconsistent act has been done, at the expiry of the period within which he or she might reasonably have been expected to do the omitted act, if it was to be done (*ibid.* para. 6(5)).

For the likely interpretation of these provisions, see the note to s.8(1), which examines the approach taken to the parallel provisions in the S.D.A., s.76, and the R.R.A., s.68.

Validity and revision of certain agreements

26.—(1) Any term in a contract for the provision of goods, facilities or services or in any other agreement is void so far as it purports to—

(a) require a person to do anything which would contravene any provision of, or made under, this Part,

(b) exclude or limit the operation of any provision of this Part, or

(c) prevent any person from making a claim under this Part.

(2) Paragraphs (b) and (c) of subsection (1) do not apply to an agreement settling a claim to which section 25 applies.

(3) On the application of any person interested in an agreement to which subsection (1) applies, a county court or a sheriff court may make such order as it thinks just for modifying the agreement to take account of the effect of subsection (1).

(4) No such order shall be made unless all persons affected have been—

(a) given notice of the application; and

(b) afforded an opportunity to make representations to the court.

(5) Subsection (4) applies subject to any rules of court providing for that notice to be dispensed with.

(6) An order under subsection (3) may include provision as respects any period before the making of the order.

General Note

This section provides that any term in a contract for the provision of goods, facilities or services or in any other agreement is void if it: (a) requires a person to contravene this Part of the

Act; (b) attempts to exclude or limit the operation of this Part of the Act; or (c) attempts to prevent a person from making a claim under this Part of the Act (subs. (1)). As usual, an exception is made in the case of an agreement to settle a claim under s.25 (subs. (2)). The court may modify a contract to take account of the effect of subs. (1), on the application of any interested person, having first notified all those affected of the application and given them an opportunity to make representations (subss. (3) to (6)). For the equivalent provisions as they apply to claims of sex and race discrimination, see the S.D.A. 1975, s.77 and the R.R.A. 1976, s.72 respectively.

Alterations to premises occupied under leases

27.—(1) This section applies where—

(a) a provider of services ("the occupier") occupies premises under a lease;

(b) but for this section, he would not be entitled to make a particular alteration to the premises; and

(c) the alteration is one which the occupier proposes to make in order to comply with a section 21 duty.

(2) Except to the extent to which it expressly so provides, the lease shall have effect by virtue of this subsection as if it provided—

(a) for the occupier to be entitled to make the alteration with the written consent of the lessor;

(b) for the occupier to have to make a written application to the lessor for consent if he wishes to make the alteration;

(c) if such an application is made, for the lessor not to withhold his consent unreasonably; and

(d) for the lessor to be entitled to make his consent subject to reasonable conditions.

(3) In this section—

"lease" includes a tenancy, sub-lease or sub-tenancy and an agreement for a lease, tenancy, sub-lease or sub-tenancy; and

"sub-lease" and "sub-tenancy" have such meaning as may be prescribed.

(4) If the terms and conditions of a lease—

(a) impose conditions which are to apply if the occupier alters the premises, or

(b) entitle the lessor to impose conditions when consenting to the occupier's altering the premises,

the occupier is to be treated for the purposes of subsection (1) as not being entitled to make the alteration.

(5) Part II of Schedule 4 supplements the provisions of this section.

General Note

This section entitles a service provider who occupies leased premises to alter those premises in order to comply with a duty to make reasonable adjustments under s.21. It is in substantially the same terms as the provisions in s.16 of the Act which entitle an employer or a trade organisation to alter leased premises, and reference should therefore be made to the notes on that section. Note, however, that under this section, if an occupier has applied in writing to the lessor for consent to alter the premises, and that consent has been refused or has been given subject to conditions, the occupier (or a disabled person who has an interest in the proposed alteration to the premises being carried out) may refer the matter to the county court, and if the court decides that the lessor's refusal, or any condition imposed by him on his consent, was unreasonable, it may make a declaration or an order authorising the occupier to make the alteration specified in the order. Any such order may also require the occupier to comply with any conditions specified therein (Sched. 4, para. 6).

Advice and assistance

28.—(1) The Secretary of State may make arrangements for the provision of advice and assistance to persons with a view to promoting the settlement of disputes arising under this Part otherwise than by recourse to the courts.

(2) Any person appointed by the Secretary of State in connection with arrangements made under subsection (1) shall have such duties as the Secretary of State may direct.

(3) The Secretary of State may pay to any person so appointed such allowances and compensation for loss of earnings as he considers appropriate.

(4) The Secretary of State may make such payments, by way of grants, in respect of expenditure incurred, or to be incurred, by any person exercising functions in accordance with arrangements made by the Secretary of State under this section as he considers appropriate.

(5) The approval of the Treasury is required for any payment under subsection (3) or (4).

General Note

This section provides for the establishment of an advisory service to offer advice and assistance to individuals alleging discrimination by those providing goods and services, and to promote the settlement of disputes. In the context of sex and race discrimination, this function may be performed by the Equal Opportunities Commission and the Commission for Racial Equality, but the National Disability Council established under Pt. VI of the Act only has the power to advise the Government; it is not empowered to provide advice, information or guidance on an individual basis to disabled persons or service providers (see the note to s.50). This service is intended to fill that gap. Advice in relation to the employment of people with disabilities will continue to be provided by the Employment Service's Placing, Assessment and Counselling Teams (PACTs) and the Advisory, Conciliation and Arbitration Service (ACAS).

The detailed nature of the advisory service to be established under this section is to be the subject of consultation, but at the time of writing it appeared that the Government were contemplating a combined approach involving a telephone helpline to provide general information to disabled people and service providers, and a "second tier" advice and assistance service which would complement the work of the existing advice agencies such as the Citizens Advice Bureaux and DIAL (the Disability Information and Advice Line Service), and would help the existing disability advisers in their work:

> "In other words, what is required is a secondary tier of advice to give help and assistance to those who have the day-to-day contact with disabled people: in essence, a team of full-time disability advisers who, whether situated centrally or regionally, will together form a pool of expertise which can be utilised to stop disputes escalating to the point where court action is necessary." (Minister of State, *Hansard*, H.L., Vol. 566, col. 1029).

Under this scheme, the existing advice agencies would continue to be the primary source of advice and assistance for disabled people and service providers. In more complicated cases, or where the parties cannot reach agreement, the guidance of the advisers could be sought, and in very difficult cases the case could be referred on to the advice service (*ibid.* col. 1030).

Part IV

Education

General Note

As originally published, the Bill did not apply to education. The right of access to goods, facilities and services in Pt. III of the Act contains an exemption in s.19(5) for education framed in very broad terms, and the Government successfully resisted Opposition attempts to include education within the range of facilities and services covered by the right of access in Pt. III. This resistance was not unexpected, given that the education of children with special educational needs and of students with learning difficulties and disabilities was tackled comparatively recently in the Education Act 1993, the Further and Higher Education Act 1992 and the Code of Practice on the Identification and Assessment of Special Educational Needs. The Government's strategy in this area, as explained in the White Paper, *Ending discrimination against disabled people*, Cm. 2729, 1995, has been to consolidate the approach of the 1992 and 1993 Acts, which attempt to strike a balance between choice, needs and resources, rather than to give disabled pupils and students a right of access to an educational institution of their choice:

> "It is an inescapable fact that, to make the best and the most efficient provision for the individual needs of pupils and students with a wide spectrum of special educational needs, a degree of planning and concentration of resources is essential. The Education Acts strike a balance between the important rights of parents and students to choice about their education and the

need to have planning and concentration of resources. That is the way in which finite resources are used to best effect. The inclusion of education in the Bill could lead to those resources being spread too thinly." (Minister for Social Security and Disabled People, *Hansard*, H.C., Standing Committee E, col. 328).

The Government was however persuaded to make some modest amendments to the Education Acts, mainly in connection with the provision of information by governing bodies and local education authorities as to arrangements and facilities for disabled pupils and students, while leaving intact the structure of the existing legislation.

One of the principal areas of controversy in this area has been whether disabled pupils should have a right to receive an integrated education in a mainstream (*i.e.* a non-special) school. Section 160 of the Education Act 1993 imposes a qualified duty to educate a child with special educational needs in an ordinary school rather than a special school, building on the integration duty previously contained in the Education Act 1981, but this duty only arises if the conditions set out in s.160(2) of the 1993 Act are satisfied. The conditions are that an integrated education must be compatible with (i) the child receiving the special educational provision which his learning difficulty calls for, (ii) the provision of efficient education for the children with whom he will be educated, and (iii) the efficient use of resources. This third condition in particular has been widely used by local education authorities as a justification for denying disabled pupils access to mainstream education, and its use has been described by the Independent Panel for Special Educational Advice as "Overused, subjective, secretive and practically unchallengeable." (*Half Measures: RADAR's Response to the Consultation Document on Government Measures to Tackle Discrimination Against Disabled People*, 1994, para. 2.21).

The duty to integrate a child with special educational needs into a mainstream school is also subject to the wishes of the child's parents. Section 160(1) of the 1993 Act provides that, subject to the conditions referred to above, a child with special educational needs must be educated in an ordinary school "unless that is incompatible with the wishes of the parent", which in effect gives a parent a veto on a child's integration into mainstream education. However, the 1993 Act does not give parents any right to choose an integrated education for their child, nor does it place any legal obligation on schools or local education authorities to take positive action to widen access for children with special educational needs. Local education authorities are merely required to "keep under review" their arrangements for special educational provision (Education Act 1993, s.159), and grant-maintained schools and local education authorities have a duty to collect information on the provision of education for children with special educational needs (*ibid.* s.21).

The 1993 Act therefore falls a long way short of giving disabled children a right of access to mainstream schools. There has been little significant change in the rate of integration of children with special educational needs into mainstream education since the duty to integrate was first introduced in 1981, and there is evidence of considerable variation across the country in the proportion of children with special educational needs who are educated in ordinary schools. Research conducted for the Centre for Studies on Integration in Education indicates that children with special educational needs are six times less likely to receive an integrated education in the London Borough of Lambeth than if they live in Barnsley or Cornwall (*ibid.* para. 2.18). A survey conducted by Coopers and Lybrand in 1993 for the Spastics Society and the National Union of Teachers to assess the extent of disabled access in schools in England and Wales found that 16 per cent of primary schools and seven per cent of secondary schools were completely inaccessible to disabled people, while 26 per cent and 10 per cent respectively reported being fully accessible; only 18 per cent of secondary schools were reported as being 75 per cent accessible, and 65 per cent of primary and 55 per cent of secondary schools had no suitably adapted toilet facilities.

Education of disabled persons

29.—(1) In section 161(5) of the Education Act 1993 (information relating to pupils with special educational needs to be included in annual report), omit the words from "and in this subsection" to the end.

(2) After section 161(5) of that Act insert—

"(6) The annual report for each county, voluntary or grant-maintained school shall include a report containing information as to—

(a) the arrangements for the admission of disabled pupils;

(b) the steps taken to prevent disabled pupils from being treated less favourably than other pupils; and

(c) the facilities provided to assist access to the school by disabled pupils.

(7) In this section—

"annual report" means the report prepared under the articles of government for the school in accordance with section 30 of the Education (No. 2) Act 1986 or, as the case may be, paragraph 8 of Schedule 6 to this Act; and

"disabled pupils" means pupils who are disabled persons for the purposes of the Disability Discrimination Act 1995."

(3) In section 1 of the Education Act 1994 (establishment of the Teacher Training Agency) add, at the end—

"(4) In exercising their functions, the Teacher Training Agency shall have regard to the requirements of persons who are disabled persons for the purposes of the Disability Discrimination Act 1995."

General Note

Section 161 of the 1993 Act places a number of duties on governing bodies in relation to pupils with special educational needs. In particular, governing bodies must "use their best endeavours" to ensure that the necessary special educational provision is made, and must ensure, so far as is reasonably practicable and subject to certain conditions, that a child with special educational needs takes part in the activities of the school together with children who do not have special educational needs. Section 161(5) provides that the annual report of the governing body must contain prescribed information about the implementation of the governing body's policy for pupils with special educational needs. Schools are required to formulate and publish information about their policy for children with special educational needs. This section adds to s.161, by providing that the annual report for each county, voluntary or grant-maintained (but not maintained special) school must in future also include information as to the arrangements for the admission of disabled pupils, the steps taken to prevent disabled pupils from being discriminated against, and the facilities provided to assist access to the school by disabled pupils (subs. (2)). As the Minister commented in introducing the new clauses in the House of Lords:

"Schools which are inaccessible to disabled pupils will have to admit it. The need to do so will be a spur for them to consider how they might become accessible cost effectively ... Schools should not merely pay lip service to the integration of disabled pupils; rather they should do everything they can to achieve genuine and full integration. I am convinced that this measure will encourage such integration, underpinned by the statutory duty to integrate pupils within mainstream schools as far as is possible." (Minister of State, *Hansard*, H.L., Vol. 564, col. 1994).

In addition, subs. (3) amends the Education Act 1994 to require the Teacher Training Agency to "have regard to the requirements of persons who are disabled persons" in exercising its functions. This falls a long way short of the equal right of access to courses of initial teacher training for suitably qualified disabled people, which was advocated by RADAR in its response to the Government's 1994 Consultation Document.

Further and higher education of disabled persons

30.—(1) The Further and Higher Education Act 1992 is amended as set out in subsections (2) to (6).

(2) In section 5 (administration of funds by further education funding councils), in subsection (6)(b), after "may" insert ", subject to subsection (7A) below,".

(3) After section 5(7) insert—

"(7A) Without prejudice to the power to impose conditions given by subsection (6)(b) above, the conditions subject to which a council gives financial support under this section to the governing body of an institution within the further education sector—

(a) shall require the governing body to publish disability statements at such intervals as may be prescribed; and

(b) may include conditions relating to the provision made, or to be made, by the institution with respect to disabled persons.

(7B) For the purposes of subsection (7A) above—

"disability statement" means a statement containing information of a prescribed description about the provision of facilities for education made by the institution in respect of disabled persons;

"disabled persons" means persons who are disabled persons for the purposes of the Disability Discrimination Act 1995; and

"prescribed" means prescribed by regulations."

(4) In section 8 (supplementary functions) add, at the end—

"(6) As soon as is reasonably practicable after the end of its financial year, each council shall make a written report to the Secretary of State on—

(a) the progress made during the year to which the report relates in the provision of further education for disabled students in their area; and

(b) their plans for the future provision of further education for disabled students in their area.

(7) In subsection (6) above—

"disabled students" means students who are disabled persons for the purposes of the Disability Discrimination Act 1995; and

"financial year" means the period of twelve months ending with 31st March 1997 and each successive period of twelve months."

(5) In section 62 (establishment of higher education funding councils), after subsection (7) insert—

"(7A) In exercising their functions, each council shall have regard to the requirements of disabled persons.

(7B) In subsection (7A) "disabled persons" means persons who are disabled persons for the purposes of the Disability Discrimination Act 1995."

(6) In section 65 (administration of funds by higher education funding councils), after subsection (4) insert—

"(4A) Without prejudice to the power to impose conditions given by subsection (3) above, the conditions subject to which a council makes grants, loans or other payments under this section to the governing body of a higher education institution shall require the governing body to publish disability statements at such intervals as may be specified.

(4B) For the purposes of subsection (4A) above—

"disability statement" means a statement containing information of a specified description about the provision of facilities for education and research made by the institution in respect of persons who are disabled persons for the purposes of the Disability Discrimination Act 1995; and

"specified" means specified in the conditions subject to which grants, loans or other payments are made by a council under this section."

(7) The Education Act 1944 is amended as set out in subsections (8) and (9).

(8) In section 41 (functions of local education authorities in respect of further education), after subsection (2) insert—

"(2A) It shall be the duty of every local education authority to publish disability statements at such intervals as may be prescribed.

(2B) For the purposes of subsection (2A) above—

"disability statement" means a statement containing information of a prescribed description about the provision of facilities for further education made by the local education authority in respect of persons who are disabled persons for the purposes of the Disability Discrimination Act 1995; and

"prescribed" means prescribed by regulations made by the Secretary of State."

(9) In section 41(7), (8) and (11), for "this section" substitute "subsections (1) and (6) above".

General Note

This section amends the Further and Higher Education Act 1992, which, *inter alia*, established the Further and Higher Education Funding Councils. Section 4(2) of the 1992 Act requires the Further Education Funding Councils for England and Wales to "have regard to the requirements of persons having learning difficulties", which includes a person who has a disability which prevents or hinders him from making use of education facilities (*ibid.* s.4(7)). Under s.5 of the 1992 Act, the Further Education Funding Councils may give financial support to the governing body of an institution "on such terms and conditions as the council think fit". Subsection (3) of this section places a duty on the funding councils to require institutions in the further education sector, as a condition of the provision of such financial support, to publish "disability statements" containing information about the provision of facilities for education for students with disabilities. Local education authorities are under a similar duty to publish disability statements in respect of facilities for further education provided by them: see subss. (7) to (9), amending the Education Act 1994, s.41. The funding councils may also make the grant of financial support subject to conditions relating to the provision made by the institution for disabled persons. The frequency and content of disability statements is to be prescribed by regulations, after consultation with the funding councils. The Government has indicated that: "Information is likely to include physical access, the provision of specialist equipment, facilities which may help students with particular disabilities, admission policies, counselling and welfare arrangements." (Minister of State, *Hansard*, H.L., Vol. 564, col. 1991). In addition, subs. (4) places a duty on the funding councils to produce an annual report to the Secretary of State on the progress made during the year in the provision of further education for students with disabilities, and their plans for future provision.

In respect of higher education, subs. (5) imposes a duty on the Higher Education Funding Councils "to have regard to the requirements of disabled persons" in exercising their functions, similar to the duty placed on the Further Education Funding Councils under s.4(2) of the 1992 Act; more significantly, as in the case of further education, subs. (6) places a duty on the Higher Education Funding Councils to make grants, loans or payments to higher education institutions conditional on the publication by the governing bodies of those institutions of disability statements containing information about the provision of facilities for education and research for students with disabilities. Unlike the provisions on further education, the frequency and content of disability statements are to be specified by the funding councils, rather than being prescribed by regulations. According to the Minister:

> "The intention is that the statements would assist disabled students and funding councils generally in understanding the provision available for education and research in the particular institution. ... The statements would thus go wider than simply including information about physical facilities. It will be a matter for the funding councils, in consultation, to determine how to specify the information needed in the statements to achieve that in a viable and cost-effective way." (Minister of State, *Hansard*, H.L., Vol. 564, col. 1993).

During the debates in the House of Lords on the scope of the disability statements, concern was expressed that the new requirements might interfere with the academic autonomy of the universities over matters such as admissions arrangements, structure and content of the curriculum, and assessment procedures. In replying, the Minister emphasised that the purpose of the disability statements is to assist disabled students to understand what provision will be available for them, not to require a university to change its admissions arrangements, modify its course structures or alter its assessment procedures in order to meet the needs of disabled students:

> "I am happy to state the Government's considered view that [the new measures] are not meant to do so and that they do not do so. Nor is it the Government's intention that the disability statements should be used to put pressure on the universities or the higher education funding councils to change policies on the curriculum or admissions. Such matters are quite properly academic matters which are the responsibility of the institutions to determine. Naturally, we hope that universities will be as receptive as they can to the needs of disabled students, and we believe that the need to set out information about their policies will help focus their attention on this issue. But it will remain for universities to determine their own policies." (Minister of State, *Hansard*, H.L., Vol. 566, col. 1036).

Further and higher education of disabled persons: Scotland

31.—(1) The Further and Higher Education (Scotland) Act 1992 is amended as follows.

(2) In section 37 (establishment of Scottish Higher Education Funding Council) after subsection (4) insert—

> "(4A) In exercising their functions, the Council shall have regard to the requirements of disabled persons.

(4B) In subsection (4A) above, "disabled persons" means persons who are disabled persons for the purpose of the Disability Discrimination Act 1995."

(3) In section 40 (administration of funds by the Council), after subsection (4) insert—

"(5) Without prejudice to the power to impose conditions given by subsection (3) above, the conditions subject to which the Council make grants, loans or other payments under this section to the governing body of an institution within the higher education sector shall require the governing body to publish disability statements at such intervals as may be specified.

(6) For the purposes of subsection (5) above—

"disability statement" means a statement containing information of a specified description about the provision of facilities for education and research made by the institution in respect of persons who are disabled persons for the purpose of the Disability Discrimination Act 1995; and

"specified" means specified in the conditions subject to which grants, loans or other payments are made by the Council under this section."

PART V

PUBLIC TRANSPORT

GENERAL NOTE

Part V of the Act contains a wide-ranging set of enabling provisions which empower the Secretary of State for Transport to establish a timetable for achieving a fully accessible public transport system through the introduction of regulations setting minimum access standards for buses, trains, taxis and other public service vehicles. As originally drafted, the Bill made no provision for access to public transport, an omission which caused widespread dismay among campaigners for disabled people's rights, many of whom argued that the right of access to employment and to goods and services conferred by the Act would be undermined if steps were not also taken to ensure that disabled people had the opportunity to travel to where those jobs, goods or services were available. The force of this argument was acknowledged in the Consultation Document on *Measures to Tackle Discrimination Against Disabled People* (July 1994), which stated that: "A fully accessible transport system and pedestrian environment are key elements for enabling disabled people to become fully integrated into society."

The Government was eventually persuaded to use the opportunity presented by the Act to tackle the question of access to public transport, and the measures contained in Pt. V were introduced into the Bill in the House of Lords. The provisions empower the Secretary of State to set minimum access standards for accessible taxis, public service vehicles and rail vehicles, with a timetable for implementation. The Government's stated intention is that the access requirements will only apply to new vehicles, in view of the cost and technical difficulty of applying them retrospectively (Minister of State, *Hansard*, H.L., Vol. 565, col. 715). The new provisions do not extend to travel by air or sea, the Government's view being that the international dimension of air and sea travel would make domestic legislation in those cases of limited value (Mr William Hague, Minister for Social Security and Disabled People, *Hansard*, H.C., Vol. 257, col. 858).

Of the 6.5 million disabled people in the U.K., 4.5 million have a mobility disability, yet progress towards accessible public transport has been slow. The Disabled Persons Transport Advisory Committee (DPTAC), an advisory body set up under the Transport Act 1985 (c. 67) to advise the Secretary of State for Transport, estimated in 1989 that between 10 and 12 per cent of the population were unable to access the public transport system adequately (*Public Transport and the Missing Six Millions: What Can be Learned?* London, DPTAC, 1989). Trains are now being designed and built to provide improved access and facilities for disabled people, but the overall position is still poor. Accommodation for wheelchair users is often restricted to one designated space per train, which means that two wheelchair users cannot travel together, and it is still commonplace for wheelchair users to be relegated to the guard's van. Lack of accessible toilet facilities on trains is a further major problem for disabled travellers. Under the Railways Act 1993 (c. 43), the operators of passenger and station services are under a duty to "have regard" to the interests of disabled travellers as a condition of being granted a licence to operate, but that Act does not impose any requirement to take positive steps to improve access. Section 70 of the 1993 Act required the Regulator to prepare and publish a code of practice for protecting the interests of disabled users of railway passenger services or station services, and to encourage the adoption and implementation of the code, but as the code of practice has no legal force there is no obligation on passenger or station operators to comply with its recommendations. The ban on people in wheelchairs from using the London underground system (except for certain above-ground stations) was removed in 1993, but access is still extremely difficult. Significant progress has been made in improving access to taxis in several major cities. So for example, in London all new licensed taxis have had to be wheelchair-accessible since 1989, and all licensed taxis are required to be wheelchair-accessible by the year 2000; similar requirements apply in Liverpool, Manchester and Edinburgh, but elsewhere the picture is more patchy. Some local authorities have adopted a policy of insisting on accessible taxis before issuing or renewing licences, but there has been no overall co-ordination of policy. The survey conducted by the Office of Population Censuses and Surveys in 1986 revealed that 1.1 million people were unable to use buses because of their disabilities. Most buses and coaches are inaccessible to wheelchair-users, and to many people with mobility restrictions, because of the height of their steps. There has however been some experimentation with wheelchair-accessible low-floor buses on urban bus-routes in London, Liverpool and Tyneside, and the Government has confirmed its commitment to ensuring that, from a date to be fixed, all new buses will be of low-floor construction, as far as is technically feasible. Most new buses already incorporate the design features contained in the Bus Specifications drawn up by DPTAC (*Making Buses More Suitable for Elderly and Ambulant Disabled People*, London, DPTAC, 1988), but they represent only a small proportion of the total number of buses in service. Ease of access to the transport system is of course a benefit to all travellers, not just those with disabilities.

The technical and financial implications for public transport operators of a requirement of fully accessible transport systems are very considerable. It may be prohibitively expensive or simply technically impracticable to require adaptations to be made to existing vehicles, although worthwhile improvements can sometimes be made at relatively little cost (*e.g.* the provision of portable ramps at railway stations). It is usually easier and more cost-effective to provide disabled access in new vehicles or facilities, or as part of a major refurbishment, a point acknowledged in the White Paper, *Ending Discrimination against Disabled People*, at para. 5.3. The Government has therefore been at pains to stress that the new access standards will only apply to new vehicles, enabling transport operators to comply with the duty to provide full access as and when vehicles are replaced (Minister of State, *Hansard*, H.L., Vol. 566, col. 463). The new measures have also been drafted so as to provide maximum flexibility in tailoring the access requirements to different modes of transport. The regulation-making powers therefore allow for the imposition of different standards and access solutions, with different time scales, to reflect the particular circumstances of different geographical areas and locations, and the wide range of modes of transport. The exclusion of existing vehicles from the accessibility requirements, coupled with the broad powers to apply different standards and to grant exemptions, means that, for certain types of transport and in certain areas, full accessibility is unlikely to be achieved until well into the next century.

Taxis

Taxi accessibility regulations

32.—(1) The Secretary of State may make regulations ("taxi accessibility regulations") for the purpose of securing that it is possible—

(a) for disabled persons—

(i) to get into and out of taxis in safety;

(ii) to be carried in taxis in safety and in reasonable comfort; and

(b) for disabled persons in wheelchairs—

(i) to be conveyed in safety into and out of taxis while remaining in their wheelchairs; and

(ii) to be carried in taxis in safety and in reasonable comfort while remaining in their wheelchairs.

(2) Taxi accessibility regulations may, in particular—

(a) require any regulated taxi to conform with provisions of the regulations as to—

(i) the size of any door opening which is for the use of passengers;

(ii) the floor area of the passenger compartment;

(iii) the amount of headroom in the passenger compartment;

(iv) the fitting of restraining devices designed to ensure the stability of a wheelchair while the taxi is moving;

(b) require the driver of any regulated taxi which is plying for hire, or which has been hired, to comply with provisions of the regulations as to the carrying of ramps or other devices designed to facilitate the loading and unloading of wheelchairs;

(c) require the driver of any regulated taxi in which a disabled person who is in a wheelchair is being carried (while remaining in his wheelchair) to comply with provisions of the regulations as to the position in which the wheelchair is to be secured.

(3) The driver of a regulated taxi which is plying for hire, or which has been hired, is guilty of an offence if—

(a) he fails to comply with any requirement imposed on him by the regulations; or

(b) the taxi fails to conform with any provision of the regulations with which it is required to conform.

(4) A person who is guilty of such an offence is liable, on summary conviction, to a fine not exceeding level 3 on the standard scale.

(5) In this section—

"passenger compartment" has such meaning as may be prescribed;

"regulated taxi" means any taxi to which the regulations are expressed to apply;

"taxi" means a vehicle licensed under—

(a) section 37 of the Town Police Clauses Act 1847, or

(b) section 6 of the Metropolitan Public Carriage Act 1869,

but does not include a taxi which is drawn by a horse or other animal.

DEFINITIONS

"disabled person": s.1(2).

"passenger compartment": subs. (5).

"regulated taxi": s.68(1); subs. (5).

"regulations": s.68(1).

"standard scale": Criminal Justice Act 1982, s.37(2).

"taxi": s.68(1); subs. (5).

"taxi accessibility regulations": s.68(1); subs. (1).

GENERAL NOTE

This is the first of eight sections in the Act concerning the accessibility of taxis. It empowers the Secretary of State for Transport to make regulations ("taxi accessibility regulations") laying down detailed specifications for taxis to ensure that they are fully accessible to all disabled persons, whether or not they are wheelchair users, and requiring taxi drivers to comply with any requirements as to the carrying and use of special equipment (*e.g.* ramps). The new requirements will generally apply only to licensed taxis (*i.e.* vehicles which are licensed as taxis under the Town Police Clauses Act 1847 (c. 89), s.37, or the Metropolitan Public Carriage Act 1869 (c. 115), s.6), not to private hire vehicles. However, in recognition of the growing trend whereby private hire companies are granted concessions to operate taxi services from certain locations (for example, as is the case at Gatwick Airport), the Secretary of State is empowered to extend the new requirements to hire car services provided under franchise agreements at ports, airports, railway stations and bus stations (s.33). The new requirements will not apply (in the first instance, at least) to existing taxis: "We have no intention of introducing the requirements over such a period as would undermine the viability of the taxi trade" (Minister of State, *Hansard*, H.L., Vol. 564, col. 2047). Section 34 makes the issue of new taxi licences (which require renewal on an annual basis) conditional on compliance with the taxi accessibility regulations, but allows a non-accessible vehicle which is already licensed as a taxi to be re-licensed, unless and until the Secretary of State decides to remove that concession. To ensure that the new requirements do not jeopardise the viability of the taxi trade in a particular area, s.35 gives the Secretary of State a broad power to make exemption regulations under which he may grant an order exempting a licensing authority from the new requirements where, because of the specific circumstances of an area, it would be inappropriate to impose the new requirements, and where to do so would result in an unacceptable reduction in the number of taxis in the area.

Requiring taxis to be accessible to passengers in wheelchairs would be of limited utility if taxi drivers were not required to carry those passengers. Section 36 therefore places the driver of a regulated taxi which has been hired by or for a disabled person in a wheelchair under a duty to carry the disabled passenger, to take steps to ensure his safety and comfort, and to assist him in getting himself and his luggage into or out of the taxi. A driver who fails to comply with these duties commits an offence, although it will not be unlawful to refuse to carry a disabled person if the circumstances are such that it would otherwise be lawful for the driver to refuse to carry that person. Drivers can seek exemption from these duties on medical grounds, or on the grounds that their physical condition makes it impossible or unreasonably difficult to comply with them. In addition, all drivers of licensed taxis (not just those who drive regulated taxis) are placed under a duty by s.37 to convey a disabled person accompanied by a guide dog or a hearing dog, without any additional charge, subject to a narrow exemption on medical grounds (*e.g.* where the driver has a medical condition such as asthma which is aggravated by dogs).

The purpose of the taxi accessibility regulations is to ensure that in due course all licensed taxis will be fully accessible to disabled persons, whether or not they are travelling in a wheelchair. Subsection (1) provides that accessibility for these purposes means ensuring that it is possible for disabled persons to get into and out of taxis in safety, and to be carried in taxis in safety and in reasonable comfort; for disabled persons in wheelchairs, these requirements must be satisfied while they remain in their wheelchairs. Significantly, the parallel provisions in s.40 concerning the accessibility of public service vehicles (for example, buses) provide that it must be possible for disabled persons to get on and off such vehicles in safety "and without unreasonable difficulty".

Subsection (2) provides that the regulations may contain detailed specifications covering, *inter alia*, the size of passenger door-openings, the floor area and amount of headroom in the passenger compartment, and the fitting of restraining devices to ensure that wheelchairs remain stable while the taxi is moving; the regulations may also require taxi drivers to comply with any requirements concerning the carrying of ramps or other equipment designed to facilitate the loading or unloading of wheelchairs, or the position in which wheelchairs must be secured. A taxi driver who fails to comply with any requirement imposed on him by the regulations, or whose taxi fails to conform with any provision of the regulations with which it is required to conform, is liable on summary conviction to a fine not exceeding level 3 on the standard scale (subss. (3) and (4)).

It seems likely that the requirement that all taxis become fully accessible will necessitate the development of a new generation of purpose-built taxi to meet the needs of the full range of people with disabilities. The currently-available designs of purpose-built taxi (the Metrocab and Fairway) can be adapted to provide access for most wheelchair users, but they are difficult for some non-wheelchair users to enter and exit, particularly those with arthritis. Ordinary saloon cars used as taxis are completely inaccessible to wheelchair users, although they can be modified (*e.g.* by fitting a swivelling passenger seat) to allow for easier access by ambulant disabled passengers. The new requirements will eventually bring to an end the use of saloon cars as licensed taxis, but the cost implications of requiring a change-over to purpose-built taxis are such that the Secretary of State is expected to allow existing non-accessible vehicles to be re-licensed for at least a 10-year period, to allow those vehicles to reach the end of their useful life (see the note to s.34). It remains to be seen whether, when that time finally comes, the cost of buying an accessible vehicle will cause owner-drivers of licensed taxis to move to the private hire sector. Ministers have indicated that the concession for existing non-accessible vehicles is unlikely to apply in areas such as London, Manchester, Liverpool and Edinburgh, where earlier target-dates for accessibility have already been set (Minister for Social Security and Disabled People, H.C., Standing Committee E, col. 447).

Taxi. With one exception (see the note to s.33), the taxi accessibility regulations apply only to vehicles licensed to ply for hire as hackney carriages under the Town Police Clauses Act 1847, s.37, or the Metropolitan Public Carriage Act 1869, s.6, not to minicabs or other private hire vehicles. The 1869 Act governs the licensing of hackney carriages in the Metropolitan Police District and the City of London, while the 1847 Act makes provision for the licensing of hackney carriages in those parts of England and Wales outside the area to which the 1869 Act applies. The 1869 Act, s.4, defines a "hackney carriage" as "any carriage for the conveyance of passengers which plies for hire" within the limits of that Act; and the London Hackney Carriage Act 1831 (c. 22), s.35, provides that a hackney carriage found standing in any street or place shall, unless actually hired, be deemed to be plying for hire. The 1847 Act, s.37, similarly defines a "hackney carriage" as a "wheeled carriage ... used in standing or plying for hire in any street..."

Plying for hire. This is not defined in the Act. In the context of the London Hackney Carriage Act 1853, s.7, it has been held that a taxi does not ply for hire while it is in motion, but only when it is standing on a taxi rank or in a street (*Hunt v. Morgan* [1949] 1 K.B. 233); a taxi which is stationary is not necessarily "standing" in a street for the purposes of the London Hackney Carriage Act 1831, s.35 (*Eldridge v. British Airports Authority* [1970] 2 Q.B. 387).

Designated transport facilities

33.—(1) In this section "a franchise agreement" means a contract entered into by the operator of a designated transport facility for the provision by the other party to the contract of hire car services—

(a) for members of the public using any part of the transport facility; and
(b) which involve vehicles entering any part of that facility.

(2) The Secretary of State may by regulations provide for the application of any taxi provision in relation to—

(a) vehicles used for the provision of services under a franchise agreement; or
(b) the drivers of such vehicles.

(3) Any regulations under subsection (2) may apply any taxi provision with such modifications as the Secretary of State considers appropriate.

(4) In this section—

"designated" means designated for the purposes of this section by an order made by the Secretary of State;

"hire car" has such meaning as may be prescribed;

"operator", in relation to a transport facility, means any person who is concerned with the management or operation of the facility;

"taxi provision" means any provision of—

(a) this Act, or
(b) regulations made in pursuance of section 20(2A) of the Civic Government (Scotland) Act 1982,

which applies in relation to taxis or the drivers of taxis; and

"transport facility" means any premises which form part of any port, airport, railway station or bus station.

DEFINITIONS

"designated": subs. (4).
"franchise agreement": subs. (1).
"hire car": subs. (4).
"operator": subs. (4).
"regulations": s.68(1).
"taxi provision": subs. (4).
"transport facility": subs. (4).

GENERAL NOTE

This section allows the accessibility requirements which apply to licensed taxis to be extended to other vehicles in certain limited circumstances. It empowers the Secretary of State to apply some or all of the taxi provisions in this Act to vehicles used for the provision of hire car services under "franchise agreements" (as defined in subs. (1)) entered into by the operators of designated transport facilities, or to the drivers of those vehicles. It is intended to address the practice whereby firms providing private hire car services are granted concessions to operate taxi services from ports, airports, railway stations and bus stations, as is the case at Gatwick Airport. Such arrangements may operate on an exclusive basis, with licensed taxis being denied the opportunity to pick up passengers from within the (privately owned) transport facility. As the 1994 Report of the House of Commons Transport Committee on *Taxis and Private Hire Vehicles* noted, such an arrangement may mean that there are no accessible vehicles available at such locations for disabled travellers. The power in this section to apply the taxi accessibility requirements to private hire vehicles in such circumstances is designed to ensure that a disabled passenger will be confident of finding an accessible taxi at a location where such a franchise agreement is in operation.

New licences conditional on compliance with taxi accessibility regulations

34.—(1) No licensing authority shall grant a licence for a taxi to ply for hire unless the vehicle conforms with those provisions of the taxi accessibility regulations with which it will be required to conform if licensed.

(2) Subsection (1) does not apply if such a licence was in force with respect to the vehicle at any time during the period of 28 days immediately before the day on which the licence is granted.

(3) The Secretary of State may by order provide for subsection (2) to cease to have effect on such date as may be specified in the order.

(4) Separate orders may be made under subsection (3) with respect to different areas or localities.

DEFINITIONS

"licensing authority": s.68(1).

"taxi": s.68(1); s.32(5).

"taxi accessibility regulations": s.68(1); s.32(1).

GENERAL NOTE

This section makes the grant of a license for a taxi to ply for hire by a licensing authority conditional on compliance with the taxi accessibility regulations (subs. (1)). In the first instance this requirement will only apply to vehicles which are newly-licensed as taxis, as subs. (2) allows a non-accessible taxi to be re-licensed where the vehicle in question was previously licensed as a taxi within 28 days of the date of issue of the new license. However, subs. (3) empowers the Secretary of State to set an end-date for this concession beyond which a non-accessible vehicle may not be re-licensed (although subs. (4) gives him the power to make separate provision for different areas or localities). As seen in the General Note to s.32, the cost implications of requiring all licensed taxis to become fully accessible are such that the Secretary of State is expected to allow existing non-accessible vehicles to be re-licensed for at least a 10-year period, to allow those vehicles to reach the end of their useful life. This concession is however unlikely to apply in areas such as London, Manchester, Liverpool and Edinburgh, where earlier target-dates for full accessibility have already been set (Minister for Social Security and Disabled People, *Hansard*, H.C., Standing Committee E, col. 447).

Licensing authority. This means, in relation to the area to which the Metropolitan Public Carriage Act 1869 applies, the Secretary of State, or the holder of any office for the time being designated by him, or in relation to any other area in England and Wales; the authority responsible for licensing taxis in that area: s.68(1).

Exemption from taxi accessibility regulations

35.—(1) The Secretary of State may make regulations ("exemption regulations") for the purpose of enabling any relevant licensing authority to apply to him for an order (an "exemption order") exempting the authority from the requirements of section 34.

(2) Exemption regulations may, in particular, make provision requiring a licensing authority proposing to apply for an exemption order—

(a) to carry out such consultations as may be prescribed;
(b) to publish the proposal in the prescribed manner;
(c) to consider any representations made to it about the proposal, before applying for the order;
(d) to make its application in the prescribed form.

(3) A licensing authority may apply for an exemption order only if it is satisfied—

(a) that, having regard to the circumstances prevailing in its area, it would be inappropriate for the requirements of section 34 to apply; and
(b) that the application of section 34 would result in an unacceptable reduction in the number of taxis in its area.

(4) After considering any application for an exemption order and consulting the Disabled Persons Transport Advisory Committee and such other persons as he considers appropriate, the Secretary of State may—

(a) make an exemption order in the terms of the application;
(b) make an exemption order in such other terms as he considers appropriate; or
(c) refuse to make an exemption order.

(5) The Secretary of State may by regulations ("swivel seat regulations") make provision requiring any exempt taxi plying for hire in an area in respect of which an exemption order is in force to conform with provisions of the regulations as to the fitting and use of swivel seats.

(6) The Secretary of State may by regulations make provision with respect to swivel seat regulations similar to that made by section 34 with respect to taxi accessibility regulations.

(7) In this section—

"exempt taxi" means a taxi in relation to which section 34(1) would apply if the exemption order were not in force;

"relevant licensing authority" means a licensing authority responsible for licensing taxis in any area of England and Wales other than the area to which the Metropolitan Public Carriage Act 1869 applies; and

"swivel seats" has such meaning as may be prescribed.

DEFINITIONS

"exemption order": subs. (1).
"exemption regulations": subs. (1).
"exempt taxi": subs. (7).
"licensing authority": s.68(1).
"prescribed": s.68(1).
"regulations": s.68(1).
"relevant licensing authority": subs. (7).
"swivel seat regulations": subs. (5).
"swivel seats": subs. (7).
"taxi": s.68(1); s.32(5).
"taxi accessibility regulations": s.68(1); s.32(1).

GENERAL NOTE

This section is designed to ensure that the imposition of the accessibility requirements does not jeopardise the viability of the taxi trade in a particular area. It empowers the Secretary of State to make exemption regulations under which he may, on the application of a relevant licensing authority, grant an order exempting that authority from the requirements of s.34. Such an application may only be made by a licensing authority where it is satisfied that, in view of the specific circumstances prevailing in its area, it would be inappropriate for those requirements to apply, and that to apply those requirements would result in an unacceptable reduction in the number of taxis in its area (subs. (3)). It would appear that both these conditions must be satisfied, but unfortunately no guidance is given as to the circumstances in which it might be considered inappropriate for the accessibility requirements to apply.

The exemption regulations may make provision as to the manner and form of an application for an exemption order, and may include a requirement for the licensing authority to carry out consultations and consider representations made to it about the proposals before applying for an order (subs. (2)). Before making a decision on an application for an exemption order, the Secretary of State must consult the Disabled Persons Transport Advisory Committee and such other persons as he considers appropriate (subs. (4)). As a concession to accessibility in areas where an exemption order is in force, the Secretary of State may make swivel seat regulations requiring exempt taxis to conform with any requirements as to the fitting and use of swivel seats (subss. (5) and (6)).

Relevant licensing authority. This is defined in subs. (7) as a licensing authority responsible for licensing taxis in any area of England and Wales, other than the area to which the Metropolitan Public Carriage Act 1869 applies, for which the Secretary of State is the licensing authority (see the note to s.34).

Disabled Persons Transport Advisory Committee. This body was established under the Transport Act 1985, s.125, to advise the Secretary of State on matters relating to the needs of disabled persons in connection with public passenger transport.

Carrying of passengers in wheelchairs

36.—(1) This section imposes duties on the driver of a regulated taxi which has been hired—

(a) by or for a disabled person who is in a wheelchair; or

(b) by a person who wishes such a disabled person to accompany him in the taxi.

(2) In this section—

"carry" means carry in the taxi concerned; and

"the passenger" means the disabled person concerned.

(3) The duties are—

(a) to carry the passenger while he remains in his wheelchair;

(b) not to make any additional charge for doing so;

(c) if the passenger chooses to sit in a passenger seat, to carry the wheelchair;

(d) to take such steps as are necessary to ensure that the passenger is carried in safety and in reasonable comfort;

(e) to give such assistance as may be reasonably required—

(i) to enable the passenger to get into or out of the taxi;

(ii) if the passenger wishes to remain in his wheelchair, to enable him to be conveyed into and out of the taxi while in his wheelchair;

(iii) to load the passenger's luggage into or out of the taxi;

(iv) if the passenger does not wish to remain in his wheelchair, to load the wheelchair into or out of the taxi.

(4) Nothing in this section is to be taken to require the driver of any taxi—

(a) except in the case of a taxi of a prescribed description, to carry more than one person in a wheelchair, or more than one wheelchair, on any one journey; or

(b) to carry any person in circumstances in which it would otherwise be lawful for him to refuse to carry that person.

(5) A driver of a regulated taxi who fails to comply with any duty imposed on him by this section is guilty of an offence and liable, on summary conviction, to a fine not exceeding level 3 on the standard scale.

(6) In any proceedings for an offence under this section, it is a defence for the accused to show that, even though at the time of the alleged offence the taxi conformed with those provisions of the taxi accessibility regulations with which it was required to conform, it would not have been possible for the wheelchair in question to be carried in safety in the taxi.

(7) If the licensing authority is satisfied that it is appropriate to exempt a person from the duties imposed by this section—

(a) on medical grounds, or

(b) on the ground that his physical condition makes it impossible or unreasonably difficult for him to comply with the duties imposed on drivers by this section,

it shall issue him with a certificate of exemption.

(8) A certificate of exemption shall be issued for such period as may be specified in the certificate.

(9) The driver of a regulated taxi is exempt from the duties imposed by this section if—

(a) a certificate of exemption issued to him under this section is in force; and

(b) the prescribed notice of his exemption is exhibited on the taxi in the prescribed manner.

DEFINITIONS

"carry": subs. (2).
"certificate of exemption": subs. (7).
"disabled person": s.1(2).
"licensing authority": s.68(1).
"passenger; the": subs. (2).
"prescribed": s.68(1).
"regulated taxi": s.68(1); s.32(5).
"standard scale": Criminal Justice Act 1982, s.37(2).
"taxi": s.68(1); s.32(5).
"taxi accessibility regulations": s.68(1); s.32(1).

GENERAL NOTE

This section places a series of duties on the driver of a regulated taxi which has been hired by or for a disabled person who is in a wheelchair, or by a person who wishes such a person to accompany him in the taxi. Thus, the driver is under a duty to carry the disabled passenger while he remains in his wheelchair, without making any additional charge for doing so, and to carry the wheelchair if the disabled passenger chooses to sit in a passenger seat. He is also under a duty to ensure that the disabled passenger is carried in safety and in reasonable comfort, and to assist him in getting himself, his luggage and his wheelchair into or out of the taxi. A driver of a regulated taxi who fails to comply with any of these duties commits an offence and is liable on summary conviction to a fine not exceeding level 3 on the standard scale. However, unless the taxi is of a certain prescribed description, drivers are not required to carry more than one person in a wheelchair, or more than one wheelchair, on any one journey, or to carry a person if the circumstances are such that it would otherwise be lawful for the driver to refuse to carry that person. It will also be a defence for a driver to show that it would not have been possible for the wheelchair in question to be carried in safety in the taxi, provided at the time of the alleged offence the taxi conformed with the relevant taxi accessibility regulations. A driver may apply to the licensing authority for exemption from these duties on medical grounds, or on the ground that his physical condition makes it impossible or unreasonably difficult for him to comply. If the licensing authority is satisfied that it is appropriate to exempt a driver on these grounds, it must issue a certificate of exemption for a period specified in the certificate. There is a right of appeal against a refusal by a licensing authority to issue an exemption certificate under this section: see s.38. To enjoy the exemption, the driver must exhibit the prescribed notice of his exemption on his taxi in the prescribed manner. The forgery, alteration or misuse, etc. of an exemption certificate or a notice of exemption under this section is an offence: see the note to s.49.

Regulated taxi. This means a taxi to which the taxi accessibility regulations are expressed to apply: see s.68(1).

Which has been hired. The duties in relation to the carrying of passengers in wheelchairs only apply where a taxi has been hired by or for a disabled person in a wheelchair, or someone wishing to accompany such a person. This section does not place any obligation on a taxi driver to accept a hiring from a disabled passenger, which might at first sight appear to be a significant oversight. However, under the general legislation concerning taxis, it is an offence for the driver of a licensed taxi which is plying for hire to refuse to carry a passenger without reasonable excuse (see in particular the London Hackney Carriage Act 1831, s.35, the London Hackney Carriage Act 1853, s.7, and Town Police Clauses Act 1847, s.53), and the introduction of the new accessibility regulations will make it difficult for the driver of a regulated taxi to claim that it was reasonable for him to refuse to carry a passenger in a wheelchair (although note the defence in subs. (6) where the accused is able to show that it would not have been possible for the wheelchair to be carried in safety in the taxi). It should also be noted that the general duty not to refuse to carry a passenger only applies when the vehicle in question is standing or plying for hire, not when it is in motion (see the note to s.32). It remains to be seen whether the duties contained in this section will make it any easier in future for a disabled person in a wheelchair to hail a moving taxi.

Carrying of guide dogs and hearing dogs

37.—(1) This section imposes duties on the driver of a taxi which has been hired—

(a) by or for a disabled person who is accompanied by his guide dog or hearing dog, or

(b) by a person who wishes such a disabled person to accompany him in the taxi.

(2) The disabled person is referred to in this section as "the passenger".

(3) The duties are—

(a) to carry the passenger's dog and allow it to remain with the passenger; and

(b) not to make any additional charge for doing so.

(4) A driver of a taxi who fails to comply with any duty imposed on him by this section is guilty of an offence and liable, on summary conviction, to a fine not exceeding level 3 on the standard scale.

(5) If the licensing authority is satisfied that it is appropriate on medical grounds to exempt a person from the duties imposed by this section, it shall issue him with a certificate of exemption.

(6) In determining whether to issue a certificate of exemption, the licensing authority shall, in particular, have regard to the physical characteristics of the taxi which the applicant drives or those of any kind of taxi in relation to which he requires the certificate.

(7) A certificate of exemption shall be issued—

(a) with respect to a specified taxi or a specified kind of taxi; and

(b) for such period as may be specified in the certificate.

(8) The driver of a taxi is exempt from the duties imposed by this section if—

(a) a certificate of exemption issued to him under this section is in force with respect to the taxi; and

(b) the prescribed notice of his exemption is exhibited on the taxi in the prescribed manner.

(9) The Secretary of State may, for the purposes of this section, prescribe any other category of dog trained to assist a disabled person who has a disability of a prescribed kind.

(10) This section applies in relation to any such prescribed category of dog as it applies in relation to guide dogs.

(11) In this section—

"guide dog" means a dog which has been trained to guide a blind person; and

"hearing dog" means a dog which has been trained to assist a deaf person.

Definitions

"certificate of exemption": subs. (5).
"disabled person": s.1(2).
"guide dog": subs. (11).
"hearing dog": subs. (11).
"licensing authority": s.68(1).
"passenger; the": subs. (2).
"prescribed": s.68(1).
"standard scale": Criminal Justice Act 1982, s.37(2).
"taxi": s.68(1); s.32(5).

General Note

This section places a duty on the driver of a licensed taxi which has been hired by or for a disabled person accompanied by his guide dog or hearing dog, or by a person who wishes such a person to accompany him in the taxi, to carry the passenger's dog and allow it to remain with the passenger, without making any additional charge for doing so. Failure to comply is an offence leading, on summary conviction, to a fine not exceeding level 3 on the standard scale. The Secretary of State may extend this duty to other prescribed categories of dogs trained to assist disabled persons. The duty is subject to an exemption where the licensing authority is satisfied, having regard to the physical characteristics of the taxi which the applicant drives, that it would be appropriate on medical grounds to issue him with a certificate of exemption for a specified period for that taxi, or for a specified kind of taxi. This might apply where for example the applicant has a medical condition such as asthma which is aggravated by dogs. There is a right of appeal against a refusal by a licensing authority to issue an exemption certificate under this section: see s.38. To benefit from the exemption, the driver must exhibit the prescribed notice of exemption on his taxi in the prescribed manner, and the certificate of exemption must relate to that taxi. The forgery, alteration or misuse, etc., of an exemption certificate or a notice of exemption under this section is an offence: see the note to s.49.

Taxi. Unlike the duty to carry passengers in wheelchairs, which is confined to the drivers of *regulated* taxis (see the note to s.36), the duty to carry guide dogs and hearing dogs applies more generally to the drivers of all licensed taxis: see s.68(1), applying for these purposes the definition of "taxi" contained in s.32 (as to which, see the note to s.32).

Which has been hired. See the note to s.36.

Appeal against refusal of exemption certificate

38.—(1) Any person who is aggrieved by the refusal of a licensing authority to issue an exemption certificate under section 36 or 37 may appeal to the appropriate court before the end of the period of 28 days beginning with the date of the refusal.

(2) On an appeal to it under this section, the court may direct the licensing authority concerned to issue the appropriate certificate of exemption to have effect for such period as may be specified in the direction.

(3) "Appropriate court" means the magistrates' court for the petty sessions area in which the licensing authority has its principal office.

DEFINITIONS

"appropriate court": subs. (3).
"licensing authority": s.68(1).

GENERAL NOTE

This section confers a right of appeal against a refusal by a licensing authority to issue an exemption certificate under ss.36 and 37. The appeal is to the local magistrates' court (the usual appeal mechanism for taxi licensing matters). Such an appeal must be brought within 28 days of the date of the refusal of the exemption certificate. On appeal, the court may direct the licensing authority to issue an exemption certificate for the period specified in the direction.

Requirements as to disabled passengers in Scotland

39.—(1) Part II of the Civic Government (Scotland) Act 1982 (licensing and regulation) is amended as follows.

(2) In subsection (4) of section 10 (suitability of vehicle for use as taxi)—

(a) after "authority" insert "—(a)"; and

(b) at the end add "; and

(b) as not being so suitable if it does not so comply."

(3) In section 20 (regulations relating to taxis etc.) after subsection (2) insert—

"(2A) Without prejudice to the generality of subsections (1) and (2) above, regulations under those subsections may make such provision as appears to the Secretary of State to be necessary or expedient in relation to the carrying in taxis of disabled persons (within the meaning of section 1(2) of the Disability Discrimination Act 1995) and such provision may in particular prescribe—

(a) requirements as to the carriage of wheelchairs, guide dogs, hearing dogs and other categories of dog;

(b) a date from which any such provision is to apply and the extent to which it is to apply; and

(c) the circumstances in which an exemption from such provision may be granted in respect of any taxi or taxi driver,

and in this subsection—

"guide dog" means a dog which has been trained to guide a blind person;

"hearing dog" means a dog which has been trained to assist a deaf person; and

"other categories of dog" means such other categories of dog as the Secretary of State may prescribe, trained to assist disabled persons who have disabilities of such kinds as he may prescribe."

DEFINITIONS

"disabled person": s.1(2).

GENERAL NOTE

This section, which amends those parts of the Civic Government (Scotland) Act 1982 (c. 45) which concern the licensing and regulation of taxis, enables the Secretary of State for Scotland to introduce regulations providing for the carrying of disabled passengers, wheelchairs, guide dogs and hearing dogs in taxis in Scotland.

Public service vehicles

PSV accessibility regulations

40.—(1) The Secretary of State may make regulations ("PSV accessibility regulations") for the purpose of securing that it is possible for disabled persons—

(a) to get on to and off regulated public service vehicles in safety and without unreasonable difficulty (and, in the case of disabled persons in wheelchairs, to do so while remaining in their wheelchairs); and

(b) to be carried in such vehicles in safety and in reasonable comfort.

(2) PSV accessibility regulations may, in particular, make provision as to the construction, use and maintenance of regulated public service vehicles including provision as to—

(a) the fitting of equipment to vehicles;

(b) equipment to be carried by vehicles;

(c) the design of equipment to be fitted to, or carried by, vehicles;

(d) the fitting and use of restraining devices designed to ensure the stability of wheelchairs while vehicles are moving;

(e) the position in which wheelchairs are to be secured while vehicles are moving.

(3) Any person who—

(a) contravenes or fails to comply with any provision of the PSV accessibility regulations,

(b) uses on a road a regulated public service vehicle which does not conform with any provision of the regulations with which it is required to conform, or

(c) causes or permits to be used on a road such a regulated public service vehicle,

is guilty of an offence.

(4) A person who is guilty of such an offence is liable, on summary conviction, to a fine not exceeding level 4 on the standard scale.

(5) In this section—

"public service vehicle" means a vehicle which is—

(a) adapted to carry more than eight passengers; and

(b) a public service vehicle for the purposes of the Public Passenger Vehicles Act 1981;

"regulated public service vehicle" means any public service vehicle to which the PSV accessibility regulations are expressed to apply.

(6) Different provision may be made in regulations under this section—

(a) as respects different classes or descriptions of vehicle;

(b) as respects the same class or description of vehicle in different circumstances.

(7) Before making any regulations under this section or section 41 or 42 the Secretary of State shall consult the Disabled Persons Transport Advisory Committee and such other representative organisations as he thinks fit.

DEFINITIONS

"disabled person": s.1(2).
"PSV accessibility regulations": s.68(1); subs. (1).
"public service vehicle": subs. (5).
"regulated public service vehicle": subs. (5).
"regulations": s.68(1).
"standard scale": Criminal Justice Act 1982, s.37(2).

General Note

This section empowers the Secretary of State for Transport to make regulations ("PSV accessibility regulations") laying down detailed specifications for the construction, use and maintenance of public service vehicles (PSVs) such as buses and coaches, to ensure that they are fully accessible to disabled persons, whether or not they are travelling in wheelchairs. Subsection (1) provides that accessibility for these purposes means ensuring that it is possible for disabled persons to get on to and off PSVs in safety and without unreasonable difficulty (those in wheelchairs must be able to do so while remaining in their wheelchairs), and to be carried in safety and in reasonable comfort. Significantly, the parallel provisions in s.32 concerning the accessibility of taxis make no reference to the difficulty of access, but simply provide that it must be possible for disabled persons to get into and out of taxis "in safety". Subsection (2) provides that the regulations may make provision as to the construction, use and maintenance of PSVs, including, *inter alia*, the design and fitting of equipment to be fitted to or carried by vehicles, the fitting and use of devices to restrain wheelchairs while the vehicle is moving, and the position in which wheelchairs must be secured. To ensure sufficient flexibility to deal with the wide range of PSVs, subs. (6) provides for different provision to be made for different classes or descriptions of vehicle, and for the same class or description of vehicle in different circumstances. "That will enable us to make regulations making different requirements for different types of vehicle over different time-scales which will ensure a smooth transition towards accessibility." (Minister of State, *Hansard*, H.L., Vol. 565, col. 716). There is also a general power in s.67 to make different provision for different areas or localities. Before making any such regulations, the Secretary of State is required by subs. (7) to consult the Disabled Persons Transport Advisory Committee, and such other "representative organisations" (not defined) as he thinks fit. A public service vehicle to which the PSV accessibility regulations apply must not be used on a road unless an accessibility certificate or an approval certificate has been issued in respect of that vehicle (see the notes to ss.41 and 42).

Failure to comply with any provision of the PSV accessibility regulations, or to use, or to cause or permit to be used, on a road a PSV which does not conform with any relevant provision of the regulations, is an offence leading on summary conviction to a fine not exceeding level 4 on the standard scale (subss. (3) and (4)). Separate provision is made for the liability in certain circumstances of the officers of a body corporate where an offence is committed by the body corporate: see the note to s.48.

The survey conducted in 1986 by the Office of Population Censuses and Surveys revealed that 1.1 million disabled people were unable to use buses, chiefly because of the height of the steps. Some progress has been made in recent years towards improving the accessibility of buses for disabled passengers, and most new buses now incorporate the design features contained in the Bus Specifications drawn up by the Disabled Persons Transport Advisory Committee (*Making Buses More Suitable for Elderly and Ambulant Disabled People*, London, DPTAC, 1988). However, these buses represent only a small proportion of the total number of buses in service, and in any event the DPTAC specifications are primarily aimed at improving access for ambulant disabled people, not for those in wheelchairs. There has however been some experimentation with wheelchair-accessible low-floor buses on urban bus-routes in London, Liverpool and Tyneside, and the Government has confirmed its commitment to ensuring that, as far as is technically feasible, all new buses will be of low-floor construction, although no implementation date has yet been fixed.

Public service vehicle. As defined in subs. (5), this means a vehicle which is adapted to carry more than eight passengers, and is a public service vehicle for the purposes of the Public Passenger Vehicles Act 1981 (c. 14). Section 1(1)(a) of the 1981 Act defines a public service vehicle as "a motor vehicle (other than a tramcar) which, being a vehicle adapted to carry more than eight passengers, is used for carrying passengers for hire or reward"; and s.1(5) of that Act provides for a number of circumstances in which a vehicle is to be treated as carrying passengers for hire or reward. The requirement in subs. (5)(a) of this section that the vehicle be adapted to carry more than eight passengers is designed to exclude PSVs falling within s.1(1)(b) of the 1981 Act (*i.e.* those which are not adapted to carry more than eight passengers) from the scope of the PSV accessibility regulations. It seems clear that in this context "adapted" is intended to mean that the vehicle is fit or suitable to carry more than eight passengers, not that it has been modified or altered to carry more than eight passengers (see *e.g. Herrmann v. Metropolitan Leather Co.* [1942] Ch. 248; *Maddox v. Storer* [1963] 1 Q.B. 451; *Burns v. Currell* [1963] 2 Q.B. 433; *Wurzal v. Addison* [1965] 2 Q.B. 131; but compare *Flower Freight Co. v. Hammond* [1963] 1 Q.B. 275; *Backer v. Secretary of State for the Environment* [1983] 2 All E.R. 1021).

Disabled Persons Transport Advisory Committee. See the note to s.35.

Accessibility certificates

41.—(1) A regulated public service vehicle shall not be used on a road unless—

(a) a vehicle examiner has issued a certificate (an "accessibility certificate") that such provisions of the PSV accessibility regulations as may be prescribed are satisfied in respect of the vehicle; or

(b) an approval certificate has been issued under section 42 in respect of the vehicle.

(2) The Secretary of State may make regulations—

(a) with respect to applications for, and the issue of, accessibility certificates;

(b) providing for the examination of vehicles in respect of which applications have been made;

(c) with respect to the issue of copies of accessibility certificates in place of certificates which have been lost or destroyed.

(3) If a regulated public service vehicle is used in contravention of this section, the operator of the vehicle is guilty of an offence and liable on summary conviction to a fine not exceeding level 4 on the standard scale.

(4) In this section "operator" has the same meaning as in the Public Passenger Vehicles Act 1981.

DEFINITIONS

"accessibility certificate": s.68(1); s.41(1)(a).
"approval certificate": s.68(1); s.42(4).
"operator": subs. (4).
"PSV accessibility regulations": s.68(1); s.40(1).
"prescribed": s.68(1).
"public service vehicle": s.40(5).
"regulated public service vehicle": s.40(5).
"regulations": s.68(1).
"standard scale": Criminal Justice Act 1982, s.37(2).

GENERAL NOTE

This section provides that a public service vehicle to which the PSV accessibility regulations apply must not be used on a road unless a vehicle examiner has issued an "accessibility certificate" in respect of that vehicle, in accordance with regulations made for the purpose by the Secretary of State under subs. (2), or an "approval certificate" has been issued in respect of the vehicle certifying that it conforms to an approved "type vehicle" (see the note to s.42). These provisions parallel the existing certification procedures for the initial fitness of public service vehicles contained in Pt. II of the Public Passenger Vehicles Act 1981, and it is intended that an accessibility certificate will be issued at the same time as a certificate of initial fitness. Regulations may be made under subs. (2) with respect to matters such as the application procedure for accessibility certificates, the examination of vehicles by vehicle examiners and the issue of duplicate certificates. There is a right of appeal to the Secretary of State against the refusal of a vehicle examiner to issue an accessibility certificate: see s.44(3). As to the fees payable in respect of an application for an accessibility certificate or an appeal under s.44, see s.45.

If a regulated PSV is used in contravention of this section, the operator of the vehicle is liable on summary conviction to a fine not exceeding level 4 on the standard scale (subs. (3)). Under the parallel provisions contained in Pt. II of the Public Passenger Vehicles Act 1981 concerning the initial fitness of public service vehicles, the operator has a defence under s.68(3) of that Act if he can prove that he took all reasonable precautions and exercised all due diligence to avoid the commission of an offence. No provision is made for any such defence under this section. The forgery, alteration or misuse, etc., of an accessibility certificate or an approval certificate is an offence, and it is also an offence for a person knowingly to make a false statement for the purpose of obtaining an accessibility certificate or an approval certificate: see the note to s.49.

Public service vehicle. See the note to s.40, above. A "regulated public service vehicle" means any public service vehicle to which the PSV accessibility regulations are expressed to apply: s.40(5).

Vehicle examiner. This refers to an examiner appointed under s.66A of the Road Traffic Act 1988 (c. 52).

Operator. Subsection (4) provides that "operator" has the same meaning as in the Public Passenger Vehicles Act 1981. Section 81(1) of the 1981 Act provides that, except in cases where a vehicle is made available by one holder of a PSV operator's licence to another under a hiring arrangement, the operator of a vehicle is; (i) the driver, if he own the vehicle; and (ii) in any other case, the person for whom the driver works (whether under a contract of employment or any other description of contract personally to do work).

Approval certificates

42.—(1) Where the Secretary of State is satisfied that such provisions of the PSV accessibility regulations as may be prescribed for the purposes of section 41 are satisfied in respect of a particular vehicle he may approve the vehicle for the purposes of this section.

(2) A vehicle which has been so approved is referred to in this section as a "type vehicle".

(3) Subsection (4) applies where a declaration in the prescribed form has been made by an authorised person that a particular vehicle conforms in design, construction and equipment with a type vehicle.

(4) A vehicle examiner may, after examining (if he thinks fit) the vehicle to which the declaration applies, issue a certificate in the prescribed form ("an approval certificate") that it conforms to the type vehicle.

(5) The Secretary of State may make regulations—

(a) with respect to applications for, and grants of, approval under subsection (1);

(b) with respect to applications for, and the issue of, approval certificates;

(c) providing for the examination of vehicles in respect of which applications have been made;

(d) with respect to the issue of copies of approval certificates in place of certificates which have been lost or destroyed.

(6) The Secretary of State may at any time withdraw his approval of a type vehicle.

(7) Where an approval is withdrawn—

(a) no further approval certificates shall be issued by reference to the type vehicle; but

(b) any approval certificate issued by reference to the type vehicle before the withdrawal shall continue to have effect for the purposes of section 41.

(8) In subsection (3) "authorised person" means a person authorised by the Secretary of State for the purposes of that subsection.

DEFINITIONS

"approval certificate": s.68(1); s.42(4).
"authorised person": subs. (8).
"prescribed": s.68(1).
"PSV accessibility regulations": s.68(1); s.40(1).
"regulations": s.68(1).
"type vehicle": subs. (2).
"vehicle examiner": s.68(1).

GENERAL NOTE

This section provides for the issue of an "approval certificate" by a vehicle examiner authorising the use of a public service vehicle on the road, where that vehicle conforms to a "type vehicle" approved by the Secretary of State for Transport under this section. This process, commonly referred to as "type approval", already exists in relation to the initial fitness of public service vehicles under Pt. II of the Public Passenger Vehicles Act 1981. Subsection (1) empowers the Secretary of State to approve a vehicle as a type vehicle where he is satisfied that it meets the relevant provisions of the PSV accessibility regulations. Where a type vehicle has been approved by the Secretary of State under subs. (1), and a declaration in the prescribed form has been made by an "authorised person" that a particular vehicle conforms in design, construction and equipment with a type vehicle (subs. (2)), a vehicle examiner may (after examining that other vehicle, if he thinks fit) issue an approval certificate that it conforms to the type vehicle (subs. (4)). The Secretary of State may make regulations with respect to applications for type approval and approval certificates, the examination of vehicles and the issue of duplicate certificates (subs. (5)). Approval of a type vehicle may be withdrawn at any time (subs. (6)), but approval certificates previously issued by reference to that type vehicle will continue to be valid (subs. (7)). Where the Secretary of State refuses an application for type approval, the applicant may ask the Secretary of State to review the decision, and in reviewing his decision the Secretary of State is required to consider any written representations made by the applicant: see s.44(1) and (2). There is also a right of appeal to the Secretary of State against the refusal of a vehicle examiner to issue an approval certificate: see s.44(3). The forgery, alteration or misuse, etc., of an approval certificate is an offence, and it is also an offence for a person knowingly to make a false statement for the purpose of obtaining an approval certificate: see the note to s.49. As to the fees payable in respect of applications for type approval or approval certificates under this section, or reviews and appeals under s.44, see s.45.

Authorised person. i.e. authorised by the Secretary of State: see subs. (8).

Special authorisations

43.—(1) The Secretary of State may by order authorise the use on roads of—

(a) any regulated public service vehicle of a class or description specified by the order, or

(b) any regulated public service vehicle which is so specified,

and nothing in section 40, 41 or 42 prevents the use of any vehicle in accordance with the order.

(2) Any such authorisation may be given subject to such restrictions and conditions as may be specified by or under the order.

(3) The Secretary of State may by order make provision for the purpose of securing that, subject to such restrictions and conditions as may be specified by or under the order, provisions of the PSV accessibility regulations apply to regulated public service vehicles of a description specified by the order subject to such modifications or exceptions as may be specified by the order.

Definitions

"PSV accessibility regulations": s.68(1); s.40(1).
"regulated public service vehicle": s.40(5).

General Note

This section empowers the Secretary of State for Transport to give special authorisation for the use on the road of specified public service vehicles which do not conform with the accessibility regulations and for which no accessibility certificate or approval certificate has been issued (subs. (1)). It also empowers the Secretary of State to modify the provisions of the PSV accessibility regulations as they apply to certain specified descriptions of public service vehicles (subs. (3)). "It provides flexibility to cater for circumstances in which an individual vehicle or class of vehicle cannot reasonably be expected to meet the full requirements of the accessibility regulations." (Minister of State, *Hansard*, H.L., Vol. 565, col. 717). An obvious example might be so-called heritage vehicles. The power to make orders under this section is exercisable by statutory instrument, unless the order applies only to a specified vehicle, or to vehicles of a specified person (see s.67(1) and (6)).

Reviews and appeals

44.—(1) Subsection (2) applies where—

(a) the Secretary of State refuses an application for the approval of a vehicle under section 42(1); and

(b) before the end of the prescribed period, the applicant asks the Secretary of State to review the decision and pays any fee fixed under section 45.

(2) The Secretary of State shall—

(a) review the decision; and

(b) in doing so, consider any representations made to him in writing, before the end of the prescribed period, by the applicant.

(3) A person applying for an accessibility certificate or an approval certificate may appeal to the Secretary of State against the refusal of a vehicle examiner to issue such a certificate.

(4) An appeal must be made within the prescribed time and in the prescribed manner.

(5) Regulations may make provision as to the procedure to be followed in connection with appeals.

(6) On the determination of an appeal, the Secretary of State may—

(a) confirm, vary or reverse the decision appealed against;

(b) give such directions as he thinks fit to the vehicle examiner for giving effect to his decision.

DEFINITIONS

"accessibility certificate": s.68(1); s.41(1)(a).
"approval certificate": s.68(1); s.42(4).
"prescribed": s.68(1).
"regulations": s.68(1).
"vehicle examiner": s.68(1).

GENERAL NOTE

This section provides for (i) a review by the Secretary of State of a decision by him to refuse an application for type approval under s.42(1) and (ii) an appeal to the Secretary of State against the refusal of a vehicle examiner to issue an accessibility certificate or an approval certificate (as to which, see the notes to ss.41 and 42).

Prescribed period; prescribed time; prescribed manner. i.e. prescribed by regulations made under this section and s.67.

Fees

45.—(1) Such fees, payable at such times, as may be prescribed may be charged by the Secretary of State in respect of—

(a) applications for, and grants of, approval under section 42(1);

(b) applications for, and the issue of, accessibility certificates and approval certificates;

(c) copies of such certificates;

(d) reviews and appeals under section 44.

(2) Any such fees received by the Secretary of State shall be paid by him into the Consolidated Fund.

(3) Regulations under subsection (1) may make provision for the repayment of fees, in whole or in part, in such circumstances as may be prescribed.

(4) Before making any regulations under subsection (1) the Secretary of State shall consult such representative organisations as he thinks fit.

DEFINITIONS

"accessibility certificate": s.68(1); s.41(1)(a).
"approval certificate": s.68(1); s.42(4).
"prescribed": s.68(1).
"regulations": s.68(1).

Rail vehicles

Rail vehicle accessibility regulations

46.—(1) The Secretary of State may make regulations ("rail vehicle accessibility regulations") for the purpose of securing that it is possible—

(a) for disabled persons—

(i) to get on to and off regulated rail vehicles in safety and without unreasonable difficulty;

(ii) to be carried in such vehicles in safety and in reasonable comfort; and

(b) for disabled persons in wheelchairs—

(i) to get on to and off such vehicles in safety and without unreasonable difficulty while remaining in their wheelchairs, and

(ii) to be carried in such vehicles in safety and in reasonable comfort while remaining in their wheelchairs.

(2) Rail vehicle accessibility regulations may, in particular, make provision as to the construction, use and maintenance of regulated rail vehicles including provision as to—

(a) the fitting of equipment to vehicles;
(b) equipment to be carried by vehicles;
(c) the design of equipment to be fitted to, or carried by, vehicles;
(d) the use of equipment fitted to, or carried by, vehicles;
(e) the toilet facilities to be provided in vehicles;
(f) the location and floor area of the wheelchair accommodation to be provided in vehicles;
(g) assistance to be given to disabled persons.

(3) If a regulated rail vehicle which does not conform with any provision of the rail vehicle accessibility regulations with which it is required to conform is used for carriage, the operator of the vehicle is guilty of an offence.

(4) A person who is guilty of such an offence is liable, on summary conviction, to a fine not exceeding level 4 on the standard scale.

(5) Different provision may be made in rail vehicle accessibility regulations—

(a) as respects different classes or descriptions of rail vehicle;
(b) as respects the same class or description of rail vehicle in different circumstances;
(c) as respects different networks.

(6) In this section—

"network" means any permanent way or other means of guiding or supporting rail vehicles or any section of it;

"operator", in relation to any rail vehicle, means the person having the management of that vehicle;

"rail vehicle" means a vehicle—

(a) constructed or adapted to carry passengers on any railway, tramway or prescribed system; and

(b) first brought into use, or belonging to a class of vehicle first brought into use, after 31st December 1998;

"regulated rail vehicle" means any rail vehicle to which the rail vehicle accessibility regulations are expressed to apply; and

"wheelchair accommodation" has such meaning as may be prescribed.

(7) In subsection (6)—

"prescribed system" means a system using a prescribed mode of guided transport ("guided transport" having the same meaning as in the Transport and Works Act 1992); and

"railway" and "tramway" have the same meaning as in that Act.

(8) The Secretary of State may by regulations make provision as to the time when a rail vehicle, or a class of rail vehicle, is to be treated, for the purposes of this section, as first brought into use.

(9) Regulations under subsection (8) may include provision for disregarding periods of testing and other prescribed periods of use.

(10) For the purposes of this section and section 47, a person uses a vehicle for carriage if he uses it for the carriage of members of the public for hire or reward at separate fares.

(11) Before making any regulations under subsection (1) or section 47 the Secretary of State shall consult the Disabled Persons Transport Advisory Committee and such other representative organisations as he thinks fit.

Definitions

"disabled person": s.1(2).
"network": subs. (6).
"operator": subs. (6).
"prescribed": s.68(1).
"prescribed system": subs. (7).
"rail vehicle": s.68(1); subs. (6).
"rail vehicle accessibility regulations": s.68(1); subs. (1).
"railway": subs. (7).
"regulated rail vehicle": s.68(1); subs. (6).
"regulations": s.68(1).
"standard scale": Criminal Justice Act 1982, s.37(2).
"tramway": subs. (7).
"wheelchair accommodation": s.46(6).

General Note

This section empowers the Secretary of State for Transport to make regulations ("rail vehicle accessibility regulations") making detailed provision as to the construction, use and maintenance of rail vehicles, to ensure that they are fully accessible to disabled persons, whether or not they are travelling in wheelchairs. The provisions are similar to those concerning the accessibility of public service vehicles contained in s.40 (see the note to that section). Subsection (1) provides that accessibility for these purposes means ensuring that it is possible for disabled persons to get on to and off rail vehicles in safety and without unreasonable difficulty, and to be carried in safety and in reasonable comfort; for disabled persons in wheelchairs, these requirements must be satisfied while they remain in their wheelchairs. The rail vehicle accessibility regulations may make provision as to the construction, use and maintenance of rail vehicles, including, *inter alia*, the design, fitting and use of equipment to be fitted to or carried by vehicles, toilet facilities, the location and floor area of the wheelchair accommodation, and the assistance to be given to disabled persons (subs. (2)). To ensure sufficient flexibility to deal with the wide range of rail vehicles and the various systems on which they operate, subs. (5) provides that different provision may be made for different classes or descriptions of rail vehicle, for the same class or description of vehicle in different circumstances, and for different networks (subs. (5)).

"That flexibility is important for a number of reasons. For example, we will want to ensure that accessibility regulations do not undermine the historic character of heritage railways ... Equally, it will allow us to look at different parts of, and different vehicles on, the London Underground to ensure that the access requirements are reasonable and practicable for such an old and largely inaccessible system. We need to be able to look at the circumstances of each system to tailor the requirements to the needs of both the industry and disabled consumers." (Minister of State, *Hansard*, H.L., Vol. 565, col. 718).

In addition, there is a general power in s.67 to make different provision for different areas or localities. Before making any regulations under this section or under s.47 (see below), the Secretary of State is required to consult the Disabled Persons Transport Advisory Committee, and such other "representative organisations" (not defined) as he thinks fit (subs. (11)). The operator of a regulated rail vehicle commits an offence, leading on summary conviction to a fine not exceeding level 4 on the standard scale, if a rail vehicle which does not conform with any provision of the rail vehicle accessibility regulations with which it is required to conform, is used for carriage (subss. (3) and (4)). "Use for carriage" in this context means use for the carriage of members of the public for hire or reward at separate fares (subs. (10)). Provision is also made for the liability in certain circumstances of the officers of a body corporate where an offence is committed by the body corporate: see the note to s.48.

Difficulty of access to the railway system has been a constant source of complaint on the part of disabled travellers. Some improvement has been made in recent years, and most new trains are now being designed and built to provide improved access and facilities for disabled people (for example, wide-entry doors, automatic doors and wheelchair-accessible toilets), but the overall position is still poor. Accommodation for wheelchair users is often restricted to one space per train, which normally has to be booked 48 hours in advance to ensure that a portable ramp is available, and it is still commonplace for wheelchair users to be relegated to the guard's van. Unstaffed stations are a further obstacle to rail travel, as many disabled people are unable to get on and off trains without assistance. Newer urban transport systems such as the Docklands Light Railway, Manchester Metrolink and Sheffield Supertram have been designed to be accessible to people with disabilities, but older systems such as the London Underground (which banned people in wheelchairs from using below-ground stations until 1993) remain inaccessible for all but the most determined and resourceful disabled travellers.

Until now, such improvements as have been made in the accessibility of rail travel have been achieved without the force of legislation. The Railways Act 1993, s.4(6) places a duty on the Regulator to "have regard" to the interests of disabled users of passenger services and station facilities, and the operators of passenger and station services are under a similar duty as a condition of their licence to operate, but the Government resisted attempts to include in the 1993 Act an obligation to take positive steps to provide access to disabled users. The Regulator has drawn up a Code of Practice, *Meeting the Needs of Disabled Passengers* (in consultation with the Disabled Persons Transport Advisory Committee), as required under s.70 of the 1993 Act, but as the code has no legal force, there is no obligation on passenger or station operators to comply with its recommendations. The measures contained in this section mark a significant break with previous practice, in that they empower the Secretary of State to set a legislative timetable for the introduction of fully accessible rail travel. As the 1995 White Paper observed (para. 5.3), the cost of achieving full accessibility retrospectively would be prohibitively expensive. The rail vehicle accessibility regulations will therefore only apply to new vehicles first brought into use, or belonging to a class of vehicle first brought into use, after December 31, 1998 (subs. (6)). The Secretary of State may determine the time when a rail vehicle is to be treated as first brought into use (subs. (8)), and whether periods of testing, etc., are to be disregarded (subs. (9)).

Railway. This has the same meaning as in the Transport and Works Act 1992 (c. 42), s.67(1), *i.e.*: "a system of transport employing parallel rails which, (a) provide support and guidance for vehicles carried on flanged wheels, and (b) form a track which either is of a gauge of at least 350 millimetres or crosses a carriageway (whether or not on the same level), but does not include a tramway".

Tramway. This has the same meaning as in the Transport and Works Act 1992, s.67(1), *i.e.*: "a system of transport used wholly or mainly for the carriage of passengers and employing parallel rails which, (a) provide support and guidance for vehicles carried on flanged wheels, and (b) are laid wholly or mainly along a street or in any other place to which the public has access (including a place to which the public has access only on making a payment)."

Guided transport. This has the same meaning as in the Transport and Works Act 1992, s.67(1), *i.e.*: "transport by vehicles guided by means external to the vehicles (whether or not the vehicles are also capable of being operated in some other way)."

Disabled Persons Transport Advisory Committee. See the note to s.35.

Exemption from rail vehicle accessibility regulations

47.—(1) The Secretary of State may by order (an "exemption order") authorise the use for carriage of any regulated rail vehicle of a specified description, or in specified circumstances, even though that vehicle does not conform with the provisions of the rail vehicle accessibility regulations with which it is required to conform.

(2) Regulations may make provision with respect to exemption orders including, in particular, provision as to—

(a) the persons by whom applications for exemption orders may be made;
(b) the form in which such applications are to be made;
(c) information to be supplied in connection with such applications;
(d) the period for which exemption orders are to continue in force;
(e) the revocation of exemption orders.

(3) After considering any application for an exemption order and consulting the Disabled Persons Transport Advisory Committee and such other persons as he considers appropriate, the Secretary of State may—

(a) make an exemption order in the terms of the application;
(b) make an exemption order in such other terms as he considers appropriate;
(c) refuse to make an exemption order.

(4) An exemption order may be made subject to such restrictions and conditions as may be specified.

(5) In this section "specified" means specified in an exemption order.

Definitions
"exemption order": subs. (1).
"rail vehicle accessibility regulations": s.68(1); s.46(1).

"regulated rail vehicle": s.68(1); s.46(6).
"regulations": s.68(1).
"specified": subs. (5).

General Note

This section empowers the Secretary of State to make an exemption order authorising the use of rail vehicles which do not comply with the rail vehicle accessibility regulations in certain specified circumstances. Before making a decision on an application for an exemption order, the Secretary of State must consult the Disabled Persons Transport Advisory Committee and such other persons as he considers appropriate (subs. (3)). It is apparently not envisaged that this power will be widely used (Minister of State, *Hansard*, H.L., Vol. 565, col. 718).

Disabled Persons Transport Advisory Committee. See the note to s.35.

Supplemental

Offences by bodies corporate etc.

48.—(1) Where an offence under section 40 or 46 committed by a body corporate is committed with the consent or connivance of, or is attributable to any neglect on the part of, a director, manager, secretary or other similar officer of the body, or a person purporting to act in such a capacity, he as well as the body corporate is guilty of the offence.

(2) In subsection (1) "director", in relation to a body corporate whose affairs are managed by its members, means a member of the body corporate.

(3) Where, in Scotland, an offence under section 40 or 46 committed by a partnership or by an unincorporated association other than a partnership is committed with the consent or connivance of, or is attributable to any neglect on the part of, a partner in the partnership or (as the case may be) a person concerned in the management or control of the association, he, as well as the partnership or association, is guilty of the offence.

General Note

This section provides for the liability of certain persons where an offence is committed by a body corporate. In such circumstances, a director, manager, secretary or other similar officer of the body corporate will be guilty of the offence committed by the body corporate, if the offence was committed with his consent or connivance, or is attributable to any neglect on his part.

Consent. "It would seem that where a director consents to the commission of an offence by his company, he is well aware of what is going on and agrees to it" (*Huckerby v. Elliott* [1970] All E.R. 189, 194, per Ashworth J.).

Connivance. This term implies acquiescence in the offence committed, or in a course of conduct reasonably likely to lead to the commission of the offence: "Where [the director] connives at the offence committed by the company he is equally well aware of what is going on but his agreement is tacit, not actively encouraging what happens but letting it continue and saying nothing about it": *Huckerby v. Elliott* (*ibid.*). In *Criminal Law: The General Part*, para. 284, Glanville Williams describes connivance in the criminal law context as requiring "knowledge (including wilful blindness) plus negligent failure to prevent."

Neglect. This term implies "failure to perform a duty which the person knows or ought to know": *Hughes, Re* [1943] Ch. 296, 298, per Simonds J. Some act or neglect on the part of a director must be shown: *Huckerby v. Elliott* (*ibid.*). As to director's duties and the extent to which a director may delegate, see *City Equitable Fire Insurance Co., Re* [1925] Ch. 407.

Other similar officer. See for example *Armour v. Skeen* [1977] IRLR 310.

Person purporting to act in such a capacity. This phrase is intended to meet the situation where the appointment of a director or other officer is defective (as in *Dean v. Hiesler* [1942] 2 All E.R. 340).

Forgery and false statements

49.—(1) In this section "relevant document" means—
(a) a certificate of exemption issued under section 36 or 37;
(b) a notice of a kind mentioned in section 36(9)(b) or 37(8)(b);

(c) an accessibility certificate; or
(d) an approval certificate.

(2) A person is guilty of an offence if, with intent to deceive, he—
(a) forges, alters or uses a relevant document;
(b) lends a relevant document to any other person;
(c) allows a relevant document to be used by any other person; or
(d) makes or has in his possession any document which closely resembles a relevant document.

(3) A person who is guilty of an offence under subsection (2) is liable—
(a) on summary conviction, to a fine not exceeding the statutory maximum;
(b) on conviction on indictment, to imprisonment for a term not exceeding two years or to a fine or to both.

(4) A person who knowingly makes a false statement for the purpose of obtaining an accessibility certificate or an approval certificate is guilty of an offence and liable on summary conviction to a fine not exceeding level 4 on the standard scale.

DEFINITIONS

"accessibility certificate": s.68(1); s.41(1)(a).
"approval certificate": s.68(1); s.42(4).
"relevant document": subs. (1).
"standard scale": Criminal Justice Act 1982, s.37(2).

GENERAL NOTE

This section makes it an offence for a person, with intent to deceive, to forge, alter or use any of the documents listed in subs. (1); to lend such a document to another person; to allow such a document to be used by another person; or to make or have in his possession a document which closely resembles such a document (subs. (2)). It is also an offence for a person knowingly to make a false statement for the purpose of obtaining an accessibility certificate or an approval certificate (subs. (4)).

With intent to deceive. As to proof of criminal intent, see the Criminal Justice Act 1967 (c. 80), s.8.

Knowingly. Mere neglect to ascertain what would have been discovered through reasonable inquiries is not tantamount to knowledge, but deliberately refraining from making inquiries can in certain circumstances constitute actual knowledge: *Roper v. Taylor's Central Garages (Exeter)* (1951) 2 T.L.R. 284, per Devlin J.

PART VI

THE NATIONAL DISABILITY COUNCIL

The National Disability Council

50.—(1) There shall be a body to be known as the National Disability Council (but in this Act referred to as "the Council").

(2) It shall be the duty of the Council to advise the Secretary of State, either on its own initiative or when asked to do so by the Secretary of State—
(a) on matters relevant to the elimination of discrimination against disabled persons and persons who have had a disability;
(b) on measures which are likely to reduce or eliminate such discrimination; and
(c) on matters related to the operation of this Act or of provisions made under this Act.

(3) The Secretary of State may by order confer additional functions on the Council.

(4) The power conferred by subsection (3) does not include power to confer on the Council any functions with respect to the investigation of any complaint which may be the subject of proceedings under this Act.

(5) In discharging its duties under this section, the Council shall in particular have regard to—

(a) the extent and nature of the benefits which would be likely to result from the implementation of any recommendation which it makes; and

(b) the likely cost of implementing any such recommendation.

(6) Where the Council makes any recommendation in the discharge of any of its functions under this section it shall, if it is reasonably practicable to do so, make an assessment of—

(a) the likely cost of implementing the recommendation; and

(b) the likely financial benefits which would result from implementing it.

(7) Where the Council proposes to give the Secretary of State advice on a matter, it shall before doing so—

(a) consult any body—

(i) established by any enactment or by a Minister of the Crown for the purpose of giving advice in relation to disability, or any aspect of disability; and

(ii) having functions in relation to the matter to which the advice relates;

(b) consult such other persons as it considers appropriate; and

(c) have regard to any representations made to it as a result of any such consultations.

(8) Schedule 5 makes further provision with respect to the Council, including provision about its membership.

(9) The power conferred on the Council by subsection (2) to give advice on its own initiative does not include power to give advice—

(a) by virtue of paragraph (a) or (b), in respect of any matter which relates to the operation of any provision of or arrangements made under—

(i) the Disabled Persons (Employment) Acts 1944 and 1958;

(ii) the Employment and Training Act 1973;

(iii) the Employment Protection (Consolidation) Act 1978; or

(iv) section 2(3) of the Enterprise and New Towns (Scotland) Act 1990; or

(b) by virtue of paragraph (c), in respect of any matter arising under Part II or section 53, 54, 56 or 61.

(10) Subsection (9) shall not have effect at any time when there is neither a national advisory council established under section 17(1)(a) of the Disabled Persons (Employment) Act 1944 nor any person appointed to act generally under section 60(1) of this Act.

DEFINITIONS

"Council; the": subs. (1).
"disability": s.1(1).
"disabled person": s.1(2).
"Minister of the Crown": s.68(1).

GENERAL NOTE

This section provides for the establishment of a National Disability Council ("NDC") to advise the Government on general issues relating to discrimination against disabled people. Separate provision is made in Sched. 8, para. 33 for a Northern Ireland Disability Council. The primary duties of the NDC will be to advise the Government: (i) on matters relating to the elimination of discrimination against disabled people; (ii) on measures to reduce or eliminate such discrimination; and (iii) on matters pertaining to the operation of the Act. The NDC also has a duty to draw up codes of practice, albeit only at the request of the Secretary of State (see s.51). However, unlike the Equal Opportunities Commission and the Commission for Racial Equality, the NDC has no power to investigate complaints of discrimination (such activity is specifically excluded by subs. (4)), to provide assistance to individuals in enforcing their rights before the courts and tribunals, or to take strategic enforcement action of its own accord. Nor will it have the responsibility for advising the Government on the employment of disabled people, the giving of advice in that area remaining (for the time being, at least) the preserve of the National Advisory Council on Employment of People with Disabilities (NACEDP), a body established under the Disabled Persons (Employment) Act 1944 (c. 10) to advise Ministers on matters relating to the employment or training of disabled people.

The limited nature of the NDC's remit when compared with bodies such as the EOC and the CRE has been a source of widespread concern among disabled rights campaigners. A number of the organisations which responded to the Government's consultation document on *Measures to Tackle Discrimination Against Disabled People* (July 1994) argued strongly that the new body should have statutory powers of enforcement like the EOC and the CRE. Concern has also been expressed over the split jurisdiction between the NDC and the NACEPD. As the Employers Forum on Disability stated in its response to the consultation document:

"The legislation must send a clear signal to employers that disability discrimination legislation is just as important as race and gender and that they should manage it accordingly. It will be very difficult for such clear messages to be effectively delivered by two sets of civil servants reporting to two different Ministers, advised by two different councils, using two separate drafted codes of practice, enforced by two different legal authorities and supported by two different local advisory arrangements."

The establishment of a statutory disability commission was proposed in the 1982 Report of the Committee on Restrictions Against Disabled People (CORAD), which recommended that there should be "a Commission with powers to investigate, conciliate and if necessary take legal action on individual complaints" (para. 4.53). Sir Peter Large, Chairman of CORAD, described the proposal for the NDC as "... a wheyfaced ghost of what is required. Not only does the proposed advisory council lack teeth but it also lacks a digestive system and a few other essential organs. It enjoys no life of its own. It acts only in response to the summonses of the Secretary of State". The NDC only has the power to advise the Government. It is no part of its function to provide advice, information or guidance on an individual basis to disabled persons, employers or service providers. Instead, s.28 of the Act empowers the Secretary of State to make arrangements for the provision of advice and assistance in relation to Pt. III of the Act (Discrimination in relation to goods, facilities, services and premises), while advice in relation to the employment of people with disabilities will continue to be provided by the Employment Service's Placing, Assessment and Counselling Teams (PACTs) and the Advisory, Conciliation and Arbitration Service (ACAS).

Subs. (7)

It is intended that the NDC will work closely with existing bodies such as the Disabled Persons Transport Advisory Committee, drawing on their expertise in particular areas (White Paper, *Ending Discrimination against Disabled People*, Cm. 2729, para. 7.3). Subs. (7) places a duty on the NDC to consult with such bodies, and to have regard to any representations made to it, before giving advice to the Secretary of State.

Subs. (8)

Schedule 5 makes detailed provision for the constitution and membership of the NDC. The Council is to have a membership of at least 10 but not more than 20 people, appointed by the Secretary of State, and drawn from people who have knowledge or experience of the needs of disabled people, or who are representatives of professional bodies or bodies representing industry or business. In appointing members of the Council, the Secretary of State must try to ensure that at least half the membership are disabled persons, persons who have had a disability, or the parents or guardians of disabled persons (para. 3). Staff are to be provided at the discretion of the Secretary of State (para. 6). Paragraph 7 empowers the Secretary of State to make regulations in relation, *inter alia*, to the commissioning of research to be undertaken on behalf of the Council, and the payment of expenses incurred by the Council.

Subss. (9) and (10)

As discussed in the General Note, the NDC is expressly precluded by subs. (9) from giving advice to the Secretary of State on matters relating to the employment and training of disabled people, the giving of advice in that area remaining the responsibility of the National Advisory Council on Employment of People with Disabilities (NACEDP), until such time as the NACEDP is wound up (see s.60(6)) and the advisory function is transferred to the NDC (subs. (10)). However, where employment matters have an impact on wider issues of discrimination, the NDC will not be precluded from discussing them:

"It is not the Government's intention that the NDC would be precluded from considering the adequacy of anti-discrimination provisions in employment where that is appropriate as an aspect of its broad overview of anti-discrimination measures." (Minister for Social Security and Disabled People, *Hansard*, H.C., Standing Committee E, col. 397).

The Government has undertaken to review the existence and constitution of NACEDP before June 1997, when the terms of office of the current NACEDP members end; if and when the NACEDP is disbanded, its advisory responsibilities will transfer automatically to the NDC by virtue of subs. (10), unless the Secretary of State has in the meantime appointed advisers under s.60(1) to advise him on national employment issues:

"[The Act's] provisions are flexible. They provide for a variety of advisory arrangements, depending on what is appropriate. For example, NACEDP could be retained indefinitely or for a particular period only. If NACEDP were to be abolished, the new advisers could be appointed on national employment issues. If no such advisers were to be appointed, then the NDC would take over that role." (Minister of State, *Hansard*., H.L., Vol. 565, col. 690).

Codes of practice prepared by the Council

51.—(1) It shall be the duty of the Council, when asked to do so by the Secretary of State—

(a) to prepare proposals for a code of practice dealing with the matters to which the Secretary of State's request relates; or

(b) to review a code and, if it considers it appropriate, propose alterations.

(2) The Secretary of State may, in accordance with the procedural provisions of section 52, issue codes of practice in response to proposals made by the Council under this section.

(3) A failure on the part of any person to observe any provision of a code does not of itself make that person liable to any proceedings.

(4) A code is admissible in evidence in any proceedings under this Act before an industrial tribunal, a county court or a sheriff court.

(5) If any provision of a code appears to a tribunal or court to be relevant to any question arising in any proceedings under this Act, it shall be taken into account in determining that question.

(6) In this section and section 52 "code" means a code issued by the Secretary of State under this section and includes a code which has been altered and re-issued.

DEFINITIONS

"code": subs. (6).

"Council; the": s.50(1).

GENERAL NOTE

This section places a duty on the NDC to prepare or review codes of practice, at the request of the Secretary of State. Unlike the Equal Opportunities Commission, the Commission for Racial Equality and the Advisory, Conciliation and Arbitration Service, all of which have the power to issue codes of practice of their own volition (under the Sex Discrimination Act 1975, s.56A; the Race Relations Act 1976, s.47, and the Trade Union and Labour Relations (Consolidation) Act 1992, s.199, respectively), the NDC may only prepare a proposal for a code of practice when asked to do so by the Secretary of State, who may approve or refuse to approve the proposal, as he thinks fit. The inability of the NDC to issue codes of practice on its own initiative has been a predictable source of criticism. The NDC will be entitled, as part of its general duty to advise on issues relevant to the elimination of discrimination, to advise the Secretary of State that a code of practice on a particular issue would be useful, or that an existing code of practice requires review or update, but in the Government's view, it would be "a shocking waste of time and money" for the Council to undertake detailed preparatory work on codes of practice if they were not then to be taken forward and submitted to Parliament (Minister for Social Security and Disabled People, *Hansard*, H.C., Standing Committee E, col. 412).

Subss. (3), (4) and (5)

These subsections contain the usual provisions concerning the significance of a failure to observe a provision of a code of practice, and the admissibility of a code of practice in legal proceedings. For the parallel provisions in relation to codes of practice issued by the EOC, CRE and ACAS, see the Sex Discrimination Act 1975, s.56A(10)); the Race Relations Act 1976, s.47(10), and the Trade Union and Labour Relations (Consolidation) Act 1992, s.207, respectively.

In any proceedings under this Act. A code of practice issued by the Secretary of State under this section is stated to be admissible in evidence in any proceedings under this Act, and not in any legal proceedings arising under other legislation in which a disability-related issue might arise.

Further provision about codes issued under section 51

52.—(1) In this section "proposal" means a proposal made by the Council to the Secretary of State under section 51.

(2) In preparing any proposal, the Council shall consult—

(a) such persons (if any) as the Secretary of State has specified in making his request to the Council; and

(b) such other persons (if any) as the Council considers appropriate.

(3) Before making any proposal, the Council shall publish a draft, consider any representations made to it about the draft and, if it thinks it appropriate, modify its proposal in the light of any of those representations.

(4) Where the Council makes any proposal, the Secretary of State may—

(a) approve it;

(b) approve it subject to such modifications as he considers appropriate; or

(c) refuse to approve it.

(5) Where the Secretary of State approves any proposal (with or without modifications), he shall prepare a draft of the proposed code and lay it before each House of Parliament.

(6) If, within the 40-day period, either House resolves not to approve the draft, the Secretary of State shall take no further steps in relation to the proposed code.

(7) If no such resolution is made within the 40-day period, the Secretary of State shall issue the code in the form of his draft.

(8) The code shall come into force on such date as the Secretary of State may appoint by order.

(9) Subsection (6) does not prevent a new draft of the proposed code from being laid before Parliament.

(10) If the Secretary of State refuses to approve a proposal, he shall give the Council a written statement of his reasons for not approving it.

(11) The Secretary of State may by order revoke a code.

(12) In this section "40-day period", in relation to the draft of a proposed code, means—

(a) if the draft is laid before one House on a day later than the day on which it is laid before the other House, the period of 40 days beginning with the later of the two days, and

(b) in any other case, the period of 40 days beginning with the day on which the draft is laid before each House,

no account being taken of any period during which Parliament is dissolved or prorogued or during which both Houses are adjourned for more than four days.

DEFINITIONS

"code": s.51(6).
"Council; the": s.50(1).
"proposal": s.52(1).
"40-day period": s.52(12).

GENERAL NOTE

This section sets out in detail the procedure for preparing a proposal for a code of practice by the NDC, the consideration of any such proposal by the Secretary of State, and the laying of a draft of the proposed code before both Houses of Parliament under the negative resolution procedure.

PART VII

SUPPLEMENTAL

Codes of practice prepared by the Secretary of State

53.—(1) The Secretary of State may issue codes of practice containing such practical guidance as he considers appropriate with a view to—

(a) eliminating discrimination in the field of employment against disabled persons and persons who have had a disability; or

(b) encouraging good practice in relation to the employment of disabled persons and persons who have had a disability.

(2) The Secretary of State may from time to time revise the whole or any part of a code and re-issue it.

(3) Without prejudice to subsection (1), a code may include practical guidance as to—

(a) the circumstances in which it would be reasonable, having regard in particular to the costs involved, for a person to be expected to make adjustments in favour of a disabled person or a person who has had a disability; or

(b) what steps it is reasonably practicable for employers to take for the purpose of preventing their employees from doing, in the course of their employment, anything which is made unlawful by this Act.

(4) A failure on the part of any person to observe any provision of a code does not of itself make that person liable to any proceedings.

(5) A code is admissible in evidence in any proceedings under this Act before an industrial tribunal, a county court or a sheriff court.

(6) If any provision of a code appears to a tribunal or court to be relevant to any question arising in any proceedings under this Act, it shall be taken into account in determining that question.

(7) In this section and section 54 "code" means a code issued by the Secretary of State under this section and includes a code which has been revised and re-issued.

(8) In subsection (1)(a), "discrimination in the field of employment" includes discrimination of a kind mentioned in section 12 or 13.

(9) In subsections (1)(b) and (3), "employment" includes contract work (as defined by section 12(6)).

DEFINITIONS

"code": subs. (7).
"disability": s.1(1).
"disabled person": s.1(2).
"discrimination in the field of employment": subs. (8).
"employment": subs. (9).

GENERAL NOTE

This section empowers the Secretary of State to issue codes of practice in relation to the employment of disabled people. Separate provision for the issue of such codes by the Secretary of State is necessary because, as discussed in the note to s.50, the NDC is precluded from advising the Secretary of State on matters relating to the employment and training of disabled people, until such time as the National Advisory Council on Employment of People with Disabilities is disbanded.

Subss. (4), (5) and (6)

See the note to s.51, subss. (3), (4) and (5).

Further provision about codes issued under section 53

54.—(1) In preparing a draft of any code under section 53, the Secretary of State shall consult such organisations representing the interests of, employers or of disabled persons in, or seeking, employment as he considers appropriate.

(2) Where the Secretary of State proposes to issue a code, he shall publish a draft of it, consider any representations that are made to him about the draft and, if he thinks it appropriate, modify his proposals in the light of any of those representations.

(3) If the Secretary of State decides to proceed with a proposed code, he shall lay a draft of it before each House of Parliament.

(4) If, within the 40-day period, either House resolves not to approve the draft, the Secretary of State shall take no further steps in relation to the proposed code.

(5) If no such resolution is made within the 40-day period, the Secretary of State shall issue the code in the form of his draft.

(6) The code shall come into force on such date as the Secretary of State may appoint by order.

(7) Subsection (4) does not prevent a new draft of the proposed code from being laid before Parliament.

(8) The Secretary of State may by order revoke a code.

(9) In this section "40-day period", in relation to the draft of a proposed code, means—

(a) if the draft is laid before one House on a day later than the day on which it is laid before the other House, the period of 40 days beginning with the later of the two days, and

(b) in any other case, the period of 40 days beginning with the day on which the draft is laid before each House,

no account being taken of any period during which Parliament is dissolved or prorogued or during which both Houses are adjourned for more than four days.

DEFINITIONS

"code": s.53(7).
"disabled person": s.1(2).
"40-day period": s.54(9).

GENERAL NOTE

The procedure which the Secretary of State is required to follow in order to issue a code of practice under s.53 differs in one important respect from the similar provisions in the Trade Union and Labour Relations (Consolidation) Act 1992 (c. 52), ss.203 *et seq.*, in that under s.204(2) of the 1992 Act, a code of practice issued by the Secretary of State must be approved by an affirmative resolution of each House of Parliament, whereas under this section the negative resolution procedure applies, with consequent reduction in the level of parliamentary scrutiny. The Secretary of State is however still required to consult with representative organisations in preparing a draft of a code, and to consider any representations made to him about the draft.

The existing Code of Good Practice on the Employment of Disabled People, originally issued by the Manpower Services Commission in 1984 and revised by the Employment Service in March 1993, is a non-statutory code, and observance of its recommendations is purely voluntary.

Victimisation

55.—(1) For the purposes of Part II or Part III, a person ("A") discriminates against another person ("B") if—

(a) he treats B less favourably than he treats or would treat other persons whose circumstances are the same as B's; and

(b) he does so for a reason mentioned in subsection (2).

(2) The reasons are that—

(a) B has—

(i) brought proceedings against A or any other person under this Act; or

(ii) given evidence or information in connection with such proceedings brought by any person; or

(iii) otherwise done anything under this Act in relation to A or any other person; or

(iv) alleged that A or any other person has (whether or not the allegation so states) contravened this Act; or

(b) A believes or suspects that B has done or intends to do any of those things.

(3) Where B is a disabled person, or a person who has had a disability, the disability in question shall be disregarded in comparing his circumstances with those of any other person for the purposes of subsection (1)(a).

(4) Subsection (1) does not apply to treatment of a person because of an allegation made by him if the allegation was false and not made in good faith.

DEFINITIONS

"disability": s.1(1).

"disabled person": s.1(2).

GENERAL NOTE

In common with the Sex Discrimination Act 1975, s.4, and the Race Relations Act 1976, s.2, this section makes it unlawful for a person to victimise another person (who need not be disabled) in connection with the exercise of rights conferred by Pts. II and III of the Act. It is unlawful for a person (A) to discriminate against another person (B) by treating B less favourably than he treats or would treat another person whose circumstances are the same as B, for any of the reasons set out in subs. (2), *i.e.*, that B has (i) brought proceedings under the Act against A or any other person; (ii) given evidence or information in connection with any proceedings brought under the Act (iii) done any other thing under the Act in relation to A or any other person; (iv) alleged that A or any other person has contravened the Act (unless that allegation was both false and not made in good faith: see subs. (4)). The provisions apply *mutatis mutandis* where A believes or suspects that B has done or intends to do any of the above.

Where the complaint is of discrimination in relation to employment under Pt. II of the Act, it seems likely that the protection against victimisation afforded by this section will be limited to events occurring during the course of employment, by analogy with *Nagarajan v. Agnew* [1994] I.R.L.R. 61 (a case under the equivalent provisions in the R.R.A.), in which the applicant unsuccessfully alleged that he had been victimised by a bad reference from his ex-manager.

Whose circumstances are the same as B's. In comparing B's circumstances with those of another person, subs. (3) requires any disability which B has, or which he had, to be disregarded.

In *Aziz v. Trinity Street Taxis* [1988] I.R.L.R. 204 (the leading case on the equivalent provisions in the R.R.A.), the Court of Appeal indicated that the correct approach is to compare the treatment of the applicant with the treatment of other persons who have not done any of the acts listed in subs. (2). See also *Cornelius v. University College of Swansea* [1987] I.R.L.R. 141 (a case under the equivalent provisions in the S.D.A.), where the Court of Appeal held that, for a claim of victimisation for bringing proceedings under the 1975 Act to succeed, the applicant would have to show that she would not have been treated in the same way had the proceedings been of an entirely different nature (an interpretation which, if correct, would considerably reduce the scope of the protection).

For a reason mentioned in subsection (2). The applicant must establish the necessary causal connection between the less favourable treatment and the fact that he has done one of the acts referred to in subs. (2). Under the equivalent provisions in the R.R.A., the Court of Appeal has confirmed that to benefit from the statutory protection against victimisation, the applicant must show that the reason for the less favourable treatment is that he has done one of the protected acts, so that if the employer, service provider, etc., can show that there was some other reason for the less favourable treatment, the necessary causal connection will not have been established and the complaint of victimisation will fail: see *Aziz v. Trinity Street Taxis* (above). In *Aziz*, the applicant's complaint failed because the respondent's action was found to have been motivated by the fact that the applicant had made secret tape recordings, and not by the fact that he had made a complaint against the company under the 1976 Act. See also *British Airways Engine Overhaul v. Francis* [1981] I.R.L.R. 9 (a case under the S.D.A.), where the applicant's complaint failed because her actions (she had made statements to the press criticising her union's policy on pursuing equal pay claims) were held by the E.A.T. not to fall within any of the four heads.

For guidance as to the proper approach to be taken in a case under the R.R.A. involving mixed motives, see *Nagarajan v. Agnew* [1994] I.R.L.R. 61:

"Where an Industrial Tribunal finds that there are mixed motives for the doing of an act, one or some but not all of which constitute unlawful discrimination, it is highly desirable for there to be an assessment of the importance from the causative point of view of the unlawful motive or motives. If the Industrial Tribunal finds that the unlawful motive or motives were of sufficient weight in the decision-making process to be treated as a cause, not the sole cause but as a cause, of the act thus motivated, there will be unlawful discrimination" (per Knox J, at p.67).

It seems very likely that a similar approach will be taken to cases involving mixed motives arising under the present Act.

Subs. (2)

Given evidence or information. In *Aziz v. Trinity Street Taxis* (above), the Court of Appeal held that the equivalent head in the R.R.A., s.2(1), applies to the giving of evidence or information by a person who is not a party to the proceedings.

Otherwise done anything under this Act. Quaere whether this would cover an employee victimised by his or her employer for refusing to discriminate against a disabled person? The wording of the present section departs from that of other anti-discrimination Acts in one important respect, in that subs. (2)(a)(iii) refers to B having "otherwise done anything under this Act", whereas the equivalent provisions in the R.R.A. and S.D.A. appear to be broader, in that they refer to the applicant having "otherwise done anything under *or by reference to* this Act" (R.R.A., s.2(1)(c); S.D.A., s.4(1)(c); emphasis added). In *Kirby v. Manpower Services Commission* [1980] I.R.L.R. 229 (a case under the R.R.A.), the applicant was disciplined by his employer for disclosing alleged instances of racial discrimination by other employers to the Commission for Racial Equality. The E.A.T. held that the applicant was not protected by s.2 of the R.R.A. because he had been disciplined for disclosing confidential information, not for making allegations of racial discrimination (see *Aziz*, above, on this point), but more significantly in view of the difference in wording discussed above, the E.A.T. considered that the applicant had not been disciplined for doing something "under" the 1976 Act, because those words imported the existence under that Act of a specific duty to act; the E.A.T. was however prepared to assume that the employee's actions might constitute something done "by reference to" the 1976 Act. The E.A.T. also held that the protection in s.2(1)(d) of the 1976 Act for those alleging a contravention of that Act did not apply on the facts, because the applicant had merely alleged that the employers *might have* contravened the Act. It remains to be seen whether a similarly narrow interpretation will be given to the present section. The point is even more important in the present context, as a person who is victimised for refusing to discriminate against another on racial grounds, and who falls outside the protection of s.2 of the 1976 Act for the reasons explained above, may nevertheless be protected under s.1 of the 1976 Act, which makes it unlawful to discriminate against a person "on racial grounds": see for example *Showboat Entertainment Centre v. Owens* [1984] I.C.R. 65, where a person dismissed for refusing to apply a colour bar was held to have been discriminated against on the grounds of *another's* colour. No such argument is available under the present Act, which makes it unlawful to discriminate against a *disabled person*, not to discriminate against a person *on grounds of disability*.

Help for persons suffering discrimination

56.—(1) For the purposes of this section—

(a) a person who considers that he may have been discriminated against, in contravention of any provision of Part II, is referred to as "the complainant"; and

(b) a person against whom the complainant may decide to make, or has made, a complaint under Part II is referred to as "the respondent".

(2) The Secretary of State shall, with a view to helping the complainant to decide whether to make a complaint against the respondent and, if he does so, to formulate and present his case in the most effective manner, by order prescribe–

(a) forms by which the complainant may question the respondent on his reasons for doing any relevant act, or on any other matter which is or may be relevant; and

(b) forms by which the respondent may if he so wishes reply to any questions.

(3) Where the complainant questions the respondent in accordance with forms prescribed by an order under subsection (2)—

(a) the question, and any reply by the respondent (whether in accordance with such an order or not), shall be admissible as evidence in any proceedings under Part II;

(b) if it appears to the tribunal in any such proceedings—
(i) that the respondent deliberately, and without reasonable excuse, omitted to reply within a reasonable period, or
(ii) that the respondent's reply is evasive or equivocal,
it may draw any inference which it considers it just and equitable to draw, including an inference that the respondent has contravened a provision of Part II.

(4) The Secretary of State may by order prescribe—
(a) the period within which questions must be duly served in order to be admissible under subsection (3)(a); and
(b) the manner in which a question, and any reply by the respondent, may be duly served.

(5) This section is without prejudice to any other enactment or rule of law regulating interlocutory and preliminary matters in proceedings before an industrial tribunal, and has effect subject to any enactment or rule of law regulating the admissibility of evidence in such proceedings.

DEFINITIONS
"complainant; the": subs. (1)(a).
"respondent; the": subs. (1)(b).

GENERAL NOTE
This section requires the Secretary of State to issue forms ("questions and replies" forms) for use by a potential complainant in order to decide whether to bring proceedings under Pt. II of the Act, and for use by the potential respondent in replying. The provisions echo those contained in the Sex Discrimination Act 1975, s.74, and the Race Relations Act 1976, s.65. Subsection (3)(b) makes it clear that a tribunal may draw adverse inferences from a failure to reply; and subs. (5) confirms that these provisions are in addition to the normal power of a tribunal to order discovery under S.I. 1993 No. 2687, Sched. 1, r.4.

Aiding unlawful acts

57.—(1) A person who knowingly aids another person to do an act made unlawful by this Act is to be treated for the purposes of this Act as himself doing the same kind of unlawful act.

(2) For the purposes of subsection (1), an employee or agent for whose act the employer or principal is liable under section 58 (or would be so liable but for section 58(5)) shall be taken to have aided the employer or principal to do the act.

(3) For the purposes of this section, a person does not knowingly aid another to do an unlawful act if—
(a) he acts in reliance on a statement made to him by that other person that, because of any provision of this Act, the act would not be unlawful; and
(b) it is reasonable for him to rely on the statement.

(4) A person who knowingly or recklessly makes such a statement which is false or misleading in a material respect is guilty of an offence.

(5) Any person guilty of an offence under subsection (4) shall be liable on summary conviction to a fine not exceeding level 5 on the standard scale.

DEFINITIONS
"act": s.68(1).
"standard scale": Criminal Justice Act 1982, s.37(2).

GENERAL NOTE
This section provides that a person who knowingly aids another person to do an act which is unlawful under this Act is himself to be treated as having committed the same kind of unlawful act. It mirrors the equivalent provisions in the Sex Discrimination Act 1975, s.42, and the Race Relations Act 1976, s.33. Its effect, when taken together with s.58 (which provides that employers and principals may be vicariously liable for the acts of their employees and agents in certain circumstances), is to enable employees or agents to be held liable for their own acts, even

though the duty not to discriminate under the Act applies only to employers or service providers. This result arises by virtue of subs. (2), which provides that an employee or agent who causes his employer or principal to be vicariously liable is deemed to have aided his employer's or principal's vicarious act. So for example, where an employer is vicariously liable under s.58 for a discriminatory act of one of his employees, the employee responsible for that discriminatory act may himself be held liable under this section for aiding the employer's breach. This will be so even if the employer is able to make out a defence under s.58(5) (*i.e.* that he took such steps as were reasonably practicable to prevent the employee's conduct), by virtue of subs. (2). As has been said in relation to the parallel provisions in the S.D.A.:

> "the intriguing result is that the employee may only be liable for aiding and abetting the employer, who in turn is only prima facie liable through being vicariously liable for the employee's acts (which, in themselves, were not directly contrary to the statute), and who may himself be able to make out a defence under s.41(3) [*i.e.* the equivalent of s.58(5)]." (Smith, Wood and Thomas, *Industrial Law*, 5th ed, 1993, at p.205).

A person can avoid liability for aiding under this section if he acts in reliance on a statement by the other person that, because of some provision of the Act, the act would not be unlawful, and it is reasonable for him to rely on that statement (subs. (3)). Anyone who knowingly or recklessly makes such a statement which is false or misleading in a material respect commits an offence, and is liable on summary conviction to a fine not exceeding level 5 on the standard scale (subss. (4) and (5)).

Knowingly. See the note to s.49.

Recklessly. On the meaning of recklessness generally in relation to statutory offences, see *R. v. Caldwell* [1982] A.C. 341. See also *Large v. Mainprize* [1989] Crim.L.R. 213.

Liability of employers and principals

58.—(1) Anything done by a person in the course of his employment shall be treated for the purposes of this Act as also done by his employer, whether or not it was done with the employer's knowledge or approval.

(2) Anything done by a person as agent for another person with the authority of that other person shall be treated for the purposes of this Act as also done by that other person.

(3) Subsection (2) applies whether the authority was—

(a) express or implied; or

(b) given before or after the act in question was done.

(4) Subsections (1) and (2) do not apply in relation to an offence under section 57(4).

(5) In proceedings under this Act against any person in respect of an act alleged to have been done by an employee of his, it shall be a defence for that person to prove that he took such steps as were reasonably practicable to prevent the employee from—

(a) doing that act; or

(b) doing, in the course of his employment, acts of that description.

DEFINITIONS

"act": s.68(1).

"employment": s.68(1).

GENERAL NOTE

This section provides for the vicarious liability of employers for acts done by their employees in the course of their employment, irrespective of whether those acts are done with the employer's knowledge or approval, and also of principals for acts done by their agents with the principal's authority. Like the previous section, it substantially mirrors the equivalent provisions in the Sex Discrimination Act 1975, s.41, and the Race Relations Act 1976, s.32. By virtue of s.57(2), an employee or agent who causes his employer or principal to be vicariously liable under this section is deemed to have aided the employer or principal to do that act, so that *both* parties may in fact be liable for the act in question (as was the case in *Read v. Tiverton District Council* [1977] I.R.L.R. 202, a case under the S.D.A., s.41; see also *Enterprise Glass v. Miles* [1990] I.C.R. 787). The point is discussed more fully in the note to s.57. An employer can however escape liability under subs. (5) if he can show that he took such steps as were reasonably practicable to prevent the employee from doing the act in question, or from doing acts of that description in the course of his employment.

Subs. (1)
In the course of his employment. The meaning of this phrase as it appears in the R.R.A., s.32, was considered in *Irving v. Post Office* [1987] I.R.L.R. 289, where the Court of Appeal held, applying *Heasmans (a firm) v. Clarity Cleaning Co.* [1987] I.R.L.R. 286, that whether an employer is vicariously liable for the unauthorised act of an employee depends on whether the employee's act was merely an unauthorised or prohibited mode of doing an authorised act, or was an act which was outside the sphere of the employee's employment. See also *Tower Boot Co. v. Jones* [1995] I.R.L.R. 529. As with common law vicarious liability, an employer is not to be held liable merely because the wrongful act in question was done during the period of the employee's employment, or because the employee's employment provided the opportunity for it to be done. Note that "employment" for these purposes includes employment of a contract personally to do any work, and is not confined to employment under a contract of service or of apprenticeship: see s.68(1).

Subs. (2)
With the authority of that other person. A principal is liable for the acts of his agent which are done with his authority, whether that authority was express or implied, and whether it was given before or after the act in question was done: see subs. (3). It is unclear whether implied authority covers ostensible authority.

Subs. (5)
Such steps as were reasonably practicable. The question of whether the employer has taken such steps as were reasonably practicable to prevent the discrimination is a question of fact for the tribunal, and the onus is on the employer to establish the defence. The meaning of this phrase as it appears in the S.D.A., s.41, was considered by the E.A.T. in *Balgobin and Francis v. Tower Hamlets London Borough* [1987] I.R.L.R. 401, a case involving allegations of sexual harassment, where the defence was held to be established where the employers had no knowledge of the discriminatory conduct complained of, but were able to show that there had been proper and adequate supervision of the staff, and that they had publicised their policy of equal opportunities (see also *Bracebridge Engineering v. Darby* [1990] I.R.L.R. 3).

Statutory authority and national security etc.

59.—(1) Nothing in this Act makes unlawful any act done—
(a) in pursuance of any enactment; or
(b) in pursuance of any instrument made by a Minister of the Crown under any enactment; or
(c) to comply with any condition or requirement imposed by a Minister of the Crown (whether before or after the passing of this Act) by virtue of any enactment.

(2) In subsection (1) "enactment" includes one passed or made after the date on which this Act is passed and "instrument" includes one made after that date.

(3) Nothing in this Act makes unlawful any act done for the purpose of safeguarding national security.

Definitions
"enactment": s.68(1); subs. (2).
"instrument": subs. (2).
"Minister of the Crown": s.68(1).

General Note
This section provides that the Act does not apply to acts done under statutory authority, or acts done for the purpose of safeguarding national security.

Subs. (1)
The effect of the provisions concerning statutory authority is to exempt from liability any act done (i) under any enactment (including an Order in Council: see s.68(1)), or (ii) under any instrument made by a Minister of the Crown under any enactment, or (iii) to comply with any condition or requirement imposed by a Minister of the Crown by virtue of any enactment, whether the authority to discriminate arises before or after the passing of the Act. This means that the obligations under the Act not to discriminate against disabled persons are subordinate to other enactments, and to conditions or requirements imposed under such enactments, which might conflict with those obligations. To use the example given by the Minister, if a health and

safety requirement is imposed on an employer to modify equipment to protect the health and safety of employees, but that modification makes that equipment impossible for a disabled employee to operate, the health and safety provisions would take precedence over those in the Act, although the employer would still have a duty under the Act to make a reasonable adjustment to allow a disabled person to continue to work in that post if at all possible (Minister for Social Security and Disabled People, *Hansard*, H.C., Standing Committee E, col. 428).

These provisions are broadly similar to those in the R.R.A., s.41(1); the provisions concerning statutory authority in the S.D.A., s.51, are however significantly different, having been amended by the Employment Act 1989 to comply with E.C. Directive 76/207 (the Equal Treatment Directive). On the position under the S.D.A., see the author's annotations to the Employment Act 1989 (c. 38), ss.1–6, *Current Law Statutes Annotated*, 1989, Vol. 3.

In pursuance of. The meaning of this phrase as it appears in equivalent provisions in the R.R.A., s.41(1)(b), was considered by the House of Lords in *Hampson v. Department of Education and Science* [1990] I.R.L.R. 302. The E.A.T. and a majority of the Court of Appeal (Balcombe L.J. dissenting) had favoured a wide interpretation, covering any act done in the exercise of a power or discretion conferred by an instrument, but the House of Lords overruled the Court of Appeal, and held that the phrase "in pursuance of", while not limited to describing an act which is done "in order" to comply with an enactment, should be interpreted narrowly as authorising only acts done in necessary performance of an express obligation contained in the instrument. Their Lordships considered that a wide interpretation of the statutory language might have undermined the object of the 1976 Act, by conferring virtual immunity on the acts of public authorities acting under statutory powers. As Lord Lowry observed:

> "almost every discretionary decision, such as that which is involved in the appointment, promotion and dismissal of individuals in, say, local government, the police, the National Health Service and the public sector of the teaching profession, is taken against a statutory background which imposes a duty on someone." (At p.307).

Condition or requirement imposed by a Minister of the Crown. In any proceedings under s.8 (Employment), or s.25 (Goods, facilities, services and premises), a certificate signed by or on behalf of a Minister of the Crown stating that the conditions or requirements specified in the certificate were imposed by a Minister and were in operation at a specified time is conclusive evidence of the facts stated, and a document purporting to be such a certificate will be deemed to be such unless the contrary is proved (Sched. 3, paras. 4 and 8).

The passing of this Act. The Disability Discrimination Act 1995 received the Royal Assent on November 8, 1995.

Subs. (2)

An act of discrimination done for the purpose of safeguarding national security is lawful. In any proceedings under s.8 (Employment), or s.25 (Goods, facilities, services and premises), a certificate signed by or on behalf of a Minister of the Crown stating that an act was done for the purpose of safeguarding national security is conclusive evidence of that fact, and a document purporting to be such a certificate will be deemed to be such unless the contrary is proved (Sched. 3, paras. 4 and 8).

PART VIII

MISCELLANEOUS

Appointment by Secretary of State of advisers

60.—(1) The Secretary of State may appoint such persons as he thinks fit to advise or assist him in connection with matters relating to the employment of disabled persons and persons who have had a disability.

(2) Persons may be appointed by the Secretary of State to act generally or in relation to a particular area or locality.

(3) The Secretary of State may pay to any person appointed under this section such allowances and compensation for loss of earnings as he considers appropriate.

(4) The approval of the Treasury is required for any payment under this section.

(5) In subsection (1) "employment" includes self-employment.

(6) The Secretary of State may by order—

(a) provide for section 17 of, and Schedule 2 to, the Disabled Persons (Employment) Act 1944 (national advisory council and district advisory committees) to cease to have effect—

(i) so far as concerns the national advisory council; or

(ii) so far as concerns district advisory committees; or

(b) repeal that section and Schedule.

(7) At any time before the coming into force of an order under paragraph (b) of subsection (6), section 17 of the Act of 1944 shall have effect as if in subsection (1), after "disabled persons" in each case there were inserted ", and persons who have had a disability," and as if at the end of the section there were added—

"(3) For the purposes of this section—

(a) a person is a disabled person if he is a disabled person for the purposes of the Disability Discrimination Act 1995; and

(b) "disability" has the same meaning as in that Act."

(8) At any time before the coming into force of an order under paragraph (a)(i) or (b) of subsection (6), section 16 of the Chronically Sick and Disabled Persons Act 1970 (which extends the functions of the national advisory council) shall have effect as if after "disabled persons" in each case there were inserted ", and persons who have had a disability," and as if at the end of the section there were added—

"(2) For the purposes of this section—

(a) a person is a disabled person if he is a disabled person for the purposes of the Disability Discrimination Act 1995; and

(b) "disability" has the same meaning as in that Act."

DEFINITIONS

"disability": s.1(1).
"disabled person": s.1(2).
"employment": s.68(1); subs. (5).

GENERAL NOTE

This section empowers the Secretary of State to appoint advisers to advise him on matters concerning the employment and self-employment of disabled persons. It also empowers him to end the current arrangements whereby Ministers are advised and assisted in matters relating to the employment and training of disabled persons by the National Advisory Council on Employment of People with Disabilities (NACEDP), and the 60 district advisory Committees for the Employment of People with Disabilities (CEPDs), established under the Disabled Persons (Employment) Act 1944 (c. 10), s.17 (see the note to s.50). Until such time as those bodies are wound up, subss. (7) and (8) apply the definition of disability contained in s.1 of this Act to s.17 of the 1944 Act and also to s.16 of the Chronically Sick and Disabled Persons Act 1970 (c. 44) (which extended the functions of NACEDP in relation to training).

The power conferred by subs. (1) is designed to give the Secretary of State greater flexibility in the appointment of bodies at national, regional and local level to advise him on employment issues relating to people with disabilities. It gives him the option of retaining the existing advisory arrangements or of bringing them to an end, either in whole or in part, and appointing people to advise him either generally (*i.e.* nationally) or in relation to a particular area or locality (subs. (2)). A further option available to the Secretary of State would of course be to transfer the general advisory function in relation to employment to the National Disability Council, although it is expressly provided in s.50(10) that this may not happen while the NACEDP remains in existence or while there are advisers appointed under subs. (1) to act generally in relation to employment. As to the relationship between NACEDP and the National Disability Council, see the note to s.50.

Subs. (6)

The power is drafted so as to allow NACEDP and the CEDPs to be wound up separately or together. Although both types of body were established under the 1944 Act, they are independent of each other and have different functions: NACEDP advises the Secretary of State on national employment and training issues relating to people with disabilities, while the CEDPs advise on local employment issues, including matters relating to the registration of disabled persons and the quota scheme under the 1944 Act (see the note to s.61).

Amendment of Disabled Persons (Employment) Act 1944

61.—(1) Section 15 of the Disabled Persons (Employment) Act 1944 (which gives the Secretary of State power to make arrangements for the provision of supported employment) is amended as set out in subsections (2) to (5).

(2) In subsection (1)—

(a) for "persons registered as handicapped by disablement" substitute "disabled persons";

(b) for "their disablement" substitute "their disability"; and

(c) for "are not subject to disablement" substitute "do not have a disability".

(3) In subsection (2), for the words from "any of one or more companies" to "so required and prohibited" substitute "any company, association or body".

(4) After subsection (2) insert—

"(2A) The only kind of company which the Minister himself may form in exercising his powers under this section is a company which is—

(a) required by its constitution to apply its profits, if any, or other income in promoting its objects; and

(b) prohibited by its constitution from paying any dividend to its members."

(5) After subsection (5) insert—

"(5A) For the purposes of this section—

(a) a person is a disabled person if he is a disabled person for the purposes of the Disability Discrimination Act 1995; and

(b) "disability" has the same meaning as in that Act."

(6) The provisions of section 16 (preference to be given under section 15 of that Act to ex-service men and women) shall become subsection (1) of that section and at the end insert—

"and whose disability is due to that service.

(2) For the purposes of subsection (1) of this section, a disabled person's disability shall be treated as due to service of a particular kind only in such circumstances as may be prescribed."

(7) The following provisions of the Act of 1944 shall cease to have effect—

(a) section 1 (definition of "disabled person");

(b) sections 6 to 8 (the register of disabled persons);

(c) sections 9 to 11 (obligations on employers with substantial staffs to employ a quota of registered persons);

(d) section 12 (the designated employment scheme for persons registered as handicapped by disablement);

(e) section 13 (interpretation of provisions repealed by this Act);

(f) section 14 (records to be kept by employers);

(g) section 19 (proceedings in relation to offences); and

(h) section 21 (application as respects place of employment, and nationality).

(8) Any provision of subordinate legislation in which "disabled person" is defined by reference to the Act of 1944 shall be construed as if that expression had the same meaning as in this Act.

(9) Subsection (8) does not prevent the further amendment of any such provision by subordinate legislation.

DEFINITIONS

"disability": s.1(1); subs. (5).

"disabled person": s.1(2); subss. (5) and (8).

"employment": s.68(1).

GENERAL NOTE

This section repeals much of the Disabled Persons (Employment) Act 1944, including the provisions relating to the register of disabled persons, the quota system which obliges employers of a certain size to employ a quota of disabled persons, the designated employment scheme whereby certain types of employment are reserved for disabled employees, and the keeping of records by employers. It also amends a number of the remaining provisions of the 1944 Act; in particular, it extends the powers of the Secretary of State under s.15 of the 1944 Act to make arrangements for the provision of supported employment, by allowing the funding of places in dividend-distributing bodies.

Subss. (1)–(5)

The supported employment programme was set up under s.15 of the 1944 Act to provide employment opportunities for severely disabled people who would otherwise be unlikely to obtain employment. The current criteria for entry to the programme are that severely disabled people should be capable of productivity within the range of 30 per cent to 80 per cent of a non-disabled worker. Around 21,800 severely disabled people are currently in supported employment, at an annual cost of about £153 million. The programme takes a variety of forms, including supported factories such as *Remploy Ltd*, which currently employs over 9,000 people, some 4,600 people in sheltered workshops run by local authorities and voluntary organisations, and over 8,000 people on the supported placement scheme, whereby local authorities and voluntary organisations help to arrange the placement of severely disabled employees in open employment (Minister of State, *Hansard*, H.L., Vol. 565, col. 708). Until now, the 1944 Act has prevented funding for supported employment from being provided to profit-distributing organisations. This is now to change, as subs. (2) allows the Secretary of State to fund supported employment in such bodies. Concern has been expressed that this development represents further evidence of creeping commercialisation in the provision of supported employment, and it has been claimed that the dividend-distributing providers may be reluctant to recruit the most severely disabled (and therefore least productive) employees because of the greater pressure on them to act like commercial enterprises (Lord Gladwin of Clee, *ibid.* col. 700). The Government has reaffirmed its commitment to the supported employment programme, and has undertaken to consult with relevant organisations before exercising the power conferred by this section (Minister of State, *ibid.* col. 708).

Restriction of publicity: industrial tribunals

62.—(1) This section applies to proceedings on a complaint under section 8 in which evidence of a personal nature is likely to be heard by the industrial tribunal hearing the complaint.

(2) The power of the Secretary of State to make regulations with respect to the procedure of industrial tribunals includes power to make provision in relation to proceedings to which this section applies for—

(a) enabling an industrial tribunal, on the application of the complainant or of its own motion, to make a restricted reporting order having effect (if not revoked earlier) until the promulgation of the tribunal's decision; and

(b) where a restricted reporting order is made in relation to a complaint which is being dealt with by the tribunal together with any other proceedings, enabling the tribunal to direct that the order is to apply also in relation to those other proceedings or such part of them as the tribunal may direct.

(3) If any identifying matter is published or included in a relevant programme in contravention of a restricted reporting order—

(a) in the case of publication in a newspaper or periodical, any proprietor, any editor and any publisher of the newspaper or periodical,

(b) in the case of publication in any other form, the person publishing the matter, and

(c) in the case of matter included in a relevant programme—

(i) any body corporate engaged in providing the service in which the programme is included, and

(ii) any person having functions in relation to the programme corresponding to those of an editor of a newspaper,

shall be guilty of an offence and liable on summary conviction to a fine not exceeding level 5 on the standard scale.

(4) Where a person is charged with an offence under subsection (3), it is a defence to prove that at the time of the alleged offence—

(a) he was not aware, and

(b) he neither suspected nor had reason to suspect,

that the publication or programme in question was of, or included, the matter in question.

(5) Where an offence under subsection (3) committed by a body corporate is proved to have been committed with the consent or connivance of, or to be attributable to any neglect on the part of—

(a) a director, manager, secretary or other similar officer of the body corporate, or

(b) a person purporting to act in any such capacity,

he as well as the body corporate is guilty of the offence and liable to be proceeded against and punished accordingly.

(6) In relation to a body corporate whose affairs are managed by its members "director", in subsection (5), means a member of the body corporate.

(7) In this section—

"evidence of a personal nature" means any evidence of a medical, or other intimate, nature which might reasonably be assumed to be likely to cause significant embarrassment to the complainant if reported;

"identifying matter" means any matter likely to lead members of the public to identify the complainant or such other persons (if any) as may be named in the order;

"promulgation" has such meaning as may be prescribed by the regulations;

"relevant programme" means a programme included in a programme service, within the meaning of the Broadcasting Act 1990;

"restricted reporting order" means an order—

(a) made in exercise of the power conferred by regulations made by virtue of this section; and

(b) prohibiting the publication in Great Britain of identifying matter in a written publication available to the public or its inclusion in a relevant programme for reception in Great Britain; and

"written publication" includes a film, a soundtrack and any other record in permanent form but does not include an indictment or other document prepared for use in particular legal proceedings.

DEFINITIONS

"director": subs. (6).
"evidence of a personal nature": subs. (7).
"identifying matter": subs. (7).
"promulgation": subs. (7).
"relevant programme": subs. (7).
"restricted reporting order": subs. (7).
"standard scale": Criminal Justice Act 1982, s.37(2).
"written publication": subs. (7).

GENERAL NOTE

This section gives the Secretary of State power to make regulations enabling an industrial tribunal to make a restricted reporting order in proceedings under s.8 of this Act where "evidence of a personal nature" is likely to be heard by the tribunal hearing the complaint. "Evidence of a personal nature" is defined in subs. (7) as evidence of a medical or other intimate nature which might reasonably be assumed to be likely to cause significant embarrassment to the complainant if reported. The effect of a restricted reporting order is to prohibit the publication in a "written publication" or a "relevant programme" (see below) of anything which would be likely to identify the complainant or any other person named in the order. In all other respects, the freedom of the media to report on the proceedings is unaffected; indeed, the media are free to report the complainant's identity once the tribunal has issued its decision, as the order only remains in force (unless revoked earlier) until the promulgation of the tribunal's decision (subs. (2)(a)). A restricted reporting order may be made on the application of the complainant or by the tribunal of its own motion; where the complaint is being dealt with by the tribunal together with other proceedings, the regulations may permit the tribunal to extend the restricted reporting order to those other proceedings (subs. (2)(b)). There are parallel provisions in s.63 with respect to the E.A.T., but the powers of the E.A.T. to make a restricted reporting order are more limited.

Contravention of a restricted reporting order is an offence punishable on summary conviction by a fine not exceeding level 5 on the standard scale. The offence may be committed, in the case of publication in a newspaper or periodical, by the proprietor, editor and publisher of that newspaper or periodical; in the case of publication in any other form, by the person publishing the material; and in the case of material broadcast in a relevant programme, by the broadcasting company and the editor of the programme (subs. 3). Where an offence by the broadcasting company is committed with the consent or connivance of or through the neglect of a director, manager, secretary or other similar officer of that company, the offence is also committed by that person (subs. (5)). It is a defence for a person charged with an offence under these provisions to show that he was not aware, and neither suspected nor had reason to suspect, that the publication or programme in question included the restricted material (subs. (4)), but it seems that ignorance of the restricted reporting order will not be a defence.

The power to make a restricted reporting order was first introduced for cases involving sexual misconduct by the Trade Union Reform and Employment Rights Act 1993, s.40, following fears that potential complainants might be deterred by the prospect of being subjected to high-profile, intrusive media coverage. Those provisions may be found in the Industrial Tribunals Rules of Procedure 1993, S.I. 1993 No. 2687, r.14, made pursuant to the E.P.(C.)A. 1978, Sched. 9, para. 1(5A). The extension of the power to make a restricted reporting order to cases involving disability discrimination is designed to cover employees with, for example, HIV or AIDS, or a history of mental illness, who might be reluctant to pursue a claim because of fears of publicity. The power to make such an order only applies to proceedings on a complaint under s.8 (*i.e.* in relation to employment); complaints under Pt. III (access to goods, facilities and services) may be dealt with under the small claims arbitration procedure, where hearings are held in private.

Restricted reporting order. This is defined in subs. (7) as an order prohibiting the publication in Great Britain, in a written publication available to the public, or a relevant programme for reception in Great Britain, of any "identifying matter", *i.e.* anything likely to lead the public to identify the complainant or any other person named in the order. It should be noted that such an order does not prohibit all reporting of the case—merely the publication in the media of anything which might identify the complainant or anyone else covered by the order.

Written publication; relevant programme. The definitions of these terms in subs. (7) are also used for the purposes of the Sexual Offences (Amendment) Act 1992 (c. 34), s.6.

Promulgation. The existing rules concerning restricted reporting orders in cases involving sexual misconduct state that "promulgation occurs on the date recorded as being the date on which the document recording the determination of the originating application was sent to the parties" (see the Industrial Tribunals Rules of Procedure 1993, r.14(5)).

Restriction of publicity: Employment Appeal Tribunal

63.—(1) This section applies to proceedings—

(a) on an appeal against a decision of an industrial tribunal to make, or not to make, a restricted reporting order, or

(b) on an appeal against any interlocutory decision of an industrial tribunal in proceedings in which the industrial tribunal has made a restricted reporting order which it has not revoked.

(2) The power of the Lord Chancellor to make rules with respect to the procedure of the Employment Appeal Tribunal includes power to make provision in relation to proceedings to which this section applies for—

(a) enabling the Tribunal, on the application of the complainant or of its own motion, to make a restricted reporting order having effect (if not revoked earlier) until the promulgation of the Tribunal's decision; and

(b) where a restricted reporting order is made in relation to an appeal which is being dealt with by the Tribunal together with any other proceedings, enabling the Tribunal to direct that the order is to apply also in relation to those other proceedings or such part of them as the Tribunal may direct.

(3) Subsections (3) to (6) of section 62 apply in relation to a restricted reporting order made by the Tribunal as they apply in relation to one made by an industrial tribunal.

(4) In subsection (1), "restricted reporting order" means an order which is a restricted reporting order for the purposes of section 62.

(5) In subsection (2), "restricted reporting order" means an order—

(a) made in exercise of the power conferred by rules made by virtue of this section; and

(b) prohibiting the publication in Great Britain of identifying matter in a written publication available to the public or its inclusion in a relevant programme for reception in Great Britain.

(6) In this section—

"complainant" means the person who made the complaint to which the proceedings before the Tribunal relate;

"identifying matter", "written publication" and "relevant programme" have the same meaning as in section 62; and

"promulgation" has such meaning as may be prescribed by the rules.

Definitions

"complainant": subs. (6).
"identifying matter": s.62(7); subs. (6).
"promulgation": subs. (6).
"relevant programme": s.62(7); subs. (6).
"restricted reporting order": s.62(7); subss. (4) and (5).
"written publication": s.62(7); subs. (6).

General Note

This section allows the Lord Chancellor to amend the Employment Appeal Tribunal Rules to enable the E.A.T. to make a restricted reporting order in the same way and to the same effect as an industrial tribunal (see the note to s.62), but in more limited circumstances. A restricted reporting order may only be made by the E.A.T. under this section in proceedings on an appeal against a decision of an industrial tribunal to make or not to make a restricted reporting order, or on an appeal against an interlocutory decision of an industrial tribunal in a case in which the tribunal made a restricted reporting order which has not been revoked (subs. (1)). The E.A.T. will not be able to make a restricted reporting order on an ordinary appeal from an industrial tribunal, even where the tribunal proceedings were subject to such an order. The thinking behind this is presumably that since the order made by the industrial tribunal would have lapsed once the tribunal issued its decision, the imposition of a further order on appeal would serve no purpose, as the identities of those involved might already have been disclosed.

In other respects, the provisions on restricted reporting orders in relation to the E.A.T. are similar to those which apply to industrial tribunals: an order may be made on the application of the complainant, or by the tribunal of its own motion, and will remain in force until the tribunal's decision is issued, unless revoked earlier (subs. (2)(a)); and where the appeal is being dealt with by the tribunal along with other proceedings, the regulations may permit the tribunal to extend the restricted reporting order to those other proceedings (subs. (2)(b)). Penalties for non-compliance are as in s.62 (see the note to that section).

The E.A.T. already has the power to make a restricted reporting order in cases involving sexual misconduct: see the Employment Appeal Tribunal Rules 1993, S.I. 1993 No. 2854, r.23, made pursuant to the E.P.(C.)A. 1978, Sched. 11, para. 18A. The power to make these rules was introduced by the Trade Union Reform and Employment Rights Act 1993, s.41.

Identifying matter; written publication; relevant programme. See the notes to s.62.

Promulgation. The existing rules concerning restricted reporting orders in cases involving sexual misconduct state that promulgation of the Tribunal's decision "means the date recorded as being the date on which the Appeal Tribunal's order finally disposing of the appeal is sent to the parties" (see the Employment Appeal Tribunal Rules 1993, r.23(9)).

Application to Crown etc.

64.—(1) This Act applies—

(a) to an act done by or for purposes of a Minister of the Crown or government department, or

(b) to an act done on behalf of the Crown by a statutory body, or a person holding a statutory office,

as it applies to an act done by a private person.

(2) Subject to subsection (5), Part II applies to service—

(a) for purposes of a Minister of the Crown or government department, other than service of a person holding a statutory office, or

(b) on behalf of the Crown for purposes of a person holding a statutory office or purposes of a statutory body,

as it applies to employment by a private person.

(3) The provisions of Parts II to IV of the 1947 Act apply to proceedings against the Crown under this Act as they apply to Crown proceedings in England and Wales; but section 20 of that Act (removal of proceedings from county court to High Court) does not apply.

(4) The provisions of Part V of the 1947 Act apply to proceedings against the Crown under this Act as they apply to proceedings in Scotland which by virtue of that Part are treated as civil proceedings by or against the Crown; but the proviso to section 44 of that Act (removal of proceedings from the sheriff court to the Court of Session) does not apply.

(5) Part II does not apply to service—

(a) as a member of the Ministry of Defence Police, the British Transport Police, the Royal Parks Constabulary or the United Kingdom Atomic Energy Authority Constabulary;

(b) as a prison officer; or

(c) for purposes of a Minister of the Crown or government department having functions with respect to defence as a person who is or may be required by his terms of service to engage in fire fighting.

(6) Part II does not apply to service as a member of a fire brigade who is or may be required by his terms of service to engage in fire fighting.

(7) It is hereby declared (for the avoidance of doubt) that Part II does not apply to service in any of the naval, military or air forces of the Crown.

(8) In this section—

"the 1947 Act" means the Crown Proceedings Act 1947;

"British Transport Police" means the constables appointed, or deemed to have been appointed, under section 53 of the British Transport Commission Act 1949;

"Crown proceedings" means proceedings which, by virtue of section 23 of the 1947 Act, are treated for the purposes of Part II of that Act as civil proceedings by or against the Crown;

"fire brigade" means a fire brigade maintained in pursuance of the Fire Services Act 1947;

"Ministry of Defence Police" means the force established under section 1 of the Ministry of Defence Police Act 1987;

"prison officer" means a person who is a prison officer within the meaning of section 127 of the Criminal Justice and Public Order Act 1994, apart from those who are custody officers within the meaning of Part I of that Act;

"Royal Parks Constabulary" means the park constables appointed under the Parks Regulation Act 1872;

"service for purposes of a Minister of the Crown or government department" does not include service in any office for the time being mentioned in Schedule 2 (Ministerial offices) to the House of Commons Disqualification Act 1975;

"statutory body" means a body set up by or under an enactment;
"statutory office" means an office so set up; and
"United Kingdom Atomic Energy Authority Constabulary" means the special constables appointed under section 3 of the Special Constables Act 1923 on the nomination of the United Kingdom Atomic Energy Authority.

Application to Parliament

65.—(1) This Act applies to an act done by or for purposes of the House of Lords or the House of Commons as it applies to an act done by a private person.

(2) For the purposes of the application of Part II in relation to the House of Commons, the Corporate Officer of that House shall be treated as the employer of a person who is (or would be) a relevant member of the House of Commons staff for the purposes of section 139 of the Employment Protection (Consolidation) Act 1978.

(3) Except as provided in subsection (4), for the purposes of the application of sections 19 to 21, the provider of services is—

(a) as respects the House of Lords, the Corporate Officer of that House; and
(b) as respects the House of Commons, the Corporate Officer of that House.

(4) Where the service in question is access to and use of any place in the Palace of Westminster which members of the public are permitted to enter, the Corporate Officers of both Houses jointly are the provider of that service.

(5) Nothing in any rule of law or the law or practice of Parliament prevents proceedings being instituted before an industrial tribunal under Part II or before any court under Part III.

Government appointments outside Part II

66.—(1) Subject to regulations under subsection (3), this section applies to any appointment made by a Minister of the Crown or government department to an office or post where Part II does not apply in relation to the appointment.

(2) In making the appointment, and in making arrangements for determining to whom the office or post should be offered, the Minister of the Crown or government department shall not act in a way which would contravene Part II if he or the department were the employer for the purposes of this Act.

(3) Regulations may provide for this section not to apply to such appointments as may be prescribed.

Regulations and orders

67.—(1) Any power under this Act to make regulations or orders shall be exercisable by statutory instrument.

(2) Any such power may be exercised to make different provision for different cases, including different provision for different areas or localities.

(3) Any such power includes power—

(a) to make such incidental, supplemental, consequential or transitional provision as appears to the Secretary of State to be expedient; and
(b) to provide for a person to exercise a discretion in dealing with any matter.

(4) No order shall be made under section 50(3) unless a draft of the statutory instrument containing the order has been laid before Parliament and approved by a resolution of each House.

(5) Any other statutory instrument made under this Act, other than one made under section 3(9), 52(8), 54(6) or 70(3), shall be subject to annulment in pursuance of a resolution of either House of Parliament.

(6) Subsection (1) does not require an order under section 43 which applies only to a specified vehicle, or to vehicles of a specified person, to be made by statutory instrument but such an order shall be as capable of being amended or revoked as an order which is made by statutory instrument.

(7) Nothing in section 34(4), 40(6) or 46(5) affects the powers conferred by subsections (2) and (3).

Interpretation

68.—(1) In this Act—

"accessibility certificate" means a certificate issued under section 41(1)(a);

"act" includes a deliberate omission;

"approval certificate" means a certificate issued under section 42(4);

"benefits", in Part II, has the meaning given in section 4(4);

"conciliation officer" means a person designated under section 211 of the Trade Union and Labour Relations (Consolidation) Act 1992;

"employment" means, subject to any prescribed provision, employment under a contract of service or of apprenticeship or a contract personally to do any work, and related expressions are to be construed accordingly;

"employment at an establishment in Great Britain" is to be construed in accordance with subsections (2) to (5);

"enactment" includes subordinate legislation and any Order in Council;

"licensing authority" means—

(a) in relation to the area to which the Metropolitan Public Carriage Act 1869 applies, the Secretary of State or the holder of any office for the time being designated by the Secretary of State; or

(b) in relation to any other area in England and Wales, the authority responsible for licensing taxis in that area;

"mental impairment" does not have the same meaning as in the Mental Health Act 1983 or the Mental Health (Scotland) Act 1984 but the fact that an impairment would be a mental impairment for the purposes of either of those Acts does not prevent it from being a mental impairment for the purposes of this Act;

"Minister of the Crown" includes the Treasury;

"occupational pension scheme" has the same meaning as in the Pension Schemes Act 1993;

"premises" includes land of any description;

"prescribed" means prescribed by regulations;

"profession" includes any vocation or occupation;

"provider of services" has the meaning given in section 19(2)(b);

"public service vehicle" and "regulated public service vehicle" have the meaning given in section 40;

"PSV accessibility regulations" means regulations made under section 40(1);

"rail vehicle" and "regulated rail vehicle" have the meaning given in section 46;

"rail vehicle accessibility regulations" means regulations made under section 46(1);

"regulations" means regulations made by the Secretary of State;

"section 6 duty" means any duty imposed by or under section 6;

"section 15 duty" means any duty imposed by or under section 15;

"section 21 duty" means any duty imposed by or under section 21;

"subordinate legislation" has the same meaning as in section 21 of the Interpretation Act 1978;

"taxi" and "regulated taxi" have the meaning given in section 32;

"taxi accessibility regulations" means regulations made under section 32(1);

"trade" includes any business;

"trade organisation" has the meaning given in section 13;

"vehicle examiner" means an examiner appointed under section 66A of the Road Traffic Act 1988.

(2) Where an employee does his work wholly or mainly outside Great Britain, his employment is not to be treated as being work at an establishment in Great Britain even if he does some of his work at such an establishment.

(3) Except in prescribed cases, employment on board a ship, aircraft or hovercraft is to be regarded as not being employment at an establishment in Great Britain.

(4) Employment of a prescribed kind, or in prescribed circumstances, is to be regarded as not being employment at an establishment in Great Britain.

(5) Where work is not done at an establishment it shall be treated as done—

(a) at the establishment from which it is done; or

(b) where it is not done from any establishment, at the establishment with which it has the closest connection.

Financial provisions

69. There shall be paid out of money provided by Parliament—

(a) any expenditure incurred by a Minister of the Crown under this Act;

(b) any increase attributable to this Act in the sums payable out of money so provided under or by virtue of any other enactment.

Short title, commencement, extent etc.

70.—(1) This Act may be cited as the Disability Discrimination Act 1995.

(2) This section (apart from subsections (4), (5) and (7)) comes into force on the passing of this Act.

(3) The other provisions of this Act come into force on such day as the Secretary of State may by order appoint and different days may be appointed for different purposes.

(4) Schedule 6 makes consequential amendments.

(5) The repeals set out in Schedule 7 shall have effect.

(6) This Act extends to Northern Ireland, but in their application to Northern Ireland the provisions of this Act mentioned in Schedule 8 shall have effect subject to the modifications set out in that Schedule.

(7) In Part II of Schedule 1 to the House of Commons Disqualification Act 1975 and in Part II of Schedule 1 to the Northern Ireland Assembly Disqualification Act 1975 (bodies whose members are disqualified) in each case insert at the appropriate places—

"The National Disability Council."

"The Northern Ireland Disability Council."

(8) Consultations which are required by any provision of this Act to be held by the Secretary of State may be held by him before the coming into force of that provision.

SCHEDULES

Section 1(1)

SCHEDULE 1

PROVISIONS SUPPLEMENTING SECTION 1

Impairment

1.—(1) "Mental impairment" includes an impairment resulting from or consisting of a mental illness only if the illness is a clinically well-recognised illness.

(2) Regulations may make provision, for the purposes of this Act—

(a) for conditions of a prescribed description to be treated as amounting to impairments;
(b) for conditions of a prescribed description to be treated as not amounting to impairments.

(3) Regulations made under sub-paragraph (2) may make provision as to the meaning of "condition" for the purposes of those regulations.

Long-term effects

2.—(1) The effect of an impairment is a long-term effect if—
(a) it has lasted at least 12 months;
(b) the period for which it lasts is likely to be at least 12 months; or
(c) it is likely to last for the rest of the life of the person affected.

(2) Where an impairment ceases to have a substantial adverse effect on a person's ability to carry out normal day-to-day activities, it is to be treated as continuing to have that effect if that effect is likely to recur.

(3) For the purposes of sub-paragraph (2), the likelihood of an effect recurring shall be disregarded in prescribed circumstances.

(4) Regulations may prescribe circumstances in which, for the purposes of this Act—
(a) an effect which would not otherwise be a long-term effect is to be treated as such an effect; or
(b) an effect which would otherwise be a long-term effect is to be treated as not being such an effect.

Severe disfigurement

3.—(1) An impairment which consists of a severe disfigurement is to be treated as having a substantial adverse effect on the ability of the person concerned to carry out normal day-to-day activities.

(2) Regulations may provide that in prescribed circumstances a severe disfigurement is not to be treated as having that effect.

(3) Regulations under sub-paragraph (2) may, in particular, make provision with respect to deliberately acquired disfigurements.

Normal day-to-day activities

4.—(1) An impairment is to be taken to affect the ability of the person concerned to carry out normal day-to-day activities only if it affects one of the following—
(a) mobility;
(b) manual dexterity;
(c) physical co-ordination;
(d) continence;
(e) ability to lift, carry or otherwise move everyday objects;
(f) speech, hearing or eyesight;
(g) memory or ability to concentrate, learn or understand; or
(h) perception of the risk of physical danger.

(2) Regulations may prescribe—
(a) circumstances in which an impairment which does not have an effect falling within sub-paragraph (1) is to be taken to affect the ability of the person concerned to carry out normal day-to-day activities;
(b) circumstances in which an impairment which has an effect falling within sub-paragraph (1) is to be taken not to affect the ability of the person concerned to carry out normal day-to-day activities.

Substantial adverse effects

5. Regulations may make provision for the purposes of this Act—
(a) for an effect of a prescribed kind on the ability of a person to carry out normal day-to-day activities to be treated as a substantial adverse effect;
(b) for an effect of a prescribed kind on the ability of a person to carry out normal day-to-day activities to be treated as not being a substantial adverse effect.

Effect of medical treatment

6.—(1) An impairment which would be likely to have a substantial adverse effect on the ability of the person concerned to carry out normal day-to-day activities, but for the fact that measures are being taken to treat or correct it, is to be treated as having that effect.

(2) In sub-paragraph (1) "measures" includes, in particular, medical treatment and the use of a prosthesis or other aid.

(3) Sub-paragraph (1) does not apply—

(a) in relation to the impairment of a person's sight, to the extent that the impairment is, in his case, correctable by spectacles or contact lenses or in such other ways as may be prescribed; or

(b) in relation to such other impairments as may be prescribed, in such circumstances as may be prescribed.

Persons deemed to be disabled

7.—(1) Sub-paragraph (2) applies to any person whose name is, both on 12th January 1995 and on the date when this paragraph comes into force, in the register of disabled persons maintained under section 6 of the Disabled Persons (Employment) Act 1944.

(2) That person is to be deemed—

(a) during the initial period, to have a disability, and hence to be a disabled person; and

(b) afterwards, to have had a disability and hence to have been a disabled person during that period.

(3) A certificate of registration shall be conclusive evidence, in relation to the person with respect to whom it was issued, of the matters certified.

(4) Unless the contrary is shown, any document purporting to be a certificate of registration shall be taken to be such a certificate and to have been validly issued.

(5) Regulations may provide for prescribed descriptions of person to be deemed to have disabilities, and hence to be disabled persons, for the purposes of this Act.

(6) Regulations may prescribe circumstances in which a person who has been deemed to be a disabled person by the provisions of sub-paragraph (1) or regulations made under sub-paragraph (5) is to be treated as no longer being deemed to be such a person.

(7) In this paragraph—

"certificate of registration" means a certificate issued under regulations made under section 6 of the Act of 1944; and

"initial period" means the period of three years beginning with the date on which this paragraph comes into force.

Progressive conditions

8.—(1) Where—

(a) a person has a progressive condition (such as cancer, multiple sclerosis or muscular dystrophy or infection by the human immunodeficiency virus),

(b) as a result of that condition, he has an impairment which has (or had) an effect on his ability to carry out normal day-to-day activities, but

(c) that effect is not (or was not) a substantial adverse effect,

he shall be taken to have an impairment which has such a substantial adverse effect if the condition is likely to result in his having such an impairment.

(2) Regulations may make provision, for the purposes of this paragraph—

(a) for conditions of a prescribed description to be treated as being progressive;

(b) for conditions of a prescribed description to be treated as not being progressive.

Section 2(2)

SCHEDULE 2

Past Disabilities

1. The modifications referred to in section 2 are as follows.

2. References in Parts II and III to a disabled person are to be read as references to a person who has had a disability.

3. In section 6(1), after "not disabled" insert "and who have not had a disability".

4. In section 6(6), for "has" substitute "has had".

5. For paragraph 2(1) to (3) of Schedule 1, substitute—

"(1) The effect of an impairment is a long-term effect if it has lasted for at least 12 months.

(2) Where an impairment ceases to have a substantial adverse effect on a person's ability to carry out normal day-to-day activities, it is to be treated as continuing to have that effect if that effect recurs.

(3) For the purposes of sub-paragraph (2), the recurrence of an effect shall be disregarded in prescribed circumstances."

Sections 8(8) and 25(6)

SCHEDULE 3

ENFORCEMENT AND PROCEDURE

PART I

EMPLOYMENT

Conciliation

1.—(1) Where a complaint is presented to an industrial tribunal under section 8 and a copy of it is sent to a conciliation officer, he shall—

(a) if requested to do so by the complainant and respondent, or

(b) if he considers that he has a reasonable prospect of success,

try to promote a settlement of the complaint without its being determined by an industrial tribunal.

(2) Where a person is contemplating presenting such a complaint, a conciliation officer shall, if asked to do so by the potential complainant or potential respondent, try to promote a settlement.

(3) The conciliation officer shall, where appropriate, have regard to the desirability of encouraging the use of other procedures available for the settlement of grievances.

(4) Anything communicated to a conciliation officer in a case in which he is acting under this paragraph shall not be admissible in evidence in any proceedings before an industrial tribunal except with the consent of the person who communicated it.

Restriction on proceedings for breach of Part II

2.—(1) Except as provided by section 8, no civil or criminal proceedings may be brought against any person in respect of an act merely because the act is unlawful under Part II.

(2) Sub-paragraph (1) does not prevent the making of an application for judicial review.

Period within which proceedings must be brought

3.—(1) An industrial tribunal shall not consider a complaint under section 8 unless it is presented before the end of the period of three months beginning when the act complained of was done.

(2) A tribunal may consider any such complaint which is out of time if, in all the circumstances of the case, it considers that it is just and equitable to do so.

(3) For the purposes of sub-paragraph (1)—

(a) where an unlawful act of discrimination is attributable to a term in a contract, that act is to be treated as extending throughout the duration of the contract;

(b) any act extending over a period shall be treated as done at the end of that period; and

(c) a deliberate omission shall be treated as done when the person in question decided upon it.

(4) In the absence of evidence establishing the contrary, a person shall be taken for the purposes of this paragraph to decide upon an omission—

(a) when he does an act inconsistent with doing the omitted act; or

(b) if he has done no such inconsistent act, when the period expires within which he might reasonably have been expected to do the omitted act if it was to be done.

Evidence

4.—(1) In any proceedings under section 8, a certificate signed by or on behalf of a Minister of the Crown and certifying—

(a) that any conditions or requirements specified in the certificate were imposed by a Minister of the Crown and were in operation at a time or throughout a time so specified, or

(b) that an act specified in the certificate was done for the purpose of safeguarding national security,

shall be conclusive evidence of the matters certified.

(2) A document purporting to be such a certificate shall be received in evidence and, unless the contrary is proved, be deemed to be such a certificate.

Part II

Discrimination in Other Areas

Restriction on proceedings for breach of Part III

5.—(1) Except as provided by section 25 no civil or criminal proceedings may be brought against any person in respect of an act merely because the act is unlawful under Part III.

(2) Sub-paragraph (1) does not prevent the making of an application for judicial review.

Period within which proceedings must be brought

6.—(1) A county court or a sheriff court shall not consider a claim under section 25 unless proceedings in respect of the claim are instituted before the end of the period of six months beginning when the act complained of was done.

(2) Where, in relation to proceedings or prospective proceedings under section 25, a person appointed in connection with arrangements under section 28 is approached before the end of the period of six months mentioned in sub-paragraph (1), the period allowed by that sub-paragraph shall be extended by two months.

(3) A court may consider any claim under section 25 which is out of time if, in all the circumstances of the case, it considers that it is just and equitable to do so.

(4) For the purposes of sub-paragraph (1)—

(a) where an unlawful act of discrimination is attributable to a term in a contract, that act is to be treated as extending throughout the duration of the contract;

(b) any act extending over a period shall be treated as done at the end of that period; and

(c) a deliberate omission shall be treated as done when the person in question decided upon it.

(5) In the absence of evidence establishing the contrary, a person shall be taken for the purposes of this paragraph to decide upon an omission—

(a) when he does an act inconsistent with doing the omitted act; or

(b) if he has done no such inconsistent act, when the period expires within which he might reasonably have been expected to do the omitted act if it was to be done.

Compensation for injury to feelings

7. In any proceedings under section 25, the amount of any damages awarded as compensation for injury to feelings shall not exceed the prescribed amount.

Evidence

8.—(1) In any proceedings under section 25, a certificate signed by or on behalf of a Minister of the Crown and certifying—

(a) that any conditions or requirements specified in the certificate were imposed by a Minister of the Crown and were in operation at a time or throughout a time so specified, or

(b) that an act specified in the certificate was done for the purpose of safeguarding national security,

shall be conclusive evidence of the matters certified.

(2) A document purporting to be such a certificate shall be received in evidence and, unless the contrary is proved, be deemed to be such a certificate.

Sections 16(5) and 27(5)

SCHEDULE 4

Premises Occupied Under Leases

Part I

Occupation by Employer or Trade Organisation

Failure to obtain consent to alteration

1. If any question arises as to whether the occupier has failed to comply with the section 6 or section 15 duty, by failing to make a particular alteration to the premises, any constraint attribu-

table to the fact that he occupies the premises under a lease is to be ignored unless he has applied to the lessor in writing for consent to the making of the alteration.

Joining lessors in proceedings under section 8

2.—(1) In any proceedings under section 8, in a case to which section 16 applies, the complainant or the occupier may ask the tribunal hearing the complaint to direct that the lessor be joined or sisted as a party to the proceedings.

(2) The request shall be granted if it is made before the hearing of the complaint begins.

(3) The tribunal may refuse the request if it is made after the hearing of the complaint begins.

(4) The request may not be granted if it is made after the tribunal has determined the complaint.

(5) Where a lessor has been so joined or sisted as a party to the proceedings, the tribunal may determine—

(a) whether the lessor has—

(i) refused consent to the alteration, or

(ii) consented subject to one or more conditions, and

(b) if so, whether the refusal or any of the conditions was unreasonable,

(6) If, under sub-paragraph (5), the tribunal determines that the refusal or any of the conditions was unreasonable it may take one or more of the following steps—

(a) make such declaration as it considers appropriate;

(b) make an order authorising the occupier to make the alteration specified in the order;

(c) order the lessor to pay compensation to the complainant.

(7) An order under sub-paragraph (6)(b) may require the occupier to comply with conditions specified in the order.

(8) Any step taken by the tribunal under sub-paragraph (6) may be in substitution for, or in addition to, any step taken by the tribunal under section 8(2).

(9) If the tribunal orders the lessor to pay compensation it may not make an order under section 8(2) ordering the occupier to do so.

Regulations

3. Regulations may make provision as to circumstances in which—

(a) a lessor is to be taken, for the purposes of section 16 and this Part of this Schedule to have—

(i) withheld his consent;

(ii) withheld his consent unreasonably;

(iii) acted reasonably in withholding his consent;

(b) a condition subject to which a lessor has given his consent is to be taken to be reasonable;

(c) a condition subject to which a lessor has given his consent is to be taken to be unreasonable.

Sub-leases etc.

4. The Secretary of State may by regulations make provision supplementing, or modifying, the provision made by section 16 or any provision made by or under this Part of this Schedule in relation to cases where the occupier occupies premises under a sub-lease or sub-tenancy.

PART II

OCCUPATION BY PROVIDER OF SERVICES

Failure to obtain consent to alteration

5. If any question arises as to whether the occupier has failed to comply with the section 21 duty, by failing to make a particular alteration to premises, any constraint attributable to the fact that he occupies the premises under a lease is to be ignored unless he has applied to the lessor in writing for consent to the making of the alteration.

Reference to court

6.—(1) If the occupier has applied in writing to the lessor for consent to the alteration and—

(a) that consent has been refused, or

(b) the lessor has made his consent subject to one or more conditions, the occupier or a disabled person who has an interest in the proposed alteration to the premises being made, may refer the matter to a county court or, in Scotland, to the sheriff.

(2) In the following provisions of this Schedule "court" includes "sheriff".

(3) On such a reference the court shall determine whether the lessor's refusal was unreasonable or (as the case may be) whether the condition is, or any of the conditions are, unreasonable.

(4) If the court determines—

(a) that the lessor's refusal was unreasonable, or

(b) that the condition is, or any of the conditions are, unreasonable,

it may make such declaration as it considers appropriate or an order authorising the occupier to make the alteration specified in the order.

(5) An order under sub-paragraph (4) may require the occupier to comply with conditions specified in the order.

Joining lessors in proceedings under section 25

7.—(1) In any proceedings on a claim under section 25, in a case to which this Part of this Schedule applies, the plaintiff, the pursuer or the occupier concerned may ask the court to direct that the lessor be joined or sisted as a party to the proceedings.

(2) The request shall be granted if it is made before the hearing of the claim begins.

(3) The court may refuse the request if it is made after the hearing of the claim begins.

(4) The request may not be granted if it is made after the court has determined the claim.

(5) Where a lessor has been so joined or sisted as a party to the proceedings, the court may determine—

(a) whether the lessor has—

(i) refused consent to the alteration, or

(ii) consented subject to one or more conditions, and

(b) if so, whether the refusal or any of the conditions was unreasonable.

(6) If, under sub-paragraph (5), the court determines that the refusal or any of the conditions was unreasonable it may take one or more of the following steps—

(a) make such declaration as it considers appropriate;

(b) make an order authorising the occupier to make the alteration specified in the order;

(c) order the lessor to pay compensation to the complainant.

(7) An order under sub-paragraph (6)(b) may require the occupier to comply with conditions specified in the order.

(8) If the court orders the lessor to pay compensation it may not order the occupier to do so.

Regulations

8. Regulations may make provision as to circumstances in which—

(a) a lessor is to be taken, for the purposes of section 27 and this Part of this Schedule to have—

(i) withheld his consent;

(ii) withheld his consent unreasonably;

(iii) acted reasonably in withholding his consent;

(b) a condition subject to which a lessor has given his consent is to be taken to be reasonable;

(c) a condition subject to which a lessor has given his consent is to be taken to be unreasonable.

Sub-leases etc.

9. The Secretary of State may by regulations make provision supplementing, or modifying, the provision made by section 27 or any provision made by or under this Part of this Schedule in relation to cases where the occupier occupies premises under a sub-lease or sub-tenancy.

Section 50(8)

SCHEDULE 5

THE NATIONAL DISABILITY COUNCIL

Status

1.—(1) The Council shall be a body corporate.

(2) The Council is not the servant or agent of the Crown and does not enjoy any status, immunity or privilege of the Crown.

Procedure

2. The Council has power to regulate its own procedure (including power to determine its quorum).

Membership

3.—(1) The Council shall consist of at least 10, but not more than 20, members.

(2) In this Schedule "member", except in sub-paragraph (5)(b), means a member of the Council.

(3) Each member shall be appointed by the Secretary of State.

(4) The Secretary of State shall appoint one member to be chairman of the Council and another member to be its deputy chairman.

(5) The members shall be appointed from among persons who, in the opinion of the Secretary of State—

(a) have knowledge or experience of the needs of disabled persons or the needs of a particular group, or particular groups, of disabled persons;

(b) have knowledge or experience of the needs of persons who have had a disability or the needs of a particular group, or particular groups, of such persons; or

(c) are members of, or otherwise represent, professional bodies or bodies which represent industry or other business interests.

(6) Before appointing any member, the Secretary of State shall consult such persons as he considers appropriate.

(7) In exercising his powers of appointment, the Secretary of State shall try to secure that at all times at least half the membership of the Council consists of disabled persons, persons who have had a disability or the parents or guardians of disabled persons.

Term of office of members

4.—(1) Each member shall be appointed for a term which does not exceed five years but shall otherwise hold and vacate his office in accordance with the terms of his appointment.

(2) A person shall not be prevented from being appointed as a member merely because he has previously been a member.

(3) Any member may at any time resign his office by written notice given to the Secretary of State.

(4) Regulations may make provision for the Secretary of State to remove a member from his office in such circumstances as may be prescribed.

Remuneration

5.—(1) The Secretary of State may pay such remuneration or expenses to any member as he considers appropriate.

(2) The approval of the Treasury is required for any payment made under this paragraph.

Staff

6. The Secretary of State shall provide the Council with such staff as he considers appropriate.

Supplementary regulation-making power

7. The Secretary of State may by regulations make provision—

(a) as to the provision of information to the Council by the Secretary of State;

(b) as to the commissioning by the Secretary of State of research to be undertaken on behalf of the Council;

(c) as to the circumstances in which and conditions subject to which the Council may appoint any person as an adviser;

(d) as to the payment by the Secretary of State, with the approval of the Treasury, of expenses incurred by the Council.

Annual report

8.—(1) As soon as is practicable after the end of each financial year, the Council shall report to the Secretary of State on its activities during the financial year to which the report relates.

(2) The Secretary of State shall lay a copy of every annual report of the Council before each House of Parliament and shall arrange for such further publication of the report as he considers appropriate.

Section 70(4)

SCHEDULE 6

CONSEQUENTIAL AMENDMENTS

Employment and Training Act 1973 (c. 50)

1. In section 12(1) of the Employment and Training Act 1973 (duty of Secretary of State to give preference to ex-service men and women in exercising certain powers in respect of disabled persons)—

(a) for "persons registered as handicapped by disablement" substitute "disabled persons"; and

(b) for the words after " "disabled person" " substitute "has the same meaning as in the Disability Discrimination Act 1995."

Employment Protection (Consolidation) Act 1978 (c. 44)

2. In section 136(1) of the Employment Protection (Consolidation) Act 1978 (appeals to Employment Appeal Tribunal), at the end insert—

"(ff) the Disability Discrimination Act 1995."

3. In paragraph 20 of Schedule 13 to that Act (reinstatement or re-engagement of dismissed employees), in sub-paragraph (3)—

(a) in the definition of "relevant complaint of dismissal", omit "or" and at the end insert "or a complaint under section 8 of the Disability Discrimination Act 1995 arising out of a dismissal";

(b) in the definition of "relevant conciliation powers", omit "or" and at the end insert "or paragraph I of Schedule 3 to the Disability Discrimination Act 1995"; and

(c) in the definition of "relevant compromise contract" for "or section" substitute "section" and at the end insert "or section 9(2) of the Disability Discrimination Act 1995".

Companies Act 1985 (c. 6)

4. In paragraph 9 of Schedule 7 to the Companies Act 1985 (disclosure in directors' report of company policy in relation to disabled persons), in the definition of "disabled person" in sub-paragraph (4)(b), for "Disabled Persons (Employment) Act 1944" substitute "Disability Discrimination Act 1995".

Local Government and Housing Act 1989 (c. 42)

5. In section 7 of the Local Government and Housing Act 1989 (all staff of a local authority etc. to be appointed on merit), in subsection (2)—

(a) paragraph (a) shall be omitted;

(b) the word "and" at the end of paragraph (d) shall be omitted; and

(c) after paragraph (e) insert—

"; and

(f) sections 5 and 6 of the Disability Discrimination Act 1995 (meaning of discrimination and duty to make adjustments)."

Enterprise and New Towns (Scotland) Act 1990 (c. 35)

6. In section 16 of the Enterprise and New Towns (Scotland) Act 1990 (duty of certain Scottish bodies to give preference to ex-service men and women in exercising powers to select disabled persons for training), in subsection (2), for "said Act of 1944" substitute "Disability Discrimination Act 1995".

Section 70(5)

SCHEDULE 7

REPEALS

Chapter	Short title	Extent of repeal
7 & 8 Geo. 6 c. 10.	The Disabled Persons (Employment) Act 1944.	Section 1. Sections 6 to 14. Section 19. Section 21. Section 22(4).
6 & 7 Eliz. 2 c. 33.	The Disabled Persons (Employment) Act 1958.	Section 2.
1970 c. 44.	The Chronically Sick and Disabled Persons Act 1970.	Section 16.
1978 c. 44.	The Employment Protection (Consolidation) Act 1978.	In Schedule 13, in paragraph 20(3), the word "or" in the definitions of "relevant complaint of dismissal" and "relevant conciliation powers".
1989 c. 42.	The Local Government and Housing Act 1989.	In section 7(2), paragraph (a) and the word "and" at the end of paragraph (d).
1993 c. 62.	The Education Act 1993.	In section 161(5), the words from "and in this subsection" to the end.

Section 70(6)

SCHEDULE 8

MODIFICATIONS OF THIS ACT IN ITS APPLICATION TO NORTHERN IRELAND

1. In its application to Northern Ireland this Act shall have effect subject to the following modifications.

2.—(1) In section 3(1) for "Secretary of State" substitute "Department".

(2) In section 3 for subsections (4) to (12) substitute—

"(4) In preparing a draft of any guidance, the Department shall consult such persons as it considers appropriate.

(5) Where the Department proposes to issue any guidance, the Department shall publish a draft of it, consider any representations that are made to the Department about the draft and, if the Department thinks it appropriate, modify its proposals in the light of any of those representations.

(6) If the Department decides to proceed with any proposed guidance the Department shall lay a draft of it before the Assembly.

(7) If, within the statutory period, the Assembly resolves not to approve the draft, the Department shall take no further steps in relation to the proposed guidance.

(8) If no such resolution is made within the statutory period, the Department shall issue the guidance in the form of its draft.

(9) The guidance shall come into force on such date as the Department may by order appoint.

(10) Subsection (7) does not prevent a new draft of the proposed guidance being laid before the Assembly.

(11) The Department may—

(a) from time to time revise the whole or any part of any guidance and re-issue it;

(b) by order revoke any guidance.

(12) In this section—

"the Department" means the Department of Economic Development;

"guidance" means guidance issued by the Department under this section and includes guidance which has been revised and re-issued;

"statutory period" has the meaning assigned to it by section 41(2) of the Interpretation Act (Northern Ireland) 1954."

3. In section 4(6) for "Great Britain" substitute "Northern Ireland".

4.—(1) In section 7(2) for "Secretary of State" substitute "Department of Economic Development".

(2) In section 7(4) to (10) for "Secretary of State" wherever it occurs substitute "Department of Economic Development", for "he" and "him" wherever they occur substitute "it" and for "his" wherever it occurs substitute "its".

(3) In section 7(9) for "Parliament" substitute "the Assembly".

5.—(1) In section 8(3) omit "or (in Scotland) in reparation".

(2) In section 8(7) for "paragraph 6A of Schedule 9 to the Employment Protection (Consolidation) Act 1978" substitute "Article 61(3) of the Industrial Relations (Northern Ireland) Order 1976".

6.—(1) In section 9(2)(a) for "a conciliation officer" substitute "the Agency".

(2) In section 9(4) in the definition of "qualified lawyer" for the words from "means" to the end substitute "means a barrister (whether in practice as such or employed to give legal advice) or a solicitor of the Supreme Court who holds a practising certificate.".

7.—(1) In section 10(1)(b) omit "or recognised body".

(2) In section 10(2)(b) for "Secretary of State" substitute "Department of Economic Development".

(3) In section 10(3) in the definition of "charity" for "1993" substitute "(Northern Ireland) 1964", omit the definition of "recognised body" and in the definition of "supported employment" for "Act 1944" substitute "Act (Northern Ireland) 1945".

(4) In section 10(4) for "England and Wales" where it twice occurs substitute "Northern Ireland".

(5) Omit section 10(5).

8.—In section 12(5) for "Great Britain" where it twice occurs substitute "Northern Ireland".

9.—(1) In section 19(3)(g) for "section 2 of the Employment and Training Act 1973" substitute "sections 1 and 2 of the Employment and Training Act (Northern Ireland) 1950".

(2) In section 19(5) for paragraph (a) substitute—

"(a) education which is funded, or secured, by a relevant body or provided at—

(i) an establishment which is funded by such a body or by the Department of Education for Northern Ireland; or

(ii) any other establishment which is a school within the meaning of the Education and Libraries (Northern Ireland) Order 1986;".

(3) For section 19(6) substitute—

"(6) In subsection (5) "relevant body" means—

(a) an education and library board;

(b) a voluntary organisation; or

(c) a body of a prescribed kind.".

10. In section 20(7) for paragraphs (b) and (c) substitute "; or

(b) functions conferred by or under Part VIII of the Mental Health (Northern Ireland) Order 1986 are exercisable in relation to a disabled person's property or affairs.".

11. In section 22(4) and (6) omit "or (in Scotland) the subject of".

12.—(1) In section 25(1) omit "or (in Scotland) in reparation".

(2) In section 25(3) for "England and Wales" substitute "Northern Ireland".

(3) Omit section 25(4).

(4) In section 25(5) omit the words from "or" to the end.

13. In section 26(3) omit "or a sheriff court".

14.—(1) In section 28 for "Secretary of State" wherever it occurs substitute "Department of Health and Social Services".

(2) In section 28(3) and (4) for "he" substitute "it".

(3) In section 28(5) for "Treasury" substitute "Department of Finance and Personnel in Northern Ireland".

15. Omit sections 29, 30 and 31.

16.—(1) In section 32(1) for "Secretary of State" substitute "Department of the Environment".

(2) In section 32(5) for the definition of "taxi" substitute—

" "taxi" means a vehicle which—

(a) is licensed under Article 61 of the Road Traffic (Northern Ireland) Order 1981 to stand or ply for hire; and

(b) seats not more than 8 passengers in addition to the driver".

17. In section 33, for "Secretary of State", wherever it occurs, substitute "Department of the Environment".

18. For section 34 substitute—

"New licences conditional on compliance with accessibility tax regulations

34.—(1) The Department of the Environment shall not grant a public service vehicle licence under Article 61 of the Road Traffic (Northern Ireland) Order 1981 for a taxi unless the vehicle conforms with those provisions of the taxi accessibility regulations with which it will be required to conform if licensed.

(2) Subsection (1) does not apply if such a licence was in force with respect to the vehicle at any time during the period of 28 days immediately before the day on which the licence is granted.

(3) The Department of the Environment may by order provide for subsection (2) to cease to have effect on such date as may be specified in the order.".

19. Omit section 35.

20. In section 36(7) for "licensing authority" substitute "Department of the Environment".

21.—(1) In section 37(5) and (6) for "licensing authority" substitute "Department of the Environment".

(2) In section 37(9) for "Secretary of State" substitute "Department of the Environment".

22.—(1) In section 38(1) for "a licensing authority" substitute "the Department of the Environment".

(2) In section 38(2) for "licensing authority concerned" substitute "Department of the Environment".

(3) In section 38(3) for the words from "the magistrates' court" to the end substitute "a court of summary jurisdiction acting for the petty sessions district in which the aggrieved person resides".

23. Omit section 39.

24.—(1) In section 40 for "Secretary of State" wherever it occurs substitute "Department of the Environment".

(2) In section 40(5) for the definition of "public service vehicle" substitute—

" "public service vehicle" means a vehicle which—

(a) seats more than 8 passengers in addition to the driver; and

(b) is a public service vehicle for the purposes of the Road Traffic (Northern Ireland) Order 1981;".

(3) In section 40(7) for the words from "the Disabled" to the end substitute "such representative organisations as it thinks fit".

25.—(1) In section 41(2) for "Secretary of State" substitute "Department of the Environment".

(2) In section 41 for subsections (3) and (4) substitute—

"(3) Any person who uses a regulated public service vehicle in contravention of this section is guilty of an offence and liable on summary conviction to a fine not exceeding level 4 on the standard scale.".

26.—(1) In section 42 for "Secretary of State" wherever it occurs substitute "Department of the Environment".

(2) In section 42(1) for "he" substitute "it".

(3) In section 42(6) for "his" substitute "its".

27. In section 43 for "Secretary of State" wherever it occurs substitute "Department of the Environment".

28.—(1) In section 44 for "Secretary of State" wherever it occurs substitute "Department of the Environment".

(2) In section 44(2) for "him" substitute "it".

(3) In section 44(6) for "he" substitute "it" and for "his" substitute "its".

29.—(1) In section 45 for "Secretary of State" wherever it occurs substitute "Department of the Environment".

(2) In section 45(2) for "him" substitute "it" and at the end add "of Northern Ireland".

(3) In section 45(4) for "he" substitute "it".

30.—(1) In section 46 for "Secretary of State" wherever it occurs substitute "Department of the Environment".

(2) In section 46(6) in the definition of "rail vehicle" for the words "on any railway, tramway or prescribed system" substitute "by rail".

(3) Omit section 46(7).

(4) In section 46(11) for the words from "the Disabled" to the end substitute "such representative organisations as it thinks fit".

31.—(1) In section 47 for "Secretary of State" wherever it occurs substitute "Department of the Environment".

(2) In section 47(3) for the words "the Disabled Persons Transport Advisory Committee and such other persons as he" substitute "such persons as it" and for "he" substitute "it".

32. Omit section 48(3).

33.—(1) In the heading to Part VI of this Act and in section 50(1) for "National Disability Council" substitute "Northern Ireland Disability Council".

(2) In section 50(2) for "the Secretary of State" in the first place where it occurs substitute "a

Northern Ireland department" and in the other place where it occurs substitute "that department".

(3) In section 50(3) for "Secretary of State" substitute "Department of Health and Social Services".

(4) In section 50(7) for "the Secretary of State" substitute "a Northern Ireland department" and after "Crown" insert "or a Northern Ireland department".

(5) In section 50(9)(a) for sub-paragraphs (i) to (iv) substitute—

"(i) the Disabled Persons (Employment) Act (Northern Ireland) 1945;

(ii) the Contracts of Employment and Redundancy Payments Act (Northern Ireland) 1965;

(iii) the Employment and Training Act (Northern Ireland) 1950;

(iv) the Industrial Relations (Northern Ireland) Orders 1976; or".

(6) In section 50(10) for the words from "time when" to the end substitute "time when—

(a) there are no committees in existence under section 17 of the Disabled Persons (Employment) Act (Northern Ireland) 1945; and

(b) there is no person appointed to act generally under section 60(1) of this Act.".

34.—(1) In section 51(1) for "the Secretary of State" substitute "any Northern Ireland department" and for "the Secretary of State's" substitute "that department's".

(2) In section 51(2) for "The Secretary of State" substitute "A Northern Ireland department".

(3) In section 51(4) for "a county court or a sheriff court" substitute "or a county court".

(4) In section 51(6) for "the Secretary of State" substitute "a Northern Ireland department".

35. For section 52 substitute—

"Further provisions about codes issued under section 51

52.—(1) In this section—

"proposal" means a proposal made by the Council to a Northern Ireland department under section 51;

"responsible department"—

(a) in relation to a proposal, means the Northern Ireland department to which the proposal is made,

(b) in relation to a code, means the Northern Ireland department by which the code is issued; and

"statutory period" has the meaning assigned to it by section 41(2) of the Interpretation Act (Northern Ireland) 1954.

(2) In preparing any proposal, the Council shall consult—

(a) such persons (if any) as the responsible department has specified in making its request to the Council; and

(b) such other persons (if any) as the Council considers appropriate.

(3) Before making any proposal the Council shall publish a draft, consider any representations made to it about the draft and, if it thinks it appropriate, modify its proposal in the light of any of those representations.

(4) Where the Council makes any proposal, the responsible department may—

(a) approve it;

(b) approve it subject to such modifications as that department thinks appropriate; or

(c) refuse to approve it.

(5) Where the responsible department approves any proposal (with or without modifications) that department shall prepare a draft of the proposed code and lay it before the Assembly.

(6) If, within the statutory period, the Assembly resolves not to approve the draft, the responsible department shall take no further steps in relation to the proposed code.

(7) If no such resolution is made within the statutory period, the responsible department shall issue the code in the form of its draft.

(8) The code shall come into force on such date as the responsible department may appoint by order.

(9) Subsection (6) does not prevent a new draft of the proposed code from being laid before the Assembly.

(10) If the responsible department refuses to approve a proposal, that department shall give the Council a written statement of the department's reasons for not approving it.

(11) The responsible department may by order revoke a code.".

36.—(1) In section 53 for "Secretary of State" wherever it occurs substitute "Department of Economic Development".

(2) In section 53(1) for "he" substitute "it".

(3) In section 53(5) for "a county court or a sheriff court" substitute "or a county court".

37. For section 54 substitute—

"**Further provisions about codes issued under section 53**

54.—(1) In preparing a draft of any code under section 53, the Department shall consult such organisations representing the interests of employers or of disabled persons in, or seeking, employment as the Department considers appropriate.

(2) Where the Department proposes to issue a code, the Department shall publish a draft of the code, consider any representations that are made to the Department about the draft and, if the Department thinks it appropriate, modify its proposals in the light of any of those representations.

(3) If the Department decides to proceed with the code, the Department shall lay a draft of it before the Assembly.

(4) If, within the statutory period, the Assembly resolves not to approve the draft, the Department shall take no further steps in relation to the proposed code.

(5) If no such resolution is made within the statutory period, the Department shall issue the code in the form of its draft.

(6) The code shall come into force on such date as the Department may appoint by order.

(7) Subsection (4) does not prevent a new draft of the proposed code from being laid before the Assembly.

(8) The Department may by order revoke a code.

(9) In this section—

"the Department" means the Department of Economic Development; and

"statutory period" has the meaning assigned to it by section 41(2) of the Interpretation Act (Northern Ireland) 1954.".

38. In section 56(2) and (4) for "Secretary of State" substitute "Department of Economic Development".

39. In section 59(1) after "Crown" where it twice occurs insert "or a Northern Ireland department".

40.—(1) In section 60(1) to (3) for "Secretary of State" wherever it occurs substitute "Department of Economic Development" and for "he" and "him" wherever they occur substitute "it".

(2) In section 60(4) for "Treasury" substitute "Department of Finance and Personnel in Northern Ireland".

(3) For section 60(6) substitute—

"(6) The Department of Economic Development may by order repeal section 17 of, and Schedule 2 to, the Disabled Persons (Employment) Act (Northern Ireland) 1945 (district advisory committees).".

(4) In section 60(7) omit "paragraph (b) of", for "1944" substitute " 1945" and omit "in each case".

(5) In section 60, omit subsection (8).

41. For section 61 substitute—

"**Amendments of Disabled Persons (Employment) Act (Northern Ireland) 1945**

61.—(1) Section 15 of the Disabled Persons (Employment) Act (Northern Ireland) 1945 (which gives the Department of Economic Development power to make arrangements for the provision of supported employment) is amended as set out in subsections (2) to (5).

(2) In subsection (1)—

(a) for "persons registered as handicapped by disablement" substitute "disabled persons";

(b) for "their disablement" substitute "their disability"; and

(c) for "are not subject to disablement" substitute "do not have a disability".

(3) In subsection (2) for the words from "any of one or more companies" to "so required and prohibited" substitute "any company, association or body".

(4) After subsection (2) insert—

"(2A) The only kind of company which the Department itself may form in exercising its powers under this section is a company which is—

(a) required by its constitution to apply its profits, if any, or other income in promoting its objects; and

(b) prohibited by its constitution from paying any dividend to its members.".

(5) After subsection (5) insert—

"(5A) For the purposes of this section—

(a) a person is a disabled person if he is a disabled person for the purposes of the Disability Discrimination Act 1995; and

(b) "disability" has the same meaning as in that Act.".

(6) The provisions of section 16 of the Act of 1945 (preference to be given under section 15 of that Act to ex-service men and women) shall become subsection (1) of that section and at the end insert—

"and whose disability is due to that service.

(2) For the purposes of subsection (1) of this section, a disabled person's disability shall be treated as due to service of a particular kind only in such circumstances as may be prescribed."

(7) The following provisions of the Act of 1945 shall cease to have effect—

(a) section 1 (definition of "disabled person");

(b) sections 2 to 4 (training for disabled persons);

(c) sections 6 to 8 (the register of disabled persons);

(d) sections 9 to 11 (obligations on employers with substantial staffs to employ quota of registered persons);

(e) section 12 (the designated employment scheme for persons registered as handicapped by disablement);

(f) section 13 (interpretation of provisions repealed by this Act);

(g) section 14 (records to be kept by employer);

(h) section 19 (proceedings in relation to offences);

(j) sections 21 and 22 (supplementary).

(8) Any statutory provision in which "disabled person" is defined by reference to the Act of 1945 shall be construed as if that expression had the same meaning as in this Act.".

42.—(1) In section 62(2) for "Secretary of State" substitute "Department of Economic Development".

(2) In section 62(7) for "Great Britain" where it twice occurs substitute "Northern Ireland".

43. Omit section 63.

44.—(1) In section 64(3) for "England and Wales" substitute "Northern Ireland".

(2) Omit section 64(4).

(3) In section 64(5)(a) omit the words from ", the British" to the end.

(4) In section 64(8)—

(a) omit the definitions of "British Transport Police", "Royal Parks Constabulary" and "United Kingdom Atomic Energy Authority Constabulary";

(b) in the definition of "the 1947 Act" at the end add "as it applies both in relation to the Crown in right of Her Majesty's Government in Northern Ireland and in relation to the Crown in right of Her Majesty's Government in the United Kingdom";

(c) in the definition of "fire brigade" for the words from "means" to the end substitute "has the same meaning as in the Fire Services (Northern Ireland) Order 1984";

(d) in the definition of "prison officer" for the words from "means" to the end substitute "means any individual who holds any post, otherwise than as a medical officer, to which he has been appointed under section 2(2) of the Prison Act (Northern Ireland) 1953 or who is a prison custody officer within the meaning of Chapter III of Part VIII of the Criminal Justice and Public Order Act 1994";

(e) in the definition of "service for purposes of a Minister of the Crown or government department" at the end add "or service as the head of a Northern Ireland department".

45. Omit section 65.

46. For section 67 substitute—

"**Regulations and orders etc.**

67.—(1) Any power under this Act to make regulations or orders shall be exercisable by statutory rule for the purposes of the Statutory Rules (Northern Ireland) Order 1979.

(2) Any such power may be exercised to make different provision for different cases, including different provision for different areas or localities.

(3) Any such power, includes power—

(a) to make such incidental, supplementary, consequential or transitional provision as appears to the Northern Ireland department exercising the power to be expedient; and

(b) to provide for a person to exercise a discretion in dealing with any matter.

(4) No order shall be made under section 50(3) unless a draft of the order has been laid before and approved by a resolution of the Assembly.

(5) Any other order made under this Act, other than an order under section 3(9), 52(8), 54(6) or 70(3), and any regulations made under this Act shall be subject to negative resolution within the meaning of section 41(6) of the Interpretation Act (Northern Ireland) 1954 as if they were statutory instruments within the meaning of that Act.

(6) Section 41(3) of the Interpretation Act (Northern Ireland) 1954 shall apply in relation to any instrument or document which by virtue of this Act is required to be laid before the Assembly as if it were a statutory instrument or statutory document within the meaning of that Act.

(7) Subsection (1) does not require an order under section 43 which applies only to a specified vehicle, or to vehicles of a specified person, to be made by statutory rule.

(8) Nothing in section 40(6) or 46(5) affects the powers conferred by subsections (2) and (3)."

47.—(1) For section 68(1) substitute—

"(1) In this Act—

"accessibility certificate" means a certificate issued under section 41(1)(a);

"act" includes a deliberate omission;

"the Agency" means the Labour Relations Agency;

"approval certificate" means a certificate issued under section 42(4);

"the Assembly" means the Northern Ireland Assembly;

"benefits", in Part II, has the meaning given in section 4(4);

"the Department of Economic Development" means the Department of Economic Development in Northern Ireland;

"the Department of the Environment" means the Department of the Environment for Northern Ireland;

"the Department of Health and Social Services" means the Department of Health and Social Services for Northern Ireland;

"employment" means, subject to any prescribed provision, employment under a contract of service or of apprenticeship or a contract personally to do work and related expressions are to be construed accordingly;

"employment at an establishment in Northern Ireland" is to be construed in accordance with subsections (2) to (5);

"enactment" means any statutory provision within the meaning of section 1(f) of the Interpretation Act (Northern Ireland) 1954;

"government department" means a Northern Ireland department or a department of the Government of the United Kingdom;

"Minister of the Crown" includes the Treasury;

"Northern Ireland department" includes (except in sections 51 and 52) the head of a Northern Ireland department;

"occupational pension scheme" has the same meaning as in the Pension Schemes (Northern Ireland) Act 1993;

"premises", includes land of any description;

"prescribed" means prescribed by regulations;

"profession" includes any vocation or occupation;

"provider of services" has the meaning given in section 19(2)(b);

"public service vehicle" and "regulated public service vehicle" have the meaning given in section 40;

"PSV accessibility regulations" means regulations made under section 40(1);

"rail vehicle" and "regulated rail vehicle" have the meaning given in section 46;

"rail vehicle accessibility regulations" means regulations made under section 46(1);

"regulations" means—

(a) in Parts I and II of this Act, section 66, the definition of "employment" above and subsections (3) and (4) below, regulations made by the Department of Economic Development;

(b) in Part V of this Act, regulations made by the Department of the Environment;

(c) in any other provision of this Act, regulations made by the Department of Health and Social Services.

"section 6 duty" means any duty imposed by or under section 6;

"section 15 duty" means any duty imposed by or under section 15;

"section 21 duty" means any duty imposed by or under section 21;

"taxi" and "regulated taxi" have the meaning given in section 32;

"taxi accessibility regulations" means regulations made under section 32(1);

"trade" includes any business;

"trade organisation" has the meaning given in section 13;

"vehicle examiner" means an officer of the Department of the Environment authorised by that Department for the purposes of sections 41 and 42.".

(2) In section 68(2) to (4) for "Great Britain" wherever it occurs substitute "Northern Ireland".

48.—(1) In section 70(3) for "Secretary of State" substitute "Department of Health and Social Services".

(2) In section 70(8) for "the Secretary of State" substitute "a Northern Ireland department" and for "him" substitute "it".

49.—(1) In Schedule 1 in paragraph 7(1) for "Act 1944" substitute "Act (Northern Ireland) 1945".

(2) In Schedule 1 in paragraph 7(7) for "1944" substitute "1945".

50.—(1) In Schedule 3 in paragraph 1—

(a) for "a conciliation officer" wherever it occurs substitute "the Agency";

(b) in sub-paragraphs (1) and (4) for "he" substitute "it";

(c) in sub-paragraph (3) for "the conciliation officer" substitute "the Agency".

(2) In Schedule 3 for paragraph 4(1) substitute—

"(1) In any proceedings under section 8—

(a) a certificate signed by or on behalf of a Minister of the Crown or a Northern Ireland department and certifying that any conditions or requirements specified in the certificate were imposed by that Minister or that department (as the case may be) and were in operation at a time or throughout a time so specified; or

(b) a certificate signed by or on behalf of the Secretary of State and certifying that an act specified in the certificate was done for the purpose of safeguarding national security,

shall be conclusive evidence of the matters certified.".

(3) In Schedule 3 in paragraph 6(1) omit "or a sheriff court".

(4) In Schedule 3 for paragraph 8(1) substitute—

"(1) In any proceedings under section 25—

(a) a certificate signed by or on behalf of a Minister of the Crown or a Northern Ireland department and certifying that any conditions or requirements specified in the certificate were imposed by that Minister or that department (as the case may be) and were in operation at a time or throughout a time so specified; or

(b) a certificate signed by or on behalf of the Secretary of State and certifying that an act specified in the certificate was done for the purpose of safeguarding national security,

shall be conclusive evidence of the matters certified.".

51.—(1) In Schedule 4 in paragraphs 2(1) and (5) and 7(1) and (5) omit "or sisted".

(2) In Schedule 4 in paragraph 4 for "Secretary of State" substitute "Department of Economic Development".

(3) In Schedule 4 in paragraph 6(1) omit "or, in Scotland, to the sheriff".

(4) In Schedule 4 omit paragraph 6(2).

(5) In Schedule 4 in paragraph 9 for "Secretary of State" substitute "Department of Health and Social Services".

52.—(1) In Schedule 5 in the heading for "National" substitute "Northern Ireland".

(2) In Schedule 5 for "Secretary of State" wherever it occurs substitute "Department of Health and Social Services".

(3) In Schedule 5 in paragraphs 3(6), 5(1), 6 and 8(2) for "he" substitute "it" and in paragraph 3(7) for "his" substitute "its".

(4) In Schedule 5 in paragraphs 5(2) and 7(d) for "Treasury" substitute "Department of Finance and Personnel in Northern Ireland".

(5) In Schedule 5 in paragraph 8(2) for "each House of Parliament" substitute "the Assembly".

53. For Schedules 6 and 7 substitute—

"SCHEDULE 6

Consequential Amendments

The Industrial Relations (Northern Ireland) Order 1976 (NI 16)

1. In Article 68(6) of the Industrial Relations (Northern Ireland) Order 1976 (reinstatement or re-engagement of dismissed employees)—

(a) in the definition of "relevant complaint of dismissal", omit "or" and at the end insert "or a complaint under section 8 of the Disability Discrimination Act 1995 arising out of a dismissal";

(b) in the definition of "relevant conciliation powers", omit "or" and at the end insert "or paragraph 1 of Schedule 3 to the Disability Discrimination Act 1995";

(c) in the definition of "relevant compromise contract" for "or Article" substitute "Article" and at the end insert "or section 9(2) of the Disability Discrimination Act 1995".

The Companies (Northern Ireland) Order 1986 (NI 6)

3. In paragraph 9 of Schedule 7 to the Companies (Northern Ireland) Order 1986 (disclosure in directors' report of company policy in relation to disabled persons) in the definition of "disabled person" in sub-paragraph (4)(b) for "Disabled Persons (Employment) Act (Northern Ireland) 1945" substitute "Disability Discrimination Act 1995".

SCHEDULE 7

REPEALS

Chapter	Short title	Extent of repeal
1945 c. 6 (N.I.)	The Disabled Persons (Employment) Act (Northern Ireland) 1945.	Sections 1 to 4. Sections 6 to 14. In section 16 the words "vocational training and industrial rehabilitation courses and", the words "courses and" and the words from "and in selecting" to "engagement". Section 19. Section 21. Section 22.
1960 c. 4 (N.I.)	The Disabled Persons (Employment) Act (Northern Ireland) 1960.	The whole Act.
1976 N.I. 16	The Industrial Relations (Northern Ireland) Order 1976.	In Article 68(6) the word "or" in the definitions of "relevant complaint of dismissal" and "relevant conciliation powers".".

INDEX

References are to sections and Schedules

MEDICAL (PROFESSIONAL PERFORMANCE) ACT 1995*

(1995 c. 51)

An Act to amend the Medical Act 1983 to make provision relating to the professional performance of registered medical practitioners and the voluntary removal of names from the register of medical practitioners; to amend section 42 of that Act; and for connected purposes.

[8th November 1995]

Parliamentary Debates

Hansard, H.C. Vol. 256, col. 1038; Vol. 258, col. 671; Vol. 261, col. 548; Vol. 265, col. 700. H.L. Vol. 564, col. 1640; Vol. 565, col. 871; Vol. 566, cols. 477, 1080, 1488.

Introduction and General Note

This Act remedies a serious defect in the ability of the medical profession to regulate itself—its inability, in general terms, to deal effectively with incompetent doctors who represent a threat to public safety.

The Act amends the Medical Act 1983 (c.54). It extends the remit of the General Medical Council ("GMC") under Part V (Professional Conduct and Fitness to Practise) of that Act to include cases where the standard of professional performance of a registered medical practitioner is seriously deficient.

Previously, the GMC was concerned solely with the maintenance of the Medical Register and ancillary matters. Its function was not concerned with maintaining standards of professional performance (except insofar as these affected registration), though it did have powers to advise medical practitioners on standards of professional conduct or medical ethics. Previously, it could act only in cases where a medical practitioner was convicted of a criminal offence, was found guilty of serious professional misconduct or his fitness to practise was found to be seriously impaired by ill health. It could not act in cases of professional incompetence except insofar as they involved professional conduct and fitness to practise. The GMC was not able to ensure that all those admitted to the register were competent to practise.

There has been widespread concern about the lack of any effective action that could be taken in cases where a doctor's general performance was seriously deficient. Only the GMC has a universal power to prevent a doctor from practising, since it maintains the Medical Register. The medical royal colleges cannot do so, as although they are concerned with maintaining and promoting medical excellence, they have limited sanctions. The National Health Service cannot either, since its sanctions are limited to the contract (of service or for services) with the doctor concerned, which can only have a local effect, and such contracts tend to be organised on a regional basis.

The Act followed the consultation paper "*Proposals for New Performance Procedures*" published by the GMC in May 1992 which was distributed widely to individuals and organisations within and outside the medical profession. It is based largely on those proposals.

There are now, therefore, three separate jurisdictions of the GMC in respect of its regulatory functions. These three jurisdictions will inevitably overlap to some extent. For example, the case of a doctor whose clinical judgment has been impaired on a number of occasions by abuse of drugs could invoke all three jurisdictions. The choice of jurisdiction would depend, of course, on the individual facts of the case and would take into consideration such factors as the attitude of the doctor and the criminality of the conduct. The procedures in respect of these jurisdictions are different and are mutually exclusive. Moreover, two (*i.e.* relating to health and professional performance) are investigative, require the co-operation of the doctor and have inquisitorial features, whereas the third (*i.e.* relating to professional conduct) is adversarial. Transfer of a case from one jurisdiction to another should not present difficulties provided it is done at an early stage. However once proceedings are under way, any proposed change from an inquisitorial process to an adversarial process could infringe the rules of natural justice. The GMC considers that such difficulties are theoretical rather than real.

The Act establishes two additional committees of the GMC to give effect to the newly created professional performance jurisdiction: the Assessment Referral Committee (ARC) and the Committee on Professional Performance (CPP).

The Act envisages the procedures proposed by the GMC in its paper "*Proposed Performance Procedures*" published on May 15, 1995. It is an investigative and consensual process which requires the co-operation of the doctor concerned. These procedures are extremely complex but in summary, consist of up to four stages. Stage I is "screening"; after inquiries by the GMC "preliminary screener" the case may be resolved or may proceed to the next stage. Stage II is

*Annotations by Anthony Barton, Solicitor and Medical Practitioner.

"assessment of performance"; in cases where the doctor refuses to have his professional performance assessed, the ARC can determine whether or not assessment is justified and can require the doctor to undergo assessment. Depending on the assessment, the case may proceed to the next stage. Stage III is "remedial action and reassessment"; remedial action includes counselling and retraining. Depending on the reassessment, the case may proceed to the next stage. Stage IV is "referral to CPP" which considers the cases not resolved by the previous procedures: for example, refusal to undergo assessment (from Stage II) and failure to respond to remedial action (from Stage III). The CPP must consider evidence, in particular the results of any assessment and any reassessment, to determine if the doctor's professional performance has been seriously deficient.

The CPP must suspend or impose conditions on a medical practitioner's registration where his standard of professional performance is found to be seriously deficient.

The GMC may make regulations which allow for the voluntary removal of a medical practitioner's name from the register, and for the restoration of a name to the register; such restoration to be subject to the approval of the GMC or one of its committees.

The Act also makes important amendments to section 42 of the Medical Act 1983 which is concerned, *inter alia*, with interim orders of suspension and conditional registration. The maximum duration of such orders is increased from two months to six months.

The Schedule contains consequential and supplementary amendments, principally to the Medical Act 1983. It makes provision for the carrying out of assessments of professional performance by Assessment Panels. It provides various powers for Assessment Panels in connection with their function of investigating professional performance.

COMMENCEMENT

The Act comes into force on an appointed day; different parts of the Act may be brought into effect on different days.

Professional performance

1. After section 36 of the Medical Act 1983 (professional misconduct and criminal offences) there shall be inserted—

"**Professional performance**

36A.—(1) Where the standard of professional performance of a fully registered person is found by the Committee on Professional Performance to have been seriously deficient, the Committee shall direct—

(a) that his registration in the register shall be suspended (that is to say, shall not have effect) during such period not exceeding twelve months as may be specified in the direction; or

(b) that his registration shall be conditional on his compliance, during such period not exceeding three years as may be specified in the direction, with the requirements so specified.

(2) Where a fully registered person, whose registration is subject to conditions imposed under any provision of this section by the Committee on Professional Performance, is judged by the Committee to have failed to comply with any of the requirements imposed on him as conditions of his registration the Committee may, if they think fit, direct that his registration in the register shall be suspended during such period not exceeding twelve months as may be specified in the direction.

(3) Where the Committee on Professional Performance have given a direction for suspension under any provision of this section the Committee may direct—

(a) that the current period of suspension shall be extended for such further period from the time when it would otherwise expire as may be specified in the direction; or

(b) that the registration of the person whose registration is suspended shall, as from the expiry (or termination under subsection (5)(b) below) of the current period of suspension, be conditional on his compliance, during such period not exceeding three years as may be specified in the direction, with such requirements so specified as the Committee think fit to impose for the protection of members of the public or in his interests;

but, subject to subsection (4) below, the Committee shall not extend any period of suspension under this section for more than twelve months at a time.

(4) The Committee on Professional Performance may make a direction extending a period of suspension indefinitely where—

(a) the period of suspension will, on the date on which the direction takes effect, have lasted for at least two years, and

(b) the direction is made not more than two months before the date on which the period of suspension would otherwise expire.

(5) Where the Committee on Professional Performance have made a direction for indefinite suspension, they—

(a) shall review the suspension when requested to do so by the person whose registration is suspended (but not until two years after the date on which the direction takes effect and not more than once in any period of two years), and

(b) having carried out such a review, may direct that the suspension be terminated.

(6) Where the Committee on Professional Performance have given a direction for conditional registration, the Committee may—

(a) direct that the current period of conditional registration shall be extended for such further period from the time when it would otherwise expire as may be specified in the direction;

(b) revoke the direction or revoke or vary any of the conditions imposed by the direction; or

(c) direct that the registration shall be suspended during such period not exceeding twelve months as may be specified in the direction;

but the Committee shall not extend any period of conditional registration under this section for more than three years at a time.

(7) Where the Committee on Professional Performance give a direction under this section for suspension or for conditional registration, or vary the conditions imposed by a direction for conditional registration, the Registrar shall forthwith serve on the person to whom the direction applies a notification of the direction or of the variation and of his right to appeal against the decision in accordance with section 40 below.

(8) In subsection (7) above the references to a direction for suspension and a direction for conditional registration include references to a direction extending a period of suspension or a period of conditional registration.

(9) While a person's registration in the register is suspended by virtue of this section he shall be treated as not being registered in the register notwithstanding that his name still appears in it.

(10) This section applies to a provisionally registered person and to a person registered with limited registration whether or not the circumstances are such that he falls within the meaning in this Act of the expression "fully registered person".".

DEFINITIONS

"Committee on Professional Performance": Sched. paras. 2(b) and 9.
"fully registered person": Medical Act 1983 s.55.
"the register": Medical Act 1983 ss.2, 30 and 55.
"Registrar": Medical Act 1983 ss.2(1) and 55.
"provisionally registered": Medical Act 1983 s.55.
"limited registration": Medical Act 1983 ss.22(2) and 55.

GENERAL NOTE

This section applies not only to fully registered persons but also to provisionally registered persons and persons with limited registration. It provides a further jurisdiction in respect of professional performance, in addition to those in respect of professional conduct and fitness to practise. It introduces the concept of a "seriously deficient standard of professional performance". This term is not defined in the Act and indeed, a proposal to measure professional performance against "published performance standards and key performance criteria" was resisted in the House of Lords. Lord Walton observed as follows:

"The problem about attempting to codify professional performance in the precise way suggested is one that is far beyond the capability of any body of medical practitioners with the legal and lay advice upon which it is likely to rely at the present time. The problem is that so many specialties exist in medicine that to attempt to lay down precise published performance standards for each of them and key performance criteria would be an incredibly difficult task." (*Hansard*, H.L. Vol. 566, col. 479)

Exactly the same difficulties of assessing medical professional standards exist in the context of common law breach of duty, whether in negligence or contract, and breach of contract, whether of service or for services. Baroness Cumberlege observed:

"It is important that a doctor knows the limits within which he should work and the standards that he should meet. It is equally important that the public should have information available so that they know what to expect . . . A doctor cannot be judged on a set of published criteria alone . . . Such criteria will be constantly changing, and a published document can soon become outdated. To require the CPP to make judgments on published standards alone would constrain it, and may act against the public interest . . . it is important that published criteria form just one aspect of its reasoning. There is a body of unpublished, but widely acknowledged, standards which also needs to be considered . . ." (*Hansard*, H.L. Vol. 566, col. 479)

The GMC provides some guidance as to what constitutes seriously deficient professional performance: ". . . so blatantly poor that patients are potentially at risk" (para. 2.1 of the GMC consultation paper, see above) and that it is concerned with professional knowledge, professional skill and professional attitudes towards patients and colleagues (*ibid.* para. 2.5). The GMC also provides guidance in its publication "*Good Medical Practice*". Although this provision can apply to single discrete acts or omissions, the Parliamentary debates contemplated repeated incidents: "a pattern of unsatisfactory conduct", "a continuous pattern of poor performance", "a pattern of serious deficiency", and "consistent incompetence" (*passim*).

The overall aim of this jurisdiction is remedial in the sense of improving a doctor's deficient standards and to protect the public (see *Hansard*, H.C. Vol. 258, col. 675). It is not intended to be punitive (*ibid.* at col. 680). It does not provide any remedy specifically for a complainant and does not appear to give a complainant any rights in private law.

Subs. (1) of s.36A

Where the CPP finds that the standard of professional performance of a doctor has been seriously deficient then it *must* (*i.e.* a statutory duty) suspend or make conditional his registration. This contrasts with the *statutory powers* provided by s.36 (professional misconduct and criminal offences) and s.37 (unfitness to practise through illness). There is no provision for removal of the doctor's name from the register though there is provision for indefinite suspension (see below). This is in keeping with the non-adversarial nature and rehabilitative purpose of the professional performance procedures.

Subs. (2) of s.36A

This subsection provides a power to suspend where there has been a breach of condition imposed under any provision of this section.

Subs. (3) of s.36A

This subsection provides additional powers where a direction for suspension has been made, so that it may be extended or the registration made conditional.

Subs. (4) of s.36A

The power of the CPP to extend the period of suspension of a doctor's registration indefinitely is novel for a GMC committee. The GMC considered that there would be a very small number of doctors whose professional performance was so seriously deficient that a period of much longer than 12 month's retraining would be needed before it would be safe to allow the doctor to resume practice. The GMC's Health Committee now also has the same powers to extend the period of suspension of a doctor's registration indefinitely (see Sched. para. 6). The Professional Conduct Committee's powers remain unchanged.

Subs. (5) of s.36A

On the termination of a period of indefinite suspension the CPP may impose conditions on the registration (see subs. 3(b) above).

Subs. (6) of s.36A

This provides additional powers where a registration is made conditional.

Subs. (7) of s.36A

The right of appeal lies only with the doctor concerned: the complainant has no right of appeal.

Subss. (9) and (10) of s.36A

The curious wording of these provisions originates from the Medical Act 1983.

Voluntary removal from the register

2. After section 31 of the Medical Act 1983 (power to make regulations with respect to the registers) there shall be inserted

"**Voluntary removal from the register**

31A.—(1) The General Council may make regulations—

(a) providing for the erasure by the Registrar from the register of medical practitioners of the name of any person, who applies, in the manner prescribed by the regulations, for his name to be erased from the register;

(b) providing for the refusal by the Registrar of applications under paragraph (a) above in such cases and circumstances as may be prescribed by the regulations;

(c) making provision (including provision requiring the approval of the General Council or of one of the statutory committees) for the restoration to the register of the name of any person whose name has been erased in accordance with regulations made in pursuance of paragraph (a) above.

(2) Regulations under this section shall not have effect until approved by order of the Privy Council.".

DEFINITIONS

"General Council" *i.e.* "General Medical Council": Medical Act 1983 ss.1(1) and 55.

"Registrar": Medical Act 1983 ss.2(1) and 55.

GENERAL NOTE

This section inserts a new section 31A into the Medical Act 1983, which enables a doctor to apply for his name to be removed from the register. Parliament had envisaged cases where a doctor's failings were considered to be beyond remedial action, for example where despite retraining there was no improvement on reassessment: the doctor might be invited to consider voluntary removal from the register. A graphic example was provided:

> "The doctor might be falling behind with the latest medical techniques, which have now become the accepted techniques. The doctor might realise that it is time to call it a day . . ." (*Hansard*, H.C. Vol. 258, col. 680).

Restoration of a doctor's name to the register would require the matter to be referred back to the relevant committee for approval.

Preliminary proceedings: interim orders

3.—(1) Section 42 of the Medical Act 1983 (preliminary proceedings as to professional misconduct and unfitness to practise) shall be amended as follows.

(2) In subsection (3), in paragraph (c) for the word "two" there shall be substituted the word "six".

(3) In subsection (4), for the words "No order for interim suspension or for interim conditional registration shall be made by the Preliminary Proceedings Committee" there shall be substituted the words "No order under subsection (3)(b) or(c) above or (6A)(b) to (d) below shall be made by any Committee".

(4) In subsection (5), for the words "If the Committee decide" there shall be substituted the words "If the Preliminary Proceedings Committee decide".

(5) In subsection (6), for the word "two" there shall be substituted the word "six".

(6) After subsection (6) there shall be inserted—

"(6A) Where an order for interim suspension or for interim conditional registration has been made in relation to any person under any provision of this section (including this subsection) the Preliminary Proceedings Committee, the Professional Conduct Committee or the Health Committee may, subject to subsection (4) above

(a) revoke the order or revoke any condition imposed by the order;
(b) vary any condition imposed by the order;
(c) if satisfied that to do so is necessary for the protection of members of the public, make an order for interim suspension; or
(d) if satisfied that to do so is necessary for the protection of members of the public or is in the interests of the person concerned, make an order that his registration shall be conditional on his compliance, during such period as is specified in the order, with such requirements so specified as the Committee think fit to impose for the protection of members of the public or in his interests.

(6B) An order under subsection (6A)(c) or (d) above—

(a) shall take effect as from a date not later than the date on which the interim suspension or interim conditional registration would otherwise come to an end; and
(b) shall specify a period not exceeding three months.

(6C) If an order is made under subsection (6A)(a) to (d) above the Registrar shall forthwith serve a notification of the order on the person to whose registration it relates.

(6D) Where an order has been made under any provision of this section, the court (within the meaning of section 38 above) may—

(a) in the case of an order for interim suspension, terminate the suspension,
(b) in the case of an order for conditional registration, revoke or vary any condition imposed by the order,
(c) in either case, substitute for the period specified in the order some other period which could have been specified in the order when it was made;

and the decision of the court on any application under this subsection shall be final.".

(7) Subsection (7) shall cease to have effect.

GENERAL NOTE

This section amends section 42 of the Medical Act 1983. Previously the maximum duration of interim orders, such as suspension or conditional registration pending full hearing by the Professional Conduct Committee or the Health Committee was two months. The purpose of such interim orders was to protect the public whilst a case was waiting to be heard. The period of two months was insufficient, since for practical reasons, a good deal more time might be needed to prepare a case. The maximum period of such orders is now six months with a power to extend by periods of up to three months.

Supplementary and consequential amendments

4. The Schedule to this Act (which makes amendments supplementary to and consequential on sections 1 to 3) shall have effect.

Expenses

5. There shall be paid out of money provided by Parliament any increase attributable to this Act in the sums payable out of money so provided by virtue of any other enactment.

Commencement

6. This Act shall come into force on such day as Her Majesty may appoint by Order in Council; and different days may be appointed for different purposes.

Short title and extent

7.—(1) This Act may be cited as the Medical (Professional Performance) Act 1995.

(2) This Act extends to Northern Ireland.

Section 4

SCHEDULE

SUPPLEMENTARY AND CONSEQUENTIAL AMENDMENTS

Medical Act 1983

1. The Medical Act 1983 shall be amended as follows.

2. In section 1(3) (committees of the General Medical Council)—

(a) for the words "shall continue to be four" there shall be substituted the words "shall be six";

(b) after the words "the Professional Conduct Committee" there shall be inserted the words ", the Assessment Referral Committee, the Committee on Professional Performance"; and

(c) after the words "assigned to them by" there shall be inserted the words "or under".

3. In section 32 (registration fees), subsection (2)(b) and the word "or" immediately before it shall cease to have effect.

4. In section 35 (General Medical Council's power to advise on conduct or ethics), after the word "conduct" there shall be inserted the words "or performance".

5. In section 36(2) (professional misconduct and criminal offences)—

(a) for the word "42(3)(c)" there shall be, substituted the word "42"; and

(b) after the words "the Preliminary Proceedings Committee" there shall be inserted the words "or the Professional Conduct Committee".

6.(1) Section 37 (unfitness to practice through illness, etc.) shall be amended as follows.

(2) In subsection (2)—

(a) for the word "42(3)(c)" there shall be substituted the word "42"; and

(b) after the words "the Preliminary Proceedings Committee" there shall be inserted the words "or the Health Committee".

(3) In subsection (3)—

(a) in paragraph (b), after the word "expiry" there shall be inserted the words "(or termination under subsection(3B)(b) below)"; and

(b) for the words "; but the Committee shall not" there shall be substituted the words "; but, subject to subsection (3A) below, the Committee shall not".

(4) After subsection (3) there shall be inserted–

"(3A) The Health Committee may give a direction extending a period of suspension indefinitely where—

(a) the period of suspension will, on the date on which the direction takes effect, have lasted for at least two years, and

(b) the direction is given not more than two months before the date on which the period of suspension would otherwise expire.

(3B) Where the Health Committee have given a direction for indefinite suspension, they—

(a) shall review the suspension when requested to do so by the person whose registration is suspended (but not until two years after the date on which the direction takes effect and not more than once in any period of two years), and

(b) having carried out such a review, may direct that the suspension be terminated.".

7.—(1) Section 38 (power to order immediate suspension after a finding of professional misconduct or unfitness to practise) shall be amended as follows.

(2) In subsection (1)—

(a) after the words "36(1) or (2)" there shall be inserted the word ", 36A";

(b) after the words "37(1) or (2) above" there shall be inserted the words ", or under rules made by virtue of paragraph 5A(3) of Schedule 4 to this Act,"; and

(c) after the words "the Professional Conduct Committee" there shall be inserted the words ", the Committee on Professional Performance".

(3) In subsection (2)—

(a) after the words "Schedule 4 to this Act" there shall be inserted the words "or in accordance with rules made by virtue of paragraph 5A(3) of that Schedule"; and

(b) after the words "section 40 below" there shall be inserted the words "or paragraph 5A(4) of that Schedule".

(4) In subsection (3), after the words "the Professional Conduct Committee" there shall be inserted the words ", the Committee on Professional Performance".

8.—(1) Section 40 (appeals) shall be amended as follows.

(2) In subsection (1), after paragraph (a) there shall be inserted—

"(aa) a decision of the Committee on Professional Performance under section 36A above giving a direction for suspension or for conditional registration or varying the conditions imposed by a direction for conditional registration; or".

(3) In subsection (3), after the word "36(6)" there shall be inserted the word ", 36A(7)".

(4) In subsection (4), after paragraph (a) there shall be inserted—

"(aa) of the Committee on Professional Performance under section 36A above;".

(5) In subsection (5), after the words "decision of the" there shall be inserted the words "Committee on Professional Performance or the".

(6) In subsection (6), after the words "the Professional Conduct Committee," there shall be inserted the words "the Committee on Professional Performance,".

(7) In subsection (7)—

(a) after the words "the Professional Conduct Committee", in each place, there shall be inserted the words ", the Committee on Professional Performance"; and

(b) in paragraph (d), after the word "36" there shall be inserted the word ", 36A".

(8) In subsection (11), after the words "the Professional Conduct Committee" there shall be inserted the words ", the Committee on Professional Performance".

9. In section 43 (proceedings before committees), after the words "the Professional Conduct Committee," there shall be inserted the words "the Assessment Referral Committee, the Committee on Professional Performance,".

10. In section 47(3) (appointments not to be held except by fully registered practitioners: effect of suspension)—

(a) after the words "registered person by" there shall be inserted the words "a direction of the Committee on Professional Performance under section 36A above or under rules made by virtue of paragraph 5A(3) of Schedule 4 to this Act,";

(b) for the words "that Committee" there shall be substituted the words "either of those Committees"; and

(c) for the words "of the Preliminary Proceedings Committee under section 42(3)(b)" there shall be substituted the words "under section 42".

11. In section 53(2) (proof of certain instruments), after the words "the Professional Conduct Committee" there shall be inserted the words ", the Committee on Professional Performance".

12. In Part III of Schedule 1 (Committees of the General Medical Council), after paragraph 21 there shall be inserted the following paragraphs—

"The Assessment Referral Committee

21A. The Assessment Referral Committee shall be constituted as provided by the General Council by rules under this paragraph.

The Committee on Professional Performance

21B. The Committee on Professional Performance shall be constituted as provided by the General Council by rules under this paragraph."

13. In that Part of that Schedule, for paragraph 23 there shall be substituted the following paragraph—

"Supplementary

23. Rules under paragraphs 21, 21B, and 22 above shall secure that a person who sits as a member of the Preliminary Proceedings Committee or the Assessment Referral Com-

mittee in proceedings on any case shall not sit as a member of the Professional Conduct Committee, the Committee on Professional Performance or the Health Committee in any subsequent proceedings on that case.".

14. In that Part of that Schedule, in paragraph 24, after the word "21" there shall be inserted the words ", 21A, 21B".

15. In paragraph 1(1) of Schedule 4 (procedure of committees) after the words "the Professional Conduct Committee" there shall be inserted the words ", for the Assessment Referral Committee, for the Committee on Professional Performance".

16. After paragraph 1(2) of that Schedule there shall be inserted—

"(2A) Rules made under this paragraph for the Assessment Referral Committee shall include provision—

(a) conferring on the Committee such functions as may be specified in the rules in relation to the handling of complaints about standards of professional performance;

(b) securing that before any case is considered by the Committee it shall have been considered by a member of the General Council appointed for the purpose by the Council and referred by that person to the Committee;

(c) securing that notice that the proceedings are to be brought shall be given, at such time and in such manner as may be specified in the rules, to the person to whose registration the proceedings relate;

(d) securing that any party to the proceedings shall, if he so requires, be entitled to be heard by the Committee;

(e) enabling any party to the proceedings to be represented by counsel or a solicitor, or (if the rules so provide and the party so elects) by a person of such other description as may be specified in the rules;

(f) requiring proceedings before the Committee to be held in private;

(g) for service on the person concerned of notice of any decision taken in relation to him by the Committee.

(2B) Rules made under this paragraph for the Committee on Professional Performance shall include provision—

(a) securing that where—

(i) proceedings relating to a person's registration have been held before the Assessment Referral Committee, and

(ii) an assessment has been carried out in accordance with a direction of that Committee,

the standard of that person's professional performance, shall, if he so requests, be considered by the Committee on Professional Performance;

(b) securing that notice that the proceedings are to be brought shall be given, at such time and in such manner as may be specified in the rules, to the person to whose registration the proceedings relate;

(c) securing that any party to the proceedings shall, if he so requires, be entitled to be heard by the Committee;

(d) enabling any party to the proceedings to be represented by counsel or a solicitor, or (if the rules so provide and the party so elects) by a person of such other description as may be specified in the rules;

(e) determining when proceedings before the Committee are to be held in public and when in private (including provision securing that proceedings are held in public if the person to whose registration they relate so requests).

17. In paragraph 2 of that Schedule (administration of oaths), after the words "the Professional Conduct Committee", in each place, there shall be inserted the words ", the Assessment Referral Committee, the Committee on Professional Performance".

18. In paragraph 3 of that Schedule (validity of proceedings)—

(a) after the words "of the Professional Conduct Committee," there shall be inserted the words "of the Assessment Referral Committee, of the Committee on Professional Performance,"; and

(b) after the words "before the Professional Conduct Committee," there shall be inserted the words "the Assessment Referral Committee, the Committee on Professional Performance,".

19. In paragraph 4 of that Schedule (transfer of cases to Health Committee)—

(a) in sub-paragraph (1), after the words "the Professional Conduct Committee" there shall be inserted the words ", the Assessment Referral Committee or the Committee on Professional Performance";

(b) in paragraphs (2) and (3), in each place, after the words "the Professional Conduct Committee" there shall be inserted the words ", the Assessment Referral Committee or, as the case may be, the Committee on Professional Performance".

20. After paragraph 5 of that Schedule there shall be inserted—

"Professional performance: assessments

5A. (1) The General Council may make rules—

(a) authorising the giving of directions by any of—

(i) the Assessment Referral Committee,

(ii) the Committee on Professional Performance,

(iii) such other persons as may be specified in, the rules,

requiring an assessment of the standard of a registered person's professional performance to be carried out;

(b) specifying circumstances in which such an assessment may be carried out otherwise than in accordance with a direction.

(2) An assessment carried out by virtue of this paragraph shall be carried out by an Assessment Panel in accordance with rules under this paragraph; and the rules shall, in particular, provide—

(a) for the constitution and proceedings of Assessment Panels;

(b) for the procedures to be followed by such panels in carrying out assessments;

(c) for the procedures to be followed following the making of a report by an Assessment Panel.

(3) Rules under this paragraph may authorise the Committee on Professional Performance to make directions of a kind which may be made under section 36A of this Act, for the suspension of or the attachment of conditions to a person's registration, where the person fails to comply with reasonable requirements imposed by an Assessment Panel for the purposes of carrying out an assessment of the standard of his professional performance in accordance with a direction of the Committee.

(4) An appeal shall lie to the court (within the meaning of section 38 of this Act) from any direction of the Committee on Professional Performance given by virtue of sub-paragraph (3) above, and on an appeal under this sub-paragraph the court may—

(a) quash the direction,

(b) substitute for the direction any other direction which the Committee could have made, or

(c) remit a case to the Committee to be disposed of in accordance with the court's directions;

and the decision of the court on any appeal under this sub-paragraph shall be final.

(5) An Assessment Panel, for the purposes of carrying out an assessment of the standard of a person's professional performance—

(a) may require the production of, inspect and take copies of any records (in whatever form they are held) arising out of or relating to the person's professional practice;

(b) where such records are kept otherwise than in legible form, may require a copy of them to be given to the panel in legible form.

(6) A person who, without reasonable excuse, obstructs an Assessment Panel in the execution of their powers under sub-paragraph (5) above shall be guilty of an offence and liable on summary conviction to a fine not exceeding level 3 on the standard scale.

(7) Nothing in this paragraph shall require or permit any disclosure of information which is prohibited by or under any other enactment; but where information is held in a form in which the prohibition operates by reason of the fact that the information is capable of identifying an individual, an Assessment Panel may, in exercising their powers under sub-paragraph (5) above, require that the information be put into a form in which it is not capable of identifying an individual.

(8) Sub-paragraphs (4) and (5) of paragraph 1 above shall apply in relation to rules made under this paragraph as they, apply in relation to rules under that paragraph.

5B. (1) A justice of the peace (including, in Scotland, a sheriff) may issue a warrant under this paragraph if satisfied by the evidence on oath of at least two members of an Assessment Panel that there are reasonable grounds for suspecting that the panel will require a warrant for the purposes of carrying out an assessment required by virtue of rules made under paragraph 5A above.

(2) A warrant under this paragraph shall authorise one or more members of the Assessment Panel (who must, if so required, produce documents identifying themselves) together with any constables—

(a) to enter any building specified in the warrant, but not a dwelling-house, using such force as is reasonably necessary for the purpose, and

(b) to search the premises for the purposes of the exercise of the powers under paragraph 5A(5) above.

(3) A warrant under this paragraph shall continue in force until the end of the period of 21 days beginning with the day on which it is issued.

(4) A person who intentionally obstructs the exercise of any rights conferred by a warrant issued under this paragraph shall be guilty of an offence and liable on summary conviction to a fine not exceeding level 3 on the standard scale.".

21. In paragraph 7 of that Schedule (legal assessors)—

(a) in sub-paragraph (1), after the words "the Professional Conduct Committee," there shall be inserted the words "the Assessment Referral Committee, the Committee on Professional Performance,"; and

(b) in sub-paragraph (4), after the words "the Professional Conduct Committee" there shall be inserted the words ", the Assessment Referral Committee, the Committee on Professional Performance".

22. In paragraph 8(1) of that Schedule (service of notifications of decisions)—

(a) after the word "36(6)," there shall be inserted the word "36A(7),"; and

(b) after the word "42(5)" there shall be inserted the words "or (6C)".

23. In paragraph 9 of that Schedule (extension of time for appealing), after the word "36(6)," there shall be inserted the word "36A(7),".

24. In paragraph 10(1) of that Schedule (taking effect of directions for erasure, suspension or conditional registration and of variations of conditions of registration)—

(a) after the words "section 36 of this Act," there shall be inserted the words "a direction for suspension or for conditional registration given by the Committee on Professional Performance under section 36A of this Act,";

(b) for the words "either Committee" there shall be substituted the words "any of those Committees"; and

(c) for the words "or 37" there shall be substituted the words ", 36A or 37".

25. In paragraph 11 of that Schedule (continuation of suspensions and conditions where supplementary direction given)—

(a) in sub-paragraph (1), after the word "36" there, shall be inserted the word ", 36A"; and

(b) in sub-paragraph (3)—

(i) after the word "36" there shall be inserted the word ", 36A"; and

(ii) for the words "that section," there shall be substituted the words "section 36 or 37 or subsection (2) or(6) of section 36A,".

26. In paragraph 12 of that Schedule (recording of directions for suspension or conditional registration), after the word "36" there shall be inserted the word ", 36A".

27. In paragraph 13 of that Schedule (meaning of "party"), after the words "the Professional Conduct Committee" there shall be inserted the words ", the Assessment Referral Committee, the Committee on Professional Performance".

National Health Service Act 1977

28. In section 29 of the National Health Service Act 1977 (arrangements and regulations for general medical services)—

(a) in subsection (8)(c), for the words "of the Preliminary Proceedings Committee of the Council under section 42(3)(b)" there shall be substituted the words "under section 42"; and

(b) after subsection (8) there shall be added—

"(9) Where the registration of a medical practitioner in the register of medical practitioners is suspended by a direction of the Committee on Professional Performance of the General Medical Council—

(a) under section 36A of the Medical Act 1983 (professional performance),

(b) under section 38(1) of that Act (order for immediate suspension), or

(c) under rules made by virtue of paragraph 5A(3) of Schedule 4 to that Act (procedure of committees),

the suspension shall not, except in so far as is provided by or determined in accordance with regulations under subsection (2) above, terminate any arrangements made with him for the provision of general medical services; but he shall not provide such services in person during the suspension.".

National Health Service (Scotland) Act 1978

29. In section 19 of the National Health Service (Scotland) Act 1978 (arrangements and regulations for general medical services)—

(a) in subsection (7)(c), for the words "of the Preliminary Proceedings Committee of the Council under section 42(3)(b)" there shall be substituted the words "under section 42"; and

(b) after subsection (7) there shall be added—

"(7A) Where the registration of a medical practitioner in the register of medical practitioners is suspended by a direction of the Committee on Professional Performance of the General Medical Council—

(a) under section 36A of the Medical Act 1983 (professional performance),

(b) under section 38(1) of that Act (order for immediate suspension), or

(c) under rules made by virtue of paragraph 5A(3) of Schedule 4 to that Act (procedure of committees),

the suspension shall not, except in so far as is provided by or determined in accordance with regulations under subsection (2) above, terminate any arrangements made with him for the provision of general medical services; but he shall not provide such services in person during the suspension.".

Health and Personal Social Services (Northern Ireland) Order 1972

30. In Article 56 of the Health and Personal Social Services (Northern Ireland) Order 1972 (arrangements and regulations for general medical services)—

(a) in paragraph (4C)(c), for the words "of the Preliminary Proceedings Committee of the Council under section 42(3)(b)" there shall be substituted the words "under section 42"; and

(b) after paragraph (4C) there shall be added—

"(4D) Where the registration of a medical practitioner in the register of medical practitioners is suspended by a direction of the Committee on Professional Performance of the General Medical Council—

(a) under section 36A of the Medical Act 1983 (professional performance),

(b) under section 38(1) of that Act (order for immediate suspension), or

(c) under rules made by virtue of paragraph 5A(3) of Schedule 4 to that Act (procedure of committees),

the suspension shall not, except in so far as is provided by or determined in accordance with regulations under subsection (2) above, terminate any arrangements made with him for the provision of general medical services; but he shall not provide such services in person during the suspension.".

Para. 3

This removes a potential loophole whereby an unscrupulous doctor could have avoided the requirement for approval of the relevant committee prior to restoration of his name to the register under s.31A(2) by *de facto* voluntary erasure under s.32(2)(b) and automatic restoration under s.32(3).

Para. 6

This amends s.37 of the Medical Act 1983 so that the Health Committee has additional powers to extend the period of suspension of a doctor's registration indefinitely.

Para. 12

This provides for the establishment of the ARC and the CPP.

Para. 16

This provides the machinery for the working of the ARC and CPP. Of interest are the provisions concerned with whether or not the proceedings before the CPP are to be public or private. Proceedings are held in public if the doctor concerned (but not the complainant) so requests. The reasons for this asymmetry is that the case concerns the doctor and whether he should continue to practise. His livelihood is at stake so under the European Convention on Human Rights he is entitled to a fair and *public* hearing. When hearings are normally to be held in private the doctor's right to a public hearing must be reserved. The Professional Conduct Committee meets in public except when it may sit *in camera*, when for example, a minor is giving evidence. The Health Committee invariably sits *in camera* (see *Hansard*, H.L. Vol. 566, col. 497).

Para. 19

This provides for the transfer of a case from the ARC or the CPP to the Health Committee.

Para. 20

This provides extensive powers of investigation for the Assessment Panel.

Para. 28

This amends the National Health Service Act 1977 (c. 49) so as to provide some protection for the livelihood of the general practitioner when suspended, but safeguarding the interests of the patients.

INDEX

References in roman type are to sections and the schedules: those in italic are to sections of the Medical Act 1983 (as amended)

MENTAL HEALTH (PATIENTS IN THE COMMUNITY) ACT 1995*

(1995 c. 52)

ARRANGEMENT OF SECTIONS

England and Wales

An Act to make provision for certain mentally disordered patients in England and Wales to receive after-care under supervision after leaving hospital; to provide for the making of community care orders in the case of certain mentally disordered patients in Scotland; to amend the law relating to mentally disordered patients absent without leave or on leave of absence from hospital; and for connected purposes. [8th November 1995]

PARLIAMENTARY DEBATES

Hansard, H.L. Vol. 562, col. 933; Vol. 563, cols. 97, 322, 1208, 1286; Vol. 564, col. 171. H.C. Vol. 262, col. 157; Vol. 264, col. 1156.

INTRODUCTION AND GENERAL NOTE

The main purpose of this Act is to provide a system of supervision of the care in the community of certain patients who have been detained in hospital in England and Wales under the Mental Health Act 1983 (c. 20) or in Scotland under the Mental Health (Scotland) Act 1984 (c. 36). In England and Wales this is to be achieved through after-care under supervision and in Scotland through community care orders. The differences between the provisions for England and Wales and those for Scotland reflect the differences between the respective mental health systems and between the 1983 Act and the 1984 Act.

The Act also extends the period during which, under the 1983 Act or the 1984 Act, certain patients who are absent without leave may be taken into custody and returned. It also removes the present six-month limit on the period for which patients detailed in hospital in England and Wales may be given leave of absence and for patients in Scotland it restricts to one year the total period of leave of absence which may be granted.

Supervised discharge and extended leave of absence form part of the 10-point plan for "a safe and successful policy of community care" for mentally ill people; announced by the Secretary of State for Health in August 1993. This announcement followed a Department of Health review of the legal powers regarding the care of mentally ill people in the community (Legal Powers on the Care of Mentally Ill People in the Community, 1993, hereinafter referred to as the "Internal Review").

The 10-point plan did not apply to Scotland. Certain elements of it, such as the establishment of supervision registers for vulnerable people, have not, so far, been taken up there. However the Scottish Office was concerned that, although arrangements for care and supervision of patients in the community generally appeared to be working well, the legality of some of those arrangements could be called into question, in particular the use by some psychiatrists of

*Annotations by Richard Jones, M.A., Solicitor and Hilary Patrick, Solicitor, Legal Adviser, the Scottish Association for Mental Health.

extended leave of absence as a way of ensuring the compulsory medical treatment of patients in the community.

The restriction of leave of absence to one year left a gap which the community care order was intended to fill.

ENGLAND AND WALES

Supervised discharge

The people for whom after-care under supervision is targeted have been described as "the small group of so-called revolving door patients. Typically, such a patient will be someone who: is compulsorily admitted to hospital for treatment for mental illness; responds to the treatment and improves; is discharged into the community with a care plan; fails to continue to comply with the care plan, and consequently deteriorates; is formally re-admitted to hospital, where the whole cycle begins again" (Internal Review, para. 2.1). The Government took the view that this group of patients, 20 or so in each Health District (*per* Mr. John Bowis M.P., Parliamentary Under-Secretary of State for Health, *Hansard*, H.C. Vol. 262, col. 183), needed "an especially high degree of supervision" (*ibid.* Standing Committee F, col. 93) if they are to live successfully in community settings.

The potential benefits to patients of an increased level of supervision was not the sole factor which prompted this legislation. The Government, it was said,

> "must never forget our obligation to reassure the public as a whole that such supervised care will be effective, because without public confidence and support, mental health policy cannot function in the interests of patients. It is a chicken-and-egg scenario—the egg of mental health policy and the chicken of supportive public opinion" (*Hansard*, H.C. Vol. 262, col. 157).

The approach that has been adopted is to produce a mechanism which requires patients who are subject to the after-care provisions contained in s.117 of the 1983 Act to receive their after-care services under supervision. "The central principle of the Bill is that supervision cannot be separated from the after-care services which it exists to support" (*per* Baroness Cumberlege, Parliamentary Under-Secretary of State for Health, *Hansard*, H.L. Vol. 564, col. 189). Such supervision will "reflect the objectives of the care programme approach and be part of a comprehensive multi-disciplinary approach to care", *ibid.* col. 1243.

The procedure for after-care under supervision set out in new ss.25A to 25J of the 1983 Act reflects the fact that it "must be health led . . . and will involve health decisions on discharge and management—largely taken by health workers, especially community psychiatric nurses" (*per* Mr. John Bowis M.P., Standing Committee F, col. 93). An application for supervision can only be made in respect of mentally disordered patients aged 16 or over who, after leaving hospital, will receive after-care services under s.117. The application is made by the patient's responsible medical officer and addressed to the Health Authority which is to be responsible (with the appropriate local authority) for providing after-care services for the patient. Before accepting the application, the Health Authority is required to consult with the local authority. The responsible medical officer must be satisfied that the application is justified by the risk of harm or serious exploitation to the patient, or by the risk to other people. Prior to submitting the application, the responsible medical officer must consult widely (consultation is a significant feature at other stages in the procedure) and find an approved social worker and a doctor to provide supporting recommendations.

The application must identify who is to be the patient's community responsible medical officer and the patient's supervisor. The community responsible medical officer, who must be approved under s.12 of the 1983 Act as having special experience in the diagnosis or treatment of mental disorder, is responsible for the medical care of the patient in the community. The supervisor, who must be a person who is professionally concerned with any of the after-care services provided to the patient, has a responsibility to ensure that the patient receives after-care services.

The application will be accompanied by a copy of the patient's after-care plan and will identify any requirements that the patient has to abide by. The requirements that can be imposed on the patient relate to place of residence and attendance for medical treatment, occupation, education or training. If a patient refuses to comply with a requirement, he can be "taken and conveyed" to the place where he is required to be.

If a patient refuses to receive after-care services, or fails to comply with a requirement, the Health Authority and local authority are required to review both services and requirements. If they consider that it might be appropriate for the patient to return to hospital for treatment under s.3 of the 1983 Act, an approved social worker will be informed.

Supervision will last for an initial period of six months, after which it may be reviewed (if the conditions for renewal are satisfied) for a further period of six months and subsequently for periods of a year at a time. The supervision will end if the community responsible medical officer so directs, or if the patient is detained under s.3 of the 1983 Act, or is received into guardianship.

Patients must be informed of their rights to apply to a Mental Health Review Tribunal for supervision to be terminated (see s.66 of the 1983 Act as amended by Sched. 1, para. 7 of this Act). A tribunal considering an application from a patient detained in hospital for treatment may, if it does not discharge the patient itself, recommend that the patient's responsible medical officer considers making an application for after-care under supervision.

It will be sometime before the effectiveness of after-care under supervision can be judged. In the meantime it is appropriate to reflect on the concerns expressed by the Internal Review that;

"legal powers can never be a substitute for properly planned and delivered services, that the solutions of choice are those which are agreed with the patient and take the maximum account of his or her wishes and aspirations, and that any legal power should be used only to the minimum extent necessary to support the achievement of its aim" (para. 8.19).

Comparison with Guardianship

The Mental Health Act Commission in its evidence to the House of Commons Health Committee's Inquiry into Supervision Orders said that in its view;

"there are sufficient powers in the Mental Health Act which, if used properly, would be able to address the needs of the majority of the identified group of patients. The problem is that they are not being utilised properly in many cases and in particular, guardianship is currently (as it has been for the last thirty years) severely under-utilised" (MHAC, May 1993, para. 4*a*).

Guardianship was also considered by the Internal Review who concluded that they "cannot see guardianship offering a ready answer to the problems of the patients with whom we have been concerned. They are, in particular, a group whose *health* care needs are of central importance, and this suggests that local authorities may not be best placed (and may find it difficult) to take the lead in their care" (para. 7.4).

Apart from the contentious power to "take and convey", the requirements that can be attached to after-care under supervision are almost identical to the powers given to a patient's guardian by s.8 of the 1983 Act. The principal difference between the two powers can be found in the procedure for making applications. As the Mental Health Act Commission has pointed out; "[in] many ways after-care under supervision can with reasonable fairness be characterised as a form of medical guardianship—the applicant is the patient's doctor and not an approved social worker and the application for its imposition is made to the relevant District Health Authority and not a Local Authority" (MHAC, Memorandum to the Secretary of State on the Mental Health (Patients in the Community) Bill 1995, p. 3).

Other distinguishing factors are: (i) while guardianship is a "freestanding" power that can be used whether or not the patient has been detained, an application for supervision can only be made in respect of detained patients who are about to leave hospital, and (ii) if a patient under guardianship refuses medical treatment for mental disorder there is a power to transfer him to hospital under r.8(3) of the Mental Health (Hospital, Guardianship and Consent to Treatment) Regulations 1983: a similar procedure does not exist for patients under supervision.

The Government's view is that guardianship is suited to patients with "a lower risk factor and fewer medical needs" than patients who will be subject to supervision which will have "a different focus from guardianship and can work alongside it" (*per* Baroness Miller, *Hansard*, H.L. Vol. 563, col. 1263). The Mental Health Act Commission has expressed the hope that "in appropriate cases doctors will not feel compelled by the new provisions to ignore the possible use of guardianship as an alternative" (MHAC, Public Position Paper on the Mental Health (Patients in the Community) Bill 1995, para. 2.5).

Jurisdiction of the Mental Health Act Commission

In its Public Position Paper on the Bill, *ibid.* the Mental Health Act Commission advocated that consideration should be given by Parliament to:

"[an] extension of its remit to patients under supervised after-care so as to enable it to ensure (so far as possible)—that the new powers are correctly exercised and applied in strict accordance with the statutory requirements, and that, by a process of observation and monitoring over the years, the use of the powers is of benefit to the patients involved and to the community into which the patients have been discharged" (para. 3.1).

Although the Government resisted various attempts that were made to amend the Bill to extend the Commission's remit, the Commission's existing remit enables it to monitor after-care under supervision as follows: (i) under s.120(1) of the 1983 Act the Secretary of State has delegated to the Commission his duty to "keep under review the exercise of the powers and the discharge of the duties conferred or imposed by this Act so far as relating to the detention of patients or to patients liable to be detained under this Act". As an application for after-care under supervision can only be made in respect of a detained patient, that part of this Act which is concerned with the making of applications comes within the Commissions remit; (ii) the Commission has the power to visit and interview detained patients who are subject to supervision applications (s.120(1)(a) of the 1983 Act); and, (iii) the Commission can investigate a complaint made by a patient or other person about the exercise of the powers of supervised discharge in so far as the complaint arises from a period when the patient was detained or liable to be detained (s.120(1)(b)(ii) of the 1983 Act).

As s.1 of this Act is incorporated into the 1983 Act, the exercise of any powers or duties conferred by s.1 can be the subject of a complaint made to the Commission.

SCOTLAND

Community care orders

As in England, community care orders are intended for the small category of people suffering from a serious mental illness, who after discharge from hospital fail to continue to take their medication or to co-operate with their care plan, often resulting in repeated re-admissions to hospital, and posing a risk both to their own health and, sometimes, to other people.

New clauses 35A to 35K are inserted in the Mental Health (Scotland) Act 1984. The responsible medical officer may apply for a community care order for a patient admitted to hospital under s.18 of the 1984 Act or under a hospital order without restrictions, if he believes the patient could be discharged from hospital provided arrangements were set up to ensure his treatment and support in the community. An application cannot be made for a community care order until the patient has been liable to detention for at least 28 days.

The application is made to the sheriff, supported by a second medical opinion and a report from a mental health officer of the local authority, setting out the care which is proposed for the patient in the community. The patient will have been consulted on the care plan, together with those most involved in his medical treatment, his nearest relative (unless the patient objects) and his principal carers, both professional and unpaid. These people will also be consulted and kept informed if there are plans to change or discharge any order which is made.

If the sheriff approves the order, it will set out the conditions which should apply to the patient and will name his "special medical officer" in the community and his "after-care officer", who will be a mental health officer from the local authority responsible for co-ordinating his social care. The sheriff may require changes in the care plan before giving his approval, and may adjourn the hearing until the necessary arrangements have been put in place. The initial order will apply for six months, after which it may be renewed by the special medical officer for six months, and, if appropriate, at yearly intervals thereafter.

The patient can appear at the hearing of the application, as can his nearest relative, and he may appeal to the sheriff against the order at any time after its renewal. Any variation in the order has to be approved by the sheriff. The patient must be consulted about any variation, but neither the patient, his carers, nearest relative or the after-care officer has the right to apply to the sheriff for a variation. The special medical officer takes the final decision whether to apply for a variation. The patient has the right to apply to the Mental Welfare Commission for Scotland for a revocation of the order.

Community care orders are not available for restricted "Secretary of State" patients, whose discharge is a matter for the Secretary of State for Scotland.

If the patient's health deteriorates following the making of a community care order, the doctors can examine him and may readmit him to hospital for assessment for up to seven days. There is no right of appeal against such a recall to hospital. The patient may be kept in hospital for a further 21 days if the responsible medical officer applies for his admission under s.18 of the 1984 Act.

The special medical officer must keep the patient's condition under review at all times and must revoke the order if he feels it is no longer necessary. Full consultation is necessary before this and he must inform the patient's nearest relative, carers and the Mental Welfare Commission of any revocation.

Background to the legislation

Some psychiatrists in Scotland have used extended leave of absence (under s.27 of the 1984 Act) as a way to ensure that patients can live in the community and continue to take their medication. A patient who has been admitted to hospital under s.18 of the Act is later allowed to live outside the hospital under the direction of the responsible medical officer. If the patient fails to take his medication or to comply with the conditions of the leave, he can be brought back to hospital immediately, being still "liable to detention" under the 1984 Act.

The numbers of patients on extended leave of absence was small (over 101 people had been on leave of absence for over 12 months at the end of 1994: Mental Welfare Commission for Scotland, *Annual Report*, 1994–5), but the Government was advised that this use of the 1984 Act was open to legal challenge.

A judgment of Sheriff Younger in 1987 (*A.B. and C.D. v. E.*, 1987 S.C.L.R. 419) cast doubt on the use of leave of absence for patients who did not require any degree of in-patient treatment. This closely followed the arguments in the English case, *R. v. Hallstrom, ex p. W. (No. 2)* [1986] 2 All E.R. 306 which (on similar wording in the 1983 Act) held that the need for in-patient treatment was a requirement for renewing the authority for detention.

Compulsory medical treatment in the community (originally proposed by the Royal College of Psychiatrists in 1987 and later rejected by them in favour of a form of compulsory supervision order) was rejected by the Department of Health Internal Review (see the general introduction to this Act on page 52–1) and also by the Scottish Office, because it "raised far reaching human rights questions" (*per* Lord James Douglas-Hamilton M.P., Minister of State, Scottish Office, *Hansard*, Standing Committee F, col. 167).

The decision to limit leave of absence to one year in Scotland has met with some opposition, notably from the Mental Welfare Commission for Scotland, the body which has "protective functions" over all people with a mental disorder who are, because of a mental disorder, unable adequately to protect themselves. In its *Annual Report* 1994–5 the Commission argued that "community care orders are flawed in that there is no sanction against non-compliance", because a patient could not be forced to take his medication.

The Government said that, in proposing the replacement of unlimited leave of absence with community care orders, it had to:

> "weigh up the issues regarding human rights and civil liberties of the individual with a mental disorder. At the same time, we cannot lose sight of the rights and liberties of the members of the public to whom we also have a duty. So far as possible, we should seek to keep any danger to the public at large to an absolute minimum. But we wish to maintain the civil liberties of the patients with mental illness as best we can." (*per* Lord Fraser of Carmyllie, Minister of State, the Scottish Office, *Hansard*, H.L. Vol. 562, col. 978).

The Scottish provisions reflect the main thrust of the conclusions of the English Department of Health's Internal Review. In particular, they emphasise the following points:

(i) The importance of a multi-disciplinary approach. While the application is made by the responsible medical officer, he is to consult fully with the patient, his nearest relative, the local authority mental health officer and any paid or informal carers of the patient. Decisions on review, renewal or revocation of the order also require such consultation.

This reflects the Government's support for the Care Programme Approach, which requires health boards and local authorities to draw up plans to show how they will provide care for people with a long term mental illness. Community care orders provide;

> "[a] statutory underpinning of the Care Programme Approach for those particularly vulnerable people with a mental disorder who, unless properly cared for, may be a risk to themselves or others. Of course, legal powers alone do not provide the answer and must be supplemented by good practice and good inter-agency working" (*per* Lord James Douglas-Hamilton, Standing Committee F, col. 130).

(ii) The need for a health led power. "Guardianship [under s.36 of the 1984 Act] is essentially an arrangement which is oriented towards social care. I believe that these sets of provisions, whether they apply in England, Wales or Scotland, are based separately: they are centred upon the health service; they are rooted in a Care Programme Approach" (*per* Lord Fraser of Carmyllie, *Hansard*, H.L. Vol. 562, col. 979).

> "Community care orders are designed to control behaviour patterns and enable somebody with medical treatment to live a fairly normal life. Guardianship is designed to look after the day-to-day affairs of somebody, perhaps because of learning difficulties or for other reasons" (*per* the Earl of Lindsay, *Hansard*, H.L. Vol. 563, col. 359).

(iii) The importance of gaining the co-operation of the patient and any carers. "We would not wish to introduce a set of arrangements which, because they necessarily contained within them a degree of coercion or compulsion, would thereby damage therapeutic relationships. That would clearly be very unsatisfactory. Ultimately, the effectiveness of the treatment and care given under the provision of the Bill will depend on the co-operation of the patient. That is why the principle of consulting the patient is so firmly enshrined. We believe that with the patients whose

needs the Bill addresses a measure of legal backing is nevertheless justified, but we do not see that as undermining the principle that treatment relies primarily on co-operation." (*per* Lord Fraser of Carmyllie, *Hansard*, H.L. Vol. 562, col. 977).

Community care orders are based on similar principles to the supervised discharge arrangements which the Act imposes for England and Wales. The general introduction on page 52–1 will, therefore, be of interest to Scottish readers. However there are differences, some reflecting the different legal and mental health systems, others more fundamental. The most important are:

(i) Power to recall to hospital. If the mental health of a patient on a community care order deteriorates so as to give cause for serious concerns about his health or safety or that of others, he may be readmitted to hospital for up to seven days for assessment, against his will if necessary. While in hospital he becomes subject to the compulsory treatment provisions of Pt. X of the 1984 Act. If the doctors decide he needs to stay in hospital, he may be kept there for a further 21 days while an application for admission is made under s.18 of the 1984 Act.

No such power is available under the English part of the Act. If a patient's mental health deteriorates while he is on supervised discharge, the doctors would have to wait to see whether his condition deteriorated further until he became detainable under the existing provisions of the 1983 Act.

(ii) Greater powers to the Mental Welfare Commission. The Mental Welfare Commission for Scotland exercises protective functions over everyone with a mental disorder who needs help, in hospital or in the community, not just detained patients, as is the case with the Mental Health Act Commission in England and Wales. The Commission is to be kept informed and notified at all stages and is given the power to discharge the patient from the community care order (mirroring its powers to discharge patients from detention under s.33(3) of the 1984 Act).

(iii) Greater freedom to the sheriff to fix conditions of order. The Act spells out the conditions which can apply to a patient subject to supervised discharge; residence, attending for medical treatment or day-care and the granting of access to certain people, such as social workers, doctors and nurses (new s.25D(3) of the 1983 Act). This is not the case in the Scottish part of the Act.

The application for an order is made to the sheriff, who can make "such orders as he thinks fit" to ensure that the patient receives medical treatment and after-care following hospitalisation. There is, therefore, greater flexibility to the sheriff to tailor the order to meet the needs of the individual. Whether this will make much difference in practice is hard to tell.

(iv) No power to take and convey in Scotland. Concern was expressed in Parliament as to whether the power to take and convey can apply in Scotland (see note to the new s.25D of the 1983 Act below). It does not appear on the face of the Act, but it was argued that it was not clear whether the sheriff could impose such a condition in a community care order.

It was not the intention of the Government that a power to take and convey to community institutions be imposed in the Scottish part of the Act. The only intention expressed in Parliament was that a person who was recalled to hospital under the reassessment provisions of s.35G could be conveyed there. Lord James Douglas-Hamilton said that: "The direction to attend hospital for reassessment in such cases [under s.35G] constitutes sufficient authority to convey a person to hospital, and an additional power to convey as proposed in England and Wales is not considered necessary." (*Hansard*, H.C. Vol. 264, col. 1173).

Need for a new Mental Health Act for Scotland

As community care for people with a mental illness develops in Scotland, the 1984 Act, which is based on admission to hospital, will become increasingly inappropriate. It was argued in Parliament that what was needed was a fundamental review of mental health law in Scotland to see how it could best meet the needs of patients and society. The author understands that such a review is now to take place. The Government spokesman, Lord Fraser of Carmyllie, said that the Government was of the view that:

> "we wish to take stock of the new powers [in the Patients in the Community Act] before considering any further fundamental changes. However, as has been pointed out more than once, it is recognised that there are, and will continue to be, changes with more and more people appropriately being treated within the community." (*Hansard*, H.L. Vol. 562, col. 979).

Abbreviations

Internal Review: Legal Powers on the Care of Mentally Ill People in the Community, 1993, Department of Health.

MHAC:	Mental Health Act Commission.
The 1983 Act:	Mental Health Act 1983 (c. 20).
The 1984 Act:	Mental Health (Scotland) Act 1984 (c. 36).

COMMENCEMENT

This Act will come into force on April 1, 1996 (s.7(2)).

England and Wales

After-care under supervision

1.—(1) After section 25 of the Mental Health Act 1983 there shall be inserted the following sections—

"After-care under supervision

Application for supervision

25A.—(1) Where a patient—

(a) is liable to be detained in a hospital in pursuance of an application for admission for treatment; and

(b) has attained the age of 16 years,

an application may be made for him to be supervised after he leaves hospital, for the period allowed by the following provisions of this Act, with a view to securing that he receives the after-care services provided for him under section 117 below.

(2) In this Act an application for a patient to be so supervised is referred to as a "supervision application"; and where a supervision application has been duly made and accepted under this Part of this Act in respect of a patient and he has left hospital, he is for the purposes of this Act "subject to after-care under supervision" (until he ceases to be so subject in accordance with the provisions of this Act).

(3) A supervision application shall be made in accordance with this section and sections 25B and 25C below.

(4) A supervision application may be made in respect of a patient only on the grounds that—

(a) he is suffering from mental disorder, being mental illness, severe mental impairment, psychopathic disorder or mental impairment;

(b) there would be a substantial risk of serious harm to the health or safety of the patient or the safety of other persons, or of the patient being seriously exploited, if he were not to receive the after-care services to be provided for him under section 117 below after he leaves hospital; and

(c) his being subject to after-care under supervision is likely to help to secure that he receives the after-care services to be so provided.

(5) A supervision application may be made only by the responsible medical officer.

(6) A supervision application in respect of a patient shall be addressed to the Health Authority which will have the duty under section 117 below to provide after-care services for the patient after he leaves hospital.

(7) Before accepting a supervision application in respect of a patient a Health Authority shall consult the local social services authority which will also have that duty.

(8) Where a Health Authority accept a supervision application in respect of a patient the Health Authority shall—

(a) inform the patient both orally and in writing—

(i) that the supervision application has been accepted; and

(ii) of the effect in his case of the provisions of this Act relating to a patient subject to after-care under supervision (including, in particular, what rights of applying to a Mental Health Review Tribunal are available);

(b) inform any person whose name is stated in the supervision application in accordance with sub-paragraph (i) of paragraph (e) of section 25B(5) below that the supervision application has been accepted; and

(c) inform in writing any person whose name is so stated in accordance with sub-paragraph (ii) of that paragraph that the supervision application has been accepted.

(9) Where a patient in respect of whom a supervision application is made is granted leave of absence from a hospital under section 17 above (whether before or after the supervision application is made), references in—

(a) this section and the following provisions of this Part of this Act; and

(b) Part V of this Act,

to his leaving hospital shall be construed as references to his period of leave expiring (otherwise than on his return to the hospital or transfer to another hospital).

General Note

This section, which should be read together with sections 25B and 25C, identifies who can be made subject to an application for after-care under supervision, who can make an application, and what grounds must be satisfied if an application is to be made.

It applies to patients who are subject to hospital orders and their equivalent made under Pt. III of the 1983 Act (Sched. 1, Pt. 1, paras. 2, 8A) but not to patients who are subject to restriction orders (s.41(3)(aa) of the 1983 Act, as inserted by Sched. 1, para. 5 of this Act).

Subs. (1)

Liable to be detained... for treatment. This is under s.3 of the 1983 Act. There is no need for the patient to have had a history of previous compulsory admissions. Although the patient must be liable to be detained at the time when the application is made, there is nothing to prevent the patient from subsequently attaining informal status. Section 117 would apply to such a patient on his eventual discharge from hospital (s.117(1)).

Age of 16 years. It might be possible to bring proceedings under s. 31 and Sched. 5, para. 5 of the Children Act 1989 (c. 41) in respect of a child under 16 who requires supervision and control in the community as a consequence of mental disorder.

An application. The application must be made before the patient leaves hospital or before his period of leave of absence under s.17 of the 1983 Act has expired. In the latter case the effect of the application is "suspended" until the leave has expired (subs. (9)).

Period allowed. See s.25G.

Subs. (2)

And he has left hospital. Although s.117 is a continuing duty in respect of any patient who may be discharged and falls within that section (*R. v. Ealing District Health Authority, ex p. Fox* [1993] 3 All E.R. 170), a supervision application does not come into effect until the patient has left hospital.

Until he ceases to be so subject. See s.25H.

Subs. (4)

Para. (a)

Severe mental impairment, psychopathic disorder and mental impairment are defined in s.1(2) of the 1983 Act.

Para. (b)

Substantial risk of serious harm. A risk of harm would not be sufficient.

Health. The risk to health can be either physical or mental.

Seriously exploited. Baroness Cumberlege, on responding to a criticism that this phase is "capable of many interpretations" said;

"[we] are trying to identify a small group of mentally disordered patients whose care in the community is less effective than it should be because of a repeating pattern in which they fail to comply with their treatment plan and then have to be readmitted to hospital. There will be mentally disordered patients who are at risk of exploitation who will fall into this group. Such risks might be that they could be lured into prostitution or that they are exposed to the risks of drug abuse" (*Hansard*, H.L. Vol. 563, col. 108). The risk of economic exploitation could be added to this list.

Para. (c)

Likely to help to secure. This convoluted formulation probably means that the responsible medical officer, having considered the general effectiveness of after-care under supervision, has concluded that the making of an application will assist the care team in their task of ensuring that the patient receives the after-care services he is deemed to need.

Subs. (5)

The responsible medical officer is the patient's responsible medical officer as defined in s.34(1) of the 1983 Act.

Subs. (6)

Health Authority. A supervision application should not be addressed to the hospital managers or to the NHS trust. The Government expects the Health Authority to delegate its function to the NHS trust providing the health care element of services. A report renewing supervision is addressed to the Health Authority *and* the local authority (s.259(3)).

Subs. (7)

Consult. A requirement that the Health Authority obtains the agreement of the local authority to the making of a supervision application was not felt to be necessary because "in practice the statement of services to be provided, which has to be submitted with the supervision application, will need to have been agreed with the local authority's representatives so far as the social services element is concerned," *per* Baroness Cumberlege (*Hansard*, H.L. Vol. 563, col. 117).

Subs. (8)

Accepts. If the Health Authority accepts the application it has a duty to secure that the patient under supervision has a community responsible medical officer and a supervisor (s.117(2A) as inserted by Sched. 1, para. 15(4) of this Act).

Para. (a)

Rights of applying to a Mental Health Review Tribunal. These are listed under s.66 of the 1983 Act, as amended by Sched. 1, para. 7 of this Act.

Para. (b)

Inform. The method to be used when informing the "lay carer" is not prescribed.

Para. (c)

Any person. The person referred to in this paragraph is the patient's nearest relative.

Subs. (9)

The rationale for this provision was explained by Baroness Cumberlege:

"[Subs. (9)] puts beyond doubt that a supervision application can be made for patients who have been granted leave of absence from hospital and who may be made subject to after-care under supervision without having first to return to hospital, once their period of liability to detention comes to an end. That has always been our policy intention. Under the existing Act patients who are on leave of absence are entitled to section 117 after-care, but remain liable to recall to hospital and are subject to the consent to treatment provisions in the Act. This means medication can be administered without their consent, although that would usually be given in hospital. When their period of detention ends, we foresee that some patients who are on their way to successful rehabilitation at the end of their period of liability to detention, but who still require supervision, could be made subject to the new power at that stage. Such after-care services would then have to be provided under supervision. The patient would have the right to appeal against the decision to a mental health review tribunal in the same way as any patient for whom a supervision application has been accepted."

Making of supervision application

25B.—(1) The responsible medical officer shall not make a supervision application unless—

(a) subsection (2) below is complied with; and

(b) the responsible medical officer has considered the matters specified in subsection (4) below.

(2) This subsection is complied with if—

(a) the following persons have been consulted about the making of the supervision application—

(i) the patient;

(ii) one or more persons who have been professionally concerned with the patient's medical treatment in hospital;

(iii) one or more persons who will be professionally concerned with the after-care services to be provided for the patient under section 117 below; and

(iv) any person who the responsible medical officer believes will play a substantial part in the care of the patient after he leaves hospital but will not be professionally concerned with any of the after-care services to be so provided;

(b) such steps as are practicable have been taken to consult the person (if any) appearing to be the nearest relative of the patient about the making of the supervision application; and

(c) the responsible medical officer has taken into account any views expressed by the persons consulted.

(3) Where the patient has requested that paragraph (b) of subsection (2) above should not apply, that paragraph shall not apply unless—

(a) the patient has a propensity to violent or dangerous behaviour towards others; and

(b) the responsible medical officer considers that it is appropriate for steps such as are mentioned in that paragraph to be taken.

(4) The matters referred to in subsection (1)(b) above are—

(a) the after-care services to be provided for the patient under section 117 below; and

(b) any requirements to be imposed on him under section 25D below.

(5) A supervision application shall state—

(a) that the patient is liable to be detained in a hospital in pursuance of an application for admission for treatment;

(b) the age of the patient or, if his exact age is not known to the applicant, that the patient is believed to have attained the age of 16 years;

(c) that in the opinion of the applicant (having regard in particular to the patient's history) all of the conditions set out in section 25A(4) above are complied with;

(d) the name of the person who is to be the community responsible medical officer, and of the person who is to be the supervisor, in relation to the patient after he leaves hospital; and

(e) the name of—

(i) any person who has been consulted under paragraph (a)(iv) of subsection (2) above; and

(ii) any person who has been consulted under paragraph (b) of that subsection.

(6) A supervision application shall be accompanied by—

(a) the written recommendation in the prescribed form of a registered medical practitioner who will be professionally concerned with the patient's medical treatment after he leaves hospital or, if no such practitioner other than the responsible medical officer will be so concerned, of any registered medical practitioner; and
(b) the written recommendation in the prescribed form of an approved social worker.

(7) A recommendation under subsection (6)(a) above shall include a statement that in the opinion of the medical practitioner (having regard in particular to the patient's history) all of the conditions set out in section 25A(4) above are complied with.

(8) A recommendation under subsection (6)(b) above shall include a statement that in the opinion of the social worker (having regard in particular to the patient's history) both of the conditions set out in section 25A(4)(b) and (c) above are complied with.

(9) A supervision application shall also be accompanied by—
(a) a statement in writing by the person who is to be the community responsible medical officer in relation to the patient after he leaves hospital that he is to be in charge of the medical treatment provided for the patient as part of the after-care services provided for him under section 117 below;
(b) a statement in writing by the person who is to be the supervisor in relation to the patient after he leaves hospital that he is to supervise the patient with a view to securing that he receives the after-care services so provided;
(c) details of the after-care services to be provided for the patient under section 117 below; and
(d) details of any requirements to be imposed on him under section 25D below.

(10) On making a supervision application in respect of a patient the responsible medical officer shall—
(a) inform the patient both orally and in writing;
(b) inform any person who has been consulted under paragraph (a)(iv) of subsection (2) above; and
(c) inform in writing any person who has been consulted under paragraph (b) of that subsection,

of the matters specified in subsection (11) below.

(11) The matters referred to in subsection (10) above are—
(a) that the application is being made;
(b) the after-care services to be provided for the patient under section 117 below;
(c) any requirements to be imposed on him under section 25D below; and
(d) the name of the person who is to be the community responsible medical officer, and of the person who is to be the supervisor, in relation to the patient after he leaves hospital.

General Note

This section requires the responsible medical officer applicant to ensure that consultation takes place, and to consider the patient's after-care plan and any requirements to be imposed on him, before making an application for after-care under supervision. It also specifies the contents of an application and the documents that must accompany it, and requires the application to be supported by recommendations from a doctor and an approved social worker. Finally, it requires the responsible medical officer to inform the patient and others that the application has been made.

Subs. (1)

Shall not. This section is mandatory.

Subs. (2)
Para. (a)

Have been consulted. The responsible medical officer need not personally undertake the consultations.

(i) *The patient.* The patient's agreement to the application is not required.

(ii) *Professionally concerned with the patient's medical treatment.* This person need not be another doctor.

(iii) *Professionally concerned with the after-care services.* The patient's potential supervisor could come within this category. As the supervisor will play a central role in the patient's care in the community, it would seem sensible to consult with him.

(iv) *Substantial part in the care of the patient.* This is a judgment for the responsible medical officer to make. A carer who would do no more than call in occasionally to "keep an eye" on the patient would not qualify.

Para. (b)

To consult. This provision is subject to subs. (3).

Nearest relative. This person has a right to make an application to a Mental Health Review Tribunal if the application is accepted (s.66(1)(ga)(i)).

Para. (c)

Taken into account. This phrase is superfluous given that "in any context the essence of consultation is the communication of a genuine invitation to give advice and a genuine consideration of that advice", *per* Webster J. in *R. v. Secretary of State for Social Services, ex p. Association of Metropolitan Authorities* [1986] 1 All E.R. 164, at p. 167.

Subs. (3)

That paragraph shall not apply. In many cases the patient's nearest relative will be a person who will play "a substantial part" in the care of the patient and will therefore have been consulted under para. (a)(iv).

Propensity to violent or dangerous behaviour. This is an unfortunate label to attach to a patient who is to be discharged into the community.

Baroness Cumberlege when responding to Baroness Jay's statement that if "people are identified as having a propensity to violent or dangerous behaviour they would appear, *prima facie*, to be unsuitable for ... release," said that she was

> "advised that the word propensity would bear its ordinary dictionary meaning of an inclination, bent, tendency or disposition. It is not possible to say in general terms how strong that propensity would need to be because the Bill deliberately leaves that to the judgment of the responsible medical officer. Clearly the responsible medical officer would wish to consider, for example, what was known about the patient's history; the seriousness of any past violence; against whom it had been directed; how the patient had responded to treatment; and how much light consultation with the nearest relative was likely to shed on the assessment of the patient's present condition and needs" (*Hansard*, H.L. Vol. 563, col. 1644).

Her Ladyship had previously stated that if "there is a serious risk of violence which could not be contained by supervision it is highly unlikely that a supervision application would be made" (*ibid.* Vol. 563, col. 1235).

Subs. (4)

After-care services to be provided. These should be described in a written after-care plan for the patient.

Any requirements to be imposed on him. As the responsible medical officer has to consider this matter before an application has been made, the after-care bodies could only realistically be expected to have given consideration to their joint power under s.25D to impose requirements if both authorities had agreed to delegate their respective duties to members of the care team who drew up the patient's after-care plan. This was the assumption made by Mr. John Bowis M.P.: "The care plan that is put in place before the supervision application is made will include any requirements that those responsible for care believe will help the patient to comply with it. Details will be attached to the application, which will have been the subject of consultation with all those concerned, including the patient." (*Hansard*, H.C. Standing Committee F, col. 83).

Subs. (5)
Para. (d)

Community responsible medical officer. As defined in s.34(1) of the 1983 Act, as amended by Sched. 1, para. 4(2) of this Act. The community responsible medical officer must be approved by the Secretary of State for the purposes of s.12 of the 1983 Act (see Sched. 1, para. 15(4) of this Act). There is nothing to prevent the same person being the patient's community responsible medical officer, responsible medical officer and supervisor; see s.34(1A) of the 1983 Act, as inserted by Sched. 1, para. 4(5) of this Act.

Supervisor. This is as defined in s.34(1) of the 1983 Act, as amended by Sched. 1, para. 4(4) of this Act. Baroness Cumberlege outlined the role and liability of the supervisor:

"The supervisor will, of course, play a crucial role in the successful working of the new power. It is he or she who will keep closely in touch with a patient, co-ordinating the care which the patient is to receive, convening meetings of the care team, alerting colleagues to any modifications that may be necessary and checking that any requirements laid upon the patient are followed. If found to be necessary, it will be the supervisor in the first instance who will invoke the power to convey the patient.

It is essential that the person who is to play this important role is identified early on and before the patient is discharged from hospital. The whole application process is founded on the understanding that there has been full consultation between the hospital responsible medical officer and the future care team and that one of the multi-disciplinary team has agreed to act as a supervisor for the patient. Indeed, the health authority could not accept an application without that degree of clarity. The nomination of the supervisor must follow from the consultation and discussion which have preceded the application and upon which the care plan has been based.

Having explained how we see the supervisor's role and how important it is to have it identified and formalised at the outset, I believe that my noble friend may have concerns about what legal liabilities this key role will attract, as he mentioned this afternoon. I think I can reassure him on that point. While the supervisor will have professional liabilities and responsibilities along with other professionals in the care team, there will be no additional liability of the kind I think my noble friend has in mind. The supervisor would, of course, be personally liable in cases involving, for example, serious professional negligence, indiscipline or the abuse of patients. But, in general, liability would fall on the bodies responsible for providing the section 117 after-care services, not the supervisor personally, just because he or she fulfils that role. This is the normal relationship between public bodies and the professional staff they employ, and in this respect the supervisor is in the same position as other professionals" (*Hansard*, H.L. Vol. 563, col. 1238).

Baroness Miller said that the Government;

"envisage the supervisor being the same person as the key worker under the care programme approach in most cases and, again, in most cases this will be a community psychiatric nurse. But we do not want to restrict who may be the supervisor ... In some cases that person might be a social worker rather than a nurse, but in others the patient's doctor might be better placed to perform the role. Nor would we want to exclude other possible but perhaps unusual arrangements such as, for example, a clinical psychologist being nominated" (*ibid.* Vol. 563, col. 1241).

Subs. (6)

Registered medical practitioner. The doctor cannot make a recommendation if he comes within the categories set out in s.25C(9).

An approved social worker. This person, who could be the patient's potential supervisor, need not have had a professional involvement with the patient's care.

Subs. (10)

Para. (b)

Inform. "We think there should be flexibility in the way [informal carers] are informed" (*per* Baroness Cumberlege, *Hansard*, H.L. Vol. 563, col. 1227).

Supervision applications: supplementary

25C.—(1) Subject to subsection (2) below, a supervision application, and the recommendation under section 25B(6)(a) above accompanying it, may describe the patient as suffering from more than one of the following forms of mental disorder, namely, mental illness, severe mental impairment, psychopathic disorder and mental impairment.

(2) A supervision application shall be of no effect unless the patient is described in the application and the recommendation under section 25B (6)(a) above accompanying it as suffering from the same form of mental disorder, whether or not he is also described in the application or the recommendation as suffering from another form.

(3) A registered medical practitioner may at any reasonable time visit a patient and examine him in private for the purpose of deciding whether to make a recommendation under section 25B(6)(a) above.

(4) An approved social worker may at any reasonable time visit and interview a patient for the purpose of deciding whether to make a recommendation under section 25B(6)(b) above.

(5) For the purpose of deciding whether to make a recommendation under section 25B(6) above in respect of a patient, a registered medical practitioner or an approved social worker may require the production of and inspect any records relating to the detention or treatment of the patient in any hospital or to any after-care services provided for the patient under section 117 below.

(6) If, within the period of 14 days beginning with the day on which a supervision application has been accepted, the application, or any recommendation accompanying it, is found to be in any respect incorrect or defective, the application or recommendation may, within that period and with the consent of the Health Authority which accepted the application, be amended by the person by whom it was made or given.

(7) Where an application or recommendation is amended in accordance with subsection (6) above it shall have effect, and shall be deemed to have had effect, as if it had been originally made or given as so amended.

(8) A supervision application which appears to be duly made and to be accompanied by recommendations under section 25B(6) above may be acted upon without further proof of—

(a) the signature or qualification of the person by whom the application or any such recommendation was made or given; or

(b) any matter of fact or opinion stated in the application or recommendation.

(9) A recommendation under section 25B(6) above accompanying a supervision application in respect of a patient shall not be given by—

(a) the responsible medical officer;

(b) a person who receives or has an interest in the receipt of any payments made on account of the maintenance of the patient; or

(c) a close relative of the patient, of any person mentioned in paragraph (a) or (b) above or of a person by whom the other recommendation is given under section 25B(6) above for the purposes of the application.

(10) In subsection (9)(c) above "close relative" means husband, wife, father, father-in-law, mother, mother-in-law, son, son-in-law, daughter, daughter-in-law, brother, brother-in-law, sister or sister-in-law.

General Note

This section requires the applicant and the doctor making the medical recommendation to state that the patient is suffering from the same form of mental disorder; provides those who make recommendations with a right to have access to the patient and to examine relevant documentation; allows for the rectification of defective application documents, and prohibits certain persons from making recommendations.

Subss. (3) and (4)

Access. Any person refusing access to the patient without reasonable cause commits an offence under s.129(1)(b) of the 1983 Act, as amended by Sched. 1, para. 19 of this Act.

Subs. (5)

Records. A person who refuses to produce records without reasonable cause commits an offence under s.129(1)(c) of the 1983 Act.

Subs. (6)

Beginning with. This includes the day on which the supervision application was accepted (*Hare v. Gocher* [1962] 2 Q.B. 641).

Incorrect or defective. Rectification cannot be used to cure a genuine deficiency which would, otherwise, invalidate the application, such as a failure by the applicant and the recommending doctor to agree on the form of the patient's mental disorder (subs. (2)).

Requirements to secure receipt of after-care under supervision

25D.—(1) Where a patient is subject to after-care under supervision (or, if he has not yet left hospital, is to be so subject after he leaves hospital), the responsible after-care bodies have power to impose any of the requirements specified in subsection (3) below for the purpose of securing that the patient receives the after-care services provided for him under section 117 below.

(2) In this Act "the responsible after-care bodies", in relation to a patient, means the bodies which have (or will have) the duty under section 117 below to provide after-care services for the patient.

(3) The requirements referred to in subsection (1) above are—

(a) that the patient reside at a specified place;

(b) that the patient attend at specified places and times for the purpose of medical treatment, occupation, education or training; and

(c) that access to the patient be given, at any place where the patient is residing, to the supervisor, any registered medical practitioner or any approved social worker or to any other person authorised by the supervisor.

(4) A patient subject to after-care under supervision may be taken and conveyed by, or by any person authorised by, the supervisor to any place where the patient is required to reside or to attend for the purpose of medical treatment, occupation, education or training.

(5) A person who demands—

(a) to be given access to a patient in whose case a requirement has been imposed under subsection (3)(c) above; or

(b) to take and convey a patient in pursuance of subsection (4) above,

shall, if asked to do so, produce some duly authenticated document to show that he is a person entitled to be given a access to, or to take and convey, the patient.

General Note

This section enables the health authority and the local authority to jointly impose certain "requirements" on a patient who is subject to after-care under supervision. The requirements are very similar to the powers given to a patient's guardian under s.8 of the 1983 Act. The major difference between guardianship powers and supervision requirements is that the latter can be enforced by means of a power to "take and convey" a reluctant patient to the place where he is required to be. This power was keenly debated in Parliament and Ministers were repeatedly called upon to explain the Government view:

"We are providing for a reserve power, as it were, which would be available to the supervisor of that small group of vulnerable, and sometimes unpredictable patients, in order to overcome a temporary unwillingness to co-operate. The power would be temporary to enable supervisors to overcome a temporary problem and assist people in complying with the terms of the care plan to which they have agreed in such a way that by the time that they have been conveyed they will, it is hoped, have resumed their agreement to co-operate with the care plan. If they continue refusing to co-operate, it will be clear that supervised discharge is not working and a patient's plan may be eligible for re-assessment. In that case, under the existing terms of the Act, the patient's case can be reconsidered" *per* Mr. John Bowis M.P. (*Hansard*, H.C. Standing Committee F, col. 94).

"Although we envisage the comparatively rare use of the power to convey a patient, we do see it as an important feature of the new provisions. It will enable a supervisor, or any person authorised by the supervisor, to take the patient to the place where he or she is required, under the terms of the supervision arrangements, to live or attend for treatment or rehabilitation. While it is true that ultimately supervision will succeed only with the patient's participation, the power to convey will give useful backing to the care team, for example where there is a temporary reluctance to co-operate. We have followed the form of the existing Mental Health

Act power for conveying a patient to hospital following an application for detention. I do not believe that this power will be misused because to do so would be so obviously self-defeating" *per* Baroness Cumberlege (*Hansard*, H.L. Vol. 563, col. 154).

"Where someone has a severe mental illness—possibly a person with schizophrenia who is not adhering to his care plan and might cause himself or others harm if not supported urgently—an immediate power is needed. It would not be practical or in the best interests of the patient to wait for the bureaucracy of an application to take its course" *per* Baroness Cumberlege (*Hansard*, H.L. Vol. 563, col. 1254).

"It is not for politicians to decide on behalf of a professional when to use the power. The professional in charge of the patient must make that decision. Perhaps the patient might have a cold, for example, on the first occasion that he showed reluctance, and the professional would not worry too much about failure to comply. If the patient subsequently refused to go for treatment or training, the supervisor might tell the patient, 'This is getting serious, you must come with me. I have the power to convey you, will you please come?' I hope that such a reminder will be sufficient. However, if the patient showed a stronger reluctance, the professional might consider using the power of conveyance. I hope that it will not be necessary to do that. The provision aims to strengthen the supervisor and protect the patient" *per* Mr. John Bowis M.P. (*Hansard*, H.C. Standing Committee F, col 96).

"[In the absence of such a power] one of two things will happen. First, the patient will be taken in for assessment each time that a risk is perceived to exist. When the conditions of the care plan are not complied with, a risk will be deemed to exist. Therefore, the patient's ability to remain in the community will be weakened. That is the first option available if there is no provision to comply with the care agreement. It means that patients could be subject to the powers to convey in the Mental Health Act 1983, which, under sections 2 or 3, mean that someone can be taken in for treatment or assessment. That will reduce a patient's potential to stay in the community. Alternatively, a second option could be chosen. A patient could be told that, however much he fails to comply with the conditions that he agreed to before he was discharged, nothing will be done about it. If he does not comply with the conditions, he will be told that there is no power halfway between leaving him in the community or taking him back in. Our proposal is designed to create a halfway stage. It will strengthen the supervisor and put a little more pressure on a patient to comply with the terms and conditions to which he agreed before a supervised discharge. I hope that will work" *per* Mr. John Bowis M.P. (*Hansard*, H.C. Vol. 262, col. 164).

The power to take and convey has generated three areas of concern: practical, legal and professional. Although subs. (4) provides the supervisor, or someone authorised by the supervisor, with a power to override a patient's objection to going to the place where he is required to be, it does not authorise the patient's detention once he has arrived at that place. There can be no implied power to detain, associated with this provision because "there is a canon of construction that Parliament is presumed not to enact legislation which interferes with the liberty of the subject without making it clear that this was its intention" (*R. v. Hallstrom, ex p. W.*; *R. v. Gardner, ex p. L.* [1986] 2 All E.R. 306, *per* McCullough J. at p. 314). Also compare this provision with s.6 of the 1983 Act which provides hospital managers with an explicit power to detain a patient who has been subject to an application for admission to hospital.

Presumably the expectation is that once the patient arrives at the place where he is required to be, he will be willing to remain there and co-operate with whatever activity is planned for him. If the patient cannot be persuaded to stay, he cannot be prevented from leaving the premises immediately after his arrival there: the take and convey power cannot be repeatedly used to take the patient back to the premises, as this would have the effect of detaining him there. As the power to take and convey is most likely to be used in respect of patients who have stopped taking their medication, and as there is no power to treat such patients without their consent once they have arrived at the place where they are to receive treatment, using this power could "be a classic case of taking a horse to water but not being able to make it drink" *per* Baroness Jay (*Hansard*, H.L. Vol. 563, col. 152).

The use of the power to take and convey the patient does not sit easily with the Government's acknowledgement that "ultimately after-care under supervision is not going to work without the co-operation of the patient," *per* Baroness Cumberlege (*Hansard*, H.L. Vol. 563, col. 1252). A number of M.P.s who spoke on the Bill reflected the view expressed by Mr. David Hinchliffe M.P. that the power to take and convey "could totally undermine the consensual relationship upon which the most successful after-care supervision is based" (*Hansard*, H.C. Vol. 262, col. 200). In particular Ms. Tessa Jowell M.P. said:

"One of the most harmful effects may be to encourage poor professional practice. As I think we all accept, good community care depends on high quality relationships, built on trust, confidence and sensitivity to a person's individual needs and circumstances. The threat or use of force can offer the short cut of gaining a person's compliance with a plan or programme. In place of the careful and diligent development of an effective relationship with the patient, a supervisor can merely call in aid his or her power to take and convey or threaten to get the police in order to use it. We are sure that that will damage community care—driving people from services rather than encouraging them to use them, especially if, as will be likely, supervisors try to get the police involved in using coercion rather than use it themselves. Many professionals are unhappy about the prospect of having these powers. Therefore, the provision may be irrelevant because, as I have said, it may simply not be used" (*Hansard*, H.C. Vol. 264, col. 1163).

On a number of occasions during the Bill's passage, the Government was pressed to confirm that the power to take and convey did not breach Arts. 5 and 8 of the European Convention for the Protection of Human Rights and Fundamental Freedoms. Such confirmation was repeatedly provided; see, for example, Mr. John Bowis M.P. at *Hansard*, H.C. Standing Committee F, col. 94. Article 5 exists to protect the freedom and security of the individual from arbitrary detention and Art. 8 provides that everyone has a right to his private and family life.

It is clear that supervision by itself is not caught by Art. 5 because the restrictions attached to after-care under supervision could not be characterised as a deprivation of liberty; see the decisions of the European Commission of Human Rights in *L. v. Sweden* (app. no. 10801/84) and *W. v. Sweden* (app. no. 12778/87). The power to take and convey is a form of psychiatric arrest and for such an arrest to be lawful under the Convention, the person concerned must be reliably shown to be of unsound mind of a nature or degree warranting detention, entailing "the establishment of a true mental disorder before a competent authority on the basis of objective expertise" (*Winterwerp v. Netherlands, The* (1979) 2 E.H.R.R. 387, para. 39).

In *X. v. United Kingdom, The* (1981) 1 B.M.L.R. 98, the court held, at pp. 112, 113, that "where a provision of domestic law is designed, among other things, to authorise emergency confinement of persons capable of presenting a damage to others, it would be impracticable to require a thorough medical examination prior to any arrest or detention". If the power to take and convey is to escape contravening the Convention by virtue of the decision in *X.*, it would need to be shown that a failure by a patient to comply with a requirement constitutes an emergency. Although it might be possible to argue that a failure by a patient to take his medication creates an emergency if such action had in the past led to the patient or others being placed at risk, it would be difficult to make a similar argument in the case of a patient who refuses to take up his place in a day centre.

Subs. (1)

Responsible after-care bodies have power to impose. This is a power which must be exercised jointly. For procedure, see the note on "Any requirements to be imposed on him" in s.25B(4). As a requirement can be imposed after the patient has left hospital, the care-team should consider this as part of their monitoring of the patient's situation.

Securing that the patient receives... after-care services. As the patient's supervisor is appointed "with a view to securing that [the patient] receives the after-care services ... provided" (s.25B(9)(b)), the supervisor's view on the imposition of requirements should always be sought.

Subs. (3)

Para. (a)

Reside at a specified place. There is no power to require that the patient resides with a particular person.

"It is simply inconceivable that health authorities or local authorities would want to make a patient live in an unacceptable place, but if the patient's agreement is stipulated in the Bill he would be able to overturn the requirement and undermine the supervised discharge arrangement simply by withdrawing his agreement" *per* Mr. John Bowis M.P. (*Hansard*, H.C. Standing Committee F, col. 88).

Para. (b)

Attend. Note that there is no requirement to reside.

Medical treatment. A patient under supervision is subject to common law rules relating to the provision of medical treatment. The power in this section "cannot be used to require the patient to accept medication in the community, and compulsory medication is no part of the Bill's provisions. I know that that is something that some, including the British Medical Association, would like, but we are advised that it would risk being in breach of our human rights convention obligations, as well as being opposed by substantial bodies of medical opinion", *per* Mr. John Bowis M.P. (*Hansard*, H.C. Vol. 262, col. 163).

Para. (c)

Access to the patient is given. If access to the patient is denied, an approved social worker will need to consider whether grounds exist for an application to be made to a magistrate under s.135(1) of the 1983 Act for a warrant to remove the patient to a place of safety. A refusal to allow access to the patient by an authorised person without reasonable cause constitutes an offence under s.129(1)(b) of the 1983 Act.

Any place where the patient is residing. This will not necessarily be the place where the patient is required to reside under para. (a).

Authorised. The authorisation should be in writing; see subs. (5).

Subs. (4)

Taken and conveyed. See the General Note to this section. If the medical condition of a patient who is reluctant to be taken and conveyed suggests that a period of hospitalisation might be appropriate, the supervisor could consider asking for an assessment to be carried out for a possible compulsory admission.

A patient being taken and conveyed is deemed to be in legal custody and the person who is conveying the patient is granted the powers of a policeman (s.137 of the 1983 Act). If the patient "escapes" during the course of his conveyance, he can be retaken by the person who was conveying him, by a policeman or by an approved social worker (s.138 of the 1983 Act). Section 138 does not provide authority for a forced entry to the place where the patient is believed to be. Both ss.137 and 138 provide authority for reasonable force to be used when conveying the patient, if this proves to be necessary.

As the use of this power will follow a refusal on the part of the patient to comply with a requirement, it will trigger a review under s.25E.

Any person authorised. The authorisation, which should be in writing (see subs. (5)), can be given to any person whom the supervisor considers suitable to perform the task. "[T]he power to convey includes the right to ask a constable to assist. However, that will not happen in many cases. I believe that telling the patient that the supervisor has the power to convey will help to overcome any temporary lack of co-operation" *per* Mr. John Bowis M.P. (*Hansard*, H.C. Standing Committee F, col. 96).

Subs. (5)

Demands. A verbal demand would be sufficient.

Duly authenticated document. This is to be authenticated by the supervisor who is the person possessing the relevant powers. It would be prudent for the supervisor to prepare such documentation for possible use during periods when he is absent from work.

Review of after-care under supervision etc.

25E.—(1) The after-care services provided (or to be provided) under section 117 below for a patient who is (or is to be) subject to after-care under supervision, and any requirements imposed on him under section 25D above, shall be kept under review, and (where appropriate) modified, by the responsible after-care bodies.

(2) This subsection applies in relation to a patient who is subject to after-care under supervision where he refuses or neglects—

(a) to receive any or all of the after-care services provided for him under section 117 below; or

(b) to comply with any or all of any requirements imposed on him under section 25D above.

(3) Where subsection (2) above applies in relation to a patient, the responsible after-care bodies shall review, and (where appropriate) modify—

(a) the after-care services provided for him under section 117 below; and

(b) any requirements imposed on him under section 25D above.

(4) Where subsection (2) above applies in relation to a patient, the responsible after-care bodies shall also—

(a) consider whether it might be appropriate for him to cease to be subject to after-care under supervision and, if they conclude that it might be, inform the community responsible medical officer; and

(b) consider whether it might be appropriate for him to be admitted to a hospital for treatment and, if they conclude that it might be, inform an approved social worker.

(5) The responsible after-care bodies shall not modify—

(a) the after-care services provided (or to be provided) under section 117 below for a patient who is (or is to be) subject to after-care under supervision; or

(b) any requirements imposed on him under section 25D above,

unless subsection (6) below is complied with.

(6) This subsection is complied with if—

(a) the patient has been consulted about the modifications;

(b) any person who the responsible after-care bodies believe plays (or will play) a substantial part in the care of the patient but is not (or will not be) professionally concerned with the after-care services provided for the patient under section 117 below has been consulted about the modifications;

(c) such steps as are practicable have been taken to consult the person (if any) appearing to be the nearest relative of the patient about the modifications; and

(d) the responsible after-care bodies have taken into account any views expressed by the persons consulted.

(7) Where the patient has requested that paragraph (c) of subsection (6) above should not apply, that paragraph shall not apply unless—

(a) the patient has a propensity to violent or dangerous behaviour towards others; and

(b) the community responsible medical officer (or the person who is to be the community responsible medical officer) considers that it is appropriate for steps such as are mentioned in that paragraph to be taken.

(8) Where the responsible after-care bodies modify the after-care services provided (or to be provided) for the patient under section 117 below or any requirements imposed on him under section 25D above, they shall—

(a) inform the patient both orally and in writing;

(b) inform any person who has been consulted under paragraph (b) of subsection (6) above; and

(c) inform in writing any person who has been consulted under paragraph (c) of that subsection,

that the modifications have been made.

(9) Where—

(a) a person other than the person named in the supervision application becomes the community responsible medical officer when the patient leaves hospital; or

(b) when the patient is subject to after-care under supervision, one person ceases to be, and another becomes, the community responsible medical officer,

the responsible after-care bodies shall comply with subsection (11) below.

(10) Where—

(a) a person other than the person named in the supervision application becomes the supervisor when the patient leaves hospital; or

(b) when the patient is subject to after-care under supervision, one person ceases to be, and another becomes, the supervisor,

the responsible after-care bodies shall comply with subsection (11) below.

(11) The responsible after-care bodies comply with this subsection if they—

(a) inform the patient both orally and in writing;

(b) inform any person who they believe plays a substantial part in the care of the patient but is not professionally concerned with the after-care services provided for the patient under section 117 below; and

(c) unless the patient otherwise requests, take such steps as are practicable to inform in writing the person (if any) appearing to be the nearest relative of the patient,

of the name of the person who becomes the community responsible medical officer or the supervisor.

GENERAL NOTE

This section requires the relevant Health Authority and local authority to keep under review and where appropriate, modify both the after-care services provided to, and any requirements imposed on, a patient who is subject to after-care under supervision. If the patient refuses to receive an after-care service or to comply with a requirement the authorities can also consider whether they should recommend to the patient's community responsible medical officer that the supervision should end, or whether they should inform an approved social worker that, in their view, he should be admitted to hospital for treatment under s.3 of the 1983 Act.

The section also requires the two authorities to inform the patient and others on a change of the patient's community responsible medical officer or supervisor.

Subs. (1)

After-care services provided ... shall be kept under review. This replicates the existing duty of the responsible after-care bodies under s.117(2).

Or to be provided. "In the great majority of cases the sequence of events will be, broadly, that the care plan will have been drawn up and agreed, the supervision application made and then accepted by the health authority, and the patient leaves hospital and returns to the community where he will be subject to after-care under supervision. However, it is possible that the care plan may need to be revised before discharge from hospital—perhaps a hostel place has fallen through, or the care team has to change. It therefore seems sensible to build in the possibility that the after-care services could be modified before the patient leaves hospital. Changes as needed could also be made to the requirements in ... section 25D. Any other approach would mean that the original care plan and requirements would take effect when the patient leaves hospital and would then need immediate review and change," *per* Baroness Cumberlege (*Hansard*, H.L. Vol. 563, cols. 1256, 1257).

Where subsection (2) ... applies. A mechanism will need to be established which will ensure that the two authorities are notified if the situation described in subs. (2) applies to a particular patient. This will presumably entail the authorities delegating their responsibilities to the care team; see the note on s.25B(4).

Modify ... the after-care services. This option is subject to the local authority's duty under s.47 of the National Health Service and Community Care Act 1990 (c. 19) to assess the social care needs of any person who appears to them to need community care services and decide in the light of the assessment whether such services should be provided. Services provided under s.117 of the 1983 Act are "community care services" under the 1990 Act (*ibid.* s.46(3)).

Modify ... any requirements. This can only be done if the two authorities agree to the modification (s.25D(1)).

Subs. (4)

Para. (a)

They conclude. A joint decision is required.

Community responsible medical officer. This person has the power to end the supervision under s.25H(1).

Para. (b)

They conclude. See note to para. (a) above.

An approved social worker. There is no requirement to inform the patient's nearest relative who is also a potential applicant under the 1983 Act. If the approved social worker is involved in the patient's care, he has an ongoing duty under s.13(1) of the 1983 Act to make an application for an admission to hospital or a guardianship application if he considers that such an application ought to be made.

Subs. (5)

Shall not. The provisions of subs. (6) are mandatory.

Subs. (6)

See the notes to s.25B(2).

Consulted. "In practice, we envisage that when the patient is subject to after-care under supervision [consultation] will fall to the supervisor", *per* Baroness Cumberlege (*op cit*, col. 1257).

Subs. (7)

See the notes to s.25B(3).

Subs. (8)

Para. (b)

Inform. This can be done either orally or in writing.

Para. (c)

Inform in writing. There is no requirement for the information to be given orally.

Reclassification of patient subject to after-care under supervision

25F.—(1) If it appears to the community responsible medical officer that a patient subject to after-care under supervision is suffering from a form of mental disorder other than the form or forms specified in the supervision application made in respect of the patient, he may furnish a report to that effect to the Health Authority which have the duty under section 117 below to provide after-care services for the patient.

(2) Where a report is so furnished the supervision application shall have effect as if that other form of mental disorder were specified in it.

(3) Unless no-one other than the community responsible medical officer is professionally concerned with the patient's medical treatment, he shall consult one or more persons who are so concerned before furnishing a report under subsection (1) above.

(4) Where a report is furnished under subsection (1) above in respect of a patient, the responsible after-care bodies shall—

(a) inform the patient both orally and in writing; and

(b) unless the patient otherwise requests, take such steps as are practicable to inform in writing the person (if any) appearing to be the nearest relative of the patient,

that the report has been furnished.

General Note

This section provides for the reclassification of the stated form of mental disorder of a patient who is subject to after-care under supervision. Reclassification has no legal consequences, as s.25A makes no distinction between the various categories of mental disorder. Either the patient or, if he has been informed of the report, the patient's nearest relative has a right to apply to a Mental Health Review Tribunal within 28 days of the report being furnished (s.66(1)(gb), (2)(d) of the 1983 Act, as amended by Sched. 1, para. 7 of this Act).

If the patient is reclassified on the renewal of the supervision, there is no need for a further report to be made under this section; see s.25G(10).

Duration and renewal of after-care under supervision

25G.—(1) Subject to sections 25H and 25I below, a patient subject to after-care under supervision shall be so subject for the period—

(a) beginning when he leaves hospital; and

(b) ending with the period of six months beginning with the day on which the supervision application was accepted,

but shall not be so subject for any longer period except in accordance with the following provisions of this section.

(2) A patient already subject to after-care under supervision may be made so subject—

(a) from the end of the period referred to in subsection (1) above, for a further period of six months; and

(b) from the end of any period of renewal under paragraph (a) above, for a further period of one year,

and so on for periods of one year at a time.

(3) Within the period of two months ending on the day on which a patient who is subject to after-care under supervision would (in default of the operation of subsection (7) below) cease to be so subject, it shall be the duty of the community responsible medical officer—

(a) to examine the patient; and

(b) if it appears to him that the conditions set out in subsection (4) below are complied with, to furnish to the responsible after-care bodies a report to that effect in the prescribed form.

(4) The conditions referred to in subsection (3) above are that—

(a) the patient is suffering from mental disorder, being mental illness, severe mental impairment, psychopathic disorder or mental impairment;

(b) there would be a substantial risk of serious harm to the health or safety of the patient or the safety of other persons, or of the patient being seriously exploited, if he were not to receive the after-care services provided for him under section 117 below;

(c) his being subject to after-care under supervision is likely to help to secure that he receives the after-care services so provided.

(5) The community responsible medical officer shall not consider whether the conditions set out in subsection (4) above are complied with unless—

(a) the following persons have been consulted—

(i) the patient;

(ii) the supervisor;

(iii) unless no-one other than the community responsible medical officer is professionally concerned with the patient's medical treatment, one or more persons who are so concerned;

(iv) one or more persons who are professionally concerned with the after-care services (other than medical treatment) provided for the patient under section 117 below; and

(v) any person who the community responsible medical officer believes plays a substantial part in the care of the patient but is not professionally concerned with the after-care services so provided;

(b) such steps as are practicable have been taken to consult the person (if any) appearing to be the nearest relative of the patient; and

(c) the community responsible medical officer has taken into account any relevant views expressed by the persons consulted.

(6) Where the patient has requested that paragraph (b) of subsection (5) above should not apply, that paragraph shall not apply unless—

(a) the patient has a propensity to violent or dangerous behaviour towards others; and

(b) the community responsible medical officer considers that it is appropriate for steps such as are mentioned in that paragraph to be taken.

(7) Where a report is duly furnished under subsection (3) above, the patient shall be thereby made subject to after-care under supervision for the further period prescribed in that case by subsection (2) above.

(8) Where a report is furnished under subsection (3) above, the responsible after-care bodies shall—

(a) inform the patient both orally and in writing—

(i) that the report has been furnished; and

(ii) of the effect in his case of the provisions of this Act relating to making a patient subject to after-care under supervision for a further period (including, in particular, what rights of applying to a Mental Health Review Tribunal are available);

(b) inform any person who has been consulted under paragraph (a)(v) of subsection (5) above that the report has been furnished; and

(c) inform in writing any person who has been consulted under paragraph (b) of that subsection that the report has been furnished.

(9) Where the form of mental disorder specified in a report furnished under subsection (3) above is a form of disorder other than that specified in the supervision application, that application shall have effect as if that other form of mental disorder were specified in it.

(10) Where on any occasion a report specifying such a form of mental disorder is furnished under subsection (3) above the community responsible medical officer need not on that occasion furnish a report under section 25F above.

General Note

This section states that the initial period of after-care under supervision can last for a maximum of six months. The patient's community responsible medical officer can, following consultation, renew the supervision for a further period of six months and thereafter for periods of one year at a time. These periods replicate the renewal periods for a patient who is detained for treatment under s.3 of the 1983 Act (see *ibid.* s.20(1)(2)). If the supervision is renewed, the notification procedure set out in subs. (7) must be followed.

Either the patient or, if he has been informed of the report, the patient's nearest relative can apply to a Mental Health Review Tribunal on a report being made under this section (s.66(1)(gc), (2)(fa) of the 1983 Act, as amended by Sched. 1, para. 7 of this Act).

Subs. (1)

Beginning when he leaves hospital. Alternatively this can be when his period of leave of absence expires (s.25A(9)).

Beginning with. This includes the day on which the supervision application was accepted (*Hare v. Gocher* [1962] 2 Q.B. 641).

Subs. (3)

To furnish to the responsible after-care bodies. Although neither the Health Authority nor the local authority have the power to discharge the patient from supervision, they will need to establish a mechanism for scrutinising the report, to ensure that it complies with this section.

Subs. (4)

The criteria for renewal replicate the grounds for making a supervision application (see s.25A(4)). If the form of mental disorder specified in the report differs from the form of mental disorder specified in the application, see subss. (8) and (9).

Subs. (5)

Shall not. This provision is mandatory. See the notes on s.25B(2).

Subs. (6)

See the notes on s.25B(3).

Subs. (8)

Responsible after-care bodies. These will presumably delegate their responsibilities under this provision to the care team; see the note on s.25B(4).

Para. (a)

Rights of applying to a Mental Health Review Tribunal. These are shown under s.66 of the 1983 Act as amended by Sched. 1, para. 7 of this Act.

Para. (b)

Inform. This can be either orally or in writing.

Para. (c)

Inform in writing. There is no requirement for the information to be given orally.

Ending or after-care under supervision

25H.—(1) The community responsible medical officer may at any time direct that a patient subject to after-care under supervision shall cease to be so subject.

(2) The community responsible medical officer shall not give a direction under subsection (1) above unless subsection (3) below is complied with.

(3) This subsection is complied with if—

(a) the following persons have been consulted about the giving of the direction—

(i) the patient;

(ii) the supervisor;

(iii) unless no-one other than the community responsible medical officer is professionally concerned with the patient's medical treatment, one or more persons who are so concerned;

(iv) one or more persons who are professionally concerned with the after-care services (other than medical treatment) provided for the patient under section 117 below; and

(v) any person who the community responsible medical officer believes plays a substantial part in the care of the patient but is not professionally concerned with the after-care services so provided;

(b) such steps as are practicable have been taken to consult the person (if any) appearing to be the nearest relative of the patient about the giving of the direction; and

(c) the community responsible medical officer has taken into account any views expressed by the persons consulted.

(4) Where the patient has requested that paragraph (b) of subsection (3) above should not apply, that paragraph shall not apply unless—

(a) the patient has a propensity to violent or dangerous behaviour towards others; and

(b) the community responsible medical officer considers that it is appropriate for steps such as are mentioned in that paragraph to be taken.

(5) A patient subject to after-care under supervision shall cease to be so subject if he—

(a) is admitted to a hospital in pursuance of an application for admission for treatment; or

(b) is received into guardianship.

(6) Where a patient (for any reason) ceases to be subject to after-care under supervision the responsible after-care bodies shall—

(a) inform the patient both orally and in writing;

(b) inform any person who they believe plays a substantial part in the care of the patient but is not professionally concerned with the after-care services provided for the patient under section 117 below; and

(c) take such steps as are practicable to inform in writing the person (if any) appearing to be the nearest relative of the patient,

that the patient has ceased to be so subject.

(7) Where the patient has requested that paragraph (c) of subsection (6) above should not apply, that paragraph shall not apply unless subsection (3)(b) above applied in his case by virtue of subsection (4) above.

General Note

This section states that after-care under supervision ends if:

(i) following consultation, a direction to that effect is made by the patient's community responsible medical officer;

(ii) the patient is detained for treatment; *or*

(iii) the patient is received into guardianship.

Supervision can also be ended by the Mental Health Review Tribunal (s.72 of the 1983 Act, as amended by Sched. 1, para. 10 of this Act), but not by the body which accepts the application for after-care under supervision (*i.e.* the Health Authority).

The ending of supervision does not effect the continuing duty of the Health Authority and the local authority under s.117 of the 1983 Act to provide after-care services, until the person concerned is no longer in need of them.

Subs. (1)

At any time. There are no circumstances that oblige the community responsible medical officer to discharge the supervision.

Subs. (2)

Shall not. The provisions of subs. (3) are mandatory.

Subs. (3)

See the notes on s.25B(2).

Subs. (4)

See the notes on s.25B(3).

Subs. (5)

Admission for treatment. A further application for after-care under supervision can be made before a patient in this category is discharged from hospital. This would not be necessary in respect of a supervised patient who is detained under s.2, because such a patient will have his supervision placed in suspension by virtue of s.25I.

Subs. (6)

The responsible after-care bodies. See the note on s.25G(8).

Para. (b)

Inform. This can be either orally or in writing.

Para. (c)

Inform in writing. There is no requirement for the nearest relative to be given the information orally.

Special provisions as to patients sentenced to imprisonment etc.

25I.—(1) This section applies where a patient who is subject to subject to after-care under supervision—

(a) is detained in custody in pursuance of any sentence or order passed or made by a court in the United Kingdom (including an order committing or remanding him in custody); or

(b) is detained in hospital in pursuance of an application for admission for assessment.

(2) At any time when the patient is detained as mentioned in subsection (1)(a) or (b) above he is not required—

(a) to receive any after-care services provided for him under section 117 below; or

(b) to comply with any requirements imposed on him under section 25D above.

(3) If the patient is detained as mentioned in paragraph (a) of subsection (1) above for a period of, or successive periods amounting in the aggregate to, six months or less, or is detained as mentioned in paragraph (b) of that subsection, and, apart from this subsection, he—

(a) would have ceased to be subject to after-care under supervision during the period for which he is so detained; or

(b) would cease to be so subject during the period of 28 days beginning with the day on which he ceases to be so detained, he shall be deemed not to have ceased, and shall not cease, to be so subject until the end of that period of 28 days.

(4) Where the period for which the patient is subject to after-care under supervision is extended by subsection (3) above, any examination and report to be made and furnished in respect of the patient under section 25G(3) above may be made and furnished within the period as so extended.

(5) Where, by virtue of subsection (4) above, the patient is made subject to after-care under supervision for a further period after the day on which (apart from subsection (3) above) he would have ceased to be so subject, the further period shall be deemed to have commenced with that day.

GENERAL NOTE

This section has the effect of placing after-care under supervision in suspense if the patient is given a custodial sentence of six months or less or is detained in hospital for assessment under s.2 of the 1983 Act. If the supervision would otherwise have lapsed during the period in hospital or custody, it is extended for 28 days after the patient's date of discharge. If the patient is given a custodial sentence of six months or more and the supervision has not lapsed during the course of his sentence, it will be re-activated on his release.

Subs. (1)

United Kingdom. This means Great Britain and Northern Ireland (Interpretation Act 1978, s.5, Sched. 1).

Application for admission for assessment. This provision was explained by Mr. John Bowis M.P.:

"As a general rule, we would expect that a patient who was subject to the new power would be readmitted only when a need for further treatment had been established. Section 3 would normally be used in preference to section 2, but we cannot be certain that section 2 will not be used in some cases. Those would include emergency admissions under section 4 which are subsequently converted to section 2. That could have the consequence of vulnerable people being returned to the community without the special support that the Bill supplies.

The amendment deals with that by extending to patients who are admitted for assessment the provision which new section 25I(1) already makes for those who are detained in custody. The effect is to put the supervision arrangements into suspense while the patient is in hospital and then to reactivate them when he or she is discharged. If the supervision would otherwise have lapsed while the patient was in hospital, it is extended for 28 days after his or her discharge." (*Hansard*, H.C. Standing Committee F, cols. 107, 108).

Subs. (3)

If a patient who is subject to after-care under supervision is detained in custody for a period of six months or less or is detained in hospital under s.2 of the 1983 Act, and the patient's supervision would have ended during the period in custody or within 28 days of his ceasing to be detained under s.2, this subsection provides that in both cases the supervision stays in place until 28 days after the patient has ceased to be detained.

Six months or less.

"The amendment does not apply to those sentenced to longer periods in custody essentially because if someone has been out of touch with the specialist services for a long period, the presumption that he or she is still suffering from the conditions which led to after-care under supervision being arranged become hard to sustain. However, if the sentence was more than six months but less than a year and supervision had not expired while the person was in custody, it would still be reactivated when he or she left prison", *per* Baroness Cumberlege (*Hansard*, H.L. Vol. 564, col. 171).

Subs. (5)

If a patient has had his period of supervision extended by virtue of subs. (3), a subsequent renewal of his supervision is deemed to have started on the day on which it would have expired if it had not been for subs. (3).

Patients moving from Scotland to England and Wales

25J.—(1) A supervision application may be made in respect of a patient who is subject to a community care order under the Mental

Health (Scotland) Act 1984 and who intends to leave Scotland in order to reside in England and Wales.

(2) Sections 25A to 25I above, section 117 below and any other provision of this Act relating to supervision applications or patients subject to after-care under supervision shall apply in relation to a patient in respect of whom a supervision application is or is to be made by virtue of this section subject to such modifications as the Secretary of State may by regulations prescribe."

(2) Schedule 1 to this Act (supplementary provisions about after-care under supervision) shall have effect.

General Note

The effect of this section and the likely content of regulations were explained by Baroness Cumberlege:

"[This section enables] an application for after-care under supervision [to] be made in respect of a patient subject to a community care order. The modifications which need to be made to the procedure to cover the fact that the patient is moving, not from being detained in hospital, but from being subject to a Scottish community care order, will be prescribed in the regulations. In practice we see this working as follows. If the care team in Scotland believes it is in the patient's best interest to move to England or Wales, it will make contact with a Section 12 approved doctor south of the Border. This is likely to be the same person who will eventually be the patient's community responsible medical officer after the transfer has taken place. This doctor will then make the application to the health authority which will have to be supported by two recommendations, one from an approved social worker and the other from a registered medical practitioner who has knowledge of the patient's history.

The significant difference from the general arrangement in Clause 1 of the Bill is that the application is made not by a doctor who has been looking after the patient in hospital, but by one who is likely to be his or her responsible medical officer in the community. So far as the supporting medical recommendation is concerned, it would obviously make sense for this to be given by the special medical officer who is the Scottish equivalent of the community responsible medical officer and that is what we expect to happen in the ordinary way. There would have to be full consultation on both sides of the Border and the transfer would take place when all concerned were ready for it to go ahead. The patient would become subject to after-care under supervision upon taking up residence in England or Wales. He or she would have an immediate right to a Mental Health Review Tribunal.

It would only be practicable to apply these provisions to patients who agree to the transfer. The new powers rely on the sanction of the patient's possible return to hospital rather than any more direct form of compulsion, so it is not feasible to legislate for patients who abscond.

Although the number of patients who are likely to be affected by such transfers is probably very small, we feel that we need this new provision to ensure that a patient does not lose the support and supervision he or she may need simply as a result of moving to the other side of the Border." (*Hansard*, H.L. Vol. 564, col. 173).

Subs. (1)

Intends to leave. The application must be made before the patient leaves Scotland.

Absence without leave

2.—(1) In section 18 of the Mental Health Act 1983 (return of patients absent without leave), for subsection (4) (which provides that a patient may not be taken into custody after the end of the period of 28 days beginning with the first day of his absence without leave) there shall be substituted the following subsection—

"(4) A patient shall not be taken into custody under this section after the later of—

(a) the end of the period of six months beginning with the first day of his absence without leave; and

(b) the end of the period for which (apart from section 21 below) he is liable to be detained or subject to guardianship;

and, in determining for the purposes of paragraph (b) above or any other provision of this Act whether a person who is or has been absent without leave is at any time liable to be detained or subject to guardianship, a report furnished under section 20 or 21B below before the first day of his absence without leave shall not be taken to have renewed the authority for his detention or guardianship unless the period of renewal began before that day."

(2) For section 21 of that Act (duration of authority for detention and guardianship: special provisions as to patients absent without leave) there shall be substituted the following sections—

GENERAL NOTE

This section makes new provision in relation to the return of absconding patients who are liable to be detained in hospital for treatment, or subject to guardianship under the 1983 Act.

Subs. (1)

This subsection replaces s.18(4) of the 1983 Act under which patients may not be taken into custody more than 28 days after the date on which they absconded. The new provision allows a patient to be taken into custody at any time up to six months from the date on which he absconded or, if later, the end of the existing authority for his detention in hospital or guardianship. It applies to patients who have been placed under hospital or guardianship orders made by a court under s.37 of the 1983 Act (*ibid.* s.40(4), Sched. 1, Pt. I, para. 2) but not to patients who have been placed under restriction orders by a court under s.41 of the 1983 Act (*ibid.* s.41(3), Sched. 1, Pt. II, para. 4(b)).

A patient cannot be taken into custody under s.18 if the period of his detention under one of the following powers in the 1983 Act has expired: admission for assessment (s.2(4)), emergency admission (s.4(4)), or the detention of an in-patient by a doctor (s.5(2)) or nurse (s.5(4)) (s.18(5)).

Mr. John Bowis M.P., explained the rationale for this provision:

"[it] ends a loophole in the 1983 Act relating to the return to hospital, or guardianship, of ... patients who are absent without leave. Restricted patients who abscond can be returned to hospital at any time, but under section 18(4), as it stands, an unrestricted patient who is not returned within 28 days simply ceases to be liable to be detained—regardless of the state of his or her mental health or the original period of detention. That is clearly unsatisfactory, so the Bill provides for an unrestricted patient to be returned to hospital or guardianship at any time up to six months from going absent without leave, or within the existing period of detention or guardianship if that is longer. Where a patient is returned after more than 28 days, his or her condition must be reassessed by the responsible medical officer. The new limits improve the protection given by the Act to detained patients and the public while taking proper account of patients' civil liberties." (*Hansard*, H.C. Vol. 262, col. 164).

The reference to the existing state of the law as representing a "loophole" or being an "anachronism" (*per* Baroness Cumberlege, *Hansard*, H.L. Vol. 562, col. 936) is hardly appropriate, because the use of such language gives the impression that the provisions of s.18(4), which have their origins in the Lunacy Act 1890 (c. 5), remained on the statute book as a result of governmental and legislative oversight. In fact, arguments for amending the existing law were examined in *A Review of the Mental Health Act 1959*, D.H.S.S., 1976, at paras. 10.4 to 10.6, and both the 28 day period and the fact that it applied both to patients who had been detained for treatment and to hospital order patients were considered in detail in the White Paper, *Review of the Mental Health Act 1959*, Cmnd. 7320, at paras. 8.18 to 8.24. At that time, the Government concluded that arguments in favour of the existing law outweighed arguments for damage.

Beginning with the first day of his absence without leave. A patient who has been granted leave of absence under s.17 of the 1983 Act can be retaken within a period of six months beginning with the first day of his absence without leave. This means that the patient can be retaken long after the expiration of his period of detention.

Subs. (2)

This subsection replaces s.21 of the 1983 Act and introduces two new sections. The new provisions extend the authority for detention or guardianship of a patient who is absent without leave for up to a week after his return and make provision for the renewal of such authority. Where the patient is taken into custody, or returns, more than 28 days after absconding, he will be reassessed within seven days of his return to establish whether detention (or guardianship) is still justified.

New ss.21, 21A and 21B apply to patients who have been placed under hospital or guardianship orders made by a court (Sched. 1, para. 1 of the 1983 Act, as amended by subs. (8), but not to patients who have been placed under restriction orders under s.41 of the 1983 Act (*ibid.* s.41(3)).

"Special provisions as to patients absent without leave

21.—(1) Where a patient is absent without leave—

(a) on the day on which (apart from this section) he would cease to be liable to be detained or subject to guardianship under this Part of this Act; or

(b) within the period of one week ending with that day,

he shall not cease to be so liable or subject until the relevant time.

(2) For the purposes of subsection (1) above the relevant time—

(a) where the patient is taken into custody under section 18 above, is the end of the period of one week beginning with the day on which he is returned to the hospital or place where he ought to be;

(b) where the patient returns himself to the hospital or place where he ought to be within the period during which he can be taken into custody under section 18 above, is the end of the period of one week beginning with the day on which he so returns himself; and

(c) otherwise, is the end of the period during which he can be taken into custody under section 18 above.

General Note

Subs. (1)

Relevant time. This allows for the patient's medical officer to examine the patient and decide whether he wishes to make a report renewing the detention or guardianship under s.20(3) or 20(6) of the 1983 Act.

Patients who are taken into custody or return within 28 days

21A.—(1) This section applies where a patient who is absent without leave is taken into custody under section 18 above, or returns himself to the hospital or place where he ought to be, not later than the end of the period of 28 days beginning with the first day of his absence without leave.

(2) Where the period for which the patient is liable to be detained or subject to guardianship is extended by section 21 above, any examination and report to be made and furnished in respect of the patient under section 20(3) or (6) above may be made and furnished within the period as so extended.

(3) Where the authority for the detention or guardianship of the patient is renewed by virtue of subsection (2) above after the day on which (apart from section 21 above) that authority would have expired, the renewal shall take effect as from that day.

General Note

If a patient who has absconded, returns to the hospital or place where he is required to be not more than 28 days after absconding, or is taken into custody during that period, the patient's medical officer can renew the detention or guardianship under s.20 without further formality.

Subs. (1)

Beginning with. This includes the first day of his absence without leave (*Hare v. Gocher* [1962] 2 Q.B. 641).

Subs. (3)

Renewal. The renewal has effect from the date when the authority for detention or guardianship would have expired if it had not been extended by new s.21.

Patients who are taken into custody or return after more than 28 days

21B.—(1) This section applies where a patient who is absent without leave is taken into custody under section 18 above, or returns himself to the hospital or place where he ought to be, later than the end of the period of 28 days beginning with the first day of his absence without leave.

(2) It shall be the duty of the appropriate medical officer, within the period of one week beginning with the day on which the patient is returned or returns himself to the hospital or place where he ought to be—

(a) to examine the patient; and

(b) if it appears to him that the relevant conditions are satisfied, to furnish to the appropriate body a report to that effect in the prescribed form;

and where such a report is furnished in respect of the patient the appropriate body shall cause him to be informed.

(3) Where the patient is liable to be detained (as opposed to subject to guardianship), the appropriate medical officer shall, before furnishing a report under subsection (2) above, consult—

(a) one or more other persons who have been professionally concerned with the patient's medical treatment; and

(b) an approved social worker.

(4) Where the patient would (apart from any renewal of the authority for his detention or guardianship on or after the day on which he is returned or returns himself to the hospital or place where he ought to be) be liable to be detained or subject to guardianship after the end of the period of one week beginning with that day, he shall cease to be so liable or subject at the end of that period unless a report is duly furnished in respect of him under subsection (2) above.

(5) Where the patient would (apart from section 21 above) have ceased to be liable to be detained or subject to guardianship on or before the day on which a report is duly furnished in respect of him under subsection (2) above, the report shall renew the authority for his detention or guardianship for the period prescribed in that case by section 20(2) above.

(6) Where the authority for the detention or guardianship of the patient is renewed by virtue of subsection (5) above—

(a) the renewal shall take effect as from the day on which (apart from section 21 above and that subsection) the authority would have expired; and

(b) if (apart from this paragraph) the renewed authority would expire on or before the day on which the report is furnished, the report shall further renew the authority, as from the day on which it would expire, for the period prescribed in that case by section 20(2) above.

(7) Where the authority for the detention or guardianship of the patient would expire within the period of two months beginning with the day on which a report is duly furnished in respect of him under subsection (2) above, the report shall, if it so provides, have effect also as a report duly furnished under section 20(3) or (6) above; and the reference in this subsection to authority includes any authority renewed under subsection (5) above by the report.

(8) Where the form of mental disorder specified in a report furnished under subsection (2) above is a form of disorder other than that specified in the application for admission for treatment or guardianship application concerned (and the report does not have effect as a report furnished under section 20(3) or (6) above), that application shall have effect as if that other form of mental disorder were specified in it.

(9) Where on any occasion a report specifying such a form of mental disorder is furnished under subsection (2) above the appropriate medical officer need not on that occasion furnish a report under section 16 above.

(10) In this section—

"appropriate medical officer" has the same meaning as in section 16(5) above;

"the appropriate body" means—

(a) in relation to a patient who is liable to be detained in a hospital, the managers of the hospital; and

(b) in relation to a patient who is subject to guardianship, the responsible local social services authority; and

"the relevant conditions" means—

(a) in relation to a patient who is liable to be detained in a hospital, the conditions set out in subsection (4) of section 20 above; and

(b) in relation to a patient who is subject to guardianship, the conditions set out in subsection (7) of that section."

(3) In section 22 of that Act (special provisions as to patients sentenced to imprisonment etc.)—

(a) in subsection (2) (detained patient in whose case application for admission for treatment or guardianship application does not cease to have effect), for the words "and 21" there shall be substituted ", 21 and 21A"; and

(b) after that subsection there shall be inserted the following subsection—

"(3) In its application by virtue of subsection (2) above section 18(4) above shall have effect with the substitution of the words "end of the period of 28 days beginning with the first day of his absence without leave." for the words from "later of" onwards."

(4) In section 40 of that Act (effect of hospital orders and guardianship orders), after subsection (5) there shall be inserted the following subsection—

"(6) Where—

(a) a patient admitted to a hospital in pursuance of a hospital order is absent without leave;

(b) a warrant to arrest him has been issued under section 72 of the Criminal Justice Act 1967; and

(c) he is held pursuant to the warrant in any country or territory other than the United Kingdom, any of the Channel Islands and the Isle of Man,

he shall be treated as having been taken into custody under section 18 above on first being so held."

(5) In section 61 of that Act (review of treatment), in subsection (1) (report on treatment and patient's condition to be given to Secretary of State), in paragraph (a) (report to be given when report furnished under section 20(3)), for the words "in respect of the patient under section 20(3) above" there shall be substituted "under section 20(3) or 21B(2) above renewing the authority for the detention of the patient".

(6) In section 66 of that Act (applications to tribunals)—

(a) in subsection (1) (cases where application may be made), after paragraph (f) there shall be inserted the following paragraphs—

"(fa) a report is furnished under subsection (2) of section 21B above in respect of a patient and subsection (5) of that section applies (or subsections (5) and (6)(b) of that section apply) in the case of the report; or

(fb) a report is furnished under subsection (2) of section 21B above in respect of a patient and subsection (8) of that section applies in the case of the report; or"; and

(b) in subsection (2) (period within which application may be made), in paragraph (d), after "(d)" there shall be inserted ", (fb)" and, in paragraph (f), for the words "of that subsection, the period" there shall be substituted "or (fa) of that subsection, the period or periods".

(7) In section 68 of that Act (duty of managers of hospitals to refer cases to tribunal), in subsection (2) (reference where detention is renewed under section 20 and three years have elapsed since last consideration of case), after "20" there shall be inserted "or 21B".

(8) In Schedule 1 to that Act (application of provisions to patients subject to hospital and guardianship orders), in Part I (patients not subject to special restrictions), in paragraph 1 (provisions applying without modification), for "21," there shall be substituted "21 to 21B,".

GENERAL NOTE

If a patient who has absconded is taken into custody, or returns to the hospital or place where he is required to be, later than 28 days after absconding, the patient's medical officer must comply with the provisions of this section if the patient's detention or guardianship is to be renewed under s.20.

Subs. (1)

Beginning with. See the note on s.21(1) above.

Subs. (2)

Appropriate medical officer, relevant considerations, appropriate body. See subs. (10) below.

Furnish to the appropriate body. Even if the unexpired period of detention or guardianship is longer than the one week provided for in this subsection. Also note subs. (4).

Cause him. The appropriate body must arrange for the patient to be informed.

Subs. (3)

Professional concerned with patient's medical treatment. This does not necessarily have to be a hospital based professional.

An approved social worker. This person need not have been involved in the patient's original admission to hospital.

Subs. (4)

This subsection states that if the patient's liability to be detained or to be subject to guardianship would have extended beyond the one week period provided for in subs. (2), the detention or guardianship will end in the absence of a report being made by the appropriate medical officer under that subsection.

Subs. (5)

If a patient's liability to be detained or to be subject to guardianship would have expired before the end of the one week period provided for in subs. (2), and a report is furnished under that provision, the period of renewal shall be the period provided for in s.20(2) of the 1983 Act. The date of the renewal is established by subs. (6).

Subs. (6)

This subsection provides that where the authority for detention or guardianship of a patient has been renewed in the circumstances set out in subs. (5), the renewal has effect from the day on which the detention or guardianship would have expired. If this renewed authority is due to expire before the day on which the report under subs. (2) is made, a further period of renewal for the prescribed period is authorised by the subs. (2) report.

Subs. (7)

This provision avoids the need for two reports renewing a patient's detention or guardianship, one under subs. (2) and the other under s.20(3) or (6), if the authority for the patient's detention or guardianship would expire within two months of the report being made under subs. (2).

Subs. (8)

If the doctor who makes a report under subs. (2) states in his report that the patient is suffering from a form of mental disorder other than that specified in the original application, this has the effect of reclassifying the patient.

Subs. (9)

Furnish a report under s.16. This provides for the reclassification of the stated form of mental disorder of a patient who is detained for treatment or subject to guardianship.

Subs. (10)

Appropriate medical officer. For guardianship patients this is the "nominated medical attendant of the patient", and for patients who are detained for treatment, it is the patient's "responsible medical officer". Both of these terms are defined in s.34(1) of the 1983 Act.

Leave of absence from hospital

3.—(1) In section 17 of the Mental Health Act 1983 (leave of absence for patient liable to be detained in a hospital under Part II of that Act), in subsection (5), the words from "; and without prejudice" to the end (which cause a patient on leave of absence to cease to be liable to be so detained six months after the beginning of his absence even though he would not otherwise have by then ceased to be so liable) shall be omitted.

(2) In Schedule 1 to that Act (application of provisions to patients subject to hospital and guardianship orders), in Part II (patients subject to special restrictions), in paragraph 3(c) (modifications of section 17(5)), for the word "six" there shall be substituted "twelve".

(3) Subsections (1) and (2) apply where leave of absence has been granted to a patient before the day on which this section comes into force (as well as where it is granted to a patient after that day).

General Note

This section amends s.17(5) of the 1983 Act to remove the limit of six months on the period for which leave of absence from hospital may be granted to detained patients. The maximum period of leave that can be granted to hospital order patients (s.37 of the 1983 Act) or to patients who have been detained for treatment (s.3 of the 1983 Act) is now equivalent to the period during which the patient can be detained. Mr. John Bowis M.P., explained:

"[This section] extends from six months to one year in England and Wales the period for which a detained patient may be given leave of absence from hospital. While the patient remains under the care of the hospital team, that time is commonly used as a preliminary period of rehabilitation, to establish whether he is ready to leave hospital care entirely. When we consulted on those proposals in 1993, there was widespread support for extending the leave of absence provision, giving a longer, more meaningful period in which to assess a patient's ability to cope with life in the community before formal discharge." (*Hansard*, H.C. Vol. 262, cols. 164, 165).

Although the members of the Department of Health's Internal Review were clear that the removal of the six-month limit "would be a simple change giving useful flexibility to ensure the continuation of care after patients were discharged", they recognised that it will not achieve this by itself. They recommended "that extended leave is operated (even if the conditions remain formally subject to the responsible medical officer's discretion) in accordance with the principles of the care programme approach. In particular ... there should always be a named key worker and a clear treatment plan negotiated with the patient and agreed with the other professionals and agencies concerned. It can *never* be acceptable for leave to be allowed to lapse without proper provision having been made for follow-up care" (para. 8.9).

Subs. (2)

This provision brings patients who are made subject to restriction orders (s.41 of the 1983 Act) into line with hospital order patients and patients who have been detained for treatment, by enabling the patient's responsible medical officer to recall the patient at any time up to 12 months from the first day of his absence on leave. The Home Secretary retains his power to recall the patient at any time.

Subs. (3)

The effect of this subsection was explained by Baroness Cumberlege:

"At present, Section 22 of the Mental Health Act 1983 states that when a patient who has been subject to imprisonment is released, he should be treated as though he were absent without leave under Section 18 of the 1983 Act. This is a legal device to provide a period of 28 days in which such patients could be returned to detention in hospital. However, as your Lordships know, Clause 2 of this Bill extends the period of time in which an absconding patient can be returned to hospital from 28 days to at least six months. An unintentional consequence of this is to extend the period of time within which a released prisoner could be returned to detention under the 1983 Act. I am sure your Lordships will agree that this is undesirable, both in its own right, and because it would be inconsistent with the provisions laid out in the earlier amendments relating to prisoners subject to supervision applications. The effect of the amendment, therefore, is to retain for the purposes of Section 22 the period of 28 days within which a person who has been released from prison may be returned to hospital. This is followed by a period of seven days during which the responsible medical officer must examine the patient and determine whether his liability to detention should be renewed." (*Hansard*, H.L. Vol. 564, col. 174).

Subs. (4)

This subsection is concerned with the taking into custody of absconding patients who have gone abroad.

Subs. (5)

Section 61. This provides for the periodic review by the Mental Health Act Commission, of treatment which is being given to detained patients either under s.57(2) of the 1983 Act (commonly psychosurgery) or s.58(3)(b) of that Act (electro-convulsive therapy or the administration of medicine three months after it was first administered to the patient).

Subs. (6)

This subsection amends s.66 of the 1983 Act by providing rights to make applications to Mental Health Review Tribunals where the authority for the detention or guardianship of patients who have been absent without leave for more than 28 days is renewed after their return.

Scotland

Community care orders

4.—(1) After section 35 of the Mental Health (Scotland) Act 1984 there shall be inserted the following sections—

"*Community care orders*

Community care orders

35A.—(1) As respects a patient who is liable to be detained in a hospital in pursuance of an application for admission the responsible medical officer may, in accordance with section 35B of this Act, make an application (in this Act referred to as a "community care application") to the sheriff for an order (in this Act referred to as a "community care order") providing that the patient shall, instead of continuing to be liable to be so detained, be subject to the conditions specified in the order, being conditions imposed with a view to ensuring that he receives—

(a) medical treatment; and

(b) after-care services provided for him under section 8 of this Act.

(2) Sections 21(1), (2)(a) and (b), (3), (4) and (5) and 113 of this Act shall apply with respect to a community care application as they apply with respect to an application for admission.

(3) The sheriff shall, as respects a community care application—

(a) make a community care order in respect of the patient, subject to the conditions set out in the application or to such other conditions as the sheriff considers appropriate; or

(b) refuse the application.

(4) A community care order shall specify—

(a) the conditions to which the patient is to be subject;

(b) the name of the medical practitioner (the "special medical officer") who is to be principally concerned with the patient's medical treatment while the order is in force, who shall be a practitioner approved for the purposes of section 20 of this Act by a Health Board as having special experience in the diagnosis or treatment of mental disorder; and

(c) the name of the person (the "after-care officer") who is to be responsible for co-ordinating the provision of the after-care services to be provided for the patient under section 8 of this Act while the order is in force, who shall be a mental health officer of the local authority which is to provide the after-care services to be so provided.

(5) The sheriff may defer the making of a community care order until such arrangements as appear to him to be necessary for the provision of medical treatment and after-care services to the patient following the making of the order have been made to the sheriff's satisfaction.

(6) If, on the date when a patient ceases to be liable to be detained in a hospital in pursuance of an application for admission, a community care application has been made in respect of him but has not been determined, his liability to be so detained shall continue until the community care order comes into force or, as the case may be, the application is refused by the sheriff.

(7) If, on the date when a patient ceases to be liable to be detained in a hospital in pursuance of an application for admission, a community care order has been made in respect of him but has not come into force, his liability to be so detained shall continue until the order comes into force.

(8) On the coming into force of a community care order in respect of a patient, he shall cease to be liable to be detained in a hospital under this Part of this Act.

(9) The responsible medical officer shall, within 7 days of the making of a community care order, send a copy of the order to—

(a) the patient and any other person who has been consulted under subsection (3)(a) or (f) or (4) of section 35B of this Act;
(b) the Mental Welfare Commission;
(c) the patient's special medical officer; and
(d) the patient's after-care officer.

(10) The patient's after-care officer shall, on receiving a copy of the community care order, take such steps as are practicable to explain to the patient, both orally and in writing—

(a) the purpose and effect of the order and of the conditions specified in it;
(b) the patient's right of appeal to the sheriff under section 35F of this Act; and
(c) that the patient may make representations to the Mental Welfare Commission,

and shall send a copy of any written explanation to any other person who has been consulted under subsection (3)(a) or (4) of section 35B of this Act.

General Note

This section defines the patients for whom community care orders may be made, and provides that the application for an order shall be made to the sheriff. If the sheriff approves the order, it will specify the conditions to which the patient will be subject and will name his "special medical officer" in the community and his "after-care officer" from the social work department. The sheriff is given the power to defer the making of an order until he is satisfied that appropriate arrangements have been met.

The order is available for patients who have been admitted to hospital under an application for admission (under s.18 of the 1984 Act). This includes patients who have been transferred to hospital by a hospital order under the Criminal Procedure (Scotland) Act 1975 (c. 21) but not patients who are subject to restriction orders, whose discharge is a question for the Secretary of State.

The equivalent English provisions (new s.25A(1)(b) of the 1983 Act) provide that supervised discharge is not available for patients under the age of 16. There is no lower age limit in the Scottish legislation.

Young people can be compulsorily admitted to hospital under the 1984 Act, although this happens rarely. (In 1993/4 eight young people were detained under s.24 of the 1984 Act and two under s.18. In 1994/5 the figures were six and one respectively. Source: the Mental Welfare Commission.) However, it was argued in Parliament that if a young person was discharged from hospital it would be better that their continued supervision be dealt with by reference to the Reporter and the Children's Panel, who would have the power to order supervision and control for children under s.70 of the Children (Scotland) Act 1995. The Government rejected this argument, saying that the rehabilitation opportunities offered by the new orders should be available to all patients.

Subs. (1)

Liable to be detained in a hospital. The patient need not be resident in hospital at the time when the application is made. He may be already living in the community under leave of absence granted by the responsible medical officer under s.27 of the 1984 Act.

In pursuance of an application for admission. Community care orders are for people who have been admitted to hospital under an application for admission made under s.18 of the 1984 Act. They are not available for people who are on emergency detention under s.24 of the 1984 Act or who are further detained under s.26. The intention is that the orders are appropriate for people with a serious, long term mental illness. The Earl of Lindsay said that:

> "We have made it clear in guidance that patients with a mild mental illness may be discharged only following agreement of a multi-disciplinary care plan which will ensure that they receive a good standard of clinical and after-care services. This is set out in the circular, *Community care in Scotland, Assessment and care management* [SW11/91]" (*Hansard*, H.L. Vol. 563, col. 1267).

Community care orders can also be made in respect of patients who are transferred to hospital under a hospital order made under ss.175 or 376 of the Criminal Procedure (Scotland) Act 1975 (see Sched. 2, para. 5(c) of this Act). The responsible medical officer may apply for a community care order within 28 days of the date of the hospital order.

Community care orders are not available to patients who have restriction orders attached to their hospital orders under ss.178 or 379 of the 1975 Act (Sched. 2, para. 4). However s.62(3) of the 1984 Act provides that if a restriction order ceases to have effect while a hospital order in respect of the patient remains in force, the patient shall be treated as if he had been admitted under a hospital order. It would then be possible for an application to be made for a community care order.

Responsible medical officer. This is defined in s.59(1) of the 1984 Act, and is usually a consultant psychiatrist.

Sheriff. See the notes to subs. (2) below.

Conditions imposed with a view to ensuring. The English equivalent provisions (new s.25D(3) of the 1983 Act) spell out the conditions which can be imposed on a patient subject to supervised discharge. The Scottish section does not limit the discretion of the sheriff. He may impose such conditions as he thinks are necessary to ensure that the patient receives medical treatment and after-care. Some concern was expressed in Parliament that the wording of the section was too vague. However certain points were made to counter-act this criticism:

(i) the conditions can only be what is necessary to ensure the patient receives medical treatment and after-care.

> "They [the conditions] would have to fall within the scope of all conditions imposed under a community care order. That is, they must be imposed with a view to ensuring that the patient receives medical treatment and after-care under s.8 of the 1984 Act." *per* the Earl of Lindsay (*Hansard*, H.L. Vol. 563, col. 1269).

The Earl of Lindsay confirmed that the kind of conditions imposed would be similar to those imposed under s.25D(3) of the 1983 Act, "... usual conditions might include attendance at various places for the purposes of education or training and a required place of residence" (*Hansard*, H.L. Vol. 564, col. 175).

Other conditions, for example a restriction on the use of alcohol, or the imposition of "no-go" areas, do not come within this wording, and could well fall foul of the European Convention on Human Rights. However, clearly the responsible medical officer and the sheriff could *advise* the patient that such limitations on behaviour might be sensible.

(ii) the sheriff must act reasonably.

(iii) the sheriff must be guided by the medical and social work reports issued under s.35B(7).

The Government has said that: "It is unlikely that a sheriff could regard as appropriate a condition which was opposed by either the special medical officer or the after-care officer." *per* the Earl of Lindsay (*Hansard*, H.L. Vol. 563, col. 1269).

However the sheriff should not take the reports at face value and if he is not satisfied that the arrangements proposed are going to ensure that the patient will receive the support he needs, he is given the power under subs. (5) to defer the making of the order until he is so satisfied.

The Government will issue guidance on the new orders, which will be made available to sheriffs *per* Mr. John Bowis M.P. (*Hansard*, H.C. Vol. 262, col. 168).

Para. (a)

Ensuring that he receives ... medical treatment. This does not mean that he can be forced to take medical treatment against his will. Subsection (8) provides that a patient for whom a community care order is made ceases to be liable to be detained in hospital under Pt. V of the 1984 Act. He therefore ceases to be liable to the compulsory treatment provisions of Pt. X of the 1984 Act, which apply, with certain exceptions, to those "liable to be detained" (s.96(1) of the 1984 Act).

> "There will be no power under community care orders to administer medication in the community without the patient's consent. I make that clear because there appears to have been some misunderstanding about what is being proposed." *per* Mr. John Bowis M.P. (*Hansard*, H.C. Vol. 262, col. 167).
>
> "The community care order is not an order to receive treatment but a way of ensuring that people receive the offer of, and are encouraged to receive, the care they need." *per* the Earl of Lindsay (*Hansard*, H.L. Vol. 563, col. 327).

Para. (b)

After-care services provided for him under section 8 of this Act. Unfortunately the 1984 Act does not define what kind of after-care services the local authority should provide or for how long they should do this.

A new system of measuring patients' needs for care in the community was introduced by the National Health Service and Community Care Act 1990. The Act amends the Social Work (Scotland) Act 1968 (c. 49) and, in a new s.12A to that Act, provides that where a "person in need" appears to require "community care services", the local authority must carry out an assessment of his needs.

There were attempts in Parliament to require that the after-care officer should provide a full community care assessment for the sheriff to see, so that he could make a decision about the adequacy of the after-care support being offered.

> *Lord Carmichael of Kelvingrove*: "If the Minister can assure me that the consultation with the sheriff will be the equivalent of the sheriff having the benefit of a full assessment, and it is not merely an untutored or an unstructured discussion, I would be happy with that ... If the noble Earl can assure us that what he is suggesting would be the equivalent of a full assessment, I would be quite happy to withdraw the amendment."
>
> *The Earl of Lindsay*: My Lords, I can reassure the noble Lord. The sheriff must be convinced that the appropriate community facilities are in place, and that the structural support is in place. Until he is convinced that is the case, he will not be in a position to grant a community care order." (*Hansard*, H.L. Vol. 563, col. 1268.)

It seems, therefore, that no distinction is being drawn by the Government between after-care services and community care services provided under the 1990 Act. The sheriff would, in any event, be entitled to ask to see the community care assessment, which the local authority is obliged to carry out under the 1990 Act. He can ask for any further information he requires under s.2(2)(a) of the 1984 Act.

Subs. (2)

Sections 21(1), 2(a) and (b), (3), (4) and (5) and 113 of this Act. These sections set out the rules for court proceedings under the 1984 Act. They have been supplemented by the Act of Sederunt (Mental Health (Scotland) Act 1984) 1986 No. 545. This deals with formal notices to the patient, fixing of hearing dates, etc. A new Act of Sederunt will be necessary to deal with such matters for this Act.

The sections specify the sheriffdom to which the application should be made, being *either* where the patient is resident *or*, if the patient is detained in hospital, where the hospital is situated. The sheriff is given the power to make further enquiries and to call witnesses.

If the application is opposed by the patient's "nearest relative" (defined in s.53 of the 1984 Act) the sheriff must give that relative, and any witnesses he calls, the opportunity to be heard. The sheriff must not withhold his approval to a community care order application without hearing from the responsible medical officer and any witnesses he may call.

The hearing may be heard in private. The sheriff should give the patient or his representative the opportunity to be heard in the proceedings, but he may exclude the patient if he is satisfied that it would not be in the interests of the patient's health or treatment that he should be present. The sheriff may appoint a curator *ad litem* to represent the patient.

The sheriff is given the same powers to administer oaths, etc., as if he were acting in his civil jurisdiction.

There were concerns expressed in Parliament that court proceedings might be unduly stressful for patients and they might be unwilling to attend and put their views. The Government said that: "A patient who is so ill as to be unable to attend a court hearing should probably not be considered for a community care order. In such circumstances, the patient should be cared for in hospital." *per* Lord James Douglas-Hamilton (*Hansard*, H.C. Vol. 264, col. 1175).

Subs. (3)
Para. (a)
Such other conditions as the sheriff considers appropriate. The conditions should be aimed at ensuring that the patient receives medical treatment or after-care services provided under s.8 of the 1984 Act.

Subs. (4)
Para. (b)
Special medical officer. This may be the responsible medical officer.

"There is nothing in the Bill as drafted which would prevent the special medical officer [and] the responsible medical officer, or the after-care officer and the patient's mental health officer from being the same person. Indeed we had envisaged that that might be so in most cases." *per* the Earl of Lindsay (*Hansard*, H.L. Vol. 563, col. 333).

Para. (c)
Mental health officer. The mental health officer is a social worker of the local authority with particular experience and qualifications in dealing with people with mental disorder (see s.9 of the 1984 Act).

Concern was expressed in Parliament that, following local government re-organisation in Scotland, some local authorities, particularly the smaller ones, might find it difficult to provide sufficient mental health officers to provide reports under the Act, or to supervise patients on community care orders, as after-care officers. The Government made it clear that:

"there is no legislative provision to prevent an after-care officer from delegating a patient's day-to-day care management to a care manager, who need not be a mental health officer." *per* Lord James Douglas-Hamilton (Standing Committee F, col. 142).

Subs. (5)
This subsection gives the sheriff the power to defer the making of a community care order. Concern was expressed whether the sheriff could require arrangements to be made which were not within the resources of either the health board or the local authority. Whilst a sheriff may not be able to impose conditions which either the special medical officer or after-care officer cannot meet, the Act makes it clear that he is able to defer the making of an order until satisfactory arrangements have been made.

Subs. (6)
his liability to be detained shall be extended. It is unfortunate that responsible medical officers are not encouraged to make applications for community care orders in good time to avoid extending the patient's detention unnecessarily.

Subs. (7)
liability to be so detained shall be extended. No time limit is imposed and the detention could be extended for a considerable time while the arrangements are being put in place.

Subs. (8)
shall cease to be liable to be detained. This has the result that the patient ceases to be liable to the consent to treatment provision of Pt. X of the 1984 Act (see s.96 of the 1984 Act).

Subs. (10)
explain. This wording contrasts with the wording used in s.110 of the 1984 Act. When a patient has been detained in hospital, the local authority are to "take such steps as are practicable to ensure that the patient understands" his legal position. Attempts were made in Parliament to apply the s.110 requirement to community care orders, but the Government rejected this, saying that: "We think there is no qualitative difference between the wording of the clause and the wording of the amendment." *per* Lord James Douglas-Hamilton (Standing Committee F, col. 144).

Community care applications

35B.—(1) A community care application may be made at any time after the expiry of the period of 28 days beginning with the day on which the patient was admitted to a hospital in pursuance of an application for admission.

(2) Before making a community care application the responsible medical officer shall—

(a) consult the persons specified in subsection (3) below; and
(b) consider the matters specified in subsection (5) below.

(3) The persons referred to in subsection (2)(a) above are—

(a) the patient and, if practicable and the patient does not object, his nearest relative;
(b) the persons who have been principally concerned with the patient's medical treatment in hospital;
(c) the medical practitioner who is to be the patient's special medical officer and the other persons who are to be concerned with the patient's medical treatment after the community care order comes into force;
(d) the person who is to be the patient's after-care officer;
(e) each other person who the responsible medical officer believes is to have a continuing professional involvement in any aspect of the after-care services which are to be provided for the patient under section 8 of this Act after the order comes into force; and
(f) any person who the responsible medical officer believes will play a substantial part in the care of the patient after the order comes into force but will not be professionally concerned with the after-care services to be so provided.

(4) If the patient has a propensity to violent or dangerous behaviour the responsible medical officer may consult the patient's nearest relative notwithstanding any objection by the patient to such consultation under subsection (3)(a) above.

(5) The matters referred to in subsection (2)(b) above are—

(a) the after-care services mentioned in subsection (3)(e) above; and
(b) the conditions which should be specified in the order with a view to ensuring that the patient receives medical treatment and such after-care services.

(6) A community care application shall be in the prescribed form and shall include—

(a) the conditions which the responsible medical officer considers should be specified in the community care order for the purpose mentioned in subsection (5)(b) above;
(b) the name of the medical practitioner who is to be the patient's special medical officer after the order comes into force;
(c) the name of the person who is to be the patient's after-care officer after the order comes into force; and
(d) subject to section 35C(1) of this Act, the period for which the responsible medical officer considers the order should have effect.

(7) A community care application shall be accompanied by—

(a) two medical recommendations, in the prescribed form and complying with subsection (8) below, one of which shall be given by a medical practitioner approved for the purposes of section 20 of this Act by a Health Board as having special experience in the diagnosis or treatment of mental disorder and the other of which shall, if practicable, be given by another medical practitioner who has previous acquaintance with the patient; and

(b) a report in the prescribed form from the person who is to be the patient's after-care officer after the order comes into force, and complying with subsection (9) below.

(8) The medical recommendations referred to in subsection (7)(a) above shall consist of statements of opinion that both the following conditions are satisfied, namely—

(a) that the patient is suffering from mental disorder of a nature or degree which makes it appropriate for him to receive medical treatment, but that the grounds set out in section 17(1) of this Act for admission to and detention in a hospital do not apply to the patient; and

(b) that the patient requires to be subject to a community care order—

(i) with a view to ensuring that he receives medical treatment and the after-care services to be provided for him under section 8 of this Act; and

(ii) in the interests of his health or safety or with a view to the protection of other persons;

and for the purposes of subsection (7)(a) above the recommendations do not comply with this subsection unless the patient is described in each of them as suffering from the same form of mental disorder (that is to say, mental illness or mental handicap), whether or not he is described in either recommendation as suffering also from the other form.

(9) The report referred to in subsection (7)(b) above shall include—

(a) information as to—

(i) the patient's social circumstances;

(ii) the after-care services which are to be provided for the patient under section 8 of this Act after the order comes into force;

(iii) the care, other than medical treatment and the after-care services so provided, which is to be provided for the patient after the order comes into force; and

(b) a statement that in the opinion of the person making the report the patient requires to be subject to a community care order—

(i) with a view to ensuring that he receives medical treatment and the after-care services to be so provided; and

(ii) in the interests of his health or safety or with a view to the protection of other persons.

(10) Before making a community care application the responsible medical officer shall take such steps as are reasonably practicable to inform any person, other than the patient, who has been consulted under subsection (3)(a) or (4) above of his right, by virtue of section 35A(2) of this Act, to be heard by the sheriff regarding the proposed community care order.

GENERAL NOTE

Before an application is made for a community care order, the responsible medical officer must carry out a full, multi-disciplinary consultation with those involved in the patient's care in hospital and those who will provide care in the community. Reports recommending the making of a community care order must then be submitted to the sheriff from two doctors (the responsible medical officer and another doctor who knows the patient) and from the after-care officer.

The medical reports submitted by the responsible medical officer must stipulate that the patient does not come within the criteria of s.17(1) of the 1984 Act (*i.e.* he does not need to be in hospital), but he does need medical treatment in the interests of his own health or safety or the protection of other people. The reports must confirm that a community care order is necessary to attempt to ensure he receives such treatment and specify the care the patient is to receive in the community.

However the community care order does *not* authorise the giving of medication to the patient without his consent. The order can ensure that the patient has access to medical treatment, as defined, and that medical practitioners have access to him, but not that he be compelled to accept the medication or treatments offered.

Subs. (1)

The community care order is available only for patients who have been admitted to hospital under s.18 of the 1984 Act. The patient must have been liable to detention for at least 28 days before an application is made. In the case of a patient who is in hospital under a hospital order, the 28 days runs from the date the order was made (Sched. 2, para. 5(c)).

Subs. (2)

Para. (a)

Consult. There were concerns that the local authority should be required to agree to the community care arrangements, rather than just be consulted about them. The Government saw this distinction as academic:

"The leading role of the medical professionals under the community care order reflects the necessarily high level of medical content. The after-care officer must nevertheless support the application for the order before it can go forward ... In effect, by the time the matter has reached the sheriff it will have become a joint application." *per* the Earl of Lindsay (*Hansard*, H.L. Vol. 563, col. 324).

Subs. (3)

Para. (a)

"*Nearest relative.* The 1984 Act contains complex rules for establishing who is entitled to be treated as the patient's nearest relative (ss.53–57).

Para. (b)

Principally concerned with the patient's medical treatment in hospital. The Scottish Home and Health Department, explaining similar wording in the 1984 Act, says that this "should invariably include the nurse in charge of the patient's ward or another nurse who has been caring for the patient. It should also include any other professional involved in the patient's treatment who may reasonably be expected to have an informed view on the suitability of the proposed form of treatment." (*Scottish Home and Health Department Notes on the [1984] Act*, para. 388.)

Para. (e)

Each other person who ... is to have a continuing professional involvement. This could include staff at day centres, or in supported accommodation projects, home helps, etc. Although the Act says "each" such person must be consulted by the responsible medical officer, presumably one representative from each such organisation suffices.

Para. (f)

Any person who ... will pay a substantial part in the care of the patient but will not be so professionally concerned. Informal and unpaid carers (often relatives of the patient) are regarded as crucial to the success of community care, and the Act requires them to be consulted at all stages of the procedure. It would be up to the responsible medical officer to decide whether a carer was providing the amount of care which would entitle him to be consulted.

Subs. (4)

Propensity to violent or dangerous behaviour. Generally, under the 1984 Act, the patient's nearest relative has the right to receive information about the patient, whether or not the patient objects. The nearest relative can consent to the patient's detention in hospital and may even apply for admission under s.18. This Act provides that the nearest relative should only be involved in community care orders "if the patient does not object" (see, for example s.35B(3)(a) and s.35C(3)(i)).

Last minute objections from relatives' organisations led to the rather strange wording of this provision. For the explanation given in the House of Lords, see comments on the new s.25B(3) of the 1983 Act, page 52–19.

Subs. (7)

Para. (a)

Previous acquaintance with the patient. This would often be the patient's G.P.

"We accept that the patient's G.P. will normally know a patient well and may, therefore, be the best person to provide the second medical report ..." *per* Lord James Douglas-Hamilton

(Standing Committee F, col. 149). However if the patient has no G.P., any doctor who knows him can be used.

Subs. (8)
Para. (a)

Mental disorder. Defined by s.1 of the 1984 Act as "mental illness or mental handicap, however caused or manifested".

Community care orders are primarily intended for people with serious mental illness. However the Government refused to say that they should not apply to people with learning disabilities or mental handicaps. Lord James Douglas-Hamilton said that: "there may be cases in which a community care order would be appropriate to a person with a learning disability, if, for example, that person had a mental illness as well." (Standing Committee F, col. 151).

Grounds set out in s.17(1). i.e. that the patient does not need to receive treatment in a hospital for his mental disorder.

It has been pointed out that there is an apparent inconsistency in the way this Act ties in with the 1984 Act. Under s.33(3) of the 1984 Act, the responsible medical officer is obliged constantly to keep the situation of the patient under review and to discharge the patient from hospital if he believes the patient should no longer be "liable to detention". This Act requires that, when he applies for a community care order, the responsible medical officer should be of the view that the patient does not need in-patient treatment. In these circumstances is the responsible medical officer not obliged immediately to discharge the patient from detention under s.33(3)?

The 1984 Act establishes different tests at the various stages of the detention process. The scheme it establishes is extended by this Act:

(i) The patient requires in-patient treatment in hospital and, in the case of certain patients, this will improve their condition or at least stop it getting worse. This test applies on admission to hospital and when the responsible medical officer renews the detention under s.30 of the 1984 Act.

(ii) The patient requires to be liable to detention. The test used for the responsible medical officer when he considers whether the detention should be discharged, and for the sheriff when he hears appeals (s.33(4) of the 1984 Act). This test applies only after an application for admission under s.18 of the 1984 Act has been approved, *i.e.* at one stage the patient must have required compulsory in-patient treatment.

Section 27 of the 1984 Act allows a person who has been detained under s.18 of the 1984 Act or a renewal under s.30 to be allowed by the responsible medical officer to leave hospital. The patient remains liable to detention and can be recalled at any time by the responsible medical officer if, for example a placement in the community does not work out or if he stops taking his medication.

(iii) The patient requires to be under a community care order. He requires medical treatment, but he does not need to receive this as a hospital in-patient. He requires a community care order to ensure he receives medical treatment and after-care.

The patient may be living on leave of absence when the community care order is applied for. Under the 1984 Act, the responsible medical officer is unable to renew the detention unless he believes the patient now requires in-patient treatment. However the responsible medical officer may believe that the patient needs continued supervision in the community. In those circumstances he would be able to apply for a community care order.

The responsible medical officer is not obliged under s.33(4) to discharge the detention at the time when he applies for the community care order because of his belief that, in the absence of a community care order, the patient will continue to need to be subject to the restraints of being liable to detention. (The author is grateful to Mr Adrian Ward, Solicitor, for raising this question.)

Medical treatment. This is defined in s.125(1) of the 1984 Act as including nursing, and care and training under medical supervision.

Subs. (9)
Para. (a)(iii)

Care, other than medical treatment and the after-care services so provided, which is to be provided. This could include help with housing or educational services, which may not be provided by the social work department, or help from a voluntary or independent care agency.

Subs. (10)

Right ... to be heard. The nearest relative has a right to be heard, and to call witnesses.

Duration and renewal of community care order

35C.—(1) Subject to section 35J of this Act and the following provisions of this section, a community care order shall have effect for such period, not exceeding 6 months, as may be specified in the order.

(2) A community care order may be renewed under this section—

(a) from the expiry of the period referred to in subsection (1) above, for a further period not exceeding 6 months;

(b) from the expiry of any period of renewal under paragraph (a) above, for a further period not exceeding one year, and so on for periods not exceeding one year at a time.

(3) The special medical officer shall, within the period of two months ending with the day on which the community care order, if not renewed, would expire—

(a) examine the patient; and

(b) consult—

(i) the patient and, if practicable and the patient does not object, his nearest relative;

(ii) the patient's after-care officer;

(iii) the other persons concerned with the patient's medical treatment or professionally concerned with any aspect of the after-care services provided for him under section 8 of this Act; and

(iv) any person who the special medical officer believes plays a substantial part in the care of the patient but is not professionally concerned with the after-care services so provided.

(4) If the patient has a propensity to violent or dangerous behaviour the responsible medical officer may consult the patient's nearest relative notwithstanding any objection by the patient to such consultation under subsection (3)(b)(i) above.

(5) If, after the examination and consultation required by subsection (3) above and any consultation under subsection (4) above, the special medical officer considers that the conditions set out in section 35B(8)(a) and (b) of this Act continue to apply to the patient, he shall send to the Mental Welfare Commission a report to that effect in the prescribed form, and the community care order shall thereby be renewed for such period as is, subject to subsection (2) above, specified in the report.

(6) The special medical officer shall notify—

(a) the patient and any other person who has been consulted under subsection (3)(b)(i) or (iv) or (4) above; and

(b) the patient's after-care officer,

of any renewal of the community care order and of the period of such renewal.

(7) Subsection (10) of section 35A of this Act shall apply in relation to a renewal of a community care order under this section as it applies in relation to a community care order made under that section, but with the substitution of references to subsections (3)(b)(i) and (4) of this section for the references to subsections (3)(a) and (4) of section 35B.

GENERAL NOTE

A community care order can last for up to six months. It may be renewed by the special medical officer for one further period of six months and thereafter for periods of one year at a time. The special medical officer must consult with the patient and all those responsible for his care before renewing the order. The Mental Welfare Commission is to be informed of the renewal of the order. The after-care officer should inform the patient and his nearest relative of the patient's right to appeal against any renewal and to apply to the Mental Welfare Commission for discharge from the order.

Subs. (1)

Six months. This should be read subject to the provisions of s.35I, which give the special medical officer the duty to discharge the patient from the community care order at any time if he thinks it is no longer necessary.

Section 22 of the 1984 Act imposes a duty on the responsible medical officer formally to review the condition of patients who are detained under s.18 within one month of their detention. There is no formal review period in this Act because: "... we do not consider this is necessary for a patient in the community. The constant review of the patient's need for a community care order should form part of good multi-disciplinary practice by the care team, and is very much a matter for guidance" *per* the Earl of Lindsay (*Hansard*, H.L. Vol. 563, col. 355.)

Subs. (4)

Propensity to violent or dangerous behaviour. See comment at s.35B(4) above.

Variation of conditions in community care order

35D.—(1) This section applies where the special medical officer, after consulting—

(a) the patient and, if practicable and the patient does not object, his nearest relative;

(b) the other persons concerned with the patient's medical treatment;

(c) the patient's after-care officer;

(d) the other persons professionally concerned with any aspect of the after-care services provided for the patient under section 8 of this Act; and

(e) any person who the special medical officer believes plays a substantial part in the care of the patient but is not professionally concerned with the after-care services so provided,

considers that the conditions specified in the order should be varied (whether by adding further conditions or deleting or amending existing conditions).

(2) If the patient has a propensity to violent or dangerous behaviour the special medical officer may consult the patient's nearest relative notwithstanding any objection by the patient to such consultation under subsection (1)(a) above.

(3) Where this section applies the special medical officer shall prepare a note, in the prescribed form, of the proposed variation of the conditions and shall send a copy of the note to—

(a) the patient and any other person who has been consulted under subsection (1)(a) or (2) above;

(b) the patient's after-care officer; and

(c) the sheriff clerk for the sheriff of the sheriffdom within which the patient is resident.

(4) If the patient wishes to object to or make representations concerning the proposed variation of the conditions he shall, within 7 days of receiving the copy of the note under subsection (3) above, so advise the sheriff clerk; and in that event the sheriff shall not approve the variation without holding a hearing.

(5) If the patient does not indicate, in accordance with subsection (4) above, that he wishes to be heard concerning the proposed variation of the conditions the sheriff shall, if he thinks fit, approve the variation without a hearing.

(6) Where a variation of conditions is approved under this section the special medical officer shall send a copy of the variation as so approved to—

(a) the patient and any other person who has been consulted under subsection (1)(a) or (e) or (2) above;

(b) the Mental Welfare Commission; and

(c) the patient's after-care officer.

(7) Subsection (10) of section 35A of this Act shall apply in relation to a variation of conditions approved under this section as it applies in relation to a community care order made under that section, but with the substitution of references to subsections (1)(a) and (2) of this section for the references to subsections (3)(a) and (4) of section 35B.

GENERAL NOTE

If, after consultation with the patient and all those involved in his treatment and care, the special medical officer believes that the order should be varied, he may notify the patient, his after-care officer and the sheriff of the proposed variation. A hearing will be held if the patient objects to the proposed variation within seven days. Otherwise the sheriff can approve the variation without a hearing.

Subs. (1)

The special medical officer. Only the special medical officer can call for a variation. The patient cannot, nor can his carer, the after-care officer or his nearest relative. They would have to request the special medical officer to consider applying for a variation.

Subs. (4)

The patient. Only the patient is given the formal right to object and so trigger a hearing. A carer or relative might oppose the variations but would have no right to insist on a hearing. However, their views will have been taken into account on consultation.

There is no form to be prescribed on which the patient should notify the sheriff that he objects to the proposed variation. It is to be hoped that the form used by the special medical officer will make it clear how the patient is to object.

Subs. (5)

Even if the patient does not object, the sheriff may hold a hearing.

Change of special medical officer or after-care officer

35E.—(1) This subsection applies where a patient's special medical officer, after consulting the persons mentioned in subsection (3) below, agrees with another medical practitioner ("the new special medical officer"), who shall be a practitioner approved for the purposes of section 20 of this Act by a Health Board as having special experience in the diagnosis or treatment of mental disorder, that the new special medical officer should, from a date so agreed, assume principal responsibility for the patient's medical treatment while the community care order is in force.

(2) This subsection applies where a patient's after-care officer, after consulting the persons mentioned in subsection (4) below, agrees with another person ("the new after-care officer", who shall be a mental health officer of the local authority which is providing (or, if different, the local authority which is to provide) the after-care services to be provided for the patient under section 8 of this Act while the community care order is in force, that the new after-care officer should, from a date so agreed, assume responsibility for co-ordinating the provision of the after-care services to be so provided.

(3) The persons referred to in subsection (1) above are—

(a) the patient and, if practicable and the patient does not object, his nearest relative;

(b) the other persons concerned or to be concerned with the patient's medical treatment (including the new special medical officer);

(c) the patient's after-care officer;

(d) the other persons professionally concerned or to be so concerned with any aspect of the after-care services provided or to be provided for the patient under section 8 of this Act; and

(e) any person who the special medical officer believes plays or is to play a substantial part in the care of the patient but is not, and will not be, professionally concerned with the after-care services so provided or to be so provided.

(4) The persons referred to in subsection (2) above are—

(a) the patient and, if practicable and the patient does not object, his nearest relative;

(b) the patient's special medical officer;

(c) the other persons concerned or to be concerned with the patient's medical treatment;

(d) the other persons professionally concerned or to be so concerned with any aspect of the after-care services provided or to be provided for the patient under section 8 of this Act (including the new after-care officer); and

(e) any person who the after-care officer believes plays or is to play a substantial part in the care of the patient but is not, and will not be professionally concerned with the after-care services so provided or to be so provided.

(5) If the patient has a propensity to violent or dangerous behaviour the special medical officer or, as the case may be, the after-care officer may consult the patient's nearest relative notwithstanding any objection by the patient to such consultation under subsection (3)(a) or, as the case may be, (4)(a) above.

(6) Where subsection (1) or (2) above applies the new special medical officer or, as the case may be, the new after-care officer shall, from the agreed date, assume responsibility as mentioned in that subsection and shall within seven days of that date intimate the change, in the prescribed form, to—

(a) the patient and any other person who has been consulted under paragraph (a) or (e) of subsection (3) or, as the case may be, (4) above or subsection (5) above;

(b) the Mental Welfare Commission; and

(c) the patient's after-care officer or, as the case may be, special medical officer.

(7) On a change of special medical officer or after-care officer by virtue of this section, the community care order shall have effect in respect of the patient as if the new special medical officer or, as the case may be, the new after-care officer had been the special medical officer or after-care officer specified in the community care order by virtue of section 35A(4) of this Act.

GENERAL NOTE

A new special medical officer or after-care officer may be appointed after the appropriate consultation process. Various people must be notified of the changes, including the patient, the Mental Welfare Commission and the patient's nearest relative (unless the patient objects).

Appeal against community care order

35F.—(1) Any patient subject to a community care order may, at any time when the order is in force following renewal under section 35C(5) of this Act, appeal to the sheriff for revocation of the order.

(2) An appeal under subsection (1) above shall be by way of summary application and shall be made to the sheriff of the sheriffdom within which the patient is resident.

(3) On an appeal under subsection (1) above—

(a) if the sheriff is satisfied that the patient—

(i) does not require to be subject to a community care order with a view to ensuring that he receives medical treatment and after-care services provided for him under section 8 of this Act; and

(ii) does not require to be subject to such an order in the interests of his health or safety or with a view to the protection of other persons,

he shall revoke the order; and

(b) in any other case, the sheriff shall refuse the appeal and affirm the order, either without amendment or subject to such variation as he considers appropriate.

(4) Where, under subsection (3)(a) above, the sheriff revokes a community care order he may order that the revocation shall have effect either immediately or from such date, not later than 28 days after the date of his decision, as he may specify.

(5) The special medical officer shall notify the patient's after-care officer of any revocation or variation of a community care order under this section.

GENERAL NOTE

The patient may appeal to the sheriff against the community care order at any time after the order has been renewed.

Subs. (3)

Para. (a)

If the sheriff is satisfied that (i) ... and (ii). Unlike the appeal against detention (s.33(4)), the test whether the conditions for a community care order apply is conjunctive, not disjunctive. The sheriff has to be satisfied both that the patient does not need supervision and that he does not need it in the interests of his own health or safety or to protect others. However the difference in the wording may not have much practical impact. It is difficult to see how a patient could "need" supervision unless for the reasons spelt out in para. (b). (The author is grateful to Mr Chris Turner, solicitor for raising this point.)

Para. (b)

Subject to such variation as he considers appropriate. "The discretion of the sheriff to vary the conditions ... must, of course, ... be exercised reasonably." *per* the Earl of Lindsay (*Hansard*, H.L. Vol. 563, col. 350).

Subs. (5)

After-care officer. It is strange that only the after-care officer is to be informed of the outcome of the appeal. Other candidates for this information could include the Mental Welfare Commission, nearest relative and carer.

Admission to hospital for reassessment

35G.—(1) This section applies where, as respects a patient in respect of whom a community care order is in force, the special medical officer, after consulting the persons mentioned in subsection (2) below, considers that the patient's mental condition—

(a) has, since the making of the order or, where the order has been renewed under section 35C(5) of this Act, the most recent renewal, deteriorated; and

(b) is, or is likely to become, such as to give grounds for serious concern regarding his health or safety or the protection of other persons.

(2) The persons referred to in subsection (1) above are—

(a) if practicable and the patient does not object, his nearest relative;

(b) the other persons concerned with the patient's medical treatment;

(c) the patient's after-care officer;

(d) the other persons professionally concerned with any aspect of the after-care services provided for the patient under section 8 of this Act; and

(e) any person who the special medical officer believes plays a substantial part in the care of the patient but is not professionally concerned with the after-care services so provided.

(3) If the patient has a propensity to violent or dangerous behaviour the special medical officer may consult the patient's nearest relative notwithstanding any objection by the patient to such consultation under subsection (2)(a) above.

(4) Where this section applies, the special medical officer shall—

(a) examine the patient and prepare a report on his condition; and

(b) arrange for another medical practitioner to carry out such an examination and provide such a report.

(5) Where both reports conclude that—

(a) the patient is suffering from mental disorder of a nature or degree which makes it appropriate for him to be admitted to and detained in a hospital for assessment, or for assessment followed by medical treatment, for at least a limited period; and

(b) he ought to be so admitted and detained in the interests of his own health or safety or with a view to the protection of other persons,

the special medical officer may, with the consent of the patient's after-care officer, direct the patient to attend a hospital specified in the direction to be admitted and detained there by virtue of this section, and the direction shall be sufficient authority for the patient's removal to the hospital so specified and for his admission to and detention in that hospital in accordance with this section.

(6) Reports under subsection (4) above and directions under subsection (5) above shall be in the prescribed form.

(7) The special medical officer shall send a copy of the reports under subsection (4) above and of the direction under subsection (5) above to—

(a) any person who has been consulted under subsection (2)(a) or (e) or (3) above;

(b) the Mental Welfare Commission;

(c) the managers of the hospital specified in the direction; and

(d) the patient's after-care officer.

(8) Subject to section 35H(4)(b) of this Act, a patient admitted to a hospital by virtue of this section may be detained there for a period not exceeding 7 days beginning with the day on which he is admitted and shall not be further detained in a hospital by virtue of this section immediately after the expiry of the period of detention.

(9) While a patient is detained in a hospital by virtue of this section the period for which, under section 35C of this Act, the community care order has effect shall continue to run but the conditions to which he is subject under the order shall not apply in relation to him.

GENERAL NOTE

If the special medical officer believes, after consulting the relevant parties, that the mental health of a patient on a community care order has deteriorated he may readmit him to hospital for reassessment. Medical reports recommending readmission should be obtained. The patient may be kept in hospital for up to seven days. The special medical officer must obtain the agreement of the after-care officer to the detention. The community care order will continue to run, but its conditions are suspended.

Subs. (1)

Para. (a)

Considers that the patient's mental condition has deteriorated. There was some discussion in Parliament as to the events which should trigger the patient's readmission to hospital. It was suggested that the trigger should be the patient's failure to comply with any condition laid out in the community care order.

However the Government was clear that while a failure to comply with any of the conditions of the order would clearly be of interest to those supervising the patient, "the trigger [for reassessment in hospital] should surely be a deterioration in his [the patient's] mental health." *per* the Earl of Lindsay (*Hansard*, H.L. Vol. 563, col. 351).

Para. (b)

Is, or is likely to become such as to give grounds for serious concern. This meets the often expressed concerns of psychiatrists that, under the 1984 Act, they cannot act to prevent a serious breakdown of the patient. Under this provision they can anticipate a future breakdown of the patient's health and return him to hospital before he becomes eligible for compulsory detention under s.24 or s.18 of the 1984 Act.

In the light of the Winterwerp judgment (see note to s.25D of the 1983 Act, above), it is interesting that the Government was advised that this provision did not fall of the European Convention on Human Rights, despite the fact that the patient is given no right to appeal against his return to hospital (see discussion between Lord Carmichael of Kelvingrove and the Earl of Lindsay, *Hansard*, H.L. Vol. 563, cols. 352–353).

Subs. (4)
Para. (b)

Another medical practitioner. This person need not be a psychiatrist.

Subs. (5)
Para. (a)

Detained in hospital for assessment. Unlike the 1983 Act, the 1984 Act did not provide for admission to hospital for assessment, although emergency detention under s.24 is used for this purpose.

The special officer may, with the consent of the after-care officer. This is the only occasion in the Act where the after-care officer is given a veto. Generally the special medical officer consults the after-care officer but takes the final decision himself. The Act does not spell out the grounds on which the after-care officer can refuse to agree to the patient's readmission to hospital.

The directions shall be sufficient authority for the patient's removal to the hospital... [and for his] admission to and detention in that hospital. The patient then becomes subject to the compulsory treatment provisions of Pt. X of the 1984 Act, being "liable to detention" within s.96 of that Act. It was argued in Parliament that where a patient was being readmitted for "reassessment" it was not appropriate compulsorily to medicate him. Compulsory medication is not available under s.24 of the 1984 Act, the emergency detention provision. The Government dismissed this. Lord James Douglas-Hamilton said that:

> "Sometimes the mental health of a community care order patient may deteriorate to the point at which it is necessary to admit that person to hospital for reassessment or reassessment followed by treatment. That could occur if the patient has failed to take the necessary medication or where he lacks insight or perception into his condition. If that is the situation, we are in no doubt that it is in the patient's best interests for clinicians to have the power to administer medication without the consent of the patient within the terms of the 1984 Act, to prevent or limit further deterioration. It is not appropriate to draw comparisons with section 24." (Standing Committee F, col. 164).

Reassessment: further provisions

35H.—(1) Where a patient is detained in a hospital by virtue of section 35G of this Act, the responsible medical officer shall—

(a) examine the patient and prepare a report, in the prescribed form, on his condition; and

(b) arrange for another medical practitioner to carry out such an examination and provide such a report.

(2) If the responsible medical officer is not a practitioner approved for the purposes of section 20 of this Act by a Health Board as having special experience in the diagnosis or treatment of mental disorder, the medical practitioner referred to in subsection (1)(b) above shall require to be such a practitioner.

(3) Where both reports conclude that the conditions set out in section 35B(8)(a) and (b) of this Act apply in relation to the patient, the patient shall, as soon as is practicable, be discharged from hospital and the conditions to which he is subject under the community care order shall again apply in relation to him.

(4) Where both reports conclude that the grounds set out in section 17(1)(a) and (b) of this Act apply in relation to the patient and, within

the period specified in section 35G(8) of this Act, an application for admission is made in respect of the patient—

(a) the community care order in respect of the patient shall cease to have effect; and

(b) the submission to the sheriff, in accordance with section 21(1) of this Act, of the application for admission shall be sufficient authority for the detention of the patient in a hospital until the expiry of a further period of 21 days immediately following the expiry of the period specified in section 35G(8).

(5) The responsible medical officer shall send to the Mental Welfare Commission copies of the reports prepared under subsection (1) above.

(6) A patient detained in a hospital by virtue of section 35G of this Act shall cease to be liable to be so detained, and the community care order in respect of him shall cease to have effect—

(a) if the period mentioned in subsection (8) of that section expires without the patient having been discharged from hospital or an application for his admission having been submitted to the sheriff; or

(b) where an application for his admission has been submitted to the sheriff within that period, if the period of 21 days mentioned in subsection (4)(b) above expires without the sheriff having approved the application.

(7) For the purposes of this section, an application for admission is submitted to the sheriff when it is lodged with his sheriff clerk.

GENERAL NOTE

Once the patient is returned to hospital he must be examined by two doctors, at least one of whom must be a psychiatrist approved by the relevant health board. If the doctors consider that the patient does not need to be detained in hospital, he should be discharged and the community care order will be reinstated. If the doctors believe that the grounds for detention, as set out in s.17 of the 1984 Act, apply to the patient, they can apply to the sheriff for the patient to be admitted under s.18 of the Act. Once the application has been made, the community care order lapses and the patient can be kept in hospital for up to 21 days. If no application for admission is made within seven days of the patient's return to hospital and he is not discharged, the community care order lapses.

Subs. (1)

Responsible medical officer. See s.59 of the 1984 Act.

Subs. (6)
Para. (b)

If the sheriff does not approve the application to detain the patient, the community care order lapses. The sheriff does not have the option to refuse the application and reinstate the community care order.

Revocation of community care order

35I.—(1) Where the special medical officer, after consulting the persons mentioned in subsection (2) below, considers that the patient—

(a) does not require to be subject to a community care order with a view to ensuring that he receives medical treatment and after-care services provided for him under section 8 of this Act; and

(b) does not require to be subject to such an order in the interests of his health or safety or with a view to the protection of other persons,

he shall revoke the order and shall notify the patient, his nearest relative (if practicable), his after-care officer, any person falling within subsection (2)(e) below and the Mental Welfare Commission of the revocation.

(2) The persons to be consulted under subsection (1) above are—

(a) the patient and, if practicable and the patient does not object, his nearest relative;

(b) the other persons concerned with the patient's medical treatment;

(c) the patient's after-care officer;

(d) the other persons professionally concerned with any aspect of the after-care services provided for the patient under section 8 of this Act; and

(e) any person who the special medical officer believes plays a substantial part in the care of the patient but is not professionally concerned with the after-care services so provided.

(3) If the patient has a propensity to violent or dangerous behaviour the special medical officer may consult the patient's nearest relative notwithstanding any objection by the patient to such consultation under subsection (2)(a) above.

(4) Where the Mental Welfare Commission consider that the patient—

(a) does not require to be subject to a community care order with a view to ensuring that he receives medical treatment and after-care services provided for him under section 8 of this Act; and

(b) does not require to be subject to such an order in the interests of his health or safety or with a view to the protection of other persons,

they shall revoke the order and shall notify the persons mentioned in subsection (5) below of the revocation.

(5) The persons to be notified under subsection (4) above are—

(a) the patient and (if practicable) his nearest relative;

(b) the patient's special medical officer;

(c) the patient's after-care officer; and

(d) any person who the Mental Welfare Commission believes plays a substantial part in the care of the patient but is not professionally concerned with the after-care services provided for the patient under section 8 of this Act.

General Note

Either the special medical officer or the Mental Welfare Commission may revoke the order. They must do so if the grounds set out in the Act no longer apply. The special medical officer should consult with all relevant parties before revocation and the nearest relative and carers should be informed.

Neither health boards nor NHS Trusts are given the power to revoke the orders. This power is available to them in respect of detention (s.33(5) of the 1984 Act), but it is not widely used.

Subs. (1)

Para. (a)

Does not require to be subject ... and (b) ... See comments on s.35F(3)(a) above.

Shall notify the patient, his nearest relative (if practicable) "Where a community care order is revoked, the nearest relative will always be informed. That is regardless of whether the revocation has been by the special medical officer or the Mental Welfare Commission and regardless of whether the nearest relative has been consulted." *per* the Earl of Lindsay (*Hansard*, H.L. Vol. 563, col. 127).

However, the nearest relative may not have been informed that the community care order was made in the first place. If the patient objects to the involvement of the relative, he will only be told of the order if the patient has a propensity to violent or dangerous behaviour (s.35A(10)).

Subs. (4)

The Mental Welfare Commission for Scotland exercises "protective functions" for everyone who is incapable of protecting their own interests because of mental disorder (s.3(1) of the 1984 Act). As in detention, the Mental Welfare Commission has the right to discharge the patient from the community care order. It does not have to carry out the same consultations as the special medical officer. The patient should be told of his right to apply to the Mental Welfare

Commission for discharge by the after-care officer (s.35A(10)). This is particularly important during the first six months of the order, when the patient has no right to appeal to the sheriff.

Patients in custody or admitted to hospital in pursuance of emergency recommendations

35J.—(1) This section applies where a patient who is subject to a community care order—

(a) is detained in custody in pursuance of any sentence or order passed or made by a court in the United Kingdom (including an order committing or remanding him in custody); or

(b) is detained in a hospital under section 24, 26 or 26A of this Act.

(2) For so long as the patient is detained as mentioned in subsection (1)(a) or (b) above the period for which, under section 35C of this Act, the community care order has effect shall continue to run but the conditions to which he is subject under that order shall not apply in relation to him.

(3) If the patient is detained as mentioned in paragraph (a) of subsection (1) above for a period of, or successive periods amounting in the aggregate to, 6 months or less, or is detained as mentioned in paragraph (b) of that subsection, and, apart from this subsection, the community care order—

(a) would have ceased to have effect during the period for which he is so detained; or

(b) would cease to have effect during the period of 28 days beginning with the day on which he ceases to be so detained,

the order shall be deemed not to have ceased, and shall not cease, to have effect until the end of that period of 28 days.

(4) Where the period for which the patient is subject to a community care order is extended by subsection (3) above, any examination and report to be made and furnished in respect of the patient under section 35C(3) and (5) of this Act may be made and furnished within the period as so extended.

(5) Where, by virtue of subsection (4) above, a community care order is renewed for a further period after the day on which (apart from subsection (3) above) the order would have ceased to have effect, the further period shall be deemed to have commenced with that day.

General Note

Where a person subject to a community care order is taken into custody, or detained in hospital under an emergency or short term detention, the community care order will continue in effect, but its conditions are suspended. If the patient is in prison for a sentence or sentences of less than six months and the community care order would have lapsed during that time, the order continues for a further 28 days after he leaves custody.

Subs. (1)

Para. (b)

Detained in hospital under section 24. Concern was expressed in Parliament that if the mental health of a patient deteriorated while he was on a community care order, the doctors would always have to use the fairly cumbersome procedure for reassessing his needs set out in s.35G of the Act if they wished to readmit him to hospital. The wording in this subsection makes it clear that, in an emergency, the provisions of s.24 can be used, followed by the use of short term detention under s.26. However it was stressed that: "It is clear that the emergency provisions are for use only in an emergency. The normal route of a community care order patient into hospital if his condition deteriorates should most definitely be by the reassessment procedure set out in new Section 35G." *per* the Earl of Courtown (*Hansard*, H.L. Vol. 566, col. 1649).

Subs. (3)

Para. (b)

28 days. The reasoning behind this amendment was explained by the Earl of Mar and Kellie, who first drew this matter to the attention of the Government:

"The few vulnerable prisoners who are subject also to community care orders will benefit from the fact that there will be a 28 day guaranteed resettlement period. Social workers and probation officers working in prisons in England and Wales will find it helpful to know that there is a community care team outside the prison waiting to receive the ex-prisoner who will once again be their patient." (*Hansard*, H.L. Vol. 564, col. 177).

Patients moving from England and Wales to Scotland

35K.—(1) A community care application may be made in respect of a patient who is subject to after-care under supervision under the Mental Health Act 1983 and who intends to leave England and Wales in order to reside in Scotland.

(2) Sections 35A to 35J of this Act shall apply in relation to a patient in respect of whom a community care application is or is to be made by virtue of this section subject to such modifications as may be prescribed."

(2) Schedule 2 to this Act (supplementary provisions about community care orders) shall have effect.

GENERAL NOTE

An application may be made for a community care order in respect of a patient who is subject to after-care under supervision in England and who wishes to move to Scotland. Regulations will spell out the rules to apply in such circumstances.

Subs. (2)

Subject to such modifications as may be prescribed. The Earl of Lindsay said that:

"It may be helpful if I reassure the House that the regulations will not produce a "fast-track" procedure by which a community care order can be made. The sheriff will continue to be involved, and we envisage that the application will require to be made by a medical practitioner approved for the purposes of Section 20 of the 1984 Act. We also envisage that the care team in England or Wales will wish to discuss the proposed transfer with those likely to be concerned with the patient in Scotland some time prior to the making of the application and that there will be the appropriate full consultation about the application." (*Hansard*, H.L. Vol. 564, col. 181).

Absence without leave

5.—(1) In section 28 of the Mental Health (Scotland) Act 1984 (return of hospital patients absent without leave), for subsection (3) (which provides that a patient may not be taken into custody after the end of the period of 28 days beginning with the first day of his absence without leave) there shall be substituted the following subsection—

"(3) A patient shall not be taken into custody under this section after the later of—

(a) the end of the period of six months beginning with the first day of his absence without leave; and

(b) the end of the period for which (apart from section 31 of this Act) he is liable to be detained;

and, in determining for the purposes of paragraph (b) above or any other provision of this Act whether a person who is or has been absent without leave is at any time liable to be detained, a report furnished under section 30 or 31B of this Act before the first day of his absence shall not be taken to have renewed the authority for his detention unless the period of renewal began before that day."

(2) In section 30(6) of that Act (right of appeal where authority for detention renewed), after the word "section" where it first occurs there shall be inserted "or section 31B of this Act".

(3) For section 31 of that Act (duration of authority for detention: special provisions as to patients absent without leave) there shall be substituted the following sections—

General Note

For the background to this section, see introduction to new s.25J of the 1983 Act, above. The case which led the Government to decide to review the law occurred in England. There had been no suggestions of problems in practice with the operation of the law in Scotland.

Under s.28 of the 1984 Act, a detained patient who is absent without leave for 28 days ceases to be liable to be detained. The new section says that a patient may be returned to hospital or guardianship at any time up to six months after going absent without leave or during the period of liability to detention or guardianship, if that is longer. If the patient returns or is returned after 28 days he must be re-examined by the responsible medical officer and/or the mental health officer within seven days and if the grounds for detention or guardianship do not then apply, the patient will be discharged.

Subs. (1)

This subsection amends s.28(3) of the 1984 Act, which provides that a patient cannot be taken into custody after having been absent without leave for 28 days. A patient can be taken into custody at any time during the first six months of his unauthorised absence or, if longer, during the period he is liable to detention under the 1984 Act.

The patient's liability to detention is determined by s.30 of the 1984 Act. If the patient goes on unauthorised leave of absence after the responsible medical officer has made the reports required by s.30(3) but before the renewal of his detention (which takes effect on the expiry of the previous detention) the renewal of his liability to detention is ineffective. The doctors will have six months from the date of his departure to retake him into detention under the new s.28(3)(a).

Subs. (3)

This inserts a new s.31, s.31A and 31B in the 1984 Act.

"Special provisions as to patients absent without leave: hospital

31.—(1) Where a patient is absent without leave—

(a) on the day on which (apart from this section) he would cease to be liable to be detained under this Part of this Act; or

(b) within the period of one week ending with that day,

he shall not cease to be so liable until the relevant time.

(2) For the purposes of subsection (1) above the relevant time—

(a) where the patient is taken into custody under section 28 of this Act, is the end of the period of one week beginning with the day on which he is returned to the hospital;

(b) where the patient returns to the hospital within the period during which he can be taken into custody under section 28 of this Act, is the end of the period of one week beginning with the day on which he so returns; and

(c) otherwise, is the end of the period during which he can be taken into custody under section 28 of this Act.

General Note

If the patient returns to custody within a week of the end of his detention, his detention can be extended to allow the doctors the time to examine him and decide whether he should still remain subject to detention under the 1984 Act.

Patients who are taken into custody or return within 28 days: hospital

31A.—(1) This section applies where a patient who is absent without leave is taken into custody under section 28 of this Act, or returns to the hospital, not later than the end of the period of 28 days beginning with the first day of his absence without leave.

(2) Where the period for which the patient is liable to be detained is extended by section 31 of this Act, any examination and report to be made and furnished in respect of the patient under section 30(3) of this Act may be made and furnished within the period as so extended.

(3) Where the authority for the detention of a patient is renewed by virtue of subsection (2) above after the day on which (apart from section 31 of this Act) that authority would have expired, the renewal shall take effect as from that day.

General Note

If a patient who has been absent without leave returns to hospital within 28 days the doctors may renew his detention under the provisions of s.30(3). They can do this so long as he is liable to detention. This period may have been extended under the new s.31(1).

Patients who are taken into custody or return after more than 28 days: hospital

31B.—(1) This section applies where a patient who is absent without leave is taken into custody under section 28 of this Act, or returns to the hospital, later than the end of the period of 28 days beginning with the first day of his absence without leave.

(2) The responsible medical officer shall, within the period of one week beginning with the day on which the patient returns, or is returned, to the hospital—

(a) examine the patient or obtain from another medical practitioner a report on the condition of the patient; and

(b) consult—

(i) such other person or persons who appear to him to be principally concerned with the patient's medical treatment; and

(ii) a mental health officer,

and thereafter assess the need for the detention of the patient to be continued; and if it appears to him that the grounds set out in section 17(1) of this Act apply to the patient he shall furnish to the managers of the hospital where the patient is liable to be detained and to the Mental Welfare Commission a report to that effect in the prescribed form, along with the report first mentioned if such a report has been obtained.

(3) Where a report under this section is furnished to them in respect of a patient, the managers of a hospital shall, unless they discharge the patient, cause him and his nearest relative to be informed.

(4) Where the patient would (apart from any renewal of the authority for his detention on or after the day on which he is returned or returns to the hospital) be liable to be detained after the end of the period of one week beginning with that day, he shall cease to be so liable at the end of that period unless a report is duly furnished in respect of him under subsection (2) above.

(5) Where the patient would (apart from section 31 of this Act) have ceased to be liable to be detained on or before the day on which a report is duly furnished in respect of him under subsection (2) above, the report shall renew the authority for his detention for the period prescribed in that case by section 30(2) of this Act.

(6) Where the authority for the detention of the patient is renewed by virtue of subsection (5) above—

(a) the renewal shall take effect as from the day on which (apart from section 31 of this Act and subsection (5) above) the authority would have expired; and

(b) if (apart from this paragraph) the renewed authority would expire on or before the day on which the report is furnished, the report shall further renew the authority, as from the day on which it would expire, for the period prescribed in that case by section 30(2) of this Act.

(7) Where the authority for the detention of the patient would expire within the period of two months beginning with the day on which a

report is duly furnished in respect of him under subsection (2) above, the report shall, if it so provides, have effect also as a report duly furnished under section 30(3) of this Act; and the reference in this subsection to authority includes any authority renewed under subsection (5) above by the report."

(4) In section 32 of that Act (special provisions as to patients sentenced to imprisonment etc: hospital)—

(a) in subsection (2) (detained person in whose case application for admission does not cease to have effect), for the words "and 31" there shall be substituted ", 31 and 31A"; and

(b) after that subsection there shall be inserted the following subsection—

"(3) In its application by virtue of subsection (2) above section 28(3) of this Act shall have effect with the substitution of the words "end of the period of 28 days beginning with the first day of his absence without leave." for the words from "later of" onwards."

(5) In section 44 of that Act (return of patients subject to guardianship absent without leave), for subsection (2) (which provides that a patient may not be taken into custody after the end of the period of 28 days beginning with the first day of his absence without leave) there shall be substituted the following subsections—

"(2) A patient shall not be taken into custody under this section after the later of—

(a) the end of the period of six months beginning with the first day of his absence without leave; and

(b) the end of the period for which (apart from section 48 of this Act) he is subject to guardianship;

and, in determining for the purposes of paragraph (b) above or any other provision of this Act whether a person who is or has been absent without leave is at any time subject to guardianship, a report furnished under section 47 or 48B of this Act before the first day of his absence shall not be taken to have renewed the authority for his guardianship unless the period of renewal began before that day."

(6) In section 47(6) of that Act (right of appeal where authority for guardianship renewed), after the word "section" where it first occurs there shall be inserted "or section 48B of this Act".

(7) For section 48 of that Act (duration of authority for guardianship: special provisions as to patients absent without leave) there shall be substituted the following sections—

General Note

Where a patient returns after 28 days, the responsible medical officer should examine him (or obtain another doctor's report) within seven days of his return to hospital. He should also consult with nurses and a mental health officer. If the grounds in s.17(1) of the Act apply to the patient, the patient's detention will be extended for either six months or a year, as prescribed by s.30(2) of the 1984 Act.

The hospital managers will report this to the patient and his nearest relative and the Mental Welfare Commission will be informed. If the s.17(1) grounds do not apply, the patient will be discharged within seven days of his return to hospital.

Subs. (4)(b)
Para. (b)

This amends s.32 of the 1984 Act. A person who is detained in custody following a court appearance for less than six months is, by s.32 of the 1984 Act, treated as if he was on unauthorised leave of absence from the first day of his release from custody. The new subs. 28(3) provides that he may be taken back to hospital at any time within 28 days of his release from custody. See note on s.35J(3)(b) for the reason for this provision.

Subs. (5)

This amends s.44 of the 1984 Act, which provides that a patient cannot be taken back into guardianship after having been absent without leave for 28 days. A patient can be taken into custody at any time during the first six months of his unauthorised absence or, if longer, during the period while he is subject to guardianship under the Act.

Section 47 of the 1984 Act determines the length of time for which a patient can be subject to guardianship. If the patient goes on unauthorised leave of absence after the responsible medical officer has made the reports required by s.47(3) but before the renewal of his guardianship (which takes effect on the expiry of the previous guardianship) the renewal of his guardianship is not effective. The doctors will then have six months from the date of his departure to retake him into custody under the new s.44(2)(a).

Subs. (7)

This inserts new sections 48, 48A and 48B in the 1984 Act.

"Special provisions as to patients absent without leave: guardianship

48.—(1) Where a patient is absent without leave—

(a) on the day on which (apart from this section) he would cease to be subject to guardianship under this Part of this Act; or

(b) within the period of one week ending with that day,

he shall not cease to be so subject until the relevant time.

(2) For the purposes of subsection (1) above the relevant time—

(a) where the patient is taken into custody under section 44 of this Act, is the end of the period of one week beginning with the day on which he is returned to the place where he ought to be;

(b) where the patient returns to the place where he ought to be within the period during which he can be taken into custody under section 44 of this Act, is the end of the period of one week beginning with the day on which he so returns; and

(c) otherwise, is the end of the period during which he can be taken into custody under section 44 of this Act.

GENERAL NOTE

If the person subject to guardianship returns to custody within a week of the end of the authority for his guardianship, the authority for the guardianship can be extended to allow the doctors time to examine him and decide whether he should still remain subject to guardianship.

Patients who are taken into custody or return within 28 days: guardianship

48A.—(1) This section applies where a patient who is absent without leave is taken into custody under section 44 of this Act, or returns to the place where he ought to be, not later than the end of the period of 28 days beginning with the first day of his absence without leave.

(2) Where the period for which the patient is subject to guardianship is extended by section 48 of this Act, any examination and report to be made and furnished in respect of the patient under section 47(3) of this Act may be made and furnished within the period as so extended.

(3) Where the authority for the guardianship of a patient is renewed by virtue of subsection (2) above after the day on which (apart from section 44 of this Act) that authority would have expired, the renewal shall take effect as from that day.

GENERAL NOTE

If a person who has been absent without leave from guardianship returns or is returned to the place where he should be within 28 days of his first absence, the authority for his guardianship can be renewed under s.47(3). This can be done so long as the authority for the guardianship is still valid. This period may have been extended under the new s.48(1).

Patients who are taken into custody or return after more than 28 days: guardianship

48B.—(1) This section applies where a patient who is absent without leave is taken into custody under section 44 of this Act, or returns to the place where he ought to be, later than the end of the period of 28 days beginning with the first day of his absence without leave.

(2) Within the period of one week beginning with the day on which the patient returns, or is returned, to the place where he ought to be—

(a) the responsible medical officer shall examine the patient or obtain from another medical practitioner a report on the condition of the patient; and, if it appears to him that the ground set out in section 36(a) of this Act continues to apply in relation to the patient, he shall furnish to such mental health officer as the local authority concerned may direct a report to that effect in the prescribed form, along with the report first mentioned if such a report has been obtained; and

(b) the mental health officer shall consider whether the ground set out in section 36(a) of this Act continues to apply in relation to the patient; and, if it appears to him it does continue so to apply, he shall furnish to the local authority concerned and to the Mental Welfare Commission a report to that effect in the prescribed form along with the report or reports furnished to him under paragraph (a) of this subsection.

(3) Where a report under this section is furnished to them in respect of a patient, the local authority shall, unless they discharge the patient, cause him, his nearest relative and his guardian to be informed.

(4) Where the patient would (apart from any renewal of the authority for his guardianship on or after the day on which he is returned or returns to the place where he ought to be) be subject to guardianship after the end of the period of one week beginning with that day, he shall cease to be so subject at the end of that period unless a report is duly furnished in respect of him under subsection (2) above.

(5) Where the patient would (apart from section 48 of this Act) have ceased to be subject to guardianship on or before the day on which a report is duly furnished in respect of him under subsection (2) above, the report shall renew the authority for his guardianship for the period prescribed in that case by section 47(2) of this Act.

(6) Where the authority for the guardianship of the patient is renewed by virtue of subsection (5) above—

(a) the renewal shall take effect as from the day on which (apart from section 48 of this Act and subsection (5) above) the authority would have expired; and

(b) if (apart from this paragraph) the renewed authority would expire on or before the day on which the report is furnished, the report shall further renew the authority, as from the day on which it would expire, for the period prescribed in that case by section 47(2) of this Act.

(7) Where the authority for the guardianship of the patient would expire within the period of two months beginning with the day on which a report is duly furnished in respect of him under subsection (2) above, the report shall, if it so provides, have effect also as a report duly furnished under section 47(3) of this Act; and the reference in this subsection to authority includes any authority renewed under subsection (5) above by the report."

(8) In section 49 of that Act (special provisions as to patients sentenced to imprisonment etc: guardianship)—

(a) in subsection (2) (detained person in whose case guardianship application does not cease to have effect), for the words "and 48" there shall be substituted ", 48 and 48A"; and

(b) after that subsection there shall be inserted the following subsection—

"(3) In its application by virtue of subsection (2) above section 44(2) of this Act shall have effect with the substitution of the words "end of the period of 28 days beginning with the first day of his absence without leave." for the words from "later of" onwards."

(9) In section 60 of that Act (effect of hospital orders), after subsection (4) there shall be inserted the following subsection—

"(5) Where—

(a) a patient admitted to a hospital in pursuance of a hospital order is absent without leave;

(b) a warrant to arrest him has been issued under section 13 of the Criminal Procedure (Scotland) Act 1975; and

(c) he is held pursuant to the warrant in any country or territory other than the United Kingdom, any of the Channel Islands and the Isle of Man,

he shall be treated as having been taken into custody under section 28 of this Act on first being so held."

(10) In section 99 of that Act (review of treatment), in subsection (1) (report on treatment and patient's condition to be given to Mental Welfare Commission), in paragraph (a) (report to be given when report furnished under section 30), for the words "in respect of the patient under section 30 of this Act" there shall be substituted "under section 30 or 31B of this Act renewing the authority for the detention of the patient".

(11) In Schedule 2 to that Act (application of Part V to patients subject to hospital or guardianship orders)—

(a) in paragraph 1 of Part I (provisions applying without modifications to patients subject to hospital order without restriction or transfer order without restriction), after "31" there shall be inserted "to 31B"; and

(b) in paragraph 1 of Part III (provisions applying without modifications to patients subject to guardianship), after "48" there shall be inserted "to 48B".

GENERAL NOTE

Where a patient returns after 28 days, the responsible medical officer should examine him within seven days of his return to hospital or obtain another doctor's report. If he thinks that the grounds set out in s.36(a) of the 1984 Act apply to the patient, he should report this to the mental health officer.

The mental health officer then considers whether he thinks the welfare grounds for guardianship apply. If he does, he reports to the local authority and to the Mental Welfare Commission and the patient's guardianship will be extended for either six months or a year, as prescribed by s.47(2) of the 1984 Act. The local authority should inform the patient, his nearest relative and the guardian. If the s.36 grounds do not apply, the patient will be discharged within seven days of his return to hospital.

Subs. (2)
Para. (b)

Whether the ground set out in section 36(a) of this Act continues to apply. This appears to be a typographical error. It refers to establishing the medical grounds for guardianship, a matter on which the mental health officer is not qualified to judge. The reports required from the mental health officer under guardianship are specified in s.36(b) of the 1984 Act. (Guidance from the Scottish Office will need to make it clear what mental health officers are to do until this error is rectified.)

Subs. (8)

This subsection amends s.49 of the 1984 Act. A person subject to guardianship who is detained in custody following a court appearance for less than six months is, by s.49 of the 1984 Act, treated as if he was on unauthorised leave of absence from the first day of his release from custody. The new subpara. 49(3) provides that he may be taken back into guardianship at any time within 28 days of his release from custody. See note on s.35J(3)(b) for the reason for this provision.

Subs. (9)

This subsection amends s.60 of the 1984 Act. A patient who is on a hospital order who leaves the U.K. and who is held on warrant outside the U.K. will be treated as having been returned to hospital on the day on which he is so held. If this is within 28 days of his first absence, the provisions of s.31A apply; if after 28 days, s.31B will apply.

Subs. (10)

This subsection amends s.99 of the 1984 Act. If the responsible medical officer renews the detention of a patient who has been absent without leave, he shall, at the time of the renewal, report to the Mental Welfare Commission on the patient's condition and on the treatment he has been given.

Leave of absence from hospital

6.—(1) Section 27 of the Mental Health (Scotland) Act 1984 (leave of absence from hospital) shall be amended in accordance with subsections (2) and (3) below.

(2) In subsection (2), after the word "may" in the second place where it occurs there shall be inserted ", subject to subsection (2A) below,".

(3) After subsection (2) there shall be inserted the following subsections—

"(2A) Subject to subsections (2B) and (2C) below, the total period of leave of absence for specified consecutive periods under this section shall not exceed 12 months.

(2B) If, on the date of expiry of leave of absence granted to a patient under this section, a community care application has been made in respect of him but has not been determined, the leave of absence shall continue until the community care order comes into force or, as the case may be, the application is refused by the sheriff.

(2C) If, on the date of expiry of leave of absence granted to a patient under this section, a community care order has been made in respect of him but has not come into force, the leave of absence shall continue until the order comes into force."

(4) In paragraph 4 of Part II of Schedule 2 to that Act (application of section 27 to hospital orders with restriction orders, etc.), at the end of sub-paragraph (b) there shall be inserted the following sub-paragraph—

"(bb) subsections (2A) to (2C) shall be omitted;".

(5) Where, on the day when this section comes into force, a patient has been absent from a hospital for more than 6 months in pursuance of leave of absence granted under section 27 of that Act, the leave may, notwithstanding subsection (3) above, be extended for a single period of not more than 6 months.

GENERAL NOTE

The clause was explained to the Commons by Lord James Douglas-Hamilton as follows:

"The clause fixes at one year the total consecutive periods of leave of absence which may be granted to a patient liable to be detained in hospital in Scotland under the 1984 Act. We are well aware that the proposal does not meet with universal approval in Scotland. It is argued that the use of leave of absence as a long-term community care and treatment option has worked reasonably well in the rehabilitation of mentally ill people in the community. We acknowledge that. However, we believe that such use of leave of absence has been placed under considerable doubt by Sheriff Younger's judgment in 1987 [*A.B. and C.D. v. E.*, 1987 S.C.L.R. 419]. We have concluded that, despite the usefulness of having open-ended leave of absence arrangements, their use on a long-term basis carries a risk of successful legal challenge. We have been advised that a lawyer is seeking to challenge the judgment." (Standing Committee F, col. 166).

This section inserts new ss.27(2A) to (2C) in the 1984 Act. Leave of absence is limited to 12 months. The leave of absence of a patient who has been on leave of absence for over six months on the date when the Act comes into force can be renewed for one further period of six months.

Specified consecutive periods. It should be noted that any attempt to bring the patient back to hospital for one or two days before starting another period of leave of absence would be likely to be held to be illegal, as was decided in *R. v. Hallstrom, ex p. W.* (No. 2) [1986] 2 All E.R. 306.

Supplementary

Short title, commencement and extent

7.—(1) This Act may be cited as the Mental Health (Patients in the Community) Act 1995.

(2) This Act shall come into force on 1st April 1996.
(3) The provisions of this Act which amend other enactments have the same extent as the enactments which they amend.

SCHEDULES

Section 1(2)

SCHEDULE 1

AFTER-CARE UNDER SUPERVISION: SUPPLEMENTARY

Records

1. In section 24 of the Mental Health Act 1983 (visiting and examination of patients), in each of subsections (2) and (4) (records) at the end there shall be inserted the words "or to any after-care services provided for the patient under section 117 below."

Regulations

2. In section 32 of that Act (regulations for purposes of Part II), in subsection (2)(c) (records etc.)—
(a) for the words "the managers of hospitals and local social services authorities" there shall be substituted "such bodies as may be prescribed by the regulations";
(b) for the words "prescribed by the regulations" there shall be substituted "so prescribed"; and
(c) after the word "guardianship" there shall be inserted "or to after-care under supervision".

Wards of court

3. In section 33 of that Act (wards of court), at the end there shall be inserted the following subsection—

"(4) Where a supervision application has been made in respect of a minor who is a ward of court, the provisions of this Part of this Act relating to after-care under supervision have effect in relation to the minor subject to any order which the court may make in the exercise of its wardship jurisdiction."

Medical officers and supervisors

4.—(1) Section 34 of that Act (interpretation) shall be amended in accordance with sub-paragraphs (2) to (5) below.
(2) In subsection (1), before the definition of "the nominated medical attendant" there shall be inserted the following definition—

" "the community responsible medical officer", in relation to a patient subject to after-care under supervision, means the person who, in accordance with section 117(2A)(a) below, is in charge of medical treatment provided for him;".

(3) In that subsection, in the definition of "the responsible medical officer"—
(a) after the word "means" there shall be inserted "(except in the phrase "the community responsible medical officer")"; and
(b) in paragraph (a), after the words "a patient" there shall be inserted "who is" and after the words "admission for treatment" there shall be inserted "or who is to be subject to after-care under supervision after leaving hospital".

(4) In that subsection, after the definition of "the responsible medical officer" there shall be inserted the following definition—

" "the supervisor", in relation to a patient subject to after-care under supervision, means the person who, in accordance with section 117(2A)(b) below, is supervising him."

(5) After that subsection there shall be inserted the following subsection—

"(1A) Nothing in this Act prevents the same person from acting as more than one of the following in relation to a patient, that is—
(a) the responsible medical officer;
(b) the community responsible medical officer; and
(c) the supervisor."

Part III patients

5. In section 41 of that Act (power of higher courts to restrict discharge from hospital of persons subject to hospital order), in subsection (3) (nature of special restrictions), after paragraph (a) there shall be inserted the following paragraph—

"(aa) none of the provisions of Part II of this Act relating to after-care under supervision shall apply;".

6. In Schedule 1 to that Act (application of provisions to patients subject to hospital and guardianship orders), in Part I (patients not subject to special restrictions)—

(a) in paragraph 1 (provisions applying without modification), for "26" there shall be substituted "25C";

(b) in paragraph 2 (provisions applying with modifications), after "23" there shall be inserted ", 25A, 25B"; and

(c) after paragraph 8 there shall be inserted the following paragraph—

"8A. In sections 25A(1)(a) and 25B(5)(a) for the words "in pursuance of an application for admission for treatment" there shall be substituted the words "by virtue of an order or direction for his admission or removal to hospital under Part III of this Act"."

Mental Health Review Tribunals

7.—(1) Section 66 of that Act (applications to tribunals) shall be amended in accordance with sub-paragraphs (2) to (4) below.

(2) In subsection (1) (cases where application may be made), after paragraph (g) there shall be inserted the following paragraphs—

"(ga) a supervision application is accepted in respect of a patient; or

(gb) a report is furnished under section 25F above in respect of a patient; or

(gc) a report is furnished under section 25G above in respect of a patient; or".

(3) In that subsection, in paragraph (i), for the words "case mentioned in paragraph (d) above, by his nearest relative" there shall be substituted "cases mentioned in paragraphs (d), (ga), (gb) and (gc), by his nearest relative if he has been (or was entitled to be) informed under this Act of the report or acceptance".

(4) In subsection (2) (period within which application may be made)—

(a) in paragraph (c), for the words "case mentioned in paragraph (c)" there shall be substituted "cases mentioned in paragraphs (c) and (ga)";

(b) in paragraph (d), for the words "and (g)" there shall be substituted ", (g) and (gb)"; and

(c) after paragraph (f) there shall be inserted the following paragraph—

"(fa) in the case mentioned in paragraph (gc) of that subsection, the further period for which the patient is made subject to after-care under supervision by virtue of the report;".

8.—(1) Section 67 of that Act (references to tribunals by Secretary of State) shall be amended in accordance with sub-paragraphs (2) and (3) below.

(2) In subsection (1) (power of Secretary of State to refer), after the word "guardianship" there shall be inserted "or to after-care under supervision".

(3) In subsection (2) (power of registered medical practitioner to require records), at the end there shall be inserted the words "or to any after-care services provided for the patient under section 117 below".

9. In section 68 of that Act (duty of managers of hospitals to refer cases to tribunal), in subsection (3) (power of registered medical practitioner to require records), at the end there shall be inserted the words "or to any after-care services provided for the patient under section 117 below".

10.—(1) Section 72 of that Act (powers of tribunal) shall be amended in accordance with sub-paragraphs (2) to (4) below.

(2) After subsection (3) there shall be inserted the following subsection—

"(3A) Where, in the case of an application to a tribunal by or in respect of a patient who is liable to be detained in pursuance of an application for admission for treatment or by virtue of an order or direction for his admission or removal to hospital under Part III of this Act, the tribunal do not direct the discharge of the patient under subsection (1) above, the tribunal may—

(a) recommend that the responsible medical officer consider whether to make a supervision application in respect of the patient; and

(b) further consider his case in the event of no such application being made."

(3) After subsection (4) there shall be inserted the following subsection—

"(4A) Where application is made to a Mental Health Review Tribunal by or in respect of a patient who is subject to after-care under supervision (or, if he has not yet left hospital, is to be so subject after he leaves hospital), the tribunal may in any case direct that the patient shall cease to be so subject (or not become so subject), and shall so direct if they are satisfied—

(a) in a case where the patient has not yet left hospital, that the conditions set out in section 25A(4) above are not complied with; or

(b) in any other case, that the conditions set out in section 25G(4) above are not complied with."

(4) In subsection (5) (power of tribunal to amend application, order or direction where satisfied that patient is suffering from a form of mental disorder different from that specified in it), after the word "discharged" there shall be inserted "or, if he is (or is to be) subject to after-care under supervision, that he cease to be so subject (or not become so subject)".

11. In section 76(1) of that Act (visiting and examination of patients)—

(a) after the word "guardianship" there shall be inserted "or to after-care under supervision (or, if he has not yet left hospital, is to be subject to after-care under supervision after he leaves hospital)"; and

(b) in paragraph (b), at the end there shall be inserted the words "or to any after-care services provided for the patient under section 117 below."

12. In section 77(3) of that Act (tribunal applications), after the word "guardianship" there shall be inserted "or when subject to after-care under supervision (or in which he is to reside on becoming so subject after leaving hospital)".

13. In section 79(6) of that Act (interpretation of Part V), after the words "a hospital" there shall be inserted ", and "the responsible medical officer" means the responsible medical officer,".

14. In Schedule 1 to that Act (application of provisions to patients subject to hospital and guardianship orders), in Part I (patients not subject to special restrictions), in paragraph 9(b) (modifications of section 66(2)), for the words from "shall be omitted" to the end there shall be substituted ", and in paragraph (d) ", (g)", shall be omitted."

After-care services

15.—(1) Section 117 of that Act (after-care services) shall be amended in accordance with sub-paragraphs (2) to (4) below.

(2) In subsection (1) (persons to whom section 117 applies), after the words "detained and" there shall be inserted "(whether or not immediately after so ceasing)".

(3) In subsection (2) (duty of authorities to provide after-care services), at the end there shall be inserted the words "; but they shall not be so satisfied in the case of a patient who is subject to after-care under supervision at any time while he remains so subject."

(4) After that subsection there shall be inserted the following subsections—

"(2A) It shall be the duty of the Health Authority to secure that at all times while a patient is subject to after-care under supervision—

(a) a person who is a registered medical practitioner approved for the purposes of section 12 above by the Secretary of State as having special experience in the diagnosis or treatment of mental disorder is in charge of the medical treatment provided for the patient as part of the after-care services provided for him under this section; and

(b) a person professionally concerned with any of the after-care services so provided is supervising him with a view to securing that he receives the after-care services so provided.

(2B) Section 32 above shall apply for the purposes of this section as it applies for the purposes of Part II of this Act."

Code of practice

16. In section 118 of that Act (code of practice), in subsection (1)(a) (guidance to medical practitioners, social workers etc.), after the word "Act" there shall be inserted "and to guardianship and after-care under supervision under this Act".

Offences

17. In section 126 of that Act (forgery, false statements etc.), in subsection (3)(b) (subsection (1) to apply to medical recommendations and reports), after the word "medical" there shall be inserted "or other".

18. In section 127 of that Act (ill-treatment of patients), after subsection (2) there shall be inserted the following subsection—

"(2A) It shall be an offence for any individual to ill-treat or wilfully to neglect a mentally disordered patient who is for the time being subject to after-care under supervision."

19. In section 129 of that Act (obstruction), in subsection (1)(b) (refusal to allow visiting, interviewing or examination by a person authorised by or under the Act), after the word "Act" there shall be inserted "or to give access to any person to a person so authorised".

Interpretation

20.—(1) Section 145 of that Act (interpretation) shall be amended in accordance with sub-paragraphs (2) and (3) below.

(2) In subsection (1)—

(a) after the definition of "patient" there shall be inserted the following definition—

" "the responsible after-care bodies" has the meaning given in section 25D above;"; and

(b) after the definition of "special hospital" there shall be inserted the following definition—

" "supervision application" has the meaning given in section 25A above;".

(3) After that subsection there shall be inserted the following subsection—

"(1A) References in this Act to a patient being subject to after-care under supervision (or to after-care under supervision) shall be construed in accordance with section 25A above."

GENERAL NOTE

Para. 3

Minor who is a ward of court. Applications for after-care under supervision can only be made in respect of persons who are over the age of 16 years (s.25A(1)).

Para. 10(3)

Application is made to a Mental Health Review Tribunal. There is no time limit within which the tribunal hearing must take place.

May in any case direct. The tribunal has a general discretion to discharge a patient who is subject to after-care under supervision in any case.

Shall so direct if satisfied. With the burden being placed on the patient to satisfy the tribunal that the conditions for an application for, or renewal of, after-care under supervision are not met. This burden will be difficult to discharge in the case of a patient who has remained stable in the community while taking medication. How will such a patient be able to convince the tribunal that the stability is not due to the effect of the medication, when the patient's responsible medical officer says that this is the case?

Para. 15(3)

They shall not be so satisfied. Under s.117 of the 1983 Act the Health Authority and local authority have a continuing duty to provide after-care services to a person to whom the section applies, until both authorities are satisfied that the person is no longer in need of such services. The authorities cannot conclude that services are no longer required while the person remains subject to after-care under supervision.

Para. 15(4)

Duty of the Health Authority. This is the Health Authority for the area where the patient is living (s.117(3) of the 1983 Act).

Section 4(2)

SCHEDULE 2

COMMUNITY CARE ORDERS: SUPPLEMENTARY

Mental Welfare Commission

1. In section 3 of the Mental Health (Scotland) Act 1984 (functions and duties of Mental Welfare Commission), in each of subsections (1) and (2)(b), after the word "guardianship" there shall be inserted "or a community care order".

2. In section 5 of that Act (duties of Secretary of State and local authorities in relation to Mental Welfare Commission), after subsection (2) there shall be inserted the following subsection—

"(3) The local authority providing after-care services under section 8 of this Act for a patient subject to a community care order shall afford the Mental Welfare Commission all facilities necessary to carry out their functions in relation to such a patient."

After-care services

3. In section 8(1) of that Act (duty of local authority to provide after-care services), at the end there shall be inserted the words "and shall (without prejudice to the foregoing) provide or arrange for the provision of after-care services for any person who is subject to a community care order".

Part VI patients

4. In section 62 of that Act (application of Act to patients subject to restriction orders), in subsection (1), after paragraph (a) there shall be inserted the following paragraph—

"(aa) none of the provisions of Part V of this Act relating to community care orders shall apply;".

5. In Schedule 2 to that Act (application of Part V to patients subject to hospital or guardianship orders), in Part I (hospital order without restriction order and transfer order without restriction)—

(a) in paragraph 1 (provisions applying without modification), after "32," there shall be inserted "35A,";

(b) in paragraph 2 (provisions applying with modifications), after "35," there shall be inserted "35B,"; and

(c) after paragraph 8 there shall be inserted the following paragraph—

"8A. In section 35B(1) for the words "an application for admission" there shall be substituted the words "an order or direction by virtue of which he is liable under Part VI of this Act to be detained."

Offences

6. In section 105 of that Act (ill-treatment of patients), after subsection (2) there shall be inserted the following subsection—

"(2A) It shall be an offence for any individual to ill-treat or wilfully neglect a patient in respect of whom a community care order is for the time being in force."

7. In section 109 of that Act (obstruction), in subsection (1), after the word "Act," there shall be inserted "or to give access to any person to a person so authorised".

Duty to inform nearest relative

8. In section 111(1) of that Act (duty of managers of hospital to inform nearest relative of discharge of patient), after the words "nearest relative" in the first place where they occur there shall be inserted "or the making of a community care order".

Code of practice

9. In section 119 of that Act (code of practice), in subsection (1)(a) (guidance to medical practitioners, mental health officers etc.), after the word "Act" there shall be inserted "guardianship under this Act and after-care services provided under section 8 of this Act for patients subject to community care orders".

Interpretation

10. In section 125(1) of that Act (interpretation), the following definitions shall be inserted in the appropriate places in alphabetical order—

" "after-care officer" has the meaning assigned to it by section 35A(4)(c) of this Act;";

" "community care application" and "community care order" have the meanings respectively assigned to them by section 35A(1) of this Act;";

" "special medical officer" has the meaning assigned to it by section 35A(4)(b) of this Act".

INDEX

References are to sections and Schedules

CRIMINAL INJURIES COMPENSATION ACT 1995*

(1995 c. 53)

ARRANGEMENT OF SECTIONS

An Act to provide for the establishment of a scheme for compensation for criminal injuries. [8th November 1995]

PARLIAMENTARY DEBATES

Hansard, H.C. Vol. 259 col. 909; Vol. 260 cols. 734–811; Vol. 262 cols. 1093–1136; Vol. 265 cols. 737–750; H.L. Vol. 565 col. 994; Vol. 566 cols. 292–344, 583–662, 673–732, 737–750, 1350–1405 and 1602–1618.

INTRODUCTION AND GENERAL NOTE

This is the Act that was forced on the Home Secretary by the decision of the House of Lords in *R. v. Secretary of State for the Home Department, ex p. Fire Brigades Union* [1995] 2 All E.R. 244. The House held by a 3:2 majority that the introduction on April 1, 1994 of a tariff replacing the common law basis for the measure of compensation under the non-statutory Criminal Injuries Compensation Scheme "the Scheme" (with 187 specified injuries valued between £1,000 and £250,000) was unlawful. The tariff was set out in a White Paper published in December 1993, *Compensating Victims of Violent Crime: Changes to the Criminal Injuries Compensation Scheme* (Cm. 2434), and was introduced against the background of ss.108–117 of the Criminal Justice Act 1988 (c. 33) which, though not in force, had, for the first time placed the Scheme on a statutory footing. In addition to the departure from the common law assessment of general damages, the tariff made no provision for loss of earnings or earning capacity, both obviously significant elements in cases of serious injury.

Sections 108–117 of the 1988 Act had resolved the constitutionally anomalous status of a Scheme that had been introduced in 1964 by written parliamentary answer (697 H.C. Debs. cols. 89–94 (June 24, 1964)). It was expressed then, and in all its subsequent revisions, to be an *ex gratia* arrangement by which the government, through the agency of the Criminal Injuries Compensation Board ("the Board") would pay compensation to specified classes of claimant. As Diplock L.J. said in the leading case, *R. v. Criminal Injuries Compensation Board, ex p. Lain* [1967] 2 Q.B. 864, "if the matter rested there no persons would have any right to obtain payment out of those moneys which would have been enforceable in courts of law or controllable by prerogative writ." But the matter did not rest there: the Board's decisions were held to be amenable to judicial review, and the only ground on which it was ever suggested that the Board could withhold payment to an eligible claimant, was if the parliamentary vote was insufficient to cover its awards.

When first established, the Scheme was modelled, with some variation, on the principles of assessment applicable in a personal injury or fatal accidents action. This remained the case through a number of revisions, including that in 1990, the most recent preceding the introduction of the tariff. Like the version to be introduced under the 1995 Act, the 1994 tariff had two main purposes: to reduce the financial burden implicit in the continuation of awards based on common law damages, and, by eliminating the need to assess each case individually, to resolve claims

* Annotations by Professor David Miers, LLM DJur; Director, Centre for Professional Legal Studies, Cardiff Law School.

more quickly and with a greater degree of clarity for the claimant. The 1994 tariff was directly at odds both with the existing Scheme and its statutory counterpart. The reason why ss.108–117 of the 1988 Act had not been brought into force was largely due to the fact that during the late 1980s the backlog of claims at the Board had become so great that it was thought that the commencement of the statutory Scheme would divert the Board's efforts to determine claims more quickly (see Home Affairs Committee, *Compensating Victims Quickly: the Administration of the Criminal Injuries Compensation Board*, 1989–90 H.C. 92).

The tariff proposals excited considerable opposition; nevertheless, they came into effect on April 1, 1994. Claims lodged with the Board by that date continued to be dealt with under the old Scheme, but it was clearly envisaged that in time there would be only one measure of compensation. This was explicit in the White Paper and it was this contradiction between the declared intentions of the executive on the one hand, and the settled intentions of Parliament on the other, that prompted the judicial review of the legality of the tariff Scheme. Speaking for the majority, Lord Browne-Wilkinson held that by bringing the tariff into effect, the Home Secretary had necessarily made it impossible for him to exercise his discretion to bring ss.108–117 of the 1988 Act into force (p. 256): "By introducing the tariff scheme he debars himself from exercising the statutory power for the purposes and on the basis which Parliament intended."

During the debates on the 1995 Bill a number of MPs and peers rebuked the Home Secretary for his decision to persist with the introduction of the 1994 scheme in the face of well founded doubts as to its legality (see for example Lords Simon and Ackner 566 H.L. Debs. cols. 297 and 307 (July 19, 1995)). The Home Secretary was unabashed, insisting that since the score was five judges all for and against him, the matter wasn't clear cut. Nevertheless, the result of the House of Lords' decision was a quickly produced framework Bill, without whose enactment the old Scheme would continue to apply. Another consequence was that all the claims decided under the tariff have had to be reassessed according to the 1990 Scheme's common law principles.

As framework legislation, the Act says virtually nothing about how the Scheme will operate. This was a matter of considerable disquiet in both Houses, where two major issues emerged. The first was that in giving authority to the Secretary of State to introduce and amend the Scheme as he saw appropriate, there was a significant attenuation of parliamentary control. When first published, the Bill provided basically that only the tariff element of the Scheme would need to be approved by Parliament; such matters as the definition of a criminal injury, eligibility and the range of qualifying persons were to be dealt with administratively. As the result of sustained pressure in the Lords, a number of important changes were made by the government. Prime among these were the amendments to clause 10 (s.11). The Secretary of State is required to seek parliamentary approval for the introduction of the entire Scheme, and any change, however minor, to the Scheme's "key" elements (see s.11(3)), will also require parliamentary approval by the affirmative resolution procedure. Changes to any other aspect of the Scheme will be subject to approval by the negative resolution procedure (see Baroness Blatch, Minister of State, Home Office 566 H.L. Debs. cols. 1610–11 (November 16, 1995)). A second major change was to bring the decisions of the Scheme's administrative officers within the jurisdiction of the Parliamentary Commissioner for Administration (s.10).

Section 1 of the Act imposes a duty on the Secretary of State to introduce a Scheme, and thereafter gives powers with regard to its detail. The second major concern that ran throughout the debates was that there is nothing in the Act concerning the Scheme's key features; for example, the criteria for claimant eligibility, the definition of a criminal injury, the range of eligible persons or the procedural arrangements for claim review and appeal. Many amendments were tabled which would have introduced into the Act the details contained in the draft Scheme that was published at the same time as the Bill in May 1995. The government resisted them all, arguing that it wished to retain the flexibility to amend the Scheme quickly, and giving "golden assurances" that the basic features of the 1990 Scheme, which were also to be found in the 1995 draft, would feature in the Scheme that would eventually be presented for parliamentary approval (see for example, Standing Committee A, cols. 57, 185 and 249–250 (June 13, 20 and 27, 1995)).

On November 16, 1995, the government laid before Parliament a draft Scheme for approval under s.11(2) of the Act. In the notes that follow, reference will be made to that draft, to illustrate the principal scope of individual sections of the Act, but they are not presented as statements of what the law will necessarily be. The unlawful 1994 tariff Scheme was, as noted, the object of a great deal of criticism concerning the heads of compensation available to qualifying applicants. In this respect the 1995 draft Scheme shows a number of significant changes from its predecessor. In particular, it makes provision for loss of earnings and of earnings capacity, and for loss of dependency in fatal cases.

COMMENCEMENT

The Act came into force on the day it received the Royal Assent.

EXTENT

The Act does not extend to Northern Ireland.

ABBREVIATION

"the draft Scheme": the draft Criminal Injuries Compensation Scheme that was laid before Parliament on November 16, 1995.

The Criminal Injuries Compensation Scheme

1.—(1) The Secretary of State shall make arrangements for the payment of compensation to, or in respect of, persons who have sustained one or more criminal injuries.

(2) Any such arrangements shall include the making of a scheme providing, in particular, for—

(a) the circumstances in which awards may be made; and

(b) the categories of person to whom awards may be made.

(3) The scheme shall be known as the Criminal Injuries Compensation Scheme.

(4) In this Act—

"adjudicator" means a person appointed by the Secretary of State under section 5(1)(b);

"award" means an award of compensation made in accordance with the provisions of the Scheme;

"claims officer" means a person appointed by the Secretary of State under section 3(4)(b);

"compensation" means compensation payable under an award;

"criminal injury", "loss of earnings" and "special expenses" have such meaning as may be specified;

"the Scheme" means the Criminal Injuries Compensation Scheme;

"Scheme manager" means a person appointed by the Secretary of State to have overall responsibility for managing the provisions of the Scheme (other than those to which section 5(2) applies); and

"specified" means specified by the Scheme.

GENERAL NOTE

This requires the Secretary of State to make arrangements for the payment of compensation for criminal injuries. Paragraph 1 of the draft Scheme indicates that the Scheme is intended to apply to claims received on or after April 1, 1996. Section 1 requires the Secretary of State to specify the circumstances under which awards shall be made, and to whom and also defines certain terms in the Act.

Subs. (1)

Paragraphs 2–5 of the draft Scheme provide for the administration of the Scheme. Claims will be determined by "claims officers" employed by the Criminal Injuries Compensation Authority. The Secretary of State will also appoint "adjudicators", who will be members of the appeals panel. Apart from determining appeals, it is intended that the Panel will advise the Secretary of State about any aspect of the Scheme as and when it seems appropriate.

Subs. (2)(a)

Paragraphs 8–12 of the draft Scheme define what will amount to qualifying criminal injuries. These are personal injuries sustained in Great Britain and directly attributable to a crime of violence, an offence of trespass on a railway, or certain kinds of law enforcement activity, provided in this last case that if accidentally sustained, the victim was taking an exceptional risk. Injuries attributable to road traffic offences continue to be excluded. A personal injury includes physical injury and any medically recognised psychiatric or psychological injury or disease. The draft Scheme maintains the provision whereby a conviction is not a precondition of eligibility.

Subs. (2)(b)

Paragraphs 6–7 of the draft Scheme set out the categories of eligible persons; but it should be noted that there are further provisions in paragraphs 14–16 and 37–38. Compensation may be paid to the person who directly sustained the injury or, where the injury was fatal, to a dependant.

DEFINITIONS

"awards": s.1(4).

"compensation": s.1(4).

"Secretary of State": "one of Her Majesty's Principal Secretaries of State", Interpretation Act 1978, Sched. 4.

Basis on which compensation is to be calculated

2.—(1) The amount of compensation payable under an award shall be determined in accordance with the provisions of the Scheme.

(2) Provision shall be made for—

(a) a standard amount of compensation, determined by reference to the nature of the injury;

(b) in such cases as may be specified, an additional amount of compensation calculated with respect to loss of earnings;

(c) in such cases as may be specified, an additional amount of compensation calculated with respect to special expenses; and

(d) in cases of fatal injury, such additional amounts as may be specified or otherwise determined in accordance with the Scheme.

(3) Provision shall be made for the standard amount to be determined—

(a) in accordance with a table ("the Tariff") prepared by the Secretary of State as part of the Scheme and such other provisions of the Scheme as may be relevant; or

(b) where no provision is made in the Tariff with respect to the injury in question, in accordance with such provisions of the Scheme as may be relevant.

(4) The Tariff shall show, in respect of each description of injury mentioned in the Tariff, the standard amount of compensation payable in respect of that description of injury.

(5) An injury may be described in the Tariff in such a way, including by reference to the nature of the injury, its severity or the circumstances in which it was sustained, as the Secretary of State considers appropriate.

(6) The Secretary of State may at any time alter the Tariff—

(a) by adding to the descriptions of injury mentioned there;

(b) by removing a description of injury;

(c) by increasing or reducing the amount shown as the standard amount of compensation payable in respect of a particular description of injury; or

(d) in such other way as he considers appropriate.

(7) The Scheme may—

(a) provide for amounts of compensation not to exceed such maximum amounts as may be specified;

(b) include such transitional provision with respect to any alteration of its provisions relating to compensation as the Secretary of State considers appropriate.

GENERAL NOTE

This sets out the basis on which compensation under the Scheme is to be determined. It provides for the payment of a standard amount of compensation by reference to the nature of the injury, calculated in accordance with a tariff prepared by the Secretary of State. Provision is also made for the payment of additional amounts of compensation in cases of fatal injury and in respect of loss of earnings or special expenses.

Subs. (2)(a)

Paragraphs 25–29 provide for non-fatal injuries to be compensated according to a tariff describing 310 injuries attracting any one of 25 levels of award, from £1,000 to £250,000.

Subs. (2)(b)

Paragraphs 30–34 of the draft Scheme provide that compensation for loss of earnings and of earning capacity shall be payable only after 28 weeks have elapsed since the date of the injury. The assessment of such loss commences at the beginning of the 28th week; it is not backdated. Loss of earnings and earning capacity to the date of the assessment are calculated in the same manner as in a personal injury action, and involve the deduction (paras. 45–47) of any occupational sick pay or pension, and any social security payments, whose payment is occasioned by the criminal injury. Where the claims officer considers that the claimant will suffer a continuing loss of earnings or of earning capacity, the draft Scheme provides a set of multipliers to be used for the assessment of those losses. They too are subject to the same deductions. The net rate of loss of earnings or of earning capacity shall not exceed 1.5 times the average weekly industrial earnings as published by the Department of Education and Employment.

Subs. (2)(c)

Paragraphs 35–36 of the draft Scheme provide for the applicant to be compensated in respect of any special expenses incurred where he has suffered a loss of earnings or of earning capacity for longer than 28 weeks. The award may include compensation for the loss of a physical aid, NHS expenses and reasonable private health treatment, and adaptations to the applicant's home. The draft Scheme also provides for unpaid carers to be compensated where they have incurred personal expense or a loss of earnings or of earning capacity as a consequence of looking after the applicant at his home.

Subs. (2)(d)

Paragraphs 37–44 of the draft Scheme provide for compensation to be paid where the victim has died. Where the victim died as a consequence of the injury, his personal action does not survive for the benefit of his estate. Funeral expenses will, subject to the matters falling within s.3, be paid to whoever incurs them (para. 37). Where the victim later dies but otherwise than in consequence of the injury, a qualifying claimant who was financially dependent upon him may be compensated if the victim would have qualified for compensation for loss of earnings or earning capacity, or for special expenses (para. 44). In cases where the victim later dies in consequence of the injury, compensation will be payable to qualifying claimants in their own right (paras. 39–43). These claimants will be the victim's dependants, defined in paragraph 38 to include a spouse or former spouse financially dependent on the deceased, a person living with the deceased as husband and wife either being married or so living together for two years at the date of death, a natural or adoptive parent, or a natural or adopted child. A single qualifying claimant receives a single (bereavement) payment of £10,000; multiple qualifying claimants receive £5,000 each. In addition, compensation for loss of dependency is payable (other than where the dependency stemmed only from social security benefits) and is calculated as in a fatal accident action, discounting the possibility of remarriage or of the prospects of remarriage.

Subs. (3)(a)

No injury that is valued at less than Level 1 (£1,000) shall qualify under the Scheme (para. 24). Paragraph 25 of the draft Scheme provides that injuries that exacerbate existing conditions shall attract compensation reflecting only the degree of exacerbation, and paragraph 27 provides that where a woman is raped she shall be awarded an additional sum of £5,000 for each child born as a result whom she intends to keep. Paragraph 26 provides that when assessing multiple injuries, the victim will receive the full award for the highest rated injury, then 10 per cent. for the second and 5 per cent. for the third highest rated.

DEFINITION

"specified": s.1(4).

Subs. (3)(b)

Paragraphs 28 and 29 provide that where the Authority identifies an injury serious enough to meet Level 1 of the tariff, but which is not described there, it may recommend its inclusion and an appropriate level of compensation. The claimant may be made an award not exceeding 50 per cent. of the recommended level. If the injury is then included in the tariff, the claimant will receive an additional award; but if it is not included, or is included at a lower level, the claimant will keep the award made.

Subs. (7)(a)

Paragraph 23 of the draft Scheme provides that the total maximum payable in respect of the same injury shall not exceed £500,000.

DEFINITIONS

"award": s.1(4).

"compensation": s.1(4).

"loss of earnings": s.1(4).

"Secretary of State": "one of Her Majesty's Principal Secretaries of State", Interpretation Act 1978, Sched 4.

"special expenses": s.1(4).

"specified": s.1(4).

"the Scheme": s.1(4).

Claims and awards

3.—(1) The Scheme may, in particular, include provision—

(a) as to the circumstances in which an award may be withheld or the amount of compensation reduced;

(b) for an award to be made subject to conditions;

(c) for the whole or any part of any compensation to be repayable in specified circumstances;

(d) for compensation to be held subject to trusts, in such cases as may be determined in accordance with the Scheme;

(e) requiring claims under the Scheme to be made within such periods as may be specified by the Scheme; and

(f) imposing other time limits.

(2) Where, in accordance with any provision of the Scheme, it falls to one person to satisfy another as to any matter, the standard of proof required shall be that applicable in civil proceedings.

(3) Where, in accordance with any provision of the Scheme made by virtue of subsection (1)(c), any amount falls to be repaid it shall be recoverable as a debt due to the Crown.

(4) The Scheme shall include provision for claims for compensation to be determined and awards and payments of compensation to be made—

(a) if a Scheme manager has been appointed, by persons appointed for the purpose by the Scheme manager; but

(b) otherwise by persons ("claims officers") appointed for the purpose by the Secretary of State.

(5) A claims officer—

(a) shall be appointed on such terms and conditions as the Secretary of State considers appropriate; but

(b) shall not be regarded as having been appointed to exercise functions of the Secretary of State or to act on his behalf.

(6) No decision taken by a claims officer shall be regarded as having been taken by, or on behalf of, the Secretary of State.

(7) If a Scheme manager has been appointed—

(a) he shall not be regarded as exercising functions of the Secretary of State or as acting on his behalf; and

(b) no decision taken by him or by any person appointed by him shall be regarded as having been taken by, or on behalf of, the Secretary of State.

GENERAL NOTE

This section provides for circumstances in which awards may be withheld or the amount of compensation reduced. It also provides for awards to be made by a scheme manager if one has been appointed or by a claims officer, and makes provision for the status of their decisions.

Subs. (1)(a)

Paragraphs 13–16 of the draft Scheme provide for circumstances under which a claims officer may reduce or withhold altogether the compensation that would otherwise be payable to an applicant. Applicants will be required to inform the police of the circumstances giving rise to the injury, and thereafter to co-operate with them, the Authority and anyone else (for example, a doctor; see paragraph 20) in connection with the application. Compensation may also be denied where the conduct of the applicant before, during or after the incident, or his criminal record, makes an award inappropriate. These provisions apply equally to claims involving fatal injuries. The claims officer may also deny compensation where the victim is living with the assailant or where, in such a case, proceedings against the assailant have not been instituted,

Subs. (1)(b)

In cases, in particular, concerning injuries to children caused by their parents, the Authority may wish to make special arrangements to defer notification of the award until the child is 18 (see paragraph 50 of the draft Scheme).

Subs. (1)(c)

Paragraph 48 provides that the applicant shall repay to the Authority any compensation received from the offender by way of damages or a compensation order. Any such sums the applicant later receives must be paid to the Authority.

Subs. (1)(d)

Compensation is normally payable as a lump sum; but paragraph 52 of the draft Scheme provides for the award to held on trust (for example, for a minor).

Subs. (1)(e)

Paragraphs 17–18 of the draft Scheme provide that an application should be made within 2 years of the date of the incident. A claims officer has discretion to waive this time limit, the burden of which lies on the applicant.

Subs. (1)(f)

Other time limits might be imposed, for example, concerning applications for reviews and appeals (paras. 59 and 66).

Subs. (2)

The civil standard applies both to the applicant making out his case, and to the claims officer (or any other employee of the Authority) determining any aspect of an application (paragraph 19). It follows that an applicant may succeed in satisfying the Authority that he did sustain a criminal injury within the scope of the Scheme, though his assailant was acquitted, for example, of an offence against the person.

Subs. (4)

It is intended that the Scheme will be managed by a Scheme Manager appointed by the Secretary of State, with applications being determined by claims officers.

Subss. (5)(b), (6) and (7)

The purpose of these provisions, which caused considerable disquiet in debate, is to separate the determination of individual applications from the Secretary of State's responsibility for the Scheme (Standing Committee A, cols. 63–72, 201–208; H.L. Vol. 566, col. 731). This separation of responsibilities reflects the present position obtaining in respect of decisions of the Criminal Injuries Compensation Board, a position which the Minister, explicitly adverting to *Pepper* v *Hart*, indicated that the government intends will be reproduced (Standing Committee A col. 201). Applicants who object to the determination in their case may seek a review (s.4), appeal to the Appeals Panel (s.5), refer maladministration to the Parliamentary Commissioner for Administration (s.11), or seek judicial review.

DEFINITIONS

"specified": s.1(4).

"Secretary of State": "one of Her Majesty's Principal Secretaries of State", Interpretation Act 1978, Sched. 4.

"the Scheme": s.1(4).
"Scheme manager": s.1(4).
"claims officers": s.1(4).
"compensation": s.1(4).
"award": s.1(4).

Reviews

4.—(1) The Scheme shall include provision for the review, in such circumstances as may be specified, of any decision taken in respect of a claim for compensation.

(2) Any such review must be conducted by a person other than the person who made the decision under review.

GENERAL NOTE

This provides that the scheme will include provision for the review of decisions taken in respect of claims for compensation, such reviews to be conducted by someone other than the person making the original decision.

Paragraphs 58–60 provide for the circumstances under which reviews will be entertained. These will principally concern the waiving of time limits, the reopening of cases, the making of an award or a reduced award, and the withholding of an award. The review must be heard by a more senior claims officer who will not be bound by the original decision. Thus an applicant who is seeking the review of an award involving a reduction because of his failure to co-operate with the police, may find that a further reduction is made because the senior claims officer takes the view that that would be appropriate.

DEFINITIONS

"the Scheme": s.1(4).
"compensation": s.1(4).
"specified": s.1(4).

Appeals

5.—(1) The Scheme shall include provision—

(a) for rights of appeal against decisions taken on reviews under provisions of the Scheme made by virtue of section 4; and
(b) for such appeals to be determined by persons ("adjudicators") appointed for the purpose by the Secretary of State.

(2) If a Scheme manager is appointed, his responsibilities shall not extend to any provision of the Scheme made by virtue of this section except so far as the provision relates to functions of persons mentioned in subsection (3)(d)(ii).

(3) The Scheme may include provision—

(a) for adjudicators to be appointed as members of a body having responsibility (in accordance with the provisions of the Scheme) for dealing with appeals;
(b) for the appointment by the Secretary of State of one of the members of that body to be its chairman;
(c) for the appointment of staff by the Secretary of State for the purpose of administering those provisions of the Scheme which relate to the appeal system;
(d) for specified functions in relation to appeals to be conferred on—
 (i) claims officers; or
 (ii) persons appointed by the Scheme manager as mentioned in section 3(4)(a).

(4) Any person appointed under this section by the Secretary of State—

(a) shall be appointed on such terms and conditions as the Secretary of State considers appropriate; but
(b) shall not be regarded as having been appointed to exercise functions of the Secretary of State or to act on his behalf.

(5) No decision taken by an adjudicator shall be regarded as having been taken by, or on behalf of, the Secretary of State.

(6) The Scheme shall include provision as to the giving of advice by adjudicators to the Secretary of State.

(7) The Secretary of State may at any time remove a person from office as an adjudicator if satisfied that—

(a) he has been convicted of a criminal offence;

(b) he has become bankrupt or has had his estate sequestrated or has made an arrangement with, or granted a trust deed for, his creditors; or

(c) he is otherwise unable or unfit to perform his duties.

(8) In Schedule 1 to the Tribunals and Inquiries Act 1992 (tribunals under the supervision of the Council on Tribunals), in the entry relating to compensation for criminal injuries substitute, for the second column—

"12. The adjudicators appointed under section 5 of the Criminal Injuries Compensation Act 1995 (c. 53).".

(9) The power conferred by section 3(1)(a) to provide for the reduction of an amount of compensation includes power to provide for a reduction where, in the opinion of the adjudicator or adjudicators determining an appeal, the appeal is frivolous or vexatious.

GENERAL NOTE

This establishes that the Scheme will include provision for appeals against decisions taken in respect of claims for compensation and provides power for a body to be established to hear such appeals. It also provides for the Secretary of State to make appointments to the appeals body.

Subs. (1)

Paragraphs 61–82 of the draft Scheme make provision for the hearing of appeals. They are to be heard by adjudicators, who will be appointed by the Secretary of State to an appeals panel. They will have no role in the making of initial decisions, and with one exception, claims officers will have no role in connection with the conduct of appeal hearings. To some appeals further provisions apply. Appeals concerning time limits and the reopening of cases will be determined by the Chairman of the appeals panel (paras. 66–68), and appeals concerning the making of awards may be referred to an oral hearing (paras. 69–78).

Subs. (2)

This precludes the Scheme manager from having any involvement in the appeals procedures, save (s.5(3)(d)(ii)) to appoint persons to assist in the presentation of some aspect of the appeal before the appeals panel (H.C. Deb. Vol. 265 col. 738).

Subss. (4) and (5)

See commentary to s.3(5)(b).

Subs. (6)

Paragraph 5 of the draft Scheme provides for the panel to advise on matters as it thinks appropriate.

Subs. (9)

This is provided for in paragraph 77 of the draft Scheme.

DEFINITIONS

"compensation": s.1(4).
"adjudicators": s.1(4).
"claims officers": s.1(4).
"the Scheme": s.1(4).
"Scheme manager": s.1(4).
"specified": s.1(4).
"Secretary of State": "one of Her Majesty's Principal Secretaries of State", Interpretation Act 1978, Sched. 4.

Reports, accounts and financial records

6.—(1) The Scheme shall include provision—

(a) for such person or persons as the Secretary of State considers appropriate to make an annual report to him; and

(b) for the report—

(i) to be made as soon as possible after the end of each financial year; and

(ii) to cover the operation of, and the discharge of functions conferred by, the Scheme during the year to which it relates.

(2) The Secretary of State shall lay before each House of Parliament a copy of every such annual report.

(3) The Scheme shall also include provision—

(a) for such person or persons as the Secretary of State considers appropriate—

(i) to keep proper accounts and proper records in relation to the accounts;

(ii) to prepare a statement of accounts in each financial year in such form as the Secretary of State may direct;

(b) requiring such a statement of accounts to be submitted to the Secretary of State at such time as the Secretary of State may direct.

(4) Where such a statement of accounts is submitted to the Secretary of State, he shall send a copy of it to the Comptroller and Auditor General as soon as is reasonably practicable.

(5) The Comptroller and Auditor General shall—

(a) examine, certify and report on any statement of accounts sent to him under subsection (4); and

(b) lay copies of the statement and of his report before each House of Parliament.

(6) In this section "financial year" means the period beginning with the day on which this section comes into force and ending with the following 31st March and each successive period of 12 months.

GENERAL NOTE

This sets out the arrangements for reports, accounts and financial records.

DEFINITIONS

"the Scheme": s.1(4).

"Secretary of State": "one of Her Majesty's Principal Secretaries of State", Interpretation Act 1978, Sched. 4.

Inalienability of awards

7.—(1) Every assignment (or, in Scotland, assignation) of, or charge on, an award and every agreement to assign or charge an award shall be void.

(2) On the bankruptcy of a person in whose favour an award is made (or, in Scotland, on the sequestration of such a person's estate), the award shall not pass to any trustee or other person acting on behalf of his creditors.

Annuities

8. After section 329B of the Income and Corporation Taxes Act 1988, insert—

"**Annuities: criminal injuries**

329C.—(1) For the purposes of this section—

(a) "a qualifying award" is an award of compensation made under the Criminal Injuries Compensation Scheme with respect to a person ("A") on terms which provide—

(i) for payments under one or more annuities purchased for A in accordance with the provisions of the Scheme to be received by A or by another person on his behalf; or

(ii) for payments under one or more annuities purchased in accordance with the provisions of the Scheme to be received and held on trust by trustees of a qualifying trust for the benefit of A; and

(b) "a qualifying trust" is a trust under which A is, during his lifetime, the sole beneficiary.

(2) Where a person receives a sum—

(a) as the annuitant under an annuity purchased for him pursuant to a qualifying award,

(b) on behalf of the annuitant under an annuity purchased for the annuitant pursuant to a qualifying award, or

(c) as a trustee to be held on trust for A under a qualifying trust, in a case where the sum is paid under the terms of an annuity purchased pursuant to a qualifying award,

the sum shall not be regarded for the purposes of income tax as income of the recipient, or as A's income, and accordingly shall be paid without any deduction under section 349(1).

(3) In this section "the Criminal Injuries Compensation Scheme" means—

(a) the scheme established by arrangements made under the Criminal Injuries Compensation Act 1995; or

(b) arrangements made by the Secretary of State for compensation for criminal injuries and in operation at any time before the commencement of that scheme."

General Note

This amends the Income and Corporation Taxes Act 1988 (C. 1) so as to enable awards paid in the form of annuities to be exempt from income tax. Section 329C(3) permits structured settlements also to be arranged for those applicants who receive qualifying awards under the provisions of the non-statutory Scheme.

Financial provisions

9.—(1) The Secretary of State may pay such remuneration, allowances or gratuities to or in respect of claims officers and other persons appointed by him under this Act (other than adjudicators) as he considers appropriate.

(2) The Secretary of State may pay, or make such payments towards the provision of, such remuneration, pensions, allowances or gratuities to or in respect of adjudicators, as he considers appropriate.

(3) The Secretary of State may make such payments by way of compensation for loss of office to any adjudicator who is removed from office under section 5(7), as he considers appropriate.

(4) Sums required for the payment of compensation in accordance with the Scheme shall be provided by the Secretary of State out of money provided by Parliament.

(5) Where a Scheme manager has been appointed, the Secretary of State may make such payments to him, in respect of the discharge of his functions in relation to the Scheme, as the Secretary of State considers appropriate.

(6) Any expenses incurred by the Secretary of State under this Act shall be paid out of money provided by Parliament.

(7) Any sums received by the Secretary of State under any provision of the Scheme made by virtue of section 3(1)(c) shall be paid by him into the Consolidated Fund.

General Note

This provides authority for the Secretary of State to fund the Scheme and to make provision for its administration out of money provided by Parliament.

Definitions

"Secretary of State": "one of Her Majesty's Principal Secretaries of State", Interpretation Act 1978, Sched. 4.

"claims officers": s.1(4).

"adjudicator": s.1(4).

"the Scheme": s.1(4).

Jurisdiction of Parliamentary Commissioner for Administration

10.—(1) In the Parliamentary Commissioner Act 1967, insert after section 11A—

"**The Criminal Injuries Compensation Scheme**

11B.—(1) For the purposes of this Act, administrative functions exercisable by an administrator of the Criminal Injuries Compensation Scheme ("Scheme functions") shall be taken to be administrative functions of a government department to which this Act applies.

(2) For the purposes of this section, the following are administrators of the Scheme—

(a) a claims officer appointed under section 3(4)(b) of the Criminal Injuries Compensation Act 1995;

(b) a person appointed under section 5(3)(c) of that Act;

(c) the Scheme manager, as defined by section 1(4) of that Act, and any person assigned by him to exercise functions in relation to the Scheme.

(3) The principal officer in relation to any complaint made in respect of any action taken in respect of Scheme functions is—

(a) in the case of action taken by a claims officer, such person as may from time to time be designated by the Secretary of State for the purposes of this paragraph;

(b) in the case of action taken by a person appointed under section 5(3)(c) of the Act of 1995, the chairman appointed by the Secretary of State under section 5(3)(b) of that Act; or

(c) in the case of action taken by the Scheme manager or by any other person mentioned in subsection (2)(c) of this section, the Scheme manager.

(4) The conduct of an investigation under this Act in respect of any action taken in respect of Scheme functions shall not affect—

(a) any action so taken; or

(b) any power or duty of any person to take further action with respect to any matters subject to investigation."

(2) In Schedule 3 to the Act of 1967 (matters not subject to investigation), insert after paragraph 6B—

"6C. Action taken by any person appointed under section 5(3)(c) of the Criminal Injuries Compensation Act 1995, so far as that action is taken at the direction, or on the authority (whether express or implied), of any person acting in his capacity as an adjudicator appointed under section 5 of that Act to determine appeals."

(3) The amendments made by this section do not affect the following provisions of this Act—

(a) section 3(5)(b);

(b) section 3(7)(b);

(c) section 5(4)(b).

GENERAL NOTE

This section, which was introduced by the Government in the Lords, meets the concerns expressed in the Commons' stages, that the decisions of claims officers, the Scheme manager, and those appointed for administering the appeals procedures of the Scheme (s.11B(2)(b) of the 1967 Act, ought to be subject to the Parliamentary Commissioner Act 1967 (C. 13) (H.C. Vol. 262 cols. 1096–1105, H.L. Vol. 566, cols. 705–707, 723).

Subs. (3)

The provisions of the Parliamentary Commissioner Act do not affect those provisions of the 1995 Act which provide that decisions taken by claims officers, the Scheme manager and those appointed for administering the appeals procedures of the Scheme are not to be regarded as taken on behalf of the Secretary of State.

DEFINITIONS

"claims officers": s.1(4).

"adjudicator": s.1(4).

"Secretary of State": "one of Her Majesty's Principal Secretaries of State", Interpretation Act 1978, Sched. 4.

"the Scheme": s.1(4).

Parliamentary control

11.—(1) Before making the Scheme, the Secretary of State shall lay a draft of it before Parliament.

(2) The Secretary of State shall not make the Scheme unless the draft has been approved by a resolution of each House.

(3) Before making any alteration to the Tariff or to any provision of the Scheme as to—

(a) any additional amount mentioned in section 2(2),

(b) the circumstances in which compensation may be payable with respect to a criminal injury of a kind for which no provision is made by the Tariff,

(c) the calculation of compensation in respect of multiple injuries,

(d) compensation payable in respect of children conceived as a result of rape,

(e) the circumstances in which an award may be withheld or compensation reduced,

(f) any limit on compensation imposed by a provision made by virtue of section 2(7)(a),

the Secretary of State shall lay before Parliament a draft of the provision as proposed to be altered.

(4) Before making any alteration to a provision of the Scheme which—

(a) gives a right of appeal, or

(b) specifies the circumstances in which an appeal is to be dealt with by a hearing,

the Secretary of State shall lay before Parliament a draft of the provision as proposed to be altered.

(5) Where the Secretary of State is required to lay a draft before Parliament under subsection (3) or (4) he shall not give effect to the proposal concerned unless the draft has been approved by a resolution of each House.

(6) Whenever any other provision of the Scheme is altered, the Secretary of State shall lay a statement of the altered provision before Parliament.

(7) If any statement laid before either House of Parliament under subsection (6) is disapproved by a resolution of that House passed before the end of the period of 40 days beginning with the date on which the statement was laid, the Secretary of State shall—

(a) make such alterations in the Scheme as appear to him to be required in the circumstances; and

(b) before the end of the period of 40 days beginning with the date on which the resolution was made, lay a statement of those alterations before Parliament.

(8) In calculating the period of 40 days mentioned in subsection (7), any period during which Parliament is dissolved or prorogued or during which both Houses are adjourned for more than 4 days shall be disregarded.

GENERAL NOTE

This section, which was substantially amended during the Lords' stages, requires the Secretary of State to seek parliamentary approval for the introduction of the Scheme and for any subsequent amendment to it (H.L. Vol. 566, cols. 595–596, 724–726, 1360–1366, 1609–1611).

Subss. (1) and (2)

These provide that the Scheme shall not come into effect until the draft, which the Secretary of State must lay before Parliament, has been approved by affirmative resolution.

Subs. (3)

This provides that where certain key elements of the tariff are to be amended, they shall not come into effect until the draft which the Secretary of State must lay before Parliament has been approved by affirmative resolution.

Subs. (3)(a)

This provides for additional amounts of compensation for loss of earnings, special expenses, and in cases of fatal injury.

Subs. (3)(b)

See commentary to s.2(2)(3)(b).

Subs. (4)

This provides that where alterations to those aspects of the Scheme affecting appeals are proposed, they shall not come into effect until the draft which the Secretary of State must lay before Parliament has been approved by affirmative resolution.

Subss. (5), (6), (7) and (8)

These provide that where any other elements of the Scheme are to be amended, they shall not come into effect until the draft which the Secretary of State must lay before Parliament has been approved by negative resolution.

DEFINITIONS

"the Scheme": s.1(4)

"Secretary of State": "one of Her Majesty's Principal Secretaries of State", Interpretation Act 1978, Sched. 4.

Repeal of the 1988 Act scheme and transitional provisions

12.—(1) Sections 108 to 117 of, and Schedules 6 and 7 to, the Criminal Justice Act 1988 (the Criminal Injuries Compensation Scheme) shall cease to have effect.

(2) The arrangements for compensation for criminal injuries in operation immediately before the passing of this Act ("the current arrangements") shall continue in force until the date on which the Scheme comes into force ("the commencement date").

(3) At any time before the commencement date, the Secretary of State may make such alterations to the current arrangements as he considers appropriate.

(4) The current arrangements shall cease to have effect on the commencement date.

(5) The Scheme may include such transitional provision ("the transitional arrangements") as the Secretary of State considers appropriate in consequence of the replacement of the current arrangements by the Scheme.

(6) The transitional arrangements may, in particular, provide for the basis on which compensation is to be calculated in cases to which the transitional arrangements apply to differ from that on which compensation is to be calculated in other cases.

(7) The repeals set out in the Schedule shall have effect.

GENERAL NOTE

This section repeals those provisions of the Criminal Justice Act 1988 that placed on a statutory footing the "common law" version of the Criminal Injuries Compensation Scheme. It also gives the Secretary of State power to continue the existing non-statutory Scheme until the commencement of the Scheme authorised by this Act.

Subss. (5) and (6)

Paragraphs 83–87 of the draft Scheme provide that applications received by April 1, 1996 will be assessed under the existing non-statutory Scheme. The Criminal Injuries Compensation

Board will cease to exist on such transfer date as the Secretary of State may direct; thereafter, paragraph 86 provides for the newly appointed panel members to take decisions formerly taken by Board members.

DEFINITIONS
"the Scheme": s.1(4)
"Secretary of State": "one of Her Majesty's Principal Secretaries of State", Interpretation Act 1978, Sched. 4.

Short title and extent

13.—(1) This Act may be cited as the Criminal Injuries Compensation Act 1995.

(2) This Act does not extend to Northern Ireland.

Section 12(7) SCHEDULE

REPEALS

Chapter	*Short title*	*Extent of repeal*
1988 c. 33.	Criminal Justice Act 1988.	Sections 108 to 117. In section 171, in subsection (2) the words from "other than" to the end and subsections (3) and (4). In section 172, in subsection (2) the words "sections 108 to 115 and 117" and in subsection (4) the words "section 116". Schedules 6 and 7.
1992 c. 53.	Tribunals and Inquiries Act 1992.	Paragraph 1 of Schedule 2.

INDEX

References are to sections and the Schedule

CONSOLIDATED FUND (No. 2) ACT 1995

(1995 c. 54)

An Act to apply certain sums out of the Consolidated Fund to the service of the years ending on 31st March 1996 and 1997.

[19th December 1995]

Parliamentary Debates
Hansard, H.C. Vol. 268, col. 1247; H.L. Vol. 567, col. 1467.

Introduction

This Act makes provision for the application of £1,915,196,000 from the Consolidated Fund for the service of the year ending March 31, 1996 and for the application of £95,393,128,000 for the service of the year ending on March 31, 1997.

Most Gracious Sovereign,

We, Your Majesty's most dutiful and loyal subjects, the Commons of the United Kingdom in Parliament assembled, towards making good the supply which we have cheerfully granted to Your Majesty in this Session of Parliament, have resolved to grant unto Your Majesty the sums hereinafter mentioned; and do therefore most humbly beseech Your Majesty that it may be enacted, and be it enacted by the Queen's most Excellent Majesty, by and with the advice and consent of the Lords Spiritual and Temporal, and Commons, in this present Parliament assembled, and by the authority of the same, as follows:—

Issue out of the Consolidated Fund for the year ending 31st March 1996

1. The Treasury may issue out of the Consolidated Fund of the United Kingdom and apply towards making good the supply granted to Her Majesty for the service of the year ending on 31st March 1996 the sum of £1,915,196,000.

Issue out of the Consolidated Fund for the year ending 31st March 1997

2. The Treasury may issue out of the Consolidated Fund of the United Kingdom and apply towards making good the supply granted to Her Majesty for the service of the year ending on 31st March 1997 the sum of £95,393,128,000.

Short title

3. This Act may be cited as the Consolidated Fund (No. 2) Act 1995.

INDEX

References are to section number

BRITISH WATERWAYS ACT 1995

(1995 c. i)

ARRANGEMENT OF SECTIONS

PART I

PRELIMINARY

PART II

ENTRY ON LAND

PART III

REGULATION AND MANAGEMENT OF INLAND WATERWAYS

PART IV

MISCELLANEOUS AND GENERAL

An Act to confer powers on the British Waterways Board to enter land and repair or maintain, or carry out other operations with respect to, the waterways owned or managed by them and other works; to confer further powers on the Board for the regulation and management of their waterways and in relation to their undertaking; to amend or repeal statutory provisions relating to the Board or their undertaking; and for other purposes. [16th January 1995]

PARLIAMENTARY PROGRESS

The Bill's progress through Parliament was as follows:

House of Lords: First Reading, January 15, 1991; Second Reading, March 28, 1991; Bill committed to an opposed committee, May 1, 1991 to July 3, 1991; Bill committed to an unopposed committee, July 18, 1991; Motion to suspend, July 18, 1991; Third Reading, January 27, 1992, March 4, 1992; Commons amendments considered, January 11, 1995.

House of Commons: First Reading, March 13, 1992; Motion to suspend, March 12, 1992; Second Reading, May 17, 1993; Bill committed to an opposed committee, June 22, 1993 to October 25, 1994; Motion to revive, January 19, 1994; Motion to suspend, October 27, 1994; Bill as amended by Committee considered, December 13, 1994; Third Reading, January 11, 1995.

INTRODUCTION

The British Waterways Board was established by the Transport Act 1962. In order to fulfil its remit, powers to enter land and repair or maintain, or carry out other operations with respect to, the inland waterways owned or managed by them, must be conferred on the Board. Further provision must also be made for the regulation and management by the Board of the inland waterways. This Act, therefore, amends or repeals certain statutory provisions relating to the Board.

Whereas—

(1) By the Transport Act 1962 the British Waterways Board (in this Act referred to as "the Board") were established:

(2) It is expedient that powers should be conferred on the Board to enter land and repair or maintain, or carry out other operations with respect to, the inland waterways owned or managed by them and other works in circumstances where it would not be reasonably practicable for such repairs, maintenance or operations to be carried out without such entry:

(3) It is expedient that further provisions should be made for the regulation and management by the Board of the inland waterways owned or managed by them and that certain statutory provisions relating to the Board or their undertaking should be amended or repealed:

(4) It is expedient that the other powers in this Act contained should be conferred upon the Board and that the other provisions in this Act contained should be enacted:

(5) The purposes of this Act cannot be effected without the authority of Parliament:

May it therefore please Your Majesty that it may be enacted, and be it enacted, by the Queen's most Excellent Majesty, by and with the advice and consent of the Lords Spiritual and Temporal, and Commons, in this present Parliament assembled, and by the authority of the same, as follows:—

PART I

PRELIMINARY

Short and collective titles

1.—(1) This Act may be cited as the British Waterways Act 1995.

(2) The British Waterways Acts 1963 to 1988 and this Act may be cited together as the British Waterways Acts 1963 to 1995.

Interpretation

2.—(1) In this Act, unless the context otherwise requires—

"the Act of 1968" means the Transport Act 1968;

"the Act of 1971" means the British Waterways Act 1971;

"the Act of 1983" means the British Waterways Act 1983;

"authorised officer" means any person duly authorised in writing by or on behalf of the Board;

"the Board" means the British Waterways Board;

"commercial waterway" and "cruising waterway" have the meanings given by section 104 of the Act of 1968;

"daily fine" means a fine for each day or part of a day on which an offence is continued after conviction thereof;

"inland waterway" means any canal or inland navigation belonging to or under the control of the Board and includes any works, lands or premises belonging to or under the control of the Board and held or used by them in connection with such canal or inland navigation;

"remainder waterway" means an inland waterway of the Board which is not for the time being a commercial waterway or a cruising waterway;

"river purification authority", in relation to Scotland, means a river purification board established under section 135 of the Local Government (Scotland) Act 1973 or an islands council;

"the specified provisions" means sections 2(2) to (5) and 4 of the Land Compensation Act 1961 or, in relation to Scotland, sections 9(2) to (5) and 11 of the Land Compensation (Scotland) Act 1963;

"the tribunal" means the Lands Tribunal or, in Scotland, the Lands Tribunal for Scotland; and

"vessel" includes any ship, boat, barge, lighter or raft and any other description of craft, whether used in navigation or not.

(2) Any reference in this Act to a Part not otherwise identified is a reference to that Part of this Act.

PART II

ENTRY ON LAND

Interpretation of Part II

3.—(1) In this Part—

"emergency operations" means relevant operations carried out pursuant to section 4 (Entry on to land in cases of emergency) of this Act;

"land", in relation to Scotland, includes an interest in land and references to entry on to land shall be construed accordingly; and any reference to land shall include a reference to salmon fishings;

"on", in relation to the carrying out of relevant operations on land, includes in, under or over;

"owner" means—

(a) in relation to any land in England and Wales, a person (other than a mortgagee not in possession) who, whether in his own right or as a trustee for any other person, is entitled to receive the rack-rent of the land or, where the land is not let at a rack-rent, would be entitled if it were so let; and

(b) in relation to any land in Scotland, the person (other than a heritable creditor not in possession) for the time being entitled to receive, or who would, if the same were let, be entitled to receive, the rents of the land, and includes a trustee, factor, tutor or curator;

"relevant operations" means—

(a) the repair, maintenance, alteration, renewal, protection or demolition of any inland waterway;

(b) the repair, maintenance, alteration, renewal or protection of any works (not forming part of any inland waterway) for the drainage of, or supply of water to, any inland waterway;

(c) any inspection, survey or investigation of any inland waterway or adjoining land, or any works such as are referred to in paragraph (b) above, for the purpose of ascertaining whether any such repair, maintenance, alteration, renewal, protection or demolition is required;

"relevant undertaker" means any of the following—

(a) the National Rivers Authority or, in Scotland, the river purification authority in whose area the land on which relevant operations are carried out or proposed to be carried out is situated;

(b) the British Coal Corporation;

(c) any of the following undertakers, that is, any—

(i) water undertaker or water authority within the meaning of the Water (Scotland) Act 1980;

(ii) sewerage undertaker or local authority within the meaning of the Sewerage (Scotland) Act 1968;

(iii) internal drainage board; or

(iv) supplier of electricity within the meaning of Part I of the Electricity Act 1989;

which has apparatus in the area where the land upon which relevant operations are carried out or proposed to be carried out is situated;

(d) any of the following undertakers, that is, any—

(i) public gas supplier within the meaning of Part I of the Gas Act 1986; or

(ii) generator or transmitter of electricity within the meaning of Part I of the Electricity Act 1989;

which has apparatus on, under or over land upon or immediately adjacent to which relevant operations are carried out or proposed to be carried out;

(e) any undertakers authorised by any enactment to carry on any water transport, canal, inland navigation, dock, harbour or pier undertaking if in any case the land on which relevant operations are carried out or porposed to be carried out is in the ownership or occupation of any such undertakers, or is immediately adjacent to any land in the ownership or occupation of any such undertakers;

(f) any telecommunications operator within the meaning of the Telecommunications Act 1984 having any telecommunication apparatus (as defined in that Act) in the area where relevant operations are carried out or proposed to be carried out; and

"road", in relation to Scotland, means any public or private road within the meaning of the Roads (Scotland) Act 1984.

(2) For the purposes of subsection (1) above, "maintenance" includes the removal, felling, cutting back or treating of any tree or other vegetation.

Entry on to land in cases of emergency

4.—(1) Where the Board have reasonable cause to believe that—

(a) the carrying out of relevant operations is necessary; and

(b) the relevant operations are required to be carried out without delay—

(i) in the case of any relevant operations consisting of any inspection, survey or investigation, for the purpose of confirming that there exists an immediate danger to persons or property and, if so, establishing the nature of the repair, maintenance, alteration, protection or demolition required to remove the danger;

(ii) in the case of any other relevant operations, for the purpose of removing or facilitating the removal of any immediate danger to persons or property; and

(c) it would not be reasonably practicable for the operations to be carried out without entry on to land (other than a highway or, in Scotland, a road) adjoining or in the vicinity of an inland waterway;

any person authorised in writing in that behalf by the Board may enter the land and carry out the operations on that land or on any adjoining land of the Board.

(2) The Board shall inform the owner and occupier of the land as soon as possible of the carrying out of emergency operations and, not more than 7 days after the entry on that land, they shall serve on such owner and occupier a notice—

(a) specifying the land upon which entry has been made and the nature of the emergency operations; and

(b) containing details of the right of the occupier to claim payment for such entry and the right of the owner and occupier to claim compensation under this Part.

Notice of entry, etc.

5.—(1) Where the Board have reasonable cause to believe that—

(a) the carrying out of relevant operations other than emergency operations is necessary; and

(b) it would not be reasonably practicable for the operations to be carried out without entry on to land (other than a highway or, in Scotland, a road) adjoining or in the vicinity of an inland waterway;

the Board may serve a notice (in this Part called "a notice of entry") in the terms prescribed in subsection (4) below.

(2) A notice of entry shall be served—

(a) on the owner of the land;

(b) on the occupier of the land, if not the owner; and

(c) on every relevant undertaker.

(3) A copy of every notice of entry shall be posted in some conspicuous place on or near the land specified in the notice not less than 28 days before entry is proposed to be made.

(4) A notice of entry—

(a) shall specify—

(i) the land on which entry is proposed to be made;

(ii) the nature of the relevant operations, the manner in which it is proposed they should be carried out and the nature of any apparatus to be placed and left on the land in connection with the relevant operations;

(iii) the date upon which it is intended that the relevant operations will commence (which shall not be earlier than the day after the last date upon which a counter-notice under subsection (5) below may be served in respect of the notice of entry) and their maximum duration; and

(iv) the hours during which the relevant operations are to be carried out;

(b) shall contain details of the rights to object to the notice (including a form of counter-notice for use by the recipient pursuant to the following provisions of this section) and to claim payment for such entry together with compensation under this Part; and

(c) shall state that it would not be reasonably practicable for the operations to be carried out without entry on the land specified in the notice.

(5)(a) A person served with a notice of entry may, within 28 days from the date on which the notice is served on him, serve on the Board a counter-notice (in this Part called "a counter-notice") stating that—

(i) he consents unconditionally to the entry by the Board on the land described in the notice and to the carrying out of the relevant operations specified in the notice, in the manner so specified ("the proposals of the notice of entry"); or

(ii) he objects to the proposals of the notice of entry on any one or more of the grounds mentioned in subection (6) below, which shall be specified in the counter-notice.

(b) If the recipient of a notice of entry does not within 28 days serve a counter-notice on the Board, he shall be deemed to have granted his consent unconditionally to the proposals of the notice of entry.

(6) The grounds upon which objection may be made to a notice of entry are—

(a) that it would be reasonably practicable for the operations mentioned in the notice to be carried out in some other way not involving entry on to the land specified in the notice;

(b) that the carrying out of the relevant operations is unnecessary;

(c) that the maximum duration of the relevant operations, as stated in the notice of entry, is excessive, having regard to the nature of the relevant operations;

(d) that there has been some informality, defect or error in, or in connection with, the notice;

(e) that the notice should lawfully have been served on another person;

(f) that the proposals of the notice of entry will interfere unreasonably with the use and enjoyment of the land by the recipient of the notice of entry and that the Board should be required to comply with the conditions specified in the counter-notice with respect to those proposals, or that the proposals should be modified in the manner specified in the counter-notice for the purpose of reducing or preventing such interference;

(g) (where the recipient is a relevant undertaker) that the proposals of the notice of entry would be detrimental to the carrying on by the recipient of its undertaking and that—

(i) having regard to the detriment entry by the Board should not be permitted; or

(ii) the Board should be required to comply with the conditions specified in the counter-notice with respect to those proposals, or that the proposals should be modified in the manner specified in the counter-notice, for the purpose of reducing or preventing such detriment.

(7) Upon receipt of a counter-notice the Board shall within 28 days—

(a) inform the recipient of the notice of entry in writing that—

(i) the notice of entry has been withdrawn (without prejudice to the right of the Board to serve a further notice of entry on the recipient or on any other person); or

(ii) the Board will accept and comply with the conditions with respect to matters such as are mentioned in subsection (6)(f) or (g) above and specified in the counter-notice or modify the proposals of the notice of entry; or

(b) where the person is a relevant undertaker, refer the counter-notice to arbitration; or

(c) in any other case, appeal against the counter-notice to a magistrates' court or, in Scotland, to the sheriff having jurisdiction over the area where the land to which the notice of entry relates is situated.

(8) On any reference to arbitration under subsection (7)(b) above the arbitrator or, in Scotland, the arbiter may have regard to any court order made on any appeal under subsection (7)(c) above relating to the proposals of the notice of entry which is the subject of the reference.

(9) On any appeal under subsection (7)(c) above, the court or the sheriff may have regard to any award of an arbitrator or, in Scotland, an arbiter made following a reference under subsection (7)(b) above relating to the proposals of the notice of entry which is the subject of the appeal.

(10) An appeal under this section shall be by way of complaint for an order or, in Scotland, by way of summary application.

(11) For the purposes of the time limit for bringing an appeal under this section, the making of the complaint or, in Scotland, the lodging of the initial writ shall be treated as the bringing of the appeal.

(12) In so far as a counter-notice is based on the ground of some informality, defect or error in or in connection with the notice of entry the court or, as the case may be, the sheriff, arbitrator or arbiter shall uphold the notice of entry if it or he is satisfied that the informality, defect or error was not a material one.

(13) On the hearing of the appeal the court or, in Scotland, the sheriff may make such order as it or he thinks fit.

(14) A person aggrieved by an order of a magistrates' court or the sheriff under this section may appeal to the Crown Court or to the sheriff principal, as the case may be.

Power to enter land and carry out relevant operations pursuant to notice of entry

6. On or after the date mentioned in the notice of entry, or, if a notice of entry is upheld on appeal (with or without modification) after service of a counter-notice, after the notice of entry has been upheld, any person authorised in writing in that behalf by the Board may enter on the land and carry out on that land or on any adjoining land of the Board the relevant operations of the nature specified in the notice during the hours and in the manner so specified.

Saving in cases of emergency

7. Nothing contained in or done under section 5 (Notice of entry, etc.) or section 6 (Power to enter land and carry out relevant operations pursuant to notice of entry) of this Act shall affect the powers of the Board under section 4 (Entry on to land in cases of emergency) of this Act to enter land and carry out emergency operations at any time.

Further provisions as to entry

8.—(1)(a) The power to carry out relevant operations includes power—

(i) to place and leave on the land apparatus for use in connection with the relevant operations in question, and to remove such apparatus; and

(ii) to carry out excavations.

(b) The nature of any apparatus and of any proposed excavations such as are referred to in paragraph (a) above shall be specified in the notice of entry in the case of relevant operations which are not emergency operations.

(c) If the Board carry out any excavation under the powers of paragraph (a)(ii) above they shall make good the surface of the land as soon as reasonably practicable after the completion of the relevant operations.

(2) In carrying out any relevant operations in pursuance of section 4 (Entry on to land in cases of emergency) of this Act, the Board shall secure that as little damage as may be is done.

(3) A person authorised by the Board to enter on land in pursuance of section 4 (Entry on to land in cases of emergency) or section 6 (Power to enter land and carry out relevant operations pursuant to notice of entry) of this Act—

(a) shall, if so required before or after entering on the land, produce evidence of his authority to enter;

(b) may take with him on to the land such other persons and such vehicles, materials and equipment as are necessary for the relevant operations;

(c) shall leave the land as effectually secured against trespassers as he found it unless the occupier of the land or his agent indicates that he does not wish the land to be so secured.

(4) As soon as reasonably practicable after the completion of any relevant operations and any making good carried out under subsection (1)(c) above the Board shall remove any apparatus, vehicles and equipment and any unused materials from the land.

(5) Nothing in this Part shall authorise the Board to—

(a) enter any building or any operational railway, tramroad or any part of a tramway laid otherwise than in a highway or, in Scotland, a road; or

(b) use or interfere with any apparatus of a relevant undertaker, unless the Board are entitled to do so otherwise than by virtue of this Part; or

(c) construct any permanent works on any land unless the Board have a sufficient right or interest in the land apart from this Part.

(6) The Board when they have entered any land pursuant to this Part shall commence the relevant operations for the purposes of which entry was made as soon as is reasonably practicable and shall complete them with all reasonable dispatch.

(7) Nothing in this Part shall authorise the Board to enter any land for the purposes of or in connection with the development of any land, being land not forming part of any inland waterway or of any works such as are mentioned in paragraph (b) of the definition of relevant operations in section 3 of this Act.

Payment for entry

9.—(1) The Board shall pay to the occupier of any land upon which entry is made in accordance with this Part a sum in respect of such entry which shall be assessed in accordance with subsections (2) and (3) below.

(2) The sum payable under subsection (1) above shall be such sum as would have been paid if the occupier had entered into an agreement with the Board granting to them rights to enter the land for such period and for such purposes as entry has been made in accordance with this Part and (where entry is made pursuant to a notice of entry) on such conditions as are specified in any counter-notice and accepted by the Board or imposed—

(a) on any reference to arbitration of a counter-notice, by an arbitrator or arbiter;
(b) on any appeal against a counter-notice, by a court or the sheriff.

(3) Part II of the Land Compensation Act 1961 or, in Scotland, Part III of the Land Compensation (Scotland) Act 1963, so far as material, shall apply to the assessment of the sum payable under subsection (1) above as though the rights deemed by subsection (2) above to be granted to the Board had been acquired by them compulsorily and in assessing that sum regard shall be had to the degree of inconvenience caused to the occupier by the entry.

(4) Nothing in this section shall require the Board to defer or suspend entry on land or the carrying out of relevant operations while any dispute as to the sum payable under subsection (1) above is determined.

(5) The rights of any person to a payment under subsection (1) above shall be without prejudice to the rights of that or any other person to recover compensation under section 10 (Compensation) of this Act.

Compensation

10. If a person suffers loss or damage in consequence of—
(a) entry on to land in accordance with this Part; or
(b) the carrying out of relevant operations in accordance with this Part; or
(c) the failure by the Board to comply with any condition—
  (i) specified in a counter-notice and accepted by the Board; or
  (ii) imposed—
    (A) on any reference to arbitration of a counter-notice, by an arbitrator or arbiter;
    (B) on any appeal against a counter-notice, by a court or the sheriff;

he shall be entitled to recover compensation for the loss or damage from the Board.

Disputes as to payments, etc.

11. Any dispute as to a person's entitlement to—
(a) a payment under section 9 (Payment for entry) of this Act; or
(b) compensation in pursuance of section 10 (Compensation) of this Act;

or as to the amount of the payment or compensation shall be determined—
(i) where the person is a relevant undertaker, and the dispute does not relate to the meaning or construction of either of the said sections of this Act, by arbitration;
(ii) in any other case, by the tribunal, and the specified provisions (which relate to the conduct of certain proceedings before the tribunal and costs) shall with necessary modifications apply in relation to the determination by the tribunal of such a dispute.

Offences under Part II

12.—(1) If a person—
(a) intentionally obstructs another person in the exercise of any power of entry conferred on the other person by this Part; or
(b) while another person is on any land in pursuance of this Part intentionally obstructs him in carrying out any emergency operations or any relevant operations specified in a notice of entry (and not superseded by any conditions accepted or modifications made under subsection (7)(a)(ii) of section 5 (Notice of entry, etc.) of this Act, or by the order of any court or the sheriff or the award of an arbitrator or arbiter), as the case may be; or
(c) without reasonable excuse removes or otherwise interferes with apparatus left on or in land in pursuance of subsection (1) of section 8 (Further provisions as to entry) of this Act;

he shall be guilty of an offence and liable, on summary conviction, to a fine—

(i) in the case of an offence of obstructing another person in the exercise of a power conferred by section 4 (Entry on to land in cases of emergency) of this Act, not exceeding level 4 on the standard scale; and

(ii) in the case of any other offence, not exceeding level 2 on the standard scale.

(2) It shall be a defence in any prosecution for an offence under subsection (1)(a) or (b) above that the person obstructed could not reasonably be identified as a person entitled to exercise powers under this Part.

(3) If a person who has entered on any land in pursuance of this Part discloses to another person information obtained by him there about a manufacturing process or trade secret, he shall be guilty of an offence and liable, on summary conviction, to a fine not exceeding the statutory maximum or, on conviction on indictment, to imprisonment for a term not exceeding two years or a fine or both.

For protection of relevant undertakers

13.—(1) The Board shall as soon as possible inform all relevant undertakers of the carrying out of emergency operations likely to affect them and shall thereafter give notice as soon as possible to the relevant undertakers of any such operations.

(2) A person authorised by the Board to enter on land in pursuance of section 6 (Power to enter land and carry out relevant operations pursuant to notice of entry) of this Act shall not exercise any of the powers of that section unless notice of his intention to do so has been served by the Board, not less than 28 days before he does so, on any relevant undertakers.

(3) This section shall have effect subject to any agreement between the Board and any relevant undertakers.

For protection of Port of London Authority

14. Nothing in this Part affects the obligation of the Board to obtain a works licence under section 66 of the Port of London Act 1968 (which relates to the licensing of works in the river Thames and adjoining waters) in respect of any operation constituting works to which that section relates.

Saving for Thames Conservancy Act 1932

15. Nothing in this Part affects the obligation of the Board to obtain a licence under Part III of the Thames Conservancy Act 1932 in respect of any operation requiring a licence under that Part.

PART III

REGULATION AND MANAGEMENT OF INLAND WATERWAYS

General terms of houseboat certificates

16.—(1) A houseboat certificate issued or renewed after the passing of this Act under the Act of 1971 shall, unless the certificate or some other document referred to in the certificate provides otherwise, be subject to the general terms set out in Schedule 1 to this Act in addition to such conditions (if any) as the Board may determine under section 14 (Registration of houseboats) of the Act of 1971.

(2) The Board shall on demand provide a copy of the general terms for the time being in force under this section to any person requiring the same and to the holder on the issue or renewal of the certificate.

(3) A houseboat certificate shall contain or refer to some other document containing the general terms and any conditions to which it is subject.

(4) The following provisions of the Act of 1971 shall cease to have effect—

(a) in section 17 (Duration of boat certificates) (which applies to the undertaking of the Board in Scotland)—

(i) the words "and a houseboat certificate" in subsection (1); and

(ii) the words "or a houseboat certificate" in subsection (2);

(b) in section 19 (Registration of transfers of pleasure boats and houseboats)—

(i) the words "or a houseboat", "or a houseboat certificate, as the case may be" and "or houseboat certificate" in subsection (1);

(ii) the words "or houseboat certificate, as the case may be" and "or houseboat" in subsection (2); and

(iii) the words "or houseboat, as the case may be" in subsection (3).

Conditions as to certificates and licences

17.—(1) In this section—

"houseboat certificate" means a houseboat certificate issued under the Act of 1971;

"insurance policy" means an insurance policy complying with Part I of Schedule 2 to this Act;

"licence" means a licence issued by the Board in respect of any vessel allowing the use of the vessel on any inland waterways;

"pleasure boat certificate" means a pleasure boat certificate issued under the Act of 1971;

"relevant consent" means a houseboat certificate, a licence or a pleasure boat certificate; and

"standards" means standards for the construction and equipment of vessels prescribed under this section and Part II of the said Schedule 2.

(2) Part I of Schedule 2 to this Act shall have effect with respect to insurance policies and Part II of that Schedule shall have effect with respect to standards.

(3) Notwithstanding anything in any enactment but subject to subsection (7) below, the Board may refuse a relevant consent in respect of any vessel unless—

(a) the applicant for the relevant consent satisfies the Board that the vessel complies with the standards applicable to that vessel;

(b) an insurance policy is in force in respect of the vessel and a copy of the policy, or evidence that it exists and is in force, has been produced to the Board; and

(c) either—

(i) the Board are satisfied that a mooring or other place where the vessel can reasonably be kept and may lawfully be left will be available for the vessel, whether on an inland waterway or elsewhere; or

(ii) the applicant for the relevant consent satisfies the Board that the vessel to which the application relates will be used bona fide for navigation throughout the period for which the consent is valid without remaining continuously in any one place for more than 14 days or such longer period as is reasonable in the circumstances.

(4) If—

(a) (subject to subsection (6) below) the vessel does not comply with the standards applicable to the vessel on the date when the consent was granted; or

(b) an insurance policy is not in force in respect of the vessel; or

(c) either—

(i) (in the case of a vessel in respect of which a relevant consent is issued pursuant to subsection (3)(c)(i) above) it appears to the

Board that a mooring or other place such as is referred to in subsection (3)(c)(i) above is not available for the vesssel; or

(ii) (in the case of a vessel in respect of which a relevant consent is issued pursuant to subsection (2)(c)(ii) above) the vessel has not in fact been used bona fide for navigation in accordance with the said subsection (3)(c)(ii);

the Board may give notice requiring the holder of the relevant consent to remedy the default within such time as may be reasonable (not being less than 28 days).

(5) If the holder of the relevant consent does not comply with any notice served pursuant to subsection (4) above then the relevant consent shall determine on the date the notice expires.

(6) Where prior to the grant of a relevant consent a certificate ("the boat safety certificate") has been issued by a person authorised by the Board so to do in respect of a vessel confirming that the vessel complies with the standards applicable to it at the date upon which the boat safety certificate is issued, subsection (4)(a) above shall have effect throughout the period for which the boat safety certificate is expressed to be valid as if for reference to the date when the consent was granted there were substituted reference to the date when the boat safety certificate was issued.

(7)(a) In this subsection—

"designated vessel" means any vessel in respect of which a relevant consent has been in force at any time during the qualifying period other than—

(i) a houseboat registered under the Act of 1971 for the first time after 31st December 1979; or

(ii) any hire pleasure boat, that is, any pleasure boat which is let, lent, hired or engaged for gift, pay, hire or reward or promise of payment or carries or conveys passengers for a charge or payment; or

(iii) any pleasure boat (not being a hire pleasure boat) adapted or used for the carriage or conveyance of passengers, being a vessel in respect of which the Board are satisfied that a multi-user licence would be appropriate; and

"the qualifying period" means the period commencing twelve months before the date of the passing of this Act and ending six months before the date of the passing of this Act.

(b) The Board shall not—

(i) before the first anniversary of the passing of this Act, in the case of any designated vessel constructed after 31st December 1970; or

(ii) before the second anniversary of the passing of this Act, in the case of any designated vessel constructed before 1st January 1971;

refuse or withdraw a relevant consent in respect of the vessel on the grounds that the vessel does not or has ceased to comply with the standards applicable to it.

(8) The Board shall not within the period expiring at the end of the sixth month after the month current at the date of the passing of this Act refuse or withdraw a relevant consent in respect of any vessel on the grounds that a mooring or other place such as is referred to in subsections (3)(c)(i) and (4)(c)(i) above is not available for the vessel.

(9) Nothing in this section shall affect any power to the Board under any other enactment to refuse or withdraw a relevant consent.

(10) Section 3 (Construction and equipment of vessels) of the Act of 1983 shall cease to have effect.

(11)(a) The refusal or withdrawal by the Board of a relevant consent in respect of any vessel on the grounds that the vessel does not comply with the standards applicable to that vessel shall not preclude the movement or use of the vessel with the consent of the Board (which shall not be unreasonably withheld) and subject to such reasonable conditions (if any) as they may determine.

(b) Without prejudice to the generality of paragraph (a) above, the Board shall not withhold their consent under this subsection to the movement or use of a vessel for the purpose of taking it to a place where it may be repaired or modified so as to comply with the standards applicable to it, or for the purpose of taking the vessel to be destroyed, unless such movement or use would give rise to the risk of obstruction or danger to navigation or to persons or property.

(c) Nothing in this section shall affect the operation of section 7 (Control of unsafe vessels) of the Act of 1983.

Obstruction by vessels

18.—(1) No person shall moor or otherwise leave a vessel on an inland waterway so as to cause obstruction or hindrance to navigation or to the free passage of persons or vehicles over and along the towing path beside the inland waterway.

(2) Any person who without reasonable excuse contravenes subsection (1) above in such a way as to cause, or give rise to the risk of, injury to any person or damage to property shall be guilty of an offence and liable on summary conviction to a fine not exceeding level 3 on the standard scale.

(3) Any vessel moored or allowed to remoor in contravention of subsection (1) above shall be deemed to be a relevant craft for the purpose of section 8 (Removal of vessels) of the Act of 1983 or, in Scotland, a vessel for the purposes of section 19 (As to vessels sunk, stranded or abandoned) of the British Transport Commission Act 1958.

Removal of vessels to permit works, etc.

19.—(1) When any vessel is moored or lying in such a position as is likely to interfere with any dredging, repairs, maintenance works, or any other works or operations of the Board, or any works or operations proposed to be carried out by any other authority or body in pursuance of any statutory functions, the Board may serve on the owner of such vessel a notice requiring him within 28 days of the date upon which the notice is served to remove the vessel for such time as the Board or such other authority or body may reasonably require for the completion of such works or operations.

(2) Where any vessel is moored or allowed to remain in contravention of a notice served under subsection (1) above the Board may without further notice remove the vessel.

(3) Where any vessel is removed by the owner or the Board pursuant to this section, the Board shall if the vessel was lawfully moored at the time of the removal make available a suitable temporary mooring for the vessel until the completion of the works or operations which required its removal.

(4) If the Board remove a vessel pursuant to subsection (2) above they shall if it was lawfully moored provide a suitable temporary mooring for the vessel and replace the same as soon as practicable after the completion of the works or operations which required its removal.

(5)(a) If the Board in exercise of the powers of this section remove a vessel to a place not readily visible from the place from which it was removed they shall serve on the owner—

(i) as soon as practicable after the removal, a notice that they have exercised the powers of this section stating the place to which the vessel has been removed; and

(ii) as soon as practicable after the replacement of the vessel, a notice that the vessel has been replaced.

(b) This subsection shall not have effect if the Board after reasonable inquiry are unable to establish the name and address of the owner or for any other sufficient reason are unable to serve the notice; and subsection (2)(d) of section 17 (Notices) of the Act of 1983 shall not apply to notices under this subsection.

(6) The removal or replacement by the Board under this section of any vessel which at the time of the removal was lawfully moored shall be at the cost and risk of the Board, and if any person suffers loss or damage in consequence of the exercise of the powers of this section in relation to any hire pleasure boat within the meaning of section 3 of the Act of 1971, he shall be entitled to recover compensation for the loss or damage from the Board.

(7) Any dispute as to a person's entitlement to compensation in pursuance of subsection (6) above or as to the amount of the compensation shall be determined by arbitration.

(8) For the purposes of this section a vessel shall not be deemed to be unlawfully moored solely by virtue of its being moored or allowed to remain in contravention of a notice served under subsection (1) above.

Provisions as to private moorings

20.—(1) Conditions attached to a certificate granted under section 21 (Control of moorings, etc.) of this Act may regulate the exercise of private rights of mooring on any inland waterway but in exercising the said powers the Board shall have due regard to the desirability of refraining from interference with private rights and established mooring practices and shall not prevent the mooring of any vessel which could lawfully have been moored pursuant to any such private right but for the exercise of such powers.

(2) A notice under section 19 (Removal of vessels to permit works, etc.) of this Act shall have effect notwithstanding any private rights of mooring.

(3) In this section "private rights of mooring" include any rights conferred by the Board or (in England or Wales) enjoyed as an incident of an interest in land.

Control of moorings, etc.

21.—(1) As from such day as the Board may by resolution appoint, no person shall, in an inland waterway specified in that resolution, construct or maintain any structure being a mooring post, gangway, landing stage or other erection or installation for any vessel unless there is in force in relation to that structure a certificate granted by the Board under this section.

(2) An application for the grant or renewal of a certificate under this section shall be made in writing and shall—

(a) give the name and address of the person responsible for the structure;
(b) specify the type of structure and its precise location;
(c) contain such other particulars as the Board may reasonably require.

(3) Upon receipt of an application made in accordance with the requirements of this section the Board shall grant, or as the case may be, renew a certificate under this section for such period not being less than 5 years as they may determine.

(4) It shall be a condition of every certificate granted under this section that the structure shall be maintained in good repair and not allowed to become unsafe or an obstruction or danger to navigation.

(5) The Board may at any time, upon giving written notice in accordance with subsection (6) below, refuse to grant or renew a certificate or, as the case may be, revoke a certificate if they are satisfied that the structure which is the subject of the application or certificate, or any part of it, is not in good repair, or is or will become unsafe or an obstruction or danger to navigation.

(6) For the purposes of subsection (5) above, written notice shall be given to the applicant for the certificate as applied for or granted and, where different, the person named in the application or, as the case may be, certificate as the person responsible for the structure.

(7) Any dispute between the Board and any applicant for, or person named in, a certificate as responsible for the structure respecting a failure or refusal by the Board to grant or renew a certificate or respecting a decision by the Board to revoke a certificate shall be determined by arbitration.

(8) Pending the determination of any reference to arbitration under this section in relation to an existing structure, there shall be deemed to be a certificate in force in relation to that structure and any failure or refusal by the Board to grant or renew a certificate in relation to the structure or a revocation of the certificate in relation to a structure shall be ignored.

(9) Nothing in this section, or in any certificate under this section, shall relieve any person of the obligation to obtain consent under section 109 of the Water Resources Act 1991 (which requires the consent of the National Rivers Authority to the erection of any structure in, over or under a watercourse which is designated as a main river).

(10) Nothing in this section shall apply to—

(a) any item of equipment designed to secure or to afford access to or from a vessel which when not in use is normally carried on board the vessel;

(b) any mooring post, erection or installation no part of which is situated on, in, under or over the waters of any inland waterway;

(c) any structure or apparatus belonging to or required by the National Rivers Authority.

(11) Nothing in this section, or in any certificate under this section, shall—

(a) entitle a person to construct or maintain any mooring post, gangway, landing stage or other erection or installation for any vessel on land in respect of which he does not hold such rights as are necessary to enable him to exercise the powers of the certificate;

(b) require the Board to grant any right or interest in any land; or

(c) prejudice the right of the Board to require any payment for any right or interest granted by them in any land to enable the said powers to be exercised.

(12) The Board may by notice require a person who contravenes this section—

(a) to remove or abate within a reasonable time specified in the notice any works to which the contravention relates and to restore the site thereof to its former condition; or

(b) in the case of any contravention of subsection (4) above, to repair or alter the structure so as to avoid such contravention;

and, if the person to whom the notice is given fails to comply with the notice, the Board may carry out the work required by the notice and recover the cost of so doing from that person.

PART IV

MISCELLANEOUS AND GENERAL

General environmental and recreational duties

22.—(1) It shall be the duty of the Board, in formulating or considering any proposals relating to their functions—

(a) so far as may be consistent with the purposes of any enactment relating to those functions, so to exercise any power conferred on them with respect to the proposals as to further the conservation and enhancement of natural beauty and the conservation of flora, fauna and geological or physiographical features of special interest;

(b) to have regard to the desirability of protecting and conserving buildings, sites and objects of archaeological, architectural, engineering or historic interest; and

(c) to take into account any effect which the proposals would have on the beauty or amenity of any rural or urban area or on any such flora, fauna, features, buildings, sites or objects.

(2) Subject to subsection (1) above, it shall be the duty of the Board, in formulating or considering any proposals relating to their functions—

(a) to have regard to the desirability of preserving for the public any freedom of access to towing paths and open land and especially to places of natural beauty;

(b) to have regard to the desirability of maintaining the availability to the public of any facility for visiting or inspecting any building, site or object of archaeological, architectural, engineering or historic interest;

(c) to take into account any effect which the proposals would have on any such freedom of access or on the availability of any such facility;

(d) to take into account the desirability of protecting for future use as cruising waterways, or as areas appropriate for other public recreational use, remainder waterways with potential for such use.

(3) It shall be the duty of the Board in determining what steps to take in performance of any duty imposed by virtue of subsection (1) or (2) above to take into account the needs of persons who are chronically sick or disabled.

(4) Nothing in this section shall require recreational facilities made available by the Board to be made available free of charge.

(5) In this section—

"building" includes a structure; and

"functions" includes powers and duties.

Amendment of section 49 of Transport Act 1968

23. Subsection (4) of section 49 of the Act of 1968 (powers with respect to land) shall be amended as follows:—

(a) in place of paragraph (b) there shall be substituted the following:—

"(b) in the case of the Waterways Board adjoins or is situated in the vicinity of any inland waterway comprised in the undertaking of that Board,";

(b) in place of "that commercial or cruising waterway" there shall be substituted "that waterway";

(c) the words "or as the case may be, the waterway services of the Waterways Board" shall be omitted; and

(d) after "can be directly used" there shall be inserted "or, as the case may be, the waterway can be conveniently used".

As to power to establish undertakings on request

24. The power of the Board under section 50(7) of the Act of 1968 to provide for any person technical advice and assistance, including research, shall include power, exercisable on the request of any such person, to establish for that person an undertaking carrying on any business in which the Board have skill or experience and, until such person is ready to manage such undertaking himself, to manage it on his behalf.

Power to appropriate parts of docks

25.—(1) In this section, "the docks" means the Ardrishaig Dock, Gloucester Docks and Sharpness Docks of the Board, or any of them.

(2) Notwithstanding anything in any statutory provision of local application, the Board may from time to time set apart and appropriate any lands, works, buildings, machinery, equipment, facilities or any other property

forming part of the docks for the exclusive, partial or preferential use and accommodation of any particular trade, activity, person, vessel or class of vessels, or goods, subject to the payment of such charges and subject to such terms, conditions and regulations as the Board think fit.

(3) Where any part of the docks is set apart and appropriated under this section no person or vessel shall make use of that part (except so far as may be authorised by the terms of the setting apart or appropriation) without the consent of a duly authorised officer of the Board and such officer may order any person or vessel making use thereof without such consent to leave or be removed and the provisions of section 58 of the Harbours, Docks and Piers Clauses Act 1847 (powers of harbour master to move vessels in harbour) shall apply with the necessary modifications to and in relation to any such vessels.

Weston Point Docks

26. As from the passing of this Act the provisions of section 33 of the Harbours, Docks and Piers Clauses Act 1847 shall cease to apply to the Board in relation to their Weston Point Docks at Runcorn in the county of Cheshire.

Provisions as to sections 25 and 26

27. Nothing in section 25 (Power to appropriate parts of docks) or section 26 (Weston Point Docks) of this Act shall authorise the Board to prevent or restrict the use by vessels of the docks (as defined in the said section 25) or the Weston Point Docks as a means of access between any two or more areas of water adjoining or in the vicinity of the docks or the Weston Point Docks, as the case may be.

Limehouse Basin

28.—(1) In this section—

"the basin" means the Limehouse Basin of the Board in the London Borough of Tower Hamlets (formerly known as Regents Canal Dock); and

"the lock" means the lock between the basin and the river Thames.

(2) For the avoidance of doubt it is hereby declared that for the purposes of any enactment the limits of jurisdiction of the Board over the basin extend to the lower gates of the lock and thence over all waters to the south of, and lying within 74 metres of an imaginary line drawn between the pivots of, the said gates.

Repeal of section 147 of Severn Navigation Act 1842

29. Section 147 (Locks to be open Night and Day) of the Act 5 & 6 Vict. (1842) intituled "An Act for improving the Navigation of the Severn from the Entrance Lock of the Gloucester and Berkeley Canal, and from the Entrance Lock of the Herefordshire and Gloucestershire Canal, in the County of Gloucester, to Gladder or Whitehouse Brook in the County of Worcester" shall cease to have effect.

River Weaver to be river waterway

30. Section 4 (Extent of Part II) of the Act of 1971 shall have effect as if there were included in Schedule 1 to that Act the following additional paragraph:—

"The river Weaver from Winsford Bridge to Shrew Bridge in the County of Cheshire.".

Notices

31.—(1) Subject to subsection (5) of section 19 (Removal of vessels to permit works, etc.) of this Act, section 17 (Notices) of the Act of 1983 shall apply to all notices authorised or required to be served on any person by or under this Act.

(2) Subsection (2)(e) of the said section 17 shall apply to notices under subsection (2) of section 4 (Entry on to land in cases of emergency) of this Act, to notices of entry under section 5 (Notice of entry, etc.) of this Act and to notices under subsection (12) of section 21 (Control of moorings, etc.) of this Act as it applies to notices under section 12 (Power to obtain particulars of persons interested in land) of the Act of 1983, as though the said section 12 applied to Scotland as well as to England and Wales.

Arbitration

32. Where under any provision of this Act any difference (other than a difference as to the meaning or construction of that provision) is to be determined by arbitration, then such difference shall be referred to and settled by a single arbitrator or, in Scotland, by a single arbiter to be agreed between the parties or, failing agreement, to be appointed on the application of either party (after notice in writing to the other), by the President of the Institution of Civil Engineers.

As to certain legal proceedings

33. Notwithstanding anything in any other enactment or rule of law, where but for this section any proceedings in respect of any provision of this Act could be instituted in the High Court, those proceedings may be instituted in the County Court.

Crown rights

34.—(1) Nothing in this Act affects prejudicially any estate, right, power, privilege, authority or exemption of the Crown including (without prejudice to the general law concerning the applicability of statutes to the Duchy of Cornwall) the Duchy of Cornwall and, in particular and without prejudice to the generality of the foregoing, nothing in this Act authorises the Board to take, use, enter upon or in any manner interfere with, any land or hereditaments or any rights of whatsoever description (including any portion of the shore or bed of the sea or of any river, channel, creek, bay or estuary)—

(a) belonging to Her Majesty in right of Her Crown and under the management of the Crown Estate Commissioners, without the consent in writing of those commissioners; or

(b) belonging to the Duchy of Cornwall or enjoyed by the possessor for the time being of the Duchy of Cornwall without the consent in writing of the Duke of Cornwall testified in writing under the seal of the said Duchy or, as the case may be, the consent in writing of two or more of such of the regular officers of the said Duchy or of such other persons as may be duly authorised under section 39 of the Duchy of Cornwall Management Act 1863; or

(c) belonging to a government department, or held in trust for Her Majesty for the purposes of a government department, without the consent in writing of that government department.

(2) A consent under subsection (1) above may be given unconditionally or subject to such conditions and upon such terms as shall be considered necessary or appropriate.

Saving for Trinity House

35. Nothing in this Act shall prejudice or derogate from the jurisdiction or authority or any of the rights or privileges of the Corporation of Trinity House of Deptford Strond.

Repeals

36. The enactments specified in columns (1) and (2) of Schedule 3 to this Act are hereby repealed to the extent mentioned in column (3) thereof.

Application to Scotland

37.—(1) Subject to subsection (2) below, this Act extends to Scotland.

(2) Nothing in this Act shall apply to Loch Lochy, Loch Oich, Loch Ness or Loch Dochfour, the boundaries of which are shown edged in red on the plan marked "The Scottish Lochs", of which five copies have been signed on behalf of the Board by Richard Jeremy Duffy, the Solicitor and Secretary to the Board, and on behalf of the Highland Regional Council by Ronald Harley Stevenson, the Chief Executive of the said Council, and deposited respectively in—

(a) the office of the Clerk of the Parliaments, House of Lords;
(b) the Private Bill Office of the House of Commons;
(c) the Department of the Environment;
(d) the principal office of the Board; and
(e) the office of the Chief Executive of the Highland Regional Council.

(3) Nothing in this Act shall prejudice the power of a river purification authority to make byelaws under section 33 of the Control of Pollution Act 1974 (control of sanitary appliances on vessels) or under section 48 of that Act (power of river purification authorities to exclude unregistered vessels from rivers, etc.).

(4) It shall be the duty of the Board, when exercising functions in relation to Scotland under any enactment, to avoid, so far as possible, causing injury to fisheries or to the stock of fish in any waters.

SCHEDULES

Section 16

SCHEDULE 1

GENERAL TERMS OF HOUSEBOAT CERTIFICATES

PART I

INTRODUCTORY

Interpretation

1. In this Schedule—

"the certificate" means the certificate relating to any houseboat;

"the holder" means the person named in a certificate as the person having control of the houseboat specified in the certificate or the assignee or personal representative (within the meaning of section 55 of the Administration of Estates Act 1925) of the person so named;

"the houseboat" means the houseboat named or otherwise identified in the certificate;

"local authority" has the meaning given by section 270 of the Local Government Act 1972 or, in relation to Scotland, section 235 of the Local Government (Scotland) Act 1973;

"moor" includes place, keep or maintain and "moored" shall be construed accordingly; and

"the site" means the mooring or other location specified in the certificate.

Application

2.—(1) Part II of this Schedule applies where—

(a) the Board own an interest in, or rights over, the site; and

(b) the site is managed by the Board or their agent.

(2) Part III of this Schedule applies to all certificates.

PART II

TERMS APPLICABLE TO SITES CONTROLLED BY BOARD

Right to moor houseboat

3. Subject to the following provisions of this Schedule the holder shall have the right to moor the houseboat at the site throughout the period of validity of the certificate.

Qualification of right to moor

4.—(1) If the interest of the Board in the site is insufficient to enable them to grant the right to moor the houseboat there for an indefinite period, the period for which that right subsists shall not extend beyond the date when the estate or interest of the Board determines.

(2) If planning permission for the use of the site as a mooring has been granted in terms such that it will expire at the end of a specified period, the period for which the right to moor the houseboat at the site subsists shall not extend beyond the date when the planning permission expires.

(3) Paragraph 3 above shall not prejudice or affect the right of the Board to move or to require the removal of the houseboat under section 19 (Removal of vessels to permit works, etc.) of this Act or any other powers available to the Board but, if they so move or require the removal of the houseboat during the period of validity of the certificate, the Board (unless they would be entitled under paragraph 6 below to determine the certificate) shall make available for it a suitable mooring or other location (which shall be broadly comparable to the site) situated as near as is practicable to the site, and shall permit the houseboat to be replaced at the site as soon as practicable after the circumstances necessitating the removal have ceased to apply.

(4) Any costs and expenses occasioned by the removal and replacement of a houseboat under sub-paragraph (3) above shall be paid by the Board.

Assignment of certificate

5. The holder shall be entitled to assign the certificate to a person (being aged 18 or over) approved by the Board whose approval shall not be unreasonably withheld.

PART III

TERMS APPLICABLE TO ALL CERTIFICATES

Determination of certificate

6.—(1) The certificate shall remain in force for the period or until the date specified therein unless—

(a) the certificate is surrendered pursuant to paragraph 8 below; or

(b) the certificate is withdrawn pursuant to section 17 (Conditions as to certificates and licences) of this Act; or

(c) the holder's interest in or other right to moor at the site (otherwise than by virtue of the certificate) ends; or

(d) the certificate is determined in accordance with sub-paragraphs (2) and (3) below.

(2) If the holder has contravened or failed to comply with any of the terms or conditions applicable to the certificate the Board may give notice requiring the holder to take or refrain from taking such action as may be necessary to remedy the contravention or non-compliance, as the case may be, within such time as may be reasonable (not being less than 28 days).

(3) If the holder does not comply with any notice served pursuant to sub-paragraph (2) above the certificate shall determine on the date on which the notice expires.

Houseboat not to be moored otherwise than in accordance with certificate

7. The holder shall not without the consent in writing of the Board moor the houseboat otherwise than at the site except where paragraph 15 below has effect.

Surrender of certificate by holder

8. The holder shall be entitled to surrender the certificate by notice in writing given to the Board not less than four weeks before the date on which the notice is to take effect.

Recovery of overpayments by holder

9. Where the certificate is surrendered in accordance with paragraph 8 above, the holder shall be entitled to recover from the Board so much of any payment made by him in pursuance of the certificate as is attributable to a period beginning after the termination.

Display of certificate

10. The certificate shall be displayed on the houseboat so as to be clearly visible from the outside of the houseboat at all times.

Holder to comply with planning law, etc.

11. The holder of a certificate shall comply in all respects with the terms of any planning permission given in relation to the houseboat and with any other enactment or byelaw in force applying to houseboats within the area in which it is moored.

Requirements of local authorities

12. The holder shall comply with the requirements of any notice served by a local authority in respect of the houseboat, and shall also comply with any limitation as to the number of persons permitted to sleep on board which may be imposed by the local authority for the area where the site is located.

Sanitary appliances

13.—(1) The holder shall ensure that no sanitary appliance which in the normal course of operation discharges, or can discharge, polluting matter into any inland waterway is used on the houseboat.

(2) The expression "polluting matter" does not include waste discharged from a sink, wash basin, bath or shower.

Sewage disposal

14. The holder shall ensure that there are available for the use of the occupants of the houseboat means for disposing of sewage arising from the occupation of the boat which are satisfactory to—

(a) the Board;
(b) in England and Wales, the National Rivers Authority;
(c) in Scotland, the river purification authority for the area where the site is located; and
(d) the local authorities for the area in which the site is located.

Movement of houseboat

15.—(1) The houseboat may be moved from place to place but while being so moved may not be navigated for hire.

(2) While the houseboat is in the course of being moved the certificate shall be deemed to be—

(i) a pleasure boat certificate for the purposes of Part II of the Act of 1971, where the houseboat is on a river waterway within the meaning of section 4 (Extent of Part II) of that Act; or
(ii) a pleasure boat licence issued by the Board, when the houseboat is on any other inland waterway;

and its use at such times shall be subject to any conditions for the time being in force for the control of pleasure boats and the holder shall comply with any requirements made by or under any enactment applicable to pleasure boats.

SCHEDULE 2

PART I

INSURANCE POLICIES AS TO VESSELS

1. An insurance policy must be issued by an insurer authorised under the Insurance Companies Act 1982 to carry on in Great Britain or in Northern Ireland insurance business of a relevant class or who has corresponding permission under the law of another member state of the European Community.

2. The policy must insure the owner of the vessel and such other person, persons or classes of persons (if any) as is or as are authorised by the owner to have control of the vessel, in respect of any liability (other than a liability specified in paragraph 3 below) which may be incurred by the owner or any such other person resulting from the presence of the vessel on any inland waterway in respect of the death of or bodily injury to any person or any damage to property.

3. The policy shall not by virtue of this Act be required—

(a) to cover liability in respect of the death, arising out of and in the course of his employment, of a person in the employment of a person insured by the policy or of bodily injury sustained by such a person arising out of and in the course of his employment;
(b) to cover liability in respect of damage to the vessel to which the policy relates;

(c) to cover liability in respect of goods carried on or in the vessel to which the policy relates, or any vessel drawn or propelled by such vessel;
(d) to cover any liability of a person in respect of damage to property in his custody or under his control;
(e) to cover any contractual liability; or
(f) to provide cover in respect of any one accident for a sum in excess of such sum as may for the time being be prescribed by the Board for the purposes of this paragraph.

PART II

STANDARDS FOR CONSTRUCTION AND EQUIPMENT OF VESSELS

1. For the purposes of section 17 (Conditions as to certificates and licences) of this Act the Board may from time to time prescribe standards for the construction of vessels to be used on inland waterways, and standards for any appliances, fittings or equipment in such vessels and for making provision with regard to the use and operation of such appliances, fittings and equipment with a view to securing the safety of passengers in such vessels and of other vessels or persons on the inland waterway, and the prevention of pollution, noise and interference with the operation of radio or television equipment.

2. Different standards may be prescribed under section 17 of this Act and this Part of this Schedule in relation to different categories of vessels, and in relation to different inland waterways or parts thereof.

3. The Board may from time to time revoke or amend any standards prescribed under section 17 of this Act and this Part of this Schedule.

4. References in this Part of this Schedule to proposed standards are to standards as proposed to be prescribed, revoked or amended under section 17 of this Act and this Part of this Schedule.

5. Without prejudice to the generality of paragraph 1 above, standards prescribed under section 17 of this Act and this Part of this Schedule may make provision—
(a) with regard to the construction, maintenance and operation of engines used for the propulsion of powered boats and to the storage and supply of fuel for such engines;
(b) requiring the provision of sufficient and effective fire extinguishers;
(c) regulating appliances for cooking, heating, lighting or refrigeration and the storage and supply of fuel for such appliances.

6. Before prescribing, revoking or amending standards under section 17 of this Act and this Part of this Schedule the Board shall—
(a) have regard to the requirements of the byelaws of any inland navigation undertakers whose waterways are contiguous with those of the Board where those byelaws deal with the subject matter of the proposed standards;
(b) take such steps as appear to the Board to be appropriate to bring the proposed standards to the attention of builders, owners and operators of vessels who are likely to be affected by them, and thereafter consider any representations made by any such persons with regard to the proposed standards;
(c) consult the Inland Waterways Amenity Advisory Council; and
(d) consult such organisations as represent a substantial number of builders, owners and operators of vessels who may be affected by the proposed standards.

7.—(1) Following the taking of the steps and the completion of the consultation required by paragraph 6 above, the Board shall—
(a) give notice to the Inland Waterways Amenity Advisory Council, and to such other organisations as were so consulted, of the date ("the prescribed date") upon which the proposed standards are to be prescribed, revoked or amended; and
(b) take such steps as appear to the Board to be appropriate to bring the proposed standards and the prescribed date to the attention of the builders, owners and operators of vessels who are likely to be affected by the standards;

unless the Board decide not to prescribe, revoke or amend the standards, in which case they shall give notice of their decision to the Inland Waterways Amenity Advisory Council and to the organisations which were so consulted.

(2) The prescribed date shall not be less than 84 days after the date of the giving of the notices and the taking of the steps required by sub-paragraph (1) above unless it is necessary to prescribe, revoke or amend the standards immediately after the completion of the consultation so as to avoid any serious risk of danger to persons or property.

8. The Board shall have regard to any advice given to them by the Inland Waterways Amenity Advisory Council as regards the nature of the steps to be taken in accordance with sub-paragraph (b) of paragraph 6 above and with sub-paragraph (1)(b) of paragraph 7 above.

9. The Inland Waterways Amenity Advisory Council shall maintain a list of organisations which claim to represent substantial numbers of builders, owners and operators of vessels who

may be affected by any proposed standards and which should thus be consulted by the Board in accordance with the duty imposed on them by sub-paragraph (d) of paragraph 6 above; and the Board shall be deemed to have complied with that duty if they consult every organisation named in the said list.

10. Standards prescribed under section 17 of this Act and this Part of this Schedule shall not apply to a vessel used wholly or mainly for the purpose of the carriage of goods on a commercial waterway while the vessel is on any such waterway.

11. The Board may on application by any person or any organisation appearing to the Board to represent a substantial number of owners or operators of such vessels as may be affected by any standards grant exemptions in writing on such conditions (if any) as the Board think fit, from the requirements of any standards in respect of any individual vessel, or any category of vessels, being a vessel or, as the case may be, a category of vessels which cannot reasonably be expected to be altered or adapted or otherwise made to comply therewith, having regard in particular to its or their traditional construction or historical character.

12. There shall be a standards appeal panel for the purpose of determining appeals under paragraph 13 below consisting of two persons appointed by the Board and three other persons of whom one each shall be appointed by—

(a) the Inland Waterways Amenity Advisory Council;

(b) in the case of any appeal relating to a narrow boat or other similar vessel normally used on canals, the Inland Waterways Association, and in the case of any other appeal, the Royal Yachting Association; and

(c) the British Marine Industries Federation.

13. Any dispute as to—

(a) any refusal or withdrawal by the Board of a relevant consent on the grounds that the vessel does not comply, or has ceased to comply, with the standards applicable to it; or

(b) any refusal by the Board of an exemption for which application is made under paragraph 11 above or any condition subject to which an exemption is granted;

shall be determined by the standards appeal panel constituted under paragraph 12 above whose decision shall be final and binding on the parties.

Section 36

SCHEDULE 3

REPEALS

Chapter (1)	Title or short title (2)	Extent of repeal (3)
5 & 6 Vict. c. xxiv (1842).	An Act for improving the Navigation of the Severn from the Entrance Lock of the Gloucester and Berkeley Canal, and from the Entrance Lock of the Herefordshire and Gloucestershire Canal, in the County of Gloucester, to Gladder or White-house Brook in the County of Worcester.	Section 147.
1971 c. xviii.	British Waterways Act 1971.	In section 17(1) to the extent that it applies to the undertaking of the Board in Scotland, the words "and a houseboat certificate". In section 17(2) to the extent that it applies to the undertaking of the Board in Scotland, the words "or a houseboat certificate". In section 19(1), the words "or a houseboat", "or a houseboat certificate, as the case may be" and "or houseboat certificate".

Chapter (1)	Title or short title (2)	Extent of repeal (3)
		In section 19(2), the words "or houseboat certificate, as the case may be" and "or houseboat". In section 19(3), the words "or houseboat, as the case may be".
1983 c. ii.	British Waterways Act 1983.	Section 3.

INDEX

References are to sections and Schedules

LETCHWORTH GARDEN CITY HERITAGE FOUNDATION ACT 1995

(1995 c. ii)

ARRANGEMENT OF SECTIONS

An Act to provide for the dissolution of Letchworth Garden City Corporation and the vesting of their undertaking in a society registered under the Industrial and Provident Societies Act 1965; to repeal the Letchworth Garden City Corporation Act 1962; and for connected purposes.
[1st May 1995]

PARLIAMENTARY PROGRESS
The Bill's progress through Parliament was as follows:
House of Commons: First Reading, January 21, 1993; Second Reading, January 28, 1993; Bill Committed, January 28, 1993; Suspended, October 28, 1993; Bill Committed to an Opposed Committee, May 11, 1994–July 19, 1994; Suspended, October 25, 1994; Bill as amended by Committee considered, November 30, 1994; Third Reading, December 6, 1994; Lords' Amendments considered by the House of Commons, April 4, 1995.
House of Lords: First Reading, December 6, 1994; Second Reading, February 8, 1995; Bill Committed, February 8, 1995; Bill Committed to an Opposed Committee, February 14 to 28, 1995; Third Reading, March 27, 1995.

INTRODUCTION

This Act provides for the transfer of the undertaking of the Letchworth Garden City Corporation, which was constituted as a corporation being a public authority by the Letchworth Garden City Corporation Act 1962, to an industrial and provident society registered under the Industrial and Provident Societies Act 1965 and for the dissolution of the Corporation.

Whereas—

(1) Letchworth Garden City Corporation (hereinafter called "the Corporation") were constituted as a corporation being a public authority by the Letchworth Garden City Corporation Act 1962:

(2) It would be of public and local advantage to transfer the undertaking of the Corporation to an industrial and provident society registered under the

Industrial and Provident Societies Act 1965 which is not a public authority and which is charitable and thereupon to dissolve the Corporation and repeal the Letchworth Garden City Corporation Act 1962:

(3) The Corporation have secured the approval of the Registrar of Friendly Societies of proposed rules for such a society which it is intended should be registered with the name "Letchworth Garden City Heritage Foundation" (hereinafter called "the Heritage Foundation"):

(4) It is expedient that other provisions of this Act be enacted:

(5) The purposes of this Act cannot be effected without the authority of Parliament:

May it therefore please Your Majesty that it may be enacted, and be it enacted, by the Queen's most Excellent Majesty, by and with the advice and consent of the Lords Spiritual and Temporal, and Commons, in this present Parliament assembled, and by the authority of the same, as follows:—

Short title

1. This Act may be cited as the Letchworth Garden City Heritage Foundation Act 1995.

Interpretation

2. In this Act, unless otherwise expressly provided or the context otherwise requires—

"the appointed day" means such day as the Corporation may appoint for the purposes of section 4(1) of this Act;

"the Corporation" means Letchworth Garden City Corporation;

"the Heritage Foundation" means the industrial and provident society to be registered under the Industrial and Provident Societies Act 1965 with the name Letchworth Garden City Heritage Foundation;

"the undertaking" means the undertaking of the Corporation.

Objects of Heritage Foundation

3. The only objects of the Heritage Foundation shall be those specified in Schedule 1 to this Act.

Transfer of undertaking

4.—(1) On such day as the Corporation may appoint, the undertaking shall vest in the Heritage Foundation by virtue of this section including—

(a) all that property vested in the Corporation which immediately before the appointed day was held by them for the purposes of the undertaking;

(b) subject to section 13 (Repeal) of this Act, all rights, liabilities and obligations of the Corporation subsisting immediately before the appointed day for the purposes of the undertaking.

(2) The Corporation shall give not less than 28 days' notice of the appointed day by advertisement in the London Gazette and in at least one local newspaper circulating in the Letchworth area.

Continuance of undertaking

5. In carrying on the undertaking transferred by section 4 (Transfer of undertaking) of this Act the Heritage Foundaction shall have regard to the maintenance of that undertaking as an entity in accordance with the principles upon which the Letchworth Garden City was founded.

Contracts of employment

6. Subsection (1)(b) of section 4 (Transfer of undertaking) and section 10 (Saving of agreements, etc.) of this Act shall apply to a contract for the employment of any person by the Corporation; and employment with the Corporation and the Heritage Foundation under any such contract shall be deemed for all puposes to be a single continuing employment.

Dissolution of Corporation

7. On the appointed day the Corporation shall be dissolved.

Final accounts of Corporation

8.—(1) The accounts of the Corporation shall be made up to the appointed day and shall be audited by an auditor appointed by the Corporation, being a person eligible for appointment as a company auditor by virtue of section 25 of the Companies Act 1989.

(2) The Heritage Foundation shall send copies of the final accounts of the Corporation and the auditor's report thereon to the North Hertfordshire District Council.

(3) The auditor's fees shall be payable by the Heritage Foundation.

(4) Any sum certified by the auditor to be due from any person to the Corporation shall be paid to the Heritage Foundation.

Books, etc., to remain evidence

9. All books and documents which, if this Act had not been passed, would have been evidence in respect of any matter for or against the Corporation shall be admissible in respect of that matter for or against the Heritage Foundation.

Saving of agreements, etc.

10. All sales, conveyances, leases, grants, assurances, deeds, contracts, bonds, agreements, notices and demands affecting the undertaking and in force immediately before the appointed day shall on and from that day be as binding and of as full force and effect in every respect and may be enforced as fully and effectively against or in favour of the Heritage Foundation as if the Heritage Foundation were a party thereto or bound thereby or entitled to the benefit thereof.

Pending actions not to abate

11. Any action, arbitration or proceeding and any cause of action, arbitration or proceeding pending or existing immediately before the appointed day by or against or in favour of the Corporation in relation to the undertaking shall not abate or be discontinued or be in anywise prejudicially affected by the transfer to the Heritage Foundation of the undertaking or by anything in this Act, but it may be continued, prosecuted and enforced by, against or in favour of the Heritage Foundation as and when it might have been continued, prosecuted and enforced by, against or in favour of the Corporation if this Act had not been passed, but not further or otherwise.

The Letchworth Commissioner

12.—(1) For the purposes of conducting independent investigations in accordance with this section there shall be a commissioner to be known as the Letchworth Commissioner.

(2) Appointments to the office of Letchworth Commissioner shall be made, and removals from that office may be made, by the President of The Law Society.

(3)(a) Subject to the provisions of this section, where a written complaint is made by or on behalf of a member of the public who claims to have sustained injustice in consequence of maladministration in connection with action taken by or on behalf of the Heritage Foundation, being action taken in the exercise of administrative functions of the Heritage Foundation, the Letchworth Commissioner may investigate that complaint.

(b) The Letchworth Commissioner shall not conduct an investigation under this section in respect of—

(i) any action in respect of which the person aggrieved has or had a right of appeal, reference or review to or before a tribunal constituted by or under any enactment;

(ii) any action in respect of which the person aggrieved has or had a right of appeal to a Minister of the Crown;

(iii) any action in respect of which the person aggrieved has or had a remedy by way of proceedings in any court of law;

(iv) any action which in the opinion of the Letchworth Commissioner affects all or most of the inhabitants of Letchworth Garden City; or

(v) without prejudice to the preceding provisions of this section, any such action or matter as is described in Part III of Schedule 2 to this Act:

Provided that, notwithstanding sub-paragraphs (i), (ii) and (iii) above, the Letchworth Commissioner may conduct an investigation notwithstanding the existence of any right or remedy there mentioned if satisfied that in the particular circumstances it is not reasonable to expect the person aggrieved to resort or have resorted to it.

(c) A complaint shall not be entertained under this section unless it is made in writing to the Letchworth Commissioner specifying the action alleged to constitute maladministration within twelve months from the day on which the person aggrieved first had notice of the matters alleged in the complaint, but the Letchworth Commissioner may conduct an investigation pursuant to a complaint not made within that period if he considers that it is reasonable to do so.

(4)(a) A complaint under this section may be made by any individual, or by any body of persons whether incorporated or not, not being—

(i) a local authority or other authority or body constituted for purposes of the public service or of local government, or for the purposes of carrying on under national ownership any industry or undertaking or part of an industry or undertaking;

(ii) any other authority or body whose members are appointed by Her Majesty or any Minister of the Crown or government department, or whose revenues consist wholly or mainly of moneys provided by Parliament.

(b) Where the person by whom a complaint might have been made under this section has died or is for any reason unable to act for himself, the complaint may be made by his personal representative or by a member of his family or by some body or individual suitable to represent him; but except as aforesaid a complaint shall not be entertained under this section unless made by the person aggrieved himself.

(5) Before proceeding to investigate a complaint, the Letchworth Commissioner shall satisfy himself that the complaint has been brought, by or on behalf of the person aggrieved, to the notice of the Heritage Foundation and that the Heritage Foundation have been afforded a reasonable opportunity to investigate, and reply to, the complaint.

(6) In determining whether to initiate, continue or discontinue an investigation, the Letchworth Commissioner shall, subject to the preceding provisions of this section, act at discretion; and any question whether a complaint is duly made under this section shall be determined by the Letchworth Commissioner.

(7) It is hereby declared that nothing in this section authorises or requires the Letchworth Commissioner to question the merits of a decision taken without maladministration by the Heritage Foundation in the exercise of a discretion vested in them.

(8) Schedule 2 to this Act, which makes further provision concerning the Letchworth Commissioner and his functions, shall have effect.

(9) In this section and Schedule 2 to this Act, unless the context otherwise requires—

"action" includes failure to act, and other expressions connoting action shall be construed accordingly;

"Letchworth Garden City" has the same meaning as in Schedule 1 to this Act;

"person aggrieved" means the person who claims or is alleged to have sustained any such injustice as in mentioned in subsection (3)(a) above;

"tribunal" includes the person constituting a tribunal consisting of one person;

and any reference to the Heritage Foundation includes a reference to the Governors and officers of the Heritage Foundation; and references to a person aggrieved include references to his personal representatives.

Repeal

13. On the appointed day the Letchworth Garden City Corporation Act 1962 shall be repealed.

Costs of Act

14. The costs, charges and expenses preliminary to, and of and incidental to, the preparing and passing of this Act shall be paid by the Corporation and may in whole or in part be defrayed out of revenue.

SCHEDULES

Section 3

SCHEDULE 1

OBJECTS OF HERITAGE FOUNDATION

1. To carry on for the benefit of the local community of Letchworth Garden City ("the local community") the industry, business or trade of—
(a) Promoting the preservation of buildings and other environmental features of beauty or historic interest within Letchworth Garden City;
(b) providing or assisting in the provision of facilities for the recreation or other leisure activity of the local community in the interests of social welfare with the object of improving their conditions of life;
(c) promoting the advancement of education and learning within Letchworth Garden City;
(d) promoting the relief of poverty and sickness within Letchworth Garden City;
(e) supporting any charitable organisation having an office or branch in Letchworth Garden City; and
(f) promoting any other charitable purposes for the benefit of the local community.

2. In this Schedule—

"Letchworth Garden City" means the whole of the estate and undertaking from time to time owned or managed by the Corporation or by the Heritage Foundation together with the environs thereof; and for this purpose "environs" means the full extent of any ecclesiastical parish in which the Corporation or the Foundation from time to time own or manage land provided that such parish includes, adjoins or is adjacent to the town of Letchworth;

"local community" means persons living or working or whose families are living or working temporarily or permanently within Letchworth Garden City and persons visiting Letchworth Garden City.

Section 12

SCHEDULE 2

THE LETCHWORTH COMMISSIONER

PART I

ADMINISTRATIVE PROVISIONS

Appointment and disqualifications

1. The Letchworth Commissioner shall be appointed for a term of five years and may not be appointed for more than two terms.

2. The Letchworth Commissioner may not be relieved of office save at his own request or on grounds of incapacity or misbehaviour and shall in any case vacate office on completing the year of service in which he attains the age of seventy years.

3. A person shall be disqualified for being appointed as, or for being, the Letchworth Commissioner if he is or has been—

(a) a Governor of the Heritage Foundation;
(b) an officer or employee of the Heritage Foundation;
(c) a resident of Letchworth Garden City;
(d) engaged in carrying on any trade or business in Letchworth Garden City, or employed in such a trade or business, provided in either case that he is or was for that purpose actually in occupation of, or employed at, premises in Letchworth Garden City; or
(e) interested in any contract with the Heritage Foundation either in his own behalf or as a member of any company, local authority or other body.

4. Any person appointed to be the Letchworth Commissioner shall be disqualified for being a Governor or officer of the Heritage Foundation.

Remuneration, etc.

5. The Heritage Foundation shall pay to or in respect of the Letchworth Commissioner such amounts by way of remuneration, pensions, allowances or gratuities, or by way of provision for any such benefits, as they may determine.

Staff and accommodation

6. The Heritage Foundation shall in addition pay the reasonable out of pocket expenses of the Letchworth Commissioner incurred in the provision of staff and accommodation.

PART II

PROCEDURE

7.—(1) Where the Letchworth Commissioner proposes to conduct an investigation he shall afford to the Heritage Foundation, and to any person who is alleged to have taken or authorised the action complained of, an opportunity to comment on any allegations contained in the complaint.

(2) Every such investigation shall be conducted in private, but except as aforesaid the procedure for conducting an investigation shall be such as the Letchworth Commissioner considers appropriate in the circumstances of the case; and (without prejudice to that generality) the Letchworth Commissioner may obtain information from such persons and in such manner, and make such inquiries, as he thinks fit, and may determine whether any person may be represented (by counsel or solicitor or otherwise) in the investigation.

(3) The Letchworth Commissioner may, if he thinks fit, require the Heritage Foundation to pay to the person by whom the complaint was made, and to any other person who attends or furnishes information for the purposes of an investigation conducted by the Letchworth Commissioner—

(a) in respect of the expenses properly incurred by them,
(b) by way of compensation for the loss of their time,

such reasonable sums as may be agreed between the Heritage Foundation and the person to whom the payment is to be made or, in default of such agreement, as may be determined by the Letchworth Commissioner.

(4) The conduct of an investigation under this Act shall not affect any action taken by the Heritage Foundation, or any power or duty of the Heritage Foundation to take further action with respect to any matters subject to the investigation.

8.—(1) The Letchworth Commissioner may for the purposes of any investigation conducted by him require any Governor or officer of the Heritage Foundation, or any other person who in his opinion is able to furnish information or produce documents relevant to the investigation, to furnish any such information or produce any such documents.

(2) For the purposes of any such investigation the Letchworth Commissioner shall have the same powers as the High Court in respect of the attendance and examination of witnesses, and in respect of the production of documents.

(3) The Letchworth Commissioner may, under sub-paragraph (1) above, require any person to furnish information concerning communications between the Heritage Foundation and any Government department, or to produce any correspondence or other documents forming part of any such written communications.

(4) No obligation to maintain secrecy or other restriction upon the disclosure of information obtained by or furnished to persons in Her Majesty's service, whether imposed by any enactment or by any rule of law, shall apply to the disclosure of information in accordance with sub-paragraph (3) above; and where that sub-paragraph applies the Crown shall not be entitled to any such privilege in respect of the production of documents or the giving of evidence as is allowed by law in legal proceedings.

(5) Nothing in sub-paragraph (1) or sub-paragraph (3) above affects—

(a) the restriction, imposed by section 11(2) of the Parliamentary Commissioner Act 1967, on the disclosure of information by the Parliamentary Commissioner or his officers; or

(b) the restriction, imposed by paragraph 16 of Schedule 13 to the National Health Service Act 1977, on the disclosure of information by the Health Service Commissioner for England or the Health Service Commissioner for Wales, or by their officers.

(6) Subject to sub-paragraph (4) above no person shall be compelled for the purposes of an investigation under this Act to give any evidence or produce any document which he could not be compelled to give or produce in civil proceedings before the High Court.

(7) To assist him in any investigation the Letchworth Commissioner may obtain advice from any person who in his opinion is qualified to give it and may require the Heritage Foundation to pay any such person such fees or allowances as the Letchworth Commissioner may determine.

(8) If any person without lawful excuse obstructs the Letchworth Commissioner in the performance of his functions under this Act, or any member of his staff assisting in the performance of those functions, or is guilty of any act or omission in relation to an investigation under this Act which, if that investigation were a proceeding in the High Court, would constitute contempt of court, the Letchworth Commissioner may certify the offence to the High Court.

(9) Where an offence is so certified, the High Court may inquire into the matter and, after hearing any witnesses who may be produced against or on behalf of the person charged with the offence, and after hearing any statement that may be offered in defence, deal with him in any manner in which the High Court could deal with him if he had committed the like offence in relation to the High Court.

(10) Nothing in sub-paragraph (8) above shall be construed as applying to the taking of any such action as is mentioned in paragraph 7(4) above.

9.—(1) Whenever the Letchworth Commissioner conducts an investigation, or decides not to conduct an investigation, he shall send a report of the results of the investigation, or as the case may be a statement of his reasons for not conducting an investigation—

(a) to the complainant, and

(b) to the Heritage Foundation.

(2) The report shall not—

(a) mention the name of any person other than the Heritage Foundation, or

(b) contain any particulars which, in the opinion of the Letchworth Commissioner, are likely to identify any person other than the Heritage Foundation and can be omitted without impairing the effectiveness of the report,

unless, after taking into account the public interest as well as the interests of the complainant and of persons other than the complainant, the Letchworth Commissioner considers it necessary to mention the name of that person or to include in the report any such particulars.

(3) Subject to the provisions of sub-paragraph (7) below, the Heritage Foundation shall for a period of three weeks make copies of the report available for inspection by the public without charge at all reasonable hours at their offices; and any person shall be entitled to take copies of, or extracts from, the report when so made available.

(4) Subject to sub-paragraph (7) below, the Heritage Foundation shall supply a copy of the report to any person on request if he pays such charge as the Heritage Foundation may reasonably require.

(5) Not later than two weeks after the report is received by the Heritage Foundation, they shall give public notice, by advertisement in newspapers and such other ways as appear to them

appropriate, that copies of the report shall be available as provided by sub-paragraphs (3) and (4) above, and shall specify the date, being a date not more than one week after public notice is first given, from which the period of three weeks will begin.

(6) If a person having the custody of a report made available for inspection as provided by sub-paragraph (3) above intentionally obstructs any person seeking to inspect the report, or to make a copy of, or extract from, the report, he shall be guilty of an offence and liable on summary conviction to a fine not exceeding level 3 on the standard scale.

(7) The Letchworth Commissioner may, if he thinks fit after taking into account the public interest as well as the interests of the complainant and of persons other than the complainant, direct that a report specified in the direction shall not be subject to the provisions of sub-paragraphs (3), (4) and (5) above.

10.—(1) Whenever the Letchworth Commissioner reports that injustice has been caused to a person aggrieved in consequence of maladministration it shall be the duty of the Heritage Foundation to consider the report and, within the period of three months beginning with the date on which they received the report or such longer period as the Letchworth Commissioner may agree in writing, to notify the Letchworth Commissioner of the action which the Heritage Foundation have taken or propose to take.

(2) If the Letchworth Commissioner—

(a) does not receive the notification required by sub-paragraph (1) above within the period allowed by or under that sub-paragraph, or

(b) is not satisfied with the action which the Heritage Foundation have taken or propose to take, or

(c) does not within a period of three months beginning with the end of the period so allowed, or such longer period as the Letchworth Commissioner may agree in writing, receive confirmation from the Heritage Foundation that they have taken action, as proposed, to the satisfaction of the Letchworth Commissioner,

he shall make a further report setting out those facts and making recommendations.

(3) Those recommendations are such recommendations as the Letchworth Commissioner thinks fit to make with respect to action which, in his opinion, the Heritage Foundation should take to remedy the injustice to the person aggrieved and to prevent similar injustice being caused in the future.

(4) Paragraph 9 above, with any necessary modifications, and sub-paragraph (1) above shall apply to a report under sub-paragraph (2) above as they apply to a report under that paragraph.

(5) If the Letchworth Commissioner—

(a) does not receive the notification required by sub-paragraph (1) above (as applied by sub-paragraph (4) above) within the period allowed by or under that sub-paragraph or is satisfied before the period allowed by that sub-paragraph has expired that the Heritage Foundation have decided to take no action, or

(b) is not satisfied with the action which the Heritage Foundation have taken or propose to take, or

(c) does not within a period of three months beginning with the end of the period allowed by or under sub-paragraph (1) above (as applied by sub-paragraph (4) above) or such longer period as the Letchworth Commissioner may agree in writing, receive confirmation from the Heritage Foundation that they have taken action, as proposed, to the satisfaction of the Letchworth Commissioner,

he may, by notice to the Heritage Foundation, require them to arrange for a statement to be published in accordance with sub-paragraphs (6) and (7) below.

(6) The statement referred to in sub-paragraph (5) above is a statement, in such form as the Heritage Foundation and the Letchworth Commissioner may agree, consisting of—

(a) details of any action recommended by the Letchworth Commissioner in his further report which the Heritage Foundation have not taken;

(b) such supporting material as the Letchworth Commissioner may require; and

(c) if the Heritage Foundation so require, a statement of the reasons for their having taken no action on, or not the action recommended in, the report.

(7) The requirements for the publication of the statement are that—

(a) publication shall be in any two editions within a fortnight of a newspaper circulating in the area of Letchworth Garden City agreed with the Letchworth Commissioner or, in default of agreement, nominated by him; and

(b) publication in the first such edition shall be arranged for the earliest practicable date.

(8) If the Heritage Foundation—

(a) fail to arrange for the publication of the statement in accordance with sub-paragraphs (6) and (7) above, or

(b) are unable, within the period of one month beginning with the date on which they received the notice under sub-paragraph (5) above, or such longer period as the Letchworth Commissioner may agree in writing, to agree with the Letchworth Commissioner the form of the statement to be published,

the Letchworth Commissioner shall arrange for such a statement as is mentioned in sub-paragraph (6) above to be published in any two editions within a fortnight of a newspaper circulating within Letchworth Garden City.

(9) The Heritage Foundation shall reimburse the Letchworth Commissioner any reasonable expenses incurred by him in performing his duty under sub-paragraph (8) above.

11. Where on consideration of any report by the Letchworth Commissioner it appears to the Heritage Foundation that a payment should be made to, or some other payment should be provided for, a person who has suffered injustice in consequence of maladministration to which the report relates, the Heritage Foundation may (notwithstanding anything in the Rules of the Heritage Foundation) incur such expenditure as appears to the Board of Management of the Heritage Foundation to be appropriate in making such a payment or providing such a benefit.

12.—(1) Any power of the Heritage Foundation to have their functions discharged by any person acting for them shall, as respects the consideration of a further report of the Letchworth Commissioner under paragraph 10(2) above, be subject to the restriction that, if it is proposed that the Heritage Foundation should take no action on, or not the action recommended in, the report, consideration of the report shall be referred to the Heritage Foundation.

(2) If when considering a further report of the Letchworth Commissioner under paragraph 10(2) above the Heritage Foundation take into consideration a report by a person or body with an interest in the Letchworth Commissioner's report, they shall not conclude their consideration of the Letchworth Commissioner's report without also having taken into consideration a report by a person or body with no interest in the Letchworth Commissioner's report.

(3) No Governor of the Heritage Foundation shall vote on any question with respect to a report or further report by the Letchworth Commissioner in which he is named and criticised by the Letchworth Commissioner.

(4) Subsection (9) of section 12 (The Letchworth Commissioner) of this Act does not apply to this paragraph.

13.—(1) For the purposes of the law of defamation the following shall be absolutely privileged:—

(a) the publication of any matter in communications between a Governor or officer of the Heritage Foundation and the Letchworth Commissioner for the purposes of this Act;

(b) the publication of any matter by the Letchworth Commissioner in communicating with a complainant for the purposes of this Act;

(c) the publication of any matter in preparing, making and sending a report or statement in accordance with paragraph 9 or paragraph 10 above, or, subject to paragraph 9(7) above, in making a report available to the public or in supplying a copy under paragraph 9(4) above;

(d) the publication of any matter by inclusion in a statement published in accordance with sub-paragraphs (5) to (8) of paragraph 10 above.

(2) Information obtained by the Letchworth Commissioner in the course of or for the purposes of an investigation under this Act shall not be disclosed except—

(a) for the purposes of the investigation and of any report to be made under paragraph 9 or paragraph 10 above;

(b) for the purposes of any proceedings for an offence under the Official Secrets Acts 1911 to 1989 alleged to have been committed in respect of information obtained, under this Act, by the Letchworth Commissioner or for an offence of perjury alleged to have been committed in the course of an investigation under this Act or for the purposes of an inquiry with a view to the taking of such proceedings; or

(c) for the purpose of any proceedings under paragraph 8(9) above;

and the Letchworth Commissioner shall not be called upon to give evidence in any proceedings (other than proceedings within sub-paragraph (b) or (c) above) of matters coming to his knowledge in the course of an investigation under this Act.

(3) A Minister of the Crown may give notice in writing to the Letchworth Commissioner with respect to any document or information specified in the notice, or any class of documents or information so specified, that in the opinion of the Minister the disclosure of that document or information, or of documents or information of that class, would be contrary to the public interest; and where such a notice is given nothing in this Act shall be construed as authorising or requiring the Letchworth Commissioner to communicate to any other person, or for any purpose, any document or information specified in the notice, or any document or information of a class so specified.

(4) Nothing in sub-paragraph (3) above shall affect the obligations imposed by paragraph 8(4) and (5) above.

(5) Where information is disclosed in accordance with paragraph 8(3) above, being information which is derived from a communication from a government department, and which has not been made public, the Letchworth Commissioner shall not without the written consent of an officer of the government department make a report which includes all or any of that information unless he has given the department not less than one month's notice in writing of his intention.

(6) The provisions of this paragraph shall apply to the Commissioners of Customs and Excise and Commissioners of Inland Revenue as they apply to a Minister of the Crown.

Part III

Matters not subject to investigation

14. The actions and matters in respect of which the Letchworth Commissioner shall not conduct an investigation are any actions or matters of the following descriptions:—

(a) The commencement or conduct of civil or criminal proceedings before any court of law.

(b) (i) Action taken in matters relating to contractual or other commercial transactions of the Heritage Foundation or any subsidiary of the Heritage Foundation within the meaning of section 736 of the Companies Act 1985, including transactions falling within sub-paragraph (ii) below but excluding transactions falling within sub-paragraph (iii) below.

(ii) The transactions mentioned in sub-paragraph (i) above as included in the matters which, by virtue of that sub-paragraph, are not subject to investigation are all transactions of the Heritage Foundation or any company in which the Heritage Foundation have an interest relating to the operation of public passenger transport, the provision of recreation or entertainment, the provision and operation of industrial establishments or the carrying on of any trade.

(iii) The transactions mentioned in sub-paragraph (i) above as not included in those matters are transactions for or relating to the acquisition or disposal of land.

(c) Action taken in respect of appointments or removals, pay, discipline, superannuation or other personnel matters.

INDEX

References are to sections and Schedules

MALVERN HILLS ACT 1995

(1994 c. iii)

ARRANGEMENT OF SECTIONS

SECT.

An Act to amend certain enactments relating to the Malvern Hills Conservators and the management of the Malvern Hills; to confer further powers on the Malvern Hills Conservators; to make further provision in relation to the Malvern Hills; and for other purposes. [28th June 1995]

PARLIAMENTARY PROGRESS

This Bill's progress through Parliament was as follows:

House of Lords: First Reading, January 19, 1993; Second Reading, March 8, 1993; Bill Committed, March 8, 1993; Bill Committed to Opposed Committee, June 28, 1993-October 18, 1993; Suspended, October 28, 1993; Unopposed Bill Committee, December 17, 1993; Third Reading, February 15, 1994; Commons' Amendments considered, May 23, 1995.

House of Commons: First Reading, February 15, 1994; Second Reading, July 19, 1994; Bill Committed, July 19, 1994; Suspended, October 25, 1994; Unopposed Bill Committee, May 3, 1995; Bill as Amended by Committee considered, May 17, 1995; Third Reading, May 23, 1995.

INTRODUCTION

This Act confers additional powers upon the Malvern Hills Conservators in relation to the lands commonly known as the Malvern Hills; these powers relate, *inter alia*, to the provision of facilities for the public, the disposal of land, the control of finances, and the management of the land.

Whereas—

(1) By the Malvern Hills Act 1884 the Malvern Hills Conservators (in this Act called "the Conservators") were incorporated and were invested with

certain powers of protection, control and management with regard to the lands in that Act specified and provision was made for restricting the user and enjoyment of the said lands:

(2) By the Malvern Hills Act 1909, the Malvern Hills Act 1924 and the Malvern Hills Act 1930 further powers were conferred upon the Conservators and further provision was made in relation to the lands under the Conservators' jurisdiction and commonly known as the Malvern Hills:

(3) Under the Malvern Hills Act 1930 it is the general duty of the Conservators except as otherwise provided in the Malvern Hills Acts 1884 to 1930 to keep the Malvern Hills unenclosed and unbuilt on as open spaces for the recreation and enjoyment of the public:

(4) The Malvern Hills have been widely known and admired for their natural beauty and have formed a centre of attraction to the inhabitants of the county of Hereford and Worcester and to visitors coming from all parts of the country for the purposes of health, recreation and enjoyment:

(5) The area of land under the Conservators' jurisdiction has increased as has the number of visitors resorting to the Malvern Hills:

(6) The existing powers of the Conservators are insufficient to enable the Conservators to make suitable provision to meet the convenience and requirements of the public, and to carry out their functions and to manage and deal with the Malvern Hills effectively and appropriately in the light of present day circumstances:

(7) It is desirable that further provision should be made enabling certain facilities to be constructed or provided on the Malvern Hills:

(8) It is expedient that further powers of protecting, controlling, regulating, managing and dealing with the Malvern Hills should be conferred upon the Conservators as in this Act provided:

(9) It is expedient that the other powers of this Act should be conferred upon the Conservators and that the other provisions contained in this Act should be enacted:

(10) The purposes of this Act cannot be effected without the authority of Parliament:

May it therefore please Your Majesty that it may be enacted, and be it enacted, by the Queen's most Excellent Majesty, by and with the advice and consent of the Lords Spiritual and Temporal, and Commons, in this present Parliament assembled, and by the authority of the same, as follows:—

Short and collective titles

1.—(1) This Act may be cited as the Malvern Hills Act 1995.

(2) The Malvern Hills Acts 1884 to 1930 and this Act may be cited together as the Malvern Hills Acts 1884 to 1995.

Interpretation

2. In this Act—

"the Act of 1884" means the Malvern Hills Act 1884;

"the Act of 1909" means the Malvern Hills Act 1909;

"the Act of 1924" means the Malvern Hills Act 1924;

"the Act of 1930" means the Malvern Hills Act 1930;

"the Board" means the Board of the Conservators;

"the Conservators" means the Malvern Hills Conservators as defined in the Act of 1930;

"domestic fowl" includes turkeys, geese, ducks, guinea fowl, peacocks and quails;

"the existing Malvern Hills" means the lands under the jurisdiction of the Conservators for the purposes of the existing Malvern Hills Acts at the time of the passing of this Act;

"the existing Malvern Hills Acts" means the Malvern Hills Acts 1884 to 1930;

"horse" includes any mare, gelding, pony, foal, colt, filly or stallion and also any ass, mule or jennet;

"the Malvern Hills" means the lands from time to time under the jurisdiction of the Conservators for the purposes of the Malvern Hills Acts;

"the Malvern Hills Acts" means the Malvern Hills Acts 1884 to 1930 and this Act.

Provision of refreshment facilities

3.—(1) (a) In the event of damage to or the destruction of the building known as St. Anne's Well the Conservators may repair, reconstruct or replace that building provided that any reconstruction or replacement shall be on the site of, and of a similar size and external character to, the existing building.

(b) The powers of this subsection shall extend in relation to any reconstruction or replacement building constructed under paragraph (a) above.

(2) The Conservators may maintain and operate a building constructed under this section and may at such a building sell meals and freshments and provide such services and facilities as are reasonably ancillary to the use of the building as a restaurant or cafeteria.

(3) The Conservators may let a building constructed under this section and may enter into and carry into effect agreements with respect to the exercise of the powers contained in subsections (1) and (2) above by any other person including the defraying of, or the making of contributions towards, the costs of the Conservators or any other person in connection with the exercise of such powers

Licensing of stalls

4. The following paragraph is hereby substituted for paragraph (g) of section 4 (Powers exerciseable over the Malvern Hills) of the Act of 1930 and the provisos thereto:—

"(g) They may grant leave or licence for any period not exceeding one year upon such terms and conditions and subject to such restrictions as they think fit to any person or persons to erect, maintain and operate temporary or mobile stalls not exceeding six in all at any one time on the Malvern Hills for the purpose of purveying food and refreshment to the public, and without prejudice to the generality of the foregoing such restrictions may relate to locations on the Malvern Hills where such a stall may be erected or from where it may be operated and the display of advertisements of any kind visible from outside the stall whether relating to any trade or business carried on at the stall or not.".

Provision of temporary lavatories

5.—(1) Subject to subsection (2) below, the Conservators may, without other sanction or authority—

(a) place or erect temporary lavatories in such positions and places on the Malvern Hills as they think fit;

(b) grant licence for any period not exceeding 14 days upon such terms and conditions as they think fit to any person to place or erect temporary lavatories in such positions and places on the Malvern Hills as the Conservators think fit and as may be specified in the licence.

(2) The powers of this section may only be exercised if the temporary lavatories are to be provided in connection with an event authorised by the Conservators which in their opinion is likely to attract such a number of people onto the Malvern Hills that such facilities will be required.

(3) Temporary lavatories placed or erected on the Malvern Hills under this section shall be removed from the Malvern Hills as soon as reasonably practicable after the event in connection with which they are provided has ended and in any case shall not remain on the Malvern Hills for a period exceeding 14 days.

As to disposal of land

6.—(1) Without prejudice to any other powers the Conservators have to sell, exchange, let, charge or otherwise dispose of land, and notwithstanding anything in the existing Malvern Hills Acts the Conservators may, with the consent of the Secretary of State, in respect of any land which—

(a) is owned by them but has not been so owned for a continuous period of more than five years;

(b) does not form part of the existing Malvern Hills;

(c) is not registered as common land or a town or village green; and

(d) the Conservators have not later than two years after the date of acquisition of it by them decided it is not desirable to retain for the benefit or recreation of the public as part of the Malvern Hills;

do any of the following:—

(i) sell the whole or any part of or the whole or any part of any interest in any such land which is not required by them;

(iii) exchange any such land which is not required by them for other land either with or without paying or receiving any money by way of equality of exchange;

(iii) let any such land subject to such terms and conditions, covenants and arrangements as they think fit;

and the provisions of section 9 (Power to adjust boundaries) of the Act of 1930 shall not apply as respects any such sale or exchange.

(2) Where land has become vested in the Conservators by virtue of a gift or bequest the powers conferred by this sectin shall not be exercisable as respects that land in any manner inconsistent with any condition attached to the gift or bequest, except with the consent of the donor or the personal representatives or trustees of the donor.

(3) Where the Conservators exercise their powers under subsection (1) above in relation to any land by letting it, all the powers under that subsection shall continue to be available to them in relation to that land on the termination of the letting whether or not, at that termination, they have owned the land for more than five years.

Provision for capital and income

7.—(1) Capital money received by the Conservators from the sale, letting, grant or other disposal of land or interests in land under the provisions of this Act may be applied by them for any purpose for which capital money may be properly applied.

(2) Any sums received by the Conservators from the sale, letting, grant or other disposal of land or interests in land under the terms of this Act other than capital money shall be treated as income of the Board and shall be used

in defraying expenses incurred by the Conservators in the execution of their powers and duties.

Power to grant easements, etc.

8. The following sections are hereby substituted for section 7 (Power to grant easements) of the Act of 1930:—

"**Power to grant easements**

7.—(1) Subject to subsection (5) below, the Conservators may grant upon such terms and conditions and for such a period as they think fit easements, rights, privileges or licences in, under or over the Malvern Hills for the provision of publc or private underground or overground services relating to water, electricity, gas, oil, telecommunications, drainage and sewerage:

Provided that it shall be a term of any such grant that the surface of any part of the Malvern Hills that may be disturbed in connection with the exercise of any easement, right, privilege or licence so granted shall be restored as soon as practicable by and at the expense of the person to whom the easement, right, privilege or licence is granted.

(2) Subject to subsection (3) below, the Conservators may with the consent of the owner exercise the powers of this section in relation to any land forming part of the Malvern Hills not owned by them as though they were the owners of that land.

(3) The consent of the owner under subsection (2) above shall not be required in any case where the owner is not known.

(4) For the purposes of this section and section 7A below the owner of land is not known where after diligent enquiry the Conservators are unable to discover his identity.

(5) (a) The Conservators shall not exercise the powers of this section for the provision of any service, other than a temporary service, overground unless—

(i) in the opinion of the Conservators it is not reasonably practicable for the service to be other than overground;

(ii) the service is to be provided to a domestic property in existence at the time of the passing of this Act; and

(iii) in the opinion of the Conservators and the local planning authority the provision of the service overground is reasonable.

(b) The Conservators shall not exercise the powers of this section for the provision of any service overground except by way of determinable licence.

Access roads

7A.—(1) Subject to subsection (2) below, the Conservators may on such terms and conditions as they think fit (including terms and conditions as to the provision and maintenance of cattle grids and other works) authorise in writing any person to construct, maintain, alter or improve roads or ways over the Malvern Hills affording vehicular or other access from any highway to land being land lying within or adjacent to any part of the Malvern Hills and appearing to the Conservators to lack satisfactory access.

(2) In granting authorisation under subsection (1) above the Conservators shall have regard to the effect of the works being so authorised on the natural aspect of the Malvern Hills and shall impose such terms and conditions as are necessary to ensure that any adverse effect is minimised.

(3) The Conservators may, on such terms and conditions as they think fit, for the purpose of or in connection with the provision of roads or

ways, grant licence to use and grant easements and rights in, under or over lands forming part of the Malvern Hills and on which roads or ways are authorised to be constructed pursuant to subsection (1) above.

(4) Subject to subsection (5) below, the Conservators may with the consent of the owner exercise the powers of this section in relation to any land forming part of the Malvern Hills not owned by them as though they were the owners of that land.

(5) The consent of the owner under subsection (4) above shall not be required in any case where the owner is not known.".

Power to provide buildings for use by the Conservators

9.—(1) The Conservators may acquire by means of purchase, lease or otherwise buildings (with or without the adjacent land) for use as their offices, for use as information centres, for the purpose of storage in connection with the carrying out of their functions and for the purpose of residential occupation by an employee of the Conservators in the interests of security of any building used by the Conservators and may furnish and equip such buildings for such purposes.

(2) At buildings acquired under this section the Conservators may sell such goods, including books, maps, souvenirs and other goods as may be reasonably ancillary to the use of the Malvern Hills by the public for enjoyment and recreation or education.

(3) Notwithstanding anything in subsection (1) (a) of section 6 (As to disposal of land) of this Act the Conservators may at any time sell, exchange or otherwise dispose of any buildings and land acquired under this section or (prior to the passing of this Act) section 53 of the Commissioners Clauses Act 1847 (power to provide offices, etc.).

(4) Residential accommodation acquired under subsection (1) above may be made available to the employee of the Conservators on such terms and conditions as the Conservators think fit.

(5) The Conservators may repair and maintain or reconstruct or extend buildings acquired under this section and may execute such works as may be necessary or expedient in connection with the furnishing and equipping of the buildings.

(6) The Conservators may let parts of buildings acquired under this section which parts are surplus to their requirements on such terms and conditions as the Conservators think fit.

Power to borrow

10.—(1) The Conservators may from time to time, with the consent of the Secretary of State and upon and subject to such terms and conditions and for such period as the Secretary of State may direct, borrow by any method or methods such sums of money as may be required by them for the purposes of this Act and the Act of 1930.

(2) Money borrowed by the Conservators may be borrowed upon the security of all or any of the revenues and property of the Conservators and the Conservators may mortgage or assign over to the persons by or on behalf of whom such money is advanced the said revenues and property or any part thereof.

(3) Notwithstanding section 101 of the Law of Property Act 1925 (powers incident to estate or interest of mortgage) or anything in any deed, where the Conservators mortgage or assign over to any person any relevant land after the passing of this Act under the powers of this section, or of section 11 of the Act of 1909 or section 32 of the Act of 1924 (powers to borrow), the mortgagee or, as the case may be, the assignee shall not have a power to sell the land or a power to cut and sell, or to contract for the cutting and sale of, timber or other trees on the land.

(4) For the purposes of this section "relevant land" means the existing Malvern Hills and any other land owned by the Conservators, other than any land and buildings acquired under section 9 (Power to provide buildings for use by the Conservators) of this Act or (prior to the passing of this Act) section 53 of the Commissioners Clauses Act 1847 (power to provide offices, etc.).

Amount for contingencies

11. Notwithstanding anything in the Act of 1884, the Act of 1909, or the Act of 1924, the Conservators may include in any percept or other demand which they may be authorised to levy or make on any local authority, or in any sum which they may request any local authority or other body to pay in any particular year, an amount for contingencies of up to 10 per cent. of the estimated expenditure for the year in respect of which the precept, demand or request is made.

Land acquisition fund

12.—(1) The Conservators may create and form a land acquisition fund and may in any particular year set aside, for credit to the land acquisition fund, from the general fund maintained by them such sum standing to the credit of the general fund as has been paid to them as a result of any precept or demand levied or made on any local authority or request made of any local authority or other body for the purpose of land acquisition during that year but which has not been required for such purpose provided that such sum set aside shall not exceed 5 per cent. of the total precept, demand or request for the Conservators' purposes generally including land acquisition in that year.

(2) Any sums so set apart for the maintenance of a land acquisition fund may from time to time be invested in any manner prescribed for the investment of trust funds and the dividends and interest arising from such investment may also be invested in the same manner so as to accumulate at compound interest for the credit of the fund.

Confirmation of byelaws and fines thereunder

13. Section 10 (Byelaws) of the Act of 1930 is hereby amended by the addition after subsection (3) of the following subsections:—

"(4) Before making any byelaws under this section the Conservators shall give notice to and consult the Central Council of Physical Recreation.

(5) Subsections (3) to (8) and (11) of section 236 and section 238 of the Local Government Act 1972 (which relate to the procedure for making, and evidence of, byelaws) shall apply to any byelaws made by the Conservators under this section as if the Conservators were a local authority and the Clerk to the Conservators were the proper officer (within the meaning of the said Act of 1972) of that local authority but, subject to subsection (6) below, the Secretary of State may confirm the byelaws with such modifications as he thinks fit.

(6) Where the Secretary of State proposes to make a modification which appears to him to be substantial, he shall inform the Conservators and require them to take any steps he considers necessary for informing persons likely to be concerned with the modification, and shall not confirm the byelaws until such period has elapsed as he thinks reasonable for consideration of, and comment upon, the proposed modification by the Conservators and by other persons who have been informed of it.

(7) Byelaws made by the Conservators under this section may provide that persons contravening the byelaws shall be liable on summary conviction to a fine not exceeding level 2 on the standard scale and, in the case of a continuing offence, a daily fine not exceeding one-tenth of the amount which is equivalent to that level.

(8) Nothing in subsection (5) above shall affect the continuance in effect of the byelaws of the Conservators made on 11th November 1982 and which came into force on 19th January 1983, and byelaw 36 thereof (which relates to fines for offences) shall have effect as from the passing into law of the Malvern Hills Act 1995 as if for the words "twenty pounds" there were substituted the words "level 2 on the standard scale" and for the words "two pounds" there were substituted the words "one-tenth of the amount which is equivalent to that level":

Provided that the amendment so made to the said byelaw 36 shall not have effect in relation to any offence committed before the passing into law of the Malvern Hills Act 1995.".

Further provision as to enforcement of byelaws

14.—(1) Where the driver of a vehicle is alleged to be guilty of an offence against any byelaw made by the Conservators which relates to the driving or parking of vehicles on the Malvern Hills—

(a) the person keeping the vehicle shall give such information as to the identity of the driver as he may be required in writing by or on behalf of the Conservators to give; and

(b) any other person shall, if required as mentioned in paragraph (a) above, give any information which it is in his power to give and which may lead to the identification of the driver.

(2) A person who fails to comply with the requirements of subsection (1) (a) above shall be guilty of an offence less he shows to the satisfaction of the court that he did not know, and could not with reasonable diligence have ascertained, who was the driver of the vehicle; and a person who fails to comply with the requirements of subsection (1) (b) above shall be guilty of an offence.

(3) A person guilty of an offence under this section shall be liable on summary conviction to a fine not exceeding level 2 on the standard scale.

Public access to the Malvern Hills

15.—(1) Subject to the provisions of the Malvern Hills Acts and compliance with all rules, regulations or byelaws relating to the Malvern Hills and for the time being in force, the public shall have a right of access to the Malvern Hills on foot and on horseback for the purpose of open-air recreation; and a person who enters on the Malvern Hills for that purpose without breaking or damaging any wall, fence, hedge, gate or other thing, or who is on the Malvern Hills for that purpose having so entered, shall not be treated as a trespasser on the Malvern Hills or incur any other liability by reason only of so entering or being on the Malvern Hills.

(2) A person entering upon the Malvern Hills in accordance with subsection (1) above is not, for the purposes of the Occupiers' Liability Act 1957, a visitor of any occupier of the Malvern Hills.

(3) Nothing in this section shall prejudice or affect the exercise of powers under any enactment whereby access to the Malvern Hills may be regulated or prohibited; and, subject to subsections (4) and (6) below, the Conservators may by notices posted in such places on the Malvern Hills as they think fit regulate or prohibit for such period as may be reasonably necessary access by all, or any part of, the public to any part of the Malvern Hills—

(a) after consultation with the Historic Buildings and Monuments Commission for England, for the protection, so far as is reasonably necessary, of any ancient monument or any area of archaeological or historical interest;

(b) for the protection and restoration of the natural beauty of the Malvern Hills and their suitability for rough grazing or recreation;

(c) for the preservation of trees on the Malvern Hills;

(d) if advised by the Nature Conservancy Council for England that regulation or prohibition of access would be desirable in the interests of protection or preservation of flora or fauna or any area of scientific interest on the Malvern Hills, for such protection or preservation, so far as is reasonably necessary;

(e) after consultation with the chief officer of police and the chief fire officer of the fire authority, for the prevention of the risk of fire on the Malvern Hills;

(f) for the prevention of accidents or injury or other damage to health at any place, which is in the opinion of the Conservators a source of danger, on the Malvern Hills;

and notwithstanding anything in the existing Malvern Hills Acts, the Conservators may post such notices and for the purposes of paragraphs (a), (b), (c), (d) and (f) above, may fence and enclose parts of the Malvern Hills for so long as may appear necessary for the attainment of the purposes of the regulation or prohibition of access; and during the currency of any such regulation or prohibition the right of access of the public shall be subject to the regulation or prohibition.

(4) In exercise of the powers of paragraphs (e) and (f) of subsection (3) above the Conservators may regulate or prohibit access by the public to, over or along any footpath or bridleway on or over the Malvern Hills but the Conservators shall not in exercise of the powers of paragraphs (a) to (d) of that subsection regulate or prohibit such access.

(5) A notice posted in accordance with this section shall include a statement of the reasons for that regulation or prohibition and of its duration.

(6) Nothing in subsection (3) above shall authorise the Conservators to regulate or prohibit access to any part of the Malvern Hills by any person bona fide going to or from any land which is accessible only over that part of the Malvern Hills.

(7) Except in case of emergency or in any case where the regulation or prohibition of access is for a period not exceeding 28 days, the Conservators shall, before exercising any of the powers conferred on them by subsection (3) above, consult with the Central Council of Physical Recreation and at least one local association, authority or other body having a substantial interest in the area to be affected by the exercise of those powers and the use of the Malvern Hills for recreational purposes.

(8) Except in case of emergency or in any case where the regulation or prohibition of access is for a period not exceeding 28 days, not less than 28 days before in any case exercising the powers of paragraph (a), (b) or (c) of subsection (3) above, the Conservators shall give notice by advertisement of the proposed regulation or prohibition of access by the public, its intended duration and the reasons for which it is proposed to be made and stating that written representations relative thereto may be notified to them within 28 days after the date of the publication of the notice, and, before giving effect to their proposals for regulating or prohibiting access, the Conservators shall consider all representations so made.

(9) The notice required by subsection (8) above shall be given in one or more newspapers which individually or together circulate throughout the county of Hereford and Worcester.

(10) The Conservators shall, on or before the date on which it is published, send a copy of any notice which is to be published in pursuance of subsection

(8) above during a specified period, of a specified description and relating to land comprised in a specified area to any person who has previously—

(a) requested the Conservators to send him copies of all such notices as so specified; and

(b) paid to the Conservators such reasonable charges as the Conservators may have specified.

(11) The Conservators may make byelaws providing that any person who, without reasonable excuse, contravenes a notice posted under subsection (3) above shall be guilty of an offence and subsections (4) to (7) of section 10 (Byelaws) of the Act 1930 shall apply to byelaws made under this subsection as if references in the said subsections (4) to (7) to "this section" included references to this subsection.

(12) Where the Conservators have exercised their powers under subsection (3) above they shall—

(a) review any continuing regulation or prohibition of access no later than one year after the regulation or prohibition was first implemented and thereafter at intervals of no more than a year;

(b) in the case of a continuing regulation or prohibition of access under paragraph (e) of that subsection, review that regulation or prohibition no later than two months after the regulation or prohibition was first implemented and thereafter at intervals of no more than two months;

(c) describe the nature and extent of the exercise of the powers in the form of an annual written report, copies of which shall be made available at the offices of the Conservators and a copy of which shall be delivered to all local authorities within whose areas the Malvern Hills lie.

Regulation of horse-riding on the Malvern Hills

16.—(1) If, in the opinion of the Conservators, it is necessary to do so to preserve the natural aspect of the Malvern Hills, or to prevent the injury or disfigurement thereof, or to protect the use of the Malvern Hills as an open space for the recreation and enjoyment of the public, they may from time to time—

(a) by notices or direction signs posted at such places on the Malvern Hills as they think fit, restrict or prohibit the riding or exercising of horses on the Malvern Hills or any part or parts of the Malvern Hills for such period as may be reasonably necessary; and

(b) give directions to the owners of horses which are, or are intended to be, let to members of the public for hire or reward as to the tracks on the Malvern Hills which those horses may use, whilst being so let, and those owners shall take all reasonable steps to ensure that only those tracks are so used.

(2) The Conservators may make byelaws providing that any person who, without the authority of the Conservators and without reasonable excuse, contravenes a notice or direction sign posted in pursuance of paragraph (a) of subsection (1) above or, without reasonable excuse, fails to comply with a direction given under paragraph (b) of the said subsection shall be guilty of an offence and subsections (4) to (7) of section 10 (Byelaws) of the Act of 1930 shall apply to byelaws made under this subsection as if references in the said subsections (4) to (7) to "this section" included references to this subsection.

(3) (a) Nothing in this section shall authorise the Conservators to restrict or prohibit the lawful use of any bridleway shown on the definitive map and statement for any area of the county of Hereford and Worcester which includes any part of the Malvern Hills.

(b) In this subsection "bridleway" shall have the meaning given by section 66 of the Wildlife and Countryside Act 1981 and "definitive map and statement'' means the definitive map and statement operative under Part III of that Act.

Designated ways

17.—(1)The Conservators may designate ways on the Malvern Hills suitable for the riding or exercising of horses and any way so designated shall be marked in such manner as shall, in the opinion of the Conservators, be necessary to give notice of the designation.

(2) A designation of a way as suitable for the riding or exercising of horses may from time to time be varied or rescinded by the Conservators.

(3) The Conservators shall consult with the Central Council of Physical Recreation—

(a) before designating a way under subsection (1) above where the Conservators propose that the designation should have effect for a period exceeding six months; and

(b) before extending any designation of a way, or making a successive designation, such that the total duration of the period for which the way will be designated will exceed six months.

New ways

18.—(1) The Conservators may, after consultation with the Central Council of Physical Recreation, make and maintain new ways and facilities on the Malvern Hills for the riding or exercising of horses and shall have power to make reasonable charges for the use of such new ways and facilities.

(2) Charges made under this section shall be computed by reference to—

(a) the reasonable cost of the construction and maintenance of the new ways and facilities; and

(b) the reasonable cost of the regulation of the use of the new ways and facilities.

(3) The amount raised by any charges made under subsection (1) above shall be wholly applied by the Conservators in undertaking the activities referred to in that subsection.

(4) Charges made under subsection (1) above may make different provision for different cases or circumstances.

Seizure of stray animals

19.—(1) The Conservators may seize and impound any animal to which this section applies, which is on the Malvern Hills in contravention of any byelaw duly made by the Conservators.

(2) The Conservators shall, within 24 hours after impounding any animal under this section, give notice of the impounding to the officer in charge of a police station and also to the owner of the animal if his identity be known to them or can reasonably be ascertained.

(3) The Conservators shall—

(a) keep a register of all animals seized by them under this section containing a brief description of each animal, the date of seizure and a statement as to whether the animal was sold or otherwise disposed of or destroyed;

(b) make the register available for public inspection at all reasonable times.

(4) If after seven clear days from the date of impounding the owner has not claimed an animal and paid all expenses incurred in seizing, impounding and maintaining it, the Conservators may sell or otherwise dispose of the animal otherwise than by destruction, and if after 14 clear days from the said date the owner has not claimed the animal and paid all such expenses the Conservators may destroy the animal in a manner to cause as little pain or distress as possible.

(5) Whilst any animal is impounded by the Conservators under this section the Conservators shall cause it to be properly fed and maintained.

(6) If any sums received on disposal of the animal are less than the expenses of the Conservators in seizing and maintaining the animal the Conservators may recover from the owner of the animal the difference.

(7) Where the Conservators dispose of any animal under subsection (4) above, they shall be accountable to the owner of the animal for any money arising from the disposal after deducting all expenses incurred by reason of its seizure, impounding, maintenance and disposal; but nothing in this subsection shall render the Conservators so accountable if they have accounted to any other person whom they reasonably believed to be the owner.

(8) The animals to which this section applies are cattle, horses, sheep, goats, pigs and domestic fowl.

Removal of placards and abandoned machinery and vehicles

20.—(1) The Conservators may remove bills, placards and signs posted or placed on any wall, railing, fence, tree, lamp post, walk, pavement or seat or elsewhere within the Malvern Hills and any other articles or things, including without prejudice to the generality of the foregoing, farm machinery placed or left on the Malvern Hills without proper authority or in contravention of any byelaw duly made by the Conservators or which appears to the Conservators to have been abandoned.

(2) (a) This subsection applies in relation to items removed under subsection (1) above other than vehicles.

(b) (i) On removal the Conservators shall impound such items as are capable of impoundment in a convenient place and if on expiry of a period of 14 days beginning with the day of removal the owner has not claimed the item and paid all expenses incurred by reason of its removal, impoundment and storage the Conservators may dispose of the item in such a manner as they think fit.

(ii) In the case of farm machinery the Conservators shall give notice of the impounding to the officer in charge of a police station and also to the owner of the machinery if his identity be known to them or can reasonably be ascertained and shall not dispose of it in accordance with sub-paragraph (i) above until the expiry of a period of 28 days beginning with the day of removal.

(3) (a) In the case of vehicles, the power of removal under this section applies only to relevant vehicles.

(b) Not less than 7 days before removing a relevant vehicle the Conservators shall cause to be affixed to the vehicle a notice stating that they propose to remove it when that period expires for disposal pursuant to subsections (5) and (6) below.

(4) On removal the Conservators may impound a relevant vehicle in a convenient place and on such impoundment shall give notice of the impounding to the officer in charge of a police station and also to the owner of the vehicle if his identity be known to them or can reasonably be ascertained.

(5) Subject to the following provisions of this section, the Conservators may, in such manner as they think fit, dispose of a relevant vehicle which has been removed under this section.

(6) The time at which the Conservators may dispose of a vehicle under subsection (5) above is as follows:—

(a) in the case of a motor vehicle on which no current licence was displayed at the time of its removal, any time after its removal;

(b) in the case of a motor vehicle on which a current licence was so displayed, any time after the licence expires;

(c) in the case of a vehicle other than a motor vehicle, any time after the expiration of a period of 28 days beginning with the day of removal.

(7) If, before the vehicle is disposed of by the Conservators in pursuance of subsections (5) and (6) above, the vehicle is claimed by a person who satisfies the Conservators that he is its owner and pays the Conservators all expenses incurred by reason of its removal, impoundment and storage, the Conservators shall permit him to remove the vehicle from their custody within the prescribed period.

(8) If in the case of any vehicle it appears to the Conservators that more than one person is or was its owner at the relevant time, such one of them as the Conservators think fit shall be treated as its owner for the purposes of subsection (7) above.

(9) The Conservators shall, in relation to the disposal, give to such persons as are prescribed by regulations under subsection (7) of section 101 of the Act of 1984 such information as is so prescribed, as if the Conservators were a competent authority within the meaning of that section and the disposal were a disposal in pursuance of that section.

(10) For the purposes of this section—

"the Act of 1984" means the Road Traffic Regulation Act 1984;

"licence", "owner" and "vehicle" have the same respective meanings as in section 101 of the Act 1984 and "motor vehicle" has the same meanings as in section 136 of that Act;

"prescribed period", in relation to removal of a vehicle from the Conservators' custody, means the period commencing on the day on which the Conservators became satisfied that the person claiming the vehicle was its owner and ending on the expiration of the seventh day after that day, or at the time when the vehicle is disposed of, whichever is the later;

"relevant vehicle" means a vehicle which appears to the Conservators to be abandoned on the Malvern Hills and which, in the case of a motor vehicle, is in their opinion in such a condition that it ought to be destroyed.

Law of Property Act

21.—(1) Subsection (4) of section 194 of the Law of Property Act 1925 (restrictions on the enclosure of commons) shall not operate to disapply the other provisions of that section from any building or fence erected or work constructed under or by virtue of this Act.

(2) For the purposes of the said section 194, land to which this Act applies which is registered under the Commons Registration Act 1965 shall be deemed—

(a) to have been subject to rights of common at the commencement of the said Act of 1925; and

(b) to remain subject to section 194 notwithstanding any express or implied extinguishment of rights of common since that date.

Local inquiries

22.—(1) The Secretary of State may cause such local inquiries to be held as he may consider necessary for the purpose of any of his functions under this Act.

(2) Subsections (2) to (5) of section 250 of the Local Government act 1972 shall apply in relation to any such inquiry as if it were an inquiry held inpursuance of subsection (1) of that section and the Conservators were a local authority.

Display of advertisements

23. For the purposes of Regulation 6 of, and Class 1A of Schedule 3 to, the Town and Country Planning (Control of Advertisements) Regulations 1992 the Conservators shall, as respects their functions under sections 15 to 17 of this Act, be deemed to be a local authority.

Saving for town and country planning

24. Any development authorised by this Act shall not be deemed for the purposes of the Town and Country Planning General Development Order 1988 (or any general order superseding that order made under section 59 of the Town and Country Planning Act 1990, or any corresponding provision of an Act repealing that section), to be development authorised by an Act which designates specifically both the nature of the development and the land upon which it may be carried out.

For protection of British Railways Board

25. Nothing in this Act shall prejudice or affect the property or rights of the British Railways Board.

Application of certain enactments

26. The enactments specified in column 1 of Schedule 1 to this Act shall apply to the Conservators in the manner specified in column 2 of that Schedule.

Amendments and repeals

27.—(1) The provisions of the Act of 1884 specified in column 1 of Part I of Schedule 2 to this Act are hereby amended as specified in column 2 of that Part.

(2) The provisions of the Act of 1924 specified in column 1 of the Part II of Schedule 2 to this Act are hereby amended as specified in column 2 of that Part.

(3) The provisions of the Act of 1930 specified in column 1 of Part III of Schedule 2 to this Act are hereby amended as specified in column 2 of that Part.

(4) The provisions of the existing Malvern Hills Acts specified in Schedule 3 to this Act are hereby repealed to the extent therein specified.

Costs of Act

28. All costs, charges and expenses of the Conservators preliminary to and of and incidental to the preparing for, obtaining and passing of this Act or otherwise in relation thereto shall be paid by the Conservators out of any moneys for the time being in their hands and not exclusively applicable to any other purposes in pursuance of existing obligations of the Conservators or out of moneys borrowed or to be borrowed by them under the provisions of the Malvern Hills Acts.

SCHEDULES

Section 26

SCHEDULE 1

Name of enactment (1)	Manner in which applied to the Conservators (2)
Part VA of and Schedule 12A to the Local Government Act 1972	Whole of Part and Schedule to apply as though the Conservators were a principal council within the meaning of Part VA and references to a committee or sub-committee of a principal council included references to any committee or sub-committee appointed by the Conservators but subject to the following modifications, namely:—

Name of enactment (1)	Manner in which applied to the Conservators (2)
	(a) The reference in section 100A (6) (c) to premises not belonging to a principal council shall be construed as a reference to premises not used as the offices of the Conservators, unless and until the Conservators acquire a building for use as their offices under section 9 of this Act. (b) The proper officer for the purposes of sections 100B, 100C and 100D shall be the Clerk to the Conservators. (c) Section 100G ((1) (a) shall apply as though after the word "ward" there was inserted the word ", parish" and after the word "represents" there were inserted the words "or body by which he was appointed".
Section 228 of the Local Government Act 1972	Section to apply with the omission of the reference to any proper officer as though the Conservators were a parish or Community Council and references in the section to a local government elector for the area of the authority shall be construed as references to a local government elector for the area of any of the local authorities from which members of the Conservators are elected or nominated.
Schedule 13 to the Defamation Act 1952	Schedule to apply as though the Conservators were a local authority and any committee or sub-committee of the Conservators were a committee of a local authority.

Section 27

SCHEDULE 2

PART I

PROVISIONS OF THE ACT OF 1884 AMENDED

Provision (1)	Amendment (2)
The Second Schedule	In the list of exceptions after the words "sections 12 to 35 inclusive" there shall be inserted "53,".

PART II

PROVISIONS OF THE ACT OF 1924 AMENDED

Provision (1)	Amendment (2)
Section 7 (Constitution of Board of Conservators)	In subsection (3) after the words "three years" where they appear for the first time there shall be inserted "or such other term, not exceeding four years, as the Board of Conservators may by resolution determine" and after the words "three years" where they appear for the second time there shall be inserted "or such other period determined by the Board of Conservators".

Provision (1)	Amendment (2)
Section 25 (Bye-laws to restrict and regulate quarrying, &c.)	In subsection (1) for the words "Section 18 (Bye-laws and proceedings) of the Act of 1884 as amended by section 13 of the Act of 1909 shall apply to any such bye-laws as if such section had been re-enacted in this Act" there shall be substituted "and subsections (4) to (8) of secton 10 (Byelaws) of the Malvern Hills Act 1930 shall apply in relation to any such byelaws as if they were byelaws made under that section".

PART III

PROVISIONS OF THE ACT OF 1930 AMENDED

Provision (1)	Amendment (2)
Section 6 (Parking places for vehicles)	In subsection (1) after the words "and other vehicles" there shall be inserted "for use by persons resorting to the Malvern Hills for the purpose of recreation and enjoyment".
Section 10 (Byelaws)	In subsection (1) after paragraph (j) there shall be inserted "(k) For preventing or regulating vehicles, including cycles, being parked, driven or ridden on any part of the Malvern Hills not set apart for that purpose; and for regulating the use of parking places on any part of the Malvern Hills set apart for parking;".

Section 27

SCHEDULE 3

REPEALS

Chapter	Enactment	Extent of repeal
1884 c. clxxv.	Malvern Hills Act 1884.	Section 18.
1909 c. xxxvii.	Malvern Hills Act 1909.	Section 13.

INDEX

References are to sections and Schedules

BELL'S BRIDGE ORDER CONFIRMATION ACT 1995

(1995 c. iv)

ARRANGEMENT OF SECTIONS

SCHEDULE

BELL'S BRIDGE

An Act to confirm a Provisional Order under the Private Legislation Procedure (Scotland) Act 1936, relating to Bell's Bridge.

[19th July 1995]

PARLIAMENTARY PROGRESS
The Bill's progress through Parliament was as follows:
House of Commons: First Reading, June 22, 1995; Bill considered by Commons, June 28, 1995; Third Reading, June 29, 1995.
House of Lords: First Reading, July 5, 1995; Bill considered by Lords, July 10, 1995; Third Reading, July 13, 1995.

INTRODUCTION
This Act makes the necessary provisions to authorise Scottish Enterprise to turn Bell's Bridge over the river Clyde into a permanent footbridge. The substance of the Order confirmed by this Act is contained in the Schedule.

Whereas the Provisional Order set forth in the Schedule hereunto annexed has been made by the Secretary of State under the provisions of the Private Legislation Procedure (Scotland) Act 1936, and it is requisite that the said Order should be confirmed by Parliament:

Be it therefore enacted by the Queen's most Excellent Majesty, by and with the advice and consent of the Lords Spiritual and Temporal, and Commons, in this present Parliament assembled, and by the authority of the same, as follows:—

Confirmation of Order in Schedule

1. The Provisional Order contained in the Schedule hereunto annexed is hereby confirmed.

Short title

2. This Act may be cited as the Bell's Bridge Order Confirmation Act 1995.

SCHEDULE

Bell's Bridge

Provisional Order to empower Scottish Enterprise to construct works to make Bell's Bridge a permanent footbridge over the river Clyde; and for related purposes.

Whereas—

(1) The Scottish Development Agency (hereinafter called "the Agency") were established by the Scottish Development Agency Act 1975 for the purposes of furthering the development of Scotland's economy and improving its environment:

(2) The Agency were empowered by a licence issued by the Clyde Port Authority on 10th October 1986 to construct a temporary footbridge now known as Bell's Bridge over the river Clyde in the city of Glasgow, linking the Scottish Exhibition Centre on the north bank of the river to a site on the south bank of the river where the third National Garden Festival was held in 1988:

(3) In accordance with the provisions of the Enterprise and New Towns (Scotland) Act 1990 Scottish Enterprise (hereinafter called "Scottish Enterprise") were established with the general functions of (amongst others) furthering the development of Scotland's economy and improvement of the environment of Scotland and by an order made thereunder all property, rights and liabilities to which the Agency were entitled or subject became property, rights and liabilities of, and vested in, Scottish Enterprise:

(4) The site of the National Garden Festival is now being developed to provide homes, a business park, a public park and a leisure and recreation area and it is expedient, and would be of public and local advantage, that Scottish Enterprise should be empowered to construct the further works by this Order provided to make permanent that footbridge, and that the other provisions of this Order should be enacted:

(5) Plans and sections showing the lines and levels of the works authorised by this Order have been deposited with the sheriff clerk of the sheriff court district of Glasgow and Strathkelvin, the said plans and sections being in this Order referred to respectively as the deposited plans and the deposited sections:

(6) The purposes aforesaid cannot be effected without an Order confirmed by Parliament under the Private Legislation Procedure (Scotland) Act 1936:

Now therefore, in pursuance of the powers contained in the said Act of 1936, the Secretary of State orders as follows:—

Short title

1. This Order may be cited as the Bell's Bridge Order 1995.

Interpretation

2.—(1) In this Order, unless the context otherwise requires—

"Bell's Bridge" means the bridge referred to as such in the Preamble to this Order (as shown on the deposited plans) or as it may from time to time be reconstructed, renewed or altered and the work;

"the level of high water" means the level of mean high-water springs;

"the limits of deviation" means the limits of deviation shown on the deposited plans;

"the navigation channel" means that part of the river Clyde in the immediate vicinity of Bell's Bridge which is 35 metres wide and which is open to navigation by vessels capable of navigating in the channel;

"the Port Authority" means Clydeport Operations Limited, a company limited by shares and registered in Scotland, formerly called Clydeport Limited, to whom the property, rights, liabilities and functions of the former Clyde Port Authority were transferred by order in accordance with a scheme of transfer made and confirmed under the provisions of Part I of the Ports Act 1991;

"tidal work" means so much of a work authorised by this Order as is on, under or over tidal waters or tidal lands below the level of high water and includes Bell's Bridge;

"the work" means the worth authorised by section 3 below, and includes any such work (including Bell's Bridge) as reconstructed, renewed or altered under that section.

(2) In the event of Strathclyde Regional Council or a successor authority as local roads authority becoming the owner of Bell's Bridge or otherwise responsible for its operation or management, any reference to "Scottish Enterprise" shall, unless the context otherwise requires, be construed as a reference to that Council or that authority.

(3) In this Order, except in section 4 below, situations, points, directions, distances or dimensions stated in any description of the work, lands or powers shall be construed as if the words "or thereabouts" were inserted after each such situation, point, direction, distance or dimension.

Power to construct work

3.—(1) Subject to the provisions of this Order Scottish Enterprise may, in the lines and situations, within the limits of deviation and according to the levels shown on the deposited sections, construct and maintain the work hereinafter described, with all necessary works and conveniences connected therewith in the parishes of Glasgow and Govan in the city of Glasgow district, that is to say:—

Tubular steel dolphins with caps, outwith the navigation channel at each side of Bell's Bridge, commencing at a point at NS256764665203 and terminating at a point at NS256851665164.

(2) Subject to the provisions of this Order Scottish Enterprise may, within the limits of deviation—

(a) maintain and operate Bell's Bridge; and

(b) reconstruct, renew of alter Bell's Bridge.

Power to deviate

4. Subject to the provisions of this Order, in the construction, reconstruction, renewal or alteration of the work Scottish Enterprise may deviate laterally from the lines or situations thereof shown on the deposited plan to the extent of the limits of deviation, and may deviate vertically from the levels shown on the deposited sections to any extent not exceeding three metres upwards and to such extent downwards as may be found necessary or convenient, but in the exercise of any of the powers granted to them by this Order Scottish Enterprise shall at all times provide in the navigation channel an opening span affording for navigation a clear width of not less than 35 metres between protective fenders and having when closed a clear headway above the level of mean high-water springs (1985) of not less than 3.73 metres being a clear headway of 5.93 metres above ordnance datum (Newlyn) throughout such width and shall not reconstruct, renew or alter Bell's Bridge otherwise than in a line or situation conforming with or parallel to that shown on the deposited plans.

Subsidiary works

5. Subject to the provision of this Order, Scottish Enterprise, for the purposes of or in connection with the work may from time to time within the limits of deviation construct and maintain all such subsidiary or incidental works and conveniences as may be necessary or expedient for the purposes of or in connection with the construction, maintenance and use of the work.

Period for completion of work and authorised extension thereof

6.—(1) Subject to subsection (2) below, if the work is not completed within two years from the coming into operation of this Order, all of the powers by this Order granted to Scottish Enterprise shall cease except as to so much of the work as shall then be completed in which event Scottish Enterprise shall cause Bell's Bridge and any other work authorised by this Order to be removed and shall restore the site thereof to its former condition.

(2) On the application of Scottish Enterprise, and whether before or after the expiration of the period referred to in subsection (1) above, the Port Authority may, by written consent, extend that period.

Tidal works not to be executed without approval of Secretary of State

7.—(1) A tidal work shall not be constructed, renewed or altered except in accordance with plans and sections approved by the Secretary of State and subject to any conditions and restrictions imposed by the Secretary of State before the work of construction, renewal or alteration is begun.

(2) If a tidal work is constructed, renewed or altered in contravention of this section—

(a) the Secretary of State may by notice in writing require Scottish Enterprise that their own expense to remove the tidal work or any part thereof and restore the site thereof to its former condition and if, on the expiration of 30 days from the date when the notice is served upon Scottish Enterprise they have failed to comply with the requirements of the notice, the Secretary of State may execute the works specified in the notice; or

(b) if it appears to the Secretary of State urgently necessary so to do, he may himself remove the tidal work or part of it and restore the site to its former condition;

and any expenditure incurred by the Secretary of State in so doing shall be recoverable from Scottish Enterprise.

Lights on tidal works during construction

8.—(1) Scottish Enterprise shall at or near a tidal work during the whole time of the construction, renewal or alteration thereof exhibit every night from sunset to sunrise such lights, if any, and take such other steps for the prevention of danger to navigation, as the Secretary of State shall from time to time direct after consultation with the Port Authority and with the sanction of the Commissioners of Northern Lighthouses.

(2) If Scottish Enterprise fail to comply in respect with a direction given under this section they shall be guilty of an offence and liable on summary conviction to a fine not exceeding the statutory maximum and on conviction on indictment to a fine.

Permanent lights on tidal works

9.—(1) After the completion of a tidal work Scottish Enterprise shall at the outer extremity thereof exhibit every night from sunset to sunrise such lights, if any, and take such other steps for preventing danger to navigation as the Port Authority with the sanction of the Commissioners of Northern Lighthouses shall from time to time direct.

(2) If Scottish Enterprise fail to comply in any respect with a direction given under this section they shall be guilty of an offence and liable on summary conviction to a fine not exceeding the statutory maximum and on conviction on indictment to a fine.

Survey of tidal works

10. The Secretary of State or the Port Authority may at any time if they deem it expedient order a survey and examination of a tidal work or of the site upon which it is proposed to construct that work and any reasonable expenditure incurred by him or the Port Authority in such survey and examination shall be recoverable from Scottish Enterprise.

Provision against danger to navigation

11.—(1) In the case of injury to or destruction or decay of a tidal work or any part thereof Scottish Enterprise shall forthwith notify the Port Authority and shall lay down such buoys, exhibit such lights and take such other steps for preventing danger to navigation as the Port Authority with the sanction of the Commissioners of Northern Lighthouses shall from time to time direct.

(2) If Scottish Enterprise fail to notify the Port Authority as required by this section or to comply in any respect with a direction given under this section they shall be guilty of an offence and liable on summary conviction to a fine not exceeding the statutory maximum and on conviction on indictment to a fine.

Abatement of works abandoned or decayed

12.—(1) Where a tidal work is abandoned or suffered to fall into decay the Secretary of State or the Port Authority may by notice in writing require Scottish Enterprise at their own expense either to repair and restore the work or any part thereof, or to remove the work and restore the site thereof to its former condition, to such an extent and within such limits as the Secretary of State or the Port Authority, as the case may be, think proper.

(2) Where a work consisting partly of a tidal work and partly of works on or over land above the level of high water is abandoned or suffered to fall into decay and that part of the work on or over land above the level of high water is in such condition as to interfere or to cause reasonable apprehension that it may interfere with the right of navigation or other public rights over the foreshore, the Secretary of State or the Port Authority, as the case may be, may include that part of the work, or any portion thereof, in any notice under this section.

(3) If, on the expiration of 30 days from the date when a notice under this section is served upon Scottish Enterprise they have failed to comply with the requirements of the notice the Secretary of State or the Port Authority, as the case may be, may execute the works specified in the notice and any expenditure incurred by them in so doing shall be recoverable from Scottish Enterprise.

Crown rights

13.—(1) Nothing in this Order shall affect prejudicially any estate, right, power, privilege, authority or exemption of the Crown and, in particular and without prejudice to the generality of the foregoing, nothing herein contained shall authorise any person to take, use, enter upon or in any manner interfere with, any land or hereditaments or any rights of whatsoever description (including any portion of the shore or bed of the sea or of any river, channel, creek, bay or estuary)—

(a) belonging to Her Majesty in right of Her Crown and under the management of the Crown Estate Commissioners, without the consent in writing of those commissioners; or

(b) belonging to a government department, or held in trust for Her Majesty for the purposes of a government department, without the consent in writing of that government department.

(2) A consent under subsection (1) above may be given unconditionally or subject to terms and conditions.

Saving for certain enactments

14. Nothing in this Order shall—

(a) affect the operation of the Control of Pollution Act 1974 or Part II of the Food and Environment Protection Act 1985; or

(b) exempt Scottish Enterprise from the provisions of Part I of the Coast Protection Act 1949.

Saving for town and country planning

15. The Town and Country Planning (Scotland) Act 1972 and any orders, regulations, rules, schemes and directions made or given thereunder and any restrictions or powers thereby imposed or conferred in relation to land shall apply and may be exercised in relation to any land notwithstanding that the development thereof is or may be authorised by this Order.

For protection of Port Authority

16. For the protection of the Port Authority and other protected parties the provisions of this section shall, unless otherwise agreed in writing between Scottish Enterprise and the Port Authority, apply and have effect—

(1) In this section "other protected parties" means the persons (other than the Port Authority) referred to in the second proviso to paragraph (13) below:

(2) Before commencing the construction of a tidal work, or any work situated on, under, over or which may affect or interfere with the river Clyde or the property of the Port Authority, including all temporary works, Scottish Enterprise shall deliver to the Port Authority for their approval (which shall not be unreasonably withheld) plans, sections and specifications of the work, and such work shall not be constructed otherwise than in accordance with such plans, sections and specifications as may be approved by the Port Authority or determined by arbitration, and all such works shall be executed to the reasonable satisfaction of the engineer of the Port Authority:

Provided that if the Port Authority fail to signify their approval or disapproval of any such plans, sections and specifications within six weeks after the receipt thereof they shall be deemed to have approved thereof:

Provided further that before commencing the construction of such a work Scottish Enterprise shall give 28 days' notice of their intention to do so to the Port Authority except in a case of emergency when such notice as is practicable shall be given:

(3) Scottish Enterprise shall allow the engineer of the Port Authority and his authorised representatives to inspect and survey all or any of the tidal works or any work on, under, over or which may effect or interfere with the river Clyde or the property of the Port Authority, while in course of construction, and shall give all reasonable facilities for so doing and shall repay to the Port Authority all expenses reasonably incurred in connection therewith:

(4) Nothing in this Order shall authorise or empower Scottish Enterprise without the previous consent of the Port Authority (which consent shall not be unreasonably withheld) to embank, encroach upon or interfere with any part of the bed, foreshore or banks of the river Clyde except as is authorised by this Order:

(5) Each tidal work shall be so executed and each operation of Scottish Enterprise so performed as in no way to obstruct or interfere with the free, uninterrupted and safe navigation of the river Clyde or the due exercise by the Port Authority of their statutory functions, and if any such obstruction or interference shall be caused or take place Scottish Enterprise shall pay to the Port Authority if injuriously affected thereby compensation in respect thereof, and shall indemnify and relieve the Port Authority in respect of all claims arising as a result of the works and operations of Scottish Enterprise:

Provided that during the execution of each tidal work and during the performance of each operation Scottish Enterprise shall comply with all directions of the Port Authority that may be given for the general safety or convenience of navigation on the river Clyde in respect of or relating to the movement and mooring of vessels or plant during or after construction of a tidal work:

(6) Each tidal work shall be so executed and each operation of Scottish Enterprise in connection therewith so performed as not to obstruct or interfere with any work of dredging and deepening the river Clyde executed by the Port Authority in the exercise of their statutory functions:

(7) Scottish Enterprise shall give immediate notice to the Port Authority of any obstruction, danger or interruption which may be occasioned by a tidal work or by the operations of Scottish Enterprise to the free passage of vessels approaching or passing under or near a tidal work, and in the event of Scottish Enterprise failing or neglecting to give such notice they shall be responsible for all loss or damage incurred by the Port Authority including loss of revenue which may be occasioned to them through such failure or neglect, and shall indemnify, free and relieve the Port Authority in respect of all claims and expenses which may be made against or incurred by the Port Authority by reason or in consequence of such failure or neglect:

(8) While any tidal work is in course of construction, reconstruction, renewal or alteration Scottish Enterprise shall repay on demand any expense reasonably incurred by the Port Authority—

(a) in taking such measures as the Port Authority deem necessary and proper for placing and maintaining buoys or other marks upon or near the tidal work and upon or near any temporary erections, appliances or obstructions which may be placed or caused by Scottish Enterprise or their contractors in or above the river Clyde and for efficiently lighting the said river in the vicinity thereof;

(b) in providing such efficient means of communication as the Port Authority deem necessary for the regulation of the passage of vessels approaching or passing under or near the tidal work and in maintaining and working the same during the construction of the tidal work until completion thereof:

(9) Except with the prior approval of the Port Authority Scottish Enterprise shall not deposit any material on the bed or foreshore of the river Clyde, and nor shall Scottish Enterprise allow any such material to fall or be washed into the said river:

(10) Scottish Enterprise shall upon reasonable notice in writing from the Port Authority requiring them so to do and in any event, whether or not notice has been given, within six months after the completion of any work remove any temporary works and materials for temporary works which may have been placed by Scottish Enterprise in the river Clyde or on the banks, bed or foreshore thereof for the construction of that work and which are no longer in use, and if Scottish Enterprise fail so to do the Port Authority may remove the same and charge Scottish Enterprise with the expense reasonably incurred by the Port Authority in so doing and Scottish Enterprise shall forthwith repay to the Port Authority any such expense:

(11) All responsibility for or in connection with Bell's Bridge and all or any of the works (both temporary and permanent) connected therewith (whether of construction or maintenance) and for loss and damage occasioned thereby shall be and remain with Scottish Enterprise. The Port Authority shall, except as hereinafter provided, in no way be responsible or answerable for any damage or injury to Bell's Bridge or any of such works or to any cycle, person, goods or things on or using or being conveyed along Bell's Bridge or to any person employed on or in connection with Bell's Bridge caused by or attributable to—

(a) the dredging and deepening (including any necessary breaking up of rock or other hard material or the removal of any obstruction including sunken vessels) or any part of the bed or foreshore of the river Clyde;

(b) the exercise of their statutory functions; or

(c) the use of the river Clyde for navigation of vessels, vessels sunk in the said river or sunken vessels being lifted, destroyed or otherwise dealt with in the said river in the manner provided in this subsection:

Provided that in the event of the Port Authority—

(i) in the course of dredging and deepening the bed and foreshore of the river Clyde encountering any boulder, block of stone or rock or obstruction the removal of which would or might cause injury to Bell's Bridge; or

(ii) being under the necessity or removing sunken vessel where such removal would or might cause injury to Bell's Bridge;

the Port Authority shall notify Scottish Enterprise before proceeding with the removal thereof and shall consult with the engineer of Scottish Enterprise as to the method to be adopted for the removal thereof. In the event of any difference arising as to the method to be adopted such difference shall be referred to arbitration, and the arbiter shall take into consideration on the one hand the safety of Bell's Bridge and on the other hand the necessity of keeping open the navigational and other facilities of the river Clyde, and any additional cost to the Port Authority in dredging and deepening or removing sunken vessels due to the adoption of such method of removal as may have been required by Scottish Enterprise or determined by the arbiter as aforesaid or such specified part of any such additional cost as the arbiter may determine shall be repayable by Scottish Enterprise and in addition Scottish Enterprise shall make good to the Port Authority any loss of revenue sustained by them and shall indemnify, free and relieve the Port Authority in respect of any claim or claims which may be made against them in consequence of the interruption of such navigational and other facilities of the said river due to the adoption of such method of removal as may have been required by Scottish Enterprise or determined by the arbiter as aforesaid:

Provided further that nothing in this subsection shall free and relieve the Port Authority in respect of liability to Scottish Enterprise for any such damage or injury which may be caused by negligence on the part of the Port Authority, their officers, servants, agents or contractors:

(12) The owners and masters of vessels shall not be liable to make good any damage which may be caused to Bell's Bridge except such as may arise from the default or wilful act of such owners or masters or their servants or agents:

(13) Scottish Enterprise shall cause Bell's Bridge to be opened at such times and for such periods as the Harbour Master or other official of the Port Authority may for the purpose of enabling the passage of vessels through the navigation channel direct upon giving to Scottish Enterprise not less than six hours' prior notice prior to the completion of the work and thereafter not less than two hours' prior notice between the hours of 8 a.m. and 8 p.m. or four hours' prior notice at all other times, notwithstanding that the use by pedestrians of Bell's Bridge may be prevented, delayed or interfered with by reason or in consequence thereof:

Provided that in cases of emergency Scottish Enterprise shall use their best endeavours to open Bell's Bridge, when requested by the Port Authority to do so in accordance with this paragraph, at shorter notice than the applicable period specified above:

Provided further that if any vessel is detained at Bell's Bridge or its passage is delayed or obstructed by reason of Scottish Enterprise failing for whatsoever reason to open Bell's Bridge after being given notice so to do in accordance with this paragraph (other than in emergency conditions arising beyond the control of Scottish Enterprise, being conditions which would prevent or render unsafe the opening of Bell's Bridge) Scottish Enterprise shall be responsible for all loss and damage suffered by the Port Authority, the owners or charterers of vessels so detained, delayed or obstructed, and the owners of their cargoes, including in the case of the Port Authority loss of revenue, which may be occasioned to them through such detention, delay or obstruction and shall indemnify and free and relieve the Port Authority in respect of all claims and expenses which may be made against or incurred by the Port Authority by reason or in consequence of such detention, delay or obstruction:

(14) (a) Scottish Enterprise shall cause Bells' Bridge to be kept in a good and safe state of maintenance, repair and working order and, subject to the proviso below, shall from time to time maintain, repair, renew, reinstate or rebuild Bell's Bridge regardless of the cause for it needing to do so;

(b) All such works of maintenance, repair renewal, reinstatement or rebuilding shall be carried out to the reasonable satisfaction of the Port Authority and shall be subject to any reasonable directions that may from time to time be given in writing by the Port Authority to Scottish Enterprise:

Provided that the Port Authority shall not unreasonably refuse or delay the grant of, or subject to unreasonable terms and conditions, a licence to Scottish Enterprise under section 25 (Licence to dredge) of the Clyde Port Authority Order 1965 to dredge any part of the bed and foreshore of the river Clyde as lies within the limits of deviation, if, in the reasonable opinion of the Port Authority, such dredging is necessary from time to time to enable Scottish Enterprise properly to perform their obligations under this paragraph, and if the application for the licence is made by Scottish Enterprise in accordance with the provisions of that section:

Provided further that nothing in this Order shall prevent Scottish Enterprise (if they so determine) from removing Bell's Bridge and, in that event, they shall as soon as reasonably practicable thereafter restore the site thereof to its former condition:

(15) If at any time after the passing of the Act confirming this Order it is agreed between Scottish Enterprise and the Port Authority after taking into account any relevant data or circumstances, or in default of agreement, it is determined by arbitration, that—

(a) any part of the river Clyde in the immediate vicinity of Bell's Bridge has silted up or has been subject to scouring; and

(b) such silting up or scouring has occurred or arisen as a result of Bell's Bridge or as a result of the construction, reconstruction, renewal or alteration of a tidal work; and

(c) for the safety or convenience of navigation or for the protection of a tidal work, such silting up or scouring should be removed or, as the case may be, made good;

Scottish Enterprise shall pay to the Port Authority any additional expense to which the Port Authority may reasonably be put in dredging the river Clyde to remove the silting up, or in making good the scouring, in so far as it is attributable to a tidal work:

(16) Scottish Enterprise shall from time to time during the construction of a tidal work and after the completion thereof provide, maintain and repair on or aground Bell's Bridge and the dolphins and piers thereof, and the works connected with the construction of any tidal work, proper fenders, jetties or other works as may in the reasonable opinion of the Port Authority be necessary or expedient for the protection of Bell's Bridge or for the safety or convenience of vessels navigating thereby but so that the width of the navigation channel shall not be reduced to less than 35 metres:

(17) (a) In the exercise of any of the powers granted to them by this Order Scottish Enterprise shall not lay any cable, wire or conduit in, under or over the navigation channel without the consent of the Port Authority:

Provided that nothing in this section shall prevent Scottish Enterprise from affixing any cable, wire or conduit to Bell's Bridge for the operational purposes of Bell's Bridge;

(b) A consent under sub-paragraph (a) above may be given subject to such terms and conditions as the Port Authority may reasonably consider necessary or appropriate:

(18) On the completion of the work Scottish Enterprise shall as soon as practicable and not more than 7 days thereafter give notice thereof to the Port Authority and shall supply to the Port Authority without payment plans, sections and cross-sections showing the situation and levels of Bell's Bridge:

(19) If there shall be any inconsistency between any plans or sections of a tidal work approved by the Port Authority or determined by arbitration under this section and the plans and sections approved by the Secretary of State under section 7 above, such tidal work shall be executed in accordance with the plans and sections so approved by the Secretary of State:

(20) (a) Any notice or direction to be given under this Order to Scottish Enterprise by the Port Authority shall be given—

(i) to the Company Secretary of Scottish Enterprise at the principal offices of Scottish Enterprise; or

(ii) in the event of Strathclyde Regional Council or a successor authority becoming the owner of Bell's Bridge or otherwise responsible for its operation or management, to the Area Engineer of Strathclyde Regional Council at Glasgow South, Roads Department, 20, India Street, Glasgow or to the appropriate engineer of that authority;

or in any such case to such other person and at such other address (being an address in Scotland) as Scottish Enterprise or Strathclyde Regional Council or a successor authority (as appropriate) may specify after giving not less than 14 days' notice thereof to the Port Authority;

(b) Any notice or other document to be given or delivered under this Order to the Port Authority by Scottish Enterprise shall be given or delivered—

(i) to the Harbour Master of the Port Authority at their Estuary Control Ocean Terminal, in the case of plans, sections and specifications to be approved by the Port Authority pursuant to paragraph (2) above; and

(ii) to the Secretary of the Port Authority at their principal offices, in any other case;

or in either case to such other person and at such other address (being an address in Scotland) as the Port Authority may specify after giving not less than 14 days' notice thereof to Scottish Enterprise:

(21) (a) Any difference arising between Scottish Enterprise and the Port Authority under this section shall be determined by an arbiter to be mutually agreed upon between the parties, or failing agreement to be appointed by the President of the Institution of Civil Engineers on the application of either party after notice in writing to the other;

(b) All proceedings conducted by such an arbiter shall take place in Scotland and be governed by the law of Scotland, and the arbiter's decision shall be final and binding on both parties;

(c) In conducting any proceedings the arbiter shall, without prejudice to any other powers available to him, have power—

(i) to direct such surveys and inspections as may in his opinion be desirable to determine the dispute in question;

(ii) to order the execution of documents, the performance of works, the carrying out of repairs and the performance of any other obligation of Scottish Enterprise under this section; and

(iii) to award damages against either party for the benefit of the other:

(22) Except as provided by this Order nothing in this Order shall prejudice or derogate from the estates, rights, interests, privileges, liberties or franchises of the Port Authority or prohibit, defeat, alter or diminish any power, authority or jurisdiction which the Port Authority do or may lawfully claim, use or exercise and in particular, but without prejudice to the generality of the foregoing, nothing herein contained shall authorise Scottish Enterprise in the exercise of the powers granted to them by this Order to take, use, enter upon or in any manner interfere with any land, hereditaments or any rights of whatsoever description (including any portion of the shore or bed of the river Clyde) belonging to the Port Authority.

Management arrangements or transfer of ownership or control

17. In the event of Scottish Enterprise entering into and carrying into effect agreements with respect to the construction, operation, management, maintenance and use of Bell's Bridge by any other person or transferring to any other person ownership and control of Bell's Bridge that person shall be subject to the same restrictions, liabilities and obligations to which Scottish Enterprise are subject under this Order and shall perform all of the duties of Scottish Enterprise under this Order.

INDEX

References are to sections and the Schedule

SHEFFIELD ASSAY OFFICE ACT 1995

(1995 c. v)

ARRANGEMENT OF SECTIONS

An Act to amend section 16 of the Hallmarking Act 1973 in its application to the Sheffield Assay Office; to extend the functions of the Office; and for other purposes incidental thereto. [19th July 1995]

PARLIAMENTARY PROGRESS

The Bill's progress through Parliament was as follows:

House of Commons: First Reading, January 24, 1994; Second Reading, March 3, 1994; Bill Committed, March 3, 1994; Suspended, October 25, 1994; Bill Committed to Unopposed Committee, December 15, 1994; Bill as Amended Considered, January 17, 1995; Third Reading, January 25, 1995; Lord's Amendments considered by the House of Commons, June 28, 1995.

House of Lords: First Reading, January 25, 1995; Second Reading, February 14, 1995; Bill Committed, February 14, 1995; Bill Committed to Unopposed Committee, May 18, 1995; Third Reading, June 14, 1995.

INTRODUCTION

This Act, *inter alia*, increases the range of activities which may be undertaken by the Sheffield Assay Office to include the analysis of materials and articles of any kind. Section 16 of the Hallmarking Act 1973 (c. 43) is amended retrospectively to validate the making of the Sheffield Assay Office Order 1978 (S.I. 1978 No. 639).

Whereas—

(1) The Sheffield Assay Office (hereinafter called "the Company"), of which the full name is The Guardians of the Standard of Wrought Plate within the Town of Sheffield, was established by the Plate Assay (Sheffield and Birmingham) Act 1772 (hereinafter called "the Act of 1772") as a corporate body for the assaying and marking of wrought silver plate:

(2) The Plate Assay (Sheffield) Act 1784 (hereinafter called "the Act of 1784") altered and amended the Act of 1772 in certain respects:

(3) By sections 47 and 48 of the Sheffield Corporation Act 1903 (hereinafter called "the Act of 1903"), the assaying of gold plate was brought within the functions of the Company:

(4) The Sheffield Assay Act 1906 (hereinafter called "the Act of 1906") made further provision for the execution of the powers and duties of the Company:

(5) Sections 47 and 48 of the Act of 1903 were subsequently replaced by sections 501 and 502 of the Sheffield Corporation (Consolidation) Act 1918, but the latter provisions were repealed by the Hallmarking Act 1973 (hereinafter called "the Act of 1973") which (*inter alia*) made fresh provision as to assay offices including provision that their functions should extend to the assaying of gold, silver and platinum and of any other metal which might be prescribed under the provisions of section 17 of that Act:

(6) The Act of 1973 also repealed the Act of 1784, and certain provisions of the Act of 1772 and of the Act of 1906, and by section 16 gave the Secretary of State power to make orders (*inter alia*) for constituting and conferring powers on assay offices:

(7) In exercise of that power, the Secretary of State made the Sheffield Assay Office Order 1978 (hereinafter called "the Order of 1978"), altering the constitution of the Company, conferring further powers upon it and making other provisions in relation to it:

(8) The Order of 1978 also repealed certain of the remaining provisions of the Act of 1772 and of the Act of 1906, made amendments to the latter Act and provided that the Act of 1772, the Act of 1906 and the Order itself might be cited together as the Sheffield Assay Office Acts and Order 1772 to 1978:

(9) The assaying of precious metals is believed to have been the earliest and, for a long time, the only form of consumer protection in the United Kingdom:

(10) It would be of public advantage if the Company could extend its activities to the independent and objective testing, examination, investigation and evaluation of materials and articles of any kind, and of firms, corporations, systems, programmes and procedures:

(11) For those reasons, and in order that it may respond to changed market conditions resulting from the Single European Market, the Company wishes to have power to carry on, in addition to the business of an assay office, the other activities described in this Act, and to have, in relation to those activities, the ancillary powers so described:

(12) Doubts have arisen as to the extent to which the making of the Order of 1978 was within the powers conferred upon the Secretary of State by section 16 of the Act of 1973, and it is desirable to set those doubts at rest, and to clarify the position for the future, by means of a retrospective amendment of that section in its application to the Company:

(13) It is expedient that such provisions should be enacted as are contained in this Act:

(14) The objects of this Act cannot be attained without the authority of Parliament:

May it therefore please Your Majesty that it may be enacted, and be it enacted, by the Queen's most Excellent Majesty, by and with the advice and consent of the Lords Spiritual and Temporal, and Commons, in this present Parliament assembled, and by the authority of the same, as follows:—

Citation

1. This Act may be cited as the Sheffield Assay Office Act 1995; and the Sheffield Assay Office Acts and Order 1772 to 1978 and this Act may be cited together as the Sheffield Assay Office Acts and Order 1772 to 1995.

Interpretation

2. In this Act, unless the subject or context otherwise requires—

"the Act of 1973" means the Hallmarking Act 1973;

"the Company" means the Sheffield Assay Office, of which the full name is The Guardians of the Standard of Wrought Plate within the Town of Sheffield;

"materials" includes liquids, gases, dusts, wastes and tangible and intangible substances of any kind; and

"the Order of 1978" means the Sheffield Assay Office Order 1978.

Section 16 of Hallmarking Act 1973

3. In its application to the Company, the Act of 1973 shall have effect, and be deemed always to have had effect, as if in section 16(1)(c)—

(a) "confer" were omitted;

(b) for "under" there were substituted "by"; and

(c) there were added at the end thereof—

"; or, on such an application, impose new duties or confer new powers on, or make alterations or additions to or omissions from the constitution of, the assay office.".

Additional activities of Company

4.—(1) In addition to the functions which it has from time to time as an assay office, the Company shall have power, in any part of the world—

(a) to undertake the provision of analytical services in relation to materials or articles of any kind, by means of chemical analysis or physical examination or testing or by any other method which is appropriate in the circumstances;

(b) to undertake investigation of the properties of materials or articles of any kind, their behaviour or likely behaviour under particular conditions, and their suitablity for particular purposes;

(c) to undertake the examination of articles of any kind for the purpose of discovering whether and to what extent they comply with standards or other criteria which are published or have been made known to the Company.

(d) to undertake the investigation of firms, corporate bodies or other persons, or of systems, programmes or procedures, for the purpose of discovering whether and to what extent they comply with standards or other criteria which are published or have been made known to the Company;

(e) to undertake the valuation, on any basis and for any purpose, of materials or articles of any kind;

(f) to undertake any other activities of a kind which the Company may consider similar to, or suitable to be carried on with, the foregoing;

(g) to undertake or instigate, or join in undertaking or instigating, and to meet or contribute towards the cost of, research into, and the provision (including manufacture) and development of, plant, equipment, technology, methodology (including systems, procedures and computer and other programmes) and materials for use in, or in connection with, any of the foregoing activities; and

(h) to undertake, or join in undertaking, the marketing of, and the provision of maintenance, advisory, technical or other services in relation to, any plant, equipment, technology, methodology (including systems, procedures and computer and other programmes) and materials or articles of any kind used or capable of use in, or in connection with—

(i) any of the activities mentioned in paragraphs (a) to (f) above, or

(ii) any of the activities carried on in the course of the business of an assay office.

(2) The Company may do anything which is calculated to facilitate or is incidental or conducive to the activities mentioned in subsection (1) above and (without prejudice to that generality) shall in particular have power—

(a) to issue certificates as to the results of any analysis, examination, test or investigation carried out under subsection (1) above;

(b) to provide advisory and supervisory services and to provide expert evidence for the purpose of legal or other proceedings;

(c) to make members of its staff available to advise on, or participate in, the formulation of standards or criteria of the kind referred to in paragraphs (c) and (d) of subsection (1) above;

(d) to register, maintain, protect and enforce in any part of the world intellectual property rights, including patents, trade marks and other marks, and to authorise the use of such intellectual property on such lawful terms and conditions as it sees fit;

(e) to promote or establish, or join in promoting or establishing, or to acquire interests in and take part in the management of, bodies corporate or unincorporate in any part of the world, having as their object, or as a main object, the carrying on of any or all of the activities mentioned in subsection (1) above;

(f) out of the income or other monies derived from such activities, to remunerate—

(i) any or all of the guardians (as defined in the Order of 1978) for work done or time spent in that capacity, and

(ii) any or all of the members of the Executive Committee (as so defined) for work done or time spent in that capacity,

in connection with such activities; and

(g) to receive grants and to acccept gifts of money or other property to be used in meeting its expenses in connection with, or in furthering, any or all of such activities.

Application of existing enactments

5.—(1) In this section references to the Company's other activities are references to the additional activities authorised by section 4 (Additional activities of Company) above or other activities which the Company is for the time being authorised to undertake in addition to its business of an assay office.

(2) Subject to the provisions of subsection (3) below, all the provisions of the Sheffield Assay Office Acts and Order 1772 to 1978 which relate to the Company and to its business of an assay office shall apply equally (so far as they are capable of doing so) to and in relation to its other activities, and to and in relation to the Company in so far as its undertaking includes them (but, save as respects the reference in article 7(2) of the Order of 1978, specific references to articles brought to be assayed shall not extend to articles received by the Company in the course of its other activities).

(3) The Company shall keep accounts in respect of its other activities separate from the accounts kept in respect of its business of an assay office and—

(a) paragraph (5) of article 10 of the Order of 1978 shall not apply to the accounts kept in respect of its other activities, and

(b) the other provisions of that article shall apply separately to or in relation to each set of accounts,

but references in this subsection to accounts do not include balance sheets and nothing in this subsection shall prevent the Company from preparing a single balance sheet in respect of the whole of its undertaking.

(4) Notwithstanding section 22(2) of the act of 1973, an order under section 16(1)(c) of that Act in relation to the Company shall, except so far as it provides otherwise or the contrary otherwise appears, apply in relation to its other activities as well as to its business of an assay office; and such an order may consist of or include provisions which apply only to the Company's other activities.

INDEX

References are to sections

BIRMINGHAM ASSAY OFFICE ACT 1995

(1995 c. vi)

Arrangement of Sections

An Act to amend section 16 of the Hallmarking Act 1973 in its application to the Birmingham Assay Office; to extend the functions of the Office; and for other purposes incidental thereto. [19th July 1995]

Parliamentary Progress

The Bill's progress through Parliament was as follows:

House of Commons: First Reading, January 24, 1995; Second Reading, January 31, 1995; Bill Committed, January 31, 1995; Bill Committed to Unopposed Committee, May 3, 1995; Bill as Amended Considered, May 17, 1995; Third Reading, May 23, 1995; Lord's Amendments considered by the House of Commons, July 18, 1995.

House of Lords: First Reading, May 23, 1995; Second Reading, June 14, 1995; Bill Committed, June 14, 1995; Bill Committed to Unopposed Committee, June 28, 1995; Third Reading, July 12, 1995.

Introduction

This Act, *inter alia*, increases the range of activities which may be undertaken by the Birmingham Assay Office to include the analysis of materials and articles of any kind. Section 16 of the Hallmarking Act 1973 (c. 43) is amended retrospectively to validate the making of the Birmingham Assay Office Order 1978 (S.I. 1989 No. 900).

Whereas—

(1) By the Plate Assay (Sheffield and Birmingham) Act 1772 (hereinafter called "the Act of 1772") a corporate body, to be known as The Guardians of the Standard of Wrought Plate, within the Town of Birmingham, was established for the assaying and marking of wrought silver plate:

(2) By the Birmingham Assay Office Act 1824 (hereinafter called "the Act of 1824") the Act 1772 was repealed so far as it related to the town of Birmingham, and within 20 miles thereof, and the present Birmingham Assay Office (hereinafter called "the Company"), of which the full name is The Guardians of the Standard of Wrought Plate in Birmingham, was established as a corporate body for receiving and assaying wrought gold and silver plate:

(3) By the Birmingham Assay Office Act 1902 (hereinafter called "the Act of 1902") certain further powers were conferred upon the Company:

(4) Certain of the provisions of the Act of 1824 were repealed by the Hallmarking Act 1973 (hereinafter called "the Act of 1973") which (*inter alia*) made fresh provision as to assay offices including provision that their functions should extend to the assaying of gold, silver, platinum and any other metal which might be prescribed under the provisions of section 17 of that Act:

(5) Section 16 of the Act of 1973 authorised the Secretary of State to make orders (*inter alia*) for constituting and conferring powers on assay offices; and in exercise of that power the Secretary of State made the Birmingham Assay Office Order 1989 (hereinafter called "the Order of 1989"), altering the constitution of the Company, conferring further powers upon it and making other provisions in relation to it:

(6) The Order of 1989 repealed certain of the remaining provisions of the Act of 1824, repealed certain provisions of the Act of 1902 and made certain amendments to both Acts; and it provided that the Act of 1824, the Act of 1902 and the Order itself might be cited together as the Birmingham Assay Office Acts and Order 1824 to 1989:

(7) The assaying of precious metals is believed to have been the earliest and, for a long time, the only form of consumer protection in the United Kingdom:

(8) It would be of public advantage if the Company could extend its activities to the independent and objective testing, examination, investigation and evaluation of materials and articles of any kind, and of firms, corporations, systems, programmes and procedures:

(9) For those reasons, and in order that it may respond to changed market conditions resulting from the Single European Market, the Company wishes to have power to carry on, in addition to the business of an assay office, the other activities described in this Act, and to have, in relation to those activities, the ancillary powers so described:

(10) Doubts have arisen as to the extent to which the making of the Order of 1989 was within the powers conferred upon the Secretary of State by section 16 of the Act of 1973, and it is desirable to set those doubts at rest, and to clarify the position for the future, by means of a retrospective amendment of that section in its application to the Company:

(11) It is expedient that such provisions should be enacted as are contained in this Act:

(12) The objects of this Act cannot be attained without the authority of Parliament:

May it therefore please Your Majesty that it may be enacted, and be it enacted, by the Queen's most Excellent Majesty, by and with the advice and consent of the Lords Spiritual and Temporal, and Commons, in this present Parliament assembled, and by the authority of the same, as follows:—

Citation

1. This Act may be cited as the Birmingham Assay Office Act 1995; and the Birmingham Assay Office Acts and Order 1824 to 1989 and this Act may be cited together as the Birmingham Assay Office Acts and Order 1824 to 1995.

Interpretation

2. In this Act, unless the subject or context otherwise requires—

"the Act of 1902" means the Birmingham Assay Office Act 1902;

"the Act of 1973" means the Hallmarking Act 1973;

"the Company" means the Birmingham Assay Office, of which the full name is The Guardians of the Standard of Wrought Plate in Birmingham;

"materials" includes liquids, gases, dusts, wastes and tangible and intangible substances of any kind; and

"the Order of 1989" means the Birmingham Assay Office Order 1989.

Section 16 of Hallmarking Act 1973

3. In its application to the Company, the Act of 1973 shall have effect, and be deemed always to have had effect, as if in section 16(1)(c)—

(a) "confer" were omitted;

(b) for "under" there were substituted "by"; and

(c) there were added at the end thereof—

"; or, on such an application, impose new duties or confer new powers on, or make alterations or additions to or omissions from the constitution of, the assay office.".

Additional activities of Company

4.—(1) In addition to the functions which it has from time to time as an assay office, the Company shall have power, in any part of the world—

(a) to undertake the provision of analytical services in relation to materials or articles of any kind, by means of chemical analysis or physical examination or testing or by any other method which is appropriate in the circumstances;

(b) to undertake investigation of the properties of materials or articles of any kind, their behaviour or likely behaviour under particular conditions, and their suitability for particular purposes;

(c) to undertake the examination of articles of any kind for the purpose of discovering whether and to what extent they comply with standards or other criteria which are published or have been made known to the Company.

(d) to undertake the investigation of firms, corporate bodies or other persons, or of systems, documentation, programmes or procedures, for the purpose of discovering whether and to what extent they comply with standards or other criteria which are published or have been made known to the Company;

(e) to undertake the valuation, on any basis and for any purpose, of materials or articles of any kind;

(f) to undertake any other activities of a kind which the Company may consider similar to, or suitable to be carried on with, the foregoing;

(g) to undertake or instigate, or join in undertaking or instigating, and to meet or contribute towards the cost of, research into, and the provisions (including manufacture) and development of, plant, equipment, technology, methodology (including systems, procedures and computer and other programmes) and materials for use in, or in connection with, any of the foregoing activities; and

(h) to undertake, or join in undertaking, the marketing of, and the provision of maintenance, advisory, technical or other services in relation to, any plant, equipment, technology, methodology (including systems, procedures and computer and other programmes) and materials or articles of any kind used or capable of use in, or in connection with—

(i) any of the activities mentioned in paragraphs (a) to (f) above, or

(ii) any of the activities carried on in the course of the business of an assay office.

(2) The Company may do anything which is calculated to facilitate or is incidental or conducive to the activities mentioned in subsection (1) above and (without prejudice to that generality) shall in particular have power—

(a) to issue certificates as to the results of any analysis, examination, test or investigation carried out under subsection (1) above;

(b) to provide advisory and supervisory services and to provide expert evidence for the purpose of legal or other proceedings;

(c) to make members of its staff available to advise on, or participate in, the formulation of standards or criteria of the kind referred to in paragraphs (c) and (d) of subsection (1) above;

(d) to register, maintain, protect and enforce in any part of the world intellectual property rights, including patents, trade marks and other marks, and to authorise the use of such intellectual property on such lawful terms and conditions as it sees fit;

(e) to promote or establish, or join in promoting or establishing, or to acquire interests in and take part in the management of, bodies corporate or unincorporate in any part of the world, having as their object, or as a main object, the carrying on of any or all of the activities mentioned in subsection (1) above; and

(f) to receive grants and to accept gifts of money or other property to be used in meeting its expenses in connection with, or in furthering, any or all of such activities.

Application and amendment of existing enactments

5.—(1) In this section references to the Company's other activities are references to the additional activities authorised by section 4 (Additional activities of Company) above or other the activities which the Company is for the time being authorised to undertake in addition to its business of an assay office.

(2) Subject to the provisions of subsections (3) and (4) below, all the provisions of the Birmingham Assay Office Acts and Order 1824 to 1989 which relate to the Company and to its business of an assay office shall apply equally (so far as they are capable of doing so) to and in relation to its other activities, and to and in relation to the Company in so far as its undertaking includes them (but, save as respects the reference in article 7 of the Order of 1989, specific references to articles brought to be assayed shall not extend to articles received by the Company in the course of its other activities).

(3) The Company shall keep accounts in respect of its other activities separate from the accounts kept in respect of its business of an assay office and—

(a) paragraph (5) of article 10 of the Order of 1989 shall not apply to the accounts kept in respect of its other activities,

(b) paragraph (8) of that article shall not apply in relation to the accounts kept in respect of its other activities, and references in that paragraph to emoluments shall not include emoluments paid for work done or time spent in connection with its other activities, and

(c) the other provisions of that article shall apply separately to or in relation to each set of accounts,

but references in this subsection to accounts do not include balance sheets and nothing in this subsection shall prevent the Company from preparing a single balance sheet in respect of the whole of its undertaking.

(4) In article 15 of the Order of 1989—

(a) in so far as the business of the Company consists of its other activities, the words "if so authorised by the British Hallmarking Council" shall not apply, and

(b) in the proviso, the reference to the principal place of business of the Company shall be taken to mean the principal place at which it carries on its business of an assay office.

(5) Notwithstanding section 22(2) of the Act of 1973, an order under section 16(1)(c) of that Act in relation to the Company shall, except so far as it provides otherwise or the contrary otherwise appears, apply in relation to its other activities as well as to its business of an assay office; and such an order may consist of or include provisions which apply only to the Company's other activities.

(6) Section 4 (Provisions as to surplus income) of the Act of 1902 is hereby amended by the substitution in subsection (1) for "1989" of "1995".

INDEX

References are to sections

LOCH LEVEN AND LOCHABER WATER POWER ORDER CONFIRMATION ACT 1995

(1995 c. vii)

ARRANGEMENT OF SECTIONS

An Act to confirm a Provisional Order under the Private Legislation Procedure (Scotland) Act 1936, relating to Loch Leven and Lochaber Water Power. [8th November 1995]

PARLIAMENTARY PROGRESS

The Bill's progress through Parliament was as follows:

House of Commons: First Reading, October 25, 1995; Bill considered by Commons, October 31, 1995; Third Reading, November 1, 1995.

House of Lords: November 1, 1995; Bill considered by Lords, November 2, 1995; Third Reading, November 6, 1995.

INTRODUCTION

This Act makes provision to dissolve the Lochaber Power Company, to transfer its undertakings to Alcan Aluminium UK Limited, and to amend the enactments relating thereto.

Whereas the Provisional Order set forth in the Schedule hereunto annexed has been made by the Secretary of State under the provisions of the Private Legislation Procedure (Scotland) Act 1936, and it is requisite that the said Order should be confirmed by Parliament:

Be it therefore enacted by the Queen's most Excellent Majesty, by and with the advice and consent of the Lords Spiritual and Temporal, and Commons, in this present Parliament assembled, and by the authority of the same, as follows:

Confirmation of Order in Schedule

1. The Provisional Order contained in the Schedule hereunto annexed is hereby confirmed.

Short title

2. This Act may be cited as the Loch Leven and Lochaber Water Power Order Confirmation Act 1995.

SCHEDULE

LOCH LEVEN AND LOCHABER WATER POWER

Provisional Order to amend the Loch Leven Water Power Act 1901, the Loch Leven Water Power (Transfer) Order 1910 and the Lochaber Water Power Acts 1921 to 1984; to enable the transfer of the undertaking of the Lochaber Power Company to Alcan Aluminium UK Limited; and for other purposes.

WHEREAS—

(1) By the Loch Leven Water Power Act 1901, the Loch Leven Water Power (Amendment) Act 1904 and the Loch Leven Water Power Order 1908 the Loch Leven Water and Electric Power Company was incorporated and authorised to construct and maintain the waterworks, electrical generating stations, pier and other works described in the said Acts and Order for the supply of water, water power and electricity within an area of supply defined in the said Act of 1901:

(2) By the Loch Leven Water Power (Transfer) Order 1910 the Loch Leven Water and Electric Power Company was authorised to sell and transfer the several portions of its undertaking to The British Aluminium Company Limited, and to two other companies incorporated for the purpose therof, and pursuant to that Order transfers of the undertaking were made by deeds and otherwise to those companies:

(3) In 1982 the whole of the issued share capital of The British Aluminium Company Limited was acquired by what is now British Alcan Aluminium plc (hereinafter referred to as "British Alcan") and following subsequent internal reorganisation the relevant undertaking of The British Aluminium Company Limited is now carried on by its subsidiary Alcan Aluminium UK Limited (hereinafter referred to as "Alcan UK"):

(4) By the Lochaber Water Power Acts 1921 to 1940 the Lochaber Power Company (hereinafter referred to as "the Power Company") was incorporated and authorised to construct and maintain electrical generating stations, waterworks and other works and was, subject to and in accordance with the provisions contained in those enactments, authorised to develop, generate, use and supply water, water hydraulic and motive power and electricity:

(5) Most of the water, water hydraulic and motive power and electricity generated by the Power Company was supplied to The British Aluminium Company Limited before its acquisition in 1982 by British Alcan and following internal reorganisation the Power Company now supplies Alcan UK:

(6) The separate existence of the Power Company is no longer necessary, practicable or administratively convenient, and it is expedient to enable the transfer of its undertaking to Alcan UK and to amend the said enactments relating thereto:

(7) In the context in which the electricity generating and supply industry operates following the enactment of the Electricity Act 1989 it is expedient that certain restrictions, limitations and provisions imposed on Alcan UK and the Power Company by the enactments relating to their respective undertakings should be removed and that the rights, benefits and powers attached to those undertakings should be clarified:

(8) It is expedient that other provisions in this Order be enacted:

(9) The purposes aforesaid cannot be effected without an Order confirmed by Parliament under the provisions of the Private Legislation Procedure (Scotland) Act 1936:

Now, therefore, in pursuance of the powers contained in the said Act of 1936, the Secretary of State orders as follows:

Short title

1.—(1) This Order may be cited as the Loch Leven and Lochaber Water Power Order 1995.

(2)(a) In respect of the Loch Leven undertaking the Acts of 1901 to 1910 and this Order may be cited together as the Loch Leven Water Power Acts 1901 to 1995;

(b) In respect of the Lochaber undertaking the Acts of 1921 to 1940 and this Order may be cited together as the Lochaber Water Power Acts 1921 to 1995.

Interpretation

2. In this Order, except where the context otherwise requires—

"the Acts of 1901 to 1910" mean the Loch Leven Water Power Act 1901, the Loch Leven Water Power (Amendment) Act 1904, the Loch Leven Water Power Order 1908 and the Loch Leven Water Power (Transfer) Order 1910;

"the Acts of 1921 to 1940" means the Lochaber Water Power Acts 1921 to 1940;

"Alcan UK" means Alcan Aluminium UK Limited or its successors or assignees;

"the appointed day" means such day as, under section 3 (Appointed day) of this Order, is appointed;

"assignation" includes an assignment;

"convey" includes the execution of any deed or other instrument or document by which (whether with or without any other procedure) any property, or any estate, interest, security or other right in or over property is constituted, completed, disponed, assigned, transmitted or discharged; and cognate expressions are to be construed accordingly;

"debenture" includes a floating charge or any instrument containing a floating charge;

"enactment" means an enactment in this Order, in the Act confirming this Order or in any general or local Act or in any order, rule or regulation made under any Act;

"existing" means existing, outstanding or in force immediately before the appointed day;

"liabilities" includes duties and obligations of every description (whether present or future, actual or contingent);

"the Lochaber undertaking" means the undertaking of the Power Company relating to the generation, use and supply of water, water hydraulic and motive power and electricity and other purposes pursuant to the Acts of 1921 to 1940;

"the Loch Leven undertaking" means the undertaking of Alcan UK relating to the generation, use and supply of water, water hydraulic and motive power and electricity and other purposes pursuant to the Acts of 1901 to 1910;

"the Power Company" means the Lochaber Power Company;

"property" means property and assets of every description (whether present or future, actual or contingent, heritable or moveable, corporeal or incorporeal), and includes property and assets held on trust or in a fiduciary capacity and securities, rights, benefits and powers of every description;

"security" includes a standard security or charge (whether legal or equitable), debenture, bill of exchange, promissory note, guarantee, lien, pledge (whether actual or constructive), hypothecation, assignation by way of security, indemnity, right of set off, undertaking or other means of securing payment or discharge of a debt or liability (whether present or future, actual or contingent);

"standard security" includes a mortgage, an assignation or disposition ex facie absolute and any agreement qualifying the same, a bond and disposition or assignation in security, a cash credit bond and disposition or assignation in security, an assignation in security and any real right or burden of whatever kind in the nature of a security; and

"undertaking" means all existing property and liabilities of whatever nature.

Appointed day

3.—(1) The directors of Alcan UK may appoint a day to be the appointed day for the purposes of this Order.

(2) Not less than 14 days before the day so appointed Alcan UK shall publish in the Edinburgh Gazette and the London Gazette notice of the day so appointed, stating that it is the appointed day for the purposes of this Order.

(3) The publication of notice of a day under subsection (2) above shall be conclusive evidence that that day is the appointed day for the purposes of this Order, and a reproduction of a page or part of a page of the Edinburgh Gazette or the London Gazette containing the notice, certified by the secretary of Alcan UK shall be evidence of the publication of the notice.

Transfer and vesting of Lochaber undertaking in Alcan UK

4.—(1) On the appointed day the Lochaber undertaking shall, by virtue of this Order and without further act or deed, be transferred to, and vest in, Alcan UK to the intent that Alcan UK shall succeed to the Lochaber undertaking as if in all respects Alcan UK were the same person in law as the Power Company.

(2) To enable Alcan UK to complete a title, if thought fit, to any property vested in it by virtue of this Order by notice of title or otherwise, or to deduce title, this Order shall be deemed to be a general disposition, conveyance or, as the case may be, assignation of such property in favour of Alcan UK.

Lochaber Power Company

5. Upon the day one year after the appointed day the Power Company shall be dissolved.

Application of enactments, documents, etc.

6. Subject to the proviso to section 7 (Contracts to be binding on or enforceable by Alcan UK) of this Order, where—

(1) any enactment other than an enactment in this Order or in the Act confirming this Order;
(2) any document whensoever made or executed; or
(3) any resolution by a company or by directors of a company;
contains any reference express or implied to the Power Company such reference shall on and after the appointed day and except where the context otherwise requires, have effect as a reference to Alcan UK.

Contracts to be binding on or enforceable by Alcan UK

7. All existing agreements, awards, contracts, conveyances, deeds, leases, licences, guarantees, bonds, indemnities, instructions and other instruments or undertakings entered into by or made with or addressed to the Power Company whether alone or with any other person and whether as principal or as agent shall on and after the appointed day be as binding and of as full force and effect in every respect against or in favour of Alcan UK and may be enforced as fully and effectually as if instead of the Power Company Alcan UK had been a party thereto, bound thereby or entitled to the benefit thereof:

Provided that no director, secretary or auditor of the Power Company shall by this Order become a director, secretary or auditor of Alcan UK.

Actions not to terminate

8.—(1) If immediately before the appointed day any claim (including any contingent claim), action, arbitration or proceeding or any cause of action, arbitration or proceeding is pending or existing against or in favour of the Power Company it shall not terminate or be discontinued or in anywise be prejudicially affected by reason of this Order but may be continued, prosecuted and enforced only by or against or in favour of Alcan UK as and when it might have been continued, prosecuted and enforced by or against or in favour of the Power Company if the Act confirming this Order had not been passed.

(2) Any judgment, decree or award obtained by or against the Power Company and not fully satisfied before the appointed day shall be enforceable only by or against Alcan UK.

(3) Nothing in this Order shall terminate or prejudicially affect the appointment of any receiver or of any administrative receiver or liquidator of the Power Company.

Documents to remain evidence

9.—(1) In subsection (2) below "documents" has the same meaning as in section 9 of the Civil Evidence (Scotland) Act 1988.

(2) All books, documents and other records which if the Lochaber undertaking had not been transferred to and vested in Alcan UK by this Order would have been admissible in evidence in respect of any matter for or against the Power Company shall be admissible in evidence in respect of the same matter for or against Alcan UK.

Transfer and vesting of interests in land and other property

10.—(1) In subsection (2) below "interest in a lease" means the interest of the lessee of land under a lease or, as the case may be, the interest of the sub-lessee of land under a sub-lease, and "reversionary interest" means the interest of a landlord in land subject to a lease or, as the case may be, the interest of the lessee of land who is the landlord under a sub-lease.

(2) The transfer and vesting of any land or other property by virtue of this Order shall not—
(a) constitute an assignation, transfer, devolution, alienation, parting with possession or other disposition or conveyance of property or of an interest in property for the purposes of any provision in any instrument, contract (whether in writing or not) or order of any court concerning that property or that interest; or
(b) give rise to any forfeiture or irritancy; or
(c) invalidate or discharge any contract or security; or
(d) operate so as to merge any interest in a lease with the reversionary interest in it.

Evidence of transfer and vesting

11.—(1) The production of a Queen's Printer's copy of the Act confirming this Order, and such evidence of publication of notice of the appointed day as is specified in subsection (3) of section 3 (Appointed day) of this Order shall, for all purposes, be conclusive evidence of the transfer of the property and liabilities of the Power Company to Alcan UK, and of the vesting thereof in Alcan UK, in accordance with the provisions of this Order.

(2) Without prejudice to the generality of subsection (1) above any document made or executed on or after the appointed day whereby Alcan UK, whether alone or jointly with any other person, purports to convey or transfer, to any person (whether for consideration or not),

or applies to be registered as the holder or proprietor of, any property held by the Power Company immediately before the appointed day, whether alone or jointly with any other person, shall be sufficient evidence that the interest of the Power Company in that property has been transferred to and vested in Alcan UK under this Order.

Loch Leven and Lochaber undertakings

12.—(1) In this section "electricity" means electricity generated by water power.

(2) Subject to—

(a) the Acts of 1901 to 1910;

(b) the Acts of 1921 to 1940; and

(c) the Electricity Act 1989;

the Loch Leven undertaking and the Lochaber undertaking shall include all necessary rights, benefits and powers to enable the use, supply or transmission of electricity by or to any person for any purpose and upon such terms and conditions as Alcan UK or the Power Company, as the case may be, see fit.

Repeals

13.—(1) The enactments specified in Part I of the Schedule to this Order are hereby repealed to the extent specified.

(2) Upon the day that the Power Company is dissolved in accordance with section 5 (Lochaber Power Company) of this Order the enactments specified in Part II of the Schedule to this Order are hereby repealed to the extent specified.

Costs of Order

14. The costs, charges and expenses preliminary to and of and incidental to the preparing for, obtaining and confirming of this Order or otherwise in relation thereto shall be paid by Alcan UK and may in whole or in part be defrayed out of revenue.

SCHEDULE

Section 13

PART I

ENACTMENTS REPEALED WITH IMMEDIATE EFFECT

Session and chapter	Short title of Act	Extent of repeal
1 Edw. 7 c. cclxx.	Loch Leven Water Power Act 1901.	In section 7, the words "within the area of supply hereinafter specified". Section 42. In section 45, the words "within the area of supply" and "without the area of supply".
10 Edw. 7 & 1 Geo. 5 c. cxxxviii.	Loch Leven Water Power (Transfer) Order Confirmation Act 1910.	In section 4(1) of the Order scheduled thereto, the words "to the Electricity Supply Company" and from the words "in bulk" to the end of the subsection.
11 & 12 Geo. 5 c. xliv.	Lochaber Water Power Act 1921.	Sections 90, 91, 92, 93 and 95. Section 110. Schedule 2.
20 & 21 Geo. 5 c. cx.	Lochaber Water Power Act 1930.	Section 11. In section 15, the words "and subsection (3)(b) of section 110 (Purchase of undertaking)".
1984 c. xxviii.	Lochaber Water Power Order Confirmation Act 1984.	The whole Act.

PART II

ENACTMENTS REPEALED ONE YEAR AFTER THE APPOINTED DAY

Session and chapter	Short title of Act	Extent of repeal
11 & 12 Geo. 5 c. xliv.	Lochaber Water Power Act 1921.	Sections 5 and 6. Sections 8 and 9. Sections 11 to 21. Sections 23 and 24. Sections 26 to 40.
1 & 2 Geo. 6 c. lxiv.	Lochaber Water Power Order Confirmation Act 1938.	Sections 9 to 24 of the Order scheduled thereto.

INDEX

References are to sections and the Schedule

ACCOMMODATION LEVEL CROSSINGS ACT 1995

(1995 c. viii)

ARRANGEMENT OF SECTIONS

An Act to make further provision with respect to offences of failing to secure gates on certain railways. [8th November 1995]

PARLIAMENTARY PROGRESS

The Bill's progress through Parliament was as follows:

House of Lords: First Reading, January 11, 1995; Second Reading, February 16, 1995; Bill committed to an unopposed committee, March 29, 1995; Third Reading, April 5, 1995.

House of Commons: First Reading, April 5, 1995; Second Reading, May 5, 1995; Bill committed, May 5, 1995; Bill committed to an unopposed committee May 17, 1995; Third Reading, October 26, 1995.

INTRODUCTION

This Act makes provision for section 49 of the Transport and Works Act 1992 (c. 42) to apply to every railway managed by Railtrack PLC. These provisions are expedient for reasons of safety and administrative convenience.

WHEREAS—

(1) Railtrack PLC (hereinafter referred to as "Railtrack") is a public limited company registered under the Companies Act 1985 to which there was transferred on 1st April 1994, under a scheme made on 30th March 1994, pursuant to section 85(1) of the Railways Act 1993 and by direction of the Secretary of State pursuant to section 85(4) of that Act, that part of the undertaking of the British Railways Board which consisted of the management of the railway network in Great Britain and related property rights and liabilities:

(2) The undertaking of Railtrack includes a number of level crossings created for the benefit of owners or occupiers of land adjoining a railway ("accommodation crossings"):

(3) Section 49 of the Transport and Works Act 1992 ("the 1992 Act") amended section 75 of the Railways Clauses Consolidation Act 1845 and section 68 of the Railways Clauses Consolidation (Scotland) Act 1845 (which make it an offence for any person to fail to shut and fasten any gate at an accommodation crossing) so as to apply these provisions to a failure to lower a barrier and to increase the fine payable for an offence under these provisions:

(4) Certain railways under the management of Railtrack were authorised by legislation passed before 1845 which accordingly did not incorporate section 75 of the Railways Clauses Consolidation Act 1845 or section 68 of the Railways Clauses Consolidation (Scotland) Act 1845 and which contain alternative provisions creating an offence of failing to shut or fasten any gate ("the pre-1845 provisions") not amended by section 49 of the 1992 Act:

(5) It is expedient for reasons of safety and administrative convenience that section 75 of the Railways Clauses Consolidation Act 1845 or section 68 of the Railways Clauses Consolidation (Scotland) Act 1845 as amended by section 49 of the 1992 Act should apply to every railway managed by Railtrack so as to create a single updated offence in relation to all accommodation crossings and that the pre-1845 provisions should cease to apply to those crossings:

(6) The pre-1845 Act provisions are, in so far as they apply to railway crossings other than accommodation crossings, now obsolete and it is accordingly expedient that they, and any other provisions which apply them to railways of Railtrack, should be repealed:

(7) The purposes of this Act cannot be effected without the authority of Parliament:

May it therefore please Your Majesty that it may be enacted, and be it enacted, by the Queen's most Excellent Majesty, by and with the advice and consent of the Lords Spiritual and Temporal, and Commons, in this present Parliament assembled and by the authority of the same, as follows:

Short title

1. This Act may be cited as the Accommodation Level Crossings Act 1995.

Application of section 75 and section 68 of Acts of 1845

2. Section 75 of the Railways Clauses Consolidation Act 1845 or, in the case of a railway in Scotland, section 68 of the Railways Clauses Consolidation (Scotland) Act 1845, shall apply to every railway of Railtrack to which it does not already apply.

Repeals

3. The enactments listed in the Schedule to this Act (being enactments which create an offence of failing to shut or fasten any gate at certain railway crossings or apply provisions creating such an offence) are hereby repealed to the extent specified in the third column of that Schedule.

Section 3

SCHEDULE

Chapter (1)	Title or short title (2)	Extent of repeal (3)
10 Geo. 4. c. lxxii (1829).	An Act for making and maintaining a Railway or Tramroad from the Town of Newcastle-upon-Tyne in the County of the Town of Newcastle-upon-Tyne to the City of Carlisle in the County of Cumberland, with a Branch there-out.	Section 151.
11 Geo. 4 & 1 Will. 4. c. lxi (1830).	An Act for making a Railway from the Cowley Hill Colliery in the Parish of Prescot to Runcorn Gap in the same Parish (with several Branches therefrom), all in the County Palatine of Lancaster; and for constructing a Wet Dock at the Termination of the said Railway at Runcorn Gap aforesaid.	Section 153.

Chapter (1)	Title or short title (2)	Extent of repeal (3)
4 & 5 Will. 4. c. xxvi (1834).	An Act for making and maintaining a Railway from Blaydon to Hebburn, with Six Branches thereout, all within the County Palatine of Durham.	Section 141.
4 & 5 Will. 4. c. lxviii (1834).	An Act for making and maintaining a Railway from Hayle in the Parish of Saint Erth in the County of Cornwall to Tresavean Mine in the Parish of Gwennap in the said County, with several Branches therefrom.	Section 131.
4 & 5 Will. 4. c. lxxxviii.	London and South-western Railway Act 1834.	Section 84.
5 & 6 Will. 4. c. lviii (1835).	An Act for making a Railway from Preston to Wyre, and for improving the Harbour of Wyre, in the County Palatine of Lancaster.	Section 66.
6 & 7 Will. 4. c. xxxii (1836).	An Act for making and maintaining a Railway from the Royal Burgh of Dundee in the County of Forfar to the Royal Burgh of Arbroath in the same County.	Section 118.
6 & 7 Will. 4. c. xxxvi (1836).	An Act for making a Railway from Bristol to Exeter, with Branches to the Towns of Bridgwater in the County of Somerset and Tiverton in the County of Devon.	Section 129.
6 & 7 Will. 4. c. lxxv (1836).	An Act for making a Railway from the London and Croydon Railway to Dover, to be called the "South-eastern Railway.".	Section 80.
6 & 7 Will. 4. c. lxxvii (1836).	An Act for making a Railway from Cheltenham and from Gloucester to join the Great Western Railway near Swindon, to be called "The Cheltenham and Great Western Union Railway," with a Branch to Cirencester.	Section 97.

Chapter (1)	Title or short title (2)	Extent of repeal (3)
6 & 7 Will. 4. c. lxxix (1836).	An Act for making a Railway from the Basin of the Kensington Canal at Kensington to join the London and Birmingham and Great Western Railways at or near Holsden Green in the County of Middlesex, and to be called "The Birmingham, Bristol, and Thames Junction Railway.".	Section 97.
6 & 7 Will. 4. c. lxxxi (1836).	An Act for making a Railway from the City of York to and into the Township of Altofts, with various Branches of Railway, all in the West Riding of the County of York or County of the said City.	Section 91.
6 & 7 Will. 4. c. lxxxii (1836).	An Act for making a Railway from Merthyr Tydfil to Cardiff, to be called "The Taff Vale Railway," with Branches.	Section 81.
6 & 7 Will. 4. c. ciii (1836).	An Act for making a Railway to form a Communication between London and Cambridge, with a view to its being extended hereafter to the Northern and Eastern Counties of England.	Section 128.
6 & 7 Will. 4. c. cx (1836).	An Act to enable the Hayle Railway Company to make certain Alterations in the Lines of such Railway, and for other purposes relating thereto.	Section 1 in so far as it applies 4 & 5 Will. 4. c. lxviii section 131.
7 Will. 4 & 1 Vict. c. xxii (1837).	An Act for making and maintaining a Railway from the Town of Lancaster to the Town of Preston in the County Palatine of Lancaster.	Section 48.
2 & 3 Vict. c. xlii (1839).	An Act to amend the Acts relating to the South-eastern Railway.	Section 1 in so far as it applies 6 & 7 Will. 4. c. lxxv section 80.
4 & 5 Vict. c. xxiv (1841).	An Act to enable the Northern and Eastern Railway Company to make certain Deviations in the Line of their Railway, and to alter and amend the several Acts relating to the said Railway.	Section 1 in so far as it applies 6 & 7 Will. 4. c. ciii section 128.

Chapter (1)	Title or short title (2)	Extent of repeal (3)
4 & 5 Vict. c. xlii (1841).	An Act to enable the Northern and Eastern Railway Company to make a Branch Line of Railway; and to alter and amend the several Acts relating to the said Railway.	Section 1 in so far as it applies 6 & 7 Will. 4. c. ciii section 128.
6 & 7 Vict. c. x (1843).	An Act for making a Railway from the Great Western Railway to the City of Oxford.	Section 329.
6 & 7 Vict. c. xxviii (1843).	An Act to enable the Northern and Eastern Railway Company to make an Extension of their present Railway; and to alter and amend the Acts relating to the said Railway.	Section 1 in so far as it applies 6 & 7 Will. 4. c. ciii section 128.
6 & 7 Vict. c. lii (1843).	An Act to enable the South-eastern Railway Company to make a Branch Railway to the Town of Maidstone.	Section 2 in so far as it applies 6 & 7 Will. 4. c. lxxv section 80.
7 & 8 Vict. c. xviii (1844).	An Act to consolidate the North Midland, Midland Counties, and Birmingham and Derby Junction Railways.	Section 239.
7 & 8 Vict. c. xxi (1844).	An Act for vesting the Leeds and Selby Railway in the York and North Midland Railway Company, and for enabling that Company to raise a further Sum of Money to complete the Purchase of such Railway.	Section 9 in so far as it applies 6 & 7 Will. 4. c. lxxxi section 91.
7 & 8 Vict. c. xxv (1844).	An Act to enable the South-eastern Railway Company to make a Railway from the said South-eastern Railway near Ashford to the City of Canterbury and the Town of Ramsgate and Margate, and to join the Canterbury and Whitstable Railway.	Section 2 in so far as it applies 6 & 7 Will. 4. c. lxxv section 80.
7 & 8 Vict. c. xxxiv.	Blackburn and Preston Railway Act 1844.	Section 337.
7 & 8 Vict. c. xxxv (1844).	An Act to enable the Northern and Eastern Railway Company to make certain Deviations in the Line of their Railway between Bishops-Stortford and Newport; and to alter and amend the Acts relating to the said Railway.	Section 1 in so far as it applies 6 & 7 Will. 4. c. ciii section 128.

Chapter (1)	Title or short title (2)	Extent of repeal (3)
7 & 8 Vict. c. xxxvii (1844).	An Act for making a Railway from the Lancaster and Preston Junction Railway at Lancaster to or near to the City of Carlisle.	Section 351.
7 & 8 Vict. c. lx (1844).	An Act for making a Railway from the Manchester and Bolton Railway in the Parish of Eccles to the Parish of Whalley, all in the County Palatine of Lancaster, to be called The Manchester, Bury and Rossendale Railway.	Section 352.
7 & 8 Vict. c. lxi (1844).	An Act for enabling the York and North Midland Railway Company to make a Railway from York to Scarborough, with a Branch to Pickering.	Section 4 in so far as it applies 6 & 7 Will. 4. c. lxxxi section 91.
7 & 8 Vict. c. lxiii.	Salisbury Branch Railway Act 1844.	Section 2 in so far as it applies 4 & 5 Will. 4. c. lxxxviii section 84.
7 & 8 Vict. c. lxiv (1844).	An Act for making a Railway from the Town and Port of Whitehaven to the Town and Port of Maryport in the County of Cumberland.	Section 347.
7 & 8 Vict. c. lxv.	Chester and Holyhead Railway Act 1844.	Section 396.
7 & 8 Vict. c. lxvii (1844).	An Act for making a Railway from the Shoreham Branch of the London and Brighton Railway to Chichester.	Section 348.
7 & 8 Vict. c. lxviii (1844).	An Act for making a Railway from Exeter to Plymouth, to be called "The South Devon Railway".	Section 381.
7 & 8 Vict. c. lxxxii (1844).	An Act for making a Railway from the Manchester and Leeds Railway to the Towns of Ashton-under-Lyne and Staly Bridge.	Section 363.
7 & 8 Vict. c. xci.	Brighton, Lewes, and Hastings Railway Act 1844.	Section 352.
8 & 9 Vict. c. lvii.	Whitby and Pickering Railway Act 1845.	Section 10 in so far as it applies 6 & 7 Will. 4. c. lxxxi section 91.
9 & 10 Vict. c. ccxli.	Hull and Selby Railway Purchase Act 1846.	Section 11 in so far as it applies 6 & 7 Will. 4. c. lxxxi section 91.
9 & 10 Vict. c. cccxxvi.	Bristol and Birmingham and Midland Railways Act 1846.	Section 9 in so far as it applies 7 & 8 Vict. c. xviii section 239.

INDEX

References are to sections and the Schedule

QUEEN MARY AND WESTFIELD COLLEGE ACT 1995

(1995 c. ix)

An Act to unite The Medical College of St. Bartholomew's Hospital in the City of London and The London Hospital Medical College with Queen Mary and Westfield College, University of London; to provide for the transfer to Queen Mary and Westfield College of rights, properties, assets and obligations of those other Colleges; and for connected and other purposes. [8th November 1995]

PARLIAMENTARY PROGRESS

The Bill's progress through Parliament was as follows:

House of Commons: First Reading, January 24, 1995; Second Reading, April 19, 1995; Bill committed, April 19, 1995; Bill committed to an unopposed committee, May 17, 1995; Third Reading, July 3, 1995.

House of Lords: First Reading, July 4, 1995; Second Reading, July 19, 1995; Bill committed, July 19, 1995; Bill committed to an opposed committee, October 17–18, 1995; Third Reading, October 30, 1995.

INTRODUCTION

This Act provides for the dissolution of the Medical College of St. Bartholomew's Hospital in the City of London, and of the London Hospital Medical College. These bodies are united with Queen Mary and Westfield College, University of London, and all rights, properties, assets and obligations are transferred to that College (subject to section 4(2)), without any conveyance, transfer, assignment or other instrument.

WHEREAS—

(1) The People's Palace Technical Schools were founded in 1887 and became the East London Technical College in 1896:

(2) As East London College the College was admited as a School of the University of London in 1907 and in 1913 established a governing body distinct from that of the People's Palace:

(3) The persons constituting the governing body of East London College were incorporated by the name of Queen Mary College by a charter granted by His late Majesty King George the Fifth on 30th November 1934:

(4) Westfield College was founded in 1882 to provide residence and instruction in a Christian context for women students preparing for the examinations of the University of London, and was admitted as a School of the University of London in 1902:

(5) The governors of Westfield College were incorporated by a charter granted by His late Majesty King George the Fifth on 19th July 1933, subsequently amended in 1964 to allow the admission of male students:

(6) A supplemental charter was granted to Westfield College on 15th September 1976, which charter redesignated the governing body as a Council, and which enjoined that the work of the College be carried on in accordance with Christian principles in a spirit of tolerance, freedom of opinion, mutual concern and community service and that facilities be provided for regular Christian worship in accordance with the doctrines of the Church of England:

(7) In 1983 and 1984 a substantial part of the Faculty of Science of Westfield College was transferred to Queen Mary College:

(8) In 1989, by virture of the Queen Mary and Westfield College Act 1989, both the said colleges merged and their rights, properties, assets and obligations were transferred to a college which was incorporated by the name of Queen Mary and Westfield College, University of London by a charter granted by Her Majesty on 1st September 1989:

(9) The governors of The Medical College of St. Bartholomew's Hospital in the City of London were incorporated by a charter granted by His late

Majesty King George the Fifth on 26th July 1921 for the purpose of constituting a Collegiate Corporation with the objects among others of acquiring and taking over property and obligations of the medical officers and lecturers of St. Bartholomew's Hospital and of the governors of that Hospital in connection with the education of students of medicine and the property held in trust for or in connection with the same purposes and of carrying on the work of the medical school of that Hospital:

(10) On 30th March 1949 The London Hospital Medical College (which had hitherto been an unincorporated general medical school of the University of London associated with the Teaching Hospital known as The London Hospital) was incorporated by a scheme pursuant to section 15 of the National Health Service Act 1946 as a body corporate, with the main objects of taking over and carrying on the former Medical College, continuing the work of medical and dental education and research previously carried on by the former Medical College and promoting research connected with or likely to advance the condition of the sciences and arts of medicine and surgery and other connected sciences and arts:

(11) Both The Medical College of St. Bartholomew's Hospital in the City of London and The London Hospital Medical College are Colleges of the University of London:

(12) It is expedient that The Medical College of St. Bartholomew's Hospital in the City of London and The London Hospital Medical College should be united with Queen Mary and Westfield College, University of London and that their rights, properties, assets and obligations should be transferred to that College with the exception of a freehold property in Charterhouse Square, London, which is to be transferred to The Medical College of St. Bartholomew's Hospital Trust:

(13) It is expedient that the other provisions contained in this Act should be enacted:

(14) And whereas the purposes of this Act cannot be effected without the authority of Parliament:

May it therefore please Your Majesty that it may be enacted, and be it enacted, by the Queen's most Excellent Majesty, by and with the advice and consent of the Lords Spiritual and Temporal, and Commons, in this present Parliament assembled and by the authority of the same, as follows:

Short title

1. This Act may be cited as the Queen Mary and Westfield College Act 1995.

Interpretation

2. In this Act, unless the subject or context otherwise requires—

"the appointed day" means 1st August 1995 or the date on which this Act is passed, whichever is later;

"the charter" means the charter incorporating the governors of The Medical College of St. Bartholomew's Hospital in the City of London, granted by His late Majesty King George the Fifth on 26th July 1921;

"the College" means Queen Mary and Westfield College, University of London;

"the Council" means the Council of the College;

"the existing bodies" means The Medical College of St. Bartholomew's Hospital in the City of London and The London Hospital Medical College, or either of them as the case may be.

Dissolution of existing bodies

3. On the appointed day—

(a) The Medical College of St. Bartholomew's Hospital in the City of London shall be dissolved and the charter shall be revoked; and

(b) The London Hospital Medical College shall be dissolved and the scheme made pursuant to section 15 of the National Health Service Act 1946 constituting the governing body of that College, defining the duties and powers of that College and providing for its management and control shall be revoked.

Transfer of property, etc.

4.—(1) Subject to subsection (2) below, all property, real and personal, of every description (including things in action) and all rights and privileges of the existing bodies which immediately before the appointed day belonged to or were vested in or exercisable by the existing bodies shall on the appointed day, without any conveyance, transfer, assignment or other instrument, be transferred to and vested in, or be exercisable by, the College for all the estate and interest therein of the existing bodies.

(2) Notwithstanding the provisions of subsection (1) above, the freehold property known as "The Medical College of St. Bartholomew's Hospital, Charterhouse Square, London EC1M 6BQ" and registered at Her Majesty's Land Registry under Title No. NGL 644815 shall on the appointed day be transferred to The Medical College of St. Bartholomew's Hospital Trust.

Transfer of obligations, etc.

5. All debts and obligations of the existing bodies shall on the appointed day be transferred and attached to the College and shall thereafter be discharged and satisfied by the College.

Savings for agreements, deeds, actions, etc.

6. Subject to subsection (2) of section 4 (Transfer of property, etc.) of this Act, all agreements, appointments, awards, contracts, deeds and other instruments, and all actions and proceedings and causes of action, which immediately before the appointed day were existing or pending in favour of, or against, the existing bodies shall on and from the appointed day continue and may be carried into effect, enforced and prosecuted by, or in favour of, or against, the College to the same extent and in like manner as if the College instead of the existing bodies had been party to, or interested in, the same respectively.

Construction of bequests, etc., and powers of trustees

7.—(1) Any scheme, will, deed or other instrument, whether made or executed before, on or after the appointed day, which contains any bequest, gift or trust or other benefit in favour of or connected with the existing bodies shall, on and after the appointed day, be read and have effect as if the College were named therein instead of the existing bodies.

(2) Without prejudice to subsection (1) above, any trustees who, immediately before the appointed day, had power, for all or any purposes relating to hospital services (including research) or to any other part of the health service associated with hospitals, to assist, support or otherwise benefit an existing body, shall, on and from that day, have power to assist, support or otherwise benefit the College as if it were a hospital for which those trustees were appointed.

(3) In this section "the health service" and "hospital" have the same meaning as in the National Health Service Act 1977.

Transfer of powers to appoint or nominate

8. Any power or right of the existing bodies or of any of their officers or employees to appoint or nominate a member of any education authority, or of the governing body of any educational, charitable or other institution, shall on the appointed day be transferred to, and may be exercised by, the College or the officer or employee of the College who in the opinion of the Council most nearly performs the functions formerly performed by the former officer or employee in question.

INDEX

References are to sections

LONDON LOCAL AUTHORITIES ACT 1995

(1995 c. x)

ARRANGEMENT OF SECTIONS

PART I

PRELIMINARY

An Act to confer further powers upon local authorities in London; and for other purposes. [8th November 1995]

PARLIAMENTARY PROGRESS

The Bill's progress through Parliament was as follows:

House of Lords: First Reading, January 19, 1993; Second Reading, February 18, 1993: Bill committed, February 18, 1993; Bill committed to an opposed committee June 7–10 1993; Motion to suspend the Bill to subsequent Sessions, October 28, 1993, October 25, 1994; Bill committed to an unopposed committee, December 12, 1994; Third Reading, February 7, 1995; Commons' amendments considered by the House of Lords, October 31, 1995.

House of Commons: First Reading, February 7, 1995; Second Reading, February 21, 1995; Bill committed, February 21, 1995; Bill committed to an opposed committee April 25, 1995–May 1, 1995; Bill as amended by the Committee considered (Report stage), October 18, 1995; Third Reading, October 31, 1995.

INTRODUCTION

This Act creates extended powers for the London borough councils, so as to make further and better provisions for improvement and development of local government services. The arrangements include the licensing and control of both near beer premises and door supervisors employed on licensed premises, and the control of parking.

WHEREAS—

(1) It is expedient that further and better provision should be made for the improvement and development of local government services in London and for the benefit of persons residing therein and that the powers of London borough councils and the Common Council of the City of London (hereinafter referred to as "'London borough councils") should be extended and amended as provided in this Act:

(2) It is expedient that arrangements for the control of parking and the enforcement of parking restrictions in London should be amended:

(3) It is expedient that London borough councils should have power to license and control near beer premises:

(4) It is expedient that London borough councils should have power to license and control door supervisors employed on licensed premises:

(5) It is expedient that the other provisions contained in this Act should be enacted:

(6) The purposes of this Act cannot be effected without the authority of Parliament:

(7) In relation to the promotion of the Bill for this Act the Westminster City Council have complied with the requirements of section 239 of the Local Government Act 1972 and the other participating councils (namely, the Common Council of the City of London and all the other London borough

councils except Tower Hamlets London Borough Council) have complied with the requirements of section 87 of the Local Government Act 1985:

May it therefore please Your Majesty that it may be enacted, and be it enacted, by the Queen's most Excellent Majesty, by and with the advice and consent of the Lords Spiritual and Temporal, and Commons, in this present Parliament assembled, and by the authority of the same, as follows, that is to say:—

PART I

PRELIMINARY

Citation and commencement

1.—(1) This Act may be cited as the London Local Authorities Act 1995.

(2) The London Local Authorities Act 1990, the London Local Authorities (No. 2) Act 1990, the London Local Authorities Act 1991, the London Local Authorities Act 1994 and this Act may together be cited as the London Local Authorities Acts 1990 to 1995.

(3) This Act, except Part V (Registration of door supervisors) and, save as otherwise provided by section 15 (Application of Part IV), Part IV (Near beer licensing) shall come into operation at the end of the period of two months beginning with the date on which it is passed.

Interpretation

2. In this Act, except as otherwise expressly provided or unless the context otherwise requires—

"the Act of 1984" means the Road Traffic Regulation Act 1984;

"the Act of 1990" means the Town and Country Planning Act 1990;

"the Act of 1991" means the Road Traffic Act 1991;

"authorised officer" means an officer of a participating council authorised by the council in writing to act in relation to the relevant provision of this Act;

"the Commissioner" means the Commissioner of Police of the Metropolis or, in the City of London, the Commissioner of the City Police;

"the fire authority" means the London Fire and Civil Defence Authority;

"participating council" means the common council of the City of London and the council of any London borough other than Tower Hamlets; and "borough" and "council" shall be construed accordingly;

"penalty charge" has the same meaning as in section 66 of the Act of 1991;

"road" has the same meaning as in section 142(1) of the Act of 1984;

"special parking area" means a special parking area designated by an order made by the Secretary of State under section 76(1) of the Act of 1991;

"traffic sign" has the same meaning as in section 64(1) of the Act of 1984.

Appointed day

3.—(1) In this Act "the appointed day" means such day as may be fixed in relation to a borough by resolution of the borough council, subject to and in accordance with the provisions of this section.

(2) Different days may be fixed under this section for the purpose of the application of different provisions of this Act to a borough.

(3) The borough council shall cause to be published in a local newspaper circulating in the borough notice—

(a) of the passing of any such resolution and of a day fixed thereby; and

(b) of the general effect of the provisions of this Act coming into operation as from that day;

and the day so fixed shall not be earlier than the expiration of three months from the publication of the said notice.

(4) Either a photostatic or other reproduction certified by the officer appointed for that purpose by the borough council to be a true reproduction of a page or part of a page of any such newspaper bearing the date of its publication and containing any such notice shall be evidence of the publication of the notice, and of the date of publication.

Part II

Parking

Stopping on or near pedestrian crossings

4.—(1) This section shall apply to any part of a road in a special parking area in the borough of a participating council within the limits of a crossing or a crossing controlled area.

(2) A driver of a vehicle shall not at any time cause it to stop on a part of a road to which this section applies and the prohibition under this subsection shall be enforceable as if it had been imposed by an order under section 6 of the Act of 1984.

(3) Nothing in this section shall prohibit the driver of a vehicle from causing it to stop within the limits of a crossing or a crossing controlled area in circumstances where doing so would not contravene regulations made or having effect as if made under section 25 of the Act of 1984.

(4)(a) No penalty charge shall be payable pursuant to subsection (2) above by the driver of a vehicle who causes it to stop contrary to that subsection in any case where—

(i) by reason of that stopping the vehicle is removed by, or under arrangements made by, a constable or traffic warden under regulations made pursuant to section 99 of the Act of 1984; or

(ii) a notice is given to the driver under section 54(2) or (4) of the Road Traffic Offenders Act 1988 in respect of any offence under section 25 of the Act of 1984 constituted by that stopping; or

(iii) notification of an intention to prosecute the driver in respect of such an offence is given by the Commissioner to the council of the borough in which the crossing is situated before the expiry of the period of 14 days, beginning with the day on which the stopping takes place.

(b) Where the driver of a vehicle causes it to stop contrary to subsection (2) above, he shall not be liable to be prosecuted in respect of any offence under section 25 of the Act of 1984 constituted by that stopping unless the case falls within sub-paragraph (i), (ii) or (iii) of paragraph (a) above.

(5) Nothing in subsection (2) above shall require the placing of any traffic signs in connection with the prohibition thereby imposed.

(6) In this section—

(a) "crossing" means a crossing for pedestrians established or having effect as if established pursuant to section 23 of the Act of 1984; and

(b) "crossing controlled area" means any area of the carriageway in the vicinity of a crossing being an area the presence and limits of which are indicated in accordance with regulations made or having effect as if made under section 25 of the Act of 1984.

Designated parking places

5.—(1) Where a designated parking place within the meaning of section 45 of the Act of 1984 exists in a special parking area in the borough of a participating council there shall exist in respect of that designated parking place a prohibited zone.

(2) The prohibited zone shall be—

(a) where the designated parking place is adjacent to the edge of the carriageway of the road, the area between two imaginary lines drawn at right angles to the edge of the carriageway from the two points where the edge of the carriageway meets the boundaries of the designated parking place and each of those lines shall extend to—

(i) the centre of the carriageway in the case where the centre of the carriageway would be crossed by those lines; or

(ii) a point 8 metres into the carriageway from each of those points in all other cases;

(b) where the designated parking place is not adjacent to the edge of the carriageway of the road, the area between two imaginary lines drawn as far apart from each other as possible at right angles to the edge of the carriageway from one edge of the carriageway to the opposite edge of the carriageway and touching the edge of the designated parking place;

but shall not include any designated parking place or any other part of a road in respect of which the waiting of vehicles is specifically authorised.

(3) There shall be a prohibition on the waiting of vehicles in a prohibited zone during any period when parking is restricted in the designated parking place in respect of which the prohibited zone exists and such prohibition shall be enforceable as if it had been imposed by an order under section 6 of the Act of 1984.

(4) Nothing in subsection (3) above shall require the placing of any traffic signs in connection with the prohibition thereby imposed.

(5) Nothing in this section shall prohibit the driver of a vehicle from causing it to stop in a prohibited zone—

(a) if the driver is prevented from proceeding by circumstances beyond his control or it is necessary for him to stop in order to avoid an accident;

(b) if the vehicle is stopped for the purpose of making a left or right turn;

(c) if the vehicle is being used for fire brigade, ambulance or police purposes;

(d) for so long as may be necessary up to a maximum of 20 minutes for the delivery or collection of goods or merchandise or the loading or unloading of the vehicle at any premises if that cannot reasonably be carried out as respects those premises without stopping in the prohibited zone;

(e) for so long as may be necessary to enable the vehicle, if it cannot be used for such purpose without stopping in the prohibited zone, to be used in connection with any building operation, demolition or excavation on the road in or in the vicinity of the prohibited zone, the collection of waste by any participating council, the removal of any obstruction to traffic, the maintenance, improvement or reconstruction of the road in or in the vicinity of the prohibited zone, or the laying, erection, alteration, repair or cleaning in or near to the prohibited zone of any traffic sign or sewer or of any main, pipe or apparatus for the supply of gas, water or electricity, or of any telegraph or telephone wires, cables, posts or supports;

(f) for so long as may be necessary for the purpose of enabling persons to board or alight from the vehicle.

Disposal of abandoned vehicles

6.—(1) Subsection (2) below shall have effect with respect to the time at which a competent authority may dispose of a vehicle under section 101 of the Act of 1984 (disposal of vehicles abandoned and removable under that

Act) where the place from which the vehicle has been removed or could at any time be removed is in the borough of a participating council or the vehicle has been delivered by the Commissioner to a participating council.

(2) In the circumstances mentioned in subsection (1) above, subsection (3) of the said section 101 shall have effect as though—

(a) at the end of paragraph (b) there were added "or after the expiry of a period of three months beginning with the removal, whichever is the sooner"; and

(b) at the end of the subsection there were added "or the expiry of a period of three months beginning with the removal, whichever is the sooner".

Recovery of unpaid penalty charges

7.—(1) The Secretary of State may make regulations for securing, subject to subsection (2) below, that—

(a) where a vehicle found in the borough of a participating council is in the custody of a competent authority under section 101 of the Act of 1984 and a person claiming the vehicle pursuant to subsection (4A) of that section is liable for the payment of any earlier penalty charge relating to that vehicle which remains unpaid, the claimant shall not be entitled to remove the vehicle from the authority's custody unless, in addition to the penalty charge and other sums specified in the said subsection (4A), he also pays the earlier penalty charge; and

(b) where a vehicle to which an immobilisation device has been fixed under section 69 of the Act of 1991 is in the borough of a participating council, there shall be no obligation to release the vehicle from that device pursuant to subsection (4) of that section unless, in addition to the charges payable under that subsection, there is paid any unpaid earlier penalty charge relating to that vehicle for the payment of which the person making payment pursuant to that subsection and, if not the same person, the person in charge of the vehicle at the time the immobilisation device was fixed, is liable.

(2) Regulations under this section—

(a) may make provision for appeals to the parking adjudicator in respect of unpaid penalty charges; and

(b) may contain such exemptions and exceptions as appear to the Secretary of State to be appropriate and shall in any event make provision whereby there is no requirement for the payment of an earlier penalty charge in order to permit the removal of a vehicle from the custody of a competent authority or, as the case may be, to secure the release of a vehicle from an immobilisation device if—

(i) representations have been made in relation to that charge to the relevant authority under section 71 of or Schedule 6 to the Act of 1991 within the period of time provided by subsection (5) of that section or paragraph 2(3) of that Schedule, as the case may be, and have not yet been considered by that authority; or

(ii) an appeal has been made in relation to that charge to the adjudicator under section 72 of or Schedule 6 to that Act within the period of time provided by subsection (1) of that section or paragraph 5(1) of that Schedule, as the case may be, and has not yet been considered by the adjudicator.

(3) Regulations under this section shall be made by statutory instrument subject to annulment in pursuance of a resolution of either House of Parliament.

(4) In this section "parking adjudicator" means a parking adjudicator appointed under section 73 of the Act of 1991.

Rounding of penalties

8. Section 66 of the Act of 1991 (which makes provision for the recovery of parking penalties in London in relation to designated parking places) shall have effect in the borough of a participating council as though after subsection (4) there were inserted the following subsection:—

"(4A) If the amount to be paid after the penalty charge has been reduced by the specified proportion under subsection (3)(d) above is not a whole number of pounds an authority may reduce the amount further to the nearest pound.".

Special temporary prohibitions

9.—(1) A participating council may, by notice, make a special temporary waiting prohibition in respect of a road or part of a road within a special parking area in the borough of that council.

(2) While a prohibition is in force the waiting of vehicles on the part of the road to which it relates shall be prohibited and that prohibition shall be enforceable as if it had been imposed by an order under section 6 of the Act of 1984.

(3) A prohibition may not—

(a) be made unless the participating council are satisfied that waiting should be prohibited for the purpose of—

(i) facilitating the holding of a special event; or

(ii) enabling members of the public to watch a special event; or

(iii) reducing the disruption to traffic likely to be caused by a special event; or

(b) last longer than three days.

(4) A notice under this section shall be displayed in a prominent place in the vicinity of the part of the road to which the prohibition relates for a period of not less than one day before the prohibition comes into effect and for the duration of the prohibition and shall—

(a) state that whilst the prohibition is in force the waiting of vehicles is prohibited in the part of the road to which the prohibition relates; and

(b) state the maximum duration of the prohibition.

(5) Subject to subsections (3) and (4) above, the Secretary of State may make regulations with respect to the procedure to be followed in connection with the giving of notice under this section including provision for notifying the public of the exercise, or proposed exercise, of the powers conferred by this section and the effect of notices made in the exercise of those powers.

(6) Any regulations under this section may make different provisions for different circumstances; and where this section or any regulations thereunder require a participating council to post a notice in a road, the council may take such steps for that purpose as they think fit, including the use for that purpose of any lamp-post, traffic sign or other structure whatsoever in the road, whether or not belonging to that authority.

(7) Regulations under this section shall be made by statutory instrument subject to annulment in pursuance of a resolution of either House of Parliament.

(8) In this section—

"prohibition" means a special temporary waiting prohibition made under subsection (1) above;

"special event" means any individual event including any sporting event, social event, entertainment or funeral which in the opinion of the participating council concerned requires a prohibition to be made for the purpose of safety, relieving traffic congestion or facilitating the holding of the event; and

"waiting" means waiting for any purpose including the delivery or collection of goods or merchandise and the loading or unloading of vehicles.

PART III

ADVERTISEMENTS, DISPLAYS, ETC.

Placards and posters

10. In its application to a participating council, section 225 of the Act of 1990 (power to remove or obliterate placards and posters) shall have effect as though subsections (3), (4) and (5) of that section were replaced by the following subsections:—

"(3) The council of a London borough may give notice in writing to a person who displays or causes to be displayed a placard or poster in respect of which they may exercise the powers conferred by subsection (1)—

(a) that in their opinion it is displayed in contravention of regulations made under section 220;

(b) requiring him to remove or obliterate it before the expiry of a period being not less than two days from the service of the notice, specified in the notice; and

(c) that if he does not do so, they intend to remove or obliterate it after the expiry of the period and recover from him the expenses reasonably incurred by them in so doing.

(4) Where a notice has been duly served under subsection (3) and the poster or placard to which it relates has not been removed or obliterated before the expiry of the period specified in the notice, the council of the London borough may remove or obliterate it and may recover from the person on whom the notice was served the expenses reasonably incurred by them in so doing; but in any proceedings for the recovery of such expenses it shall be for the council to show that the poster or placard was displayed in contravention of regulations made under section 220.

(5) If a poster or placard is removed or obliterated pursuant to a notice under this section and within 28 days thereof another poster or placard is displayed on the same premises, in addition to the power under the foregoing provisions of this section the council of the London borough may serve a notice under subsection (3) on the owner or occupier of the premises on which the poster or placard is displayed, and subsection (4) shall, subject to subsection (6) apply to that person.

(6) In its application to a case in which a notice is served on any person under subsection (5), subsection (4) shall have effect with the omission of the right to recover from that person the expenses of removal or obliteration.

(7) If a poster or placard is removed or obliterated pursuant to a notice under this section, the council of the London borough may exhibit a notice in the vicinity of the place where the poster or placard was displayed, stating that the display of an advertisement in contravention of regulations made under section 220 is a criminal offence punishable by a fine under section 224.

(8) A notice under subsection (7) may not be exhibited without the consent of the occupier of the premises, unless he cannot after reasonable enquiry be identified.

(9) Without prejudice to the generality of subsection (3), a person shall be deemed to display or cause to be displayed a placard or poster for the purposes of that subsection if the placard or poster gives publicity to his goods, trade, business or other concerns except when the placard or poster is displayed on a hoarding or other structure designed for the display of advertisements.".

Unauthorised advertisement hoardings, etc.

11.—(1) This section applies to a hoarding or other structure used, or designed or adapted for use, for the display of advertisements including a movable structure, fitments used to support a hoarding or other structure and a structure which itself is an advertisement, other than such a structure for which deemed or express consent has been granted under the Act of 1990 or regulations made thereunder or for which no such consent for such use is required or which was erected before 1st April 1990.

(2) Where there is in their area a hoarding or structure to which this section applies, a participating council may serve notice under this section on any person who appears to them to be responsible for the erection or maintenance thereof or, if after reasonable enquiry they have been unable to ascertain the name and address of such person, may affix a notice under this section to the hoarding or structure or exhibit a notice in the vicinity of the place where the hoarding or structure is fixed and serve a copy on the occupier of the land unless after reasonable enquiry he cannot be identified.

(3) A notice under this section shall require the removal of the hoarding or structure to which it relates within a period, being not less than 21 days after the date of the notice, specified in the notice, and shall state the effect of subsection (4) below.

(4) If a notice under subsection (2) above is not complied with before the expiry of the period specified in the notice, the participating council may—

(a) enter on the land;

(b) remove the hoarding or structure and its fitments and dispose of them; and

(c) recover from the person on whom the notice was served the reasonable expenses incurred by them in so doing unless he satisfies them that he was not responsible for the erection, and is not responsible for the maintenance of the hoarding or structure.

(5) Where, in the exercise of a right of entry conferred under subsection (4), damage is caused to land or chattels other than the hoarding or structure and its fitments, compensation may be recovered from the participating council by any person suffering the damage.

(6) Nothing in subsection (4) above shall authorise entry into a building.

Defacement of buildings

12.—(1) Where there is a sign to which this subsection applies in the borough of a participating council on a surface to which this section applies, if that council consider it to be detrimental to the amenity of the area or offensive, they may—

(a) serve on the occupier of the premises which include the surface; or

(b) if there appears to be no occupier of the premises which include the surface, affix to the surface;

a notice under this section, requiring the occupier or in the case of paragraph (b) above the occupier or owner to remove or obliterate the sign within a period specified in the notice, being not less than 14 days after the service or affixation of the notice.

(2) A sign to which subsection (1) of this section applies includes any writing, letter, picture, device or representation, other than an advertisement within the meaning of the Act of 1990.

(3) A person on whom notice has been served under subsection (1)(a) above, or the occupier or owner of premises which include a surface to which a notice has been affixed under subsection (1)(b) above may appeal to a magistrates' court on any of the following grounds:—

(a) that the sign is not detrimental to the amenity of the area and is not offensive;

(b) that there has been some informality, defect or error in, or in connection with, the notice;

(c) in the case of a notice under subsection (1)(a) above, that the notice should have been served on another person.

(4) If and in so far as an appeal under this section is based on the ground of some informality, defect or error in, or in connection with, the notice, the court shall dismiss the appeal, if it is satisfied that the informality, defect or error was not a material one.

(5) Where the grounds upon which an appeal under this section is brought include a ground specified in subsection (3)(c) above, the appellant shall serve a copy of his notice of appeal on each other person referred to therein.

(6) Subject to such right of appeal as aforesaid, if the person required by the notice to remove or obliterate the sign fails to do so within the time thereby limited, the council may themselves remove or obliterate the sign.

(7) Where there is a sign to which this subsection applies in the borough of a participating council on a surface to which this section applies and the owner or occupier of the premises which include that surface requests that council to remove or obliterate that sign, the council may do so and they may recover from the said owner or occupier the expenses reasonably incurred by them in so doing.

(8) A sign to which subsection (7) of this section applies includes any writing, letter, picture, device or representation, and any advertisement within the meaning of the Act of 1990, other than an advertisement for the display of which deemed or express consent has been granted under the Act of 1990 or regulations made thereunder.

(9) A surface to which this section applies is the surface of any building, wall, fence or other structure or erection, where that surface is readily visible from a place to which the public have access.

For protection of British Railways Board, Railtrack PLC, British Waterways Board and London Regional Transport

13.—(1) Subsection (5B) of section 225 of the Act of 1990 (as amended by section 10 (Placards and posters) of this Act) shall have effect in relation to any notice under that subsection served on a protected party in pursuance of subsection (5D) of that section as if for the period of two days specified in subsection (5B) there were substituted the period of 28 days.

(2) Subsections (3) to (5) below apply where a participating council propose to exercise any power (hereinafter referred to as a "relevant power") conferred by section 225 of the Act of 1990 (as amended by the said section 10) or section 11 (Unauthorised advertisement hoardings, etc.) or 12 (Defacement of buildings) of this Act to enter on any operational land of a protected party or to remove or obliterate a poster, placard, hoarding, structure or sign on that land or on any premises or surface of any such land.

(3) Before exercising the relevant power the participating council shall serve not less than 28 days' notice in writing of their intention so to do on the relevant protected party specifying the placard, poster, hoarding, structure or sign concerned and its location.

(4) The protected party on whom a notice under subsection (3) above is served may within the period of 28 days beginning with the day on which the notice is served serve a counter-notice on the participating council specifying conditions subject to which the relevant power is to be exercised, being reasonable conditions which are necessary or expedient in the interests of safety or the efficient and economic operation of the transport undertaking concerned or (where the protected party is the British Waterways Board) for the protection of any works, apparatus or other property not vested in the protected party which are lawfully present on, in, under or over the land upon which entry is proposed to be made.

(5) Where a counter-notice is served under subsection (4) above the relevant power may only be exercised subject to and in accordance with the conditions in the counter-notice.

(6) Before exercising any power conferred by section 225 of the Act of 1990 (as amended by the said section 10) or the said section 12 of this Act to remove or obliterate a placard, poster or sign from any surface on a bus shelter or other street furniture of a protected party (not being situated on operational land of the protected party), the participating council shall serve not less than 28 days' notice in writing of their intention so to do on the protected party specifying the bus shelter or other street furniture concerned.

(7) Nothing in this section shall be taken as prejudicing the operation of section 225(1) of the Act of 1990.

(8) In this section—

"operational land" has the same meaning as in the Act of 1990; and

"protected party" means the British Railways Board, Railtrack PLC, the British Waterways Board or London Regional Transport or any of their subsidiaries (as defined by section 736 of the Companies Act 1985).

PART IV

NEAR BEER LICENSING

Interpretation of Part IV

14. In this Part of this Act—

"the Act of 1964" means the Licensing Act 1964;

"near beer premises" means any premises, vehicle, vessel or stall used for a business which—

(a) consists to a significant degree in—

(i) the sale to customers for consumption on the premises of liquid refreshments which include in their trade description any of the following words:—beer, lager, pils, shandy, cider, wine, champagne, cocktail, sherry, gin, brandy, whisky, vodka or other words which imply that the liquid refreshment contains or can reasonably be expected to contain alcohol; or

(ii) the sale to customers for consumption on the premises of liquid refreshments which consist of any beverage commonly expected to contain alcohol or calculated to represent any alcoholic beverage; and

(b) offers, expressly or by implication, whether on payment of a fee or not, either or both of the following:—

(i) the provision of companions for customers on the premises; or

(ii) the provision of live entertainment on the premises;

but does not include any such premises in which the sale to customers for consumption of intoxicating liquor is provided exemption or saving from the provisions of the Act of 1964 by virtue of section 199 of that Act or in respect of which there is in force—

(A) a justices' on-licence within the meaning of section 1(2) of the Act of 1964;

(B) a licence granted by the council under Schedule 12 to the London Government Act 1963, section 21 (Licensing of public exhibitions, etc.) of the Greater London Council (General Powers) Act 1966 or the Private Places of Entertainment (Licensing) Act 1967;

(C) a licence granted by the council under the Theatres Act 1968 for the performance of plays;

(D) a licence granted by the council under the Cinemas Act 1985;
(E) a licence granted by licensing justices under section 148 (licences for seamen's canteens authorising the holding of retailer's on-licences) of the Act of 1964;
(F) a permission granted by licensing justices under section 1 (grant of occasional permissions) of the Licensing (Occasional Permissions) Act 1983;
(G) an occasional licence granted under section 180 (consent to grant of occasional licence) of the Act of 1964;

during the hours permitted by such licence or, in the case of premises to which sub-paragraph (A) above applies, until the expiration of 30 minutes after the end of the hours permitted by such licence:

Provided that the premises are in use wholly or mainly and bona fide for the purpose authorised by such licence; and

does not include any such premises in respect of which there is in force a licence under Part II of the Gaming Act 1968;

"occupier" in relation to any premises means an occupier who is—
(a) the freeholder; or
(b) a lessee; or
(c) a tenant holding a tenancy of at least one year in duration.

Application of Part IV

15. This Part of this Act applies to the City of Westminster as from the date of commencement and to the boroughs of all other participating councils as from the appointed day.

Licensing

16.—(1) No premises shall be used in the borough as near beer premises except under and in accordance with a near beer licence granted under this section by the council.

(2) The council may grant to an applicant and from time to time, renew or transfer a near beer licence on such terms and conditions and subject to such restrictions as may be specified.

(3) Without prejudice to the generality of subsection (2) above, such conditions may relate to—
(a) the maintenance of public order and safety;
(b) the hours of opening and closing the premises for use as near beer premises to ensure that nuisance is not likely to be caused to residents in the neighbourhood;
(c) the display of advertisements on or near the near beer premises and the prohibition of touting in any form;
(d) the display of prices of goods and services offered on the premises;
(e) the number of persons who may be allowed to be on the premises at any time;
(f) the taking of proper precautions against fire, and the maintenance in proper order of means of escape in case of fire, fire-fighting equipment and means of lighting, sanitation and ventilation of the premises;
(g) the maintenance in safe condition of means of heating the premises.

(4) Provided it has not been cancelled or revoked the near beer licence shall remain in force for 18 months or such shorter period specified in the near beer licence as the council may think fit.

Applications under Part IV

17.—(1) The occupier of premises in the borough may apply for the grant, renewal or transfer of a near beer licence, and shall not later than the day the application is made send a copy to the Commissioner and a copy to the fire authority and, subject to subsection (2) below, no such application shall be considered by the council unless the applicant complies with this subsection.

(2) The council may in such cases as they think fit, after consulting with the Commissioner and the fire authority, consider an application for the grant, renewal or transfer of a near beer licence notwithstanding that the applicant has failed to comply with subsection (1) above.

(3) In considering any application for the grant, renewal or transfer of a near beer licence the council shall have regard to any observations submitted to them by the Commissioner or by the fire authority within 28 days of the making of the application and may have regard to any observations submitted by him or them thereafter.

(4) An applicant for the grant, renewal, transfer or variation of a near beer licence shall furnish such particulars and give such other notices, including the public advertisement of the application, as the council may by regulation prescribe.

(5) Regulations under subsection (4) above may, inter alia, prescribe the procedure for determining applications.

(6) An applicant for the grant, renewal or transfer of a near beer licence shall pay a reasonable fee determined by the council.

(7) Where, before the date of expiry of a near beer licence, an application has been made for its renewal or transfer, the near beer licence shall be deemed to remain in force, or as the case may require, to have effect with any necessary modifications until the determination of the application by the council or the withdrawal of the application.

Refusal of licence

18.—(1) The council may refuse to grant, renew or transfer a near beer licence on any of the following grounds:—

(a) the premises are not structurally suitable for the purpose;

(b) there is a likelihood of nuisance being caused by reason of the conduct, management or situation of the premises or the character of the relevant locality or the use to which any premises in the vicinity are put;

(c) the persons concerned or intended to be concerned in the conduct or management of the premises as a near beer establishment could be reasonably regarded as not being fit and proper persons to hold such a licence;

(d) the premises are not provided with satisfactory means of lighting, sanitation and ventilation;

(e) the means of heating the premises are not safe;

(f) proper precautions against fire on the premises are not being taken;

(g) satisfactory means of escape in case of fire and suitable fire-fighting equipment are not provided on the premises; or

(h) the applicant has failed to comply with the requirements of subsection (4) or (6) of section 17 (Applications under Part IV) of this Act.

(2) The council shall not refuse an application without giving the applicant an opportunity to appear before the committee or sub-committee determining the application.

(3) The council may not delegate to an officer their function of refusing an application under this Part of this Act.

(4) Where the council refuse to grant, renew or transfer a licence, they shall, if required to do so by the applicant or holder of the licence, give him a statement in writing of the reasons for their decision within 7 days of his requiring them to do so.

Transmission and cancellation of near beer licences

19.—(1) In the event of the death of the holder of a near beer licence, the person carrying on at the place in respect of which the near beer licence was granted the function to which the near beer licence relates shall be deemed to be the holder of the near beer licence unless and until the near beer licence is transferred to some other person.

(2) The council may, at the written request of the holder of a near beer licence, cancel the near beer licence.

Power to prescribe standard terms, conditions and restrictions under Part IV

20.—(1) The council may make regulations prescribing standard conditions applicable to all, or any class of near beer licences, that is to say terms, conditions and restrictions on or subject to which such near beer licences, or near beer licences of that class are in general to be granted, renewed or transferred by them.

(2) Where the council have made regulations under this section, every such near beer licence granted, renewed or transferred by them shall be deemed to have been so granted, renewed or transferred subject to any standard conditions applicable to it unless those standard conditions have been expressly excluded or amended.

Provisional grant of near beer licences

21.—(1) Where application is made to the council for the grant of a near beer licence in respect of premises which are to be, or are in the course of being constructed, extended or altered or improved and the council are satisfied that the premises would if completed in accordance with plans or proposals deposited in pursuance of the requirements of the council be such that they would grant the near beer licence, the council may grant the near beer licence subject to a condition that it shall be of no effect until confirmed by them.

(2) The council shall, on application being made for the appropriate variation of the near beer licence, confirm any near beer licence granted by virtue of subsection (1) above if and when they are satisfied that the premises have been completed in accordance with the plans or proposals referred to in the said subsection (1) or in accordance with those plans or proposals as modified with the approval of the council.

Variation of near beer licences

22.—(1) The holder of a near beer licence may at any time apply to the council for a variation in the terms, conditions or restrictions on or subject to which the near beer licence is held.

(2) The person making an application for such a variation of licence shall on making the application pay to the council such reasonable fee as the council may fix.

(3) The council may—

(a) make the variation specified in the application;

(b) make that variation together with such further variation consequent thereon as the council may determine; or

(c) refuse the application:

Provided that no variation relating to fire safety conditions shall be made under this section before the fire authority have been consulted.

Appeals under Part IV

23.—(1) Any of the following persons, that is to say:—

(a) an applicant for the grant, renewal or transfer of a near beer licence whose application is refused;

(b) an applicant for the grant, renewal or transfer of a near beer licence who is aggrieved by any term, condition or restriction on or subject to which the near beer licence is granted, renewed or transferred;

(c) an applicant for the variation of the terms, conditions or restrictions on or subject to which a near beer licence is held whose application is refused;

(d) an applicant for the variation of the terms, conditions or restrictions on or subject to which a near beer licence is held who is aggrieved by any term, condition or restriction contained in a further variation made consequent on the variation applied for;

(e) a holder of any such near beer licence whose near beer licence is revoked under section 24 (Enforcement under Part IV) of this Act;

may at any time before the expiration of the period of 21 days beginning with the relevant date appeal to the magistrates' court acting for the petty sessions area in which the premises are situated by way of complaint for an order.

(2) In this section "the relevant date" means the date on which the person in question is notified in writing of the refusal of his application, the imposition of the terms, conditions or restrictions by which he is aggrieved or the revocation of his near beer licence, as the case may be.

(3) An appeal by either party against the decision of the magistrates' court under this section may be brought to the Crown Court.

(4) On an appeal to the magistrates' court or to the Crown Court under this section the court may make such order as it thinks fit and it shall be the duty of the council to give effect to such order.

(5) Where any near beer licence is revoked under the said section 24 of this Act or an application for the renewal of such a near beer licence is refused, the near beer licence shall be deemed to remain in force—

(a) until the time for bringing an appeal under this section has expired and, if such an appeal is duly brought, until the determination or abandonment of the appeal; and

(b) where an appeal relating to the refusal of an application for such a renewal is successful until the licence is renewed by the council.

(6) Where any near beer licence is renewed under section 16 (Licensing) of this Act and the council specify any term, condition or restriction which was not previously specified in relation to that licence, the near beer licence shall be deemed to be free of it until the time for bringing an appeal under this section has expired and, if such an appeal is duly brought, until the determination or abandonment of the appeal.

(7) Where the holder of a licence makes an application under section 22 (Variation of near beer licences) of this Act and the council make the variation applied for together with a further variation, then the licence shall continue as it was before the application—

(a) until the time for bringing an appeal under this section against any term, condition or restriction contained in the further variation has expired; and

(b) where any such appeal is brought, until the determination or abandonment of the appeal.

Enforcement under Part IV

24.—(1) If any occupier or other person concerned in the conduct or management of premises in the borough which are not currently licensed by the council under this Part of this Act—

(a) uses them as near beer premises; or

(b) permits them to be so used knowing or having reasonable cause to suspect that they are not currently so licensed;

he shall be guilty of an offence and shall be liable on summary conviction to a fine not exceeding level 5 on the standard scale or to imprisonment for a term not exceeding three months or to both.

(2) If any premises in respect of which a near beer licence is in force are used as near beer premises otherwise than in accordance with the terms, con-

ditions or restrictions on or subject to which the near beer licence is held then the holder of the licence or other person concerned in the conduct or management of the premises shall be guilty of an offence and liable on summary conviction to a fine not exceeding level 5 on the standard scale.

(3) Subject to section 23 (Appeals under Part IV) of this Act, the council may revoke a near beer licence if its holder is convicted of an offence under subsection (2) above.

Powers of entry under Part IV

25.—(1) Any authorised officer (on production, if so required, of a duly authenticated document of his authority) or any police officer may at all reasonable times enter upon, inspect and examine any premises used, or which he has reasonable cause to believe are—

(a) used or intended to be used as a near beer premises either without the requisite near beer licence; or

(b) used in contravention of the terms, conditions or restrictions on or subject to which a near beer licence is granted;

and may do all things reasonably necessary for the purpose of ascertaining whether an offence has been committed.

(2) Subsections (2), (3) and (4) of section 287 of the Public Health Act 1936 shall apply in respect of entry to premises for the purposes of subsection (1) above as they apply to entry to premises for the purposes of subsection (1) of that section.

(3) An officer of the fire authority authorised by the fire authority in writing to act in relation to this Part of this Act may at all reasonable times enter upon, inspect and examine premises which are licensed under this Part of this Act to ascertain whether conditions attached to the licence by virtue of section 16(3)(f) (Licensing) of this Act are being complied with.

(4) Any person who intentionally obstructs any person acting in the exercise of his powers under this section shall be guilty of an offence and shall be liable on summary conviction to a fine not exceeding level 3 on the standard scale.

Seizure

26.—(1) Any police officer who enters any premises by virtue of the powers contained in subsection (1) of section 25 (Powers of entry under Part IV) of this Act or any authorised officer who enters any premises under the authority of a warrant granted under subsection (2) of the said section 25 of this Act may seize and remove any apparatus or equipment or other thing whatsoever found on the premises which he has reasonable cause to believe may be liable to be forfeited under section 43 of the Powers of Criminal Courts Act 1973.

(2)(a) The following provisions of this subsection shall have effect where any apparatus or equipment or any other thing is seized under subsection (1) above and references in those provisions to proceedings are to proceedings in respect of the alleged offence in relation to which the article or thing is seized.

(b) Subject to paragraphs (c) and (d) below, at the conclusion of the proceedings the apparatus, equipment or thing shall be returned to the premises from which it was seized unless the court orders it to be forfeited under any enactment.

(c) If no proceedings are instituted before the expiration of a period of 28 days beginning with the date of seizure, or any proceedings instituted within that period are discontinued, at the expiration of that period or, as the case may be, on the discontinuance of the proceedings, the apparatus, equipment or thing shall, subject to paragraph (d) below, be returned to the premises from which it was seized.

(d) Where, at the time at which any apparatus, equipment or thing falls to be returned under paragraph (b) or (c) above, the premises from which it was seized have ceased to be occupied or the occupier of the premises appears to the council to be different from the person who occupied the premises at the time of seizure the council may, instead of returning it to the premises apply to a magistrates' court for an order as to the manner in which it should be dealt with.

Application to existing premises

27. Where near beer premises exist on the date this Part of this Act comes into force in the borough in which the near beer premises are situated and application for a near beer licence is made in respect of those premises within four weeks of that date those premises may lawfully continue to be used as near beer premises until the determination or withdrawal of that application and if an appeal is lodged until the determination or abandonment of the appeal.

Amendment of London Local Authorities Act 1990

28. Section 4 (Interpretation of Part II) of the London Local Authorities Act 1990 is hereby amended by the deletion, in the definition of night café, of the words "or the Private Places of Entertainment (Licensing) Act 1967" and the substitution of ", the Private Places of Entertainment (Licensing) Act 1967 or section 16 (Licensing) of the London Local Authorities Act 1995".

PART V

REGISTRATION OF DOOR SUPERVISORS

Interpretation of Part V

29. In this Part of this Act—

"door supervisor" means any person employed at or near the entrance to licensed premises to ascertain or satisfy himself as to the suitability of customers to be allowed on those premises or to maintain order on those premises;

"licensed premises" means any premises in respect of which there is in force for the time being a justices' on-licence within the meaning of section 1(2) of the Licensing Act 1964 or an occasional licence within the meaning of section 180(1) of that Act or any premises in respect of which there is in force a licence under Schedule 12 to the London Government Act 1963, the Private Places of Entertainment (Licensing) Act 1967 or Part IV (Near beer licensing) of this Act but does not include any such premises—

(a) in respect of which there is in force a licence—

(i) under the Cinemas Act 1985; or

(ii) under Part IV of the Licensing Act 1964:

Provided that the premises to which such licence relates are in use wholly or mainly and bona fide for the purpose authorised by such licence; or

(b) in respect of which there is in force—

(i) a licence under the Theatres Act 1968; or

(ii) letters patent of the Crown by virtue of which it is lawful for those premises to be used for the public performance of plays without a licence under the Theatres Act 1968,

except when a play as defined in the said Act of 1968 is not being performed and the premises are being used for a purpose for which a licence is required under Schedule 12 to the London Government Act 1963 or under the Private Places of Entertainment (Licensing) Act 1967 other than a concert of classical music; or

(c) which are being used exclusively and bona fide by a club registered or licensed under Part II of the Licensing Act 1964 and to which a certificate under section 79 of that Act does not apply; or

(d) in respect of which there is in force a licence under Part II of the Gaming Act 1968; or

(e) which are kept open wholly or mainly and bona fide as a tenpin bowling establishment; or

(f) (i) which are structurally adapted and bona fide used, or intended to be used, for the purpose of habitually providing the customary main meal at midday or in the evening, or both, for the accommodation of persons frequenting the premises; or

(ii) which are bona fide used, or intended to be used for the purpose of habitually providing for reward board and lodging, including breakfast and one other at least of the customary main meals; or

(g) which from time to time are by resolution of the borough council excluded from the operation of this Part of this Act;

"registration" means registration as a door supervisor under section 31 (Registration of door supervisors) of this Act.

Application of Part V

30. This Part of this Act applies to the borough of a participating council as from the appointed day.

Registration of door supervisors

31. As from the appointed day no person may be employed on licensed premises as a door supervisor unless he holds a valid current registration from the council.

Power to register

32.—(1) The council may register an applicant and from time to time renew a registration on such terms and conditions and subject to such restrictions as may be specified.

(2) Without prejudice to the generality of subsection (1) above, such conditions may relate to—

(a) the wearing of an identification card whilst on duty;

(b) an obligation to notify the council of any arrest or prosecution of the door supervisor for a crime of violence or dishonesty during the period of registration;

(c) training.

(3) Provided it has not been cancelled or revoked the registration shall remain in force for three years or such shorter period as the council may think fit.

Applications under Part V

33.—(1) An applicant for registration as a door supervisor or for renewal of a registration shall not later than the day the application is made send a copy of any application document to the Commissioner and, subject to subsection (2) below, no such application shall be considered by the council unless the applicant complies with this subsection and consents to the disclosure to the council by the police of the record of his criminal convictions other than spent convictions within the meaning of the Rehabilitation of Offenders Act 1974.

(2) The council may, in such cases as they think fit, after consulting with the Commissioner consider an application for the grant or renewal of a regis-

tration notwithstanding that the applicant has failed to comply with subsection (1) above.

(3) In considering any application for the grant or renewal of a registration the council shall have regard to any observations submitted to them by the Commissioner within 28 days of the making of the application and may have regard to any observations submitted by him thereafter.

(4) An applicant for the grant or renewal of registration shall furnish such particulars as the council may by regulation prescribe.

(5) Regulations under subsection (4) above may, inter alia, prescribe the procedure for determining applications.

(6) An applicant for the grant or renewal of a registration shall pay a reasonable fee determined by the council:

Provided that where the holder of a valid current registration from a council under this Part of this Act applies for registration by another council, that council may not charge a fee greater than one-quarter of the fee payable by an applicant who is not the holder of a valid current registration.

(7) Where, before the date of expiry of a registration, an application has been made for its renewal the registration shall be deemed to remain in force, or as the case may require, to have effect with any necessary modifications until the determination of the application by the council or the withdrawal of the application.

Refusal of registration

34.—(1) The council may refuse to grant or renew a registration on any of the following grounds:—

(a) the applicant could be reasonably regarded as not being a fit and proper person to hold a registration;
(b) the applicant has received insufficient training;
(c) the applicant has made a material statement which he knew to be false in a material particular in connection with his application;
(d) the applicant has failed to comply with the requirements of subsection (4) or (6) of section 33 (Applications under Part V) of this Act.

(2) The council shall not refuse an application or revoke a registration without giving the applicant or holder an opportunity to appear before the committee, sub-committee or officer determining the matter.

(3) Where the council refuse to grant or renew a registration, they shall, if required to do so by the applicant or holder of the registration, give him a statement in writing of the reasons for their decision within 7 days of his requiring them to do so.

Cancellation

35. The council may, at the written request of the holder of a registration, cancel that registration.

Revocation

36.—(1) The council may revoke a registration on any of the grounds included in section 34 (Refusal of registration) of this Act.

(2) Where the council consider that a registration could be revoked under subsection (1) above they may instead of revoking it attach additional conditions to the registration.

Power to prescribe standard terms, conditions and restrictions under Part V

37.—(1) The council may make regulations prescribing standard conditions applicable to all registrations that is to say terms, conditions and restrictions on or subject to which such registrations are in general to be granted or renewed by them.

(2) Where the council have made regulations under this section, every such registration granted or renewed by them shall be deemed to have been so granted or renewed subject to the standard conditions unless those standard conditions have been expressly excluded or amended.

Appeals under Part V

38.—(1) Any of the following persons, that is to say:—
(a) an applicant for the grant or renewal of a registration whose application is refused;
(b) a holder of any such registration who is aggrieved by any term, condition or restriction on or subject to which the registration is held; or
(c) a holder of any such registration whose registration is revoked under section 36 (Revocation) of this Act;

may at any time before the expiration of the period of 21 days beginning with the relevant date appeal to the magistrates' court acting for the petty sessions area in which the council's offices concerned with registration are situated by way of complaint for an order.

(2) In this section "the relevant date" means either the date on which the person in question or his representative is informed orally of the refusal of his application, the imposition of the terms, conditions or restrictions by which he is aggrieved or the revocation of his registration, as the case may be, or 7 days after the date when such notification was posted to him by first class pre-paid letter, whichever is the earlier.

(3) An appeal by either party against the decision of the magistrates' court under this section may be brought to the Crown Court.

(4) On an appeal to the magistrates' court or to the Crown Court under this section the court may make such order as it thinks fit and it shall be the duty of the council to give effect to such order.

(5) Where any registration is revoked under section 36 (Revocation) of this Act or an application for the renewal of such a registration is refused, the registration shall be deemed to remain in force—
(a) until the time for bringing an appeal under this section has expired and, if such an appeal is duly brought, until the determination or abandonment of the appeal;
(b) where an appeal relating to the refusal of an application for such a renewal is successful until the licence is renewed by the council; and
(c) where any registration is renewed under section 32 (Power to register) of this Act and the council specify any term, condition or restriction which was not previously specified in relation to that licence or such a condition or restriction is imposed under section 32(2) of this Act the registration shall be deemed to be free of it until the time for bringing an appeal under this section has expired and, if such an appeal is duly brought, until the determination or abandonment of the appeal.

Enforcement under Part V

39.—(1) If the holder of a licence in respect of licensed premises, or any person concerned in the conduct or management of such premises, employs a person as a door supervisor who is not currently registered with the council he shall be guilty of an offence and shall be liable on summary conviction to a fine not exceeding level 5 on the standard scale.

(2) Any person who is employed on licensed premises as a door supervisor without being currently registered with the council shall be guilty of an offence and shall be liable on summary conviction to a fine not exceeding level 4 on the standard scale.

(3) Any person who—

(a) contravenes any of the conditions of his registration; or

(b) resists or intentionally obstructs any person in the execution of his duties under this Part of this Act; or

(c) in connection with his application for registration makes a statement which he knows to be false in a material particular,

shall be guilty of an offence and shall be liable on summary conviction to a fine not exceeding level 4 on the standard scale.

Powers of entry under Part V

40.—(1) Any authorised officer (on production, if so required, of a duly authenticated document of his authority) or any police officer may at all reasonable times enter upon any premises where he has reasonable cause to believe—

(a) persons are being employed or are acting as door supervisors who have not been registered by the council; or

(b) door supervisors are contravening any of the conditions of the registration,

and may do all things reasonably necessary for the purpose of ascertaining whether an offence has been committed.

(2) Subsections (2), (3) and (4) of section 287 of the Public Health Act 1936 shall apply in respect of entry to premises for the purpose of this section as they apply to entry to premises for the purposes of subsection (1) of that section.

Confidentiality

41.—(1) A person who discloses information which he has obtained by virtue of this Part of this Act and which relates to the affairs of any particular business shall be guilty of an offence unless he does so—

(a) with the consent of the person for the time being carrying on the business; or

(b) in the exercise of functions under this Part of this Act.

(2) A person guilty of an offence under this section shall be liable—

(a) on summary conviction, to a fine not exceeding the statutory maximum; and

(b) on conviction on indictment, to imprisonment not exceeding two years or a fine or both.

Application to existing door supervisors

42. Persons who are employed as door supervisors on the appointed day and who apply for registration within four weeks of that day may lawfully continue to be employed as door supervisors until the determination or withdrawal of their application and if an appeal is lodged until the determination or abandonment of the appeal.

Defence of due diligence

43.—(1) In proceedings for an offence under any provision of this Part of this Act except subsections (2) and (3) of section 39 (Enforcement under Part V) of this Act it shall be a defence for the person charged to prove that he took all reasonable precautions and exercised all due diligence to avoid the commission of the offence.

(2) If in any case the defence provided under subsection (1) above involves the allegation that the commission of the offence was due to the act or default of another person the person charged shall not, without leave of the court, be entitled to rely on that defence unless, within a period ending 7 clear days before the hearing, he has served on the prosecutor a notice in writing giving

such information as was then in his possession, identifying, or assisting in the identification of, that other person.

PART VI

MISCELLANEOUS

Appointment of deputies

44.—(1) A participating council may appoint one or more members of the council to act as deputy to the member appointed by them to the fire authority, and shall notify that authority of any such appointment and, if more than one appointment is made, of the order of priority as between each such deputy.

(2) If a member appointed to the fire authority ceases to be a member of that authority the appointment of any deputy under this section by the participating council which appointed that member shall continue to have full effect, as if the member had continued to be a member.

(3) If the member appointed to the fire authority is not present at a meeting of that authority or at part of such a meeting, the deputy or one of the deputies to that member, duly notified to the authority under subsection (1) above, may attend that meeting or that part of that meeting in his place as if he were the member appointed to that authority.

(4) Where a participating council have appointed more than one deputy under subsection (1) above, the right of a deputy under subsection (3) above shall be exercisable in accordance with the order of priority notified by the appointing council.

(5) The enactments referred to in the Schedule to this Act shall apply to deputies appointed under this section as if they were appointed under Part IV of the Local Government Act 1985.

(6) A participating council may appoint one or more members of the council to act as deputy to the member appointed by them to the London Waste Regulation Authority, and the foregoing provisions of this section shall apply with the necessary modifications in respect of such appointment.

(7) Notwithstanding anything in subsection (3) above a deputy may not preside at a meeting of the fire authority.

Cinema licence fees

45. Section 3(8) of the Cinemas Act 1985 (which relates to the grant, etc., of licences for film exhibitions) in its application to a participating council shall have effect as though—

(a) after the word "cases" in both places where that word occurs there were inserted the words "or areas"; and

(b) at the end there were inserted the words "and may make provision for different fees in the case of grants from those in the case of renewals".

Application of London Local Authorities Act 1991 to City of London

46. Part III (Entertainment) of the London Local Authorities Act 1991 shall apply to the City of London as if it were a London borough and the Common Council were the council of that borough.

Special treatment: acupuncture, etc.

47. When a participating council have appointed a day for the purposes of Part II (Special treatment premises) of the London Local Authorities Act 1991, they may serve notice on any person registered by them under section 19 (Acupuncturists, tattooists and cosmetic piercers) of the Greater London

Council (General Powers) Act 1981 notifying him of the repeal of that section and terminating his registration under that section from a date specified in the notice, being not less than six months after the date of service of the notice.

Offences by bodies corporate

48.—(1) Where an offence under this Act committed by a body corporate is proved to have been committed with the consent or connivance of, or to be attributable to any neglect on the part of, any director, manager, secretary or other similar officer of the body corporate or any person who was purporting to act in any such capacity, he, as well as the body corporate, shall be guilty of that offence and shall be liable to be proceeded against and punished accordingly.

(2) Where the affairs of a body corporate are managed by its members subsection (1) above shall apply to the acts and defaults of a member in connection with his function of management as if he were a director of the body corporate.

Section 44

SCHEDULE

PART I

ENACTMENTS APPLIED TO DEPUTY MEMBERS

Public Bodies Corrupt Practices Act 1889.
Local Government Act 1972: sections 80, 81, 82, 84, 94 to 98, 100G, 116, 140 and 174.
Local Government Act 1974: sections 29, 30(3A) and 32.
Local Government (Miscellaneous Provisions) Act 1976: section 39.
Employment Protection (Consolidation) Act 1978: section 29.
Local Government Finance Act 1982: section 16.
Local Government Act 1985: sections 31, 32(1), 32(1A), 32(5), 35 and 36.
Local Government and Housing Act 1989: sections 12 and 18(1)(b).

PART II

ENACTMENTS APPLIED TO DEPUTY MEMBERS WHEN DEPUTISING

Local Government Act 1972: Schedule 12 paragraphs 6, 39 to 43.
Local Government Finance Act 1992: section 106.

INDEX

References are to sections and the Schedule

CHURCH OF SCOTLAND (PROPERTY AND ENDOWMENTS) AMENDMENT ORDER CONFIRMATION ACT 1995

(1995 c. xi)

An Act to confirm a Provisional Order under the Private Legislation Procedure (Scotland) Act 1936, relating to Church of Scotland (Property and Endowments) Amendment. [19th December 1995]

PARLIAMENTARY PROGRESS

The Bill's progress through Parliament was as follows:

House of Commons: First Reading, December 6, 1995; Bill considered by Commons, December 12, 1995; Third Reading, December 13, 1995.

House of Lords: First Reading, December 14, 1995; Bill considered by Lords, December 18, 1995; Third Reading, December 19, 1995.

INTRODUCTION

Statutory stipulations contained, *inter alia*, in the Church of Scotland (Property and Endowments) Amendment Act 1933 (c. 44) have become increasingly difficult to interpret and to apply and their existence is no longer considered to be in the general interest of the Church. This Act is therefore introduced to increase the discretionary powers of the General Assembly of the Church of Scotland, in relation to certain property and endowments of the Church.

WHEREAS the Provisional Order set forth in the Schedule hereunto annexed has been made by the Secretary of State under the provisions of the Private Legislation Procedure (Scotland) Act 1936, and it is requisite that the said Order should be confirmed by Parliament:

Be it therefore enacted by the Queen's most Excellent Majesty, by and with the advice and consent of the Lords Spiritual and Temporal, and Commons, in this present Parliament assembled, and by the authority of the same, as follows:—

Confirmation of Order in Schedule

1. The Provisional Order contained in the Schedule hereunto annexed is hereby confirmed.

Short title

2. This Act may be cited as the Church of Scotland (Property and Endowments) Amendment Order Confirmation Act 1995.

SCHEDULE

CHURCH OF SCOTLAND (PROPERTY AND ENDOWMENTS) AMENDMENT

Provisional Order to amend the Church of Scotland (Property and Endowments) Act 1925 and the Church of Scotland (Property and Endowments) Amendment Act 1933, and to modify the effect of certain Orders made under the Churches (Scotland) Act 1905, so as to increase the discretionary powers of the General Assembly of the Church of Scotland in relation to certain property and endowments of the Church.

WHEREAS—

(1) The supreme legislative, judicial and administrative Court of the Church of Scotland (hereinafter referred to as "the Church") is the General Assembly of the Church (hereinafter referred to as "the General Assembly"):

(2) By the Church of Scotland (General Trustees) Order 1921, the Church of Scotland General Trustees (hereinafter referred to as "the General Trust-

ees") were incorporated with power to purchase, acquire, hold and sell, feu or otherwise dispose of lands and other property heritable and moveable and borrow on the security thereof, and with all other privileges of a body corporate:

(3) By the Church of Scotland (Property and Endowments) Act 1925 (hereinafter referred to as "the Act of 1925") provisions were made in relation to the property and 1endowments of the Church and further powers and duties were conferred and imposed on the General Trustees:

(4) By the Church of Scotland (Property and Endowments) Amendment Act 1933 (hereinafter referred to as "the Act of 1933") the Act of 1925 was amended and further provision was made in relation to the property and endowments of the Church:

(5) By the Church of Scotland (Property and Endowments) Amendment Act 1957 (hereinafter referred to as "the Act of 1957") an alteration was made in the meaning of section 36 of the Act of 1925:

(6) By the Church of Scotland (Property and Endowments) Amendment Order 1978 (hereinafter referred to as "the Order of 1978"), added powers of delegation were conferred (largely through amendment of the Act of 1925 and the Act of 1933) on the General Assembly and a further power of delegation was so conferred:

(7) Section 36 of the Act of 1925 and sections 3(2), 6 and 8(2) of the Act of 1933, as amended by the Order of 1978, contain provisions which, while giving to the General Assembly (or any body to which it may delegate the necessary powers) a residual discretion as to the application of the property there described, stipulate that such property shall be appropriated or applied in the first place to meet the proper requirements of the parish there designated (or, in the case of the said section 36, of that parish or its neighbourhood); and section 34(1) of the Act of 1925 and section 8(1) of the Act of 1933, in requiring that the property there described be applied in accordance with, or subject to, the said section 36, embody stipulations to similar effect:

(8) Section 3(2) of the Act of 1933 contains a further stipulation to the effect that the power to sell or otherwise dispose of certain assets shall be subject to the approval of the presbytery of the bounds; and proviso (ii) to that subsection contains a further stipulation that the transfer of certain assets in the way there specified shall be subject to the like approval of the presbytery of the bounds and of the kirk session:

(9) By the Churches (Scotland) Act 1905 (hereinafter referred to as "the Act of 1905") a Commission was established with power by order to allocate church property between the Free Church and the United Free Church in Scotland, now united within the Church, and a number of orders made under the Act of 1905—

(*a*) have contained a stipulation that the property comprised in the order shall be used for the purposes of and in connection with the particular United Free Church of Scotland Congregation named in the order, and

(*b*) have contained a further stipulation that the proceeds of the sale or other disposition of such property shall be held and applied for those purposes.

(10) Much reorganisation has taken place, and many changes have occurred, since the stipulations mentioned in paragraphs (7) and (9) above were first imposed; those stipulations have become increasingly difficult both to interpret and to apply; and it is considered that their existence is no longer in the general interest of the Church:

(11) It is therefore expedient that those stipulations should (with certain exceptions relating to property comprised in an order made under the Act of 1905) be repealed and that the application of all the property to which they apply should be at the discretion of the General Assembly (or any body to which it may delegate the necessary powers):

(12) For similar reasons it is no longer appropriate that the statutory stipulations mentioned in paragraph (8) above should apply to the disposal or transfer of the assets there mentioned, and it is expedient that those stipulations also should be repealed:

(13) In seeking the changes mentioned above, the General Trustees act with the authority and the active approval of the General Assembly:

(14) The purposes aforesaid cannot be effected without an Order confirmed by Parliament under the provisions of the Private Legislation Procedure (Scotland) Act 1936:

Now, therefore, in pursuance of the powers contained in the said Act of 1936, the Secretary of State orders as follows:—

Citation and commencement

1.—(1) This Order may be cited as the Church of Scotland (Property and Endowments) Amendment Order 1995; and the Act of 1925, the Act of 1933, the Act of 1957, the Order of 1978 and this Order may be cited together as the Church of Scotland (Property and Endowments) Acts and Orders 1925 to 1995.

(2) This Order shall come into force on a date to be appointed by the General Trustees.

(3) Before the date so appointed the General Trustees shall publish in the Edinburgh Gazette notice of the date appointed, stating that it is the date appointed for the commencement of this Order.

Repeals and amendments

2.—(1) In section 36 of the Act of 1925 (requirements of parish to be first charge on endowments), the words beginning "in the first place" and ending "part of a general fund at the disposal of the General Assembly or any body to which the General Assembly may delegate the necessary powers" are repealed and replaced by "for such ends, uses and purposes as the General Assembly, or any body to which the General Assembly may delegate the necessary powers, may direct".

(2) In subsection (2) of section 3 of the Act of 1933 (non-statutory properties and endowments of quoad sacra parishes), the words "and to the approval of the presbytery of the bounds" are repealed; the words beginning "to apply the proceeds" and ending "fully met" are repealed and replaced by "the proceeds thereof"; and the words in proviso (ii) ", with the like approval of the presbytery of the bounds and of the kirk session of the parish concerned," are repealed.

(3) In section 6 of the Act of 1933 (power to dispose of certain churches and manses erected under the New Parishes (Scotland) Act 1844), the words beginning "in the first place" and ending "fully met shall be applied" are repealed.

(4) In section 8 of the Act of 1933 (application of properties and endowments on suppression or union of quoad sacra parishes), the words in subsection (1) ", subject to the provisions of section thirty-six of the principal Act," are repealed; and the words in subsection (2) beginning ", in the first place" and ending "fully met shall be applied" are repealed.

Orders made under Churches (Scotland) Act 1905

3.—(1) In this section "relevant property" means property which was allocated, by an order made under the Act of 1905, to the United Free Church of Scotland to be used for the purposes of and in connection with a Congregation of that Church, but not including property which was at 30th October 1900 held by trustees upon titles which did not give to the General Assembly of the Free Church of Scotland any powers of regulation and direction as to its management and disposal.

(2) Nowithstanding anything contained in the order, or in the Act of 1905, relevant property, and any property which represents it, and the proceeds of sale of relevant property and of any such representative property, shall be appropriated for such ends, uses and purposes as the General Assembly, or any body to which the General Assembly may delegate the necessary powers, may direct.

(3) Nothing in this section shall prejudice or affect—

(*a*) the terms of any trust, stipulation, condition or other requirement imposed by a donor or testator, appropriating property or its proceeds to some special Church purposes (as that term is used in the Act of 1905), or

(*b*) any patrimonial right or interest of a superior or other third party—

(i) conferred by or reserved under any writ recorded in the Register of Sasines; or

(ii) registered in the Land Register of Scotland.

INDEX

References are to sections, recitals (in italic) and Schedule

TEAM AND GROUP MINISTRIES MEASURE 1995

(1995 No. 1)

ARRANGEMENT OF CLAUSES

PART I

AMENDMENT OF PASTORAL MEASURE 1983

A Measure passed by the General Synod of the Church of England to make further provision with respect to team and group ministries.

[28th June 1995]

PART I

AMENDMENT OF PASTORAL MEASURE 1983

Team ministries

1.—(1) Section 20 of the Pastoral Measure 1983 (establishment of team ministries) shall have effect subject to the following amendments.

(2) In subsection (1) in paragraph (b) for the words "licence or permission of the bishop" there shall be substituted the words "a provision contained in a licence or permission of the bishop".

(3) In subsection (2) for the words from the beginning to "specified in the scheme" there shall be substituted the words "The office of rector in a team ministry shall be held by each holder thereof for the specified term of years".

(4) In subsection (3) for the words from "such term of years" to "bishop's licence" there shall be substituted the words "the specified term of years".

(5) After subsection (3) there shall be inserted—

"(3A) A person ordained to the office of deacon who is authorised under subsection (1)(b) by licence of the bishop—

(a) to serve in a team ministry as a member of the team; and

(b) for the purposes of the team ministry to perform, so far as consistent with the office of deacon, all such offices and services as may be performed by an incumbent,

shall serve for the specified term of years; and any such person shall, during that term, have the same security of tenure of his office as an incumbent of a benefice, and shall not be affected by a vacancy in the benefice of the rector.

(3B) Any other person who is authorised under subsection (1)(b) by licence of the bishop to serve in a team ministry as a member of the team shall serve for a term of years to be specified in the licence, but no person shall be authorised as aforesaid unless he has been nominated for that purpose by the rector with the consent of a majority of the other members of the team and of each parochial church council concerned:

Provided that it shall not be necessary for the person concerned to be nominated for that purpose by the rector as aforesaid where that person is authorised to serve in a team ministry for a period immediately following a period of service in the team ministry.".

(6) In subsection (6)—

(a) after the word "ministry" there shall be inserted the words "or for which a deacon to whom subsection (3A) applies is authorised to serve in a team ministry";

(b) for the words "length of the original term" there shall be substituted the words "specified term of years";

(c) for the words "or vicar concerned" there shall be substituted the words ", vicar or deacon concerned".

(7) After subsection (8) there shall be inserted—

"(8A) A pastoral scheme establishing a team ministry or, subject to the scheme, the bishop's licence may assign to any member of the team who is not a member of the team chapter a special responsibility for pastoral care in respect of a part of the area of the benefice, so far as consistent with that member's office; and, if any such provision as aforesaid is made by the bishop's licence, it may (subject to the scheme) be varied or revoked by a subsequent licence under seal.".

(8) In subsection (9) after the words "vicars in a team ministry" there shall be inserted the words "and deacons in a team ministry to whom subsection (3A) applies".

(9) After subsection (9) there shall be inserted—

"(9A) The Ecclesiastical Offices (Age Limit) Measure 1975 shall apply to deacons in a team ministry to whom subsection (3A) applies as if they were vicars in the team ministry and, accordingly, no person shall be capable of being authorised by licence of the bishop to serve in a team ministry as such a deacon if at the time of the issue of the licence he has attained the age of seventy years.".

(10) In subsection (10) for the words from "shall preside" to the end there shall be substituted the words ", unless a pastoral scheme otherwise provides, the rector shall preside, except that if he requests otherwise or is absent a deputy chairman appointed by the meeting shall preside".

(11) After subsection (10) there shall be inserted—

"(10A) Any member of the team in a team ministry may, by notice in writing, request the rector to convene a team meeting under subsection (10) to be held within the period of twenty-eight days following the service of the notice; and, if the rector fails to comply with such a request, that member may himself convene the meeting.".

(12) At the end there shall be inserted—

"(13) Where the rector in a team ministry established for any benefice receives a statutory notice concerning ecclesiastical property in the benefice, he shall—

(a) keep every member of the team informed of matters arising from the notice;

(b) afford every member of the team an opportunity to express views thereon before taking any action in response to the notice; and

(c) have regard to those views before taking any such action.

(14) Where a benefice for which a team ministry is established becomes vacant the bishop may appoint a person holding the office of vicar in the team ministry to act as rector in the team ministry for the purposes of subsections (3B), (7) and (10), and any person so appointed shall be deemed to hold the office of rector in the team ministry for the purposes of those subsections while the benefice remains vacant.

(15) In this section "specified term of years" in relation to a team ministry means such term of years as may for the time being be specified for the team ministry for the purposes of subsections (2), (3) and (3A) by a pastoral scheme or pastoral order; and in the case of a team ministry for which no term of years is so specified seven years shall be deemed to be the specified term of years for the purposes of those subsections.

(16) In this section—

"ecclesiastical property" has the same meaning as in section 12(3) of the Acquisition of Land Act 1981;

"statutory notice" means a notice given in pursuance of any enactment or of any instrument made under an enactment.".

(13) Section 20 of the 1983 Measure, as amended by this section, is set out in Schedule 1 to this Measure.

Team ministries established under Pastoral Measure 1968

2. After section 20 of the 1983 Measure there shall be inserted—

"**Team ministries established under 1968 Measure**

20A.—(1) Subject to the following provisions of this section, in the case of a team ministry established for the area of any benefice under a pastoral scheme made and confirmed by Order in Council under the Pastoral Measure 1968 (referred to in this section as "a 1968 Measure team ministry"), the scheme shall be deemed to contain provisions of the kind referred to in section 20(1)(b), that is to say, provisions for the pastoral care of persons in that area by those who are to share the cure of souls therein together with all other persons who are from time to time authorised by licence or permission of the bishop to serve in that area as members of the team.

(2) The persons who are to share the cure of souls in the said area shall constitute the team chapter, and the team chapter together with the other persons deemed to be referred to in the scheme by virtue of subsection (1) shall constitute the team.

(3) The pastoral committee of each diocese shall, as soon as possible after the passing of the Team and Group Ministries Measure 1995, send to the secretary of the parochial church council of every parish comprised in the area of a benefice in the diocese for which a 1968 Measure team ministry is established a notice stating that written representations to the effect that subsections (1) and (2) should not apply to the team ministry may be made to the pastoral committee within the period of six months immediately following the date on which the notice was sent, and require him to affix a copy on or near the principal door of every

church in the parish and every building licensed by the bishop for public worship in the parish.

(4) Subsections (1) and (2) shall not apply to any team ministry until the expiration of the period of six months immediately following the date on which the notice referred to in subsection (3) was sent to the parishes concerned and if, within the said period of six months, written representations as aforesaid with respect to a 1968 Measure team ministry are received by a pastoral committee—

(a) the pastoral committee shall forthwith refer the representations to the Commissioners, and the Commissioners shall then as soon as possible consider the representations and determine whether or not subsections (1) and (2) are to apply to the team ministry; and

(b) subsections (1) and (2) shall not apply to the team ministry unless and until the Commissioners determine that they are to apply to it."

Alteration of team and group ministries

3.—(1) Section 22 of the 1983 Measure (provisions which may be included in pastoral scheme) shall have effect subject to the following amendments.

(2) In subsection (1)—

(a) after paragraph (b) there shall be inserted—

"(bb) alter a team ministry by providing for the right of presentation of the rector to be transferred to a patronage board constituted by the scheme or to the diocesan board of patronage;

(bbb) alter a team ministry by providing for the vicars therein to be chosen by the body entitled to present the rector, in accordance with paragraph 2(1) of Schedule 3;";

(b) for paragraph (c) there shall be substituted—

"(c) with the consent of the rector or vicar concerned, change the office of a rector in a team ministry from a freehold office to an office held for the specified term of years or alter the term of years for which an office of rector or vicar in a team ministry is held to accord with the specified term of years;";

(c) after paragraph (c) there shall be inserted—

"(cc) specify the term of years (for which certain members of a team are to hold office or serve) for the purposes of section 20(2), (3) and (3A);".

(3) At the end there shall be inserted—

"(3) In this section "specified term of years" has the same meaning as in section 20.".

Compensation

4.—(1) Section 26 of the 1983 Measure (compensation of clergy) shall have effect subject to the following amendments.

(2) That section shall be renumbered as subsection (1) thereof.

(3) At the end there shall be inserted—

"(2) Subsection (1) (and Schedule 4) shall have effect in relation to a deacon to whom section 20(3A) applies as it has effect in relation to a vicar in a team ministry.".

Pastoral orders

5.—(1) Section 37 of the 1983 Measure (powers exercisable by pastoral order) shall have effect subject to the following amendments.

(2) That section shall be re-numbered as subsection (1) thereof.

(3) For paragraph (e) there shall be substituted—

"(e) the power to—

(i) assign a special cure of souls or other responsibilities to vicars in team ministries under section 20(8);

(ii) assign to any member of a team who is not a member of the team chapter a special responsibility for pastoral care, so far as consistent with that member's office, under section 20(8A);

(iii) specify the term of years (for which certain members of a team are to hold office or serve) for the purposes of section 20(2), (3) and (3A) under section 22(1)(cc);

(iv) alter a team ministry or change the office of a rector or vicar in a team ministry under section 22(1)(b) or (c);

(v) alter a team ministry under section 22(1)(bb) or (bbb);

(vi) alter a group ministry under section 22(1)(e);

(vii) provide for supplementary, consequential or transitional matters under section 22(1)(f);".

(4) At the end there shall be inserted—

"(2) In the case of a team ministry established for the area of any benefice under a pastoral scheme made and confirmed by Order in Council under the Pastoral Measure 1968, being a team ministry in respect of which the Commissioners have determined under section 20A that subsections (1) and (2) of that section are not to apply, a pastoral order may apply those subsections to the team ministry.".

Supplementary provisions re pastoral schemes and orders

6.—(1) Schedule 3 to the 1983 Measure (supplementary provisions applicable to matters arising out of pastoral schemes and orders) shall have effect subject to the following amendments.

(2) In paragraph 1—

(a) in sub-paragraph (7) after the words "Subject to" there shall be inserted the words "sub-paragraph (7)(a) and";

(b) after sub-paragraph (7) there shall be inserted—

"(7A)(a) This sub-paragraph applies to every vicar in a team ministry and every member of a team to whom section 20(3A) applies or to whom a special responsibility for pastoral care is assigned under section 20(8A).

(b) Every person to whom this sub-paragraph applies shall have the right to attend at the meetings of the patronage board or the diocesan board of patronage, as the case may be, at which the person to be presented as rector of the team ministry is considered and chosen and shall be entitled between them to one vote, which shall be exercised by such one of them or such two or more of them (acting unanimously or by a majority) as may be present at any such meeting.";

(c) at the end there shall be inserted—

"(13) Sub-paragraphs (3) to (11) shall apply in relation to a pastoral scheme or order altering a team ministry under section 22(1)(bb) or 37(e)(v) as they apply in relation to a pastoral scheme establishing a team ministry.".

(3) In paragraph 2—

(a) in sub-paragraph (2) the words "and every vicar therein" shall be omitted;

(b) for sub-paragraph (3) there shall be substituted—

"(3)(a) This sub-paragraph applies to every vicar in a team ministry and every member of a team to whom section 20(3A) applies or to whom a special responsibility for pastoral care is assigned under section 20(8A).

(b) Where such a scheme provides as aforesaid, every person to whom this sub-paragraph applies shall have the right to attend at the meetings referred to in sub-paragraph (2) and shall be entitled between them to one vote, which shall be exercised by such one of them or such two or more of them (acting unanimously or by a majority) as may be present at any such meeting.";

(c) after sub-paragraph (5) there shall be inserted—

"(6)(a) The body or other persons who are entitled to choose a person to be a vicar in a team ministry shall not make to any person an offer of appointment as such until the making of the offer to the person in question has been approved by the parish representatives.

(b) If, before the expiration of the period of two weeks beginning with the date on which the said body or other persons sent to the parish representatives a request for them to approve under this sub-paragraph the making of the offer to the person named in the request, no notice is received from any representative of his refusal to approve the making of the offer, the representatives shall be deemed to have given their approval under this sub-paragraph.

(c) If any parish representative refuses to approve under this sub-paragraph the making of the offer to the person named in the request, the representative shall notify the said body or other persons in writing of the grounds on which the refusal is made.

(d) Where approval of an offer is refused under this sub-paragraph, the said body or other persons may request the archbishop of the province in which the benefice in question is to review the matter and if, after review, the archbishop authorises the said body or other persons to make the offer in question, that offer may be made accordingly.

(7) In sub-paragraph (6) the expression "parish representatives" means two lay members of the parochial church council concerned appointed by that council to act as representatives of the council in connection with the selection of vicars in the team ministry.

(8) Sub-paragraphs (2), (3), (5) and (6) shall apply in relation to a pastoral scheme or order altering a team ministry under section 22(1)(bbb) or section 37(e)(v) as they apply in relation to a pastoral scheme establishing a team ministry.".

(4) In paragraph 11 in sub-paragraph (3) for the words from ", the trusts" to the end there shall be substituted the words "or, where a special cure of souls is not so assigned, a special responsibility for pastoral care in respect of such a part of that area is assigned to a member of the team under section 20(8A), the trusts of the charity or the constitution of the corporation shall have effect with the substitution for the incumbent of that benefice of that vicar or that member, as the case may be, but, except as aforesaid those trusts and that constitution shall (where necessary) have effect with the substitution for that incumbent of any such member of the team as may be nominated for the purposes of this sub-paragraph by the bishop of the diocese concerned.".

PART II

AMENDMENT OF OTHER ENACTMENTS

Diocesan Boards of Finance Measure 1925

7. In section 3 of the Diocesan Boards of Finance Measure 1925 (exercise of powers, etc. by Diocesan Boards of Finance) at the beginning there shall be inserted the figure "(1)" and at the end there shall be inserted—

"(2) A Diocesan Board of Finance for any diocese constituted under this Measure proposing to alter or dispose of any house occupied by a member of the team in a team ministry established for a benefice in the diocese shall—

(a) keep that member informed of matters arising from the proposal;

(b) afford that member an opportunity to express views before taking any action to implement the proposal; and
(c) have regard to those views before taking any such action.".

Parsonages Measure 1938

8.—(1) The Parsonages Measure 1938 shall have effect subject to the following amendments.

(2) In section 1 (powers of selling parsonage houses, etc.) in subsection (3) at the end of paragraph (iii) the word "or" shall be omitted and after that paragraph there shall be inserted—

"(iiia) in cases where the property proposed to be disposed of is occupied by a member of the team in a team ministry, without that member's consent; or".

(3) In section 2A (power to divide and improve parsonage houses during vacancy in benefice) after subsection (1) there shall be inserted—

"(1A) Where the residence house of a benefice is occupied by a member of the team in a team ministry, the sequestrators shall not carry out any work authorised under this section without that member's consent.".

(4) In section 3 (provisions as to exercise of foregoing powers) at the end there shall be inserted—

"(4) An incumbent or bishop proposing to exercise any of the powers conferred on him by any of the foregoing sections of this Measure in respect of the residence house of a benefice for which a team ministry is established shall, if the house is or is to be occupied by the incumbent,—

(a) keep every member of the team informed of matters arising from the proposal;
(b) afford every member of the team an opportunity to express views thereon before taking any action to implement the proposal; and
(c) have regard to those views before taking any such action.".

Parochial Church Councils (Powers) Measure 1956

9. In section 6 of the Parochial Church Council (Powers) Measure 1956 (supplementary provisions relating to certain property) after subsection (3) there shall be inserted—

"(3A) Where any property which is occupied by a member of the team in a team ministry is vested in the diocesan authority pursuant to subsection (2) of this section and the council proposes to alter or dispose of the property or any part thereof, the council shall—

(a) keep that member informed of matters arising from the proposal;
(b) afford that member an opportunity to express views thereon before taking any action to implement the proposal; and
(c) have regard to those views before taking any such action.".

Churchwardens (Appointment and Resignation) Measure 1964

10. In section 13 of the Churchwardens (Appointment and Resignation) Measure 1964 (interpretation) the word "minister" shall be omitted and at the end there shall be inserted—

" "minister" has the same meaning as that assigned to that expression in rule 44(1) of the Church Representation Rules except that, where a special responsibility for pastoral care in respect of the parish in question has been assigned to a member of the team in a team ministry under section 20(8A) of the Pastoral Measure 1983 but a special cure of souls in respect of the parish has not been assigned to a vicar in the team ministry by a scheme under that Measure or by his licence from the bishop, it means that member.".

Church Representation Rules

11. In the Church Representation Rules contained in Schedule 3 to the Synodical Government Measure 1969 in Appendix II (general provisions relating to parochial church councils) in paragraph 1 (officers of the council) at the end there shall be inserted—

"(h) For the purposes of this paragraph, where a special cure of souls in respect of a parish has been assigned to a vicar in a team ministry, or where there has been no such assignment but a special responsibility for pastoral care in respect of the parish has been assigned to a member of the team under section 20(8A) of the Pastoral Measure 1983, that vicar or that member, as the case may be, shall be deemed to be the minister unless incapacitated by absence or illness or any other cause, in which case the rector in the team ministry shall be deemed to be the minister.".

Sharing of Church Buildings Act 1969

12. In section 1 of the Sharing of Church Buildings Act 1969 (agreements for sharing church buildings) in subsection (3) at the end of paragraph (a) there shall be inserted—

"and, where a team ministry is established for the benefice comprising that parish,—

(i) any vicar in the team ministry to whom a special cure of souls in respect of the parish has been assigned by a scheme under the Pastoral Measure 1983 or by his licence from the bishop; or

(ii) any member of the team to whom a special responsibility for pastoral care in respect of the parish has been assigned under section 20(8A) of that Measure, the parish not being one in respect of which a special cure of souls has been assigned as mentioned in paragraph (i) above".

Deaconesses and Lay Ministry Measure 1972

13. In the Deaconesses and Lay Ministry Measure 1972 after section 1 there shall be inserted—

"**Provision with respect to licensing for fixed term**

1A. Without prejudice to section 7(1) of the Church of England (Legal Aid and Miscellaneous Provisions) Measure 1988, it shall be lawful for the General Synod to provide by Canon for empowering the bishop of a diocese, in the case of a benefice in his diocese in respect of which a team ministry is established,—

(a) to grant a licence to any of the persons mentioned in subsection (1) of section 1 above to serve in the area of the benefice for such term of years as may be specified in the licence; and

(b) to revoke such a licence summarily and without further process before the expiration of the term so specified for such cause and subject to such conditions as the Canon may provide.".

Endowments and Glebe Measure 1976

14.—(1) The Endowments and Glebe Measure 1976 shall have effect subject to the following amendments.

(2) In section 20 (powers of Diocesan Boards of Finance to deal with diocesan glebe land) after subsection (6) there shall be inserted—

"(6A) Where a transaction is in respect of diocesan glebe land situated in the area of a benefice for which a team ministry is established, subsection (5) above shall have effect in relation to every vicar in the team ministry and, in the case of a house occupied by a member of the team, in relation to that member as it has effect in relation to the incumbent of the benefice.".

(3) In section 32 (provisions for transfer of parsonage land to Diocesan Board of Finance) in subsection (2) at the end there shall be inserted—

"and, in the case of a benefice in respect of which a team ministry is established, every member of the team".

Church of England (Legal Aid and Miscellaneous Provisions) Measure 1988

15. In section 7 of the Church of England (Legal Aid and Miscellaneous Provisions) Measure 1988 (provisions as to licences of ministers, deaconesses, lay workers and readers)—

(a) in subsection (1) at the beginning there shall be inserted the words "Subject to subsection (1A) below,";

(b) after subsection (1) there shall be inserted—

"(1A)(a) In the case of a deacon to whom section 20(3A) of the Pastoral Measure 1983 applies, a licence shall not be revoked by a bishop unless the bishop is satisfied that there has been a serious breakdown of the pastoral relationship between that deacon and the parishioners concerned or he is unable by reason of age or infirmity to discharge his pastoral duties adequately.

(b) In this subsection the reference to a serious breakdown of the pastoral relationship between a deacon and the parishioners concerned shall be construed in accordance with section 19A of the Incumbents (Vacation of Benefices) Measure 1977.".

Care of Churches and Ecclesiastical Jurisdiction Measure 1991

16. In section 31 of the Care of Churches and Ecclesiastical Jurisdiction Measure 1991 (interpretation) in the definition of "minister" in subsection (1) after paragraph (a) there shall be inserted—

"(aa) in a case where a special responsibility for pastoral care in respect of the parish has been assigned to a member of the team in a team ministry under section 20(8A) of that Measure but a special cure of souls in respect of the parish has not been assigned as mentioned in paragraph (a) above, that member;".

Church of England (Miscellaneous Provisions) Measure 1992

17.—(1) Section 1 of the Church of England (Miscellaneous Provisions) Measure 1992 (sequestration) shall have effect subject to the following amendments.

(2) In subsection (1) after the word "shall" (where it first appears) there shall be inserted the words ", subject to subsection (1A) below,".

(3) After subsection (1) there shall be inserted—

"(1A) In the case of a benefice in respect of which a team ministry is established, subsection (1) above shall have effect as if for the words "rural dean" there were substituted the words "ministers in the team ministry":

Provided that the bishop of the diocese concerned, if he considers that any of the ministers in the team ministry should not be a sequestrator of the benefice, may direct accordingly.

(1B) In subsection (1A) above "minister" in relation to a team ministry means a person—
- (a) who is a vicar in the team ministry; or
- (b) to whom a special responsibility for pastoral care in respect of a part of the benefice has been assigned under section 20(8A) of the Pastoral Measure 1983, that part of the benefice not being a part in respect of which a special cure of souls has been assigned to a vicar in the team ministry by a scheme under that Measure or by his licence from the bishop.".

PART III

GENERAL

Transitional provisions

18. The transitional provisions in Schedule 2 to this Measure shall have effect.

Extent

19.—(1) Subject to subsection (2) below this Measure shall extend to the whole of the provinces of Canterbury and York except the Channel Islands and the Isle of Man, but the provisions thereof may be applied to the Channel Islands as defined in the Channel Islands (Church Legislation) Measures 1931 and 1957, or either of them, in accordance with those Measures and if an Act of Tynwald or an instrument made in pursuance of an Act of Tynwald so provides, shall extend to the Isle of Man subject to such exceptions, adaptations or modifications as may be specified in the Act of Tynwald or instrument.

(2) The power to apply the provisions of this Measure to the Channel Islands shall not apply to sections 8, 9 and 12.

Citation, commencement and interpretation

20.—(1) This Measure may be cited as the Team and Group Ministries Measure 1995.

(2) Section 2 of this Measure shall come into operation on the date on which this Measure is passed, and the other provisions of this Measure shall come into operation on such date as the Archbishops of Canterbury and York may jointly appoint; and different dates may be appointed for different provisions.

(3) In this Measure "the 1983 Measure" means the Pastoral Measure 1983.

SCHEDULES

Section 1(13)

SCHEDULE 1

SECTION 20 OF THE PASTORAL MEASURE 1983, AS AMENDED

Establishment of team ministries

20.—(1) A pastoral scheme may make provision for the establishment of a team ministry for the area of any benefice, and such a scheme shall provide—
- (a) for the sharing of the cure of souls in that area by the incumbent of the benefice which, if it is not or would not otherwise be a rectory, shall be a rectory and one or more other ministers who shall have the title of vicar and a status equal to that of an incumbent of a benefice; and
- (b) for the pastoral care of persons in that area by those who are to share the cure of souls therein together with all other persons who are from time to time authorised by a provision contained in a licence or permission of the bishop to serve in that area as members of the team.

The persons who are to share the cure of souls in the said area shall constitute the team chapter, and the team chapter together with the other persons referred to in the scheme by virtue of paragraph (b) of this subsection shall constitute the team.

(2) The office of rector in a team ministry shall be held by each holder thereof for the specified term of years; but the fact that the office is held for a term of years shall not affect its other attributes as a benefice and, in particular, the rector shall be a corporation sole and as such hold the property of the benefice during his term of office.

(3) The office of vicar in a team ministry shall be an ecclesiastical office constituted by the scheme and shall be held by each holder thereof for the specified term of years; and the vicar shall, during that term, have the same security of tenure of his office as an incumbent of a benefice, and shall not be affected by a vacancy in the benefice of the rector.

(3A) A person ordained to the office of deacon who is authorised under subsection (1)(b) by licence of the bishop—

(a) to serve in a team ministry as a member of the team; and
(b) for the purposes of the team ministry to perform, so far as consistent with the office of deacon, all such offices and services as may be performed by an incumbent,

shall serve for the specified term of years; and any such person shall, during that term, have the same security of tenure of his office as an incumbent of a benefice, and shall not be affected by a vacancy in the benefice of the rector.

(3B) Any other person who is authorised under subsection (1)(b) by licence of the bishop to serve in a team ministry as a member of the team shall serve for a term of years to be specified in the licence, but no person shall be authorised as aforesaid unless he has been nominated for that purpose by the rector with the consent of a majority of the other members of the team and of each parochial church council concerned:

Provided that it shall not be necessary for the person concerned to be nominated for that purpose by the rector as aforesaid where that person is authorised to serve in a team ministry for a period immediately following a period of service in the team ministry.

(4) A pastoral scheme establishing a team ministry may designate the first rector (who may be the existing incumbent) or the first holder of any office of vicar but, subject to any such provision,—

(a) the rector shall be presented or collated to the benefice, as the circumstances require, in accordance with paragraph 1 of Schedule 3 and the provisions of the scheme made thereunder;
(b) the vicar or vicars shall be chosen in accordance with paragraph 2 of that Schedule, shall be appointed to the office by licence of the bishop under seal and, unless the bishop otherwise directs, shall be publicly admitted in a church in the area.

(5) Where a pastoral scheme designates a person as the first holder of the office of vicar in a team ministry, the bishop shall offer to issue a licence appointing him to the office, and if that person does not accept the offer within one month after it is made to him, the designation shall cease to have effect.

(6) The term of years for which the office of rector or vicar in a team ministry or for which a deacon to whom subsection (3A) applies is authorised to serve in a team ministry is held may, subject to any provision in a pastoral scheme, be extended by licence of the bishop under seal for a further term or further terms not exceeding, in the case of any one extension, the specified term of years, but any such extension shall be personal to the rector, vicar or deacon concerned and not affect the term of office of subsequent holders.

(7) The rector in a team ministry shall have a general responsibility for the cure of souls in the area of the benefice, which may be subject to any special cure or special responsibility given to a vicar as hereinafter provided, and shall be responsible for the leadership of the team; and the scheme may make further provision as to the relationship of the rector and other members of the team ministry.

(8) A vicar in a team ministry shall by virtue of his office, but subject to his licence, have authority to perform in the area of the benefice all such offices and services as may be performed by an incumbent, and the scheme or, subject to the scheme, the bishop's licence may—

(a) assign to a vicar a special cure of souls in respect of a part of the said area and, if appropriate, the name of vicar of a church in that part;
(b) assign to a vicar a special responsibility for a particular pastoral function;
(c) provide that any such special cure or responsibility shall be independent of the rector's general responsibility;
(d) assign to a vicar a general responsibility to be shared with the rector for a cure of souls in the area as a whole;

and, if any such provision as aforesaid is made by the bishop's licence, it may (subject to the scheme) be varied or revoked, with the consent of the rector and the vicar concerned, by a subsequent licence under seal.

(8A) A pastoral scheme establishing a team ministry or, subject to the scheme, the bishop's licence may assign to any member of the team who is not a member of the team chapter a special responsibility for pastoral care in respect of a part of the area of the benefice, so far as consistent with that member's office; and, if any such provision as aforesaid is made by the bishop's licence, it may (subject to the scheme) be varied or revoked by a subsequent licence under seal.

(9) The Ecclesiastical Jurisdiction Measures 1963 and 1974 shall apply to vicars in a team ministry and deacons in a team ministry to whom subsection (3A) applies as if they were incumbents of the benefice for the area of which the team ministry is established.

(9A) The Ecclesiastical Offices (Age Limit) Measure 1975 shall apply to deacons in a team ministry to whom subsection (3A) applies as if they were vicars in the team ministry and, accordingly, no person shall be capable of being authorised by licence of the bishop to serve in a team ministry as such a deacon if at the time of the issue of the licence he has attained the age of seventy years.

(10) The rector in a team ministry shall convene meetings of the team at regular intervals for the purpose of discussing and reaching a common mind on all matters of general concern or special interest to the team ministry and, unless a pastoral scheme otherwise provides, the rector shall preside, except that if he requests otherwise or is absent a deputy chairman appointed by the meeting shall preside.

(10A) Any member of the team in a team ministry may, by notice in writing, request the rector to convene a team meeting under subsection (10) to be held within the period of twenty-eight days following the service of the notice; and, if the rector fails to comply with such a request, that member may himself convene the meeting.

(11) Sub-paragraphs (1), (2), (3), (5) and (6) of paragraph 4 of Schedule 3 shall apply to parochial church meetings and parochial church councils in the area of a benefice for which a team ministry is established, and for the election of district church councils and churchwardens, and, if the area comprises more than one parish, for establishing a team council and empowering that council to exercise certain powers.

(12) Where two or more benefices are, or are to be, held in plurality, and a team ministry is established or is to be established for the area of one of those benefices, a pastoral scheme may provide for extending the operation of the team ministry, so long as the plurality continues, to the area of any other benefice so held, and subsections (7), (8) and (11) and the provisions of Schedule 3 therein referred to shall have effect as if the references to the area of the benefice were references to the combined area of the benefices concerned.

(13) Where the rector in a team ministry established for any benefice receives a statutory notice concerning ecclesiastical property in the benefice, he shall—

(a) keep every member of the team informed of matters arising from the notice;
(b) afford every member of the team an opportunity to express views thereon before taking any action in response to the notice; and
(c) have regard to those views before taking any such action.

(14) Where a benefice for which a team ministry is established becomes vacant the bishop may appoint a person holding the office of vicar in the team ministry to act as rector in the team ministry for the purposes of subsections (3B), (7) and (10), and any person so appointed shall be deemed to hold the office of rector in the team ministry for the purposes of those subsections while the benefice remains vacant.

(15) In this section "specified term of years" in relation to a team ministry means such term of years as may for the time being be specified for the team ministry for the purposes of subsections (2), (3) and (3A) by a pastoral scheme or pastoral order; and in the case of a team ministry for which no term of years is so specified seven years shall be deemed to be the specified term of years for the purposes of those subsections.

(16) In this section—

"ecclesiastical property" has the same meaning as in section 12(3) of the Acquisition of Land Act 1981;

"statutory notice" means a notice given in pursuance of any enactment or of any instrument made under an enactment.

Section 18

SCHEDULE 2

Transitional Provisions

1. The provisions of section 1 above shall not affect the freehold tenure or term of office or service of any person who—

(a) is a member of a team in a team ministry immediately before the coming into operation of those provisions; or

(b) has been designated as the rector in a team ministry by a pastoral scheme made by the Church Commissioners and confirmed by Order in Council under Part I of the 1983 Measure before the coming into operation of those provisions,

but, except as provided above, the provisions of this Measure shall have effect notwithstanding any provision to the contrary in a pastoral scheme or pastoral order.

2. A provision which could not have been made by a pastoral scheme under the 1983 Measure as in force before the coming into operation of section 3 above shall not be included in a pastoral scheme which is pending at the coming into operation of that section.

3. A provision which could not have been made by a pastoral order under the 1983 Measure as in force before the coming into operation of section 5 above shall not be included in a pastoral order which is pending at the coming into operation of that section.

4. For the purposes of this Schedule a pastoral scheme or pastoral order shall be deemed to be pending at the coming into operation of a provision of this Measure if it has at least reached the following stage of the procedure applicable to that scheme or order, that is to say the submission to the Church Commissioners of proposals—

(a) under section 3(9) or 14(1) of the 1983 Measure; or

(b) under the said section 3(9) as applied by section 13(5) of that Measure.

5. Nothing in this Schedule shall be taken as prejudicing the application of sections 16 and 17 of the Interpretation Act 1978.

CHURCH OF ENGLAND (MISCELLANEOUS PROVISIONS) MEASURE 1995

(1995 No. 2)

ARRANGEMENT OF SECTIONS

A Measure passed by the General Synod of the Church of England to make it lawful for Church of Ireland ministers to officiate in England; to provide for the appointment of lay canons in the Cathedral Church of Christ in Oxford; to enable the designation of archdeacon emeritus to be conferred; to amend the law relating to the resignation of deans, residentiary canons and archdeacons; to amend section 27 of the Ecclesiastical Commissioners Act 1840, section 6 of the Church Commissioners Measure 1947, the Schedule to the Church Funds Investment Measure 1958, section 21 of the Clergy Pensions Measure 1961, sections 2, 3 and 27 of and Schedule 1 to the Ecclesiastical Jurisdiction Measure 1963, section 20 of the Parochial Registers and Records Measure 1978, sections 9, 44, 51 and 87 of and Schedule 1 to the Pastoral Measure 1983, section 8 of the Church of England (Miscellaneous Provisions) Measure 1983 and section 6 of the Care of Churches and Ecclesiastical Jurisdiction Measure 1991; to amend certain enactments in connection with the procedure of the General Synod; and for purposes connected therewith. [19th July 1995]

Ministers of Church of Ireland

1. It shall be lawful for persons admitted to Holy Orders by a bishop of the Church of Ireland, whether or not they hold or have held any benefice or preferment in England, to officiate in England in a church or chapel belonging to the Church of England, if invited to do so by the minister having the cure of souls of the church or chapel, without notifying the bishop of the diocese in which the church or chapel is situate for the same period and subject to the same conditions as would be applicable to them if they had been admitted to Holy Orders by the bishop of a diocese in the Church of England.

Provisions relating to Christ Church Oxford

2.—(1) It shall be lawful for the constitution and statutes of the foundation known as the Cathedral Church of Christ in Oxford to provide for the appointment of not more than two lay canons and to specify the functions of such lay canon or canons.

(2) No such lay canon shall be appointed unless the person concerned is—
(a) a communicant member of the Church of England; or
(b) a member of a church to which the Church of England (Ecumenical Relations) Measure 1988 applies and is entitled lawfully to take part in public worship in accordance with the forms of service and practice of the Church of England.

(3) The regius professorship of ecclesiastical history which, pursuant to section 6 of the Ecclesiastical Commissioners Act 1840, was annexed to a canonry in the chapter of the said Cathedral Church may, notwithstanding the provisions of that Act, be held either by a residentiary canon in the said chapter or by a lay canon appointed pursuant to subsection (1) above.

Designation of archdeacon emeritus

3. The bishop of a diocese may confer the designation of archdeacon emeritus upon any person who retires immediately after holding the office of archdeacon.

Resignation of certain office holders

4. Where a dean, residentiary canon or archdeacon wishes to resign it shall not be necessary to proceed by way of a deed, but any such resignation shall be in writing, duly signed and witnessed and sent—
(a) in the case of a dean, to Her Majesty;
(b) in the case of a residentiary canon where the canonry is in the direct patronage of Her Majesty, to Her Majesty;
(c) in the case of any other residentiary canon, to the diocesan bishop concerned; and
(d) in the case of an archdeacon, to the diocesan bishop concerned.

Amendment of Ecclesiastical Commissioners Act 1840

5. In section 27 of the Ecclesiastical Commissioners Act 1840 (qualification of deans, archdeacons and canons)—
(a) after the word "dean," there shall be inserted the word "provost,";
(b) for the words "priest's orders" there shall be substituted the words "holy orders and, in the case of a dean, provost or archdeacon, be in priest's orders at the time of the appointment".

Amendment of Church Commissioners Measure 1947

6. In section 6 of the Church Commissioners Measure 1947 for paragraph (b) (Assets Committee) there shall be substituted the following paragraph—
"(b) the Assets Committee shall comprise—
(i) the First Church Estates Commissioner;
(ii) one Commissioner, being a clerk in holy orders appointed for three years by the Board;
(iii) not less than three nor more than five lay Commissioners appointed for three years by the Archbishop of Canterbury; and
(iv) not less than one nor more than three Commissioners appointed for three years by the Archbishop of Canterbury, after consultation with the Board, from among the twenty clerks in holy orders and laymen appointed as Commissioners by the General Synod;

the persons referred to in sub-paragraphs (iii) and (iv) above being persons who in the opinion of the Archbishop are well qualified to assist in the management of the assets of the Commissioners,".

Amendment of Church Funds Investment Measure 1958

7. The Scheme contained in the Schedule to the Church Funds Investment Measure 1958 shall have effect subject to the amendments specified in the Schedule to this Measure.

Amendment of Clergy Pensions Measure 1961

8. In section 21 of the Clergy Pensions Measure 1961 (constitution of Board)—

(a) in paragraph (a) of subsection (3) the words from "of whom eight" to the end shall be omitted;

(b) in subsection (5) for the words from "Standing Committee" to the end there shall be substituted the words "General Synod in such manner as the Synod may from time to time determine".

Amendment of Ecclesiastical Jurisdiction Measure 1963

9. The Ecclesiastical Jurisdiction Measure 1963 shall have effect subject to the following amendments—

(a) in section 2 (judge of consistory court) in paragraph (5) the words "and subscribe" and "and subscription" shall be omitted;

(b) in section 3 (judges of the Arches and Chancery Courts)—

(i) in paragraphs (6) and (7) the words "and subscribe" shall be omitted;

(ii) in paragraph (8) the words "and subscription" shall be omitted;

(c) in section 27 (power of chancellor to nominate trial judge in lieu of himself) in subsection (2) the words "and subscribe" shall be omitted;

(d) in Schedule 1 (which sets out the form of the oaths to be taken by all judges) the words "AND SUBSCRIBED, AND DECLARATION TO BE MADE AND SUBSCRIBED," and the words "AND SUBSCRIBED" (where they appear elsewhere) shall be omitted.

Amendment of Parochial Registers and Records Measure 1978

10. In section 20 of the Parochial Registers and Records Measure 1978 (searches of certain register books) at the end there shall be inserted the following subsection—

"(6) This section shall so far as applicable and with the necessary modifications, apply in relation to the custody or deposit of register books of baptisms, burials or marriages provided for any cathedral or collegiate church or any other church or chapel which does not belong to a parish.".

Amendment of Pastoral Measure 1983

11. The Pastoral Measure 1983 shall have effect subject to the following amendments—

(a) in section 9 (confirmation of schemes by Order in Council) in subsection (4) after paragraph (d) there shall be inserted the word "or" and the following paragraphs—

"(e) no person has duly made written representations with respect to the draft scheme; or

(f) written representations with respect to the draft scheme have been duly made but it has not been practicable to serve any notice under subsection (1)(a),";

(b) in section 44 (appointment of Churches Conservation Trust) in subsection (5) after paragraph (a) there shall be inserted the following paragraph—

"(aa) to acquire property (including rights of way) where the Trust considers that to do so would assist it in the exercise of its powers under paragraph (a);";

(c) in section 51 (contents of redundancy schemes) in subsection (9) for the words from "being a church" to "in the case of that church" there shall be substituted the words "and the Commissioners are satisfied that a new church or place of worship is to be provided in the area of the benefice in which the first-mentioned church is situated to take the place of that church";

(d) in section 87 (general interpretation) at the end there shall be inserted the following subsection—

"(5) Any reference in this Measure to the demolition of a building shall be construed as including a reference to the demolition of part thereof.";

(e) in Schedule 1 (constitution and procedure of the pastoral committee of a diocese) in paragraph 3 after the words "suffragan bishop in the diocese" there shall be inserted the words "(not being a suffragan bishop appointed to act as a provincial episcopal visitor for the purposes of the Episcopal Ministry Act of Synod 1993)".

Amendment of Church of England (Miscellaneous Provisions) Measure 1983

12. In section 8 of the Church of England (Miscellaneous Provisions) Measure 1983 (discharge of certain functions of bishop)—

(a) in subsection (1)(a) after the words "from his diocese" there shall be inserted the words "or by reason of his forthcoming translation to another see";

(b) in subsection (2) the words "which shall not be longer than six months" shall be omitted.

Amendment of Care of Churches and Ecclesiastical Jurisdiction Measure 1991

13. In section 6 of the Care of Churches and Ecclesiastical Jurisdiction Measure 1991 (provisions relating to trees in churchyards)—

(a) in subsection (1) for the word "churchyards" there shall be substituted the words "a churchyard which the council is liable to maintain";

(b) in subsection (2)—

(i) for the words "maintainable by a parochial church council" there shall be substituted the words "which a parochial church council is liable to maintain";

(ii) for the words "maintainable by the council" there shall be substituted the words "which the council is liable to maintain".

Amendment of various enactments in connection with General Synod procedure

14. In the following enactments, that is to say—

section 6(4A) of the Clergy Pensions (Amendment) Measure 1972;
sections 2(3) and 6(4) of the Ecclesiastical Fees Measure 1986;
section 38(5) of the Patronage (Benefices) Measure 1986;
section 27(3) of the Care of Churches and Ecclesiastical Jurisdiction Measure 1991;
section 9(5) of the Incumbents (Vacation of Benefices) (Amendment) Measure 1993;

in paragraph (b) in each case the words from "and at least" to the end of that paragraph shall be omitted.

Short title, commencement and extent

15.—(1) This Measure may be cited as the Church of England (Miscellaneous Provisions) Measure 1995.

(2) This Measure shall come into force on such date as the Archbishops of Canterbury and York may jointly appoint; and different dates may be appointed for different provisions.

(3) Subject to subsections (4) and (5) below this Measure shall extend to the whole of the provinces of Canterbury and York, except the Channel Islands and the Isle of Man.

(4) This Measure (except section 2) may be applied to the Channel Islands, as defined in the Channel Islands (Church Legislation) Measures 1931 and 1957, or either of them, in accordance with those Measures.

(5) Sections 6 and 8 above shall extend to the Isle of Man and, if an Act of Tynwald or an instrument made under an Act of Tynwald so provides, the remainder of this Measure except sections 2 and 5 shall extend to the Isle of Man subject to such modifications, if any, as may be specified in such Act of Tynwald or other instrument.

Section 8

SCHEDULE

Amendment of Church Funds Investment Measure 1958

1. The Scheme contained in the Schedule to the Church Funds Investment Measure 1958 shall be amended as follows.

2. In paragraph 1 (definitions)—

(a) after the definition of "Diocesan Authority" there shall be inserted the following definition—

" "Dividend Record Date" means, as regards any Investment Fund, a valuation date on which the income of that Investment Fund is allocated for distribution or accumulation in accordance with this Scheme;";

(b) after the definition of "The Holder of a Share" there shall be inserted the following definition—

" "Income Reserve" means an Income Reserve created under sub-paragraph (4) of paragraph 11 hereof;";

(c) in the definition of "The Measure" for the figure "1957" there shall be substituted the figure "1958".

3. In paragraph 6 (shares in Investment Funds)—

(a) for sub-paragraph (1) there shall be substituted the following sub-paragraphs—

"(1) For convenience in recording the respective interests of the Holders of the Contributing Funds in an Investment Fund each Investment Fund shall comprise Shares of either or both of two classes, namely—

(a) Income Shares, in respect of which attributable income shall be distributed or retained (or both distributed and retained) in the Income Reserve in accordance with this Scheme; and

(b) Accumulation Shares, in respect of which attributable income shall be accumulated by investment as capital of the Investment Fund in accordance with this Scheme.

(1A) Where an Investment Fund comprises both Income Shares and Accumulation Shares, each class of Shares shall be referable to one of two parts of the value of the Investment Fund.

(1B) Each Income Share shall represent an equal undivided part of the beneficial interest in the Investment Fund or, as the case may be, that part of the value of the Investment Fund to which Income Shares are referable.

(1C) Each Accumulation Share shall represent an equal undivided part of the beneficial interest in the Investment Fund or, as the case may be, that part of the value of the Investment Fund to which Accumulation Shares are referable.

(1D) Such Shares shall be recorded in the names of the Holders for the time being of the Contributing Funds in books to be kept for that purpose by the Central Board. The number of Shares so recorded may comprise decimal parts of a Share to two places of decimals and reference in this Scheme to a number of Shares shall be construed as including references to a number which comprises such decimal parts.";

(b) after sub-paragraph (3) there shall be inserted the following sub-paragraph—

"(3A) The Central Board may at any time sub-divide the Shares of either class.".

4. In paragraph 7 (initial contributions: division into Shares)—

(a) after the words "number of Shares" there shall be inserted the words "of each class";

(b) after the words "Such Shares" there shall be inserted the words "shall be denominated as Income Shares or as Accumulation Shares and the number of such Shares".

5. In paragraph 8 (subsequent contributions and withdrawals)—

(a) in sub-paragraph (1)—

(i) for the words "one or more complete Shares" there shall be substituted the words "a number of Shares of either or both classes";

(ii) after the words "number of Shares" there shall be inserted the words "of the relevant class or classes";

(b) in sub-paragraph (2) after the words "value of the" there shall be inserted the word "relevant";

(c) in sub-paragraph (3)—

(i) after the words "Holder of Shares" there shall be inserted the words "of either class";

(ii) after the words "basic value of the Share or Shares" there shall be inserted the words "of either class";

(iii) after the words "basic value of a Share" there shall be inserted the words "of the class concerned";

(iv) after the words "Investment fund the number of Shares" there shall be inserted the words "of the class concerned";

(v) after the words "and the number of Shares" there shall be inserted the words "of the class concerned";

(vi) after the words "reduced by the number of" there shall be inserted the word "such";

(d) in sub-paragraph (5)—

(i) after the word "Shares" there shall be inserted the words "of each class";

(ii) after the words "amount per Share" in both places where they occur there shall be inserted the words "of the same class".

6. After paragraph 8 there shall be inserted the following paragraph—

"CONVERSION

8A. Where an Investment Fund comprises two classes of Shares and subject to compliance with such conditions as the Central Board may from time to time prescribe with regard to the notice to be given on conversion, the Central Board shall at the request of the Holder of any Share in an Investment Fund at any valuation date convert such number of Shares of either class recorded as held by the Holder as the Holder may require into Shares of the other class, being Shares which on that valuation date are of the basic value determined in accordance with this Scheme as nearly as possible equal to the basic value so determined of the Shares being converted. The proportion of the value of the Investment Fund attributable to each class of Shares shall immediately after that valuation date be adjusted accordingly.".

7. In paragraph 9 (valuations)—

(a) in sub-paragraph (1)—

(i) after the words "Investment Fund" there shall be inserted the words "and each class of Shares therein";

(ii) for the words "in advance each valuation date" there shall be substituted the words "the frequency of valuation dates";

(iii) for the words "to be valued on that date" there shall be substituted the word "concerned";

(b) in sub-paragraph (2)—

(i) after the words "of an Investment Fund" there shall be inserted the words "or of either class of Share therein";

(ii) for the words "on the valuation date as published in relation to the relevant Stock Exchange" there shall be substituted the words "on the relevant Stock Exchange on the valuation date";

(iii) for the words "no published price" there shall be substituted the words "no such price available";

(iv) for the words "there is a published price" there shall be substituted the words "such price is available";

(c) after sub-paragraph (2) there shall be inserted the following sub-paragraph—

"(2A) The amount of the Income Reserve referred to in sub-paragraph (4) of paragraph 11 hereof shall be included in that part of the value of the Investment Fund that is attributable to Income Shares only and shall be available for distribution to Holders of Income Shares only,";

(d) for sub-paragraph (3) there shall be substituted the following sub-paragraph—

"(3) On any valuation date, the basic value of a Share of either class shall be arrived at by—

(a) calculating the value of the Investment Fund or, where there are two classes of Shares, that part of the value of the Investment Fund attributable to Shares of the class concerned on the basis—

(i) that the value of the Investment Fund, excluding the amount of the Income Reserve, shall be apportioned between the two classes of Share in the same proportion as they bore to each other immediately after the previous valuation date, subject only, in the case of a valuation date which is also a Dividend Record Date, to adjustment for any income determined to be distributed or transferred to the Income Reserve or accumulated; and

(ii) that the amount of the Income Reserve shall be dealt with in accordance with sub-paragraph (2A) above;

(b) dividing the same by the number of Shares of the class concerned into which the Investment Fund is divided; and

(c) rounding off the resulting figure to the nearest 0.01p.".

8. In paragraph 10 (certificates as to value)—

(a) after the words "of an Investment Fund" there shall be inserted the words "or of either class of Shares therein";

(b) after the words "of a Share" there shall be inserted the words "of either class".

9. In paragraph 11 (income)—

(a) in sub-paragraph (2) at the end there shall be inserted the words "(in respect of Income Shares) and for allocation (in respect of Accumulation Shares) in accordance with sub-paragraphs (5) and (6) of this paragraph";

(b) for sub-paragraph (3) there shall be substituted the following sub-paragraphs—

"(3) In respect of each Dividend Record Date the Central Board shall determine the amount of the income and the apportionment of it between Income and Accumulation Shares in accordance with the relative proportion in terms of value that each class of Share bears to the total value of that Investment Fund (excluding the amount of the Income Reserve) on the Dividend Record Date before the issue or cancellation of Shares (if any) and subject to sub-paragraph (4)(d) of this paragraph.

(4)(a) For the purpose of avoiding fluctuations in the amounts of income distributed in respect of Income Shares, the Central Board may create out of the income attributable to Income Shares and maintain in the accounts of the Investment Fund an Income Reserve in accordance with the provisions of this sub-paragraph.

(b) The Central Board may deduct from the amount of income determined to be available to be distributed in respect of Income Shares under sub-paragraph (7) of this paragraph for any distribution period not more than half of that amount; and where they do so they shall credit to the Income Reserve the amount deducted.

(c) The Central Board may add to the net income to be distributed in respect of Income Shares all or any part of the amount of the Income Reserve.

(d) Any income attributable to the amount of the Income Reserve shall be treated as income of the Income Shares and dealt with accordingly.

(5) Each distribution of income attributable to Income Shares shall be made as soon as practicable after the Dividend Record Date in question to the Holders of the Income Shares in proportion to the numbers of such Shares recorded in their names on that Dividend Record Date (before the recording of any new contribution or withdrawals on such Dividend Record Date) and the amount determined to be distributed but not yet withdrawn from the Investment Fund (but not the amount determined to be transferred to the Income Reserve) shall be treated as a charge on the Investment Fund and shall accordingly be deducted in arriving at the value of the Investment Fund on and after that Dividend Record Date.

(6) Each allocation of income attributable to Accumulation Shares shall be made on or as soon as practicable after the Dividend Record Date in question and as of that Dividend Record Date shall become capital and shall be retained as part of the Investment Fund.

(7) The amounts available for distribution or allocation under sub-paragraphs (5) or (6) of this paragraph shall be circulated by the Central Board adjusting the income of an Investment Fund by—

(i) adding the aggregate amount of the Income Element (as hereinafter determined) included in contributions to the Investment Fund on the issue of Shares during the distribution period concerned;

(ii) subtracting the aggregate amount of the Income Element included in the amounts paid during such distribution period on the withdrawal of Shares by the Holders; and

(iii) subtracting the aggregate amount of costs and expenses for the distribution period to be deducted in accordance with this Scheme.

For the purpose of this sub-paragraph, the Income Element included in an issue of Shares means that element of the amount of cash or value of other assets transferred to the Investment Fund which for the purpose of securing equality of treatment between the Holders of Shares falls to be treated by the Central Board as income of the Investment Fund for the distribution period within which such issue of Shares takes effect; and the Income Element included in the amount payable on a withdrawal of Shares means that element of the amount of cash paid (or value of the assets transferred) on a withdrawal which falls to be treated by the Central Board as a payment out of the income of the Investment Fund for the distribution period within which occurs the valuation date on or as of which the Shares are withdrawn."

10. In paragraph 12 (costs and expenses) for the words "retain out of" there shall be substituted the words "deduct from".

11. In paragraph 14 (accounts and information)—

(a) after the words "the amount per" there shall be inserted the word "Income";

(b) after the words "distribute as income" there shall be inserted the words "and the amount of income per Accumulation Share which the Central Board had as on that date determined to allocate";

(c) after the words "determined to distribute" there shall be inserted the words "or allocate";

(d) after the words "pursuant to" there shall be inserted the words "sub-paragraphs (1) and (2) of".

12. In paragraph 16 (holding of investments) the words "trust corporation as" shall be omitted.

13. In paragraph 18 (winding up of an Investment Fund) for the words "in proportion to their holdings of such Shares" there shall be substituted the words "(without prejudice to sub-paragraph (3) of paragraph 9 hereof) in proportion to the value of the Investment Fund represented by the Shares held by each such Holder".

CURRENT LAW STATUTES 1995

COMMENCEMENT DIARY

This table notes alphabetically by statute the commencement of statutes from January 1995 as initiated by Orders and by statutory provisions. This is up to date to **March 11, 1996** (Orders received). The full texts of the Orders can be found in the Commencement Orders section of Current Law Statutes.

Act Affected	Provision Brought Into Force	Commencement Date	Authority
Activity Centres (Young Persons' Safety) Act 1995 (c. 15)	All provisions	August 28, 1995	s.5
Agricultural Tenancies Act 1995 (c. 8)	All provisions	September 1, 1995	s.41(2)
Appropriation Act 1995 (c. 19)	All provisions	July 19, 1995	Royal Assent
Antarctic Act 1994 (c. 15)	ss.1 and 2, ss.8–32, s.33 (part), ss.34–36	November 1, 1995	S.I. 1995 No. 2748 (c. 58)
Atomic Energy Authority Act 1995 (c. 37)	All provisions	November 8, 1995	Royal Assent
Building Societies (Joint Account Holders) Act 1995 (c. 5)	All provisions	May 1, 1995	Royal Assent
Carers (Recognition and Services) Act 1995 (c. 12)	All provisions	April 1, 1996	s.5(2)
Charities Act 1992 (c. 41)	Pt. II (ss.58–64) [except that for the purposes of exercising the power to make regulations under ss.59 or 64 it shall come into force on November 28, 1994]	March 1, 1995	S.I. 1994 No. 3023 (C.69)
Charities Act 1993 (c. 10)	ss.41–49 (for the purposes only of making orders or regulations under those sections)	October 15, 1995	S.I. 1995 No. 2695 (C.54)

Act Affected	Provision Brought Into Force	Commencement Date	Authority
Charities Act 1993 (c. 10)	All remaining provisions (ss.41–49, 69, Sched. 6, para. 21(3))	March 1, 1996	S.I. 1995 No. 2695 (C.54)
Charities (Amendment) Act 1995 (c. 45)	All provisions	November 8, 1995	Royal Assent
Child Support Act 1995 (c. 34)	ss.29, 30(1)–(4)(6)	July 19, 1995	s.30(3)
Child Support Act 1995 (c. 34)	ss.18–21, 23 (part), 26(1)–(3)(4)(b)(5) (6), 27, 28, 30(5) (part), Sched. 3, paras. 2, 3(2), 4, 8, 10, 14, 15, 16, 19	September 4, 1995	S.I. 1995 No. 2302 (C.46)
Child Support Act 1995 (c. 34)	s.12(1), (5) (part), (7) (part), 23 (part), 24, 25, 26(4)(c), 30(5), Sched. 3, para. 1 (part), 3(1), 11, 12	October 1, 1995	S.I. 1995 No. 2302 (C.46)
Child Support Act 1995 (c. 34)	Pt. I: ss.16, 17, para. 18 of Sched. 3 (part), 30(5) (part) Pt. II: ss.9 (part), 11, 12 (remainder), 13, 14, 15	December 18, 1995 January 22, 1996	S.I. 1995 No. 3262 (C.76) S.I. 1995 No. 3262 (C.76)
Children (Scotland) Act 1995 (c. 36)	s.105(1)(2)(6)–(10)	July 19, 1995	s.105(1)(b)
Children (Scotland) Act 1995 (c. 36)	s.1(1) to (3) (part), 15, 35, 37, 99, 103, 104, 105(4) (part), 105(5) (part), Scheds. 4 (part), 5 (part)	November 1, 1995	S.I. 1995 No. 2787 (C.57) (s.205)
Civil Evidence (Family Mediation) (Scotland) Act 1995 (c. 6)	All provisions	February 19, 1996	S.I. 1996 No. 125 (C.2) (S.9)
Coal Industry Act 1994 (c. 21)	s.24	January 31, 1995	S.I. 1995 No. 159 (C.7)
Coal Industry Act 1994 (c. 21)	Sched. 11, Pt. III (part)	March 1, 1995	S.I. 1995 No. 273 (C.9)
Coal Industry Act 1994 (c. 21)	s.67(8) (part), Sched. 11, Pt. III (part)	June 30, 1995	S.I. 1995 No. 1507 (C.32)

Act Affected	Provision Brought Into Force	Commencement Date	Authority
Coal Industry Act 1994 (c. 21)	s.23(1)(a)(b)(c)(d) (Appointed day)	June 30, 1995	S.I. 1995 No. 1507 (C.32)
Commonwealth Development Corporation Act 1995 (c. 9)	All provisions	June 28, 1995	Royal Assent
Companies Act 1989 (c. 40)	ss.140(1)–(6), 145 (part), 212 (part), Sched. 19, para. 20, Sched. 24 (part)	July 3, 1995	S.I. 1995 No. 1352 (C.27)
Companies Act 1989 (c. 40)	ss.171, 176, 181	July 4, 1995	S.I. 1995 No. 1591 (C.34)
Consolidated Fund Act 1995 (c. 2)	All provisions	March 23, 1995	Royal Assent
Consolidated Fund (No. 2) Act 1995 (c. 54)	All provisions	December 19, 1995	Royal Assent
Courts and Legal Services Act 1990 (c. 41)	s.82	March 6, 1995	S.I. 1995 No. 641 (C.16)
Criminal Appeal Act 1995 (c. 35)	ss.1, 2, 4, 6, 7 (part), 26–28, 29 (part), 30, 31 (part), 32–34, Sched. 2: paras. 1, 2, 4(1)–(3), 4(5), 5, 6, 12(1)–(4), 12(6), 15, 17 Sched. 3 (part)	January 1, 1996	S.I. 1995 No. 3061 (C.69)
Criminal Injuries Compensation Act 1995 (c. 53)	All provisions	November 8, 1995	Royal Assent
Criminal Justice Act 1991 (c. 53)	ss.12, 13	January 9, 1995	S.I. 1994 No. 3191 (C.77)
Criminal Justice Act 1993 (c. 36)	ss.24(12)–(15) (Scotland only), 27, 28 (both England & Wales only), 36–43 (all N.I. only), Sched. 5, paras. 3, 17(2) (3) (6) (7), Sched. 6, (part) (all N.I. only)	February 3, 1995	S.I. 1995 No. 43 (C.3)
Criminal Justice Act 1993 (c. 36)	s.79(13) (part), Sched. 5, para. 1	August 14, 1995	S.I. 1995 No. 1958 (C.39)

Act Affected	Provision Brought Into Force	Commencement Date	Authority
Criminal Justice and Public Order Act 1994 (c. 33)	ss.16, 151, 168 (part), Sched. 9, paras. 34, 41, Sched. 10, paras. 40, 64 (part), 69, Sched. 11 (part)	January 9, 1995	S.I. 1994 No. 3192 (C.78)
Criminal Justice and Public Order Act 1994 (c. 33)	s.52	January 11, 1995	S.I. 1994 No. 3258 (C.82)
Criminal Justice and Public Order Act 1994 (c. 33)	s.53	February 2, 1995	S.I. 1995 No. 24 (C.1)
Criminal Justice and Public Order Act 1994 (c. 33)	ss.17, 18, 23, 24, 31–33, 40–43, 46–51, 64(1)–(3) (in part), 66(6) (10)–(13), 67(3)–(5) (8) (9), 72–74, 84–88, 91, 92, 102–117, 129–133, 134(1) (2), (3) (part), (4)–(6), 135–141, 152–155, 157, 160–164, 168 (part), 169, 170, Scheds. 6, 8, 9 (part), 10 (part), 11 (part)	February 3, 1995	S.I. 1995 No. 127 (C.4)
Criminal Justice and Public Order Act 1994 (c. 33)	ss.25–30, 34–39, 54–60, 62, 64(4)(5) (6), 66(1)–(5), (7)–(9), 67(1)(2)(6) (7), 118–125, 156, 168 (part), Scheds. 3, 7, 9, para. 37(3), Sched. 10, paras. 1–3, 5, 6, 10, 15, 19–23, 32–34, 41–44, 48, 51, 54–58, 61, 62, 67, 71, Sched. 11 (part)	April 10, 1995	S.I. 1995 No. 721 (C.19)
Criminal Justice and Public Order Act 1994 (c. 33)	s.19	May 30, 1995	S.I. 1995 No. 1378 (C.29)
Criminal Justice and Public Order Act 1994 (c. 33)	s.134(3) (remainder)	June 1, 1995	S.I. 1995 No. 127 (C.4)
Criminal Justice and Public Order Act 1994 (c. 33)	ss.75, 76, Sched. 10, para. 53	August 24, 1995	S.I. 1995 No. 1957 (C.38)

Act Affected	Provision Brought Into Force	Commencement Date	Authority
Criminal Justice and Public Order Act 1994 (c. 33)	ss.45, 168 (part, remainder), Sched. 5, Sched. 10, para. 65	September 4, 1995	S.I. 1995 No. 1957 (C.38)
Criminal Justice and Public Order Act 1994 (c. 33)	s.89	November 1, 1995	S.I. 1995 No. 1957 (C.38)
Criminal Justice (Scotland) Act 1995 (c.20)	ss.22(1)(3)(4)(7)(9), 35, 42, 43, 65, 117(1) (part), (2) (part), 118, Sched. 6, para. 87, Sched. 7, Pt. 1 (part)	September 26, 1995	S.I. 1995 No. 2295 (C.45) (S.171)
Criminal Law (Consolidation) (Scotland) Act 1995 (c. 39)	All provisions	April 1, 1996	s.53(2)
Criminal Procedure (Consequential Provisions) (Scotland) 1995 (c. 40)	All provisions	April 1, 1996	s.7(2)
Criminal Procedure (Scotland) Act 1995 (c. 46)	All provisions	April 1, 1996	s.309(2)
Crown Agents Act 1995 (c. 24)	All provisions	July 19, 1995	Royal Assent
Deregulation and Contracting Out Act 1994 (c. 40)	ss.8, 11, 19, 35, 36(1), 39 (part), 51, 58, 62, 64, 67, 68 (part), 81 (part), Scheds. 7, 10, 11, paras. 1 (part), 2 (part), Sched. 14, para. 1 (part), Sched. 17 (part)	January 3, 1995	S.I. 1994 No. 3188 (C.76)
Deregulation and Contracting Out Act 1994 (c. 40)	ss.7, 9, 10, 12, 15, 16, 17, 20, 21, 31, 39 (part), Pt. II (ss.69–79), 81 (part), Scheds. 2–4, 8, 9, 11 (part), 17 (part)	January 3, 1995	s.82(2)
Deregulation and Contracting Out Act 1994 (c. 40)	s.60	April 1, 1995	S.I. 1994 No. 3188 (C.76)

Act Affected	Provision Brought Into Force	Commencement Date	Authority
Deregulation and Contracting Out Act 1994 (c. 40)	ss.13(1)(2) (part), 39 (part), Scheds. 5, 6, paras. 1 (part), 2 (part), Sched. 11, para. 6	July 1, 1995	S.I. 1995 No. 1433 (C.31)
Deregulation and Contracting Out Act 1994 (c. 40)	ss.13(2) (remainder), 39 (part), Scheds. 6 (remainder), 11, para. 10	November 1, 1995	S.I. 1995 No. 1433 (C.31)
Deregulation and Contracting Out Act 1994 (c. 40)	All remaining provisions	January, 1, 1996	S.I. 1995 No. 2835 (C.68)
Disability Discrimination Act 1995 (c. 50)	s.70(1), (2), (3), (6), (8)	November 8, 1995	s.70(2)
Disability Discrimination Act 1995 (c. 50)	ss.50, 51, 52, Sched. 5	January 1, 1996	S.I. 1995 No. 3330 (C.78)
Drug Trafficking Act 1994 (c. 37)	All provisions	February 3, 1995	s.69(2)
Education Act 1993 (c. 35)	ss.279 (remainder), 307(1) (part) (3) (part), Sched. 19, paras. 103, 104, 107 (part), Sched. 21	April 1, 1995	S.I. 1994 No. 1558 (C.28)
Education Act 1994 (c. 30)	s.22(3)–(5)	April 1, 1995	S.I. 1994 No. 2204 (C.46)
Environment Act 1995 (c. 25)	ss.74, 125, Sched. 22, paras. 76(8)(a), 135	July 19, 1995	Royal Assent, s.125(3)
Environment Act 1995 (c. 25)	ss.1, 3(2)–(8), 4, 7, 9, 12, 37(1)(2)(9), 38–40, 43–52, 56, 120(1) (part) (4)–(6), 121–124	July 28, 1995	S.I. 1995 No. 1983 (C.40)
Environment Act 1995 (c. 25)	Pt.III (except s.78), Sched. 7, para. 7(2), Sched. 10	September 19, 1995	s.125(2)
Environment Act 1995 (c. 25)	ss.41 (part), 42, 57 (part), s.58 (part), 93–95, 97–103, 105 (part), 116 (part), 120(1) (part) (3) (part)	September 21, 1995	S.I. 1995 No. 1983 (C.40)
Environment Act 1995 (c. 25)	ss.20, 21, 22, 23, 30, 31, 32, 36, 59 (part), 120(1) (part)	October 12, 1995	S.I. 1995 No. 2649 (C.52) (S.199)

Act Affected	Provision Brought Into Force	Commencement Date	Authority
Environment Act 1995 (c. 25)	s.96(1), (5), (6), Scheds. 13, 14 (part), ss. 96(2), 96(4) (part), 120(3) (part)	November 1, 1995	S.I. 1995 No. 2765 (C.56)
Environment Act 1995 (c. 25)	s.78 (part), Sched. 10, para. 32(2) (part)	November 23, 1995	S.I. 1995 No. 2950 (C.65)
Environment Act 1995 (c. 25)	s.78 (part), s.115(1) (part), s.115(2) (part), s.115 (3), (4), (6) (part)	April 1, 1996	S.I. 1995 No. 2950 (C.65)
Environment Act 1995 (c. 25)	ss.5(2), (5), 41 (part), 55(7)–(10), 80, 87–89, 90 (part), 91, 105 (part), 117, 118(1)–(3), (4) (part), (5) (part), (6), 119, 120(1) (part), (3) (part), Scheds. 11, paras. 2, 3, 5, Sched. 15, paras. 3, 5(1), Sched. 22, paras. 2, 13, 36, 37(2)(b), 43, 44, 67, 102, 103, 232(1), Sched. 24 (part)	February 1, 1996	S.I. 1996 No. 186 (C.3)

Act Affected	Provision Brought Into Force	Commencement Date	Authority
Environment Act 1995 (c. 25)	ss.2, 3(1), 5(1), (3), (4), 6, 8, 10, 11, 13–19, 25–29, 33–35, 37(3)–(8), 41 (remainder), 53, 54, 55(1)–(6), 81, 92, 104, 105 (part), 106–114, 115 (remainder), 120(1) (part), (2) (part), (3) (part), Sched. 15, paras. 1, 2, 4, 5(2), (3), 6–12, 14(2), (3), 6–12, 14(2), (3), 15, 16, 18, 19, 21–24, Sched. 22 paras. 1, 3, 5–12, 14, 17–27(a), 28, 29(1) (remainder), 29(2)–(20), 21(9)(ii), (23)–(25), (27)–(35), 30, 32–35, 37(3), (5)–(8), 40, 41, 45, 46(1)–(4), (6)–(11), 47–50, 51(4), 52, 54–66, 68(1), (2) (part), (3), (4), (6), (70)(1), (2), 72(2), 73(1), (2) (part) (3)–(6), 74 (part), 75, 76(2), (4)–(7), (8)(b), 77, 78, 80(3), 82 (remainder), 83–87, 90, 93, 94, 96–101, 103 (remainder), 104–132, 133(2), 134, 136, 140, 141, 144–146, 148–152, 154–160, 164–168, 171–181, 184, 185, 187 (2), 188–191, 193–212, 213(a), (4)(5), 214–222, 223(1)(a) (b) (2), 224–231, 233, Sched. 23, paras. 1–6, 8–10, 12, 13, 14(1)–(4), (7), (8) (part), 16–24, Sched. 24 (part)	April 1, 1996	S.I. 1996 No. 186 (C.3)
Environment Act 1995 (c. 25)	ss.105 (part), 120(2) (part) (3) (part)	January 1, 1999	S.I. 1995 No. 1988 (C.40)

Act Affected	Provision Brought Into Force	Commencement Date	Authority
Environmental Protection Act 1990 (c. 43)	ss.33 (remainder) (part), 35–40 (remainder) (part), 42 (remainder) (part), 43 (remainder) (part), 44 (part), 57 (part), 162(1) (part) (2) (part)	April 1, 1995 [see full text of S.I.]	S.I. 1994 No. 1096 (C.18) as amended by S.I. 1994 Nos. 2487 (C.49) and 3234 (C.81)
Environmental Protection Act 1990 (c. 43)	s.62	August 11, 1995	S.I. 1995 No. 2152 (C.43)
European Communities (Finance) Act 1995 (c. 1)	All provisions	January 16, 1995	Royal Assent
Finance Act 1989 (c. 26)	s.165(2)	May 20, 1995	S.I. 1994 No. 2508 (C.50)
Finance Act 1993 (c. 34)	s.4(2)(b)(d)(3)	January 1, 1995	S.I. 1994 No. 2968 (C.67)
Finance Act 1993 (c. 34)	s.165	March 23, 1995	S.I. 1994 No. 3224 (C.79)
Finance Act 1993 (c. 34)	s.11	December 1, 1995	S.I. 1994 No. 2715 (C.55)
Finance Act 1994 (c. 9)	Pt. I, Chap. II, (ss.7–19) Scheds. 4, 5, 26, Pt. III (all in remainder)	January 1, 1995	S.I. 1994 No. 2679 (C.59)
Finance Act 1994 (c. 9)	Pt. IV, Chap. II (ss.147–177)	March 23, 1995	S.I. 1994 No. 3225 (C.80)
Finance Act 1994 (c. 9)	subs. (3), (4)(b) of s.105	January 1, 1996	S.I. 1995 No. 3125 (C.72)
Finance Act 1995 (c. 4)	All provisions	May 1, 1995	Royal Assent
Finance Act 1995 (c. 4)	s.24 (Appointed day)	June 1, 1995	S.I. 1995 No. 1374 (C.28)
Finance Act 1995 (c. 4)	Sched. 12, para. 4(3) (Appointed day)	July 31, 1995	S.I. 1995 No. 1778 (C.35)
Finance Act 1995 (c. 4)	s.20	December 1, 1995	S.I. 1995 No. 2892 (C.61)
Finance Act 1995 (c. 4)	s.82	January 2, 1996	S.I. 1995 No. 2933 (C.63)
Financial Services Act 1986 (c. 60)	s.212(3), Sched. 17 (part)	June 19, 1995	S.I. 1995 No. 1538 (C.33)

Act Affected	Provision Brought Into Force	Commencement Date	Authority
Friendly Societies Act 1992 (c. 40)	s.31 (part)	January 1, 1995	S.I. 1993 No. 3226 (C.65)
Friendly Societies Act 1992 (c. 40)	s.31 (remainder)	April 1, 1995	S.I. 1994 No. 2543 (C.51)
Gas Act 1995 (c. 45)	ss.18, 8(2), 11(1)–(5), 13, 17(1), (2), (5) (part) Sched. 5, 6 (part)	November 8, 1995	s.18(2)
Gas Act 1995 (c. 45)	Remaining provisions	March 1, 1996	S.I. 1996 No. 218 (C.4)
Goods Vehicles (Licensing of Operators) Act 1995 (c. 23)	All provisions except s.50, Sched. 5	January 1, 1996	S.I. 1995 No. 2181 (C.44)
Health Authorities Act 1995 (c. 17)	s.1(1), 2(1), 4(1), Scheds. 1, 2 (all in part for the purposes of making regulations)	June 28, 1995	s.8(1)
Health Authorities Act 1995 (c. 17)	s.1(2), s.2(2)(3), s.3, s.4(2), ss.5(1) (part), (2), 6, 7, 8, 9, 10, Sched. 3 (part)	June 28, 1995	Royal Assent
Health Authorities Act 1995 (c. 17)	s.1(1), 2(1), 4(1), 5(1) (remainder), Scheds. 1, 2, 3 (remainder)	April 1, 1996	s.1(2), 2(3), 4(2), 5(2)
Home Energy Conservation Act 1995 (c. 10)	ss.3(1) and 4(1), (2)	January 15, 1996	S.I. 1995 No. 3340 (C.79)
Home Energy Conservation Act 1995 (c. 10)	Remaining provisions	April 1, 1996	S.I. 1995 No. 3340 (C.79)
Hong Kong (Overseas Public Servants) Act 1996 (c. 2)	All provisions	February 29, 1996	Royal Assent
Humber Bridge (Debts) Act 1996 (c. 1)	All provisions	February 29, 1996	Royal Assent
Income and Corporation Taxes Act 1988 (c. 1)	s.737A	May 1, 1995	S.I. 1995 No. 1007 (C.25)
Income and Corporation Taxes Act 1988 (c. 1)	s.51A	January 2, 1996	S.I. 1995 No. 2932 (C.62)

Act Affected	Provision Brought Into Force	Commencement Date	Authority
Insurance Companies (Reserves) Act 1995 (c. 29)	ss.2, 4	July 19, 1995	Royal Assent
Jobseekers Act 1995 (c. 18)	ss.39, 41(1)(2)(3)(6)	June 28, 1995	s.41(2)
Jobseekers Act 1995 (c. 18)	ss.9(13), 19(10)(a), 35, 36, 37, Sched. (part), 27, 34(3) (part), (7) (part), 28, (part) ss.28 (remainder), 29, 30, Sched. 3 (part) ss.27, 34(3), (7) (remainder)	December 12, 1995 April 1, 1996 April 6, 1996	S.I. 1995 No. 3228 (C.75)
Judicial Pensions and Retirement Act 1993 (c. 8)	All provisions	March 31, 1995	S.I. 1995 No. 631 (C.15)
Landlord and Tenant (Covenants) Act 1995 (c. 30)	All provisions	January 1, 1996	S.I. 1995 No. 2963 (C.66)
Land Registers (Scotland) Act 1996 (c. 14)	All provisions	April 1, 1996	S.I. 1996 No. 94 (C.1) (S.4)
Land Registration (Scotland) Act 1979 (c. 33)	ss.2(1)(2), 3(3) [for the purposes of the County of Fife]	April 1, 1995	S.I. 1994 No. 2588 (C.56) (S.124)
Law of Property (Miscellaneous Provisions) Act 1994 (c. 36)	s.21(1) so far as it relates to Sched. 1, para. 2	February 15, 1995	S.I. 1995 No. 145 (C.6)
Law of Property (Miscellaneous Provisions) Act 1994 (c. 36)	All remaining provisions	July 1, 1995	S.I. 1995 No. 1317 (C.26)
Law Reform (Miscellaneous Provisions) (Scotland) Act 1990 (c. 40)	ss.56–59 (remainder)	April 3, 1995	S.I. 1995 No. 364 (C.10) (S.14)
Law Reform (Succession) Act 1995 (c. 41)	All provisions	November 8, 1995	Royal Assent
Licensing (Sunday Hours) Act 1995 (c. 33)	All provisions	August 6, 1995	S.I. 1995 No. 1930 (C.37)

Act Affected	Provision Brought Into Force	Commencement Date	Authority
Local Government and Housing Act 1989 (c. 42)	s.71(1) (part) (4) (remainder) (5) (part) (6) (remainder) (8) (remainder)	April 1, 1995	S.I. 1995 No. 841 (C.20)
Local Government etc. (Scotland) Act 1994 (c. 39)	ss.8–11, 13–17, 24, 34, 38, 40, 44, 47, 49, 50, 51(3), 60, 97 (remainder), 101, 104, 113–115, 124, 126, 137 (remainder), 141, 143, 146–151, 165–167, 170, 172, 173, 175, 179, 180 (part), 182, Scheds. 5, 13 (part), 14 (part)	January 4, 1995	S.I. 1994 No. 2850 (C.63)
Local Government etc. (Scotland) Act 1994 (c. 39)	ss.153, 160, 161, 180(2) (part), Sched. 14 (part)	January 4, 1995	S.I. 1994 No. 3150 (C.74) (S.174)
Local Government etc. (Scotland) Act 1994 (c. 39)	ss.91–96, Sched. 11	March 10, 1995	S.I. 1995 No. 702 (C.18) (S.60)
Local Government etc. (Scotland) Act 1994 (c. 39)	ss.164(1)(2), 168, 180 (part), Sched. 13, paras. 72(1)(2), 92(25), Sched. 14 (part)	April 1, 1995	S.I. 1995 No. 702 (C.18) (S.60)
Local Government etc. (Scotland) Act 1994 (c. 39)	ss.152, 154, 155, 156, 158, 159, 162(1), 180 (part), Sched. 13, paras. 57, 60(4), 67(1) (2) (5), 100 (2) (4) (5), Sched. 14 (part)	April 1, 1995	S.I. 1994 No. 3150 (C.74) (S.174)
Local Government etc. (Scotland) Act 1994 (c. 39)	ss.2, 3, 4, 18, 19, 23, 25–29, 36, 39, 42, 43, 55, 56, 59, 127(1) (part) (2), 128–131, 133–136, 138, 169, 177(1) (part) (2) (part) (3) (part), 180 (part), 181 (remainder), 183(3) (6), Sched. 3, Sched. 12, Sched. 13, paras. 27(3)(p), 100(6)(a) (i)	April 6, 1995	S.I. 1995 No. 702 (C.18) (S.60)

Act Affected	Provision Brought Into Force	Commencement Date	Authority
Local Government etc. (Scotland) Act 1994 (c. 39)	ss.62, 63, 64, 65(2), 66, 73, 74, 76, 77, 79(1)–(3)(5), 81, 83–90, 98, 116, 118(1), 120(1), 122, 123, 177(1) (part) (2) (part), 180 (part), Scheds. 7, 8, 13, para. 75(25)(b)	July 17, 1995	S.I. 1995 No. 1898 (C.36) (S.141)
Local Government etc. (Scotland) Act 1994 (c. 39)	s.58 [only for specified purposes]	August 1, 1995	S.I. 1995 No. 702 (C.18) (S.60)
Local Government etc. (Scotland) Act 1994 (c. 39)	ss.67, 68(1), (4), (5), 69, 70, 71, 171 (part), 177 (remaining), Sched. 9	October 30, 1995	S.I. 1995 No. 2866 (C.60) (S.209)
Local Government etc. (Scotland) Act 1994 (c. 39)	s.180(1) (part), Sched. 13, paras. 162(1) and (2)	December 22, 1995	S.I. 1995 No. 3326 (C.77) (S.246)
Local Government etc. (Scotland) Act 1994 (c. 39)	ss.171 (remaining), 176	April 1, 1996	S.I. 1995 No. 2866 (C.60) (S.209)
Local Government etc. (Scotland) Act 1994 (c. 39)	ss.20, 33, 52, Sched. 6	April 1, 1996	S.I. 1995 No. 702 (C.18) (S.60)
Local Government Finance Act 1992 (c. 14)	s.110(2)(3)	March 31, 1995	S.I. 1994 No. 3152 (C.75) (S.176)
Local Government Finance Act 1992 (c. 14)	Sched. 13, para. 37(1)	April 1, 1995	S.I. 1994 No. 3152 (C.75) (S.176)
Local Government (Wales) Act 1994 (c. 19)	s.39(1)	February 1, 1995	S.I. 1995 No. 103 (C.5)
Local Government (Wales) Act 1994 (c. 19)	ss.1(5) (part) (8) (part), 2, 4, 17 (part), 66(5) (part), (6) (part), (7) (part), (8) (part), Sched. 15, para. 6, Sched. 16, para. 68 (6), (7) (part), (8)(9)(13)–(16)(19), Sched. 17, paras. 7, 8, Sched. 18 (part)	March 20, 1995	S.I. 1995 No. 546 (C.13)

Act Affected	Provision Brought Into Force	Commencement Date	Authority
Local Government (Wales) Act 1994 (c. 19)	ss.1(3) (part) (5)(6) (8), 5, 14, 15, 18(1)–(6), 19, 20(4) (part), 22(1) (part) (4) (part), 23(2)–(6), 25, 26, 42, 44, 45, 51, 53, 56, 57, 58, 59, 60, 66(5) (part) (6) (part) (7) (part) (8) (part), Sched. 2, paras. 8, 9, Sched. 6, paras. 2, 3, 4, 11, 12, 21, 23, 24(1)(b), Sched. 7, para. 1, Sched. 10, para. 14, Sched. 15, paras. 3, 20, 23, 26, 55, Sched. 16, paras. 57(1)–(5), 82(1)–(4), (5) (part), 84–86, 88, 96, 97, 106, Sched. 17, paras. 2, 3, 5, 10–14, 18–23, Sched. 18 (part)	April 3, 1995	S.I. 1995 No. 852 (C.22)
Local Government (Wales) Act 1994 (c. 19)	Pt. I s.1(3) (part), (5) (part), (8) (part), para. 13 of Sched. 2 (part) Pt. II para. 24 (10)(b) (part), (17)(a) (part) of Sched. 6, s.20 (part) para. 27(4) of Sched. 7 (part), s.22(1) (part) para. 3(2) of Sched. 8 (part), s.22(2) (part) Pt. VII para. 10(1), 52, 58–61 of Sched. 15 (part), s.66(5) (part) para. 12, 26, 98 of Sched. 16 (part), s.66(6) (part) Sched. 18 (part), s.66(8) (part)	October 1, 1995	S.I. 1995 No. 2490 (C.49)
Local Government (Wales) Act 1994 (c. 19)	Sched. 17, para. 18(2)	January 1, 1996	S.I. 1995 No. 2816 (C.59)
Local Government (Wales) Act 1994 (c. 19)	Sched. 16, para. 54(2), s.66(6) (part)	January 1, 1996	S.I. 1995 No. 3178 (C.73)

Act Affected	Provision Brought Into Force	Commencement Date	Authority
Local Government (Wales) Act 1994 (c. 19)	s.66(8) (part), Sched. 1 (part)	January 1, 1996	S.I. 1995 No. 3198 (C.73)
Local Government (Wales) Act 1994 (c. 19)	ss.1(3) (part), (5), (6), (8), 8, 9, 10, 11, 12, 13, 16, Sched. 2, paras. 1, 2, 3, 7, 10, 11, 12, ss.18(7), 20(1), (2), (3), 23(1), Scheds. 4, 5, ss.49, 50, Sched. 16, para. 54(2), s.66(6) (part)	April 1, 1996	S.I. 1995 No. 3198 (C.73)
Local Government (Wales) Act 1994 (c. 19)	ss.62, 66(7) (part), Sched. 17, paras. 15, 17	April 1, 1996	S.I. 1995 No. 3198 (C.73)
Local Government (Wales) Act 1994 (c. 19)	ss.17, 20(4) (part), 21, 22(1) (part), (2) (part), (3) (part), (4) (part), (5) (part), (6), 61, 66(5) (part), (6) (part), (7) (part), (8) (part), Sched. 6, paras. 1, 13–17, 19, 20, 22, 24(2)–(10) (9), 24(11)–(16), 24(17)(b)–27, Sched. 7, paras. 1–27(3), 28–43, Sched. 8, paras. 1–3(1), 3(3)–(11), Sched. 9, paras. 1–16, 17(1) (part), (2), (3), 17(5)–18, Sched. 10, paras. 1–10, 11(2)–13, Sched. 11, paras. 1, 2, 3(3)–(5), Sched. 15, paras. 2, 4, 5, 8(1)–(4), 9(1)–(4)(a), 10(2)–11(1), 12(a), 13–17, 21, 22, 24, 25, 27–51, 53, 54, 56, 62–66, Sched. 16, paras. 1–10, 13–25, 27–40(2)(a), 40(3)–54(1), 55, 56, 58–66, 68(1)–(5), 68(7) (part), 68(10)–(12), (17), (18), (20), 69, 71–81, 82(5) (part), 82(6)–83, 87, 89–92, 94, 95, 99–105, 107–109, Sched. 17, para. 16, Sched. 18 (part)	April 1, 1996	S.I. 1996 No. 396 (C.7)

Act Affected	Provision Brought Into Force	Commencement Date	Authority
Marriage Act 1994 (c. 34)	ss.2(1) (part), (2), 3	January 1, 1995	S.I. 1994 No. 3116 (C.73)
Marriage Act 1994 (c. 34)	s.1(2) (3), Sched. (all in part)	February 24, 1995	S.I. 1995 No. 424 (C.11)
Marriage Act 1994 (c. 34)	s.1(1) (2) (remainder), (3) (remainder), 2(1) (remainder), Sched. (remainder)	April 1, 1995	S.I. 1995 No. 424 (C.11)
Medical (Professional Performance) Act 1995 (c. 51)	ss.3, 4 (part), 5, 6, 7(1), (2) (part), Sched. paras. 1 (part), 4, 5, 6, 10(c), 22(b), 28(a), 29(a), 30(a)	May 1, 1996	S.I. 1996 No. 271 (C.5)
Mental Health (Patients in the Community) Act 1995 (c. 52)	All provisions	April 1, 1996	s.7(2)
Merchant Shipping Act 1970 (c. 36)	ss.51, 100(3) (part), Sched. 5 (part)	May 1, 1995	S.I. 1995 No. 965 (C.24)
Merchant Shipping Act 1970 (c. 36)	s.100(3) (part), Sched. 5 (part)	August 1, 1995	S.I. 1995 No. 1426 (C.30)
Merchant Shipping Act 1995 (c. 21)	All provisions	January 1, 1996	s.316(2)
Merchant Shipping (Salvage and Pollution) Act 1994 (c. 28)	ss.1, 2, 4, 10(3) (part), Scheds. 1, 2, 4 (part)	January 1, 1995	S.I. 1994 No. 2971 (C.68)
Motor Cycle Noise Act 1987 (c. 34)	All provisions	August 1, 1996	S.I. 1995 No. 2367 (C.47)
National Health Service (Amendment) Act 1995 (c. 31)	ss.13, 14(1)(3)–(6)	July 19, 1995	Royal Assent
National Health Service (Amendment) Act 1995 (c. 31)	ss.1, 2 (part), 3, 4, 5, 6, 14(2) (part)	December 21, 1995	S.I. 1995 No. 3090 (C.70)
National Health Service (Amendment) Act 1995 (c. 31)	ss.7 (part), 8 (part), 9, 10, 11, 12, 14(2), Sched. (part)	January 1, 1996	S.I. 1995 No. 3214 (C.74) (S.240)

Act Affected	Provision Brought Into Force	Commencement Date	Authority
National Health Service and Community Care Act 1990 (c. 19)	ss.36(1) (remainder), 66(2) (part), Scheds. 7 (remainder), 10 (part)	April 1, 1995	S.I. 1994 No. 2658 (C.57) (S.136)
Northern Ireland (Remission of Sentences) Act 1995 (c. 47)	All provisions	November 17, 1995	S.I. 1995 No. 2945 (C.64)
Offshore Safety Act 1992 (c. 15)	ss.2(3)(b) (part), (c) (part), 3(3)(b) (part), 7(2) (part)	March 1, 1996	S.I. 1996 No. 487 (C.8)
Olympic Symbol etc. (Protection) Act 1995 (c. 32)	All provisions	September 20, 1995	S.I. 1995 No. 2472 (C.48)
Pensions Act 1995 (c. 26)	ss.168, 170, 171, 179, Sched. 7 (part)	July 19, 1995	s.180(2)
Pensions Act 1995 (c. 26)	ss.90, 156, 169, 172, 173 (part), 174 (part), 175 (part), Sched. 6, para. 1	October 2, 1995	S.I. 1995 No. 2548 (C.51)
Pensions Act 1995 (c. 26)	ss.62–66, 120 (part), 121 (part), 124 (part), 174 (part), 175 (part) [for the purposes only of authorising making of regs. under ss.63(5), 64(2), 66(4)]	December 4, 1995	S.I. 1995 No. 3104 (C.71)
Pensions Act 1995 (c. 26)	ss.39, 117 (part), 121 (part), 124 (part)	January 1, 1996	S.I. 1995 No. 3104 (C.71)
Pensions Act 1995 (c. 26)	ss.62–66, 120 (part), 121 (part), 124 (part), 174 (part), 175 (part)	January 1, 1996	S.I. 1995 No. 3104 (C.71)
Pensions Act 1995 (c. 26)	paras. 29, 32–37, 39(b), 42, 44(a)(i), 47 of Sched. 3 (part), s.122 (part)	January 1, 1996	S.I. 1995 No. 3104 (C.71)
Planning and Compensation Act 1991 (c. 34)	ss.44, 46, 61 (part), 84(6) (part), Scheds. 13 (part), 19 (part)	February 3, 1995	S.I. 1994 No. 3292 (C.84) (S.191)
Planning and Compensation Act 1991 (c. 34)	ss.59, 61 (part), 80 (part), 84(6) (part), Sched. 11, Sched. 13, para. 40(2), Sched. 18, Pt. 1 (part)	August 30, 1995	S.I. 1995 No. 2045 (C.42) (S.150)

Act Affected	Provision Brought Into Force	Commencement Date	Authority
Police and Magistrates' Courts Act 1994 (c. 29)	ss.48 (part), 51 (part), 52(1)(3) (part), 53(1), 55(1) (part), 56, 57, 58, 59 (part), 62, 63(1)(6) (7)(b) (9)(b), 93 (part), Sched. 9, Pt. I (part)	January 1, 1995	S.I. 1994 No. 3075 (C.72) (S.163)
Police and Magistrates' Courts Act 1994 (c. 29)	Sched. 8, para. 19(1) (2)	February 3, 1995	S.I. 1995 No. 42 (C.2)
Police and Magistrates' Courts Act 1994 (c. 29)	ss.1–12, 14–16, 20, 21, 23, 24, 26, 29–31, 39(2)(3), 40, 43, 44 (part), 45, 93 (part), Scheds. 1, 2, 4, 5, paras. 2–7, 9, 10(2), 13, 14, 15, 17–20, 22, 23, 24(a), 29, 30, 35–38, Sched. 9, Pt. I (part)	April 1, 1995	S.I. 1994 No. 3262 (C.83)
Police and Magistrates' Courts Act 1994 (c. 29)	s.59 (remainder)	April 1, 1995	S.I. 1994 No. 3075 (C.72) (S.163)
Police and Magistrates' Courts Act 1994 (c. 29)	ss.47(2)(a), 48, 53(2), 59, 60, 63(2) (4) (5) (7) (all in remainder), 93 (part), Sched. 9, Pt. I (part)	April 1, 1995	S.I. 1995 No. 492 (C.12) (S.34)
Police and Magistrates' Courts Act 1994 (c. 29)	ss.79 (remainder), 93 (part) (remainder)	April 1, 1995	S.I. 1995 No. 685 (C.17)
Police and Magistrates' Courts Act 1994 (c. 29)	ss.72, 73, 75–77, 80, 81, 83(1)(2) (part), 84, 88(6), 91(1) (part) (2)(3), 93 (part) [see Order for transitional provisions]	April 1, 1995	S.I. 1995 No. 685 (C.17)
Police and Magistrates' Courts Act 1994 (c. 29)	ss.47(1), (2), (4), (5), 63(9)(a), 93 (part), Sched. 9, Pt. I (part)	December 13, 1995	S.I. 1995 No. 3003 (C.67)
Police and Magistrates' Courts Act 1994 (c. 29)	s.51 (remainder)	January 1, 1996	S.I. 1994 No. 3075 (C.72) (S.163)
Police and Magistrates' Courts Act 1994 (c. 29)	ss.47(1)–(5), 49, 54, 63(9), 64 (all in remainder), 93 (part), Sched. 9, Pt. I	April 1, 1996	S.I. 1995 No. 492 (C.12) (S.34)

Act Affected	Provision Brought Into Force	Commencement Date	Authority
Prisoners (Return to Custody) Act 1995 (c. 16)	All provisions	September 5, 1995	S.I. 1995 No. 2021 (C.41)
Private International Law (Miscellaneous Provisions) Act 1995 (c. 42)	Part II (ss.5–8)	January 8, 1996	s.16(2)
Proceeds of Crime Act 1995 (c. 11)	ss.14, 16	June 28, 1995	s.16(4)
Proceeds of Crime Act 1995 (c. 11)	All remaining provisions	November 1, 1995	S.I. 1995 No. 2650 (C.53)
Proceeds of Crime (Scotland) Act 1995 (c. 43)	All provisions	April 1, 1996	s.50(2)
Requirements of Writing (Scotland) Act 1995 (c. 7)	All provisions	August 1, 1995	s.15(2)
Sale and Supply of Goods Act 1994 (c. 35)	All provisions	January 3, 1995	s.8(2)
Sale of Goods (Amendment) Act 1994 (c. 32)	All provisions	January 3, 1995	s.3(3)
Sale of Goods (Amendment) Act 1995 (c. 28)	All provisions	September 19, 1995	s.3(2)
Shipping and Trading Interests (Protection) Act 1995 (c. 22)	All provisions	January 1, 1996	s.9(4)
Social Security (Incapacity for Work) Act 1994 (c. 18)	s.8(1)(3)(4)	April 6, 1995	S.I. 1994 No. 2926 (C.65)
Social Security (Incapacity for Work) Act 1994 (c. 18)	ss.2(1)(5), 3(1), 5, 6, 9(1)(2)(3), 10(1)(3) [For all purposes other than the making of regulations]	April 13, 1995	S.I. 1994 No. 2926 (C.65)
Social Security (Incapacity for Work) Act 1994 (c. 18)	ss.1, 2(2) (4) (6), 3(2), 10(2), 11, 13, Scheds. 1, 2	April 13, 1995	S.I. 1994 No. 2926 (C.65)

Act Affected	Provision Brought Into Force	Commencement Date	Authority
South Africa Act 1995 (c. 3)	All provisions	March 23, 1995	Royal Assent
State Hospitals (Scotland) Act 1994 (c. 16)	All provisions	April 1, 1995	S.I. 1995 No. 576 (C.14) (S.45)
Statute Law (Repeals) Act 1995 (c. 44)	All provisions	November 8, 1995	Royal Assent
Town and Country Planning (Costs of Inquiries etc.) Act 1995 (c. 49)	All provisions	November 8, 1995	Royal Assent
Trade Union Reform and Employment Rights Act 1993 (c. 19)	ss.45 (remainder), 46, 49(2) (part), 51 (part), Sched. 8, paras. 1, 3–5, 8, 9, 33, 34, Sched. 10 (part) [for all other purposes]	April 1, 1995	S.I. 1993 No. 2503 (C.52)
Trade Union Reform and Employment Rights Act 1993 (c. 19)	ss.7(2) (3), 51 (part), Sched. 10 (part)	April 1, 1996	S.I. 1993 No. 1908 (C.34)
Wild Mammals (Protection) Act 1996 (c. 3)	All provisions	April 29, 1996	s.7(2)

SUPREME COURT OF NORTHERN IRELAND

THE CRIMINAL JUSTICE AND PUBLIC ORDER ACT 1994 (COMMENCEMENT NO. 4) ORDER 1995

(S.I. 1995 No. 24 (C. 1))

Made - - - - - - *9th January 1995*

INTRODUCTION

This Order brings into force, on February 2, 1995, s.53 of the Criminal Justice and Public Order Act 1994 (c. 33). Section 53 amends the Criminal Appeal (Northern Ireland) Act 1980 (c. 47) to provide for a formal review of the assessment by the Master (Taxing Office) of the expenses allowed to a solicitor or counsel in criminal proceedings in the Court of Appeal and to allow for an appeal by the solicitor or counsel or the Lord Chancellor to the High Court against a decision of the Master (Taxing Office) on such a review.

The Lord Chancellor, in exercise of the powers conferred on him by section 172(2) of the Criminal Justice and Public Order Act 1994 (c. 33), hereby makes the following Order:—

1. This Order may be cited as the Criminal Justice and Public Order Act 1994 (Commencement No. 4) Order 1995.

2. Section 53 of the Criminal Justice and Public Order Act 1994 (Expenses in criminal appeals in Northern Ireland Court of Appeal) shall come into force on 2 February 1995.

Dated 9th January 1995 *Mackay of Clashfern,* C.

MAGISTRATES' COURTS

THE POLICE AND MAGISTRATES' COURTS ACT 1994 (COMMENCEMENT NO. 6 AND TRANSITIONAL PROVISIONS) ORDER 1995

(S.I. 1995 No. 42 (C. 2))

Made - - - - -	*12th January 1995*
Laid - - - - -	*12th January 1995*
Coming into force - - -	*3rd February 1995*

INTRODUCTION

This Order brings into force, on February 3, 1995, provisions of the Police and Magistrates' Courts Act 1994 (c. 29) which amend s.59(1) of the Justices of the Peace Act 1979 (c. 55) to enable grants to be paid to local authorities in respect of compensation for loss of office or employment or loss or diminution of emoluments by justices' clerks and their assistants.

The Lord Chancellor, in exercise of the powers conferred on him by section 94(2) and (5) of the Police and Magistrates' Courts Act 1994 (c. 29), hereby makes the following Order—

1.—(1) This Order may be cited as the Police and Magistrates' Courts Act 1994 (Commencement No. 6 and Transitional Provisions) Order 1995.

(2) This Order shall come into force on 3rd February 1995.

2. Subject to article 3, paragraph 19(1) and (2) of the Schedule to the Police and Magistrates' Courts Act 1994 (amendments of section 59(1) of the Justices of the Peace Act 1979 (c. 55)) shall come into force by virtue of this Order.

3. Section 59(1) of the Justices of the Peace Act 1979 as amended by paragraph 19(1) and (2) of Schedule 8 of the Police and Magistrates' Courts Act 1994 shall apply as regards the net cost to a responsible authority in any year of its functions under the Justices of the Peace Act 1949 (Compensation) Regulations 1978 (S.I. 1978/1682, as varied by S.I. 1995/41) only in respect of decisions on claims for compensation made by a determining authority under those Regulations on or after 3rd February 1995.

Dated 12th January 1995 *Mackay of Clashfern,* C.

CRIMINAL LAW, ENGLAND AND WALES
CRIMINAL LAW, SCOTLAND
CRIMINAL LAW, NORTHERN IRELAND

THE CRIMINAL JUSTICE ACT 1993 (COMMENCEMENT NO. 8) ORDER 1995

(S.I. 1995 No. 43 (C. 3))

Made - - - - - 11th January 1995

INTRODUCTION

This Order brings into force, on February 3, 1995 various provisions of the Criminal Justice Act 1993 (c. 36) relating to, *inter alia*, confiscation orders, postponed determinations, revised assessments, statements, etc., relevant to making confiscation orders, variation of orders, provision of information, availability of powers and satisfaction of orders, defendants who have died or absconded and compensation.

In exercise of the powers conferred on me by section 78(3) and (4) of the Criminal Justice Act 1993 (c. 36), I hereby make the following Order:

1. This Order may be cited as the Criminal Justice Act 1993 (Commencement No. 8) Order 1995.

2. The provisions of the Criminal Justice Act 1993 ("the 1993 Act") referred to in the left-hand column of the Schedule to this Order (which relate to the matters described in the right-hand column of the Schedule) shall come into force on 3rd February 1995.

3.—(1) So far as relating to the following provisions of the 1993 Act, namely, sections 27 and 28, this Order extends to England and Wales only.

(2) So far as relating to section 24(12) to (15), this Order extends to Scotland only.

(3) So far as relating to the following provisions of the 1993 Act, namely—

(a) sections 36 to 43; and

(b) paragraph 3 and paragraph 17(2) to (3) and (6) to (7) of Schedule 5 and Schedule 6 so far as it relates to the Northern Ireland (Emergency Provisions) Act 1991 (c. 24),

this Order extends to Northern Ireland only.

Michael Howard
One of Her Majesty's
Principal Secretaries of State

Home Office
11th January 1995

Article 2 SCHEDULE

PROVISIONS OF THE CRIMINAL JUSTICE ACT 1993 COMING INTO FORCE ON 3RD FEBRUARY 1995

Provisions of the Act	*Subject matter of provisions*
Section 24(12) to (15)	Miscellaneous amendments
Section 27	Confiscation orders
Section 28	Postponed determinations
Section 36	Confiscation orders
Section 37	Revised assessments
Section 38	Statements, etc. relevant to making confiscation orders
Section 39	Provision of information

Provisions of the Act	Subject matter of provisions
Section 40	Variation of confiscation orders
Section 41	Availability of powers and satisfaction of orders
Section 42	Defendant who has died or absconded
Section 43	Compensation
Schedule 5, paragraphs 3 and 17(2), (3), (6) and (7)	Consequential amendments
Schedule 6, so far as it relates to sections 48(3) and 51(3) of the Northern Ireland (Emergency Provisions) Act 1991	Repeals and Revocations

CRIMINAL LAW, ENGLAND AND WALES
CRIMINAL LAW, SCOTLAND
CRIMINAL LAW, NORTHERN IRELAND

THE CRIMINAL JUSTICE AND PUBLIC ORDER ACT 1994 (COMMENCEMENT NO. 5 AND TRANSITIONAL PROVISIONS) ORDER 1995

(S.I. 1995 No. 127 (C. 4))

Made - - - - - 19th January 1995

INTRODUCTION

This Order brings into force, on February 3, 1995, various provisions of the Criminal Justice and Public Order Act 1994 (c. 33) relating to, *inter alia*, young offenders, child testimony, intimidation of witnesses, serious fraud and cross-border enforcement.

In exercise of the powers conferred upon him by section 172(2) and (3) of the Criminal Justice and Public Order Act 1994 (c. 33), the Secretary of State hereby makes the following Order:

1. This Order may be cited as the Criminal Justice and Public Order Act 1994 (Commencement No. 5 and Transitional Provisions) Order 1995.

2.—(1) Subject to paragraphs (2) and (3) below, the provisions of the Criminal Justice and Public Order Act 1994 ("the 1994 Act") referred to in the left-hand column of Schedule 1 to this Order (which relate to the matters described in the right-hand column of that Schedule) shall come into force on 3rd February 1995.

(2) Schedule 2 (transitional provisions) shall have effect in relation to the coming into force of the provisions of the 1994 Act specified therein.

(3) The coming into force on 3rd February 1995 of section 134(3) of the 1994 Act shall have effect only for the purpose of the making of rules under section 18(3A) of the Prisons (Scotland) Act 1989 (c. 45), and the said section 134(3) shall otherwise come into force on 1st June 1995.

3.—(1) Subject to the following provisions, this Order extends to England and Wales only.

(2) So far as relating to the following provisions of the 1994 Act, namely sections 47(3), 49, 64(1) to (3), 66(6) and (10) to (13), 67(3), (4), (5), (8) and (9), 157(1), 163, 169 and 170, this Order also extends to Scotland.

(3) So far as relating to the following provisions, namely sections 88, 91 and 92, 136 to 141, 157(2), (3), (4), (5) and (9), 161, 162, 164 and 168, this Order extends to the United Kingdom.

(4) So far as relating to sections 102(1) to (3), 104, 105 and 117, so far as those provisions relate to the transfer of prisoners to or from premises situated in a part of the British Islands outside Scotland, this Order extends to that part of those Islands, but otherwise so far as relating to Chapter II of Part VIII this Order extends to Scotland only.

(5) So far as relating to the following provisions, namely sections 47(4), 84(5) to (7), 87, Part IX, sections 152(2), 153, 157(7) and section 160(2), this Order extends to Scotland only.

(6) So far as relating to the following provisions, namely sections 84(8) to (11), 85(4) to (6), 86(2) and 157(8), this Order extends to Northern Ireland only.

(7) So far as relating to the amendment, repeal or revocation of any enactment by Schedule 9, 10 or 11, this Order has the same extent as that amendment, repeal or revocation.

Michael Howard
One of Her Majesty's
Principal Secretaries of State

Home Office
19th January 1995

Article 2(1) SCHEDULE 1

PROVISIONS OF THE CRIMINAL JUSTICE AND PUBLIC ORDER ACT 1994 COMING INTO FORCE ON 3RD FEBRUARY 1995

Provisions of the Act	*Subject matter of provisions*
Section 17	Maximum length of detention for young offenders.
Section 18	Accommodation of young offenders sentenced to custody for life.
Section 23	Arrest of young persons in breach of conditions of remand.
Section 24	Police detention of young persons.
Sections 31 to 33	Evidence: imputations on character and corroboration.
Sections 40 to 43	Juries.
Section 46	Criminal damage: summary trial.
Section 47	Fines: deduction from income support.
Section 48	Sentencing: guilty pleas.
Section 49	Publication of reports in young offender cases.
Section 50	Child testimony.
Section 51	Intimidation, etc. of witnesses, jurors, etc.
Section 64(1) to (3), so far as relating to powers conferred on a constable by section 63	Supplementary powers of entry.
Section 66(6) and (10) to (13) and section 67(3), (4), (5), (8) and (9)	Power of court to forfeit sound equipment and retention and charges for seized property.
Sections 72 to 74	Squatters.
Sections 84 to 87	Obscene publications and indecent photographs of children.
Sections 88 and 91	Video recordings.
Section 92	Obscene, offensive or annoying telephone calls: increase in penalty.
Sections 102 to 117 and Schedule 6	Scottish prisons.
Sections 129 to 135	Miscellaneous amendments: Scotland.
Sections 136 to 141	Cross-border enforcement.
Section 152	Powers of search by authorised employees in prisons.
Section 153	Prohibited articles in Scottish prisons.
Section 154	Offence of causing intentional harassment, alarm or distress.
Section 155	Offence of racially inflammatory publication, etc. to be arrestable.
Section 157 and Schedule 8	Increase in penalties for certain offences.
Section 160	Constabulary powers in United Kingdom waters.
Section 161	Procuring disclosure of, and selling, computer-held personal information.
Section 162	Access to computer material by constables and other enforcement officers.
Section 163	Local authority powers to provide closed-circuit television.
Section 164	Serious fraud.
Section 168, to the extent necessary to bring into force the provisions of Schedules 9, 10 and 11 to the extent specified respectively below.	Minor and consequential amendments and repeals.

Provisions of the Act	*Subject matter of provisions*
Section 169	Power of the Secretary of State to make payments or grants in relation to crime prevention, etc.
Section 170	Security costs at party conferences.
Schedule 9, to the extent specified in Appendix A below.	Minor amendments.
Schedule 10, to the extent specified in Appendix B below.	Consequential amendments.
Schedule 11, to the extent specified in Appendix C below.	Repeals.

APPENDIX A

PROVISIONS OF SCHEDULE 9 COMING INTO FORCE ON 3RD FEBRUARY 1995

All the provisions of Schedule 9 so far as not already in force, save for paragraphs 37(3) and 38.

APPENDIX B

PROVISIONS OF SCHEDULE 10 COMING INTO FORCE ON 3RD FEBRUARY 1995

The following paragraphs of Schedule 10: paragraphs 7, 8, 11, 13, 14, 17, 18, 25, 27, 28, 29, 31, 37, 38, 45, 47, 52, 63 (so far as not already in force), 64 (so far as not already in force) and 68.

APPENDIX C

PROVISIONS OF SCHEDULE 11 COMING INTO FORCE ON 3RD FEBRUARY 1995

The provisions of Schedule 11, so far as not already in force, so far as it relates to the following enactments:

Indictable Offences Act 1848 (c. 42)
Sexual Offences Act 1956 (c. 69)
Children and Young Persons Act 1963 (c. 37)
Police (Scotland) Act 1967 (c. 77)
Children and Young Persons Act 1969 (c. 54)
Police Act 1969 (c. 63)
Police Act (Northern Ireland) 1970 (c. 9) (N.I.)
Juries Act 1974 (c. 23)
Rehabilitation of Offenders Act 1974 (c. 53)
Criminal Law Act 1977 (c. 45), section 38
Protection of Children Act 1978 (c. 37)
Magistrates' Courts Act 1980 (c. 43), sections 22(1) and 38(2)(b)
Criminal Justice Act 1982 (c. 48), section 12(6), (7) and (11)
Video Recordings Act 1984 (c. 39)
Prisons (Scotland) Act 1989 (c. 45)
Broadcasting Act 1990 (c. 42)
Northern Ireland (Emergency Provisions) Act 1991 (c. 24)
Criminal Justice Act 1991 (c. 53)
Parole Board (Transfer of Functions) Order 1992 (S.I. 1992/1829)
Video Recordings Act 1993 (c. 24)
Criminal Justice Act 1993 (c. 36)

Article 2(2)

SCHEDULE 2

TRANSITIONAL PROVISIONS

1. Section 23 shall only have effect in relation to a person remanded as therein mentioned on or after 3rd February 1995.

2. Sections 31 and 50 and paragraph 33 of Schedule 9 shall not apply—

(i) to trials, or to proceedings before courts-martial under the Army Act 1955 (c. 18), or the Air Force Act 1955 (c. 19), or before courts-martial or disciplinary courts under the Naval Discipline Act 1957 (c. 53) or before Standing Civilian Courts established under the Armed Forces Act 1976 (c. 52); or

(ii) to applications to the Crown Court for the dismissal of charges contained in a notice of transfer given under section 4 of the Criminal Justice Act 1987 (c. 38) or section 53 of the Criminal Justice Act 1991 (c. 53); or

(iii) to proceedings before magistrates' courts acting as examining justices,

which began before 3rd February 1995.

3. Section 129 shall apply only in the case of a person who is arrested or is detained under section 2(1) of the Criminal Justice (Scotland) Act 1980 (c. 62) or section 48 of the Criminal Justice (Scotland) Act 1987 (c. 41) on or after 3rd February 1995.

4. Where a case has been referred to the Parole Board for Scotland before 1st June 1995, section 134(3) shall not apply for the purposes of any proceedings of that Board on or after that date in dealing with that case on that reference.

5. The amendments made by paragraph 15 of Schedule 9 shall apply in relation to offenders convicted (but not sentenced) before 3rd February 1995 as they apply in relation to offenders convicted after that date.

6. Paragraph 40 of Schedule 9 shall not apply in relation to any sentence passed before 3rd February 1995.

7. Without prejudice to any express provision in that behalf contained in the 1994 Act the increases in penalties brought into force by this Order (including the amendments made by section 17), and paragraph 50 of Schedule 9, do not apply to offences committed before 3rd February 1995.

LOCAL GOVERNMENT, ENGLAND AND WALES

THE RESIDUARY BODY FOR WALES (APPOINTED DAY) ORDER 1995

(S.I. 1995 No. 103 (C. 5))

Made - - - - - *18th January 1995*

INTRODUCTION

This Order appoints February 1, 1995 as the day on which the Residuary Body for Wales is to be established. The Order is made under the Local Government (Wales) Act 1994 (c. 19) which creates unitary authorities in Wales which will carry out the functions of existing district and county councils.

The Secretary of State for Wales, in exercise of the power conferred on him by section 39(1) of the Local Government (Wales) Act 1994 (c. 19) and of all other powers enabling him in that behalf, hereby makes the following Order:

1. This Order may be cited as the Residuary Body for Wales (Appointed Day) Order 1995.

2. The day appointed for the establishment of the Residuary Body for Wales or Corff Gweddilliol Cymru is 1st February 1995.

Signed by authority of the Secretary of State for Wales

18th January 1995

Gwilym Jones
Parliamentary Under Secretary of State
Welsh Office

LAND

THE LAW OF PROPERTY (MISCELLANEOUS PROVISIONS) ACT 1994 (COMMENCEMENT NO. 1) ORDER 1995

(S.I. 1995 No. 145 (C. 6))

Made - - - - - - *24th January 1995*

INTRODUCTION

This Order brings into force, on February 15, 1995, an amendment to the Land Registration Act 1925 (c. 21) which enables the Lord Chancellor to make rules for prescribing the effect of covenants implied by virtue of the 1994 Act in dispositions of registered land.

The Lord Chancellor, in exercise of the powers conferred on him by section 23 of the Law of Property (Miscellaneous Provisions) Act 1994 (c. 36) hereby makes the following Order:

1. This Order may be cited as the Law of Property (Miscellaneous Provisions) Act 1994 (Commencement No. 1) Order 1995.

2. Section 21(1) of the Law of Property (Miscellaneous Provisions) Act 1994 (consequential amendments), so far as it relates to paragraph 2 of Schedule 1 to the Act, shall come into force on 15th February 1995.

24th January 1995 *Mackay of Clashfern*, C.

COAL INDUSTRY

THE COAL INDUSTRY ACT 1994 (COMMENCEMENT NO. 4) ORDER 1995

(S.I. 1995 No. 159 (C. 7))

Made - - - - - 23rd January 1995

INTRODUCTION

This Order brings into force, on January 31, 1995, s.24 of the Coal Industry Act 1994 (c. 21) (abolition of the Domestic Coal Consumers' Council).

The Secretary of State, in exercise of the powers conferred on him by section 68(4) of the Coal Industry Act 1994 (c. 21), and of all other powers enabling him in that behalf, hereby makes the following Order:

Citation and interpretation

1.—(1) This Order may be cited as the Coal Industry Act 1994 (Commencement No. 4) Order 1995.

(2) In this Order "the Act" means the Coal Industry Act 1994.

Provision coming into force on 31st January 1995

2. Section 24 of the Act shall come into force on 31st January, 1995.

Charles Wardle

23rd January 1995

Parliamentary Under Secretary for Industry and Energy, Department of Trade and Industry

POLICE

THE POLICE AND MAGISTRATES' COURTS ACT 1994 (COMMENCEMENT NO. 5 AND TRANSITIONAL PROVISIONS) (AMENDMENT) ORDER 1995

(S.I. 1995 No. 246 (C. 8))

Made - - - - -	*1st February 1995*
Laid before Parliament - -	*10th February 1995*
Coming into force - - -	*14th March 1995*

INTRODUCTION

This Order amends two transitional provisions in the Police and Magistrates' Courts Act 1994 (Commencement No. 5 and Transitional Provisions) Order 1994 (S.I. 1994 No. 3262 (C. 83)), concerning reports to be issued by the new police authorities on the policing of their areas and loans incurred by old police authorities.

The Secretary of State, in exercise of powers conferred on him by section 94(1), (5) and (6) of the Police and Magistrates' Courts Act 1994 (c. 29), hereby makes the following Order:

1.—(1) This Order may be cited as the Police and Magistrates' Courts Act 1994 (Commencement No. 5 and Transitional Provisions) (Amendment) Order 1995.

(2) This Order shall come into force on 14th March 1995.

2.—(1) The Police and Magistrates' Courts Act 1994 (Commencement No. 5 and Transitional Provisions) Order 1994 (S.I. 1994 No. 3262 (C. 83)) shall be amended in accordance with paragraphs (2) and (3) below.

(2) In article 4(2) (which provides that the commencement of section 4C of the Police Act 1964 (c. 48; Section 4C was inserted by section 4 of the Police and Magistrates' Courts Act 1994) shall not apply in respect of the financial year ending on 31st March 1994) for the words "March 1994" there shall be substituted the words "March 1995".

(3) In article 11(4) (which provides for the calculation of an increase in loan debt in specified financial years by reference to the issue of certain supplementary credit approvals)—

(a) before the word "issued" there shall be inserted "used by the council and ";

(b) in sub-paragraph (a), for the words "the council" there shall be substituted "a local authority";

(c) after the words "ceiling of the" there shall be inserted "relevant", and

(d) for the words "such functions" there shall be substituted "its police authority functions".

Home Office
1st February 1995

David Maclean
Minister of State

COAL INDUSTRY

THE COAL INDUSTRY ACT 1994 (COMMENCEMENT NO. 5) ORDER 1995

(S.I. 1995 No. 273 (C. 9))

Made - - - - - - 4th February 1995

INTRODUCTION

This Order brings into force on March 1, 1995, some repeals specified in Pt. III of Sched. 11 to the Coal Industry Act 1994 (c. 21). The repeals brought into force relate to the Coal Industry Nationalisation Act 1946 (c. 59), the Coal Consumers' Councils (Northern Irish Interests) Act 1962 (c. 22) and the Chronically Sick and Disabled Persons Act 1970 (c. 44).

The Secretary of State, in exercise of the powers conferred on him by section 68(4) and (5)(a) of the Coal Industry Act 1994 (c. 21), and of all other powers enabling him in that behalf, hereby makes the following Order:

Citation and interpretation

1.—(1) This Order may be cited as the Coal Industry Act 1994 (Commencement No. 5) Order 1995.

(2) In this Order "the Act" means the Coal Industry Act 1994.

Provision coming into force on 1st March 1995

2. Part III of Schedule 11 to the Act shall, so far as it relates to the repeals set out in the Schedule to this Order, come into force on 1st March 1995.

Charles Wardle
Parliamentary Under Secretary
for Industry and Energy,
4th February 1995 Department of Trade and Industry

SCHEDULE

REPEALS TAKING EFFECT ON 1ST MARCH 1995

Chapter	*Short title*	*Extent of repeal*
9 & 10 Geo. 6, c. 59.	The Coal Industry Nationalisation Act 1946.	Section 4, other than subsection (6). Section 4(6), except for the purpose of the determination and payment of remuneration, allowances and expenses as mentioned therein relating to the time before 1st March 1995.

Chapter	*Short title*	*Extent of repeal*
10 & 11 Eliz. 2, c. 22.	The Coal Consumers' Councils (Northern Irish Interests) Act 1962.	The whole Act, other than section 2. Section 2, except for the purpose of the payment of any increase as mentioned therein relating to the time before 1st March 1995.
1970 c. 44.	The Chronically Sick and Disabled Persons Act 1970.	In section 14(1), the words "and the Domestic Coal Consumers' Council".

EVIDENCE
HIGH COURT OF JUSTICIARY, SCOTLAND
SHERIFF COURT, SCOTLAND

THE LAW REFORM (MISCELLANEOUS PROVISIONS) (SCOTLAND) ACT 1990 (COMMENCEMENT NO. 13) ORDER 1995

(S.I. 1995 No. 364 (C. 10) (S.14))

Made - - - - - *13th February 1995*

INTRODUCTION

This Order brings into force on April 3, 1995, ss.56–59 of the Law Reform (Miscellaneous Provisions) (Scotland) Act 1990 (c. 40), insofar as those sections are not already in force. Previously (by S.I. 1991 No. 2151) the sections were brought into force for proceedings in certain sittings of the High Court of Justiciary and in certain sheriff courts, but they are now brought into force for proceedings for other sittings of the High Court and other sheriff courts.

The Secretary of State, in exercise of the powers conferred on him by section 75(2) of the Law Reform (Miscellaneous Provisions) (Scotland) Act 1990 (c. 40) and of all other powers enabling him in that behalf, hereby makes the following Order:

Citation

1. This Order may be cited as the Law Reform (Miscellaneous Provisions) (Scotland) Act 1990 (Commencement No. 13) Order 1995.

Commencement

2. Sections 56 to 59 (evidence by children in criminal trials) of the Law Reform (Miscellaneous Provisions) (Scotland) Act 1990 shall, in so far as they are not then in force (sections 56 to 59 were commenced by S.I. 1991/2151 with effect from 30 September 1991 only for proceedings in certain sittings of the High Court of Justiciary and in certain sheriff courts), come into force on 3rd April 1995.

James Douglas-Hamilton
Parliamentary Under Secretary of State,
Scottish Office

St Andrew's House, Edinburgh
13th February 1995

MARRIAGE

THE MARRIAGE ACT 1994 (COMMENCEMENT NO. 2) ORDER 1995

(S.I. 1995 No. 424 (C. 11))

Made - - - - - *23rd February 1995*

INTRODUCTION

This Order brings into force on February 24, 1995 and April 1, 1995, the remaining provisions of the Marriage Act 1994 (c. 34). These provisions, *inter alia*, enable the Secretary of State to make regulations in connection with the approval of premises by local authorities for use as a venue for civil marriages and allow civil marriages to take place on approved premises.

In exercise of the powers conferred by section 3(2) of the Marriage Act 1994 (c. 34), I hereby make the following Order:

Citation and interpretation

1.—(1) This Order may be cited as the Marriage Act 1994 (Commencement No. 2) Order 1995.

(2) In this Order "the Act" means the Marriage Act 1994.

Appointed days

2.—(1) 24th February 1995 is the day appointed for the coming into force of the following provisions of the Act—

(a) section 1(2) of the Act (approval of premises—marriages on approved premises) so far as it inserts sections 46A and 46B(2) in the Marriage Act 1949 (c. 76);

(b) section 1(3) of and the Schedule to the Act (approved premises: consequential amendments) so far as it inserts section 51(1A) in the Marriage Act 1949.

(2) 1st April 1995 is the day appointed for the coming into force of the following provisions of the Act—

(a) section 1(1) (solemnization of marriages on premises approved by local authorities);

(b) section 1(2) (marriages on approved premises), so far as not already in force on that date;

(c) section 1(3) of and the Schedule to the Act (approved premises: consequential amendments), so far as not already in force on that date;

(d) section 2(1) (registration districts in which marriages may be solemnized), so far as not already in force on that date.

Virginia Bottomley
One of Her Majesty's Principal Secretaries of State
Department of Health

23rd February 1995

POLICE

THE POLICE AND MAGISTRATES' COURTS ACT 1994 (COMMENCEMENT NO. 7 AND TRANSITIONAL PROVISIONS) (SCOTLAND) ORDER 1995

(S.I. 1995 No. 492 (C. 12) (S. 34))

Made - - - - - -	*28th February 1995*
Laid before Parliament - - -	*10th March 1995*
Coming into force - - - -	*1st April 1995*

INTRODUCTION

This Order brings into force on April 1, 1995 and April 1, 1996, for specified purposes, various provisions of Pt. II of the Police and Magistrates' Courts Act 1994 (c. 29). The provisions concern, *inter alia*, assignment of ranks, assistant chief constables, fixed term appointments, civilian employees and regulations as to retirement of certain constables. Transitional provision in relation to the abolition of the ranks of deputy chief constable and chief superintendent is also made.

The Secretary of State, in exercise of the powers conferred on him by section 94(1), (4) and (5) of the Police and Magistrates' Courts Act 1994 (c. 29) and of all other powers enabling him in that behalf, hereby makes the following Order:

Citation, commencement and interpretation

1.—(1) This Order may be cited as the Police and Magistrates' Courts Act 1994 (Commencement No. 7 and Transitional Provisions) (Scotland) Order 1995.

(2) This Order shall come into force on 1st April 1995.

(3) In this Order—

"the 1967 Act" means the Police (Scotland) Act 1967 (c. 77); and

"the 1994 Act" means the Police and Magistrates' Courts Act 1994.

Provisions of the 1994 Act coming into force on 1st April 1995

2. The provisions of the 1994 Act which are specified in column 1 of Schedule 1 to this Order, and described by reference to the subject matter in column 2 of that Schedule, shall, insofar as not then in force, come into force on 1st April 1995 but, where a particular purpose is specified in relation to any provision in column 3 of that Schedule, that provision shall come into force on that day only for that purpose.

Provisions of the 1994 Act coming into force on 1st April 1996

3. The provisions of the 1994 Act which are specified in column 1 of Schedule 2 to this Order, and described by reference to the subject matter in column 2 of that Schedule, shall, insofar as not then in force, come into force on 1st April 1996 but, where a particular purpose is specified in relation to any provision in column 3 of that Schedule, that provisions shall come into force on that day only for that purpose.

Transitional provision

4.—(1) Any person who on 1st April 1995 would hold the rank of deputy chief constable in a police force maintained under section 1 of the 1967 Act (section 1 was amended by the Local Government (Scotland) Act 1973 (c. 65), section 146) but for the commencement by this Order of the provisions of the 1994 Act abolishing that rank shall hold the rank of assistant chief constable in that force.

(2) Any person who on 1st April 1995 would hold the rank of chief superintendent in a police force maintained under section 1 of the 1967 Act but for the commencement by this Order of the provisions of the 1994 Act abolishing that rank shall hold the rank of superintendent in that force.

Fraser of Carmyllie
Minister of State,
Scottish Office

St Andrew's House, Edinburgh
28th February 1995

Article 2 SCHEDULE 1

PROVISIONS OF THE 1994 ACT WHICH WILL COME INTO FORCE ON 1ST APRIL 1995

Column 1 *Provision*	*Column 2* *Subject matter*	*Column 3* *Extent of commencement*
Section 47(2)(a)	Assignment of ranks	
Section 48	Assistant chief constables	
Section 53(2)	Fixed term appointments etc.	
Section 59	Common services	
Section 60	Constables engaged on service outside their force	
Section 63(2), (4), (5), and (7)	Other amendments of 1967 Act	
Section 93	Repeals	Only so far as it relates to the entries in Schedule 9, Part I specified below.
Schedule 9, Part I	Repeals	1. Only so far as extending to Scotland, the entry in relation to the Police (Overseas Service) Act 1945. 2. The following entries in respect of the 1967 Act:— In section 6(2), the words "a deputy chief constable". In section 7(1), the words "deputy chief constable," and ", chief superintendent and". In section 31, in each of subsections (2) and (4), the words "or deputy". 3. Only so far as extending to Scotland, the entry in relation to the Police Act 1969. 4. Only so far as extending to Scotland, the entry in relation to the Police Pensions Act 1976. 5. Only so far as extending to Scotland, the entry in relation to the Overseas Development and Cooperation Act 1980.

Article 3

SCHEDULE 2

PROVISIONS OF THE 1994 ACT WHICH WILL COME INTO FORCE ON 1ST APRIL 1996

Column 1 *Provision*	*Column 2* *Subject matter*	*Column 3* *Extent of commencement*
Section 47(1)	Establishments of police forces	
Section 47(2)	Assignment of ranks	
Section 47(3)	Appointment of police cadets	
Section 47(4)	Extra policing of locality where works are being constructed	
Section 47(5)	Regulations as to retirement of certain constables	
Section 49	Civilian employees	
Section 54	Power of Secretary of State to give directions to police authorities	
Section 63(9)	Other amendments of 1967 Act	
Section 64	Delegation of functions of Scottish police authorities	
Section 93	Repeals	Only so far as it relates to the entries in Schedule 9, Part I specified below.
Schedule 9, Part I	Repeals	The following entries in respect of the 1967 Act:— Section 7(2). In section 8(1), the words "and subject to the approval of the police authority and the Secretary of State as to numbers". In section 14(1), the words "(whether by the appointment of temporary constables or otherwise)". In section 26, in subsection (2)(d), the words "or temporary";. In section 51(1), the definitions of "regular constable", "special constable" and "temporary constable".

LOCAL GOVERNMENT, ENGLAND AND WALES

WALES

THE LOCAL GOVERNMENT (WALES) ACT 1994 (COMMENCEMENT NO. 3) ORDER 1995

(S.I. 1995 No. 546 (C. 13))

Made - - - - - - 27th January 1995

INTRODUCTION

This Order brings into force, on March 20, 1995, provisions of the Local Government (Wales) Act 1994 (c. 19) relating to the ordinary elections of councillors for the new Welsh county and county borough councils, the combination of polls at such elections with the ordinary elections of councillors for communities and the filling of casual vacancies occurring in the new Welsh counties and county boroughs after May 4, 1995.

Article 8, para. (4) was substituted by the Local Government (Wales) Act 1994 (Commencement No. 3) (Amendment) Order 1995 (S.I. 1995 No. 851 (C. 21)).

The Secretary of State for Wales, in exercise of the powers conferred on him by sections 63(5) and 66(3) of the Local Government (Wales) Act 1994 (c. 19), hereby makes the following Order:—

1. This Order may be cited as the Local Government (Wales) Act 1994 (Commencement No. 3) Order 1995.

2. In this Order—

"the 1972 Act" means the Local Government Act 1972 (c. 70);

"the 1983 Act" means the Representation of the People Act 1983 (c. 2);

"the 1994 Act" means the Local Government (Wales) Act 1994;

"the 1995 ordinary elections" means the ordinary elections of councillors for new principal areas and for communities to be held on 4th May 1995;

"existing council" means a county or district council which will cease to exist as a result of the 1994 Act;

"new principal area" means a county or county borough which is established by the 1994 Act;

"new principal council" means the council of a new principal area.

3. Subject to articles 4 to 8 the provisions of Parts I, II and VII of, and Schedules 15, 16, 17 and 18 to, the 1994 Act which are specified in the Schedule to this Order shall come into force on 20th March 1995.

4. The provisions of section 1(5) and (8) of the 1994 Act brought into force by this Order shall have effect only for the interpretation of sections 21, 25, 26, 79, 80 and 270(1) and (3) of the 1972 Act, and section 17 of the 1994 Act.

5. Subject to paragraph (4) of article 8, the provisions of section 17 of the 1994 Act brought into force by this Order shall have effect only in relation to the following legislative provisions—

Regulation 97(5) of the Representation of the People Regulations 1986 (S.I. 1986/1081);

Rule 4 of the Local Elections (Principal Areas) Rules 1986 (S.I. 1986/2214. Rule 4 was substituted by the Local Elections (Principal Areas) (Amendment) Rules 1990 S.I. 1990/158), Rule 4 in and the appendix of Forms to Schedule 2 to those Rules, Schedule 3 to those Rules and paragraphs 8, 18 and 24 of Schedule 4 to those Rules (Schedules 2, 3 and 4 were amended by the Local Elections (Principal Areas) (Amendment) Rules 1987 S.I. 1987/261 and by S.I. 1990/158 referred to above);

Rule 4 of the Local Elections (Parishes and Communities) Rules 1986 (S.I. 1986/2215), paragraphs 4 and 20 of Schedule 3 to those Rules and paragraph 22 of Schedule 4 to those Rules;
Articles 2 and 4 of the Local Elections (Principal Areas) (Welsh Forms) Order 1987 (S.I. 1987/562);
The Local Elections (Principal Areas) (Declaration of Acceptance of Office) Order 1990 (S.I. 1990/932);
Article 2 of the Local Elections (Declaration of Acceptance of Office) (Welsh Forms) Order 1991 (S.I. 1991/1169).

6. The provisions of sections 21, 25(2), 26 and 270(1) of the 1972 Act in force immediately prior to the commencement of sections 1(5), (8), 2 and 4 of the 1994 Act shall continue to have effect in relation to the administration of local government in Wales before 1st April 1996.

7. The provisions of sections 31(1), 35(1) and 36(3) of the 1983 Act in force immediately prior to the commencement of paragraph 68(6), (7) and (8) of Schedule 16 to the 1994 Act shall continue to have effect in relation to electoral matters concerning existing councils.

8.—(1) In relation to the commencement of paragraph 68(6) of Schedule 16 to the 1994 Act, the power contained in section 31(1A) of the 1983 Act for the division of an electoral division into polling districts shall, for the 1995 ordinary elections, be exercisable by the existing council which appointed the returning officer for the area in question (see S.I. 1995/151: the Returning Officers (Principal Areas: Wales) Order 1995 which designates certain existing councils to appoint returning officers for the 1995 ordinary elections of councillors for the new principal areas).

(2) In relation to the commencement of paragraph 68(8) of Schedule 16 to the 1994 Act, the references in section 36(3AB) of the 1983 Act to elections to fill casual vacancies shall not apply in respect of casual vacancies occurring prior to 1st April 1996.

(3) In relation to the commencement of paragraph 68(16) of Schedule 16 to the 1994 Act—

(a) the provision in section 36(6) of the 1983 Act whereby a council for a local government area other than a community may be required to advance expenses in relation to an election shall, for the 1995 ordinary elections, apply to the existing council which appointed the returning officer for the area in question;

(b) the reference in regulation 96(2) of the Representation of the People Regulations 1986 (Regulation 96(2) was amended by S.I. 1990/520: the Representation of the People (Amendment) Regulations 1990) to the proper officer of the local authority for which the election was held shall, in relation to the 1995 ordinary elections, be construed as a reference to the person who is deemed to be the proper officer of that authority under paragraph 4 of Schedule 5 to the 1972 Act (Schedule 5 to the 1972 Act was substituted by section 3 of, and Schedule 3 to, the 1994 Act) and any documents held by a person in accordance with this provision shall be transferred by him to the custody of the proper officer of the new principal council upon the appointment of that officer;

(c) the references in Parts IV and V of Schedule 2 to the Local Elections (Principal Areas) Rules 1986 (Rule 46 in Part V was amended by S.I. 1990/158; the Local Elections (Principal Areas) (Amendment) Rules 1990) to the proper officer of the council for which the election is held shall, in relation to the 1995 ordinary elections and until such officer is duly appointed, be construed as references to the person who is deemed to be the proper officer of that council under paragraph 4 of Schedule 5 to the 1972 Act, and any documents held by a person in accordance with this provision shall be transferred by him to the custody of the proper officer of the new principal council upon the appointment of that officer.

[(4) In relation to the commencement of section 17 of the 1994 Act, the provision in paragraph (1) of rule 4 in Schedule 2 to the Local Elections (Principal Areas) Rules 1986 which restricts the place which the returning officer may fix for the delivery of nomination papers to the offices of the council of the district in which the electoral area wholly or mainly lies shall not have effect in relation to the 1995 ordinary elections.]

Signed by authority of the Secretary of State

Gwilym Jones
Parliamentary Under Secretary of State
Welsh Office

27th February 1995

Article 3

SCHEDULE

PROVISIONS OF PARTS I, II AND VII OF, AND SCHEDULES 15, 16, 17 AND 18 TO, THE 1994 ACT COMING INTO FORCE ON 20TH MARCH 1995

Provision of the 1994 Act	*Subject matter*
Section 1(5)	Definition of "local authority".
Section 1(8)	Definition of "principal area".
Section 2	Constitution of new principal councils in Wales.
Section 4	Election of councillors.
Section 17	General provision for transfer of functions.
Paragraph 6 of Schedule 15 and section 66(5) so far as it relates thereto	Minor and consequential amendments of the 1972 Act.
Paragraph 68(6), (7) (but not in respect of paragraph (b) of the new section 35(1A) of the 1983 Act), (8), (9), (13) to (16) and (19) of Schedule 16 and section 66(6) so far as it relates thereto	Consequential amendments to the 1983 Act.
Paragraphs 7 and 8 of Schedule 17 and section 66(7) so far as it relates thereto	Transitional provisions.
In Schedule 18 the repeals to sections 35(1) and 36(3)(b) of the 1983 Act, and section 66(8) so far as it relates thereto	Consequential repeals.

NATIONAL HEALTH SERVICE, SCOTLAND

THE STATE HOSPITALS (SCOTLAND) ACT 1994 COMMENCEMENT ORDER 1995

(S.I. 1995 No. 576 (C. 14) (S. 45))

Made - - - - - *3rd March 1995*

INTRODUCTION

This Order brings into force on April 1, 1995 the provisions of the State Hospitals (Scotland) Act 1994 (c. 16) which substitute a new s.102 of the National Health Service (Scotland) Act 1978 (c. 29) in relation to the provision, control and management of state hospitals in Scotland. Powers to make orders under the 1978 Act are now exercisable for the purpose of constituting Special Health Boards in relation to state hospitals.

The Secretary of State in exercise of the powers conferred on him by section 3(2) of the State Hospitals (Scotland) Act 1994 (c. 16) and of all other powers enabling him in that behalf, hereby makes the following Order:

Citation

1. This Order may be cited as the State Hospitals (Scotland) Act 1994 Commencement Order 1995.

Appointed Day

2. The State Hospitals (Scotland) Act 1994 shall come into force on 1st April 1995.

Fraser of Carmyllie
Minister of State,
Scottish Office

St Andrew's House, Edinburgh
3rd March 1995

PENSIONS

THE JUDICIAL PENSIONS AND RETIREMENT ACT 1993 (COMMENCEMENT) ORDER 1995

(S.I. 1995 No. 631 (C. 15))

Made - - - - - 7th March 1995

INTRODUCTION

This Order brings the Judicial Pensions and Retirement Act 1993 (c. 8), which makes provision with respect to, *inter alia*, pensions and other benefits in certain judicial and senior public investigative offices and retirement ages, into force on March 31, 1995.

The Lord Chancellor, and, in relation to judicial offices whose jurisdiction is exercised exclusively in Scotland, the Secretary of State, in exercise of the powers conferred on them by section 31(2) of the Judicial Pensions and Retirement Act 1993 (c. 8) (by virtue of section 31(2) the power to make this order is vested in "the appropriate Minister" which expression is defined in section 30(1) as (a) in relation to any judicial office whose jurisdiction is exercised exclusively in Scotland, the Secretary of State, or (b) subject to (a), the Lord Chancellor), hereby make the following Order—

Title and commencement

1. This Order may be cited as the Judicial Pensions and Retirement Act 1993 (Commencement) Order 1995.

2. The Judicial Pensions and Retirement Act 1993 shall come into force on 31st March 1995.

Dated 6th March 1995 *Mackay of Clashfern*, C.

Ian Lang
One of Her Majesty's Principal
Dated 7th March 1995 Secretaries of State

LEGAL SERVICES

THE COURTS AND LEGAL SERVICES ACT 1990 (COMMENCEMENT NO. 10) ORDER 1995

(S.I. 1995 No. 641 (C. 16))

Made - - - - - *6th March 1995*

INTRODUCTION

This Order brings into force forthwith s.82 of the Courts and Legal Services Act 1990 (c. 41) which amends the Judicial Pensions Act 1981 (c. 20) allowing Regulations to be made entitling a member of a judicial pension scheme to make voluntary contributions towards the cost of the provision of additional benefits under the scheme.

The Lord Chancellor, in exercise of the powers conferred on him by section 124(3) of the Courts and Legal Services Act 1990 (c. 41), hereby makes the following Order—

1. This Order may be cited as the Courts and Legal Services Act 1990 (Commencement No. 10) Order 1995.

2. Section 82 of the Courts and Legal Services Act 1990 shall come into force forthwith.

Dated 6th March 1995 *Mackay of Clashfern*, C.

MAGISTRATES' COURTS

THE POLICE AND MAGISTRATES' COURTS ACT 1994 (COMMENCEMENT NO. 8 AND TRANSITIONAL PROVISIONS) ORDER 1995

(S.I. 1995 No. 685 (C. 17))

Made - - - - - -	*8th March 1995*
Laid before Parliament - - -	*10th March 1995*
Coming into force	
all provisions except article 5(2) and (3)	*1st April 1995*
article 5(2) - - - -	*1st October 1995*
article 5(3) - - - -	*1st January 1996*

INTRODUCTION

This Order brings into force most of the remaining provisions of Part IV (relating to magistrates' courts) of the Police and Magistrates' Courts Act 1994 (c. 29), Sched. 8 (minor and consequential amendments) and Part II of Sched. 9 (repeals) on April 1, 1995. The Order also makes transitional provisions.

The Lord Chancellor, in exercise of the powers conferred on him by section 94(2), (4), (5) and (7) of the Police and Magistrates' Courts Act 1994 (c. 29), hereby makes the following Order:

Citation and commencement

1.—(1) This Order may be cited as the Police and Magistrates' Courts Act 1994 (Commencement No. 8 and Transitional Provisions) Order 1995.

(2) This Order, except for article 5(2) and (3), shall come into force on 1st April 1995.

(3) Article 5(2) shall come into force on 1st October 1995.

(4) Article 5(3) shall come into force on 1st January 1996.

Interpretation

2. In this Order—

"the 1979 Act" means the Justices of the Peace Act 1979 (c. 55);

"the 1994 Act" means the Police and Magistrates' Courts Act 1994.

Magistrates' courts committee for inner London area

3. Section 79 of the 1994 Act (section 79 and section 93 so far as it related to the repeal of section 35 of the 1979 Act were brought into force by S.I. 1994/2594 for the purpose only of enabling a magistrates' courts committee for the inner London area to be constituted in accordance with S.I. 1994/2811) (magistrates' courts committee for inner London area) and section 93, so far as it relates to the entry in Part II of Schedule 9 in respect of section 35 of the 1979 Act, shall come into force for all remaining purposes on 1st April 1995.

Commencement of provisions on 1st April 1995

4. Subject to articles 5 and 6, the following provisions of the 1994 Act shall come into force on 1st April 1995—

(a) section 72 (supplementary provisions as to magistrates' courts committees);

(b) section 73 (general powers and duties of magistrates' courts committees);

(c) section 75 (justices' chief executives, justices' clerks and staff);

(d) section 76 (appointment and removal of justices' clerks);

(e) section 77 (justices' chief executives and justices' clerks to be employed under contracts of service);

(f) section 80 (organisation of justices' clerks in inner London area);
(g) section 81 (division of work in inner London area);
(h) section 83(1) (administrative and financial arrangements for magistrates' courts);
(i) section 83(2) so far as it applies to section 57 of the 1979 Act;
(j) section 84 (local authority land appropriated to magistrates' courts purposes);
(k) section 88(6) (default powers);
(l) section 91(1) (magistrates' courts: minor and consequential amendments), so far as it relates to the entries in Parts I and II of Schedule 8 referred to in article 7 below;
(m) section 91(2) and (3);
(n) section 93 (repeals) so far as it relates to the entries in Part II of Schedule 9 (magistrates' courts: repeals) referred to in article 8 below.

Commencement of provisions for certain areas on 1st April 1995, 1st October 1995 and 1st January 1996

5.—(1) Section 72(6) of the 1994 Act shall come into force on 1st April 1995 only in relation to the magistrates' courts committee for the inner London area.

(2) Section 72(6) of the 1994 Act so far as it inserts section 22(9) to (11) in the 1979 Act shall come into force on 1st October 1995, except in relation to the magistrates' courts committee for the inner London area.

(3) Section 72(6) of the 1994 Act so far as it inserts section 22(8) in the 1979 Act shall come into force on 1st January 1996, except in relation to the magistrates' courts committee for the inner London area.

(4) Section 75 of the 1994 Act so far as it inserts section 24D(5) in the 1979 Act shall come into force on 1st April 1995, except in relation to appointments of justices' chief executives by the magistrates' courts committees for Hampshire, Kent and Lincolnshire.

(5) Section 83(1) of the 1994 Act (which substitutes new sections 55 and 56 in the 1979 Act) shall come into force on 1st April 1995, except in relation to the inner London area.

(6) Section 91(1) of the 1994 Act, so far as it gives effect to paragraph 19(1) and (3) of Schedule 8 to the 1994 Act, and paragraph 19(1) and (3) of that Schedule, so far as it substitutes in subsection (8) of section 59 of the 1979 Act a new definition of responsible authority for the purposes of that section, shall come into force on 1st April 1995, except in relation to the inner London area.

Transitional provisions

6.—(1) A person appointed clerk to a magistrates' courts committee under section 22(1) of the 1979 Act or holding office as clerk under section 22(2) of the 1979 Act on 31st March 1995 may continue in that appointment until the magistrates' courts committee have appointed a justices' chief executive in accordance with section 24D(1) of the 1979 Act.

(2) Until the repeal of section 58 of the 1979 Act by section 83(2) and section 93 and Part II of Schedule 9 to the 1994 Act the Receiver for the metropolitan police district shall be—

(a) the paying authority for the purposes of section 53 of the 1979 Act (section 53 was amended by paragraph 18 of Schedule 8 and Part II of Schedule 9 to the 1994 Act) (indemnification of justices and justices' clerks) in respect of a justice or justices' clerk acting for the inner London area;
(b) the paying authority and the responsible authority for the purposes of section 82 of the Road Traffic Offenders Act 1988 (c. 53; section 82 was amended by paragraph 32 of Schedule 8 to the 1994 Act) (accounting

for fixed penalties: England and Wales) in relation to the magistrates' courts committee for the inner London area;

(c) the paying authority for the purposes of section 76 of the Criminal Justice Act 1991 (c. 53; section 76 was amended by paragraph 33 of Schedule 8 to the 1994 Act. Paragraph 33(5) of Schedule 8 is not yet in force) (provision of court security officers) in relation to the magistrates' courts committee for the inner London area and the provisions of subsections (3) and (4) of that section shall not apply.

Magistrates' courts: minor and consequential amendments

7.—(1) The entries in Part I of Schedule 8 (amendments of the 1979 Act) referred to in paragraph (l) of article 4 above are—

(a) paragraph 5 (amendment of section 22);
(b) paragraph 10 (amendment of section 26);
(c) paragraph 11 (amendment of section 27);
(d) paragraph 12 (amendment of section 28);
(e) paragraph 13 (amendment of section 30);
(f) paragraph 14 (amendment of section 32);
(g) paragraph 15 (insertion of section 34B);
(h) paragraph 16 (omission of sections 36 and 36A);
(i) paragraph 18 (amendment of section 53);
(j) paragraph 19(1) and (3) (substitution of section 59(8));
(k) paragraph 20 (amendment of section 62);
(l) paragraph 21 (amendment of section 63).

(2) The entries in Part II of Schedule 8 (amendments of other enactments) referred to in paragraph (l) of article 4 above are—

(a) paragraph 25 (section 15 of the Superannuation (Miscellaneous Provisions) Act 1967 (c. 28);
(b) paragraph 26 (paragraph 47 of Schedule 2 to the Pensions (Increase) Act 1971 (c. 56);
(c) paragraph 27 (paragraph (d) of Schedule 6 to the Pensions (Increase) Act 1971);
(d) paragraph 28 (Group B of Part I of Schedule 1 to the Juries Act 1974) (c. 23);
(e) paragraph 29 (section 30 of the Domestic Proceedings and Magistrates' Courts Act 1978) (c. 22);
(f) paragraph 30 (section 70 of the Magistrates' Courts Act 1980) (c. 43);
(g) paragraph 31 (section 145 of the Magistrates' Courts Act 1980);
(h) paragraph 32 (section 82 of the Road Traffic Offenders Act 1988);
(i) paragraph 33(1) to (4) and (6) (section 76 of the Criminal Justice Act 1991);
(j) paragraph 34 (section 77 of the Criminal Justice Act 1991).

Repeals

8. The entries in Part II of Schedule 9 (repeals: magistrates' courts) referred to in paragraph (n) of article 4 above are—

(a) section 48 of the Reserve and Auxiliary Forces (Protection of Civil Interests) Act 1951 (14 & 15 Geo. 6 c. 65);
(b) paragraph 29 of Part II of Schedule 3 to the Administration of Justice Act 1964 (c. 42);
(c) paragraph 2(2) of Schedule 2 to the Gaming Act 1968 (c. 65);
(d) Group B of Part I of Schedule 1 to the Juries Act 1974;
(e) section 22(2) of the 1979 Act;
(f) section 26(1), (2), (4) and (5) of the 1979 Act;
(g) section 27(1) to (5) and (7) and (9) of the 1979 Act;
(h) section 28(1A)(b) and (c) of the 1979 Act;
(i) section 30(1) of the 1979 Act;

(j) sections 36 to 38 of the 1979 Act;
(k) section 53(6) of the 1979 Act;
(l) section 57 of the 1979 Act;
(m) section 63(2) and (4) of the 1979 Act;
(n) section 68(7) of the Magistrates' Courts Act 1980;
(o) section 141(3) of the Magistrates' Courts Act 1980;
(p) section 145(1)(d) of the Magistrates' Courts Act 1980;
(q) section 12(4)(a), (5), (6), (8)(c) and (9) of the Local Government Act 1985 (c. 51);
(r) sections 164(3) and 165 of the Criminal Justice Act 1988 (c. 33);
(s) section 10(3) to (5) of the Courts and Legal Services Act 1990 (c. 41);
(t) paragraph 25(4)(c) of Schedule 18 to the Courts and Legal Services Act 1990;
(u) section 76(3) of the Criminal Justice Act 1991;
(v) section 79 of the Criminal Justice Act 1991 so far as it applies to section 55(2) of the 1979 Act;
(w) section 93(1) of the Criminal Justice Act 1991;
(x) paragraphs 40(2)(k) and 41(2)(c) of Schedule 11 to the Criminal Justice Act 1991.

Dated 8th March 1995 *Mackay of Clashfern*, C.

LOCAL GOVERNMENT, SCOTLAND

WATER SUPPLY, SCOTLAND

THE LOCAL GOVERNMENT ETC. (SCOTLAND) ACT 1994 (COMMENCEMENT NO. 3) ORDER 1995

(S.I. 1995 No. 702 (C. 18) (S. 60))

Made - - - - - - 8th March 1995

INTRODUCTION

This Order brings into force, on various dates in 1995 and 1996, various provisions of the Local Government *etc.* (Scotland) Act 1994 (c. 39). Transitional provision is also made in consequence of the commencement of s.168 in connection with certain existing local authority funds.

The Secretary of State, in exercise of the powers conferred on him by section 184 of the Local Government etc. (Scotland) Act 1994 (c. 39) and of all other powers enabling him in that behalf, hereby makes the following Order:

Citation and interpretation

1.—(1) This Order may be cited as the Local Government etc. (Scotland) Act 1994 (Commencement No. 3) Order 1995.

(2) In this Order, "the Act" means the Local Government etc. (Scotland) Act 1994.

Days appointed

2. 10th March 1995 is the day appointed for the coming into force of the following provisions of the Act:—

(a) section 91 (transfer of property, rights and liabilities to new authorities);
(b) section 92 (transfer schemes: general);
(c) section 93 (preparations for transfer of functions etc. to new authorities);
(d) section 94 (power to require provision of information and assistance as respects transfer schemes);
(e) section 95 (supplementary provision as to transfer schemes);
(f) section 96 (transfer schemes: exemption from stamp duty and stamp duty reserve tax); and
(g) Schedule 11 (water and sewerage transfer schemes).

3. Subject to article 8 below, 1st April 1995 is the day appointed for the coming into force of the following provisions of the Act:—

(a) section 164(1) and (2) (power of authorities to incur expenditure not otherwise authorised);
(b) section 168 (Direct Labour Organisation/Direct Services Organisation Accounts);
(c) section 180, so far as it relates to the provisions of Schedules 13 and 14 to the Act specified in paragraphs (d) and (e) below;
(d) in Schedule 13 (minor and consequential amendments)—
    (i) paragraph 72(1) and (2); and
    (ii) paragraph 92(25); and
(e) the repeals in Schedule 14 to the Act specified in Schedule 1 to this Order.

4.—(1) Subject to paragraph (2) and article 7 below, 6th April 1995 is the day appointed for the coming into force of the provisions of the Act specified in Schedule 2 to this Order.

(2) The commencement of section 127(1) of the Act by paragraph (1) above shall not extend to—

(a) the transfer of functions referred to therein; or
(b) the provision that section 36(1) of the Social Work (Scotland) Act 1968 (c. 49) shall cease to have effect.

5.—(1) Subject to paragraph (2) below, 1st August 1995 is the day appointed for the coming into force of section 58 of the Act.

(2) The commencement of section 58 by virtue of paragraph (1) above is only for the purpose of enabling a new local authority to enter into an agreement thereunder with any other new local authority for the carrying out of an activity or service on and after 1st April 1996.

(3) In this article, "new local authority" means—

(a) a council in respect of which an ordinary election of councillors takes place on 6th April 1995 in terms of section 5(2) of the Act;
(b) an Islands Council;
(c) a residuary body; and
(d) a joint board.

6. 1st April 1996 is the day appointed for the coming into force of the following provisions of the Act:—

(a) section 20 (joint committees and joint boards);
(b) section 33 (structure plans);
(c) section 52 (Tweed Fisheries Commissioners); and
(d) Schedule 6 (New Schedule 1 to the Tweed Fisheries Act 1969 (c. xxiv)).

Saving and transitional provision

7. The amendments made to sections 36 and 38 of the Fire Services Act 1947 (c. 41; section 36 was also amended by the Water (Scotland) Act 1980 (c. 45), Schedule 10; section 38 was also amended by the Roads (Scotland) Act 1984 (c. 54), Schedule 9, paragraph 34(5) and by the New Roads and Street Works Act 1991 (c. 22); Schedule 8, paragraph 99(3)) by section 147(5) and (6) of the Local Government (Scotland) Act 1973 (c. 65) shall, notwithstanding the commencement of section 36 of the Act by virtue of article 4(1) above, continue to have effect.

8. A DLO reserve fund established by a local authority under paragraph 22(1)(c) of Schedule 3 to the Local Government (Scotland) Act 1975 (c. 30. Paragraph 22(1)(c) of Schedule 3 was inserted by the Local Government Act 1988 (c. 9), Schedule 6, paragraph 11(2)(b)) which is in existence on 31st March 1995 shall be treated for all purposes as if it were a DLO/DSO fund established by that authority at 1st April 1995 under section 15A of the said Act of 1975, inserted by section 168 of the Act and commenced by virtue of article 3 above.

George Kynoch
Parliamentary Under Secretary of State,
Scottish Office

St Andrew's House, Edinburgh
8th March 1995

Article 3(e) SCHEDULE 1

REPEALS IN SCHEDULE 14 TO THE ACT COMING INTO FORCE ON 1ST APRIL 1995

Chapter	*Short Title*	*Extent of Repeal*
1973 c. 65	The Local Government (Scotland) Act 1973	In section 83(4B)(d), the word "Economic". In section 96(5), the words from ", so however that" to "31st March 1976". In section 100(3), the words from "and to an additional fine" to the end.
1975 c. 21	The Criminal Procedure (Scotland) Act 1975	In Schedule 7D, paragraph 59.
1975 c. 30	The Local Government (Scotland) Act 1975	In Schedule 3, in paragraph 22, in sub-paragraph (1), head (c) and paragraph 24A.
1988 c. 9	The Local Government Act 1988	In Schedule 6, in paragraph 11, the words from "and", where it first occurs, to the end.
1992 c. 14	The Local Government Finance Act 1992	In Schedule 7, paragraph 1(6).

Article 4(1) SCHEDULE 2

PROVISIONS OF THE ACT COMING INTO FORCE ON 6TH APRIL 1995

1. Section 2 (constitution of councils).
2. Section 3 (Orkney, Shetland and Western Isles).
3. Section 4 (convener and depute convener).
4. Section 18 (residuary bodies).
5. Section 19 (property commission).
6. Section 23 (duty to prepare decentralisation schemes).
7. Section 25 (financing of new authorities prior to 1st April 1996).
8. Section 26 (valuation lists).
9. Section 27 (valuation areas and authorities and appointment of assessors etc.).
10. Section 28 (valuation rolls).
11. Section 29 (valuation appeal panels and committees).
12. Section 36 (fire services).
13. Section 39 (roads authority for boundary bridges).
14. Section 42 (power to secure management of traffic control system).
15. Section 43 (guidance as to exercise of traffic powers).
16. Section 55 (restrictions on disposal of assets and entering into contracts by existing authorities).
17. Section 56 (duty of existing authorities and assessors to provide information to new authorities).
18. Section 59 (local Acts and instruments).
19. Section 127 (the Principal Reporter).
20. Section 128 (the Scottish Children's Reporter Administration).
21. Section 129 (appeal against dismissal of Principal Reporter and other officers).
22. Section 130 (annual report of Principal Reporter).
23. Section 131 (delegation of Principal Reporter's functions).
24. Section 133 (ancillary powers of Administration).
25. Section 134 (directions by the Secretary of State).
26. Section 135 (government grants to the Administration).
27. Section 136 (reports, accounts etc. of the Administration).
28. Section 138 (property etc.: application of Chapter 3 of Part I).
29. Section 169 (Statements of support services costs).
30. Subsections (1) and (2) of section 177 so far as those subsections relate to the entry in Part II of Schedule 1 to the House of Commons Disqualification Act 1975 (c. 24) concerning the Scottish Children's Reporter Administration and section 177(1) and (3), so far as relating to those parts of section 177(3) not already in force (Parliamentary disqualification).

31. Section 180, so far as it relates to the provisions of Schedule 13 to the Act specified in paragraph 36 below.

32. Section 181, so far as not already in force (consequential and supplementary provisions).

33. Section 183(3) and (6) (translation of references).

34. Schedule 3 (residuary bodies).

35. Schedule 12 (status, constitution and proceedings of the Scottish Children's Reporter Administration).

36. In Schedule 13 (minor and consequential amendments)—

(a) paragraph 27(3)(p); and

(b) paragraph 100(6)(a)(i).

CRIMINAL LAW, ENGLAND AND WALES
CRIMINAL LAW, SCOTLAND
CRIMINAL LAW, NORTHERN IRELAND

THE CRIMINAL JUSTICE AND PUBLIC ORDER ACT 1994 (COMMENCEMENT NO. 6) ORDER 1995

(S.I. 1995 No. 721 (C. 19))

Made - - - - - *11th March 1995*

INTRODUCTION

This Order brings into force on April 10, 1995, various provisions of the Criminal Justice and Public Order Act 1994 (c. 33) relating to, *inter alia*, bail, inferences from the accused's silence, the powers of the police to take body samples and powers to stop and search in anticipation of violence.

In exercise of the powers conferred upon him by section 172(2) of the Criminal Justice and Public Order Act 1994 (c. 33), the Secretary of State hereby makes the following Order:

1. This Order may be cited as the Criminal Justice and Public Order Act 1994 (Commencement No. 6) Order 1995.

2. The provisions of the Criminal Justice and Public Order Act 1994 referred to in the left-hand column of the Schedule to this Order (which relate to the matters described in the right-hand column) shall come into force on 10th April 1995.

Home Office
11th March 1995

Michael Howard
One of Her Majesty's Principal Secretaries of State

SCHEDULE

PROVISIONS OF THE CRIMINAL JUSTICE AND PUBLIC ORDER ACT 1994 COMING INTO FORCE ON 10TH APRIL 1995

Provisions of the Act	*Subject matter of provisions*
Sections 25 to 30 and Schedule 3	Bail
Sections 34 to 39	Inferences from accused's silence
Sections 54 to 59	Powers of police to take body samples
Section 60	Powers to stop and search in anticipation of violence
Sections 62, 64(4), (5) and (6), 66(1) to (5) and (7) to (9) and 67(1), (2), (6) and (7)	Public order
Sections 118 to 125 and Schedule 7	Northern Ireland prisoner escorts
Section 156	Prohibition on use of cells from embryos or foetuses
Section 168, to the extent necessary to bring into force the provisions of Schedules 9, 10 and 11 to the extent specified respectively below	Minor and consequential amendments and repeals
Schedule 9, paragraph 37(3)	Minor amendments
Schedule 10 to the extent specified in Appendix A below	Consequential amendments
Schedule 11, to the extent specified in Appendix B below	Repeals

APPENDIX A

PROVISIONS OF SCHEDULE 10 COMING INTO FORCE ON 10TH APRIL 1995

The following paragraphs of Schedule 10: paragraphs 1, 2, 3, 5, 6, 10, 15, 19 to 23, 32 to 34, 41 to 44, 48, 51, 54 to 58, 61, 62, 67 and 71.

APPENDIX B

PROVISIONS OF SCHEDULE 11 COMING INTO FORCE ON 10TH APRIL 1995

The provisions of Schedule 11, so far as it relates to the following enactments:
Criminal Evidence Act 1898 (c. 36)
Criminal Evidence Act (Northern Ireland) 1923 (c. 9 (N.I.))
Bail Act 1976 (c. 63)
Police and Criminal Evidence Act 1984 (c. 60)
Criminal Evidence (Northern Ireland) Order 1988 (S.I. 1988/1987 (N.I. 20))

LOCAL GOVERNMENT, ENGLAND AND WALES

THE LOCAL GOVERNMENT AND HOUSING ACT 1989 (COMMENCEMENT NO. 17) ORDER 1995

(S.I. 1995 No. 841 (C. 20))

Made - - - - - 20th March 1995

INTRODUCTION

This Order brings into force on April 1, 1995, certain provisions of s.71 of the Local Government and Housing Act 1989 (c. 42). Section 71 relates to minor interests held by local authorities in limited companies.

The Secretary of State, in exercise of the powers conferred on him by section 195(2) and (3) of the Local Government and Housing Act 1989 (c. 42) and of all other powers enabling him in that behalf, hereby makes the following Order:

Citation and interpretation

1.—(1) This Order may be cited as the Local Government and Housing Act 1989 (Commencement No. 17) Order 1995.

(2) In this Order "the Act" means the Local Government and Housing Act 1989.

Commencement of section 71

2. Subject to article 3 the following provisions of section 71 of the Act, in so far as not already in force, shall come into force on 1st April 1995:

(a) subsection (1), for the purposes only of subsections (4) to (6);
(b) subsections (4), (6) and (8);
(c) subsection (5), for the purposes only of paragraph (a) of that subsection.

Transitional provision

3. Nothing in article 2 shall have effect to apply the requirements of subsections (4) and (5) of section 71 of the Act before 1st July 1995 in relation to any company formed on or before 31st March 1995.

Authorised by the Secretary of State
to sign in that behalf

David Curry
Minister of State,
Department of the Environment

20th March 1995

LOCAL GOVERNMENT, ENGLAND AND WALES

WALES

THE LOCAL GOVERNMENT (WALES) ACT 1994 (COMMENCEMENT NO. 3) (AMENDMENT) ORDER 1995

(S.I. 1995 No. 851 (C. 21))

Made - - - - - - 15th March 1995
Coming into force - - - - 20th March 1995

INTRODUCTION

This Order substitutes art. 8, para. (4), of the Local Government (Wales) Act 1994 (Commencement No. 3) Order 1995 (S.I. 1995 No. 546 (C. 13)). Article 8(4) contained a transitional provision whereby the partial commencement by that Order of s.17 of the Local Government (Wales) Act 1994 (c. 19) was not to apply to r.4 of Sched. 2 to the Local Elections (Principal Areas) Rules 1986 (S.I. 1986 No. 2214) at the first elections to the new authorities established by the 1994 Act. Article 8(4) provided for nomination papers to be delivered at the offices of the existing council which nominated the returning officer. For reasons of the possible inconvenience that this could cause, the present amendment is made whereby the restriction to district council offices is removed.

The Secretary of State for Wales, in exercise of the powers conferred on him by sections 63(5) and 66(3) of the Local Government (Wales) Act 1994 (c. 19), and of all other powers enabling him in that behalf, hereby makes the following Order:—

1. This Order may be cited as the Local Government (Wales) Act 1994 (Commencement No. 3) (Amendment) Order 1995 and shall come into force on 20th March 1995.

2. In article 8 of the Local Government (Wales) Act 1994 (Commencement No. 3) Order 1995 (S.I. 1995/546), for paragraph (4) there shall be substituted the following paragraph:—

> "(4) In relation to the commencement of section 17 of the 1994 Act, the provision in paragraph (1) of rule 4 in Schedule 2 to the Local Elections (Principal Areas) Rules 1986 which restricts the place which the returning officer may fix for the delivery of nomination papers to the offices of the council of the district in which the electoral area wholly or mainly lies shall not have effect in relation to the 1995 ordinary elections."

Signed by authority of the Secretary of State for Wales

Gwilym Jones
Parliamentary Under Secretary of State,
15th March 1995 Welsh Office

LOCAL GOVERNMENT, ENGLAND AND WALES

WALES

THE LOCAL GOVERNMENT (WALES) ACT 1994 (COMMENCEMENT NO. 4) ORDER 1995

(S.I. 1995 No. 852 (C. 22))

Made - - - - - *23rd March 1995*

INTRODUCTION

This Order brings into force on April 3, 1995, various provisions of the Local Government (Wales) Act 1994 (c. 19) including provisions relating to change of status from county to county borough, joint and special planning boards in Wales, fire services, transfers of staff, control of disposals and contracts and amendments and repeals.

The Secretary of State for Wales, in exercise of the powers conferred upon him by sections 63(5) and 66(3) of the Local Government (Wales) Act 1994 (c. 19), hereby makes the following Order:—

Citation

1. This Order may be cited as the Local Government (Wales) Act 1994 (Commencement No. 4) Order 1995.

Interpretation

2. In this Order—

"the 1972 Act" means the Local Government Act 1972 (c. 70);

"the 1990 Act" means the Town and Country Planning Act 1990 (c. 8);

"the 1994 Act" means the Local Government (Wales) Act 1994; and

"old authority" means a county or district council which will cease to exist as a result of the 1994 Act.

Commencement of certain provisions of Part I of the 1994 Act

3.—(1) Subject to paragraphs (2) and (3) the provisions of Part I of, and Schedule 2 to, the 1994 Act which are specified in Schedule 1 to this Order shall come into force on 3rd April 1995.

(2) The provisions of section 1(5), (6) and (8) of the 1994 Act (section 1(5), (6) and (8) of the 1994 Act has already been brought partially into force by S.I. 1994/2790: the Local Government (Wales) Act 1994 (Commencement No. 2) Order 1994. In addition section 1(5) and (8) of the 1994 Act has been brought partially into force by S.I. 1995/546: the Local Government (Wales) Act 1994 (Commencement No. 3) Order 1995) brought into force by this Order shall have effect for the interpretation of the 1972 Act only to such extent as provisions of that Act fall to be applied in consequence of the bringing into force of provisions of the 1994 Act.

(3) The provisions of section 270(1) and 245A of the 1972 Act (section 245A of the 1972 Act was inserted by section 160 of, and paragraph 6 of Schedule 8 to, the Local Government and Housing Act 1989 (c. 42) in force immediately prior to the commencement of sections 1(5), (6) and (8), and 5 of the 1994 Act shall continue to have effect in relation to the administration of local government in Wales before 1st April 1996.

Commencement of certain provisions of Part II of the 1994 Act

4.—(1) Subject to paragraphs (2) to (6) the provisions of Part II of, and Schedules 6, 7 and 10 to, the 1994 Act which are specified in Schedule 2 to this Order shall come into force on 3rd April 1995.

(2) Until 1st April 1996 the provisions of section 18(1) to (6) of the 1994 Act brought into force by this Order shall have effect only for the purpose of any order made under section 2(1B) of the 1990 Act (section 2(1B) of the 1990 Act is inserted by section 19(1) of the 1994 Act) or, as the case may be, paragraph 3A(1) of Schedule 17 to the 1972 Act (paragraph 3A(1) of Schedule 17 to the 1972 Act is inserted by section 19(2) of the 1994 Act).

(3) The provisions of section 1 of the 1990 Act in force immediately prior to the commencement of section 18(1) to (6) of the 1994 Act shall continue to have effect in relation to the exercise of local planning authority functions by each old authority.

(4) The provisions of paragraph 21A of Schedule 17 to the 1972 Act (paragraph 21(A) of Schedule 17 to the 1972 Act was inserted by section 7 of, and paragraph 5(8) of Schedule 3 to, The Local Government Act 1985 (c. 51)) in force immediately prior to the commencement of paragraph 12 of Schedule 6 to the 1994 Act shall continue to have effect in relation to the discharge of planning and countryside functions in national parks in Wales before 1st April 1996.

(5) The provisions of paragraph 1 of Schedule 7 to the 1994 Act brought into force by this Order shall have effect only for the interpretation of paragraph 18 of Schedule 17 to the 1994 Act and only to such extent as will allow action to be taken thereunder for the purpose of identifying the relevant highway authority in readiness for its assumption of full highway authority functions on 1st April 1996.

(6) The provisions of section 1 of the Highways Act 1980 (c. 66) in force immediately prior to the commencement of paragraph 1 of Schedule 7 to the 1994 Act shall continue to have effect in relation to the discharge of local highway authority functions in Wales before 1st April 1996.

Commencement of Part III of the 1994 Act

5. The provisions of Part III of the 1994 Act shall come into force on 3rd April 1995.

Commencement of Part IV of the 1994 Act

6.—(1) Subject to paragraphs (2) to (5) the provisions of Part IV of, and Schedule 12 to, the 1994 Act shall come into force on 3rd April 1995.

(2) The provisions of section 1(2) of the Local Government Finance Act 1992 (c. 14) in force immediately prior to the commencement of section 35 of the 1994 Act shall continue to have effect so far as is necessary for the purposes of section 35(3) of the 1994 Act.

(3) Nothing in paragraph 1 of Schedule 12 to the 1994 Act shall affect the operation of section 148 of the 1972 Act in relation to an old authority.

(4) Nothing in paragraph 2 of Schedule 12 to the 1994 Act shall affect the operation of Part VI of the Local Government Finance Act 1988 (c. 41) in relation to an old authority.

(5) Nothing in paragraphs 4, 5, 6 and 8 of Schedule 12 shall affect the operation of sections 32, 33, 35 and 62 of the Local Government Finance Act 1992 in relation to an old authority.

Commencement of Part V of the 1994 Act

7. The provisions of Part V of the 1994 Act which are specified in Schedule 3 to this Order shall come into force on 3rd April 1995.

Commencement of certain provisions of Part VI of the 1994 Act

8. The provisions of Part VI of the 1994 Act which are specified in Schedule 4 to this Order shall come into force on 3rd April 1995.

Commencement of certain provisions of Part VII of the 1994 Act

9.—(1) Subject to paragraphs (2) to (5) the provisions of Part VII of, and Schedules 15, 16, 17 and 18 to, the 1994 Act which are specified in Schedule 5 to this Order shall come into force on 3rd April 1995.

(2) The provisions of sections 74, 101 and 249 of the 1972 Act in force immediately prior to the commencement of paragraphs 20, 26 and 55 of Schedule 15 to the 1994 Act shall continue to have effect in relation to an old authority.

(3) The provisions of section 20(1) of the Local Government, Planning and Land Act 1980 (c. 65) in force immediately prior to the commencement of paragraph 57(3) of Schedule 16 shall continue to have effect in relation to an old authority.

(4) Until 1st April 1996 the provisions of paragraph 82(1), (2) and (3) of Schedule 16 to the 1994 Act brought into force by this Order shall have effect only for the purpose of any order made under section 4A of the Coroners Act 1988 (section 4A of the Coroners Act 1988 is inserted by section 66(6) of, and paragraph 82(5) of Schedule 16 to, the 1994 Act).

(5) The provisions of sections 1, 2 and 4 of the Coroners Act 1988 (c. 13) in force immediately prior to the commencement of paragraph 82(1), (2), (3) and (4) of Schedule 16 to the 1994 Act shall continue to have effect in relation to coroners in Wales before 1st April 1996.

Signed by authority of the Secretary of State for Wales

Gwilym Jones
Parliamentary Under Secretary of State
Welsh Office

23rd March 1995

Article 3(1) SCHEDULE 1

PROVISIONS OF PART I OF, AND SCHEDULE 2 TO, THE 1994 ACT COMING INTO FORCE ON 3RD APRIL 1995

Provision of the 1994 Act	*Subject Matter*
Section 1(5)	Definition of "local authority".
Section 1(6)	Definition of "local government area".
Section 1(8)	Definition of "principal area".
Section 5	Change of status from county to county borough.
Section 14	Consultation with community councils.
Section 15	Elections of community councillors.
Paragraphs 8 and 9 of Schedule 2 and section 1(3) so far as it relates thereto	Meaning of "Wales".

Article 4(1) SCHEDULE 2

PROVISIONS OF PART II OF, AND SCHEDULES 6, 7 AND 10 TO, THE 1994 ACT COMING INTO FORCE ON 3RD APRIL 1995

Provision of the 1994 Act	*Subject Matter*
Section 18(1) to (6)	New principal councils to be local planning authorities in Wales.
Section 19	Joint and special planning boards in Wales.
Section 23(2) to (6)	Fire services.
Section 25	Provision of services by one new principal council for another.
Section 26	Service delivery plans.
Paragraphs 2, 3, 4, 11, 12, 21, 23 and 24(1)(b) of Schedule 6 and section 20(4) so far as it relates thereto	Miscellaneous amendments relating to provision for joint and special planning boards.
Paragraph 1 of Schedule 7 and section 22(1) so far as it relates thereto	General provision for determining the highway authority.
Paragraph 14 of Schedule 10 and section 22(4) so far as it relates thereto	Local authority plans for community care services.

Article 7 SCHEDULE 3

PROVISIONS OF PART V OF THE 1994 ACT COMING INTO FORCE ON 3RD APRIL 1995

Provision of the 1994 Act	*Subject Matter*
Section 42	Transfers of staff.
Section 44	Redundancy payments.
Section 45	Other compensation payments.

Article 8 SCHEDULE 4

PROVISIONS OF PART VI OF THE 1994 ACT COMING INTO FORCE ON 3RD APRIL 1995

Provision of the 1994 Act	*Subject Matter*
Section 51	Control of disposals and contracts.
Section 53	Continuity of exercise of functions.
Section 56	Transitional agreements as to property and finance.
Section 57	Local Acts and instruments.
Section 58	Modification etc. of local Acts and instruments.
Section 59	Existing joint boards and committees and port health districts.

Article 9(1)

SCHEDULE 5

PROVISIONS OF PART VII OF, AND SCHEDULES 15, 16, 17 AND 18 TO, THE 1994 ACT COMING INTO FORCE ON 3RD APRIL 1995

Provision of the 1994 Act	*Subject Matter*
Section 60	Records.
Paragraphs 3, 20, 23, 26 and 55 of Schedule 15 and section 66(5) so far as it relates thereto	Minor and consequential amendments of the 1972 Act.
Paragraphs 57(1) to (5), 82(1) to (4), 82(5) (but only in respect of subsections (1), (2), (7), (9) and (10) of the new section 4A of the Coroners Act 1988), 84, 85, 86, 88, 96, 97 and 106 of Schedule 16 and section 66(6) so far as it relates thereto	Other consequential amendments.
Paragraphs 2, 3, 5, 10 to 14 and 18 to 23 of Schedule 17 and section 66(7) so far as it relates thereto	Savings and transitional provisions.
In Schedule 18 the repeals to section 74(3) and (4) of the 1972 Act, sections 4(7) and 20(1)(a) of the Local Government, Planning and Land Act 1980, and sections 1(3) and 2(1) of the 1990 Act, and section 66(8) so far as it relates thereto	Consequential repeals.

POLICE

THE POLICE AND MAGISTRATES' COURTS ACT 1994 (COMMENCEMENT NO. 5 AND TRANSITIONAL PROVISIONS) (AMENDMENT NO. 2) ORDER 1995

(S.I. 1995 No. 899 (C. 23))

Made - - - - -	*27th March 1995*
Laid before Parliament	*30th March 1995*
Coming into force	*31st March 1995*

INTRODUCTION

This Order makes further amendments to art. 11(4) of the Police and Magistrates' Courts Act 1994 (Commencement No. 5 and Transitional Provisions) Order 1994 (S.I. 1994 No. 3262) which has been amended by the Police and Magistrates' Courts Act 1994 (Commencement No. 5 and Transitional Provisions) (Amendment) Order 1995 (S.I. 1995 No. 246). The amendments made refer to the increase in the council's credit ceiling by virtue of the use of supplementary credit approvals in place of the existing reference to the amounts of all supplementary credit approvals used by the council and allow regard to be had to all credit approvals issued in respect of the financial year ending on March 31, 1995.

The Secretary of State in exercise of the powers conferred on him by section 94(1), (5) and (6) of the Police and Magistrates' Courts Act 1994 (c. 29), hereby makes the following Order:

1.—(1) This Order may be cited as the Police and Magistrates' Courts Act 1994 (Commencement No. 5 and Transitional Provisions) (Amendment No. 2) Order 1995.

(2) This Order shall come into force on 31st March 1995.

2. In article 11(4) of the Police and Magistrates' Courts Act 1994 (Commencement No. 5 and Transitional Provisions) Order 1994 (S.I. 1994/3262 (C. 83), as amended by the Police and Magistrates' Courts Act 1994 (Commencement No. 5 and Transitional Provisions) (Amendment) Order 1995 (S.I. 1995/246))—

(a) for the words "the amounts of all the supplementary credit approvals used by the council and" there shall be substituted "all increases in the council's credit ceiling in that year by virtue of the use by the council of supplementary credit approvals"; and

(b) for sub-paragraph (b) there shall be substituted

"(b) for a period beginning in a financial year ending on 31st March in the years 1991 to 1995,".

Home Office

27th March 1995

David Maclean
Minister of State

MERCHANT SHIPPING

THE MERCHANT SHIPPING ACT 1970 (COMMENCEMENT NO. 11) ORDER 1995

(S.I. 1995 No. 965 (C. 24))

Made - - - - - *29th March 1995*

INTRODUCTION

This Order brings into force, on May 1, 1995, s.51 of the Merchant Shipping Act 1970 (c. 36) which relates to the restriction on employment of persons under 18 on board ship. Repeals of other enactments relating to seamen which have been superseded by later legislation are also brought into force on that date.

The Secretary of State for Transport, in exercise of powers conferred by section 101(4) of the Merchant Shipping Act 1970 (c. 36; section 101(4) was amended by section 37(7) of the Merchant Shipping Act 1979 (c. 39)) and now vested in him (see S.I. 1970/1537), and of all other powers enabling him in that behalf, hereby makes the following Order:—

1. This Order may be cited as the Merchant Shipping Act 1970 (Commencement No. 11) Order 1995.

2. The provisions of the Merchant Shipping Act 1970 specified in the first column of the Schedule to this Order (which relate to the matters specified in the second column of the Schedule) shall come into force on 1st May 1995.

Signed by authority of
the Secretary of State for Transport

Goschen
Parliamentary Under Secretary of State
Department of Transport

29th March 1995

Article 2 SCHEDULE

PROVISIONS COMING INTO FORCE ON 1ST MAY 1995

Provisions of the Act	*Subject matter of provisions*
Section 51	Restriction on employment of persons under 18 on board ship.
In section 100, subsection (3) so far as it relates to the provisions of Schedule 5 brought into force by this Schedule	Repeals.
Schedule 5, so far as it relates to the repeals set out in the Appendix to this Schedule	Enactments repealed.

APPENDIX TO SCHEDULE

REPEALS TAKING EFFECT ON 1ST MAY 1995

Chapter	*Short Title*	*Extent of Repeal*
1894 c. 60.	The Merchant Shipping Act 1894.	Part II to the extent that it is not already repealed. Sections 369, 413, 415, 416 and 417. In section 676, in subsection (1), in paragraph (b), the words "Second and" and the words from "including" to the end of the paragraph, and paragraphs (d) and (f). In section 677, paragraph (a), in paragraph (b) the words from "and the remuneration" to the end of the paragraph, and paragraph (e). In section 721, the word "Second". In section 722, subsection (2)(a). Schedules 5 and 6.
1906 c. 48.	The Merchant Shipping Act 1906.	Section 56.
1925 c. 65.	The Employment of Women, Young Persons and Children Act 1920.	In section 1, subsections (2) and (5), and in subsection (6) the sub-paragraph beginning "This section so far as it relates to employment in a ship" and, in the sub-paragraph following it, the words "or in any ship" and paragraphs (b) and (d).
1925 c. 42.	The Merchant Shipping (International Labour Convention) 1925.	The whole Act.
1950 c. 9.	The Merchant Shipping Act 1950.	Section 3, to the extent it is not already repealed.
1967 c. 26.	The Merchant Shipping Act 1967.	The whole Act.

INCOME TAX

THE INCOME AND CORPORATION TAXES ACT 1988, SECTION 737A, (APPOINTED DAY) ORDER 1995

(S.I. 1995 No. 1007 (C. 25))

Made - - - - - 5th April 1995

INTRODUCTION

This Order provides for s.737A of the Income and Corporation Taxes Act 1988 (c. 1), which makes provision relating to the sale and repurchase of securities, to apply in relation to agreements to sell U.K. equities and U.K. securities entered into on or after the day on which the Finance Act 1995 is passed.

The Treasury, in exercise of the powers conferred on them by section 737B(9) of the Income and Corporation Taxes Act 1988 (c. 1; sections 737A and 737B were inserted by section 122 of the Finance Act 1994 (c. 9)), hereby make the following Order:

1. This Order may be cited as the Income and Corporation Taxes Act 1988, section 737A, (Appointed Day) Order 1995.

2. The day appointed for the purposes of section 737A of the Income and Corporation Taxes Act 1988 in relation to agreements to sell United Kingdom equities and United Kingdom securities entered into on or after that day is the day on which the Finance Act 1995 is passed.

Derek Conway
Andrew Mitchell
Two of the Lords Commissioners
of Her Majesty's Treasury

5th April 1995

LAND

THE LAW OF PROPERTY (MISCELLANEOUS PROVISIONS) ACT 1994 (COMMENCEMENT NO. 2) ORDER 1995

(S.I. 1995 No. 1317 (C. 26))

Made - - - - - *16th May 1995*

INTRODUCTION

This Order brings into force on July 1, 1995, the remaining provisions of the Law of Property (Miscellaneous Provisions) Act 1994 (c. 36). S.I. 1995 No. 145 brought into force s.21(1) insofar as it relates to Sched. 1, para. 2, on February 15, 1995.

The Lord Chancellor, in exercise of the powers conferred on him by section 23 of the Law of Property (Miscellaneous Provisions) Act 1994 (c. 36) hereby makes the following Order—

1. This Order may be cited as the Law of Property (Miscellaneous Provisions) Act 1994 (Commencement No. 2) Order 1995.

2. The provisions of the Law of Property (Miscellaneous Provisions) Act 1994 not already in force shall come into force on 1st July 1995.

Dated 16th May 1995 *Mackay of Clashfern, C.*

COMPANIES

THE COMPANIES ACT 1989 (COMMENCEMENT NO. 15 AND TRANSITIONAL AND SAVINGS PROVISIONS) ORDER 1995

(S.I. 1995 No. 1352 (C. 27))

Made - - - - - - *20th May 1995*

INTRODUCTION

This Order brings into force on July 3, 1995, various provisions of the Companies Act 1989 (c. 40) which amend ss.463 and 464 of the Companies Act 1985 (c. 6) relating to floating charges in Scotland, insert a new s.744A (index of defined expressions) into the 1985 Act and make some repeals. The Order also contains transitional and saving provisions.

The Secretary of State, in exercise of his powers under section 215(2) and (3) of the Companies Act 1989 (c. 40), hereby makes the following Order:

Citation

1. This Order may be cited as the Companies Act 1989 (Commencement No. 15 and Transitional Savings Provisions) Order 1995.

Interpretation

2.—(1) In this Order:—

"the 1985 Act" means the Companies Act 1985 (c. 6);
"the 1986 Act" means the Insolvency Act 1986 (c. 45);
"the 1989 Act" means the Companies Act 1989,

and, unless the context otherwise requires, any expression used in this Order which is also used in Part XVIII of the 1985 Act shall have the same meaning as in that Part.

(2) Any reference in this Order to an instrument to which article 5, 6 or 7 of this Order applies is a reference to:—

(a) an instrument creating a floating charge which is executed by a company before 3rd July 1995, and
(b) an instrument of alteration under section 466 of the 1985 Act which is executed by all the parties thereto before that date.

Provisions of the 1989 Act commenced by this Order

3. Subject to articles 4 to 8 of this Order, the following provisions of the 1989 Act shall come into force on 3rd July 1995, namely:—

(a) section 140(1) to (6);
(b) paragraph 20 of Schedule 19, together with section 145 so far as it extends to that paragraph; and
(c) section 212 and Schedule 24 insofar as is necessary to effect the repeal of—

(i) the word "and" at the end of section 464(5)(c) of the 1985 Act; and

(ii) the definition of "annual return" in section 744 of the 1985 Act.

Transitional and Savings Provisions

4. The amendment made to section 463(1) of the 1985 Act by section 140(1) of the 1989 Act shall not apply to any floating charge created by a company where the commencement of the winding up of the company takes place before 3rd July 1995.

5. The amendment made to section 464(1)(b) of the 1985 Act by section 140(3) of the 1989 Act shall not have effect with respect to any provision such as is mentioned in section 464(1)(b) of the 1985 Act which is contained in an instrument to which this article applies by virtue of article 2(2) of this Order.

6. Section 464(1A) of the 1985 Act, which is inserted into that Act by section 140(4) of the 1989 Act, shall not have effect with respect to any provision such as is mentioned in section 464(1)(a) of the 1985 Act which is contained in an instrument to which this article applies by virtue of article 2(2) of this Order.

7. Section 464(3) of the 1985 Act, as substituted by section 140(5) of the 1989 Act, shall not have effect with respect to an instrument to which this article applies by virtue of article 2(2) of this Order.

8. The amendment made to section 464(5) of the 1985 Act by section 140(6) of the 1989 Act shall only have effect in any case where, on or after 3rd July 1995, a holder of the floating charge has received intimation in writing of the registration (whether that registration was before, on or after that date) of another floating charge as mentioned in section 464(5) of the 1985 Act.

Jonathan Evans,
Parliamentary Under-Secretary of State,
Department of Trade and Industry

20th May 1995

VALUE ADDED TAX

THE FINANCE ACT 1995, SECTION 24, (APPOINTED DAY) ORDER 1995

(S.I. 1995 No. 1374 (C. 28))

Made - - - - - 25th May 1995

INTRODUCTION

This Order appoints June 1, 1995 as the day on which s.32 of the Value Added Tax Act 1994 (c. 23) (relief on supply of certain secondhand goods) shall cease to have effect.

The Commissioners of Customs and Excise, in exercise of the powers conferred on them by section 24(2) of the Finance Act 1995 (c. 4) and of all other powers enabling them in that behalf, hereby make the following Order:

1. This Order may be cited as the Finance Act 1995, section 24, (Appointed Day) Order 1995.

2. The day appointed as the day on which section 32 of the Value Added Tax Act 1994 (c. 23) shall cease to have effect is 1st June 1995.

New King's Beam House
22 Upper Ground
LONDON
SE1 9PJ

Leonard Harris

25th May 1995 Commissioner of Customs and Excise

CHILDREN AND YOUNG PERSONS

THE CRIMINAL JUSTICE AND PUBLIC ORDER ACT 1994 (COMMENCEMENT NO. 7) ORDER 1995

(S.I. 1995 No. 1378 (C. 29))

Made - - - - - 24th May 1995

INTRODUCTION

This Order brings into force on May 30, 1995, s.19 of the Criminal Justice and Public Order Act 1994 (c. 33) which makes provision relating to the extension of kinds of secure accommodation.

In exercise of the powers conferred upon her by section 172(2) of the Criminal Justice and Public Order Act 1994 (c. 33), the Secretary of State hereby makes the following Order:

1. This Order may be cited as the Criminal Justice and Public Order Act 1994 (Commencement No. 7) Order 1995.

2. Section 19 of the Criminal Justice and Public Order Act 1994 (extension of kinds of secure accommodation for certain young persons) shall come into force on 30th May 1995.

Virginia Bottomley
One of Her Majesty's Principal Secretaries of State
Department of Health

24th May 1995

MERCHANT SHIPPING

THE MERCHANT SHIPPING ACT 1970 (COMMENCEMENT NO. 12) ORDER 1995

(S.I. 1995 No. 1426 (C. 30))

Made - - - - - *1st June 1995*

INTRODUCTION

This Order brings into force s.100(3) of and Schedule 5 to the Merchant Shipping Act 1970 (c. 36), both insofar as they relate to the repeal of s.5 of the Aliens Restriction (Amendment) Act 1919 (c. 92) (masters, chief engineers and skippers of British vessels to be British subjects).

The Secretary of State for Transport, in exercise of powers conferred by section 101(4) of the Merchant Shipping Act 1970(c. 36; section 101(4) was amended by section 37(7) of the Merchant Shipping Act 1979 (c. 39)) and now vested in him (S.I. 1970/1537), and of all other powers enabling him in that behalf, hereby makes the following Order:

1. This Order may be cited as the Merchant Shipping Act 1970 (Commencement No. 12) Order 1995.

2. The provisions of the Merchant Shipping Act 1970 specified in the first column of the Schedule to this Order (which relate to the matters specified in the second column of the Schedule) shall come into force on 1st August 1995.

Signed by the authority of the
Secretary of State for Transport

Goschen
Parliamentary Under Secretary of State,
Department of Transport

1st June 1995

SCHEDULE **Article 2**

PROVISIONS COMING INTO FORCE ON 1ST AUGUST 1995

Provisions of the Act	*Subject matter of provisions*
In section 100, subjection (3) so far as it relates to the provisions of Schedule 5 brought into force by this Schedule	Repeals.
Schedule 5, so far as it relates to the repeals set out in the Appendix to this Schedule	Enactments repealed.

APPENDIX TO SCHEDULE

REPEALS TAKING EFFECT ON 1ST AUGUST 1995

Chapter	*Short title*	*Extent of repeal*
1919 c. 92	The Aliens Restriction (Amendment) Act 1919	Section 5

DEREGULATION

THE DEREGULATION AND CONTRACTING OUT ACT 1994 (COMMENCEMENT NO.3) ORDER 1995

(S.I. 1995 No. 1433 (C. 31))

Made - - - - - 27th May 1995

INTRODUCTION

This Order, *inter alia*, brings into force on July 1, 1995, provisions of the Deregulation and Contracting Out Act 1994 (c. 40) amending the Companies Act 1985 (c. 6) and the Company Directors Disqualification Act 1986 (c. 46), relating to the procedure for the directors of a non-trading private company to apply to the registrar of companies for the company's name to be struck off the register.

The Secretary of State, in exercise of the powers conferred on him by section 82(4) of the Deregulation and Contracting Out Act 1994 (c. 40) and of all other powers enabling him in that behalf, hereby makes the following Order:

1. This Order may be cited as the Deregulation and Contracting Out Act 1994 (Commencement No. 3) Order 1995.

2. The provisions of the Deregulation and Contracting Out Act 1994 specified in article 3 below shall come into force on 1st July 1995.

3. The provisions referred to in article 2 above are—

(a) section 13(1) and Schedule 5 (striking off of non-trading private companies registered in Great Britain);

(b) section 13(2) and paragraphs 1 and 2 of Schedule 6 (striking off of non-trading private companies registered in Northern Ireland), insofar as is necessary to enable regulations to be made under Articles 603B(6)(f) and 603C(2)(f) of the Companies (Northern Ireland) Order 1986 (S.I. 1986/1032 (N.I. 6));

(c) section 39 (Chapter II: consequential amendments) so far as relating to section 2(1) of the Company Directors Disqualification Act 1986 (c. 46); and

(d) in Schedule 11 (miscellaneous deregulatory provisions: consequential amendments), paragraph 6.

4. Insofar as they are not yet in force, the provisions of the Deregulation and Contracting Out Act 1994 specified in article 5 below shall come into force on 1st November 1995.

5. The provisions referred to in article 4 above are—

(a) section 13(2) and Schedule 6;

(b) section 39 so far as relating to Article 5(1) of the Companies (Northern Ireland) Order 1989 (1989 N.I. 18)); and

(c) in Schedule 11, paragraph 10.

Jonathan Evans
Parliamentary Under-Secretary of State,
for Corporate and Consumer Affairs,
Department of Trade and Industry

27th May 1995

COAL INDUSTRY

THE COAL INDUSTRY ACT 1994 (COMMENCEMENT NO. 6) AND MEMBERSHIP OF THE BRITISH COAL CORPORATION (APPOINTED DAY) ORDER 1995

(S.I. 1995 No. 1507 (C. 32))

Made - - - - - 8th June 1995

INTRODUCTION

This Order appoints June 30, 1995 for the purposes of s.23(1) of the Coal Industry Act 1994 (c. 21), concerning the membership of the British Coal Corporation. It also brings into force on that date related appeals.

The Secretary of State, in exercise of the powers conferred upon him by sections 23(1), 68(4) and (5)(a) of the Coal Industry Act 1994 (c. 21), and of all other powers enabling him in that behalf, hereby makes the following Order:—

Citation and interpretation

1.—(1) This Order may be cited as the Coal Industry Act 1994 (Commencement No. 6) and Membership of the British Coal Corporation (Appointed Day) Order 1995.

(2) In this Order "the Act" means the Coal Industry Act 1994.

Provisions coming into force on 30th June 1995

2. The following provisions shall come into force on 30th June 1995:

(a) section 67(8) of the Act, so far as it relates to provisions coming into force by virtue of this Order; and

(b) Part III of Schedule 11 to the Act so far as it relates to the repeals set out in the Schedule to this Order.

Appointed day for the purposes of section 23(1) of the Act

3. The day appointed for the purposes of section 23(1)(a), (b), (c) and (d) of the Act is 30th June 1995.

Tim Eggar,
Minister for Industry and Energy,
Department of Trade and Industry

8th June 1995

SCHEDULE

REPEALS TAKING EFFECT ON 30TH JUNE 1995

Chapter	*Short title*	*Extent of repeal*
9 & 10 Geo. 6. c. 59.	The Coal Industry Nationalisation Act 1946.	In section 2— (a) in subsection (2), the words "less than eight nor"; (b) in subsection (3), the words "from amongst" onwards; and (c) subsection (5).
12 & 13 Geo. 6. c. 53.	The Coal Industry Act 1949.	Section 1(2) and (4).

FINANCIAL SERVICES

THE FINANCIAL SERVICES ACT 1986 (COMMENCEMENT) (NO. 13) ORDER 1995

(S.I. 1995 No. 1538 (C. 33))

Made - - - - - 14th June 1995

INTRODUCTION

This Order brings into force on June 19, 1995, various provisions of the Financial Services Act 1986 (c. 60), to the extent necessary to repeal Part III of and Sched. 3 to the Companies Act 1985 (c. 6) for all purposes other than the interpretation of various other provisions of the 1985 Act.

The Treasury in exercise of their powers under section 211(1) of the Financial Services Act 1986 (c. 60) hereby make the following Order—

Citation and interpretation

1.—(1) This Order may be cited as the Financial Services Act 1986 (Commencement) (No. 13) Order 1995.

(2) In this Order "the Act" means the Financial Services Act 1986.

Provisions brought into force

2. Section 212(3) of and Schedule 17 to the Act shall come into force on 19th June 1995 to the extent necessary to repeal—

(a) Part III of and Schedule 3 to the Companies Act 1985 (c. 6), and in Schedule 22 to that Act the entry relating to Part III, and in Schedule 24 to that Act the entries relating to sections 56(4), 61, 64(5), 70(1) and 78(1), for all remaining purposes except—

(i) sections 58, 59 and 60 of the Companies Act 1985, in so far as it is necessary for the purposes of sections 81, 83, 246 and 744 of that Act; and

(ii) paragraph 2 of Schedule 3 to the Companies Act 1985, in so far as it is necessary for the purposes of section 83(1)(a) of that Act; and

(iii) section 62 of the Companies Act 1985, in so far as it is necessary for purposes of section 744 of that Act; and

(b) the corresponding provisions of the Companies (Northern Ireland) Order 1986 (No. 1032 (N.I. 6)), for corresponding purposes.

Derek Conway
Timothy Kirthope
14th June 1995 — Two of the Lords Commissioners of Her Majesty's Treasury

COMPANIES

THE COMPANIES ACT 1989 (COMMENCEMENT NO. 16) ORDER 1995

(S.I. 1995 No. 1591 (C. 34))

Made - - - - - - *21st June 1995*

INTRODUCTION

This Order brings into force on July 4, 1995, ss.171, 176 and 181 of the Companies Act 1989 (c. 40). These provisions relate to settlement arrangements provided by the Bank of England, the power to make provision about certain charges and the power to apply provisions of the Act to certain cases.

The Treasury, in exercise of the powers conferred by section 215(2) of the Companies Act 1989 (c. 40) that are now vested in them (by virtue of article 2(2)(c)(i) of the Financial Services (Transfer of Functions) Order 1992 (S.I. 1992/1315), the functions originally vested in the Secretary of State under section 215(2) of the Companies Act 1989, so far as it relates to the bringing into force of any provisions of Part VII of that Act, have been transferred to the Treasury), hereby make the following Order:—

1. This Order may be cited as the Companies Act 1989 (Commencement No. 16) Order 1995.

2. Sections 171, 176 and 181 of the Companies Act 1989 shall come into force on 4th July 1995.

Timothy Kirkhope
Timothy Wood
Two of the Lords Commissioners of
Her Majesty's Treasury

21st June 1995

INCOME TAX

THE FINANCE ACT 1995 (CONTRACTUAL SAVINGS SCHEMES) (APPOINTED DAY) ORDER 1995

(S.I. 1995 No. 1778 (C. 35))

Made - - - - - *12th July 1995*

INTRODUCTION

This Order appoints July 31, 1995 as the day from which the amendments to s.326 of the Income and Corporation Taxes Act 1988 (c. 1) made by the Finance Act 1995 (c. 4) will apply to new contractual savings schemes certified under s.326 of the 1988 Act by the Treasury.

The Treasury, in exercise of the powers conferred on them by section 65 of and paragraph 4(3) of Schedule 12 to the Finance Act 1995 (c. 4) and of all other powers enabling them in that behalf, hereby make the following Order:

1. This Order may be cited as the Finance Act 1995 (Contractual Savings Schemes) (Appointed Day) Order 1995.

2. The day appointed under paragraph 4(3) of Schedule 12 to the Finance Act 1995 is 31st July 1995.

Derek Conway
Andrew Mackay
Two of the Lords Commissioners
of Her Majesty's Treasury

12th July 1995

INCOME TAX

WATER SUPPLY, SCOTLAND

THE LOCAL GOVERNMENT ETC. (SCOTLAND) ACT 1994 (COMMENCEMENT NO. 4) ORDER 1995

(S.I. 1995 No. 1898 (C. 36) (S. 141))

Made - - - - - - *14th July 1995*

INTRODUCTION

This Order brings into force on July 17, 1995, various provisions in Pt. II of the Local Government etc. (Scotland) Act 1994 (c. 39), for example, those provisions relating to new water and sewerage authorities, charges schemes, duties and powers relating to finance and acquisition of land by agreement. The Order also brings into force on the same date some other related provisions.

The Secretary of State, in exercise of the powers conferred on him by section 184(2) of the Local Government etc. (Scotland) Act 1994 (c. 39) and of all other powers enabling him in that behalf, hereby makes the following Order:

Citation and interpretation

1.—(1) This Order may be cited as the Local Government etc. (Scotland) Act 1994 (Commencement No. 4) Order 1995.

(2) In this Order, "the Act" means the Local Government etc. (Scotland) Act 1994.

Day appointed

2. 17th July 1995 is the day appointed for the coming into force of—

(a) the provisions of the Act specified in column 1 of the Schedule to this Order (which relate to the matters specified in column 2 of that Schedule);

(b) subsections (1) and (2) of section 177 of the Act, so far as those subsections relate to the entries in Part II of the House of Commons Disqualification Act 1975 (c. 24) concerning the East of Scotland Water Authority, the North of Scotland Water Authority and the West of Scotland Water Authority;

(c) section 180 of the Act, so far as it relates to the provision in Schedule 13 to the Act specified in paragraph (d) below; and

(d) in Schedule 13 to the Act, paragraph 75(25)(b).

George Kynoch
Parliamentary Under-Secretary of State,
Scottish Office

St. Andrew's House, Edinburgh
14th July 1995

Article 2(a)

SCHEDULE

PROVISIONS OF THE ACT COMING INTO FORCE ON 17TH JULY 1995

Column 1 *Provision of the Act*	*Column 2* *Subject matter*
Section 62	New water and sewerage authorities
Section 63	Alteration of water areas and sewerage areas
Section 64	Maps of areas
Section 65(2)	General duties of Secretary of State and of new authorities

Column 1 *Provision of the Act*	*Column 2* *Subject matter*
Section 66	Codes of practice for new water and sewerage authorities
Section 73	Duty of new authorities as respects Natural Heritage Area or area of special interest
Section 74	Charges for services provided
Section 76	Charges schemes
Section 77	Publication of summary of charges scheme
Section 79(1) to (3) and (5)	Collection of charges by local authority
Section 81	Reduced charges
Section 83	Duties and powers relating to finance
Section 84	Financing and borrowing
Section 85	Guarantees
Section 86	Directions as to payment and investment
Section 87	Accounts
Section 88	Audit of accounts
Section 89	Subsidiary powers of new authorities
Section 90	Dissolution of Central Scotland Water Development Board
Section 98	Acquisition of land by agreement
Section 116	Power of Secretary of State to give directions to new authorities
Section 118(1)	Provision of information, etc.
Section 120(1)	Duty of new authorities to collaborate
Section 122	Supply of goods and services to new authorities by local authorities
Section 123	Power to require local authorities and assessors to supply information to new authorities
Schedule 7	Constitution and proceedings etc. of a new water and sewerage authority
Schedule 8	Water and sewerage areas

LICENSING (LIQUOR)

THE LICENSING (SUNDAY HOURS) ACT 1995 (COMMENCEMENT) ORDER 1995

(S.I. 1995 No. 1930 (C. 37))

Made - - - - - 20th July 1995

INTRODUCTION

This Order brings all provisions of the Licensing (Sunday Hours) Act 1995 (c. 33) into force on August 6, 1995.

The Secretary of State, in exercise of the power conferred upon him by section 5 of the Licensing (Sunday Hours) Act 1995 (c. 33), hereby makes the following Order:

1. This Order may be cited as the Licensing (Sunday Hours) Act 1995 (Commencement) Order 1995.

2. The Licensing (Sunday Hours) Act 1995 shall come into force on 6th August 1995.

Home Office
20th July 1995

Nicholas Baker
Parliamentary Under-Secretary of State

CRIMINAL LAW, ENGLAND AND WALES
CRIMINAL LAW, SCOTLAND
CRIMINAL LAW, NORTHERN IRELAND

THE CRIMINAL JUSTICE AND PUBLIC ORDER ACT 1994 (COMMENCEMENT NO. 8 AND TRANSITIONAL PROVISIONS) ORDER 1995

(S.I. 1995 No. 1957 (C. 38))

Made - - - - - 23rd July 1995

INTRODUCTION

This Order brings into force various provisions of the Criminal Justice and Public Order Act 1994 (c. 33) making provisions relating to squatters, interim possession orders and powers of entry, extension of procedures for guilty pleas and video recordings and restriction of exemptions and repeals.

In exercise of the powers conferred on him by section 172(2) and (3) of the Criminal Justice and Public Order Act 1994 (c. 33), the Secretary of State hereby makes the following Order:

1. This Order may be cited as the Criminal Justice and Public Order Act 1994 (Commencement No. 8 and Transitional Provisions) Order 1995.

2. In this Order any reference to a section or a schedule is a reference to a section of or, as the case may be, a schedule to, the Criminal Justice and Public Order Act 1994.

3. Sections 75 and 76 and paragraph 53 of Schedule 10 (squatters: interim possession orders: power of entry) shall come into force on 24th August 1995.

4. Section 45, Schedule 5 and paragraph 65 of Schedule 10 (extension of procedures for guilty pleas) shall come into force on 4th September 1995.

5.—(1) Subject to paragraph (2) below, section 89 (video recordings: restriction of exemptions) shall come into force on 1st November 1995.

(2) Paragraph (1) above does not apply in relation to a video work of which a video recording has been supplied or offered for supply prior to 1st November 1995.

(3) In this article "video work" and "video recording" have the same meaning as in the Video Recordings Act 1984 (c. 39).

6. Section 168 shall, so far as it is not already in force, come into force on 4th September 1995 to the extent necessary to bring into force on that date the provisions of Schedule 11 (repeals) so far as it relates to the following enactments:

Prosecution of Offences Act 1985 (c. 23)
Criminal Justice Act 1988 (c. 33): sections 25, 34 and 160.

Home Office
23rd July 1995

Michael Howard
One of Her Majesty's Principal Secretaries of State

CRIMINAL LAW, ENGLAND AND WALES
CRIMINAL LAW, SCOTLAND
CRIMINAL LAW, NORTHERN IRELAND

THE CRIMINAL JUSTICE ACT 1993 (COMMENCEMENT NO. 9) ORDER 1995

(S.I. 1995 No. 1958 (C. 39))

Made - - - - - *22nd July 1995*

INTRODUCTION

This Order brings into force Sched. 5, para. 1, to the Criminal Justice Act 1993 (c. 36), which provides for consequential amendments, on August 14, 1995.

In exercise of the powers conferred upon him by section 78(3) and (4) of the Criminal Justice Act 1993 (c. 36), the Secretary of State hereby makes the following Order:

1. This Order may be cited as the Criminal Justice Act 1993 (Commencement No. 9) Order 1995.

2. Paragraph 1 of Schedule 5 to the Criminal Justice Act 1993 (Consequential Amendments) together with, to the extent necessary to commence that paragraph, section 79(13) of that Act, shall come into force on 14th August 1995.

3. This Order extends to England and Wales only.

Home Office
22nd July 1995

David Maclean
Minister of State

ENVIRONMENTAL PROTECTION

THE ENVIRONMENT ACT 1995 (COMMENCEMENT NO. 1) ORDER 1995

(S.I. 1995 No. 1983 (C. 40))

Made - - - - - - *21st July 1995*

INTRODUCTION

This Order brings various provisions of the Environment Act 1995 (c. 25) into force. Provisions relating, *inter alia*, to the Environment Agency, schemes for the transfer of property, rights of and liabilities to the Agency, the principal aim and objectives of the Agency, general environmental and recreational duties, codes of practice with respect to those duties and environment protection advisory committees are brought into force on July 28, 1995.

Provisions relating to the approval of charging schemes, producer responsibility, hedgerows, grants for purposes conducive to conservation, consultation before making or modifying certain subordinate legislation for England, grants in connection with drainage works and sea fisheries are brought into force on September 21, 1995.

Finally, provisions relating to the provision of screens to protect salmon and migatory trout are brought into force on January 1, 1999.

The Secretary of State, in exercise of his powers under section 125(2) of the Environment Act 1995 (c. 25), hereby makes the following Order:

Citation

1. This Order may be cited as the Environment Act 1995 (Commencement No. 1) Order 1995.

Provisions coming into force on 28th July 1995

2. The following provisions of the Environment Act 1995 shall come into force on 28th July 1995—

section 1;
section 3(2) to (8);
section 4;
section 7;
section 9;
section 12
section 37(1), (2) and (9);
sections 38 to 40;
sections 43 to 52;
section 56;
section 120(1) in so far as it—

(a) confers power on the Secretary of State and the Minister to make regulations; or
(b) relates to paragraphs 4, 31, 42, 213(1), (2)(b) and (3) and 223(1)(c) of Schedule 22;

section 120(4) to (6);
sections 121 to 124.

Provisions coming into force on 21st September 1995

3. The following provisions of the Environment Act 1995 shall come into force on 21st September 1995—

section 41 in so far as it confers power to make schemes imposing charges;
section 42;
sections 57 and 58, in so far as the amendments made by those sections—

(a) confer power on the Secretary of State to make regulations or orders, give directions or issue guidance; or
(b) make provision with respect to the exercise of any such power;

sections 93 to 95;
sections 97 to 103;
section 105 in so far as it relates to paragraphs 25 and 26(1) of Schedule 15;
section 166 in so far as it relates to paragraphs 2(1) to (3) of Schedule 21;
section 120(1) in so far as it relates to the following provisions of Schedule 22—

(a) paragraphs 37(1) and (4), 38, 39, 76(1) and (3), 80(1) and (2), 133(1), 137 to 139, 147, 153, 182, 187(1) and 192;

(b) paragraphs 82(1) and (5) and 162, in so far as the amendments made by those provisions—

(i) confer power on the Secretary of State to make regulations; or

(ii) make provision with respect to the exercise of any such power;

section 130(3) in so far as it relates to the repeal in Schedule 24 of sections 68, 69(5), 126(6) and 129(4) of the Water Resources Act 1991 (c. 57).

Provisions coming into force on 1st January 1999

4. The following provisions of the Environment Act 1995 shall come into force on 1st January 1999—
section 105 in so far as it relates to paragraphs 13, 14(1) and (4), 17, 20 and 26(2) of Schedule 15;
section 120(2) in so far as it relates to paragraph 14(5) and (6) of Schedule 23 and to the definitions of "grating" and "the substitution date" in paragraph 14(8) of that Schedule;
section 120(3) in so far as it relates to the repeals made in Schedule 24 in relation to sections 30 and 41(1) of the Salmon and Freshwater Fisheries Act 1975 (c. 51).

Signed by authority of
Secretary of State for the Environment
21st July 1995

David Curry
Minister of State,
Department of the Environment

CHILDREN AND YOUNG PERSONS
CRIMINAL LAW, ENGLAND AND WALES
POLICE

THE PRISONERS (RETURN TO CUSTODY) ACT 1995 (COMMENCEMENT) ORDER 1995

(S.I. 1995 No. 2021 (C. 41))

Made - - - - - 28th July 1995

INTRODUCTION

This Order brings all provisions of the Prisoners (Return to Custody) Act 1995 (c. 16) into force on September 5, 1995.

In exercise of the powers conferred upon me by section 3(2) of the Prisoners (Return to Custody) Act 1995 (c. 16), I hereby make the following Order:

1. This Order may be cited as the Prisoners (Return to Custody) Act 1995 (Commencement) Order 1995.

2. The Prisoners (Return to Custody) Act 1995 shall come into force on 5th September 1995.

Home Office *Michael Howard*
28th July 1995 One of Her Majesty's Principal Secretaries of State

TOWN AND COUNTRY PLANNING, SCOTLAND

THE PLANNING AND COMPENSATION ACT 1991 (COMMENCEMENT NO. 18 AND TRANSITIONAL PROVISION) (SCOTLAND) ORDER 1995

(S.I. 1995 No. 2045 (C. 42) (S. 150))

Made - - - - - *31st July 1995*

INTRODUCTION

This Order brings into force s.59 of and Sched. 11 to the Planning and Compensation Act 1991 (c. 34), which deal with simplified planning zones and which apply to Scotland, on August 30, 1995. Other miscellaneous provisions relating to Scotland are also brought into force, with the result that the only provisions of the Act relating to Scotland that are not in force after that date are Sched. 19, Pt. IV, repeals relating to s.101(1) and (2) of the Town and Country Planning Act 1972 (c. 52) and Sched. 13, para. 44.

The Secretary of State, in exercise of the powers conferred on him by section 84(2) and (3) of the Planning and Compensation Act 1991 (c. 34) and of all other powers enabling him in that behalf, hereby makes the following Order:

Citation

1. This Order may be cited as the Planning and Compensation Act 1991 (Commencement No. 18 and Transitional Provision) (Scotland) Order 1995.

Interpretation

2. In this Order—

"the 1972 Act" means the Town and Country Planning (Scotland) Act 1972 (c. 52);

"the 1991 Act" means the Planning and Compensation Act 1991.

Provisions coming into force on 30th August 1995

3. The following provisions of the 1991 Act shall come into force on 30th August 1995:—

section 59;

section 61 insofar as it relates to the provision of Schedule 13 referred to below;

section 80 insofar as it relates to the provisions of Schedule 18 referred to below;

section 84(6) insofar as it gives effect to the repeals in Part IV of Schedule 19 specified in the Schedule to this Order;

Schedule 11;

in Schedule 13 paragraph 40(2); and

in Schedule 18 the entries in Part I in respect of sections 56J(8) and 56K(12) of the 1972 Act.

Transitional provision

4. The amendments to Schedule 6A to the 1972 Act brought into force by this Order shall not apply with respect to any proposals for the making or alteration of a simplified planning zone scheme which are or have been made available for inspection in accordance with paragraphs 5 or 6 of Schedule 6A to the 1972 Act before the coming into force of this Order but where that scheme or that alteration of a scheme has not yet come into operation on that date.

George Kynoch
Parliamentary Under-Secretary of State,
Scottish Office

St Andrew's House, Edinburgh
31st July 1995

Article 3

SCHEDULE

REPEALS IN PART IV OF SCHEDULE 19 (REPEALS: SCOTLAND)

Chapter	*Short Title*	*Extent of Repeal*
1972 c. 52	Town and Country Planning (Scotland) Act 1972	Section 61(6). In Schedule 6A, in paragraph 12(2)(e), the words from "for the purpose" to "5(3)". In Schedule 7, in paragraph 2(1)(c), the words "and (3)". Schedules 12 to 15.

ENVIRONMENTAL PROTECTION

THE ENVIRONMENTAL PROTECTION ACT 1990 (COMMENCEMENT NO. 17) ORDER 1995

(S.I. 1995 No. 2152 (C. 43))

Made - - - - - 10th August 1995

INTRODUCTION

This Order brings s.62 of the Environmental Protection Act 1990 (c. 43), which enables the Secretary of State to make special provision by regulations with respect to certain dangerous or intractable waste, into force on August 11, 1995.

The Secretary of State, in exercise of his powers under section 164(3) of the Environmental Protection Act 1990 (c. 43), hereby makes the following Order:

Citation

1. This Order may be cited as the Environmental Protection Act 1990 (Commencement No.17) Order 1995.

Provisions coming into force on 11th August 1995

2. Section 62 of the Environmental Protection Act 1990 shall come into force on 11th August 1995.

Signed by authority of the Secretary of State

Paul Beresford
Parliamentary Under-Secretary of State
10th August 1995 Department of the Environment

ROAD TRAFFIC

THE GOODS VEHICLES (LICENSING OF OPERATORS) ACT 1995 (COMMENCEMENT AND TRANSITIONAL PROVISIONS) ORDER 1995

(S.I. 1995 No. 2181 (C. 44))

Made - - - - - - 21st August 1995

INTRODUCTION

This Order brings into force on January 1, 1996, almost all provisions of the Goods Vehicles (Licensing of Operators) Act 1995 (c. 23). The 1995 Act consolidates Pt. V of the Transport Act 1968 (c. 73) and related provisions concerning goods vehicle operator licensing. Section 50 of, and Sched. 5 to, the 1995 Act which are not yet in force, relate to consignment notes.

The Secretary of State for Transport, in exercise of the powers conferred by section 61 of the Goods Vehicles (Licensing of Operators) Act 1995 (c. 23), hereby makes the following Order:—

1. This Order may be cited as the Goods Vehicles (Licensing of Operators) Act 1995 (Commencement and Transitional Provisions) Order 1995.

2. The Goods Vehicles (Licensing of Operators) Act 1995, except section 50 and Schedule 5, shall come into force on the 1st January 1996.

3. The Schedule to this Order (transitional provisions) shall have effect.

Signed by authority of the Secretary of State

Steven Norris
Parliamentary Under Secretary of State,
21st August 1995 Department of Transport

Article 3 THE SCHEDULE

TRANSITIONAL PROVISIONS

Interpretation

1. In this Schedule—

"the 1968 Act" means the Transport Act 1968 (c. 73. Section 67 was amended by the Road Traffic Act 1974 (c. 50), Sch. 4, para. 3. Section 68 was amended by the Goods Vehicles (Operators' Licences, Qualifications and Fees) Regulations 1984 (S.I. 1984/176) reg. 36. Section 69 was amended by the Transport Act 1982 (c. 49) ("the 1982 Act"), Sch. 4, Part II, para. 7. Section 69A to 69G were inserted by the 1982 Act, Sch. 4, Part I. Part V is repealed by the Goods Vehicles (Licensing of Operators) Act 1995, Sch. 8. Other amendments have been made which are not relevant for the purposes of this instrument. Prospective amendments were made by the Deregulation and Contracting Out Act 1994 (c. 40) (see explanatory note).

"the 1995 Act" means the Goods Vehicles (Licensing of Operators) Act 1995;

"the appointed day" means 1st January 1996;

"existing licence" means an operator's licence within the meaning of Part V of the 1968 Act which was in force immediately before the appointed day; and "old-style licence" means an existing licence in respect of which no direction has been given under paragraph 10 below.

Licences with expiry dates before the appointed day

2.—(1) This paragraph applies to an existing licence if—

(a) on the date that the licence was due to expire proceedings were pending before the traffic commissioner on an application by the holder of the licence for the grant to him of a new licence in substitution therefor; and

(b) the licence was in force immediately before the appointed day by virtue of that application and section 67(4) of the 1968 Act.

(2) An existing licence to which this paragraph applies shall, unless previously revoked or otherwise terminated under any provision of the 1995 Act or any other statutory provision, terminate upon the requirements of sub-paragraph (3) below being met.

(3) The requirements of this sub-paragraph are that—

(a) the application, and

(b) any appeal under (or having effect as an appeal under) section 37 of the 1995 Act arising out of that application,

are disposed of.

(4) Section 16(2) of the 1995 Act shall have effect subject to this paragraph.

Prematurely terminated licences

3.—(1) This paragraph applies to an existing licence if—

(a) a traffic commissioner has, before the appointed day, given a direction under section 69 of the 1968 Act that an existing licence be terminated on a date earlier than that on which it would otherwise expire under section 67 of that Act; and

(b) the date specified in the direction as the date on which the licence is to terminate is on or after the appointed day.

(2) Subject to sub-paragraph (3), an existing licence to which this paragraph applies shall, unless previously revoked or otherwise terminated under any provision of the 1995 Act or any other statutory provision, terminate on the date specified in the direction as the date on which the licence is to terminate.

(3) If, on the date on which an existing licence is due to expire by virtue of sub-paragraph (2) above, proceedings are pending before the traffic commissioner on an application by the holder of that licence for the grant to him of a new licence in substitution therefor, the existing licence shall, subject to its revocation or other termination under any provision of the 1995 Act or any other statutory provision, continue in force until—

(a) the application, and

(b) any appeal under section 37 of the 1995 Act arising out of the application,

are disposed of.

(4) Section 16(2) of the 1995 Act shall have effect subject to this paragraph.

Statements of intent

4. Where—

(a) the holder of an old-style licence had made or procured to be made—

(i) for the purposes of his application for the licence, or

(ii) for the purposes of an application for the variation of the licence,

a statement of intent in writing; and

(b) the application was determined before the appointed day,

the statement shall, for the purposes of the 1995 Act, have effect on and after the appointed day as if it were an undertaking recorded in the licence.

Authorised vehicles

5.—(1) Section 5 of the 1995 Act (which replaces section 61 of the 1968 Act) shall have effect in relation to an old style licence as if for subsection (1) there were substituted—

"(1) Subject to subsection (2) of this section, the vehicles authorised to be used under an operator's licence shall be—

(a) such motor vehicles, being vehicles in the lawful possession of the holder of the licence as are specified in the licence;

(b) trailers from time to time in the lawful possession of the holder of the licence, not exceeding at any time such maximum number as is specified in the licence;

(c) unless the licence does not permit the addition of vehicles under this paragraph and subject to subsection (6) of this section, motor vehicles not exceeding such maximum number as is specified in the licence, being vehicles in the lawful possession of the holder of the licence.

For the purposes of paragraphs (b) and (c) of this subsection different types of trailers or different types of motor vehicles, as the case may be, may be distinguished in a licence and a maximum number may be specified in the licence for trailers or vehicles of each type.".

(2) Section 5(2) and (3) of the 1995 Act shall not have effect in relation to an old-style licence.

(3) Subject to sub-paragraph (4) below, section 5(6) of the 1995 Act shall have effect in relation to an old-style licence as if for the words "subsection (1)" there were substituted the words "subsection (1)(c)".

(4) In section 5(6) of the 1995 Act, the words "and has paid him a prescribed fee" shall not have effect in relation to a notice given to the traffic commissioner under section 61(3) of the 1968 Act before the appointed day.

(5) In section 5(7) of the 1995 Act, the words "and the prescribed fee has been duly paid under subsection (6)" shall not have effect in relation to a notice to the traffic commissioner under section 61(3) of the 1968 Act before the appointed day.

(6) Section 6 of the 1995 Act shall not have effect in relation to an old-style licence.

Variation of old-style licences

6. Section 17 of the 1995 Act (which amongst other things replaces section 68 of the 1968 Act) shall have effect in relation to an old-style licence as if—

(a) for subsection 1(a) to (f) there were substituted—

"(a) that additional vehicles be specified therein;

(aa) that the maximum number of trailers or of motor vehicles specified in the licence under (or having effect as specified in the licence under) paragraph (b) or (c) of section 5(1) of the 1995 Act (as substituted by paragraph 5 of the Schedule to the Goods Vehicles (Licensing of Operators) Act 1995 (Commencement and Transitional Provisions) Order 1995) be increased;

(ab) if the licence does not permit the addition of vehicles under paragraph (c) of the said section 5(1) (as so substituted), that it shall so permit and that a maximum be specified under that paragraph accordingly;

(b) that vehicles specified therein be removed therefrom or that any such maximum as is mentioned in paragraph (aa) of this subsection be reduced;";

(b) for subsection (1)(h), there were substituted—

"(h) that—

(i) any statement of intent which, by virtue of paragraph 4 of the Schedule to the Goods Vehicles (Licensing of Operators) Act 1995 (Commencement and Transitional Provisions) Order 1995 has effect as if it were an undertaking recorded in the licence, cease to have such effect, or

(ii) any undertaking recorded in the licence be varied or removed;";

(c) in subsection (4), paragraph (a) was omitted.

Publication of notices of applications for licences made before the appointed day

7. Section 11 of the 1995 Act (which replaces section 69E of the 1968 Act in part) shall have effect in relation to an application for a licence made before the appointed day as if subsection (3) were omitted.

Publication of notices of applications for the variation of licences made before the appointed day

8.—(1) Section 18 of the 1995 Act (which replaces section 69E of the 1968 Act in part) shall not have effect in relation to an application made before the appointed day for the variation of a licence unless notice of the application has been (or has the effect of having been) published under section 17(3) of the 1995 Act.

(2) Section 18 of the 1995 Act shall have effect in relation to an application made before the appointed day of which notice has been published as mentioned in sub-paragraph (1) above as if—

(a) for subsections (1) and (2) there were substituted the following subsection—

"(1) The traffic commissioner to whom an application for the variation of an operator's licence is made shall refuse the application without considering the merits unless he is satisfied that subsection (3) has been complied with in respect of each locality affected by the application."; and

(b) subsection (4) were omitted.

Publication of notices of applications for the variation of old-style licences made on or after the appointed day

9.—(1) Section 18 of the 1995 Act (which replaces section 69E of the 1968 Act in part) shall not have effect in relation to an application made on or after the appointed day for the variation of an old-style licence unless notice of the application has been (or has the effect of having been) published under section 17(3) of the 1995 Act.

(2) Section 18 of the 1995 Act shall have effect in relation to an application for a variation of an old-style licence made on or after the appointed day of which notice has been published as mentioned in sub-paragraph (1) above as if for paragraphs (a) and (b) there were substituted—

"(a) any direction under section 17(1)(a) (as substituted by paragraph 6 of the Goods Vehicles (Licensing of Operators) Act 1995 (Commencement and Transitional Provisions) Order 1995) that additional vehicles be specified in the licence;

(aa) any direction under section 17(1)(aa) (as so substituted) that a maximum number specified in the licence be increased;

(ab) any direction under section 17(1)(ab) (as so substituted);".

Conversion of old-style licences

10.—(1) The traffic commissioner by whom an old-style licence was issued may at any time after the appointed day vary the licence by directing—

(a) that any maximum number specified in the licence under (or having effect as specified in the licence under) section 5(1)(b) or (c) of the 1995 Act (as substituted by paragraph 5 above) shall cease to have effect;

(b) that a provision such as is mentioned in section 5(2) of the 1995 Act be included in the licence;

(c) that a maximum number of motor vehicles be specified in the licence in accordance with section 6(1)(a) of the 1995 Act;

(d) that a maximum number of trailers be specified in the licence in accordance with section 6(2)(a) of the 1995 Act;

(e) that a provision such as is mentioned in section 6(1)(b) or (2)(b) of the 1995 Act be included in the licence;

(f) that any statement having effect as an undertaking by virtue of paragraph 4 above immediately before the direction or a statement to the like effect be recorded in the licence as an undertaking; or

(g) that an alteration of any other description be made which appears to the traffic commissioner to be consequential to the coming into force of the 1995 Act;

or any two or more of those things; and paragraph 5 of this Schedule shall be disregarded for the purposes of paragraphs (b) to (e) above.

(2) The powers under sub-paragraph (1) above shall be exercised in such a way as appears to the traffic commissioner—

(a) to put the licence into a form that would have been appropriate had the 1995 Act been in force at the time it was granted; and

(b) to leave the holder of the licence in the same position as he was immediately before the licence is varied or as near to that position as is practicable using those powers while meeting the requirements of paragraph (a) above.

(3) If it appears to a traffic commissioner that an old-style licence is in a form that would have been appropriate had the 1995 Act been in force at the time it was granted, he may at any time after the appointed day give a direction that no variation is to be made to the licence under this paragraph.

(4) A traffic commissioner shall not exercise his powers under this paragraph without first giving the holder of the licence an opportunity to make representations to the commissioner with respect to the proposed variation.

Revocation etc. of old-style licences

11. Section 26 of the 1995 Act (which replaces section 69 of the 1968 Act) shall have effect in relation to an old-style licence as if in subsection (11) for paragraphs (b) and (c) there were substituted—

"(b) that the maximum number of trailers or of motor vehicles specified in the licence in pursuance of (or having effect as specified in the licence in pursuance of) section 5(1)(b) or (c) of the 1995 Act (as substituted by paragraph 5 of the Schedule to the Goods Vehicles (Licensing of Operators) Act 1995 (Commencement and Transitional Provisions) Order 1995) be reduced;

(c) that the addition of vehicles under the said section 5(1)(c) (as so substituted) be no longer permitted;".

Periods of review of operating centres

12.—(1) Subject to sub-paragraph (2) below, section 30(2) of the 1995 Act shall not have effect in relation to an existing licence, but in relation to such a licence, the periods of review for the purposes of the 1995 Act are—

(a) the period—

(i) beginning with the date specified in the licence as the date on which it came into force, and

(ii) ending at the end of the last day that the licence would have continued in force by virtue of section 67(2) of the 1968 Act had neither the Deregulation and Contracting Out Act 1994 (c. 40) nor the 1995 Act been passed; and

(b) each consecutive period of five years.

(2) Sections 30, 31 and 32 of the 1995 Act shall not have effect in relation to a licence to which paragraph 2 or 3 above applies.

Removal of operating centres on review

13.—(1) This paragraph has effect where a person at any time—

(a) after the date that this Order is made, and

(b) before the appointed day,

makes representations to the traffic commissioner as to the unsuitability of a relevant place on environmental grounds for continued use as an operating centre for vehicles used under any operator's licence; and for the purposes of this sub-paragraph a relevant place is a place specified in an operator's licence issued by the traffic commissioner.

(2) If the representations comply with paragraphs (a) and (b) of regulation 18 of the Goods Vehicles (Operators' Licences, Qualifications and Fees) Regulations 1984 (S.I. 1984/176; relevant amending instrument is S.I. 1987/841), the representations shall for the purposes of section 31 of the 1995 Act—

(a) be deemed to comply with the requirements of subsection (5)(a) of that section; and

(b) have effect as if that section had been in force at the time the representations are made.

(3) Representations made on or before the date that this Order is made shall be disregarded for the purposes of section 31 of the 1995 Act.

Fees

14. Nothing in section 45(3) of the 1995 Act shall in any circumstances affect the validity of—

(a) any decision made;

(b) any direction given;

(c) any licence issued; or

(d) any variation effected,

before the appointed day.

CRIMINAL LAW, SCOTLAND

THE CRIMINAL JUSTICE (SCOTLAND) ACT 1995 (COMMENCEMENT NO. 1, TRANSITIONAL PROVISIONS AND SAVINGS) ORDER 1995

(S.I. 1995 No. 2295 (C. 45) (S. 171))

Made - - - - - - *31st August 1995*

INTRODUCTION

This Order brings into force various provisions of the Criminal Justice (Scotland) Act 1995 (c. 20), which relate, *inter alia*, to routine evidence, supervised attendance orders, leave to appeal and legal aid in criminal appeals, on September 26, 1995. Transitional and savings provisions are also made.

The Secretary of State, in exercise of the powers conferred upon him by section 118(2) and (3) of the Criminal Justice (Scotland) Act 1995 (c. 20) and of all other powers enabling him in that behalf, hereby makes the following Order:

Citation and interpretation

1. This Order may be cited as the Criminal Justice (Scotland) Act 1995 (Commencement No. 1, Transitional Provisions and Savings) Order 1995.

2. In this Order—
"the Act" means the Criminal Justice (Scotland) Act 1995; and
"the 1975 Act" means the Criminal Procedure (Scotland) Act 1975 (c. 21).

Commencement of Provisions

3.—(1) This Article has effect subject to the provisions of Articles 4 to 6 below.

(2) The provisions of the Act which are specified in column 1 of the Schedule to this Order shall, insofar as they are not then in force, come into force on 26th September 1995 but, where a particular purpose in relation to any such provision is specified in column 2 of that Schedule, that provision shall come into force on that day only for that purpose.

Transitional Provisions and Savings

4. Section 35 of the Act shall not affect the powers of a court in relation to an offence committed before 26th September 1995.

5. Section 42 of the Act shall not apply in relation to an appeal where the person was, before 26th September 1995, convicted of or, as the case may be, found to have committed the offence.

6. Section 65 of the Act and the repeal, in Part I of Schedule 7 to the Act, of words in section 25(2) of the Legal Aid (Scotland) Act 1986 (c. 47) shall not apply in the case of an application for criminal legal aid in respect of an appeal under section 228(1) or 442(1)(a) of the 1975 Act where the person was, before 26th September 1995, convicted of or, as the case may be, found to have committed the offence.

James Douglas-Hamilton
Minister of State,
Scottish Office

St Andrew's House, Edinburgh
31st August 1995

Article 3(2)

SCHEDULE

THE PROVISIONS OF THE ACT WHICH COME INTO FORCE ON 26TH SEPTEMBER 1995

Column 1 *Provisions of the Act*	*Column 2* *Purpose*
Section 22(1), (3), (4), (7) and (9)	
Section 35	
Section 42	
Section 43	
Section 65	
Section 117(1)	Only for the purpose of bringing into force the provisions of Schedule 6 to the Act specified in column 1 below
Section 117(2)	Only for the purpose of bringing into force the repeals in Schedule 7 to the Act which are referred to in column 1 below
Section 118	
Paragraph 87 of Schedule 6 to the Act	
In part I of Schedule 7 to the Act, the repeals listed in the Table below	

TABLE

REPEALS

Chapter	*Short Title*	*Extent of repeal*
1975 c. 21	The Criminal Procedure (Scotland) Act 1975	Section 256.
1980 c. 62	The Criminal Justice (Scotland) Act 1980	In section 26, in subsection (2), the word "summary" and the words from "In the foregoing" to the end.
1986 c. 47	The Legal Aid (Scotland) Act 1986	In section 25(2), the words "the Board is satisfied".

FAMILY LAW

CHILD SUPPORT

THE CHILD SUPPORT ACT 1995 (COMMENCEMENT NO. 1) ORDER 1995

(S.I. 1995 No. 2302 (C. 46))

Made - - - - - 4th September 1995

INTRODUCTION

This Order brings into force various provisions of the Child Support Act 1995 (c. 34). The provisions include those relating to the deferral of the right to apply for maintenance assessment, disputed parentage and repayment of overpaid child support maintenance which come into force on September 4, 1995, and those relating to reviews on change of circumstances, repayment of overpaid child support maintenance and compensation payments which come into force on October 1, 1995.

The Secretary of State for Social Security, in exercise of the power conferred upon him by section 30(4) of the Child Support Act 1995 (c. 34), hereby makes the following Order:

Citation and interpretation

1.—(1) This Order may be cited as the Child Support Act 1995 (Commencement No. 1) Order 1995.

(2) In this Order, unless the context otherwise requires, references to sections, Schedules and paragraphs of a Schedule are references to sections of, Schedules to, and paragraphs of a Schedule to the Child Support Act 1995.

Appointed days

2.—(1) The day appointed for the coming into force of the provisions specified in Part I of the Schedule to this Order is 4th September 1995.

(2) The day appointed for the coming into force of the provisions specified in Part II of the Schedule to this Order is 1st October 1995.

Signed by authority of the Secretary of State for Social Security.

Andrew Mitchell
Department of Social Security

4th September 1995

Article 2

SCHEDULE

PART I

PROVISIONS COMING INTO FORCE ON 4TH SEPTEMBER 1995

Provisions of the Child Support Act 1995	*Subject Matter*
Section 18	Deferral of right to apply for maintenance assessment
Section 19	Non-referral of applications for maintenance assessments
Section 20	Disputed parentage
Section 21	Fees for scientific tests

Provisions of the Child Support Act 1995	*Subject Matter*
Section 23, in the respects specified below— insertion of section 41B(1), (2) and (7) into the Child Support Act 1991 (c. 48)	Repayment of overpaid child support maintenance
Section 26(1), (2), (3), (4)(b), (5) and (6)	Regulations and orders
Section 27	Interpretation
Section 28	Financial provisions
Schedule 3 in respects specified below and section 30(5), so far as it relates to them— paragraphs 2, 3(2), 4, 8, 10, 14, 15, 16 and 19	Minor and consequential amendments

PART II

PROVISIONS COMING INTO FORCE ON 1ST OCTOBER 1995

Provisions of the Child Support Act 1995	*Subject Matter*
Section 12(1), (5) (for the purpose only of the making of regulations under section 17(5) of the Child Support Act 1991 substituted by it) and (7) (for the purpose only of the making of regulations under section 17(7) of the Child Support Act 1991 added by it)	Reviews on change of circumstances
Section 23, in the respects specified below— insertion of section 41B(3), (4), (5), (6), (8) and (9) into the Child Support Act 1991	Repayment of overpaid child support maintenance
Section 24	Compensation payments
Section 25	Payment of benefit where maintenance payments collected by Secretary of State
Section 26(4)(c)	Regulations and orders
Schedule 3 in the respects specified below and section 30(5), so far as it relates to them— paragraph 1 in respect of the insertion of paragraph (ae) into section 617(2) of the Income and Corporation Taxes Act 1988 (c. 1) (social security and other benefits which are not treated as income for purposes of the Income Tax Acts) and paragraphs 3(1), 11 and 12	Minor and consequential amendments

ROAD TRAFFIC

THE MOTOR CYCLE NOISE ACT 1987 (COMMENCEMENT) ORDER 1995

(S.I. 1995 No. 2367 (C. 47))

Made - - - - - *30th August 1995*

INTRODUCTION

This Order brings the Motor Cycle Noise Act 1987 (c. 34) into force on August 1, 1996.

The Secretary of State for Transport, in exercise of the powers conferred by section 2(3) of the Motor Cycle Noise Act 1987 (c. 34), hereby makes the following Order:

1. This Order may be cited as the Motor Cycle Noise Act 1987 (Commencement) Order 1995.

2. The Motor Cycle Noise Act 1987 shall come into force on 1st August 1996.

Signed by authority of the
Secretary of State for Transport

Steven Norris
Parliamentary Under Secretary of State,
Department of Transport

30th August 1995

TRADE MARKS COMMERCIAL PROPERTY

THE OLYMPIC SYMBOL ETC. (PROTECTION) ACT 1995 (COMMENCEMENT) ORDER 1995

(S.I. 1995 No. 2472 (C. 48))

Made - - - - - *19th September 1995*

INTRODUCTION

This Order brings the Olympic Symbol etc. (Protection) Act 1995 (c. 32) into force on September 20, 1995.

The Secretary of State, in exercise of the powers conferred on her by section 19(2) of the Olympic Symbol etc. (Protection) Act 1995 (c. 32) and of all other powers enabling her in that behalf hereby makes the following Order:

1. This Order may be cited as The Olympic Symbol etc. (Protection) Act 1995 (Commencement) Order 1995.

2. The Olympic Symbol etc. (Protection) Act 1995 shall come into force on 20th September 1995.

Virginia Bottomley

19th September 1995 Secretary of State for National Heritage

LOCAL GOVERNMENT, ENGLAND AND WALES WALES

THE LOCAL GOVERNMENT (WALES) ACT 1994 (COMMENCEMENT NO. 5) ORDER 1995

(S.I. 1995 No. 2490 (C. 49))

Made - - - - - *26th September 1995*

INTRODUCTION

This Order brings into force on October 1, 1995 various provisions of the Local Government (Wales) Act 1994 and provides, *inter alia*, for minor and consequential amendments of the Town and Country Planning Act 1990 (c. 8).

The Secretary of State for Wales, in exercise of the powers conferred upon him by sections 63(5) and 66(3) of the Local Government (Wales) Act 1994 (c. 19), hereby makes the following Order:

Citation

1. This Order may be cited as the Local Government (Wales) Act 1994 (Commencement No. 5) Order 1995.

Interpretation

2. In this Order—

"the 1972 Act" means the Local Government Act 1972 (c. 70);

"the 1982 Act" means the Local Government Finance Act 1982 (c. 32);

"the 1994 Act" means the Local Government (Wales) Act 1994.

Commencement of certain provisions of Part I of the 1994 Act

3.—(1) Subject to paragraphs (2) to (4) the provisions of Part I of, and Schedule 2 to, the 1994 Act which are specified in Schedule 1 to this Order shall come into force on 1st October 1995.

(2) The provisions of section 1(5) of the 1994 Act brought into force by this Order shall have effect only for the interpretation of "local authority" in Part III of the 1982 Act (By virtue of section 36(2) of the 1982 Act, section 270 of the 1972 Act (general interpretation, which includes the definition of "local authority", is applied for the interpretation of Part III of the 1982 Act sections 11–36)).

(3) Until 1st April 1996 "local authority" in Part III of the 1982 Act shall be interpreted as including the district and county councils in Wales created as a result of the 1972 Act, as originally enacted.

(4) The provisions of section 1(8) of the 1994 Act brought into force by this Order shall have effect only for the interpretation of section 65(4) of, and paragraph 2 of Schedule 7 to, the Environment Act 1995 (c. 25; by virtue of section 79(1) of that Act "principal area" has the same meaning as in the 1972 Act).

Commencement of certain provisions of Part II of the 1994 Act

4.—(1) Subject to paragraphs (2) and (3) the provisions of Part II of, and Schedules 6, 7 and 8 to, the 1994 Act which are specified in Schedule 2 to this Order shall come into force on 1st October 1995.

(2) Until 1st April 1996 the amendments made by paragraph 3(2) of Schedule 8 to the 1994 Act shall have effect only for the purposes of enabling a scheme to be made under section 63 of the Rent Act 1977 (c. 42) (schemes for appointment of rent officers) in relation to the new local government structure provided for by the 1994 Act.

(3) The provisions of section 62 of the Rent Act 1977 as in force immediately before the commencement of paragraph 3(2) of Schedule 8 to the 1994 Act shall continue to have effect in relation to the provision of the rent officer service in Wales until 1st April 1996.

Commencement of certain provisions of Part VII of the 1994 Act

5.—(1) Subject to paragraphs (2) to (6) the provisions of Part VII of, and Schedules 15, 16 and 18 to, the 1994 Act which are specified in Schedule 3 to this Order shall come into force on 1st October 1995.

(2) Until 1st April 1996 the amendments made by paragraph 12 of Schedule 16 to the 1994 Act shall have effect only for the purposes of enabling a local scheme to be made under section 14 of the Registration Service Act 1953 (c. 37) (preparation, submission and approval of local schemes) in relation to the new local government structure provided for by the 1994 Act.

(3) The provisions of section 21 of the Registration Service Act 1953 as in force immediately before the commencement of paragraph 12 of Schedule 16 to the 1994 Act shall continue to have effect in relation to the provision of the registration service in Wales until 1st April 1996.

(4) Until 1st April 1996 the amendments made by paragraph 26 of Schedule 16 shall have effect only for the purposes of enabling an order to be made under section 1 of the Sea Fisheries Regulation Act 1966 (c. 38) (sea fisheries districts and committees) in relation to the new local government structure provided for by the 1994 Act.

(5) The provision of the Sea Fisheries Regulation Act 1966 as in force immediately before the commencement of paragraph 26 of Schedule 16 to the 1994 Act shall continue to have effect in respect of any existing sea fisheries district and local fisheries committee in Wales until 1st April 1996.

(6) The amendments made by paragraph 98 of Schedule 16 to the 1994 Act shall have effect only in relation to any financial year beginning on or after 1st April 1996.

Signed by authority of the Secretary of State for Wales

Gwilym Jones
Parliamentary Under Secretary of State,
Welsh Office

26th September 1995

SCHEDULE 1 **Article 3(1)**

PROVISIONS OF PART I OF, AND SCHEDULE 2 TO, THE 1994 ACT COMING INTO FORCE ON 1ST OCTOBER 1995

Provision of the 1994 Act	Subject Matter
Section 1(5)	Definition of "local authority".
Section 1(8)	Definition of "principal area".
Paragraph 13 of Schedule 2 and section 1(3) so far as it relates thereto	Definition of "county" for the purposes of the Parliamentary Constituencies Act 1986 (c. 56).

SCHEDULE 2 **Article 4(1)**

PROVISIONS OF PART II OF, AND SCHEDULES 6, 7 AND 8 TO, THE 1994 ACT COMING INTO FORCE ON 1ST OCTOBER 1995

Provision of the 1994 Act	Subject Matter
Paragraph 24(10(b) and (17)(a) of Schedule 6 and section 20(4) so far as it relates thereto	Minor and consequential amendments of the Town and Country Planning Act 1990 (c. 8)
Paragraph 27(4) of Schedule 7 and section 22(1) so far as it relates thereto	Highways.
Paragraph 3(2) of Schedule 8 and section 22(2) so far as it relates thereto	Registration areas for registration of rents.

SCHEDULE 3 **Article 5(1)**

PROVISIONS OF PART VII OF, AND SCHEDULES 15, 16 AND 18 TO, THE 1994 ACT COMING INTO FORCE ON 1ST OCTOBER 1995

Provision of the 1994 Act	Subject Matter
Paragraphs 10(1), 52 and 58 to 61 of Schedule 15 and section 66(5) so far as it relates thereto	Minor and consequential amendments of the 1972 Act.
Paragraphs 12, 26, and 98 of Schedule 16 and section 66(6) so far as it relates thereto	Consequential amendments to the Registration Service Act 1953, the Sea Fisheries Regulation Act 1966 and the Local Government Finance Act 1992 (c. 14).
In Schedule 18 the repeals of Part IV of Schedule 4 and Schedule 10 to the 1972 Act, and the repeals to paragraph 8 of Schedule 8 and paragraph 3(2)(b) and (c) of Schedule 11 to that Act; and section 66(8) so far as it relates thereto	Consequential repeals.

LAND REGISTRATION, SCOTLAND

THE LAND REGISTRATION (SCOTLAND) ACT 1979 (COMMENCEMENT NO. 9) ORDER 1995

(S.I. 1995 No. 2547 (C. 50) (S. 184))

Made - - - - - 25th September 1995

INTRODUCTION

This Order brings into force on April 1, 1996 certain provisions of the Land Registration (Scotland) Act 1979 (c. 33), in the areas of the County of Aberdeen and the County of Kincardine. Provisions are made for the circumstances by which an interest in land shall be registrable, and for certain persons to obtain a real right only by registration.

The Secretary of State, in exercise of the powers conferred on him by section 30(2) of the Land Registration (Scotland) Act 1979 (c. 33) and of all other powers enabling him in that behalf, hereby makes the following Order:

1. This Order may be cited as the Land Registration (Scotland) Act 1979 (Commencement No. 9) Order 1995.

2. Sections 2(1) and (2) and 3(3) of the Land Registration (Scotland) Act 1979 shall come into force on 1st April 1996 in the areas, for the purpose of registration of writs, of the County of Aberdeen and the County of Kincardine.

James Douglas-Hamilton
Minister of State,
Scottish Office

St Andrew's House, Edinburgh
25th September 1995

PENSIONS

THE PENSIONS ACT 1995 (COMMENCEMENT NO. 1) ORDER 1995

(S.I. 1995 No. 2548 (C. 51))

Made - - - - - *29th September 1995*

INTRODUCTION

This Order brings into force on October 2, 1995, various provisions of the Pensions Act 1995 (c. 26), including those relating to unpaid contributions in cases of insolvency, employment of staff by the Pensions Ombudsman and disclosure of information by public service pension schemes.

The Secretary of State for Social Security, in exercise of the powers conferred on him by section 180(1) of the Pensions Act 1995 (c. 26) and of all other powers enabling him in that behalf, hereby makes the following Order:

Citation and interpretation

1. This Order may be cited as the Pensions Act 1995 (Commencement No. 1) Order 1995.

Appointed day

2. The day appointed for the coming into force of the following provisions of the Pensions Act 1995 is 2nd October 1995—

section 90 (unpaid contributions in cases of insolvency);
section 156 (employment of staff by the Pensions Ombudsman);
section 169 (extensions of Pensions Appeal Tribunals Act 1943 (c. 49));
section 172, and sections 174 and 175 in so far as they relate to that section, (information about public service schemes);
paragraph 1 of Schedule 6, and section 173 in so far as it relates to that paragraph, (amendment to the Public Records Act 1958 (c. 51)).

Signed by authority of the Secretary of State for Social Security.

Oliver Heald
Parliamentary Under-Secretary of State,
Department of Social Security

29th September 1995

ENVIRONMENTAL PROTECTION

THE ENVIRONMENT ACT 1995 (COMMENCEMENT NO. 2) ORDER 1995

(S.I. 1995 No. 2649 (C. 52) (S. 199))

Made - - - - - *5th October 1995*

INTRODUCTION

This Order brings into force on October 12, 1995, various provisions of the Environment Act 1995 (c. 25) which are primarily concerned with, or related to, establishment of the Scottish Environment Protection Agency.

The Secretary of State, in exercise of the powers conferred on him by section 125(3) of the Environment Act 1995 (c. 25), hereby makes the following Order:

Citation

1. This Order may be cited as the Environment Act 1995 (Commencement No. 2) Order 1995.

Provisions coming into force on 12th October 1995

2. The following provisions of the Environment Act 1995 shall come into force on 12th October 1995—

(a) section 20 (the Scottish Environment Protection Agency);
(b) section 21 (transfer of functions to SEPA);
(c) section 22 (transfer of property, rights and liabilities to SEPA);
(d) section 23 (functions of staff commission);
(e) section 30 (records held by SEPA);
(f) section 31 (guidance on sustainable development and other aims and objectives);
(g) section 32 (general environmental and recreational duties);
(h) section 36 (codes of practice with respect to environmental and recreational duties);
(i) section 59 (abandoned mines: Scotland), in so far as the amendments made by that section confer power on the Secretary of State to make regulations; and
(j) section 12(1) (minor and consequential amendments), in so far as it relates to the following provisions of Schedule 22—
   (i) paragraph 15;
   (ii) sub-paragraphs (1) and (22) of paragraph 29, in so far as the amendments made by those provisions confer power on the Secretary of State to make regulations;
   (iii) sub-paragraphs (1) to (3) and (5) of paragraph 51; and
   (iv) paragraph 53.

James Douglas-Hamilton
Minister of State,
Scottish Office

St Andrew's House, Edinburgh
5th October 1995

ENVIRONMENTAL PROTECTION

THE ENVIRONMENT ACT 1995 (COMMENCEMENT NO. 2) ORDER 1995

(S.I. 1995 No. 2649 (C. 57) (S. 195))

Made . . . . 5th October 1995

[illegible]

The [illegible] [illegible] [illegible] [illegible] [illegible] [illegible] [illegible] [illegible] [illegible] [illegible] [illegible] [illegible] Scottish [illegible] [illegible] [illegible].

The Secretary of State, in exercise of the powers conferred on him by section 125(3) of the Environment Act 1995 (c. 25), hereby makes the following Order:

Citation

1. This Order may be cited as the Environment Act 1995 (Commencement No. 2) Order 1995.

Provisions coming into force on 12th October 1995

2. The following provisions of the Environment Act 1995 shall come into force on 12th October 1995:—

(a) section 20 (the Scottish Environment Protection Agency);
(b) section 21 (transfer of functions to SEPA);
(c) section 22 (transfer of property, rights and liabilities to SEPA);
(d) section 23 (functions of staff of commission);
(e) section [illegible] ([illegible] to SEPA);
(f) section 31 (guidance on sustainable development and other aims and objectives);
(g) section 32 (general environmental and recreational duties);
(h) section 36 (codes of practice with respect to environmental and recreational duties);
(i) section 59 ([illegible]) in so far as the amendments made by that section confer power on the Secretary of State to make regulations; and
(j) section 120(1) (minor and consequential amendments) in so far as it relates to the following provisions of Schedule 22—
(i) paragraph [illegible];
(ii) sub-paragraphs (1) and (2) of paragraph 29, in so far as the amendments made by those provisions confer power on the Secretary of State to make regulations;
(iii) sub-paragraphs (1) to (3) and (5) of paragraph 31; and
(iv) paragraph 38.

James Douglas-Hamilton
Minister of State,
Scottish Office

St Andrew's House, Edinburgh
5th October 1995

CRIMINAL LAW, ENGLAND AND WALES

THE PROCEEDS OF CRIME ACT 1995 (COMMENCEMENT) ORDER 1995

(S.I. 1995 No. 2650 (C. 53))

Made - - - - - *7th October 1995*

INTRODUCTION

This Order brings into force on November 1, 1995 all remaining provisions of the Proceeds of Crime Act 1995 (c. 11).

The Secretary of State, in exercise of the powers conferred on him by section 16(3) of the Proceeds of Crime Act 1995 (c. 11), hereby makes the following Order:

1. This Order may be cited as the Proceeds of Crime Act 1995 (Commencement) Order 1995 and extends to England and Wales only.

2. The provisions of the Proceeds of Crime Act 1995 (save for section 14 (enforcement in UK of overseas forfeiture and restraint orders) and section 16 (short title, interpretation, commencement and extent) which came into force on the passing of that Act) shall come into force on 1st November 1995.

Home Office
7th October 1995

David Maclean
Minister of State

CHARITIES

THE CHARITIES ACT 1993 (COMMENCEMENT AND TRANSITIONAL PROVISIONS) ORDER 1995

(S.I. 1995 No. 2695 (C. 54))

Made - - - - - - *14th October 1995*

INTRODUCTION

This Order brings into force on March 1, 1996, the remaining provisions of the Charities Act 1993 (c. 10). These are Part VI (ss.41–49) and s.69 and Sched. 6, para. 21(3) which relate to charity accounts, reports and returns and make provision for the investigation of accounts of charitable companies. Part VI is brought into force on October 15, 1995 for the purposes only of making orders or regulations under that Part. The Order also makes transitional provisions.

The Secretary of State, in pursuance of sections 86(3)(b) and 99(2) of the Charities Act 1993 (c. 10), hereby makes the following Order:

1. This Order may be cited as the Charities Act 1993 (Commencement and Transitional Provisions) Order 1995.

2. Subject to articles 3 and 4 below, Part VI and section 69 of, and paragraph 21(3) of Schedule 6 to, the Charities Act 1993 shall come into force on 1st March 1996.

3. Without prejudice to section 13 of the Interpretation Act 1978 (c. 30) and for the purposes only of making any order or regulations under any of the provisions of Part VI of the Charities Act 1993, that Part shall come into force on the day after the day on which this Order is made.

4. No requirement imposed by section 42, 43, 45, 46(5) or 48 of the Charities Act 1993 in respect of a financial year of a charity shall apply in relation to any financial year which begins before 1st March 1996.

Home Office
14th October 1995

Blatch
Minister of State

CHARITIES

THE CHARITIES ACT 1993 (COMMENCEMENT AND TRANSITIONAL PROVISIONS) ORDER 1995

(S.I. 1995 No. 2695 (C. 54))

Made [illegible] *October 1995*

INTRODUCTION

This Order brings into force on 1st March 1996 the remaining provisions of the Charities Act 1993 (c. 10). These are Part VI (ss.41 to 49) and [illegible] which relate to charity accounts, reports and returns and make provision for the investigation of accounts [illegible]. Part VI was brought into force on [illegible] October 1995 for the purposes [illegible] made under that Part. The Order also makes transitional provisions.

The Secretary of State, in pursuance of sections 99(3)(?) and 99(?) of the Charities Act 1993 (a), hereby makes the following Order:—

1. This Order may be cited as the Charities Act 1993 (Commencement and Transitional Provisions) Order 1995.

2. Subject to articles 3 and 4 below, Part VI and section [illegible] of Schedule 6 to the Charities Act 1993 shall come into force on 1st March 1996.

3. Without prejudice to section 13 of the Interpretation Act 1978 (b), for the purposes of making any order or regulations under any of the provisions of Part VI of the Charities Act 1993 that Part shall come into force on the day after the day on which this Order is made.

4. No requirement imposed by section 41, 42, 43 or 45 of the Charities Act 1993 shall have effect in relation to any financial year of a charity which began before 1st March 1996.

Home Office
[illegible] October 1995

Blatch
Minister of State

CUSTOMS AND EXCISE

THE FINANCE ACT 1993, SECTION 11, (APPOINTED DAY) ORDER 1995

(S.I. 1995 No. 2715 (C. 55))

Made - - - - - 9th November 1995

INTRODUCTION

This Order appoints December 1, 1995 as the day on which section 11 of the Finance Act 1993 (c. 34) becomes effective. The Hydrocarbon Oil Duties Act 1979 (c. 5) is amended by the insertion of section 6A. This section, *inter alia*, charges a duty of excise on the chargeable use of any non-hydrocarbon oil liquid used as a fuel for an engine, motor or other machinery.

The Treasury, in excercise of the powers conferred on them by section 11 of the Finance Act 1993 (c. 34) and of all other powers enabling them in that behalf, hereby make the following Order:

1. This Order may be cited as the Finance Act 1993, section 11, (Appointed Day) Order 1995.

2. The day appointed as the day on which section 11 of the Finance Act 1993 comes into force is 1st December 1995.

Bowen Wells
David Willetts
Two of the Lords Commissioners
of Her Majesty's Treasury

9th November 1995

TOWN AND COUNTRY PLANNING, ENGLAND AND WALES

THE ENVIRONMENT ACT 1995 (COMMENCEMENT NO. 3) ORDER 1995

(S.I. 1995 No. 2765 (C. 56))

Made - - - - - 24th October 1995

INTRODUCTION

This Order brings into force on November 1, 1995 various provisions of the Environment Act 1995 (c. 25), relating to mineral planning permission in England and Wales. The Order also brings into force on the same day s.96(4) and s.120(3) both insofar as they relate to the repeal of s.105 and its related Schedule 24 of the Town and Country Planning Act 1990 (c. 8) (reviews by mineral planning authorities).

The Secretary of State, in exercise of his powers under section 125(3) of the Environment Act 1995 (c. 25), hereby makes the following Order:

Citation

1. This Order may be cited as the Environment Act 1995 (Commencement No. 3) Order 1995.

Provisions coming into force on 1st November 1995

2. The following provisions of the Environment Act 1995 shall come into force on 1st November 1995–

section 96(1), (5) and (6) and Schedules 13 and 14 in so far as they apply in relation to England and Wales;

section 96(2);

section 96(4) in so far as it relates to section 105 of the Town and Country Planning Act 1990 (c. 8. Section 105 of the Act of 1990 was substituted by section 21 of, and Schedule 1, paragraph 7 to, the Planning and Compensation Act 1991 c. 34) ceasing to have effect;

section 120(3) in so far as it relates to the repeal in Schedule 24 of section 105 of the Town and Country Planning Act 1990.

Signed by authority of the Secretary of State

Paul Beresford
Parliamentary Under-Secretary of State,
24th October 1995 Department of the Environment

CHILDREN AND YOUNG PERSONS
COURT OF SESSION, SCOTLAND
EDUCATION, SCOTLAND
FAMILY LAW
LEGAL AID AND ADVICE, SCOTLAND
REGISTRATION OF BIRTHS, DEATHS, MARRIAGES, ETC.
SHERIFF COURT, SCOTLAND

THE CHILDREN (SCOTLAND) ACT 1995 (COMMENCEMENT NO. 1) ORDER 1995

(S.I. 1995 No. 2787 (C. 57) (S. 205))

Made - - - - - 24th October 1995

INTRODUCTION

This Order brings into force on November 1, 1995 the provisions contained in the Schedule to the Children (Scotland) Act 1995 (c. 36). These provisions relate, *inter alia*, to the legal capacity of children under the age of 16 years and the disqualification of certain persons from registration as a child minder, or as a provider of day care for children.

The Secretary of State, in exercise of the powers conferred upon him by section 105(1) of the Children (Scotland) Act 1995 (c. 36) and of all other powers enabling him in that behalf, hereby makes the following Order:

Citation

1. This Order may be cited as the Children (Scotland) Act 1995 (Commencement No. 1) Order 1995.

Interpretation

2. In this Order "the Act" means the Children (Scotland) Act 1995.

Commencement

3. The provisions of the Act which are specified in column 1 of the Schedule to this Order shall come into force on 1st November 1995, but, where a particular purpose in relation to any such provision is specified in column 2 of that Schedule, that provision shall come into force on that day only for that purpose.

James Douglas-Hamilton
Minister of State,
Scottish Office

St Andrew's House, Edinburgh
24th October 1995

SCHEDULE

Article 3

PROVISIONS OF THE ACT WHICH COME INTO FORCE ON 1ST NOVEMBER 1995

Column 1 *Provisions of the Act*	*Column 2* *Purpose*
Section 1(1) to (3)	Only for the purpose of bringing into force sections 15 and 103 and paragraph 12 of Schedule 4 to the Act
Section 15	
Section 35	
Section 37	
Section 99	
Section 103	
Section 104	
Section 105(4)	Only for the purpose of bringing into force the provisions of Schedule 4 to the Act specified in column 1 below
Section 105(5)	Only for the purpose of bringing into force the repeals in Schedule 5 to the Act which are referred to in column 1 below
In Schedule 4, paragraphs 12, 13, 18(1) and (2), 40(b), 45 and 53(1) and (3)	
In Schedule 5, the repeal specified in the Table below	

TABLE

REPEALS

Chapter	*Short title*	*Extent of repeal*
1965 c. 49	The Registration of Births, Deaths and Marriages (Scotland) Act 1965	In section 43, in subsection (3) the words from "In this" to the end; and subsection (10)

ANTARCTICA

THE ANTARCTIC ACT 1994 (COMMENCEMENT) ORDER 1995

(No. 2748 (C. 58))

Made - - - - - 9th October 1995

INTRODUCTION

This Order brings into force on November 1, 1995 the following provisions of the Antarctic Act 1994 (c. 15): ss.1, 2, 8–32, 33 (except insofar as it relates to the repeal of certain provisions of the Antarctic Treaty Act 1967 (c. 65) connected with specially protected areas), and ss.34–36.

The Secretary of State, in exercise of the powers conferred upon him by section 35 of the Antarctic Act 1994 (c. 15), and all other powers enabling him in that behalf, hereby makes the following Order:

Citation

1. This Order may be cited as the Antarctic Act 1994 (Commencement) Order 1995.

Commencement of certain provisions of the Antarctic Act 1994

2. The following provisions of the Antarctic Act 1994 shall come into force on 1st November 1995—

Sections 1 and 2

Sections 8 to 32

Section 33, except in respect of the repeal of Sections 6, 7(2)(b) and (7), 8, 9, 10 and 11 of the Antarctic Treaty Act 1967 (c. 65).

Malcolm Rifkind
Secretary of State for Foreign and Commonwealth Affairs

9th October 1995

HIGHWAYS, ENGLAND AND WALES
WALES

THE BOUNDARY BRIDGES (WALES) (APPOINTED DAY) ORDER 1995

(S.I. 1995 No. 2816 (C. 59))

Made - - - - - 24th October 1995

INTRODUCTION

This Order appoints January 1, 1996 as the day before which the new councils established by the Local Government (Wales) Act 1994 (c. 19), are to agree which of them shall be the highway authority for a cross border highway bridge.

The Secretary of State for Wales, in exercise of the powers conferred on him by paragraph 18(2) of Schedule 17 to the Local Government (Wales) Act 1994 (c. 19) and of all other powers enabling him in that behalf, hereby makes the following Order:—

1. This Order may be cited as the Boundary Bridges (Wales) (Appointed Day) Order 1995.

2. The appointed day for the purposes of paragraph 18(2) of Schedule 17 to the Local Government (Wales) Act 1994 is 1st January 1996.

Signed by authority of the Secretary of State for Wales

Gwilym Jones
Parliamentary Under-Secretary of State,
Welsh Office

24th October 1995

LOCAL GOVERNMENT, SCOTLAND
WATER SUPPLY, SCOTLAND

THE LOCAL GOVERNMENT (SCOTLAND) ACT 1994 (COMMENCEMENT NO. 5) ORDER 1995

(S.I. 1995 No. 2866 (C. 60) (S. 209))

Made - - - - - *25th October 1995*

INTRODUCTION

This Order brings into force on October 30, 1995 certain provisions of the Local Government etc. (Scotland) Act 1994 (c. 39), which relate to the Scottish Water and Sewerage Customers Council, and to local authorities' powers of economic development. Provisions are also brought into force on January 1, 1996, relating to local authorities' powers of economic development and tourist-related activities.

The Secretary of State, in exercise of the powers conferred on him by section 184(2) of the Local Government etc. (Scotland) Act 1994 (c. 39) and of all other powers enabling him in that behalf, hereby makes the following Order:

Citation and interpretation

1.—(1) This Order may be cited as the Local Government etc. (Scotland) Act 1994 (Commencement No. 5) Order 1995.

(2) In this Order—

"the Act" means the Local Government etc. (Scotland) Act 1994;

"the 1973 Act" means the Local Government (Scotland) Act 1973 (c. 65); and

"local authority" means—

(a) a council in respect of which an ordinary election of councillors took place on 6th April 1995 in terms of section 5(2) of the Act; and

(b) the islands councils of Orkney, Shetland and the Western Isles.

Days appointed

2. 30th October 1995 is the day appointed for the coming into force of the following provisions of the Act:—

(a) section 67 (Scottish Water and Sewerage Customers Council);

(b) section 68(1), (4) and (5) (functions of Customers Council);

(c) section 69 (power of Customers Council to require information);

(d) section 70 (annual reports by, and information from, Customers Council);

(e) section 71 (funding of Customers Council);

(f) section 171 (economic development), only for the purposes of enabling—

(i) a local authority to comply with their duties under section 171A(5) of the 1973 Act before the beginning of the financial year starting on 1st April 1996; and

(ii) the Secretary of State to approve under section 171A(6) of the 1973 Act the proposals submitted by the local authority under subsection (5) of that section;

(g) section 177 (Parliamentary disqualification), so far as not already in force; and

(h) Schedule 9 (constitution and proceedings etc. of the Scottish Water and Sewerage Customers Council).

3. 1st April 1996 is the day appointed for the coming into force of the following provisions of the Act:—

(a) section 171 (economic development), so far as not already in force; and

(b) section 176 (powers to carry on tourism-related activities).

George Kynoch
Parliamentary Under Secretary of State,
Scottish Office

St Andrew's House, Edinburgh
25th October 1995

CUSTOMS AND EXCISE

THE FINANCE ACT 1995, SECTION 20, (APPOINTED DAY) ORDER 1995

(S.I. 1995 No. 2892 (C. 61))

Made - - - - - 9th November 1995

INTRODUCTION

This Order appoints December 1, 1995 as the day on which section 20 of the Finance Act 1995 (c. 4) shall have effect. The Customs and Excise Management Act 1979 (c. 2) is amended to provide for the recovery of overpaid excise duty.

The Commissioners of Customs and Excise, in exercise of other powers conferred upon them by section 20 of the Finance Act 1995 (c. 4) and of all other powers enabling them in that behalf, hereby make the following Order:

1. This Order may be cited as the Finance Act 1995, section 20, (Appointed Day) Order 1995.

2. The provisions of section 20 of the Finance Act 1995 shall have effect in relation to payments made on or after 1st December 1995.

New King's Beam House
22 Upper Ground
London SE1 9PJ

9th November 1995

D. J. Howard
Commissioner of Customs and Excise

INCOME TAX

THE INCOME AND CORPORATION TAXES ACT 1988, SECTION 51A, (APPOINTED DAY) ORDER 1995

(S.I. 1995 No. 2932 (C. 62))

Made - - - - - - *15th November 1995*

INTRODUCTION

This Order brings into force on January 2, 1996, section 51A of the Income and Corporation Taxes Act 1988 (c. 1). Section 51A was inserted by s.77 of the Finance Act 1995 (c. 4) and provides, *inter alia*, that in certain circumstances, income tax shall not be deducted from payments of interest on gilt-edged securities.

The Treasury, in exercise of the powers conferred on them by section 51A(10) of the Income and Corporation Taxes Act 1988 (c. 1; section 51A was inserted by section 77 of the Finance Act 1995 (c. 4)), hereby make the following Order:

1. This Order may be cited as the Income and Corporation Taxes Act 1988, section 51A, (Appointed Day) Order 1995.

2. The day appointed for the purposes of section 51A of the Income and Corporation Taxes Act 1988 is 2nd January 1996.

Simon Burns
David Willetts
Two of the Lords Commissioners
of Her Majesty's Treasury

15th November 1995

INCOME TAX

THE FINANCE ACT 1995, SECTION 82, (APPOINTED DAY) ORDER 1995

(S.I. 1995 No. 2933 (C. 63))

Made - - - - - *15th November 1995*

INTRODUCTION

This Order provides that section 82 of the Finance Act 1995 (c. 4), will have effect, in relation to any payments made on or after January 2, 1996, which concern manufactured interest on gilt-edged securities.

The Treasury, in exercise of the powers conferred on them by section 82(4) of the Finance Act 1995 (c. 4), hereby make the following Order:

1. This Order may be cited as the Finance Act 1995, section 82, (Appointed Day) Order 1995.

2. The day appointed for the purposes of section 82 of the Finance Act 1995 is 2nd January 1996.

Simon Burns
David Willetts
Two of the Lord Commissioners
of Her Majesty's Treasury

15th November 1995

1996 c.64

INCOME TAX

[illegible]

[illegible]

[illegible]

NORTHERN IRELAND

THE NORTHERN IRELAND (REMISSION OF SENTENCES) ACT 1995 (COMMENCEMENT) ORDER 1995

(S.I. 1995 No. 2945 (C. 64))

Made - - - - - - *10th November 1995*

INTRODUCTION

This Order brings the Northern Ireland (Remission of Sentences) Act 1995 into force on November 17, 1995.

In exercise of the power conferred on me by section 2 of the Northern Ireland (Remission of Sentences) Act 1995 (c. 47), I hereby make the following Order:

1. This Order may be cited as the Northern Ireland (Remission of Sentences) Act 1995 (Commencement) Order 1995.

2. The Northern Ireland (Remission of Sentences) Act 1995 shall come into force on 17th November 1995.

Northern Ireland Office
10th November 1995

P. B. B. Mayhew
One of Her Majesty's Principal Secretaries of State

COUNTRYSIDE

THE ENVIRONMENT ACT 1995 (COMMENCEMENT NO. 4 AND SAVING PROVISIONS) ORDER 1995

(S.I. 1995 No. 2950 (C. 65))

Made - - - - - - *16th November 1995*

INTRODUCTION

This Order brings into force on November 23, 1995 certain provisions of the Environment Act 1995 (c. 25). Paragraph 32(2) inserts a new section 2(1D) into the Town and Country Planning Act 1990 (c. 8). The effect of this is to prevent a united district for a joint planning board being constituted for a National Park, where a National Park authority is already established. Further provisions are brought into force on April 1, 1996 creating amendments to National Parks.

The Secretary of State, in exercise of his powers under section 125(3) and (4) of the Environment Act 1995 (c. 25), hereby makes the following Order:

Citation and Interpretation

1.—(1) This Order may be cited as the Environment Act 1995 (Commencement No. 4 and Saving Provisions) Order 1995.

(2) In this Order—

"the 1995 Act" means the Environment Act 1995.

Provisions coming into force on 23rd November 1995

2.—(1) Subject to paragraph (2), the following provisions of the 1995 Act shall come into force on the 23rd November 1995—

Section 78 insofar as it relates to paragraphs 1, 2 (except sub-paragraphs (2) and (9)(b)), 3 to 7, 8(2), 9, 10(1) and (3), 11, 12, 14, 15, 17 to 19, 21, 23 to 26, 28 to 31 (Paragraph 30 of Schedule 10 amends paragraph 2(6) of Schedule 8 to the Electricity Act 1989 (c. 29). Amendment to the said paragraph 2(6) of Schedule 8 is also made by paragraph 22 of Schedule 6 to the Local Government (Wales) Act 1994 (c. 19). The 1994 amendment has not yet been brought into force. Consequently, sub-paragraph (3) of the said paragraph 30 applies and not sub-paragraph (4) or (5) thereof. The said paragraph 2(6) of Schedule 8 to the 1989 Act was also amended by the Planning (Consequential Provisions) Act 1990 (c. 10) Schedule 2 paragraph 83(1)), 32(1) to (13) and (15) to (18), 33(1) to (5), 34, 35 (insofar as it adds to section 35(5) of the Local Government Finance Act 1992 (c. 14) the words, "or (c) a National Park authority in relation to a National Park in Wales"), 36, 37 and 38(1) of Schedule 10;

(2) The commencement of sub-paragraph (2) of paragraph 32 of Schedule 10 to the 1995 Act shall not affect the constitution of a united district for a National Park (or any area which by virtue of paragraph 3 of Schedule 17 to the Local Government Act 1972 (c. 70) is treated as a united district) where such a district is in being immediately before the commencement of the said sub-paragraph; and such a district shall continue to be constituted until such time as is provided for in an order under section 63 of the 1995 Act (establishment of National Park authorities) or section 2 of the Town and Country Planning Act 1990 (c. 8) (joint planning boards) or Part I of Schedule 17 to the Local Government Act 1972 (discharge of planning and countryside functions in National Parks).

Provisions coming into force on 1st April 1996

3.—(1) Subject to paragraph (2), the following provisions of the 1995 Act shall come into force on 1st April 1996—

Section 78 insofar as it relates to paragraphs 2(2) and (9)(b), 8(1), and (3), 13, 16, 20 and 22(3), (4)(a) and (b) and (5) of Schedule 10;
Section 115(1) insofar as it relates to the other provisions of section 115 brought into force by this article;
Section 115(2) insofar as it relates to Part III of the 1995 Act;
Section 115(3), (4) and (6) insofar as it relates to the provisions of section 115(2) brought into force by this article.

(2) The provisions of sections 42 and 51(2)(c) of the Wildlife and Countryside Act 1981 (c. 69. Sections 42 and 51(2)(c) of the Act of 1981 were amended by Schedule 3 paragraph 7(4) to the Local Government Act 1985 (c. 51)) as in force immediately before the commencement of paragraph 22(3) and (5) of Schedule 10 to the 1995 Act shall continue to have effect in relation to any National Park (for the meaning of National Park, see section 5(3) of the National Parks and Access to the Countryside Act 1949 (c. 97)) for which the local planning authority is not a National Park authority established by order under section 63 of the 1995 Act.

Signed by authority of the Secretary of State for Wales

Gwilym Jones
Parliamentary Under Secretary of State,
Welsh Office

16th November 1995

LANDLORD AND TENANT, ENGLAND AND WALES

THE LANDLORD AND TENANT (COVENANTS) ACT 1995 (COMMENCEMENT) ORDER 1995

(S.I. 1995 No. 2963 (C. 66))

Made - - - - - *9th November 1995*

INTRODUCTION

This Order appoints January 1, 1996 as the day on which the provisions of the Landlord and Tenant (Covenants) Act 1995 (c. 30) shall have effect. The Act, *inter alia*, makes provision with respect to rights and liabilities arising under tenancy covenants.

The Lord Chancellor, in exercise of the powers conferred on him by section 31 of the Landlord and Tenant (Covenants) Act 1995 (c. 30) hereby makes the following Order:

1. This Order may be cited as the Landlord and Tenant (Covenants) Act 1995 (Commencement) Order 1995.

2. The Landlord and Tenant (Covenants) Act 1995 shall come into force on 1st January 1996.

Dated 9th November 1995 *Mackay of Clashfern, C.*

POLICE

THE POLICE AND MAGISTRATES' COURTS ACT 1994 (COMMENCEMENT NO. 9 AND AMENDMENT) ORDER 1995

(S.I. 1995 No. 3003 (C. 67))

Made - - - - - *14th November 1995*

Coming into force - - - *13th December 1995*

INTRODUCTION

This Order provides, *inter alia*, for the provisions of section 47(1), (2), (4) and (5) of the Police and Magistrates' Courts Act 1994 (c. 29) relating to the constitution of police forces in Scotland, to be brought into force on December 13, 1995.

The Secretary of State, in exercise of the powers conferred on him by section 94(1) and (4) of the Police and Magistrates' Courts Act 1994 (c. 29) and of all other powers enabling him in that behalf, hereby makes the following Order:

Citation and commencement

1. This Order may be cited as the Police and Magistrates' Courts Act 1994 (Commencement No. 9 and Amendment) Order 1995 and shall come into force on 13th December 1995.

Provisions of the Act coming into force on 13th December 1995

2. The provisions of the 1994 Act which are specified in column 1 of the Schedule to this Order, and described by reference to the subject matter in column 2 of that Schedule, shall, insofar as not then in force, come into force on 13th December 1995 but, where a particular purpose is specified in relation to any provision in column 3 of that Schedule, that provision shall come into force on that day only for that purpose.

Amendments

3. Schedule 2 to the Police and Magistrates' Courts Act 1994 (Commencement No. 7 and Transitional Provisions) (Scotland) Order 1995 (S.I. 1995/492) is amended by the omission of—

(a) the entries in relation to—
  (i) section 47(1) (Establishments of police forces);
  (ii) section 47(2) (Assignment of ranks);
  (iii) section 47(4) (Extra policing of locality where works are being constructed); and
  (iv) section 47(5) (Regulations as to retirement of certain constables); and

(b) in relation to the entry in respect of Schedule 9, Part I, the references to repeals in sections 7(2), 14(1), 26 and 51(1) of the Police (Scotland) Act 1967.

Michael Forsyth
One of Her Majesty's Principal Secretaries of State

St Andrew's House, Edinburgh
14th November 1995

Article 2 SCHEDULE

PROVISIONS OF THE 1994 ACT WHICH COME INTO FORCE ON 13TH DECEMBER 1995

Column 1 *Provisions*	*Column 2* *Subject matter*	*Column 3* *Extent of commencement*
Section 47(1)	Establishments of police forces	
Section 47(2)	Assignment of ranks	
Section 47(4)	Extra policing of locality where works are being constructed	
Section 47(5)	Regulations as to retirement of certain constables	
Section 63(9)(a)	Interpretation	
Section 93	Repeals	Only so far as it relates to the entries in Schedule 9, Part I specified below.
Schedule 9, Part I	Repeals	1. The following entries in respect of the Police (Scotland) Act 1967 (c. 77): Section 7(2) In section 14(1) the words "(whether by the appointment of temporary constables or otherwise)". In section 26, in subsection (2)(d), the words "or temporary". In section 51(1), the definitions of "regular constable", "special constable" and "temporary constable". 2. The following entry in respect of the Police and Criminal Evidence Act 1984 (c. 60): In Schedule 4, in paragraph 11, sub-paragraph (a)(ii) and sub-paragraph (b)(iii) and the word "or" immediately preceding it.

DEREGULATION

THE DEREGULATION AND CONTRACTING OUT ACT 1994 (COMMENCEMENT NO. 4 AND TRANSITIONAL PROVISIONS) ORDER 1995

(S.I. 1995 No. 2835 (C. 68))

Made - - - - - - *2nd November 1995*

INTRODUCTION

This Order brings into force on January 1, 1996 the remaining provisions of the Deregulation and Contracting Out Act 1994 (c. 40), including, *inter alia*, provisions which relate to public service vehicle operator licensing.

The Secretary of State, in exercise of the powers conferred on him by section 82(4) and (5) of the Deregulation and Contracting Out Act 1994 (c. 40. Chapter III of Part I and Schedules 12 and 13 are prospectively repealed by the Goods Vehicles (Licensing of Operators) Act 1995 (c. 23)), hereby makes the following Order:

1. This Order may be cited as the Deregulation and Contracting Out Act 1994 (Commencement No. 4 and Transitional Provisions) Order 1995.

2. The Deregulation and Contracting Out Act 1994, so far as it has not been brought into force before, or is not brought into force as part of the Goods Vehicles (Licensing of Operators) Act 1995 (c. 23) on 1st January 1996 shall come into force on that day.

3. The Schedule to this Order (transitional provisions) shall have effect.

Signed by authority of the Secretary of State

Steven Norris
Parliamentary Under Secretary of State,
Department of Transport

2nd November 1995

THE SCHEDULE **Article 3**

TRANSITIONAL PROVISIONS

Interpretation

1. In this Schedule—

"the 1981 Act" means the Public Passenger Vehicles Act 1981 (c. 14. Section 4 is substituted by the Transport Act 1985 (c. 67) ("the 1985 Act"), s.3(2). Section 15 is amended by the 1985 Act, Sch. 2, Part II, para. 4(1) and (6) and by section 61 of the Deregulation and Contracting Out Act 1994 (c. 40) ("the 1994 Act"). Section 16 is amended by the 1985 Act, s.24, Sch. 2, Part II, para. 4(1) and (7), Sch. 7, para. 21(1) and (4) and Sch. 8 and by the 1994 Act, s.59, Sch. 14, para. 4 and Sch. 17. Section 17 is amended by the 1985 Act, Sch. 2, para. 4(1) and (8) and Sch. 7, para. 21(1) and (6) and by the 1994 Act, ss.59 and 62, Sch. 14, para. 5 and Sch. 8. Section 50 is substituted by the 1985 Act, s.31 and amended by the 1994 Act, s.65 and Sch. 14, para. 7 and Sch. 17. Section 52 is amended by the Metropolitan Traffic Area (Transfer of Functions) Order 1984 (S.I. 1984/31), by the 1985 Act, Sch. 2, Part II, para. 4(1) and (14) and Sch. 8, the Road Traffic (Driver Licensing and Information System) Act 1989 (c. 22), Sch. 6 and by the 1984 Act, s.66. Other amendments have been made which are not relevant to this Order);

"the 1994 Act" means the Deregulation and Contracting Out Act 1994;

"the appointed day" means 1st January 1996;

"existing licence" means a PSV operator's licence which was in force immediately before the appointed day;

"PSV operator's licence" has the same meaning as in the 1981 Act;
"old-style licence" means an existing licence in respect of which no direction has been given under paragraph 6 below.

Licences with expiry dates prior to the appointed day

2.—(1) This paragraph applies to an existing licence if—

(a) on the date that the licence was due to expire, proceedings were pending before the traffic commissioner on an application by the holder of the licence for the grant to him of a new licence in substitution for it; and

(b) the licence was in force immediately before the appointed day by virtue of that application and section 15(3) or (4) or 50(2) of the 1981 Act.

(2) Subject to paragraph (4) below, an existing licence to which this paragraph applies shall, unless previously revoked or otherwise terminated under any provision of the 1981 Act or any other statutory provision, terminate upon the requirements of sub-paragraph (3) below being met.

(3) The requirements of this sub-paragraph are that—

(a) the application, and

(b) any appeal under section 50 of the 1981 Act arising out of the application,

are disposed of.

(4) Section 15(4) of the 1981 Act as it was in force immediately before the appointed day shall, notwithstanding anything in the 1994 Act, continue to have effect in relation to an existing licence to which this paragraph applies.

(5) Section 15(2) of the 1981 Act shall, on and after the appointed day, have effect subject to this paragraph.

Prematurely terminated licences

3.—(1) This paragraph applies to an existing licence if—

(a) a traffic commissioner has before the appointed day curtailed the period of validity of the licence under section 17(2) of the 1981 Act; and

(b) the expiry date of the licence is the appointed day or any day thereafter.

(2) Subject to sub-paragraphs (3) and (4) below, an existing licence to which this paragraph applies shall, unless previously revoked or otherwise terminated under any provision of the 1981 Act or any other statutory provision, terminate on the expiry date.

(3) If, immediately before an existing licence is due to expire by virtue of sub-paragraph (2) above, proceedings are pending before the traffic commissioner on an application by the holder of that licence for the grant to him of a new licence in substitution for it, the existing licence shall, subject to its revocation or other termination under any provision of the 1981 Act or any other statutory provision, continue in force until—

(a) the application, and

(b) any appeal under section 50 of the 1981 Act arising out of the application,

are disposed of.

(4) Section 15(4) of the 1981 Act as it was in force immediately before the appointed day shall, notwithstanding anything in the 1994 Act, continue to have effect in relation to an existing licence to which this paragraph applies.

(5) For the purposes of this paragraph, the expiry date of a licence that has, before the appointed day, been curtailed under subsection (2) of section 17 of the 1981 Act is the date on which it would have expired by virtue of the curtailment had the 1994 Act not been passed and no application were made for a licence in substitution for it.

(6) Section 15(2) of the 1981 Act shall, on and after the appointed day, have effect subject to this paragraph.

Statements of intent

4.—(1) Where—

(a) the holder of an old-style licence had made or procured to be made—

(i) for the purposes of his application for the licence, or

(ii) for the purposes of an application for the variation of the licence,

a statement of intent in writing; and

(b) the application was determined before the appointed day,

the statement shall for the purposes of the 1981 Act, on and after the appointed day, have effect as if it were an undertaking recorded in the licence.

Variation of an old-style licence

5. Section 16(6) of the 1981 Act shall, on and after the appointed day, have effect in relation to an old-style licence as if after paragraph (c), there were inserted—

"or

(d) direct that any statement of intent which by virtue of paragraph 4 of the Schedule to the Deregulation and Contracting Out Act 1994 (Commencement No. 4 and Transitional Provisions) Order 1995 has effect as if it were an undertaking recorded in the licence, cease to have such effect.".

Conversion of old-style licences

6.—(1) The traffic commissioner by whom an old-style licence was issued may at any time after the appointed day vary the licence by directing—

(a) that any statement of intent having effect as an undertaking by virtue of paragraph 4 above immediately before the variation, or a statement that appears to the traffic commissioner to be to the like effect, be recorded as an undertaking in the licence; or

(b) that an alteration of any other description be made which appears to the traffic commissioner to be consequential to the coming into force of the 1994 Act;

or both of those things.

(2) The powers under paragraph (1) above shall be exercised in such a way as appears to the traffic commissioner—

(a) to put the licence into a form that would have been appropriate had the 1994 Act been in force at the time it was granted; and

(b) to leave the holder of the licence in the same position as he was immediately before the licence is varied or as near to that position as is practicable using those powers while meeting the requirements of paragraph (a) above.

(3) A traffic commissioner shall not exercise his powers under this paragraph without first giving the holder of the licence an opportunity to make representations to the commissioner with respect to the proposed variation.

Fees

7. Nothing in sections 52(2A), (2B) or (2D) of the 1981 Act shall in any circumstances affect the validity, on or after the appointed day, of—

(a) any decision made;

(b) any licence granted;

(c) any variation effected; or

(d) any disc issued,

before the appointed day.

CRIMINAL LAW, ENGLAND AND WALES
CRIMINAL LAW, NORTHERN IRELAND

THE CRIMINAL APPEAL ACT 1995 (COMMENCEMENT NO. 1 AND TRANSITIONAL PROVISIONS) ORDER 1995

(S.I. 1995 No. 3061 (C. 69))

Made - - - - - 27th November 1995

INTRODUCTION

This Order allows for certain provisions of the Criminal Appeal Act 1995 (c. 35) to be brought into force on January 1, 1996.

In exercise of the powers conferred on him by section 32 of the Criminal Appeal Act 1995 (c. 35), the Secretary of State hereby makes the following Order:

1. This Order may be cited as the Criminal Appeal Act 1995 (Commencement No. 1 and Transitional Provisions) Order 1995.

2. In this Order, "the 1968 Act" means the Criminal Appeal Act 1968 (c. 19), "the 1980 Act" means the Criminal Appeal (Northern Ireland) Act 1980 (c. 47) and "the 1995 Act" means the Criminal Appeal Act 1995.

3. The following provisions of the 1995 Act shall, subject to article 4 below, come into force on 1 January 1996:

(a) sections 1, 2, 4, and 6;
(b) section 7, except to the extent that section 44A of the 1968 Act and section 47A of the 1980 Act, as inserted by that section, relate to references by the Criminal Cases Review Commission;
(c) sections 26 to 28;
(d) section 29, so far as is necessary to bring into force Schedules 2 and 3 to the extent specified below;
(e) section 30;
(f) section 31, except for subsection (1)(a);
(g) sections 32 to 34;
(h) in Schedule 2: paragraphs 1, 2, 4(1) to (3), 4(5), 5, 6, 12(1) to (4), 12(6), 15 and 17;
(i) Schedule 3, so far as it relates to the following enactments:
  (i) section 23(3) of the 1968 Act;
  (ii) the Courts-Martial (Appeals) Act 1968 (c. 20);
  (iii) the Criminal Law Act 1977 (c. 45);
  (iv) the Magistrates' Courts Act 1980 (c. 43);
  (v) sections 16(1) and 25(3) of the 1980 Act;
  (vi) the Supreme Court Act 1981 (c. 54);
  (vii) the Criminal Justice Act 1988 (c.33);
  (viii) Paragraph 3(1) of Schedule 3 to the Criminal Procedure (Insanity and Unfitness to Plead) Act 1991 (c. 25).

4. The following provisions shall continue to have effect, in the circumstances described below, as if this Order had not been made:

(a) sections 1, 12 and 15 of the 1968 Act and sections 1, 12(1) and 13A(2) of the 1980 Act so far as they relate to a conviction, verdict or finding occurring before 1 January 1996;

(b) sections 2, 13, 16 and 23 of the 1968 Act, sections 2, 12(2), 12(3), 13A(3), 13A(4) and 25 of the 1980 Act, section 110 of the Army Act 1955 (c. 18), section 110 of the Air Force Act 1955 (c. 19) and sections 12 and 28 of the Courts-Martial (Appeals) Act 1968 so far as they relate to an appeal where the hearing begins before 1 January 1996.

Michael Howard
One of Her Majesty's Principal
Secretaries of State

Home Office
27th November 1995

NATIONAL HEALTH SERVICE, ENGLAND AND WALES

THE NATIONAL HEALTH SERVICE (AMENDMENT) ACT 1995 (COMMENCEMENT NO. 1 AND SAVING) ORDER 1995

(S.I. 1995 No. 3090 (C. 70))

Made - - - - - 30th November 1995

INTRODUCTION

This Order brings into force on November 21, 1995 certain provisions of the National Health Service (Amendment) Act 1995 (c. 31). The provisions which are effective relate, *inter alia*, to the powers of the National Health Service Tribunal for doctors and dentists, and amendments are made to the National Health Service Act 1977 (c. 49) concerning the constitution of the Tribunal.

The Secretary of State for Health, in exercise of powers conferred on him by section 14(3) and (4) of the National Health Service (Amendment) Act 1995 (c. 31) and of all other powers enabling him in that behalf, hereby makes the following Order:—

Citation and Interpretation

1.—(1) This Order may be cited as the National Health Service (Amendment) Act 1995 (Commencement No. 1 and Saving) Order 1995.

(2) In this Order—

"the 1977 Act" means the National Health Service Act 1977 (c. 49); and

"the 1995 Act" means the National Health Service (Amendment) Act 1995.

Appointed day

2.—(1) Subject to paragraph (2) and article 3, 21st December 1995 is the day appointed for the coming into force of the provisions of the 1995 Act specified in column 1 of the Schedule to this Order (the subject matter of each provision being mentioned in column 2).

(2) Sections 1 and 2 of the 1995 Act shall come into force for the purpose of amending the 1977 Act in relation to general medical services and general dental services only.

Saving

3. Where before 21st December 1995—

(a) an appeal has been made to the Secretary of State under section 46(3) of the 1977 Act; or

(b) an application has been made to the Secretary of State for a direction under section 47 of, or paragraph 8 of Schedule 14 to, the 1977 Act,

the 1977 Act shall have effect in relation to that appeal or that application as if section 3 or (as the case may be) section 4 of the 1995 Act (and, in the Schedule to the 1995 Act, the associated repeals relating to sections 46(3), 47 and 49 of the 1977 Act) had not come into force.

Stephen Dorell

30th November 1995 Secretary of State for Health

Article 2 SCHEDULE

PROVISIONS OF THE 1995 ACT COMING INTO FORCE ON 21ST DECEMBER 1995

(1) Provision of the Act	(2) *Subject matter*
Section 1, for the purposes specified in article 2(2) of this Order	Disqualified practitioners: engagement in provision of services by others (England and Wales)
Section 2, for the purposes specified in article 2(2) of this Order	Interim suspension of practitioners (England and Wales)
Section 3	Appeals against disqualification: removal of appeal to Secretary of State (England and Wales)
Section 4	Removal of disqualification (England and Wales)
Section 5	Procedure relating to disqualification (England and Wales)
Section 6	Constitution of the Tribunal (England and Wales)
Section 14(2), so far as it relates to the provisions of the Schedule brought into force by this Order	Repeal of provisions specified in the Schedule
In the Schedule, the entries relating to the National Health Service Act 1977 and the Health Authorities Act 1995	Repeals

PENSIONS

THE PENSIONS ACT 1995 (COMMENCEMENT NO. 2) ORDER 1995

(S.I. 1995 No. 3104 (C. 71))

Made - - - - - *30th November 1995*

INTRODUCTION

This Order brings into force certain provisions of the Pensions Act 1995 (c. 26). Section 39 which concerns the exercise of powers by member trustees, and sections 62 to 66 concerning equal treatment become effective on January 1, 1996. Provisions for the purposes of making regulations in relation thereto, come into force on December 4, 1995.

The Secretary of State for Social Security, in exercise of the powers conferred on him by section 180(1) of the Pensions Act 1995 (c. 26) and of all other powers enabling him in that behalf, hereby makes the following Order:

Citation and interpretation

1.—(1) This Order may be cited as the Pensions Act 1995 (Commencement No. 2) Order 1995.

(2) In this Order references to sections and Schedules are references to sections of, and Schedules to, the Pensions Act 1995.

Appointed day

2.—(1) The day appointed for the coming into force of section 39 (exercise of powers by member trustees), and sections 117, 121 and 124, insofar as they relate to that section, is 1st January 1996.

(2) The day appointed for the coming into force of sections 62 to 66 (equal treatment) and sections 117, 120, 121, 124, 174 and 175 insofar as they relate to those sections—

(a) for the purpose only of authorising the making of regulations under sections 63(5), 64(2) and (3) and 66(4), is 4th December 1995; and

(b) for all other purposes, is 1st January 1996.

(3) The day appointed for the coming into force of paragraphs 29, 32 to 37, 39(b), 42, 44(a)(i) and 47 of Schedule 3 (repeal of section 118 of the Pension Schemes Act 1993 (c. 48): equal access), and section 122 insofar as it relates to these paragraphs, is 1st January 1996.

Signed by authority of the Secretary of State for Social Security.

Oliver Heald
Parliamentary Under-Secretary of State,
Department of Social Security

30th November 1995

INCOME TAX

THE FINANCE ACT 1994, SECTION 105, (APPOINTED DAY) ORDER 1995

(S.I. 1995 No. 3125 (C. 72))

Made - - - - - *4th December 1995*

INTRODUCTION

This Order provides for subss. (3) and (4)(b) of s.105 of the Finance Act 1994 (c. 9) to come into force on January 1, 1996. Subsection (3) provides that certain provisions of the Income and Corporation Taxes Act 1988 (c. 1) which relate to retirement benefit schemes, will cease to be effective. Subsection (4)(b) amends s.98 of the Taxes Management Act 1970 (c. 9) to reflect new information powers.

The Treasury, in exercise of the powers conferred on them by section 105(5) of the Finance Act 1994(c. 9), hereby make the following Order:

1. This Order may be cited as the Finance Act 1994, section 105, (Appointed Day) Order 1995.

2. The day appointed for the coming into force of subsections (3) and (4)(b) of section 105 of the Finance Act 1994 is 1st January 1996.

Simon Burns
Bowen Wells
Two of the Lords Commissioners
of Her Majesty's Treasury

4th December 1995

LOCAL GOVERNMENT, ENGLAND AND WALES

WALES

THE LOCAL GOVERNMENT (WALES) ACT 1994 (COMMENCEMENT NO. 6) ORDER 1995

(S.I. 1995 No. 3198 (C. 73))

Made - - - - - *7th December 1995*

INTRODUCTION

This Order allows for certain provisions of the Local Government (Wales) Act 1994 (c. 19) to be brought into force on January 1, 1996 and April 1, 1996. The sections which shall become effective on these dates are listed in the Schedules to this Order and include, *inter alia*, the definition of 'local authority' in s.1(5).

The Secretary of State for Wales, in exercise of the powers conferred upon him by sections 63(5) and 66(3) of the Local Government (Wales) Act 1994 (c. 19), hereby makes the following Order:

Citation

1. This Order may be cited as the Local Government (Wales) Act 1994 (Commencement No. 6) Order 1995.

Interpretation

2. In this Order "the 1994 Act" means the Local Government (Wales) Act 1994.

Commencement of certain provisions of Part I of the 1994 Act

3. The provisions of Part I of, and Schedule 2 to, the 1994 Act which are specified in Schedule 1 to this Order shall come into force on 1st April 1996.

Commencement of certain provisions of Part II of the 1994 Act

4. The provisions of Part II of, and Schedules 4 and 5 to, the 1994 Act which are specified in Schedule 2 to this Order shall come into force on 1st April 1996.

Commencement of certain provisions of Part VI of the 1994 Act

5. The provisions of Part VI of the 1994 Act which are specified in Schedule 3 to this Order shall come into force on 1st April 1996.

Commencement of certain provisions of Part VII of the 1994 Act

6.—(1) Subject to paragraph (2) the provisions of Part VII of, and Schedules 16 and 18 to, the 1994 Act which are specified in Schedule 4 to this Order shall come into force on 1st January 1996.

(2) Until 1st April 1996 the meaning of "local authority" in paragraph 5A(4) of Schedule 2 to the European Parliamentary Elections Act 1978 (c. 10)(paragraph 5A was inserted by the Parliamentary Constituencies Act 1986 (c. 56), section 7 and Schedule 3, paragraph 5(6).) shall, in relation to Wales, be interpreted as including the district and county councils created as a result of the Local Government Act 1972 (c. 70), as originally enacted.

(3) The provisions of Part VII of, and Schedule 17 to, the 1994 Act which are specified in Schedule 5 to this Order shall come into force on 1st April 1996.

Signed by authority of the Secretary of State for Wales

Gwilym Jones
Parliamentary Under-Secretary of State,
Welsh Office

7th December 1995

Article 3

SCHEDULE 1

PROVISIONS OF PART I OF, AND SCHEDULE 2 TO, THE 1994 ACT COMING INTO FORCE ON 1ST APRIL 1996

Provision of the 1994 Act	*Subject matter*
Section 1(5)	Definition of "local authority".
Section 1(6)	Definition of "local government area".
Section 1(8)	Definition of "principal area".
Section 8	Community meetings and continuation of community councils.
Section 9	Establishment, dissolution and grouping etc. of community councils.
Section 10	Community councils for groups of communities.
Section 11	Community councils for groups of communities; dissolution.
Section 12	Community councils: supplemental provisions.
Section 13	Constitution and powers of community councils.
Section 16	Community having the status of a town.
Paragraphs 1 to 3, 6, 7 and 10 to 12 of Schedule 2, and section 1(3) so far as it relates thereto	Provisions applying to preserved counties.

Article 4

SCHEDULE 2

PROVISIONS OF PART II OF, AND SCHEDULES 4 AND 5 TO, THE 1994 ACT COMING INTO FORCE ON 1ST APRIL 1996

Provision of the 1994 Act	*Subject matter*
Section 18(7) and all provisions of Schedule 4	Exercise of planning functions in Wales.
Section 20(1)	Application of Chapter I of the Town and Country Planning Act 1990 (c. 8) in relation to Wales.
Section 20(2)	Application of Chapter I of the Town and Country Planning Act 1990 in relation to Wales: transitional provisions.
Section 20(3) and all provisions of Schedule 5	Unitary development plans in Wales.
Section 23(1)	Fire authorities in Wales.

Article 5

SCHEDULE 3

PROVISIONS OF PART VI OF THE 1994 ACT COMING INTO FORCE ON 1ST APRIL 1996

Provisions of the 1994 Act	*Subject matter*
Section 49	Charities.
Section 50	Welsh Church funds.

Article 6(1)

SCHEDULE 4

PROVISIONS OF PART VII, AND SCHEDULES 16 AND 18 TO, THE 1994 ACT COMING INTO FORCE ON 1ST JANUARY 1996

Provision of the 1994 Act	*Subject matter*
Paragraph 54(2) of Schedule 16 and section 66(6) so far as it relates thereto	Consequential amendments to the European Parliamentary Elections Act 1978.
In Schedule 18 the repeal to paragraph 5A(4)(a) of Schedule 2 to the European Parliamentary Elections Act 1978; and section 66(8) so far as it relates thereto	Consequential repeal.

Article 6(3)

SCHEDULE 5

PROVISIONS OF PART VII, AND SCHEDULE 17 TO, THE 1994 ACT COMING INTO FORCE ON 1ST APRIL 1996

Provision of the 1994 Act	*Subject matter*
Section 62	Sheriffs.
Paragraphs 15 and 17 of Schedule 17, and section 66(7) so far as it relates thereto	Transitional Provisions: Planning

NATIONAL HEALTH SERVICE, SCOTLAND

THE NATIONAL HEALTH SERVICE (AMENDMENT) ACT 1995 (COMMENCEMENT NO. 2 AND SAVING) (SCOTLAND) ORDER 1995

(S.I. 1995 No. 3214 (C. 74) (S.240))

Made - - - - - 7th December 1995

INTRODUCTION

This Order allows certain provisions of the National Health Service (Amendment) Act 1995 (c. 31) to be brought into force on January 1, 1996. The provisions relate, *inter alia*, to the power of the National Health Service Tribunal to direct the interim suspension of a doctor or dentist providing family health services under the National Health Service (Scotland) Act 1978 (c. 29).

The Secretary of State in exercise of the powers conferred on him by section 14(3) and (4) of the National Health Service (Amendment) Act 1995 (c. 31) and of all other powers enabling him in that behalf, hereby makes the following Order:

Citation and interpretation

1.—(1) This Order may be cited as the National Health Service (Amendment) Act 1995 (Commencement No. 2 and Saving) (Scotland) Order 1995.

(2) In this Order—

"the 1978 Act" means the National Health Service (Scotland) Act 1978(c. 29);

"the 1995 Act" means the National Health Service (Amendment) Act 1995.

Appointed day

2.—(1) Subject to paragraph (2) and article 3 below, 1st January 1996 is the day appointed for the coming into force of the provisions of the 1995 Act specified in column 1 of the Schedule to this Order (the subject matter of each provision being mentioned in column 2).

(2) Sections 7 and 8 of the 1995 Act shall come into force for the purpose of amending the 1978 Act in relation to general medical services and general dental services only.

Saving

3. Where before 1st January 1996—

(a) an appeal has been made to the Secretary of State under section 29(4) of the 1978 Act; or

(b) an application has been made to the Secretary of State for a direction under section 30 of, or paragraph 6 of Schedule 15 to, the 1978 Act,

the 1978 Act shall have effect in relation to that appeal or that application as if section 9 or (as the case may be) section 10 of the 1995 Act (and, in the Schedule to the 1995 Act, the associated repeals relating to sections 29(4), 30 and 32 of the 1978 Act) had not come into force.

James Douglas-Hamilton
Minister of State,
Scottish Office

St Andrew's House, Edinburgh
7th December 1995

Article 2 SCHEDULE

PROVISIONS OF THE ACT COMING INTO FORCE ON 1ST JANUARY 1996

(1) *Provision of the Act*	*(2)* *Subject matter*
Section 7, for the purposes specified in article 2(2) of this Order	Disqualified practitioners: engagement in provision of services by others (Scotland).
Section 8, for the purposes specified in article 2(2) of this Order	Interim suspension of practitioners (Scotland).
Section 9	Appeals against disqualification: removal of appeal to Secretary of State (Scotland).
Section 10	Removal of disqualification (Scotland).
Section 11	Procedure relating to disqualification (Scotland).
Section 12	Constitution of the Tribunal (Scotland).
Section 14(2), so far as it relates to the provisions of the Schedule brought into force by this Order	Repeal of provisions specified in the Schedule.
In the Schedule, the entries relating to the National Health Service (Scotland) Act 1978	Repeals.

SOCIAL SECURITY

THE JOBSEEKERS ACT 1995 (COMMENCEMENT NO. 1) ORDER 1995

(S.I. 1995 No. 3228 (C. 75))

Made - - - - - 11th December 1995

INTRODUCTION

This Order provides, *inter alia*, for the coming into force on January 1, 1996 of section 29 in the Jobseekers Act 1995 (c. 18), which relates to the making of pilot schemes. Further provisions in section 28 relating to expedited claims for housing benefit and council tax benefit are to come into force on April 1, 1996, and provisions relating to finance are to come into force on April 6, 1996.

The Secretary of State, in exercise of the powers conferred upon him by section 41(2) and (3) of the Jobseekers Act 1995 (c. 18) and of all other powers enabling him in that behalf, hereby makes the following Order:

Citation and interpretation

1.—(1) This Order may be cited as the Jobseekers Act 1995 (Commencement No. 1) Order 1995.

(2) In the Order, unless the context otherwise requires, references to sections and Schedules are references to sections of and Schedules to the Jobseekers Act 1995.

Appointed days

2. The day appointed for the coming into force of—
(a) sections 9(13) (meaning of employment officer), 19(10)(a) (meaning of employment officer), 35 (interpretation), 36 (regulations and orders) and 37 (parliamentary control) is 12th December 1995;
(b) the provisions specified in the Schedule to this Order for the purpose only of authorising the making of regulations is 12th December 1995;
(c) sections 27 and 34(3) and (7) (employment of long-term unemployed: deductions by employers)—
  (i) for the purpose only of authorising the making of regulations, is 12th December 1995; and
  (ii) for all other purposes is 6th April 1996;
(d) section 28 (expedited claims for housing benefit and council tax benefit and the exchange of information)—
  (i) for the purpose only of authorising the making of regulations, is 12th December 1995; and
  (ii) for all other purposes is 1st April 1996;
(e) section 29 (pilot schemes) is 1st January 1996;
(f) section 30 (grants for resettlement places) and the repeals in Schedule 3 relating to section 30 of and Schedule 5 to the Supplementary Benefits Act 1976 and section 41(5) in so far as it relates to them, is 1st April 1996;

(g) sections 33 (inspection), 34 (offences), 38(1)(b) and (5) (financial arrangements) and Schedule 2, paragraph 41 (questions for adjudication by the Secretary of State) and section 41(5) in so far as it relates to it, is 6th April 1996.

Signed by authority of the Secretary of State for Social Security.

Roger Evans
Parliamentary Under-Secretary of State,
Department of Social Security

11th December 1995

Article 2(b) SCHEDULE

PROVISIONS COMING INTO FORCE ON 12TH DECEMBER 1995

Provisions of the Jobseekers Act 1995	*Subject matter*
Section 2(1)(c) and (4)(b)	Contribution conditions for a jobseeker's allowance.
Section 3(1)(f)(iii), (2), (3) and (4).	The income-based conditions.
Section 4(1)(b), (2), (4), (5) and (12).	Amounts payable by way of a jobseeker's allowance.
Section 5(3).	Duration of contribution-based jobseeker's allowance.
Section 6(2), (3), (4), (5), (7) and (8)	Availability for employment.
Section 7(2), (3), (4), (5), (6) and (8).	Actively seeking employment.
Section 8.	Attendance, information and evidence.
Section 9(1), (8), (10), (11) and (12).	The Jobseeker's Agreement.
Section 10(1), (6)(c) and (7).	Variation of Jobseeker's Agreement.
Section 11(2), (5), (7) and (8).	Jobseeker's Agreement: reviews and appeals.
Section 12.	Income and capital: general.
Section 13.	Income and capital: income-based jobseeker's allowance.
Section 15(1), (2)(d), (5) and (6).	Effect of trade dispute on other claimants.
Section 17(1).	Reduced payments.
Section 19(2), (4), (7), (8) and (10)(c).	Circumstances in which a jobseeker's allowance is not payable.
Section 20(3), (4), (5), (6), (7) and (8).	Exemptions from section 19.
Section 21 and Schedule 1.	Supplementary Provisions.
Section 22.	Members of the Forces.
Section 23(1), (3) and (4).	Recovery of sums in respect of maintenance.
Section 26.	Back to Work Bonus.
Section 31.	Termination of Awards.
Section 40.	Transitional Provisions.
Schedule 2, paragraph 30(5) and section 41(4) in so far as it refers to it.	Prescribed categories of persons for the purpose of income support.

FAMILY LAW

CHILD SUPPORT

THE CHILD SUPPORT ACT 1995 (COMMENCEMENT NO. 2) ORDER 1995

(S.I. 1995 No. 3262 (C. 76))

Made - - - - - *15th December 1995*

INTRODUCTION

This Order brings into force certain provisions of the Child Support Act 1995 (c. 34). Provisions which relate to, *inter alia*, child support appeal tribunals, come into force on December 18, 1996. The provisions which come into force on January 22, 1996 relate to, *inter alia*, the cancellation of maintenance assessments on review.

The Secretary of State for Social Security, in exercise of the power conferred upon him by section 30(4) of the Child Support Act 1995 (c. 34), hereby makes the following Order:

Citation and interpretation

1.—(1) This Order may be cited as the Child Support Act 1995 (Commencement No. 2) Order 1995.

(2) In this Order, unless the context otherwise requires, references to sections, Schedules and paragraphs of a Schedule are references to sections of, Schedules to, and paragraphs of a Schedule to the Child Support Act 1995.

Appointed days

2.—(1) The day appointed for the coming into force of the provisions specified in Part I of the Schedule to this Order is 18th December 1995.

(2) The day appointed for the coming into force of the provisions specified in Part II of the Schedule to this Order is 22nd January 1996.

Signed by authority of the Secretary of State for Social Security.

A. J. B. Mitchell
Parliamentary Under-Secretary of State,
Department of Social Security

15th December 1995

Article 2

SCHEDULE

PART I

PROVISIONS COMING INTO FORCE ON 18TH DECEMBER 1995

Provisions of the Child Support Act 1995	*Subject matter*
Section 16	Lapse of appeals to child support appeal tribunals.
Section 17	Determination of questions other than by Child Support Commissioners.
Paragraph 18 of Schedule 3 and section 30(5) so far as it relates to that paragraph	Minor and consequential amendments—expenses of persons required to attend proceedings before a Child Support Commissioner.

PART II

PROVISIONS COMING INTO FORCE ON 22ND JANUARY 1996

Provisions of the Child Support Act 1995	*Subject matter*
Section 9, in respect of insertion of section 281(4) into the Child Support Act 1991 (c. 48)	Transitional provisions.
Section 11	Reviews: interim maintenance assessments.
Section 12 in so far as it is not already in force	Reviews on change of circumstances.
Section 13	Continuation of reviews under section 18 of the Child Support Act 1991.
Section 14	Cancellation of maintenance assessments on review.
Section 15	Reviews at instigation of child support officers.

LOCAL GOVERNMENT, SCOTLAND

PRISONS

THE LOCAL GOVERNMENT ETC. (SCOTLAND) ACT 1994 (COMMENCEMENT NO. 6 AND SAVING) ORDER 1995

(S.I. 1995 No. 3326 (C. 77) (S.246))

Made - - - - - 15th December 1995

INTRODUCTION

This Order brings into effect s.180(1) on December 22, 1995, so far as it amends the Prisons (Scotland) Act 1989 (c. 45) in relation to visiting committees. The Order also brings into force other provisions of the 1989 Act as a consequence of the changes in local authorities on April 1, 1996.

The Secretary of State, in exercise of the powers conferred on him by section 184(2) and (3) of the Local Government etc. (Scotland) Act 1994 (c. 39) and of all other powers enabling him in that behaf, hereby makes the following Order:

Citation and interpretation

1.—(1) This Order may be cited as the Local Government etc. (Scotland) Act 1994 (Commencement No. 6 and Saving) Order 1995.

(2) In this Order—

"the Act" means the Local Government etc. (Scotland) Act 1994.

Days appointed

2. Subject to article 4 below, 22nd December 1995 is the day appointed for the coming into force of the following provisions of the Act—

(a) section 180(1), so far as it relates to the provision in Schedule 13 to the Act specified in paragraph (b) below;

(b) in Schedule 13 to the Act, paragraph 162(1) and (2).

3. 1st April 1996 is the day appointed for the coming into force of the following provisions of the Act—

(a) section 180, so far as it relates to the provisions of Schedules 13 and 14 to the Act specified in paragraphs (b) and (c) below;

(b) in Schedule 13 to the Act, paragraph 162(3) and (4) and

(c) the repeals in Schedule 14 to the Act specified in the Schedule to this Order.

Saving

4. Notwithstanding article 2 above, until 1st April 1996 paragraph 162(2) of Schedule 13 to the Act shall not apply in relation to any visiting committee constituted before 22nd December 1995 by rules made under section 39, as read with section 8(1), of the Prisons (Scotland) Act 1989 (c. 45; section 39 was amended by the Prisoners and Criminal Proceedings (Scotland) Act 1993 (c. 9), sections 24 and 25, Schedule 5, paragraph 6(6) and Schedule 7 and by the Criminal Justice and Public Order Act 1994 (c. 33), sections 116(4) and 130(4); section 39 is to be read with sections 8(1) and (2), 11(1), 12 (as amended by the 1993 Act, Schedule 5, paragraph 6(2)), 14(1) (as amended by the 1993 Act, Schedule 5, paragraph 6(3)), 19(3) and (4) (as amended by the

1993 Act, Schedule 5, paragraph 6(4)), 24 (which was repealed by the 1993 Act, Schedule 7 but was saved by Schedule 6 to that Act in relation to any "existing prisoner" within the meaning specified in paragraph 1 of Schedule 6) and 41; section 39 was extended by the Courts-Martial (Appeals) Act 1968 (c. 20), section 52 (as amended by the 1989 Act, Schedule 2, Paragraph 10)).

George Kynoch
Parliamentary Under-Secretary of State,
Scottish Office

St Andrew's House, Edinburgh
15th December 1995

Article 3(c)

SCHEDULE

REPEALS IN SCHEDULE 14 TO THE ACT COMING INTO FORCE ON 1ST APRIL 1966

Chapter	*Short title*	*Extent of repeal*
1989 c. 45	The Prisons (Scotland) Act 1989	In section 14(2), the words "region or islands", where secondly occurring and, in section 16(2), the words "district or islands", in both places where they occur.

DISABLED PERSONS

THE DISABILITY DISCRIMINATION ACT 1995 (COMMENCEMENT NO. 1) ORDER 1995

(S.I. 1995 No. 3330 (C. 78))

Made - - - - - 28th December 1995

INTRODUCTION

This Order brings into force on January 1, 1996, ss.50, 51, and 52 of, and Sched. 5 to the Disability Discrimination Act 1995 (c. 50) which provide for the establishment and functions of the National Disability Council.

The Secretary of State for Social Security, in exercise of the power conferred by section 70(3) of the Disability Discrimination Act 1995 (c. 50), hereby makes the following Order:

Citation

1. This Order may be cited as the Disability Discrimination Act 1995 (Commencement No. 1) Order 1995.

Commencement of sections 50, 51 and 52 of, and Schedule 5 to, the Disability Discrimination Act 1995

2. The day appointed for the coming into force of sections 50, 51 and 52 of, and Schedule 5 to, the Disability Discrimination Act 1995 is 1st January 1996.

Signed by authority of the Secretary of State for Social Security.

A. J. B. Mitchell
Parliamentary Under-Secretary of State,
Department of Social Security

28th December 1995

ENERGY CONSERVATION

ENGLAND

THE HOME ENERGY CONSERVATION ACT 1995 (COMMENCEMENT NO. 2) (ENGLAND) ORDER 1995

(S.I. 1995 No. 3340 (C. 79))

Made - - - - - 29th December 1995

INTRODUCTION

This Order provides for ss.3(1) and 4(1) and (2) of the Home Energy Conservation Act 1995 (c. 10) to come into effect on January 15, 1996 and for the remainder of the Act, as it relates to England, to be brought into force on April 1, 1996.

The Secretary of State for the Environment, as respects England, in exercise of the powers conferred upon him by section 9(2) and (3) of the Home Energy Conservation Act 1995 (c. 10) and of all other powers enabling him in that behalf, hereby makes the following Order:

Citation

1. This Order may be cited as the Home Energy Conservation Act 1995 (Commencement No. 2) (England) Order 1995.

Commencement

2.—(1) Subject to paragraph (2), the Home Energy Conservation Act 1995 shall come into force on 1st April 1996.

(2) Sections 3(1) and 4(1) and (2) of that Act shall come into force on 15th January 1996.

Application

3. This Order shall apply in relation only to energy conservation authorities whose areas are in England.

Signed by authority of the Secretary of State

Robert Jones
Minister of State,
Department of the Environment

29th December 1995

CURRENT LAW STATUTES

NUMERICAL TABLE OF STATUTORY INSTRUMENTS 1995

This table details in numerical order Statutory Instruments released in 1995. The table is up to date to **March 11, 1996**. For brief digests of Statutory Instruments see the Current Law Monthly Digest. A list of 1996 SIs follows the 1995 table.

1 (S. 1).....National Health Service (Optical Charges and Payments) (Scotland) Amendment Regulations 1995
2................Plymouth Hospitals National Health Service Trust (Transfer of Trust Property) Order 1995
10................Criminal Justice Act 1988 (Reviews of Sentencing) Order 1995
11................Pigs (Records, Identification and Movement) Order 1995
12................Bovine Animals (Records, Identification and Movement) Order 1995
13................Enzootic Bovine Leukosis (Amendment) Order 1995
14................Beef Special Premium (Amendment) Regulations 1995
15................Suckler Cow Premium (Amendment) Regulations 1995
16................Fertilisers (Amendment) Regulations 1995
17................A23 Trunk Road (Brighton Road, Croydon) (Prohibition of Right Turn and U-Turn) Order 1995
21................Community Charges (Administration and Enforcement) (Amendment) Regulations 1995
22................Council Tax (Administration and Enforcement) (Amendment) Regulations 1995
23................Local Government Changes for England (Council Tax and Non-Domestic Rating, Demand Notices) Regulations 1995
24 (C. 1).....Criminal Justice and Public Order Act 1994 (Commencement No. 4) Order 1995
25................Industrial Training Levy (Construction Board) Order 1995
26................Industrial Training Levy (Engineering Construction Board) Order 1995
31................Employment Protection (Part-time Employees) Regulations 1995
33................Borough of Trafford (Eastern Spine Canal Bridge) Scheme 1993 Confirmation Instrument 1995
34................National Health Service (Optical Charges and Payments) Amendment Regulations 1995
35................Occupational and Personal Pension Schemes (Miscellaneous Amendments) Regulations 1995
38................Borough of Trafford (A5063 Trafford/White City Gyratory System Canal Bridges) Scheme 1993 Confirmation Instrument 1995
39................Food Protection (Emergency Prohibitions) (Radioactivity in Sheep) (England) (Partial Revocation) Order 1995
40................Apple Orchard Grubbing Up (Amendment) Regulations 1995
41................Justices of the Peace Act 1949 (Compensation) (Variation) Regulations 1995
42 (C. 2).....Police and Magistrates' Courts Act 1994 (Commencement No. 6 and Transitional Provisions) Order 1995
43 (C. 3).....Criminal Justice Act 1993 (Commencement No. 8) Order 1995
44................District of Bromsgrove (Electrical Arrangements) Order 1995
45................Education (Special Educational Needs) (Prescribed Forms) (Welsh Forms) Regulations 1995
46................Food Protection (Emergency Prohibitions) (Radioactivity in Sheep) (Wales) (Partial Revocation) Order 1995

48................Food Protection (Emergency Prohibitions) (Radioactivity in Sheep) Partial Revocation Order 1995
49................Home Energy Efficiency Grants (Amendment) Regulations 1995
51................Education (National Curriculum) (Attainment Targets and Programmes of Study in English) Order 1995
52................Education (National Curriculum) (Attainment Targets and Programmes of Study Mathematics) Order 1995
53................Education (National Curriculum) (Attainment Targets and Programmes of Study in Science) Order 1995
54................Education (National Curriculum) (Attainment Targets and Programmes of Study in History) (England) Order 1995
55................Education (National Curriculum) (Attainment Targets and Programmes of Study in Geography) (England) Order 1995
56................Education (National Curriculum) (Attainment Targets and Programmes of Study in Technology) Order 1995
57................Education (National Curriculum) (Attainment Targets and Programmes of Study in Modern Foreign Languages) Order 1995
58................Education (National Curriculum) (Attainment Targets and Programmes of Study in Art) (England) Order 1995
59................Education (National Curriculum) (Attainment Targets and Programmes of Study in Music) (England) Order 1995
60................Education (National Curriculum) (Attainment Targets and Programmes of Study in Physical Education) Order 1995
61................Education (Schools Conducted by Education Associations) (Amendment) Regulations 1995
68................Electricity (Non-Fossil Fuel Sources) (England and Wales) (Amendment) Order 1995
69................Education (National Curriculum) (Attainment Targets and Programmes of Study in Welsh) Order 1995
70................Education (National Curriculum) (Attainment Targets and Programmes of Study in Music) (Wales) Order 1995
71................Education (National Curriculum) (Attainment Targets and Programmes of Study in Art) (Wales) Order 1995
72................Education (National Curriculum) (Attainment Targets and Programmes of Study in Geography) (Wales) Order 1995
73................Education (National Curriculum) (Attainment Targets and Programmes of Study in History) (Wales) Order 1995
74................Social Security (Widow's Benefit and Retirement Pensions) Amendment Regulations 1995
77................Infant Formula and Follow-on Formula Regulations 1995
79................Hartlepools Water Company (Constitution and Regulation) Order 1995
80................National Health Service (General Medical Services) Amendment Regulations 1995
82................City Hospitals Sunderland National Health Service Trust (Transfer of Property) Order 1995
83................Derbyshire Royal Infirmary National Health Trust (Transfer of Trust Property) Order 1995
84................North Tyneside Health Care National Health Service Trust (Transfer of Trust Property) Order 1995
85................Southport and Formby Community Health Services National Health Service Trust (Transfer of Trust Property) Order 1995
86................West Lancashire National Health Service Trust (Transfer of Trust Property) Order 1995

87................Wrightington Hospital National Health Service Trust (Transfer of Trust Property) Order 1995
88................Princess Royal Hospital National Health Service Trust (Establishment) Amendment Order 1995
89................Priority Healthcare Wearside National Health Service Trust (Transfer of Trust Property) Order 1995
90................Pilgrim Health National Health Service Trust (Transfer of Trust Property) Order 1995
91................Royal Hull Hospital National Health Service Trust (Establishment) Amendment Order 1995
92................Cumbria Ambulance Service National Health Service Trust (Establishment) Amendment Order 1995
99................Teddington Memorial Hospital National Health Service Trust (Establishment) Amendment Order 1995
100................Hill Livestock (Compensatory Allowances) (Amendment) Regulations 1995
101................Residuary Body for Wales (Capital Finance) Regulations 1995
102................Residuary Body for Wales (Miscellaneous Provisions) Order 1995
103 (C. 5).....Residuary Body for Wales (Appointed Day) Order 1995
115................Local Government Reorganisation (Wales) (Consequential Amendments) Order 1995
117................North Hampshire Hospitals National Health Service Trust (Establishment) Amendment Order 1995
121................Council Tax and Non-Domestic Rating (Demand Notices) (England) Amendment Regulations 1995
122................Gaming (Bingo) Act (Variation of Monetary Limit) Order 1995
123................Child Support (Miscellaneous Amendments) Regulations 1995
124................A205 Trunk Road (Richmond and Wandsworth) Red Route Experimental Traffic Order 1995
125................A205 Trunk Road (Hounslow) Red Route (Bus Lanes) Experimental Traffic Order 1995
126................A205 Trunk Road (Hounslow) Red Route Experimental Traffic Order 1995
127 (C. 4).....Criminal Justice and Public Order Act 1994 (Commencement No. 5 and Transitional Provisions) Order 1995
128................Local Government Reorganisation (Wales) (Special Grant) Order 1995
131................Welfare of Animals During Transport (Amendment) Order 1995
132 (S. 2).....Lyon Court and Office Fees (Variation) Order 1995
137 (S. 3).....Police (Scotland) Amendment Regulations 1995
140................Land Registration Rules 1995
141................West Wales Ambulance National Health Service Trust (Establishment) Order 1995
142................Cardiff Community Healthcare National Health Service Trust (Establishment) Order 1995
143................University Dental Hospital National Health Service Trust (Establishment) Order 1995
144................Telecommunications Terminal Equipment (Amendment) Regulations 1995
145 (C. 6).....Law of Property (Miscellaneous Provisions) Act 1994 (Commencement No. 1) Order 1995
150................Financial Assistance for Environmental Purposes Order 1995
151................Returning Officers (Principal Areas: Wales) Order 1995
152................Value Added Tax (General) (Amendment) Regulations 1995
157................Merchant Shipping (Hours of Work) Regulations 1995

158................Motorways Traffic (England and Wales) (Amendment) Regulations 1995
159 (C. 7).....Coal Industry Act 1994 (Commencement No. 4) Order 1995
160................Council Tax (Demand Notices) (Wales) (Amendment) Regulations 1995
161................Local Government Finance (Miscellaneous Provisions) (England) Order 1995
162................Legal Aid Advisory Committee (Dissolution) Order 1995
164 (S. 4).....Valuation Timetable (Scotland) Order 1995
165 (S. 5).....National Health Service (General Medical and Pharmaceutical Services) (Scotland) Amendment Regulations 1995
168................Mackerel (Specified Sea Areas) (Prohibition of Fishing) Order 1995
171................Friendly Societies (Taxation of Transfers of Business) Regulations 1995
178................Education (Financial Delegation to Schools) (Mandatory Exceptions) Regulations 1995
182................Public Telecommunications System Designation (AT&T Communications (UK) Ltd) Order 1995
183................Education (Welsh Agricultural College Higher Education Corporation) (Dissolution) Order 1995
184................Surplus Food Regulations 1995
185................Public Service Vehicles (Lost Property) (Amendment) Regulations 1995
186................Public Service Vehicles (Conduct of Drivers, Inspectors, Conductors and Passengers) (Amendment) Regulations 1995
187................Cleveland (Structural Change) Order 1995
188 (S. 6).....Housing Revenue Account General Fund Contribution Limits (Scotland) Order 1995
189................Environmentally Sensitive Areas (North Peak) Designation (Amendment) Order 1995
190................Environmentally Sensitive Areas (Clun) Designation (Amendment) Order 1995
191................Environmentally Sensitive Areas (Test Valley) Designation (Amendment) Order 1995
192................Environmentally Sensitive Areas (South West Peak) Designation (Amendment) Order 1995
193................Environmentally Sensitive Areas (Lake District) Designation (Amendment) Order 1995
194................Environmentally Sensitive Areas (Suffolk River Valley) Designation (Amendment) Order 1995
195................Environmentally Sensitive Areas (Exmoor) Designation (Amendment) Order 1995
196................Environmentally Sensitive Areas (South Wessex Downs) Designation (Amendment) Order 1995
197................Environmentally Sensitive Areas (Avon Valley) Designation (Amendment) Order 1995
198................Environmentally Sensitive Areas (Breckland) Designation (Amendment) Order 1995
199................Environmentally Sensitive Areas (North Kent Marshes) Designation (Amendment) Order 1995
200................Environmentally Sensitive Areas (Cotswold Hills) Designation (Amendment) Order 1995
201................Public Supply Contracts Regulations 1995
202................Financial Services Act 1986 (Miscellaneous Exemptions) Order 1995
203................A11 Trunk Road (Thetford Bypass Slips Roads) (Trunking) Order 1995
204................Toys (Safety) Regulations 1995

205 (L. 1).....High Court and County Courts Jurisdiction (Amendment) Order 1995
206 (L. 2).....County Court Remedies (Amendment) Regulations 1995
207................Veterinary Surgeons and Veterinary Practitioners (Registration) (Amendment) Regulations Order of Council 1995
208................Education (School Financial Statements) (Prescribed Particulars etc.) Regulations 1995
209................Council Tax (Transitional Reduction Scheme) (England) Regulations 1995
210................Mortgage Indemnities (Recognised Bodies) Order 1995
211................Housing (Right to Buy) (Priority of Charges) Order 1995
212................Local Government Changes for England (Non-Domestic Rating, Collection and Enforcement and Discretionary Relief) Regulations 1995
213................Valuation for Rating (Former Enterprise Zones) Regulations 1995
214 (S. 7).....Local Government Superannuation (Scotland) Amendment Regulations 1995
215................Police Regulations 1995
216................Income Tax (Employments) (Amendment) Regulations 1995
217................Income Tax (Sub-Contractors in the Construction Industry) (Amendment) Regulations 1995
219................Cardiff–Glan Conway Trunk Road (A470) (Cancoed to Minffordd Improvement) Order 1995
220................Chester–Bangor Trunk Road (A55) (Aber Improvement) Detrunking Order 1995
231................Leeds City Council (M1–A1 Link Road/East Leeds Radical (A63) Junction Connecting Roads) Scheme 1993 Confirmation Instrument 1995
232................Telecommunications (Registers) Order 1995
234................Local Authorities (Alteration of Requisite Calculations and Funds) Regulations 1995
235................Billing Authorities (Anticipation of Precepts) (Amendment) Regulations 1995
236................Fruit Juices and Fruit Nectars (England, Wales and Scotland) (Amendment) Regulations 1995
238................Overseas Service (Pensions Supplement) Regulations 1995
239 (S. 8).....Non-Domestic Rating (Telecommunications and Canals) (Scotland) Order 1995
242................Environmentally Sensitive Areas Designation (Wales) (Amendment) Order 1995
243................Environmentally Sensitive Areas (Cambrian Mountains) Designation (Amendment) Order 1995
244................Wireless Telegraphy (Licence Charges) (Amendment) Regulations 1995
246 (C. 8).....Police and Magistrates' Courts Act 1994 (Commencement No. 5 and Transitional Provisions) (Amendment) Order 1995
247................Local Government Changes for England (Community Charge and Council Tax, Administration and Enforcement) Regulations 1995
248 (S. 9).....Land Registration (Scotland) Amendment Rules 1995
254................Dairy Produce Quotas (Amendment) Regulations 1995
255................Coal Industry (Abolition of Domestic Coal Consumers Council) Order 1995
260................Local Land Charges (Amendment) Rules 1995
261................Council for the Central Laboratory of the Research Councils Order 1995
262................European Communities (Designation) Order 1995

263................Health and Safety at Work etc. Act 1974 (Application Outside Great Britain) Order 1995
264................Child Abduction and Custody (Parties to Conventions) (Amendment) Order 1995
265................European Communities (Definition of Treaties) (The Agreement Establishing the World Trade Organisation) Order 1995
266................World Trade Organisation (Immunities and Privileges) Order 1995
267................Public Health (Ships and Aircraft) (Isle of Man) (Revocation) Order 1995
268................Wireless Telegraphy (Isle of Man) Order 1995
270................Somerset County Council (Bridgwater Northern Distributor Road Bridge) Scheme 1992 Confirmation Instrument 1995
271................Dual-Use and Related Goods (Export Control) Regulations 1995
273 (C. 9).....Coal Industry Act 1994 (Commencement No. 5) Order 1995
278................Insolvency of Employer (Excluded Classes) Regulations 1995
279................Value Added Tax (Buildings and Land) Order 1995
280................Value Added Tax (Construction of Buildings) Order 1995
281................Value Added Tax (Input Tax) (Amendment) Order 1995
282................Value Added Tax (Land) Order 1995
283................Value Added Tax (Protected Buildings) Order 1995
284................Non-Domestic Rating (Demand Notices) (Wales) (Amendment) Regulations 1995
288................Waste Management Licensing (Amendment etc.) Regulations 1995
289................Isle of Wight (Staff Transfer) Order 1995
291................Value Added Tax (Payments on Account) (Amendment) Order 1995
292................Food Protection (Emergency Prohibitions) (Oil and Chemical Pollution of Fish) (No. 2) Order 1993 (Partial Revocation No. 4) Order 1995
293................Food Protection (Emergency Prohibitions) (Oil and Chemical Pollution of Fish) (No. 2) Order 1993 (Partial Revocation No. 4) Order 1995
296................A3 Trunk Road (Kingston By-Pass, Kingston Upon Thames and Merton) (40 m.p.h. Speed Limit) Order 1995
297................Town and Country Planning (Use Classes) (Amendment) Order 1995
298................Town and Country Planning General Development (Amendment) Order 1995
299................A638 Trunk Road (King Royd Lane, Brackenhill Common, Ackworth to District Boundary, South Elmsall) (Detrunking) Order 1995
300................National Health Service Pension Scheme Regulations 1995
301................Brent and Harrow Health Authority (Transfer of Trust Property) Order 1995
302................Approved Probation and Bail Hostel Rules 1995
304................Genetically Modified Organisms (Deliberate Release) Regulations 1995
305................Public Service Vehicles (Conditions of Fitness, Equipment, Use and Certification) (Amendment) Regulations 1995
307 (S. 10)...Scottish Land Court (Fees) Order 1995
308 (S. 11)...Lands Tribunal for Scotland (Amendment) (Fees) Rules 1995
309................Medicines (Advisory Board on the Registration of Homoeopathic Products) Order 1995
310................Social Security (Incapacity Benefit) (Transitional) Regulations 1995

311................Social Security (Incapacity for Work) (General) Regulations 1995
312 (S. 12)...Non-Domestic Rate (Scotland) Order 1995
320................A3 Trunk Road (Malden Way, Kingston-Upon-Thames) (Prescribed Routes) Order 1995
321................Gaming Act (Variation of Fees) Order 1995
322................Gaming (Bingo) Act (Fees) (Amendment) Order 1995
323................Lotteries (Gaming Board Fees) Order 1995
324................Nottingham City Hospital National Health Service Trust (Transfer of Trust Property) Order 1995
331................Greater London and Surrey (County and London Borough Boundaries) Order 1995
335................A3 Trunk Road (Wandsworth) Red Route (Clearway) Experimental Traffic Order 1995
336................A3 Trunk Road (Merton) Red Route Experimental Traffic Order 1995
337................A3 Trunk Road (Kingston Upon Thames) Red Route (Clearway) Experimental Traffic Order 1995
338................A3 Trunk Road (Merton) Red Route (Clearway) Experimental Traffic Order 1995
339................A3 Trunk Road (Kingston Upon Thames) Red Route Experimental Traffic Order 1995
340 (S. 13)...Local Government (Compensation for Redundancy or Premature Retirement on Reorganisation) (Scotland) Regulations 1995
341................Carlisle Hospitals National Health Service Trust (Transfer of Trust Property) Order 1995
342................Guild Community Healthcare National Health Service Trust (Transfer of Trust Property) Order 1995
343................Hounslow and Spelthorne Community and Mental Health National Health Service Trust (Transfer of Trust Property) Order 1995
344................Lancashire Ambulance Service National Health Service Trust (Transfer of Trust Property) Order 1995
345................Preston Acute Hospitals National Health Service Trust (Transfer of Trust Property) Order 1995
346................Richmond, Twickenham and Roehampton Healthcare National Health Service Trust (Transfer of Property) Order 1995
347................St Albans and Hemel Hempstead National Health Service Trust (Transfer of Trust Property) Order 1995
348................Trafford Healthcare National Health Service Trust (Transfer of Property) Order 1995
351................Lloyd's Underwriters (Tax) Regulations 1995
352................Lloyd's Underwriters (Tax) (1992–93 to 1996–97) Regulations 1995
353................Lloyd's Underwriters (Special Reserve Funds) Regulations 1995
356................Milk Development Council Order 1995
360................Plastic Materials and Articles in Contact with Food (Amendment) Regulations 1995
361................Meat (Hygiene, Inspection and Examinations for Residues) (Charges) Regulations 1995
362................Agricultural Processing and Marketing Grant Regulations 1995
363................Valuation and Community Charge Tribunals (Amendment) (England) Regulations 1995
364 (C. 10) (S. 14) Law Reform (Miscellaneous Provisions) (Scotland) Act 1990 (Commencement No. 13) Order 1995

365 (S. 15)...National Health Service Superannuation Scheme (Scotland) Regulations 1995
366 (S. 16)...Mines and Quarries (Rateable Values) (Scotland) Order 1995
367 (S. 17)...Water Undertakings (Rateable Values) (Scotland) Order 1995
368 (S. 18)...British Gas plc (Rateable Values) (Scotland) Order 1995
369 (S. 19)...Electricity Generation Lands (Rateable Values) (Scotland) Order 1995
370 (S. 20)...Electricity Transmission Lands (Rateable Values) (Scotland) Order 1995
371 (S. 21)...Electricity Generators (Rateable Values) (Scotland) Order 1995
372 (S. 22)...Electricity Generators (Aluminium) (Rateable Values) (Scotland) Order 1995
373 (S. 23)...Electricity Distribution Lands (Rateable Values) (Scotland) Order 1995
374 (S. 24)...Formula Valuation (Revocations) (Scotland) Order 1995
375 (S. 25)...Docks and Harbours (Rateable Values) (Scotland) Amendment Order 1995
376................Recreation Grounds (Revocation of Parish Council Byelaws) Order 1995
377................Land Registration (Implied Covenants for Title) Rules 1995
378................Bolton Hospitals National Health Service Trust (Transfer of Trust Property) Order 1995
379................Burton Hospitals National Health Service Trust (Transfer of Trust Property) Order 1995
380................Central Nottinghamshire Healthcare National Health Service Trust (Transfer of Trust Property) Order 1995
381................Community Healthcare Bolton National Health Service Trust (Transfer of Trust Property) Order 1995
382................East Surrey Learning Disability and Mental Health Service National Health Service Trust (Transfer of Trust Property) Order 1995
383................Greenwich Healthcare National Health Service Trust (Transfer of Trust Property) Order 1995
384................King's Mill Centre for Health Care Services National Health Service Trust (Transfer of Trust Property) Order 1995
385................Lincoln Hospitals National Health Service Trust (Transfer of Trust Property) Order 1995
386................Premier Health National Health Service Trust (Transfer of Trust Property) Order 1995
387................Surrey Ambulance Service National Health Service Trust (Transfer of Trust Property) Order 1995
389................Leeds Development Corporation (Planning Functions) Order 1995
390................Leeds Development Corporation (Transfer of Property, Rights and Liabilities) Order 1995
391 (S. 26)...Local Government Finance (Scotland) Order 1995
392 (S. 27)...Revenue Support Grant (Scotland) Order 1995
394................National Health Service Trusts (Originating Capital Debt) (Wales) Order 1995
401................Local Government Residuary Body (England) Order 1995
402................Local Government Changes for England (Property Transfer and Transitional Payments) Regulations 1995
405................A63 Trunk Road (South Cave Interchange Slip Roads) (Trunking) Order 1995
406................A63 Trunk Road (Welton Interchange Slip Roads) (Trunking) Order 1995
407................National Health Service Trusts (Originating Capital Debt) Order 1995

408................Exchange Gains and Losses (Transitional Provisions) (Amendment) Regulations 1995
414 (S. 28)...National Health Service (Pharmaceutical Services) (Scotland) Regulations 1995
415................Fireworks (Safety) (Revocation) Regulations 1995
416 (S. 29)...National Health Service (General Medical Services) (Scotland) Regulations 1995
417................Town and Country Planning (Environmental Assessment and Permitted Development) Regulations 1995
418................Town and Country Planning (General Permitted Development) Order 1995
419................Town and Country Planning (General Development Procedure) Order 1995
421................Bristol City Docks Harbour Revision Order 1995
422................Bristol City Docks (No. 2) Harbour Revision Order 1995
424 (C. 11)...Marriage Act 1994 (Commencement No. 2) Order 1995
425................A64 Trunk Road (Bramham Crossroads) Order 1994 (Variation) Order 1995
426................M1–A1 Link Road (Belle Isle to Bramham Crossroads Section and Connecting Roads) Scheme 1994 (Variation) Scheme 1995
428................Non-Automatic Weighing Machines and Non-Automatic Weighing Instruments (Amendment) Regulations 1995
430................Railway Pensions (Substitution and Miscellaneous Provisions) Order 1995
432................A65 Trunk Road (Chelker Bends Improvement) Order 1995
433................A15 (Brigg and Redbourne Bypass) (Trunking) Order 1995
441................Dual-Use and Related Goods (Export Control) (Suspension) Regulations 1994
442................Gaming Licence Duty (Games) Order 1995
443................National Assistance (Sums for Personal Requirements) Regulations 1995
444................National Health Service (Dental Charges) Amendment Regulations 1995
445................Personal Injuries (Civilians) Amendment Scheme 1995
447................Income Tax (Employments) (Amendment No. 2) Regulations 1995
448................Income Tax (Sub-contractors in the Construction Industry) (Amendment No. 2) Regulations 1995
449................Medical Devices (Consultation Requirements) (Fees) Regulation 1995
450................Police and Criminal Evidence Act 1984 (Codes of Practice) (No. 3) Order 1995
451................Rail Crossing Extinguishment and Diversion Orders, the Public Path Orders and the Definitive Maps and Statements (Amendment) Regulations 1995
469 (S. 30)...Housing Support Grant (Scotland) Variation Order 1995
470 (S. 31)...Housing Support Grant (Scotland) Order 1995
471 (S. 32)...Edinburgh College of Art (Scotland) Order of Council 1995
473................Glan Clwyd District General Hospital National Health Service Trust (Transfer of Trust Property) Order 1995
474................Gofal Cymuned Clwydian Community Care National Health Service Trust (Transfer of Property) Order 1995
475................Wrexham Maelor Hospital National Health Service Trust (Transfer of Trust Property) Order 1995
476................Environmental Protection (Waste Recycling Payments) (Amendment) Regulations 1995
477................Broadgreen Hospital National Health Service Trust Dissolution Order 1995

478................Fosse Health, Leicestershire Community National Health Service Trust Dissolution Order 1995
479................Royal Liverpool University Hospital National Health Service Trust Dissolution Order 1995
480................St James's University Hospital National Health Service Trust Dissolution Order 1995
481................Weybourne Community National Health Service Trust Dissolution Order 1995
482................Disability Working Allowance and Income Support (General) Amendment Regulations 1995
483................Certification Officer (Amendment of Fees) Regulations 1995
484 (S. 33)...Spirit Drinks (Scotland) Amendment Regulations 1995
485................A5 Trunk Road (Priorslee–Gailey) (Detrunking) Order 1995
490................Antarctic Regulations 1995
492 (C. 12) (S. 34) Police and Magistrates' Courts Act 1994 (Commencement No. 7 and Transitional Provisions) Scotland Order 1995
493................Avon (Structural Change) Order 1995
494................Offshore Installations (Safety Zones) Regulations 1995
495................Port of Folkstone Licensing (Liquor) Order 1995
496................Port of Ramsgate Licensing (Liquor) Order 1995
497................Civil Aviation (Navigation Services Charges) Regulations 1995
501................Education (Grants for Education Support and Training) (Wales) Regulations 1995
502................Carmarthen and District National Health Service Trust (Transfer of Trust Property) Order 1995
503................Derwen National Health Service Trust (Transfer of Trust Property) Order 1995
504................Ceredigion and Mid Wales National Health Service Trust (Transfer of Trust Property) Order 1995
505................Llanelli Dinefwr National Health Service Trust (Transfer of Trust Property) Order 1995
506................Misuse of Drugs (Licence Fees) (Amendment) Regulations 1995
509................Coal Industry Act 1984 (British Coal Corporation) Extinguishment of Loans Order 1995
510................Marriages (Approved Premises) Regulations 1995
511................Housing Benefit and Council Tax Benefit (Amendment) Regulations 1995
512................Statutory Sick Pay Percentage Threshold Order 1995
513................Statutory Sick Pay Percentage Threshold Order 1995 (Consequential) Regulations 1995
514................Social Security (Contributions) Amendment Regulations 1995
515................Guaranteed Minimum Pensions Increase Order 1995
516................Income-Related Benefits Schemes (Miscellaneous Amendments) Regulations 1995
517 (S. 35)...Local Government Act 1988 (Defined Activities) (Exemption of Development Corporations) (Scotland) Order 1995
518 (S. 36)...Non-Domestic Rating (Unoccupied Property) (Scotland) Amendment Regulations 1995
519................Barking Barrage Order 1995
520................Local Government Changes for England (Staff) Regulations 1995
521................Value Added Tax Act 1994 (Interest on Tax) (Prescribed Rate) Order 1995

522................Education (Individual Pupils' Achievements) (Information) (Wales) (Amendment) Regulations 1995
524................Occupational and Personal Pension Schemes (Levy) Regulations 1995
525................Merchant Shipping (Light Dues) (Amendment) Regulations 1995
526................Plant Breeders' Rights (Herbaceous Perennials) Scheme 1995
527................Plant Breeders' Rights (Miscellaneous Ornamental Plants) Scheme 1995
528................Plant Breeders' Rights (Trees, Shrubs and Woody Climbers) (Variation) Scheme 1995
529................Plant Breeders' Rights (Sweet Peas) Scheme 1995
530................Plant Breeders' Rights (Vegetables) (Including Field Beans and Field Peas) (Variation) Scheme 1995
531................Local Government Changes for England (Housing Benefit and Council Tax Benefit) Regulations 1995
532................Education (School Financial Statements) (Prescribed Particulars, etc.) (Amendment) Regulations 1995
533................National Health Service (Determination of Districts) (No. 2) Order 1995
534................National Health Service (District Health Authorities) (No. 2) Order 1995
535................Local Authorities (Capital Finance) (Rate of Discount for 1995/96) Regulations 1995
536................Greater London and Surrey (County and London Borough Boundaries) (Variation) Order 1995
537 (S. 37)...Bovine Offal (Prohibition) (Scotland) Amendment Regulations 1995
538 (S. 38)...Central Regional Council (Prohibition of Swimming, Bathing *etc.* in Reservoirs) Byelaws Extension Order 1995
539................Fresh Meat (Hygiene and Inspection) Regulations 1995
540................Poultry Meat, Farmed Game Bird Meat and Rabbit Meat (Hygiene and Inspection) Regulations 1995
541................Medicines (Homeopathic Medicinal Products for Human Use) Amendment Regulations 1995
542................Legal Aid in Criminal and Care Proceedings (General) (Amendment) Regulations 1995
543................Education (Grants) (Travellers and Displaced Persons) (Amendment) Regulations 1995
546 (C. 13)...Local Government (Wales) Act 1994 (Commencement No. 3) Order 1995
547................Police (Amendment) Regulations 1995
548 (S. 39)...Non-Domestic Rates (Levying) (Scotland) Regulations 1995
549................Non-Domestic Rating (Unoccupied Property) (Amendment) Regulations 1995
550................Building Societies (Liquid Asset) (Amendment) Regulations 1995
551................Road Vehicles (Construction and Use) (Amendment) Regulations 1995
552................British Citizenship (Designated Service) (Amendment) Order 1995
553................Local Authorities (Members' Allowances) (Amendment) Regulations 1995
554................Financial Assistance for Environmental Purposes (No. 2) Order 1995
555................Prosecution of Offences (Custody Time Limits) (Amendment) Regulations 1995
556................Local Government (Promotion of Economic Development) (Amendment) Regulations 1995

558................National Health Service (General Ophthalmic Services) Amendment Regulations 1995
559................Social Security Benefits Up-Rating Order 1995
560................Housing Benefit and Council Tax Benefit (Miscellaneous Amendments) Regulations 1995
561................Social Security (Contributions) (Re-Rating and National Insurance Fund Payments) Regulations 1995
562................National Health Service (Determination of Districts) Order 1995
563................National Health Service (District Health Authorities) Order 1995
564................United Leeds Teaching Hospitals National Health Service Trust (Transfer of Trust Property) Regulations 1995
565................Wolverley National Health Service Trust (Transfer of Trust Property) Order 1995
566................Statutory Maternity Pay (Compensation of Employers) Amendment Regulations 1995
567................North Wales Ambulance National Health Service Trust (Transfer of Trust Property) Order 1995
568................Gwynedd Hospitals National Health Service Trust (Transfer of Trust Property) Order 1995
569................Gwynedd Community Health National Health Service Trust (Transfer of Trust Property) Order 1995
570................Local Government Reorganisation (Wales) (Transitional Provisions) Order 1995
571 (S. 40)...Gaming Act (Variation of Fees) (Scotland) Order 1995
572 (S. 41)...Valuation Appeal Committee (Procedure in Appeals under the Valuation Acts) (Scotland) Regulations 1995
573 (S. 42)...Valuation Roll and Valuation Notice (Scotland) Amendment Order 1995
574 (S. 43)...State Hospitals Board for Scotland Order 1995
575 (S. 44)...Mental Health (State Hospital Management Committee, State Hospital, Carstairs) (Scotland) Transfer and Dissolution Order 1995
576 (C. 14) (S. 45) State Hospitals (Scotland) Act 1994 Commencement Order 1995
577 (S. 46)...National Health Service Trusts (Originating Capital Debt) (Scotland) Order 1995
578................Licensed Betting Offices (Amendment) Regulations 1995
579................Betting, Gaming and Lotteries Act 1963 (Schedule 4) (Amendment) Order 1995
580................Social Security Benefits Up-Rating Regulations 1995
581................Social Security (Industrial Injuries) (Dependency) (Permitted Earnings Limits) Order 1995
585 (L. 3).....Magistrates' Courts (Amendment) Rules 1995
586................Insolvency (Amendment) Rules 1995
587................Education (Grant-Maintained Schools) (Finance) (Wales) Regulations 1995
589................Companies Act 1985 (Audit Exemption) (Amendment) Regulations 1995
590................Local Government Changes for England Regulations 1995
596 (S. 47)...Police (Scotland) Amendment (No. 2) Regulations 1995
597 (S. 48)...Council Tax (Discounts) (Scotland) Amendment Regulations 1995
598 (S. 49)...Council Tax (Exempt Dwellings) (Scotland) Amendment Order 1995
599 (S. 50)...Council Tax (Discounts) (Scotland) Amendment Order 1995
600................Humberside (Structural Change) Order 1995
601................Teacher Training Agency (Additional Functions) Order 1995
602................Education (Teachers) (Amendment) Regulations 1995

603................Education (Bursaries for Teacher Training) (Amendment) Regulations 1995
604................Education (University Commissioners) Order 1995
605................Education (Grants for Education Support and Training) (England) Regulations 1995
606................Plant Breeders' Rights (Fees) (Amendment) Regulations 1995
607................Seeds (National Lists of Varieties) (Fees) (Amendment) Regulations 1995
608................Norfolk and Suffolk Broads (Extension of Byelaws) Order 1995
609................Non-Domestic Rating (Alteration of Lists and Appeals) (Amendment) Regulations 1995
610................North Yorkshire (District of York) (Structural and Boundary Changes) Order 1995
611................Capital Allowances (Corresponding Northern Ireland Grants) Order 1995
612................Sugar Beet (Research and Education) Order 1995
613................Bovine Offal (Prohibition) (Amendment) Regulations 1995
614................Animal By-Products (Identification) Regulations 1995
615................Common Agricultural Policy (Wine) Regulations 1995
616................Road Traffic (Special Parking Area) (London Borough of Redbridge) (Amendment) Order 1995
617................Road Traffic (Special Parking Area) (Royal Borough of Kingston-upon-Thames) (Amendment) Order 1995
618................Road Traffic (Special Parking Area) (London Borough of Sutton) (Amendment) Order 1995
619................Council Tax (Discount Disregards and Exempt Dwellings) (Amendments) Order 1995
620................Council Tax (Liability for Owners and Additional Provisions for Discount Disregards) (Amendment) Regulations 1995
621................Family Health Services Appeal Authority (Establishment and Constitution) Order 1995
622................Family Health Services Appeal Authority Regulations 1995
623................Local Government Changes for England (Non-Domestic Rating, Alteration of Lists and Appeals) Regulations 1995
624................Local Government Changes for England (Community Charge and Council Tax, Valuation and Community Charge Tribunals and Alteration of Lists and Appeals) Regulations 1995
625................Housing Benefit, Council Tax Benefit and Income Support (Amendment) Regulations 1995
626................Housing Benefit and Council Tax Benefit (Miscellaneous Amendments) (No. 2) Regulations 1995
627................Education (London Residuary Body) (Property Transfer) (Modification and Amendment) Order 1995
628................Education (Ballot Expenditure) Regulations 1995
629................Education (Payment for Special Educational Needs Supplies) (Amendment) Regulation 1995
630................Research Councils (Transfer of Property etc.) Order 1995
631 (C. 15)...Judicial Pensions and Retirement Act 1993 (Commencement) Order 1995
632................Judicial Pensions (Miscellaneous) Regulations 1995
633................Judicial Pensions (Qualifying Judicial Offices etc.) (City of London) Order 1995
634................Judicial Pensions (Preservation of Benefits) Order 1995
635................Judicial Pensions (Appeals) Regulations 1995
636................Judicial Pensions (Transfer Between Judicial Pension Schemes) Regulations 1995

637................Judicial Pensions (Transfer of Accrued Benefits) Regulations 1995
638................Judicial Pensions (Contributions) Regulations 1995
639................Judicial Pensions (Additional Voluntary Contributions) Regulations 1995
640................Judicial Pensions (Additional Benefits for Disregard Earnings) Regulations 1995
641 (C. 16)...Courts and Legal Services Act 1990 (Commencement No. 10) Order 1995
642................National Health Service (Travelling Expenses and Remission of Charges) Amendment Regulations 1995
643................National Health Service (Charges for Drugs and Appliances) Amendment Regulations 1995
644................National Health Service (Pharmaceutical Services) Amendment Regulations 1995
645 (S. 51) ...Charities (Exemption from Accounting Requirements) (Scotland) Amendment Regulations 1995
646 (S. 52) ...Registration of Births, Deaths, Marriages and Divorces (Fees) (Scotland) Amendment Regulations 1995
647 (S. 53) ...Police (Discipline) (Miscellaneous Amendments) (Scotland) Regulations 1995
650................Defence Evaluation and Research Agency Trading Fund Order 1995
651................Local Authorities (Discretionary Expenditure Limits) (England) Order 1995
652................Value Added Tax (Supply of Pharmaceutical Goods) Order 1995
653................Value Added Tax (Transport) Order 1995
654................Natural History Museum (Authorised Repositories) Order 1995
655................Wireless Telegraphy (Television Licence Fees) (Amendment) Regulations 1995
675................Northern Ireland (Loans) (Increase of Limit) Order 1995
677 (S. 54) ...Local Government, Planning and Land Act 1980 (Competition) (Scotland) Regulations 1995
678 (S. 55) ...Local Government (Exemption from Competition) (Scotland) Order 1995
679................Road Traffic (Special Parking Areas) (London Borough of Lambeth) (Amendment) Order 1995
680................Road Traffic (Special Parking Area) (London Borough of Merton) (Amendment) Order 1995
685 (C. 17)...Police and Magistrates' Courts Act 1994 (Commencement No. 8 and Transitional Provisions) Order 1995
686................Justices' Chief Executives and Justices' Clerks (Appointment) Regulations 1995
687................Electricity (Standards of Performance) (Amendment) Regulations 1995
688................Insurance (Fees) Regulations 1995
689................Public Service Vehicles (Operators' Licences) (Amendment) Regulations 1995
691................National Health Service (Optical Charges and Payments) Amendment (No. 2) Regulations 1995
692................Electricity Supply Industry (Rateable Values) (Amendment) Order 1995
693................National Health Service (Fund-Holding Practices) Amendment Regulations 1995
694................Time Off for Public Duties Order 1995
698 (S. 56) ...National Health Service (Expenses of Audit) (Scotland) Regulations 1995

699 (S. 57)...National Health Service (Charges of Drugs and Appliances) (Scotland) Amendment Regulations 1995
700 (S. 58)...National Health Service (Travelling Expenses and Remission of Charges) (Scotland) Amendment Regulations 1995
701 (S. 59)...Local Authorities etc. (Allowances) (Scotland) Amendment Regulations 1995
702 (C. 18)...(S. 60) Local Government etc. (Scotland) Act 1994 (Commencement No. 3) Order 1995
703 (S. 61)...National Health Service (Dental Charges) (Scotland) Amendment Regulations 1995
704 (S. 62)...National Health Service (General Ophthalmic Services) (Scotland) Amendment Regulations 1995
705 (S. 63)...National Health Service (Optical Charges and Payments) (Scotland) Amendment (No. 2) Regulations 1995
706 (S. 64)...Police (Common Police Services) (Scotland) Revocation Order 1995
707 (S. 65)...Common Police Services (Scotland) Order 1995
708................Pensions Increase (Review) Order 1995
709................Friendly Societies (General Charge and Fees) Regulations 1995
710................Friendly Societies Act 1992 (Transitional and Consequential Provisions) Regulations 1995
711................Building Societies (General Charge and Fees) Regulations 1995
712................Industrial and Provident Societies (Credit Unions) (Amendment of Fees) Regulations 1995
713................Industrial and Provident Societies (Amendment of Fees) Regulations 1995
714................Social Security (Contributions) Amendment (No. 2) Regulations 1995
721 (C. 19)...Criminal Justice and Public Order Act 1994 (Commencement No. 6) Order 1995
722................Police (Disposal of Sound Equipment) Regulations 1995
723................Police (Retention and Disposal of Vehicles) Regulations 1995
730................Social Security (Contributions) Amendment (No. 3) Regulations 1995
731................Welfare of Animals (Slaughter or Killing) Regulations 1995
732................Spirit Drinks (Amendment) Regulations 1995
734................Companies (Welsh Language Forms and Documents) (Amendment) Regulations 1995
735................Measuring Equipment (Capacity Measures and Testing Equipment) Regulations 1995
736................Companies (Forms) (Amendment) Regulations 1995
737................Road Vehicles (Construction and Use) (Amendment) Regulations 1995
738................Offshore Installations and Pipeline Works (Management and Administration) Regulations 1995
739................European Parliamentary (United Kingdom Representatives) Pensions (Additional Voluntary Contributions Scheme) (No. 2) Order 1995
740 (S. 66)...Stornoway Harbour Revision Order 1995
741 (S. 67)...Law Hospital National Health Service Trust (Establishment) Amendment Order 1995
742 (S. 68)...Royal Infirmary of Edinburgh National Health Service Trust (Establishment) Amendment Order 1995
743................Offshore Installations (Prevention of Fire and Explosion, and Emergency Response) Regulations 1995
744................Registration of Births, Deaths and Marriages (Miscellaneous Amendments) Regulations 1995

745................Cardiff-Glan Conwy Trunk Road (A470) (Felinfach By-Pass) Order 1995
746................Workmen's Compensation (Supplementation) (Amendment) Scheme 1995
747................Combined Probation Areas (Essex) Order 1995
748................County Council of Humberside (River Hull Bridge) Scheme 1994 Confirmation Instrument 1995
749 (S. 69)...Registered Establishments (Fees) (Scotland) Order 1995
750 (S. 70)...Local Government (Superannuation and Compensation for Premature Retirement) (Scotland) Amendment Regulations 1995
751................European Communities (Designation) (No. 2) Order 1995
752................Intelligence Services Act 1994 (Dependent Territories) Order 1995
753................Health Service Commissioner (Family Health Services Appeal Authority) Order 1995
754 (N.I. 1)..Appropriation (Northern Ireland) Order 1995
755 (N.I. 2)..Children (Northern Ireland) Order 1995
756................Children (Northern Ireland Consequential Amendments) Order 1995
757 (N.I. 3)..Children's Evidence (Northern Ireland) Order 1995
758 (N.I. 4)..Fair Employment (Amendment) (Northern Ireland) Order 1995
759 (N.I. 5)..Local Government (Miscellaneous Provisions) (Northern Ireland) Order 1995
760................Prevention of Terrorism (Temporary Provisions) Act 1989 (Enforcement of External Orders) Order 1995
761 (N.I. 6)..Wildlife (Amendment) (Northern Ireland) Order 1995
762................Double Taxation Relief (Taxes on Income) (Azerbaijan) Order 1995
763................Double Taxation Relief (Taxes on Income) (Malta) Order 1995
764................Double Taxation Relief (Taxes on Income) (Republic of Ireland) Order 1995
765................Double Taxation Relief (Taxes on Income) (Spain) Order 1995
766................Naval, Military and Air Forces etc. (Disablement and Death) Service Pensions Amendment Order 1995
767................Social Security (Reciprocal Agreements) Order 1995
768................Trustee Investments (Additional Powers) Order 1995
769................Glan-y-Mor National Health Service Trust (Establishment) Order 1995
770................University Hospital of Wales Health-Care National Health Service Trust (Establishment) Order 1995
789 (S. 71)...Local Government (Application of Enactments) (Scotland) Order 1995
791................National Health Service Trusts (Originating Capital Debt) Amendment Order 1995
792................Homewood National Health Service Trust Dissolution Order 1995
795................Legal Advice and Assistance (Amendment) Regulations 1995
796................Legal Aid in Criminal and Care Proceedings (General) (Amendment) (No. 2) Regulations 1995
797................Civil Legal Aid (Assessment of Resources) (Amendment) Regulations 1995
798................Local Government Changes for England (Capital Finance) Regulations 1995
799................Medicines (Medicated Animal Feeding Stuffs) (Amendment) Regulations 1995

801................United Leeds Teaching Hospitals National Health Service Trust Dissolution Order 1995
802 (S. 72)...Licensed Betting Offices (Scotland) Amendment Regulations 1995
816................Prevention of Terrorism (Temporary Provisions) Act 1989 (Continuance) Order 1995
817................Local Government (Compensation for Redundancy and Premature Retirement) (Amendment) Regulations 1995
818................Registration of Births and Deaths (Welsh Language) (Amendment) Regulations 1995
819................A638 Trunk Road (Doncaster Road Railway Bridge, Agbrigg, to Junction with B6273 Garmil Lane, West of Wragby) (Detrunking) Order 1995
828................Local Government Act 1988 (Defined Activities) (Exemption) (Sports and Leisure Management, Catering and Maintenance of Ground) Order 1995
829................Social Security (Incapacity Benefit) (Consequential and Transitional Amendments and Savings) Regulations 1995
830................Elections (Welsh Forms) Order 1995
837................London Cab Order 1995
838................Housing Renovation etc. Grants (Reduction of Grant) (Amendment) Regulations 1995
839................Housing Renovation etc. Grants (Prescribed Forms and Particulars) (Amendment) Regulations 1995
840 (S. 73)...Local Government (Education Administration) (Compensation for Redundancy of Premature Retirement on Reorganisation) (Scotland) Regulations 1995
841 (C. 20)...Local Government Act and Housing Act 1989 (Commencement No. 17) Order 1995
842................Newham Community Health Services National Health Service Trust (Establishment) Order 1995
843................City and Hackney Community Services National Health Service Trust (Establishment) Order 1995
844................University Hospital Birmingham Services National Health Service Trust (Establishment) Order 1995
845................Royal Orthopaedic Hospital National Health Service Trust (Establishment) Order 1995
846................Wolverley National Health Service Trust Dissolution Order 1995
847................Tower Hamlets Healthcare National Health Service Trust (Establishment) Order 1995
848................Surrey Heartlands National Health Service Trust (Establishment) Order 1995
849................Local Authorities (Companies) Order 1995
850................Local Authorities (Capital Finance and Approval Investments) (Amendment) Regulations 1995
851................Local Government (Wales) Act 1994 (Commencement No. 3) (Amendment) Order 1995
852 (C. 22)...Local Government (Wales) Act 1994 (Commencement No. 4) Order 1995
853................Income Tax (Employments) (Incapacity Benefit) Regulations 1995
854................Housing (Change of Landlord) (Payment of Disposal Cost by Instalments) (Amendment) Regulations 1995
855................Miners' Welfare Act 1952 (Transfer of Functions of Coal Industry Social Welfare Organisation) Order 1995
857................Housing Renovation etc. Grants (Prescribed Forms and Particulars) (Welsh Forms and Particulars) (Amendment) Regulations 1995
858................National Assistance (Assessment of Resources) (Amendment) Regulations 1995

861................Welsh Highland Railway (Transfer) Light Railway Order 1995
866................National Health Service (Injury Benefits) Regulations 1995
870................A312 Trunk Road (The Parkway, Hounslow) (50 mph Speed Limit) Order 1995
871................Medicines (Fixing of Fees Relating to Medicinal Products for Human Use) Amendment Order 1995
872................Housing Benefit and Council Tax Benefit (Subsidy) Order 1995
874................Housing Benefit and Council Tax Benefit (Subsidy) Amendment Regulations 1995
886................Fish Health (Amendment) Regulations 1995
887................Plant Protection Products Regulations 1995
888................Plant Protection Products (Fees) Regulations 1995
889................Road Traffic Accidents (Payments for Treatment) Order 1995
890................Farm and Conservation Grant (Variation) Scheme 1995
891 (S. 74)...Heather Moorland (Livestock Extensification) (Scotland) Regulations 1995
899 (C. 23)...Police and Magistrates' Courts Act 1994 (Commencement No. 5 and Transitional Provisions) (Amendment No. 2) Order 1995
900................Local Government Superannuation (Limitation on Earnings and Reckonable Service) Regulations 1995
901................Local Government Superannuation (Equality and Maternity Absence) Regulations 1995
903................Education (School Curriculum and Assessment Authority) (Transfer of Functions) Order 1995
904................Moorland (Livestock Extensification) Regulations 1995
907................Third Country Fishing (Enforcement) Order 1995
908................Sea Fishing (Enforcement of Community Quota Measures) Order 1995
909................Electricity (Class Exemptions from the Requirement for a Licence) (No. 2) Order 1995
910 (S. 75)...Prisons (Scotland) Act 1989 (Release of Prisoners etc.) Order 1995
911 (S. 76)...Prisoners and Criminal Proceedings (Scotland) Act 1993 (Release of Prisoners etc.) Order 1995
912 (S. 77)...Local Authorities etc. (Allowances) (Scotland) Regulations 1995
913................Value Added Tax (General) (Amendment) (No. 2) Regulations 1995
916................Leeds Development Corporation (Area and Constitution) Order 1995
917................Profit-Related Pay (Shortfall Recovery) Regulations 1995
918................Llandough Hospital National Health Service Trust (Change of Name) Order 1995
924................Education (Individual Pupils' Achievements) (Information) (Amendment) Regulations 1995
925................Motor Vehicles (Type Approval and Approval Marks) (Fees) Regulations 1995
926................Gaming Act (Variation of Monetary Limits) Order 1995
927................Gaming Clubs (Hours and Charges) (Amendment) Regulations 1995
928................Amusements with Prizes (Variation of Monetary Limits) Order 1995
929 (S. 78)...The Railtrack PLC (Rateable Values) (Scotland) Order 1995
930 (S. 79)...British Railways Board (Rateable Values) (Scotland) Order 1995
932................Portsmouth Hospitals National Health Service Trust (Transfer of Trust Property) Order 1995

933................Portsmouth Health Care National Health Service Trust (Transfer of Trust Property) Order 1995
934................Hereford Hospitals National Health Trust (Transfer of Trust Property) Order 1995
935................Dartford and Gravesham National Service Trust (Transfer of Trust Property) Order 1995
936................Education (Grant-maintained and Grant-maintained Special Schools) (Finance) Regulations 1995
937................Winchester and Eastleigh Healthcare National Health Service Trust (Transfer of Trust Property) Order 1995
938................Stoke Mandeville Hospital National Health Service Trust (Transfer of Trust Property) Order 1995
939................Ministry of Defence Police (Police Committee) Regulations 1995
941................Public Telecommunications System Designation (Liberty Communications Limited) Order 1995
948................Legal Advice in Contempt Proceeding (Remuneration) Regulations 1995
949................Legal Advice and Assistance (Amendment) (No. 2) Regulations 1995
950................Legal Advice and Assistance at Police Stations (Remuneration) (Amendment) Regulations 1995
951................Legal Advice and Assistance (Duty Solicitor) (Remuneration) (Amendment) Regulations 1995
952................Legal Aid in Criminal and Care Proceedings (Costs) (Amendment) Regulations 1995
957................Value Added Tax (Special Provisions) (Amendment) Order 1995
958................Value Added Tax (Treatment of Transactions) Order 1995
960................Environmentally Sensitive Areas (Exmoor) Designation (Amendment) (No. 2) Order 1995
961................Non-Domestic Rating (Chargeable Amounts) (Amendment) Regulations 1995
962................Electricity Supply Industry (Rateable Values) (Amendment) Order 1995
963................Local Government Superannuation (Miscellaneous Provisions) Regulations
964 (S. 80)...Stornoway (Ferry Terminal) Harbour Revision Order 1995
965 (C. 24)...Merchant Shipping Act 1970 (Commencement No. 11) Order 1995
966................Leeds Development Corporation (Dissolution) Order 1995
967................Nurses, Midwives and Health Visitors (Periodic Registration) Amendment Rules Approval Order 1995
968................East Surrey Hospital and Community Healthcare National Health Service Trust (Change of Name) Order 1995
969 (L. 4).....County Court (Amendment) Rules 1995
970 (L. 5).....County Court (Forms) (Amendment) Rules 1995
971................Justices of the Peace (Size and Chairmanship of Bench) Rules 1995
972................Merchant Shipping (Employment of Young Persons) Regulations 1995
979................Injuries in War (Shoe Employments) Compensation (Amendment) Scheme 1995
983................Prison (Amendment) Rules 1995
984................Young Offender Institution (Amendment) Rules 1995
987................Social Security (Incapacity to Work) Miscellaneous Amendments Regulations 1995
990................Street Works (Registers, Notices, Directions and Designations) (Amendment) Regulations 1995
991................Public Record Office (Fees) Regulations 1995

992 (S. 81)...Strathclyde Regional Council Prevention of Water Pollution (Mill Glen, Busbie Muir, Munnoch, Caaf, Knockendon, Glenburn, Pundeavon, Cuffhill, Kirkleegreen) Byelaws Extension Order 1995
993................Hyde Park and Regent's Park (Vehicle Parking) Regulations 1995
994 (S. 82)...Strathclyde Regional Council Prevention of Water Pollution (Skelmorlie Lower, Skelmorlie Upper, Skelmorlie Intakes, Outerwards, Greeto Intake, Haylie, Millport Lower, Millport Upper) Byelaws Extension Order 1995
996................Robert Jones and Agnes Hunt Orthopaedic and District Hospital National Health Service Trust (Establishment) Amendment Order 1995
997................Local Government Act 1988 (Defined Activities) (Exemption) (Breckland District Council) Order 1995
1002................Premium Savings Bonds (Amendment) Regulations 1995
1003................Social Security (Contributions) Amendment (No. 4) Regulations 1995
1004................Civil Aviation (Route Charges for Navigation Services) (Amendment) Regulations 1995
1006................Building Societies (Commercial Assets) Order 1995
1007 (C. 25)...Income and Corporation Taxes Act 1988, section 737A, (Appointed Day) Order 1995
1009................A5 Trunk Road (Junctions 18 (M1) to A5/A5 Road Junction) Order 1995
1011................Weights and Measures (Guernsey and Alderney) Order 1995
1012................N-nitrosamines and N-nitrosatable Substances in Elastomer or Rubber Teats and Dummies (Safety) Regulations 1995
1013................Contracting Out (Functions in Relation to the Registration of Companies) Order 1995
1014................Measuring Equipment (Liquid Fuel and Lubricants) Regulations 1995
1015................Education (School Teachers' Pay and Conditions) Order 1995
1019................Local Government Pension Scheme Regulations 1995
1020 (S. 83)...Gaming Act (Variation of Monetary Limits) (Scotland) Order 1995
1021 (S. 84)...Amusements with Prizes (Variation of Monetary Limits) (Scotland) Order 1995
1022 (S. 85)...Gaming Clubs (Hours and Charges) (Scotland) Amendment Regulations 1995
1023 (S. 86)...Act of Sederunt (Rules of the Court of Session 1994 Amendment) (Shorthand Writers' Fees) 1995
1024 (S. 87)...Act of Sederunt (Fees of Shorthand Writers in the Sheriff Court) (Amendment) 1995
1030................Antarctic Act 1994 (Overseas Territories) Order 1995
1031................Child Abduction and Custody (Parties to Conventions) (Amendment) (No. 2) Order 1995
1032................United Nations Arms Embargoes (Dependent Territories) Order 1995
1033................Antarctic Act 1994 (Guernsey) Order 1995
1034................Antarctic Act 1994 (Jersey) Order 1995
1035................Antarctic Act 1994 (Isle of Man) Order 1995
1036................Parliamentary Constituencies (Wales) Order 1995
1037 (S. 90)...Parliamentary Constituencies (Scotland) Order 1995
1038................Air Navigation Order 1995
1039................Local Government Reorganisation (Wales) (Limitation of Compensation) Regulations 1995
1040................Local Government (Wales) (Service Agency Agreements) Regulations 1995

1041................Local Government Reorganisation (Wales) (Capital Finance) Order 1995
1042................Local Government Reorganisation (Wales) (Transitional Provisions No. 2) Order 1995
1043................Local Authorities (Closure of Accounts) (Wales) Order 1995
1044 (S. 88)...Civil Legal Aid (Scotland) (Fees) Amendment Regulations 1995
1045................Child Support and Income Support (Amendment) Regulations 1995
1046................Excise Goods (Drawback) Regulations 1995
1047................Charities (The Bridge House Estates) Order 1995
1048................A61 Trunk Road (Tankersley Roundabout, Birdwell to Old County Borough Boundary, Barnsley) (Detrunking) Order 1995
1053................Personal and Occupational Pension Schemes (Pensions Ombudsman) (Procedure) Rules 1995
1054................Civil Aviation (Air Travel Organisers' Licensing) Regulations 1995
1055................Local Government Changes for England (No. 2) Regulations 1995
1057 (S. 89)...Police Cadets (Scotland) Amendment Regulations 1995
1063................Portsmouth (Camber Dock) Harbour Revision Order 1995
1065 (S. 91)...Civil Legal Aid (Scotland) Amendment Regulations 1995
1066 (S. 92)...Advice and Assistance (Scotland) Amendment Regulations (No. 3) Order 1995
1067................Free Zone (Humberside) Designation (Variation) Order 1995
1069................Value Added Tax (General) (Amendment) (No. 3) Regulations 1995
1070................Social Security Revaluation of Earnings Factors Order 1995
1071................London Regional Transport (Penalty Fares) Act 1992 (Activating No. 2) Order 1995
1081................Wireless Telegraphy (Short Range Devices) (Exemption) (Amendment) Regulations 1995
1085................Financial Assistance for Environmental Purposes (No. 3) Order 1995
1086................Dairy Products (Hygiene) Regulations 1995
1088................South and East Wales Ambulance National Health Service Trust (Transfer of Trust Property) Order 1995
1089................Morriston Hospital National Health Service Trust (Transfer of Trust Property) Order 1995
1090................Nevill Hall and District National Health Service Trust (Transfer of Trust Property) Order 1995
1091................St Michaels Mead Natural Gas Pipelines Order 1995
1092................Charities (Trustee Investment Act 1961) Order 1995
1093................Air Navigation (General) (Amendment) Regulations 1995
1094................M25 Motorway (Junctions 10–15) (Variable Speed Limits) Regulations 1995
1107................East Glamorgan National Health Service Trust (Transfer of Trust Property) Order 1995
1116................Medicines (Products for Human Use—Fees) Regulations 1995
1121................North Wales Ambulance National Health Service Trust (Transfer of Trust Property) (No. 2) Order 1995
1122................Dairy Products (Hygiene) (Charges) Regulations 1995
1123................Special Trustees for the Royal Free Hospital (Transfer of Trust Property) Order 1995
1124................Camden and Islington Community Health Services National Health Service Trust (Transfer of Trust Property) Order 1995

1125................Whittington Hospital National Health Service Trust (Transfer of Trust Property) Order 1995
1126................Special Trustees for the Middlesex Hospital (Transfer of Trust Property) Order 1995
1127................North Yorkshire Health Authority (Transfer of Trust Property) Order 1995
1128................Royal London Homeopathic Hospital National Health Service Trust (Transfer of Trust Property) Order 1995
1129................Special Trustees for University College Hospital (Transfer of Trust Property) Order 1995
1130................London Priority Route (Amendment) Order 1995
1139................Town and Country Planning (Crown Land Applications) Regulations 1995
1142................Returning Officers (Parliamentary Constituencies) (Wales) Order 1995
1143................Welfare Food (Amendment) Regulations 1995
1144................A23 Trunk Road (Streatham High Road, Lambeth) (Prohibition of Use of Gaps in Central Reserve) Order 1995
1151................Dual-Use and Related Goods (Export Control) (Suspension No. 2) Regulations 1995
1152................Social Security (Recoupment) (Prolongation of Period for Furnishing of Certificate of Total Benefit) Order 1995
1153................A19 Trunk Road (New Park Bends Improvement) Order 1995
1154................Street Works (Registers, Notices, Directions and Designations) (Amendment No. 2) Regulations 1995
1157................Redundancy Payments Local Government (Modification) (Amendment) Order 1995
1158................A4 Trunk Road (Great West Road, Hounslow) (Prohibition of U-turns) Order 1995
1159................Moorland (Livestock Extensification) (Wales) Regulations 1995
1161................Local Government Reorganisation (Wales) (Transitional Provisions No. 3) Order 1995
1162................Motor Vehicles (Driving Licences) (Large Goods and Passenger-Carrying Vehicles) (Amendment) Regulations 1995
1163................Companies Act 1989 Part II (Consequential Amendment) Regulations 1995
1164................Vaccine Damage Payments (Specified Disease) Order 1995
1165................A1 Trunk Road (Islington) Red Route Traffic Order 1993 Variation Order 1995
1166................A1 Trunk Road (Islington) Red Route (Prohibition of U-Turns) Traffic Order 1995
1181................London Cab (No. 2) Order 1995
1182................Local Government Act 1988 (Defined Activities) (Exemption) (Housing Management) (England) Order 1995
1184................Income Tax (Building Societies) (Dividends and Interest) (Amendment) Regulations 1995
1185................Lloyd's Underwriters (Special Reserve Funds) (Amendment) Regulations 1995
1186................Electrical Equipment for Explosive Atmosphere (Certification) (Amendment) Regulations 1995
1187................Building Societies (Aggregation) (Amendment) Rules 1995
1188................Building Societies (Designation of Qualifying Bodies) Order 1995
1189................Building Societies (Provision of Services) Order 1995
1200................Motor Vehicles (Driving Licences) (Amendment) Regulations 1995
1201................Road Vehicles (Construction and Use) (Amendment) (No. 3) Regulations 1995
1202................Education (London Residuary Body) (Property Transfer) (Modification and Amendment) (No. 2) Order 1995

1203................Customs Traders (Accounts and Records) Regulations 1995
1210................Merchant Shipping (Survey and Certification) Regulations 1995
1211................Life Assurance (Apportionment of Receipts of Participating Funds) (Applicable Percentage) (Amendment) Order 1995
1212................Income Tax (Interest Relief) (Housing Associations) (Amendment) Regulations 1995
1213................Income Tax (Interest Relief) (Amendment) Regulations 1995
1214................Mackerel (Specified Sea Areas) (Prohibition of Fishing) (No. 2) Order 1995
1215................Occupational Pension Schemes (Equal Access to Membership) Amendment Regulations 1995
1216................Air Passenger (Extended Schemes) Regulations 1995
1217................Banking Co-ordination (Second Council Directive) (Amendment) Regulations 1995
1218................Motor Cars (Driving Instruction) (Amendment) Regulations 1995
1219 (S. 93)...Air Navigation (Geneva) (Amendment) Regulations 1995
1220 (S. 94)...Advice and Assistance (Financial Conditions) (Scotland) Regulations 1995
1221 (S. 95)...Civil Legal Aid (Financial Conditions) (Scotland) Regulations 1995
1222 (S. 96)...Criminal Legal Aid (Scotland) (Prescribed Proceedings) Amendment Regulations 1995
1223................Income Tax (Employments) (Amendment No. 3) Regulations 1995
1224................British Museum (Authorised Repositories) Order 1995
1228................British Railways (Marylebone Diesel Depot) Order 1995
1229................Social Fund Maternity and Funeral Expenses (General) Amendment Regulations 1995
1232................Glan Hafren National Health Service Trust (Transfer of Trust Property) Order 1995
1233................Powys Health Care National Health Service Trust (Transfer of Trust Property) Order 1995
1234................South and East Wales Ambulance National Health Service Trust (Transfer of Trust Property) Order 1995
1235................Bexley Community Health National Health Service Trust (Change of Name) Order 1995
1236................Foxfield Light Railway Order 1995
1239................Pipe-lines (Inquiries Procedure) Rules 1995
1240................Education (Mandatory Awards) (Amendment) Regulations 1995
1241................Education (Fees and Awards) (Amendment) Regulations 1995
1242................North East Worcestershire Community Health Care National Health Service Trust (Transfer of Trust Property) Order 1995
1243................Mancunian Community Health National Health Service Trust (Transfer of Trust Property) Order 1995
1244................Wirral Community Healthcare National Health Service Trust (Transfer of Trust Property) Order 1995
1245................Havering Hospitals National Health Service Trust (Transfer of Trust Property) Order 1995
1246................BHB Community Health Care National Health Service Trust (Transfer of Trust Property) Order 1995
1247................Haringey Health Care National Health Service Trust (Transfer of Trust Property) Order 1995
1248................South Durham Health Care National Health Service Trust (Transfer of Trust Property) Order 1995
1249................Dewsbury Health Care National Health Service Trust (Transfer of Trust Property) Order 1995

1250................Consumer Credit (Exempt Agreements) (Amendment) Order 1995
1251................Gas (Meters) (Amendment) Regulations 1995
1257................Stanwood Bay Oyster Fishery (Variation) Order 1995
1258................Calshot Oyster Fishery (Variation) Order 1995
1259................Westcountry Ambulance Services National Health Service Trust (Transfer of Trust Property) Order 1995
1260................Bishop Auckland Hospitals National Health Service Trust (Transfer of Trust Property) Order 1995
1261................Darlington Memorial Hospital National Health Service Trust (Transfer of Trust Property) Order 1995
1262................Worthing and Southlands Hospitals National Health Service Trust (Transfer of Trust Property) Order 1995
1263................Mid Essex Community and Mental Health National Health Service Trust (Transfer of Trust Property) Order 1995
1264................New Possibilities National Health Service Trust (Transfer of Trust Property) Order 1995
1265................Salisbury Health Care National Health Service Trust (Transfer of Trust Property) Order 1995
1266................Financial Services Act 1986 (Investment Advertisements) (Exemptions) Order 1995
1267................Value Added Tax (Input Tax) (Amendment) (No. 2) Order 1995
1268................Value Added Tax (Special Provisions) Order 1995
1269................Value Added Tax (Cars) (Amendment) Order 1995
1271 (S. 97)...Education (Fees and Awards) (Scotland) Amendment Regulations 1995
1272 (S. 98)...Local Review Committee (Scotland) Revocation Rules 1995
1273 (S. 99)...Parole Board (Scotland) Rules 1995
1280................Value Added Tax (General) (Amendment) (No. 4) Regulations 1995
1283................Income Tax (Mandatory Awards) (Amendment) Regulations 1995
1284................Income Tax (Employments) (Amendment No. 4) Regulations 1995
1289................Civil Aviation Authority (Borrowing Powers) Orders 1995
1290................Goods Vehicles (International Road Haulage Permits) (Revocation) Regulations 1995
1293................Superannuation (Admission to the Principal Civil Service Pension Scheme) Order 1995
1294................Department of Trade and Industry (Fees) (Amendment) Order 1995
1295................Child Abduction and Custody (Parties to Conventions) (Amendment) (No. 3) Order 1995
1296................Air Navigation (Isle of Man) (Revocation) Order 1995
1297................Civil Aviation (Isle of Man) (Revocation) Order 1995
1298................European Convention on Cinematographic Co-production (Amendment) Order 1995
1299................Hovercraft (Application of Enactment) (Amendment) Order 1995
1300................Northampton and Lamport Light Railway Order 1995
1301................Birmingham City Council (Birmingham and Fazeley Canal Bridge) Scheme 1994 Confirmation Instrument 1995
1310................City Council of Sheffield (Inner Ring Road — Stage 1A Bridge) Scheme 1994 Confirmation Instrument 1995
1311................Durham County Ambulance Service National Health Service Trust (Establishment) Amendment Order 1995
1317 (C. 26)...Law of Property (Miscellaneous Provisions) Act 1994 (Commencement No. 2) Order 1995
1322................Motor Vehicles (Type Approval) (Great Britain) (Amendment) Regulations 1995

1323................Motor Vehicles (Type Approval for Goods Vehicles) (Great Britain) (Amendment) Regulations 1995
1324................Income Tax (Manufactured Overseas Dividends) (Amendment) Regulations 1995
1325................Amalgamation of the Holme Common, River Burn and Stiffkey River Internal Drainage Boards Order 1995
1326................Local Government Changes for England and Local Government Act 1988 (Competition) (Miscellaneous Amendment) Regulations 1995
1330................Public Trustees (Notices Affecting Land) (Title on Death) Regulations 1995
1331................Wireless Telegraphy (Licence Charges) Regulations 1995
1332................Heathrow Express Railway (Transfer) Order 1995
1333................Road Traffic (Special Parking Area) (Royal Borough of Kingston upon Thames) (Amendment No. 2) Order 1995
1334................Road Traffic (Special Parking Area) (London Borough of Sutton) (Amendment No. 2) Order 1995
1335................Road Traffic (Special Parking Area) (London Borough of Redbridge) (Amendment No. 2) Order 1995
1336................Local Government (Direct Service Organisations) (Competition) (Amendment) Regulations 1995
1339................Income-related Benefits Schemes (Miscellaneous Amendments) (No. 2) Order 1995
1340 (S. 100).Local Authorities (Staff Transfer) (Scotland) Order 1995
1341................Middlesbrough College (Incorporation) Order 1995
1342................Middlesbrough College (Government) Regulations 1995
1343................Teesside Tertiary College (Incorporation) Order 1995
1344................Teesside Tertiary College (Government) Regulations 1995
1351................Fair Trading Act (Amendment) (Newspaper Mergers) Order 1995
1352 (C. 27)...Companies Act 1989 (Commencement No. 15 and Transitional and Savings Provisions) Order 1995
1354................Land Registration (No. 2) Rules 1995
1355................Land Charges (Amendment) Rules 1995
1356................Building Regulations (Amendment) Regulations 1995
1357................Wolverhampton Borough Council (Wednesfield Way) (Bridge over the Wyrley and Essington Canal) Scheme 1994 Confirmation Instrument 1995
1358................Plant Health (Great Britain) (Amendment) Order 1995
1370................Deposit-takers (Interest Payments) (Discretionary or Accumulation Trusts) Regulations 1995
1371................Motor Vehicles (Off Road Events) Regulations 1995
1372 (S. 101).Dairy Products (Hygiene) (Scotland) Regulations 1995
1373 (S. 102).Inshore Fishing (Prohibition of Fishing for Cockles) (Scotland) Order 1995
1374 (C. 28)...Finance Act 1995, section 24, (Appointed Day) Order 1995
1375................Public Telecommunication System Designation (Mercury Personal Communications Limited) Order 1995
1376................Measuring Instruments (EEC Requirements) (Fees) (Amendment) Regulations 1995
1377................Local Government (Direct Labour Organisations) (Competition) (Amendment) (Crown Courts) Regulations 1995
1378 (C. 29)...Criminal Justice and Public Order Act 1994 (Commencement No. 7) Order 1995
1379................Curfew Order (Responsible Officer) (City of Manchester, Reading and Norfolk) Order 1995
1384................Medicines (Products Other Than Veterinary Drugs) (Prescription Only) Amendment Order 1995
1385................Value Added Tax (Special Provisions) Order 1995 (Amendment) Order 1995

1386................Contracting Out (Functions of the Official Receiver) Order 1995
1387................Building (Approved Inspectors etc.) (Amendment) Regulations 1995
1388 (S. 103).Food Protection (Emergency Prohibitions) (Paralytic Shellfish Poisoning) Order 1995
1395 (S. 104).Act of Sederunt (Fees of Solicitors in the Sheriff Court) (Amendment) 1995
1396 (S. 105).Act of Sederunt (Rules of the Court of Session 1994 Amendment No. 2) (Fees of Solicitors) 1995
1397................Vehicle Excise Duty (Designation of Small Islands) Order 1995
1398................Children (Secure Accommodation) Amendment Regulations 1995
1412................Feedingstuffs Regulations 1995
1413................A41 Trunk Road (Detrunking of Slip Roads Between the A41 and the A51, Chester) Order 1995
1422 (S. 106).Food Protection (Emergency Prohibitions) (Paralytic Shellfish Poisoning) (No. 2) Order 1995
1423................Companies (Fees) (Amendment) Regulations 1995
1424................Dual-Use and Related Goods (Export Control) (Amendment) Regulations 1995
1425................Public Trustee (Fees) (Amendment) Order 1995
1426 (C. 30)...Merchant Shipping Act 1970 (Commencement No. 12) Order 1995
1427................Merchant Shipping (Officer Nationality) Regulations 1995
1428................Fishing Vessels (Certification of Deck Officers and Engineer Officers) (Amendment) Regulations 1995
1429................Merchant Shipping (Certification of Deck and Marine Engineer Officers) (Amendment) Regulations 1995
1430................Counterfeit and Pirated Goods (Customs) Regulations 1995
1431................Passenger Transport Executives (Capital Finance) (Amendment) Order 1995
1433 (C. 31)...Deregulation and Contracting Out Act 1994 (Commencement No. 3) Order 1995
1434................Hydrocarbons Licensing Directive Regulations 1995
1435................Petroleum (Production) (Seaward Areas) (Amendment) Regulations 1995
1436................Petroleum (Production) (Landward Areas) Regulations 1995
1437................Road Traffic Act 1991 (Amendment of Section 76(3)) Order 1995
1438................Civil Aviation (Route Charges for Navigation Services) (Second Amendment) Regulations 1995
1439................Home-Grown Cereals Authority (Rate of Levy) Order 1995
1440................Extraction of Solvents in Food (Amendment) Regulations 1995
1441................Price Marking (Amendment) Order 1995
1442................Credit Institutions (Protection of Depositors) Regulations 1995
1443................Pensions for Dependants of the Prime Minister or Speaker (Designated Provisions) Regulations 1995
1444................Trade Marks (EC Measures Relating to Counterfeit Goods) Regulations 1995
1445................Copyright (EC Measures Relating to Pirated Goods and Abolition of Restrictions on the Import of Goods) Regulations 1995
1446................Suckler Cow Premium (Amendment) (No. 2) Regulations 1995
1447................Counterfeit and Pirated Goods (Consequential Provisions) Regulations 1995

1453................Further Education (Attribution of Surpluses and Deficits) (Margaret Danyers College) Regulations 1995
1454................Coal Industry (Restructuring Grants) Order 1995
1455................Vehicle Excise (Design Weight Certificate) Regulations 1995
1456................Goods Vehicles (Plating and Testing) (Amendment) Regulations 1995
1457................Motor Vehicles (Tests) (Amendment) Regulations 1995
1458................Road Vehicles (Construction and Use) (Amendment) (No. 4) Regulations 1995
1459................Inheritance Tax (Delivery of Accounts) (Scotland) Regulations 1995
1460................Inheritance Tax (Delivery of Accounts) (Northern Ireland) Regulations 1995
1461................Inheritance Tax (Delivery of Accounts) Regulations 1995
1462................Northampton Community Healthcare National Health Service Trust (Transfer of Trust Property) Order 1995
1463................Northampton General Hospital National Health Service Trust (Transfer of Trust Property) Order 1995
1464................Royal Wolverhampton Hospitals National Health Service Trust (Transfer of Trust Property) Order 1995
1465................Norfolk and Norwich Health Care National Health Service Trust (Transfer of Trust Property) Order 1995
1466................Leicestershire Ambulance and Paramedic Service National Health Service Trust (Transfer of Trust Property) Order 1995
1467................Alexandra Health Care National Health Service Trust (Transfer of Trust Property) Order 1995
1468................Derbyshire Ambulance Service National Health Service Trust (Transfer of Trust Property) Order 1995
1469................Calderdale Healthcare National Health Service Trust (Establishment) Amendment Order 1995
1470................Road Vehicles (Registration and Licensing) (Amendment) Regulations 1995
1471................Road Vehicles (Registration and Licensing) (Amendment) Regulations (Northern Ireland) 1995
1472................Isles of Scilly Sea Fisheries District (Variation) Order 1995
1474................Kent and Essex Sea Fisheries District (Variation) Order 1995
1475................Police (Discipline) (Amendment) Regulations 1995
1476 (S. 107) .Roads (Transitional Powers) (Scotland) Order 1995
1477................Coal Industry (Coal Mining Successor Companies Target Investment Limit) Order 1995
1478................Cosmetic Products (Safety) (Amendment) Regulations 1995
1479................Companies (Forms) (No. 2) Regulations 1995
1480................Companies (Welsh Language Forms and Documents) (No. 2) Regulations 1995
1481................Hill Livestock (Compensatory Allowances) (Amendment) (No. 2) Regulations 1995
1482................Cereal Seeds (Amendment) Regulations 1995
1483................Pesticides (Maximum Residue Levels in Crops, Food and Feeding Stuffs) (Amendment) Regulations 1995
1488................Goods Vehicles (Operators' Licences, Qualifications and Fees) (Amendment) Regulations 1995
1489................Norwich Community Health Partnership National Health Service Trust (Transfer of Trust Property) Order 1995
1490................Norfolk Mental Health Care National Health Service Trust (Transfer of Trust Property) Order 1995
1491................Leicestershire Mental Health Service National Health Service Trust (Transfer of Trust Property) Order 1995
1492................Bury Health Care National Health Service Trust (Transfer of Trust Property) Order 1995

1493................Cumbria Ambulance Service National Health Service Trust (Transfer of Trust Property) Order 1995
1494................North Lakeland Healthcare National Health Service Trust (Transfer of Trust Property) Order 1995
1495................Value Added Tax (Tour Operators) (Amendment) Order 1995
1497................Local Government Superannuation (Gratuities) Regulations 1995
1502................Asian Development Bank (Extension of Limit on Guarantees) Order 1995
1503................Asian Development Bank (Further Payment to Capital Stock) Order 1995
1506................British Coal Corporation (Change of Quorum) Regulations 1995
1507 (C. 32)...Coal Industry Act 1994 (Commencement No. 6) and Membership of the British Coal Corporation (Appointed Day) Order 1995
1508................Companies (Welsh Language Forms and Documents) (No. 3) Regulations 1995
1509................Companies (Disqualification Orders) (Amendment) Regulations 1995
1510................Local Government Reorganisation (Wales) (Consequential Amendments No. 2) Order 1995
1513................Motor Cycle (EC Type Approval) Regulations 1995
1514................Pneumoconiosis etc. (Workers' Compensation) (Payment of Claims) (Amendment) Regulations 1995
1515 (S. 108).Local Government (Qualifications of Assessors) (Scotland) Order 1995
1520................Companies Act 1985 (Disclosure of Remuneration for Non-Audit Work) (Amendment) Regulations 1995
1522................Greater Manchester Passenger Transport Authority (Increase in Number of Members) Order 1995
1526................Local Authorities (Capital Finance) (Amendment) Regulations 1995
1527 (S. 109).Fraserburgh Harbour Revision Order 1995
1534................West Yorkshire Metropolitan Ambulance Service National Health Service Trust (Transfer of Property) Order 1995
1536................Financial Services Act 1986 (Investment Advertisements) (Exemptions) (No. 2) Order 1995
1537................Public Offers of Securities Regulations 1995
1538 (C. 33)...Financial Services Act 1986 (Commencement) (No. 13) Order 1995
1539................Personal Equity Plan (Amendment) Regulations 1995
1540................Section 19 Minibus (Designated Bodies) (Amendment) Order 1995
1541................Transport and Works (Assessment of Environmental Effects) Regulations 1995
1544................Eggs (Marketing Standards) Regulations 1995
1545................Council Tax Limitation (England) (Maximum Amounts) Order 1995
1551................Double Taxation Relief (Manufactured Overseas Dividend) (Amendment) Regulations 1995
1554................Education (Grant-maintained and Grant-maintained Special Schools) (Finance) (Amendment) Regulations 1995
1555................Betting and Gaming Duties (Payment) Regulations 1995
1556................Dwr Cymru Cyfyngedig (Pipelaying and Other Works) (Code of Practice) Order 1995

1560 (S. 110) .Food Protection (Emergency Prohibitions) (Paralytic Shellfish Poisoning) (No. 3) Order 1995
1561................Education (School Performance Information) (England) (Amendment) Regulations 1995
1566................Northern Ireland (Emergency and Prevention of Terrorism Provisions) (Continuance) Order 1995
1567................Offshore Installations (Safety Zones) (No. 2) Order 1995
1568................Ridge Danyers College (Incorporation) Order 1995
1569................Ridge Danyers College (Government) Regulations 1995
1570................Social Security (Contributions) Amendment (No. 5) Regulations 1995
1571 (S. 111) .National Health Service (Fund-Holding Practices) (Scotland) Amendment Regulations 1995
1572 (S. 112) .Building (Procedure) (Scotland) Amendment Regulations 1995
1574................Education (National Curriculum) (Exceptions) (Wales) Regulations 1995
1575................Offshore Installations (Safety Zones) (No. 3) Order 1995
1576................Fisheries and Aquaculture Structures (Grants) Regulations 1995
1581................Local Government Act 1988 (Defined Activities) (Exemption) (Hart District Council) Order 1995
1582 (L. 6).....County Court (Amendment No. 2) Rules 1995
1583 (L. 7).....County Court (Forms) (Amendment No. 2) Rules 1995
1587................Insurance Premium Tax (Amendment) Regulations 1995
1588................Walsgrave Hospitals National Health Service Trust (Transfer of Trust Property) Order 1995
1589................Kettering General Hospital National Health Service Trust (Transfer of Trust Property) Order 1995
1590................Tavistock and Portman National Health Service Trust (Transfer of Trust Property) Order 1995
1591 (C. 34)...Companies Act 1989 (Commencement No. 16) Order 1995
1593................A3 Trunk Road (Kingston Vale, Kingston Upon Thames) (Prescribed Routes) Order 1995
1594................Kent County Council (Hale Street Medway Bridge) Scheme 1994 Confirmation Instrument 1995
1596 (S. 113) .Act of Sederunt (Registration Appeal Court) 1995
1597................A312 Trunk Road (The Parkway, Hounslow) (Prescribed Routes) Order 1995
1598................Prison (Amendment) (No. 2) Rules 1995
1599................Young Offender Institution (Amendment) (No. 2) Rules 1995
1602................East Wiltshire Health Care National Health Service Trust (Transfer of Trust Property) Order 1995
1603................Rockingham Forest National Health Service Trust (Transfer of Trust Property) Order 1995
1604................Swindon and Marlborough National Health Service Trust (Transfer of Trust Property) Order 1995
1609................Fishing Vessels (Safety Improvements) (Grants) Scheme 1995
1610................Fishing Vessels (Decommissioning) Scheme 1995
1611................Food Protection (Emergency Prohibitions) (Paralytic Shellfish Poisoning) Order 1995 (No. 4) Order 1995
1612................Personal Pension Schemes (Appropriate Schemes) Amendment Regulations 1995
1613................Social Security (Income Support and Claims and Payments) Amendment Regulations 1995
1614 (S. 114) .Adoption (Designation of Overseas Adoptions) (Variation) (Scotland) Order 1995
1615................Parliamentary Commissioner Order 1995

1616................Child Abduction and Custody (Parties to Conventions) (Amendment) (No. 4) Order 1995
1617................Consular Fees Order 1995
1618................European Communities (Definition of Treaties) (Partnership and Co-operation Agreement between the European Communities and their Member States and the Russian Federation) Order 1995
1619................European Communities (Definition of Treaties) (Partnership and Co-operation Agreement between the European Communities and their Member States and the Ukraine) Order 1995
1620................Extradition (Drug Trafficking) (Falkland Islands and Gibraltar) Order 1995
1621................South Georgia and South Sandwich Islands Order 1995
1622 (N.I. 7)..Armagh Observatory and Planetarium (Northern Ireland) Order 1995
1623 (N.I. 8)..Arts Council (Northern Ireland) Order 1995
1624................European Convention on Extradition Order 1990 (Amendment) Order 1995
1625 (N.I. 9)..Historic Monuments and Archaeological Objects (Northern Ireland) Order 1995
1626................Parliamentary Constituencies (England) Order 1995
1627 (N.I. 10)Ports (Amendment) (Northern Ireland) Order 1995
1628................Education (Inspectors of Schools in Wales) Order 1995
1629................Gas Appliances (Safety) Regulations 1995
1630................Food Protection (Emergency Prohibitions) (Paralytic Shellfish Poisoning) Order 1995 Partial Revocation Order 1995
1642................Rent Officers (Additional Functions) Order 1995
1643 (S. 115).Rent Officers (Additional Functions) (Scotland) Order 1995
1644................Housing Benefit (General) Amendment Regulations 1995
1645................National Lottery Charities Board (Increase in Membership) Order 1995
1648................Package Travel, Package Holidays and Package Tours (Amendment) Regulations 1995
1649................Children (Allocation of Proceedings) (Amendment) Order 1995
1655................Buying Agency Trading Fund (Extension) Order 1995
1657................Dudley Priority Health National Health Service Trust (Transfer of Trust Property) Order 1995
1658................Lincolnshire County Council (B1003/A57 Rope Walk to Carholme Road, Lincoln, Fossdyke Navigation and Brayford Pool Bridge) Scheme 1995 Confirmation Instrument 1995
1665................Buying Agency Trading Fund (Extension) Order 1995
1666................Value Added Tax (Input Tax) (Amendment) (No. 3) Order 1995
1667................Value Added Tax (Cars) (Amendment) (No. 2) Order 1995
1668................Value Added Tax (Supply of Services) (Amendment) Order 1995
1669................Gaming (Small Charges) (Amendment) Order 1995
1670 (S. 116).Teachers' Superannuation (Scotland) Amendment Regulations 1995
1671................Active Implantable Medical Devices (Amendment and Transitional Provisions) Regulations 1995
1673................Education (Special Educational Needs) (Amendment) Regulations 1995
1674................Conditional Fee Agreements Order 1995
1675................Conditional Fee Agreements Regulations 1995
1676................Commissioners for Oaths (Prescribed Bodies) Regulations 1995
1677................Severn Bridge (Amendment) Regulations 1995

1678................Non-Domestic Rating (Chargeable Amounts) (Amendment No. 2) Regulations 1995
1679................Non-Domestic Rating (Police Authorities) Order 1995
1680................Pensions Increase (Civil Service Compensation Scheme 1994) Regulations 1995
1681................Pensions Increase (Pension Schemes for Derek Compton Lewis) Regulations 1995
1682................Pensions Increase (Pension Scheme for Mr Allan David Green) Regulations 1995
1683................Pensions Increase (Civil Service Supplementary (Earnings Cap) Pension Scheme 1994) Regulations 1995
1684................Department of Transport (Fees) (Amendment) Order 1995
1688................Education (Grant) (Bishop Perowne High School) Regulations 1995
1692................A12 Trunk Road (Redbridge) (No. 1) Red Route Experimental Traffic Order 1995
1693................A316 Trunk Road (Hounslow) Red Route Traffic Order 1995
1694................A316 Trunk Road (Richmond) (No. 1) Red Route Experimental Traffic Order 1995
1695................A12 Trunk Road (Redbridge) Red Route Experimental Traffic Order 1995
1696................A1400 Trunk Road (Redbridge) Red Route Experimental Traffic Order 1995
1697................A316 Trunk Road (Richmond) Red Route (Clearway) Traffic Order 1995
1698................A316 Trunk Road (Hounslow) Red Route (Clearway) Traffic Order 1995
1699................A406 Trunk Road (Newham and Barking and Dagenham) Red Route Experimental Traffic Order 1995
1700................A13 Trunk Road (Barking and Dagenham) Red Route Experimental Traffic Order 1995
1701................A13 Trunk Road (Newham) Red Route Experimental Traffic Order 1995
1702................A10 Trunk Road (Haringey) Red Route Experimental Traffic Order 1995
1703................A13 Trunk Road (Havering) Red Route Experimental Traffic Order 1995
1704................Education (Funding for Teacher Training) Designation Order 1995
1705................Education (Funding for Teacher Training) Designation Order 1995
1706................Football Spectators (Seating) Order 1995
1707................Local Government Act 1988 (Defined Activities) (Exemption) (Allerdale Borough Council, St Edmundsbury Borough Council and Uttlesford District Council) Order 1995
1708................Nitrate Sensitive Areas (Amendment) Regulations 1995
1709................Royal Orthopaedic Hospital National Health Service Trust (Establishment) Amendment Order 1995
1710................Acklam Sixth Form College, Middlesbrough and Kirby College of Further Education, Middlesbrough (Dissolution) Order 1995
1711................Longlands College of Further Education, Middlesbrough and Marton Sixth Form College, Middlesbrough (Dissolution) Order 1995
1712 (S. 117) .St. Mary's Music School (Aided Places) Regulations 1995
1713 (S. 118) .Education (Assisted Places) (Scotland) Regulations 1995
1714................Food Protection (Emergency Prohibitions) (Paralytic Shellfish Poisoning) (No. 5) Order 1995
1716................International Carriage of Perishable Foodstuffs (Amendment) Regulations 1995

1717................Industrial Tribunals (Enforcement of Orders under the Civil Jurisdiction and Judgments Act 1982) (Scotland) Regulations 1995
1729................Foreign Companies (Execution of Documents) (Amendment) Regulations 1995
1730................Insurance Companies (Taxation of Reinsurance Business) Regulations 1995
1731................Mancunian Community Health National Health Service Trust (Transfer of Trust Property) (No. 2) Order 1995
1732................South Manchester University Hospitals National Health Service Trust (Transfer of Trust Property) Order 1995
1733................Tameside and Glossop Acute Services National Health Service Trust (Transfer of Trust Property) Order 1995
1734................Tameside and Glossop Community and Priority Services National Health Service Trust (Transfer of Trust Property) Order 1995
1735................Gloucestershire Royal National Health Service Trust (Transfer of Trust Property) Order 1995
1736................North Manchester Healthcare National Health Service Trust (Transfer of Trust Property) Order 1995
1737................Food Protection (Emergency Prohibitions) (Paralytic Shellfish Poisoning) (No. 6) Order 1995
1738................Arable Area Payments Regulations 1995
1739 (S. 119).Education Authority Bursaries (Scotland) Regulations 1995
1742................Social Security Benefits (Miscellaneous Amendments) Regulations 1995
1743................Education (School Teachers' Pay and Conditions) (No. 2) Order 1995
1747................Cleveland (Further Provisions) Order 1995
1748................Local Government Changes for England (Miscellaneous Provisions) Regulations 1995
1749................Combined Probations Areas (Greater Manchester) Order 1995
1750 (S. 120).Gaming (Small Charges) (Scotland) (Variation) Order 1995
1751 (S. 121).Transcripts of Criminal Proceedings (Scotland) Amendment Order 1995
1752................Training for Work (Scottish Enterprise and Highlands and Islands Enterprise Programmes) Order 1995
1755................Equine Viral Arteritis Order 1995
1763................Food Safety (General Food Hygiene) Regulations 1995
1766................South Kent Community Healthcare National Health Service Trust (Transfer of Trust Property) Order 1995
1767................South Kent Hospitals National Health Service Trust (Transfer of Trust Property) Order 1995
1768................Birmingham Heartlands Hospital National Health Service Trust (Transfer of Trust Property) Order 1995
1769................Buckinghamshire (Borough of Milton Keynes) (Structural Change) Order 1995
1770................East Sussex (Boroughs of Brighton and Hove) (Structural Change) Order 1995
1771................Dorset (Boroughs of Poole and Bournemouth) (Structural Change) Order 1995
1772................Durham (Borough of Darlington) (Structural Change) Order 1995
1773................Derbyshire (City of Derby) (Structural Change) Order 1995
1774................Wiltshire (Borough of Tamesdown) (Structural Change) Order 1995
1775................Hampshire (Cities of Portsmouth and Southampton) (Structural Change) Order 1995
1776................Bedfordshire (Borough of Luton) (Structural Change) Order 1995

1777................Traveller's Reliefs (Fuel and Lubricants) Order 1995
1778 (C. 35)...Finance Act 1995 (Contractual Savings Schemes) (Appointed Day) Order 1995
1779................Staffordshire (City of Stoke-on-Trent) (Structural and Boundary Changes) Order 1995
1780................Training for Work (Miscellaneous Provisions) Order 1995
1801................Social Security (Adjudication) Regulations 1995
1802................Merchant Shipping and Fishing Vessels (Medical Stores) Regulations 1995
1803................Merchant Shipping (Ships' Doctors) Regulations 1995
1804................Units of Measurement Regulations 1995
1805................County Council of Norfolk (Reconstruction of Welney Suspension Bridge) Scheme 1994 Confirmation Instrument 1995
1872................Building Societies (Limits on Transactions with Directors) Order 1995
1873................Building Societies (Non-Retail Funds and Deposits) (Limit on Election) Order 1995
1874................Building Societies (Mergers) (Amendment) Regulations 1995
1875 (S. 122).Act of Adjournal (Consolidation Amendment) (Supervised Release Orders) 1995
1876 (S. 123).Act of Sederunt (Proceedings in the Sheriff Court under the Debtors (Scotland) Act 1987) (Amendment) 1995
1877 (S. 124).Act of Sederunt (Consumer Credit Act 1974) 1985 (Amendment) 1995
1878 (S. 125).Local Government (Transitional Provisions) (Scotland) Order 1995
1879 (S. 126).Aberdeen and Grampian Tourist Board Scheme Order 1995
1880 (S. 127).Angus and City of Dundee Tourist Board Scheme Order 1995
1881 (S. 128).Argyll, the Isles, Loch Lomond, Stirling and Trossachs Tourist Board Scheme Order 1995
1882 (S. 129).Ayrshire and Arran Tourist Board Scheme Order 1995
1883 (S. 130).Dumfries and Galloway Tourist Board Scheme Order 1995
1884 (S. 131).Edinburgh and Lothians Tourist Board Scheme Order 1995
1885 (S. 132).Greater Glasgow and Clyde Valley Tourist Board Scheme Order 1995
1886 (S. 133).Highlands of Scotland Tourist Board Scheme Order 1995
1887 (S. 134).Kingdom of Fife Tourist Board Scheme Order 1995
1888 (S. 135).Orkney Tourist Board Scheme Order 1995
1889 (S. 136).Perthshire Tourist Board Scheme Order 1995
1890 (S. 137).Scottish Borders Tourist Board Scheme Order 1995
1891 (S. 138).Shetland Tourist Board Scheme Order 1995
1892 (S. 139).Western Isles Tourist Board Scheme Order 1995
1893................Merchant Shipping (Fees) Regulations 1995
1894 (S. 140).Local Government (Relevant Date) (Scotland) Order 1995
1895................Northern Ireland Act 1974 (Interim Period Extension) Order 1995
1896................Northern Ireland (Emergency Provisions) Act 1991 (Codes of Practice) Order 1995
1897................Civil Courts (Amendment) Order 1995
1898 (C. 36) (S. 141) Local Government etc. (Scotland) Act 1994 (Commencement No. 4) Order 1995
1900................Merchant Shipping (Seaman's Documents) (Amendment) Regulations 1995
1904................Education (School Performance Information) (Wales) Regulations 1995
1907................Non-automatic Weighing Instruments (EEC Requirements) Regulations 1995
1909 (L. 8).....Magistrates' Courts (Forms) (Amendment) Rules 1995

1910................Medway National Health Service Trust (Transfer of Trust Property) Order 1995
1911................Kent Ambulance National Health Service Trust (Transfer of Trust Property) Order 1995
1912................Mid Kent Healthcare National Health Service Trust (Transfer of Trust Property) Order 1995
1913................North Kent Healthcare National Health Service Trust (Transfer of Trust Property) Order 1995
1914................Royal Victoria Infirmary and Associated Hospitals National Health Service Trust (Transfer of Trust Property) Order 1995
1915................Local Government Act 1988 (Competition) (Defined Activities) Order 1995
1916................Friendly Societies (Modification of the Corporation Tax Acts) (Amendment) Regulations 1995
1924................Broadcasting (Restrictions on the Holding of Licences) (Amendment) Order 1995
1925................Broadcasting (Independent Productions) (Amendment) Order 1995
1927................Ridge College, Stockport and Margaret Danyers College (Dissolution) Order 1995
1928................Specified Bovine Offal Order 1995
1929................Tax-exempt Special Savings Account (Amendment) Regulations 1995
1930 (C. 37)...Licensing (Sunday Hours) Act 1995 (Commencement) Order 1995
1945 (S. 142) .Fees in the Registers of Scotland Order 1995
1946................A30 Trunk Road (Kennards House Junction Improvement and Slip Roads) Order 1995
1947................Satellite Communications Services Regulations 1995
1948................Local Government Elections (Changes to the Franchise and Qualification of Members) Regulations 1995
1950................Waste Management Licensing (Amendment No. 2) Regulations 1995
1953................Employment Protection (Increase of Limits) Order 1995
1954................Housing Benefit (Permitted Totals) Order 1995
1955................Bovine Offal (Prohibition) (England, Wales and Scotland) (Revocation) Regulations 1995
1956................Offshore Installations (Safety Zones) (No. 4) Order 1995
1957 (C. 38)...Criminal Justice and Public Order Act 1994 (Commencement No. 8 and Transitional Provision) Order 1995
1958 (C. 39)...Criminal Justice Act 1993 (Commencement No. 9) Order 1995
1959................Legal Officers (Annual Fees) Order 1995
1960................Parochial Fees Order 1995
1961................Ecclesiastical Judges and Legal Officers (Fees) Order 1995
1962................European Convention on Extradition Order 1990 (Amendment) (No. 2) Order 1995
1963................European Convention on Cinematographic Co-production (Amendment) (No. 2) Order 1995
1964................Army, Air Force and Naval Discipline Acts (Continuation) Order 1995
1965................Naval Medical Compassionate Fund (Amendment) Order 1995
1966................Misuse of Drugs Act 1971 (Modification) Order 1995
1967................Drug Trafficking Act 1994 (Enforcement of Northern Ireland Confiscation Orders) Order 1995
1968................Criminal Justice Act 1988 (Enforcement of Northern Ireland Confiscation Orders) Order 1995
1969 (N.I. 11) Appropriation (No. 2) (Northern Ireland) Order 1995
1970................Air Navigation (No. 2) Order 1995

1971 (S. 143) .Strathclyde Passenger Transport Area (Designation) Order 1995
1972 (S. 144) .Local Government Act 1988 (Defined Activities) (Competition) (Scotland) Amendment Regulations 1995
1973................Local Government Act 1988 (Defined Activities) (Cleaning of Police Buildings) (England and Wales) Regulations 1995
1974................Local Government Reorganisation (Capital Money) (Greater London) (Amendment) Order 1995
1978................Value Added Tax (Refund of Tax) Order 1995
1979................Venture Capital Trust Regulations 1995
1980 (N.I. 12) Trade Union and Labour Relations (Northern Ireland) Order 1995
1981................Local Authorities (Payment of Levy on Disposals) Regulations 1995
1982................Local Authorities (Capital Finance and Approved Investments) (Amendment No. 2) Regulations 1995
1983 (C. 40)...Environment Act 1995 (Commencement) (No. 1) Order 1995
1984 (S. 145) .A87 Extension (Skye Bridge Crossing) Special Road Regulations 1995
1985................Local Government Pension Scheme (Local Government Reorganisation in Wales) Regulations 1995
1986................Contracting Out (Highway Functions) Order 1995
1987................Legal Advice and Assistance (Scope) (Amendment) Regulations 1995
1988................Export and Investment Guarantees (Limit on Foreign Currency Commitments) Order 1995
1989................Plant Health (Forestry) (Great Britain) (Amendment) Order 1995
1990................Safety of Sport Grounds (Designation) Order 1995
1991................Dudley Group of Hospitals National Health Service Trust (Transfer of Trust Property) Order 1995
1992................Furness Hospitals National Health Service Trust (Transfer of Trust Property) Order 1995
1993................Severn National Health Service Trust (Transfer of Trust Property) Order 1995
1994................South Cumbria Community and Mental Health National Health Service Trust (Transfer of Trust Property) Order 1995
1995................Westmorland Hospitals National Health Service Trust (Transfer of Trust Property) Order 1995
2004................Teachers' Superannuation (Amendment) Regulations 1995
2005................Mines Miscellaneous Health and Safety Provisions Regulations 1995
2006................Local Government (Publication of Staffing Information) (England) Regulations 1995
2007 (S. 146) .Western Isles Islands Council (Various Harbours Jurisdiction and Byelaws) Harbour Revision Order 1995
2015................Children (Short-term Placements) (Miscellaneous Amendments) Regulations 1995
2016................Education (Assisted Places) Regulations 1995
2017................Education (Assisted Places) (Incidental Expenses) Regulations 1995
2018................Education (Grants) (Music, Ballet and Choir Schools) Regulations 1995
2019................Sex Discrimination (Designated Educational Establishments) (Revocation) Order 1995
2020................Police (Amendment No. 2) Regulations 1995
2021 (C. 41)...Prisoners (Return to Custody) Act 1995 (Commencement) Order 1995
2034................Church of England (Legal Aid) Rules 1995

2036................Quarries Miscellaneous Health and Safety Provisions Regulations 1995
2037................North East London Education Association Order 1995
2038................Borehole Sites and Operations Regulations 1995
2042 (S. 147) .Warble Fly (Scotland) Amendment Order 1995
2043 (S. 148) .Town and Country Planning (Simplified Planning Zones) (Scotland) Regulations 1995
2044 (S. 149) .Town and Country Planning (Simplified Planning Zones) (Scotland) Order 1995
2045 (C. 42) (S. 150) Planning and Compensation Act 1991 (Commencement No. 18 and Transitional Provision) (Scotland) Order 1995
2046................Food Protection (Emergency Prohibitions) (Paralytic Shellfish Poisoning) (No. 6) Order 1995 Revocation Order 1995
2047................Misuse of Drugs (Designation) (Variation) Order 1995
2048................Misuse of Drugs (Amendment) Regulations 1995
2049................Financial Markets and Insolvency (Money Market) Regulations 1995
2050................Income Tax (Dealers in Securities) (Tradepoint) Regulations 1995
2051................Stamp Duty Reserve Tax (Tradepoint) Regulations 1995
2052................Income Tax (Manufactured Dividends) (Tradepoint) Regulations 1995
2053................Mortgage Indemnities (Recognised Bodies) (No. 2) Order 1995
2054................Repeal of Offensive Trades or Businesses Provisions Order 1995
2056 (S. 151) .Charities (Dormant Accounts) (Scotland) Regulations 1995
2059................Dartford-Thurrock Crossing Tolls Order 1995
2060................Dartford-Thurrock Crossing (Amendment) Regulations 1995
2061................Returning Officers (Parliamentary Constituencies) (England) Order 1995
2065................Education (Further Education Institutions Information) (England) Regulations 1995
2066................Housing (Right to Buy) (Priority of Charges) (No. 2) Order 1995
2067................A43 Trunk Road (Whitfield Turn to Brackley Hatch Dualling) (Detrunking) Order 1995
2068................A43 Trunk Road (Whitfield Turn to Brackley Hatch Dualling and Slip Roads) Order 1995
2070................Education (School Information) (Wales) (Amendment) Regulations 1995
2071................Education (National Curriculum) (Assessment Arrangements for the Core Subjects) (Key Stage 1) (England) Order 1995
2072................Education (National Curriculum) (Assessment Arrangements for the Core Subjects) (Key Stage 2) (England) Order 1995
2073................Education (National Curriculum) (Assessment Arrangements for the Core Subjects) (Key Stage 3) (England) Order 1995
2074................Local Government Act 1988 (Security Work) (Exemption) (England) Order 1995
2075................Motor Vehicles (Driving Licences) (Large Goods and Passenger Carrying Vehicles) (Amendment) (No. 2) Regulations 1995
2076................Motor Vehicles (Driving Licences) (Amendment) (No. 2) Regulations 1995

2087................Education (Wyvern College, Salisbury) (Exemption from Pay and Conditions Orders) Order 1995
2088................National Lottery etc. Act 1993 (Amendment of Section 23) Order 1995
2089................Education (Pupil Registration) Regulations 1995
2090................Education (School Attendance Order) Regulations 1995
2091................Rhondda College (Dissolution) Order 1995
2092................Companies (Summary Financial Statement) Regulations 1995
2093................Patents Rules 1995
2095................Nitrate Sensitive Areas (Amendment) (No. 2) Regulations 1995
2100................Local Government Act 1988 (Competition) (Personnel Services) (Fire and Civil Defence Authorities) (England) Regulations 1995
2101................Local Government Act 1988 (Competition) (Personnel Services) (England) Regulations 1995
2109................Fire Services (Appointments and Promotion) (Amendment) Regulations 1995
2110 (S. 152).Fire Services (Appointments and Promotion) (Scotland) Amendment Regulations 1995
2124................London–Fishguard Trunk Road (A40) (Fishguard Western By-Pass) Order 1995
2125................Agricultural Holdings (Units of Production) Order 1995
2128................Street Works (Registers, Notices, Directions and Designations) (Amendment No. 3) Regulations 1995
2129................Central Manchester Healthcare National Health Service Trust (Transfer of Trust Property) Order 1995
2131 (S. 153).Police (Scotland) Amendment (No. 3) Regulations 1995
2142................Oswestry Light Railway Order 1995
2143................Great Central (Nottingham) Railway Order 1995
2144................Civil Aviation (Canadian Navigation Services) Regulations 1995
2145................Swansea Bay Mussel Fishery Order 1995
2146................Dolgellau to South of Birkenhead Trunk Road (A494) (Improvement at Nantclwyd Bridge) Order 1995
2147................Medicines (Administration of Radioactive Substances) Amendment Regulations 1995
2148................Wild Game Meat (Hygiene and Inspection) Regulations 1995
2149................Greater Manchester Ambulance Service National Health Service Trust (Transfer of Trust Property) Order 1995
2150................Warwickshire Ambulance Service National Health Service Trust (Transfer of Trust Property) Order 1995
2151................Distraint by Collectors (Fees, Costs and Charges) (Amendment) Regulations 1995
2152 (C. 43)...Environmental Protection Act 1990 (Commencement No. 17) Order 1995
2162................Social Security (Attendance and Disability Living Allowances) Amendment Regulations 1995
2164................Patents (Fees) Rules 1995
2165................Registered Designs (Fees) Rules 1995
2168................M4 Motorway (Severn Bridge) (Speed Limit) Regulations 1995
2181 (C. 44)...Goods Vehicles (Licensing of Operators) Act 1995 (Commencement and Transitional Provisions) Order 1995
2182................A650 Trunk Road (Crossflatts Roundabout to Keighley Road Roundabout) (Detrunking) Order 1995
2192................Social Security (Unemployment, Sickness and Invalidity Benefit) Amendment Regulations 1995

2193 (S. 154) .Conon Salmon Fishery District Designation Order 1995
2194 (S. 155) .Alness Salmon Fishery District Designation Order 1995
2195................Land Drainage Improvement Works (Assessment of Environmental Effects) (Amendment) Regulations 1995
2200................Food Safety (Temperature Control) Regulations 1995
2201................County Council of the Royal County of Berkshire (A329(M) Loddon Bridge Connecting Road) Special Road Scheme 1995 Confirmation Instrument 1995
2202................Rural Development Grants (Agriculture) (No. 2) Regulations 1995
2206 (L. 9).....Rules of the Supreme Court (Amendment) 1995
2207................Education (National Curriculum) (Assessment Arrangements for English, Welsh, Mathematics and Science) (Key Stage 1) (Wales) Order 1995
2208................Education (National Curriculum) (Assessment Arrangements for English, Welsh, Mathematics and Science) (Key Stage 2) (Wales) Order 1995
2209................Education (National Curriculum) (Assessment Arrangements for English, Welsh, Mathematics and Science) (Key Stage 3) (Wales) Order 1995
2210................Road Vehicles (Construction and Use) (Amendment) (No. 5) Regulations 1995
2211 (S. 156) .Aberdeen and Grampian Tourist Board Scheme Amendment Order 1995
2212 (S. 157) .Angus and City of Dundee Tourist Board Scheme Amendment Order 1995
2213 (S. 158) .Argyll, the Isles, Loch Lomond, Stirling and Trossachs Tourist Board Scheme Amendment Order 1995
2214 (S. 159) .Scottish Borders Tourist Board Scheme Amendment Order 1995
2215................A12 Trunk Road (Eastern Avenue, Redbridge) (Prescribed Route) Order 1995
2216................A3 Trunk Road (Beverley Way, Merton) (Prohibition of Left Turn) Order 1995
2232 (S. 160) .Ayrshire and Arran Tourist Board Scheme Amendment Order 1995
2233 (S. 161) .Dumfries and Galloway Tourist Board Scheme Amendment Order 1995
2234 (S. 162) .Edinburgh and Lothians Tourist Board Scheme Amendment Order 1995
2235 (S. 163) .Greater Glasgow and Clyde Valley Tourist Board Scheme Amendment Order 1995
2236 (S. 164) .Highlands of Scotland Tourist Board Scheme Amendment Order 1995
2237 (S. 165) .Kingdom of Fife Tourist Board Scheme Amendment Order 1995
2238 (S. 166) .Orkney Tourist Board Scheme Amendment Order 1995
2239 (S. 167) .Perthshire Tourist Board Scheme Amendment Order 1995
2240 (S. 168) .Shetland Tourist Board Scheme Amendment Order 1995
2241 (S. 169) .Western Isles Tourist Board Scheme Amendment Order 1995
2245................A13 Trunk Road (Tower Hamlets) Red Route Experimental Traffic Order 1995
2246................A406 Trunk Road (Enfield) Red Route Experimental Traffic Order 1995
2248................Stonebridge Housing Action Trust (Transfer of Property) Order 1995
2249................Local Government Pension Scheme (Pensionable Remuneration Amendment) Regulations 1995

2258................Town and Country Planning (Environmental Assessment and Unauthorised Development) Regulations 1995
2259................Town and Country Planning (Determination of Appeals by Appointed Persons) (Prescribed Classes) (Amendment) Regulations 1995
2260................East Midlands Enterprise Zones (Mansfield) (Designation) Order 1995
2261 (S. 170).Royal Scottish Academy of Music and Drama (Scotland) Order of Council 1995
2262................Acquisition of Land (Rate of Interest After Entry) Regulations 1995
2287................Income Support (General) Amendment and Transitional Regulations 1995
2288................Gaming Act (Variation of Monetary Limits) (No. 2) Order 1995
2294................Civil Aviation Authority (Economic Regulation of Airports) (Northern Ireland) Regulations 1995
2295 (C. 45) (S. 171) Criminal Justice (Scotland) Act 1995 (Commencement No. 1, Transitional Provisions and Savings) Order 1995
2302 (C. 46)...Child Support Act 1995 (Commencement No. 1) Order 1995
2303................Income-related Benefits Schemes and Social Security (Claims and Payments) (Miscellaneous Amendments) Regulations 1995
2306................Residuary Body for Wales (Levies) Regulations 1995
2307................National Health Service (Optical Charges and Payments) Amendment (No. 3) Regulations 1995
2319 (S. 172).Legal Aid in Contempt of Court Proceedings (Scotland) Amendment Regulations 1995
2320 (S. 173).Criminal Legal Aid (Scotland) Amendment Regulations 1995
2321................Medicines Act 1968 (Amendment) Regulations 1995
2322................Northern Birmingham Community Health National Health Service Trust (Transfer of Trust Property) Order 1995
2323................Northern Birmingham Mental Health National Health Service Trust (Transfer of Trust Property) Order 1995
2324................South Warwickshire Mental Health National Health Service Trust (Transfer of Trust Property) Order 1995
2325................Fosse Health, Leicester Community National Health Service Trust (Transfer of Trust Property) Order 1995
2326................Worcester Royal Infirmary National Health Service Trust (Transfer of Trust Property) Order 1995
2327................City Hospital National Health Service Trust (Transfer of Trust Property) Order 1995
2328................Motor Vehicles (EC Type Approval) (Amendment) Regulations 1995
2329................Civil Aviation (Route Charges for Navigation Services) (Third Amendment) Regulations 1995
2351................Customs Reviews and Appeals (Binding Tariff Information) Regulations 1995
2352................National Health Service (Travelling Expenses and Remission of Charges) Amendment No. 2 Regulations 1995
2356................Electricity Act 1989 (Disclosure of Information) (Director General of Electricity Supply for Northern Ireland) Order 1995
2357................Construction Plant and Equipment (Harmonisation of Noise Emission Standards) (Amendment) Regulations 1995
2360 (S. 174).Gaming Act (Variation of Monetary Limits) (Scotland) (No. 2) Order 1995

2361 (S. 175) .Rent Officers (Additional Functions) (Scotland) Amendment Order 1995
2363................Offshore Installations (Safety Zones) (No. 5) Order 1995
2364................Medicines (Products for Animal Use—Fees) Regulations 1995
2365................Rent Officers (Additional Functions) (Amendment) Order 1995
2367 (C. 47)...Motor Cycle Noise Act 1987 (Commencement) Order 1995
2368................Local Government Changes for England (School Reorganisation and Admissions) Regulations 1995
2369 (S. 176) .National Health Service (Optical Charges and Payments) (Scotland) Amendment (No. 3) Regulations 1995
2370................Motor Cycle Silencer and Exhaust Systems Regulations 1995
2372................Magistrates' Courts Committees (Berkshire and Oxfordshire) Amalgamation Order 1995
2373................Magistrates' Courts Committees (Bradford, Kirklees and Wakefield) Amalgamation Order 1995
2374................Betting and Gaming Duties Act 1981 (Monetary Amounts) Order 1995
2375................Magistrates' Courts Committees (Gwent, Mid Glamorgan and South Glamorgan) Amalgamation Order 1995
2376................Magistrates' Courts Committees (Clwyd and Gwynedd) Amalgamation Order 1995
2377................West Herts Community Health National Health Service Trust (Transfer of Trust Property) Order 1995
2378................Mount Vernon and Watford Hospitals National Health Service Trust (Transfer of Trust Property) Order 1995
2379................East Surrey Learning Disability and Mental Health Service National Health Service Trust (Change of Name) Order 1995
2380 (S. 177) .Shetland Islands Council (West Burrafirth) Harbour Revision Order 1995
2381 (S. 178) .National Health Service (Travelling Expenses and Remission of Charges) (Scotland) Amendment (No. 2) Regulations 1995
2382 (S. 179) .Tay River Purification Board (Ordie Burn) Control Order 1995
2383................Greater Manchester (Light Rapid Transit System) (Land Acquisition) Order 1995
2395................Radioactive Substances (Hospitals) Exemption (Amendment) Order 1995
2396................Veterinary Surgeons (Examination of Commonwealth and Foreign Candidates) (Amendment) Regulations Order of Council 1995
2397................Veterinary Surgeons (Practice by Students) (Amendment) Regulations Order of Council 1995
2411................Rhondda Health Care National Health Service Trust (Transfer of Trust Property) Order 1995
2425................Food Protection (Emergency Prohibitions) (Paralytic Shellfish Poisoning) (Nos. 2, 3 and 4) Orders 1995 Partial Revocation Order 1995
2427................Spring Traps Approval Order 1995
2428................Animals and Animal Products (Import and Export) Regulations 1995
2434................West Midlands Ambulance Service National Health Service Trust (Transfer of Trust Property) Order 1995
2435................Mental Health Services of Salford National Health Service Trust (Transfer of Trust Property) Order 1995

2436................Taxes (Interest Rate) (Amendment) Regulations 1995
2437................Third Country Fishing (Enforcement) (Amendment) Order 1995
2438................Motor Vehicles (Tests) (Amendment) (No. 2) Regulations 1995
2439................Animals (Post-Import Control) Order 1995
2443................A20 Trunk Road (Greenwich) Red Route Experimental Traffic Order 1995
2444................A2 Trunk Road (Bexley) Red Route Experimental Traffic Order 1995
2445................A20 Trunk Road (Bexley and Bromley) Red Route Experimental Traffic Order 1995
2446................Trafford Park Railway Order 1995
2448................Glanusk Park (Crickhowell)–Llyswen Trunk Road (A479) (Dderw Improvement) Order 1995
2449................Local Government Act 1988 (Defined Activities) (Cleaning of Police Buildings) (Exemption) (England and Wales) Order 1995
2450................Electricity Generating Stations (Gas Contracts) Order 1995
2451................Local Government Changes (Rent Act) Regulations 1995
2454................London South Circular Trunk Road (A205) (Catford Hill, Lewisham) (Prescribed Routes) Order 1995
2455 (S. 180) .Valuation Timetable (Scotland) Amendment Order 1995
2456................Local Government (Assistance for Political Groups) (Remuneration) Order 1995
2457................National Health Service Supplies Authority (Transfer of Trust Property) Order 1995
2458................Chinnor and Princes Risborough Railway (Extension) Order 1995
2459................National Blood Authority (Transfer of Trust Property) Order 1995
2472 (C. 48)...Olympic Symbol etc. (Protection) Act 1995 (Commencement) Order 1995
2473................Olympics Association Right (Appointment of Proprietor) Order 1995
2474................Airport Byelaws (Designation) Order 1995
2475................Aerodromes (Designation) (Detention and Sale of Aircraft) Order 1995
2478................Bovine Embyro (Collection, Production and Transfer) Regulations 1995
2479................Bovine Embryo (Collection, Production and Transfer) (Fees) Regulations 1995
2480................Education (School Information) (England) (Amendment) Regulations 1995
2481................Food Protection (Emergency Prohibitions) (Paralytic Shellfish Poisoning) Order 1995 and (Nos. 4 and 5) Orders 1995 Revocation Order 1995
2484................Local Government Act 1988 (Defined Activities) (Specified Periods) (England) Regulations 1995
2487................Medical Devices Fees Regulations 1995
2488................Hallmarking (International Convention) (Amendment) Order 1995
2489................Footwear (Indication of Composition) Labelling Regulations 1995
2490 (C. 49)...Local Government (Wales) Act 1994 (Commencement No. 5) Order 1995
2491................Mid Glamorgan Ambulance National Health Service Trust (Transfer of Trust Property) Order 1995

2492................Velindre Hospital National Health Service Trust (Transfer of Trust Property) Order 1995
2493................Cardiff Community Healthcare National Health Service Trust (Transfer of Trust Property) Order 1995
2494................University Dental Hospital National Health Service Trust (Transfer of Trust Property) Order 1995
2495................Llandough Hospital and Community National Health Service Trust (Transfer of Trust Property) Order 1995
2496................South and East Wales Ambulance National Health Service Trust (Transfer of Trust Property) (No. 3) Order 1995
2497................George Eliot Hospital National Health Service Trust (Transfer of Trust Property) Order 1995
2498................Merchant Shipping (Reporting Requirements for Ships Carrying Dangerous or Polluting Goods) Regulations 1995
2499 (S. 181) .Local Authorities (Property Transfer) (Scotland) Order 1995
2500 (S. 182) .Local Government Property Commission (Scotland) Order 1995
2501................Low Moor Tramway Light Railway Order 1995
2507 (S. 183) .Motorways Traffic (Scotland) Regulations 1995
2517................Police (Discipline) (Amendment No. 2) Regulations 1995
2518................Value Added Tax Regulations 1995
2519................A2 Trunk Road (Bexley) Red Route (Clearway) Traffic Order 1995
2520................A2 Trunk Road (Greenwich) Red Route (Clearway) Traffic Order 1995
2521................A10 Trunk Road (Enfield) Red Route (Clearway) Traffic Order 1995
2523................A12 Trunk Road (Redbridge and Barking and Dagenham) Red Route (Clearway) Traffic Order 1995
2524................A13 Trunk Road (Barking and Dagenham and Newham) Red Route (Clearway) Traffic Order 1995
2525................A13 Trunk Road (Havering) Red Route (Clearway) Traffic Order 1995
2526................A13 Trunk Road (Newham) Red Route (Clearway) Traffic Order 1995
2527................A20 Trunk Road (Bexley and Bromley) Red Route (Clearway) Traffic Order 1995
2528................A20 Trunk Road (Greenwich) Red Route (Clearway) Traffic Order 1995
2530................A102 Trunk Road (Tower Hamlets) Red Route (Clearway) Traffic Order 1995
2532................A406 Trunk Road (Enfield) Red Route (Clearway) Traffic Order 1995
2533................A406 Trunk Road (Redbridge) Red Route (Clearway) Traffic Order 1995
2534................A406 Trunk Road (Newham, Redbridge and Barking and Dagenham Red Route (Clearway) Traffic Order 1995
2535................A406 Trunk Road (Waltham Forest) Red Route (Clearway) Traffic Order 1995
2536................A1400 Trunk Road (Redbridge) Red Route (Clearway) Traffic Order 1995
2546................Local Government Act 1988 (Defined Activities) (Competition) (Amendment) (England) Regulations 1995
2547 (C. 50) (S. 184) Land Registration (Scotland) Act 1979 (Commencement No. 9) Order 1995
2548 (C. 51)...Pensions Act 1995 (Commencement No. 1) Order 1995
2549................Artificial Insemination of Cattle (Animal Health) (England and Wales) (Amendment) Regulations 1995

2550................Video Recordings (Labelling) (Amendment) Regulations 1995
2551................Video Recordings (Review of Determinations) Order 1995
2552................Combined Probation Areas (Northumbria) Order 1995
2553................Combined Probation Areas (North Wales) Order 1995
2554................Combined Probation Areas (West Yorkshire) Order 1995
2555................Outer London Probation Areas (North East London) Order 1995
2556 (S. 185).Artificial Insemination of Cattle (Animal Health) (Scotland) Amendment Regulations 1995
2558................Social Security (Credits) Amendment Regulations
2559................Social Security (Effect of Family Credit on Earnings Factors) Regulations 1995
2561................Local Authorities (Calculation of Council Tax Base) (Wales) Regulations 1995
2562................Local Authorities (Precepts) (Wales) Regulations 1995
2563................Local Government Reorganisation (Wales) (Transitional Provisions No. 4) Order 1995
2581................Surrey Heartlands National Health Service Trust (Transfer of Trust Property) Order 1995
2587................Collective Redundancies and Transfer of Undertakings (Protection of Employment) (Amendment) Regulations 1995
2588................The Wireless Telegraphy (Citizens' Band and Amateur Apparatus) (Various Provisions) (Amendment) Order 1995
2589 (S. 186).Valuation Joint Boards (Scotland) Order 1995
2594................Education (Teachers) (Amendment) (No. 2) Regulations 1995
2606................Social Security (Graduated Retirement Benefit) Amendment Regulations 1995
2607................Measuring Instruments (EC Requirements) (Electrical Energy Meters) Regulations 1995
2618 (L. 9).....Crown Court (Amendment) Rules 1995
2619 (L. 10)...Magistrates' Courts (Amendment) (No. 2) Rules 1995
2620................Social Fund Cold Weather Payments (General) Amendment Regulations 1995
2621................Immigration (Transit Visa) (Amendment) Order 1995
2622................Probation (Amendment) Rules 1995
2624................Dearne Valley Enterprise Zones (Designation) Order 1995
2625................East Midlands Enterprise Zones (North East Derbyshire) (Designation) Order 1995
2626................Local Authorities (Goods and Services) (Public Bodies) (Meat Hygiene) Order 1995
2627 (L. 11)...County Court Fees (Amendment) Order 1995
2628 (L. 12)...Family Proceedings Fees (Amendment) Order 1995
2629 (L. 13)...Supreme Court Fees (Amendment) Order 1995
2630................The Mental Health Act Commission (Amendment) Regulations 1995
2631................Amusement Machine Licence Duty Regulations 1995
2632 (S. 187).North Eastern Combined Fire Services Area Administrative Scheme Order 1995
2633 (S. 188).Northern Combined Fire Services Area Administrative Scheme Order 1995
2634 (S. 189).South Eastern Combined Fire Services Area Administrative Scheme Order 1995
2635 (S. 190).Central Combined Fire Services Area Administration Scheme Order 1995

2636 (S. 191) .Mid and South Western Combined Fire Services Area Administration Scheme Order 1995
2637 (S. 192) .Mid Eastern Combined Fire Services Area Administration Scheme Order 1995
2638 (S. 193) .Central Scotland Combined Police Area Amalgamation Scheme Order 1995
2639 (S. 194) .The Grampian Combined Police Area Amalgamation Scheme Order 1995
2640 (S. 195) .Lothian and Borders Combined Police Area Amalgamation Scheme Order 1995
2641 (S. 196) .Northern Combined Police Area Amalgamation Scheme Order 1995
2642 (S. 197) .Strathclyde Combined Police Area Amalgamation Scheme Order 1995
2643 (S. 198) .Tayside Combined Police Area Amalgamation Scheme Order 1995
2644................Statutory Nuisance (Appeals) Regulations 1995
2645................Blyth Harbour Act 1986 (Amendment) Order 1995
2646................Health and Safety (Fees) Regulations 1995
2647................The Judicial Pensions (Guaranteed Minimum Pension etc.) Order 1995
2648................The Pensions Commutation (Amendment) Regulations 1995
2649 (C. 52) (S. 199) The Environmental Act 1995 (Commencement No. 2) Order 1995
2650 (C. 53)...The Proceeds of Crime Act 1995 (Commencement) Order 1995
2651................Marketing of Ornamental Plant Material Regulations 1995
2652................Marketing of Vegetable Plant Material Regulations 1995
2653................Marketing of Fruit Plant Material Regulations 1995
2654................The Protection of Wrecks (Designation No. 1) Order 1995
2655................Plant Variety Rights Office (Extension of Functions) Regulations 1995
2682 (S. 200) .River Nith Salmon Fishery District (Baits and Lures) Regulations 1995
2683 (S. 201) .River Arkaig, Loch Arkaig and Associated Waters Protection Order 1995
2685................A23 Trunk Road (Croydon) Red Route (Bus Lanes) Experimental Traffic Order 1995
2686................A23 Trunk Road (Croydon) Red Route (Prescribed Route No. 1) Experimental Traffic Order 1995
2687................A23 Trunk Road (Croydon) Red Route Experimental Traffic Order 1995
2688................A205 Trunk Road (Richmond) Temporary Restriction of Traffic Order 1995
2689................A23 Trunk Road (Croydon) Red Route (Clearway) Experimental Traffic Order 1995
2691................Cheshire Community Healthcare National Health Service Trust (Transfer of Trust Property) Order 1995
2695 (C. 54)...Charities Act 1993 (Commencement and Transitional Provisions) Order 1995
2696................Charities Act 1993 (Substitution of Sums) Order 1995
2697................Kent Ambulance National Health Service Trust (Establishment) Amendment Order 1995
2698................West Cheshire National Health Service Trust (Transfer of Trust Property) Order 1995
2699................Social Security (Canada) Order 1995
2700................Air Navigation (Hong Kong) Order 1995

2701................Air Navigation (Overseas Territories) (Amendment) Order 1995
2702 (N.I. 13)Child Support (Northern Ireland) Order 1995
2703................European Convention on Extradition Order 1990 (Amendment) (No. 3) Order 1995
2704 (N.I. 14)Health and Personal Social Services (Amendment) (Northern Ireland) Order 1995
2705 (N.I. 15)Jobseekers (Northern Ireland) Order 1995
2706................Double Taxation Relief (Taxes on Income) (Belarus) Order 1995
2707................The Double Taxation Relief (Taxes on Income) (Bolivia) Order 1995
2708................The Reciprocal Enforcement of Foreign Judgments (Canada) (Amendment) Order 1995
2709................Reciprocal Enforcement of Maintenance Orders (United States of America) Order 1995
2713................Civil Aviation (Canadian Navigation Services) (Second Amendment) Regulations 1995
2715 (C. 55)...Finance Act 1993, section 11, (Appointed Day) Order 1995
2716................Other Fuel Substitutes (Rates of Excise Duty etc.) Order 1995
2717................Other Fuel Substitutes (Payment of Excise Duty etc.) Regulations 1995
2720................Housing (Welfare Services) (Wales) Order 1995
2723................Companies Act 1989 Part II (Consequential Amendment) (No. 2) Regulation 1995
2724................Charities (Accounts and Reports) Regulations 1995
2729................Employment Code of Practice (Industrial Action Ballots and Notice to Employers) Order 1995
2730................The European Convention on Cinematographic Co-production (Amendment) (No. 3) Order 1995
2737................The National Health Service (Charges for Drugs and Appliances) Amendment (No. 2) Regulations 1995
2738................The East Midlands Enterprise Zones (Bassetlaw) (Designation) Order 1995
2739 (S. 202) .National Health Service (Charges for Drugs and Appliances) (Scotland) Amendment (No. 2) Regulations 1995
2741................Antarctic (Amendment) Regulations 1995
2742 (S. 203) .Environmental Protection (Determination of Enforcing Authority etc.) (Scotland) Amendment Regulations 1995
2744................A205 Trunk Road (Richmond and Wandsworth) Red Route Experimental Traffic Order 1995 Amendment Order 1995
2746................A205 Trunk Road (Upper Richmond Road West) Red Route (Prescribed Route No. 1) Experimental Traffic Order 1995
2748 (C. 58)...Antarctic Act 1994 (Commencement) Order 1995
2749................Kidderminster Health Care National Health Service Trust (Transfer of Trust Property) Order 1995
2750................Public Telecommunication System Designation (Orange Personal Communications Services Limited) Order 1995
2758................East Midlands Enterprise Zones (Ashfield) (Designation) Order 1995
2765 (C. 56)...Environment Act 1995 (Commencement No. 3) Order 1995
2766 (S. 204) .Local Government (Application of Enactments) (Scotland) (No. 2) Order 1995
2767................Control of Dogs on Roads Orders (Procedure) (England and Wales) Regulations 1995
2768................Police Federation (Amendment) Regulations 1995
2769................Traffic Signs General (Amendment) Directions 1995

2778................Hill Livestock (Compensatory Allowances) (Amendment) (No. 3) Regulations 1995
2779................Sheep Annual Premium (Amendment) Regulations 1995
2780................Arable Area Payments (Amendment) Regulations 1995
2781................Trafford Healthcare National Health Service Trust (Transfer of Trust Property) (No. 2) Order 1995
2782................Approval of Codes of Management Practice (Residential Property) Order 1995
2783................National Health Service Trusts (Originating Capital Debt) (Wales) (No. 2) Order 1995
2786................General Medical Council (Registration (Fees) (Amendment) Regulations) Order of Council 1995
2787 (C. 57) (S. 205) Children (Scotland) Act 1995 (Commencement No. 1) Order 1995
2791 (S. 206) .Acquisition of Land (Rate of Interest after Entry) (Scotland) Regulations 1995
2792................Income-related Benefits Schemes Amendment (No. 2) Regulations 1995
2793................Housing Benefit (Permitted Totals) and Council Tax Benefit (Permitted Total) (Pensions for War Widows) Amendment Order 1995
2794................Local Government Act 1988 (Sports and Leisure Management, Cleaning of Buildings and Repair and Maintenance of Vehicles) (Exemption) Order 1995
2795................Offshore Installations (Safety Zones) (No. 6) Order 1995
2796................Local Government Changes for England (Property Transfer and Transitional Payments) (Amendment) Regulations 1995
2797................Gwent Community Health National Health Service Trust (Establishment) Amendment Order 1995
2800................National Health Service Litigation Authority (Establishment and Constitution) Order 1995
2801................National Health Service Litigation Authority Regulations 1995
2802 (L. 14)...Magistrates' Courts (Reciprocal Enforcement of Maintenance Orders) (United States of America) Rules 1995
2803................National Parks Authorities (Wales) Order 1995
2808................Medicines (Exemption from Licences) (Clinical Trials) Order 1995
2809................Medicines (Exemption from Licences and Certificates) (Clinical Trials) Order 1995
2811................Morriston Hospital National Health Service Trust Property) (No. 2) Order 1995
2812................East Durham Enterprise Zones (Designation) Order 1995
2813................Local Government Act 1988 (Competition) (Information Technology) (England) Regulations 1995
2814 (S. 207) .Teachers' Superannuation (Additional Voluntary Contributions) (Scotland) Regulations 1995
2815................Lottery Duty (Instant Chances) Regulations 1995
2816 (C. 59)...Boundary Bridges (Wales) (Appointed Day) Order 1995
2823................Housing (Change of Landlord) (Payment of Disposal Cost by Instalments) (Amendment No. 2) Regulations 1995
2825................Wildlife and Countryside Act 1981 (Amendment) Regulations 1995
2835 (C. 68)...Deregulation and Contracting Out Act 1994 (Commencement No. 4 and Transitional Provisions) Order 1995
2836................Meat (Hygiene, Inspection and Examinations for Residues) (Charges) (Amendment) Regulations 1995

2837................Local Government Reorganisation (Compensation for Loss of Remuneration) Regulations 1995
2838 (L. 15)...County Court (Amendment No. 3) Rules 1995
2839 (L. 16)...County Court (Forms) (Amendment No. 3) Rules 1995
2840................Curfew Order (Responsible Officer) (Berkshire, Greater Manchester and Norfolk) Order 1995
2861................Export Refunds (Administrative Penalties) (Rate of Interest) Regulations 1995
2862................Local Government Changes for England (Finance) (Amendment) Regulations 1995
2863................Towns and Country Planning (Minerals) Regulations 1995
2864................Police Areas (Wales) Order 1995
2865 (S. 208) .Local Government (Compensation for Reduction of Remuneration on Reorganisation) (Scotland) Regulations 1995
2866 (C. 60) (S. 209) Local Government etc. (Scotland) Act 1994 (Commencement No. 5) Order 1995
2867................Parliamentary Pensions (Amendment) Regulations 1995
2868................Housing Benefit (General) Amendment (No. 2) Regulations 1995
2869................Goods Vehicles (Licensing of Operators) Regulations 1995
2870................Escape and Rescue from Mines Regulations 1995
2871................Habitat (Salt-Marsh) (Amendment) Regulations 1995
2874 (S. 210) .Seed Potatoes originating in the Netherlands (Notification) (Scotland) Order 1995
2875................Christie Hospital National Health Service Trust (Transfer of Trust Property) Order 1995
2876................Gibralter Point (Area of Special Protection) Order 1995
2877................Tribunals and Inquiries (Antarctic Tribunal) Order 1995
2878 (S. 211) .Diligence against Earnings (Variation) (Scotland) Regulations 1995
2879................Trunk Road (A3) (Robin Hood Way Service Road, Kingston Upon Thames) (Restriction of Entry) Order 1982 (Variation) Order 1995
2880................Sale of Registration Marks Regulations 1995
2889................Local Government Changes for England (Collection Fund Surpluses and Deficits) Regulations 1995
2891................Habitat (Salt-Marsh) (Correction to Amendment) Regulations 1995
2892 (C. 61)...Finance Act 1995, section 20, (Appointed Day) Order 1995
2893................Revenue Traders (Accounts and Records) (Amendment) Regulations 1995
2894................Local Government Changes for England (Designation of Authorities) Order 1995
2895................Local Government Changes for England (Payments to Designated Authorities) (Minimum Reserve Provisions) 1995
2896 (S. 212) .Sporting Grounds and Sporting Events (Designation) (Scotland) Amendment Order 1995
2897 (L. 17)...Rules of the Supreme Court (Amendment No. 2) 1995
2899................Bristol Development Corporation (Planning Functions) Order 1995
2900................Bristol Development Corporation (Transfer of Property, Rights and Liabilities) Order 1995
2901................Local Government Act 1988 (Defined Activities) (Exemption) (Fire Services) (England and Wales) Regulations 1995
2902................Taxation of Income from Land (Non-residents) Regulations 1995

2906................Insurance Brokers (Registration) Act 1977 (Amendment) Order 1995
2907................Child Support Commissioners (Procedure) (Amendment) Regulations 1995
2908................Public Service Vehicles (Operators' Licences) Regulations 1995
2909................Public Service Vehicles (Operators' Licences) (Fees) Regulations 1995
2910................Local Authorities (Funds) (England) (Amendment) Regulations 1995
2911................Products of Animal Origin (Import and Export) (Amendment) Regulations 1995
2912................Registered Designs Rules 1995
2913................Registered Designs (Fees) (No. 2) Rules 1995
2914................Consumer Credit (Exempt Agreements) (Amendment) (No. 2) Order 1995
2915................Local Government Act 1988 (Defined Activities) (Exemption) (Stockton-on-Tees Borough Council) Order 1995
2916................Local Government Act 1988 (Competition) (Financial Services) (England) Regulations 1995
2917................Foreign Satellite Service Proscription Order 1995
2922................Animal Health Orders (Divisional Veterinary Manager Amendment) Order 1995
2923................Health and Safety Information for Employees (Modifications and Repeals) Regulations 1995
2927................Social Security (Income Support, Claims and Payments and Adjudication) Amendment Regulations 1995
2928................Immigration (Registration with Police) (Amendment) Registration 1995
2929................Plant Health (Great Britain) (Amendment) (No. 2) Order 1995
2930................Road Traffic (Special Parking Area) (London Borough of Croydon) (Amendment) Order 1995
2932 (C. 62)...Income and Corporation Taxes Act 1988, section 51A, (Appointed Day), Order 1995
2933 (C. 63)...Finance Act 1995, section 82, (Appointed Day) Order 1995
2934................Income Tax (Gilt-edged Securities) (Gross Payments of Interest) Regulations 1995
2935................Social Security (Invalid Care Allowance) Amendment Regulations 1995
2943................Civil Aviation (Aerial Advertising) Regulations 1995
2944................Sole, Plaice, Cod and Haddock (Specified Sea Areas) (Prohibition of Fishing) Order 1995
2945 (C. 64)...Northern Ireland (Remission of Sentences) Act 1995 (Commencement) Order 1995
2946................Statistics of Trade (Customs and Excise) (Amendment) Regulations 1995
2947................Plant Breeders' Rights (Fees) (Amendment) (No. 2) Regulations 1995
2950 (C. 65)...Environment Act 1995 (Commencement No. 4 and Saving Provisions) Order 1995
2951................Combined Probation Areas (Hertfordshire) Order 1995
2952................Forge Lane, Horbury Level Crossing Order 1995
2953................Local Government Pension Scheme (Augmentation) Regulations 1995
2956................County Council of Staffordshire (Trent and Mersey Canal) Bridge Scheme 1994 Confirmation Instrument 1994

2958................Stockport Healthcare National Health Service Trust (Transfer of Trust Property) Order 1995
2959................Stockport Acute Services National Health Service Trust (Transfer of Trust Property) Order 1995
2960 (S. 213).College of Further Education (Changes of Name) (Scotland) Order 1995
2961................Judicial Pensions (Contributions) (Amendment) Regulations 1995
2962................Land Registration (District Registries) Order 1995
2963 (C. 66)...Landlord and Tenant (Covenants) Act 1995 (Commencement) Order 1995
2964................Landlord and Tenant (Covenants) Act 1995 (Notices) Regulations 1995
2965................A30 Trunk Road (Great South West Road, Hounslow) (Temporary Restriction of Traffic) Order 1995
2966................A41 Trunk Road (Baker Street) (Temporary Restriction of Traffic) Order 1995
2967................A501 Trunk Road (Fitzroy Street) (Temporary Restriction of Traffic) Order 1995
2971 (S. 214).Western Isles Islands Council (Leverburgh) Harbour Revision Order 1995
2983................European Communities (Designation) (No. 3) Order 1995
2984................Ministerial and Other Salaries Order 1995
2985................Transfer of Functions (Science) Order 1995
2986................Transfer of Functions (Education and Employment) Order 1995
2987................Copyright (Application to Other Countries) (Amendment) Order 1995
2988................Designs (Convention Countries) (Amendment) Order 1995
2989................Patents (Convention Countries) (Amendment) Order 1995
2990................Performance (Reciprocal Protection) (Convention Countries) Order 1995
2991 (N.I. 16)Financial Provisions (Northern Ireland) Order 1995
2992................Parliamentary Constituencies (Northern Ireland) Order 1995
2993 (N.I. 17)Police (Amendment) (Northern Ireland) Order 1995
2994 (N.I. 18)Road Traffic (Northern Ireland) Order 1995
2995................Transfer of Functions (European Parliamentary Pay and Pensions) Order 1995
2996................Local Government Act 1988 (Defined Activities, Exemptions) (Wales) (Amendment) Order 1995
2997................Trade Marks (Claims to Priority from Relevant Countries) (Amendment) Order 1995
2998................Exempt Charities Order 1995
2999................Value Added Tax (Refund of Tax) (No. 2) Order 1995
3000................Goods Vehicles (Licensing of Operators) (Fees) Regulations 1995
3001 (S. 215).Police (Scotland) Amendment (No. 4) Regulations 1995
3002 (S. 216).Designation of Structure Plan Areas (Scotland) Order 1995
3003 (C. 67)...Police and Magistrates' Courts Act 1994 (Commencement No. 9 and Amendment) Order 1995
3018................Potatoes Originating in the Netherlands Order 1995
3019................National Park Authorities (Levies) (Wales) Regulations 1995
3021................Occupational Pensions (Revaluation) Order 1995
3022................Company and Business Names (Amendment) Regulations 1995
3023................Dundee Port Authority Transfer Scheme 1995 Confirmation Order 1995
3024 (S. 217).Soft Fruit Plants (Scotland) Revocation Order 1995

3025 (S. 218) .Police Grant (Scotland) Amendment Order 1995
3026 (S. 219) .Strathclyde Passenger Transport Authority (Constitution, Membership and Transitional and Consequential Provisions) Order 1995
3028................National Blood Authority (Transfer of Trust Property) (No. 2) Order 1995
3029................Medicines (Pharmacies) (Applications for Registration and Fees) Amendment Regulations 1995
3031................Income Tax (Indexation) Order 1995
3032................Inheritance Tax (Indexation) Order 1995
3033................Capital Gains Tax (Annual Exempt Amount) Order 1995
3034................Retirement Benefits Schemes (Indexation of Earnings Cap) Order 1995
3035................Income Tax (Cash Equivalents of Car Fuel Benefits) Order 1995
3036................Manufactured Payments and Transfer of Securities (Tax Relief) Regulations 1995
3037................Value Added Tax (Increase of Registration Limits) Order 1995
3038................Value Added Tax (Place of Supply of Services) (Amendment) Order 1995
3039................Value Added Tax (Ships and Aircraft) Order 1995
3040................Value Added Tax (Increase of Consideration for Fuel) Order 1995
3041................Value Added Tax (Tax Free Shops) Order 1995
3042................Value Added Tax (Treatment of Transactions) (Tradings Stamps) Order 1995
3043................Value Added Tax (Trading Stamps) Regulations 1995
3044................Travellers' Allowances Amendment Order 1995
3047 (S. 220) .Annual Close Time (River Eachaig Salmon Fishery District) Order 1995
3048 (S. 221) .Town and Country Planning (Limit of Annual Value) (Scotland) Order 1995
3051................Road Vehicles (Construction and Use) (Amendment) (No. 6) Regulations 1995
3052................Motor Vehicles (Authorisation of Special Types) (Amendment) Order 1995
3054................National Assistance (Assessment of Resources) (Amendment No. 2) Regulations 1995
3055................Social Security (Claims and Payments) Amendment Regulations 1995
3056................Valuation Tribunals (Wales) Regulations 1995
3057................Kensington and Chelsea and Hammersmith and Fulham (London Borough Boundaries) Order 1995
3058................A102 Trunk Road (Blackwall Tunnel Approach, Greenwich) (Tunnel Avenue Slip Road) Order 1995
3059................Beer (Amendment) Regulations 1995
3060................Export of Goods (Control) Amendment Order 1995
3061 (C. 69)...Criminal Appeal Act 1995 (Commencement No. 1 and Transitional Provisions) Order 1995
3062................Friendly Societies (Activities of a Subsidiary) Order 1995
3063................Building Societies (Designation of Qualifying Bodies) (No. 2) Order 1995
3064................Building Societies (Liquid Asset) (Amendment) (No. 2) Regulations 1995
3065................Building Societies (Accounts and Related Provisions) (Amendment) Regulations 1995
3066................Building Societies (Syndicated Lending) Order 1995

3067................Occupational and Personal Pension Schemes (Miscellaneous Amendments) (No. 2) Regulations 1995
3068 (S. 222).New Town (East Kilbride) (Transfer of Property, Rights and Liabilities) Order 1995
3069 (S. 223).Act of Serundunt (Lands Valuation Appeal Court) 1995
3070 (S. 224).Motorways Traffic (Scotland) Amendment Regulations 1995
3090 (C. 70)...National Health Service (Amendment) Act 1995 (Commencement No. 1 and Saving) Order 1995
3091................National Health Service (Service Committees and Tribunal) Amendment Regulations 1995
3092................National Health Service (General Dental Services) Amendment Regulations 1995
3093................National Health Service (General Medical Services) Amendment (No. 2) Regulations 1995
3094 (S. 225).Act of Sederunt (Fees of Messengers-at-Arms) 1995
3095 (S. 226).Act of Sederunt (Fees of Sheriff Officers) 1995
3096 (S. 227).Environmentally Sensitive Areas (Breadalbane) Designation (Amendment) Order 1995
3097 (S. 228).Environmentally Sensitive Areas (Loch Lomond) Designation (Amendment) Order 1995
3098................London Docklands Development Corporation (Alteration of Boundaries) Order 1995
3099................Financial Assistance for Environmental Purposes (No. 4) Order 1995
3100................A12 Trunk Road (Colchester Road, Havering) (Prescribed Routes) Order 1995
3103................Retirement Benefits Schemes (Information Powers) Regulations 1995
3104 (C. 71)...Pensions Act 1995 (Commencement No. 2) Order 1995
3105................Local Government (Changes for the Registration Service in Avon, Cleveland, Humberside and North Yorkshire) Order 1995
3106................Local Government (Registration Service in Wales) Order 1995
3107................Traffic Signs (Amendment) Regulations and General Directions 1995
3108................Local Government Act 1988 (Defined Activities) (Competition) (Supervision of Parking) (Amendment) (England) Regulations 1995
3109 (S. 229).Mallaig Harbour Revision Order 1995
3113................Special Educational Needs Tribunal Regulations 1995
3114................Local Government Changes for England (Local Management of Schools) Regulations 1995
3116................Spreadable Fats (Marketing Standards) Regulations 1995
3117................Measuring Equipment (Liquid Fuel Delivered from Road Tankers) (Amendment) Regulations 1995
3118................Local Government Act 1988 (Defined Activities) (Specified Periods) (England) (Amendment) Regulations 1995
3119................War Pensions Committees (Amendment) Regulations 1995
3122................Haddock (Specified Sea Areas) (Prohibition of Fishing) Order 1995
3123................Sweeteners in Food Regulations 1995
3124................Colours in Food Regulations 1995
3125 (C. 72)...Finance Act 1994, section 105 (Appointed Day) Order 1995
3126................County Council of Clwyd (River Dee Estuary Bridge) (Variation) Scheme 1995
3127................Avon Fire Services (Combination Scheme) Order 1995
3128................Merchant Shipping (Port State Control) Regulations 1995

3129................Restrictive Trade Practices (Standards and Arrangements) (Goods) Order 1995
3130................Restrictive Trade Practices (Standards and Arrangements) (Services) Order 1995
3131................Cleveland Fire Services (Combination Scheme) Order 1995
3132................Humberside Fire Services (Combination Scheme) Order 1995
3133................North Yorkshire Fire Services (Combinations Scheme) Order 1995
3134................Insurance Companies (Pension Business) (Transitional Provisions) (Amendment) Regulations 1995
3139................A40 Trunk Road (Ealing) Red Route (Clearway) Traffic Order 1995
3142................A406 Trunk Road (Brent) Red Route (Clearway) Traffic Order 1995
3143................A406 Trunk Road (Brent) Red Route Experimental Traffic Order 1995
3145................Criminal Justice Act 1988 (Confiscation Orders) Order 1995
3146................Air Quality Standards (Amendment) Regulations 1995
3147................Value Added Tax (Amendment) Regulations 1995
3148................Rent Officers (Additional Functions) (Amendment No. 2) Order 1995
3149................Approval of Codes of Management Practice (Residential Property) (No. 2) Order 1995
3150................Local Government Reorganisation (Wales) (Finance) (Miscellaneous Amendments and Transitional Provisions) Order 1995
3151................Housing Benefit (Permitted Totals) Amendment Order 1995
3152................Social Security (Unemployment, Sickness and Invalidity Benefit) Amendment (No. 2) Regulations 1995
3153................Land Registration (No. 3) Rules 1995
3154................Land Registration (Overriding Leases) Rules 1995
3155 (S. 230) .Water Byelaws (Loch an Sgoltaire) Extension Order 1995
3156 (S. 231) .Marriage (Prescription of Forms) (Scotland) Amendment Regulations 1995
3157 (S. 232) .Registration of Births, Still-births, Deaths and Marriages (Prescription of Forms) (Scotland) Amendment Regulations 1995
3158 (S. 233) .Adopted Children Register and Parental Order Register (Form of Entry) (Scotland) Regulations 1995
3159................Hounslow (Various Roads) Traffic Order 1969 (Variation) Order 1995
3160................Civil Aviation (Route Charges for Navigation Services) Regulations 1995
3161................Civil Aviation (Joint Financing) (Amendment) Regulations 1995
3162................Registration of Births, Deaths and Marriages (Fees) Order 1995
3163................Reporting of Injuries, Diseases and Dangerous Occurrences Regulations 1995
3164................A40 Trunk Road (Hillingdon) Red Route (Clearway) Traffic Order 1995
3168................A501 Trunk Road (Euston Road and Osnaburgh Street, Camden and Westminster) Red Route (Prescribed Route and Prohibited Turn No. 1) Experimental Traffic Order 1995
3173 (L. 21)...Civil Courts (Amendment) (No. 2) Order 1995
3174................Medicines (Products Other Than Veterinary Drugs) (Prescription Only) Amendment (No. 2) Order 1995
3175................Community Trade Mark (Fees) Regulations 1995

3176 (S. 234) .Fire Services (Notification of Establishment Schemes) (Scotland) Regulations 1995
3177 (S. 235) .Non-Domestic Rating Contributions (Scotland) Amendment Regulations 1995
3180................Electromagnetic Compatibility (Amendment) Regulations 1995
3181................Non-Domestic Rating Contributions (England) (Amendment) Regulations 1995
3182................Sussex Ambulance Service National Health Service Trust (Transfer of Trust Property) Order 1995
3183................Occupational Pension Schemes (Equal Treatment) Regulations 1995
3184................Revenue Support Grant (Specified Bodies) (Amendment) Regulations 1995
3185 (S. 236) .Rent Officers (Additional Functions) (Scotland) Amendment (No. 2) Order 1995
3186................Agricultural Wages Committees (Areas) (England) Order 1995
3187................Miscellaneous Food Additives Regulations 1995
3188................Railtrack (Swinedyke Level Crossing) Order 1995
3189................Fresh Meat (Hygiene and Inspection) (Amendment) Regulations 1995
3192................Retirement Age of General Commissioners Order 1995
3193................Medicines (Veterinary Drugs) (Pharmacy and Merchants' List) (Amendment) Order 1995
3198 (C. 73)...Local Government (Wales) Act 1994 (Commencement No. 6) Order 1995
3199 (S. 237) .National Health Service (General Medical Services) (Scotland) Amendment Regulations 1995
3200 (S. 238) .National Health Service (General Dental Services) (Scotland) Amendment Regulations 1995
3201 (S. 239) .National Health Service (Service Committees and Tribunal) (Scotland) Amendment Regulations 1995
3202................Bread and Flour Regulations 1995
3203................City of Sunderland College (Incorporation) Order 1995
3204................City of Sunderland College (Government) Regulations 1995
3205................Minced Meat and Meat Preparations (Hygiene) Regulations 1995
3207................European Communities (Designation) (No. 4) Order 1995
3208................European Specialist Medical Qualifications Order 1995
3209................Extradition (Torture) (Bermuda) Order 1995
3210 (N.I. 19) Street Works (Northern Ireland) Order 1995
3211 (N.I. 20) Polygamous Marriages (Northern Ireland) Order 1995
3212 (N.I. 21) Agriculture (Conservation Grants) (Northern Ireland) Order 1995
3213 (N.I. 22) Pensions (Northern Ireland) Order 1995
3214 (C. 74) (S. 240) National Health Service (Amendment) Act 1995 (Commencement No. 2 and Saving) (Scotland) Order 1995
3215................Medicines (Sale or Supply) (Miscellaneous Provisions) Amendment Regulations 1995
3216................Medicines (Products Other than Veterinary Drugs) (General Sale List) Amendment Order 1995
3217................Police and Criminal Evidence Act 1984 (Application to Customs and Excise) (Amendment) Order 1995
3218................North Wales Fire Services (Combination Scheme) Order 1995
3219................Income Tax (Stock Lending) (Amendment No. 2) Regulations 1995

3220................Sale and Repurchase of Securities (Modification of Enactments) Regulations 1995
3221................Income Tax (Manufactured Interest) (Amendment) Regulations 1995
3222................Value Added Tax (Imported Goods) Relief (Amendment) Order 1995
3223................Insurance Companies (Gilt-edged Securities) (Periodic Accounting for Tax on Interest) Regulations 1995
3224................Gilt-edged Securities (Periodic Accounting for Tax on Interest) Regulations 1995
3225................Lloyd's Underwriters (Gilt-edged Securities) (Periodic Accounting for Tax on Interest) Regulations 1995
3228 (C. 75)...Jobseekers Act 1995 (Commencement No. 1) Order 1995
3229................Mid and West Wales Fire Services (Combination Scheme) Order 1995
3230................South Wales Fire Services (Combination Scheme) Order 1995
3231................Deregulation (Greyhound Racing) Order 1995
3232................Dog Racecourse Totalisator Regulations 1995
3233................Deregulation (Building Societies) Order 1995
3234................Health and Safety (Repeals and Revocations) Regulations 1995
3235................Non-Domestic Rating Contributions (Wales) (Amendment) Regulations 1995
3236................Finance Act 1995, section 63(2), (Appointed Day) Order 1995
3237................Insurance Companies (Overseas Life Assurance Business) (Compliances) Regulations 1995
3238................Insurance Companies (Overseas Life Assurance Business) (Tax Credit) Regulations 1995
3239................Tax-Exempt Special Savings Account (Relevant European Institutions) Regulations 1995
3240................Cheese and Cream Regulations 1995
3241................Cycle Racing on Highways (Amendment) Regulations 1995
3243................Church Representation Rules (Amendment) Resolution 1995
3244................Misuse of Drugs (Amendment) (No. 2) Regulations 1995
3245................Saithe (Specified Sea Areas) (Prohibition of Fishing) Order 1995
3246................Specified Bovine Offal (Amendment) Order 1995
3247................Environmental Protection (Prescribed Processes and Substances) (Amendment) Regulations 1995
3248................Insurance Companies (Amendment) Regulations 1995
3249................Export of Goods (Control) (Amendment No. 2) Order 1995
3252 (S. 241).Water Undertakings (Rateable Values) (Scotland) (No. 2) Order 1995
3253 (S. 242).Docks and Harbours (Rateable Values) (Scotland) Amendment (No. 2) Order 1995
3254................Severn Bridges Tolls Order 1995
3256................Hinchingbrooke Health Care National Health Service Trust (Transfer of Trust Property) Order 1995
3257................Kent and Sussex Weald National Health Service Trust (Transfer of Trust Property) Order 1995
3258................Mid Kent Healthcare National Health Service Trust (Transfer of Trust Property) Order 1995
3259................Weald of Kent Community National Health Service Trust (Transfer of Trust Property) Order 1995
3260................Queen Victoria Hospital National Health Service Trust (Transfer of Trust Property) Order 1995
3261................Child Support (Miscellaneous Amendments) (No. 2) Regulations 1995
3262 (C. 76)...Child Support Act 1995 (Commencement No. 2) Order 1995

3263................Child Support (Compensation for Recipients of Family Credit and Disability Working Allowance) Regulations 1995
3264................Local Government Changes (Rent Act Registration Areas) Order 1995
3265................Child Support (Miscellaneous Amendments) (No. 3) Regulations 1995
3266................City of Manchester (Mancunian Way A635(M) and A57(M) Mancunian Way Slip Roads) Special Road Scheme 1992 Confirmation Instrument 1995
3267................Food (Miscellaneous Revocations and Amendments) Regulations 1995
3269................Bristol Development Corporation (Area and Constitution) Order 1995
3270................M27 South Coast Motorway (Ower–Chilworth Section) Connecting Roads Scheme 1970 Variation Scheme (No. 2) 1995
3271................Financial Services Act 1986 (Investment Services) (Extension of Scope of Act) Order 1995
3272................Uncertified Securities Regulations 1995
3273................Financial Services Act 1986 (European Regulated Markets) (Exemption) Order 1995
3274................Vocational Training (Public Financial Assistance and Disentitlement to Tax Relief) (Amendment) Regulations 1995
3275................Investment Services Regulations 1995
3276................Jobseeker's Allowance (Transitional Provisions) Regulations 1995
3277 (L. 18)...County Court (Amendment No. 4) Rules 1995
3278 (L. 19)...County Court (Forms) (Amendment No. 4) Rules 1995
3280................National Health Service (Fund-holding Practices) (Functions of Family Health Services Authorities) Regulations 1995
3281................Attendance Centre Rules 1995
3282................Income-related Benefits Schemes (Widows' etc. Pensions Disregards) Amendment Regulations 1995
3283................Combined Probation Areas (Oxfordshire and Buckinghamshire) Order 1995
3284................Combined Probation Areas (Greater Manchester) (No. 2) Order 1995
3285................Sandwell Healthcare National Health Service Trust (Transfer of Trust Property) Order 1995
3287................Personal Equity Plan (Amendment No. 2) Regulations 1995
3293................Cod and Whiting (Specified Sea Areas) (Prohibition of Fishing) Order 1995
3294 (S. 243).Local Government (Superannuation and Compensation for Redundancy or Premature Retirement) (Scotland) Amendment Regulations 1995
3295 (S. 244).Rural Diversification Programme (Scotland) Regulations 1995
3297................Duration of Copyright and Rights in Performances Regulations 1995
3298................Dual-Use and Related Goods (Export Control) (Amendment No. 2) Regulations 1995
3299................Electrical Contracting (London Exhibitions Halls) Order 1995
3302................Local Government Act 1988 (Competition) (Legal and Construction etc. Services) (Police Authorities) Regulations 1995
3303................Local Government Act 1988 (Defined Activities) (Exemptions) (Police Authorities) Order 1995
3304................Local Authorities (Expenditure Powers) Order 1995

3316 (L. 20)...Rules of the Supreme Court (Amendment No. 3) 1995
3320................Income Support (General) Amendment Regulations 1995
3321................Education (Mandatory Awards) Regulations 1995
3322................Non-Domestic Rating (Chargeable Amounts) (Amendment No. 3) Regulations 1995
3323................Bristol Development Corporation (Dissolution) Order 1995
3325................Olympics Association Right (Infringement Proceedings) Regulations 1995
3326 (C. 77) (S. 246) Local Government etc. (Scotland) Act 1994 (Commencement No. 6 and Saving) Order 1995
3328 (S. 245).Roads (Transitional Powers) (Scotland) Amendment Order 1995
3329................Sole (Specified Sea Areas) (Prohibition of Fishing) Order 1995
3330 (C. 78)...Disability Discrimination Act 1995 (Commencement No. 1) Order 1995
3336................Town and Country Planning (General Development Procedure) (Welsh Forms) Order 1995
3340 (C. 79)...Home Energy Conservation Act 1995 (Commencement No. 2) (England) Order 1995
3342................Motor Vehicles (Designation of Approval Marks) (Amendment) Regulations 1995
3345 (S. 247).Act of Sederunt (Reciprocal Enforcement of Maintenance Orders) (United States of America) 1995

CURRENT LAW STATUTES

NUMERICAL TABLE OF STATUTORY INSTRUMENTS 1996

This table details in numerical order Statutory Instruments released in 1996. The table is up to date to **March 11, 1996**. For brief digests of Statutory Instruments see the Current Law Monthly Digest.

1................Insurance Companies (Pensions Business) (Transitional Provisions) (Amendment) Regulations 1996
2................Sea Fishing (Enforcement of Community Control Measures) (Amendment) Order 1996
5................Occupational Pension Schemes (Deficiency on Winding Up etc.) Amendment Regulations 1996
11................National Disability Council Regulations 1996
15................Weymouth Harbour Revision Order 1996
16................Road Vehicles (Construction and Use) (Amendment) Regulations 1996
21................Friendly Societies (Gilt-Edged Securities) (Periodic Accounting for Tax on Interest) Regulations 1996
22................Civil Aviation (Canadian Navigation Services) (Third Amendment) Regulations 1996
24................Town and Country Planning (Costs of Inquiries etc.) (Standard Daily Amount) Regulations 1996
25................Plant Health (Great Britain) (Amendment) Order 1996
26................Plant Health (Licence Fees) (England and Wales) Regulations 1996
27................Hill Livestock (Compensatory Allowances) (Amendment) Regulations 1996
28................Sheep and Goats (Records, Identification and Movement) Order 1996
29................Food Protection (Emergency Prohibitions) (Radioactivity in Sheep) (Wales) (Partial Revocation) Order 1996
30................Social Security (Persons from Abroad) Miscellaneous Amendments Regulations 1996
31................Food Protection (Emergency Prohibitions) (Radioactivity in Sheep) Partial Revocation Order 1996
32 (S. 1).....Prisons and Young Offenders Institutions (Scotland) Amendment Rules 1996
33................National Blood Authority (Transfer of Trust Property) Order 1996
34................National Blood Authority (Transfer of Trust Property) (No. 2) Order 1996
35................King's Mill Centre for Health Care Services National Health Trust (Transfer of Trust Property) Order 1996
43................Local Government Changes for England (Valuation and Community Charge Tribunals) Regulations 1996
48................Sheep Annual Premium and Suckler Cow Premium Quotas (Re-assessment of Eligibility) Regulations 1996
49................Sheep Annual Premium (Amendment) Regulations 1996
52................Judicial Pensions (Additional Voluntary Contributions) (Amendment) Regulations 1996
53................Kent County Council (Wainscott Northern Bypass) Motorway Scheme 1992 Confirmation Instrument 1996
54................Taxes (Interest Rate) (Amendment) Regulations 1996
56................Local Government Reorganisation (Wales) (Council Tax Reduction Scheme) Order 1996

57 (S. 2).....Upper Spey and Associated Waters Protection (Renewal) Order 1993 Variation Order 1996
58 (S. 3).....River Tay Catchment Area Protection (Renewal) Order 1993 Variation Order 1996
60................East of Abercynon–East of Dowlais Trunk Road (A4060) (Improvement of Mountain Hare to Dowlais Top) Order 1996
61................River Teign Mussel Fishery (Variation) (Oysters) Order 1996
62................Food Protection (Emergency Prohibitions) (Radioactivity in Sheep) (England) (Partial Revocation) Order 1996
63................A30 Trunk Road (Hounslow and Hillingdon) Red Route (Clearway) Traffic Order 1996
64................A41 Trunk Road (Barnet) Red Route (Prescribed Route) Experimental Traffic Order 1996
68................Civil Courts (Amendment) Order 1996
71................Leeds City Council (Leeds Inner Ring Road Stages 6 and 7 (A61) to M1 Motorway (Junction 46) Connecting Road) Scheme 1994 Confirmation Instrument 1996
72................Leeds City Council (M1 Motorway Junction 46 Slip Road Connecting Road) Scheme 1992 Confirmation Instrument 1996
73................Leeds City Council (Hunslet Viaduct) Scheme 1992 Confirmation Instrument 1996
74................City of Stoke-on-Trent (Lichfield Street Canal Bridge) Scheme, 1995 Confirmation Instrument 1996
75................Merchant Shipping (Distress Signals and Prevention of Collisions) Regulations 1996
76................Civil Aviation Act (Investigation of Accidents) Regulations 1996
88................Local Government Reorganisation (Wales) (Finance) Order 1996
90................London Ambulance Service National Health Service Trust (Establishment) Order 1996
91................Sussex Ambulance Service National Health Service Trust (Transfer of Trust Property) Order 1996
92................Hull and Holderness Community Health National Health Service Trust (Transfer of Trust Property) Order 1996
94 (C.I.) (S. 4) Land Registers (Scotland) Act 1995 (Commencement) Order 1996
95 (S. 5).....Non-domestic Rate (Scotland) Order 1996
97................Offshore Installations (Safety Zones) Order 1996
98................A1 Trunk Road (Haringey) Red Route Traffic Order 1993 Experimental Variation Order 1996
99................A1 Trunk Road (Islington) Red Route Traffic Order 1993 Experimental Variation No. 3 Order 1996
101................Industrial Training Levy (Construction Board) Order 1996
102................Industrial Training Levy (Engineering Construction Board) Order 1996
103 (S. 6).....Non-Domestic Rates (Levying) (Scotland) Regulations 1996
106................Tyne Riverside Enterprise Zones (North Tyneside) (Designation) (No. 1) Order 1996
107................Vehicle Excise Duty (Immobilisation, Removal and Disposal of Vehicles) Regulations 1996
111................Education (Grant Maintained Special Schools) (Amendment) Regulations 1996
115 (S. 7).....Housing Revenue Account General Fund Contribution Limits (Scotland) Order 1996
120 (S. 8).....Glasgow School of Art (Scotland) Order of Council 1996

124................North Staffordshire Combined Healthcare National Health Service Trust (Transfer of Trust Property) Order 1996
125 (C. 2) (S. 9) Civil Evidence (Family Mediation) (Scotland) Act 1995 (Commencement and Transitional Provision) Order 1996
127................Worthing and Southlands Hospitals National Health Service Trust (Transfer of Trust Property) Order 1996
131................Goods Vehicles (Authorisation of International Journeys) (Fees) Regulations 1996
137 (S. 10)...Valuation Appeal Panels and Committees (Scotland) Regulations 1996
138................Local Government Act 1988 (Defined Activities) (Exemption) (Royal Borough of Kingston-upon-Thames) Order 1996
139 (S. 11)...Scottish Environment Protection Agency (Transfer Date) Order 1996
140 (S. 12)...Act of Sederunt (Civil Evidence (Family Mediation)) 1996
141 (S. 13)...Coast Protection (Notices) (Scotland) Amendment Regulations 1996
142................Tameside (Ashton Northern By-pass Stage 1 Ashton-Under-Lyne) (Special Roads) Scheme 1994 Confirmation Instrument 1996
146................Health Authorities (Wales) Establishment Order 1996
147................Merchant Shipping (Delegation of Type Approval) Regulations 1996
148................Gateshead Hospitals National Health Service Trust (Transfer of Trust Property) Order 1996
149................Gateshead Healthcare National Health Service Trust (Transfer of Trust Property) Order 1996
154................Local Government Act 1988 (Competition) (Housing Management) (Rossendale) Regulations 1996
156................National Savings Stock Register (Amendment) Regulations 1996
158................County Council of Norfolk (Reconstruction of Acle Wey Bridge) Scheme 1995 Confirmation Instrument 1996
159................County Council of Norfolk (Reconstruction of Acle Wey Bridge—Temporary Bridge) Scheme 1995 Confirmation Instrument 1996
160................Sea Fish Industry Authority (Levy) Regulations 1995 Confirmation Order 1996
161................Mortgage Indemnities (Recognised Bodies) Order 1996
162................Housing (Right to Buy) (Priority of Charges) Order 1996
163................Road Vehicles (Construction and Use) (Amendment) (No. 2) Regulations 1996
164................Air Passenger Duty (Prescribed Rates of Interest) (Amendment) Order 1996
165................Value Added Tax Act 1994 (Interest on Tax) (Prescribed Rate) Order 1996
166................Insurance Premium Tax (Prescribed Rates of Interest) (Amendment) Order 1996
167................Public Services Vehicles (Carrying Capacity) (Amendment) Regulations 1996
175................Local Authorities (Alteration of Requisite Calculations) Regulations 1996
176................Local Government Changes for England (Council Tax) (Transitional Reduction) Regulations 1996
177 (S. 14)...National Health Service (General Dental Services) (Scotland) Regulations 1996

178................Contracting Out (Administration of the Teachers' Superannuation Scheme) Order 1996
179................Local Government (Wales) (Alternative Community Names) (Prescribed Steps) Regulations 1996
180................Charities (Exception from Registration) Regulations 1996
182................Social Security (Adjudication) and Child Support Amendment Regulations 1996
183................Local Government Reorganisation (Wales) (Charities) Order 1996
184................Housing (Change of Landlord) (Payment of Disposal Cost by Instalments) (Amendment) Regulations 1996
185................Local Government Pension Scheme (Appropriation Pension Fund) Regulations 1996
186 (C. 3).....Environment Act 1995 (Commencement No. 5) Order 1996
187................Land Registration Fees Order 1996
189................Companies Act 1985 (Miscellaneous Accounting Amendments) Regulations 1996
190................Copyright (Certification of Licensing Scheme for Educational Recording of Broadcasts) (Open University Educational Enterprises Limited) (Amendment) Order 1996
191................Copyright (Certification of Licensing Scheme for Educational Recording of Broadcasts and Cable Programmes) (Educational Recording Agency Limited) (Amendment) Order 1996
192................Equipment and Protective Systems Intended for Use in Potentially Explosive Atmospheres Regulations 1996
193................Social Security (Back to Work Bonus) Regulations 1996
194................Housing Benefit, Supply of Information and Council Tax Benefit (Amendment) Regulations 1996
195................Employer's Contributions Re-imbursement Regulations 1996
197................Newlyn Pier and Harbour (Revision of Constitution of Commissioners) Order 1996
201................A38 Trunk Road (A3064 St Budeaux Bypass Slip Roads) (Trunking) Order 1996
205................Education (Grant) (Henrietta Barnett School) (Amendment) Regulations 1996
206................Income Support (General) (Jobseeker's Allowance Consequential Amendments) Regulations 1996
207................Jobseeker's Allowance Regulations 1996
208................Local Government Act 1988 (Defined Activities) (Exemption) (London Borough of Hillingdon Council) Order 1996
210................Value Added Tax (Amendment) Regulations 1996
211................Motor Vehicles (Driving Licences) (Amendment) Regulations 1996
212................Motor Vehicles (Driving Licences) (Large Goods and Passenger Carrying Vehicles) (Amendment) Regulations 1996
218 (C. 4).....Gas Act 1995 (Appointed Day and Commencement) Order 1996
219................Gas Act 1995 (Transitional Provisions and Savings) (No. 1) Order 1996
211 (S. 15)...Police (Promotion) (Scotland) Regulations 1996
223................Income Tax (Building Societies) (Dividends and Interest) (Amendment) Regulations 1996
232................Central Manchester Development Corporation (Planning Functions) Order 1996
233................Central Manchester Development Corporation (Transfer of Property, Rights and Liabilities) Order 1996

234................Environment Agency (Transfer Date) Order 1996
235................Education (Grants for Education Support and Training: Nursery Education) (England) Regulations 1996
236 (S. 16)...Act of Sederunt (Fees of Solicitors in the Sheriff Court) (Amendment) 1996
237 (S. 17)...Act of Sederunt (Rules of the Court of Session Amendment No. 1) (Fees of Solicitors) 1996
238 (S. 18)...Act of Sederunt (Copyright, Designs and Patents) (Amendment) 1996
239................Community Drivers' Hours (Passenger and Goods Vehicles) (Temporary Exception) Regulations 1996
240................Drivers' Hours (Passenger and Goods Vehicles) (Exemption) Regulations 1996
243................Child Support Commissioners (Procedure) (Amendment) Regulations 1996
244................Carriage by Air (Sterling Equivalent) Order 1996
247................Sea Fishing (Enforcement of Community Quota Measures) Order 1996
248................Fishing Boats (European Economic Community) Designation (Variation) Order 1996
249................Hinckley College (Dissolution) Order 1996
251................National Health Service (Clinical Negligence Scheme) Regulations 1996
252................Gas Act 1995 (Consequential Modifications of Subordinate Legislation) Order 1996
253................Co-operation of Insolvency Courts (Designation of Relevant Countries) Order 1996
255................Bridgend and District National Health Service Trust (Dissolution) Order 1996
256................Glan Hafren National Health Service Trust (Dissolution) Order 1996
257................Bridgend and District National Health Service Trust (Establishment) Order 1996
258................Glan Hafren National Health Service Trust (Establishment) Order 1996
259................North Glamorgan National Health Service Trust (Establishment) Order 1996
262................Partnerships (Unrestricted Size) No. 11 Regulations 1996
263................Charter Trustees Regulations 1996
264................A316 Trunk Road (Richmond) (No. 2) Red Route Experimental Traffic Order 1996
265................Local Government Act 1988 (Defined Activities) (Specified Periods) (Wales) Regulations 1996
266................European Communities (Designation) Order 1996
267................European Communities (Definition of Treaties) (Statute of the European Schools) Order 1996
268................Bosnia and Herzegovina (High Representative) Order 1996
269................Child Abduction and Custody (Parties to Conventions) (Amendment) Order 1996
270................International Sea Bed Authority (Immunities and Privileges) Order 1996
271 (C. 5).....Medical (Professional Performance) Act 1995 (Commencement No. 1) Order 1996
272................International Tribunal for the Law of the Sea (Immunities and Privileges) Order 1996

273................Transfer of Functions (Registration and Statistics) Order 1996
274 (NI. 1)...Education (Northern Ireland) Order 1996
275 (NI. 2)...Gas (Northern Ireland) Order 1996
276................Crown Office (Forms and Proclamations Rules) (Amendment) Order 1996
277 (NI. 3)...County Courts (Amendment) (Northern Ireland) Order 1996
278................Criminal Justice Act 1988 (Designated Countries and Territories) (Amendment) Order 1996
279................Extradition (Designated Commonwealth Countries) Order 1991 (Amendment) Order 1996
280................Merchant Shipping (Categorisation of Registries of Overseas Territories) (Gibraltar) Order 1996
281................Merchant Shipping (Gibraltar Colours) Order 1996
282................Merchant Shipping (Prevention of Pollution) (Law of the Sea Convention) Order 1996
283................Combined Probation Areas (Shropshire) Order 1996
284................Combined Probation Areas (Gwent and Mid Glamorgan) Order 1996
285................A1 Trunk Road (Barnet) (50 mph Speed Limit) Order 1996
293 (S. 19)...Fossil Fuel Levy (Scotland) Regulations 1996
294................Mental Health (After-care under Supervision) Regulations 1996
295................Mental Health (Patients in the Community) (Transfers from Scotland) Regulations 1996
306 (S. 20)...Educational Endowments (Fife Region) Transfer Scheme Order 1996
307 (S. 21)...Educational Endowments (Highlands Region) Transfer Scheme Order 1996
308 (S. 22)...Education Endowments (Borders Region) Transfer Scheme Order 1996
311................Non-Domestic Rating (Demand Notices) (Wales) (Amendment) Regulations 1996
312................Local Government Changes for England (Property Transfer and Transitional Payments) (Amendment) Regulations 1996
313................Transfer of Functions (Foreign Service Allowance) Order 1996
314................Mental Health Review Tribunal (Amendment) Rules 1996
315................Companies (Revision of Defective Accounts and Report) (Amendment) Regulations 1996
316................Wireless Telegraphy (Cordless Telephone Apparatus) (Exemption) Regulations 1996
323 (C. 6) (S. 23) Local Government etc. (Scotland) Act 1994 (Commencement No. 7 and Savings) Order 1996
324 (S. 24)...West Glasgow Hospitals University National Health Service Trust (Establishment) (Amendment) Order 1996
326 (S. 26)...Domestic Sewerage Charges (Reduction) (Scotland) Regulations 1996
330................Local Government Changes for England (Miscellaneous Provision) Regulations 1996
333................Local Government Changes for England (Council Tax) (Transitional Reduction) (Amendment) Regulations 1996
334................Education (Grants for Education Support and Training) (Wales) Regulations 1996
336................Potato Marketing Scheme (Commencement of Revocation Period) Order 1996

337................Agricultural Holdings (Fee) Regulations 1996
341................Health and Safety (Safety Signs and Signals) Regulations 1996
342................Local Authorities (Goods and Services) (Public Bodies) (Trunk Roads) Order 1996
344................Welsh Church Act Funds (Designation and Specification) Order 1996
345................Deregulation (Fair Trading Act 1973) (Amendment) (Merger Reference Time Limits) Order 1996
346................Deregulation (Restrictive Trade Practices Act 1976) (Amendment) (Variation of Exempt Agreements) Order 1996
347................Deregulation (Restrictive Trade Practices Act 1976) (Amendment) (Time Limits) Order 1996
349................Restrictive Trade Practices (Non-notifiable Agreements) (E.C. Block Exemptions) Order 1996
350................National Health Service Trusts (Originating Capital Debt) Order 1996
351................North Durham Acute Hospitals (Transfer of Trust Property) Order 1996
352................Community Health Care: North Durham National Health Service Trust (Transfer of Trust Property) Order 1996
353................Education (Grants for Nursery Education) (England) Regulations 1996
357................Trunk Road (A4) (Great West Road, Hounslow) (Restriction of Traffic) Order 1984 (Variation) Order 1996
360................Education (School Premises) Regulations 1996
372................Redundancy Payments (Local Government) (Modification) (Amendment) Order 1996
374................Animals, Meat and Meat Products (Examination for Residues and Maximum Residue Limits) (Amendment) Regulations 1996
375................Human Fertilisation and Embryology (Statutory Storage Period for Embryos) Regulations 1996
378................East Riding of Yorkshire District Council (Staff Transfer) Order 1996
379................Wireless Telegraphy (Television Licence Fees) (Amendment) Regulations 1996
380................Coventry Healthcare National Health Service Trust (Transfer of Trust Property) Order 1996
383................South Tyneside Health Care National Health Service Trust (Transfer of Trust Property) Order 1996
384................North Lincolnshire District Council (Staff Transfer) Order 1996
386................North East Lincolnshire District Council (Staff Transfer) Order 1996
387................South Gloucestershire District Council (Staff Transfer) Order 1996
388................North Yorkshire (District of York) (Staff Transfer) Order 1996
389................National Health Service (Dental Charges) Amendment Regulations 1996
391................National Assistance (Sums for Personal Requirements) Regulations 1996
395................Education (Financial Delegation to Schools) (Mandatory Exceptions) (Revocation and Amendment) Regulations 1996

396 (C. 7).....Local Government (Wales) Act 1994 (Commencement No.7) Order 1996
397................Humberside (Staff Transfer) Order 1996
398................Cleveland (Staff Transfer) Order 1996
400................Avon (Staff Transfer) Order 1996
401................University College London Hospitals National Health Service Trust (Establishment) Order 1996
408................North Lincolnshire and East Riding of Yorkshire District Councils (Staff Transfer) Order 1996
410................National Health Service (Travelling Expenses and Remission of Charges) Amendment Regulations 1996
422................Electricity and Pipe-line Works (Assessment of Environmental Effects) (Amendment) Regulations 1996
423................East Glamorgan National Health Service Trust (Transfer of Trust Property) Order 1996
424................Llandough Hospital and Community National Health Service Trust (Transfer of Trust Property) Order 1996
425................Social Security (Industrial Injuries and Diseases) (Miscellaneous Amendments) Regulations 1996
428................Noise Insulation (Railways and Other Guided Transport Systems) Regulations 1996
433................National Health Service (Appointment of Consultants) (Wales) Continuation and Transitional Provisions Order 1996
438................Sex Discrimination and Equal Pay (Miscellaneous Amendments) Regulations 1996
443................A57 Trunk Road (Rotherham/Sheffield Boundary to Swallownest Roundabout) (Detrunking) Order 1996
446................Local Government Changes for England (Miscellaneous Provision) Order 1996
455................Local Government Changes for England (Staff) (Amendment) Regulations 1996
456................Local Government (Compensation for Redundancy) (Amendment) Regulations 1996
462................Income-related Benefits Schemes (Miscellaneous Amendments) Regulations 1996
468................Lotteries (Gaming Board Fees) Order 1996
487 (C. 8).....Offshore Safety Act 1992 (Commencement No. 2) Order 1996
504................Council Tax and Non-Domestic Rating (Demand Notices) (England) Amendment Regulations 1996

ALPHABETICAL TABLE OF STATUTES

This is an alphabetical table of statutes from 1700–1995. It comprises a listing of Acts printed in the edition of the Record Commissioners known as Statutes of the Realm so far as it extends (1713), the Acts printed in Ruffhead's Edition so far as it extends (1785) and thereafter all Acts printed by the King's or Queen's Printer as Public Acts or (since 1797) Public General Acts. It should be noted that from 1797 Public Acts were divided into two series, Public General and Public Local and Personal Acts, prior to that date Acts which might now be classified as local were included in the definition Public Acts. Such Acts are therefore included in this list. For 1996 statutes see the most recent table in the Contents section of the Service File.

Abandonment of Animals Act 1960 (c.43)
Abandonment of Railways Act 1850 (c.83)
Abandonment of Railways Act 1869 (c.114)
Aberbrothock Beer Duties Act 1737 (c.4)
Aberbrothock Beer Duties Act 1763 (c.28)
Aberbrothock Beer Duties Act 1787 (c.46)
Aberdare Canal Act 1793 (c.95)
Aberdeen Beer Duties Act 1730 (c.13)
Aberdeen Commissary Court Records Act 1721 (c.28)
Aberdeen Harbour Act 1772 (c.29)
Aberdeen Harbour Act 1795 (c.41)
Aberdeen Harbour Act 1796 (c.68)
Aberdeen: Harbour Improvement Act 1797 (c.101)
Aberdeen Improvements Act 1795 (c.76)
Aberdeen Records Act 1722 (c.25)
Aberdeen Roads Act 1795 (c.161)
Abergavenny: Improvement Act 1794 (c.106)
Abergele and Rhydlan: Drainage Act 1794 (c.110)
Aberystwyth Harbour Act 1780 (c.26)
Abingdon: Improvement Act 1794 (c.89)
Abingdon to Swinford Roads Act 1768 (c.61)
Abingdon to Trowbridge Canal Act 1795 (c.52)
Abnormal Importations (Customs Duties) Act 1931 (c.1)
Abolition of Domestic Rates Etc. (Scotland) Act 1987 (c.47)
Abolition of Offices in Courts of Law Act 1845 (c.78)
Abolition of Slave Trade Act 1807 (c.36)
Abolition of Slavery Act 1836 (c.5)
Abolition of Slavery Act 1836 (c.16)
Abolition of Slavery Act 1836 (c.82)
Abolition of Slavery Act 1837 (c.3)
Abolition of Slavery Act 1838 (c.19)
Abolition of Slavery Act 1841 (c.18)
Abortion Act 1967 (c.87)
Absconding Debtors Act 1870 (c.76)
Access to Health Records Act 1990 (c.23)
Access to Medical Reports Act 1988 (c.28)
Access to Mountains Act 1939 (c.30)
Access to Neighbouring Land Act 1992 (c.23)
Access to Personal Files Act 1987 (c.37)
Accession Declaration Act 1910 (c.29)
Accessories and Abettors Act 1861 (c.94)
Accommodation Agencies Act 1953 (c.23)
Account of Civil List Revenues Act 1815 (c.15)
Accountant General in Chancery Act 1804 (c.82)
Accountant General of Court of Chancery Act 1813 (c.14)
Accounting for Certain Debentures Act 1706 (c.33)
Accounts, etc., of Barrack Master General Act 1807 (c.13)
Accounts of Barrack Office Act 1808 (c.89)
Accounts of Colonial Revenues Act 1814 (c.184)
Accounts of Expenditure in France Act 1814 (c.98)
Accounts of Expenditure in West Indies Act 1808 (c.91)
Accounts of Paymaster General Act 1808 (c.49)
Accumulations Act 1800 (c.98)
Accumulations Act 1892 (c.58)
Achurch Parish Church 1778 (c.9)
Acknowledgement of Deeds by Married Women Act 1854 (c.75)
Acknowledgement of Deeds by Married Women (Ireland) Act 1878 (c.23)
Acquisition of Land Act 1981 (c.67)
Acquisition of Land (Assessment of Compensation) Act 1919 (c.57)
Acquisition of Land (Assessment of Compensation) (Scotland) Act 1931 (c.11)
Acquisition of Land (Authorisation Procedure) Act 1946 (c.49)
Acquisition of Land (Authorisation Procedure) (Scotland) Act 1947 (c.42)
Act of Marriage 1929 (c.36)
Act of Settlement 1700 (c.2)
Act of Uniformity 1662 (c.4)
Act of Uniformity Amendment Act 1872 (c.35)
Actions Against Certain Spiritual Persons Act 1803 (c.34)
Actions Against Spiritual Persons Act 1813 (c.6)
Actions, etc., for Buying Oak Bark, etc. Act 1806 (c.152)
Actions for Gaming Act 1844 (c.3)
Actions for Gaming Act 1844 (c.58)
Activity Centres (Young Persons' Safety) Act 1995 (c.15)

Acts of Common Council, London Act 1745 (c.8)
Acts of Parliament (Commencement) Act 1793 (c.13)
Acts of Parliament (Expiration) 1808 (c.106)
Acts of Parliament (Mistaken References) Act 1837 (c.60)
Acts of Parliament Numbering and Citation Act 1962 (c.34)
Adam Buildings Act 1772 (c.75)
Aden, Perim and Kuria Muria Islands Act 1967 (c.71)
Addenbrooke's Hospital, Cambridge Act 1767 (c.99)
Adderbury and Oxford Road Act 1797 (c.170)
Addingham to Black Lane End Road Act 1781 (c.99)
Additional Income Tax Act 1884 (c.1)
Additional Taxes Act 1795 (c.14)
Admeasurement of Coals Act 1780 (c.34)
Administration Act 1868 (c.90)
Administration of Estates Act 1798 (c.87)
Administration of Estates Act 1869 (c.46)
Administration of Estates Act 1925 (c.23)
Administration of Estates Act 1971 (c.25)
Administration of Estates (Probate) Act 1800 (c.72)
Administration of Estates (Small Payments) Act 1965 (c.32)
Administration of Intestates' Estates Act 1856 (c.94)
Administration of Justice Act 1705 (c.3)
Administration of Justice Act 1813 (c.24)
Administration of Justice Act 1920 (c.81)
Administration of Justice Act 1925 (c.28)
Administration of Justice Act 1928 (c.26)
Administration of Justice Act 1932 (c.55)
Administration of Justice Act 1956 (c.46)
Administration of Justice Act 1960 (c.65)
Administration of Justice Act 1964 (c.42)
Administration of Justice Act 1965 (c.2)
Administration of Justice Act 1968 (c.5)
Administration of Justice Act 1969 (c.58)
Administration of Justice Act 1970 (c.31)
Administration of Justice Act 1973 (c.15)
Administration of Justice Act 1977 (c.38)
Administration of Justice Act 1982 (c.53)
Administration of Justice Act 1985 (c.61)
Administration of Justice (Appeals) Act 1934 (c.40)
Administration of Justice (Emergency Provisions) Act 1939 (c.78)
Administration of Justice (Emergency Provisions) Act 1939 (c.105)
Administration of Justice (Emergency Provisions) (Scotland) Act 1939 (c.79)
Administration of Justice (Emergency Provisions) (Scotland) Act 1979 (c.19)
Administration of Justice in Certain Boroughs Act 1836 (c.105)
Administration of Justice (Judges and Pensions) Act 1960 (c.3)
Administration of Justice (Miscellaneous Provisions) Act 1933 (c.36)
Administration of Justice (Miscellaneous Provisions) Act 1938 (c.63)
Administration of Justice, New South Wales, etc. Act 1838 (c.50)
Administration of Justice (Pensions) Act 1950 (c.11)
Administration of Justice (Scotland) Act 1809 (c.119)
Administration of Justice (Scotland) Act 1933 (c.41)
Administration of Justice (Scotland) Act 1948 (c.10)
Administration of Justice (Scotland) Act 1972 (c.59)
Administration of Justice, West Indies Act 1836 (c.17)
Admiralty and Prize Courts Act 1810 (c.118)
Admiralty and War Office Regulation Act 1878 (c.53)
Admiralty Court Act 1840 (c.65)
Admiralty Court Act 1861 (c.10)
Admiralty, etc. Acts Repeal Act 1865 (c.112)
Admiralty, etc., Courts, (Scotland) Act 1786 (c.47)
Admiralty Jurisdiction (Indian) Act 1860 (c.88)
Admiralty Lands Act 1843 (c.58)
Admiralty Lands and Works Act 1864 (c.57)
Admiralty Offences Act 1826 (c.38)
Admiralty Offences Act 1844 (c.2)
Admiralty Offences (Colonial) Act 1849 (c.96)
Admiralty Offences (Colonial) Act 1860 (c.122)
Admiralty Pensions Act 1921 (c.39)
Admiralty Powers etc. Act 1865 (c.124)
Admiralty Suits Act 1868 (c.78)
Admission of Vassals (Scotland) Act 1751 (c.20)
Adoption Act 1950 (c.26)
Adoption Act 1958 (c.5)
Adoption Act 1960 (c.59)
Adoption Act 1964 (c.57)
Adoption Act 1968 (c.53)
Adoption Act 1976 (c.36)
Adoption of Children Act 1926 (c.29)
Adoption of Children Act 1949 (c.98)
Adoption of Children (Regulation) Act 1939 (c.27)
Adoption of Children (Scotland) Act 1930 (c.37)
Adoption of Children (Workmen's Compensation) Act 1934 (c.34)
Adoption (Scotland) Act 1978 (c.28)
Adulteration of Coffee Act 1718 (c.11)
Adulteration of Food and Drugs Act 1872 (c.74)
Adulteration of Hops Act 1733 (c.19)
Adulteration of Seeds Act 1869 (c.112)
Adulteration of Seeds Act 1878 (c.17)
Adulteration of Tea Act 1730 (c.14)
Adulteration of Tea Act 1776 (c.29)
Adulteration of Tea and Coffee Act 1724 (c.30)

Advance by Bank of England Act 1781 (c.60)
Advance by Bank of England Act 1816 (c.7)
Advance by Bank of England Act 1816 (c.14)
Advance from Bank of England Act 1808 (c.3)
Advance of Money to Foreign States Act 1729 (c.5)
Advance of Unclaimed Dividends, etc. Act 1808 (c.4)
Advance of Unclaimed Dividends, etc. Act 1816 (c.97)
Advance Petroleum Revenue Tax Act 1986 (c.68)
Advance to Boyed, Benfield and Co. Act 1805 (c.78)
Advances by Bank of Ireland Act 1811 (c.35)
Advances for Public Works Act 1837 (c.51)
Advances for Public Works Act 1838 (c.88)
Advances for Public Works Act 1840 (c.10)
Advances for Public Works Act 1842 (c.9)
Advances for Public Works Act 1861 (c.80)
Advances for Public Works Act 1862 (c.30)
Advances for Railways (Ireland) Act 1847 (c.73)
Advances to County of Mayo Acts 1854 (c.110)
Advertisements (Hire Purchase) Act 1957 (c.41)
Advertisements (Hire-Purchase) Act 1967 (c.42)
Advertisements Regulation Act 1907 (c.27)
Advertisements Regulation Act 1925 (c.52)
Advertising Stations (Rating) Act 1889 (c.27)
Advowsons Act 1707 (c.18)
Aerial Navigation Act 1911 (c.4)
Aerial Navigation Act 1913 (c.22)
Affidavits in County of Durham Act 1763 (c.21)
Affidavits in County of Lancaster Act 1743 (c.7)
Affiliation Orders Act 1914 (c.6)
Affiliation Orders Act 1952 (c.41)
Affiliation Orders (Increase of Maximum Payment) Act 1918 (c.49)
Affiliation Proceedings Act 1957 (c.55)
Affiliation Proceedings (Amendment) Act 1972 (c.49)
Affirmation by Quakers Act 1701 (c.4)
Affirmations Act 1861 (c.66)
Affirmations by Quakers etc. Act 1859 (c.10)
Affirmations (Scotland) Act 1855 (c.25)
Affirmations (Scotland) Act 1865 (c.9)
African Company Act 1711 (c.34)
African Company Act 1750 (c.49)
African Company Act 1751 (c.40)
African Company Act 1783 (c.65)
African Slave Trade Act 1862 (c.40)
African Slave Trade Act 1862 (c.90)
African Slave Trade Treaty Act 1863 (c.34)
Age of Legal Capacity (Scotland) Act 1991 (c.50)
Age of Majority (Scotland) Act 1969 (c.39)
Age of Marriage Act 1929 (c.36)
Agent General for Volunteers, etc. Act 1812 (c.152)
Agent General for Volunteers, etc. Act 1815 (c.170)
Aggravated Vehicle-Taking Act 1992 (c.11)
Agricultural and Technical Instruction (Ireland) - Northern Irish Act 1899 (c.50)
Agricultural and Forestry Associations Act 1962 (c.29)
Agricultural and Forestry (Financial Provisions) Act 1991 (c.33)
Agricultural Children Act 1873 (c.67)
Agricultural Credits Act 1923 (c.34)
Agricultural Credits Act 1928 (c.43)
Agricultural Credits Act 1931 (c.35)
Agricultural Credits (Scotland) Act 1929 (c.13)
Agricultural Development Act 1939 (c.48)
Agricultural Development (Ploughing up of Land) Act 1946 (c.32)
Agricultural Gangs Act 1867 (c.130)
Agricultural Holdings Act 1900 (c.50)
Agricultural Holdings Act 1906 (c.56)
Agricultural Holdings Act 1908 (c.28)
Agricultural Holdings Act 1913 (c.21)
Agricultural Holdings Act 1914 (c.7)
Agricultural Holdings Act 1923 (c.9)
Agricultural Holdings Act 1948 (c.63)
Agricultural Holdings Act 1984 (c.41)
Agricultural Holdings Act 1986 (c.5)
Agricultural Holdings (Amendment) Act 1990 (c.15)
Agricultural Holdings (Amendment) (Scotland) Act 1983 (c.46)
Agricultural Holdings (England) Act 1875 (c.92)
Agricultural Holdings (England) Act (1875) Amendment Act 1876 (c.74)
Agricultural Holdings (England) Act 1883 (c.61)
Agricultural Holdings (Notices to Quit) Act 1977 (c.12)
Agricultural Holdings (Scotland) Act 1883 (c.62)
Agricultural Holdings (Scotland) Act 1889 (c.20)
Agricultural Holdings (Scotland) Act 1908 (c.64)
Agricultural Holdings (Scotland) Act 1923 (c.10)
Agricultural Holdings (Scotland) Act 1949 (c.75)
Agricultural Holdings (Scotland) Amendment Act 1910 (c.30)
Agricultural Improvement Grants Act 1959 (c.31)
Agricultural Land (Removal of Surface Soil) Act 1953 (c.10)
Agricultural Land Sales (Restriction of Notice to Quit) Act 1919 (c.63)
Agricultural Land (Utilisation) Act 1931 (c.41)
Agricultural Marketing Act 1931 (c.42)
Agricultural Marketing Act 1933 (c.31)
Agricultural Marketing Act 1949 (c.38)
Agricultural Marketing Act 1958 (c.47)

Agricultural Marketing Act 1983 (c.3)
Agricultural Marketing (No. 2) Act 1933 (c.1)
Agricultural (Miscellaneous Provisions) Act 1949 (c.37)
Agricultural (Miscellaneous Provisions) Act 1950 (c.17)
Agricultural Mortgage Corporation Act 1956 (c.38)
Agricultural Mortgage Corporation Act 1958 (c.2)
Agricultural Produce (Grading and Marking) Act 1928 (c.19)
Agricultural Produce (Grading and Marking) Amendment Act 1931 (c.40)
Agricultural Rates Act 1896 (c.16)
Agricultural Rates Act, 1896, etc., Continuance Act 1901 (c.13)
Agricultural Rates Act, 1896, etc., Continuance Act 1905 (c.8)
Agricultural Rates Act 1923 (c.39)
Agricultural Rates Act 1929 (c.26)
Agricultural Rates (Additional Grant) Continuance Act 1925 (c.10)
Agricultural Rates, Congested Districts, and Burgh Land Tax Relief (Scotland) 1896 (c.37)
Agricultural Research Act 1955 (c.28)
Agricultural Research etc. (Pensions) Act 1961 (c.9)
Agricultural Returns Act 1925 (c.39)
Agricultural Statistics Act 1979 (c.13)
Agricultural Tenancies Act 1995 (c.8)
Agricultural Training Board Act 1982 (c.9)
Agricultural Training Board Act 1985 (c.36)
Agricultural Training Board Act 1987 (c.29)
Agricultural Wages Act 1948 (c.47)
Agricultural Wages (Regulation) Act 1924 (c.37)
Agricultural Wages (Regulation) Act 1947 (c.15)
Agricultural Wages (Regulation) Amendment Act 1939 (c.17)
Agricultural Wages (Regulation) (Scotland) Act 1937 (c.53)
Agricultural Wages (Regulation) (Scotland) Act 1939 (c.27)
Agricultural Wages (Scotland) Act 1949 (c.30)
Agriculture Act 1920 (c.76)
Agriculture Act 1937 (c.70)
Agriculture Act 1947 (c.48)
Agriculture Act 1957 (c.57)
Agriculture Act 1958 (c.71)
Agriculture Act 1967 (c.22)
Agriculture Act 1970 (c.40)
Agriculture Act 1986 (c.49)
Agriculture Act 1993 (c.37)
Agriculture (Amendment) Act 1921 (c.17)
Agriculture (Amendment) Act 1923 (c.25)
Agriculture (Amendment) Act 1984 (c.20)
Agriculture and Horticulture Act 1964 (c.28)
Agriculture and Technical Instruction (Ireland) Act 1902 (c.3)
Agriculture and Technical Instruction (Ireland) (No. 2) Act 1902 (c.33)
Agriculture (Artificial Insemination) Act 1946 (c.29)
Agriculture (Calf Subsidies) Act 1952 (c.62)
Agriculture (Emergency Payments) Act 1947 (c.32)
Agriculture (Fertilisers) Act 1952 (c.15)
Agriculture (Improvement of Roads) Act 1955 (c.20)
Agriculture (Miscellaneous Provisions) Act 1940 (c.14)
Agriculture (Miscellaneous Provisions) Act 1941 (c.50)
Agriculture (Miscellaneous Provisions) Act 1943 (c.16)
Agriculture (Miscellaneous Provisions) Act 1944 (c.28)
Agriculture (Miscellaneous Provisions) Act 1949 (c.37)
Agriculture (Miscellaneous Provisions) Act 1950 (c.17)
Agriculture (Miscellaneous Provisions) Act 1954 (c.39)
Agriculture (Miscellaneous Provisions) Act 1963 (c.11)
Agriculture (Miscellaneous Provisions) Act 1968 (c.34)
Agriculture (Miscellaneous Provisions) Act 1972 (c.62)
Agriculture (Miscellaneous Provisions) Act 1976 (c.55)
Agriculture (Miscellaneous War Provisions) Act 1940 (c.14)
Agriculture (Miscellaneous War Provisions) (No.2) Act 1940 (c.50)
Agriculture Mortgage Corporation Act 1956 (c.38)
Agriculture (Ploughing Grants) Act 1952 (c.35)
Agriculture (Poisonous Substances) Act 1952 (c.60)
Agriculture (Safety, Health and Welfare Provisions) Act 1956 (c.49)
Agriculture (Scotland) Act 1948 (c.45)
Agriculture (Small Farmers) Act 1959 (c.12)
Agriculture (Spring Traps) (Scotland) Act 1969 (c.26)
Agriculture and Horticulture Act 1964 (c.28)
Aid to Government of France Act 1794 (c.9)
Aid to Russia, etc. Act 1813 (c.13)
AIDS Control Act 1987 (c.33)
Air Corporations Act 1949 (c.91)
Air Corporations Act 1960 (c.13)
Air Corporations Act 1962 (c.5)
Air Corporations Act 1966 (c.11)
Air Corporations Act 1967 (c.33)
Air Corporations Act 1968 (c.30)
Air Corporations Act 1969 (c.43)
Air Corporations Act 1971 (c.5)
Air Force Act 1955 (c.19)
Air Force (Constitution) Act 1917 (c.51)
Air Force Reserve Act 1950 (c.33)

Air Force Reserve (Pilots and Observers) Act 1934 (c.5)
Air Guns and Shot Guns, etc. Act 1962 (c.49)
Air Ministry (Heston and Kenley Aerodromes Extension) Act 1939 (c.59)
Air Ministry (Kenley Common Acquisition) Act 1922 (c.40)
Air Navigation Act 1919 (c.3)
Air Navigation Act 1920 (c.80)
Air Navigation Act 1936 (c.44)
Air Navigation Act 1947 (c.18)
Air Navigation (Financial Provisions) Act 1938 (c.33)
Air Raid Precaution (Postponement of Financial Investigations) Act 1941 (c.10)
Air Raid Precautions Act 1937 (c.6)
Air Transport (Subsidy Agreements) Act 1930 (c.30)
Air Travel Reserve Fund Act 1975 (c.36)
Aircraft and Shipbuilding Industries Act 1977 (c.3)
Aire and Calder, Navigation Act 1774 (c.96)
Airports Act 1986 (c.31)
Airport Authority Act 1965 (c.16)
Airports Authority Act 1972 (c.8)
Airports Authority Act 1975 (c.78)
Airways Corporations Act 1949 (c.57)
Alcoholic Liquor Duties Act 1979 (c.4)
Alderney Harbour (Transfer) Act 1874 (c.92)
Alderney (Transfer of Property etc.) Act 1923 (c.15)
Alford to Cowbridge Road Act 1784 (c.62)
Aldwork Bridge, Ure Act 1772 (c.87)
Alehouses Act 1753 (c.31)
Alehouses Act 1756 (c.12)
Alexander Wilson (Provost of Edinburgh) Act 1736 (c.34)
Alice Holt Forest Act 1812 (c.72)
Aliens Act 1746 (c.44)
Aliens Act 1793 (c.4)
Aliens Act 1794 (c.82)
Aliens Act 1795 (c.24)
Aliens Act 1796 (c.109)
Aliens Act 1797 (c.92)
Aliens Act 1798 (c.50)
Aliens Act 1798 (c.77)
Aliens Act 1800 (c.24)
Aliens Act 1802 (c.92)
Aliens Act 1803 (c.155)
Aliens Act 1814 (c.155)
Aliens Act 1815 (c.54)
Aliens Act 1816 (c.86)
Aliens Act 1844 (c.66)
Aliens Act 1847 (c.83)
Aliens Act 1848 (c.20)
Aliens Act 1905 (c.13)
Aliens' Employment Act 1955 (c.18)
Aliens Restriction Act 1914 (c.12)
Aliens Restriction (Amendment) Act 1919 (c.92)
Alkali Act 1863 (c.124)
Alkali Act 1874 (c.43)
Alkali Act Perpetuation Act 1868 (c.36)
Alkali, etc., Works Regulation Act 1881 (c.37)
Alkali, etc., Works Regulation Act 1892 (c.30)
Alkali, etc., Works Regulation Act 1906 (c.14)
Alkali, etc., Works Regulation (Scotland) Act 1951 (c.21)
All Saints' Church, Newcastle Act 1786 (c.117)
All Saints' Church, Southampton Act 1791 (c.71)
All Saints' Church, Southampton Act 1793 (c.101)
Allied Forces Act 1939 (c.51)
Allied Powers (Maritime Courts) Act 1941 (c.21)
Allied Powers (War Service) Act 1942 (c.29)
Alloa Beer Duties Act 1754 (c.35)
Alloa Harbour Act 1786 (c.13)
Allotments Act 1887 (c.48)
Allotments Act 1890 (c.65)
Allotments Act 1922 (c.51)
Allotments Act 1925 (c.61)
Allotments Act 1950 (c.31)
Allotments and Cottage Gardens Compensation for Crops Act 1887 (c.26)
Allotments Extension Act 1882 (c.80)
Allotments Rating Exemption Act 1891 (c.33)
Allotments (Scotland) Act 1892 (c.54)
Allotments (Scotland) Act 1922 (c.52)
Allotments (Scotland) Act 1926 (c.5)
Allotments (Scotland) Act 1950 (c.38)
Allowance for Mint Prosecutions Act 1772 (c.52)
Allowance of Duty to Meux & Co. Act 1815 (c.189)
Allowance to Brewers Act 1785 (c.73)
Allowance to Distillers (Scotland) Act 1790 (c.39)
Allowances to Foreign Officers Act 1815 (c.126)
Allowing Time for First Meetings Act 1757 (c.13)
Alteration of Terms in Scotland Act 1708 (c.15)
Altrincham and Warrington Roads Act 1796 (c.145)
Alvingham, Lincoln, Navigation Act 1763 (c.39)
Amendment of c.10 of this Session Act 1800 (c.19)
Amendment of cc.26, 28 of this Session Act 1808 (c.71)
Amendment of c.29 of this Session Act 1793 (c.51)
American and European Payments (Financial Provisions) Act 1949 (c.17)
American Colonies Act 1766 (c.12)
American Loan Act 1915 (c.81)
American Loyalists Act 1783 (c.80)
American Loyalists Act 1785 (c.76)
American Loyalists Act 1786 (c.68)
American Loyalists Act 1787 (c.39)
American Loyalists Act 1788 (c.44)
American Loyalists Act 1789 (c.62)

American Loyalists Act 1790 (c.34)
American Prizes Act 1813 (c.63)
American Rebellion Act 1774 (c.39)
American Rebellion Act 1774 (c.45)
American Rebellion Act 1778 (c.13)
American Treaty Commissioners Act 1803 (c.135)
Amlwch Harbour Act 1793 (c.125)
Anatomy Act 1832 (c.75)
Anatomy Act 1871 (c.16)
Anatomy Act 1984 (c.14)
Anchors and Chain Cables Act 1899 (c.23)
Ancient Monument Act 1931 (c.16)
Ancient Monuments and Archaeological Areas Act 1979 (c.46)
Ancient Monuments Consolidation and Amendment Act 1913 (c.32)
Ancient Monuments Protection Act 1882 (c.73)
Ancient Monuments Protection Act 1900 (c.34)
Ancient Monuments Protection Act 1910 (c.3)
Ancient Monuments Protection (Ireland) Act 1892 (c.46)
Andover Canal Act 1789 (c.72)
Anglesey: Drainage, etc. Act 1788 (c.71)
Anglesey: Drainage Act 1790 (c.59)
Anglesey Roads Act 1765 (c.56)
Anglo-French Convention Act 1904 (c.33)
Anglo-French Treaty (Defence of France) Act 1919 (c.34)
Anglo-German Agreement Act 1890 (c.32)
Anglo-Italian Treaty (East African Territories) Act 1925 (c.9)
Anglo-Persian Oil Company (Acquisition of Capital) Act 1914 (c.37)
Anglo-Persian Oil Company (Acquisition of Capital) (Amendment) Act 1919 (c.86)
Anglo-Persian Oil Company (Payment of Calls) Act 1922 (c.26)
Anglo-Portuguese Commercial Treaty Act 1914 (c.1)
Anglo-Portuguese Commercial Treaty Act 1916 (c.39)
Anglo-Turkish (Armaments Credit) Agreement 1938 (c.60)
Anglo-Venezuelan Treaty (Island of Patos) Act 1942 (c.17)
Anguilla Act 1971 (c.63)
Anguilla Act 1980 (c.67)
Animal Boarding Establishments Act 1963 (c.43)
Animal Health Act 1981 (c.22)
Animal Health and Welfare Act 1984 (c.40)
Animals Act 1948 (c.35)
Animals Act 1971 (c.22)
Animals (Anaesthetics) Act 1919 (c.54)
Animals (Cruel Poisons) Act 1962 (c.26)
Animals (Restriction of Importation) Act 1964 (c.61)
Animals (Scientific Procedures) Act 1986 (c.14)
Animals (Scotland) Act 1987 (c.9.)
Annoyance Jurors, Westminster Acts 1861 (c.78)
Annual Revision of Rateable Property (Ireland) Amendment Act 1860 (c.4)
Annual Turnpike Acts Continuance Act 1850 (c.79)
Annual Turnpike Acts Continuance Act 1851 (c.37)
Annual Turnpike Acts Continuance Act 1853 (c.135)
Annual Turnpike Acts Continuance Act 1854 (c.58)
Annual Turnpike Acts Continuance Act 1859 (c.51)
Annual Turnpike Acts Continuance Act 1860 (c.73)
Annual Turnpike Acts Continuance Act 1861 (c.64)
Annual Turnpike Acts Continuance Act 1862 (c.72)
Annual Turnpike Acts Continuance Act 1863 (c.94)
Annual Turnpike Acts Continuance Act 1864 (c.75)
Annual Turnpike Acts Continuance Act 1865 (c.107)
Annual Turnpike Acts Continuance Act 1866 (c.105)
Annual Turnpike Acts Continuance Act 1867 (c.121)
Annual Turnpike Acts Continuance Act 1867 (c.129)
Annual Turnpike Acts Continuance Act 1868 (c.99)
Annual Turnpike Acts Continuance Act 1869 (c.90)
Annual Turnpike Acts Continuance Act 1870 (c.73)
Annual Turnpike Acts Continuance Act 1871 (c.115)
Annual Turnpike Acts Continuance Act 1872 (c.85)
Annual Turnpike Acts Continuance Act 1873 (c.90)
Annual Turnpike Acts Continuance Act 1874 (c.95)
Annual Turnpike Acts Continuance Act 1876 (c.39)
Annual Turnpike Acts Continuance Act 1877 (c.64)
Annual Turnpike Acts Continuance Act 1878 (c.62)
Annual Turnpike Acts Continuance Act 1879 (c.46)
Annual Turnpike Acts Continuance Act 1880 (c.12)
Annual Turnpike Acts Continuance Act 1881 (c.31)
Annual Turnpike Acts Continuance Act 1882 (c.52)
Annual Turnpike Acts Continuance Act 1883 (c.21)
Annual Turnpike Acts Continuance Act 1884 (c.52)

Annual Turnpike Acts Continuance Act 1885 (c.37)
Annuities Act 1704 (c.2)
Annuities Act 1799 (c.29)
Annuities Act 1799 (c.30)
Annuities, etc. Act 1702 (c.14)
Annuities, etc. Act 1704 (c.14)
Annuities (Ireland) Act 1807 (c.21)
Annuities (Prince of Wales, etc.) Act 1863 (c.1)
Annuities to Branches of Royal Family Act 1807 (c.39)
Annuities to Duke and Princess Mary of Cambridge Act 1850 (c.77)
Annuities to Duke, etc., of York 1792 (c.13)
Annuities to Duke of Sussex etc. Act 1802 (c.48)
Annuities to Lady Abercromby, etc. Act 1801 (c.59)
Annuities to Princesses Act 1812 (c.57)
Annuities to Retired Judges (Scotland) Act 1814 (c.94)
Annuities to Royal Family Act 1806 (c.145)
Annuity, Duchess of Mecklenburgh Strelitz Act 1843 (c.25)
Annuity, Duke of Albany Act 1882 (c.5)
Annuity, Duke of Edinburgh Act 1866 (c.8)
Annuity, Duke of Marlborough; Pension Act 1706 (c.6)
Annuity, etc., to Duke of Wellington Act 1814 (c.161)
Annuity (Heirs of Sir T. Clarges) Act 1799 (c.84)
Annuity, Lady Mayo Act 1872 (c.56)
Annuity (Lady of Havelock) Act 1858 (c.2)
Annuity (Lord Amherst) Act 1803 (c.159)
Annuity (Lord and Lady Raglan) Act 1855 (c.64)
Annuity, Lord Exmouth Act 1814 (c.164)
Annuity, Lord Gough Act 1846 (c.32)
Annuity Lord Hardinge Act 1846 (c.31)
Annuity (Lord Napier) Act 1868 (c.91)
Annuity (Lord Rodney) Act 1793 (c.77)
Annuity (Penn's Descendants) Act 1790 (c.46)
Annuity, Princess Beatrice Act 1885 (c.24)
Annuity, Princess Helena Act 1866 (c.7)
Annuity, Princess Mary of Cambridge Act 1866 (c.48)
Annuity, Princess Royal Act 1857 (c.2)
Annuity (Sir H. Brand) Act 1884 (c.1)
Annuity Tax in Edinburgh and Montrose Act 1860 (c.50)
Annuity Tax in Edinburgh and Montrose, etc. Act 1870 (c.87)
Annuity to Admiral Duckworth Act 1806 (c.40)
Annuity to Admiral Saumanez Act 1803 (c.37)
Annuity to Brook Watson, Esq. Act 1786 (c.93)
Annuity to Brook Watson, Esq. Act 1788 (c.43)
Annuity to Dr. Willis Act 1790 (c.44)
Annuity to Duchess of Brunswick Wolfenbuttel Act 1808 (c.59)
Annuity to Duke and Duchess of Edinburgh Act 1873 (c.80)
Annuity to Duke of Atholl, etc. Act 1805 (c.123)
Annuity to Duke of Brunswick Act 1810 (c.37)
Annuity to Duke of Clarence Act 1791 (c.34)
Annuity to Duke of Connaught Act 1871 (c.64)
Annuity to Duke of Gloucester Act 1785 (c.53)
Annuity to Duke of St. Albans Act 1788 (c.41)
Annuity to Duke of Wellington, etc. Act 1810 (c.8)
Annuity to Duke of Wellington, etc. Act 1812 (c.37)
Annuity to Family of Lord Kilwarden Act 1804 (c.76)
Annuity to Family of Sir G. Carlton Act 1788 (c.42)
Annuity to Lady Elgin Act 1864 (c.31)
Annuity to Lady Maria Carlton Act 1786 (c.88)
Annuity to Lady Nelson Act 1806 (c.4)
Annuity to Lord Beresford, etc. Act 1814 (c.162)
Annuity to Lord Camperdown Act 1797 (c.22)
Annuity to Lord Collingwood, etc. Act 1806 (c.13)
Annuity to Lord Combermere, etc. Act 1814 (c.163)
Annuity to Lord Hill Act 1814 (c.165)
Annuity to Lord Hutchinson, etc. Act 1802 (c.113)
Annuity to Lord Keane, etc. Act 1841 (c.1)
Annuity to Lord Lynedoch Act 1814 (c.166)
Annuity to Lord Nelson, etc. Act 1798 (c.1)
Annuity to Lord Rodney Act 1783 (c.86)
Annuity to Lord Rodney Act 1806 (c.147)
Annuity to Lord St. Vincent Act 1797 (c.21)
Annuity to Lord St. Vincent Act 1806 (c.50)
Annuity to Lord Walsingham Act 1815 (c.18)
Annuity to Major-Gen. Sir J. Stuart Act 1807 (c.4)
Annuity to Prince Leopold Act 1874 (c.65)
Annuity to Prince of Wales, etc. Act 1803 (c.26)
Annuity to Princess Alice Act 1861 (c.15)
Annuity to Princess Louise Act 1871 (c.1)
Annuity to Princess of Wales Act 1814 (c.160)
Annuity to Right Hon. Charles Shaw Lefevre Act 1857 (c.9)
Annuity to Sir G.A. Elliott Act 1783 (c.85)
Annuity to Sir J. Marriott Act (c.58)
Annuity to Sir J. Skynner Act 1787 (c.12)
Annuity to Sir R. Strachan Act 1806 (c.5)
Annuity to Sir Sidney Smith Act 1801 (c.5)
Annuity to Sir W.F. Williams Act 1856 (c.30)
Annuity to Viscount Lake, etc. Act 1808 (c.13)
Anstruther Easter Beer Duties Act 1748 (c.10)
Anstruther Easter Beer Duties Act 1775 (c.48)
Anstruther Union Harbour Act 1860 (c.39)
Antarctic Act 1994 (c.15)
Antarctic Minerals Act 1989 (c.21)

Antarctic Treaty Act 1967 (c.65)
Anthrax Prevention Act 1919 (c.23)
Antigua and Barbuda Act 1859 (c.13)
Anwick: Inclosure Act 1791 (c.93)
"Anzac" (Restriction on Trade Use of Word) Act 1916 (c.51)
Apothecaries Act 1702 (c.5)
Apothecaries Act 1815 (c.194)
Apothecaries Act Amendment Act 1874 (c.34)
Appeal (Forma Pauperis) Act 1893 (c.22)
Appeal in Revenue Cases (Ireland) Act 1812 (c.78)
Appeals on Civil Bills, Dublin Act 1848 (c.34)
Appellate Jurisdiction Act 1876 (c.59)
Appellate Jurisdiction Act 1887 (c.70)
Appellate Jurisdiction Act 1908 (c.51)
Appellate Jurisdiction Act 1913 (c.21)
Appellate Jurisdiction Act 1929 (c.8)
Appellate Jurisdiction Act 1947 (c.11)
Application of Bounties on Linen, etc. Act 1812 (c.96)
Application of Highway Rates to Turnpikes Act 1841 (c.59)
Appointment Act 1834 (c.22)
Appointment of a Judge at Bombay Act 1864 (c.16)
Appointment of Judges in Vacation Act 1799 (c.113)
Appointment of Revising Barristers Act 1872 (c.84)
Appointment of Superintending Magistrates, etc. Act 1814 (c.131)
Appointment of Vice-Chancellor Act 1851 (c.4)
Appointments in Cathedral Churches Act 1839 (c.14)
Apportionment Act 1820 (c.108)
Apportionment Act 1834 (c.22)
Apportionment Act 1870 (c.35)
Appraisers Licences Act 1806 (c.43)
Apprehension of Certain Offenders Act 1853 (c.118)
Apprehension of Endorsed Warrants Act 1750 (c.55)
Apprehension of Housebreakers Act 1706 (c.31)
Apprehension of Offenders Act 1804 (c.92)
Apprehension of Offenders Act 1814 (c.186)
Apprehension of Offenders Act 1843 (c.34)
Apprentices Act 1814 (c.96)
Apprentices (Settlement) Act 1757 (c.11)
Apprenticeship Indentures Act 1801 (c.22)
Appropriation Act 1775 (c.12)
Appropriation Act 1775 (c.42)
Appropriation Act 1776 (c.47)
Appropriation Act 1776 (c.49)
Appropriation Act 1778 (c.54)
Appropriation Act 1779 (c.71)
Appropriation Act 1780 (c.62)
Appropriation Act 1781 (c.57)
Appropriation Act 1782 (c.67)
Appropriation Act 1783 (c.78)
Appropriation Act 1784 (c.44)
Appropriation Act 1786 (c.61)
Appropriation Act 1787 (c.33)
Appropriation Act 1788 (c.26)
Appropriation Act 1789 (c.61)
Appropriation Act 1790 (c.32)
Appropriation Act 1791 (c.41)
Appropriation Act 1792 (c.35)
Appropriation Act 1793 (c.72)
Appropriation Act 1794 (c.49)
Appropriation Act 1795 (c.120)
Appropriation Act 1796 (c.126)
Appropriation Act 1797 (c.144)
Appropriation Act 1798 (c.90)
Appropriation Act 1799 (c.114)
Appropriation Act 1800 (c.14)
Appropriation Act 1802 (c.120)
Appropriation Act 1803 (c.162)
Appropriation Act 1804 (c.110)
Appropriation Act 1805 (c.129)
Appropriation Act 1806 (c.149)
Appropriation Act 1807 (c.76)
Appropriation Act 1808 (c.148)
Appropriation Act 1809 (c.128)
Appropriation Act 1810 (c.115)
Appropriation Act 1811 (c.117)
Appropriation Act 1812 (c.154)
Appropriation Act 1813 (c.136)
Appropriation Act 1814 (c.167)
Appropriation Act 1815 (c.187)
Appropriation Act 1835 (c.80)
Appropriation Act 1836 (c.98)
Appropriation Act 1837 (c.79)
Appropriation Act 1838 (c.111)
Appropriation Act 1839 (c.89)
Appropriation Act 1840 (c.112)
Appropriation Act 1841 (c.11)
Appropriation Act 1841 (c.53)
Appropriation Act 1842 (c.121)
Appropriation Act 1843 (c.99)
Appropriation Act 1844 (c.104)
Appropriation Act 1845 (c.130)
Appropriation Act 1846 (c.116)
Appropriation Act 1848 (c.126)
Appropriation Act 1849 (c.98)
Appropriation Act 1850 (c.107)
Appropriation Act 1851 (c.101)
Appropriation Act 1852 (c.82)
Appropriation Act 1853 (c.110)
Appropriation Act 1854 (c.121)
Appropriation Act 1855 (c.129)
Appropriation Act 1856 (c.105)
Appropriation Act 1857 (c.20)
Appropriation Act 1857 (c.69)
Appropriation Act 1858 (c.107)
Appropriation Act 1859 (c.23)
Appropriation Act 1859 (c.55)
Appropriation Act 1860 (c.131)
Appropriation Act 1861 (c.103)
Appropriation Act 1862 (c.71)
Appropriation Act 1863 (c.99)
Appropriation Act 1865 (c.123)
Appropriation Act 1866 (c.91)

Appropriation Act 1867 (c.120)
Appropriation Act 1868 (c.85)
Appropriation Act 1869 (c.93)
Appropriation Act 1870 (c.96)
Appropriation Act 1871 (c.89)
Appropriation Act 1872 (c.87)
Appropriation Act 1873 (c.79)
Appropriation Act 1874 (c.56)
Appropriation Act 1875 (c.78)
Appropriation Act 1876 (c.60)
Appropriation Act 1877 (c.61)
Appropriation Act 1878 (c.65)
Appropriation Act 1879 (c.51)
Appropriation Act 1880 (c.13)
Appropriation Act 1881 (c.56)
Appropriation Act 1882 (c.71)
Appropriation Act 1883 (c.50)
Appropriation Act 1884 (c.73)
Appropriation Act 1885 (c.64)
Appropriation Act 1886 (c.26)
Appropriation Act 1887 (c.50)
Appropriation Act 1888 (c.61)
Appropriation Act 1889 (c.70)
Appropriation Act 1890 (c.72)
Appropriation Act 1891 (c.55)
Appropriation Act 1892 (c.33)
Appropriation Act 1893 (c.60)
Appropriation Act 1894 (c.59)
Appropriation Act 1895 (c.6)
Appropriation Act 1895 (c.31)
Appropriation Act 1896 (c.46)
Appropriation Act 1897 (c.67)
Appropriation Act 1898 (c.61)
Appropriation Act 1899 (c.1)
Appropriation Act 1899 (c.49)
Appropriation Act 1900 (c.2)
Appropriation Act 1900 (c.57)
Appropriation Act 1901 (c.21)
Appropriation Act 1902 (c.27)
Appropriation Act 1903 (c.32)
Appropriation Act 1904 (c.17)
Appropriation Act 1905 (c.17)
Appropriation Act 1906 (c.26)
Appropriation Act 1907 (c.20)
Appropriation Act 1908 (c.30)
Appropriation Act 1909 (c.5)
Appropriation Act 1910 (c.14)
Appropriation Act 1911 (c.15)
Appropriation Act 1912 (c.7)
Appropriation Act 1913 (c.27)
Appropriation Act 1913 (c.35)
Appropriation Act 1914 (c.24)
Appropriation Act 1915 (c.77)
Appropriation Act 1916 (c.71)
Appropriation Act 1917 (c.52)
Appropriation Act 1918 (c.56)
Appropriation Act 1919 (c.88)
Appropriation Act 1921 (c.46)
Appropriation Act 1922 (c.3)
Appropriation Act 1922 (c.32)
Appropriation Act 1923 (c.35)
Appropriation Act 1924 (c.31)
Appropriation Act 1925 (c.57)
Appropriation Act 1926 (c.23)
Appropriation Act 1927 (c.11)
Appropriation Act 1928 (c.18)
Appropriation Act 1929 (c.22)
Appropriation Act 1930 (c.27)
Appropriation Act 1931 (c.29)
Appropriation Act 1931 (c.50)
Appropriation Act 1933 (c.34)
Appropriation Act 1934 (c.44)
Appropriation Act 1935 (c.28)
Appropriation Act 1936 (c.37)
Appropriation Act 1937 (c.55)
Appropriation Act 1938 (c.47)
Appropriation Act 1939 (c.46)
Appropriation Act 1939 (c.52)
Appropriation Act 1941 (c.38)
Appropriation Act 1942 (c.27)
Appropriation Act 1943 (c.31)
Appropriation Act 1944 (c.25)
Appropriation Act 1944 (c.30)
Appropriation Act 1946 (c.65)
Appropriation Act 1947 (c.52)
Appropriation Act 1948 (c.50)
Appropriation Act 1949 (c.48)
Appropriation Act 1950 (c.16)
Appropriation Act 1951 (c.44)
Appropriation Act 1952 (c.38)
Appropriation Act 1953 (c.35)
Appropriation Act 1954 (c.45)
Appropriation Act 1955 (c.16)
Appropriation Act 1956 (c.55)
Appropriation Act 1957 (c.63)
Appropriation Act 1959 (c.59)
Appropriation Act 1960 (c.45)
Appropriation Act 1961 (c.59)
Appropriation Act 1962 (c.45)
Appropriation Act 1963 (c.26)
Appropriation Act 1964 (c.62)
Appropriation Act 1965 (c.23)
Appropriation Act 1966 (c.3)
Appropriation Act 1967 (c.59)
Appropriation Act 1968 (c.43)
Appropriation Act 1969 (c.31)
Appropriation Act 1970 (c.25)
Appropriation Act 1971 (c.67)
Appropriation Act 1972 (c.56)
Appropriation Act 1973 (c.40)
Appropriation Act 1974 (c.2)
Appropriation Act 1975 (c.44)
Appropriation Act 1976 (c.43)
Appropriation Act 1977 (c.35)
Appropriation Act 1978 (c.57)
Appropriation Act 1979 (c.24)
Appropriation Act 1980 (c.54)
Appropriation Act 1981 (c.51)
Appropriation Act 1982 (c.40)
Appropriation Act 1983 (c.27)
Appropriation Act 1983 (c.48)
Appropriation Act 1984 (c.44)
Appropriation Act 1985 (c.55)
Appropriation Act 1986 (c.42)
Appropriation Act 1987 (c.17)
Appropriation Act 1988 (c.38)

Appropriation Act 1989 (c.25)
Appropriation Act 1990 (c.28)
Appropriation Act 1991 (c.32)
Appropriation Act 1992 (c.22)
Appropriation Act 1993 (c.33)
Appropriation Act 1994 (c.24)
Appropriation Act 1995 (c.19)
Appropriation Acts Amendment Act 1842 (c.1)
Appropriation, etc. Act 1785 (c.60)
Appropriation, etc. Act 1801 (c.84)
Appropriation (No. 2) Act 1902 (c.30)
Appropriation (No. 2) Act 1910 (c.38)
Appropriation (No. 2) Act 1915 (c.86)
Appropriation (No. 2) Act 1921 (c.63)
Appropriation (No. 2) Act 1925 (c.78)
Appropriation (No. 2) Act 1926 (c.33)
Appropriation (No. 2) Act 1927 (c.25)
Appropriation (No. 2) Act 1931 (c.50)
Appropriation (No. 2) Act 1939 (c.63)
Appropriation (No. 2) Act 1941 (c.43)
Appropriation (No. 2) Act 1942 (c.33)
Appropriation (No. 2) Act 1943 (c.41)
Appropriation (No. 2) Act 1944 (c.37)
Appropriation (No. 2) Act 1955 (c.3)
Appropriation (No. 2) Act 1966 (c.26)
Appropriation (No. 2) Act 1970 (c.48)
Appropriation (No. 2) Act 1974 (c.31)
Appropriation (No. 2) Act 1979 (c.51)
Appropriation (No. 2) Act 1983 (c.48)
Appropriation (No. 2) Act 1987 (c.50)
Appropriation (No. 2) Act 1992 (c.47)
Appropriation (No. 3) Act 1942 (c.34)
Appropriation of Certain Duties Act 1799 (c.11)
Appropriation of Revenue Act 1700 (c.12)
Appropriation (Session 2) Act 1880 (c.40)
Appropriation (Session 2) Act 1886 (c.1)
Arbitration Act 1889 (c.49)
Arbitration Act 1934 (c.14)
Arbitration Act 1950 (c.27)
Arbitration Act 1975 (c.3)
Arbitration Act 1979 (c.42)
Arbitration Clauses (Protocol) Act 1924 (c.39)
Arbitration (Foreign Awards) Act 1930 (c.15)
Arbitration (International Investment Disputes) Act 1966 (c.41)
Arbitration (Masters and Workmen) Act 1872 (c.46)
Arbitration (Scotland) Act 1894 (c.13)
Arbitrations Act 1844 (c.93)
Archbishops' etc., House of Residence Act 1839 (c.18)
Archbishops' Palace, Dublin Act 1804 (c.63)
Archdeaconries and Rural Deaneries Act 1874 (c.63)
Archdeaconry of Cornwall Act 1897 (c.9)
Archdeaconry of London (Additional Endowment) Act 1897 (c.45)
Archdeaconry of Rochester Act 1861 (c.131)
Architects Registration Act 1938 (c.54)
Architects (Registration) Act 1931 (c.33)
Architects (Registration) Act 1934 (c.38)
Argentine Treaty Act 1842 (c.40)
Argyll Roads and Bridges Act 1775 (c.63)
Argyllshire Valuation Act 1748 (c.29)
Architects Registration (Amendment) Act 1969 (c.42)
Argyllshire Valuation Act 1748 (c.29)
Arklow Harbour Act 1882 (c.13)
Armed Forces Act 1966 (c.45)
Armed Forces Act 1971 (c.33)
Armed Forces Act 1976 (c.52)
Armed Forces Act 1981 (c.55)
Armed Forces Act 1986 (c.21)
Armed Forces Act 1991 (c.62)
Armed Forces (Conditions of Service) Act 1939 (c.68)
Armed Forces (Housing Loans) Act 1949 (c.77)
Armed Forces (Housing Loans) Act 1953 (c.3)
Armed Forces (Housing Loans) Act 1958 (c.1)
Armed Forces (Housing Loans) Act 1965 (c.9)
Armorial Bearings Act 1798 (c.53)
Armorial Bearings Act 1799 (c.8)
Arms and Gunpowder (Ireland) Act 1807 (c.8)
Arms and Gunpowder (Ireland) Act 1836 (c.39)
Arms and Gunpowder (Ireland) Act 1838 (c.71)
Arms Control and Disarmament (Inspections) Act 1991 (c.41)
Arms Control and Disarmament (Privileges and Immunities) Act 1988 (c.2)
Arms, etc. (Ireland) Act 1843 (c.74)
Arms (Ireland) Act 1810 (c.109)
Arms (Ireland) Act 1813 (c.78)
Army Act 1774 (c.54)
Army Act 1811 (c.106)
Army Act 1812 (c.27)
Army Act 1812 (c.120)
Army Act 1881 (c.58)
Army Act 1955 (c.18)
Army Act 1992 (c.39)
Army (Amendment) Act 1915 (c.26)
Army (Amendment) No. 2 Act 1915 (c.58)
Army and Air Force Act 1961 (c.52)
Army and Air Force (Annual) Act 1921 (c.9)
Army and Air Force (Annual) Act 1922 (c.6)
Army and Air Force (Annual) Act 1923 (c.3)
Army and Air Force (Annual) Act 1924 (c.5)
Army and Air Force (Annual) Act 1925 (c.25)
Army and Air Force (Annual) Act 1926 (c.6)
Army and Air Force (Annual) Act 1927 (c.7)
Army and Air Force (Annual) Act 1928 (c.7)
Army and Air Force (Annual) Act 1929 (c.20)
Army and Air Force (Annual) Act 1930 (c.22)
Army and Air Force (Annual) Act 1931 (c.14)
Army and Air Force (Annual) Act 1932 (c.22)
Army and Air Force (Annual) Act 1933 (c.11)
Army and Air Force (Annual) Act 1934 (c.11)
Army and Air Force (Annual) Act 1935 (c.17)
Army and Air Force (Annual) Act 1936 (c.14)

Army and Air Force (Annual) Act 1937 (c.26)
Army and Air Force (Annual) Act 1938 (c.20)
Army and Air Force (Annual) Act 1939 (c.17)
Army and Air Force (Annual) Act 1940 (c.18)
Army and Air Force (Annual) Act 1941 (c.17)
Army and Air Force (Annual) Act 1942 (c.15)
Army and Air Force (Annual) Act 1943 (c.15)
Army and Air Force (Annual) Act 1944 (c.18)
Army and Air Force (Annual) Act 1945 (c.22)
Army and Air Force (Annual) Act 1946 (c.47)
Army and Air Force (Annual) Act 1947 (c.25)
Army and Air Force (Annual) Act 1948 (c.28)
Army and Air Force (Annual) Act 1949 (c.28)
Army and Air Force (Annual) Act 1950 (c.3)
Army and Air Force (Annual) Act 1951 (c.24)
Army and Air Force (Annual) Act 1952 (c.24)
Army and Air Force (Annual) Act 1953 (c.31)
Army and Air Force (Annual) Act 1954 (c.35)
Army and Air Force (Women's Service) Act 1948 (c.21)
Army and Navy Act 1797 (c.6)
Army and Navy Act 1798 (c.4)
Army and Navy Act 1800 (c.16)
Army and Navy Act 1800 (c.29)
Army and Navy Act 1800 (c.100)
Army and Navy Act 1807 (c.15)
Army and Navy Audit Act 1889 (c.31)
Army (Annual) Act 1882 (c.7)
Army (Annual) Act 1883 (c.6)
Army (Annual) Act 1884 (c.8)
Army (Annual) Act 1885 (c.8)
Army (Annual) Act 1886 (c.8)
Army (Annual) Act 1887 (c.2)
Army (Annual) Act 1888 (c.4)
Army (Annual) Act 1889 (c.3)
Army (Annual) Act 1890 (c.4)
Army (Annual) Act 1891 (c.5)
Army (Annual) Act 1892 (c.2)
Army (Annual) Act 1893 (c.4)
Army (Annual) Act 1894 (c.3)
Army (Annual) Act 1895 (c.7)
Army (Annual) Act 1896 (c.2)
Army (Annual) Act 1897 (c.3)
Army (Annual) Act 1898 (c.1)
Army (Annual) Act 1899 (c.3)
Army (Annual) Act 1900 (c.5)
Army (Annual) Act 1901 (c.2)
Army (Annual) Act 1902 (c.2)
Army (Annual) Act 1903 (c.4)
Army (Annual) Act 1904 (c.5)
Army (Annual) Act 1905 (c.2)
Army (Annual) Act 1906 (c.2)
Army (Annual) Act 1907 (c.2)
Army (Annual) Act 1908 (c.2)
Army (Annual) Act 1909 (c.3)
Army (Annual) Act 1910 (c.6)
Army (Annual) Act 1911 (c.3)
Army (Annual) Act 1912 (c.5)
Army (Annual) Act 1913 (c.2)
Army (Annual) Act 1914 (c.2)
Army (Annual) Act 1915 (c.25)
Army (Annual) Act 1916 (c.5)
Army (Annual) Act (1916) Amendment 1917 (c.10)
Army (Annual) Act 1917 (c.9)
Army (Annual) Act 1918 (c.6)
Army (Annual) Act 1919 (c.11)
Army Chaplains Act 1868 (c.83)
Army (Conditions of Enlistment) Act 1957 (c.50)
Army (Courts of Inquiry) Act 1916 (c.33)
Army Discipline and Regulation Act 1879 (c.33)
Army Discipline and Regulation (Annual) Act 1880 (c.9)
Army Discipline and Regulation (Annual) Act 1881 (c.9)
Army Enlistment Act 1849 (c.73)
Army Enlistment Act 1855 (c.4)
Army Enlistment Act 1858 (c.55)
Army Enlistment Act 1867 (c.34)
Army in Ireland Act 1768 (c.13)
Army Pensions Act 1830 (c.41)
Army Pensions Act 1914 (c.83)
Army Prize Money Act 1814 (c.86)
Army Prize Money Act 1848 (c.103)
Army Prize (Shares of Deceased) Act 1864 (c.36)
Army Reserve Act 1950 (c.32)
Army Reserve Act 1962 (c.10)
Army Reserve Act 1969 (c.23)
Army Schools Act 1891 (c.16)
Army (Supply of Food, Forage and Stores) Act 1914 (c.26)
Army (Suspension of Sentences) Act 1915 (c.23)
Army (Suspension of Sentences) Amendment Act 1916 (c.103)
Army (Transfer) Act 1915 (c.43)
Arrangements Between Debtors and Creditors Act 1844 (c.70)
Arranmore Polling District Act 1878 (c.75)
Arrears of Crown, etc., Rents (Ireland) Act 1816 (c.71)
Arrears of Crown Rents (Ireland) Act 1811 (c.91)
Arrears of Rent (Ireland) Act 1882 (c.47)
Arrest for Debtors Act 1851 (c.52)
Arrest in Personal Actions (Ireland) Act 1841 (c.17)
Arsenic Act 1851 (c.13)
Art Act 1866 (c.16)
Art Unions Act 1846 (c.48)
Art Unions Indemnity Act 1844 (c.109)
Art Unions Indemnity Act 1845 (c.57)
Arthur Jenkins Indemnity Act 1941 (c.1)
Articles of Commerce (Returns, &c.) Act 1914 (c.65)
Artificers Act 1718 (c.27)
Artificers etc. Act 1749 (c.13)
Artificial Cream Act 1929 (c.32)
Artillery and Rifle Ranges Act 1885 (c.36)
Artillery Corps, etc. Act 1795 (c.83)
Artizans and Labourers Dwellings Act 1868 (c.130)
Artizans and Labourers Dwellings Act (1868) Amendment 1879 (c.64)

Artizans' and Labourers' Dwellings Improvement Act 1875 (c.36)
Artizans and Labourers Dwellings Improvement Act 1879 (c.63)
Artizans and Labourers Dwellings Improvement (Scotland) Act 1875 (c.49)
Artizans and Labourers Dwellings Improvement (Scotland) Act 1880 (c.2)
Artizans' Dwellings Act (1868) Amendment Act (1879) Amendment 1880 (c.8)
Artizans Dwellings Act 1882 (c.54)
Arun, Sussex: Navigation Act 1785 (c.100)
Arundel: Improvement Act 1785 (c.90)
Ascertaining of Strength of Spirits Act 1791 (c.44)
Ashburton Roads Act 1776 (c.79)
Assaulting a Privy Counsellor Act 1710 (c.21)
Assaults (Ireland) Act 1814 (c.181)
Assaults (Ireland) Act 1815 (c.88)
Assaults (Ireland) Act 1839 (c.77)
Assaults (Ireland) Act 1844 (c.23)
Assaults (Ireland) Act 1849 (c.38)
Assaults with Intent to Rob Act 1733 (c.21)
Assay of Imported Watch-Cases (Existing Stocks Exemption) Act 1907 (c.8)
Assay of Plate Act 1702 (c.3)
Assessed Rates Act 1879 (c.10)
Assessed Taxes Act 1791 (c.5)
Assessed Taxes Act 1805 (c.13)
Assessed Taxes Act 1805 (c.105)
Assessed Taxes Act 1806 (c.78)
Assessed Taxes Act 1810 (c.104)
Assessed Taxes Act 1811 (c.72)
Assessed Taxes Act 1812 (c.93)
Assessed Taxes Act 1812 (c.147)
Assessed Taxes Act 1816 (c.66)
Assessed Taxes Act 1837 (c.61)
Assessed Taxes Act 1840 (c.38)
Assessed Taxes Act 1841 (c.26)
Assessed Taxes Act 1845 (c.36)
Assessed Taxes Act 1851 (c.33)
Assessed Taxes Act 1854 (c.1)
Assessed Taxes Composition Act 1850 (c.96)
Assessed Taxes and Income Tax Act 1846 (c.56)
Assessed Taxes, etc. Act 1839 (c.35)
Assessed Taxes, etc. (Ireland) Act 1807 (c.11)
Assessed Taxes, etc. (Ireland) Act 1816 (c.57)
Assessed Taxes (Ireland) Act 1807 (c.21)
Assessed Taxes (Ireland) Act 1808 (c.42)
Assessed Taxes (Ireland) Act 1815 (c.61)
Assessed Taxes (Ireland) Act 1815 (c.67)
Assessed Taxes (Ireland) Act 1815 (c.140)
Assessed Taxes, Property Tax and Duty on Pensions and Offices of Profit Act 1844 (c.46)
Assessionable Manors Award Act 1848 (c.83)
Assessment of Taxes Act 1808 (c.141)
Assessments in Edinburgh Act 1861 (c.27)
Assessor of Public Undertakings (Scotland) Act 1934 (c.22)
Assise and Making of Bread, London Act 1797 (c.98)
Assise of Bread Act 1798 (c.62)
Assise of Fuel Act 1710 (c.20)
Assise of Fuel Act 1711 (c.5)
Assistant Postmaster-General Act 1909 (c.14)
Assizes Act 1839 (c.72)
Assizes and Quarter Sessions Act 1908 (c.41)
Assizes for Cornwall Act 1715 (c.45)
Assizes (Ireland) Act 1825 (c.51)
Assizes (Ireland) Act 1835 (c.26)
Assizes (Ireland) Act 1850 (c.85)
Assizes (Ireland) Act 1850 (c.88)
Assizes Relief Act 1889 (c.12)
Association of County Councils (Scotland) Act 1946 (c.77)
Assurance Companies Act 1909 (c.49)
Assurance Companies Act 1946 (c.28)
Assurance Companies (Winding Up) Act 1933 (c.9)
Assurance Companies (Winding Up) Act 1935 (c.45)
Assurance on French Ships Act 1747 (c.4)
Asthall to Buckland Road Act 1777 (c.105)
Asylum and Immigration Appeals Act 1993 (c.23)
Asylums and Certified Institutions (Officers Pensions) Act 1918 (c.33)
Asylums' Officers Superannuation Act 1909 (c.48)
Atomic Energy Act 1946 (c.80)
Atomic Energy Act 1989 (c.7)
Atomic Energy Authority Act 1954 (c.32)
Atomic Energy Authority Act 1959 (c.5)
Atomic Energy Authority Act 1971 (c.11)
Atomic Energy Authority Act 1986 (c.3)
Atomic Energy Authority Act 1995 (c.37)
Atomic Energy Authority (Special Constables) Act 1976 (c.23)
Atomic Energy Authority (Weapons Group) Act 1973 (c.4)
Atomic Energy (Miscellaneous Provisions) Act 1981 (c.48)
Atomic Weapons Establishment Act 1991 (c.46)
Attachment of Earnings Act 1971 (c.32)
Attachment of Goods (Ireland) Act 1850 (c.73)
Attainder of Bishop of Rochester Act 1722 (c.17)
Attainder of David Ogilvy: Disabilities Removed on Pardon Act 1783 (c.34)
Attainder of Duke of Ormonde Act 1714 (c.17)
Attainder of Earl of Kellie and Others Act 1745 (c.26)
Attainder of Earl of Mar and Others Act 1715 (c.32)
Attainder of Earl of Marischal and Others Act 1715 (c.42)

Attainder of George Kelley Act 1722 (c.16)
Attainder of John Plunket Act 1722 (c.15)
Attainder of Thomas Forster and Others Act 1715 (c.53)
Attainder of Viscount Bolingbroke Act 1714 (c.16)
Attempted Rape Act 1948 (c.19)
Attendance of Witnesses Act 1854 (c.34)
Attorneys Act 1809 (c.28)
Attorneys and Solicitors Act 1728 (c.23)
Attorneys and Solicitors Act 1732 (c.27)
Attorneys and Solicitors Act (1860) Amendment 1872 (c.81)
Attorneys and Solicitors Act 1870 (c.28)
Attorneys and Solicitors Act 1874 (c.68)
Attorneys and Solicitors (Ireland) Act 1866 (c.84)
Auction Duties Act 1815 (c.142)
Auction Duties, etc. Act 1779 (c.56)
Auction Duties (Ireland) Act 1807 (c.17)
Auction Duties (Ireland) Act 1814 (c.82)
Auction Duty Act 1792 (c.41)
Auction Duty Act 1807 (c.65)
Auction Duty Act 1812 (c.53)
Auction Duty, etc. Act 1790 (c.26)
Auctioneers Act 1845 (c.15)
Auctioneers' Licences Act 1776 (c.50)
Auctions (Bidding Agreements) Act 1927 (c.12)
Auctions (Bidding Agreements) Act 1969 (c.56)
Auctions Duties (Ireland) Act 1809 (c.100)
Audit (Local Authorities) Act 1927 (c.31)
Audit (Local Authorities etc.) Act 1922 (c.14)
Audit of Accounts Act 1813 (c.100)
Audit of Accounts, etc. Act 1813 (c.150)
Audit of Military Accounts (Ireland) Act 1812 (c.51)
Audit of Public Accounts Act 1780 (c.40)
Audit of Public Accounts Act 1780 (c.45)
Audit of Public Accounts Act 1780 (c.54)
Audit of Public Accounts Act 1782 (c.50)
Audit of Public Accounts Act 1784 (c.13)
Audit of Public Accounts Act 1785 (c.52)
Audit of Public Accounts Act 1785 (c.68)
Audit of Public Accounts Act 1786 (c.67)
Audit of Public Accounts Act 1794 (c.59)
Audit of Public Accounts Act 1805 (c.55)
Audit of Public Accounts Act 1806 (c.141)
Audit of Public Accounts (Ireland) Act 1812 (c.52)
Auditing of Public Accounts Act 1805 (c.91)
Auditing of Public Accounts Act 1809 (c.95)
Auditing of the Public Accounts Act 1783 (c.68)
Auditor of the Exchequer Act (1806) (c.1)
Auditors of Land Revenue Act 1799 (c.83)
Augmentation of Benefices Act 1854 (c.84)
Augmentation of 60th Regiment Act 1797 (c.13)
Augmentation of 60th Regiment Act 1799 (c.104)
Augmentation of 60th Regiment Act 1813 (c.12)
Australia Act 1986 (c.2)
Australian Colonies Act 1801 (c.44)
Australian Colonies Duties Act 1873 (c.22)
Australian Colonies Duties Act 1895 (c.3)
Australian Colonies, Waste Lands Act 1842 (c.36)
Australian Constitution (Public Record Copy) Act 1990 (c.17)
Australian Constitutions Act 1842 (c.76)
Australian Constitutions Act 1844 (c.74)
Australian Constitutions Act 1850 (c.59)
Australian Constitutions Act 1862 (c.11)
Australian Passengers Act 1861 (c.52)
Australian States Constitution Act 1907 (c.7)
Australian Waste Lands Act 1855 (c.56)
Austrian Loan Guarantee Act 1931 (c.5)
Austrian State Treaty Act 1955 (c.1)
Auxiliary Air Force and Air Force Reserve Act 1924 (c.15)
Auxiliary and Reserve Forces Act 1949 (c.96)
Auxiliary Forces Act 1953 (c.50)
Average Price of Brown Sugar Act 1809 (c.43)
Aviation and Maritime Security Act 1990 (c.31)
Aviation Security Act 1982 (c.36)
Axminster Roads Act 1754 (c.32)
Aylesbury Gaol and Shire Hall: Rate in Buckinghamshire Act 1736 (c.10)
Aylesbury to West Wycombe Road Act 1795 (c.149)
Ayre and Lamark Roads Act 1771 (c.90)
Ayr Bridge Act 1785 (c.37)
Ayr (County) Roads Act 1797 (c.162)
Ayr Harbour Act 1772 (c.22)
Ayr Harbour Act 1794 (c.99)
Ayr Roads Act 1757 (c.57)
Ayr Roads Act 1767 (c.106)
Ayr Roads Act 1774 (c.109)
Ayr Roads Act 1789 (c.79)
Ayr Roads Act 1791 (c.95)
Ayr Roads Act 1791 (c.107)
Ayr Roads Act 1792 (c.121)

Backing of Warrants (Republic of Ireland) Act 1965 (c.45)
Bacon Industry Act 1938 (c.71)
Bacon Industry (Amendment) Act 1939 (c.10)
Badgers Act 1973 (c.57)
Badgers Act 1991 (c.36)
Badgers (Further Protection) Act 1991 (c.35)
Badgers (Protection) Act 1992 (c.51)
Bagshot to Hertford Bridge Hill Road Act 1777 (c.84)
Bagshot to Winchester Road Act 1773 (c.88)
Bahama Islands (Constitution) Act 1963 (c.56)
Bahama Islands Trade Act 1812 (c.99)
Bahamas Independence Act 1973 (c.27)
Bail Act 1898 (c.7)
Bail Act 1976 (c.63)
Bail (Amendment) Act 1993 (c.26)

Bail Bonds Act 1808 (c.58)
Bail etc. (Scotland) Act 1980 (c.4)
Bail in Cases of Forgery, etc. (Scotland) Act 1835 (c.73)
Bail in Criminal Cases (Scotland) Act 1724 (c.26)
Bail in Criminal Cases (Scotland) Act 1799 (c.49)
Bail in Error Act 1845 (c.68)
Bail in Error Act 1853 (c.32)
Bail (Scotland) Act 1888 (c.36)
Bails Act 1869 (c.38)
Bakehouse Regulation Act 1863 (c.40)
Baking Industry (Hours of Work) Act 1938 (c.41)
Baking Industry (Hours of Work) Act 1954 (c.57)
Baking Trade Act 1810 (c.73)
Baking Trade, Dublin Act 1802 (c.8)
Balby to Worksop Road Act 1765 (c.67)
Balby to Worksop Road Act 1787 (c.84)
Bale and Dolgelly Roads Act 1796 (c.147)
Ballot Act 1872 (c.33)
Banbury Church Act 1790 (c.72)
Banbury Road Act 1780 (c.67)
Banbury to Lutterworth Road Act 1785 (c.128)
Bancroft's Patent Act 1785 (c.38)
Bangladesh Act 1973 (c.49)
Bank Act 1892 (c.48)
Bank Charter Act 1844 (c.32)
Bank Holiday (Ireland) Act 1903 (c.1)
Bank Holidays Act 1871 (c.17)
Bank Notes (Scotland) Act 1765 (c.49)
Bank Notes Act 1833 (c.83)
Bank Notes Act 1841 (c.50)
Bank Notes Act 1852 (c.2)
Bank Notes Act 1853 (c.2)
Bank Notes Forgery Act 1801 (c.57)
Bank Notes (Forgery) Act 1805 (c.89)
Bank Notes Forgery (Scotland) Act 1820 (c.92)
Bank Notes (Ireland) Act 1864 (c.78)
Bank Notes (Scotland) Act 1765 (c.49)
Bank Notes (Scotland) Act 1845 (c.38)
Bank of Ayr Act 1774 (c.21)
Bank of Bombay Failure Commissioners Act 1868 (c.63)
Bank of England Act 1694 (c.20)
Bank of England Act 1696 (c.20)
Bank of England Act 1707 (c.59)
Bank of England Act 1708 (c.30)
Bank of England Act 1709 (c.1)
Bank of England Act 1710 (c.7)
Bank of England Act 1716 (c.8)
Bank of England Act 1727 (c.8)
Bank of England Act 1728 (c.3)
Bank of England Act 1741 (c.13)
Bank of England Act 1745 (c.6)
Bank of England Act 1750 (c.4)
Bank of England Act 1784 (c.32)
Bank of England Act 1785 (c.83)
Bank of England Act 1791 (c.33)
Bank of England Act 1800 (c.28)
Bank of England Act 1833 (c.98)
Bank of England Act 1854 (c.1)
Bank of England Act 1861 (c.3)
Bank of England Act 1946 (c.27)
Bank of England (Advance) Act 1816 (c.96)
Bank of England Buildings Act 1764 (c.49)
Bank of England: Buildings Act 1766 (c.76)
Bank of England (Election of Directors) Act 1872 (c.34)
Bank of England Notes Act 1773 (c.79)
Bank of England Notes Act 1797 (c.28)
Bank of England Site Act 1793 (c.15)
Bank of England Stock Act 1796 (c.90)
Bank of Ireland Act 1808 (c.103)
Bank of Ireland Act 1860 (c.31)
Bank of Ireland Act 1865 (c.16)
Bank of Ireland Advances Act 1837 (c.59)
Bank of Ireland Advances Act 1838 (c.81)
Bank of Ireland Advances Act 1839 (c.91)
Bank of Ireland Charter Act 1872 (c.5)
Bank of Ireland, Transfer of Stocks Act 1862 (c.21)
Bank of Scotland Act 1774 (c.32)
Bank of Scotland Act 1784 (c.12)
Bank of Scotland Act 1792 (c.25)
Bank of Scotland Act 1794 (c.19)
Bank Post Bills Composition (Ireland) Act
Bank (Scotland) Act 1797 (c.40)
Bank (Scotland) Act 1797 (c.137)
Bankers' Books Evidence Act 1876 (c.48)
Bankers' Books Evidence Act 1879 (c.11)
Bankers' Composition Act 1856 (c.20)
Bankers' Composition (Scotland) Act 1853 (c.63)
Bankers' (Scotland) Act 1854 (c.73)
Bankers' Debt Act 1703 (c.9)
Bankers (Ireland) Act 1845 (c.37)
Bankers (Northern Ireland) Act 1928 (c.15)
Banking Act 1979 (c.37)
Banking Act 1987 (c.22)
Banking and Financial Dealings Act 1971 (c.80)
Banking Companies' (Shares) Act 1867 (c.29)
Banking Copartnerships Act 1864 (c.32)
Bankrupt and Insolvent Act 1857 (c.60)
Bankruptcy Act 1621 (c.18)
Bankruptcy Act 1716 (c.12)
Bankruptcy Act 1836 (c.27)
Bankruptcy Act 1839 (c.29)
Bankruptcy Act 1839 (c.86)
Bankruptcy Act 1842 (c.122)
Bankruptcy Act 1845 (c.48)
Bankruptcy Act 1852 (c.77)
Bankruptcy Act 1854 (c.119)
Bankruptcy Act 1861 (c.134)
Bankruptcy Act 1862 (c.99)
Bankruptcy Act 1869 (c.71)
Bankruptcy Act 1883 (c.52)
Bankruptcy Act 1890 (c.71)
Bankruptcy Act 1914 (c.59)
Bankruptcy (Agricultural Labourers' Wages) Act 1886 (c.28)

Bankruptcy Amendment Act 1868 (c.104)
Bankruptcy (Amendment) Act 1926 (c.7)
Bankruptcy and Cessio (Scotland) Act 1881 (c.22)
Bankruptcy and Deeds of Arrangement Act 1913 (c.34)
Bankruptcy and Real Securities (Scotland) Act 1857 (c.19)
Bankruptcy Appeals (County Courts) Act 1884 (c.9)
Bankruptcy Court Act 1853 (c.81)
Bankruptcy (Discharge and Closure) Act 1887 (c.66)
Bankruptcy Disqualification Act 1871 (c.50)
Bankruptcy, etc. Act 1847 (c.102)
Bankruptcy, etc. (Ireland) Act 1859 (c.62)
Bankruptcy Frauds and Disabilities (Scotland) Act 1884 (c.16)
Bankruptcy (Ireland) Act 1836 (c.14)
Bankruptcy (Ireland) Act 1837 (c.48)
Bankruptcy (Ireland) Act 1849 (c.107)
Bankruptcy (Ireland) Amendment Act 1872 (c.58)
Bankruptcy Law Consolidation Act 1849 (c.106)
Bankruptcy (Office Accommodation) Act 1885 (c.47)
Bankruptcy (Office Accommodation) Act 1886 (c.12)
Bankruptcy Repeal and Insolvent Court Act 1869 (c.83)
Bankruptcy (Scotland) Act 1839 (c.41)
Bankruptcy (Scotland) Act 1853 (c.53)
Bankruptcy (Scotland) Act 1856 (c.79)
Bankruptcy (Scotland) Act 1875 (c.26)
Bankruptcy (Scotland) Act 1913 (c.20)
Bankruptcy (Scotland) Act 1985 (c.66)
Bankruptcy (Scotland) Act 1993 (c.6)
Bankruptcy (Scotland) Amendment Act 1860 (c.33)
Bankrupts Act 1705 (c.4)
Bankrupts Act 1706 (c.22)
Bankrupts Act 1711 (c.25)
Bankrupts Act 1718 (c.24)
Bankrupts Act 1720 (c.19)
Bankrupts Act 1720 (c.31)
Bankrupts Act 1731 (c.30)
Bankrupts Act 1742 (c.27)
Bankrupts Act 1745 (c.32)
Bankrupts Act 1763 (c.33)
Bankrupts Act 1772 (c.47)
Bankrupts Act 1794 (c.57)
Bankrupts Act 1797 (c.124)
Bankrupts Act 1806 (c.135)
Bankrupts (England) and (Ireland) Act 1809 (c.121)
Bankrupts, etc. Act 1763 (c.36)
Bankrupts Release Act 1848 (c.86)
Banks (Scotland) Act 1797 (c.62)
Baptismal Fees Abolition Act 1872 (c.36)
Barbados Independence Act 1966 (c.37)
Barbed Wire Act 1893 (c.32)
Barking Act 1786 (c.115)
Barmouth Harbour Act 1797 (c.50)
Barnsley Canal Act 1793 (c.110)
Barnsley Canal Act 1793 (c.115)
Barnstaple Roads Act 1763 (c.35)
Barnstaple Roads Act 1783 (c.31)
Barrack Lane, Windsor Act 1867 (c.109)
Barracks Act 1890 (c.25)
Barristers Admission (Ireland) Act 1885 (c.20)
Barristers Admission, Stamp Duty Act 1874 (c.19)
Barristers (Qualifications for Office) Act 1961 (c.44)
Barthomley Church, Chester Act 1789 (c.11)
Basingstoke Canal Act 1778 (c.75)
Basingstoke Canal Act 1793 (c.16)
Basingstoke Roads Act 1797 (c.169)
Basingstoke to Winchester Road Act 1795 (c.162)
Basses Lights Act 1869 (c.77)
Basses Lights Act 1872 (c.55)
Bastard Children Act 1732 (c.31)
Bastard Children Act 1839 (c.85)
Bastards Act 1810 (c.51)
Bastards (Scotland) Act 1836 (c.22)
Bastardy Act 1809 (c.68)
Bastardy Act 1845 (c.10)
Bastardy Act 1923 (c.23)
Bastardy (Ireland) Act 1863 (c.21)
Bastardy Laws Act Amendment 1872 (c.65)
Bastardy Laws Amendment Act 1873 (c.9)
Bastardy Orders Act 1880 (c.32)
Bastardy (Witness Process) Act 1929 (c.38)
Bath City Prison Act 1871 (c.46)
Bath Highway, Streets, etc. Act 1707 (c.42)
Bath Highway, Streets, etc. Act 1720 (c.19)
Bath Hospital Act 1738 (c.31)
Bath Hospital Act 1779 (c.23)
Bath: Improvement Act 1766 (c.70)
Bath: Improvement Act 1789 (c.73)
Bath Roads Act 1757 (c.67)
Bath Roads Act 1758 (c.51)
Bath Roads Act 1760 (c.31)
Bath Roads Act 1793 (c.144)
Bath Roads, Streets, etc. Act 1738 (c.20)
Bath (Streets, Buildings, Watch etc.) 1757 (c.65)
Baths and Washhouses Act 1846 (c.74)
Baths and Washhouses Act 1847 (c.61)
Baths and Washhouses Act 1878 (c.14)
Baths and Washhouses Act 1882 (c.30)
Baths and Washhouses Act 1896 (c.59)
Baths and Washhouses Act 1899 (c.29)
Baths and Washhouses (Ireland) Act 1846 (c.87)
Bathwick Roads and Bridges, etc. Act 1769 (c.95)
Battersea Bridge Act 1766 (c.66)
Battersea Bridge and Embankment, etc. Act 1846 (c.39)
Battersea Parish Church Act 1774 (c.95)
Battersea Park Act 1846 (c.38)
Battersea Park Act 1851 (c.77)

Battersea Park Act 1853 (c.47)
Battle-axe Guards (Ireland) Act 1813 (c.54)
Bawtry to Markham Road Act 1793 (c.136)
Bawtry by Selby Road Act 1793 (c.166)
Beaconsfield and Redhill Road Act 1750 (c.32)
Beaconsfield and Stokenchurch Road Act 1759 (c.37)
Beaconsfield to Stokenchurch Road Act 1775 (c.70)
Beaconsfield to Stokenchurch Road Act 1794 (c.142)
Beccles: Improvement Act 1796 (c.51)
Bedford and Buckingham Highways Act 1708 (c.25)
Bedford and Buckingham Highways Act 1709 (c.25)
Bedford and Buckingham Roads Act 1727 (c.10)
Bedford and Buckingham Roads Act 1754 (c.21)
Bedford and Buckingham Roads Act 1754 (c.34)
Bedford and Buckingham Roads Act 1780 (c.68)
Bedford and Buckingham Roads Act 1790 (c.114)
Bedford and Hertford Roads Act 1742 (c.42)
Bedford and Hertford Roads Act 1775 (c.72)
Bedford and Hertford Roads Act 1786 (c.130)
Bedford and Hertford Roads Act 1795 (c.163)
Bedford and Hunts. Roads Act 1770 (c.83)
Bedford and Hunts. Roads Act 1791 (c.96)
Bedford and Northants Roads Act 1754 (c.33)
Bedford and Woburn Road Act 1796 (c.151)
Bedford Level Act 1754 (c.19)
Bedford Level Act 1756 (c.9)
Bedford Level Act 1772 (c.9)
Bedford Level Act 1780 (c.25)
Bedford Level Act 1783 (c.25)
Bedford Level Act 1789 (c.22)
Bedford Level Act 1796 (c.73)
Bedford Level and Swaffham Drainage Act 1767 (c.53)
Bedford Level: Drainage Act 1757 (c.18)
Bedford Level: Drainage Act 1771 (c.78)
Bedford Level: Drainage Act 1772 (c.40)
Bedford Level: Drainage Act 1772 (c.45)
Bedford Level: Drainage Act 1772 (c.49)
Bedford Level: Drainage Act 1775 (c.12)
Bedford Level: Drainage Act 1777 (c.65)
Bedford Level: Drainage Act 1779 (c.24)
Bedford Level: Drainage Act 1796 (c.33)
Bedford Roads Act 1731 (c.26)
Bedford Roads Act 1772 (c.89)
Bedford Roads Act 1772 (c.107)
Bedford Roads Act 1777 (c.94)
Bedford Roads Act 1793 (c.178)
Bedford: Poor Relief Act 1794 (c.98)
Bedford to Kimbolton Road Act 1795 (c.148)
Bedfordshire and Buckinghamshire Roads Act 1706 (c.4)
Bedfordshire and Buckinghamshire Roads Act 1739 (c.9)
Bedfordshire and Hertfordshire Roads Act 1763 (c.27)
Bedfordshire Highways Act 1706 (c.13)
Bedfordshire Roads Act 1724 (c.20)
Bedfordshire Roads Act 1736 (c.24)
Bedfordshire Roads Act 1753 (c.41)
Bee Pest Prevention (Ireland) Act 1908 (c.34)
Beef and Veal Customs Duties Act 1937 (c.8)
Beer Act 1761 (c.14)
Beer Act 1816 (c.58)
Beer and Malt (Ireland) Act 1809 (c.57)
Beer Dealers Retail Licences Act 1880 (c.6)
Beer Dealers, Retail Licences (Amendment) Act 1882 (c.34)
Beer, Devon, Harbour Act 1792 (c.92)
Beer Duties, Borrowstoness Act 1743 (c.21)
Beer Duties, Borrowstoness Act 1767 (c.90)
Beer Duties: Borrowstoness Act 1794 (c.91)
Beer, etc., Licences (Great Britain) Act 1816 (c.113)
Beer Licences Regulation (Ireland) Act 1877 (c.4)
Beer Retailers etc., Retail Licences (Ireland) Act 1900 (c.30)
Beerhouse Act 1840 (c.61)
Beerhouse Act 1870 (c.111)
Beerhouses (Ireland) Act 1864 (c.35)
Beerhouses (Ireland) Act (1864) Amendment 1871 (c.111)
Bees Act 1980 (c.12)
Behring Sea Award Act 1894 (c.2)
Belfast Borough Extension Act 1853 (c.114)
Belfast Commission Act 1886 (c.4)
Belfast Constabulary Act 1866 (c.46)
Belfast Custom House Act 1852 (c.30)
Belize Act 1981 (c.52)
Benefice (Ireland) Act 1865 (c.82)
Benefices Act 1807 (c.75)
Benefices Act 1808 (c.5)
Benefices Act 1898 (c.48)
Benefices (England) Act 1803 (c.84)
Benefices (England) Act 1803 (c.109)
Benefices (Ireland) Act 1808 (c.66)
Benefices (Ireland) Act 1860 (c.72)
Benefices (Scotland) Act 1843 (c.61)
Benefit Building Societies Act 1836 (c.32)
Benthall Bridge, Severn Act 1776 (c.17)
Berkshire Act 1751 (c.21)
Berkshire and Oxford Roads Act 1765 (c.55)
Berkshire and Southampton Roads Act 1772 (c.78)
Berkshire and Southampton Roads Act 1794 (c.141)
Berkshire and Wiltshire Roads Act 1770 (c.100)
Berkshire and Wiltshire Roads Act 1771 (c.97)
Berkshire and Wiltshire Roads Act 1781 (c.91)
Berkshire and Wiltshire Roads Act 1781 (c.101)

Berkshire and Wiltshire Roads Act 1793 (c.138)
Berkshire Highways Act 1713 (c.28)
Berkshire, Oxford, Buckinghamshire and Hertford Roads Act 1787 (c.81)
Berkshire Roads Act 1732 (c.16)
Berkshire Roads Act 1738 (c.11)
Berkshire Roads Act 1746 (c.6)
Berkshire Roads Act 1751 (c.21)
Berkshire Roads Act 1756 (c.77)
Berkshire Roads Act 1756 (c.81)
Berkshire Roads Act 1771 (c.70)
Berkshire Roads Act 1772 (c.104)
Berkshire Roads Act 1778 (c.99)
Berkshire Roads Act 1783 (c.100)
Berkshire Roads Act 1790 (c.106)
Berkshire Roads Act 1791 (c.105)
Berkshire Roads Act 1794 (c.132)
Bermuda Constitution Act 1967 (c.63)
Bermondsey, etc.: Streets Act 1785 (c.23)
Bermondsey (Poor Relief) Act 1757 (c.45)
Bermondsey: Poor Relief Act 1791 (c.19)
Bermuda Trade Act 1813 (c.50)
Berwick and Durham Roads Act 1793 (c.185)
Berwick-on-Tweed Act 1836 (c.103)
Berwick Roads Act 1753 (c.82)
Berwick Roads Act 1766 (c.73)
Berwick Roads Act 1772 (c.97)
Berwick Roads Act 1779 (c.79)
Berwick Roads Act 1781 (c.91)
Berwick Roads Act 1787 (c.89)
Berwick Roads Act 1792 (c.149)
Berwickshire County Town Act 1903 (c.5)
Berwickshire Courts Act 1853 (c.27)
Bethnal Green and Shoreditch: Improvement Act 1793 (c.88)
Bethnal Green: Completion of Church and Poor Relief Act 1745 (c.15)
Bethnal Green: Parish Act 1742 (c.28)
Bethnal Green: Poor Relief Act 1763 (c.40)
Bethnal Green: Poor Relief Act 1772 (c.53)
Bethnal Green Road Act 1756 (c.43)
Bethnal Green Road Act 1767 (c.105)
Betting Act 1853 (c.119)
Betting Act 1874 (c.15)
Betting and Gaming Act 1960 (c.60)
Betting and Gaming Duties Act 1972 (c.25)
Betting and Gaming Duties Act 1981 (c.63)
Betting and Loans (Infants) Act 1892 (c.4)
Betting and Lotteries Act 1934 (c.58)
Betting Duties Act 1963 (c.3)
Betting, Gaming and Lotteries Act 1963 (c.2)
Betting, Gaming and Lotteries Act 1964 (c.78)
Betting, Gaming and Lotteries (Amendment) Act 1969 (c.17)
Betting, Gaming and Lotteries (Amendment) Act 1971 (c.26)
Betting, Gaming and Lotteries (Amendment) Act 1980 (c.18)
Betting, Gaming and Lotteries (Amendment) Act 1984 (c.25)
Betting, Gaming and Lotteries (Amendment) Act 1985 (c.18)
Betting (Juvenile Messengers) (Scotland) Act 1928 (c.27)
Betting Levy Act 1961 (c.17)
Beverley and Kexby Bridge Road Act 1764 (c.76)
Beverley Improvement Act 1726 (c.4)
Beverley Improvement Act 1744 (c.13)
Beverley to Kexby Bridge Road Act 1785 (c.110)
Bewdley Bridge Act 1795 (c.78)
Bewdley Roads Act 1753 (c.39)
Bewdley Roads Act 1774 (c.112)
Bicester and Aylesbury Road Act 1770 (c.72)
Bicester Roads Act 1793 (c.180)
Bicester to Aylesbury Road Act 1791 (c.101)
Bicester to Aynho Road Act 1791 (c.103)
Bideford Roads Act 1764 (c.87)
Bideford Roads Act 1785 (c.119)
Bigamy Act 1795 (c.67)
Billiards (Abolition of Restrictions) Act 1987 (c.19)
Bill Chamber Procedure Act 1857 (c.18)
Bill of Exchange Act 1702 (c.8)
Bill of Exchange Act 1704 (c.8)
Bill of Exchange Act 1776 (c.30)
Bill of Exchange Act 1800 (c.42)
Bill of Exchange Act 1808 (c.88)
Bill of Exchange (Scotland) Act 1772 (c.72)
Bill of Sale Act 1891 (c.35)
Billeting of Civilians Act 1917 (c.20)
Bills and Notes Metropolis Act 1852 (c.1)
Bills and Notes Metropolis Act 1863 (c.2)
Bills Confirming Provisional Orders Act 1870 (c.1)
Bills of Exchange Act 1836 (c.58)
Bills of Exchange Act 1871 (c.74)
Bills of Exchange Act 1878 (c.13)
Bills of Exchange Act 1882 (c.61)
Bills of Exchange Act 1914 (c.82)
Bills of Exchange Act (1882) Amendment Act 1932 (c.44)
Bills of Exchange (Crossed Cheques) Act 1906 (c.17)
Bills of Exchange, etc. Act 1783 (c.7)
Bills of Exchange (Ireland) Act 1828 (c.24)
Bills of Exchange (Ireland) Act 1862 (c.23)
Bills of Exchange (Ireland) Act 1864 (c.7)
Bills of Exchange (Scotland) Act 1772 (c.72)
Bills of Exchange (Time of Noting) Act 1917 (c.48)
Bills of Lading Act 1855 (c.111)
Bills of Sale Act 1854 (c.36)
Bills of Sale (Ireland) Act 1854 (c.55)
Bills of Sale Act 1866 (c.96)
Bills of Sale Act 1878 (c.31)
Bills of Sale Act (1878) Amendment Act 1882 (c.43)
Bills of Sale Act 1890 (c.53)
Bills of Sale (Ireland) Act 1879 (c.50)
Bills of Sale (Ireland) Act (1879) Amendment Act 1883 (c.7)
Bingo Act 1992 (c.10)
Biological Standards Act 1975 (c.4)

Biological Weapons Act 1974 (c.6)
Birkenhead Enfranchisement Act 1861 (c.112)
Birmingham and Chesterfield Roads Act 1786 (c.149)
Birmingham and Stratford Roads Act 1825 (c.6)
Birmingham and Wednesbury Roads Act 1726 (c.14)
Birmingham Canal Act 1769 (c.53)
Birmingham Canal, Navigation Act 1768 (c.38)
Birmingham Canal, Navigation Act 1771 (c.67)
Birmingham Canal, Navigation Act 1783 (c.92)
Birmingham Canal, Navigation Act 1784 (c.4)
Birmingham Canal: Navigation Act 1785 (c.99)
Birmingham Canal: Navigation Act 1792 (c.81)
Birmingham Canal: Navigation Act 1794 (c.25)
Birmingham Canal: Navigation Act 1794 (c.87)
Birmingham Chapels Act 1772 (c.64)
Birmingham: Improvement Act 1769 (c.83)
Birmingham: Improvement Act 1772 (c.36)
Birmingham Police Act 1839 (c.88)
Birmingham: Poor Relief Act 1783 (c.54)
Birmingham to Edghill Road Act 1757 (c.58)
Birmingham to Stratford Roads Act 1725 (c.6)
Birmingham to Stratford Road Act 1771 (c.74)
Birmingham and Wednesbury Roads Act 1726 (c.14)
Birmingham Canal, Navigation Act 1784 (c.4)
Birstall to Huddersfield Roads Act 1786 (c.140)
Births and Deaths Registration Act 1836 (c.86)
Births and Deaths Registration Act 1837 (c.22)
Births and Deaths Registration Act 1858 (c.25)
Births and Deaths Registration Act 1874 (c.88)
Births and Deaths Registration Act 1901 (c.26)
Births and Deaths Registration Act 1926 (c.48)
Births and Deaths Registration Act 1947 (c.12)
Births and Deaths Registration Act 1953 (c.20)
Births and Deaths Registration (Ireland) Act 1880 (c.13)
Bishop of Calcutta Act 1874 (c.13)
Bishop of Quebec Act 1852 (c.53)
Bishopric of Bristol Act 1884 (c.66)
Bishopric of Bristol Amendment Act 1894 (c.21)
Bishopric of Bristol Amendment Act 1896 (c.29)
Bishopric of Christ Church, New Zealand Act 1852 (c.88)
Bishopric of St. Albans Act 1875 (c.34)
Bishopric of Southwark and Birmingham Act 1904 (c.30)
Bishopric of Truro Act 1876 (c.54)
Bishoprics Act 1878 (c.68)
Bishoprics, etc., in West Indies Act 1842 (c.4)
Bishoprics of Bradford and Coventry Act 1918 (c.57)
Bishoprics of Sheffield, Chelmsford and for the County of Suffolk Act 1913 (c.36)
Bishoprics of Southwark and Birmingham Act 1904 (c.30)
Bishops in Foreign Countries Act 1841 (c.6)
Bishops of London and Durham Act 1856 (c.115)
Bishops Trusts Substitution Act 1858 (c.71)
Bishops Resignation Act 1869 (c.111)
Bishops Resignation Act 1875 (c.19)
Bishops Resignation Act Continuance 1872 (c.40)
Bishopsgate: Poor Relief Act 1795 (c.61)
Black Game in Somerset and Devon Act 1810 (c.67)
Blackburn and Addingham Road Act 1796 (c.137)
Blackburn Roads Act 1776 (c.75)
Blackburn Roads Act 1796 (c.144)
Blackburn to Burscough Bridge Road Act 1793 (c.134)
Blackfriars Bridge Act 1756 (c.86)
Blackfriars Bridge Act 1756 (c.86)
Blackfriars Bridge (Sunday Tolls) Act 1786 (c.37)
Blackfriars Sewer Act 1795 (c.131)
Blackheath, etc., Small Debts Act 1770 (c.29)
Blackwater Bridge Act 1867 (c.57)
Blackwater Bridge Act 1873 (c.46)
Blackwater Bridge Debt Act 1873 (c.47)
Blandford Forum (Rebuilding after the Fire) Act 1731 (c.16)
Bleaching and Dyeing Works Act 1860 (c.78)
Bleaching and Dyeing Works Act Amendment Act 1863 (c.38)
Bleaching and Dyeing Works Act Ext. 1864 (c.98)
Bleaching Powder Act 1815 (c.38)
Bleaching Works Act 1862 (c.8)
Blind Persons Act 1938 (c.11)
Blind Voters Act 1933 (c.27)
Bloomsbury Churches Act 1730 (c.19)
Bloomsbury: Poor Relief Act 1774 (c.62)
Bloomsbury: Poor Relief Act 1774 (c.108)
Blything, Suffolk: Poor Relief, etc. Act 1764 (c.56)
Blything, Suffolk (Poor Relief, Guardians, etc.) Act 1793 (c.126)
Board of Agriculture Act 1889 (c.30)
Board of Agriculture and Fisheries Act 1903 (c.31)
Board of Agriculture and Fisheries Act 1909 (c.15)

Board of Education Act 1899 (c.33)
Board of Education (Scotland) Act 1877 (c.38)
Board of Trade Act 1909 (c.23)
Board of Trade Arbitrations etc. Act 1874 (c.40)
Boards of Guardians (Default) Act 1926 (c.20)
Boards of Management of Poor Law District Schools (Ireland) Act 1892 (c.41)
Bodies Corporate (Joint Tenancy) Act 1899 (c.20)
Bodmin Canal Act 1797 (c.29)
Bodmin Gaol Act 1778 (c.17)
Bodmin Roads Act 1769 (c.69)
Bodmin Roads Act 1786 (c.129)
Bogs (Ireland) Act 1811 (c.122)
Bogs (Ireland) Act 1812 (c.74)
Boiler Explosions Act 1882 (c.22)
Boiler Explosions Act 1890 (c.35)
Bolton and Nightingale's Road Act 1763 (c.31)
Bolton and Nightingale's Road Act 1763 (c.40)
Bolton and St. Helens Road Act 1796 (c.149)
Bolton, Blackburn and Twisey Roads Act 1797 (c.173)
Bolton Grammar School Act 1788 (c.81)
Bolton Police Act 1839 (c.95)
Bombay Civil Fund Act 1882 (c.45)
Bonded Corn Act 1842 (c.92)
Bonded Corn Act 1845 (c.103)
Bonded Warehouses Act 1805 (c.87)
Bonded Warehouses Act 1848 (c.122)
Bonding of Coffee, etc. Act 1807 (c.48)
Bonding of Spirits Act 1806 (c.27)
Bonding of Spirits (Ireland) Act 1804 (c.104)
Bonding of Sugar Act 1804 (c.36)
Bonding of Wine Act 1803 (c.103)
Bonding of Wines Act 1803 (c.14)
Bonding Warehouses Act 1806 (c.137)
Bonding Warehouses (Ireland) Act 1808 (c.32)
Bonded Warehouses (Ireland) Act 1810 (c.38)
Bonds of East India Company Act 1803 (c.3)
Booth's Charity, Salford Act 1776 (c.55)
Booth's Patent Act 1792 (c.73)
Borders Rivers (Prevention of Pollution) Act 1951 (c.7)
Borough and Local Courts of Record Act 1872 (c.86)
Borough and Watch Rates Act 1845 (c.110)
Borough Charters Confirmation Act 1842 (c.111)
Borough Clerks of the Peace (Ireland) Act 1868 (c.98)
Borough Constables Act 1883 (c.44)
Borough Coroners (Ireland) Act 1860 (c.74)
Borough Councillors (Alteration of Number) Act 1925 (c.11)
Borough Courts (England) Act 1839 (c.27)
Borough Electors Act 1868 (c.41)
Borough Fund in Certain Boroughs Act 1836 (c.104)
Borough Funds Act 1872 (c.91)
Borough Funds Act 1903 (c.14)
Borough Funds (Ireland) Act 1888 (c.53)
Borough Justices Act 1850 (c.91)
Borough of Hanley Act 1857 (c.10)
Borough Police Act 1848 (c.14)
Borough Quarter Sessions Act 1877 (c.17)
Borough Rates (England) Act 1854 (c.71)
Borough Recorders' Deputies Act 1869 (c.23)
Borough Watch Rates Act 1839 (c.28)
Boroughbridge and Darlington Road Act 1744 (c.8)
Boroughs, Relief from County Expenditure Act 1849 (c.82)
Borrowing (Control and Guarantees) Act 1946 (c.58)
Borrowstoness Canal Act 1783 (c.5)
Bosmere and Claydon, Suffolk (Poor Relief) Act 1764 (c.57)
Boston: Improvement Act 1792 (c.80)
Boston Pilotage Act 1776 (c.23)
Boston Pilotage Act 1792 (c.79)
Boston: Streets Act 1776 (c.25)
Boston Water Supply Act 1711 (c.44)
Botswana Independence Act 1966 (c.23)
Boundaries of Burghs Extension (Scotland) Act 1857 (c.70)
Boundaries of Burghs Extension (Scotland) Act 1861 (c.36)
Boundary Act 1868 (c.46)
Boundary Commissions Act 1992 (c.55)
Boundary Survey (Ireland) Act 1854 (c.17)
Boundary Survey (Ireland) Act 1857 (c.45)
Boundary Survey (Ireland) Act 1859 (c.8)
Bounties Act 1779 (c.27)
Bounties Act 1780 (c.40)
Bounties Act 1783 (c.21)
Bounties Act 1795 (c.21)
Bounties Act 1796 (c.56)
Bounties Act 1801 (c.13)
Bounties Act 1801 (c.34)
Bounties Act 1801 (c.92)
Bounties Act 1802 (c.59)
Bounties and Drawbacks Act 1805 (c.24)
Bounties and Drawbacks Act 1808 (cc.16, 17)
Bounties, etc., on Sugar Act 1809 (cc.10, 11)
Bounties, etc., on Sugar Act 1812 (c.15)
Bounties, etc., on Sugar Act 1813 (c.24)
Bounties for Destroying Spanish Ships Act 1785 (c.29)
Bounties for Destroying Spanish Ships Act 1786 (c.35)
Bounties (Great Britain) Act 1807 (c.29)
Bounties on Exportation Act 1744 (c.25)
Bounties on Importation Act 1800 (c.10)
Bounties on Importation Act 1800 (c.29)
Bounties on Pilchards Act 1812 (c.42)
Bounties on Sugar Act 1807 (c.22)
Bounties on Sugar Act 1808 (c.12)

Bounty for Taking L'Amazone Act 1784 (c.28)
Bounty of Exportation Act 1766 (c.45)
Bounty of Raw Sugar Act 1810 (c.9)
Bounty on British Calicoes Act 1807 (c.64)
Bounty on British Sail Cloth Exported Act 1797 (c.30)
Bounty on Certain Linens Exported Act 1799 (c.28)
Bounty on Cordage Exported Act 1786 (c.85)
Bounty on Corn Act 1780 (c.31)
Bounty on Corn, etc. Act 1750 (c.56)
Bounty on Exportation Act 1797 (c.76)
Bounty on Exportation Act 1806 (c.99)
Bounty on Exportation Act 1810 (c.40)
Bounty on Hemp Act 1779 (c.37)
Bounty on Importation Act 1800 (c.35)
Bounty on Pilchards Act 1797 (c.94)
Bounty on Pilchards Act 1799 (c.65)
Bounty on Pilchards Act 1808 (c.68)
Bounty on Rye Act 1800 (c.53)
Bounty on Silk Manufactures Act 1806 (c.110)
Bounty on Sugar Act 1816 (c.19)
Bounty on Sugar, etc. Act 1806 (c.109)
Bounty to Garrison of Gibraltar Act 1783 (c.16)
Bounty upon Importation Act 1763 (c.26)
Board of Trade (Parliamentary Secretary) Act 1867 (c.72)
Bourn, Lincs.: Navigation Act 1780 (c.22)
Bradford and Wakefield Road Act 1753 (c.83)
Bradford-on-Avon (Additional Overseer) Act 1783 (c.20)
Bradford to Idle Canal Act 1771 (c.89)
Bradford, Yorks: Water Supply Act 1790 (c.63)
Branding of Herrings (Northumberland) Act 1891 (c.28)
Brandon and Sams Cut Drain: Drainage Act 1757 (c.35)
Brandon and Waveney: Navigation Act 1750 (c.12)
Brazilian Slave Trade Repeal Act 1869 (c.2)
Bread Act 1762 (c.6)
Bread Act 1762 (c.11)
Bread Act 1772 (c.62)
Bread Act 1793 (c.37)
Bread Act 1836 (c.37)
Bread Acts Amendment Act 1922 (c.28)
Bread (Ireland) Act 1838 (c.28)
Brecknock and Abergavenny Canal Act 1793 (c.96)
Brecknock Forest Act 1815 (c.190)
Brecknock Water Supply Act 1776 (c.56)
Brecon Roads Act 1767 (c.60)
Brecon Roads Act 1772 (c.105)
Brecon Roads Act 1787 (c.75)
Brecon Roads Act 1793 (c.154)
Breeding of Dogs Act 1973 (c.60)
Breeding of Dogs Act 1991 (c.64)
Brent Bridge to Plymouth Road Act 1777 (c.81)
Brentford Road Act 1791 (c.124)
Bretton Woods Agreements Act 1945 (c.19)
Brewers' Licensing Act 1850 (c.67)
Brewn Roads Act 1772 (c.105)
Bribery at Elections Act 1842 (c.102)
Brick Duties Repeal Act 1850 (c.9)
Brick Making Act 1725 (c.35)
Brickmaking Act 1728 (c.15)
Brickmaking Act 1730 (c.22)
Bricks and Tiles Act 1770 (c.49)
Bricks and Tiles Act 1776 (c.42)
Bridewell Hospital Act 1780 (c.27)
Bridgeford Lane, Notts. to Kettering Road 1754 (c.39)
Bridges Act 1670 (c.12)
Bridges Act 1702 (c.12)
Bridges Act 1740 (c.33)
Bridges Act 1803 (c.59)
Bridges Act 1812 (c.110)
Bridges Act 1814 (c.90)
Bridges Act 1815 (c.143)
Bridges Act 1850 (c.64)
Bridges Act 1929 (c.33)
Bridges (Ireland) Act 1843 (c.42)
Bridges (Ireland) Act 1850 (c.4)
Bridges (Ireland) Act 1851 (c.21)
Bridges (Ireland) Act 1867 (c.50)
Bridges (Ireland) Act 1875 (c.46)
Bridges (Ireland) Act 1813 (c.77)
Bridges (Scotland) Act 1813 (c.117)
Bridgewell Hospital Act 1783 (c.27)
Bridgnorth Bridge Act 1797 (c.58)
Bridgnorth Church Act 1792 (c.30)
Bridgwater and Beverly Disfranchisement Act 1870 (c.21)
Bridgwater Canal Act 1795 (c.44)
Bridgwater Markets Act 1779 (c.36)
Bridgwater: Navigation Act 1794 (c.105)
Bridgwater Roads Act 1730 (c.34)
Bridgwater Roads Act 1779 (c.100)
Bridlington Pier Act 1715 (c.49)
Bridlington Pier Act 1718 (c.10)
Bridlington Pier Act 1789 (c.23)
Bridlington Piers Act 1720 (c.16)
Bridlington Piers Act 1753 (c.10)
Bridlington Roads Act 1767 (c.89)
Bridport, Dorset, Harbour Act 1721 (c.11)
Bridport: Improvement Act 1785 (c.91)
Brighton: Streets Act 1772 (c.34)
Brine Pumping (Compensation for Subsidence) Act 1891 (c.40)
Bringing of Coals, etc., to London, etc. Act 1805 (c.128)
Bringing of Coals, etc., to London Act 1807 (c.34)
Bringing of Coals, etc., to London, etc. Act 1808 (c.95)
Bringing of Coals, etc., to London, etc. Act 1810 (c.110)
Bringing of Coals, etc., to London Act 1811 (c.29)
Bringing of Coals, etc., to London, etc. Act 1817 (c.114)
Bringing of Coals to London, etc. Act 1806 (c.104)

Bringing of Coals to London, etc. Act 1813 (c.135)
Bringing of Coals to London, etc. 1815 (c.175)
Bringing of Coals to London, etc. Act 1816 (c.124)
Bristol and Exeter Railway Act 1836 (c.36)
Bristol Bridge Act 1759 (c.52)
Bristol Bridge Act 1786 (c.111)
Bristol: Building Act 1788 (c.66)
Bristol Charities Act 1858 (c.30)
Bristol Charities Act 1858 (c.31)
Bristol Churches Act 1750 (c.37)
Bristol Dock Act 1776 (c.33)
Bristol Gaol Act 1792 (c.82)
Bristol Guildhall, etc. Act 1788 (c.67)
Bristol Hospitals Act 1744 (c.38)
Bristol: Improvement Act 1788 (c.65)
Bristol Museum Act 1766 (c.18)
Bristol (Nightly Watch) Act 1755 (c.32)
Bristol, Paving, etc. Act 1748 (c.20)
Bristol, Poor Relief Act 1713 (c.32)
Bristol (Poor Relief) Act 1757 (c.56)
Bristol Roads Act 1726 (c.12)
Bristol Roads Act 1730 (c.22)
Bristol Roads Act 1748 (c.28)
Bristol Roads Act 1779 (c.117)
Bristol Roads Act 1797 (c.178)
Bristol Streets Act 1766 (c.34)
Bristol Theatre Act 1778 (c.8)
Bristol Watch Act 1756 (c.47)
British Aerospace Act 1980 (c.26)
British Airways Board Act 1977 (c.13)
British Calicoes Act 1811 (c.33)
British Caribbean Federation Act 1956 (c.63)
British Coal and British Rail (Transfer Proposals) Act 1993 (c.2)
British Columbia Act 1866 (c.67)
British Columbia Boundaries Act 1863 (c.83)
British Columbia Government Act 1858 (c.99)
British Columbia Government Act 1870 (c.66)
British Columbia (Loan) Act 1892 (c.52)
British Council and Commonwealth Institute Superannuation Act 1986 (c.51)
British Empire Exhibition (Amendment) Act 1922 (c.25)
British Empire Exhibition (Guarantee) Act 1920 (c.74)
British Empire Exhibition (Guarantee) Act 1925 (c.26)
British Ferries Society Act 1799 (c.100)
British Film Institute Act 1949 (c.35)
British Fisheries Act 1795 (c.56)
British Fisheries Act 1798 (c.58)
British Fisheries Act 1800 (c.85)
British Fisheries Act 1804 (c.86)
British Fisheries Act 1806 (c.34)
British Fisheries Act 1806 (c.156)
British Fisheries Act 1807 (c.51)
British Fisheries Act 1808 (c.86)
British Fisheries Act 1810 (c.54)
British Fisheries, etc. Act 1802 (c.79)
British Fisheries Society Act 1786 (c.106)
British Fishing Boats Act 1983 (c.8)
British Forces in India Act 1862 (c.27)
British Guiana Act 1928 (c.5)
British Honduras (Court of Appeal) Act 1881 (c.36)
British Hydrocarbon Oils Production Act 1934 (c.4)
British Industries Fair (Guarantees and Grants) Act 1954 (c.26)
British Kaffrania Act 1865 (c.5)
British Law Ascertainment Act 1859 (c.63)
British Leyland Act 1975 (c.43)
British Library Act 1972 (c.54)
British Mercantile Marine Uniform Act 1919 (c.62)
British Museum Act 1700 (c.7)
British Museum Act 1706 (c.30)
British Museum Act 1753 (c.22)
British Museum Act 1766 (c.18)
British Museum Act 1805 (c.127)
British Museum Act 1807 (c.36)
British Museum Act 1816 (c.99)
British Museum Act 1839 (c.10)
British Museum Act 1878 (c.55)
British Museum Act 1902 (c.12)
British Museum Act 1924 (c.23)
British Museum Act 1930 (c.46)
British Museum Act 1931 (c.34)
British Museum Act 1932 (c.34)
British Museum Act 1938 (c.62)
British Museum Act 1946 (c.56)
British Museum Act 1955 (c.23)
British Museum Act 1962 (c.18)
British Museum Act 1963 (c.24)
British Museum (Purchase of Land) Act 1894 (c.34)
British Nationality Act 1730 (c.21)
British Nationality Act 1772 (c.21)
British Nationality Act 1948 (c.56)
British Nationality Act 1958 (c.10)
British Nationality Act 1964 (c.22)
British Nationality Act 1965 (c.34)
British Nationality Act 1981 (c.61)
British Nationality and Status of Aliens Act 1918 (c.38)
British Nationality and Status of Aliens Act 1922 (c.44)
British Nationality and Status of Aliens Act 1933 (c.49)
British Nationality and Status of Aliens Act 1943 (c.14)
British Nationality (Falkland Islands) Act 1983 (c.6)
British Nationality (Hong Kong) Act 1990 (c.34)
British Nationality (No. 2) Act 1964 (c.54)
British North America Act 1840 (c.35)
British North America Act 1867 (c.3)
British North America Act 1870 (c.28)
British North America Act 1871 (c.28)
British North America Act 1886 (c.35)
British North America Act 1907 (c.11)
British North America Act 1915 (c.45)

British North America Act 1916 (c.19)
British North America Act 1930 (c.26)
British North America Act 1939 (c.36)
British North America Act 1940 (c.36)
British North America Act 1943 (c.30)
British North America Act 1946 (c.63)
British North America Act 1949 (c.22)
British North America Act 1951 (c.32)
British North America Act 1960 (c.2)
British North America Act 1964 (c.73)
British North America (No. 2) Act 1949 (c.81)
British North America (Quebec) Act 1774 (c.83)
British Overseas Airways Act 1939 (c.61)
British Railways Board (Finance) Act 1991 (c.63)
British Sailcloth, etc. Act 1793 (c.49)
British Settlements Act 1887 (c.54)
British Settlements Act 1945 (c.7)
British Settlements in Africa, etc. Act 1764 (c.44)
British Shipbuilders Act 1983 (c.15)
British Shipbuilders (Borrowing Powers) Act 1983 (c.58)
British Shipbuilders (Borrowing Powers) Act 1986 (c.19)
British Shipbuilders (Borrowing Powers) Act 1987 (c.52)
British Shipping (Assistance) Act 1935 (c.7)
British Shipping (Continuance of Subsidy) Act 1936 (c.12)
British Shipping (Continuance of Subsidy) Act 1937 (c.21)
British Ships Act 1772 (c.26)
British Ships Captured by the Enemy Act 1808 (c.70)
British Ships (Transfer Restriction) Act 1915 (c.21)
British Ships (Transfer Restriction) Act 1916 (c.42)
British Standard Time Act 1968 (c.45)
British Steel Act 1988 (c.35)
Btitish Subjects Act 1751 (c.39)
British Subjects in China Act 1843 (c.80)
British Sugar Industry (Assistance) Act 1931 (c.35)
British Sugar (Subsidy) Act 1925 (c.12)
British Sugar (Subsidy) Act 1934 (c.39)
British Sugar (Subsidy) Act 1935 (c.37)
British Technology Group Act 1991 (c.66)
British Telecommunications Act 1981 (c.38)
British White Herring Fishery Act 1811 (c.101)
British White Herring Fishery Act 1812 (c.153)
British White Herring Fishery Act 1814 (c.102)
Brixton: Small Debts Act 1757 (c.23)
Broadcasting Act 1980 (c.64)
Broadcasting Act 1981 (c.68)
Broadcasting Act 1987 (c.10)
Broadcasting Act 1990 (c.42)
Broadstairs Pier Act 1792 (c.86)
Brokers, Bristol Act 1730 (c.31)
Bromsgrove and Birmingham Roads Act 1776 (c.15)
Bromsgrove to Birmingham Road Act 1790 (c.101)
Brown Linen Manufacture (Ireland) Act 1815 (c.25)
Brunei and Maldives Act 1985 (c.3)
Brunei Appeals Act 1989 (c.36)
Bruntisland Beer Duties Act 1746 (c.26)
Bruntisland Beer Duties Act 1776 (c.20)
Bruntisland Beer Duties Act 1794 (c.8)
Bruton Roads Act 1756 (c.50)
Bubble Schemes, Colonies Act 1740 (c.37)
Bubwith Bridge Act 1793 (c.106)
Buckingham and Hanwell Road Act 1792 (c.134)
Buckingham and Middlesex Roads Act 1779 (c.83)
Buckingham and Oxford Roads Act 1770 (c.58)
Buckingham and Oxford Roads Act 1785 (c.127)
Buckingham to Banbury Road Act 1791 (c.133)
Buckingham to Hanwell Road Act 1769 (c.52)
Buckingham to Warmington Road Act 1743 (c.43)
Buckinghamshire and Oxford Roads Act 1769 (c.88)
Buckinghamshire and Oxford Roads Act 1791 (c.136)
Buckinghamshire Assizes Act 1747 (c.12)
Buckinghamshire Assizes Act 1849 (c.6)
Buckinghamshire Highways Act 1722 (c.13)
Buckinghamshire Roads Act 1720 (c.24)
Buckinghamshire Roads Act 1735 (c.11)
Buckinghamshire Roads Act 1735 (c.21)
Buckinghamshire Roads Act 1741 (c.5)
Buckinghamshire Roads Act 1741 (c.6)
Buckinghamshire Roads Act 1759 (c.43)
Buckinghamshire Roads Act 1767 (c.61)
Buckinghamshire Roads Act 1777 (c.82)
Bude Canal Act 1774 (c.53)
Building Act 1984 (c.55)
Building Control Act 1966 (c.27)
Building Materials and Housing Act 1945 (c.20)
Building of Churches, etc. (Ireland) Act 1809
Building of Churches, London and Westminster Act 1714 (c.23)
Building Restrictions (War-Time Contraventions) Act 1946 (c.35)
Building (Scotland) Act 1959 (c.24)
Building (Scotland) Act 1970 (c.38)
Building Sites for Religious and Other Purposes Act 1868 (c.44)
Building Societies Act 1874 (c.42)
Building Societies Act 1875 (c.9)
Building Societies Act 1877 (c.63)
Building Societies Act 1884 (c.41)
Building Societies Act 1894 (c.47)
Building Societies Act 1939 (c.55)

Building Societies Act 1960 (c.64)
Building Societies Act 1962 (c.37)
Building Societies Act 1986 (c.53)
Building Societies (Joint Account Holders) Act 1995 (c.5)
Bunhill Fields Burial Ground Act 1867 (c.38)
Burford Charities Act 1861 (c.22)
Burford to Preston Road Act 1780 (c.76)
Burgesses Qualification (Scotland) Act 1876 (c.12)
Burgesses (Scotland) Act 1860 (c.47)
Burgh Council Elections (Scotland) Act 1853 (c.26)
Burgh Customs (Scotland) Act 1870 (c.42)
Burgh Gas Supply (Scotland) Amendment Act 1918 (c.45)
Burgh Harbours (Scotland) Act 1853 (c.93)
Burgh Police (Amendment) (Scotland) Act 1964 (c.33)
Burgh Police, etc. (Scotland) Act 1847 (c.39)
Burgh Police (Scotland) Act 1892 (c.55)
Burgh Police (Scotland) Act 1892, Amendment 1894 (c.18)
Burgh Police (Scotland) Act 1893 (c.25)
Burgh Police (Scotland) Act 1903 (c.33)
Burgh Police (Scotland) Amendment Act 1911 (c.51)
Burgh Registers (Scotland) Act 1926 (c.50)
Burgh, Scotland (Petty Customs) Act 1879 (c.13)
Burgh Sewerage, Drainage and Water Supply (Scotland) Act 1901 (c.24)
Burgh Trading Act 1846 (c.17)
Burgh Voters' Registration (Scotland) Act 1856 (c.58)
Burgh Wards (Scotland) Act 1876 (c.25)
Burghs Gas Supply (Scotland) Act 1876 (c.49)
Burghs Gas Supply (Scotland) Act 1893 (c.52)
Burghs of Barony (Scotland) Act 1795 (c.122)
Burghs (Scotland) Act 1852 (c.33)
Burglaries, etc. Act 1706 (c.9)
Burglary Act 1837 (c.86)
Burglary Act 1896 (c.57)
Burial Act 1852 (c.85)
Burial Act 1853 (c.134)
Burial Act 1854 (c.87)
Burial Act 1855 (c.128)
Burial Act 1857 (c.81)
Burial Act 1859 (c.1)
Burial Act 1860 (c.64)
Burial Act 1862 (c.100)
Burial Act 1871 (c.33)
Burial Act 1900 (c.15)
Burial Act 1906 (c.44)
Burial and Registration Acts (Doubts Removal) Act 1881 (c.2)
Burial Boards (Contested Elections) Act 1885 (c.21)
Burial Grounds (Ireland) Act 1856 (c.98)
Burial Grounds (Ireland) Act 1860 (c.76)
Burial Grounds (Scotland) Act 1855 (c.68)
Burial Grounds (Scotland) Act, 1855, Amendment Act 1881 (c.27)
Burial Grounds (Scotland) Act 1857 (c.42)
Burial Grounds (Scotland) Amendment Act 1886 (c.21)
Burial in Burghs (Scotland) Act 1866 (c.46)
Burial (Ireland) Act 1868 (c.103)
Burial Laws Amendment Act 1880 (c.41)
Burial of Drowned Persons Act 1808 (c.75)
Burial of Drowned Persons Act 1886 (c.20)
Burma Independence Act 1947 (c.3)
Burma Legislature Act 1946 (c.57)
Burning of Buildings, etc. Act 1837 (c.89)
Burning of Farm Buildings Act 1844 (c.62)
Burning of Houses (Dublin) Act 1841 (c.10)
Burning of Land (Ireland) Act 1814 (c.115)
Burnley Roads Act 1795 (c.146)
Burnt Fen (Northampton): Drainage Act 1797 (c.89)
Bursledon Bridge, Southampton Act 1797 (c.131)
Burton-upon-Trent and Derby Road Act 1753 (c.59)
Burton-upon-Trent and Derby Road Act 1764 (c.51)
Burton-upon-Trent: Improvement Act 1779 (c.39)
Burtry Ford to Burnstone Road 1794 (c.125)
Bury and Bolton Roads Act 1797 (c.174)
Bury and Stratton Road Act 1755 (c.35)
Bury St. Edmunds (Poor Relief) Act 1749 (c.21)
Bury to Church Kirk Canal Act 1794 (c.77)
Burying in Woollen Act 1814 (c.108)
Bus Fuel Grants Act 1966 (c.46)
Bushey Heath to Aylesbury Road Act 1783 (c.93)
Business Names Act 1985 (c.7)
Butter and Cheese Trade Act 1844 (c.48)
Butter and Margarine Act 1907 (c.21)
Butter Trade (Ireland) Act 1812 (c.134)
Butter Trade (Ireland) Act 1813 (c.46)
Buxton and Manchester Road Act 1753 (c.53)
Buxton to Manchester Road Act 1729 (c.4)
Buxton to Manchester Road Act 1748 (c.12)
Byron's Shorthand Act 1741 (c.23)

Cable and Broadcasting Act 1984 (c.46)
Cable and Wireless Act 1946 (c.82)
Caddington Church Act 1740 (c.26)
Caithness Roads Act 1793 (c.120)
Calder and Hebb: Navigation Act 1769 (c.71)
Calder Canal Act 1774 (c.13)
Calder Navigation Act 1757 (c.72)
Caldey Island Act 1990 (c.44)
Caldon Canal Act 1797 (c.36)
Caledonian and Crinan Canals Amendment Act 1860 (c.46)
Caledonian Canal Act 1803 (c.102)
Caledonian Canal Act 1804 (c.62)
Caledonian Canal Act 1840 (c.41)

Caledonian Canal Act 1848 (c.54)
Caledonian Canal Act 1857 (c.27)
Calendar Act 1750 (c.30)
Calendar (New Style) Act 1750 (c.23)
Callington Roads Act 1764 (c.48)
Camberwell and Peckham: Streets Act 1776 (c.26)
Camberwell, Bristol and Nottingham Elections (Validation) Act 1946 (c.43)
Camberwell: Streets Act 1787 (c.52)
Cambrics Act 1744 (c.36)
Cambrics Act 1747 (c.26)
Cambridge and Arrington Roads Act 1797 (c.179)
Cambridge and Ely Roads Act 1763 (c.36)
Cambridge and Newmarket Road Act 1763 (c.30)
Cambridge and Norfolk Roads Act 1770 (c.97)
Cambridge Commissioners Act 1873 (c.73)
Cambridge: Improvement Act 1788 (c.64)
Cambridge: Improvement Act 1794 (c.104)
Cambridge Roads Act 1723 (c.12)
Cambridge Roads Act 1724 (c.14)
Cambridge Roads Act 1730 (c.37)
Cambridge Roads Act 1755 (c.36)
Cambridge Roads Act 1765 (c.74)
Cambridge Roads Act 1765 (c.76)
Cambridge Roads Act 1765 (c.79)
Cambridge Roads Act 1766 (c.84)
Cambridge Roads Act 1773 (c.110)
Cambridge Roads Act 1790 (c.94)
Cambridge Roads Act 1792 (c.129)
Cambridge to Royston Road Act 1793 (c.130)
Cambridge University Act 1856 (c.88)
Cambridge University Act 1858 (c.11)
Cambridge University, etc. Act 1859 (c.34)
Cambridgeshire Roads Act 1730 (c.24)
Cambridgeshire Roads Act 1741 (c.16)
Camps Act 1939 (c.22)
Camps Act 1945 (c.26)
Canada Act 1775 (c.40)
Canada Act 1982 (c.11)
Canada Civil List Act 1847 (c.71)
Canada Company's Amendment Act 1856 (c.23)
Canada Copyright Act 1875 (c.53)
Canada Defences Loan Act 1870 (c.82)
Canada Loan Guarantee Act 1842 (c.118)
Canada (Ontario Boundary) Act 1889 (c.28)
Canada (Public Works) Loan Act 1873 (c.45)
Canada Railway Loan Act 1867 (c.16)
Canada (Rupert's Land) Loan Act 1869 (c.101)
Canada Union Act 1848 (c.56)
Canadian Speaker (Appointment of Deputy) Act 1895 (c.3)
Canadian Stock Stamp Act 1874 (c.26)
Canal Boats Act 1877 (c.60)
Canal Boats Act 1884 (c.75)
Canal, Carmarthen Act 1766 (c.55)
Canal Carriers Act 1845 (c.42)
Canal (Carriers) Act 1847 (c.94)
Canal Tolls Act 1845 (c.28)
Canals (Continuance of Charging Powers) Act 1922 (c.27)
Canals (Continuance of Charging Powers) Act 1924 (c.2)
Canals, etc. (Scotland) Act 1806 (c.155)
Canals (Ireland) Act 1816 (c.55)
Canals (Offences) Act 1840 (c.50)
Canals Protection (London) Act 1898 (c.16)
Canals: Trent and Mersey Act 1797 (c.81)
Cancer Act 1939 (c.13)
Canterbury Association (New Zealand) Act 1850 (c.70)
Canterbury Association (New Zealand) Act 1851 (c.84)
Canterbury: Church of St. Andrew Act 1763 (c.49)
Canterbury: Poor Relief Act 1727 (c.20)
Canterbury: Streets Act 1787 (c.14)
Canterbury to Whitstable Road Act 1783 (c.97)
Canvey Island, Sea Defences Act 1792 (c.23)
Cape of Good Hope (Advance) Act 1885 (c.7)
Cape of Good Hope Trade Act 1796 (c.21)
Cape of Good Hope Trade Act 1806 (c.30)
Cape of Good Hope Trade Act 1807 (c.11)
Cape of Good Hope Trade Act 1808 (c.105)
Cape of Good Hope Trade Act 1809 (c.17)
Cape of Good Hope Trade Act 1816 (c.8)
Cape Race Lighthouse Act 1886 (c.13)
Cape Rock Lighthouse (Scotland) Act 1806 (c.132)
Capital Allowances Act 1968 (c.3)
Capital Allowances Act 1990 (c.1)
Capital Expenditure (Money) Act 1904 (c.21)
Capital Gains Tax Act 1979 (c.14)
Capital Punishment, etc. Act 1823 (c.46)
Capital Punishment Abolition Act 1835 (c.81)
Capital Punishment Abolition Act 1836 (c.4)
Capital Punishment Amendment Act 1868 (c.24)
Capital Punishment (Ireland) Act 1842 (c.28)
Capital Transfer Tax Act 1984 (c.51)
Captive Birds Shooting (Prohibition) Act 1921 (c.13)
Captures Act 1776 (c.40)
Car Tax (Abolition) Act 1992 (c.58)
Car Tax Act 1983 (c.53)
Caravan Sites Act 1968 (c.52)
Caravan Sites and Control of Development Act 1960 (c.62)
Caravans (Standard Community Charge and Rating) Act 1991 (c.2)
Cardiff Bay Barrage Act 1993 (c.42)
Cardiff: Improvement Act 1774 (c.9)
Cardigan Roads Act 1770 (c.55)
Cardigan Roads Act 1791 (c.97)
Care and Treatment of Lunatics Act 1853 (c.96)
Care, etc., of Lunatics Act 1841 (c.4)
Care of King During His Illness, etc. Act 1811 (c.1)
Care of King's Estate During His Illness Act 1812 (c.14)

Carers (Recognition and Services) Act 1995 (c.12)
Carlford, Suffolk: Poor Relief Act 1756 (c.79)
Carlford, Suffolk (Poor Relief) Act 1764 (c.58)
Carlisle and Eamont Bridge Road Act 1753 (c.40)
Carlisle and Newcastle Road Act 1750 (c.25)
Carlton Bridge, Yorks. Act 1774 (c.63)
Carmarthen and Pembroke Roads Act 1763 (c.34)
Carmarthen: Improvement Act 1792 (c.104)
Carmarthen Roads Act 1765 (c.76)
Carmarthen Roads Act 1779 (c.102)
Carmarthen Roads Act 1779 (c.103)
Carmarthen Roads Act 1783 (c.33)
Carmarthen Roads Act 1786 (c.150)
Carmarthen Roads Act 1788 (c.109)
Carmarthen Roads Act 1792 (c.156)
Carnarvon Harbour Act 1793 (c.123)
Carnarvon Roads Act 1769 (c.77)
Carnarvon Roads Act 1795 (c.143)
Carriage and Deposit of Dangerous Goods Act 1866 (c.69)
Carriage by Air Act 1931 (c.36)
Carriage by Air Act 1961 (c.27)
Carriage by Air and Road Act 1979 (c.28)
Carriage by Air (Supplementary Provisions) Act 1962 (c.43)
Carriage by Railway Act 1972 (c.33)
Carriage Duties Act 1795 (c.109)
Carriage of Corn, etc. Act 1702 (c.20)
Carriage of Goods by Road Act 1965 (c.37)
Carriage of Goods by Sea Act 1924 (c.22)
Carriage of Goods by Sea Act 1971 (c.19)
Carriage of Goods by Sea Act 1992 (c.50)
Carriage of Gunpowder (Great Britain) Act 1814 (c.152)
Carriage of Passengers by Road Act 1974 (c.35)
Carriers Act 1830 (c.68)
Carriers Act Amendment Act 1865 (c.94)
Carrying of Knives etc. (Scotland) Act 1993 (c.13)
Carts on Highways Act 1744 (c.33)
Casting Away of Vessels, etc. Act 1803 (c.113)
Castle Stewart and Nairn Road Assessment Act 1860 (c.37)
Casual Poor Act 1882 (c.36)
Catering Wages Act 1943 (c.24)
Cathedral Acts Amendment 1873 (c.39)
Cathedral Churches, etc. Act 1853 (c.35)
Cathedral Statutes Act 1707 (c.75)
Cathedrals Act 1864 (c.70)
Catterick Bridge to Durham Road Act 1788 (c.90)
Cattle Assurance Act 1866 (c.34)
Cattle Disease Act 1866 (c.15)
Cattle Disease (Ireland) Act 1866 (c.4)
Cattle Disease (Ireland) Act 1876 (c.51)
Cattle Disease (Ireland) Acts Amendment 1874 (c.6)
Cattle Disease (Ireland) Amendment Act 1872 (c.16)
Cattle Diseases (Ireland) Amendment Act 1870 (c.36)
Cattle Disease Prevention Amendment Act 1866 (c.110)
Cattle Diseases Prevention Act 1866 (c.2)
Cattle Distemper, Vagrancy, Marshalsea Prison Act 1753 (c.34)
Cattle Industry Act 1936 (c.46)
Cattle Industry (Emergency Provisions) Act 1934 (c.54)
Cattle Industry (Emergency Provisions) Act 1935 (c.12)
Cattle Industry (Emergency Provisions) (No. 2) Act 1935 (c.39)
Cattle sheds in Burghs (Scotland) Act 1866 (c.17)
Cattle Stealing Act 1740 (c.6)
Cattle Stealing Act 1741 (c.34)
Cattle Theft (Scotland) Act 1747 (c.34)
Catwater Harbour and Sutton Pool, Plymouth Act 1709 (c.4 (b))
Causey, Yarmouth to Caistor Act 1723 (c.8)
Cawdle Fen. etc. Drainage Act 1737 (c.34)
Cayman Islands Act 1863 (c.31)
Cayman Islands and Turks and Caicos Islands Act 1958 (c.13)
Celluloid and Cinematograph Film Act 1922 (c.35)
Cemeteries Clauses Act 1847 (c.65)
Census Act 1800 (c.15)
Census Act 1841 (c.7)
Census Act 1841 (c.9)
Census Act 1860 (cc.61, 62)
Census Act 1880 (c.37)
Census Act 1920 (c.41)
Census (Confidentiality) Act 1991 (c.6)
Census (England) Act 1870 (c.107)
Census (England and Wales) Act 1890 (c.61)
Census (Great Britain) Act 1811 (c.6)
Census (Great Britain) Act 1840 (c.99)
Census, Great Britain Act 1850 (c.53)
Census (Great Britain) Act 1900 (c.4)
Census (Great Britain) Act 1910 (c.27)
Census (Ireland) Act 1812 (c.133)
Census (Ireland) Act 1815 (c.120)
Census (Ireland) Act 1840 (c.100)
Census (Ireland) Act 1850 (c.44)
Census (Ireland) Act 1870 (c.80)
Census (Ireland) Act 1880 (c.28)
Census (Ireland) Act 1890 (c.46)
Census (Ireland) Act 1900 (c.6)
Census (Ireland) Act 1910 (c.11)
Census of Production Act 1906 (c.49)
Census of Production Act 1917 (c.2)
Census of Production Act 1939 (c.15)
Census (Scotland) Act 1860 (c.98)
Census (Scotland) Act 1870 (c.108)
Census (Scotland) Act 1880 (c.38)
Census (Scotland) Act 1890 (c.38)
Central Criminal Court Act 1837 (c.77)
Central Criminal Court Act 1846 (c.24)
Central Criminal Court Act 1856 (c.16)
Central Criminal Court (Prisons) Act 1881 (c.64)

Central Criminal Lunatic Asylum (Ireland) Act 1845 (c.107)
Cereals Marketing Act 1965 (c.14)
Certain Export Duties Repeal Act 1845 (c.7)
Certain Mutinous Crews Act 1797 (c.71)
Certain Parliamentary Grants Act 1801 (c.73)
Certificates for Killing Hares Act 1791 (c.21)
Certificates of Attorneys, etc. Act 1804 (c.59)
Cessio (Scotland) Act 1836 (c.56)
Cestui que Vie Act 1707 (c.72)
Ceylon Independence Act 1947 (c.7)
Chaff-Cutting Machines (Accidents) Act 1897 (c.60)
Chain Cable and Anchor Act 1864 (c.27)
Chain Cable and Anchor Act 1871 (c.101)
Chain Cable and Anchor Act 1872 (c.30)
Chain Cables and Anchors Act 1874 (c.51)
Chairman of District Councils Act 1896 (c.22)
Chairman of Quarter Sessions (Ireland) Act 1858 (c.88)
Chairman of Quarter Sessions (Ireland) Jurisdiction Act 1876 (c.71)
Chairman of Traffic Commissioners etc. (Tenure of Office) Act 1937 (c.52)
Chancel Repairs Act 1931 (c.20)
Chancery Amendment Act 1858 (c.27)
Chancery and Common Law Offices (Ireland) Act 1867 (c.129)
Chancery Appeal Court (Ireland) Act 1856 (c.92)
Chancery Court Act 1838 (c.54)
Chancery (Ireland) Act 1834 (c.78)
Chancery (Ireland) Act 1835 (c.16)
Chancery (Ireland) Act 1851 (c.15)
Chancery (Ireland) Act 1867 (c.44)
Chancery of Lancaster Act 1890 (c.23)
Chancery Receivers (Ireland) Act 1856 (c.77)
Chancery Regulation Act 1862 (c.42)
Chancery Regulation (Ireland) Act 1862 (c.46)
Chancery Rules and Orders Act 1860 (c.128)
Chancery Taxing Master (Ireland) Act 1845 (c.115)
Channel Tunnel Act 1987 (c.53)
Channel Tunnel (Initial Finance) Act 1973 (c.66)
Chapel of Ease, Yarmouth Act 1713 (c.16(d))
Chapels of Ease Act 1836 (c.31)
Chapels of Ease, etc. (Ireland) Act 1849 (c.99)
Chaplains in Gaols, etc. (England) Act 1815 (c.48)
Chaplains in the Navy (1820) (c.106)
Charge of Certain Annuities Act 1813 (c.156)
Charge of Loan Act 1807 (c.55)
Charge of Loan Act 1811 (c.61)
Charges of Loan, etc., of Present Session Act 1810 (c.71)
Charge of Loans Act 1809 (c.92)
Charging Orders Act 1979 (c.53)
Charitable Corporation Act 1732 (c.2)
Charitable Corporation (Arrangements with Creditors) Act 1732 (c.36)
Charitable Corporation (Claims and Disputes) Act 1731 (c.31)
Charitable Corporation Frauds Act 1731 (c.3)
Charitable Corporation Lottery Act 1733 (c.11)
Charitable Corporation Lottery Act 1734 (c.14)
Charitable Donations and Bequest (Ireland) Act 1867 (c.54)
Charitable Donations and Bequests (Ireland) Act 1844 (c.97)
Charitable Donations and Bequests (Ireland) Act 1871 (c.102)
Charitable Donations Registration Act 1812 (c.102)
Charitable Funds Investment Act 1870 (c.34)
Charitable Loan Societies (Ireland) Act 1844 (c.38)
Charitable Loan Societies (Ireland) Act 1900 (c.25)
Charitable Loan Societies (Ireland) Act 1906 (c.23)
Charitable Pawn Offices (Ireland) Act 1842 (c.75)
Charitable Trust (Recovery) Act 1891 (c.17)
Charitable Trustees Incorporation Act 1872 (c.24)
Charitable Trusts Act 1853 (c.137)
Charitable Trusts Act 1860 (c.136)
Charitable Trusts Act 1862 (c.112)
Charitable Trusts Act 1869 (c.110)
Charitable Trusts Act 1887 (c.49)
Charitable Trusts Act 1914 (c.56)
Charitable Trusts Act 1925 (c.27)
Charitable Trusts Amendment Act 1855 (c.124)
Charitable Trusts Deeds Enrolment Act 1866 (c.57)
Charitable Trusts (Places of Religious Worship) Amendment Act 1894 (c.35)
Charitable Trusts (Validation) Act 1954 (c.58)
Charitable Uses Act 1735 (c.36)
Charitable Uses Act 1861 (c.9)
Charitable Uses Act 1862 (c.17)
Charities Act 1960 (c.58)
Charities Act 1985 (c.20)
Charities Act 1992 (c.41)
Charities Act 1993 (c.10)
Charities (Amendment) Act 1995 (c.48)
Charities (Enrolment of Deeds) Act 1864 (c.13)
Charities (Fuel Allotments) Act 1939 (c.26)
Charities Inquiries Commission Expenses Act 1837 (c.4)
Charities Inquiries (England) Act 1835 (c.71)
Charities of John Pierrepont Act 1708 (c.10)
Charities of Thomas Guy Act 1724 (c.12)
Charities Procedure Act 1812 (c.101)
Charities (Service of Notice) Act 1851 (c.56)
Charity Inquiries Expenses Act 1892 (c.15)
Charity Lands Act 1863 (c.106)
Charles Beattie Indemnity Act 1956 (c.27)
Charles Radcliffe's Estates Act 1788 (c.63)

Charlwood and Horley Act 1974 (c.11)
Charter Trustees Act 1985 (c.45)
Chartered and Other Bodies (Resumption of Elections) Act 1945 (c.6)
Chartered and Other Bodies (Temporary Provisions) Act 1939 (c.119)
Chartered and Other Bodies (Temporary Provisions) Act 1941 (c.19)
Chartered Associations (Protection of Names and Uniforms) Act 1926 (c.26)
Chartered Companies Act 1837 (c.73)
Chartered Companies Act 1884 (c.56)
Charterhouse Governors (Quorum) Act 1721 (c.29)
Charterhouse Square: Rates Act 1742 (c.6)
Chatham and Sheerness Stipendiary Magistrate Act 1867 (c.63)
Chatham and Sheerness Stipendiary Magistrate Act 1929 (c.30)
Chatham Dockyard Act 1861 (c.41)
Chatham Fortifications Act 1780 (c.49)
Chatham: Improvement Act 1776 (c.58)
Chatham Lands Purchase Act 1857 (c.30)
Chatham Roads Act 1797 (c.155)
Chatham: Streets Act 1772 (c.18)
Cheap Trains Act 1883 (c.34)
Cheap Trains and Canal Carriers Act 1858 (c.75)
Checkweighing in Various Industries Act 1919 (c.51)
Chelmsford and Blackwater Canal Act 1793 (c.93)
Chelmsford Gaol Act 1770 (c.28)
Chelmsford: Improvement Act 1789 (c.44)
Chelmsford Roads Act 1794 (c.137)
Chelsea and Greenwich Out-Pensioners Act 1847 (c.54)
Chelsea and Greenwich Out-Pensioners, etc. Act 1848 (c.84)
Chelsea and Kilmainham Hospitals Act 1826 (c.16)
Chelsea Bridge Act 1858 (c.66)
Chelsea Hospital Act 1755 (c.1)
Chelsea Hospital Act 1812 (c.109)
Chelsea Hospital Act 1815 (c.125)
Chelsea Hospital Act 1843 (c.31)
Chelsea Hospital Act 1858 (c.18)
Chelsea Hospital Act 1876 (c.14)
Chelsea Hospital Out-Pensioners Act 1842 (c.70)
Chelsea Hospital Out-Pensioners Act 1843 (c.95)
Chelsea Hospital Purchase Act 1855 (c.21)
Chelsea and Greenwich Hospitals Act 1815 (c.133)
Chelsea Pensions (Abolition of Poundage) Act 1847 (c.4)
Cheltenham Roads Act 1785 (c.125)
Cheltenham: Streets Act 1786 (c.116)
Chequers Estate Act 1917 (c.55)
Chequers Estate Act 1958 (c.60)
Cheques Act 1957 (c.36)
Cheques Act 1992 (c.32)
Cheshire Roads Act 1730 (c.3)
Cheshire Roads Act 1753 (c.62)
Cheshire Roads Act 1774 (c.100)
Cheshire Roads Act 1781 (c.82)
Cheshire Roads Act 1786 (c.139)
Chest of Greenwich Act 1806 (c.101)
Chester and Derby Roads Act 1770 (c.97)
Chester and Derby Roads Act 1789 (c.93)
Chester and Derby Roads Act 1790 (c.88)
Chester and Lancaster Roads Act 1770 (c.89)
Chester and Stafford Roads Act 1783 (c.101)
Chester and Stafford Roads Act 1788 (c.104)
Chester and Whitchurch Roads Act 1778 (c.86)
Chester Courts Act 1867 (c.36)
Chester Highways Act 1705 (c.26)
Chester: Improvement Act 1788 (c.82)
Chester, Lancaster and Yorks. Roads Act 1765 (c.100)
Chester Lighthouse Act 1776 (c.61)
Chester–Nantwich Canal Act 1772 (c.75)
Chester (Poor Relief, etc.) Act 1762 (c.45)
Chester Roads Act 1753 (c.84)
Chester Roads Act 1765 (c.98)
Chester Roads Act 1769 (c.65)
Chester Roads Act 1777 (c.76)
Chester Roads Act 1779 (c.113)
Chester Roads Act 1787 (c.93)
Chester Roads Act 1788 (c.111)
Chester Roads Act 1789 (c.99)
Chester Roads Act 1791 (c.125)
Chester Theatre Act 1776 (c.14)
Chester to Birmingham Road Act 1759 (c.51)
Chesterfield to Stockwith (Trent) Canal Act 1771 (c.75)
Chesterfield to Worksop Road Act 1786 (c.152)
Chevening Estate Act 1959 (c.49)
Chevening Estate Act 1987 (c.20)
Chichester Paving and Improvement Act 1791 (c.63)
Chichester: Poor Relief, etc. Act 1753 (c.100)
Chief Justice's Salary Act 1851 (c.41)
Chief Superintendent in China Act 1859 (c.9)
Child Abduction Act 1984 (c.37)
Child Abduction and Custody Act 1985 (c.60)
Child Benefit Act 1975 (c.61)
Child Care Act 1980 (c.5)
Child Stealing Act 1814 (c.101)
Child Support Act 1991 (c.48)
Child Support Act 1995 (c.34)
Children Act 1908 (c.67)
Children Act 1921 (c.4)
Children Act 1948 (c.43)
Children Act 1958 (c.65)
Children Act 1972 (c.44)
Children Act 1975 (c.72)
Children Act 1989 (c.41)
Children Act (1908) Amendment Act 1910 (c.25)
Children and Young Persons Act 1931 (c.46)
Children and Young Persons Act 1932 (c.46)

Children and Young Persons Act 1933 (c.12)
Children and Young Persons Act 1938 (c.40)
Children and Young Persons Act 1956 (c.24)
Children and Young Persons Act 1963 (c.37)
Children and Young Persons Act 1969 (c.54)
Children and Young Persons Act 1952 (c.50)
Children and Young Persons (Amendment) Act 1986 (c.28)
Children and Young Persons (Harmful Publications) Act 1955 (c.28)
Children and Young Persons (Protection from Tobacco) Act 1991 (c.23)
Children and Young Persons (Scotland) Act 1931 (c.47)
Children and Young Persons (Scotland) Act 1937 (c.37)
Children (Employment Abroad) Act 1913 (c.7)
Children (Scotland) Act 1995 (c.36)
Children's Dangerous Performances Act 1879 (c.34)
Children's (Employment Abroad) Act 1930 (c.21)
Children's Homes Act 1982 (c.20)
Chimney Sweepers Act 1788 (c.48)
Chimney Sweepers Act 1875 (c.70)
Chimney Sweepers Act 1894 (c.51)
Chimney Sweepers Acts (Repeal) Act 1938 (c.58)
Chimney Sweepers and Chimneys Regulation Act 1840 (c.85)
Chimney Sweepers Regulations Act 1864 (c.37)
China (Currency Stabilisation) Act 1939 (c.14)
China Indemnity (Application) Act 1925 (c.41)
China Indemnity (Application) Act 1931 (c.7)
Chinese Passengers Act 1855 (c.104)
Chippenham Roads Act 1726 (c.13)
Chiropractors Act 1994 (c.17)
Cholera, etc. Protection (Ireland) Act 1884 (c.69)
Cholera Hospitals (Ireland) Act 1883 (c.48)
Cholera Hospitals (Ireland) Act 1884 (c.59)
Cholera Hospitals (Ireland) Act 1885 (c.39)
Cholera Hospitals (Ireland) Act 1893 (c.13)
Chorley and Rufford Chapels, Lancaster Act 1793 (c.24)
Christ Church, Oxford Act 1867 (c.76)
Christ Church, Surrey Act 1737 (c.21)
Christ College of Brecknock Act 1853 (c.82)
Christchurch, Middlesex Act 1772 (c.38)
Christchurch, Middlesex: Improvement Act 1788 (c.60)
Christchurch, Middlesex: Light and Watch Act 1737 (c.35)
Christchurch, Stepney: Poor Relief Act 1753 (c.98)
Christchurch, Stepney: Poor Relief Act 1778 (c.74)
Christchurch, Surrey: Improvement Act 1791 (c.61)
Christchurch, Surrey, Streets Act 1793 (c.90)
Christmas Islands Act 1958 (c.25)
Chronically Sick and Disabled Persons Act 1970 (c.44)
Chronically Sick and Disabled Persons (Amendment) Act 1976 (c.49)
Chronically Sick and Disabled Persons (Northern Ireland) Act 1978 (c.53)
Chronically Sick and Disabled Persons (Scotland) Act 1972 (c.51)
Church at Coventry Act 1733 (c.27)
Church at Gravesend Act 1730 (c.20)
Church at Limerick Act 1844 (c.89)
Church at Woolwich Act 1731 (c.4)
Church, Buckingham Act 1776 (c.32)
Church Building Act 1818 (c.45)
Church Building Act 1819 (c.134)
Church Building Act 1822 (c.72)
Church Building Act 1824 (c.103)
Church Building Act 1827 (c.72)
Church Building Act 1831 (c.38)
Church Building Act 1832 (c.61)
Church Building Act 1837 (c.75)
Church Building Act 1838 (c.107)
Church Building Act 1839 (c.49)
Church Building Act 1840 (c.60)
Church Building Act 1845 (c.70)
Church Building Act 1848 (c.37)
Church Building Act 1851 (c.97)
Church Building Act 1854 (c.32)
Church Building Acts Amendment Act 1871 (c.82)
Church Building (Banns and Marriages) Act 1844 (c.56)
Church Building (Burial Service in Chapels) Act 1846 (c.68)
Church Building Commission Act 1848 (c.71)
Church Building Commission Act 1854 (c.14)
Church Building Commissioners (Transfer of Powers) Act 1856 (c.55)
Church Building etc. (Ireland) Act 1808 (c.65)
Church Building (Ireland) Act 1814 (c.117)
Church Discipline Act 1840 (c.86)
Church in Sheffield Act 1739 (c.12)
Church in Strand on Maypole Site: Stepney Advowsons Act 1712 (c.17)
Church, Macclesfield Act 1779 (c.7)
Church of Abthorpe and Foxcoate, Northants Act 1736 (c.21)
Church of Allhallows, City Act 1765 (c.65)
Church of Allhallows, City Act 1766 (c.75)
Church of All Saints, Worcester Act 1737 (c.5)
Church of England 1706 (c.8)
Church of England Act 1966 (c.2)
Church of England Assembly (Powers) Act 1919 (c.76)
Church of Ireland Act 1858 (c.59)
Church of Ireland Act 1863 (c.123)
Church of Ireland Acts Repeal Act 1851 (c.71)
Church of Ireland Act 1851 (c.72)
Church of Scotland Act 1921 (c.29)
Church of Scotland, etc. Act 1748 (c.21)
Church of Scotland Courts Act 1863 (c.47)
Church of Scotland (Property and Endowments) Act 1925 (c.33)

Civil Defence Act 1949 (c.5)
Civil Defence (Armed Forces) Act 1954 (c.66)
Civil Defence (Electricity Undertakings) Act 1954 (c.19)
Civil Defence (Suspension of Powers) Act 1945 (c.12)
Civil Evidence Act 1968 (c.64)
Civil Evidence Act 1972 (c.30)
Civil Evidence Act 1995 (c.38)
Civil Evidence (Family Mediation) (Scotland) Act 1995 (c.6)
Civil Evidence (Scotland) Act 1988 (c.32)
Civil Imprisonment (Scotland) Act 1882 (c.42)
Civil Jurisdiction and Judgments Act 1982 (c.27)
Civil Jurisdiction and Judgments Act 1991 (c.12)
Civil Liability (Contribution) Act 1978 (c.47)
Civil List Act 1714 (c.1)
Civil List Act 1727 (c.1)
Civil List Act 1760 (c.1)
Civil List Act 1776 (c.21)
Civil List Act 1785 (c.61)
Civil List Act 1804 (c.80)
Civil List Act 1837 (c.2)
Civil List Act 1901 (c.4)
Civil List Act 1910 (c.28)
Civil List Act 1936 (c.15)
Civil List Act 1937 (c.32)
Civil List Act 1952 (c.37)
Civil List Act 1972 (c.7)
Civil List Act 1975 (c.82)
Civil List and Secret Service Money Act 1782 (c.82)
Civil List Audit Act 1816 (c.46)
Civil List, During King's Illness Act 1812 (c.6)
Civil List (Ireland) Act 1805 (c.76)
Civil Procedure Acts Repeal 1879 (c.59)
Civil Protection in Peacetime Act 1986 (c.22)
Civil Rights of Convicts Act 1828 (c.32)
Civil Service, India Act 1837 (c.70)
Civil Service (Management Functions) Act 1992 (c.61)
Civil Service Superannuation Act 1857 (c.37)
Clackmannan and Perth Roads Act 1794 (c.139)
Clackmannan and Perth Roads Act 1797 (c.166)
Clan Gregour (Scotland) Act 1775 (c.29)
Clandestine Marriages Act 1753 (c.33)
Clandestine Running of Goods, etc. Act 1810 (c.10)
Clapham Church Act 1774 (c.12)
Clapham: Streets Act 1785 (c.88)
Claremont Estate Purchase (Grant of Life Interest) Act 1816 (c.115)
Clean Air Act 1956 (c.52)
Clean Air Act 1968 (c.62)
Clean Air Act 1993 (c.11)
Clean Rivers (Estuaries and Tidal Waters) Act 1960 (c.54)
Cleansing of Persons Act 1897 (c.31)
Clearance of Vessels, London Act 1811 (c.24)
Clergy Discipline Act 1892 (c.32)
Clergy Endowments (Canada) Act 1791 (c.31)
Clergy Ordination Act 1804 (c.43)
Clergy Reserves in Canada Act 1840 (c.78)
Clergy Residences Repair Act 1776 (c.53)
Clergy Residences Repair Act 1781 (c.66)
Clergymen Ordained Abroad Act 1863 (c.121)
Clerical Disabilities Act 1870 (c.91)
Clerical Subscription Act 1865 (c.122)
Clerkenwell Church Act 1788 (c.10)
Clerkenwell: Poor Relief Act 1775 (c.23)
Clerkenwell: Poor Relief Act 1783 (c.44)
Clerkenwell: Streets Act 1774 (c.24)
Clerkenwell: Streets Act 1777 (c.63)
Clerkenwell: Watching, etc. Act 1771 (c.33)
Clerk of Assize (Ireland) Act 1821 (c.54)
Clerk of the Crown (Ireland) Act 1832 (c.48)
Clerk of the Council Act 1859 (c.1)
Clerk of the Crown in Chancery Act 1844 (c.77)
Clerk of the Hanaper Act 1749 (c.25)
Clerks of Assize, etc. Act 1869 (c.89)
Clerks of Session (Scotland) Regulation Act 1889 (c.54)
Clerks of Session (Scotland) Regulation Act 1913 (c.23)
Clerks of the Peace (Removal) Act 1864 (c.65)
Cloth Manufacture Act 1733 (c.25)
Cloth Manufacture Act 1737 (c.28)
Cloth Manufacture Act 1740 (c.35)
Cloth Manufacturer Act 1724 (c.24)
Cloth Manufacture, Yorkshire Act 1765 (c.51)
Cloth Manufacture, Yorkshire Act 1766 (c.23)
Clothing of the Army, etc. Act 1810 (c.107)
Clubs (Temporary Provisions) Act 1915 (c.84)
Clyde Bridge Act 1758 (c.62)
Clyde Marine Society Act 1786 (c.109)
Clyde, Navigation Act 1774 (c.103)
Coaches, Bond Street Act 1792 (c.62)
Coadjutors to Bishops in Ireland Act 1812 (c.62)
Coal Act 1938 (c.52)
Coal Act 1943 (c.38)
Coal (Concurrent Leases) Act 1942 (c.19)
Coal Consumers' Councils (Northern Irish Interests) Act 1962 (c.22)
Coal Duty, Dublin Act 1811 (c.11)
Coal Duty, London Act 1845 (c.101)
Coal Industry Act 1949 (c.53)
Coal Industry Act 1951 (c.41)
Coal Industry Act 1956 (c.61)
Coal Industry Act 1960 (c.17)
Coal Industry Act 1961 (c.5)
Coal Industry Act 1962 (c.6)
Coal Industry Act 1965 (c.82)
Coal Industry Act 1967 (c.91)
Coal Industry Act 1971 (c.16)
Coal Industry Act 1973 (c.8)
Coal Industry Act 1975 (c.56)

Coal Industry Act 1977 (c.39)
Coal Industry Act 1980 (c.50)
Coal Industry Act 1982 (c.15)
Coal Industry Act 1983 (c.60)
Coal Industry Act 1985 (c.27)
Coal Industry Act 1987 (c.3)
Coal Industry Act 1990 (c.3)
Coal Industry Act 1992 (c.17)
Coal Industry Act 1994 (c.21)
Coal Industry Commission Act 1919 (c.1)
Coal Industry Nationalisation Act 1946 (c.59)
Coal Industry (No. 2) Act 1949 (c.79)
Coal Loading: Newcastle and Sunderland Act 1766 (c.22)
Coal Loading: Newcastle and Sunderland Act 1772 (c.22)
Coal Measurement, London Act 1776 (c.13)
Coal Metage, etc., London Act 1766 (c.23)
Coal Mines Act 1855 (c.107)
Coal Mines Act 1862 (c.79)
Coal Mines Act 1886 (c.40)
Coal Mines Act 1911 (c.50)
Coal Mines Act 1914 (c.22)
Coal Mines Act 1919 (c.48)
Coal Mines Act 1926 (c.17)
Coal Mines Act 1930 (c.34)
Coal Mines Act 1931 (c.27)
Coal Mines Act 1932 (c.29)
Coal Mines (Check Weigher) Act 1894 (c.52)
Coal Mines Control Agreement (Confirmation) Act 1918 (c.56)
Coal Mines (Decontrol) Act 1921 (c.6)
Coal Mines (Employment of Boys) Act 1937 (c.62)
Coal Mines Inspection Act 1850 (c.100)
Coal Mines (Minimum Wage) Act 1912 (c.2)
Coal Mines Regulation Act 1872 (c.76)
Coal Mines Regulation Act 1887 (c.58)
Coal Mines Regulation Act (1887) Amendment 1903 (c.7)
Coal Mines Regulation Act 1896 (c.43)
Coal Mines Regulation Act 1908 (c.57)
Coal Mines Regulation (Amendment) Act 1917 (c.8)
Coal Mines (Weighing of Minerals) Act 1905 (c.9)
Coal Mining (Subsidence) Act 1950 (c.23)
Coal Mining (Subsidence) Act 1957 (c.59)
Coal Mining Subsidence Act 1991 (c.45)
Coal (Registration of Ownership) Act 1937 (c.56)
Coal Trade Act 1710 (c.30)
Coal Trade Act 1730 (c.26)
Coal Trade Act 1730 (c.30)
Coal Trade Act 1788 (c.53)
Coal Trade Act 1836 (c.109)
Coal Trade, London Act 1745 (c.35)
Coal Trade, London Act 1758 (c.27)
Coal Trade, London Act 1786 (c.83)
Coal Trade, London Act 1796 (c.61)
Coal Trade: Westminster Act 1766 (c.35)
Coal Trade, Westminster Act 1786 (c.108)
Coal Vendors Act 1843 (c.2)
Coalport Bridge over Severn (Tolls, etc.) Act 1776 (c.12)
Coals Act 1743 (c.35)
Coals, Newcastle Act 1782 (c.32)
Coalwhippers, London Act 1851 (c.78)
Coalwhippers, Port of London Act 1846 (c.36)
Coast Protection Act 1939 (c.39)
Coast Protection Act 1949 (c.74)
Coast Trade Act 1792 (c.50)
Coastal Flooding (Emergency Provisions) Act 1953 (c.18)
Coastguard Act 1925 (c.88)
Coastguard Service Act 1856 (c.83)
Coasting Trade Act 1805 (c.81)
Coasting Trade Act 1854 (c.5)
Coatbridge and Springburn Elections (Validation) Act 1945 (c.3)
Cobham, Leatherhead and Godalming Bridges Act 1782 (c.17)
Cockburnspath Bridge, Berwick Act 1789 (c.42)
Cockermouth and Workington Road Act 1779 (c.105)
Cockerton Bridge to Staindrop Road Act 1793 (c.146)
Cockfighting Act 1952 (c.59)
Cocos Islands Act 1955 (c.5)
Codbreck Brook, Navigation Act 1767 (c.95)
Coffee and Cocoa-Nuts Act 1783 (c.79)
Coffee, etc. Act 1812 (c.149)
Coffee, etc. Act 1814 (c.47)
Coin Act 1732 (c.26)
Coin Act 1774 (c.70)
Coin Act 1816 (c.68)
Coin Act 1849 (c.41)
Coinage Act 1708 (c.24)
Coinage Act 1859 (c.30)
Coinage Act 1870 (c.10)
Coinage Act 1889 (c.58)
Coinage Act 1891 (c.72)
Coinage Act 1893 (c.1)
Coinage Act 1946 (c.74)
Coinage Act 1971 (c.24)
Coinage (Colonial Offences) Act 1853 (c.48)
Coinage Duties Act 1730 (c.12)
Coinage Duties Act 1738 (c.5)
Coinage Duties Act 1745 (c.14)
Coinage Duties Act 1760 (c.16)
Coinage Duties Act 1769 (c.25)
Coinage Duties, etc. Act 1754 (c.11)
Coinage in American Plantations Act 1707 (c.57)
Coinage Offences Act 1861 (c.99)
Coinage Offences Act 1936 (c.16)
Colewort Barracks, Portsmouth Act 1860 (c.49)
Collecting Societies and Industrial Assurance Companies Act 1896 (c.26)
Collection of Charity Money Act 1705 (c.25)
Collection of Malt Duties, etc. Act 1805 (c.53)
Collection of Revenue, etc. (Ireland) Act 1803 (c.98)
Collection of Revenue (Ireland) Act 1803 (c.43)

Collection of Revenue (Ireland) Act 1803 (c.97)
Collection of Revenue (Ireland) Act 1804 (c.105)
Collection of Revenues (Ireland) Act 1802 (c.36)
College Charter Act 1871 (c.63)
College of Physicians (Ireland) Act 1862 (c.15)
Collegiate Church of Manchester Act 1728 (c.29)
Collieries and Mines Act 1800 (c.77)
Collieries (Ireland) Act 1807 (c.45)
Colliers Act 1775 (c.28)
Colliers (Scotland) Act 1799 (c.56)
Collingham to York Road Act 1792 (c.142)
Colneis and Carlford Hundreds, Suffolk: Poor Relief Act 1790 (c.22)
Colne Oyster Fishery Act 1757 (c.71)
Colne River, Essex: Navigation Act 1718 (c.31)
Colonial Acts Confirmation Act 1863 (c.84)
Colonial Acts Confirmation Act 1894 (c.72)
Colonial Acts Confirmation Act 1901 (c.29)
Colonial Affidavits Act 1859 (c.12)
Colonial and Other Territories (Divorce Jurisdiction) Act 1950 (c.20)
Colonial Attorneys Relief Act 1857 (c.39)
Colonial Attorneys Relief Act 1874 (c.41)
Colonial Attorneys Relief Amendment Act 1884 (c.24)
Colonial Bishops Act 1852 (c.52)
Colonial Bishops Act 1853 (c.49)
Colonial Boundaries Act 1895 (c.34)
Colonial Branch Mint Act 1866 (c.65)
Colonial Clergy Act 1874 (c.77)
Colonial Copyright Act 1847 (c.95)
Colonial Courts of Admiralty Act 1890 (c.27)
Colonial Development Act 1929 (c.5)
Colonial Development and Welfare Act 1939 (c.40)
Colonial Development and Welfare Act 1944 (c.20)
Colonial Development and Welfare Act 1949 (c.49)
Colonial Development and Welfare Act 1950 (c.4)
Colonial Development and Welfare Act 1955 (c.6)
Colonial Development and Welfare Act 1959 (c.71)
Colonial Docks Loans Act 1865 (c.106)
Colonial Duties Act 1842 (c.49)
Colonial Fortifications Act 1877 (c.23)
Colonial Governors (Pensions) Act 1865 (c.113)
Colonial Governors (Pensions) Act 1872 (c.29)
Colonial Inland Post Office Act 1849 (c.66)
Colonial Laws Validity Act 1865 (c.63)
Colonial Leave of Absence Act 1782 (c.75)
Colonial Letters Patent Act 1863 (c.76)
Colonial Loans Act 1899 (c.36)
Colonial Loans Act 1949 (c.50)
Colonial Loans Act 1952 (c.1)
Colonial Loans Act 1962 (c.41)
Colonial Marriages Act 1865 (c.64)
Colonial Marriages (Deceased Wife's Sister) Act 1906 (c.30)
Colonial Naval Defence Act 1865 (c.14)
Colonial Naval Defence Act 1909 (c.19)
Colonial Naval Defence Act 1931 (c.9)
Colonial Naval Defence Act 1949 (c.18)
Colonial Officers (Leave of Absence) Act 1894 (c.17)
Colonial Offices Act 1830 (c.4)
Colonial Prisoners Removal Act 1869 (c.10)
Colonial Prisoners Removal Act 1884 (c.31)
Colonial Probates Act 1892 (c.6)
Colonial Probates (Protected States and Mandated Territories) Act 1927 (c.43)
Colonial Shipping Act 1868 (c.129)
Colonial Solicitors Act 1900 (c.14)
Colonial Stock Act 1877 (c.59)
Colonial Stock Act 1892 (c.35)
Colonial Stock Act 1900 (c.62)
Colonial Stock Act 1934 (c.47)
Colonial Stock Act 1948 (c.1)
Colonial Trade Act 1730 (c.28)
Colonial Trade Act 1734 (c.19)
Colonial Trade Act 1738 (c.30)
Colonial Trade Act 1760 (c.9)
Colonial Trade Act 1763 (c.27)
Colonial Trade Act 1768 (c.22)
Colonial Trade Act 1769 (c.27)
Colonial Trade Act 1812 (c.98)
Colonial War Risks Insurance (Guarantees) Act 1941 (c.35)
(Colonies) Evidence Act 1843 (c.22)
Colony of New York Act 1770 (c.35)
Colouring of Porter Act 1811 (c.87)
Combination of Workmen Act 1796 (c.111)
Combinations of Workmen Act 1801 (c.38)
Combination of Workmen Act 1859 (c.34)
Commerce with Certain Countries Act 1721 (c.8)
Commerce with Spain Act 1739 (c.27)
Commerce with Sweden Act 1716 (c.1)
Commerce with United States Act 1816 (c.15)
Commerce with United States Act 1816 (c.51)
Commercial Treaty with Portugal Act 1811 (c.47)
Commissariat Accounts Act 1821 (c.121)
Commissary Court of Edinburgh Act 1815 (c.97)
Commissary Court of Edinburgh, etc. Act 1836 (c.41)
Commissioners Clauses Act 1847 (c.16)
Commissioners for Oaths Act 1853 (c.78)
Commissioners for Oaths Act 1855 (c.42)
Commissioners for Oaths Act 1889 (c.10)
Commissioners for Oaths Act 1891 (c.50)
Commissioners for Oaths Amendment Act 1890 (c.7)

Commissioners for Oaths, Bail in Error, etc. Act 1859
Commissioners for Oaths, Bail in Error, etc. Act 1859 (c.16)
Commissioners for Oaths (Ireland) Act 1872 (c.75)
Commissioners for Oaths (Prize Proceedings) Act 1907 (c.25)
Commissioners of Customs Act 1845 (c.85)
Commissioners of Sewers (City of London) Act 1708 (c.32)
Commissioners of Supply Meetings (Scotland) Act 1865 (c.38)
Commissioners of Supply (Scotland) Act 1856 (c.93)
Commissioners of Supply (Scotland) Act 1857 (c.11)
Commissioners of the Treasury Act 1807 (c.20)
Commissioners of Woods (Audit) Act 1844 (c.89)
Commissioners of Woods (Thames Piers) Act 1879 (c.73)
Commissioners of Works Act 1852 (c.28)
Commissioners of Works Act 1894 (c.23)
Commissions of Sewers Act 1708 (c.33)
Commissions of the Peace Continuance Act 1837 (c.1)
Commissions to Foreign Protestants Act 1756 (c.5)
Commissions and Salaries of Judges Act 1760 (c.23)
Commission of Assize in County Palatine of Lancaster Act 1855 (c.45)
Common Informers Act 1951 (c.39)
Common Land (Rectification of Registers) Act 1989 (c.18)
Common Law Chambers Act 1867 (c.68)
Common Law Courts Act 1852 (c.73)
Common Law Courts (Fees) Act 1865 (c.45)
Common Law Courts (Fees and Salaries) Act 1866 (c.101)
Common Law Courts (Ireland) Act 1851 (c.17)
Common Law Offices (Ireland) Act 1844 (c.107)
Common Law Procedure Act 1838 (c.45)
Common Law Procedure Act 1852 (c.76)
Common Law Procedure Act 1854 (c.125)
Common Law Procedure Act 1860 (c.126)
Common Law Procedure Act 1864 (c.28)
Common Law Procedure Amendment (Ireland) Act 1853 (c.113)
Common Law Procedure Amendment (Ireland) Act 1856 (c.102)
Common Law Procedure Amendment (Ireland) Act 1870 (c.109)
Common Law Procedure (Ireland) Act 1855 (c.7)
Common Law Procedure (Ireland) Act 1860 (c.82)
Common Lodging House Act 1853 (c.41)
Common Lodging Houses Act 1851 (c.28)
Common Lodging Houses (Ireland) Act 1860 (c.26)
Common Pleas of Lancaster Act 1794 (c.46)
Common Pleas of Lancaster Act 1800 (c.105)
Common Pleas at Lancaster Amendment Act 1869 (c.37)
Common Recoveries, etc. Act 1740 (c.20)
Commonable Rights Compensation Act 1882 (c.15)
Commons Act 1876 (c.56)
Commons Act 1879 (c.37)
Commons Act 1899 (c.30)
Commons Act 1908 (c.44)
Commons (Expenses) Act 1878 (c.56)
Commons Registration Act 1965 (c.64)
Commonwealth Development Act 1963 (c.40)
Commonwealth Development Corporation Act 1978 (c.2)
Commonwealth Development Corporation Act 1982 (c.54)
Commonwealth Development Corporation Act 1986 (c.25)
Commonwealth Development Corporation Act 1995 (c.9)
Commonwealth Immigrants Act 1962 (c.21)
Commonwealth Immigration Act 1968 (c.9)
Commonwealth (India (Consequential) Provisions) Act 1949 (c.92)
Commonwealth Institute Act 1958 (c.16)
Commonwealth of Australia Constitution Act 1900 (c.12)
Commonwealth Scholarships Act 1959 (c.6)
Commonwealth Scholarships (Amendment) Act 1963 (c.6)
Commonwealth Secretariat Act 1966 (c.10)
Commonwealth Settlement Act 1957 (c.8)
Commonwealth Settlement Act 1962 (c.17)
Commonwealth Settlement Act 1967 (c.31)
Commonwealth Teachers Act 1960 (c.40)
Commonwealth Telecommunications Act 1968 (c.24)
Commonwealth Telegraphs Act 1949 (c.39)
Communications from Marylebone to Charing Cross Act 1813 (c.121)
Community Care (Residential Accommodation) Act 1992 (c.49)
Community Charges (General Reduction) Act 1991 (c.9)
Community Charges (Substitute Setting) Act 1991 (c.8)
Community Health Councils (Access to Information) Act 1988 (c.24)
Community Land Act 1975 (c.77)
Community Service by Offenders (Scotland) Act 1978 (c.49)
Companies Act 1862 (c.89)
Companies Act 1867 (c.131)
Companies Act 1877 (c.26)
Companies Act 1879 (c.76)
Companies Act 1880 (c.19)
Companies Act 1883 (c.28)
Companies Act 1886 (c.23)

Companies Act 1898 (c.26)
Companies Act 1900 (c.48)
Companies Act 1907 (c.50)
Companies Act 1908 (c.12)
Companies Act 1913 (c.25)
Companies Act 1928 (c.45)
Companies Act 1929 (c.23)
Companies Act 1947 (c.47)
Companies Act 1948 (c.38)
Companies Act 1967 (c.81)
Companies Act 1976 (c.69)
Companies Act 1980 (c.22)
Companies Act 1981 (c.62)
Companies Act 1985 (c.6)
Companies Act 1989 (c.40)
Companies (Beneficial Interests) Act 1983 (c.50)
Companies Clauses Act 1863 (c.118)
Companies Clauses Act 1869 (c.48)
Companies Clauses Consolidation Act 1845 (c.16)
Companies Clauses Consolidation Act 1888 (c.48)
Companies Clauses Consolidation Act 1889 (c.37)
Companies Clauses Consolidation (Scotland) Act 1845 (c.17)
Companies (Colonial Registers) Act 1883 (c.30)
Companies (Consolidation) Act 1908 (c.69)
Companies Consolidation (Consequential Provisions) Act 1985 (c.9)
Companies (Converted Societies) Act 1910 (c.23)
Companies (Defence) Act 1939 (c.75)
Companies (Floating Charges and Receivers) (Scotland) Act 1972 (c.67)
Companies (Floating Charges) (Scotland) Act 1961 (c.46)
Companies (Foreign Interests) Act 1917 (c.18)
Companies (Memorandum of Association) Act 1890 (c.62)
Companies (Particulars as to Directors) Act 1917 (c.28)
Companies (Winding-up) Act 1890 (c.63)
Companies (Winding-up) Act 1893 (c.58)
Company Directors (Disqualification) Act 1986 (c.46)
Company Seals Act 1864 (c.19)
Company Securities (Insider Dealing) Act 1985 (c.8)
Compassionate List of the Navy, etc. Act 1809 (c.45)
Compensation (Defence) Act 1939 (c.75)
Compensation for Injuries to Mills etc. Act 1801 (c.24)
Compensation for Works at Portsmouth Act 1815 (c.123)
Compensation of Displaced Officers (War Service) Act 1945 (c.10)
Compensation to American Loyalists, etc. Act 1788 (c.40)
Compensation to Patentee Officers (Ireland) Act 1808 (c.108)
Competency of Witnesses Act 1787 (c.29)
Competition Act 1980 (c.21)
Competition and Service (Utilities) Act 1992 (c.43)
Completing St. Paul's, etc. Act 1702 (c.12)
Completion of Somerset House Act 1780 (c.40)
Composition for a Certain Crown Debt Act 1770 (c.12)
Composition for a Crown Debt Act 1774 (c.35)
Composition for a Crown Debt Act 1775 (c.19)
Composition for a Crown Debt Act 1776 (c.31)
Composition for a Crown Debt Act 1776 (c.49)
Composition for a Crown Debt Act 1779 (c.77)
Composition for a Crown Debt Act 1784 (c.14)
Composition for a Crown Debt Act 1801 (c.60)
Compound Householders Act 1851 (c.14)
Comptroller of the Exchequer, etc. Act 1865 (c.93)
Compulsory Church Date Abolition 1868 (c.109)
Compulsory Purchase Act 1965 (c.56)
Compulsory Purchase (Vesting Declarations) Act 1981 (c.66)
Computer Misuse Act 1990 (c.18)
Concealment of Birth (Scotland) Act 1809 (c.14)
Concessionary Travel for Handicapped Persons (Scotland) Act 1980 (c.29)
Conciliation Act 1896 (c.30)
Concorde Aircraft Act 1973 (c.7)
Confirmation and Probate Amendment Act 1859 (c.30)
Confirmation of Certain Marriages Act 1781 (c.53)
Confirmation of Certain Marriages Act 1858 (c.46)
Confirmation of Certain Marriages Act 1889 (c.38)
Confirmation of Certain Proceedings Act 1842 (c.43)
Confirmation of Executors (Scotland) Act 1823 (c.98)
Confirmation of Executors (Scotland) Act 1858 (c.56)
Confirmation of Executors (War Service) (Scotland) Act 1917 (c.27)
Confirmation of Executors (War Service) (Scotland) Act 1939 (c.41)
Confirmation of Executors (War Service) (Scotland) Act 1940 (c.41)
Confirmation of Marriages Act 1853 (c.122)
Confirmation of Marriages Act 1854 (c.88)
Confirmation of Marriages Act 1855 (c.66)

Confirmation of Marriages Act 1856 (c.70)
Confirmation of Marriages Act 1857 (c.29)
Confirmation of Marriages Act 1859 (c.24)
Confirmation of Marriages Act 1859 (c.64)
Confirmation of Marriages Act 1860 (c.1)
Confirmation of Marriages Act 1861 (c.16)
Confirmation of Marriages, Blakedown Chapel Act 1868 (c.113)
Confirmation of Marriages (Cove Chapel) Act 1873 (c.1)
Confirmation of Marriages on Her Majesty's Ships Act 1879 (c.29)
Confirmation of Provision Order (Land Drainage) Act 1867 (c.22)
Confirmation of Provisional Orders, Turnpike Trusts Act 1867 (c.66)
Confirmation of Sales etc., by Trustees Act 1862 (c.108)
Confirmation to Small Estates (Scotland) Act 1979 (c.22)
Congenital Disabilities (Civil Liability) Act 1976 (c.28)
Congested Districts Board (Ireland) Act 1893 (c.35)
Congested Districts Board (Ireland) Act 1894 (c.50)
Congested Districts Board (Ireland) Act 1899 (c.18)
Congested Districts Board (Ireland) Act 1901 (c.34)
Congested Districts (Scotland) Act 1897 (c.53)
Conjugal Rights (Scotland) Amendment Act 1861 (c.86)
Conjugal Rights (Scotland) Amendment Act 1874 (c.31)
Consecration of Bishops Abroad Act 1786 (c.84)
Consecration of Churchyards Act 1867 (c.133)
Consecration of Churchyards Act 1868 (c.47)
Conservation of Seals Act 1970 (c.30)
Conservation of Wild Creatures and Wild Plants Act 1975 (c.48)
Consolidated Annuities (Ireland) Act 1853 (c.75)
Consolidated Fund Act 1806 (c.44)
Consolidated Fund Act 1816 (c.98)
Consolidated Fund Act 1947 (c.17)
Consolidated Fund Act 1950 (c.1)
Consolidated Fund Act 1951 (c.12)
Consolidated Fund Act 1952 (c.16)
Consolidated Fund Act 1953 (c.6)
Consolidated Fund Act 1954 (c.22)
Consolidated Fund Act 1955 (c.3)
Consolidated Fund Act 1956 (c.32)
Consolidated Fund Act 1957 (c.7)
Consolidated Fund Act 1958 (c.7)
Consolidated Fund Act 1960 (c.10)
Consolidated Fund Act 1963 (c.1)
Consolidated Fund Act 1965 (c.1)
Consolidated Fund Act 1966 (c.1)
Consolidated Fund Act 1968 (c.1)
Consolidated Fund Act 1969 (c.3)
Consolidated Fund Act 1970 (c.1)
Consolidated Fund Act 1971 (c.1)
Consolidated Fund Act 1972 (c.13)
Consolidated Fund Act 1973 (c.1)
Consolidated Fund Act 1974 (c.1)
Consolidated Fund Act 1975 (c.1)
Consolidated Fund Act 1976 (c.2)
Consolidated Fund Act 1977 (c.1)
Consolidated Fund Act 1978 (c.7)
Consolidated Fund Act 1979 (c.20)
Consolidated Fund Act 1980 (c.14)
Consolidated Fund Act 1981 (c.4)
Consolidated Fund Act 1982 (c.8)
Consolidated Fund Act 1983 (c.1)
Consolidated Fund Act 1984 (c.1)
Consolidated Fund Act 1985 (c.1)
Consolidated Fund Act 1986 (c.4)
Consolidated Fund Act 1987 (c.8)
Consolidated Fund Act 1988 (c.6)
Consolidated Fund Act 1989 (c.2)
Consolidated Fund Act 1990 (c.4)
Consolidated Fund Act 1991 (c.7)
Consolidated Fund Act 1992 (c.1)
Consolidated Fund Act 1993 (c.4)
Consolidated Fund Act 1994 (c.4)
Consolidated Fund Act 1995 (c.2)
Consolidated Fund (Civil List Provisions) Act 1951 (c.50)
Consolidated Fund (No. 1) Act 1879 (c.2)
Consolidated Fund (No. 1) Act 1880 (c.5)
Consolidated Fund (No. 1) Act 1881 (c.1)
Consolidated Fund (No. 1) Act 1882 (c.1)
Consolidated Fund (No. 1) Act 1883 (c.2)
Consolidated Fund (No. 1) Act 1884 (c.2)
Consolidated Fund (No. 1) Act 1884 (c.4)
Consolidated Fund (No. 1) Act 1886 (c.4)
Consolidated Fund (No. 1) Act 1887 (c.1)
Consolidated Fund (No. 1) Act 1888 (c.1)
Consolidated Fund (No. 1) Act 1889 (c.1)
Consolidated Fund (No. 1) Act 1890 (c.1)
Consolidated Fund (No. 1) Act 1891 (c.6)
Consolidated Fund (No. 1) Act 1892 (c.3)
Consolidated Fund (No. 1) Act 1893 (c.3)
Consolidated Fund (No. 1) Act 1894 (c.1)
Consolidated Fund (No. 1) Act 1895 (c.4)
Consolidated Fund (No. 1) Act 1896 (c.3)
Consolidated Fund (No. 1) Act 1897 (c.4)
Consolidated Fund (No. 1) Act 1898 (c.3)
Consolidated Fund (No. 1) Act 1899 (c.2)
Consolidated Fund (No. 1) Act 1900 (c.1)
Consolidated Fund (No. 1) Act 1901 (c.1)
Consolidated Fund (No. 1) Act 1902 (c.1)
Consolidated Fund (No. 1) Act 1903 (c.3)
Consolidated Fund (No. 1) Act 1904 (c.1)
Consolidated Fund (No. 1) Act 1905 (c.1)
Consolidated Fund (No. 1) Act 1906 (c.1)
Consolidated Fund (No. 1) Act 1907 (c.1)
Consolidated Fund (No. 1) Act 1908 (c.1)
Consolidated Fund (No. 1) Act 1909 (c.1)
Consolidated Fund (No. 1) Act 1910 (c.4)
Consolidated Fund (No. 1) Act 1911 (c.1)
Consolidated Fund (No. 1) Act 1912 (c.1)

Consolidated Fund (No. 1) Act 1913 (c.1)
Consolidated Fund (No. 1) Act 1914 (c.1)
Consolidated Fund (No. 1) Act 1916 (c.1)
Consolidated Fund (No. 1) Act 1917 (c.1)
Consolidated Fund (No. 1) Act 1918 (c.1)
Consolidated Fund (No. 1) Act 1919 (c.5)
Consolidated Fund (No. 1) Act 1921 (c.2)
Consolidated Fund (No. 1) Act 1922 (c.1)
Consolidated Fund (No. 1) Act 1923 (c.1)
Consolidated Fund (No. 1) Act 1924 (c.2)
Consolidated Fund (No. 1) Act 1925 (c.8)
Consolidated Fund (No. 1) Act 1926 (c.1)
Consolidated Fund (No. 1) Act 1927 (c.2)
Consolidated Fund (No. 1) Act 1928 (c.1)
Consolidated Fund (No. 1) Act 1928 (c.2)
Consolidated Fund (No. 1) Act 1929 (c.10)
Consolidated Fund (No. 1) Act 1932 (c.1)
Consolidated Fund (No. 1) Act 1932 (c.14)
Consolidated Fund (No. 1) Act 1934 (c.3)
Consolidated Fund (No. 1) Act 1935 (c.4)
Consolidated Fund (No. 1) Act 1936 (c.8)
Consolidated Fund (No. 1) Act 1937 (c.7)
Consolidated Fund (No. 1) Act 1938 (c.9)
Consolidated Fund (No. 1) Act 1939 (c.12)
Consolidated Fund (No. 1) Act 1940 (c.11)
Consolidated Fund (No. 1) Act 1941 (c.6)
Consolidated Fund (No. 1) Act 1943 (c.4)
Consolidated Fund (No. 1) Act 1944 (c.1)
Consolidated Fund (No. 1) Act 1944 (c.4)
Consolidated Fund (No. 1) Act 1945 (c.4)
Consolidated Fund (No. 1) Act 1946 (c.33)
Consolidated Fund (No. 1) Act 1948 (c.18)
Consolidated Fund (No. 1) Act 1949 (c.24)
Consolidated Fund (No. 1) (Session 2) Act 1880 (c.3)
Consolidated Fund (No. 1) (Session 2) Act 1914 (c.6)
Consolidated Fund (No. 1) (Session 2) Act 1931 (c.1)
Consolidated Fund (No. 1) (Session 2) Act 1941 (c.2)
Consolidated Fund (No. 2) Act 1879 (c.7)
Consolidated Fund (No. 2) Act 1881 (c.8)
Consolidated Fund (No. 2) Act 1882 (c.4)
Consolidated Fund (No. 2) Act 1883 (c.5)
Consolidated Fund (No. 2) Act 1884 (c.15)
Consolidated Fund (No. 2) Act 1885 (c.6)
Consolidated Fund (No. 2) Act 1886 (c.7)
Consolidated Fund (No. 2) Act 1887 (c.14)
Consolidated Fund (No. 2) Act 1888 (c.16)
Consolidated Fund (No. 2) Act 1889 (c.2)
Consolidated Fund (No. 2) Act 1890 (c.28)
Consolidated Fund (No. 2) Act 1891 (c.27)
Consolidated Fund (No. 2) Act 1892 (c.20)
Consolidated Fund (No. 2) Act 1893 (c.16)
Consolidated Fund (No. 2) Act 1894 (c.7)
Consolidated Fund (No. 2) Act 1895 (c.15)
Consolidated Fund (No. 2) Act 1896 (c.7)
Consolidated Fund (No. 2) Act 1898 (c.32)
Consolidated Fund (No. 2) Act 1900 (c.3)
Consolidated Fund (No. 2) Act 1901 (c.6)
Consolidated Fund (No. 2) Act 1905 (c.6)
Consolidated Fund (No. 2) Act 1909 (c.2)
Consolidated Fund (No. 2) Act 1910 (c.9(a))
Consolidated Fund (No. 2) Act 1911 (c.5)
Consolidated Fund (No. 2) Act 1913 (c.5)
Consolidated Fund (No. 2) Act 1915 (c.33)
Consolidated Fund (No. 2) Act 1916 (c.3)
Consolidated Fund (No. 2) Act 1917 (c.7)
Consolidated Fund (No. 2) Act 1918 (c.11)
Consolidated Fund (No. 2) Act 1919 (c.49)
Consolidated Fund (No. 2) Act 1921 (c.3)
Consolidated Fund (No. 2) Act 1922 (c.3)
Consolidated Fund (No. 2) Act 1924 (c.4)
Consolidated Fund (No. 2) Act 1929 (c.10)
Consolidated Fund (No. 2) Act 1930 (c.14)
Consolidated Fund (No. 2) Act 1931 (c.10)
Consolidated Fund (No. 2) Act 1933 (c.3)
Consolidated Fund (No. 2) Act 1935 (c.10)
Consolidated Fund (No. 2) Act 1936 (c.11)
Consolidated Fund (No. 2) Act 1937 (c.20)
Consolidated Fund (No. 2) Act 1939 (c.39)
Consolidated Fund (No. 2) Act 1941 (c.9)
Consolidated Fund (No. 2) Act 1942 (c.12)
Consolidated Fund (No. 2) Act 1943 (c.11)
Consolidated Fund (No. 2) Act 1944 (c.17)
Consolidated Fund (No. 2) Act 1945 (c.4)
Consolidated Fund (No. 2) Act 1957 (c.10)
Consolidated Fund (No. 2) Act 1958 (c.18)
Consolidated Fund (No. 2) Act 1961 (c.12)
Consolidated Fund (No. 2) Act 1962 (c.11)
Consolidated Fund (No. 2) Act 1963 (c.8)
Consolidated Fund (No. 2) Act 1964 (c.17)
Consolidated Fund (No. 2) Act 1965 (c.8)
Consolidated Fund (No. 2) Act 1967 (c.6)
Consolidated Fund (No. 2) Act 1968 (c.15)
Consolidated Fund (No. 2) Act 1969 (c.9)
Consolidated Fund (No. 2) Act 1970 (c.12)
Consolidated Fund (No. 2) Act 1971 (c.14)
Consolidated Fund (No. 2) Act 1972 (c.23)
Consolidated Fund (No. 2) Act 1973 (c.10)
Consolidated Fund (No. 2) Act 1974 (c.12)
Consolidated Fund (No. 2) Act 1975 (c.12)
Consolidated Fund (No. 2) Act 1976 (c.84)
Consolidated Fund (No. 2) Act 1977 (c.52)
Consolidated Fund (No. 2) Act 1978 (c.59)
Consolidated Fund (No. 2) Act 1979 (c.56)
Consolidated Fund (No. 2) Act 1980 (c.68)
Consolidated Fund (No. 2) Act 1981 (c.70)
Consolidated Fund (No. 2) Act 1983 (c.5)
Consolidated Fund (No. 2) Act 1984 (c.61)
Consolidated Fund (No. 2) Act 1985 (c.11)
Consolidated Fund (No. 2) Act 1986 (c.67)
Consolidated Fund (No. 2) Act 1987 (c.54)
Consolidated Fund (No. 2) Act 1988 (c.55)
Consolidated Fund (No. 2) Act 1989 (c.46)
Consolidated Fund (No. 2) Act 1990 (c.46)
Consolidated Fund (No. 2) Act 1991 (c.10)
Consolidated Fund (No. 2) Act 1992 (c.21)
Consolidated Fund (No. 2) Act 1993 (c.7)
Consolidated Fund (No. 2) Act 1994 (c.41)
Consolidated Fund (No. 2) Act 1995 (c.54)
Consolidated Fund (No. 2) (Session 2) Act 1880 (c.30)
Consolidated Fund (No. 3) Act 1879 (c.14)
Consolidated Fund (No. 3) Act 1881 (c.15)

Consolidated Fund (No. 3) Act 1882 (c.8)
Consolidated Fund (No. 3) Act 1883 (c.13)
Consolidated Fund (No. 3) Act 1885 (c.14)
Consolidated Fund (No. 3) Act 1888 (c.26)
Consolidated Fund (No. 3) Act 1889 (c.15)
Consolidated Fund (No. 3) Act 1893 (c.28)
Consolidated Fund (No. 3) Act 1894 (c.29)
Consolidated Fund (No. 3) Act 1915 (c.53)
Consolidated Fund (No. 3) Act 1916 (c.16)
Consolidated Fund (No. 3) Act 1917 (c.17)
Consolidated Fund (No. 3) Act 1918 (c.37)
Consolidated Fund (No. 3) Act 1930 (c.18)
Consolidated Fund (No. 3) Act 1939 (c.52)
Consolidated Fund (No. 3) Act 1941 (c.26)
Consolidated Fund (No. 3) Act 1942 (c.22)
Consolidated Fund (No. 3) Act 1943 (c.20)
Consolidated Fund (No. 3) Act 1944 (c.20)
Consolidated Fund (No. 3) Act 1945 (c.13)
Consolidated Fund (No. 3) Act 1951 (c.1)
Consolidated Fund (No. 3) Act 1953 (c.2)
Consolidated Fund (No. 3) Act 1971 (c.79)
Consolidated Fund (No. 3) Act 1972 (c.78)
Consolidated Fund (No. 3) Act 1974 (c.15)
Consolidated Fund (No. 3) Act 1975 (c.79)
Consolidated Fund (No. 3) Act 1983 (c.57)
Consolidated Fund (No. 3) Act 1985 (c.74)
Consolidated Fund (No. 3) Act 1987 (c.55)
Consolidated Fund (No. 3) Act 1991 (c.68)
Consolidated Fund (No. 3) Act 1992 (c.59)
Consolidated Fund (No. 3) Act 1993 (c.52)
Consolidated Fund (No. 4) Act 1879 (c.20)
Consolidated Fund (No. 4) Act 1881 (c.50)
Consolidated Fund (No. 4) Act 1882 (c.28)
Consolidated Fund (No. 4) Act 1883 (c.23)
Consolidated Fund (No. 4) Act 1893 (c.46)
Consolidated Fund (No. 4) Act 1915 (c.80)
Consolidated Fund (No. 4) Act 1916 (c.30)
Consolidated Fund (No. 4) Act 1917 (c.33)
Consolidated Fund (No. 4) Act 1974 (c.57)
Consolidated Fund (No. 5) Act 1916 (c.48)
Consolidated Fund (No. 5) Act 1917 (c.49)
Consolidated Fund (Permanent Charges Redemption) Act 1873 (c.57)
Consolidated Fund (Permanent Charges Redemption) Act 1883 (c.1)
Consolidation of Enactments (Procedure) Act 1949 (c.33)
Conspiracy and Protection of Property Act 1875 (c.86)
Constables Expenses Act 1801 (c.78)
Constables Near Public Works (Scotland) Act 1845 (c.3)
Constables Protection Act 1750 (c.44)
Constables (Scotland) Act 1875 (c.47)
Constabulary and Police (Ireland) Act 1883 (c.14)
Constabulary and Police (Ireland) Act 1914 (c.54)
Constabulary and Police (Ireland) Act 1916 (c.59)
Constabulary and Police (Ireland) Act 1918 (c.53)
Constabulary and Police (Ireland) Act 1919 (c.68)
Constabulary (Ireland) Act 1836 (c.13)
Constabulary (Ireland) Act 1846 (c.97)
Constabulary (Ireland) Act 1848 (c.72)
Constabulary (Ireland) Act 1851 (c.85)
Constabulary (Ireland) Act 1857 (c.17)
Constabulary (Ireland) Act 1859 (c.22)
Constabulary (Ireland) Act 1866 (c.103)
Constabulary (Ireland) Act 1875 (c.44)
Constabulary (Ireland) Act 1877 (c.20)
Constabulary (Ireland) Act 1897 (c.64)
Constabulary (Ireland) Act 1908 (c.60)
Constabulary (Ireland) Act 1922 (c.55)
Constabulary (Ireland) Amendment Act 1865 (c.70)
Constabulary (Ireland) Amendment) Act 1870 (c.83)
Constabulary (Ireland) Amendment Act 1882 (c.63)
Constabulary (Ireland) (Consular Advances) Act 1825 (c.87)
Constabulary (Ireland) (No. 2) Act 1836 (c.36)
Constabulary (Ireland) Redistribution Act 1885 (c.12)
Consular Conventions Act 1949 (c.29)
Consular Fees Act 1980 (c.23)
Consular Marriage Act 1868 (c.61)
Consular Marriages Act 1849 (c.68)
Consular Relations Act 1968 (c.18)
Consular Salaries and Fees Act 1891 (c.36)
Consuls in Ottoman Dominions Act 1836 (c.78)
Consumer Arbitration Agreements Act 1988 (c.21)
Consumer Credit Act 1974 (c.39)
Consumer Protection Act 1961 (c.40)
Consumer Protection Act 1971 (c.15)
Consumer Protection Act 1987 (c.43)
Consumer Safety Act 1978 (c.38)
Consumer Safety (Amendment) Act 1986 (c.29)
Consumption of Malt Liquors (Ireland) Act 1810 (c.46)
Contagious Diseases Act 1866 (c.35)
Contagious Diseases Act 1869 (c.96)
Contagious Diseases Acts Repeal 1886 (c.10)
Contagious Diseases (Animals) Act 1853 (c.62)
Contagious Diseases, Animals Act 1856 (c.101)
Contagious Diseases (Animals) Act 1867 (c.125)
Contagious Diseases (Animals) Act 1869 (c.70)
Contagious Diseases (Animals) Act 1878 (c.74)
Contagious Diseases (Animals) Act 1884 (c.13)
Contagious Diseases (Animals) Act 1886 (c.32)
Contagious Diseases (Animals) Act 1892 (c.47)

Contagious Diseases (Animals) Act 1893 (c.43)
Contagious Diseases (Animals) (Pleuro pneumonia) Act 1890 (c.14)
Contagious Diseases (Animals) (Scotland) Act 1875 (c.75)
Contagious Diseases (Animals) Transfer of Parts of Districts Act 1884 (c.47)
Contagious Diseases (Ireland) Amendment Act 1868 (c.80)
Contagious Diseases of Sheep Act 1858 (c.62)
Contagious Diseases Prevention Act 1864 (c.85)
Contagious Disorders (Sheep), etc. Act 1848 (c.107)
Contempt of Court Act 1981 (c.49)
Continental Shelf Act 1964 (c.29)
Continental Shelf Act 1989 (c.35)
Contingencies Fund Act 1970 (c.56)
Contingencies Fund Act 1974 (c.18)
Contingent Remainders Act 1877 (c.33)
Continuance etc. of Acts Act 1735 (c.18)
Continuance etc., of Acts Act 1757 (c.42)
Continuance etc. of Acts Act 1763 (c.25)
Continuance of Acts Act 1702 (c.13)
Continuance of Acts Act 1706 (c.34)
Continuance of Acts Act 1711 (c.24(e))
Continuance of Acts Act 1718 (c.25)
Continuance of Acts Act 1726 (c.27)
Continuance of Acts Act 1734 (c.18)
Continuance of Acts Act 1737 (c.18)
Continuance of Acts Act 1740 (c.34)
Continuance of Acts Act 1746 (c.47)
Continuance of Acts Act 1750 (c.57)
Continuance of Acts Act 1756 (c.28)
Continuance of Acts Act 1759 (c.16)
Continuance of Acts Act 1797 (c.9)
Continuance of Acts Act 1780 (cc.4, 5)
Continuance of Acts Act 1799 (c.9)
Continuance of Acts Act 1799 (c.12)
Continuance of Acts Act 1799 (c.38)
Continuance of Acts Act 1801 (c.45)
Continuance of Acts, etc. Act 1722 (c.8)
Continuance of Acts, etc. Act 1723 (c.17)
Continuance of Acts, etc. Act 1724 (c.29)
Continuance of Acts, etc. Act 1739 (c.28)
Continuance of Acts, etc. Act 1749 (c.26)
Continuance of Acts, etc. Act 1753 (c.32)
Continuance of Acts, etc. Act 1754 (c.18)
Continuance of Acts, etc. Act 1757 (c.1)
Continuance of Acts. etc. Act 1757 (c.35)
Continuance of Certain Duties, etc. Act 1708 (c.31)
Continuance of Certain Laws Act 1772 (c.56)
Continuance of Certain Laws, etc. Act 1771 (c.51)
Continuance of Criminal Law Act 1722 Act 1725 (c.30)
Continuance of Laws Act 1734 (c.21)
Continuance of Laws Act 1763 (c.11)
Continuance of Laws Act 1763 (c.12)
Continuance of Laws Act 1766 (c.44)
Continuance of Laws Act 1768 (c.1)
Continuance of Laws Act 1774 (c.67)
Continuance of Laws Act 1774 (c.80)
Continuance of Laws Act 1774 (c.86)
Continuance of Laws Act 1776 (c.44)
Continuance of Laws Act 1776 (c.54)
Continuance of Laws Act 1778 (c.45)
Continuance of Laws Act 1779 (c.22)
Continuance of Laws Act 1780 (c.19)
Continuance of Laws Act 1782 (c.13)
Continuance of Laws Act 1783 (c.6)
Continuance of Laws Act 1786 (c.53)
Continuance of Laws Act 1786 (c.80)
Continuance of Laws Act 1787 (c.36)
Continuance of Laws Act 1788 (cc.23, 24)
Continuance of Laws Act 1789 (c.55)
Continuance of Laws Act 1790 (c.18)
Continuance of Laws Act 1791 (c.43)
Continuance of Laws Act 1792 (c.36)
Continuance of Laws Act 1793 (c.40)
Continuance of Laws Act 1794 (c.36)
Continuance of Laws Act 1795 (c.38)
Continuance of Laws Act 1796 (c.40)
Continuance of Laws Act 1796 (c.108)
Continuance of Laws Act 1797 (c.35)
Continuance of Laws Act 1797 (c.99)
Continuance of Laws Act 1800 (c.5)
Continuance of Laws Act 1800 (c.20)
Continuance of Laws Act 1803 (c.4)
Continuance of Laws Act 1803 (c.29)
Continuance of Laws Act 1805 (c.80)
Continuance of Laws Act 1806 (c.29)
Continuance of Laws, etc. Act 1714 (c.26)
Continuance of Laws, etc. Act 1742 (c.26)
Continuance of Laws, etc. Act 1748 (c.46)
Contract (India Office) Act 1903 (c.11)
Contracts (Applicable Law) Act 1990 (c.36)
Contracts of Employment Act 1963 (c.49)
Contracts of Employment Act 1972 (c.53)
Controlled Drugs (Penalties) Act 1985 (c.39)
Control of Employment Act 1939 (c.104)
Control of Food Premises (Scotland) Act 1977 (c.28)
Control of Liquid Fuel Act 1967 (c.57)
Control of Office and Industrial Development Act 1965 (c.33)
Control of Office Development Act 1977 (c.40)
Control of Pollution Act 1974 (c.40)
Control of Pollution (Amendment) Act 1989 (c.14)
Control of Smoke Pollution Act 1989 (c.17)
Controverted Elections Act 1788 (c.52)
Controverted Elections Act 1796 (c.59)
Controverted Elections Act 1801 (c.101)
Controverted Elections Act 1802 (c.84)
Controverted Elections Act 1802 (c.106)
Controverted Elections Act 1807 (c.1)
Controverted Elections Act 1813 (c.71)
Controverted Elections Act 1841 (c.58)
Controverted Elections Act 1842 (c.73)
Controverted Elections Act 1843 (c.47)
Controverted Elections Act 1844 (c.103)

Controverted Elections, etc. Act 1792 (c.1)
Controverted Elections (Ireland) Act 1807 (c.14)
County Rates Act 1738 (c.29)
Convention (Ireland) Act Repeal 1879 (c.28)
Convention of Royal Burghs (Scotland) Act 1879 (c.27)
Convention of Royal Burghs (Scotland) Act 1879, Amendment Act 1895 (c.6)
Convention with United States Act 1855 (c.77)
Conversion of India Stock Act 1887 (c.11)
Conveyance by Release Without Lease Act 1841 (c.21)
Conveyance of Mails Act 1893 (c.38)
Conveyance of Prisoners (Ireland) Act 1815 (c.158)
Conveyance of Prisoners (Ireland) Act 1837 (c.6)
Conveyance of Real Property Act 1845 (c.119)
Conveyancers (Ireland) Act 1864 (c.8)
Conveyancing Act 1881 (c.41)
Conveyancing Act 1882 (c.39)
Conveyancing Act 1911 (c.37)
Conveyancing Amendment (Scotland) Act 1938 (c.24)
Conveyancing and Feudal Reform (Scotland) Act 1970 (c.35)
Conveyancing and Law of Property Act 1892 (c.13)
Conveyancing (Scotland) Act 1874 (c.94)
Conveyancing (Scotland) Act, 1874, Amendment 1879 (c.40)
Conveyancing (Scotland) Act 1924 (c.27)
Conveyancing (Scotland) Acts (1874 and 1879) Amendment 1887 (c.69)
Convict Prisons Act 1850 (c.39)
Convict Prisons Act 1853 (c.121)
Convict Prisons Abroad Act 1859 (c.25)
Convict Prisons Act 1854 (c.76)
Convict Prisons Returns Act 1876 (c.42)
Convicted Prisoners Removal, etc. Act 1853
Conway's Patent Kiln Act 1795 (c.68)
Conwy Tunnel (Supplementary Powers) Act 1983 (c.7)
Co-operative Development Agency 1978 (c.21)
Co-operative Development Agency and Industrial Development Act 1984 (c.57)
Copyhold Act 1843 (c.23)
Copyhold Act 1852 (c.51)
Copyhold Act 1887 (c.73)
Copyhold Act 1894 (c.46)
Copyhold Commission Act 1846 (c.53)
Copyhold Commission Act 1847 (c.101)
Copyhold Commission Act 1858 (c.53)
Copyhold Commission Cont. Act 1860 (c.81)
Copyhold, etc., Commission Act 1853 (c.124)
Copyhold, etc., Commission Act 1855 (c.52)
Copyhold, etc., Commission Act 1857 (c.8)
Copyhold, etc., Commission Cont. Act 1862 (c.73)
Copyhold Lands Act 1844 (c.55)
Copyholds Act 1722 (c.29)
Copyholds Act 1853 (c.57)
Copyholds Act 1858 (c.94)
Copyright Act 1709 (c.21(i))
Copyright Act 1775 (c.53)
Copyright Act 1798 (c.71)
Copyright Act 1801 (c.107)
Copyright Act 1814 (c.156)
Copyright Act 1836 (c.110)
Copyright Act 1842 (c.45)
Copyright Act 1911 (c.46)
Copyright Act 1956 (c.74)
Copyright Act 1956 (Amendment) Act 1982 (c.35)
Copyright (Amendment) Act 1983 (c.42)
Copyright (British Museum) Act 1915 (c.38)
Copyright (Computer Software) Amendment Act 1985 (c.41)
Copyright, Designs and Patents Act 1988 (c.48)
Copyright (Musical Compositions) Act 1882 (c.40)
Copyright (Musical Compositions) Act 1888 (c.17)
Copyright of Designs Act 1839 (c.13)
Copyright of Designs Act 1839 (c.17)
Copyright of Designs Act 1842 (c.100)
Copyright of Designs Act 1843 (c.65)
Copyright of Designs Act 1850 (c.104)
Copyright of Designs Act 1858 (c.70)
Copyright of Designs Act 1861 (c.73)
Copyright of Designs Act 1875 (c.93)
Cordage for Shipping Act 1785 (c.56)
Cork Infirmary Act 1861 (c.29)
Corn Act 1731 (c.12)
Corn Act 1766 (c.17)
Corn Act 1770 (c.39)
Corn Act 1774 (c.64)
Corn Act 1780 (c.50)
Corn Accounts and Returns Act 1864 (c.87)
Corn Duties Act 1847 (c.1)
Corn, etc. Act 1801 (c.13)
Corn Exportation Act 1737 (c.22)
Corn Production Act 1917 (c.46)
Corn Production Acts (Repeal) Act 1921 (c.48)
Corn Production (Amendment) Act 1918 (c.36)
Corn Rents Act 1963 (c.14)
Corn Returns Act 1882 (c.37)
Corn Sales Act 1921 (c.35)
Corneal Grafting Act 1952 (c.28)
Corneal Tissue Act 1986 (c.18)
Cornwall and Devon Roads Act 1770 (c.87)
Cornwall and Devon Roads Act 1777 (c.79)
Cornwall Duchy Act 1760 (c.11)
Cornwall Duchy Act 1793 (c.78)
Cornwall Duchy Act 1810 (c.6)
Cornwall Roads Act 1759 (c.42)
Cornwall Roads Act 1760 (c.27)
Cornwall Roads Act 1760 (c.32)
Cornwall Roads Act 1762 (c.46)

Cornwall Roads Act 1763 (c.52)
Cornwall Roads Act 1781 (c.78)
Cornwall Roads Act 1781 (c.90)
Cornwall Roads Act 1782 (c.104)
Cornwall Roads Act 1783 (c.27)
Cornwall Roads Act 1785 (c.108)
Cornwall Roads Act 1785 (c.114)
Cornwall Submarine Mines Act 1858 (c.109)
Coroners Act 1751 (c.29)
Coroners Act 1836 (c.89)
Coroners Act 1843 (c.12)
Coroners Act 1843 (c.83)
Coroners Act 1844 (c.92)
Coroners Act 1887 (c.71)
Coroners Act 1892 (c.56)
Coroners Act 1921 (c.30)
Coroners Act 1954 (c.31)
Coroners Act 1980 (c.38)
Coroners Act 1988 (c.13)
Coroners (Amendment) Act 1926 (c.59)
Coroners (Emergency Provisions) Act 1917 (c.19)
Coroners (Emergency Provisions Continuance) Act 1922 (c.2)
Coroners' Inquests, Bail Act 1859 (c.33)
Coroners' Inquests Expenses Act 1837 (c.68)
Coroners (Ireland) Act 1846 (c.37)
Coroners (Ireland) Act 1881 (c.35)
Coroners (Ireland) Act 1908 (c.37)
Coroners' Juries Act 1983 (c.31)
Corporate Bodies' Contracts Act 1960 (c.46)
Corporation of Dublin Act 1850 (c.55)
Corporations Act 1718 (c.6)
Correspondence with Enemies Act 1704 (c.13)
Correspondence with Enemies Act 1793 (c.27)
Correspondence with Foreign Parts Act 1801 (c.11)
Correspondence with James the Pretender (High Treason) Act 1701 (c.3)
Corrupt and Illegal Practices Prevention Act 1883 (c.51)
Corrupt and Illegal Practices Prevention Act 1895 (c.40)
Corrupt Practice (Municipal Elections) Act 1872 (c.60)
Corrupt Practices Act 1856 (c.84)
Corrupt Practices Act 1858 (c.87)
Corrupt Practices Act 1859 (c.48)
Corrupt Practices Act 1861 (c.122)
Corrupt Practices Act 1862 (c.109)
Corrupt Practices 1854 Act, Continuation Act 1860 (c.99)
Corrupt Practices at Elections Act 1735 (c.38)
Corrupt Practice Commission Expenses Act 1869 (c.21)
Corrupt Practices at Parliamentary Elections Act 1728 (c.24)
Corrupt Practices, Dublin City 1869 (c.65)
Corrupt Practices Prevention Act 1854 (c.102)
Corrupt Practices Prevention Act 1863 (c.29)
Corrupt Practices (Suspension of Election) Act 1882 (c.68)
Corrupt Practices (Suspension of Elections) Act 1881 (c.42)
Corrupt Practices (Suspension of Elections) Act 1883 (c.46)
Corrupt Practices (Suspension of Elections) Act 1884 (c.78)
Corruption of Blood Act 1814 (c.145)
Corsham to Bath Easton Bridge Road Act 1779 (c.112)
Cosford, Suffolk: Poor Relief Act 1779 (c.30)
Cosham to Chichester Road Act 1762 (c.84)
Cosham to Chichester Road Act 1783 (c.32)
Costs Act 1803 (c.46)
Costs in Criminal Cases Act 1952 (c.48)
Costs in Criminal Cases Act 1908 (c.15)
Costs in Criminal Cases Act 1973 (c.14)
Costs of Action of Trespass Act 1840 (c.24)
Costs of Leases Act 1958 (c.52)
Cottier Tenant (Ireland) Act 1856 (c.65)
Cottingham, Yorks: Inclosure Act 1791 (c.20)
Cotton Act 1954 (c.24)
Cotton Association (Emergency Action) Act 1915 (c.69)
Cotton (Centralised Buying) Act 1947 (c.26)
Cotton Cloth Factories Act 1889 (c.62)
Cotton Cloth Factories Act 1897 (c.58)
Cotton Industry Act 1923 (c.22)
Cotton Industry Act 1928 (c.11)
Cotton Industry Act 1933 (c.30)
Cotton Industry Act 1938 (c.15)
Cotton Industry Act 1939 (c.9)
Cotton Industry Act 1959 (c.48)
Cotton Industry (Reorganisation) Act 1939 (c.54)
Cotton Industry (Reorganisation) (Postponement) Act 1939 (c.116)
Cotton Manufacture (Scotland) Act 1803 (c.151)
Cotton Manufacturing Industry (Temporary Provisions) Act 1934 (c.30)
Cotton Spinning Industry Act 1936 (c.21)
Cotton Spinning (Re-equipment Subsidy) Act 1948 (c.31)
Cotton Statistics Act 1868 (c.33)
Cotton Trade (Ireland) Act 1813 (c.75)
Council of India Act 1876 (c.7)
Council of India Act 1907 (c.35)
Council of India Reduction Act 1889 (c.65)
Councils of Conciliation Act 1867 (c.105)
Counter Inflation Act 1973 (c.9)
Counter Inflation (Temporary Provisions) Act 1972 (c.74)
Counterfeit Currency (Convention) Act 1935 (c.25)
Counterfeit Dollars and Tokens Act 1804 (c.71)
Counterfeit Medal Act 1883 (c.45)
Counterfeiting Act 1702 (c.3)
Counterfeiting Bank of England Tokens Act 1811 (c.110)
Counterfeiting Bank of Ireland Silver Tokens, etc. Act 1805 (c.42)

Counterfeiting Coin Act 1741 (c.28)
Counterfeiting Coin Act 1797 (c.126)
Counterfeiting, etc., of Gold Coin Act 1772 (c.71)
Counterfeiting of Bank of Ireland Tokens Act 1813 (c.106)
Counterfeiting of Copper Coin Act 1771 (c.40)
Counterfeiting of Tokens, etc. Act 1808 (c.31)
Counterfeiting of Tokens, etc. Act 1812 (c.138)
Countervailing Duties Act 1802 (c.27)
Countervailing Duties Act 1804 (c.27)
Countervailing Duties (Ireland) Act 1807 (c.18)
Countervailing Duties on Spirit Mixtures, etc. Act 1836 (c.72)
Countervailing Duty Act 1803 (c.154)
Counties and Boroughs (Ireland) Act 1840 (c.109)
Counties (Detached Parts) Act 1839 (c.82)
Counties (Detached Parts) Act 1844 (c.61)
Counties of Cities Act 1798 (c.52)
Counties of Cities Act 1811 (c.100)
Counties of Drogheda and Meath Act 1845 (c.121)
Countryside Act 1968 (c.41)
Countryside (Scotland) Act 1967 (c.86)
Countryside (Scotland) Act 1981 (c.44)
County and Borough Councils (Qualification) Act 1914 (c.21)
County and Borough Police Act 1856 (c.69)
County and Borough Police Act 1859 (c.32)
County and Borough Police Act 1919 (c.84)
County and City of Dublin Grand Juries Act 1873 (c.65)
County Boundaries (Ireland) Act 1872 (c.48)
County Bridges Act 1841 (c.49)
County Bridges Loans Extension Act 1880 (c.5)
County Buildings Act 1837 (c.24)
County Buildings Act 1847 (c.28)
County Buildings (Loans) Act 1872 (c.7)
County Cessation (Ireland) Act 1848 (c.32)
County Cessation (Ireland) Act 1849 (c.36)
County Cessation (Ireland) Act 1850 (c.1)
County Cessation (Ireland) Act 1859 (c.23)
County Cessation (Ireland) Act 1861 (c.58)
County Common Juries Act 1910 (c.17)
County Contributions to Prisons, etc. Act 1861 (c.12)
County Coroners Act 1860 (c.116)
County Council Association Expenses (Amendment) Act 1937 (c.27)
County Council (Elections) Act 1891 (c.68)
County Councils Association Expenses Act 1890 (c.3)
County Councils Association Expenses (Amendment) Act 1947 (c.13)
County Councils Association (Scotland) Expenses Act 1894 (c.5)
County Councils (Bills in Parliament) Act 1903 (c.9)
County Councils (Elections) Amendment Act 1900 (c.13)
County Councils Mortgages Act 1909 (c.38)
County Court Amendment (Ireland) Act 1882 (c.29)
County Court Appeals (Ireland) Act 1889 (c.48)
County Court (Buildings) Act 1870 (c.15)
County Court (Costs and Salaries) Act 1882 (c.57)
County Court Districts (England) Act 1858 (c.74)
County Court Judges Act 1859 (c.57)
County Court Judges (Retirement Pensions and Deputies) Act 1919 (c.70)
County Court Jurisdiction in Lunacy (Ireland) Act 1880 (c.39)
County Court (Penalties for Contempt) Act 1983 (c.45)
County Courts Act 1849 (c.101)
County Courts Act 1850 (c.61)
County Courts Act 1852 (c.54)
County Courts Act 1854 (c.16)
County Courts Act 1856 (c.108)
County Courts Act 1857 (c.36)
County Courts Act 1866 (c.14)
County Courts Act 1867 (c.142)
County Courts Act 1875 (c.50)
County Courts Act 1888 (c.43)
County Courts Act 1903 (c.42)
County Courts Act 1919 (c.73)
County Courts Act 1924 (c.17)
County Courts Act 1934 (c.53)
County Courts Act 1955 (c.8)
County Courts Act 1959 (c.22)
County Courts Act 1984 (c.28)
County Courts Admiralty Jurisdiction Act 1868 (c.71)
County Courts Admiralty Jurisdiction Amendment Act 1869 (c.51)
County Courts (Amendment) Act 1934 (c.17)
County Courts (Equity Jurisdiction) Act 1865 (c.99)
County Courts (Expenses) Act 1887 (c.3)
County Courts (Investment) Act 1900 (c.47)
County Courts (Jurisdiction) Act 1963 (c.5)
County Courts Westminster and Southwark Act 1859 (c.8)
County Debentures Act 1873 (c.35)
County Dublin Baronies Act 1838 (c.115)
County Dublin Grand Jury Act 1844 (c.106)
County Dublin Surveyors Act 1897 (c.2)
County Elections Act 1788 (c.36)
County Elections Act 1789 (c.13)
County Elections Act 1789 (c.18)
County Elections (Ireland) Act 1862 (c.62)
County Elections (Scotland) Act 1853 (c.28)
County Electors Act 1888 (c.10)
County Fermanagh Baronies Act 1837 (c.82)
County General Assessment (Scotland) Act 1868 (c.82)
County Infirmaries (Ireland) Act 1805 (c.111)
County Infirmaries (Ireland) Act 1807 (c.50)

County Infirmaries (Ireland) Act 1814 (c.62)
County Institutions (Ireland) Act 1838 (c.116)
County Law Procedure Act 1848 (c.31)
County of Clare Treasurer Act 1838 (c.104)
County of Dublin Jurors and Voters' Revision Act 1884 (c.35)
County of Durham Coroners Act 1837 (c.64)
County of Hertford Act 1878 (c.50)
County of Hertford and Liberty of St. Albans Act 1874 (c.45)
County of Roscommon Act 1840 (c.76)
County of Sussex Act 1865 (c.37)
County Officers and Courts (Ireland) Act 1877 (c.56)
County Officers and Courts (Ireland) Amendment Act 1885 (c.71)
County Palatine of Chester Act 1787 (c.43)
County Police Act 1839 (c.93)
County Police Act 1840 (c.88)
County Police Act 1856 (c.2)
County Property Act 1858 (c.92)
County Property Act 1871 (c.14)
County Rate Act 1866 (c.78)
County Rates Act 1815 (c.51)
County Rates Act 1816 (c.49)
County Rates Act 1844 (c.33)
County Rates Act 1845 (c.111)
County Rates Act 1852 (c.81)
County Rates (England) Act 1858 (c.33)
County Rates Within Boroughs Act 1849 (c.65)
County Surveyors, etc. (Ireland) Act 1861 (c.63)
County Surveyors (Ireland) Act 1862 (c.106)
County Surveyors (Ireland) Act 1893 (c.49)
County Surveyors (Ireland) Act 1900 (c.18)
County Surveyors Superannuation (Ireland) - Northern Irish Act 1875 (c.56)
County, Town and Parish Councils (Qualification) (Scotland) Act 1914 (c.39)
County Treasurers (Ireland) Act 1837 (c.54)
County Treasurers (Ireland) Act 1838 (c.53)
County Treasurers (Ireland) Act 1867 (c.46)
County Voters Registration Act 1865 (c.36)
County Votes Registration (Scotland) Act 1861 (c.83)
County Works (Ireland) Act 1846 (c.2)
County Works (Ireland) Act 1846 (c.78)
Court Funds Act 1829 (c.13)
Court House (Ireland) Act 1813 (c.131)
Court Houses (Ireland) Act 1815 (c.89)
Court Houses (Ireland) Act 1840 (c.102)
Court Houses (Ireland) Act 1841 (c.31)
Court-martial on Admiral Keppel Act 1779 (c.6)
Court of Admiralty Act 1854 (c.78)
Court of Admiralty (Ireland) Act 1867 (c.114)
Court of Admiralty (Ireland) Amendment Act 1876 (c.28)
Court of Appeal in Chancery Act 1867 (c.64)
Court of Appeal in Chancery Act 1868 (c.11)
Court of Bankruptcy (Ireland) Officers and Clerks Act 1881 (c.23)
Court of Chancery Act 1738 (c.24)
Court of Chancery Act 1763 (c.32)
Court of Chancery Act 1765 (c.28)
Court of Chancery Act 1769 (c.19)
Court of Chancery Act 1774 (c.43)
Court of Chancery Act 1806 (c.129)
Court of Chancery Act 1840 (c.94)
Court of Chancery Act 1841 (c.5)
Court of Chancery Act 1841 (c.52)
Court of Chancery Act 1842 (c.103)
Court of Chancery Act 1845 (c.105)
Court of Chancery Act 1848 (c.10)
Court of Chancery Act 1851 (c.83)
Court of Chancery Act 1852 (c.87(a))
Court of Chancery Act 1854 (c.100)
Court of Chancery Act 1855 (c.134)
Court of Chancery Act 1860 (c.149)
Court of Chancery and Exchequer Funds (Ireland) Act 1868 (c.88)
Court of Chancery Act 1852 (c.80)
Court of Chancery (England) Act 1850 (c.35)
Court of Chancery (England) Act 1853 (c.98)
Court of Chancery Examiners Act 1853 (c.22)
Court of Chancery (Funds) Act 1872 (c.44)
Court of Chancery (Ireland) Act 1823 (c.61)
Court of Chancery (Ireland) Act 1836 (c.74)
Court of Chancery (Ireland) Reg. Act 1850 (c.89)
Court of Chancery of Lancaster Act 1850 (c.43)
Court of Chancery of Lancaster Act 1854 (c.82)
Court of Chancery of Lancaster Act 1952 (c.49)
Court of Chancery of Lancaster (Amendment) Act 1961 (c.38)
Court of Chancery (Officers) Act 1867 (c.87)
Court of Chancery Offices Act 1848 (c.94)
Court of Chancery Procedure Act 1852 (c.86)
Court of Common Pleas Act 1850 (c.75)
Court of Common Pleas Act 1862 (c.96)
Court of Exchequer Chamber (Ireland) Act 1857 (c.6)
Court of Exchequer, Equity Side Act 1836 (c.112)
Court of Exchequer (Ireland) Act 1816 (c.122)
Court of Exchequer (Ireland) Act 1855 (c.50)
Court of Exchequer (Scotland) Act 1806 (c.154)
Court of Exchequer (Scotland) Act 1836 (c.73)
Court of Justice Act Act 1866 (c.63)
Court of Justiciary (Scotland) Act 1864 (c.30)
Court of Justiciary (Scotland) Act 1868 (c.95)
Court of Pleas of Durham Act 1839 (c.16)
Court of Probate Act 1857 (c.77)
Court of Probate Act 1858 (c.95)
Court of Probate Act (Ireland) 1859 (c.31)
Court of Probate (Ireland) Act 1861 (c.111)
Court of Queen's Bench Act 1843 (c.20)
Court of Session Act 1723 (c.19)
Court of Session Act 1808 (c.151)
Court of Session Act 1810 (c.112)

Court of Session Act 1813 (c.64)
Court of Session Act 1821 (c.38)
Court of Session Act 1825 (c.120)
Court of Session Act 1830 (c.69)
Court of Session Act 1838 (c.86)
Court of Session Act 1839 (c.36)
Court of Session Act 1850 (c.36)
Court of Session Act 1857 (c.56)
Court of Session Act 1868 (c.100)
Court of Session Act 1988 (c.36)
Court of Session Adjournment Act 1762 (c.27)
Court of Session Consignations (Scotland) Act 1895 (c.19)
Court of Session (Extracts) Act 1916 (c.49)
Court of Session (No. 2) Act 1838 (c.118)
Court of Session (Records) Act 1815 (c.70)
Court of Session (Scotland) Act 1745 (c.7)
Courts Act 1672 (c.40)
Courts Act 1971 (c.23)
Courts and Legal Services Act 1990 (c.41)
Courts Baron of High Peak and Castleton Act 1759 (c.31)
Courts Baron, Sheffield Act 1756 (c.37)
Courts (Colonial) Jurisdiction Act 1874 (c.27)
Courts (Emergency Powers) Act 1914 (c.78)
Courts (Emergency Powers) Act 1917 (c.25)
Courts (Emergency Powers) Act 1919 (c.64)
Courts (Emergency Powers) Act 1939 (c.67)
Courts (Emergency Powers) Act 1940 (c.37)
Courts (Emergency Powers) Act 1943 (c.19)
Courts (Emergency Powers) (Amendment) Act 1916 (c.13)
Courts (Emergency Powers) Amendment Act 1942 (c.36)
Courts (Emergency Powers) (Ireland) Act 1914 (c.19)
Courts (Emergency Power) (No. 2) Act 1916 (c.18)
Courts (Emergency Powers) (Scotland) Act 1939 (c.113)
Courts (Emergency Powers) (Scotland) Act 1944 (c.6)
Courts in Prince of Wales Island and India Act 1855 (c.93)
Courts in Wales and Chester Act 1732 (c.14)
Courts-Martial (Appeals) Act 1951 (c.46)
Courts-Martial (Appeals) Act 1968 (c.20)
Courts-Martial, East Indies Act 1760 (c.14)
Courts-Martial in India Act 1844 (c.18)
Courts-Martial on Troops of East India Company Act 1810 (c.87)
Courts, Newfoundland Act 1791 (c.29)
Courts, Newfoundland Act 1792 (c.46)
Courts, Newfoundland Act 1793 (c.76)
Courts, Newfoundland Act 1795 (c.25)
Courts, Newfoundland Act 1796 (c.37)
Courts, Newfoundland Act 1799 (c.16)
Courts, Newfoundland, etc. Act 1794 (c.44)
Courts of Common Law, Sittings Act 1838 (c.32)
Courts of Exchequer Act 1799 (c.67)
Courts of Judicature, India Act 1839 (c.34)
Courts of Justice (Additional Site) Act 1871 (c.57)
Courts of Justice Building Act 1865 (c.48)
Courts of Justice Building Amendment Act 1880 (c.29)
Courts of Justice, Canada Act 1803 (c.138)
Courts of Justice Concentration (Site) Act 1865 (c.49)
Courts of Justice (Salaries and Funds) Act 1869 (c.91)
Courts of Law Fees Act 1867 (c.122)
Courts of Law Fees (Scotland) Act 1868 (c.55)
Courts of Law Fees (Scotland) Act 1895 (c.14)
Covent Garden Market Act 1961 (c.49)
Covent Garden Market (Financial Provisions) Act 1977 (c.2)
Coventry Act 1842 (c.110)
Coventry Canal Act 1768 (c.36)
Coventry Canal Act 1786 (c.20)
Coventry Canal Act 1786 (c.30)
Coventry Freemen, etc. Act 1781 (c.54)
Coventry Gaol Act 1768 (c.40)
Coventry Grammar School Act 1864 (c.41)
Coventry Improvement Act 1763 (c.41)
Coventry–Oxford Canal Act 1775 (c.9)
Coventry Roads Act 1796 (c.133)
Coventry: Streets Act 1790 (c.77)
Coventry to Oxford Canal Act 1769 (c.70)
Coventry to Oxford Canal Act 1794 (c.103)
Coventry to Ticknall Canal Act 1794 (c.93)
Cowgil Parish; Marriages Confirmation, Park Gate Chapel Act 1869 (c.30)
Cowley's Charity Act 1858 (c.81)
Cran Measures Act 1908 (c.17)
Cranbourne Street Act 1864 (c.111)
Cranford and Maidenhead Road Act 1726 (c.31)
Credit-Sale Agreements (Scotland) Act 1961 (c.56)
Credit Unions Act 1979 (c.34)
Cremation Act 1902 (c.8)
Cremation Act 1952 (c.31)
Crew of a Certain Foreign Vessel Act 1786 (c.8)
Crewkerne Roads Act 1765 (c.61)
Crewkerne Roads Act 1786 (c.123)
Crime and Outrage (Ireland) Act 1850 (c.106)
Crime and Outrage (Ireland) Act 1852 (c.66)
Crime and Outrage (Ireland) Act 1853 (c.72)
Crime and Outrage (Ireland) Act 1854 (c.92)
Crimes and Outrage (Ireland) Act 1855 (c.112)
Criminal and Dangerous Lunatics (Scotland) Amendment Act 1871 (c.55)
Criminal Appeal Act 1907 (c.23)
Criminal Appeal Act 1964 (c.43)
Criminal Appeal Act 1966 (c.31)
Criminal Appeal Act 1968 (c.19)
Criminal Appeal Act 1995 (c.35)
Criminal Appeal (Amendment) Act 1908 (c.46)

Criminal Appeal (Northern Ireland) Act 1930 (c.45)
Criminal Appeal (Northern Ireland) Act 1968 (c.21)
Criminal Appeal (Northern Ireland) Act 1980 (c.47)
Criminal Appeal (Scotland) Act 1926 (c.15)
Criminal Appeal (Scotland) Act 1927 (c.26)
Criminal Attempts Act 1981 (c.47)
Criminal Costs (Dublin) Act 1815 (c.91)
Criminal Court, Norfolk Island Act 1794 (c.45)
Criminal Court, Norfolk Island Act 1795 (c.18)
Criminal Damage Act 1971 (c.48)
Criminal Evidence Act 1898 (c.36)
Criminal Evidence Act 1965 (c.20)
Criminal Evidence Act 1979 (c.16)
Criminal Injuries Compensation Act 1995 (c.53)
Criminal Injuries (Ireland) Act 1919 (c.14)
Criminal Jurisdiction Act 1802 (c.85)
Criminal Jurisdiction Act 1975 (c.59)
Criminal Justice Act 1855 (c.126)
Criminal Justice Act 1856 (c.118)
Criminal Justice Act 1925 (c.86)
Criminal Justice Act 1948 (c.58)
Criminal Justice Act 1961 (c.39)
Criminal Justice Act 1965 (c.26)
Criminal Justice Act 1967 (c.80)
Criminal Justice Act 1972 (c.71)
Criminal Justice Act 1982 (c.48)
Criminal Justice Act 1987 (c.38)
Criminal Justice Act 1988 (c.33)
Criminal Justice Act 1991 (c.53)
Criminal Justice Act 1993 (c.36)
Criminal Justice Administration Act 1851 (c.55)
Criminal Justice Administration Act 1914 (c.58)
Criminal Justice Administration Act 1956 (c.34)
Criminal Justice Administration Act 1962 (c.15)
Criminal Justice Administration (Amendment) Act 1959 (c.41)
Criminal Justice Administration (Postponement) Act 1914 (c.9)
Criminal Justice (Amendment) Act 1925 (c.13)
Criminal Justice (Amendment) Act 1981 (c.27)
Criminal Justice and Public Order Act 1994 (c.33)
Criminal Justice (International Co-operation) Act 1990 (c.5)
Criminal Justice (Scotland) Act 1949 (c.94)
Criminal Justice (Scotland) Act 1963 (c.39)
Criminal Justice (Scotland) Act 1980 (c.62)
Criminal Justice (Scotland) Act 1987 (c.41)
Criminal Justice (Scotland) Act 1995 (c.20)
Criminal Law Act 1722 (c.22)
Criminal Law Act 1772 (c.31)
Criminal Law Act 1776 (c.43)
Criminal Law Act 1778 (c.62)
Criminal Law Act 1779 (c.54)
Criminal Law Act 1781 (cc.68, 69)
Criminal Law Act 1782 (c.40)
Criminal Law Act 1782 (c.58)
Criminal Law Act 1826 (c.64)
Criminal Law Act 1967 (c.58)
Criminal Law Act 1977 (c.45)
Criminal Law Amendment Act 1867 (c.35)
Criminal Law Amendment Act 1871 (c.32)
Criminal Law Amendment Act 1880 (c.45)
Criminal Law Amendment Act 1885 (c.69)
Criminal Law Amendment Act 1912 (c.20)
Criminal Law Amendment Act 1922 (c.56)
Criminal Law Amendment Act 1928 (c.42)
Criminal Law Amendment Act 1951 (c.36)
Criminal Law and Procedure (Ireland) Act 1887 (c.20)
Criminal Law (Consolidation) (Scotland) Act 1995 (c.39)
Criminal Law (Ireland) Act 1828 (c.54)
Criminal Law (Scotland) Act 1829 (c.38)
Criminal Law (Scotland) Act 1830 (c.37)
Criminal Lunatic Asylums Act 1860 (c.75)
Criminal Lunatics Act 1800 (c.94)
Criminal Lunatics Act 1838 (c.14)
Criminal Lunatics Act 1867 (c.12)
Criminal Lunatics Act 1869 (c.78)
Criminal Lunatics Act 1884 (c.64)
Criminal Lunatics (Ireland) Act 1838 (c.27)
Criminal Lunatics (Scotland) Act 1935 (c.32)
Criminal Procedure Act 1694 (c.43)
Criminal Procedure Act 1701 (c.6)
Criminal Procedure Act 1848 (c.46)
Criminal Procedure Act 1851 (c.100)
Criminal Procedure Act 1853 (c.30)
Criminal Procedure Act 1865 (c.18)
Criminal Procedure (Attendance of Witnesses) Act 1965 (c.69)
Criminal Procedure (Consequential Provisions) (Scotland) Act 1995 (c.40)
Criminal Procedure (Insanity) Act 1964 (c.84)
Criminal Procedure (Insanity and Unfitness to Plead) Act 1991 (c.25)
Criminal Procedure (Right of Reply) Act 1964 (c.34)
Criminal Procedure (Scotland) Act 1887 (c.35)
Criminal Procedure (Scotland) Act 1921 (c.50)
Criminal Procedure (Scotland) Act 1938 (c.48)
Criminal Procedure (Scotland) Act 1965 (c.39)
Criminal Procedure (Scotland) Act 1975 (c.21)
Criminal Procedure (Scotland) Act 1995 (c.46)
Criminal Prosecutions Fees (Ireland) Act 1809 (c.101)
Criminal Statutes Repeal Act 1861 (c.95)
Crinan Canal Act 1793 (c.104)
Crinan Canal Act 1805 (c.85)
Cripplegate: Church Building Act 1732 (c.21)

Crofter Forestry (Scotland) Act 1991 (c.18)
Crofters Commission (Delegation of Powers) Act 1888 (c.63)
Crofters Common Grazings Regulation Act 1891 (c.41)
Crofters Common Grazings Regulation Act 1908 (c.50)
Crofters Holdings (Scotland) Act 1886 (c.29)
Crofters Holdings (Scotland) Act 1887 (c.24)
Crofters (Scotland) Act 1955 (c.21)
Crofters (Scotland) Act 1961 (c.58)
Crofters (Scotland) Act 1993 (c.44)
Crofting Reform (Scotland) Act 1976 (c.21)
Cromarty Harbour Act 1785 (c.39)
Cromford Bridge to Langley Mill Road Act 1786 (c.124)
Cromford Canal Act 1789 (c.74)
Crossbows Act 1987 (c.32)
Crossed Cheques Act 1876 (c.81)
Crossford Bridge and Altrincham Road Act 1796 (c.143)
Crown Agents Act 1979 (c.43)
Crown Agents Act 1995 (c.24)
Crown Agents (Amendment) Act 1986 (c.43)
Crown Appointments, Colonies Act 1846 (c.91)
Crown Cases Act 1848 (c.78)
Crown Debt from Late Right Hon. R. Rigby Act 1794 (c.66)
Crown Debt of Abraham Goldsmid, etc. Act 1812 (c.75)
Crown Debtors Act 1785 (c.35)
Crown Debts Act 1541 (c.39)
Crown Debts Act 1801 (c.90)
Crown Debts Act 1824 (c.111)
Crown Debts and Judgments Act 1860 (c.115)
Crown Estate Act 1956 (c.73)
Crown Estate Act 1961 (c.55)
Crown Land, Revenues Act 1854 (c.68)
Crown Lands Act 1702 (c.1)
Crown Lands Act 1775 (c.33)
Crown Lands Act 1784 (c.57)
Crown Lands Act 1800 (c.78)
Crown Lands Act 1806 (c.151)
Crown Lands Act 1810 (c.65)
Crown Lands Act 1814 (c.70)
Crown Lands Act 1841 (c.1)
Crown Lands Act 1845 (c.99)
Crown Lands Act 1848 (c.102)
Crown Lands Act 1851 (c.42)
Crown Lands Act 1852 (c.62)
Crown Lands Act 1853 (c.56)
Crown Lands Act 1855 (c.16)
Crown Lands Act 1866 (c.62)
Crown Lands Act 1873 (c.36)
Crown Lands Act 1885 (c.79)
Crown Lands Act 1894 (c.43)
Crown Lands Act 1906 (c.28)
Crown Lands Act 1913 (c.8)
Crown Lands Act 1927 (c.23)
Crown Lands Act 1936 (c.47)
Crown Lands Act 1943 (c.7)
Crown Lands at Byfleet, Weybridge, etc., Surrey Act 1804 (c.25)
Crown Lands at Catterick and Tunstall, Yorkshire Act 1790 (c.51)
Crown Lands at Egham, Exchange King and David Jebb Act 1807 (c.77)
Crown Lands at Enfield, Middlesex Act 1776 (c.17)
Crown Lands at North Scotland Yard, Middlesex Act 1785 (c.98)
Crown Lands at Richmond, Surrey Act 1772 (c.35)
Crown Lands at Richmond, Surrey Act 1772 (c.59)
Crown Lands at Shilston Bay, Devon Act 1805 (c.116)
Crown Lands (Copyholds) Act 1851 (c.46)
Crown Lands, Escheats Act 1807 (c.24)
Crown Lands (Forfeited Estates) Act 1715 (c.50)
Crown Lands—Forfeited Estates Act 1717 (c.8)
Crown Lands—Forfeited Estates Act 1718 (c.22)
Crown Lands—Forfeited Estates Act 1719 (c.24)
Crown Lands—Forfeited Estates Act 1720 (c.22)
Crown Lands—Forfeited Estates Act 1726 (c.28)
Crown Lands—Forfeited Estates Act 1727 (c.21)
Crown Lands—Forfeited Estates Act 1728 (c.33)
Crown Lands—Forfeited Estates Act 1744 (c.37)
Crown Lands—Forfeited Estates Act 1746 (c.41)
Crown Lands—Forfeited Estates Act 1748 (c.52)
Crown Lands—Forfeited Estates Act 1751 (c.41)
Crown Lands, Forfeited Estates Act 1757 (c.16)
Crown Lands, Forfeited Estates Act 1762 (c.17)
Crown Lands—Forfeited Estates Act 1774 (c.22)
Crown Lands—Forfeited Estates Act 1794 (c.101)
Crown Lands—Forfeited Estates Act 1795 (c.69)
Crown Lands (Forfeited Estates): Greenwich Hospital Act 1737 (c.30)
Crown Lands, Forfeited Estates in Ireland Act 1793 (c.46)
Crown Lands, Forfeited Estates (Ireland) Act 1702 (c.18(a))
Crown Lands, Forfeited Estates (Ireland) Act 1702 (c.25)
Crown Lands, Forfeited Estates (Ireland) Act 1706 (c.25)
Crown Lands, Forfeited Estates (Ireland) Act 1778 (c.61)

Crown Lands Grant to Jame's Archbald Stuart Act 1772 (c.44)
Crown Lands—Greenwich Hospital Act 1778 (c.29)
Crown Lands in Fenchurch Street London Act 1772 (c.19)
Crown Lands in Holborn, London Act 1772 (c.43)
Crown Lands in Meath to Vest in Gerald Fitzgerald Act 1771 (c.56)
Crown Lands in Northamptonshire, Grant to Earl of Exeter Act 1796 (c.63)
Crown Lands in Northamptonshire, Grant to Earl of Upper Ossory Act 1795 (c.40)
Crown Lands in Northamptonshire, Grant to Earl of Westmorland Act 1796 (c.62)
Crown Lands in Privy Garden, Westminster Act 1792 (c.24)
Crown Lands (Ireland) Act 1822 (c.63)
Crown Lands - New Forest Act 1800 (c.86)
Crown Land Revenues, etc. Act 1786 (c.87)
Crown Lands, Savoy Act 1771 (c.4)
Crown Lands (Scotland) Act 1833 (c.69)
Crown Lands: Taxation Act 1801 (c.47)
Crown Lessees (Protection of Sub-Tenants) Act 1952 (c.40)
Crown Office Act 1860 (c.54)
Crown Office Act 1877 (c.41)
Crown Office Act 1890 (c.2)
Crown Pensioners Disqualification Act 1715 (c.56)
Crown Pre-Emption of Lead Ore Act 1815 (c.134)
Crown Private Estate Act 1800 (c.88)
Crown Private Estates Act 1862 (c.37)
Crown Private Estates Act 1873 (c.61)
Crown Proceedings Act 1947 (c.44)
Crown Proceedings (Armed Forces) Act 1987 (c.25)
Crown Land Revenues Act 1794 (c.75)
Crown Revenues (Colonies) Act 1852 (c.39)
Crown Suits Act 1769 (c.16)
Crown Suits Act 1855 (c.90)
Crown Suits Act 1861 (c.62)
Crown Suits, etc. Act 1865 (c.104)
Crown Suits (Isle of Man) Act 1862 (c.14)
Crown Suits (Scotland) Act 1857 (c.44)
Croydon Parish Church Act 1760 (c.38)
Cruelty to Animals Act 1849 (c.92)
Cruelty to Animals Act 1854 (c.60)
Cruelty to Animals Act 1876 (c.77)
Cruelty to Animals (Ireland) Act 1837 (c.66)
Cruelty to Animals (Scotland) Act 1850 (c.92)
Cruelty to Animals (Scotland) Act 1895 (c.13)
Cultivation, etc. of Trees Act 1766 (c.36)
Cultivation of Madder Act 1765 (c.18)
Cumberland and Westmorland Roads Act 1762 (c.81)
Cumberland and Westmorland Roads Act 1783 (c.108)
Cumberland Roads Act 1749 (c.40)
Cumberland Roads Act 1753 (c.37)
Cumberland Roads Act 1753 (c.49)
Cumberland Roads Act 1767 (c.83)
Cumberland Roads Act 1778 (c.108)
Cumberland Roads Act 1779 (c.97)
Cumberland Roads Act 1789 (c.97)
Cumberland Roads Act 1794 (c.143)
Cunard Agreement (Money) Act 1904 (c.22)
Cunard (Insurance) Agreement Act 1931 (c.2)
Curates, etc. Act 1796 (c.83)
Curragh of Kildare Act 1868 (c.60)
Curragh of Kildare Act 1870 (c.74)
Currency Act 1982 (c.3)
Currency Act 1983 (c.9)
Currency and Bank Notes Act 1914 (c.14)
Currency and Bank Notes Act 1928 (c.13)
Currency and Bank Notes Act 1939 (c.7)
Currency and Bank Notes Act 1954 (c.12)
Currency and Bank Notes (Amendment) Act 1914 (c.72)
Currency (Defence) Act 1939 (c.64)
Curriers, etc. Act 1738 (c.25)
Cursitor Baron of the Exchequer Act 1856 (c.86)
Custody of Children Act 1891 (c.3)
Custody of Children (Scotland) Act 1939 (c.4)
Custody of Infants Act 1839 (c.54)
Custody of Infants Act 1873 (c.12)
Custody of Insane Persons Act 1816 (c.117)
Custody of Napoleon Buonaparte Act 1816 (c.22)
Customs Act 1719 (c.12)
Customs Act 1722 (c.21)
Customs Act 1772 (c.50)
Customs Act 1772 (c.60)
Customs Act 1724 (c.7)
Customs Act 1736 (c.30)
Customs Act 1753 (c.12)
Customs Act 1763 (c.9)
Customs Act 1763 (c.22)
Customs Act 1766 (c.20)
Customs Act 1766 (c.28)
Customs Act 1766 (c.41)
Customs Act 1766 (c.45)
Customs Act 1766 (c.50)
Customs Act 1767 (c.58)
Customs Act 1768 (c.23)
Customs Act 1770 (c.17)
Customs Act 1770 (c.30)
Customs Act 1770 (c.43)
Customs Act 1775 (c.34)
Customs Act 1775 (c.35)
Customs Act 1775 (c.37)
Customs Act 1776 (c.12)
Customs Act 1776 (c.27)
Customs Act 1776 (c.41)
Customs Act 1776 (c.42)
Customs Act 1776 (c.43)
Customs Act 1776 (c.48)
Customs Act 1778 (c.4)
Customs Act 1778 (cc.24, 25)
Customs Act 1778 (c.27)
Customs Act 1778 (c.40)
Customs Act 1778 (c.58)

Customs Act 1779 (c.29)
Customs Act 1779 (c.41)
Customs Act 1779 (c.62)
Customs Act 1780 (c.7)
Customs Act 1780 (c.16)
Customs Act 1780 (c.25)
Customs Act 1780 (c.30)
Customs Act 1780 (c.32)
Customs Act 1782 (c.20)
Customs Act 1782 (c.21)
Customs Act 1782 (c.28)
Customs Act 1782 (c.49)
Customs Act 1782 (c.61)
Customs Act 1783 (c.11)
Customs Act 1783 (c.56)
Customs Act 1783 (c.74)
Customs Act 1784 (c.9)
Customs Act 1784 (c.16)
Customs Act 1784 (c.49)
Customs Act 1785 (c.25)
Customs Act 1785 (c.69)
Customs Act 1786 (c.42)
Customs Act 1786 (c.104)
Customs Act 1788 (c.27)
Customs Act 1788 (c.33)
Customs Act 1789 (c.59)
Customs Act 1789 (c.60)
Customs Act 1789 (c.64)
Customs Act 1790 (c.4)
Customs Act 1791 (c.15)
Customs Act 1791 (c.26)
Customs Act 1792 (c.32)
Customs Act 1792 (c.43)
Customs Act 1792 (c.54)
Customs Act 1793 (c.48)
Customs Act 1793 (c.70)
Customs Act 1793 (c.81)
Customs Act 1794 (c.51)
Customs Act 1794 (c.70)
Customs Act 1795 (c.20)
Customs Act 1796 (c.15)
Customs Act 1796 (cc.78, 79)
Customs Act 1796 (c.110)
Customs Act 1797 (c.110)
Customs Act 1798 (c.86)
Customs Act 1799 (c.61)
Customs Act 1800 (c.51)
Customs Act 1800 (c.59)
Customs Act 1800 (c.60)
Customs Act 1801 (c.87)
Customs Act 1801 (c.89)
Customs Act 1801 (c.94)
Customs Act 1802 (c.95)
Customs Act 1803 (c.68)
Customs Act 1803 (c.70)
Customs Act 1803 (c.128)
Customs Act 1803 (c.131)
Customs Act 1804 (c.53)
Customs Act 1805 (c.18)
Customs Act 1805 (c.29)
Customs Act 1805 (cc.44, 45)
Customs Act 1805 (c.88)
Customs Act 1805 (c.103)
Customs Act 1806 (c.150)
Customs Act 1807 (c.51)
Customs Act 1807 (c.61)
Customs Act 1808 (c.9)
Customs Act 1808 (c.26)
Customs Act 1808 (c.28)
Customs Act 1808 (cc.56, 57)
Customs Act 1808 (c.67)
Customs Act 1809 (c.46)
Customs Act 1809 (c.65)
Customs Act 1809 (c.98)
Customs Act 1810 (c.77)
Customs Act 1811 (c.52)
Customs Act 1811 (c.55)
Customs Act 1811 (c.71)
Customs Act 1811 (c.96)
Customs Act 1812 (c.2)
Customs Act 1812 (c.60)
Customs Act 1812 (c.89)
Customs Act 1812 (c.117)
Customs Act 1812 (c.141)
Customs Act 1813 (cc.26, 27)
Customs Act 1813 (c.29)
Customs Act 1813 (c.33)
Customs Act 1813 (c.47)
Customs Act 1813 (c.104)
Customs Act 1813 (c.105)
Customs Act 1814 (c.14)
Customs Act 1814 (c.50)
Customs Act 1814 (cc.64–66)
Customs Act 1814 (c.69)
Customs Act 1814 (c.77)
Customs Act 1814 (c.103)
Customs Act 1814 (c.122)
Customs Act 1815 (cc.22, 23)
Customs Act 1815 (c.24)
Customs Act 1815 (cc.32, 33)
Customs Act 1815 (c.36)
Customs Act 1815 (c.52)
Customs Act 1815 (c.95)
Customs Act 1815 (c.135)
Customs Act 1815 (c.163)
Customs Act 1815 (c.174)
Customs Act 1815 (c.181)
Customs Act 1816 (c.77)
Customs Act 1816 (c.93)
Customs Act 1835 (c.66)
Customs Act 1836 (c.60)
Customs Act 1838 (c.113)
Customs Act 1840 (c.19)
Customs Act 1840 (c.95)
Customs Act 1842 (c.47)
Customs Act 1843 (c.84)
Customs Act 1844 (c.16)
Customs Act 1844 (c.43)
Customs Act 1844 (c.73)
Customs Act 1845 (c.12)
Customs Act 1845 (c.84)
Customs Act 1845 (c.86)
Customs Act 1845 (c.92)
Customs Act 1846 (c.24)
Customs Act 1846 (c.58)
Customs Act 1846 (c.94)

Customs Act 1846 (c.102)
Customs Act 1847 (c.24)
Customs Act 1849 (c.90)
Customs Act 1850 (c.95)
Customs Act 1851 (c.62)
Customs Act 1853 (c.54)
Customs Act 1853 (c.106)
Customs Act 1854 (cc.28, 29)
Customs Act 1854 (c.122)
Customs Act 1855 (c.21)
Customs Act 1856 (c.75)
Customs Act 1857 (c.15)
Customs Act 1857 (c.62)
Customs Act 1858 (c.12)
Customs Act 1858 (c.16)
Customs Act 1859 (c.37)
Customs Act 1860 (c.22)
Customs Act 1860 (c.36)
Customs Act 1867 (c.82)
Customs Amendment Act 1842 (c.56)
Customs Amendment Act 1886 (c.41)
Customs and Excise Act 1711 (c.19)
Customs and Excise Act 1782 (c.66)
Customs and Excise Act 1787 (c.13)
Customs and Excise Act 1804 (c.67)
Customs and Excise Act 1806 (c.38)
Customs and Excise Act 1809 (c.116)
Customs and Excise Act 1814 (cc.120, 121)
Customs and Excise Act 1815 (c.118)
Customs and Excise Act 1816 (c.85)
Customs and Excise Act 1857 (c.61)
Customs and Excise Act 1952 (c.44)
Customs and Excise Duties (General Reliefs) Act 1979 (c.3)
Customs and Excise (Ireland) Act 1804 (c.103)
Customs and Excise (Ireland) Act 1805 (c.108)
Customs and Excise (Ireland) Act 1806 (c.58)
Customs and Excise (Ireland) Act 1807 (c.48)
Customs and Excise (Ireland) Act 1808 (c.62)
Customs and Excise (Ireland) Act 1816 (c.20)
Customs and Excise Management Act 1979 (c.2)
Customs and Excise Warehousing Act 1869 (c.103)
Customs and Income Tax Act 1871 (c.21)
Customs and Inland Revenue Act 1861 (c.20)
Customs and Inland Revenue Act 1863 (c.22)
Customs and Inland Revenue Act 1867 (c.23)
Customs and Inland Revenue Act 1870 (c.32)
Customs and Inland Revenue Act 1872 (c.20)
Customs and Inland Revenue Act 1873 (c.18)
Customs and Inland Revenue Act 1874 (c.16)
Customs and Inland Revenue Act 1875 (c.23)
Customs and Inland Revenue Act 1876 (c.16)
Customs and Inland Revenue Act 1878 (c.15)
Customs and Inland Revenue Act 1879 (c.21)
Customs and Inland Revenue Act 1880 (c.14)
Customs and Inland Revenue Act 1881 (c.12)
Customs and Inland Revenue Act 1882 (c.41)
Customs and Inland Revenue Act 1883 (c.10)
Customs and Inland Revenue Act 1884 (c.25)
Customs and Inland Revenue Act 1885 (c.51)
Customs and Inland Revenue Act 1886 (c.18)
Customs and Inland Revenue Act 1887 (c.15)
Customs and Inland Revenue Act 1888 (c.8)
Customs and Inland Revenue Act 1889 (c.7)
Customs and Inland Revenue Act 1890 (c.8)
Customs and Inland Revenue Act 1891 (c.25)
Customs and Inland Revenue Act 1892 (c.16)
Customs and Inland Revenue Act 1893 (c.7)
Customs and Inland Revenue Amendment Act 1877 (c.10)
Customs and Inland Revenue Buildings (Ireland) - Northern Irish Act 1882 (c.17)
Customs Buildings Act 1879 (c.36)
Customs Consolidation Act 1853 (c.107)
Customs Consolidation Act 1860 (c.110)
Customs Consolidation Act 1876 (c.36)
Customs Consolidation Act, 1876, Amendment 1887 (c.7)
Customs Consolidation Act, 1876, Amendment 1890 (c.56)
Customs Duties Act 1811 (cc.67, 68)
Customs Duties (Dumping and Subsidies) Act 1957 (c.18)
Customs Duties (Dumping and Subsidies) Act 1969 (c.16)
Customs Duties (Dumping and Subsidies) Amendment Act 1968 (c.33)
Customs Duties, etc. Act 1763 (c.15)
Customs, etc. Act 1721 (c.18)
Customs, etc. Act 1727 (c.17)
Customs, etc. Act 1728 (c.18)
Customs, etc. Act 1736 (c.27)
Customs, etc. Act 1765 (cc.29–32)
Customs, etc. Act 1765 (c.45)
Customs, etc. Act 1766 (cc.46, 47)
Customs, etc. Act 1766 (c.52)
Customs, etc. Act 1769 (c.35)
Customs, etc. Act 1769 (c.41)
Customs, etc. Act 1784 (c.7)
Customs, etc. Act 1798 (c.76)
Customs, etc. Act 1813 (c.36)
Customs, etc. Act 1814 (c.171)
Customs, etc. Act 1815 (cc.82, 83)
Customs, etc. Act 1816 (c.29)
Customs, etc. (Ireland) Act 1812 (c.76)
Customs, etc., Revenues Act 1725 (c.28)
Customs, etc., Revenues Act 1765 (c.43)
Customs, Excise and Taxes Act 1804 (c.26)
Customs (Exportation Prohibition) Act 1914 (c.64)
Customs (Exportation Restriction) Act 1914 (c.2)
Customs (Exportation Restriction) Act 1915 (c.52)
Customs (Import Deposits) Act 1968 (c.74)
Customs (Import Deposits) Act 1969 (c.64)
Customs, Inland Revenue, and Savings Banks Act 1877 (c.13)
Customs (Ireland) Act 1806 (c.87)
Customs (Ireland) Act 1807 (c.12)
Customs (Ireland) Act 1808 (c.80)
Customs (Isle of Man) Act 1870 (c.12)

Customs (Isle of Man) Tariff Act 1874 (c.46)
Customs (Manchester Bonding) Act 1850 (c.84)
Customs (Officers) Act 1881 (c.30)
Customs Refined Sugar Duties, Isle of Man Act 1870 (c.43)
Customs Rotulorum (Ireland) Act 1831 (c.17)
Customs Seizures Act 1790 (c.43)
Customs Sugar Duties (Isle of Man) Act 1873 (c.29)
Customs Tariff Act 1855 (c.97)
Customs Tariff Act 1876 (c.35)
Customs (War Powers) Act 1915 (c.31)
Customs (War Powers) Act 1916 (c.102)
Customs (War Powers) (No. 2) Act 1915 (c.71)
Customs (Wine Duty) Act 1888 (c.14)
Cutlery Trade Act 1819 (c.7)
Cycle Tracks Act 1984 (c.38)
Cyprus Act 1960 (c.52)
Czecho-Slovakia (Financial Assistance) Act 1939 (c.6)
Czecho-Slovakia (Financial Claims and Refugees) Act 1940 (c.4)
Czecho-Slovakia (Restrictions on Banking Accounts etc.) Act 1939 (c.11)

Dalkeith Beer Duties Act 1759 (c.53)
Dalkeith Beer Duties Act 1782 (c.18)
Damages (Scotland) Act 1976 (c.13)
Damages (Scotland) Act 1993 (c.5)
Damaging of Hides Act 1801 (c.53)
Dangerous Dogs Act 1989 (c.30)
Dangerous Dogs Act 1991 (c.65)
Dangerous Drugs Act 1925 (c.74)
Dangerous Drugs Act 1931 (c.14)
Dangerous Drugs Act 1951 (c.48)
Dangerous Drugs Act 1964 (c.36)
Dangerous Drugs Act 1965 (c.15)
Dangerous Drugs Act 1967 (c.82)
Dangerous Drugs (Amendment) Act 1950 (c.7)
Dangerous Drugs and Poisons (Amendment) Act 1923 (c.5)
Dangerous Litter Act 1971 (c.35)
Dangerous Performances Act 1897 (c.52)
Dangerous Vessels Act 1985 (c.22)
Dangerous Wild Animals Act 1976 (c.38)
Danube Works Loan Act 1868 (c.126)
Darby Court, Westminster Act 1845 (c.104)
Dartford and Strood Road Act 1760 (c.40)
Dartford Roads Act 1766 (c.98)
Dartford Roads Act 1788 (c.84)
Dartford–Thurrock Crossing Act 1988 (c.20)
Data Protection Act 1984 (c.35)
Day Industrial Schools (Scotland) Act 1893 (c.12)
Deal Act 1711 (c.43)
Deal Chapel of Ease Act 1711 (c.43)
Deal: Improvement Act 1791 (c.64)
Deal: Improvement Act 1796 (c.45)
Dealers in Excisable Articles Act 1805 (c.52)
Dean and Chapter Act 1868 (c.19)
Dean and New Forests Act 1808 (c.72)
Dean Forest (Encroachments) Act 1838 (cc.39–41)
Dean Forest Act 1861 (c.40)
Dean Forest (Mines) Act 1838 (c.43)
Dean Forest (Mines) Act 1871 (c.85)
Dean Forest (Mines) Act 1871 (c.85)
Dean Forest Roads Act 1796 (c.131)
Deanery of Manchester Act 1906 (c.19)
Deans and Canons Resignation Act 1872 (c.8)
Dean's Yard, Westminster Act 1755 (c.54)
Death Duties (Killed in War) Act 1914 (c.76)
Debenture Stock Act 1871 (c.27)
Debt of City of Edinburgh, etc. Act 1838 (c.55)
Debtors Act 1869 (c.62)
Debtors Act 1878 (c.54)
Debtors and Creditors Act 1860 (c.147)
Debtors and Imprisonment Act 1758 (c.28)
Debtors Imprisonment Act 1758 (c.28)
Debtors (Ireland) Act 1840 (c.105)
Debtors (Ireland) Act 1872 (c.57)
Debtors, Middlesex Act 1785 (c.45)
Debtors' Prison, Devonshire Act 1753 (c.57)
Debtors Relief Act 1793 (c.5)
Debtors Relief Act 1801 (c.64)
Debtors Relief Act 1812 (c.34)
Debtors (Scotland) Act 1838 (c.114)
Debtors (Scotland) Act 1880 (c.34)
Debtors (Scotland) Act 1987 (c.18)
Debts Clearing Offices Act 1948 (c.2)
Debts Clearing Offices and Import Restrictions Act 1934 (c.31)
Debts Due to Swiss Government Act 1798 (c.45)
Debts Due to the Army Act 1702 (c.24)
Debts Due to the Army Act 1711 (c.38)
Debts Due to the Army Act 1714 (c.24)
Debts Due to the Army Act 1715 (c.35)
Debts Due to the Army Act 1716 (c.17)
Debts Due to the Army Act 1720 (c.30)
Debts Due to the Army, etc. Act 1701 (c.1)
Debts Due to the Army, etc. Act 1717 (c.9)
Debts Due to the Army, etc. Act 1718 (c.14)
Debts Due to the Army, etc. Act 1719 (c.17)
Debts Due to the United Provinces, etc. Act 1797 (c.28)
Debts of East India Company Act 1812 (c.121)
Debts of Traders Act 1807 (c.74)
Debts Recovery Act 1839 (c.60)
Debts Recovery Act 1848 (c.87)
Debts Recovery (Scotland) Act 1867 (c.96)
Debts Securities (Scotland) Act 1856 (c.91)
Deceased Brother's Widow's Marriage Act 1921 (c.24)
Deceased Wife's Sister's Marriage Act 1907 (c.47)
Decimal Currency Act 1967 (c.47)
Decimal Currency Act 1969 (c.19)
Declaration by Quakers, etc. Act 1837 (c.5)
Declaration of Title Act 1862 (c.67)

Declarations by Quakers, etc. on Acceptance of Offices Act 1838 (c.15)
Declarations Before Taking Office Act 1866 (c.22)
Deeds of Arrangement Act 1887 (c.57)
Deeds of Arrangement Act 1914 (c.47)
Deeds of Arrangement Amendment Act 1890 (c.24)
Deep Sea Mining (Temporary Provisions) Act 1981 (c.53)
Deeping Fen Drainage Act 1737 (c.39)
Deeping Fens Act 1774 (c.23)
Deer Act 1963 (c.36)
Deer Act 1980 (c.49)
Deer Act 1987 (c.28)
Deer Act 1991 (c.54)
Deer (Amendment) (Scotland) Act 1967 (c.37)
Deer (Amendment) (Scotland) Act 1982 (c.19)
Deer (Scotland) Act 1959 (c.40)
Deer Stealers Act 1718 (c.15)
Deer Stealing (England) Act 1802 (c.107)
Deer Stealing (England) Act 1811 (c.120)
Defacing the Coin Act 1853 (c.102)
Defamation Act 1952 (c.66)
Defective Premises Act 1972 (c.35)
Defence Act 1842 (c.94)
Defence Act 1854 (c.67)
Defence Act 1859 (c.12)
Defence Act 1860 (c.112)
Defence Act 1865 (c.65)
Defence Act Amendment Act 1864 (c.89)
Defence Acts Amendment Act 1873 (c.72)
Defence (Barracks) Act 1935 (c.26)
Defence Contracts Act 1958 (c.38)
Defence Loans Act 1937 (c.13)
Defence Loans Act 1939 (c.8)
Defence of the Realm Act 1797 (c.27)
Defence of the Realm Act 1803 (c.55)
Defence of the Realm Act 1803 (c.120)
Defence of the Realm Act 1803 (c.125)
Defence of the Realm Act 1804 (c.95)
Defence of the Realm Act 1806 (c.90)
Defence of the Realm Act 1808 (c.107)
Defence of the Realm Act 1914 (c.29)
Defence of the Realm (Acquisition of Land) Act 1916 (c.63)
Defence of the Realm (Acquisition of Land) Act 1920 (c.79)
Defence of the Realm (Amendment) Act 1915 (c.34)
Defence of the Realm (Amendment) (No. 2) Act 1915 (c.37)
Defence of the Realm (Amendment) (No. 3) Act 1915 (c.42)
Defence of the Realm (Beans, Peas and Pulse Orders) Act 1918 (c.12)
Defence of the Realm Consolidation Act 1914 (c.8)
Defence of the Realm (Employment Exchanges) Act 1918 (c.58)
Defence of the Realm (England) Act 1803 (c.82)
Defence of the Realm (England) Act 1803 (c.123)
Defence of the Realm, etc. Act 1803 (c.96)
Defence of the Realm, etc. Act 1804 (c.56)
Defence of the Realm, etc. Act 1804 (c.66)
Defence of the Realm, etc. Act 1804 (c.74)
Defence of the Realm (Food Profits) Act 1918 (c.9)
Defence of the Realm (Ireland) Act 1803 (c.85)
Defence of the Realm (Ireland) Act 1806 (c.63)
Defence of the Realm, London Act 1803 (c.101)
Defence of the Realm, London Act 1804 (c.96)
Defence of the Realm, London Act 1806 (c.144)
Defence of the Realm (No. 2) Act 1914 (c.63)
Defence of the Realm (Scotland) Act 1803 (c.83)
Defence of the Realm (Scotland) Act 1803 (c.124)
Defence (Transfer of Functions) Act 1964 (c.15)
Defranchisement of Sudbury Act 1844 (c.53)
Delamere Forest Act 1856 (c.13)
Delay Act 1387 (c.10)
Delay of Cause After Issue Joined Act 1740 (c.17)
Demise of Parts of Rolls Estate Act 1836 (c.49)
Demise of the Crown Act 1727 (c.5)
Demise of the Crown Act 1830 (c.43)
Demise of the Crown Act 1837 (c.31)
Demise of the Crown Act 1901 (c.5)
Denbigh and Carnarvon Roads Act 1757 (c.69)
Denbigh and Flint Roads Act 1769 (c.45)
Denbigh and Flint Roads Act 1790 (c.110)
Denbigh, Flint and Carnarvon Roads Act 1758 (c.55)
Denbigh, Flint and Carnarvon Roads Act 1779 (c.109)
Denbigh, Flint and Carnarvon Roads Act 1780 (c.97)
Denbigh, Flint, Salop. and Chester Roads Act 1767 (c.104)
Denbigh Roads Act 1756 (c.68)
Denbigh Roads Act 1762 (c.77)
Denbigh Roads Act 1763 (c.43)
Denbigh Roads Act 1777 (c.111)
Denbigh Roads Act 1788 (c.112)
Denbigh to Rutland Road Act 1781 (c.80)
Dentists Act 1878 (c.33)
Dentists Act 1921 (c.21)
Dentists Act 1923 (c.36)
Dentists Act 1956 (c.29)
Dentists Act 1957 (c.28)
Dentists Act 1983 (c.38)
Dentists Act 1984 (c.24)
Dentists (Amendment) Act 1973 (c.31)
Denver, etc., Drainage, Norfolk Act 1771 (c.72)

Denver, etc. (Norfolk and Cambridge) Drainage Act 1748 (c.16)
Deodands Act 1846 (c.62)
Department of Science and Art Act 1875 (c.68)
Department of Scientific and Industrial Research Act 1956 (c.58)
Department of Technical Co-operation Act 1961 (c.30)
Dependency of Ireland on Great Britain Act 1719 (c.5)
Deposit of Poisonous Waste Act 1972 (c.21)
Depredations on the Thames Act 1800 (c.87)
Depredations on the Thames Act 1807 (c.37)
Depredations on the Thames Act 1814 (c.187)
Deputy Lieutenants Act 1918 (c.19)
Deputy Speaker Act 1855 (c.84)
Derby and Cheshire Roads Act 1792 (c.128)
Derby and Chester Roads Act 1782 (c.107)
Derby and Leicester Roads Act 1794 (c.120)
Derby and Nottinghamshire Roads Act 1757 (c.60)
Derby and Nottinghamshire Roads Act 1764 (c.67)
Derby and Nottinghamshire Roads Act 1780 (c.74)
Derby and Nottinghamshire Roads Act 1790 (c.113)
Derby and Sheffield Roads Act 1756 (c.82)
Derby and Stafford Roads Act 1766 (c.79)
Derby and Stafford Roads Act 1787 (c.87)
Derby and Uttoxeter Road Act 1763 (c.57)
Derby and Yorkshire Roads Act 1764 (c.65)
Derby and Yorkshire Roads Act 1776 (c.73)
Derby and Yorkshire Roads Act 1779 (c.99)
Derby Bridge Act 1788 (c.77)
Derby Canal Act 1793 (c.102)
Derby Gaol Act 1756 (c.48)
Derby: Improvement Act 1792 (c.78)
Derby, Leicester and Warwick Roads Act 1759 (c.47)
Derby, Leicester and Warwick Roads Act 1781 (c.92)
Derby Roads Act 1737 (c.33)
Derby Roads Act 1743 (c.20)
Derby Roads Act 1759 (c.33)
Derby Roads Act 1764 (c.82)
Derby Roads Act 1766 (c.69)
Derby Roads Act 1766 (c.80)
Derby Roads Act 1766 (c.87)
Derby Roads Act 1777 (c.92)
Derby Roads Act 1777 (c.101)
Derby Roads Act 1785 (c.121)
Derby Roads Act 1786 (c.151)
Derby Roads Act 1788 (c.89)
Derby Roads Act 1793 (c.152)
Derby Roads Act 1795 (c.154)
Derby to Newcastle-under-Lyme Road Act 1758 (c.60)
Derbyshire Roads Act 1724 (c.13)
Derbyshire Roads Act 1738 (c.12)
Derbyshire Roads Act 1758 (c.43)
Derbyshire Roads Act 1759 (c.39)
Derbyshire Roads Act 1769 (c.81)
Derbyshire Roads Act 1779 (c.87)
Derbyshire Roads Act 1781 (c.81)
Derbyshire Roads Act 1781 (c.83)
Deregulation and Contracting Out Act 1994 (c.40)
Derelict Land Act 1982 (c.42)
Derelict Vessels (Report) Act 1896 (c.12)
Deritend and Bordesley, Warwick: Improvement Act 1791 (c.17)
Deritend Bridge, Birmingham: Rebuilding Act 1788 (c.70)
Derwent (Yorks.) Navigation Act 1702 (c.14)
Desertion of Seamen Act 1797 (c.73)
Design Copyright Act 1968 (c.68)
Designing and Printing of Linens, etc. Act 1787 (c.38)
Designing and Printing of Linens, etc. Act 1789 (c.19)
Destruction of Coal Works Act 1739 (c.21)
Destruction of Deer (England) Act 1718 (c.28)
Destruction of Prisons by Rioters Act 1780 (c.1)
Destruction of Property (S.) Act 1789 (c.46)
Destruction of Stocking Frames, etc. Act 1812 (c.16)
Destruction of Stocking Frames, etc. Act 1813 (c.42)
Destruction of Turnpikes, etc. Act 1727 (c.19)
Destruction of Turnpikes, etc. Act 1731 (c.33)
Destruction of Turnpikes, etc. Act 1734 (c.20)
Destructive Imported Animals Act 1932 (c.12)
Destructive Insects Act 1877 (c.68)
Destructive Insects and Pests Act 1907 (c.4)
Destructive Insects and Pests Act 1927 (c.32)
Detached Parts of Counties (England) Act 1858 (c.68)
Detached Portions of Counties (Ireland) Act 1871 (c.106)
Determination of Needs Act 1941 (c.11)
Development and Road Improvement Funds Act 1909 (c.47)
Development and Road Improvement Funds Act 1910 (c.7)
Development Board for Rural Wales Act 1991 (c.1)
Development Land Tax Act 1976 (c.24)
Development (Loan Guarantees and Grants) Act 1929 (c.7)
Development of Inventions Act 1948 (c.60)
Development of Inventions Act 1954 (c.20)
Development of Inventions Act 1958 (c.3)
Development of Inventions Act 1965 (c.21)
Development of Inventions Act 1967 (c.32)
Development of Rural Wales Act 1976 (c.75)
Development of Tourism Act 1969 (c.51)
Devizes Road Act 1784 (c.65)
Devizes Roads Act 1797 (c.154)
Devizes: Streets Act 1780 (c.36)
Devon Bridges Act 1757 (c.47)
Devon: Canal Act 1796 (c.46)

Devon, Dorset and Somerset Roads Act 1792 (c.144)
Devon Gaol Act 1787 (c.59)
Devon (Poor Relief) Act 1772 (c.18)
Devon Roads Act 1755 (c.49)
Devon Roads Act 1757 (c.51)
Devon Roads Act 1758 (c.52)
Devon Roads Act 1758 (c.68)
Devon Roads Act 1760 (c.34)
Devon Roads Act 1762 (c.50)
Devon Roads Act 1762 (c.64)
Devon Roads Act 1763 (c.38)
Devon Roads Act 1765 (cc.69, 70)
Devon Roads Act 1767 (c.62)
Devon Roads Act 1772 (c.86)
Devon Roads Act 1772 (c.93)
Devon Roads Act 1780 (c.79)
Devon Roads Act 1781 (c.84)
Devon Roads Act 1783 (c.26)
Devon Roads Act 1784 (c.63)
Devon Roads Act 1784 (c.67)
Devon Roads Act 1787 (c.74)
Devon Roads Act 1791 (c.117)
Devon, Shire Hall Act 1772 (c.16)
Devonshire: Poor Relief Act 1769 (c.82)
Dewsbury to Elland Road Act 1758 (c.54)
Dewsbury to Elland Road Act 1779 (c.88)
Diet of Soldiers on a March Act 1813 (c.83)
Differential Duties on Foreign Ships Act 1852 (c.47)
Dindings Agreement (Approval) Act 1934 (c.55)
Diocesan Boundaries Act 1871 (c.14)
Diocesan Boundaries Act 1872 (c.14)
Diocese of Norwich Act 1848 (c.61)
Diplomatic and Consular Premises Act 1987 (c.46)
Diplomatic and Other Privileges Act 1971 (c.64)
Diplomatic Immunities (Commonwealth Countries and Republic of Ireland) Act 1951 (c.18)
Diplomatic Immunities (Conferences with Commonwealth Countries and Republic of Ireland) Act 1961 (c.11)
Diplomatic Immunities Restriction Act 1955 (c.22)
Diplomatic Privileges Act 1708 (c.12)
Diplomatic Privileges Act 1964 (c.81)
Diplomatic Privileges (Extension) Act 1941 (c.7)
Diplomatic Privileges (Extension) Act 1944 (c.44)
Diplomatic Privileges (Extension) Act 1946 (c.66)
Diplomatic Privileges (Extension) Act 1950 (c.7)
Diplomatic Relations with See of Rome Act 1848 (c.108)
Diplomatic Salaries, etc. Act 1869 (c.43)
Directors' Liability Act 1890 (c.64)
Disability Discrimination Act 1995 (c.50)
Disability (Grants) Act 1993 (c.14)
Disability Living Allowance and Disability Working Allowance Act 1991 (c.21)
Disabled Men (Facilities for Employment) (Master and Servant) Act 1919 (c.22)
Disabled Persons Act 1981 (c.43)
Disabled Persons Act 1986 (c.33)
Disabled Persons (Employment) Act 1944 (c.10)
Disabled Persons (Employment) Act 1958 (c.33)
Disabled Persons (Northern Ireland) Act 1989 (c.10)
Disarming the Highlands, etc. Act 1745 (c.39)
Disarming the Highlands, etc. Act 1753 (c.29)
Discharge of a Crown Debt Act 1788 (c.32)
Discharge of Certain Imprisoned Debtors Act 1808 (c.123)
Discharge to Lady A. Jekyll's Executors Act 1772 (c.53)
Discharged Prisoners Act 1774 (c.20)
Discharged Prisoners' Aid Act 1862 (c.44)
Discharged Soldiers, etc. Act 1748 (c.44)
Discontinuance of Duties Act 1757 (c.7)
Discontinuance of Duties Act 1757 (c.14)
Discontinuance of Duties Act 1758 (c.12)
Discontinuance of Duties Act 1770 (c.8)
Discontinuance of Portsdown Fair, Southampton Act 1862 (c.34)
Discount on Newspapers Act 1809 (c.50)
Discovery of Longitude at Sea Act 1713 (c.14)
Discovery of Longitude at Sea Act 1762 (c.14)
Discovery of Longitude at Sea Act 1762 (c.18)
Discovery of Longitude at Sea Act 1765 (c.11)
Discovery of Longitude at Sea Act 1765 (c.20)
Discovery of Longitude at Sea Act 1770 (c.34)
Discovery of Longitude at Sea Act 1774 (c.66)
Discovery of Longitude at Sea Act 1790 (c.14)
Discovery of Longitude at Sea Act 1815 (c.75)
Discovery of Longitude at Sea, etc. Act 1803 (c.118)
Discovery of Longitude at Sea, etc. Act 1806 (c.77)
Discovery of Longitude at Seas Act 1753 (c.25)
Discovery of North-West Passage Act 1744 (c.17)
Discovery of Northern Passage Act 1776 (c.6)
Disease Among Cattle Act 1772 (c.51)
Diseased Sheep, etc. Act 1798 (c.65)
Diseases of Animals Act 1894 (c.57)
Diseases of Animals Act 1896 (c.15)
Diseases of Animals Act 1903 (c.43)
Diseases of Animals Act 1909 (c.26)

Diseases of Animals Act 1910 (c.20)
Diseases of Animals Act 1922 (c.8)
Diseases of Animals Act 1923 (c.3)
Diseases of Animals Act 1925 (c.63)
Diseases of Animals Act 1927 (c.13)
Diseases of Animals Act 1935 (c.31)
Diseases of Animals Act 1950 (c.36)
Diseases of Animals Act 1975 (c.40)
Diseases of Animals (Ireland) Act 1914 (c.40)
Diseases of Fish Act 1937 (c.33)
Diseases of Fish Act 1983 (c.30)
Diseases Prevention Act 1855 (c.116)
Diseases Prevention (Metropolis) Act 1883 (c.35)
Disfranchisement of Freemen, Great Yarmouth Act 1848 (c.24)
Disfranchisement of St. Alban's Act 1852 (c.9)
Disorderly Houses Act 1751 (c.36)
Dispensary Committees (Ireland) Act 1896 (c.10)
Dispensary Houses (Ireland) Act 1879 (c.25)
Disposal of Ulysses Fitzmaurice's Intestate Estate Act 1774 (c.40)
Disposal of Uncollected Goods Act 1952 (c.43)
Disposition of Copyhold Estates by Will Act 1815 (c.192)
Disputes Between Masters and Workmen Act 1800 (c.90)
Dissolved Boards of Management and Guardians Act 1870 (c.2)
Distemper Amongst Cattle Act 1745 (c.5)
Distemper Amongst Cattle Act 1746 (c.4)
Distemper Amongst Cattle Act 1749 (c.23)
Distemper Amongst Cattle Act 1750 (c.31)
Distemper Amongst Cattle Act 1754 (c.14)
Distemper Amongst Cattle Act 1755 (c.18)
Distemper Amongst Cattle Act 1757 (c.20)
Distemper Amongst Cattle Act 1770 (c.4)
Distemper Amongst Cattle Act 1770 (c.45)
Distillation Act 1757 (c.10)
Distillation Act 1757 (c.15)
Distillation Act 1759 (c.9)
Distillation, etc. Act 1702 (c.14)
Distillation, etc. Act 1774 (c.73)
Distillation, etc. of Spirits (Ireland) Act 1813 (c.52)
Distillation from Corn, etc. Act 1812 (c.118)
Distillation from Corn Prohibition, etc. Act 1812 (c.7)
Distillation from Wheat, etc. Act 1799 (c.7)
Distillation from Wheat, etc. Act 1800 (c.21)
Distillation from Wheat, etc., Prohibition Act 1795 (c.20)
Distillation from Wheat (Ireland) Act 1801 (c.15)
Distillation (Ireland) Act 1812 (c.47)
Distillation of Spirits Act 1803 (c.11)
Distillation of Spirits Act 1805 (c.100)
Distillation of Spirits Act 1808 (c.118)
Distillation of Spirits Act 1809 (c.7)
Distillation of Spirits Act 1809 (c.24)
Distillation of Spirits Act 1810 (c.5)
Distillation of Spirits Act 1812 (c.3)
Distillation of Spirits from Sugar Act 1847 (c.6)
Distillation of Spirits from Sugar, etc. Act 1848 (c.100)
Distillation of Spirits (Ireland) Act 1813 (c.145)
Distillation of Spirits (Ireland) Act 1813 (c.148)
Distillation of Spirits (Ireland) Act 1814 (c.150)
Distillation of Spirits (Ireland) Act 1815 (c.151)
Distillation of Spirits (Ireland) Act 1816 (c.112)
Distillation of Spirits (Scotland) Act 1808 (c.10)
Distillation of Spirits (Scotland) Act 1810 (c.79)
Distillation of Spirits (Scotland) Act 1813 (c.9)
Distilleries, etc. Act 1793 (c.61)
Distillers Act 1746 (c.39)
Distillers Act 1779 (c.50)
Distillers of Spirits Act 1811 (c.42)
Distress (Costs) Act 1817 (c.93)
Distress for Rates Act 1849 (c.14)
Distress for Rent Act 1737 (c.19)
Distress for Rent Act 1960 (c.12)
Distressed Unions Advances (Ireland) Act 1850 (c.14)
Distressed Unions (Ireland) Act 1852 (c.68)
Distresses Under Justices' Warrants Act 1754 (c.20)
Distribution of Certain Monies Act 1803 (c.39)
Distribution of Industry Act 1944 (c.36)
Distribution of Industry (Industrial Finance) Act 1958 (c.41)
District Auditors Act 1879 (c.6)
District Church Tithes Act 1865 (c.42)
District Councillors and Guardians (Term of Office) Act 1900 (c.16)
District Councils (Water Supply Facilities) Act 1897 (c.44)
District Courts and Prisons Act 1842 (c.53)
District Courts and Prisons Act 1844 (c.50)
District Courts (Scotland) Act 1975 (c.20)
Distribution of Germany Enemy Property Act 1949 (c.85)
Distribution of Industry Act 1950 (c.8)
Disused Burial Grounds Act 1884 (c.72)
Disused Burial Grounds (Amendment) Act 1981 (c.18)
Disused Public Buildings (Ireland) Act 1808 (c.113)
Divided Parishes and Poor Law Amendment Act 1876 (c.61)
Divided Parishes and Poor Law Amendment Act 1882 (c.58)
Dividends Act 1978 (c.54)
Dividends and Stock Act 1869 (c.104)
Dividends and Stock Act 1870 (c.47)
Division of Deanery of St. Burian Act 1850 (c.76)

Divorce Amendment Act 1868 (c.77)
Divorce (Insanity and Desertion) Act 1958 (c.54)
Divorce Jurisdiction, Court Fees and Legal Aid (Scotland) Act 1983 (c.12)
Divorce Reform Act 1969 (c.55)
Divorce (Scotland) Act 1938 (c.50)
Divorce (Scotland) Act 1964 (c.91)
Divorce (Scotland) Act 1976 (c.39)
Dock Work Regulation Act 1976 (c.79)
Dock Workers (Pensions) Act 1960 (c.39)
Dock Workers (Regulation of Employment) Act 1946 (c.22)
Docking and Nicking of Horses Act 1949 (c.70)
Docks and Harbours Act 1966 (c.28)
Docks and Ordnance Service Act 1804 (c.79)
Docks, etc., at Chatham, etc. Act 1806 (c.130)
Dockyard Act 1865 (c.25)
Dockyard Ports Regulation Act 1865 (c.125)
Dockyard Services Act 1986 (c.52)
Dockyards, etc., Protection Act 1772 (c.24)
Dockyards Protection Act Amendment Act 1863 (c.30)
Doctrine of the Trinity Act 1813 (c.160)
Documentary Evidence Act 1868 (c.37)
Documentary Evidence Act 1882 (c.9)
Documentary Evidence Act 1895 (c.9)
Dog Licences Act 1959 (c.55)
Dog Licences Act 1867 (c.5)
Dog Racecourse Betting (Temporary Provisions) Act 1947 (c.20)
Dog Stealing Act 1770 (c.18)
Dog Stealing Act 1845 (c.47)
Dogs Act 1865 (c.60)
Dogs Act 1871 (c.56)
Dogs Act 1906 (c.32)
Dogs (Amendment) Act 1928 (c.21)
Dogs Amendment Act 1938 (c.21)
Dogs (Ireland) Act 1862 (c.59)
Dogs (Ireland) Act 1867 (c.116)
Dogs (Protection of Livestock) Act 1953 (c.28)
Dogs Regulation (Ireland) Act 1865 (c.50)
Dogs Regulation (Ireland) Act 1919 (c.81)
Dogs (Scotland) Act 1863 (c.100)
Domestic and Appellate Proceedings (Restriction of Publicity) Act 1968 (c.63)
Domestic Proceedings and Magistrates' Courts Act 1978 (c.22)
Domestic Violence and Matrimonial Proceedings Act 1976 (c.50)
Domicile Act 1861 (c.121)
Domicile and Matrimonial Proceedings Act 1973 (c.45)
Dominica Act 1938 (c.10)
Dominica Loan Act 1860 (c.57)
Dominica Loan Act 1867 (c.91)
Doncaster and Tadcaster Road Act 1740 (c.28)
Doncaster Road and Bridges Act 1795 (c.158)
Doncaster Roads Act 1785 (c.104)
Doncaster: Small Debts, Lighting, etc. Act 1763 (c.40)
Doncaster to Bawtry Road Act 1776 (c.71)
Doncaster to Chester Road Act 1789 (c.98)
Donnington to Southall Canal Act 1788 (c.73)
Dorchester Bridge and Causeway Act 1745 (c.24)
Dorchester: Streets Act 1776 (c.27)
Dorset and Devon Roads Act 1757 (c.43)
Dorset and Devon Roads Act 1765 (c.75)
Dorset and Somerset Roads Act 1765 (c.102)
Dorset and Somerset Roads Act 1767 (c.82)
Dorset and Wilts: Canal Act 1796 (c.47)
Dorset, Devon and Somerset Roads Act 1777 (c.89)
Dorset, etc., Roads Act 1762 (c.61)
Dorset Roads Act 1758 (c.50)
Dorset Roads Act 1760 (c.24)
Dorset Roads Act 1766 (c.68)
Dorset Roads Act 1766 (c.92)
Dorset Roads Act 1769 (c.47)
Dorset Roads Act 1777 (c.103)
Dorset Roads Act 1782 (c.101)
Dorset Roads Act 1788 (c.91)
Dorset Roads Act 1790 (c.95)
Dover and Rye Harbours Act 1764 (c.72)
Dover, Deal and Sandwich Road Act 1797 (c.156)
Dover Harbour Act 1703 (c.7)
Dover Harbour Act 1717 (c.13)
Dover Harbour Act 1722 (c.30)
Dover Harbour Act 1737 (c.7)
Dover Harbour Act 1757 (c.8)
Dover Harbour Act 1786 (c.11)
Dover Harbour Act 1794 (c.112)
Dover Streets Act 1778 (c.76)
Doveridge Roads, Derby Act 1769 (c.59)
Downpatrick Election Committee Act 1815 (c.98)
Drafts on Bankers Act 1856 (c.25)
Drafts on Bankers Act 1858 (c.79)
Drainage and Improvement of Land (Ireland) Act 1866 (c.40)
Drainage and Improvement of Land (Ireland) Act 1892 (c.65)
Drainage and Improvement of Land, Supplemental (Ireland) Act 1865 (c.13)
Drainage and Improvement of Land, Supplemental (Ireland) Act 1865 (c.50)
Drainage and Improvement of Land, Supplemental (Ireland) Act 1867 (c.43)
Drainage and Improvement of Lands Amendment (Ireland) Act 1865 (c.52)
Drainage and Improvement of Lands Amendment (Ireland) Act 1869 (c.72)
Drainage and Improvement of Lands Amendment (Ireland) Act 1872 (c.31)
Drainage and Improvement of Lands Amendment (Ireland) Act 1874 (c.32)
Drainage and Improvement of Lands (Ireland) Act 1853 (c.130)
Drainage and Improvement of Lands (Ireland) Act 1855 (c.110)

Drainage and Improvement of Lands (Ireland) Act 1863 (c.88)
Drainage and Improvement of Lands (Ireland) Act 1864 (c.72)
Drainage and Improvement of Lands (Ireland) Act 1878 (c.59)
Drainage and Improvement of Lands (Ireland) Act 1880 (c.27)
Drainage and Improvement of Lands Supplemental Act 1866 (c.61)
Drainage and Improvement of Lands, Supplemental (Ireland) Act 1864 (c.107)
Drainage and Improvement of Lands, Supplemental (Ireland) Act 1867 (c.139)
Drainage: Cambridge, Isle of Ely Act 1772 (c.26)
Drainage, etc. (Ireland) Act 1847 (c.106)
Drainage (Ireland) Act 1842 (c.89)
Drainage (Ireland) Act 1846 (c.4)
Drainage (Ireland) Act 1847 (c.79)
Drainage (Ireland) Act 1856 (c.62)
Drainage: Isle of Ely Act 1772 (c.27)
Drainage Haddenham Level Act 1726 (c.18)
Drainage Maintenance Act 1866 (c.49)
Drainage of Bogs, etc. (Ireland) Act 1809 (c.102)
Drainage of Lands Act 1849 (c.100)
Drainage Rates Act 1958 (c.37)
Drainage Rates Act 1962 (c.39)
Drainage Rates Act 1963 (c.10)
Drainage Rates (Disabled Persons) Act 1986 (c.17)
Dramatic and Musical Performers' Protection Act 1925 (c.46)
Dramatic and Musical Performers' Protection Act 1958 (c.44)
Dramatic and Musical Performers' Protection Act 1972 (c.32)
Drawback Act 1795 (c.98)
Drawback Act 1795 (c.110)
Drawback Act 1796 (c.106)
Drawback Act 1806 (c.114)
Drawback Act 1807 (c.49)
Drawback, etc. on Glass Act 1812 (c.77)
Drawback of Duties Act 1795 (c.39)
Drawback of Duty on Coals Act 1811 (c.83)
Drawback on Chocolate Act 1812 (c.11)
Drawback on Coals Act 1813 (c.18)
Drawback on Linens Act 1805 (c.98)
Drawback on Paper Act 1814 (c.153)
Drawback on Wines Act 1813 (c.44)
Drawbacks Act 1802 (c.17)
Drawbacks Act 1802 (c.60)
Drawbacks Act 1803 (c.5)
Drawbacks Act 1803 (c.10)
Drawbacks Act 1807 (c.20)
Drawbacks Act 1807 (c.62)
Drawbacks Act 1808 (c.43)
Drawbacks and Bounties Act 1795 (c.18)
Drawbacks and Bounties Act 1802 (c.11)
Drawbacks and Bounties Act 1805 (c.93)
Drawbacks, etc. Act 1798 (c.61)
Drawbacks, etc. (Ireland) Act 1805 (c.23)
Drawbacks, etc., on Sugar Act 1811 (c.12)
Drawbacks, etc. on Tobacco, etc. Act 1815 (c.129)
Drawbacks (Ireland) Act 1806 (c.14)
Drawbacks (Ireland) Act 1807 (c.19)
Drawbacks on Paper Act 1814 (c.106)
Drawbacks on Spirits Act 1811 (c.121)
Drawbacks upon Sugar Act 1806 (c.10)
Drayton and Edgehill Road Act 1753 (c.78)
Drill Grounds Act 1886 (c.5)
Driving of Cattle, Metropolis Act 1774 (c.87)
Driving of Cattle, Metropolis Act 1781 (c.67)
Droitwich Roads Act 1768 (c.39)
Drought Act 1976 (c.44)
Drouly Fund Act 1838 (c.89)
Drugging of Animals Act 1876 (c.13)
Drugs (Prevention of Misuse) Act 1964 (c.64)
Drug Trafficking Act 1994 (c.37)
Drug Trafficking Offences Act 1986 (c.32)
Drury Lane Theatre Act 1776 (c.13)
Dublin Amended Carriage Act 1854 (c.45)
Dublin Amended Carriage Act 1855 (c.65)
Dublin and Other Roads Turnpikes Abolition Act 1855 (c.69)
Dublin Baronies Act 1842 (c.96)
Dublin Carriage Act 1853 (c.112)
Dublin, Collection of Rates Act 1849 (c.91)
Dublin Collector-General of Rates Act 1870 (c.11)
Dublin Corporation Act 1849 (c.85)
Dublin Corporation Act 1850 (c.81)
Dublin Foundling Hospital 1814 (c.128)
Dublin, Four Courts Act 1858 (c.84)
Dublin General Post Office Act 1808 (c.48)
Dublin General Post Office Act 1809 (c.70)
Dublin Grand Jury Act 1845 (c.81)
Dublin Harbour Act 1815 (c.191)
Dublin Harbour Act 1816 (c.62)
Dublin Hospitals Act 1856 (c.110)
Dublin, Hotels and Restaurants Act 1910 (c.33)
Dublin Improvement Act 1849 (c.97)
Dublin Improvement Act 1861 (c.26)
Dublin Justices Act 1840 (c.103)
Dublin Justices Act 1875 (c.20)
Dublin National Gallery Act 1865 (c.71)
Dublin Parliamentary Revising Act 1853 (c.58)
Dublin Paying, etc., Inquiry Act 1806 (c.68)
Dublin, Phoenix Park Act 1860 (c.42)
Dublin Police Act 1836 (c.29)
Dublin Police Act 1837 (c.25)
Dublin Police Act 1839 (c.78)
Dublin Police Act 1842 (c.24)
Dublin Police Act 1848 (c.113)
Dublin Police Act 1859 (c.52)
Dublin Police District Act 1838 (c.63)
Dublin Police Magistrates Act 1808 (c.140)
Dublin, Public Offices Site Act 1903 (c.16)
Dublin, Purchase of Land Act 1841 (c.16)
Dublin Reconstruction Act 1916 (c.66)
Dublin Record Office Act 1814 (c.63)
Dublin Revising Barristers Act 1857 (c.68)

Duties, etc. Act 1743 (c.31)
Duties, etc., India Act 1814 (c.105)
Duties, etc. (Ireland) Act 1803 (c.92)
Duties, etc., on Coffee, etc. Act 1802 (c.83)
Duties, etc., on Foreign Liquors, etc. Act 1812 (c.159)
Duties, etc., on Glass, etc. Act 1815 (c.113)
Duties, etc., on Glass (Ireland) Act 1814 (c.87)
Duties, etc., on Malt, etc. (Ireland) Act 1807 (c.40)
Duties, etc., on Soap Act 1816 (c.44)
Duties, etc., on Sugar, etc. Act 1803 (c.42)
Duties, etc., on Tobacco (Ireland) Act 1813 (c.73)
Duties in American Colonies Act 1765 (c.12)
Duties in American Colonies Act 1766 (c.11)
Duties (Logwood, etc.) Act 1766 (c.47)
Duties of Customs Act 1845 (c.90)
Duties of Customs and Tonnage Act 1802 (c.43)
Duties of Prisage and Butlerage (Ireland) Act (c.94)
Duties on Auctioneers, etc. Act 1803 (c.130)
Duties on Auctions (Ireland) Act 1808 (c.63)
Duties on Beer, etc. Act 1802 (c.38)
Duties on Beetroot Sugar Act 1837 (c.57)
Duties on Bricks Act 1839 (c.24)
Duties on Bricks and Tiles Act 1784 (c.24)
Duties on Bricks and Tiles Act 1785 (c.66)
Duties on Bricks and Tiles Act 1794 (c.15)
Duties on Buckwheat, etc. Act 1847 (c.3)
Duties on Calicoes, etc. Act 1807 (c.47)
Duties on Candles Act 1784 (c.36)
Duties on Candles Act 1792 (c.7)
Duties on Cape Wines Act 1813 (c.84)
Duties on Carriages, etc. (Ireland) Act 1813 (c.59)
Duties on Certain Goods Act 1806 (c.42)
Duties on Certain Licences Act 1784 (c.41)
Duties on Certain Licences Act 1808 (c.143)
Duties on Certain Woods, etc. Act 1811 (c.43)
Duties on Cider, etc. Act 1766 (c.14)
Duties on Cinnamon, etc. Act 1798 (c.68)
Duties on Cinnamon, etc. Act 1802 (c.24)
Duties on Cinnamon, etc. Act 1808 (c.18)
Duties on Clocks and Watches Act 1797 (c.108)
Duties on Coach Makers' Licences, etc. 1785 (c.49)
Duties on Coals, etc. Act 1785 (c.54)
Duties on Coals, etc. Act 1812 (c.9)
Duties on Copper and Lead Act 1848 (c.127)
Duties on Corn Act 1842 (c.14)
Duties on Corn, etc. Act 1847 (c.64)
Duties on Distillation Act 1800 (c.73)
Duties on Distilleries Act 1797 (c.11)
Duties on Distilleries Act 1797 (c.31)
Duties on Distilleries Act 1799 (c.31)
Duties on Distilleries (Scotland) Act 1799 (c.78)
Duties on Distilleries (Scotland), etc. Act 1796 (c.17)
Duties on Dogs Act 1796 (c.124)
Duties on East India Goods Act 1707 (c.37)
Duties on Epsom Salts Act 1815 (c.162)
Duties on Foreign Cambrics, etc. Act 1741 (c.29)
Duties on Foreign Hops Act 1800 (c.82)
Duties on Foreign Packets Act 1816 (c.9)
Duties on Game Certificates Act 1803 (c.23)
Duties on Glass Act 1795 (c.114)
Duties on Glass Act 1805 (c.122)
Duties on Glass Act 1811 (c.69)
Duties on Glass Act 1812 (c.54)
Duties on Glass Act 1813 (c.109)
Duties on Glass Act 1839 (c.25)
Duties on Glass Act 1840 (c.22)
Duties on Glass, etc. Act 1800 (c.45)
Duties on Glass, etc. (Ireland) Act 1814 (c.7)
Duties on Glass (Great Britain) Act 1814 (c.97)
Duties on Glass (Great Britain) Act 1816 (c.1)
Duties on Hair Powder, etc. Act 1800 (c.32)
Duties on Hats, etc., Repeal (Ireland) Act 1811 (c.60)
Duties on Hides, etc. Act 1815 (c.105)
Duties on Hides, etc. (Ireland) Act 1813 (c.60)
Duties on Hops Act 1800 (c.4)
Duties on Horse Dealers' Licences Act 1795 (c.17)
Duties on Horses Act 1784 (c.31)
Duties on Horses Act 1795 (cc.15, 16)
Duties on Horses Act 1797 (c.106)
Duties on Horses and Carriage Act 1789 (c.49)
Duties on Horses, etc. Act 1802 (c.100)
Duties on Horses Let for Hire Act 1853 (c.88)
Duties on Houses, etc. Act 1779 (c.59)
Duties on Houses, etc. Act 1786 (c.79)
Duties on Importation, etc. Act 1791 (c.42)
Duties on Income Act 1799 (c.13)
Duties on Income Act 1799 (c.22)
Duties on Income Act 1799 (c.42)
Duties on Income Act 1799 (c.72)
Duties on Income Act 1800 (c.49)
Duties on Income Act 1800 (c.96)
Duties on Kid Skins Act 1800 (c.63)
Duties on Killing Game Act 1814 (c.141)
Duties on Leather Act 1815 (c.102)
Duties on Linens Act 1784 (c.40)
Duties on Linens Act 1785 (c.72)
Duties on Madder Act 1816 (c.69)
Duties on Mahogany, etc. Act 1812 (c.36)
Duties on Malt Act 1803 (c.16)
Duties on Malt Act 1805 (c.1)
Duties on Malt Act 1806 (c.2)
Duties on Malt Act 1807 (c.3)
Duties on Malt, etc. Act 1780 (c.35)
Duties on Malt, etc. Act 1795 (c.1)
Duties on Malt, etc. Act 1796 (c.1)
Duties on Malt, etc. Act 1797 (c.4)
Duties on Malt, etc. Act 1801 (c.1)
Duties on Malt, etc. Act 1802 (c.3)
Duties on Malt, etc. Act 1805 (c.22)
Duties on Malt, etc. Act 1808 (c.2)

Duties on Malt, etc. Act 1809 (c.1)
Duties on Malt, etc. Act 1810 (c.1)
Duties on Malt, etc. Act 1811 (c.2)
Duties on Malt, etc. Act 1812 (c.1)
Duties on Malt, etc. Act 1812 (c.15)
Duties on Malt, etc. Act 1813 (c.2)
Duties on Malt, etc. Act 1814 (c.3)
Duties on Malt, etc. Act 1816 (c.3)
Duties on Malt, etc. Act 1816 (c.43)
Duties on Malt (Ireland) Act 1815 (c.99)
Duties on Norway Timber Act 1811 (c.93)
Duties on Offices and Pensions Act 1836 (c.97)
Duties on Paper Act 1805 (c.106)
Duties on Paper Act 1839 (c.23)
Duties on Paper (Ireland) Act 1815 (c.112)
Duties on Paper (Ireland) Act 1816 (c.78)
Duties on Pensions, etc. Act 1798 (c.3)
Duties on Pensions, etc. Act 1799 (c.3)
Duties on Pensions, etc. Act 1801 (c.2)
Duties on Pensions, etc. Act 1802 (c.4)
Duties on Pensions, etc. Act 1803 (c.17)
Duties on Pensions, etc. Act 1805 (c.2)
Duties on Pensions, etc. Act 1806 (c.3)
Duties on Pensions, etc. Act 1807 (c.4)
Duties on Plate Act 1797 (c.24)
Duties on Post Horses, etc. Act 1785 (c.51)
Duties on Property, etc. Act 1816 (c.65)
Duties on Property, etc. (Great Britain) Act 1815 (c.53)
Duties on Rape Seed, etc. Act 1816 (c.75)
Duties on Rape Seed, etc. Act 1816 (c.79)
Duties on Rum, etc. Act 1802 (c.20)
Duties on Rum, etc. Act 1841 (c.8)
Duties on Salt Act 1703 (c.16)
Duties on Salt Act 1795 (c.19)
Duties on Salt Act 1798 (c.43)
Duties on Salt, etc. Act 1706 (c.29)
Duties on Scotch Distilleries Act 1795 (c.59)
Duties on Servants Act 1780 (c.31)
Duties on Servants Act 1785 (c.43)
Duties on Servants Act 1785 (c.70)
Duties on Servants Act 1791 (c.3)
Duties on Servants Act 1797 (c.107)
Duties on Servants Act 1798 (c.80)
Duties on Servants, etc. Act 1797 (c.41)
Duties on Servants, etc. Act 1802 (c.37)
Duties on Shops Act 1785 (c.30)
Duties on Shops Act 1786 (c.9)
Duties on Shops Act 1789 (c.9)
Duties on Smalts, etc. Act 1783 (c.75)
Duties on Soap Act 1839 (c.63)
Duties on Soap Act 1840 (c.49)
Duties on Soap, etc. Act 1776 (c.52)
Duties on Spanish Red Wine Act 1805 (c.67)
Duties on Spirit Licences Act 1787 (c.30)
Duties on Spirit Mixtures, etc. Act 1842 (c.25)
Duties on Spirits Act 1784 (c.46)
Duties on Spirits Act 1795 (c.89)
Duties on Spirits Act 1799 (c.8)
Duties on Spirits Act 1808 (c.115)
Duties on Spirits Act 1808 (c.119)
Duties on Spirits Act 1811 (c.59)
Duties on Spirits Act 1843 (c.49)
Duties on Spirits Act 1845 (c.65)
Duties on Spirits Act 1848 (c.60)
Duties on Spirits and Coffee Act 1808 (cc.121, 122)
Duties on Spirits, etc. Act 1794 (cc.3, 4)
Duties on Spirits, etc. Act 1842 (c.15)
Duties on Spirits, etc. Act 1853 (c.37)
Duties on Spirits, etc. (Scotland) Act 1815 (c.155)
Duties on Spirits, etc. (Scotland) Act 1816 (c.106)
Duties on Spirits (Great Britain) Act 1813 (c.147)
Duties on Spirits (Ireland) Act 1806 (c.56)
Duties on Spirits (Ireland) Act 1806 (c.88)
Duties on Spirits (Ireland) Act 1807 (c.17)
Duties on Spirits (Ireland) Act 1808 (c.81)
Duties on Spirits (Ireland) Act 1809 (c.73)
Duties on Spirits (Ireland) Act 1810 (c.15)
Duties on Spirits (Ireland) Act 1812 (c.46)
Duties on Spirits (Ireland) Act 1812 (c.48)
Duties on Spirits (Ireland) Act 1814 (c.88)
Duties on Spirits (Ireland) Act 1815 (c.111)
Duties on Spirits (Ireland) Act 1816 (c.111)
Duties on Spirits (Scotland) Act 1814 (c.172)
Duties on Spirituous Liquors (Ireland) Act 1805 (c.104)
Duties on Starch Act 1779 (c.40)
Duties on Starch Act 1786 (c.51)
Duties on Starch and Soap Act 1784 (c.48)
Duties on Stills, etc. (Scotland) Act 1806 (c.102)
Duties on Stone Bottles Act 1812 (c.139)
Duties on Sugar Act 1813 (c.62)
Duties on Sugar Act 1845 (c.13)
Duties on Sugar Act 1865 (c.95)
Duties on Sugar Act 1867 (c.10)
Duties on Sugar, etc. Act 1799 (c.63)
Duties on Sugar, etc. Act 1800 (c.48)
Duties on Sugar, etc. Act 1802 (c.47)
Duties on Sweets, etc. (Ireland) Act 1815 (c.110)
Duties on Tea, etc. (American Plantations) Act 1766 (c.46)
Duties on Tobacco Act 1785 (c.81)
Duties on Tobacco Act 1811 (c.56)
Duties on Tobacco and Snuff Act 1789 (c.68)
Duties on Waggons, etc. Act 1783 (c.66)
Duties on Wagons, etc. Act 1792 (c.4)
Duties on Wash Made From Sugar Act 1800 (c.61)
Duties on Wheat, etc. Act 1843 (c.29)
Duties on Windows, etc. Act 1802 (c.34)
Duties on Wines, etc. Act 1783 (c.76)
Duties on Wines, etc. Act 1796 (c.123)
Duties on Worts or Wash Act 1808 (c.152)
Duties on Worts, Spirits, etc. Act 1791 (c.1)
Duties on Worts, Wash, etc. Act 1794 (c.2)
Duties upon Candles Act 1784 (c.11)
Duties upon East India Goods Act 1814 (c.10)
Duties upon Malt, etc. Act 1798 (c.2)
Duties upon Malt, etc. Act 1799 (c.2)

Duties upon Silks Act 1808 (c.117)
Duty of Spirits, Newfoundland Act 1812 (c.106)
Duty on Almanacks Act 1781 (c.56)
Duty on Coffee, etc., Warehoused Act 1807 (c.52)
Duty on Copper Act 1811 (c.31)
Duty on Corks Act 1816 (c.34)
Duty on Cotton Stuffs, etc. Act 1774 (c.72)
Duty on Foreign Spirits Act 1815 (c.164)
Duty on Hair Powder Act 1795 (c.49)
Duty on Hats Act 1796 (c.125)
Duty on Hats, etc., Repeal (Great Britain) Act 1811 (c.70)
Duty on Hawkers, etc. Act 1789 (c.26)
Duty on Hops Act 1805 (c.94)
Duty on Horses Act 1797 (c.134)
Duty on Horses Act 1801 (c.9)
Duty on Houses Act 1806 (c.36)
Duty on Lead (Great Britain) Act 1816 (c.18)
Duty on Linen Act 1811 (c.44)
Duty on Malt Act 1812 (c.9)
Duty on Malt (Ireland) Act 1804 (c.28)
Duty on Malt (Ireland) Act 1813 (c.74)
Duty on Malt (Ireland) Act 1816 (c.59)
Duty on Oil, etc. Act 1816 (c.118)
Duty on Paper Act 1816 (c.103)
Duty on Paper Hangings, etc. (Ireland) Act 1815 (c.106)
Duty on Pensions, etc. Act 1800 (c.8)
Duty on Pensions, etc. Act 1800 (c.31)
Duty on Racehorses Act 1856 (c.82)
Duty on Racehorses Act 1857 (c.16)
Duty on Rice Act 1812 (c.10)
Duty on Salt Act 1812 (c.107)
Duty on Salt Act 1813 (c.21)
Duty on Servants Act 1778 (c.30)
Duty on Silk Handkerchiefs Act 1815 (c.93)
Duty on Spanish Red Wines Act 1805 (c.107)
Duty on Spirits Act 1788 (c.4)
Duty on Spirits (Ireland) Act 1813 (c.94)
Duty on Spirits (Ireland) Act 1815 (c.139)
Duty on Stage Carriages Act 1839 (c.66)
Duty on Sugar Act 1809 (c.61)
Duty on Sugar, etc. Act 1810 (c.61)
Duty on Taxed Carts Act 1798 (c.93)
Duty on Tiles Act 1815 (c.176)
Duty on Tobacco Act 1794 (c.55)
Duty on Tobacco and Snuff Act 1790 (c.40)
Duty on Woollen Goods Act 1805 (c.82)
Duty on Worts, etc. Act 1801 (c.5)
Dwelling-houses for the Working Classes (Scotland) Act 1855 (c.88)
Dyeing Trade Act 1726 (c.24)
Dyeing Trade (Frauds) Act 1783 (c.15)
Dyers Act 1776 (c.33)
Dyestuffs (Import Regulations) Act 1920 (c.77)
Dyestuffs (Import Regulations) Act 1934 (c.6)
Dygart Beer Duties Act 1753 (c.44)

Ealing Church Act 1738 (c.7)
Ealing Roads Act 1767 (c.75)
Earl of Clanriccard's Estates Act 1708 (c.29)
Earldom of Mar Act 1885 (c.48)
East Africa Loans Act 1926 (c.62)
East Africa Loans (Amendment) Act 1931 (c.21)
East African Protectorates (Loans) Act 1914 (c.38)
East and West Flegg: Poor Relief Act 1775 (c.13)
East Greenwich Church: Burial Act 1751 (c.11)
East Grinstead Church Act 1790 (c.79)
East India Act 1797 (c.142)
East India Annuity Funds Act 1874 (c.12)
East India Company Act 1707 (c.71)
East India Company Act 1711 (c.35)
East India Company Act 1730 (c.14)
East India Company Act 1767 (c.49)
East India Company Act 1767 (c.57)
East India Company Act 1768 (c.11)
East India Company Act 1769 (c.24)
East India Company Act 1770 (c.47)
East India Company Act 1772 (c.7)
East India Company Act 1772 (c.9)
East India Company Act 1772 (c.63)
East India Company Act 1772 (c.64)
East India Company Act 1775 (c.44)
East India Company Act 1776 (c.8)
East India Company Act 1776 (c.51)
East India Company Act 1779 (c.61)
East India Company Act 1780 (c.56)
East India Company Act 1780 (c.58)
East India Company Act 1780 (c.70)
East India Company Act 1781 (c.65)
East India Company Act 1782 (c.51)
East India Company Act 1783 (c.2)
East India Company Act 1783 (c.3)
East India Company Act 1783 (c.36)
East India Company Act 1783 (c.83)
East India Company Act 1784 (c.25)
East India Company Act 1784 (c.34)
East India Company Act 1786 (c.16)
East India Company Act 1786 (c.57)
East India Company Act 1788 (c.8)
East India Company Act 1788 (c.29)
East India Company Act 1793 (c.52)
East India Company Act 1796 (c.120)
East India Company Act 1797 (c.31)
East India Company Act 1797 (c.74)
East India Company Act 1799 (c.89)
East India Company Act 1803 (c.48)
East India Company Act 1803 (c.63)
East India Company Act 1803 (c.137)
East India Company Act 1806 (c.85)
East India Company Act 1807 (c.41)
East India Company Act 1810 (c.86)
East India Company Act 1811 (c.75)
East India Company Act 1812 (c.10)
East India Company Act 1812 (c.135)
East India Company Act 1813 (c.155)
East India Company Act 1815 (c.64)
East India Company Bonds Act 1811 (c.64)

East India Company (Money) Act 1794 (c.41)
East India Company Stock Act 1786 (c.62)
East India Company Stock Act 1789 (c.65)
East India Company (Stock) Act 1791 (c.11)
East India Company (Stock) Act 1793 (c.47)
East India Company, Warehouses Act 1787 (c.48)
East India Company's Officers Superannuation Act 1897 (c.10)
East India Contracts Act 1870 (c.59)
East India Irrigation and Canal Act 1869 (c.7)
East India Unclaimed Stock Act 1885 (c.25)
East India Loan Act 1859 (c.11)
East India Loan Act 1860 (c.130)
East India Loan Act 1861 (c.25)
East India Loan Act 1861 (c.118)
East India Loan Act 1869 (c.106)
East India Loan Act 1873 (c.32)
East India Loan Act 1874 (c.3)
East India Loan Act 1877 (c.51)
East India Loan Act 1879 (c.60)
East India Loan Act 1885 (c.28)
East India Loan Act 1893 (c.70)
East India Loan Act 1898 (c.13)
East India Loan (East Indian Railway Debentures) Act 1880 (c.10)
East India Loan (Great Indian Peninsular Railway Debentures) Act 1901 (c.25)
East India Loan (No. 2) Act 1859 (c.39)
East India Loans Act 1858 (c.3)
East India Loans Act 1908 (c.54)
East India Loans Act 1923 (c.31)
East India Loans Act 1937 (c.14)
East India Loans (Railway and Irrigation) Act 1922 (c.9)
East India Loans (Railways) Act 1905 (c.19)
East India Loans (Railways and Irrigation) Act 1910 (c.5)
East India Merchants: Land for Warehouses etc. Act 1796 (c.127)
East India Merchants: Purchase of Land in City, etc. Act 1796 (c.119)
East India Prize Goods Act 1804 (c.72)
East India Stock Act 1860 (c.102)
East India Stock Dividend Redemption Act 1873 (c.17)
East India Trade Act 1774 (c.34)
East India Trade Act 1813 (c.34)
East India Trade Act 1813 (c.35)
East India Trade Act 1840 (c.56)
East India Trade, etc. Act 1814 (c.134)
East India Unclaimed Stock Act 1885 (c.25)
East Indian Loan (Annuities) Act 1879 (c.61)
East Indian Railway (Redemption of Annuities) Act 1879 (c.43)
East Indian Railway (Redemption of Annuities) Act 1881 (c.53)
East Indies Act 1791 (c.40)
East Kent: Drainage Act 1776 (c.62)
East Stonehouse Chapel Act 1787 (c.17)
East Tarbet Harbour Act 1707 (c.79(b))
Easter Act 1928 (c.35)
Eccles, Appointments Suspension Act 1836 (c.67)
Ecclesiastical Appointments Suspension Act 1838 (c.108)
Ecclesiastical Assessments (Scotland) Act 1900 (c.20)
Ecclesiastical Buildings and Glebes (Scotland) Act 1868 (c.96)
Ecclesiastical Commissioners Act 1836 (c.77)
Ecclesiastical Commissioners Act 1840 (c.113)
Ecclesiastical Commissioners Act 1840, Amendment 1885 (c.55)
Ecclesiastical Commissioners Act 1841 (c.39)
Ecclesiastical Commissioners Act 1847 (c.108)
Ecclesiastical Commissioners Act 1850 (c.94)
Ecclesiastical Commissioners Act 1860 (c.124)
Ecclesiastical Commissioners Act 1866 (c.111)
Ecclesiastical Commissioners Act 1868 (c.114)
Ecclesiastical Commissioners Act 1873 (c.64)
Ecclesiastical Commissioners Act 1875 (c.71)
Ecclesiastical Commissioners Act 1885 (c.31)
Ecclesiastical Commissioners (Exchange of Patronage) Act 1853 (c.50)
Ecclesiastical Commissioners (Superannuation) Act 1865 (c.68)
Ecclesiastical Commissioners (Takenhill Rectory) Act 1885 (c.31)
Ecclesiastical Courts Act 1813 (c.127)
Ecclesiastical Courts Act 1840 (c.93)
Ecclesiastical Courts Act 1844 (c.68)
Ecclesiastical Courts Act 1854 (c.47)
Ecclesiastical Courts Act 1855 (c.41)
Ecclesiastical Courts and Registries (Ireland) Act 1864 (c.54)
Ecclesiastical Courts Jurisdiction Act 1860 (c.32)
Ecclesiastical Dilapidations Act 1871 (c.43)
Ecclesiastical Dilapidations Act 1872 (c.96)
Ecclesiastical Districts in Forest of Dean Act 1842 (c.65)
Ecclesiastical Fees Act 1867 (c.135)
Ecclesiastical Fees Act 1875 (c.76)
Ecclesiastical Houses of Residence Act 1842 (c.26)
Ecclesiastical Jurisdiction Act 1842 (c.58)
Ecclesiastical Jurisdiction Act 1843 (c.60)
Ecclesiastical Jurisdiction Act 1847 (c.98)
Ecclesiastical Jurisdiction Act 1848 (c.67)
Ecclesiastical Jurisdiction Act 1849 (c.39)
Ecclesiastical Jurisdiction Act 1850 (c.47)
Ecclesiastical Jurisdiction Act 1851 (c.29)
Ecclesiastical Jurisdiction Act 1852 (c.17)
Ecclesiastical Jurisdiction Act 1853 (c.108)
Ecclesiastical Jurisdiction Act 1854 (c.65)

Ecclesiastical Jurisdiction Act 1855 (c.75)
Ecclesiastical Jurisdiction Act 1857 (c.10)
Ecclesiastical Jurisdiction Act 1858 (c.50)
Ecclesiastical Jurisdiction Act 1859 (c.45)
Ecclesiastical Leases Act 1800 (c.41)
Ecclesiastical Leases Act 1836 (c.20)
Ecclesiastical Leases Act 1842 (c.27)
Ecclesiastical Leases Act 1861 (c.104)
Ecclesiastical Leases Act 1862 (c.52)
Ecclesiastical Leases Act 1865 (c.57)
Ecclesiastical Leases Act 1765 (c.17)
Ecclesiastical Leases (Amendment) Act 1836 (c.64)
Ecclesiastical Leases (Isle of Man) Act 1866 (c.81)
Ecclesiastical Leasing Act 1842 (c.108)
Ecclesiastical Leasing Act 1858 (c.57)
Ecclesiastical Patronage (Ireland) Act 1845 (c.51)
Ecclesiastical Patronage (Ireland) Act 1848 (c.78)
Ecclesiastical Patronage (Ireland) Act 1848 (c.67)
Ecclesiastical Preferments (England) Act 1839 (c.55)
Ecclesiastical Proctors (Ireland) Act 1814 (c.68)
Ecclesiastical Property (Ireland) Act 1855 (c.28)
Ecclesiastical Property Valuation (Ireland) Act 1851 (c.74)
Ecclesiastical Services (Omission of Account on War) Act 1917 (c.5)
Ecclesiastical Suits Act 1787 (c.44)
Ecclesiastical Tithe Rentcharges (Rates) Act 1922 (c.58)
Ecclesiastical Titles Act 1851 (c.60)
Ecclesiastical Titles Act 1871 (c.53)
Ecclesiastical Unions, etc. (Ireland) Act 1848 (c.41)
Economy (Miscellaneous Provisions) Act 1926 (c.9)
Eddystone Lighthouse Act 1705 (c.7)
Eddystone Lighthouse Act 1709 (c.17)
Eden River, Cumberland (Temporary Tolls for Improvement) Act 1721 (c.14)
Edinburgh and Glasgow Roads Act 1757 (c.55)
Edinburgh and Leith Road Act 1750 (c.35)
Edinburgh and Linlithgow Roads Act 1764 (c.86)
Edinburgh Beer Duties Act 1716 (c.5)
Edinburgh Beer Duties Act 1722 (c.14)
Edinburgh Beer Duties Act 1727 (c.22)
Edinburgh Beer Duties Act 1751 (c.9)
Edinburgh Bridewell Act 1791 (c.57)
Edinburgh Bridges and Highways Act 1713 (c.30)
Edinburgh Buildings Act 1753 (c.36)
Edinburgh College of Surgeons Act 1787 (c.65)
Edinburgh Debt Act 1844 (c.20)
Edinburgh, etc., Roads Act 1795 (c.150)
Edinburgh General Register House Act 1896 (c.24)
Edinburgh: Improvement Act 1772 (c.15)
Edinburgh: Improvement Act 1786 (c.113)
Edinburgh: Improvement Act 1787 (c.51)
Edinburgh: Improvements Act 1766 (c.27)
Edinburgh, Linlithgow and Lanark Roads, etc. Act 1792 (c.120)
Edinburgh Roads Act 1755 (c.39)
Edinburgh Roads Act 1783 (c.18)
Edinburgh Roads Act 1789 (c.105)
Edinburgh (Slaughter of Animals) Act 1782 (c.52)
Edinburgh: Streets Act 1771 (c.36)
Edinburgh: Streets Act 1785 (c.28)
Edinburgh University Property Arrangement Act 1861 (c.90)
Edinburgh University (Transfer of Patronage) Act 1897 (c.13)
Edinburgh Water Act 1756 (c.74)
Edington, Somerset Drainage, etc. Act 1790 (c.58)
Education Act 1901 (c.11)
Education Act 1901 (Renewal) 1902 (c.19)
Education Act 1902 (c.42)
Education Act 1918 (c.39)
Education Act 1921 (c.51)
Education Act 1936 (c.41)
Education Act 1944 (c.31)
Education Act 1946 (c.50)
Education Act 1959 (c.60)
Education Act 1962 (c.12)
Education Act 1964 (c.82)
Education Act 1967 (c.3)
Education Act 1968 (c.17)
Education Act 1973 (c.16)
Education Act 1975 (c.2)
Education Act 1976 (c.81)
Education Act 1979 (c.49)
Education Act 1980 (c.20)
Education Act 1981 (c.60)
Education Act 1986 (c.40)
Education Act 1993 (c.35)
Education Act 1994 (c.30)
Education (Administrative Provisions) Act 1907 (c.43)
Education (Administrative Provisions) Act 1909 (c.29)
Education (Administrative Provisions) Act 1911 (c.32)
Education (Amendment) Act 1986 (c.1)
Education (Amendment) (Scotland) Act 1984 (c.6)
Education and Local Taxation Account (Scotland) Act 1892 (c.51)
Education (Choice of Employment) Act 1910 (c.37)
Education Code (1890) (c.22)
Education (Compliance with Conditions of Grants) Act 1919 (c.41)
Education (Deaf Children) Act 1937 (c.25)
Education Department Act 1856 (c.116)
Education (Emergency) Act 1939 (c.111)

Education (Emergency) (Scotland) Act 1939 (c.112)
Education Endowments (Scotland) Act 1931 (c.5)
Education (Exemptions) (Scotland) Act 1947 (c.36)
Education (Fees and Awards) Act 1983 (c.40)
Education (Grants and Awards) Act 1984 (c.11)
Education (Handicapped Children) Act 1970 (c.52)
Education (Institution Children) Act 1923 (c.38)
Education (Ireland) Act 1806 (c.122)
Education (Local Authorities) Act 1931 (c.6)
Education (Local Authority Default) Act 1904 (c.18)
Education (London) Act 1903 (c.24)
Education (Mentally Handicapped Children) (Scotland) Act 1974 (c.27)
Education (Milk) Act 1971 (c.74)
Education (Miscellaneous Provisions) Act 1948 (c.40)
Education (Miscellaneous Provisions) Act 1953 (c.33)
Education (Necessity of Schools) Act 1933 (c.29)
Education (Northern Ireland) Act 1978 (c.13)
Education (No. 2) Act 1968 (c.37)
Education (No. 2) Act 1986 (c.61)
Education of Blind and Deaf Children (Scotland) Act 1890 (c.43)
Education of Defective Children (Scotland) Act 1906 (c.10)
Education of Pauper Children Act 1855 (c.34)
Education (Provision of Meals) Act 1906 (c.57)
Education (Provision of Meals) Act 1914 (c.20)
Education (Provision of Meals) (Ireland) Act 1914 (c.35)
Education (Provision of Meals) (Ireland) Act 1916 (c.10)
Education (Provision of Meals) (Ireland) Act 1917 (c.53)
Education (Provision of the Working Balances) Act 1903 (c.10)
Education Reform Act 1988 (c.40)
Education (School-Leaving Dates) Act 1976 (c.5)
Education (School Milk) Act 1970 (c.14)
Education (Schools) Act 1992 (c.38)
Education (Scotland) Act 1872 (c.62)
Education (Scotland) Act 1878 (c.78)
Education (Scotland) Act 1883 (c.56)
Education (Scotland) Act 1897 (c.62)
Education (Scotland) Act 1901 (c.9)
Education (Scotland) Act 1908 (c.63)
Education (Scotland) Act 1913 (c.12)
Education (Scotland) Act 1918 (c.48)
Education (Scotland) Act 1925 (c.89)
Education (Scotland) Act 1928 (c.28)
Education (Scotland) Act 1930 (c.36)
Education (Scotland) Act 1936 (c.42)
Education (Scotland) Act 1942 (c.5)
Education (Scotland) Act 1944 (c.37)
Education (Scotland) Act 1945 (c.37)
Education (Scotland) Act 1946 (c.72)
Education (Scotland) Act 1949 (c.19)
Education (Scotland) Act 1956 (c.75)
Education (Scotland) Act 1962 (c.47)
Education (Scotland) Act 1963 (c.21)
Education (Scotland) Act 1965 (c.7)
Education (Scotland) Act 1969 (c.49)
Education (Scotland) Act 1971 (c.42)
Education (Scotland) Act 1973 (c.59)
Education (Scotland) Act 1976 (c.20)
Education (Scotland) Act 1980 (c.44)
Education (Scotland) Act 1981 (c.58)
Education (Scotland) (Glasgow Electoral Division) Act 1913 (c.13)
Education (Scotland) (Provision of Meals) Act 1914 (c.68)
Education (Scotland) (Superannuation) Act 1919 (c.17)
Education (Scotland) (Superannuation) Act 1922 (c.48)
Education (Scotland) (Superannuation) Act 1924 (c.13)
Education (Scotland) (Superannuation) Act 1925 (c.55)
Education (Scotland) (War Service Superannuation) Act 1914 (c.67)
Education (Scotland) (War Service Superannuation) Act 1939 (c.96)
Education (Small Population Grants) Act 1915 (c.95)
Education (Student Loans) Act 1990 (c.6)
Education (Work Experience) Act 1973 (c.23)
Educational Endowments (Ireland) Act 1885 (c.78)
Educational Endowments (Scotland) Act 1882 (c.59)
Educational Endowments (Scotland) Act 1928 (c.30)
Educational Endowments (Scotland) Act 1935 (c.5)
Edw. Whitaker, Public Accountant Act 1702 (c.16)
Effects of Residents in France Act 1794 (c.79)
Egham and Bagshot Roads Act 1727 (c.6)
Egham and Bagshot Road Act 1738 (c.16)
Egham and Bagshot Road Act 1763 (c.47)
Egyptian Loan Act 1885 (c.11)
Egyptians Act 1783 (c.51)
Eire (Confirmation of Agreements) Act 1938 (c.25)
Eisteddfod Act 1959 (c.32)
Ejectment and Distress (Ireland) Act 1846 (c.111)
Elders Widows' Fund (India) Act 1878 (c.47)
Elected Authorities (Northern Ireland) Act 1989 (c.3)
Election Commissioners Act 1852 (c.57)
Election Commissioners Act 1949 (c.90)
Election Commissioners Expenses Act 1871 (c.61)

Election (Hours of Poll) Act 1884 (c.34)
Election in the Recess Act 1863 (c.20)
Election (Ireland) Act 1862 (c.92)
Election of Members During Recess Act 1858 (c.110)
Election of Members for Cheshire Act 1846 (c.44)
Election of Representative Peers (Ireland) Act 1882 (c.26)
Election Petitions Act 1794 (c.83)
Election Petitions Act 1839 (c.38)
Election Petitions Act 1848 (c.98)
Election Petitions Act 1865 (c.8)
Election Recognizances Act 1848 (c.18)
Elections and Jurors Act 1945 (c.21)
Elections and Registration Act 1915 (c.76)
Elections (Fraudulent Conveyance) Act 1711 (c.31)
Elections (Hours of Poll) Act 1885 (c.10)
Elections in Recess Act 1863 (c.20)
Elections (Northern Ireland) Act 1985 (c.2)
Elections (Scotland) (Corrupt and Illegal Practices) Act 1890 (c.55)
Elections (Welsh Forms) Act 1964 (c.31)
Electoral Disabilities (Military Service) Removal Act 1900 (c.8)
Electoral Disabilities (Naval and Military Service) Removal Act 1914 (c.25)
Electoral Disabilities Removal Act 1891 (c.11)
Electoral Registers Act 1949 (c.86)
Electoral Registers Act 1953 (c.8)
Electric Lighting Act 1882 (c.56)
Electric Lighting Act 1888 (c.12)
Electric Lighting Act 1909 (c.34)
Electric Lighting (Clauses) Act 1899 (c.19)
Electric Lighting (Scotland) Act 1890 (c.13)
Electric Lighting (Scotland) Act 1902 (c.35)
Electricity Act 1947 (c.54)
Electricity Act 1957 (c.48)
Electricity Act 1972 (c.17)
Electricity Act 1989 (c.29)
Electricity (Amendment) Act 1961 (c.8)
Electricity and Gas Act 1963 (c.59)
Electricity (Borrowing Powers) Act 1959 (c.20)
Electricity (Borrowing Powers) (Scotland) Act 1962 (c.7)
Electricity (Financial Provisions) Act 1982 (c.56)
Electricity (Financial Provisions) (Scotland) Act 1976 (c.61)
Electricity (Financial Provisions) (Scotland) Act 1982 (c.56)
Electricity (Financial Provisions) (Scotland) Act 1988 (c.37)
Electricity Reorganisation (Scotland) Act 1954 (c.60)
Electricity (Scotland) Act 1969 (c.1)
Electricity (Scotland) Act 1979 (c.11)
Electricity (Supply) Act 1919 (c.100)
Electricity (Supply) Act 1922 (c.46)
Electricity (Supply) Act 1926 (c.51)
Electricity (Supply) Act 1928 (c.4)
Electricity (Supply) Act 1933 (c.46)
Electricity Supply Act 1935 (c.3)
Electricity Supply (Meters) Act 1936 (c.20)
Electricity Supply (Meters) Act 1952 (c.32)
Elementary Education Act 1870 (c.75)
Elementary Education Act 1873 (c.86)
Elementary Education Act 1876 (c.79)
Elementary Education Act 1880 (c.23)
Elementary Education Act 1891 (c.56)
Elementary Education Act 1897 (c.16)
Elementary Education Act 1900 (c.53)
Elementary Education Act Amendment Act 1872 (c.27)
Elementary Education Amendment Act 1903 (c.13)
Elementary Education (Blind and Deaf Children) Act 1893 (c.42)
Elementary Education (Defective and Epileptic Children) Act 1899 (c.32)
Elementary Education (Defective and Epileptic Children) Act 1914 (c.45)
Elementary Education (Election) Act 1871 (c.94)
Elementary Education (Elections) Act 1872 (c.59)
Elementary Education (Fee Grant) Act 1916 (c.35)
Elementary Education (Industrial Schools) Act 1879 (c.48)
Elementary Education (Orders) Act 1874 (c.90)
Elementary Education (School Attendance) Act 1893 (c.51)
Elementary Education (School Attendance) Act (1893) Amendment 1899 (c.13)
Elementary Education (Wenlock) Act 1874 (c.39)
Elementary School Teachers (Superannuation) Act 1898 (c.57)
Elementary School Teachers (Superannuation) Act 1912 (c.12)
Elementary School Teachers Superannuation (Isle of Man) Act 1900 (c.38)
Elementary School Teachers Superannuation (Jersey) Act 1900 (c.40)
Elementary School Teachers (War Service Superannuation) Act 1914 (c.66)
Elgin Beer Duties Act 1721 (c.7)
Elizabeth Taylor's Patent Act 1776 (c.18)
Elland and Leeds Road Act 1753 (c.61)
Elland to Leeds Road Act 1777 (c.87)
Elland to Leeds Road Act 1795 (c.159)
Elland to Leeds Road Act 1740 (c.25)
Ellesmere and Chester Canal Act 1793 (c.91)
Ellesmere and Chester Canal Act 1796 (c.71)
Ellesmere and Chester Canal Act 1796 (c.96)
Ellesmere, Salop: Poor Relief Act 1791 (c.78)
Elloe, Lincoln: Small Debts Act 1775 (c.64)
Elver Fishing Act 1876 (c.34)
Ely Roads Act 1740 (c.14)
Embezzlement Act 1799 Act (c.85)
Embezzlement Act 1814 (c.60)

Embezzlement by Bankers, etc. Act 1812 (c.63)
Embezzlement by Collectors Act 1810 (c.59)
Embezzlement (Ireland) Act 1811 (c.38)
Embezzlement of Naval, etc., Stores Act 1812 (c.12)
Embezzlement of Public Stores Act 1800 (c.89)
Embezzlement of Public Stores Act (c.126)
Embezzlement of Public Stores Act 1815 (c.127)
Emergency Laws (Miscellaneous Provisions) Act 1947 (c.10)
Emergency Laws (Miscellaneous Provisions) Act 1953 (c.47)
Emergency Laws (Re-enactments and Repeals) Act 1964 (c.60)
Emergency Laws (Repeal) Act 1959 (c.19)
Emergency Laws (Transitional Provisions) Act 1946 (c.26)
Emergency Powers Act 1920 (c.55)
Emergency Powers Act 1964 (c.38)
Emergency Powers (Defence) Act 1939 (c.20)
Emergency Powers (Defence) Act 1939 (c.62)
Emergency Powers (Defence) Act 1944 (c.31)
Emergency Powers (Defence) (No. 2) Act 1939 (c.45)
Emergency Powers (Isle of Man—Defence) Act 1943 (c.36)
Emigration from Scotland Act 1851 (c.91)
Empire Settlement Act 1922 (c.13)
Empire Settlement Act 1937 (c.18)
Empire Settlement Act 1952 (c.26)
Employers and Workmen Act 1875 (c.90)
Employers' Liability Act 1880 (c.42)
Employers' Liability Act 1888 (c.58)
Employers' Liability (Compulsory Insurance) Act 1969 (c.57)
Employers' Liability (Defective Equipment) Act 1969 (c.37)
Employers' Liability Insurance Companies Act 1907 (c.46)
Employment Act 1980 (c.42)
Employment Act 1982 (c.46)
Employment Act 1988 (c.19)
Employment Act 1989 (c.38)
Employment Act 1990 (c.38)
Employment Agencies Act 1973 (c.35)
Employment and Training Act 1948 (c.46)
Employment and Training Act 1973 (c.50)
Employment and Training Act 1981 (c.57)
Employment (Continental Shelf) Act 1978 (c.46)
Employment Medical Advisory Service Act 1972 (c.28)
Employment of Children Act 1903 (c.45)
Employment of Children Act 1973 (c.24)
Employment of Poor Act 1847 (c.87)
Employment of Poor, etc. (I.) Act 1847 (c.80)
Employment of Women Act 1907 (c.10)
Employment of Women and Young Persons Act 1936 (c.24)
Employment of Women, Young Persons and Children Act 1920 (c.65)
Employment Protection Act 1975 (c.71)
Employment Protection (Consolidation) Act 1978 (c.44)
Employment Subsidies Act 1978 (c.6)
Encouragement of Manufacturers Act 1723 (c.11)
Encouragement of Seamen, etc. Act 1803 (c.160)
Endangered Species (Import and Export) Act 1976 (c.72)
Endowed Institutions (Scotland) Act 1869 (c.39)
Endowed Institutions (Scotland) Act 1878 (c.48)
Endowed School Acts Continuance 1879 (c.66)
Endowed Schools Act 1813 (c.107)
Endowed Schools Act 1860 (c.11)
Endowed Schools Act 1869 (c.56)
Endowed Schools Act 1868 (c.32)
Endowed Schools Act 1869 (c.56)
Endowed Schools Act 1873 (c.87)
Endowed Schools Act 1874 (c.87)
Endowed Schools Inquiries (Ireland) Act 1855 (c.59)
Endowed Schools (Ireland) Act 1813 (c.107)
Endowed Schools (Masters) Act 1908 (c.39)
Endowed Schools (Time of Address) Act 1873 (c.7)
Endowed Schools (Vested Interests) Act Continued 1875 (c.29)
Enduring Power of Attorney Act 1985 (c.29)
Enemy Property Act 1953 (c.52)
Energy Act 1976 (c.76)
Energy Act 1983 (c.25)
Energy Conservation Act 1981 (c.17)
Enfranchisement of Copyholds Act 1841 (c.35)
English Industrial Estates Corporation Act 1981 (c.13)
Engraving Copyright Act 1734 (c.13)
Engraving Copyright Act 1766 (c.38)
Enlargement of Time for First Meetings Act 1757 (c.34)
Enlargement of Time for First Meetings Act 1759 (c.14)
Enlargement of Times for Executing Acts Act 1757 (c.37)
Enlargement of Times for Executing Acts Act 1765 (c.15)
Enlistment Act 1794 (c.43)
Enlistment of Foreigners Act 1804 (c.75)
Enlistment of Foreigners Act 1806 (c.23)
Enlistment of Foreigners Act 1815 (c.85)
Enlistment of Foreigners Act 1837 (c.29)
Enlistment of Foreigners Act 1855 (c.2)
Enlistment of Persons Transferred from the Indian Forces Act 1861 (c.74)
Enlistment in Foreign Service Act 1713 (c.10)

Entail Act 1838 (c.70)
Entail Amendment Act 1848 (c.36)
Entail Amendment Act 1853 (c.94)
Entail Amendment (Scotland) Act 1868 (c.84)
Entail Amendment (Scotland) Act 1875 (c.61)
Entail Amendment (Scotland) Act 1878 (c.28)
Entail Cottages Act 1860 (c.95)
Entail Improvement Act 1770 (c.51)
Entail Powers Act 1836 (c.42)
Entail (Scotland) Act 1882 (c.53)
Entail (Scotland) Act 1914 (c.43)
Entail Sites Act 1840 (c.48)
Entailed Estates Act 1800 (c.56)
Entailed Lands, etc. (Scotland) Act 1841 (c.24)
Enterprise and New Towns (Scotland) Act 1990 (c.35)
Entertainments Duty Act 1958 (c.9)
Entertainments (Increased Penalties) Act 1990 (c.20)
Environment Act 1995 (c.25)
Environment and Safety Information Act 1988 (c.30)
Environmental Protection Act 1990 (c.43)
Epidemic and Other Diseases Prevention Act 1883 (c.59)
Episcopal and Capitular Estates Act 1851 (c.104)
Episcopal and Capitular Estates Act 1854 (c.116)
Episcopal and Capitular Estates Act 1857 (c.74)
Episcopal and Capitular Estates Act 1859 (c.46)
Episcopal Church (Scotland) Act 1864 (c.94)
Episcopal Church (Scotland) Act 1964 (c.12)
Episcopal, etc., Estates Management Act 1856 (c.74)
Episcopal Jurisdiction (England) Act 1839 (c.9)
Episcopal Meeting Houses (Scotland) Act 1745 (c.38)
Epping and Ongar Road Act 1742 (c.19)
Epping and Ongar Road Act 1769 (c.63)
Epping Forest Act 1871 (c.93)
Epping Forest Act 1873 (c.5)
Epping Forest Act 1875 (c.6)
Epping Forest Act 1876 (c.3)
Epping Forest Act Amendment 1872 (c.95)
Equal Pay Act 1970 (c.41)
Equity Procedure Act 1731 (c.25)
Equivalent Act 1714 (c.27)
Equivalent Act 1716 (c.14)
Equivalent Company Act 1850 (c.63)
Equivalent Money Act 1707 (c.51)
Equivalent Money Act 1713 (c.12)
Erasures in Deeds (Scotland) Act 1836 (c.33)
Erection of Cottages Act 1775 (c.32)
Erection of Lighthouses Act 1786 (c.101)
Erection of Lighthouses Act 1788 (c.25)
Erection of Lighthouses Act 1789 (c.52)
Erewash Canal Act 1777 (c.69)
Erewash Canal Act 1790 (c.56)
Erskine Bridge Tolls Act 1968 (c.4)
Escape of Debtors from Prison Act 1702 (c.6)
Escheat (Procedure) Act 1887 (c.53)
Escrick Church, Yorks Act 1781 (c.76)
Essential Buildings and Plant (Repair of War Damage) Act 1939 (c.74)
Essential Commodities Reserves Act 1938 (c.51)
Essex and Hertfordshire Roads Act 1743 (c.9)
Essex and Hertfordshire Roads Act 1769 (c.51)
Essex and Hertfordshire Roads Act 1791 (c.99)
Essex Roads Act 1702 (c.10)
Essex Roads Act 1723 (c.9)
Essex Roads Act 1725 (c.23)
Essex Roads Act 1746 (c.7)
Essex Roads Act 1763 (c.58)
Essex Roads Act 1787 (c.69)
Essex Roads Act 1793 (c.145)
Essex Roads Act 1793 (c.149)
Essex Shire House Act 1789 (c.8)
Essex, Suffolk and Hertford Roads Act 1765 (c.60)
Established Church Act 1713 (c.7)
Estate Agents Act 1979 (c.38)
Estate of Benjamin Hopkins Act 1795 (c.103)
Estate of Hugh Naish Act 1737 (c.38)
Estates Held for the Barrack Service Act 1805 (c.69)
Estates of Duke of Wellington Act 1839 (c.4)
Estates of Grenada and St. Vincent Traders Act 1806 (c.157)
Estates of Grenada and St. Vincent Traders Act 1806 (c.158)
Estates of Intestates, etc. Act 1852 (c.3)
Estates of Lunatics Act 1803 (c.75)
Estates Vest in Heirs, etc., of Mortgages Act 1838 (c.69)
Estreats Act 1716 (c.15)
European Assembly Elections Act 1978 (c.10)
European Assembly Elections Act 1981 (c.8)
European Assembly (Pay and Pensions) Act 1979 (c.50)
European Coal and Steel Community Act 1955 (c.4)
European Communities Act 1972 (c.68)
European Communities (Amendment) Act 1986 (c.58)
European Communities (Amendment) Act 1993 (c.32)
European Communities (Finance) Act 1985 (c.64)
European Communities (Finance) Act 1988 (c.46)
European Communities (Finance) Act 1995 (c.1)
European Communities (Greek Accession) Act 1979 (c.57)
European Communities (Spanish and Portuguese Accession) Act 1985 (c.75)

European Economic Area Act 1993 (c.51)
European Forces (India) Act 1860 (c.100)
European Free Trade Association Act 1960 (c.19)
European Monetary Agreement Act 1959 (c.11)
European Parliamentary Elections Act 1993 (c.41)
European Payments Union (Financial Provisions) Act 1950 (c.8)
European Troops in India Act 1859 (c.27)
European Union (Accessions) Act 1994 (c.38)
Everton, etc. (Nottinghamshire): Drainage, etc. Act 1796 (c.99)
Evesham Roads Act 1727 (c.11)
Evesham Roads Act 1778 (c.93)
Evesham Roads Act 1789 (c.103)
Evicted Tenants (Ireland) Act 1907 (c.56)
Evicted Tenants (Ireland) Act 1908 (c.22)
Eviction (Ireland) Act 1848 (c.47)
Evidence Act 1791 (c.35)
Evidence Act 1840 (c.26)
Evidence Act 1843 (c.85)
Evidence Act 1845 (c.113)
Evidence Act 1851 (c.99)
Evidence Act 1870 (c.49)
Evidence Act 1877 (c.14)
Evidence Act 1938 (c.28)
Evidence (Amendment) Act 1853 (c.83)
Evidence (Amendment) Act 1915 (c.94)
Evidence and Powers of Attorney Act 1940 (c.28)
Evidence and Powers of Attorney Act 1943 (c.18)
Evidence by Commission Act 1843 (c.82)
Evidence by Commission Act 1859 (c.20)
Evidence by Commission Act 1885 (c.74)
Evidence (Colonial Statutes) Act 1907 (c.16)
Evidence (Foreign, Dominion and Colonial Documents) Act 1933 (c.4)
Evidence Further Amendment Act 1869 (c.68)
Evidence Further Amendment Act 1874 (c.64)
Evidence Ireland Act 1815 (c.157)
Evidence (Proceedings in Other Jurisdictions) Act 1975 (c.34)
Evidence (Scotland) Act 1840 (c.59)
Evidence (Scotland) Act 1852 (c.27)
Evidence (Scotland) Act 1853 (c.20)
Evidence (Scotland) Act 1866 (c.112)
Examination of Drugs Act 1723 (c.20)
Excessive Loading of Vehicles, London and Westminster Act 1719 (c.6)
Exchange Control Act 1947 (c.14)
Exchange, Crown and Eton College Act 1842 (c.78)
Exchange Equalisation Account Act 1933 (c.18)
Exchange Equalisation Account Act 1937 (c.41)
Exchange Equalisation Account Act 1979 (c.30)
Exchange of American Prisoners Act 1782 (c.10)
Exchange of Crown Advowsons Act 1848 (c.57)
Exchange of Crown Lands in Perthshire Act 1766 (c.33)
Exchange of Ecclesiastical Patronage Act 1859 (c.9)
Exchequer Act 1728 (c.6)
Exchequer and Audit Departments Act 1866 (c.39)
Exchequer and Audit Departments Act 1921 (c.52)
Exchequer and Audit Departments Act 1950 (c.3)
Exchequer and Audit Departments Act 1957 (c.45)
Exchequer and Audit Departments (Temporary Provisions) Act 1939 (c.101)
Exchequer and Treasury Bills Act 1885 (c.44)
Exchequer Bills Act 1700 (c.1)
Exchequer Bills Act 1786 (c.97)
Exchequer Bills Act 1787 (c.23)
Exchequer Bills Act 1793 (c.29)
Exchequer Bills Act 1796 (cc.29, 30)
Exchequer Bills Act 1798 (c.91)
Exchequer Bills Act 1799 (c.6)
Exchequer Bills Act 1800 (c.33)
Exchequer Bills Act 1800 (c.109)
Exchequer Bills Act 1802 (c.41)
Exchequer Bills Act 1803 (c.60)
Exchequer Bills Act 1803 (c.148)
Exchequer Bills Act 1804 (c.73)
Exchequer Bills Act 1805 (c.27)
Exchequer Bills Act 1806 (c.93)
Exchequer Bills Act 1807 (c.28)
Exchequer Bills Act 1808 (c.7)
Exchequer Bills Act 1808 (cc.53, 54)
Exchequer Bills Act 1808 (c.97)
Exchequer Bills Act 1808 (c.114)
Exchequer Bills Act 1809 (cc.2, 3)
Exchequer Bills Act 1809 (c.52)
Exchequer Bills Act 1809 (c.93)
Exchequer Bills Act 1809 (c.114)
Exchequer Bills Act 1810 (cc.2, 3)
Exchequer Bills Act 1810 (cc.69, 70)
Exchequer Bills Act 1810 (cc.113, 114)
Exchequer Bills Act 1811 (cc.3, 4)
Exchequer Bills Act 1811 (c.15)
Exchequer Bills Act 1811 (cc.53, 54)
Exchequer Bills Act 1811 (c.85)
Exchequer Bills Act 1811 (c.112)
Exchequer Bills Act 1812 (cc.4, 5)
Exchequer Bills Act 1812 (c.16)
Exchequer Bills Act 1812 (c.86)
Exchequer Bills Act 1812 (c.114)
Exchequer Bills Act 1812 (c.164)
Exchequer Bills Act 1813 (c.18)
Exchequer Bills Act 1813 (cc.26, 27)
Exchequer Bills Act 1813 (c.39)
Exchequer Bills Act 1813 (c.42)
Exchequer Bills Act 1813 (cc.118, 119)
Exchequer Bills Act 1813 (c.161)

Exchequer Bills Act 1814 (cc.4, 5)
Exchequer Bills Act 1814 (c.53)
Exchequer Bills Act 1814 (cc.79, 80)
Exchequer Bills Act 1814 (c.188)
Exchequer Bills Act 1815 (cc.148, 149)
Exchequer Bills Act 1816 (c.4)
Exchequer Bills Act 1816 (c.28)
Exchequer Bills Act 1816 (c.54)
Exchequer Bills Act 1836 (c.2)
Exchequer Bills Act 1836 (c.113)
Exchequer Bills Act 1837 (c.16)
Exchequer Bills Act 1837 (c.38)
Exchequer Bills Act 1838 (c.12)
Exchequer Bills Act 1838 (c.26)
Exchequer Bills Act 1838 (c.93)
Exchequer Bills Act 1839 (c.8)
Exchequer Bills Act 1839 (c.90)
Exchequer Bills Act 1840 (c.12)
Exchequer Bills Act 1840 (c.106)
Exchequer Bills Act 1841 (c.19)
Exchequer Bills Act 1842 (c.21)
Exchequer Bills Act 1842 (c.66)
Exchequer Bills Act 1842 (c.86)
Exchequer Bills Act 1842 (c.115)
Exchequer Bills Act 1843 (c.17)
Exchequer Bills Act 1844 (c.14)
Exchequer Bills Act 1845 (c.23)
Exchequer Bills Act 1845 (c.129)
Exchequer Bills Act 1846 (c.15)
Exchequer Bills Act 1847 (c.19)
Exchequer Bills Act 1848 (c.16)
Exchequer Bills Act 1849 (c.20)
Exchequer Bills Act 1850 (c.10)
Exchequer Bills Act 1850 (c.22)
Exchequer Bills Act 1851 (c.9)
Exchequer Bills Act 1852 (c.10)
Exchequer Bills Act 1853 (c.25)
Exchequer Bills Act 1854 (c.3)
Exchequer Bills Act 1854 (c.12)
Exchequer Bills Act 1855 (c.8)
Exchequer Bills Act 1856 (c.19)
Exchequer Bills Act 1857 (c.17)
Exchequer Bills Act 1858 (c.13)
Exchequer Bills Act 1859 (c.22)
Exchequer Bills Act 1860 (c.20)
Exchequer Bills Act 1861 (c.5)
Exchequer Bills Act 1862 (c.3)
Exchequer Bills and Bonds Act 1855 (c.130)
Exchequer Bills and Bonds Act 1856 (c.44)
Exchequer Bills and Bonds Act 1866 (c.25)
Exchequer Bills and Bonds Act 1877 (c.5)
Exchequer Bills and Bonds Act 1878 (c.2)
Exchequer Bills and Bonds Act 1879 (c.62)
Exchequer Bills and Bonds Act 1880 (c.16)
Exchequer Bills and Bonds (Session 2) Act 1880 (c.21)
Exchequer Bills (Great Britain) Act 1815 (c.196)
Exchequer Bonds Act 1858 (c.14)
Exchequer Bonds Act 1862 (c.13)
Exchequer Bonds Act 1863 (c.16)
Exchequer Bonds Act 1864 (c.74)
Exchequer Bonds Act 1865 (c.29)
Exchequer Bonds Act 1867 (c.31)
Exchequer Bonds Act 1868 (c.27)
Exchequer Bonds Act 1869 (c.22)
Exchequer Bonds Act 1870 (c.41)
Exchequer Bonds Act 1871 (c.52)
Exchequer Bonds Act 1873 (c.54)
Exchequer Bonds Act 1876 (c.1)
Exchequer Bonds Act 1878 (c.7)
Exchequer Bonds and Bills Act 1854 (c.23)
Exchequer Bonds and Bills Act 1860 (c.132)
Exchequer Bonds and Bills (No. 2) Act 1878 (c.64)
Exchequer Bonds (No. 1) Act 1879 (c.3)
Exchequer Bonds (No. 2) Act 1878 (c.22)
Exchequer Court (Ireland) Act 1843 (c.55)
Exchequer Court (Ireland) Act 1843 (c.78)
Exchequer Court (Scotland) Act 1707 (c.53)
Exchequer Court (Scotland) Act 1779 (c.38)
Exchequer Court (Scotland) Act 1837 (c.65)
Exchequer Court (Scotland) Act 1856 (c.56)
Exchequer Equitable Jurisdiction (Ireland) Act 1850 (c.51)
Exchequer, etc., Courts (Scotland) Act 1790 (c.17)
Exchequer Extra Receipts Act 1868 (c.9)
Exchequer (Ireland) Act 1814 (c.83)
Excisable Goods on the Thames Act 1803 (c.115)
Excisable Liquors (Scotland) Act 1804 (c.55)
Excise Act 1719 (c.21)
Excise Act 1758 (c.29)
Excise Act 1772 (c.46)
Excise Act 1781 (c.55)
Excise Act 1781 (c.64)
Excise Act 1783 (c.70)
Excise Act 1785 (c.22)
Excise Act 1785 (c.47)
Excise Act 1785 (c.74)
Excise Act 1786 (c.59)
Excise Act 1786 (c.64)
Excise Act 1786 (cc.73, 74)
Excise Act 1786 (c.77)
Excise Act 1788 (c.37)
Excise Act 1788 (c.46)
Excise Act 1789 (c.63)
Excise Act 1790 (c.37)
Excise Act 1793 (c.59)
Excise Act 1795 (cc.10–13)
Excise Act 1795 (c.13)
Excise Act 1795 (c.97)
Excise Act 1795 (c.116)
Excise Act 1796 (c.14)
Excise Act 1798 (c.42)
Excise Act 1798 (c.54)
Excise Act 1800 (c.23)
Excise Act 1801 (c.91)
Excise Act 1802 (c.93)
Excise Act 1802 (c.96)
Excise Act 1803 (c.69)
Excise Act 1803 (c.81)
Excise Act 1803 (c.129)
Excise Act 1804 (c.49)
Excise Act 1805 (c.30)

Excise Act 1806 (c.39)
Excise Act 1806 (c.75)
Excise Act 1806 (c.112)
Excise Act 1806 (cc.138, 139)
Excise Act 1807 (c.27)
Excise Act 1807 (c.37)
Excise Act 1809 (c.63)
Excise Act 1809 (c.77)
Excise Act 1809 (c.80)
Excise Act 1809 (c.81)
Excise Act 1811 (c.32)
Excise Act 1812 (c.58)
Excise Act 1812 (c.61)
Excise Act 1812 (c.94)
Excise Act 1812 (c.128)
Excise Act 1813 (cc.56, 57)
Excise Act 1813 (c.88)
Excise Act 1813 (c.103)
Excise Act 1814 (c.73)
Excise Act 1814 (c.148)
Excise Act 1814 (c.183)
Excise Act 1815 (c.27)
Excise Act 1815 (c.30)
Excise Act 1815 (c.35)
Excise Act 1815 (c.62)
Excise Act 1815 (c.63)
Excise Act 1816 (c.17)
Excise Act 1816 (c.104)
Excise Act 1816 (c.108)
Excise Act 1836 (c.52)
Excise Act 1840 (c.17)
Excise Act 1848 (c.118)
Excise Act 1854 (c.27)
Excise Act 1855 (c.94)
Excise Act 1858 (c.15)
Excise Act 1860 (c.113)
Excise and Customs Act 1815 (c.66)
Excise and Stamps Act 1808 (c.41)
Excise and Stamps (Ireland) Act 1807 (c.14)
Excise and Taxes (Ireland) Act 1805 (c.19)
Excise Duties Act 1780 (c.17)
Excise Duties Act 1789 (c.45)
Excise Duties Act 1794 (c.33)
Excise Duties Act 1855 (c.22)
Excise Duties Act 1856 (c.34)
Excise Duties Act 1862 (c.84)
Excise Duties and Drawbacks Act 1807 (c.63)
Excise Duties and Licences (Ireland) Act 1815 (c.19)
Excise Duties and Taxes (Ireland) Act 1807 (c.18)
Excise Duties (Surcharges or Rebates) Act 1979 (c.8)
Excise Duty on Malt Act 1863 (c.3)
Excise Duty on Malt Act 1865 (c.66)
Excise, etc. Act 1811 (c.95)
Excise, etc. (Great Britain) Act 1807 (c.30)
Excise, etc. Act 1816 (c.30)
Excise (Great Britain) Act 1809 (c.117)
Excise (Ireland) Act 1807 (c.35)
Excise (Ireland) Act 1808 (c.82)
Excise (Ireland) Act 1809 (c.33)
Excise Incorporation (Scotland) Act 1835 (c.72)
Excise Laws, Glass Act 1792 (c.40)
Excise Management Act 1841 (c.20)
Excise Officers Act 1810 (c.44)
Excise Officers Allowance Act 1812 (c.81)
Excise on Spirits Act 1860 (c.129)
Excise (Scotland) Act 1793 (c.69)
Exclusive Trading (Ireland) Act 1846 (c.76)
Execution Act 1844 (c.96)
Execution (Ireland) Act 1848 (c.28)
Execution of Diligence (Scotland) Act 1926 (c.16)
Execution of Sentences (Scotland) Act 1730 (c.32)
Execution of Trusts (Emergency Provisions) Act 1939 (c.114)
Execution of Trusts (War Facilities) Act 1914 (c.13)
Execution of Trusts (War Facilities) Amendment Act 1915 (c.70)
Executions for Murder Act 1836 (c.30)
Executors (Scotland) Act 1900 (c.55)
Exemption from Coal Duty Act 1787 (c.21)
Exemption from Duties Act 1809 (c.44)
Exemption from Impressment Act 1739 (c.17)
Exemption from Toll Act 1812 (c.145)
Exemption of Bankers from Penalties Act 1813 (c.139)
Exercise Act 1723 (c.10)
Exercise Act 1727 (c.16)
Exercise of Trade by Soldiers Act 1784 (c.6)
Exercise of Trade by Soldiers, etc. Act 1802 (c.69)
Exercise of Trades by Soldiers, etc. Act 1816 (c.67)
Exercises of Trades Act 1712 (c.14)
Exercising Ground, Chatham Act 1808 (c.101)
Exeter: Lighting, etc. Act 1760 (c.28)
Exeter (Poor Relief) Act 1757 (c.53)
Exeter: Poor Relief Act 1774 (c.61)
Exeter: Poor Relief Act 1785 (c.21)
Exeter: Poor Relief Act 1788 (c.76)
Exeter Roads Act 1753 (c.74)
Exeter Roads Act 1756 (c.55)
Exeter Roads Act 1769 (c.93)
Exeter Roads Act 1770 (c.73)
Exeter Roads, etc. Act 1773 (c.109)
Exeter: Small Debts Act 1772 (c.27)
Exhibition Medals Act 1863 (c.119)
Exmoor Forest Act 1815 (c.138)
Ex-Officio Justice of the Peace (Scotland) Act 1898 (c.20)
Expenditure, etc., of Office of Works, etc. Act 1812 (c.41)
Expenditure in the West Indies Act 1800 (c.22)
Expenses of Fortifications for Protecting Royal Arsenals (No. 1) Act 1867 (c.24)
Expenses of Fortifications for Protecting Royal Arsenals (No. 2) Act 1867 (c.145)
Expenses of H.M. Forces, India Act 1791 (c.10)

Expenses of Prince Regent Act 1812 (c.7)
Expiring Laws Act 1922 (c.50)
Expiring Laws Act 1925 (c.76)
Expiring Laws Act 1931 (c.2)
Expiring Laws Act 1969 (c.61)
Expiring Laws Continuance Act 1841 (c.7)
Expiring Laws Continuance Act 1863 (c.95)
Expiring Laws Continuance Act 1864 (c.84)
Expiring Laws Continuance Act 1865 (c.119)
Expiring Laws Continuance Act 1866 (c.102)
Expiring Laws Continuance Act 1867 (c.143)
Expiring Laws Continuance Act 1868 (c.111)
Expiring Laws Continuance Act 1869 (c.85)
Expiring Laws Continuance Act 1870 (c.103)
Expiring Laws Continuance Act 1871 (c.95)
Expiring Laws Continuance Act 1872 (c.88)
Expiring Laws Continuance Act 1873 (c.75)
Expiring Laws Continuance Act 1874 (c.76)
Expiring Laws Continuance Act 1875 (c.72)
Expiring Laws Continuance Act 1876 (c.69)
Expiring Laws Continuance Act 1877 (c.67)
Expiring Laws Continuance Act 1878 (c.70)
Expiring Laws Continuance Act 1879 (c.67)
Expiring Laws Continuance Act 1880 (c.48)
Expiring Laws Continuance Act 1881 (c.70)
Expiring Laws Continuance Act 1882 (c.64)
Expiring Laws Continuance Act 1883 (c.40)
Expiring Laws Continuance Act 1884 (c.53)
Expiring Laws Continuance Act 1885 (c.59)
Expiring Laws Continuance Act 1886 (c.5)
Expiring Laws Continuance Act 1887 (c.63)
Expiring Laws Continuance Act 1888 (c.38)
Expiring Laws Continuance Act 1889 (c.67)
Expiring Laws Continuance Act 1890 (c.49)
Expiring Laws Continuance Act 1891 (c.60)
Expiring Laws Continuance Act 1892 (c.60)
Expiring Laws Continuance Act 1893 (c.59)
Expiring Laws Continuance Act 1894 (c.48)
Expiring Laws Continuance Act 1895 (c.1)
Expiring Laws Continuance Act 1896 (c.39)
Expiring Laws Continuance Act 1897 (c.54)
Expiring Laws Continuance Act 1898 (c.47)
Expiring Laws Continuance Act 1899 (c.34)
Expiring Laws Continuance Act 1900 (c.37)
Expiring Laws Continuance Act 1901 (c.33)
Expiring Laws Continuance Act 1902 (c.32)
Expiring Laws Continuance Act 1903 (c.40)
Expiring Laws Continuance Act 1904 (c.29)
Expiring Laws Continuance Act 1905 (c.21)
Expiring Laws Continuance Act 1906 (c.51)
Expiring Laws Continuance Act 1907 (c.34)
Expiring Laws Continuance Act 1908 (c.18)
Expiring Laws Continuance Act 1909 (c.46)
Expiring Laws Continuance Act 1910 (c.36)
Expiring Laws Continuance Act 1911 (c.22)
Expiring Laws Continuance Act 1912 (c.18)
Expiring Laws Continuance Act 1913 (c.15)
Expiring Laws Continuance Act 1914 (c.23)
Expiring Laws Continuance Act 1915 (c.63)
Expiring Laws Continuance Act 1916 (c.29)
Expiring Laws Continuance Act 1917 (c.38)
Expiring Laws Continuance Act 1918 (c.21)
Expiring Laws Continuance Act 1919 (c.39)
Expiring Laws Continuance Act 1920 (c.73)
Expiring Laws Continuance Act 1921 (c.53)
Expiring Laws Continuance Act 1923 (c.37)
Expiring Laws Continuance Act 1924 (c.1)
Expiring Laws Continuance Act 1926 (c.49)
Expiring Laws Continuance Act 1927 (c.34)
Expiring Laws Continuance Act 1928 (c.3)
Expiring Laws Continuance Act 1929 (c.12)
Expiring Laws Continuance Act 1931 (c.4)
Expiring Laws Continuance Act 1932 (c.2)
Expiring Laws Continuance Act 1933 (c.48)
Expiring Laws Continuance Act 1934 (c.57)
Expiring Laws Continuance Act 1935 (c.4)
Expiring Laws Continuance Act 1936 (c.4)
Expiring Laws Continuance Act 1937 (c.1)
Expiring Laws Continuance Act 1938 (c.1)
Expiring Laws Continuance Act 1939 (c.1)
Expiring Laws Continuance Act 1941 (c.3)
Expiring Laws Continuance Act 1942 (c.1)
Expiring Laws Continuance Act 1943 (c.1)
Expiring Laws Continuance Act 1944 (c.2)
Expiring Laws Continuance Act 1945 (c.9)
Expiring Laws Continuance Act 1947 (c.1)
Expiring Laws Continuance Act 1948 (c.3)
Expiring Laws Continuance Act 1949 (c.71)
Expiring Laws Continuance Act 1950 (c.1)
Expiring Laws Continuance Act 1951 (c.3)
Expiring Laws Continuance Act 1952 (c.5)
Expiring Laws Continuance Act 1953 (c.9)
Expiring Laws Continuance Act 1954 (c.69)
Expiring Laws Continuance Act 1955 (c.22)
Expiring Laws Continuance Act 1957 (c.2)
Expiring Laws Continuance Act 1958 (c.4)
Expiring Laws Continuance Act 1959 (c.4)
Expiring Laws Continuance Act 1960 (c.4)
Expiring Laws Continuance Act 1961 (c.4)
Expiring Laws Continuance Act 1962 (c.3)
Expiring Laws Continuance Act 1963 (c.58)
Expiring Laws Continuance Act 1964 (c.94)
Expiring Laws Continuance Act 1965 (c.77)
Expiring Laws Continuance Act 1966 (c.40)
Expiring Laws Continuance Act 1967 (c.89)
Expiring Laws Continuance Act 1968 (c.76)
Expiring Laws Continuance Act 1970 (c.58)
Explosive Substances Act 1883 (c.3)
Explosives Act 1875 (c.17)
Explosives Act 1923 (c.17)
Explosives (Age of Purchase) Act 1976 (c.26)
Export and Investment Guarantees Act 1991 (c.67)
Export Duty Act 1804 (c.57)
Export Guarantees Act 1937 (c.61)
Export Guarantees Act 1939 (c.5)
Export Guarantees Act 1944 (c.9)
Export Guarantees Act 1948 (c.54)
Export Guarantees Act 1949 (c.14)
Export Guarantees Act 1952 (c.21)
Export Guarantees Act 1957 (c.23)
Export Guarantees Act 1959 (c.63)
Export Guarantees Act 1967 (c.11)
Export Guarantees Act 1968 (c.26)
Export Guarantees Act 1975 (c.38)
Export Guarantees Amendment Act 1975 (c.19)

Export Guarantees and Overseas Investment Act 1978 (c.18)
Export Guarantees and Payments Act 1970 (c.14)
Export Guarantees and Payments Act 1970 (c.15)
Export of Salted Beef, etc. (Ireland) Act 1807 (c.10)
Exportation Act 1705 (c.19)
Exportation Act 1707 (c.44)
Exportation Act 1709 (c.2)
Exportation Act 1709 (c.7)
Exportation Act 1730 (c.29)
Exportation Act 1740 (c.3)
Exportation Act 1753 (c.11)
Exportation Act 1753 (c.15)
Exportation Act 1756 (cc.15, 16)
Exportation Act 1757 (c.1)
Exportation Act 1757 (c.9)
Exportation Act 1757 (c.37)
Exportation Act 1758 (c.8)
Exportation Act 1759 (c.15)
Exportation Act 1759 (c.28)
Exportation Act 1768 (c.24)
Exportation Act 1769 (c.1)
Exportation Act 1770 (c.1)
Exportation Act 1770 (c.10)
Exportation Act 1770 (c.31)
Exportation Act 1770 (c.38)
Exportation Act 1771 (c.37)
Exportation Act 1771 (c.39)
Exportation Act 1772 (cc.1, 2)
Exportation Act 1774 (c.5)
Exportation Act 1774 (c.10)
Exportation Act 1774 (c.11)
Exportation Act 1774 (c.26)
Exportation Act 1774 (c.71)
Exportation Act 1775 (c.5)
Exportation Act 1776 (c.28)
Exportation Act 1776 (c.37)
Exportation Act 1778 (c.16)
Exportation Act 1780 (c.37)
Exportation Act 1780 (c.46)
Exportation Act 1783 (c.14)
Exportation Act 1783 (c.81)
Exportation Act 1785 (c.5)
Exportation Act 1785 (c.62)
Exportation Act 1785 (c.67)
Exportation Act 1786 (c.2)
Exportation Act 1786 (c.76)
Exportation Act 1786 (c.89)
Exportation Act 1788 (c.16)
Exportation Act 1788 (c.38)
Exportation Act 1788 (c.45)
Exportation Act 1792 (c.2)
Exportation Act 1792 (c.9)
Exportation Act 1793 (c.3)
Exportation Act 1794 (c.34)
Exportation Act 1795 (c.5)
Exportation Act 1796 (c.53)
Exportation Act 1797 (c.10)
Exportation Act 1797 (c.29)
Exportation Act 1797 (c.125)
Exportation Act 1798 (c.67)
Exportation Act 1799 (c.26)
Exportation Act 1799 (c.96)
Exportation Act 1800 (c.1)
Exportation Act 1800 (c.2)
Exportation Act 1800 (c.91)
Exportation Act 1801 (c.21)
Exportation Act 1803 (c.49)
Exportation Act 1803 (c.105)
Exportation Act 1804 (c.22)
Exportation Act 1804 (c.70)
Exportation Act 1804 (c.101)
Exportation Act 1806 (c.11)
Exportation Act 1806 (c.17)
Exportation Act 1806 (c.115)
Exportation Act 1806 (c.116)
Exportation Act 1807 (c.9)
Exportation Act 1807 (c.30)
Exportation Act 1807 (c.49)
Exportation Act 1808 (c.29)
Exportation Act 1808 (cc.33–35)
Exportation Act 1808 (c.44)
Exportation Act 1808 (c.69)
Exportation Act 1809 (c.23)
Exportation Act 1809 (cc.30, 31)
Exportation Act 1810 (c.26)
Exportation Act 1810 (c.34)
Exportation Act 1810 (c.60)
Exportation Act 1810 (c.63)
Exportation Act 1810 (c.64)
Exportation Act 1811 (c.50)
Exportation Act 1811 (c.57)
Exportation Act 1812 (c.25)
Exportation Act 1812 (c.45)
Exportation Act 1812 (c.140)
Exportation Act 1813 (c.7)
Exportation Act 1813 (c.30)
Exportation Act 1813 (cc.31, 32)
Exportation Act 1813 (c.38)
Exportation Act 1813 (c.40)
Exportation Act 1813 (c.45)
Exportation Act 1813 (c.98)
Exportation Act 1813 (c.125)
Exportation Act 1814 (c.57)
Exportation Act 1814 (c.100)
Exportation Act 1814 (c.127)
Exportation Act 1814 (c.142)
Exportation Act 1814 (c.185)
Exportation Act 1815 (c.180)
Exportation Act 1815 (c.183)
Exportation Act 1816 (c.76)
Exportation Act 1816 (c.92)
Exportation Act 1816 (c.109)
Exportation Act 1816 (c.127)
Exportation and Importation Act 1768 (cc.1–3)
Exportation and Importation Act 1795 (c.3)
Exportation and Importation Act 1795 (c.4)
Exportation and Importation Act 1796 (c.7)
Exportation and Importation Act 1797 (c.83)
Exportation and Importation Act 1803 (c.12)
Exportation and Importation Act 1804 (c.65)
Exportation and Importation Act 1805 (c.33)

Exportation and Importation Act 1808 (c.27)
Exportation and Importation Act 1811 (c.14)
Exportation and Importation Act 1811 (c.86)
Exportation and Importation Act 1813 (c.67)
Exportation and Importation Act 1815 (c.31)
Exportation and Importation Act 1815 (c.37)
Exportation and Importation (Great Britain) Act 1810 (cc.18, 19)
Exportation and Importation (Ireland) Act 1810 (cc.16, 17)
Exportation, etc. Act 1716 (c.21)
Exportation, etc. Act 1749 (c.14)
Exportation, etc. Act 1758 (c.2)
Exportation, etc. Act 1769 (c.28)
Exportation etc. Act 1771 (c.1)
Exportation, etc. Act 1778 (c.55)
Exportation, etc. Act 1784 (c.50)
Exportation, etc. Act 1801 (c.36)
Exportation, etc. Act 1808 (c.22)
Exportation (Ireland) Act 1807 (c.58)
Exportation (Ireland) Act 1809 (c.76)
Exportation of Arms Act 1900 (c.44)
Exportation of Army Clothing Act 1775 (c.45)
Exportation of Gunpowder Act 1803 (c.52)
Exportation of Horses Act 1914 (c.15)
Exportation of Horses Act 1937 (c.42)
Exportations, etc. Act 1704 (c.7)
Exportations, etc. Act 1780 (c.59)
Exportations, etc. Act 1802 (cc.12, 13)
Exports Act 1786 (c.40)
Exports Act 1787 (c.31)
Extension of Polling Hours Act 1913 (c.6)
Extradition Act 1843 (cc.75, 76)
Extradition Act 1845 (c.120)
Extradition Act 1862 (c.70)
Extradition Act 1866 (c.121)
Extradition Act 1870 (c.52)
Extradition Act 1873 (c.60)
Extradition Act 1895 (c.33)
Extradition Act 1906 (c.15)
Extradition Act 1931 (c.39)
Extradition Act 1932 (c.39)
Extradition Act 1989 (c.33)
Extraordinary Tithe Act 1897 (c.23)
Extraordinary Tithe Redemption Act 1886 (c.54)
Extra-Parochial Places Act 1857 (c.19)
Eyemouth Harbour Act 1797 (c.49)
Eynsham Bridge Act 1767 (c.68)

Fabrics (Misdescription) Act 1913 (c.17)
Factories Act 1802 (c.73)
Factories Act 1937 (c.67)
Factories Act 1844 (c.15)
Factories Act 1847 (c.29)
Factories Act 1850 (c.54)
Factories Act 1853 (c.104)
Factories Act 1856 (c.38)
Factories Act 1948 (c.55)
Factories Act 1959 (c.67)
Factories Act 1961 (c.34)
Factors Act 1842 (c.39)
Factors Act 1889 (c.45)
Factors Acts Amendment 1877 (c.39)
Factors (Scotland) Act 1890 (c.40)
Factory Act 1874 (c.44)
Factory Acts Extension Act 1864 (c.48)
Factory Acts Extension Act 1867 (c.103)
Factory and Workshop Act 1870 (c.62)
Factory and Workshop Act 1871 (c.104)
Factory and Workshop Act 1878 (c.16)
Factory and Workshop Act 1883 (c.53)
Factory and Workshop Act 1891 (c.75)
Factory and Workshop Act 1895 (c.37)
Factory and Workshop Act 1901 (c.22)
Factory and Workshop Act 1907 (c.39)
Factory and Workshop Amendment (Scotland) Act 1888 (c.22)
Factory and Workshop (Cotton Cloth Factories) Act 1911 (c.21)
Factory and Workshop (Cotton Cloth Factories) Act 1929 (c.15)
Failure of Corn Crop Act 1783 (c.53)
Fair Employment (Northern Ireland) Act 1976 (c.25)
Fair Employment (Northern Ireland) Act 1989 (c.32)
Fair Trading Act 1973 (c.41)
Fairs Act 1868 (c.51)
Fairs Act 1871 (c.12)
Fairs Act 1873 (c.37)
Fairs and Market Act 1850 (c.23)
Fairs (Ireland) Act 1868 (c.12)
Falmouth Gaol Act 1865 (c.103)
False Alarms of Fire Act 1895 (c.28)
False Oaths (Scotland) Act 1933 (c.20)
False Personation Act 1874 (c.36)
False Weights and Scales Act 1770 (c.44)
Falsification of Accounts Act 1875 (c.24)
Families of Militiamen Act 1793 (c.8)
Families of Militiamen Act 1795 (c.81)
Families of Militiamen, etc. Act 1794 (c.47)
Families of Militiamen, etc. Act 1796 (c.114)
Family Allowances Act 1944 (c.41)
Family Allowances Act 1965 (c.53)
Family Allowances and National Insurance Act 1952 (c.29)
Family Allowances and National Insurance Act 1956 (c.50)
Family Allowances and National Insurance Act 1959 (c.18)
Family Allowances and National Insurance Act 1961 (c.6)
Family Allowances and National Insurance Act 1963 (c.10)
Family Allowances and National Insurance Act 1967 (c.90)
Family Allowances and National Insurance Act 1968 (c.40)
Family Income Supplements Act 1970 (c.55)
Family Law Act 1986 (c.55)
Family Law Reform Act 1969 (c.46)
Family Law Reform Act 1987 (c.42)
Family Law (Scotland) Act 1985 (c.37)
Family of Rt. Hon. S. Perceval Act 1812 (c.67)

Family Provision Act 1966 (c.35)
Farm and Garden Chemicals Act 1967 (c.50)
Farm Land and Rural Development Act 1988 (c.16)
Farnborough and Seven Oaks Road Act 1796 (c.128)
Farnborough to Seven Oaks Road Act 1773 (c.92)
Farnhurst, Chichester and Delkey Road Act 1797 (c.148)
Farriers (Registration) Act 1975 (c.35)
Farriers (Registration) (Amendment) Act 1977 (c.31)
Farringdon to Burford Road 1771 (c.84)
Fatal Accidents Act 1846 (c.93)
Fatal Accidents Act 1864 (c.95)
Fatal Accidents Act 1959 (c.65)
Fatal Accidents Act 1976 (c.30)
Fatal Accidents and Sudden Deaths Inquiry (Scotland) Act 1906 (c.35)
Fatal Accidents and Sudden Deaths Inquiry (Scotland) Act 1976 (c.14)
Fatal Accidents (Damages) Act 1908 (c.7)
Fatal Accidents Inquiry (Scotland) Act 1895 (c.36)
Faversham (Improvement) Act 1789 (c.69)
Faversham, Portsmouth, Plymouth Fortifications Act 1786 (c.94)
Federal Council of Australasia Act 1885 (c.60)
Federation of Malaya Independence Act 1957 (c.60)
Fee-Farm Rents (Ireland) Act 1851 (c.20)
Fees, etc., in Public Offices (Ireland) Act 1807 (c.41)
Fees etc., in Public Offices, etc. (Ireland) Act 1811 (c.81)
Fees for Pardons Act 1818 (c.29)
Fees in Public Offices, etc. Act 1809 (c.51)
Fees in Public Offices, etc. (Ireland) Act 1810 (c.81)
Fees in Public Offices, etc. (Ireland) Act 1812 (c.92)
Fees (Increase) Act 1923 (c.4)
Fees of Coroners (Ireland) Act 1810 (c.30)
Fees, Officers of the Exchequer Act 1786 (c.99)
Fees, Port of London, etc. Act 1806 (c.82)
Felony Act 1819 (c.27)
Felony Act 1841 (c.22)
Felony and Piracy Act 1772 (c.20)
Fencibles Act 1793 (c.36)
Fen Drainage Act 1749 (c.18)
Fen Drainage Act 1758 (c.13)
Fen Drainage Act 1774 (c.16)
Fen Drainage Act 1775 (c.65)
Fen Drainage Act 1776 (c.64)
Ferries (Acquisition by Local Authorities) Act 1919 (c.75)
Ferrybridge and Boroughbridge Road Act 1753 (c.77)
Fertilisers and Feeding Stuffs Act 1893 (c.56)
Fertilisers and Feeding Stuffs Act 1906 (c.27)
Fertilisers and Feeding Stuffs Act 1926 (c.45)
Festival of Britain (Additional Loans) Act 1951 (c.47)
Festival of Britain (Sunday Opening) Act 1951 (c.14)
Festival of Britain (Supplementary Provisions) Act (c.102)
Festival Pleasure Gardens 1952 (c.13)
Feudal Casualties (Scotland) Act 1914 (c.48)
Fever (Ireland) Act 1846 (c.6)
Fever (Ireland) Act 1847 (c.22)
Fever (Ireland) Act 1848 (c.131)
Field Monuments Act 1972 (c.43)
Fife (Country) Roads Act 1797 (c.180)
Fife Roads Act 1772 (c.83)
Fife Roads Act 1790 (c.93)
Fife Roads and Bridges Act 1774 (c.31)
Fifield, St. John's and Newbridge Road Act 1763 (c.29)
Fiji Independence Act 1970 (c.50)
Fiji Marriage Act 1878 (c.61)
Film Levy Finance Act 1981 (c.16)
Films Act 1960 (c.57)
Films Act 1964 (c.52)
Films Act 1966 (c.48)
Films Act 1970 (c.26)
Films Act 1979 (c.9)
Films Act 1980 (c.41)
Films Act 1985 (c.21)
Finance Act 1894 (c.30)
Finance Act 1895 (c.16)
Finance Act 1896 (c.28)
Finance Act 1897 (c.24)
Finance Act 1898 (c.10)
Finance Act 1899 (c.9)
Finance Act 1900 (c.7)
Finance Act 1901 (c.7)
Finance Act 1902 (c.7)
Finance Act 1903 (c.8)
Finance Act 1904 (c.7)
Finance Act 1905 (c.4)
Finance Act 1906 (c.8)
Finance Act 1907 (c.13)
Finance Act 1908 (c.16)
Finance (1909–10) Act 1910 (c.8)
Finance Act 1910 (c.35)
Finance Act 1911 (c.48)
Finance Act 1912 (c.8)
Finance Act 1913 (c.30)
Finance Act 1914 (c.10)
Finance Act 1915 (c.62)
Finance Act 1916 (c.24)
Finance Act 1917 (c.31)
Finance Act 1918 (c.15)
Finance Act 1919 (c.32)
Finance Act 1920 (c.18)
Finance Act 1921 (c.32)
Finance Act 1922 (c.17)
Finance Act 1923 (c.14)
Finance Act 1924 (c.21)
Finance Act 1925 (c.36)
Finance Act 1926 (c.22)
Finance Act 1927 (c.10)

Finance Act 1928 (c.17)
Finance Act 1929 (c.21)
Finance Act 1930 (c.28)
Finance Act 1931 (c.25)
Finance Act 1931 (c.28)
Finance Act 1932 (c.25)
Finance Act 1933 (c.19)
Finance Act 1934 (c.32)
Finance Act 1935 (c.24)
Finance Act 1936 (c.34)
Finance Act 1937 (c.54)
Finance Act 1938 (c.46)
Finance Act 1939 (c.41)
Finance Act 1940 (c.29)
Finance Act 1941 (c.30)
Finance Act 1942 (c.21)
Finance Act 1943 (c.28)
Finance Act 1944 (c.23)
Finance Act 1945 (c.24)
Finance Act 1946 (c.64)
Finance Act 1947 (c.35)
Finance Act 1948 (c.49)
Finance Act 1949 (c.47)
Finance Act 1950 (c.15)
Finance Act 1951 (c.43)
Finance Act 1952 (c.33)
Finance Act 1953 (c.34)
Finance Act 1954 (c.44)
Finance Act 1955 (c.15)
Finance Act 1956 (c.54)
Finance Act 1957 (c.49)
Finance Act 1958 (c.56)
Finance Act 1959 (c.58)
Finance Act 1960 (c.44)
Finance Act 1961 (c.36)
Finance Act 1962 (c.44)
Finance Act 1963 (c.25)
Finance Act 1964 (c.49)
Finance Act 1965 (c.25)
Finance Act 1966 (c.18)
Finance Act 1967 (c.54)
Finance Act 1968 (c.44)
Finance Act 1969 (c.32)
Finance Act 1970 (c.24)
Finance Act 1971 (c.68)
Finance Act 1972 (c.41)
Finance Act 1973 (c.51)
Finance Act 1974 (c.30)
Finance Act 1975 (c.7)
Finance Act 1976 (c.40)
Finance Act 1977 (c.36)
Finance Act 1978 (c.42)
Finance Act 1979 (c.25)
Finance Act 1980 (c.48)
Finance Act 1981 (c.35)
Finance Act 1982 (c.39)
Finance Act 1983 (c.28)
Finance Act 1984 (c.43)
Finance Act 1985 (c.54)
Finance Act 1986 (c.41)
Finance Act 1987 (c.16)
Finance Act 1988 (c.39)
Finance Act 1989 (c.26)
Finance Act 1990 (c.29)
Finance Act 1991 (c.31)
Finance Act 1992 (c.20)
Finance Act 1993 (c.34)
Finance Act 1994 (c.9)
Finance Act 1995 (c.4)
Finance (Exchequer Bonds) Amendment Act 1916 (c.36)
Finance (Income Tax Reliefs) Act 1977 (c.53)
Finance (New Duties) Act 1916 (c.11)
Finance (No. 2) Act 1915 (c.89)
Finance (No. 2) Act 1931 (c.49)
Finance (No. 2) Act 1939 (c.109)
Finance (No. 2) Act 1940 (c.48)
Finance (No. 2) Act 1945 (c.13)
Finance (No. 2) Act 1947 (c.9)
Finance (No. 2) Act 1955 (c.17)
Finance (No. 2) Act 1964 (c.92)
Finance (No. 2) Act 1975 (c.45)
Finance (No. 2) Act 1979 (c.47)
Finance (No. 2) Act 1983 (c.49)
Finance (No. 2) Act 1987 (c.51)
Finance (No. 2) Act 1992 (c.48)
Finance (Session 2) Act 1914 (c.7)
Financial Emergency Enactments (Cont.) Act 1931 (c.13)
Financial Powers (U.S.A. Securities) Act 1941 (c.36)
Financial Services Act 1986 (c.60)
Findhorn Harbour Act 1778 (c.70)
Finding of the Longitude at Sea Act 1776 (c.48)
Finding of the Longitude at Sea Act 1780 (c.52)
Finding of the Longitude at Sea Act 1780 (c.61)
Fine Arts Copyright Act 1862 (c.68)
Fine or Imprisonment (Scotland and Ireland) Act 1899 (c.11)
Fines Act 1833 (c.99)
Fines Act (Ireland) 1851 (c.90)
Fines Act (Ireland) 1851, Amendment Act 1874 (c.72)
Fines Act (Ireland) 1874 (c.72)
Fines and Penalties (Ireland) Act 1839 (c.92)
Fines and Recoveries Act 1833 (c.74)
Fines and Recoveries Act 1842 (c.32)
Fines and Recoveries Act 1848 (c.70)
Fines and Recoveries (Ireland) Act 1834 (c.82)
Fines by Justices Act 1801 (c.85)
Fines, etc. (Ireland) Act 1838 (c.99)
Fines, etc. (Ireland) Act 1843 (c.56)
Fines (Ireland) Act 1851 (c.90)
Fines on Stills Act 1810 (c.100)
Finsbury Square Act 1791 (c.90)
Finsbury Square (Paving, Watching, etc.) Act 1795 (c.45)
Fire Brigade Pensions Act 1925 (c.47)
Fire Brigade Pensions Act 1929 (c.35)
Fire Brigades Act 1938 (c.72)
Fire Insurance Duty Act 1782 (c.48)
Fire Precautions Act 1971 (c.40)

Fire Precautions (Loans) Act 1973 (c.11)
Fire Prevention (Metropolis) Act 1774 (c.78)
Fire Safety and Safety of Places of Sport Act 1987 (c.27)
Fire Service College Board (Abolition) Act 1982 (c.13)
Fire Services Act 1947 (c.41)
Fire Services Act 1951 (c.27)
Fire Services Act 1959 (c.44)
Fire Services (Emergency Provisions) Act 1941 (c.22)
Firearms Act 1813 (c.115)
Firearms Act 1815 (c.59)
Firearms Act 1934 (c.16)
Firearms Act 1937 (c.12)
Firearms Act 1965 (c.44)
Firearms Act 1968 (c.27)
Firearms Act 1982 (c.31)
Firearms (Amendment) Act 1936 (c.39)
Firearms (Amendment) Act 1988 (c.45)
Firearms (Amendment) Act 1992 (c.31)
Firearms (Amendment) Act 1994 (c.31)
Firearms and Imitation Firearms (Criminal Use) Act 1933 (c.50)
Fires Prevention Act 1785 (c.77)
Fires Prevention Act 1838 (c.75)
Fireworks Act 1951 (c.58)
Fireworks Act 1964 (c.23)
First Meetings of Certain Commissioners Act 1786 (c.95)
First Meetings of Commissioners Act 1808 (c.133)
First Meetings of Commissioners, etc. Act 1776 (c.36)
First Meetings of Commissioners, etc. Act 1779 (c.55)
First Meetings of Commissioners, etc. Act 1782 (c.74)
First Offenders Act 1958 (c.31)
First Offenders (Scotland) Act 1960 (c.23)
First Public Health Supplemental Act 1852 (c.41)
Fish Act 1705 (c.8)
Fish Act 1714 (c.18)
Fish Act 1756 (c.39)
Fish Act 1759 (c.27)
Fish Act 1796 (c.118)
Fish Act 1801 (c.3)
Fish Act 1801 (c.99)
Fish Carriage Act 1762 (c.15)
Fish Market, Westminster Act 1748 (c.49)
Fish, Newfoundland, etc. Act 1801 (c.77)
Fish Teinds (Scotland) Act 1864 (c.33)
Fisheries Act 1780 (c.60)
Fisheries Act 1785 (c.65)
Fisheries Act 1786 (c.41)
Fisheries Act 1786 (c.81)
Fisheries Act 1787 (c.10)
Fisheries Act 1891 (c.37)
Fisheries Act 1955 (c.7)
Fisheries Act 1981 (c.29)
Fisheries Close Season (Ireland) Act 1895 (c.29)
Fisheries, Continuance of Laws Act 1801 (c.97)
Fisheries, Convention with France Act 1839 (c.96)
Fisheries, Convention with France Act 1840 (c.69)
Fisheries, Convention with France Act 1842 (c.63)
Fisheries (Dynamite) Act 1877 (c.65)
Fisheries in Greenland Seas, etc. Act 1799 (c.101)
Fisheries (Ireland) Act 1807 (c.22)
Fisheries (Ireland) Act 1842 (c.106)
Fisheries (Ireland) Act 1844 (c.108)
Fisheries (Ireland) Act 1845 (c.108)
Fisheries (Ireland) Act 1846 (c.3)
Fisheries (Ireland) Act 1846 (c.114)
Fisheries (Ireland) Act 1848 (c.92)
Fisheries (Ireland) Act 1850 (c.88)
Fisheries (Ireland) Act 1869 (c.92)
Fisheries (Ireland) Act 1901 (c.38)
Fisheries (Ireland) Act 1909 (c.25)
Fisheries (Norfolk and Suffolk) Act 1896 (c.18)
Fisheries (Oyster, Crab and Lobster) Act 1877 (c.42)
Fisheries (Oyster, Crab and Lobster) Act (1877) Amendment 1884 (c.26)
Fisheries (Scotland) Act 1726 (c.30)
Fisheries (Scotland) Act 1756 (c.23)
Fisheries (Severn and Verniew) Act 1778 (c.33)
Fishery Act 1791 (c.22)
Fishery Act 1794 (c.22)
Fishery Board (Scotland) Act 1882 (c.78)
Fishery Boards (Scotland) Extension of Powers Act 1894 (c.14)
Fishery Convention with France Act 1855 (c.101)
Fishery Harbours Act 1915 (c.48)
Fishery Harbours (Continuance of Powers) Act 1917 (c.39)
Fishery (Ireland) Act 1888 (c.30)
Fishery Limits Act 1964 (c.72)
Fishery Limits Act 1976 (c.86)
Fishery Treaty with United States Act 1855 (c.3)
Fishguard Roads Act 1791 (c.106)
Fishhouse Bridge Lancashire Act 1750 (c.36)
Fishing Vessel Grants Act 1967 (c.35)
Fishing Vessels (Safety Provisions) Act 1970 (c.27)
Flax and Cotton Manufactures Act 1789 (c.54)
Flax and Hemp Seed (Ireland) Act 1810 (c.82)
Flax Companies (Financial Assistance) Act 1918 (c.24)
Flax, etc., Manufacture Act 1783 (c.77)
Flax, etc. Manufacture (Great Britain) Act 1815 (c.178)
Flax Seed (Ireland) Act 1809 (c.29)
Fleet Ditch Act 1732 (c.22)

Flint and Carnarvon Roads Act 1779 (c.107)
Flint Canal Act 1788 (c.72)
Flint Roads Act 1769 (c.45)
Flint Roads Act 1771 (c.69)
Flint Roads Act 1788 (c.101)
Flintshire Roads Act 1763 (c.44)
Flood Prevention (Scotland) Act 1961 (c.41)
Folkestone: Improvement Act 1796 (c.49)
Folkestone Parish Church Act 1766 (c.63)
Food Act 1984 (c.30)
Food and Drugs Act 1938 (c.56)
Food and Drugs Act 1955 (c.16)
Food and Drugs (Amendment) Act 1954 (c.67)
Food and Drugs (Amendment) Act 1981 (c.26)
Food and Drugs (Amendment) Act 1982 (c.26)
Food and Drugs (Control of Food Premises) Act 1976 (c.37)
Food and Drugs (Milk) Act 1970 (c.3)
Food and Drugs (Milk and Dairies) Act 1944 (c.29)
Food and Drugs (Milk and Dairies and Artificial Cream) Act 1950 (c.35)
Food and Drugs (Scotland) Act 1956 (c.30)
Food and Environment Protection Act 1985 (c.48)
Food Safety Act 1990 (c.16)
Foods and Drugs (Adulteration) Act 1928 (c.31)
Foodstuffs (Prevention of Exploitation) Act 1931 (c.51)
Football (Offences) Act 1991 (c.19)
Football Spectators Act 1989 (c.37)
Forces Act 1922 (c.11)
Forces of East India Company Act 1799 (c.109)
Forces of East India Company Act 1805 (c.36)
Forces of East India Company Act 1812 (c.122)
Forcible Entry Act 1381 (c.7)
Forcible Entry Act 1429 (c.9)
Forcible Entry Act 1588 (c.1588)
Forcible Entry Act 1623 (c.15)
Forcible Entry (Ireland) Act 1786 (c.24)
Forehoe, Norfolk (Borrowing Powers of Guardians) Act 1783 (c.29)
Forehoe, Norfolk (Guardians' Borrowing Powers) Act 1789 (c.4)
Forehoe, Norfolk: Poor Relief Act 1776 (c.9)
Foreign and Protestants Naturalization Act 1708 (c.5)
Foreign Compensation Act 1950 (c.12)
Foreign Compensation Act 1962 (c.4)
Foreign Compensation Act 1969 (c.20)
Foreign Compensation (Amendment) Act 1993 (c.16)
Foreign Corporations Act 1991 (c.44)
Foreign Deserters Act 1852 (c.26)
Foreign Enlistment Act 1735 (c.30)
Foreign Enlistment Act 1756 (c.17)
Foreign Enlistment Act 1870 (c.90)
Foreign Judgments (Reciprocal Enforcement) Act 1933 (c.13)
Foreign Jurisdiction Act 1844 (c.94)
Foreign Jurisdiction Act 1875 (c.85)
Foreign Jurisdiction Act 1878 (c.67)
Foreign Jurisdiction Act 1890 (c.37)
Foreign Jurisdiction Act 1913 (c.16)
Foreign Jurisdiction Act Amendment Act 1865 (c.16)
Foreign Jurisdiction Act Amendment Act 1866 (c.87)
Foreign Jurisdiction Act Foreign Law Ascertainment Act 1861 (c.11)
Foreign Law Ascertainment Act 1861 (c.11)
Foreign Limitation Periods Act 1984 (c.16)
Foreign Marriage Act 1891 (c.74)
Foreign Marriage Act 1892 (c.23)
Foreign Marriage Act 1947 (c.33)
Foreign Marriage (Amendment) Act 1988 (c.44)
Foreign Prison-Made Goods Act 1897 (c.63)
Foreign Protestants Naturalization Act 1714 (c.29)
Foreign Service Act 1943 (c.35)
Foreign Service Act 1960 (c.11)
Foreign Ships Act 1797 (c.63)
Foreign Ships, etc. Act 1805 (c.32)
Foreign Tribunals Evidence Act 1856 (c.113)
Forest of Dean Act 1836 (c.3)
Forest of Dean Act 1844 (c.13)
Forest of Dean (Poor Relief) Act 1842 (c.48)
Forestalling, Regrating, etc. Act 1844 (c.24)
Forestry Act 1919 (c.58)
Forestry Act 1921 (c.61)
Forestry Act 1927 (c.6)
Forestry Act 1944 (c.35)
Forestry Act 1947 (c.21)
Forestry Act 1951 (c.61)
Forestry Act 1967 (c.10)
Forestry Act 1979 (c.21)
Forestry Act 1981 (c.39)
Forestry Act 1986 (c.30)
Forestry Act 1991 (c.43)
Forestry (Sale of Land) (Scotland) Act 1963 (c.23)
Forestry (Transfer of Woods) Act 1923 (c.21)
Forfar Roads Act 1789 (c.20)
Forfar Roads Act 1794 (c.100)
Forfeited and Unclaimed Prize Money Act 1811 (c.104)
Forfeited Estates Act 1703 (c.61)
Forfeited Estates—Derwentwater Estate Act 1731 (c.23)
Forfeited Estates, etc. Act 1718 (c.23)
Forfeited Estates—Greenwich Hospital Act 1734 (c.29)
Forfeited Estates (Ireland) Act 1705 (c.11)
Forfeited Estates (Ireland) Act 1703 (c.19)
Forfeited Estates (Ireland) etc. Act 1703 (c.21)
Forfeited Estates (Scotland) Act 1774 (c.65)
Forfeited Estates, Scotland Act 1786 (c.27)

Forfeited Estates (Time for Claims) Act 1716 (c.20)
Forfeiture Act 1870 (c.23)
Forfeiture Act 1982 (c.34)
Forfeiture upon Attainder of Treason Act 1799 (c.93)
Forged Exchequer Bills Act 1842 (c.11)
Forged Exchequer Bills Act 1843 (c.1)
Forged Transfers Act 1891 (c.43)
Forged Transfers Act 1892 (c.36)
Forgeries and Frauds in Bank Transfers Act 1793 (c.30)
Forgery Act 1733 (c.22)
Forgery Act 1778 (c.18)
Forgery Act 1797 (c.122)
Forgery Act 1830 (c.66)
Forgery Act 1837 (c.84)
Forgery Act 1861 (c.98)
Forgery Act 1870 (c.58)
Forgery Act 1913 (c.27)
Forgery and Counterfeiting Act 1981 (c.45)
Forgery of Bank of Ireland Notes, etc. Act 1809 (c.13)
Forgery of Banknotes Act 1801 (c.39)
Forgery of Foreign Bills Act 1803 (c.139)
Form of Deeds Act (Scotland) 1856 (c.89)
Former Enemy Aliens (Disabilities Removal) Act 1925 (c.43)
Forms of Pleading Act 1838 (c.100)
Forms of Pleading in High Court Act 1855 (c.26)
Forsyth's Indemnity Act 1866 (c.20)
Fort Marlborough in India Act 1802 (c.29)
Fort of Senegal Act 1763 (c.20)
Fort William in Bengal Act 1786 (c.25)
Fort William Pulp and Paper Mills Act 1963 (c.15)
Forth and Clyde and Monkland Canal Act 1790 (c.73)
Forth and Clyde Canal (Extinguishment of Rights of Navigation) Act 1962 (c.16)
Forth and Clyde Navigation Act 1768 (c.63)
Forth and Clyde, Navigation Act 1771 (c.62)
Forth and Clyde, Navigation Act 1773 (c.104)
Forth and Clyde: Navigation Act 1784 (c.59)
Forth and Clyde: Navigation Act 1787 (c.20)
Forth and Clyde: Navigation Act 1787 (c.55)
Fortifications Act 1708 (c.26)
Fortifications Act 1709 (c.23)
Fortifications Act 1757 (cc.38, 39)
Fortifications (Expenses) Act 1869 (c.76)
Fortifications for Royal Arsenals, etc. Act 1863 (c.80)
Fortifications for Royal Arsenals, etc. Act 1864 (c.109)
Fortifications - Portsmouth Act 1722 (c.32)
Fortifications - Portsmouth and Dover Act 1806 (c.105)
Fortifications, Portsmouth and Dover Act 1809 (c.39)
Fortifications, Royal Arsenals, etc. Act 1865 (c.61)
Fosdyke Bridge Act 1984 (c.17)
Foss, York: Navigation Act 1793 (c.99)
Foster Children Act 1980 (c.6)
Foster Children (Scotland) Act 1984 (c.56)
Foston Bridge and Witham Common Road Act 1725 (c.16)
Founding Hospital Act 1739 (c.29)
Foundling Hospital, Dublin Act 1801 (c.50)
Four and a Half Per Cent, Duties Repeal Act 1838 (c.92)
Four Courts Library Act 1894 (c.4)
Four Courts Marshalsea Discontinuance Act 1874 (c.21)
Four Courts Marshalsea (Ireland) Act 1842 (c.95)
Foyle College Act 1874 (c.79)
Frame Work Knitters Act 1766 (c.29)
Frampton Mansel Marriage Act 1868 (c.23)
Franchise Prisons Abolition Act 1858 (c.22)
Frauds by Boatmen and Others, etc. Act 1809 (c.122)
Frauds by Boatmen, etc. Act 1813 (c.87)
Frauds by Boatmen in Cinque Ports, etc. Act 1808 (c.130)
Frauds by Journeymen Shoemakers Act 1722 (c.27)
Frauds by Workmen Act 1748 (c.27)
Frauds by Workmen Act 1777 (c.56)
Frauds, etc., in Woollen Manufacturers Act 1774 (c.25)
Frauds in Excise Revenue Act 1791 (c.21)
Frauds in Excise Revenue Act 1792 (c.8)
Frauds in Manufacture of Clocks, etc. Act 1754 (c.7)
Frauds in Manufacture of Sweets Act 1815 (c.177)
Frauds in the Public Revenues, etc. Act 1738 (c.72)
Frauds of Workmen Act 1739 (c.8)
Frauds on Exportation Act 1810 (c.53)
Fraudulent Bankrupts (Scotland) Act 1827 (c.20)
Fraudulent Mediums Act 1951 (c.33)
Free Fishers of Whitstable Act 1793 (c.42)
Free Ports Act 1796 (c.55)
Free Ports Act 1797 (c.77)
Free Ports Act 1800 (c.23)
Free Ports, Jamaica Act 1774 (c.41)
Free Ports, West Indies, etc. Act 1766 (c.49)
Freeman (Admission) Act 1763 (c.15)
Freshwater and Salmon Fisheries (Scotland) Act 1976 (c.22)
Freshwater Fish (Scotland) Act 1902 (c.29)
Freshwater Fisheries Act 1878 (c.39)
Freshwater Fisheries Act 1884 (c.11)
Freshwater Fisheries Act 1886 (c.2)
Friendly and Industrial and Provident Societies Act 1968 (c.55)
Friendly Societies Act 1793 (c.54)
Friendly Societies Act 1795 (c.111)
Friendly Societies Act 1803 (c.111)
Friendly Societies Act 1809 (c.125)
Friendly Societies Act 1840 (c.73)
Friendly Societies Act 1846 (c.27)

Friendly Societies Act 1850 (c.115)
Friendly Societies Act 1852 (c.65)
Friendly Societies Act 1854 (c.101)
Friendly Societies Act 1855 (c.63)
Friendly Societies Act 1858 (c.101)
Friendly Societies Act 1860 (c.13)
Friendly Societies Act 1860 (c.58)
Friendly Societies Act 1875 (c.60)
Friendly Societies Act 1879 (c.9)
Friendly Societies Act 1887 (c.56)
Friendly Societies Act 1888 (c.66)
Friendly Societies Act 1889 (c.22)
Friendly Societies Act 1893 (c.30)
Friendly Societies Act 1895 (c.26)
Friendly Societies Act 1896 (c.25)
Friendly Societies Act 1908 (c.32)
Friendly Societies Act 1916 (c.54)
Friendly Societies Act 1924 (c.11)
Friendly Societies Act 1955 (c.19)
Friendly Societies Act 1971 (c.66)
Friendly Societies Act 1974 (c.46)
Friendly Societies Act 1981 (c.50)
Friendly Societies Act 1984 (c.62)
Friendly Societies Act 1992 (c.40)
Friendly Societies Amendment Act 1876 (c.32)
Friendly Society Amendment Act 1885 (c.27)
Friendly Societies Discharge Act 1854 (c.56)
Friendly Societies (Ireland) Act 1809 (c.58)
Friendly Societies (Quinquennial Returns) Act 1882 (c.35)
Frivolous Arrests Act 1725 (c.29)
Frivolous Arrests Act 1811 (c.124)
Frivolous Suits Act 1772 (c.51)
Frivolous Suits Act 1841 (c.28)
Frogmore House Act 1841 (c.2)
Frome Roads Act 1757 (c.39)
Frome Roads Act 1772 (c.94)
Frome Roads Act 1797 (c.175)
Fuel and Electricity (Control) Act 1973 (c.67)
Fugitive Offenders Act 1881 (c.69)
Fugitive Offenders Act 1967 (c.68)
Fugitive Offenders (Protected States) Act 1915 (c.39)
Fulbourne Church Act 1775 (c.49)
Fulham and Putney Bridge Act 1725 (c.36)
Fulham Bridge Act 1727 (c.18)
Fulham Roads Act 1730 (c.34)
Fulham Roads Act 1749 (c.16)
Fund for Fire Victims in Edinburgh Act 1727 (c.22)
Furnished Houses (Rent Control) Act 1946 (c.34)
Furnished Lettings (Rent Allowances) Act 1973 (c.6)
Further and Higher Education Act 1992 (c.13)
Further and Higher Education (Scotland) Act 1992 (c.37)
Further Education Act 1985 (c.47)

Gainsborough Bridge Act 1787 (c.15)
Gainsborough Church Act 1735 (c.22)
Gainsborough Church Act 1740 (c.15)
Gainsborough: Improvement Act 1769 (c.21)
Gainsborough: Inclosure Act 1796 (c.101)
Gainsborough Inclosure, etc. Act 1795 (c.82)
Galashiels Act 1867 (c.85)
Galashiels and Selkirk Act 1872 (c.47)
Galway Harbour Act 1859 (c.28)
Galway Harbour Act 1867 (c.56)
Gambia Independence Act 1964 (c.93)
Game Act 1706 (c.16)
Game Act 1710 (c.27)
Game Act 1716 (c.11)
Game Act 1721 (c.19)
Game Act 1755 (c.12)
Game Act 1762 (c.19)
Game Act 1766 (c.21)
Game Act 1770 (c.19)
Game Act 1773 (c.80)
Game Act 1796 (c.39)
Game Act 1796 (c.54)
Game Act 1831 (c.32)
Game Act 1970 (c.13)
Game Birds (Ireland) Act 1874 (c.11)
Game Certificates Act 1784 (c.43)
Game Certificates Act 1785 (c.50)
Game Certificates (Ireland) Act 1842 (c.81)
Game (England) Act 1772 (c.55)
Game Laws (Amendment) Act 1960 (c.36)
Game Laws Amendment (Scotland) Act 1877 (c.28)
Game Laws (England); Local Taxes, etc. (Scotland) Act 1836 (c.65)
Game Licences Act 1860 (c.90)
Game (Scotland) Act 1750 (c.34)
Game (Scotland) Act 1772 (c.54)
Game Trespass (Ireland) Act 1864 (c.67)
Gamekeepers Act 1808 (c.93)
Gaming Act 1710 (c.19)
Gaming Act 1738 (c.28)
Gaming Act 1739 (c.19)
Gaming Act 1744 (c.34)
Gaming Act 1802 (c.119)
Gaming Act 1845 (c.109)
Gaming Act 1892 (c.9)
Gaming Act 1922 (c.19)
Gaming Act 1968 (c.65)
Gaming Act (Northern Ireland) 1845 (c.109)
Gaming (Amendment) Act 1973 (c.12)
Gaming (Amendment) Act 1982 (c.22)
Gaming (Amendment) Act 1980 (c.8)
Gaming (Amendment) Act 1986 (c.11)
Gaming (Amendment) Act 1987 (c.11)
Gaming (Amendment) Act 1990 (c.26)
Gaming (Bingo) Act 1985 (c.35)
Gaming Houses Act 1854 (c.38)
Gaming Machines (Scotland) Act 1917 (c.23)
Gaming Transactions Act 1844 (c.7)
Gaol Fees Abolition Act 1815 (c.50)
Gaol Fees Abolition Act 1845 (c.114)
Gaols Act 1772 (c.58)
Gaols Act 1784 (c.54)
Gaols Act 1789 (c.67)
Gaols Act 1791 (c.46)

Garrotters Act 1863 (c.44)
Gas Act 1948 (c.67)
Gas Act 1960 (c.27)
Gas Act 1965 (c.36)
Gas Act 1972 (c.60)
Gas Act 1980 (c.37)
Gas Act 1986 (c.44)
Gas Act 1995 (c.45)
Gas and Electricity Act 1968 (c.39)
Gas and Electricity (Borrowing Powers) Act 1954 (c.52)
Gas and Steam Vehicles (Excise Duties) Act 1939 (c.6)
Gas and Water Works Facilities Act 1870 (c.70)
Gas and Water Works Facilities Act, 1870, Amendment 1873 (c.89)
Gas (Borrowing Powers) Act 1965 (c.60)
Gas (Exempt Supplies) Act 1993 (c.1)
Gas Levy Act 1981 (c.3)
Gas (Standard of Calorific Power) Act 1916 (c.25)
Gas Undertakings Act 1929 (c.24)
Gas Undertakings Act 1931 (c.40)
Gas Undertakings Act 1934 (c.28)
Gasworks Clauses Act 1847 (c.15)
Gasworks Clauses Act 1871 (c.41)
General Board of Health Act 1856 (c.85)
General Board of Health Act 1857 (c.38)
General Board of Health Continuance Act 1855 (c.115)
General de Lancey (Crown Claims) Act 1807 (c.69)
General de Lancey (Estates and Crown Claims) Act 1811 (c.102)
General Dealers (Ireland) Act 1903 (c.44)
General Pardon Act (c.19)
General Pardon Act 1707 (c.22)
General Pardon Act 1720 (c.29)
General Pardon Act 1746 (c.52)
General Pier and Harbour Act 1861 (c.45)
General Pier and Harbour Act, 1861, Amendment Act 1862 (c.19)
General Police and Improvement (Scotland) Act 1862 (c.101)
General Police and Improvement (Scotland) Act, 1862, Amendment Act 1877 (c.22)
General Police and Improvement (Scotland) Act, 1862, Amendment Act 1889 (c.51)
General Police and Improvement (Scotland) Act 1865 (c.7)
General Police and Improvement (Scotland) Act 1882 (c.6)
General Police and Improvement (Scotland) Amendment Act 1878 (c.30)
General Police and Improvement (Scotland) Supplemental Act 1863
General Police and Improvement (Scotland) Supplemental Act 1865 (c.7)
General Police and Improvement (Scotland) Supplemental Act 1866 (c.93)
General Police and Improvement (Scotland) Supplemental Act 1867 (c.79)
General Prisons (Ireland) Act 1877 (c.49)
General Rate Act 1967 (c.9)
General Rate Act 1970 (c.19)
General Rate Act 1975 (c.5)
General Rate (Public Utilities) Act 1977 (c.11)
General Register House, Edinburgh Act 1847 (c.20)
General Register Office Act 1852 (c.25)
Geneva Convention Act 1911 (c.20)
Geneva Convention Act 1937 (c.15)
Geneva Conventions Act 1957 (c.52)
Geneva Conventions (Amendment) Act 1995 (c.27)
Genocide Act 1969 (c.12)
Geological Survey Act 1845 (c.63)
German Conventions Act 1955 (c.2)
German Reparation (Recovery) Act 1921 (c.5)
Ghana (Consequential Provisions) Act 1960 (c.41)
Ghana Independence Act 1957 (c.6)
Gibraltar Lighthouse, etc. Act 1838 (c.66)
Gifts for Churches Act 1803 (c.108)
Gifts for Churches Act 1811 (c.115)
Glamorgan, Llansamlett–Llangevelach Bridge, River Tawey Act 1778 (c.68)
Glamorgan Roads Act 1764 (c.88)
Glamorgan Roads Act 1771 (c.77)
Glamorgan Roads Act 1779 (c.110)
Glamorgan Roads Act 1785 (c.122)
Glamorgan Roads Act 1793 (c.133)
Glamorganshire Canal Act 1796 (c.69)
Glamorganshire Election Act 1815 (c.72)
Glasgow and Dumbarton Roads Act 1772 (c.106)
Glasgow and Renfrew Road Act 1797 (c.161)
Glasgow and Renfrew Roads Act 1794 (c.140)
Glasgow and Shotts Road Act 1753 (c.81)
Glasgow Beer Duties Act 1715 (c.44)
Glasgow Beer Duties Act 1725 (c.27)
Glasgow Beer Duties Act 1735 (c.31)
Glasgow Beer Duties Act 1755 (c.29)
Glasgow Boundaries Act 1871 (c.68)
Glasgow (Improvement) Act 1768 (c.16)
Glasgow: Improvement Act 1793 (c.124)
Glasgow Parliamentary Divisions Act 1896 (c.17)
Glasgow Roads Act 1753 (c.90)
Glasgow Roads Act 1754 (c.27)
Glasgow Roads Act 1766 (c.82)
Glasgow Roads Act 1774 (c.102)
Glasgow Roads Act 1774 (c.105)
Glasgow Roads Act 1788 (c.92)
Glasgow Roads Act 1792 (c.152)
Glasgow Roads Act 1792 (c.154)
Glasgow Roads Act 1793 (c.160)
Glasgow Roads Act 1793 (c.174)
Glasgow Roads Act 1795 (c.155)
Glass Duties Act 1787 (c.28)
Glass Duties Act 1794 (c.27)
Glass Duties Act 1835 (c.77)
Glass Duties Act 1838 (c.44)

Glass Duties Repeal Act 1845 (c.6)
Glass, etc., Duties Act 1813 (c.70)
Glebe Exchange Act 1815 (c.147)
Glebe Exchange Act 1816 (c.52)
Glebe Houses (Ireland) Act 1803 (c.158)
Glebe (Ireland) Act 1851 (c.73)
Glebe Lands Act 1888 (c.20)
Glebe Lands Leasing Powers (Ireland) Act 1857 (c.47)
Glebe Lands, Representative Church Body, Ireland, Act 1875 (c.42)
Glebe Lands (Scotland) Act 1866 (c.71)
Glebe Loan Act 1870 (c.112)
Glebe Loan Act 1871 (c.100)
Glebe Loan (Ireland) Acts Amendment 1880 (c.2)
Glebe Loan (Ireland) Acts Amendment 1883 (c.8)
Glebe Loan (Ireland) Acts Amendment 1886 (c.6)
Glebe Loan (Ireland) Amendment Act 1875 (c.30)
Glebe Loan (Ireland) Amendment Act 1878 (c.6)
Glebe Loan (Ireland) Amendments Act 1871 (c.100)
Gloucester and Berkeley Canal Act 1793 (c.97)
Gloucester and Berkeley Canal Act 1797 (c.54)
Gloucester and Crickley Hull Road Act 1760 (c.30)
Gloucester and Hereford Roads Act 1746 (c.31)
Gloucester and Hereford Roads Act 1759 (c.34)
Gloucester and Hereford Roads Act 1769 (c.50)
Gloucester and Oxford Road Act 1750 (c.28)
Gloucester and Oxford Roads Act 1768 (c.41)
Gloucester and Oxford Roads Act 1787 (c.77)
Gloucester and Warwick Roads Act 1755 (c.47)
Gloucester and Wiltshire Roads Act 1756 (c.56)
Gloucester and Wiltshire Roads Act 1757 (c.61)
Gloucester and Wiltshire Roads Act 1762 (c.74)
Gloucester and Wiltshire Roads Act 1779 (c.118)
Gloucester and Wiltshire Roads Act 1792 (c.153)
Gloucester and Worcester Roads Act 1764 (c.79)
Gloucester and Worcester Roads Act 1794 (c.135)
Gloucester Gaol Act 1781 (c.74)
Gloucester Gaol Act 1785 (c.10)
Gloucester (Poor Relief, etc.) Act 1764 (c.60)
Gloucester Roads Act 1742 (c.21)
Gloucester Roads Act 1742 (c.22)
Gloucester Roads Act 1745 (c.18)
Gloucester Roads Act 1746 (c.23)
Gloucester Roads Act 1751 (c.13)
Gloucester Roads Act 1756 (c.58)
Gloucester Roads Act 1770 (c.74)
Gloucester Roads Act 1778 (c.102)
Gloucester Roads Act 1779 (c.93)
Gloucester Roads Act 1779 (c.115)
Gloucester Roads Act 1780 (c.70)
Gloucester Roads Act 1780 (c.84)
Gloucester Roads Act 1780 (c.93)
Gloucester Roads Act 1783 (c.104)
Gloucester Roads Act 1787 (c.68)
Gloucester Roads Act 1787 (c.78)
Gloucester Roads Act 1792 (c.146)
Gloucester Roads Act 1795 (c.140)
Gloucester Streets Act 1749 (c.15)
Gloucester to Stroud Road Act 1778 (c.98)
Gloucester Water Supply Act 1740 (c.11)
Gloucestershire Highways Act 1722 (c.31)
Gloucestershire Roads Act 1725 (c.24)
Gloucestershire Roads Act 1741 (c.15)
Gloucestershire Roads Act 1756 (c.51)
Gloucestershire Roads Act 1757 (c.54)
Gloucestershire Roads Act 1757 (c.64)
Gloucestershire Roads Act 1757 (c.65)
Gloucestershire Roads Act 1757 (c.70)
Gloucestershire Roads Act 1769 (c.58)
Gloucestershire Roads Act 1774 (c.111)
Gloucestershire Roads Act 1783 (c.106)
Gloucestershire: Small Debts Act 1792 (c.77)
Glove Duties Act 1785 (c.55)
Godmanchester to Cambridge Road Act 1793 (c.156)
Godstone to Highgate Road Act 1766 (c.58)
Gold and Silver (Export Control, etc.) Act 1920 (c.70)
Gold and Silver Thread Act 1702 (c.11)
Gold and Silver Thread Act 1741 (c.20)
Gold and Silver Thread Act 1788 (c.7)
Gold and Silver Wares Act 1844 (c.22)
Gold and Silver Wares Act 1854 (c.96)
Gold Currency Act 1812 (c.5)
Gold Currency Act 1814 (c.52)
Gold Currency and Bank Notes Act 1811 (c.127)
Gold Currency, etc. Act 1812 (c.50)
Gold Plate (Standard) Act 1798 (c.69)
Gold Standard Act 1925 (c.29)
Gold Standard (Amendment) Act 1931 (c.46)
Golden Square (Rates) Act 1750 (c.27)
Goodman's Fields Act 1778 (c.50)
Goods and Services (Price Control) Act 1941 (c.31)
Goods in Neutral Ships Act 1802 (c.80)
Goods Vehicles (Licensing of Operators) Act 1995 (c.23)
Gordon Memorial College at Khartoum Act 1899 (c.16)
Gosport: Improvement Act 1763 (c.56)
Goswell St., Middlesex Act 1780 (c.48)
Government and Other Stocks (Emergency Provisions) Act 1939 (c.100)

Government Annuities Act 1838 (c.49)
Government Annuities Act 1853 (c.45)
Government Annuities Act 1873 (c.44)
Government Annuities Act 1882 (c.51)
Government Annuities Act 1929 (c.29)
Government Annuities (Investments) Act 1864 (c.46)
Government Contractors Act 1815 (c.195)
Government of Burma Act 1935 (c.3)
Government of Burma (Temporary Provisions) Act 1944 (c.30)
Government of India Act 1800 (c.79)
Government of India Act 1833 (c.85)
Government of India Act 1853 (c.95)
Government of India Act 1854 (c.77)
Government of India Act 1858 (c.106)
Government of India Act 1859 (c.41)
Government of India Act 1865 (c.17)
Government of India Act 1869 (c.97)
Government of India Act 1870 (c.3)
Government of India Act 1912 (c.6)
Government of India Act 1915 (c.61)
Government of India Act 1919 (c.101)
Government of India Act 1935 (c.2)
Government of India Act 1935 (c.42)
Government of India (Aden) Act 1929 (c.2)
Government of India Amendment Act 1911 (c.25)
Government of India Amendment Act 1916 (c.37)
Government of India Amendment Act 1933 (c.23)
Government of India (Amendment) Act 1939 (c.66)
Government of India (Civil Services) Act 1925 (c.83)
Government of India (Indian Navy) Act 1927 (c.8)
Government of India (Leave of Absence) Act 1924 (c.28)
Government of India (Reprinting) Act 1935 (c.1)
Government of India (Statutory Commission) Act 1927 (c.24)
Government of Ireland Act 1914 (c.90)
Government of Ireland Act 1920 (c.67)
Government of New South Wales and Van Diemen's Land Act 1866 (c.74)
Government of New Zealand Act 1846 (c.103)
Government of Newfoundland Act 1847 (c.44)
Government of Northern Ireland (Loan Guarantee) Act 1922 (c.24)
Government of Soudan Loan Act 1919 (c.43)
Government of the Soudan Loan Act 1913 (c.10)
Government of the Soudan Loan Act 1914 (c.9)
Government of the Soudan Loan (Amendment) Act 1922 (c.15)
Government of New Zealand Act 1848 (c.5)
Government Offices Security Act 1810 (c.85)
Government Offices Security Act 1836 (c.28)
Government Offices Security Act 1838 (c.61)
Government Offices (Security) Act 1875 (c.64)
Government Trading Act 1990 (c.30)
Government Trading Funds Act 1973 (c.63)
Government War Obligations Act 1914 (c.11)
Government War Obligations Act 1915 (c.96)
Government War Obligations Act 1916 (c.70)
Government War Obligations Act 1918 (c.28)
Government War Obligations Act 1919 (c.44)
Governors, etc., of West Indies Islands Act 1794 (c.35)
Governors' Pension Act 1956 (c.64)
Governors' Pensions Act 1957 (c.62)
Grain Between Great Britain and Ireland Act 1806 (c.97)
Grammar Schools Act 1840 (c.77)
Grand Canal Branches (Ireland) Act 1844 (c.98)
Grand Canal (Ireland) Act 1813 (c.143)
Grand Junction Canal Act 1793 (c.80)
Grand Junction Canal Act 1794 (c.24)
Grand Junction Canal (No. 1) Act 1795 (c.8)
Grand Junction Canal (No. 2) Act 1795 (c.43)
Grand Junction Canal (No. 3) Act 1795 (c.85)
Grand Junction Canal (No. 4) Act 1795 (c.25)
Grand Juries Act 1856 (c.54)
Grand Juries (Ireland) Act 1843 (c.32)
Grand Juries (Suspension) Act 1917 (c.4)
Grand Jury Cess. Act 1846 (c.60)
Grand Jury Cess. Dublin Act 1838 (c.51)
Grand Jury Cess. (Dublin) Act 1851 (c.65)
Grand Jury Cess. (Ireland) Act 1848 (c.26)
Grand Jury Cess. (Ireland) Act 1849 (c.32)
Grand Jury Cess. (Ireland) Act 1850 (c.82)
Grand Jury Cess. (Ireland) Act 1853 (c.13)
Grand Jury Cess. (Ireland) Act 1857 (c.7)
Grand Jury (Ireland) Act 1816 (c.87)
Grand Jury (Ireland) Act 1836 Amendment 1908 (c.29)
Grand Jury (Ireland) Act 1836 (c.116)
Grand Jury (Ireland) Act 1837 (c.2)
Grand Jury (Ireland) Act 1838 (c.37)
Grand Jury (Ireland) Act 1853 (c.136)
Grand Jury (Ireland) Act 1856 (c.63)
Grand Jury (Ireland) Act 1857 (c.15)
Grand Jury (Ireland) Act 1872 (c.42)
Grand Jury (Ireland) Act 1873 (c.34)
Grand Jury (Ireland) Act 1895 (c.8)
Grand Jury Presentments (Ireland) Act 1842 (c.77)
Grand Jury Presentments (Ireland) Act 1843 (c.71)
Grant of Administration (Bonds) Act 1919 (c.26)
Grant of Feu Duties to John Francis Erskine Act 1815 (c.188)
Grant of Frogmore, etc. Act 1807 (c.45)
Grant of Manor of Corsham to Paul Methuen Act 1770 (c.13)
Grant of Military, etc. Commissions Act 1857 (c.4)

Grant to Duke of Marlborough Act 1704 (c.4)
Grant to J. Palmer, Esq. (Post Office Services) Act 1813 (c.157)
Grant to the House of Orange Act 1803 (c.149)
Grantham Canal Act 1793 (c.94)
Grantham Canal Act 1797 (c.30)
Grantham Town Hall Act 1787 (c.61)
Grants for Glebe Houses (I.) Act 1807 (c.23)
Grants of Life Annuities Act 1776 (c.26)
Grants of Officers Act 1812 (c.40)
Grants of Offices in Reversion, etc. Act 1808 (c.50)
Grants of Pensions Act 1811 (c.21)
Grants to George Keith Act 1760 (c.15)
Graves End: Streets Act 1772 (c.15)
Grease Butter from Ireland Act 1763 (c.20)
Great and Little Botton: Improvement Act 1792 (c.71)
Great Farringdon to Burford Road Act 1792 (c.150)
Great Grimsby (Lincoln) Harbour Act 1796 (c.98)
Great Marlow to Stokenchurch Road Act 1791 (c.135)
Great Seal Act 1851 (c.82)
Great Seal Act 1880 (c.10)
Great Seal Act 1884 (c.30)
Great Seal (Offices) Act 1874 (c.81)
Great Sessions in Wales Act 1768 (c.14)
Great Torrington Roads Act 1765 (c.58)
Great Torrington Roads Act 1786 (c.128)
Great Tower Hill: Improvement, etc. Act 1797 (c.87)
Great Yarmouth Haven Act 1749 (c.6)
Great Yarmouth: Improvement Act 1772 (c.14)
Great Yarmouth: Improvement Act 1785 (c.36)
Great Yarmouth Pier Act (c.10)
Greek Loan Act 1864 (c.40)
Greek Loan Act 1898 (c.4)
Greek Loan Guarantee Act 1836 (c.94)
Greek Marriages Act 1884 (c.20)
Greenland and Whale Fishery Act 1771 (c.38)
Greenland, etc., Fishery Act 1782 (c.19)
Greenland Fishery Act 1723 (c.16)
Greenland Fishery Act 1731 (c.78)
Greenland Fishery Act 1804 (c.23)
Greenland Trade Act 1702 (c.10)
Greenland Whale Fisheries Act 1802 (c.22)
Greenland Whale Fisheries Act 1815 (c.39)
Greenland Whale Fisheries, etc. Act (c.20)
Greenland Whale Fishery Act 1803 (c.32)
Greenland Whale Fishery Act 1805 (c.9)
Greenland Whale Fishery Act 1806 (c.9)
Greenland Whale Fishery Act 1810 (c.11)
Greenock Beer Duties Act 1750 (c.38)
Greenock: Improvement Act 1789 (c.43)
Greenock: Water Supply, etc. Act 1772 (c.28)
Greenwich Hospital Act 1728 (c.7)
Greenwich Hospital Act 1744 (c.31)
Greenwich Hospital Act 1751 (c.42)
Greenwich Hospital Act 1776 (c.24)
Greenwich Hospital Act 1806 (c.100)
Greenwich Hospital Act 1807 (c.52)
Greenwich Hospital Act 1814 (c.110)
Greenwich Hospital Act 1815 (c.56)
Greenwich Hospital Act 1829 (c.25)
Greenwich Hospital Act 1850 (c.24)
Greenwich Hospital Act 1865 (c.89)
Greenwich Hospital Act 1869 (c.44)
Greenwich Hospital Act 1870 (c.100)
Greenwich Hospital Act 1872 (c.67)
Greenwich Hospital Act 1883 (c.32)
Greenwich Hospital Act 1885 (c.42)
Greenwich Hospital Act 1898 (c.24)
Greenwich Hospital Act 1921 (c.41)
Greenwich Hospital Act 1942 (c.35)
Greenwich Hospital Act 1947 (c.5)
Greenwich Hospital Act 1967 (c.74)
Greenwich Hospital Act 1990 (c.13)
Greenwich Hospital (Disused Burial Ground) Act 1925 (c.58)
Greenwich Hospital, etc. Act 1711 (c.27)
Greenwich Hospital (Provision for Widows) Act 1863 (c.67)
Greenwich Markets Act 1849 (c.28)
Greenwich Out-Pensioners Act 1763 (c.16)
Grenada and St. Vincent Traders Act (c.11)
Grenada and St. Vincent Traders Act 1800 (c.27)
Grenada and St. Vincent Traders Act 1803 (c.40)
Grenada and St. Vincent Traders Act 1803 (c.104)
Grenada and St. Vincent Traders Act 1808 (c.135)
Gresham College, etc. Act 1768 (c.32)
Grey Seals Protection Act 1914 (c.3)
Grey Seals Protection Act 1931 (c.23)
Grosvenor Square: Paving, etc. Act 1774 (c.52)
Ground Game Act 1880 (c.47)
Ground Game (Amendment) Act 1906 (c.21)
Groundhurst Roads Act 1768 (c.35)
Growth of Coffee Act 1731 (c.24)
Growth of Coffee Act 1745 (c.23)
Growth of Coffee, etc. Act 1750 (c.35)
Growth of Hemp and Flax Act 1781 (c.58)
Growth of Raw Silk Act 1749 (c.20)
Guarantee by Companies Act 1867 (c.108)
Guard Dogs Act 1975 (c.50)
Guardians (Ireland) Act 1849 (c.4)
Guardianship Act 1973 (c.29)
Guardianship and Maintenance of Infants Act 1951 (c.56)
Guardianship of Infants Act 1886 (c.27)
Guardianship of Infants Act 1925 (c.45)
Guardianship of Minors Act 1971 (c.3)
Guardianship (Refugee Children) Act 1944 (c.8)
Guildford and Arundel Road Act 1757 (c.60)
Guildford and Farnham Road Act 1757 (c.78)
Guildford Hospital Act 1861 (c.32)

Guildford Streets Act 1758 (c.58)
Guildford to Farnham Road Act 1780 (c.96)
Gun Barrel Proof Act 1978 (c.9)
Gun Licence Act 1870 (c.57)
Gunpowder Act 1772 (c.61)
Gunpowder Act Amendment Act 1862 (c.98)
Gunpowder and Fireworks Act 1860 (c.139)
Gunpowder and Fireworks Act 1861 (c.130)
Gunpowder in Mersey Act 1851 (c.67)
Gunpowder Mill, Tonbridge Act 1772 (c.13)
Guyana Independence Act 1966 (c.14)
Guyana Republic Act 1970 (c.18)

Habeas Corpus Act 1679 (c.2)
Habeas Corpus Act 1803 (c.140)
Habeas Corpus Act 1804 (c.102)
Habeas Corpus Act 1816 (c.100)
Habeas Corpus Act 1862 (c.20)
Habeas Corpus (Ireland) Act 1868 (c.7)
Habeas Corpus Suspension Act 1707 (c.67)
Habeas Corpus Suspension Act 1715 (c.30)
Habeas Corpus Suspension Act 1722 (c.1)
Habeas Corpus Suspension Act 1743 (c.6)
Habeas Corpus Suspension Act 1745 (c.1)
Habeas Corpus Suspension Act 1745 (c.17)
Habeas Corpus Suspension Act 1746 (c.1)
Habeas Corpus Suspension Act 1776 (c.9)
Habeas Corpus Suspension Act 1778 (c.1)
Habeas Corpus Suspension Act 1779 (c.1)
Habeas Corpus Suspension Act 1780 (c.2)
Habeas Corpus Suspension Act 1782 (c.1)
Habeas Corpus Suspension Act 1794 (c.54)
Habeas Corpus Suspension Act 1795 (c.3)
Habeas Corpus Suspension Act 1797 (c.36)
Habeas Corpus Suspension Act 1799 (c.15)
Habeas Corpus Suspension Act 1799 (c.44)
Habeas Corpus Suspension Act 1800 (c.20)
Habeas Corpus Suspension Act 1800 (c.32)
Habeas Corpus Suspension Act 1801 (c.26)
Habeas Corpus Suspension, etc. Act 1714 (c.8)
Habeas Corpus Suspension (Ireland) Act 1803 (c.8)
Habeas Corpus Suspension (Ireland) Act 1801 (c.15)
Habeas Corpus Suspension (Ireland) Act 1803 (c.116)
Habeas Corpus Suspension (Ireland) Act 1805 (c.4)
Habeas Corpus Suspension (Ireland) Act 1848 (c.35)
Habeas Corpus Suspension (Ireland) Act 1849 (c.2)
Habeas Corpus Suspension (Ireland) Act 1866 (c.1)
Habeas Corpus Suspension (Ireland) Act 1866 (c.119)
Habeas Corpus Suspension (Ireland) Act 1867 (c.1)
Habeas Corpus Suspension (Ireland) Act 1867 (c.25)
Habitual Criminals Act 1869 (c.99)
Habitual Drunkards Act 1879 (c.19)
Hackney Carriages Act 1815 (c.159)
Hackney Carriages, Metropolis Act 1838 (c.79)
Hackney Chairs Act 1712 (c.15)
Hackney Chairs, etc. Act 1759 (c.25)
Hackney Coach Fares Act 1808 (c.87)
Hackney Coaches Act 1771 (c.24)
Hackney Coaches Act 1772 (c.49)
Hackney Coaches Act 1784 (c.27)
Hackney Coaches Act 1786 (c.72)
Hackney Coaches Act 1792 (c.47)
Hackney Coaches Act 1804 (c.88)
Hackney Coaches Act 1814 (c.147)
Hackney Coaches, etc. Act 1715 (c.57)
Hackney Coaches, etc., London Act 1800 (c.47)
Hackney Coaches, Metropolis Act 1802 (c.78)
Hackney Coachmen Act 1771 (c.28)
Hackney (Poor Relief etc.) Act 1764 (c.43)
Haddington County Roads Act 1749 (c.17)
Haddington Roads Act 1769 (c.74)
Haddington Roads Act 1793 (c.163)
Hagley and Birmingham Road Act 1753 (c.47)
Haileybury College Act 1838 (c.22)
Haileybury College Act 1855 (c.52)
Hainault Forest Act 1851 (c.43)
Hainault Forest (Allotment of Commons) Act 1858 (c.37)
Hair Powder Certificates, etc. Act 1795 (c.112)
Hairdressers' and Barbers' Shops (Sunday Closing) Act 1930 (c.35)
Hairdressers (Registration) Act 1964 (c.89)
Half-Pay and Pensions Act 1807 (c.25)
Half Pay of Officers, etc. 1815 (c.131)
Halifax and Sheffield Road Act 1797 (c.160)
Halifax Church Act 1795 Act (c.71)
Halifax to Manchester Canal Act 1794 (c.78)
Halifax to Sheffield Road Act 1777 (c.106)
Halifax to Sheffield Road Act 1793 (c.142)
Halifax: Water Supply Act 1762 (c.40)
Halifax: (Water Supply, etc.) Act 1768 (c.44)
Hallamshire Cutlers Act 1791 (c.58)
Halliwell and Finsbury Drainage Act 1778 (c.66)
Hallmarking Act 1973 (c.43)
Hall-marking of Foreign Plate Act 1904 (c.6)
Hall-marking of Foreign Plate Act 1939 (c.36)
Hamilton Bridge Act 1770 (c.93)
Hampshire and Berkshire Roads Act 1766 (c.86)
Hampshire and Dorset Roads Act 1762 (c.57)
Hampshire and Dorset Roads Act 1780 (c.92)
Hampshire and Wiltshire Fisheries Act 1797 (c.95)
Hampshire and Wiltshire Roads Act 1774 (c.104)
Hampshire, Kent, Sussex—Fortifications Act 1762 (c.37)
Hampshire, Kent, Sussex—Fortifications Act 1763 (c.35)

Hampshire Roads Act 1741 (c.14)
Hampshire Roads Act 1757 (c.73)
Hampshire Roads Act 1757 (c.74)
Hampshire Roads Act 1765 (c.95)
Hampstead Roads Act 1753 (c.80)
Hampstead: Streets Act 1775 (c.58)
Hampton Court Bridge Act 1749 (c.37)
Hampton to Staines Road Act 1773 (c.105)
Hampton to Staines Road Act 1793 (c.135)
Hanbury Church Act 1793 (c.45)
Hanley Chapel, Stafford Act 1787 (c.62)
Hans Town, Chelsea: Improvement Act 1790 (c.76)
Happing and Tunstead, Norfolk: Poor Relief Act 1785 (c.27)
Harbour Loans Act 1866 (c.30)
Harbour of Colombo Loan Act 1874 (c.24)
Harbour of Galle Loan Act 1869 (c.105)
Harbour of Howth Act 1805 (c.113)
Harbour of Leith Act 1800 (c.57)
Harbour of Leith Act 1805 (c.114)
Harbour Transfer Act 1865 (c.100)
Harbours Act 1745 (c.22)
Harbours Act 1814 (c.159)
Harbours Act 1964 (c.40)
Harbours (Amendment) Act 1970 (c.53)
Harbours and Passing Tolls etc. Act 1861 (c.47)
Harbours Development (Scotland) Act 1972 (c.64)
Harbours, Docks and Piers Clauses Act 1847 (c.27)
Harbours, Docks and Piers (Temporary Increase of Charges) Act 1922 (c.23)
Harbours (Ireland) Act 1805 (c.64)
Harbours (Loans) Act 1972 (c.16)
Harbours, Piers and Ferries (Scotland) Act 1937 (c.28)
Harbours, Piers and Ferries (Scotland) Act 1953 (c.11)
Harbours, Piers and Ferries (Scotland) Act 1972 (c.29)
Harbours (Scotland) Act 1982 (c.17)
Harbours Transfer Act 1862 (c.69)
Hardington and Old Stratford Road Act 1768 (c.52)
Hares Act 1848 (c.29)
Hares Preservation Act 1892 (c.8)
Hares Preservation (Ireland) Act 1879 (c.23)
Hares (Scotland) Act 1848 (c.30)
Harrogate to Ripon Road Act 1794 (c.121)
Hartlepool Pilotage Order Confirmation Act 1864 (c.58)
Hartley's Patent (Fire Prevention) Act 1776 (c.6)
Hartsmere, etc., Suffolk: Poor Relief Act 1779 (c.13)
Harvey's Charity, Folkestone Act 1858 (c.29)
Harwich, etc., Election Act 1842 (c.31)
Harwich Harbour Act 1863 (c.71)
Harwich Harbour Act 1864 (c.102)
Harwich Harbour Act 1865 (c.120)
Hastings: Improvement Act 1789 (c.27)
Hat Duties Act 1803 (c.22)
Hat Duties, etc. Act 1784 (c.51)
Hat Manufacture Act 1731 (c.22)
Hat Manufacture Act 1784 (c.21)
Hatfield Chase Act 1783 (c.13)
Hatfield Chase: Drainage Act 1787 (c.53)
Hawford–Droitwich Canal Act 1768 (c.37)
Hawkers Act 1717 (c.6)
Hawkers Act 1785 (c.78)
Hawkers Act 1810 (c.41)
Hawkers Act 1812 (c.108)
Hawkers Act 1888 (c.33)
Hawkers and Pedlars Act 1795 (c.91)
Hawkers (Scotland) Act 1815 (c.71)
Hay and Straw Act 1796 (c.88)
Hay and Straw Act 1856 (c.114)
Hay Bridge Over Wye Act 1756 (c.73)
Haydon, Chapel, Northumberland Act 1795 (c.47)
Heage to Duffield Road Act 1793 (c.177)
Health and Medicines Act 1988 (c.49)
Health and Safety at Work etc. Act 1974 (c.37)
Health and Social Security Act 1984 (c.48)
Health and Social Services and Social Security Adjudications Act 1983 (c.41)
Health Authorities Act 1995 (c.17)
Health of Prisoners Act 1774 (c.59)
Health Resorts and Watering Places Act 1921 (c.27)
Health Resorts and Watering Places Act 1936 (c.48)
Health Resorts, etc. (Ireland) Act 1909 (c.32)
Health Service Commissioners Act 1993 (c.46)
Health Service Joint Consultative Committees (Access to Information) Act 1986 (c.24)
Health Services Act 1976 (c.83)
Health Services Act 1980 (c.53)
Health Services and Public Health Act 1968 (c.46)
Health Visiting and Social Work (Training) Act 1962 (c.33)
Hearing Aid Council Act 1968 (c.50)
Hearing Aid Council (Amendment) Act 1989 (c.12)
Hearing Aid Council (Extension) Act 1975 (c.39)
Heather Burning (Scotland) Act 1926 (c.30)
Heating Appliances (Fireguards) Act 1952 (c.42)
Heavy Commercial Vehicles (Controls and Regulations) Act 1973 (c.44)
Hedon Haven Act 1774 (c.106)
Heir Apparent's Establishment Act 1795 (c.125)
Hemingbrough to Market Weighton Road Act 1793 (c.159)
Hemlingford Riots Act 1793 (c.39)
Hemp and Flax Act 1770 (c.40)
Hemp and Flax Act 1786 (c.43)
Henley Grammar School Act 1778 (c.41)

Henley Improvement Act 1795 (c.79)
Henley to Oxford Road Act 1781 (c.97)
Henley-upon-Thames Bridge Act 1780 (c.33)
Hereditary Revenues Act 1856 (c.43)
Hereford and Bedford Roads Act 1769 (c.64)
Hereford and Gloucester Roads Act 1764 (c.62)
Hereford and Gloucester Roads Act 1789 (c.104)
Hereford and Salop Roads Act 1758 (c.66)
Hereford and Worcester Roads Act 1782 (c.100)
Hereford Cathedral Act 1792 (c.87)
Hereford (City) Roads Act 1730 (c.18)
Hereford, Radnor and Salop Roads Act 1778 (c.111)
Hereford Roads Act 1748 (c.15)
Hereford Roads Act 1748 (c.18)
Hereford Roads Act 1748 (c.26)
Hereford Roads Act 1751 (c.56)
Hereford Roads Act 1756 (c.65)
Hereford Roads Act 1770 (c.91)
Hereford Roads Act 1773 (c.95)
Hereford Roads Act 1773 (c.96)
Hereford Roads Act 1767 (c.67)
Hereford Roads Act 1769 (c.90)
Hereford Roads Act 1781 (c.105)
Hereford Roads Act 1782 (c.108)
Hereford Roads Act 1782 (c.112)
Hereford Roads Act 1784 (c.69)
Hereford Roads Act 1789 (c.108)
Hereford Roads Act 1791 (c.114)
Hereford Roads Act 1791 (c.130)
Hereford Roads Act 1794 (c.119)
Hereford Roads, etc. Act 1759 (c.58)
Hereford Streets Act 1774 (c.38)
Herefordshire and Gloucestershire Canal Act 1791 (c.89)
Herefordshire Roads Act 1740 (c.13)
Herefordshire Roads Act 1741 (c.17)
Heritable Jurisdictions (Scotland) Act 1746 (c.43)
Heritable Securities (Scotland) Act 1845 (c.31)
Heritable Securities (Scotland) Act 1847 (c.50)
Heritable Securities (Scotland) Act 1854 (c.62)
Heritable Securities (Scotland) Act 1860 (c.80)
Heritable Securities (Scotland) Act 1894 (c.44)
Herring Fisheries (Scotland) Act 1858 (c.69)
Herring Fisheries (Scotland) Act 1860 (c.92)
Herring Fisheries (Scotland) Act 1865 (c.22)
Herring Fisheries (Scotland) Act 1867 (c.52)
Herring Fishery Act 1749 (c.24)
Herring Fishery Act 1753 (c.9)
Herring Fishery Act 1755 (c.14)
Herring Fishery Act 1757 (c.30)
Herring Fishery Act 1765 (c.22)
Herring Fishery Act 1772 (c.58)
Herring Fishery Act 1851 (c.26)
Herring Fishery Barrels Act 1874 (c.25)
Herring Fishery (Scotland) Act 1808 (c.110)
Herring Fishery (Scotland) Act 1815 (c.94)
Herring Fishery (Scotland) Act 1889 (c.23)
Herring Fishery (Scotland) Act Amendment 1890 (c.10)
Herring Fishing (Branding) Act 1913 (c.9)
Herring Industry Act 1935 (c.9)
Herring Industry Act 1938 (c.42)
Herring Industry Act 1944 (c.32)
Hertford and Bedford Roads Act 1757 (c.43)
Hertford and Bedford Roads Act 1769 (c.87)
Hertford and Bedford Roads Act 1790 (c.115)
Hertford and Broadwater Road Act 1757 (c.45)
Hertford and Bucks. Roads Act 1762 (c.63)
Hertford and Cambridge Roads Act 1769 (c.86)
Hertford and Middlesex Roads Act 1791 (c.108)
Hertford and Ware Roads Act 1732 (c.15)
Hertford and Ware Roads Act 1753 (c.56)
Hertford Church Act 1765 (c.94)
Hertford College Act 1874 (c.55)
Hertford Highways Act 1721 (c.9)
Hertford: Improvement Act 1788 (c.75)
Hertford Prison Act 1775 (c.25)
Hertford Roads Act 1762 (c.48)
Hertford Roads Act 1771 (c.57)
Hertford Roads Act 1778 (c.90)
Hertford Roads Act 1778 (c.94)
Hertford Roads Act 1782 (c.91)
Hertford Roads Act 1783 (c.25)
Hertford Shire-House Act 1768 (c.58)
Hertfordshire and Gloucestershire Canal Act 1793 (c.119)
Hertfordshire and Huntingdonshire Highways Act 1713 (c.33)
Hertfordshire and Huntingdonshire Roads Act 1765 (c.77)
Hertfordshire and Huntingdonshire Roads Act 1790 (c.89)
Hertfordshire and Middlesex Roads Act 1770 (c.107)
Hertfordshire Highways Act 1706 (c.14)
Hertfordshire Highways Act 1710 (c.14)
Hertfordshire Highways Act 1719 (c.20)
Hertfordshire Roads Act 1724 (c.11)
Hertfordshire Roads Act 1725 (c.10)
Hertfordshire Roads Act 1726 (c.32)
Hertfordshire Roads Act 1731 (c.10)
Hertfordshire Roads Act 1732 (c.24)
Hertfordshire Roads Act 1742 (c.16)
Hertfordshire Roads Act 1763 (c.26)
Hexham Bridge Act 1778 (c.44)
Hexham: Inclosure Act 1792 (c.110)
Hexham to Alston Road Act 1778 (c.116)
Hides and Skins Act 1769 (c.39)
High Constables Act 1869 (c.47)
High Court and County Court (Judges) Act 1950 (c.4)
High Court of Admiralty Act 1859 (c.6)
High Court of Admiralty (E.) Act 1840 (c.66)

High Court of Justiciary (Scotland) Act 1892 (c.21)
High Highlands Act 1823 (c.79)
High Peak Mining Customs and Mineral Courts. Act 1851 (c.94)
Highgate and Chipping Barnet Road Act 1720 (c.18)
Highgate and Chipping Barnet Road Act 1763 (c.37)
Highgate and Hampstead Highways Act 1721 (c.5)
Highgate and Hampstead Roads Act 1734 (c.28)
Highgate and Hampstead Roads Act 1756 (c.88)
Highgate and Hampstead Roads Act 1776 (c.76)
Highgate and Hampstead Roads Act 1780 (c.78)
Highgate: Streets Act 1775 (c.43)
Highland Road and Bridges (Scotland) Act (c.43)
Highland Roads and Bridges Act 1851 (c.66)
Highland Roads and Bridges Act 1862 (c.105)
Highland Schools Act 1838 (c.87)
Highland Schools Act 1873 (c.53)
Highland Services Act 1715 (c.54)
Highlands and Islands Air Services (Scotland) Act 1980 (c.19)
Highlands and Islands Development (Scotland) Act 1965 (c.46)
Highlands and Islands Development (Scotland) Act 1968 (c.51)
Highlands and Islands (Medical Service) Additional Grant Act 1929 (c.13)
Highlands and Islands (Medical Service) Grant Act 1913 (c.26)
Highlands and Islands Shipping Services Act 1960 (c.31)
Highland Roads and Bridges Act 1862 (c.105)
Highland Services Act 1715 (c.54)
Highway Accounts Returns Act 1879 (c.39)
Highway Act 1794 (c.64)
Highway Act 1835 (c.50)
Highway Act 1841 (c.51)
Highway Act 1845 (c.71)
Highway Act 1863 (c.61)
Highway Act 1864 (c.101)
Highway Act Amendment 1885 (c.13)
Highway (Railway Crossing) Act 1839 (c.45)
Highway Rate Assessment and Expenditure Act 1882 (c.27)
Highway Rates Act 1836 (c.63)
Highway Rates Act 1839 (c.81)
Highway Rates Act 1840 (c.98)
Highway Rates Act 1843 (c.59)
Highway Rates Act 1845 (c.59)
Highway Rates Act 1846 (c.49)
Highway Rates Act 1847 (c.93)
Highway Rates Act 1848 (c.66)
Highway Rates Act 1849 (c.54)
Highway Rates Act 1850 (c.58)
Highway Rates Act 1851 (c.30)
Highway Rates Act 1852 (c.19)
Highway Rates Act 1853 (c.66)
Highway Rates Act 1854 (c.52)
Highway Rates Act 1860 (c.67)
Highway (Scotland) Act 1718 (c.30)
Highway (Scotland) Act 1771 (c.53)
Highway (Scotland) Act 1803 (c.80)
Highways Act 1707 (c.56)
Highways Act 1710 (c.23)
Highways Act 1714 (c.11)
Highways Act 1715 (c.52)
Highways Act 1718 (c.12)
Highways Act 1733 (c.9)
Highways Act 1742 (c.29)
Highways Act 1749 (c.28)
Highways Act 1750 (c.43)
Highways Act 1753 (c.28)
Highways Act 1765 (c.38)
Highways Act 1766 (c.42)
Highways Act 1766 (c.43)
Highways Act 1768 (c.5)
Highways Act 1773 (c.78)
Highways Act 1794 (c.74)
Highways Act 1839 (c.40)
Highways Act 1854 (c.69)
Highways Act 1862 (c.61)
Highways Act 1959 (c.25)
Highways Act 1971 (c.41)
Highways Act 1980 (c.66)
Highways (Amendment) Act 1965 (c.30)
Highways (Amendment) Act 1986 (c.13)
Highways and Bridges Act 1891 (c.63)
Highways and Locomotives (Amendment) Act 1878 (c.77)
Highways and Turnpike Roads Act 1753 (c.30)
Highways and Turnpike Roads Act 1755 (c.17)
Highways and Turnpike Roads Act 1757 (cc.27, 28)
Highways (England) Act 1814 (c.109)
Highways, etc. (England) Act 1815 (c.68)
Highways, etc. (Scotland) Act 1845 (c.41)
Highways (Ireland) Act 1805 (c.43)
Highways (Ireland) Act 1805 (c.96)
Highways (Ireland) Act 1806 (c.134)
Highways (Ireland) Act 1809 (c.84)
Highways (Ireland) Act 1810 (c.29)
Highways (Ireland) Act 1811 (c.40)
Highways (Ireland) Act 1811 (c.92)
Highways (Ireland) Act 1813 (c.76)
Highways (Ireland) Act 1813 (c.146)
Highways (Ireland) Act 1814 (c.135)
Highways (Isle of Wight) Act 1881 (c.72)
Highways (Miscellaneous Provisions) Act 1961 (c.63)
Highways, Old Stratford to Dunchurch Act 1757 (c.77)
Highways (Provision of Cattle Grids) Act 1950 (c.24)
Highways Returns Act 1849 (c.35)

Highways, South Wales Act 1851 (c.16)
Highways, South Wales Act 1854 (c.7)
Highworth, Wiltshire (Workhouse and Additional Overseer) Act 1789 (c.29)
Hijacking Act 1971 (c.70)
Hill Farming Act 1946 (c.73)
Hill Farming Act 1954 (c.23)
Hill Farming Act 1956 (c.72)
Hill Farming Act 1985 (c.32)
Hill to Lyde Way Road Act 1782 (c.109)
Hinckley and Coventry Road Act 1756 (c.66)
Hinckley and Coventry Road Act 1762 (c.69)
Hinckley to Melbourne Common Road Act 1774 (c.110)
Hire-Purchase Act 1938 (c.53)
Hire-Purchase Act 1954 (c.51)
Hire-Purchase Act 1964 (c.53)
Hire-Purchase Act 1965 (c.66)
Hire-Purchase (Scotland) Act 1965 (c.67)
Historic Buildings and Ancient Monuments Act 1953 (c.49)
Hockliffe to Stony Stratford Road Act 1786 (c.143)
Holborn: Improvement Act 1766 (c.100)
Holborn: Poor Relief Act 1770 (c.79)
Holborn: Poor Relief Act 1770 (c.80)
Holderness: Drainage Act 1774 (c.107)
Holderness to Beverley Road Act 1782 (c.90)
Holdings of County Courts Act 1732 (c.23)
Holidays Extension Act 1875 (c.13)
Holidays With Pay Act 1938 (c.70)
Holloway Prison Act 1852 (c.70)
Holy Island: Inclosure Act 1791 (c.92)
Holy Trinity Church, Bristol Act 1785 (c.95)
Holyhead Banks (Ireland) Act 1850 (c.111)
Holyhead Harbour Act 1810 (c.93)
Holyhead Harbour Act 1816 (c.84)
Holyhead Harbour Act 1847 (c.76)
Holyhead Harbour Railway Act 1859 (c.60)
Holyhead Harbours Act 1854 (c.44)
Holyhead Old Harbour Road Act 1874 (c.30)
Holyhead Road Act 1861 (c.28)
Holyhead Roads Act 1775 (c.69)
Holyhead Roads Act 1815 (c.152)
Holyhead Roads Act 1840 (c.104)
Home Counties (Music and Dancing) Licensing Act 1926 (c.31)
Home Energy Conservation Act 1995 (c.10)
Home Guard Act 1951 (c.8)
Home Purchase Assistance and Housing Corporation Guarantee Act 1978 (c.27)
Home Safety Act 1961 (c.20)
Homes Insulation Act 1978 (c.48)
Homicide Act 1957 (c.11)
Honiton: Improvement Act 1790 (c.25)
Honorary Freedom of Boroughs Act 1885 (c.29)
Honourable Lady Hylton-Foster's Annuity Act 1965 (c.70)
Hong Kong Act 1985 (c.15)
Hop (Prevention of Frauds) Act 1866 (c.37)
Hop Trade Act 1800 (c.81)
Hop Trade Act 1814 (c.123)
Hops Act 1774 (c.68)
Hops Act 1808 (c.134)
Hops Marketing Act 1982 (c.5)
Horse Breeding Act 1918 (c.13)
Horse Breeding Act 1958 (c.43)
Horse Duty Act 1811 (c.76)
Horse Patrol, Metropolis Act 1836 (c.50)
Horse Racing Act 1840 (c.5)
Horserace Betting Levy Act 1969 (c.14)
Horserace Betting Levy Act 1981 (c.30)
Horserace Totalisator and Betting Levy Boards Act 1972 (c.69)
Horses (Protective Headgear for Young Riders) Act 1990 (c.25)
Horsham Roads Act 1792 (c.115)
Horsleytown Parish Act 1732 (c.11)
Horticultural Produce Act 1986 (c.20)
Horticultural Products (Emergency Customs Duties) Act 1931 (c.3)
Horticultural Produce (Sales on Commission) Act 1926 (c.39)
Horticulture Act 1960 (c.22)
Horticulture (Special Payments) Act 1974 (c.5)
Hosiery Act 1845 (c.77)
Hosiery Manufacture (Wages) Act 1874 (c.48)
Hospital Complaints Procedure Act 1985 (c.42)
Hospital Endowments (Scotland) Act 1953 (c.41)
Hospital Endowments (Scotland) Act 1971 (c.8)
Hospitals and Infirmaries (Ireland) Act 1806 (c.95)
Hospitals (Ireland) Act 1807 (c.44)
Hospitals (Ireland) Act 1809 (c.36)
Hospitals (Ireland) Act 1814 (c.112)
Hotel Proprietors Act 1956 (c.62)
Hours of Employment (Conventions) Act 1936 (c.22)
House and Window Duties Act 1766 (c.38)
House Duties Act (c.105)
House Duty Act 1778 (c.26)
House Duty (Ireland) Act 1814 (c.132)
House Letting and Rating (Scotland) Act 1911 (c.53)
House Letting and Rating (Scotland) Act 1920 (c.8)
House Occupiers Disqualification Removal Act 1878 (c.3)
House Occupiers Disqualification Removal (Scotland) Act 1878 (c.5)
House Occupiers in Counties Disqualification Removal (Scotland) Act 1880 (c.6)
House of Commons Act 1800 (c.92)
House of Commons Act 1855 (c.10)
House of Commons Act 1859 (c.5)
House of Commons (Administration) Act 1978 (c.36)
House of Commons (Clergy Disqualification) Act 1801 (c.63)
House of Commons (Commissions in H.M.'s Forces) Act 1914 (c.3)

House of Commons Cost Taxation Act 1847 (c.69)
House of Commons Costs Taxation Act 1879 (c.17)
House of Commons Disqualification Act 1741 (c.22)
House of Commons (Disqualification) Act 1782 (c.45)
House of Commons Disqualification Act 1957 (c.20)
House of Commons Disqualification Act 1975 (c.24)
House of Commons Disqualification (Declaration of Law) Act 1931 (c.13)
House of Commons Disqualification (Declaration of Law) Act 1935 (c.38)
House of Commons Disqualification (Temporary Provisions) Act 1941 (c.8)
House of Commons Disqualifications (Temporary Provisions) Act 1943 (c.10)
House of Commons Disqualification (Temporary Provisions) Act 1944 (c.11)
House of Commons (Disqualifications) Act 1801 (c.52)
House of Commons (Disqualifications) Act 1813 (c.16)
House of Commons (Electors) Act 1786 (c.100)
House of Commons (Indemnification of Certain Members) Act 1949 (c.46)
House of Commons Members' Fund Act 1939 (c.49)
House of Commons Members' Fund Act 1948 (c.36)
House of Commons Members' Fund Act 1957 (c.24)
House of Commons Members' Fund Act 1960 (c.50)
House of Commons Members' Fund Act 1962 (c.53)
House of Commons Members' Fund and Parliamentary Pensions Act 1981 (c.7)
House of Commons Officers Act 1834 (c.70)
House of Commons (Offices) Act 1812 (c.11)
House of Commons Offices Act 1846 (c.77)
House of Commons Offices Act 1849 (c.72)
House of Commons Offices Act 1856 (c.1)
House of Commons Qualification Act 1838 (c.48)
House of Commons (Redistribution of Seats) Act 1944 (c.41)
House of Commons (Redistribution of Seats) Act 1947 (c.10)
House of Commons (Redistribution of Seats) Act 1949 (c.66)
House of Commons (Redistribution of Seats) Act 1958 (c.26)
House of Commons (Redistribution of Seats) Act 1979 (c.15)
House of Commons (Service in His Majesty's Forces) Act 1939 (c.85)
House of Commons (Speaker) Act 1832 (c.105)
House of Correction Act (1852) (c.70)
House of Lords Costs Taxation Act 1849 (c.78)
House of Lords Oath Act 1843 (c.6)
House Purchase and Housing Act 1959 (c.33)
House Purchase Assistance and Housing Corporation Guarantee Act 1978 (c.27)
House Tax Act 1803 (c.161)
House Tax Act 1808 (c.55)
House Tax Act 1851 (c.36)
House Tax Act 1871 (c.103)
House to House Collections Act 1939 (c.44)
Houses of Correction Act 1782 (c.64)
Houses of Correction Act 1784 (c.55)
Houses of Industry, etc. (I.) Act 1841 (c.41)
Houses of Parliament Act 1806 (c.89)
Houses of Parliament Act 1810 (c.119)
Houses of Parliament Act 1837 (c.7)
Houses of Parliament Act 1867 (c.40)
Housing Act 1914 (c.31)
Housing Act 1921 (c.19)
Housing Act 1925 (c.14)
Housing Act 1930 (c.39)
Housing Act 1935 (c.40)
Housing Act 1936 (c.51)
Housing Act 1949 (c.60)
Housing Act 1952 (c.53)
Housing Act 1957 (c.56)
Housing Act 1961 (c.65)
Housing Act 1964 (c.56)
Housing Act 1969 (c.33)
Housing Act 1971 (c.76)
Housing Act 1974 (c.44)
Housing Act 1980 (c.51)
Housing Act 1985 (c.68)
Housing Act 1988 (c.50)
Housing (Agricultural Population) (Scotland) Act 1938 (c.38)
Housing (Agricultural Population) (Scotland) Act 1943 (c.22)
Housing (Amendment) Act 1973 (c.5)
Housing (Amendment) (Scotland) Act 1965 (c.40)
Housing (Amendment) (Scotland) Act 1970 (c.5)
Housing (Amendment) (Scotland) Act 1976 (c.11)
Housing (Amendment) (Scotland) Act 1981 (c.72)
Housing and Building Control Act 1984 (c.29)
Housing and Planning Act 1986 (c.63)
Housing and Town and Development (Scotland) Act 1957 (c.38)
Housing Associations Act 1985 (c.69)
Housing (Consequential Provisions) Act 1985 (c.71)
Housing Defects Act 1984 (c.50)
Housing (Emergency Powers) Act 1939 (c.73)
Housing, etc. Act 1923 (c.24)
Housing Finance Act 1972 (c.47)
Housing Finance (Special Provisions) Act 1975 (c.67)

Housing (Financial and Miscellaneous Provisions) Act 1946 (c.48)
Housing (Financial Provisions) Act 1924 (c.35)
Housing (Financial Provisions) Act 1933 (c.15)
Housing (Financial Provisions) Act 1938 (c.16)
Housing (Financial Provisions) Act 1958 (c.42)
Housing (Financial Provisions) (Scotland) Act 1933 (c.16)
Housing (Financial Provisions) (Scotland) Act 1946 (c.54)
Housing (Financial Provisions) (Scotland) Act 1967 (c.20)
Housing (Financial Provisions) (Scotland) Act 1968 (c.31)
Housing (Financial Provisions) (Scotland) Act 1972 (c.46)
Housing (Financial Provisions) (Scotland) Act 1978 (c.14)
Housing (Homeless Persons) Act 1977 (c.48)
Housing (Ireland) Act 1919 (c.45)
Housing (No. 2) Act 1914 (c.52)
Housing (No. 2) (Amendment) Act 1914 (c.71)
Housing of the Working Classes Act 1885 (c.72)
Housing of the Working Classes Act 1890 (c.70)
Housing of the Working Classes Act, 1890, Amendment (Scotland) 1892 (c.22)
Housing of the Working Classes Act, 1890, Amendment (Scotland) 1896 (c.31)
Housing of the Working Classes Act 1894 (c.55)
Housing of the Working Classes Act 1900 (c.59)
Housing of the Working Classes Act 1903 (c.39)
Housing of the Working Classes Act 1908 (c.61)
Housing of the Working Classes (Ireland) Act 1893 (c.33)
Housing of the Working Classes (Ireland) Act 1896 (c.11)
Housing of the Working Classes (Ireland) Act 1908 (c.61)
Housing Rents and Subsidies Act 1975 (c.6)
Housing Rents and Subsidies (Scotland) Act 1975 (c.28)
Housing Repairs and Rents Act 1954 (c.53)
Housing (Repairs and Rents) (Scotland) Act 1954 (c.50)
Housing (Revision of Contributions) Act 1929 (c.6)
Housing (Rosyth Dockyard) Act 1915 (c.49)
Housing (Rural Authorities) Act 1931 (c.39)
Housing (Rural Workers) Act 1926 (c.56)
Housing (Rural Workers) Act 1942 (c.32)
Housing (Rural Workers) Amendment Act 1931 (c.22)
Housing (Rural Workers) Amendment Act 1938 (c.35)
Housing (Scotland) Act 1920 (c.71)
Housing (Scotland) Act 1921 (c.33)
Housing (Scotland) Act 1925 (c.15)
Housing (Scotland) Act 1930 (c.40)
Housing (Scotland) Act 1935 (c.41)
Housing (Scotland) Act 1944 (c.39)
Housing (Scotland) Act 1949 (c.61)
Housing (Scotland) Act 1950 (c.34)
Housing (Scotland) Act 1952 (c.63)
Housing (Scotland) Act 1962 (c.28)
Housing (Scotland) Act 1966 (c.49)
Housing (Scotland) Act 1969 (c.34)
Housing (Scotland) Act 1974 (c.45)
Housing (Scotland) Act 1986 (c.65)
Housing (Scotland) Act 1987 (c.26)
Housing (Scotland) Act 1988 (c.43)
Housing (Slum Clearance Compensation) Act 1965 (c.81)
Housing Subsidies Act 1956 (c.33)
Housing Subsidies Act 1967 (c.29)
Housing (Temporary Accommodation) Act 1944 (c.36)
Housing (Temporary Accommodation) Act 1945 (c.39)
Housing (Temporary Accommodation) Act 1947 (c.6)
Housing (Temporary Provisions) Act 1944 (c.33)
Housing, Town Planning etc. Act 1919 (c.35)
Housing, Town Planning, etc. Act 1909 (c.44)
Housing, Town Planning, etc. (Scotland) Act 1919 (c.60)
Housing (Underground Rooms) Act 1959 (c.34)
Hovercraft Act 1968 (c.59)
Howth Harbour Act 1810 (c.72)
Howth Harbour Act 1863 (c.72)
Hubberston and Pill, Pembroke: Docks and Piers Act 1790 (c.55)
Huddersfield Burial Ground Act 1852 (c.41)
Huddersfield Burial Ground Act 1855 (c.89)
Huddersfield Roads Act 1788 (c.103)
Huddersfield to Ashton-under-Lyne Canal Act 1794 (c.53)
Hudson's Bay Company Act 1868 (c.105)
Hue and Cry Act 1734 (c.16)
Hue and Cry Act 1748 (c.24)
Hull: Drainage Act 1792 (c.109)
Hull: Improvement Act 1795 (c.46)
Hull, Poor Relief Act 1741 (c.10)
Hulmes Chapel and Chelpord Road Act 1797 (c.157)
Human Fertilisation and Embryology Act 1990 (c.37)
Human Fertilisation and Embryology (Disclosure of Information) Act 1992 (c.54)
Human Organ Transplants Act 1989 (c.31)
Human Tissue Act 1961 (c.54)
Hundred Foot River and Ouse: Bedford Level Act 1756 (c.22)
Hungerford to Leckford Road Act 1793 (c.168)

Huntingdon Clergy Charity Act 1775 (c.24)
Huntingdon: Drainage Act 1772 (c.39)
Huntingdon: Improvement Act 1785 (c.9)
Huntingdon Roads Act 1755 (c.26)
Huntingdon Roads Act 1765 (c.51)
Huntingdonshire and Cambridgeshire Roads Act 1744 (c.23)
Huntingdonshire and Northamptonshire Roads Act 1750 (c.59)
Huntingdonshire and Northamptonshire Roads Act 1771 (c.80)
Huntingdonshire Roads Act 1727 (c.4)
Huntingdonshire Roads Act 1757 (c.51)
Huntingdonshire Roads Act 1774 (c.118)
Huntingdonshire Roads Act 1779 (c.86)
Huntingdonshire Roads Act 1790 (c.103)
Hyde Park Act 1842 (c.19)
Hyde Park (Underground Parking) Act 1961 (c.26)
Hydrocarbon Oil (Customs and Excise) Act 1971 (c.12)
Hydrocarbon Oil Duties Act 1979 (c.5)
Hydrocarbon Oil Duties (Temporary Increase) Act 1956 (c.2)
Hydro-Electric Development (Scotland) Act 1943 (c.32)
Hydro-Electric Undertaking (Valuation for Rating) (Scotland) Act 1944 (c.34)
Hydro-Electricity Development (Scotland) Act 1952 (c.22)
Hydrogen Cyanide (Fumigation) Act 1937 (c.45)
Hypnotism Act 1952 (c.46)
Hypothec Abolition (Scotland) Act 1880 (c.12)
Hypothec Amendment (Scotland) Act 1867 (c.42)

Idiots Act 1886 (c.25)
Ilfracombe Harbour Act 1730 (c.19)
Illegal Trawling (Scotland) Act 1934 (c.18)
Illegitimate Children (Scotland) Act 1930 (c.33)
Illicit Distillation (Ireland) Act 1813 (c.32)
Illicit Distillation (Ireland) Act 1831 (c.55)
Illicit Distillation (Ireland) Act 1857 (c.40)
Immature Spirits (Restriction) Act 1915 (c.46)
Immigration Act 1971 (c.77)
Immigration Act 1988 (c.14)
Immigration Appeals Act 1969 (c.21)
Immigration (Carriers' Liability) Act 1987 (c.24)
Immoral Traffic (Scotland) Act 1902 (c.11)
Imperial Defence Act 1888 (c.32)
Imperial Institute (Management) Act 1916 (c.8)
Imperial Telegraphs Act 1929 (c.7)
Imperial Telegraphs Act 1938 (c.57)
Imperial War Graves Endowment Fund Act 1926 (c.14)
Imperial War Museum Act 1920 (c.16)
Imperial War Museum Act 1955 (c.14)
Import and Export Control Act 1990 (c.45)
Import and Export Duties Act 1802 (c.117)
Import Duties Act 1931 (c.8)
Import Duties Act 1958 (c.6)
Import Duties (Emergency Provisions) Act 1939 (c.97)
Import Duty Act 1804 (c.85)
Import, Export and Customs Powers (Defence) Act 1939 (c.69)
Import of Live Fish (England and Wales) Act 1980 (c.27)
Import of Live Fish (Scotland) Act 1978 (c.35)
Importation Act 1702 (c.8)
Importation Act 1702 (cc. 21, 22)
Importation Act 1703 (c.15)
Importation Act 1704 (c.9)
Importation Act 1706 (c.19)
Importation Act 1707 (c.60)
Importation Act 1711 (c.36)
Importation Act 1712 (c.9)
Importation Act 1714 (c.15)
Importation Act 1715 (c.40)
Importation Act 1719 (c.14)
Importation Act 1721 (c.12)
Importation Act 1726 (c.5)
Importation Act 1726 (c.25)
Importation Act 1728 (c.9)
Importation Act 1730 (c.12)
Importation Act 1730 (c.15)
Importation Act 1731 (c.9)
Importation Act 1732 (c.7)
Importation Act 1738 (c.36)
Importation Act 1740 (c.36)
Importation Act 1743 (c.36)
Importation Act 1753 (c.8)
Importation Act 1755 (c.21)
Importation Act 1757 (c.3)
Importation Act 1763 (c.6)
Importation Act 1763 (c.28)
Importation Act 1765 (c.1)
Importation Act 1765 (c.3)
Importation Act 1765 (c.10)
Importation Act 1765 (c.48)
Importation Act 1766 (cc.11, 12)
Importation Act 1766 (c.13)
Importation Act 1766 (c.19)
Importation Act 1766 (c.22)
Importation Act 1766 (c.30)
Importation Act 1766 (c.43)
Importation Act 1768 (c.9)
Importation Act 1769 (c.4)
Importation Act 1769 (c.9)
Importation Act 1770 (c.2)
Importation Act 1771 (c.8)
Importation Act 1771 (c.41)
Importation Act 1771 (cc.49, 50)
Importation Act 1772 (c.7)
Importation Act 1772 (cc.32, 33)
Importation Act 1772 (c.67)
Importation Act 1774 (c.9)
Importation Act 1774 (c.74)
Importation Act 1775 (c.1)
Importation Act 1775 (c.7)

Importation Act 1776 (c.8)
Importation Act 1776 (c.35)
Importation Act 1776 (c.41)
Importation Act 1778 (c.56)
Importation Act 1779 (c.28)
Importation Act 1780 (c.6)
Importation Act 1781 (c.62)
Importation Act 1782 (c.7)
Importation Act 1782 (c.30)
Importation Act 1782 (c.38)
Importation Act 1782 (c.72)
Importation Act 1782 (c.78)
Importation Act 1783 (c.1)
Importation Act 1783 (cc.9, 10)
Importation Act 1783 (c.14)
Importation Act 1788 (c.39)
Importation Act 1789 (c.16)
Importation Act 1790 (c.28)
Importation Act 1790 (c.41)
Importation Act 1791 (c.37)
Importation Act 1791 (c.38)
Importation Act 1792 (c.49)
Importation Act 1793 (c.63)
Importation Act 1794 (c.50)
Importation Act 1795 (c.4)
Importation Act 1795 (c.15)
Importation Act 1795 (c.100)
Importation Act 1795 (c.115)
Importation Act 1795 (c.117)
Importation Act 1796 (c.8)
Importation Act 1796 (c.81)
Importation Act 1796 (c.113)
Importation Act 1797 (c.3)
Importation Act 1797 (c.25)
Importation Act 1797 (c.72)
Importation Act 1797 (c.84)
Importation Act 1799 (c.27)
Importation Act 1799 (c.75)
Importation Act 1799 (c.87)
Importation Act 1799 (c.95)
Importation Act 1799 (c.98)
Importation Act 1799 (c.111)
Importation Act 1799 (c.112)
Importation Act 1800 (c.11)
Importation Act 1800 (c.18)
Importation Act 1800 (c.25)
Importation Act 1800 (c.83)
Importation Act 1800 (c.107)
Importation Act 1801 (c.7)
Importation Act 1801 (c.16)
Importation Act 1801 (c.37)
Importation Act 1801 (c.41)
Importation Act 1801 (c.93)
Importation Act 1802 (c.44)
Importation Act 1804 (cc.29, 30)
Importation Act 1806 (c.74)
Importation Act 1806 (c.103)
Importation Act 1806 (c.113)
Importation Act 1806 (c.117)
Importation Act 1806 (c.121)
Importation Act 1807 (c.24)
Importation Act 1807 (cc.25, 26)
Importation Act 1807 (c.27)
Importation Act 1807 (c.67)
Importation Act 1808 (c.11)
Importation Act 1808 (c.19)
Importation Act 1808 (cc.23, 24)
Importation Act 1808 (c.125)
Importation Act 1809 (c.9)
Importation Act 1809 (c.16)
Importation Act 1809 (cc.25, 26)
Importation Act 1809 (c.60)
Importation Act 1809 (c.105)
Importation Act 1810 (c.55)
Importation Act 1810 (c.80)
Importation Act 1811 (c.48)
Importation Act 1811 (c.58)
Importation Act 1811 (c.62)
Importation Act 1812 (c.18)
Importation Act 1812 (c.33)
Importation Act 1812 (c.119)
Importation Act 1813 (c.34)
Importation Act 1813 (c.37)
Importation Act 1813 (c.41)
Importation Act 1814 (c.51)
Importation Act 1814 (c.124)
Importation Act 1814 (c.125)
Importation Act 1815 (c.26)
Importation Act 1815 (c.34)
Importation Act 1815 (c.86)
Importation Act 1816 (c.2)
Importation Act 1816 (cc.25, 26)
Importation Act 1816 (c.36)
Importation Act 1816 (c.37)
Importation Act 1840 (c.32)
Importation Act 1844 (c.100)
Importation Act 1847 (c.2)
Importation Act 1847 (c.86)
Importation and Exportation Act 1766 (cc.1–5)
Importation and Exportation Act 1772 (cc. 1–5)
Importation and Exportation Act 1772 (cc.69, 70)
Importation and Exportation Act 1772 (cc.72, 73)
Importation and Exportation Act 1787 (c.27)
Importation and Exportation Act 1789 (c.58)
Importation and Exportation Act 1790 (c.1)
Importation and Exportation Act 1790 (c.29)
Importation and Exportation Act 1790 (c.42)
Importation and Exportation Act 1791 (c.4)
Importation and Exportation Act 1791 (c.30)
Importation and Exportation Act 1791 (c.47)
Importation and Exportation Act 1792 (c.37)
Importation and Exportation Act 1793 (c.50)
Importation and Exportation Act 1793 (c.65)
Importation and Exportation Act 1797 (c.39)
Importation and Exportation Act 1799 (c.88)
Importation and Exportation Act 1800 (c.58)
Importation and Exportation Act 1804 (c.109)
Importation and Exportation Act 1805 (c.57)
Importation and Exportation Act 1805 (c.86)
Importation and Exportation Act 1807 (c.34)
Importation and Exportation Act 1810 (cc.12, 13)

Importation and Exportation Act 1810 (c.21)
Importation and Exportation Act 1812 (c.8)
Importation and Exportation Act 1812 (c.69)
Importation and Exportation Act 1812 (c.79)
Importation and Exportation Act 1813 (c.55)
Importation and Exportation Act 1814 (c.81)
Importation and Exportation Act 1814 (c.129)
Importation and Exportation Act 1815 (c.117)
Importation and Exportation (Ireland) Act 1807 (c.1)
Importation and Exportation (Ireland) Act 1807 (c.16)
Importation and Exportation (Ireland) Act 1810 (c.97)
Importation, etc. Act 1750 (c.32)
Importation, etc. Act 1766 (c.28)
Importation, etc. Act 1766 (c.36)
Importation, etc. Act 1780 (c.45)
Importation, etc. Act 1801 (c.68)
Importation, etc. Act 1804 (c.35)
Importation, etc. Act 1804 (c.89)
Importation, etc. Act 1806 (c.53)
Importation, etc. Act 1809 (c.18)
Importation, etc. Act 1809 (c.22)
Importation, etc. Act 1812 (c.2)
Importation, etc. Act 1812 (c.20)
Importation, etc. Act 1814 (cc.8, 9)
Importation, etc. Act 1814 (c.111)
Importation, Exportation, etc. Act 1805 (c.26)
Importation in Neutral Vessel, etc. Act 1803 (c.153)
Importation into Isle of Man Act 1813 (c.110)
Importation into Quebec Act 1763 (c.19)
Importation into Quebec Act 1766 (c.42)
Importation into Scotland Act 1740 (c.7)
Importation (Ireland) Act 1807 (c.31)
Importation of Animals Act 1922 (c.5)
Importation of Arms, etc. (Ireland) Act 1841 (c.25)
Importation of Milk Act 1983 (c.37)
Importation of Pedigree Animals Act 1925 (c.30)
Importation of Plumage (Prohibition) Act 1921 (c.16)
Importation of Prize Goods Act 1711 (c.30)
Importation of Silk Act 1779 (c.9)
Imprisonment for Debt (Scotland) Act 1835 (c.70)
Imprisonment for Debts Abroad Act 1801 (c.106)
Imprisonment of Certain Traitors Act 1702 (c.23)
Imprisonment of Certain Traitors Act 1714 (c.7)
Imprisonment of Certain Traitors Act 1727 (c.4)
Imprisonment of Debtors, etc. Act 1786 (c.38)
Imprisonment (Temporary Provisions) Act 1980 (c.57)
Imprisonment with Hard Labour Act 1813 (c.162)
Improvement at Westminster Act 1814 (c.154)
Improvement of Commons Act 1801 (c.20)
Improvement of Land Act 1864 (c.114)
Improvement of Land Act 1899 (c.46)
Improvement of Land Act (1899) Amendment Act 1925 (c.48)
Improvement of Land (Scotland) Act 1893 (c.34)
Improvement of Lands (Ecclesiastical Benefices) Act 1854 (c.67)
Improvement of Live Stock (Licensing of Bulls) Act 1931 (c.43)
Improvements, Metropolis Act 1844 (c.1)
Incapacitated Bishops Act 1843 (c.62)
Incest Act 1567 (c.14)
Incest and Related Offences (Scotland) Act 1986 (c.36)
Incitement to Disaffection Act 1934 (c.56)
Incitement to Mutiny Act 1797 (c.70)
Incitement to Mutiny Act 1814 (c.158)
Inciting to Mutiny, etc. Act 1815 (c.171)
Inclosure Act 1773 (c.81)
Inclosure Act 1801 (c.109)
Inclosure Act 1836 (c.115)
Inclosure Act 1840 (c.31)
Inclosure Act 1845 (c.118)
Inclosure Act 1846 (c.70)
Inclosure Act 1852 (c.79)
Inclosure Act 1854 (c.97)
Inclosure Act 1857 (c.31)
Inclosure Act 1866 (c.94)
Inclosure Act 1867 (c.20)
Inclosure Act 1867 (c.71)
Inclosure, etc., Expenses Act 1868 (c.89)
Inclosures Act 1846 (c.16)
Inclosures Act 1846 (c.117)
Inclosures Act 1847 (c.25)
Income and Corporation Taxes Act 1970 (c.10)
Income and Corporation Taxes Act 1988 (c.1)
Income and Corporation Taxes (No. 2) Act 1970 (c.54)
Income Tax Act 1803 (c.122)
Income Tax Act 1804 (c.37)
Income Tax Act 1804 (c.83)
Income Tax Act 1805 (c.15)
Income Tax Act 1805 (c.49)
Income Tax Act 1805 (c.110)
Income Tax Act 1806 (c.65)
Income Tax Act 1842 (c.35)
Income Tax Act 1844 (c.38)
Income Tax Act 1845 (c.4)
Income Tax Act 1846 (c.81)
Income Tax Act 1871 (c.5)
Income Tax Act 1873 (c.8)
Income Tax Act 1918 (c.40)
Income Tax Act 1944 (c.32)
Income Tax Act 1952 (c.10)
Income Tax Assessment Act 1870 (c.4)
Income Tax (Employments) Act 1943 (c.45)
Income Tax, etc. Act 1810 (c.106)
Income Tax (Foreign Dividends) Act 1842 (c.80)
Income Tax Management Act 1964 (c.37)

Income Tax (Offices and Employment) Act 1944 (c.12)
Income Tax Procedure (Emergency Provisions) Act 1939 (c.99)
Income Tax (Public Offices) Act 1872 (c.82)
Income Tax (Repayment of Post-War Credits) Act 1959 (c.28)
Income Tax Repeal, etc. Act 1802 (c.42)
Increase of Rent and Mortgage Interest (Restrictions) Act 1919 (c.7)
Increase of Rent and Mortgage Interest (Restrictions) Act 1920 (c.17)
Increase of Rent and Mortgage Interest (Restrictions) Act 1935 (c.13)
Increase of Rent and Mortgage Interest (Restrictions) Act 1938 (c.26)
Increase of Rent and Mortgage Interest Restrictions Act 1923 (c.7)
Increase of Rent and Mortgage Interest (War Restrictions) Act 1915 (c.97)
Increase of Rent, etc. (Amendment) Act 1918 (c.7)
Increase of Rent, etc. (Amendment) Act 1919 (c.90)
Increased Assessments Act 1861 (c.27)
Incumbents Act 1868 (c.117)
Incumbents and Benefices Loans Extension Act 1881 (c.25)
Incumbents of Benefices Loans Act 1887 (c.8)
Incumbents of Benefices Loans Extension Act 1886 (c.34)
Incumbents of Benefices Loans Extension Act 1896 (c.13)
Incumbents Resignation Act 1871 (c.44)
Incumbents Resignation Act, 1871, Amendment 1887 (c.23)
Indecent Advertisements (Amendment) Act 1970 (c.47)
Indecent Advertisements Act 1889 (c.18)
Indecent Displays (Control) Act 1981 (c.42)
Indecency with Children Act 1960 (c.33)
Indemnity Act 1715 (c.39)
Indemnity Act 1727 (c.23)
Indemnity Act 1728 (c.31)
Indemnity Act 1730 (c.6)
Indemnity Act 1732 (c.4)
Indemnity Act 1733 (c.10)
Indemnity Act 1734 (c.4)
Indemnity Act 1734 (c.17)
Indemnity Act 1735 (c.6)
Indemnity Act 1736 (c.13)
Indemnity Act 1737 (c.31)
Indemnity Act 1738 (c.6)
Indemnity Act 1739 (c.6)
Indemnity Act 1740 (c.18)
Indemnity Act 1742 (c.30)
Indemnity Act 1754 (c.13)
Indemnity Act 1755 (c.3)
Indemnity Act 1755 (c.24)
Indemnity Act 1757 (c.9)
Indemnity Act 1763 (c.31)
Indemnity Act 1765 (c.4)
Indemnity Act 1766 (c.7)
Indemnity Act 1766 (c.31)
Indemnity Act 1766 (c.51)
Indemnity Act 1768 (c.6)
Indemnity Act 1769 (c.12)
Indemnity Act 1770 (c.42)
Indemnity Act 1771 (c.18)
Indemnity Act 1772 (c.12)
Indemnity Act 1772 (c.31)
Indemnity Act 1772 (c.76)
Indemnity Act 1774 (c.47)
Indemnity Act 1775 (c.17)
Indemnity Act 1776 (c.37)
Indemnity Act 1776 (c.50)
Indemnity Act 1778 (c.39)
Indemnity Act 1779 (c.47)
Indemnity Act 1780 (c.47)
Indemnity Act 1782 (c.55)
Indemnity Act 1783 (c.30)
Indemnity Act 1784 (c.58)
Indemnity Act 1785 (c.82)
Indemnity Act 1786 (c.98)
Indemnity Act 1787 (c.40)
Indemnity Act 1788 (c.22)
Indemnity Act 1789 (c.40)
Indemnity Act 1790 (c.12)
Indemnity Act 1791 (c.8)
Indemnity Act 1791 (c.27)
Indemnity Act 1793 (c.12)
Indemnity Act 1794 (c.12)
Indemnity Act 1795 (c.50)
Indemnity Act 1796 (c.11)
Indemnity Act 1796 (c.57)
Indemnity Act 1797 (c.14)
Indemnity Act 1797 (c.93)
Indemnity Act 1799 (c.17)
Indemnity Act 1800 (c.19)
Indemnity Act 1800 (c.31)
Indemnity Act 1801 (c.66)
Indemnity Act 1802 (c.6)
Indemnity Act 1802 (c.23)
Indemnity Act 1803 (c.7)
Indemnity Act 1805 (c.6)
Indemnity Act 1806 (c.7)
Indemnity Act 1807 (c.5)
Indemnity Act 1807 (c.3)
Indemnity Act 1807 (c.35)
Indemnity Act 1808 (c.40)
Indemnity Act 1809 (c.15)
Indemnity Act 1810 (c.4)
Indemnity Act 1811 (cc.17, 18)
Indemnity Act 1811 (c.98)
Indemnity Act 1812 (c.26)
Indemnity Act 1813 (c.5)
Indemnity Act 1815 (c.17)
Indemnity Act 1816 (c.33)
Indemnity Act 1836 (c.7)
Indemnity Act 1837 (c.12)
Indemnity Act 1838 (c.16)
Indemnity Act 1840 (c.16)
Indemnity Act 1841 (c.11)
Indemnity Act 1842 (c.10)
Indemnity Act 1843 (c.9)

Indemnity Act 1844 (c.10)
Indemnity Act 1845 (c.24)
Indemnity Act 1846 (c.13)
Indemnity Act 1847 (c.18)
Indemnity Act 1866 (c.116)
Indemnity Act 1867 (c.88)
Indemnity as to Certain Books Act 1809 (c.69)
Indemnity, etc. Act 1735 (c.26)
Indemnity for Certain Acts Act 1801 (c.46)
Indemnity for Certain Orders of Council Act 1805 (c.97)
Indemnity (Ireland) Act 1801 (c.49)
Indemnity (Ireland) Act 1802 (c.53)
Indemnity (Ireland) Act 1803 (c.77)
Indemnity, Masters in Chancery Act 1724 (c.2)
Indemnity (O. in C., West Indies Importation) Act 1812 (c.12)
Indemnity of Innkeepers Act 1774 (c.60)
Indemnity, Suppression of Riots Act 1780 (c.63)
Indemnity to Certain Governors Act 1836 (c.48)
Indemnity to Certain Governors, etc. Act 1795 (c.57)
Indemnity to Certain Persons Act 1838 (c.112)
Indemnity to Certain Printers Act 1801 (c.80)
Indemnity to Governor of Surinam Act 1800 (c.108)
Indemnity to Governors of West Indies Act 1796 (c.32)
Indemnity to Governors of West Indies Act 1797 (c.64)
Indemnity to Governors of West Indies Act 1798 (c.72)
Indemnity to Governors of West Indies Act 1799 (c.57)
Indemnity to Printers Act 1800 (c.95)
Indemnity to Proprietors, etc., of Newspapers Act 1792 (c.61)
Indemnity, West Indies Act 1800 (c.76)
Independent Broadcasting Authority Act 1973 (c.19)
Independent Broadcasting Authority Act 1974 (c.16)
Independent Broadcasting Authority Act 1978 (c.43)
Independent Broadcasting Authority Act 1979 (c.35)
Independent Broadcasting Authority (No. 2) Act 1974 (c.42)
India and Burma (Emergency Provisions) Act 1940 (c.33)
India and Burma (Existing Laws) Act 1937 (c.9)
India and Burma (Miscellaneous Amendments) Act 1940 (c.5)
India and Burma (Postponement of Elections) Act 1941 (c.44)
India and Burma (Temporary and Miscellaneous Provisions) Act 1942 (c.39)
India (Attachment of States) Act 1944 (c.14)
India (Central Government and Legislature) Act 1946 (c.39)
India (Consequential Provisions) Act 1949 (c.92)
India (Estate Duty) Act 1945 (c.7)
India (Federal Court Judges) Act 1942 (c.7)
India Government, etc. Act 1807 (c.68)
India Home (Appointments) Act 1875 (c.73)
India (Home Charges Arrears) Act 1882 (c.79)
India (Inam Lands) Act 1869 (c.29)
India Independence Act 1947 (c.30)
India Military Funds Act 1866 (c.18)
India (Miscellaneous Provisions) Act 1944 (c.38)
India Office Auditor Act 1881 (c.63)
India Officers' Salaries Act 1837 (c.47)
India Pay (Temporary Abatements) Act 1933 (c.7)
India (Proclamations of Emergency) Act 1946 (c.23)
India Stock Certificate Act 1863 (c.73)
India Stock Dividends Act 1871 (c.29)
India Stock (Powers of Attorney) Act 1880 (c.11)
India Stock Transfer Act 1862 (c.7)
Indian Advance Act 1879 (c.45)
Indian and Colonial Divorce Jurisdiction Act 1926 (c.40)
Indian and Colonial Divorce Jurisdiction Act 1939 (c.35)
Indian Army Pension Deficiency Act 1885 (c.67)
Indian Bishops Act 1842 (c.119)
Indian Bishops Act 1871 (c.62)
Indian Church Act 1927 (c.40)
Indian Civil Service (Temporary Provisions) Act 1915 (c.87)
Indian Councils Act 1869 (c.98)
Indian Councils Act 1871 (c.34)
Indian Councils Act 1874 (c.91)
Indian Councils Act 1892 (c.14)
Indian Councils Act 1904 (c.26)
Indian Councils Act 1909 (c.4)
Indian Divorce Act 1945 (c.5)
Indian Divorces (Validity) Act 1921 (c.18)
Indian Franchise Act 1945 (c.2)
Indian Guaranteed Railways Act 1879 (c.41)
Indian High Courts Act 1911 (c.18)
Indian High Courts Act 1922 (c.20)
Indian Independence Act 1947 (c.30)
Indian Loan Act 1881 (c.54)
Indian Marine Service Act 1884 (c.38)
Indian Pay (Temporary Abatements) Act 1931 (c.7)
Indian Pay (Temporary Abatements) Act 1934 (c.8)
Indian Presidency Towns Act 1815 (c.84)
Indian Prize Money Act 1866 (c.47)
Indian Prize Money Act 1868 (c.38)
Indian Railway Companies Act 1868 (c.26)
Indian Railway Companies Act 1873 (c.43)
Indian Railways Act 1894 (c.12)

Indian Railways Act Amendment 1906 (c.9)
Indian Salaries and Allowances Act 1880 (c.3)
Indian Securities Act 1860 (c.5)
Indictable Offences Act 1848 (c.42)
Indictable Offences Act Amendment 1868 (c.107)
Indictments Act 1915 (c.90)
Indus Basin Development Fund Act 1960 (c.1)
Industrial and Providence Societies Act 1952 (c.17)
Industrial and Providence Societies Act 1961 (c.28)
Industrial and Provident Societies Act 1867 (c.117)
Industrial and Provident Societies Act 1871 (c.80)
Industrial and Provident Societies Act 1876 (c.45)
Industrial and Provident Societies Act 1893 (c.39)
Industrial and Provident Societies Act 1894 (c.8)
Industrial and Provident Societies Act 1965 (c.12)
Industrial and Provident Societies Act 1967 (c.48)
Industrial and Provident Societies Act 1975 (c.41)
Industrial and Provident Societies Act 1978 (c.34)
Industrial and Provident Societies (Amendment) Act 1895 (c.30)
Industrial and Provident Societies (Amendment) Act 1913 (c.31)
Industrial and Provident Societies (Amendment) Act 1928 (c.4)
Industrial and Providence Societies (Amendment) Act 1954 (c.43)
Industrial Assurance Act 1923 (c.8)
Industrial Assurance and Friendly Societies Act 1929 (c.28)
Industrial Assurance and Friendly Societies Act 1948 (c.39)
Industrial Assurance and Friendly Societies Act 1948 (Amendment) Act 1958 (c.27)
Industrial Assurance and Friendly Societies (Emergency Protection from Forfeiture) Act 1940 (c.10)
Industrial Assurance (Juvenile Societies) Act 1926 (c.35)
Industrial Common Ownership Act 1976 (c.78)
Industrial Courts Act 1919 (c.69)
Industrial Development Act 1966 (c.34)
Industrial Development Act 1982 (c.52)
Industrial Development Act 1985 (c.25)
Industrial Development (Ships) Act 1970 (c.2)
Industrial Diseases (Notification) Act 1981 (c.25)
Industrial Expansion Act 1968 (c.32)
Industrial Injuries and Diseases (Northern Ireland Old Cases) Act 1975 (c.17)
Industrial Injuries and Diseases (Old Cases) Act 1967 (c.34)
Industrial Injuries and Diseases (Old Cases) Act 1975 (c.16)
Industrial Organisations and Development Act 1947 (c.40)
Industrial Relations Act 1971 (c.72)
Industrial Reorganisation Corporation Act 1966 (c.50)
Industrial Schools Act 1866 (c.118)
Industrial Schools Act Amendment 1880 (c.15)
Industrial Schools Acts Amendment 1894 (c.33)
Industrial Schools (Ireland) Act 1868 (c.25)
Industrial Schools (Ireland) Act 1885 (c.19)
Industrial Training Act 1954 (c.16)
Industrial Training Act 1964 (c.16)
Industrial Training Act 1982 (c.10)
Industrial Training Act 1986 (c.15)
Industry Act 1971 (c.17)
Industry Act 1972 (c.63)
Industry Act 1975 (c.68)
Industry Act 1979 (c.32)
Industry Act 1980 (c.33)
Industry Act 1981 (c.6)
Industry Act 1982 (c.18)
Industry (Amendment) Act 1976 (c.73)
Inebriates Act 1888 (c.19)
Inebriates Act 1898 (c.60)
Inebriates Act 1899 (c.35)
Inebriates Amendment (Scotland) Act 1900 (c.28)
Infant Felons Act 1840 (c.90)
Infant Life (Preservation) Act 1929 (c.34)
Infant Life Protection Act 1872 (c.38)
Infant Life Protection Act 1897 (c.57)
Infant Suitors in Equity Entitled to Stock Act 1812 (c.32)
Infant Trustees and Mortgages Act 1763 (c.16)
Infanticide Act 1922 (c.18)
Infanticide Act 1938 (c.36)
Infants Property Act 1830 (c.65)
Infants Relief Act 1874 (c.62)
Infants' Settlements Act 1855 (c.43)
Infectious Diseases (Notification) Act 1889 (c.72)
Infectious Diseases (Notification) Extension Act 1899 (c.8)
Infectious Diseases (Prevention) Act 1890 (c.34)
Infeftment Act 1845 (c.35)
Inferior Courts Act 1779 (c.70)
Inferior Courts Act 1844 (c.19)
Inferior Courts Judgments Extension Act 1882 (c.31)
Informal Attestation of Certain Deeds Act 1814 (c.168)
Information in Nature of Quo Warranto Act 1792 (c.58)

Inhabited House Duties Act 1791 (c.2)
Inhabited House, etc., Duties Act 1797 (c.40)
Inheritance (Family Provision) Act 1938 (c.45)
Inheritance (Provision for Family and Dependants) Act 1975 (c.63)
Inheritance Tax (Formerly Capital Transfer Tax) Act 1984 (c.51)
Injured Animals Act 1894 (c.22)
Injured Animals Act 1907 (c.5)
Injuries in War (Compensation) Act 1914 (c.30)
Injuries in War Compensation Act 1914 (Session 2) (c.18)
Injuries in War (Compensation) Act 1915 (c.24)
Inland Excise and Taxes (Ireland) Act 1812 (c.97)
Inland Fisheries (Ireland) Act 1838 (c.76)
Inland Navigation (Ireland) Act 1813 (c.144)
Inland Navigation (Ireland) Act 1815 (c.182)
Inland Revenue Act 1866 (c.64)
Inland Revenue Act 1868 (c.124)
Inland Revenue Act 1880 (c.20)
Inland Revenue Buildings Act 1881 (c.10)
Inland Revenue Regulation Act 1890 (c.21)
Inland Revenue Repeal Act 1870 (c.99)
Inner Urban Areas Act 1978 (c.50)
Innkeepers Act 1878 (c.38)
Inquiries by Board of Trade Act 1872 (c.18)
Inquiry into Certain Frauds and Abuses Act 1802 (c.16)
Inquiry into Fees, Public Offices Act 1785 (c.19)
Inquiry into Fees, Public Offices Act 1786 (c.66)
Inquiry into Fees, Public Offices Act 1787 (c.35)
Inquiry into Military Departments Act 1805 (c.47)
Inquiry into Military Departments Act 1807 (c.33)
Inquiry into Military Departments Act 1808 (c.61)
Inquiry into Military Departments Act 1809 (c.111)
Inquiry into Military Expenditure, etc. Act 1811 (c.19)
Inquiry into Naval Departments Act 1805 (c.46)
Inquiry into Public Expenditure Act 1805 (c.70)
Inquiry into Public Offices (Ireland) Act 1804 (c.106)
Inquiry into Public Offices (Ireland) Act (c.65)
Inquiry into Public Offices (Ireland) Act 1813 (c.130)
Inrolment of Grants of Annuities Act (c.141)
Insane Prisoners Act 1840 (c.54)
Inshore Fishing Industry Act 1945 (c.11)
Inshore Fishing (Scotland) Act 1984 (c.26)
Inshore Fishing (Scotland) Act 1994 (c.27)
Insolvency Act 1976 (c.60)
Insolvency Act 1985 (c.65)
Insolvency Act 1986 (c.45)
Insolvency Act 1994 (c.7)
Insolvency (No. 2) Act 1994 (c.12)
Insolvency Services (Accounting and Investment) Act 1970 (c.8)
Insolvent Act 1812 (c.163)
Insolvent Debtors Act 1839 (c.39)
Insolvent Debtors Act 1842 (c.116)
Insolvent Debtor's Discharge Act 1794 (c.69)
Insolvent Debtor's Discharge Act 1795 (c.88)
Insolvent Debtors, East Indies Act 1836 (c.47)
Insolvent Debtors (England) Act 1813 (c.23)
Insolvent Debtors (England) Act 1813 (c.102)
Insolvent Debtors (England) Act 1816 (c.102)
Insolvent Debtors (England) Act 1836 (c.44)
Insolvent Debtors, etc., Relief Act 1774 (c.77)
Insolvent Debtors, India Act 1840 (c.80)
Insolvent Debtors, India Act 1846 (c.14)
Insolvent Debtors (Ireland) Act 1810 (c.47)
Insolvent Debtors (Ireland) Act 1813 (c.138)
Insolvent Debtors (Ireland) Act 1814 (c.114)
Insolvent Debtors (Ireland) Act 1816 (c.126)
Insolvent Debtors (Ireland) Act 1836 (c.23)
Insolvent Debtors (Ireland) Act 1840 (c.14)
Insolvent Debtors (Ireland) Act 1840 (c.107)
Insolvent Debtors (Ireland) Act 1841 (c.47)
Insolvent Debtors Relief Act 1702 (c.19)
Insolvent Debtors Relief Act 1703 (c.10)
Insolvent Debtors' Relief Act 1711 (c.29)
Insolvent Debtors' Relief Act 1724 (c.21)
Insolvent Debtors' Relief Act 1728 (c.20)
Insolvent Debtors' Relief Act 1730 (c.27)
Insolvent Debtors' Relief Act 1737 (c.9)
Insolvent Debtors' Relief Act 1755 (c.13)
Insolvent Debtors' Relief Act 1765 (c.41)
Insolvent Debtors' Relief Act 1769 (c.26)
Insolvent Debtors Relief Act 1776 (c.38)
Insolvent Debtors Relief Act 1781 (c.63)
Insolvent Debtors Relief Act 1801 (c.70)
Insolvent Debtors Relief Act 1804 (c.108)
Insolvent Debtors Relief Act 1805 (c.3)
Insolvent Debtors Relief Act 1806 (c.108)
Insolvent Debtors Relief Act 1809 (c.54)
Insolvent Debtors Relief Act 1809 (c.115)
Insolvent Debtors Relief Act 1812 (c.13)
Insolvent Debtors Relief Act 1812 (c.165)
Insolvent Debtors Relief (England) Act 1811 (c.125)
Insolvent Debtors Relief (England) Act 1812 (c.6)
Insolvent Debtors Relief (England) Act 1813 (c.28)
Insolvent Debtors' Relief, etc. Act 1719 (c.22)
Insolvent Debtors Relief, etc. Act 1778 (c.52)
Insolvent Debtors Relief (Ireland) Act 1811 (c.123)
Insurance Brokers (Registration) Act 1977 (c.46)
Insurance Companies Act 1958 (c.72)
Insurance Companies Act 1974 (c.49)
Insurance Companies Act 1980 (c.25)

Insurance Companies Act 1981 (c.31)
Insurance Companies Act 1982 (c.50)
Insurance Companies Amendment Act 1973 (c.58)
Insurance Companies Reserves Act 1995 (c.29)
Insurance Contracts (War Settlement) Act 1952 (c.56)
Insurance (Fees) Act 1985 (c.46)
Insurances on Ships, etc. Act 1785 (c.44)
Insurrection and Disturbances (Ireland) Act 1807 (c.13)
Intelligence Services Act 1994 (c.13)
Interception of Communications Act 1985 (c.56)
Interchange of Grain Between Great Britain and Ireland Act 1807 (c.7)
Intercourse Between Jamaica and St. Domingo Act 1812 (c.3)
Intercourse with St. Helena Act 1816 (c.23)
Interest on Damages (Scotland) Act 1958 (c.61)
Interest on Damages (Scotland) Act 1971 (c.31)
Intermediate Education (Ireland) Act 1878 (c.66)
Intermediate Education (Ireland) Act 1882 (c.69)
Intermediate Education (Ireland) Act 1900 (c.43)
Intermediate Education (Ireland) Act 1913 (c.29)
Intermediate Education (Ireland) Act 1914 (c.41)
Interments (Felo de se) Act 1882 (c.19)
International Bank and Monetary Fund Act 1959 (c.17)
International Carriage of Perishable Foodstuffs Act 1976 (c.58)
International Cocoa Agreement Act 1973 (c.46)
International Copyright Act 1838 (c.59)
International Copyright Act 1844 (c.12)
International Copyright Act 1875 (c.12)
International Copyright Act 1886 (c.33)
International Development Association Act 1960 (c.35)
International Development Association Act 1964 (c.13)
International Finance Corporation Act 1955 (c.5)
International Finance, Trade and Aid Act 1977 (c.6)
International Headquarters and Defence Organisations Act 1964 (c.5)
International Monetary Arrangements Act 1983 (c.51)
International Monetary Fund Act 1962 (c.20)
International Monetary Fund Act 1968 (c.58)
International Monetary Fund Act 1970 (c.49)
International Monetary Fund Act 1979 (c.29)
International Organisations Act 1968 (c.48)
International Organisations Act 1981 (c.9)
International Organisations (Immunities and Privileges) Act 1950 (c.14)
International Parliamentary Organisations (Registration) Act 1989 (c.19)
International Road Haulage Permits Act 1975 (c.46)
International Sugar Organisation Act 1973 (c.68)
International Transport Conventions Act 1983 (c.14)
Internationally Protected Persons Act 1978 (c.17)
Interpleader (Ireland) Act 1846 (c.64)
Interpretation Act 1889 (c.63)
Interpretation Act 1978 (c.30)
Interpretation of Terms Act 1837 (c.39)
Intestate Husband's Estate (Scotland) Act 1911 (c.10)
Intestate Husband's Estate (Scotland) Act 1919 (c.9)
Intestate Husband's Estate (Scotland) Act 1959 (c.21)
Intestate Moveable Succession (Scotland) Act 1919 (c.61)
Intestates Act 1873 (c.52)
Intestates Act 1875 (c.27)
Intestates' Estates Act 1884 (c.71)
Intestates' Estates Act 1890 (c.29)
Intestates' Estates Act 1952 (c.64)
Intestates' Widows and Children (Scotland) Act 1875 (c.41)
Institute of Management (Customs) Act 1951 (c.51)
Intoxicating Liquor (Sales to Persons Under Eighteen) Act 1923 (c.28)
Intoxicating Liquor (Temporary Restriction) Act 1914 (c.77)
Intoxicating Liquors (Ireland) Act 1906 (c.39)
Intoxicating Liquors (Licences Suspension) Act 1871 (c.88)
Intoxicating Liquors (Sale to Children) Act 1886 (c.56)
Intoxicating Liquors (Sale to Children) Act 1901 (c.27)
Intoxicating Substances (Supply) Act 1985 (c.26)
Inventories (Scotland) Act 1816 (c.107)
Inverness and Elgin County Boundaries Act 1870 (c.16)
Inverness Beer Duties Act 1718 (c.17)
Inverness Beer Duties Act 1737 (c.16)
Inverness Gaol Act 1788 (c.69)
Inverness Roads Act 1793 (c.118)
Investment and Building Grants Act 1971 (c.51)
Investment of Certain Money Act 1808 (c.21)
Investments of Trust Funds Act 1867 (c.132)
Ionian Islands Commissioners Act 1868 (c.128)
Ipswich and Stowmarket Navigation Act 1790 (c.57)
Ipswich and Stowmarket Navigation Act 1793 (c.20)

Ipswich and Yaxley Roads Act 1793 (c.128)
Ipswich: Improvement Act 1793 (c.92)
Ipswich: Improvement, etc. Act 1797 (c.44)
Iran (Temporary Powers) Act 1980 (c.28)
Ireland Act 1949 (c.41)
Ireland (Confirmation of Agreement) Act 1925 (c.77)
Ireland Development Grant Act 1903 (c.23)
Irish and Scotch Paupers Removal Act 1837 (c.10)
Irish Appeals Act 1780 (c.28)
Irish Appeals Act 1783 (c.28)
Irish Bankrupt and Insolvent Act 1857 (c.60)
Irish Charges Act 1801 (c.32)
Irish Church Act 1869 (c.42)
Irish Church Act Amendment Act 1881 (c.71)
Irish Church Act (1869) Amendment Act 1872 (c.90)
Irish Church Amendment Act 1872 (c.13)
Irish Constabulary Act 1874 (c.80)
Irish Education Act 1892 (c.42)
Irish Education Act 1893 (c.41)
Irish Free State (Agreement) Act 1922 (c.4)
Irish Free State (Confirmation of Agreement) Act 1924 (c.41)
Irish Free State (Confirmation of Agreement) Act 1929 (c.4)
Irish Free State (Consequential Provisions) Act 1922 (c.2)
Irish Free State Constitution Act 1922 (c.1)
Irish Free State Land Purchase (Loan Guarantee) Act 1924 (c.3)
Irish Free State (Special Duties) Act 1931 (c.30)
Irish Handloom Weavers Act 1909 (c.21)
Irish Land Act 1903 (c.37)
Irish Land Act 1904 (c.34)
Irish Land Act 1907 (c.38)
Irish Land Act 1909 (c.42)
Irish Land (Provisions for Sailors and Soldiers) Act 1919 (c.82)
Irish Lighthouses Act 1811 (c.66)
Irish Loans Act 1880 (c.44)
Irish Mariners, etc. Act 1802 (c.61)
Irish Militia Act 1805 (c.38)
Irish Militia Act 1806 (c.124)
Irish Militia Act 1807 (c.6)
Irish Police Constables (Naval and Military Service) Act 1914 (c.84)
Irish Police (Naval and Military Service) Act 1915 (c.32)
Irish Presbyterian Church Act 1871 (c.24)
Irish Railways (Confirmation of Agreement) Act 1919 (c.78)
Irish Reformatory Schools Act 1868 (c.59)
Irish Reproductive Loan Fund Act 1883 (c.33)
Irish Reproductive Loan Fund Amendment Act 1882 (c.16)
Irish Sailors and Soldiers Land Trust Act 1952 (c.58)
Irish Sailors and Soldiers Land Trust Act 1967 (c.67)
Irish Sailors and Soldiers Land Trust Act 1987 (c.48)
Irish Tobacco Act 1907 (c.3)
Irish Universities Act 1908 (c.38)
Iron and Steel Act 1949 (c.72)
Iron and Steel Act 1953 (c.15)
Iron and Steel Act 1967 (c.17)
Iron and Steel Act 1969 (c.45)
Iron and Steel Act 1972 (c.12)
Iron and Steel Act 1975 (c.64)
Iron and Steel Act 1981 (c.46)
Iron and Steel Act 1982 (c.25)
Iron and Steel (Amendment) Act 1976 (c.41)
Iron and Steel (Amendment) Act 1978 (c.41)
Iron and Steel (Borrowing Powers) Act 1981 (c.2)
Iron and Steel (Financial Provisions) Act 1960 (c.26)
Irvine Beer Duties Act 1735 (c.27)
Island of Rockall Act 1972 (c.2)
Isle of Axholme: Inclosure, etc. Act 1795 (c.107)
Isle of Ely and Norfolk Roads Act 1767 (c.100)
Isle of Ely: Drainage Act 1757 (c.19)
Isle of Ely: Drainage Act 1772 (c.20)
Isle of Ely: Drainage Act 1791 (c.81)
Isle of Ely: Drainage Act 1792 (c.108)
Isle of Ely: Drainage Act 1795 (c.48)
Isle of Ely: Drainage Act 1797 (c.96)
Isle of Ely, etc.: Drainage Act 1772 (c.19)
Isle of Ely, etc.: Drainage Act 1772 (c.60)
Isle of Ely, etc.: Drainage Act 1775 (c.66)
Isle of Ely: Small Debts Act 1778 (c.36)
Isle of Ely to Ramsey Road Act 1794 (c.127)
Isle of Man Act 1780 (c.42)
Isle of Man 1865 (c.28)
Isle of Man Act 1958 (c.11)
Isle of Man Act 1979 (c.58)
Isle of Man (Church Building and New Parishes) Act 1897 (c.33)
Isle of Man (Customs) Act 1810 (c.42)
Isle of Man (Customs) Act 1887 (c.5)
Isle of Man (Customs) Act 1888 (c.7)
Isle of Man (Customs) Act 1892 (c.28)
Isle of Man (Customs) Act 1895 (c.38)
Isle of Man (Customs) Act 1898 (c.27)
Isle of Man (Customs) Act 1899 (c.39)
Isle of Man (Customs) Act 1900 (c.31)
Isle of Man (Customs) Act 1901 (c.32)
Isle of Man (Customs) Act 1902 (c.23)
Isle of Man (Customs) Act 1903 (c.35)
Isle of Man (Customs) Act 1904 (c.25)
Isle of Man (Customs) Act 1905 (c.16)
Isle of Man (Customs) Act 1906 (c.18)
Isle of Man (Customs) Act 1907 (c.26)
Isle of Man (Customs) Act 1908 (c.9)
Isle of Man (Customs) Act 1909 (c.45)
Isle of Man (Customs) Act 1910 (c.18)
Isle of Man (Customs) Act 1911 (c.14)
Isle of Man (Customs) Act 1912 (c.9)
Isle of Man (Customs) Act 1913 (c.18)
Isle of Man (Customs) Act 1914 (c.19)
Isle of Man (Customs) Act 1915 (c.67)
Isle of Man (Customs) Act 1916 (c.27)
Isle of Man (Customs) Act 1917 (c.35)

Isle of Man (Customs) Act 1918 (c.41)
Isle of Man (Customs) Act 1919 (c.74)
Isle of Man (Customs) Act 1921 (c.40)
Isle of Man (Customs) Act 1922 (c.36)
Isle of Man (Customs) Act 1923 (c.26)
Isle of Man (Customs) Act 1924 (c.24)
Isle of Man (Customs) Act 1925 (c.56)
Isle of Man (Customs) Act 1926 (c.27)
Isle of Man (Customs) Act 1927 (c.20)
Isle of Man (Customs) Act 1928 (c.38)
Isle of Man (Customs) Act 1929 (c.1)
Isle of Man (Customs) Act 1930 (c.42)
Isle of Man (Customs) Act 1931 (c.16)
Isle of Man (Customs) Act 1931 (c.34)
Isle of Man (Customs) Act 1931 (c.41)
Isle of Man (Customs) Act 1933 (c.40)
Isle of Man (Customs) Act 1934 (c.46)
Isle of Man (Customs) Act 1935 (c.34)
Isle of Man (Customs) Act 1936 (c.45)
Isle of Man (Customs) Act 1937 (c.64)
Isle of Man (Customs) Act 1938 (c.68)
Isle of Man (Customs) Act 1939 (c.49)
Isle of Man (Customs) Act 1939 (c.53)
Isle of Man (Customs) Act 1941 (c.32)
Isle of Man (Customs) Act 1942 (c.25)
Isle of Man (Customs) Act 1943 (c.37)
Isle of Man (Customs) Act 1944 (c.27)
Isle of Man (Customs) Act 1945 (c.14)
Isle of Man (Customs) Act 1946 (c.69)
Isle of Man (Customs) Act 1947 (c.50)
Isle of Man (Customs) Act 1948 (c.61)
Isle of Man (Customs) Act 1949 (c.58)
Isle of Man (Customs) Act 1950 (c.19)
Isle of Man (Customs) Act 1952 (c.51)
Isle of Man (Customs) Act 1953 (c.44)
Isle of Man (Customs) Act 1954 (c.54)
Isle of Man (Customs) Act 1955 (c.17)
Isle of Man Customs Duties Act 1867 (c.86)
Isle of Man (Detention) Act 1941 (c.16)
Isle of Man Harbours Act 1771 (c.52)
Isle of Man Harbours Act 1814 (c.143)
Isle of Man Harbours Act 1840 (c.63)
Isle of Man Harbours Act 1872 (c.23)
Isle of Man Harbours Act 1874 (c.8)
Isle of Man Harbours Act 1883 (c.9)
Isle of Man Harbours Act 1884 (c.7)
Isle of Man Harbours Act 1911 (c.33)
Isle of Man (Harbours) Act 1947
Isle of Man Harbours Amendment Act 1864 (c.62)
Isle of Man Loans Act 1880 (c.8)
Isle of Man Loans Act 1931 (c.38)
Isle of Man (Officers) Act 1876 (c.43)
Isle of Man (Officers) Act 1882 (c.46)
Isle of Man Purchase Act 1765 (c.26)
Isle of Man Smuggling Act 1810 (c.62)
Isle of Man Trade Act 1798 (c.63)
Isle of Man Trade Act 1801 (c.54)
Isle of Man Trade Act 1802 (c.98)
Isle of Man Trade Act 1845 (c.94)
Isle of Man (War Legislation) Act 1914 (c.62)
Isle of Man (War Legislation) Act 1939 (c.86)
Isle of Wight, Carriage Rates Act 1783 (c.19)
Isle of Wight Guardians Act 1776 (c.53)
Isle of Wight: Poor Relief Act 1771 (c.43)
Islington: Poor Relief, etc. Act 1776 (c.5)
Islington: Poor Relief, etc. Act 1795 (c.147)
Isolation Hospitals Act 1893 (c.68)
Isolation Hospitals Act 1901 (c.8)
Issue and Payment of Exchequer Bills Act 1808 (c.1)
Issue, etc., of Gold and Silver Tokens Act 1813 (c.19)
Issue, etc., of Gold and Silver Tokens Act 1813 (c.114)
Issue of Bank Notes (Scotland) Act 1797 (c.2)
Issue of Bank Notes (Scotland) Act 1799 (c.10)
Issue of Bank Notes (Scotland) Act 1799 (c.25)
Issue of Bank Notes (Scotland) Act 1799 (c.48)

Jamaica Act 1866 (c.12)
Jamaica and St. Domingo Act 1812 (c.35)
Jamaica Independence Act 1962 (c.40)
Jamaica Loan Act 1854 (c.54)
Jamaica Loan Act 1862 (c.55)
Jamaica Loans Act 1869 (c.69)
James Watt's Fire Engines Patent Act 1775 (c.61)
Japanese Treaty of Peace Act 1951 (c.6)
Jedburgh Beer Duties Act 1720 (c.25)
Jeremy's Ferry Bridge, River Lee Act 1778 (c.10)
Jersey and Guernsey (Financial Provisions) Act 1947 (c.2)
Jews Act 1860 (c.63)
Jews Relief Act 1858 (c.49)
Joanna Stephens' Reward (Cure for Stone) Act 1738 (c.23)
Job Release Act 1977 (c.8)
Jobseekers Act 1995 (c.18)
John F. Kennedy Memorial Act 1964 (c.85)
John Whitehill, Esq Act 1782 (c.69)
John Whitehill, Esq Act 1783 (c.19)
John Wilkinson's Estate Act 1794 (c.67)
John Yeldham's Estate Act 1797 (c.47)
Joint Stock Banking Companies Act 1839 (c.68)
Joint Stock Banking Companies Act 1842 (c.85)
Joint Stock Banking Companies Act 1857 (c.49)
Joint Stock Banks Act 1838 (c.96)
Joint Stock Banks Act 1844 (c.113)
Joint Stock Banks Act 1856 (c.100)
Joint Stock Banks Act 1858 (c.91)
Joint Stock Banks (Scotland) Act 1856 (c.3)
Joint Stock Banks (Scotland) and (Ireland) Act 1846 (c.75)
Joint Stock Companies Act 1840 (c.111)
Joint Stock Companies Act 1844 (cc.110, 111)
Joint Stock Companies Act 1847 (c.78)

Joint Stock Companies Act 1848 (c.45)
Joint Stock Companies Act 1849 (c.108)
Joint Stock Companies Act 1856 (c.47)
Joint Stock Companies Act 1857 (c.14)
Joint Stock Companies Act 1857 (c.80)
Joint Stock Companies Act 1858 (c.60)
Joint Stock Companies Arrangements Act 1870 (c.104)
Joint Stock Companies (Ireland) Act 1845 (c.98)
Joint Stock Companies Winding-up Amendment Act 1857 (c.78)
Journeymen Tailors Act 1720 (c.13)
Journeymen Tailors, London Act 1768 (c.17)
Judges Jurisdiction Act 1870 (c.6)
Judges' Lodgings Act 1839 (c.69)
Judges' Lodgings (Ireland) Act 1801 (c.88)
Judges' Pensions Act 1799 (c.110)
Judges' Pensions Act 1813 (c.153)
Judges' Pensions (India and Burma) Act 1948 (c.4)
Judges' Pensions (Ireland) Act 1814 (c.95)
Judges' Pensions (Scotland) Act 1808 (c.145)
Judges' Remuneration Act 1954 (c.27)
Judges' Remuneration Act 1965 (c.61)
Judges' Salaries Act 1765 (c.47)
Judges' Salaries Act 1872 (c.51)
Judgment Mortgage (Ireland) Act 1850 (c.29)
Judgment Mortgage (Ireland) Act 1858 (c.105)
Judgment of Death Act 1823 (c.48)
Judgments Act 1838 (c.110)
Judgments Act 1839 (c.11)
Judgments Act 1840 (c.82)
Judgments Act 1855 (c.15)
Judgments Act 1864 (c.112)
Judgments Extension Act 1868 (c.54)
Judgments (Ireland) Act 1844 (c.90)
Judgments (Ireland) Act 1849 (c.95)
Judgments Registry Act 1871 (c.72)
Judgments Registry (Ireland) Act 1850 (c.74)
Judgments Registry (Ireland) Act 1871 (c.72)
Judgments, Wales and Counties Palatine Act 1721 (c.25)
Judicature (Northern Ireland) Act 1978 (c.23)
Judicature (Rule Committee) Act 1909 (c.11)
Judicial Committee Act 1833 (c.41)
Judicial Committee Act 1843 (c.38)
Judicial Committee Act 1844 (c.69)
Judicial Committee Act 1845 (c.30)
Judicial Committee Act 1871 (c.91)
Judicial Committee Act 1881 (c.3)
Judicial Committee Act 1915 (c.92)
Judicial Committee Amendment Act 1895 (c.44)
Judicial Factors Act 1849 (c.51)
Judicial Factors (Scotland) Act 1880 (c.4)
Judicial Factors (Scotland) Act 1889 (c.39)
Judicial Offices (Salaries and Pensions) Act 1957 (c.46)
Judicial Officers (Salaries, etc.) Act 1952 (c.12)
Judicial Pensions Act 1959 (c.9)
Judicial Pensions Act 1981 (c.20)
Judicial Pensions and Retirement Act 1993 (c.8)
Judicial Proceedings (Regulation of Reports) Act 1926 (c.61)
Judicial Ratifications (Scotland) Act 1836 (c.43)
Judicial Statistics (Scotland) Act 1869 (c.33)
Judicial Trustees Act 1896 (c.35)
Juries Act 1730 (c.7)
Juries Act 1730 (c.25)
Juries Act 1756 (c.19)
Juries Act 1825 (c.50)
Juries Act 1862 (c.107)
Juries Act 1870 (c.77)
Juries Act 1871 (c.2)
Juries Act 1871 (c.65)
Juries Act 1918 (c.23)
Juries Act 1922 (c.11)
Juries Act 1949 (c.27)
Juries Act 1954 (c.41)
Juries Act 1974 (c.23)
Juries Detention Act 1897 (c.18)
Juries (Disqualification) Act 1984 (c.34)
Juries (Emergency Provisions) Act 1920 (c.78)
Juries (Emergency Provisions) (Renewal) Act 1921 (c.36)
Juries, etc. Act 1750 (c.18)
Juries (Ireland) Act 1839 (c.48)
Juries (Ireland) Act 1845 (c.67)
Juries (Ireland) Act 1868 (c.75)
Juries (Ireland) Act 1871 (c.65)
Juries (Ireland) Act 1872 (c.25)
Juries (Ireland) Act 1873 (c.27)
Juries (Ireland) Act 1874 (c.28)
Juries (Ireland) Act 1875 (c.37)
Juries (Lighthouse Keepers' Exemption) Act 1869 (c.36)
Juries Procedure (Ireland) Act 1876 (c.78)
Juries (Scotland) Act 1826 (c.8)
Jurisdiction in Homicides Act 1862 (c.65)
Jurisdiction in Rating Act 1877 (c.11)
Jurisdiction in Siam Act 1857 (c.75)
Jurors Act 1587 (c.54)
Jurors Affirmation (Scotland) Act 1868 (c.39)
Jurors (Enrolment of Women) (Scotland) Act 1920 (c.53)
Jurors (Ireland) Amendment Act 1894 (c.49)
Jurors Prize Money Act 1868 (c.38)
Jurors Qualification (Ireland) Act 1876 (c.21)
Jurors (Scotland) Act 1745 (c.9)
Jurors (Scotland) Act 1825 (c.22)
Jury Trials Amendment (Scotland) Act 1910 (c.31)
Jury Trials (Scotland) Act 1815 (c.42)
Jury Trials (Scotland) Act 1819 (c.35)
Jury Trials (Scotland) Act 1837 (c.14)
Jury Trials (Scotland) Act 1854 (c.59)
Jury Trials (Scotland) Act 1859 (c.7)
Justice of Assize Act 1809 (c.91)
Justice of Assizes Act 1850 (c.25)

Justice of the Peace Act 1906 (c.16)
Justice of the Peace, Metropolis Act 1811 (c.119)
Justice of the Peace, the Metropolis Act 1792 (c.53)
Justices Act 1753 (c.27)
Justices' Clerks Act 1877 (c.43)
Justices' Clerks' Fees Act 1753 (c.14)
Justices' Clerks' Fees (Middlesex) Act 1754 (c.16)
Justices Commitment Act 1741 (c.24)
Justices Commitment Act 1743 (c.5)
Justices (Ireland) Act 1842 (c.46)
Justices (Ireland) Act 1843 (c.8)
Justices Jurisdiction Act 1742 (c.18)
Justices Jurisdiction Act 1852 (c.38)
Justices of Assize Act 1738 (c.27)
Justices of Assize Act 1839 (c.22)
Justices of the Peace Act 1361 (c.1)
Justices of the Peace Act 1661 (c.38)
Justices of the Peace Act 1788 (c.49)
Justices of the Peace Act 1867 (c.115)
Justices of the Peace Act 1906 (c.16)
Justices of the Peace Act 1949 (c.101)
Justices of the Peace Act 1965 (c.28)
Justices of the Peace Act 1968 (c.69)
Justices of the Peace Act 1979 (c.55)
Justices of the Peace in Metropolis Act 1837 (c.37)
Justices of the Peace, Nottingham Act 1803 (c.45)
Justices of the Peace Small Debt (Scotland) Act 1825 (c.48)
Justices of the Peace Small Debt (Scotland) Act 1849 (c.34)
Justices Oaths Act 1766 (c.9)
Justices Proceedings Confirmation (Sussex) Act 1864 (c.100)
Justices Protection Act 1803 (c.141)
Justices Protection Act 1848 (c.44)
Justices Protection (Ireland) Act 1849 (c.16)
Justices Qualification Act 1731 (c.18)
Justices Qualification Act 1744 (c.20)
Justices' Qualification Act 1760 (c.13)
Justices Qualification Act 1871 (c.18)
Justices Qualification Act 1875 (c.54)
Justices Quorum Act 1766 (c.21)
Justices (Scotland) Act 1856 (c.48)
Justices (Supplement List) Act 1941 (c.27)
Justiciary and Circuit Courts (Scotland) Act 1783 (c.45)
Justiciary Court (Scotland) Act 1868 (c.95)
Justiciary Courts (Scotland) Act 1814 (c.67)
Justiciary (Scotland) Act 1848 (c.79)
Juvenile Convict Prison (Ireland) Act 1856 (c.24)
Juvenile Courts (Metropolis) Act 1920 (c.68)
Juvenile Offenders Act 1847 (c.82)
Juvenile Offenders (Ireland) Act 1848 (c.59)

Keeper of Holyrood Park, etc. Act 1843 (c.64)
Keeping, etc., of Gunpowder Act 1748 (c.38)
Keeping, etc., of Gunpowder Act 1771 (c.35)
Keeping of Gunpowder Act 1718 (c.26)
Keeping of Gunpowder Act 1724 (c.23)
Keeping of Gunpowder Act 1741 (c.32)
Keighley to Bradford Road Act 1795 (c.135)
Keighley to Halifax Road Act 1795 (c.151)
Keighley to Kirby Kendal Road Act 1778 (c.113)
Kelso Beer Duties Act 1758 (c.56)
Kelso Beer Duties Act 1780 (c.11)
Kennet and Avon: Canal Act 1796 (c.44)
Kennington Common Act 1852 (c.29)
Kensington, Chelsea and Fulham: Improvements Act 1767 (c.101)
Kensington, Chelsea and Fulham Roads (Toll Continuation) Act 1740 (c.16)
Kensington, Chelsea and Fulham Roads (Tolls) Act 1725 (c.37)
Kensington: Improvement Act 1795 (c.74)
Kensington: Poor Relief Act 1777 (c.64)
Kensington Road Act 1795 (c.142)
Kensington Station and North and South London Junction Railway Act 1872 (c.80)
Kent and Surrey Roads Act 1765 (c.68)
Kent and Surrey Roads Act 1770 (c.62)
Kent and Surrey Roads Act 1781 (c.100)
Kent and Surrey Roads Act 1787 (c.70)
Kent and Surrey Roads Act 1792 (c.151)
Kent and Sussex Roads Act 1740 (c.12)
Kent and Sussex Roads Act 1762 (c.67)
Kent and Sussex Roads Act 1766 (c.56)
Kent and Sussex Roads Act 1767 (c.84)
Kent and Sussex Roads Act 1767 (c.86)
Kent and Sussex Roads Act 1770 (c.108)
Kent and Sussex Roads Act 1772 (c.92)
Kent and Sussex Roads Act 1787 (c.80)
Kent and Sussex Roads Act 1788 (c.85)
Kent and Sussex Roads Act 1789 (c.85)
Kent, Devon Fortifications Act 1794 (c.76)
Kent Fortifications Act 1797 (c.66)
Kent Roads Act 1724 (c.5)
Kent Roads Act 1724 (c.15)
Kent Roads Act 1730 (c.15)
Kent Roads Act 1735 (c.7)
Kent Roads Act 1737 (c.37)
Kent Roads Act 1743 (c.4)
Kent Roads Act 1748 (c.4)
Kent Roads Act 1748 (c.8)
Kent Roads Act 1751 (c.8)
Kent Roads Act 1753 (c.68)
Kent Roads Act 1754 (c.26)
Kent Roads Act 1759 (c.40)
Kent Roads Act 1762 (c.65)
Kent Roads Act 1762 (c.76)
Kent Roads Act 1764 (c.78)
Kent Roads Act 1765 (c.63)
Kent Roads Act 1765 (c.71)
Kent Roads Act 1766 (c.91)
Kent Roads Act 1766 (c.93)
Kent Roads Act 1767 (c.91)
Kent Roads Act 1767 (c.103)
Kent Roads Act 1769 (c.43)
Kent Roads Act 1769 (c.49)

Kent Roads Act 1769 (c.76)
Kent Roads Act 1769 (c.78)
Kent Roads Act 1769 (c.92)
Kent Roads Act 1773 (c.98)
Kent Roads Act 1773 (c.114)
Kent Roads Act 1776 (c.69)
Kent Roads Act 1782 (c.98)
Kent Roads Act 1782 (c.102)
Kent Roads Act 1785 (c.103)
Kent Roads Act 1785 (c.112)
Kent Roads Act 1786 (c.132)
Kent Roads Act 1786 (c.134)
Kent Roads Act 1786 (c.145)
Kent Roads Act 1788 (c.93)
Kent Roads Act 1789 (c.84)
Kent Roads Act 1789 (c.100)
Kent Roads Act 1790 (c.90)
Kent Roads Act 1791 (c.94)
Kent Roads Act 1792 (c.117)
Kent Roads Act 1793 (c.162)
Kent Roads Act 1793 (c.183)
Kent Roads Act 1795 (c.165)
Kent: Small Debts Act 1783 (c.8)
Kent: Small Debts Act 1786 (c.18)
Kent: Small Debts Act 1786 (c.22)
Kent: Small Debts Act 1786 (c.118)
Kent, Sussex Fortifications Act 1780 (c.10)
Kentish Town: Footpath Act 1771 (c.59)
Kenya Divorces (Validity) Act 1922 (c.10)
Kenya Independence Act 1963 (c.54)
Kenya Republic Act 1965 (c.5)
Kettering and Newport Pagnell Road Act 1754 (c.31)
Kettering to Newport Pagnell Roads Act 1773 (c.92)
Kettering to Newport Pagnell Road Act 1781 (c.103)
Kew Bridge (Building and Tolls) Act 1782 (c.42)
Kidderminster Church Act 1785 (c.94)
Kidderminster Roads Act 1777 (c.75)
Kidderminster: Small Debts Act 1772 (c.66)
Kilburn Road Act 1779 (c.120)
Kilmainham Hospital Act 1815 (c. 136)
Kilmainham Hospital Pensions Act 1807 (c.5)
Kilmainham Hospital (Pensions Commutation) Act 1813 (c.154)
Kimbolton Road Act 1755 (c.33)
Kincardine (County) Roads Act 1796 (c.132)
Kinghorn Beer Duties Act 1748 (c.13)
Kinghorn Beer Duties Act 1774 (c.28)
King's Bench Prison Act 1754 (c.17)
King's Bench Prison: Poor Relief Act 1783 (c.23)
King's Lynn: Pilotage Act 1772 (c.30)
King's Lynn: Small Debts Act 1770 (c.20)
Kingsholm District Act 1871 (c.54)
Kingston to Sheetbridge Road Act 1792 (c.119)
Kingston-upon-Hull: Improvement Act 1755 (c.27)
Kingston-upon-Hull: Improvement Act 1762 (c.70)
Kingston-upon-Hull: Improvement Act 1764 (c.74)
Kingston-upon-Hull: Improvement Act 1783 (c.55)
Kingston-upon-Hull Port Act 1774 (c.56)
Kingston-upon-Hull Roads Act 1744 (c.4)
Kingston-upon-Hull Roads Act 1767 (c.70)
Kingston-upon-Hull Roads Act 1788 (c.95)
Kingston-upon-Hull: Small Debts Act 1762 (c.38)
Kingston-upon-Thames: Streets Act 1772 (c.61)
Kingston-upon-Thames to Street Bride Road Act 1768 (c.56)
Kingstown and Dublin Harbours Act 1838 (c.36)
Kingstown Harbour Act 1836 (c.117)
Kingstown Harbour Act 1865 (c.67)
Kingstown Township Act 1898 (c.52)
Kinross and Alloa Road Act 1797 (c.171)
Kirby Kendal and Kirkby Ireleth Road Act 1763 (c.33)
Kirby Kendal to Kirkby Ireleth Road Act 1783 (c.23)
Kirby, Westmorland: Small Debts Act 1764 (c.41)
Kiribati Act 1979 (c.27)
Kirkby Lonsdale and Milnthorpe Road Act 1797 (c.165)
Kirkcaldy Beer Duties Act 1741 (c.8)
Kirkcaldy Beer Duties Act 1757 (c.69)
Kirkcaldy Beer Duties Act 1791 (c.82)
Kirkcudbright Roads Act 1780 (c.24)
Kirkcudbright Roads Act (c.153)
Knackers Act 1786 (c.71)
Knackers Act 1844 (c.87)
Knaresborough and Greenhammerton Road Act 1771 (c.65)
Knaresborough Inclosure Act 1789 (c.76)
Knaresborough: Water Supply Act 1764 (c.93)

L.C.C. (Money) Act 1890 (c.41)
L.C.C. (Money) Act 1891 (c.62)
Labour Bureaux (London) Act 1902 (c.13)
Labour Exchange Act 1909 (c.7)
Labourers' Cottages and Allotments (Ireland) Act 1882 (c.60)
Labourers (Ireland) Act 1883 (c.60)
Labourers (Ireland) Act 1885 (c.77)
Labourers (Ireland) Act 1886 (c.59)
Labourers (Ireland) Act 1891 (c.71)
Labourers (Ireland) Act 1892 (c.7)
Labourers (Ireland) Act 1896 (c.53)
Labourers (Ireland) Act 1906 (c.37)
Labourers (Ireland) Act 1911 (c.19)
Labourers (Ireland) Act 1914 (c.32)
Labourers (Ireland) Act 1918 (c.20)
Labourers (Ireland) Act 1919 (c.55)
Labouring Classes Lodging Houses and Dwellings (Ireland) Act 1866 (c.44)
Lairy Embankment (Plymouth) Act 1802 (c.32)

Lambeth Water Works Act 1785 (c.89)
Lanark and Hamilton Roads Act 1792 (c.122)
Lanark and Renfrew Roads Act 1789 (c.92)
Lanark Prisons Act 1868 (c.50)
Lanark Roads Act 1772 (c.82)
Lanark Roads Act 1792 (c.124)
Lancashire Roads Act 1730 (c.31)
Lancashire Roads Act 1774 (c.99)
Lancashire Roads Act 1784 (c.68)
Lancaster and Westmorland Roads Act 1782 (c.88)
Lancaster Bridge Act 1782 (c.57)
Lancaster Canal Act 1793 (c.107)
Lancaster County Clerk Act 1871 (c.73)
Lancaster: Drainage Act 1779 (c.33)
Lancaster Marsh: Drainage Act 1795 (c.11)
Lancaster Palatine Courts Act 1794 (c.58)
Lancaster Roads Act 1771 (c.91)
Lancaster Roads Act 1785 (c.106)
Lancaster Roads Act 1789 (c.107)
Lancaster Roads Act 1789 (c.110)
Lancaster Roads Act 1792 (c.139)
Lancaster Roads Act 1793 (c.181)
Lancaster Roads Act 1795 (c.144)
Land at Snaith Yorks. Act 1773 (c.85)
Land Charges Act 1900 (c.26)
Land Charges Act 1925 (c.22)
Land Charges Act 1972 (c.61)
Land Charges Registration and Searches Act 1888 (c.51)
Land Clauses Consolidation Act 1845 (c.18)
Land Clauses Consolidation Acts Amendment Act 1860 (c.106)
Land Clauses (Umpire) Act 1883 (c.15)
Land Commisssion Act 1967 (c.1)
Land Commission (Dissolution) Act 1971 (c.18)
Land Commissioners (Ireland) Salaries Act 1892 (c.45)
Land Compensation Act 1961 (c.33)
Land Compensation Act 1967 (c.1)
Land Compensation Act 1973 (c.26)
Land Compensation (Scotland) Act 1963 (c.51)
Land Compensation (Scotland) Act 1973 (c.56)
Land Drainage Act 1845 (c.56)
Land Drainage Act 1914 (c.4)
Land Drainage Act 1918 (c.17)
Land Drainage Act 1926 (c.24)
Land Drainage Act 1929 (c.8)
Land Drainage Act 1930 (c.44)
Land Drainage Act 1961 (c.48)
Land Drainage Act 1976 (c.70)
Land Drainage Act 1991 (c.59)
Land Drainage Act 1994 (c.25)
Land Drainage (Amendment) Act 1976 (c.17)
Land Drainage (Rating) Act 1743 (c.37)
Land Drainage (Scotland) Act 1930 (c.20)
Land Drainage (Scotland) Act 1935 (c.19)
Land Drainage (Scotland) Act 1941 (c.13)
Land Drainage (Scotland) Act 1958 (c.24)
Land Drainage Supplemental (No. 2) Act 1866 (c.80)
Land Drained at Great Carlton, Lincolnshire Act 1792 (c.91)
Land for Ordnance Services Act 1803 (cc. 65, 66)
Land for Prisons (Ireland) Act 1847 (c.26)
Land Law (Ireland) Act 1881 (c.49)
Land Law (Ireland) Act 1887 (c.33)
Land Law (Ireland) Act 1888 (c.13)
Land Law (Ireland) Act, 1888, Amendment 1889 (c.59)
Land Law (Ireland) Act 1896 (c.47)
Land Law (Ireland) Act 1881 (c.49)
Land Law (Ireland) Act 1887 (c.33)
Land Powers (Defence) Act 1958 (c.30)
Land Registers (Scotland) Act 1868 (c.64)
Land Registers (Scotland) Act 1995 (c.14)
Land Registration Act 1925 (c.21)
Land Registration Act 1936 (c.26)
Land Registration Act 1966 (c.39)
Land Registration Act 1986 (c.26)
Land Registration Act 1988 (c.3)
Land Registration and Land Charges Act 1971 (c.54)
Land Registration (Scotland) Act 1979 (c.33)
Land Registry Act 1862 (c.53)
Land Registry Act 1886 (c.1)
Land Registry (Middlesex Deeds) Act 1891 (c.64)
Land Registry (New Buildings) Act 1900 (c.19)
Land Revenue of the Crown Act 1815 (c.55)
Land Revenues of the Crown Act 1790 (c.50)
Land Settlement Amendment Act 1921 (c.43)
Land Settlement (Facilities) Act 1919 (c.59)
Land Settlement (Facilities) Amendment Act 1925 (c.85)
Land Settlement (Scotland) Act 1919 (c.97)
Land Settlement (Scotland) Act 1934 (c.35)
Land Tax Act 1702 (c.1)
Land Tax Act 1704 (c.1)
Land Tax Act 1705 (c.1)
Land Tax Act 1707 (c.35)
Land Tax Act 1708 (c.1)
Land Tax Act 1710 (c.1)
Land Tax Act 1711 (c.1)
Land Tax Act 1712 (c.1)
Land Tax Act 1713 (c.1)
Land Tax Act 1714 (c.1)
Land Tax Act 1715 (c.31)
Land Tax Act 1717 (c.1)
Land Tax Act 1718 (c.1)
Land Tax Act 1719 (c.1)
Land Tax Act 1720 (c.4)
Land Tax Act 1721 (c.1)
Land Tax Act 1723 (c.1)
Land Tax Act 1724 (c.1)
Land Tax Act 1725 (c.1)
Land Tax Act 1726 (c.1)
Land Tax Act 1727 (c.5)
Land Tax Act 1728 (c.4)
Land Tax Act 1729 (c.1)
Land Tax Act 1730 (c.4)
Land Tax Act 1732 (c.10)

Land Tax Act 1733 (c.7)
Land Tax Act 1734 (c.23)
Land Tax Act 1735 (c.3)
Land Tax Act 1736 (c.3)
Land Tax Act 1737 (c.14)
Land Tax Act 1746 (c.2)
Land Tax Act 1757 (c.4)
Land Tax Act 1757 (c.7)
Land Tax Act 1771 (c.5)
Land Tax Act 1772 (c.3)
Land Tax Act 1772 (c.8)
Land Tax Act 1774 (c.1)
Land Tax Act 1774 (c.17)
Land Tax Act 1775 (c.3)
Land Tax Act 1775 (c.26)
Land Tax Act 1776 (c.1)
Land Tax Act 1776 (c.4)
Land Tax Act 1776 (c.14)
Land Tax Act 1778 (c.2)
Land Tax Act 1778 (c.23)
Land Tax Act 1780 (c.2)
Land Tax Act 1780 (c.3)
Land Tax Act 1780 (c.23)
Land Tax Act 1782 (c.2)
Land Tax Act 1782 (c.9)
Land Tax Act 1783 (c.3)
Land Tax Act 1783 (c.4)
Land Tax Act 1783 (c.10)
Land Tax Act 1785 (c.4)
Land Tax Act 1785 (c.20)
Land Tax Act 1786 (c.3)
Land Tax Act 1786 (c.54)
Land Tax Act 1786 (c.103)
Land Tax Act 1786 (c.105)
Land Tax Act 1786 (c.121)
Land Tax Act 1787 (c.5)
Land Tax Act 1787 (c.47)
Land Tax Act 1788 (c.2)
Land Tax Act 1789 (c.6)
Land Tax Act 1790 (c.2)
Land Tax Act 1790 (c.13)
Land Tax Act 1791 (c.6)
Land Tax Act 1791 (c.14)
Land Tax Act 1792 (c.5)
Land Tax Act 1792 (c.23)
Land Tax Act 1793 (c.7)
Land Tax Act 1794 (c.8)
Land Tax Act 1795 (c.2)
Land Tax Act 1795 (c.17)
Land Tax Act 1796 (c.2)
Land Tax Act 1796 (c.89)
Land Tax Act 1797 (c.5)
Land Tax Act 1797 (c.26)
Land Tax Act 1797 (c.35)
Land Tax Act 1797 (c.128)
Land Tax Act 1800 (c.68)
Land Tax Act 1805 (c.48)
Land Tax Act 1808 (c.102)
Land Tax Act 1809 (c.55)
Land Tax Act 1809 (c.67)
Land Tax Act 1813 (c.142)
Land Tax Act 1814 (c.190)
Land Tax Act 1842 (c.37)
Land Tax, Assessed Tax, and Income Tax Act 1843 (c.24)
Land Tax Certificates Forgery Act 1812 (c.143)
Land Tax Commissioners Act 1798 (c.48)
Land Tax Commissioners Act 1844 (c.79)
Land Tax Commissioners Act 1867 (c.51)
Land Tax Commissioners Act 1906 (c.52)
Land Tax Commissioners Act 1927 (c.16)
Land Tax Commissioners Act 1937 (c.18)
Land Tax Commissioners (Appointment) Act 1836 (c.80)
Land Tax Commissioners (Appointment) Act 1838 (c.57)
Land Tax Commissioners (Appointment) Act 1866 (c.59)
Land Tax Commissioners (Appointment) Act 1869 (c.64)
Land Tax Commissioners (Appointment) Act 1874 (c.18)
Land Tax Commissioners (Names) Act 1879 (c.52)
Land Tax Commissioners (Names) Act 1881 (c.16)
Land Tax Commissioners Names Act 1886 (c.47)
Land Tax Commissioners Names Act 1893 (c.27)
Land Tax Commissioners Names Act 1899 (c.25)
Land, Tax, etc. Act 1806 (c.107)
Land, Tax, etc. Act 1815 (c.150)
Land Tax, Forfeited Estates, etc. Act 1702 (c.6)
Land Tax Perpetuation Act 1798 (c.60)
Land Tax Redemption Act 1799 (c.10)
Land Tax Redemption Act 1799 (c.21)
Land Tax Redemption Act 1799 (c.40)
Land Tax Redemption Act 1799 (c.43)
Land Tax Redemption Act 1799 (c.108)
Land Tax Redemption Act 1800 (c.28)
Land Tax Redemption Act 1800 (c.30)
Land Tax Redemption Act 1801 (c.72)
Land Tax Redemption Act 1802 (c.116)
Land Tax Redemption Act 1803 (c.51)
Land Tax Redemption Act 1805 (c.77)
Land Tax Redemption Act 1806 (c.133)
Land Tax Redemption Act 1810 (c.58)
Land Tax Redemption Act 1812 (c.80)
Land Tax Redemption Act 1813 (c.123)
Land Tax Redemption Act 1814 (c.173)
Land Tax Redemption Act 1837 (c.17)
Land Tax Redemption Act 1838 (c.58)
Land Tax Redemption, etc. Act 1798 (c.6)
Land Tenure Reform (Scotland) Act 1974 (c.38)
Land Transfer Act 1875 (c.87)
Land Transfer Act 1897 (c.65)
Landed Estates Court (Ireland) Act 1858 (c.72)
Landed Estates Court (Ireland) Act 1866 (c.99)
Landed Property Improvement (Ireland) Act 1847 (c.32)

Landing of Merchandise Act 1796 (c.82)
Landlord and Tenant Act 1709 (c.18(i))
Landlord and Tenant Act 1730 (c.28)
Landlord and Tenant Act 1871 (c.92)
Landlord and Tenant Act 1927 (c.36)
Landlord and Tenant Act 1954 (c.56)
Landlord and Tenant Act 1959 (c.64)
Landlord and Tenant Act 1962 (c.50)
Landlord and Tenant Act 1985 (c.70)
Landlord and Tenant Act 1987 (c.31)
Landlord and Tenant Act 1988 (c.26)
Landlord and Tenant (Covenants) Act 1995 (c.30)
Landlord and Tenant (Ireland) Act 1870 (c.46)
Landlord and Tenant (Ireland) Act 1871 (c.92)
Landlord and Tenant (Ireland) Act 1872 (c.32)
Landlord and Tenant Law Amendment Act Ireland 1860 (c.154)
Landlord and Tenant (Licensed Premises) Act 1990 (c.39)
Landlord and Tenant (Rent Control) Act 1949 (c.40)
Landlord and Tenant (Requisitioned Land) Act 1942 (c.13)
Landlord and Tenant (Requisitioned Land) Act 1944 (c.5)
Landlord and Tenant (Temporary Provisions) Act 1958 (c.68)
Landlord and Tenant (War Damage) Act 1939 (c.72)
Landlord and Tenant (War Damage) (Amendment) Act 1941 (c.41)
Lands at Sheerness and Chatham Act 1816 (c.74)
Lands Clauses Consolidation Act 1845 (c.18)
Lands Clauses Consolidation Act 1869 (c.18)
Lands Clauses Consolidation (Scotland) Act 1845 (c.19)
Lands Clauses (Taxation of Costs) Act 1895 (c.11)
Lands for Ordnance Services, Woolwich Act 1802 (c.89)
Lands for Ordnance Services, Woolwich Act 1803 (c.35)
Lands for the Defence of the Realm Act 1809 (c.112)
Lands of Earl of Pembroke Act 1783 (c.61)
Lands Tribunal Act 1949 (c.42)
Lands Valuation Amendment (Scotland) Act 1982 (c.57)
Lands Valuation (Scotland) Act 1854 (c.91)
Lands Valuation (Scotland) Act 1857 (c.58)
Lands Valuation (Scotland) Amendment Act 1895 (c.41)
Lands Valuation (Scotland) Amendment Act 1902 (c.25)
Lane End Chapel, Stoke upon Trent 1792 (c.88)
Langbaurgh Coroners Act 1873 (c.81)
Lapworth to Kingswood Canal Act 1795 (c.72)
Larceny Act 1808 (c.129)
Larceny Act 1868 (c.116)
Larceny Act 1896 (c.52)
Larceny Act 1901 (c.10)
Larceny Act 1916 (c.50)
Larceny (Advertisements) Act 1870 (c.65)
Late Earl of Seaforth Act 1734 (c.22)
Late Night Refreshment Houses Act 1969 (c.53)
Latent Damage Act 1986 (c.37)
Launceston: Poor Relief Act 1784 (c.17)
Launceston Roads Act 1781 (c.86)
Law Agents and Notaries Public (Scotland) Act 1891 (c.30)
Law Agents Apprenticeship (War Service) (Scotland) Act 1914 (c.20)
Law Agents Apprenticeship (War Service) (Scotland) Act 1919 (c.24)
Law Agents (Scotland) Act 1873 (c.63)
Law Agents (Scotland) Act Amendment 1896 (c.49)
Law and Procedure (Emergency Provisions) (Ireland) Act 1916 (c.46)
Law Commissions Act 1965 (c.22)
Law Costs (Ireland) Act 1823 (c.89)
Law of Commons Amendment Act 1893 (c.57)
Law of Distress Amendment Act 1888 (c.21)
Law of Distress Amendment Act 1895 (c.24)
Law of Distress Amendment Act 1908 (c.53)
Law of Distress and Small Debts (Ireland) Act 1888 (c.47)
Law of Distress and Small Debts (Ireland) Act 1893 (c.36)
Law of Libel Amendment Act 1888 (c.64)
Law of Property Act 1922 (c.16)
Law of Property Act 1925 (c.20)
Law of Property Act 1969 (c.59)
Law of Property Act (Postponement) Act 1924 (c.4)
Law of Property Amendment Act 1859 (c.35)
Law of Property Amendment Act 1860 (c.38)
Law of Property (Amendment) Act 1924 (c.5)
Law of Property (Amendment) Act 1926 (c.11)
Law of Property (Amendment) Act 1926 (c.14)
Law of Property (Amendment) Act 1929 (c.9)
Law of Property (Entailed Interests) Act 1931 (c.27)
Law of Property (Joint Tenants) Act 1964 (c.63)
Law of Property (Miscellaneous Provisions) Act 1989 (c.34)
Law of Property (Miscellaneous Provisions) Act 1994 (c.36)
Law Officers Act 1944 (c.25)
Law Officers' Fees Act 1872 (c.70)
Law Reform (Contributory Negligence) Act 1945 (c.28)
Law Reform (Damages and Solatium) (Scotland) Act 1962 (c.42)
Law Reform (Diligence) (Scotland) Act 1973 (c.22)

Law Reform (Enforcement of Contracts) Act 1954 (c.34)
Law Reform (Frustrated Contracts) Act 1943 (c.40)
Law Reform (Husband and Wife) Act 1962 (c.48)
Law Reform (Husband and Wife) (Scotland) Act 1984 (c.15)
Law Reform (Jurisdiction in Delict) (Scotland) Act 1971 (c.55)
Law Reform (Limitation of Actions etc.) Act 1954 (c.36)
Law Reform (Married Women and Tortfeasors) Act 1935 (c.30)
Law Reform (Miscellaneous Provisions) Act 1934 (c.41)
Law Reform (Miscellaneous Provisions) Act 1949 (c.100)
Law Reform (Miscellaneous Provisions) Act 1970 (c.33)
Law Reform (Miscellaneous Provisions) Act 1971 (c.43)
Law Reform (Miscellaneous Provisions) (Scotland) Act 1940 (c.42)
Law Reform (Miscellaneous Provisions) (Scotland) Act 1966 (c.19)
Law Reform (Miscellaneous Provisions) (Scotland) Act 1968 (c.70)
Law Reform (Miscellaneous Provisions) (Scotland) Act 1980 (c.55)
Law Reform (Miscellaneous Provisions) (Scotland) Act 1985 (c.73)
Law Reform (Miscellaneous Provisions) (Scotland) Act 1990 (c.40)
Law Reform (Parent and Child) (Scotland) Act 1986 (c.9)
Law Reform (Personal Injuries) Act 1948 (c.41)
Law Reform (Personal Injuries) Amendment Act 1948 (c.7)
Law Reform (Personal Injuries) Amendment Act 1953 (c.7)
Law Reform (Succession) Act 1995 (c.41)
Laws Continuation, etc. Act 1739 (c.18)
Laws in Wales Act 1542 (c.39)
Laying of Documents before Parliament (Interpretation) Act 1948 (c.59)
Lazarets Act 1772 (c.57)
Lead Paint (Protection Against Poisoning) Act 1926 (c.37)
Lease of Exeter Castle Act 1710 (c.24)
Leasehold Property Act and Long Leases (Scotland) Act Extension Act 1953 (c.12)
Leasehold Property (Repairs) Act 1938 (c.34)
Leasehold Property (Temporary Provisions) Act 1951 (c.38)
Leasehold Reform Act 1967 (c.88)
Leasehold Reform Act 1979 (c.44)
Leasehold Reform, Housing and Urban Development Act 1993 (c.28)
Leases and Sales of Settled Estates Amendment Act 1874 (c.33)
Leases for Schools (Ireland) Act 1881 (c.65)
Leases (Ireland) Act 1846 (c.112)
Leases of Episcopal Lands (Ireland) Act 1813 (c.92)
Leasing-making, etc. (Scotland) Act 1837 (c.5)
Leasing-making (Scotland) Act 1825 (c.47)
Leasing Powers Amendment Act for Religious Purposes in Ireland Act 1875 (c.11)
Leasing Powers for Religious Worship in Ireland Act 1855 (c.39)
Leatherhead and Guildford Road Act 1757 (c.77)
Lecturers and Parish Clerks Act 1844 (c.59)
Lectures Copyright Act 1835 (c.65)
Ledbury Highways Act 1720 (c.23)
Ledbury Roads Act 1793 (c.132)
Leddon and Clavering, Norfolk: Poor Relief Act 1764 (c.90)
Leeds and Blackburn Roads Act 1781 (c.102)
Leeds and Halifax Roads Act 1740 (c.32)
Leeds and Halifax Roads Act 1751 (c.55)
Leeds and Halifax Roads Act 1783 (c.94)
Leeds and Harrogate Road Act 1796 (c.138)
Leeds and Liverpool Canal Act 1770 (c.114)
Leeds and Liverpool Canal Act 1783 (c.47)
Leeds and Wakefield Road Act 1770 (c.61)
Leeds Bridge Act 1759 (c.54)
Leeds Church Act 1792 (c.89)
Leeds Coal Supply Act 1779 (c.11)
Leeds Coal Supply Act 1793 (c.86)
Leeds Corporation (Consolidation) Act 1905 (c.1)
Leeds: Lighting, etc. Act 1755 (c.41)
Leeds to Liverpool Canal Act 1790 (c.65)
Leeds to Liverpool Canal Act 1794 (c.94)
Leeds to Otley Road Act 1781 (c.98)
Leeds to Sheffield Road Act 1760 (c.33)
Leeds to Wakefield Road Act 1792 (c.131)
Leeds University Act 1904 (c.12)
Leeds: Water Supply Act 1790 (c.68)
Leeward Islands Act 1871 (c.107)
Leeward Islands Act 1956 (c.23)
Legacy Duty Act 1796 (c.52)
Legacy Duty Act 1797 Act (c.135)
Legacy Duty Act 1799 (c.73)
Legacy Duty Act 1805 (c.28)
Legal Advice and Assistance Act 1972 (c.50)
Legal Aid Act 1960 (c.28)
Legal Aid Act 1964 (c.30)
Legal Aid Act 1974 (c.4)
Legal Aid Act 1979 (c.26)
Legal Aid Act 1982 (c.44)
Legal Aid Act 1988 (c.34)
Legal Aid and Advice Act 1949 (c.51)
Legal Aid and Solicitors (Scotland) Act 1949 (c.63)
Legal Aid (Scotland) Act 1967 (c.43)
Legal Aid (Scotland) Act 1986 (c.47)
Legal Practitioners Act 1875 (c.79)
Legal Practitioners Act 1876 (c.66)
Legal Practitioners (Ireland) Act 1876 (c.44)
Legal Proceedings Against Enemies Act 1915 (c.36)

Legal Rate of Interest Act 1774 (c.79)
Legislative Council for Canada Act 1854 (c.118)
Legislative Council of Canada Act 1859 (c.10)
Legislative Council, New Zealand Act 1868 (c.57)
Legitimacy Act 1926 (c.60)
Legitimacy Act 1959 (c.73)
Legitimacy Act 1976 (c.31)
Legitimacy Declaration Act 1858 (c.93)
Legitimacy Declaration Act (Ireland) 1868 (c.20)
Legitimation (Re-registration of Births) Act 1957 (c.39)
Legitimation (Scotland) Act 1968 (c.22)
Leicester and Derby Roads Act 1759 (c.46)
Leicester and Notts. Roads Act 1762 (c.82)
Leicester and Stafford Roads Act 1753 (c.85)
Leicester and Stafford Roads Act 1779 (c.85)
Leicester and Warwick Roads Act 1754 (c.42)
Leicester and Warwick Roads Act 1781 (c.85)
Leicester Navigation Act 1791 (c.65)
Leicester Navigation Act 1797 (c.51)
Leicester Road Act 1725 (c.5)
Leicester Roads Act 1745 (c.10)
Leicester Roads Act 1753 (c.46)
Leicester Roads Act 1757 (c.44)
Leicester Roads Act 1759 (c.41)
Leicester Roads Act 1764 (c.84)
Leicester Roads Act 1769 (c.91)
Leicester Roads Act 1776 (c.81)
Leicester Roads Act 1777 (c.108)
Leicester Roads Act 1779 (c.90)
Leicester Roads Act 1781 (c.89)
Leicester Roads Act 1783 (c.107)
Leicester Roads Act 1785 (c.113)
Leicester Roads Act 1788 (c.100)
Leicester Roads Act 1790 (c.92)
Leicester to Peterborough Road Act 1754 (c.30)
Leicester, Warwick and Coventry Roads Act 1762 (c.80)
Leicestershire and Northamptonshire Union Canal Act 1793 (c.98)
Leicestershire Roads Act 1757 (c.49)
Leicestershire Roads Act 1762 (c.54)
Leicestershire Roads Act 1771 (c.88)
Leigh and Deerhurst Canal Act 1792 (c.83)
Leith and Bruntisland Ferries, etc. Act 1792 (c.93)
Leith Harbour Act 1754 (c.8)
Leith Harbour Act 1788 (c.58)
Leith Harbour and Docks Act 1847 (c.114)
Leith Harbour and Docks Act 1860 (c.48)
Leominster Canal Act 1791 (c.69)
Leominster Canal Act 1796 (c.70)
Leominster Roads Act 1728 (c.13)
Leominster Roads Act 1777 (c.85)
Leominster Roads Act 1797 (c.176)
Lesotho Independence Act 1966 (c.24)
Letter Stealing (Scotland) Act 1836 (c.21)
Letters of Marque Act 1801 (c.76)
Letters Patent for Inventions Act 1835 (c.83)
Levant Trade Act 1753 (c.18)
Level Crossings Act 1983 (c.16)
Lewes and Brighton Road Act 1770 (c.64)
Lewes and Eastbourne Road Act 1758 (c.67)
Lewes: Improvement Act 1791 (c.86)
Lewes to Brighton Road Act 1791 (c.115)
Lewis (Estates and Crown Claims) Act 1806 (c.131)
Lewisham Church Act 1774 (c.93)
Liabilities (War-Time Adjustment) Act 1941 (c.24)
Liabilities (War-Time Adjustment) Act 1944 (c.40)
Liabilities (War-Time Adjustment) (Scotland) Act 1944 (c.29)
Liability for War Damage (Miscellaneous Provisions) Act 1939 (c.102)
Liardet's Cement Patent Act 1776 (c.29)
Libel Act 1792 (c.60)
Libel Act 1843 (c.96)
Libel Act 1845 (c.75)
Libel (Ireland) Act 1868 (c.69)
Liberties Act 1836 (c.87)
Liberties Act 1850 (c.105)
Liberty of Ely Act 1837 (c.53)
Liberty of Religious Worship Act 1855 (c.86)
Libraries Offences Act 1898 (c.53)
Licences for Retailing Beer, etc. Act 1784 (c.30)
Licence to J. Porter etc. to Import Silk Act 1740 (c.4)
Licensed Premises (Exclusion of Certain Persons) Act 1980 (c.32)
Licensed Premises in New Towns 1952 (c.65)
Licensing (Abolition of State Management) Act 1971 (c.65)
Licensing Act 1842 (c.44)
Licensing Act 1872 (c.94)
Licensing Act 1874 (c.49)
Licensing Act 1902 (c.28)
Licensing Act 1904 (c.23)
Licensing Act 1906 (c.42)
Licensing Act 1921 (c.42)
Licensing Act 1949 (c.59)
Licensing Act 1953 (c.46)
Licensing Act 1961 (c.61)
Licensing Act 1964 (c.26)
Licensing Act 1988 (c.17)
Licensing (Airports) Act 1956 (c.37)
Licensing (Alcohol Education and Research) Act 1981 (c.28)
Licensing (Amendment) Act 1967 (c.51)
Licensing (Amendment) Act 1976 (c.18)
Licensing (Amendment) Act 1977 (c.26)
Licensing (Amendment) Act 1980 (c.40)
Licensing (Amendment) Act 1981 (c.40)
Licensing (Amendment) Act 1985 (c.40)
Licensing (Amendment) Act 1989 (c.20)
Licensing Amendment (Scotland) Act 1897 (c.50)

Licensing (Amendment) (Scotland) Act 1992 (c.18)
Licensing (Amendment) (Scotland) Act 1993 (c.20)
Licensing (Certificates in Suspense) (Scotland) Act 1967 (c.14)
Licensing (Consolidation) Act 1910 (c.24)
Licensing (Evidence) Act 1884 (c.29)
Licensing (Ireland) Act 1836 (c.38)
Licensing (Ireland) Act 1855 (c.62)
Licensing (Ireland) Act 1860 (c.35)
Licensing (Ireland) Act 1874 (c.69)
Licensing (Ireland) Act 1902 (c.18)
Licensing (Ireland) Act 1905 (c.3)
Licensing (Low Alcohol Drinks) Act 1990 (c.21)
Licensing (Occasional Permissions) Act 1983 (c.24)
Licensing of Alehouses Act 1792 (c.59)
Licensing (Permitted Hours) Act 1934 (c.26)
Licensing Planning (Temporary Provisions) Act 1944 (c.15)
Licensing Planning (Temporary Provisions) Act 1946 (c.53)
Licensing (Restaurant Meals) Act 1987 (c.2)
Licensing (Retail Sales) Act 1988 (c.25)
Licensing (Scotland) Act 1903 (c.25)
Licensing (Scotland) Act 1959 (c.51)
Licensing (Scotland) Act 1962 (c.51)
Licensing (Scotland) Act 1969 (c.13)
Licensing (Scotland) Act 1976 (c.66)
Licensing (Seamen's Canteens) Act 1954 (c.11)
Licensing (Sunday Hours) Act 1995 (c.33)
Lichfield Roads Act 1728 (c.5)
Lieutenancy Clerks Allowances Act 1887 (c.36)
Life Annuities Act 1808 (c.142)
Life Annuities Act 1809 (c.104)
Life Assurance Act 1774 (c.48)
Life Assurance Companies Act 1870 (c.61)
Life Assurance Companies Act 1871 (c.58)
Life Assurance Companies Act 1872 (c.41)
Life Insurance Companies (Payment into Court) Act 1896 (c.8)
Life Insurance (Ireland) Act 1866 (c.42)
Life Peerages Act 1958 (c.21)
Light Locomotives (Ireland) Act 1903 (c.2)
Light Railways Act 1896 (c.48)
Light Railways Act 1912 (c.19)
Light Railways Commissioners (Salaries) Act 1901 (c.36)
Light Railways (Ireland) Act 1889 (c.66)
Light Railways (Ireland) Act 1893 (c.50)
Light Silver Coin Act 1774 (c.42)
Lighthouses Act 1836 (c.79)
Lighthouses (Ireland) Act 1810 (c.95)
Lighting, etc., of Cities (Ireland) Act 1807 (c.42)
Lighting of Towns (Ireland) Act 1857 (c.12)
Lights on Vehicles Act 1907 (c.45)
Limehouse, Stepney Parish Act 1730 (c.17)
Limehouse, Stepney: Streets Act 1782 (c.87)
Limerick Harbour Act 1867 (c.53)
Limitation Act 1939 (c.21)
Limitation Act 1963 (c.47)
Limitation Act 1975 (c.54)
Limitation Act 1980 (c.58)
Limitation Amendment Act 1980 (c.24)
Limitation (Enemies and War Prisoners) Act 1945 (c.16)
Limitation of Action Act 1843 (c.54)
Limitation of Time (Ireland) (Canal Companies) Act 1815 (c.90)
Limitations of Actions and Costs Act 1842 (c.97)
Limited Liability Act 1855 (c.133)
Limited Owners Reservoirs and Water Supply Further Facilities Act 1877 (c.31)
Limited Owners Residence Act 1870 (c.56)
Limited Owners Residences Act (1870) Amendment Act 1871 (c.84)
Limited Partnerships Act 1907 (c.24)
Limited Penalties Act 1864 (c.110)
Lincoln and Northampton Roads Act 1757 (c.68)
Lincoln and Northamptonshire Roads Act 1765 (c.106)
Lincoln and Nottinghamshire Roads Act 1758 (c.57)
Lincoln and Nottinghamshire Roads Act 1766 (c.83)
Lincoln and Nottinghamshire Roads Act 1767 (c.78)
Lincoln and Nottinghamshire Roads Act 1767 (c.79)
Lincoln and Nottinghamshire Roads Act 1780 (c.73)
Lincoln and Nottinghamshire Roads Act 1782 (c.94)
Lincoln and Nottinghamshire Roads Act 1787 (c.71)
Lincoln and Peterborough Roads Act 1756 (c.85)
Lincoln and Rutland Roads Act 1762 (c.73)
Lincoln and Rutland Roads Act 1786 (c.159)
Lincoln (City) Roads Act 1738 (c.10)
Lincoln (City) Roads Act 1797 (c.168)
Lincoln: Drainage Act 1777 (c.70)
Lincoln: Drainage Act 1785 (c.14)
Lincoln: Drainage Act 1787 (c.66)
Lincoln: Drainage Act 1789 (c.32)
Lincoln: Drainage Act 1789 (c.70)
Lincoln: Drainage Act 1793 (c.116)
Lincoln: Drainage Act 1797 (c.67)
Lincoln: Drainage, etc. Act 1794 (c.102)
Lincoln: Improvement Act 1791 (c.80)
Lincoln: Poor Relief Act 1796 (c.102)
Lincoln Roads Act 1738 (c.8)
Lincoln Roads Act 1756 (c.84)
Lincoln Roads Act 1758 (c.44)
Lincoln Roads Act 1764 (c.53)
Lincoln Roads Act 1764 (c.80)
Lincoln Roads Act 1765 (c.73)
Lincoln Roads Act 1765 (c.88)
Lincoln Roads Act 1765 (c.96)

Lincoln Roads Act 1777 (c.109)
Lincoln Roads Act 1778 (c.104)
Lincoln Roads Act 1780 (c.75)
Lincoln Roads Act 1783 (c.34)
Lincoln Roads Act 1785 (c.123)
Lincoln Roads Act 1786 (c.137)
Lincoln Roads Act 1786 (c.138)
Lincoln Roads Act 1786 (c.141)
Lincoln Roads Act 1786 (c.146)
Lincoln Roads Act 1793 (c.150)
Lincoln: Small Debts Act 1778 (c.43)
Lincoln's Inn Fields Rate Act 1734 (c.26)
Lincolnshire Coroners Act 1899 (c.48)
Lincolnshire: Small Debts Act 1777 (c.62)
Lincolnshire: Small Debts Act 1778 (c.34)
Lincolnshire: Small Debts Act 1779 (c.43)
Linen and Hemp Manufacturers Act 1750 (c.31)
Linen and Hempen Manufacturers (Scotland) Act 1726 (c.26)
Linen, etc., Manufacturers (Ireland) Act 1850 (c.48)
Linen, etc., Manufacturers (Ireland) Act 1852 (c.13)
Linen, etc., Manufacturers (Ireland) Act 1853 (c.103)
Linen, etc., Manufacturers (Ireland) Act 1854 (c.46)
Linen, etc., Manufacturers (Ireland) Act 1859 (c.25)
Linen Manufacture (Ireland) Act 1802 (c.75)
Linen Manufacture (Ireland) Act 1804 (c.42)
Linen Manufacture (Ireland) Act 1804 (c.69)
Linen Manufacture, (Scotland) Act (c.23)
Linen Manufacture (Scotland) Act 1753 (c.20)
Linen Manufacturers, etc. (Ireland) Act 1838 (c.52)
Linen Manufacturers (Ireland) Act 1844 (c.47)
Linen (Trade Marks) Act 1743 (c.30)
Linen (Trade Marks) Act 1744 (c.24)
Linens, etc. Act 1794 (c.23)
Linlithgow and Stirling Roads Act 1790 (c.108)
Linlithgow Beer Duties Act 1732 (c.18)
Linlithgow Roads Act 1771 (c.79)
Linlithgow Roads Act 1781 (c.79)
Linlithgow Roads Act 1790 (c.105)
Linlithgow Roads and Bridges Act 1779 (c.12)
Liqueur Act 1848 (c.121)
Liquidation Act 1868 (c.68)
Lis. Pendens Act 1867 (c.47)
Liston, Essex Roads Act 1790 (c.84)
Litchfield Roads Act 1743 (c.24)
Literary and Scientific Institution Act 1854 (c.112)
Literary Copyright Act 1842 (c.45)
Litigants in Person (Costs and Expenses) Act 1975 (c.47)
Litter Act 1958 (c.34)
Litter Act 1983 (c.35)
Little Bowden to Rockingham Road Act 1793 (c.143)
Little Cumbrae Lighthouse Act 1756 (c.20)
Littlehampton Harbour Act 1732 (c.12)
Littlehampton Harbour Act 1793 (c.100)
Liverpool, Admiralty District Registrar Act 1970 (c.45)
Liverpool and Prescot Road Act 1725 (c.21)
Liverpool and Preston Road Act 1771 (c.93)
Liverpool Church Act 1792 (c.76)
Liverpool Churches Act 1767 (c.80)
Liverpool Court of Passage Act 1896 (c.21)
Liverpool Courts of Passage Act 1893 (c.37)
Liverpool Dock Act 1737 (c.32)
Liverpool Docks Act 1709 (c.8)
Liverpool Harbour Act 1762 (c.86)
Liverpool Harbour Act 1785 (c.15)
Liverpool, Improvement Act 1749 (c.24)
Liverpool: Improvement Act 1762 (c.68)
Liverpool: Improvement Act 1786 (c.12)
Liverpool: Improvement Act 1788 (c.13)
Liverpool Note Issue Act 1793 (c.31)
Liverpool Rectory Act 1786 (c.15)
Liverpool Theatre Act 1771 (c.16)
Liverpool to Preston Road Act 1786 (c.126)
Livestock Industry Act 1937 (c.50)
Livestock Rearing Act 1951 (c.18)
Llandilo Rhynws Bridge Act 1784 (c.66)
Llandovery Bridge Act 1773 (c.111)
Llanfyllin Market House Act 1789 (c.24)
Llangollen International Musical Eisteddfod Act 1967 (c.49)
Llanyblodwell to Newtown Canal Act 1794 (c.39)
Lloyd's Signal Stations Act 1888 (c.29)
Loan Act 1901 (c.12)
Loan Act 1902 (c.4)
Loan from Bank of England Act 1815 (c.16)
Loan Societies Act 1840 (c.110)
Loan Societies Act 1841 (c.55)
Loan Societies Act 1842 (c.5)
Loan Societies Act 1843 (c.41)
Loan Societies Act 1844 (c.54)
Loan Societies Act 1845 (c.60)
Loan Societies Act 1846 (c.52)
Loan Societies Act 1848 (c.64)
Loan Societies Act 1849 (c.37)
Loan Societies Act 1850 (c.45)
Loan Societies Act 1851 (c.31)
Loan Societies Act 1852 (c.15)
Loan Societies Act 1853 (c.109)
Loan Societies Act 1857 (c.41)
Loan Societies Act 1858 (c.19)
Loan Societies Act 1863 (c.56)
Loan Societies (Ireland) Act 1836 (c.55)
Loan Societies (Ireland) Act 1838 (c.78)
Loan Societies (Ireland) Act 1843 Amendment Act 1872 (c.17)
Loan to Emperor of Germany Act 1795 (c.93)
Loan to Emperor of Germany Act 1797 (c.59)
Loan to South Australia Act 1841 (c.13)
Loans for Erection of Workhouses Act 1802 (c.74)

Loans for Erection of Workhouses Act 1803 (c.110)
Loans for Parsonages, etc. (Ireland) Act 1803 (c.106)
Loans for Public Works (Ireland) Act 1846 (c.85)
Loans for Public Works (Ireland) Act 1846 (c.108)
Loans for Public Works (Ireland) Act 1851 (c.51)
Loans for Relief of Certain Merchants Act 1799 (c.5)
Loans for Schools, etc. (Ireland) Act 1884 (c.22)
Loans (Incumbents of Benefices) Amendment Act 1918 (c.42)
Loans of Exchequer Bills Act 1771 (c.25)
Loans of Exchequer Bills Act 1792 (cc.15, 16)
Loans of Exchequer Bills Act 1798 (cc.82–84)
Loans of Exchequer Bills Act 1799 (cc.68–71)
Loans or Exchequer Bills Act 1793 (cc.17, 18)
Loans or Exchequer Bills Act 1774 (c.69)
Loans or Exchequer Bills Act 1775 (c.38)
Loans or Exchequer Bills Act 1776 (c.35)
Loans or Exchequer Bills Act 1776 (c.38)
Loans or Exchequer Bills Act 1776 (c.45)
Loans or Exchequer Bills Act 1776 (c.51)
Loans or Exchequer Bills Act 1778 (c.38)
Loans or Exchequer Bills Act 1778 (c.57)
Loans or Exchequer Bills Act 1778 (c.64)
Loans or Exchequer Bills Act 1779 (cc.63, 64)
Loans or Exchequer Bills Act 1779 (c.73)
Loans or Exchequer Bills Act 1780 (cc.41, 42)
Loans or Exchequer Bills Act 1780 (c.43)
Loans or Exchequer Bills Act 1780 (c.53)
Loans or Exchequer Bills Act 1780 (c.57)
Loans or Exchequer Bills Act 1781 (c.59)
Loans or Exchequer Bills Act 1782 (c.36)
Loans or Exchequer Bills Act 1782 (c.76)
Loans or Exchequer Bills Act 1783 (c.12)
Loans or Exchequer Bills Act 1783 (c.72)
Loans or Exchequer Bills Act 1783 (c.84)
Loans or Exchequer Bills Act 1784 (c.33)
Loans or Exchequer Bills Act 1784 (c.52)
Loans or Exchequer Bills Act 1785 (cc.11, 12)
Loans or Exchequer Bills Act 1785 (c.33)
Loans or Exchequer Bills Act 1786 (cc.32, 33)
Loans or Exchequer Bills Act 1787 (c.24)
Loans or Exchequer Bills Act 1788 (cc.18,19)
Loans or Exchequer Bills Act 1789 (cc.34, 35)
Loans or Exchequer Bills Act 1790 (cc.15, 16)
Loans or Exchequer Bills Act 1790 (c.24)
Loans or Exchequer Bills Act 1791 (cc.48–50)
Loans or Exchequer Bills Act 1794 (cc.28, 29)
Loans or Exchequer Bills Act 1794 (c.62)
Loans or Exchequer Bills Act 1795 (cc.21, 22)
Loans or Exchequer Bills Act 1795 (c.37)
Loans or Exchequer Bills Act 1796 (c.31)
Loans or Exchequer Bills Act 1797 (c.8)
Loans or Exchequer Bills Act 1797 (c.20)
Loans or Exchequer Bills Act 1797 (c.114)
Loans or Exchequer Bills Act 1799 (c.4)
Loans or Exchequer Bills Act 1799 (c.18)
Loans or Exchequer Bills Act 1799 (c.33)
Loans or Exchequer Bills Act 1799 (c.41)
Loans or Exchequer Bills Act 1800 (cc.102–104)
Loans or Exchequer Bills Act 1801 (c.9)
Loans or Exchequer Bills Act 1801 (cc.81–83)
Loans or Exchequer Bills Act 1802 (c.5)
Loans or Exchequer Bills Act 1802 (c.17)
Loans or Exchequer Bills Act 1802 (c.21)
Loans or Exchequer Bills Act 1802 (cc.110, 111)
Loans or Exchequer Bills Act 1803 (c.15)
Loans or Exchequer Bills Act 1803 (c.36)
Loans or Exchequer Bills Act 1803 (c.93)
Loans or Exchequer Bills Act 1803 (cc.146, 147)
Loans or Exchequer Bills Act 1804 (c.31)
Loans or Exchequer Bills Act 1804 (cc.45, 46)
Loans or Exchequer Bills Act 1804 (c.81)
Loans or Exchequer Bills Act 1805 (c.7)
Loans or Exchequer Bills Act 1806 (c.6)
Loans or Exchequer Bills Act 1806 (cc.25, 26)
Loans or Exchequer Bills Act 1806 (c.41)
Loans or Exchequer Bills Act 1807 (c.2)
Loans or Exchequer Bills Act 1807 (cc.6, 7)
Loans or Exchequer Bills Act 1807 (c.73)
Loans or Exchequer Bills Act 1812 (c.137)
Loans or Exchequer Bills, etc. Act 1805 (cc.118–120)
Loans to A. Houston and Co., etc. Act 1800 (c.101)
Loans to Grenada and St. Vincent Traders Act 1796 (c.27)
Loans to Grenada and St. Vincent Traders Act 1799 (c.13)
Lobsters (Scotland) Act 1735 (c.33)
Local Acts, Preliminary Inquiries Act 1846 (c.106)
Local Acts, Preliminary Inquiries Act 1848 (c.129)
Local and Personal (Durham University) Act 1861 (c.82)
Local and Personal (Inverness Bridge (Treasury Grant)) Act 1855 (c.113)
Local and Personal (River Suck Drainage) Act 1890 (c.12)
Local Authorities (Admission of the Press to Meetings) Act 1908 (c.43)
Local Authorities (Disqualification Relief) Act 1914 (c.10)
Local Authorities (Emergency Provisions) Act 1923 (c.6)
Local Authorities (Emergency Provisions) Act 1924 (c.29)
Local Authorities (Emergency Provisions) Act 1926 (c.10)
Local Authorities (Emergency Provisions) Act 1928 (c.9)
Local Authorities (Expenditure on Special Purposes) (Scotland) Act 1961 (c.32)
Local Authorities (Expenditure Powers) Act 1983 (c.52)

Local Authorities (Expenses) Act 1887 (c.72)
Local Authorities (Expenses) Act 1956 (c.36)
Local Authorities (Financial Provisions) Act 1921 (c.67)
Local Authorities (Goods and Services) Act 1970 (c.39)
Local Authorities (Historic Buildings) Act 1962 (c.36)
Local Authorities (Ireland) (etc.) Act 1911 (c.35)
Local Authorities (Land) Act 1963 (c.29)
Local Authorities Loans Act 1945 (c.18)
Local Authorities Loans (Scotland) Act 1891 (c.34)
Local Authorities Loans (Scotland) Act, 1891, Amendment 1893 (c.8)
Local Authorities Loans (Scotland) Act 1924 (c.36)
Local Authorities' Mutual Investment Trust Act 1968 (c.25)
Local Authorities (Publicity) Act 1931 (c.17)
Local Authorities (Qualification of Members) Act 1971 (c.7)
Local Authorities (Restoration of Works Powers) Act 1977 (c.47)
Local Authorities (Treasury Powers) Act 1906 (c.33)
Local Authority Social Services Act 1970 (c.42)
Local Bankruptcy (Ireland) Act 1888 (c.44)
Local Commissioners Relief Act 1838 (c.65)
Local Education Authorities (Medical Treatment) Act 1909 (c.13)
Local Elections and Register of Electors (Temporary Provisions) Act 1939 (c.115)
Local Elections and Register of Electors (Temporary Provisions) Act 1940 (c.3)
Local Elections and Register of Electors (Temporary Provisions) Act 1941 (c.3)
Local Elections and Register of Electors (Temporary Provisions) Act 1941 (c.49)
Local Elections and Register of Electors (Temporary Provisions) Act 1942 (c.38)
Local Elections and Register of Electors (Temporary Provisions) Act 1943 (c.2)
Local Elections and Register of Electors (Temporary Provisions) Act 1944 (c.3)
Local Elections (Expenses) Act 1919 (c.13)
Local Elections (Service Abroad) Act 1945 (c.1)
Local Employment Act 1960 (c.18)
Local Employment Act 1963 (c.19)
Local Employment Act 1970 (c.7)
Local Employment Act 1972 (c.5)
Local (Forfeited Estates: Scotland) Act 1789 (c.28)
Local Government Act 1858 (c.98)
Local Government Act 1888 (c.41)
Local Government Act 1894 (c.73)
Local Government Act 1897 (c.1)
Local Government Act 1929 (c.17)
Local Government Act 1933 (c.51)
Local Government Act 1948 (c.26)
Local Government Act 1958 (c.55)
Local Government Act 1966 (c.42)
Local Government Act 1972 (c.70)
Local Government Act 1974 (c.7)
Local Government Act 1978 (c.39)
Local Government Act 1985 (c.51)
Local Government Act 1986 (c.10)
Local Government Act 1987 (c.44)
Local Government Act 1988 (c.9)
Local Government Act 1992 (c.19)
Local Government (Access to Information) Act 1985 (c.43)
Local Government (Adjustments) Act 1913 (c.19)
Local Government (Adjustments) (Scotland) Act 1914 (c.74)
Local Government (Allotments and Land Cultivation) (Ireland) Act 1917 (c.30)
Local Government (Amendment) Act 1863 (c.17)
Local Government (Amendment) Act 1993 (c.27)
Local Government and Housing Act 1989 (c.42)
Local Government and Miscellaneous Financial Provisions (Scotland) Act 1958 (c.64)
Local Government and Other Officers' Superannuation Act 1922 (c.59)
Local Government and Other Officers Superannuation (Temporary Provisions) Act 1933 (c.43)
Local Government and Planning (Amendment) Act 1981 (c.41)
Local Government and Planning (Scotland) Act 1982 (c.43)
Local Government Board Act 1871 (c.70)
Local Government Board (Ireland) Act 1872 (c.69)
Local Government Board (Ireland) Amendment Act 1881 (c.28)
Local Government Boundaries Act 1871 (c.70)
Local Government (Boundaries) Act 1887 (c.61)
Local Government (Boundary Commission) Act 1944 (c.38)
Local Government Boundary Commission (Dissolution) Act 1949 (c.83)
Local Government (Clerks) Act 1931 (c.45)
Local Government (County Boroughs and Adjustments) Act 1926 (c.38)
Local Government (Determination of Differences) Act 1896 (c.9)
Local Government (Development and Finance) (Scotland) Act 1964 (c.67)
Local Government (Elections) Act 1896 (c.1)
Local Government Elections Act 1956 (c.43)
Local Government (Elections) (No. 2) Act 1896 (c.4)
Local Government (Emergency Provisions) Act 1916 (c.12)
Local Government Emergency Provisions (No. 2) Act 1916 (c.55)

Local Government etc. (Scotland) Act 1994 (c.39)
Local Government Finance Act 1982 (c.32)
Local Government Finance Act 1987 (c.6)
Local Government Finance Act 1988 (c.41)
Local Government Finance Act 1992 (c.14)
Local Government Finance and Valuation Act 1991 (c.51)
Local Government Finance (Publicity for Auditors' Reports) Act 1991 (c.15)
Local Government (Financial Provisions) Act 1937 (c.22)
Local Government (Financial Provisions) Act 1941 (c.33)
Local Government (Financial Provisions) Act 1946 (c.24)
Local Government (Financial Provisions) Act 1963 (c.46)
Local Government (Financial Provisions) (Scotland) Act 1937 (c.29)
Local Government (Financial Provisions) (Scotland) Act 1941 (c.45)
Local Government (Financial Provisions) (Scotland) Act 1946 (c.25)
Local Government (Financial Provisions) (Scotland) Act 1954 (c.13)
Local Government (Financial Provisions) (Scotland) Act 1963 (c.12)
Local Government (Financial Provisions etc.) (Scotland) Act 1962 (c.9)
Local Government (Footpath and Open Spaces) (Scotland) Act 1970 (c.28)
Local Government (General Exchequer Contributions) Act 1933 (c.8)
Local Government Grants (Social Need) Act 1969 (c.2)
Local Government (Hours of Poll) Act 1938 (c.59)
Local Government (Interim Provisions) Act 1984 (c.53)
Local Government (Ireland) Act 1871 (c.109)
Local Government (Ireland) Act 1898 (c.37)
Local Government (Ireland) Act (1898) Amendment 1906 (c.31)
Local Government (Ireland) Act 1900 (c.63)
Local Government (Ireland) Act 1901 (c.28)
Local Government (Ireland) Act 1902 (c.38)
Local Government (Ireland) Act 1919 (c.19)
Local Government (Ireland) (No. 2) Act 1900 (c.41)
Local Government (Joint Committees) Act 1897 (c.40)
Local Government (Members' Travelling Expenses) Act 1937 (c.36)
Local Government (Miscellaneous Provisions) Act 1953 (c.26)
Local Government (Miscellaneous Provisions) Act 1976 (c.57)
Local Government (Miscellaneous Provisions) Act 1982 (c.30)
Local Government (Miscellaneous Provisions) (Scotland) Act 1981 (c.23)
Local Government Act 1898 (c.37)
Local Government (Omnibus Shelters and Queue Barriers) (Scotland) Act 1958 (c.50)
Local Government (Overseas Assistance) Act 1993 (c.25)
Local Government (Pecuniary Interests) Act 1964 (c.77)
Local Government (Pecuniary Interests) (Scotland) Act 1966 (c.7)
Local Government, Planning and Land Act 1980 (c.65)
Local Government (Records) Act 1962 (c.56)
Local Government (Scotland) Act 1889 (c.50)
Local Government (Scotland) Act 1894 (c.58)
Local Government (Scotland) Act, 1894, Amendment 1895 (c.1)
Local Government (Scotland) Act 1908 (c.62)
Local Government (Scotland) Act 1929 (c.25)
Local Government (Scotland) Act 1939 (c.28)
Local Government (Scotland) Act 1947 (c.43)
Local Government (Scotland) Act 1951 (c.15)
Local Government (Scotland) Act 1965 (c.41)
Local Government (Scotland) Act 1966 (c.51)
Local Government (Scotland) Act 1973 (c.65)
Local Government (Scotland) Act 1975 (c.30)
Local Government (Scotland) Act 1978 (c.4)
Local Government (Scotland) Act 1947 (Amendment) Act 1965 (c.41)
Local Government Staffs (War Service) Act 1939 (c.94)
Local Government (Stock Transfer) Act 1895 (c.32)
Local Government (Street Works) (Scotland) (Amendment) Act 1956 (c.40)
Local Government Superannuation Act 1937 (c.68)
Local Government Superannuation Act 1939 (c.18)
Local Government Superannuation Act 1953 (c.25)
Local Government Superannuation (Scotland) Act 1937 (c.69)
Local Government Supplemental Act 1859 (c.31)
Local Government Supplemental Act 1860 (c.44)
Local Government Supplemental Act 1861 (c.39)
Local Government Supplemental Act 1862 (c.25)
Local Government Supplemental Act 1863 (c.32)
Local Government Supplemental Act 1864 (c.26)
Local Government Supplemental Act 1865 (c.24)
Local Government Supplemental Act 1866 (c.24)
Local Government Supplemental Act 1867 (c.21)
Local Government Supplemental (No. 2) Act 1859 (c.11)
Local Government Supplemental (No. 2) Act 1860 (c.118)

Local Government Supplemental (No. 2) Act 1861 (c.128)
Local Government Supplemental (No. 2) Act 1863 (c.64)
Local Government Supplemental (No. 2) Act 1864 (c.83)
Local Government Supplemental (No. 2) Act 1865 (c.25)
Local Government Supplemental (No. 2) Act 1866 (c.79)
Local Government Supplemental (No. 3) Act 1865 (c.41)
Local Government Supplemental (No. 3) Act 1866 (c.106)
Local Government Supplemental (No. 3) Act 1867 (c.49)
Local Government Supplemental (No. 4) Act 1865 (c.110)
Local Government Supplemental (No. 4) Act 1866 (c.107)
Local Government Supplemental (No. 5) Act 1865 (c.108)
Local Government Supplemental (No. 5) Act 1867 (c.83)
Local Government Supplemental (No. 6) Act 1867 (c.123)
Local Government (Termination of Reviews) Act 1967 (c.18)
Local Government (Transfer of Powers) Act 1903 (c.15)
Local Government (Wales) Act 1994 (c.19)
Local Land Charges Act 1975 (c.76)
Local Light Dues Reduction Act 1876 (c.27)
Local Loans Act 1875 (c.83)
Local Loans Sinking Funds Act 1885 (c.30)
Local Militia Ballot Suspension Act 1816 (c.38)
Local Militia (England) Act 1808 (c.111)
Local Militia (England) Act 1809 (c.40)
Local Militia (England) Act 1812 (c.38)
Local Militia (England) Act 1813 (c.28)
Local Militia (Exemption) Act 1812 (c.116)
Local Militia (Great Britain) Act 1809 (c.82)
Local Militia (Great Britain) Act 1813 (c.19)
Local Militia (Great Britain) Act 1815 (c.76)
Local Militia (Ireland) Act 1813 (c.48)
Local Militia Pay (Great Britain) Act 1814 (c.176)
Local Militia Pay (Great Britain) Act 1815 (c.166)
Local Militia Pay (Great Britain) Act 1816 (c.45)
Local Militia (Scotland) Act 1808 (c.150)
Local Militia (Scotland) Act 1809 (c.48)
Local Militia (Scotland) Act 1812 (c.68)
Local Officers Superannuation (Ireland) Act 1869 (c.79)
Local (Redstone Bridge, Severn) Act 1773 (c.113)
Local Registration of Title (Ireland) Act 1891 (c.66)
Local Registration of Title (Ireland) Act 1909 (c.36)
Local Registration of Title (Ireland) Amendment Act 1908 (c.58)
Local (Rutland Roads) Act 1773 (c.108)
Local Stamp Act 1869 (c.49)
Local Tax Act 1731 (c.5)
Local Taxation Account (Scotland) Act 1898 (c.56)
Local Taxation (Customs and Excise) Act 1890 (c.60)
Local Taxation (Ireland) Estate Duty Act 1896 (c.41)
Local Taxation Returns Act 1860 (c.51)
Local Taxation Returns Act 1877 (c.66)
Local Taxation Returns (Scotland) Act 1881 (c.6)
Local (Westminster Streets) Act 1765 (c.13)
Locomotive Act 1861 (c.70)
Locomotive Threshing Engines Act 1894 (c.37)
Locomotives Act 1865 (c.83)
Locomotives Act 1898 (c.29)
Locomotives Amendment (Scotland) Act 1878 (c.58)
Locomotives on Highways Act 1896 (c.36)
Lodgers' Goods Protection Act 1871 (c.79)
Lodgers' Goods Protection Societies Act 1871 (c.80)
Lodging Houses Act 1851 (c.34)
Lodgings of Justices of Assize Act 1799 (c.46)
Loes and Wilford, Suffolk: Poor Relief Act 1791 (c.72)
Lombs's Silk Engines Act 1731 (c.8)
London Act 1532 (c.16)
London and Hertford Hospitals Act 1795 (c.104)
London and Holyhead Road Act 1836 (c.35)
London Assurance Act 1796 (c.27)
London Barbers and Surgeons Act 1744 (c.15)
London Bridge Act 1756 (c.40)
London Bridge Act 1757 (c.20)
London Bridge Act 1762 (c.30)
London Bridge Act 1771 (c.26)
London Bridge Act 1842 (c.64)
London Bridge Approaches Act 1848 (c.124)
London Bridge Approaches Act 1850 (c.103)
London Bridge Approaches Fund Act 1847 (c.115)
London Brokers Relief Act 1870 (c.60)
London Brokers Relief Act 1884 (c.3)
London Cab Act 1896 (c.27)
London Cab Act 1968 (c.7)
London Cab Act 1973 (c.20)
London Cab and Stage Carriage Act 1907 (c.55)
London, City Road Act 1760 (c.26)
London, City Road Act 1783 (c.102)
London Coal and Wine Duties Cont. Act 1863 (c.46)
London Coal and Wine Duties Cont. Act 1868 (c.17)
London Coal Duties Abolition Act 1889 (c.17)

London: Coal Trade Act 1786 (c.14)
London Council (Money) Act 1889 (c.61)
London County Council Electors Qualification Act 1900 (c.29)
London County Council (General Powers) Act 1947 (c.45)
London County Council (Improvements) Act 1962 (c.49)
London Diocese Act 1863 (c.36)
London Docks (Warehousing of Goods) Act (c.100)
London Electric Lighting Areas Act 1904 (c.13)
London Electric Lighting Areas Act 1904 (c.13)
London (Equalization of Rates) Act 1894 (c.53)
London Flour Company Act 1800 (c.97)
London Government Act 1899 (c.14)
London Government Act 1939 (c.40)
London Government Act 1950 (c.22)
London Government Act 1963 (c.33)
London Government Act 1967 (c.5)
London Hackney Carriage Act 1831 (c.22)
London Hackney Carriage Act 1853 (c.33)
London Hackney Carriage (No. 2) Act 1853 (c.127)
London Hackney Carriages Act 1843 (c.86)
London Hackney Carriages Act 1850 (c.7)
London Hospitals Act 1782 (c.77)
London Institution (Transfer) Act 1912 (c.13)
London Militia Act 1795 (c.27)
London Militia Act 1796 (c.91)
London Museum Site Act 1868 (c.8)
London Naval Treaty Act 1930 (c.48)
London Naval Treaty Act 1937 (c.65)
London Park and Works Act 1887 (c.34)
London Passenger Transport Act 1933 (c.14)
London Paving and Lighting Act 1766 (c.26)
London Regional Transport Act 1984 (c.32)
London Regional Transport (Amendment) Act 1985 (c.10)
London Roads Act 1839 (c.80)
London Street Lighting Act 1743 (c.29)
London Streets Act 1762 (c.21)
London: Streets Act 1771 (c.54)
London: Streets Act 1772 (c.17)
London Streets Act 1772 (c.69)
London: Streets Act 1775 (c.54)
London: Streets Act 1776 (c.22)
London: Streets Act 1776 (c.23)
London: Streets Act 1778 (c.71)
London: Streets Act 1778 (c.73)
London: Streets Act 1782 (c.84)
London (Streets and Sewers) Act 1793 (c.75)
London Streets, City Act 1759 (c.30)
London: Thames Embankment Act 1771 (c.34)
London Traffic Act 1924 (c.34)
London Widening of Passages etc. Act 1766 (c.27)
Londonderry School Act 1808 (c.77)
Long Leases (Scotland) Act 1954 (c.49)
Long Leases (Temporary Provisions) (Scotland) Act 1951 (c.28)
Longitude and Latitude Act 1740 (c.39)
Longitude at Sea Act 1796 (c.107)
Lord Alcester's Grant Act 1883 (c.16)
Lord Blessington's Will Act 1772 (c.17)
Lord Chancellor of Ireland Act 1802 (c.105)
Lord Chancellor (Tenure of Office and Discharge of Ecclesiastical Functions) Act 1974 (c.25)
Lord Chancellor's Augmentation Act 1863 (c.120)
Lord Chancellor's Pension Act 1832 (c.111)
Lord Clerk Register (Scotland) Act 1861 (c.81)
Lord Clerk Register (Scotland) Act 1879 (c.44)
Lord Dundonald's Patent (Tar, Pitch, etc.) Act 1785 (c.42)
Lord High Commission (Church of Scotland) Act 1959 (c.8)
Lord High Commissioner (Church of Scotland) Act 1948 (c.30)
Lord High Commissioner (Church of Scotland) Act 1974 (c.19)
Lord Napier Act 1869 (c.3)
Lord Napier's Salary Act 1869 (c.3)
Lord Nelson, Purchase of Estate for Act 1815 (c.96)
Lord Powerscourt's Mansion Act 1807 (c.78)
Lord Wolseley's Grant Act 1883 (c.17)
Lords Justices Act 1837 (c.72)
Losses During Rebellion in Ireland Act 1805 (c.79)
Losses from Cession of East Florida Act 1786 (c.75)
Losses from Cession of East Florida Act 1788 (c.31)
Lost Property (Scotland) Act 1965 (c.27)
Lotteries Act 1710 (c.6)
Lotteries Act 1721 (c.2)
Lotteries Act 1787 (c.41)
Lotteries Act 1790 (c.30)
Lotteries Act 1802 (c.54)
Lotteries Act 1803 (c.91)
Lotteries Act 1804 (c.93)
Lotteries Act 1805 (c.74)
Lotteries Act 1806 (c.148)
Lotteries Act 1807 (c.9)
Lotteries Act 1808 (c.139)
Lotteries Act 1809 (c.94)
Lotteries Act 1810 (c.94)
Lotteries Act 1811 (c.113)
Lotteries Act 1812 (c.19)
Lotteries Act 1812 (c.125)
Lotteries Act 1813 (c.93)
Lotteries Act 1814 (c.74)
Lotteries Act 1815 (c.73)
Lotteries Act 1816 (c.61)
Lotteries Act 1836 (c.66)
Lotteries Act 1845 (c.74)
Lotteries Act 1975 (c.58)
Lotteries (Amendment) Act 1984 (c.9)

Lotteries and Amusements Act 1976 (c.32)
Lotteries and Gaming Act 1962 (c.55)
Lotteries (Ireland) Act 1780 (c.14)
Lottery Act 1771 (c.47)
Lottery Act 1785 (c.59)
Lottery Act 1786 (c.65)
Lottery Act 1787 (c.1)
Lottery Act 1788 (c.21)
Lottery Act 1789 (c.33)
Lottery Act 1791 (c.53)
Lottery Act 1792 (c.28)
Lottery Act 1793 (c.62)
Lottery Act 1794 (c.40)
Lottery Act 1795 (c.36)
Lottery Act 1796 (c.104)
Lottery Act 1797 (c.113)
Lottery Act 1798 (c.75)
Lottery Act 1799 (c.91)
Lottery Act 1800 (c.52)
Lottery Act 1801 (c.6)
Lottery Act 1801 (c.27)
Lottery Office Keepers Act 1779 (c.21)
Lottery Office Keepers Act 1782 (c.47)
Lottery Regulations Act 1802 (c.104)
Lough Corrib Act 1850 (c.112)
Lough Corrib Navigation Act 1874 (c.71)
Loughborough: Navigation Act 1766 (c.94)
Loughborough Navigation Act 1776 (c.65)
Louth, Lincoln, Roads Act 1770 (c.109)
Louth Roads Act 1780 (c.94)
Lower Canada Government Act 1838 (c.9)
Lower Canada Government Act 1839 (c.53)
Lower Ouse: Navigation Act 1791 (c.76)
Ludlow and Monk's Bridge Road Act 1750 (c.29)
Ludlow Roads Act 1756 (c.59)
Ludlow Roads Act 1779 (c.114)
Ludlow, Salop: Improvement Act 1793 (c.25)
Lunacy Act 1771 (c.20)
Lunacy Act 1842 (c.84)
Lunacy Act 1855 (c.13)
Lunacy Act 1890 (c.5)
Lunacy Act 1891 (c.65)
Lunacy Act 1908 (c.47)
Lunacy Act 1911 (c.40)
Lunacy Act 1922 (c.60)
Lunacy Act Amendment Act 1865 (c.80)
Lunacy Acts Amendment 1885 (c.52)
Lunacy Acts Amendment 1889 (c.41)
Lunacy Acts Amendments Act 1826 (c.111)
Lunacy Acts Amendments Act 1862 (c.111)
Lunacy Board (Scotland) Act 1864 (c.59)
Lunacy Board (Scotland) Salaries and Clerks Act 1900 (c.54)
Lunacy Districts (Scotland) Act 1887 (c.39)
Lunacy (Ireland) Act 1867 (c.118)
Lunacy (Ireland) Act 1901 (c.17)
Lunacy Regulation Act 1853 (c.70)
Lunacy Regulation Act 1855 (c.105)
Lunacy Regulation Act 1862 (c.86)
Lunacy Regulation Act 1871 (c.22)
Lunacy Regulation Amendment Act 1882 (c.82)
Lunacy Regulation (Ireland) Act 1871 (c.22)
Lunacy (Scotland) Act 1857 (c.71)
Lunacy (Scotland) Act 1862 (c.54)
Lunacy (Scotland) Act 1866 (c.51)
Lunacy (Vacating of Seats) Act 1886 (c.16)
Lunatic Asylums Act 1842 (c.87)
Lunatic Asylums Act 1853 (c.97)
Lunatic Asylums Act 1856 (c.87)
Lunatic Asylums, etc. Act 1846 (c.84)
Lunatic Asylums (Ireland) Act 1846 (c.79)
Lunatic Asylums (Ireland) Act 1846 (c.115)
Lunatic Asylums (Ireland) Act 1849 (c.56)
Lunatic Asylums (Ireland) Act 1851 (c.45)
Lunatic Asylums (Ireland) Act 1875 (c.67)
Lunatic Asylums (Ireland) Accounts Audit Act 1868 (c.97)
Lunatic Asylums Loans (Ireland) Act 1878 (c.24)
Lunatic Asylums Repayment of Advances (Ireland) Act 1855 (c.109)
Lunatic Asylums, Superannuations (Ireland) Act 1856 (c.99)
Lunatic Paupers or Criminals Act 1808 (c.96)
Lunatic Paupers, etc. (England) Act 1811 (c.79)
Lunatics Act 1730 (c.10)
Lunatics Act 1838 (c.73)
Lunatics Act 1845 (c.100)
Lunatics Act 1845 (c.126)
Lunatics Removal (India) Act 1851 (c.81)
Lunatics (Scotland) Act 1858 (c.89)
Lunatics (Scotland) Act 1867 (c.55)
Luton and St. Albans Road Act 1726 (c.17)
Luton and St. Albans Road Act 1742 (c.23)
Lying-in Hospitals Act 1773 (c.82)
Lyme Regis Roads Act 1770 (c.59)
Lymington Roads Act 1765 (c.59)
Lymington Roads Act 1786 (c.156)
Lyon King of Arms Act 1867 (c.17)

Macclesfield and Buxton Road Act 1958 (c.41)
Macclesfield to Buxton Road Act 1780 (c.91)
Macclesfield Grammar School Act 1774 (c.51)
Madder Act 1957 (c.12)
Madhouses Act 1774 (c.49)
Madhouses Act 1779 (c.15)
Madhouses Act 1786 (c.91)
Magdalen Hospital, London Act 1769 (c.31)
Magistrates' Courts Act 1952 (c.55)
Magistrates' Courts Act 1957 (c.29)
Magistrates' Courts Act 1980 (c.43)
Magistrates' Courts (Appeals from Binding Over Orders) Act 1956 (c.44)
Maidenhead and Reading, etc. Roads Act 1727 (c.3)
Maidenhead Bridge Act 1772 (c.41)
Maidenhead, Reading etc. Roads Act 1763 (c.46)
Maidenhead Road Act 1743 (c.19)
Maidenhead Roads Act 1779 (c.84)

Maidstone Gaol, Kent (Expenses) Act 1735 (c.12)
Maidstone, Kent: Improvement Act 1791 (c.62)
Maidstone: Poor Relief Act 1780 (c.22)
Maidstone to Ashford Road Act 1973 (c.173)
Maidstone to Cranbrook Road Act 1759 (c.57)
Maidstone to Cranbrook Road Act 1768 (c.43)
Mail to Spain Act 1793 (c.60)
Mail Ships Act 1902 (c.36)
Maintenance Agreements Act 1957 (c.35)
Maintenance Enforcement Act 1991 (c.17)
Maintenance of Church of England Act 1706 (c.8)
Maintenance of Live Stock Act 1915 (c.65)
Maintenance Orders Act 1950 (c.37)
Maintenance Orders Act 1958 (c.39)
Maintenance Orders Act 1968 (c.36)
Maintenance Orders (Facilities for Enforcement) Act 1920 (c.33)
Maintenance Orders (Reciprocal Enforcement) Act 1972 (c.18)
Maintenance Orders (Reciprocal Enforcement) Act 1992 (c.56)
Making of Bread Act 1957 (c.29)
Making of Indigo Act 1755 (c.25)
Making of indigo, etc. 1770 (c.37)
Making of Sail Cloth Act 1741 (c.35)
Malawi Independence 1964 (c.46)
Malaysia Act 1963 (c.35)
Malaysian Act 1963 (c.60)
Malicious Communications Act 1988 (c.27)
Malicious Damage Act 1812 (c.130)
Malicious Damage Act 1861 (c.97)
Malicious Damage Act 1964 (c.76)
Malicious Damage (Scotland) Act 1816 (c.125)
Malicious Injury Act 1769 (c.29)
Mall Approach (Improvement) Act 1914 (c.28)
Malmesbury Roads Act 1778 (c.114)
Malt Duties, etc. Act 1714 (c.2)
Malt Duties, etc. Act 1725 (c.4)
Malt Duties, etc. Act 1759 (c.7)
Malt Duties Act 1762 (c.13)
Malt Duties Act 1762 (c.2)
Malt Duties Act 1766 (c.6)
Malt Duties Act 1768 (c.4)
Malt Duties Act 1769 (c.2)
Malt Duties Act 1770 (c.5)
Malt Duties Act 1772 (c.6)
Malt Duties Act 1772 (c.6)
Malt Duties Act 1837 (c.49)
Malt Duties Act 1971 (c.2)
Malt Duties Act 1774 (c.2)
Malt Duties Act 1775 (c.2)
Malt Duties Act 1776 (c.1)
Malt Duties Act 1776 (c.2)
Malt Duties Act 1778 (c.3)
Malt Duties Act 1779 (c.3)
Malt Duties Act 1780 (c.3)
Malt Duties Act 1780 (c.4)
Malt Duties Act 1782 (c.3)
Malt Duties Act 1782 (c.4)
Malt Duties Act 1783 (c.64)
Malt Duties Act 1783 (c.1)
Malt Duties Act 1785 (c.2)
Malt Duties Act 1786 (c.6)
Malt Duties Act 1788 (c.1)
Malt Duties Act 1789 (c.10)
Malt Duties Act 1790 (c.3)
Malt Duties Act 1791 (c.2)
Malt Duties Act 1791 (c.7)
Malt Duties Act 1791 (c.6)
Malt Duties Act 1791 (c.18)
Malt Duties Act 1793 (c.11)
Malt Duties Act 1794 (c.7)
Malt, etc. Duties Act 1765 (c.2)
Malta Constitution Act 1932 (c.43)
Malta Independence Act 1964 (c.86)
Malta (Letters Patent) Act 1936 (c.29)
Malta (Reconstruction) Act 1947 (c.9)
Malta Republic Act 1975 (c.31)
Malton and Pickering Road Act 1765 (c.108)
Manchester and Oldham Canal Act 1792 (c.84)
Manchester-Oldham Canal Act 1974 (c.26)
Manchester and Salford: Improvement Act 1792 (c.69)
Manchester and Stockport Canal Act 1793 (c.21)
Manchester, Bolton and Bury Canal Act 1791 (c.68)
Manchester Canal Act 1794 (c.37)
Manchester Church Act 1753 (c.45)
Manchester Church Act 1769 (c.60)
Manchester, Church Building 1708 (c.28)
Manchester General Improvement Act 1851 (c.119)
Manchester Improvement Act 1765 (c.81)
Manchester: Poor Relief Act 1790 (c.81)
Manchester Roads Act 1731 (c.10)
Manchester Roads Act 1749 (c.5)
Manchester Roads Act 1771 (c.82)
Manchester Roads Act 1772 (c.88)
Manchester, School Mills Act 1758 (c.61)
Manchester Square: Improvement Act 1789 (c.5)
Manchester: Streets Act 1776 (c.63)
Manchester Theatre Act 1775 (c.47)
Manchester to Buxton Road Act 1793 (c.171)
Manchester to Chester Roads Act 1793 (c.139)
Manchester to Wilmslow Road Act 1793 (c.170)
Mandated and Trust Territories Act 1947 (c.8)
Manning of the Navy, etc. Act 1793 (c.66)
Manning of the Navy Act 1795 (c.5)
Manning of the Navy Act 1795 (c.9)
Manning of the Navy Act 1795 (c.19)
Manning of the Navy Act 1795 (c.29)
Manoeuvres Act 1958 (c.7)
Mansfield and Chesterfield Road Act 1958 (c.37)

Mansfield to Chesterfield Road Act 1780 (c.72)
Manufacture of Cambrics 1763 (c.37)
Manufacture of Hats Act 1776 (c.55)
Manufacture of Leather Act 1784 (c.19)
Manufacture of Ounce Thread Act 1788 (c.17)
Manufacture of Sail Cloth Act 1730 (c.27)
Manufacture of Sail Cloth Act 1735 (c.37)
Manufacture of Serges, etc. Act 1719 (c.13)
Manufacture of Serges, etc. Act 1723 (c.18)
Maplin Development Act 1973 (c.64)
Maplin Development Authority (Dissolution) Act 1976 (c.51)
Mar Peerage Restoration Act 1824 (c.59)
March, Cambridge, Isle of Ely: Drainage Act 1957 (c.36)
Margate Pier Act 1724 (c.3)
Margate Theatre Act 1786 (c.29)
Marine and Aviation Insurance (War Risks) Act 1952 (c.57)
Marine Duty Act 1791 (c.17)
Marine, etc. Broadcasting Offences Act 1967 (c.41)
Marine Insurance Act 1745 (c.37)
Marine Insurance Act 1788 (c.56)
Marine Insurance Act 1906 (c.41)
Marine Insurance (Gambling Policies) Act 1909 (c.12)
Marine Mutiny Act 1755 (c.11)
Marine Mutiny Act 1757 (c.11)
Marine Mutiny Act 1757 (c.6)
Marine Mutiny Act 1757 (c.9)
Marine Mutiny Act 1759 (c.8)
Marine Mutiny Act 1760 (c.8)
Marine Mutiny Act 1761 (c.12)
Marine Mutiny Act 1762 (c.3)
Marine Mutiny Act 1763 (c.8)
Marine Mutiny Act 1765 (c.6)
Marine Mutiny Act 1766 (c.10)
Marine Mutiny Act 1766 (c.13)
Marine Mutiny Act 1768 (c.12)
Marine Mutiny Act 1769 (c.7)
Marine Mutiny Act 1770 (c.7)
Marine Mutiny Act 1771 (c.7)
Marine Mutiny Act 1772 (c.5)
Marine Mutiny Act 1772 (c.11)
Marine Mutiny Act 1774 (c.4)
Marine Mutiny Act 1775 (c.4)
Marine Mutiny Act 1776 (c.7)
Marine Mutiny Act 1776 (c.4)
Marine Mutiny Act 1778 (c.5)
Marine Mutiny Act 1779 (c.8)
Marine Mutiny Act 1780 (c.13)
Marine Mutiny Act 1780 (c.9)
Marine Mutiny Act 1782 (c.5)
Marine Mutiny Act 1782 (c.7)
Marine Mutiny Act 1783 (c.17)
Marine Mutiny Act 1785 (c.3)
Marine Mutiny Act 1786 (c.7)
Marine Mutiny Act 1788 (c.3)
Marine Mutiny Act 1789 (c.3)
Marine Mutiny Act 1790 (c.7)
Marine Mutiny Act 1791 (c.9)
Marine Mutiny Act 1793 (c.6)
Marine Mutiny Act 1794 (c.6)
Marine Mutiny Act 1795 (c.7)
Marine Mutiny Act 1840 (c.8)
Marine Society Act 1772 (c.67)
Marine Works (Ireland) Act 1902 (c.24)
Marines Act 1792 (c.67)
Maritime Conventions Act 1911 (c.57)
Market Harborough and Brampton Road Act 1751 (c.57)
Market Harborough and Brampton Road Act 1754 (c.28)
Market Harborough and Brampton Road Act 1759 (c.38)
Market Harborough to Coventry Road Act 1755 (c.40)
Market Harborough to Coventry Road Act 1779 (c.82)
Market Harborough to Loughborough Road Act 1793 (c.176)
Market Weighton Act 1772 (c.37)
Markets and Fairs Clauses Act 1847 (c.14)
Markets and Fairs (Weighing of Cattle) Act 1887 (c.27)
Markets and Fairs (Weighing of Cattle) Act 1891 (c.70)
Markets and Fairs (Weighing of Cattle) Act 1926 (c.21)
Marriage Act 1939 (c.33)
Marriage Act 1949 (c.76)
Marriage Act 1983 (c.32)
Marriage Act 1949 (Amendment) 1954 (c.47)
Marriage Act 1994 (c.34)
Marriage Acts Amendment Act 1958 (c.29)
Marriage Confirmation Act 1830 (c.18)
Marriage (Enabling) Act 1960 (c.29)
Marriage (Extension of Hours) Act 1934 (c.13)
Marriage Law (Ireland) Amendment Act 1873 (c.16)
Marriage (Members of His Majesty's Forces) Act 1941 (c.47)
Marriage (Naval, Military and Air Force Chapels) Act 1932 (c.31)
Marriage Notice (Scotland) Act 1878 (c.43)
Marriage of British Subjects (Facilities) Act 1915 (c.40)
Marriage of British Subjects (Facilities) Amendment 1916 (c.21)
Marriage of Lunatics Act 1941 (c.30)
Marriage (Prohibited Degrees of Relationship) Act 1931 (c.31)
Marriage (Prohibited Degrees of Relationship) Act 1986 (c.16)
Marriage (Registrar General's Licence Act 1970 (c.34)
Marriage (Registration of Buildings) Act 1990 (c.33)
Marriage (Scotland) Act 1834 (c.28)
Marriage (Scotland) Act 1916 (c.7)
Marriage (Scotland) Act 1939 (c.34)
Marriage (Scotland) Act 1942 (c.20)

Marriage (Scotland) Act 1956 (c.70)
Marriage (Scotland) Act 1977 (c.15)
Marriage (Scotland) Emergency Provisions Act 1940 (c.30)
Marriage (Secretaries of Synagogues) Act 1959 (c.13)
Marriage (Wales) Act 1986 (c.7)
Marriage (Wales and Monmouthshire) Act 1962 (c.32)
Marriage with Foreigners Act 1906 (c.40)
Marriages (Confirmation) Act 1804 (c.77)
Marriages (Confirmation) Act 1808 (c.127)
Marriages (Confirmation) Act 1825 (c.92)
Marriages in Japan (Validity) Act 1912 (c.15)
Marriages (Ireland) Act 1844 (c.81)
Marriages (Ireland) Act 1846 (c.72)
Marriages (Ireland) Act 1918 (c.2)
Marriages Legalisation Act 1901 (c.23)
Marriages Legalisation Act 1903 (c.26)
Marriages (Validity) Act 1939 (c.35)
Marriages Validity (Provisional Orders) Act 1924 (c.20)
Married Women (Maintenance) Act 1920 (c.63)
Married Women (Restraint Upon Anticipation) Act 1949 (c.78)
Married Women's Policies of Assurance Act 1880 (c.26)
Married Women's Policies of Assurance (Scotland) (Amendment) Act 1980 (c.56)
Married Women's Property Act 1882 (c.75)
Married Women's Property Act 1907 (c.18)
Married Women's Property Act 1908 (c.27)
Married Women's Property Act 1964 (c.19)
Married Women's Property (Scotland) Act 1881 (c.21)
Married Women's Property (Scotland) Act 1920 (c.64)
Married Women's Reversionary Interests Act 1857 (c.57)
Marshall Aid Commemoration Act 1953 (c.39)
Marshall Scholarships Act 1959 (c.3)
Marylebone Act 1783 (c.110)
Marylebone: Improvement Act 1768 (c.46)
Marylebone Road Act 1720 (c.26)
Marylebone Road Act 1734 (c.8)
Maryport Harbour Act 1748 (c.6)
Maryport Harbour Act 1756 (c.57)
Maryport Harbour Act 1791 (c.23)
Master and Servant Act 1889 (c.24)
Matches and Mechanical Lighters Duties Act 1979 (c.6)
Maternity and Child Welfare Act 1918 (c.29)
Maternity Services (Scotland) Act 1937 (c.30)
Matrimonial and Family Proceedings Act 1984 (c.42)
Matrimonial Causes Act 1907 (c.12)
Matrimonial Causes Act 1923 (c.19)
Matrimonial Causes Act 1937 (c.57)
Matrimonial Causes Act 1950 (c.25)
Matrimonial Causes Act 1963 (c.45)
Matrimonial Causes Act 1965 (c.72)
Matrimonial Causes Act 1967 (c.56)
Matrimonial Causes Act 1973 (c.18)
Matrimonial Causes and Marriage Law (Ireland) Amendment Act 1871 (c.49)
Matrimonial Causes (Dominions Troops) Act 1919 (c.28)
Matrimonial Causes (Property and Maintenance) Act 1958 (c.35)
Matrimonial Causes (War Marriages) Act (c.43)
Matrimonial Homes Act 1967 (c.75)
Matrimonial Homes Act 1983 (c.19)
Matrimonial Homes and Property Act 1981 (c.24)
Matrimonial Homes (Family Protection) (Scotland) 1981 (c.59)
Matrimonial Proceedings and Property Act 1970 (c.45)
Matrimonial Proceedings (Children) Act 1958 (c.40)
Matrimonial Proceedings (Magistrates' Courts) Act 1960 (c.48)
Matrimonial Proceedings (Polygamous Marriages) Act 1972 (c.38)
Matrimonial Proceedings (Transfers) Act 1988 (c.18)
Mauritius Independence Act 1968 (c.8)
Mauritius Loan (Guarantee) Act 1931 (c.26)
Mauritius Republic Act 1992 (c.45)
Measurement of Coal Wagons, etc. Act 1775 (c.27)
Medical Act 1858 (c.90)
Medical Act 1860 (c.66)
Medical Act 1876 (c.41)
Medical Act 1886 (c.48)
Medical Act 1950 (c.29)
Medical Act 1956 (c.76)
Medical Act 1969 (c.40)
Medical Act 1978 (c.12)
Medical Act 1983 (c.54)
Medical Act (1886) Amendment 1904 (c.14)
Medical Act 1956 (Amendment) Act 1958 (c.58)
Medical Act (Royal College of Surgeons of England) 1875 (c.43)
Medical Act (University of London) 1873 (c.55)
Medical and Dentists Acts Amendment Act 1927 (c.39)
Medical Practitioners and Pharmacists Act 1947 (c.11)
Medical (Professional Performance) Act 1995 (c.51)
Medical Qualifications (Amendment) Act 1991 (c.38)
Medicinal Products: Prescription by Nurses, etc. Act 1992 (c.28)
Medicine Duties Act 1785 (c.79)
Medicines Act 1968 (c.67)
Medicines Act 1971 (c.69)
Mediterranean Passes Act 1730 (c.18)
Medway Fisheries Act 1757 (c.21)
Medway: Navigation Act 1792 (c.105)

Medway Oyster Fishery Act 1728 (c.19)
Melton Mowbray to Grantham Road Act 1780 (c.95)
Members of Local Authorities Relief Act 1900 (c.46)
Memorials of Grants of Annuities Act 1822 (c.92)
Mental Deficiency Act 1913 (c.28)
Mental Deficiency Act 1927 (c.33)
Mental Deficiency Act 1938 (c.43)
Mental Deficiency (Amendment) Act 1925 (c.53)
Mental Deficiency and Lunacy (Amendment) Act 1919 (c.85)
Mental Deficiency (Scotland) Act 1940 (c.8)
Mental Health Act 1959 (c.72)
Mental Health Act 1983 (c.20)
Mental Health (Amendment) Act 1975 (c.29)
Mental Health (Amendment) Act 1982 (c.51)
Mental Health (Amendment) Act 1994 (c.6)
Mental Health (Amendment) (Scotland) Act 1983 (c.39)
Mental Health (Detention) (Scotland) Act 1991 (c.47)
Mental Health (Patients in the Community) Act 1995 (c.52)
Mental Health (Scotland) Act 1960 (c.61)
Mental Health (Scotland) Act 1984 (c.36)
Mental Treatment Act 1930 (c.23)
Mercantile Law Amendment Act 1856 (c.97)
Mercantile Law Amendment (Scotland) Act 1856 (c.60)
Mercers Company, London Act 1751 (c.7)
Mercers Company, London Act 1764 (c.50)
Mercers, London Act 1747 (c.32)
Merchandise Marks Act 1911 (c.31)
Merchandise Marks Act 1926 (c.53)
Merchandise Marks Act 1953 (c.48)
Merchandise Marks (Ireland) Act 1909 (c.24)
Merchant Seamen Act 1728 (c.36)
Merchant Seamen Act 1746 (c.38)
Merchant Seamen Act 1762 (c.31)
Merchant Seamen (Payment of Wages and Rating) Act 1880 (c.16)
Merchant Shipping Act 1786 (c.86)
Merchant Shipping Act 1791 (c.39)
Merchant Shipping Act 1794 (c.68)
Merchant Shipping Act 1872 (c.73)
Merchant Shipping Act 1894 (c.60)
Merchant Shipping Act 1906 (c.48)
Merchant Shipping Act 1907 (c.52)
Merchant Shipping Act 1911 (c.42)
Merchant Shipping Act 1921 (c.28)
Merchant Shipping Act 1937 (c.23)
Merchant Shipping Act 1948 (c.44)
Merchant Shipping Act 1950 (c.9)
Merchant Shipping Act 1952 (c.14)
Merchant Shipping Act 1954 (c.18)
Merchant Shipping Act 1964 (c.47)
Merchant Shipping Act 1965 (c.47)
Merchant Shipping Act 1967 (c.26)
Merchant Shipping Act 1970 (c.36)
Merchant Shipping Act 1974 (c.43)
Merchant Shipping Act 1979 (c.39)
Merchant Shipping Act 1981 (c.11)
Merchant Shipping Act 1983 (c.13)
Merchant Shipping Act 1984 (c.5)
Merchant Shipping Act 1988 (c.12)
Merchant Shipping Act 1995 (c.21)
Merchant Shipping Acts (Amendment) 1923 (c.40)
Merchant Shipping (Amendment) Act 1920 (c.2)
Merchant Shipping (Carriage of Munitions to Spain) Act 1936 (c.1)
Merchant Shipping (Certificates) Act 1914 (c.42)
Merchant Shipping (Convention) Act 1914 (c.50)
Merchant Shipping (Equivalent Provisions) Act 1925 (c.37)
Merchant Shipping (International Labour Convention) Act 1925 (c.42)
Merchant Shipping (Liability of Shipowners and Others) Act 1900 (c.32)
Merchant Shipping (Liability of Shipowners and Others) Act 1958 (c.62)
Merchant Shipping (Line-throwing Appliances) Act 1928 (c.40)
Merchant Shipping (Liner Conferences) Act 1982 (c.37)
Merchant Shipping (Load Lines) Act 1967 (c.27)
Merchant Shipping (Mercantile Marine Fund) Act 1898 (c.44)
Merchant Shipping (Minicoy Lighthouse) 1960 (c.42)
Merchant Shipping (Oil Pollution) Act 1971 (c.59)
Merchant Shipping (Registration, etc.) Act 1993 (c.22)
Merchant Shipping (Safety and Load Line Conventions) Act 1932 (c.9)
Merchant Shipping (Safety Convention) Act 1949 (c.43)
Merchant Shipping (Safety Convention) Act 1977 (c.24)
Merchant Shipping (Salvage and Pollution) Act 1994 (c.28)
Merchant Shipping (Scottish Fishing Boats) Act 1920 (c.39)
Merchant Shipping (Seamen's Allotment) Act 1911 (c.8)
Merchant Shipping (Salvage) Act 1916 (c.41)
Merchant Shipping (Salvage) Act 1940 (c.43)
Merchant Shipping (Spanish Frontiers Observation) Act 1937 (c.19)
Merchant Shipping (Stevedores and Trimmers) Act 1911 (c.41)
Merchant Shipping (Superannuation Contributions) Act 1937 (c.4)
Merchant Shipping (Wireless Telegraphy) Act 1919 (c.38)
Merioneth Roads Act 1777 (c.96)
Merioneth Roads Act 1969 (c.56)
Mersey Canal Act 1775 (c.20)

Methylated Spirits (Sale by Retail) (Scotland) Act 1937 (c.48)
Metropolis Gas Act 1860 (c.125)
Metropolis Gas Act 1861 (c.79)
Metropolis Water Act 1899 (c.41)
Metropolis Water Act 1902 (c.41)
Metropolitan Ambulances Act 1909 (c.17)
Metropolitan Board of Works (Money) Act 1884 (c.50)
Metropolitan Board of Works (Money) Act 1886 (c.44)
Metropolitan Buildings Act 1772 (c.73)
Metropolitan Improvements (Funds) Act 1904 (c.2)
Metropolitan Magistrates' Courts Act 1959 (c.45)
Metropolitan Police Act 1829 (c.44)
Metropolitan Police Act 1838 (c.47)
Metropolitan Police Act 1839 (c.47)
Metropolitan Police Act 1856 (c.2)
Metropolitan Police Act 1860 (c.135)
Metropolitan Police Act 1884 (c.17)
Metropolitan Police Act 1886 (c.22)
Metropolitan Police Act 1912 (c.4)
Metropolitan Police Act 1918 (c.61)
Metropolitan Police Act 1933 (c.33)
Metropolitan Police Act 1958 (c.48)
Metropolitan Police (Borrowing Powers) Act 1935 (c.16)
Metropolitan Police (Borrowing Powers) Act 1952 (c.19)
Metropolitan Police (Commission) Act 1906 (c.6)
Metropolitan Police (Courts) Act 1839 (c.71)
Metropolitan Police (Courts) Act 1897 (c.26)
Metropolitan Police (Employment in Scotland) Act (c.44)
Metropolitan Police (Receiver) Act 1867 (c.39)
Metropolitan Police (Staff Superannuation and Police Fund) Act 1931 (c.12)
Metropolitan Streets Act 1903 (c.17)
Mevagissey Pier, Cornwall Act 1775 (c.62)
Michaelmas Term Act 1750 (c.48)
Middlesex and Essex Roads Act 1785 (c.124)
Middlesex and Hertford Highways Act 1711 (c.3)
Middlesex and Hertford Roads Act 1730) (c.10)
Middlesex and Hertford Roads Act 1743 (c.14)
Middlesex and Hertford Roads Act 1770 (c.71)
Middlesex and Hertford Roads Act 1772 (c.84)
Middlesex and Hertfordshire Roads Act 1748 (c.14)
Middlesex and Surrey Roads Act 1791 (c.134)
Middlesex Deeds Act 1940 (c.34)
Middlesex Gaol Act 1786 (c.55)
Middlesex Highways Act 1711 (c.4)
Middlesex Highways Act 1723 (c.6)
Middlesex Registry Act 1708 (c.20)
Middlesex (Registry of Deeds) Act 1751 (c.4)
Middlesex Road Act 1767 (c.88)
Middlesex Roads Act 1733 (c.26)
Middlesex Roads Act 1741 (c.9)
Middlesex Roads Act 1767 (c.102)
Middlesex Roads Act 1778 (c.84)
Middlesex Roads Act 1789 (c.96)
Middlesex Roads Act 1794 (c.131)
Middlesex Roads Act 1937 (c.6)
Middlesex Sessions Act 1792 (c.48)
Middlesex Sessions House Act 1778 (c.67)
Midwives Act 1902 (c.17)
Midwives Act 1918 (c.43)
Midwives Act 1926 (c.32)
Midwives Act 1936 (c.40)
Midwives Act 1951 (c.53)
Midwives (Amendment) Act (c.13)
Midwives (Ireland) Act 1918 (c.59)
Midwives (Scotland) Act 1915 (c.91)
Midwives (Scotland) Act 1927 (c.17)
Midwives (Scotland) Act 1951 (c.54)
Milbank New Church Act 1728 (c.15)
Mile End Night Watch Act 1777 (c.66)
Milford Fortifications Act 1758 (c.26)
Milford Haven Conservancy Act 1958 (c.23)
Milford to Portsmouth Road Act 1764 (c.63)
Milford to Portsmouth Road Act 1787 (c.95)
Milk (Special Designations) Act (c.34)
Military Aircraft (Loans) Act 1966 (c.15)
Military and Air Forces (Prolongation of Service) Act 1939 (c.90)
Military Lands Act 1900 (c.56)
Military Lands Act 1903 (c.47)
Military Manoeuvres Act 1911 (c.44)
Military Service Act 1916 (c.104)
Military Service Act 1918 (c.66)
Military Service (No. 2) Act 1918 (c.5)
Military Service (Review of Exceptions) Act 1917 (c.12)
Military Service (Session 2) 1916 (c.15)
Military Training Act 1939 (c.25)
Military Tramways Act 1887 (c.65)
Military Works Act 1901 (c.40)
Military Works Act 1903 (c.29)
Militia Act 1700 (c.8)
Militia Act 1701 (c.17)
Militia Act 1702 (c.15(d))
Militia Act 1703 (c.14(e))
Militia Act 1704 (c.15(l))
Militia Act 1705 (c.10)
Militia Act 1706 (c.28)
Militia Act 1707 (c.63)
Militia Act 1708 (c.23)
Militia Act 1709 (c.22)
Militia Act 1710 (c.31)
Militia Act 1712 (c.8)
Militia Act 1766 (c.15)
Militia Act 1786 (c.107)
Militia Act 1714 (c.14)
Militia Act 1733 (c.23)
Militia Act 1745 (c.2)
Militia Act 1757 (c.25)

Militia Act 1757 (c.26)
Militia Act 1758 (c.20)
Militia Act 1759 (c.2)
Militia Act 1759 (c.2)
Militia Act 1762 (c.20)
Militia Act 1763 (c.17)
Militia Act 1765 (c.36)
Militia Act 1769 (c.40)
Militia Act 1771 (c.32)
Militia Act 1776 (c.3)
Militia Act 1778 (c.14)
Militia Act 1779 (c.76)
Militia Act 1780 (c.8)
Militia Act 1780 (c.44)
Militia Act 1780 (c.7)
Militia Act 1780 (c.18)
Militia Act 1782 (c.6)
Militia Act 1782 (c.62)
Militia Act 1794 (c.81)
Militia Act 1802 (c.90)
Militia Act 1882 (c.49)
Militia and Yeomanry Act 1901 (c.14)
Militia and Yeomanry Act 1902 (c.39)
Militia (City of London) Act 1820 (c.100)
Militia, Derbyshire Act 1795 (c.16)
Militia, etc. Act 1711 (c.33)
Militia, etc. Act 1713 (c.9(c))
Militia, etc. Act 1778 (c.59)
Militia, etc. Act 1779 (c.72)
Militia Pay Act 1757 (c.30)
Militia Pay Act 1758 (c.21)
Militia Pay Act 1759 (c.24)
Militia Pay Act 1760 (c.22)
Militia Pay Act 1762 (c.35)
Militia Pay Act 1762 (c.10)
Militia Pay Act 1763 (c.30)
Militia Pay Act 1765 (c.34)
Militia Pay Act 1768 (c.20)
Militia Pay Act 1770 (c.9)
Militia Pay Act 1772 (c.13)
Militia Pay Act 1772 (c.23)
Militia Pay Act 1774 (c.18)
Militia Pay Act 1775 (c.8)
Militia Pay Act 1776 (c.19)
Militia Pay Act 1776 (c.10)
Militia Pay Act 1779 (c.19)
Militia Pay Act 1780 (c.13)
Militia Pay Act 1780 (c.21)
Militia Pay Act 1782 (c.24)
Militia Pay Act 1783 (c.35)
Militia Pay Act 1785 (c.8)
Militia Pay Act 1786 (c.69)
Militia Pay Act 1788 (c.11)
Militia Pay Act 1789 (c.15)
Militia Pay Act 1790 (c.9)
Militia Pay Act 1791 (c.16)
Militia Pay Act 1791 (c.26)
Militia Pay Act 1793 (c.19)
Militia Pay Act 1794 (c.16)
Militia Pay Act 1794 (c.30)
Militia Pay, etc. Act 1766 (c.30)
Militia Pay, etc. Act 1766 (c.17)
Militia Pay, etc. Act 1783 (c.13)
Militia (Scotland) Act 1802 (c.91)
Militia (Storehouse) Act 1882 (c.12)
Militia, Sussex Act 1793 (c.79)
Milk Act 1934 (c.51)
Milk (Amendment) 1937 (c.66)
Milk and Dairies Act 1914 (c.49)
Milk and Dairies Act Postponement Act 1915 (c.59)
Milk and Dairies (Amendment) 1922 (c.54)
Milk and Dairies (Consolidation) Act 1915 (c.66)
Milk and Dairies (Scotland) Act 1914 (c.46)
Milk (Cessation of Production) Act 1985 (c.4)
Milk (Extension and Amendment) 1938 (c.61)
Milk (Extension of Temporary Provisions) Act 1936 (c.9)
Milk Industry Act 1939 (c.46)
Milk (Special Designations) Act 1949 (c.34)
Mine Adventurers of England Act (c.26(d))
Minehead Harbour Act 1700 (c.9)
Minehead Harbour Act 1711 (c.32)
Minehead Harbour Act 1770 (c.26)
Minehead Harbour Act 1937 (c.8)
Minehead Roads Act 1786 (c.136)
Mineral Exploration and Investment Grants Act 1972 (c.9)
Mineral Workings Act 1951 (c.60)
Mineral Workings Act 1971 (c.71)
Mineral Workings Act 1985 (c.12)
Mineral Workings (Offshore Installations) Act 1971 (c.61)
Miners Welfare Act 1952 (c.23)
Mines Accidents (Rescue and Aid) Act 1910 (c.15)
Mines and Quarries Act 1954 (c.70)
Mines and Quarries Act 1969 (c.10)
Mines and Quarries (Tips) Act 1969 (c.10)
Mines Management Act 1971 (c.20)
Mines (Prohibition of Child Labour Underground) Act 1900 (c.21)
Mines (Working Facilities) Act 1934 (c.27)
Mines (Working Facilities and Support) Act 1923 (c.20)
Mines (Working Facilities and Support) Act 1966 (c.4)
Mines (Working Facilities and Support) Act 1974 (c.36)
Mining Industry Act 1920 (c.50)
Mining Industry Act 1926 (c.28)
Mining Industry (Amendment) Act 1939 (c.45)
Mining Industry (Welfare Fund) Act 1925 (c.80)
Mining Industry (Welfare Fund) Act 1931 (c.23)
Mining Industry (Welfare Fund) Act 1934 (c.9)
Mining Industry (Welfare Fund) Act 1939 (c.9)
Mining Industry (Welfare Fund) Act 1943 (c.3)
Minister of Agriculture and Fisheries Act 1919 (c.91)
Minister of Food (Continuance) Act 1920 (c.47)
Minister of Health Act 1919 (c.21)

Minister of Pensions 1916 (c.65)
Minister of the Crown Act 1964 (c.98)
Minister of Transport Act 1919 (c.50)
Ministerial and Other Pensions and Salaries Act 1991 (c.5)
Ministerial and other Salaries Act 1971 (c.3)
Ministerial and other Salaries Act 1975 (c.27)
Ministerial Salaries Act 1946 (c.55)
Ministerial Salaries Act 1957 (c.47)
Ministerial Salaries and Members' Pensions Act 1965 (c.11)
Ministerial Salaries Consolidation 1965 (c.58)
Ministeries of Munitions and Shipping (Cessation) Act 1921 (c.8)
Ministers of the Crown Act 1951 (c.9)
Ministers of the Crown Act 1964 (c.98)
Ministers of the Crown Act 1974 (c.21)
Ministers of the Crown Act 1975 (c.26)
Ministers of the Crown (Parliamentary Secretaries) Act 1960 (c.6)
Ministers of the Crown (Parliamentary Under-Secretaries) Act 1951 (c.9)
Ministers of the Crown (Transfer of Functions) Act 1964 (c.31)
Ministers Widows Fund (Scotland) Act 1779 (c.20)
Ministry of Civil Aviation Act 1945 (c.21)
Ministry of Defence Police Act 1987 (c.4)
Ministry of Food (Financial Powers) Act 1949 (c.15)
Ministry of Fuel and Power Act 1945 (c.19)
Ministry of Materials Act 1951 (c.42)
Ministry of Munitions Act 1915 (c.51)
Ministry of Munitions Act 1918 (c.60)
Ministry of National Insurance Act 1944 (c.46)
Ministry of National Service Act 1917 (c.6)
Ministry of Religion (Removal of Disqualifications) Act 1925 (c.54)
Ministry of Social Security Act 1966 (c.20)
Ministry of Supply Act 1939 (c.38)
Ministry of the Crown Act 1937 (c.38)
Ministry of the Crown and House of Commons Disqualification Act 1942 (c.11)
Ministry of the Crown (Emergency Appointments) Act 1939 (c.77)
Ministry of the Crown (Transfer of Functions) Act 1946 (c.31)
Ministry of the Crown (Treasury Secretaries) Act 1947 (c.5)
Ministry of Town and Country Planning Act 1943 (c.5)
Ministry of Transport Act 1919 (c.50)
Ministry of Works Act 1942 (c.23)
Minority of Heir to the Crown Act 1765 (c.27)
Minority of Successor to Crown Act 1750 (c.24)
Minors' Contracts Act 1987 (c.13)
Mint Prosecutions Expenses Act 1776 (c.46)
Miscellaneous Financial Provisions Act 1946 (c.40)
Miscellaneous Financial Provisions Act 1950 (c.21)
Miscellaneous Financial Provisions Act 1955 (c.6)
Miscellaneous Financial Provisions Act 1968 (c.75)
Miscellaneous Financial Provisions Act 1983 (c.29)
Mischief by Fire 1724 (c.28)
Mischiefs by Fire 1708 (c.17)
Mischiefs from Fire 1707 (c.58)
Misrepresentation Act 1967 (c.7)
Misuse of Drugs Act 1971 (c.38)
Mitford and Launditch, Norfolk: Poor Relief Act 1775 (c.59)
Mobile Homes Act 1975 (c.49)
Mobile Homes Act 1983 (c.34)
Mock Auctions Act 1961 (c.47)
Money Payments (Justices Procedure) Act 1935 (c.46)
Moneylenders Act 1900 (c.51)
Moneylenders Act 1911 (c.38)
Moneylenders Act 1927 (c.21)
Moneylenders (Crown Agents) Act 1975 (c.81)
Monkland, Glasgow: Navigation, etc. Act 1770 (c.105)
Monmouth and Gloucester Roads Act 1757 (c.44)
Monmouth Roads Act 1755 (c.31)
Monmouth Roads Act 1770 (c.106)
Monmouth Roads Act 1777 (c.96)
Monmouth Roads Act 1793 (c.169)
Monmouthshire Canal: Navigation Act 1792 (c.102)
Monopolies and Mergers Act 1965 (c.50)
Monopolies and Restrictive Practices Commission (Inquiry and Control) Act 1948 (c.66)
Monopolies and Restrictive Practices Commission Act 1953 (c.51)
Montgomery: Poor Relief Act 1792 (c.96)
Montgomery, Salop and Denbigh Roads Act 1788 (c.96)
Montrose Beer Duties Act 1719 (c.7)
Montrose Beer Duties Act 1732 (c.5)
Montrose Beer Duties Act 1769 (c.57)
Montrose Bridge Act 1792 (c.38)
Morden College Kent Act 1771 (c.10)
Morpeth and Elsdon Road Act 1751 (c.33)
Morpeth to Elsdon Road Act 1778 (c.107)
Morrison's Haven and Fort, East Lothian (repair) 1708 (c.27)
Mortmain and Charitable Uses Act 1888 (c.42)
Mortgage Act 1733 (c.20)
Mortuaries (Bangor, etc.) Abolition Act 1713 (c.6)
Mortuaries (Chester) Act 1755 (c.6)
Moss Troopers Act 1700 (c.6)
Moss Troopers Act 1712 (c.10)
Motor Car Act 1903 (c.36)
Motor Car (International Circulation) Act 1909 (c.37)
Motor-Cycle Crash-Helmets (Religious Exemption) Act 1976 (c.62)

Motor-Cycle Crash-Helmets (Restriction of Liability) Act 1985 (c.28)
Motor-Cycle Noise Act 1987 (c.34)
Motor Spirit (Regulations) Act 1948 (c.34)
Motor Vehicles (International Circulation) Act 1952 (c.39)
Motor Vehicles (Passenger Insurance) Act 1971 (c.36)
Motor Vehicles (Safety Equipment for Children) Act 1991 (c.14)
Motor Vehicles (Wearing of Rear Seat Belts by Children) Act 1988 (c.23)
Mr Speaker Clifton Brown's Retirement Act 1951 (c.2)
Mr Speaker King's Retirement Act 1970 (c.13)
Mr Speaker Morrison's Retirement Act 1959 (c.1)
Mr Speaker's Retirement Act 1904 (c.5)
Mr Speaker's Retirement Act 1921 (c.10)
Mr Speaker's Retirement Act 1928 (c.16)
Much Wenlock Roads Act 1756 (c.60)
Much Wenlock Roads Act 1778 (c.89)
Multilateral Investment Guarantee Agency Act 1988 (c.8)
Municipal Corporations Act 1882 (c.50)
Municipal Corporations Act 1883 (c.18)
Municipal Corporations Amendment 1906 (c.12)
Municipal Corporations Amendment 1910 (c.19)
Municipal Corporations (Audit) Act 1933 (c.28)
Municipal Corporations (Ireland) Act 1840 (c.108)
Municipal Corporations (Mandamus) Act 1772 (c.21)
Municipal Elections Act 1924 (c.4)
Municipal Elections (Corrupt and Illegal Practices) Act 1884 (c.70)
Municipal Elections (Corrupt and Illegal Practices) Act 1911 (c.7)
Municipal Offices Act 1710 (c.25)
Municipal Rate (Edinburgh) Act 1868 (c.42)
Municipal Savings Banks (War Loan Investment) Act 1916 (c.47)
Munitions (Liability for Explosion) Act 1916 (c.61)
Munitions of War Act 1915 (c.54)
Munitions of War Act 1917 (c.45)
Munitions of War Amendment 1916 (c.99)
Murder (Abolition of Death Penalty) Act 1965 (c.71)
Murder Act 1728 (c.21)
Murder Act 1751 (c.37)
Murders Abroad Act 1817 (c.53)
Murderers of Captain Porteous Act 1735 (c.35)
Museums and Galleries Admission Charges Act 1972 (c.73)
Museums and Gymnasiums Act 1891 (c.22)
Museum of London Act 1965 (c.17)
Museum of London Act 1986 (c.8)
Museums and Galleries Act 1992 (c.44)
Musical Copyright Act 1906 (c.36)
Musical (Summary Proceedings) Copyright Act 1902 (c.15)
Mutford and Lothingland, Suffolk (Poor Relief) Act 1764 (c.89)
Mutiny Act 1701 (c.2)
Mutiny Act 1702 (c.20)
Mutiny Act 1703 (c.17)
Mutiny Act 1704 (c.5)
Mutiny Act 1705 (c.22)
Mutiny Act 1706 (c.18)
Mutiny Act 1707 (c.74)
Mutiny Act 1708 (c.4)
Mutiny Act 1709 (c.6)
Mutiny Act 1710 (c.9)
Mutiny Act 1711 (c.13)
Mutiny Act 1712 (c.13)
Mutiny Act 1713 (c.4)
Mutiny Act 1714 (c.3)
Mutiny Act 1714 (c.9)
Mutiny Act 1715 (c.34)
Mutiny Act 1716 (c.2)
Mutiny Act 1717 (c.4)
Mutiny Act 1718 (c.5)
Mutiny Act 1719 (c.3)
Mutiny Act 1720 (c.6)
Mutiny Act 1721 (c.3)
Mutiny Act 1722 (c.4)
Mutiny Act 1723 (c.3)
Mutiny Act 1724 (c.6)
Mutiny Act 1725 (c.3)
Mutiny Act 1726 (c.2)
Mutiny Act 1727 (c.2)
Mutiny Act 1728 (c.2)
Mutiny Act 1729 (c.2)
Mutiny Act 1730 (c.2)
Mutiny Act 1731 (c.2)
Mutiny Act 1732 (c.3)
Mutiny Act 1733 (c.2)
Mutiny Act 1734 (c.2)
Mutiny Act 1735 (c.2)
Mutiny Act 1736 (c.2)
Mutiny Act 1737 (c.2)
Mutiny Act 1738 (c.2)
Mutiny Act 1739 (c.10)
Mutiny Act 1740 (c.9)
Mutiny Act 1741 (c.4)
Mutiny Act 1742 (c.14)
Mutiny Act 1743 (c.16)
Mutiny Act 1744 (c.7)
Mutiny Act 1745 (c.11)
Mutiny Act 1746 (c.11)
Mutiny Act 1747 (c.6)
Mutiny Act 1747 (c.13)
Mutiny Act 1748 (c.5)
Mutiny Act 1749 (c.4)
Mutiny Act 1750 (c.6)
Mutiny Act 1751 (c.2)
Mutiny Act 1753 (c.5)
Mutiny Act 1754 (c.5)
Mutiny Act 1755 (c.4)
Mutiny Act 1756 (c.3)

Mutiny Act 1757 (c.6)
Mutiny Act 1757 (c.5)
Mutiny Act 1758 (c.5)
Mutiny Act 1759 (c.6)
Mutiny Act 1760 (c.6)
Mutiny Act 1761 (c.11)
Mutiny Act 1762 (c.7)
Mutiny Act 1763 (c.3)
Mutiny Act 1765 (c.7)
Mutiny Act 1766 (c.8)
Mutiny Act 1766 (c.10)
Mutiny Act 1768 (c.7)
Mutiny Act 1769 (c.7)
Mutiny Act 1770 (c.3)
Mutiny Act 1770 (c.15)
Mutiny Act 1771 (c.6)
Mutiny Act 1772 (c.4)
Mutiny Act 1772 (c.10)
Mutiny Act 1774 (c.3)
Mutiny Act 1775 (c.6)
Mutiny Act 1776 (c.2)
Mutiny Act 1776 (c.3)
Mutiny Act 1778 (c.4)
Mutiny Act 1779 (c.16)
Mutiny Act 1780 (c.12)
Mutiny Act 1782 (c.4)
Mutiny Act 1783 (c.17)
Mutiny Act 1783 (c.24)
Mutiny Act 1783 (c.52)
Mutiny Act 1783 (c.11)
Mutiny Act 1785 (c.6)
Mutiny Act 1786 (c.10)
Mutiny Act 1788 (c.12)
Mutiny Act 1789 (c.2)
Mutiny Act 1790 (c.6)
Mutiny Act 1791 (c.13)
Mutiny Act 1791 (c.19)
Mutiny Act 1793 (c.9)
Mutiny Act 1794 (c.13)
Mutiny Act 1795 (c.6)
Mutiny, America Act 1765 (c.33)
Mutiny, America Act 1768 (c.19)
Mutiny, East Indies Act 1754 (c.9)
Mutiny in America Act 1766 (c.18)
Mutiny in America Act 1767 (c.55)
Mutiny in America Act 1769 (c.18)
Mutiny in America Act 1771 (c.11)
Mutiny in America Act 1772 (c.12)
Mutiny in America Act 1773 (c.24)
Mutiny in America Act 1774 (c.6)
Mutiny in America Act 1775 (c.15)
Mutiny in America Act 1776 (c.11)

Namibia Act 1991 (c.4)
Nantwich Canal Act 1777 (c.67)
Nantwich Canal Act 1778 (c.21)
Nantwich to Chester Road Act 1789 (c.91)
Nar: Navigation Act 1750 (c.19)
National Assistance Act 1948 (c.29)
National Assistance Act 1948 (Amendment) Act 1962 (c.24)
National Assistance Act 1959 (c.52)
National Assistance (Amendment) Act 1951 (c.57)
National Assistance (Amendment) Act 1959 (c.30)
National Audit Act 1983 (c.44)
National Coal Board (Additional Powers) Act 1966 (c.47)
National Coal Board (Finance) Act 1976 (c.1)
National Debt Act 1714 (c.2)
National Debt Act 1714 (c.12)
National Debt Act 1714 (c.19)
National Debt Act 1714 (c.21)
National Debt Act 1716 (c.7)
National Debt Act 1716 (c.9)
National Debt Act 1717 (c.10)
National Debt Act 1718 (c.3)
National Debt Act 1718 (c.9)
National Debt Act 1718 (c.19)
National Debt Act 1719 (c.4)
National Debt Act 1719 (c.10)
National Debt Act 1720 (c.5)
National Debt Act 1721 (c.1)
National Debt Act 1721 (c.20)
National Debt Act 1721 (c.22)
National Debt Act 1722 (cc.5, 6)
National Debt Act 1722 (c.12)
National Debt Act 1723 (c.5)
National Debt Act 1724 (c.17)
National Debt Act 1726 (c.3)
National Debt Act 1726 (c.21)
National Debt Act 1730 (c.16)
National Debt Act 1730 (c.5)
National Debt Act 1730 (c.9)
National Debt Act 1731 (c.17)
National Debt Act 1732 (c.28)
National Debt Act 1735 (c.34)
National Debt Act 1736 (c.17)
National Debt Act 1737 (c.27)
National Debt Act 1741 (c.19)
National Debt Act 1742 (cc.12, 13)
National Debt Act 1743 (c.18)
National Debt Act 1744 (c.9)
National Debt Act 1745 (c.12)
National Debt Act 1746 (c.3)
National Debt Act 1746 (c.10)
National Debt Act 1747 (c.2)
National Debt Act 1748 (c.23)
National Debt Act 1749 (c.1)
National Debt Act 1749 (c.16)
National Debt Act 1750 (c.2)
National Debt Act 1750 (c.11)
National Debt Act 1751 (c.25)
National Debt Act 1751 (c.27)
National Debt Act 1753 (c.1)
National Debt Act 1753 (c.23)
National Debt Act 1755 (c.15)
National Debt Act 1756 (c.7)
National Debt Act 1757 (c.19)
National Debt Act 1758 (c.22)
National Debt Act 1759 (c.12)
National Debt Act 1760 (c.7)
National Debt Act 1761 (cc.9, 10)
National Debt Act 1762 (c.9)

National Debt Act 1762 (c.12)
National Debt Act 1763 (c.18)
National Debt Act 1763 (c.25)
National Debt Act 1765 (c.16)
National Debt Act 1765 (c.23)
National Debt Act 1765 (c.42)
National Debt Act 1766 (c.21)
National Debt Act 1766 (c.39)
National Debt Act 1766 (cc.24–26)
National Debt Act 1768 (c.29)
National Debt Act 1768 (c.31)
National Debt Act 1770 (c.36)
National Debt Act 1770 (c.46)
National Debt Act 1772 (c.63)
National Debt Act 1774 (c.76)
National Debt Act 1775 (c.41)
National Debt Act 1776 (c.46)
National Debt Act 1778 (c.22)
National Debt Act 1779 (c.18)
National Debt Act 1782 (c.8)
National Debt Act 1782 (c.34)
National Debt Act 1783 (c.35)
National Debt Act 1784 (c.10)
National Debt Act 1784 (c.37)
National Debt Act 1784 (c.39)
National Debt Act 1785 (c.32)
National Debt Act 1785 (c.71)
National Debt Act 1786 (c.34)
National Debt Act 1789 (c.37)
National Debt Act 1793 (c.28)
National Debt Act 1793 (c.32)
National Debt Act 1794 (c.1)
National Debt Act 1794 (c.21)
National Debt Act 1795 (c.14)
National Debt Act 1795 (c.23)
National Debt Act 1795 (c.32)
National Debt Act 1958 (c.6)
National Debt Act 1972 (c.65)
National Debt (Conversion of Stock) Act 1884 (c.23)
National Debt (No. 2) Act 1749 (c.22)
National Debt Reduction Act 1724 (c.9)
National Debt Reduction Act 1786 (c.31)
National Economy Act 1931 (c.48)
National Film Finance Corporation Act 1981 (c.15)
National Fire Service Regulations (Indemnity) Act 1944 (c.35)
National Galleries of Scotland Act 1906 (c.50)
National Galleries of Scotland Act 1959 (c.61)
National Gallery and St. James's Park Act 1911 (c.23)
National Gallery and Tate Gallery Act 1954 (c.65)
National Gallery Enlargement Act 1866 (c.83)
National Gallery Enlargement Act 1867 (c.41)
National Gallery (Overseas Loans) Act 1935 (c.18)
National Gallery (Purchase of Adjacent Land) Act 1901 (c.16)
National Health (Hospital Boards) Act 1964 (c.32)
National Health Insurance Act 1918 (c.62)
National Health Insurance Act 1919 (c.36)
National Health Insurance Act 1920 (c.10)
National Health Insurance Act 1921 (c.25)
National Health Insurance Act 1922 (c.38)
National Health Insurance Act 1924 (c.38)
National Health Insurance Act 1928 (c.14)
National Health Insurance Act 1936 (c.32)
National Health Insurance (Amendment) Act 1937 (c.24)
National Health Insurance (Amendment) Act 1938 (c.14)
National Health Insurance and Contributory Pensions Act 1932 (c.52)
National Health Insurance and Contributory Pensions Act 1935 (c.44)
National Health Insurance and Contributory Pensions (Emergency Provisions) Act 1939 (c.84)
National Health Insurance, Contributory Pensions and Workmen's Compensation Act 1941 (c.39)
National Health Insurance (Cost of Medical Benefit) Act 1924 (c.10)
National Health Insurance (Juvenile Contributors and Young Persons) Act 1937 (c.3)
National Health Insurance (Prolongation of Insurance) Act 1921 (c.66)
National Health Insurance (Prolongation of Insurance) Act 1931 (c.5)
National Health Insurance (Prolongation of Insurance) Act 1932 (c.6)
National Health Service Act 1946 (c.81)
National Health Service Act 1951 (c.31)
National Health Service Act 1952 (c.25)
National Health Service Act 1961 (c.19)
National Health Service Act 1966 (c.8)
National Health Service Act 1977 (c.49)
National Health Service (Amendment) Act 1949 (c.93)
National Health Service (Amendment) Act 1957 (c.44)
National Health Service (Amendment) Act 1986 (c.66)
National Health Service (Amendment) Act 1995 (c.31)
National Health Service and Community Care Act 1990 (c.19)
National Health Service Contributions Act 1957 (c.34)
National Health Service Contributions Act 1961 (c.13)
National Health Service Contributions Act 1965 (c.54)
National Health Service Contributions Act 1970 (c.16)
National Health Service (Family Planning) Act 1967 (c.39)
National Health Service (Family Planning) Amendment Act 1972 (c.72)
National Health Service (Hospital Boards) Act 1964 (c.32)
National Health Service (Invalid Direction) Act 1980 (c.15)

National Health Service Reorganisation Act 1973 (c.32)
National Health Service (Scotland) Act 1947 (c.27)
National Health Service (Scotland) Act 1972 (c.58)
National Health Service (Scotland) Act 1978 (c.29)
National Health Service (Vocational Training) Act 1976 (c.59)
National Heritage Act 1980 (c.17)
National Heritage Act 1983 (c.47)
National Heritage (Scotland) Act 1985 (c.16)
National Insurance Act 1911 (c.55)
National Insurance Act 1913 (c.37)
National Insurance Act 1946 (c.67)
National Insurance Act 1947 (c.37)
National Insurance Act 1949 (c.56)
National Insurance Act 1951 (c.34)
National Insurance Act 1953 (c.29)
National Insurance Act 1955 (c.29)
National Insurance Act 1956 (c.47)
National Insurance Act 1957 (c.26)
National Insurance Act 1959 (c.47)
National Insurance Act 1960 (c.5)
National Insurance Act 1963 (c.7)
National Insurance Act 1965 (c.51)
National Insurance Act 1966 (c.6)
National Insurance Act 1967 (c.73)
National Insurance Act 1969 (c.4)
National Insurance Act 1969 (c.44)
National Insurance Act 1971 (c.50)
National Insurance Act 1972 (c.57)
National Insurance Act 1974 (c.14)
National Insurance &c Act 1964 (c.96)
National Insurance and Supplementary Benefit Act 1973 (c.42)
National Insurance (Amendment) Act 1972 (c.36)
National Insurance, etc. Act 1969 (c.4)
National Insurance (Industrial) Act 1953 (c.43)
National Insurance (Industrial Injuries) Act 1946 (c.62)
National Insurance (Industrial Injuries) Act 1948 (c.42)
National Insurance (Industrial Injuries) Act 1965 (c.52)
National Insurance (Industrial Injuries) (Amendment) Act 1967 (c.25)
National Insurance Land Purchase (Winding-up) Act 1935 (c.21)
National Insurance (Miscellaneous Provisions) Act 1928 (c.24)
National Insurance (Miscellaneous Provisions) Act 1932 (c.11)
National Insurance (Miscellaneous Provisions) Act 1945 (c.12)
National Insurance (Navy and Army) Act (c.81)
National Insurance (Navy and Army) (Session 2) Act 1914 (c.15)
National Insurance (No. 2) Act 1957 (c.1)
National Insurance (Old Persons' and Widows' Pensions and Attendance Allowance) Act 1970 (c.51)
National Insurance (Pt. I Amendment) Act 1915 (c.29)
National Insurance (Pt. I Amendment) Act 1917 (c.15)
National Insurance (Pt. II Amendment) Act 1914 (c.57)
National Insurance (Pt. II Amendment) Act 1914 (c.27)
National Insurance (Pt. II) (Munition Workers) Act 1916 (c.20)
National Insurance Regulations (Validation) Act 1972 (c.4)
National Insurance Surcharge Act 1976 (c.85)
National Insurance Surcharge Act 1982 (c.55)
National Insurance (Temporary Employment in Agriculture) Act 1916 (c.53)
National Insurance (Unemployment) Act 1918 (c.63)
National Insurance (Unemployment) Act 1919 (c.77)
National Library of Scotland Act 1925 (c.73)
National Loans Act 1939 (c.117)
National Loans Act 1940 (c.3)
National Loans Act 1941 (c.18)
National Loans Act 1942 (c.14)
National Loans Act 1943 (c.13)
National Loans Act 1944 (c.19)
National Loans Act 1945 (c.23)
National Loans Act 1968 (c.13)
National Loans (No. 2) Act 1940 (c.23)
National Lottery etc. Act 1993 (c.39)
National Maritime Museum Act 1934 (c.43)
National Maritime Museum Act 1989 (c.8)
National Mod (Scotland) Act 1969 (c.41)
National Museum of Antiquities of Scotland Act 1954 (c.14)
National Parks and Access to the Countryside Act 1949 (c.97)
National Portrait Gallery Act 1889 (c.25)
National Registration Act 1915 (c.60)
National Registration Act 1939 (c.91)
National Registration (Amendment) Act 1918 (c.60)
National Savings Bank Act 1971 (c.29)
National Service Act 1941 (c.15)
National Service Act 1942 (c.3)
National Service Act 1947 (c.31)
National Service Act 1948 (c.64)
National Service Act 1950 (c.30)
National Service Act 1955 (c.11)
National Service (Amendment) Act 1948 (c.6)
National Service (Armed Forces) Act 1939 (c.81)
National Service (Armed Forces) Act 1940 (c.22)
National Service (Channel Islands) Act 1940 (c.24)
National Service (Foreign Countries) Act 1942 (c.30)

National Service (No. 2) Act 1941 (c.4)
National Service (Release of Conscientious Objectors) Act 1946 (c.38)
National Theatre Act 1949 (c.16)
National Theatre Act 1969 (c.11)
National Theatre Act 1974 (c.55)
National Theatre and Museum of London Act 1973 (c.2)
Nationalised Industries Loans Act 1958 (c.19)
Natural Heritage (Scotland) Act 1991 (c.28)
Natural-born Children of Aliens Act 1776 (c.52)
Naturalisation Act 1711 (c.9)
Naturalisation Act 1714 (c.4)
Naturalisation Act 1739 (c.7)
Naturalisation Act 1762 (c.25)
Naturalisation Act 1763 (c.4)
Naturalisation Act 1772 (c.25)
Naturalisation Act 1774 (c.84)
Naturalisation of Jews Act 1753 (c.26)
Naturalisation of Jews Act 1754 (c.1)
Nature Conservancy Council Act 1973 (c.54)
Naval Agency and Distribution Act 1864 (c.24)
Naval and Marine Forces (Temporary Release from Service) Act 1941 (c.4)
Naval and Marine Pay and Pensions Act 1865 (c.73)
Naval and Marine Reserves Pay Act 1957 (c.32)
Naval and Military War Pensions, etc. Act 1915 (c.83)
Naval and Military War Pensions, etc. (Admin. Expenses) Act 1917 (c.14)
Naval and Military War Pension, etc. (Committees) Act 1917 (c.54)
Naval and Military War Pensions, etc. (Expenses) Act 1916 (c.4)
Naval and Military War Pensions, etc. (Transfer of Powers) Act 1917 (c.37)
Naval Billeting, etc. Act 1914 (c. 70)
Naval Courts-Martial Act 1779 (c.17)
Naval Discipline Act 1909 (c.41)
Naval Discipline Act 1915 (c.30)
Naval Discipline Act 1917 (c.34)
Naval Discipline Act 1922 (c.37)
Naval Discipline Act 1957 (c.53)
Naval Discipline (Amendment) Act 1938 (c.64)
Naval Discipline (Amendment) Act 1941 (c.29)
Naval Discipline (Delegation of Powers) Act 1916 (c.17)
Naval Discipline (Delegation of Powers) Act 1917 (c.11)
Naval Discipline (Dominion Naval Forces) Act 1911 (c.47)
Naval Discipline (No. 2) Act 1915 (c.73)
Naval Enlistment Act 1884 (c.46)
Naval Establishments in British Possessions Act 1909 (c.18)
Naval Forces Act 1903 (c.6)
Naval Forces (Enforcement of Maintenance Liabilities) Act (c.24)
Naval Forces (Extension of Services) Act 1944 (c.13)
Naval Forces (Service on Shore) Act 1916 (c.101)
Naval Knights of Windsor (Dissolution) Act 1892 (c.34)
Naval Lands (Volunteers) Act 1908 (c.25)
Naval Marriages Act 1908 (c.26)
Naval Marriages Act 1915 (c.35)
Naval Medical Compassionate Fund Act 1915 (c.28)
Naval, Military and Air Force Service Act 1919 (c.15)
Naval Pensions Act 1884 (c.44)
Naval Prize Act 1739 (c.4)
Naval Prize Act 1743 (c.34)
Naval Prize Act 1746 (c.24)
Naval Prize Act 1758 (c.25)
Naval Prize Act 1772 (c.25)
Naval Prize Act 1864 (c.25)
Naval Prize Act 1918 (c.30)
Naval Prize Act 1928 (c.36)
Naval Prize etc. Act 1756 (c.34)
Naval Prize Money Act 1820 (c.85)
Naval Prize (Procedure) Act 1916 (c.2)
Naval Reserve Act 1900 (c.52)
Naval Reserve (Mobilisation) Act 1900 (c.17)
Naval Reserve (Officers) Act 1926 (c.41)
Naval Stores Act 1745 (c.36)
Naval Volunteers Act 1853 (c.73)
Naval Works Act 1901 (c.39)
Naval Works Act 1903 (c.22)
Naval Works Act 1904 (c.20)
Navigation Act 1703 (c.6)
Navigation Act 1755 (c.16)
Navigation Act 1756 (c.11)
Navigation Act 1776 (c.20)
Navigation Act 1776 (c.34)
Navigation Act 1778 (c.6)
Navigation Act 1779 (c.14)
Navigation Act 1780 (c.19)
Navigation Act 1782 (c.16)
Navigation, Norfolk Act 1754 (c.12)
Navru Island Agreement Act 1920 (c.27)
Navy Act 1705 (c.6)
Navy Act 1727 (c.14)
Navy Act 1740 (c.38)
Navy Act 1744 (c.35)
Navy Act 1747 (c.11)
Navy Act 1748 (c.33)
Navy Act 1756 (c.27)
Navy Act 1756 (c.10)
Navy Act 1762 (c.16)
Navy Act 1769 (c.30)
Navy Act 1779 (c.67)
Navy Act 1779 (c.75)
Navy Act 1780 (c.23)
Navy Act 1780 (c.15)
Navy Act 1786 (c.63)
Navy Act 1791 (c.33)
Navy Act 1791 (c.34)

Navy and Marines Act 1795 (c.28)
Navy and Marines (Wills) Act 1914 (c.17)
Navy and Marines (Wills) Act 1930 (c.38)
Navy and Marines (Wills) Act 1939 (c.87)
Navy and Marines (Wills) Act 1953 (c.24)
Navy and Victualling Bills Act 1794 (c.56)
Navy, Army and Air Force Reserves Act 1954 (c.10)
Navy, Army and Air Force Reserves Act 1959 (c.10)
Navy, Army and Air Force Reserves Act 1964 (c.11)
Navy, etc. Act 1714 (c.25)
Navy, etc. Act 1780 (c.11)
Navy (Pledging of Certificates, etc.) Act 1914 (c.89)
Neath Canal Act 1791 (c.85)
Negotiations of Certain Bonds Act 1782 (c.11)
Negotiations of Notes and Bills 1775 (c.51)
Negotiations of Notes and Bills Act 1802 (c.1)
Nether Knutsford Church Act 1740 (c.5)
New Forest Act 1949 (c.69)
New Forest Act 1964 (c.83)
New Forest Act 1970 (c.21)
Newfoundland (Consequential Provisions) Act 1949 (c.5)
New Hebrides Act 1980 (c.16)
New Malton, Yorks. (Searching, Sealing, etc. of Butter) Act 1743 (c.8)
New Method of Tanning Act 1794 (c.63)
New Ministries Act 1917 (c.44)
New Ministries and Secretaries Act 1916 (c.68)
New Office of Excise Act 1770 (c.32)
New Palace Yard, Westminster 1706 (c.15)
New Parishes Act 1843 (c.37)
New Parishes Act 1844 (c.94)
New Parishes Act 1856 (c.104)
New Parishes Acts and Church Building Acts Amendment Act 1869 (c.94)
New Parishes Acts and Church Building Acts Amendment Act 1884 (c.65)
New Roads and Street Works Act 1991 (c.22)
New Sarum: Poor Relief Act 1770 (c.81)
New Shoreham Harbour Act 1759 (c.35)
New Shoreham Harbour Act 1789 (c.21)
New Streets Act 1951 (c.40)
New Streets Act 1951 (Amendment) Act 1957 (c.33)
New Towns Act 1946 (c.68)
New Towns Act 1952 (c.27)
New Towns Act 1953 (c.38)
New Towns Act 1955 (c.4)
New Towns Act 1958 (c.12)
New Towns Act 1959 (c.62)
New Towns Act 1965 (c.59)
New Towns Act 1966 (c.44)
New Towns Act 1969 (c.5)
New Towns Act 1971 (c.81)
New Towns Act 1975 (c.42)
New Towns Act 1977 (c.23)
New Towns Act 1980 (c.36)
New Towns Act 1981 (c.64)
New Towns Act 1982 (c.7)
New Towns (No. 2) Act 1964 (c.68)
New Towns (Amendment) Act 1976 (c.68)
New Towns (Amendment) Act 1994 (c.5)
New Towns and Urban Development Corporations Act 1985 (c.5)
New Towns (Scotland) Act 1968 (c.16)
New Towns (Scotland) Act 1977 (c.16)
New Valuation Lists (Postponement) Act 1952 (c.4)
New Woodstock, Kiddington, etc. Roads Act 1757 (c.48)
New Zealand Constitution (Amendment) 1947 (c.4)
Newbury and Marlborough Roads Act 1744 (c.12)
Newbury to Bath Canal Act 1794 (c.90)
Newbury to Marlborough Road Act 1725 (c.8)
Newcastle and Gateshead Bridge Act 1788 (c.78)
Newcastle and Sunderland: Coals Act 1790 (c.78)
Newcastle: Improvement Act 1763 (c.55)
Newcastle (Sale of Coal by Measured Keel) Act 1791 (c.36)
Newcastle: Streets Act 1786 (c.39)
Newcastle to Buckton Burn Road Act 1794 (c.130)
Newcastle to Carlisle Road Act 1786 (c.160)
Newfoundland Act 1933 (c.2)
Newfoundland (Consequential Provisions) Act 1950 (c.5)
Newfoundland Fisheries Act 1775 (c.31)
Newfoundland Fisheries Act 1786 (c.26)
Newfoundland Fisheries Act 1788 (c.35)
Newgate Gaol Delivery Act 1785 (c.18)
Newgate Gaol and Session House Act 1778 (c.48)
Newhaven Bridge Act 1783 (c.21)
Newhaven Harbour Act 1730 (c.17)
Newmarket and Cambridge Road Act 1763 (c.32)
Newmarket to Cambridge Road Act 1775 (c.68)
Newspaper Duty Act 1772 (c.65)
Newspaper Libel and Registration Act 1881 (c.60)
Newspapers, Printers and Reading Rooms Repeal Act 1869 (c.24)
Newport, Isle of Wight: Improvement Act 1786 (c.119)
Niall Macpherson Indemnity 1954 (c.29)
Nigeria Independence Act 1960 (c.55)
Nigeria (Remission of Payments) Act 1937 (c.63)
Nigeria Republic Act 1963 (c.57)
Night Poaching Act 1828 (c.69)
Night Watch Westminster Act (c.15)
Nisi Prius, Middlesex Act 1725 (c.31)
Nith Fisheries Act 1792 (c.94)
Noise Abatement Act 1960 (c.68)
Noise and Statutory Nuisance Act 1993 (c.40)

Nonconformist Relief Act 1779 (c.44)
Non-Domestic Rating Act 1992 (c.46)
Non-Domestic Rating Act 1993 (c.17)
Non-Domestic Rating Act 1994 (c.3)
Non-Ferrous Metal Industry Act 1917 (c.67)
Norfolk and Suffolk Broads Act 1988 (c.4)
Norfolk: Drainage Act 1783 (c,9)
Norfolk Highways Act 1708 (c.8)
Norfolk: Improvement Act 1725 (c.15)
Norfolk Roads Act 1765 (c.83)
Norfolk Roads Act 1765 (c.101)
Norfolk Roads Act 1767 (c.76)
Norfolk Roads Act 1770 (c.54)
Norfolk Roads Act 1770 (c.85)
Norfolk Roads Act 1770 (c.86)
Norfolk Roads Act 1786 (c.127)
Norfolk Roads Act 1790 (c.87)
Norfolk Roads Act 1790 (c.104)
Norfolk Roads Act 1791 (c.100)
Norfolk Roads Act 1791 (c.112)
Norfolk Roads Act 1791 (c.113)
Norfolk Roads Act 1792 (c.148)
Norfolk Roads Act 1792 (c.158)
Norfolk Roads Act 1794 (c.114)
North American Fisheries Act 1819 (c.38)
North Atlantic Shipping Act 1934 (c.10)
North Kyme Drainage Act 1788 (c.14)
North River, Norfolk: Navigation Act 1772 (c.37)
North Shields to Newcastle Road Act 1774 (c.115)
North Shields: Water Supply Act 1786 (c.110)
Northampton and Lincoln Roads Act 1756 (c.76)
Northampton and Lincoln Roads Act 1776 (c.72)
Northampton and Oxford Roads Act 1778 (c.87)
Northampton and Warwick Roads Act 1724 (c.25)
Northampton Highways Act (c.9)
Northampton: Improvement Act 1778 (c.79)
Northampton Roads Act 1748 (c.17)
Northampton Roads Act 1749 (c.8)
Northampton Roads Act 1753 (c.88)
Northampton Roads Act 1754 (c.23)
Northampton Roads Act 1778 (c.112)
Northampton Roads Act 1781 (c.94)
Northampton Roads Act 1783 (c.28)
Northampton Roads Act 1794 (c.126)
Northern Ireland Act 1929 (c.14)
Northern Ireland Act 1947 (c.37)
Northern Ireland Act 1955 (c.8)
Northern Ireland Act 1962 (c.30)
Northern Ireland Act 1972 (c.10)
Northern Ireland Act 1974 (c.28)
Northern Ireland Act 1982 (c.38)
Northern Ireland Assembly Act 1973 (c.17)
Northern Ireland Assembly Disqualifications Act 1975 (c.25)
Northern Ireland (Border Poll) Act 1972 (c.77)
Northern Ireland Compensation (for Compulsory Purchase) Act 1957 (c.14)
Northern Ireland Constitution Act 1973 (c.36)
Northern Ireland Constitution (Amendment) Act 1973 (c.69)
Northern Ireland (Emergency Provisions) Act 1973 (c.53)
Northern Ireland (Emergency Provisions) Act 1978 (c.5)
Northern Ireland (Emergency Provisions) Act 1987 (c.30)
Northern Ireland (Emergency Provisions) Act 1991 (c.24)
Northern Ireland (Emergency Provisions) Amendment Act 1975 (c.62)
Northern Ireland (Emergency Provisions) (Amendment) Act 1977 (c.34)
Northern Ireland (Financial Provisions) Act 1972 (c.76)
Northern Ireland (Foyle Fisheries) Act 1952 (c.11)
Northern Ireland Land Act 1925 (c.34)
Northern Ireland Land Act 1929 (c.14)
Northern Ireland Land Purchase (Winding Up) Act 1935 (c.21)
Northern Ireland (Loans) Act 1975 (c.83)
Northern Ireland (Loans) Act 1985 (c.76)
Northern Ireland (Miscellaneous Provisions) Act 1928 (c.24)
Northern Ireland (Miscellaneous Provisions) Act 1932 (c.11)
Northern Ireland (Miscellaneous Provisions) Act 1945 (c.12)
Northern Ireland (Remission of Sentences) Act 1995 (c.47)
Northern Ireland (Temporary Provisions) Act 1972 (c.22)
Northern Ireland (Young Persons) Act 1974 (c.33)
Northern Roads, London Act 1735 (c.39)
Northumberland Fishery Act 1789 (c.25)
Northumberland and Durham Roads Act 1792 (c.145)
Northumberland Roads Act 1746 (c.9)
Northumberland Roads Act 1748 (c.7)
Northumberland Roads Act 1748 (c.9)
Northumberland Roads Act 1751 (c.18)
Northumberland Roads Act 1751 (c.46)
Northumberland Roads Act 1751 (c.48)
Northumberland Roads Act 1757 (c.52)
Northumberland Roads Act 1776 (c.68)
Northumberland Roads Act 1776 (c.83)
Northumberland Roads Act 1778 (c.83)
Northumberland Roads Act 1778 (c.115)
Northumberland Roads Act 1779 (c.95)
Norton Folley, Middlesex, Lighting etc. Act 1758 (c.49)
Norwich Assizes Act 1746 (c.21)
Norwich and Swaffham Road Act 1770 (c.67)
Norwich and Thetford Road Act 1725 (c.22)
Norwich and Thetford Road Act 1746 (c.16)
Norwich and Watton Road Act 1770 (c.77)
Norwich Mayors, Sheriffs, etc. 1922 (c.9)
Norwich Roads Act 1790 (c.86)
Norwich to Bixley Roads Act 1790 (c.85)

Norwich to New Buckingham Road Act 1772 (c.95)
Norwich to Scole Bridge Road Act 1969 (c.66)
Norwich to Scole Bridge Road Act 1772 (c.76)
Norwich to Thetford Road Act 1792 (c.111)
Norwich to Swaffham Road Act 1792 (c.112)
Norwich to Yarmouth Road Act 1969 (c.68)
Norwich Water Act 1790 (c.21)
Norwich Workhouse Act 1711 (c.15)
Notice of Accidents Act 1906 (c.53)
Notification of Births Act 1907 (c.40)
Notification of Births (Extension) Act 1915 (c.64)
Nottingham Roads Act 1770 (c.92)
Nottingham Roads Act 1774 (c.101)
Nottingham Roads Act 1785 (c.107)
Nottingham and Derby Road Act 1758 (c.38)
Nottingham and Derby Roads Act 1764 (c.83)
Nottingham and Derby Roads Act 1765 (c.90)
Nottingham and Derby Roads Act 1783 (c.24)
Nottingham and Derby Roads Act 1788 (c.87)
Nottingham and Derby Roads Act 1788 (c.99)
Nottingham and Leicester Highways Act 1721 (c.13)
Nottingham and Leicester Roads Act 1737 (c.3)
Nottingham and Leicester Roads Act 1754 (c.22)
Nottingham and Lincoln Roads Act 1765 (c.85)
Nottingham Canal Act 1792 (c.100)
Nottingham, Leicester, Rutland and Northampton Roads Act 1780 (c.81)
Nottingham: Lighting etc. Act 1762 (c.47)
Nottingham Roads Act 1765 (c.54)
Nottingham Roads Act 1791 (c.131)
Nottingham Roads Act 1791 (c.132)
Nottingham, Shire Hall Act 1769 (c.62)
Nottingham to Mansfield Road Act 1787 (c.76)
Nuclear Industry (Finance) Act 1977 (c.7)
Nuclear Industry (Finance) Act 1981 (c.71)
Nuclear Installations Act 1959 (c.46)
Nuclear Installations Act 1965 (c.57)
Nuclear Installations Act 1969 (c.18)
Nuclear Installations (Amendment) Act 1965 (c.6)
Nuclear Materials (Offences) Act 1983 (c.18)
Nuclear Safeguards and Electricity (Finance) Act 1978 (c.25)
Nuisances Removal (Scotland) Act 1856 (c.103)
Nullity of Marriage Act 1971 (c.44)
Nurseries and Child Minders Regulation Act 1948 (c.53)
Nurses Act 1943 (c.17)
Nurses Act 1945 (c.6)
Nurses Act 1949 (c.73)
Nurses Act 1957 (c.15)
Nurses Act 1964 (c.44)
Nurses Act 1969 (c.47)
Nurses Registration Act 1919 (c.94)
Nurses Registration (Ireland) Act 1919 (c.96)
Nurses Registration (Scotland) Act 1919 (c.95)
Nurses (Scotland) Act 1943 (c.33)
Nurses (Scotland) Act 1949 (c.95)
Nurses (Scotland) Act (c.55)
Nurses Agencies Act 1957 (c.16)
Nurses (Amendment) Act 1961 (c.14)
Nurses, Midwives and Health Visitors Act 1979 (c.36)
Nurses, Midwives and Health Visitors Act 1992 (c.16)
Nurses (Scotland) Act 1951 (c.55)
Nursing Homes Act 1963 (c.13)
Nursing Homes Act 1975 (c.37)
Nursing Homes Registration Act 1927 (c.38)
Nursing Homes Registration (Scotland) Act 1938 (c.73)

OECD Support Fund Act 1975 (c.80)
Oakham Canal Act 1793 (c.103)
Oakhampton Roads Act 1782 (c.92)
Oaths, etc. Act 1714 (c.3)
Oaths Act 1775 (c.39)
Oaths Act 1838 (c.105)
Oaths Act 1888 (c.46)
Oaths Act 1909 (c.39)
Oaths Act 1961 (c.21)
Oaths Act 1978 (c.19)
Oaths and Evidence (Overseas Authorities) (Land) Act 1963 (c.27)
Oaths at Parliamentary Elections Act 1794 (c.84)
Oaths of Justices of the Peace Act 1745 (c.13)
Obscene Publications Act 1857 (c.83)
Obscene Publications Act 1959 (c.66)
Obscene Publications Act 1964 (c.74)
Observance of Lord's Day by Bakers Act 1794 (c.61)
Obtaining Money by False Pretences, etc. Act 1757 (c.24)
Occasional Licences and Young Persons 1956 (c.42)
Occupiers' Liability Act 1957 (c.31)
Occupiers' Liability Act 1984 (c.3)
Occupier's Liability (Scotland) Act 1960 (c.30)
Odiham to Farnham Roads Act 1789 (c.89)
Offences Against Customs and Excise Laws Act 1935 (c.35)
Offences Against Customs or Excise Act 1745 (c.34)
Offences Against Excise Laws Act 1758 (c.17)
Offences Against Excise Laws Act 1791 (c.10)
Offences Against the Person Act 1861 (c.100)
Offences Against Persons and Property Act 1936 (c.32)
Offences at Sea Act 1806 (c.54)
Offenders (Conveyance) Act 1753 (c.3)

Offices Act 1960 (c.47)
Office and Oath Act 1867 (c.75)
Offices of Court of Chancery Act 1792 (c.42)
Offices, Shops and Railway Premises Act 1963 (c.41)
Officers of Inland Revenue Act (1849) (c.58)
Officer of Late Wine Licences Office Act 1791 (c.28)
Officers of the Royal Naval Reserve Act 1863 (c.69)
Official Secrets Act 1911 (c.28)
Official Secrets Act 1920 (c.75)
Official Secrets Act 1939 (c.121)
Official Secrets Act 1989 (c.6)
Official Solicitor Act 1919 (c.30)
Offshore Petroleum Development (Scotland) Act 1975 (c.8)
Offshore Safety Act 1992 (c.15)
Offshore Safety (Protection against Victimisation) Act 1992 (c.24)
Oil and Gas (Enterprise) Act 1982 (c.23)
Oil and Pipelines Act 1985 (c.62)
Oil in Navigable Waters Act 1922 (c.39)
Oil Burners (Standards) Act 1960 (c.53)
Oil in Navigable Waters Act 1963 (c.28)
Oil in Navigable Waters Act 1955 (c.25)
Oil in Navigable Waters Act 1971 (c.21)
Oil in Tobacco Act 1900 (c.35)
Oil Taxation Act 1975 (c.22)
Oil Taxation Act 1983 (c.56)
Okehampton Roads Act 1759 (c.36)
Old Age and Widows Pensions Act 1940 (c.13)
Old Age Pensions Act 1908 (c.40)
Old Age Pensions Act 1911 (c.16)
Old Age Pensions Act 1919 (c.102)
Old Age Pensions Act 1924 (c.33)
Old Age Pensions Act 1936 (c.31)
Old Age and Widows' Pensions Act 1940 (c.13)
Old Brentford Bridge Act 1757 (c.63)
Old Brentford Bridge Act 1757 (c.46)
Old Palace Yard Act 1966 (c.32)
Old Shoreham, Bridge, Sussex Act 1780 (c.35)
Old Stratford to Dunchurch Road Act 1757 (c.57)
Old Stratford to Dunchurch Road Act 1775 (c.73)
Old Street Road Act 1753 (c.87)
Old Street Road Act 1756 (c.44)
Old Street Road Act 1772 (c.99)
Old Street Road Act 1789 (c.82)
Old Swineford: Small Debts Act 1776 (c.19)
Oldham to Alton Road Act 1793 (c.182)
Olympic Symbol etc. (Protection) Act 1995 (c.32)
Opencast Coal Act 1958 (c.69)
Open Spaces Act 1887 (c.32)
Open Spaces Act 1906 (c.25)
Open Space Act 1986 (c.38)
Opticians Act 1958 (c.32)
Opticians Act 1989 (c.44)
Orders, etc. of the Master of the Rolls Act 1730 (c.30)
Ordination of Aliens Act 1783 (c.35)
Ordnance Board Transfer Act 1855 (c.117)
Ordnance Factories and Military Services Act 1984 (c.59)
Ordnance Property Act 1821 (c.69)
Orkney and Shetland Small Piers and Harbours Act 1896 (c.32)
Orphans, London Act 1947 (c.29)
Osborne Estate Act 1902 (c.37)
Osborne Estate Act 1914 (c.36)
Osteopaths Act 1993 (c.21)
Oswestry: Poor Relief Act 1791 (c.24)
Ottawa Agreements Act 1932 (c.53)
Ouse: Navigation Act 1790 (c.52)
Ouse: Navigation Act 1790 (c.83)
Outdoor Relief (Friendly Societies) Act 1904 (c.32)
Outer Space Act 1986 (c.38)
Output of Beer (Restriction) Act 1916 (c.26)
Output of Beer (Restriction) Amendment Act 1916 (c.57)
Ouze Navigation Act 1731 (c.15)
Overseas Aid Act 1966 (c.21)
Overseas Aid Act 1968 (c.57)
Overseas Development and Co-operation Act 1980 (c.63)
Overseas Development and Service Act 1965 (c.38)
Overseas Investment and Export Guarantees Act 1972 (c.40)
Overseas Pensions Act 1973 (c.21)
Overseas Resources Act 1969 (c.36)
Overseas Resources Development Act 1947 (c.15)
Overseas Resources Development Act 1949 (c.65)
Overseas Resources Development Act 1951 (c.20)
Overseas Resources Development Act 1954 (c.71)
Overseas Resources Development Act 1956 (c.71)
Overseas Resources Development Act 1958 (c.15)
Overseas Resources Development Act 1959 (c.23)
Overseas Resources Development Act 1969 (c.36)
Overseas Service Act 1958 (c.14)
Overseas Service Act 1961 (c.10)
Overseas Superannuation Act 1991 (c.16)
Overseas Trade Act 1929 (c.12)
Overseas Trade Act 1930 (c.31)
Overseas Trade Act 1934 (c.12)
Overseas Trade (Credits and Insurance) Act 1920 (c.29)
Overseas Trade (Credits and Insurance) Amendment Act 1921 (c.26)
Overseas Trade Department (Secretary) Act 1918 (c.3)
Overseas Trade Guarantees Act 1939 (c.47)

Oxford and Berkshire Roads Act 1778 (c.81)
Oxford and Buckinghamshire Roads Act 1755 (c.42)
Oxford and Buckinghamshire Roads Act 1781 (c.77)
Oxford and Fifield Road Act 1767 (c.66)
Oxford and Gloucester Roads Act 1743 (c.10)
Oxford and Gloucester Roads Act 1730 (c.23)
Oxford and Gloucester Roads Act 1753 (c.70)
Oxford and Gloucester Roads Act 1765 (c.80)
Oxford and Gloucester Roads Act 1791 (c.111)
Oxford and Leicester Roads Act 1765 (c.105)
Oxford and Northampton Roads Act 1791 (c.128)
Oxford, Gloucester and Nottingham Roads Act 1770 (c.101)
Oxford: Improvement Act 1771 (c.19)
Oxford: Improvements Act 1780 (c.47)
Oxford: Poor Relief Act 1771 (c.14)
Oxford Roads Act 1750 (c.21)
Oxford Roads Act 1768 (c.34)
Oxford Roads Act 1771 (c.73)
Oxford Roads Act 1777 (c.88)
Oxford Roads Act 1778 (c.91)
Oxford Roads Act 1781 (c.87)
Oxford Roads Act 1789 (c.90)
Oxfordshire Roads Act 1739 (c.15)
Oxfordshire Roads Act 1730 (c.21)
Oxfordshire Roads Act 1757 (c.48)
Oxfordshire Roads Act 1762 (c.41)
Oyster and Mussel Fisheries Orders Confirmation Act 1869 (No. 2) (c.31)
Oyster Fisheries Act 1791 (c.51)

Pacific Cable Act 1901 (c.31)
Pacific Cable Act 1911 (c.36)
Pacific Cable Act 1924 (c.19)
Pacific Cable Act 1927 (c.9)
Pacific Cable Amendment Act 1902 (c.26)
Pacific Islands Protection Act 1875 (c.51)
Pacific Islands Regulations (Validation) Act 1916 (c.9)
Packing, etc. of Butter Act 1798 (c.73)
Paddington Churchyard Act 1753 (c.43)
Paddington (Improvement) Act 1763 (c.50)
Paddington Parish Church Act 1788 (c.74)
Paddington Parish Church Act 1793 (c.43)
Paisley Beer Duties Act 1753 (c.96)
Pakistan Act 1973 (c.48)
Pakistan Act 1974 (c.34)
Pakistan Act 1990 (c.14)
Pakistan (Consequential Provisions) Act 1956 (c.31)
Palestine Act 1948 (c.27)
Palestine Loan Act 1934 (c.33)
Pangbourn Bridge Act 1792 (c.97)
Paper Bills of Credit Act 1763 (c.34)
Paper Bills of Credit, American Colonies Act 1951 (c.53)
Paper Currency in America Act 1772 (c.57)
Paper Duties Act 1780 (c.24)
Paper Duties Act 1784 (c.18)
Paper Duties Act 1786 (c.78)
Paper Duties Act 1794 (c.20)
Papists Act 1715 (c.55)
Papists Act 1716 (c.18)
Papists Act 1722 (c.24)
Papists Act 1723 (c.4)
Papists Act 1732 (c.5)
Papists Act 1734 (c.25)
Papists Act 1737 (c.11)
Papists Act 1738 (c.14)
Papists Act 1740 (c.21)
Papists Act 1745 (c.16)
Papists Act 1753 (c.24)
Papists Act 1755 (c.10)
Papists Act 1757 (c.21)
Papists Act 1759 (c.13)
Papists Act 1762 (c.26)
Papists Act 1763 (c.38)
Papists Act 1766 (c.34)
Papists Act 1772 (c.10)
Papists Act 1774 (c.37)
Papists Act 1776 (c.45)
Papists Act 1778 (c.46)
Papists Act 1778 (c.60)
Papists Act 1780 (c.51)
Papists Act 1782 (c.23)
Papists Act 1783 (c.22)
Papists Act 1783 (c.16)
Papists Act 1787 (c.42)
Papists Act 1788 (c.47)
Papists Act 1789 (c.36)
Papists Act 1790 (c.19)
Papua New Guinea, Western Samoa and Nauru (Miscellaneous Provisions) Act 1980 (c.2)
Parish Apprentices Act 1778 (c.47)
Parish Apprentices Act 1792 (c.57)
Parish Church of St. Marylebone Act 1770 (c.112)
Parish Councils Act 1957 (c.42)
Parish Councils and Burial Authorities (Miscellaneous Provisions) Act 1970 (c.29)
Parish of The Trinity, Coventry Act 1779 (c.57)
Parish Officers Act 1793 (c.55)
Parish: Spittlefields, Stepney Act 1727 (c.10)
Park Lane Improvement Act 1958 (c.63)
Parking Act 1989 (c.16)
Parks Regulation Act 1872 (c.15)
Parks Regulation (Amendment) Act 1926 (c.36)
Parks Regulation (Amendment) Act 1974 (c.29)
Parliament Act 1710 (c.5)
Parliament Act 1712 (cc.5,6)
Parliament Act 1712 (c.16)
Parliament Act 1775 (c.36)
Parliament Act 1780 (c.1)

Parliament Act 1780 (c.50)
Parliament Act 1780 (c.43)
Parliament Act 1782 (c.29)
Parliament Act 1782 (c.41)
Parliament Act 1911 (c.13)
Parliament Act 1949 (c.103)
Parliament of Canada Act 1875 (c.38)
Parliament and Local Elections Act 1916 (c.44)
Parliament and Local Elections Act 1917 (c.13)
Parliament and Local Elections Act 1918 (c.22)
Parliament and Local Elections (No.2) Act 1917 (c.50)
Parliament and Registration Act 1916 (c.100)
Parliament (Elections and Meeting) Act 1943 (c.48)
Parliament (Qualification of Women) Act 1918 (c.47)
Parliamentary and Health Service Commissioners Act 1987 (c.39)
Parliamentary and Other Pensions Act 1972 (c.48)
Parliamentary and Other Pensions Act 1987 (c.45)
Parliamentary and Other Pensions and Salaries Act 1976 (c.48)
Parliamentary Commissioner Act 1967 (c.13)
Parliamentary Commissioner Act 1994 (c.14)
Parliamentary Commissioner (Consular Complaints) Act 1981 (c.11)
Parliamentary Constituencies Act 1986 (c.56)
Parliamentary Corporate Bodies Act 1992 (c.27)
Parliamentary Documents Deposit Act 1837 (c.83)
Parliamentary Elections Act 1734 (c.30)
Parliamentary Elections Act 1742 (c.11)
Parliamentary Elections Act 1744 (c.18)
Parliamentary Elections Act 1745 (c.28)
Parliamentary Elections Act 1757 (c.14)
Parliamentary Elections Act 1763 (c.24)
Parliamentary Elections Act 1770 (c.16)
Parliamentary Elections Act 1770 (c.41)
Parliamentary Elections Act 1771 (c.42)
Parliamentary Elections Act 1774 (c.15)
Parliamentary Elections Act 1774 (c.58)
Parliamentary Elections Act 1774 (c.81)
Parliamentary Elections Act 1780 (c.17)
Parliamentary Elections Act 1785 (c.84)
Parliamentary Elections Act 1790 (c.35)
Parliamentary Elections Act 1793 (c.64)
Parliamentary Elections Act 1795 (c.65)
Parliamentary Elections Act 1868 (c.125)
Parliamentary Elections, Cricklade Act 1782 (c.31)
Parliamentary Elections (Fraudulent Conveyances) Act 1739 (c.20)
Parliamentary Elections, New Shoreham Act 1771 (c.55)
Parliamentary Elections, Norwich 1730 (c.8)
Parliamentary Elections (Returning Officers) Act (1875) Amendment Act 1886 (c.57)
Parliamentary Elections Corrupt Practices Act 1879 (c.75)
Parliamentary Elections (Scotland) Act (c.16)
Parliamentary Elections (Soldiers) Act 1919 (c.10)
Parliamentary Electors (War-time Registration) Act 1944 (c.24)
Parliamentary Papers Act 1840 (c.9)
Parliamentary Pensions Act 1978 (c.56)
Parliamentary Pensions etc. Act 1984 (c.52)
Parliamentary Privilege Act 1770 (c.50)
Parliamentary Privilege Act 1937 (c.24)
Parliamentary Witnesses Act 1858 (c.78)
Parliamentary Witnesses Oaths Act 1871 (c.83)
Parochial Libraries Act 1708 (c.14)
Parochial Registers Act 1812 (c.146)
Parsonages Act 1838 (c.23)
Parsonages Act 1911 (c.29)
Participation Agreements Act 1978 (c.1)
Partition Act 1868 (c.40)
Partnership Act 1890 (c.39)
Parton, Cumberland, Harbour Act 1724 (c.16)
Parton Harbour, Cumberland Act 1731 (c.13)
Partridges Act 1799 (c.34)
Party Processions (Ireland) Act 1832 (c.118)
Party Processions (Ireland) Act 1844 (c.63)
Passage from Charing Cross Act 1757 (c.36)
Passenger Ships Act 1845 (c.14)
Passenger Vehicles (Experimental Areas) Act 1977 (c.21)
Patent Law Amendment Act 1852 (c.83)
Patents Act 1901 (c.18)
Patents Act 1902 (c.34)
Patents Act 1949 (c.87)
Patents Act 1957 (c.13)
Patents Act 1977 (c.37)
Patents and Designs Act 1907 (c.29)
Patents and Designs Act 1908 (c.4)
Patents and Designs Act 1914 (c.18)
Patents and Designs Act 1919 (c.80)
Patents and Designs Act 1927 (c.3)
Patents and Designs Act 1932 (c.32)
Patents and Designs Act 1942 (c.6)
Patents and Designs Act 1946 (c.44)
Patents and Designs Act 1949 (c.62)
Patents and Designs (Amendment) Act 1907 (c.28)
Patents and Designs (Limits of Time) Act 1939 (c.32)
Patents and Designs (Partial Suspension) Act 1915 (c.85)
Patents and Designs (Renewals, Extensions and Fees) Act 1961 (c.25)
Patents, Designs and Marks Act 1986 (c.39)
Patents, Designs and Trade Marks Act 1883 (c.57)
Patents, Designs and Trade Marks (Temporary Rules) Act 1914 (c.27)
Patents, Designs and Trade Marks (Temporary Rules) Amendment 1914 (c.73)

Patents, Designs, Copyright and Trade Marks (Emergency) Act 1939 (c.107)
Patents etc. (International Conventions) Act 1938 (c.29)
Patriotic Fund Act 1866 (c.120)
Patriotic Fund Reorganisation Act 1903 (c.20)
Pauper Children (Ireland) Act 1902 (c.16)
Paving, etc. of London Act 1768 (c.21)
Pawnbrokers Act 1784 (c.42)
Pawnbrokers Act 1785 (c.48)
Pawnbrokers Act 1787 (c.37)
Pawnbrokers Act 1788 (c.50)
Pawnbrokers Act 1789 (c.57)
Pawnbrokers Act 1791 (c.52)
Pawnbrokers Act 1793 (c.53)
Pawnbrokers Act 1872 (c.93)
Pawnbrokers Act 1922 (c.5)
Pawnbrokers Act 1960 (c.24)
Paymaster General Act 1782 (c.81)
Paymaster General Act 1783 (c.50)
Paymaster General Act 1835 (c.35)
Paymaster General Act 1848 (c.55)
Paymaster General, Balance, etc. Act 1780 (c.48)
Payment of Certain Regiments Act 1705 (c.12)
Payment of Charges of Constables Act 1778 (c.19)
Payment of Creditors (Scotland) Act 1780 (c.41)
Payment of Creditors (Scotland) Act 1783 (c.18)
Payment of Creditors (Scotland) Act 1789 (c.5)
Payment of Creditors (Scotland) Act 1793 (c.74)
Payment of Creditors (Scotland) Act 1804 (c.24)
Payment of Creditors (Scotland) Act 1813 (c.65)
Payment of Lace Makers' Wages Act 1779 (c.49)
Payment of Wages Act 1960 (c.37)
Pedlars Act 1871 (c.96)
Peebles Road Act 1753 (c.93)
Peebles Road Act 1771 (c.85)
Peebles Road Act 1775 (c.71)
Peebles Roads Act 1792 (c.123)
Peerage Act 1963 (c.48)
Pembroke Gaol Act 1779 (c.46)
Pembroke Road Act 1771 (c.96)
Pembroke Roads Act 1788 (c.102)
Pembroke Roads Act 1790 (c.91)
Pembroke Roads Act 1791 (c.102)
Pembroke Roads Act 1791 (c.109)
Pembroke Roads Act 1791 (c.126)
Penal Servitude Act 1891 (c.69)
Penal Servitude Act 1926 (c.58)
Penalties for Drunkenness Act 1962 (c.52)
Penicillin Act 1947 (c.29)
Penicillin (Merchant Ships) 1951 (c.13)
Penitentiary for Convicts Act 1794 (c.84)
Penny Post Act 1794 (c.17)
Pension Duties Act 1720 (c.27)
Pension Duties Act 1725 (c.2)
Pension Duties Act 1757 (c.22)
Pension Duties Act 1758 (c.33)
Pension Schemes Act 1993 (c.48)
Pension Schemes (Northern Ireland) Act 1993 (c.49)
Pensioners and Family Income Supplement Payments Act 1972 (c.75)
Pensioners' Payments Act 1974 (c.54)
Pensioners Payments Act 1977 (c.51)
Pensioners Payments Act 1978 (c.58)
Pensioners' Payments and National Insurance Act 1973 (c.61)
Pensioners' Payments and National Insurance Contributions Act 1972 (c.80)
Pensioners' Payments and Social Security Act 1979 (c.48)
Pensions Act 1839 (c.51)
Pensions Act 1995 (c.26)
Pensions and Determination of Needs Act 1943 (c.27)
Pensions and Yeomanry Pay Act 1884 (c.55)
Pensions Appeal Tribunals Act 1943 (c.39)
Pensions Appeal Tribunals Act 1949 (c.12)
Pensions Commutation Act 1871 (c.36)
Pensions Commutation Act 1882 (c.44)
Pensions Commutation Act 1984 (c.7)
Pensions (Governors of Dominions, etc.) Act 1911 (c.24)
Pensions (Governors of Dominions, etc.) Act 1929 (c.16)
Pensions (Governors of Dominions, etc.) Act 1936 (c.25)
Pensions (Governors of Dominions, etc.) Act 1947 (c.12)
Pensions (Governors of Dominions, etc.) Amendment 1913 (c.26)
Pensions (Increase) Act 1920 (c.36)
Pensions (Increase) Act 1924 (c.32)
Pensions (Increase) Act 1944 (c.21)
Pensions (Increase) Act 1946 (c.7)
Pensions (Increase) Act 1952 (c.45)
Pensions (Increase) Act 1954 (c.25)
Pensions (Increase) Act 1956 (c.39)
Pensions (Increase) Act 1962 (c.2)
Pensions (Increase) Act 1965 (c.78)
Pensions (Increase) Act 1969 (c.7)
Pensions (Increase) Act 1971 (c.56)
Pensions (Increase) Act 1974 (c.9)
Pensions (India, Pakistan and Burma) Act 1955 (c.22)
Pensions (Mercantile Marine) Act 1942 (c.26)
Pensions (Miscellaneous Provisions) Act 1990 (c.7)
Pensions (Navy, Army, Air Force and Mercantile Marine) Act 1939 (c.83)
Pensions to Seamen, etc. Act 1814 (c.1)
Performers' Protection Act 1963 (c.53)
Performers' Protection Act 1972 (c.32)
Performing Animals (Regulation) Act 1925 (c.38)

Perjury Act 1727 (c.25)
Perjury Act 1911 (c.6)
Perpetuation and Amendment of Acts 1904 (c.16)
Perpetuation, etc. of Acts 1708 (c.25)
Perpetuation of Acts, etc. Act 1719 (c.19)
Perpetuation of Testimony Act 1842 (c.69)
Perpetuation of Various Laws Act 1732 (c.37)
Perpetuities and Accumulations Act 1964 (c.55)
Persons Going Armed or Disguised Act 1758 (c.18)
Persons Going Armed and Disguised Act 1754 (c.15)
Personal Injuries (Emergency Provisions) Act 1939 (c.82)
Persuading Soldiers to Desert, etc. Act 1715 (c.47)
Perth: Highways and Bridge Act 1785 (c.13)
Perth Roads Act 1753 (c.91)
Perth Roads Act 1765 (c.89)
Perth Roads Act 1789 (c.17)
Perth Roads Act 1793 (c.158)
Pesticides (Fees and Enforcement) Act 1989 (c.27)
Pests Act 1954 (c.68)
Pet Animals Act 1951 (c.35)
Pet Animals Act 1951 (Amendment) Act 1983 (c.26)
Peterborough: Streets Act 1790 (c.66)
Petersham: Streets Act 1772 (c.42)
Petersfield Highways Act 1710 (c.33(f))
Petersfield to Portsmouth Road Act 1725 (c.19)
Petroleum Act 1879 (c.47)
Petroleum Act 1926 (c.25)
Petroleum Act 1975 (c.74)
Petroleum Act 1987 (c.12)
Petroleum (Amendment) 1928 (c.21)
Petroleum and Submarine Pipelines Act 1975 (c.74)
Petroleum (Consolidation) Act 1928 (c.32)
Petroleum (Production) Act 1918 (c.52)
Petroleum (Production) Act 1934 (c.36)
Petroleum Revenue Tax Act 1980 (c.1)
Petroleum Royalties (Relief) Act 1983 (c.59)
Petroleum Royalties (Relief) and Continental Shelf Act 1989 (c.1)
Petroleum Royalties (Relief) Act 1983 (c.59)
Petroleum (Transfer of Licences) Act 1936 (c.27)
Petty Sessions Act 1849 (c.18)
Petty Sessions Clerks and Fines (Ireland) Act 1878 (c.69)
Petty Sessions (Ireland) Act 1851 (c.93)
Petty Sessions Clerk (Ireland) (Amendment) Act 1901 (c.22)
Pharmacy Act 1929 (c.31)
Pharmacy Act 1953 (c.19)
Pharmacy Act 1954 (c.61)
Pharmacy and Medicines Act 1941 (c.42)
Pharmacy and Poisons Act 1933 (c.25)
Pharmacy and Poisons (Amendment) Act 1964 (c.35)
Physical Training and Recreation Act 1937 (c.46)
Physical Training and Recreation Act 1958 (c.36)
Piccadilly Act 1844 (c.88)
Piccadilly; Watering Act 1775 (c.57)
Pig Industry Levy Act 1983 (c.4)
Pilchard Fisheries Act 1791 (c.45)
Pilchard Fishery Act 1785 (c.58)
Pilchard Fishery Act 1786 (c.45)
Pilchard Fishery, Cornwall Act 1776 (c.36)
Pillory Abolition Act 1816 (c.138)
Pilotage Act 1716 (c.13)
Pilotage Act 1731 (c.20)
Pilotage Act 1913 (c.31)
Pilotage Act 1983 (c.21)
Pilotage Act 1987 (c.21)
Pilotage Authorities (Limitation of Liability) Act 1936 (c.36)
Pipelines Act 1962 (c.58)
Piracy Act 1717 (c.11)
Piracy Act 1721 (c.24)
Piracy Act 1744 (c.30)
Piracy Act 1837 (c.88)
Pistols Act 1903 (c.18)
Pittenweem Beer Duties Act 1719 (c.9)
Places of Religious Worship Act 1812 (c.155)
Places of Worship (Enfranchisement) Act 1920 (c.56)
Places of Worship Registration Act 1855 (c.81)
Planning and Compensation Act 1991 (c.34)
Planning (Consequential Provisions) Act 1990 (c.11)
Planning (Hazardous Substances) Act 1990 (c.10)
Planning Inquiries (Attendance of Public) Act 1982 (c.21)
Planning (Listed Buildings and Conservation Areas) Act 1990 (c.9)
Plant Health Act 1967 (c.8)
Plant Varieties Act 1983 (c.17)
Plant Varieties and Seeds Act 1964 (c.14)
Plantation Trade etc., Act 1741 (c.31)
Plate Act 1696 (c.8)
Plate Assay Act 1700 (c.3)
Plate Assay (Sheffield) Act 1784 (c.20)
Plate Assay (Sheffield and Birmingham) Act 1772 (c.52)
Plate Duties Act 1784 (c.53)
Plate (Duties, Drawbacks) Act 1785 (c.64)
Plate Duty Act 1719 (c.11)
Plate (Duty on Dealer's Licence) Act 1757 (c.32)
Plate (Duty on Dealer's Licence) Act 1757 (c.24)
Plate Glass Manufacture Act 1772 (c.38)
Plate (Offences) Act 1738 (c.26)
Plate (Offences) Act 1772 (c.59)
Plate (Scotland) Act 1836 (c.69)
Plays and Wine Licences 1736 (c.28)
Pleading Act 1711 (c.28)
Pleading in Misdemeanour Act 1819 (c.4)

Pluralities Act 1838 (c.106)
Pluralities Act 1850 (c.98)
Pluralities Act 1887 (c.68)
Pluralities of Living Act 1801 (c.102)
Plymouth and Portsmouth Fortifications Act 1758 (c.30)
Plymouth Dock Act 1766 (c.102)
Plymouth Dock to Torpoint: Ferry Act 1790 (c.61)
Plymouth: Fortifications Act 1774 (c.50)
Plymouth Fortifications Act 1781 (c.61)
Plymouth Fortifications Act 1782 (c.12)
Plymouth Improvement Act 1770 (c.14)
Plymouth Improvement Act 1772 (c.8)
Plymouth: Poor Relief Act 1758 (c.59)
Plymouth: Poor Relief Act 1786 (c.19)
Plymouth: Poor Relief etc, Act 1781 (c.72)
Plymouth, Sheerness, Gravesend, Tilbury-Fortifications Act 1780 (c.38)
Plymouth: Streets Act 1774 (c.8)
Plymouth Water Supply Act 1793 (c.85)
Plymouth Workhouse 1707 (c.46(d))
Pneumoconiosis and Byssinosis Benefit Act 1951 (c.4)
Pneumoconiosis etc. (Workers' Compensation) Act 1979 (c.41)
Poaching Prevention Act 1862 (c.114)
Poisons Act 1972 (c.66)
Poisons and Pharmacy Act 1908 (c.55)
Polehampton Estates Act 1885 (c.40)
Police Act 1909 (c.40)
Police Act 1919 (c.46)
Police Act 1964 (c.48)
Police Act 1969 (c.63)
Police Act 1972 (c.39)
Police Act 1976 (c.46)
Police and Criminal Evidence Act 1984 (c.60)
Police and Firemen (War Service) Act 1939 (c.103)
Police and Firemen (War Service) Act 1944 (c.22)
Police and Magistrates' Courts Act 1994 (c.29)
Police (Appeals) Act 1927 (c.19)
Police (Appeals) Act 1943 (c.8)
Police Army Act 1946 (c.46)
Police Constables (Naval and Military Service) Act 1914 (c.80)
Police Constables (Naval and Military Service) Act 1917 (c.36)
Police (Emergency Provisions) Act 1915 (c.41)
Police Factories, etc. (Miscellaneous Provisions) Act 1916 (c.31)
Police Federation Act 1959 (c.38)
Police Federations Act 1962 (c.25)
Police Federation Act 1961 (c.51)
Police, Fire and Probation Officers' Remuneration Act 1956 (c.1)
Police (His Majesty's Inspectors of Constabulary) Act 1945 (c.11)
Police (Liverpool Inquiry) Act 1909 (c.35)
Police Magistrates (Superannuation) Act 1915 (c.74)
Police Magistrates Superannuation Amendment Act 1929 (c.37)
Police Negotiating Board Act 1980 (c.10)
Police Officers (Central Service) Act 1989 (c.11)
Police (Overseas Service) Act 1945 (c.17)
Police (Pensions) Act 1918 (c.51)
Police (Pensions) Act 1921 (c.31)
Police Pensions Act 1926 (c.34)
Police Pensions Act 1948 (c.24)
Police Pensions Act 1961 (c.35)
Police Pensions Act 1976 (c.35)
Police (Property) Act 1897 (c.30)
Police Revenue and Consolidated Fund Charges Act 1854 (c.94)
Police (Scotland) Act 1857 (c.72)
Police (Scotland) Act 1856 (c.26)
Police (Scotland) Act 1890 (c.67)
Police (Scotland) Act 1946 (c.71)
Police (Scotland) Act 1966 (c.52)
Police (Scotland) Act 1967 (c.77)
Police (Scotland) Act (1890) Amendment Act 1910 (c.10)
Police (Scotland) (Limit of Age) Act 1914 (c.69)
Police Reservists Act 1902 (c.10)
Police Reservists (Allowances) Act 1900 (c.9)
Police Reservists (Allowances) Act 1914 (c.34)
Police (Superannuation) Act 1906 (c.7)
Police (Superannuation) Act 1908 (c.5)
Police (Weekly Rest Day) Act 1910 (c.13)
Police (Weekly Rest Day) (Scotland) Act 1914 (c.8)
Policing of Airports Act 1974 (c.41)
Policyholders Protection Act 1975 (c.75)
Polish Resettlement Act 1947 (c.19)
Polling Arrangements (Parliamentary Boroughs) Act 1908 (c.14)
Polling Districts (County Councils) Act 1908 (c.13)
Polling Districts and Registration of Voters (Ireland) Act 1908 (c.35)
Ponies Act 1969 (c.28)
Pool Betting Act 1954 (c.33)
Pool Competitions Act 1971 (c.57)
Pool Harbour Act 1756 (c.10)
Poole Roads Act 1756 (c.52)
Poole Roads Act 1757 (c.52)
Poole Roads Act 1757 (c.66)
Poole Roads Act 1777 (c.104)
Poole to Blandford Road Act 1777 (c.86)
Poor Act 1762 (c.22)
Poor Act 1766 (c.39)
Poor Act 1776 (c.40)
Poor Act 1793 (c.35)
Poor Act 1912 (c.18)
Poor Apprentices Act 1780 (c.36)
Poor Law Act 1927 (c.14)
Poor Law Act 1930 (c.17)
Poor Law Act 1934 (c.59)
Poor Law Amendment Act 1844 (c.101)

Poor Law (Amendment) Act 1938 (c.23)
Poor Law Authorities (Transfer of Property) Act 1904 (c.20)
Poor Law (Dissolution of School Districts and Adjustments) Act 1903 (c.19)
Poor Law Emergency Provisions (Scotland) Act 1921 (c.64)
Poor Law Emergency Provisions (Scotland) Act 1927 (c.3)
Poor Law Emergency Provisions Continuance (Scotland) Act 1924 (c.9)
Poor Law Emergency Provisions Continuance (Scotland) Act 1925 (c.35)
Poor Law, Hull Act 1709 (c.24)
Poor Law Officers' Superannuation Act 1896 (c.50)
Poor Law (Scotland) Act 1934 (c.52)
Poor Persons 1495 (c.12)
Poor Prisoners' Defence Act 1903 (c.38)
Poor Prisoners' Defence Act 1930 (c.32)
Poor Prisoners Relief Act 1737 (c.20)
Poor Prisoners (Scotland) Act 1825 (c.62)
Poor Rate Act 1743 (c.3)
Poor Rate Exemption Act 1833 (c.30)
Poor Relief Act 1722 (c.7)
Poor Relief Act 1743 (c.38)
Poor Relief Act 1769 (c.37)
Poor Relief (Deserted Wives and Children) Act 1718 (c.8)
Poor Relief: Gloucester Act 1726 (c.19)
Poor Relief (Ireland) Act 1838 (c.56)
Poor Relief (Ireland) Act 1849 (c.104)
Poor Relief (Ireland) Act 1900 (c.45)
Poor Relief (Ireland) Act 1914 (c.14)
Poor Removal Act 1900 (c.23)
Poor, Staffordshire Act 1791 (c.20)
Population (Statistics) Act 1938 (c.13)
Population (Statistics) Act 1960 (c.32)
Porcelain Patent Act 1775 (c.52)
Port Glasgow Harbour Act 1772 (c.16)
Port of Liverpool Act 1766 (c.61)
Port of London (Financial Assistance) Act 1980 (c.31)
Portman Square: Improvement Act 1782 (c.85)
Ports Act 1991 (c.52)
Ports (Finance) Act 1985 (c.30)
Ports (Financial Assistance) Act 1981 (c.21)
Ports (Reduction of Debt) Act 1983 (c.22)
Portsea Chapel Act 1787 (c.64)
Portsea Common Chapel Act 1753 (c.58)
Portsea: Improvement Act 1792 (c.103)
Portsmouth, Chatham Fortifications Act 1782 (c.80)
Portsmouth, Chatham Fortifications Act 1783 (c.71)
Portsmouth, Faversham Fortifications Act 1783 (c.87)
Portsmouth Improvement Act 1768 (c.62)
Portsmouth, Plymouth Fortifications Act 1784 (c.29)
Portsmouth: Streets Act 1776 (c.59)
Portsmouth Water Supply (Farlington) Act 1740 (c.43)
Possession of Mortgaged Land (Emergency Provisions) Act 1939 (c.108)
Postage Act 1730 (c.33)
Postage Act 1763 (c.24)
Postage Act 1765 (c.25)
Postage Act 1782 (c.70)
Postage Act 1783 (c.69)
Postage Act 1784 (c.8)
Postage Act 1787 (c.9)
Postage Act 1794 (c.18)
Postage Act 1796 (c.18)
Postage Act 1805 (c.11)
Postage Act 1805 (c.21)
Post Fines Act 1758 (c.14)
Post Horse Duties Act 1787 (c.26)
Post Horse Duties Act 1790 (c.23)
Post Horse Duties Act 1793 (c.71)
Post Horse Duties Act 1796 (c.84)
Post Office Act 1748 (c.25)
Post Office Act 1904 (c.14)
Post Office Act 1908 (c.48)
Post Office Act 1913 (c.11)
Post Office Act 1918 (c.10)
Post Office Act 1953 (c.36)
Post Office Act 1961 (c.15)
Post Office Act 1969 (c.48)
Post Office Act 1977 (c.44)
Post Office (Amendment) Act 1935 (c.15)
Post Office and Telegraph Act 1915 (c.82)
Post Office and Telegraph Act 1920 (c.40)
Post Office and Telegraph Act 1940 (c.25)
Post Office and Telegraph (Money) Act 1928 (c.37)
Post Office and Telegraph (Money) Act 1931 (c.20)
Post Office and Telegraph (Money) Act 1935 (c.14)
Post Office and Telegraph (Money) Act 1937 (c.51)
Post Office and Telegraph (Money) Act 1939 (c.42)
Post Office and Telegraph (Money) Act 1942 (c.24)
Post Office and Telegraph (Money) Act 1946 (c.51)
Post Office and Telegraph (Money) Act 1947 (c.16)
Post Office and Telegraph (Money) Act 1950 (c.2)
Post Office and Telegraph (Money) Act 1952 (c.34)
Post Office and Telegraph (Money) Act 1953 (c.4)
Post Office and Telegraph (Money) Act 1955 (c.14)
Post Office and Telegraph (Money) Act 1957 (c.5)
Post Office and Telegraph (Money) Act 1950 (c.2)
Post Office (Banking Services) Act 1976 (c.10)
Post Office (Borrowing Powers) Act 1967 (c.15)

Post Office (Borrowing Powers) Act 1972 (c.79)
Post Office (Data Processing Service) Act 1967 (c.62)
Post Office (Literature for the Blind) Act 1906 (c.22)
Post Office (Money Orders) Act 1903 (c.12)
Post Office (Money Orders) Act 1906 (c.4)
Post Office Offences and Isle of Man Postage Act 1767 (c.50)
Post Office (Parcels) Act 1922 (c.49)
Post Office (Pneumatic Tubes Acquisition) Act 1922 (c.43)
Post Office (Protection) Act 1884 (c.76)
Post Office (Revenues) Act 1710 (c.11(p))
Post Office Savings Bank Act 1908 (c.8)
Post Office Savings Bank Act 1954 (c.62)
Post Office Savings Bank Act 1965 (c.12)
Post Office Savings Bank (Public Trustee) Act 1908 (c.52)
Post Office (Subway) Act 1966 (c.25)
Post Office Works Act 1959 (c.43)
Post Roads in Scotland Act 1951 (c.28)
Post Works Loans Act 1957 (c.4)
Postponement of Enactments (Miscellaneous Provisions) Act 1939 (c.2)
Postponement of Payments Act 1914 (c.11)
Postponement of Polling Day Act 1945 (c.40)
Pot and Pearl Ashes Act 1750 (c.51)
Poultry Act 1911 (c.11)
Powers of Attorney Act 1971 (c.27)
Powers of Criminal Courts Act 1973 (c.62)
Prescription Act 1832 (c.71)
Prescription and Limitation (Scotland) Act 1973 (c.52)
Prescription and Limitation (Scotland) Act 1984 (c.45)
Prescription (Scotland) Act 1987 (c.36)
Presentation of Benefices Act 1713 (c.13)
Preservation of Fish and Conies Act 1965 (c.14)
Preservation of House Doves, etc. Act 1762 (c.29)
Preservation of Roads Act 1740 (c.42)
Preservation of Timber Act 1772 (c.33)
Preservation of Timber Trees Act 1715 (c.48)
Preservation of Timber Trees Act 1766 (c.48)
Preservation of Timber Trees (Scotland) Act 1719 (c.16)
Preservation of Trees, America Act 1710 (c.22)
Preservation of Woods, America Act 1728 (c.35)
President of the Board of Trade 1932 (c.21)
Presteigne Road Act 1756 (c.94)
Preston Bridge Act 1757 (c.55)
Prestonpans Beer Duties Act 1753 (c.79)
Prestonpans Beer Duties Act 1757 (c.52)
Presumption of Death (Scotland) Act 1977 (c.27)
Presumption of Life Limitation (Scotland) Act 1891 (c.29)
Prevention and Treatment of Blindness (Scotland) Act 1938 (c.32)
Prevention of Corruption Act 1906 (c.34)
Prevention of Corruption Act 1916 (c.64)
Prevention of Crimes Act 1871 (c.112)
Prevention of Crime Act 1908 (c.59)
Prevention of Crime Act 1953 (c.14)
Prevention of Cruelty to Children Act 1904 (c.15)
Prevention of Damage by Pests Act 1949 (c.55)
Prevention of Damage by Rabbits 1939 (c.43)
Prevention of Eviction Act 1924 (c.18)
Prevention of Fraud (Investments) Act 1939 (c.16)
Prevention of Fraud (Investments) Act 1958 (c.45)
Prevention of Offences Act 1851 (c.19)
Prevention of Oil Pollution Act 1971 (c.60)
Prevention of Oil Pollution Act 1986 (c.6)
Prevention of Terrorism (Temporary Provisions) Act 1974 (c.55)
Prevention of Terrorism (Temporary Provisions) Act 1976 (c.8)
Prevention of Terrorism (Temporary Provisions Act 1984 (c.8)
Prevention of Terrorism (Temporary Provisions) Act 1989 (c.4)
Prevention of Violence (Temporary Provisions) Act 1939 (c.50)
Previous Conviction Act 1836 (c.111)
Price Commission Act 1977 (c.33)
Price Commission (Amendment) Act 1979 (c.1)
Price Control and Other Orders (Indemnity) Act 1951 (c.59)
Price Control (Regulation of Disposal of Stocks) Act 1943 (c.47)
Price of Coal (Limitation) Act 1915 (c.75)
Prices Act 1974 (c.24)
Prices Act 1975 (c.32)
Prices and Incomes Act 1966 (c.33)
Prices and Incomes Act 1967 (c.53)
Prices and Incomes Act 1968 (c.42)
Prices of Goods Act 1939 (c.118)
Princess Elizabeth's and Duke of Edinburgh's Annuities Act 1947 (c.14)
Printer's Imprint Act 1961 (c.31)
Prison Act 1952 (c.52)
Prison Officers (Pensions) Act (c.9)
Prison Security Act 1992 (c.25)
Prisoners and Criminal Proceedings (Scotland) Act 1993 (c.9)
Prisoners of War (Escape) Act 1812 (c.156)
Prisoners (Return to Custody) Act 1995 (c.16)
Prisoners (Temporary Discharge for Ill-Health) Act 1913 (c.4)
Prisons (Ireland) Act 1819 (c.100)
Prisons (Ireland) Act 1907 (c.19)
Prisons (Scotland) Act 1839 (c.42)
Prisons (Scotland) Act 1844 (c.34)
Prisons (Scotland) Act 1904 (c.35)
Prisons (Scotland) Act 1909 (c.27)

Prisons (Scotland) Act 1926 (c.57)
Prisons (Scotland) Act 1952 (c.61)
Prisons (Scotland) Act 1989 (c.45)
Private International Law (Miscellaneous Provisions) Act 1995 (c.42)
Private Legislation Procedure (Scotland) Act 1933 (c.37)
Private Legislation Procedure (Scotland) Act 1936 (c.52)
Private Place of Entertainment (Licensing) Act 1967 (c.19)
Private Street Works Act 1961 (c.24)
Prize Act 1939 (c.65)
Prize Act 1948 (c.9)
Prize Causes Act 1797 (c.38)
Prize Courts Act 1915 (c.57)
Prize Courts (Procedure) Act 1914 (c.13)
Prize Goods Act 1803 (c.134)
Prize Salvage Act 1943 (c.7)
Prize Salvage Act 1944 (c.7)
Probate and Legacy Duties Act 1808 (c.149)
Probate and Legacy Duties (Ireland) Act 1814 (c.92)
Probate Duty Act 1801 (c.86)
Probate Duty Act 1859 (c.36)
Probate Duty Act 1860 (c.15)
Probate Duty Act 1861 (c.92)
Probate Duty (Ireland) Act 1816 (c.56)
Probates and Letters of Administration Act (Ireland) 1857 (c.79)
Probation of Offenders Act 1907 (c.17)
Probation of Offenders (Scotland) Act 1931 (c.30)
Probation Officers (Superannuation) Act 1947 (c.38)
Probation Service Act 1993 (c.47)
Proceedings Against Estates Act 1970 (c.17)
Proceeds of Crime Act 1995 (c.11)
Proceeds of Crime (Scotland) Act 1995 (c.43)
Professional Cavalry Act 1796 (c.23)
Professions Supplementary to Medicine Act 1960 (c.66)
Profiteering Act 1919 (c.66)
Profiteering Amendment Act 1920 (c.13)
Profiteering (Cont.) Act 1919 (c.87)
Profits Tax Act 1949 (c.64)
Prohibition of Female Circumcision Act 1985 (c.38)
Prolongation of Parliament Act 1940 (c.53)
Prolongation of Parliament Act 1941 (c.48)
Prolongation of Parliament Act 1942 (c.37)
Prolongation of Parliament Act 1943 (c.46)
Prolongation of Parliament Act 1944 (c.45)
Promissory Oaths Act 1868 (c.72)
Promissory Oaths Act 1871 (c.48)
Property Misdescriptions Act 1991 (c.29)
Property Services Agency and Crown Suppliers Act 1990 (c.12)
Prosecution of Offences Act 1879 (c.22)
Prosecution of Offences Act 1884 (c.58)
Prosecution of Offences Act 1908 (c.3)
Prosecution of Offences Act 1979 (c.31)
Prosecution of Offences Act 1985 (c.23)
Protection Against Cruel Tethering Act 1988 (c.31)
Protection from Eviction Act 1964 (c.97)
Protection from Eviction Act 1977 (c.43)
Protection of Aircraft Act 1973 (c.47)
Protection of Animals Act 1911 (c.27)
Protection of Animals Act 1934 (c.21)
Protection of Animals Act (1911) Amendment 1921 (c.14)
Protection of Animals (Amendment) 1927 (c.27)
Protection of Animals (Amendment) Act 1954 (c.40)
Protection of Animals (Amendment) Act 1988 (c.29)
Protection of Animals (Anaesthetics) Act 1954 (c.46)
Protection of Animals (Anaesthetics) Act 1964 (c.39)
Protection of Animals (Cruelty to Dogs) Act 1933 (c.17)
Protection of Animals (Cruelty to Dogs) (Scotland) Act 1934 (c.25)
Protection of Animals (Penalties) Act 1987 (c.35)
Protection of Animals (Scotland) Act 1912 (c.14)
Protection of Animals (Scotland) Act, 1912, Amendment Act 1921 (c.22)
Protection of Animals (Scotland) Act 1993 (c.15)
Protection of Birds Act 1925 (c.31)
Protection of Birds Act 1933 (c.52)
Protection of Birds Act 1954 (c.30)
Protection of Birds Act 1967 (c.46)
Protection of Birds Act 1954 (Amendment) Act 1964 (c.59)
Protection of Birds (Amendment) Act 1976 (c.42)
Protection of Children Act 1978 (c.37)
Protection of Children (Tobacco) Act 1986 (c.34)
Protection of Depositors Act 1963 (c.16)
Protection of Lapwings Act 1928 (c.2)
Protection of Military Remains Act 1986 (c.35)
Protection of Trading Interests Act 1980 (c.11)
Protection of Wrecks Act 1973 (c.33)
Provident Nominations and Small Intestacies Act 1883 (c.47)
Provisional Collection of Taxes 1913 (c.3)
Provisional Collection of Taxes Act 1968 (c.2)
Provisional Order Confirmation (Turnpikes) Act 1854 (c.51)
Provisional Order Confirmation (Turnpikes) Act 1855 (c.102)
Provisional Order Confirmation (Turnpikes) Act 1857 (c.9)
Provisional Order Confirmation (Turnpikes) Act 1858 (c.80)
Provisional Order Confirmation (Turnpikes) Act 1859 (c.33)

Provisional Order Confirmation (Turnpikes) Act 1860 (c.70)
Provisional Orders Confirmation (Turnpikes) Act 1862 (c.69)
Provisional Order Confirmation (Turnpikes) Act 1863 (c.98)
Provisional Order Confirmation (Turnpikes) Act 1864 (c.79)
Provisional Order (Marriages) Act 1904 (c.23)
Public Accounts Act 1804 (c.58)
Public Accounts and Charges Act 1891 (c.24)
Public and Other Schools (War Conditions) Act 1941 (c.20)
Public Authorities (Allowances) Act 1961 (c.43)
Public Authorities and Bodies (Loans) Act 1916 (c.69)
Public Bodies (Admission to Meetings) Act 1960 (c.67)
Public Bodies Corrupt Practices Act 1889 (c.69)
Public Buildings Expenses Act 1903 (c.41)
Public Buildings Expenses Act 1913 (c.14)
Public Entertainment Act 1875 (c.21)
Public Expenditure and Receipts Act 1968 (c.14)
Public Health Act 1875 (c.55)
Public Health Act 1904 (c.16)
Public Health Act 1908 (c.6)
Public Health Act 1925 (c.71)
Public Health Act 1936 (c.49)
Public Health Act (London) Act 1936 (c.50)
Public Health Act 1961 (c.64)
Public Health Acts Amendment Act 1890 (c.59)
Public Health Acts Amendment Act 1907 (c.53)
Public Health (Borrowing Powers) (Ireland) Act (c.35)
Public Health (Cleansing of Shellfish) Act 1932 (c.28)
Public Health (Coal Mine Refuse) Act 1939 (c.58)
Public Health (Coal Mine Refuse) (Scotland) Act 1939 (c.23)
Public Health (Confirmation of Byelaws) Act 1884 (c.12)
Public Health (Control of Disease) Act 1984 (c.22)
Public Health (Drainage of Trade Premises) Act 1937 (c.40)
Public Health (Interments) Act 1879 (c.31)
Public Health (Ireland) Act 1878 (c.52)
Public Health (Ireland) Act 1896 (c.54)
Public Health (Ireland) Act 1900 (c.10)
Public Health (Ireland) Act 1911 (c.12)
Public Health (Laboratory Service) Act 1960 (c.49)
Public Health (Laboratory Service) Act 1979 (c.23)
Public Health (London) Act 1936 (c.50)
Public Health (Medical Treatment, etc.) (Ireland) Act 1919 (c.16)
Public Health (Notification of Births) Act 1965 (c.42)
Public Health (Officers) Act 1921 (c.23)
Public Health Officers (Deputies) Act 1957 (c.19)
Public Health (Prevention and Treatment of Disease) Act 1913 (c.23)
Public Health (Prevention, etc. of Disease) (Ireland) Act 1917 (c.40)
Public Health (Recurring Nuisances) Act 1969 (c.25)
Public Health (Regulations as to Food) Act 1907 (c.32)
Public Health (Scotland) Act 1897 (c.38)
Public Health (Scotland) Amendment Act 1907 (c.30)
Public Health (Scotland) Act (1897) Amendment 1911 (c.30)
Public Health (Scotland) Amendment 1925 (c.75)
Public Health (Scotland) Act 1945 (c.15)
Public Health (Smoke Abatement) Act 1926 (c.43)
Public Health (Tuberculosis) Act 1921 (c.12)
Public Health (Water and Sewerage) (Scotland) Act 1935 (c.36)
Public Lavatories (Turnstiles) Act 1963 (c.32)
Public Lending Right Act 1979 (c.10)
Public Libraries Act 1884 (c.37)
Public Libraries Act 1901 (c.19)
Public Libraries Act 1919 (c.93)
Public Libraries (etc.) Act (Ireland) Act 1911 (c.9)
Public Libraries Act (Ireland) 1855 (c.40)
Public Libraries and Museums Act 1964 (c.75)
Public Libraries Consolidation (Scotland) Act 1887 (c.42)
Public Libraries (Ireland) Amendment Act 1877 (c.15)
Public Libraries (Ireland) Act 1894 (c.38)
Public Libraries (Ireland) Act 1902 (c.20)
Public Libraries (Ireland) Act 1920 (c.25)
Public Libraries (Scotland) Act 1894 (c.20)
Public Libraries (Scotland) Act 1899 (c.5)
Public Libraries (Scotland) Act 1920 (c.45)
Public Libraries (Scotland) Act 1955 (c.27)
Public Meeting Act 1908 (c.66)
Public Notaries (Articled Clerks) Act 1919 (c.25)
Public Notaries (Ireland) Act 1821 (c.36)
Public Notaries (War Service of Articled Clerks) Act 1946 (c.79)
Public Officers Protection (Ireland) Act 1803 (c.143)
Public Offices Fees Act 1879 (c.58)
Public Offices (Site) Act 1947 (c.45)
Public Order Act 1936 (c.6)
Public Order Act 1963 (c.52)
Public Order Act 1986 (c.64)
Public Parks (Scotland) Act 1878 (c.8)
Public Passenger Vehicles Act 1981 (c.14)
Public Records Act 1958 (c.51)

Public Records Act 1967 (c.44)
Public Records (Scotland) Act 1937 (c.43)
Public Registers and Records (Scotland) Act 1948 (c.57)
Public Registers and Records (Scotland) Act 1949 (c.11)
Public Roads (Ireland) Act 1911 (c.45)
Public Schools Act 1868 (c.118)
Public Schools (Eton College Property) Act 1873 (c.62)
Public Service Vehicles (Arrest of Offenders) Act 1975 (c.53)
Public Service Vehicles (Travel Concessions) Act 1955 (c.26)
Public Stores Act 1875 (c.25)
Public Trustee Act 1906 (c.55)
Public Trustee and Administration of Funds Act 1986 (c.57)
Public Trustee (Fees) Act 1957 (c.12)
Public Trustee (General Deposit Fund) Act 1939 (c.51)
Public Utilities Street Works Act 1950 (c.39)
Public Utility Companies (Capital Issues) Act 1920 (c.9)
Public Utility Transfers and Water Charges Act 1988 (c.15)
Public Works Facilities Act 1930 (c.50)
Public Works (Festival of Britain) Act 1949 (c.26)
Public Works Loans Act 1900 (c.36)
Public Works Loans Act 1901 (c.35)
Public Works Loans Act 1902 (c.22)
Public Works Loans Act 1903 (c.28)
Public Works Loans Act 1904 (c.22)
Public Works Loans Act 1904 (c.36)
Public Works Loans Act 1906 (c.29)
Public Works Loans Act 1907 (c.36)
Public Works Loans Act 1908 (c.23)
Public Works Loans Act 1909 (c.6)
Public Works Loans Act 1910 (c.21)
Public Works Loans Act 1911 (c.17)
Public Works Loans Act 1912 (c.11)
Public Works Loans Act 1913 (c.22)
Public Works Loans Act 1914 (c.33)
Public Works Loans Act 1915 (c.68)
Public Works Loans Act 1916 (c.28)
Public Works Loans Act 1917 (c.32)
Public Works Loans Act 1918 (c.27)
Public Works Loans Act 1919 (c.52)
Public Works Loans Act 1920 (c.61)
Public Works Loans Act 1921 (c.54)
Public Works Loans Act 1922 (c.33)
Public Works Loans Act 1923 (c.29)
Public Works Loans Act 1924 (c.26)
Public Works Loans Act 1925 (c.62)
Public Works Loans Act 1926 (c.2)
Public Works Loans Act 1927 (c.1)
Public Works Loans Act 1928 (c.5)
Public Works Loans Act 1930 (c.49)
Public Works Loans Act 1931 (c.47)
Public Works Loans Act 1932 (c.42)
Public Works Loans Act 1934 (c.48)
Public Works Loans Act 1935 (c.5)
Public Works Loans Act 1937 (c.11)
Public Works Loans Act 1939 (c.2)
Public Works Loans Act 1941 (c.14)
Public Works Loans Act 1944 (c.16)
Public Works Loans Act 1946 (c.41)
Public Works Loans Act 1947 (c.13)
Public Works Loans Act 1948 (c.48)
Public Works Loans Act 1949 (c.82)
Public Works Loans Act 1950 (c.5)
Public Works Loans Act 1951 (c.5)
Public Works Loans Act 1952 (c.3)
Public Works Loans Act 1953 (c.6)
Public Works Loans Act 1955 (c.11)
Public Works Loans Act 1956 (c.65)
Public Works Loans Act 1964 (c.9)
Public Works Loans Act 1965 (c.63)
Public Works Loans Act 1966 (c.16)
Public Works Loans Act 1967 (c.61)
Public Works Loans (No. 2) Act 1927 (c.28)
Public Works Loans (No. 2) Act 1937 (c.7)
Punishment of Incest Act 1908 (c.45)
Purchase of Land (Ireland) Act 1885 (c.73)
Purchase of Land (Ireland) Act 1891 (c.48)
Purchase of Land (Ireland) Act 1901 (c.3)
Purchase of Land (Ireland) (No. 2) Act 1901 (c.30)
Purchase Tax Act 1963 (c.9)

Quail Protection Act 1937 (c.5)
Quakers and Moravians Act 1833 (c.49)
Quakers and Moravians Act 1838 (c.77)
Qualification of Women (County and Borough Councils) Act 1907 (c.33)
Qualification of Women (County and Town Councils) Act 1907 (c.48)
Quarantine Act 1797 (c.33)
Quarantine Act 1800 (c.80)
Quarantine Act 1805 (c.10)
Quarantine Act 1810 (c.20)
Quarantine Act 1811 (c.46)
Quarantine Act 1825 (c.78)
Quarantine Act (Great Britain) Act 1806 (c.98)
Quarantine, etc., Act 1800 (c.30)
Quarries Act 1894 (c.42)
Quarry (Fencing) Act 1887 (c.19)
Quarter Sessions Act 1814 (c.84)
Quarter Sessions Act 1837 (c.4)
Quarter Sessions Act 1842 (c.38)
Quarter Sessions Act 1849 (c.45)
Quarter Sessions Act 1894 (c.6)
Quarter Sessions (Ireland) Act 1845 (c.80)
Quarter Sessions Jurors (Ireland) Act 1897 (c.20)
Quarter Sessions (London) Act 1896 (c.55)
Quartering of Soldiers Act 1795 (c.64)
Quartering of Soldiers Act 1796 (c.36)
Quartering of Soldiers Act 1797 (c.32)
Quartering of Soldiers Act 1797 (c.41)
Quartering of Soldiers Act 1799 (c.36)
Quartering of Soldiers Act 1800 (c.39)
Quartering of Soldiers Act 1801 (c.35)

Quartering of Soldiers Act 1802 (c.108)
Quartering of Soldiers Act 1803 (c.41)
Quartering of Soldiers Act 1804 (c.38)
Quartering of Soldiers Act 1805 (c.37)
Quartering of Soldiers Act 1806 (c.126)
Quartering of Soldiers Act 1807 (c.54)
Quartering of Soldiers Act 1808 (c.39)
Quartering of Soldiers Act 1809 (c.37)
Quartering of Soldiers Act 1810 (c.28)
Quartering of Soldiers Act 1810 (c.96)
Quartering of Soldiers Act 1811 (c.28)
Quartering of Soldiers Act 1812 (c.43)
Quartering of Soldiers Act 1813 (c.43)
Quartering of Soldiers Act 1814 (c.55)
Quartering of Soldiers Act 1815 (c.154)
Quartering of Soldiers Act 1816 (c.32)
Quartering of Soldiers Act 1817 (c.78)
Quartering of Soldiers Act 1818 (c.22)
Quartering of Soldiers Act 1819 (c.26)
Quartering of Soldiers Act 1820 (c.38)
Quartering of Soldiers Act 1821 (c.25)
Quartering of Soldiers Act 1822 (c.20)
Quartering of Soldiers Act 1823 (c.20)
Quartering of Soldiers Act 1824 (c.31)
Quartering of Soldiers Act 1825 (c.20)
Quartering of Soldiers Act 1826 (c.14)
Quartering of Soldiers Act 1826 (c.24)
Quartering of Soldiers Act 1828 (c.8)
Quartering of Soldiers Act 1828 (c.9)
Quays, etc. Between Tower and London Bridge Act 1832 (c.66)
Quebec Act 1774 (c.88)
Quebec Act 1852 (c.53)
Quebec Civil Government Charges Act 1831 (c.23)
Queen Anne's Bounty Act 1714 (c.10)
Queen Anne's Bounty Act 1803 (c.107)
Queen Anne's Bounty Act 1805 (c.84)
Queen Anne's Bounty Act 1838 (c.20)
Queen Anne's Bounty Act 1840 (c.20)
Queen Anne's Bounty (Superannuation) Act 1870 (c.89)
Queen's Bench (Ireland) Procedure Act 1872 (c.28)
Queen Caroline's Servants' Pension Act 1822 (c.98)
Queen's Colleges (Ireland) Act 1845 (c.66)
Queen's Prison Act 1842 (c.22)
Queen's Prison Act 1848 (c.7)
Queen's Prison Act 1860 (c.60)
Queen's Prison Discontinuance Act 1862 (c.104)
Queen's Remembrance Act 1859 (c.21)
Queensferry, Firth of Forth: Finance Act 1814 (c.138)

Rabies Act 1974 (c.17)
Race Relations Act 1965 (c.73)
Race Relations Act 1968 (c.71)
Race Relations Act 1976 (c.74)
Race Relations (Remedies) Act 1994 (c.10)
Racecourse Betting Act 1928 (c.41)
Racecourse Licensing Act 1879 (c.18)
Radioactive Material (Road Transport) Act 1991 (c.27)
Radioactive Substances Act 1948 (c.37)
Radioactive Substances Act 1960 (c.34)
Radioactive Substances Act 1993 (c.12)
Radiological Protection Act 1970 (c.46)
Rag Flock Act 1911 (c.52)
Rag Flock Act (1911) Amendment Act 1928 (c.39)
Rag Flock and Other Filling Materials Act 1951 (c.63)
Railways Act 1848 (c.3)
Railways Act 1974 (c.48)
Railway and Canal Commission (Abolition) Act 1949 (c.11)
Railway and Canal Commission (Consents) Act 1922 (c.47)
Railway and Canal Traffic Act 1854 (c.31)
Railway and Canal Traffic Act 1888 (c.25)
Railway and Canal Traffic Act 1892 (c.44)
Railway and Canal Traffic Act 1894 (c.54)
Railway and Canal Traffic Act 1913 (c.29)
Railway and Canal Traffic (Provisional Orders) Amendment Act 1891 (c.12)
Railway Assessors (Scotland) Superannuation Act 1897 (c.12)
Railway Clauses Act 1863 (c.92)
Railway Companies Act 1867 (c.127)
Railway Companies Act 1868 (c.79)
Railway Companies Act 1875 (c.31)
Railway Companies (Accounts and Returns) Act 1911 (c.34)
Railway Companies Arbitration Act 1859 (c.59)
Railway Companies (Ireland) Act 1867 (c.138)
Railway Companies (Ireland) Temporary Advances Act 1866 (c.95)
Railway Companies (Ireland) Temporary Advances Act 1868 (c.94)
Railway Companies Meetings Act 1869 (c.6)
Railway Companies Mortgage Trans. (Scotland) Act 1861 (c.50)
Railway Companies' Powers Act 1864 (c.120)
Railway Companies (Scotland) Act 1867 (c.126)
Railway Companies Securities Act 1866 (c.108)
Railway Employment (Prevention of Accidents) Act 1900 (c.27)
Railway Fires Act 1904 (c.11)
Railway Freight Rebates Act 1936 (c.2)
Railway Freight Rebates Act 1943 (c.23)
Railway Passenger Duty Act 1917 (c.3)
Railway Regulation Act 1851 (c.64)
Railway Regulation Act 1893 (c.29)
Railway Regulation Act (Returns of Signal Arrangements, Working &c.) Act 1873 (c.76)
Railway Returns (Continuous Brakes) Act 1878 (c.20)

Railways Act 1921 (c.55)
Railways Act 1993 (c.43)
Railways (Agreement) Act 1935 (c.6)
Railways Agreement (Powers) Act 1941 (c.5)
Railways and Canals Act 1860 (c.41)
Railways (Authorisation of Works) Act 1923 (c.30)
Railways Clauses Act 1863 (c.92)
Railways Clauses Consolidation Act 1845 (c.20)
Railways Clauses Consolidation (Scotland) Act 1845 (c.33)
Railways Commission Act 1846 (c.105)
Railway Companies Dissolution 1846 (c.28)
Railways Construction Amendment (Ireland) Act 1880 (c.31)
Railways Construction Facilities Act 1864 (c.121)
Railways (Conveyance of Mails) Act 1838 (c.98)
Railways (Electrical Power) Act 1903 (c.30)
Railways Employment (Prevention of Accidents) Act 1900 (c.27)
Railways (Extension of Time) Act 1868 (c.18)
Railway Fires Act 1905 (c.11)
Railway Fires Act (1905) Amendment Act 1923 (c.27)
Railways (Ireland) Act 1856 (c.72)
Railways (Ireland) Act 1858 (c.34)
Railways (Ireland) Act 1864 (c.71)
Railways (Ireland) Act 1867 (c.104)
Railways (Ireland) Act 1890 (c.52)
Railways (Ireland) Act 1896 (c.34)
Railway Passenger Duty Act 1842 (c.79)
Railway Passenger Duty Act 1847 (c.42)
Railways (Powers and Construction) Acts, 1864, Amendment Act 1870 (c.19)
Railways (Private Sidings) Act 1904 (c.19)
Railway Regulation Act 1840 (c.97)
Railway Regulation Act 1842 (c.55)
Railway Regulation Act 1844 (c.85)
Railway Regulation (Gauge) Act 1846 (c.57)
Railway Rolling Stock Protection Act 1872 (c.50)
Railway (Sales and Leases) Act 1845 (c.96)
Railways Act 1921 (c.55)
Railways Act (Ireland) 1851 (c.70)
Railways Act (Ireland) 1860 (c.97)
Railways (Private Sidings) Act 1904 (c.19)
Railways (Settlement of Claims) Act 1921 (c.59)
Railways Traverse Act 1868 (c.70)
Railways (Valuation for Rating) Act 1930 (c.24)
Railways (Valuation for Rating) Act 1946 (c.61)
Ramsey (Huntingdonshire): Drainage, etc. Act 1796 (c.72)
Ramsgate Harbour Act 1797 (c.86)
Ramsgate: Improvement Act 1796 (c.43)
Ranges Act 1891 (c.54)
Rate in Aid of Distressed Unions Act 1849 (c.24)
Rate Rebate Act 1973 (c.28)
Rate of Interest Act 1821 (c.51)
Rate of Interest Act 1822 (c.47)
Rate Support Grants Act 1986 (c.54)
Rate Support Grants Act 1987 (c.5)
Rate Support Grants Act 1988 (c.51)
Rateable Property (Ireland) Act 1846 (c.110)
Rates Act 1984 (c.33)
Rates of Carriage of Goods Act 1827 (c.39)
Rates (Proceedings for Recovery) Act 1914 (c.85)
Rating Act 1874 (c.54)
Rating Act 1966 (c.9)
Rating Act 1971 (c.39)
Rating and Valuation Act 1925 (c.90)
Rating and Valuation Act 1928 (c.8)
Rating and Valuation Act 1932 (c.18)
Rating and Valuation Act 1937 (c.60)
Rating and Valuation Act 1957 (c.17)
Rating and Valuation Act 1959 (c.36)
Rating and Valuation Act 1961 (c.45)
Rating and Valuation (Air-Raid Works) Act 1938 (c.65)
Rating and Valuation (Air-Raid Works) (Scotland) Act 1938 (c.66)
Rating and Valuation (Amendment) (Scotland) Act 1984 (c.31)
Rating and Valuation (Apportionment) Act 1928 (c.44)
Rating and Valuation (Miscellaneous Provisions) Act 1955 (c.9)
Rating and Valuation (No. 2) Act 1932 (c.33)
Rating and Valuation (Postponement of Valuations) Act 1938 (c.19)
Rating and Valuation (Postponement of Valuations) Act 1940 (c.12)
Rating and Valuation (Scotland) Act 1952 (c.47)
Rating (Caravan Sites) Act 1976 (c.15)
Rating (Charity Shops) Act 1976 (c.45)
Rating (Disabled Persons) Act 1978 (c.40)
Rating Exemption (Scotland) Act 1874 (c.20)
Rating (Interim Relief) Act 1964 (c.18)
Rating of Small Tenements Act 1850 (c.99)
Rating of Small Tenements Act 1851 (c.39)
Rating (Revaluation Rebates) (Scotland) Act 1985 (c.33)
Rating (Scotland) Act 1926 (c.47)
Rating (Scotland) Amendment Act 1928 (c.6)
Rating (War Damage Insurance) Act 1941 (c.25)
Rating (War Damages) (Scotland) Act 1941 (c.25)
Rats and Mice (Destruction) Act 1919 (c.72)
Reading Charities Act 1861 (c.23)
Ready Money Football Betting Act 1920 (c.52)
Real Estate Charges Act 1854 (c.113)
Real Estate Charges Act 1867 (c.69)
Real Etate Charges Act 1877 (c.34)
Real Property Act 1845 (c.106)
Real Property Limitation Act 1833 (c.27)
Real Property Limitation Act 1837 (c.28)

Real Property Limitation Act 1874 (c.57)
Real Rights Act 1693 (c.22)
Rebuilding of London Bridge Act 1823 (c.50)
Recall of Army and Air Force Pensions Act 1948 (c.8)
Recaptured British-built Ships Act 1809 (c.41)
Receipt and Remittance of Taxes, etc. Act 1831 (c.18)
Receipt Stamps Act 1828 (c.27)
Receiver General of Stamps Act 1806 (c.76)
Receivers of Crown Rents Act 1816 (c.16)
Receivers of Stolen Goods, etc., Act 1822 (c.24)
Recess Elections Act 1784 (c.26)
Recess Elections Act 1975 (c.66)
Reclamation of Lands, etc. Act 1842 (c.105)
Reclamation of Lands, etc. (Ireland) Act 1831 (c.57)
Recognition of Divorces and Legal Separations Act 1971 (c.53)
Recognition of Trusts Act 1987 (c.14)
Recognizances (Ireland) Act 1809 (c.83)
Recognizances (Ireland) Act 1817 (c.56)
Record of Title (Ireland) Act 1865 (c.88)
Recorded Delivery Service Act 1962 (c.27)
Recorders' Courts of Quarter Sessions Act 1837 (c.19)
Recorders, Magistrates and Clerks of the Peace Act 1888 (c.23)
Recorders, Stipendiary Magistrates and Clerks of the Peace Act 1906 (c.46)
Recoveries in Copyhold, etc. Courts Act 1807 (c.8)
Recovery of Advowsons in Ireland Act 1844 (c.27)
Recovery of Alimony (Ireland) Act 1867 (c.11)
Recovery of Possession by Landlords Act 1820 (c.87)
Recovery of Small Tithes Act 1826 (c.15)
Recovery of Tenements, etc. (Ireland) Act 1816 (c.88)
Recovery of Tenements, etc. (Ireland) Act 1818 (c.39)
Recovery of Tenements (Ireland) Act 1820 (c.41)
Recovery of Tithes (Ireland) Act 1832 (c.41)
Recovery of Wages (Ireland) Act 1814 (c.116)
Recovery of Wages (Ireland) Act 1849 (c.15)
Recreation Grounds Act 1859 (c.27)
Recreational Charities Act 1958 (c.17)
Rectifying of Spirits (Ireland) Act 1807 (c.19)
Rectory of Ewelme Act 1871 (c.23)
Rectory of Ledbury Act 1855 (c.92)
Red Sea and India Telegraph Company Act 1861 (c.4)
Red Sea and India Telegraph Company Act 1862 (c.39)
Redemption of Rent (Ireland) Act 1891 (c.57)
Redemption of Standard Securities (Scotland) Act 1971 (c.45)
Redistribution of Seats Act 1885 (c.23)
Redistribution of Seats (Ireland) Act 1918 (c.65)
Redstone Bridge, Severn Act 1795 (c.108)
Reduction of Annuity Tax Act 1867 (c.107)
Reduction of Duty on Rum Act 1863 (c.102)
Reduction of National Debt 1809 (c.64)
Reduction of National Debt Act 1822 (c.9)
Reduction of National Debt Act 1858 (c.38)
Reduction of National Debt Act 1860 (c.71)
Reductions Ex Capite Lecti Abolished Act 1871 (c.81)
Redundancy Fund Act 1981 (c.5)
Redundancy Payments Act 1965 (c.62)
Redundancy Rebates Act 1969 (c.8)
Redundancy Rebates Act 1977 (c.22)
Redundant Churches and Other Religious Buildings Act 1969 (c.22)
Re-election of Ministers Act 1915 (c.50)
Re-election of Ministers Act 1916 (c.22)
Re-election of Ministers Act 1919 (c.2)
Re-election of Ministers Act (1919) Amendment 1926 (c.19)
Re-election of Ministers (No.2) Act 1916 (c.56)
Referendum Act 1975 (c.33)
Refined Sugar Bounties Act 1824 (c.35)
Reformatory and Industrial Schools Act 1891 (c.23)
Reformatory and Industrial Schools Acts Amendment Act 1872 (c.21)
Reformatory and Industrial Schools (Channel Islands Children) Act 1895 (c.17)
Reformatory and Industrial Schools (Manx Children) Act 1884 (c.40)
Reformatory, etc. Schools Act 1856 (c.109)
Reformatory Institutions (Ireland) Act 1881 (c.29)
Reformatory Schools Act 1856 (c.28)
Reformatory Schools Act 1866 (c.117)
Reformatory Schools Act 1893 (c.15)
Reformatory Schools Act 1893 (c.48)
Reformatory Schools Act 1899 (c.12)
Reformatory Schools (England) Act 1854 (c.74)
Reformatory Schools (England) Act 1857 (c.55)
Reformatory Schools (Ireland) Act 1858 (c.103)
Refreshment Houses Act 1860 (c.27)
Refreshment Houses Act 1964 (c.88)
Refreshment Houses Act 1967 (c.38)
Refreshment Houses (Ireland) Act 1860 (c.107)
Refuse Disposal (Amenity) Act 1978 (c.3)
Regency Act 1830 (c.2)
Regency Act 1840 (c.52)
Regency Act 1910 (c.26)
Regency Act 1937 (c.16)
Regency Act 1943 (c.42)
Regency Act 1953 (c.1)
Regency Act Amendment Act 1838 (c.24)
Regent's Park, Regent Street Act 1851 (c.95)
Regent's Park, Regent Street, etc. Act 1817 (c.24)

Regent's Park, Regent Street, etc. Act 1824 (c.100)
Regent's Park, Regent Street, etc. Act 1831 (c.29)
Regent's Park, Regent Street, etc. Act 1832 (c.56)
Regent's Quadrant Colonnade Act 1848 (c.50)
Regent Street, etc. Act 1825 (c.38)
Regent Street Act 1828 (c.64)
Regent Street Act 1829 (c.61)
Regent Street, Caslton Place Act 1826 (c.77)
Regent Street, etc. Act 1828 (c.70)
Regiment of Cornwall and Devon Miners Act 1798 (c.74)
Regimental Accounts Act 1808 (c.128)
Regimental Benefit Societies Act 1849 (c.71)
Regimental Charitable Funds Act 1935 (c.11)
Regimental Debts Act 1863 (c.57)
Regimental Debts Act 1893 (c.5)
Regimental Debts (Deposit of Wills) (Scotland) Act 1919 (c.89)
Regimental Exchange Act 1875 (c.16)
Regional Commissioners Act 1939 (c.76)
Regional Development Grants (Termination) Act 1988 (c.11)
Register of Sasines Act 1828 (c.19)
Register of Sasines (Scotland) Act 1987 (c.23)
Registered Designs Act 1949 (c.88)
Registered Establishments (Scotland) Act 1987 (c.40)
Registered Homes Act 1984 (c.23)
Registered Homes (Amendment) Act 1991 (c.20)
Registering of British Vessels Act 1845 (c.89)
Registering of Vessels Act 1823 (c.41)
Registers of Sasines (Scotland) Act 1848 (c.74)
Registrar General (Scotland) Act 1920 (c.69)
Registration Acceleration Act 1894 (c.32)
Registration Act 1885 (c.15)
Registration Act 1908 (c.21)
Registration Amendment (Ireland) Act 1868 (c.112)
Registration Amendment (Scotland) Act 1885 (c.)
Registration Appeals (Ireland) Act 1885 (c.66)
Registration (Ireland) Act 1898 (c.2)
Registration of Aliens Act 1836 (c.11)
Registration of Assurances (Ireland) Act 1850 (c.72)
Registration of Births and Deaths (Ireland) Act 1863 (c.11)
Registration of Births, Deaths and Marriages (Army) Act 1879 (c.8)
Registration of Births, Deaths and Marriages (Scotland) Act 1854 (c.80)
Registration of Births, Deaths and Marriages (Scotland) Act 1855 (c.29)
Registration of Births, Deaths and Marriages (Scotland) Act 1860 (c.85)
Registration of Births, Deaths and Marriages (Scotland) Act 1965 (c.49)
Registration of Births, Deaths and Marriages (Scotland) Amendment Act 1910 (c.32)
Registration of Births, Deaths and Marriages (Scotland) (Amendment) Act 1934 (c.19)
Registration of Births, Deaths and Marriages (Special Provisions) Act 1957 (c.58)
Registration of Births, etc. Act 1836 (c.1)
Registration of Burials Act 1864 (c.97)
Registration of Business Names Act 1916 (c.58)
Registration of Certain Writs (Scotland) Act 1891 (c.9)
Registration of Clubs (Ireland) Act 1904 (c.9)
Registration of County Electors (Extension of Time) Act 1889 (c.19)
Registration of County Voters (Ireland) Act 1864 (c.22)
Registration of Deeds (Ireland) Act 1864 (c.76)
Registration of Electors 1891 (c.18)
Registration of Leases (Scotland) Act 1857 (c.26)
Registration of Leases (Scotland) Amendment Act 1877 (c.36)
Registration of Marriages (Ireland) Act 1863 (c.90)
Registration of Still-Births (Scotland) Act 1938 (c.55)
Registration of Voters (Ireland) Act 1973 (c.30)
Registration Service Act 1953 (c.37)
Registry Courts (Ireland) Amendment Act 1879 (c.71)
Registry, etc. of Colonial Slaves Act 1819 (c.120)
Registry of Admiralty Court Act 1813 (c.151)
Registry of Boats, etc. Act 1795 (c.58)
Registry of Deeds Act 1822 (c.116)
Registry of Deeds Act 1832 (c.87)
Registry of Deeds Act 1875 (c.5)
Registry of Deeds, etc. (Ireland) Act 1828 (c.57)
Registry of Deeds Office (Ireland) Holidays Act 1883 (c.20)
Registry of Ships Act 1796 (c.112)
Registry of Ships Built in India Act 1815 (c.116)
Registry of Wool Act 1821 (c.81)
Regrating and Ingrossing of Oaken Bark Act 1807 (c.53)
Regular and Elders' Widows' Funds Act 1897 (c.11)
Regulation of Factories Act 1834 (c.1)
Regulation of Railways Act 1868 (c.119)
Regulation of Railways Act 1871 (c.78)
Regulation of Railways Act 1873 (c.48)
Regulation of Railways Acts, 1873 and 1874, Continuance Act 1879 (c.56)
Regulation of Railways Act 1889 (c.57)
Regulation of the Forces Act 1871 (c.86)
Regulation of the Forces Act 1881 (c.57)

Rehabilitation of Offenders Act 1974 (c.53)
Reinstatement in Civil Employment Act 1944 (c.15)
Reinstatement in Civil Employment Act 1950 (c.10)
Reinsurance (Acts of Terrorism) Act 1993 (c.18)
Released Persons (Poor Law Relief) Act 1907 (c.14)
Relief as to Transferable Stocks, etc. Act 1812 (c.158)
Relief of Bankers Act 1824 (c.73)
Relief of Certain Bishops Act 1843 (c.57)
Relief of Certain Curates (England) Act 1803 (c.2)
Relief of Certain Incumbents Act 1824 (c.89)
Relief of Debtors Act 1799 (c.50)
Relief of Debtors in Prison Act 1812 (c.160)
Relief of Discharged Soldiers and Sailors Act 1803 (c.61)
Relief of Distress Act 1849 (c.63)
Relief of Distress (Ireland) Act 1880 (c.4)
Relief of Distress (Ireland) Amendment Act 1880 (c.14)
Relief of Distressed Unions (Ireland) Act 1883 (c.24)
Relief of Families of Militiamen Act 1803 (c.47)
Relief of Families of Militiamen (Scotland) Act 1809 (c.90)
Relief of Families of Militiamen (Ireland) Act 1811 (c.78)
Relief of Families of Militiamen Act 1812 (c.28)
Relief of Insolvent Debtors Act 1797 (c.112)
Relief of Prisoners Act 1797 (c.85)
Relief of Prisoners for Debt Act 1809 (c.6)
Relief of the Poor Act 1795 (c.23)
Relief of the Poor Act 1810 (c.50)
Relief of the Poor Act 1812 (c.73)
Relief of Revenue Prisoners Act 1795 (c.96)
Relief of Rutson & Company Act 1820 (c.30)
Relief of Sailors Abroad Act 1818 (c.38)
Relief of Shipwrecked Mariners, etc. Act 1814 (c.126)
Relief of Stress (Ireland) Act 1849 (c.5)
Relief of Traders for Grenada, etc. Act (c.127)
Relief to Chelsea, etc. Pensioners Act 1825 (c. 27)
Relief to Holders of Certain Securities Act 1818 (c.93)
Religious Congregations, etc. (Scotland) Act 1850 (c.13)
Religious Disabilities Act 1846 (c.59)
Remedies Against the Hundred (England) Act 1827 (c.31)
Remission of Penalties Act 1859 (c.32)
Remission of Penalties Act 1875 (c.80)
Remission of Rates (London) Act 1940 (c.32)
Removal of Goods Act 1812 (c.142)
Removal of Goods for Exportation, etc. Act 1808 (c.126)
Removal of Indictments into King's Bench Act 1835 (c.33)
Removal of Offensive Matter Act 1906 (c.45)
Removal of Prisoners in Custody Act 1854 (c.115)
Removal of Slaves Act 1820 (c.50)
Removal of Wool Act 1814 (c.78)
Removal of Wrecks Act 1877 (c.16)
Removal of Wrecks Act, 1877, Amendment Act 1889 (c.5)
Removal Terms Act 1886 (c.50)
Removal Terms (Burghs) (Scotland) Act 1881 (c.39)
Removal Terms (Scotland) Act, 1886, Amendment Act 1890 (c.36)
Remuneration, Charges and Grants Act 1975 (c.57)
Remuneration of Teachers Act 1963 (c.20)
Remuneration of Teachers Act 1965 (c.3)
Remuneration of Teachers (Scotland) Act 1967 (c.36)
Renewable Leasehold Conversion Act 1849 (c.105)
Renewable Leasehold Conversion (Ireland) Act 1868 (c.62)
Renewal of Leases (Ireland) Act 1838 (c.62)
Rent Act 1957 (c.25)
Rent Act 1965 (c.75)
Rent Act 1968 (c.23)
Rent Act 1974 (c.51)
Rent Act 1977 (c.42)
Rent (Agricultural) Amendment Act 1977 (c.17)
Rent (Agriculture) Act 1976 (c.80)
Rent (Amendment) Act 1985 (c.24)
Rent and Mortgage Interest Restrictions Act 1923 (c.32)
Rent and Mortgage Interest Restriction Act 1939 (c.71)
Rent and Mortgage Interest Restrictions (Amendment) Act 1933 (c.32)
Rent and Mortgage Interest (Restrictions Continuance) Act 1925 (c.32)
Rent (Control of Increases) Act 1969 (c.62)
Rent of Furnished Houses Control (Scotland) Act 1943 (c.44)
Rent Rebate Act 1973 (c.28)
Rent Restrictions (Notices of Increase) Act 1923 (c.13)
Rent (Scotland) Act 1971 (c.28)
Rent (Scotland) Act 1984 (c.58)
Rentcharges Act 1977 (c.30)
Rents of the Rolls Estate, etc. Act 1820 (c.107)
Reorganisation of Offices (Scotland) Act 1928 (c.34)
Reorganisation of Offices (Scotland) Act 1939 (c.20)
Repair of Blenheim Palace Act 1840 (c.43)
Repair of Roads and Bridges (Ireland) Act 1825 (c.101)
Repair of War Damage Act 1941 (c.34)
Repatriation of Prisoners Act 1984 (c.47)
Repayment of Advances (Ireland) Act 1852 (c.16)

Repayment of Certain Loans Act 1802 (c.39)
Repayment of Duty in Certain Cases Act 1810 (c.39)
Repeal of Acts Concerning Importation Act 1822 (cc.41, 42)
Repeal of 39 Eliz. c.17 Act 1812 (c.31)
Repeal of 41 Geo. 3 (Great Britain) 1801 (c.4)
Repeal of Certain Duties Act 1800 (c.69)
Repeal of Certain Duties Act 1824 (c.22)
Repeal, etc. of Certain Duties Act 1802 (c.103)
Repeal of a Certain Tax Act 1801 (c.100)
Repeal of Obsolete Statutes Act 1856 (c.64)
Repeal of Part of 15 Geo.3.c.31 Act 1850 (c.80)
Repeal of Salt Duties Act 1824 (c.65)
Repeal of Sir J. Barnard's Act 1860 (c.28)
Repeal of Nore Tolls Act 1859 (c.29)
Representation of the People Act 1832 (c.45)
Representation of the People Act 1832 (c.88)
Representation of the People Act 1867 (c.102)
Representation of the People Act 1884 (c.3)
Representation of the People Act 1918 (c.64)
Representation of the People Act 1920 (c.15)
Representation of the People Act 1921 (c.34)
Representation of the People Act 1922 (c.12)
Representation of the People Act 1945 (c.5)
Representation of the People Act 1948 (c.65)
Representation of the People Act 1949 (c.68)
Representation of the People Act 1968 (c.15)
Representation of the People Act 1969 (c.15)
Representation of the People Act 1974 (c.10)
Representation of the People Act 1977 (c.9)
Representation of the People Act 1978 (c.32)
Representation of the People Act 1979 (c.40)
Representation of the People Act 1980 (c.3)
Representation of the People Act 1981 (c.34)
Representation of the People Act 1983 (c.2)
Representation of the People Act 1985 (c.50)
Representation of the People Act 1989 (c.28)
Representation of the People Act 1990 (c.32)
Representation of the People Act 1991 (c.11)
Representation of the People Act 1993 (c.29)
Representation of the People (Amendment) Act 1918 (c.50)
Representation of the People Amendment Act 1957 (c.43)
Representation of the People Amendment Act 1958 (c.9)
Representation of the People (Armed Forces) Act 1976 (c.29)
Representation of the People (Equal Franchise) Act 1928 (c.12)
Representation of the People (Ireland) Act 1850 (c.69)
Representation of the People (Ireland) Act 1861 (c.60)
Representation of the People (Ireland) Act 1868 (c.49)
Representation of the People (No. 2) Act 1920 (c.35)
Representation of the People (No. 2) Act 1922 (c.41)
Representation of the People (No. 2) Act 1974 (c.13)
Representation of the People (Reading University) Act 1928 (c.25)
Representation of the People (Returning Officers' Expenses) Act 1919 (c.8)
Representation of the People (Scotland) Act 1832 (c.65)
Representation of the People (Scotland) Act 1868 (c.48)
Representative Peers (Ireland) Act 1857 (c.33)
Representative Peers (Scotland) Act 1847 (c.52)
Representative Peers (Scotland) Act 1851 (c.87)
Representative Peers (Scotland) Act 1852 (c.35)
Reprisals Against Foreign Ships, etc. Act 1808 (c.132)
Reproductive Loan Fund Act 1874 (c.86)
Republic of Gambia Act 1970 (c.37)
Republic of South Africa (Temporary Provisions) Act 1961 (c.23)
Requirements of Writing (Scotland) Act 1995 (c.7)
Requisitioned Houses Act 1960 (c.20)
Requisitioned Houses and Housing (Amendment) Act 1955 (c.24)
Requisitioned Land and War Works Act 1945 (c.43)
Requisitioned Land and War Works Act 1947 (c.17)
Requisitioned Land and War Works Act 1948 (c.17)
Resale Prices Act 1964 (c.58)
Resale Prices Act 1976 (c.53)
Rescue Act 1821 (c.88)
Reserve and Auxiliary Forces Act 1939 (c.24)
Reserve and Auxiliary Forces (Protection of Civil Interests) Act 1951 (c.65)
Reserve and Auxiliary Forces (Training) Act 1951 (c.23)
Reserve Force Act 1859 (c.42)
Reserve Force Act 1867 (c.110)
Reserve Forces Act 1870 (c.67)
Reserve Forces Act 1882 (c.48)
Reserve Forces Act 1890 (c.42)
Reserve Forces Act 1899 (c.40)
Reserve Forces Act 1900 (c.62)
Reserve Forces Act 1906 (c.11)
Reserve Forces Act 1937 (c.17)
Reserve Forces Act 1966 (c.30)
Reserve Forces Act 1980 (c.9)
Reserve Forces Act 1982 (c.14)
Reserve Forces and Militia Act 1898 (c.9)
Reserve Forces (Safeguard of Employment) Act 1985 (c.17)
Reservoirs Act 1975 (c.23)
Reservoirs (Safety Provisions) Act 1930 (c.51)
Residence in France During the War Act 1798 (c.79)

Residence of Incumbents Act 1869 (c.109)
Residence on Benefices, etc. (England) Act 1814 (c.175)
Residence on Benefices, etc. (England) Act 1816 (c.6)
Residence on Benefices, etc. (England) Act 1816 (c.123)
Residence on Benefices, etc. (England) Act 1817 (c.99)
Resident Magistrates and Police Commissioners Salaries Act 1874 (c.23)
Resident Magistrates (Belfast) Act 1911 (c.58)
Resident Magistrates (Ireland) Act 1920 (c.38)
Resident Magistrates (Ireland) Act 1853 (c.60)
Residential Homes Act 1980 (c.7)
Resignation Bonds Act 1827 (c.25)
Responsibility of Shipowners Act 1813 (c.159)
Restoration of Order in Ireland Act 1920 (c.31)
Restoration of Order In Ireland (Indemnity) Act 1923 (c.12)
Restoration of Pre-War Practices Act 1919 (c.42)
Restoration of Pre-War Trade Practices Act 1942 (c.9)
Restoration of Pre-War Trade Practices Act 1950 (c.9)
Restriction of Advertisement (War Risks Insurance) Act 1939 (c.120)
Restriction of Offensive Weapons Act 1959 (c.37)
Restriction of Ribbon Development (Temporary Development) Act 1943 (c.34)
Restrictions of Ribbon Development Act 1935 (c.47)
Restriction on Cash Payments Act 1797 (c.1)
Restriction on Cash Payments Act 1797 (c.45)
Restriction on Cash Payments Act 1797 (c.91)
Restriction on Cash Payments Act 1802 (c.40)
Restriction on Cash Payments Act 1802 (c.45)
Restriction on Cash Payments Act 1803 (c.1)
Restriction on Cash Payments Act 1803 (c.18)
Restriction on Cash Payments Act 1803 (c.44)
Restriction on Cash Payments Act 1814 (c.99)
Restriction on Cash Payments Act 1814 (c.130)
Restriction on Cash Payments Act 1815 (c.28)
Restriction on Cash Payments Act 1815 (c.41)
Restriction on Cash Payments Act 1816 (c.40)
Restriction on Cash Payments Act 1816 (c.48)
Restriction on Cash Payments Act 1818 (c.37)
Restriction on Cash Payments Act 1818 (c.60)
Restriction on Cash Payments (Ireland) Act 1804 (c.21)
Restrictive Practices Court Act 1976 (c.33)
Restrictive Trade Practices Act 1956 (c.68)
Restrictive Trade Practices Act 1968 (c.66)
Restrictive Trade Practices Act 1976 (c.34)
Restrictive Trade Practices Act 1977 (c.19)
Restrictive Trade Practices (Stock Exchange) Act 1984 (c.2)
Resumption of Cash Payments Act 1819 (c.49)
Resumption of Cash Payments Act 1819 (c.99)
Retail Brewers Act 1828 (c.68)
Retail Meat Dealers' Shops (Sunday Closing) Act 1936 (c.30)
Retailing of Spirits (Scotland) Act 1818 (c.13)
Retail of Sweets, etc. Act 1834 (c.77)
Retired Officers (Civil Employment) Act 1919 (c.40)
Retirement of Officers on Half Pay Act 1811 (c.103)
Retirement of Officers on Half Pay Act 1812 (c.151)
Retirement of Teachers (Scotland) Act 1976 (c.65)
Return of Persons Committed, etc. Act 1815 (c.49)
Returning Officers Act 1854 (c.57)
Returning Officers (Scotland) Act 1886 (c.58)
Returning Officers (Scotland) Act 1891 (c.49)
Returning Officers (Scotland) Act 1977 (c.14)
Returns to Secretary of State Act 1858 (c.67)
Revenue Act 1845 (c.76)
Revenue Act 1862 (c.22)
Revenue Act 1863 (c.33)
Revenue Act 1865 (c.30)
Revenue Act 1866 (c.36)
Revenue Act 1867 (c.114)
Revenue Act 1867 (c.90)
Revenue Act 1868 (c.28)
Revenue Act 1869 (c.14)
Revenue Act 1883 (c.55)
Revenue Act 1884 (c.62)
Revenue Act 1889 (c.42)
Revenue Act 1898 (c.46)
Revenue Act 1903 (c.46)
Revenue Act 1906 (c.20)
Revenue Act 1909 (c.43)
Revenue Act 1911 (c.2)
Revenue Act 1968 (c.11)
Revenue Buildings, Liverpool Act 1832 (c.14)
Revenue Departments Accounts Act 1861 (c.93)
Revenue, Friendly Societies and National Debt Act 1882 (c.72)
Revenue (Ireland) Act 1806 (c.106)

Revenue (Ireland) Act 1821 (c.90)
Revenue Inquiry Act 1824 (c.7)
Revenue (No. 1) Act 1861 (c.21)
Revenue (No. 1) Act 1864 (c.18)
Revenue (No. 2) Act 1861 (c.91)
Revenue (No. 2) Act 1864 (c.56)
Revenue (No. 2) Act 1865 (c.96)
Revenue of Scotland Act 1718 (c.20)
Revenue Officers' Disabilities Act 1868 (c.73)
Revenue Officers' Disabilities Removal Act 1874 (c.22)
Revenue Offices (Scotland) Holidays Act 1880 (c.17)
Revenue Solicitors Act 1828 (c.25)
Revenue (Transfer of Charges) Act 1856 (c.59)
Revenues of Archbishopric of Armagh Act 1864 (c.81)
Reverend J. G. MacManaway's Indemnity Act 1951 (c.29)
Reverter of Sites Act 1987 (c.15)
Review of Justices' Decisions Act 1872 (c.26)
Revising Barristers Act 1866 (c.54)
Revising Barristers Act 1873 (c.70)
Revising Barristers Act 1874 (c.53)
Revising Barristers Act 1885 (c.57)
Revising Barristers Act 1886 (c.42)
Revising Barristers (Ireland) Act 1886 (c.43)
Revision of the Army and Air Force Acts (Transitional Provisions) Act 1955 (c.20)
Revival of Expired Laws, etc. Jamaica Act 1839 (c.26)
Rhodesia and Nyasaland Federation Act 1953 (c.30)
Rhodesia and Nyasaland Act 1963 (c.34)
Richmond Lunatic Asylum Act 1815 (c.107)
Richmond Lunatic Asylum Act 1830 (c.22)
Richmond Lunatic Asylum Act 1831 (c.13)
Richmond Penitentiary, etc. Act 1836 (c.51)
Richmond to Lancaster Road Act 1795 (c.157)
Riding Establishments Act 1939 (c.56)
Riding Establishments Act 1964 (c.70)
Riding Establishments Act 1970 (c.32)
Rifle Volunteer Grounds Act 1860 (c.140)
Rifle Volunteer Grounds Act 1862 (c.41)
Right of Light Act 1959 (c.56)
Rights of Entry (Gas and Electricity Boards) Act 1954 (c.21)
Rights of Way Act 1932 (c.45)
Rights of Way Act 1990 (c.24)
Rights of Way Near Aldershot Camp Act 1856 (c.66)
Riot Act 1714 (c.5)
Riot (Damages) Act 1886 (c.38)
Riotous Assemblies (Scotland) Act 1822 (c.33)
River Boards Act 1948 (c.32)
River Itchin: Navigation Act 1795 (c.86)
River Ivel: Navigation Act 1795 (c.105)
River Liffey, Dublin Act 1833 (c.26)
River Ness Act 1855 (c.113)
River Navigation Improvement (Ireland) Act 1914 (c.55)
River Ouze: Navigation Act 1795 (c.77)
River Poddle Act 1840 (c.58)
River Thames and Isis: Navigation Act 1795 (c.106)
Rivers Pollution Prevention Act 1876 (c.75)
Rivers Pollution Prevention Act 1893 (c.31)
Rivers Pollution Prevention (Border Councils) Act 1898 (c.34)
Rivers (Prevention of Pollution) Act 1951 (c.64)
Rivers (Prevention of Pollution) Act 1961 (c.50)
Rivers (Prevention of Pollution) (Scotland) Act 1951 (c.66)
Rivers (Prevention of Pollution) (Scotland) Act 1965 (c.13)
Road and Rail Traffic Act 1933 (c.53)
Road Haulage Wages Act 1938 (c.44)
Road Safety Act 1967 (c.30)
Road Traffic Act 1930 (c.43)
Road Traffic Act 1934 (c.50)
Road Traffic Act 1937 (c.44)
Road Traffic Act 1956 (c.67)
Road Traffic Act 1959 (c.16)
Road Traffic Act 1960 (c.16)
Road Traffic Act 1962 (c.59)
Road Traffic Act 1964 (c.45)
Road Traffic Act 1967 (c.21)
Road Traffic Act 1972 (c.20)
Road Traffic Act 1974 (c.50)
Road Traffic Act 1988 (c.52)
Road Traffic Act 1991 (c.40)
Road Traffic (Amendment) Act 1931 (c.32)
Road Traffic (Amendment) Act 1960 (c.51)
Road Traffic (Amendment) Act 1967 (c.70)
Road Traffic and Roads Improvement Act 1960 (c.63)
Road Traffic (Consequential Provisions) Act 1988 (c.54)
Road Traffic (Disqualification) Act 1970 (c.23)
Road Traffic (Driving Instruction by Disabled Persons) Act 1993 (c.31)
Road Traffic (Driver Licensing and Information Systems) Act 1989 (c.22)
Road Traffic (Drivers' Ages and Hours of Work) Act 1976 (c.3)
Road Traffic (Driving Instruction) Act 1967 (c.79)
Road Traffic (Driving Instruction) Act 1984 (c.13)
Road Traffic (Driving Licences) Act 1936 (c.23)
Road Traffic (Driving Licences) Act 1946 (c.8)
Road Traffic (Driving Licences) Act 1983 (c.43)
Road Traffic (Driving of Motor Cycles) Act 1960 (c.69)
Road Traffic (Foreign Vehicles) Act 1972 (c.27)
Road Traffic (New Drivers) Act 1995 (c.13)
Road Traffic Offenders Act 1988 (c.53)
Road Traffic (Production of Documents) Act 1985 (c.34)

Road Traffic Regulation Act 1967 (c.76)
Road Traffic Regulation Act 1984 (c.27)
Road Traffic Regulation (Parking) Act 1986 (c.27)
Road Traffic Regulation (Special Events) Act 1994 (c.11)
Road Traffic (Temporary Restrictions) Act 1991 (c.26)
Road Transport Lighting Act 1927 (c.37)
Road Transport Lighting Act 1953 (c.21)
Road Transport Lighting Act 1957 (c.51)
Road Transport Lighting Act 1967 (c.55)
Road Transport Lighting (No. 2) Act (c.22)
Road Transport Lighting (Amendment) Act 1958 (c.22)
Roads Act 1920 (c.72)
Roads Amendment Act 1880 (c.7)
Roads and Bridges (Scotland) Act 1848 (c.40)
Roads and Bridges (Scotland) Act 1878 (c.51)
Roads and Bridges (Scotland) Amendment Act 1892 (c.12)
Roads and Bridges (Scotland) Act 1878 Amendment Act 1888 (c.9)
Roads and Streets in Police Burghs (Scotland) Act 1891 (c.32)
Roads and Streets in Police Burghs (Scotland) Act 1925 (c.82)
Roads between London and Holyhead Act 1819 (c.48)
Roads, etc. (Ireland) Act 1827 (c.23)
Roads, etc. (Ireland) Act 1829 (c.40)
Roads, etc. (Scotland) Act 1833 (c.33)
Roads (Ireland) Act 1835 (c.31)
Roads Improvement Act 1925 (c.68)
Roads in Lanarkshire, etc. Act 1823 (c.10)
Roads (London to Chirk) Act 1820 (c.70)
Roads (Scotland) Act 1970 (c.20)
Roads (Scotland) Act 1984 (c.54)
Roasted Malt for Colouring Beer Act 1842 (c.30)
Robbery from the Person Act 1837 (c.87)
Rochdale Canal Company Act 1798 (c.49)
Rochdale Road Act 1795 (c.160)
Rochdale and Bury Road Act 1797 (c.145)
Rochdale and Bury and Sudden Roads Act 1797 (c.146)
Rochdale to Bury Road Act 1794 (c.124)
Rochdale Vicarage Act 1866 (c.86)
Rochdale Vicarage Appointment Act 1865 (c.117)
Rock Salt Act 1811 (c.82)
Roe Deer (Close Seasons) Act 1977 (c.4)
Rogue Money Act (Scotland) 1839 (c.65)
Roll of Valuation (1748) (c.29)
Rolls Estate Act 1837 (c.46)
Rolls-Royce (Purchase) Act 1971 (c.9)
Roman Catholic Act 1844 (c.102)
Roman Catholic Charities Act 1831 (c.115)
Roman Catholic Charities Act 1856 (c.76)
Roman Catholic Charities Act 1857 (c.76)
Roman Catholic Charities Act 1858 (c.51)
Roman Catholic Charities Act 1859 (c.50)
Roman Catholic Charities Act 1860 (c.134)
Roman Catholic Relief Act 1791 (c.32)
Roman Catholic Relief Act 1803 (c.30)
Roman Catholic Relief Act 1813 (c.128)
Roman Catholic Relief Act 1829 (c.7)
Roman Catholic Relief Act 1926 (c.55)
Roosevelt Memorial Act 1946 (c.83)
Ropeworks Act 1846 (c.40)
Rothwell Gaol Act 1845 (c.72)
Royal and Parliamentary Titles Act 1927 (c.4)
Royal Arsenals, etc. Act 1862 (c.78)
Royal Assent Act 1967 (c.23)
Royal Burghs (Scotland) Act 1822 (c.91)
Royal Burghs (Scotland) Act 1833 (c.76)
Royal Burghs, etc. (Scotland) Act 1834 (c.87)
Royal Canal Act 1818 (c.35)
Royal Canal Company Act 1813 (c.101)
Royal Exchange Assurance Act 1796 (c.26)
Royal Household, etc., Act 1812 (c.8)
Royal Irish Constabulary Act 1873 (c.74)
Royal Irish Constabulary (Widows' Pensions) Act 1954 (c.17)
Royal (Late Indian) Ordinance Corps Act 1874 (c.61)
Royal Marines Act 1820 (c.91)
Royal Marines Act 1847 (c.63)
Royal Marines Act 1857 (c.1)
Royal Marines Act 1914 (c.16)
Royal Marines Act 1916 (c.23)
Royal Marines Act 1939 (c.88)
Royal Marines Act 1946 (c.4)
Royal Marines Act 1948 (c.25)
Royal Military Asylum, Chelsea Act 1854 (c.61)
Royal Military Asylum Chelsea (Transfer) Act 1884 (c.32)
Royal Military Canal Act 1837 (c.20)
Royal Military Canal Act 1867 (c.140)
Royal Military Canal Act 1872 (c.66)
Royal Naval Asylum Act 181 (c.105)
Royal Naval Asylum, etc. Act 1825 (c.26)
Royal Naval Reserve Act 1902 (c.5)
Royal Naval Reserve Act 1927 (c.18)
Royal Naval Reserve (Volunteer) Act 1859 (c.40)
Royal Naval Reserve Volunteer Act 1896 (c.33)
Royal Naval Volunteer Reserve Act 1917 (c.22)
Royal Naval Volunteer Reserve Act 1942 (c.18)
Royal Niger Company Act 1899 (c.43)
Royal Patriotic Fund Corporation Act 1949 (c.10)
Royal Pavilion, Brighton, etc. Act 1849 (c.102)
Royal Scottish Museum (Extension) Act 1912 (c.16)
Royal Signature by Commission Act 1830 (c.23)
Royal Tithes Act 1876 (c.10)
Royal Titles Act 1901 (c.15)

Royal Titles Act 1952 (c.9)
Royal University of Ireland Act 1881 (c.52)
Rules Publication Act 1893 (c.66)
Rural Water Supplies Act 1934 (c.7)
Rural Water Supplies and Sewerage Act 1944 (c.26)
Rural Water Supplies and Sewerage Act 1951 (c.45)
Rural Water Supplies and Sewerage Act 1955 (c.13)
Rural Water Supplies and Sewerage Act 1961 (c.29)
Rural Water Supplies and Sewerage Act 1965 (c.80)
Rural Water Supplies and Sewerage Act 1971 (c.49)
Rural Water Supplies and Sewerage (No. 2) Act 1955 (c.15)
Rural Water Supplies and Sewerage (Scotland) Act 1969 (c.6)
Russian Dutch Loan Act 1815 (c.115)
Russian Dutch Loan Act 1832 (c.81)
Russian Dutch Loan Act 1891 (c.26)
Russian Goods (Import Prohibition) Act 1933 (c.10)
Russian Government Securities Act 1854 (c.123)
Ruthin Charities Act 1863 (c.59)
Rye Harbour Act 1797 (c.130)

Sacramental Test Act 1828 (c.17)
Sacramental Test (Ireland) Act 1832 (c.7)
Sailcloth Manufacture, etc. Act 1805 (c.68)
Safety at Sea Act 1986 (c.23)
Safety of Sports Grounds Act 1975 (c.52)
Safeguarding of Industries Act 1921 (c.47)
Safeguarding of Industries (Customs Duties) Act 1925 (c.79)
Sailors and Soldiers (Gifts for Land Settlement) Act 1916 (c.60)
Salaries of Bishops, etc. in West Indies Act 1826 (c.4)
Salaries of Chief Baron, etc. Act 1809 (c.127)
Salaries of County Officers (Ireland) Act 1823 (c.43)
Salaries of County Officers (Ireland) Act 1824 (c.93)
Salaries of Judges (Scotland) Act 1806 (c.49)
Salaries of Scotch Judges Act 1800 (c.55)
Salary of Lord Lieutenant Act 1811 (c.89)
Salary of Sir J. Lawrence Act 1864 (c.2)
Salcey Forest Act 1825 (c.132)
Sale and Supply of Goods Act 1994 (c.35)
Sale of Advowsons Act 1856 (c.50)
Sale of Beer Act 1795 (c.113)
Sale of Beer, etc. on Sunday Act 1848 (c.49)
Sale of Beer, etc. Act 1854 (c.79)
Sale of Bread, etc. Act 1800 (c.16)
Sale of Bread Act 1800 (c.71)
Sale of Bread Act 1800 (c.18)
Sale of Bread Act 1801 (c.12)
Sale of Butter Act 1796 (c.86)
Sale of Certain Lands in Worcester Act 1819 (c.137)
Sale of Certain Stock Act 1812 (c.148)
Sale, etc. of Certain Stocks Act 1829 (c.48)
Sale of Church Patronages Belonging to Municipal Corporations Act 1838 (c.31)
Sale of Crown Lands Act 1826 (c.51)
Sale of Crown Rents (Ireland) Act 1806 (c.123)
Sale of Crown Rents, etc. (Ireland) Act 1807 (c.16)
Sale of Exhausted Parish Lands Act 1876 (c.62)
Sale of Farming Stock Act 1816 (c.50)
Sale of Fish Act 1834 (c.20)
Sale of Food and Drugs Act 1875 (c.63)
Sale of Food and Drugs Act 1899 (c.51)
Sale of Food and Drugs Act 1927 (c.5)
Sale of Food and Drugs Amendment Act 1879 (c.30)
Sale of Food (Weights and Measures) Act 1926 c.63)
Sale of Gas Act 1859 (c.66)
Sale of Gas Act 1860 (c.146)
Sale of Gas (Scotland) Act 1864 (c.96)
Sale of Goods Act 1893 (c.71)
Sale of Goods Act 1979 (c.54)
Sale of Goods (Amendment) Act 1994 (c.32)
Sale of Goods (Amendment) Act 1995 (c.28)
Sale of Hares (Ireland) Act 1863 (c.19)
Sale of H. M.'s Bakehouse in Windsor Act 1862 (c.57)
Sale of Horseflesh, etc. Regulation Act 1889 (c.11)
Sale of Land by Auction Act 1867 (c.48)
Sale of Liquors by Retail (Ireland) Act 1807 (c.12)
Sale of Liquors on Sunday Act 1878 (c.72)
Sale of Mill Sites, etc. (Ireland) Act 1863 (c.42)
Sale of Muriate of Potash, etc. Act 1813 (c.97)
Sale of Offices Act 1809 (c.126)
Sale of Post Office Buildings Act 1831 (c.27)
Sale of Prize Ship Constantia Maria Act 1808 (c.147)
Sale of Spirits Act 1862 (c.38)
Sale of Spirits (England) Act 1820 (c.76)
Sale of Spirits, etc. (Ireland) Act 1839 (c.79)
Sale of Spirituous Liquors Act 1805 (c.50)
Sale of Spirituous Liquors, etc. Act 1813 (c.137)
Sale of Tea Act 1922 (c.29)
Sale of Venison (Scotland) Act 1968 (c.38)
Sale of Wine, etc. Act 1801 (c.48)
Sale of Workhouses Act 1821 (c.56)
Sales of Reversions Act 1867 (c.4)
Salmon Act 1696 (c.35)
Salmon Act 1986 (c.62)
Salmon Acts Amendment Act 1863 (c.10)
Salmon Acts Amendment Act 1870 (c.33)
Salmon and Fisheries Act 1965 (c.68)
Salmon and Freshwater Fisheries Act 1886 (c.39)

Salmon and Freshwater Fisheries Act 1892 (c.50)
Salmon and Freshwater Fisheries Act 1907 (c.15)
Salmon and Freshwater Fisheries Act 1921 (c.38)
Salmon and Freshwater Fisheries Act 1923 (c.16)
Salmon and Freshwater Fisheries Act 1923 (Amendment) Act 1964 (c.27)
Salmon and Freshwater Fisheries Act 1935 (c.43)
Salmon and Freshwater Fisheries Act 1972 (c.37)
Salmon and Freshwater Fisheries Act 1975 (c.51)
Salmon and Freshwater Fisheries (Amendment) Act 1929 (c.39)
Salmon and Freshwater Fisheries (Protection) (Scotland) Act 1951 (c.26)
Salmon Fisheries Act 1843 (c.33)
Salmon Fisheries Act 1848 (c.52)
Salmon Fisheries (England) Act 1818 (c.43)
Salmon Fisheries (Scotland) Act 1828 (c.39)
Salmon Fisheries (Scotland) Act 1844 (c.95)
Salmon Fisheries (Scotland) Act 1862 (c.97)
Salmon Fisheries (Scotland) Act 1863 (c.50)
Salmon Fisheries (Scotland) Act 1864 (c.118)
Salmon Fisheries (Scotland) Act 1868 (c.123)
Salmon Fishery Act 1861 (c.109)
Salmon Fishery Act 1865 (c.121)
Salmon Fishery Act 1873 (c.71)
Salmon Fishery Act 1876 (c.19)
Salmon Fishery Commissioners Act 1873 (c.13)
Salmon Fishery (Ireland) Act 1863 (c.114)
Salmon Fishery (Ireland) Act 1869 (c.9)
Salmon Fishery Law Amendment Act 1879 (c.26)
Salop Roads Act 1794 (c.123)
Salop Roads Act 1797 (c.172)
Salop and Hereford Roads Act 1794 (c.122)
Salt Duties Act 1798 (c.89)
Salt Duties Act 1799 (c.77)
Salt Duties Act 1805 (c.14)
Salt Duties Act 1813 (c.22)
Salt Duty Act 1813 (c.124)
Salt Duty Act 1815 (c.179)
Salt Duty Act 1816 (c.94)
Saltcoates Harbour 1797 (c.132)
Saltpetre Act 1800 (c.38)
Sand-Grouse Protection Act 1888 (c.55)
Sandhurst Act 1862 (c.33)
Sanitary Act 1866 (c.90)
Sanitary Act 1868 (c.115)
Sanitary Act 1870 (c.53)
Sanitary Act 1873 (c.78)
Sanitary Act, 1866, Amendment (Ireland) Act 1869 (c.108)
Sanitary Act (Dublin) Amendment Act 1870 (c.106)
Sanitary Inspectors (Change of Designation) Act 1956 (c.66)
Sanitary Law Amendment Act 1874 (c.89)
Sanitary Law (Dublin) Amendment Act 1875 (c.95)
Sanitary Loans Act 1869 (c.100)
Sardinia Loan Act 1855 (c.17)
Sardinian Loan Act 1856 (c.39)
Satisfied Terms Act 1845 (c.112)
Saving Banks Act 1824 (c.62)
Saving Bank Act 1828 (c.92)
Saving Bank Act 1833 (c.14)
Saving Bank Act 1835 (c.57)
Saving Bank Act 1844 (c.83)
Saving Banks Act 1852 (c.60)
Saving Banks Act 1880 (c.36)
Saving Banks Act 1887 (c.40)
Savings Banks Act 1891 (c.21)
Savings Bank Act 1893 (c.69)
Savings Bank Act 1904 (c.8)
Savings Banks Act 1920 (c.12)
Savings Banks Act 1929 (c.27)
Savings Banks Act 1949 (c.13)
Savings Banks and Friendly Societies Act 1854 (c.50)
Savings Banks (Barrister) Act 1876 (c.52)
Savings Bank (Charitable Societies) Act 1859 (c.53)
Savings Bank (England) Act 1817 (c.130)
Savings Bank (England) Act 1818 (c.48)
Savings Bank (England) Act 1820 (c.83)
Savings Bank Investment Act 1863 (c.25)
Savings Bank Investment Act 1866 (c.5)
Savings Bank Investment Act 1869 (c.59)
Savings Bank (Ireland) Act 1817 (c.105)
Savings Bank (Ireland) Act 1848 (c.133)
Savings Bank (Ireland) Act 1850 (c.110)
Savings Banks (Ireland) Act 1859 (c.17)
Savings Banks (Ireland) Cont. Act 1862 (c.75)
Savings Bank (Scotland) Act 1819 (c.62)
School Board Conference Act 1897 (c.32)
School Boards Act 1885 (c.38)
School Boards (Scotland) Act 1988 (c.47)
School Crossing Patrols Act 1953 (c.45)
School Districts Act 1850 (c.11)
School Grants Act 1855 (c.131)
School of Physic (Ireland) Amendment Act 1867 (c.9)
School Sites Act 1841 (c.38)
School Sites Act 1844 (c.37)
School Sites Act 1849 (c.49)
School Sites Act 1851 (c.24)
School Sites Act 1852 (c.49)
School Sites (Ireland) Act 1810 (c.32)
School Teachers Pay and Conditions Act 1991 (c.49)
School Teachers (Superannuation) Act 1918 (c.55)
School Teachers (Superannuation) Act 1922 (c.42)
School Teachers (Superannuation) Act 1924 (c.12)

Schools for Science and Art Act 1891 (c.61)
Science and Technology Act 1965 (c.4)
Scientific Societies Act 1843 (c.36)
Scotch and Irish Paupers Act 1840 (c.27)
Scotch and Irish Paupers Removal Act 1844 (c.42)
Scotch Distilleries Act 1797 (c.102)
Scotch Distilleries Act 1798 (c.92)
Scotch Whisky Act 1988 (c.22)
Scotland Act 1978 (c.51)
Scottish Board of Health Act 1919 (c.20)
Scottish Development Agency Act 1975 (c.69)
Scottish Development Agency Act 1987 (c.56)
Scottish Episcopal and other Clergy Act 1840 (c.33)
Scottish Episcopalians Act 1711 (c.10)
Scottish Episcopalians Relief Act 1792 (c.63)
Scottish Fisheries Advisory Council Act 1941 (c.1)
Scottish Land Court Act 1938 (c.31)
Scottish Land Court Act 1993 (c.45)
Scottish Universities (Emergency Powers) Act 1915 (c.78)
Scrabster Harbour Act 1841 (c.1)
Scrap Metal Dealers Act 1964 (c.69)
Sculpture Copyright Act 1814 (c.56)
Sea and Coast Fisheries Fund (Ireland) Act 1884 (c.21)
Sea Birds Preservation Act 1869 (c.17)
Sea Fish (Conservation) Act 1967 (c.84)
Sea Fish (Conservation) Act 1992 (c.60)
Sea Fish Industry Act 1938 (c.30)
Sea Fish Industry Act 1951 (c.30)
Sea Fish Industry Act 1959 (c.7)
Sea Fish Industry Act 1962 (c.31)
Sea Fish Industry Act 1970 (c.11)
Sea Fish Industry Act 1973 (c.3)
Sea Fish Industry Act 1980 (c.35)
Sea Fisheries Act 1817 (c.69)
Sea Fisheries Act 1843 (c.79)
Sea Fisheries Act 1868 (c.45)
Sea Fisheries Act 1875 (c.15)
Sea Fisheries Act 1883 (c.22)
Sea Fisheries Act 1884 (c.27)
Sea Fisheries Act 1967 (c.83)
Sea Fisheries Act 1968 (c.77)
Sea Fisheries (Clam and Bait Beds) Act 1881 (c.11)
Sea Fisheries (Compensation) (Scotland) Act 1959 (c.27)
Sea Fisheries (Ireland) Act 1818 (c.94)
Sea Fisheries (Ireland) Act 1883 (c.26)
Sea Fisheries Regulation Act 1888 (c.54)
Sea Fisheries Regulation Act 1966 (c.38)
Sea Fisheries (Regulation) Expenses Act 1930 (c.41)
Sea Fisheries Regulation (Scotland) Act 1895 (c.42)
Sea Fisheries (Scotland) Act 1810 (c.108)
Sea Fisheries (Scotland) Application of Penalties Act 1907 (c.42)
Sea Fisheries (Scotland) Act 1810 (c.108)
Sea Fisheries (Scotland) Amendment Act 1885 (c.70)
Sea Fisheries (Shellfish) Act 1967 (c.83)
Sea Fisheries (Shellfish) Act 1973 (c.30)
Sea Fisheries (Shellfish) Regulation Act 1894 (c.26)
Sea Fisheries (Wildlife Conservation) Act 1992 (c.36)
Sea Fishing Boats (Scotland) Act 1886 (c.53)
Sea Fishing Industry Act 1933 (c.45)
Sea Insurances (Stamping of Policies) Amendment Act 1876 (c.6)
Seal Fisheries (North Pacific) Act 1895 (c.21)
Seal Fisheries (North Pacific) Act 1912 (c.10)
Seal Fishery Act 1875 (c.18)
Seal Fishery (Behring's Sea) Act 1891 (c.19)
Seal Fishery (North Pacific) Act 1893 (c.23)
Seal Office in Courts of Queen's Bench and Common Pleas Act 1845 (c.34)
Seamen Act 1836 (c.15)
Seamen's and Soldiers' False Characters Act 1906 (c.5)
Seamen's Clothing Act 1869 (c.57)
Seamen's Fund Winding-up Act 1851 (c.102)
Seamen's Hospital Society Act 1832 (c.9)
Seamen's Savings Bank Act 1856 (c.41)
Seats for Shop Assistants Act 1899 (c.21)
Second Session (Explanation) Act 1899 (c.3)
Secret Service Money (Repeal) Act 1886 (c.2)
Secretary at War Abolition Act 1863 (c.12)
Secretary for Scotland Act 1885 (c.61)
Secretary for Scotland Act 1887 (c.52)
Secretary for Scotland Act 1889 (c.16)
Secretary for State 1904 (c.27)
Secretaries of State Act 1926 (c.18)
Securities (Validation) Act 1940 (c.55)
Securities (Validation) Act 1942 (c.10)
Security of Public Officers Act 1812 (c.66)
Security of Rents, Durham Act 1830 (c.11)
Security Service Act 1989 (c.5)
Seditious Meetings Act 1795 (c.8)
Seditious Meetings Act 1817 (c.19)
Seditious Meetings Act 1846 (c.33)
Seditious Meetings, etc. Act 1819 (c.6)
Seditious Meetings Prevention Act 1801 (c.30)
Seed Potatoes and Seed Oats Supply (Ireland) Act 1908 (c.19)
Seed Potatoes Supply (Ireland) Act 1891 (c.1)
Seed Potatoes Supply (Ireland) Act 1891 (c.7)
Seed Potatoes Supply (Ireland) Act 1895 (c.2)
Seed Potatoes Supply (Ireland) Act 1906 (c.3)
Seed Supply and Potato Spraying (Ireland) Act 1898 (c.50)
Seed Supply (Ireland) Act 1880 (c.1)
Seeds Act 1920 (c.54)
Seeds Amendment Act 1925 (c.66)

Sees of St. Asaph and Bangor Act 1842 (c.112)
Seizure of Arms Act 1819 (c.2)
Seizure of Crops (Ireland) Act 1863 (c.62)
Selective Employment Payments Act 1966 (c.32)
Self-Governing Schools etc. (Scotland) Act 1989 (c.39)
Senior Member of Council, India Act 1860 (c.87)
Senior Public Elementary Schools (Liverpool) Act (c.60)
Sentence of Death (Expectant Mothers) Act 1931 (c.24)
Separatists' Affirmations Act 1833 (c.82)
Sequestration Act 1849 (c.67)
Sequestration Act 1871 (c.45)
Sergeants at Law Act 1825 (c.95)
Servants' Characters Act 1792 (c.56)
Servants' Wages (Ireland) Act 1807 (c.43)
Service of Heirs (Scotland) Act 1847 (c.47)
Service of Process (Justices) Act 1933 (c.42)
Service of Process out of the Jurisdiction (England and Ireland) Act 1832 (c.33)
Service of Process out of the Jurisdiction (England and Ireland) Act 1834 (c.82)
Session Court (Scotland) Act 1810 (c.31)
Session of the Peace, Dublin Act 1843 (c.81)
Sessions Houses, Westminster, etc. Act 1804 (c.61)
Sessions of the Peace, Westminster Act 1828 (c.9)
Settled Estates Act 1840 (c.55)
Settled Estates Act 1856 (c.120)
Settled Estates Act 1858 (c.77)
Settled Estates Act 1876 (c.30)
Settled Estates Act 1877 (c.18)
Settled Estates Act Amendment Act 1864 (c.45)
Settled Land Act 1882 (c.38)
Settled Land Act 1884 (c.18)
Settled Land Act 1889 (c.36)
Settled Land Act 1890 (c.69)
Settled Land Act 1925 (c.18)
Settled Land Acts (Amendment) Act 1887 (c.30)
Settled Land and Trustee Acts (Courts General Powers) Act 1943 (c.25)
Settled Land (Ireland) Act 1847 (c.46)
Settlement of Estate on Lord Nelson Act 1813 (c.134)
Settlement of the Poor (England) Act 1819 (c.50)
Settlements on Coast of Africa and Falkland Islands Act 1843 (c.13)
Severn Bridge Tolls Act 1965 (c.24)
Severn Bridge Act 1992 (c.3)
Sewage Utilisation Act 1865 (c.75)
Sewage Utilisation Act 1867 (c.113)
Sewerage (Scotland) Act 1968 (c.47)
Sewers Act 1833 (c.22)
Sewers Act 1841 (c.45)
Sewers Act 1849 (c.50)
Sex Discrimination Act 1975 (c.65)
Sex Discrimination Act 1986 (c.59)
Sex Disqualification (Removal) Act 1919 (c.71)
Sexual Offences Act 1956 (c.69)
Sexual Offences Act 1967 (c.60)
Sexual Offences Act 1985 (c.44)
Sexual Offences Act 1993 (c.30)
Sexual Offences (Amendment) Act 1976 (c.82)
Sexual Offences (Amendment) Act 1992 (c.34)
Sexual Offences (Scotland) Act 1976 (c.67)
Seychelles Act 1976 (c.19)
Shannon Act 1874 (c.60)
Shannon Act 1885 (c.41)
Shannon Navigation Act 1839 (c.61)
Shannon Navigation Act 1847 (c.74)
Sharing of Church Buildings Act 1969 (c.38)
Sheep and Cattle Disease Prevention Act 1850 (c.71)
Sheep, etc. Diseases Act 1851 (c.69)
Sheep, etc. Disorders Prevention Act 1852 (c.11)
Sheep Stealers (Ireland) Act 1849 (c.30)
Sheep Stocks Valuation (Scotland) Act 1937 (c.34)
Sheffield University Act 1914 (c.4)
Sheriff and Sheriff Clerk of Chancery (Scotland) Act 1854 (c.72)
Sheriff Court Houses Act 1860 (c.79)
Sheriff Court Houses (Scotland) Act 1866 (c.53)
Sheriff Court Houses (Scotland) Amendment Act 1884 (c.42)
Sheriff Courts and Legal Officers (Scotland) Act 1927 (c.35)
Sheriff Courts (Civil Jurisdiction and Procedure) (Scotland) Act 1963 (c.22)
Sheriff Courts Consignations (Scotland) Act 1893 (c.44)
Sheriff Courts (Scotland) Act 1825 (c.23)
Sheriff Courts (Scotland) Act 1838 (c.119)
Sheriff Courts (Scotland) Act 1853 (c.80)
Sheriff Courts (Scotland) Act 1870 (c.86)
Sheriff Courts (Scotland) Act 1876 (c.70)
Sheriff Courts (Scotland) Act 1877 (c.50)
Sheriff Courts (Scotland) Act 1907 (c.51)
Sheriff Courts (Scotland) Act 1913 (c.28)
Sheriff Courts (Scotland) Act 1939 (c.98)
Sheriff Courts (Scotland) Act 1971 (c.58)
Sheriff Courts (Scotland) Amendment 1914 (c.5)
Sheriff Courts (Scotland) Extracts Act 1892 (c.17)
Sheriff Deputies, etc. Act 1799 (c.66)
Sheriff of Lanarkshire Act 1887 (c.41)
Sheriff of Selkirkshire Act 1832 (c.101)
Sheriff of Westmoreland Act 1849 (c.42)
Sheriff of Westmoreland Act 1850 (c.30)
Sheriff Substitute (Scotland) Act 1875 (c.81)
Sheriffs Act 1817 (c.68)
Sheriffs Act 1887 (c.55)

Sheriffs Fees Act 1837 (c.55)
Sheriffs (Ireland) Act 1835 (c.55)
Sheriffs (Ireland) Act 1920 (c.26)
Sheriffs of Edinburgh and Lanark Act 1822 (c.49)
Sheriffs' Pension (Scotland) Act 1961 (c.42)
Sheriffs (Scotland) Act 1853 (c.92)
Sheriff's Substitute Act 1864 (c.106)
Sheriff's Tenure of Office (Scotland) Act 1898 (c.8)
Sheriffs, Wales Act 1845 (c.11)
Sherwood Forest Act 1818 (c.100)
Shipbuilding Act 1979 (c.59)
Shipbuilding Act 1982 (c.4)
Shipbuilding Act 1985 (c.14)
Shipbuilding Credit Act 1964 (c.7)
Shipbuilding Industry Act 1967 (c.40)
Shipbuilding Industry Act 1968 (c.6)
Shipbuilding Industry Act 1971 (c.46)
Shipbuilding (Redundancy Payments) Act 1978 (c.11)
Shipowners' Liability for Losses by Fire Act 1836 (c.61)
Shipowners' Negligence (Remedies) Act 1904 (c.10)
Shipping Act 1795 (c.80)
Shipping Act 1799 (c.32)
Shipping Act 1816 (c.114)
Shipping and Trading Interests (Protection) Act 1995 (c.22)
Shipping Casualties Investigations Act 1879 (c.72)
Shipping Dues Exemption Act 1867 (c.15)
Shipping Dues Exemption Act Amendment Act 1869 (c.52)
Shipping Duties Exemption Act 1870 (c.50)
Shipping, etc. Act 1845 (c.88)
Shipping Offences Act 1793 (c.67)
Shipping under Treaties of Commerce Act 1826 (c.5)
Ships and Aircraft (Transfer Restriction) Act 1939 (c.70)
Shoeburyness Artillery Rangers Act 1862 (c.36)
Shooting Hares (Scotland) Act 1808 (c.94)
Shop Clubs Act 1902 (c.21)
Shop Hours Act 1892 (c.62)
Shop Hours Act 1893 (c.67)
Shop Hours Act 1895 (c.5)
Shop Hours Act 1904 (c.31)
Shop Hours Regulation Act 1886 (c.55)
Shops Act 1911 (c.54)
Shops Act 1912 (c.3)
Shops Act 1913 (c.24)
Shops Act 1934 (c.42)
Shops Act 1936 (c.28)
Shops Act 1950 (c.28)
Shops (Airports) Act 1962 (c.35)
Shops (Early Closing) Act 1920 (c.58)
Shops (Early Closing) Act (1920) Amendment Act 1921 (c.60)
Shops (Early Closing Days) Act 1965 (c.35)
Shops (Hours of Closing) Act 1928 (c.33)
Shops (Sunday Trading Restrictions) Act 1936 (c.53)
Shorncliffe Military Canal, etc. Act 1807 (c.70)
Short Titles Act 1892 (c.10)
Short Titles Act 1896 (c.14)
Shrewsbury and Holyhead Road Act 1845 (c.73)
Shrewsbury Improvement Act 1756 (c.78)
Shrewsbury to Bangor Road Act 1835 (c.21)
Shrewsbury to Holyhead Act 1819 (c.30)
Shubenaccasie Canal, Nova Scotia Act 1830 (c.34)
Siam and Straits Settlement Jurisdiction Act 1870 (c.55)
Sierra Leone Act 1853 (c.86)
Sierra Leone Company Act 1807 (c.44)
Sierra Leone Independence Act 1961 (c.16)
Sierra Leone Offences Act 1861 (c.31)
Sierra Leone Republic Act 1972 (c.1)
Sikes' Hydrometer Act 1816 (c.140)
Silk, etc. Bounties Act 1821 (c.91)
Silk Duties Act 1828 (c.23)
Silk Manufacture Act 1811 (c.7)
Silk Manufacture, etc. Act 1821 (c.11)
Silk Manufacture (Ireland) Act 1810 (c.27)
Silk Manufactures Act 1809 (c.20)
Silk Manufactures Act 1824 (c.21)
Silk Manufactures Act 1824 (c.66)
Silk Weavers Act 1845 (c.128)
Silver Coin Act 1798 (c.59)
Silver Plate Act 1790 (c.31)
Simony Act 1588 (c.6)
Singapore Act 1966 (c.29)
Sinking Fund Act 1875 (c.45)
Sir H. Pottinger's Annuity Act 1845 (c.49)
Sir J. Soane's Museum Act 1862 (c.9)
Sir John Port's Charity, Repton Act 1867 (c.99)
Sir R. Hitcham's Charity Act 1863 (c.58)
Site for Docks, etc. Dublin Act 1819 (c.82)
Site for Record Office (Ireland) Act 1826 (c.13)
Sites for Schoolrooms Act 1836 (c.70)
Sites of Parish Churches (Ireland) Act 1813 (c.66)
Six Clerks in Chancery (Ireland) Act 1813 (c.129)
Slander of Women Act 1891 (c.51)
Slate Mines (Gunpowder) Act 1882 (c.3)
Slaughter of Animals Act 1914 (c.75)
Slaughter of Animals Act 1933 (c.39)
Slaughter of Animals Act 1958 (c.8)
Slaughter of Animals (Amendment) Act 1951 (c.49)
Slaughter of Animals (Amendment) Act 1954 (c.59)
Slaughter of Animals (Pigs) Act 1953 (c.27)
Slaughter of Animals (Scotland) Act 1928 (c.29)
Slaughter of Animals (Scotland) Act 1949 (c.52)
Slaughter of Animals (Scotland) Act 1980 (c.13)

Slaughter of Poultry Act 1967 (c.24)
Slaughterhouses Act 1954 (c.42)
Slaughterhouses Act 1958 (c.70)
Slaughterhouses Act 1974 (c.3)
Slaughterhouses etc. (Metropolis) Act 1874 (c.67)
Slave Trade Act 1795 (c.90)
Slave Trade Act 1797 (c.104)
Slave Trade Act 1797 (c.118)
Slave Trade Act 1798 (c.88)
Slave Trade Act 1799 (c.80)
Slave Trade Act 1806 (c.52)
Slave Trade Act 1806 (c.119)
Slave Trade Act 1811 (c.23)
Slave Trade Act 1813 (c.112)
Slave Trade Act 1814 (c.59)
Slave Trade Act 1818 (c.36)
Slave Trade Act 1818 (c.49)
Slave Trade Act 1818 (c.85)
Slave Trade Act 1818 (c.98)
Slave Trade Act 1819 (c.97)
Slave Trade Act 1824 (c.17)
Slave Trade Act 1824 (c.113)
Slave Trade Act 1828 (c.84)
Slave Trade Act 1833 (c.72)
Slave Trade Act 1835 (cc.60, 61)
Slave Trade Act 1836 (c.81)
Slave Trade Act 1837 (c.62)
Slave Trade Act 1843 (c.46)
Slave Trade Act 1843 (c.98)
Slave Trade Act 1844 (c.26)
Slave Trade Act 1848 (c.116)
Slave Trade Act 1849 (c.84)
Slave Trade Act 1873 (c.88)
Slave Trade Act 1876 (c.46)
Slave Trade, Brazil Act 1845 (c.122)
Slave Trade Convention with Brazil Act 1827 (c.74)
Slave Trade (East African Courts) Act 1873 (c.59)
Slave Trade (East African Courts) Act 1879 (c.38)
Slave Trade Jurisdiction (Zanzibar) Act 1869 (c.75)
Slave Trade (Muscat) Act 1848 (c.128)
Slave Trade Suppression Act 1838 (c.47)
Slave Trade Suppression Act 1838 (c.102)
Slave Trade Suppression Act 1839 (c.57)
Slave Trade Suppression Act 1839 (c.73)
Slave Trade Suppression Act 1840 (c.64)
Slave Trade Suppression Act 1842 (c.42)
Slave Trade Suppression Act 1842 (c.59)
Slave Trade Suppression Act 1842 (c.91)
Slave Trade Suppression Act 1842 (c.101)
Slave Trade Suppression Act 1842 (c.114)
Slave Trade Suppression, African Treaty Act 1855 (c.85)
Slave Trade Suppression, Netherlands Act 1819 (c.16)
Slave Trade Suppression, Portugal Act 1819 (c.17)
Slave Trade Suppression Treaties with Sohar and New Grenada Act 1853 (cc.16, 17)
Slave Trade Suppression Treaty with Spain Act 1836 (c.6)
Slave Trade Suppression Treaty with Venezuela Act 1840 (c.67)
Slave Trade Treaties Act 1838 (cc.39–41)
Slave Trade Treaties Act 1838 (cc.83, 84)
Slave Trade Treaties Act 1843 (cc.50–53)
Slave Trade Treaties with Bolivia, Texas, Uruguay Act 1843 (cc.14-16)
Slave Trade, Treaty with Sweden Act 1827 (c.54)
Slavery Abolition Act 1833 (c.73)
Sligo and Cashel Disfranchisement Act 1870 (c.38)
Slough Roads Act 1796 (c.140)
Slum Clearance (Compensation) Act 1956 (c.57)
Small Debt Amendment (Scotland) Act 1889 (c.26)
Small Debt (Scotland) Act 1837 (c.41)
Small Debt (Scotland) Act 1924 (c.16)
Small Debt (Scotland) Act 1932 (c.38)
Small Debts Act 1795 (c.123)
Small Debts Act 1845 (c.127)
Small Debts Recovery (Ireland) Act 1837 (c.43)
Small Debts (Scotland) Act 1800 (c.46)
Small Debts (Scotland) Act 1825 (c.24)
Small Debts (Scotland) Act 1829 (c.55)
Small Dwellings Acquisition Act 1899 (c.44)
Small Estates (Representation) Act 1961 (c.37)
Small Holdings Act 1892 (c.31)
Small Holdings Act 1910 (c.34)
Small Holdings and Allotments Act 1907 (c.54)
Small Holdings and Allotments Act 1908 (c.36)
Small Holdings and Allotments Act 1926 (c.52)
Small Holding Colonies Act 1916 (c.38)
Small Holding Colonies (Amendment) Act 1918 (c.26)
Small Landholders and Agricultural Holdings (Scotland) Act 1931 (c.44)
Small Landholders (Scotland) Act 1911 (c.49)
Small Livings Act 1806 (c.60)
Small Lotteries and Gaming Act 1956 (c.45)
Small Lotteries and Gaming Act 1959 (c.35)
Small Penalties Act 1865 (c.127)
Small Penalties (Ireland) Act 1873 (c.82)
Small Tenements Recovery Act 1838 (c.74)
Small Testate Estates (Scotland) Act 1876 (c.24)
Smithfield Market Act 1851 (c.61)
Smoke Abatement, London Act 1853 (c.128)
Smoke Abatement, London Act 1856 (c.107)
Smoke Detectors Act 1991 (c.37)
Smoke Nuisance (Scotland) Act 1857 (c.73)
Smoke Nuisance (Scotland) Act 1865 (c.102)
Smoke of Furnaces (Scotland) Act 1861 (c.17)

Smugglers' Families Act 1830 (c.10)
Smuggling Act 1795 (c.31)
Smuggling Act 1802 (c.82)
Smuggling Act 1803 (c.157)
Smuggling Act 1805 (c.121)
Smuggling Act 1807 (c.66)
Smuggling Act 1819 (c.121)
Smuggling Act 1822 (c.110)
Smuggling Act 1834 (c.13)
Smuggling Customs Regulations etc. Act 1809 (c.62)
Smuggling, etc. Act 1805 (c.99)
Smuggling, etc. Act 1808 (c.84)
Smuggling, etc. Act 1818 (c.76)
Smuggling, etc. Act 1820 (c.43)
Soap Duty Allowances Act 1835 (c.15)
Soap Duties Act 1839 (c.32)
Soap Duties Allowances Act 1842 (c.16)
Soap Duties Allowances Act 1844 (c.51)
Soap Duties Allowances Act 1847 (c.41)
Soap Duties Allowances Act 1849 (c.40)
Soap Duties Allowances Act 1851 (c.59)
Soap Duties Repeal Act 1853 (c.39)
Social Fund (Maternity and Funeral Expenses) Act 1987 (c.7)
Social Security Act 1971 (c.73)
Social Security Act 1973 (c.38)
Social Security Act 1975 (c.14)
Social Security Act 1979 (c.18)
Social Security Act 1980 (c.30)
Social Security Act 1981 (c.33)
Social Security Act 1985 (c.53)
Social Security Act 1986 (c.50)
Social Security Act 1988 (c.7)
Social Security Act 1989 (c.24)
Social Security Act 1990 (c.27)
Social Security Act 1993 (c.3)
Social Security Administration Act 1992 (c.5)
Social Security Administration (Northern Ireland) Act 1992 (c.8)
Social Security Amendment Act 1974 (c.58)
Social Security and Housing Benefits Act 1982 (c.24)
Social Security and Housing Benefits Act 1983 (c.36)
Social Security Benefits Act 1975 (c.11)
Social Security (Consequential Provisions) Act 1975 (c.18)
Social Security (Consequential Provisions) Act 1992 (c.6)
Social Security (Consequential Provisions) (Northern Ireland) Act 1992 (c.9)
Social Security (Contributions) Act 1981 (c.1)
Social Security (Contributions) Act 1982 (c.2)
Social Security (Contributions) Act 1991 (c.42)
Social Security (Contributions) Act 1994 (c.1)
Social Security Contributions and Benefits Act 1992 (c.4)
Social Security Contributions and Benefits (Northern Ireland) Act 1992 (c.7)
Social Security (Incapacity for Work) Act 1994 (c.18)
Social Security (Miscellaneous Provisions) Act 1977 (c.5)
Social Security (Mortgage Interest Payments) Act 1992 (c.33)
Social Security (Northern Ireland) Act 1975 (c.15)
Social Security (No. 2) Act 1980 (c.39)
Social Security Pensions Act 1975 (c.60)
Social Services (Northern Ireland Agreement) Act 1949 (c.23)
Social Work (Scotland) Act 1968 (c.49)
Social Work (Scotland) Act 1972 (c.24)
Societies' Borrowing Powers Act 1898 (c.15)
Societies (Miscellaneous Provisions) Act 1940 (c.19)
Societies (Suspension of Meetings) Act 1917 (c.16)
Sodor and Man Act 1838 (c.30)
Solicitor (Ireland) Act 1822 (c.16)
Solicitors Act 1837 (c.56)
Solicitors Act 1843 (c.73)
Solicitors Act 1860 (c.127)
Solicitors Act 1877 (c.25)
Solicitors Act 1888 (c.65)
Solicitors Act 1894 (c.9)
Solicitors Act 1899 (c.4)
Solicitors Act 1906 (c.24)
Solicitors Act 1919 (c.56)
Solicitors Act 1922 (c.57)
Solicitors Act 1928 (c.22)
Solicitors Act 1932 (c.37)
Solicitors Act 1933 (c.24)
Solicitors Act 1934 (c.45)
Solicitors Act 1936 (c.35)
Solicitors Act 1941 (c.46)
Solicitors Act 1950 (c.6)
Solicitors Act 1957 (c.27)
Solicitors Act 1965 (c.31)
Solicitors Act 1974 (c.47)
Solicitors (Amendment) Act 1956 (c.41)
Solicitors (Amendment) Act 1959 (c.42)
Solicitors (Amendment) Act 1974 (c.26)
Solicitors (Articled Clerks) Act 1918 (c.16)
Solicitors (Articled Clerks) Act 1919 (c.27)
Solicitors (Clerks) Act 1839 (c.33)
Solicitors (Clerks) Act 1844 (c.86)
Solicitors (Disciplinary Committee) Act 1939 (c.110)
Solicitors (Emergency Provisions) Act 1940 (c.15)
Solicitors (Examination) Act 1917 (c.43)
Solicitors (Ireland) Act 1821 (c.48)
Solicitors (Ireland) Act 1849 (c.53)
Solicitors (Ireland) Act 1861 (c.68)
Solicitors (Ireland) Act 1898 (c.17)
Solicitors, Public Notaries, etc. Act 1949 (c.21)
Solicitors Remuneration Act 1881 (c.44)
Solicitors (Scotland) Act 1933 (c.21)
Solicitors (Scotland) Act 1958 (c.28)
Solicitors (Scotland) Act 1965 (c.29)
Solicitors (Scotland) Act 1976 (c.6)
Solicitors (Scotland) Act 1980 (c.46)

Solicitors (Scotland) Act 1988 (c.42)
Solitary Confinement Act 1837 (c.90)
Solomon Islands Act 1978 (c.15)
Solvent Abuse (Scotland) Act 1983 (c.33)
Somerset: Canal Act 1796 (c.48)
Somerset House Act 1853 (c.8)
Somerset House Act 1984 (c.21)
Somerset House (King's College Lease) Act 1873 (c.4)
Somersham Rectory Act 1882 (c.81)
Sound Broadcasting Act 1972 (c.31)
Sound Dues Redemption Act 1857 (c.12)
South Africa Act 1877 (c.47)
South Africa Act 1909 (c.9)
South Africa Act 1962 (c.23)
South Africa Act 1995 (c.3)
South African Loans and War Contribution Act 1903 (c.27)
South African Offences Act 1863 (c.35)
South American Loans Guarantee Act 1852 (c.4)
South Australia Act 1834 (c.95)
South Australia Act 1842 (c.61)
South Australia Government Act 1838 (c.60)
South Indian Railway Purchase Act 1890 (c.6)
South Sea Company Act 1807 (c.23)
South Sea Company Act 1815 (c.57)
South Sea Company Act 1820 (c.2)
South Sea Company's Privileges Act 1815 (c.141)
South Sea Trade Act 1821 (c.60)
South Wales Bridges Act 1881 (c.14)
South Wales Highways Act 1860 (c.68)
South Wales Highway Act Amendment Act 1878 (c.34)
South Wales Turnpike Roads Act 1847 (c.72)
South Wales Turnpike Roads Amendment Act 1882 (c.67)
South Wales Turnpike Trusts Amendment Act 1875 (c.35)
Southampton to New Sarum Canal Act 1795 (c.51)
Southampton, Portsmouth and Sheet Bridge Roads Act 1796 (c.135)
Southern Rhodesia Act 1965 (c.76)
Southern Rhodesia Act 1979 (c.52)
Southern Rhodesia (Constitution) Act 1961 (c.2)
Southern Whale Fisheries Act 1795 (c.92)
Southern Whale Fisheries Act 1797 (c.121)
Southern Whale Fisheries Act 1798 (c.57)
Southern Whale Fisheries Act 1808 (c.124)
Southern Whale Fishery Act 1802 (c.18)
Southern Whale Fishery Act 1802 (c.114)
Southern Whale Fishery Act 1803 (c.90)
Southern Whale Fishery Act 1805 (c.96)
Southern Whale Fishery Act 1811 (c.34)
Southern Whale Fishery Act 1812 (c.103)
Southern Whale Fishery Act 1813 (c.111)
Southern Whale Fishery Act 1815 (c.45)
Southern Whale Fishery Act 1819 (c.113)
Spalding Road Act 1795 (c.166)
Special Acts (Extension of Time) Act 1915 (c.72)
Special Areas (Amendment) Act 1937 (c.31)
Special Areas (Development and Improvement) Act 1935 (c.1)
Special Areas Reconstruction (Agreement) Act 1936 (c.19)
Special Commission Act 1888 (c.35)
Special Commission (Belfast Prison) Act 1918 (c.44)
Special Commission (Dardanelles and Mesopotamia) Act 1916 (c.34)
Special Constables Act 1831 (c.41)
Special Constables Act 1835 (c.43)
Special Constables Act 1838 (c.80)
Special Constables Act 1914 (c.61)
Special Constables Act 1923 (c.11)
Special Constables (Ireland) Act 1832 (c.108)
Special Constables (Ireland) Act 1845 (c.46)
Special Constables (Scotland) Act 1914 (c.53)
Special Constables (Scotland) Act 1915 (c.47)
Special Enactments (Extension of Time) Act 1940 (c.16)
Special Juries Act 1898 (c.6)
Special Roads Act 1949 (c.32)
Spencer Perceval's Pensions Act 1813 (c.122)
Spirit, etc. Licences (Ireland) Act 1806 (c.70)
Spirit Licences Act 1799 (c.86)
Spirit of Wine Act 1855 (c.38)
Spirit Trade Act 1814 (c.149)
Spirits Act 1805 (c.39)
Spirits Act 1832 (c.74)
Spirits Act 1860 (c.114)
Spirits Act 1880 (c.24)
Spirits (Ireland) Act 1809 (c.99)
Spirits (Ireland) Act 1815 (c.104)
Spirits (Ireland) Act 1844 (c.82)
Spirits (Ireland) Act 1845 (c.64)
Spirits (Ireland) Act 1849 (c.17)
Spirits (Ireland) Act 1854 (c.89)
Spirits (Ireland) Act 1855 (c.103)
Spirits (Scotland): Spirits (Ireland) Act 1832 (c.29)
Spirits (Strength Ascertainment) Act 1818 (c.28)
Spiritual Duties Act 1839 (c.30)
Spitalfields and Shoreditch New Street Act 1853 (c.52)
Spitalfields Improvements Act 1850 (c.109)
Sporting Events (Control of Alcohol etc.) Act 1985 (c.57)
Sporting Events (Control of Alcohol etc.) (Amendment) Act 1992 (c.57)
Sporting Lands Rating (Scotland) Act 1886 (c.15)
Spray Irrigation (Scotland) Act 1964 (c.90)
Spring Assizes Act 1879 (c.1)
Spring Guns Act 1827 (c.18)
Sri Lanka Republic Act 1972 (c.55)

St. Albans Bribery Commission Act 1851 (c.106)
St. Albans Roads Act 1794 (c.113)
St. Briavels Small Debts Court Act 1842 (c.83)
St. Bride's Church, City Act 1796 (c.35)
St. David's College Act 1824 (c.101)
St. Helena Act 1833 (c.85)
St. John's Church, Hackney Act 1795 (c.70)
St. John's, Newfoundland Act 1820 (c.51)
St. John's, Newfoundland, etc. Act 1811 (c.45)
St. Martin Outwich Church, City Act 1796 (c.103)
St. Mary Magdalen Hospital, Bath Act 1856 (c.45)
St. Mary Somerset's Church, London Act 1868 (c.127)
St. Marylebone: Improvement Act 1795 (c.73)
St. Marylebone Rectory, Purchase of Act 1817 (c.98)
St. Michael, Cornhill: Building Act 1716 (c.5)
St. Pancras: Improvements, etc. Act 1797 (c.80)
St. Paul, Covent Garden: Church Rebuilding Act 1796 (c.65)
St. Vincent and Grenada Constitution Act 1876 (c.47)
Stables at Windsor Castle Act 1839 (c.20)
Stafford Election Act 1833 (c.20)
Stafford Election Act 1836 (c.10)
Stafford Roads Act 1770 (c.113)
Staffordshire Potteries Stipendiary Justice Act 1839 (c.15)
Stage Carriages Act 1832 (c.120)
Stage Coach duties Act 1796 (c.16)
Stage Coaches, etc. Act 1806 (c.136)
Stage Coaches, etc. (Great Britain) Act 1810 (c.48)
Stage Coaches, etc. (Ireland) Act 1810 (c.32)
Stage Coaches (Scotland) Act 1820 (c.4)
Stamford to Greetham Road Act 1795 (c.152)
Stamp Act 1795 (c.30)
Stamp Act 1795 (c.55)
Stamp Act 1795 (c.63)
Stamp Act 1796 (c.19)
Stamp Act 1796 (c.80)
Stamp Act 1797 (c.60)
Stamp Act 1797 (c.90)
Stamp Act 1797 (c.111)
Stamp Act 1797 (c.136)
Stamp Act 1798 (c.56)
Stamp Act 1798 (c.85)
Stamp Act 1799 (c.39)
Stamp Act 1799 (c.92)
Stamp Act 1799 (c.107)
Stamp Act 1804 (c.98)
Stamp Act 1815 (c.184)
Stamp Act 1853 (c.59)
Stamp Act 1854 (c.83)
Stamp Act 1864 (c.90)
Stamp Act 1870 (c.97)
Stamp Act 1891 (c.39)
Stamp Duties Act 1828 (c.49)
Stamp Duties Act 1848 (c.9)
Stamp Duties Act 1850 (c.97)
Stamp Duties Act 1860 (c.111)
Stamp Duties, etc. (Ireland) Act 1812 (c.87)
Stamp Duties (Court of Chancery) (Ireland) Act 1823 (c.78)
Stamp Duties (Ireland) Act 1815 (c.100)
Stamp Duties (Ireland) Act 1826 (c.20)
Stamp Duties in Law Proceedings (Ireland) Act 1821 (c.112)
Stamp Duties (Ireland) Act 1842 (c.82)
Stamp Duties (Ireland) Act 1850 (c.114)
Stamp Duties Management Act 1870 (c.98)
Stamp Duties Management Act 1891 (c.38)
Stamp Duties on Cards and Dice Act 1828 (c.18)
Stamp Duties on Newspapers Act 1836 (c.76)
Stamp Duty Composition (Ireland) Act 1867 (c.89)
Stamp Duty on Certain Leases Act 1870 (c.44)
Stamp Duty (Temporary Provisions) Act 1992 (c.2)
Stamps Act 1800 (c.84)
Stamps Act 1801 (c.58)
Stamps Act 1802 (c.99)
Stamps Act 1803 (c.21)
Stamps Act 1803 (cc.126, 127)
Stamps Act 1810 (c.35)
Stamps Act 1813 (c.108)
Stamps Act 1814 (c.144)
Stamps Act 1815 (c.101)
Stamps Act 1821 (c.55)
Stamps Act 1822 (c.117)
Stamps Act 1824 (c.41)
Stamps Act 1825 (c.41)
Stamps Act 1826 (c.44)
Stamps Act 1832 (c.91)
Stamps Act 1833 (c.23)
Stamps Act 1834 (c.57)
Stamps Act 1838 (c.85)
Stamps Act 1840 (c.79)
Stamps Act 1841 (c.34)
Stamps Act 1843 (c.72)
Stamps Act 1844 (c.21)
Stamps Act 1845 (c.2)
Stamps Act 1849 (c.80)
Stamps Act 1851 (c.18)
Stamps Act 1852 (c.21)
Stamps Act 1856 (c.22)
Stamps Act 1856 (c.81)
Stamps Act 1858 (c.20)
Stamps Act 1858 (c.24)
Stamps Act 1871 (c.4)
Stamps and Excise Act 1836 (c.45)
Stamps and Taxes Act 1835 (c.20)
Stamps, etc. Act 1833 (c.97)
Stamps (Great Britain) Act 1814 (c.133)
Stamps (Ireland) Act 1804 (c.68)
Stamps (Ireland) Act 1805 (c.20)

Stamps (Ireland) Act 1805 (c.51)
Stamps (Ireland) Act 1806 (c.35)
Stamps (Ireland) Act 1806 (c.64)
Stamps (Ireland) Act 1807 (c.50)
Stamps (Ireland) Act 1810 (c.76)
Stamps (Ireland) Act 1812 (c.126)
Stamps (Ireland) Act 1814 (c.118)
Stamps (Ireland) Act 1815 (cc.78, 79)
Stamps (Ireland) Act 1815 (c.80)
Stamps (Ireland) Act 1815 (c.81)
Stamps on Fire Insurances Act 1828 (c.13)
Standards of Weights, Measures and Coinage Act 1866 (c.82)
Stanhope and Wolsingham Rectories Act 1858 (c.58)
Stannaries Act 1836 (c.106)
Stannaries Act 1839 (c.58)
Stannaries Act 1855 (c.32)
Stannaries Act 1869 (c.19)
Stannaries Act 1887 (c.43)
Stannaries Court (Abolition) Act 1896 (c.45)
Stannaries Court of Cornwall Act 1834 (c.42)
Starch and Soap Duties Allowances Act 1822 (c.25)
State Hospitals (Scotland) Act 1994 (c.16)
State Immunity Act 1978 (c.33)
State of Singapore Act 1958 (c.59)
Statement of Rates Act 1919 (c.31)
Statistics of Trade Act 1947 (c.39)
Status of Aliens Act 1914 (c.17)
Statute Duty Act 1804 (c.52)
Statute of Frauds Amendment Act 1828 (c.14)
Statute of Westminster Act 1932 (c.4)
Statute Law (Repeals) Act 1969 (c.52)
Statute Law (Repeals) Act 1971 (c.52)
Statute Law (Repeals) Act 1973 (c.39)
Statute Law (Repeals) Act 1974 (c.22)
Statute Law (Repeals) Act 1975 (c.10)
Statute Law (Repeals) Act 1976 (c.16)
Statute Law (Repeals) Act 1977 (c.18)
Statute Law (Repeals) Act 1978 (c.45)
Statute Law (Repeals) Act 1981 (c.19)
Statute Law (Repeals) Act 1986 (c.12)
Statute Law (Repeals) Act 1989 (c.43)
Statute Law (Repeals) Act 1993 (c.50)
Statute Law (Repeals) Act 1995 (c.44)
Statute Law Revision Act 1861 (c.101)
Statute Law Revision Act 1863 (c.125)
Statute Law Revision Act 1867 (c.59)
Statute Law Revision Act 1870 (c.69)
Statute Law Revision Act 1871 (c.116)
Statute Law Revision Act 1872 (c.63)
Statute Law Revision Act 1873 (c.91)
Statute Law Revision Act 1874 (c.35)
Statute Law Revision Act 1875 (c.66)
Statute Law Revision Act 1878 (c.79)
Statute Law Revision Act 1883 (c.39)
Statute Law Revision Act 1887 (c.59)
Statute Law Revision Act 1888 (c.3)
Statute Law Revision Act 1890 (c.33)
Statute Law Revision Act 1891 (c.67)
Statute Law Revision Act 1892 (c.19)
Statute Law Revision Act 1893 (c.14)
Statute Law Revision Act 1894 (c.56)
Statute Law Revision Act 1898 (c.22)
Statute Law Revision Act 1908 (c.49)
Statute Law Revision Act 1927 (c.42)
Statute Law Revision Act 1948 (c.62)
Statute Law Revision Act 1950 (c.6)
Statute Law Revision Act 1953 (c.5)
Statute Law Revision Act 1958 (c.46)
Statute Law Revision Act 1959 (c.68)
Statute Law Revision Act 1960 (c.56)
Statute Law Revision Act 1963 (c.30)
Statute Law Revision Act 1964 (c.79)
Statute Law Revision Act 1966 (c.5)
Statute Law Revision Act 1969 (c.52)
Statute Law Revision Act 1971 (c.52)
Statute Law Revision and Civil Procedure Act 1881 (c.59)
Statute Law Revision and Civil Procedure Act 1883 (c.49)
Statute Law Revision (Consequential Repeals) Act 1965 (c.55)
Statute Law Revision (Ireland) Act 1872 (c.98)
Statute Law Revision (Ireland) Act 1878 (c.57)
Statute Law Revision (Ireland) Act 1879 (c.24)
Statute Law Revision (Isle of Man) Act 1991 (c.61)
Statute Law Revision (Northern Ireland) Act 1973 (c.55)
Statute Law Revision (Northern Ireland) Act 1976 (c.12)
Statute Law Revision (Northern Ireland) Act 1980 (c.59)
Statute Law Revision (No. 2) Act 1872 (c.97)
Statute Law Revision (No. 2) Act 1874 (c.96)
Statute Law Revision (No. 2) Act 1888 (c.57)
Statute Law Revision (No. 2) Act 1890 (c.51)
Statute Law Revision (No. 2) Act 1893 (c.54)
Statute Law Revision (Scotland) Act 1906 (c.38)
Statute Law Revision (Scotland) Act 1964 (c.80)
Statute Law Revision (Substituted Enactments) Act 1876 (c.20)
Statute of Frauds 1677 (c.3)
Statute of Frauds Amendment Act 1828 (c.14)
Statute of Westminster 1931 (c.4)
Statutes (Definition of Time) Act 1880 (c.9)
Statutory Commissioners Act 1823 (c.35)
Statutory Companies (Redeemable Stock) Act 1915 (c.44)
Statutory Corporations (Financial Provisions) Act 1974 (c.8)
Statutory Corporations (Financial Provisions) Act 1975 (c.55)
Statutory Declarations Act 1835 (c.62)
Statutory Gas Companies (Electricity Supply Powers) Act 1925 (c.44)
Statutory Instruments Act 1946 (c.36)

Statutory Orders (Special Procedure) Act 1945 (c.18)
Statutory Orders (Special Procedure) Act 1965 (c.43)
Statutory Salaries Act 1937 (c.35)
Statutory Salaries (Restoration) Act 1934 (c.24)
Statutory Sick Pay Act 1991 (c.3)
Statutory Sick Pay Act 1994 (c.2)
Statutory Undertakings (Temporary Increase of Charges) Act 1918 (c.34)
Statutory Water Companies Act 1991 (c.58)
Stealing from Bleaching Grounds (Ireland) Act 1811 (c.39)
Stealing from Gardens Act 1826 (c.69)
Stealing in Shops, etc. Act 1820 (c.117)
Stealing of Linen, etc. Act 1811 (c.41)
Stealing of Records, etc. Act 1824 (c.30)
Stealing Property from Mines Act 1816 (c.73)
Steam Engines Furnaces Act 1821 (c.41)
Steam Navigation Act 1846 (c.100)
Steam Navigation Act 1848 (c.81)
Steam Navigation Act 1851 (c.79)
Steam Trawling (Ireland) Act 1889 (c.74)
Steam Whistles Act 1872 (c.61)
Steeping of Barley Act 1801 (c.31)
Stepney: Improvements, Poor Relief Act 1797 (c.79)
Still-Birth (Definition) Act 1992 (c.29)
Still Licences Act 1846 (c.90)
Stipendiary Curates Act 1813 (c.149)
Stipendiary Magistrate, Manchester Act 1813 (c.72)
Stipendiary Magistrate, Manchester and Salford Act 1854 (c.20)
Stipendiary Magistrate, Staffs Act 1846 (c.65)
Stipendiary Magistrates Act 1858 (c.73)
Stipendiary Magistrates Act 1863 (c.97)
Stipendiary Magistrates Act 1869 (c.34)
Stipendiary Magistrates Jurisdiction (Scotland) Act 1897 (c.48)
Stipendiary Magistrate for Manchester Act 1844 (c.30)
Stirling Roads Act 1794 (c.138)
Stirling, Dumbarton and Perth Roads Act 1794 (c.129)
Stockbridge Roads Act 1797 (c.149)
Stockbrokers (Ireland) Act 1868 (c.31)
Stockbrokers (Ireland) Act 1918 (c.46)
Stock Exchange (Completion of Bargains) Act 1976 (c.47)
Stock Transfer Act 1963 (c.18)
Stock Transfer Act 1982 (c.41)
Stocks, etc. of Lunatics Act 1821 (c.15)
Stoke Poges Hospital Act 1856 (c.111)
Stoke to Newcastle Canal Act 1795 (c.87)
Straits Settlements Act 1866 (c.115)
Straits Settlements and Johore Territorial Waters (Agreement) Act 1928 (c.23)
Straits Settlements (Ecclesiastic) Act 1869 (c.88)
Straits Settlements Offences Act 1874 (c.38)
Straits Settlements (Repeal) Act 1946 (c.37)
Stratified Ironstone Mines (Gunpowder) Act 1881 (c.26)
Stratford and Long Compton Hill Roads Act 1797 (c.152)
Street Betting Act 1906 (c.43)
Street Collections Regulations (Scotland) Act 1915 (c.88)
Street from Coventry Street to Long Acre Act 1841 (c.12)
Street Offences Act 1959 (c.57)
Street Playgrounds Act 1938 (c.37)
Submarine Telegraph Act 1885 (c.49)
Submarine Telegraph Act 1886 (c.3)
Subscriptions to Loan Act 1797 (c.82)
Subscriptions to Loan Act 1847 (c.36)
Substitution of Punishments for Death Act 1841 (c.56)
Succession Duty Act 1853 (c.51)
Succession (Scotland) Act 1964 (c.41)
Succession (Scotland) Act 1973 (c.25)
Succession to the Crown Act 1707 (c.41)
Sudan (Special Payments) Act 1955 (c.11)
Sudbury Bribery Commission Act 1843 (c.97)
Sudbury Disfranchisement Act 1842 (c.52)
Sudbury Disfranchisement Act 1843 (c.11)
Suez Canal (Shares) Act 1876 (c.67)
Suffragan Bishops Act 1898 (c.11)
Suffragans Nomination Act 1888 (c.56)
Sugar Act 1956 (c.48)
Sugar Bounties, etc. Act 1811 (c.13)
Sugar Convention Act 1903 (c.21)
Sugar Duties Act 1828 (c.36)
Sugar Duties Act 1829 (c.39)
Sugar Duties Act 1830 (c.50)
Sugar Duties Act 1831 (c.23)
Sugar Duties Act 1832 (c.22)
Sugar Duties Act 1832 (c.95)
Sugar Duties Act 1834 (c.5)
Sugar Duties Act 1836 (c.26)
Sugar Duties Act 1837 (c.27)
Sugar Duties Act 1838 (c.33)
Sugar Duties Act 1839 (c.21)
Sugar Duties Act 1840 (c.23)
Sugar Duties Act 1840 (c.57)
Sugar Duties Act 1841 (c.29)
Sugar Duties Act 1842 (c.34)
Sugar Duties Act 1843 (c.27)
Sugar Duties Act 1844 (c.28)
Sugar Duties Act 1845 (c.5)
Sugar Duties Act 1846 (c.29)
Sugar Duties Act 1846 (c.41)
Sugar Duties Act 1846 (c.63)
Sugar Duties Act 1848 (c.97)
Sugar Duties Act 1854 (c.30)
Sugar Duties (Ireland) Act 1820 (c.80)
Sugar Duties and Exchequer Bills Act 1835 (c.12)
Sugar, etc. Act 1820 (c.64)
Sugar in Brewing Act 1847 (c.5)
Sugar Industry Act 1942 (c.16)
Sugar Industry (Reorganisation) Act 1936 (c.18)
Suicide Act 1961 (c.60)

Suits Against Spiritual Persons Act 1814 (c.54)
Summary Convictions, etc. Act 1824 (c.18)
Summary Convictions (Ireland) Act 1834 (c.93)
Summary Convictions (Ireland) Act 1849 (c.70)
Summary Jurisdiction Act 1848 (c.43)
Summary Jurisdiction Act 1857 (c.43)
Summary Jurisdiction Act 1863 (c.77)
Summary Jurisdiction Act 1879 (c.49)
Summary Jurisdiction Act 1884 (c.43)
Summary Jurisdiction Act 1899 (c.22)
Summary Jurisdiction (Appeals) Act 1933 (c.38)
Summary Jurisdiction Cinque Ports, etc. Act 1864 (c.80)
Summary Jurisdiction (Ireland) Act 1850 (c.102)
Summary Jurisdiction (Ireland) Act 1851 (c.92)
Summary Jurisdiction (Ireland) Act 1862 (c.50)
Summary Jurisdiction (Ireland) Act 1908 (c.24)
Summary Jurisdiction (Ireland) Act 1918 (c.18)
Summary Jurisdiction (Ireland) Amendment Act 1871 (c.76)
Summary Jurisdiction (Married Women) Act 1895 (c.39)
Summary Jurisdiction over Children (Ireland) Act 1884 (c.19)
Summary Jurisdiction (Process) Act 1881 (c.24)
Summary Jurisdiction (Scotland) Act 1881 (c.33)
Summary Jurisdiction (Scotland) Act 1908 (c.65)
Summary Jurisdiction (Scotland) Act 1909 (c.28)
Summary Jurisdiction (Scotland) Act 1954 (c.48)
Summary Jurisdiction (Separation and Maintenance) Act 1925 (c.51)
Summary Proceedings Act 1822 (c.23)
Summary Procedure (Domestic Proceedings) Act 1937 (c.58)
Summary Procedure on Bills of Exchange Act 1855 (c.67)
Summary Procedure on Bills of Exchange (Ireland) Act 1861 (c.43)
Summary Procedure (Scotland) Act 1864 (c.53)
Summary Prosecutions Appeals (Scotland) Act 1875 (c.62)
Summer Time Act 1916 (c.14)
Summer Time Act 1922 (c.22)
Summer Time Act 1925 (c.64)
Summer Time Act 1947 (c.16)
Summer Time Act 1972 (c.6)
Summons and Process Servers' Fees (Ireland) Act 1919 (c.4)
Sunday and Ragged Schools (Exemption from Rating) Act 1869 (c.40)
Sunday Cinema Act 1972 (c.19)
Sunday Closing (Wales) Act 1881 (c.61)
Sunday Entertainments Act 1932 (c.51)
Sunday Observance Act 1833 (c.31)
Sunday Observation Prosecution Act 1871 (c.87)
Sunday Performances (Temporary Regulation) Act 1931 (c.52)
Sunday Theatre Act 1972 (c.26)
Sunday Trading Act 1994 (c.20)
Sunderland Pilotage Order Confirmation Act 1865 (c.59)
Superannuation Act 1834 (c.24)
Superannuation Act 1859 (c.26)
Superannuation Act 1860 (c.89)
Superannuation Act 1866 (c.68)
Superannuation Act 1872 (c.12)
Superannuation Act 1875 (c.4)
Superannuation Act 1876 (c.53)
Superannuation Act 1881 (c.43)
Superannuation Act 1884 (c.57)
Superannuation Act 1887 (c.67)
Superannuation Act 1892 (c.40)
Superannuation Act 1909 (c.10)
Superannuation Act 1914 (c.86)
Superannuation Act 1935 (c.23)
Superannuation Act 1946 (c.60)
Superannuation Act 1949 (c.44)
Superannuation Act 1950 (c.2)
Superannuation Act 1957 (c.37)
Superannuation Act 1965 (c.74)
Superannuation Act 1972 (c.11)
Superannuation Allowances Act 1824 (c.104)
Superannuation Act Amendment Act 1834 (c.45)
Superannuation Acts Amendment Act 1873 (c.23)
Superannuation Amendment Act 1965 (c.10)
Superannuation and Other Trust Funds (Validation) Act 1927 (c.41)
Superannuation, etc. Act 1828 (c.79)
Superannuation (Diplomatic Service) Act 1929 (c.11)
Superannuation (Ecclesiastical Commissioners and Queen Anne's Bounty) Act 1914 (c.5)
Superannuation (Ecclesiastical Commissioners and Queen Anne's Bounty) Act 1933 (c.47)
Superannuation (Mercantile Marine Fund Officers) Act 1877 (c.44)
Superannuation (Metropolis) Act 1866 (c.31)
Superannuation (Miscellaneous Provisions) Act 1948 (c.33)
Superannuation (Miscellaneous Provisions) Act 1967 (c.28)
Superannuation Post Office and War Office Act 1876 (c.68)
Superannuation (President of Industrial Court) Act 1954 (c.37)
Superannuation (Prison Officers) Act 1919 (c.67)

Superannuation Schemes (War Service) Act 1940 (c.26)
Superannuation (Various Services) Act 1938 (c.13)
Superannuation (War Department) Act 1890 (c.18)
Superintending Magistrates, etc. (Ireland) Act 1814 (c.13)
Superintending Magistrates, etc. (Ireland) Act 1817 (c.22)
Superior Courts (Officers) Act 1837 (c.30)
Supplemental Customs Consolidation Act 1855 (c.96)
Supplemental War Loan Act 1900 (c.61)
Supplemental War Loan (No. 2) Act 1900 (c.1)
Supplementary Benefits Act 1976 (c.71)
Supplementary Benefit (Amendment) Act 1976 (c.56)
Supplementary Militia Act 1797 (c.18)
Supplementary Militia Act 1797 (c.19)
Supplementary Militia Act 1799 (c.14)
Supplies and Services (Defence Purposes) Act 1951 (c.25)
Supplies and Services (Extended Purpose) Act 1947 (c.55)
Supplies and Services (Translation Powers) Act 1945 (c.10)
Supply Act 1820 (c.10)
Supply Act 1821 (c.4)
Supply Act 1821 (c.7)
Supply Act 1823 (c.6)
Supply Act 1823 (c.21)
Supply Act 1824 (c.3)
Supply Act 1824 (c.42)
Supply Act 1825 (c.1)
Supply Act 1825 (c.14)
Supply Act 1826 (c.1)
Supply Act 1827 (c.16)
Supply Act 1827 (c.42)
Supply Act 1828 (c.1)
Supply Act 1828 (c.10)
Supply Act 1828 (c.19)
Supply Act 1828 (c.28)
Supply Act 1828 (c.30)
Supply Act 1829 (c.3)
Supply Act 1830 (c.1)
Supply Act 1830 (c.2)
Supply Act 1830 (c.4)
Supply Act 1830 (c.28)
Supply Act 1831 (cc.9–10)
Supply Act 1831 (c.28)
Supply Act 1832 (c.1)
Supply Act 1832 (c.6)
Supply Act 1832 (c.30)
Supply Act 1832 (c.55)
Supply Act 1833 (c.18)
Supply Act 1834 (c.2)
Supply Act 1834 (c.12)
Supply Act 1835 (c.3)
Supply Act 1835 (c.9)
Supply Act 1836 (c.1)
Supply Act 1836 (c.18)
Supply Act 1837 (c.6)
Supply Act 1837 (c.11)
Supply Act 1838 (c.11)
Supply Act 1838 (c.21)
Supply Act 1839 (c.2)
Supply Act 1839 (c.6)
Supply Act 1840 (c.4)
Supply Act 1840 (c.7)
Supply Act 1841 (c.4)
Supply Act 1842 (c.8)
Supply Act 1843 (c.5)
Supply Act 1843 (c.87)
Supply Act 1844 (c.6)
Supply Act 1845 (c.1)
Supply Act 1846 (c.7)
Supply Act 1846 (c.47)
Supply Act 1847 (c.8)
Supply Act 1848 (c.4)
Supply Act 1848 (c.33)
Supply Act 1849 (c.3)
Supply Act 1849 (c.44)
Supply Act 1850 (c.3)
Supply Act 1851 (c.3)
Supply Act 1852 (c.1)
Supply Act 1853 (c.12)
Supply Act 1853 (c.31)
Supply Act 1854 (c.2)
Supply Act 1854 (c.21)
Supply Act 1855 (cc.5, 6)
Supply Act 1855 (c.37)
Supply Act 1856 (c.4)
Supply Act 1856 (c.7)
Supply Act 1857 (c.4)
Supply Act 1858 (cc.5, 6)
Supply Act 1858 (c.17)
Supply Act 1859 (cc.6, 7)
Supply Act 1859 (c.2)
Supply Act 1860 (cc.2, 3)
Supply Act 1860 (c.12)
Supply Act 1860 (c.25)
Supply Act 1860 (c.103)
Supply Act 1861 (c.2)
Supply Act 1861 (c.6)
Supply Act 1861 (c.19)
Supply Act 1862 (cc.1, 2)
Supply Act 1862 (c.31)
Supply Act 1863 (c.6)
Supply Act 1863 (c.15)
Supply Act 1864 (cc.5, 6)
Supply Act 1864 (c.11)
Supply Act 1864 (c.73)
Supply Act 1865 (c.4)
Supply Act 1865 (c.10)
Supply Act 1866 (c.6)
Supply Act 1866 (c.13)
Supply Act 1867 (c.4)
Supply Act 1867 (c.7)
Supply Act 1867 (c.30)
Supply Act 1867 (c.1)
Supply Act 1868 (c.10)
Supply Act 1868 (c.13)
Supply Act 1868 (c.16)
Supply Act 1869 (c.1)

Supply Act 1869 (c.8)
Supply Act 1870 (c.5)
Supply Act 1870 (c.31)
Supply Act 1871 (cc.6, 7)
Supply Act 1871 (c.20)
Supply Act 1871 (c.51)
Supply Act 1872 (c.1)
Supply Act 1872 (c.11)
Supply Act 1872 (c.37)
Supply Act 1873 (c.26)
Supply Act 1873 (c.3)
Supply Act 1874 (cc.1, 2)
Supply Act 1874 (c.10)
Supply Act 1875 (cc.1, 2)
Supply Act 1875 (c.10)
Supply Act 1876 (c.2)
Supply Act 1876 (c.4)
Supply Act 1876 (c.15)
Supply Act 1877 (c.1)
Supply Act 1877 (c.6)
Supply Act 1877 (c.12)
Supply Act 1877 (c.24)
Supply Act 1878 (c.1)
Supply Act 1878 (c.9)
Supply Act 1878 (c.21)
Supply Act 1878 (c.45)
Supply, etc., Act 1742 (c.25)
Supply of Goods and Services Act 1982 (c.29)
Supply of Goods (Implied Terms) Act 1973 (c.13)
Supply of Seamen Act 1803 (c.64)
Supply of Water in Bulk Act 1934 (c.15)
Supply Powers Act 1975 (c.9)
Support of Captured Slaves Act 1815 (c.172)
Support of Commercial Credit (Ireland) Act 1820 (c.39)
Support of Commercial Credit (Ireland) Act 1822 (c.22)
Support of Commercial Credit (Ireland) Act 1822 (c.118)
Support of Commercial Credit (Ireland) Act 1823 (c.42)
Suppression of Insurrections (Ireland) Act 1822 (c.1)
Suppression of Insurrections (Ireland) Act 1822 (c.80)
Suppression of Insurrection, etc. (Ireland) Act 1810 (c.78)
Suppression of Rebellion Act 1801 (c.14)
Suppression of Rebellion Act 1801 (c.61)
Suppression of Rebellion Act 1801 (c.104)
Suppression of Rebellion, etc. Act 1803 (c.117)
Suppression of Rebellion, etc. (Ireland) Act 1803 (c.9)
Suppression of Rebellion, etc. (Ireland) Act 1803 (c.117)
Suppression of Terrorism Act 1978 (c.26)
Supreme Court Act 1981 (c.54)
Supreme Court Act (Northern Ireland) 1942 (c.2)
Supreme Court (England) Act 1850 (c.16)
Supreme Court (England) Act 1864 (c.15)
Supreme Court (Ireland) Act 1850 (c.18)
Supreme Court (Ireland) Act 1850 (c.19)
Supreme Court (Ireland) (Master of the Rolls) Act 1815 (c.114)
Supreme Court, Madras Act 1830 (c.75)
Supreme Court (Northern Ireland) Act 1942 (c.2)
Supreme Court of Judicature Act 1873 (c.66)
Supreme Court of Judicature Act 1875 (c.77)
Supreme Court of Judicature Act 1877 (c.9)
Supreme Court of Judicature Act 1881 (c.68)
Supreme Court of Judicature Act 1884 (c.61)
Supreme Court of Judicature Act 1890 (c.44)
Supreme Court of Judicature Act 1891 (c.53)
Supreme Court of Judicature Act 1899 (c.6)
Supreme Court of Judicature Act 1902 (c.31)
Supreme Court of Judicature Act 1910 (c.12)
Supreme Court of Judicature (Amendment) Act 1935 (c.2)
Supreme Court of Judicature (Amendment) Act 1938 (c.67)
Supreme Court of Judicature (Amendment) Act 1944 (c.9)
Supreme Court of Judicature (Amendment) Act 1948 (c.20)
Supreme Court of Judicature (Amendment) Act 1959 (c.39)
Supreme Court of Judicature (Circuit Officers) Act 1946 (c.78)
Supreme Court of Judicature (Commencement) Act 1874 (c.83)
Supreme Court of Judicature (Consolidation) Act 1925 (c.49)
Supreme Court of Judicature (Funds, etc.) Act 1883 (c.29)
Supreme Court of Judicature Act (Ireland) Act 1877 (c.57)
Supreme Court of Judicature (Ireland) Act 1882 (c.70)
Supreme Court of Judicature (Ireland) Act 1887 (c.6)
Supreme Court of Judicature (Ireland) Act 1897 (c.17)
Supreme Court of Judicature (Ireland) Act 1907 (c.44)
Supreme Court of Judicature (Ireland) Act 1877, Amendment Act 1878 (c.27)
Supreme Court of Judicature (Ireland) Amendment Act 1888 (c.27)
Supreme Court of Judicature (Ireland) (No. 2) Act 1897 (c.66)
Supreme Court of Judicature of Northern Ireland 1926 (c.44)
Supreme Court of Judicature (London Causes) Act 1891 (c.14)
Supreme Court of Judicature (Officers) Act 1878 (c.35)
Supreme Court of Judicature (Officers) Act 1879 (c.78)
Supreme Court of Judicature (Procedure) Act 1894 (c.16)
Supreme Court Officers (Pensions) Act 1954 (c.38)

Supreme Court Officers (Retirement, Pensions, etc.) Act 1921 (c.56)
Surrey Act 1856 (c.61)
Surrogacy Arrangements Act 1985 (c.49)
Survey Act 1870 (c.13)
Survey, Great Britain Act 1851 (c.22)
Survey (Great Britain) Continuance Act 1875 (c.32)
Suspension of Certain Appointments Act 1837 (c.71)
Suspensory Act 1914 (c.88)
Swansea Harbour Act 1796 (c.93)
Swaziland Independence Act 1968 (c.56)
Sydney Branch Mint Act 1863 (c.74)

Tancred's Charities 1871 (c.117)
Tanganyika Agricultural Corporation Act 1957 (c.54)
Tanganyika and British Honduras Loans Act 1932 (c.17)
Tanganyika Independence Act 1961 (c.1)
Tanganyika Republic Act 1962 (c.1)
Tanners, Curriers, Shoemakers, etc. Act 1808 (c.60)
Tanners' Indemnity, etc. Act 1799 (c.54)
Taking of Hostages Act 1982 (c.28)
Tanzania Act 1969 (c.29)
Tattooing of Minors Act 1969 (c.24)
Tavistock Canal Act 1796 (c.67)
Taxation Act 1797 (c.16)
Taxation Act 1798 (c.81)
Taxation Act 1801 (c.8)
Taxation Act 1801 (c.10)
Taxation Act 1801 (c.33)
Taxation Act 1801 (c.40)
Taxation Act 1801 (c.42)
Taxation Act 1801 (c.44)
Taxation Act 1801 (c.51)
Taxation Act 1801 (c.62)
Taxation Act 1801 (c.69)
Taxation Act 1801 (c.71)
Taxation Act 1801 (c.74)
Taxation Act 1801 (c.75)
Taxation Act 1805 (c.5)
Taxation Act 1806 (c.84)
Taxation of Chargeable Gains Act 1992 (c.12)
Taxation of Colonies Act 1778 (c.12)
Taxes Act 1797 (c.69)
Taxes Act 1803 (c.99)
Taxes Act 1805 (c.71)
Taxes Act 1810 (c.105)
Taxes Act 1821 (c.113)
Taxes Act 1856 (c.80)
Taxes Management Act 1880 (c.19)
Taxes Management Act 1970 (c.9)
Taxes on Carriages, etc., (Ireland) Act 1809 (c.75)
Taxes (Regulation of Remuneration) Act 1891 (c.13)
Taxes (Regulation of Remuneration) Amendment Act 1892 (c.25)
Taxes (Scotland) Act 1803 (c.150)
Taxes (Scotland) Act 1805 (c.95)
Taxes (Scotland) 1812 (c.95)
Taxes (Scotland) Act 1815 (c.161)
Taxing Masters (Ireland) Act 1848 (c.132)
Taxing Officer (Ireland) Act 1853 (c.55)
Tea Duties Act 1833 (c.101)
Tea Duties Act 1835 (c.32)
Tea Duties Act 1855 (c.9)
Teachers of Nursing Act 1967 (c.16)
Teachers of Schools (Ireland) Act 1844 (c.8)
Teachers' Pay and Conditions Act 1987 (c.1)
Teachers' (Superannuation) Act 1925 (c.59)
Teachers' (Superannuation) Act 1928 (c.10)
Teachers' (Superannuation) Act 1933 (c.22)
Teachers' (Superannuation) Act 1935 (c.35)
Teachers' (Superannuation) Act 1937 (c.47)
Teachers' (Superannuation) Act 1945 (c.14)
Teachers' Superannuation Act 1965 (c.83)
Teachers' Superannuation Act 1967 (c.12)
Teachers' Superannuation (Scotland) Act 1968 (c.12)
Teachers' Superannuation (War Service) Act 1939 (c.95)
Teaching Council (Scotland) Act 1965 (c.19)
Teaching Council (Scotland) Act 1970 (c.2)
Technical and Industrial Institutions Act 1892 (c.29)
Technical Instruction Act 1889 (c.76)
Technical Instruction Act 1891 (c.4)
Technical Instruction Amendment (Scotland) Act 1892 (c.63)
Technical Schools (Scotland) Act 1887 (c.64)
Teinds Act 1808 (c.138)
Teinds Act 1810 (c.84)
Teinds Act 1824 (c.72)
Telecommunications Act 1984 (c.12)
Telegraph Act 1869 (c.73)
Telegraph Act 1870 (c.88)
Telegraph Act 1873 (c.83)
Telegraph Act 1885 (c.58)
Telegraph Act 1954 (c.28)
Telegraph Act 1863 (c.112)
Telegraph Act 1868 (c.110)
Telegraph Act 1878 (c.76)
Telegraph Act 1892 (c.59)
Telegraph Act 1899 (c.38)
Telegraph Act 1943 (c.26)
Telegraph Act 1949 (c.80)
Telegraph Act 1951 (c.37)
Telegraph Act 1962 (c.14)
Telegraph Act Amendment Act 1866 (c.3)
Telegraph (Arbitration) Act 1909 (c.20)
Telegraph (Construction) Act 1908 (c.33)
Telegraph (Construction) Act 1911 (c.39)
Telegraph (Construction) Act 1916 (c.40)
Telegraph (Isle of Man) Act 1889 (c.34)
Telegraph (Money) Act 1871 (c.75)
Telegraph (Money) Act 1876 (c.5)
Telegraph (Money) Act 1896 (c.40)
Telegraph (Money) Act 1898 (c.33)
Telegraph (Money) Act 1904 (c.3)
Telegraph (Money) Act 1907 (c.6)

Telegraph (Money) Act 1913 (c.24)
Telegraph (Money) Act 1920 (c.37)
Telegraph (Money) Act 1921 (c.57)
Telegraph (Money) Act 1922 (c.45)
Telegraph (Money) Act 1924 (c.25)
Telegraph (Money) Act 1925 (c.65)
Telegraphs (Money) Act 1877 (c.30)
Telephone Act 1951 (c.52)
Telephone Transfer Act 1911 (c.26)
Telephone Transfer Amendment Act 1911 (c.56)
Television Act 1954 (c.55)
Television Act 1963 (c.50)
Television Act 1964 (c.21)
Temperance (Scotland) Act 1913 (c.33)
Temple Balsall Hospital Act 1861 (c.24)
Temple Bar, etc. Act 1795 (c.126)
Temporary Migration of Children (Guardianship) Act 1941 (c.23)
Temporary Removal of Convicts Act 1823 (c.82)
Tenancy of Shops (Scotland) Act 1949 (c.25)
Tenancy of Shops (Scotland) Act 1964 (c.50)
Tenants Compensation 1890 (c.57)
Tenants' Rights, etc. (Scotland) Act 1980 (c.52)
Tenants' Rights, etc. (Scotland) Amendment Act 1980 (c.61)
Tenants' Rights, etc. (Scotland) Amendment Act 1984 (c.18)
Tension's Charity Act 1860 (c.43)
Tenures Abolition Act 1660 (c.24)
Term and Quarter Days (Scotland) Act 1990 (c.22)
Termination of the Present War (Definition) Act 1918 (c.59)
Terms and Conditions of Employment Act 1959 (c.26)
Territorial and Reserve Forces Act 1907 (c.9)
Territorial Army and Militia Act 1921 (c.37)
Territorial Sea Act 1987 (c.49)
Territorial Waters Jurisdiction Act 1878 (c.73)
Test Abolition Act 1867 (c.62)
Textile Manufacturers (Ireland) Act 1840 (c.91)
Textile Manufacturers (Ireland) Act 1842 (c.68)
Textile Manufacturers (Ireland) Act 1867 (c.60)
Thames: Ballastage Act 1795 (c.84)
Thames and Isis, Navigation Act 1771 (c.45)
Thames and Severn Canal Act 1796 (c.34)
Thames Conservancy Act 1864 (c.113)
Thames Embankment Act 1852 (c.71)
Thames Embankment Act 1853 (c.87)
Thames Embankment Act 1862 (c.93)
Thames Embankment Act 1863 (c.75)
Thames Embankment Act 1873 (c.40)
Thames Embankment, etc. (Loans) Act 1864 (c.61)
Thames Embankment, etc. (Loans) Act 1868 (c.43)
Thames Navigation Act 1866 (c.89)
Thames Preservation Act 1885 (c.76)
Thatched House Court and Little St. James's Street, Westminster Act 1843 (c.19)
The Chest at Chatham Act 1803 (c.119)
Theatres Act 1843 (c.68)
Theatres Act 1968 (c.54)
Theatres Trust Act 1976 (c.27)
Theatres Trust (Scotland) Act 1978 (c.24)
Theatrical Employers Act 1928 (c.46)
Theatrical Employers Registration Act 1925 (c.50)
Theatrical Employers Registration (Amendment) Act 1928 (c.46)
Theft Act 1968 (c.60)
Theft Act 1978 (c.31)
Theft of Turnips, etc. Act 1802 (c.67)
Therapeutic Substances Act 1925 (c.60)
Therapeutic Substances Act 1953 (c.32)
Therapeutic Substances Act 1956 (c.25)
Thermal Insulation (Industrial Buildings) Act 1957 (c.40)
Third Parties (Rights against Insurers) Act 1930 (c.25)
Thirlage Act 1799 (c.55)
Thirsk Roads Act 1794 (c.118)
Thomas Macklin's Paintings Act 1797 (c.133)
Thread Lace Manufacture (England) Act 1806 (c.81)
Threatening Letters Act 1825 (c.19)
Threatening Letters, etc. Act 1847 (c.66)
Threshing Machines Act 1878 (c.12)
Threshing Machines, Remedies for Damage Act 1832 (c.72)
Timber (Ireland) Act 1888 (c.37)
Timber Ships Act 1845 (c.45)
Timber Ships, America Act 1842 (c.17)
Timber Ships, British North America Act 1839 (c.44)
Timber Ships, British North America Act 1840 (c.36)
Time (Ireland) Act 1916 (c.45)
Time of Service in the Army Act 1847 (c.37)
Timeshare Act 1992 (c.35)
Tithe Act 1832 (c.100)
Tithe Act 1836 (c.71)
Tithe Act 1837 (c.69)
Tithe Act 1838 (c.64)
Tithe Act 1839 (c.62)
Tithe Act 1840 (c.15)
Tithe Act 1842 (c.54)
Tithe Act 1846 (c.73)
Tithe Act 1847 (c.104)
Tithe Act 1860 (c.93)
Tithe Act 1878 (c.42)
Tithe Act 1891 (c.8)
Tithe Act 1918 (c.54)
Tithe Act 1925 (c.87)
Tithe Act 1936 (c.43)
Tithe Act 1951 (c.62)
Tithe Annuities Apportionment Act 1921 (c.20)
Tithe Arrears Act 1839 (c.3)
Tithe Commutation Acts Amendment Act 1873 (c.42)

Tithe Composition Act 1837 (c.58)
Tithe Compositions (Ireland) Act 1836 (c.95)
Tithe Compositions (Ireland) Act 1841 (c.37)
Tithe Compositions (Ireland) Act 1841 (c.6)
Tithe (Ireland) Act 1840 (c.13)
Tithe Rentcharge (Ireland) Act 1838 (c.109)
Tithe Rentcharge (Ireland) Act 1848 (c.80)
Tithe Rentcharge (Ireland) Act 1900 (c.58)
Tithe Rentcharge (Rates) Act 1899 (c.17)
Tithe Rentcharge Redemption Act 1885 (c.32)
Tithes Act 1841 (c.36)
Tithes Prescription Act 1834 (c.83)
Tithes Rating Act 1851 (c.50)
Title Act 1846 (c.73)
Title Act 1925 (c.87)
Title Act 1936 (c.43)
Title Act 1951 (c.62)
Tin Duties Act 1838 (c.120)
Titles Deprivation Act 1917 (c.47)
Titles to Land Consolidation (Scotland) Act 1868 (c.101)
Titles to Land Consolidation (Scotland) Amendment Act 1869 (c.116)
Titles to Land (Scotland) Act 1858 (c.76)
Titles to Land (Scotland) Act 1860 (c.143)
Tobacco Act 1840 (c.18)
Tobacco Act 1842 (c.93)
Tobacco Cultivation Act 1831 (c.13)
Tobacco Growing (Scotland) Act 1908 (c.10)
Tobacco Products Duty Act 1979 (c.7)
Tokens Act 1812 (c.157)
Tokens Act 1813 (c.4)
Tokens Act 1817 (c.46)
Tokens Act 1817 (c.113)
Tokens Act 1825 (c.98)
Tokyo Convention Act 1967 (c.52)
Tolls for Certain Carriages Act 1813 (c.82)
Tolls (Ireland) Act 1817 (c.108)
Tonga Act 1970 (c.22)
Tonnage Duties Act 1822 (c.48)
Tonnage, etc. of Ships Act 1835 (c.56)
Tonnage Rates (Port of London) Act 1834 (c.32)
Tonnage of Steam Vessels Act 1819 (c.5)
Tortola Trade Act 1802 (c.102)
Tortola Trade, etc. Act 1803 (c.133)
Tortola Trade Act 1806 (c.72)
Torts (Interference with Goods) Act 1977 (c.32)
Tourism (Overseas Promotion) (Scotland) Act 1984 (c.4)
Tourism (Overseas Promotion) (Wales) Act 1992 (c.26)
Towcaser to Hardington Road Act 1795 (c.153)
Tower Burial Ground Act 1811 (c.116)
Tower Hamlets Militia Act 1797 (c.75)
Town and Country Amenities Act 1974 (c.32)
Town and Country Planning Act 1932 (c.48)
Town and Country Planning Act 1943 (c.5)
Town and Country Planning Act 1944 (c.47)
Town and Country Planning Act 1947 (c.51)
Town and Country Planning Act 1953 (c.16)
Town and Country Planning Act 1954 (c.72)
Town and Country Planning Act 1959 (c.53)
Town and Country Planning Act 1962 (c.38)
Town and Country Planning Act 1963 (c.17)
Town and Country Planning Act 1968 (c.72)
Town and Country Planning Act 1969 (c.30)
Town and Country Planning Act 1971 (c.78)
Town and Country Planning Act 1984 (c.10)
Town and Country Planning Act 1990 (c.8)
Town and Country Planning (Amendment) Act 1951 (c.19)
Town and Country Planning (Amendment) Act 1972 (c.42)
Town and Country Planning (Amendment) Act 1977 (c.29)
Town and Country Planning (Amendment) Act 1985 (c.52)
Town and Country Planning (Compensation) Act 1985 (c.19)
Town and Country Planning (Costs of Inquiries etc.) Act 1995 (c.49)
Town and Country Planning (Interim Development) Act 1943 (c.29)
Town and Country Planning (Interim Development) (Scotland) Act 1943 (c.43)
Town and Country Planning (Minerals) Act 1981 (c.36)
Town and Country Planning Regulations (London) (Indemnity) Act 1970 (c.57)
Town and Country Planning (Scotland) Act 1932 (c.49)
Town and Country Planning (Scotland) Act 1945 (c.33)
Town and Country Planning (Scotland) Act 1947 (c.53)
Town and Country Planning (Scotland) Act 1954 (c.73)
Town and Country Planning (Scotland) Act 1959 (c.70)
Town and Country Planning (Scotland) Act 1972 (c.52)
Town and Country Planning (Scotland) Act 1977 (c.10)
Town and Country (Scotland) Act 1969 (c.30)
Town Council and Local Bds. Act 1880 (c.17)
Town Councils (Scotland) Act 1900 (c.49)
Town Councils (Scotland) Act 1903 (c.34)
Town Councils (Scotland) Act 1923 (c.41)
Town Development Act 1952 (c.54)
Town Gardens Protection Act 1863 (c.13)
Town Planning Act 1925 (c.16)
Town Planning (Scotland) Act 1925 (c.17)
Town Police Clauses Act 1847 (c.89)
Town Police Clauses Act 1889 (c.14)
Town Tenants (Ireland) Act 1906 (c.54)
Towns Improvements Clauses Act 1847 (c.34)
Towns Improvement (Ireland) Act 1854 (c.103)
Towyn Trewan Common Act 1963 (c.4)
Trade Act 1807 (c.38)
Trade Act 1814 (c.72)

Trade Act 1822 (cc.44,45)
Trade, America, etc. Act 1817 (c.29)
Trade, American Colonies and West Indies Act 1823 (c.2)
Trade Between Bermuda and America Act 1817 (c.28)
Trade Between Great Britain and Ireland Act 1802 (c.14)
Trade Between Great Britain and Ireland Act 1803 (c.78)
Trade Between Europe and British America Act 1809 (c.47)
Trade Between Ireland and East Indies Act 1808 (c.30)
Trade Boards Act 1909 (c.22)
Trade Boards Act 1918 (c.32)
Trade Boards and Road Haulage Wages (Emergency Provisions) Act 1940 (c.7)
Trade Descriptions Act 1968 (c.29)
Trade Descriptions Act 1972 (c.34)
Trade Disputes Act 1906 (c.47)
Trade Disputes Act 1965 (c.48)
Trade Disputes and Trade Unions Act 1927 (c.22)
Trade Disputes and Trade Unions Act 1946 (c.52)
Trade During Hostilities Act 1803 (c.57)
Trade, East Indies and Mediterranean Act 1817 (c.36)
Trade, Europe and American Colonies Act 1811 (c.97)
Trade Facilities Act 1921 (c.65)
Trade Facilities Act 1924 (c.8)
Trade Facilities Act 1925 (c.13)
Trade Facilities Act 1926 (c.3)
Trade Facilities and Loans Guarantee Act 1922 (c.4)
Trade in Grain, etc. Act 1802 (c.35)
Trade in Spirits Act 1815 (c.132)
Trade in Spirits Act 1816 (c.105)
Trade in Spirits Act 1817 (c.72)
Trade in Spirits Act 1818 (c.26)
Trade in Spirits Act 1819 (c.75)
Trade in Spirits Act 1820 (c.77)
Trade Marks Act 1904 (c.15)
Trade Marks Act 1905 (c.15)
Trade Marks Act 1914 (c.16)
Trade Marks Act 1919 (c.79)
Trade Marks Act 1938 (c.22)
Trade Marks Act 1994 (c.26)
Trade Marks (Amendment) Act 1937 (c.49)
Trade Marks (Amendment) Act 1984 (c.19)
Trade Marks Registration Act 1875 (c.91)
Trade Marks Registration Amendment Act 1876 (c.33)
Trade Marks, Registration etc. Act 1877 (c.37)
Trade of British Possessions Act 1845 (c.93)
Trade of Canada Act 1812 (c.55)
Trade of Demerara, etc. Act 1816 (c.91)
Trade of Malta, etc. Act 1814 (c.182)
Trade of Malta, Act 1815 (c.29)
Trade of Nova Scotia, etc. Act 1809 (c.49)
Trade of West Indies Act 1812 (c.100)
Trade of West Indies Act 1814 (c.48)
Trade of West Indies, etc. Act 1814 (c.49)
Trade to the Levant Sea Act 1799 (c.99)
Trade Union Act 1871 (c.31)
Trade Union Act Amendment Act 1876 (c.22)
Trade Union Act 1913 (c.30)
Trade Union Act 1984 (c.49)
Trade Union (Amalgamation) Act 1917 (c.24)
Trade Union (Amalgamations, etc.) Act 1964 (c.24)
Trade Union and Labour Relations Act 1974 (c.52)
Trade Union and Labour Relations (Amendment) Act 1976 (c.7)
Trade Union and Labour Relations (Consolidation) Act 1992 (c.52)
Trade Union Commissions Act 1967 (c.8)
Trade Union Commissions Act Extension 1867 (c.74)
Trade Union (Provident Funds) Act 1893 (c.2)
Trade Union Funds Protection Act 1869 (c.61)
Trade Union Reform and Employment Rights Act 1993 (c.19)
Trade with America Act 1795 (c.26)
Trade with America Act 1796 (c.58)
Trade with America Act 1801 (c.95)
Trade with America Act 1808 (c.85)
Trade with British Possession Act 1831 (c.24)
Trade with French Colonies Act 1815 (c.146)
Trade with India Act 1797 (c.117)
Trade with New South Wales Act 1819 (c.122)
Trade with South America Act 1808 (c.109)
Trade with United States Act 1797 (c.37)
Trade with United States Act 1809 (c.59)
Trade with United States Act 1815 (c.193)
Trade of Tanners and Curriers Act 1816 (c.110)
Trading Partnerships Act 1841 (c.14)
Trading Representations (Disabled Persons) Act 1958 (c.49)
Trading Representations (Disabled Persons) Amendment Act 1972 (c.45)
Trading Stamps Act 1964 (c.71)
Trading with the Enemy Act 1914 (c.87)
Trading with the Enemy Act 1939 (c.89)
Trading with the Enemy Amendment Act 1914 (c.12)
Trading with the Enemy Amendment Act 1915 (c.79)
Trading with the Enemy Amendment Act 1916 (c.105)
Trading with the Enemy (Amendment) Act 1918 (c.31)
Trading with the Enemy and Export of Prohibited Goods Act 1916 (c.52)
Trading with the Enemy (Copyright) Act 1916 (c.32)
Trading with the Enemy (Extension of Powers) Act 1915 (c.98)
Trafalgar Estates Act 1947 (c.34)

Trafalgar Square Act 1844 (c.60)
Traffic Calming Act 1992 (c.30)
Tralee Navigation and Harbour Act 1844 (c.99)
Tralee Navigation Loan Act 1841 (c.46)
Tramway Act (1865) (c.74)
Tramways Act 1870 (c.78)
Tramways and Public Companies Act 1884 (c.5)
Tramways and Public Companies (Ireland) Act 1883 (c.43)
Tramways and Public Companies (Ireland) Amendment Act 1884 (c.28)
Tramways (Ireland) Act 1860 (c.152)
Tramways (Ireland) Act 1895 (c.20)
Tramways (Ireland) Act 1900 (c.60)
Tramways (Ireland) Amendment Act 1861 (c.102)
Tramways (Ireland) Amendment Act 1871 (c.114)
Tramways (Ireland) Amendment Act 1881 (c.17)
Tramways (Ireland) Amendment Act 1891 (c.42)
Tramways (Scotland) Act 1861 (c.69)
Tramways (Temporary Increase of Charges) Act 1920 (c.14)
Transfer of Aids Act 1853 (c.6)
Transfer of Property Act 1844 (c.76)
Transfer of Railways (Ireland) Act 1891 (c.2)
Transfer of Uster Canal Act 1865 (c.109)
Transfer of Balance of Fees Act 1830 (c.1)
Transfer of Contracts, etc. Act 1816 (c.31)
Transfer of Public Funds Act 1821 (c.73)
Transfer of Scotch Excise Charity, etc. Act (c.82)
Transfer of Singapore to East India Company, etc., Act 1824 (c.108)
Transfer of Stock Act 1800 (c.36)
Transfer of Stock (Ireland) Act 1820 (c.5)
Transfer of Stock of Hertford College Act 1816 (c.95)
Transfer of Stocks Act 1817 (c.79)
Transfer of Stocks Act 1818 (c.80)
Transfer of Trust Estates Act 1830 (c.60)
Transfer of Trust Estates, etc. (Ireland) Act 1826 (c.43)
Transfer of Works (Ireland) Act 1856 (c.37)
Transfer to Admiralty of Postal Contracts Act 1837 (c.3)
Transferrence of Lands (Scotland) Act 1847 (cc.48, 49)
Transitional Payments Act (Determination of Need) Act 1932 (c.54)
Transitional Payments Prolongation (Unemployed Persons) Act 1932 (c.19)
Transmission of Moveable Property (Scotland) Act 1862 (c.85)
Transport Act 1947 (c.49)
Transport Act 1953 (c.13)
Transport Act 1962 (c.46)
Transport Act 1968 (c.73)
Transport Act 1978 (c.55)
Transport Act 1980 (c.34)
Transport Act 1981 (c.56)
Transport Act 1982 (c.49)
Transport Act 1983 (c.10)
Transport Act 1985 (c.67)
Transport Act 1962 (Amendment) Act 1981 (c.32)
Transport and Works Act 1992 (c.42)
Transport (Borrowing Papers) Act 1954 (c.10)
Transport (Borrowing Papers) Act 1959 (c.16)
Transport Charges, etc. (Miscellaneous Provisions) Act 1954 (c.64)
Transport (Disposal of Road Haulage Property) Act 1956 (c.56)
Transport (Finance) Act 1982 (c.6)
Transport Finances Act 1966 (c.17)
Transport (Financial Provisions) Act 1977 (c.20)
Transport (Grants) Act 1972 (c.15)
Transport Holding Company Act 1968 (c.10)
Transport Holding Company Act 1972 (c.14)
Transport (London) Act 1969 (c.35)
Transport (London) Amendment Act 1969 (c.60)
Transport Police (Jurisdiction) Act 1994 (c.8)
Transport (Railway Finances) Act 1957 (c.9)
Transport (Scotland) Act 1989 (c.23)
Transportation Act 1799 (c.51)
Transportation Act 1802 (c.15)
Transportation Act 1802 (c.28)
Transportation, etc. Act 1806 (c.28)
Transportation Act 1813 (c.39)
Transportation Act 1813 (c.30)
Transportation Act 1815 (c.156)
Transportation Act 1816 (c.27)
Transportation Act 1819 (c.101)
Transportation Act 1821 (c.6)
Transportation Act 1824 (c.84)
Transportation Act 1825 (c.69)
Transportation Act 1830 (c.39)
Transportation Act 1834 (c.67)
Transportation Act 1843 (c.7)
Transportation Act 1846 (c.26)
Transportation Act 1847 (c.67)
Transportation (Ireland) Act 1849 (c.27)
Transvaal Loan (Guarantee) Act 1907 (c.37)
Travel Concessions Act 1964 (c.95)
Travel Concessions (London) Act 1982 (c.12)
Trawling in Prohibited Areas Prevention Act 1909 (c.8)
Treachery Act 1940 (c.21)
Treason Act 1708 (c.21)
Treason Act 1746 (c.30)
Treason Act 1795 (c.7)
Treason Act 1800 (c.93)
Treason Act 1814 (c.146)
Treason Act 1817 (c.6)
Treason Act 1842 (c.51)
Treason Act 1945 (c.44)
Treason Felony Act 1848 (c.12)
Treason (Ireland) Act 1821 (c.24)

Treason (Ireland) Act 1854 (c.26)
Treason in Scotland Act 1714 (c.20)
Treason Outlawries (Scotland) Act 1748 (c.48)
Treasurer of the Navy Act 1807 (c.56)
Treasurer of the Navy Act 1808 (c.8)
Treasurer of the Navy, etc. Act 1817 (c.121)
Treasurer of the Navy Act 1821 (c.74)
Treasurer of the Navy Act 1830 (c.42)
Treasurers of Counties (Ireland) Act 1855 (c.74)
Treasury Bills Act 1806 (c.32)
Treasury Bills Act 1807 (c.10)
Treasury Bills Act 1877 (c.2)
Treasury Bills Act 1899 (c.2)
Treasury Bills (Ireland) Act 1803 (c.114)
Treasury Bills (Ireland) Act 1804 (c.97)
Treasury Bills (Ireland) Act 1807 (c.72)
Treasury Bills (Ireland) Act 1808 (c.112)
Treasury Bills (Ireland) Act 1809 (c.79)
Treasury Bills (Ireland) Act 1810 (c.98)
Treasury Bills (Ireland) Act 1811 (c.5)
Treasury Bills (Ireland) Act 1811 (c.88)
Treasury Bills (Ireland) Act 1812 (c.90)
Treasury Bills (Ireland) Act 1812 (c.113)
Treasury Bills (Ireland) Act 1813 (c.80)
Treasury Bills (Ireland) Act 1814 (c.75)
Treasury Bills (Ireland) Act 1815 (c.40)
Treasury Bills (Ireland) Act 1816 (cc.41, 42)
Treasury Bills (Ireland) Act 1816 (c.47)
Treasury Bills (Ireland) Act 1817 (c.81)
Treasury Bills (Ireland) Act 1818 (c.87)
Treasury Bills (Ireland) Act 1819 (c.132)
Treasury Bills (Ireland) Act 1820 (c.46)
Treasury Bills (Ireland) Act 1821 (c.80)
Treasury Chest Fund Act 1861 (c.127)
Treasury Chest Fund Act 1873 (c.56)
Treasury Chest Fund Act 1877 (c.45)
Treasury Chest Fund Act 1893 (c.18)
Treasury Instruments (Signature) Act 1849 (c.89)
Treasury of the Ordnance Act 1806 (c.45)
Treasury Solicitor Act 1876 (c.18)
Treasury (Temporary Borrowing) Act 1910 (c.1)
Treaties of Peace (Austria and Bulgaria) Act 1920 (c.6)
Treaties of Peace (Italy, Roumania, Bulgaria, Hungary and Finland) Act 1947 (c.23)
Treaties of Washington Act 1922 (c.21)
Treaty of Commerce, etc. with America Act 1805 (c.35)
Treaty of Commerce, etc. with America Act 1806 (c.16)
Treaty of Commerce, etc. with America Act 1807 (c.2)
Treaty of Commerce, etc. with America Act 1808 (c.6)
Treaty of Peace Act 1919 (c.33)
Treaty of Peace (Hungary) Act 1921 (c.11)
Treaty of Peace (Turkey) Act 1924 (c.7)
Treaty of Washington Act 1872 (c.45)
Treaty with Hayti Act 1842 (c.41)
Treaty with United States 1797 (c.97)
Treaty with United States Act 1819 (c.54)
Trees Act 1970 (c.43)
Trent and Markham Bridges Act 1837 (c.15)
Trespass (Scotland) Act 1865 (c.56)
Trial of Felonies in Certain Boroughs Act 1834 (c.27)
Trial of Lunatics Act 1883 (c.38)
Trial of Offences (Ireland) Act 1833 (c.79)
Trial of Peers (Scotland) Act 1825 (c.66)
Trials for Felony Act 1836 (c.114)
Trials of Murders, etc., in Honduras Act 1819 (c.44)
Tribunals and Inquiries Act 1958 (c.66)
Tribunals and Inquiries Act 1966 (c.43)
Tribunals and Inquiries Act 1971 (c.62)
Tribunals and Inquiries Act 1992 (c.53)
Tribunals of Inquiry (Evidence) Act 1921 (c.7)
Trinidad and Tobago Act 1887 (c.44)
Trinidad and Tobago Independence Act 1962 (c.54)
Trinidad and Tobago Republic Act 1976 (c.54)
Trinity College, Dublin Act 1855 (c.82)
Trout (Scotland) Act 1845 (c.26)
Trout (Scotland) Act 1860 (c.45)
Trout (Scotland) Act 1933 (c.35)
Truck Act 1831 (c.37)
Truck Act 1837 (c.37)
Truck Act 1896 (c.44)
Truck Act 1940 (c.38)
Truck Amendment Act 1887 (c.46)
Truck Commission Act 1870 (c.105)
Trunk Roads Act 1936 (c.5)
Trunk Roads Act 1946 (c.30)
Truro Bishopric and Chapter Acts Amendment Act 1887 (c.12)
Truro Chapter Act 1878 (c.44)
Trust Investment Act 1889 (c.32)
Trust Property, Escheat Act 1834 (c.23)
Trust (Scotland) Amendment Act 1884 (c.63)
Trustee Act 1850 (c.60)
Trustee Act 1852 (c.55)
Trustee Act 1888 (c.59)
Trustee Act 1893 (c.53)
Trustee Act 1925 (c.19)
Trustee Act 1893 Amendment Act 1894 (c.10)
Trustee Appointment Act 1850 (c.28)
Trustee Appointment Act 1869 (c.26)
Trustee Churches (Ireland) Act 1884 (c.10)
Trustee Investments Act 1961 (c.62)
Trustee Savings Banks Act 1863 (c.87)
Trustee Savings Banks Act 1887 (c.47)
Trustee Savings Banks Act 1918 (c.4)
Trustee Savings Banks Act 1946 (c.6)
Trustee Savings Banks Act 1954 (c.63)
Trustee Savings Banks Act 1957 (c.8)
Trustee Savings Banks Act 1969 (c.50)
Trustee Savings Banks Act 1976 (c.4)
Trustee Savings Banks Act 1978 (c.16)
Trustee Savings Banks Act 1981 (c.65)
Trustee Savings Banks Act 1985 (c.58)

Trustee Savings Banks (Pensions) Act 1954 (c.12)
Trustee Savings Banks (Special Investments) Act 1934 (c.37)
Trustee (War Damage Insurance) Act 1941 (c.28)
Trustees Appointment Act 1890 (c.19)
Trustees Relief Act 1847 (c.96)
Trustees Relief Act 1849 (c.74)
Trustees Relief (Ireland) Act 1848 (c.68)
Trustees Savings Banks Act 1968 (c.6)
Trusts (Scotland) Act 1861 (c.84)
Trusts (Scotland) Act 1867 (c.97)
Trusts (Scotland) Act 1897 (c.8)
Trusts (Scotland) Act 1898 (c.42)
Trusts (Scotland) Act, 1867, Amendment Act 1887 (c.18)
Trusts (Scotland) Amendment Act 1891 (c.44)
Trustee (Scotland) Act 1910 (c.22)
Trusts (Scotland) Act 1921 (c.58)
Trusts (Scotland) Act 1961 (c.57)
Tuberculosis Prevention (Ireland) Act 1908 (c.56)
Tuberculosis Prevention (Ireland) Act 1913 (c.25)
Tumultuous Petitioning Act 1661 (c.5)
Tumultuous Risings (Ireland) Act 1831 (c.44)
Tunnel Between Devonport and Keyham Act 1854 (c.15)
Turbary (Ireland) Act 1891 (c.45)
Turkish Loan Act 1855 (c.99)
Turks and Caicos Islands Act 1873 (c.6)
Turnpike Acts Act 1843 (c.69)
Turnpike Acts Continuance 1800 (c.26)
Turnpike Acts Continuance Act 1831 (c.6)
Turnpike Acts Continuance Act 1834 (c.10)
Turnpike Acts Continuance Act 1835 (c.49)
Turnpike Acts Continuance Act 1836 (c.62)
Turnpike Acts Continuance Act 1837 (c.18)
Turnpike Acts Continuance Act 1838 (c.68)
Turnpike Acts Continuance Act 1839 (c.31)
Turnpike Acts Continuance Act 1840 (c.45)
Turnpike Acts Continuance Act 1841 (c.9)
Turnpike Acts Continuance Act 1842 (c.60)
Turnpike Acts Continuance Act 1845 (c.53)
Turnpike Acts Continuance Act 1848 (c.96)
Turnpike Acts Continuance Act 1849 (c.87)
Turnpike Acts Continuance Act 1857 (c.24)
Turnpike Acts Continuance Act 1858 (c.63)
Turnpike Acts Continuance Act 1866 (c.105)
Turnpike Acts Continuance (Ireland) Act 1851 (c.44)
Turnpike Acts, Great Britain Act 1844 (c.41)
Turnpike Acts, Great Britain Act 1846 (c.51)
Turnpike Acts, Great Britain Act 1847 (c.105)
Turnpike Acts, Great Britain Act 1852 (c.58)
Turnpike Acts, Great Britain Act 1855 (c.98)
Turnpike Acts, Great Britain Act 1856 (c.49)
Turnpike Acts (Ireland) Act 1838 (c.72)
Turnpike Acts (Ireland) Act 1842 (c.23)
Turnpike Acts (Ireland) Act 1843 (c.21)
Turnpike Acts (Ireland) Act 1844 (c.36)
Turnpike Acts (Ireland) Act 1845 (c.125)
Turnpike Acts (Ireland) Act 1848 (c.73)
Turnpike Acts (Ireland) Act 1849 (c.47)
Turnpike Acts (Ireland) Act 1852 (c.22)
Turnpike Acts (Ireland) Act 1853 (c.76)
Turnpike Acts (Ireland) Act 1854 (c.42)
Turnpike Acts (Ireland) Act 1855 (c.83)
Turnpike Acts, Ireland, Continuance Act 1836 (c.40)
Turnpike Acts, Ireland, Continuance Act 1840 (c.46)
Turnpike Acts, Ireland, Continuance Act 1850 (c.34)
Turnpike Acts, Ireland, Continuance Act 1856 (c.71)
Turnpike Debts Act 1852 (c.33)
Turnpike Roads Act 1815 (c.119)
Turnpike Roads Act 1817 (c.37)
Turnpike Roads Act 1822 (c.126)
Turnpike Roads Act 1823 (c.95)
Turnpike Roads Act 1824 (c.69)
Turnpike Roads Act 1827 (c.24)
Turnpike Roads Act 1828 (c.77)
Turnpike Roads (England) Act 1853 (c.135)
Turnpike Roads (England) Act 1854 (c.58)
Turnpike Roads in Yorkshire Act 1852 (c.45)
Turnpike Roads (Ireland) Act 1834 (c.91)
Turnpike Roads (Ireland) Act 1841 (c.6)
Turnpike Roads (Ireland) Act 1846 (c.89)
Turnpike Roads (Ireland) Act 1847 (c.35)
Turnpike Roads (Scotland) Act 1823 (c.49)
Turnpike Roads (Scotland) Act 1831 (c.43)
Turnpike Roads (Scotland) Act 1849 (c.31)
Turnpike Roads (Tolls on Lime) Act 1823 (c.16)
Turnpike Roads Trusts Act 1820 (c.95)
Turnpike Tolls Act 1835 (c.18)
Turnpike Tolls Act 1839 (c.46)
Turnpike Tolls Act 1840 (c.51)
Turnpike Tolls Act 1841 (c.33)
Turnpike Tolls (Allowance of Wagon Weights) Act 1834 (c.81)
Turnpike Trusts Act 1856 (c.12)
Turnpike Trusts Arrangements Act 1867 (c.66)
Turnpike Trusts Arrangements Act 1868 (c.66)
Turnpike Trusts Arrangements Act 1872 (c.72)
Turnpike Trusts: Making of Provisional Orders Act 1851 (c.38)
Turnpike Trusts Relief Act 1861 (c.46)
Turnpike Trusts Returns Act 1833 (c.80)
Turnpike Trusts, South Wales Act 1845 (c.61)
Turnpikes Abolition (Ireland) Act 1857 (c.16)
Turnpikes Act 1831 (c.25)
Turnpikes Act 1832 (c.124)
Turnpikes Act 1840 (c.39)
Turnpikes Acts Continuation Act 1849 (c.87)
Turnpikes (Provisional Orders Confirmation) Act 1865 (c.91)
Turnpikes (Provisional Orders Confirmation) Act 1866 (c.92)

Turnpikes (Provisional Orders Confirmation) Act 1870 (c.22)
Turnpikes, South Wales Act 1844 (c.91)
Tuvalu Act 1978 (c.20)
Tweed Fisheries Act 1797 (c.48)
Tyne Pilotage Order Confirmation Act 1865 (c.44)
Tyne Pilotage Order Confirmation Act 1867 (c.78)

Uganda Act 1964 (c.20)
Uganda Railway Act 1896 (c.38)
Uganda Railway Act 1900 (c.11)
Uganda Railway Act 1902 (c.40)
Ugandan Independence Act 1962 (c.57)
Ulster Defence Regiment Act 1969 (c.65)
Ulster Defence Regiment Act 1973 (c.34)
Ulster Society 1704 (c.19)
Ulverstone Canal Act 1793 (c.105)
Unclaimed Prize Money, etc. Act 1812 (c.132)
Under Secretaries of State Act 1929 (c.9)
Under Secretary of State Indemnity Act 1864 (c.21)
Underground Works (London) Act 1956 (c.59)
Unemployed Workers' Dependants (Temporary Provisions) Act 1921 (c.62)
Unemployed Workmen Act 1904 (c.18)
Unemployment Act 1934 (c.29)
Unemployment and Family Allowances (Northern Ireland Agreement) Act 1946 (c.3)
Unemployment Assistance (Emergency Powers) Act 1939 (c.93)
Unemployment Assistance (Temporary Provisions) Act 1935 (c.6)
Unemployment Assistance (Temporary Provisions) (Amendment) Act 1937 (c.10)
Unemployment Assistance (Temporary Provisions) (Extension) Act 1936 (c.7)
Unemployment Assistance (Temporary Provisions) (No. 2) Act 1935 (c.22)
Unemployment Insurance Act 1920 (c.30)
Unemployment Insurance Act 1921 (c.1)
Unemployment Insurance Act 1922 (c.7)
Unemployment Insurance Act 1923 (c.2)
Unemployment Insurance Act 1924 (c.1)
Unemployment Insurance Act 1925 (c.69)
Unemployment Insurance Act 1926 (c.12)
Unemployment Insurance Act 1927 (c.30)
Unemployment Insurance Act 1928 (c.1)
Unemployment Insurance Act 1929 (c.3)
Unemployment Insurance Act 1930 (c.16)
Unemployment Insurance Act 1931 (c.8)
Unemployment Insurance Act 1935 (c.8)
Unemployment Insurance Act 1938 (c.8)
Unemployment Insurance Act 1939 (c.29)
Unemployment Insurance Act 1940 (c.44)
Unemployment Insurance (Agriculture) Act 1936 (c.13)
Unemployment Insurance (Crediting of Contributions) Act 1935 (c.33)
Unemployment Insurance (Emergency Powers) Act 1939 (c.92)
Unemployment Insurance (Expiring Enactments) Act 1933 (c.26)
Unemployment Insurance (Eire Volunteers) Act 1946 (c.76)
Unemployment Insurance (Increase of Benefit) Act 1944 (c.42)
Unemployment Insurance (Northern Ireland Agreement) Act 1926 (c.4)
Unemployment Insurance (Northern Ireland Agreement) Act 1929 (c.18)
Unemployment Insurance (No. 2) Act 1921 (c.15)
Unemployment Insurance (No. 2) Act 1922 (c.30)
Unemployment Insurance (No. 2) Act 1924 (c.30)
Unemployment Insurance (No. 2) Act 1930 (c.19)
Unemployment Insurance (No. 2) Act 1931 (c.25)
Unemployment Insurance (No. 3) Act 1924 (c.6)
Unemployment Insurance (No. 3) Act 1930 (c.47)
Unemployment Insurance (No. 3) Act 1931 (c.36)
Unemployment Insurance (No. 4) Act 1931 (c.3)
Unemployment Insurance (Temporary Provisions Amendment) 1920 (c.82)
Unemployment Insurance (Transitional Provisions Amendment) Act 1929 (c.19)
Unemployment (Northern Ireland Agreement) Act 1936 (c.10)
Unemployment Relief Works 1920 (c.57)
Unfair Contract Terms Act 1977 (c.50)
Unfunded Debt Act 1761 (c.7)
Unfunded Debt Act 1765 (c.19)
Unfunded Debt Act 1766 (c.15)
Unfunded Debt Act 1766 (c.16)
Unfunded Debt Act 1768 (c.18)
Unfunded Debt Act 1769 (c.15)
Unfunded Debt Act 1770 (c.11)
Unfunded Debt Act 1772 (c.39)
Unfunded Debt Act 1772 (c.66)
Unfunded Debt Act 1801 (c.4)
Uniform Laws on International Sales Act 1967 (c.45)
Uniformity of Worship Act 1749 (c.28)
Uniforms Act 1894 (c.45)
Union and Parish Property Act 1837 (c.50)
Union Assessment Act 1880 (c.7)
Union Assessment Committee Act 1862 (c.103)
Union Assessment Committee Amendment Act 1864 (c.39)
Union Between England and Scotland Act 1702 (c.8)
Union Chargeability Act 1865 (c.79)

Union Loans Act 1869 (c.45)
Union of Benefices Act 1860 (c.142)
Union of Benefices Act 1898 (c.23)
Union of Benefices Act 1919 (c.98)
Union of Benefices Acts Amendment Act 1871 (c.90)
Union of Benefices, etc. Act 1855 (c.127)
Union of England and Scotland 1704 (c.6)
Union of England and Scotland 1705 (c.15)
Union of Parishes Act 1827 (c.43)
Union of Parishes, etc. (Ireland) Act 1832 (c.67)
Union of Turnpike Trusts Act 1849 (c.46)
Union Officers (Ireland) Act 1872 (c.89)
Union Officers (Ireland) Act 1885 (c.80)
Union Officers Superannuation (Ireland) Act 1865 (c.26)
Union Relief Aid Act 1862 (c.110)
Union Relief Aid Act 1863 (c.91)
Union Relief Aid Continuance Act 1863 (c.4)
Union Relief Aid Continuance Act 1864 (c.10)
Union with Ireland Act 1800 (c.67)
Union with Scotland Act 1706 (c.11)
Union with Scotland (Amendment) Act 1707 (c.40)
United Nations Act 1946 (c.45)
United Parishes (Scotland) Act 1868 (c.30)
United Parishes (Scotland) Act 1876 (c.11)
United States of America Veterans' Pensions (Administration) Act 1949 (c.45)
United States of America (Visiting Forces) Act 1942 (c.31)
Universities Act 1825 (c.97)
Universities and College (Emergency Powers) Act 1914 (c.22)
Universities and College (Emergency Provisions) Act 1939 (c.106)
Universities and College Estates Act 1858 (c.44)
Universities and College Estates Act 1898 (c.55)
Universities and College Estates Act 1925 (c.24)
Universities and College Estates Act 1964 (c.51)
Universities and College Estates Act Extension Act 1860 (c.59)
Universities and College Estates Amendment Act 1880 (c.46)
Universities and Colleges (Trust) Act 1943 (c.9)
Universities Election Act 1868 (c.65)
Universities Elections Amendment (Scotland) Act 1881 (c.40)
Universities of Oxford and Cambridge Act 1859 (c.19)
Universities of Oxford and Cambridge Act 1877 (c.48)
Universities of Oxford and Cambridge Act 1880 (c.11)
Universities of Oxford and Cambridge Act 1923 (c.33)
Universities (Scotland) Act 1853 (c.89)
Universities (Scotland) Act 1858 (c.83)
Universities (Scotland) Act 1859 (c.24)
Universities (Scotland) Act 1862 (c.28)
Universities (Scotland) Act 1889 (c.55)
Universities (Scotland) Act 1922 (c.31)
Universities (Scotland) Act 1932 (c.26)
Universities (Scotland) Act 1966 (c.13)
Universities Tests Act 1871 (c.26)
University Education (Ireland) Act 1879 (c.65)
University Elections Act 1861 (c.53)
University of Dublin Registration Act 1842 (c.74)
University of Dublin Tests 1873 (c.21)
University of Durham Act 1908 (c.20)
University of Durham Act 1935 (c.29)
University of Liverpool Act 1904 (c.11)
University of London Act 1898 (c.62)
University of London Act 1899 (c.24)
University of London Act 1926 (c.46)
University of London Medical Graduates Act 1854 (c.114)
University of Oxford Act 1869 (c.20)
University of St. Andrews Act 1746 (c.32)
University of St. Andrews Act 1953 (c.40)
University of Wales Act 1902 (c.14)
University of Wales (Medical Graduates) Act 1911 (c.43)
Universities (Wine Licences) Act 1743 (c.40)
Unlawful Combinations (Ireland) Act 1803 (c.86)
Unlawful Combinations (Ireland) Act 1814 (c.180)
Unlawful Combinations (Ireland) Act 1848 (c.89)
Unlawful Combinations of Workmen Act 1799 (c.81)
Unlawful Combinations of Workmen Act 1800 (c.106)
Unlawful Distillation, etc. (Ireland) Act 1814 (c.12)
Unlawful Drilling Act 1819 (c.1)
Unlawful Games Act 1728 (c.28)
Unlawful Oaths Act 1797 (c.123)
Unlawful Oaths Act 1810 (c.102)
Unlawful Oaths Act 1812 (c.104)
Unlawful Oaths Act 1823 (c.87)
Unlawful Oaths (Ireland) Act 1810 (c.102)
Unlawful Oaths (Ireland) Act 1844 (c.78)
Unlawful Oaths (Ireland) Act 1845 (c.55)
Unlawful Oaths (Ireland) Act 1851 (c.48)
Unlawful Oaths (Ireland) Act 1856 (c.78)
Unlawful Oaths (Ireland) Act 1862 (c.32)
Unlawful Pawning Act 1786 (c.92)
Unlawful Societies Act 1799 (c.79)
Unlawful Societies (Ireland) Act 1839 (c.74)
Unlawful Weights (Ireland) Act 1824 (c.110)
Unreasonable Withholding of Food Supplies Act 1914 (c.51)
Unsolicited Goods and Services Act 1971 (c.30)
Unsolicited Goods and Services (Amendment) Act 1975 (c.13)

Urban Development Corporations (Financial Limits) Act 1987 (c.57)
Use of Clarke's Hydrometer Act 1802 (c.97)
Use of Corn in Distillation of Spirits, etc. Act 1800 (c.3)
Use of Fine Flow Act 1801 (cc.1, 2)
Use of Fire on Steamboats Act 1828 (c.11)
Use of Highland Dress Act 1782 (c.63)
Use of Horsehides etc. Act 1800 (c.66)
Use of Plate Act 1769 (c.11)
Use of Rice in Distillation Act 1856 (c.51)
Use of Salt Duty Free, etc. Act 1800 (c.21)
Use of Sugar in Brewing Act 1800 (c.62)
Use of Sugar in Brewing Act 1812 (c.1)
Use of Sugar in Brewing Act 1812 (c.65)
Use of Wheat in Making Starch Act 1800 (c.25)
Usury Act 1713 (c.15)
Usury Act 1837 (c.80)
Usury Act 1839 (c.37)
Usury Act 1840 (c.83)
Usury Act 1841 (c.54)
Usury Act 1843 (c.45)
Usury Act 1845 (c.102)
Usury Act 1850 (c.56)
Usury Laws Repeal Act 1854 (c.90)
Uttoxeter to Stoke Road Act 1793 (c.131)
Uxbridge: Streets Act 1785 (c.16)

Vacant Ecclesiastical Dignities, etc. Act 1835 (c.30)
Vaccination Act 1840 (c.29)
Vaccination Act 1841 (c.32)
Vaccination Act 1853 (c.100)
Vaccination Act 1867 (c.84)
Vaccination Act 1871 (c.98)
Vaccination Act 1874 (c.75)
Vaccination Act 1898 (c.49)
Vaccination Act 1907 (c.31)
Vaccination Acts Amendment Act 1861 (c.59)
Vaccination Amendment (Ireland) Act 1868 (c.87)
Vaccination Amendment (Ireland) Act 1879 (c.70)
Vaccination (Ireland) Act 1858 (c.64)
Vaccination (Ireland) Act 1863 (c.52)
Vaccination (Scotland) Act 1863 (c.108)
Vaccination (Scotland) Act 1907 (c.49)
Vaccine Damage Payments Act 1979 (c.17)
Vagrance (Ireland) Amendment Act 1865 (c.33)
Vagrancy Act 1824 (c.83)
Vagrancy Act 1838 (c.38)
Vagrancy Act 1898 (c.39)
Vagrancy Act 1935 (c.20)
Vagrancy (England) Act 1822 (c.40)
Vagrancy (Ireland) Act 1847 (c.84)
Vagrant Act Amendment Act 1868 (c.52)
Vagrant Act Amendment Act 1873 (c.38)
Vagrants Act 1706 (c.32)
Vagrants Act 1713 (c.26)
Vagrants Act 1739 (c.24)
Vagrants Act 1821 (c.64)
Vagrants and Criminals Act 1787 (c.11)
Validation of Acts of Hate, Chief Justice of Bombay Act 1858 (c.32)
Validation of Elections Act 1955 (c.10)
Validation of Elections (No. 2) Act 1955 (c.12)
Validation of Elections (No. 3) Act 1955 (c.13)
Validation of Elections (Northern Ireland) Act 1956 (c.35)
Validation of War-time Leases Act 1944 (c.34)
Validity of Certain Contracts Act 1838 (c.10)
Validity of Certain Oaths Act 1812 (c.21)
Validity of Certain Orders in Council, etc. Act 1808 (c.37)
Validity of Certain Proceedings, etc. Act 1854 (c.37)
Validity of Proceedings in the House of Commons Act 1855 (c.33)
Valuation and Rating (Exempted Classes) (Scotland) Act 1976 (c.64)
Valuation and Rating (Scotland) Act 1956 (c.60)
Valuation (Ireland) Act 1834 (c.55)
Valuation (Ireland) Act 1852 (c.63)
Valuation (Ireland) Act 1853 (c.7)
Valuation (Ireland) Act 1854 (c.8)
Valuation (Ireland) Act 1864 (c.52)
Valuation (Ireland) Act 1901 (c.37)
Valuation (Ireland) Amendment Act 1874 (c.70)
Valuation (Metropolis) Act 1869 (c.67)
Valuation Metropolis Amendment Act 1884 (c.5)
Valuation Metropolis Amendment Act 1925 (c.40)
Valuation of Lands (Ireland) Act 1826 (c.62)
Valuation of Lands (Ireland) Act 1831 (c.51)
Valuation of Lands (Ireland) Act 1832 (c.73)
Valuation of Lands (Ireland) Act 1836 (c.84)
Valuation for Rating Act 1953 (c.42)
Valuation for Rating (Scotland) Act 1970 (c.4)
Valuation of Lands (Scotland) Acts Amendment Act 1894 (c.36)
Valuation of Lands (Scotland) Amendment Act 1867 (c.80)
Valuation of Lands (Scotland) Amendment Act 1879 (c.42)
Valuation of Lands (Scotland) Amendment Act 1887 (c.51)
Value Added Tax Act 1983 (c.55)
Value Added Tax Act 1994 (c.23)
Van Diemen's Land Act 1842 (c.3)
Van Diemen's Land Co. Act 1825 (c.39)
Van Diemen's Land Co. Act 1847 (c.57)
Vancouver's Island Act 1849 (c.48)
Variation of Trusts Act 1958 (c.53)
Vehicle and Driving Licences Act 1969 (c.27)
Vehicle Excise and Registration Act 1994 (c.22)
Vehicles (Excise) Act 1949 (c.89)
Vehicles (Excise) Act 1962 (c.13)
Vehicles (Excise) Act 1971 (c.10)

Vendor and Purchaser Act 1874 (c.78)
Venereal Disease Act 1917 (c.21)
Vessels Built at Malta, etc. Act 1820 (c.9)
Vessels Protection Act 1967 (c.85)
Vesting in Crown of Lands at Sandhurst Act 1812 (c.124)
Vestries Act 1818 (c.69)
Vestries Act 1819 (c.85)
Vestries Act 1831 (c.60)
Vestries Act 1850 (c.57)
Vestries Act 1853 (c.65)
Vesty Cess Abolition Act 1864 (c.17)
Veterinary Surgeons Act 1881 (c.62)
Veterinary Surgeons Act 1948 (c.52)
Veterinary Surgeons Act 1966 (c.36)
Veterinary Surgeons Act (1881) Amendment 1920 (c.20)
Veterinary Surgeons Amendment 1900 (c.24)
Veterinary Surgeons (Irish Free State Agreement) Act 1932 (c.10)
Vexatious Actions Act 1896 (c.51)
Vexatious Actions (Scotland) Act 1898 (c.35)
Vexatious Arrests Act 1747 (c.3)
Vexatious Arrests Act 1817 (c.101)
Vexatious Indictments Act 1859 (c.17)
Vice-Admiralty Courts Act 1816 (c.82)
Vice-Admiralty Courts Act 1832 (c.51)
Vice-Admiralty Courts Act 1863 (c.24)
Vice-Admiralty Courts Act Amendment Act 1867 (c.45)
Victoria Constitution Act 1855 (c.55)
Victoria Park Act 1842 (c.20)
Victoria Park Act 1872 (c.53)
Victoria University Act 1888 (c.45)
Victualling Establishment, Plymouth Act 1824 (c.49)
Video Recordings Act 1984 (c.39)
Video Recordings Act 1993 (c.24)
Vinegar Act 1844 (c.25)
Viscount Hardinge's Annuity Act 1846 (c.21)
Visiting Forces Act 1952 (c.67)
Visiting Forces (British Commonwealth) Act 1933 (c.6)
Voluntary Conveyances Act 1893 (c.21)
Voluntary Hospitals (Paying Patients) Act 1936 (c.17)
Voluntary Schools Act 1897 (c.5)
Volunteer Act 1863 (c.65)
Volunteer Act 1869 (c.81)
Volunteer Act 1895 (c.23)
Volunteer Act 1897 (c.47)
Volunteer Act 1900 (c.39)
Volunteer Act 1916 (c.62)
Volunteers Act 1780 (c.37)
Volunteers Act 1782 (c.79)
Volunteers Act 1861 (c.126)
Volunteers and Local Militia Act 1809 (c.113)
Volunteers and Yeomanry (Great Britain) Act 1803 (c.18)
Volunteer Corps Act 1794 (c.31)

Wadeshill and Royston Road Act 1796 (c.129)
Wages Act 1708 (c.16)
Wages Act 1986 (c.48)
Wages and Prize Money, etc. in the Navy Act 1809 (c.108)
Wages Arrestment Act 1845 (c.39)
Wages Arrestment Limitation (Amendment) (Scotland) Act 1960 (c.21)
Wages Arrestment Limitation (Scotland) Act 1870 (c.63)
Wages Attachment Abolition Act 1870 (c.30)
Wages Councils Act 1945 (c.17)
Wages Councils Act 1948 (c.7)
Wages Councils Act 1959 (c.69)
Wages Councils Act 1979 (c.12)
Wages Councils (Northern Ireland) Act 1945 (c.21)
Wages, etc. of Artificers, etc. Act 1813 (c.40)
Wages of Artificers, etc. Act 1820 (c.93)
Wages of Certain Deceased Seamen Act 1819 (c.59)
Wages of Merchant Seamen Act 1819 (c.58)
Wages (Temporary Regulations) Act 1918 (c.61)
Wages (Temporary Regulations) Extension Act 1919 (c.18)
Wakefield Church Act 1791 (c.74)
Wakefield, etc. Roads Act 1740 (c.19)
Wakefield and Halifax Roads Act 1793 (c.129)
Wakefield and Sheffield Road Act 1797 (c.159)
Wakefield (Improvement) Act 1771 (c.44)
Wakefield: Improvement Act 1796 (c.50)
Wakefield Roads Act 1778 (c.85)
Wakefield to Abberford Road Act 1789 (c.86)
Wakefield to Abberford Road Act 1793 (c.179)
Wakefield to Austerlands Road Act 1758 (c.48)
Wakefield to Sheffield Road Act 1778 (c.105)
Walcot, Somerset: Improvement Act 1793 (c.89)
Wales Act 1978 (c.52)
Wales and Berwick Act 1746 (c.42)
Wales, Chester, etc. (Courts) Act 1793 (c.68)
Wallingford: Improvement Act 1795 (c.75)
Walmer Vesting Act 1863 (c.54)
Walmore and Bearce Commons, Forest of Dean Act 1866 (c.70)
Walton - Shepperton Bridge (Building and Tolls) Act 1746 (c.22)
Walton - Shepperton Bridge (Rebuilding and Tolls) Act 1780 (c.32)
Wangford, Suffolk: Poor Relief Act 1764 (c.91)
Wapping, Stepney Act 1728 (c.30)
Wapping, Stepney: Poor Relief Act 1782 (c.35)
Wapping, Stepney: Poor Relief, etc. Act 1783 (c.32)
Wapping, Stepney: Improvement Act 1782 (c.86)
War Charges (Validity) Act 1925 (c.6)

War Charities Act 1916 (c.43)
War Charities Act 1940 (c.31)
War Charities Act (Scotland) 1919 (c.12)
War Crimes Act 1991 (c.13)
War Damage Act 1941 (c.12)
War Damage Act 1943 (c.21)
War Damage Act 1949 (c.36)
War Damage Act 1964 (c.25)
War Damage Act 1965 (c.18)
War Damage (Amendment) Act 1942 (c.28)
War Damages (Amendment) Act 1943 (c.12)
War Damage (Clearance Payments) Act 1960 (c.25)
War Damage (Extension of Risk Period) Act 1941 (c.37)
War Damage (Public Utility Undertakings, etc.) Act 1949 (c.36)
War Damage to Land (Scotland) Act 1939 (c.80)
War Damage to Land (Scotland) Act 1941 (c.40)
War Damage (Valuation Appeals) Act 1945 (c.8)
War Damaged Sites Act 1949 (c.84)
War Department Property Act 1938 (c.49)
War Department Stores Act 1867 (c.128)
War Department Tramway (Devon) Act 1865 (c.74)
War Emergency Laws (Continuance) Act 1920 (c.5)
War Loan Act 1900 (c.2)
War Loan Act 1914 (c.60)
War Loan Act 1915 (c.55)
War Loan Act 1916 (c.67)
War Loan Act 1917 (c.41)
War Loan Act 1918 (c.25)
War Loan Act 1919 (c.37)
War Loan (Redemption) Act 1910 (c.2)
War Loan (Supplemental Provisions) Act 1915 (c.93)
War Memorials (Local Authorities' Powers) Act 1923 (c.18)
War Office Act 1879 (c.17)
War Orphans Act 1942 (c.8)
War Pensions Act 1920 (c.23)
War Pensions Act 1921 (c.49)
War Pensions (Administrative Provisions) Act 1918 (c.57)
War Pensions (Administrative Provisions) Act 1919 (c.53)
War Risks Insurance Act 1939 (c.57)
War Risks (Insurance by Truskes) Act 1916 (c.6)
War Service Canteens (Disposal of Surplus) Act 1922 (c.53)
War Stores (Commission) Act 1904 (c.7)
Warden of Fleet Prison Act 1728 (c.32)
Warden of the Fleet Prison Act 1819 (c.64)
Wareham and Purbeck Roads Act 1786 (c.122)
Wareham: Improvement Act 1763 (c.54)
Warehoused British Spirits Act 1867 (c.27)
Warehoused Goods Act 1809 (c.106)
Warehoused Tobacco, etc. Act 1793 (c.57)
Warehousing of British Compounded Spirits Act 1865 (c.98)
Warehousing of British Spirits Act 1864 (c.12)
Warehousing of Foreign Goods, Manchester Act 1844 (c.31)
Warehousing of Goods Act 1799 (c.59)
Warehousing of Goods Act 1803 (c.132)
Warehousing of Goods Act 1823 (c.24)
Warehousing of Goods Act 1845 (c.91)
Warehousing of Spirits (Ireland) Act 1812 (c.30)
Warehousing of Wines, etc. Act 1795 (c.118)
Warminster Roads Act 1726 (c.16)
Warminster Roads Act 1742 (c.5)
Warminster Roads Act 1765 (c.62)
Warminster Roads Act 1792 (c.141)
Warrants of Attorney Act 1822 (c.39)
Warrants of Attorney Act 1843 (c.66)
Warrick Election Act 1834 (c.17)
Warrington and Wigan Road Act 1726 (c.10)
Warrington and Wigan Road Act 1770 (c.70)
Warrington to Wigan Road Act 1746 (c.8)
Warrington to Wigan Road Act 1793 (c.164)
Warwick and Birmingham Canal Act 1793 (c.38)
Warrington and Birmingham Canal Act 1796 (c.42)
Warwick and Gloucester Roads Act 1773 (c.97)
Warwick and Gloucester Roads Act 1791 (c.116)
Warwick and Napton Canal Act 1794 (c.38)
Warwick and Napton Canal Act 1796 (c.95)
Warwick and Northampton Road Act 1765 (c.107)
Warwick Assizes Act 1854 (c.35)
Warwick, etc. Roads Act 1739 (c.5)
Warwick to Northampton Road Act 1776 (c.80)
Warwick and Northampton Roads Act 1781 (c.106)
Warwick and Northamptonshire Roads Act 1759 (c.44)
Warwick and Oxford Roads Act 1755 (c.46)
Warwick and Oxford Roads Act 1780 (c.69)
Warwick and Worcester Roads Act 1754 (c.36)
Warwick and Worcester Roads Act 1767 (c.81)
Warwick and Worcester Roads Act 1780 (c.71)
Warwick and Worcester Roads Act 1781 (c.88)
Warwick Bridge Act 1788 (c.9)
Warwick Gaol Act 1777 (c.58)
Warwick, Stafford and Worcester Roads Act 1794 (c.117)
Warwick Roads Act 1723 (c.15)
Warwick Roads Act 1730 (c.9)
Warwick Roads Act 1738 (c.18)
Warwick Roads Act 1739 (c.22)
Warwick Roads Act 1742 (c.20)

Warwick Roads Act 1743 (c.12)
Warwick Roads Act 1744 (c.32)
Warwick Roads Act 1753 (c.73)
Warwick Roads Act 1760 (c.36)
Warwick Roads Act 1767 (c.77)
Warwick Roads Act 1770 (c.63)
Warwick Roads Act 1770 (c.69)
Warwick Roads Act 1770 (c.94)
Warwick Roads Act 1772 (c.91)
Warwick Roads Act 1780 (c.80)
Warwick Roads Act 1785 (c.115)
Warwick Roads Act 1788 (c.107)
Warwick Roads Act 1791 (c.98)
Warwick Roads Act 1792 (c.116)
Warwick Roads Act 1794 (c.115)
Warwick Roads Act 1794 (c.116)
Warwick Shire Hall Act 1757 (c.56)
Warwick, Stafford and Worcester Roads Act 1772 (c.110)
Warwick, Worcester and Stafford Roads Act 1787 (c.73)
Warwickshire and Northamptonshire Roads 1736 (c.11)
Warwickshire Roads Act 1744 (c.19)
Washington Treaty (Claims) Act 1875 (c.52)
Waste Lands, Australia Act 1846 (c.104)
Waste Lands, Van Diemen's Land Act 1845 (c.95)
Watch Rates in Boroughs Act 1840 (c.28)
Watching: City of London Act 1736 (c.22)
Watching: Holborn Act 1736 (c.25)
Watching, St. Margaret and St. John, Westminster 1735 (c.17)
Watching, St. Martin's in the Fields Act 1735 (c.8)
Watching, St. Paul (Covent Garden) 1735 (c.13)
Watching, Westminster 1735 (c.19)
Watchett (Somerset) Harbour Act 1707 (c.69)
Watchett (Somerset) Harbour Act 1720 (c.14)
Watchett Harbour Act 1770 (c.24)
Water Act 1945 (c.42)
Water Act 1948 (c.22)
Water Act 1958 (c.67)
Water Act 1973 (c.37)
Water Act 1981 (c.12)
Water Act 1983 (c.23)
Water Act 1989 (c.15)
Water Charges Act 1976 (c.9)
Water Charges Equalisation Act 1977 (c.41)
Water Companies (Regulation of Powers) Act 1887 (c.21)
Water Consolidation (Consequential Provisions) Act 1991 (c.60)
Water (Fluoridation) Act 1985 (c.63)
Water Industry Act 1991 (c.60)
Water Measure of Fruit 1702 (c.9)
Water Officers Compensation Act 1960 (c.15)
Water Rate Definition Act 1885 (c.34)
Water Resources Act 1963 (c.38)
Water Resources Act 1968 (c.35)
Water Resources Act 1971 (c.34)
Water Resources Act 1991 (c.57)
Water (Scotland) Act 1946 (c.42)
Water (Scotland) Act 1949 (c.31)
Water (Scotland) Act 1967 (c.78)
Water (Scotland) Act 1980 (c.45)
Water Supplies (Exceptional Shortage Orders) Act 1934 (c.20)
Water Supply, London Act 1747 (c.8)
Water Undertakings (Modification of Charges) Act 1921 (c.44)
Waterbeach Level (Cambridge, Isle of Ely): Drainage Act 1797 (c.88)
Waterbeach Level: Drainage Act 1790 (c.74)
Waterbeach Level, Northampton: Drainage Act 1740 (c.24)
Waterford Hospital Act 1839 (c.19)
Waterfront House of Industry Act 1838 (c.13)
Waterloo Subscription Fund Act 1819 (c.34)
Waterworks Clauses Act 1847 (c.17)
Waterworks Clauses Act 1863 (c.93)
Watford Churchyard and Workhouse Act 1772 (c.28)
Wear Coal Trade Act 1792 (c.29)
Wear Navigation Act 1758 (c.64)
Wear Navigation Act 1758 (c.65)
Wearmouth and Tyne Bridge Road Act 1796 (c.136)
Wedding Rings Act 1855 (c.60)
Wednesfield Chapel Act 1746 (c.27)
Weedon Barracks Act 1804 (c.78)
Weeds Act 1959 (c.54)
Weeds and Agricultural Seeds (Ireland) Act 1909 (c.31)
Weights and Measures Act 1795 (c.102)
Weights and Measures Act 1797 (c.143)
Weights and Measures Act 1815 (c.43)
Weights and Measures Act 1824 (c.74)
Weights and Measures Act 1825 (c.12)
Weights and Measures Act 1834 (c.49)
Weights and Measures Act 1855 (c.72)
Weights and Measures Act 1859 (c.56)
Weights and Measures Act 1862 (c.76)
Weights and Measures Act 1878 (c.49)
Weights and Measures Act 1889 (c.21)
Weights and Measures Act 1893 (c.19)
Weights and Measures Act 1904 (c.28)
Weights and Measures Act 1936 (c.38)
Weights and Measures Act 1963 (c.31)
Weights and Measures Act 1979 (c.45)
Weights and Measures Act 1985 (c.72)
Weights and Measures (Amendment) Act 1926 (c.8)
Weights and Measures, Dublin Act 1867 (c.94)
Weights and Measures etc. Act 1976 (c.77)
Weights and Measures (Ireland) Act 1860 (c.119)
Weights and Measures (Leather Measurement) Act 1919 (c.29)
Weights and Measures (Metric System) Act 1897 (c.46)
Weights and Measures (Northern Ireland) Act 1967 (c.6)

Weights and Measures (Purchase) Act 1892 (c.18)
Weights and Measures, Sale of Coal (Scotland) Act 1936 (c.54)
Weights in Sales of Bullion Act 1853 (c.29)
Weights for Coin in the Mint Act 1774 (c.92)
Weights for Coin in the Mint Act 1775 (c.30)
Welfare of Animals at Slaughter Act 1991 (c.30)
Welford and Leicester Road Act 1765 (c.78)
Welford Bridge to Milston Lane Road Act 1786 (c.148)
Wellingborough and Northampton Road Act 1797 (c.167)
Wellington Museum Act 1947 (c.46)
Wells Harbour Act 1769 (c.8)
Wells Roads Act 1753 (c.76)
Wells, Somerset: Improvement Act 1779 (c.31)
Welsh Cathedrals Act 1843 (c.77)
Welsh Church Act 1914 (c.91)
Welsh Church (Amendment) Act 1938 (c.39)
Welsh Church (Burial Grounds) Act 1945 (c.27)
Welsh Church (Temporalities) Act 1919 (c.65)
Welsh Courts Act 1942 (c.40)
Welsh Development Agency Act 1975 (c.70)
Welsh Development Agency Act 1988 (c.5)
Welsh Development Agency Act 1991 (c.69)
Welsh Intermediate Education Act 1889 (c.40)
Welsh Language Act 1967 (c.66)
Welsh Language Act 1993 (c.38)
Welsh National Opera Company 1971 (c.37)
Wendover and Buckingham Road Act 1766 (c.71)
Wern and Bron-y-Garth Road Act 1797 (c.151)
Wesleyan Methodists (Appointments During the War) Act 1917 (c.29)
West Africa Offences Act 1871 (c.8)
West Coast of Africa and Falkland Islands Act 1860 (c.121)
West Coast of Africa Possessions Act 1821 (c.28)
West Cowgate and Alemouth Road Act 1797 (c.163)
West Highland Railway Guarantee Act 1896 (c.58)
West India Island Relief Act 1845 (c.50)
West India Islands Relief Act 1840 (c.40)
West India Loans Act 1848 (c.38)
West India Loans Act 1855 (c.71)
West India Loans Act 1879 (c.16)
West India Relief Commissioners Act 1856 (c.35)
West Indian Bishops, etc. Act 1825 (c.88)
West Indian Court of Appeal Act 1919 (c.47)
West Indian Courts of Appeal Act 1850 (c.15)
West Indian Incumbered Estates Act 1854 (c.117)
West Indian Incumbered Estates Act 1858 (c.96)
West Indian Incumbered Estates Act 1862 (c.45)
West Indian Incumbered Estates Act 1864 (c.108)
West Indian Islands Relief Act 1844 (c.17)
West Indian Islands (Telegraph) Act 1924 (c.14)
West Indian Loans Act 1848 (c.130)
West Indian Mortgages Act 1772 (c.14)
West Indian Prisons Act 1838 (c.67)
West Indies Act 1806 (c.80)
West Indies Act 1962 (c.19)
West Indies Act 1967 (c.4)
West Indies (Encumbered Estates) Act 1872 (c.9)
West Indies (Encumbered Estates) Act 1886 (c.36)
West Indies Relief Act 1843 (c.63)
West Indies (Salaries) Act 1868 (c.120)
West Riding Inclosures Act 1712 (c.4)
West Riding: Small Debts Act 1780 (c.65)
West Riding: Small Debts Act 1793 (c.84)
Westbury, Wilts (Additional Oversees) Act 1786 (c.23)
Western Australia Constitution Act 1890 (c.26)
Western Australia Government Act 1835 (c.14)
Western Australia Government Act 1836 (c.68)
Western Australia Government Act 1838 (c.46)
Western Australia Government Act 1841 (c.43)
Western Australia Government Act 1842 (c.88)
Western Australia Government Act 1844 (c.57)
Western Australia Government Act 1846 (c.35)
Western Highlands and Islands (Transport Services) Act 1928 (c.6)
Western Highlands and Islands (Scotland) Works Act 1891 (c.58)
Westminster Act 1756 (c.25)
Westminster Act 1757 (c.17)
Westminster 1861 (c.78)
Westminster Abbey Act 1888 (c.11)
Westminster Bridge Act 1735 (c.29)
Westminster Bridge Act 1736 (c.16)
Westminster Bridge Act 1737 (c.25)
Westminster Bridge Act 1738 (c.33)
Westminster Bridge Act 1739 (c.16)
Westminster Bridge Act 1740 (c.40)
Westminster Bridge Act 1741 (c.26)
Westminster Bridge Act 1743 (c.32)
Westminster Bridge Act 1744 (c.29)
Westminster Bridge Act 1756 (c.38)
Westminster Bridge Act 1757 (c.34)
Westminster Bridge Act 1853 (c.46)
Westminster Bridge Act 1859 (c.58)
Westminster Bridge Act 1864 (c.88)
Westminster Corn and Grain Market Act 1757 (c.25)

Westminster Election Act 1813 (c.152)
Westminster Fish Market Act 1790 (c.54)
Westminster Fish Market Act 1802 (c.19)
Westminster: Improvement Act 1778 (c.72)
Westminster: Improvement Act 1787 (c.54)
Westminster: Improvements Act 1790 (c.53)
Westminster, Improvements Act 1821 (c.45)
Westminster, King's Street Act 1753 (c.101)
Westminster Market Act 1749 (c.14)
Westminster Offices Act 1855 (c.95)
Westminster Offices Act 1859 (c.19)
Westminster Offices Act 1861 (c.33)
Westminster Offices Act 1862 (c.74)
Westminster Offices Act 1864 (c.51)
Westminster Offices Act 1865 (c.31)
Westminster Offices Act 1865 (c.32)
Westminster Parliamentary Elections Act 1811 (c.126)
Westminster Parliamentary Elections Act 1819 (c.2)
Westminster Streets Act 1728 (c.11)
Westminster Streets Act 1763 (c.39)
Westminster Streets Act 1765 (c.50)
Westminster Streets Act 1777 (c.61)
Westminster: Streets Act 1782 (c.44)
Westminster: Streets Act 1783 (c.42)
Westminster: Streets Act 1783 (c.43)
Westminster: Streets Act 1783 (c.89)
Westminster: Streets Act 1783 (c.90)
Westminster: Streets Act 1786 (c.102)
Westminster: Watching Act 1774 (c.90)
Westminster: Watching Act 1786 (c.112)
Westminster (Water Supply) Act 1721 (c.26)
Westmoreland Canals Act 1792 (c.101)
Westmoreland Gaol, etc. Act 1776 (c.54)
Westmoreland Roads Act 1742 (c.3)
Westmoreland Roads Act 1760 (c.43)
Westmoreland Roads Act 1753 (c.67)
Westmoreland Roads Act 1758 (c.69)
Westmoreland Roads Act 1779 (c.106)
Westmoreland Roads Act 1779 (c.108)
Westmoreland Roads Act 1780 (c.88)
Westmoreland Roads Act 1782 (c.111)
Westmoreland and Yorkshire Roads Act 1784 (c.70)
Wetherby to Grassington Road Act 1758 (c.71)
Wetherby to Grassington Road Act 1774 (c.98)
Wetherby to Knaresborough Road Act 1783 (c.103)
Wexford Grand Jury Act 1867 (c.77)
Weyhill and Lyde Way Road Act 1762 (c.60)
Weymouth Harbour Act 1748 (c.22)
Weymouth: Improvement Act 1776 (c.57)
Weymouth: Water Supply Act 1797 (c.129)
Whale Fishery Act 1732 (c.33)
Whale Fishery Act 1748 (c.45)
Whale Fishery Act 1755 (c.20)
Whale Fishery Act 1763 (c.22)
Whale Fishery Act 1768 (c.27)
Whale Fishery, etc. Act 1776 (c.47)
Whale Fisheries Act 1789 (c.53)
Whale Fisheries (Scotland) Act 1907 (c.41)
Whale Fisheries (Scotland) Act Amendment 1922 (c.34)
Whales Fisheries (Ireland) Act 1908 (c.31)
Whaling Industry (Regulation) Act 1934 (c.49)
Wharves Between London Bridge and Temple Act 1821 (c.89)
Wheat Act 1932 (c.24)
Wheat (Amendment) Act 1939 (c.37)
Whichwood Disafforesting Act 1853 (c.36)
Whichwood Disafforesting Act 1856 (c.32)
Whipping Act 1820 (c.57)
Whipping Act 1862 (c.18)
Whipping of Female Offenders, Abolition Act 1817 (c.75)
Whitby Harbour Act 1734 (c.10)
Whitby Harbour Act 1749 (c.39)
Whitby Harbour Act 1766 (c.81)
Whitby Harbour Act 1780 (c.12)
Whitby Harbour Act 1796 (c.121)
Whitby: Improvement Act 1764 (c.73)
Whitby: Improvement Act 1789 (c.12)
Whitby Piers 1702 (c.13)
Whitby Piers Act 1708 (c.7)
Whitby Roads Act 1785 (c.111)
Whitchurch, Salop: Poor Relief Act 1792 (c.85)
White Cross and Beverley Roads Act 1760 (c.42)
White Fish and Herring Industries Act 1948 (c.51)
White Fish and Herring Industries Act 1953 (c.17)
White Fish and Herring Industries Act 1957 (c.22)
White Fish and Herring Industries Act 1961 (c.18)
White Herring Fisheries Act 1771 (c.31)
White Herring Fishery Act 1779 (c.26)
White Herring Fishery (Scotland) Act 1821 (c.79)
White Herring Fishery (Scotland) Act 1861 (c.72)
White Phosphorus Matches Prohibition Act 1908 (c.42)
Whitechapel Highways Act 1721 (c.30)
Whitechapel: Improvement Act 1778 (c.37)
Whitechapel: Improvement Act 1778 (c.80)
Whitechapel (Poor Relief) Act 1763 (c.53)
Whitechapel: Poor Relief Act 1766 (c.74)
Whitechapel Roads Act 1736 (c.36)
Whitechapel, Stepney: Improvement Act 1793 (c.82)
Whitechapel: Streets Act 1783 (c.91)
Whitechapel to Aldermaston Road Act 1770 (c.88)
Whitehaven Harbour Act 1708 (c.9)
Whitehaven Harbour Act 1710 (c.17)
Whitehaven Harbour Improvement Act 1739 (c.14)
Whitehaven Harbour Impovement Act 1760 (c.44)

Whitehaven Harbour Improvement Act 1762 (c.87)
Whitehaven: Improvement Act 1788 (c.61)
Whitgift, Yorks (Drainage) Act 1793 (c.108)
Whitney Bridge, Hereford Act 1797 (c.56)
Whitney Bridge, Wye Act 1780 (c.27)
Whittlesey Drainage Act 1797 (c.68)
Whittlewood Disafforesting Act 1853 (c.42)
Whittlewood Forest Act 1824 (c.99)
Wicklow Harbour Act 1897 (c.55)
Wide Streets and Coal Trade, Dublin Act 1809 (c.72)
Wide Streets, Dublin Act 1811 (c.10)
Widows', Orphans' and Old Age Contributory Pensions Act 1925 (c.70)
Widows', Orphans' and Old Age Contributory Pensions Act 1929 (c.10)
Widows', Orphans' and Old Age Contributory Pensions Act 1931 (c.19)
Widows', Orphans' and Old Age Contributory Pensions Act 1936 (c.33)
Widows', Orphans' and Old Age Contributory Pensions (Voluntary Contributors) Act 1937 (c.39)
Wigan to Preston Road Act 1726 (c.9)
Wigan to Preston Road Act 1779 (c.92)
Wigan to Preston Road Act 1795 (c.145)
Wigan: Water Supply Act 1764 (c.75)
Wiggenhall Drainage Act 1757 (c.32)
Wigtown Roads Act 1778 (c.7)
Wild Animals in Captivity Protection Act 1900 (c.33)
Wild Animals in Captivity Protection (Scotland) Act 1909 (c.33)
Wild Birds (Duck and Geese) Protection Act 1939 (c.19)
Wild Birds Protection Act 1880 (c.35)
Wild Birds Protection Act 1881 (c.51)
Wild Birds Protection Act 1894 (c.24)
Wild Birds (Protection) Act 1896 (c.56)
Wild Birds Protection Act 1902 (c.6)
Wild Birds Protection Act 1904 (c.4)
Wild Birds Protection Act 1908 (c.11)
Wild Birds Protection (St. Kilda) Act 1904 (c.10)
Wild Creatures and Forest Laws Act 1971 (c.47)
Wilden Ferry Bridge Act 1757 (c.59)
Wildlife and Countryside Act 1981 (c.69)
Wildlife and Countryside (Amendment) Act 1985 (c.31)
Wildlife and Countryside (Amendment) Act 1991 (c.39)
Wildlife and Countryside (Service of Notices) Act 1985 (c.59)
Will of Sir Joseph Jekyll Act 1746 (c.34)
Willian Preston Indemnity Act 1925 (c.7)
Wills Act 1703 (c.5)
Wills Act 1751 (c.6)
Wills Act 1837 (c.26)
Wills Act 1861 (c.114)
Wills Act 1963 (c.44)
Wills Act 1968 (c.28)
Wills Act Amendment Act 1852 (c.24)
Wills, etc. of Seamen, etc. Act 1815 (c.60)
Wills (Soldiers and Sailors) Act 1918 (c.58)
Wiltshire Highways 1706 (c.26)
Wiltshire Highways Act 1707 (c.76)
Wiltshire Highways Act 1713 (c.17)
Wiltshire Highways Act 1728 (c.12)
Wiltshire Roads Act 1724 (c.27)
Wiltshire Roads Act 1725 (c.7)
Wiltshire Roads Act 1725 (c.11)
Wiltshire Roads Act 1736 (c.6)
Wiltshire Roads Act 1740 (c.29)
Wiltshire Roads Act 1742 (c.10)
Wiltshire Roads Act 1743 (c.23)
Wiltshire Roads Act 1743 (c.27)
Wiltshire Roads Act 1744 (c.14)
Wiltshire Roads Act 1750 (c.9)
Wiltshire Roads Act 1751 (c.5)
Wiltshire Roads Act 1751 (c.12)
Wiltshire Roads Act 1753 (c.42)
Wiltshire Roads Act 1755 (c.44)
Wiltshire Roads Act 1756 (c.67)
Wiltshire Roads Act 1757 (c.41)
Wiltshire Roads Act 1757 (c.68)
Wiltshire Roads Act 1758 (c.63)
Wiltshire Roads Act 1760 (c.37)
Wiltshire Roads Act 1762 (c.49)
Wiltshire Roads Act 1762 (c.51)
Wiltshire Roads Act 1762 (c.59)
Wiltshire Roads Act 1762 (c.66)
Wiltshire Roads Act 1766 (c.57)
Wiltshire Roads Act 1768 (c.49)
Wiltshire Roads Act 1769 (c.48)
Wiltshire Roads Act 1769 (c.73)
Wiltshire Roads Act 1771 (c.81)
Wiltshire Roads Act 1772 (c.74)
Wiltshire Roads Act 1772 (c.85)
Wiltshire Roads Act 1773 (c.101)
Wiltshire Roads Act 1777 (c.72)
Wiltshire Roads Act 1777 (c.98)
Wiltshire Roads Act 1779 (c.111)
Wiltshire Roads Act 1780 (c.82)
Wiltshire Roads Act 1780 (c.98)
Wiltshire Roads Act 1783 (c.30)
Wiltshire Roads Act 1783 (c.111)
Wiltshire Roads Act 1788 (c.86)
Wiltshire Roads Act 1790 (c.96)
Wiltshire Roads Act 1790 (c.98)
Wiltshire Roads Act 1791 (c.121)
Wiltshire Roads Act 1792 (c.114)
Wiltshire Roads Act 1795 (c.136)
Wiltshire and Berkshire Roads Act 1757 (c.66)
Wiltshire, Dorset and Somerset Roads Act 1753 (c.60)
Wiltshire, Dorset and Somerset Roads Act 1756 (c.92)
Wiltshire, Dorset and Somerset Roads Act 1756 (c.54)
Wiltshire and Dorset Roads Act 1777 (c.83)
Wiltshire, Dorset and Somerset Roads Act 1779 (c.94)
Wiltshire and Gloucester Roads Act 1751 (c.59)

Wiltshire and Gloucester Roads 1778 (c.103)
Wiltshire and Hampshire Roads 1764 (c.47)
Wiltshire and Somerset Roads Act 1751 (c.17)
Wiltshire and Somerset Roads Act 1751 (c.52)
Wiltshire and Somerset Roads Act 1751 (c.24)
Wiltshire and Somerset Roads Act 1757 (c.46)
Wiltshire and Somerset Roads Act 1768 (c.49)
Wiltshire and Somerset Roads Act 1777 (c.93)
Wiltshire and Somerset Roads Act 1777 (c.99)
Wiltshire and Somerset Roads Act 1792 (c.137)
Wiltshire and Somerset Roads Act 1793 (c.155)
Wiltshire and Southampton Roads Act 1753 (c.66)
Wiltshire and Southampton Roads Act 1756 (c.45)
Wiltshire and Southampton Roads Act 1782 (c.110)
Wincanton Roads 1756 (c.49)
Winchester: Improvement Act 1771 (c.9)
Window Duties Act 1747 (c.10)
Window Duties Act 1753 (c.17)
Window Duties Act 1761 (c.8)
Window Duties (Scotland) Act 1817 (c.128)
Window Duty (Ireland) Act 1810 (c.75)
Windows Duties Act 1796 (c.117)
Windsor Bridge Act 1735 (c.15)
Windsor Castle Act 1848 (c.53)
Windsor Forest Act 1806 (c.143)
Windsor Forest Act 1813 (c.158)
Windsor Forest Act 1815 (c.122)
Windsor Forest Act 1816 (c.132)
Windsor Forest Boundary Commission Act 1807 (c.46)
Windsor Forest Road Act 1758 (c.46)
Windsor Lands Act 1702 (c.27)
Windward Islands Appeal Court Act 1889 (c.33)
Wine and Beerhouse Act 1869 (c.27)
Wine and Beerhouse Amendment Act 1870 (c.29)
Wine, etc. Duties Act 1825 (c.13)
Wine Licences Act 1758 (c.19)
Winfrith Heath Act 1957 (c.61)
Winter Assizes Act 1876 (c.57)
Winter Assizes Act 1877 (c.46)
Winterbourne Parish Act 1841 (c.42)
Wireless Telegraph (Blind Person' Facilities) Act 1926 (c.54)
Wireless Telegraphy Act 1904 (c.24)
Wireless Telegraphy Act 1906 (c.13)
Wireless Telegraphy Act 1949 (c.54)
Wireless Telegraphy Act 1955 (c.10)
Wireless Telegraphy Act 1967 (c.72)
Wireless Telegraphy (Explanation) Act 1925 (c.67)
Wireless Telegraphy (Validation of Charges) Act 1954 (c.2)
Wisbech Canal Act 1794 (c.92)
Wisbech Roads Act 1786 (c.133)
Witchcraft Act 1735 (c.5)
Witchcraft, etc. (Ireland) Act 1821 (c.18)
Witford, etc. Suffolk: Poor Relief Act 1765 (c.97)
Witham Drainage Act 1762 (c.32)
Witnesses Act 1806 (c.37)
Witnesses' Indemnity, Penryn Act 1828 (c.13)
Witnesses on Petitions Act 1801 (c.105)
Witnesses on Trial for Treason 1702 (c.9)
Witnesses (Public Inquiries) Protection Act 1892 (c.64)
Witney to Chanfield Road Act 1793 (c.137)
Wiveliscombe Roads Act 1786 (c.135)
Wolverhampton Church Act 1755 (c.34)
Wolverhampton: Improvements Act 1776 (c.25)
Wolverhampton Parish Act 1848 (c.95)
Wolverhampton Roads Act 1772 (c.101)
Wolverhampton Roads 1747 (c.25)
Wolverhampton Roads Act 1793 (c.147)
Wolverhampton Roads Act 1794 (c.133)
Wolverhampton Roads Act 1796 (c.146)
Women and Young Persons (Employment in Lead Processes) Act 1920 (c.62)
Woods and Forest Act 1803 (c.31)
Woods and Forests Act 1806 (c.142)
Woodstock, Oxford, Roads Act 1784 (c.61)
Wool Act 1738 (c.21)
Wool Act 1780 (c.55)
Wool Duties, etc. Act 1824 (c.47)
Woolcombers Act 1795 (c.124)
Woollen Cloths Act 1707 (c.43)
Woollen Cloths Act 1708 (c.13)
Woollen, etc. Manufacturers Act 1710 (c.32)
Woollen, etc. Manufacturers 1735 (c.4)
Woollen, etc. Manufactures Act 1720 (c.7)
Woollen, etc. Manufactures, Bedfordshire Act 1785 (c.40)
Woollen, etc. Manufactures, Norfolk Act 1791 (c.56)
Woollen Manufacturers Act 1702 (c.22)
Woollen Manufacture Act 1711 (c.26)
Woollen Manufacture Act 1714 (c.15)
Woollen Manufacture Act 1715 (c.41)
Woollen Manufactures Act 1725 (c.34)
Woollen Manufactures Act 1726 (c.23)
Woollen Manufactures Act 1731 (c.21)
Woollen Manufacture Act 1756 (c.33)
Woollen Manufactures Act 1757 (c.12)
Woollen Manufactures Act 1803 (c.136)
Woollen Manufacture Act 1804 (c.64)
Woollen Manufacture Act 1805 (c.83)
Woollen Manufacture Act 1806 (c.18)
Woollen Manufacture Act 1807 (c.43)
Woollen Manufacture Act 1808 (c.131)
Woollen Manufacture Act 1809 (c.109)
Woollen Manufacture Act 1810 (c.83)
Woollen Manufactures, Suffolk Act 1784 (c.3)

Woollen Trade Act 1833 (c.28)
Woolmer Forest Act 1812 (c.71)
Woolmer Forest Act 1855 (c.46)
Woolwich Church Act 1738 (c.9)
Woolwich Dockyard Act 1833 (c.65)
Woolwich Fortifications Act 1780 (c.46)
Worcester Roads Act 1725 (c.14)
Worcester Roads Act 1736 (c.5)
Worcester Roads act 1743 (c.13)
Worcester Roads Act 1753 (c.50)
Worcester Roads Act 1759 (c.50)
Worcester Roads Act 1767 (c.65)
Worcester Roads Act 1782 (c.95)
Worcester Roads Act 1783 (c.98)
Worcester Roads Act 1788 (c.88)
Worcester Roads Act 1789 (c.102)
Worcester Roads Act 1793 (c.175)
Worcester Roads Act 1795 (c.133)
Worcester and Birmingham Canal Act 1791 (c.59)
Worcester Bridge Act 1769 (c.84)
Worcester Bridge Act 1779 (c.42)
Worcester to Droitwich Road Act 1725 (c.20)
Worcester: Improvement Act 1770 (c.22)
Worcester: Poor Relief, Burial Ground and Hopmarket 1703 (c.8)
Worcester: Poor Relief, Burial Ground and Hopmarket Act 1730 (c.23)
Worcester: Poor Relief, Burial Ground and Hopmarket Act 1730 (c.25)
Worcester: Poor Relief, Burial Ground and Hopmarket Act 1792 (c.99)
Worcester and Salop Roads Act 1762 (c.78)
Worcester and Salop Roads Act 1763 (c.51)
Worcester, Salop and Stafford Roads Act 1790 (c.102)
Worcester: Streets Act 1780 (c.21)
Worcester and Warwick Roads Act 1767 (c.68)
Worcester and Warwick Roads Act 1771 (c.92)
Worcester and Warwick Roads Act 1773 (c.106)
Worcester and Warwick Roads Act 1773 (c.107)
Worcester and Warwick Roads Act 1788 (c.115)
Worcester and Warwick Roads Act 1789 (c.106)
Worcester and Warwick Roads Act 1792 (c.140)
Worcester and Warwick Roads Act 1794 (c.136)
Worcester, Warwick and Gloucester Roads Act 1757 (c.64)
Worcester: Water Supply, etc., Act 1771 (c.13)
Worcestershire Highways Act 1713 (c.27)
Worcestershire Roads Act 1748 (c.43)
Worcestershire Roads Act 1751 (c.60)
Worcestershire Roads Act 1755 (c.48)
Worcestershire Roads Act 17776 (c.78)
Worcestershire Roads Act 1779 (c.89)
Worcestershire, Staffordshire, Shropshire Roads Act 1781 (c.93)
Workhouses Act 1790 (c.49)
Workhouse Act 1816 (c.129)
Workhouses (Ireland) Act 1849 (c.86)
Workhouse Sites Act 1857 (c.13)
Workhouse, Westminster Act 1772 (c.34)
Working Classes Dwellings Act 1890 (c.16)
Working Men's Dwellings Act 1874 (c.59)
Working of Jews on Sunday Act 1871 (c.19)
Workmen's Compensation Act 1897 (c.37)
Workmen's Compensation Act 1900 (c.22)
Workmen's Compensation Act 1906 (c.58)
Workmen's Compensation Act 1909 (c.16)
Workmen's Compensation Act 1923 (c.42)
Workmen's Compensation Act 1925 (c.84)
Workmen's Compensation Act 1926 (c.42)
Workmen's Compensation Act 1931 (c.18)
Workmen's Compensation Act 1943 (c.6)
Workmen's Compensation (Amendment) Act 1938 (c.27)
Workmen's Compensation and Benefit (Amendment) Act 1965 (c.79)
Workmen's Compensation and Benefit (Byssinosis) Act 1940 (c.56)
Workmen's Compensation and Benefit (Supplementation) Act 1956 (c.51)
Workmen's Compensation (Coal Mines) Act 1934 (c.23)
Workmen's Compensation (Illegal Employment) Act 1918 (c.8)
Workmen's Compensation (Pneumoconiosis) Act 1945 (c.16)
Workmen's Compensation (Silicosis) Act 1918 (c.14)
Workmen's Compensation (Silicosis) Act 1924 (c.40)
Workmen's Compensation (Silicosis and Asbestosis) Act 1930 (c.29)
Workmen's Compensation (Supplementary Allowances) Act 1940 (c.47)
Workmen's Compensation (Supplementation) Act 1951 (c.22)
Workmen's Compensation (Temporary Increase) Act 1943 (c.49)
Workmen's Compensation (Transfer of Funds) Act 1927 (c.15)
Workmen's Compensation (War Addition) Act 1917 (c.42)
Workmen's Compensation (War Addition) Amendment Act 1919 (c.83)
Works and Public Buildings Act 1874 (c.84)
Works of Utility, etc. Indemnity Act 1858 (c.102)
Workshop Regulation Act 1867 (c.146)
Worksop and Attercliffe Road Act 1764 (c.52)
Worksop and Attercliffe Road Act 1786 (c.125)
Worsley Brook: Navigation Act 1736 (c.9)
Worstead Act 1776 (c.11)
Wreak and Eye: Navigation Act 1791 (c.77)
Wreck and Salvage Act 1846 (c.99)
Wrecking (Ireland) Act 1803 (c.79)

Wrexham to Barnhill Road Act 1782 (c.105)
Writ of Subpoena Act 1805 (c.92)
Writs Execution (Scotland) Act 1877 (c.40)
Writs of Assistance Act 1814 (c.46)
Writs of Error Act 1718 (c.13)
Writs of Error Act 1825 (c.96)
Writs of Execution Act 1833 (c.67)
Writs of Mandamus Act 1843 (c.67)
Writs Registration (Scotland) Act 1868 (c.34)

Yarmouth Coal Import Duties 1706 (c.10)
Yarmouth Coal Import Duties (Privileges of Freemen, etc.) 1782 (c.22)
Yarmouth Haven Act 1746 (c.40)
Yarmouth Haven and Pier Repairs 1702 (c.7)
Yarmouth Naval Hospital Act 1931 (c.15)
Yarmouth Naval Hospital Transfer Act 1957 (c.3)
Yarmouth: Small Debts Act 1757 (c.24)
Yarmouth to Gorleston Road Act 1775 (c.67)
Yarmouth to Gorleston Road Act 1795 (c.132)
Yaxley: Drainage Act 1772 (c.46)
Yeomanry Act 1804 (c.54)
Yeomanry Act 1817 (c.44)
Yeomanry Act 1826 (c.58)
Yeomanry (Accounts) Act 1804 (c.94)
Yeomanry Cavalry Act 1798 (c.51)
Yeomanry (Ireland) Act 1802 (c.68)
Yeomanry (Training) Act 1816 (c.39)
Yeomanry and Volunteers Act 1802 (c.66)
Yeomanry and Volunteers Act 1803 (c.121)
Yeomanry Corps, etc. (Ireland) Act 1814 (c.178)
Yeomanry Corps (Ireland) Act 1816 (c.72)
Yeomanry Corps (Ireland) Act 1818 (c.40)
Yeomanry Corps (Ireland) Act 1820 (c.48)
Yeomanry Corps (Ireland) Act 1823 (c.15)
Yeomanry Corps (Ireland) Act 1828 (c.30)
Yeomanry, etc. Act 1806 (c.125)
York and Boroughbridge Road Act 1749 (c.38)
York and Boroughbridge Road Act 1771 (c.66)
York and Boroughbridge Road Act 1797 (c.149)
York and Durham Roads Act 1753 (c.95)
York Buildings Company, Sale of Scottish Estates Act 1776 (c.24)
York Buildings: Rates Act 1756 (c.90)
York Butter Trade Supervision Act 1721 (c.27)
York House and Victoria Park Act 1841 (c.27)
York: Lighting and Watching Act 1763 (c.48)
York Roads Act 1765 (c.99)
York Roads Act 1792 (c.155)
Yorkshire Registries Act 1884 (c.54)
Yorkshire Registries Amendment Act 1884 (c.4)
Yorkshire Registries Amendment Act 1885 (c.26)
Yorkshire Roads Act 1740 (c.23)
Yorkshire Roads Act 1742 (c.7)
Yorkshire Roads Act 1743 (c.22)
Yorkshire Roads Act 1743 (c.25)
Yorkshire Roads Act 1744 (c.6)
Yorkshire Roads Act 1744 (c.16)
Yorkshire Roads Act 1748 (c.39)
Yorkshire Roads Act 1751 (c.47)
Yorkshire Roads Act 1751 (c.53)
Yorkshire Roads Act 1751 (c.58)
Yorkshire Roads Act 1755 (c.50)
Yorkshire Roads Act 1756 (c.71)
Yorkshire Roads Act 1756 (c.83)
Yorkshire Roads Act 1757 (c.54)
Yorkshire Roads Act 1758 (c.70)
Yorkshire Roads Act 1759 (c.55)
Yorkshire Roads Act 1760 (c.35)
Yorkshire Roads Act 1762 (c.71)
Yorkshire Roads Act 1764 (c.66)
Yorkshire Roads Act 1764 (c.69)
Yorkshire Roads Act 1765 (c.72)
Yorkshire Roads Act 1766 (c.59)
Yorkshire Roads Act 1766 (c.62)
Yorkshire Roads Act 1767 (c.71)
Yorkshire Roads Act 1768 (c.54)
Yorkshire Roads Act 1769 (c.54)
Yorkshire Roads Act 1769 (c.75)
Yorkshire Roads Act 1769 (c.79)
Yorkshire Roads Act 1771 (c.63)
Yorkshire Roads Act 1771 (c.68)
Yorkshire Roads Act 1771 (c.71)
Yorkshire Roads Act 1774 (c.117)
Yorkshire Roads Act 1777 (c.73)
Yorkshire Roads Act 1777 (c.77)
Yorkshire Roads Act 1777 (c.78)
Yorkshire Roads Act 1777 (c.80)
Yorkshire Roads Act 1777 (c.102)
Yorkshire Roads Act 1778 (c.96)
Yorkshire Roads Act 1780 (c.86)
Yorkshire Roads Act 1780 (c.89)
Yorkshire Roads Act 1781 (c.96)
Yorkshire Roads Act 1782 (c.97)
Yorkshire Roads Act 1783 (c.29)
Yorkshire Roads Act 1783 (c.95)
Yorkshire Roads Act 1786 (c.142)
Yorkshire Roads Act 1786 (c.144)
Yorkshire Roads Act 1787 (c.86)
Yorkshire Roads Act 1788 (c.106)
Yorkshire Roads Act 1788 (c.108)
Yorkshire Roads Act 1788 (c.110)
Yorkshire Roads Act 1789 (c.109)
Yorkshire Roads Act 1790 (c.99)
Yorkshire Roads Act 1792 (c.132)
Yorkshire Roads Act 1792 (c.133)
Yorkshire Roads Act 1792 (c.136)
Yorkshire Roads Act 1793 (c.157)
Yorkshire Roads Act 1794 (c.134)
Yorkshire and Chester Roads Act 1767 (c.94)
Yorkshire and Derby Roads Act 1757 (c.62)
Yorkshire and Derby Roads Act 1768 (c.47)
Yorkshire and Derby Roads Act 1771 (c.76)
Yorkshire and Derby Roads Act 1779 (c.96)
Yorkshire and Derby Roads Act 1795 (c.164)
Yorkshire, Derby and Chester Roads Act 1793 (c.140)

Yorkshire and Derbyshire Roads Act 1793 (c.184)
Yorkshire and Durham Roads Act 1746 (c.28)
Yorkshire and Durham Roads Act 1748 (c.32)
Yorkshire and Durham Roads Act 1755 (c.51)
Yorkshire and Durham Roads Act 1756 (c.80)
Yorkshire and Durham Roads Act 1760 (c.41)
Yorkshire and Durham Roads Act 1779 (c.80)
Yorkshire and Durham Roads Act 1782 (c.93)
Yorkshire and Durham Roads Act 1792 (c.118)
Yorkshire and Durham Roads Act 1792 (c.135)
Yorkshire and Lancaster Roads Act 1755 (c.59)
Yorkshire and Lancaster Roads Act 1755 (c.60)
Yorkshire and Lancaster Roads Act 1756 (c.91)
Yorkshire and Lancaster Roads Act 1759 (c.48)
Yorkshire and Lancaster Roads Act 1777 (c.90)
Yorkshire and Nottinghamshire Roads Act 1766 (c.67)
Yorkshire and Westmorland Roads Act 1753 (c.86)
Yorkshire and Westmorland Roads Act 1791 (c.122)
Yorkshire Coroners Act 1897 (c.39)
Yorkshire: Drainage Act 1789 (c.78)
Yorkshire (East Riding) Land Registry Act 1707 (c.62)
Yorkshire (North Riding) Land Registry Act 1734 (c.6)
Yorkshire: Small Debts Act 1776 (c.15)
Yorkshire (West Riding) Land Registry Act 1703 (c.4)
Yorkshire (West Riding) Land Registry 1706 (c.20)
Youghal Rectory Act 1827 (c.26)
Young Persons (Employment) Act 1938 (c.69)
Young Persons (Employment) Act 1964 (c.66)
Youthful Offenders Act 1855 (c.87)
Youthful Offenders Act 1901 (c.20)
Youthful Offenders, Great Britain Act 1854 (c.86)
Yule Vacance Act 1711 (c.22)
Yule Vacance Act 1714 (c.28)

Zambia Independence Act 1964 (c.65)
Zanzibar Act 1963 (c.55)
Zanzibar Indemnity Act 1894 (c.31)
Zimbabwe Act 1979 (c.60)
Zoo Licensing Act 1981 (c.37)

CURRENT LAW
LEGISLATION CITATOR 1995

This is the sixth part of the Current Law Legislation Citator 1995 and is up to date to December 11, 1995 (orders received). It comprises in a single table:

(i) Statutes passed between January 1 and December 11, 1995;
(ii) Statutes affected during this period by Statute or Statutory Instrument;
(iii) Statutes judicially considered during this period;
(iv) Statutes repealed and amended during this period;
(v) Statutes under which Statutory Instruments have been made during this period.

(S.) Amendments relating to Scotland only.

[Please Note: where legislation has been consolidated by a subsequent Act this is denoted by **C.** followed by the section/Schedule of the Act where the relevant provision can now be found.]

ACTS OF THE PARLIAMENT OF SCOTLAND

CAP.

37. Subscription of Deeds Act 1540.
repealed: 1995, c. 7, sch. 5 (S.).

18. Subscription of Deeds Act 1579.
repealed: 1995, c. 7, sch. 5 (S.).

47. Lyon King of Arms Act 1672.
repealed in pt.: 1995, c. 7, sch. 5 (S.).

5. Subscription of Deeds Act 1681.
repealed: 1995, c. 7, sch. 5 (S.).

CAP.

13. Real Rights Act 1693.
see *Sharp* v. *Thomson*, 1995 S.L.T. 837.

15. Deeds Act 1696.
repealed: 1995, c. 7, sch. 5 (S.).

25. Blank Bonds and Trusts Act 1696.
repealed: 1995, c. 7, sch. 5 (S.).

4. Registration Act 1698.
repealed: 1995, c. 7, sch. 5 (S.).

ACTS OF THE PARLIAMENTS OF ENGLAND, GREAT BRITAIN AND THE UNITED KINGDOM

CAP.

29 Car. 2 (1677)

3. Statute of Frauds 1677.
see *Firstpost Homes* v. *Johnson*, *The Times*, August 14, 1995, C.A.
s. 4, see *State Bank of India* v. *Kaur, The Times*, April 24, 1995, Sir Stephen Brown.

2 Will. & Mar. (1689)

2. Bill of Rights Act 1689.
art. 9, see *Allason* v. *Haines, The Times*, July 25, 1995, Owen J.

11 Will. 3 (1698)

12. An Act to Punish Governors of Plantations in this Kingdom for Crimes Committed by them in the Plantations.
repealed: 1995, c. 44, sch. 1.

CAP.

6 Anne (1706)

11. Union with Scotland Act 1706.
art. XIX, see *R.* v. *Commissioner of Police of the Metropolis, ex p. Bennett* [1995] 3 All E.R. 248, D.C.

4 Geo. 3 (1764)

8. Bank of England Act 1716.
repealed: 1995, c. 44, sch. 1.

49. An Act to enable the Governor and Company of the Bank of England to purchase houses and ground for opening a Passage for Carriages, from Cornhill to the Bank, and making more commodious several other Passages leading thereto; and for enlarging the Buildings of the said Bank and making the same more commodious.
repealed: 1995, c. 44, sch. 1.

CAP.

5 Geo. 3 (1765)

91. An Act for vesting certain Glebe lands belonging to the rectory of the Parish Church of Saint Christopher in the City of London, in the Governor and Company of the Bank of England; and for Recompence to the Rector of the said Parish, and his successors, in lieu thereof; and for obviating certain Doubts in an Act passed in the Thirty Third Year of the Reign of His Late Majesty, for widening certain Streets, Lanes and Passages, within the City of London.
repealed: 1995, c. 44, sch. 1.

6 Geo. 3 (1766)

76. An Act to enable the Governor and Company of the Bank of England to purchase certain Houses and Ground contiguous and near to the Bank; and for making certain avenues leading thereto more commodious.
repealed: 1995, c. 44, sch. 1.

7 Geo. 3 (1767)

36. An Act for dividing and inclosing the open fields, meadows, common pastures and commonable lands lying south of the turnpike road leading from Nottingham to Alfreton within the liberties and townships of Lenton and Radford in the county of Nottingham.
repealed: 1995, c. 44, sch. 1.

9 Geo. 3 (1769)

62. An Act to rebuild the shire hall of the county of Nottingham; and for using the guildhall of the town and county of Nottingham for the purposes of a shire hall in the meantime.
repealed: 1995, c. 44, sch. 1.

13 Geo. 3 (1773)

96. An Act for the sale of certain charity estates therein mentioned, and to apply the money to arise therefrom in the buildings of a town hall and shambles in the town of Newark-upon-Trent; and in the purchasing of lands and hereditaments for enlarging the churchyard of the said town and for opening the avenues thereto; and for laying out the residue of the money in purchasing other lands, to be settled to the charitable uses therein mentioned.
repealed: 1995, c. 44, sch. 1.

CAP.

14 Geo. 3 (1774)

48. Life Assurance Act 1774.
s. 1, see *Fuji Finance Inc.* v. *Aetna Life Insurance Co.* [1994] 4 All E.R. 1025, Sir Donald Nicholls, V-C.

21 Geo. 3 (1781)

71. An Act for vesting the Parish Church of Saint Christopher le Socks, in the City of London, and the Materials and Site thereof and of the Churchyard thereto adjoining, in the Governor and Company of the Bank of England, and their successors for ever; and for uniting the said Parish to the Parish of Saint Lothbury, in the said City.
repealed: 1995, c. 44, sch. 1.

33 Geo. 3 (1793)

15. An Act to enable the Governor and Company of the Bank of England to purchase certain Houses and Ground contiguous to the Bank of England.
repealed: 1995, c. 44, sch. 1.

34 Geo. 3 (1794)

1. An Act for rebuilding the town of Warwick and for determining the differences touching houses burnt or demolished by reason of the late dreadful fire there.
repealed: 1995, c. 44, sch. 1.

35 Geo. 3 (1795)

87. An Act for dividing, allotting and inclosing the open and common fields, meadows, closes, commonable lands, pastures, commons and waste grounds within the several parishes of Saint Paul, Saint Peter and Saint Cuthbert, in the town of Bedford, in the county of Bedford.
repealed: 1995, c. 44, sch. 1.

36 Geo. 3 (1796)

114. An Act for dividing and inclosing the forest, commons and waste lands within the liberties and townships of Lenton and Radford in the county of Nottingham.
repealed: 1995, c. 44, sch. 1.

CAP.

36 Geo. 3 (1796)

152. **An Act for raising, maintaining and keeping in repair the road from the north end of the bridge, commonly called the Old Trent Bridge, to the west end of Saint Mary's churchyard by way of Hollow Stone, in the parish of Saint Mary, in the town of Nottingham, and for erecting and maintaining such and so many flood bridges upon the said road as may be necessary to carry off the flood water, and for widening and improving the entrance into the town of Nottingham by way of Hollow Stone.**
repealed (except s. 52): 1995, c. 44, sch. 1.

37 Geo. 3 (1797)

53. **An Act for dividing, allotting and inclosing, the pen and common fields, pastures, commons and waste grounds within the Parish of St. Mary, in the town of Bedford in the county of Bedford.**
repealed: 1995, c. 44, sch. 1.

42 Geo. 3 (1802)

85. **Criminal Jurisdiction Act 1802.**
s. 1, repealed in pt.: 1995, c. 44, sch. 1.

48 Geo. 3 (1808)

128. **Regimental Accounts Act 1808.**
repealed: 1995, c. 44, sch. 1.

57 Geo. 3 (1817)

93. **Distress (Costs) Act 1817.**
repealed: 1995, c. 44, sch. 1.

60 Geo. 3 & 1 Geo. 4 (1819)

1. **Unlawful Drilling Act 1819.**
s. 1, repealed in pt.: 1995, c. 44, sch. 1.
s. 1, amended: 1995, c. 44, sch. 2.

3 Geo. 4 (1822)

33. **Riotous Assemblies (Scotland) Act 1822.**
s. 10, amended: 1994 c. 39, sch. 13 (S.).

CAP.

6 Geo. 4 (1825)

22. **Jurors (Scotland) Act 1825.**
s. 3, amended: 1995, c. 40, sch. 4, 1995, c. 20, s. 3.

8 Geo. 4 (1827)

17. **Distress (Costs) Act 1827.**
repealed: 1995, c. 44, sch. 1.

9 Geo. 4 (1828)

69. **Night Poaching Act 1828.**
s. 1, amended: 1995, c. 40, sch. 2 (S.).

11 Geo. 4 & 1 Will. 4 (1830)

69. **Court of Session Act 1830.**
s. 18, repealed: 1995, c. 40, sch. 5 (S.).

7 Will. 4 & 1 Vict. (1837)

26. **Wills Act 1837.**
s. 18A, repealed in pt.: 1995, c. 41, sch.
s. 18A, amended: 1995, c. 41, s. 3.

1 & 2 Vict. (1837–38)

110. **Judgments Act 1838.**
ss. 17, 18, see *Kuwait Airways Corp.* v. *Iraq Airways Co.* (No. 2) [1994] 1 Lloyd's Rep. 284, C.A.

2 & 3 Vict. (1839)

28. **An Act for inclosing certain lands called the West Croft and Burton Leys, in the parish of Saint Mary in the town and county of Nottingham.**
repealed: 1995, c. 44, sch. 1.

32. **An Act for inclosing, allotting and improving certain open fields in the parish of Saint Mary in the town and county of the town of Nottingham.**
repealed (except ss. 28, 32, 53, 55–58): 1995, c. 44, sch. 2.

7 & 8 Vict. (1844)

7. **An Act for altering and amending [the Act 2 & 3 Vict. c. 28].**
repealed: 1995, c. 44, sch. 1.

8 & 9 Vict. (1845)

7. **An Act for inclosing lands in the parish of Saint Mary in the town and county of Nottingham in the town of Nottingham.**
repealed (except ss. 53, 54, 59, 70, 97–99, 173–175: 1995, c. 44, sch. 1.

CAP.

8 & 9 Vict. (1845)—cont.

19. Lands Clauses Consolidation (Scotland) Act 1845.
s. 7, repealed in pt.: 1995, c. 36, schs. 4, 5.
s. 7, amended: 1995, c. 36, sch. 4.
s. 67, repealed in pt.: 1995, c. 36, schs. 4, 5.
s. 69, repealed in pt.: 1995, c. 36, schs. 4, 5.
s. 70, amended: 1995, c. 36, sch. 4.
schs. A, B, amended: 1995, c. 7, sch. 4.

35. Infeftment Act 1845.
schs. A, B, amended: 1995, c. 7, sch. 4 (S.).

109. Gaming Act 1845.
see *Morgan Grenfell & Co.* v. *Welwyn Hatfield District Council (Islington London Borough Council, Third Party)* [1995] 1 All E.R. 1, Hobhouse J.

113. Evidence Act 1845.
s. 4, repealed: 1995, c. 44, s. 1.

10 & 11 Vict. (1847)

27. Harbour, Docks and Piers Clauses Act 1847.
s. 7, amended: 1994, c. 39, sch. 13 (S.).
s. 8, amended: 1994, c. 39, sch. 13 (S.).
s. 30, see *R.* v. *Coventry City Council, ex p. Phoenix Aviation* [1995] 3 All E.R. 37, D.C.
s. 40, see *R.* v. *Coventry City Council, ex p. Phoenix Aviation.*
s. 83, amended: order 95/2007.

34. Town Improvement Clauses Act 1847.
ss. 64, 65, repealed: S.R. 1995 No. 759.

89. Town Police Clauses Act 1847.
s. 37, see *R.* v. *Leeds City Council, ex p. Mellor* [1993] C.O.D. 352, Hutchison J.

12 & 13 Vict. (1849)

51. Judicial Factors (Scotland) Act 1849.
s. 1, repealed in pt.: 1995, c. 36, sch. 5.
s. 10, repealed in pt.: 1995, c. 36, sch. 4.
s. 10, amended: 1995, c. 36, sch. 4.
s. 25, repealed in pt.: 1995, c. 36, sch. 5.
s. 27, repealed in pt.: 1995, c. 36, schs. 4, 5.
s. 31, repealed in pt.: 1995, c. 36, schs. 4, 5.
s. 32, repealed in pt.: 1995, c. 36, schs. 4, 5.
s. 33, repealed in pt.: 1995, c. 36, schs. 4, 5.
s. 34, repealed in pt.: 1995, c. 36, schs. 4, 5.
s. 34A, amended: 1995, c. 36, sch. 4.
s. 36, repealed in pt.: 1995, c. 36, schs. 4, 5.

CAP.

12 & 13 Vict. (1849)—cont.

51. Judicial Factors (Scotland) Act 1849—*cont.*
s. 37, repealed in pt.: 1995, c. 36, schs. 4, 5.
s. 40, repealed in pt.: 1995, c. 36, schs. 4, 5.

15 & 16 Vict. (1852)

69. Public Health Supplemental Act 1852 (No. 2).
s. 5, repealed in pt.: 1995, c. 44, sch. 1.

17 & 18 Vict. (1854)

91. Lands Valuation (Scotland) Act 1854.
s. 42, regs. 94/3199.
s. 42, amended: 1994, c. 39, s. 152.
s. 43, added: 1994, c. 39, s. 152.

103. Towns Improvement (Ireland) Act 1854.
s. 38, repealed in pt.: S.R. 1995 No. 759.

120. Merchant Shipping Repeal Act 1854.
s. 7, repealed: 1995, c. 21, sch. 12.
s. 7, C.: 1995, c. 21, sch. 14.

18 & 19 Vict. (1855)

68. Burial Grounds (Scotland) Act 1855.
ss. 4, 9, amended: 1994, c. 39, sch. 13.
s. 10, 11, repealed in pt.: 1994, c. 39, schs. 13, 14.

19 & 20 Vict. (1856)

56. Exchequer Court (Scotland) Act 1856.
s. 24, see *Meekison* v. *Uniroyal Engelbert Tyres* (Sh.Ct.), 1995 S.C.L.R. 273.

20 & 21 Vict. (1857)

26. Registration of Leases (Scotland) Act 1857.
schs. A–D, F–H, amended: 1995, c. 7, sch. 4.

44. Crown Suits (Scotland) Act 1857.
ss. 1, 4, 5, see *Advocate (Lord)* v. *Black* (O.H.), 1994 S.C.L.R. 925.

24 & 25 Vict. (1861)

100. Offences against the Person Act 1861.
see *R.* v. *Bills, The Times*, March 1, 1995, C.A.
s. 18, see *R.* v. *Fairbairn (Philip Joseph)* (94/4116/Y5), January 27, 1995, C.A.; see *R.* v. *Baker* [1994] Crim.L.R. 444, C.A.; *R.* v. *Maxwell* (1994) J.P.N. 877, C.A.
s. 20, see *R.* v. *Pearson* [1994] Crim.L.R. 534, C.A.; *R.* v. *Wright (Gary Wayne)* (95/0759/W3), April 4, 1995, C.A.; *R.* v. *Maxwell* (1994) J.P.N. 877, C.A.
s. 47, see *R.* v. *Maxwell* (1994) J.P.N. 877, C.A.
s. 53, amended: S.R. 1995 No. 755.
s. 55, amended: S.R. 1995 No. 755.

CAP.

25 & 26 Vict. (1862)

19. General Pier and Harbour Act 1861 Amendment Act 1862.
s. 21, amended: 1995, c. 21, sch. 13.

85. Transmission of Moveable Property (Scotland) Act 1862.
schs. A, B, C, amended: 1995, c. 7, sch. 4.

26 & 27 Vict. (1863)

32. Local Government Supplemental Act 1863.
sch., repealed in pt.: 1995, c. 44, sch. 1.

27 & 28 Vict. (1864)

114. Improvement of Land Act 1864.
s. 18, repealed in pt.: 1995, c. 36, sch. 5 (S.).
s. 21, repealed in pt.: 1995, c. 36, sch. 5 (S.).
s. 24, amended: 1995, c. 36, sch. 4 (S.).

28 & 29 Vict. (1865)

18. Criminal Procedure Act 1865.
see *R.* v. *Derby Magistrates Court, ex p. B., The Times*, October 25, 1995, H.L.

73. Naval and Marine Pay and Pensions Amendment Act 1865.
s. 3, order 95/766.

107. Local Government Supplemental Act 1866 (No. 4).
sch., repealed in pt.: 1995, c. 44, sch. 1.

108. Local Government Supplemental Act 1865 (No. 5).
sch., amended: 1995, c. 44, sch. 1.

30 & 31 Vict. (1867)

17. Lyon King of Arms Act 1867.
sch. B, amended: order 95/132.

31 & 32 Vict. (1868)

45. Sea Fisheries Act 1868.
s. 26, substituted: 1995, c. 21, sch. 13.

64. Land Registers (Scotland) Act 1868.
s. 4, amended: 1994, c. 14, s. 1.
s. 6, repealed in pt.: 1995, c. 14, s. 1.

101. Titles to Land (Consolidation) Act 1868.
s. 120, see *Scotlife Home Loans (No. 2)* v. *Muir* (Sh.Ct.), 1994 S.C.L.R. 791.
ss. 139, 149, repealed: 1995, c. 7, sch. 5.
schs. B, FF, GG, J, NN, amended: 1995, c. 7, sch. 4.

119. Regulation of Railways Act 1868.
s. 22, order 95/2458.

123. Salmon Fisheries (Scotland) Act 1868.
s. 20, see *Brady* v. *Procurator Fiscal, Stonehaven, The Times*, February 27, 1995.

CAP.

32 & 33 Vict. (1869)

115. Metropolitan Public Carriage Act 1869.
s. 6, order 95/837.
s. 9, order 95/1181.

33 & 34 Vict. (1870)

52. Extradition Act 1870.
s. 2, orders 94/2794; 95/1620, 1962.
s. 3, see *T.* v. *Secretary of State for the Home Department* [1995] Imm. A.R. 142, C.A.
s. 21, orders 94/2794; 95/1620, 1962.

90. Foreign Enlistment Act 1870.
s. 33, repealed: 1995, c. 44, sch. 1.

34 & 35 Vict. (1871)

69. Medicines Act 1871.
s. 1, order 95/871.

36 & 37 Vict. (1873)

12. Custody of Infants Act 1873.
repealed: S.R. 1995 No. 755.

88. Slave Trade Act 1873.
s. 26, amended: 1995, c. 21, sch. 13.

37 & 38 Vict. (1874)

81. Great Seal (Offices) Act 1874.
s. 4, repealed in pt.: 1995, c. 44, sch. 1.
s. 7, repealed: 1995, c. 44, sch. 1.

94. Conveyancing (Scotland) Act 1874.
ss. 38–41, repealed: 1995, c. 7, sch. 5.
s. 51, amended: 1995, c. 44, sch. 1.
schs. C, F, G, I, L, M, N, amended: 1995, c. 7, sch. 4.

38 & 39 Vict. (1875)

16. Regimental Exchange Act 1875.
repealed: 1995, c. 44, sch. 1.

17. Explosives Act 1875.
ss. 58, 98, 101, amended: 1995, c. 21, sch. 13.
ss. 110, 111, amended: 1994, c. 39, sch. 13 (S.).

22. Trade Marks Act 1875.
see *Al Bassam Trade Mark* [1994] R.P.C. 315, Aldous J.

86. Conspiracy and Protection of Property Act 1875.
s. 7, see *D.P.P.* v. *Todd*, *The Independent*, May 5, 1995, D.C.

40 & 41 Vict. (1877)

59. Colonial Stock Act 1877.
s. 4, amended: 1995, c. 7, sch. 4 (S.).
s. 6, amended: 1995, c. 7, sch. 4 (S.).

42 & 43 Vict. (1879)

11. Bankers' Books Evidence Act 1879.
s. 6, amended: 1995, c. 40, sch. 4 (S.).

CAP.

43 & 44 Vict. (1880)

4. Judicial Factors (Scotland) Act 1880.
s. 3, repealed in pt.: 1995, c. 36, schs. 4, 5.

46 & 47 Vict. (1883)

3. Explosive Substances Act 1883.
s. 8, amended: 1995, c. 21, sch. 13.

57. Patents, Designs and Trade Marks Act 1883.
ss. 62, 71, 75, see *Al Bassam Trade Mark* [1994] R.P.C. 315, Aldous J.

47 & 48 Vict. (1884)

55. Pensions and Yeomanry Pay Act 1884.
s. 2, order 95/766.

48 & 49 Vict. (1885)

49. Submarine Telegraph Act 1885.
s. 5, amended: 1995, c. 21, sch. 13.
s. 6, repealed in pt.: 1995, c. 44, sch. 1.
s. 7, amended: 1995, c. 21, sch. 13.

69. Criminal Law Amendment Act 1885.
s. 7, amended: S.R. 1995 No. 755.
s. 10, repealed in pt.: S.R. 1995 No. 755.
s. 10, amended: S.R. 1995 No. 755.

72. Houses of the Working Classes Act 1885.
repealed: 1995, c. 44, sch. 1.

49 & 50 Vict. (1886)

15. Sporting Lands Rating (Scotland) Act 1886.
repealed: 1994, c. 39, sch. 14.

27. Guardianship of Infants Act 1886.
repealed: S.R. 1995 No. 755.

50 & 51 Vict. (1887)

35. Criminal Procedure (Scotland) Act 1887.
repealed: 1995, c. 40, sch. 5.
s. 3, repealed: 1995, c. 20, sch. 7.
s. 3, amended: 1995, c. 20, sch. 6.
schs. A, C: 1995, c. 46, sch. 2.
schs. D, E, N, O, repealed: 1995, c. 20, sch. 6.

42. Public Libraries Consolidation (Scotland) Act 1887.
s. 2, amended: 1994, c. 39, sch. 13.

54. British Settlements Act 1887.
orders 95/1030, 1621.

55. Sheriffs Act 1887.
s. 38, amended: regs. 95/1748.
sch. 2A, added: regs. 95/1748.

CAP.

52 & 53 Vict. (1889)

69. Public Bodies Corrupt Practices Act 1889.
see *R.* v. *Bowden (Terence) (93/6974/X2)*, February 24, 1995, C.A.

53 & 54 Vict. (1890)

37. Foreign Jurisdiction Act 1890.
order 95/1030.
sch. 1, amended: 1995, c. 21, sch. 13.

54 & 55 Vict. (1891)

3. Custody of Children Act 1891.
repealed: S.R. 1995 No. 755.

37. Fisheries Act 1891.
s. 2, amended: 1995, c. 21, sch. 13.

39. Stamp Act 1891.
see *Nisbet* v. *Shepherd* [1994] BCC 91, C.A.
s. 54, see *Peter Bone* v. *I.R.C.*, *The Independent (C.S.)*, September 4, 1995, Vinelott J.

40. Brine Pumping (Compensation for Subsidence) Act 1891.
repealed: 1995, c. 44, sch. 1.

50. Commissioner for Oaths Act 1891.
s. 1, amended: 1995, c. 21, sch. 13.

55 & 56 Vict. (1892)

9. Gaming Act 1892.
s. 1, see *Morgan Grenfell & Co.* v. *Welwyn Hatfield District Council (Islington London Borough Council, Third Party)* [1995] 1 All E.R. 1, Hobhouse J.

17. Sheriff Courts (Scotland) Extracts Act 1892.
s. 7, see *Main* v. *Reid* (Sh.Ct.), 1994 S.C.L.R. 948.

35. Colonial Stock Act 1892.
s. 2, sch., amended: 1995, c. 7, sch. 4 (S.).

43. Military Lands Act 1892.
s. 17, 1995, c. 40, sch. 2 (S.).

54. Allotments (Scotland) Act 1892.
s. 16, amended: 1994, c. 39, sch. 13.

56 & 57 Vict. (1893–94)

60. Merchant Shipping Act 1894.
s. 692, amended: regs. 95/1802.

CAP.

57 & 58 Vict. (1894)

44. Heritable Securities (Scotland) Act 1894.
s. 13, amended: 1995, c. 36, sch. 4.

60. Merchant Shipping Act 1894.
s. 66, repealed: 1995, c. 21, sch. 12.
s. 76, repealed: 1995, c. 21, sch. 12.
s. 76, C.: 1995, c. 21, sch. 14.
s. 82, repealed: 1995, c. 21, sch. 12.
s. 82, C.: 1995, c. 21, sch. 14.
s. 84, repealed: 1995, c. 21, sch. 12.
s. 84, C.: 1995, c. 21, sch. 14.
s. 256, C.: 1995, c. 21, sch. 14.
s. 267, repealed (prosp.): regs. 95/1210.
ss. 271–283, repealed (prosp.): regs. 95/1210.
s. 287, repealed: 1995, c. 21, sch. 12.
s. 287, C.: 1995, c. 21, sch. 14.
s. 288, repealed: 1995, c. 21, sch. 12.
s. 288, C.: 1995, c. 21, sch. 14.
s. 363, repealed: regs. 95/1210.
s. 422, repealed: 1995, c. 21, sch. 12.
s. 422, C.: 1995, c. 21, sch. 14.
s. 430, continued in force (temp.): 1995, c. 21, sch. 14.
s. 449, repealed: 1995, c. 21, sch. 12.
s. 449, C.: 1995, c. 21, sch. 14.
s. 458, repealed: 1995, c. 21, sch. 12.
s. 503, see *Hamburg Star, The* [1994] 1 Lloyd's Rep. 399, Clarke J.
s. 510, repealed: 1995, c. 21, sch. 12.
s. 510, C.: 1995, c. 21, sch. 14.
s. 511, repealed: 1995, c. 21, sch. 12.
s. 511, C.: 1995, c. 21, sch. 14.
s. 512, repealed: 1995, c. 21, sch. 12.
s. 512, C.: 1995, c. 21, sch. 14.
s. 513, repealed: 1995, c. 21, sch. 12.
s. 513, C.: 1995, c. 21, sch. 14.
s. 515, repealed: 1995, c. 21, sch. 12.
s. 515, C.: 1995, c. 21, sch. 14.
s. 516, repealed: 1995, c. 21, sch. 12.
s. 516, C.: 1995, c. 21, sch. 14.
s. 518, repealed: 1995, c. 21, sch. 12.
s. 518, C.: 1995, c. 21, sch. 14.
s. 519, repealed: 1995, c. 21, sch. 12.
s. 519, C.: 1995, c. 21, sch. 14.
s. 520, repealed: 1995, c. 21, sch. 12.
s. 520, C.: 1995, c. 21, sch. 14.
s. 521, repealed: 1995, c. 21, sch. 12.
s. 521, C.: 1995, c. 21, sch. 14.
s. 522, repealed: 1995, c. 21, sch. 12.
s. 522, C.: 1995, c. 21, sch. 14.
s. 523, repealed: 1995, c. 21, sch. 12.
s. 523, C.: 1995, c. 21, sch. 14.
s. 524, repealed: 1995, c. 21, sch. 12.
s. 524, C.: 1995, c. 21, sch. 14.
s. 525, repealed: 1995, c. 21, sch. 12.
s. 525, C.: 1995, c. 21, sch. 14.
s. 527, repealed: 1995, c. 21, sch. 12.
s. 527, C.: 1995, c. 21, sch. 14.
s. 530, repealed: 1995, c. 21, sch. 12.
s. 530, C.: 1995, c. 21, sch. 14.
s. 531, repealed: 1995, c. 21, sch. 12.
s. 531, C.: 1995, c. 21, sch. 14.
s. 532, repealed: 1995, c. 21, sch. 12.

CAP.

57 & 58 Vict. (1894)—cont.

60. Merchant Shipping Act 1894—*cont.*
s. 532, C.: 1995, c. 21, sch. 14.
s. 533, repealed: 1995, c. 21, sch. 12.
s. 533, C.: 1995, c. 21, sch. 14.
s. 534, repealed: 1995, c. 21, sch. 12.
s. 534, C.: 1995, c. 21, sch. 14.
s. 535, repealed: 1995, c. 21, sch. 12.
s. 535, C.: 1995, c. 21, sch. 14.
s. 536, repealed: 1995, c. 21, sch. 12.
s. 536, C.: 1995, c. 21, sch. 14.
s. 537, repealed: 1995, c. 21, sch. 12.
s. 537, C.: 1995, c. 21, sch. 14.
s. 551, repealed: 1995, c. 21, sch. 12.
s. 551, C.: 1995, c. 21, sch. 14.
s. 552, repealed: 1995, c. 21, sch. 12.
s. 552, C.: 1995, c. 21, sch. 14.
s. 553, repealed: 1995, c. 21, sch. 12.
s. 553, C.: 1995, c. 21, sch. 14.
s. 555, repealed: 1995, c. 21, sch. 12.
s. 555, C.: 1995, c. 21, sch. 14.
s. 556, repealed: 1995, c. 21, sch. 12.
s. 556, C.: 1995, c. 21, sch. 14.
s. 557, repealed: 1995, c. 21, sch. 12.
s. 557, C.: 1995, c. 21, sch. 14.
s. 566, repealed: 1995, c. 21, sch. 12.
s. 566, C.: 1995, c. 21, sch. 14.
s. 567, repealed: 1995, c. 21, sch. 12.
s. 567, C.: 1995, c. 21, sch. 14.
s. 568, repealed: 1995, c. 21, sch. 12.
s. 568, C.: 1995, c. 21, sch. 14.
s. 569, repealed in pt.: 1995, c. 21, sch. 12.
s. 569, C.: 1995, c. 21, sch. 14.
s. 570, repealed: 1995, c. 21, sch. 12.
s. 570, C.: 1995, c. 21, sch. 14.
s. 571, repealed: 1995, c. 21, sch. 12.
s. 571, C.: 1995, c. 21, sch. 14.
s. 634, repealed: 1995, c. 21, sch. 12.
s. 634, C.: 1995, c. 21, sch. 14.
s. 635, repealed: 1995, c. 21, sch. 12.
s. 635, C.: 1995, c. 21, sch. 14.
s. 636, repealed: 1995, c. 21, sch. 12.
s. 636, C.: 1995, c. 21, sch. 14.
s. 638, repealed: 1995, c. 21, sch. 12.
s. 638, C.: 1995, c. 21, sch. 14.
s. 639, repealed: 1995, c. 21, sch. 12.
s. 639, C.: 1995, c. 21, sch. 14.
s. 642, repealed: 1995, c. 21, sch. 12.
s. 643, repealed: 1995, c. 21, sch. 12.
s. 643, C.: 1995, c. 21, sch. 14.
s. 643A, repealed: 1995, c. 21, sch. 12.
s. 643A, C.: 1995, c. 21, sch. 14.
s. 647, repealed: 1995, c. 21, sch. 12.
s. 647, C.: 1995, c. 21, sch. 14.
s. 648, repealed: 1995, c. 21, sch. 12.
s. 648, C.: 1995, c. 21, sch. 14.
s. 649, repealed: 1995, c. 21, sch. 12.
s. 649, C.: 1995, c. 21, sch. 14.
s. 650, repealed: 1995, c. 21, sch. 12.
s. 650, C.: 1995, c. 21, sch. 14.
s. 651, repealed: 1995, c. 21, sch. 12.
s. 651, C.: 1995, c. 21, sch. 14.

CAP.

57 & 58 Vict. (1894)—cont.

60. Merchant Shipping Act 1894—*cont.*
s. 652, repealed: 1995, c. 21, sch. 12.
s. 652, C.: 1995, c. 21, sch. 14.
s. 653, repealed: 1995, c. 21, sch. 12.
s. 653, C.: 1995, c. 21, sch. 14.
s. 654, repealed: 1995, c. 21, sch. 12.
s. 654, C.: 1995, c. 21, sch. 14.
s. 655, repealed: 1995, c. 21, sch. 12.
s. 655, C.: 1995, c. 21, sch. 14.
s. 656, repealed: 1995, c. 21, sch. 12.
s. 656, C.: 1995, c. 21, sch. 14.
s. 657, repealed (Northern Ireland only): 1995, c. 21, sch. 12.
s. 658, repealed: 1995, c. 21, sch. 12.
s. 658, C.: 1995, c. 21, sch. 14.
s. 659, repealed: 1995, c. 21, sch. 12.
s. 659, C.: 1995, c. 21, sch. 14.
s. 660, repealed: 1995, c. 21, sch. 12.
s. 660, C.: 1995, c. 21, sch. 14.
s. 662, repealed: 1995, c. 21, sch. 12.
s. 662, C.: 1995, c. 21, sch. 14.
s. 662A, C.: 1995, c. 21, sch. 14.
s. 662B, repealed: 1995, c. 21, sch. 12.
s. 662B, C.: 1995, c. 21, sch. 14.
s. 664, repealed: 1995, c. 21, sch. 12.
s. 664, C.: 1995, c. 21, sch. 14.
s. 666, repealed: 1995, c. 21, sch. 12.
s. 666, C.: 1995, c. 21, sch. 14.
s. 667, repealed: 1995, c. 21, sch. 12.
s. 667, C.: 1995, c. 21, sch. 14.
s. 668, repealed: 1995, c. 21, sch. 12.
s. 668, amended: 1994, c. 39, sch. 13 (S.).
s. 668, C.: 1995, c. 21, sch. 14.
s. 669, repealed: 1995, c. 21, sch. 12.
s. 669, C.: 1995, c. 21, sch. 14.
s. 676, repealed: 1995, c. 21, sch. 12.
s. 676, C.: 1995, c. 21, sch. 14.
s. 677, repealed: 1995, c. 21, sch. 12.
s. 677, C.: 1995, c. 21, sch. 14.
s. 679, repealed: 1995, c. 21, sch. 12.
s. 679, C.: 1995, c. 21, sch. 14.
s. 680, repealed: 1995, c. 21, sch. 12.
s. 680, C.: 1995, c. 21, sch. 14.
s. 681, repealed: 1995, c. 21, sch. 14.
s. 681, C.: 1995, c. 21, sch. 14.
s. 683, repealed: 1995, c. 21, sch. 12.
s. 683, C.: 1995, c. 21, sch. 14.
s. 684, repealed: 1995, c. 21, sch. 12.
s. 684, C.: 1995, c. 21, sch. 14.
s. 685, repealed: 1995, c. 21, sch. 12.
s. 685, C.: 1995, c. 21, sch. 14.
s. 686, repealed: 1995, c. 21, sch. 12.
s. 686, C.: 1995, c. 21, sch. 14.
s. 687, repealed: 1995, c. 21, sch. 12.
s. 687, C.: 1995, c. 21, sch. 14.
s. 687A, repealed: 1995, c. 21, sch. 12.
s. 687A, C.: 1995, c. 21, sch. 14.
s. 687B, repealed: 1995, c. 21, sch. 12.
s. 687B, C.: 1995, c. 21, sch. 14.
s. 688, repealed: 1995, c. 21, sch. 12 (S.).
s. 689, repealed: 1995, c. 21, sch. 12.
s. 689, C.: 1995, c. 21, sch. 14.

CAP.

57 & 58 Vict. (1894)—cont.

60. Merchant Shipping Act 1894—*cont.*
s. 691, repealed: 1995, c. 21, sch. 12.
s. 692, repealed: 1995, c. 21, sch. 12.
s. 692, amended: regs. 95/157, 1210, 1802.
s. 692, C.: 1995, c. 21, sch. 14.
s. 693, repealed: 1995, c. 21, sch. 12.
s. 693, C.: 1995, c. 21, sch. 14.
s. 695, repealed: 1995, c. 21, sch. 12.
s. 695, C.: 1995, c. 21, sch. 14.
s. 696, repealed: 1995, c. 21, sch. 12.
s. 696, C.: 1995, c. 21, sch. 14.
s. 697, repealed: 1995, c. 21, sch. 12.
s. 697, C.: 1995, c. 21, sch. 14.
s. 702, repealed: 1995, c. 21, sch. 12.
s. 703, repealed: 1995, c. 21, sch. 12.
s. 703, C.: 1995, c. 21, sch. 14.
s. 710, repealed: 1995, c. 21, sch. 12.
s. 710, C.: 1995, c. 21, sch. 14.
s. 711, repealed: 1995, c. 21, sch. 12.
s. 712, repealed: 1995, c. 21, sch. 12.
s. 713, repealed: 1995, c. 21, sch. 12.
s. 713, C.: 1995, c. 21, sch. 14.
s. 714, repealed: 1995, c. 21, sch. 12.
s. 714, C.: 1995, c. 21, sch. 14.
s. 715, repealed: 1995, c. 21, sch. 12.
s. 715, C.: 1995, c. 21, sch. 14.
s. 717, repealed: 1995, c. 21, sch. 12.
s. 717, C.: 1995, c. 21, sch. 14.
s. 718, repealed: 1995, c. 21, sch. 12.
s. 718, C.: 1995, c. 21, sch. 14.
s. 720, repealed: 1995, c. 21, sch. 12.
s. 720, C.: 1995, c. 21, sch. 14.
s. 721, repealed: 1995, c. 21, sch. 12.
s. 721, C.: 1995, c. 21, sch. 14.
s. 722, repealed: 1995, c. 21, sch. 12.
s. 722, C.: 1995, c. 21, sch. 14.
s. 723, repealed: 1995, c. 21, sch. 12.
s. 723, C.: 1995, c. 21, sch. 14.
s. 724, repealed: 1995, c. 21, sch. 12.
s. 724, C.: 1995, c. 21, sch. 14.
s. 726, repealed: 1995, c. 21, sch. 12.
s. 726, C.: 1995, c. 21, sch. 14.
s. 727, repealed: 1995, c. 21, sch. 12.
s. 728, repealed: 1995, c. 21, sch. 12.
s. 728, C.: 1995, c. 21, sch. 14.
s. 731, repealed: 1995, c. 21, sch. 12.
s. 732, repealed: 1995, c. 21, sch. 12.
s. 732, C.: 1995, c. 21, sch. 14.
s. 735, repealed: 1995, c. 21, sch. 12.
s. 735, continued in force (pt.): 1995, c. 21, sch. 14.
s. 736, repealed: 1995, c. 21, sch. 12.
s. 738, repealed in pt.: 1995, c. 21, sch. 12.
s. 738, C.: 1995, c. 21, sch. 14.
s. 739, repealed: 1995, c. 21, sch. 12.
s. 739, C.: 1995, c. 21, sch. 14.
s. 741, repealed: 1995, c. 21, sch. 12.
s. 742, repealed: 1995, c. 21, sch. 12.
s. 742, C.: 1995, c. 21, sch. 14.
s. 743, repealed: 1995, c. 21, sch. 12.
s. 745, repealed: 1995, c. 21, sch. 12.

CAP.

57 & 58 Vict. (1894)—cont.

60. Merchant Shipping Act 1894—*cont.*
s. 745, C.: 1995, c. 21, sch. 14.
s. 746, repealed: 1995, c. 21, sch. 12.
s. 747, repealed: 1995, c. 21, sch. 12.
sch. 4, amended: regs. 95/1210.
sch. 17, repealed: 1995, c. 21, sch. 12.
sch. 19, repealed: 1995, c. 21, sch. 12.

58 & 59 Vict. (1895)

14. Courts of Law Fees (Scotland) Act 1895.
s. 2, orders 94/498, 3266, 3265; 95/307.
21. Seal Fisheries (North Pacific) Act 1895.
ss. 1, 2, 3, amended: 1995, c. 21, sch. 13.

59 & 60 Vict. (1896)

14. Short Titles Act 1896.
s. 1, repealed: 1995, c. 44, sch. 1.
sch. 1, repealed: 1995, c. 44, sch. 1.
sch. 2, repealed in pt.: 1995, c. 44, sch. 1.
48. Light Railway Act 1896.
s. 7, orders 95/861, 1236, 1300, 2142.
s. 9, order 95/861.
ss. 10, 11, 12, 18, orders 95/861, 1236, 1300, 2142.
s. 11, orders 95/861, 1236.
s. 12, orders 95/861, 1236.
s. 18, order 95/1236.
s. 24, order 95/861.

60 & 61 Vict. (1897)

21. Mersey Channels Act 1897.
repealed: 1995, c. 21, sch. 12.
30. Police (Property) Act 1897.
see *R.* v. *Basildon Justices, ex p. Holding and Barnes* [1994] RA 157, Schiemann J.
38. Public Health (Scotland) Act 1897.
s. 12, amended: 1994, c. 39, sch. 13.
ss. 16–26, repealed: 1995, c. 25, sch. 24.
ss. 36–37, repealed: 1995, c. 25, sch. 24.
59. Merchant Shipping Act 1897.
repealed: 1995, c. 21, sch. 12.

61 & 62 Vict. (1898)

36. Criminal Evidence Act 1898.
s. 1, see *R.* v. *Marsh* [1994] Crim.L.R. 52, C.A.; *R.* v. *McLeod* [1994] 1 W.L.R. 1500, C.A.; *Fearon* v. *D.P.P., The Independent*, April 24, 1995, D.C.; *R.* v. *Stanton* [1994] Crim.L.R. 834, C.A.
44. Merchant Shipping (Mercantile Marine Fund) Act 1898.
s. 1, repealed: 1995, c. 21, sch. 12.
s. 1, continued in force (pt.): 1995, c. 21, sch. 14.
s. 1A, repealed: 1995, c. 21, sch. 12.

CAP.

61 & 62 Vict. (1898)—cont.

44. Merchant Shipping (Mercantile Marine Fund) Act 1898—*cont.*
s. 2, repealed in pt.: 1995, c. 21, sch. 12.
ss. 2A, 2B, repealed: 1995, c. 21, sch. 12.
s. 5, regs. 95/525.
s. 5, repealed in pt.: 1995, c. 21, sch. 12.
s. 5, C.: 1995, c. 21, sch. 14.
s. 9, repealed: 1995, c. 21, sch. 12.
sch. 3, repealed in pt.: 1995, c. 21, sch. 12.

63 & 64 Vict. (1900)

32. Merchant Shipping (Liability of Shipowners and Others) Act 1900.
s. 2, repealed: 1995, c. 21, sch. 12.
s. 2, C.: 1995, c. 21, sch. 14.
s. 3, repealed: 1995, c. 21, sch. 12.
s. 3, C.: 1995, c. 21, sch. 14.
ss. 4–5, repealed: 1995, c. 21, sch. 12.
55. Executors (Scotland) Act 1900.
ss. 6, 7, see *Dagleish* v. *Swanston* (Sh.Ct.), 1994 S.C.L.R. 920.

5 Edw. 7 (1905)

15. Trade Marks Act 1905.
ss. 12, 20, 42, see *Al Bassam Trade Mark* [1994] R.P.C. 315, Aldous J.

6 Edw. 7 (1906)

14. Alkali, & c., Works Regulation Act 1906.
ss. 1, 2, amended: 1995, c. 25, sch. 22.
s. 9, repealed in pt.: 1995, c. 25, sch. 24.
s. 9, amended: 1995, c. 25, sch. 22.
ss. 22, 23, amended: 1995, c. 25, sch. 22.
s. 25, repealed: 1995, c. 25, schs. 22, 24.
s. 27, repealed in pt.: 1995, c. 25, sch. 24.
s. 27, amended: 1995, c. 25, sch. 22.
s. 28, repealed in pt.: 1995, c. 25, schs. 22, 24.
41. Marine Insurance Act 1906.
ss. 17, 18, 20, see *Pan Atlantic Insurance Co.* v. *Pine Top Insurance Co.* [1994] 3 W.L.R. 677, H.L.
ss. 18, 19, see *PCW Syndicates* v. *PCW Reinsurers, The Independent*, September 8, 1995, C.A.
s. 39, see *Lombard Insurance Co.* v. *Kin Yuen Co.; Pab, The, Lloyd's List*, July 25, 1995, C.A.
48. Merchant Shipping Act 1906.
ss. 13, 21, 22, repealed (prosp.): regs. 95/1210.
s. 72, repealed: 1995, c. 21, sch. 12; regs. 95/1210.
ss. 75, 76, repealed: 1995, c. 21, sch. 12.
s. 78, repealed: 1995, c. 21, sch. 12.
s. 78, C.: 1995, c. 21, sch. 14.
ss. 79–80, repealed: 1995, c. 21, sch. 12.
ss. 84–86, repealed: 1995, c. 21, sch. 12.
55. Public Trustee Act 1906.
s. 5, see *Duxbury's Settlement Trusts, Re*, [1995] 1 W.L.R. 425, C.A.

CAP.

7 Edw. 7 (1907)

29. Patents and Designs Act 1907.

s. 32A, see *Gerber Garment Technology* v. *Lectra Systems* [1994] F.S.R. 471, Aldous J.

51. Sheriff Courts (Scotland) Act 1907.

see *Ritchie* v. *Cleary (Sh.Ct.)*, 1995 S.C.L.R. 561.

s. 3, see *Thomson* v. *Proctor (Sh.Ct.)*, 1995 S.C.L.R. 648.

s. 4, Act of Sederunt 95/1395.

s. 5, repealed in pt.: 1995, c. 36, sch. 5.

s. 35, sch., repealed in pt.: 1995, c. 7, sch. 5.

s. 38, repealed in pt.: 1995, c. 36, sch. 5.

s. 40, Act of Sederunt 94/3267.

Sched., see *Fairbairn* v. *Welsh* (Sh.Ct.), 1994 S.C.L.R. 942; *Burtonport Fishermen's Co-op* v. *Sans Unkles* (Sh.Ct.), 1994 S.C.L.R. 844; *Gracey* v. *Sykes* (Sh.Ct.), 1994 S.C.L.R. 909; *Gordon* v. *Mayfair Homes* (Sh.Ct.), 1994 S.C.L.R. 862; *R.* v. *R.* (Sh.Ct.), 1994 S.C.L.R. 849; *Scotlife Home Loans (No. 2)* v. *Muir* (Sh.Ct.), 1994 S.C.L.R. 967; *Muir* v. *Stewart* (Sh.Ct.), 1994 S.C.L.R. 935; *Colvin* v. *Montgomery Preservations*, 1995 S.L.T. (Sh.Ct.) 15; *Taylor* v. *Stakis*, 1995 S.L.T. (Sh.Ct.) 14; *Bell* v. *John Davidson (Pipes)*, 1995 S.L.T. (Sh.Ct.) 18; *Forbes* v. *Johnstone*, 1995 S.L.T. 158; *Rae* v. *Calor Gas*, 1995 S.L.T. 244; *Welsh (Andrew)* v. *Thornhome Services* (Sh.Ct.), 1994 S.C.L.R. 1021; *Morran* v. *Glasgow Council of Tenants' Associations* (Sh.Ct.), 1994 S.C.L.R. 1065; *Mahoney* v. *Officer* (Sh.Ct.), 1994 S.C.L.R. 1059; *Ritchie* v. *Maersk Co.* (Sh.Ct.), 1994 S.C.L.R. 1038; *Ampliflaire* v. *The Chisholme Institute* (Sh.Ct.), 1995 S.C.L.R. 11; *Matthews* v. *Scottish Legal Board* (Sh.Ct.), 1995 S.C.L.R. 184; *Winter (David) & Sons* v. *George Craig & Sons* (I.H.), 1995 S.C.L.R. 109; *Wagon Finance* v. *O'Lone* (Sh.Ct.), 1995 S.C.L.R. 149; *Mellor* v. *Towle* (Sh.Ct.), 1995 S.C.L.R. 76; *D.T.Z. Debenham Thorpe* v. *I. Henderson Transport Services*, 1995 S.L.T. 553; *Price* v. *Fernando* (Sh.Ct.), 1990 S.C.L.R. 23; *Weatherall* v. *Jack* (Sh.Ct.), 1995 S.C.L.R. 189; *Grimes* v. *Grimes* (Sh.Ct.), 1995 S.C.L.R. 268; *Nicolson* (Sh.Ct.), 1995 S.C.L.R. 389; *McGowan* v. *Cartner* (Sh.Ct.), 1995 S.C.L.R. 312; *Group 4 Total Security* v. *Jaymarke Developments* (Sh.Ct.), 1995 S.C.L.R. 303; *Blair Bryden Partnership (The)* v. *Adair* (Sh.Ct.), 1995

CAP.

7 Edw. 7 (1907)—cont.

51. Sheriff Courts (Scotland) Act 1907—*cont.*

S.C.L.R. 358; *De Melo* v. *Bazazi*, 1995 S.L.T. (Sh.Ct.) 57; *McVinnie* v. *McVinnie (Sh.Ct.)*, 1995 S.C.L.R. 480; *Strathclyde Business Park (Management)* v. *Cochrane*, 1995 S.L.T. (Sh.Ct.) 69; *Heritage House* v. *Brown (Sh.Ct.)*, 1995 S.C.L.R. 783; *Napier Co. (Arbroath)* v. *Frangos (Sh.Ct.)*, 1995 S.C.L.R. 804; *Hart* v. *Thorntons, W.S. (Sh.Ct.)*, 1995 S.C.L.R. 642.

53. Public Health Acts Amendment Act 1907.

s. 7, see *Wirral Metropolitan Borough Council* v. *Smith (Derek) (CO/3206/94; CO/3229/93)*, March 17, 1995, Laws J.

s. 21, S.R. 1995 No. 759.

55. London Cab and Stage Carriage Act 1907.

s. 1, order 95/1181.

8 Edw. 7 (1908)

36. Small Holdings and Allotments Act 1908.

ss. 23, 32, see *R.* v. *Secretary of State for the Environment, ex p. Gosforth Allotments and Gardens Association (CO/294/94)*, May 23, 1995, Laws J.

s. 47, amended: 1995, c. 8, sch.

45. Punishment of Incest Act 1908.

s. 1, S.R. 1995 No. 755.

53. Law of Distress Amendment Act 1908.

s. 4, amended: 1995, c. 8, sch.

s. 4, see *Salford Van Hire (Contracts)* v. *Bocholt Developments, The Times*, April 22, 1995, C.A.

66. Public Meeting Act 1908.

s. 1, amended: 1995, c. 40, sch. 2 (S.).

1 & 2 Geo. 5 (1911)

6. Perjury Act 1911.

s. 13, see *R.* v. *Carroll* (1994) 99 Cr.App.R. 381, C.A.

27. Protection of Animals Act 1911.

s. 1, see *RSPCA* v. *Isaacs* [1994] Crim. L.R. 517, D.C.

57. Maritime Conventions Act 1911.

s. 1, repealed: 1995, c. 21, sch. 12.

s. 1, C.: 1995, c. 21, sch. 14.

s. 2, repealed: 1995, c. 21, sch. 12.

s. 2, C.: 1995, c. 21, sch. 14.

s. 3, repealed: 1995, c. 21, sch. 12.

s. 3, C.: 1995, c. 21, sch. 14.

s. 4, repealed in pt.: 1995, c. 21, sch. 12.

s. 5, repealed: 1995, c. 21, sch. 12.

s. 6, repealed: 1995, c. 21, sch. 12.

s. 7, repealed: 1995, c. 21, sch. 12.

s. 8, repealed: 1995, c. 21, sch. 12.

CAP.

1 & 2 Geo. 5 (1911)—cont.

57. Maritime Conventions Act 1911—*cont.*
s. 8, C.: 1995, c. 21, sch. 14.
s. 9, repealed: 1995, c. 21, sch. 12.
s. 9, C.: 1995, c. 21, sch. 14.
s. 10, repealed: 1995, c. 21, sch. 12.

2 & 3 Geo. 5 (1912–13)

10. Seal Fisheries (North Pacific) Act 1912.
s. 3, amended: 1995, c. 21, sch. 12.

14. Protection of Animals (Scotland) Act 1912.
s. 1, amended: 1995, c. 40, sch. 2.
s. 7, amended: 1995, c. 40, sch. 2.

4 & 5 Geo. 5 (1914)

18. War Compensation Act 1914.
s. 1, scheme 95/979.

48. Feudal Casualties (Scotland) Act 1914.
s. 8, repealed in pt.: 1995, c. 7, sch. 5.
schs. B, C, amended: 1995, c. 7, sch. 4.

58. Criminal Justice Administration Act 1914.
s. 28, repealed: 1995, c. 40, sch. 5 (S.).

59. Bankruptcy Act 1914.
ss. 37, 38, see *Dennis (A Bankrupt), Re* [1995] 3 W.L.R. 367, C.A.

5 & 6 Geo. 5 (1914–15)

90. Indictments Act 1915.
s. 5, see *R.* v. *C.* [1994] Crim.L.R. 590, C.A.; *R.* v. *Wells* [1995] 159 J.P. 243, C.A.

7 & 8 Geo. 5 (1917–18)

51. Air Force (Constitution) Act 1917.
s. 2, order 95/766.

9 & 10 Geo. 5 (1919)

62. Mercantile Marine Uniform Act 1919.
repealed: 1995, c. 21, sch. 12.
s. 1, C.: 1995, c. 21, sch. 14.

76. Church of England Assembly (Powers) Act 1919
see *R.* v. *Ecclesiastical Committee of Both Houses of Parliament, ex p. The Church Society* [1994] C.O.D. 319, D.C.
s. 3, see *R.* v. *Ecclesiastical Committee of Both Houses of Parliament and the Archbishops of Canterbury and York, ex p. The Church Society* (1994) 6 Admin. L.R. 670, D.C.

92. Aliens Restriction (Amendment) Act 1919.
s. 5, repealed: order 95/1426; 1995, c. 21, sch. 12.

CAP.

10 & 11 Geo. 5 (1920)

2. Merchant Shipping (Amendment) Act 1920.
repealed: 1995, c. 21, sch. 12.
s. 1, C.: 1995, c. 21, sch. 14.

20. Imperial War Museum Act 1920.
sch., amended: 1995, c. 3, sch.

33. Maintenance Orders (Facilities for Enforcement) Act 1920.
s. 4A, repealed in pt.: S.R. 1995 No. 755.
s. 4A, amended: S.R. 1995 No. 755.
s. 11, repealed in pt.: S.R. 1995 No. 755.
s. 11, amended: S.R. 1995 No. 755.

39. Merchant Shipping (Scottish Fishing Boats) Act 1920.
repealed: 1995, c. 21, sch. 12.

41. Census Act 1920.
s. 9, amended: 1994, c. 39, sch. 13 (S.).

43. Firearms Act 1920.
repealed: 1995, c. 44, sch. 1.

65. Employment of Women, Young Persons and Children Act 1920.
s. 16, amended: S.R. 1995 No. 755.

11 & 12 Geo. 5 (1921)

7. Tribunals of Enquiry (Evidence) Act 1921.
s. 1, repealed: 1995, c. 44, sch. 1.

28. Merchant Shipping Act 1921.
s. 2, repealed: 1995, c. 21, sch. 12.
s. 2, C.: 1995, c. 21, sch. 14.
s. 3, repealed: 1995, c. 21, sch. 12.
s. 3, C.: 1995, c. 21, sch. 14.
s. 4, repealed: 1995, c. 21, sch. 12.

29. Church of Scotland Act 1921.
sch., see *Logan* v. *Presbytery of Dumbarton*, *The Times*, May 23, 1995.

58. Trusts (Scotland) Act 1921.
s. 2, amended: 1995, c. 36, schs. 4, 5.
s. 32, see *Governors of Dollar Academy Trust* v. *Lord Advocate* (O.H.), 1995 S.L.T. 596.
schs. A, B, amended: 1995, c. 7, sch. 4.

12 & 13 Geo. 5 (1922)

35. Celluloid and Cinematograph Film Act 1922.
s. 10, amended: 1994, c. 39, sch. 13 (S.).

51. Allotments Act 1922.
ss. 3, 6, amended: 1995, c. 8, sch.

52. Allotments (Scotland) Act 1922.
s. 19, amended: 1994, c. 39, sch. 13.

14 & 15 Geo. 5 (1924)

27. Conveyancing (Scotland) Act 1924.
s. 18, repealed in pt.: 1995, c. 7, sch. 5.
schs. B, E, G, H, amended: 1995, c. 7, sch. 4.
sch. I, repealed in pt.: 1995, c. 7, sch. 5.
schs. K, L, N, amended: 1995, c. 7, sch. 4.

CAP.

15 & 16 Geo. 5 (1924–25)

18. Settled Land Act 1925.
s. 1, *Costello* v. *Costello* [1994] N.P.C. 32, C.A.

19. Trustee Act 1925.
s. 26, amended: 1995, c. 30, sch. 1.
s. 51, amended: 1995, c. 21, sch. 13.
s. 54, rules 94/3046.

20. Law of Property Act 1925.
s. 26, see *Crawley Borough Council* v. *Ure, The Times*, February 23, 1995, C.A.
s. 30, see *Abbey National* v. *Moss* [1994] 1 F.L.R. 307, C.A.
s. 40, see *Firstpost Homes* v. *Johnson, The Times*, August 14, 1995, C.A.
s. 53, see *Ivin* v. *Blake (Property: Beneficial Interest)* [1995] 1 F.L.R. 70, C.A.; *United Bank of Kuwait* v. *Sahib* [1995] 2 All E.R. 973, Chadwick, J.
s. 56, see *Shaw's Application, Re* [1995] 68 P. & C.R. 591, Lands Tribunal.
s. 63, see *Brackenbank Lodge* v. *Peart* (1994) 67 P. & C.R. 249, C.A.
s. 65, see *Ingram* v. *I.R.C., The Times*, May 23, 1995, Ferris J.
s. 77, repealed in pt.: 1995, c. 30, sch. 1.
s. 77, amended: 1995, c. 30, sch. 1.
s. 78, see *Caerns Motor Services* v. *Texaco* [1995] 1 All E.R. 247, H.H.J. Paul Baker Q.C. sitting as a deputy judge.
s. 81, see *Midland Bank* v. *Greene* [1995] 1 F.C.R. 365, Judge Rich, Q.C. sitting as a deputy judge.
s. 84, see *Severn Trent Waters Application*, (1993) 67 P.&C.R. 236, Lands Tribunal; *Beechwood Homes' Application, Re* [1994] 28 EG 128, C.A.; *Shaw's Application, Re* [1995] 68 P. & C.R. 591, Lands Tribunal.
s. 99, amended: 1995, c. 8, s. 31.
s. 109, see *Sargent* v. *Customs and Excise Commissioners, The Times*, February 23, 1995, C.A.
s. 141, see *Caerns Motor Services* v. *Texaco* [1995] 1 All E.R. 247, H.H.J. Paul Baker Q.C. sitting as a deputy judge.
s. 146, see *The Keepers of the Possessions Revenues and Goods of the Free Grammar School of John Lyon* v. *Christopher James*, December 2, 1994; H.H.J. Butter Q.C.; Central London County Ct.
s. 193, see *Hanning* v. *Top Deck Travel Group* (1993) (1994) 68 P.&C.R. 14, C.A.
s. 196, see *Wandsworth London Borough Council* v. *Atwell, The Times*, April 22, 1995, C.A.
s. 199, see *B.* v. *B. (P. Intervening) (No. 2)* [1995] 1 F.L.R. 374, C.A.

21. Land Registration Act 1925.
s. 24, repealed in pt.: 1995, c. 30, sch. 1.
s. 38, rules 95/377.

CAP.

15 & 16 Geo. 5 (1924–25)—cont.

21. Land Registration Act 1925—*cont.*
ss. 55, 56, see *Clark* v. *Chief Land Registrar*; *Chancery* v. *Ketteringham* [1994] 3 W.L.R. 593, C.A.
s. 70, see *Overseas Investment Services* v. *Simcobuild Construction, The Times*, April 21, 1995, C.A.
s. 82, see *Hayes* v. *Nwajiaku* [1994] N.P.C. 93, Mr. John Cherryman, Q.C.
s. 83, see *Clark* v. *Chief Land Registrar*; *Chancery* v. *Ketteringham* [1994] 3 W.L.R. 593, C.A.; *Hayes* v. *Nwajiaku* [1994] N.P.C. 93, Mr. John Cherryman, Q.C.
s. 112, rules 95/1354.
s. 144, rules 95/140, 377, 1354.

23. Administration of Estates Act 1925.
s. 46, amended: 1995, c. 41, s. 1.
s. 47, repealed in pt.: 1995, c. 41, s. 1, sch.
s. 49, repealed in pt.: 1995, c. 41, s. 1, sch.

38. Performing Animals (Regulation) Act 1925.
s. 6, amended: 1994, c. 39, sch. 13 (S.).

58. Greenwich Hospital (Disused Burial Ground) Act 1925.
repealed: 1995, c. 44, sch. 1.

61. Allotments Act 1925.
s. 8, see *R.* v. *Secretary of State for the Environment, ex p. Gosforth Allotments and Gardens Association (CO/294/94)*, May 23, 1995, Laws J.

86. Criminal Justice Act 1925.
s. 47, see *R.* v. *Shortland, The Times*, May 23, 1995, C.A.

16 & 17 Geo. 5 (1926)

16. Execution of Diligence (Scotland) Act 1926.
s. 6, Acts of Sederunt 94/3267, 3268.

36. Parks Regulation (Amendment) Act 1926.
s. 2, regs. 94/432, 95/993.

17 & 18 Geo. 5 (1927)

36. Landlord and Tenant Act 1927.
s. 17, amended: 1995, c. 8, sch.
s. 19, amended: 1995, c. 8, sch., 1995, c. 30, s. 22.

18 & 19 Geo. 5 (1928)

19. Agricultural Produce (Grading and Marking) Act 1928.
s. 8, amended: 1994, c. 39, sch. 13 (S.).

32. Petroleum (Consolidation) Act 1928.
s. 24, amended: 1994, c. 39, sch. 13 (S.).

43. Agricultural Credits Act 1928.
s. 5, amended: 1995, c. 8, sch.

CAP.

19 & 20 Geo. 5 (1929)

25. Local Government (Scotland) Act 1929.
s. 29, amended: 1994, c. 39, sch. 13.

20 & 21 Geo. 5 (1930)

20. Land Drainage (Scotland) Act 1930.
s. 2, 1995, c. 40, sch. 2.

25. Third Parties (Rights against Insurers) Act 1930.
see *Cox* v. *Bankside Members Agency* (LTA 94/6391/B; LTA 94/7098/B; LTA 94/7124/B), November 29, 1994, C.A.
s. 1, see *Airmuscle* v. *Spitting Image Productions* [1994] R.P.C. 604, Patents County Court.

28. Finance Act 1930.
s. 42, repealed in pt.: 1995, c. 4, sch. 29.
s. 42, amended: 1995, c. 4, s. 149.

43. Road Traffic Act 1930.
ss. 108, 109, 119, amended: 1994, c. 39, sch. 13 (S.).

21 & 22 Geo. 5 (1930–31)

28. Finance Act 1931.
sch. 2, amended: 1995, c. 25, sch. 10.

22 & 23 Geo. 5 (1931–32)

4. Statute of Westminster 1931.
s. 5, repealed: 1995, c. 21, sch. 12.

9. Merchant Shipping (Safety and Load Lines Conventions) Act 1932.
s. 5, repealed in pt.: 1995, c. 21, sch. 12.
s. 8, repealed: 1995, c. 21, sch. 12; regs. 95/1210.
s. 9, repealed: regs. 95/1210.
s. 24, repealed: 1995, c. 21, sch. 12.
s. 24, C.: 1995, c. 21, sch. 14.
s. 62, repealed in pt.: 1995, c. 21, sch. 12.
s. 69, repealed: 1995, c. 21, sch. 12.
ss. 73–74, repealed: 1995, c. 21, sch. 12.
sch. 1, repealed: 1995, c. 21, sch. 12.

23 & 24 Geo. 5 (1932–33)

6. Visiting Forces (British Commonwealth) Act 1933.
s. 4, amended: 1995, c. 3, sch.

12. Children and Young Persons Act 1933.
s. 7, see *Hereford and Worcester County Council* v. *T&S Stores* [1995] 93 L.G.R. 98, D.C.
s. 39, see *R. (A Minor) (Wardships: Restrictions on Publication), Re* [1994] 3 W.L.R. 36, C.A.; *Crook, Re* [1995] 1 W.L.R. 139, C.A.; *R.* v. *Inner London Crown Court, ex p. Barnes (Anthony), The Times*, August 7, 1995, D.C.; *R.* v. *Cambridge and Huntingdon Health Authority, ex p. B. (No. 2), The Times*, October 27, 1995, C.A.

CAP.

23 & 24 Geo. 5 (1932–33)—cont.

12. Children and Young Persons Act 1933—*cont.*
s. 53, see *R.* v. *Onslow-Macauley (Jeremy); R.* v. *Stockton (Paul Jonathan); R.* v. *English (Stuart James)* (94/5628/W5; 94/5857/W5), January 16, 1995, C.A.; *R.* v. *Baxter* [1994] 15 Cr.App. R. (S.) 609, C.A.; *R.* v. *Probert* [1994] 15 Cr.App. R. (S.) 891, C.A.; *R.* v. *Iqbal, The Times*, September 5, 1995, C.A.; *R.* v. *Coffey* [1994] 15 Cr.App. R. (S.) 754, C.A.; *R.* v. *Suleman (Simon)* [1994] 15 Cr.App. R. (S.) 848, C.A.; *R.* v. *Edgell (Robert Benjamin)* [1994] 15 Cr.App. R. (S.) 509, C.A.; *R.* v. *Basid, The Times*, October 19, 1995, C.A.
s. 55, see *D.* v. *D.P.P., The Independent*, April 4, 1995, D.C.

20. False Oaths (Scotland) Act 1933.
ss. 1, 2, 3, C.: 1995, c. 39, s. 44.
s. 4, 1995, c. 39, s. 44.
s. 5, C.: 1995, c. 39, s. 46.
s. 6, C.: 1995, c. 39, s. 45.
s. 7, C.: 1995, c. 39, s. 46.

36. Administration of Justice (Miscellaneous Provisions) Act 1933.
s. 2, see *R.* v. *Cooper, The Times*, November 22, 1994, C.A.; *R.* v. *Wells, The Times*, December 14, 1994, C.A.; *R.* v. *C.* [1995] 159 J.P. 205, C.A.; *R.* v. *Wells* [1995] 159 J.P. 243, C.A.

41. Administration of Justice (Scotland) Act 1933.
Sched., Act of Sederunt 94/3267.

44. Church of Scotland (Property and Endowments) (Amendment) Act 1933.
s. 2, amended: 1994, c. 39, sch. 13.
s. 13, repealed: 1995, c. 7, sch. 5.

24 & 25 Geo. 5 (1933–34)

21. Protection of Animals Act 1934.
s. 2, amended: 1995, c. 40, sch. 2 (S.).

36. Petroleum (Production) Act 1934.
s. 6, regs. 95/1435, 1436.

49. Whaling Industry (Regulations) Act 1934.
s. 17, amended: 1995, c. 21, sch. 13.

26 Geo. 5 & 1 Edw. 8 (1935–36)

6. Public Order Act 1936.
s. 7, amended: 1995, c. 40, sch. 2 (S.).

49. Public Health Act 1936.
ss. 107, 108, repealed: order 95/2054.
s. 229, repealed: 1995, c. 45, sch. 4.

CAP.

26 Geo. 5 & 1 Edw. 8 (1935–36)—cont.

49. Public Health Act 1936—*cont.*
s. 309, repealed in pt.: 1995, c. 44, sch. 1.
s. 315, repealed: 1995, c. 44, sch. 1.
s. 326, repealed in pt.: 1995, c. 44, sch. 1.
s. 343, amended: 1995, c. 21, sch. 13.

52. Private Legislation Procedure (Scotland) Act 1936.
s. 11, amended: 1994, c. 39, sch. 13.

1 Edw. 8 & 1 Geo. 6 (1936–37)

16. Regency Act 1937.
s. 2, repealed in pt.: 1995, c. 44, sch. 1.

28. Harbours, Piers and Ferries (Scotland) Act 1937.
s. 11, amended: order 95/2007.
s. 31, amended: 1994, c. 39, sch. 13.

37. Children and Young Persons (Scotland) Act 1937.
s. 12, amended: 1995, c. 36, sch. 4 (S.).
s. 12, see *McD.* v. *Orr*, 1994 S.C.C.R. 645.
s. 15, amended: 1995, c. 36, sch. 4 (S.).
s. 22, amended: 1995, c. 36, sch. 4 (S.).
s. 27, repealed in pt.: 1995, c. 36, schs. 4 (S.), 5 (S.).
s. 27, amended: 1995, c. 36, sch. 4 (S.).
s. 46, amended: 1995, c. 40, sch. 2.
s. 63, added: 1995, c. 40, sch. 4.
s. 103, added: 1995, c. 40, sch. 4.
s. 110, amended: 1995, c. 39, sch. 13; 1995, c. 36, sch. 4 (S.).

40. Public Health (Drainage of Trade Premises) Act 1937.
s. 14, amended: 1995, c. 21, sch. 13.

43. Public Records (Scotland) Act 1937.
ss. 5, 14, amended: 1994, c. 39, sch. 13.

48. Methylated Spirits (Sale by Retail) (Scotland) Act 1937.
s. 6, amended: 1994, c. 39, sch. 13.

57. Diseases of Fish Act 1937.
s. 8, amended: 1995, c. 25, sch. 15.

59. Cinematograph Films (Animals) Act 1937.
s. 1, amended: 1995, c. 40, sch. 2 (S.).

1 & 2 Geo. 6 (1937–38)

13. Superannuation (Various Services) Act 1938.
sch., amended: 1995, c. 21, sch. 13.

22. Trade Marks Act 1938.
s. 1, see *St. Trudo Trade Mark* [1995] F.S.R. 345, Ferris J.
s. 2, see *Al Bassam Trade Mark* [1994] R.P.C. 315, Aldous J.
s. 4, see *International Business Machines Corp.* v. *Phoenix International (Computers)* (1994) R.P.C. 251, Ferris J.; *Fisons* v. *Norton Healthcare* [1994] F.S.R. 745, Aldous J.

CAP.

1 & 2 Geo. 6 (1937–38)—cont.

22. Trade Marks Act 1938—*cont.*
s. 7, see *Silicon Graphics* v. *Indigo Graphic Systems (U.K.)* [1994] F.S.R. 403, Knox J.
s. 9, see *Jockey Trade Mark* [1994] F.S.R. 269, Trade Marks Registry; *Club Trade Mark* [1994] R.P.C. 527, Trade Mark Registry; *Profitmaker Trade Mark* [1994] R.P.C. 613, Sir Hugh Laddie, Q.C.
ss. 10, 11, see *Al Bassam Trade Mark* [1994] R.P.C. 315, Aldous J.; *Jockey Trade Mark* [1994] F.S.R. 269, Trade Marks Registry.
s. 11, see *Silicon Graphics* v. *Indigo Graphic Systems (U.K.)* [1994] F.S.R. 403, Knox J.
s. 12, see *Jockey Trade Mark* [1994] F.S.R. 269, Trade Marks Registry; *Fisons* v. *Norton Healthcare* [1994] F.S.R. 745, Aldous J.
s. 17, see *Al Bassam Trade Mark* [1994] R.P.C. 315, Aldous J.
s. 18, see *St. Trudo Trade Mark* [1995] F.S.R. 345, Ferris J.
s. 22, see *Al Bassam Trade Mark* [1994] R.P.C. 315, Aldous J.
s. 25, see *St. Trudo Trade Mark* [1995] F.S.R. 345, Ferris J.
s. 26, see *Al Bassam Trade Mark* [1994] R.P.C. 315, Aldous J.; *Fisons* v. *Norton Healthcare* [1994] F.S.R. 745, Aldous J.; *St. Trudo Trade Mark* [1995] F.S.R. 345, Ferris J.
s. 27, see *St. Trudo Trade Mark* [1995] F.S.R. 345, Ferris J.
ss. 28, 31, see *Fisons* v. *Norton Healthcare* [1994] F.S.R. 745, Aldous J.; *Al Bassam Trade Mark* [1994] R.P.C. 315, Aldous J.
ss. 32, 33, see *St. Trudo Trade Mark* [1995] F.S.R. 345, Ferris J.
s. 40, rules 94/2582.
s. 40, see *Al Bassam Trade Mark* [1994] R.P.C. 315, Aldous J.; *St. Trudo Trade Mark* [1995] F.S.R. 345, Ferris J.
ss. 50, 54, 55, see *St. Trudo Trade Mark* [1995] F.S.R. 345, Ferris J.
s. 58B, amended: 1995, c. 20, sch. 6 (S.); 1995, c. 40, sch. 4 (S.).
s. 68, regs. 94/2582.
s. 68, see *Al Bassam Trade Mark* [1994] R.P.C. 315, Aldous J.; *Fisons* v. *Norton Healthcare* [1994] F.S.R. 745, Aldous J.

28. Evidence Act 1938.
ss. 1, 2, repealed: 1995, c. 38, sch. 2.
s. 6, repealed in pt.: 1995, c. 38, sch. 2.

34. Leasehold Property (Repairs) Act 1938.
s. 7, amended: 1995, c. 8, sch.

CAP.

1 & 2 Geo. 6 (1937–38)—cont.

54. Architects Registration Act 1938.
s. 3, amended: 1995, c. 40, sch. 2 (S.).

73. Nursing Homes Registration (Scotland) Act 1938.
s. 4, repealed in pt.: 1995, c. 36, sch. 5.
s. 8, amended: 1995, c. 40, sch. 2.

2 & 3 Geo. 6 (1938–39)

20. Reorganisation of Offices (Scotland) Act 1939.
s. 1, repealed in pt.: 1995, c. 7, sch. 5.

31. Civil Defence Act 1939.
s. 62, amended: 1994, c. 39, sch. 13 (S.).

65. Prize Act 1939.
s. 4, repealed in pt.: 1995, c. 44, sch. 1.

69. Import, Export and Customs Powers (Defence) Act 1939.
s. 1, orders 94/1191, 2711, 2972.

72. Landlord and Tenant (War Damage) Act 1939.
ss. 6, 15, repealed in pt.: 1995, c. 44, sch. 1.

75. Compensation (Defence) Act 1939.
s. 17, amended: 1995, c. 21, sch. 13.

82. Personal Injuries (Emergency Provisions) Act 1939.
ss. 1, 2, scheme 95/445.

83. Pensions (Navy, Army, Air Force and Mercantile Marine) Act 1939.
s. 4, amended: 1995, c. 21, sch. 13.
s. 6, repealed: 1995, c. 21, sch. 12.
s. 10, amended: 1995, c. 21, sch. 13.

89. Trading with the Enemy Act 1939.
s. 17, repealed in pt.: 1995, c. 44, sch. 1.

107. Patents, Designs, Copyright and Trade Marks (Emergency) Act 1939.
ss. 1, 2, repealed in pt.: 1995, c. 44, sch. 1.

4 & 5 Geo. 6 (1940–41)

13. Land Drainage (Scotland) Act 1941.
s. 2, 1995, c. 40, sch. 2 (S.).
s. 7, amended: 1994, c. 39, sch. 13.

41. Landlord and Tenant (War Damage) (Amendment) Act 1941.
ss. 1, 2, repealed in pt.: 1995, c. 44, sch. 1.
ss. 3–9, repealed: 1995, c. 44, sch. 1.
ss. 10, 11, repealed in pt.: 1995, c. 44, sch. 1.
s. 16, repealed: 1995, c. 44, sch. 1.
s. 17, repealed in pt.: 1995, c. 44, sch. 1.
sch. 1, repealed in pt.: 1995, c. 44, sch. 1.

5 & 6 Geo. 6 (1941–42)

17. Anglo-Venezuelan Treaty (Island of Patos) Act 1942.
repealed: 1995, c. 44, sch. 1.

6 & 7 Geo. 6 (1942–43)

49. Pensions Appeal Tribunal Act 1943.
ss. 1, 7, 10, 12, amended: 1995, c. 26, s. 169.

CAP.

7 & 8 Geo. 6 (1943–44)

7. Prize Salvage Act 1944.
s. 2, repealed in pt.: 1995, c. 44, sch. 1.

10. Disabled Persons (Employment) Act 1944.
ss. 1, 6–14, repealed: 1995, c. 44, sch. 7.
s. 15, amended: 1995, c. 50, s. 61.
s. 17, repealed: 1995, c. 50, s. 60.
ss. 19, 21, repealed: 1995, c. 44, sch. 7.
s. 22, repealed in pt.: 1995, c. 50, sch. 7.

26. Rural Water Supplies and Sewerage Act 1944.
repealed: 1994, c. 39, sch. 14.

31. Education Act 1944.
see *E. (A Minor)* v. *Dorset County Council*; *Christmas* v. *Hampshire County Council*; *Keating* v. *Bromley London Borough Council* [1994] 3 W.L.R. 853, C.A.
s. 8, see *X. (Minors)* v. *Bedfordshire County Council* [1995] 3 W.L.R. 152, H.L.
s. 14, see *Hampstead Garden Suburb Institute, Re, The Times*, April 13, 1995, Carnwath J.
ss. 33, 34, see *X. (Minors)* v. *Bedfordshire County Council* [1995] 3 W.L.R. 152, H.L.
s. 39, see *R.* v. *Essex County Council, ex p. C.* [1994] 1 F.C.R. 773, C.A.
s. 41, amended: 1995, c. 50, s. 30.
s. 55, regs. 95/2070.
s. 55, see *R.* v. *Essex County Council, ex p. C.* [1994] 1 F.C.R. 773, C.A.
ss. 70, 76, see *R.* v. *Essex County Council, ex p. C.* [1994] 1 F.C.R. 773, C.A.
s. 100, regs. 95/2018.

9 & 10 Geo. 6 (1945–46)

7. British Settlements Act 1945.
orders 95/1030, 1621.

15. Public Health (Scotland) Act 1945.
s. 1, 1995, c. 40, sch. 2 (S.).
s. 1, amended: 1994, c. 39, sch. 13; 1995, c. 21, sch. 13.

28. Law Reform (Contributory Negligence) Act 1945.
s. 1, see *Barclays Bank* v. *Fairclough Building* [1994] 3 W.L.R. 1057, C.A.; *Fowles* v. *Bedfordshire County Council* (QBENF 93/1384/C), May 17, 1995, C.A.
s. 4, see *Barclays Bank* v. *Fairclough Building* [1994] 3 W.L.R. 1057, C.A.

45. United Nations Act 1946.
s. 1, orders 94/2673, 2674, 2675, 2676; 95/1032.
s. 1, repealed in pt.: 1995, c. 44, sch. 1.

59. Coal Industry Nationalisation Act 1946.
s. 2, repealed in pt.: orders 95/1506, 1507.
s. 46, see *R.* v. *British Coal Corp. and Secretary of State for Trade and Industry, ex p. Price* [1994] IRLR 72, C.A.

CAP.

10 & 11 Geo. 6 (1946–47)

7. Ceylon Independence Act 1947.
sch. 1, repealed: 1995, c. 21, sch. 12.

19. Polish Resettlement Act 1947.
s. 4, amended: 1995, c. 17, sch. 1.

39. Statistics of Trade Act 1947.
s. 9, amended: 1995, c. 45, sch. 4.
s. 9A, added: 1995, c. 25, sch. 22.

40. Industrial Organisation and Development Act 1947.
ss. 1–6, 14, sch. 2, order 95/356.

41. Fire Services Act 1947.
s. 5, amended: 95/187, 600, 610.
s. 10, amended: orders 95/187, 600, 610, 1769, 1770, 1771, 1772, 1773, 1774, 1775, 1776, 1779.
s. 14, 1995, c. 40, sch. 2 (S.).
s. 15, repealed in pt.: 1994, c. 39, sch. 13 (S.).
s. 15, amended: 1994, c. 39, sch. 13 (S.).
s. 18, regs. 95/2109, 2110.
s. 30, 1995, c. 40, sch. 2 (S.).
s. 31, amended: 1995, c. 40, sch. 2 (S.).
s. 36, repealed in pt.: 1994, c. 39, sch. 13 (S.).
s. 38, amended: 1994, c. 39, sch. 13 (S.).

42. Acquisition of Land (Authorisation Procedure) (Scotland) Act 1947.
s. 7, amended: 1994, c. 39, sch. 13.
sch. 1, regs. 94/3097.

43. Local Government (Scotland) Act 1947.
s. 237, repealed in pt: 1994, c. 39, sch. 14.
ss. 243–243B, 244, repealed: 1994, c. 39, sch. 14.

44. Crown Proceedings Act 1947.
s. 2, see *Wood* v. *Lord Advocate* (Sh.Ct.), 1994 S.C.L.R. 1034.
s. 5, repealed: 1995, c. 21, sch. 12.
s. 5, C.: 1995, c. 21, sch. 14.
s. 6, repealed: 1995, c. 21, sch. 12.
s. 6, C.: 1995, c. 21, sch. 14.
s. 7, repealed: 1995, c. 21, sch. 12.
s. 7, C.: 1995, c. 21, sch. 14.
s. 8, repealed: 1995, c. 21, sch. 12.
s. 8, C.: 1995, c. 21, sch. 14.
s. 19, see *St. Martin's Property Investment* v. *Philips Electronics (U.K.); Secretary of State for the Environment (Third Party)* [1994] 3 W.L.R. 1074, Rattee J.
s. 24, amended: 1995, c. 42, s. 4.
s. 30, repealed: 1995, c. 21, sch. 12.
s. 30, C.: 1995, c. 21, sch. 14.
s. 38, amended: 1995, c. 21, sch. 13.
s. 43, see *Wood* v. *Lord Advocate* (Sh.Ct.), 1994 S.C.L.R. 1034.

11 & 12 Geo. 6 (1947–48)

26. Local Government Act 1948.
s. 145, amended: 1994, c. 39, sch. 13 (S.).

29. National Assistance Act 1948.
see *R.* v. *Cleveland County Council, ex p. Ward* [1994] C.O.D. 222, D.C.

CAP.

11 & 12 Geo. 6 (1947–48)—cont.

29. National Assistance Act 1948—*cont.*
s. 21, see *R.* v. *Brent London Borough, ex p. S* [1994] 1 FLR 203, C.A.; *R.* v. *Wandsworth London Borough Council, ex p. Beckwith, The Independent*, April 21, 1995, Popplewell J.; *R.* v. *Avon County Council, ex p. M.* [1994] 2 F.L.R. 1006, Henry J.; *R.* v. *Newcastle upon Tyne City Council, ex p. Dixon* (1994) 92 L.G.R. 169, Auld J.
s. 22, amended: regs. 95/443, 858 (S.).
s. 26, amended: 1995, c. 17, sch. 1.
s. 26, see *R.* v. *Newcastle upon Tyne City Council, ex p. Dixon* (1994) 92 L.G.R. 169, Auld J.
s. 33, amended: 1994, c. 39, sch. 13 (S.).
s. 33, repealed in pt.: 1994, c. 39, sch. 14 (S.).
s. 35, regs. 94/826.
s. 36, see *R.* v. *Brent London Borough, ex p. S.* [1994] 1 FLR 203, C.A.
ss. 47, 48, 50, amended: 1994, c. 39, sch. 13 (S.).
s. 55, amended: 1995, c. 40, sch. 2.
s. 64, regs. 94/826.
s. 65, amended: 1994, c. 39, sch. 13 (S.).
sch. 3, repealed in pt.: 1994, c. 39, sch. 14 (S.).
sch. 6, repealed in pt.: 1995, c. 17, sch. 3.
sch. 6, amended: 1995, c. 17, sch. 1.

37. Radioactive Substances Act 1948.
s. 8, 1995, c. 40, sch. 2 (S.).

38. Companies Act 1948.
s. 75, see *Nisbet* v. *Shepherd* [1994] BCC 91, C.A.
s. 242, see *Brown* v. *Dickson*, 1995 S.L.T. 354.
sch. 1, see *William Steward (Holdings), Re* [1994] BCC 284, C.A.

40. Education (Miscellaneous Provisions) Act 1948.
s. 4, regs. 95/2089.

44. Merchant Shipping Act 1948.
s. 5, repealed: 1995, c. 21, sch.
s. 5, C.: 1995, c. 21, sch. 14.

45. Agriculture (Scotland) Act 1948.
ss. 50, 50A, 1995, c. 40, sch. 2 (S.).

53. Nurseries and Childminders Regulation Act 1948.
s. 5, see *T. (A Minor)* v. *Surrey County Council* [1994] 4 All E.R. 577, Scott-Baker J.

56. British Nationality Act 1948.
s. 3, amended: 1995, c. 21, sch. 13.
ss. 6, 7, see *R.* v. *Secretary of State for the Home Department, ex p. Muru* [1994] Imm.A.R. 574, Schiemann J.

58. Criminal Justice Act 1948.
s. 1, C.: 1995, c. 21, sch. 14.

62. Statute Law Revision Act 1948.
s. 5, sch. 2, repealed: 1995, c. 44, sch. 1.

63. Agricultural Holdings Act 1948.
sch. 6, 1995, c. 42, s. 4.

CAP.

12, 13 & 14 Geo. 6 (1948–49)

5. Civil Defence Act 1948.
s. 4A, added: 1994, c.39, sch. 13 (S.).
s. 9, amended: 1994, c. 39, sch. 13 (S.).

29. Consular Conventions Act 1949.
s. 5, repealed: 1995, c. 21, sch. 12.
s. 5, C.: 1995, c. 21, sch. 14.

30. Agricultural Wages (Scotland) Act 1949.
s. 4, see *Teviot Scientific Publications* v. *McLeod*, 1995 S.C.C.R. 188.

34. Merchant Shipping Act 1949.
ss. 3, 21, 28, continued in force (temp.): 1995, c. 21, sch. 14.
s. 22, C.: 1995, c. 21, sch. 14.

42. Lands Tribunal Act 1949.
s. 3, rules 94/497 (S.); 95/308 (S.).
s. 50, rules 95/308 (S.).

43. Merchant Shipping (Safety Convention) Act 1949.
ss. 7–14, repealed: regs. 95/1210.
s. 15, repealed (prosp.): regs. 95/1210.
s. 17, repealed: regs. 95/1210.
s. 22, repealed: 1995, c. 21, sch. 12.
s. 22, C.: 1995, c. 21, sch. 14.
s. 25, repealed: 1995, c. 21, sch. 12.
s. 25, C.: 1995, c. 21, sch. 14.
ss. 26, 31, repealed: regs. 95/1210.
s. 32, repealed: 1995, c. 21, sch. 12.
s. 33, regs. 95/1893.
s. 33, C.: 1995, c. 21, sch. 14.
s. 34, repealed: 1995, c. 21, sch. 12.
s. 35, repealed in pt.: 1995, c. 21, sch. 12; regs. 95/1210.
s. 36, repealed: 1995, c. 21, sch. 12.
s. 37, C.: 1995, c. 21, sch. 14.
sch. 1, repealed in pt.: 1995, c. 21, sch. 12.
sch. 2, C.: 1995, c. 21, sch. 14.

53. Coal Industry Act 1949.
s. 1, repealed in pt.: order 95/1507.

54. Wireless Telegraphy Act 1949.
s. 1, regs. 95/1081.
s. 2, regs. 95/244, 655, 1331.
s. 3, regs. 95/1081.
s. 19, amended: 1995, c. 21, sch. 13.
s. 20, order 95/268.
s. 170, amended: order 95/268.
s. 172, repealed in pt.: order 95/268.

70. Docking and Nicking of Horses Act 1949.
ss. 1, 2, 1995, c. 40, sch. 2 (S.).

74. Coast Protection Act 1949.
s. 1, amended: 1994, c. 39, sch. 13 (S.).
s. 20, repealed in pt.: 1994, c. 39, sch. 14 (S.).
s. 20, amended: 1994, c. 39, sch. 14 (S.).
ss. 22, 45, amended: 1994, c. 39, sch. 13 (S.).
s. 49, amended: 1995, c. 21, sch. 13.

76. Marriage Act 1949.
s. 35, order 94/3116.

CAP.

12, 13 & 14 Geo. 6 (1948–49)—cont.

76. Marriage Act 1949—*cont.*
ss. 46A, 46B, 51, regs. 95/510.
ss. 55, 74, regs. 95/744.

87. Patents Act 1949.
s. 22, see *Sundstrand Corp.* v. *Safe Flight Instrument Corp.* [1994] F.S.R. 599, Patents County Ct.
s. 30, see *Chiron Corp.* v. *Organon Teknika (No. 5)*; *Same* v. *Murex Diagnostics (No. 5)* [1994] F.S.R. 258, Patents Ct.
s. 32, see *Sundstrand Corp.* v. *Safe Flight Instrument Corp.* [1994] F.S.R. 599, Patents County Ct.; *Glaverbel SA* v. *British Coal Corp.* [1995] F.S.R. 254, C.A.; *Assidoman Multipack (formerly Multipack Wraparound Systems)* v. *The Mead Corp.* [1995] F.S.R. 225, Aldous J.; *Lesaffre's Patent* [1994] R.P.C. 521, C.A.
s. 62, see *Gerber Garment Technology* v. *Lectra Systems* [1994] F.S.R. 471, Aldous J.

88. Registered Designs Act 1949.
s. 1, see *R.* v. *Registered Designs Appeal Tribunal, ex p. Ford Motor Company* [1995] 1 W.L.R. 18, H.L.; *Breville Europe* v. *Thorn EMI Domestic Appliances* [1995] F.S.R. 77, Falconer J.
s. 1, amended: 1995, c. 32, s. 13.
s. 2, see *Breville Europe* v. *Thorn EMI Domestic Appliances* [1995] F.S.R. 77, Falconer J.
s. 8, amended: 1995, c. 21, sch. 13.
s. 36, rules 95/2165.
s. 37, order 94/3219.
s. 40, rules 95/2165.
s. 44, rules 95/2165.
s. 44, see *R.* v. *Registered Designs Appeal Tribunal, ex p. Ford Motor Company* [1995] 1 W.L.R. 18, H.L.

94. Criminal Justice (Scotland) Act 1949.
repealed: 1995, c. 40, sch. 5.
sch. 7, repealed: 1995, c. 20, sch. 6.

97. National Parks and Access to the Countryside Act 1949.
s. 5, amended: 1995, c. 25, s. 61.
s. 6, repealed in pt.: 1995, c. 25, sch. 24.
s. 6, amended: 1995, c. 25, sch. 10.
s. 7, amended: 1995, c. 25, sch. 10.
s. 9, amended: 1995, c. 25, sch. 10.
s. 11, repealed: 1995, c. 25, sch. 24.
s. 11A, repealed in pt.: 1995, c. 25, sch. 24.
s. 11A, added: 1995, c. 25, s. 62.
s. 12, repealed in pt.: 1995, c. 25, sch. 24.
s. 12, amended: 1995, c. 25, sch. 10.
s. 13, repealed in pt.: 1995, c. 25, sch. 24.
s. 21, repealed in pt.: 1994, c. 39, sch. 14 (S.).
s. 52, amended: 1995, c. 25, sch. 10.
s. 88, substituted: 1995, c. 25, sch. 10.

CAP.

12, 13 & 14 Geo. 6 (1948–49)—cont.

97. National Parks and Access to the Countryside Act 1949—*cont.*
s. 90, see *R.* v. *Dyfed County Council, ex p. Manson* [1994] N.P.C. 27, Harrison J.
s. 99, amended: 1994, c. 39, sch. 13 (S.).
s. 111A, repealed in pt.: 1995, c. 25, sch. 24.
s. 114, amended: 1995, c. 25, sch. 10.
sch. 1, amended: 1995, c. 25, sch. 10.

14 Geo. 6 (1950)

9. Merchant Shipping Act 1950.
ss. 7–8, repealed: 1995, c. 21, sch. 12.

27. Arbitration Act 1950.
s. 4, see *Alfred McAlpine Construction* v. *Unex Corp.* [1994] N.P.C. 16, C.A.; *Excess Insurance Co.* v. *Mander (C.L.), Lloyd's List*, May 18, 1995, D.C.
s. 12, see *Gidrxslme Shipping Co.* v. *Tantomar-Transportes Martimos LDA* [1995] 1 W.L.R. 299, Colman J.; *Sokana Industries* v. *Freyre & Co.* [1994] 2 Lloyd's Rep. 57, Colman J.
s. 20, substituted: 1995, c. 42, s. 3.
s. 26, see *Gidrxslme Shipping Co.* v. *Tantomar-Transportes Martimos LDA* [1995] 1 W.L.R. 299, Colman J.
s. 27, see *Fordgate Bingley* v. *Argyll Stores* [1994] 39 EG 135, Nicholas Stewart, Q.C. sitting as a deputy judge.
s. 29, repealed in pt.: 1995, c. 21, sch. 12.

28. Shops Act 1950.
see *R.* v. *Kirklees Metropolitan Borough Council, ex p. Tesco Stores* (1994) 92 L.G.R. 279 D.C.; *R.* v. *Lincoln City Council, ex p. Wickes Building Supplies* (1994) 92 L.G.R. 215, D.C.
s. 73, amended: 1994, c. 39, sch. 13 (S.).
s. 74, see *Ritz Video* [1995] N.P.C. 12, C.A.

37. Maintenance Orders Act 1950.
ss. 10, 11, repealed: order 95/756.
s. 12, amended: order 95/756.
s. 13, repealed in pt.: order 95/756.
s. 15, repealed in pt.: order 95/756.
s. 15, amended: order 95/756.
ss. 16, 18, 25, amended: order 95/756.

38. Allotments (Scotland) Act 1950.
ss. 9, 13, amended: 1994, c. 39, sch. 13.

14 & 15 Geo. 6 (1950–51)

35. Pet Animals Act 1951.
s. 7, amended: 1994, c. 39, sch. 13 (S.).

63. Rag Flock and other Filling Materials Act 1951.
s. 36, amended: 1994, c. 39, sch. 13 (S.).

CAP.

14 & 15 Geo. 6 (1950–51)—cont.

65. Reserve and Auxiliary Forces (Protection of Civil Interests) Act 1951.
s. 8, repealed in pt.: 1995, c. 36, sch. 5 (S.).
s. 15, amended: 1995, c. 17, sch. 1.
s. 27, amended: 1995, c. 8, sch.
s. 61, repealed in pt.: 1995, c. 17, sch. 3.

66. Rivers (Prevention of Pollution) (Scotland) Act 1951.
Part II, repealed: 1995, c. 25, schs. 22, 24.
ss. 6, 12, 13, 16, amended: 1994, c. 39, sch. 13.
s. 17, repealed: 1995, c. 25, schs. 22, 24.
s. 17, amended: 1994, c. 29, sch. 13.
s. 18, repealed in pt.: 1995, c. 25, sch. 24.
s. 18, amended: 1995, c. 25, sch. 22.
s. 19, repealed in pt.: 1995, c. 25, sch. 24.
s. 19, amended: 1994, c. 39, sch. 13; 1995, c. 25, sch. 22.
s. 21, 1995, c. 40, sch. 2 (S.).
s. 29, amended: 1995, c. 21, sch. 13.
s. 35, repealed in pt.: 1995, c. 25, sch. 24.
s. 35, amended: 1994, c. 39, sch. 13; 1995, c. 25, sch. 22.

15 & 16 Geo. 6 & 1 Eliz. 2 (1951–52)

23. Miners' Welfare Act 1952.
ss. 12, 15, order 95/855.

46. Hypnotism Act 1952.
s. 2, amended: 1994, c. 39, sch. 13 (S.).

52. Prison Act 1952.
see *R.* v. *Secretary of State for the Home Department, ex p. Briggs, The Independent*, September 26, 1995, D.C.
s. 47, rules 94/3194, 3195; 95/983, 984, 1598, 1599.
s. 47, see *R.* v. *Secretary of State for the Home Department, ex p. O'Dhuibhir, The Times*, October 26, 1995, D.C.

59. Cockfighting Act 1952.
s. 1, 1995, c. 40, sch. 2 (S.).

64. Intestates' Estates Act 1952.
s. 3, repealed in pt.: 1995, c. 41, sch.

67. Visiting Forces Act 1952.
ss. 1, 8, amended: 1995, c. 3, sch.

1 & 2 Eliz. 2 (1952–53)

14. Prevention of Crime Act 1953.
s. 1, repealed: 1995, c. 40, sch. 5 (S.).
s. 1, see *McKee* v. *MacDonald*, 1995 S.C.C.R. 513.

20. Births and Deaths Registration Act 1953.
ss. 5, 9, 10, 10A, 11, 39, regs. 95/818.

28. Dogs (Protection of Livestock) Act 1953.
s. 1, 1995, c. 40, sch. 2 (S.).

CAP.

1 & 2 Eliz. 2 (1952–53)—cont.

33. Education (Miscellaneous Provisions) Act 1953.
s. 6, see *R.* v. *Kent County Council, ex p. W (A Minor) (Special Educational Needs), The Times*, March 3, 1995, Turner J.

36. Post Office Act 1953.
s. 29, amended: 1995, c. 21, sch. 13.
s. 51, amended: 1994, c. 39, sch. 13 (S.).
s. 56, amended: 1995, c. 40, sch. 2 (S.).

37. Registration Service Act 1953.
s. 15, modified: order 95/867.
s. 20, regs. 95/744.
s. 60, regs. 95/744.

47. Emergency Laws (Miscellaneous Provisions) Act 1953.
s. 5, amended: 1994, c. 39, sch. 13 (S.).

2 & 3 Eliz. 2 (1953–54)

21. Rights of Entry (Gas and Electricity Boards) Act 1954.
ss. 1, 2, amended: 1995, c. 45, sch. 4.

40. Protection of Animals (Amendment) Act 1954.
s. 2, see *R.S.P.C.A.* v. *Miller* [1994] C.O.D. 364, Div. Ct.

48. Summary Jurisdiction (Scotland) Act 1954.
repealed: 1995, c. 40, sch. 5.
s. 76, C.: 1995, c. 46, s. 305.
sch. 2, repealed in pt.: 1995, c. 20, sch. 7.
sch. 2, C.: 1995, c. 46, sch. 5.
sch. 3, repealed: 1995, c. 20, schs. 6, 7.

49. Long Leases (Scotland) Act 1954.
s. 4, amended: 1994, c. 39, sch. 13.
sch. 4, amended: 1995, c. 7, sch. 4.

56. Landlord and Tenant Act 1954.
s. 34, amended: 1995, c. 30, sch. 1.
s. 35, amended: 1995, c. 30, sch. 1.
s. 43, amended: 1995, c. 8, sch.
s. 57, amended: 1995, c. 17, sch. 1.
s. 69, amended: 1995, c. 25, sch. 10.

64. Transport Charges etc. (Miscellaneous Provisions) Act 1954.
s. 6, amended: 1994, c. 39, sch. 13 (S.).

68. Pests Act 1954.
s. 12, amended: 1995, c. 40, sch. 2 (S.).

70. Mines and Quarries Act 1954.
s. 151, repealed in pt.: 1995, c. 25, sch. 24.
s. 182, amended: 1995, c. 36, sch. 4 (S.).

3 & 4 Eliz. 2 (1954–55)

13. Rural Water Supplies and Sewerage Act 1955.
repealed: 1994, c. 39, sch. 14.

18. Army Act 1955.
s. 21, sch. 5A, amended: 1994, c. 39, sch. 13 (S.).
s. 62, substituted: 1995, c. 38, sch. 1.
s. 110, amended: 1995, c. 35, sch. 2.

CAP.

3 & 4 Eliz. 2 (1954–55)—cont.

18. Army Act 1955—*cont.*
s. 150, S.R. 1995 No. 755.
s. 151, amended: order 95/756.
s. 215, S.R. 1995 No. 755.
s. 225, amended: 1995, c. 3, sch.
sch. 5A, amended: 1994, c. 39, sch. 13 (S.).

19. Air Force Act 1955.
s. 62, substituted: 1995, c. 19, sch. 1.
s. 110, amended: 1995, c. 35, sch. 2.
s. 150, S.R. 1995 No. 755.
s. 151, amended: order 95/756.
s. 212, sch. 5A, amended: 1994, c. 39, sch. 13 (S.).
s. 223, amended: 1995, c. 3, sch.
sch. 5A, amended: 1994, c. 39, sch. 13 (S.).

4 & 5 Eliz. 2 (1955–56)

46. Administration of Justice Act 1956.
s. 47, repealed in pt.: 1995, c. 21, sch. 12.
s. 47, amended: 1995, c. 21, sch. 13.
s. 48, amended: 1995, c. 21, sch. 13.
s. 49, repealed in pt.: 1995, c. 21, sch. 12.
sch. 1, repealed: 1995, c. 21, sch. 12.
sch. 1, amended: 1995, c. 21, sch. 13.

60. Valuation and Rating (Scotland) Act 1956.
s. 1, repealed: 1994, c. 39, sch. 14.
s. 3, repealed: 1994, c. 39, s. 162, sch. 14.
s. 6, amended: orders 94/2072, 3256; 95/366, 367, 368, 369, 370, 371, 372.
s. 6A, order 95/239.
s. 6A, added: 1994, c. 39, s. 161.
s. 7, see *Ballantyne* v. *Assessor for Tayside Region*, 1992 S.C. 351.
s. 8A, see *East Kilbride Development Corporation* v. *Assessor for Strathclyde Region*, 1995 S.L.T. (Lands Tr.) 27.
s. 13, order 95/2455.
s. 22, order 95/164.
s. 22A, repealed: 1994, c. 39, sch. 14.
s. 42, orders 95/164, 2455.
s. 43, repealed in pt.: 1994, c. 39, s. 162, sch. 14.
s. 43, amended: 1994, c. 39, sch. 13.

69. Sexual Offences Act 1956.
ss. 10, 11, see *R.* v. *Pickford* [1994] 3 W.L.R. 1022, C.A.
s. 32, see *R.* v. *Tuck* [1994] Crim.L.R. 375, C.A.

74. Copyright Act 1956.
s. 2, see *Bookmakers' Afternoon Greyhound Services* v. *Wilf Gilbert (Staffordshire)* [1994] F.S.R. 723, Aldous J.; *Waterlow Publishers* v. *Rose* [1995] F.S.R. 207, C.A.; *Breville Europe* v. *Thorn EMI Domestic Appliances* [1995] F.S.R. 77, Falconer J.

CAP.

4 & 5 Eliz. 2 (1955–56)—cont.

74. Copyright Act 1956—*cont.*
s. 3, see *Breville Europe* v. *Thorn EMI Domestic Appliances* [1995] F.S.R. 77, Falconer J.
s. 4, see *Waterlow Publishers* v. *Rose* [1995] F.S.R. 207, C.A.
s. 9, see *Anacon Corp.* v. *Environmental Research Technology* [1994] F.S.R. 659, Jacob J.
s. 20, see *Waterlow Publishers* v. *Rose* [1995] F.S.R. 207, C.A.
s. 48, see *Bookmakers' Afternoon Greyhound Services* v. *Wilf Gilbert (Staffordshire)* [1994] F.S.R. 659, Jacob J.; *Waterlow Publishers* v. *Rose* [1995] F.S.R. 207, C.A.; *Breville Europe* v. *Thorn EMI Domestic Appliances* [1995] F.S.R. 77, Falconer J.
s. 49, see *Bookmakers' Afternoon Greyhound Services* v. *Wilf Gilbert (Staffordshire)* [1994] F.S.R. 659, Jacob J.; *Waterlow Publishers* v. *Rose* [1995] F.S.R. 207, C.A.

5 & 6 Eliz. 2 (1957)

6. Ghana Independence Act 1957.
sch. 1, repealed in pt.: 1995, c. 21, sch. 12.
sch. 2, repealed in pt.: 1995, c. 21, sch. 12.

11. Homicide Act 1957.
s. 2, see *R.* v. *Sanderson (Lloyd)* [1994] 98 Cr.App.R. 325, C.A.
s. 3, see *R.* v. *Cox (Andrew Mark), The Times*, April 12, 1995, C.A.; *R.* v. *Morhall* [1995] 3 W.L.R. 330, H.L.

31. Occupiers' Liability Act 1957.
s. 2, see *Staples* v. *West Dorset District Council, The Times*, April 28, 1995, C.A.

52. Geneva Conventions Act 1957.
s. 1, amended: 1995, c. 27, s. 1.
s. 6, repealed in pt.: 1995, c. 27, s. 5.
s. 6, amended: 1995, c. 27, s. 2.
s. 6A, added: 1995, c. 27, s. 3.
s. 7, amended: 1995, c. 27, s. 4.
s. 8, repealed in pt.: 1995, c. 27, s. 5.
schs. 5, 6, added: 1995, c. 27, sch.

53. Naval Discipline Act 1957.
s. 35, substituted: 1995, c. 53, sch. 1.
s. 101, repealed in pt.: S.R. 1995 No. 755.
s. 124, repealed in pt.: S.R. 1995 No. 755.
s. 128G, see *Legrove* v. *Legrove* [1994] 2 F.L.R. 119, C.A.
sch. 4A, amended: 1994, c. 39, sch. 13 (S.).

59. Coal Mining (Subsidence) Act 1957.
ss. 1, 2, 3, 6, see *British Coal Corp.* v. *Ellistown Pipes* [1994] RVR 81, C.A.

6 & 7 Eliz. 2 (1957–58)

24. Land Drainage (Scotland) Act 1958.
s. 11, 1995, c. 40, sch. 2 (S.).

CAP.

6 & 7 Eliz. 2 (1957–58)—cont.

24. Land Drainage (Scotland) Act 1958—*cont.*
sch. 1, amended: 1994, c. 39, sch. 13.

33. Disabled Persons (Employment) Act 1958.
s. 3, amended: 1994, c. 39, sch. 13 (S.).

40. Matrimonial Proceedings (Children) Act 1958.
ss. 8, 9, repealed: 1995, c. 36, sch. 5 (S.).
s. 10, repealed: 1995, c. 36, sch. 5 (S.).
s. 10, amended: 1994, c. 39, sch. 13 (S.).
s. 11, amended: 1995, c. 36, sch. 4 (S.).
s. 12, repealed: 1995, c. 36, sch. 5 (S.).
s. 13, amended: 1995, c. 39, sch. 5 (S.).

47. Agricultural Marketing Act 1958.
Pt. 1, amended: 94/2922.
s. 2, sch. 1, order 94/2404.

49. Trading Representations (Disabled Persons) Act 1958.
s. 1, amended: 1994, c. 39, sch. 13 (S.).

51. Public Records Act 1958.
s. 2, regs. 95/991.
sch. 1, repealed in pt.: 1995, c. 26, sch. 7.
sch. 1, amended: 1995, c. 17, sch. 1; 1995, c. 25, sch. 22; 1995, c. 26, schs. 5, 6; 1995, c. 35, sch. 2.

62. Merchant Shipping (Liability of Shipowners) Act 1958.
see *Hamburg Star, The* [1994] 1 Lloyd's Rep. 399, Clarke J.

64. Local Government and Miscellaneous Financial Provisions (Scotland) Act 1958.
s. 7, repealed: 1994, c. 39, sch. 14.

69. Opencast Coal Act 1958.
s. 4, regs. 94/3097.
s. 7, amended: 1995, c. 25, sch. 22.
s. 14, amended: 1995, c. 8, sch.
s. 14B, added: 1995, c. 8, sch.
s. 15A, regs. 94/3097.
s. 24, amended: 1995, c. 8, sch.
s. 25A, added: 1995, c. 8, sch.
ss. 26, 28, amended: 1995, c. 8, sch.
s. 49, regs. 94/3097.
s. 51, sch. 7, amended: 1995, c. 8, sch.
s. 58, amended: 1995, c. 25, sch. 22.

7 & 8 Eliz. 2 (1958–59)

24. Building (Scotland) Act 1959.
ss. 2, 4, regs. 95/1572.
s. 29, amended: 1994, c. 39, sch. 13.
sch. 3, regs. 95/1572.

40. Deer (Scotland) Act 1959.
s. 25A, repealed in pt.: 1994, c. 39, sch. 13.
s. 25A, amended: 1994, c. 39, sch. 13.
s. 25D, repealed in pt.: 1994, c. 39, sch. 13.
ss. 25D, 25E, amended: 1994, c. 39, sch. 13.
sch. 1, repealed in pt.: 1995, c. 7, sch. 5 (S.).

CAP.

7 & 8 Eliz. 2 (1958–59)—cont.

57. Street Offences Act 1959.
s. 1, see *D.P.P.* v. *Bull* [1994] 4 All E.R. 411, D.C.

72. Mental Health Act 1959.
see *C. (Adult Patient) (Access: Jurisdiction), Re* [1994] 1 F.C.R. 705, Eastham J.

8 & 9 Eliz. 2 (1959–60)

16. Road Traffic Act 1960.
s. 232, amended: 1995, c. 23, sch. 7.
s. 233, repealed: 1995, c. 23, sch. 8.
s. 233, C.: 1995, c. 23, sch. 8.
s. 235, repealed: 1995, c. 23, sch. 8.
s. 235, C.: 1995, c. 23, sch. 8.
s. 244, repealed in pt.: 1995, c. 23, sch. 8.
s. 244, amended: 1995, c. 23, sch. 7.
s. 244, C.: 1995, c. 23, sch. 8.
s. 247, C.: 1995, c. 23, sch. 8.
s. 255, C.: 1995, c. 23, sch. 8.
s. 263, repealed: 1995, c. 23, sch. 8.
s. 263, C.: 1995, c. 23, sch. 8.
s. 265, repealed: 1995, c. 23, sch. 8.
s. 269, C.: 1995, c. 23, sch. 8.

34. Radioactive Substances Act 1960.
ss. 6, 8, see *R.* v. *Inspectorate of Pollution, ex p. Greenpeace (No. 2)*; *sub nom. R.* v. *H.M. Inspectorate of Pollution, ex p. Greenpeace (No. 2)* [1994] 4 All E.R. 329, Otton J.

52. Cyprus Act 1960.
sch., repealed in pt.: 1995, c. 21, sch. 12.

55. Nigeria Independence Act 1960.
sch. 1, repealed: 1995, c. 21, sch. 12.
sch. 2, repealed: 1995, c. 21, sch. 12.

62. Caravan Sites and Control of Development Act 1960.
s. 21, substituted: 1995, c. 4, s. 39.
s. 24, repealed in pt.: 1994, c. 39, sch. 14 (S.); 1995, c. 25, sch. 24.
s. 24, amended: 1994, c. 39, sch. 13 (S.).
s. 29, amended: 1995, c. 4, s. 39.
s. 29, see *Carter* v. *Secretary of State for the Environment* [1994] EG 124, C.A.

65. Administration of Justice Act 1960.
s. 2, see *Conlon (John Francis), Re* (CO/3778/94), March 2, 1995, D.C.
s. 12, see *Official Solicitor* v. *News Group Newspapers* [1994] 2 F.L.R. 174, Connell J.
sch. 2, amended: S.R. 1995 No. 755.

67. Public Bodies (Admission to Meetings) Act 1960.
sch., amended: 1995, c. 17, sch. 1.

9 & 10 Eliz. 2 (1960–61)

1. Tanganyika Independence Act 1961.
sch. 1, repealed: 1995, c. 21, sch. 12.
sch. 2, repealed: 1995, c. 21, sch. 12.

16. Sierra Leone Independence Act 1961.
sch. 2, repealed: 1995, c. 21, sch. 12.
sch. 3, repealed: 1995, c. 21, sch. 12.

CAP.

9 & 10 Eliz. 2 (1960–61)—cont.

27. Carriage by Air Act 1961.
s. 1, sch. 1, see *Abnett* v. *British Airways (I.H.)*, 1995 S.C.L.R. 654.
s. 9, order 95/1297.

33. Land Compensation Act 1961.
s. 5, see *Kolbe House Society* v. *Department of Transport* [1995] P. & C.R. 569, Lands Tribunal; *Maidstone Borough Council* v. *Secretary of State for the Environment and Kent County Council* [1995] NPC 121, C.A.
s. 14, see *Maidstone Borough Council* v. *Secretary of State for the Environment and Kent County Council* [1995] NPC 121, C.A.
s. 17, see *Maidstone Borough Council* v. *Secretary of State for the Environment and Kent County Council (REF/43/1991)* 34 R.V.R. 226, Lands Tribunal.
ss. 18, 21, see *Maidstone Borough Council* v. *Secretary of State for the Environment and Kent County Council* [1995] NPC 121, C.A.
s. 31, see *Williams* v. *Blaenau Gwent Borough Council* [1994] 40 EG 139, H.H.J. Marder, Q.C.
ss. 39, 55, amended: 1995, c. 25, sch. 10.

34. Factories Act 1961.
ss. 14, 16, see *McMeechan* v. *Uniroyal Engelbert Tyres*, 1994 S.L.T. (Sh.Ct.) 69.
s. 29, see *Scott* v. *E.D.C. Pipework Services* (O.H.), 1995 S.L.T. 561; *Mains* v. *Uniroyal Englebert Tyres*, *The Scotsman*, June 14, 1995; *The Times*, September 29, 1995.
s. 65, see *Gerrard* v. *Staffordshire Potteries* [1995] I.C.R. 502, C.A.
s. 127, regs. 94/3140.
s. 176, amended: 1994, c. 39, sch. 13 (S.); 1995, c. 21, sch. 13; 1995, c. 36, sch. 4 (S.).

41. Flood Prevention (Scotland) Act 1961.
s. 1, amended: 1994, c. 39, sch. 13.
ss. 4, 12, repealed in pt.: 1994, c. 39, schs. 13, 14.
s. 15, amended: 1994, c. 39, sch. 13.

42. Sheriffs' Pensions (Scotland) Act 1961.
s. 9A, regs. 95/635.

54. Human Tissue Act 1961.
s. 1, amended: 1995, c. 17, sch. 1.

62. Trustee Investments Act 1961.
ss. 2, 4, amended: order 95/1092.
s. 11, amended: 1995, c. 25, sch. 10.
s. 12, order 95/768.
s. 17, amended: order 95/1092.
sch. 1, amended: order 95/768.
sch. 2, amended: order 95/1092.

10 & 11 Eliz. 2 (1961–62)

9. Local Government (Financial Provisions etc.) (Scotland) Act 1962.
s. 4, amended: 1994, c. 39, sch. 13.

CAP.

10 & 11 Eliz. 2 (1961–62)—cont.

9. Local Government (Financial Provisions etc.) (Scotland) Act 1962—*cont.*
s. 4, see *Coalburn Miners' Welfare and Charitable Society* v. *Strathclyde Regional Council* (O.H.), 1994 S.C.L.R. 1089.

12. Education Act 1962.
s. 1, regs. 94/3043, 3044; 95/1240.
s. 1, see *R.* v. *London Borough of Bexley, ex p. Jones* [1994] C.O.D. 393, Leggatt J.
s. 2, see *R.* v. *Warwickshire County Council, ex p. Williams, The Independent*, February 15, 1995, Schiemann J.
s. 4, regs. 94/3043, 3044; 95/1240.
sch. 1, regs. 94/3044.

21. Commonwealth Immigrants Act 1962.
s. 2, see *Miah (Nazmul)* v. *Secretary of State for the Home Department* [1995] Imm AR 24, C.A.

23. South Africa Act 1962.
ss. 1, 2, sch. 2, repealed in pt.: 1995, c. 3, sch.
sch. 3, repealed in pt.: 1995, c. 3, sch.; 1995, c. 21, sch. 12.
sch. 4, repealed in pt.: 1995, c. 3, sch.

26. Animal (Cruel Poisons) Act 1962.
s. 1, 1995, c. 40, sch. 2 (S.).

30. Northern Ireland Act 1962.
s. 25, repealed in pt.: 1995, c. 21, sch. 12.

40. Jamaica Independence Act 1962.
sch. 1, repealed in pt.: 1995, c. 21, sch. 12.
sch. 2, repealed in pt.: 1995, c. 21, sch. 12.

43. Carriage by Sea (Supplementary Provisions) Act 1962.
s. 5, order 95/1297.

47. Education (Scotland) Act 1962.
s. 145, amended: 1994, c. 39, sch. 13; 1995, c. 36, sch. 4.

54. Trinidad and Tobago Independence Act 1962.
sch. 1, repealed in pt.: 1995, c. 21, sch. 12.
sch. 3, repealed in pt.: 1995, c. 21, sch. 12.

57. Uganda Independence Act 1962.
sch. 1, repealed in pt.: 1995, c. 21, sch. 12.
sch. 2, repealed in pt.: 1995, c. 21, sch. 12.

58. Pipelines Act 1962.
s. 7, order 95/1091.
s. 39, amended: 1995, c. 21, sch. 13.
s. 58, amended: 1995, c. 45, sch. 4.
s. 58A, added: 1995, c. 45, sch. 4.
s. 58B, added: 1995, c. 45, sch. 4.

1963

2. Betting, Gaming and Lotteries Act 1963.
s. 10, regs. 95/578, 802 (S.); order 95/579.
s. 28, 1995, c. 40, sch. 2 (S.).
s. 52, amended: 1995, c. 40, sch. 2 (S.).

CAP.

1963—cont.

2. Betting, Gaming and Lotteries Act 1963—*cont.*
s. 55, regs. 95/578.
sch. 1, amended: 1994, c. 39, sch. 13 (S.).
sch. 1, see *Ladbroke Racing (Strathclyde)* v. *William Hill (Scotland)* (O.H.) 1995 S.L.T. 134.
sch. 2, amended: 1994, c. 39, sch. 13 (S.).
sch. 3, amended: 1994, c. 39, sch. 13 (S.); order 95/579.
sch. 4, regs. 95/578.
sch. 4, amended: order 95/579.
sch. 5A, repealed in pt.: regs. 95/31.

11. Agriculture (Miscellaneous Provisions) Act 1963.
s. 22, amended: 1995, c. 8, sch.

12. Local Government (Financial Provisions) (Scotland) Act 1963.
s. 7, amended: 1994, c. 39, sch. 13.
s. 15, regs. 95/672.
s. 15, amended: 1994, c. 39, sch. 13.
ss. 18, 26, amended: 1994, c. 39, sch. 13.

18. Stock Transfer Act 1963.
s. 2, repealed in pt.: 1995, c. 7, sch. 5 (S.).

24. British Museum Act 1963.
s. 10, orders 95/654, 1224.
sch. 3, amended: orders 95/654, 1224.

25. Finance Act 1963.
s. 55, see *Glenrothes Development Corporation* v. *I.R.C.*, 1994 S.L.T. 1310.

33. London Government Act 1963.
see *Willowcell* v. *Westminster City Council, The Times*, April 14, 1995, C.A.
sch. 12, *Barking and Dagenham London Borough Council* v. *Bass Taverns* [1993] C.O.D. 453, D.C.

41. Office, Shops and Railway Premises Act 1963.
s. 84, amended: 1995, c. 3, sch.

43. Animal Boarding Establishments Act 1963.
s. 5, amended: 1994, c. 39, sch. 13 (S.).

54. Kenya Independence Act 1963.
sch. 1, repealed in pt.: 1995, c. 21, sch. 12.
sch. 2, repealed in pt.: 1995, c. 21, sch. 12.

55. Zanzibar Act 1963.
sch. 1, repealed in pt.: 1995, c. 21, sch. 12.

1964

9. Public Works Loans Act 1964.
s. 6, amended: 1994, c. 39, sch. 13 (S.).

14. Plant Varieties and Seeds Act 1964.
ss. 1, 3, 4, 5, 7, schemes 95/526, 527, 528, 529, 530, 537.
s. 9, regs. 95/606.
s. 16, regs. 94/676; 95/607, 1482; order 94/2592.
s. 25, 1995, c. 40, sch. 2 (S.).
s. 27, 1995, c. 40, sch. 2 (S.).
s. 36, regs. 94/676; 95/606, 607, 1482; order 94/2592.

CAP.

1964—cont.

14. Plant Varieties and Seeds Act 1964—*cont.*
s. 38, order 94/2592; schemes 95/526, 527, 528, 529, 530, 537.
sch. 3, schemes 95/526, 527, 528, 529, 530.
15. Defence (Transfer of Functions) Act 1964.
ss. 1, 3, C.: 1995, c. 21, sch. 14.
26. Licensing Act 1964.
orders 95/495, 496.
s. 10, see *Breslin* v. *West Yorkshire Police, The Independent*, July 24, 1995, Popplewell J.
s. 20A, see *Buchanan* v. *Gresswell, The Independent*, May 30, 1995, Keene J.
s. 51, amended: 1995, c. 33, sch. 1.
s. 60, repealed in pt.: 1995, c. 33, sch. 2.
s. 60, amended: 1995, c. 33, s. 1, sch. 1.
s. 62, amended: 1995, c. 33, s. 2.
s. 67A, amended: 1995, c. 33, s. 3.
s. 68, amended: 1995, c. 33, sch. 1.
s. 81A, see *Chief Constable of West Midlands Police* v. *Marsden, The Times*, May 2, 1995, Owen J.
s. 86A, orders 95/495, 496.
s. 87A, amended: 1995, c. 33, sch. 1.
s. 158, repealed: 1995, c. 21, sch. 12.
s. 160, see *D.P.P.* v. *McVitie (James Francis)* (CO 552/94), October 17, 1994, D.C.
s. 182, see *Waltham Forest London Borough Council* v. *Loizou* (FC395/5990/F), May 22, 1995, C.A.
27. Merchant Shipping Act 1964.
ss. 1, 3, 4, 5, 7, 12, 13, repealed: regs. 95/1210.
s. 17, repealed in pt.: regs. 95/1210.
28. Agriculture and Horticulture Act 1964.
s. 20, 1995, c. 40, sch. 2 (S.).
40. Harbours Act 1964.
s. 14, orders 94/3162; 95/421, 422, 740 (S.), 964 (S.), 1063, 1527 (S.), 2007, 2380.
s. 29, repealed in pt.: 1995, c. 21, sch. 12.
s. 29, C.: 1995, c. 21, sch. 14.
s. 30, repealed in pt.: 1995, c. 21, sch. 12.
s. 30, C.: 1995, c. 21, sch. 14.
s. 35, repealed: 1995, c. 21, sch. 12.
s. 35, C.: 1995, c. 21, sch. 14.
s. 57, amended: 1995, c. 21, sch. 13.
sch. 3, order 95/1063.
sch. 3, amended: 1994, c. 39, sch. 13 (S.).
41. Succession (Scotland) Act 1964.
s. 21, amended: 1995, c. 7, sch. 4.
s. 21A, added: 1995, c. 7, sch. 4.
s. 32, substituted: 1995, c. 7, sch. 4.
sch. 1, amended: 1995, c. 7, sch. 4.
46. Malawi Independence Act 1964.
schs. 1, 2, repealed: 1995, c. 21, sch. 12.
47. Merchant Shipping Act 1964.
s. 9, repealed: 1995, c. 21, sch. 12.
s. 11, repealed: 1995, c. 21, sch. 12.

CAP.

1964—cont.

47. Merchant Shipping Act 1964—*cont.*
s. 16, repealed: 1995, c. 21, sch. 12.
s. 16, C.: 1995, c. 21, sch. 14.
ss. 19, 20, repealed: 1995, c. 21, sch. 12.
48. Police Act 1964.
ss. 4A, 4B, orders 95/600, 610.
s. 21A, order 95/2864.
s. 21C, order 95/2864.
s. 33, regs. 95/215, 1475.
s. 46, regs. 95/215.
s. 51, see *Hourihane* v. *Commissioner of Police of the Metropolis, The Times*, December 27, 1994, C.A.; *Connolly* v. *Dale, The Times*, July 13, 1995, D.C.
s. 52, see *Kerr* v. *D.P.P.* [1994] 158 J.P. 1048, D.C.
sch. 1A, amended: orders 95/493, 600, 610, 1747, 1769, 1770, 1771, 1772, 1773, 1774, 1775, 1776, 1779, 2864.
sch. 1B, amended: orders 95/187, 600, 610, 1769, 1770, 1771, 1772, 1773, 1774, 1775, 1776, 1779.
sch. 5, see *R.* v. *Secretary of State for the Home Department, ex p. Cooke* [1993] C.O.D. 331, D.C.
67. Local Government (Development and Finance) (Scotland) Act 1964.
s. 16, amended: 1994, c. 39, sch. 13.
70. Riding Establishments Act 1964.
s. 6, amended: 1994, c. 39, sch. 13 (S.).
80. Statute Law Revision (Scotland) Act 1964.
repealed: 1995, c. 44, sch. 1.
81. Diplomatic Privileges Act 1964.
sch. 1, see *Abidi* v. *Secretary of State for the Home Department* [1994] Imm.A.R. 532, C.A.
86. Malta Independence Act 1964.
schs. 1, 2, repealed in pt.: 1995, c. 21, sch. 12.
93. Gambia Independence Act 1964.
schs. 1, 2, repealed in pt.: 1995, c. 21, sch. 12.

1965

4. Science and Technology Act 1965.
s. 1, order 95/261.
s. 3, order 95/630.
12. Industrial and Provident Societies Act 1965.
see *Halifax Building Society* v. *Chamberlain Martin & Spurgeon*; *Same* v. *Meridian Housing Association* [1994] EGCS 41, Arden J.
s. 34, repealed in pt.: 1995, c. 7, sch. 5 (S.).
s. 36, repealed: 1995, c. 7, sch. 5 (S.).
s. 61, 1995, c. 40, sch. 2 (S.).
ss. 70, 71, regs. 95/712, 713.
sch. 3, amended: 1995, c. 7, sch. 4.
sch. 4, amended: 1995, c. 7, sch. 4.

CAP.

1965—cont.

13. Rivers (Prevention of Pollution) (Scotland) Act 1965.
s. 10, repealed in pt.: 1995, c. 25, sch. 24.
s. 10, amended: 1995, c. 25, sch. 22.
s. 11, amended: 1995, c. 40, sch. 2 (S.).

14. Cereals Marketing Act 1965.
ss. 13, 23, 24, order 95/1439.

18. War Damage Act 1965.
s. 1, repealed in pt.: 1995, c. 44, sch. 1.

32. Administration of Estates (Small Payments) Act 1965.
s. 1, amended: regs. 95/300.

36. Gas Act 1965.
Part II, amended: 1995, c. 45, sch. 4.
s. 28, amended: 1994, c. 39, sch. 13.
s. 32, amended: 1995, c. 45, sch. 4.
sch. 2, amended: 1995, c. 45, sch. 4.
sch. 6, amended: 1995, c. 39, sch. 13.

37. Carriage of Goods by Road Act 1965.
see *G.I. Cicatiello Srl* v. *Anglo European Shipping Services* [1994] 1 Lloyd's Rep. 678, H.H.J. Matt-Johnson; *Aqualon (U.K.)* v. *Vallana Shipping Corp.* [1994] 1 Lloyd's Rep. 669, Mance J.

45. Backing of Warrants (Republic of Ireland) Act 1965.
s. 2, see *Conlon (John Francis), Re* (CO/3778/94), March 2, 1995, D.C.
s. 8, amended: 1995, c. 20, sch. 6 (S.); 1995, c. 40, sch. 4 (S.).

47. Merchant Shipping Act 1965.
s. 1, C.: 1995, c. 21, sch. 14.
sch. 1, C.: 1995, c. 21, sch. 14.

49. Registration of Births, Deaths and Marriages (Scotland) Act 1965.
s. 5, substituted in pt.: 1994, c. 39, s. 51.
s. 14, amended: 1995, c. 36, s. 99.
s. 17, repealed in pt.: 1994, c. 39, sch. 14.
s. 18, amended: 1995, c. 36, s. 99.
s. 20, repealed in pt.: 1994, c. 39, sch. 14.
s. 20, amended: 1995, c. 36, sch. 4.
s. 25, repealed in pt.: 1995, c. 36, sch. 14.
s. 40, regs. 95/3151.
s. 40, repealed in pt.: 1994, c. 39, sch. 14.
s. 43, regs. 94/3151.
s. 43, repealed in pt.: 1995, c. 36, sch. 5; order 95/2787.
s. 43, amended: 1995, c. 36, sch. 4.
s. 47, regs. 95/646.
s. 53, amended: 1995, c. 36, sch. 4.
s. 54, regs. 94/3151; 95/646.
s. 56, regs. 94/3151; 95/646.
s. 56, amended: 1995, c. 36, sch. 4.
schs. 3, 5, repealed in pt.: 1994, c. 39, sch. 14.

51. National Insurance Act 1965.
s. 36, amended: order 95/559; regs. 95/2606.

56. Compulsory Purchase Act 1965.
s. 4, repealed in pt.: order 95/2383.
s. 11, amended: order 95/2383.

CAP.

1965—cont.

57. Nuclear Installations Act 1965.
s. 3, repealed in pt.: 1995, c. 25, sch. 24.
s. 3, amended: 1995, c. 25, sch. 22.
ss. 4, 5, 26, amended: 1995, c. 25, sch. 22.

64. Commons Registration Act 1965.
ss. 1, 4, 6, see *Dynevor (Lord)* v. *Richardson* [1994] 3 W.L.R. 1091, Knox J.
ss. 13, 14, 22, see *R.* v. *Hereford and Worcester County Council, ex p. Ind Coope (Oxford and West)*, October 26, 1994; Brooke J.

69. Criminal Procedure (Attendance of Witnesses) Act 1965.
s. 2, see *Morrow, Geach and Thomas* v. *D.P.P., Secretary of State for Health and Social Security and British Pregnancy Advisory Service* [1994] Crim.L.R. 58, D.C.

71. Murder (Abolition of Death Penalty) Act 1965.
s. 1, see *R.* v. *Leaney, The Times*, April 12, 1995, C.A.

1966

18. Finance Act 1966.
s. 2, amended: 1995, c. 21, sch. 13.

19. Law Reform (Miscellaneous Provisions) (Scotland) Act 1966.
s. 8, amended: 1995, c. 36, sch. 4.

36. Veterinary Surgeon Act 1966.
s. 11, regs. 95/207.

38. Sea Fisheries Regulation Act 1966.
s. 1, orders 95/1472, 1474.
s. 1, amended: 1995, c. 25, sch. 12.
s. 2, amended: 1995, c. 25, s. 102, sch. 10.
s. 5A, added: 1995, c. 25, s. 102.
s. 8, amended: 1995, c. 25, s. 102.
s. 18, amended: 1995, c. 25, sch. 12.

39. Land Registration Act 1966.
repealed: 1995, c. 44, sch. 1.

51. Local Government (Scotland) Act 1966.
s. 6, amended: 1994, c. 39, s. 157.
s. 11, substituted: 1994, c. 39, s. 166.
s. 18, amended: 1995, c. 45, sch. 3.
s. 24, regs. 94/3200 (S.); 95/518.
s. 24, substituted: 1994, c. 39, s. 154.
s. 24A, regs. 94/3200 (S.); 95/518.
s. 24A, added: 1994, c. 39, s. 155.
s. 24B, amended: 1994, c. 39, s. 155.
s. 25, amended: 1994, c. 39, sch. 13.
s. 25A, added: 1994, c. 39, s. 156.
ss. 44, 46, sch. 3, amended: 1994, c. 39, sch. 13.

1967

8. Plant Health Act 1967.
ss. 2, 3, orders 94/3093, 3094; 95/1353, 1989.
s. 4, order 95/1358.
s. 5, amended: 1994, c. 39, sch. 13 (S.).

CAP.

1967—cont.

9. General Rate Act 1967.
ss. 9, 72, 79, see *R.* v. *Newham Borough Council*, ex p. *Barking and Dagenham London Borough Council*; *R.* v. *Newham London Borough Council*, ex p. *University of East London* [1994] RA 13, Potts J.
s. 104, see *Trull* v. *Restormel Borough Council* [1994] 34 R.V.R. 122, Latham J.
sch. 11, order 94/3106.

10. Forestry Act 1967.
s. 24, 1995, c. 40, sch. 2 (S.).
s. 39, repealed in pt.: 1995, c. 7, sch. 5 (S.).
s. 40, amended: 1994, c. 39, sch. 13 (S.).
ss. 46, 48, 1995, c. 40, sch. 2 (S.).

13. Parliamentary Commissioner Act 1967.
s. 4, order 95/1615.
s. 11B, added: 1995, c. 53, s. 10.
sch. 1, regs. 95/635 (S.), 637.
sch. 2, repealed in pt.: 1995, c. 25, sch. 24.
sch. 2, amended: 1995, c. 25, sch. 22; 1995, c. 26, sch. 1.
sch. 3, repealed in pt.: 1995, c. 17, sch. 3; 1995, c. 35, sch. 3.
sch. 3, amended: 1995, c. 17, sch. 1.

22. Agriculture Act 1967.
s. 50, repealed in pt.: 1995, c. 25, sch. 24.
s. 50, amended: 1995, c. 25, sch. 10.

24. Slaughter of Poultry Act 1967.
s. 8, amended: 1994, c. 39, sch. 13 (S.).

27. Merchant Shipping (Load Lines) Act 1967.
ss. 1–9, 10–24, 27, 30–32, repealed: 1995, c. 21, sch. 12.
s. 30, C.: 1995, c. 21, sch. 14.

41. Marine etc. Broadcasting (Offences) Act 1967.
s. 10, order 95/268.
sch. 16, amended: order 95/268.

48. Industrial and Provident Societies Act 1967.
s. 7, regs. 95/712, 713.
s. 8, order 95/1297.

54. Finance Act 1967.
s. 27, amended: 1995, c. 4, s. 149.

58. Criminal Law Act 1967.
sch. 2, repealed in pt.: 1995, c. 44, sch. 1.

64. Anchor and Chain Cables Act 1967.
s. 1, continued in force (temp.): 1995, c. 21, sch. 14.

71. Aden, Perim and Kuria Muria Islands Act 1967.
repealed (with savings): 1995, c. 44, schs. 1, 2.

72. Wireless Telegraphy Act 1967.
ss. 13, 15, order 95/268.

77. Police (Scotland) Act 1967.
s. 1, order 95/492.
s. 1, amended: 1994, c. 39, sch. 13.
ss. 2, 18, amended: 1994, c. 39, sch. 13.

CAP.

1967—cont.

77. Police (Scotland) Act 1967—*cont.*
s. 19, repealed in pt.: 1994, c. 39, sch. 14.
s. 19, amended: 1994, c. 39, sch. 13.
s. 20, substituted: 1994, c. 39, s. 35.
s. 21, amended: 1994, c. 39, sch. 13.
s. 21A, repealed: 1994, c. 39, sch. 14.
s. 21B, added: 1994, c. 39, s. 34.
ss. 22, 23, amended: 1994, c. 39, sch. 13.
s. 26, regs. 94/3039; 95/137, 596, 647, 2131.
s. 26, amended: 1994, c. 39, sch. 13.
ss. 26A, 26B, 26C, amended: 1994, c. 39, sch. 13.
s. 27, regs. 95/1057.
ss. 32, 32A, amended: 1994, c. 39, sch. 13.
s. 36, orders 95/706, 707.
s. 41, 1995, c. 40, sch. 2.
ss. 43, 44, 1995, c. 40, sch. 2.
s. 48, orders 95/706.
s. 51, sch. 2, amended: 1994, c. 39, sch. 13.
s. 111, regs. 95/1057.
sch. 6, regs. 94/3039.

78. Water (Scotland) Act 1967.
repealed: 1994, c. 39, sch. 14.

80. Criminal Justice Act 1967.
s. 3, see *Morrow, Geach and Thomas* v. *D.P.P., Secretary of State for Health and Social Security and British Pregnancy Advisory Service* [1994] Crim.L.R. 58, D.C.
s. 6, see *R.* v. *Baker* [1994] Crim.L.R. 444, C.A.
s. 11, see *R.* v. *Carnegie; R.* v. *Webber* [1994] Crim.L.R. 591, C.A.
s. 67, see *R.* v. *Davies*, *The Times*, December 30, 1994, C.A.; *R.* v. *Governor of Styal Prison, ex p. Mooney*, *The Times*, May 17, 1995, D.C.
s. 69, repealed in pt.: 1995, c. 20, sch. 7 (S.).
s. 69, amended: 1995, c. 20, sch. 6 (S.).

83. Sea Fisheries (Shellfish) Act 1967.
s. 1, orders 94/2329; 95/1257, 1258, 2145.
s. 7, 1995, c. 40, sch. 2 (S.).

84. Sea Fish (Conservation) Act 1967.
s. 1, amended: 1995, c. 21, sch. 13.
ss. 4, 4A, 4B, order 94/2813.
s. 5, orders 94/3273; 95/168, 1214.
s. 5, amended: 1995, c. 21, sch. 13.
s. 5A, added: 1995, c. 25, s. 103.
s. 15, orders 94/3273; 95/168, 1214.
s. 18, amended: 1995, c. 25, sch. 15.
s. 22, orders 94/3273; 95/168, 1214.
s. 22, amended: 1995, c. 21, sch. 13.

86. Countryside (Scotland) Act 1967.
ss. 46, 48A, amended: 1994, c. 39, sch. 13.
s. 49, repealed in pt.: 1994, c. 39, schs. 13, 14.
ss. 50, 54, amended: 1994, c. 39, sch. 13.
ss. 63, 65, repealed in pt.: 1994, c. 39, schs. 13, 14.
s. 78, amended: 1994, c. 39, sch. 13.

CAP.

1967—cont.

87. Abortion Act 1967.
s. 2, 1995, c. 40, sch. 2 (S.).

88. Leasehold Reform Act 1967.
see *Hynes* v. *Twinsectra*, *The Times*, March 8, 1995, C.A.
s. 1, amended: 1995, c. 8, sch.
s. 1, see *Duke of Westminster* v. *Birrane* [1995] 2 W.L.R. 270, C.A.
s. 2, see *Duke of Westminster* v. *Birrane* [1995] 2 W.L.R. 270, C.A.
s. 9, see *Covent Garden Group* v. *Naiva* (1994) 27 H.L.R. 295, C.A.
s. 21, see *Covent Garden Group* v. *Naiva* (1994) 27 H.L.R. 295, C.A.
s. 28, amended: 1995, c. 17, sch. 1; 1995, c. 25, sch. 10.

1968

5. Administration of Justice Act 1968.
s. 1, amended: order 94/3217.

7. London Cab Act 1968.
s. 1, order 95/1181.

14. Public Expenditure and Receipts Act 1968.
order 95/889.
s. 5, sch. 3, orders 94/3257; 95/132 (S.), 889.

16. New Towns (Scotland) Act 1968.
ss. 1A, amended: 1994, c. 39, sch. 13.
s. 34, repealed in pt.: 1994, c. 39, sch. 14.
ss. 35, 36, 47, sch. 1, amended: 1994, c. 39, sch. 13.
sch. 2, repealed in pt.: 1995, c. 7, sch. 5.

18. Consular Relations Act 1968.
ss. 13, 15, amended: 1995, c. 21, sch. 13.

19. Criminal Appeal Act 1968.
see *R.* v. *Hiley, The Times*, March 10, 1995, C.A.
s. 1, amended: 1995, c. 35, s. 1.
s. 2, amended: 1995, c. 35, s. 2.
s. 2, see *R.* v. *Cox (Andrew Mark), The Times*, April 12, 1995, C.A.; *R.* v. *Johl* [1994] Crim.L.R. 522, C.A.; *R.* v. *Young (Stephen)* [1995] 2 W.L.R. 430, C.A.; *R.* v. *Hitchens (Wayne)* (94/4674/Z4), February 13, 1995, C.A.; *R.* v. *Foran (Martin)* (92/5629/W1), February 24, 1995, C.A.; *R.* v. *Brook (Malcolm) and Sheffield (John)* (95/0307/W5; 95/0308/W5), July 14, 1995, C.A.
s. 5, amended: 1995, c. 35, sch. 2.
s. 7, see *R.* v. *Khan (Ashrouf Bryan)* (94/7266/Z2), March 8, 1995, C.A.
s. 8, see *R.* v. *Murphy, The Times*, February 28, 1995, C.A.
s. 11, see *R.* v. *Guppy*; *Same* v. *Marsh* [1994] Crim.L.R. 614, C.A.
s. 12, amended: 1995, c. 35, s. 2.
s. 13, amended: 1995, c. 35, s. 1.
s. 15, amended: 1995, c. 35, s. 1.

CAP.

1968—cont.

19. Criminal Appeal Act 1968—*cont.*
s. 16, amended: 1995, c. 35, s. 2.
s. 17, repealed: 1995, c. 35, sch. 3.
s. 17, see *R.* v. *Foran (Martin)* (92/5629/W1), February 24, 1995, C.A.; *R.* v. *Secretary of State for the Home Department, ex p. Hickey (No. 2)* [1995] 1 All E.R. 490, D.C.
s. 19, see *R.* v. *Ofori (Noble Julius)*; *R.* v. *Tackie (Nazar)* (1994) 99 Cr.App.R. 219, C.A.
s. 23, repealed in pt.: 1995, c. 35, sch. 3.
s. 23, amended: 1995, c. 35, s. 4, sch. 2.
s. 23, see *R.* v. *Guppy*; *Same* v. *Marsh* [1994] Crim.L.R. 614, C.A.; *R.* v. *Gilfoyle, The Times*, October 31, 1995, C.A.
s. 23A, added: 1995, c. 35, s. 5.
s. 29, amended: 1995, c. 35, sch. 2.
s. 31, see *R.* v. *Ahmed (Asim Naseer), The Times*, July 11, 1995, C.A.
s. 31A, added: 1995, c. 35, s. 6.
s. 33, see *R.* v. *Tang, The Times*, May 23, 1995, C.A.
s. 34, see *R.* v. *Dalton* [1995] 2 W.L.R. 377, C.A.
s. 44A, added: 1995, c. 35, s. 7.
s. 45, amended: 1995, c. 35, sch. 2.
s. 50, see *R.* v. *Leaney, The Times*, April 12, 1995, C.A.
s. 51, see *R.* v. *Ofori (Noble Julius)*; *R.* v. *Tackie (Nazar)* [1994] 99 Cr.App.R. 219, C.A.

20. Courts-Martial (Appeals) Act 1968.
s. 12, amended: 1995, c. 35, sch. 2.
s. 28, repealed in pt.: 1995, c. 35, sch. 3.
s. 28, amended: 1995, c. 35, sch. 2.

27. Firearms Act 1968.
s. 8, see *R.* v. *Bull (Adrian William)* (1994) 99 Cr.App.R. 193, C.A.
s. 26, order 94/2614.
s. 31, see *R.* v. *Bull (Adrian William)* (1994) 99 Cr.App.R. 193, C.A.
s. 43, order 94/2615.

29. Trade Descriptions Act 1968.
see *R.* v. *Piper, The Times*, March 2, 1995, C.A.; *R.* v. *Manchester Magistrates' Courts, ex p. Kaymanesh* [1994] 15 Cr.App.R. (S.) 838, C.A.
s. 1, see *Reynolds* v. *Hamilton*, 1994 S.C.C.R. 760; *R.* v. *Shrewsbury Crown Court, ex p. Venables* [1994] Crim.L.R. 61, D.C.; *R.* v. *South Tyneside Justices, ex p. Mill Garages, The Times*, April 17, 1995, Keene J.; *Roberts* v. *Leonard, The Times*, May 10, 1995, D.C.
s. 2, amended: regs. 94/3144.
s. 14, see *Ashley* v. *Sutton London Borough Council, The Times*, December 8, 1994, D.C.

CAP.

1968—cont.

29. Trade Descriptions Act 1968—*cont.*
s. 19, see *R.* v. *South Tyneside Justices, ex p. Mill Garages, The Times*, April 17, 1995, Keene J.
s. 24, see *Gale* v. *Dixon Stores Group* (1994) 6 Admin.L.R. 497, D.C.

34. Agriculture (Miscellaneous Provisions) Act 1968.
s. 7, amended: 1995, c. 40, sch. 2 (S.).
s. 12, amended: 1995, c. 8, sch.

36. Merchant Shipping Act 1968.
ss. 43, 99, order 95/1438.

38. Sale of Venison (Scotland) Act 1968.
ss. 1, 2, 1995, c. 40, sch. 2 (S.).

41. Countryside Act 1968.
s. 4, amended: 1995, c. 25, sch. 10.
s. 6, repealed in pt.: 1995, c. 25, sch. 24.
s. 12, amended: 1995, c. 25, sch. 10.
s. 13, repealed in pt.: 1995, c. 25, sch. 24.
s. 13, amended: 1995, c. 21, sch. 13; 1995, c. 25, sch. 10.
s. 40, repealed: 1995, c. 25, sch. 24.
s. 42, repealed in pt.: 1995, c. 25, sch. 24.
s. 47A, repealed in pt.: 1995, c. 25, sch. 24.

44. Finance Act 1968.
sch. 19, see *NAP Holdings U.K.* v. *Whittles (Inspector of Taxes), The Times*, November 22, 1994, H.L.

45. Firearms Act 1968.
s. 27, rules 94/3198 (S.).

46. Health Services and Public Health Act 1968.
s. 63, amended: 1994, c. 39, sch. 13 (S.); 1995, c. 17, sch. 1.
s. 64, amended: 1994, c. 39, sch. 13 (S.); 1995, c. 17, sch. 1.
s. 71, repealed in pt.: 1994, c. 39, sch. 14 (S.).

47. Sewerage (Scotland) Act 1968.
ss. 1–4, amended: 1994, c. 39, sch. 13.
s. 3A, added: 1994, c. 39, s. 101.
s. 10, substituted: 1994, c. 39, s. 102.
ss. 6–7, 11–16, amended: 1994, c. 39, sch. 13.
s. 16A, added: 1994, c. 39, sch. 13.
s. 18, repealed in pt.: 1994, c. 39, schs. 13, 14.
ss. 20–23, amended: 1994, c. 39, sch. 13.
ss. 37A–37B, added: 1994, c. 39, s. 103.
s. 38, repealed in pt.: 1995, c. 25, sch. 24.
s. 38, amended: 1995, c. 39, sch. 13; 1995, c. 25, sch. 22.
s. 39, amended: 1995, c. 39, sch. 13.
s. 40, repealed in pt.: 1994, c. 39, schs. 13, 14.
s. 44, 1995, c. 40, sch. 2.
s. 47, repealed (with savings): 1994, c. 39, s. 179, sch. 14.
s. 48, amended: 1995, c. 40, sch. 2.
s. 48, amended: 1994, c. 39, sch. 13.
s. 49, repealed: 1995, c. 25, sch. 24.

CAP.

1968—cont.

47. Sewerage (Scotland) Act 1968—*cont.*
s. 50, amended: 1995, c. 40, sch. 2.
s. 50, amended: 1994, c. 39, s. 104.
s. 51, amended: 1994, c. 39, sch. 13.
s. 52, repealed: 1994, c. 39, schs. 13, 14.
s. 55, substituted: 1995, c. 25, sch. 21.
s. 59, repealed in pt.: 1995, c. 25, sch. 24.
s. 59, amended: 1994, c. 39, sch. 13; 1995, c. 25, sch. 22.

48. International Organisations Act 1968.
s. 10, order 95/266.

49. Social Work (Scotland) Act 1968.
Part III, repealed in pt.: 1995, c. 36, sch. 5.
Part V, repealed in pt.: 1995, c. 36, sch. 5.
s. 1, amended: 1994, c. 39, sch. 13; 1995, c. 36, sch. 4.
s. 1, amended: 1994, c. 39, sch. 13.
s. 2, repealed in pt.: 1994, c. 39, sch. 14.
s. 3, substituted: 1994, c. 39, s. 45.
s. 4, amended: 1995, c. 36, sch. 4.
s. 5, repealed in pt.: 1995, c. 36, sch. 5.
s. 5, amended: 1994, c. 39, sch. 13; 1995, c. 36, sch. 4; 1995, c. 40, sch. 4.
s. 5A, repealed in pt.: 1994, c. 39, sch. 14.
s. 5A, amended: 1994, c. 39, sch. 13.
s. 5B, repealed in pt.: 1995, c. 36, sch. 5.
s. 5B, amended: 1994, c. 39, sch. 13; 1995, c. 36, sch. 4.
s. 6, amended: 1995, c. 40, sch. 2.
s. 6, repealed in pt.: 1995, c. 36, sch. 4.
s. 6, amended: 1995, c. 36, sch. 4.
s. 6A, amended: 1994, c. 39, sch. 13; 1995, c. 40, sch. 4.
s. 6B, inserted: 1995, c. 36, s. 100.
s. 9, amended: 1995, c. 36, sch. 4.
s. 10, amended: 1994, c. 39, sch. 13; 1995, c. 36, sch. 4.
s. 11, amended: 1994, c. 39, sch. 13; 1995, c. 36, sch. 4.
s. 12, amended: 1995, c. 36, sch. 4.
s. 13, amended: 1994, c. 39, sch. 13.
s. 15, repealed: 1995, c. 36, sch. 5.
s. 15, see *R.* v. *R.* (Sh.Ct.), 1994 S.C.L.R. 849.
s. 16, repealed: 1995, c. 36, sch. 5.
s. 16, see *R.* v. *R.* (Sh.Ct.), 1994 S.C.L.R. 849.
ss. 17–19, repealed: 1995, c. 36, sch. 5.
s. 20, repealed: 1995, c. 36, sch. 5.
s. 20, see *R.* v. *R.* (Sh.Ct.), 1994 S.C.L.R. 849.
s. 20A, amended: 1994, c. 39, sch. 13.
ss. 21, 22, repealed: 1995, c. 36, sch. 5.
s. 23, repealed: 1995, c. 36, s. 28, sch. 5.
s. 24, repealed: 1995, c. 36, sch. 5.
s. 25, repealed: 1995, c. 36, s. 30, sch. 5.
s. 26, repealed: 1995, c. 36, sch. 5.
s. 27, amended: 1994, c. 39, sch. 13; 1995, c. 20, s. 66; 1995, c. 40, sch. 4.
s. 28, amended: 1995, c. 36, sch. 4.

CAP.

1968—cont.

49. Social Work (Scotland) Act 1968—*cont.*
s. 29, amended: 1995, c. 36, sch. 4.
s. 30, see *T.* v. *Watson*, 1994 S.C.L.R. 1084.
s. 31, repealed: 1995, c. 40, sch. 5.
s. 31, C.: 1995, c. 46, s. 42.
s. 32, see *D.* v. *Kelly (I.H.)*, 1995 S.L.T. 1220.
s. 33, amended: 1994, c. 39, sch. 13.
s. 34, repealed in pt.: 1994, c. 39, sch. 14.
s. 34, amended: 1994, c. 39, sch. 13.
s. 36, repealed in pt.: 1994, c. 39, s. 138, sch. 13.
s. 36, amended: 1994, c. 39, s. 138, sch. 13.
s. 38, amended: 1994, c. 39, sch. 13.
s. 39, amended: 1994, c. 39, s. 139.
s. 42, see *L.Petrs.*, (1st Div.), *The Times*, April 21, 1995.
s. 44, amended: 1994, c. 39, sch. 13.
s. 47, amended: 1994, c. 39, sch. 13.
s. 47, see *Stirling* v. *D. (I.H.)*, 1995 S.C.L.R. 460.
s. 48, see *Stirling* v. *D. (I.H.)*, 1995 S.C.L.R. 460.
s. 49, see *M.* v. *Kennedy*, 1995 S.L.T. 123.
ss. 50, 54, 58A, 58B, 58C, amended: 1994, c. 39, sch. 13.
s. 59, amended: 1995, c. 36, sch. 4.
s. 60, 1995, c. 40, sch. 2.
s. 61, amended: 1995, c. 40, sch. 2.
s. 61, repealed: 1995, c. 36, s. 34.
s. 61A, substituted: 1995, c. 36, s. 34.
s. 62, amended: 1995, c. 40, sch. 2.
s. 62A, added: 1995, c. 36, s. 34.
s. 64A, amended: order 95/749.
s. 65, amended: 1995, c. 40, sch. 2.
s. 67, substituted: 1995, c. 36, s. 34.
s. 68, amended: 1995, c. 36, sch. 4.
s. 72, amended: order 95/756.
s. 73, amended: 1994, c. 39, sch. 13.
s. 74, amended: order 95/576.
s. 75, amended: 1994, c. 39, sch. 13; order 95/576.
s. 76, repealed in pt.: 1994, c. 39, sch. 14.
s. 76, amended: 1994, c. 39, schs. 3, 13; order 95/576.
s. 78, amended: 1995, c. 18, sch. 2; 1995, c. 36, sch. 4.
s. 78A, amended: 1995, c. 36, sch. 4.
s. 79, amended: 1995, c. 36, sch. 4.
s. 80, amended: 1995, c. 36, sch. 4.
s. 82, amended: 1995, c. 36, sch. 4.
s. 83, amended: 1995, c. 36, sch. 4.
s. 83A, added: 1995, c. 36, sch. 4.
s. 86, amended: 1995, c. 36, sch. 4.
s. 87, regs. 95/858.
s. 87, amended: 1995, c. 36, sch. 4; regs. 94/826; 95/443.
s. 88, repealed: 1995, c. 36, schs. 4, 5.
s. 90, order 95/749.
s. 90, repealed in pt.: 1995, c. 36, schs. 4, 5.

CAP.

1968—cont.

49. Social Work (Scotland) Act 1968—*cont.*
s. 94, order 95/749.
s. 94, repealed in pt.: 1995, c. 36, schs. 4, 5.
s. 94, amended: order 95/756.
s. 94, see *T.* v. *Watson*, 1994 S.C.L.R. 1084.
s. 97, repealed in pt.: 1995, c. 36, schs. 4, 5.
sch. 2, amended: 1995, c. 36, sch. 4.

52. Caravan Sites Act 1968.
s. 6, see *R.* v. *South Hams District Council, ex p. Gibb*; *Same* v. *Gloucestershire County Council, ex p. Davies*; *Same* v. *Dorset County Council, ex p. Rolls* [1994] 3 W.L.R. 1151, C.A.; *Waverley Borough Council* v. *Marney* [1995] 93 L.G.R. 86, C.A.; *R.* v. *Avon County Council, ex p. Hills* [1995] 27 H.L.R. 411, Harrison J.
s. 16, see *R.* v. *South Hams District Council, ex p. Gibb*; *Same* v. *Gloucestershire County Council, ex p. Davies*; *Same* v. *Dorset County Council, ex p. Rolls* [1994] 3 W.L.R. 1151, C.A.

54. Theatres Act 1968.
s. 6, amended: 1995, c. 40, sch. 2 (S.).
s. 18, amended: 1994, c. 39, sch. 13 (S.).

59. Hovercraft Act 1968.
order 95/1299.
s. 1, repealed in pt.: 1995, c. 25, sch. 24.
s. 1, amended: 1995, c. 21, sch. 13.

60. Theft Act 1968.
s. 3, see *R.* v. *Gallasso (Lesley Caroline)* (1994) 98 Cr.App.R. 284, C.A.
s. 5, see *R.* v. *Dubar* [1994] 1 W.L.R. 1484, Ct.M.A.C.
s. 6, see *D.P.P.* v. *Lavender* [1994] Crim.L.R. 297, D.C.; *R.* v. *Fernandes*, *The Times*, April 22, 1995, C.A.
s. 12A, see *R.* v. *Sherwood*; *R.* v. *Button* [1995] RTR 60, C.A.
s. 20, see *R.* v. *Johl* [1994] Crim.L.R. 522, C.A.
s. 25, see *In the Matter of McAngus* [1994] Crim.L.R. 602, D.C.
s. 27, see *R.* v. *Hacker*, *The Times*, November 21, 1994, H.L.

64. Civil Evidence Act 1968.
Part 1, repealed in pt.: 1995, c. 38, sch. 2.
ss. 1, 2, see *St. Trudo Trade Mark* [1995] F.S.R. 345, Ferris J.
s. 9, repealed in pt. (with savings): 1995, c. 38, s. 7.
s. 11, see *Brinks* v. *Abu Saleh*, *The Times*, May 12, 1995, Rimer J.
s. 12, amended: order 95/756.
s. 18, see *St. Trudo Trade Mark* [1995] F.S.R. 345, Ferris J.

65. Gaming Act 1968.
order 95/321.
see *R.* v. *South Westminster Licensing Justices, ex p. Aspinall's Club* [1993] C.O.D. 335, Auld J.

CAP.

1968—cont.

65. Gaming Act 1968—*cont.*
s. 8, amended: 1995, c. 40, sch. 2 (S.).
s. 8, see *Bass Inns & Taverns* v. *Glasgow District Licensing Board (I.H.)*, 1995 S.C.L.R. 415.
s. 13, regs. 94/2899.
s. 14, regs. 94/958; 95/1022.
s. 15, regs. 94/2899.
ss. 20, 21, amended: orders 94/956; 95/926, 1020 (S.).
s. 31, amended: orders 95/2288, 2360.
s. 34, amended: orders 95/2288, 2360.
s. 34, see *R.* v. *Chichester Crown Court, ex p. Forte* (CO/1583/93), February 23, 1995, Brooke J.
s. 40, order 95/1750.
s. 43, amended: 1995, c. 38, sch. 1.
s. 44, amended: 1994, c. 39, sch. 13 (S.).
s. 48, amended: orders 95/321, 571 (S.).
s. 51, regs. 94/958, 2899; 95/1022.
s. 51, orders 94/956; 957; 95/321, 571 (S.), 926, 1020 (S.), 1750, 2288, 2360.
schs. 2, 9, amended: 1994, c. 39, sch. 13 (S.).

67. Medicines Act 1968.
order 95/309.
s. 4, order 94/3120.
s. 7, order 94/2986.
ss. 9, 10, amended: regs. 94/2987.
ss. 18, 24, 34, regs. 94/3143.
s. 35, order 95/2809.
s. 38, regs. 94/3143.
s. 40, regs. 95/799.
s. 47, regs. 94/2852.
s. 57, order 94/3169.
s. 58, order 94/3016, 3050; 95/1384.
ss. 75, 76, regs. 94/2936.
s. 103, regs. 95/1802.
ss. 106–107, amended: regs. 94/3144.
ss. 108–114, applied: regs. 94/2987.
s. 108, order 94/2852.
s. 108, amended: regs. 94/3144.
s. 109, order 94/2852.
s. 109, amended: 1994, c. 39, sch. 13 (S.); regs. 94/3144.
s. 110, order 94/2852.
s. 110, amended: regs. 94/3144.
s. 111, order 94/2852.
s. 111, amended: regs. 94/3144.
s. 112, order 94/2852.
s. 112, amended: regs. 94/3144.
s. 113, order 94/2852.
s. 113, amended: regs. 94/3144.
s. 114, order 94/2852.
s. 114, amended: regs. 94/3144.
ss. 115, 116, 118, amended: regs. 94/3144.
s. 119, amended: regs. 94/3144.
s. 119, applied: regs. 94/2987.
ss. 121–127, amended: regs. 94/3144.
s. 129, orders 94/3016, 3050, 3120, 3169; 95/1384; regs. 94/2852, 2936, 3143; 95/799, 2809.

CAP.

1968—cont.

67. Medicines Act 1968—*cont.*
s. 130, amended: regs. 94/3119.
sch. 3, amended: regs. 94/3144.

73. Transport Act 1968.
Part V, repealed: 1995, c. 23, sch. 8.
s. 9, amended: 1994, c. 39, sch. 13 (S.).
s. 9A, repealed in pt.: 1994, c. 39, schs. 13, 14 (S.).
ss. 9B, 10, amended: 1994, c. 39, sch. 13 (S.).
s. 13, substituted: 1994, c. 39, s. 41 (S.).
s. 13A, added: 1994, c. 39, s. 163 (S.).
ss. 34, 56, amended: 1994, c. 39, sch. 13 (S.).
s. 58, amended: 1995, c. 23, sch. 7.
s. 59, C.: 1995, c. 23, sch. 8.
s. 60, regs. 95/1488.
s. 60, C.: 1995, c. 23, sch. 8.
s. 61, C.: 1995, c. 23, sch. 8.
s. 61A, C.: 1995, c. 23, sch. 8.
s. 62, C.: 1995, c. 23, sch. 8.
s. 63, amended: 1994, c. 39, sch. 13 (S.).
s. 63, C.: 1995, c. 23, sch. 8.
s. 64B, C.: 1995, c. 23, sch. 8.
s. 64, C.: 1995, c. 23, sch. 8.
s. 64A, C.: 1995, c. 23, sch. 8.
s. 66, C.: 1995, c. 23, sch. 8.
s. 67, C.: 1995, c. 23, sch. 8.
s. 67A, C.: 1995, c. 23, sch. 8.
s. 68, C.: 1995, c. 23, sch. 8.
s. 68A, C.: 1995, c. 23, sch. 8.
s. 69, C.: 1995, c. 23, sch. 8.
s. 69A, C.: 1995, c. 23, sch. 8.
s. 69B, C.: 1995, c. 23, sch. 8.
s. 69C, C.: 1995, c. 23, sch. 8.
s. 69D, C.: 1995, c. 23, sch. 8.
s. 69E, C.: 1995, c. 23, sch. 8.
s. 69G, C.: 1995, c. 23, sch. 8.
s. 69I, C.: 1995, c. 23, sch. 8.
s. 70, C.: 1995, c. 23, sch. 8.
s. 71, C.: 1995, c. 23, sch. 8.
s. 81, C.: 1995, c. 23, sch. 8.
s. 82, C.: 1995, c. 23, sch. 8.
s. 83, C.: 1995, c. 23, sch. 8.
s. 84, C.: 1995, c. 23, sch. 8.
s. 85, C.: 1995, c. 23, sch. 8.
s. 85A, C.: 1995, c. 23, sch. 8.
s. 86, C.: 1995, c. 23, sch. 8.
s. 87, C.: 1995, c. 23, sch. 8.
s. 89, regs. 95/1488.
s. 89, C.: 1995, c. 23, sch. 8.
s. 91, regs. 95/1488.
s. 91, C.: 1995, c. 23, sch. 8.
s. 92, C.: 1995, c. 23, sch. 8.
s. 95, see *Prime* v. *Hosking* (CO 2703/94), December 12, 1994, D.C.
s. 97, see *R.* v. *Sheffield Crown Court, ex p. Aubrey* (CO2712/93), March 8, 1995, Balcombe J.
s. 97A, added: 1995, c. 40, sch. 2 (S.).
s. 115, amended: 1994, c. 39, sch. 13 (S.).
s. 121, regs. 95/1236, 1300.
ss. 123, 124, sch. 5, amended: 1994, c. 39, sch. 13 (S.).

CAP.

1968—cont.

73. Transport Act 1968—*cont.*
s. 157, C.: 1995, c. 23, sch. 8.
s. 158, repealed in pt.: 1995, c. 23, sch. 8.
s. 158, amended: 1995, c. 23, sch. 7.
s. 159, C.: 1995, c. 23, sch. 8.
s. 166, C.: 1995, c. 23, sch. 8.
s. 233, C.: 1995, c. 23, sch. 8.
ss. 263, 265, repealed: 1995, c. 23, sch. 8.
sch. 8A, C.: 1995, c. 23, sch. 8.
sch. 10, C.: 1995, c. 23, sch. 8.

77. Sea Fisheries Act 1968.
s. 8, amended: 1995, c. 21, sch. 13.
s. 13, amended: 1995, c. 40, sch. 4 (S.).
ss. 17, 19, amended: 1995, c. 21, sch. 13.

1969

10. Mines and Quarries (Tips) Act 1969.
s. 11, amended: 1994, c. 39, sch. 13 (S.).

21. Immigration Appeals Act 1969.
s. 20, see *Miah (Nazmul)* v. *Secretary of State for the Home Department* [1995] Imm AR 24, C.A.

27. Driver and Vehicle Licensing Act 1969.
s. 27, amended: 1995, c. 38, sch. 1.
sch. 2, C.: 1995, c. 23, sch. 8.

29. Tanzania Act 1969.
s. 6, repealed in pt.: 1995, c. 44, sch. 1.

46. Family Law Reform Act 1969.
s. 7, see *J. (Minors) (Care: Care Plan), Re* [1994] 1 FLR 253, Wall J.; *R. (Minors) (Care Proceedings: Care Plan), Re* [1994] 2 F.C.R. 136, Wall J.
s. 20, see *C.B. (A Minor) (Blood Tests), Re* [1994] 2 F.L.R. 762, Wall J.; *E. (Parental Responsibility: Blood Tests), Re* [1995] 1 F.L.R. 392, C.A.; *G. (A Minor) (Blood Test), Re* [1994] 1 F.L.R. 495, M. Horowitz, Q.C.; *C.G. (A Minor) (Blood Tests), Re* [1994] 2 F.C.R. 889, Michael Horowitz, Q.C. sitting as a deputy judge.
s. 21, see *C.B. (A Minor) (Blood Tests), Re* [1994] 2 F.L.R. 762, Wall J.; *E. (Parental Responsibility: Blood Tests), Re* [1995] 1 F.L.R. 392, C.A.; *G. (A Minor) (Blood Test), Re* [1994] 1 F.L.R. 495, M. Horowitz, Q.C.; *C.G. (A Minor) (Blood Tests), Re* [1994] 2 F.C.R. 889, Michael Horowitz, Q.C. sitting as a deputy judge.
s. 23, see *C.B. (A Minor) (Blood Tests), Re* [1994] 2 F.L.R. 762, Wall J.

48. Post Office Act 1969.
s. 3, C.: 1995, c. 21, sch. 14.
s. 7, amended: 1995, c. 45, sch. 4.
s. 86, amended: 1994, c. 39, sch. 13 (S.); 1995, c. 17, sch. 1.
sch. 9, repealed in pt.: 1995, c. 44, sch. 1.

54. Children and Young Persons Act 1969.
see *W. (Minors), Re* (95/5739/F; 95/0390/F; 95/0391/F), July 19, 1995, C.A.

CAP.

1969—cont.

54. Children and Young Persons Act 1969—*cont.*
ss. 1, 2, see *X. (Minors)* v. *Bedfordshire County Council* [1995] 3 W.L.R. 152, H.L.
s. 25, amended and repealed in pt.: order 95/756.
s. 32, amended: 1995, c. 16, s. 2; order 95/756.
sch. 5, repealed in pt.: 1995, c. 36, schs. 4 (S.), 5 (S.).

57. Employers' Liability (Compulsory Insurance) Act 1969.
s. 1, regs. 94/3301.
s. 1, amended: regs. 95/738.
s. 1, see *Richardson* v. *Pitt-Stanley* [1995] 2 W.L.R. 26, C.A.
s. 2, repealed: regs. 95/738.
s. 3, amended: 1994, c. 39, sch. 13 (S.); 1995, c. 25, sch. 10.
s. 4, amended: regs. 95/738.
s. 5, 1995, c. 40, sch. 2 (S.).
s. 5, see *Richardson* v. *Pitt-Stanley* [1995] 2 W.L.R. 26, C.A.
s. 5A, added: regs. 95/738.
s. 6, regs. 94/3301.

1970

2. Conveyancing and Feudal Reform (Scotland) Act 1970.
s. 2, see *McCarthy & Stone (Developments)* v. *Smith*, 1995 S.L.T. (Lands Tr.) 19.
ss. 9, 53, sch. 2 see *Bennett* v. *Beneficial Bank* (O.H.), 1995 S.C.L.R. 284.

6. Rural Water Supplies and Sewerage (Scotland) Act 1970.
repealed: 1994, c. 39, sch. 14.

9. Taxes Management Act 1970.
s. 7, amended: 1995, c. 4, ss. 103, 115.
s. 8, amended: 1995, c. 4, s. 104.
s. 8A, amended: 1995, c. 4, ss. 103, 104.
s. 9, amended: 1995, c. 4, ss. 104, 115.
s. 9, repealed in pt.: 1995, c. 4, sch. 29.
s. 10, see *Earlspring Properties* v. *Guest* [1995] S.T.C. 479, C.A.
s. 11A, repealed in pt.: 1995, c. 4, sch. 29.
s. 11A, amended: 1995, c. 4, s. 115.
s. 11AA, amended: 1995, c. 4, s. 104.
s. 12AA, amended: 1995, c. 4, ss. 104, 115.
s. 12AB, amended: 1995, c. 4, s. 104.
s. 12B, repealed in pt.: 1995, c. 4, sch. 29.
s. 12B, amended: 1995, c. 4, s. 105.
s. 13, see *Fawcett* v. *Special Commissioners and Lancaster Farmers Auction Mart Co.* [1995] STC 61, Rattee J.
s. 15, substituted: 1995, c. 4, s. 106.
s. 20C, see *R.* v. *Hunt* [1995] STC 819, C.A.
s. 20D, amended: 1995, c. 38, sch. 1.

CAP.

1970—cont.

9. Taxes Management Act 1970—*cont.*
s. 27, amended: 1995, c. 4, sch. 17.
s. 30B, amended: 1995, c. 4, s. 115.
s. 31, amended: 1995, c. 4, sch. 17.
s. 33, amended: regs. 95/352.
s. 42, repealed in pt.: 1995, c. 4, sch. 29.
s. 42, amended: 1995, c. 4, s. 107.
s. 43, amended: regs. 95/352.
s. 49, see *R.* v. *Hastings and Bexhill General Commissioners and Inland Revenue Commissioners, ex p. Goodacre* [1994] S.T.C. 799, Schiemann J.
s. 50, see *Cassell* v. *Crutchfield* [1995] STC 663, Blackburne J.
s. 51, see *Khan* v. *Newport General Commissioners and I.R.C.* [1994] S.T.C. 972, Knox J.; *Stoll* v. *High Wycombe General Commissioners and I.R.C.* [1995] STC 91, Harman J.
s. 53, see *Stoll* v. *High Wycombe General Commissioners and I.R.C.* [1995] STC 91, Harman J.
s. 56, see *Sutherland* v. *Gustar (Inspector of Taxes)* [1994] 3 W.L.R. 735, C.A.; *Esslemont* v. *Marshall (Inspector of Taxes)* [1994] S.T.C. 813, Judge Paul Baker, Q.C.
s. 58, see *I.R.C.* v. *McGuckian*; *McGuckian* v. *I.R.C.* [1994] S.T.C. 888, C.A.N.I.
s. 59A, amended: 1995, c. 4, s. 108, sch. 17.
s. 59B, amended: 1995, c. 4, s. 115.
s. 59C, amended: 1995, c. 4, s. 109.
s. 61, regs. 95/2151.
s. 67, amended: 1995, c. 4, s. 156.
ss. 78–85, repealed: 1995, c. 4, sch. 29.
s. 86, substituted: 1995, c. 4, s. 110.
s. 86, see *Billingham (Inspector of Taxes)* v. *Myers* [1994] S.T.C. 1016, Knox J.
s. 87A, amended: 1995, c. 4, sch. 24.
s. 88, see *Billingham (Inspector of Taxes)* v. *Myers* [1994] S.T.C. 1016, Knox J.; *Earlspring Properties* v. *Guest* [1995] S.T.C. 479, C.A.
s. 91, amended: 1995, c. 4, sch. 24.
s. 98, amended: 1995, c. 4, ss. 57, 71, 73, 78, 97, schs. 8, 17.
s. 100B, amended: 1995, c. 4, s. 115.
s. 103A, amended: 1995, c. 4, s. 115.
s. 107A, added: 1995, c. 4, s. 103.
s. 109, see *Earlspring Properties* v. *Guest* [1995] S.T.C. 479, C.A.
s. 115, see *Sinclair* v. *I.R.C.* [1995] 65 TC 94, W.A. Blackburne, Q.C.
s. 115A, added: 1995, c. 4, sch. 28.
s. 118, amended: 1995, c. 4, s. 103.
ss. 181, 183, 187, 188, see *Allan* v. *I.R.C.*, 1995 S.L.T. 771.
s. 393, see *R.* v. *I.R.C., ex p. Unilever* [1994] S.T.C. 841, MacPherson of Cluny J.

CAP.

1970—cont.

9. Taxes Management Act 1970—*cont.*
s. 432, amended: 1995, c. 4, sch. 8.
s. 434, amended: 1995, c. 4, sch. 8.
s. 436, amended: 1995, c. 4, sch. 8.
sch. 1A, amended: 1995, c. 4, sch. 17.
sch. 3A, added: 1995, c. 4, sch. 28.

10. Income and Corporation Taxes Act 1970.
s. 130, see *Vodafone Cellular* v. *Shaw* [1995] S.T.C. 353, Jacob J.
s. 247, see *Kelsall* v. *Stipplechoice* [1995] S.T.C. 681, C.A.
s. 267A, amended: regs. 95/171.
s. 273, see *NAP Holdings U.K.* v. *Whittles (Inspector of Taxes)*, *The Times*, November 22, 1994, H.L.
s. 286, see *Earlspring Properties* v. *Guest* [1995] S.T.C. 479, C.A.

27. Fishing Vessels (Safety Provisions) Act 1970.
s. 1, repealed: 1995, c. 21, sch. 12.
s. 2, repealed in pt.: 1995, c. 21, sch. 12; regs. 95/1210.
ss. 3–5, 7, 9–11, repealed: 1995, c. 21, sch. 12.

30. Conservation of Seals Act 1970.
s. 5, 1995, c. 40, sch. 2 (S.).

31. Administration of Justice Act 1970.
s. 36, see *Tipton* v. *Coseley Building Society* [1994] EGCS 120, C.A.; *Abbey National* v. *Mewton*, July 12, 1995, C.A.; *National Provincial Building Society* v. *Ahmed* (CCRTF 94/1635/E), May 5, 1995, C.A.; *Abbey National Mortgages* v. *Bernard* [1995] NPC 118, C.A.
s. 40, see *North Yorkshire Trading Standards Department* v. *Williams*, *The Times*, November 22, 1994, D.C.
s. 44A, added: 1995, c. 42, s. 1.
sch. 4, amended: 1995, c. 26, sch. 5.

33. Chronically Sick and Disabled Persons Act 1970.
s. 16, repealed: 1995, c. 50, sch. 7.

35. Conveyancing and Feudal Reform (Scotland) Act 1970.
s. 19, see *Bank of Scotland* v. *Flett* (Sh.Ct.), 1995 S.C.L.R. 591.
s. 44, repealed: 1995, c. 7, sch. 5.
schs. 2, 4, 5, 9, amended: 1995, c. 7, sch. 4.

36. Merchant Shipping Act 1970.
Commencement order: 95/965.
Commencement order: 95/1426.
s. 1, repealed: 1995, c. 21, sch. 12.
s. 1, see *Hellyer Brothers* v. *Atkinson and Dickinson* [1994] IRLR 88, C.A.
s. 1, C.: 1995, c. 12, sch. 14.
s. 2, repealed: 1995, c. 21, sch. 12.
s. 2, C.: 1995, c. 12, sch. 14.
s. 3, repealed: 1995, c. 21, sch. 12.
s. 3, C.: 1995, c. 12, sch. 14.
s. 4, repealed: 1995, c. 21, sch. 12.
s. 4, C.: 1995, c. 12, sch. 14.

CAP.

1970—cont.

36. Merchant Shipping Act 1970—*cont.*
s. 5, repealed: 1995, c. 21, sch. 12.
s. 5, C.: 1995, c. 12, sch. 14.
s. 7, repealed: 1995, c. 21, sch. 12.
s. 7, C.: 1995, c. 12, sch. 14.
s. 8, repealed: 1995, c. 21, sch. 12.
s. 8, C.: 1995, c. 12, sch. 14.
s. 9, repealed: 1995, c. 21, sch. 12.
s. 9, C.: 1995, c. 12, sch. 14.
s. 10, repealed: 1995, c. 21, sch. 12.
s. 10, C.: 1995, c. 12, sch. 14.
s. 11, repealed: 1995, c. 21, sch. 12.
s. 11, C.: 1995, c. 12, sch. 14.
s. 12, repealed: 1995, c. 21, sch. 12.
s. 12, C.: 1995, c. 12, sch. 14.
s. 13, repealed: 1995, c. 21, sch. 12.
s. 13, C.: 1995, c. 12, sch. 14.
s. 14, repealed: 1995, c. 21, sch. 12.
s. 14, C.: 1995, c. 12, sch. 14.
s. 15, repealed: 1995, c. 21, sch. 12.
s. 15, C.: 1995, c. 12, sch. 14.
s. 16, repealed: 1995, c. 21, sch. 12.
s. 16, C.: 1995, c. 12, sch. 14.
s. 17, repealed: 1995, c. 21, sch. 12.
s. 17, C.: 1995, c. 12, sch. 14.
s. 18, repealed: 1995, c. 21, sch. 12.
s. 18, C.: 1995, c. 12, sch. 14.
s. 20, repealed: 1995, c. 21, sch. 12.
s. 20, C.: 1995, c. 12, sch. 14.
s. 22, repealed: 1995, c. 21, sch. 12.
s. 22, C.: 1995, c. 12, sch. 14.
s. 25, repealed: 1995, c. 21, sch. 12.
s. 25, C.: 1995, c. 12, sch. 14.
s. 26, repealed: 1995, c. 21, sch. 12.
s. 26, C.: 1995, c. 12, sch. 14.
s. 27, repealed: 1995, c. 21, sch. 12.
s. 27, C.: 1995, c. 12, sch. 14.
s. 28, repealed: 1995, c. 21, sch. 12.
s. 30, repealed: 1995, c. 21, sch. 12.
s. 30, C.: 1995, c. 21, sch. 14.
s. 32, repealed: 1995, c. 21, sch. 12.
s. 32, C.: 1995, c. 21, sch. 14.
s. 33, repealed: 1995, c. 21, sch. 12.
s. 33, C.: 1995, c. 21, sch. 14.
s. 39, repealed: 1995, c. 21, sch. 12.
s. 39, C.: 1995, c. 21, sch. 14.
s. 40, repealed: 1995, c. 21, sch. 12.
s. 40, C.: 1995, c. 21, sch. 14.
s. 41, repealed: 1995, c. 21, sch. 12.
s. 41, C.: 1995, c.21, sch. 14.
s. 43, regs. 95/1427, 1429.
s. 43, repealed: 1995, c. 21, sch. 12.
s. 43, C.: 1995, c. 21, sch. 14.
s. 44, repealed: 1995, c. 21, sch. 12.
s. 44, C.: 1995, c. 21, sch. 14.
s. 45, repealed: 1995, c. 21, sch. 12.
s. 45, C.: 1995, c. 21, sch. 14.
s. 46, repealed: 1995, c. 21, sch. 12.
s. 46, C.: 1995, c. 21, sch. 14.
s. 47, repealed: 1995, c. 21, sch. 12.
s. 47, C.: 1995, c. 21, sch. 14.
s. 48, repealed: 1995, c. 21, sch. 12.
s. 48, C.: 1995, c. 21, sch. 14.

CAP.

1970—cont.

36. Merchant Shipping Act 1970—*cont.*
s. 49, repealed: 1995, c. 21, sch. 12.
s. 49, C.: 1995, c. 21, sch. 14.
s. 50, repealed: 1995, c. 21, sch. 12.
s. 50, C.: 1995, c. 21, sch. 14.
s. 51, regs. 95/972.
s. 51, repealed: 1995, c. 21, sch. 12.
s. 51, C.: 1995, c. 21, sch. 14.
s. 52, repealed: 1995, c. 21, sch. 12.
s. 52, C.: 1995, c. 21, sch. 14.
s. 53, repealed: 1995, c. 21, sch. 12.
s. 53, C.: 1995, c. 21, sch. 14.
s. 54, repealed: 1995, c. 21, sch. 12.
s. 56, repealed: 1995, c. 21, sch. 12.
s. 56, C.: 1995, c. 21, sch. 14.
s. 57, repealed: 1995, c. 21, sch. 12.
s. 57, C.: 1995, c. 21, sch. 14.
s. 58, repealed: 1995, c. 21, sch. 12.
s. 58, C.: 1995, c. 21, sch. 14.
s. 59, repealed: 1995, c. 21, sch. 12.
s. 59, C.: 1995, c. 21, sch. 14.
s. 60, repealed: 1995, c. 21, sch. 12.
s. 60, C.: 1995, c. 21, sch. 14.
s. 61, repealed: 1995, c. 21, sch. 12.
s. 61, C.: 1995, c. 21, sch. 14.
s. 62, repealed: 1995, c. 21, sch. 12.
s. 62, C.: 1995, c. 21, sch. 14.
s. 63, repealed: 1995, c. 21, sch. 12.
s. 63, C.: 1995, c. 21, sch. 14.
s. 64, repealed: 1995, c. 21, sch. 12.
s. 64, C.: 1995, c. 21, sch. 14.
s. 67, repealed: 1995, c. 21, sch. 12.
s. 67, C.: 1995, c. 21, sch. 14.
s. 68, repealed: 1995, c. 21, sch. 12.
s. 68, C.: 1995, c. 21, sch. 14.
s. 69, repealed: 1995, c. 21, sch. 12.
s. 69, C.: 1995, c. 21, sch. 14.
s. 70, repealed: 1995, c. 21, sch. 12.
s. 70, C.: 1995, c. 21, sch. 14.
s. 71, regs. 95/1900.
s. 71, repealed: 1995, c. 21, sch. 12.
s. 71, C.: 1995, c. 21, sch. 14.
s. 72, repealed: 1995, c. 21, sch. 12.
s. 72, C.: 1995, c. 21, sch. 14.
s. 74, repealed: 1995, c. 21, sch. 12.
s. 74, C.: 1995, c. 21, sch.14.
s. 75, repealed: 1995, c. 21, sch. 12.
s. 75A, C.: 1995, c. 21, sch. 14.
s. 76, repealed: 1995, c. 21, sch. 12.
s. 76, C.: 1995, c. 21, sch. 14.
s. 77, repealed: 1995, c. 21, sch. 12.
s. 77, C.: 1995, c. 21, sch. 14.
s. 78, repealed: 1995, c. 21, sch. 12.
s. 78, C.: 1995, c. 21, sch. 14.
s. 79, repealed: 1995, c. 21, sch. 12.
s. 79, C.: 1995, c. 21, sch. 14.
s. 80, repealed: 1995, c. 21, sch. 12.
s. 81, repealed: 1995, c. 21, sch. 12.
s. 81, C.: 1995, c. 21, sch. 14.
s. 82, repealed: 1995, c. 21, sch. 12.
s. 82, C.: 1995, c. 21, sch. 14.
s. 83, repealed: 1995, c. 21, sch. 12.
s. 83, C.: 1995, c. 21, sch. 14.

CAP.

1970—cont.

36. Merchant Shipping Act 1970—*cont.*
s. 86, repealed: 1995, c. 21, sch. 12.
s. 86, C.: 1995, c. 21, sch. 14.
s. 88, repealed: 1995, c. 21, sch. 12.
s. 91, repealed: 1995, c. 21, sch. 12.
s. 92, regs. 95/1427.
s. 95, repealed: 1995, c. 21, sch. 12.
s. 95, C.: 1995, c. 21, sch. 14.
s. 96, repealed: 1995, c. 21, sch. 12.
s. 96, C.: 1995, c. 21, sch. 14.
s. 97, repealed: 1995, c. 21, sch. 12.
s. 97, C.: 1995, c. 21, sch. 14.
s. 98, repealed: 1995, c. 21, sch. 12.
s. 99, regs. 95/972, 1429.
s. 99, repealed: 1995, c. 21, sch. 12.
s. 99, C.: 1995, c. 21, sch. 14.
s. 100, repealed: 1995, c. 21, sch. 12.
s. 101, order 95/965; regs. 95/972.
s. 101, repealed: 1995, c. 21, sch. 12.
sch. 1, repealed: 1995, c. 21, sch. 12.
sch. 2, repealed: 1995, c. 21, sch. 12.
sch. 3, repealed: 1995, c. 21, sch. 12.
sch. 3, C.: 1995, c. 21, sch. 14.
sch. 4, repealed: 1995, c. 21, sch. 14.
sch. 5, repealed: 1995, c. 21, sch. 12.

39. Local Authorities (Goods and Services) Act 1970.
s. 1, amended: 1994, c. 39, sch. 13 (S.).

40. Agriculture Act 1970.
ss. 28, 29, schemes 94/3002; 95/890.
s. 66, regs. 94/502, 2510; 95/16, 49.
s. 66, amended: regs. 95/1412.
s. 67, amended: 1994, c. 39, sch. 13 (S.).
s. 68, regs. 94/502, 2510; 95/49, 1412.
s. 69, regs. 94/502, 2510; 95/16, 49.
s. 69, amended: regs. 95/1412.
s. 70, regs. 94/502, 2510; 95/16, 49, 1412.
s. 73, regs. 94/502.
s. 74, regs. 94/502, 2510; 95/16, 49, 1412.
s. 74A, regs. 94/502, 2510; 95/16, 49, 1412.
s. 82, amended: regs. 95/1412.
s. 84, regs. 94/502, 2510; 95/49, 1412.
s. 86, regs. 94/502; 95/49.
s. 92, repealed in pt.: 1995, c. 25, sch. 24.
s. 92, amended: 1994, c. 39, sch. 13 (S.); 1995, c. 25, sch. 22.
s. 94, amended: 1994, c. 39, sch. 13 (S.); 1995, c. 25, sch. 22.
s. 98, amended: 1995, c. 25, sch. 22.

41. Equal Pay Act 1970.
s. 1, see *Ratcliffe* v. *North Yorkshire County Council* [1995] IRLR 439, H.L.
s. 6, amended: 1995, c. 26, s. 66.

42. Local Authorities Social Services Act 1970.
s. 7B, see *R.* v. *Avon County Council, ex p. M.* [1994] 2 F.L.R. 1006, Henry J.
s. 7D, see *R.* v. *Brent London Borough, ex p. S.* [1994] 1 FLR 203, C.A.; *R.* v. *Devon County Council, ex p. Baker*; *R.* v. *Durham County Council, ex p. Curtis* [1995] 1 All E.R. 73, C.A.

CAP.

1970—cont.

42. Local Authorities Social Services Act 1970—*cont.*
s. 7E, see *R.* v. *Secretary of State for Health, ex p. Alcohol Recovery Project* [1993] C.O.D. 344, D.C.
sch. 1, amended: 1995, c. 12, s. 1.

44. Chronically Sick and Disabled Persons Act 1970.
s. 2, see *R.* v. *Gloucestershire County Council, ex p. Mahfood*, *The Times*, June 21, 1995, D.C.; *R.* v. *Bexley London Borough Council, ex p. B.*, July 31, 1995, Latham J.
s. 18, amended: 1995, c. 36, sch. 4 (S.).
s. 21, amended: 1994, c. 39, s. 13(S.).
s. 29, amended: 1995, c. 36, sch. 4 (S.).

50. Fiji Independence Act 1970.
schs. 1, 2, repealed in pt.: 1995, c. 21, sch. 12.

1971

3. Guardianship of Minors Act 1971.
s. 11B, see *B.* v. *B. (Periodical Payments: Transitional Provisions)* [1995] 1 FLR 459, Douglas Brown J.

10. Vehicles (Excise) Act 1971.
s. 26, see *R.* v. *Macrae* [1994] Crim.L.R. 363, C.A.

19. Carriage of Goods by Sea Act 1971.
s. 1, amended: 1995, c. 21, sch. 13.
s. 1A, added: 1995, c. 21, sch. 13.

22. Animals Act 1971.
ss. 2, 11, see *Hunt* v. *Wallis* [1994] P.I.Q.R. P128, Pill J.

32. Attachment of Earnings Act 1971.
s. 24, amended: 1995, c. 12, sch. 13.
s. 27, C.: 1995, c. 21, sch. 14.
sch. 2, amended: 1995, c. 26, sch. 5.

33. Armed Forces Act 1971.
s. 26, repealed: 1995, c. 38, sch. 2.

38. Misuse of Drugs Act 1971.
see *The Queen* v. *Secretary of State for the Home Department, ex p. Evans Medical* (C–324/95), March 28, 1995, ECJ.
s. 5, see *Lockhart* v. *Hardie*, 1994 S.C.C.R. 722.
s. 7, regs. 95/305, 2048.
s. 10, regs. 95/305, 2048.
s. 23, see *Gavin* v. *Normand*, 1995 S.C.C.R. 209; *Black (Michael David)* v. *D.P.P.* (CO 877–95), May 11, 1995, Mitchell J.
s. 30, regs. 95/506.
s. 31, regs. 95/305, 506, 3048.
s. 37, regs. 95/506.
s. 37, see *R.* v. *Harris, The Times*, August 3, 1995, C.A.
sch. 4, amended: 1995, c. 40, schs. 1, 2.

40. Fire Precautions Act 1971.
s. 40, repealed in pt.: 1995, c. 17, sch. 3.
s. 43, amended: 1994, c. 39, sch. 13 (S.).

CAP.

1971—cont.

41. Highways Act 1971.
s. 18, see *CIN Properties* v. *Rawlins (Martin)*, February 1, 1995, C.A.

48. Criminal Damage Act 1971.
s. 1, see *R.* v. *Webster*; *R.* v. *Warwick* [1995] 2 All E.R. 168, C.A.
s. 5, see *Johnson* v. *D.P.P.* [1994] Crim. L.R. 673, D.C.

49. Rural Water Supplies and Sewerage Act 1971.
repealed: 1994, c. 39, sch. 14 (S.).

56. Pensions (Increase) Act 1971.
s. 1, amended: regs. 95/238.
s. 3, repealed in pt.: 1995, c. 26, sch. 7.
s. 3, amended: 1995, c. 26, s. 171.
s. 5, regs. 95/1680, 1681, 1682, 1683.
ss. 6, 8, 9, amended: regs. 95/238.
ss. 11, 11A, 12, 13, regs. 95/238.
s. 17, amended: regs. 95/238.

58. Sheriff Courts (Scotland) Act 1971.
s. 12, see *Stewart* v. *Secretary of State for Scotland* (O.H.), 1995 S.L.T. 895.
s. 32, Act of Sederunt 94/2805, 3066.
s. 32, amended: 1995, c. 36, sch. 4.
s. 37, amended: 1995, c. 36, sch. 4.
ss. 38, 45, see *Thomson* v. *Proctor* (Sh.Ct.), 1995 S.C.L.R. 648.

59. Merchant Shipping (Oil Pollution) Act 1971.
repealed: 1995, c. 21, sch. 12.
s. 1, C.: 1995, c. 21, sch. 14.
s. 1A, C.: 1995, c. 21, sch. 14.
s. 2, C.: 1995, c. 21, sch. 14.
s. 3, C.: 1995, c. 21, sch. 14.
s. 4, C.: 1995, c. 21, sch. 14.
s. 5, C.: 1995, c. 21, sch. 14.
s. 6, C.: 1995, c. 21, sch. 14.
s. 7, C.: 1995, c. 21, sch. 14.
s. 8, C.: 1995, c. 21, sch. 14.
s. 9, C.: 1995, c. 21, sch. 14.
s. 10, C.: 1995, c. 21, sch. 14.
s. 11, C.: 1995, c. 21, sch. 14.
s. 12, C.: 1995, c. 21, sch. 14.
s. 13, C.: 1995, c. 21, sch. 14.
s. 14, C.: 1995, c. 21, sch. 14.
s. 15, C.: 1995, c. 21, sch. 14.
s. 16, C.: 1995, c. 21, sch. 14.
s. 17, C.: 1995, c. 21, sch. 14.
s. 19, C.: 1995, c. 21, sch. 14.
s. 19A, C.: 1995, c. 21, sch. 14.
s. 20, C.: 1995, c. 21, sch. 14.
s. 23, C.: 1995, c. 21, sch. 14.
s. 24, C.: 1995, c. 21, sch. 14.
s. 26, C.: 1995, c. 21, sch. 14.
s. 27, C.: 1995, c. 21, sch. 14.
s. 29, C.: 1995, c. 21, sch. 14.
s. 32, C.: 1995, c. 21, sch. 14.

60. Prevention of Oil Pollution Act 1971.
s. 1, C.: 1995, c. 21, sch. 14.
s. 1A, C.: 1995, c. 21, sch. 14.

CAP.

1971—cont.

60. Prevention of Oil Pollution Act 1971—*cont.*
s. 2, repealed in pt.: 1995, c. 21, sch. 12.
s. 2, C.: 1995, c. 21, sch. 14.
s. 2A, C.: 1995, c. 21, sch. 14.
s. 3, C.: 1995, c. 21, sch. 14.
s. 3A, C.: 1995, c. 21, sch. 14.
s. 4, C.: 1995, c. 21, sch. 14.
s. 5, repealed: 1995, c. 21, sch. 12.
s. 5, C.: 1995, c. 21, sch. 14.
s. 6, repealed in pt.: 1995, c. 21, sch. 12.
s. 6, C.: 1995, c. 21, sch. 14.
s. 7, repealed: 1995, c. 21, sch.12.
s. 7, C.: 1995, c. 21, sch. 14.
s. 8, repealed in pt.: 1995, c. 21, sch. 12.
s. 8, C.: 1995, c. 21, sch. 14.
s. 9, C.: 1995, c. 21, sch. 14.
s. 10, repealed: 1995, c. 21, sch. 12.
s. 10, C.: 1995, c. 21, sch. 14.
s. 11, repealed in pt.: 1995, c. 21, sch. 12.
s. 11, C.: 1995, c. 21, sch. 14.
s. 11A, added: 1995, c. 25, sch. 22.
s. 12, repealed: 1995, c. 21, sch. 12.
s. 12, C.: 1995, c. 21, sch. 14.
s. 13, repealed: 1995, c. 21, sch. 12.
s. 13, C.: 1995, c. 21, sch. 14.
s. 14, repealed: 1995, c. 21, sch. 12.
s. 14, C.: 1995, c. 21, sch. 14.
s. 15, repealed: 1995, c. 21, sch. 12.
s. 15, C.: 1995, c. 21, sch. 14.
s. 16, repealed: 1995, c. 21, sch. 12.
s. 16, C.: 1995, c. 21, sch. 14.
s. 17, repealed: 1995, c. 21, sch. 12.
s. 18, repealed in pt.: 1995, c. 21, sch. 12.
s. 18, C.: 1995, c. 21, sch. 14.
s. 19, repealed in pt.: 1995, c. 21, sch. 12.
s. 19, C.: 1995, c. 21, sch. 14.
s. 19A, repealed: 1995, c. 21, sch. 12.
s. 20, repealed: 1995, c. 21, sch. 12.
s. 20, C.: 1995, c. 21, sch. 14.
s. 21, repealed: 1995, c. 21, sch. 12.
s. 23, repealed in pt.: 1995, c. 21, sch. 12.
s. 24, repealed: 1995, c. 21, sch. 12.
s. 25, repealed in pt.: 1995, c. 21, sch. 12.
s. 27, repealed in pt.: 1995, c. 21, sch. 12.
s. 27, C.: 1995, c. 21, sch. 14.
s. 29, repealed in pt.: 1995, c. 21, sch. 12.
s. 30, repealed in pt.: 1995, c. 21, sch. 12.
s. 30, C.: 1995, c. 21, sch. 14.

61. Mineral Workings (Offshore Installations) Act 1971.
s. 1, repealed: regs. 95/738.
s. 3, repealed in pt.: regs. 95/738.
ss. 4, 5, repealed: regs. 95/738.
ss. 9, 11, 12, repealed in pt.: regs. 95/738.

68. Finance Act 1971.
s. 44, see *Melluish (Inspector of Taxes)* v. *BMI (No. 3)*, *The Times*, October 16, 1995, H.L.

69. Medicines Act 1971.
s. 1, regs. 95/1116.
s. 1, amended: regs. 94/3144.

CAP.

1971—cont.

69. Medicines Act 1971—*cont.*
ss. 3, 4, 7, 23, 58, 58A, 59–61, 92, 103, 107–116, 118–119, 121–127, 129, schs. 3, 5–7, amended: regs. 94/3144.

71. Supplementary Benefits Act 1971.
s. 30, repealed: 1995, c. 18, s. 30.
sch. 5, repealed: 1995, c. 18, s. 30.

77. Immigration Act 1971.
see *R.* v. *Secretary of State for the Home Department, ex p. Rizrani (Dyleman)* (CO 195/95), March 9, 1995, McCullough J.; *R.* v. *Secretary of State for the Home Department, ex p. Fawehinmi*, January 23, 1995; Dyson J.; *R.* v. *Secretary of State for the Home Department, ex p. T.* [1995] 1 FLR 293, C.A.
s. 1, see *R.* v. *Immigration Appeal Tribunal, ex p. Sunsara (Nargis)* [1995] Imm.A.R. 15, Ognall J.; *Miah (Nazmul)* v. *Secretary of State for the Home Department* [1995] Imm.A.R. 24, C.A.
s. 3, see *Social Security Decision No. R(IS) 9/94*; *Ofori (Michael)* v. *Secretary of State for the Home Department* [1995] Imm.A.R. 34, C.A.; *R.* v. *Secretary of State for the Home Department, ex p. Payne (Harry Oluwagbohunmi)* [1995] Imm.A.R. 48, Sedley J.; *Secretary of State for the Home Department, ex p. Kazmi (Syed Majid)* [1995] Imm.A.R. 74, Dyson J.; *Secretary of State for the Home Department* v. *Yasin (Mohammed)* [1995] Imm.A.R. 118, C.A.; *R.* v. *Secretary of State for the Home Department, ex p. Ekewuba (Napolean Chibuike)* [1995] Imm.A.R. 89, Harrison J.; *R.* v. *Immigration Appeal Tribunal, ex p. Cheung (Wai Kwan)* [1995] Imm.A.R. 104, Popplewell J.; *R.* v. *Secretary of State for the Home Department, ex p. Odaro* (CO/669/95), March 16, 1995, D.C.; *Tongo (Bridget)* v. *Secretary of State for the Home Department* [1995] Imm.A.R. 109, C.A.; *R.* v. *Secretary of State for the Home Department, ex p. Ofori* [1994] A.R. 581, Macpherson J.
s. 4, see *Secretary of State for the Home Department, ex p. Kazmi (Syed Majid)* [1995] Imm.A.R. 74, Dyson J.; *Abidi* v. *Secretary of State for the Home Department* [1994] Imm.A.R. 532, C.A.
s. 8, repealed in pt.: 1995, c. 44, sch. 1.
s. 8, see *Abidi* v. *Secretary of State for the Home Department* [1994] Imm.A.R. 532, C.A.
s. 13, see *Secretary of State for the Home Department, ex p. Kazmi (Syed Majid)* [1995] Imm.A.R. 74, Dyson J.

CAP.

1971—cont.

77. Immigration Act 1971—*cont.*
s. 15, see *Secretary of State for the Home Department* v. *Yasin (Mohammed)* [1995] Imm.A.R. 118, C.A.
s. 19, see *R.* v. *Secretary of State for the Home Department, ex p. Roberts* [1994] Imm.A.R. 504, Popplewell J.; *R.* v. *Immigration Appeal Tribunal, exp. Nalongo* [1994] Imm.A.R. 536, Macpherson J.; *R.* v. *Immigration Appeal Tribunal, ex p. Singh* [1994] Imm.A.R. 513, Auld J.
s. 20, see *Gnanavarathan (Pitchaippah)* v. *Special Ajudicator*; *Norbert (Sebastian)* v. *Same* [1995] Imm.A.R. 64, C.A.
s. 21, see *R.* v. *Immigration Appeal Tribunal, ex p. Ali (Omar Mohammed)* [1995] Imm.A.R. 45, Sedley J.
s. 33, sch. 2, see *R.* v. *Secretary of State for the Home Department, ex p. Khan*; *Same* v. *Same, ex p. Virk*; *Same* v. *Same, ex p. Singh*; *Same* v. *Same, ex p. Taggar*; *sub nom. R.* v. *Immigration Officer, ex p. Khan, The Times*, January 25, 1995, Dyson J.
sch. 2, see *R.* v. *Secretary of State for the Home Department, ex p. Virk, The Times*, October 13, 1995, D.C.; *Odishu* v. *Immigration Appeal Tribunal* [1994] Imm.A.R. 475, C.A.
sch. 3, see *R.* v. *Ofori (Noble Julius)*; *R.* v. *Tackie (Nazar)* (1994) 99 Cr.App.R. 219, C.A.; *Mahmod, Re* [1994] C.O.D. 404, Laws J.; *Ali (Akin)* v. *Secretary of State for the Home Department* [1994] Imm.A.R. 489, C.A.

78. Town and Country Planning Act 1971.
ss. 22, 23, 25, 27, 29, 33, 34, see *Handoll* v. *Warner Goodman Streat (A Firm), The Times*, December 26, 1994, C.A.
s. 52, see *Williamson's Application, Re* [1994] 68 P.&C.R. 384, Lands Tribunal.
s. 53, see *Tidman* v. *Reading Borough Council* [1994] N.P.C. 136, Burton J.
s. 87, see *Handoll* v. *Warner Goodman Streat (A Firm), The Times*, December 26, 1994, C.A.
s. 89, see *R.* v. *Collett; Same* v. *Furminger; Same* v. *Nazari; Same* v. *Pope; Same* v. *Banbari* [1994] Crim.L.R. 607, C.A.

1972

6. Summer Time Act 1972.
s. 2, order 94/2798.

11. Superannuation Act 1972.
s. 1, order 95/1293.
s. 1, amended: 1995, c. 26, sch. 1.

CAP.

1972—cont.

11. Superannuation Act 1972—*cont.*
s. 7, regs. 94/3026, 3221; 95/214, 750 (S.), 900, 901, 963, 1019; 95/1497, 1985, 2249.
s. 9, regs. 94/2774, 2876, 2924; 95/1497, 2004.
s. 10, regs. 95/300, 365, 866.
s. 12, regs. 94/2774, 2876, 2924, 3026; 95/300, 365, 866, 901, 963, 1019, 1497, 1670, 2004.
s. 13, regs. 95/635 (S.), 637.
s. 17, repealed: 1995, c. 12, sch. 12.
s. 17, C.: 1995, c. 12, sch. 14.
s. 24, regs. 94/3025, 3068 (S.); 95/340 (S.), 750 (S.), 817, 840 (S.).
sch. 3, regs. 94/2774, 2876, 2924; 95/300, 866, 2004.

18. Maintenance Orders (Reciprocal Enforcement) Act 1972.
s. 2, amended: order 95/2709.
s. 3, repealed in pt.: S.R. 1995 No. 755.
s. 3, amended: S.R. 1995 No. 755.
s. 4, repealed in pt.: 1995, c. 36, sch. 5 (S.).
s. 5, substituted: order 95/2709.
s. 5, amended: S.R. 1995 No. 755.
s. 6, amended: order 95/2709.
s. 7, repealed in pt.: S.R. 1995 No. 755.
s. 7, see *McIntyre* v. *McIntyre* (Sh.Ct.), 1995 S.C.L.R. 765.
s. 8, amended: S.R. 1995 No. 755; order 95/2709.
s. 8, see *McIntyre* v. *McIntyre* (Sh.Ct.), 1995 S.C.L.R. 765.
s. 9, amended: S.R. 1995 No. 755; order 95/2709.
ss. 10, 11, amended: order 95/2709.
s. 12, substituted: order 95/2709.
ss. 13–16, amended: order 95/2709.
s. 17, repealed in pt.: S.R. 1995 No. 755.
s. 17, amended: S.R. 1995 No. 755.
s. 18, amended: S.R. 1995 No. 755.
s. 19, amended: order 95/2709.
s. 21, amended: order 95/2709.
s. 22, repealed in pt.: 1995, c. 3, sch.
s. 27B, amended: order 95/756.
s. 28C, substituted: S.R. 1995 No. 755.
s. 28D, added: S.R. 1995 No. 755.
s. 28E, added: S.R. 1995 No. 755.
s. 29, substituted: S.R. 1995 No. 755.
s. 29A, substituted: S.R. 1995 No. 755.
s. 29B, added: S.R. 1995 No. 755.
s. 30, repealed in pt.: S.R. 1995 No. 755.
s. 35A, substituted: S.R. 1995 No. 755.
s. 36, amended: S.R. 1995 No. 755.
s. 38A, repealed in pt.: S.R. 1995 No. 755.
s. 38A, amended: S.R. 1995 No. 755.
s. 40, order 95/2709.
sch. 1, amended: 1995, c. 35, sch. 2.

CAP.

1972—cont.

20. Road Traffic Act 1972.
sch. 7, C.: 1995, c. 23, sch. 8.

24. Social Work (Scotland) Act 1972.
repealed: 1995, c. 36, sch. 5.

27. Road Traffic (Foreign Vehicles) Act 1972.
s. 3, amended: 1995, c. 40, sch. 2 (S.).
s. 3, see *Glaverbvel SA* v. *British Coal Corp.* [1995] F.S.R. 254, C.A.
s. 4, amended: 1995, c. 23, sch. 7.
sch. 2, amended: 1995, c. 23, sch. 7.

30. Civil Evidence Act 1972.
s. 1, repealed: 1995, c. 38, sch. 2.
s. 2, repealed in pt.: 1995, c. 38, sch. 2.
s. 3, repealed in pt.: 1995, c. 38, sch. 2.
s. 5, amended: 1995, c. 38, sch. 1.
s. 6, repealed in pt.: 1995, c. 38, sch. 2.

38. Matrimonial Proceedings (Polygamous Marriages) Act 1972.
s. 2, amended: 1995, c. 42, sch.

42. Town and Country Planning (Amendment) Act 1972.
s. 10C, amended: 1994, c. 39, sch. 13 (S.).

48. Parliamentary and Other Pensions Act 1972.
s. 27, amended: 1995, c. 26, s. 170; regs. 95/1443.

49. Affiliation Proceedings (Amendment) Act 1972.
s. 2, S.R. 1995 No. 755.
s. 4, S.R. 1995 No. 755.

51. Administration of Justice (Scotland) Act 1972.
s. 1, see *Union Carbide Corporation* v. *B.P. Chemicals*, *The Times*, April 18, 1995.

52. Town and Country Planning (Scotland) Act 1972.
s. 4, repealed in pt.: 1994, c. 39, sch. 14.
s. 4, amended: 1994, c. 39, sch. 4.
s. 4A, added: 1994, c. 39, s. 33.
s. 5, repealed in pt.: 1994, c. 39, sch. 14.
s. 5, amended: 1994, c. 39, s. 33, sch. 4.
s. 6, amended: 1994, c. 39, sch. 4.
s. 6A, added: 1994, c. 39, sch. 4.
s. 7, amended: 1994, c. 39, sch. 4.
s. 8, repealed in pt.: 1994, c. 39, sch. 14.
s. 9, amended: 1994, c. 39, sch. 4.
s. 11, amended: 1995, c. 49, s. 3.
s. 15, repealed in pt.: 1994, c. 39, sch. 14.
s. 15, amended: 1994, c. 39, sch. 4.
s. 17, amended: 1994, c. 39, sch. 4.
s. 21, order 94/3293, 3294.
s. 21E, order 95/2044.
s. 22, order 94/3293.
s. 22, repealed in pt.: 1994, c. 39, sch. 14.
s. 24, order 94/3293.
s. 25, repealed in pt.: 1994, c. 39, sch. 14.
s. 26, order 94/3293.
s. 28, order 94/3293.
s. 28, repealed in pt.: 1994, c. 39, sch. 14.
s. 32, order 94/3293.

CAP.

1972—cont.

52. Town and Country Planning (Scotland) Act 1972—*cont.*
s. 32, repealed in pt.: 1994, c. 39, sch. 14.
s. 33, order 94/3293.
s. 34, order 94/3293.
s. 49G, repealed: 1994, c. 39, sch. 14.
ss. 50, 52, 56F, 56K, repealed in pt.: 1994, c. 39, sch. 14.
s. 61, repealed in pt.: order 95/2045.
s. 83B, see *Barn Properties* v. *Secretary of State for Scotland* (I.H.), 1995 S.C.L.R. 113.
s. 84A, repealed: 1994, c. 39, sch. 14.
ss. 84AA, 85, see *Barn Properties* v. *Secretary of State for Scotland* (I.H.), 1995 S.C.L.R. 113.
s. 87A, repealed in pt.: 1994, c. 39, sch. 14.
s. 102, repealed in pt.: 1994, c. 39, sch. 14.
s. 102, amended: 1994, c. 39, sch. 4.
s. 169, repealed in pt.: 1994, c. 39, sch. 14.
ss. 201, 202, amended: 1994, c. 39, sch. 4.
s. 229A, repealed in pt.: 1994, c. 39, sch. 14.
ss. 242, 243, amended: 1994, c. 39, sch. 4.
s. 251A, repealed: 1995, c. 25, s. 96, sch. 24.
ss. 254, 265, repealed in pt.: 1994, c. 39, sch. 14.
s. 273, order 94/3293; regs. 95/2043.
s. 275, regs. 95/2043.
s. 275, amended: 1994, c. 39, sch. 4.
sch. 4, 1994, c. 39, s. 33.
sch. 6A, regs. 95/2043.
sch. 6A, repealed in pt.: order 95/2045.
sch. 6A, amended: 1995, c. 49, s. 3.
sch. 7, repealed in pt.: order 95/2045.
sch. 7, amended: 1995, c. 25, sch. 22.
schs. 12–15, repealed: order 95/2045.
sch. 21, repealed in pt.: 1994, c. 39, sch. 14.

61. Land Charges Act 1972.
ss. 10, 16, 17, regs. 95/1355.

62. Agriculture (Miscellaneous Provisions) Act 1972.
s. 20, order 94/3094; 95/1358.

63. Industry Act 1972.
s. 12, amended: 1995, c. 12, sch. 13.

65. National Debt Act 1972.
s. 3, regs. 94/3277.
s. 11, regs. 95/1002.

66. Poisons Act 1972.
s. 8, 1995, c. 40, sch. 2 (S.).
s. 11, amended: 1994, c. 39, sch. 13 (S.).

68. European Communities Act 1972.
s. 1, order 95/265.
s. 1, see *Monckton* v. *Lord Advocate* (O.H.), 1995 S.L.T. 1201.
s. 1, amended: 1995, c. 1, s. 1.

CAP.

1972—cont.

68. European Communities Act 1972—*cont.*
s. 2, regs. 94/105 (corrected by regs. 94/899), 417, 452, 476, 486, 502, 672, 1056, 1291, 1292, 1293, 2286, 2287, 2326, 2349, 2448, 2716, 2740, 2741, 2782, 2783, 2842 (S.), 2853, 2867, 2894, 2914, 2919, 2986, 2987, 3051, 3076, 3080, 3083, 3085 (S.), 3096 (S.), 3098, 3099, 3100, 3101, 3102, 3117, 3119, 3129, 3130, 3131, 3132, 3133, 3142, 3144, 3159, 3246, 3247, 3260, 3270; 95/12, 14, 15, 22, 31, 33, 40, 46, 52, 60, 93, 100, 105, 113, 116, 122, 134, 144, 168, 172, 174, 183, 184, 201, 204, 226, 239, 245, 246, 254, 271, 275, 278, 305, 318, 357, 360, 371, 372, 381, 382, 396, 417, 428, 441, 484 (S.), 504, 539, 541, 615, 652, 731, 732, 799, 886, 887, 888, 904, 1151, 1159, 1186, 1215, 1217, 1290, 1412, 1424, 1428, 1429, 1430, 1434, 1442, 1444, 1445, 1446, 1447, 1481, 1483, 1486, 1513, 1541, 1544, 1576, 1618, 1619, 1648, 1671, 1708, 1802, 1804, 1907, 1947, 1948, 1970, 2043, 2095, 2195, 2202, 2258, 2321, 2357, 2370, 2825; orders 94/2867, 2986, 2987, 3003, 3017, 3276; 95/262, 288, 751, 768, 1029, 1038, 1159.
s. 2, see *R.* v. *Secretary of State for Employment, ex p. Seymour-Smith and Perez* [1994] IRLR 448, D.C.; *Biggs* v. *Somerset County Council* [1995] IRLR 452, E.A.T.; *R.* v. *Secretary of State for Employment, ex p. Seymour-Smith and Perez* [1995] IRLR 464, C.A.
s. 11, amended: 1995, c. 40, sch. 4 (S.).
s. 68, see *R.* v. *Knightsbridge Crown Court, ex p. O'Grady; Same* v. *Same, ex p. Gallagher* [1993] C.O.D. 456, D.C.

70. Local Government Act 1972.
orders 95/44, 536.
s. 2, order 95/600.
s. 2, amended: order 95/493.
s. 51, 95/536.
s. 55, order 95/3168.
s. 69, 95/536.
s. 74, amended: regs. 95/1748.
s. 79, amended: regs. 95/1948.
s. 80, amended: 1995, c. 25, sch. 10.
s. 89, amended: order 95/1769.
s. 101, order 95/600.
s. 101, repealed in pt.: 1995, c. 25, sch. 24.
s. 111, see *Morgan Grenfell & Co.* v. *Sutton London Borough Council, The Times*, March 23, 1995, Clarke J.; *Credit Suisse* v. *Waltham Forest London Borough Council* [1994] N.P.C. 137, Gatehouse J.
s. 113, amended: 1995, c. 17, sch. 1.

CAP.

1972—cont.

70. Local Government Act 1972—*cont.*
s. 120, see *R.* v. *Somerset County Council, ex p. Fewings*, *The Times*, March 23, 1995, C.A.; *R.* v. *Somerset County Council, ex p. Fewings* [1995] 1 W.L.R. 1037, C.A.
s. 137, order 95/651.
s. 137, amended: regs. 94/2825.
s. 148, amended: regs. 94/2825.
ss. 173, 175, regs. 94/553, 615.
s. 179, C.: 1995, c. 23, sch. 8.
s. 184, repealed in pt.: 1995, c. 25, sch. 24.
s. 184, amended: 1995, c. 25, sch. 10.
s. 219, amended: regs. 95/1748.
s. 223, repealed in pt.: 1995, c. 25, sch. 24.
s. 223, amended: 1995, c. 25, sch. 22.
s. 243, repealed in pt.: 1995, c. 44, sch. 1.
s. 261, amended: 1995, c. 17, sch. 1.
ss. 236–238, order 95/1063.
s. 250, order 95/1063.
s. 262, order 95/376.
s. 266, 95/536.
s. 270, regs. 94/615.
sch. 5, orders 94/2843; 95/151.
sch. 16, repealed in pt.: 1995, c. 25, sch. 24.
sch. 17, repealed in pt.: 1995, c. 25, sch. 24.
sch. 17, amended: order 95/187.

71. Criminal Justice Act 1972.
see *R.* v. *Basildon Justices, ex p. Holding and Barnes* [1994] RA 157, Schiemann J.
s. 3, regs. 94/3044.

1973

16. Education Act 1973.
s. 3, regs. 94/3044.

18. Matrimonial Causes Act 1973.
see *Thomas* v. *Thomas, The Independent*, May 4, 1995, C.A.
s. 1, see *Lawlor* v. *Lawlor* [1995] 1 F.C.R. 412, C.A.
s. 9, see *Manchanda* v. *Manchanda*, *The Times*, May 28, 1995, C.A.
s. 11, amended: 1995, c. 42, sch.
s. 16, see *P.* v. *P. (Ouster: Decree Nisi of Nullity)* [1994] 2 FLR 400, C.A.
s. 23, see *L.* v. *L. (Lump Sum: Interest)* [1994] 2 FLR 324, Ewbank J.; *T.* v. *S. (Financial Provision for Children)* [1994] 1 F.C.R. 743, Johnson J.; *Belcher* v. *Belcher* [1995] 2 F.C.R. 143, C.A.
s. 24, see *Brooks* v. *Brooks* [1995] 3 W.L.R. 141, H.L.
s. 25, see *F.* v. *F. (Divorce: Insolvency; Annulment of Bankruptcy Order)* [1994] 1 F.L.R. 358, Thorpe J.; *L.* v. *L. (Financial Provision)* [1994] 1 F.C.R. 134, Thorpe J.; *A.* v. *A. (Financial Provision: Conduct)* [1995] 1 F.L.R. 345,

CAP.

1973—cont.

18. Matrimonial Causes Act 1973—*cont.*
Thorpe J.; *B.* v. *M. (Child Support: Revocation of Order)* [1994] 1 F.L.R. 342, H.H.J. Bryant; *A.* v. *A. (A Minor: Financial Provision)* [1994] 1 F.L.R. 657, Ward J.; *S.* v. *S. (Financial Provision) (Post-Divorce Cohabitation)* [1994] F.L.R. 228, Douglas Brown J.; *Baker* v. *Baker* (95/0103/F), April 11, 1995, C.A.; *Perks* v. *Perks*, April 28, 1995, deputy District Judge Freeman, Wolverhampton County Ct.; *Van G.* v. *Van G. (Financial Provision: Millionaires' Defence)* [1995] 1 FLR 328, Ewbank J.
s. 25B–25D, added: 1995, c. 26, s. 166.
s. 27, see *R.* v. *Crewe and Nantwich Justices, ex p. Burton* [1993] C.O.D. 460, D.C.
s. 29, see *T.* v. *S. (Financial Provision for Children)* [1994] 1 F.C.R. 743, Johnson J.
s. 31, see *B.* v. *M. (Child Support: Revocation of Order)* [1994] 1 F.L.R. 342, H.H.J. Bryant.; *Richardson* v. *Richardson* (No. 2) [1994] 2 F.C.R. 826, Thorpe J.; *Cornick* v. *Cornick* [1994] 2 F.C.R. 1189, Hale J.; *Penrose* v. *Penrose* [1994] 2 F.C.R. 1167, C.A.
s. 37, see *B.* v. *B. (P. Intervening) (No. 2)* [1995] 1 F.L.R. 374, C.A.; *Langley* v. *Langley* [1994] 1 F.L.R. 383, C.A.
s. 47, amended: 1995, c. 42, sch.
s. 50, see *Children Act 1989 (Taxation of Costs), Re* [1994] 2 F.L.R. 934, Cazalet J.

21. Overseas Pensions Act 1973.
s. 1, regs. 95/238.

23. Education (Work Experience) Act 1973.
s. 1, amended: 1995, c. 12, sch. 13.

24. Employment of Children Act 1973.
s. 2, amended: 1995, c. 36, sch. 4 (S.).

26. Land Compensation Act 1973.
see *Faragher* v. *Gerber* [1994] EGCS 122, H.H.J. Lachs, sitting as a deputy judge.
s. 1, *Blower* v. *Suffolk County Council* (1994) 67 P. & C.R. 228.
s. 4, see *Allen* v. *Department of Transport* (1994) 68 P.&C.R. 347, Lands Tribunal.
s. 9, see *Williamson* v. *Cumbria County Council* (1994) 68 P.&C.R. 367, Lands Tribunal.
s. 37, amended: 1995, c. 8, sch.
s. 46, see *Glossop Sectional Buildings* v. *Sheffield Development Corp.* [1994] N.P.C. 102, C.A.

27. Bahamas Independence Act 1973.
s. 3, repealed in pt.: 1995, c. 44, sch. 1.
schs. 1, 2, repealed in pt.: 1995, c. 21, sch. 12.

CAP.

1973—cont.

28. Magistrates Causes Act 1973.
s. 28, see *B.* v. *B. (Consent Order: Variation)* [1995] 1 F.L.R. 9, Thorpe J.
s. 31, see *Masefield* v. *Alexander (Lump Sum: Extension of Time)* [1995] 1 F.L.R. 100, C.A.

29. Guardianship Act 1973.
repealed: 1995, c. 36, sch. 5 (S.).

32. National Health Service Reorganisation Act 1973.
repealed: 1995, c. 15, sch. 1.

35. Employment Agencies Act 1973.
s. 13, amended: 1994, c. 39, sch. 13 (S.); 1995, c. 25, sch. 10.

36. Northern Ireland Constitution Act 1973.
s. 38, amended: order 95/756.

41. Fair Trading Act 1973.
see *R.* v. *Manchester Magistrates' Courts, ex p. Kaymanesh* [1994] C.O.D. 380, D.C.
ss. 48, 49, 52, *R.* v. *Monopolies and Mergers Commission, ex p. National House Building Council* (1994) 6 Admin.L.R. 161, Auld J.
s. 58, amended: order 95/1351.
ss. 64, 69, 75, orders 94/2877, 2953.
s. 129, amended: 1995, c. 40, sch. 4 (S.).
sch. 5, repealed in pt.: 1995, c. 45, sch. 7.

43. Hallmarking Act 1973.
s. 16, amended: 1995, c. v, s. 3; 1995, c. vi, s. 3.

45. Domicile and Matrimonial Proceedings Act 1973.
s. 7, see *Spence* v. *Spence* (O.H.), March 9, 1994.
s. 10, repealed in pt.: 1995, c. 36, sch. 4 (S.).
s. 10, amended: 1995, c. 36, sch. 4 (S.).
sch. 1, see *R.* v. *R. (Divorce: Stay of Proceedings)* [1995] 1 F.C.R. 745, Ewbank J.
sch. 3, amended: 1995, c. 36, sch. 4 (S.).

49. Bangladesh Act 1973.
sch., repealed in pt.: 1995, c. 21, sch. 12.

50. Employment and Training Act 1973.
s. 12, amended: 1995, c. 50, sch. 6.

51. Finance Act 1973.
s. 56, regs. 95/449, 925, 1376.

52. Prescription and Limitation (Scotland) Act 1973.
s. 5, repealed in pt.: c. 7, sch. 5.
s. 6, see *Ductform Ventilation (Fife)* v. *Andrews-Weatherfoil* (O.H.), 1995 S.L.T. 88; *Reid* v. *Beaton* (Sh.Ct.), 1995 S.C.L.R. 382.
ss. 8, 14, see *Porteous's Exrs.* v. *Ferguson* (O.H.), 1995 S.L.T. 649.
s. 17, see *Ferla* v. *Secretary of State for Scotland* (O.H.), March 2, 1994.

CAP.

1973—cont.

52. Prescription and Limitation (Scotland) Act 1973—*cont.*
s. 19A, see *Ferla* v. *Secretary of State for Scotland* (O.H.), March 2, 1994; *Johnston* v. *Thomson* (O.H.), 1995 S.C.L.R. 554; *Tomkinson* v. *Broughton Brewery* (Sh.Ct.), 1995 S.C.L.R. 570.
sch. 1, repealed in pt.: 1995, c. 7, sch. 5.
sch. 1, see *Reid* v. *Beaton* (Sh.Ct.), 1995 S.C.L.R. 382.
sch. 2, see *Porteous's Exrs.* v. *Ferguson* (O.H.), 1995 S.L.T. 649.

56. Land Compensation (Scotland) Act 1973.
ss. 35, 80, amended: 1995, c. 36, sch. 4.

60. Breeding of Dogs Act 1973.
s. 5, amended: 1994, c. 39, sch. 13 (S.).

62. Powers of Criminal Court Act 1973.
ss. 1A, 1B, 1C, 13, 22, 23, 24, 25, see *R.* v. *Moore* [1995] 2 W.L.R. 728, C.A.
s. 8, see *R.* v. *Cousin (David Peter)* [1994] 15 Cr.App.R. (S.) 516, C.A.
s. 30, C.: 1995, c. 23, sch. 8.
s. 31, see *R.* v. *Szajber* [1994] Crim.L.R. 43, C.A.
s. 35, see *R* v. *Guppy; Same* v. *Marsh* [1994] Crim.L.R. 614, C.A.; *R.* v. *Crutchley*; *R.* v. *Tonks* [1994] 15 Cr.App.R. (S.) 627, C.A.; *D.P.P.* v. *Scott* [1995] 159 J.P. 261, D.C.

63. Government Trading Funds Act 1973.
ss. 1, 2, 2A, 6, orders 95/650, 1666.

65. Local Government (Scotland) Act 1973.
ss. 1, 2, 3, 3A, 4, 5, 11, repealed: 1994, c. 39, sch. 14.
ss. 14, 16, amended: 1994, c. 39, sch. 13.
s. 17, see *East Kilbride District Council* v. *Secretary of State for Scotland* (O.H.), 1995 S.L.T. 1238.
s. 20, amended: 1995, c. 39, sch. 13.
s. 23, substituted: 1994, c. 39, sch. 13.
ss. 24, 28, amended: 1994, c. 39, sch. 13.
s. 29, amended: regs. 95/1948.
s. 30, amended: order 95/789.
s. 31, amended: 1994, c. 39, sch. 13.
s. 38, amended: 1994, c. 39, sch. 13; order 95/789.
s. 45, regs. 95/701, 912.
s. 47, regs. 95/912.
s. 47, amended: 1994, c. 39, sch. 13.
s. 49A, regs. 95/701, 912.
ss. 50B, 50K, amended: 1994, c. 39, sch. 13.
s. 54, amended: 1994, c. 39, s. 53.
s. 55, amended: 1994, c. 39, sch. 13.
s. 56, amended: 1994, c. 39, sch. 13; 1995, c. 36, sch. 4.
s. 59, amended: order 95/789.
ss. 62A, 62B, 62C, added: 1994, c. 39, s. 20.
s. 63, amended: 1994, c. 39, sch. 13.

CAP.

1973—cont.

65. Local Government (Scotland) Act 1973—*cont.*
s. 63A, added: 1994, c. 39, sch. 13.
s. 67, amended: 1994, c. 39, sch. 13; order 95/789.
ss. 70, 71, amended: 1994, c. 39, s. 182.
s. 79, amended: order 95/789.
s. 83, repealed in pt.: 1994, c. 39, sch. 13.
s. 83, amended: 1994, c. 39, s. 164, sch. 13.
ss. 84, 87, amended: 1994, c. 39, sch. 13.
s. 88, amended: 1994, c. 39, s. 140.
s. 90, substituted: 1994, c. 39, s. 176.
ss. 92, 93, 94, amended: 1994, c. 39, sch. 13.
s. 98, regs. 95/698.
ss. 100, 102, 103, amended: 1994, c. 39, sch. 13.
s. 106, repealed in pt.: 1994, c. 39, s. 90.
s. 122A, added: 1994, c. 39, s. 170.
s. 123, substituted: 1994, c. 39, sch. 13.
s. 124, substituted: 1994, c. 39, s. 31.
s. 126, substituted: 1994, c. 39, sch. 13.
s. 127, repealed: 1994, c. 39, sch. 14.
ss. 128, 130, amended: 1994, c. 39, sch. 13.
ss. 131, 132, repealed: 1994, c. 39, sch. 14.
ss. 133, 134, amended: 1994, c. 39, sch. 13.
s. 135, amended: 1994, c. 39, sch. 13.
s. 135A, repealed: 1995, c. 25, sch. 24.
s. 135A, amended: 1994, c. 39, s. 37, sch. 13.
ss. 137, 138, 140, 142, 143, repealed: 1994, c. 39, schs. 13, 14.
ss. 145, 146, amended: 1994, c. 39, sch. 13.
s. 147, substituted: 1994, c. 39, s. 36.
s. 150, substituted: 1994, c. 39, sch. 13.
ss. 153, 154, repealed in pt.: 1994, c. 39, sch. 13.
ss. 154A, 154B, repealed: 1994, c. 39, sch. 14.
s. 159, repealed: 1994, c. 39, schs. 13, 14.
s. 161, repealed: 1994, c. 30, sch. 13.
s. 168, repealed: 1994, c. 39, schs. 13, 14.
s. 169, repealed in pt.: 1994, c. 39, sch. 13.
ss. 170, 170A, 170B, amended: 1994, c. 39, sch. 13.
s. 171, repealed: 1994, c. 39, sch. 13.
ss. 171A–171C, added: 1994, c. 39, s. 171.
s. 172, substituted: 1994, c. 39, sch. 13.
ss. 173, 174, 176, 177, 179, 181, 183, repealed: 1994, c. 39, sch. 14.
s. 188, substituted: 1994, c. 39, sch. 13.
s. 190, amended: 1994, c. 39, sch. 13; order 95/789.
s. 194, repealed in pt.: 1995, c. 7, sch. 5.
s. 200, repealed: 1994, c. 39, s. 54; 1995, c. 25, sch. 24.
s. 201, amended: 1994, c. 39, sch. 13.
s. 202, repealed in pt.: 1994, c. 39, sch. 13.
s. 206, amended: 1994, c. 39, sch. 13.
s. 211, amended: 1994, c. 39, s. 21.
ss. 222–225, repealed: 1994, c. 39, sch. 14.
s. 226, repealed: 1994, c. 39, schs. 13, 14.

CAP.

1973—cont.

65. Local Government (Scotland) Act 1973—*cont.*
s. 230, repealed: 1994, c. 39, sch. 13.
s. 235, regs. 95/512, 701, 912.
s. 235, amended: 1994, c. 39, sch. 13; order 95/789.
schs. 1, 2, repealed: 1994, c. 39, sch. 14.
sch. 5, substituted: 1994, c. 39, sch. 13.
sch. 7, amended: 1994, c. 39, sch. 13; order 95/789.
sch. 8, repealed in pt.: 1995, c. 7, sch. 5.
sch. 10, repealed: 1994, c. 39, sch. 14.
sch. 12, regs. 95/701.
schs. 13, 14, amended and repealed in pt.: 1994, c. 39, sch. 14.
sch. 16, repealed in pt.: 1995, c. 25, sch. 24.
sch. 17, amended: 1994, c. 39, sch. 14.
sch. 18, repealed in pt.: 1995, c. 23, sch. 8.
sch. 25, repealed in pt.: 1995, c. 36, sch. 5.
sch. 25, amended: 1995, c. 36, sch. 4.
sch. 27, repealed in pt.: 1995, c. 25, sch. 24; 1995, c. 36, schs. 4, 5.
sch. 27, C.: 1995, c. 12, sch. 14.

1974

7. Local Government Act 1974.
s. 7, repealed in pt.: 1995, c. 25, sch. 24.
s. 25, amended: 1995, c. 25, schs. 7, 22.
s. 26, amended: 1995, c. 25, sch. 7.
s. 34, amended: 1995, c. 25, sch. 7.

23. Juries Act 1974.
sch. 1, amended: 1995, c. 35, sch. 2.

24. Prices Act 1974.
s. 4, S.R. 1995 No. 231; order 95/1441.

28. Northern Ireland Act 1974.
ss. 16, 17, C.: 1995, c. 21, sch. 14.
sch. 1, S.R. 1995 Nos. 754, 755, 756, 757, 758, 759, 1625, 2705.

37. Health and Safety at Work Act 1974.
regs. 95/2038.
see *R.* v. *Secretary of State for Employment, ex p. National Association of Colliery Overman, Deputies and Shotfirers* [1994] C.O.D. 218, D.C.
Pt. 1, amended: 94/3246.
s. 2, regs. 94/3247.
s. 3, order 94/3246.
s. 3, see *R.* v. *Board of Trustees of the Science Museum* [1994] IRLR 35, C.A.; *R.* v. *Associated Octel* [1994] IRLR 540, C.A.; *Gotech Industrial and Environmental Services* v. *Friel*, 1995 S.C.C.R. 22; *R.* v. *British Steel* [1995] IRLR 310, C.A.
s. 4, see *Geotechnics* v. *Robbins (Inspector of Factories)* (CO 470/95), May 2, 1995, Curtis J.
s. 11, regs. 94/3140, 3246; 95/738.
s. 15, regs. 94/2865, 3140, 3246, 3247; regs. 95/738, 743.

CAP.

1974—cont.

37. Health and Safety at Work Act 1974—*cont.*

ss. 20, 21, 22, see *R.* v. *Board of Trustees of the Science Museum* [1994] IRLR 25, C.A.

s. 28, repealed in pt.: 1995, c. 25, sch. 24.

s. 28, amended: 1994, c. 39, sch. 13 (S.); 1995, c. 25, schs. 10, 22.

s. 33, 1995, c. 40, sch. 2 (S.).

s. 33, see *R.* v. *Board of Trustees of the Science Museum* [1994] IRLR 25, C.A.

s. 34, amended: regs. 94/3260.

s. 38, amended: 1995, c. 25, sch. 22.

s. 40, see *R.* v. *Associated Octel* [1994] IRLR 540, C.A.

s. 46, see *Health and Safety Executive* v. *George Tancocks Garage (Exeter)* [1993] C.O.D. 284, D.C.

s. 47, regs. 94/2865.

s. 50, regs. 94/3140, 3246.

s. 52, regs. 94/3246.

s. 53, amended: 1994, c. 39, sch. 13 (S.).

s. 60, amended: 1995, c. 17, sch. 1.

s. 80, regs. 94/3247.

s. 82, regs. 94/3140, 3246, 3247; 95/738, 743.

s. 84, order 95/263.

sch. 1, regs. 94/2865.

sch. 3, regs. 94/3140, 3246, 3247; 95/738.

sch. 9, amended: regs. 94/3246.

schs. 20, 22, repealed: 1994, c. 39, sch. 14 (S.).

39. Consumer Credit Act 1974.

ss. 11, 12, see *Renton* v. *Hendersons Garage (Nairn) and United Dominions Trust* [1994] CCLR 29, Sheriff Principal D.J. Risk, Q.C.

s. 16, order 95/1250.

s. 75, see *Renton* v. *Hendersons Garage (Nairn) and United Dominions Trust* [1994] CCLR 29, Sheriff Principal D.J.Risk Q.C.

ss. 129, 136, see *Murie McDougall* v. *Sinclair* 1994 S.L.T. (Sh.Ct.) 74; *J. & J. Securities* v. *Lee* [1994] CCLR 44, H.H.J. Mettyear sitting as a deputy judge; *First National Bank* v. *Colman and Colman* [1994] CCLR 39, H.H.J. Morrell sitting as a deputy judge; *J. & J. Securities* v. *Ewart and Ewart* [1994] CCLR 51, H.H.J. Townend sitting as a deputy judge; *Southern and District Finance* v. *Barnes, The Times*, April 19, 1995, Leggatt L.J.

s. 182, order 95/1250.

s. 189, amended: 1994, c. 39, sch. 13 (S.).

40. Control of Pollution Act 1974.

see *R.* v. *Canterbury Crown Court, ex p. Kent County Council* [1994] Env. L.R. D3, D.C.

s. 2, regs. 94/1056.

CAP.

1974—cont.

40. Control of Pollution Act 1974—*cont.*

s. 3, see *Thanet District Council* v. *Kent County Council* [1993] C.O.D. 308, D.C.; *Gotech Industrial and Environmental Services* v. *Friel*, 1995 S.C.C.R. 22.

s. 4, see *Gotech Industrial and Environmental Services* v. *Friel*, 1995 S.C.C.R. 22.

s. 5, repealed in pt.: 1995, c. 25, sch. 24.

s. 5, amended: 1995, c. 25, sch. 22.

s. 6, amended: 1995, c. 25, sch. 22.

s. 7, repealed in pt.: 1995, c. 25, sch. 24.

s. 7, amended: 1995, c. 25, sch. 22.

s. 8, amended: 1995, c. 25, sch. 22.

s. 9, repealed in pt.: 1995, c. 25, sch. 24.

s. 9, amended: 1995, c. 25, sch. 22.

ss. 10, 11, 16, amended: 1995, c. 25, sch. 22.

s. 16, see *McDonald* v. *H.L. Friel & Son*, 1995 S.C.C.R. 461.

s. 30, regs. 94/1056.

s. 30, repealed in pt.: 1995, c. 25, sch. 24.

s. 30, see *Gotech Industrial and Environmental Services* v. *Friel*, 1995 S.C.C.R. 22.

s. 30A, repealed in pt.: 1995, c. 25, schs. 22, 24.

s. 30A, amended: 1995, c. 25, sch. 22 (S.).

s. 30C, repealed in pt.: 1995, c. 25, sch. 24.

s. 30C, amended: 1995, c. 25, sch. 22 (S.).

s. 30D, amended: 1995, c. 25, sch. 22 (S.).

ss. 30F–30J, added: 1995, c. 25, sch. 16 (S.).

ss. 30Y–30Z, added: 1995, c. 25, s. 59 (S.).

s. 31, repealed in pt.: 1995, c. 25, sch. 16 (S.), sch. 24.

s. 31, amended: 1995, c. 25, schs. 16, 22 (S.).

s. 31A, amended: 1995, c. 25, sch. 22.

s. 31B, amended: 1995, c. 25, sch. 16 (S.).

s. 31D, repealed in pt.: 1995, c. 25, sch. 22 (S.), 24.

s. 32, repealed: 1995, c. 25, sch. 24.

s. 32, amended: 1994, c. 39, sch. 13 (S.).

s. 33, repealed in pt.: 1995, c. 25, sch. 22 (S.), sch. 24.

s. 33, amended: 1995, c. 25, sch. 22.

s. 34, repealed in pt.: 1995, c. 25, sch. 24.

s. 34, amended: 1995, c. 25, schs. 16 (S.), 19, 22 (S.).

s. 35, amended: 1995, c. 25, sch. 22 (S.).

s. 36, amended: 1994, c. 39, sch. 13 (S.); 1995, c. 25, sch. 22 (S.).

s. 37, amended: 1995, c. 25, sch. 22 (S.).

s. 38, amended: 1995, c. 25, sch. 22 (S.).

s. 38A, amended: 1995, c. 25, sch. 22 (S.).

s. 39, amended: 1995, c. 25, schs. 16 (S.), 22 (S.).

s. 40, repealed in pt.: 1995, c. 25, sch. 24.

s. 40, amended: 1995, c. 25, sch. 22 (S.).

CAP.

1974—cont.

40. Control of Pollution Act 1974—*cont.*
s. 41, repealed in pt.: 1995, c. 25, sch. 24.
s. 41, amended: 1995, c. 25, sch. 22 (S.).
ss. 42A, 42B, repealed in pt.: 1995, c. 25, sch. 22 (S.).
s. 46, repealed in pt.: 1995, c. 25, schs. 22 (S.), 24.
s. 46, amended: 1995, c. 25, sch. 22 (S.).
s. 46A, added: 1995, c. 25, sch. 22 (S.).
s. 46B, added: 1995, c. 25, sch. 22 (S.).
s. 46C, added: 1995, c. 25, sch. 22 (S.).
s. 46D, added: 1995, c. 25, sch. 22 (S.).
s. 47, repealed in pt.: 1995, c. 25, schs. 22 (S.), 24.
s. 47, amended: 1995, c. 25, sch. 22 (S.).
s. 48, repealed in pt.: 1995, c. 25, schs. 22 (S.), 24.
s. 48, amended: 1995, c. 25, sch. 22 (S.).
s. 49, repealed in pt.: 1995, c. 25, sch. 22 (S.).
s. 49, amended: 1995, c. 25, sch. 22 (S.).
s. 49A, added: 1995, c. 25, sch. 22 (S.).
s. 49B, added: 1995, c. 25, sch. 22 (S.).
s. 50, repealed in pt.: 1995, c. 25, schs. 22 (S.), 24.
s. 50, amended: 1995, c. 25, sch. 22 (S.).
s. 51, amended: 1995, c. 25, sch. 22 (S.).
s. 53, repealed in pt.: 1995, c. 25, schs. 22 (S.), 24.
s. 54, repealed in pt.: 1995, c. 25, sch. 24.
s. 55, repealed in pt.: 1995, c. 25, sch. 24.
s. 55, amended: 1994, c. 39, sch. 13 (S.).
s. 56, repealed in pt.: 1995, c. 25, schs. 22 (S.), 24.
s. 56, amended: 1995, c. 25, sch. 16 (S.).
s. 57, repealed in pt.: 1995, c. 25, sch. 24.
s. 58, repealed: 1995, c. 25, sch. 24.
s. 58, see *Meri Mate* v. *City of Dundee District Council* (Sh.Ct.), 1994 S.C.L.R. 960.
s. 58A, repealed: 1995, c. 25, sch. 24.
s. 58B, repealed: 1995, c. 25, sch. 24.
s. 59, repealed: 1995, c. 25, sch. 24.
s. 59A, repealed: 1995, c. 25, sch. 24.
s. 62, amended: 1994, c. 39, sch. 13 (S.); 1995, c. 25, sch. 22.
s. 69, repealed in pt.: 1995, c. 25, sch. 24.
s. 73, repealed in pt.: 1995, c. 25, sch. 24.
s. 73, amended: 1994, c. 39, sch. 13 (S.).
s. 74, repealed in pt.: 1995, c. 25, sch. 24.
s. 85, see *McDonald* v. *H.L. Friel & Son*, 1995 S.C.C.R. 461.
s. 87, repealed in pt.: 1995, c. 25, sch. 16 (S.), 24.
s. 87, amended: 1995, c. 25, sch. 16 (S.).
s. 90, amended: 1995, c. 25, sch. 22 (S.).
s. 91, repealed in pt.: 1995, c. 25, sch. 24.
s. 91, amended: 1995, c. 25, sch. 22 (S.).
s. 91, see *Gotech Industrial and Environmental Services* v. *Friel*, 1995 S.C.C.R. 22.
s. 93, amended: 1995, c. 25, sch. 19.
s. 96, repealed in pt.: 1995, c. 25, sch. 24.

CAP.

1974—cont.

40. Control of Pollution Act 1974—*cont.*
s. 96, amended: 1995, c. 25, sch. 22 (S.).
s. 98, amended: 1994, c. 39, sch. 13 (S.); 1995, c. 25, sch. 22 (S.).
s. 104, regs. 94/1056.
s. 104, repealed in pt.: 1995, c. 25, schs. 22 (S.), 24.
s. 105, amended: 1995, c. 25, schs. 21, 22 (S.).
s. 106, repealed in pt.: 1994, c. 39, sch. 13 (S.); 1995, c. 25, sch. 24.
s. 106, amended: 1994, c. 39, sch. 13 (S.).
sch. 1A, amended: 1994, c. 39, sch. 13 (S.); 1995, c. 25, sch. 22 (S.).
sch. 3, repealed in pt.: 1995, c. 25, sch. 24.

43. Merchant Shipping Act 1974.
s. 1, order 94/2788.
s. 1, repealed: 1995, c. 21, sch. 12.
ss. 2–8A, repealed: 1995, c. 21, sch. 12.
ss. 14, 15: repealed: 1995, c. 22, sch.
ss. 16–18, repealed: 1995, c. 21, sch. 12.
s. 19, repealed in pt.: 1995, c. 21, sch. 12.
ss. 21, 23, 24, schs. 1, 5, repealed: 1995, c. 21, sch. 12.

46. Friendly Societies Act 1974.
s. 104, regs. 95/709.

47. Solicitors Act 1974.
see *R.* v. *Law Society, ex p. Bratsky Lesopromyshlenny Complex* (CO-2776-94B), November 17, 1994, Tucker J.
s. 12, see *R.* v. *Solicitors Complaints Bureau, ex p. Curtin* (1994) 6 Admin. L.R. 657, C.A.
s. 22, amended: 1995, c. 8, s. 35.
s. 70, see *Debtor, A (Nos. 833 and 835 of 1993)*, Re, [1994] N.P.C. 82, Vinelott J.
s. 79, see *R.* v. *Solicitors Complaints Bureau, ex p. Curtin* (1994) 6 Admin. L.R. 657, C.A.
sch. 1, see *Solicitor, A (No. S2700 of 1995), Re, The Times*, July 11, 1995, Blackburne J., *Solicitor, Re, The Independent*, (C.S.), September 4, 1995, Walker J.; *Giles* v. *Law Society, The Times*, October 20, 1995, C.A.

50. Road Traffic Act 1974.
s. 16, repealed: 1995, c. 23, sch. 8.
sch. 4, repealed: 1995, c. 23, sch. 8.
sch. 4, C.: 1995, c. 23, sch. 8.
see *Biggs* v. *Somerset County Council, The Times*, July 17, 1995, E.A.T.

53. Rehabilitation of Offenders Act 1974.
s. 3, amended: 1995, c. 36, sch. 4 (S.).
s. 5, repealed in pt.: 1995, c. 36, sch. 5 (S.).
s. 5, amended: 1995, c. 36, sch. 4 (S.).
s. 7, repealed in pt.: 1995, c. 36, schs. 4 (S.), 5, (S.).
s. 7, amended: 1995, c. 36, sch. 4 (S.).

CAP.

1975

3. Arbitration Act 1975.
see *Aectra Refining and Manufacturing* v. *Exmar* [1994] 1 W.L.R. 1634, C.A.
s. 1, see *Rimeco Riggelsen & Metal Co.* v. *Queenborough Rolling Mill Co.* (QBCMI 94/0087/B), November 9, 1994, C.A.; *Daval Aciers D'Usinor et De Sacilor* v. *Armare Srl.*; *Nerano, The* [1994] 2 Lloyd's Rep. 50, Clarke J.

7. Finance Act 1975.
s. 38, see *Lady Fox's Executors* v. *I.R.C.* [1994] 38 EG 156, C.A.; *Walton's Executors* v. *I.R.C.* [1994] 38 EG 161, Lands Tribunal.

14. Social Security Act 1975.
ss. 45, 49, see *Social Security Decision* No. R(S) 6/94.
s. 59, order 95/708.
s. 126A, amended: order 95/559.
s. 165A, see *Johnson* v. *Chief Adjudication Officer (No. 2)* [1995] 2 All E.R. (E.C.) 258, ECJ.

15. Social Security (Northern Ireland) Act 1975.
sch. 10, S.R. 1995 No. 210.

20. District Courts (Scotland) Act 1975.
s. 1A, amended: 1994, c. 39, sch. 13.
s. 2, repealed: 1995, c. 40, sch. 5.
s. 2, amended: 1994, c. 39, s. 48.
s. 2, C.: 1995, c. 46, s. 6.
s. 3, C.: 1995, c. 46, s. 7.
s. 4, C.: 1995, c. 46, s. 8.
s. 6, repealed: 1995, c. 40, sch. 5.
s. 6, C.: 1995, c. 46, s. 6.
s. 7, repealed in pt.: 1994, c. 39, schs. 13, 14.
s. 18, repealed in pt.: 1994, c. 39, sch. 14.
s. 26, amended: 1994, c. 39, sch. 13.
sch. 1, repealed: 1995, c. 40, sch. 5.

21. Criminal Procedure (Scotland) Act 1975.
repealed: 1995, c. 40, sch. 5.
s. 2, C.: 1995, c. 46, s. 3.
s. 3, C.: 1995, c. 46, s. 4.
s. 4, C.: 1995, c. 46, s. 9.
s. 6, amended: 1995, c. 20, sch. 6.
s. 6, C.: 1995, c. 46, s. 11.
s. 7, C.: 1995, c. 46, s. 11.
s. 8, C.: 1995, c. 46, s. 3.
s. 9, C.: 1995, c. 46, s. 12.
ss. 10, 11, C.: 1995, c. 46, s. 288.
s. 12, C.: 1995, c. 46, s. 34.
s. 14, repealed: 1995, c. 36, schs. 4, 5.
s. 14, amended: 1995, c. 20, sch. 6.
s. 15, repealed in pt.: 1995, c. 20, s. 9.
s. 15, C.: 1995, c. 46, s. 297.
s. 15A, added: 1995, c. 20, sch. 6.
s. 15A, C.: 1995, c. 46, s. 296.
s. 16, C.: 1995, c. 46, s. 297.
s. 18, amended: 1995, c. 20, sch. 6.
s. 18, C.: 1995, c. 46, s. 21.
s. 19, amended: 1995, c. 20, sch. 6.
s. 19, C.: 1995, c. 46, ss. 17, 35.

CAP.

1975—cont.

21. Criminal Procedure (Scotland) Act 1975—*cont.*
s. 20, repealed in pt.: 1995, c. 20, schs. 6, 7.
s. 20, C.: 1995, c. 46, s. 35.
s. 20A, amended: 1995, c. 20, s. 10.
s. 20A, C.: 1995, c. 46, s. 36.
ss. 20A, see *Dempsey* v. *H.M. Advocate*, 1995 S.C.C.R. 431.
s. 20B, amended: 1995, c. 20, sch. 6.
s. 20B, see *Robertson* v. *H.M. Advocate*, 1995 S.C.C.R. 152.
s. 20B, C.: 1995, c. 46, ss. 37, 38.
s. 21, C.: 1995, c. 46, s. 39.
s. 22, C.: 1995, c. 46, s. 40.
s. 23, amended: 1995, c. 20, sch. 6; 1995, c. 36, sch. 4.
s. 23, C.: 1995, c. 46, s. 51.
s. 25, C.: 1995, c. 46, s. 52.
s. 26, repealed in pt.: 1995, c. 20, schs. 6, 7.
s. 26, C.: 1995, c. 46, s. 23.
s. 27, C.: 1995, c. 46, s. 23.
s. 28, C.: 1995, c. 46, s. 23.
s. 28A, added: 1995, c. 20, s. 3.
s. 28A, C.: 1995, c. 46, s. 26.
s. 30, C.: 1995, c. 46, ss. 28, 30.
s. 30A, added: 1995, c. 20, s. 3.
s. 30A, C.: 1995, c. 46, s. 31.
s. 31, repealed in pt.: 1995, c. 20, sch. 6.
s. 32, C.: 1995, c. 46, s. 33.
s. 33, repealed in pt.: 1995, c. 20, sch. 7.
s. 35, C.: 1995, c. 46, s. 24.
s. 37, amended: 1995, c. 36, sch. 4.
s. 37, C.: 1995, c. 46, s. 45.
s. 39, amended: 1995, c. 36, sch. 4.
s. 39, C.: 1995, c. 46, s. 42.
s. 40, C.: 1995, c. 46, s. 42.
s. 41, C.; 1995, c. 46, s. 64.
s. 42, substituted: 1995, c. 20, sch. 6.
s. 42, C.: 1995, c. 46, s. 287.
s. 43, C.: 1995, c. 46, sch. 3.
s. 43, repealed (with savings): 1995, c. 40, sch. 6.
s. 44, C.: 1995, c. 46, sch. 3.
s. 45, repealed (with savings): 1995, c. 40, sch. 6.
s. 46, repealed (with savings): 1995, c. 40, sch. 6.
s. 47, repealed (with savings): 1995, c. 40, sch. 6.
s. 48, C.: 1995, c. 46, sch. 3.
s. 48A, added: 1995, c. 20, sch. 6.
s. 48A, C.: 1995, c. 46, sch. 3.
s. 48B, added: 1995, c. 20, sch. 6.
s. 48B, C.: 1995, c. 46, sch. 3.
ss. 48C, 48D, added: 1995, c. 20, sch. 6.
s. 49, C.: 1995, c. 46, sch. 3.
s. 50, amended: 1995, c. 20, sch. 6.
s. 50, C.: 1995, c. 46, sch. 3.
s. 51, C.: 1995, c. 46, sch. 3.

CAP.

1975—cont.

21. Criminal Procedure (Scotland) Act 1975—*cont.*

s. 52, repealed (with savings): 1995, c. 40, sch. 6.
s. 53, repealed (with savings): 1995, c. 40, sch. 6.
s. 54, repealed (with savings): 1995, c. 40, sch. 6.
s. 54, amended: 1995, c. 20, sch. 6.
s. 54, C.: 1995, c. 46, sch. 3.
s. 55, C.: 1995, c. 46, sch. 3.
s. 55, repealed (with savings): 1995, c. 40, sch. 6.
s. 56, C.: 1995, c. 46, ss. 302, 303.
s. 56, repealed (with savings): 1995, c. 40, sch. 6.
s. 57, C.: 1995, c. 46, s. 64.
s. 57, repealed (with savings): 1995, c. 40, sch. 6.
s. 58, C.: 1995, c. 46, s. 66.
s. 59, C.: 1995, c. 46, sch. 3.
s. 60, C.: 1995, c. 46, sch. 3.
s. 60A, added: 1995, c. 20, sch. 6.
s. 60A, C.: 1995, c. 46, sch. 3.
s. 61, C.: 1995, c. 46, sch. 3.
s. 62, repealed: 1995, c. 20, schs. 6, 7.
s. 63, C.: 1995, c. 46, s. 294, sch. 3.
s. 64, C.: 1995, c. 46, sch. 3.
s. 65, C.: 1995, c. 46, sch. 3.
s. 66, C.: 1995, c. 46, sch. 3.
s. 67, see *Young* v. *H.M. Advocate*, 1995 S.C.C.R 213.
s. 68, repealed: 1995, c. 20, sch. 6.
s. 69, repealed in pt.: 1995, c. 20, sch. 7.
s. 69, amended: 1995, c. 20, sch. 6.
s. 69, C.: 1995, c. 46, s. 66.
s. 70, C.: 1995, c. 46, s. 66.
s. 71, C.: 1995, c. 46, s. 66.
s. 72, amended: 1995, c. 20, sch. 6.
s. 72, C.: 1995, c. 46, s. 66.
s. 73, repealed in pt.: 1995, c. 20, schs. 6, 7.
s. 73, C.: 1995, c. 46, s. 66.
s. 74, C.: 1995, c. 46, ss. 34, 70.
s. 75, amended: 1995, c. 20, s. 13.
s. 75, C.: 1995, c. 46, s. 66.
s. 75A, added: 1995, c. 20, s. 13.
s. 75A, C.: 1995, c. 46, s. 71.
s. 76, amended: 1995, c. 20, s. 13.
s. 76, C.: 1995, c. 46, ss. 72, 73, 102.
s. 76A, amended: 1995, c. 20, s. 13.
s. 76A, C.: 1995, c. 46, s. 74.
s. 77, amended: 1995, c. 20, sch. 6.
s. 77, C.: 1995, c. 46, s. 80.
s. 77A, C.: 1995, c. 46, s. 80.
s. 78, amended: 1995, c. 20, sch. 6.
s. 78 see *Robertson* v. *H.M. Advocate*, 1995 S.C.C.R. 152.
s. 78, C.: 1995, c. 46, ss. 66, 68.
s. 79, amended: 1995, c. 20, sch. 6.
s. 79, C.: 1995, c. 46, s. 67.
s. 80, amended: 1995, c. 20, sch. 6.

CAP.

1975—cont.

21. Criminal Procedure (Scotland) Act 1975—*cont.*

s. 80, C.: 1995, c. 46, s. 67.
s. 81, amended: 1995, c. 20, sch. 6.
s. 81, C.: 1995, c. 46, s. 67.
s. 82, amended: 1995, c. 20, s. 11, sch. 6.
s. 82, C.: 1995, c. 46, s. 78.
s. 82A, C.: 1995, c. 46, s. 67.
s. 84, amended: 1995, c. 20, s. 23.
s. 84A, added: 1995, c. 20, s. 12.
s. 84A, C.: 1995, c. 46, s. 257.
s. 85, substituted: 1995, c. 20, sch. 6.
s. 85, C.: 1995, c. 46, s. 84.
s. 86, C.: 1995, c. 46, s. 84.
s. 89, C.: 1995, c. 46, s. 84.
s. 90, C.: 1995, c. 46, s. 84.
s. 91, C.: 1995, c. 46, s. 84.
s. 92, C.: 1995, c. 46, s. 84.
s. 93, amended: 1995, c. 20, sch. 6.
s. 93, C.: 1995, c. 46, s. 84.
s. 94, C.: 1995, c. 46, s. 84.
s. 95, C.: 1995, c. 46, s. 84.
s. 96, C.: 1995, c. 46, s. 85.
s. 97, C.: 1995, c. 46, ss. 85, 140A.
s. 98, C.: 1995, c. 46, s. 85.
s. 99, C.: 1995, c. 46, s. 85.
s. 100, repealed in pt.: 1995, c. 20, sch. 6.
s. 100, C.: 1995, c. 46, s. 85.
s. 101, amended: 1995, c. 20, s. 15.
s. 101, see *X. Petr.*, 1995 S.C.C.R. 407; *Beattie* v. *H.M. Advocate*, 1995 S.L.T. 946; *C.* v. *Forsyth*, 1995 S.L.T. 905.
s. 101, C.: 1995, c. 46, s. 65.
s. 103, amended: 1995, c. 20, sch. 6.
s. 103, C.: 1995, c. 46, ss. 70, 77.
s. 104, C.: 1995, c. 46, s. 195.
s. 108, amended: 1995, c. 20, sch. 6.
s. 108, C.: 1995, c. 46, ss. 72, 79.
s. 109, C.: 1995, c. 46, s. 73.
s. 109, repealed (with savings): 1995, c. 40, sch. 6.
s. 110, repealed: 1995, c. 20, schs. 6, 7.
s. 111, C.: 1995, c. 46, s. 82.
s. 111, repealed (with savings): 1995, c. 40, sch. 6.
s. 111A, C.: 1995, c. 46, s. 75.
s. 112, C.: 1995, c. 46, s. 3.
s. 113, C.: 1995, c. 46, s. 1.
s. 114, C.: 1995, c. 46, s. 2.
s. 114A, added: 1995, c. 20, sch. 6.
s. 114A, C.: 1995, c. 46, s. 83.
s. 123, C.: 1995, c. 46, s. 96.
s. 124, C.: 1995, c. 46, s. 77.
s. 124, repealed (with savings): 1995, c. 40, sch. 6.
s. 125, substituted: 1995, c. 20, sch. 6.
s. 125, C.: 1995, c. 46, s. 88.
s. 127, repealed in pt.: 1995, c. 20, sch. 7.
s. 127, amended: 1995, c. 20, sch. 6.
s. 127, C.: 1995, c. 46, s. 81.
s. 128, amended: 1995, c. 20, s. 30.

CAP.

1975—cont.

21. Criminal Procedure (Scotland) Act 1975—*cont.*

s. 128, C.: 1995, c. 46, s. 87.
s. 129, amended: 1995, c. 20, sch. 6.
s. 129, C.: 1995, c. 46, s. 88.
s. 130, repealed in pt.: 1995, c. 20, s. 8, sch. 7.
s. 130, C.: 1995, c. 46, s. 86.
s. 131, C.: 1995, c. 46, s. 88.
s. 132, repealed in pt.: 1995, c. 20, schs. 6, 7.
s. 132, C.: 1995, c. 46, s. 88.
s. 133, C.: 1995, c. 46, s. 88.
s. 134, amended: 1995, c. 20, sch. 6.
s. 134, C.: 1995, c. 46, s. 90.
s. 135, amended: 1995, c. 20, sch. 6.
s. 135, C.: 1995, c. 46, ss. 88, 89.
s. 136, C.: 1995, c. 46, s. 91.
s. 137, C.: 1995, c. 46, s. 88.
s. 137A, C.: 1995, c. 46, s. 95.
s. 138, C.: 1995, c. 46, s. 264.
s. 139, C.: 1995, c. 46, s. 265.
s. 139A, C.: 1995, c. 46, s. 267.
s. 140, C.: 1995, c. 46, s. 267.
s. 140A, repealed in pt.: 1995, c. 20, schs. 6, 7.
s. 141, repealed in pt.: 1995, c. 20, s. 9, sch. 7.
s. 141, amended: 1995, c. 20, s. 24.
s. 141, C.: 1995, c. 46, s. 266.
s. 141, see *Dempsey* v. *H.M. Advocate*, 1995 S.C.C.R. 431.
s. 141A, amended: 1995, c. 20, s. 28.
s. 141A, C.: 1995, c. 46, s. 274.
s. 141B, C.: 1995, c. 46, s. 275.
s. 141ZA, added: 1995, c. 20, s. 9.
s. 141ZA, C.: 1995, c. 46, s. 270.
s. 142, substituted: 1995, c. 20, sch. 6.
s. 142, C.: 1995, c. 46, s. 266.
s. 143, C.: 1995, c. 46, s. 264.
s. 144, repealed: 1995, c. 20, schs. 6, 7.
s. 145, repealed in pt.: 1995, c. 20, schs. 6, 7.
s. 145, C.: 1995, c. 46, s. 92.
s. 146, repealed: 1995, c. 20, sch. 6.
s. 147, see *Young* v. *H.M. Advocate*, 1995 S.C.C.R. 418.
s. 147, C.: 1995, c. 46, s. 263.
s. 148, amended: 1995, c. 20, sch. 6.
s. 148, C.: 1995, c. 46, s. 263.
s. 148A, C.: 1995, c. 46, s. 263.
s. 149, C.: 1995, c. 46, s. 268.
s. 149A, C.: 1995, c. 46, s. 269.
s. 150, repealed in pt.: 1995, c. 20, sch. 7.
s. 150, amended: 1995, c. 20, sch. 6.
s. 150, C.: 1995, c. 46, s. 256.
s. 151, amended: 1995, c. 20, sch. 6.
s. 151, C.: 1995, c. 46, s. 278.
s. 152, C.: 1995, c. 46, s. 98.
s. 153, repealed in pt.: 1995, c. 20, schs. 6, 7.

CAP.

1975—cont.

21. Criminal Procedure (Scotland) Act 1975—*cont.*

s. 153, see *Love* v. *H.M. Advocate*, 1995 S.C.C.R. 501.
s. 153, C.: 1995, c. 46, s. 99.
s. 154, C.: 1995, c. 46, s. 100.
s. 155, C.: 1995, c. 46, s. 100.
s. 155A, C.: 1995, c. 46, s. 99.
s. 156, repealed in pt.: 1995, c. 20, schs. 6, 7.
s. 156, C.: 1995, c. 46, s. 102.
s. 157, repealed in pt.: 1995, c. 20, sch. 6.
s. 157, C.: 1995, c. 46, s. 102.
s. 158, C.: 1995, c. 46, s. 102.
s. 159, repealed in pt.: 1995, c. 20, schs. 6, 7.
s. 159, C.: 1995, c. 46, s. 101.
s. 160, repealed in pt.: 1995, c. 20, schs. 6, 7.
s. 160, see *Robertson* v. *H.M. Advocate*, 1995 S.C.C.R. 550.
s. 160, C.: 1995, c. 46, s. 101.
s. 161, C.: 1995, c. 46, s. 101.
s. 162, amended: 1995, c. 20, s. 29, sch. 6.
s. 162, C.: 1995, c. 46, ss. 285, 286.
s. 163, repealed: 1995, c. 20, sch. 7.
s. 164, C.: 1995, c. 46, s. 285.
s. 165, C.: 1995, c. 46, s. 50.
s. 166, amended: 1995, c. 20, sch. 6.
s. 166, C.: 1995, c. 46, s. 50.
s. 167, C.: 1995, c. 46, s. 50.
s. 168, repealed in pt.: 1995, c. 36, schs. 4, 5.
s. 168, amended: 1994, c. 39, sch. 13.
s. 168, C.: 1995, c. 46, s. 48.
s. 169, see *Caledonian Newspapers, Petrs.*, 1995 S.C.C.R. 576.
s. 169, C.: 1995, c. 46, s. 47.
s. 170, C.: 1995, c. 46, s. 41.
s. 171, amended: 1995, c. 36, sch. 4.
s. 171, C.: 1995, c. 46, s. 46.
s. 172, C.: 1995, c. 46, s. 50.
s. 173, amended: 1994, c. 39, sch. 13; 1995, c. 36, s. 49.
s. 173, C.: 1995, c. 46, s. 49.
s. 174, repealed in pt.: 1995, c. 20, sch. 7.
s. 174, amended: 1995, c. 20, s. 47, sch. 6.
s. 174, C.: 1995, c. 46, s. 54.
s. 174A, C.: 1995, c. 46, ss. 53.
s. 174ZA, added: 1995, c. 20, s. 49.
s. 174ZA, C.: 1995, c. 46, s. 55.
s. 174ZB, added: 1995, c. 20, s. 49.
s. 174ZB, C.: 1995, c. 46, s. 56.
s. 174ZC, added: 1995, c. 20, s. 50.
s. 174ZC, C.: 1995, c. 46, s. 57.
s. 174ZD, added: 1995, c. 20, s. 51.
s. 174ZD, C.: 1995, c. 46, s. 62.
s. 174ZE, added: 1995, c. 20, s. 52.
s. 174ZE, C.: 1995, c. 46, s. 63.
s. 175, C.: 1995, c. 46, ss. 52, 58.
s. 176, amended: 1995, c. 20, sch. 6.
s. 176, C.: 1995, c. 46, s. 61.

CAP.

1975—cont.

21. Criminal Procedure (Scotland) Act 1975—*cont.*

s. 177, amended: 1995, c. 36, schs. 4, 5.
s. 177, C.: 1995, c. 46, s. 58.
s. 178, repealed in pt.: 1995, c. 20, s. 54, sch. 7.
s. 178, amended: 1995, c. 20, sch. 6.
s. 178, C.: 1995, c. 46, s. 59.
s. 179, amended: 1995, c. 20, sch. 6.
s. 179, C.: 1995, c. 46, s. 201.
s. 179A, added: 1995, c. 20, s. 37.
s. 179A, C.: 1995, c. 46, s. 203.
s. 180, amended: 1995, c. 20, s. 55.
s. 180, C.: 1995, c. 46, s. 200.
s. 182A, added: 1995, c. 20, sch. 6.
s. 182A, C.: 1995, c. 46, s. 227.
s. 183, repealed in pt.: 1995, c. 20, sch. 7.
s. 183, amended: 1995, c. 20, s. 38, sch. 6.
s. 183, C.: 1995, c. 46, ss. 228, 229.
s. 184, amended: 1995, c. 20, s. 39.
s. 184, C.: 1995, c. 46, s. 230.
s. 185, C.: 1995, c. 46, s. 231.
s. 186, repealed in pt.: 1995, c. 20, schs. 6, 7.
s. 186, C.: 1995, c. 46, s. 232.
s. 187, amended: 1995, c. 20, s. 40.
s. 187, C.: 1995, c. 46, s. 233.
s. 188, C.: 1995, c. 46, s. 234.
s. 190, repealed: 1995, c. 20, schs. 6, 7.
s. 191, C.: 1995, c. 46, s. 247.
s. 191, repealed in pt.: 1995, c. 20, schs. 6, 7.
s. 192, repealed in pt.: 1995, c. 20, schs. 6, 7.
s. 192, C.: 1995, c. 46, s. 203.
s. 193, C.: 1995, c. 46, s. 199.
s. 193A, C.: 1995, c. 46, s. 211.
s. 194, amended: 1995, c. 20, s. 9.
s. 194, C.: 1995, c. 46, ss. 211, 213, 214, 215, 216, 217, 218, 219, 220, 221, 222, 223.
s. 196, repealed in pt.: 1995, c. 20, schs. 6, 7.
s. 196, C.: 1995, c. 46, s. 211.
s. 203, C.: 1995, c. 46, s. 211.
s. 205, C.: 1995, c. 46, s. 205.
s. 206, see *F.* v. *H.M. Advocate*, 1994 S.C.C.R. 711.
s. 206, C.: 1995, c. 46, s. 208.
s. 207, C.: 1995, c. 46, s. 207.
s. 212A, added: 1995, c. 20, s. 36.
s. 212A, C.: 1995, c. 46, s. 209.
s. 215, C.: 1995, c. 46, s. 295.
s. 216, C.: 1995, c. 46, s. 293.
s. 217, amended: 1995, c. 20, s. 33.
s. 217A, C.: 1995, c. 46, s. 196.
s. 218, see *Young* v. *H.M. Advocate*, 1995 S.C.C.R. 418.
s. 218, C.: 1995, c. 46, s. 210.
s. 219, C.: 1995, c. 46, s. 202.
s. 222, repealed (with savings): 1995, c. 40, sch. 6.
s. 223, repealed: 1995, c. 20, schs. 6, 7.
s. 223A, C.: 1995, c. 46, s. 248.
s. 224, C.: 1995, c. 46, s. 254.
s. 225, repealed: 1995, c. 20, schs. 6, 7.
s. 226, repealed: 1995, c. 20, sch. 7.
s. 227, repealed: 1995, c. 20, sch. 7.
s. 227A, C.: 1995, c. 46, s. 299.
s. 228, amended: 1995, c. 20, s. 42.
s. 228, see *Reid* v. *H.M. Advocate*, 1994 S.C.C.R. 755; *MacKenzie* v. *H.M. Advocate*, 1995 S.C.C.R. 141; *Church* v. *H.M. Advocate*, 1995, S.L.T. 604; *Elliott* v. *H.M. Advocate*, 1995 S.LT. 612; *Advocate (H.M.)* v. *Bell*, 1995 S.C.C.R. 244.
s. 228, C.: 1995, c. 46, ss. 4, 106.
s. 228A, see *Advocate H.M.* v. *McPhee*, 1994 S.L.T. 1292.
s. 228A, see *Advocate, H.M.* v. *McAllister*, 1995 S.C.C.R. 545.
s. 228A, C.: 1995, c. 46, s. 108.
s. 230, C.: 1995, c. 46, s. 130.
s. 230A, added: 1995, c. 20, s. 42.
s. 230A, C.: 1995, c. 46, s. 107.
s. 231, amended: 1995, c. 20, sch. 6.
s. 231, C.: 1995, c. 46, s. 109.
s. 233, C.: 1995, c. 46, s. 110.
s. 234, C.: 1995, c. 46, s. 115.
s. 235, repealed in pt.: 1995, c. 20, schs. 6, 7.
s. 235, C.: 1995, c. 46, s. 114.
s. 236A, repealed in pt.: 1995, c. 20, sch. 6.
s. 236A, C.: 1995, c. 46, s. 113.
s. 236B, C.: 1995, c. 46, s. 111.
s. 236C, repealed in pt.: 1995, c. 20, schs. 6, 7.
s. 237, repealed: 1995, c. 20, schs. 6, 7.
s. 238, repealed in pt.: 1995, c. 20, sch. 7.
s. 238, amended: 1995, c. 20, s. 5, sch. 6.
s. 238, C.: 1995, c. 46, s. 112.
s. 239, repealed in pt.: 1995, c. 20, schs. 6, 7.
s. 239, C.: 1995, c. 46, s. 117.
s. 240, repealed in pt.: 1995, c. 20, schs. 6, 7.
s. 240, C.: 1995, c. 46, s. 117.
s. 241, C.: 1995, c. 46, s. 117.
s. 242, C.: 1995, c. 46, s. 117.
s. 242A, C.: 1995, c. 46, s. 117.
s. 243, C.: 1995, c. 46, s. 117.
s. 244, see *McIntosh, Petr.*, 1995 S.L.T. 796.
s. 244, C.: 1995, c. 46, s. 116.
s. 245, amended: 1995, c. 20, s. 43.
s. 245, C.: 1995, c. 46, s. 103.
s. 246, repealed: 1995, c. 20, sch. 7.
s. 246, amended: 1995, c. 20, sch. 6.
s. 247, C.: 1995, c. 46, s. 103.
s. 249, C.: 1995, c. 46, s. 103.

CAP.

1975—cont.

21. Criminal Procedure (Scotland) Act 1975—*cont.*

s. 250, C.: 1995, c. 46, s. 103.
s. 251, C.: 1995, c. 46, s. 105.
s. 252, see *Tarbett* v. *H.M. Advocate*, 1994 S.C.C.R. 867; *Beattie* v. *H.M. Advocate*, 1995 S.L.T. 275; *Church* v. *H.M. Advocate*, 1995, S.L.T. 604; *Elliott* v. *H.M. Advocate*, 1995 S.L.T. 612.
s. 252, C.: 1995, c. 46, s. 104.
s. 253, C.: 1995, c. 46, s. 104.
s. 254, repealed in pt.: 1995, c. 20, sch. 6.
s. 254, see *B.* v. *H.M. Advocate*, 1995 S.L.T. 961.
s. 254, C.: 1995, c. 46, s. 118.
s. 254A, added: 1995, c. 20, s. 34.
s. 254A, C.: 1995, c. 46, ss. 118, 197.
s. 254B, added: 1995, c. 20, s. 34.
s. 254B, C.: 1995, c. 46, s. 118.
s. 255, amended: 1995, c. 20, s. 46.
s. 255, C.: 1995, c. 46, s. 119.
s. 256, repealed: order 95/2295.
s. 256, repealed: 1995, c. 20, schs. 6, 7.
s. 257, amended: 1995, c. 20, sch. 6.
s. 257, C.: 1995, c. 46, s. 120.
s. 258, C.: 1995, c. 46, s. 120.
s. 259, repealed in pt.: 1995, c. 20, schs. 6, 7.
s. 260, C.: 1995, c. 46, s. 120.
s. 261, C.: 1995, c. 46, s. 120.
s. 262, see *McIntosh, Petr.*, 1995 S.L.T. 796.
s. 262, C.: 1995, c. 46, s. 124.
s. 263, repealed in pt.: 1995, c. 20, sch. 6.
s. 263, see *Beattie* v. *H.M. Advocate*, 1995 S.L.T. 275.
s. 263, C.: 1995, c. 46, s. 124.
s. 263A, amended: 1995, c. 20, sch. 6.
s. 263A, C.: 1995, c. 46, s. 123.
s. 264, repealed in pt.: 1995, c. 20, sch. 6.
s. 264, amended: 1995, c. 20, sch. 6.
s. 264, C.: 1995, c. 46, s. 121.
s. 265, repealed in pt.: 1995, c. 20, schs. 6, 7.
s. 265, amended: 1995, c. 20, sch. 6.
s. 265, C.: 1995, c. 46, s. 122.
s. 266, C.: 1995, c. 46, s. 128.
s. 267, C.: 1995, c. 46, s. 128.
s. 268, amended: 1995, c. 20, sch. 6.
s. 268, C.: 1995, c. 46, s. 125.
s. 269, amended: 1995, c. 20, sch. 6.
s. 269, C.: 1995, c. 46, s. 126.
s. 270, repealed in pt.: 1995, c. 20, schs. 6, 7.
s. 270, C.: 1995, c. 46, s. 106.
s. 271, C.: 1995, c. 46, s. 127.
s. 272, repealed: 1995, c. 20, schs. 6, 7.
s. 273, repealed: 1995, c. 20, sch. 7.
s. 274, repealed in pt.: 1995, c. 20, sch. 6.
s. 274, C.: 1995, c. 46, s. 93.
s. 275, C.: 1995, c. 46, s. 94.

CAP.

1975—cont.

21. Criminal Procedure (Scotland) Act 1975—*cont.*

s. 276, repealed: 1995, c. 20, schs. 6, 7.
s. 277, repealed in pt.: 1995, c. 20, sch. 7.
s. 277, C.: 1995, c. 46, s. 129.
s. 278, C.: 1995, c. 46, s. 305.
s. 279, C.: 1995, c. 46, s. 132.
s. 280, C.: 1995, c. 46, s. 60.
s. 280A, C.: 1995, c. 46, s. 131.
s. 282, repealed in pt.: 1995, c. 20, schs. 6, 7.
s. 282A, C.: 1995, c. 46, s. 301.
s. 282B, C.: 1995, c. 46, s. 301.
s. 283, amended: 1995, c. 20, sch. 6.
s. 283, C.: 1995, c. 46, s. 133.
s. 283A, C.: 1995, c. 46, s. 292.
s. 284, C.: 1995, c. 46, s. 7.
s. 285, C.: 1995, c. 46, s. 7.
s. 286, C.: 1995, c. 46, s. 7.
s. 288, see *Howdle* v. *Beattie*, 1995 S.C.C.R. 349.
s. 288A, see *Advocate H.M.* v. *May*, 1995 S.C.C.R. 365.
s. 289, C.: 1995, c. 46, s. 5.
s. 289B, C.: 1995, c. 46, s. 225.
s. 289D, repealed in pt.: 1995, c. 20, schs. 6, 7.
s. 289D, C.: 1995, c. 46, s. 225.
s. 289G, C.: 1995, c. 46, s. 225.
s. 289GB, C.: 1995, c. 46, s. 226.
s. 290, C.: 1995, c. 46, s. 5.
s. 294, C.: 1995, c. 46, s. 22.
s. 295, C.: 1995, c. 46, s. 22.
s. 296, repealed in pt.: 1995, c. 20, sch. 6; 1995, c. 36, schs. 4, 5.
s. 296, amended: 1994, c. 39, sch. 13.
s. 296, C.: 1995, c. 46, s. 43.
s. 298, C.: 1995, c. 46, s. 23.
s. 299, C.: 1995, c. 46, s. 30.
s. 299A, added: 1995, c. 20, s. 3.
s. 299A, C.: 1995, c. 46, s. 31.
s. 300, repealed in pt.: 1995, c. 20, schs. 6, 7.
s. 300, C.: 1995, c. 46, s. 32.
s. 303, C.: 1995, c. 46, s. 168.
s. 304, amended: 1995, c. 36, sch. 4.
s. 304, C.: 1995, c. 46, s. 45.
s. 305, substituted: 1995, c. 20, sch. 6.
s. 305, C.: 1995, c. 46, s. 17.
s. 306, C.: 1995, c. 46, s. 42.
s. 307, amended: 1995, c. 36, sch. 4.
s. 307, C.: 1995, c. 46, s. 42.
s. 308, C.: 1995, c. 46, s. 42.
s. 309, repealed in pt.: 1995, c. 20, schs. 6, 7.
s. 309, C.: 1995, c. 46, ss. 172, 296.
s. 310, repealed in pt.: 1995, c. 20, schs. 6, 7.
s. 310, amended: 1995, c. 20, sch. 6.
s. 310, C.: 1995, c. 46, s. 134.
s. 310A, added: 1995, c. 20, s. 63.
s. 310A, C.: 1995, c. 46, s. 133.

CAP.

1975—cont.

21. Criminal Procedure (Scotland) Act 1975—*cont.*
- s. 311, repealed in pt.: 1995, c. 20, schs. 6, 7.
- s. 311, see *Turner* v. *Russell*, 1995, S.C.C.R. 488.
- s. 311, C.: 1995, c. 46, s. 138.
- s. 312, amended: 1995, c. 20, sch. 6.
- s. 312, C.: 1995, c. 46, ss. 138, 294, sch. 3.
- s. 312, see *Ross* v. *Simpson*, 1994 S.C.C.R. 847.
- s. 313, repealed: 1995, c. 20, schs. 6, 7.
- s. 314, repealed in pt.: 1995, c. 20, schs. 6, 7.
- s. 314, amended: 1995, c. 20, sch. 6.
- s. 314, C.: 1995, c. 46, ss. 137, 139.
- s. 315, repealed in pt.: 1995, c. 20, sch. 6.
- s. 315, C.: 1995, c. 46, s. 140.
- s. 316, amended: 1995, c. 20, sch. 6.
- s. 316, C.: 1995, c. 46, s. 141.
- s. 317, C.: 1995, c. 46, s. 232.
- s. 318, repealed in pt.: 1995, c. 20, schs. 6, 7.
- s. 318, C.: 1995, c. 46, s. 216.
- s. 319, repealed in pt.: 1995, c. 20, schs. 6, 7.
- s. 319, C.: 1995, c. 46, s. 141.
- s. 320, C.: 1995, c. 46, s. 156.
- s. 321, repealed in pt.: 1995, c. 20, schs. 6, 7.
- s. 321, amended: 1995, c. 20, sch. 6.
- s. 321, C.: 1995, c. 46, ss. 135, 156.
- s. 323, repealed in pt.: 1995, c. 20, sch. 7; 1995, c. 36, sch. 5.
- s. 323, amended: 1995, c. 20, sch. 6.
- s. 324, C.: 1995, c. 46, s. 297.
- s. 326, C.: 1995, c. 46, s. 297.
- s. 327, amended: 1995, c. 20, s. 9.
- s. 327, C.: 1995, c. 46, s. 297.
- s. 329, amended: 1995, c. 20, sch. 6.
- s. 329, C.: 1995, c. 46, s. 51.
- s. 330, C.: 1995, c. 46, s. 52.
- s. 331, repealed in pt.: 1995, c. 20, sch. 7.
- s. 331, amended: 1995, c. 20, s. 62.
- s. 331, C.: 1995, c. 46, s. 136.
- s. 331A, C.: 1995, c. 46, s. 147.
- s. 331B, added: 1995, c. 20, s. 30.
- s. 331B, C.: 1995, c. 46, s. 151.
- s. 332, C.: 1995, c. 46, s. 171.
- s. 333, C.: 1995, c. 46, s. 143.
- s. 333A, C.: 1995, c. 46, s. 145.
- s. 333B, added: 1995, c. 20, s. 12.
- s. 333B, C.: 1995, c. 46, s. 257.
- s. 334, see *Allan* v. *McKay*, 1994 S.C.C.R. 726; *Sutterfield* v. *O'Brien*, 1995 S.C.C.R. 483.
- s. 334, C.: 1995, c. 46, ss. 144, 174.
- s. 335, repealed in pt.: 1995, c. 20, schs. 6, 7.
- s. 336, repealed: 1995, c. 20, schs. 6, 7.
- s. 336, see *Allan* v. *MacKay*, 1994 S.C.C.R. 726.
- s. 337, C.: 1995, c. 46, s. 146.
- s. 337A, repealed in pt.: 1995, c. 20, sch. 7.
- s. 337A, amended: 1995, c. 20, s. 14.
- s. 337A, C.: 1995, c. 46, s. 148.
- s. 337B, added: 1995, c. 20, s. 31.
- s. 337B, C.: 1995, c. 46, s. 153.
- s. 338, C.: 1995, c. 46, s. 150.
- s. 338A, C.: 1995, c. 46, s. 152.
- s. 339, C.: 1995, c. 46, s. 149.
- s. 340, amended: 1995, c. 20, sch. 6.
- s. 340, C.: 1995, c. 46, s. 263.
- s. 341, C.: 1995, c. 46, s. 265.
- s. 342, C.: 1995, c. 46, s. 265.
- s. 342A, C.: 1995, c. 46, s. 267.
- s. 343, C.: 1995, c. 46, s. 267.
- s. 344, repealed in pt.: 1995, c. 20, sch. 7.
- s. 344, C.: 1995, c. 46, s. 155.
- s. 345, repealed: 1995, c. 20, sch. 7.
- s. 346, repealed in pt.: 1995, c. 20, sch. 7.
- s. 346, amended: 1995, c. 20, s. 24.
- s. 346, C.: 1995, c. 46, ss. 266, 274.
- s. 346A, amended: 1995, c. 20, s. 28.
- s. 346B, C.: 1995, c. 46, s. 275.
- s. 346ZA, C.: 1995, c. 46, s. 270.
- s. 347, C.: 1995, c. 46, ss. 266, 267.
- s. 348, C.: 1995, c. 46, s. 264.
- s. 349, C.: 1995, c. 46, s. 263.
- s. 349A, C.: 1995, c. 46, s. 263.
- s. 350, C.: 1995, c. 46, s. 268.
- s. 350A, C.: 1995, c. 46, s. 269.
- s. 352, C.: 1995, c. 46, s. 278.
- s. 353, C.: 1995, c. 46, s. 154.
- s. 354, repealed in pt.: 1995, c. 20, sch. 7.
- s. 354, C.: 1995, c. 46, s. 256.
- s. 355, C.: 1995, c. 46, s. 162.
- s. 356, repealed in pt.: 1995, c. 20, sch. 7.
- s. 356, C.: 1995, c. 46, s. 166.
- s. 357, repealed in pt.: 1995, c. 20, sch. 7.
- s. 357, amended: 1995, c. 20, s. 24.
- s. 357, C.: 1995, c. 46, ss. 285, 286.
- s. 358, C.: 1995, c. 46, s. 285.
- s. 359, see *Macaulay* v. *Wilson*, 1995 S.C.C.R. 133.
- s. 359, C.: 1995, c. 46, s. 157.
- s. 360, repealed: 1995, c. 20, schs. 6, 7.
- s. 360A, repealed in pt.: 1995, c. 20, sch. 6.
- s. 360A, C.: 1995, c. 46, s. 158.
- s. 361, C.: 1995, c. 46, s. 50.
- s. 362, amended: 1995, c. 20, sch. 6.
- s. 362, C.: 1995, c. 46, s. 50.
- s. 363, C.: 1995, c. 46, s. 50.
- s. 364, repealed in pt.: 1995, c. 36, schs. 4, 5.
- s. 364, amended: 1994, c. 39, sch. 13.
- s. 364, C.: 1995, c. 46, s. 48.
- s. 366, repealed in pt.: 1995, c. 20, schs. 6, 7.
- s. 366, amended: 1995, c. 20, sch. 6.
- s. 366, C.: 1995, c. 46, s. 142.
- s. 367, C.: 1995, c. 46, s. 142.

CAP.

1975—cont.

21. Criminal Procedure (Scotland) Act 1975—*cont.*
s. 368, amended: 1995, c. 36, sch. 4.
s. 368, C.: 1995, c. 46, s. 46.
s. 369, C.: 1995, c. 46, s. 41.
s. 370, C.: 1995, c. 46, s. 142.
s. 371, C.: 1995, c. 46, s. 50.
s. 372, C.: 1995, c. 46, s. 49.
s. 373, C.: 1995, c. 46, s. 49.
s. 374, C.: 1995, c. 46, s. 47.
s. 375, amended: 1995, c. 20, ss. 47, 48, sch. 6.
s. 375, C.: 1995, c. 46, s. 54.
s. 375A, C.: 1995, c. 46, s. 53.
s. 375ZA, added: 1995, c. 20, s. 49.
s. 375ZA, C.: 1995, c. 46, s. 55.
s. 375ZB, added: 1995, c. 46, s. 53.
s. 375ZB, C.: 1995, c. 46, s. 56.
s. 375ZC, added: 1995, c. 20, s. 50.
s. 375ZC, C.: 1995, c. 46, s. 57.
s. 375ZD, added: 1995, c. 20, s. 51.
s. 375ZD, C.: 1995, c. 46, s. 62.
s. 375ZE, added: 1995, c. 20, s. 52.
s. 375ZE, C.: 1995, c. 46, s. 63.
s. 376, repealed in pt.: 1995, c. 20, schs. 6, 7.
s. 376, amended: 1995, c. 20, sch. 6.
s. 376, C.: 1995, c. 46, ss. 52, 58.
s. 377, amended: 1995, c. 20, sch. 6.
s. 377, C.: 1995, c. 46, s. 61.
s. 378, repealed in pt.: 1995, c. 36, sch. 5.
s. 378, amended: 1995, c. 36, sch. 4.
s. 378, C.: 1995, c. 46, s. 58.
s. 379, repealed in pt.: 1995, c. 20, s. 54, sch. 7.
s. 379, amended: 1995, c. 20, sch. 6.
s. 379, C.: 1995, c. 46, s. 59.
s. 380, amended: 1995, c. 20, sch. 6.
s. 380, see *Burns* v. *Lees*, 1994 S.C.C.R. 780; *Hunter* v. *Carmichael*, 1995 S.L.T. 449.
s. 380, C.: 1995, c. 46, s. 201.
s. 380A, added: 1995, c. 20, s. 37.
s. 380A, C.: 1995, c. 46, s. 203.
s. 381, amended: 1995, c. 20, s. 55.
s. 384, repealed in pt.: 1995, c. 20, s. 38, sch. 7.
s. 384, amended: 1995, c. 20, s. 38, sch. 6.
s. 385, amended: 1995, c. 20, s. 39.
s. 385, C.: 1995, c. 46, s. 230.
s. 386, C.: 1995, c. 46, s. 231.
s. 387, repealed in pt.: 1995, c. 20, schs. 6, 7.
s. 387, C.: 1995, c. 46, s. 232.
s. 388, C.: 1995, c. 46, s. 233.
s. 389, C.: 1995, c. 46, s. 234.
s. 391, repealed: 1995, c. 20, sch. 7.
s. 392, repealed in pt.: 1995, c. 20, schs. 6, 7.
s. 392, C.: 1995, c. 46, s. 247.
s. 393, repealed in pt.: 1995, c. 20, schs. 6, 7.

CAP.

1975—cont.

21. Criminal Procedure (Scotland) Act 1975—*cont.*
s. 394, C.: 1995, c. 46, s. 199.
s. 395, see *Tonner* v. *Hamilton*, 1995 S.C.C.R. 469.
s. 395, C.: 1995, c. 46, ss. 211, 212.
s. 395A, C.: 1995, c. 46, s. 213.
s. 396, repealed in pt.: 1995, c. 20, schs. 6, 7.
s. 396, C.: 1995, c. 46, s. 214.
s. 397, C.: 1995, c. 46, s. 215.
s, 398, repealed in pt.: 1995, c. 20, sch. 6.
s. 398, C.: 1995, c. 46, s. 216.
s. 399, C.: 1995, c. 46, s. 214.
s. 400, C.: 1995, c. 46, s. 217.
s. 401, C.: 1995, c. 46, s. 218.
s. 402, repealed in pt.: 1995, c. 20, schs. 6, 7.
s. 403, amended: 1995, c. 20, s. 67.
s. 403, C.: 1995, c. 46, s. 222.
s. 404, C.: 1995, c. 46, s. 223.
s. 406, repealed in pt.: 1995, c. 20, schs. 6, 7.
s. 406, C.: 1995, c. 46, s. 216.
s. 407, amended: 1995, c. 20, s. 35.
s. 407, C.: 1995, c. 46, s. 219.
s. 408, amended: 1995, c. 20, sch. 6.
s. 408, C.: 1995, c. 46, s. 224.
s. 409, C.: 1995, c. 46, ss. 220, 305.
s. 411, C.: 1995, c. 46, s. 221.
s. 412, C.: 1995, c. 46, s. 211.
s. 412A, added: 1995, c. 20, s. 35.
s. 412A, C.: 1995, c. 46, s. 236.
s. 412B, added: 1995, c. 20, s. 35.
s. 412B, C.: 1995, c. 46, s. 237.
s. 413, amended: 1994, c. 39, sch. 13; 1995, c. 36, sch. 4.
s. 413, repealed in pt.: 1995, c. 20, schs. 6, 7; 1995, c. 36, schs. 4, 5.
s. 413, amended: 1995, c. 20, sch. 6.
s. 413, C.: 1995, c. 46, s. 44.
s. 415, C.: 1995, c. 46, s. 207.
s. 424, C.: 1995, c. 46, s. 169.
s. 425, C.: 1995, c. 46, s. 206.
s. 426, C.: 1995, c. 46, s. 295.
s. 427, C.: 1995, c. 46, s. 164.
s. 428, C.: 1995, c. 46, s. 293.
s. 429, C.: 1995, c. 46, s. 165.
s. 430, repealed in pt.: 1995, c. 20, schs. 6, 7.
s. 430, amended: 1995, c. 20, s. 33.
s. 430, C.: 1995, c. 46, s. 167.
s. 430A, C.: 1995, c. 46, s. 196.
s. 432, repealed in pt.: 1995, c. 20, schs. 6, 7.
s. 432, C.: 1995, c. 46, s. 202.
s. 433, C.: 1995, c. 46, s. 167.
s. 434, C.: 1995, c. 46, s. 167.
s. 435, repealed: 1995, c. 20, schs. 6, 7.
s. 436, repealed: 1995, c. 20, schs. 6, 7.
s. 437, C.: 1995, c. 46, s. 254.
s. 439A, added: 1995, c. 20, s. 41.

CAP.

1975—cont.

21. Criminal Procedure (Scotland) Act 1975—*cont.*
s. 439A, C.: 1995, c. 46, s. 300.
s. 440, repealed in pt.: 1995, c. 20, schs. 6, 7.
s. 440, C.: 1995, c. 46, s. 163.
s. 441, repealed in pt.: 1995, c. 20, schs. 6, 7.
s. 441, C.: 1995, c. 46, s. 163.
s. 441, see *Normand* v. *Walker*, 1995 S.L.T. 94.
s. 442, amended: 1995, c. 20, s. 42.
s. 442, C.: 1995, c. 46, s. 175.
s. 442B, C.: 1995, c. 46, s. 175.
s. 442ZA, added: 1995, c. 20, s. 42.
s. 442ZA, C.: 1995, c. 46, s. 180.
s. 443, C.: 1995, c. 46, s. 60.
s. 443A, amended: 1995, c. 20, sch. 6.
s. 443A, C.: 1995, c. 46, s. 193.
s. 444, amended: 1995, c. 20, sch. 6.
s. 444, see *Crowe, Petr.*, 1994 S.C.C.R. 784; *Leonard, Petr.*, 1995 S.C.C.R. 39.
s. 444, C.: 1995, c. 46, ss. 176, 181.
s. 446, amended: 1995, c. 20, sch. 6.
s. 446, C.: 1995, c. 46, s. 177.
s. 447, see *Leonard, Petr.*, 1995 S.C.C.R. 39.
s. 447, C.: 1995, c. 46, s. 178.
s. 448, C.: 1995, c. 46, s. 179.
s. 449, C.: 1995, c. 46, s. 184.
s. 450, C.: 1995, c. 46, s. 176.
s. 451, amended: 1995, c. 20, s. 45, sch. 6.
s. 451, C.: 1995, c. 46, s. 194.
s. 451A, added: 1995, c. 20, s. 43.
s. 451A, C.: 1995, c. 46, s. 173.
s. 452, see *Normand* v. *Walker*, 1995 S.L.T. 94; *Anderson* v. *Macleod*, 1995 S.C.C.R. 395.
s. 452, C.: 1995, c. 46, s. 182.
s. 452A, C.: 1995, c. 46, s. 183.
s. 452B, C.: 1995, c. 46, s. 185.
s. 453, repealed in pt.: 1995, c. 20, sch. 7.
s. 453, amended: 1995, c. 20, sch. 6.
s. 453, C.: 1995, c. 46, ss. 188, 189.
s. 453A, C.: 1995, c. 46, s. 191.
s. 453AA, added: 1995, c. 20, s. 42.
s. 453AA, C.: 1995, c. 46, s. 187.
s. 453B, amended: 1995, c. 20, sch. 6.
s. 453B, C.: 1995, c. 46, s. 186.
s. 453C, C.: 1995, c. 46, s. 189.
s. 453D, amended: 1995, c. 20, sch. 6.
s. 453D, C.: 1995, c. 46, s. 190.
s. 453E, see *Pratt* v. *H.M. Advocate*, 1994 S.C.C.R. 881.
s. 453E, C.: 1995, c. 46, s. 192.
s. 454, repealed in pt.: 1995, c. 20, schs. 6, 7.
s. 454, see *Macaulay* v. *Wilson*, 1995 S.C.C.R. 133; *Sutterfield* v. *O'Brien*, 1995 S.C.C.R. 483.
s. 454, C.: 1995, c. 46, s. 192.
s. 455, C.: 1995, c. 46, s. 192.

CAP.

1975—cont.

21. Criminal Procedure (Scotland) Act 1975—*cont.*
s. 455A, added: 1995, c. 20, s. 34.
s. 455A, C.: 1995, c. 46, ss. 189, 197.
s. 456, C.: 1995, c. 46, s. 170.
s. 457A, C.: 1995, c. 46, s. 292.
s. 457, repealed: 1995, c. 20, schs. 6, 7.
s. 457ZA, added: 1995, c. 20, sch. 6.
s. 457ZA, C.: 1995, c. 46, s. 305.
s. 458, C.: 1995, c. 46, s. 308.
s. 459, C.: 1995, c. 46, s. 308.
s. 462, repealed in pt.: 1995, c. 20, schs. 6, 7.
s. 462, amended: 1994, c. 39, sch. 13; 1995, c. 20, s. 39, sch. 6.
s. 462, C.: 1995, c. 46, s. 307.
sch. 1, C.: 1995, c. 46, sch. 1.
sch. 3, repealed in pt.: 1995, c. 20, sch. 7.
sch. 5, amended: 1995, c. 39, sch. 13; 1995, c. 20, sch. 6.
sch. 5, C.: 1995, c. 46, sch. 3.
sch. 5A, C.: 1995, c. 46, sch. 3.
sch. 7, C.: 1995, c. 46, s. 220.
sch. 7A, C.: 1995, c. 46, sch. 10.
sch. 7D, repealed in pt.: 1994, c. 39, sch. 14.

22. Oil Taxation Act 1975.
s. 6, amended: 1995, c. 4, s. 146.
sch. 2, see *Elf Enterprise Caledonia* v. *I.R.C.* [1994] S.T.C. 785, Sir Donald Nicholls, V-C.
sch. 8, amended: 1995, c. 4, s. 147.
sch. 8, repealed in pt.: 1995, c. 4, sch. 29.

23. Reservoirs Act 1975.
s. 2, amended: 1994, c. 39, sch. 13 (S.).

24. House of Commons Disqualification Act 1975.
ss. 65–67, repealed: 1994, c. 39, s. 179 (S.).
ss. 76H, 109, repealed in pt.: 1994, c. 39, s. 179 (S.).
sch. 1, repealed in pt.: 1994, c. 39, sch. 14 (S.); 1995, c. 17, sch. 2; 1995, c. 25, sch. 24; 1995, c. 26, schs. 5, 7.
sch. 1, amended: 1994, c. 39, s. 177, sch. 13 (S.); 1995, c. 17, sch. 1; 1995, c. 24, s. 12; 1995, c. 25, sch. 22; 1995, c. 26, sch. 1; 1995, c. 35, sch. 2; 1995, c. 37, sch. 2.

25. Northern Ireland Assembly Disqualification Act 1975.
sch. 1, repealed in pt.: 1995, c. 24, sch. 2; 1995, c. 25, sch. 24; 1995, c. 26, schs. 5, 7.
sch. 1, amended: 1995, c. 25, sch. 22; 1995, c. 26, sch. 1.

26. Ministers of the Crown Act 1975.
s. 1, order 95/269.

27. Ministerial and other Salaries Act 1975.
s. 1, order 94/3206.
sch. 1, substituted: order 94/3206.

30. Local Government (Scotland) Act 1975.
s. 1, repealed in pt.: 1994, c. 39, sch. 14.

CAP.

1975—cont.

30. Local Government (Scotland) Act 1975—*cont.*
s. 2, amended: 1994, c. 39, sch. 13; orders 94/911, 913, 2068, 2069, 2071, 2072, 2073, 2074, 2075, 2076, 2077, 2078, 2079, 2080, 2081; 95/366, 367, 368, 369, 370, 371, 372, 373, 929, 930.
s. 3, order 95/573.
s. 3, amended: orders 94/911, 2068, 2069, 2071, 2073, 2074, 2075, 2076, 2077, 2078, 2079, 2080, 2081; 95/367, 368, 369, 370, 373, 929, 930.
s. 4, repealed: 1994, c. 39, sch. 14.
s. 6, orders 94/911, 912, 913, 2068, 2069, 2071, 2072, 2073, 2074, 2075, 2076, 2077, 2078, 2079, 2080, 2081; 95/366, 367, 368, 369, 370, 371, 372, 373, 374, 375, 929, 930.
s. 6, repealed in pt.: 1994, c. 39, sch. 14.
s. 6, amended: 1994, c. 39, ss. 157, 160.
s. 7, repealed in pt.: 1994, c. 39, sch. 14.
s. 7A, order 95/64.
s. 7A, repealed in pt.: 1994, c. 39, sch. 14.
s. 7A, amended: 1994, c. 39, sch. 13.
s. 7B, order 95/312.
s. 7B, amended: 1994, c. 39, sch. 13.
s. 15A, added: 1994, c. 39, s. 168.
s. 16, repealed in pt.: 1995, c. 25, sch. 24.
s. 16, amended: 1995, c. 25, sch. 22.
s. 23, repealed in pt.: 1994, c. 39, sch. 13; 1995, c. 25, sch. 24; 1995, c. 36, sch. 4.
s. 23, repealed in pt.: 1994, c. 39, sch. 14.
s. 23, amended: 1994, c. 39, sch. 13.
s. 27, amended: 1994, c. 39, sch. 14.
s. 28, amended: 1994, c. 39, sch. 14; order 95/789.
s. 29A, repealed in pt.: 1994, c. 39, sch. 14.
s. 35, orders 94/911, 912, 2068, 2069, 2071, 2073, 2074, 2075, 2076, 2077, 2078, 2079, 2080; 95/366, 367, 368, 369, 370, 371, 372, 373, 374, 375, 573, 929, 930.
s. 37, orders 94/911, 912, 2068, 2069, 2071, 2073, 2074, 2075, 2076, 2077, 2078, 2079, 2080; 95/366, 367, 368, 369, 370, 371, 372, 373, 374, 375, 573, 929, 930.
s. 37, amended: 1994, c. 39, sch. 13.
sch. 3, repealed in pt.: 1994, c. 39, s. 168, sch. 14; 1995, c. 25, sch. 24.
sch. 3, amended: 1994, c. 39, sch. 13; 1995, c. 25, sch. 22.

35. Evidence (Proceedings in Other Jurisdictions) Act 1975.
sch. 1, C.: 1995, c. 39, s. 44 (S.).

36. Air Travel Reserve Fund Act 1975.
repealed: 1995, c. 44, sch. 1.

42. Children Act 1975.
ss. 47–49, repealed: 1995, c. 36, sch. 4 (S.).
s. 50, amended: 1995, c. 36, sch. 4 (S.).

CAP.

1975—cont.

42. Children Act 1975—*cont.*
s. 51, amended: 1995, c. 36, sch. 4 (S.).
s. 52, amended: 1995, c. 36, sch. 4 (S.).
s. 53, repealed: 1995, c. 36, sch. 4 (S.).
s. 55, amended: 1995, c. 36, sch. 4 (S.).
ss. 73–84, 89, 99, 100, 102, 103, amended: 1995, c. 36, sch. 4 (S.).
s. 105, amended: 1995, c. 36, s. 94 (S.).
s. 107, amended: 1995, c. 36, sch. 4 (S.).
sch. 3, repealed in pt.: 1995, c. 36, sch. 4 (S.).

46. International Road Haulage Permits Act 1975.
s. 1, regs. 95/1290.
s. 1, amended: 1995, c. 23, sch. 7.
s. 3, repealed: 1995, c. 23, sch. 8.
s. 3, C.: 1995, c. 23, sch. 8.
sch. 4, repealed: 1994, c. 39, sch. 14.

50. Guard Dogs 1975.
s. 7, amended: 1994, c. 39, sch. 13 (S.).

51. Salmon and Freshwater Fisheries Act 1975.
s. 5, repealed in pt.: 1995, c. 25, sch. 24.
s. 5, amended: 1995, c. 25, sch. 12.
ss. 6, 8, 9, amended: 1995, c. 25, sch. 12.
s. 10, repealed in pt.: 1995, c. 25, sch. 24.
s. 10, amended: 1995, c. 25, sch. 15.
s. 11, amended: 1995, c. 25, sch. 15.
s. 14, substituted: 1995, c. 25, sch. 15.
s. 15, repealed in pt.: 1995, c. 25, sch. 24.
s. 15, amended: 1995, c. 25, sch. 15.
ss. 17, 18, amended: 1995, c. 25, sch. 15.
s. 30, repealed in pt.: 1995, c. 25, sch. 24.
s. 30, amended: 1995, c. 25, sch. 15.
s. 35, amended: 1995, c. 25, sch. 15.
s. 37A, added: 1995, c. 25, s. 104.
ss. 35, 39, amended: 1995, c. 25, sch. 15.
s. 41, repealed in pt.: 1995, c. 25, sch. 24.
s. 41, amended: 1995, c. 25, sch. 15.
s. 43, sch. 1, amended: 1995, c. 25, sch. 15.
sch. 4, 1995, c. 40, sch. 2 (S.).

52. Safety of Sports Grounds Act 1975.
s. 1, order 95/1990.
s. 17, amended: 1994, c. 39, sch. 13 (S.).
s. 18, order 95/1990.

56. Coal Industry Act 1975.
s. 2, sch. 1, see *British Coal Corp.* v. *Ellistown Pipes* [1994] RVR 81, C.A.

60. Social Security Pensions Act 1975.
s. 61, amended: 1995, c. 26, sch. 5.
s. 61B, repealed in pt.: 1995, c. 26, schs. 5, 7.
s. 64, amended: 1995, c. 26, sch. 5.

63. Inheritance (Provisions for Family and Dependants) Act 1975.
see *Stock* v. *Brown* [1994] 1 F.L.R. 840, Thorpe J.
s. 1, amended: 1995, c. 41, s. 2.
s. 1, see *Jennings (Dec'd), Re* [1994] 3 W.L.R. 67, C.A.

CAP.

1975—cont.

63. Inheritance (Provisions for Family and Dependants) Act 1975—*cont.*
s. 2, see *Jennings (Dec'd), Re* [1994] 3 W.L.R. 67, C.A.
s. 3, amended: 1995, c. 41, s. 2.
s. 3, see *Jennings (Dec'd), Re* [1994] 3 W.L.R. 67, C.A.
s. 21, repealed: 1995, c. 38, sch. 2.

65. Sex Discrimination Act 1975.
see *Ratcliffe* v. *North Yorkshire County Council, The Times*, July 7, 1995, H.L.; *Webb* v. *EMO Air Cargo (U.K.) (No. 2), The Times*, October 20, 1995, H.L.
s. 1, see *Burrett* v. *West Birmingham Health Authority* [1994] IRLR 7, E.A.T.; *R.* v. *Secretary of State for Employment, ex p. Seymour-Smith and Perez* [1994] IRLR 448, D.C.; *Stewart* v. *Cleveland Guest (Engineering)* [1994] IRLR 440, E.A.T.; *Meade-Hill* v. *British Council, The Times*, April 14, 1995, Millett L.J.; *British Coal Corporation* v. *Smith*; *Smith* v. *Safeway* [1995] I.C.R. 472, E.A.T.; *Ratcliffe* v. *North Yorkshire County Council* [1995] IRLR 439, H.L.; *London Underground* v. *Edwards* [1995] ICR 574, E.A.T.; *Meade-Hill and National Union of Civil and Public Servants* v. *British Council* [1995] IRLR 478, C.A.
s. 4, repealed in pt.: 1994, c. 33, s. 33, sch. 11.
s. 4, amended: 1995, c. 26, s. 66.
s. 4, see *Waters* v. *Commissioner of Police of the Metropolis* [1995] I.C.R. 510, E.A.T.
s. 5, see *Stewart* v. *Cleveland Guest (Engineering)* [1994] IRLR 440, C.A.
s. 6, amended: 1995, c. 26, s. 66.
s. 6, see *Meade-Hill* v. *British Council, The Times*, April 14, 1995, Millett L.J.; *Stewart* v. *Cleveland Guest (Engineering)* [1994] 440, E.A.T.; *Waters* v. *Commissioner of Police of the Metropolis* [1995] I.C.R. 510, E.A.T.; *Leighton* v. *Michael, The Times*, October 26, 1995, E.A.T.; *Meade-Hill and National Union of Civil and Public Servants* v. *British Council*]1995] IRLR 478, C.A.
s. 13, see *Khan* v. *General Medical Council* [1994] IRLR 646, C.A.
ss. 22, 23, repealed in pt.: 1994, c. 33, s. 33, sch. 11.
s. 24, order 95/2019.
s. 41, see *Waters* v. *Commissioner of Police of the Metropolis* [1995] I.C.R. 510, E.A.T.
s. 57, see *London Fire and Civil Defence Authority* v. *Betty* [1994] IRLR 384, E.A.T.

CAP.

1975—cont.

65. Sex Discrimination Act 1975—*cont.*
s. 63, see *Khan* v. *General Medical Council* [1994] IRLR 646, C.A.
s. 65, see *Harvey* v. *Institute of Motor Industry* [1995] IRLR 416, E.A.T.; *R.* v. *Secretary of State for Employment, ex p. Seymour-Smith and Perez* [1995] IRLR 464, C.A.; *Ministry of Defence* v. *Cannock* [1994] IRLR 589, E.A.T.
s. 66, see *Ministry of Defence* v. *Cannock* [1994] IRLR 589, E.A.T.
s. 77, see *Meade-Hill and National Union of Civil and Public Servants* v. *British Council* [1995] IRLR 478, C.A.
s. 81, order 95/2019.
s. 85, substituted and repealed in pt.: regs. 94/3276.
s. 85, see *Ministry of Defence* v. *Cannock* [1994] IRLR 589, E.A.T.

70. Welsh Development Agency Act 1975.
ss. 1, 15, amended: 1995, c. 25, sch. 10.
s. 16, repealed in pt.: 1995, c. 25, sch. 24.

71. Employment Protection Act 1975.
ss. 99, 100, 101, see *MSF* v. *GEC Ferranti (Defence Systems) (No. 2.)* [1994] IRLR 113, E.A.T.

72. Children Act 1975.
s. 47, repealed: 1995, c. 36, sch. 5 (S.).
s. 47, see *D.* v. *Grampian Regional Council*, 1995 S.L.T. 519.
s. 48, Act of Sederunt 94/2901 (S.).
s. 48, repealed: 1995, c. 36, sch. 5 (S.).
s. 49, repealed: 1995, c. 36, sch. 5 (S.).
s. 49, see *R.* v. *R.* (Sh.Ct.), 1994 S.C.L.R. 849.
s. 53, repealed: 1995, c. 36, sch. 5 (S.).
ss. 73–84, amended: 1995, c. 36, sch. 4 (S.).
s. 99, repealed: 1995, c. 36, sch. 5 (S.).
s. 99, amended: 1994, c. 39, sch. 13 (S.).
ss. 100, 102, 103, 105, repealed: 1995, c. 36, sch. 5 (S.).
s. 107, sch. 3, repealed in pt.: 1995, c. 36, sch. 5 (S.).

74. Petroleum and Submarine Pipe-Lines Act 1975.
s. 18, amended: 1995, c. 7, sch. 4 (S.).
s. 45, C.: 1995, c. 21, sch. 14.

76. Local Land Charges Act 1975.
ss. 1, 2, amended: 1995, c. 25, sch. 10.
s. 14, rules 95/260.

83. Northern Ireland (Loans) Act 1975.
s. 1, order 95/675.

1976

3. Road Traffic (Drivers' Ages and Hours of Work) Act 1976.
s. 2, repealed in pt.: 1995, c. 23, sch. 8.
s. 2, C.: 1995, c. 23, sch. 8.

12. Adoption Act 1976.
s. 6, see *E. (Adoption: Freeing Order), Re* [1995] 1 F.L.R. 382, C.A.; *G (Adoption: Illegal Placement) Re* [1995] 1 F.L.R. 403, C.A.

CAP.

1976—cont.

12. Adoption Act 1976—*cont.*

s. 11, see *G. (Adoption: Illegal Placement) Re* [1995] 1 F.L.R. 403, C.A.

s. 12, see *S. (A Minor) (Adoption Order: Conditions), Re* [1995] 2 All E.R. 122, C.A.; *G. (Adoption: Illegal Placement) Re* [1995] 1 F.L.R. 403, C.A.

s. 13, see *G. (Adoption: Illegal Placement) Re* [1995] 1 F.L.R. 403, C.A.

s. 18, see *E. (Adoption: Freeing Order), Re* [1995] 1 F.L.R. 382, C.A.

ss. 22, 24, 57, see *G. (Adoption: Illegal Placement) Re* [1995] 1 F.L.R. 403, C.A.

14. Fatal Accidents and Sudden Deaths Inquiry (Scotland) Act 1976.

s. 2, amended: 1995, c. 40, sch. 4 (S.).

s. 6, see *Smith* v. *Lord Advocate* (O.H.), 1995 S.L.T. 379.

19. Seychelles Act 1976.

sch., repealed in pt.: 1995, c. 21, sch. 12.

21. Crofting Reform (Scotland) Act 1976.

s. 1, see *MacMillan* v. *MacKenzie*, 1995 S.L.T. (Land Ct.) 7.

22. Freshwater and Salmon Fisheries (Scotland) Act 1976.

s. 1, order 94/3302.

s. 1, amended: 1995, c. 40, sch. 4 (S.).

25. Fair Employment (Northern Ireland) Act 1976.

s. 26, order S.R. 1995 No. 240.

ss. 26, 56, amended: S.R. 1995 No. 758.

30. Fatal Accidents Act 1976.

s. 1, see *R.* v. *Criminal Injuries Compensation Board, ex p. Barrett* (1994) 1 F.L.R. 587, Latham J.; *Shepherd* v. *Post Office, The Times*, June 15, 1995, C.A.

32. Lotteries and Amusements Act 1976.

amended: order 95/323.

s. 16, amended: orders 95/928, 1021 (S.).

s. 16, see *Matchurban* v. *Kyle and Carrick District Council (No. 2)* (I.H.), 1995 S.L.T. 1211.

s. 18, orders 95/323, 928, 1021 (S.).

s. 23, amended: 1994, c. 39, sch. 13 (S.).

s. 24, orders 95/323, 928, 1021 (S.).

sch. 1, amended: 1994, c. 39, sch. 13 (S.).

sch. 2A, amended: 95/323.

sch. 3, amended: 1994, c. 39, sch. 13 (S.).

sch. 3, see *Matchurban* v. *Kyle and Carrick District Council (No. 2)* (I.H.), 1995 S.L.T. 1211.

34. Restrictive Trade Practices Act 1976.

s. 1, see *Mackie & Dewar* v. *Director General of Fair Trading* (R.P.C.), 1995 S.L.T. 1028.

s. 9, see *Associated Dairies* v. *Baines* [1995] I.C.R. 296, Sir John Vinelott.

s. 26, see *Mackie & Dewar* v. *Director General of Fair Trading* (R.P.C.), 1995 S.L.T. 1028.

CAP.

1976—cont.

34. Restrictive Trade Practices Act 1976—*cont.*

s. 35, see *Director General of Fair Trading* v. *Pioneer Concrete (U.K.); sub nom. Supply of Ready Mixed Concrete (No. 2), Re* [1994] 3 W.L.R. 1249, H.L.

ss. 39, 41, amended: 1995, c. 40, sch. 4 (S.).

sch. 3, see *Associated Dairies* v. *Baines* [1995] I.C.R. 296, Sir John Vinelott.

36. Adoption Act 1976.

s. 2, amended: 1995, c. 17, sch. 1.

s. 6, see *P. (A Minor) (Removal of Child for Adoption), Re* [1994] 2 F.C.R. 537, Miss Mary Hogg, Q.C. sitting as a High Court Judge; *C.* v. *Salford City Council* [1994] 2 F.L.R. 926, Hale J.; *T. and E. (Proceedings: Conflicting Interests), Re* [1995] 1 F.L.R. 581, Wall J.

s. 12, see *R. (A Minor) (Adoption: Contact Order) Re* [1994] 1 F.C.R. 104, C.A.

s. 14, see *A.B. (A Minor) (Adoption; Unmarried Couple), Re, The Times*, August 10, 1995, Cazalet J.

s. 16, see *R. (A Minor) (Adoption: Contact Order) Re* [1994] 1 F.C.R. 104, C.A.; *P. (Minors) (Adoption: Freeing Order), Re* [1994] 2 F.C.R. 1306, C.A.

s. 18, see *R. (A Minor) (Adoption: Contact Order) Re* [1994] 1 F.C.R. 104, C.A.

s. 19, see *R. (A Minor) (Adoption: Contact Order) Re* [1994] 1 F.C.R. 104, C.A.

ss. 22, 30–32, see *P. (A Minor) (Removal of Child for Adoption), Re* [1994] 2 F.C.R. 537, Miss Mary Hogg, Q.C. sitting as a High Court Judge.

s. 63, repealed in pt.: order 94/3138.

s. 67, sch. 1, regs. 94/2981.

s. 72, see *C. (A Minor) (Adoption: Parties), Re, The Times*, June 1, 1995, C.A.

sch. 2, see *P. (A Minor) (Removal of Child for Adoption), Re* [1994] 2 F.C.R. 537, Miss Mary Hogg, Q.C. sitting as a High Court Judge.

38. Dangerous Wild Animals Act 1976.

s. 7, amended: 1994, c. 39, sch. 13 (S.).

50. Domestic Violence and Matrimonial Proceedings Act 1976.

see *Khan* v. *Khan* (LTA 94/6904/F), October 26, 1994, C.A.

s. 2, see *McCann* v. *Wright, The Times*, July 10, 1995, C.A.

57. Local Government (Miscellaneous Provisions) Act 1976.

s. 44, amended: 1995, c. 25, sch. 22.

s. 46, see *Kingston upon Hull City Council* v. *Wilson, The Times*, July 25, 1995, Buxton J.; *Adur District Council* v. *Fry* (CO 25/95), April 7, 1995, Kay J.

CAP.

1976—cont.

57. Local Government (Miscellaneous Provisions) Act 1976—*cont.*

s. 48, see *R.* v. *Leeds City Council, ex p. Hendry* (1994) 6 Admin.L.R. 439, Latham J.

58. International Carriage of Perishable Foodstuffs Act 1976.

s. 12, amended: 1995, c. 40, sch. 4 (S.).
s. 15, amended: 1995, c. 38, sch. 1.

63. Bail Act 1976.

see *C. (Secure Accommodation: Bail), Re* [1994] 2 F.L.R. 922, Hollis J.; *R.* v. *Starkey (Darren)* (1994) 15 Cr.App.R. (S.) 576, C.A.

66. Licensing (Scotland) Act 1976.

ss. 1, 3, repealed in pt.: 1994, c. 39, schs. 13, 14.
s. 5, repealed in pt.: 1994, c. 39, schs. 13, 14.
s. 5, see *Glasgow Licensing Board* v. *Din* (I.H.), 1995 S.C.L.R. 290.
s. 7, repealed in pt.: 1994, c. 39, sch. 14.
s. 13, see *Lowther* v. *Perth and Kinross District Licensing Board* (O.H.), 1995 S.L.T. 241; 1994 S.C.L.R. 1107.
ss. 16, 16A, see *Pagliocca* v. *City of Glasgow District Licensing Board*, 1995 S.L.T. 180.
s. 17, see *Pagliocca* v. *City of Glasgow District Licensing Board*, 1995 S.L.T. 180; *Glasgow District Licensing Board* v. *Din* (I.H.), 1995 S.C.L.R. 290.
s. 18, see *Robertson* v. *City of Edinburgh District Licensing Board*, 1995 S.L.T. 107.
s. 23, amended: 1994, c. 39, sch. 13.
s. 25, see *Chaudry* v. *Edinburgh District Licensing Board* (O.H.), 1995 S.C.L.R. 423.
s. 31, see *Basra* v. *Cunninghame District Licensing Board*, 1995 S.L.T. 1013.
ss. 105, 120, 139, amended: 1994, c. 39, sch. 13.

67. Sexual Offences (Scotland) Act 1976.

s. 1, C.: 1995, c. 39, s. 7.
s. 2, C.: 1995, c. 39, s. 7.
s. 2A, C.: 1995, c. 39, s. 1.
s. 2B, C.: 1995, c. 39, s. 2.
s. 2C, C.: 1995, c. 39, s. 3.
s. 2D, C.: 1995, c. 39, s. 4.
s. 3, C.: 1995, c. 39, s. 5.
s. 4, repealed in pt.: 1995, c. 20, schs. 6, 7.
s. 4, amended: 1995, c. 20, sch. 6.
s. 4, C.: 1995, c. 39, s. 5.
s. 5, C.: 1995, c. 39, s. 6.
s. 6, C.: 1995, c. 39, s. 15.
s. 8, orders 95/533, 562, 563.
s. 8, substituted: 1995, c. 17, s. 1.
s. 8, C.: 1995, c. 39, s. 8.
s. 9, C.: 1995, c. 39, s. 8.
s. 10, C.: 1995, c. 39, s. 9.
s. 11, C.: 1995, c. 38, s. 10.
s. 12, C.: 1995, c. 39, s. 11.

CAP.

1976—cont.

67. Sexual Offences (Scotland) Act 1976—*cont.*

s. 13, C.: 1995, c. 39, s. 11.
s. 14, C.: 1995, c. 39, s. 12.
s. 15, C.: 1995, c. 39, s. 14.
s. 17, C.: 1995, c. 39, s. 7.
s. 18, C.: 1995, c. 39, s. 16.
s. 19, C.: 1995, c. 39, s. 17.
s. 36, amended: 1995, c. 36, sch. 4.
s. 38, C.: 1995, c. 39, s. 31.
s. 39, C.: 1995, c. 39, s. 32.
s. 40, C.: 1995, c. 39, s. 33.
s. 40A, C.: 1995, c. 39, s. 34.
s. 41, C.: 1995, c. 39, s. 35.
s. 42, C.: 1995, c. 39, s. 36.
s. 42A, C.: 1995, c. 39, s. 37.
s. 43, C.: 1995, c. 39, s. 38.
s. 43A, C.: 1995, c. 39, s. 39.
s. 43B, C.: 1995, c. 39, s. 40.
s. 44, repealed in pt.: 1995, c. 36, sch. 4.
s. 44, amended: 1995, c. 36, sch. 4.
s. 44, C.: 1995, c. 39, s. 41.
s. 46A, C.: 1995, c. 39, s. 42.
s. 47, C.: 1995, c. 39, s. 43.
s. 48, C.: 1995, c. 39, s. 24.
s. 49, C.: 1995, c. 39, s. 25.
s. 50, C.: 1995, c. 39, s. 26.
s. 51, C.: 1995, c. 39, s. 27.
s. 52, C.: 1995, c. 39, s. 28.
s. 53, C.: 1995, c. 39, s. 29.
s. 54, C.: 1995, c. 39, s. 30.
s. 65B, repealed in pt.: 1995, c. 36, sch. 4.
s. 65B, amended: 1995, c. 36, sch. 4.
s. 135, repealed in pt.: 1995, c. 36, sch. 4.
s. 135, amended: 1995, c. 36, sch. 4.
sch. 1, C.: 1995, c. 46, s. 46, sch. 1.
sch. 2, C.: 1995, c. 46, sch. 1.

70. Land Drainage Act 1976.

s. 8, see *Dear* v. *Thames Water* 33 Con LR 43, H.H.J. Bowsher Q.C. sitting as a deputy judge.
s. 72, see *Barribal* v. *Everett* [1994] EGCS 62, C.A.

71. Supplementary Benefits Act 1976.

s. 30, repealed: 1995, c. 18, sch. 3.
sch. 5, repealed: 1995, c. 18, sch. 3.
sch. 6, repealed in pt.: 1995, c. 17, sch. 3.
sch. 7, repealed in pt.: 1995, c. 17, sch. 3.

74. Race Relations Act 1976.

s. 1, see *Chapman* v. *Simon* [1994] IRLR 124 C.A.; *Nagarajan* v. *Agnew*; *Same* v. *Swiggs and London Regional Transport* v. *Nagarajan* [1994] IRLR 61, E.A.T.; *Khan* v. *General Medical Council* [1994] IRLR 646, C.A.; *R.* v. *Bradford Metropolitan Borough Council, ex p. Ali (Sikander)* (1994) 6 Admin.L.R. 589, Jowitt J.; *Barclays Bank* v. *Kapur (No. 2)* [1995] IRLR 87, C.A.; *Quarcoopome* v. *Sock Shop Holdings* [1995] IRLR 353, E.A.T.

CAP.

1976—cont.

74. Race Relations Act 1976—*cont.*

s. 2, see *Nagarajan* v. *Agnew; Same* v. *Swiggs and London Regional Transport* v. *Nagarajan* [1994] IRLR 61, E.A.T.

s. 3, see *R.* v. *Bradford Metropolitan Borough Council, ex p. Ali (Sikander)* (1994) 6 Admin.L.R. 589, Jowitt J.

s. 4, see *Nagarajan* v. *Agnew; Same* v. *Swiggs and London Regional Transport* v. *Nagarajan* [1994] IRLR 61, E.A.T.; *Chapman* v. *Simon* [1994] 1 IRLR 124, C.A.; *Cardiff Womens Aid* v. *Hartup* [1994] IRLR 390, E.A.T.; *Post Office* v. *Adekeye, The Times*, February 23, 1995, E.A.T.; *Post Office* v. *Adekeye (No. 2)* [1995] IRLR 297, E.A.T.; *Barclays Bank* v. *Kapur (No. 2)* [1995] IRLR 87, C.A.

s. 12, see *Khan* v. *General Medical Council* [1994] IRLR 646, C.A.

s. 19A, repealed in pt.: 1995, c. 25, sch. 24.

s. 19A, amended: 1995, c. 25, sch. 10.

s. 20, see *CIN Properties* v. *Rawlins (Martin)*, February 1, 1995, C.A.

s. 29, see *Cardiff Womens Aid* v. *Hartup* [1994] IRLR 390, E.A.T.

ss. 32, 33, see *Nagarajan* v. *Agnew; Same* v. *Swiggs and London Regional Transport, Swiggs and London Regional Transport* v. *Nagarajan* [1994] IRLR 61, E.A.T.

s. 38, see *Cardiff Womens Aid* v. *Hartup* [1994] IRLR 390, E.A.T.

s. 53, see *Khan* v. *General Medical Council* [1994] IRLR 646, C.A.

s. 54, see *Chapman* v. *Simon* [1994] IRLR 124, C.A.; *Cardiff Womens Aid* v. *Hartup* [1994] IRLR 390, E.A.T.; *Khan* v. *General Medical Council* [1994] IRLR 646, C.A.

s. 56, see *Chapman* v. *Simon* [1994] IRLR 124, C.A.

s. 63, see *Cardiff Womens Aid* v. *Hartup* [1994] IRLR 390, E.A.T.

s. 68, see *Post Office* v. *Adekeye (No. 2)* [1995] IRLR 297, E.A.T.; *Quarcoopome* v. *Sock Shop Holdings* [1995] IRLR 353, E.A.T.

s. 71, amended: 1994, c. 39, sch. 13 (S.); 1995, c. 25, sch. 10.

s. 75, see *Khan* v. *General Medical Council* [1994] IRLR 646, C.A.; *R.* v. *Secretary of State for Social Security, ex p. Nessa* (1995) 7 Admin.L.R. 402, Auld J.

s. 78, see *Post Office* v. *Adekeye (No. 2)* [1995] IRLR 297, E.A.T.

75. Development of Rural Wales Act 1976.

ss. 1, 4, 8, sch. 3, amended: 1995, c. 25, sch. 10.

CAP.

1976—cont.

76. Energy Act 1976.

ss. 9, 12, amended: 1995, c. 45, sch. 4.

s. 14, order 95/2450.

80. Rent (Agriculture) Act 1976.

s. 5, amended: 1995, c. 25, sch. 10.

s. 9, sch. 2, amended: 1995, c. 8, sch.

82. Sexual Offences (Amendment) Act 1976.

s. 1, see *R.* v. *Gardiner* [1994] Crim.L.R. 455, C.A.

s. 2, see *R.* v. *Ahmed and Khan* [1994] Crim.L.R. 669, C.A.; *R.* v. *Barnes* [1994] Crim.L.R. 691, C.A.

86. Fishery Limits Act 1976.

s. 8, amended: 1995, c. 21, sch. 13.

1977

3. Aircraft and Shipbuilding Industry Act 1977.

sch. 2, amended: 1995, c. 12, sch. 13.

5. Social Security (Miscellaneous Provisions) Act 1977.

ss. 12, 24, order 95/766.

15. Marriage (Scotland) Act 1977.

s. 24, amended: 1995, c. 40, sch. 4 (S.).

18. Statute Law (Repeals) Act 1977.

s. 3, repealed: 1995, c. 44, sch. 1.

sch. 3, repealed: 1995, c. 44, sch. 1.

24. Merchant Shipping (Safety Convention) Act 1977.

s. 1, C.: 1995, c. 21, sch. 14.

27. Presumption of Death (Scotland) Act 1977.

s. 15, Act of Sederunt 94/2901.

36. Finance Act 1977.

s. 40, see *NAP Holdings U.K.* v. *Whittles (Inspector of Taxes), The Times*, November 22, 1994, H.L.

37. Patents Act 1977.

rules 95/2093.

s. 1, see *Biogen Inc.* v. *Medeva* (CHANF 93/1659/B), October 27, 1994, C.A.; *Chiron Corp.* v. *Organon Teknika (No. 3); Same* v. *Murex Diagnostics (No. 3)* [1994] F.S.R. 202, Patents County Ct.

s. 2, see *Biogen Inc.* v. *Medeva* (CHANF 93/1659/B), October 27, 1994, C.A.; *Chiron Corp.* v. *Organon Teknika (No. 3); Same* v. *Murex Diagnostics (No. 3)* [1994] F.S.R. 202, Patents County Ct.; *Molnlycke A.B.* v. *Procter & Gamble (No. 5)* [1994] R.P.C. 49, C.A.; *Merrell Dow Pharmaceuticals* v. *H.N. Norton & Co* [1994] R.P.C. 1, Patents Ct.

s. 3, see *Biogen Inc.* v. *Medeva* (CHANF 93/1659/B), October 27, 1994, C.A.; *Chiron Corp.* v. *Organon Teknika (No. 3); Same* v. *Murex Diagnostics (No. 3)* [1994] F.S.R. 202, Patents County Ct.; *Molnlycke A.B.* v. *Procter & Gamble (No. 5)* [1994] R.P.C. 49, C.A.

CAP.

1977—cont.

37. Patents Act 1977—*cont.*

s. 4, see *Biogen Inc.* v. *Medeva* (CHANF 93/1659/B), October 27, 1994, C.A.; *Chiron Corp.* v. *Organon Teknika (No. 3); Same* v. *Murex Diagnostics (No. 3)* [1994] F.S.R. 202.

s. 5, order 94/3220.

s. 6, see *Beloit Technologies* v. *Valmet Paper Machinery*, *The Times*, May 12, 1995, Jacob J.

s. 14, see *Chiron Corp.* v. *Organon Teknika (No. 5)*; *Same* v. *Murex Diagnostics* [1994] F.S.R. 258, Patents Ct.; *Chiron Corp.* v. *Organon Teknika (No. 3)*; *Same* v. *Murex Diagnostics (No. 3)* [1994] F.S.R. 202, Patents County Ct.; *McManus's Application* [1994] F.S.R. 558, Patents Ct.

s. 28, see *Continental Manufacturing & Sales' Patent* [1994] R.P.C. 535, Aldous J.

s. 31, amended: 1995, c. 7, sch. 4 (S.).

s. 44, see *Chiron Corp.* v. *Organon Teknika (No. 3)*; *Same* v. *Murex Diagnostics (No. 3)* [1994] F.S.R. 202, Patents County Ct.; *Chiron Corp.* v. *Organon Teknika (No. 4)*; *Same* v. *Murex Diagnostics (No. 4)* [1994] F.S.R. 252, Patents Ct.; *Chiron Corp.* v. *Murex Diagnostics (No. 8)* [1995] F.S.R. 309, C.A.

s. 46, see *Research Corp's Supplementary Protection Certificate* [1994] R.P.C. 667, Aldous J.

s. 60, see *Chiron Corp.* v. *Organon Teknika (No. 3); Same v. Murex Diagnostics (No. 3)* [1994] F.S.R. 202, Patents County Ct.; *Assidoman Multipack (formerly Multipack Wraparound Systems)* v. *The Mead Corp.* [1995] F.S.R. 225, Aldous J.; *Merrell Dow Pharmaceuticals* v. *HN Norton & Co.*, *The Times*, October 27, 1995, H.L.

s. 62, see *Gerber Garment Technology* v. *Lectra Systems* [1994] F.S.R. 471, Aldous J.; *Chiron Corp.* v. *Organon Teknika (No. 7)*; *Chiron Corp.* v. *Murex Diagnostics (No. 7)* [1994] F.S.R. 458, Aldous J.

s. 63, see *Gerber Garment Technology* v. *Lectra Systems* [1994] F.S.R. 471, Aldous J.; *Chiron Corp.* v. *Organon Teknika (No. 7)*; *Chiron Corp.* v. *Murex Diagnostics (No. 7)* [1994] F.S.R. 458, Aldous J.

s. 67, see *Chiron Corp.* v. *Organon Teknika (No. 3); Same* v. *Murex Diagnostics (No. 3)* [1994] F.S.R. 202, Patents County Ct.

s. 68, see *Molnlycke A.B.* v. *Procter & Gamble (No. 5)* [1994] R.P.C. 49, C.A.

CAP.

1977—cont.

37. Patents Act 1977—*cont.*

s. 70, see *Brain* v. *Ingledew Brown Bennison & Garrett, The Independent*, April 18, 1995, Jacob J.

s. 71, see *Sundstrand Corp.* v. *Safe Flight Instrument Corp.* [1994] F.S.R. 599, Patents County Ct.

s. 72, see *Chiron Corp.* v. *Organon Teknika (No. 5)*; *Same* v. *Murex Diagnostics (No. 5)* [1994] F.S.R. 258, Patents Ct.; *Chiron Corp.* v. *Organon Teknika (No. 3)*; *Same* v. *Murex Diagnostics (No. 3)* [1994] F.S.R. 202, Patents County Ct.; *Hong Kong Toy Centre* v. *Tomy U.K.* [1994] F.S.R. 593, Aldous J.; *Assidoman Multipack (formerly Multipack Wraparound Systems)* v. *The Mead Corp.* [1995] F.S.R. 225, Aldous J.

s. 74, see *Chiron Corp.* v. *Organon Teknika (No. 5)*; *Same* v. *Murex Diagnostics (No. 5)* [1994] F.S.R. 258, Patents Ct.

s. 75, see *Chiron Corp.* v. *Organon Teknika (No. 5)*; *Same* v. *Murex Diagnostics (No. 5)* [1994] F.S.R. 258, Patents Ct.; *Gerber Garment Technology* v. *Lectra Systems* [1994] F.S.R. 471, Aldous J.; *Chiron Corp.* v. *Organon Teknika (No. 7)*; *Chiron Corp.* v. *Murex Diagnostics (No. 7)* [1994] F.S.R. 458, Aldous J.

s. 76, see *Chiron Corp.* v. *Organon Teknika (No. 5)*; *Same* v. *Murex Diagnostics (No. 5)* [1994] F.S.R. 258, Patents Ct.; *Gerber Garment Technology* v. *Lectra Systems* [1994] F.S.R. 471, Aldous J.; *Chiron Corp.* v. *Organon Teknika (No. 7)*; *Chiron Corp.* v. *Murex Diagnostics (No. 7)* [1994] F.S.R. 458, Aldous J.

s. 90, order 94/3220.

s. 123, rules 95/2164.

s. 124, order 94/3220.

s. 125, see *Chiron Corp.* v. *Organon Teknika (No. 3)*; *Same* v. *Murex Diagnostics (No. 3)* [1994] F.S.R. 202, Patents County Ct.; *PLG Research* v. *Ardon Intl.* [1995] F.S.R. 116, C.A.

s. 130, see *Chiron Corp.* v. *Organon Teknika (No. 3)*; *Same* v. *Murex Diagnostics (No. 3)* [1994] F.S.R. 202, Patents County Ct.; *Chiron Corp.* v. *Organon Teknika (No. 5)*; *Same* v. *Murex Diagnostics (No. 5)* [1994] F.S.R. 258, Patents Ct.; *Assidoman Multipack (formerly Multipack Wraparound Systems)* v. *The Mead Corp.* [1995] F.S.R. 225, Aldous J.

sch. 1, see *Research Corp's Supplementary Protection Certificate* [1994] R.P.C. 667, Aldous J.

CAP.

1977—cont.

42. Rent Act 1977.

see *Elitestone* v. *Morris* (CCRTF 95/0238/G; CCRTF 95/0247/G), July 28, 1995, C.A.

s. 2, see *Johnson* v. *Felton* (1994) 27 H.L.R. 265, C.A.

s. 10, substituted: 1995, c. 8, sch.

s. 12, see *Barnett* v. *O'Sullivan* [1994] 1 W.L.R. 1667, C.A.

s. 14, amended: 1995, c. 25, sch. 10.

s. 62, amended: regs. 95/2451.

s. 63, amended: regs. 95/2451.

s. 70, see *Spath Holme* v. *Chairman of the Greater Manchester and Lancashire Rent Assessment Committee* (1994) 27 H.L.R. 243, D.C.

s. 83, amended: regs. 95/2451.

s. 98, see *Lipton* v. *Whitworth* (1994) 26 H.L.R. 293, C.A.

s. 124, amended: regs. 95/2451.

s. 137, amended: 1995, c. 8, sch.

s. 137, see *Keepers and Governors of the Free Grammar School of John Lyon* v. *James, The Times*, July 7, 1995, C.A.

s. 149, amended: regs. 95/2451.

sch. 5, see *Lipton* v. *Whitworth* [1993] [1994] 26 H.L.R. 293, C.A.; *White* v. *Jones* [1993] 26 H.L.R. 477, C.A.

sch. 15, see *White* v. *Jones* [1993] 26 H.L.R. 477, C.A.; *O'Brien* v. *Secretary of State for the Environment and Fenland District Council* (1994) 68 P.&C.R. 314, Hidden J.

43. Protection from Eviction Act 1977.

s. 1, see *R.* v. *Mitchell* [1994] Crim.L.R. 66, C.A.

s. 3, see *R.* v. *Kensington and Chelsea Royal London Borough Council, ex p. Amarfio, The Times*, April 22, 1995, C.A.; *Mohamed* v. *Manek and Kensington and Chelsea Royal Borough* (1995) 27 H.L.R. 439, C.A.

s. 8, amended: 1995, c. 8, sch.

45. Criminal Law Act 1977.

s. 44, repealed: 1995, c. 35, sch. 3.

s. 47, see *R.* v. *Vince* (1994) 15 Cr.App.R. (S.) 657, C.A.

s. 137, see *The Keepers of the Possessions Revenues and Goods of the Free Grammar School of John Lyon* v. *Christopher James*, December 2, 1994; H.H.J. Butter Q.C.; Central London County Ct.

schs. 6, 7, repealed: 1995, c. 40, sch. 5 (S.).

sch. 11, C.: 1995, c. 39, s. 12 (S.); 1995, c. 46, s. 7 (S.).

46. Insurance Brokers (Registration) Act 1977.

ss. 27, 28, order 94/2569, 3069.

49. National Health Service Act 1977.

orders 95/474, 477, 479, 480, 481, 846, 1107, 1226.

CAP.

1977—cont.

49. National Health Service Act 1977—*cont.*

see *R.* v. *Secretary of State for Health, ex p. Manchester Local Medical Committee* (CO/3306/93; CO/189/94), March 28, 1995, Collins J.

s. 8, orders 95/533, 562, 563.

s. 8, substituted: 1995, c. 17, s. 1.

s. 10, substituted: 1995, c. 17, s. 1.

s. 11, order 95/621.

s. 11, amended: 1995, c. 17, sch. 1.

s. 12, amended: 1995, c. 17, sch. 1.

s. 13, regs. 95/622.

s. 13, repealed in pt.: 1995, c. 17, sch. 3.

s. 13, amended: 1995, c. 17, sch. 1.

s. 14, repealed: 1995, c. 17, sch. 1, sch. 3.

s. 15, regs. 94/3130; 95/80, 692.

s. 15, repealed in pt.: 1995, c. 17, sch. 3.

s. 15, amended: 1995, c. 17, sch. 1.

s. 16, regs. 95/622.

s. 16, substituted: 1995, c. 17, sch. 1.

s. 17, regs. 95/622.

s. 17, substituted: 1995, c. 17, sch. 1.

s. 18, regs. 95/622.

s. 18, repealed in pt.: 1995, c. 17, s. 3, sch. 3.

s. 18, amended: 1995, c. 17, sch. 1.

s. 19, repealed in pt.: 1995, c. 17, sch. 3.

s. 19, amended: 1995, c. 17, sch. 1.

s. 20, amended: 1995, c. 17, sch. 1.

s. 22, repealed in pt.: 1995, c. 17, sch. 3.

s. 22, amended: 1995, c. 17, sch. 1.

s. 23, amended: 1995, c. 17, sch. 1.

s. 26, amended: 1995, c. 17, sch. 1.

s. 27, amended: 1995, c. 17, sch. 1.

s. 28, amended: 1995, c. 17, sch. 1.

s. 28A, amended: 1995, c. 17, sch. 1.

s. 29, regs. 94/2620, 3130; 95/80.

s. 29, amended: 1995, c. 17, sch. 1; 1995, c. 51, sch.

s. 30, amended: 1995, c. 17, sch. 1.

s. 31, amended: 1995, c. 17, sch. 1.

s. 32, regs. 94/3130.

s. 32, amended: 1995, c. 17, sch. 1.

s. 33, regs. 95/80.

s. 33, amended: 1995, c. 17, sch. 1.

s. 34, amended: 1995, c. 17, sch. 1.

s. 35, amended: 1995, c. 17, sch. 1.

s. 36, amended: 1995, c. 17, sch. 1.

s. 37, amended: 1995, c. 17, sch. 1.

s. 38, regs. 95/588.

s. 38, amended: 1995, c. 17, sch. 1.

s. 39, amended: 1995, c. 17, sch. 1.

s. 41, regs. 95/644.

s. 41, amended: 1995, c. 17, sch. 1.

s. 42, regs. 95/622, 644.

s. 42, amended: 1995, c. 17, sch. 1.

s. 43, regs. 95/644.

s. 43, amended: 1995, c. 17, sch. 1.

s. 44, amended: 1995, c. 17, sch. 1.

s. 45, amended: 1995, c. 17, sch. 1.

s. 46, repealed in pt.: 1995, c. 31, sch.

CAP.

1977—cont.

49. National Health Service Act 1977—*cont.*

s. 46, amended: 1995, c. 17, sch. 1, 1995, c. 31, ss. 1, 2, 3.
s. 47, repealed in pt.: 1995, c. 31, sch.
s. 47, amended: 1995, c. 31, s. 4.
s. 49, repealed in pt.: 1995, c. 31, sch.
s. 49, amended: 1995, c. 31, s. 5.
s. 49A, 49B, 49C, 49D, 49E, added: 1995, c. 31, s. 2.
s. 51, amended: 1995, c. 17, sch. 1.
s. 54, amended: 1995, c. 17, sch. 1.
s. 56, amended: 1995, c. 17, sch. 1.
s. 65, amended: 1995, c. 17, sch. 1.
s. 77, regs. 95/643.
s. 79A, regs. 95/444, 530.
s. 83, amended: 1995, c. 17, sch. 1.
s. 83A, regs. 95/642.
s. 83A, amended: 1995, c. 17, sch. 1.
s. 85, amended: 1995, c. 17, sch. 1.
s. 90, amended: 1995, c. 17, sch. 1.
s. 91, amended: 1995, c. 17, sch. 1.
s. 92, orders 94/2950, 2952, 2988, 2989, 2990, 2991; 95/473, 475, 502, 503, 504, 505, 564, 565, 567, 568, 569, 932, 933, 934, 935, 937, 938, 1088, 1089, 1090, 1121, 1123, 1124, 1125, 1126, 1127, 1128, 1129, 1232, 1233, 1234, 1242, 1243, 1244, 1245, 1246, 1247, 1248, 1249, 1259, 1260, 1261, 1262, 1263, 1264, 1265, 1462, 1463, 1465, 1466, 1467, 1468, 1489, 1490, 1491, 1492, 1493, 1534, 1589, 1590, 1602, 1603, 1604, 1657, 1731, 1732, 1733, 1735, 1736, 1766, 1767, 1768, 1910, 1911, 1912, 1913, 1914, 1991, 1992, 1993, 1994, 1995, 2129, 2149, 2150, 2307, 2322, 2323, 2324, 2325, 2326, 2327, 2352, 2434, 2435; regs. 94/1571, 1572, 1573, 1574, 1576, 2521, 2687, 2688, 2689, 2691, 2692, 2693, 2694, 2695, 2696, 2697, 2698, 2708, 2709.
s. 92, amended: 1995, c. 17, sch. 1.
s. 93, repealed in pt.: 1995, c. 17, sch. 3.
s. 96, amended: 1995, c. 17, sch. 1.
s. 96A, repealed in pt.: 1995, c. 17, sch. 3.
s. 96A, amended: 1995, c. 17, sch. 1.
s. 97, substituted: 1995, c. 17, sch. 1.
s. 97A, substituted: 1995, c. 17, sch. 1.
s. 97B, repealed: 1995, c. 17, sch. 1, sch. 3.
s. 98, repealed in pt.: 1995, c. 17, sch. 3.
s. 98, amended: 1995, c. 17, sch. 1.
s. 99, amended: 1995, c. 17, sch. 1.
s. 103, amended: 1995, c. 17, sch. 1.
s. 104, amended: 1995, c. 17, sch. 1.
s. 105, amended: 1995, c. 17, sch. 1.
s. 107, regs. 95/635.
s. 124, repealed in pt.: 1995, c. 17, sch. 3.
s. 124, amended: 1995, c. 17, sch. 1.
s. 126, regs. 94/2522, 2619, 2620, 2690, 3130; 95/34, 80, 477, 478, 479, 480, 481, 558, 622, 642, 643, 644, 691, 692, 693,

CAP.

1977—cont.

49. National Health Service Act 1977—*cont.*

791, 792; orders 95/2, 83, 84, 85, 86, 87, 88, 89, 90, 91, 92, 99, 141, 142, 143, 533, 562, 563, 621, 801, 846, 918, 968, 996, 1311, 1709.
s. 126, repealed in pt.: 1995, c. 17, sch. 3.
s. 126, amended: 1995, c. 17, sch. 1.
s. 128, repealed in pt.: 1995, c. 17, sch. 3.
s. 128, amended: 1995, c. 17, sch. 1.
sch. 5, order 95/621; sch. 5, regs. 95/622.
sch. 5, repealed in pt.: 1995, c. 17, sch. 3.
sch. 5, amended: 1995, c. 17, sch. 1.
sch. 6, repealed in pt.: 1995, c. 17, sch. 3.
sch. 6, amended: 1995, c. 17, sch. 1.
sch. 7, repealed in pt.: 1995, c. 17, sch. 3.
sch. 7, amended: 1995, c. 17, sch. 1.
sch. 9, amended: 1995, c. 17, sch. 1; 1995, c. 31, sch. 9.
sch. 12, regs. 94/530, 2619; 95/34, 444, 691.
sch. 14, repealed in pt.: 1995, c. 17, sch. 3.
sch. 14, amended: 1995, c. 17, sch. 1.
sch. 15, repealed in pt.: 1995, c. 17, sch. 3.

50. Unfair Contract Terms Act 1977.

s. 11, see *Edmund Murray* v. *BSP International Foundations* 33 Con LR 1, C.A.
s. 20, sch. 2, see *Knight Machinery (Holdings)* v. *Rennie*, 1995 S.L.T. 166

1978

2. Commonwealth Development Corporation Act 1978.

s. 3, order 1994/2880.
s. 9A, amended: 1995, c. 9, s. 1.
s. 10, repealed in pt.: 1995, c. 9, sch.
s. 10, amended: 1995, c. 9, s. 1.
s. 12, amended: 1995, c. 9, s. 2.
s. 13, substituted: 1995, c. 9, s. 3.
sch. 1, amended: 1995, c. 9, s. 3.

3. Refuse Disposal (Amenity) Act 1978.

s. 2, amended: 1995, c. 40, sch. 4 (S.).
s. 11, amended: 1994, c. 39, sch. 13 (S.).

8. Civil Aviation Act 1978.

repealed: 1995, c. 44, sch. 1.

10. European Parliamentary Elections Act 1978.

schs. 1, 2, amended: 1994, c. 39, sch. 13 (S.).

15. Solomon Islands Act 1978.

s. 6, repealed in pt.: 1995, c. 44, sch. 1.
sch., repealed in pt.: 1995, c. 21, sch. 12.

19. Oaths Act 1978.

ss. 4, 5, 6, see *Vitalis* v. *CPS* (CO–1154–95), May 23, 1995, Forbes J.

20. Tuvalu Act 1978.

schs. 1, 2, repealed in pt.: 1995, c. 21, sch. 12.

22. Domestic Proceedings and Magistrates' Courts Act 1978.

ss. 20, 29, see *P.* v. *P. (Periodical Payments: Appeals)* [1995] 1 FLR 563, Bracewell J.

CAP.

1978—cont.

23. Judicature (Northern Ireland) Act 1978.
S.R. 1995 No. 290.
s. 46, amended: 1995, c. 12, sch. 13.
ss. 48, 51, S.R. 1995 No. 757.
s. 55, S.R. 1995 No. 2, 576.
s. 116, S.R. 1995 Nos. 217, 218, 219, 220, 221, 222.
sch. 5, S.R. 1995 No. 755.

26. Suppression of Terrorism Act 1978.
s. 8, order 94/2978.

28. Adoption (Scotland) Act 1978.
s. 1, repealed in pt.: 1995, c. 36, sch. 5.
s. 1, amended: 1995, c. 36, sch. 2.
s. 2, repealed in pt.: 1995, c. 36, sch. 5.
s. 2, amended: 1994, c. 39, sch. 13.
s. 3, repealed in pt.: 1995, c. 36, sch. 5.
s. 3, amended: 1995, c. 36, s. 94, sch. 2.
s. 6, amended: 1995, c. 36, s. 95.
s. 6A, added: 1995, c. 36, s. 96.
s. 8, repealed: 1995, c. 36, schs. 2, 5.
s. 9, amended: 1995, c. 36, sch. 2.
s. 11, amended: 1995, c. 36, sch. 2.
s. 12, repealed in pt.: 1995, c. 36, sch. 5.
s. 12, amended: 1995, c. 36, s. 97, sch. 2.
s. 14, repealed in pt.: 1995, c. 36, schs. 2, 5.
s. 14, amended: 1995, c. 36, sch. 2.
s. 15, repealed in pt.: 1995, c. 26, schs. 2, 5.
s. 15, amended: 1995, c. 36, sch. 2.
s. 16, repealed in pt.: 1995, c. 36, schs. 2, 5.
s. 16, amended: 1995, c. 36, sch. 2.
s. 18, amended: 1995, c. 36, sch. 2.
s. 18, see *D.* v. *Grampian Regional Council*, 1995 S.L.T. 519.
s. 19, amended: 1995, c. 36, sch. 2.
s. 20, amended: 1995, c. 36, sch. 2.
s. 21, amended: 1995, c. 36, sch. 2.
s. 22A, inserted: 1995, c. 36, sch. 2.
s. 24, amended: 1995, c. 36, sch. 2.
s. 25, amended: 1995, c. 36, sch. 2.
s. 25A, added: 1995, c. 36, sch. 2.
s. 26, repealed: 1995, c. 36, sch. 5.
s. 27, amended: 1995, c. 36, sch. 2.
s. 28, repealed in pt.: 1995, c. 36, schs. 2, 5.
s. 28, amended: 1995, c. 36, sch. 2.
ss. 32–33, repealed: 1995, c. 36, schs. 2, 5.
s. 37, repealed: 1995, c. 36, schs. 2, 5.
s. 37, amended: 1995, c. 40, sch. 4 (S.).
s. 39, amended: 1995, c. 36, s. 97.
s. 45, amended: 1995, c. 36, sch. 2.
s. 51, repealed in pt.: 1995, c. 36, schs. 2, 5.
s. 51, amended: 1995, c. 36, sch. 2.
ss. 51A–51B, added: 1995, c. 36, sch. 2.
s. 58, amended: 1995, c. 36, sch. 2.
s. 59, amended: 1995, c. 36, sch. 2.
s. 59, Acts of Sederunt 94/2805, 2806, 2901.
s. 60, repealed: 1995, c. 36, schs. 2, 5.

CAP.

1978—cont.

28. Adoption (Scotland) Act 1978—*cont.*
s. 65, repealed in pt.: 1995, c. 36, sch. 5.
s. 65, amended: 1994, c. 39, sch. 13; 1995, c. 36, s. 94, sch. 2.
sch. 1, regs. 94/3147.

29. National Health Service (Scotland) Act 1978.
s. 2, orders 95/414, 416, 574, 1571.
s. 12, repealed in pt.: regs. 95/31.
s. 12A, orders 94/2994, 2995, 2996, 2997, 2998, 2999, 3000, 3001; 95/741, 742.
s. 12E, order 95/577.
s. 12G, order 94/3254.
s. 16, order 95/574.
s. 16A, amended: 1994, c. 39, sch. 13; repealed in pt.: 1994, c. 39, sch. 14.
s. 16B, order 95/574.
s. 17A, repealed in pt.: 1995, c. 17, sch. 3.
s. 17A, amended: 1995, c. 17, sch. 1.
s. 17B, amended: 1995, c. 17, sch. 1.
s. 19, amended: 1995, c. 51, sch.
s. 22, regs. 94/3130.
s. 23, regs. 95/414, 416.
s. 24, regs. 95/414.
s. 26, regs. 95/704, 705.
s. 29, repealed in pt.: 1995, c. 31, sch.
s. 29, amended: 1995, c. 31, ss. 7, 9.
s. 30, repealed in pt.: 1995, c. 31, sch.
s. 30, amended: 1995, c. 31, s. 10.
ss. 28, 28A, regs. 95/414, 416.
s. 32, repealed in pt.: 1995, c. 31, sch.
s. 32, amended: 1995, c. 31, s. 11.
ss. 32A, 32B, 32C, 32D, 32E, added: 1995, c. 31, s. 8.
s. 34, regs. 95/414, 416.
ss. 36, 37, 42, order 95/574.
s. 43, regs. 95/414, 416.
ss. 47, 48, order 95/574.
s. 69, regs. 95/699.
s. 70, regs. 95/1, 703, 705, 2369.
ss. 71, 71A, regs. 95/703.
s. 75, regs. 95/699.
s. 75A, regs. 95/700, 2381.
s. 79, order 95/574.
s. 79, repealed in pt.: 1995, c. 7, sch. 5.
s. 87A, amended: 1995, c. 17, sch. 1.
s. 87B, amended: 1995, c. 17, sch. 1.
s. 87D, amended: 1995, c. 17, sch. 1.
s. 91, regs. 95/635, 637.
s. 102, order 95/574.
s. 105, orders 95/416, 574; regs. 95/165, 414, 416, 699, 700, 703, 704, 705, 884, 3130.
s. 106, regs. 95/414, 416.
s. 108, order 95/416; regs. 94/884, 2624; 95/1, 414, 416, 700, 703, 704, 705.
s. 108, repealed in pt.: 1994, c. 39, sch. 13.
s. 108, amended: 1994, c. 39, sch. 13.
sch. 1, regs. 95/414; order 95/574.
sch. 1, repealed in pt.: 1995, c. 7, sch. 5.
sch. 2, regs. 95/414, 416.
sch. 5, repealed in pt.: 1995, c. 7, sch. 5.
schs. 6, 7, regs. 95/703.

CAP.

1978—cont.

29. National Health Service (Scotland) Act 1978—*cont.*

sch. 7A, orders 94/2994, 2995, 2996, 2997, 2998, 2999, 3000, 3001, 3038; 95/574, 741, 742.
sch. 7A, amended: 1995, c. 17, sch. 1.
sch. 8, amended: 1995, c. 31, s. 12.
sch. 9, regs. 95/414, 416.
sch. 11, regs. 95/1, 705.
sch. 15, repealed in pt.: 1995, c. 17, sch. 3.
sch. 15, amended: 1995, c. 17, sch. 1, 1995, c. 31, s. 10.
sch. 16, repealed: 1995, c. 40, sch. 5.
sch. 16, C.: 1995, c. 46, s. 307.

30. Interpretation Act 1978.

s. 7, see *Kayanga (Christine Resty)* v. *Secretary of State for the Home Department* [1995] Imm.A.R. 123, C.A.
s. 16, see *Harvey* v. *Institute of Motor Industry* [1995] IRLR 416, E.A.T.; *B.* v. *B. (Periodical Payments: Transitional Provisions)* [1995] 1 FLR 459, Douglas Brown, J.
s. 17, C.: 1995, c. 23, sch. 8.
s. 115, see *Starke* v. *I.R.C.*, *The Times*, May 29, 1995, C.A.
sch. 1, amended: 1995, c. 40, sch. 4 (S.).
sch. 1, see *Gotech Industrial and Environmental Services* v. *Friel*, 1995 S.C.C.R. 22.
sch. 2, repealed in pt.: 1995, c. 17, sch. 3.

33. State Immunity Act 1978.

s. 2, see *London Branch of the Nigerian Universities Commission* v. *Bastians* [1995] I.C.R. 358, E.A.T.
ss. 12, 14, see *Kuwait Airways Corp.* v. *Iraqi Airways Co.*, *The Times*, July 25, 1995, H.L.

44. Employment Protection (Consolidation) Act 1978.

order 95/1953.
see *Biggs* v. *Somerset County Council*, *The Times*, July 17, 1995, E.A.T.; *South Durham Health Authority* v. *Unison* [1995] I.C.R. 495, E.A.T.
s. 5, repealed in pt.: regs. 95/31.
s. 23, see *Associated Newspapers* v. *Wilson*; *Associated British Ports* v. *Palmer* [1995] I.C.R. 406, H.L.; *Department of Transport* v. *Gallacher* [1994] I.C.R. 967, C.A.
s. 29, amended: order 95/694; 1995, c. 17, sch. 1.
s. 29, modified: order 95/694.
s. 33, see *Philip Hodges* v. *Kell* [1994] IRLR 568, E.A.T.
s. 45, order 94/2930.
s. 45, see *Philip Hodges* v. *Kell* [1994] IRLR 568, E.A.T.
s. 47, see *Philip Hodges* v. *Kell* [1994] IRLR 568, E.A.T.

CAP.

1978—cont.

44. Employment Protection (Consolidation) Act 1978—*cont.*

s. 49, see *Clark* v. *Secretary of State for Employment* [1995] I.C.R. 673, E.A.T.
s. 54, see *Mediguard Services* v. *Thame* [1994] IRLR 504, E.A.T.; *Warren* v. *Wylie and Wylie* [1994] IRLR 316, Industrial Tribunal; *Milligan* v. *Securicor Cleaning* [1995] IRLR 288, E.A.T.; *Biggs* v. *Somerset County Council* [1995] IRLR 452, E.A.T.
s. 55, see *Greenaway Harrison* v. *Wiles* [1994] IRLR 380, E.A.T.; *Newman* v. *Polytechnic of Wales Students Union* [1995] IRLR 72, E.A.T.; *Patel* v. *Nagesan* [1995] IRLR 370, C.A.
s. 56, see *Philip Hodges* v. *Kell* [1994] IRLR 568, E.A.T.
s. 57, see *Cabaj* v. *Westminster City Council* [1994] IRLR 530, E.A.T.; *London Fire and Civil Defence Authority* v. *Betty* [1994] IRLR 384, E.A.T.; *Boulton & Paul* v. *Arnold* [1994] IRLR 532, E.A.T.; *Catamaran Cruises* v. *Williams* [1994] IRLR 386, E.A.T.; *Baxter* v. *Limb* [1994] IRLR 572, C.A.; *Philip Hodges* v. *Kell* [1994] IRLR, E.A.T.; *Duffy* v. *Yeomans & Partners* [1994] IRLR 642, C.A.; *Securicor Guarding* v. *R.* [1994] IRLR 633, E.A.T.; *British Railways Board* v. *Jackson* [1994] IRLR 235, C.A.; *Milligan* v. *Securicor Cleaning* [1995] IRLR 288, E.A.T.; *Eaton* v. *King* [1995] IRLR 75, E.A.T.; *FDR* v. *Holloway* [1995] IRLR 400, E.A.T.; *British Aerospace* v. *Green* [1995] IRLR 433, C.A.; *Dundon* v. *GPT* [1995] IRLR 403, E.A.T.
s. 58, see *Discount Tobacco & Confectionery* v. *Armitage* [1995] I.C.R. 431, E.A.T.
s. 59, see *O'Dea* v. *ISC Chemicals* (EATRF 94/0722/B), July 28, 1995, *The Times*, August 4, 1995, C.A.; *Dundon* v. *GPT* [1995] IRLR 403, E.A.T.
s. 60A, amended: 1995, c. 26, sch. 3.
s. 62, see *Lewis and Britton* v. *E. Mason & Sons* [1994] IRLR 4, E.A.T.; *Baxter* v. *Limb* [1994] IRLR 572, C.A.
s. 64, see *R.* v. *Secretary of State for Employment, ex p. Seymour-Smith and Perez* [1994] IRLR 448, D.C.; *Mediguard Services* v. *Thame* [1994] IRLR 504, E.A.T.; *Secretary of State for Education and Science* v. *Birchall* [1994] IRLR 630, E.A.T.; *Clifford* v. *Devon County Council* [1994] IRLR 628, E.A.T.; *Warren* v. *Wylie and*

CAP.

1978—cont.

44. Employment Protection (Consolidation) Act 1978—*cont.*
Wylie [1994] IRLR 316, Industrial Tribunal; *Gale* v. *Northern General Hospital National Health Service Trust* [1994] IRLR 292, C.A.
ss. 69, 70, see *Port of London Authority* v. *Payne* [1994] IRLR 9, C.A.
s. 71, amended: 1995, c. 26, sch. 3.
s. 71, see *Port of London Authority* v. *Payne* [1994] IRLR 9, C.A.
s. 72, amended: 1995, c. 26, sch. 3.
s. 72, see *Port of London Authority* v. *Payne* [1994] IRLR 9, C.A.
s. 73, amended: 1995, c. 26, sch. 3.
s. 73, see *Lock* v. *Connell Estate Agents* [1994] IRLR 444, E.A.T.
s. 74, see *Boulton & Paul* v. *Arnold* [1994] IRLR 532, E.A.T.; *Lock* v. *Connell Estate Agents* [1994] IRLR 444, E.A.T.; *Derwent Coachworks* v. *Kirby* [1994] IRLR 639, E.A.T.
s. 75, see *Derwent Coachworks* v. *Kirby* [1994] IRLR 639, E.A.T.
s. 75A, see *Port of London Authority* v. *Payne* [1994] IRLR 9, C.A.
s. 77, amended: 1995, c. 26, sch. 3.
s. 77A, amended: 1995, c. 26, sch. 3.
s. 79, see *Boorman* v. *Allmakes*, *The Times*, April 21, 1995, C.A.
s. 81, see *Bass Leisure* v. *Thomas* [1994] IRLR 104, E.A.T; *Baxter* v. *Limb* [1994] IRLR 572, C.A.
s. 82, see *Bass Leisure* v. *Thomas* [1994] IRLR 104, E.A.T.
s. 83, see *Hellyer Brothers* v. *Atkinson and Dickinson* [1994] IRLR 88, C.A.; *Bass Leisure* v. *Thomas* [1994] IRLR 104, E.A.T.
s. 91, see *Baxter* v. *Limb* [1994] IRLR 572, C.A.
s. 92, see *Mediguard Services* v. *Thame* [1994] IRLR 504, E.A.T.
s. 122, see *Secretary of State for Employment* v. *Stone* [1994] I.C.R. 761, E.A.T.; *Clark* v. *Secretary of State for Employment, The Times*, April 7, 1995, E.A.T.
s. 127, see *Secretary of State for Employment* v. *Stone* [1994] I.C.R. 761, E.A.T.
s. 132, amended: 1995, c. 18, sch. 2.
s. 133, amended: 1995, c. 26, sch. 3.
s. 136, amended: 1995, c. 26, sch. 3.
s. 138, amended: 1995, c. 26, sch. 3.
s. 141, amended: regs. 95/278.
s. 146, repealed in pt.: regs. 95/31.
s. 149, order 95/1157.
s. 149, repealed in pt.: regs. 95/31.
s. 153, see *Secretary of State for Education and Science* v. *Birchall* [1994] IRLR 630, E.A.T.

CAP.

1978—cont.

44. Employment Protection (Consolidation) Act 1978—*cont.*
s. 154, orders 95/694, 1157.
sch. 3, see *Clark* v. *Secretary of State for Employment* [1995] I.C.R. 673, E.A.T.
sch. 9, see *R.* v. *Secretary of State for the Foreign & Commonwealth Office, ex p. Vidler* [1993] C.O.D. 305, Popplewell J.
sch. 11, see *Bass Leisure* v. *Thomas* [1994] IRLR 104, E.A.T.
sch. 13, repealed in pt.: 1995, c. 50, sch. 7; regs. 95/31, 520.
sch. 13, amended: 1995, c. 50, sch. 6; regs. 95/31, 520.
sch. 13, see *Mediguard Services* v. *Thame* [1994] IRLR 504, E.A.T.; *Clifford* v. *Devon County Council* [1994] IRLR 628, E.A.T.
sch. 15, see *Biggs* v. *Somerset County Council* [1995] IRLR 452, E.A.T.

45. Statute Law (Repeals) Act 1978.
s. 2, sch. 3, repealed: 1995, c. 44, sch. 1.

47. Civil Liability (Contributions) Act 1978.
see *Hamburg Star, The* [1994] 1 Lloyd's Rep. 399, Clarke J.; *Prekookeanska Plovidba* v. *Felstar Shipping Corp. and Setramar Srl and STC Scantrade A.B. (Third Party)*; *Carnivalm, The* [1944] 2 Lloyd's Rep. 14, C.A.
ss. 1, 6, see *Friends' Provident Life Office* v. *Hillier Parker May & Bowden, The Times*, April 15, 1995, C.A.

49. Community Service by Offenders (Scotland) Act 1978.
s. 1, repealed: 1995, c. 40, sch. 5.
s. 1, amended: 1995, c. 20, sch. 6.
s. 2, repealed: 1995, c. 40, sch. 5.
s. 2, amended: 1994, c. 39, sch. 13; 1995, c. 20, sch. 6.
s. 3, repealed: 1995, c. 40, sch. 5.
s. 4, repealed: 1995, c. 40, sch. 5.
s. 4, amended: 1995, c. 29, sch. 6.
s. 5, repealed: 1995, c. 40, sch. 5.
s. 5A, added: 1995, c. 29, sch. 6.
s. 6, repealed: 1995, c. 40, sch. 5.
s. 7, repealed: 1995, c. 40, sch. 5.
s. 8, repealed: 1995, c. 40, sch. 5.
s. 10, repealed: 1995, c. 40, sch. 5.
s. 11, repealed: 1995, c. 40, sch. 5.
s. 12, repealed: 1995, c. 40, sch. 5.
s. 12, amended: 1994, c. 39, sch. 13.
s. 13, repealed: 1995, c. 40, sch. 5.
s. 15, repealed: 1995, c. 40, sch. 5.
sch. 2, repealed: 1995, c. 40, sch. 5.

50. Inner Urban Areas Act 1978.
s. 1, repealed in pt.: 1994, c. 39, sch. 14 (S.).
s. 1, amended: 1994, c. 39, sch. 13 (S.).
s. 2, repealed in pt.: 1994, c. 39, sch. 14 (S.).

CAP.

1978—cont.

50. Inner Urban Areas Act 1978—*cont.*
s. 2, amended: 1994, c. 39, sch. 13 (S.).
s. 7, repealed in pt.: 1994, c. 39, sch. 14 (S.).
s. 7, amended: 1994, c. 39, sch. 13 (S.).

53. Chronically Sick and Disabled Persons (Northern Ireland) Act 1978.
s. 14, regs. 95/332.

1979

2. Customs and Excise Management Act 1979.
s. 1, amended: 1995, c. 21, sch. 13.
s. 8, amended: 1995, c. 21, sch. 13.
s. 13, order 95/1777.
s. 75A, repealed in pt.: 1995, c. 38, sch. 2.
s. 118, repealed in pt.: 1995, c. 38, sch. 2.
s. 137A, regs. 95/2893.
s. 17, amended: 1995, c. 4, s. 20.
s. 17, see *BSC Footwear Supplies* v. *Customs and Excise Commissioners, The Independent*, June 19, 1995, Robert Walker J.
s. 78, see *R.* v. *Lucien, The Times*, March 3, 1995, C.A.
s. 93, regs. 95/1046.
s. 100A, orders 1994/2898; 95/1067.
s. 102, see *Department of Transport* v. *Ladd, The Times*, May 29, 1995, D.C.
s. 137A, added: 1995, c. 4, s. 20.
s. 139, see *Air Canada* v. *United Kingdom, The Times*, May 13, 1995, European Ct. H.R.
sch. 1, amended: 1995, c. 21, sch. 14.

3. Customs and Excise Duties (General Reliefs) Act 1979.
s. 15, amended: 1995, c. 40, sch. 4 (S.).

4. Alcoholic Liquor Duties Act 1979.
s. 1, order 94/2904.
s. 1, repealed in pt.: 1995, c. 4, sch. 29.
s. 1, amended: 1995, c. 4, s. 1.
s. 2, repealed in pt.: 1995, c. 4, sch. 29.
s. 4, repealed in pt.: 1995, c. 4, sch. 29.
s. 4, amended: 1995, c. 4, sch. 2; 1995, c. 40, sch. 4 (S.).
s. 5, amended: 1995, c. 4, s. 3.
s. 6A, repealed in pt.: 1995, c. 4, sch. 29.
s. 9, repealed: 1995, c. 4, sch. 2.
s. 10, amended: 1995, c. 4, sch. 2.
s. 24, amended: 1995, c. 4, sch. 2.
s. 36, amended: 1995, c. 4, s. 3.
s. 45, repealed in pt.: 1995, c. 4, sch. 29.
s. 59, amended: 1995, c. 4, s. 1.
s. 60, repealed in pt.: 1995, c. 4, sch. 29.
s. 62, amended: 1995, c. 4, s. 3.
s. 63, repealed in pt.: 1995, c. 4, sch. 29.
s. 75, amended: 1995, c. 4, sch. 2.
s. 77, repealed in pt.: 1995, c. 4, sch. 29.
s. 77, amended: 1995, c. 4, sch. 2.
s. 78, substituted: 1995, c. 4, sch. 2.
s. 79, amended: 1995, c. 4, sch. 2.
s. 80, amended: 1995, c. 4, sch. 2.
sch. 1, amended: 1995, c. 4, s. 2.

CAP.

1979—cont.

5. Hydrocarbon Oil Duties Act 1979.
s. 6, amended: 1995, c. 4, ss. 6, 7.
s. 8, repealed in pt.: 1995, c. 4, sch. 29.
s. 8, amended: 1995, c. 4, s. 6.
ss. 11, 14, amended: 1995, c. 4, s. 6.
s. 19, amended: 1995, c. 21, sch. 13.
s. 27, repealed in pt.: 1995, c. 4, sch. 29.
s. 27, amended: 1995, c. 4, s. 8; 1995, c. 40, sch. 4 (S.).
s. 97, amended: 1995, c. 4, s. 21.
sch. 1, substituted: 1995, c. 4, s. 8.
sch. 6, repealed in pt.: 1995, c. 23, sch. 8.
sch. 6, C.: 1995, c. 23, sch. 8.
sch. 13, amended: 1995, c. 4, s. 8.

7. Tobacco Products Duty Act 1979.
sch. 1, amended: 1995, c. 7, ss. 10, 11.

14. Capital Gains Tax Act 1979.
s. 29A, see *Whitehouse* v. *Ellam* [1995] S.T.C. 503, Vinelott J.
ss. 78, 85, 87, 88, see *NAP Holdings U.K.* v. *Whittles* (Inspector of Taxes), *The Times*, November 22, 1994, H.L.

16. Criminal Evidence Act 1979.
s. 1, repealed: 1995, c. 40, sch. 5 (S.).
s. 1, C.: 1995, c. 46, s. 266 (S.).

17. Vaccine Damage Payments Act 1979.
s. 1, order 95/1164.

27. Kiribati Act 1979.
sch., repealed in pt.: 1995, c. 21, sch. 12.

33. Land Registration (Scotland) Act 1979.
Commencement order: order 95/2547.
ss. 2, 3, order 95/2547.
s. 27, rules 95/248.

34. Credit Unions Act 1979.
s. 31, regs. 95/712.
s. 31, amended: 1995, c. 40, sch. 4 (S.).

36. Nurses, Midwives and Health Visitors Act 1979.
s. 16, amended: 1995, c. 17, sch. 1.
s. 22, order 95/967.

38. Estate Agents Act 1979.
s. 33, amended: 1995, c. 40, sch. 4 (S.).

39. Merchant Shipping Act 1979.
Commencement order: 94/2789.
s. 9, C.: 1995, c. 21, sch. 14.
ss. 14–16, C.: 1995, c. 21, sch. 14.
s. 17, see *Hamburg Star, The* [1994] 1 Lloyd's Rep. 399, Clarke J.
s. 17, C.: 1995, c. 21, sch. 14.
ss. 18, 19, repealed: 1995, c. 21, sch. 12.
s. 20, C.: 1995, c. 21, sch. 14.
s. 20A, C.: 1995, c. 21, sch. 14.
s. 21, regs. 94/3245; 95/157, 1210, 1802, 1803.
s. 21, C.: 1995, c. 21, sch. 14.
s. 22, regs. 95/157, 1210, 1802, 1803.
s. 22, C.: 1995, c. 21, sch. 14.
s. 23, C.: 1995, c. 21, sch. 14.
s. 24, C.: 1995, c. 21, sch. 14.
s. 25, C.: 1995, c. 21, sch. 14.
s. 27, C.: 1995, c. 21, sch. 14.
s. 28, C.: 1995, c. 21, sch. 14.

CAP.

1979—cont.

39. Merchant Shipping Act 1979.
s. 30, C.: 1995, c. 21, sch. 14.
s. 34, C.: 1995, c. 21, sch. 14.
s. 37, C.: 1995, c. 21, sch. 14.
s. 38, C.: 1995, c. 21, sch. 14.
s. 38, continued in force (pt.): 1995, c. 21, sch. 14.
s. 39, C.: 1995, c. 21, sch. 14.
s. 40, repealed in pt.: 1995, c. 22, sch.
ss. 41–42, repealed in pt.: 1995, c. 21, sch. 12.
s. 43, repealed in pt.: 1995, c. 21, sch. 12.
s. 43, C.: 1995, c. 21, sch. 14.
s. 45, repealed: 1995, c. 21, sch. 12.
s. 45, C.: 1995, c. 21, sch. 14.
s. 48, repealed: 1995, c. 21, sch. 12.
s. 49, repealed: 1995, c. 21, sch. 12.
s. 49, C.: 1995, c. 21, sch. 14.
s. 50, repealed: 1995, c. 21, sch. 12.
s. 51, repealed: 1995, c. 21, sch. 12.
s. 52, order 95/2789.
s. 52, repealed: 1995, c. 21, sch. 12.
s. 118A, amended: 1995, c. 40, sch. 4 (S.).
s. 118C, amended: 1995, c. 40, sch. 4 (S.).
s. 118D, amended: 1995, c. 40, sch. 4 (S.).
s. 171, amended: 1995, c. 40, sch. 4 (S.).
s. 193, repealed (prosp.): 1995, c. 21, sch. 12.
sch. 3, repealed: 1995, c. 21, sch. 12.
sch. 3, C.: 1995, c. 21, sch. 14.
sch. 4, order 94/3049.
sch. 4, repealed: 1995, c. 21, sch. 12.
sch. 4, C.: 1995, c. 21, sch. 14.
sch. 5, repealed: 1995, c. 21, sch. 12.
sch. 5, C.: 1995, c. 21, sch. 14.
sch. 6, repealed: 1995, c. 21, sch. 21.
sch. 7, repealed: 1995, c. 21, sch. 12.
sch. 7, C.: 1995, c. 21, sch. 14.
ss. 1, 7, regs. 95/1514.

42. Arbitration Act 1979.
s. 1, *Secretary of State for the Environment* v. *Euston Centre Investments* [1994] 3 W.L.R. 1081, C.A.

43. Crown Agents Act 1979.
s. 1, repealed in pt.: 1995, c. 24, sch. 2.
ss. 2–24, repealed: 1995, c. 24, sch. 2.
s. 25, amended: 1995, c. 24, s. 11.
s. 27, repealed in pt.: 1995, c. 24, sch. 2.
s. 28, repealed: 1995, c. 24, sch. 2.
s. 30, repealed in pt.: 1995, c. 24, sch. 2.
s. 31, repealed in pt.: 1995, c. 24, sch. 2.
sch. 1, repealed in pt.: 1995, c. 24, sch. 2.
sch. 2, repealed in pt.: 1995, c. 24, sch. 2.
sch. 3, repealed in pt.: 1995, c. 44, sch. 1.
sch. 4, repealed in pt.: 1995, c. 24, sch. 2.
sch. 5, repealed in pt.: 1995, c. 24, sch. 2.
sch. 5, amended, 1995, c. 24, s. 11.

46. Ancient Monuments and Archaeological Areas Act 1979.
s. 59, amended: 1995, c. 40, sch. 4 (S.).
s. 61, amended: 1995, c. 40, sch. 4 (S.).

CAP.

1979—cont.

50. European Parliament (Pay and Pensions) Act 1979.
s. 4, order 95/739.
s. 6, repealed in pt.: 1995, c. 26, schs. 5, 7.

53. Charging Orders Act 1979.
s. 2, see *Clarke* v. *Chief Land Registrar*; *Chancery* v. *Ketteringham* [1994] 3 W.L.R. 593, C.A.

54. Sale of Goods Act 1979.
s. 14, see *Renton* v. *Hendersons Garage (Nairn) and United Dominions Trust* [1994] CCLR 29, Sheriff Principal D.J. Risk, Q.C.; *Boyter* v. *Thomson* [1995] 3 W.L.R. 36, H.L.
s. 16, amended: 1995, c. 28, s. 1.
s. 16, see *Ellis, Son and Vidler, Re sub nom. Stapylton Fletcher, Re; Ellis, Son and Vidler, Re* [1994] BCC 532, H.H.J. Paul Baker, Q.C.
s. 18, amended: 1995, c. 28, s. 1.
ss. 20A, 20B, added: 1995, c. 28, s. 1.
s. 61, amended: 1995, c. 28, s. 2.

55. Justices of the Peace Act 1979.
regs. 95/686.
s. 18, rules 95/571.
s. 21, regs. 94/2811.
s. 55, amended: 1995, c. 26, sch. 5.
s. 64, amended: 1995, c. 25, sch. 10.
sch. para 13, regs. 95/41.

58. Isle of Man Act 1979.
s. 1, amended: order 94/3041.
s. 5, amended: 1995, c. 40, sch. 4 (S.).

60. Zimbabwe Act 1979.
s. 4, amended: 1995, c. 44, sch. 1.

1980

2. Papua New Guinea, Western Samoa and Nauru (Miscellaneous Provisions) Act 1980.
s. 1, repealed in pt.: 1995, c. 44, sch. 1.
sch., repealed in pt.: 1995, c. 21, sch. 12.

4. Bail etc. (Scotland) Act 1980.
repealed: 1995, c. 40, sch. 5.
s. 1, amended: 1995, c. 20, s. 1.
s. 1, C.: 1995, c. 46, ss. 24, 30.
s. 2, C.: 1995, c. 46, s. 25.
s. 2, see *Reilly* v. *H.M. Advocate*, 1995 S.C.C.R. 45.
s. 3, C.: 1995, c. 46, ss. 27, 28.
s. 3, amended: 1995, c. 20, s. 1.
s. 4, C.: 1995, c. 46, s. 29.
s. 5, C.: 1995, c. 46, s. 201.
s. 7, C.: 1995, c. 46, s. 21.
s. 8, C.: 1995, c. 46, s. 22.
s. 9, C.: 1995, c. 46, s. 43.
s. 10, amended: 1994, c. 39, sch. 13.
s. 10, C.: 1995, c. 46, s. 8.
sch. 1, C.: 1995, c. 46, ss. 30, 135, 146.
sch. 2, C.: 1995, c. 46, s. 146.

5. Child Care Act 1980.
ss. 1, 2, 18, see *X. (Minors)* v. *Bedfordshire County Council* [1995] 3 W.L.R. 152, H.L.

CAP.

1980—cont.

9. Reserve Forces Act 1980.
s. 130, amended: regs. 95/1748.
s. 131, repealed in pt.: 1994, c. 39, sch. 14.
s. 131, amended: 1994, c. 39, sch. 13.
s. 133, amended: 1994, c. 39, sch. 13.
s. 144, amended: 1995, c. 40, sch. 4 (S.).
s. 156, schs. 7, 8, amended: 1994, c. 39, sch. 13.

10. Police Negotiating Board Act 1980.
s. 2, regs. 94/3049 (S.); 95/137 (S.), 95/215.

11. Protection of Trading Interests Act 1980.
s. 3, amended: 1995, c. 40, sch. 4 (S.).

13. Slaughter of Animals (Scotland) Act 1980.
s. 22, amended: 1994, c. 39, sch. 13.

16. New Hebrides Act 1980.
s. 3, amended: S.R. 1995 No. 1625.
sch. 1, repealed in pt.: 1995, c. 21, sch. 12.

20. Education Act 1980.
s. 6, see *R.* v. *Bradford Metropolitan Borough Council, ex p. Ali (Sikander)* (1994) 6 Admin. L.R. 589, Jowitt J.
s. 7, see *R.* v. *Bradford Metropolitan Borough Council, ex p. Ali (Sikander)* (1994) 6 Admin. L.R. 589, Jowitt J.; *R.* v. *Kingsbury, ex p. Northampton Education Department* [1994] C.O.D. 114, C.A.
s. 8, regs. 95/1904, 2070.
s. 9, see *R.* v. *Kingsbury, ex p. Northampton Education Department* [1994] C.O.D. 114, C.A.
s. 17, regs. 95/2016.
s. 18, regs. 95/2017.
s. 22, amended: 1995, c. 18, sch. 2.
s. 35, regs. 95/1904, 2016, 2017, 2070.

21. Competition Act 1980.
s. 11, amended: 1994, c. 39, s. 72 (S.).
s. 19, amended: 1995, c. 40, sch. 4 (S.).

23. Consular Fees Act 1980.
s. 1, orders 94/3202; 95/1617.

25. Insurance Companies Act 1980.
sch. 3, repealed in pt.: S.R. 1995 No. 755; 1995, c. 44, sch. 1.

30. Social Security Act 1980.
sch. 4, repealed in pt.: 1995, c. 17, sch. 3.

31. Limitation Act 1980.
ss. 8, 9, see *British Coal Corp.* v. *Ellistown Pipes* [1994] RVR 81, C.A.

32. Licensed Premises (Exclusion of Certain Persons) Act 1980.
s. 1, amended: 1995, c. 40, sch. 4 (S.).

34. Transport Act 1980.
s. 52, order 94/2388.
ss. 52B, 52D, orders 94/2388; 95/430.
s. 66, repealed in pt.: 1995, c. 23, sch. 8.
sch. 4, repealed in pt.: 1995, c. 23, sch. 8.
sch. 4, C.: 1995, c. 23, sch. 8.

CAP.

1980—cont.

39. Self-Governing Schools etc. (Scotland) Act 1980.
s. 21, amended: 1994, c. 39, s. 143; order 94/3149.
s. 3, see *Annan* v. *Roberts*, 1995 S.C.C.R. 361.

43. Magistrates' Courts Act 1980.
s. 3A, added: 1995, c. 12, sch. 13.
s. 9, see *R.* v. *Basildon Justices, ex p. Holding and Barnes* [1994] RA 157, Schiemann J.
s. 19, see *R.* v. *Ipswich Justices, ex p. Callaghan, The Times*, April 3, 1995, D.C.; *R.* v. *Manchester Magistrates' Courts, ex p. Kaymanesh* (1994) 15 Cr.App.R. (S.) 838, C.A.
s. 22, see *R.* v. *Kieran (Martin Christopher)* (95/545/Y2), February 14, 1995, C.A.
s. 38, see *R.* v. *Sheffield Crown Court and Stipendiary Magistrate, ex p. D.P.P.* (1994) 15 Cr.App.R. (S.) 768, C.A.; *R.* v. *Manchester Magistrates' Courts, ex p. Kaymanesh* (1994) 15 Cr.App.R. (S.) 838, C.A.
s. 53, see *R.* v. *Basildon Justices, ex p. Holding and Barnes* [1994] RA 157, Schiemann J.
s. 54, see *R.* v. *Erewash Borough Council and Ilkeston Justices, ex p. Smedbury and Smedbury* [1994] RVR 60, Auld J.
s. 97, see *R.* v. *Reading Justices, ex p. Berkshire County Council, The Times*, May 5, 1995, D.C.; *R.* v. *Nottingham Justices, ex p. Fraser, The Times*, May 13, 1995, D.C.
s. 106, see *R.* v. *Sinclair (Beverley), The Times*, April 7, 1995, C.A.
s. 111, see *P.* v. *P. (Periodical Payments: Appeals), The Times*, December 19, 1994; *R.* v. *Herefordshire Magistrates, ex p. Hereford and Worcester City Council* (CO/90/95), February 13, 1995, Brooke J.
s. 115, see *Hourihane* v. *Commissioner of Police of the Metropolis, The Times*, December 27, 1994, C.A.
s. 137, order 94/3250.
s. 137, see *R.* v. *Liverpool Justices, ex p. R.M. Broudie & Co* [1994] C.O.D. 436, D.C.
s. 142, repealed in pt.: 1995, c. 35, sch. 3.
s. 142, amended: 1995, c. 35, s. 26.
s. 144, rules 94/3154, 3156.
sch. 6, amended: order 94/3250; 1995, c. 18, sch. 2.
sch. 7, repealed in pt.: 1995, c. 38, sch. 2.
sch. 7, C.: 1995, c. 12, sch. 14; 1995, c. 46, s. 215.

44. Education (Scotland) Act 1980.
ss. 4, 6, repealed in pt.: 1994, sch. 39, schs. 13, 14.
s. 22D, amended: 1994, c. 39, s. 144.
s. 23, amended: 1994, c. 39, s. 32.

CAP.

1980—cont.

44. Education (Scotland) Act 1980—*cont.*
s. 35, see *Ross* v. *Simpson*, 1994 S.C.C.R. 847.
s. 43, amended: 1995, c. 40, sch. 2.
s. 36, amended: 1995, c. 36, sch. 4.
s. 36, see *Ross* v. *Simpson*, 1994 S.C.C.R. 847.
s. 43, 1995, c. 40, sch. 2.
s. 44, repealed in pt.: 1995, c. 36, sch. 5.
s. 44, amended: 1995, c. 36, sch. 4.
s. 49, regs. 94/3148; 95/1739.
ss. 50, 51, amended: 1994, c. 39, s. 145.
s. 53, amended: 1995, c. 18, sch. 2.
s. 65B, repealed in pt.: 1995, c. 36, schs. 4, 5.
s. 65B, amended: 1995, c. 36, sch. 4.
s. 66, amended: 1995, c. 40, sch. 2.
s. 73, regs. 94/3148; 95/1712.
s. 74, regs. 94/3148.
ss. 75A, 75B, regs. 95/1713.
s. 78, repealed in pt.: 1994, c. 39, schs. 13, 14.
ss. 98, 101; 1995, c. 40, sch. 2.
s. 86, repealed in pt.: 1994, c. 39, sch. 14.
s. 98, amended: 1995, c. 40, sch. 2.
s. 101, amended: 1995, c. 40, sch. 2.
s. 105, see *Governors of Dollar Academy Trust* v. *Lord Advocate* (O.H.), 1995, S.L.T. 596.
ss. 112, 122, amended: 1994, c. 39, sch. 13.
s. 123, amended: 1995, c. 12, sch. 13.
s. 125A, added: 1995, c. 36, s. 35.
s. 135, repealed in pt.: 1995, c. 36, schs. 4, 5.
s. 135, amended: 1994, c. 39, sch. 13; 1995, c. 36, sch. 4.
sch. A1, amended: 1994, c. 39, sch. 13.

45. Water (Scotland) Act 1980.
s. 1, substituted: 1994, c. 39, s. 65.
s. 2, amended: order 94/3308.
ss. 3–5, repealed: 1994, c. 39, schs. 13, 14.
s. 6, amended: 1994, c. 39, sch. 13.
s. 9, amended: 1994, c. 39, s. 105.
s. 9A, amended: 1994, c. 39, sch. 13.
s. 10, repealed in pt.: 1994, c. 39, schs. 13, 14.
s. 10, amended: order 94/3308.
s. 11, repealed in pt.: 1994, c. 39, schs. 13, 14.
s. 12, substituted: 1994, c. 39, s. 106.
s. 13, repealed in pt.: 1994, c. 39, schs. 13, 14.
s. 13A, added: 1994, c. 39, s. 107.
s. 15, repealed: 1994, c. 39, schs. 13, 14.
s. 16, repealed in pt.: 1994, c. 39, schs. 13, 14.
s. 17, repealed in pt.: 1994, c. 39, schs. 13, 14.
s. 17, amended: order 94/3308.
s. 18, repealed in pt.: 1994, c. 39, schs. 13, 14.

CAP.

1980—cont.

45. Water (Scotland) Act 1980—*cont.*
s. 20, repealed: 1994, c. 39, schs. 13, 14.
s. 21, substituted: 1994, c. 39, s. 108.
s. 22, repealed in pt.: 1994, c. 39, schs. 13, 14.
s. 23, repealed in pt.: 1994, c. 39, schs. 13, 14.
s. 23, amended: 1994, c. 39, s. 109.
s. 24, amended: 1994, c. 39, s. 110.
s. 24A, added: 1994, c. 39, s. 111.
s. 25, repealed in pt.: 1994, c. 39, schs. 13, 14.
s. 26, amended: 1994, c. 39, sch. 13.
ss. 27, 28, repealed in pt.: 1994, c. 39, schs. 13, 14.
s. 29, order 94/3308.
s. 29, repealed in pt.: 1994, c. 39, schs. 13, 14.
s. 30, repealed: 1994, c. 39, schs. 13, 14.
s. 31, amended: 1995, c. 25, sch. 22.
s. 33, repealed in pt.: 1995, c. 39, schs. 13, 14; 1995, c. 25, sch. 24.
s. 33, amended: 1995, c. 25, sch. 22.
s. 35, repealed in pt.: 1994, c. 39, schs. 13, 14.
s. 38, repealed in pt.: 1994, c. 39, schs. 13, 14.
s. 38, amended: 1995, c. 40, sch. 2.
ss. 40–46, repealed: 1994, c. 39, schs. 13, 14.
s.41A, substituted: 1994, c. 39, s. 112.
s. 47, repealed in pt.: 1994, c. 39, schs. 13, 14.
ss. 48, 49, repealed: 1994, c. 39, schs. 13, 14.
s. 54, repealed in pt.: 1994, c. 39, schs. 13, 14.
s. 55, amended: 1994, c. 39, sch. 13.
s. 58, repealed in pt.: 1994, c. 39, schs. 13, 14.
ss. 60, 61, repealed: 1994, c. 39, schs. 13, 14.
s. 63, repealed in pt.: 1994, c. 39, schs. 13, 14.
ss. 64–67, repealed: 1994, c. 39, schs. 13, 14.
s. 68, repealed in pt.: 1994, c. 39, sch. 13.
s. 69, amended: 1994, c. 39, schs. 13, 14.
ss. 70–71, repealed in pt.: 1994, c. 39, schs. 13, 14.
s. 72, orders 95/992, 1994.
s. 72, amended: 1995, c. 40, sch. 2.
s. 72, repealed in pt.: 1994, c. 39, schs. 13, 14.
s. 73, repealed in pt.: 1994, c. 39, schs. 13, 14.
s. 75, amended: 1995, c. 40, sch. 4.
s. 76, repealed in pt.: 1994, c. 39, schs. 13, 14.
s. 76F, amended: 1994, c. 39, s. 114.

CAP.

1980—cont.

45. Water (Scotland) Act 1980—*cont.*
ss. 76H, 76I, 76J, 76L, repealed in pt.: 1994, c. 39, schs. 13, 14.
ss. 80–92, repealed: 1994, c. 39, schs. 13, 14.
s. 93, amended: 1995, c. 40, sch. 2.
ss. 93, 94, amended: 1995, c. 25, sch. 19.
s. 100, amended: 1994, c. 39, sch. 13.
s. 101, amended: 1994, c. 39, s. 115.
s. 103, repealed in pt.: 1994, c. 39, schs. 13, 14.
ss. 104, 106, amended: 1994, c. 39, sch. 13.
s. 107, orders 94/3308, 3309.
s. 107, repealed in pt.: 1994, c. 39, schs. 13, 14.
s. 109, repealed in pt.: 1994, c. 39, schs. 13, 14.
s. 109, repealed in pt.: 1995, c. 25, sch. 24.
s. 109, amended: 1995, c. 25, sch. 22.
s. 110A, added: 1995, c. 25, sch. 21.
sch. 1, repealed in pt.: 1994, c. 39, schs. 13, 14; 1995, c. 25, sch. 24.
sch. 1, amended: 1995, c. 25, sch. 22.
schs. 2, 3, repealed in pt.: 1994, c. 39, schs. 13, 14.
sch. 4, order 94/3308.
sch. 4, amended: 1994, c. 39, sch. 13.
sch. 4, amended: 1995, c. 40, sch. 2; 1995, c. 45, sch. 4.
schs. 7, 8, repealed: 1994, c. 39, schs. 13, 14.
sch. 10, repealed in pt.: 1994, c. 39, sch. 14.

46. Solicitors (Scotland) Act 1980.
s. 25A, amended: 1995, c. 40, sch. 4.
ss. 41, 42, see *Law Society of Scotland, Council of the* v. *McKinnie* (I.H.), 1995 S.C.L.R. 53.
sch. 1, repealed in pt.: 1995, c. 7, sch. 5.

47. Criminal Appeal (Northern Ireland) Act 1980.
s. 1, amended: 1995, c. 35, s. 1.
s. 12, amended: 1995, c. 35, ss. 1, 2.
s. 13A, amended: 1995, c. 35, s. 1, 2.
s. 14, repealed: 1995, c. 35, sch. 3.
s. 16, repealed in pt.: 1995, c. 35, sch. 3.
s. 16, amended: 1995, c. 35, sch. 2.
s. 25, repealed in pt.: 1995, c. 35, sch. 3.
s. 25, amended: 1995, c. 35, s. 4, sch. 2.
s. 25A, added: 1995, c. 35, s. 5.
s. 26, amended: 1995, c. 35, sch. 2.
s. 29, amended: 1995, c. 35, sch. 2.
s. 44, repealed in pt.: 1995, c. 35, sch. 3.
s. 45, amended: 1995, c. 35, sch. 2.
s. 47A, added: 1995, c. 35, s. 7.

48. Finance Act 1980.
sch. 17, amended: 1995, c. 4, s. 148.

50. Coal Industry Act 1980.
s. 2, amended: order 95/509.

51. Housing Act 1980.
sch. 22, see *Naiva (Khatim)* v. *Covent Garden Group* [1994] N.P.C. 131, C.A.

CAP.

1980—cont.

52. Criminal Justice (Scotland) Act 1980.
s. 26, see *Duffy* v. *Normand*, 1995 S.C.C.R. 538.

53. Health Services Act 1980.
s. 1, repealed in pt.: 1995, c. 17, sch. 3.
s. 6, repealed in pt.: 1995, c. 17, sch. 3.
sch. 1, repealed in pt.: 1995, c. 17, sch. 3.

55. Law Reform (Miscellaneous Provisions) (Scotland) Act 1980.
s. 1, amended: 1995, c. 20, s. 7; 1995, c. 40, sch. 4 (S.).
s. 2, C.: 1995, c. 46, s. 85.
sch. 2, C.: 1995, c. 46, ss. 84, 86.

58. Limitation Act 1980.
s. 2, see *S.* v. *W.*, *The Times*, December 26, 1994, C.A.
s. 5, see *Kleinwort Benson* v. *South Tyneside Metropolitan Borough Council* [1994] 4 All E.R. 972, Hobhouse J.
s. 9, see *Farmizer (Products), Re*, *The Independent*, June 19, 1995, Blackburne J.
s. 11, see *S.* v. *W.*, *The Times*, December 26, 1994, C.A.; *Dobbie* v. *Medway Health Authority* [1994] 1 W.L.R. 1234, C.A.
s. 14, see *S.* v. *W.*, *The Times*, December 26, 1994, C.A.; *Colegrove* v. *Smyth* [1994] 5 Med. LR 111, Buckley J.; *Dobbie* v. *Medway Health Authority* [1994] 1 W.L.R. 1234, C.A.; *Baig* v. *City and Hackney Health Authority* [1994] 5 Med. LR 221, Rougier J.; *Smith (Michael John)* v. *West Lancashire Health Authority* (CCRTF 94/1240/C), June 8, 1995, C.A.
s. 14A, see *Hallam-Eames* v. *Merrett Syndicates*, *The Times*, January 25, 1995, C.A.; *Spencer-Ward* v. *Humberts* [1994] NPC 105, C.A.; *Wilson* v. *Le Fevre Wood & Royale*, *The Independent*, October 12, 1995, C.A.; *Heathcote and Heathcote* v. *David Marks & Co.*, December 13, 1994; Buckley J.; Manchester District Registry.
s. 29, see *Kleinwort Benson* v. *South Tyneside Metropolitan Borough Council* [1994] 4 All E.R. 972, Hobhouse J.
s. 32, see *Sheldon* v. *R.H.M. Outhwaite (Underwriting Agencies)* [1994] 3 W.L.R. 999, C.A.
s. 33, see *S.* v. *W.*, *The Times*, December 26, 1994, C.A.; *Hallam-Eames* v. *Merrett Syndicates*, *The Times*, January 25, 1995, C.A.; *Dobbie* v. *Medway Health Authority* [1994] 1 W.L.R. 1234, C.A.; *Baig* v. *City and Hackney Health Authority* [1994] 5 Med. LR 221, Rougier J.; *Barrand* v. *British Cellophane*, *The Times*, February 16, 1995, C.A.

CAP.

1980—cont.

58. Limitation Act 1980—*cont.*

s. 35, see *Welsh Development Agency* v. *Redpath Dorman Long* [1994] 4 All E.R. 10, C.A.

62. Criminal Justice (Scotland) Act 1980.

s. 1, repealed: 1995, c. 40, sch. 5.
s. 2, amended: 1995, c. 20, s. 59.
s. 2, repealed: 1995, c. 40, sch. 5.
s. 2, C.: 1995, c. 46, s. 14.
s. 3, amended: 1995, c. 36, sch. 4.
s. 3, repealed: 1995, c. 40, sch. 5.
s. 3, C.: 1995, c. 46, ss. 14, 15.
s. 4, repealed: 1995, c. 40, sch. 5.
s. 5, repealed: 1995, c. 40, sch. 5.
s. 5, C.: 1995, s. 46, s. 16.
s. 6, repealed: 1995, c. 40, sch. 5.
s. 6, C.: 1995, c. 46, ss. 36, 37.
s. 7, repealed: 1995, c. 40, sch. 5.
s. 7, amended: 1995, c. 20, s. 60.
s. 7, C.: 1995, c. 46, s. 7.
s. 9, repealed: 1995, c. 40, sch. 5.
s. 9, see *Gilmour, Petr.*, 1994 S.C.C.R. 872.
s. 9, C.: 1995, c. 46, s. 291.
s. 10, repealed: 1995, c. 40, sch. 5.
s. 11, repealed: 1995, c. 40, sch. 5.
s. 11, C.: 1995, c. 46, ss. 137, 139.
s. 12, repealed: 1995, c. 40, sch. 5.
s. 13, repealed: 1995, c. 40, sch. 5.
s. 13, C.: 1995, c. 46, s. 78.
s. 14, repealed: 1995, c. 40, sch. 5.
s. 14, C.: 1995, c. 46, ss. 65, 147.
s. 15, repealed: 1995, c. 40, sch. 5.
s. 15, C.: 1995, c. 46, s. 148.
s. 16, repealed: 1995, c. 40, sch. 5.
s. 17, C.: 1995, c. 46, s. 150.
s. 18, repealed: 1995, c. 40, sch. 5.
s. 18, C.: 1995, c. 46, s. 152.
s. 19, repealed: 1995, c. 40, sch. 5.
s. 19, C.: 1995, c. 46, ss. 97, 160.
s. 20, repealed: 1995, c. 40, sch. 5.
s. 20, C.: 1995, c. 46, s. 299.
s. 21, repealed: 1995, c. 40, sch. 5.
s. 21, C.: 1995, c. 46, s. 92.
s. 22, repealed: 1995, c. 40, sch. 5.
s. 22, C.: 1995, c. 46, s. 47.
s. 23, repealed: 1995, c. 40, sch. 5.
s. 24, repealed: 1995, c. 40, sch. 5.
s. 24, C.: 1995, c. 46, s. 100.
s. 25, repealed: 1995, c. 40, sch. 5.
s. 25, repealed: 1995, c. 40, sch. 5.
s. 26, repealed in pt.: 1995, c. 20, sch. 7; order 95/2295.
s. 26, amended: 1995, c. 20, s. 22, sch. 6.
s. 26, see *Donnelly* v. *Schrickel*, 1994 S.C.C.R. 640; *Allan* v. *Ingram*, 1995 S.C.C.R. 390; *Duffy* v. *Normand*, 1995 S.L.T. 1264.
s. 26, repealed: 1995, c. 40, sch. 5.
s. 26, C.: 1995, c. 46, ss. 280, 281.

CAP.

1980—cont.

62. Criminal Justice (Scotland) Act 1980—*cont.*

ss. 27–29, repealed: 1995, c. 40, sch. 5.
s. 30, repealed: 1995, c. 40, sch. 5.
s. 30, C.: 1995, c. 46, s. 269.
s. 31, repealed: 1995, c. 40, sch. 5.
s. 32, repealed: 1995, c. 40, sch. 5.
s. 32, C.: 1995, c. 46, s. 272.
s. 32A, C.: 1995, c. 46, s. 273.
s. 33, repealed: 1995, c. 40, sch. 5.
s. 34, repealed: 1995, c. 40, sch. 5.
s. 35, repealed: 1995, c. 40, sch. 5.
s. 35, C.: 1995, c. 46, s. 131.
s. 36, repealed: 1995, c. 40, sch. 5.
s. 36, C.: 1995, c. 46, s. 174.
s. 37, repealed: 1995, c. 40, sch. 5.
s. 37, C.: 1995, c. 46, s. 123.
s. 38, repealed: 1995, c. 40, sch. 5.
s. 38, C.: 1995, c. 46, s. 5.
s. 39, repealed: 1995, c. 40, sch. 5.
s. 39, C.: 1995, c. 46, s. 289.
s. 40, repealed: 1995, c. 40, sch. 5.
s. 40, C.: 1995, c. 46, s. 166.
s. 41, repealed: 1995, c. 40, sch. 5.
s. 41, C.: 1995, c. 46, s. 204.
s. 42, C.: 1995, c. 46, s. 204.
s. 43, repealed: 1995, c. 40, sch. 5.
s. 43, C.: 1995, c. 46, s. 205.
s. 44, C.: 1995, c. 46, s. 208.
s. 45, repealed in pt.: 1995, c. 40, sch. 5.
s. 45, C.: 1995, c. 46, s. 207.
s. 46, repealed: 1995, c. 40, sch. 5.
s. 46, C.: 1995, c. 46, ss. 199, 232.
s. 47, repealed: 1995, c. 40, sch. 5.
s. 47, C.: 1995, c. 46, ss. 213–222, 224.
s. 48, repealed: 1995, c. 40, sch. 5.
s. 49, repealed: 1995, c. 40, sch. 5.
s. 49, C.: 1995, c. 46, s. 213.
s. 50, repealed: 1995, c. 40, sch. 5.
s. 50, C.: 1995, c. 46, s. 219.
s. 52, repealed: 1995, c. 40, sch. 5.
s. 52, C.: 1995, c. 46, s. 222.
s. 53, repealed: 1995, c. 40, sch. 5.
s. 54, repealed: 1995, c. 40, sch. 5.
s. 54, C.: 1995, c. 46, s. 202.
s. 58, repealed: 1995, c. 40, sch. 5.
s. 58, C.: 1995, c. 46, s. 249.
s. 59, repealed: 1995, c. 40, sch. 5.
s. 59, C.: 1995, c. 46, s. 249.
s. 60, repealed: 1995, c. 40, sch. 5.
s. 60, C.: 1995, c. 46, s. 249.
s. 61, repealed: 1995, c. 40, sch. 5.
s. 61, C.: 1995, c. 46, s. 250.
s. 62, repealed: 1995, c. 40, sch. 5.
s. 62, C.: 1995, c. 46, s. 250.
s. 63, repealed: 1995, c. 40, sch. 5.
s. 63, C.: 1995, c. 46, s. 250.
s. 64, repealed: 1995, c. 46, s. 251.
s. 64, C.: 1995, c. 46, s. 251.
s. 65, repealed: 1995, c. 40, sch. 5.
s. 66, repealed: 1995, c. 40, sch. 5.
s. 66, C.: 1995, c. 46, s. 252.
s. 67, repealed: 1995, c. 40, sch. 5.

CAP.

1980—cont.

62. Criminal Justice (Scotland) Act 1980—*cont.*

s. 68, C.: 1995, c. 39, s. 18; 1995, c. 46, 106.
s. 69, C.: 1995, c. 39, s. 19.
s. 70, C.: 1995, c. 39, s. 19.
s. 70A, C.: 1995, c. 39, s. 19.
s. 71, C.: 1995, c. 39, s. 19.
s. 72, C.: 1995, c. 39, s. 20.
s. 72A, C.: 1995, c. 39, s. 20.
s. 73, C.: 1995, c. 39, s. 20.
s. 74, C.: 1995, c. 39, s. 20.
s. 75, C.: 1995, c. 39, s. 21.
s. 76, C.: 1995, c. 39, s. 22.
s. 77, C.: 1995, c. 39, s. 23.
ss. 78–80, repealed: 1995, c. 40, sch. 5.
Part V, repealed: 1995, c. 40, sch. 5.
sch. 1, repealed: 1995, c. 40, sch. 5.
sch. 1, amended: 1995, c. 25, sch. 22.
sch. 1, see *Donnelly* v. *Schrickel*, 1994 S.C.C.R. 640.
sch. 2, repealed: 1995, c. 40, sch. 5; 1995, c. 46, s. 106.
sch. 2, C.: 1995, c. 46, ss. 59, 60, 104, 106, 109–113, 116–121, 123, 124, 126, 127, 129, 131.
sch. 3, repealed: 1995, c. 40, sch. 5.
sch. 3, C.: 1995, c. 46, ss. 175, 177, 178, 179, 181–186, 189, 190, 191, 192, 194, 195.
sch. 4, repealed: 1995, c. 40, sch. 5.
sch. 4, repealed in pt.: 1995, c. 20, sch. 7.
sch. 4, C.: 1995, c. 46, ss. 66–70, 72, 74, 77, 79.
sch. 5, C.: 1995, c. 46, s. 112.
sch. 7, repealed in pt.: 1995, c. 36, sch. 5; 1995, c. 40, sch. 5.
sch. 7, amended: 1995, c. 36, sch. 4.
sch. 7, C.: 1995, c. 46, ss. 17, 23, 47, 49, 66, 67, 75, 85, 105, 106, 108, 109, 110, 111, 117, 125, 142, 144, 155, 169, 201, 210, 212, 215, 218, 220, 292, 308.
sch. 8, C.: 1995, c. 46, ss. 93, 97, 99, 103, 104, 115, 117, 118, 120, 127, 129, 137, 178.

63. Overseas Development and Co-operation Act 1980.

s. 1, see *R.* v. *Secretary of State for Foreign and Commonwealth Affairs, ex p. World Development Movement* [1995] 1 W.L.R. 386, D.C.
s. 7, order 95/1502.
sch. 1, amended: 1995, c. 17, sch. 1.

65. Local Government, Planning and Land Act 1980.

s. 2, amended: 1994, c. 39, sch. 13 (S.).
s. 3, regs. 94/2677; 95/2006.
s. 7, regs. 95/677 (S.).
s. 8, repealed in pt.: 1994, c. 39, schs. 13, 14 (S.).
s. 9, regs. 94/677 (S.); 95/1366, 1377.

CAP.

1980—cont.

65. Local Government, Planning and Land Act 1980—*cont.*

s. 16, see *R.* v. *Bowden (Terence)* (93/6974/X2), February 24, 1995, C.A.
s. 20, repealed in pt.: 1994, c. 39, schs. 13, 14 (S.).
s. 23, regs. 95/677 (S.).
s. 32, amended: 1994, c. 39, s. 158 (S.).
s. 52, repealed in pt.: 1995, c. 25, sch. 24.
s. 69, amended: 1994, c. 39, s. 158 (S.).
s. 87, regs. 94/3269.
s. 87, repealed in pt.: 1994, c. 39, sch. 14 (S.).
s. 103, repealed in pt.: 1995, c. 25, sch. 24.
s. 103, amended: 1995, c. 25, sch. 10.
s. 120, amended: 1994, c. 39, sch. 14 (S.).
ss. 134, 135, order 95/916.
s. 148, orders 95/384, 389, 2899.
s. 148, repealed in pt.: 1994, c. 39, sch. 14 (S.).
s. 148, amended: 1994, c. 39, sch. 14 (S.).
s. 149, orders 95/384, 389, 2899.
s. 165, amended: 1994, c. 39, sch. 13 (S.).
s. 165A, order 95/390.
s. 167, amended: 1995, c. 40, sch. 4 (S.).
sch. 2, repealed in pt.: 1995, c. 25, sch. 24.
schs. 19, 20, 21, amended: 1995, c. 25, sch. 10.
sch. 26, order 95/916.
sch. 32, amended: 1994, c. 39, s. 159 (S.), sch. 14 (S.).

66. Highways Act 1980.

regs. 95/451.
confirmation instrument 95/1301.
see *Estate of Kingsley* v. *Secretary of State for Transport* [1994] C.O.D. 358, D.C.
s. 16, confirmation instrument 95/2201.
s. 18, repealed in pt.: 1995, c. 44, sch. 1.
s. 25, repealed in pt.: 1995, c. 25, sch. 24.
s. 27, repealed in pt.: 1995, c. 25, sch. 24.
s. 29, repealed in pt.: 1995, c. 25, sch. 24.
s. 31, see *Ward* v. *Durham County Council* [1994] EGCS 39, C.A.
s. 35, see *CIN Properties* v. *Rawlins (Martin)*, February 1, 1995, C.A.
s. 38, see *Overseas Investment Services* v. *Simcobuild Construction, The Times*, April 21, 1995, C.A.
s. 41, see *Misell* v. *Essex County Council* (1995) 93 L.G.R. 108, Colman J.
s. 56, see *R.* v. *Herefordshire Magistrates, ex p. Hereford and Worcester City Council* (CO/90/95), February 13, 1995, Brooke J.
s. 58, see *Misell* v. *Essex County Council* (1995) 93 L.G.R. 108, Colman J.; *Allen* v. *Newcastle City Council*, June 29, 1995, Mr Recorder Hirst, Newcastle-upon-Tyne County Ct.
s. 72, repealed in pt.: 1995, c. 25, sch. 24.

CAP.

1980—cont.

66. Highways Act 1980—*cont.*
s. 96, see *Paterson* v. *Humberside County Council, The Times*, April 19, 1995, D.C.
s. 106, confirmation instrument 95/1301, 1357.
s. 108, confirmation instrument 95/1357.
s. 116, see *Westley* v. *Hertfordshire County Council* (CO/2517/94), March 29, 1995, Collins J.
s. 118, repealed in pt.: 1995, c. 25, sch. 24.
s. 137, see *R.* v. *Hereford and Worcester County Council, ex p. Smith (Tommy)* [1994] C.O.D. 129, C.A.; *Carey* v. *Chief Constable of Avon and Somerset, The Times*, April 7, 1995, C.A.
s. 149, see *Cornwall County Council* v. *Blewett* [1994] C.O.D. 46, D.C.
sch. 2, confirmation instruments 95/1301, 1357.

67. Anguilla Act 1980.
ss. 1, 2, repealed in pt.: 1995, c. 44, sch. 1.

1981

10. Merchant Shipping Act 1981.
repealed: 1995, c. 21, sch. 12.

14. Public Passenger Vehicles Act 1981.
s. 5, amended: 1994, c. 39, sch. 13 (S.).
s. 10, regs. 93/3012.
s. 14A, regs. 95/689.
s. 14A, amended: 1994, c. 39, sch. 13 (S.).
s. 25, regs. 95/186.
s. 52, regs. 93/3012.
s. 59, regs. 95/689.
s. 60, regs. 93/3012; 94/3271, 3272; 95/185, 689.
s. 82, sch. 1, amended: 1994, c. 39, sch. 13 (S.).
sch. 7, repealed in pt.: 1995, c. 23, sch. 8.

20. Judicial Pensions Act 1981.
s. 14A, amended: 1995, c. 26, sch. 5.
s. 32A, regs. 95/635 (S.).
s. 33A, regs. 95/639.

22. Animal Health Act 1981.
s. 1, orders 94/2627, 2770 (S.), 2920, 2965, 3141, 3249; 95/11, 13, 131, 1755, 2042.
s. 7, orders 94/2965, 3141, 3249; 95/11, 12, 131.
s. 8, orders 94/2627, 3141, 3249; 95/11, 12, 131, 1755, 2042.
s. 8, see *R.* v. *Secretary of State for Education, ex p. E.* (CO/362/95), June 21, 1995, Hidden J.
s. 10, order 94/2920.
s. 11, order 94/2627.
s. 15, orders 94/2627, 2770 (S.), 3141; 95/13, 1755, 2042.
s. 17, order 94/3141.
s. 23, orders 94/2965, 3141.
s. 25, orders 94/3141; 95/12.

CAP.

1981—cont.

22. Animal Health Act 1981—*cont.*
s. 35, order 95/12.
s. 37, order 94/3249; 95/131.
ss. 38, 39, order 94/3249.
ss. 49, 65, amended: 1995, c. 21, sch. 13.
s. 50, amended: 1994, c. 39, sch. 13 (S.).
s. 73, see *Ken Lane Transport* v. *North Yorkshire County Council, The Times*, May 22, 1995, D.C.
s. 83, orders 94/2627, 3141, 3249; 95/11, 12.
s. 87, orders 94/2920, 3249.
s. 87, amended: orders 94/2627, 3141.
s. 88, order 95/1755.
s. 88, amended: orders 94/2627, 3141.
s. 92, amended: 1995, c. 40, sch. 4 (S.).

23. Local Government (Miscellaneous Provisions) (Scotland) Act 1981.
ss. 6, 11, 27, repealed: 1994, c. 39, sch. 14 (S.).
schs. 2, 3, repealed in pt.: 1994, c. 39, sch. 14 (S.).

29. Fisheries Act 1981.
s. 15, schemes 95/1609, 1610.
s. 30, orders 95/907, 908.

35. Finance Act 1981.
s. 80, see *De Rothschild* v. *Lawrenson* [1995] S.T.C. 623, C.A.
s. 107, amended: 1994, c. 39, sch. 13 (S.).

37. Zoo Licensing Act 1981.
s. 1, amended: 1994, c. 39, sch. 13 (S.).

45. Forgery and Counterfeiting Act 1981.
s. 1, see *R.* v. *Macrae* [1994] Crim.L.R. 363, C.A.
s. 9, see *R.* v. *Jeraj* [1994] Crim.L.R. 595, C.A.
s. 10, see *R.* v. *Macrae* [1994] Crim.L.R. 363, C.A.; *R.* v. *Mellon (Basil)* (92/3682/W4), March 9, 1995, C.A.
s. 12, repealed in pt.: 1995, c. 23, sch. 8.
s. 12, C.: 1995, c. 23, sch. 8.
s. 26, repealed: 1995, c. 40, sch. 5 (S.).
s. 26, C.: 1995, c. 46, sch. 9 (S.).

47. Criminal Attempts Act 1981.
s. 9, see *C. (A Minor)* v. *D.P.P.* [1995] 2 W.L.R. 383, H.L.

49. Contempt of Court Act 1981.
see *R.* v. *Westminster City Council, ex p. Castelli; R.* v. *Same, ex p. Tristram-Garcia, The Times*, August 14, 1995, Latham J.
ss. 1, 2, see *Advocate (H.M.)* v. *Caledonian Newspapers; Advocate (H.M.)* v. *Scottish Daily Record and Sunday Mail*, 1995 S.C.C.R. 330.
s. 8, see *R.* v. *Young (Stephen)* [1995] 2 W.L.R. 430, C.A.
s. 12, see *R.* v. *Powell (Paul Baden)* (1994) 98 Cr.App.R. 224, C.A.
s. 14, see *Delaney* v. *Delaney, The Times*, November 2, 1995, C.A.
s. 15, amended: 1995, c. 40, sch. 4 (S.).

CAP.

1981—cont.

52. Belize Act 1981.
s. 4, repealed in pt.: 1995, c. 44, sch. 1.
schs. 1, 2, repealed in pt.: 1995, c. 21, sch. 12.

53. Deep Sea Mining (Temporary Provisions) Act 1981.
s. 1, repealed in pt.: 1995, c. 44, sch. 1.

54. Supreme Court Act 1981.
s. 1, see *Huggett* v. *Secretary of State for the Environment; Wendy Fair Markets* v. *Same; Bello* v. *Same, The Times*, March 1, 1995, C.A.
s. 2, amended: order 94/3217.
s. 18, rules 95/2206.
s. 18, see *Northampton Health Authority* v. *The Official Solicitor and the Governors of St. Andrews Hospital* [1994] 1 FLR 162, C.A.; *Prout* v. *British Gas* [1994] F.S.R. 160, C.A.; *J. (A Minor) (Contact) Re*, [1994] 1 F.L.R. 729, C.A.
s. 19, see *Smith* v. *Glennon* [1994] 5 Med. LR 218, C.A.
s. 20, see *Hamburg Star, The* [1994] 1 Lloyd's Rep. 399, Clarke J.
s. 20, amended: 1995, c. 21, sch. 13.
s. 24, amended: 1995, c. 21, sch. 13.
s. 28A, see *Waldie (Darren)* v. *D.P.P.* (CO3183/94), March 6, 1995, Pill J.
s. 29, see *R.* v. *Maidstone Crown Court, ex p. Clark, The Times*, December 19, 1994, D.C.; *R.* v. *Southwark Crown Court, ex p. Ward* (1995) 7 Admin. L.R. 395, D.C.; *R.* v. *Southwark Crown Court, ex p. Tawfick* (1995) 7 Admin. L.R. 410, D.C.; *R.* v. *Chester Crown Court, ex p. Cheshire County Council, The Times*, October 23, 1995, D.C.
s. 31, see *R.* v. *Secretary of State for Foreign and Commonwealth Affairs, ex p. World Development Movement* [1995] 1 W.L.R. 386, D.C.
s. 35, see *Guardian Ocean Cargoes, Transorient Ship Cargoes, Middle East Agents S.A.L. and Med Line SA* v. *Banco Do Brasil (Nos. 1 and 3)* [1994] 2 Lloyd's Rep. 152, C.A.
s. 35A, see *Mathew (Thomas)* v. *T.M. Sutton* [1994] 1 W.L.R. 1455, Chadwick J.; *Cox* v. *Bankside Members Agency, The Times*, January 27, 1995, Phillips J.
s. 37, see *Gidrxslme Shipping Co.* v. *Tantomar-Transportes Martimos LDA* [1995] 1 W.L.R. 299, Colman J.; *Department of Social Security* v. *Butler, The Times*, August 11, 1995, C.A.
s. 38, see *Escalus Properties* v. *Robinson, The Times*, April 21, 1995, C.A.; *Sinclair Gardens Investments (Kensington)* v. *Walsh (Patrick), Folan (Bridie)*

CAP.

1981—cont.

54. Supreme Court Act 1981—*cont.*
and Bristol & West Building Society (CCRFT 93/1371/E; 94/0082/E; 94/0084/E; QBENI 94/0210E), March 30, 1995, C.A.
s. 42, see *Ewing (No. 2), ex p.* [1994] 1 W.L.R. 1553, C.A.; *Mephistopheles Debt Collection Service (A Firm)* v. *Lotay* [1994] 1 W.L.R. 1064, C.A.
s. 46A, added: 1995, c. 21, sch. 13.
s. 47, see *R.* v. *Dunham, The Times*, November 2, 1995, C.A.
s. 48, amended: 1995, c. 35, sch. 2.
s. 49, see *Hamed El Chiaty & Co (t/a Travers Nile Cruise Lines)* v. *Thomas Cook Group; Nile Rhapsody, The* [1994] 1 Lloyd's Rep. 382, C.A.
s. 50, see *Chiron Corp.* v. *Organon Teknika (No. 10); Chiron Corp.* v. *Murex Diagnostics (No. 10)* [1995] F.S.R. 325, Aldous J.
s. 51, rules 95/2206.
s. 51, see *Thistleton* v. *Hendricks* 32 Con LR 123, H.H.J. Hicks, Q.C.; *McDonald* v. *Horn* [1995] 1 All E.R. 961, C.A.; *C.* v. *C. (Wasted Costs Order)* [1994] 2 F.L.R. 34, Ewbank J.; *Bell Fruit Manufacturing Co.* v. *Twin Falcon* [1995] F.S.R. 144, Ford J.; *Murphy* v. *Young & Co's Brewery, Lloyd's List*, August 16, 1995, D.C.; *R.* v. *Darlington Borough Council, ex p. Association of Darlington Taxi Owners* [1994] C.O.D. 424, Auld J.; *R.* v. *Horsham District Council, ex p. Wenman* [1995] 1 W.L.R. 680, Brooke J.
s. 54, see *Dunlop* v. *Secretary of State for the Environment, The Times*, May 5, 1995, D.C.
s. 69, see *Taylor* v. *Anderton (Police Complaints Authority Intervening)* [1995] 1 W.L.R. 447, C.A.
s. 72, see *Coca-Cola Co.* v. *Gilbey, The Independent*, October 10, 1995, Lightman J.
s. 84, rules 94/1480, 3153; 95/2206.
s. 86, rules 94/1480, 3153.
s. 99, orders 94/1536, 2626, 2893.
s. 104, order 94/3079.
s. 153, repealed in pt.: 1995, c. 21, sch. 12.
sch. 5, repealed in pt.: 1995, c. 21, sch. 12; 1995, c. 35, sch. 3.
sch. 5, C.: 1995, c. 21, sch. 14.

55. Armed Forces Act 1981.
s. 14, amended: order 95/756.

59. Matrimonial Homes (Family Protection) (Scotland) Act 1981.
s. 17, amended: 1995, c. 40, sch. 4.
s. 22, amended: 1995, c. 36, sch. 4.

60. Education Act 1981.
see *E. (A Minor)* v. *Dorset County Council; Christmas* v. *Hampshire*

CAP.

1981—cont.

60. Education Act 1981—*cont.*
County Council; *Keating* v. *Bromley London Borough Council* [1994] 3 W.L.R. 853, C.A.
s. 1, see *R.* v. *Wiltshire County Court, ex p. D.* [1994] 1 F.C.R. 172, Potts J.
s. 2, see *R.* v. *Essex County Council, ex p. C.* [1994] 1 F.C.R. 773, C.A.; *X. (Minors)* v. *Bedfordshire County Council* [1995] 3 W.L.R. 152, H.L.
s. 4, see *X. (Minors)* v. *Bedfordshire County Council* [1995] 3 W.L.R. 152, H.L.
s. 5, see *R.* v. *Wiltshire County Court, ex p. D.* [1994] 1 F.C.R. 172, Potts J.; *X. (Minors)* v. *Bedfordshire County Council* [1995] 3 W.L.R. 152, H.L.
s. 7, see *R.* v. *Cumbria County Council, ex p. B.*, *The Times*, December 26, 1994, Schiemann J.; *R.* v. *Kent County Council, ex p. W. (A Minor) (Special Educational Needs)*, *The Times*, March 3, 1995, Turner J.; *R.* v. *Wiltshire County Court, ex p. D.* [1994] 1 F.C.R. 172, Potts J.; *R.* v. *Essex County Council, ex p. C.* [1994] 1 F.C.R. 773, C.A.; *X. (Minors)* v. *Bedfordshire County Council* [1995] 3 W.L.R. 152, H.L.
s. 8, see *R.* v. *Wiltshire County Court, ex p. D.* [1994] 1 F.C.R. 172, Potts J.
s. 15, see *R.* v. *Essex County Council, ex p. C.* [1994] 1 F.C.R. 773, C.A.
sch. 1, see *R.* v. *Essex County Council, ex p. C.* [1994] 1 F.C.R. 773, C.A.

61. British Nationality Act 1981.
s. 2, order 95/552.
s. 37, see *R.* v. *Secretary of State for the Home Department, ex p. Muru* [1994] Imm.A.R. 574, Schiemann J.
s. 51, C.: 1995, c. 21, sch. 14.
s. 53, repealed in pt.: 1995, c. 44, sch. 1.
sch. 7, C.: 1995, c. 21, sch. 14.

63. Betting and Gaming Duties Act 1981.
s. 7, amended: 1995, c. 4, s. 12.
s. 12, regs. 95/1555.
s. 13, amended: order 95/442.
s. 16, regs. 95/1555.
s. 20, regs. 95/1555.
s. 21, amended: 1995, c. 4, sch. 3.
s. 22, amended: 1995, c. 4, sch. 3; order 95/2374.
ss. 23, 24, 25, amended: 1995, c. 4, sch. 3.
s. 25A, added: 1995, c. 4, sch. 3.
s. 26, amended: 1995, c. 4, sch. 3.
s. 26, see *R.* v. *Customs & Excise Commissioners, ex p. Ferrymatics*, *The Times*, February 23, 1995, Ognall J.
ss. 28, 29, repealed in pt.: 1995, c. 4, sch. 29.
ss. 31, 32, amended: 1995, c. 4, sch. 3.

CAP.

1981—cont.

63. Betting and Gaming Duties Act 1981—*cont.*
s. 33, repealed in pt.: 1995, c. 4, sch. 29.
s. 33, amended: 1995, c. 4, sch. 3; 1995, c. 40, sch. 4 (S.).
sch. 2, regs. 95/1555.
sch. 3, amended: order 94/2967; 1995, c. 4, sch. 3; regs. 95/1555; order 95/2374.
sch. 4, repealed in pt.: 1995, c. 4, sch. 29.
sch. 4, amended: 1995, c. 4; order 95/2374.

67. Acquisition of Land Act 1981.
ss. 10–12, 15, regs. 94/3097.
s. 17, repealed in pt.: 1995, c. 25, sch. 24.
s. 17, amended: 1995, c. 25, sch. 10.
ss. 22, 29, regs. 94/3097.
sch. 1, rules 94/3264.
sch. 3, repealed in pt.: 1995, c. 25, sch. 24.
sch. 3, amended: 1995, c. 25, sch. 10.

69. Wildlife and Countryside Act 1981.
regs. 95/451.
s. 1, see *Forsyth* v. *Cardle* 1994 S.C.C.R. 769.
s. 3, order 95/2876.
s. 4, amended: regs. 95/2825.
s. 16, amended: regs. 95/2825.
s. 26, order 95/2876.
s. 27, amended: 1994, c. 39, sch. 13 (S.); regs. 95/2825.
s. 36, amended: 1994, c. 39, sch. 13 (S.).
s. 39, repealed in pt.: 1995, c. 25, sch. 24.
s. 39, amended 1995, c. 25, sch. 10.
ss. 41, 42, amended: 1995, c. 25, sch. 10.
s. 44, repealed in pt.: 1995, c. 25, sch. 24.
s. 46, repealed: 1995, c. 25, sch. 24.
s. 52, repealed in pt.: 1995, c. 25, schs. 10, 24.
s. 52, amended: 1995, c. 25, sch. 10.
s. 53, see *O'Keefe* v. *Secretary of State for the Environment and Isle of Wight District Council* [1994] N.P.C. 94, Pill J.; *R.* v. *Secretary of State for the Environment, ex p. Bagshaw and Norton* (1995) 68 P. & C.R. 402, Owen J.
s. 54, sch. 15, see *Shropshire County Council's Reclassification Order* (Ref: FPS/A3200/8/7) (1994) P.A.D. 843; *O'Keefe* v. *Secretary of State for the Environment and Isle of Wight District Council* [1994] N.P.C. 94, Pill J.

1982

16. Civil Aviation Act 1982.
s. 2, regs. 95/1054.
s. 10, amended: order 95/1289.
s. 30, repealed in pt.: 1994, c. 39, schs. 13, 14 (S.).
s. 36, amended: 1994, c. 39, sch. 13 (S.).
s. 48, repealed in pt.: 1995 c. 44, sch. 1.
s. 60, orders 95/1038, 1296.
s. 60, repealed in pt.: 1995, c. 44, sch. 1.
s. 61, orders 95/1038, 1296.

CAP.

1982—cont.

16. Civil Aviation Act 1982—*cont.*
s. 64, repealed in pt.: 1995, c. 44, sch. 1.
s. 65, repealed in pt.: 1995, c. 44, sch. 1.
s. 69, repealed in pt.: c. 44, sch. 1.
s. 70, repealed in pt.: 1995, c. 44, sch. 1.
s. 71, regs. 95/1054.
s. 73, regs. 94/503, 3055, 3071; 95/497, 1004, 1438, 2144.
s. 74, regs. 94/3055, 3071; 95/497.
s. 75, amended: 1995, c. 21, sch. 13.
s. 77, orders 95/1038, 1296.
s. 84, repealed in pt.: 1995, c. 44, sch. 1
s. 86, amended: 1995, c. 21, sch. 13.
s. 88, amended: 1994, c. 39, sch. 13 (S.).
s. 97, repealed in pt.: 1995, c. 21, sch. 12.
s. 97, amended: 1995, c. 21, sch. 13.
s. 101, order 95/1038.
s. 102, orders 94/3071; 95/1038, 1296.
s. 105, amended: 1994, c. 39, sch. 13 (S.); 1995, c. 40, sch. 4 (S).
s. 108, order 95/1297.
sch. 1, regs. 95/1054.
sch. 14, repealed in pt.: 1995, c. 44, sch. 1.
sch. 15, repealed in pt.: 1995, c. 44, sch. 1.

23. Oil and Gas (Enterprise) Act 1982.
s. 19, amended: 1995, c. 7, sch. 4 (S.).
s. 27, amended: 1995, c. 21, sch. 13.
s. 28, amended: 1995, c. 21, sch. 13; 1995, c. 40, sch. 4 (S).

25. Iron and Steel Box Act 1982.
s. 37, amended: 1995, c. 40, sch. 4 (S).

27. Civil Jurisdiction and Judgments Act 1982.
see *Denby* v. *Hellenic Mediterranean Line Co.* [1994] 1 Lloyd's Rep. 320, Rix J.
s. 5, S.R. 1995 No. 755.
s. 18, amended: 1995, c. 20, sch. 6 (S.); 1995, c. 40, sch. 4 (S).
s. 25, see *Balkanbank* v. *Taher* [1994] 4 All E.R. 239, C.A.
s. 27, see *G.* v. *Caledonian Newspapers* (O.H.), 1995 S.L.T. 559.
s. 28, see *Union Carbide Corporation* v. *B.P. Chemicals*, *The Times*, April 18, 1995.
s. 31, amended: 1995, c. 21, sch. 13.
s. 32, repealed in pt.: 1995, c. 21, sch. 12.
s. 32, amended: 1995, c. 21, sch. 13.
s. 48, Act of Sederunt 94/2901 (S.).
sch. 1, see *Leyland DAF (No. 2), Re*; *Talbot* v. *Edcrest* [1994] BCC 166, C.A.; *K.* v. *B. (Brussels Convention)* [1994] 1 FLR 267, Wall J.; *Balkanbank* v. *Taher* [1994] 4 All E.R. 239, C.A.; *Maciej Rataj, The* [1995] All E.R. (E.C.) 229, E.C.J.
sch. 4, see *Kleinwort Benson* v. *City of Glasgow District Council* (C-346/93), *The Times*, April 17, 1995, C.A.
sch. 5, amended: order 95/756.
sch. 9, amended: 1995, c. 36, sch. 4 (S.).

CAP.

1982—cont.

29. Supply of Goods and Services Act 1982.
s. 91, see *John Elliott (Contracts)* v. *Byrne Bros. (Formwork)* 31 Con LR 89, H.H.J. Newey Q.C.

30. Local Government (Miscellaneous Provisions) Act 1982.
s. 33, repealed in pt.: 1995, c. 25, sch. 24.
s. 33, see *Overseas Investment Services* v. *Simcobuild Construction*, *The Times*, April 21, 1995, C.A.
s. 41, repealed in pt.: 1995, c. 25, sch. 24.
s. 45, repealed in pt.: 1995, c. 25, sch. 24.
sch. 3, see *Willowcell* v. *Westminster City Council*, *The Times*, April 14, 1995, C.A.; *Westminster City Council* v. *North*, *The Independent*, April 27, 1995, D.C.

32. Local Government Finance Act 1982.
s. 12, amended: 1995, c. 17, sch. 1; 1995, c. 25, sch. 7.
s. 15, see *West Wiltshire District Council* v. *Garland and Cond* [1995] 2 W.L.R. 439, C.A.
s. 22, amended: order 95/401.
s. 23, regs. 94/3018.
s. 28A, repealed in pt.: 1995, c. 17, sch. 3.
s. 36, amended: 1995, c. 25, sch. 7.
s. 153, repealed in pt.: 1995, c. 24, sch. 2.

36. Aviation Security Act 1982.
s. 38, amended: 1995, c. 40, sch. 4 (S.).
s. 39, order 95/1297.

41. Stock Transfer Act 1982.
s. 5, repealed in pt.: 1994, c. 39, sch. 14 (S.).
sch. 1, amended: 1994, c. 39, sch. 13 (S.).

42. Derelict Land Act 1982.
s. 1, repealed in pt.: 1995, c. 25, sch. 24.

43. Local Government and Planning (Scotland) Act 1982.
ss. 4, 6–7, repealed: 1994, c. 39, sch. 14.
s. 9, substituted: 1994, c. 39, sch. 13.
s. 14, repealed in pt.: 1994, c. 39, sch. 14.
s. 14, amended: 1994, c. 39, sch. 13.
s. 16, amended: 1994, c. 39, sch. 13.
s. 17, substituted: 1994, c. 39, sch. 13.
ss. 18, 24–28, amended: 1994, c. 39, sch. 13.
s. 27, repealed in pt.: 1994, c. 39, sch. 14.
s. 30, amended: 1994, c. 39, sch. 13.
ss. 30–34, repealed: 1994, c. 39, sch. 14.
s. 50, repealed in pt.: 1994, c. 39, sch. 14.
s. 56, repealed: 1994, c. 39, sch. 14.
s. 67, amended: 1994, c. 39, sch. 13.
sch. 1, repealed in pt.: 1994, c. 39, schs. 13, 14.
sch. 3, repealed in pt.: 1994, c. 39, sch. 14.

45. Civic Government (Scotland) Act 1982.
s. 2, amended: 1994, c. 39, sch. 13.
s. 3, see *Monklands District Independent Taxi Owners Association* v. *Monklands District Council* (O.H.), 1995 S.C.L.R. 547; *Monklands District Council* v. *McGhee*, 1995 S.L.T. (Sh.Ct.) 52.

CAP.

1982—cont.

45. Civic Government (Scotland) Act 1982—*cont.*

s. 7, see *Buchmann* v. *Normand*, 1994 S.C.C.R. 929.
s. 9, amended (temp.): order 95/1878.
s. 9, see *Scanlan* v. *City of Edinburgh District Council*, 1995 S.L.T. (Sh.Ct.) 89.
s. 38, amended: 1995, c. 12, sch. 13.
s. 41, see *Scanlan* v. *City of Edinburgh District Council*, 1995 S.L.T. (Sh.Ct.) 89.
s. 45, amended: 1994, c. 39, sch. 13.
ss. 51, 52, amended: 1995, c. 40, sch. 4 (S.).
s. 58, see *Phillips* v. *Macleod*, 1995 S.C.C.R. 319.
ss. 62, 64, amended: 1994, c. 39, sch. 13.
ss. 87, 89, repealed in pt.: 1994, c. 39, schs. 13, 14.
ss. 90–92, 95–97, 119–120, amended: 1994, c. 39, sch. 13.
s. 121, repealed in pt.: 1994, c. 39, schs. 13, 14.
s. 121, amended: 1994, c. 39, s. 141.
s. 122, repealed in pt.: 1994, c. 39, schs. 13, 14.
s. 122, amended: 1994, c. 39, sch. 13.
s. 123, amended: 1994, c. 39, sch. 13.
s. 133, amended: 1994, c. 39, sch. 13.
sch. 1, see *Glasgow District Council (City of)* v. *Doyle*, Extra Division, November 26, 1993; *Monklands District Independent Taxi Owners Association* v. *Monklands District Council* (O.H.), 1995 S.C.L.R. 547.
sch. 2, amended: 1994, c. 39, sch. 13.

46. Employment Act 1982.

sch. 2, regs. 95/31.
sch. 3, repealed in pt.: 1995, c. 24, sch. 2.

48. Criminal Justice Act 1982.

s. 1, see *R.* v. *Grimsby Justices, ex p. Hogg* (1994) 158 J.P. 1053, Macpherson, J.
s. 1B, see *R.* v. *Smithyman (Daniel Ian Ronald)* (1993) 14 Cr.App.R. (S.) 263, C.A.; *R.* v. *Foran, The Times*, June 1, 1995, C.A.; *R.* v. *Starkey (Darren)* (1994) 15 Cr.App.R. (S.) 576, C.A.; *R.* v. *Edgell (Robert Benjamin)* (1994) 15 Cr.App.R. (S.) 509, C.A.; *R.* v. *Venison* (1994) 15 Cr.App.R. (S.) 624, C.A.
s. 15, repealed in pt.: 1995, c. 21, schs. 12, 24.
s. 49, repealed: 1995, c. 21, sch. 12.
s. 81, schs. 7, 14, repealed in pt.: 1995, c. 21, sch. 12.
Part IV, repealed: 1995, c. 40, sch. 5 (S).
sch. 6, repealed: 1995, c. 40, sch. 5 (S.).
sch. 7, repealed: 1995, c. 40, sch. 5 (S.).
sch. 7, C.: 1995, c. 46, s. 7.

49. Transport Act 1982.

s. 8, amended: 1995, c. 23, sch. 7.
s. 40, repealed: 1995, c. 40, sch. 5 (S.).

CAP.

1982—cont.

49. Transport Act 1982—*cont.*

s. 52, repealed: 1995, c. 23, sch. 8.
s. 70, amended: 1995, c. 18, sch. 2.
s. 76, repealed in pt.: 1995, c. 23, sch. 8.
sch. 4, repealed 1995, c. 23, sch. 8.
sch. 4, C.: 1995, c. 23, sch. 8.
sch. 5, repealed in pt.: 1995, c. 23, sch. 8.
sch. 5, C.: 1995, c. 23, sch. 8.

50. Insurance Companies Act 1982.

s. 2, amended: regs. 94/3132.
s. 2, see *Company (No. 007816 of 1994), Re, The Times*, October 13, 1995, D.C.
s. 14, amended: 1995, c. 40, sch. 4 (S.).
s. 15, amended: regs. 94/3132.
s. 5, regs. 94/3133.
ss. 11, 12, amended: regs. 94/3132.
ss. 17, 18, 20, 21, regs. 94/3133.
s. 31, amended: regs. 94/3132.
s. 32, regs. 94/3133.
s. 32, amended: 1995, c. 29, s. 1.
s. 33, regs. 94/3133.
s. 34A, added: 1995, c. 29, s. 1.
s. 35, regs. 94/3133.
s. 35A, amended: regs. 94/3132.
s. 49, see *NRG Victory Reinsurance, Re* [1995] 1 All E.R. 533, Lindsay J.
ss. 52A, 52B, amended: regs. 94/3132.
s. 62, regs. 94/3133.
s. 68, amended: 1995, c. 29, s. 2.
s. 71, amended: 1995, c. 40, sch. 4 (S.).
s. 74, see *Company (No. 007816 of 1994), Re, The Times*, October 13, 1995, D.C.
s. 75, amended: regs. 94/3132.
s. 78, regs. 94/3133.
s. 81, amended: 1995, c. 40, sch. 4 (S.).
s. 90, regs. 94/3133.
ss. 92, 94, amended: 1995, c. 40, sch. 4 (S.).
s. 94A, regs. 95/688.
s. 96, regs. 94/3133; 95/688.
s. 96, amended: regs. 94/3132.
s. 96A, amended: regs. 94/3132.
s. 97, regs. 94/3133; 95/688.
sch. 2B, repealed in pt.: 1995, c. 26, schs. 5, 7.
sch. 2B, amended: regs. 94/3132; 1995, c. 26, sch. 3.
schs. 2C, 2E, amended: regs. 94/3132.
sch. 5, repealed in pt.: S.R. 1995 No. 755; repealed in pt.: 1995, c. 44, sch. 1.

52. Industrial Development Act 1982.

sch. 1, amended: 1995, c. 40, sch. 4 (S.).

53. Administration of Justice Act 1982.

s. 10, amended: 1995, c. 18, sch. 2.
s. 15, see *Mathew (Thomas)* v. *T.M. Sutton* [1994] 1 W.L.R. 1455, Chadwick J.
s. 21, see *Watson* v. *National Children's Homes, The Times*, October 31, 1995, Colyer J.

54. Commonwealth Development Corporation Act 1982.

s. 3, repealed: 1995, c. 9, sch.

CAP.

1983

2. Representation of the People Act 1983.
s. 2, amended: regs. 95/1948.
s. 8, amended: 1994, c. 39, sch. 13 (S.); order 94/3255 (S.).
s. 10, amended: 1994, c. 39, sch. 13 (S.).
s. 18, repealed in pt.: 1994, c. 39, sch. 14 (S.).
s. 18, amended: 1994, c. 39, s. 142 (S.).
s. 24, orders 95/1142, 2061.
s. 25, repealed in pt.: 1994, c. 39, sch. 14 (S.).
s. 25, amended: 1994, c. 39, sch. 13 (S.).
s. 28, order 95/1142.
s. 31, order 94/3255.
s. 31, repealed in pt.: 1994, c. 39, sch. 14 (S.).
s. 31, amended: 1994, c. 39, sch. 13 (S.).
ss. 41, 42, amended: 1994, c. 39, sch. 14 (S.).
s. 43, amended: 1994, c. 39, s. 6 (S.).
s. 45, amended: order 95/789.
s. 52, amended: 1994, c. 39, sch. 13 (S.).
s. 54, amended: order 94/3255.
s. 57, Act of Sederunt 95/1596.
s. 67, amended: order 94/3255.
s. 75, see *Walker* v. *Unison* (O.H.) 1995 S.C.L.R. 786.
ss. 82, 96, amended: 1994, c. 39, sch. 13 (S.).
s. 128, see *Absalom* v. *Gillett* [1995] 1 W.L.R. 128, D.C.
ss. 131, 134, amended: order 94/3255.
s. 136, see *Absalom* v. *Gillett* [1995] 1 W.L.R. 128, D.C.
s. 191, see *R.* v. *Corp. of London, ex p. Matson, The Independent*, September 27, 1995, C.A.
s. 200, amended: order 94/3255.
s. 202, amended: regs. 95/1948.
s. 204, repealed in pt.: 1994, c. 39, sch. 14 (S.).
s. 204, amended: 1994, c. 39, sch. 13 (S.).

6. British Nationality (Falkland Islands) Act 1983.
s. 5, repealed in pt.,: 1995, c. 44, sch. 1.

8. British Fishing Boats Act 1983.
s. 9, amended: 1995, c. 21, sch. 13.

12. Divorce Jurisdiction, Court Fees and Legal Aid (Scotland) Act 1983.
schs. 1, 2, Act of Sederunt 94/3267.

16. Level Crossing Act 1983.
s. 1, amended: 1994, c. 39, sch. 13 (S.).

19. Matrimonial Homes Act 1983.
s. 1, see *Brown* v. *Brown* [1994] 1 FLR 233, C.A.; *P.* v. *P. (Ouster: Decree Nisi of Nullity)* [1994] 2 FLR 400, C.A.; *M. (Minors) (Disclosure of Evidence), Re* [1994] 1 F.L.R. 760, C.A.
s. 10, amended: 1995, c. 42, sch.

20. Mental Health Act 1983.
s. 3, see *L.B.* v. *Croydon District Health Authority* [1995] 1 F.C.R. 332, Thorpe J.

CAP.

1983—cont.

20. Mental Health Act 1983—*cont.*
s. 4, see *S. (A Minor), Re* (95/0039/F; 94/0040/F) March 13, 1994, C.A.
s. 17, repealed in pt.: 1995, c. 52, s. 3.
s. 18, amended: 1995, c. 52, s. 2.
ss. 21, 21A, 21B, 22, substituted: 1995, c. 52, s. 2.
s. 23, amended: 1995, c. 17, sch. 1.
s. 24, amended: 1995, c. 17, sch. 1.
ss. 25A, 25B, 25C, 25D, 25E, 25F, 25G, 25H, 25I, added: 1995, c. 52, s. 1.
s. 32, amended: 1995, c. 17, sch. 1; 1995, c. 17, sch. 1; 1995, c. 52, sch. 1.
ss. 33, 34, amended: 1995, c. 52, sch. 1.
s. 39, repealed in pt.: 1995, c. 17, sch. 3.
s. 39, amended: 1995, c. 17, sch. 1.
s. 40, amended: 1995, c. 52, s. 2.
s. 41, amended: 1995, c. 52, sch. 1.
s. 50, see *R.* v. *Secretary of State for the Home Department, ex p. H.*; *R.* v. *Same, ex p. Hickey*; *sub nom. R.* v. *Secretary of State for the Home Department, ex p. T* [1994] 3 W.L.R. 1110, C.A.; *R.* v. *Wilson, ex p. Williamson, The Independent*, April 19, 1995, Tucker J.
ss. 57, 58, see *L.B.* v. *Croydon District Health Authority* [1995] 1 F.C.R. 332, Thorpe J.
s. 61, amended: 1995, c. 52, s. 2.
s. 63, see *B.* v. *Croydon Health Authority* [1995] 2 W.L.R. 294, C.A.; *South West Hertfordshire Health Authority* v. *K.B.* [1994] 2 F.C.R. 1051, Ewbank J.
s. 65, amended: 1995, c. 17, sch. 1.
ss. 66, 67, amended: 1995, c. 52, sch. 1.
s. 68, amended: 1995, c. 52, s. 2, sch. 1.
s. 72, amended: 1995, c. 52, sch. 1.
s. 76, amended: 1995, c. 52, sch. 1.
s. 77, amended: 1995, c. 52, sch. 1.
s. 79, amended: 1995, c. 17, sch. 1; 1995, c. 52, sch. 1.
s. 106, rules 94/3046, 3047.
s. 107, rules 94/3046.
s. 108, rules 94/3046, 3047.
s. 117, amended: 1995, c. 17, sch. 1; 1995, c. 52, sch. 1.
s. 118, amended: 1995, c. 52, sch. 1.
s. 121, amended: 1995, c. 17, sch. 1.
s. 126, amended: 1995, c. 52, sch. 1.
s. 127, amended: 1995, c. 52, sch. 1.
s. 134, amended: 1995, c. 17, sch. 1.
s. 139, amended: 1995, c. 17, sch. 1.
s. 140, amended: 1995, c. 17, sch. 1.
s. 143, amended: 1995, c. 17, sch. 1.
s. 145, amended: 1995, c. 52, sch. 1.
s. 145, see *L.B.* v. *Croydon District Health Authority* [1995] 1 F.C.R. 332, Thorpe J.
sch. 1, amended: 1995, c. 52, ss. 2, 3, sch. 1.
sch. 4, repealed in pt.: 1995, c. 17, sch. 3.
sch. 5, repealed in pt.: 1995, c. 17, sch. 3.

CAP.

1983—cont.

30. Diseases of Fish Act 1983.
s. 9, amended: 1995, c. 25, sch. 15.

33. Solvent Abuse (Scotland) Act 1983.
repealed: 1995, c. 36, sch. 5.

35. Litter Act 1983.
s. 4, repealed in pt.: 1995, c. 25, sch. 24.
s. 4, substituted: 1994, c. 39, sch. 13 (S.).
ss. 6, 10, repealed in pt.: 1995, c. 25, sch. 24.

39. Mental Health (Amendment) (Scotland) Act 1983.
s. 22, C.: 1995, c. 46, s. 59.
s. 34, C.: 1995, c. 46, ss. 53, 60.
s. 35, C.: 1995, c. 46, s. 61.
sch. 2, C.: 1995, c. 46, s. 59.
sch. 3, C.: 1995, c. 46, s. 58.

40. Education (Fees and Awards) Act 1983.
ss. 1, 2, regs. 94/3042; 95/1241.
ss. 25, 28, 29, 40, see *Khan* v. *General Medical Council* [1994] IRLR 646, C.A.
sch. 1, rules 94/3171.
sch. 4, rules 94/3298.

41. Health and Social Services and Social Security Adjudications Act 1983.
s. 7, repealed: 1995, c. 36, sch. 5 (S.).
s. 8, repealed: 1995, c. 36, sch. 5 (S.).
sch. 2, repealed in pt.: 1995, c. 36, sch. 5 (S.); order 95/756.
sch. 2, amended: 1995, c. 36, sch. 4 (S.).
sch. 2, C.: 1995, c. 46, s. 42.
sch. 5, repealed in pt.: 1995, c. 17, sch. 3.
sch. 9, repealed in pt.: 1995, c. 17, sch. 3.

53. Car Tax Act 1983.
sch. 1, amended: 1995, c. 40, sch. 4 (S.).

54. Medical Act 1983.
s. 1, amended: 1995, c. 51, sch.
s. 19, see *R.* v. *General Medical Council, ex p. Virik*, *The Times*, October 31, 1995, C.A.
ss. 25, see *Khan* v. *General Medical Council* [1994] IRLR 646, C.A.; *R.* v. *General Medical Council, ex p. Virik*, *The Times*, October 31, 1995, C.A.
ss. 28, 29, see *Khan* v. *General Medical Council* [1994] IRLR 646, C.A.
s. 31A, added: 1995, c. 51, s. 2.
s. 32, repealed in pt.: 1995, c. 51, sch.
s. 35, amended: 1995, c. 51, sch.
s. 36, amended: 1995, c. 51, sch.
s. 36A, added: 1995, c. 51, s. 1.
s. 37, amended: 1995, c. 51, sch.
s. 38, amended: 1995, c. 51, sch.
s. 40, amended: 1995, c. 51, sch.
s. 40, see *Khan* v. *General Medical Council* [1994] IRLR 646, C.A.
s. 42, amended: 1995, c. 51, s. 3.
s. 43, amended: 1995, c. 51, sch.
s. 47, amended: 1995, c. 51, sch.
s. 53, amended: 1995, c. 51, sch.
sch. 1, rules 94/3171.

CAP.

1983—cont.

54. Medical Act 1983—*cont.*
sch. 1, amended: 1995, c. 51, sch.
sch. 4, rules 94/3298.
sch. 4, amended: 1995, c. 51, sch.

55. Value Added Tax Act 1983.
see *R.* v. *Dealy*, *The Times*, December 13, 1994, C.A.; *House* v. *Customs and Excise Commissioners*, *The Times*, October 20, 1995, C.A.
s. 3, see *Virgin Atlantic Airways* v. *Customs and Excise Commissioners*, *The Times*, February 16, 1995, Turner J.
s. 4, see *Marios Chippery* v. *Customs and Excise Commissioners* [1994] V.A.T.T.R. 125, Manchester Tribunal.
s. 5, see *Customs and Excise Commissioners* v. *Richmond Theatre Management* [1995] S.T.C. 257, Dyson J.
s. 10, see *Customs and Excise Commissioners* v. *Tron Theatre*, 1995 S.L.T. 1021.
s. 14, see *Dean and Chapter of Hereford Cathedral* v. *Customs and Excise Commissioners* [1994] V.A.T.T.R. 159, London Tribunal.
ss. 16, 17, see *Customs and Excise Commissioners* v. *Link Housing Association*, 1992 S.C. 508.
s. 32, see *Metropolitan Borough of Wirral* v. *Customs and Excise Commissioners* [1995] S.T.C. 597, Potts J.
s. 39, see *R.* v. *Northamptonshire Magistrates, ex p. Customs and Excise Commissioners* [1994] C.O.D. 392, D.C.; *R.* v. *Dealy* [1995] 1 W.L.R. 658, C.A.
s. 40, see *John Dee* v. *Customs and Excise Commissioners*, *The Times*, July 20, 1995, C.A.; *RMSG* v. *Customs and Excise Commissioners* [1994] V.A.T.T.R. 167, London Tribunal; *Dollar Land (Feltham)* v. *Customs and Excise Commissioners* [1995] S.T.C. 414, Judge J.
sch. 4, see *Customs and Excise Commissioners* v. *Granton Marketing* [1995] S.T.C. 510, Tucker J.
sch. 5, see *Customs and Excise Commissioners* v. *Link Housing Association*, 1992 S.C. 508; *Customs and Excise Commissioners* v. *Colour Offset* [1995] S.T.C. 95, May J.; *Virgin Atlantic Airways* v. *Customs and Excise Commissioners* [1995] S.T.C. 341, Turner J.; *Customs and Excise Commissioners* v. *David Lewis Centre* [1995] S.T.C. 485, Owen J.; *Marchday Holdings* v. *Customs and Excise Commissioners* [1994] V.A.T.T.R. 253, London Tribunal; *Customs and Excise Commissioners* v. *Arbib* [1995] S.T.C. 490, Latham J.

CAP.

1983—cont.

55. Value Added Tax Act 1983—*cont.*
sch. 6, see *Customs and Excise Commissioners* v. *Annabel's Casino* [1995] S.T.C. 225, Schiemann J.; *Feehan* v. *Customs and Excise Commissioners* [1995] S.T.C. 75, Hidden J.; *Harpur Group* v. *Customs and Excise Commissioners* [1994] V.A.T.T.R. 180, London Tribunal; *Customs and Excise Commissioners* v. *Reed Personnel Services* [1995] S.T.C. 588, Laws J.; *Customs and Excise Commissioners* v. *Leightons* [1995] S.T.C. 458, McCullogh J.
sch. 7, see *Customs and Excise Commissioners* v. *Croydon Hotel and Leisure Company, The Times*, June 1, 1995, Popplewell J.; *Customs and Excise Commissioner* v. *Post Office, The Independent*, June 19, 1995, Potts J.

1984

5. Merchant Shipping Act 1984.
s. 1, repealed in pt.: 1995, c. 21, sch. 12.
s. 2, repealed in pt.: 1995, c. 21, sch. 12.
s. 3, repealed in pt.: 1995, c. 21, sch. 12.
s. 4, repealed in pt.: 1995, c. 21, sch. 12.
s. 4, amended: regs. 95/1210.
s. 4, C.: 1995, c. 21, sch. 14.
s. 5, repealed in pt.: 1995, c. 21, sch. 12.
s. 5, amended: regs. 95/1210.
s. 5, C.: 1995, c. 21, sch. 14.
s. 6, repealed in pt.: 1995, c. 21, sch. 21.
s. 7, repealed in pt.: 1995, c. 21, sch. 12.
s. 8, repealed in pt.: 1995, c. 21, sch. 12.
s. 9, repealed in pt.: 1995, c. 21, sch. 12.
s. 10, repealed in pt.: 1995, c. 21, sch. 12.
s. 11, repealed in pt.: 1995, c. 21, sch. 12.
s. 12, repealed in pt.: 1995, c. 21, sch. 12.
s. 13, repealed in pt.: 1995, c. 21, sch. 12.
s. 14, repealed in pt.: 1995, c. 21, sch. 12.
s. 287, amended: regs. 95/1210.
sch. 1, repealed in pt.: 1995, c. 21, sch. 12.
sch. 2, repealed in pt.: 1995, c. 21, sch. 12.

11. Education (Grants and Awards) Act 1984.
ss. 1, 3, regs. 94/612, 2446; 95/501, 605, 1705.

12. Telecommunications Act 1984.
s. 3A, order 95/268.
s. 7, orders 95/182, 941, 1375.
s. 9, orders 94/2654; 95/182, 941, 1375.
ss. 19, 21, 23, order 95/232.
s. 24, order 94/3163.
s. 62, regs. 95/993.
ss. 74, 75, 76, modified: order 95/268.
s. 77, repealed: order 95/268.
s. 79, amended: order 95/268.
s. 80, repealed: order 95/268.
s. 81, repealed: order 95/268.
s. 81, amended: 1995, c. 40, sch. 4 (S.).
s. 83, repealed in pt.: order 95/268.

CAP.

1984—cont.

12. Telecommunications Act 1984—*cont.*
s. 84, regs. 95/1081.
s. 84, repealed in pt.: order 95/268.
ss. 85, 88, 91, 92, amended: order 95/268.
ss. 97, 98, amended: 1994, c. 39, sch. 13 (S.).
s. 102, order 95/268.
s. 106, amended: order 95/268.
s. 108, order 95/268.
s. 109, amended: order 95/268.
sch. 3, amended: 1995, c. 20, sch. 6 (S.); 1995, c. 40, sch. 4 (S.).

15. Law Reform (Husband and Wife) (Scotland) Act 1984.
s. 3, repealed in pt.: 1995, c. 36, sch. 5.

20. Mental Health Act 1984.
s. 41, see *R.* v. *Nwohia, The Times*, May 18, 1995, C.A.

22. Public Health (Control of Disease) Act 1984.
s. 1, amended: 1995, c. 17, sch. 1.
s. 11, amended: 1995, c. 17, sch. 1.
s. 12, amended: 1995, c. 17, sch. 1.
s. 13, amended: 1995, c. 17, sch. 1.
s. 37, amended: 1995, c. 17, sch. 1.
s. 39, amended: 1995, c. 17, sch. 1.
s. 41, amended: 1995, c. 17, sch. 1.
ss. 53, 74, amended: 1995, c. 21, sch. 13.
s. 76, order 95/292.
sch. 2, repealed in pt.: 1995, c. 17, sch. 3.

24. Dentists Act 1984.
sch. 5, repealed in pt.: 1995, c. 17, sch. 3.

26. Inshore Fishing (Scotland) Act 1984.
s. 1, order 95/1373.
s. 2A, added: 1995, c. 25, s. 103.
s. 9, amended: 1995, c. 21, sch. 13.

27. Road Traffic Regulation Act 1984.
orders 95/219, 220, 338, 870, 1009, 1166.
s. 1, amended: 1995, c. 25, sch. 22.
s. 6, amended: 1995, c. 25, sch. 22.
s. 8, see *TNT Express (U.K.)* v. *Richmond upon Thames London Borough Council, The Times*, June 27, 1995, Waller J.; *Post Office* v. *Richmond upon Thames London Borough Countil* [1995] R.T.R. 28, D.C.
s. 17, regs. 95/158, 2168, 2507.
s. 19, amended: 1994, c. 39, sch. 13 (S.).
s. 26, repealed in pt.: 1994, c. 39, sch. 14 (S.).
ss. 32, 37, 44, 45, amended: 1994, c. 39, sch. 13 (S.).
s. 55, see *R.* v. *Camden London Borough Council, ex p. Cran, The Times*, January 25, 1995, McCullough J.
s. 62, regs. 94/432.
s. 100, amended: 1994, c. 39, sch. 13 (S.).
s. 110, amended: 1995, c. 40, sch. 4 (S.).
s. 121, amended: 1994, c. 39, sch. 13 (S.).
s. 122, amended: 1995, c. 25, sch. 22.
s. 133, amended: 1995, c. 21, sch. 13.
sch. 9, see *R.* v. *Camden London Borough Council, ex p. Cran, The Times*, January 25, 1995, McCullough J.

CAP.

1984—cont.

27. Road Traffic Regulation Act 1984—*cont.*
sch. 13, repealed in pt.: 1995, c. 23, sch. 8.
sch. 13, C.: 1995, c. 23, sch. 8; C.: 1995, c. 46, sch. 9 (S.).

28. County Courts Act 1984.
rules 94/2110.
see *Preston Borough Council* v. *Riley, The Times*, April 19, 1995, C.A.
s. 2, orders 94/1536, 2626, 2893; 95/1897.
s. 6, orders 94/1536, 2626, 2893.
s. 27, repealed in pt.: 1995, c. 12, sch. 12.
ss. 27, 30, 31, amended: 1995, c. 12, sch. 13.
s. 38, regs. 95/206.
s. 40, see *Walters* v. *Newton*, February 2, 1994; H.H.J. Irvine; Oxford County Ct.
s. 53, see *Hipwood* v. *Gloucester Health Authority, The Times*, February 21, 1995, C.A.
s. 60, amended: 1995, c. 25, sch. 10.
s. 66, see *Grant* v. *Travellers Cheque Associates, The Times*, April 19, 1995, C.A.; *Duffus and Duffus* v. *Chief Constable of Derbyshire*, March 14, 1995, H.H.J. Styler, Derby County Ct.
s. 74, amended: 1995, c. 42, s. 2.
s. 75, rules 95/1582, 1583.
s. 75, see *Walters* v. *Newton*, February 2, 1994; H.H.J. Irvine; Oxford County Ct.
ss. 112, 113, 114, 115, 117, see *Preston Borough Council* v. *Riley* [1995] R.A. 277, C.A.
s. 138, see *Melview Properties* v. *Personal Representatives of Dr Klinger (Dec'd)*, October 12, 1995, Recorder Hill-Smith, Central London Ct.
s. 147, see *Walters* v. *Newton*, February 2, 1994; H.H.J. Irvine; Oxford County Ct.
sch. 2, repealed in pt.: 1995, c. 38, sch. 2.

30. Food Act 1984.
s. 68, order 95/612.

31. Rating and Valuation (Amendment) (Scotland) Act 1984.
ss. 6, 7, repealed: 1994, c. 39, sch. 14.
sch. 2, repealed in pt.: 1994, c. 39, sch. 14.

32. London Regional Transport Act 1984.
s. 50, amended: 1995, c. 26, sch. 4.
s. 62, amended: 1995, c. 23, sch. 7.

35. Data Protection Act 1984.
s. 1, see *Data Protection Registrar* v. *Griffin* [1993] C.O.D. 283, D.C.
s. 5, see *Data Protection Registrar* v. *Amnesty International (British Section), The Times*, November 23, 1994, D.C.; *Data Protection Registrar* v. *Griffin* [1993] C.O.D. 283, D.C.
s. 19, see *Data Protection Registrar* v. *Griffin* [1993] C.O.D. 283, D.C.

36. Mental Health (Scotland) Act 1984.
s. 3, amended: 1995, c. 52, sch. 2.

CAP.

1984—cont.

36. Mental Health (Scotland) Act 1984—*cont.*
s. 5, amended: 1995, c. 52, sch. 2.
s. 7, amended: regs. 95/443.
s. 8, amended: 1995, c. 52, sch. 2.
s. 10, repealed in pt.: 1995, c. 36, sch. 5.
s. 10, amended: 1995, c. 36, sch. 4.
s. 27, amended: 1995, c. 52, s. 6.
s. 28, amended: 1995, c. 52, s. 5.
s. 30, amended: 1995, c. 52, s. 5.
ss. 31, 31A, substituted: 1995, c. 52, s. 5.
s. 32, amended: 1995, c. 52, s. 5.
ss. 35A–35K, added: 1995, c. 52, s. 4.
s. 44, amended: 1995, c. 52, s. 5.
s. 47, amended: 1995, c. 52, s. 5.
ss. 488, 48A, 48B, substituted: 1995, c. 52, s. 5.
s. 54, amended: 1995, c. 36, sch. 4.
s. 55, repealed in pt.: 1995, c. 36, schs. 4, 5.
s. 55, amended: 1995, c. 36, sch. 4.
s. 60, amended: 1995, c. 40, sch. 4; 1995, c. 52, s. 5.
s. 61, amended: 1995, c. 40, sch. 4 (S.).
s. 62, amended: 1995, c. 40, sch. 4; 1995, c. 52, sch. 2.
s. 67, repealed in pt.: 1995, c. 20, sch. 7.
s. 67, amended: 1995, c. 20, sch. 6.
s. 69, amended: 1995, c. 20, sch. 6; 1995, c. 40, sch. 4.
s. 71, amended: 1995, c. 20, sch. 6; 1995, c. 40, sch. 4.
ss. 73, amended: 1995, c. 20, sch. 6; 1995, c. 40, sch. 4.
s. 76, amended: 1995, c. 40, sch. 4.
s. 91, order 95/575.
s. 99, amended: 1995, c. 52, s. 5.
s. 105, amended: 1995, c. 52, sch. 2.
s. 109, amended: 1995, c. 52, sch. 2.
s. 111, amended: 1995, c. 52, sch. 2.
s. 119, amended: 1995, c. 52, sch. 2.
s. 121A, added: 1995, c. 40, sch. 4.
s. 125, amended: 1995, c. 20, sch. 6; 1995, c. 40, sch. 4; 1995, c. 52, sch. 2.
sch. 2, amended: 1995, c. 52, ss. 5, 6, sch. 2.
sch. 3, C.: 1995, c. 46, ss. 52, 53, 58, 59, 61.
sch. 5, C.: 1995, c. 39, s. 13.

37. Child Abduction Act 1984.
s. 2, see *R.* v. *Leather (John Holdsworth)* (1994) 98 Cr.App.R. 179, C.A.
s. 6, amended: 1995, c. 36, sch. 4 (S.).

39. Video Recordings Act 1984.
ss. 1, 2, see *Kent County Council* v. *Multi Media Marketing (Canterbury), The Times*, May 9, 1995, D.C.
s. 16C, amended: 1995, c. 40, sch. 4 (S.).
s. 20, repealed: 1995, c. 40, sch. 5 (S.).
s. 20, C.: 1995, c. 46, sch. 9 (S.).

40. Animal Health Act 1984.
s. 10, regs. 95/2556.

CAP.

1984—cont.

42. Matrimonial and Family Proceedings Act 1984.
s. 13, see *Hewitson* v. *Hewitson* [1995] 2 W.L.R. 287, C.A.
ss. 28, 29, see *Tahir* v. *Tahir (No. 2)*, (O.H.), 1995 S.L.T. 451.
s.40, order 94/2890, 3155.
s. 40, see *Children Act 1989 (Taxation of Costs), Re* [1994] 2 F.L.R. 934, Cazalet J.
s. 45, repealed S.R. 1995 No. 755.
s. 46, see *Children Act 1989 (Taxation of Costs), Re* [1994] 2 F.L.R. 934, Cazalet J.
s. 48, repealed in pt.: S.R. 1995 No. 755.
Part III, see *M.* v. *M (Financial Provision after Foreign Divorce)* [1994] 1 F.L.R. 399, Thorpe J.; *R.* v. *R. (Divorce: Stay of Proceedings)* [1995] 1 F.C.R. 745, Ewbank J.

46. Cable and Broadcasting Act 1984.
sch. 5, S.R. 1995 No. 755.
sch. 5, C.: 1995, c. 46, s. 47.

47. Repatriation of Prisoners Act 1984.
s. 5, amended: 1995, c. 21, sch. 13.
sch., amended: 1995, c. 40, sch. 4 (S.).

48. Health and Social Security Act 1984.
s. 5, repealed in pt.: 1995, c. 17, sch. 3.
s. 6, repealed in pt.: 1995, c. 17, sch. 3.
sch. 3, repealed in pt.: 1995, c. 17, sch. 3.

49. Trade Union Act 1984.
ss. 10, 11, see *West Midlands Travel* v. *Transport and General Workers' Union* [1994] IRLR 578, C.A.

51. Inheritance Tax Act 1984.
regs. 95/1459 (S.)
s. 8, order 94/3011.
s. 21, see *Bennett* v. *I.R.C.*, February 13, 1995, Lightman J.
s. 59, amended: 1995, c. 4, s. 52.
s. 115, see *Starke* v. *I.R.C.*, *The Times*, May 29, 1995, C.A.
s. 116, repealed in pt.: 1995, c. 4, sch. 29.
s. 116, amended: 1995, c. 4, s. 155.
s. 158, order 94/3214.
s. 230, S.R. 1995 No. 1625.
s. 256, regs. 95/1459 (S.), 1460, 1461.
sch. 1, substituted: order 94/3214.

54. Roads (Scotland) Act 1984.
s. 4, repealed in pt.: 1994, c. 39, sch. 14.
s. 9, amended: 1994, c. 39, sch. 13.
s. 12A, added: 1994, c. 39, sch. 13.
s. 12B, order 95/1476.
s. 12B, added: 1994, c. 39, sch. 13.
s. 12C, order 95/1476.
s. 12C, added: 1994, c. 39, sch. 13.
ss. 12D, 12F, added: 1994, c. 39, sch. 13.
s. 38, order 95/1476.
s. 55, amended: 1994, c. 39, sch. 13.
s. 81A, added: 1994, c. 39, s. 39.
s. 93, amended: 1994, c. 39, sch. 13.
s. 95, repealed in pt.: 1994, c. 39, sch. 14.

CAP.

1984—cont.

54. Roads (Scotland) Act 1984—*cont.*
s. 95, amended: 1994, c. 39, sch. 14.
ss. 97, 112, 113, amended: 1994, c. 39, sch. 13.
s. 113A, added: 1994, c. 39, s. 147.
ss. 135, amended: 1994, c. 39, sch. 13.
s. 143, order 95/1476.
s. 143, amended: 1994, c. 39, sch. 13.
s. 151, amended: 1994, c. 39, s. 146, sch. 13.
sch. 1, amended: 1994, c. 39, s. 148.
sch. 9, repealed in pt.: 1995, c. 25, sch. 24.
sch. 9, C.: 1995, c. 39, s. 47.

55. Building Act 1984.
ss. 1, 16, 17 regs. 95/1387.
s. 24, repealed in pt.: regs. 95/1387.
ss. 35, 47, 49–52, sch. 1. regs. 95/1387.

56. Foster Children (Scotland) Act 1984.
s. 2, repealed in pt.: 1995, c. 36, schs. 4, 5.
s. 2, amended: 1994, c. 39, sch. 13; 1995, c. 36, sch. 4.
s. 3, amended: 1995, c. 36, sch. 4.
s. 7, amended: 1995, c. 36, sch. 4; 1995, c. 40, sch. 4 (S.).
s. 12, amended: 1995, c. 36, sch. 4.
s. 13, amended: 1995, c. 36, sch. 4; 1995, c. 40, sch. 4 (S.).
s. 21, amended: 1995, c. 36, sch. 4.

58. Rent (Scotland) Act 1984.
ss. 5, 43, 62, 63, amended: 1994, c. 39, sch. 13.
s. 115, amended: 1995, c. 40, sch. 4.

60. Police and Criminal Evidence Act 1984.
see *Whelehan* v. *D.P.P.* [1995] RTR 177, C.A.
s. 8, see *R.* v. *Central Criminal Court, ex p. Propend Finance Property* [1994] C.O.D. 386, D.C.
s. 9, see *R.* v. *Southampton Crown Court, ex p. J. and P.* [1993] C.O.D. 286, D.C.; *R.* v. *Kiffin* [1994] Crim.L.R. 449, C.A.
s. 10, see *R.* v. *Southampton Crown Court, ex p. J. and P.* [1993] C.O.D. 286, D.C.; *R.* v. *R.* [1994] 4 All E.R. 260, C.A.
ss. 11, 14, see *R.* v. *Southampton Crown Court, ex p. J. and P.* [1993] C.O.D. 286, D.C.
s. 17, amended: 1995, c. 16, s. 2.
s. 18, see *R.* v. *Wright* [1994] Crim.L.R. 55, C.A.
s. 19, see *R.* v. *Southwark Crown Court, ex p. Sorsky Defries, The Times*, July 21, 1995, D.C.
s. 49, see *R.* v. *Governor of Styal Prison, ex p. Mooney, The Times*, May 17, 1995, D.C.
s. 54, order 94/3262.
s. 55, see *R.* v. *Hughes (Patrick)* [1994] 1 W.L.R. 876, C.A.
s. 60, order 95/450.

CAP.

1984—cont.

60. Police and Criminal Evidence Act 1984—*cont.*

s. 60, see *R.* v. *Campbell* [1994] Crim.L.R. 357, C.A.; *R.* v. *Bayliss (Roy Alfred)* (1994) Cr.App.R. 235, C.A.; *R.* v. *Shah* [1994] Crim.L.R. 125, C.A.; *R.* v. *W.* [1994] Crim.L.R. 130, C.A.

s. 64, see *R.* v. *Nathaniel, The Times*, April 6, 1995, C.A.

s. 66, order 95/450.

s. 66, see *R.* v. *Smith (Wallace)* [1994] 1 W.L.R. 1398, C.A.

s. 67, order 95/450.

s. 67, see *R.* v. *Rutherford; Same* v. *Palmer* (1994) 98 Cr.App.R. 191, C.A.

s. 69, see *R.* v. *Taplin (Gary)* (94/2913/X4), February 28, 1995, C.A.; *Ashton* v. *D.P.P., The Times*, July 14, 1995, D.C.

s. 72, amended: 1995, c. 38, sch. 1.

s. 73, see *R.* v. *Hacker, The Times*, November 21, 1994, H.L.

s. 74, see *R.* v. *Buckingham* [1994] Crim.L.R. 283, C.A.; *R.* v. *Potamitis* [1994] Crim.L.R. 434, C.A.; *R.* v. *Garrity and Nugent* [1994] Crim.L.R. 828, C.A.

s. 75, amended: 1995, c. 40, sch. 1 (S.).

s. 75, see *R.* v. *Garrity and Nugent* [1994] Crim.L.R. 828, C.A.

s. 76, see *R.* v. *Paris, Abdullahi and Miller* [1994] Crim.L.R. 361, C.A.; *R.* v. *Goddard* [1994] Crim.L.R. 46, C.A.; *R.* v. *Smith (Wallace)* [1994] 1 W.L.R. 1398, C.A.; *Hackney London Borough* v. *G.* [1994] 2 F.C.R. 216, Wall J.; *R.* v. *L.* [1994] Crim.L.R. 839, C.A.; *R.* v. *Conway* [1994] Crim.L.R. 838, C.A.

s. 77, see *R.* v. *Kenny* [1994] Crim.L.R. 284, C.A.

s. 78, see *Williams and O'Hare* v. *D.P.P.* [1994] 98 Cr.App.R. 209, D.C.; *R.* v. *Joseph* [1994] Crim.L.R. 48, C.A.; *R.* v. *Wright* [1994] Crim.L.R. 131, C.A.; *North Yorkshire Trading Standards Department* v. *Williams, The Times*, November 22, 1994, D.C.; *R.* v. *Goddard* [1994] Crim.L.R. 46, C.A.; *Braham* v. *D.P.P., The Times*, December 29, 1994, D.C.; *R.* v. *Hughes (Patrick)* [1994] 1 W.L.R. 876, C.A.; *R.* v. *Smith (Wallace)* [1994] 1 W.L.R. 1398, C.A.; *R.* v. *Okafor (Stephen)* [1994] 99 Cr.App.R. 97, C.A.; *Worsley (Trevor James)* v. *D.P.P.* (CO-1679-92), November 11, 1994, D.C.; *R.* v. *Nathaniel, The Times*, April 6, 1995, C.A.; *R.* v. *Neil* [1994] Crim.L.R. 441, C.A.; *C. (Restraint Orders: Identification), Re, The Times*, April 21, 1995, Ognall J.; *R.* v. *Governor of Belmarsh Prison, ex p. Francis, The Times*, April 12, 1995, D.C.; *R.* v. *Nathaniel (Lonsdale)* (94/1743/X3), March 8, 1995, C.A.; *R.* v. *Lampeter Magistrates' Court, ex p. R.S.P.C.A.* (C.O. 2905/94), May 1, 1995, Curtis J.; *R.* v. *L.* [1994] Crim.L.R. 839, C.A.; *R.* v. *Lowe* [1994] Crim.L.R. 837, C.A.; *R.* v. *Conway* [1994] Crim.L.R. 838, C.A.; *R.* v. *Garrity and Nugent* [1994] Crim.L.R. 828, C.A.

s. 94, order 94/3262.

s. 101, regs. 95/1475.

s. 118, see *R.* v. *Hughes (Patrick)* [1994] 1 W.L.R. 876, C.A.

s. 118, amended: 1995, c. 38, sch. 1.

See, *R.* v. *Pattemore* [1994] Crim.L.R. 836, C.A.

sch. 1, see *R.* v. *Central Criminal Court, ex p. Propend Finance Property* [1994] C.O.D. 386, D.C.

sch. 3, see *R.* v. *Medway Magistrates' Courts, ex p. Goddard* [1995] RTR 206, D.C.

68. Housing Act 1984.

ss. 43, 45, 573, amended: 1995, c. 25, sch. 10.

1985

3. Brunei and Maldives Act 1985.

sch., repealed in pt.: 1995, c. 21, sch. 12.

6. Companies Act 1985.

s. 2, repealed in pt.: 1995, c. 7, sch. 5 (S.).

s. 6, regs. 95/736.

s. 7, repealed in pt.: 1995, c. 7, sch. 5 (S.).

s. 9A, amended: 1995, c. 29, s. 3.

ss. 10, 12, regs. 95/734, 736.

s. 24, see *Nisbet* v. *Shepherd* [1994] BCC 91, C.A.

s. 30, regs. 95/736.

s. 36B, substituted: 1995, c. 7, sch. 4 (S.).

ss. 38, 39, 40, amended: 1995, c. 7, sch. 4.

ss. 43, 49, 51, 53, 54, 117, regs. 95/736.

s. 178, see *Barclays Bank* v. *British & Commonwealth Holdings, The Times*, August 10, 1995, C.A.

s. 183, see *Nisbet* v. *Shepherd* [1994] BCC 91, C.A.

ss. 186, 188, amended: 1995, c. 7, sch. 4.

s. 190, regs. 95/736.

s. 245, regs. 95/2092.

s. 249D, amended: regs. 95/589.

s. 251, regs. 95/2092.

s. 257, regs. 94/2879; 95/589.

s. 266, regs. 95/736.

ss. 287, 288, regs. 95/734, 736.

s. 317, see *Neptune (Vehicle Washing Equipment)* v. *Fitzgerald* [1995] 3 W.L.R. 108, Lightman J.

CAP.

1985—cont.

6. Companies Act 1985—*cont.*
s. 318, regs. 95/736.
s. 320, see *Duckwari* v. *Offerventure* [1994] NPC 109, C.A.
ss. 325, 353, regs. 95/736.
s. 359, see *Jenice* v. *Dan* [1994] BCC 43, Mr. R. Titheridge, Q.C. sitting as a deputy judge.
s. 363, regs. 95/736.
s. 371, see *Whitchurch Insurance Consultants, Re* [1994] BCC 1, Harman J.; *British Union for the Abolition of Vivisection, Re, The Times*, March 3, 1995, Rimer J.
s. 390B, regs. 95/1520.
s. 391, regs. 95/736.
s. 395, see *Lovell Construction* v. *Independent Estates (In Liquidation)* [1994] 1 BCLC 31, Mr. Fox-Andrews, sitting as a deputy judge; *Ian Chisholm Textiles* v. *Griffiths* [1994] BCC 96, Mr. David Neuberger, Q.C. sitting as deputy judge.
s. 425, see *RMCA Reinsurance, Re* [1994] BCC 378, Morrit J.
s. 440, amended: 1995, c. 40, sch. 4 (S.).
s. 449, amended: 1995, c. 26, sch. 3.
s. 459, see *Whitchurch Insurance Consultants, Re* [1994] BCC 1, Harman J.; *BSB Holdings, Re, The Times*, August 2, 1995, Arden J.
s. 462, repealed in pt.: 1995, c. 7, sch. 5 (S.).
s. 462, see *Sharp* v. *Thomson*, 1995 S.L.T. 837.
s. 651, see *Stanhope Pension Trust* v. *Registrar of Companies*; *sub nom Forte's (Manufacturing), Re*; *Stanhope Pensions Trust* v. *Registrar of Companies* [1994] BCC 84, C.A.; *Townreach (No. 002081 of 1994), Re*; *Principle Business Machines, Re* [1994] 3 W.L.R. 983, Paul Baker Q.C.
ss. 652, 653, see *McShane* v. *Comet Group* (Sh.Ct.), 1994 S.C.L.R. 1077.
s. 708, regs. 95/1423.
s. 709, amended: 1995, c. 38, sch. 1.
s. 710B, regs. 95/734.
s. 717, amended: regs. 95/1163.
s. 726, see *Unisoft Group, Re*; *Saunderson Holdings* v. *Unisoft Group* [1994] BCC 11, C.A.; *Airmuscle* v. *Spitting Image Productions* [1994] R.P.C. 604, Patents County Court; *Metric Modules International* v. *Laughton Construction Co.* (Sh.Ct.), 1995 S.C.L.R. 676.
s. 727, see *D'Jan of London, Re*; *Copp* v. *D'Jan* [1994] 1 BCLC 561, Hoffmann L.J.
s. 731, amended: 1995, c. 40, sch. 4 (S.).
s. 734, amended: 1995, c. 40, sch. 4 (S.).

CAP.

1985—cont.

6. Companies Act 1985—*cont.*
s. 744, regs. 95/734, 736.
sch. 2, amended: 1995, c. 26, sch. 5.
sch. 7, amended: 1995, c. 50, sch. 6.
sch. 13, regs. 95/736.

8. Child Abduction and Custody Act 1985.
s. 8, see *P. (A Minor) (Child Abduction: Declaration), Re, The Times*, February 16, 1995, C.A.

9. Companies Consolidation (Consequential Provisions) Act 1985.
s. 11, amended: 1995, c. 7, sch. 4.
sch. 2, repealed in pt.: 1995, c. 24, sch. 2; 1995, c. 31, sch. 8.
sch. 2, C.: 1995, c. 21, sch. 14.

13. Cinemas Act 1985.
s. 21, amended: 1994, c. 39, sch. 13 (S.).

16. National Heritage (Scotland) Act 1985.
sch. 1, repealed in pt.: 1995, c. 7, sch. 5.

21. Films Act 1985.
sch. 1, orders 94/3218, 3222; 95/1298, 1963.

22. Dangerous Vessels Act 1984.
s. 2, amended: 1995, c. 21, sch. 13.
s. 4, repealed in pt.: 1995, c. 21, sch. 12.

23. Prosecution of Offences Act 1985.
s. 16, see *R.* v. *Sheffield Crown Court, ex p. Aubrey* (CO2712/93), March 8, 1995, Balcombe J.
s. 21, amended: 1995, c. 35, sch. 2.
s. 22, order 95/555.
s. 22, see *R.* v. *Central Criminal Court, ex p. Behbehani* [1994] Crim.L.R. 352, D.C.; *R.* v. *Maidstone Crown Court, ex p. Clark, The Times*, December 19, 1994, D.C.; *R.* v. *Folkestone Magistrates' Court, ex p. Bradley* [1994] C.O.D. 138, D.C.; *R.* v. *Cardiff Crown Court, ex p. Reeves, The Independent*, August 21, 1995, D.C.; *R.* v. *Maidstone Crown Court, ex p. Clark* [1995] 1 W.L.R. 831, D.C.
s. 23, see *R.* v. *D.P.P., ex p. Thom, The Times*, December 21, 1994, D.C.
s. 29, order 95/555.

35. Gaming (Bingo) Act 1985.
order 95/322.
s. 2, order 95/122.

37. Family Law (Scotland) Act 1985.
s. 1, see *Watson* v. *Watson* (Sh.Ct.) 1994 S.C.L.R. 1097; *Drummond* v. *Drummond, The Scotsman*, March 1, 1995.
s. 2, amended: 1995, c. 36, sch. 4.
s. 3, see *MacDonald* v. *MacDonald* (O.H.), 1995 S.L.T. 72.
s. 4, see *Semple* v. *Semple* (Sh.Ct.), 1995 S.C.L.R. 569.
s. 7, see *Drummond* v. *Drummond, The Scotsman*, March 1, 1995.
s. 8, amended: 1995, c. 26, s. 167.

CAP.

1985—cont.

37. Family Law (Scotland) Act 1985—*cont.*
- s. 8, see *Maclue* v. *Maclue* (Sh.Ct.) 1994 S.C.C.R. 933; *Tahir* v. *Tahir (No. 2)*, (O.H.), 1995 S.L.T. 451; *Crosbie* v. *Crosbie* (Sh.Ct.), 1995 S.C.L.R. 399; *Jacques* v. *Jacques*, 1995 S.L.T. 963.
- s. 9, see *Tahir* v. *Tahir (No. 2)*, (O.H.), 1995 S.L.T. 451; *McCormick* v. *McCormick* (O.H.), 1994 S.C.L.R. 958; *Stephen* v. *Stephen* (Sh.Ct.), 1995 S.C.L.R. 175.
- s. 10, amended: 1995, c. 26, s. 167.
- s. 10, see *Crosbie* v. *Crosbie* (Sh.Ct.), 1995 S.C.L.R. 399; *Stephen* v. *Stephen* (Sh.Ct.), 1995 S.C.L.R. 175; *Jacques* v. *Jacques*, 1995 S.L.T. 963.
- s. 12A, added: 1995, c. 26, s. 167.
- s. 14, see *MacDonald* v. *MacDonald* (O.H.), 1995 S.L.T. 72; *Maclue* v. *Maclue* (Sh.Ct.), 1994 S.C.C.R. 933; *Jacques* v. *Jacques*, 1995 S.L.T. 963.
- s. 18, see *Tahir* v. *Tahir (No. 2)*, (O.H.), 1995 S.L.T. 451; *Mayor* v. *Mayor* (O.H.), 1995 S.L.T. 1097.
- s. 21, repealed in pt.: 1995, c. 36, sch. 5.
- s. 27, see *Semple* v. *Semple* (Sh.Ct.), 1995 S.C.L.R. 569.

42. Hospital Complaints Procedure Act 1985.
- s. 1, amended: 1995, c. 17, sch. 1.
- s. 1A, repealed: 1995, c. 17, schs. 1, 3.

44. Sexual Offences Act 1985.
- see *R.* v. *B. (Carl)* (1993) 14 Cr.App.R. (S.) 774, C.A.; *R.* v. *R. (Paul Brian)* (1993) 14 Cr.App.R. (S) 772, C.A.

48. Food and Environment Protection Act 1985.
- s. 1, orders 95/1388 (S.), 1560 (S.); 95/1611, 1630 (S.), 1714, 1737, 2046.
- s. 1, S.R. 1994 No. 489; orders 95/39, 292.
- s. 7, S.R. 1995 No. 234.
- s. 16, regs. 95/32.
- s. 24, S.R. 1994 No. 489; regs. 95/32; orders 95/292; 1388 (S.), 1422 (S.), 1560 (S.), 1611, 1630 (S.), 1714, 1737, 2046.
- s. 24, amended: 1995, c. 21, sch. 13.
- s. 25, S.R. 1995 No. 234.
- s. 26, order 94/3205.

49. Surrogacy Arrangements Act 1985.
- s. 1, S.R. 1995 No. 755.
- s. 4, amended: 1995, c. 40, sch. 4 (S.).

51. Local Government Act 1985.
- s. 29, order 95/1522.
- s. 67, order 94/3104.
- s. 77, order 95/1974.
- s. 101, order 94/2812.
- s. 103, order 95/1522.
- sch. 3, repealed in pt.: 1995, c. 25, sch. 24.
- sch. 10, amended: order 95/1522.

CAP.

1985—cont.

54. Finance Act 1985.
- s. 10, amended: 1995, c. 38, schs. 1, 2.
- s. 15, amended: 1995, c. 4, s. 32.
- s. 50, repealed: 1995, c. 4, sch. 29.
- s. 69, see *Jarmin (Inspector of Taxes)* v. *Rawlings*, *The Times*, December 13, 1994, Knox J.
- sch. 17, see *Melluish (Inspector of Taxes)* v. *BMI (No. 3)*, *The Times*, October 16, 1995, H.L.

56. Interception of Communications Act 1985.
- ss. 1, 9, 10, see *R.* v. *Governor of Belmarsh Prison, ex p. Martin* [1995] 1 W.L.R. 412, D.C.

57. Sporting Events (Control of Alcohol etc.) Act 1985.
- s. 10, C.: 1995, c. 39, ss. 18, 23.

60. Child Abduction and Custody Act 1985.
- see *B. (Child Abduction: Habitual Residence), Re* [1994] 2 F.L.R. 915, Ewbank J.
- s. 2, orders 94/3201; 95/1031, 1616.
- s. 5, see *A.* v. *A. (Abduction: Jurisdiction)* [1995] 1 F.L.R. 341, Wilson J.
- s. 9, repealed in pt.: order 95/756.
- s. 9, amended: 1995, c. 36, sch. 4 (S.); order 95/756.
- s. 13, orders 94/2792; 95/264, 1295.
- ss. 15, 16, see *M. (Child Abduction) (European Convention), Re* [1994] 1 F.L.R. 551, Rattee J.
- s. 20, repealed in pt.: order 95/756.
- s. 20, amended: 1995, c. 36, sch. 4 (S.); order 95/756.
- s. 25, repealed in pt.: 1995, c. 36, schs. 4 (S.), 5 (S.); order 95/756.
- s. 27, amended: 1994, c. 39, sch. 13 (S.); order 95/756.
- s. 28, order 94/2799.
- sch. 1, see *Soucie* v. *Soucie* (O.H.), 1995 S.L.T. 414; *Seroka* v. *Bellah* (O.H.), 1995 S.L.T. 204; *M. (A. Minor) (Child Abduction), Re* [1994] 1 F.L.R. 391, C.A.; *McKiver* v. *McGiver* (O.H.), 1995 S.L.T. 790; *N. (Child Abduction: Jurisdiction), Re* [1995] 5–6 F.L.R. 96, Wilson J.; *F. (A Minor), Re* [1995] 3 W.L.R. 339, C.A.; *Bordera* v. *Bordera* (O.H.), 1995 S.L.T. 1176.
- sch. 2, see *M. (Child Abduction), (European Convention), Re* [1994] 1 F.L.R. 551, Rattee J.
- sch. 3, repealed in pt.: 1995, c. 36. schs. 4 (S.): order 95/756.
- sch. 3, amended: 1995, c. 36, sch. 4 (S.); order 95/756.

63. Water (Fluoridation) Act 1985.
- s. 1, amended: 1994, c. 39, sch. 13 (S.).
- s. 3, repealed: 1994, c. 39, schs. 13, 14 (S.).
- s. 4, amended: 1994, c. 39, sch. 13 (S.); repealed in pt.: 1994, c. 39, sch. 14 (S.).
- s. 5, amended: 1994, c. 39, sch. 13 (S.).

CAP.

1985—cont.

65. Insolvency Act 1985.
s. 218, see *Secretary of State for Employment* v. *Stone* [1994] I.C.R. 761, E.A.T.
ss. 282, 285, see *F.* v. *F. (Divorce: Insolvency; Annulment of Bankruptcy Order)* [1994] 1 F.L.R. 358, Thorpe J.
sch. 8, repealed in pt.: 1995, c. 23, sch. 8.

66. Bankruptcy (Scotland) Act 1985.
s. 5, repealed in pt.: 1995, c. 40, sch. 5.
s. 5, amended: 1995, c. 20, sch. 6; 1995, c. 40, sch. 4.
s. 7, repealed in pt.: 1995, c. 40, sch. 5.
s. 7, amended: 1995, c. 20, sch. 6; 1995, c. 40, sch. 4.
s. 31, amended: 1995, c. 18, sch. 2; 1995, c. 26, sch. 3.
s. 31, see *Law Society of Scotland, Council of the* v. *McKinnie* (I.H.), 1995 S.C.L.R. 53.
s. 32, amended: 1995, c. 26, sch. 3.
s. 32, see *Mulvey* v. *Secretary of State for Social Security* (O.H.), 1995 S.C.L.R. 102.
s. 33, see *Law Society of Scotland, Council of the* v. *McKinnie* (I.H.), 1995 S.C.L.R. 53.
s. 36, see *Mulvey* v. *Secretary of State for Social Security* (O.H.), 1995 S.C.L.R. 102.
ss. 36A–36C, added: 1995, c. 26, s. 95.
s. 40, see *Gourlay's T.R.* v. *Gourlay*, 1995 S.L.T. (Sh.Ct.).
ss. 41, 42, see *Law Society of Scotland, Council of the* v. *Andrew* (I.H.), 1995 S.C.L.R. 48.
s. 48, see *Mulvey* v. *Secretary of State for Social Security* (O.H.), 1995 S.C.L.R. 102.
s. 51, see *Law Society of Scotland, Council of the* v. *McKinnie* (I.H.), 1995 S.C.L.R. 53.
s. 54, see *Mulvey* v. *Secretary of State for Social Security* (O.H.), 1995 S.C.L.R. 102.
s. 55, amended: 1995, c. 20, s. 68; 1995, c. 40, sch. 4.
s. 55, see *Mulvey* v. *Secretary of State for Social Security* (O.H.), 1995 S.C.L.R. 102.
s. 68, amended: 1995, c. 40, sch. 4.
s. 70, amended: 1995, c. 45, sch. 3.

67. Transport Act 1985.
s. 3, repealed in pt.: 1995, c. 23, sch. 8; 1995, c. 31, sch. 8.
s. 6, regs. 94/3271, 3272.
s. 16, see *R.* v. *Leeds City Council, ex p. Mellor* [1993] C.O.D. 352, Hutchison J.
s. 19, order 95/1540.
ss. 35, 39, 89, repealed in pt.: 1995, c. 44, sch. 1.
s. 93, amended: 1994, c. 39, sch. 13 (S.); 1995, c. 26, sch. 4.

CAP.

1985—cont.

67. Transport Act 1985—*cont.*
s. 134, regs. 94/3271, 3272.
sch. 4, repealed in pt.: 1995, c. 23, sch. 8; 1995, c. 31, sch. 8.
sch. 4, amended: 1995, c. 23, sch. 7.

68. Housing Act 1985.
see *R.* v. *Sandwell Metropolitan Council, ex p. Thomas* (1994) 158 L.G.Rev. 203, Potts J.
s. 22, see *R.* v. *London Borough of Newham, ex p. Watkins* [1993] 26 H.L.R. 434, D.C.; *R.* v. *Islington London Borough, ex p. Aldabbagh* (1994) 27 H.L.R. 271, D.C.
ss. 27, 28, see *Murray* v. *Aslam* (1994) 27 H.L.R. 284, C.A.
s. 58, see *R.* v. *Wandsworth Borough Council, ex p. Oteng* [1993] 26 H.L.R. 413, C.A.; *R.* v. *Kensington and Chelsea Royal London Borough Council, ex p. Ben-el-Mabrouk, The Times*, June 22, 1995, C.A.; *R.* v. *Brent London Borough Council, ex p. Awua, The Times*, July 7, 1995; *R.* v. *Islington London Borough Council, ex p. Hassan (Bashir)* (CO/2004/94), January 18, 1995, Roger Toulson, Q.C.(*R.* v. *Brent London Borough Council, ex p. Awua* [1995] 3 W.L.R. 215, H.L.
s. 59, *R.* v. *Kensington and Chelsea Royal London Borough Council, ex p. Amarfio, The Times*, April 22, 1995, C.A.; *R.* v. *Bristol City Council, ex p. Bradic, The Times*, July 27, 1995, C.A.; *R.* v. *Sheffield City Council, ex p. Leek* [1994] C.O.D. 412, C.A.
s. 60, see *R.* v. *Wandsworth London Borough Council, ex p. Hawthorne* [1994] 1 W.L.R. 1442, C.A.; *R.* v. *Barking and Dagenham London Borough Council, ex p. Okuneye, The Times*, February 17, 1995, Sir Louis Blom-Cooper, Q.C. sitting as a deputy judge; *R.* v. *Brent London Borough Council, ex p. Awua, The Times*, July 7, 1995; *R.* v. *Islington London Borough Council, ex p. Hassan (Bashir)* (CO/2004/94), January 18, 1995, Roger Toulson, Q.C.; *R.* v. *Havant Borough Council, ex p. Marten* (CO/3110/94), January 19, 1995, Roger Toulson, Q.C.; *R.* v. *Brent London Borough Council, ex p. Awua* [1995] 3 W.L.R. 215, H.L.
s. 61, see *R.* v. *Slough Borough Council, ex p. Khan, The Times*, January 30, 1995, Mr. Roger Toulson, Q.C. sitting as a deputy judge.
ss. 62, 63, see *R.* v. *Northavon District Council, ex p. Palmer, The Times*, August 1, 1994, C.A.

CAP.

1985—cont.

68. Housing Act 1985—*cont.*

s. 64, see *R.* v. *Southwark London Borough Council, ex p. Dagou* (CO/3090/94), February 7, 1995, Sir Louis Blom-Cooper, Q.C.; *R.* v. *Islington London Borough Council, ex p. Hind, The Independent*, October 23, 1995 (C.S.), C.A.; *R.* v. *Brent London Borough Council, ex p. Baruwa* (CO/1388/94), July 20, 1995, Roger Henderson, Q.C.

s. 65, see *R.* v. *London Borough of Brent, ex p. MacWan* [1994] 26 H.L.R. 528, C.A.; *R.* v. *Wandsworth London Borough Council, ex p. Crooks, The Times*, April 12, 1995, Sir Louis Blom-Cooper, Q.C.; *R.* v. *Brent London Borough Council, ex p. Awua* [1995] 3 W.L.R. 215, H.L.; *R.* v. *Southwark London Borough Council, ex p. Dagou* (CO/3090/94), February 7, 1995, Sir Louis Blom-Cooper, Q.C.

s. 67, see *R.* v. *Southwark London Borough Council, ex p. Dagou* (CO/3090/94), February 7, 1995, Sir Louis Blom-Cooper, Q.C.

s. 69, see *R.* v. *Southwark London Borough Council, ex p. Dagou* (CO/3090/94), February 7, 1995, Sir Louis Blom-Cooper, Q.C.; *R.* v. *Camden London Borough Council, ex p. Spencer* (CO/2758/94), February 13, 1995, Carnwath J.; *R.* v. *Brent London Borough Council, ex p. Baruwa* (CO/1388/94), July 20, 1995, Roger Henderson, Q.C.

s. 72, see *R.* v. *Hertsmere Borough Council, ex p. Woolgar, The Times*, May 10, 1995, Sir Louis Blom-Cooper.

s. 76, amended: 1994, c. 39, sch. 13 (S).

s. 79, see *Basingstoke and Deane Borough Council* v. *Paice* (1995) 27 H.L.R. 433, C.A.

s. 84, see *Green* v. *Sheffield City Council; sub nom. Sheffield City Council* v. *Green* (1993) (1994) 26 H.L.R. 349, C.A.

s. 156, order 95/2066.

s. 156, amended: order 95/211.

s. 176, regs. 94/2931, 2932.

s. 270, see *R.* v. *Lambeth London Borough Council, ex p. Sarkbrook, The Times*, December 14, 1994, Jowitt J.

s. 276, 317, see *Johnson* v. *Felton* (1994) 27 H.L.R. 265, C.A.

s. 352, see *R.* v. *Kensington and Chelsea Royal London Borough Council, ex p. Ben-el-Mabrouk, The Times*, June 22, 1995, C.A.

ss. 442, 443, order 95/210.

s. 444, orders 95/210, 2053.

s. 573, repealed in pt.: 1995, c. 25, sch. 24.

CAP.

1985—cont.

68. Housing Act 1985—*cont.*

ss. 612, 622, see *Johnson* v. *Felton* (1994) 27 H.L.R. 265, C.A.

Pt. III, see *R.* v. *Newham London Borough Council, ex p. Ugbo* [1994] 26 H.L.R. 263, Sir Louis Blom-Cooper, Q.C.; *R.* v. *Croydon London Borough Council, ex p. Graham* [1994] 26 H.L.R. 286, C.A.; *R.* v. *Wandsworth London Borough Council, ex p. Onwudiwe* [1994] 26 H.L.R. 302, C.A.; *R.* v. *London Borough of Tower Hamlets, ex p. Khalique* [1994] 26 H.L.R. 517, Sedley J.; *R.* v. *Brent London Borough Council, ex p. Awua* [1994] 26 H.L.R. 539, C.A.; *R.* v. *London Borough of Newham, ex p. Gentle* [1993] 26 H.L.R. 466, Andrew Collins, Q.C.; *R.* v. *Royal London Borough of Kensington and Chelsea, ex p. Kassam* [1993] 26 H.L.R. 455, Andrew Collins, Q.C.; *R.* v. *Westminster City Council, ex p. Castelli (No. 2), The Times*, October 20, 1995, Roger Henderson, Q.C.; *R.* v. *London Borough of Newham, ex p. Laronde* (1994) 27 H.L.R. 215, D.C.; *R.* v. *Brent London Borough Council, ex p. Baruwa* (CO/1388/94), July 20, 1995, Roger Henderson, Q.C.; *R.* v. *Ealing London Borough, ex p. Denny* (1995) 27 H.L.R. 424, C.A.; *Ortiz* v. *City of Westminster* (1993) 27 H.L.R. 364, C.A.; *R.* v. *Tower Hamlets London Borough, ex p. Khatun* (1993) 27 H.L.R. 344, C.A.

Pt. V, *see R. v. Secretary of State for the Environment, ex p. West Oxfordshire District Council* [1993] 26 H.L.R. 417, Hutchinson J.

Pt. XV, see *R.* v. *Parker* [1994] 26 H.L.R. 508, C.A.

sch. 1, amended: 1995, c. 8, sch.

sch. 2, see *Green* v. *Sheffield City Council; sub nom. Sheffield City Council* v. *Green* (1993) (1994) 26 H.L.R. 349, C.A.

sch. 4, amended: 1994, c. 39, sch. 13 (S.).

sch. 5, see *R.* v. *Secretary of State for the Environment, ex p. West Oxfordshire District Council* (1993) 26 H.L.R. 417, Hutchinson J.

69. Housing Associations Act 1985.

see *Morgan Grenfell & Co.* v. *Sutton London Borough Council, The Times*, March 23, 1995, Clarke J.

s. 4, amended: order 94/2895.

s. 48, amended: order 94/2895.

s. 54, repealed in pt.: 1994, c. 39, schs. 13, 14 (S.).

ss. 104, 106, amended: 1994, c. 39, sch. 14 (S.).

70. Landlord and Tenant Act 1985.

s. 11, see *Joyce* v. *Liverpool City Council; Wynee* v. *Same, The Times*, May 2, 1995, C.A.

CAP.

1985—cont.

70. Landlord and Tenant Act 1985—*cont.*
s. 14, amended: 1995, c. 8, sch.
s. 19, see *Iperion Investments Corp.* v. *Broadwalk House Residents*, *The Times*, December 16, 1994, C.A.; *Abbotts Heath Management* v. *Sinclair Gardens Investments* [1995] N.P.C. 19, Mayor's and City of London Court.
s. 20C, see *Iperion Investments Corp.* v. *Broadwalk House Residents*, *The Times*, December 16, 1994, C.A.
s. 58, amended: 1995, c. 25, sch. 10.

72. Weights and Measures Act 1985.
ss. 1, 3, amended (prosp.): order 94/2867.
s. 5, regs. 95/735, 1014.
s. 8, amended (prosp.): orders 94/2866, 2867.
s. 10, regs. 95/735.
s. 11, order 95/1011; regs. 95/735, 1014.
s. 12, regs. 95/1014.
s. 15, regs. 95/428, 735.
s. 22, orders 94/2866, 2868.
s. 24, order 94/2868.
s. 27, amended (prosp.): order 94/2867.
s. 86, regs. 94/2866, 2868; 95/428, 735, 1014.
s. 94, regs. 95/735, 1014; order 95/1011.
sch. 1, amended (prosp.): order 94/2867.
sch. 3, amended (prosp.): order 94/2866.
schs. 5, 11, amended (prosp.): order 94/2867.

73. Law Reform (Miscellaneous Provisions) (Scotland) Act 1985.
s. 5, see *Blythswood Investments (Scotland)* v. *Clydesdale Electrical Stores (In Receivership)* (O.H.), 1995 S.L.T. 150.
s. 8, see *Bank of England* v. *Brunswick Developments* (1987), First Division, January 26, 1995; *McClymont* v. *McCubbin* (I.H.) 1995 S.L.T. 1995.
s. 9, see *McClymont* v. *McCubbin* (I.H.) 1995 S.L.T. 1995.
s. 21, repealed: 1995, c. 40, sch. 5.
s. 21, C.: 1995, c. 46, s. 8.
ss. 36, 37, repealed: 1995, c. 40, sch. 5.
s. 40, repealed: 1995, c. 40, sch. 5.
s. 43, repealed: 1995, c. 40, sch. 5.
s. 45, repealed: 1995, c. 40, sch. 5.
sch. 2, C.: 1995, c. 46, ss. 14, 79, 84.
schs. 3, 4, repealed in pt.: 1995, c. 40, sch. 5.

76. Northern Ireland (Loans) Act 1985.
s. 1, order 95/675.

1986

2. Australia Act 1986.
s. 4, repealed: 1995, c. 21, sch. 12.

5. Agricultural Holdings Act 1986.
s. 26, see *Omnivale* v. *Boldan* [1994] EGCS 63, C.A.; *Robinson* v. *Moody* [1994] 37 EG 154, C.A.; *Pennell*

CAP.

1986—cont.

5. Agricultural Holdings Act 1986—*cont.*
(Harold) v. *Payne (George Rodney)* (FC3/94/7963/F); (CRTI 94/0115/F), November 25, 1994, C.A.
s. 36, see *Welby* v. *Casswell* [1994] 35 EG 126, Popplewell J.
sch. 3, see *Omnivale* v. *Boldan* [1994] EGCS 63, C.A.; *Pennell (Harold)* v. *Payne (George Rodney)* (FC3/94/7963/F); (CRTI 94/0115/F), November 25, 1994, C.A.
sch. 6, amended: 1995, c. 8, sch.
sch. 11, amended: 1995, c. 42, s. 4.
sch. 14, repealed in pt.: 1995, c. 8, s. 31.

6. Prevention of Oil Pollution Act 1986.
repealed: 1995, c. 21, sch. 12.
s. 1, C.: 1995, c. 21, sch. 14.

9. Law Reform (Parent and Child) (Scotland) Act 1986.
s. 1, amended: 1995, c. 36, sch. 4.
s. 2, repealed: 1995, c. 36, sch. 5.
s. 2, see *Greig* v. *Greig* (Sh.Ct.) 1995 S.C.L.R. 789.
s. 3, repealed: 1995, c. 36, sch. 5.
s. 3, see *R.* v. *R.* (Sh.Ct.), 1994 S.C.L.R. 849; *D.* v. *Grampian Regional Council*, 1995 S.L.T. 519; *F.* v. *F.* (Sh.Ct.), 1995 S.C.L.R. 189; *Greig* v. *Greig* (Sh.Ct.) 1995 S.C.L.R. 789.
s. 4, repealed: 1995, c. 36, sch. 5.
s. 6, amended: 1995, c. 36, sch. 4.
s. 8, repealed in pt.: 1995, c. 36, sch. 5.
s. 9, see *D.* v. *Grampian Regional Council*, 1995 S.L.T. 519.
sch. 1, repealed in pt.: 1995, c. 36, sch. 5.

10. Local Government Act 1986.
s. 6, amended: 1994, c. 39, sch. 13 (S.).

14. Animals (Scientific Procedures) Act 1986.
s. 26, amended: 1995, c. 40, sch. 4 (S.).

22. Civil Protection in Peacetime 1986.
s. 1, amended: 1994, c. 39, sch. 13 (S.).
s. 146, amended: 1994, c. 39, sch. 13 (S.).

23. Safety at Sea Act 1986.
ss. 7–10, repealed: 1995, c. 21, sch. 12.
s. 7, C.: 1995, c. 21, sch. 14.
s. 8, repealed: 1995, c. 21, sch. 12.
s. 9, repealed: 1995, c. 21, sch. 12.
s. 9, C.: 1995, c. 21, sch. 14.
s. 10, repealed: 1995, c. 21, sch. 12.
s. 10, C.: 1995, c. 21, sch. 14.
s. 11, repealed: 1995, c. 21, sch. 12.
s. 11, C.: 1995, c. 21, sch. 14.
ss. 12–13, 15, repealed: 1995, c. 21, sch. 12.

24. Disabled Persons (Services, Consultation and Representation) Act 1986.
s. 2, amended: 1995, c. 17, sch. 1.
s. 7, repealed in pt.: 1995, c. 17, sch. 3.
s. 7, amended: 1995, c. 17, sch. 1; 1995, c. 40, sch. 4 (S.).
s. 16, amended: 1995, c. 17, sch. 1.

CAP.

1986—cont.

29. Consumer Safety (Amendment) Act 1986.
ss. 7, 10, amended: 1995, c. 40, sch. 4 (S.).

31. Airports Act 1986.
s. 12, amended: 1994, c. 39, sch. 13 (S.).
s. 35, order 95/1038.

32. Drug Trafficking Offences Act 1986.
see *Welch* v. *United Kingdom*, *The Times*, February 15, 1995, E.C.H.R.; *Londono, Re, The Times*, July 11, 1995, C.A.; *R.* v. *Dunham*, *The Times*, November 2, 1995, C.A.; *R.* v. *Gregory*, *The Times*, October 31, 1995, C.A.; *R.* v. *Basid*, *The Times*, October 19, 1995, C.A.; *R.* v. *Callan (Terrence Paul)* (1994) 15 Cr.App.R. (S.) 574, C.A.; *R.* v. *Wiggins (Mark Douglas)* (1994) 15 Cr.App.R. (S.) 558, C.A.
s. 4, see *R.* v. *Walbrook; Same* v. *Glasgow* [1994] Crim.L.R. 613, C.A.
s. 5, see *R.* v. *Hussain, The Independent*, July 24, 1995, C.A.
s. 38, see *R.* v. *Walbrook; Same* v. *Glasgow* [1994] Crim.L.R. 613, C.A.

33. Disabled Persons (Services, Consultation and Representation) Act 1986.
s. 1, amended: 1995, c. 36, sch. 4 (S.).
s. 2, amended: 1994, c. 39, sch. 13 (S.); 1995, c. 36, sch. 4 (S.).
s. 4, see *R.* v. *Bexley London Borough Council, ex p. B.*, July 31, 1995, Latham J.
s. 8, amended: 1995, c. 12, s. 2.
s. 13, amended: 1995, c. 36, sch. 4 (S.).
s. 16, repealed in pt.: 1994, c. 39, sch. 13 (S.); 1995, c. 36, sch. 5 (S.).
s. 16, amended: 1994, c. 39, sch. 14 (S.); 1995, c. 36, sch. 4 (S.).

35. Protection of Military Remains Act 1986.
s. 9, amended: 1995, c. 21, sch. 13.

36. Incest and Related Offences (Scotland) Act 1986.
s. 1, C.: 1995, c. 39, ss. 1–4.
sch. 1, repealed in pt.: 1995, c. 20, sch. 7.
sch. 1, C.: 1995, c. 39, s. 5; 1995, c. 46, ss. 46, 136.

41. Finance Act 1986.
s. 14, see *Customs and Excise Commissioners* v. *Bessimeh, The Independent*, August 28, 1995, D.C.
s. 102, see *Ingram* v. *I.R.C.* [1995] S.T.C. 564, Ferris J.

43. Crown Agents (Amendment) Act 1986.
repealed: 1995, c. 24, sch. 2.

44. Gas Act 1986.
s. 4, substituted: 1995, c. 45, s. 1.
s. 4A, added: 1995, c. 45, s. 1.
s. 5, substituted: 1995, c. 45, s. 1.
s. 6, repealed: 1995, c. 45, sch. 6.
s. 6A, substituted: 1995, c. 45, s. 4.
s. 7, substituted: 1995, c. 45, s. 5.

CAP.

1986—cont.

44. Gas Act 1986—*cont.*
s. 7A, added: 1995, c. 45, s. 6.
s. 7B, added: 1995, c. 45, s. 7.
s. 8, substituted: 1995, c. 45, s. 8.
s. 8A, added: 1995, c. 45, s. 9.
s. 8A, repealed in pt.: 1995, c. 45, schs. 3, 6.
s. 8A, amended: 1995, c. 45, sch. 3.
s. 8AA, added: 1995, c. 45, sch. 3.
s. 9, substituted: 1995, c. 45, sch. 3.
s. 10, substituted: 1995, c. 45, sch. 3.
s. 11, substituted: 1995, c. 45, sch. 3.
s. 12, substituted: 1995, c. 45, sch. 3.
s. 13, substituted: 1995, c. 45, sch. 3.
ss. 14, 14A, repealed: 1995, c. 45, sch. 3.
s. 15, repealed: 1995, c. 45, sch. 6.
s. 15A, amended: 1995, c. 45, sch. 3.
s. 15B, repealed: 1995, c. 45, sch. 3.
s. 16, substituted: 1995, c. 45, sch. 3.
s. 17, regs. 95/1251.
s. 17, substituted: 1995, c. 45, sch. 3.
s. 18, amended: 1995, c. 45, sch. 3.
s. 18A, substituted: 1995, c. 45, sch. 3.
s. 19, substituted: 1995, c. 45, sch. 3.
s. 20, repealed: 1995, c. 45, schs. 3, 6.
s. 21, amended: 1995, c. 45, sch. 3.
s. 22, repealed: 1995, c. 45, sch. 3.
s. 22A, added: 1995, c. 45, sch. 3.
s. 23, substituted: 1995, c. 45, sch. 3.
s. 24, amended: 1995, c. 45, sch. 3.
s. 25, amended: 1995, c. 45, sch. 3.
s. 26, amended: 1995, c. 45, sch. 3.
s. 27, substituted: 1995, c. 45, sch. 3.
s. 27A, added: 1995, c. 45, sch. 3.
s. 29, amended: 1995, c. 45, sch. 3.
s. 30, amended: 1995, c. 45, sch. 3.
s. 31, amended: 1995, c. 45, sch. 3.
s. 32, repealed in pt.: 1995, c. 45, sch. 6.
s. 32, amended: 1995, c. 45, sch. 3.
s. 32A, amended: 1995, c. 45, sch. 3.
s. 33, repealed in pt.: 1995, c. 45, sch. 3.
s. 33, amended: 1995, c. 45, sch. 3.
s. 33A, repealed in pt. (prosp.): 1995, c. 45, schs. 3, 6.
s. 33A, amended: 1995, c. 45, sch. 3.
s. 33B, repealed in pt. (prosp.): 1995, c. 45, sch. 3.
s. 33B, amended: 1995, c. 45, sch. 3.
s. 33B, added: 1995, c. 45, sch. 3.
s. 33C, repealed in pt. (prosp.): 1995, c. 45, sch. 3.
s. 33C, amended: 1995, c. 45, sch. 3.
s. 33D, repealed in pt. (prosp.): 1995, c. 45, sch. 3.
s. 33D, amended: 1995, c. 45, sch. 3.
s. 33E, repealed in pt. (prosp.): 1995, c. 45, sch. 3.
s. 33E, amended: 1995, c. 45, sch. 3.
s. 34, amended: 1995, c. 45, sch. 3.
s. 35, amended: 1995, c. 45, sch. 3.
s. 36, amended: 1995, c. 45, sch. 3.
s. 36A, added: 1995, c. 45, sch. 3.
s. 36B, added: 1995, c. 45, sch. 3.

CAP.

1986—cont.

44. Gas Act 1986—*cont.*

s. 37, substituted: 1995, c. 45, sch. 3.
s. 38, repealed in pt.: 1995, c. 45, sch. 6.
s. 38, amended: 1995, c. 45, sch. 3.
s. 38A, added: 1995, c. 45, sch. 3.
s. 39, amended: 1995, c. 45, sch. 3.
s. 40, repealed: 1995, c. 45, sch. 3.
s. 42, amended: 1995, c. 45, sch. 3.
s. 43, amended: 1995, c. 45, sch. 3.
s. 46, repealed in pt.: 1995, c. 45, schs. 3, 6.
s. 46, amended: 1995, c. 45, sch. 3.
s. 47, amended: 1995, c. 45, sch. 3.
s. 48, regs. 95/1251.
s. 48, repealed in pt.: 1995, c. 45, sch. 3.
s. 48, amended: 1995, c. 45, sch. 3.
s. 62, repealed in pt.: 1995, c. 45, s. 11, sch. 6.
s. 62, amended: 1995, c. 45, s. 11.
s. 63, repealed: 1995, c. 45, sch. 6.
s. 64, repealed in pt.: 1995, c. 45, s. 11, sch. 6.
sch. 1, amended: 1995, c. 45, sch. 3.
sch. 2B, added: 1995, c. 45, sch. 2.
sch. 3, amended: 1995, c. 45, sch. 3.
sch. 4, amended: 1995, c. 45, sch. 3.
sch. 5, repealed: 1995, c. 45, sch. 6.
sch. 7, repealed in pt.: 1995, c. 45, sch. 6.
sch. 7, amended: 1994, c. 39, sch. 13 (S.).

45. Insolvency Act 1986.

see *Cranley Mansions, Re*; *Saigol* v. *Goldstein* [1994] EGCS 95, Ferris J.; *Lally* v. *I.R.C.* (94/6921/C), March 30, 1995, C.A.
s. 5, see *R.A. Securities* v. *Mercantile Credit Co.* [1994] N.P.C. 76, Jacob J.; *Company (No. 003932 of 1995), Re, The Times*, July 25, 1995, Knox J.
s. 7, see *Leisure Study Group*, *Re* [1994] 2 BCLC 65, Harman J.
s. 11, see *AGB Research*, *Re* [1994] N.P.C. 56, Vinelott J.
s. 19, see *Powdrill* v. *Watson; Talbot* v. *Cadge; Talbot* v. *Grundy* [1995] 2 W.L.R. 312, H.L.
s. 35, see *Butlers Wharf, Re, The Times*, April 17, 1995, D.C.
s. 40, see *New Bullas Trading*, *Re* [1994] BCC 36, C.A.
s. 44, see *Powdrill* v. *Watson; Talbot* v. *Cadge; Talbot* v. *Grundy* [1995] 2 W.L.R. 312, H.L.
s. 53, amended: 1995, c. 7, sch. 4.
s. 54, see *Sharp* v. *Thomson*, 1995 S.L.T. 837.
s. 114, see *Company, A (No. 006341 of 1992), ex p. B, Re* [1994] BCLC 225, Paul Baker Q.C.
s. 117, orders 94/1536, 2626, 2893.
s. 122, see *Securum Finance* v. *Camswell* [1994] BCC 434, H.H.J. Weeks.

CAP.

1986—cont.

45. Insolvency Act 1986—*cont.*

s. 124, see *Pentagin Technologies International* v. *Express Company Secretaries, The Times*, April 7, 1995, C.A.; *Tottenham Hotspur* v. *Edennote* [1995] 1 BCLC 65, Rattee J.
s. 124A, see *Applied Database*, *Re, The Times*, February 27, 1995, Lightman J.; *Company (No. 007816 of 1994)*, *Re, The Times*, October 13, 1995, D.C.
s. 127, see *Barn Crown*, *Re* [1994] BCC 381, H.H.J. Rich, Q.C.
ss. 164, 165, see *Grovewood* v. *James Capel & Co* [1994] 4 All E.R. 417, Lightman J.
s. 178, see *Hindcastle* v. *Barbara Attenborough Associates* [1994] 4 All E.R. 129, C.A.
s. 181, see *Vedmay*, *Re* (1995) 69 P. & C.R. 247, Mr Gavin Lightman, Q.C. sitting as a deputy judge.
s. 195, see *Leigh Estates (U.K.)*, *Re* (1994) BCC 292, Mr. Richard Sykes, Q.C. sitting as a depty judge.
s. 212, see *D'Jan of London*, *Re*; *Copp* v. *D'Jan* [1994] 1 BCLC 561, Hoffmann L.J.
s. 214, see *Hydrodam (Corby) (In Liquidation)*, *Re* [1994] BCC 161, Millett J.; *D'Jan of London*, *Re*; *Copp* v. *D'Jan* [1994] 1 BCLC 561, Hoffmann L.J.; *Farmizer (Products), Re, The Independent*, June 19, 1995, Blackburne J.
ss. 216, 217, see *Thorne* v. *Silverleaf* [1994] BCC 109, C.A.
s. 233, repealed in pt.: 1995, c. 45. sch. 6.
s. 233, amended: 1995, c. 45, sch. 4.
s. 236, see *Arrows (No. 4)*, *Re*; *sub nom. Hamilton* v. *Naviede and Director of the Serious Fraud Office* [1994] 3 W.L.R. 656, H.L.; *Kingscroft Insurance*, *Re* [1994] BCC 343, Harman J.; *McIsaac* v. *Wilson, Petrs.* (O.H.), January 13, 1994.
s. 237, see *McIsaac* v. *Wilson, Petrs.* (O.H.), January 13, 1994.
s. 239, see *Secretary of State for Trade and Industry* v. *Gray*, *The Times*, November 24, 1994, C.A.
s. 242, see *Rankin* v. *Meek* (O.H.), 1995 S.L.T. 526.
s. 245, see *Power* v. *Sharp Investments* [1994] 1 BCLC 111, C.A.
s. 257, see *Bradley-Hole (A Bankrupt), Re* [1995] 1 W.L.R. 1097, Rimer J.
s. 260, see *Bradley-Hole (A Bankrupt), Re* [1995] 1 W.L.R. 1097, Rimer J.
s. 262, see *Debtor, A. (No. 87 of 1993) (No. 2), Re, The Times*, August 7, 1995, D.C.
s. 268, see *Debtor, A (No. 340 of 1992), Re, The Times*, March 6, 1995, C.A.; *Sinclair* v. *I.R.C.* (1995) 65 TC 94, W.A. Blackburne, Q.C.

CAP.

1986—cont.

45. Insolvency Act 1986—*cont.*

s. 310, amended: 1995, c. 26, sch. 3.
s. 323, see *Stein* v. *Blake, The Times*, May 19, 1995, H.L.; *Bank of Credit and Commerce Intl. SA (No. 3)* [1994] BCC 462, Rattee J.; *Stein* v. *Blake* [1995] 2 All E.R. 961, H.L.
ss. 342A–342C, added: 1995, c. 26, s. 95.
s. 366, see *Albert* v. *Albert* (94/0828/f), January 11, 1995, C.A.
s. 372, repealed in pt.: 1995, c. 45, schs. 4, 6.
s. 372, amended: 1995, c. 45, sch. 4.
s. 382, see *Wisepark, Re* [1994] BCC 221, Evans-Lombe J.; *Bradley-Hole (A Bankrupt), Re* [1995] 1 W.L.R. 1097, Rimer J.
s. 383, see *Wisepark, Re* [1994] BCC 221, Evans-Lombe, J.
s. 374, orders 94/1536, 2626, 2893.
s. 386, amended: 1995, c. 4, s. 17.
ss. 411, 412, rules 95/586.
s. 420, order 94/2421.
s. 423, see *Menzies* v. *National Bank of Kuwait SAK* [1994] BCC 119, CA.; *Chohan* v. *Saggar* [1994] BCC 134, C.A.; *Midland Bank* v. *Wyatt* [1994] EGCS 113, Ms D.E.M. Young Q.C.; *Pinewood Joinery* v. *Starelm Properties* [1994] BCC 569, H.H.J. Moseley, Q.C.; *Barclays Bank* v. *Eustice, The Times*, August 3, 1995, C.A.; *Alsop Wilkinson* v. *Neary* [1995] 1 All E.R. 431, Lightman J.; *Agricultural Mortgage Corp.* v. *Woodward* [1995] 1 BCLC 1, C.A.
s. 425, see *Chohan* v. *Saggar* [1994] BCC 134, C.A.
s. 431, amended: 1995, c. 40, sch. 4 (S.).
sch. 4, see *Grovewood* v. *James Capel & Co.* [1994] 4 All E.R. 417, Lightman J.

46. Company Directors Disqualification Act 1986.

s. 1, see *Secretary of State for Trade and Industry* v. *Palfreman* (O.H.), 1995 S.L.T. 156; *Brian Sheridan Cars, Re, The Independent*, August 21, 1995, D.C.
s. 6, see *Packaging Direct, Re*; *Jones* v. *Secretary of State for Trade and Industry* [1994] BCC 313, Jacob J.; *Secretary of State for Trade and Industry* v. *Gray, The Times*, November 24, 1994, C.A.; *Dicetrade, Re*; *Secretary of State for Trade and Industry* v. *Worth* [1994] BCC 371, C.A.; *Secretary of State for Trade and Industry* v. *Palfreman* (O.H.), 1995 S.L.T. 156; *Secretary of State for Trade and Industry* v. *Lovat* (Sh.Ct.), 1995 S.C.C.R. 180; *Richborough Furniture, Re, The Independent*, August 21, 1995, District Judge Lloyd, Q.C.

CAP.

1986—cont.

46. Company Directors Disqualification Act 1986—*cont.*

s. 7, see *Philipp & Lion, Re* [1994] BCC 261, Arden J.; *Packaging Direct, Re*; *Jones* v. *Secretary of State for Trade and Industry* [1994] BCC 313, Jacob J.; *Polly Peck International, Re*; *sub nom. Secretary of State for Trade and Industry* v. *Ellis* [1994] 1 BCLC 661, Jonathan Parker J.; *Dicetrade, Re*; *Secretary of State for Trade and Industry* v. *Worth* [1994] BCC 371, C.A.; *Official Receiver* v. *B* [1994] 2 BCLC 1, H.H.J. Paul Baker, Q.C. sitting as a deputy judge; *Secretary of State for Trade and Industry* v. *Lovat* (Sh.Ct.), 1995 S.C.C.R. 180.
s. 8, amended: 1995, c. 40, sch. 4 (S.).
ss. 11, 13, see *R.* v. *Brockley* [1994] BCC 131, C.A.
s. 16, see *Rex Williams Leisure (in administration), Re* [1994] 3 W.L.R. 745, C.A.; *Secretary of State for Trade and Industry* v. *Lovat* (Sh.Ct.), 1995 S.C.C.R. 180.
s. 17, see *Dicetrade, Re*; *Secretary of State for Trade and Industry* v. *Worth* [1994] BCC 371, C.A.; *Secretary of State for Trade and Industry* v. *Bannister* (FC395/5635/B), July 19, 1995, C.A.
s. 18, regs. 95/1509.
s. 21, order 94/2421.

47. Legal Aid (Scotland) Act 1986.

s. 8, amended: 1995, c. 18, sch. 2.
s. 9, regs. 95/1219.
s. 11, regs. 95/1220.
s. 11, amended: 1995, c. 18, sch. 2.
s. 14, see *Scottish Legal Aid Board's Reference (No. 1 of 1995)* (Sh.Ct.) (Notes), 1995 S.C.L.R. 760; *McTear* v. *Scottish Legal Aid Board* (O.H.), 1995 S.C.L.R. 611.
s. 18, see *MacDonald* v. *Tarn*, 1994 S.L.C.R. 150; *Mackenzie* v. *Lothian and Borders Police* (O.H.), 1995 S.C.L.R. 737.
s. 19, see *Learmonth* v. *Learmonth* (Sh.Ct.), 1995 S.C.L.R. 768.
s. 21, regs. 95/1222.
s. 21, amended: 1995, c. 40, sch. 4.
s. 22, amended: 1995, c. 20, s. 64; 1995, c. 40, sch. 4.
s. 23, amended: 1995, c. 40, sch. 4.
s. 25, repealed in pt. (with savings): order 95/2295.
s. 25, amended: 1995, c. 20, s. 64; 1995, c. 40, sch. 4.
s. 29, substituted: 1995, c. 36, s. 92.
s. 30, amended: 1995, c. 20, s. 64; 1995, c. 40, sch. 4.
s. 33, regs. 95/1044.

CAP.

1986—cont.

47. Legal Aid (Scotland) Act 1986—*cont.*
s. 35, amended: 1995, c. 40, sch. 4.
s. 36, regs. 95/1044, 1065, 1066, 1219, 1221, 1222, 2319, 2320.
s. 37, regs. 95/1065, 1066, 1219, 1220.
s. 41, amended: 1995, c. 36, sch. 4.
s. 42, regs. 95/1065, 1066.
sch. 1, repealed in pt.: 1995, c. 7, sch. 5.

48. Wages Act 1986.
see *J. Sainsbury* v. *Moger* [1994] I.C.R. 800, E.A.T.
s. 1, see *Davies* v. *Hotpoint* [1994] IRLR 538, E.A.T.; *Bruce* v. *Wiggins Teape (Stationery)* [1994] IRLR 536, E.A.T.; *Morgan* v. *West Glamorgan County Council* [1995] IRLR 68, E.A.T.
s. 7, see *Bruce* v. *Wiggins Teape (Stationery)* [1994] IRLR 536, E.A.T.
s. 8, see *Davies* v. *Hotpoint* [1994] IRLR 538, E.A.T.; *Bruce* v. *Wiggins Teape (Stationery)* [1994] IRLR 536, E.A.T.; *Yemm* v. *British Steel* [1994] IRLR 117, E.A.T.; *Morgan* v. *West Glamorgan County Council* [1995] IRLR 68, E.A.T.

49. Agriculture Act 1986.
s. 18, orders 94/238, 239, 3067 (S.); 95/189, 190, 191, 192, 193, 194, 195, 196, 197, 198, 199, 200.
s. 30, amended: 1995, c. 12, sch. 13.
sch. 1, see *Creear* v. *Fearon* [1994] N.P.C. 93, C.A.

50. Social Security Act 1986.
ss. 24, 25, 26, see *C. (A Minor) (Contribution Notice), Re* [1994] 1 FLR 111, Ward J.
s. 27, see *Social Security Decision No. R (IS) 14/94.*
s. 53, see *Chief Adjudication Officer* v. *Sherriff, The Times*, May 10, 1995, C.A.
s. 56, amended: 1995, c. 40, sch. 4 (S.).
s. 63, amended: order 95/559.
sch. 10, repealed in pt.: order 95/756.

53. Building Societies Act 1986.
s. 2, regs. 95/711.
s. 7, amended: order 95/1873.
s. 18, orders 94/2457; 95/1188.
s. 18, amended: orders 95/1006, 1188.
s. 19, order 95/1006.
s. 20, rules 94/2458; orders 95/1006, 1187.
s. 21, regs. 95/550.
s. 24, amended: regs. 95/1442.
s. 25, amended: regs. 95/1442.
s. 25A, added: regs. 95/1442.
s. 26, amended: regs. 95/1442.
s. 27, amended: regs. 95/1442.
s. 28, amended: regs. 95/1442.
s. 29, amended: regs. 95/1442.
s. 29A, added: regs. 95/1442.
s. 34, order 95/1189.
s. 43, amended: regs. 95/1442.

CAP.

1986—cont.

53. Building Societies Act 1986.
s. 53, repealed in pt.: 1995, c. 26, sch. 7.
s. 53, amended: 1995, c. 26, sch. 3.
ss. 64, 65, amended: order 95/1872.
s. 100, see *Cheltenham & Gloucester Building Society* v. *Building Societies Commission* [1994] 4 All E.R. 65, Sir Donald Nicholls, V-C.; *Building Societies Commission* v. *Halifax Building Society* [1995] 3 All E.R. 193, Chadwick J.
s. 102A, added: 1995, c. 5, s. 1.
s. 111, amended: 1995, c. 40, sch. 4 (S.).
s. 116, regs. 95/711.
s. 119, amended: order 95/1442.
s. 151, see *Dick* v. *Walkingshaw*, 1995 S.C.C.R. 307.
sch. 1, rules 95/1187.
sch. 6, amended: regs. 95/1442.
sch. 8, amended: order 95/1189.
sch. 11, repealed: regs. 95/2723.

55. Family Law Act 1986.
s. 1, repealed in pt.: order 95/756.
s. 1, amended: order 95/756; 1995, c. 36, sch. 4 (S.).
s. 1, see *S. (A Minor) (Contact: Jurisdiction), Re* [1995] 2 F.C.R. 162, Thorpe J.
ss. 2, 3, 5, see *S. (A Minor) (Contact: Jurisdiction), Re* [1995] 2 F.C.R. 162, Thorpe J.
ss. 8, 9, 10, see *Dorward* v. *Dorward* (Sh.Ct.), 1994 S.C.C.R. 928.
s. 13, amended: 1995, c. 36, sch. 4 (S.).
s. 15, repealed in pt.: 1995, c. 36, sch. 5 (S.).
s. 15, amended: 1995, c. 36, sch. 4 (S.).
s. 15, see *S. (Residence Order: Jurisdiction), Re* [1995] 1 F.C.R. 497, Bracewell J.; *S.* v. *S. (Custody Jurisdiction)* [1995] 1 F.L.R. 155, Bracewell J.
s. 17, repealed in pt.: 1995, c. 36, sch. 5 (S.).
s. 17, amended: 1995, c. 36, sch. 4 (S.).
s. 19, substituted: S.R. 1995 No. 755.
s. 19A, substituted: S.R. 1995 No. 755.
s. 20, repealed in pt.: S.R. 1995 No. 755.
s. 20, amended: S.R. 1995 No. 755.
s. 21, repealed: S.R. 1995 No. 755.
s. 23, amended: S.R. 1995 No. 755.
s. 24, substituted: S.R. 1995 No. 755.
s. 26, substituted: 1995, c. 36, sch. 4 (S.).
s. 33, amended: 1995, c. 36, sch. 4 (S.).
s. 34, amended: order 95/756.
s. 35, repealed in pt.: S.R. 1995 No. 755; 1995, c. 36, sch. 5.
s. 35, amended: 1995, c. 36, sch. 4 (S.).
s. 42, repealed in pt.: order 95/756.
s. 42, amended: order 95/756; 1995, c. 36, sch. 4 (S.).
s. 43, order 94/2800.

CAP.

1986—cont.

55. Family Law Act 1986—*cont.*
ss. 44, 45, see *Berkovits* v. *Grinberg, Attorney-General Intervening* [1995] 1 FLR 477, Wall J.
s. 46, see *D.* v. *D. (Recognition of Foreign Divorce)* [1994] 1 FLR 38, Wall J.; *Berkovits* v. *Grinberg, Attorney-General Intervening* [1995] 1 FLR 477, Wall J.
s. 54, see *R.* v. *Investors Compensation Scheme, ex p. Bowden, The Times*, July 18, 1995, H.L.
s. 55, see *Berkovits* v. *Grinberg, Attorney-General Intervening* [1995] 1 FLR 477, Wall J.
s. 58, orders 95/1266, 1536.
s. 66, repealed: S.R. 1995 No. 755.
s. 69, repealed in pt.: S.R. 1995 No. 755.
s. 205A, orders 95/1266, 1536.
sch. 1, repealed in pt.: S.R. 1995 No. 755.

56. Parliamentary Constituencies Act 1986.
s. 4, orders 95/1036, 1037 (S.), 1626.
s. 6, amended: 1994, c. 39, sch. 13 (S.).

60. Financial Services Act 1986.
s. 10, see *R.* v. *Insurance Ombudsman, ex p. Aegon Life Insurance* [1994] C.O.D. 426, D.C.
s. 46, order 95/202.
s. 54, see *R.* v. *Securities and Investments Board, ex p. Sun Life Assurance Society, The Independent*, October 5, 1995, Sedley J.
s. 57, orders 95/1266, 1536.
s. 58, orders 95/1266, 1536.
s. 179, see *Melton Medes* v. *Securities and Investments Board* [1995] 2 W.L.R. 247, Lightman J.
s. 180, amended: 1995, c. 26, sch.
s. 187, see *Melton Medes* v. *Securities and Investments Board* [1995] 2 W.L.R. 247, Lightman J.
s. 203, amended: 1995, c. 40, sch. 4 (S.).
s. 205A, orders 95/1266, 1536.
s. 211, order 95/1538.

61. Education (No. 2) Act 1986.
s. 7, amended: 1995, c. 17, sch. 1.
s. 50, regs. 95/603.
s. 51, order 94/3251.
s. 63, order 94/3251; regs. 95/603.

62. Salmon Act 1986.
s. 37, amended: 1995, c. 25, sch. 15.
sch. 1, orders 95/2193, 2194.

64. Public Order Act 1986.
s. 4, see *R.* v. *Notman* [1994] Crim.L.R. 518, C.A.
s. 5, see *Morrow, Geach and Thomas* v. *D.D.P.*; *Secretary of State for Health and Social Security and British Pregnancy Advisory Service* [1994] Crim.L.R. 58, D.C.; *Hourihane* v. *Commissioner of Police of the Metropolis, The Times*, December 27, 1994, C.A.

CAP.

1986—cont.

64. Public Order Act 1986—*cont.*
s. 10, repealed in pt.: 1995, c. 21, sch. 12.
s. 10, C.: 1995, c. 21, sch. 14.
sch. 1, C.: 1995, c. 39, ss. 19, 20, 21.

1987

3. Coal Industry Act 1987.
s. 3, order 95/1454.

4. Ministry of Defence Police Act 1987.
s. 1, regs. 95/939.

12. Petroleum Act 1987.
s. 22, order 95/1956.
s. 23, amended: 1995, c. 21, sch. 13.

18. Debtors (Scotland) Act 1987.
s. 1, amended: 1994, c. 39, sch. 13.
s. 73, amended: 1995, c. 12, sch. 13.
s. 103, see *Frost* v. *Bulman*, 1995 S.C.L.R. 579.
s. 106, amended: 1994, c. 39, sch. 13.
schs. 2, 5, amended: 1994, c. 39, sch. 13.
sch. 6, C.: 1995, c. 21, sch. 14; 1995, c. 46, s. 221.

21. Pilotage Act 1987.
ss. 21, 31, amended: 1995, c. 21, sch. 13.

22. Banking Act 1987.
s. 5, amended: regs. 95/1442.
s. 9, see *R.* v. *Smith (Wallace)* [1994] 1 W.L.R. 1398, C.A.
s. 11, see *R.* v. *Smith (Wallace)* [1994] 1 W.L.R. 1398, C.A.
s. 11, amended: regs. 95/1442.
s. 12, amended: regs. 95/1442.
s. 13, see *Shah* v. *Governor and Company of the Bank of England* [1994] 3 Bank L.R. 205, Vinelott, J.
s. 27, see *Shah* v. *Governor and Company of the Bank of England* [1994] 3 Bank L.R. 205, Vinelott, J.
s. 47, see *R.* v. *Smith (Wallace)* [1994] 1 W.L.R. 1398, C.A.
s. 50, amended: regs. 95/1442.
s. 51, amended: regs. 95/1442.
s. 52, amended: regs. 95/1442.
s. 53, amended: regs. 95/1442.
s. 57, amended: regs. 95/1442.
s. 58, amended: regs. 95/1442.
s. 59, substituted: regs. 95/1442.
s. 61, amended: regs. 95/1442.
s. 62, amended: regs. 95/1442.
s. 65, amended: regs. 95/1442.
s. 84, repealed in pt.: 1995, c. 26, sch. 7.
s. 84, amended: 1995, c. 26, sch. 3; regs. 94/3132.
ss. 97, 98, amended: 1995, c. 40, sch. 4 (S.).
sch. 2, repealed in pt.: 1995, c. 24, sch. 2.
sch. 3, see *R.* v. *Smith (Wallace)* [1994] 1 W.L.R. 1398, C.A.; *Shah* v. *Governor and Company of the Bank of England* [1994] 3 Bank L.R. 205, Vinelott J.
sch. 6, repealed in pt.: 1995, c. 24, sch. 2.

CAP.

1987—cont.

26. Housing (Scotland) Act 1987.
ss. 27, 31, 33, see *McMillan* v. *Kyle and Carrick District Council* (O.H.), 1995 S.C.L.R. 365.
s. 48, see *Edinburgh District Council, City of* v. *Sinclair* (Sh.Ct.) 1995 S.C.L.R. 194.
ss. 53, 54, amended: 1995, c. 7, sch. 4.
s. 61, repealed in pt.: 1994, c. 39, sch. 14.
s. 61, amended: 1994, c. 39, sch. 13; 1995, c. 36, sch. 4.
s. 61, see *Kelly* v. *City of Dundee District Council*, 1994 S.L.T. 1268; *Houston* v. *East Kilbride Development Corporation*, 1995 S.L.T. (Lands Tr.) 12; *Ross and Cromarty District Council* v. *Patience* (I.H.), 1995 S.C.L.R. 488.
s. 64, amended: 1994, c. 39, sch. 13.
s. 64, see *Ross and Cromarty District Council* v. *Patience* (I.H.), 1995 S.C.L.R. 488.
s. 70, amended: 1994, c. 39, sch. 13.
s. 73B, amended: 1995, c. 26, sch. 4.
s. 83, see *McMillan* v. *Kyle and Carrick District Council* (O.H.), 1995 S.C.L.R. 365.
ss. 191, 192, order 94/430.
s. 193, order 95/469.
s. 204, order 95/188.
s. 212, repealed in pt.: 1994, c. 39, sch. 14.
s. 229, order 94/3253.
ss. 300, 338, sch. 3, amended: 1994, c. 39, sch. 13.
sch. 10, see *Quinn* v. *Monklands District Council* (Sh.Ct.), 1995 S.C.L.R. 393; *Fyfe* v. *Scottish Homes* (Sh.Ct.), 1995 S.C.L.R. 209.
schs. 15, 23, repealed in pt.: 1994, c. 39, sch. 14.

27. Fire Safety and Safety of Places of Sport Act 1987.
s. 41, amended: 1994, c. 39, sch. 13 (S.).

31. Landlord and Tenant Act 1987.
s. 48, see *Rogan* v. *Woodfield Building Services* [1994] EGCS 145, C.A.

33. AIDS (Control) Act 1987.
s. 1, repealed in pt.: 1995, c. 17, sch. 3.
s. 1, amended: 1995, c. 17, sch. 1.
sch., repealed in pt.: 1995, c. 17, sch. 3.
sch., amended: 1995, c. 17, sch. 1.

34. Motor Cycle Noise Act 1987.
Commencement order: 95/2367.
s. 1, regs. 95/2370.
s. 2, order 95/2367.

37. Access to Personal Files Act 1987.
sch. 2, amended: 1994, c. 39, sch. 13 (S.).

38. Criminal Justice Act 1987.
ss. 4, 6, see *R.* v. *Salford Magistrates' Court*, ex p. *Gallagher* [1993] C.O.D. 491, D.C.
s. 7, see *R.* v. *Jennings (Malcolm), Johnson (Charles), Mullins (Alex)* [1994] 98 Cr.App.R. 308, C.A.

CAP.

1987—cont.

38. Criminal Justice Act 1987—*cont.*
s. 8, see *R.* v. *Central Criminal Court, ex p. Guney* [1995] 1 W.L.R. 576, C.A.
s. 9, see *R.* v. *Smithson* [1994] 1 W.L.R. 1052, C.A.
s. 236, see *Arrows (No. 4), Re; sub nom. Hamilton* v. *Naviede and Director of the Serious Fraud Office* [1994] 3 W.L.R. 656, H.L.

40. Registered Establishments (Scotland) Act 1987.
In force; order dated September 26, 1988.

41. Criminal Justice (Scotland) Act 1987.
s. 1, repealed in pt.: 1995, c. 20, sch. 7.
s. 1, amended: 1995, c. 20, sch. 5.
s. 1, C.: 1995, c. 43, ss. 1, 8, 49.
s. 2, substituted: 1995, c. 20, sch. 5.
s. 2, C.: 1995, c. 43, s. 10.
s. 3, repealed in pt.: 1995, c. 20, schs. 5, 7.
s. 3, C.: 1995, c. 43, s. 3.
s. 4, amended: 1995, c. 20, sch. 5.
s. 5, repealed in pt.: 1995, c. 20, schs. 5, 7.
s. 5, amended: 1995, c. 20, sch. 5.
s. 5, C.: 1995, c. 43, ss. 4, 49.
s. 6, repealed in pt.: 1995, c. 20, sch. 7.
s. 6, amended: 1995, c. 20, sch. 5.
s. 6, C.: 1995, c. 43, ss. 6, 7.
s. 6A, added: 1995, c. 20, sch. 5.
s. 6A, C.: 1995, c. 43, s. 11.
s. 6B, added: 1995, c. 20, sch. 5.
s. 6B, C.: 1995, c. 43, s. 13.
s. 7, repealed in pt.: 1995, c. 20, sch. 7.
s. 7, amended: 1995, c. 20, sch. 5.
s. 7, C.: 1995, c. 43, s. 14.
s. 7A, added: 1995, c. 20, sch. 5.
s. 7A, C.: 1995, c. 43, s. 45.
s. 8, substituted: 1995, c. 20, sch. 5.
s. 8, C.: 1995, c. 43, ss. 28, 29, 49.
s. 9, substituted: 1995, c. 20, sch. 5.
s. 9, C.: 1995, c. 43, s. 31.
s. 10, C.: 1995, c. 43, s. 28.
s. 11, repealed in pt.: 1995, c. 20, sch. 7.
s. 11, amended: 1995, c. 20, sch. 5.
s. 11A, added: 1995, c. 20, sch. 5.
s. 11A, C.: 1995, c. 43, s. 33.
s. 12, repealed in pt.: 1995, c. 20, sch. 7.
s. 12, amended: 1995, c. 20, sch. 5.
s. 12, C.: 1995, c. 43, s. 28.
s. 13, amended: 1995, c. 20, sch. 5.
s. 13, C.: 1995, c. 43, sch. 1.
s. 14, repealed in pt.: 1995, c. 20, sch. 7.
s. 14, amended: 1995, c. 20, sch. 5.
s. 14, C.: 1995, c. 43, sch. 1.
s. 15, C.: 1995, c. 43, sch. 1.
s. 16, amended: 1995, c. 20, sch. 5.
s. 16, C.: 1995, c. 43, sch. 1.
s. 17, amended: 1995, c. 20, sch. 5.
s. 17, C.: 1995, c. 43, sch. 1.
s. 18, amended: 1995, c. 20, sch. 5.
s. 18, C.: 1995, c. 43, sch. 1.

CAP.

1987—cont.

41. Criminal Justice (Scotland) Act 1987—*cont.*

s. 19, amended: 1995, c. 20, sch. 5.
s. 19, C.: 1995, c. 43, sch. 1.
s. 20, amended: 1995, c. 20, sch. 5.
s. 20, C.: 1995, c. 43, sch. 1.
s. 21, C.: 1995, c. 43, sch. 1.
s. 22, C.: 1995, c. 43, sch. 1.
s. 23, repealed in pt.: 1995, c. 20, sch. 7.
s. 23, amended: 1995, c. 20, sch. 5.
s. 24, amended: 1995, c. 20, sch. 5.
s. 24, C.: 1995, c. 43, sch. 1.
s. 25, substituted: 1995, c. 20, sch. 5.
s. 25, C.: 1995, c. 43, s. 12.
s. 26, repealed in pt.: 1995, c. 20, sch. 7.
s. 26, amended: 1995, c. 20, sch. 5.
s. 26, C.: 1995, c. 43, s. 17, sch. 1.
s. 27, C.: 1995, c. 43, s. 35.
s. 28, C.: 1995, c. 43, s. 36.
s. 28A, added: 1995, c. 20, sch. 5.
s. 28A, C.: 1995, c. 43, s. 37.
s. 28B, added: 1995, c. 20, sch. 5.
s. 28B, C.: 1995, c. 43, s. 38.
s. 29, C.: 1995, c. 43, s. 39.
s. 30, repealed in pt.: 1995, c. 20, sch. 7.
s. 30, amended: 1995, c. 20, sch. 5.
s. 30, C.: 1995, c. 43, s. 40.
s. 30A, C.: 1995, c. 43, s. 41.
s. 32, amended: 1995, c. 20, sch. 5.
s. 32, C.: 1995, c. 43, s. 43.
s. 33, amended: 1995, c. 20, sch. 5.
s. 33, C.: 1995, c. 43, sch. 2.
s. 34, amended: 1995, c. 20, sch. 5.
s. 34, C.: 1995, c. 43, sch. 2.
s. 35, amended: 1995, c. 20, sch. 5.
s. 35, C.: 1995, c. 43, sch. 2.
s. 36, amended: 1995, c. 20, sch. 5.
s. 36, C.: 1995, c. 43, sch. 2.
s. 37, amended: 1995, c. 20, sch. 5.
s. 37, C.: 1995, c. 43, sch. 2.
s. 37A, added: 1995, c. 20, sch. 5.
s. 37A, C.: 1995, c. 43, s. 46.
s. 41, repealed in pt.: 1995, c. 20, sch. 7.
s. 41, amended: 1995, c. 20, sch. 5.
s. 44, amended: 1995, c. 20, sch. 5.
s. 45, C.: 1995, c. 43, s. 47; 1995, c. 46, s. 109.
s. 46, C.: 1995, c. 43, s. 48.
s. 47, repealed in pt.: 1995, c. 20, sch. 7.
s. 47, amended: 1995, c. 20, sch. 5.
s. 47, C.: 1995, c. 43, ss. 17, 29, 49, sch. 2.
s. 49, amended: 1995, c. 36, sch. 4.
s. 56, repealed: 1995, c. 40, sch. 5.
s. 56, amended: 1995, c. 20, s. 61.
s. 56, C.: 1995, c. 46, ss. 302, 303.
s. 57, repealed: 1995, c. 40, sch. 5.
s. 57, C.: 1995, c. 46, s. 2.
s. 58, repealed: 1995, c. 40, sch. 5.
s. 58, C.: 1995, c. 46, ss. 3, 195.
s. 59, repealed: 1995, c. 40, sch. 5.
s. 59, C.: 1995, c. 46, s. 44.
s. 60, repealed: 1995, c. 40, sch. 5.

CAP.

1987—cont.

41. Criminal Justice (Scotland) Act 1987—*cont.*

s. 60, amended: 1995, c. 20, sch. 6.
s. 61, repealed: 1995, c. 40, sch. 5.
s. 61, C.: 1995, c. 46, s. 272.
s. 62, repealed: 1995, c. 40, sch. 5.
s. 62, C.: 1995, c. 46, ss. 32, 51, 146.
s. 63, repealed: 1995, c. 40, sch. 5.
s. 63, C.: 1995, c. 46, s. 267.
s. 64, repealed: 1995, c. 40, sch. 5.
s. 64, C.: 1995, c. 46, s. 293.
s. 65, repealed: 1995, c. 40, sch. 5.
s. 65, C.: 1995, c. 46, s. 228.
s. 66, repealed: 1995, c. 40, sch. 5.
s. 66, C.: 1995, c. 46, s. 226.
s. 67, repealed: 1995, c. 40, sch. 5.
s. 68, repealed: 1995, c. 40, sch. 5; 1995, c. 46, s. 193.
s. 68, C.: 1995, c. 46, s. 121.
s. 72, C.: 1995, c. 39, s. 53.
Part 1, repealed: 1995, c. 40, sch. 5.
sch. 1, repealed in pt.: 1995, c. 40, sch. 5.
sch. 1, C.: 1995, c. 46, ss. 10, 14, 84, 103, 228, 268, 295.
sch. 2, C.: 1995, c. 46, s. 124.

42. Family Law Reform Act 1987.

s. 4, see *P. (A Minor) (Parental Responsibility Order), Re* [1994] 1 F.L.R. 578, Wilson J.
s. 23, see *C.B. (A Minor) (Blood Tests), Re* [1994] 2 F.L.R. 762, Wall J.

43. Consumer Protection Act 1987.

see *Balding* v. *Lew Ways*, *The Times*, March 9, 1995, D.C.
s. 10, amended: 1995, c. 45, sch. 4.
s. 10, see *P&M Supplies (Essex)* v. *Walsall Metropolitan Borough Council* [1994] Crim.L.R. 580, D.C.
s. 11, regs. 94/2844, 3017, 3117, 3260; 95/204, 415, 1671.
s. 11, amended: 1995, c. 45, sch. 4.
s. 17, amended: 1995, c. 40, sch. 4 (S.).
s. 19, amended: regs. 94/3144.
s. 20, see *Berkshire County Council* v. *Olympic Holidays* [1994] 158 J.P.N. 337, D.C.; *MFI Furniture Centres* v. *Hibbert, The Times*, July 21, 1995, C.A.
s. 26, regs. 94/3248.
s. 27, regs. 94/3017.
s. 27, see *Snape* v. *Mulvenna*, *The Times*, December 28, 1994, D.C.

47. Abolition of Domestic Rates etc. (Scotland) Act 1987.

s. 2, see *Central Region, Assessor for* v. *Springbank Garden Residents Association*, 1992 S.C. 346.
sch. 2, amended: 1995, c. 18, sch. 2.
sch. 4, orders 94/529; 95/392.

51. Finance (No. 2) Act 1987.

s. 102, order 95/871, 1294.
sch. 6, repealed in pt.: 1995, c. 4, sch. 29.

CAP.

1987—cont.

53. Channel Tunnel Act 1987.
s. 11, orders 94/3286; 95/3286.
sch. 7, amended: 1995, c. 21, sch. 13.

1988

1. Income and Corporation Taxes Act 1988.
Commencement order: 95/1007.
order 95/2052.
s. 1, amended: 1995, c. 4, s. 35; order 94/3012.
s. 3, repealed in pt.: 1995, c. 4, sch. 29.
s. 12, amended: 1995, c. 4, sch. 9; order 95/171.
s. 15, repealed in pt.: 1995, c. 4, sch. 6.
s. 15, amended: 1995, c. 4, s. 39.
s. 18, amended: 1995, c. 4, sch. 6.
s. 18, see *Deeny* v. *Gooda Walker (No. 2)*, *The Times*, October 19, 1995, C.A.; *Alongi* v. *I.R.C.* (1994) 64 TC 304, C.A.
s. 19, see *Wilcock (Inspector of Taxes)* v. *Eve* [1995] S.T.C. 18, Carnwath J.; *Nichols* v. *Gibson (Inspector of Taxes)* [1994] S.T.C. 1029, Sir John Vinelott.
s. 19AA, amended: 1995, c. 4, sch. 8.
ss. 22, 23, repealed: 1995, c. 4, schs. 6, 29.
ss. 25, 26, repealed in pt.: 1995, c. 4, sch. 6.
s. 27, amended: 1995, c. 4, sch. 6.
ss. 28, 29, repealed in pt.: 1995, c. 4, sch. 6.
s. 30, amended: 1995, c. 4, sch. 6.
s. 31, repealed in pt.: 1995, c. 4, sch. 6.
s. 32, amended: 1995, c. 4, sch. 6.
ss. 33, 33A, 33B, repealed in pt.: 1995, c. 4, sch. 6.
s. 34, repealed in pt.: 1995, c. 4, sch. 29.
s. 34, amended: 1995, c. 4, sch. 6.
ss. 35, 36, 37, amended: 1995, c. 4, sch. 6.
ss. 40, 41, repealed in pt.: 1995, c. 4, sch. 6.
s. 42A, added: 1995, c. 4, s. 40.
s. 43, repealed: 1995, c. 4, sch. 29.
ss. 51A, 51B, added: 1995, c. 4, s. 77.
s. 65, amended: 1995, c. 4, s. 41.
s. 65A, added: 1995, c. 4, s. 41.
s. 72, amended: 1995, c. 4, s. 121.
s. 73, repealed: 1995, c. 4, sch. 29.
s. 73, amended: 1995, c. 4, s. 115.
s. 74, repealed in pt.: 1995, c. 4, sch. 29.
s. 75, repealed in pt.: 1995, c. 4, sch. 29.
s. 75, amended: 1995, c. 4, sch. 8.
s. 76, amended: 1995, c. 4, sch. 8.
s. 82, amended: 1995, c. 4, sch. 6.
s. 86, amended: 1995, c. 4, sch. 8.
s. 87, amended: 1995, c. 4, sch. 6.
s. 96, amended: 1995, c. 4, sch. 6; order 95/352.

CAP.

1988—cont.

1. Income and Corporation Taxes Act 1988—*cont.*
s. 97, see *Cala Homes (South)* v. *Alfred McAlpine Homes East*, *The Independent*, October 30, 1995 (C.S.), Laddie J.
s. 98, amended: 1995, c. 4, sch. 6.
s. 100, amended: 1995, c. 4, s. 140.
s. 105, amended: 1995, c. 4, s. 90.
s. 109A, added: 1995, c. 4, s. 90.
s. 110, amended: 1995, c. 4, s. 90.
s. 110A, added: 1995, c. 4, s. 124.
s. 112, amended: 1995, c. 4, s. 125.
s. 114, repealed in pt.: 1995, c. 4, sch. 29.
s. 114, amended: 1995, c. 4, s. 125.
s. 115, repealed in pt.: 1995, c. 4, sch. 29.
s. 115, amended: 1995, c. 4, s. 125.
s. 119, repealed in pt.: 1995, c. 4, sch. 29.
s. 119, amended: 1995, c. 4, s. 145.
s. 121, amended: 1995, c. 4, s. 145.
s. 125, amended: 1995, c. 4, sch. 17.
s. 129, regs. 95/1283.
s. 129, repealed in pt.: 1995, c. 4, sch. 29.
s. 129, amended: 1995, c. 4, s. 84.
s. 129A, added: 1995, c. 4, s. 85.
ss. 141, 142, amended: 1995, c. 4, ss. 91, 93.
s. 148, see *Wilcock (Inspector of Taxes)* v. *Eve* [1995] S.T.C. 18, Carnwath J.; *Nichols* v. *Gibson (Inspector of Taxes)* [1994] S.T.C. 1029, Sir John Vinelott.
s. 151A, added: 1995, c. 18, sch. 2.
s. 152, amended: 1995, c. 18, sch. 2.
s. 153, amended: 1995, c. 4, s. 91.
s. 154, see *Wilcock (Inspector of Taxes)* v. *Eve* [1995] S.T.C. 18, Carnwath J.
s. 155, amended: 1995, c. 4, s. 93.
s. 156, amended: 1995, c. 4, s. 91.
s. 157, see *I.R.C.* v. *Quigley*, 1995 S.L.T. 1052.
s. 157A, added: 1995, c. 4, s. 43.
s. 158, regs. 95/447.
s. 158, amended: 1995, c. 4, s. 43.
s. 158, substituted: 94/3010.
s. 160, repealed in pt.: 1995, c. 4, sch. 29.
s. 160, amended: 1995, c. 4, s. 45.
s. 167, amended: 1995, c. 4, s. 43.
s. 168A, amended: 1995, c. 4, s. 44.
s. 168AA, added: 1995, c. 4, s. 44.
s. 184, amended: regs. 95/1163.
s. 187, repealed in pt.: 1995, c. 26, sch. 7.
s. 187, amended: 1995, c. 26, sch. 4.
s. 188, see *Wilcock (Inspector of Taxes)* v. *Eve* [1995] S.T.C. 18, Carnwath J.; *Nichols* v. *Gibson (Inspector of Taxes)* [1994] S.T.C. 1029, Sir John Vinelott.
s. 200A, added: 1995, c. 4, s. 93.
s. 201AA, added: 1995, c. 4, s. 91.
s. 203, regs. 95/216, 853, 917, 1223, 1284.
s. 204, amended: 1995, c. 18, sch. 2.
s. 205, substituted: 1995, c. 4, s. 111.
s. 206, repealed in pt.: 1995, c. 4, s. 111, sch. 29.
s. 209, repealed in pt.: 1995, c. 4, sch. 29.

CAP.

1988—cont.

1. Income and Corporation Taxes Act 1988—*cont.*

s. 209, amended: 1995, c. 4, s. 87.
s. 212, amended: 1995, c. 4, s. 87.
s. 238, amended: 1995, c. 4, sch. 8.
s. 239, see *Savacentre* v. *I.R.C.*, *The Times*, June 2, 1995, C.A.
s. 241, repealed in pt.: 1995, c. 4, sch. 29.
s. 241, amended: 1995, c. 4, sch. 8.
s. 242, amended: 1995, c. 4, sch. 8.
s. 242, repealed in pt.: 1995, c. 4, sch. 29.
s. 246D, amended: 1995, c. 4, s. 76.
s. 257, order 94/3012.
s. 257, amended: 1995, c. 4, s. 35; order 94/3012.
ss. 257A, 257C, amended: order 94/3012.
ss. 267B, 267BB, 257D, 265, amended: regs. 95/352.
s. 289, amended: 1995, c. 4, s. 68.
ss. 292, 293, amended: 1995, c. 4, s. 66.
s. 305, amended: 1995, c. 4, ss. 66, 68.
s. 306, amended: regs. 95/352.
s. 326, amended: 1995, c. 4, sch. 12.
s. 326A, amended: 1995, c. 4, s. 63.
s. 326BB, added: 1995, c. 4, s. 62.
s. 326C, regs. 95/1929.
s. 326C, amended: 1995, c. 4, s. 62.
s. 326D, added: 1995, c. 4, s. 63.
s. 329A, added: 1995, c. 4, s. 142.
s. 329B, added: 1995, c. 4, s. 142.
s. 329C, added: 1995, c. 53, s. 8.
s. 332A, added: 1995, c. 4, s. 71.
s. 333, regs. 95/1539.
s. 333A, added: 1995, c. 4, s. 64.
s. 338, amended: 1995, c. 4, sch. 7.
s. 338A, added: 1995, c. 4, sch. 7.
s. 339, amended: 1995, c. 4, sch. 17.
s. 347A, repealed in pt.: 1995, c. 4, sch. 29.
s. 347A, amended: 1995, c. 4, sch. 17.
s. 347B, amended: 1995, c. 18, sch. 2.
s. 348, repealed in pt.: 1995, c. 4, sch. 29.
s. 349, repealed in pt.: 1995, c. 4, sch. 29.
s. 353, repealed in pt.: 1995, c. 4, sch. 29.
s. 353, amended: 1995, c. 4, s. 42.
s. 354, repealed in pt.: 1995, c. 4, sch. 29.
s. 355, repealed in pt.: 1995, c. 4, sch. 29.
s. 355, amended: 1995, c. 4, s. 42.
s. 356, amended: 1995, c. 4, s. 42.
s. 356A, repealed in pt.: 1995, c. 4, sch. 29.
s. 356B, amended: 1995, c. 4, s. 42; regs. 95/352.
s. 356D, repealed in pt.: 1995, c. 4, sch. 29.
s. 357, repealed in pt.: 1995, c. 4, sch. 29.
s. 357A, amended: 1995, c. 4, s. 42.
s. 357B, amended: 1995, c. 4, s. 42.
s. 357C, amended: 1995, c. 4, s. 42.
s. 358, repealed in pt.: 1995, c. 4, sch. 29.
s. 360A, amended: 1995, c. 4, sch. 17.
s. 366, repealed in pt.: 1995, c. 4, sch. 29.
s. 368, amended: 1995, c. 4, sch. 6.
s. 370, repealed in pt.: 1995, c. 4, sch. 29.

CAP.

1988—cont.

1. Income and Corporation Taxes Act 1988—*cont.*

s. 374A, added: 1995, c. 4, s. 112.
s. 375, regs. 95/1212, 1213.
s. 375, amended: 1995, c. 4, s. 112.
s. 375A, added: 1995, c. 4, sch. 6.
s. 378, regs. 95/1212, 1213.
s. 379A, added: 1995, c. 4, sch. 6.
ss. 380, 381, amended: regs. 95/352.
s. 385, see *Richardson* v. *Jenkins* [1995] STC 95, Rattee J.
s. 393, see *Nuclear Electric* v. *Bradley (Inspector of Taxes)*, *The Times*, October 27, 1995, C.A.
s. 401, repealed in pt.: 1995, c. 4, sch. 29.
s. 401, amended: 1995, c. 4, s. 120, sch. 6.
s. 417, amended: 1995, c. 4, sch. 17.
s. 431, repealed in pt.: 1995, c. 4, sch. 29.
s. 431, amended: 1995, c. 4, s. 52, sch. 8.
s. 431B, added: 1995, c. 4, sch. 8.
s. 431C, regs. 95/1730.
s. 431C, added: 1995, c. 4, sch. 8.
s. 431D, added: 1995, c. 4, sch. 8.
s. 431E, added: 1995, c. 4, sch. 8.
s. 431F, added: 1995, c. 4, sch. 8.
ss. 432, 432A, 432B, amended: 1995, c. 4, sch. 8.
s. 432C, repealed in pt.: 1995, c. 4, sch. 29.
s. 432C, amended: 1995, c. 4, sch. 8.
s. 432D, amended: 1995, c. 4, sch. 8.
s. 432E, order 95/1211.
s. 432E, amended: 1995, c. 4, sch. 8.
ss. 432F, 432ZA, added: 1995, c. 4, sch. 8.
s. 434, repealed in pt.: 1995, c. 4, sch. 29.
s. 434, amended: 1995, c. 4, sch. 8.
s. 434A, substituted: 1995, c. 4, sch. 8.
ss. 434B, 434C, 434D, 434E, added: 1995, c. 4, sch. 8.
s. 436, amended: 1995, c. 4, sch. 8.
s. 437, repealed in pt.: 1995, c. 4, sch. 29.
s. 438, amended: 1995, c. 4, sch. 8.
s. 439A, regs. 95/1730.
ss. 439A, 439B, added: 1995, c. 4, sch. 8.
s. 440, amended: 1995, c. 4, schs. 8, 9; regs. 95/171.
s. 440A, amended: 1995, c. 4, sch. 8.
s. 440B, added: 1995, c. 4, sch. 8.
s. 441, repealed in pt.: 1995, c. 4, sch. 29.
s. 441, amended: 1995, c. 4, sch. 8.
s. 441A, amended: 1995, c. 4, sch. 8.
s. 441B, added: 1995, c. 4, sch. 8.
s. 442A, regs. 95/1730.
s. 442A, added: 1995, c. 4, sch. 8.
s. 444, amended: regs. 95/171.
s. 444A, amended: 1995, c. 4, schs. 8, 9.
s. 444C, repealed in pt.: 1995, c. 4, sch. 29.
s. 460, amended: 1995, c. 4, sch. 10.
s. 463, regs. 95/171, 1916.
s. 464, amended: 1995, c. 4, sch. 10.
s. 474, repealed in pt.: 1995, c. 4, sch. 29.
s. 474, amended: 1995, c. 4, sch. 8.
s. 475, repealed in pt.: 1995, c. 4, sch. 29.

CAP.

1988—cont.

1. Income and Corporation Taxes Act 1988—*cont.*

s. 475, amended: 1995, c. 4, sch. 8.
s. 477A, regs. 95/1184.
s. 481, repealed in pt.: 1995, c. 4, sch. 29.
s. 481, amended: 1995, c. 4, s. 86.
s. 482, regs. 95/1370.
s. 482, amended: 1995, c. 4, s. 86.
s. 503, amended: 1995, c. 4, sch. 6.
s. 505, amended: 1995, c. 4, s. 138, sch. 17.
s. 505, see *Muir (William) (Bond 9) Employees' Share Scheme Trs.* v. *I.R.C.*, 1995 S.L.T. 225.
s. 510A, repealed in pt.: 1995, c. 4, sch. 29.
s. 519A, repealed in pt.: 1995, c. 17, sch. 3.
s. 519A, amended: 1995, c. 17, sch. 1.
s. 536, repealed in pt.: 1995, c. 4, s. 115, sch. 29.
s. 537B, repealed in pt.: 1995, c. 4, s. 115, sch. 29.
s. 547, amended: 1995, c. 4, ss. 56, 76.
s. 552, amended: 1995, c. 4, s. 57.
s. 553, amended: 1995, c. 4, ss. 55, 56, 76.
s. 559, repealed in pt.: 1995, c. 4, sch. 29.
s. 559, amended: 1995, c. 4, s. 139, sch. 27.
s. 560, amended: 1995, c. 4, sch. 27.
s. 561, repealed in pt.: 1995, c. 4, sch. 29.
s. 561, amended: 1995, c. 4, sch. 27.
s. 562, repealed in pt.: 1995, c. 4, sch. 29.
s. 562, amended: 1995, c. 4, sch. 27.
s. 563, repealed: 1995, c. 4, schs. 27, 29.
s. 565, amended: 1995, c. 4, sch. 27.
s. 566, regs. 95/217, 488.
s. 566, amended: 1995, c. 4, sch. 27.
s. 574, amended: regs. 95/352.
ss. 577, 579, amended: 1995, c. 4, sch. 6.
s. 587, see *Esslemont* v. *Marshall (Inspector of Taxes)* [1994] S.T.C. 813, Judge Paul Baker, Q.C.
ss. 588, 589A, amended: 1995, c. 4, sch. 6.
s. 590C, order 94/3009.
s. 591, amended: 1995, c. 4, s. 59.
ss. 591C, 591D, added: 1995, c. 4, s. 61.
s. 599, amended: 1995, c. 4, s. 59.
s. 617, amended: 1995, c. 18, sch. 2; 1995, c. 34, sch. 3.
s. 619, see *Koenigsberger* v. *Mellor* [1995] S.T.C. 547, C.A.
s. 623, see *Koenigsberger* v. *Mellor* [1995] S.T.C. 547, C.A.
ss. 630, 633, amended: 1995, c. 4, sch. 11.
s. 634A, added: 1995, c. 4, sch. 11.
ss. 635, 636, amended: 1995, c. 4, sch. 11.
s. 636A, added: 1995, c. 4, sch. 11.
ss. 637, 637A, substituted: 1995, c. 4, sch. 11.
ss. 638, 640, 643, 648B, amended: 1995, c. 4, sch. 11.
s. 649, amended: 1995, c. 26, sch. 5.
s. 659B, added: 1995, c. 4, s. 59.
ss. 660–676, substituted: 1995, c. 4, s. 74, schs. 17, 29.

CAP.

1988—cont.

1. Income and Corporation Taxes Act 1988—*cont.*

s. 677, amended: 1995, c. 4, sch. 17.
ss. 678, 679, 680, 681, repealed in pt.: 1995, c. 4, sch. 29.
s. 682A, added: 1995, c. 4, sch. 17.
ss. 683–685, repealed in pt.: 1995, c. 4, sch. 29.
ss. 683–685, substituted: 1995, c. 4, s. 74, sch. 17.
ss. 686, 687, amended: 1995, c. 4, sch. 17.
s. 689, repealed: 1995, c. 4, sch. 17.
ss. 692, 694, amended: 1995, c. 4, sch. 6.
s. 695, repealed in pt.: 1995, c. 4, sch. 29.
s. 695, amended: 1995, c. 5, sch. 17.
ss. 696, 697, 698, amended: 1995, c. 4, sch. 17.
s. 699A, added: 1995, c. 4, s. 76.
s. 700, amended: 1995, c. 4, sch. 17.
s. 701, amended: 1995, c. 4, s. 76, sch. 17.
s. 710, amended: 1995, c. 4, s. 87.
s. 720, amended: 1995, c. 4, sch. 17.
s. 724, amended: 1995, c. 4, sch. 8.
s. 727A, added: 1995, c. 4, s. 79.
s. 728, amended: 1995, c. 4, s. 79.
s. 730, see *I.R.C.* v. *McGuckian; McGuckian* v. *I.R.C.* [1994] S.T.C. 888, C.A.N.I.
ss. 730A, 730B, added: 1995, c. 4, s. 80.
s. 731, amended: 1995, c. 4, s. 81.
s. 732, regs. 95/2050.
s. 737, amended: 1995, c. 4, s. 82.
ss. 737A, 737B, order 95/1007.
s. 737C, amended: 1995, c. 4, s. 80.
s. 737D, added: 1995, c. 4, s. 83.
s. 739, see *I.R.C.* v. *McGuckian; McGuckian* v. *I.R.C.* [1994] S.T.C. 888, C.A.N.I.; *I.R.C.* v. *Willoughby* [1995] S.T.C. 143, C.A.
ss. 740, 741, see *I.R.C.* v. *Willoughby* [1995] S.T.C. 143, C.A.
s. 745, amended: 1995, c. 4, sch. 17.
s. 747, amended: 1995, c. 4, sch. 25.
s. 747A, added: 1995, c. 4, sch. 25.
ss. 748, 750, amended: 1995, c. 4, sch. 25.
s. 759, amended: 1995, c. 4, s. 134.
ss. 768B, 768C, added: 1995, c. 4, sch. 26.
s. 769, amended: 1995, c. 4, sch. 26.
s. 779, repealed in pt.: 1995, c. 4, sch. 29.
s. 779, amended: 1995, c. 4, sch. 6.
s. 783, amended: 1995, c. 4, sch. 17.
s. 788, orders 94/3207, 3208, 3209, 3210, 3211, 3212, 3213, 3215, 3216; 95/762, 763, 764, 765.
s. 821, repealed in pt.: 1995, c. 4, sch. 29.
s. 825, see *Savacentre* v. *I.R.C.*, *The Times*, June 2, 1995, C.A.
s. 826, amended: 1995, c. 4, sch. 24.
s. 832, amended: 1995, c. 4, sch. 6.
s. 839, amended: 1995, c. 4, sch. 17.
s. 842A, amended: 1994, c. 39, sch. 13 (S.); 1995, c. 4, s. 144.

CAP.

1988—cont.

1. Income and Corporation Taxes Act 1988—*cont.*
s. 842AA, added: 1995, c. 4, s. 70.
sch. 3, repealed in pt.: 1995, c. 4, s. 115, sch. 29.
sch. 4, amended: 1995, c. 4, s. 87.
sch. 5A, added: 1995, c. 4, s. 85.
sch. 7, amended: 1995, c. 4, s. 45.
sch. 8, amended: 1995, c. 4, ss. 136, 137.
sch. 8, repealed in pt.: 1995, c. 4, sch. 29.
sch. 9, amended: 1995, c. 4, s. 137.
schs. 9, 14, repealed in pt.: 1995, c. 4, sch. 29.
sch. 15, repealed in pt.: 1995, c. 4, sch. 29.
sch. 15, amended: 1995, c. 4, ss. 55, 71, sch. 10.
sch. 15A, added: 1995, c. 4, sch. 12.
sch. 15B, added: 1995, c. 4, s. 71.
sch. 19AA, amended: order 94/3278; 1995, c. 4, sch. 8.
sch. 19AB, regs. 94/3036.
sch. 19AC, amended: 1995, c. 4, schs. 8, 9.
sch. 19AC, repealed in pt.: 1995, c. 4, sch. 29.
sch. 23A, regs. 95/1324.
sch. 23A, amended: 1995, c. 4, s. 82.
sch. 24, repealed in pt.: 1995, c. 4, sch. 29.
sch. 24, amended: 1995, c. 4, sch. 25.
sch. 28, repealed in pt.: 1995, c. 4, sch. 29.
sch. 28A, added: 1995, c. 4, sch. 26.
sch. 28B, added: 1995, c. 4, s. 70.
schs. 29, 30, repealed in pt.: 1995, c. 4, sch. 29.

4. Norfolk and Suffolk Broads Act 1988.
s. 23, order 95/608.
s. 25, amended: 1995, c. 21, sch. 13.
sch. 3, amended: 1995, c. 25, sch. 10.
sch. 6, repealed in pt.: 1995, c. 25, sch. 24.

7. Social Security Act 1988.
s. 13, regs. 95/1143.

9. Local Government Act 1988.
Commencement order: 94/2790.
s. 1, orders 95/115, 678 (S.).
s. 1, repealed in pt.: 1994, c. 39, sch. 13 (S.).
s. 1, amended: 1994, c. 39, sch. 13 (S.); 1995, c. 25, sch. 8.
s. 2, orders 94/3084, 3107, 3161, 3189, 3190; 95/517 (S.), 678 (S.), 828, 997, 1182.
s. 2, amended: 1995, c. 39, sch. 13 (S.).
s. 2, see *Earl* v. *Huntingdonshire District Council* [1994] RA 91, Judge J.
ss. 4, 5, order 95/678 (S.).
s. 6, order 95/678 (S.); regs. 95/1326, 1973, 3164, 3165, 3166.
s. 8, regs. 94/3165; 95/1336, 1973.
ss. 9, 10, 11, order 95/678 (S.).
s. 13, see *South Norfolk District Council* v. *Norfolk Valuation and Community Charge Tribunal and Emerson*; *Birmingham City Council* v. *Birmingham Valuation and Community Charge Tribunal and Adamson* [1994] RVR 64, Latham J.

CAP.

1988—cont.

9. Local Government Act 1988—*cont.*
s. 15, orders 94/3084, 3107 (S.), 3161, 3189, 3190; 95/517 (S.), 678 (S.), 828, 997, 1182, 1326; regs. 94/3164, 3165, 3166; 95/1184, 1515, 1707, 2074, 2449.
s. 15, amended: 1994, c. 39, sch. 13 (S.).
s. 16, see *Earl* v. *Huntingdonshire District Council* [1994] RA 91, Judge J.
s. 18, amended: 1995, c. 25, sch. 8.
s. 24, amended: 1994, c. 39, sch. 13 (S.).
s. 30, see *South Norfolk District Council* v. *Norfolk Valuation and Community Charge Tribunal and Emerson*; *Birmingham City Council* v. *Birmingham Valuation and Community Charge Tribunal and Adamson* [1994] RVR 64, Latham J.
s. 33, amended: 1995, c. 25, sch. 8.
s. 58, regs. 94/3279.
ss. 63, 66, order 94/2790.
ss. 74, 89, 91, 92, regs. 94/2825.
s. 140, orders 94/3280, 3281, 3282, 3283, 3284.
s. 143, orders 94/3280, 3281, 3282, 3283, 3284; regs. 94/3279.
sch. 1, see *Earl* v. *Huntingdonshire District Council* [1994] RA 91, Judge J.
sch. 2, repealed in pt.: 1994, c. 39, sch. 14 (S.); 1995, c. 25, sch. 24.
sch. 2, amended: 1994, c. 39, sch. 13 (S.); 1995, c. 25, sch. 8.
sch. 6, orders 94/3280, 3281, 3282, 3283, 3284.
sch. 6, repealed in pt.: 1994, c. 39, sch. 14 (S.).

12. Merchant Shipping Act 1988.
ss. 11, 26–30, C.: 1995, c. 21, sch. 14.
s. 30A, see *Ullapool Harbour Trustees* v. *Secretary of State for Transport* (O.H.), *The Scotsman*, April 13, 1995.
ss. 31, 32, 35, C.: 1995, c. 21, sch. 14.
ss. 38, 39, 40, repealed: 1995, c. 22, sch.
ss. 44–47, 52, 53, schs. 1, 4–6, C.: 1995, c. 21, sch. 14.

13. Coroners Act 1988.
ss. 8, 11, see *R.* v. *Inner West London Coroner, ex p. Dallaglio* [1994] 4 All E.R. 139, C.A.
s. 13, see *R.* v. *H.M. Attorney-General, ex p. Ferrante, The Independent*, April 3, 1995, C.A.
s. 16, see *R.* v. *Inner West London Coroner, ex p. Dallaglio* [1994] 4 All E.R. 139, C.A.

17. Licensing Act 1988.
s. 1, repealed in pt.: 1995, c. 33, sch. 2.
s. 5, see *Chief Constable of West Midlands Police* v. *Marsden, The Times*, May 2, 1995, Owen J.
sch. 1, repealed in pt.: 1995, c. 33, sch. 2.

CAP.

1988—cont.

20. Dartford-Thurrock Crossing Act 1988.
s. 17, regs. 95/2059.
s. 19, amended: 1995, c. 17, sch. 1.
ss. 25, 26, 44, 46, regs. 95/2060.

24. Community Health Councils (Access to Information) Act 1988.
s. 1, repealed in pt.: 1995, c. 17, sch. 3.
s. 1, amended: 1995, c. 17, sch. 1.

32. Civil Evidence (Scotland) Act 1988.
s. 2, Acts of Sederunt 94/2805, 3066.
s. 2, see *Davies* v. *McGuire* (O.H.), 1995 S.L.T. 755; *McVinnie* v. *McVinnie* (Sh.Ct.), 1995 S.C.L.R. 480.
ss. 3, 4, see *Davies* v. *McGuire* (O.H.), 1995 S.L.T. 755.
s. 6, see *McIlveney* v. *Donald* (Sh.Ct.), 1995 S.C.L.R. 802.
s. 9, repealed in pt.: 1995, c. 36, schs. 4, 5.
s. 9, amended: 1995, c. 36, sch. 4.

33. Criminal Justice Act 1988.
ss. 8, 11, 16, see *R.* v. *Inner West London Coroner, ex p. Dallaglio* [1994] 4 All E.R. 139, C.A.
s. 23, see *R.* v. *Setz-Dempsey and Richardson* (1994) 98 Cr.App.R. 23, C.A.; *R.* v. *Jiminez-Paez (Carmenza)* (1994) 98 Cr.App.R. 239, C.A.; *R.* v. *Kennedy*; *Same* v. *Burrell* (1994) Crim.L.R. 50, C.A.; *R.* v. *Serdeiro (Roberto Newton Amaraz)* (93/0317/Z5), January 17, 1995, C.A.; *R.* v. *Maloney* [1994] Crim.L.R. 525, C.A.; *R.* v. *Castillo*, *The Times*, November 2, 1995, C.A.
s. 24, see *R.* v. *Foxley*, *The Independent*, April 3, 1995, C.A.; *R.* v. *Carrington* [1994] Crim.L.R. 438, C.A.; *R.* v. *Rock* [1994] Crim.L.R. 843, C.A.
s. 25, see *R.* v. *Setz-Dempsey and Richardson* (1994) 98 Cr.App.R. 23, C.A.
s. 26, *ibid.*; *R.* v. *Kennedy*; *Same* v. *Burrell* (1994) Crim.L.R. 50, C.A.
s. 32, amended: 1995, c. 35, sch. 2.
s. 32A, amended: 1995, c. 35, sch. 2.
s. 32A, see *R.* v. *Hawkins (Stephen Arthur)* (94/5793/X4), February 20, 1995, C.A.; *R.* v. *Rawlings* [1995] 1 All E.R. 580, C.A.
s. 35, order 95/10.
s. 38, see *R.* v. *Lynsey (Jonathan Simon)* (94/5487/X2), March 2, 1995, C.A.
s. 39, see *R.* v. *Nottingham Crown Court, ex p. D.P.P.*, *The Independent*, July 24, 1995, D.C.
s. 40, see *R.* v. *Kieran (Martin Christopher)* (95/545/Y2), February 14, 1995, C.A.; *R.* v. *Lynsey (Jonathan Simon)* (94/5487/X2), March 2, 1995, C.A.
s. 41, see *R.* v. *Avey* [1994] RTR 419, C.A.

CAP.

1988—cont.

33. Criminal Justice Act 1988—*cont.*
s. 71, repealed in pt.: 1995, c. 11, sch. 2.
s. 71, amended: 1995, c. 11, s. 1.
s. 71, see *R.* v. *Tighe*, *The Times*, September 5, 1995, C.A.; *R.* v. *Crutchley*; *R.* v. *Tonks* (1994) 15 Cr.App.R. (S.) 627, C.A.
s. 72, repealed in pt.: 1995, c. 11, sch. 1.
s. 72A, amended: 1995, c. 11, sch. 1.
s. 72AA, added: 1995, c. 11, s. 2.
s. 73, amended: 1995, c. 11, s. 3.
s. 73, see *R.* v. *Crutchley*; *R.* v. *Tonks* (1994) 15 Cr.App.R. (S.) 627, C.A.
s. 73A, added: 1995, c. 11, s. 4.
s. 74, amended: 1995, c. 20, sch. 6 (S.); 1995, c. 40, sch. 4 (S.).
s. 74A, added: 1995, c. 11, s. 5.
s. 74B, added: 1995, c. 11, s. 6.
s. 74C, added: 1995, c. 11, s. 7.
s. 75, amended: 1995, c. 11, s. 8.
s. 75A, added: 1995, c. 11, s. 9.
s. 76, amended: 1995, c. 11, s. 8.
s. 77, amended: 1995, c. 20, sch. 6 (S.); 1995, c. 40, sch. 4 (S.).
s. 80, amended: 1995, c. 11, s. 8.
s. 83, amended: 1995, c. 11, s. 10.
s. 84, amended: 1995, c. 11, s. 8.
s. 89, amended: 1995, c. 20, sch. 6 (S.); 1995, c. 40, sch. 4 (S.).
s. 90, repealed: 1995, c. 20, sch. 7 (S.).
s. 91, repealed: 1995, c. 20, sch. 7 (S.).
s. 92, repealed: 1995, c. 20, sch. 7 (S.).
s. 93, repealed: 1995, c. 20, sch. 7 (S.).
s. 93E, amended: 1995, c. 20, sch. 6 (S.).
s. 93G, added: 1995, c. 11, s. 11.
s. 93I, added: 1995, c. 11, s. 12.
s. 93J, added: 1995, c. 11, s. 13.
s. 95, repealed: 1995, c. 20, sch. 7 (S.).
s. 102, amended: 1995, c. 11, s. 8, sch. 1.
ss. 108–117, repealed: 1995, c. 53, s. 12, sch.
ss. 108–117, see *R.* v. *Secretary of State for the Home Department, ex p. Fire Brigades Union, The Times*, April 6, 1995, H.L.
s. 133, repealed in pt.: 1995, c. 35, sch. 3.
s. 133, amended: 1995, c. 35, s. 28, sch. 2.
s. 133, see *R.* v. *Secretary of State for the Home Department, ex p. Bateman and Howse* [1995] 7 Admin. L.R. 175, C.A.
s. 159, see *R.* v. *Salih*; *Section 159 of the Criminal Justice Act 1988, Re, The Times*, December 31, 1994, C.A.
s. 171, see *R.* v. *Secretary of State for the Home Department, ex p. Fire Brigades Union* [1995] 2 W.L.R. 1, C.A.
s. 171, repealed: 1995, c. 3, sch.
s. 172, repealed: 1995, c. 53, sch.

CAP.

1988—cont.

33. Criminal Justice Act 1988—*cont.*
sch. 2, amended: 1995, c. 38, sch. 1.
sch. 5, C.: 1995, c. 43, s. 49.
schs. 6, 7, repealed: 1995, c. 53, s. 12, sch.
sch. 8, C.: 1995, c. 39, s. 47 (S.).
sch. 15, C.: 1995, c. 39, ss. 28, 30, 31, 46 (S.).

34. Legal Aid Act 1988.
regs. 95/542, 797.
s. 8, regs. 94/2768; 95/1987.
s. 9, regs. 95/795.
s. 14, regs. 94/2798.
s. 15, regs. 95/797.
s. 15, see *B. and H. (Minors) (Costs: Legal Aid), Re* [1994] 1 F.L.R. 327, Ward J.; *A.B.* v. *John Wyeth & Brother* [1994] P.I.Q.R. P109, C.A.
s. 16, regs. 95/797.
s. 16, see *Brookes* v. *Harris*, *The Times*, April 22, 1995, Ferris J.
s. 17, see *Parr* v. *Smith* [1995] 2 All E.R. 1031, C.A.; *A.B.* v. *John Wyeth & Brother* [1994] P.I.Q.R. P109, C.A.; *Barker* v. *Rye*, September 20, 1995, H.H.J. Hamilton, Derby County Ct.
s. 18, see *Lewis* v. *Lewis*, February 21, 1995; H.H.J. Wilson sitting as a deputy judge; *Keller* v. *Keller and Legal Aid Board* [1995] 1 F.L.R. 259, C.A.
s. 21, amended: 1995, c. 35, sch. 2.
s. 21, regs. 95/796.
s. 25, regs. 95/948, 952.
s. 31, see *Knight (Lola Elaine)* v. *Lambeth London Borough Council* (CCRT/94/0330/E), November 28, 1994, C.A.; *B. and H. (Minors) (Costs: Legal Aid), Re* [1994] 1 F.L.R. 327, Ward J.; *Connelly* v. *Ritz Corp.*, *The Independent*, September 29, 1995, C.A.
s. 32, see *B. and H. (Minors) (Costs: Legal Aid), Re* [1994] 1 F.L.R. 327, Ward J.
s. 34, regs. 94/3136, 3303; 95/542, 795, 796, 797, 948, 949, 950, 951, 952.
s. 35, amended: order 95/162.
s. 36, order 95/162.
s. 43, regs. 94/2768, 3136, 3303; 95/542, 795, 796, 797, 948, 949, 950, 951, 952, 1987.
Part 5, see *R.* v. *Liverpool Justices, ex p. R.M. Broudie & Co.* [1994] C.O.D. 436, D.C.

36. Court of Session Act 1988.
s. 5, Act of Sederunt 94/2806, 2901, 3268; 95/1396.
s. 5, amended: 1995, c. 36, sch. 4.
s. 9, see *McMartin* v. *Gindha* (O.H.), 1995 S.L.T. 523; *Davidson* v. *Moodie* (O.H.), 1995 S.L.T. 545.
s. 20, repealed in pt.: 1995, c. 36, sch. 5.

CAP.

1988—cont.

36. Court of Session Act 1988—*cont.*
s. 40, see *Houston* v. *British Broadcasting Corporation* (I.H.), 1995 S.L.T. 1305.
ss. 46, 47, see *Overgate Centre* v. *William Low Supermarkets* (O.H.), *The Times*, December 16, 1994.

39. Finance Act 1988.
s. 28, repealed: 1995, c. 4, sch. 29.
s. 109, see *De Rothschild* v. *Lawrenson* [1995] S.T.C. 623, C.A.
s. 115, see *NAP Holdings U.K.* v. *Whittles (Inspector of Taxes)*, *The Times*, November 22, 1994, H.L.
s. 127, amended: 1995, c. 38, sch. 1.
schs. 1, 3, repealed in pt.: 1995, c. 4, sch. 29.
sch. 6, amended: order 95/352.
sch. 10, see *De Rothschild* v. *Lawrenson* [1995] S.T.C. 623, C.A.

40. Education Reform Act 1988.
orders 95/1202, 2071.
s. 4, orders 94/2227, 2228; 95/51, 52, 53, 54, 55, 56, 57, 58, 59, 60, 69, 70, 71, 72, 1574, 2071, 2072, 2073, 2207, 2208, 2209.
s. 22, regs. 94/959; 95/522, 924, 1571.
s. 38, regs. 95/178.
s. 42, regs. 94/323; 95/208, 532.
s. 52, see *R.* v. *Secretary of State for Wales, ex p. Gwent County Council* [1994] 34 R.V.R. 214, C.A.
s. 61, see *R.* v. *Governors of Astley High School, ex p. Northumberland County Council* [1994] C.O.D. 27, Macpherson J.
ss. 79, 81, 82, see *R.* v. *Secretary of State for Wales, ex p. Gwent County Council* [1994] 34 R.V.R. 214, C.A.
s. 110, amended: 1995, c. 18, sch. 2.
ss. 121, 126, 235, see *R.* v. *Newham London Borough Council, ex p. Barking and Dagenham London Borough Council, ex p. University of East London* [1994] RA 13, Potts J.
s. 128, order 95/183.
s. 148, see *Morgan* v. *West Glamorgan County Council* [1995] I.R.L.R. 68, E.A.T.
s. 151, see *Morgan* v. *West Glamorgan County Council* [1995] I.R.L.R. 68, E.A.T.
s. 187, orders 94/3078, 3105; 95/627, 1202.
s. 210, regs. 95/543.
s. 218, regs. 95/602, 2089.
s. 231, order 95/627, 1202.
s. 232, regs. 94/323, 959; 95/522, 532, 543, 602; orders 94/2227, 2228, 3078, 3105; 95/51, 52, 53, 54, 55, 56, 57, 59, 60, 69, 70, 71, 72, 178, 627, 924, 1561, 2073, 2207, 2208, 2209.

CAP.

1988—cont.

40. Education Reform Act 1988—*cont.*
s. 235, see *R.* v. *Newham London Borough Council, ex p. Barking and Dagenham London Borough Council, ex p. University of East London* [1994] RA 13, Potts J.
sch. 11, orders 94/3106; 95/604.

41. Local Government Finance Act 1988.
s. 2, order 95/1915.
s. 2, see *Codner* v. *Wiltshire Valuation and Community Charge Tribunal* [1994] 34 R.V.R. 169, Laws J.
ss. 9, 22, see *Preston Borough Council* v. *Riley* [1995] RA 277, C.A.
ss. 41, 43, see *Hackney London Borough Council* v. *Mott and Fairman* [1994] RA 381, Auld J.
s. 45, see *Hackney London Borough Council* v. *Mott and Fairman* [1994] RA 381, Auld J.; *Kingston upon Thames London Borough Council* v. *Marlow*, *The Times*, October 25, 1995, D.C.
s. 50, see *Ford* v. *Burnley Borough Council*, *The Times*, March 6, 1995, Pill J.
s. 53, order 94/3121, 3131.
s. 55, regs. 95/609, 363.
s. 55, see *Hackney London Borough Council* v. *Mott and Fairman* [1994] RA 381, Auld J.
s. 58, regs. 94/3279, 3285; 95/961, 1678.
s. 64, regs. 94/3122, 3123; order 95/1679.
s. 64, see *Williams* v. *Bristol District Valuation Officer and Avon Valuation Tribunal* [1995] RA 189, Collins J.
s. 65, regs. 94/3122, 3123.
s. 66, see *Williams* v. *Bristol District Valuation Officer and Avon Valuation Tribunal* [1995] RA 189, Collins J.
s. 74, repealed in pt.: 1995, c. 25, sch. 24.
s. 74, amended: regs. 94/2825.
ss. 78, 78A, 82, 83, see *R.* v. *Secretary of State for Wales, ex p. Gwent County Council* [1994] 34 R.V.R. 214, C.A.
ss. 89, 91, 92, amended: regs. 94/2825.
s. 99, regs. 94/2924.
s. 108, amended: 1995, c. 20, sch. 6 (S.).
s. 111, amended: regs. 95/1445.
s. 128, repealed in pt.: 1994, c. 39, sch. 14 (S.).
s. 140, regs. 94/2964, 3122, 3125, 3139; 95/284, 363, 961; orders 94/3121, 3282, 3283, 3285.
s. 141, see *R.* v. *Secretary of State for Wales, ex p. Gwent County Council* [1994] 34 R.V.R. 214, C.A.
s. 143, regs. 94/2680, 2964, 3121, 3139, 3279; 95/21, 121, 284, 363, 609, 961, 1678; orders 94/3282, 3283, 3285.
s. 146, regs. 94/2964, 3125; 95/284.
s. 162, amended: 1995, c. 21, sch. 13.

CAP.

1988—cont.

41. Local Government Finance Act 1988—*cont.*
s. 199, amended: 1995, c. 20, sch. 6 (S.).
s. 210, amended: 1995, c. 21, sch. 13.
s. 213, amended: 1995, c. 32, s. 14.
s. 235, see *Gale* v. *Northern General Hospital National Health Service Trust* [1994] I.R.L.R. 292, C.A.
sch. 2, see *Preston Borough Council* v. *Riley* [1995] RA 277, C.A.
sch. 4, amended: 1995, c. 18, sch. 2.
sch. 4, see *Preston Borough Council* v. *Riley* [1995] RA 277, C.A.
sch. 5, amended: 1995, c. 12, sch. 13.
sch. 6, orders 94/213, 2680, 3121, 3282, 3283, 3285; regs. 95/213, 961.
sch. 8, regs. 94/3125, 3139; see *R.* v. *Secretary of State for Wales, ex p. Gwent County Council* [1994] 34 R.V.R. 214, C.A.
sch. 9, regs. 95/284.
sch. 11, regs. 95/363.
sch. 12, repealed in pt.: c. 39, sch. 14 (S.).

43. Housing (Scotland) Act 1988.
s. 12, see *Milnbank Housing Association* v. *Murdoch*, 1995 S.L.T. (Sh.Ct.) 12.
s. 43, amended: 1994, c. 39, sch. 13.
s. 43, see *Milnbank Housing Association* v. *Murdoch*, 1995 S.L.T. (Sh.Ct.) 12.
s. 45, amended: 1994, c. 39, sch. 13.
s. 55, repealed in pt.: 1994, c. 39, sch. 14.
s. 56, amended: 1994, c. 39, sch. 13.
s. 57, repealed in pt.: 1994, c. 39, sch. 14.
s. 57, amended: 1994, c. 39, sch. 14.
ss. 58, 63, see *Waverley Housing Trust* v. *Roxburgh District Council*, 1995 S.L.T. (Lands Tr.) 2.
s. 70, orders 94/3108; 95/2361.
sch. 1, repealed in pt.: 1995, c. 7, sch. 5.
sch. 4, amended: 1994, c. 39, sch. 13.
sch. 4, see *Milnbank Housing Association* v. *Murdoch*, 1995 S.L.T. (Sh.Ct.) 12.

45. Firearms (Amendment) Act 1988.
s. 15, order 94/2615.
ss. 23, 53, 57, rules 94/3198.

46. European Communities (Finance) Act 1988.
repealed: 1995, c. 1, s. 2.

47. School Boards (Scotland) Act 1988.
s. 5, amended: 1994, c. 39, sch. 13.
s. 22, repealed in pt.: 1994, c. 39, sch. 14.
s. 22, amended: 1995, c. 36, sch. 4.
sch. 2, repealed in pt.: 1994, c. 39, sch. 14.

48. Copyright, Designs and Patents Act 1988.
ss. 1, 3, see *Ibcos Computers* v. *Barclays Mercantile Highland Finance* [1994] F.S.R. 274, Jacob J.
s. 16, see *Ibcos Computers* v. *Barclays Mercantile Highland Finance* [1994] F.S.R. 274, Jacob J.; *Abkco Music & Records Inc* v. *Music Collection International* (FC2 94/6973/B; Chani 93/

CAP.

1988—cont.

48. Copyright, Designs and Patents Act 1988—*cont.*
0063/B), November 7, 1994, C.A.; *Anacon Corp.* v. *Environmental Research Technology* [1994] F.S.R. 659, Jacob J.; *Hutchinson Personal Communications* v. *Hook Advertising* [1995] F.S.R. 365, Blackburne J.
s. 17, see *Ibcos Computers* v. *Barclays Mercantile Highland Finance* [1994] F.S.R. 274, Jacob J.
s. 22, see *Linpac Mouldings* v. *Eagleton Direct Export* [1994] F.S.R. 545, C.A.
s. 23, see *Linpac Mouldings* v. *Eagleton Direct Export* [1994] F.S.R. 545, C.A.; *Hutchinson Personal Communications* v. *Hook Advertising* [1995] F.S.R. 365, Blackburne J.
s. 30, see *Thames & Hudson* v. *Design and Artists Copyright Society* [1995] F.S.R. 153, Evans-Lombe J.
ss. 74, 75, see *Gale* v. *Northern General Hospital National Health Service Trust* [1994] I.R.L.R. 292, C.A.
s. 97, see *Bookmakers' Afternoon Greyhound Services* v. *Wilf Gilbert (Staffordshire)* [1994] F.S.R. 723, Aldous J.
s. 107, see *Thames & Hudson* v. *Design and Artists Copyright Society* [1995] F.S.R. 153, Evans-Lombe J.
s. 108, amended: 1995, c. 40, sch. 4 (S.).
s. 110, see *Thames & Hudson* v. *Design and Artists Copyright Society* [1995] F.S.R. 153, Evans-Lombe J.
s. 111, Act of Sederunt 94/2901 (S.).
s. 111, amended: regs. 95/1445.
s. 119, amended: 1995, c. 40, sch. 4 (S.).
s. 121, order 94/3040.
s. 178, see *Anacon Corp.* v. *Environmental Research Technology* [1994] F.S.R. 659, Jacob J.
ss. 204, 231, Act of Sederunt 94/2901 (S.).
s. 292, see *Bell Fruit Manufacturing Co.* v. *Twin Falcon* [1995] F.S.R. 144, Ford J.
s. 298, see *British Sky Broadcasting Group* v. *Lyons (David)* [1995] F.S.R. 357, Aldous J.

49. Health and Medicines Act 1988.
s. 8, order 95/416 (S.).
s. 16, repealed in pt.: 1995, c. 17, sch. 3.

50. Housing Act 1988.
regs. 95/854.
s. 4, amended: 94/2895.
s. 5, see *Lower Street Properties (Formerly Mirod Estates)* v. *Jones*, March 6, 1995, Assistant Recorder J. Phillips; Worthing County Ct.
s. 8, see *Kelsey Housing Association* v. *King, The Times*, August 8, 1995, C.A.

CAP.

1988—cont.

50. Housing Act 1988—*cont.*
s. 20, see *R.* v. *Newham London Borough Council, ex p. Ugbo* [1994] 26 H.L.R. 263, Sir Louis Blom-Cooper, Q.C.
s. 21, see *Lower Street Properties (Formerly Mirod Estates)* v. *Jones*, March 6, 1995, Assistant Recorder J. Phillips; Worthing County Ct.
ss. 27, 28, see *Sampson* v. *Wilson* [1994] 26 H.L.R. 486, H.H.J. Roger Cooke.
s. 48, order 94/2895.
s. 74, order 95/2248.
s. 75, order 95/2248.
s. 97, amended: 1995, c. 38, sch. 1.
s. 101, 1995, c. 8, sch.
ss. 104, 111, 112, 114, regs. 94/2916.
s. 121, orders 95/1642, 2365.
sch. 1, amended: 1995, c. 25, sch. 10.
sch. 17, C.: 1995, c. 43, sch. 2.

52. Road Traffic Act 1988.
order 95/737.
s. 1, see *R.* v. *Woodward (Terence)* [1995] 1 W.L.R. 375, C.A.
ss. 2, 3, see *Rodger* v. *Normand*, 1994 S.C.C.R. 861.
s. 2A, see *R.* v. *Woodward (Terence)* [1995] 1 W.L.R. 375, C.A.
s. 3, see *Rodger* v. *Normand*, 1994 S.C.C.R. 861.
s. 3A, see *R.* v. *Harrison (Alan)* (1994) 15 Cr.App.R. (S.) 546, C.A.
s. 5, see *D.P.P.* v. *Johnson* [1994] Crim.L.R. 601, D.C.; *D.P.P.* v. *Davis; Same* v. *Pittaway* [1994] Crim.L.R. 600, D.C.; *Baldwin* v. *D.P.P., The Times*, May 13, 1995, D.C.; *D.P.P.* v. *Harris* [1994] J.P.N. 896, Q.B.; *Drake* v. *D.P.P.* [1994] RTR 411, D.C.; *R.* v. *Burton upon Trent Justices, ex p. Woolley* [1995] RTR 139, C.A.; *R.* v. *Medway Magistrates' Courts, ex p. Goddard* [1995] RTR 206, D.C.; *D.P.P.* v. *Johnson* [1994] J.P.N. 891, Q.B.; *Williamson* v. *Crowe*, 1995 S.L.T. 959; *D.P.P.* v. *Johnson (David)* [1995] RTR 9, D.C.; *D.P.P.* v. *Harris (Nigel)* [1995] RTR 100, D.C.
s. 6, regs. 95/925.
s. 6, see *R.* v. *Moore (Frank)* [1994] RTR 360, C.A.; *MacKenzie* v. *Hingston*, 1995 S.C.C.R. 386.
s. 7, see *Worsley (Trevor James)* v. *D.P.P.* (CO-1679-92), November 11, 1994, D.C.; *D.P.P.* v. *Shuker (Thomas John)* (CO 2822/94), March 7, 1995, Balcombe J.; *Smyth* v. *D.P.P., The Times*, June 21, 1995, D.C.; *Chadburn (Lorraine)* v. *D.P.P.* (C 3803/94), March 8, 1995, Balcombe L.J.; *R.* v. *Moore (Frank)* [1994] RTR 360, C.A.

CAP.

1988—cont.

52. Road Traffic Act 1988—*cont.*

s. 8, see *Baldwin* v. *D.P.P., The Times*, May 13, 1995, D.C.
s. 9, see *R.* v. *Burton upon Trent Justices, ex p. Woolley* [1995] RTR 139, C.A.
s. 13A, regs. 95/1371.
s. 20, see *Pickard* v. *Carmichael*, 1995 S.C.C.R. 76.
ss. 27, 33, 39, amended: 1994, c. 39, sch. 13 (S.), 2210.
s. 41, regs. 94/3270; 95/305, 551, 737, 1201.
s. 45, amended: 1994, c. 39, sch. 13 (S.).
s. 54, regs. 95/1322, 1323.
ss. 61, 63, regs. 95/1222.
s. 66A, amended: 1995, c. 23, sch. 7.
s. 67B, amended: 1995, c. 39, sch. 13 (S.).
s. 73, amended: 1995, c. 23, sch. 7.
s. 85, repealed in pt.: 1995, c. 23, sch. 8.
s. 85, amended: 1995, c. 23, sch. 7.
s. 86, repealed in pt.: 1995, c. 23, sch. 8.
s. 86, amended: 1995, c. 23, sch. 7.
s. 88, amended: 1995, c. 13, sch. 2.
s. 89, regs. 95/100, 200, 2076.
s. 91, regs. 95/1162.
s. 97, amended: 1995, c. 13, sch. 2.
s. 103, see *Henderson* v. *Hamilton*, 1995 S.C.C.R. 413.
s. 105, regs. 95/100, 1162, 1200, 2075, 2076.
s. 108, regs. 95/100, 1162, 1200, 2075, 2076.
s. 108, see *Small* v. *D.P.P.* [1995] RTR 95, D.C.
s. 124, amended: 1994, c. 39, sch. 13 (S.).
s. 125, regs. 95/1218.
s. 127, regs. 95/1218.
s. 132, regs. 95/1218.
s. 141, regs. 95/1218.
s. 143, see *MacDonald* v. *Howdle*, 1995 S.C.C.R. 216; *McCulloch* v. *Heywood*, 1995 S.C.C.R. 221; *Henderson* v. *Hamilton*, 1995 S.C.C.R. 413.
s. 144, amended: 1994, c. 39, sch. 13 (S.); 1995, c. 21, sch. 13; 1995, c. 25, sch. 10.
s. 147, *McCulloch* v. *Heywood*, 1995 S.C.C.R. 221.
s. 152, see *Orme* v. *Ferguson* (Sh.Ct.), 1995 S.C.L.R. 752.
ss. 157, 158, amended: order 95/889.
s. 159, amended: 1995, c. 17, sch. 1.
s. 163, see *Normand* v. *McKellar*, 1995 S.L.T. 798.
s. 172, see *Souter* v. *Lees*, 1995 S.C.C.R. 33.
s. 173, see *R.* v. *Aworinde, The Times*, April 25, 1995, C.A.
s. 192, regs. 95/116, 1200, 2076.
s. 192, see *Severn Trent Water* v. *Williams and the Motor Insurers' Bureau*, March 8, 1995, District Judge Rhodes, Watford County Ct.
s. 195, regs. 95/1371.
sch. 2, amended: 1994, c. 39, sch. 13 (S.).

53. Road Traffic Offenders Act 1988.

see *Secretary of State for Trade and Industry* v. *Bannister* (FC395/5635/B), July 19, 1995, C.A.
s. 6, amended: 1995, c. 40, sch. 4 (S.).
s. 6, see *Gray* v. *Normand*, 1994 S.C.C.R. 794.
s. 13, amended: 1995, c. 38, sch. 1.
s. 15, see *Johnson (Anthony Harold)* v. *D.P.P.* (CO 1241/94), October 13, 1994, D.C.
s. 16, see *Macaulay* v. *Wilson*, 1995 S.C.C.R. 133.
s. 19, amended: 1995, c. 20, sch. 6 (S.).
s. 20, amended: 1995, c. 20, sch. 6 (S.).
s. 24, amended: 1995, c. 40, sch. 4 (S.).
s. 28, see *Nicholson* v. *Westwater*, 1995 S.C.C.R. 428.
s. 31, repealed in pt.: 1995, c. 20, schs. 6 (S.), 7 (S.).
s. 31, amended: 1995, c. 40, sch. 4 (S.).
s. 31, see *Nicholson* v. *Westwater*, 1995 S.C.C.R. 428.
s. 32, repealed in pt.: 1995, c. 20, sch. 7 (S.).
s. 32, amended: 1995, c. 40, sch. 4 (S.).
s. 33A, added: 1995, c. 20, sch. 6 (S.).
s. 35, see *Howdle* v. *Davidson*, 1994 S.C.C.R. 751.
s. 42, see *R.* v. *Liverpool Crown Court, ex p. McCann* [1995] RTR 23, D.C.
s. 47, amended: 1995, c. 13, sch. 2 (S.).
s. 57, amended: 1995, c. 13, sch. 2 (S.).
s. 60, repealed in pt.: 1995, c. 40, sch. 5.
s. 60, amended: 1995, c. 40, sch. 4 (S.).
s. 64, amended: 1995, c. 40, sch. 4 (S.).
s. 77, amended: 1995, c. 13, sch. 2 (S.).
s. 89, amended: 1995, c. 40, sch. 4 (S.).
sch. 1, amended: 1995, c. 13, sch. 2 (S.).

54. Road Traffic (Consequential Provisions) Act 1988.

s. 60, repealed: 1995, c. 40, sch. 5 (S.).
sch. 3, repealed in pt.: 1995, c. 23, sch. 8.
sch. 3, C.: 1995, c. 23, sch. 8; 1995, c. 46, s. 302.

1989

2. Law of Property (Miscellaneous Provisions) Act 1989.

s. 2, see *Hooper* v. *Sherman* (CCRTF 93/1144/C), November 30, 1994, C.A.

3. Elected Authorities (Northern Ireland) Act 1989.

s. 1, amended: regs. 95/1948.
s. 10, amended: regs. 95/1948.

CAP.

1989—cont.

4. Prevention of Terrorism (Temporary Provisions) Act 1989.
s. 15, amended: 1995, c. 40, sch. 4 (S.).
s. 27, orders 95/816, 1566.
s. 295, amended: 1995, c. 40, sch. 4 (S.).
Pt. VIII, see *R.* v. *Bristol City Council, ex p. Bailey and Bailey* (1994) 27 H.L.R. 307, D.C.
sch. 4, order 95/760.
sch. 4, amended: 1995, c. 11, s. 14; 1995, c. 20, sch. 6 (S.), 7 (S.); 1995, c. 40, sch. 4 (S.).

5. Security Service Act 1989.
ss. 5, 6, amended: order 94/2955.
s. 7, order 94/2955.
ss. 11, 12, amended: order 94/2955.

10. Disabled Persons (Northern Ireland) Act 1989.
s. 1, S.R. 1995 No. 755.
s. 2, S.R. 1995 No. 755.
s. 11, repealed in pt.: S.R. 1995 No. 755.

14. Control of Pollution (Amendment) Act 1989.
s. 1, regs. 94/1056.
s. 1, see *Cormick Transport Services, Re* (CO-776-95), May 24, 1995, McCowan L.J.
s. 2, regs. 94/1056.
s. 2, repealed in pt.: 1995, c. 25, sch. 24.
s. 2, amended: 1995, c. 25, sch. 22.
s. 6, amended: 1995, c. 25, sch. 22.
s. 7, repealed in pt.: 1995, c. 25, sch. 24.
s. 7, amended: 1995, c. 25, schs. 19, 22.
s. 8, regs. 94/1056.
s. 9, regs. 94/1056.
s. 9, amended: 1995, c. 25, sch. 22.
s. 10A, added: 1995, c. 25, s. 118.
s. 11, repealed in pt.: 1995, c. 25, s. 118, sch. 25.

15. Water Act 1989.
s. 107, see *National Rivers Authority* v. *Yorkshire Water Services* [1994] 3 W.L.R. 1202, H.L.; *National Rivers Authority* v. *Wright Engineering Co.* [1994] 4 All E.R. 281, D.C.
s. 108, see *National Rivers Authority* v. *Yorkshire Water Services* [1994] 3 W.L.R. 1202, H.L.
s. 148, see *Att.-Gen's Reference (No. 2 of 1994)* [1994] 1 W.L.R. 1579, C.A.
schs. 1, 17, repealed in pt.: 1995, c. 25, sch. 24.
sch. 25, repealed in pt.: 1994, c. 39, sch. 14 (S.); 1995, c. 25, sch. 24.

18. Common Land (Rectification of Registers) Act 1989.
s. 1, see *Land at Mooredge Farm* [1994] N.P.C. 65, Warner J.

22. Road Traffic (Driver Licensing and Information Systems) Act 1989.
sch. 5, amended: 1995, c. 45, sch. 4.

24. Social Security Act 1989.
s. 5, C.: 1995, c. 21, sch. 14.

CAP.

1989—cont.

24. Social Security Act 1989—*cont.*
s. 29, repealed in pt.: 1995, c. 26, schs. 5, 7.
sch. 5, repealed in pt.: 1995, c. 26, schs. 5, 7.
sch. 7, repealed in pt.: 1995, c. 44, sch. 1.

26. Finance Act 1989.
s. 24, see *Computeach International* v. *Customs and Excise Commissioners* [1994] V.A.T.T.R. 237, Manchester Tribunal.
s. 29, amended: 1995, c. 4, s. 20.
s. 59, amended: 1995, c. 4, sch. 17.
s. 60, repealed in pt.: 1995, c. 4, sch. 29.
s. 60, amended: 1995, c. 4, sch. 17.
s. 83, substituted: 1995, c. 4, sch. 8.
s. 83A, added: 1995, c. 4, sch. 8.
s. 88, amended: 1995, c. 4, sch. 8.
s. 102, amended: 1995, c. 4, sch. 24.
ss. 108, 109, 170, repealed in pt.: 1995, c. 4, sch. 29.
ss. 178, 182, repealed in pt.: 1995, c. 4, sch. 29.
sch. 5, amended: 1995, c. 4, s. 137.
schs. 6, 8, repealed in pt.: 1995, c. 4, sch. 29.
sch. 8A, repealed in pt.: 1995, c. 4, sch. 29.
sch. 8A, amended: 1995, c. 4, sch. 8.

29. Electricity Act 1989.
see *R.* v. *Secretary of State for Trade and Industry, ex p. Duddridge, The Times*, October 26, 1995, C.A.
s. 3, amended: 1995, c. 25, sch. 22.
s. 5, order 95/909.
s. 22, see *Norweb* v. *Dixon, The Times*, February 24, 1995, Dyson J.
s. 23, see *R.* v. *Director General of Electricity Supply, ex p. Redrow Homes (Northern), The Times*, February 21, 1995, Schiemann J.
s. 29, regs. 94/3021.
s. 32, orders 94/3259, 3275; 95/68.
s. 32, amended: 1995, c. 25, sch. 22.
s. 39, regs. 95/687.
s. 57, amended: order 95/2356.
s. 60, regs. 94/3021; 95/687.
s. 111, order 95/909.
sch. 4, amended: 1995, c. 25, sch. 22; 1995, c. 45, sch. 4.
sch. 5, repealed in pt.: 1994, c. 39, sch. 14 (S.).
sch. 5, amended: 1994, c. 39, sch. 13 (S.).
sch. 6, see *Norweb* v. *Dixon, The Times*, February 24, 1995, Dyson J.
sch. 8, repealed in pt.: 1995, c. 25, sch. 24.
sch. 8, amended: 1995, c. 25, sch. 10.

32. Fair Employment (Northern Ireland) Act 1989.
s. 6, order S.R. 1995 No. 240.
s. 25, order 95/10.

CAP.

1989—cont.

33. Extradition Act 1989.
see *Dokleja, Re; R. v. Bow Street Stipendiary Magistrate, ex p. Dokleja* [1994] C.O.D. 207, D.C.
s. 4, orders 94/2794, 2796, 3203; 95/1620, 1624.
s. 9, see *Lander, Re (CO-1031-94)*, December 14, 1994, D.C.
s. 10, amended: 1995, c. 40, sch. 4 (S.).
s. 11, see *Lander, Re* (CO-1031-94), December 14, 1994, D.C.
s. 22, orders 94/2794; 95/1620.
s. 30, orders 94/2794; 95/1620.
s. 37, orders 94/2794; 95/1620.
sch. 1, see *Sariq (Avishalom), Re* [1993] C.O.D. 472, D.C.

34. Law of Property (Miscellaneous Provisions) Act 1989.
s. 2, see *Commission for the New Towns* v. *Cooper (Great Britain) (Formerly Coopind U.K.), The Times*, March 3, 1995, C.A.; *Firstpost Homes* v. *Johnson, The Times*, August 14, 1995, C.A.

37. Football Spectators Act 1989.
s. 11, order 95/1706.

39. Self-Governing Schools etc. (Scotland) Act 1989.
s. 21, order 94/3149.
s. 21, substituted: 1994, c. 39, s. 143.

40. Companies Act 1989.
Commencement orders: 95/1352, 1591.
s. 44, amended: 1995, c. 40, sch. 4 (S.).
s. 50, regs. 95/1163.
s. 87, amended: 1995, c. 26, sch. 3.
s. 91, amended: 1995, c. 40, sch. 4 (S.).
s. 130, regs. 95/1729.
s. 171, regs. 95/2049.
s. 176, regs. 95/2049.
s. 181, regs. 95/2049.
s. 186, regs. 95/2049.
s. 215, orders 95/1352, 1591.
s. 652A, regs. 95/1480.
s. 652D, regs. 95/1480.
Pt. II, see *R. v. Institute of Chartered Accountants in England and Wales, ex p. Brindle* [1994] BCC 297, C.A.
sch. 10, repealed in pt.: 1995, c. 24, sch. 2.
sch. 18, repealed in pt.: 1995, c. 23, sch. 8.

41. Children Act 1989.
see *W. (Minors) (Removal from Jurisdiction), Re* [1994] 1 F.C.R. 842, Thorpe J.; *P. (A Minor) (Removal of Child for Adoption), Re* [1994] 2 F.C.R. 537, Miss Mary Hogg, Q.C. sitting as High Court Judge; *W. (Minors) (Removal from Jurisdiction), Re* [1994] 1 F.C.R. 842, Thorpe J.
s. 1, see *C. (Minors) (Access: Attendance of Court Welfare Officer), Re, The Times*, November 21, 1994, C.A.; *M.*

CAP.

1989—cont.

41. Children Act 1989—*cont.*
(A Minor) (Appeal) (No. 2), Re [1994] 1 FLR 59, C.A.; *J. (Minors) (Care: Care Plan), Re* [1994] 1 FLR 253; Wall J.; *S. (Minors) (Abduction), Re* [1994] 1 FLR 297, C.A.; *S.C. (A Minor) (Leave to Seek Residence Orders), Re* [1994] 1 FLR 96, Booth J.; *C. (A Minor) (Leave to Seek Section 8 Orders), Re* [1994] 1 FLR 26, Johnson J.; *O. (Minors) (Leave to Seek Residence Order), Re* [1994] 1 FLR 172, Ewbank J.; *H. (A Minor) (Contact), Re* [1994] 2 F.C.R. 419, C.A.; *S. (A Minor), Re* (95/0039/F; 94/0040/F) March 13, 1994, C.A.; *B. (Minors) (Removal from Jurisdiction), Re* [1994] 2 F.C.R. 309, C.A.; *R. (Minors) (Care Proceedings: Care Plan), Re* [1994] 2 F.C.R. 136, Wall J.; *Oldham Metropolitan Borough Council* v. *E.* [1994] 1 FLR 568, C.A.; *B. (Minors) (Care Proceedings), Re* [1994] 1 F.C.R. 471, Hollings J.; *W. (A Minor) (Interim Care Order), Re* [1994] 2 FLR 892, C.A.; *C. (A Minor) (Interim Care), Re* [1994] 1 F.C.R. 447, Balcombe L.J. sitting as a judge of the Family Division; *Y. (Child Orders: Restricting Applications), Re* [1994] 2 FLR 699, Thorpe J.; *H. (A Minor) (Contact), Re* [1994] 2 F.C.R. 419, C.A.; *D.H. (A Minor) (Child Abuse), Re* [1994] 1 FLR 679, Wall J.; *E. (Parental Responsibility: Blood Tests), Re* [1995] 1 FLR 392, C.A.; *P. (A Minor) (Parental Responsibility Order), Re* [1994] 1 FLR 578, Wilson J.; *G. (A Minor) (Parental Responsibility Order), Re* [1994] 1 FLR 504, C.A.; *B. (Minors) (Removal from Jurisdiction), Re* [1994] 2 F.C.R. 309, C.A.; *H. (A Minor) (Shared Residence Order), Re* [1994] 1 FLR 717, C.A.; *C.* v. *Salford City Council* [1994] 2 FLR 926, Hale J.; *M.* v. *Birmingham City Council* [1994] 2 FLR 141, Stuart-White J.; *M. (A Minor) (Secure Accommodation Order), Re* [1995] 2 W.L.R. 302, C.A.; *S. (Care Order: Criminal Proceedings), Re* [1995] 1 FLR 151, C.A.; *M. (Minors) (Contact), Re* [1995] 1 F.C.R. 753; *F.* v. *R. (Contact: Justices' Reasons)* [1995] 1 FLR 227, Wall J.; *M. (A Minor), Re* [1995] 5–6 FLR 108, C.A.; *A. (A Minor) (Supervision Order: Extension), Re* [1995] 1 All E.R. 401, C.A. *T. and E. (Proceedings: Conflicting Interests), Re* [1995] 1 FLR 581, Wall J.; *H.* v. *H. (Residence Order: Leave to Remove from Jurisdiction) (Note)* [1995] 1 FLR 529, C.A.

CAP.

1989—cont.

41. Children Act 1989—*cont.*

s. 2, see *P. (A Minor) (Parental Responsibility Order), Re* [1994] 1 FLR 578, Wilson J.; *G. (A Minor) (Parental Responsibility Order), Re* [1994] 1 FLR 504, C.A.

s. 3, see *F. (Minors), Re* (1993) (1994) 26 H.L.R. 354, C.A.; *Oldham Metropolitan Borough Council* v. *E.* [1994] 1 FLR 568, C.A.; *G. (A Minor) (Parental Responsibility Order), Re* [1994] 1 FLR 504, C.A.; *H. (A Minor) (Shared Residence Order), Re* [1994] 1 FLR 717, C.A.

s. 4, regs. 94/3157.

s. 4, see *S. (A Minor) (Parental Responsibility), Re, The Times*, February 22, 1995, C.A.; *E. (Parental Responsibility: Blood Tests), Re* [1995] 1 FLR 392, C.A.; *P. (A Minor) (Parental Responsibility Order), Re* [1994] 1 FLR 578, Wilson J.; *G. (A Minor) (Parental Responsibility Order), Re* [1994] 1 FLR 504, C.A.; *G. (A Minor) (Blood Test), Re* [1994] 1 FLR 495, M. Horowitz, Q.C.; *H. (A Minor) (Shared Residence Order), Re* [1994] 1 FLR 717, C.A.

s. 6, amended: 1995, c. 41, s. 4.

s. 7, see *K. (A Minor) (Contact: Psychiatric Report), Re, The Times*, April 13, 1995, C.A.; *W.* v. *Wakefield City Council* [1994] 2 F.C.R. 564, Wall J.; *A. and B. (Minors) (No. 2), Re* [1995] 1 FLR 351, Wall J.; *B.* v. *B. (Child Abuse: Contact)* [1994] 2 FLR 713, Wall J.; *W.* v. *Wakefield City Council* [1995] 1 FLR 170, Wall J.

s. 8, see *M. (A Minor) (Contact: Conditions), Re* [1994] 1 FLR 272, Wall J.; *S.C. (A Minor) (Leave to Seek Section 8 Orders), Re* [1994] 1 FLR 26, Johnson J.; *O. (Minors) (Leave to Seek Residence Order), Re* [1994] 1 FLR 172, Ewbank J.; *F. (Minors), Re* (1993) (1994) 26 H.L.R. 354, C.A.; *O. (A Minor) (Contact: Imposition of Conditions), Re, The Times*, March 17, 1995, C.A.; *R. (A Minor) (Adoption: Contact Order) Re* [1994] 1 F.C.R. 104, C.A.; *E. (Adoption: Freeing Order), Re* [1995] 1 FLR 382, C.A.; *W.* v. *Wakefield City Council* [1994] 2 F.C.R. 564, Wall J.; *D.H. (A Minor) (Child Abuse), Re* [1994] 1 FLR 679, Wall J.; *J. (A Minor) (Contact) Re*, [1994] 1 FLR 729, C.A.; *C.* v. *Salford City Council* [1994] 2 FLR 926, Hale J.; *A.* v. *A. (Minors) (Shared Residence Order)* [1994] 1 FLR 669, C.A.; *E. (Adopted Child: Contact: Leave), Re* [1995] 1 FLR 57, Thorpe J.; *H. (Minors) (Prohibited Steps Order), Re* [1995] 1 W.L.R. 667, C.A.; *F.* v. *Cambridgeshire County Council* [1995] 1 FLR 516, Stuart-White J.

s. 9, amended: 1995, c. 38, sch. 1.

s. 9, see *D.H. (A Minor) (Child Abuse), Re* [1994] 1 FLR 679, Wall J.; *C.* v. *Salford City Council* [1994] 2 FLR 926, Hale J.; *B. (A Minors) (Contact), Re* [1994] 2 FLR 1, C.A.

s. 10, see *S.C. (A Minor) (Leave to Seek Residence Orders), Re* [1994] 1 FLR 96, Booth J.; *C. (A Minor) (Leave to Seek Section 8 Orders), Re* [1994] 1 FLR 26, Johnson J.; *A. (A Minor) (Contact Application: Grandparent), Re, The Times*, March 6, 1995, C.A.; *W.* v. *Wakefield City Council* [1994] 2 F.C.R. 564, Wall J.; *H. (Contact: Principles), Re* [1994] 2 FLR 969, C.A.; *C.* v. *Salford City Council* [1994] 2 FLR 926, Hale J.; *E. (Adopted Child: Contact: Leave), Re* [1995] 1 FLR 57, Thorpe J.; *R.* v. *Secretary of State for the Home Department, ex p. T.* [1995] 1 FLR 293, C.A.; *F. and R. (Section 8 Order: Grandparent's Application), Re* [1995] 1 FLR 524, Cazalet J.

s. 11, see *M. (A Minor) (Contact: Conditions), Re* [1994] 1 FLR 272, Wall J.; *O. (A Minor) (Contact: Imposition of Conditions), Re, The Times*, March 17, 1995, C.A.; *D.H. (A Minor) (Child Abuse), Re* [1994] 1 FLR 679, Wall J.; *A. and B. (Minors) (No. 2), Re* [1995] 1 FLR 351, Wall J.; *H. (A Minor) (Shared Residence Order), Re* [1994] 1 FLR 717, C.A.; *J. (A Minor) (Residence), Re* [1994] 1 FLR 369, Singer J.; *A.* v. *A. (Minors) (Shared Residence Order)* [1994] 1 FLR 669, C.A.; *A.B. (A Minor) (Adoption: Unmarried Couple), Re, The Times*, August 10, 1995, Cazalet J.

s. 12, see *S.C. (A Minor) (Leave to Seek Residence Orders), Re* [1994] 1 FLR 96, Booth J.

s. 13, see *E. (Parental Responsibility: Blood Tests), Re* [1995] 1 FLR 392, C.A.; *P. (A Minor) (Parental Responsibility Order), Re* [1994] 1 FLR 578, Wilson J.

s. 15, see *F. (Minors), Re* (1993) (1994) 26 H.L.R. 354, C.A.; *T.* v. *S. (Financial Provision for Children)* [1994] 1 F.C.R. 743, Johnson J.

s. 16, see *D.H. (A Minor) (Child Abuse), Re* [1994] 1 FLR 679, Wall J.; *B.* v. *B. (Child Abuse: Contact)* [1994] 2 FLR 713, Wall J.

s. 17, amended: 1995, c. 18, sch. 2.

s. 17, see *R.* v. *Brent London Borough Council, ex p. S.* [1994] 1 FLR 203, C.A.; *R.* v. *Kingston-upon-Thames*

CAP.

1989—cont.

41. Children Act 1989—*cont.*

Royal Borough, ex p. T. [1994] 1 FLR 798, Ward J.; *R.* v. *Barnet London Borough Council, ex p. B.* [1994] 1 FLR 592, Auld J.; *Oldham Metropolitan Borough Council* v. *E.* [1994] 1 FLR 568, C.A.; *T. (Accommodation by Local Authority), Re* [1995] 1 FLR 159, Johnson J.; *Sawyers* v. *Brent London Borough* [1994] C.O.D. 416, C.A.; *R.* v. *Bexley London Borough Council, ex p. B.*, July 31, 1995, Latham J.; *X. (Minors)* v. *Bedfordshire County Council* [1995] 3 W.L.R. 152, H.L.; *R.* v. *Avon County Council, ex p. Hills* [1995] 27 H.L.R. 411, Harrison J.

s. 19, amended: 1995, c. 17, sch. 1.

s. 19, see *R.* v. *Barnet London Borough Council, ex p. B.* [1994] 1 FLR 592, Auld J.

s. 20, see *R.* v. *Kingston-upon-Thames Royal Borough, ex p. T.* [1994] 1 FLR 798, Ward J.; *R.* v. *Barnet London Borough Council, ex p. B.* [1994] 1 FLR 592, Auld J.; *Birmingham City Council* v. *D.; Birmingham City Council* v. *M.* [1994] 2 FLR 502, Thorpe J.; *C. (Secure Accommodation: Bail), Re* [1994] 2 FLR 922, Hollis J.

s. 21, amended: 1995, c. 17, sch. 1.

s. 21, see *R.* v. *Barnet London Borough Council, ex p. B.* [1994] 1 FLR 592, Auld J.

s. 22, see *R.* v. *Brent London Borough Council, ex p. S.* [1994] 1 FLR 203, C.A.; *Birmingham City Council* v. *D.; Birmingham City Council* v. *M.* [1994] 2 FLR 502, Thorpe J.; *R.* v. *Barnet London Borough Council, ex p. B.* [1994] 1 FLR 592, Auld J.; *C.* v. *Salford City Council* [1994] 2 FLR 926, Hale J.; *C. (Secure Accommodation: Bail), Re* [1994] 2 FLR 922, Hollis J.; *Sawyers* v. *Brent London Borough* [1994] C.O.D. 416, C.A.

s. 23, see *R.* v. *Brent London Borough Council, ex p. S.* [1994] 1 FLR 203, C.A.; *T. (A Minor) (Care or Supervision Orders), Re* [1994] 1 FLR 96, Booth J.; *Birmingham City Council* v. *D.; Birmingham City Council* v. *M.* [1994] 2 FLR 502, Thorpe J.; *R.* v. *Barnet London Borough Council, ex p. B.* [1994] 1 FLR 592, Auld J.; *C.* v. *Salford City Council* [1994] 2 FLR 926, Hale J.; *Sawyers* v. *Brent London Borough* [1994] C.O.D. 416, C.A.

s. 24, see *R.* v. *Barnet London Borough Council, ex p. B.* [1994] 1 FLR 592, Auld J.; *Birmingham City Council* v. *D.; Birmingham City Council* v. *M.* [1994] 2 FLR 502, Thorpe J.

CAP.

1989—cont.

41. Children Act 1989—*cont.*

s. 24, amended: 1995, c. 17, sch. 1.

s. 25, regs. 95/1398.

s. 25, see *C. (Secure Accommodation: Bail), Re* [1994] 2 FLR 922, Hollis J.; *C.* v. *Humberside County Council* [1994] 2 FLR 759, Bracewell J.; *A.E.* v. *Staffordshire County Council* [1995] 2 F.C.R. 84, Kirkwood J.; *M.* v. *Birmingham City Council* [1994] 2 FLR 141, Stuart-White J.; *M. (A Minor) (Secure Accommodation Order), Re* [1995] 2 W.L.R. 302, C.A.; *M. (A Minor), Re* [1995] 5–6 FLR 108, C.A.

s. 26, regs. 95/1398.

s. 26, see *R.* v. *Brent London Borough, ex p. S.* [1994] 1 FLR 203, C.A.; *R.* v. *Kingston-upon-Thames Royal Borough, ex p. T.* [1994] 1 FLR 798, Ward J.; *R.* v. *Barnet London Borough Council, ex p. B.* [1994] 1 FLR 592, Auld J.; *Sawyers* v. *Brent London Borough* [1994] C.O.D. 416, C.A.

s. 27, amended: 1995, c. 17, sch. 1.

s. 27, see *R.* v. *Brent London Borough, ex p. S.* [1994] 1 FLR 203, C.A.

s. 29, amended: 1995, c. 17, schs. 1, 2.

s. 31, amended: 1995, c. 36, sch. 4 (S.).

s. 31, see *M. (A Minor) (Appeal) (No. 2), Re* [1994] 1 FLR 59, C.A.; *J. (Minors) (Care: Care Plan), Re* [1994] 1 FLR 253, Wall J.; *E. (A Minor) (Care Order: Contact), Re* [1994] 1 FLR 146, C.A.; *T. (A Minor) (Care or Supervision Order), Re* [1994] 1 FLR 146, C.A.; *G. (A Minor) (Care Order: Threshold Conditions), Re; sub nom. G. (A Minor) (Care Proceedings), Re* [1994] 3 W.L.R. 1211, Wall J.; *R. (Minors) (Care Proceedings: Care Plan), Re* [1994] 2 F.C.R. 136, Wall J.; *Birmingham City Council* v. *D.; Birmingham City Council* v. *M.* [1994] 2 FLR 502, Thorpe J.; *Hackney London Borough* v. *G.* [1994] 2 F.C.R. 216, Wall J.; *B. (Minors) (Care Proceedings), Re* [1994] 1 F.C.R. 471, Hollings J.; *W. (A Minor) (Interim Care Order), Re* [1994] 2 FLR 892, C.A.; *C. (A Minor) (Interim Care), Re* [1994] 1 F.C.R. 447, Balcombe L.J. sitting as a judge of the Family Division; *D.H. (A Minor) (Child Abuse), Re* [1994] 1 FLR 679, Wall J.; *S. (Minors) (Inherent Jurisdiction: Ouster), Re* [1994] 1 FLR 623, Connell J.; *F. (A Minor), Re* (94/6637/f; 94/7325/F; 94/0986/F), January 30, 1995, C.A.; *M.* v. *Warwickshire County Council* [1994] 2 FLR 593, Thorpe J.; *R. and G. (Minors) (Interim Care or Supervision Orders), Re* [1994] 1 FLR 793, Ewbank J.; *H. (A Minor) (Care or*

CAP.

1989—cont.

41. Children Act 1989—*cont.*
Residence Order), Re [1994] 2 FLR 80, Hollis J.; *M.* v. *Birmingham City Council* [1994] 2 FLR 141, Stuart-White J.; *A. (A Minor) (Supervision Order: Extension), Re* [1995] 1 W.L.R. 482, C.A.; *C. (A Minor), Re, The Independent*, August 7, 1995, Douglas Brown J.; *M. (A Minor) (Care Proceedings: Appeal), Re* [1995] 1 F.C.R. 417, C.A.; *X. (Minors)* v. *Bedfordshire County Council* [1995] 3 W.L.R. 152, H.L.; *L. (A Minor), Re*, May 22, 1995, C.A.; *A. (A Minor) (Supervision Order: Extension), Re* [1995] 1 All E.R. 401, C.A.

s. 32, see *A. and B. (Minors) (No. 2), Re* [1995] 1 FLR 351, Wall J.

s. 33, see *G. (A Minor) (Parental Responsibility Order), Re* [1994] 1 FLR 504, C.A.; *S. (A Minor) (Care: Contact Order), Re* [1994] 2 FLR 222, C.A.

s. 34, see *E. (A Minor) (Care Order: Contact), Re* [1994] 1 FLR 146, C.A.; *M. (Minors in Care) (Contact: Grandmother's Application), Re, The Times*, April 21, 1995, C.A.; *E. (Adoption: Freeing Order), Re* [1995] 1 FLR 382, C.A.; *B. (Minors) (Care Proceedings), Re* [1994] 1 F.C.R. 471, Hollings J.; *N. (Contested Care Application), Re* [1994] 2 FLR 992, Thorpe J.; *Y. (Child Orders: Restricting Applications), Re* [1994] 2 FLR 699, Thorpe J.; *S. (Minors) (Inherent Jurisdiction: Ouster), Re* [1994] 1 FLR 623, Connell J.; *O. (A Minor) (Wasted Costs Application), Re* [1994] 2 FLR 842, Connell J.; *Boyle* v. *United Kingdom* [1994] 2 F.C.R. 822, European Ct. H.R.; *S. (A Minor) (Care: Contact Order), Re* [1994] 2 FLR 222, C.A.; see *B. (A Minors) (Contact), Re* [1994] 2 FLR 1, C.A.; *F.* v. *Cambridgeshire County Council* [1995] 1 FLR 516, Stuart-White J.

s. 35, see *A. (A Minor) (Supervision Order: Extension), Re* [1995] 1 W.L.R. 482, C.A.

s. 37, see *R.* v. *Kingston-upon-Thames Royal Borough, ex p. T.* [1994] 1 FLR 798, Ward J.; *R. (Minors) (Care Proceedings: Care Plan), Re* [1994] 2 F.C.R. 136, Wall J.; *W.* v. *Wakefield City Council* [1994] 2 F.C.R. 564, Wall J.; *CE (Section 37 Direction), Re* [1995] 1 FLR 26, Wall J.

s. 38, see *J. (Minors) (Care: Care Plan), Re* [1994] 1 FLR 253, Wall J.; *F. (A Minor) (Care Order: Procedure), Re* [1994] 1 FLR 240, Wall J.; *R. (Minors) (Care Proceedings: Care Plan), Re* [1994] 2 F.C.R. 136, Wall J.; *S.* v. *Merton London Borough* [1994] 1 F.C.R. 186, Ward J.; *S. (Minors) (Inherent Jurisdiction: Ouster), Re* [1994] 1 FLR 623, Connell J.; *R. and G. (Minors) (Interim Care or Supervision Orders), Re* [1994] 1 FLR 793, Ewbank J.; *HIV Tests (Note), Re* [1994] 2 FLR 116, Singer J.; *M.* v. *Birmingham City Council* [1994] 2 FLR 141, Stuart-White J.; *A. (A Minor) (Supervision Order: Extension), Re* [1995] 1 W.L.R. 482, C.A.; *L. (A Minor), Re*, May 22, 1995, C.A.

s. 39, see *S.C. (A Minor) (Leave to Seek Residence Orders), Re* [1994] 1 FLR 96, Booth J.; *W. (A Minor) (Interim Care Order), Re* [1994] 2 FLR 892, C.A.; *C. (A Minor) (Interim Care), Re* [1994] 1 F.C.R. 447, Balcombe L.J. sitting as a judge of the Family Division; *T. and E. (Proceedings: Conflicting Interests), Re* [1995] 1 FLR 581, Wall J.

s. 40, see *M. (A Minor) (Appeal: Interim Care Order) (No. 1), Re* [1994] 1 FLR 54, C.A.

s. 41, see *S.C. (A Minor) (Leave to Seek Residence Orders), Re* [1994] 1 FLR 96, Booth J.; *W.* v. *Wakefield City Council* [1994] 2 F.C.R. 564, Wall J.; *W. (A Minor) (Contact), Re* [1994] 1 FLR 843, Wall J.; *M. (Minors) (Care Proceedings: Child's Wishes), Re* [1994] 1 FLR 749, Wall J.; *CE (Section 37 Direction), Re* [1995] 1 FLR 26, Wall J.

s. 42, see *T. (A Minor) (Guardian Ad Litem: Case Record), Re* [1994] 1 FLR 632, C.A.

s. 47, amended: 1995, c. 17, sch. 1.

s. 51, amended: 1995, c. 36, sch. 4 (S.).

s. 79, amended: 1995, c. 36, sch. 4 (S.).

s. 80, amended: 1995, c. 17, sch. 1.

s. 81, see *R.* v. *Barnet London Borough Council, ex p. B.* [1994] 1 FLR 592, Auld J.

s. 84, see *R.* v. *Brent London Borough, ex p. S.* [1994] 1 FLR 203, C.A.; *R.* v. *Barnet London Borough Council, ex p. B.* [1994] 1 FLR 592, Auld J.; *Sawyers* v. *Brent London Borough* [1994] C.O.D. 416, C.A.

s. 85, amended: 1995, c. 17, sch. 1.

s. 91, see *Hackney London Borough* v. *G.* [1994] 2 F.C.R. 216, Wall J.; *Y. (Child Orders: Restricting Applications), Re* [1994] 2 FLR 699, Thorpe J.; *W. (Minors) (Sexual Abuse: Standard of Proof), Re* [1994] 1 FLR 419, C.A.; *G. (A Minor) (Parental Responsibility Order), Re* [1994] 1

CAP.

1989—cont.

41. Children Act 1989—*cont.*
FLR 504, C.A.; *O. (A Minor) (Wasted Costs Application), Re* [1994] 2 FLR 842, Connell J.; *B. (A Minors) (Contact), Re* [1994] 2 FLR 1, C.A.; *S. (A Minor), Re* (CCFMI 94/1097/F), May 1, 1995, C.A.; *N. (A Minor) (Section 91(4) of the Children Act 1989), Re*, October 5, 1995, C.A.
s. 92, see *C. (A Minor) (Contribution Notice), Re* [1994] 1 FLR 111, Ward J.
s. 94, see *P.* v. *P. (Periodical Payments: Appeals), The Times*, December 19, 1994, Bracewell J.; *S.* v. *Merton London Borough* [1994] 1 F.C.R. 186, Ward J.; *P. (A Minor) (Parental Responsibility Order), Re* [1994] 1 FLR 578, Wilson J.; *J. (A Minor) (Residence), Re* [1994] 1 FLR 369, Singer J.; *M. (Section 94 Appeals), Re* [1995] 1 FLR 546, C.A.; *R.* v. *High Peak Magistrates' Court, ex p. B.* [1995] 1 FLR 568, Cazalet J.; *B.* v. *B. (Periodical Payments: Transitional Provisions)* [1995] 1 FLR 459, Douglas Brown J.
s. 98, see *A. and B. (Minors) (No. 2), Re* [1995] 1 FLR 351, Wall J.; *K. (Minors) (Care Proceedings: Disclosure), Re* [1994] 2 F.C.R. 805, Booth J.
s. 100, see *Birmingham City Council* v. *D.; Birmingham City Council* v. *M.* [1994] 2 FLR 502, Thorpe J.; *S. (Minors) (Inherent Jurisdiction: Ouster), Re* [1994] 1 FLR 623, Connell J.; *Devon County Council* v. *S.* [1994] 1 FLR 355, Thorpe J.; *Devon County Council* v. *S.* [1995] 1 All E.R. 243, Thorpe J.
s. 104, regs. 94/3157; 95/1398.
s. 105, repealed in pt.: 1995, c. 17, sch. 3.
s. 105, amended: 1995, c. 17, schs. 1, 2.
s. 105, see *A.* v. *A (A Minor: Financial Provision)* [1994] 1 FLR 657, Ward J.; *C.* v. *Salford City Council* [1994] 2 FLR 926, Hale J.; *S. (A Minor) (Care: Contact Order), Re* [1994] 2 FLR 222, C.A.
Pt. IV, see *L.* v. *L. (Minors) (Separate Representation)* [1994] 1 FLR 156, C.A.
sch. 1, see *C. (A Minor) (Contribution Notice), Re* [1994] 1 FLR 111, Ward J.; *F. (Minors), Re* (1993) (1994) 26 H.L.R. 354, C.A.; *T.* v. *S. (Financial Provision for Children)* [1994] 1 F.C.R. 743, Johnson J.; *A.* v. *A. (A Minor: Financial Provision)* [1994] 1 FLR 657, Ward J.; *D. (A Minor), Re* (LTA 94/6672/F), April 6, 1995, C.A. *B.* v. *B. (Periodical Payments: Transitional Provisions)* [1995] 1 FLR 459, Douglas Brown J.
sch. 2, amended: 1995, c. 18, sch. 2.
sch. 2, see *R.* v. *Brent London Borough Council, ex p. S.* [1994] 1 FLR 203, C.A.; see *C. (A Minor) (Contribution Notice), Re* [1994] 1 FLR 111, Ward J.; *G. (Minors) (Care: Leave to Place Outside Jurisdiction), Re* [1994] 2 FLR 301, Thorpe J.; *R.* v. *Barnet London Borough Council, ex p. B.* [1994] 1 FLR 592, Auld J.
sch. 3, see *T. (A Minor) (Care or Supervision Order), Re* [1994] 1 FLR 103, C.A.; *W. (A Minor) (Interim Care Order), Re* [1994] 2 FLR 892, C.A.; *C. (A Minor) (Interim Care), Re* [1994] 1 F.C.R. 447, Balcombe L.J. sitting as a judge of the Family Division; *M.* v. *Warwickshire County Council* [1994] 2 FLR 593, Thorpe J.; *R. and G. (Minors) (Interim Care or Supervision Orders), Re* [1994] 1 FLR 793, Ewbank J.; *H. (Supervision Order), Re* [1994] 2 FLR 979, Bracewell J.; *A. (A Minor) (Supervision Order: Extension), Re* [1995] 1 All E.R. 401, C.A.
sch. 5, regs. 95/1398.
sch. 6, regs. 95/2015.
sch. 8, amended: 1995, c. 36, sch. 4 (S.).
sch. 9, amended: 1995, c. 36, s. 37.
sch. 10, see *C. (Minor) (Adoption: Parties), Re, The Times*, June 1, 1995, C.A.
sch. 11, order 94/3138.
sch. 13, repealed in pt.: S.R. 1995 No. 755; 1995, c. 36, sch. 5; order 95/756.
sch. 14, see *W. (Minors) (Sexual Abuse: Standard of Proof), Re* [1994] 1 FLR 419, C.A.; *B. (A Minors) (Contact), Re* [1994] 2 FLR 1, C.A.; *B.* v. *B. (Periodical Payments: Transitional Provisions)* [1995] 1 FLR 459, Douglas Brown J.

42. Local Government and Housing Act 1989.
Commencement order: 95/841.
regs. 95/838, 839.
s. 2, repealed in pt.: 1994, c. 39, schs. 13, 14 (S.).
s. 2, amended: order 95/789.
s. 4, regs. 94/2825; 95/101.
s. 4, amended: 1994, c. 39, schs. 13, 14; order 95/789.
s. 5, repealed in pt.: 1994, c. 39, schs. 13, 14; 1995, c. 25, sch. 24.
s. 5, amended: order 95/789.
s. 7, amended: 1995, c. 50, sch. 13.
s. 7, repealed in pt.: 1995, c. 50, sch. 7.
s. 8, amended: *ibid.*, sch. 13 (S.).
s. 9, amended: 1994, c. 39, sch. 13 (S.); repealed in pt.: 1994, c. 39, sch. 14 (S.).
s. 13, repealed in pt.: 1995, c. 25, sch. 24.
s. 14, repealed in pt.: 1994, c. 39, sch. 13 (S.).
s. 14, amended: 1994, c. 39, sch. 13 (S.); 1995, c. 36, sch. 4 (S.).
s. 18, order 95/615; regs. 95/701 (S.), 912 (S.).

CAP.

1989—cont.

42. Local Government and Housing Act 1989—*cont.*
s. 18, amended: order 95/789.
s. 21, repealed in pt.: 1995, c. 25, sch. 24.
s. 21, amended: 1994, c. 39, sch. 13 (S.); 1995, c. 25, sch. 10.
s. 31, amended: 1994, c. 39, sch. 13 (S.).
s. 39, order 95/849, 1431.
s. 39, repealed in pt.: 1995, c. 25, sch. 24.
s. 39, amended: 1995, c. 25, sch. 10; regs. 94/2825; 95/101.
s. 40, regs. 95/850.
s. 43, amended: regs. 95/101, 1041.
ss. 45, 46, amended: order 95/1041.
s. 48, regs. 95/101.
s. 49, amended: regs. 95/535, 850.
s. 51, regs. 95/850.
s. 53, amended: orders 95/1041; 95/105.
s. 54, order 95/1041.
s. 56, amended: orders 95/105.
s. 58, regs. 95/101.
ss. 59, 61, regs. 95/850, 1526.
ss. 64, 66, regs. 95/850.
s. 67, order 95/849.
s. 67, repealed in pt.: 1995, c. 25, sch. 24.
s. 67, amended: 1995, c. 25, schs. 8, 10.
ss. 70, 71, order 95/849.
s. 86, amended: regs. 94/2825.
ss. 102, 137, 138, regs. 94/2765; 95/857.
s. 151, amended: 1994, c. 39, sch. 13 (S.).
s. 152, repealed in pt.: 1995, c. 25, sch. 24.
s. 152, 1994, c. 39, sch. 13 (S.); amended: 1995, c. 25, sch. 8.
s. 155, amended and repealed in pt.: 1994, c. 39, sch. 13 (S.).
ss. 157, 170, amended: 1994, c. 39, sch. 13 (S.).
s. 190, order 95/615; regs. 95/101, 701 (S.), 850, 857, 912 (S.).
s. 191, regs. 95/850, 857.
s. 195, order 95/841.
sch. 1, repealed in pt.: 1994, c. 39, sch. 14 (S.); 1995, c. 25, sch. 24.
sch. 3, amended: regs. 95/101, 850; order 95/1041.
sch. 6, repealed in pt.: 1994, c. 39, sch. 13 (S.).
sch. 11, repealed in pt.: 1994, c. 39, sch. 13 (S.); 1995, c. 36, sch. 5.

44. Opticians Act 1989.
s. 3, order 94/2579.
s. 16, amended: order 94/3327.
s. 37, repealed in pt.: 1995, c. 17, sch. 3.

45. Prisons (Scotland) Act 1989.
s. 8, amended: 1994, c. 39, sch. 13.
s. 11, amended: 1995, c. 40, sch. 4.
s. 14, repealed in pt.: 1994, c. 39, sch. 14.
s. 14, amended: 1994, c. 39, sch. 13.
s. 16, amended: 1994, c. 39, sch. 13.
s. 18, rules 95/1272, 1273.
s. 21, amended: 1995, c. 40, sch. 4.
ss. 22, 28, amended: order 95/910.
s. 39, amended: 1995, c. 40, sch. 4.
s. 40, amended: 1995, c. 20, s. 69; 1995, c. 40, sch. 4.

CAP.

1989—cont.

45. Prisons (Scotland) Act 1989—*cont.*
s. 40A, amended: 1995, c. 40, sch. 4.
s. 43, amended: 1995, c. 40, sch. 4.
sch. 2, C.: 1995, c. 46, s. 208.

1990

1. Capital Allowances Act 1990.
s. 2, see *Gray (Inspector of Taxes)* v. *Seymours Garden Centre (Horticulture), The Times*, May 31, 1995, C.A.
ss. 3, 4, amended: 1995, c. 4, s. 99.
s. 9, repealed in pt.: 1995, c. 4, sch. 29.
s. 9, amended: 1995, c. 4, sch. 6.
s. 10D, added: 1995, c. 4, s. 100.
s. 11, amended: regs. 95/352.
s. 15, amended: 1995, c. 4, sch. 6.
s. 18, amended: 1995, c. 4, ss. 99, 101.
s. 20, amended: 1995, c. 4, s. 99.
s. 21, amended: 1995, c. 4, s. 99.
s. 25, amended: regs. 95/352.
s. 28, substituted: 1995, c. 4, sch. 8.
s. 29, amended: 1995, c. 4, sch. 6.
ss. 31, 33, amended: regs. 95/352.
s. 33A, added: 1995, c. 4, s. 94.
s. 33B, added: 1995, c. 4, s. 94.
s. 33C, added: 1995, c. 4, s. 95.
ss. 33D, 33E, added: 1995, c. 4, s. 96.
s. 33F, added: 1995, c. 4, s. 97.
ss. 37, 53, 55, amended: regs. 95/352.
ss. 67, 73, amended: 1995, c. 4, sch. 6.
s. 77, amended: regs. 95/352.
s. 92, repealed in pt.: 1995, c. 4, sch. 29.
s. 92, amended: 1995, c. 4, sch. 6.
s. 129, amended: regs. 95/352.
s. 132, repealed in pt.: 1995, c. 4, sch. 29.
s. 132, amended: 1995, c. 4, sch. 6.
s. 141, amended: regs. 95/352.
s. 151, amended: 1995, c. 4, s. 100.
s. 152A, amended: 1995, c. 4, sch. 9; regs. 95/171.
s. 153, order 95/611.
s. 156, amended: 1995, c. 4, s. 99.
s. 161, amended: 1995, c. 4, s. 41.

5. Criminal Justice (International Co-operation) Act 1990.
s. 3, see *R.* v. *Central Criminal Court, ex p. Hunt, The Times*, February 21, 1995, D.C.
s. 5, order 95/1709.
s. 5, amended: 1995, c. 21, sch. 13.
s. 7, see *R.* v. *Southwark Crown Court, ex p. Sorsky Defries, The Times*, July 21, 1995, D.C.; *R.* v. *Central Criminal Court, ex p. Propend Finance Property* [1994] C.O.D. 386, D.C.
s. 9, amended: 1995, c. 11, s. 14; 1995, c. 20, sch. 6 (S.); 1995, c. 40, sch. 4 (S.).
s. 15, repealed: 1995, c. 40, sch. 5 (S.).
s. 15, amended: 1995, c. 20, sch. 6 (S.).
s. 17, repealed: 1995, c. 20, schs. 6 (S.), 7 (S.).
s. 25, see *R.* v. *Uxbridge Magistrates' Court, ex p. Henry* [1994] Crim.L.R. 581, D.C.

CAP.

1990—cont.

5. Criminal Justice (International Co-operation) Act 1990—*cont.*

sch. 1, amended: 1995, c. 40, sch. 4 (S.).
sch. 4, repealed: 1995, c. 40, sch. 5 (S.).

6. Education (Student Loans) Act 1990.

s. 1, sch. 2, regs. 94/3045.

8. Town and Country Planning Act 1990.

s. 1, repealed in pt.: 1995, c. 25, sch. 24.
s. 1, amended: 1995, c. 25, sch. 10.
s. 2, repealed in pt.: 1995, c. 25, sch. 24.
s. 2, amended: 1995, c. 25, sch. 22.
s. 4, repealed: 1995, c. 25, sch. 24.
s. 4A, repealed in pt.: 1995, c. 25, sch. 24.
s. 4A, added: 1995, c. 25, s. 67.
s. 35, see *Landmatch* v. *Secretary of State for the Environment and Suffolk County Council and Forest Heath District Council; sub nom. Landmatch* v. *Secretary of State for the Environment; R.* v. *Same, ex p. Landmatch* (1993) (1994) 68 P.&C.R. 149, Mr Malcolm Spence, Q.C., sitting as a deputy judge; *Alfred McAlpine Homes (North)* v. *Secretary of State for the Environment* [1994] N.P.C. 138, C.A.
s. 35A, see *Landmatch* v. *Secretary of State for the Environment and Suffolk County Council and Forest Heath District Council; sub nom. Landmatch* v. *Secretary of State for the Environment; R.* v. *Same, ex p. Landmatch* (1993) (1994) 68 P.&C.R. 149, Mr Malcolm Spence, Q.C., sitting as a deputy judge.
s. 36, orders 95/600, 610.
s. 36, amended: order 95/187.
s. 37, orders 95/600, 610.
s. 37, amended: orders 95/187, 493, 1769, 1770, 1771, 1772, 1773, 1774, 1775, 1776, 1779.
s. 38, order 95/600.
s. 38, amended: orders 95/493, 610, 1769, 1770, 1771, 1772, 1773, 1774, 1775, 1776, 1779.
s. 50, orders 95/600, 610.
s. 54, see *David Wilson Homes (Southern)* v. *South Somerset District Council and Secretary of State for the Environment* [1994] J.P.L. 63, C.A.; *Gateshead Metropolitan Borough Council* v. *Secretary of the State for the Environment, Evans of Leeds and Safeway* [1994] J.P.L. 55, Roy Vandermeer, Q.C., sitting as a deputy judge.
s. 54A, see *Crawley Borough Council* v. *Lynton* (1994) 9 P.A.D. 199; *Elmbridge Borough Council* v. *Secretary of State for the Environment* [1994] J.P.L. 242, Roy Vandermeer, Q.C., sitting as a deputy judge; *Spelthorne Borough Council* v. *Secretary of State for the Environment* (1994) 68 P.&C.R. 211, Mr. David Keene, Q.C., sitting as a deputy judge; *Trustees of the Viscount Folkestone 1963 Settlement (Coop)* v. *Secretary of State for the Environment* (1994) 68 P.&C.R. 241, Mr. Gerald Moriarty, Q.C., sitting as a deputy judge; *St. George Developments and Kew Riverside Developments* v. *Secretary of State for the Environment and Richmond London Borough Council* [1994] NPC 121, Mr. N. McCleod, Q.C., sitting as a deputy judge; *St George Developments* v. *Secretary of State for the Environment* [1994] 3 P.L.R. 33, Sir Nigel Macleod, Q.C. sitting as a deputy judge.
s. 55, see *Croydon London Borough Council* v. *Gladden* [1994] 1 PLR 30, C.A.
s. 59, orders 94/678, 2595; 95/298, 389, 418, 419, 2899.
s. 60, orders 94/678, 2595; 95/298, 418.
s. 61, orders 94/2595; 95/298, 419.
s. 65, orders 94/678, 2595.
s. 65, amended: 1995, c. 8, sch.
s. 70, see *David Wilson Homes (Southern)* v. *South Somerset District Council and Secretary of State for the Environment* [1994] J.P.L. 63, C.A.; *Elmbridge Borough Council* v. *Secretary of State of the Environment* [1994] J.P.L. 242, Roy Vandermeer, Q.C., sitting as a deputy judge; *Tesco Stores* v. *Secretary of State for the Environment*, *The Times*, May 13, 1995, H.L.; *Tesco Stores* v. *Environment Secretary* [1995] 1 W.L.R. 759, H.L.
s. 71, orders 95/418, 419.
s. 72, amended: regs. 95/1139.
s. 73, order 95/419.
s. 73, see *Swale Borough Council* v. *Secretary of State for the Environment and Wards Construction (Medway)* [1994] J.P.L. 236, Mr. Moriarty, Q.C., sitting as a deputy judge; *R.* v. *Secretary of State for the Environment, ex p. Corby Borough Council* [1994] 1 PLR 38, Pill J.; *Sevenoaks District Council* v. *Secretary of State for the Environment and Geer* (1994) 69 P. & C.R. 87, Gerald Moriaty, Q.C. sitting as a deputy judge.
s. 73A, see *Sevenoaks District Council* v. *Secretary of State for the Environment and Geer* (1994) 69 P. & C.R. 87, Gerald Moriaty, Q.C. sitting as a deputy judge.
s. 74, orders 94/678, 2595; 95/418, 419.
s. 77, order 95/419.

CAP.

1990—cont.

8. Town and Country Planning Act 1990—*cont.*

s. 77, see *Crawley Borough Council* v. *Lynton* (1994) 9 P.A.D. 199; *Wycombe District Council* v. *McAlpine* (1994) 9 P.A.D. 166.

s. 78, see *Wyre Forest District Council* v. *British Telecommunications* (1994) 9 P.A.D. 157; *North West Leicestershire District Council* v. *Hutchison Microtel* (1994) 9 P.A.D. 252; *Epping Forest District Council* v. *Greys Milking Sheep* (refs: T/APP/J1535/A/94/232621/P5 and /235371/P5) (1994) 9 P.A.D. 754; *Worcester City Council* v. *Worcester Consolidated Municipal Charity* (Ref: T/APP/D1835/A/94/234623/P2) (1994) 9 P.A.D. 723; *Walsall Metropolitan Borough Council* v. *West Midlands Cooperative Council* (Ref: T/APP/V4630/A/93/229927/P7) (1994) 9 P.A.D. 677; *Hounslow London Borough Council* v. *McDonalds Restaurant* (Ref: T/APP/F5540/A/93/23041P5) (1994) 9 P.A.D. 646; *St. George Developments* v. *Secretary of State for the Environment* [1994] 3 P.L.R. 33, Sir Nigel Macleod, Q.C. sitting as a deputy judge.

s. 79, order 95/419.

s. 90, amended: 1995, c. 25, sch. 10.

s. 101, amended: 1995, c. 25, sch. 10.

s. 105, repealed: 1995, c. 25, s. 96, sch. 24.

s. 106, see *South Oxfordshire District Council* v. *Secretary of State for the Environment* [1994] N.P.C. 57, Sir Graham Eyre, Q.C.; *Epping Forest District Council* v. *Greys Milking Sheep* (refs: T/APP/J1535/A/94/232621/P5 and /235371/P5) (1994) 9 P.A.D. 754; *R.* v. *South Northamptonshire District Council, ex p. Crest Homes* (1995) 93 L.G.R. 205, C.A.; *T.* v. *Thurrock Borough Council, ex p. Tesco Stores* (1994) 92 L.G.R. 321, Schiemann J.

s. 137, see *Cook and Woodham* v. *Winchester City Council* (1994) 69 P. & C.R. 99, Lands Tribunal.

s. 147A, added: 1995, c. 25, s. 67.

s. 150, see *Jones Son & Vernon* v. *Sandwell Metropolitan Borough Council* (1995) 68 P. & C.R. 563, Lands Tribunal.

s. 169, amended: 1995, c. 25, sch. 10.

s. 170, amended: 1995, c. 25, sch. 10.

s. 171C, see *R.* v. *Teignbridge District Council, ex p. Teignmouth Quay Company*, *The Times*, December 31, 1994, Judge J.

CAP.

1990—cont.

8. Town and Country Planning Act 1990—*cont.*

s. 172, see *Bruce* v. *Secretary of State for the Environment*, *The Times*, November, 17, 1994, C.A.; *Newbury District Council* v. *Marsh* (1994) 92 L.G.R. 195, C.A.

s. 174, see *Camden London Borough Council* v. *Thresh* (1994) 9 P.A.D. 182; *Wycombe District Council* v. *McAlpine* (1994) 9 P.A.D. 166; *McAlpine (David)* v. *Secretary of State for the Environment* (CO/3417/93), November 14, 1994, Nigel MacLeod, Q.C.; *Maidstone District Council* v. *O'Neill* (Ref: T/APP/C/93/U2335/630325) (1994) 9 P.A.D. 747; *Three Rivers District Council* v. *Greenshields* (Ref: T/APP/C/92/P1490/622002) (1994) 9 P.A.D. 577; *Surrey County Council* v. *Foss* (Ref: T/APP/C/93/B3600/629193) (1994) 9 P.A.D. 670.

s. 179, see *R.* v. *Beaconsfield Magistrates, ex p. South Buckinghamshire District Council* [1993] C.O.D. 357, D.C.; *R.* v. *Wicks, The Times*, April 19, 1995, C.A.; *R.* v. *Briscoe* (1994) 15 Cr.App.R. (S.) 699, C.A.

s. 187B, see *Croydon London Borough Council* v. *Gladden* [1994] 1 PLR 30, C.A.; *Runnymede Borough Council* v. *Harwood*; *sub nom. Harwood* v. *Runnymede Borough Council* [1994] 1 PLR 22, C.A.

s. 188, order 95/419.

ss. 191, 192, see *Bailey (Alan Charles)* v. *Secretary of State for the Environment* (QBCOF 93/0405/D), December 15, 1994, C.A.

ss. 193, 196, order 95/419.

s. 199, see *Evans* v. *Waverley Borough Council, The Times*, July 18, 1995, C.A.

s. 206, see *HB Investments* v. *Secretary of State for the Environment* [1994] J.P.L. 45, C.A.

ss. 220, 224, see *Gillingham Borough Council* v. *Cock* [1993] C.O.D. 355, D.C.

s. 228, see *Regalbourne* v. *East Lindsey District Council* [1994] RA 1, C.A.; *Elmbridge Borough Council* v. *Secretary of State for the Environment* [1994] J.P.L. 242, Roy Vandermeer, Q.C., sitting as a deputy judge; *Low* v. *Secretary of State for Wales and Glyndwr D.C.* [1994] J.P.L. 45, C.A.; *HB Investments* v. *Secretary of State for the Environment* [1994] J.P.L. 45, C.A.; *Murphy* v. *Secretary of State for the Environment and Torfaen Borough Council* [1994] J.P.L. 156, David

CAP.

1990—cont.

8. Town and Country Planning Act 1990—*cont.*

Widdicombe, Q.C., sitting as a deputy judge; *Carter* v. *Secretary of State for the Environment and Mid-Sussex District Council* [1994] J.P.L. 145, Roy Vandermeer, Q.C., sitting as a deputy judge.

s. 233, see *R.* v. *Thurrock Borough Council, ex p. Blue Circle Industries* (1994) 69 P. & C.R. 79, C.A.

s. 244, repealed in pt.: 1995, c. 25, sch. 24.

s. 244A, added: 1995, c. 25, sch. 8.

s. 252, repealed in pt.: c. 44, sch. 1.

s. 252, amended: 1995, c. 25, sch. 10; 1995, c. 45, sch. 4.

s. 253, amended: 1995, c. 25, sch. 10.

s. 259, regs. 95/451.

s. 262, amended: 1995, c. 45, sch. 4.

s. 265, amended: 1995, c. 45, sch. 4.

s. 285, see *R.* v. *Avon County Council, ex p. Valentine* [1994] EGCS 71, C.A.

s. 287, see *Swan Hill Developments* v. *Southend-on-Sea Borough Council* [1994] 3 P.L.R. 14, Mr Malcolm Spence, Q.C. sitting as a deputy judge.

s. 288, see *Ravebuild* v. *Secretary of State for the Environment* (CO/2675/94), November 21, 1994, Jeremy Sullivan, Q.C.; *O'Brien* v. *Secretary of State for the Environment and Fenland District Council* (1994) 68 P.&C.R. 314, Hidden J.; *Morbaine* v. *Secretary of State for the Environment and South Northampton District Council* (1995) 68 P. & C.R. 525, Mr David Widdicombe, Q.C. sitting as a deputy judge; *British Broadcasting Corp., Vodaphone Orange Personal Communications* v. *Secretary of State for the Environment and Bristol City Council* (CO/798/95), August 18, 1995, R. Purchas, Q.C.; *South Northamptonshire District Council* v. *Secretary of State for the Environment* [1995] NPC 45, C.A.

s. 289, see *Huggett* v. *Secretary of State for the Environment; Wendy Fair Markets* v. *Same; Bello* v. *Same, The Times*, March 1, 1995, C.A.

s. 299, regs. 95/1139.

s. 303A, added: 1995, c. 49, s.1.

ss. 305, 306, 330, amended: 1995, c. 25, sch. 10.

s. 333, orders 94/678, 2595; 95/389, 418, 419, 2899; regs. 95/451, 1139, 2259.

s. 333, amended: 1995, c. 25, sch. 10.

s. 336, regs. 95/2259.

s. 336, amended: 1995, c. 25, sch. 10; 1995, c. 45, sch. 4.

sch. 1, repealed in pt.: 1995, c. 25, sch. 24.

sch. 1, amended: 1995, c. 25, sch. 10.

sch. 5, amended: 1995, c. 25, sch. 22.

CAP.

1990—cont.

8. Town and Country Planning Act 1990—*cont.*

sch. 6, amended: 1995, c. 25, sch. 22.

sch. 6, see *South Northamptonshire District Council* v. *Secretary of State for the Environment* [1995] NPC 45, C.A.

sch. 8, amended: 1995, c. 25, sch. 10.

sch. 9, see *R.* v. *Secretary of State for Wales, ex p. Mid-Glamorgan County Council, The Times*, February 10, 1995, C.A.

sch. 13, amended: 1995, c. 25, sch. 10.

sch. 14, regs. 95/451.

sch. 14, repealed in pt.: 1995, c. 44, sch. 1.

sch. 14, amended: 1995, c. 25, sch. 10.

9. Planning (Listed Buildings and Conservation Areas) Act 1990.

s. 8, see *R.* v. *Secretary of State for the Environment, ex p. South Northamptonshire District Council, The Times*, March 9, 1995, C.A.

s. 27, see *Shimizu (U.K.)* v. *Westminster City Council* (1994) 20 E.G. 154, Lands Tribunal.

s. 32, amended: 1995, c. 25, sch. 10.

s. 39, see *O'Brien* v. *Secretary of State for the Environment and Fenland District Council* (1994) 68 P.&C.R. 314, Hidden J.

s. 66, repealed in pt.: 1995, c. 25, sch. 24.

s. 66, see *Heatherington (U.K.)* v. *Secretary of State for the Environment* (1995) 6 P. & C.R. 374, David Keene Q.C. sitting as a deputy judge.

s. 72, see *Sherwood* v. *Secretary of State for the Environment and Islington London Borough Council* (CO/1075/95), August 16, 1995, R. Purchas, Q.C.

s. 74, see *Kent County Council* v. *Secretary of State for the Environment and Canterbury City Council* (1995) 68 P. & C.R. 520, Mr Gerald Moriaty, Q.C. sitting as a deputy judge.

s. 79, amended: 1995, c. 25, sch. 10.

s. 93, amended: 1995, c. 25, sch. 10.

sch. 2, amended: 1995, c. 25, sch. 10.

sch. 4, repealed in pt.: 1995, c. 25, sch. 24.

sch. 4, amended: 1995, c. 25, sch. 10.

10. Planning (Hazardous Substance) Act 1990.

s. 3, repealed in pt.: 1995, c. 25, sch. 24.

11. Planning (Consequential Provisions) Act 1990.

sch. 2, repealed in pt.: 1995, c. 23, sch. 8; 1995, c. 25, sch. 24.

sch. 2, C.: 1995, c. 23, sch. 8.

15. Water Act 1990.

s. 107, see *Attorney-General's Reference (No. 1 of 1994), Re* (94/0097/S1), January 19, 1995, C.A.

CAP.

1990—cont.

16. Food Safety Act 1990.
regs. 95/1955.
s. 1, amended: regs. 94/3144.
s. 5, regs. 95/539, 540.
s. 5, amended: 1994, c. 39, sch. 13 (S.).
s. 6, regs. 94/2782, 2783; 95/77, 360, 484 (S.), 537 (S.), 539, 540, 613, 614, 1086, 1122, 1372 (S.), 1544, 1763, 2200.
s. 12, see *East Kilbride District Council* v. *King* (Sh.Ct.), 1994 S.C.L.R. 950.
s. 16, regs. 94/1486, 2628, 2782, 2783, 3082; 95/77, 236, 360, 539, 540, 613, 614, 1029, 1086, 1440; orders 94/3082; 95/1372 (S.).
s. 17, regs. 94/2782, 2783, 3082; 95/77, 236, 360, 361, 484 (S.), 539, 540, 732, 1029, 1086, 1440; orders 94/3082; 95/1372 (S.).
s. 18, regs. 94/2782, 2783.
s. 19, regs. 95/539, 540, 1029, 1086; orders 95/1372 (S.), 2148.
s. 21, see *Cow & Gate Nutricia* v. *Westminster City Council, The Independent*, April 24, 1995, D.C.
s. 26, regs. 94/3082; 95/77, 360, 539, 540, 613, 614, 1029, 1086, 1440; orders 94/1486, 3082, 1372 (S.), 1544, 1763, 2200.
ss. 27, 28, amended: 1994, c. 39, sch. 13 (S.); regs. 94/867.
s. 31, regs. 95/360; order 95/1372 (S.).
s. 37, regs. 95/539, 540, 1029.
s. 37, amended: regs. 94/3082; 95/1086.
s. 37, see *East Kilbride District Council* v. *King* (Sh.Ct.), 1994 S.C.L.R. 950.
s. 38, see *East Kilbride District Council* v. *King* (Sh.Ct.), 1994 S.C.L.R. 950.
s. 45, regs. 94/3082; 95/361; order 95/1372 (S.).
s. 48, regs. 94/2782, 2783, 3082; 95/77, 360, 361, 539, 540, 613, 614, 1029, 1086, 1440; orders 94/1486, 3082; 95/1372 (S.), 1544, 1763, 2200.
s. 49, regs. 94/2628, 2782, 2783; 95/539, 540, 1029.
sch. 1, regs. 94/2628, 2782; 95/539, 540, 613, 1029, 1086; order 94/3082.

18. Computer Misuse Act 1990.
s. 13, amended: 1995, c. 40, sch. 4 (S.).

19. National Health Service and Community Care Act 1990.
see *R.* v. *Brent London Borough, ex p. S.* [1994] 1 FLR 203, C.A.; *R.* v. *Cleveland County Council, ex p. Ward* [1994] C.O.D. 222, D.C.
s. 1, repealed in pt.: 1995, c. 17, sch. 3.
s. 1, amended: 1995, c. 17, sch. 1.
s. 2, repealed in pt.: 1995, c. 17, sch. 3.
s. 3, repealed in pt.: 1995, c. 17, sch. 3.
s. 3, amended: 1995, c. 17, sch. 1.
s. 4, repealed in pt.: 1995, c. 17, sch. 3.
s. 4, amended: 1995, c. 17, sch. 1.
s. 5, orders 94/3173, 3174, 3175, 3176, 3177, 3178, 3179, 3180, 3181, 3182, 3183, 3184, 3185, 3186, 3197; 95/88, 92,

CAP.

1990—cont.

19. National Health Service and Community Care Act 1990—*cont.*
99, 141, 142, 143, 477, 478, 479, 480, 481, 769, 770, 792, 801, 842, 843, 844, 845, 846, 847, 848, 918, 968, 996.
s. 5, amended: 1995, c. 17, sch. 1.
s. 6, amended: 1995, c. 17, sch. 1.
s. 6, see *Gale* v. *Northern General Hospital National Health Service Trust* [1994] I.R.L.R. 292, C.A.
s. 7, repealed in pt.: regs. 95/31.
s. 7, amended: 1995, c. 17, sch. 1.
s. 8, amended: 1995, c. 17, sch. 1.
s. 9, orders 95/394, 407, 791.
s. 9, repealed in pt.: 1995, c. 17, sch. 3.
s. 11, repealed in pt.: 1995, c. 17, sch. 3.
s. 12, repealed in pt.: 1995, c. 17, sch. 3.
s. 13, repealed: 1995, c. 17, sch. 3.
s. 14, regs. 95/693.
s. 14, repealed in pt.: 1995, c. 17, sch. 3.
s. 14, amended: 1995, c. 17, sch. 1.
s. 15, regs. 95/693.
s. 15, repealed in pt.: 1995, c. 17, sch. 3.
s. 15, amended: 1995, c. 17, sch. 1.
s. 16, repealed in pt.: 1995, c. 17, sch. 3.
s. 16, amended: 1995, c. 17, sch. 1.
s. 17, repealed in pt.: 1995, c. 17, sch. 3.
s. 17, amended: 1995, c. 17, sch. 1.
s. 18, amended; 1995, c. 17, sch. 1.
s. 19, repealed: 1995, c. 17, sch. 3.
s. 20, repealed in pt.: 1995, c. 17, sch. 3.
s. 20, amended: 1995, c. 17, sch. 1.
s. 21, amended: 1995, c. 17, sch. 1.
s. 23, repealed in pt.: 1995, c. 17, sch. 3.
s. 25, repealed in pt.: 1995, c. 17, sch. 3.
s. 26, repealed in pt.: 1995, c. 17, sch. 3.
s. 46, repealed in pt.: 1995, c. 17, sch. 3.
s. 46, amended: 1995, c. 17, sch. 1.
s. 47, amended: 1995, c. 17, sch. 1.
s. 47, see *R.* v. *Gloucestershire County Council, ex p. Mahfood, The Times*, June 21, 1995, D.C.; *R.* v. *Avon County Council, ex p. M.* [1994] 2 F.L.R. 1006, Henry J.
s. 49, amended: 1995, c. 17, sch. 1.
s. 50, see *R.* v. *Avon County Council, ex p. M.* [1994] 2 F.L.R. 1006, Henry J.
s. 59, repealed in pt.: 1995, c. 17, sch. 3.
s. 60, repealed in pt.: 1995, c. 17, sch. 3.
s. 60, amended: 1995, c. 17, sch. 1.
s. 62, repealed in pt.: 1995, c. 17, sch. 3.
s. 62, amended: 1995, c. 17, sch. 1.
s. 67, order 94/2773.
s. 126, orders 95/304, 1709.
sch. 1, repealed in pt.: 1995, c. 17, sch. 3.
sch. 2, orders 94/3173, 3174, 3175, 3176, 3177, 3178, 3179, 3180, 3181, 3182, 3183, 3184, 3185, 3186, 3197; 95/769, 770, 846.
sch. 2, repealed in pt.: 1995, c. 17, sch. 3.
sch. 2, amended: orders 95/141, 142, 143, 842, 843, 844, 845, 847, 848; 1995, c. 17, sch. 1.
sch. 9, C.: 1995, c. 46, s. 307.

CAP.

1990—cont.

23. Access to Health Records Act 1990.
s. 1, amended: 1995, c. 17, sch. 1.
s. 3, amended: 1995, c. 36, sch. 4 (S.).
s. 4, amended: 1995, c. 36, sch. 4 (S.).
s. 5, amended: 1995, c. 36, sch. 4 (S.).
s. 7, repealed in pt.: 1995, c. 17, sch. 3.
s. 11, amended: 1995, c. 17, sch. 1; 1995, c. 36, sch. 4 (S.).

25. Horses (Protective Headgear for Young Riders) Act 1990.
s. 12, amended: 1995, c. 36, sch. 4 (S.).

26. Gaming (Amendment) Act 1990.
s. 2, repealed in pt.: 1995, c. 38, sch. 2.

27. Social Security Act 1990.
s. 15, regs. 95/49.

29. Finance Act 1990.
s. 8, repealed: 1995, c. 4, sch. 29.
s. 25, amended: 1995, c. 4, sch. 17.
s. 45, repealed in pt.: 1995, c. 4, sch. 29.
s. 82, repealed: 1995, c. 4, sch. 29.
ss. 115–120, repealed: 1995, c. 4, s. 159, sch. 29.
s. 128, regs. 95/925.
sch. 6, repealed in pt.: 1995, c. 4, sch. 29.
sch. 8, amended: regs. 95/171.

31. Aviation and Maritime Security Act 1990.
ss. 14, 15, 35, 45, 46, amended: 1995, c. 21, sch. 13.
s. 51, repealed: 1995, c. 21, sch. 12.
s. 51, sch. 3, repealed in pt.: c. 21, sch. 12.
sch. 3, C.: 1995, c. 21, sch. 14.

35. Enterprise and New Towns (Scotland) Act 1990.
s. 9, amended: 1995, c. 45, sch. 4.
s. 16, amended: 1995, c. 50, sch. 6.
ss. 21, 36, amended: 1994, c. 39, sch. 13.
sch. 1, repealed in pt.: 1995, c. 7, sch. 5.

36. Contracts (Applicable Law) Act 1990.
Art. 4, see *Bank of Baroda* v. *Vysya Bank* [1994] 2 Lloyd's Rep. 86, Mance J.

37. Human Fertilisation and Embryology Act 1990.
s. 30, reg. 94/2767.
s. 30, amended: rules 95/48.
s. 45, reg. 94/2767.

38. Employment Protection Act 1990.
sch. 2, see *Secretary of State for Employment* v. *Stone* [1994] I.C.R. 761, E.A.T.

40. Law Reform (Miscellaneous Provisions) (Scotland) Act 1990.
Commencement order: 95/364.
s. 12, regs. 95/2056.
s. 20, amended: 1995, c. 40, sch. 4.
s. 56, repealed: 1995, c. 40, sch. 5.
s. 56, repealed in pt.: 1995, c. 20, sch. 7.
s. 56, amended: 1995, c. 20, sch. 6.
s. 56, see *Brotherston* v. *H.M. Advocate*, 1995 S.C.C.R. 613.
s. 57, repealed: 1995, c. 40, sch. 5.

CAP.

1990—cont.

40. Law Reform (Miscellaneous Provisions) (Scotland) Act 1990—*cont.*
s. 58, repealed in pt.: 1995, c. 20, sch. 7.
s. 58, amended: 1995, c. 20, sch. 6.
s. 58, see *Brotherston* v. *H.M. Advocate*, 1995 S.C.C.R. 613.
s. 60, C.: 1995, c. 46, s. 4.
s. 62, repealed: 1995, c. 40, sch. 5.
s. 62, amended: 1994, c. 39, sch. 13; 1995, c. 20, s. 35.
s. 63, C.: 1995, c. 43, ss. 40, 41.
s. 70, see *MacKay* v. *Murphy*, 1995 S.L.T. (Sh.Ct.) 30.
s. 75, order 95/364.
sch. 4, C.: 1995, c. 43, s. 49.
sch. 6, repealed: 1995, c. 40, sch. 5.
sch. 6, amended: 1994, c. 39, sch. 13; 1995, c. 20, sch. 6.
sch. 8, repealed in pt.: 1995, c. 7, sch. 5.
sch. 8, C.: 1995, c. 39, s. 22; 1995, c. 43, s. 6.

41. Courts and Legal Services Act 1990.
Commencement order: 95/641.
s. 1, order 95/205.
s. 27, see *R.* v. *Southwark Crown Court, ex p. Tawfick* (1995) 7 Admin. L.R. 410, D.C.
s. 58, amended: order 95/1674.
ss. 113, 119, regs. 95/1676.
s. 124, order 95/641.
sch. 10, repealed in pt.: 1995, c. 21, sch. 12.
sch. 10, C.: 1995, c. 21, sch. 14.

42. Broadcasting Act 1990.
s. 13, order 94/3172.
s. 92, see *R.* v. *Radio Authority, ex p. Bull, The Times*, July 20, 1995, D.C.
s. 143, see *R.* v. *British Broadcasting Complaints Commission, ex p. Granada Television, The Times*, December 16, 1994, C.A.; *R.* v. *Broadcasting Complaints Commission, ex p. British Broadcasting Corp.* [1994] 6 Admin. L.R. 714, D.C.
s. 146, see *R.* v. *Broadcasting Complaints Commission, ex p. Granada Television, The Times*, December 16, 1994, C.A.
s. 150, see *R.* v. *Broadcasting Complaints Commission, ex p. British Broadcasting Corp.* [1994] 6 Admin. L.R. 714, D.C.
s. 200, order 94/3172.
s. 204, order 95/268.
sch. 2, amended: 1994, c. 39, sch. 13 (S.); orders 95/1924, 1925.
sch. 2, see *R.* v. *Radio Authority, ex p. Guardian Media Group; R.* v. *Radio Authority, ex p. Trans World Communications* [1995] 1 W.L.R. 334, Schiemann J.
sch. 20, S.R. 1995 No. 755.
sch. 20, C.: 1995, c. 46, s. 47.
sch. 22, S.R. 1995 No. 755.

CAP.

1990—cont.

43. Environmental Protection Act 1990.
Commencement orders: 94/2854, 3234.
see *Gateshead Metropolitan Borough Council* v. *Secretary of State for the Environment and Northumbrian Water Group* [1994] 1 PLR 85, C.A.
s. 1, amended: 1995, c. 25, sch. 22.
s. 4, repealed in pt.: 1995, c. 25, sch. 24.
s. 4, amended: 1994, c. 39, sch. 13 (S.); 1995, c. 25, sch. 22.
s. 5, repealed: 1995, c. 25, sch. 24.
s. 6, amended: 1995, c. 25, sch. 22.
s. 7, repealed in pt.: 1995, c. 25, sch. 24.
s. 7, amended: 1995, c. 25, sch. 22.
s. 8, repealed in pt.: 1995, c. 25, sch. 24.
s. 8, amended: 1995, c. 25, sch. 22.
s. 10, amended: 1995, c. 25, sch. 22.
s. 11, amended: 1995, c. 25, sch. 22.
s. 13, amended: 1995, c. 25, sch. 22.
s. 15, amended: 1995, c. 25, sch. 22.
ss. 16–18, repealed in pt.: 1995, c. 25, schs. 22, 24.
s. 19, amended: 1995, c. 25, sch. 22.
s. 20, repealed in pt.: 1995, c. 25, sch. 24.
s. 20, amended: 1995, c. 25, sch. 22.
s. 22, amended: 1995, c. 25, sch. 22.
s. 23, repealed in pt.: 1995, c. 25, sch. 24.
s. 23, amended: 1995, c. 25, sch. 22.
s. 27, amended: 1995, c. 25, sch. 22.
s. 28, repealed in pt.: 1995, c. 25, sch. 24.
s. 28, amended: 1995, c. 25, sch. 22.
s. 29, regs. 94/1056; 95/288.
s. 30, repealed in pt.: 1995, c. 25, schs. 22, 24.
s. 30, amended: 1994, c. 39, sch. 13 (S.); 1995, c. 25, sch. 22.
s. 31, repealed: 1995, c. 25, sch. 24.
s. 33, regs. 94/1056; 95/288, 1950.
s. 33, repealed in pt.: 1995, c. 25, sch. 24.
s. 33, amended: 1995, c. 25, sch. 22.
s. 34, amended: 1995, c. 25, sch. 22.
s. 35, regs. 94/1056.
s. 35, amended: 1995, c. 25, sch. 22.
s. 35A, added: 1995, c. 25, sch. 22.
s. 36, regs. 94/1056.
s. 36, repealed in pt.: 1994, c. 39, sch. 13 (S.); 1995, c. 25, sch. 24.
s. 36, amended: 1994, c. 39, sch. 13 (S.); 1995, c. 25, sch. 22.
s. 36A, added: 1995, c. 25, sch. 22.
s. 37, repealed in pt.: 1995, c. 25, sch. 24.
s. 37, amended: 1995, c. 25, sch. 22.
s. 37A, added: 1995, c. 25, sch. 22.
s. 38, amended: 1995, c. 25, sch. 22.
s. 39, repealed in pt.: 1994, c. 39, sch. 14 (S.); 1995, c. 25, sch. 24.
s. 39, amended: 1994, c. 39, sch. 13 (S.); 1995, c. 25, sch. 22.
s. 40, regs. 94/1056.
s. 40, amended: 1995, c. 25, sch. 22.
s. 41, repealed: 1995, c. 25, schs. 22, 24.
s. 42, repealed in pt.: 1995, c. 25, sch. 24.
s. 42, amended: 1995, c. 25, sch. 22.

CAP.

1990—cont.

43. Environmental Protection Act 1990—*cont.*
s. 43, regs. 94/1056.
s. 43, repealed in pt.: 1995, c. 25, sch. 24.
s. 43, amended: 1995, c. 25, sch. 22.
s. 44, substituted: 1995, c. 25, sch. 19.
ss. 44A–44B, added: 1995, c. 25, s. 92.
s. 45, regs. 94/1056.
s. 45, amended: 1994, c. 39, sch. 13 (S.).
s. 50, regs. 94/1056.
s. 50, repealed: 1995, c. 25, schs. 22, 24.
s. 52, regs. 95/476.
s. 53, repealed in pt.: 1994, c. 39, sch. 14 (S.).
s. 53, amended: 1994, c. 39, sch. 13 (S.).
s. 54, regs. 94/1056.
s. 54, repealed: 1995, c. 25, sch. 24.
s. 54, amended: 1994, c. 39, sch. 13 (S.).
s. 61, repealed: 1995, c. 25, schs. 22, 24.
s. 62, amended: 1995, c. 25, sch. 22.
s. 63, amended: 1995, c. 25, sch. 22.
s. 64, regs. 94/1056.
s. 64, repealed in pt.: 1995, c. 25, sch. 24.
s. 64, amended: 1995, c. 25, sch. 22.
s. 66, amended: 1995, c. 25, sch. 22.
s. 67, repealed: 1995, c. 25, schs. 22, 24.
ss. 68–70, repealed: 1995, c. 25, schs. 22, 24.
s. 71, repealed in pt.: 1995, c. 25, schs. 19, 22, 24.
s. 71, amended: 1995, c. 25, sch. 22.
s. 72, repealed: 1995, c. 25, schs. 22, 24.
s. 74, regs. 94/1056; 95/288, 1950.
s. 75, regs. 94/1056; 95/288.
s. 75, repealed in pt.: 1995, c. 25, schs. 22, 24.
s. 75, amended: 1995, c. 25, sch. 22.
s. 76, substituted: 1995, c. 25, s. 118.
ss. 78A–78YC, added: 1995, c. 25, s. 57.
s. 79, repealed in pt.: 1995, c. 25, sch. 24.
s. 79, amended: 1995, c. 25, schs. 17 (S.), 22.
s. 80, amended: 1995, c. 25, sch. 17 (S.).
s. 80, see *R.* v. *Tunbridge Wells Justices, ex p. Tunbridge Wells Borough Council* (CO/2962/94), May 1, 1995, Simon Brown L.J.
s. 81, amended: 1995, c. 25, sch. 17 (S.).
s. 81A, amended: 1995, c. 25, sch. 17 (S.).
s. 82, amended: 1995, c. 25, sch. 17 (S.).
s. 82, see *Carr* v. *Hackney London Borough Council, The Times*, March 9, 1995, McKinnon J.
s. 83, repealed: 1995, c. 25, sch. 24.
s. 84, order 95/2054.
s. 86, amended: 1994, c. 39, sch. 13 (S.).
s. 87, see *Westminster City Council* v. *Riding, The Times*, July 31, 1995, D.C.
s. 88, repealed in pt.: 1994, c. 39, schs. 13, 14 (S.); 1995, c. 25, sch. 24.
ss. 90, 92, 93, 95, repealed in pt.: 1994, c. 39, schs. 13, 14 (S.).
s. 99, amended: 1994, c. 39, sch. 13 (S.).
ss. 111, 122, regs. 95/304.

CAP.

1990—cont.

43. Environmental Protection Act 1990—*cont.*
s. 141, repealed: 1995, c. 25, schs. 22, 24.
s. 143, repealed: 1995, c. 25, schs. 22, 24.
s. 148, repealed: 1995, c. 21, sch. 12.
s. 148, C.: 1995, c. 21, sch. 14.
s. 149, amended: 1994, c. 39, sch. 13 (S.).
s. 153, orders 95/150, 554.
s. 153, amended: order 95/1085.
s. 161, amended: 1995, c. 25, sch. 22.
s. 164, orders 94/2854, 3234; 95/2152.
sch. 1, amended: 1995, c. 25, sch. 22.
sch. 2, repealed in pt.: 1995, c. 25, schs. 22, 24.
sch. 2A, added: 1995, c. 25, sch. 12.
sch. 2B, added: 1995, c. 25, sch. 22.
sch. 3, amended: 1995, c. 25, sch. 17 (S.).
sch. 8, repealed in pt.: 1995, c. 25, sch. 24.
sch. 14, repealed in pt.: 1995, c. 21, sch. 12.
sch. 14, C.: 1995, c. 21, sch. 14.
sch. 15, repealed in pt.: 1995, c. 23, sch. 8; 1995, c. 25, sch. 24.
sch. 15, C.: 1995, c. 23, sch. 8.

44. Caldey Island Act 1990.
s. 3, repealed in pt.: 1995, c. 17, sch. 3.
s. 4, repealed in pt.: 1995, c. 17, sch. 3.

1991

22. New Roads and Street Works Act 1991.
s. 27, amended: 1994, c. 39, s. 148 (S.).
s. 53, regs. 95/990.
s. 64, regs. 95/1154, 2128.
s. 104, regs. 95/990, 2128.
ss. 108, 109, amended: 1994, c. 39, sch. 13 (S.).
s. 112, amended: 1994, c. 39, s. 149.
s. 148, amended: 1994, c. 39, sch. 13 (S.).
s. 153, repealed in pt.: 1994, c. 39, schs. 13, 14 (S.).
s. 164, amended: 1994, c. 39, sch. 13 (S.).

23. Children and Young Persons (Protection From Tobacco) Act 1991.
s. 6, amended: 1994, c. 39, sch. 13 (S.).

24. Northern Ireland (Emergency Provisions) Act 1991.
s. 50, amended: 1995, c. 20, sch. 6 (S.); 1995, c. 40, sch. 4 (S.).
s. 69, order 95/1566.

25. Criminal Procedure (Insanity and Unfitness to Plead) Act 1991.
sch. 3, repealed in pt.: 1995, c. 35, sch. 3.

28. National Heritage (Scotland) Act 1991.
s. 7, repealed in pt.: 1995, c. 45, sch. 6.
s. 7, amended: 1995, c. 45, sch. 4.
s. 15, order 95/2382.
s. 15, repealed in pt.: 1995, c. 25, sch. 24.
s. 15, amended: 1995, c. 25, sch. 22.
s. 17, order 95/2382.
ss. 17, 18: amended: 1995, c. 25, sch. 22.
s. 20, amended: 1994, c. 39, sch. 13.
s. 22, repealed in pt.: 1995, c. 39, schs. 13, 14.

CAP.

1991—cont.

28. National Heritage (Scotland) Act 1991—*cont.*
s. 24, repealed in pt.: 1995, c. 39, schs. 13, 14.
s. 24, amended: 1995, c. 25, sch. 22.
s. 26A, added: 1995, c. 25, sch. 22.
sch. 1, repealed in pt.: 1995, c. 7, sch. 5.
sch. 2, repealed in pt.: 1995, c. 25, sch. 24.
sch. 5, repealed in pt.: 1995, c. 25, sch. 24.
sch. 6, repealed in pt.: 1995, c. 25, sch. 24.
sch. 6, amended: 1995, c. 25, sch. 22.
sch. 7, repealed in pt.: 1994, c. 39, schs. 13, 14.
sch. 8, repealed in pt.: 1994, c. 39, sch. 14; 1995, c. 25, sch. 24.
sch. 8, amended: 1994, c. 39, sch. 13; 1995, c. 25, sch. 22.
sch. 10, repealed in pt.: 1995, c. 25, sch. 24.

29. Age of Legal Capacity (Scotland) Act 1991.
sch. 1, repealed in pt.: 1995, c. 4, sch. 29.

31. Finance Act 1991.
s. 72, amended: order 95/352.
s. 81, repealed: 1995, c. 4, sch. 29.
schs. 2, 7, 15, repealed in pt.: 1995, c. 4, sch. 29.

34. Planning and Compensation Act 1991.
Commencement orders: 94/3292 (S.); 95/2045 (S.).
s. 44, order 94/3292 (S.).
s. 54A, see *Houghton* v. *Secretary of State for the Environment* [1995] N.P.C. 2, Mr M. Spence, Q.C.
s. 84, orders 94/3292 (S.); 95/2045 (S.).
sch. 4, repealed in pt.: 1995, c. 25, sch. 24.
sch. 13, repealed in pt.: 1994, c. 39, sch. 14 (S.); order 94/3292.

40. Road Traffic Act 1991.
s. 32, see *R.* v. *Miller (Jason Mark)* (1994) 15 Cr.App.R. (S.) 505, C.A.
s. 37, repealed: 1995, c. 20, sch. 6 (S.), 7 (S.).
s. 39, C.: 1995, c. 46, s. 248.
s. 50, order 95/1130.
s. 58, orders 95/124, 125, 126.
s. 76, orders 95/616, 617, 618, 679, 1333, 1334.
s. 76, amended: order 95/1437.
s. 77, orders 95/616, 617, 618, 679, 1333, 1334.
sch. 3, amended: 1994, c. 39, sch. 13 (S.).
sch. 4, repealed in pt.: 1995, c. 23, sch. 8.
sch. 4, C.: 1995, c. 23, sch. 8.

45. Coal Mining Subsidence Act 1991.
ss. 1, 2, see *British Coal Corporation* v. *Netherlee Trust Trustees*, 1995 S.L.T. 1038.
s. 21, amended: 1995, c. 8, sch.
ss. 25, 29, regs. 94/2564.
s. 31, see *British Coal Corp.* v. *Ellistown Pipes* [1994] RVR 81, C.A.
s. 36, regs. 94/3064.
s. 46, regs. 94/2565.

CAP.

1991—cont.

45. Coal Mining Subsidence Act 1991—*cont.*
s. 47, amended: 1994, c. 39, sch. 13 (S.).
s. 50, regs. 94/2563, 2564, 2566, 3064.
sch. 3, amended: 1995, c. 8, sch.

48. Child Support Act 1991.
regs. 95/123, 1045.
see *C. (A Minor) (Contribution Notice), Re* [1994] 1 FLR 111, Ward J.; *Department of Social Security* v. *Butler, The Times*, August 11, 1995, C.A.
s. 2, see *R.* v. *Secretary of State for Social Security, The Times*, January 30, 1995, Thorpe J.
s. 3, amended: 1995, c. 36, sch. 4 (S.).
s. 4, amended: 1995, c. 34, s. 18.
s. 5, repealed in pt.: 1995, c. 36, sch. 5 (S.).
s. 5, amended: 1995, c. 36, sch. 4 (S.).
s. 6, amended: 1995, c. 18, sch. 2.
s. 7, amended: 1995, c. 34, s. 18.
s. 8, regs. 95/1045.
s. 8, see *B.* v. *M. (Child Support: Revocation of Order)* [1994] 1 F.L.R. 342, H.H.J. Bryant.
s. 9, amended: 1995, c. 34, s. 18.
s. 10, regs. 95/1045.
s. 11, amended: 1995, c. 34, s. 19.
s. 12, regs. 95/1045.
s. 12, amended: 1995, c. 34, s. 11.
s. 14, regs. 95/1045.
s. 14, amended: 1995, c. 18, sch. 2; 1995, c. 34, sch. 3.
s. 16, regs. 95/1045.
s. 17, regs. 95/1045.
s. 17, amended: 1995, c. 34, s. 12.
s. 18, regs. 95/1045.
s. 18, amended: 1995, c. 34, ss. 13, 14, sch. 3.
s. 19, substituted: 1995, c. 34, s. 15.
s. 20, amended: 1995, c. 34, sch. 3.
s. 20A, added: 1995, c. 34, s. 16.
s. 21, regs. 95/1045.
s. 24, amended: 1995, c. 34, sch. 3.
s. 25, amended: 1995, c. 34, sch. 3.
s. 26, amended: order 95/756.
s. 27, amended: 1995, c. 34, s. 20.
s. 27A, added: 1995, c. 34, s. 21.
s. 28, amended: 1995, c. 34, s. 20.
s. 28A, added: 1995, c. 34, s. 1.
s. 28B, added: 1995, c. 34, s. 2.
s. 28C, added: 1995, c. 34, s. 3.
s. 28D, added: 1995, c. 34, s. 4.
s. 28E, added: 1995, c. 34, s. 5.
s. 28F, added: 1995, c. 34, s. 6.
s. 28G, added: 1995, c. 34, s. 7.
s. 28H, added: 1995, c. 34, s. 8.
s. 28I, added: 1995, c. 34, s. 9.
s. 29, regs. 95/1045.
s. 30, amended: 1995, c. 34, sch. 3.
s. 32, regs. 95/1045.
s. 33, amended: 1995, c. 34, sch. 3.
s. 41, regs. 95/1045.
s. 41, amended: 1995, c. 34, sch. 3.

CAP.

1991—cont.

48. Child Support Act 1991—*cont.*
s. 41A, added: 1995, c. 34, s. 22.
s. 41B, added: 1995, c. 34, s. 23.
s. 42, regs. 95/1045.
s. 43, regs. 95/1045.
s. 46, regs. 95/1045.
s. 46, amended: 1995, c. 18, schs. 2, 3.
s. 47, regs. 95/1045.
s. 47, amended: 1995, c. 18, schs. 2, 3.
s. 48, amended: 1995, c. 34, sch. 3.
s. 51, regs. 95/1045.
s. 52, regs. 95/1045.
s. 52, amended: 1995, c. 34, sch. 3.
s. 54, regs. 95/1045.
s. 54, repealed in pt.: 1995, c. 36, schs. 4 (S.), 5 (S.).
s. 54, amended: 1995, c. 18, schs. 2, 3; 1995, c. 36, sch. 4 (S.).
s. 57, regs. 95/1045.
sch. 1, regs. 95/1045.
sch. 1, amended: 1995, c. 18, sch. 2.
sch. 3, amended: 1995, c. 34, sch. 3.
sch. 4, amended: 1995, c. 34, s. 17, sch. 3.
sch. 4A, added: 1995, c. 34, sch. 1.
sch. 4B, added: 1995, c. 34, sch. 2.
sch. 5, amended: 1995, c. 34, sch. 3.

49. School Teachers' Pay and Conditions Act 1991.
s. 2, orders 95/1015, 1743.
s. 3, order 95/2087.
s. 5, order 95/1015.

50. Age of Legal Capacity (Scotland) Act 1991.
ss. 1, 2, amended: 1995, c. 36, sch. 4.
s. 5, repealed in pt.: 1995, c. 36, sch. 5.
s. 5, amended: 1995, c. 36, sch. 4.
s. 9, repealed in pt.: 1995, c. 36, sch. 5.
sch. 1, repealed in pt.: 1995, c. 36, sch. 5.

52. Ports Act 1991.
s. 15A, added: 1995, c. 4, s. 159.
ss. 31–34, repealed: 1995, c. 21, sch. 12.
s. 31, C.: 1995, c. 21, sch. 14.
s. 32, repealed: 1995, c. 21, sch. 12.
s. 32, C.: 1995, c. 21, sch. 14.
s. 33, repealed: 1995, c. 21, sch. 12.
s. 33, C.: 1995, c. 21, sch. 14.
s. 34, repealed: 1995, c. 21, sch. 12.
s. 34, C.: 1995, c. 21, sch. 14.
s. 36, repealed in pt.: 1995, c. 21, sch. 12.
s. 36, C.: 1995, c. 21, sch. 14.
s. 41, repealed in pt.: 1994, c. 4, sch. 29; 1995, c. 21, sch. 12.
s. 42, repealed in pt.: 1995, c. 21, sch. 12.

53. Criminal Justice Act 1991.
Commencement orders: 94/3191; 95/43.
see *R.* v. *Ipswich Justices, ex p. Best* (1993) 14 Cr.App.R. (S.) 685, D.C.
s. 1, see *R.* v. *Crawford* (1993) 14 Cr.App.R. (S.) 782, C.A.; *R.* v. *Bibby* [1994] Crim.L.R. 610, C.A.; *R.* v. *Wise (Frank William)* (94/7181/W4), April 4, 1995, C.A.; *R.* v. *Creasey* (1994) 15 Cr.App.R. (S.) 671, C.A.

CAP.

1991—cont.

53. Criminal Justice Act 1991—*cont.*

s. 2, see *R.* v. *Cini, The Times*, February 17, 1995, C.A.; *R.* v. *Ely* [1994] Crim.L.R. 539, C.A.; *R.* v. *Gardiner* [1994] Crim.L.R. 539, C.A.; *R.* v. *Fleming* [1994] Crim.L.R. 541, C.A.; *R.* v. *Richart, The Times*, April 14, 1995, C.A.; *R.* v. *Bibby* [1994] Crim.L.R. 610, C.A.; *R.* v. *Chapman* [1994] Crim.L.R. 609, C.A.; *R.* v. *Hashi* [1994] Crim.L.R. 618, C.A.; *R.* v. *Ragg, The Times*, May 13, 1995, C.A.; *R.* v. *Dootson* [1994] Crim.L.R. 702, C.A.; *R.* v. *Oudkerk* [1994] Crim.L.R. 700, C.A.; *R.* v. *Walsh* [1994] Crim.L.R. 701, C.A.; *R.* v. *Creasey* (1994) 15 Cr.App.R. (S.) 671, C.A.; *R.* v. *L. (Henry George)* (1994) 15 Cr.App.R. (S.) 501, C.A.; *R.* v. *Watford* (1994) 15 Cr.App.R. (S.) 730, C.A.; *R.* v. *Cochrane* (1994) 15 Cr.App.R. (S.) 708, C.A.

s. 3, see *R.* v. *Ely* [1994] Crim.L.R. 539, C.A.

s. 5, *R.* v. *Vince* (1994) 15 Cr.App.R. (S.) 657, C.A.

s. 8, see *R.* v. *Moore* [1995] 2 W.L.R. 728, C.A.

s. 12, order 95/1379.

s. 24, amended: 1995, c. 18, schs. 2, 3; 1995, c. 40, sch. 4 (S.).

s. 24, see *R.* v. *Gardiner (Dean Norman William)* (1994) 15 Cr.App.R. (S.) 747, C.A.; *R.* v. *Swain* (1994) 15 Cr.App.R. (S.) 765, C.A.; *R.* v. *Fleming* (1994) 15 Cr.App.R. (S.) 861, C.A.; *R.* v. *Murrey (Michael)* (1994) 15 Cr.App.R. (S.) 567, C.A.

s. 25, see *R.* v. *Manchester Magistrates' Court, ex p. Kaymanesh* [1994] C.O.D. 380, D.C.

s. 29, see *R.* v. *Utip (Doreen)* (1993) 14 Cr.App.R. (S.) 746, C.A.; *R.* v. *Reynolds (Glenn William)* (1993) 14 Cr.App.R. (S.) 694, C.A.; *R.* v. *Dootson* [1994] Crim.L.R. 702, C.A.

s. 30, order 95/1379.

s. 31, see *R.* v. *Richart, The Times*, April 14, 1995, C.A.; *R.* v. *Bibby* [1994] Crim.L.R. 610, C.A.; *R.* v. *Chapman* [1994] Crim.L.R. 609, C.A.; *R.* v. *Ragg, The Times*, May 13, 1995, C.A.; *R.* v. *Cochrane* (1994) 15 Cr.App.R. (S.) 708, C.A.

s. 32, see *R.* v. *Parole Board, ex p. Gittens* [1994] C.O.D. 441, D.C.; *R.* v. *Secretary of State for the Home Department, ex p. Edwards* [1994] C.O.D. 443, D.C.

s. 34, see *R.* v. *Fox (Michael), The Times*, November 24, 1994, C.A.; *R.* v. *Leaney, The Times*, April 12, 1995, C.A.; *R.* v. *Dalton* [1995] 2 W.L.R. 377, C.A.; *R.* v. *Secretary of State for the Home Department, ex p. Norney, The Independent*, October 4, 1995, Dyson J.; *R.* v. *Parole Board, ex p. Gittens* [1994] C.O.D. 441, D.C.; *R.* v. *Secretary of State for the Home Department, ex p. Edwards* [1994] C.O.D. 443, D.C.

s. 40, see *R.* v. *Foran, The Times*, June 1, 1995, C.A.

s. 44, see *R.* v. *Barker (John Humphrey)* (94/5971/Z5), March 3, 1995, C.A.

s. 51, see *R.* v. *Governor of Styal Prison, ex p. Mooney, The Times*, May 17, 1995, D.C.

s. 60, see *R.* v. *Croydon Youth Court, ex p. G. (A Minor), The Times*, May 3, 1995, Leggatt L.J.; *Liverpool City Council* v. *B.* [1995] 1 W.L.R. 505, D.C.

s. 78, order 95/43.

s. 102, order 94/3191 *R.* v. *Evans (Marcus Anthony)* (1993) 14 Cr.App.R. (S.) 751, C.A.

sch. 2, see *Caton* v. *Community Service Office, The Times*, February 27, 1995, D.C.; *R.* v. *Cousin (David Peter)* (1994) 15 Cr.App.R. (S.) 516, C.A.

sch. 3, repealed in pt.: order 95/756; 1995, c. 40, sch. 5 (S.).

sch. 3, amended: 1995, c. 20, sch. 6 (S.).

sch. 10, regs. 94/3193.

sch. 12, see *R.* v. *Vince* (1994) 15 Cr.App.R. (S.) 657, C.A.

55. Agricultural Holdings (Scotland) Act 1991.

ss. 21, 24, see *O'Donnell* v. *Heath*, 1995 S.L.T. (Land Ct.) 15.

s. 60, see *Hill* v. *Wildfowl Trust (Holdings)* (Sh.Ct.), 1995 S.C.L.R. 778.

s. 61, see *Maciver* v. *Broadland Properties Estates*, 1995 S.L.T. (Land Ct.) 9.

56. Water Industry Act 1991.

s. 3, amended: 1995, c. 25, sch. 22.

s. 4, repealed in pt.: 1995, c. 25, sch. 24.

s. 4, amended: 1995, c. 25, sch. 10.

s. 5, amended: 1995, c. 25, sch. 22.

s. 19, see *R.* v. *Secretary of State for the Environment, ex p. Friends of the Earth, The Times*, June 8, 1995, C.A.

s. 40, amended: 1995, c. 25, sch. 22.

s. 40A, amended: 1995, c. 25, sch. 22.

s. 68, see *R.* v. *Secretary of State for the Environment, ex p. Friends of the Earth, The Times*, June 8, 1995, C.A.

s. 71, amended: 1995, c. 25, sch. 22.

s. 87, amended: 1995, c. 17, sch. 1.

s. 89, amended: 1995, c. 17, sch. 1.

ss. 93A–93D, added: 1995, c. 25, sch. 22.

s. 101A, added: 1995, c. 25, sch. 22.

s. 110A, amended: 1995, c. 25, sch. 22.

s. 120, amended: 1995, c. 25, sch. 22.

CAP.

1991—cont.

56. Water Industry Act 1991—*cont.*
s. 121, amended: 1995, c. 21, sch. 13.
s. 123, amended: 1995, c. 25, sch. 22.
s. 127, amended: 1995, c. 25, sch. 22.
s. 130, amended: 1995, c. 25, sch. 22.
s. 131, amended: 1995, c. 25, sch. 22.
s. 132, repealed in pt.: 1995, c. 25, sch. 24.
s. 132, amended: 1995, c. 25, sch. 22.
s. 133, amended: 1995, c. 25, sch. 22.
s. 134, amended: 1995, c. 25, sch. 22.
s. 135A, added: 1995, c. 25, sch. 22.
s. 142, amended: 1995, c. 25, sch. 22.
s. 143, amended: 1995, c. 25, sch. 22.
s. 151, added: 1995, c. 25, sch. 22.
s. 151, repealed: 1995, c. 25, sch. 24.
s. 161, amended: 1995, c. 25, sch. 22.
s. 166, amended: 1995, c. 25, sch. 22.
s. 171, repealed in pt.: 1995, c. 25, sch. 24.
s. 182, order 95/1556.
s. 184, amended: 1995, c. 25, sch. 22.
s. 202, amended: 1995, c. 25, sch. 22.
s. 206, repealed in pt.: 1995, c. 25, schs. 22, 24.
s. 209, amended: 1995, c. 25, sch. 22.
s. 215, amended: 1995, c. 25, sch. 22.
s. 217, amended: 1995, c. 25, sch. 22.
s. 219, repealed in pt.: 1995, c. 25, sch. 24.
s. 219, amended: 1995, c. 21, sch. 13; c. 25, sch. 22.
s. 221, substituted: 1995, c. 25, sch. 21.
s. 222, substituted: 1995, c. 25, s. 118.
sch. 7, amended: 1995, c. 17, sch. 1.
sch. 11, amended: 1995, c. 25, sch. 22.
sch. 13, amended: 1995, c. 25, sch. 22.

57. Water Resources Act 1991.
ss. 1–14, repealed in pt.: 1995, c. 25, schs. 22, 24.
s. 15, amended: 1995, c. 25, sch. 22.
s. 16, repealed: 1995, c. 25, sch. 24.
s. 16, amended: 1995, c. 25, sch. 22.
s. 17, repealed: 1995, c. 25, sch. 24.
s. 17, amended: 1995, c. 25, schs. 10, 22.
s. 18, repealed: 1995, c. 25, sch. 24.
s. 18, amended: 1995, c. 25, sch. 22.
s. 19, repealed: 1995, c. 25, sch. 24.
s. 19, amended: 1995, c. 25, sch. 22.
s. 20, amended: 1995, c. 25, sch. 22.
s. 21, amended: 1995, c. 25, sch. 22.
s. 22, amended: 1995, c. 21, sch. 13.
s. 25, amended: 1995, c. 25, s. 103.
s. 34, repealed in pt.: 1995, c. 25, sch. 24.
s. 43, amended: 1995, c. 25, sch. 22.
s. 45, repealed in pt.: 1995, c. 25, sch. 24.
s. 50, amended: 1995, c. 25, sch. 22.
s. 58, repealed in pt.: 1995, c. 25, schs. 22, 24.
s. 68, repealed: 1995, c. 25, schs. 22, 24.
s. 69, repealed in pt.: 1995, c. 25, schs. 22, 24.
s. 72, amended: 1995, c. 25, s. 100.
s. 73, repealed in pt.: 1995, c. 25, sch. 22.
s. 79A, added: 1995, c. 25, sch. 22.
s. 80, amended: 1995, c. 25, sch. 22.

CAP.

1991—cont.

57. Water Resources Act 1991—*cont.*
s. 85, see *National Rivers Authority* v. *Alfred McAlpine Homes East* [1994] 4 All E.R. 286; D.C.; *C.P.C. (U.K.)* [1994] NPC 112, C.A.
s. 89, amended: 1995, c. 25, s. 60.
s. 90A, added: 1995, c. 25, sch. 22.
s. 90B, added: 1995, c. 25, sch. 22.
s. 91, repealed in pt.: 1995, c. 25, sch. 24.
s. 91, amended: 1995, c. 25, sch. 22.
ss. 91A–91B, added: 1995, c. 25, s. 58.
s. 105, repealed: 1995, c. 25, schs. 22, 24.
s. 110, repealed: 1995, c. 25, sch. 22.
s. 113, repealed in pt.: 1995, c. 25, sch. 24.
s. 113, amended: 1995, c. 25, s. 100.
s. 114, repealed: 1995, c. 25, schs. 22, 24.
s. 115, amended: 1995, c. 25, schs. 15, 21.
s. 117, repealed: 1995, c. 25, schs. 22, 24.
s. 118, amended: 1995, c. 25, sch. 22.
s. 119, amended: 1995, c. 25, sch. 22.
ss. 121–124, repealed: 1995, c. 25, schs. 22, 24.
s. 126, repealed in pt.: 1995, c. 25, schs. 22, 24.
s. 129, repealed in pt.: 1995, c. 25, sch. 24.
ss. 131–132, repealed: 1995, c. 25, schs. 22, 24.
s. 142, amended: 1995, c. 25, sch. 21.
s. 144, repealed in pt.: 1995, c. 25, sch. 24.
s. 146, repealed: 1995, c. 25, schs. 22, 24.
s. 147, amended: 1995, c. 25, s. 101.
ss. 150–153, repealed: 1995, c. 25, schs. 22, 24.
s. 154, amended: 1995, c. 25, sch. 22.
s. 156, amended: 1995, c. 25, sch. 22.
s. 157, amended: 1995, c. 25, sch. 22.
s. 158, amended: 1995, c. 25, sch. 22.
s. 161, amended: 1995, c. 25, sch. 22.
ss. 161A–161D, added: 1995, c. 25, sch. 22.
s. 162, amended: 1995, c. 25, sch. 22.
s. 166, amended: 1995, c. 25, sch. 22.
s. 169, amended: 1995, c. 25, sch. 22.
s. 172, amended: 1995, c. 25, sch. 22.
s. 174, amended: 1995, c. 25, sch. 22.
s. 187, repealed: 1995, c. 25, schs. 22, 24.
s. 190, repealed in pt.: 1995, c. 25, sch. 24.
s. 190, amended: 1995, c. 25, sch. 22.
ss. 191A–191B, added: 1995, c. 25, sch. 22.
s. 196, repealed: 1995, c. 25, schs. 22, 24.
s. 202, repealed: 1995, c. 25, schs. 22, 24.
s. 204, repealed: 1995, c. 25, sch. 22.
s. 206, repealed in pt.: 1995, c. 25, sch. 24.
s. 206, amended: 1995, c. 25, sch. 19.
s. 209, repealed in pt.: 1995, c. 25, sch. 24.
ss. 213–215, repealed: 1995, c. 25, schs. 22, 24.
s. 218, repealed: 1995, c. 25, sch. 22.
ss. 219, repealed: 1995, c. 25, sch. 22.
s. 221, amended: 1995, c. 25, sch. 22.
s. 222, substituted: 1995, c. 25, sch. 21.
s. 224, substituted: 1995, c. 25, s. 118.

CAP.

1991—cont.

57. Water Resources Act 1991—*cont.*
sch. 1, repealed: 1995, c. 25, schs. 22, 24.
schs. 3–4, repealed: 1995, c. 25, schs. 22, 24.
sch. 5, amended: 1995, c. 25, sch. 22.
sch. 10, substituted: 1995, c. 25, sch. 22.
sch. 25, amended: 1995, c. 25, sch. 15.

58. Statutory Water Companies Act 1991.
ss. 12, 14, order 95/79.

59. Land Drainage Act 1991.
amended: 1995, c. 25, sch. 22.
s. 3, orders 95/1325, 2851.
s. 12, amended: 1995, c. 21, sch. 13.
s. 23, amended: 1995, c. 25, sch. 22.
s. 59, amended: 1995, c. 25, s. 101.
s. 61C, repealed in pt.: 1995, c. 25, sch. 24.
s. 61C, amended: 1995, c. 25, sch. 10.
s. 61F, added: 1995, c. 25, sch. 22.
s. 72, repealed in pt.: 1995, c. 25, sch. 24.
s. 72, amended: 1995, c. 21, sch. 13.
s. 74, amended: 1995, c. 21, sch. 21.
s. 75, substituted: 1995, c. 25, s. 118.

60. Water Consolidation (Consequential Provisions) Act 1991.
sch. 1, repealed in pt.: 1995, c. 25, sch. 24.

62. Armed Forces Act 1991.
s. 1, order 95/1964.
s. 16, see *Legrove* v. *Legrove* [1994] 2 F.L.R. 119, C.A.
s. 17, amended: 1995, c. 36, sch. 4 (S.); order 95/756.
s. 18, amended: 1995, c. 36, sch. 4 (S.); order 95/756.
s. 20, amended: order 95/756.
s. 21, amended: 1995, c. 36, sch. 4 (S.); order 95/756.
s. 23, amended: 1995, c. 36, sch. 4 (S.); order 95/756.
sch. 2, repealed in pt.: 1995, c. 40, sch. 5 (S.).
sch. 2, C.: 1995, c. 46, s. 253.

65. Dangerous Dogs Act 1991.
see *R.* v. *Secretary of State for the Home Office, ex p. James (Nicola)* [1994] C.O.D. 167, D.C.
s. 3, see *Swinlay* v. *Crowe*, 1995 S.L.T. 34; *Tierney* v. *Valentine*, 1994 S.C.C.R. 697; *R.* v. *Rawlings* [1994] Crim.L.R. 433, C.A.; *R.* v. *Trafford Magistrates Court, ex p. Riley (Robertina)* (CO/1603/95), March 16, 1995, Balcombe L.J.
s. 4, amended: 1995, c. 40, sch. 4 (S.).
s. 5, see *R.* v. *Bezzina*; *Same* v. *Codling*; *Same* v. *Elvin* [1994] 1 W.L.R. 1057, C.A.
s. 10, see *Tierney* v. *Valentine*, 1994 S.C.C.R. 697.
s. 35, see *R.* v. *Bezzina*; *Same* v. *Codling*; *Same* v. *Elvin* [1994] 1 W.L.R. 1057, C.A.

CAP.

1991—cont.

67. Export and Investment Guarantees Act 1991.
s. 6, amended: order 95/1988.

1992

3. Severn Bridges Act 1992.
s. 9, order 94/3158.

4. Social Security Contributions and Benefits Act 1992.
order 95/767; regs. 95/580, 1045.
see *Graham* v. *Secretary of State for Social Security*, *The Times*, September 25, 1995, ECJ.
s. 1, regs. 94/1553.
s. 3, regs. 94/1003, 1553, 2945; 95/1570.
s. 5, regs. 94/3196; 95/714.
s. 9, amended: regs. 95/561.
s. 11, regs. 94/1553.
s. 11, amended: regs. 95/561.
ss. 13, 15, 18, amended: regs. 95/561.
s. 20, repealed in pt.: 1995, c. 18, sch. 3.
s. 20, amended: 1995, c. 26, sch. 4.
s. 21, repealed in pt.: 1995, c. 18, sch. 3.
s. 22, amended: 1995, c. 18, sch. 2.
s. 23, amended: 1995, c. 26, s. 134.
s. 25, repealed: 1995, c. 18, sch. 3.
s. 25, amended: 1995, c. 26, sch. 4.
s. 25A, regs. 95/1742, 2192.
s. 25A, repealed: 1995, c. 18, sch. 3.
s. 25B, repealed: 1995, c. 18, sch. 3.
s. 26, repealed: 1995, c. 18, sch. 3.
s. 27, repealed: 1995, c. 18, sch. 3.
s. 28, repealed: 1995, c. 18, sch. 3.
s. 28, amended: 1994, c. 39, sch. 13 (S.).
2. 29, repealed: 1995, c. 18, sch. 3.
s. 30, repealed: 1995, c. 18, sch. 3.
s. 30B, regs. 94/2946.
s. 30B, amended: 1995, c. 26, sch. 4.
ss. 30C, 30D, regs. 94/2946.
s. 30E, regs. 94/1553, 2946.
s. 34, see *R.* v. *Secretary of State for the Home Department, ex p. H.*; *R.* v. *Same, ex p. Hickey*; *sub nom. R.* v. *Secretary of State for the Home Department, ex p. T.* [1994] 3 W.L.R. 1110, C.A.
s. 35, regs. 94/1882.
s. 35, see *R.* v. *Secretary of State for the Home Department, ex p. H.*; *R.* v. *Same, ex p. Hickey*; *sub nom. R.* v. *Secretary of State for the Home Department, ex p. T.* [1994] 3 W.L.R. 1110, C.A.
s. 41, amended: 1995, c. 26, sch. 4.
s. 44, amended: 1995, c. 26, s. 128; order 95/559.
s. 45A, added: 1995, c. 26, s. 127.
s. 46, amended: 1995, c. 26, sch. 4.
s. 47, amended: order 95/559.
ss. 48A–48C, added: 1995, c. 26, sch. 4.
s. 49, substituted: 1995, c. 26, sch. 3.
s. 50, amended: order 95/559.
s. 50, substituted: 1995, c. 26, sch. 3.
s. 51A, inserted: 1995, c. 26, sch. 4.

CAP.

1992—cont.

4. Social Security Contributions and Benefits Act 1992—*cont.*

s. 52, amended: 1995, c. 26, sch. 4.
s. 53, repealed: 1995, c. 26, schs. 4, 7.
s. 54, repealed in pt.: 1995, c. 26, schs. 4, 7.
s. 54, amended: 1995, c. 26, s. 134, sch. 4.
s. 57, regs. 95/580.
s. 58, amended: 1994, c. 39, sch. 13 (S.).
s. 60, amended: 1995, c. 26, sch. 4.
s. 61, amended: 1995, c. 18, sch. 2.
s. 61A, added: amended: 1995, c. 26, s. 133.
s. 62, regs. 95/2606.
s. 62, amended: 1995, c. 26, s. 131, sch. 4.
s. 67, regs. 95/2162.
s. 68, order 94/2947.
s. 70, see *R.* v. *Maidstone Borough Council, ex p. Bunce* (1994) H.L.R. 375, Brooke J.
s. 72, regs. 95/2162.
s. 78, amended: 1995, c. 26, sch. 4.
s. 80, regs. 94/2945.
s. 80, repealed in pt.: 1995, c. 18, sch. 3.
s. 80, amended: order 95/559.
s. 82, repealed in pt.: 1995, c. 18, sch. 3.
s. 82, amended: 1995, c. 18, sch. 2.
s. 83, substituted: 1995, c. 26, sch. 4.
s. 83A, added: 1995, c. 26, sch. 4.
s. 84, substituted: 1995, c. 26, sch. 4.
s. 85, amended: 1995, c. 26, sch. 4.
s. 86A, regs. 94/2945; order 95/829.
s. 86A, amended: order 95/559.
s. 87, regs. 94/2945.
s. 87, amended: order 95/559; 1995, c. 18, sch. 2.
s. 88, amended: 1995, c. 26, sch. 4.
s. 89, regs. 94/2945.
s. 90, regs. 94/2945; 95/580.
s. 91, amended: 1995, c. 18, sch. 2.
s. 113, regs. 95/580.
s. 114, regs. 94/2945.
s. 114, amended: 1995, c. 26, sch. 4.
s. 116, regs. 94/1553; 95/714.
s. 116, amended: 1995, c. 18, sch. 2.
s. 117, regs. 95/514.
s. 119, regs. 95/714.
s. 121, regs. 95/74.
s. 121, amended: 1995, c. 42, sch.
s. 122, regs. 94/1553, 2945, 2946; 95/580, 1003, 1570.
s. 122, amended: 1995, c. 18, sch. 2; 1995, c. 26, s. 134, sch. 4.
s. 123, regs. 95/511, 516, 560, 625, 626, 1339, 1644, 1742, 2303.
s. 123, amended: 1994, c. 39, sch. 13 (S.).
s. 123, see *R.* v. *North Cornwall District Council, ex p. Singer*; *Same* v. *Same, ex p. Barrett*; *Same* v. *Same, ex p. Bateman*]1994] 26 H.L.R. 360, D.C.; *R.* v. *Manchester City Council, ex p. Harcup* [1993] 26 H.L.R. 402, D.C.
s. 124, regs. 95/2303.
s. 124, repealed in pt.: 1995, c. 18, sch. 3.

CAP.

1992—cont.

4. Social Security Contributions and Benefits Act 1992—*cont.*

s. 124, amended: 1995, c. 18, sch. 2.
s. 125, repealed: 1995, c. 18, sch. 3.
s. 126, amended: 1995, c. 18, sch. 2.
s. 127, amended: 1995, c. 18, sch. 2.
s. 128, regs. 95/516, 1339.
s. 128, amended: 1995, c. 18, sch. 2.
s. 129, regs. 95/482, 516, 1339, 2303.
s. 129, amended: 1995, c. 18, sch. 2.
s. 130, regs. 95/626, 1644, 1742, 2303.
s. 130, see *R.* v. *Stoke City Council, ex p. Highgate Projects* [1994] C.O.D. 414, D.C.; *R.* v. *Sheffield City Council Housing Benefit Review Board, ex p. Smith* [1995] L.G.R. 139, Blackburne J.
s. 131, regs. 95/625, 626.
s. 134, see *R.* v. *Stoke City Council, ex p. Highgate Projects* [1994] C.O.D. 414, D.C.
s. 135, regs. 94/3061; 95/482, 516, 560, 626, 1045, 1613, 2287, 2303.
s. 136, regs. 95/511, 560, 626, 1339, 1613, 1742, 2303.
s. 137, regs. 94/3061; 95/482, 511, 516, 560, 626, 1045, 1613, 1644, 1742, 2287, 2303.
s. 137, repealed in pt.: 1994, c. 39, schs. 13, 14.
s. 137, amended: 1995, c. 18, sch. 2.
s. 138, regs. 95/1229.
s. 138, see *R.* v. *Chance, ex p. Smith, The Times*, January 28, 1995, D.C.; *R.* v. *Social Fund Inspector, ex p. Connick* [1994] C.O.D. 75, D.C.; *R.* v. *Social Fund Inspector, ex p. Connick* [1994] C.O.D. 75, D.C.
s. 147, amended: 1995, c. 42, sch.
s. 149, amended: 1995, c. 26, sch. 4.
s. 150, amended: 1995, c. 26, s. 132, sch. 6.
s. 157, amended: order 95/559.
s. 159A, orders 95/512, 513.
s. 163, orders 95/513.
s. 163, repealed in pt.: 1995, c. 18, sch. 3.
ss. 167, 171, regs. 94/1882; 95/566.
s. 171A, regs. 95/829, 987.
s. 171B, regs. 95/829.
s. 171C, regs. 95/311, 987; order 95/829.
s. 171D, regs. 95/311, 987; order 95/829.
s. 171E, regs. 95/311, 987; order 95/829.
s. 175, orders 95/482, 512, 581, 714, 825; regs. 94/1553, 1882, 2946, 3061; 95/74, 482, 511, 514, 516, 560, 566, 580, 626.
s. 175, regs. 95/1003, 1045, 1143, 1229, 1339, 1570, 1613, 1742, 2287, 2606.
s. 189, regs. 94/3196.
sch. 1, regs. 94/1553.
sch. 1, amended: 1995, c. 26, s. 148, sch. 5.
sch. 3, repealed in pt.: 1995, c. 18, schs. 3, 7.
sch. 3, amended: 1995, c. 26, s. 129, s. 134, sch. 4.
sch. 4, repealed in pt.: 1995, c. 18, sch. 3.

CAP.

1992—cont.

4. Social Security Contributions and Benefits Act 1992—*cont.*

sch. 4, amended: order 95/559.
sch. 5, repealed in pt.: 1995, c. 26, schs. 4, 7.
sch. 5, amended: 1995, c. 26, sch. 4; order 95/559.
sch. 7, amended: 1995, c. 18, sch. 2; orders 95/559, 581.
sch. 8, scheme 95/746.
sch. 8, amended: order 95/559.
sch. 11, repealed in pt.: 1995, c. 18, sch. 3.
sch. 12, repealed in pt.: 1995, c. 18, sch. 3.
sch. 12, see *R.* v. *Secretary of State for the Home Department, ex p. H.*; *R.* v. *Same, ex p. Hickey; sub nom. R.* v. *Secretary of State for the Home Department, ex p. T.* [1994] 3 W.L.R. 1110, C.A.
sch. 13, amended: 1995, c. 18, sch. 2.

5. Social Security Administration Act 1992.

regs. 95/559, 580, 1801.
see *R.* v. *Social Fund Inspector, ex p. Tuckwood* (CO-3807-94), April 27, 1995.
s. 1, amended: 1995, c. 18, sch. 2.
s. 5, regs. 94/2943; 95/511, 560, 625, 1613, 1644, 2303.
s. 5, amended: 1995, c. 18, sch. 2.
s. 6, regs. 95/511, 560, 625, 2303.
s. 15A, regs. 94/2944; 95/1613.
s. 15A, amended: 1994, c. 39, sch. 13 (S.); 1995, c. 18, sch. 2.
s. 17, repealed in pt.: 1995, c. 18, sch. 3.
s. 17, amended: order 95/512; 1995, c. 18, sch. 2.
s. 20, repealed in pt.: 1995, c. 18, sch. 3.
s. 20, amended: 1995, c. 18, sch. 2.
ss. 23, 24, see *Kuganathan* v. *Chief Adjudication Officer, The Times*, March 1, 1995, C.A.
s. 25, amended: 1995, c. 18, sch. 2.
s. 59, regs. 94/2975; 95/987.
s. 61, regs. 94/2686.
s. 61, amended: 1995, c. 18, sch. 2.
s. 61A, regs. 95/311.
s. 63, regs. 95/511, 987, 1644.
s. 63, amended: 1995, c. 18, s. 28.
s. 66, see *R.* v. *Social Fund Inspector, ex p. Ledicott, The Times*, May 24, 1995, Sedley J.
s. 68, amended: 1995, c. 18, sch. 2.
s. 70, repealed in pt.: 1995, c. 18, sch. 3.
s. 70, amended: 1995, c. 18, sch. 2.
s. 71, repealed in pt.: 1995, c. 18, sch. 3.
s. 71, amended: 1995, c. 18, s. 32, sch. 2.
s. 71A, added: 1995, c. 18, s. 18.
s. 73, amended: order 95/559; 1995, c. 18, sch. 2.
s. 74, amended: 1995, c. 18, sch. 2.
s. 74A, added: 1995, c. 34, s. 25.
ss. 75, 76, regs. 95/511.
ss. 75, 76, modified: regs. 95/531.

CAP.

1992—cont.

5. Social Security Administration Act 1992—*cont.*

s. 78, amended: 1995, c. 18, s. 32, sch. 2.
s. 78, see *Mulvey* v. *Secretary of State for Social Security* (O.H.), 1995 S.C.L.R. 102.
s. 81, amended: 1995, c. 18, sch. 2.
s. 96, order 95/1152.
s. 105, amended: 1995, c. 18, sch. 2.
s. 110, amended: 1995, c. 18, sch. 2; 1995, c. 26, sch. 5.
s. 115, amended: 1995, c. 18, sch. 2.
s. 116, amended: 1995, c. 18, sch. 2; 1995, c. 40, sch. 4 (S.).
s. 117, amended: 1995, c. 18, sch. 2.
s. 120, amended: 1995, c. 26, sch. 5.
s. 122, amended: 1995, c. 18, sch. 2.
s. 124, amended: 1995, c. 18, sch. 2.
s. 125, amended: 1995, c. 18, sch. 2.
s. 126, order 94/559.
s. 126, amended: 1995, c. 18, sch. 2.
s. 127, regs. 95/626.
s. 127, amended: 1995, c. 18, sch. 2.
s. 127, modified: regs. 95/531.
s. 128, regs. 95/626.
s. 128, amended: 1995, c. 18, sch. 2.
s. 128, modified: regs. 95/531.
s. 128A, added: 1995, c. 18, s. 28.
s. 134, order 95/2793.
s. 135, regs. 95/531.
s. 135, modified: order 95/872.
s. 136, regs. 95/1644.
s. 137, regs. 95/874.
s. 138, amended: 1994, c. 39, sch. 13 (S.).
s. 139, order 95/2793.
s. 140, regs. 95/531, 874.
s. 140, modified: order 95/872.
ss. 141, 142, 145, 147, order 95/512.
s. 148, order 95/1070.
s. 148, amended: 1995, c. 26, s. 128.
s. 149, amended: order 95/512.
s. 150, order 95/559; regs. 95/580, 2606.
s. 150, amended: 1995, c. 18, sch. 2; 1995, c. 26, s. 131.
s. 155, regs. 95/580, 2606.
s. 155, amended: 1995, c. 26, s. 131.
s. 156, substituted: 1995, c. 26, s. 130.
s. 159A, added: 1995, c. 18, s. 24.
s. 160A, added: 1995, c. 18, s. 25.
s. 164, amended: 1995, c. 18, sch. 2.
s. 166, amended: 1995, c. 18, sch. 2.
s. 170, amended: 1995, c. 18, sch. 2, 1995, c. 34, sch. 3.
s. 176, order 95/872.
s. 177, amended: 1995, c. 18, sch. 2.
s. 178, amended: 1995, c. 18, sch. 2.
s. 179, orders 94/2802; 95/767, 2699.
s. 179, amended: 1995, c. 18, sch. 2.
s. 180, amended: 1995, c. 18, sch. 2.
s. 187, amended: 1995, c. 18, sch. 2.
s. 189, orders 95/561, 872, 2793; regs. 94/2686, 2943, 2944; 95/561, 580, 626, 872, 874, 1613, 1644, 2303, 2606.
s. 190, order 95/559.

CAP.

1992—cont.

5. Social Security Administration Act 1992—*cont.*
s. 191, regs. 95/580, 874, 1644.
s. 191, repealed in pt.: 1994, c. 39, schs. 13, 14 (S.).
s. 191, amended: 1994, c. 39, sch. 13 (S.); 1995, c. 18, sch. 2; 1995, c. 26, sch. 4.
sch. 3, regs. 94/2975.
sch. 4, amended: 1995, c. 18, sch. 2; 1995, c. 26, schs. 5, 7.
sch. 9, scheme 95/746.

7. Social Security Contributions and Benefits (Northern Ireland) Act 1992.
s. 3, S.R. 1994 No. 485; regs. 95/146, 257.
s. 5, S.R. 1994 No. 484; regs. 95/88.
s. 17, regs. 95/91.
s. 20, repealed in pt.: S.R. 1995 No. 2705.
s. 21, repealed in pt.: S.R. 1995 No. 2705.
s. 22, amended: S.R. 1995 No. 2705.
s. 25, repealed: S.R. 1995 No. 2705.
s. 25A, regs. 95/341.
s. 25A, repealed: S.R. 1995 No. 2705.
s. 25B, repealed: S.R. 1995 No. 2705.
ss. 26–30, repealed: S.R. 1995 No. 2705.
ss. 30E, 57, regs. 95/72.
s. 61, amended: S.R. 1995 No. 2705.
s. 67, regs. 95/59.
s. 68, S.R. 1994 No. 462.
s. 72, regs. 95/59.
s. 80, S.R. 1994 No. 485.
s. 80, repealed in pt.: S.R. 1995 No. 2705.
s. 82, repealed in pt.: S.R. 1995 No. 2705.
s. 82, amended: S.R. 1995 No. 2705.
s. 84, amended: S.R. 1995 No. 2705.
s. 86A, S.R. 1994 No. 485; regs. 95/150.
s. 87, S.R. 1994 No. 485.
s. 87, amended: S.R. 1995 No. 2705.
s. 89, S.R. 1994 No. 485.
s. 90, S.R. 1994 No. 485; regs. 95/72.
s. 91, amended: S.R. 1995 No. 2705.
s. 113, regs. 95/72, 150.
s. 114, S.R. 1994 No. 485.
s. 116, regs. 94/1553; 95/714.
s. 116, amended: S.R. 1995 No. 2705.
s. 117, regs. 95/61.
s. 119, regs. 95/88.
s. 120, S.R. 1994 No. 13; regs. 95/13.
s. 121, S.R. 1994 No. 485; regs. 95/150.
s. 121, amended: S.R. 1995 No. 2705.
s. 122, regs. 95/64, 67, 84, 86, 89, 101, 129, 301, 350, 367, S.R. 1995 No. 223.
s. 123, regs. 95/67, 367.
s. 123, repealed in pt.: S.R. 1995 No. 2705.
s. 123, amended: S.R. 1995 No. 2705.
s. 124, repealed: S.R. 1995 No. 2705.
s. 125, amended: S.R. 1995 No. 2705.
s. 126, amended: S.R. 1995 No. 2705.
s. 127, regs. 95/86, S.R. 1995 No. 223.
s. 127, amended: S.R. 1995 No. 2705.
s. 128, regs. 95/67, 86, 367.
s. 128, amended: S.R. 1995 No. 2705.

CAP.

1992—cont.

7. Social Security Contributions and Benefits (Northern Ireland) Act 1992—*cont.*
s. 129, regs. 95/84, 129.
s. 131, regs. 95/67, 84, 86, 89, 101, 129, 301, 367.
s. 132, regs. 95/64, 84, 89, 129, 301, 367, S.R. 1995 No. 223.
s. 133, regs. 95/86, 89, 101, 367, S.R. 1995 No. 223.
s. 133, amended: S.R. 1995 No. 2705.
s. 134, S.R. 1995 No. 190; regs. 95/387.
s. 139, S.R. 1995 No. 755.
s. 155A, order 95/69, 70.
s. 158, repealed (with savings): S.R. 1994 No. 512.
s. 159, repealed (with savings): S.R. 1994 No. 512; order 95/70.
s. 159A, repealed (with savings): S.R. 1994 No. 512.
s. 163, order 95/74.
s. 165, S.R. 1994 No. 484.
s. 167A, regs. 95/41, 149.
s. 167B, regs. 95/41.
s. 167C, regs. 95/41, 149.
s. 167D, regs. 95/41, 149.
s. 167E, regs. 95/41, 149.
s. 171, regs. 95/64, 89, 101, 301, 367.
s. 175, S.R. 1994 No. 512.
s. 176, S.R. 1994 No. 512.
sch. 1, regs. 95/91.
sch. 1, amended: S.R. 1994 No. 512.
sch. 3, repealed in pt.: S.R. 1995 No. 2705.
sch. 4, repealed in pt.: S.R. 1995 No. 2705.
sch. 7, regs. 95/72, 73.
sch. 7, amended: S.R. 1995 No. 2705.
sch. 8, regs. 95/102.
sch. 11, repealed in pt.: S.R. 1995 No. 2705.
sch. 12, repealed in pt.: S.R. 1995 No. 2705.
sch. 13, amended: S.R. 1995 No. 2705.

8. Social Security Administration (Northern Ireland) Act 1992.
s. 1, amended: S.R. 1995 No. 2705.
s. 5, S.R. 1994 No. 456; regs. 95/64, 89, 150, 301.
s. 5, amended: S.R. 1995 No. 2705.
s. 13A, S.R. 1994 No. 456, 457; regs. 95/301.
s. 13A, amended: S.R. 1995 No. 2705.
s. 15, regs. 95/293.
s. 15, repealed in pt.: S.R. 1995 No. 2705.
s. 15, amended: S.R. 1995 No. 2705.
s. 18, regs. 95/293.
s. 18, repealed in pt.: S.R. 1995 No. 2705.
s. 18, amended: S.R. 1995 No. 2705.
ss. 20, 21, regs. 95/293.
ss. 23, 24, 25, 28, 29, 30; regs. 95/293.

CAP.

1992—cont.

8. Social Security Administration (Northern Ireland) Act 1992—*cont.*

ss. 30B, 30C, 30D, 30E, S.R. 1994 No. 456.
ss. 31, 32, 33, 43, 44, 45, 46, 48, 53; regs. 95/293.
s. 56, regs. 95/293.
s. 56, amended: S.R. 1995 No. 2705.
s. 57, S.R. 1994 No. 468; regs. 95/149, 293.
s. 59, regs. 95/150, 293.
s. 59A, regs. 95/41, 149.
s. 61, regs. 95/64.
s. 66, amended: S.R. 1995 No. 2705.
s. 68, regs. 95/293.
s. 68, repealed in pt.: S.R. 1995 No. 2705.
s. 68, amended: S.R. 1995 No. 2705.
s. 69, repealed in pt.: S.R. 1995 No. 2705.
s. 69, amended: S.R. 1995 No. 2705.
s. 69A, added: S.R. 1995 No. 2705.
s. 70, repealed: S.R. 1995 No. 2705.
s. 71, regs. 95/59.
s. 71, amended: S.R. 1995 No. 2705.
s. 72, amended: S.R. 1995 No. 2705.
s. 73, regs. 95/64.
s. 74, S.R. 1995 No. 755.
s. 74, amended: S.R. 1995 No. 2705.
s. 77, amended: S.R. 1995 No. 2705.
s. 100, amended: S.R. 1995 No. 2705.
s. 101, repealed in pt.: S.R. 1995 No. 755.
s. 104, amended: S.R. 1995 No. 2705.
s. 110, amended: S.R. 1995 No. 2705.
s. 111, amended: S.R. 1995 No. 2705.
s. 116, amended: S.R. 1995 No. 2705.
s. 118, amended: S.R. 1995 No. 2705.
s. 119, amended: S.R. 1995 No. 2705.
s. 120, regs. 95/129.
s. 120, amended: S.R. 1995 No. 2705.
s. 129, order 95/79.
s. 130, order 95/169.
s. 131, S.R. 1994 No. 474.
s. 132, order 95/71.
s. 135, regs. 95/72.
s. 139, regs. 95/293.
s. 139A, added: S.R. 1995 No. 2705.
s. 140A, added: S.R. 1995 No. 2705.
s. 144, amended: S.R. 1995 No. 2705.
s. 149, amended: S.R. 1995 No. 2705.
s. 153, amended: S.R. 1995 No. 2705.
s. 154, amended: S.R. 1995 No. 2705.
s. 155, order 95/110.
s. 155, amended: S.R. 1995 No. 2705.
s. 156, amended: S.R. 1995 No. 2705.
s. 163, amended: S.R. 1995 No. 2705.
s. 165, sch. 3, sch. 7, regs. 95/293.
s. 167, amended: S.R. 1995 No. 2705.

9. Social Security (Consequential Provisions) (Northern Ireland) Act 1992.

sch. 2, repealed in pt.: S.R. 1995 No. 755.
sch. 3, S.R. 1994 No. 474.

CAP.

1992—cont.

12. Taxation of Chargeable Gains Act 1992.

s. 3, order 94/3008.
s. 6, repealed in pt.: 1995, c. 4, sch. 29.
s. 7, repealed: 1995, c. 4, s. 115, sch. 29.
s. 16, amended: 1995, c. 4, s. 113.
s. 59, repealed in pt.: 1995, c. 4, sch. 29.
s. 65, amended: 1995, c. 4, s. 114.
s. 77, substituted: 1995, c. 4, sch. 17.
s. 78, amended: 1995, c. 5, sch. 17.
s. 79, repealed in pt.: 1995, c. 4, sch. 29.
s. 79, amended: 1995, c. 5, sch. 17.
s. 97, amended: 1995, c. 5, sch. 17.
s. 100, amended: 1995, c. 4, s. 72.
s. 117, amended: 1995, c. 4, s. 50.
ss. 127, 135, see *Nap Holdings U.K.* v. *Whittles (Inspector of Taxes)* [1994] S.T.C. 979, H.L.
s. 150, amended: 1995, c. 4, s. 69.
s. 150A, amended: 1995, c. 4, sch. 13.
ss. 150B, 150C, added: 1995, c. 4, sch. 13.
s. 151, amended: 1995, c. 4, s. 64.
ss. 151A, 151B, added: 1995, c. 4, s. 72.
s. 163, see *Jarmin (Inspector of Taxes)* v. *Rawlings* [1994] S.T.C. 1005, Knox J.
ss. 164A, 164F, amended: 1995, c. 4, ss. 46, 47.
ss. 164FF, 164FG, added: 1995, c. 4, s. 47.
s. 164I, amended: 1995, c. 4, s. 46.
s. 170, regs. 94/3228.
s. 171, see *Nap Holdings U.K.* v. *Whittles (Inspector of Taxes)* [1994] S.T.C. 979, H.L.
s. 175, repealed in pt.: 1995, c. 4, sch. 29.
s. 175, amended: 1995, c. 4, s. 48.
s. 179, amended: 1995, c. 4, s. 49.
s. 201, repealed in pt.: 1995, c. 4, sch. 29.
s. 209, regs. 95/352.
s. 211, amended: 1995, c. 4, sch. 9.
s. 212, amended: 1995, c. 4, s. 134, sch. 8.
s. 213, amended: 1995, c. 4, sch. 9; regs. 95/171.
s. 214, amended: regs. 95/171.
s. 214A, amended: 1995, c. 4, schs. 8, 9; regs. 95/171.
s. 222, see *Honour (Inspector of Taxes)* v. *Norris* (1994) 64 TC 599, Vinelott J.
s. 239A, added: 1995, c. 4, s. 61.
s. 241, amended: 1995, c. 4, sch. 6.
s. 247, amended: 1995, c. 4, s. 48.
s. 257, amended: 1995, c. 4, s. 72.
s. 260, amended: 1995, c. 4, s. 72, sch. 13.
s. 263A, added: 1995, c. 4, s. 80.
s. 271, amended: 1995, c. 4, s. 84.
s. 286, amended: 1995, c. 4, sch. 17.
s. 288, amended: 1995, c. 4, s. 72.
sch. 5B, added: 1995, c. 4, sch. 13.
sch. 7B, amended: 1995, c. 4, sch. 9.
sch. 8, amended: 1995, c. 4, s. 41, sch. 6.
sch. 9, order 94/2656.
sch. 10, repealed in pt.: 1995, c. 4, sch. 29.

CAP.

1992—cont.

13. Further and Higher Education Act 1992.
ss. 5, 8, amended: 1995, c. 50, s. 30.
s. 20, regs. 95/1342, 1344.
s. 21, regs. 95/1342, 1344.
s. 27, order 95/1927, 1929, 2091.
s. 50, regs. 95/2065.
s. 51, orders 94/2979; 95/1341, 1342, 1343, 1344, 1927.
s. 61, regs. 95/1342, 1344.
ss. 62, 65, amended: 1995, c. 50, s. 30.
s. 89, regs. 95/1342, 1344, 2065.
sch. 4, regs. 95/1342, 1344.

14. Local Government Finance Act 1992.
Commencement order: 94/3152.
orders 95/234, 619.
ss. 1, 3, see *Williams* v. *Bristol District Valuation Officer and Avon Valuation Tribunal* [1995] RA 189, Collins J.
s. 8, regs. 95/620.
s. 13, regs. 95/209.
s. 19, order 94/3054.
ss. 21–24, see *Williams* v. *Bristol District Valuation Officer and Avon Valuation Tribunal* [1995] RA 189, Collins J.
s. 24, regs. 95/363.
s. 26, order 94/3054.
s. 30, amended: 1994, c. 39, sch. 13 (S.).
s. 32, regs. 95/234.
s. 32, amended: regs. 95/234.
s. 32, see *R.* v. *Secretary of State for Wales, ex p. Gwent County Council* [1994] 34 R.V.R. 214, C.A.
s. 33, regs. 95/234.
s. 33, see *R.* v. *Secretary of State for Wales, ex p. Gwent County Council* [1994] 34 R.V.R. 214, C.A.
s. 35, repealed in pt.: 1995, c. 25, sch. 24.
s. 35, amended: 1995, c. 25, sch. 10.
s. 40, see *R.* v. *Secretary of State for Wales, ex p. Gwent County Council* [1994] 34 R.V.R. 214, C.A.
s. 41, regs. 95/235.
s. 43, regs. 95/234.
s. 43, see *R.* v. *Secretary of State for Wales, ex p. Gwent County Council* [1994] 34 R.V.R. 214, C.A.
s. 44, amended: regs. 95/234.
s. 54, see *R.* v. *Secretary of State for Wales, ex p. Gwent County Council* [1994] 34 R.V.R. 214, C.A.
s. 55, amended: regs. 94/2825.
s. 55, see *R.* v. *Secretary of State for Wales, ex p. Gwent County Council* [1994] 34 R.V.R. 214, C.A.
s. 56, amended: regs. 94/2825.
s. 56, see *R.* v. *Secretary of State for Wales, ex p. Gwent County Council* [1994] 34 R.V.R. 214, C.A.
s. 57, order 95/1545.
s. 72, order 95/598.
s. 74, repealed in pt.: 1994, c. 39, sch. 14 (S.).

CAP.

1992—cont.

14. Local Government Finance Act 1992—*cont.*
s. 80, regs. 94/3170 (S.).
s. 80, amended: 1994, c. 39, sch. 13 (S.).
s. 81, amended: 1994, c. 39, sch. 13 (S.).
s. 84, regs. 94/3170 (S.).
s. 84, amended: 1994, c. 39, sch. 13 (S.).
ss. 85, 86, 87, repealed in pt.: 1994, c. 39, sch. 13 (S.).
s. 90, repealed in pt.: 1994, c. 39, sch. 14 (S.).
s. 90, amended: 1994, c. 39, sch. 13 (S.).
s. 91, amended: 1994, c. 39, sch. 13 (S.).
s. 93, repealed in pt.: 1994, c. 39, sch. 14 (S.).
s. 94, repealed in pt.: 1994, c. 39, sch. 14 (S.).
s. 94, amended: 1994, c. 39, sch. 13 (S.).
s. 94A, added: 1994, c. 39, s. 24 (S.).
s. 95, repealed: 1994, c. 39, sch. 14 (S.).
ss. 97, 99, 107, repealed in pt.: 1994, c. 39, sch. 14 (S.).
ss. 97, 99, 107, amended: 1994, c. 39, sch. 13 (S.).
s. 108A, added: 1994, c. 39, s. 167 (S.).
ss. 109, 111, amended: 1994, c. 39, sch. 13 (S.).
s. 112, repealed in pt.: 1994, c. 39, sch. 14 (S.).
s. 113, orders 95/22, 121, 160, 161, 209, 597, 599; regs. 94/3146 (S.), 3170 (S.); 95/234, 235, 620.
s. 114, order 95/161.
s. 116, regs. 94/3146 (S.), 3170 (S.); 95/160, 597.
s. 119, order 94/3152.
Part 1, orders 95/600, 610.
sch. 1, orders 95/597, 620.
sch. 2, regs. 94/3170 (S.); 95/22, 121, 160.
sch. 2, repealed in pt.: 1994, c. 39, sch. 14 (S.).
sch. 3, amended: 1994, c. 39, sch. 13 (S.).
sch. 4, regs. 95/22.
sch. 4, repealed in pt.: 1995, c. 18, sch. 3.
sch. 4, amended: 1995, c. 18, sch. 2
sch. 7, repealed in pt.: 1994, c. 39, sch. 14 (S.).
sch. 8, repealed in pt.: 1994, c. 39, sch. 14 (S.); 1995, c. 18, sch. 3.
sch. 8, amended: 1994, c. 39, sch. 13 (S.); 1995, c. 18, sch. 2.
sch. 9, repealed in pt.: 1994, c. 39, sch. 14 (S.).
sch. 11, order 95/598.
sch. 11, repealed in pt.: 1994, c. 39, sch. 14 (S.).
sch. 12, order 94/528 (S.); regs. 94/3146 (S.).
sch. 12, amended: 1994, c. 39, sch. 13 (S.).
sch. 12, order 95/391 (S.).
sch. 13, repealed in pt.: 1994, c. 39, sch. 14 (S.); 1995, c. 25, sch. 24.

15. Offshore Safety Act 1992.
s. 2, repealed in pt.: 1995, c. 45, sch. 6.

CAP.

1992—cont.

19. Local Government Act 1992.
regs. 95/624.
s. 9, orders 95/600, 610; regs. 95/1336.
s. 13, see *R.* v. *Secretary of State for the Environment, ex p. Lancashire County Council*; *Same* v. *Same, ex p. Derbyshire County Council* [1994] 4 All E.R. 165, C.A.
s. 15, orders 95/187, 493, 600, 610, 1769, 1770, 1771, 1772, 1773, 1774, 1775, 1776, 1779.
s. 17, orders 95/187, 289, 493, 600, 610, 1747, 1769, 1770, 1771, 1772, 1773, 1774, 1775, 1776, 1779; regs. 94/867.
s. 18, regs. 94/2825; orders 95/187, 493, 600, 610, 1769, 1770, 1771, 1772, 1773, 1774, 1775, 1776, 1779.
s. 19, regs. 94/867, 2825, 3223; 95/23, 212, 247, 402, 520, 531, 590, 623, 624, 798, 1326, 1748, 2451; orders 94/3054, 3115, 3167.
s. 22, order 95/401.
s. 26, regs. 94/2825; 95/23, 212, 402, 520, 531, 590, 623, 624, 798, 1326, 1748, 2451; orders 94/3054, 3115, 3223; 95/187, 247, 289, 401, 493, 531, 600, 601, 610, 1747, 1769, 1770, 1771, 1772, 1773, 1774, 1775, 1776, 1779.
s. 30, amended: 1994, c. 39, sch. 13 (S.).
ss. 32, 41, 50, 54, amended: order 95/161.

35. Timeshare Act 1992.
s. 11, amended: 1995, c. 40, sch. 4 (S.).

37. Further and Higher Education (Scotland) Act 1992.
s. 27, orders 1995/1710, 1711.
s. 37, amended: 1995, c. 50, s. 31.
s. 40, amended: 1995, c. 50, s. 31.
s. 45, order 95/471.
s. 45, order of council 95/2261.
s. 60, order 95/471.
s. 60, order of council 95/2261.

38. Education (Schools) Act 1992.
s. 5, order 94/2957.
ss. 16, 19; regs. 95/1561, 1904, 2070.

40. Friendly Societies Act 1992.
Commencement order: 94/2543.
s. 1, regs. 94/1984.
s. 2, regs. 95/709.
s. 64, amended: 1995, c. 26, sch. 3.
s. 107, amended: 1995, c. 40, sch. 4 (S.).
s. 114, regs. 95/709.
s. 115, amended: regs. 95/710.
s. 123, regs. 95/710.
s. 126, order 94/2543.

41. Charities Act 1992.
Commencement order: 94/3023.
ss. 59, 64, 77, orders 94/3023, 3024.
s. 79, order 94/3023.

42. Transport and Works Act 1992.
s. 1, orders 94/1532; 95/1228, 2143, 2383, 2446, 2458.
ss. 3, order 95/619.
s. 5, orders 94/1532; 95/619, 1228, 2143, 2383.

CAP.

1992—cont.

42. Transport and Works Act 1992—*cont.*
s. 6, orders 95/1228, 1332, 2446, 2458.
s. 13, orders 95/2446, 2458.
s. 14, amended: regs. 95/1541.
sch. 1, orders 95/244, 2458.

43. Competition and Services (Utilities) Act 1992.
ss. 15, 16, 19, 38, repealed: 1995, c. 45, sch. 6.
s. 53, repealed in pt.: 1995, c. 45, sch. 6.
sch. 1, repealed in pt.: 1995, c. 45, sch. 6.

48. Finance (No. 2) Act 1992.
s. 2, regs. 95/1046.
s. 10, amended: 1995, c. 4, sch. 6.
ss. 19, 23, repealed in pt.: 1995, c. 4, sch. 29.
s. 27, repealed: 1995, c. 4, sch. 29.
s. 65, amended: 1995, c. 4, sch. 8.
sch. 9, repealed in pt.: 1995, c. 4, sch. 29.

52. Trade Union and Labour Relations (Consolidation) Act 1992.
s. 1, see *National Union of Mineworkers (Yorkshire Area)* v. *Millward* [1995] I.C.R. 482, E.A.T.
ss. 3, 6, regs. 95/483.
s. 37, see *Harrison* v. *Kent County Council* [1995] I.C.R. 434, E.A.T.
s. 41, see *D.P.P.* v. *Todd, The Independent*, May 5, 1995, D.C.
s. 45A, amended: 1995, c. 40, sch. 4 (S.).
ss. 46, 48, see *Douglas* v. *GPMU* [1995] IRLR 426, Morison J.
s. 50, see *National Union of Mineworkers (Yorkshire Area)* v. *Millward* [1995] I.C.R. 482, E.A.T.
s. 58, amended: 1995, c. 26, sch. 4.
s. 100B, see *National Union of Mineworkers (Yorkshire Area)* v. *Millward* [1995] I.C.R. 482, E.A.T.
ss. 108, 124, regs. 95/483.
s. 137, see *Harrison* v. *Kent County Council, The Times*, March 8, 1995, E.A.T.
ss. 152, 153, see *O'Dea* v. *ISC Chemicals* (EATRF 94/0722/B), July 28, 1995, C.A.
s. 159, order 95/1953.
ss. 188, 189, 195, see *R.* v. *British Coal Corp. and Secretary of State for Trade and Industry, ex p. Price* [1994] IRLR 72, C.A.
ss. 219, 226, 226A, 234A, see *Blackpool and the Flyde College* v. *National Association of Teachers in Further and Higher Education* [1994] IRLR 227, C.A.
s. 281, repealed: regs. 95/31.
s. 293, regs. 95/483.
sch. 1, amended: 1995, c. 17, sch. 1.
sch. 2, repealed in pt.: 1995, c. 24, sch. 2; 1995, c. 31, sch. 8.
sch. 2, C.: 1995, c. 23, sch. 8.

CAP.

1992—cont.

53. Tribunals and Inquiries Act 1992.
rules 95/1239.
s. 7, repealed in pt.: 1995, c. 26, schs. 5, 7.
s. 7, amended: 1995, c. 26, sch. 3.
s. 8, rules 95/1053; regs. 94/2849, 2896; 95/1045, 1801; order 95/1029.
s. 9, rules 94/3263, 3264; 95/1239.
s. 10, repealed in pt.: 1995, c. 26, schs. 5, 7.
s. 11, see *Strathclyde Regional Council* v. *Gallagher*, *The Times*, March 6, 1995; *R.* v. *London Value Added Tax and Duties Tribunal, ex p. Conoco* (LTA 95/5861/D; LTA96/6060/D), July 19, 1995, C.A.
s. 13, order 95/2877.
s. 13, repealed in pt.: 1995, c. 26, schs. 5, 7.
s. 14, repealed in pt.: 1995, c. 26, schs. 5, 7.
s. 14, amended: 1995, c. 26, sch. 3.
sch. 1, orders 94/2849, 2896; rules 94/3264.
sch. 1, repealed in pt.: 1995, c. 26, schs. 5, 7.
sch. 1, amended: 1994, c. 39, sch. 13 (S.); 1995, c. 26, sch. 3; 1995, c. 36, sch. 4 (S.), 1995, c. 53, s. 5; order 95/2877.
sch. 2, repealed in pt.: 1995, c. 53, sch. 2.

56. Maintenance Orders (Reciprocal Enforcement) Act 1992.
sch. 1, repealed in pt.: S.R. 1995 No. 755.

59. Consolidated Fund (No. 3) Act 1992.
repealed: 1995, c. 19, sch. C.

1993

1. Gas (Exempt Supplies) Act 1993.
Commencement order: 94/2568.
ss. 1, 2, repealed: 1995, c. 45, sch. 6.
s. 4, order 94/2568.

3. Social Security Act 1993.
s. 2, order 95/561.

4. Consolidated Fund Act 1993.
repealed: 1995, c. 19, sch. C.

7. Consolidated Fund (No. 2) Act 1993.
repealed: 1995, c. 19, sch. C.

8. Judicial Pensions and Retirement Act 1993.
Commencement order: 95/631.
s. 1, orders 95/632, 633.
ss. 2, 3, order 95/632.
s. 9, orders 95/638, 640.
s. 10, regs. 95/639.
s. 12, regs. 95/636, 639.
s. 13, repealed in pt.: 1995, c. 26, schs. 5, 7.
s. 19, regs. 95/640.
s. 20, order 95/635 (S.).
s. 21, order 95/633.
s. 23, orders 95/637, 639.
s. 26, amended: 1995, c. 21, sch. 13.

CAP.

1993—cont.

8. Judicial Pensions and Retirement Act 1993—*cont.*
s. 29, orders 95/633, 636, 639.
s. 31, order 95/631.
sch. 1, amended: order 95/633.
sch. 2, regs. 95/637, 639.
sch. 5, amended: 1995, c. 21, sch. 13.
sch. 6, repealed in pt.: 1995, c. 21, sch. 12.
sch. 6, C.: 1995, c. 21, sch. 14.
sch. 7, amended: 1995, c. 21, sch. 13.

9. Prisoners and Criminal Proceedings (Scotland) Act 1993.
s. 1, amended: order 95/911.
s. 2, see *F.* v. *H.M. Advocate*, 1994 S.C.C.R. 711.
ss. 5, 6, amended: 1995, c. 40, sch. 4.
s. 7, amended: 1995, c. 40, sch. 4.
s. 7, see *F.* v. *H.M. Advocate*, 1994 S.C.C.R. 711.
s. 8, repealed: 1995, c. 40, sch. 5.
s. 8, C.: 1995, c. 46, s. 44.
s. 11, amended: 1995, c. 20, sch. 6.
s. 12, amended: order 95/911.
s. 14, repealed in pt.: 1995, c. 40, sch. 5.
s. 14, amended: 1995, c. 40, sch. 4.
s. 14, C.: 1995, c. 46, s. 209.
s. 15, amended: 1995, c. 40, sch. 4.
s. 16, amended: 1995, c. 20, sch. 6.
s. 16, see *Advocate (H.M.)* v. *Donnachie*, 1994 S.C.C.R. 937; *Lynch* v. *Normand*, 1995 S.C.C.R. 404.
s. 17, amended: order 95/911.
s. 18, amended: 1994, c. 39, sch. 13; 1995, c. 20, sch. 6.
s. 20, order 95/911.
s. 27, amended: 1994, c. 39, sch. 13; 1995, c. 40, sch. 4.
s. 28, repealed: 1995, c. 40, sch. 5.
s. 28, repealed in pt.: 1995, c. 20, s. 50, sch. 7.
s. 28, C.: 1995, c. 46, s. 18.
s. 28A, added: 1995, c. 20, s. 58.
s. 28A, C.: 1995, c. 46, s. 19.
s. 28B, added: 1995, c. 20, s. 58.
s. 28B, C.: 1995, c. 46, s. 20.
s. 29, repealed: 1995, c. 40, sch. 5.
s. 30, repealed: 1995, c. 40, sch. 5.
s. 30, C.: 1995, c. 46, s. 272.
s. 31, C.: 1995, c. 46, s. 277.
s. 32, C.: 1995, c. 46, s. 273.
s. 33, repealed in pt.: 1995, c. 20, schs. 6, 7.
s. 33, amended: 1995, c. 20, sch. 6.
s. 34, amended: 1995, c. 20, sch. 6.
ss. 37–39, repealed: 1995, c. 40, sch. 5.
s. 40, repealed: 1995, c. 40, sch. 5.
s. 40, C.: 1995, c. 46, ss. 99, 158.
s. 41, repealed: 1995, c. 50, sch. 5.
s. 41, C.: 1995, c. 46, s. 210.
s. 42, repealed: 1995, c. 50, sch. 5.
s. 42, C.: 1995, c. 46, s. 108.
s. 43, repealed: 1995, c. 40, sch. 5; 1995, c. 46, s. 188.
s. 46, repealed in pt.: 1995, c. 40, sch. 5.

CAP.

1993—cont.

9. Prisoners and Criminal Proceedings (Scotland) Act 1993—*cont.*
s. 46, amended: 1995, c. 40, sch. 4.
sch. 3, repealed: 1995, c. 40, sch. 5.
sch. 3, repealed in pt.: 1995, c. 36, sch. 5.
sch. 3, amended: 1995, c. 20, sch. 6; 1995, c. 36, sch. 4.
sch. 4, repealed: 1995, c. 40, sch. 5.
sch. 5, repealed in pt.: 1995, c. 20, sch. 7; 1995, c. 40, sch. 5.
sch. 5, C.: 1995, c. 46, ss. 44, 110, 111, 117, 120, 122, 125, 126, 144, 145, 186, 189.
sch. 6, amended: 1995, c. 36, sch. 4.
sch. 7, C.: 1995, c. 46, s. 14.

10. Charities Act 1993.
Commencement order: 95/2695.
s. 5, amended: order 95/2696.
s. 17, order 95/1047.
s. 42, amended: order 95/2696.
s. 43, amended: order 95/2696.
s. 70, order 95/1092.
s. 86, order 95/2695.
s. 96, amended: 1995, c. 48, s. 1.
s. 99, order 95/2695.
sch. 2, order 94/2956.

11. Clean Air Act 1993.
s. 2, amended: 1995, c. 25, sch. 22.
s. 2, see *O'Fee* v. *Copeland Borough Council, The Times*, April 22, 1995, D.C.
s. 3, repealed in pt.: 1995, c. 25, sch. 24.
s. 17, repealed: 1995, c. 25, sch. 24.
s. 19, amended: 1995, c. 25, sch. 22.
s. 42, repealed in pt.: 1995, c. 25, sch. 24.
s. 46, amended: 1995, c. 21, sch. 13.
s. 51, repealed in pt.: 1995, c. 25, sch. 24.
s. 59, amended: 1995, c. 25, sch. 22.
s. 60, amended: 1995, c. 25, sch. 22.
s. 63, amended: 1995, c. 25, sch. 22.
s. 64, amended: 1994, c. 39, sch. 13 (S.); 1995, c. 21, sch. 13.
s. 64, see *O'Fee* v. *Copeland Borough Council, The Times*, April 22, 1995, D.C.
sch. 3, repealed in pt.: 1995, c. 25, sch. 24.

12. Radioactive Substances Act 1993.
amended: 1995, c. 25, sch. 22.
ss. 4–5, repealed in pt.: 1995, c. 25, sch. 24.
ss. 4–5, amended: 1995, c. 25, sch. 22.
s. 7, amended: 1995, c. 25, sch. 22.
s. 8, S.R. 1995 No. 296.
s. 8, amended: 1995, c. 25, s. 22.
s. 10, amended: 1995, c. 25, s. 22.
s. 11, S.R. 1995 No. 296.
s. 13, see *R.* v. *Secretary of State for the Environment, ex p. Greenpeace* [1994] 3 All E.R. 352, Potts J.
s. 15, S.R. 1995 No. 296.
s. 16, repealed in pt.: 1995, c. 25, sch. 24.
s. 16, amended: 1995, c. 25, sch. 22.
s. 16, see *R.* v. *Secretary of State for the Environment, ex p. Greenpeace* [1994] 3 All E.R. 352, Potts J.

CAP.

1993—cont.

12. Radioactive Substances Act 1993—*cont.*
s. 17, repealed in pt.: 1995, c. 25, sch. 24.
s. 17, amended: 1995, c. 25, sch. 22.
s. 18, repealed in pt.: 1995, c. 25, sch. 24.
s. 20, repealed in pt.: 1995, c. 25, sch. 24.
s. 20, amended: 1995, c. 25, sch. 22.
s. 21, repealed in pt.: 1995, c. 25, sch. 24.
s. 21, amended: 1995, c. 25, sch. 22.
s. 22, repealed in pt.: 1995, c. 25, sch. 24.
s. 22, amended: 1995, c. 26, sch. 22.
s. 23, amended: 1995, c. 26, sch. 22.
s. 24, amended: 1995, c. 26, sch. 22.
s. 24, see *R.* v. *Secretary of State for the Environment, ex p. Greenpeace* [1994] 3 All E.R. 352, Potts J.
s. 25, repealed in pt.: 1995, c. 25, sch. 24.
s. 25, amended: 1995, c. 26, sch. 22.
s. 26, repealed in pt.: 1995, c. 25, sch. 24.
s. 26, amended: 1995, c. 26, sch. 22.
s. 27, amended: 1995, c. 26, sch. 22.
s. 28, repealed: 1995, c. 25, sch. 24.
s. 28, amended: 1995, c. 26, sch. 22.
s. 30, amended: 1995, c. 26, sch. 22.
s. 31, repealed: 1995, c. 25, sch. 24.
s. 31, amended: 1995, c. 26, sch. 22.
ss. 32, 34, amended: 1995, c. 25, sch. 22.
s. 34A, added: 1995, c. 25, sch. 19.
s. 35, repealed: 1995, c. 25, sch. 24.
s. 35, amended: 1995, c. 25, sch. 22.
s. 38, amended: 1995, c. 25, sch. 22.
s. 39, repealed in pt.: 1995, c. 25, sch. 24.
s. 39, amended: 1995, c. 25, sch. 22.
s. 40, amended: 1995, c. 25, sch. 22.
s. 42, repealed in pt.: 1995, c. 25, sch. 24.
s. 42, amended: 1995, c. 25, sch. 22.
s. 43, repealed: 1995, c. 25, sch. 24.
s. 43, amended: 1995, c. 25, sch. 22.
s. 47, repealed in pt.: 1995, c. 25, sch. 24.
s. 47, amended: 1994, c. 39, sch. 13 (S.); 1995, c. 25, sch. 22.
s. 48, repealed in pt.: 1995, c. 25, sch. 24.
sch. 2, repealed: 1995, c. 25, sch. 25.
sch. 3, repealed in pt.: 1995, c. 25, sch. 24.
sch. 3, amended: 1995, c. 25, schs. 17, 22.

13. Carrying of Knives (Scotland) Act 1993.
s. 1, see *Stewart* v. *Friel*, 1995 S.C.C.R. 492.
s. 2, C.: 1995, c. 39, s. 50.
ss. 68, 69, repealed: 1995, c. 40, sch. 5.
sch. 5, repealed in pt.: 1995, c. 40, sch. 5.

19. Trade Union Reform and Employment Rights Act 1993.
s. 52, sch. 9, order 94/1365.
sch. 11, repealed in pt.: regs. 95/31.

22. Merchant Shipping (Registration, etc.) Act 1993.
repealed: 1995, c. 21, sch. 12.
sch. 4, regs. 95/972, 1983.

23. Asylum and Immigration Appeals Act 1993.
see *R.* v. *Immigration Appeal Tribunal, ex p. Sandralingam, The Times*, October 30, 1995, C.A.

CAP.

1993—cont.

23. Asylum and Immigration Appeals Act 1993—*cont.*

s. 1, see *Murugendran* v. *Secretary of State for the Home Department* [1994] Imm.A.R. 559, C.A.; *Kalunga* v. *Secretary of State for the Home Department* [1994] Imm.A.R. 585, C.A.

s. 3, see *R.* v. *Secretary of State for the Home Department, ex p. Tabed* [1994] Imm.A.R. 468, Sedley J.

s. 6, see *R.* v. *Governor of Wolds Prison, ex p. Samateh, The Times*, April 17, 1995, C.A.; *Kalunga* v. *Secretary of State for the Home Department* [1994] Imm.A.R. 585, C.A.

s. 8, see *Secretary of State for the Home Department, ex p. Kazmi (Syed Majid)* [1995] Imm.A.R. 74, Dyson J.; *Gnanavarathan (Pitchaippah)* v. *Special Ajudicator; Norbert (Sebastian)* v. *Same* [1995] Imm.A.R. 64, C.A.; *R.* v. *Secretary of State for the Home Department, ex p. Fahmi* [1994] Imm.A.R. 447, Jowitt J.; *Kalunga* v. *Secretary of State for the Home Department* [1994] Imm.A.R. 585, C.A.; *T.* v. *Secretary of State for the Home Department* [1995] 2 All E.R. 1042, C.A.; *R.* v. *Secretary of State for the Home Department, ex p. Singh, The Independent*, October 17, 1995, Carnwath J.

sch. 2, see *Gnanavarathan (Pitchaippah)* v. *Special Ajudicator; Norbert (Sebastian)* v. *Same* [1995] Imm.A.R. 64, C.A.; *R.* v. *Special Ajudicator, ex p. Abudine (Mohammed Said Ahmed)* [1995] Imm.A.R. 60, Sedley J.; *Hassan* v. *Secretary of State for the Home Department* [1994] Imm.A.R. 492, C.A.; *Kalunga* v. *Secretary of State for the Home Department* [1994] Imm.A.R. 585, C.A.

25. Local Government (Overseas Assistance) Act 1993.

s. 1, repealed in pt.: 1995, c. 25, sch. 24.

s. 1, amended: 1994, c. 39, sch. 13 (S.); 1995, c. 25, sch. 10.

28. Leasehold Reform, Housing and Urban Development Act 1993.

see *Treryn Heights, Godalming, Re*, October 19, 1994, Mr. B. Perrin; *South Eastern Rent Assessment Panel*; *Waitt* v. *Morris* (LON/NL/3) [1994] 39 EG 140, Leasehold Valuation Tribunal.

s. 11, amended: 1995, c. 38, sch. 1.

s. 127, amended: order 95/2720.

s. 128, order 95/2720.

s. 136, regs. 95/1981.

33. Appropriation Act 1993.

repealed: 1995, c. 19, sch. C.

34. Finance Act 1993.

Commencement orders: 94/2968, 3224, 3228.

CAP.

1993—cont.

34. Finance Act 1993—*cont.*

s. 4, order 94/2968.

s. 8, repealed: 1995, c. 4, sch. 29.

s. 16, repealed in pt.: 1995, c. 4, sch. 29.

s. 62A, added: 1995, c. 4, s. 88.

s. 63, repealed in pt.: 1995, c. 4, sch. 29.

s. 63, amended: 1995, c. 4, s. 88.

ss. 64–66, amended: 1995, c. 4, s. 88.

ss. 93, 94, 95, regs. 94/3230.

s. 96, repealed: 1995, c. 4, sch. 29.

ss. 99, 100, repealed in pt.: 1995, c. 4, sch. 29.

s. 126, amended: order 94/3233.

s. 128, amended: 1995, c. 4, sch. 24.

s. 129, repealed in pt.: 1995, c. 4, sch. 29.

s. 129, amended: 1995, c. 4, sch. 24.

s. 136, regs. 94/3232.

s. 141, amended: regs. 94/3228.

s. 143, regs. 94/3228.

s. 148, regs. 94/3229.

s. 153, amended: 1995, c. 4, sch. 24.

s. 164, regs. 94/3226, 3227, 3228, 3229; 95/408.

s. 165, order 94/3224; regs. 94/3226.

s. 167, regs. 94/3226, 3227, 3228, 3229, 3232; 95/408; order 94/3224.

s. 168, regs. 94/3231.

s. 168, amended: 1995, c. 4, s. 52.

s. 168A, added: 1995, c. 4, sch. 25.

s. 171, see *Deeny* v. *Gooda Walker (No. 2), The Times*, October 19, 1995, C.A.

ss. 179, 179A, regs. 95/351.

s. 182, regs. 95/351, 352, 353, 1185.

s. 182, amended: 1995, c. 4, s. 83.

s. 184, regs. 95/351, 352, 353.

sch. 6, repealed in pt.: 1995, c. 4, sch. 29.

sch. 16, regs. 94/3226, 3227; 95/408.

sch. 17, amended: 1995, c. 4, sch. 24.

sch. 20, amended: order 95/353.

sch. 20, amended: 1995, c. 4, s. 143.

35. Education Act 1993.

s. 36, regs. 95/628.

s. 81, regs. 95/587, 936, 1554.

s. 82, regs. 95/587, 936.

s. 83, regs. 95/587, 936.

s. 84, regs. 95/936.

s. 88, regs. 95/587.

s. 89, regs. 95/587.

s. 90, regs. 95/587.

s. 94, regs. 95/587, 936.

ss. 118, 119–124, regs. 94/2896.

s. 127, regs. 94/2281.

s. 153, regs. 95/2070.

s. 162, regs. 94/650; 95/629.

s. 166, amended: 1995, c. 17, sch. 1.

s. 168, regs. 95/45.

s. 172, regs. 95/1673.

s. 176, amended: 1995, c. 17, sch. 1.

s. 187, regs. 94/2281.

s. 192, regs. 95/2090.

s. 218, order 95/2037.

s. 220, order 95/2037.

ss. 223, 301, order 94/2849.

CAP.

1993—cont.

35. Education Act 1993—*cont.*
s. 228, regs. 95/61.
s. 252, order 95/903.
s. 298, regs. 95/2070.
s. 301, regs. 94/650, 2849; 95/587, 628, 629, 936, 1554, 1673, 2070.
sch. 9, regs. 95/1673.
sch. 10, regs. 95/45.
sch. 18, regs. 95/602, 2070.
sch. 19, repealed in pt.: 1995, c. 36, sch. 5.

36. Criminal Justice Act 1993.
Commencement order: 95/43, 1958.
s. 17, C.: 1995, c. 39, s. 37 (S.).
s. 19, C.: 1995, c. 39, ss. 38, 39, 40 (S.).
s. 20, C.: 1995, c. 39, s. 34 (S.).
s. 22, C.: 1995, c. 43, s. 39 (S.).
s. 24, C.: 1995, c. 43, s. 49 (S.).
s. 26, C.: 1995, c. 43, s. 36 (S.).
ss. 68, 69, repealed: 1995, c. 40, sch. 5 (S.).
s. 78, orders 95/43, 1958.
sch. 4, C.: 1995, c. 39, s. 42 (S.).
sch. 5, repealed: 1995, c. 40, sch. 5 (S.).

37. Agriculture Act 1993.
s. 1, orders 94/2900 (S.), 2921.
ss. 11, 14, regs. 94/2759.
s. 21, order 94/2922.
s. 52, amended: 1995, c. 40, sch. 4 (S.).
s. 62, regs. 94/2640, 2759.
sch. 2, order 94/2640.

38. Welsh Language Act 1993.
s. 6, repealed in pt.: 1995, c. 17, sch. 3.
s. 6, amended: 1995, c. 17, sch. 1; 1995, c. 25, sch. 10.
s. 25, orders 94/2736, 2889; 95/534.
s. 26, regs. 94/2981; orders 95/284, 734, 830, 1508.
s. 27, orders 94/2736, 2889; 95/830.

39. National Lottery etc. Act 1993.
Commencement order: 94/2659.
s. 23, repealed: 95/2088.
s. 29, order 95/2088.
s. 60, order 95/1645.
s. 65, order 94/2659.

40. Noise and Statutory Nuisance Act 1993.
s. 6, repealed: 1995, c. 25, sch. 24.
ss. 8, 9, amended: 1994, c. 39, sch. 13 (S.).
s. 13, repealed in pt.: 1995, c. 25, sch. 24.
sch. 1, repealed: 1995, c. 25, sch. 24.

43. Railways Act 1993.
Commencement order: 94/2142.
s. 37, see *Highland Regional Council* v. *British Railways Board, (I.H.), The Times*, November 6, 1994.
s. 136, amended: 1994, c. 39, sch. 13 (S.).
s. 148, amended: 1995, c. 40, sch. 4 (S.).
s. 151, amended: 1994, c. 39, sch. 13 (S.); repealed in pt.: 1994, c. 39, schs. 13, 14 (S.).
s. 154, order 94/2142.
sch. 11, orders 94/2388; 95/430.

CAP.

1993—cont.

44. Crofters (Scotland) Act 1993.
s. 12, see *Ross* v. *Barr's Trs.*, 1994 S.L.C.R. 60.
s. 13, see *Fraser* v. *MacKintosh*, 1994 S.L.C.R. 38.
s. 20, see *Dunbari (Sir G.C.D.S.) Trs.* v. *Crofters Sharing in Winless Common Grazings*, 1994 S.L.C.R. 89.
sch. 1, repealed in pt.: 1995, c. 7, sch. 5.

45. Scottish Land Court Act 1993.
sch. 1, see *Maciver* v. *Broadland Properties Estates* [1995] S.L.T. (Land Ct.) 9.

46. Health Service Commissioner Act 1993.
s. 2, orders 94/2954; 95/753.
s. 2, repealed in pt.: 1995, c. 17, sch. 3.
s. 2, amended: 1995, c. 17, sch. 1.
s. 6, amended: 1995, c. 17, sch. 1.
s. 14, amended: 1995, c. 17, sch. 1.

47. Probation Service Act 1993.
s. 2, orders 94/3313, 3314, 3315; 95/747, 1749.
s. 27, rules 95/302.

48. Pension Schemes Act 1993.
s. 2, regs. 95/1215.
s. 2, repealed: 1995, c. 26, schs. 5, 7.
ss. 3, 4, repealed: 1995, c. 26, schs. 5, 7.
s. 5, order 95/634.
s. 5, repealed: 1995, c. 26, schs. 5, 7.
s. 6, amended: 1995, c. 26, schs. 3, 5.
s. 7, repealed in pt.: 1995, c. 26, schs. 5, 7.
s. 7, amended: 1995, c. 26, s. 136.
s. 8, order 95/634.
s. 8, repealed in pt.: 1995, c. 26, schs. 5, 7.
s. 8, amended: 1995, c. 26, 136, sch. 5.
s. 9, regs. 95/35, 1612.
s. 9, repealed in pt.: 1995, c. 26, sch. 5.
s. 9, amended: 1995, c. 26, s. 136, sch. 5.
s. 10, amended: 1995, c. 26, sch. 5.
s. 11, amended: 1995, c. 26, sch. 5.
ss. 12A–12D, added: 1995, c. 26, 136.
s. 13, repealed in pt.: 1995, c. 26, schs. 5, 7.
s. 14, amended: 1995, c. 26, schs. 5, 7.
s. 15, amended: order 95/559.
s. 16, amended: 1995, c. 26, sch. 5.
s. 17, amended: 1995, c. 26, sch. 5; order 95/559.
s. 19, regs. 95/35.
s. 20, regs. 95/635.
s. 22, repealed: 1995, c. 26, schs. 5, 7.
s. 23, regs. 95/35.
s. 23, amended: 1995, c. 26, schs. 5, 7.
s. 24, repealed: 1995, c. 26, schs. 5, 7.
s. 25, repealed in pt.: 1995, c. 26, schs. 5, 7.
s. 25, amended: 1995, c. 26, sch. 5.
s. 26, regs. 95/35.
s. 28, repealed in pt.: 1995, c. 26, schs. 5, 7.
s. 28, amended: 1995, c. 26, ss. 142, 146, sch. 5.
ss. 28A–28B, added: 1995, c. 26, s. 143.

CAP.

1993—cont.

48. Pension Schemes Act 1993—*cont.*
s. 29, regs. 95/35.
s. 29, amended: 1995, c. 26, s. 144, sch. 5.
s. 30, amended: 1995, c. 26, sch. 5.
s. 31, regs. 95/35.
s. 31, repealed in pt.: 1995, c. 26, sch. 7.
s. 32A, added: 1995, c. 26, s. 146.
s. 33A, added: 1995, c. 26, s. 147.
s. 34, repealed in pt.: 1995, c. 26, schs. 5, 7.
s. 34, amended: 1995, c. 26, sch. 5.
ss. 35–36, repealed: 1995, c. 26, schs. 5, 7.
s. 37, substituted: 1995, c. 26, sch. 5.
s. 38, repealed in pt.: 1995, c. 26, schs. 5, 7.
s. 38, amended: 1995, c. 26, sch. 5.
s. 40, amended: 1995, c. 26, s. 137.
s. 41, amended: 1995, c. 26, s. 137.
s. 42, amended: 1995, c. 26, s. 137, sch. 5.
ss. 42A–42B, added: 1995, c. 26, s. 137.
s. 43, amended: 1995, c. 26, sch. 5.
s. 44, amended: 1995, c. 26, s. 164.
s. 45, repealed in pt.: 1995, c. 26, schs. 5, 7.
s. 45, amended: 1995, c. 26, s. 138.
s. 45A, added: 1995, c. 26, s. 138.
s. 45B, added: 1995, c. 26, s. 139.
s. 46, amended: 1995, c. 26, schs. 4, 5.
s. 48, repealed in pt.: 1995, c. 26, sch. 7.
s. 48, amended: 1995, c. 26, s. 140.
s. 48A, added: 1995, c. 26, s. 140.
s. 49, substituted: 1995, c. 26, sch. 4.
s. 50, repealed in pt.: 1995, c. 26, sch. 7.
s. 50, amended: 1995, c. 26, sch. 5.
s. 51, amended: 1995, c. 26, sch. 5.
s. 52, repealed in pt.: 1995, c. 26, schs. 5, 7.
s. 52, amended: 1995, c. 26, sch. 5.
s. 53, repealed in pt.: 1995, c. 26, sch. 5.
s. 53, amended: 1995, c. 26, sch. 5.
s. 54, repealed in pt.: 1995, c. 26, schs. 5, 7.
s. 54, amended: 1995, c. 26, sch. 5.
s. 55, repealed in pt.: 1995, c. 26, schs. 5, 7.
s. 56, repealed in pt.: 1995, c. 26, schs. 5, 7.
s. 56, amended: 1995, c. 26, sch. 5.
s. 57, amended: 1995, c. 26, sch. 5.
s. 58, repealed in pt.: 1995, c. 26, schs. 5, 7.
s. 59, repealed: 1995, c. 26, schs. 5, 7.
s. 60, repealed in pt.: 1995, c. 26, schs. 5, 7.
s. 60, amended: 1995, c. 26, sch. 5.
s. 61, repealed in pt.: 1995, c. 26, sch. 5.
s. 61, amended: 1995, c. 26, sch. 5.
s. 62, repealed in pt.: 1995, c. 26, sch. 7.
s. 63, repealed in pt.: 1995, c. 26, schs. 5, 7.
s. 64, repealed: 1995, c. 26, schs. 5, 7.
s. 65, repealed: 1995, c. 26, schs. 5, 7.
s. 66, repealed: 1995, c. 26, schs. 5, 7.

CAP.

1993—cont.

48. Pension Schemes Act 1993—*cont.*
s. 67, amended: 1995, c. 26, sch. 5.
s. 68, amended: 1995, c. 26, sch. 5.
s. 73, regs. 95/35.
ss. 77–80, repealed: 1995, c. 26, schs. 3, 7.
s. 84, repealed in pt.: 1995, c. 26, schs. 5, 7.
s. 93, amended: 1995, c. 26, s. 152.
s. 93A, added: 1995, c. 26, s. 153.
s. 94, amended: 1995, c. 26, s. 154.
s. 95, amended: 1995, c. 26, sch. 6.
s. 96, amended: 1995, c. 26, sch. 5.
s. 97, amended: 1995, c. 26, sch. 6.
s. 98, amended: 1995, c. 26, sch. 6.
s. 99, amended: 1995, c. 26, sch. 6.
ss. 102–108, repealed: 1995, c. 26, schs. 3, 7.
s. 109, amended: 1995, c. 26, s. 55.
s. 110, repealed in pt.: 1995, c. 26, sch. 7.
s. 110, amended: 1995, c. 26, s. 53.
s. 112, repealed: 1995, c. 26, schs. 3, 7.
s. 113, regs. 95/35.
s. 114, repealed: 1995, c. 26, schs. 3, 7.
s. 116, repealed: 1995, c. 26, schs. 3, 7.
s. 118, regs. 95/1215.
s. 118, repealed: 1995, c. 26, schs. 3, 7.
ss. 119–122, repealed: 1995, c. 26, schs. 3, 7.
s. 124, amended: 1995, c. 26, s. 90.
s. 129, repealed in pt.: 1995, c. 26, schs. 3, 5, 7.
s. 132, repealed in pt.: 1995, c. 26, schs. 3, 5, 7.
s. 133, repealed: 1995, c. 26, schs. 3, 5, 7.
s. 134, repealed: 1995, c. 26, schs. 3, 5, 7.
s. 135, repealed: 1995, c. 26, schs. 5, 7.
ss. 136, repealed in pt.: 1995, c. 26, s. 161, sch. 7.
s. 137, repealed in pt.: 1995, c. 26, s. 161, sch. 7.
s. 138, repealed in pt.: 1995, c. 26, s. 161, sch. 7.
s. 139, repealed in pt.: 1995, c. 26, s. 161, sch. 7.
s. 140, repealed in pt.: 1995, c. 26, s. 161, sch. 7.
s. 141, order 95/634.
s. 141, repealed in pt.: 1995, c. 26, s. 161, sch. 7.
s. 142, repealed in pt.: 1995, c. 26, s. 161, sch. 7.
s. 143, repealed in pt.: 1995, c. 26, s. 161, sch. 7.
s. 144, repealed: 1995, c. 26, schs. 3, 7.
s. 145, repealed in pt.: 1995, c. 26, sch. 7.
s. 145, amended: 1995, c. 26, s. 156, sch. 6.
s. 146, amended: 1995, c. 26, s. 157.
s. 146, see *Century Life* v. *Pensions Ombudsman*, *The Times*, May 23, 1995, Dyson J.
s. 147, amended: 1995, c. 26, s. 157.
s. 148, amended: 1995, c. 26, s. 157.
s. 149, rules 95/1053.

CAP.

1993—cont.

48. Pension Schemes Act 1993—*cont.*
s. 149, repealed in pt.: 1995, c. 26, sch. 7.
s. 149, amended: 1995, c. 26, ss. 157, 158, 159.
s. 150, amended: 1995, c. 26, s. 157.
s. 151, amended: 1995, c. 26, ss. 157, 159, sch. 6.
s. 151A, added: 1995, c. 26, s. 160.
s. 153, regs. 95/1215.
s. 153, repealed in pt.: 1995, c. 26, schs. 3, 7.
s. 154, amended: 1995, c. 26, sch. 3.
s. 155, repealed in pt.: 1995, c. 26, schs. 5, 7.
s. 155, amended: 1995, c. 26, sch. 5.
s. 158, repealed in pt.: 1995, c. 26, schs. 5, 7.
s. 158, amended: 1995, c. 26, sch. 5.
s. 158A, added: 1995, c. 26, sch. 6.
s. 159, amended: 1995, c. 26, sch. 3.
s. 162, regs. 95/35.
s. 163, amended: 1995, c. 26, sch. 5.
s. 164, repealed in pt.: 1995, c. 26, schs. 5, 6, 7.
s. 165, amended: 1995, c. 26, sch. 5.
s. 166, repealed in pt.: 1995, c. 26, schs. 5, 6, 7.
s. 168, substituted: 1995, c. 26, s. 155.
s. 168A, added: 1995, c. 26, s. 155.
s. 170, repealed in pt.: 1995, c. 26, schs. 3, 5, 7.
s. 170, amended: 1995, c. 26, sch. 5.
s. 171, amended: 1995, c. 26, sch. 5.
ss. 172–173, repealed: 1995, c. 26, schs. 5, 7.
s. 174, amended: 1995, c. 26, sch. 5.
s. 175, regs. 95/524.
s. 175, substituted: 1995, c. 26, s. 165.
s. 176, amended: 1995, c. 26, sch. 5.
s. 177, repealed in pt.: 1995, c. 26, schs. 5, 6, 7.
s. 178, repealed in pt.: 1995, c. 26, schs. 5, 6, 7.
s. 178, amended: 1995, c. 26, sch. 3.
s. 181, regs. 95/35, 524, 1215, 1612.
s. 181, repealed in pt.: 1995, c. 26, schs. 5, 6, 7.
s. 181, amended: 1995, c. 26, schs. 3, 4, 5.
s. 182, regs. 95/35, 524, 1215, 1612.
s. 182, repealed in pt.: 1995, c. 26, schs. 5, 7.
s. 183, repealed in pt.: 1995, c. 26, schs. 3, 5, 6, 7.
s. 183, amended: 1995, c. 26, sch. 3.
s. 185, repealed in pt.: 1995, c. 26, schs. 3, 5, 7.
s. 185, amended: 1995, c. 26, sch. 5.
s. 186, repealed in pt.: 1995, c. 26, schs. 5, 7.
s. 186, amended: 1995, c. 26, s. 155.
s. 192, repealed in pt.: 1995, c. 26, schs. 5, 7.
Part III, order 95/1070.
sch. 1, repealed: 1995, c. 26, schs. 5, 7.

CAP.

1993—cont.

48. Pension Schemes Act 1993—*cont.*
sch. 2, repealed in pt.: 1995, c. 26, schs. 5, 7.
sch. 2, amended: 1995, c. 26, s. 141, sch. 5.
sch. 3, regs. 94/2891.
sch. 4, amended: 1995, c. 26, sch. 5.
sch. 6, repealed in pt.: 1995, c. 26, schs. 5, 7.
sch. 7, repealed in pt.: 1995, c. 26, schs. 3, 7.
sch. 8, repealed in pt.: 1995, c. 26, sch. 7.
sch. 9, repealed in pt.: 1995, c. 26, sch. 7.
sch. 9, amended: 1995, c. 26, sch. 6.

49. Pension Schemes (Northern Ireland) Act 1993.
s. 5, regs. 95/7, 266.
ss. 15, 19, 22, 25, 27, 35, 69, regs. 95/7.
s. 105, order 95/62.
s. 109, regs. 95/7.
s. 137, S.R. 1995 No. 634; orders 95/388, 389.
s. 145, rules 95/167.
s. 158, sch. 1, regs. 95/7.
s. 170, regs. 95/65.

51. European Economic Area Act 1993.
s. 3, regs. 95/484, 732.

52. Consolidated Fund (No. 3) Act 1993.
repealed: 1995, c. 19, sch. C.

54. Finance Act 1993.
sch. 21, amended: 1995, c. 38, sch. 1.

62. Education Act 1993.
s. 161, repealed in pt.: 1995, c. 50, sch. 7.
s. 161, amended: 1995, c. 50, s. 29.

1994

2. Statutory Sick Pay Act 1994.
s. 3, order 95/512.

9. Finance Act 1994.
Commencement orders: 94/2679, 3225.
s. 7, regs. 95/2351.
s. 10, repealed in pt.: 1995, c. 38, sch. 2.
s. 14, regs. 95/2351.
s. 14, amended: 1995, c. 4, s. 20.
s. 21, regs. 95/1203.
ss. 22, 25, amended: 1995, c. 40, sch. 4 (S.).
s. 30, amended: 1995, c. 4, s. 15.
s. 39, amended: regs. 94/1216.
s. 53, regs. 95/1587.
s. 53, amended: 1995, c. 4, sch. 5.
s. 53, repealed in pt.: 1995, c. 4, sch. 29.
s. 53A, regs. 95/1587.
s. 53A, added: 1995, c. 4, sch. 5.
ss. 59, 73, amended: 1995, c. 4, sch. 5.
s. 110, amended: 1995, c. 4, s. 117.
s. 139, amended: 1995, c. 4, s. 141.
s. 143, repealed in pt.: 1995, c. 4, sch. 29.
s. 147, order 94/3225.
s. 150, amended: order 94/3233.
s. 175, amended: 1995, c. 4, s. 132.
s. 176, repealed in pt.: 1995, c. 4, sch. 29.

CAP.

1994—cont.

9. **Finance Act 1994**—*cont.*
s. 177, order 94/3233.
s. 177, amended: 1995, c. 4, s. 52.
s. 198, repealed: 1995, c. 4, s. 116, sch. 29.
s. 209, amended: 1995, c. 4, s. 209.
s. 210, amended: 1995, c. 4, s. 119.
s. 213, amended: 1995, c. 4, s. 102.
s. 215, amended: 1994, c. 4, s. 117.
s. 215, repealed in pt.: 1995, c. 4, sch. 29.
s. 218, amended: 1995, c. 4, s. 102.
s. 227, regs. 95/351.
s. 229, regs. 95/351.
s. 229, amended: 1995, c. 4, s. 83.
s. 230, regs. 95/351.
schs. 3, 4, repealed in pt.: 1995, c. 4, sch. 29.
sch. 5, repealed in pt.: 1995, c. 4, sch. 29.
sch. 5, amended: 1995, c. 4, sch. 3.
sch. 6, amended: 1995, c. 4, s. 16.
sch. 7, amended: 1995, c. 4, sch. 5; 1995, c. 40, sch. 4 (S.).
sch. 7, regs. 95/1587.
schs. 9, 16, repealed in pt.: 1995, c. 4, sch. 29.
sch. 17, repealed in pt.: 1995, c. 4, sch. 29.
sch. 18, amended: 1995, c. 4, sch. 8.
sch. 20, amended: 1995, c. 4, s. 122.
sch. 24, repealed in pt.: regs. 95/31.

13. **Intelligence Services Act 1994.**
Commencement order: 94/2734.
ss. 5, 11, amended: order 95/752.
s. 12, order 94/2955; 95/752.

15. **Antarctic Act 1994.**
Commencement order: 95/2748.
s. 3, amended: orders 95/1030, 1033, 1034, 1035.
s. 4, amended: order 95/1030.
s. 5, amended: order 95/1030, 1034.
ss. 9, 10, 11, regs. 95/490.
s. 13, amended: order 95/1030.
s. 14, regs. 95/490.
s. 15, regs. 95/490.
s. 15, amended: order 95/1030.
s. 17, amended: orders 95/1033, 1034, 1035.
s. 18, amended: order 95/1030.
s. 20, amended: orders 95/1034, 1035.
s. 21, amended: orders 95/1033, 1034, 1035.
ss. 22, 23, amended: orders 95/1030, 1033, 1034, 1035.
s. 24, amended: order 95/1035.
s. 25, regs. 95/490.
s. 28, substituted: order 95/1035.
s. 29, regs. 95/490.
ss. 31, 32, amended: orders 95/1033, 1034, 1035.
s. 32, regs. 95/490.
s. 34, orders 95/1030, 1033, 1034, 1035.
s. 35, orders 95/1035, 2748.

16. **State Hospitals (Scotland) Act 1994.**
Commencement order: 95/576.
s. 3, order 95/576.

CAP.

1994—cont.

18. **Social Security (Incapacity for Work) Act 1994.**
regs. 94/2975; order 95/559.
s. 2, order 94/559; regs. 94/2976.
s. 3, regs. 94/2976.
s. 4, regs. 95/310, 987.
s. 6, regs. 95/311.
s. 7, regs. 95/310, 987.
s. 12, regs. 94/2943, 2947; 95/310, 482, 626; order 95/829, 987.
s. 90, amended: regs. 94/2945.
sch. 1, repealed in pt.: 1995, c. 18, schs. 3, 7.

19. **Local Government (Wales) Act 1994.**
Commencement order: 94/2790; 95/546, 851, 852, 2816.
order 95/102; regs. 95/1040.
s. 17, order 95/2816.
s. 19, repealed in pt.: 1995, c. 25, sch. 24.
s. 39, order 95/103.
s. 45, regs. 95/1039.
s. 54, orders 94/3124; 95/102, 115, 128, 570, 1041, 1042, 1161, 1510.
s. 59, repealed in pt.: 1995, c. 25, sch. 24.
s. 63, orders 94/2790; 95/102, 115, 546, 570, 851, 852.
s. 65, order 92/2790.
s. 66, orders 95/102, 546, 570, 851, 852.
sch. 5, repealed in pt.: 1995, c. 25, sch. 24.
sch. 6, repealed in pt.: 1995, c. 25, sch. 24.
sch. 6, amended: 1995, c. 25, sch. 10.
sch. 7, C.: 1995, c. 23, sch. 8.
sch. 9, repealed in pt.: 1995, c. 25, sch. 24.
sch. 9, amended: 1995, c. 25, sch. 22.
sch. 10, repealed in pt.: 1995, c. 17, sch. 3.
sch. 11, repealed in pt.: 1995, c. 25, sch. 24.
sch. 15, repealed in pt.: 1995, c. 25, sch. 24.
sch. 16, repealed in pt.: 1995, c. 25, sch. 24; 1995, c. 45, sch. 6.
sch. 17, order 95/1043.
sch. 17, repealed in pt.: 1995, c. 25, sch. 24.

20. **Sunday Trading Act 1994.**
sch. 1, amended: order 95/3286.
sch. 4, repealed in pt.: regs. 95/31.

21. **Coal Industry Act 1994.**
Commencement orders: 94/2552, 3063; 95/159, 273, 1507.
s. 7, order 94/2553.
s. 16, order 95/1477.
s. 20, order 95/509.
s. 22, regs. 94/2576, 2577, 2973, 2974; 95/509.
s. 23, order 95/1507.
s. 24, order 95/255.
s. 45, regs. 94/2565.
s. 46, regs. 94/2563.
s. 47, reg. 94/2566.

CAP.

1994—cont.

21. Coal Industry Act 1994—*cont.*

s. 54, regs. 94/2595; orders 95/418, 419.
s. 67, orders 94/2567, 2645, 3062, 3065, 3081.
s. 68, orders 94/2552, 3063; 95/159, 273, 1507.
sch. 5, regs. 94/2576, 2577, 2973, 2974.
sch. 7, regs. 94/2562.
sch. 10, regs. 94/2564, 2565.

22. Vehicle Excise and Registration Act 1994.

ss. 3, 4, order 94/3095.
s. 7, regs. 94/3296, 3297.
s. 7, amended: 1995, c. 4, sch. 4.
ss. 11, 13, amended: 1995, c. 4, sch. 4.
s. 14, regs. 94/3296, 3297.
ss. 15, 16, amended: 1995, c. 4, sch. 4.
s. 17, repealed in pt.: 1995, c. 4, sch. 29.
s. 17, amended: 1995, c. 4, sch. 4.
s. 19A, added: 1995, c. 4, sch. 4.
s. 20, amended: 1995, c. 4, sch. 4.
s. 21, amended: 1995, c. 4, sch. 4.
s. 22, amended: 1995, c. 4, sch. 4.
s. 26, regs. 94/2976, 2977.
s. 31, repealed in pt.: 1995, c. 4, schs. 4, 29.
s. 32, amended: 1995, c. 40, sch. 4 (S.).
s. 32A, added: 1995, c. 4, sch. 4.
s. 35A, added: 1995, c. 4, sch. 4.
s. 36, amended: 1995, c. 4, sch. 4.
s. 37, repealed in pt.: 1995, c. 4, schs. 4, 29.
ss. 39, 40, amended: 1995, c. 4, sch. 4.
s. 41, repealed in pt.: 1995, c. 4, schs. 4, 29.
s. 41, amended: 1995, c. 40, sch. 4 (S.).
s. 45, amended: 1995, c. 4, sch. 4.
s. 48, amended: 1995, c. 40, sch. 4 (S.).
s. 52, amended: 1995, c. 4, sch. 4; 1995, c. 38, sch. 1.
s. 57, regs. 94/3296, 3297.
s. 60, amended: 1995, c. 4, sch. 4.
s. 60A, added: 1995, c. 4, sch. 4.
s. 61, amended: 1995, c. 4, sch. 4.
s. 61A, added: 1995, c. 4, sch. 4.
s. 62, repealed in pt.: 1995, c. 4, sch. 29.
sch. 1, order 95/1397.
sch. 1, repealed in pt.: 1995, c. 4, sch. 29.
sch. 1, amended: 1995, c. 4, s. 18, sch. 4.
sch. 2, repealed in pt.: 1995, c. 4, sch. 29.
sch. 2, amended: 1995, c. 4, sch. 4.
sch. 2A, added: 1995, c. 4, sch. 4.

23. Value Added Tax Act 1994.

s. 2, amended: 1995, c. 4, s. 21.
s. 5, orders 95/958, 1268, 1269, 1385, 1668.
s. 5, see *Patrick* v. *Customs and Excise Commissioners* [1994] V.A.T.T.R. 247, London Tribunal.
s. 11, order 95/1268.
s. 18, amended: 1995, c. 4, s. 29.
s. 21, amended: 1995, c. 4, s. 22.
s. 25, orders 95/281, 1267, 1666.

CAP.

1994—cont.

23. Value Added Tax Act 1994—*cont.*

s. 26, regs. 94/3015; 95/1069.
s. 28, order 95/291.
s. 30, orders 94/3014; 95/280, 283, 652, 653; regs. 95/1280.
s. 30, amended: 1995, c. 4, s. 28.
s. 31, order 94/2969; 95/282, 1978.
s. 32, repealed: regs. 95/1374.
s. 33, order 95/1978.
s. 33, amended: 1995, c. 21, sch. 13.
s. 33, see *Haringey London Borough Council* v. *Customs and Excise Commissioners, The Independent*, June 19, 1995, Dyson J.
s. 35, amended: 1995, c. 4, s. 33.
s. 37, regs. 95/913.
s. 39, see *R.* v. *Dayan (Abraham)* (1994) 15 Cr.App. R. (S.) 223, C.A.
s. 43, order 95/1268.
s. 43, amended: 1995, c. 4, s. 25.
s. 47, repealed in pt.: 1995, c. 4, sch. 29.
s. 47, amended: 1995, c. 4, s. 23.
s. 50A, orders 95/1268, 1269.
s. 50A, added: 1995, c. 4, s. 24.
s. 51, order 94/3013; 95/279.
s. 51A, added: 1995, c. 4, s. 26.
s. 53, order 95/1268.
s. 57, amended: 1995, c. 4, s. 30.
s. 67, amended: 1995, c. 4, s. 32.
s. 67, see *Cohen* v. *Customs and Excise Commissioners* [1994] V.A.T.T.R. 290, London Tribunal; *Jordan* v. *Customs and Excise Commissioners* [1994] V.A.T.T.R. 286, London Tribunal.
s. 70, see *Cohen* v. *Customs and Excise Commissioners* [1994] V.A.T.T.R. 290, London Tribunal; *Jordan* v. *Customs and Excise Commissioners* [1994] V.A.T.T.R. 286, London Tribunal.
s. 74, order 94/2542.
s. 74, amended: order 95/521.
s. 81, amended: 1995, c. 4, s. 27.
s. 84, amended: 1995, c. 4, s. 31.
s. 84, repealed in pt.: 1995, c. 4, sch. 29.
s. 93, regs. 95/152.
s. 95, amended; order 94/3128.
s. 96, orders 94/2969, 3014; 95/280, 283, 652, 1510.
s. 96, amended: 1995, c. 38, schs. 1, 2.
sch. A1, added: 1995, c. 4, s. 21.
sch. 1, amended: order 94/2905.
sch. 1, see *Ying Luong (A Partnership)* v. *Customs and Excise Commissioners* [1994] V.A.T.T.R. 349, Manchester Tribunal.
sch. 3, amended: order 94/2905.
sch. 4, amended: 1995, c. 4, s. 33.
sch. 8, repealed in pt.: 1995 S.R. No. 1625.
sch. 8, amended: orders 95/280, 283, 652, 653; 1995 S.R. No. 1625; 1995, c. 17, sch. 1.

CAP.

1994—cont.

23. Value Added Tax Act 1994—*cont.*

sch. 8, see *Customs and Excise Commissioners* v. *Colour, The Independent*, February 13, 1995, May J.; *Customs and Excise Commissioners* v. *David Lewis Centre, The Independent*, May 1, 1995, Owen J.; *Customs and Excise Commissioner* v. *Arbib, The Independent*, May 30, 1995, Latham J.; *Customs and Excise Commissioner* v. *Wellington Private Hospital, The Independent*, May 30, 1995, Jowitt J.; *Ashworth* v. *Customs and Excise Commissioner* [1994] V.A.T.T.R. 275, London Tribunal; *Hardy* v. *Customs and Excise Commissioners* [1994] V.A.T.T.R. 302, Manchester Tribunal.
sch. 9, see *Nell Gwynn House Maintenance Fund Trustees* v. *Customs and Excise Commissioners* [1994] S.T.C. 995, Popplewell J.; *Arts Council of Great Britain* v. *Customs and Excise Commissioners* [1994] V.A.T.T.R. 313, London Tribunal; *Ashworth* v. *Customs and Excise Commissioner* [1994] V.A.T.T.R. 275, London Tribunal.
sch. 10, amended: 1995, c. 4, sch. 10; order 95/3013; 95/279.
sch. 11, regs. 95/152, 1069; orders 95/1268, 1269.
sch. 11, amended: 1995, c. 40, sch. 4 (S.).
sch. 11, see *Primback* v. *Customs and Excise Commissioners* [1994] S.T.C. 957, May J.
sch. 12, rules 94/2617.
sch. 13, repealed in pt.: 1995, c. 4, sch. 29.
sch. 13, amended: 1995, c. 4, s. 33.
sch. 14, amended: 1995, c. 4, s. 33.

26. Trade Marks Act 1994.

s. 4, order 94/2583.
s. 4, amended: 1995, c. 32, s. 13.
s. 13, order 94/2583.
s. 19, Act of Sederunt 94/29091 (S.), 3066 (S.).
ss. 24, 34, 35, 36, 39, order 94/2883.
ss. 40, 41, rules 94/2581, 2583.
ss. 43, 44, 45, 63, rules 94/2583.
s. 64, rules 94/2583.
s. 64, see *St. Trudo Trade Mark* [1995] F.S.R. 345, Ferris J.
ss. 65–67, rules 94/2582.
s. 68, rules 94/2581, 2583.
ss. 69, 76, 78, rules 94/2583.
s. 79, rules 94/2584.
ss. 80, 81, 82, 88, rules 94/2583.
s. 89, amended: regs. 95/1444.
s. 90, regs. 94/2625.
s. 96, amended: 1995, c. 40, sch. 4 (S.).
s. 97, amended: 1995, c. 32, s. 11.
s. 98, amended: 1995, c. 32, s. 12; 1995, c. 40, sch. 4 (S.).

CAP.

1994—cont.

26. Trade Marks Act 1994—*cont.*

s. 105, see *St. Trudo Trade Mark* [1995] F.S.R. 345, Ferris J.
schs. 1, 2, rules 94/2583.
sch. 3, rules 94/2583.
sch. 3, see *St. Trudo Trade Mark* [1995] F.S.R. 345, Ferris J.

28. Merchant Shipping (Salvage and Pollution) Act 1994.

Commencement order: 94/2971.
repealed: 1995, c. 21, sch. 12.
ss. 1–7, 9, C.: 1995, c. 21, sch. 14.
s. 10, order 94/2971.
s. 10, C.: 1995, c. 21, sch. 14.
schs. 1, 3. C.: 1995, c. 21, sch. 14.
sch. 4, continued in force (pt.): 1995, c. 21, sch. 14.
schs. 4, 5. C.: 1995, c. 21, sch. 14.

29. Police and Magistrates' Courts Act 1994.

Commencement orders: 94/2594, 3075 (S.), 3262 (corrected by order 95/246); 95/42, 89, 246, 492 (S.), 685.
s. 28, orders 95/600, 610, 1769, 1770, 1771, 1772, 1773, 1774, 1775, 1776, 1779.
s. 31, order 94/2969.
s. 52, regs. 94/3039 (S.).
s. 69, order 95/2376.
s. 94, orders 94/3075 (S.), 3262; 95/42, 89, 246, 492 (S.), 685.
s. 96, order 94/2969.

30. Education Act 1994.

s. 1, amended: 1995, c. 50, s. 29.
s. 4, order 95/1704.
s. 16, order 95/601.
s. 17, order 94/2463.
s. 23, order 94/2463; 95/601, 1704.

32. Drug Trafficking Act 1994.

ss. 4, 6, 18, 26, amended: 1995, c. 20, sch. 6 (S.).

33. Criminal Justice and Public Order Act 1994.

Commencement orders: 94/2935, 3192, 3258, 3262; 95/24, 127, 721, 1378, 1957.
see *R.* v. *Iqbal, The Times*, September 5, 1995, C.A.
s. 25, amended: 1995, c. 40, sch. 4 (S.).
s. 32, see *R.* v. *Makanjuola, The Times*, May 17, 1995, C.A.
s. 35, see *R.* v. *Cowan, The Times*, October 13, 1995, C.A.
s. 47, repealed in pt.: 1995, c. 40, sch. 5 (S.).
s. 51, amended: 1995, c. 35, sch. 2.
s. 67, regs. 95/723.
s. 77, see *R.* v. *Wealden District Council, ex p. Wales*; *R.* v. *Same, ex p. Stratford*; *R.* v. *Lincolnshire County Council, ex p. Atkinson, The Times*, September 22, 1995, Sedley J.
ss. 78, 79, order 95/1042.
s. 94, order 94/3262.

CAP.

1994—cont.

33. Criminal Justice and Public Order Act 1994—*cont.*

s. 102, amended: 1995, c. 40, sch. 4 (S.).
s. 104, amended: 1995, c. 40, sch. 4 (S.).
s. 117, amended: 1995, c. 40, sch. 4 (S.).
s. 129, repealed in pt.: 1995, c. 40, sch. 5 (S.).
s. 129, C.: 1995, c. 39, ss. 24, 25 (S.); 1995, c. 46, s. 14 (S.).
s. 132, repealed: 1995, c. 40, sch. 5 (S.).
s. 138, amended: 1995, c. 40, sch. 4 (S.).
ss. 145, 146, C.: 1995, c. 39, s. 13 (S.).
s. 157, repealed in pt.: 1995, c. 40, sch. 5 (S.).
s. 164, C.: 1995, c. 39, s. 28 (S.).
s. 172, orders 94/2935, 3192, 3258; 95/24, 127, 721, 1378, 1957.
sch. 10, repealed in pt.: 1995, c. 20, sch. 7.

34. Marriage Act 1994.

Commencement order: 94/3116; 95/424.
s. 3, orders 94/3116; 95/424.

36. Law of Property (Miscellaneous Provisions) Act 1994.

Commencement orders: 95/145, 1317.
s. 19, regs. 95/1330.
s. 23, orders 95/145, 1317.

37. Drug Trafficking Act 1994.

see *R.* v. *Dunham*, *The Times*, November 2, 1995, C.A.
s. 4, amended: 1995, c. 40, sch. 4 (S.).
s. 6, amended: 1995, c. 40, sch. 4 (S.).
s. 10, amended: 1995, c. 42, s. 4.
s. 18, amended: 1995, c. 40, sch. 4 (S.).
s. 26, amended: 1995, c. 40, sch. 4 (S.).
s. 37, repealed in pt.: 1995, c. 40, sch. 4 (S.).
s. 37, amended: 1995, c. 40, sch. 5 (S.).
s. 48, amended: 1995, c. 40, sch. 4 (S.).
sch. 1, C.: 1995, c. 43, ss. 3, 14, 35, 36 (S.).

39. Local Government etc. (Scotland) Act 1994.

Commencement orders: 94/3150; 95/702, 1898.
s. 2, amended: 1995, c. 25, sch. 22.
s. 8, order 95/1340.
s. 12, order 94/2958 (S.).
s. 15, order 95/2499.
s. 19, order 94/2500.
s. 27, order 95/1515.
s. 37, repealed: 1995, c. 25, sch. 24.
s. 40, order 95/1971.
s. 54, repealed in pt.: 1995, c. 25, sch. 24.
s. 55, order 95/1894.
s. 97, order 95/1340.
s. 125A, added: 1995, c. 25, sch. 21.
ss. 127, 128, 130, amended: 1995, c. 40, sch. 4 (S.).
s. 128, amended: 1995, c. 36, sch. 4.
s. 130, amended: 1995, c. 36, sch. 4.
s. 132, amended: 1995, c. 36, sch. 4.
s. 137, order 95/1340.
s. 139, repealed: 1995, c. 36, sch. 5.
s. 153, regs. 95/548.
s. 165, repealed in pt.: 1995, c. 25, sch. 24.

CAP.

1994—cont.

39. Local Government etc. (Scotland) Act 1994—*cont.*

s. 172, orders 95/1879, 1880, 1881, 1882, 1883, 1884, 1885, 1886, 1887, 1888, 1889, 1890, 1891, 1892, 2211, 2212, 2213, 2214, 2232, 2236, 2237, 2238, 2239, 2240, 2241.
s. 172, repealed in pt.: 1995, c. 7, sch. 5.
s. 173, orders 95/2211, 2212, 2213, 2214, 2232, 2236, 2237, 2238, 2239, 2240, 2241.
s. 181, orders 94/3255; 95/1878, 2499, 2766.
s. 184, orders 94/3150; 95/702, 1898.
s. 235, amended (temp.): 1995, c. 21, sch. 14.
sch. 3, repealed in pt.: 1995, c. 7, sch. 5.
sch. 7, repealed in pt.: 1995, c. 7, sch. 5.
sch. 8, amended: 1995, c. 21, sch. 12.
sch. 12, repealed in pt.: 1995, c. 7, sch. 5.
sch. 13, repealed in pt.: 1995, c. 7, sch. 5; 1995, c. 21, sch. 12; 1995, c. 23, sch. 8; 1995, c. 25, schs. 22, 24; 1995, c. 36, sch. 5; 1995, c. 45, sch. 6.
sch. 13, C.: 1995, c. 21, sch. 14; 1995, c. 23, sch. 8; 1995, c. 46, ss. 49, 232.

40. Deregulation and Contracting Order Act 1994.

Commencement orders: 94/488, 1433, 3037, 3188.
s. 2, amended: 1995, c. 40, sch. 4 (S.).
ss. 44–49, 55, C.: 1995, c. 23, sch. 8.
s. 69, order 95/1386.
s. 82, order 95/1433.
s. 82, orders 94/488, 3037, 3188; 95/1433.
Part 1, repealed in pt.: 1995, c. 23, sch. 8.
sch. 12, repealed: 1995, c. 23, sch. 8.
sch. 12, C.: 1995, c. 23, sch. 8.
sch. 13, repealed: 1995, c. 23, sch. 8.
sch. 13, C.: 1995, c. 23, sch. 8.
sch. 16, repealed in pt.: 1995, c. 45, sch. 6.

68. Merchant Shipping (Salvage and Pollution) Act 1994.

Commencement order: 94/2971.
s. 10, order 94/2971.

1995

1. European Communities (Finance) Act 1995.

Royal Assent, January 16, 1995.

2. Consolidated Fund Act 1995.

Royal Assent, March 23, 1995.

3. South Africa Act 1995.

Royal Assent, March 23, 1995.

4. Finance Act 1995.

Royal Assent, May 1, 1995.
Commencement orders: 95/1778, 2892.
s. 20, order 95/2892.
s. 24, order 95/1374.
s. 65, order 95/1778.

CAP.

1995—cont.

4. Finance Act 1995—*cont.*
s. 73, regs. 95/1979.
sch. 4, amended: 1995, c. 38, sch. 2.
sch. 8, regs. 95/1730.
sch. 12, order 95/1778.

5. Building Societies (Joint Account Holders) Act 1995.
Royal Assent, May 1, 1995.

6. Civil Evidence (Family Mediation) (Scotland) Act 1995.
Royal Assent, May 1, 1995.
s. 2, amended: 1995, c. 36, sch. 4.

7. Requirements of Writing (Scotland) Act 1995.
Royal Assent, May 1, 1995.

8. Agricultural Tenancies Act 1995.
Royal Assent, May 9, 1995.

9. Commonwealth Development Corporation Act 1995.
Royal Assent, June 28, 1995.

10. Home Energy Conservation Act 1995.
Royal Assent, June 28, 1995.

11. Proceeds of Crime Act 1995.
Royal Assent, June 28, 1995.
Commencement order: 95/2650.
s. 16, order 95/2640.

12. Carers (Recognition and Services) Act 1995.
Royal Assent, June 28, 1995.

13. Road Traffic (New Drivers) Act 1995.
Royal Assent, June 28, 1995.

14. Land Registers (Scotland) Act 1995.
Royal Assent, June 28, 1995.

15. Activity Centres (Young Persons' Safety) Act 1995.
Royal Assent, June 28, 1995.

16. Prisoners (Return to Custody) Act 1995.
Royal Assent, June 28, 1995.
Commencement order: 95/2021.
s. 3, order 95/2021.

17. Health Authorities Act 1995.
Royal Assent, June 28, 1995.
sch. 1, repealed in pt.: 1995, c. 31, sch.

18. Jobseekers Act 1995.
Royal Assent, June 28, 1995.

19. Appropriation Act 1995.
Royal Assent, July 19, 1995.

20. Criminal Justice (Scotland) Act 1995.
Royal Assent, July 19, 1995.
Commencement order: 95/2295.
repealed (prosp.): 1995, c. 40, sch. 5.
s. 2, C.: 1995, c. 46, s. 27.
s. 3, C.: 1995, c. 46, s. 27.
s. 5, C.: 1995, c. 46, s. 112.
s. 9, C.: 1995, c. 46, s. 297.
s. 10, C.: 1995, c. 46, s. 36.
s. 11, order 95/2295.
s. 11, C.: 1995, c. 46, s. 78.
s. 12, C.: 1995, c. 46, s. 257.
s. 13, C.: 1995, c. 46, ss. 73, 74.
s. 14, C.: 1995, c. 46, s. 148.
s. 16, C.: 1995, c. 46, s. 258.

CAP.

1995—cont.

20. Criminal Justice (Scotland) Act 1995—*cont.*
s. 17, C.: 1995, c. 46, s. 259.
s. 18, C.: 1995, c. 46, s. 260.
s. 19, C.: 1995, c. 46, s. 261.
s. 20, amended: 1995, c. 36, sch. 4.
s. 20, C.: 1995, c. 46, s. 262.
s. 21, C.: 1995, c. 46, s. 276.
s. 22, C.: 1995, c. 46, ss. 280, 281.
s. 23, C.: 1995, c. 46, s. 68.
s. 24, C.: 1995, c. 46, ss. 101, 266, 270.
s. 25, C.: 1995, c. 46, s. 282.
s. 26, C.: 1995, c. 46, s. 283.
s. 27, C.: 1995, c. 46, s. 284.
s. 28, C.: 1995, c. 46, s. 274.
s. 29, C.: 1995, c. 46, s. 286.
s. 30, C.: 1995, c. 46, ss. 87, 151.
s. 31, C.: 1995, c. 46, s. 153.
s. 33, C.: 1995, c. 46, s. 196.
s. 34, C.: 1995, c. 46, ss. 189, 197.
s. 35, C.: 1995, c. 46, ss. 235, 236, 237, sch. 7.
s. 36, C.: 1995, c. 46, s. 209.
s. 37, C.: 1995, c. 46, s. 203.
s. 38, C.: 1995, c. 46, ss. 228, 229.
s. 39, C.: 1995, c. 46, ss. 230, 307.
s. 40, C.: 1995, c. 46, ss. 233, 241.
s. 41, C.: 1995, c. 46, s. 300.
s. 42, C.: 1995, c. 46, ss. 106, 110, 182, 187.
s. 43, C.: 1995, c. 46, s. 103.
s. 44, C.: 1995, c. 46, s. 298.
s. 46, C.: 1995, c. 46, ss. 119, 183, 185.
s. 48, C.: 1995, c. 46, s. 54.
s. 49, C.: 1995, c. 46, ss. 55, 56.
s. 50, C.: 1995, c. 46, s. 57.
s. 55, C.: 1995, c. 46, s. 200.
s. 56, C.: 1995, c. 46, s. 304.
s. 57, C.: 1995, c. 46, s. 306.
s. 58, C.: 1995, c. 46, ss. 18, 19.
s. 60, C.: 1995, c. 46, s. 7.
s. 61, C.: 1995, c. 46, s. 302.
s. 62, C.: 1995, c. 46, s. 136.
s. 67, C.: 1995, c. 46, s. 222.
s. 70, see *Bennett* v. *H.M. Advocate*, 1995 S.L.T. 761.
s. 101, see *McCulloch* v. *H.M. Advocate*, 1995 S.L.T. 918.
s. 108, see *Bennett* v. *H.M. Advocate*, 1995 S.L.T. 761.
sch. 2, C.: 1995, c. 46, sch. 4.
sch. 6, C.: 1995, c. 46, ss. 11, 17, 37, 44, 47, 51, 54, 58, 61, 66, 67, 69, 77, 78, 79, 81, 84, 85, 88, 89, 93, 97, 99, 102, 106, 113, 114, 117, 118, 120, 121, 122, 124, 125, 126, 129, 133–142, 148, 149, 150, 155–159, 163, 166, 167, 172, 173, 175, 186, 188, 190, 192, 193, 194, 201, 202, 211, 214, 216, 224, 227, 228, 231, 238, 239, 247, 256, 263, 271, 277, 285, 287, 296, 305, schs. 3, 6, 7.

CAP.

1995—cont.

21. Merchant Shipping Act 1995.
Royal Assent, July 19, 1995.

22. Shipping and Trading Interests (Protection) Act 1995.
Royal Assent, July 19, 1995.

23. Goods Vehicles (Licensing of Operators) Act 1995.
Royal Assent, July 19, 1995.
Commencement order: 95/2181.
s. 61, order 95/2181.

24. Crown Agents Act 1995.
Royal Assent, July 19, 1995.

25. Environment Act 1995.
Royal Assent, July 19, 1995.
Commencement orders: 95/1983, 2649, 2765.
s. 8, repealed in pt.: 1995, c. 25, sch. 24.
s. 125, orders 95/1983, 2649, 2765.
sch. 10, repealed in pt.: 1995, c. 25, sch. 24.
sch. 11, repealed in pt.: 1995, c. 25, sch. 24.
sch. 22, repealed in pt.: 1995, c. 25, sch. 24.

26. Pensions Act 1995.
Royal Assent, July 19, 1995.
s. 100, amended: 1995, c. 40, sch. 4 (S.).
s. 131, regs. 95/2606.

27. Geneva Conventions (Amendments) Act 1995.
Royal Assent, July 19, 1995.

28. Sale of Goods (Amendment) Act 1995.
Royal Assent, July 19, 1995.

29. Insurance Companies (Reserves) Act 1995.
Royal Assent, July 19, 1995.

30. Landlord and Tenant (Covenants) Act 1995.
Royal Assent, July 19, 1995.

31. National Health Service (Amendment) Act 1995.
Royal Assent, July 19, 1995.

32. Olympic Symbol etc. (Protection) Act 1995.
Royal Assent, July 19, 1995.
Commencement order: 95/2472.
s. 19, order 95/2472.

33. Licensing (Sunday Hours) Act 1995.
Royal Assent, July 19, 1995.
Royal Assent, July 19, 1995.
Commencement order: 95/1930.
s. 5 order 95/1930.

34. Child Support Act 1995.
Royal Assent, July 19, 1995.
Commencement order: 95/2302.
s. 30, order 95/2302.

35. Criminal Appeal Act 1995.
Royal Assent, July 19, 1995.

36. Children (Scotland) Act 1995.
Royal Assent, July 19, 1995.

CAP.

1995—cont.

36. Children (Scotland) Act 1995—*cont.*
Commencement order: 95/2787.
s. 45, amended: 1995, c. 40, sch. 4.
s. 49, repealed: 1995, c. 40, sch. 5.
s. 50, amended: 1995, c. 40, sch. 4.
ss. 52, 53, amended: 1995, c. 40, sch. 4.
s. 63, amended: 1995, c. 40, sch. 4.
s. 78, amended: 1995, c. 40, sch. 4.
s. 105, order 95/2787.
s. 164, C.: 1995, c. 39, ss. 27, 28.
sch. 3, C.: 1995, c. 39, s. 25.
sch. 4, repealed: 1995, c. 40, sch. 5.
sch. 4, C.: 1995, c. 46, ss. 43, 44, 45, 46, 48, 51, 58.

37. Atomic Energy Authority Act 1995.
Royal Assent, November 8, 1995.

38. Civil Evidence Act 1995.
Royal Assent, November 8, 1995.

39. Criminal Law (Consolidation) (Scotland) Act 1995.
Royal Assent, November 8, 1995.

40. Criminal Procedure (Consequential Provisions) (Scotland) Act 1995.
Royal Assent, November 8, 1995.

41. Law Reform (Succession) Act 1995.
Royal Assent, November 8, 1995.

42. Private International Law (Miscellaneous Provisions) Act 1995.
Royal Assent, November 8, 1995.

43. Proceeds of Crime (Scotland) Act 1995.
Royal Assent, November 8, 1995.

44. Statute Law (Repeals) Act 1995.
Royal Assent, November 8, 1995.

45. Gas Act 1995.
Royal Assent, November 8, 1995.

46. Criminal Procedure (Scotland) Act 1995.
Royal Assent, November 8, 1995.

47. Northern Ireland (Remission of Sentences) Act 1995.
Royal Assent, November 8, 1995.

48. Charities (Amendment) Act 1995.
Royal Assent, November 8, 1995.

49. Town and Country Planning (Costs of Inquiries etc.) Act 1995.
Royal Assent, November 8, 1995.

50. Disability Discrimination Act 1995.
Royal Assent, November 8, 1995.
ss. 3, 4, 7, 8, 9, 10, 12, 19, 20, 22, 25, 26, 28, 29–48, 50–54, 56, 59–65, 67, 68, 70, sch. 1, schs. 3–7, modified in respect of NI: 1995, c. 50, sch. 8.

51. Medical (Professional Performance) Act 1995.
Royal Assent, November 8, 1995.

52. Mental Health (Patients in the Community) Act 1995.
Royal Assent, November 8, 1995.

53. Criminal Injuries Compensation Act 1995.
Royal Assent, November 8, 1995.

54. Consolidated Fund Act 1995.
Royal Assent, December 19, 1995.

CURRENT LAW
STATUTORY INSTRUMENT CITATOR 1995

This is the sixth part of the Statutory Instrument Citator 1995. It details how Statutory Instruments have been affected by other Statutory Instruments and by Acts and also notes where the provisions of Statutory Instruments have been judicially considered.

The material is arranged in chronological order, by year. This Part is up to date to December 14, 1995 (materials received in house).

NO.

1901

799. Order in Council apply the provisions of the Patents Etc. Act to the Republic of Honduras 1901.
revoked: ord. 94/3219, art. 3 (designs), ord. 94/3220, art. 3 (patents).

1915

769. Standing Orders and Regulations for the Constitution and Government of the Naval Medical Compassionate Fund Order in Council 1915.
art. 2, substituted: ord. 95/1965, art. 2.
art. 5, amended: ord. 95/61965, art. 2.
art. 11, amended: ord. 95/1965, art. 2.
Sch., Pt. II, substituted: ord. 95/1965, art. 2.

1925

1093. Land Registration Rules 1925.
rule 60, amended: rules 95/140, rule 2.
rule 76, substituted: rules 95/377, rule 2.
rule 76A, inserted: rules 95/377, rule 3.
rule 77, amended: rules 95/377, rule 4.
rule 77A, inserted: rules 95/377, rule 5.
rule 115, amended: rules 95/377, rule 6.
rule 117, amended: rules 95/377, rule 7.
rule 124, amended: rules 95/140, rule 3.
rule 179, substituted: rules 95/1354, rule 3.
rule 180, substituted: rules 95/1354, rule 4.
rule 239, substituted: rules 95/140, rule 2.
rule 323, substituted: rules 95/140, rule 2.

1349. Markets, Sales and Lairs Order 1925.
Whole Order (to extent that it relates to pigs) revoked: Order 95/11, Sch. 8.

NO.

1926

546. Markets, Sales and Lairs (Amendment) Order 1926.
Whole Order (to extent that it relates to pigs) revoked: Order 95/11, Sch. 8.

1927

290. Animals (Miscellaneous Provisions) Order 1927.
art. 9 amended: Order 95/11, art. 19.

982. Markets, Sales and Lairs (Amendment) Order 1927.
Whole Order (to extent that it relates to pigs) revoked: Order 95/11, Sch. 8.

1929

993. Petroleum (Mixtures) Order 1929.
amended by 1994 No. 3247.

1933

789. Milk Marketing Scheme 1933.
referred to: regs. 94/2759, reg. 2.

933. North Norfolk Rivers Catchment Board (Stiffkey River Drainage District) Order 1933.
referred to: ord. 95/1325, Sch. 1.

1934

1346. London Cab Order 1934.
referred to: ord. 95/837, art. 2.
referred to: ord. 95/1268, art. 2.
para. 40, amended: Ord. 95/1181, art. 3.

1474. North Norfolk Rivers Catchment Board (River Burn Drainage District) Order 1934.
referred to: ord. 95/1325, Sch. 1.

NO.

1938

574. Local Government Superannuation (Administration) Regulations 1938.
applied regs. 95/1019, reg. M4.

767. Patents Etc. (Convention Countries) (No. 1) Order 1938.
revoked: ord. 94/3219, art. 3 (designs), ord. 94/3220, art. 3 (patents).

768. Patents Etc. (Convention Countries) (No. 2) Order 1938.
revoked: ord. 94/3219, art. 3 (designs), ord. 94/3220, art. 3 (patents).

1944

1470. School Attendance Order Regulations 1944.
revoked: regs. 95/2090, reg. 2.

1946

170. Patents Etc. (Luxembourg) Order 1946.
revoked: ord. 94/3219, art. 3 (designs), ord. 94/3220, art. 3 (patents).

1948

104. Patents Etc. (Union of South Africa) (Convention) Order 1948.
revoked: ord. 94/3219, art. 3 (designs), ord. 94/3220, art. 3 (patents).

872. Patents etc. (Austria) (Convention) Order 1948.
revoked: ord. 94/3219, art. 3 (designs), ord. 94/3220, art. 3 (patents).

960. Ice Cream (Scotland) Regulations 1948.
reg. 1A, inserted: regs. 95/1372, reg. 24.

1006. Patents etc. (Spanish Colonies) (Convention) Order 1948.
revoked: ord. 94/3219, art. 3 (designs), ord. 94/3220, art. 3 (patents).

1131. Local Government Superannuation (England and Scotland) Regulations 1948.
reg. 15, applied: regs. 95/1019, Sch. A1.

1220. Probation Officers (Superannuation) Order 1948.
art. 1, applied: regs. 95/1019, Sch. B5.

1949

631. Local Government Superannuation (England and Scotland) Regulations 1949.
reg. 15, applied: regs. 95/1019, Sch. A1.

2224. Dry Cleaning Special Regulations 1949.
amended by 1994 No. 3247.

2338. Patents etc. (Singapore) Order 1949.
revoked: ord. 94/3219, art. 3 (designs), ord. 94/3220, art. 3 (patents).

NO.

1950

522. Patents Etc. (Israel) (Convention) Order 1950.
revoked: ord. 94/3219, art. 3 (designs), ord. 94/3220, art. 3 (patents).

1653. Patents Etc. (Dominican Republic) (Convention) Order 1950.
revoked: ord. 94/3219, art. 3 (designs), ord. 94/3220, art. 3 (patents).

1952

437. Poultry Pens, Fittings and Receptacles (Disinfection) Order 1952.
revoked: ord. 94/3141, art. 15.

784. North Norfolk Rivers Catchment Board (Reconstitution of the Stiffkey River Internal Drainage Board) Order 1952.
referred to: ord. 95/1325, Sch. 1.

819. North Norfolk Rivers Catchment Board (Reconstitution of the River Burn Internal Drainage Board) Order 1952.
referred to: ord. 95/1325, Sch. 1.

1032. Civil Aviation Act (Isle of Man) Order 1952.
revoked: ord. 95/1297, art. 2.

1689. Factories (Testing of Aircraft Engines and Accessories) Special Regulations 1952.
amended by 1994 No. 3247.

1215. The Double Taxation Relief (Taxes on Income) (Guernsey) Order 1952.
amended by 1994 No. 3209.

1216. The Double Taxation Relief (Taxes on Income) (Jersey) Order 1952.
amended by 1994 No. 3210.

2107. Patents Etc. (Indonesia) (Convention) Order 1952.
revoked: ord. 94/3219, art. 3 (designs), ord. 94/3220, art. 3 (patents).

1953

394. Patents Etc. (Ceylon) (Convention) Order 1953.
revoked: ord. 94/3219, art. 3 (designs), ord. 94/3220, art. 3 (patents).

884. National Insurance and Industrial Injuries (Reciprocal Agreement with Italy) Order 1953.
modified: ord. 95/767, art. 2.

971. Patents Etc. (Finland) (Convention) Order 1953.
revoked: ord. 94/3219, art. 3 (designs), ord. 94/3220, art. 3 (patents).

1048. Local Government Superannuation (Benefits) Regulations 1954.
referred to: regs. 95/1019, Sch. A1.

1192. Local Government Superannuation (Administration) Regulations 1954.
applied: regs. 95/1019, reg. M4.

NO.

1953—cont.

1211. Local Government (Reckoning of Service on Transfer) Regulations 1954.
reg. 5, applied: regs. 95/1019, Sch. A1.

1250. Local Government Superannuation (England and Scotland) Regulations 1954.
reg. 15, applied: regs. 95/1019, Sch. A1.

1899. Patents Etc. (Greece) (Convention) Order 1953.
revoked: ord. 94/3219, art. 3 (designs), ord. 94/3220, art. 3 (patents).

1955

420. National Insurance and Industrial Injuries (Luxembourg) Order 1955.
modified: ord. 95/767, art. 2.

874. National Insurance and Industrial Injuries (Netherlands) Order 1955.
modified: ord. 95/767, art. 2.

1041. Local Government Superannuation (Benefits) Regulations 1954.
referred to: regs. 95/1019, Sch. A1.

1205. The Double Taxation Relief (Taxes on Income) (Isle of Man) Order 1955.
amended by 1994 No. 3208.

1956

11. Poultry Premises and Vehicles (Disinfection) Order 1956.
revoked: ord. 94/3141, art. 15.

357. Pupils' Registration Regulations 1956.
revoked: regs. 95/2089, reg. 3.

919. Milk and Dairies (Channel Islands and South Devon Milk) Regulations 1956.
revoked: regs. 95/1086, reg. 23.

1003. Patents Etc. (Monaco) (Convention) Order 1956.
revoked: ord. 94/3219, art. 3 (designs), ord. 94/3220, art. 3 (patents).

1897. National Insurance and Industrial Injuries (Malta) Order 1956.
modified: ord. 95/767, art. 2.

1957

600. Patents Etc. (Vietnam) (Convention) Order 1957.
revoked: ord. 94/3219, art. 3 (designs), ord. 94/3220, art. 3 (patents).

1879. National Insurance and Industrial Injuries (Israel) Order 1957.
modified: ord. 95/767, art. 2.

1958

263. Patents Etc. (Federation of Rhodesia and Nyasaland) (Convention) Order 1958.
revoked: ord. 94/3219, art. 3 (designs), ord. 94/3220, art. 3 (patents).

NO.

1958—cont.

597. National Insurance and Industrial Injuries (France) Order 1958.
modified: ord. 95/767, art. 2.

771. Family Allowances, National Insurance and Industrial Injuries (Yugoslavia) Order 1958.
modified: ord. 95/767, art. 2.

772. National Insurance and Industrial Injuries (Malta) Order 1958.
modified: ord. 95/767, art. 2.

1053. Patents Etc. (Republic of Haiti) (Convention) Order 1958.
revoked: ord. 94/3219, art. 3 (designs), ord. 94/3220, art. 3 (patents).

1054. Patents Etc. (Republic of Ireland) (Convention) Order 1958.
revoked: ord. 94/3219, art. 3 (designs), ord. 94/3220, art. 3 (patents).

1263. Family Allowances, National Insurance and Industrial Injuries (Yugoslavia) Order 1958.
modified: ord. 95/767, art. 2.

1344. Live Poultry (Movement Records) Order 1958.
revoked: ord. 94/3141, art. 15.

1442. Fowl Pest (Infected Area Restrictions) Amendment Order 1958.
revoked: ord. 94/3141, art. 15.

1486. Coal-Mining Subsidence (Land Drainage) Regulations 1958.
revoked: regs. 94/3064, reg. 2.

1611. Fowl Pest (Infected Areas Restrictions) Order 1958.
revoked: ord. 94/3141, art. 15.

1971. Slaughter of Pigs (Anaesthesia) Regulations 1958.
revoked: regs. 95/731, reg. 28.

1959

277. Milk and Dairies (General) Regulations 1959.
applied: regs. 95/1086, reg. 14.
Sch., revoked: regs. 95/1086, reg. 23.
Pts II–VI, revoked: regs. 95/1086, reg. 23.
Pts. VIII–X, revoked: regs. 95/1086, reg. 23.

364. Schools Regulations 1959.
reg. 16, applied: regs. 94/3044, reg. 12.

413. Food Hygiene (Scotland) Regulations 1959.
reg. 3, amended: regs. 95/1372, reg. 24.

734. Ice Cream (Heat Treatment etc.) Regulations 1959.
reg. 2B, inserted: regs. 95/1086, reg. 24.

2298. Argyll County Council (Loch Poit Na H-I) Water Order 1959.
revoked: ord. 94/3308, art. 4.

NO.

1960

105. Movement of Animals (Records) Order 1960.
amended by 1995 No. 11.
amended by 1995 No. 12.

201. Patents Etc. (Iran) (Convention) Order 1960.
revoked: ord. 94/3219, art. 3 (designs) ,ord. 94/3220, art. 3 (patents).

211. Family Allowances, National Insurance and Industrial Injuries (Denmark) Order 1960.
modified: ord. 95/767, art. 2.

437. Patents Etc. (The Republic of San Marino) (Convention) Order 1960.
revoked: ord. 94/3219, art. 3 (designs), ord. 94/3220, art. 3 (patents).

707. National Insurance and Industrial Injuries (Republic of Ireland) Order 1960.
modified: ord. 95/767, art. 2.

1103. National Insurance (Non-participation Assurance of Equivalent Pension Benefits) Regulations 1960.
reg. 2, applied: regs. 95/1019, reg. D19.

1602. Food Hygiene (Docks, Carriers, etc.) Regulations 1960.
reg. 4A, amended: regs. 94/3082, reg. 24, regs. 95/539, reg. 26, regs. 95/540, reg. 27.

1651. Patents Etc. (United Arab Republic) (Convention) Order 1960.
revoked: ord. 94/3219, art. 3 (designs), ord. 94/3220, art. 3 (patents).

1932. Shipbuilding and Ship-repairing Regulations 1960.
amended by 1994 No. 3247.

1958. Patents Etc. (Vatican City) (Convention) Order 1960.
revoked: ord. 94/3219, art. 3 (designs), ord. 94/3220, art. 3 (patents).

2331. Skimmed Milk with Non-Milk Fat Regulations 1960.
reg. 2, amended: regs. 95/77, reg. 24.
reg. 3, amended: regs. 95/77, reg. 24.
Sch. 1, Pt. I, amended: regs. 95/77, reg. 24.
Sch. 2, revoked: regs. 95/77, reg. 24.

2437. Skimmed Milk with Non-Milk Fat (Scotland) Regulations 1960.
reg. 2, amended: regs. 95/77, reg. 24.
reg. 3, amended: regs. 95/77, reg. 24.
Sch. 1, Pt. I, amended: regs. 95/77, reg. 24.
Sch. 2, revoked: regs. 95/77, reg. 24.

1961

575. Civil Aviation (Licensing) Act 1960 (Isle of Man) Order 1961.
revoked: ord. 95/1297, art. 2.

584. Family Allowances, National Insurance and Industrial Injuries (Turkey) Order 1961.
modified: ord. 95/767, art. 2.

NO.

1961—cont.

1202. Family Allowances, National Insurance and Industrial Injuries (Germany) Order 1961.
modified: ord. 95/767, art. 2.

1441. National Health Service (Superannuation) Regulations 1961.
referred to: regs. 95/866, reg. 2.

1493. Movement of Animals (Records) Amendment Order 1961.
amended by 1995 No. 11.
amended by 1995 No. 12.

1580. Construction (General Provisions) Regulations 1961.
regs. 5, 6, revoked: regs. 94/3140, reg. 24.

1962

401. Antarctic Treaty Order in Council 1962.
revoked: ord. 95/1030, art. 3.

435. Argyll County Council (Allt au Fhireoin, Bunessam) Water Order 1962.
revoked: ord. 94/3308, art. 4.

560. East Suffolk and Norfolk River Board (Holme Common Internal Drainage District) Order 1962.
referred to: ord. 95/1325, Sch. 1.

1083. Patents Etc. (Iceland) (Convention) Order 1962.
revoked: ord. 94/3219, art. 3 (designs), ord. 94/3220, art. 3 (patents).

1963

286. The Swine Fever Order 1963.
amended by 1995 No. 11.

366. Patents Etc. (Cuba) (Convention) Order 1963.
revoked: ord. 94/3219, art. 3 (designs), ord. 94/3220, art. 3 (patents).

510. London Traffic (40 M.P.H. Speed Limit) (No. 1) Order 1963.
revoked: ord. 95/296, art. 5.

1326. Patents Etc. (US Dependencies and Tanganyika) (Convention) Order 1963.
revoked: ord. 94/3219, art. 3 (designs), ord. 94/3220, art. 3 (patents).

1487. Patents Etc. (Nigeria and Congo (Brazzaville)) (Convention) Order 1963.
revoked: ord. 94/3219, art. 3 (designs), ord. 94/3220, art. 3 (patents).

1710. Weights and Measures Regulations 1963.
reg. 1, amended: regs. 95/735, reg. 1.
reg. 3, revoked: regs. 95/735, reg. 1.
reg. 5, amended: regs. 95/735, reg. 1.
reg. 6, amended: regs. 95/735, reg. 1.
Pts. III, IV, revoked: regs. 95/735, reg. 1.
Sch. 1, Pt. II, revoked: regs. 95/735, reg. 1.

NO.

1963—cont.

1757. Patents Etc. (Ivory Coast) (Convention) Order 1963.
revoked: ord. 94/3219, art. 3 (designs), ord. 94/3220, art. 3 (patents).

1919. Patents Etc. (Central African Republic, Chad, Laos, Upper Volta and Roumania) (Convention) Order 1963.
revoked: ord. 94/3219, art. 3 (designs), ord. 94/3220, art. 3 (patents).

1956. Poultry Pens, Fittings and Receptacles (Disinfection) (Amendment) Order 1963.
revoked: ord. 94/3141, art. 15.

2082. Patents Etc. (Malagasy and Senegal) (Convention) Order 1963.
revoked: ord. 94/3219, art. 3 (designs), ord. 94/3220, art. 3 (patents).

1964

265. Patents Etc. (Gabon) (Convention) Order 1964.
revoked: ord. 94/3219, art. 3 (designs), ord. 94/3220, art. 3 (patents).

388. Prison Rules 1964.
amended by 1994 No. 3195.
rule 3, amended: rules 95/983, rule 2.
rule 6, substituted: rules 95/983, rule 2.
rule 50, amended: rules 95/983, rule 2.
rule 52, amended: rules 95/983, rule 2.

692. Patents Etc. (Cameroon) (Convention) Order 1964.
revoked: ord. 94/3219, art. 3 (designs), ord. 94/3220, art. 3 (patents).

977. Patents Etc. (Mauritania) (Convention) Order 1964.
revoked: ord. 94/3219, art. 3 (designs), ord. 94/3220, art. 3 (patents).

988. Patents Etc. (Niger) (Convention) Order 1964.
revoked: ord. 94/3219, art. 3 (designs), ord. 94/3220, art. 3 (patents).

1196. Patents Etc. (Trinidad and Tobago) (Convention) Order 1964.
revoked: ord. 94/3219, art. 3 (designs), ord. 94/3220, art. 3 (patents).

2007. Pensions (Polish Forces) Scheme 1964.
referred to: rules 94/3046, rule 86.

1965

221. Construction (Notice of Operations and Works) Order 1965.
revoked: regs. 94/3140, reg. 24.

321. Rules of Court of Session 1965.
rule 89A(1)(c), see *Cowie* v. *Atlantic Drilling Co. (I.H.)*, 1995 S.C.L.R. 335.
rule 89B, see *Struthers* v. *British Alcan Rolled Products (O.H.)*, 1995 S.L.T. 142.
rule 269(b): introduction, para. (4), see *X* v. *Dumfries and Galloway Regional Council*, 1994 S.L.T. 1285.

NO.

1965—cont.

537. Superannuation (Inner London Magistrates' Courts) Regulations 1965.
reg. 2, applied: regs. 95/1019, Sch. B3.

621. London Authorities (Superannuation) Order 1965.
art. 14, applied: regs. 95/1019, Sch. C1.
art. 15, applied: regs. 95/1019, Sch. C1.

1123. Patents Etc. (Union of Soviet Socialist Republics) (Convention) Order 1965.
revoked: ord. 94/3219, art. 3 (designs), ord. 94/3220, art. 3 (patents).

1304. Patents Etc. (Uganda and Kenya) (Convention) Order 1965.
revoked: ord. 94/3219, art. 3 (designs), ord. 94/3220, art. 3 (patents).

1711. Patents Etc. (Philippines) (Convention) Order 1965.
revoked: ord. 94/3219, art. 3 (designs), ord. 94/3220, art. 3 (patents).

1776. Rules of the Supreme Court 1965.
ord. 1,
rule 2(1), see *R.* v. *Darlington Borough Council, ex p. Association of Darlington Taxi Owners* [1994] C.O.D. 424, Auld J.
ord. 3,
rule 2(1)(2), see *Bevan Ashford* v. *Malin* [1995] IRLR 360, E.A.T.
rule 5, see *Woodhouse* v. *McDonald Young and the Motor Insurers Bureau* [1994] P.I.Q.R. P446, C.A.
rule 5(1), see *Regalbourne* v. *East Lindsey District Council* [1994] R.A. 1, C.A.
ord. 5,
rule 4, see *Cox* v. *Bankside Members Agency (LTA 94/6391/B; LTA 94/7098/B; LTA 94/7124/B)*, November 29, 1994, C.A.
ord. 10,
rule 1(2)(3), see *Woodhouse* v. *McDonald Young and the Motor Insurers Bureau* [1994] P.I.Q.R. P446, C.A.
ord. 11,
rule 1 (Hong Kong), see *Mercedes-Benz AG* v. *Leiduck, The Times*, August 11, 1995, P.C.
rule 1, see *Unilever* v. *Chefaro Proprietaries* [1994] F.S.R. 135, C.A.
rule 1(1)(d), see *Bank of Baroda* v. *Vysya Bank* [1994] 2 Lloyd's Rep. 86, Mance J.; *Gulf Bank KSC* v. *Mitsubishi Heavy Industries* [1994] 1 Lloyd's Rep. 323, Hobhouse J.
ord. 12,
rule 8, see *Unilever* v. *Chefaro Proprietaries* [1994] F.S.R. 135, C.A.

NO.

1965—cont.

1776. Rules of the Supreme Court 1965—*cont.*

ord. 14,

see *Brinks* v. *Abu-Saleh, The Times*, January 30, 1995, Jacob J.; *Bristol and West Building Society* v. *Brandon, The Times*, March 9, 1995, Coleman J.; *Chiron Corp.* v. *Murex Diagnostics (No. 9)* [1995] F.S.R. 318, Aldous J.; *Credit Suisse* v. *Waltham Forest London Borough Council* [1994] N.P.C. 137, Gatehouse J.; *Gillette U.K.* v. *Edenwest* [1994] R.P.C. 279, Blackburne J.; *Linpac Mouldings* v. *Eagleton Direct Export* [1994] F.S.R. 545, C.A.

rule 1, amended: rules 95/2206, rule 44, see *Bergin* v. *David Wickes Television* [1994] P.I.Q.R. P167, C.A.

rule 3(1), see *Trafalgar House Construction (Regions)* v. *General Surety and Guarantee Co.* [1995] 3 W.L.R. 204, H.L.

rule 4, see *Bergin* v. *David Wickes Television* [1994] P.I.Q.R. P167, C.A.

ord. 14A,

see *International Business Machines Corp.* v. *Phoenix International (Computers)* [1994] R.P.C. 251, Ferris J.; *Merrell Dow Pharmaceuticals* v. *H. N. Norton & Co.* [1994] R.P.C. 1, Patents Court.

ord. 15,

rule 5, see *International Business Machines Corp.* v. *Phoenix International (Computers)* [1994] R.P.C. 251, Ferris J.

rule 6, see *Balkanbank* v. *Taher (No. 4), The Times*, April 14, 1995, Clarke J.

rule 6(1), see *R.* v. *Darlington Borough Council, ex p. Association of Darlington Taxi Owners* [1994] C.O.D. 424, Auld J.

rule 6(2)(b), see *Stanhope Pension Trust* v. *Registrar of Companies*; *sub nom. Forte's (Manufacturing), Re*; *Stanhope Pension Trust* v. *Registrar of Companies* [1994] BCC 84, C.A.

rule 6(3), see *Albert* v. *Albert (94/0828/F)*, January 11, 1995, C.A.

rule 7, see *Industrie Chimiche Italia Centrale* v. *Alexander G. Tsvaliris & Sons Maritime Co., The Times*, August 8, 1995, Mance J.

rule 7(2), see *Yorkshire Regional Health Authority* v. *AMEC Building* [1994] 10 Const. L.J. 336, Lloyd J.

NO.

1965—cont.

1776. Rules of the Supreme Court 1965—*cont.*

ord. 15—*cont.*

rule 12, see *R.* v. *Darlington Borough Council, ex p. Association of Darlington Taxi Owners* [1994] C.O.D. 424, Auld J.

rule 16, see *C. (Adult Patient) (Access: Jurisdiction), Re* [1994] 1 F.C.R. 705, Eastham J.; *R.* v. *British Coal Corp., and Secretary of State for Trade and Industry, ex p. Price* [1994] IRLR 72, C.A.

ord. 17,

rule 1(2), see *St. Martin's Property Investment* v. *Philips Electronics (U.K.); Secretary of State for the Environment (Third Party)* [1994] 3 W.L.R. 1074, Rattee J.

rule 9(1), see *St. Martin's Property Investment* v. *Philips Electronics (U.K.); Secretary of State for the Environment (Third Party)* [1994] 3 W.L.R. 1074, Rattee J.

rule 13(1), see *St Martin's Property Investment* v. *Philips Electronics (U.K.); Secretary of State for the Environment (Third Party)* [1994] 3 W.L.R. 1074, Rattee J.

ord. 18,

rule 19, see *A.B.* v. *John Wyeth & Brother* [1994] P.I.Q.R. P109, C.A.; *Chiron Corp.* v. *Organon Teknika (No. 6)*; *Chiron Corp.* v. *Murex Diagnostics (No. 6)* [1994] F.S.R. 448, Aldous J.; *Chiron Corp.* v. *Organon Teknika (No. 5)*; *Same* v. *Murex Diagnostics (No. 5)* [1994] F.S.R. 258, Patents Ct.; *Chiron Corp.* v. *Murex Diagnostics (No. 2)* [1994] F.S.R. 187, C.A.; *Elguzouli-Daf* v. *Commissioner of Police of the Metropolis*; *McBreaty* v. *Minister of Defence, The Times*, November 23, 1994, C.A.; *International Business Machines Corp.* v. *Phoenix International (Computers)* [1994] R.P.C. 251, Ferris J.; *Loughridge (Thomas)* v. *Go Gas Co. (LTA 94/6607/E)*, December 1, 1994, C.A.; *Port* v. *Auger*; *sub nom Port (A Bankrupt) (No. 56 of 1987), Re*; *Port* v. *Auger* [1994] 1 W.L.R. 862, Harman J.; *Unisoft Group (No. 3), Re* [1994] 1 BCLC 609, Harman J.

rule 19(1), see *Hutchison Personal Communications* v. *Hook Advertising* [1995] F.S.R. 365, Blackburne J.

NO.

1965—cont.

1776. Rules of the Supreme Court 1965—*cont.*
ord. 19,
rule 4(2)(b), see *Box* v. *Webb, MJL Morsch, Third Party*, October 5, 1994; District Judge Cotterill; Coventry Cty. Ct. [*Ex rel. Griffiths and Co., Solicitors*].
rule 7, see *International Business Machines Corp.* v. *Phoenix International (Computers)* [1994] R.P.C. 251, Ferris J.
ord. 20,
rule 5, see *Chiron Corp.* v. *Organon Teknika (No. 4)*; *Same* v. *Murex Diagnostics (No. 4)* [1994] F.S.R. 252, Patents Ct.
rule 5(5), see *Welsh Development Agency* v. *Redpath Dorman Long* [1994] 4 All E.R. 10, C.A.
rule 8(1), see *R.* v. *Darlington Borough Council, ex p. Association of Darlington Taxi Owners* [1994] C.O.D. 424, Auld J.
ord. 21,
rule 3, see *Albright & Wilson* v. *S.B. Chemicals* [1994] R.P.C. 608, Aldous J.; *Britannia Life Association of Scotland* v. *Smith (LTA 95/5225/B)*, June 8, 1995, C.A.
ord. 23,
rule 1, see *C.A. Envis* v. *Thakkar*, *The Times*, May 2, 1995, Kennedy L.J.
rule 1(1), see *Unisoft Group, Re*; *Saunderson Holdings* v. *Unisoft Group* [1994] BCC 11, C.A.
rule 1(1)(a), see *Little Olympian Each Ways, Re* [1994] 4 All E.R. 561, Lindsay J.
ord. 24,
see *Cox* v. *Bankside Members Agency (LTA 94/6391/B; LTA 94/7098/B; LTA 94/7124/B)*, November 29, 1994, C.A.
rule 1, see *Baldock* v. *Addison* [1994] F.S.R. 665, Lightman J.
rule 2, see *Baldock* v. *Addison* [1994] F.S.R. 665, Lightman J.
rule 2(5), see *Baldock* v. *Addison* [1995] 1 All E.R. 437, Lightman J.
rule 3, see *Baldock* v. *Addison* [1994] F.S.R. 665, Lightman J.; *R.* v. *Secretary of State for Foreign and Commonwealth Affairs, ex p. World Development Movement* [1995] 1 W.L.R. 386, D.C.
rule 5, see *Helitune* v. *Stewart Hughes* [1994] F.S.R. 422, Ferris J.

NO.

1965—cont.

1776. Rules of the Supreme Court 1965—*cont.*
ord. 24—*cont.*
rule 8, see *Baldock* v. *Addison* [1994] F.S.R. 665, Lightman J.; *Helitune* v. *Stewart Hughes* [1994] F.S.R. 422, Ferris J.; *R.* v. *Secretary of State for Foreign and Commonwealth Affairs, ex p. World Development Movement* [1995] 1 W.L.R. 386, D.C.
ord. 25,
rule 8, amended: rules 95/2206, rule 36.
ord. 26,
rule 3(i), see *Jones* v. *Swift Structures*, April 19, 1995; D.D.J. Perry; Romford County Ct.
ord. 27,
rule 3, see *International Business Machines Corp.* v. *Phoenix International (Computers)* [1994] R.P.C. 251, Ferris J.
ord. 28,
rule 7, see *Balkanbank* v. *Taher (No. 3)* [1995] 1 W.L.R. 1067, C.A.
rule 7(1), see *Balkanbank* v. *Taher* [1994] 4 All E.R. 239, C.A.
rule 10, substituted: rules 95/2206, rule 37.
ord. 29,
rule 1, amended: rules 95/2206, rule 38.
rule 9, see *Harris (Barbara)* v. *Ellen*, December 21, 1994, C.A.
rule 11, see *Campfil* v. *Barclays Bank*, *The Times*, February 24, 1995, C.A.
ord. 30,
rule 3, see *Alliance & Leicester Building Society* v. *Edgestop (No. 2)*, *The Times*, May 24, 1995, C.A.
rule 3(2)(b), see *Alliance & Leicester Building Society* v. *Edgestop (LTA 94/5856/B)*, November 23, 1994, C.A.
ord. 32,
rule 4, see *Hawthorne* v. *Hawthorne (LTA 94/6840/F)*, November 30, 1994, C.A.
rule 6, see *R.* v. *Customs and Excise Commissioners, ex p. Eurotunnel*, *The Independent*, February 17, 1995, H.L.
rule 11, see *Smith* v. *Glennon* [1994] 5 MedLR218, C.A.
ord. 33,
see *Deeny* v. *Gooda Walker (No. 2)*, *The Times*, May 5, 1995, Phillips J.
ord. 35,
rule 2, see *R.* v. *Newcastle Under Lyme Justices, ex p. Massey* [1994] 1 W.L.R. 1684, D.C.

NO.

1965—cont.

1776. Rules of the Supreme Court 1965—*cont.*
ord. 38,
rule 1, see *St. Trudo Trade Mark* [1995] F.S.R. 345, Ferris J.
rule 2, see *St. Trudo Trade Mark* [1995] F.S.R. 345, Ferris J.
rule 3(2) see *R.* v. *Horseferry Road Magistrates' Court, ex p. Bennett* [1994] C.O.D. 321, D.C.
rule 4, see *Rawlinson* v. *Westbrook, The Times*, January 25, 1995, C.A.
rule 13, see *A. and B. (Minors) (No. 2), Re* [1995] 1 F.L.R. 351, Wall J.
rule 21(1), see *St. Trudo Trade Mark* [1995] F.S.R. 345, Ferris J.
rule 21(4), see *St. Trudo Trade Mark* [1995] F.S.R. 345, Ferris J.
ord. 40,
see *K. (A Minor) (Contact: Psychiatric Report), Re, The Times*, April 13, 1995, C.A.
ord. 41,
rule 5, see *St. Trudo Trade Mark* [1995] F.S.R. 345, Ferris J.
rule 5(2), see *Deutsche Ruckversicherung AG* v. *Walbrook Insurance Co.; Group Josire (Formerly Known as Group Josi Reassurance SA)* v. *Same* [1994] 4 All E.R. 181, Phillips J.
ord. 42,
rule 3, see *Kuwait Airways Corp.* v. *Iraq Airways Co. (No. 2)* [1994] 1 Lloyd's Rep. 284, C.A.
rule 3(2), see *Pounds* v. *Pounds* [1994] 1 W.L.R. 1535, C.A.
ord. 50,
rules 1, 2, 3, 4, see *Clark* v. *Chief Land Registrar; Chancery* v. *Ketteringham* [1994] 3 W.L.R. 593, C.A.
ord. 52,
rule 1(2), see *Peach Grey & Co.* v. *Sommers, The Times*, February 16, 1995, D.C.
ord. 53,
see *Venice Simplon Orient Express Inc.'s Applications* [1995] F.S.R. 103, High Court of the Republic of Singapore, Selvan J.
rule 3(2), see *R.* v. *Tottenham Magistrates' Courts, ex p. Gleaves* [1993] C.O.D. 332, D.C.
rule 3(7), see *R.* v. *Darlington Borough Council, ex p. Association of Darlington Taxi Owners* [1994] C.O.D. 424, Auld J.; *R.* v. *Secretary of State for Foreign and Commonwealth Affairs, ex p. World Development Movement* [1995] 1 W.L.R. 386, D.C.

NO.

1965—cont.

1776. Rules of the Supreme Court 1965—*cont.*
ord. 53—*cont.*
rule 4, see *R.* v. *Customs and Excise Commissioners, ex p. Eurotunnel, The Independent*, February 17, 1995, H.L.
rule 5, see *R.* v. *Liverpool City Council, ex p. Muldoon*; *R.* v. *Rent Officer Service, ex p. Kelly, The Times*, April 18, 1995, C.A.
rule 5(3), see *R.* v. *Sandwell Metropolitan Borough Council, ex p. Lyn* [1994] C.O.D. 431, Popplewell J.
rule 6(4), see *R.* v. *Sandwell Metropolitan Borough Council, ex p. Lyn* [1994] C.O.D. 431, Popplewell J.
rule 7, see *R.* v. *Erewash Borough Council and Ilkestone Justices, ex p. Smedburg and Smedburg* [1994] RVR 60, Auld J.
rule 9(4), see *R.* v. *Highbury Corner Magistrates' Court, ex p. Uchendu* [1994] R.A. 51, Laws J.
ord. 55,
rule 1, see *S.* v. *Merton London Borough* [1994] 1 F.C.R. 186, Ward J.
rule 4(2), see *Regalbourne* v. *East Lindsey District Council* [1994] R.A. 1, C.A.
rule 7(2), see *S.* v. *Merton London Borough* [1994] 1 F.C.R. 186, Ward J.
ord. 58,
rule 1, see *Savill* v. *Southend Health Authority, The Times*, December 28, 1994, C.A.
rule 2, amended: rules 95/2206, rule 7.
rule 3, see *Savill* v. *Southend Health Authority, The Times*, December 28, 1994, C.A.
ord. 59,
see *Kuwait Airways Corp.* v. *Iraq Airways Co. (No. 2)* [1994] 1 Lloyd's Rep. 284, C.A.
rule 1, see *Palmeria Properties* v. *Bennett (LTA 94/6729/E)*, October 26, 1994, C.A.
rule 10(2), see *Laltimer* v. *Cumbria County Council* [1994] P.I.Q.R. P395, C.A.
rule 13, amended: rules 95/2206, rule 8.
rule 14, see *R.* v. *Secretary of State for the Home Department, ex p. Parry (FC3 94/5261/D)*, November 2, 1994, C.A.
rule 14(3), see *Ewing (No. 2), ex p.* [1994] 1 W.L.R. 1553, C.A.
rule 24, inserted: rules 95/2206, rule 3.

NO.

1965—cont.

1776. Rules of the Supreme Court 1965—*cont.*

ord. 61,

rule 3, see *Ozanne* v. *Hertfordshire County Council* [1995] 35 RVR 40, C.A.

rule 4, revoked: rules 95/2206, rule 4, see *Ozanne* v. *Hertfordshire County Council* [1995] 35 RVR 40, C.A.

ord. 62,

applied: rules 94/3046, rule 89.

rule 7, see *Alliance & Leicester Building Society* v. *Edgestop (No. 2)*, *The Times*, May 24, 1995, C.A.

rule 8(2), see *Blackman* v. *Pryor*, June 28, 1994, Ognall J.

rule 10(1), see *R.* v. *Newcastle Under Lyme Justices, ex p. Massey* [1994] 1 W.L.R. 1684, D.C.

rule 12, see *Children Act 1989 (Taxation of Costs), Re* [1994] 2 F.L.R. 934, Cazalet J.

rule 15, amended: rules 95/2206, rule 11.

rule 15A, inserted: rules 95/2206, rule 12.

rule 16, amended: rules 95/2206, rule 13.

rule 29, amended: rules 95/2206, rule 14.

Append. 2, amended: rules 95/2206, rule 50.

ord. 63,

Append. 3, amended: rules 95/2206, rule 39.

ord. 65,

rule 3(1), see *Kuwait Airways Corp.* v. *Iraqi Airways Co., The Times*, July 25, 1995, H.L.; [1995] 1 W.L.R. 1147, H.L.

ord. 73,

rule 5(9), see *Acada Chemicals* v. *Empresa Nacional Pesquera SA* [1994] 1 Lloyd's Rep. 428, Colman J.

rule 7, see *Sokona Industries* v. *Freyre & Co.* [1994] 2 Lloyd's Rep. 57, Colman J.

ord. 79,

rule 9, amended: rules 95/2206, rule 40.

Append. A, amended: rules 95/2206, rule 41.

ord. 80,

rule 2, see *L.* v. *L. (Minors) (Separate Representation)* [1994] 1 F.L.R. 156, C.A.

ord. 86, rule 8, inserted: rules 95/2206, rule 43.

ord. 87, rule 2(4), (5), see *Venice Simplon Orient Express Inc.'s Applications* [1995] F.S.R. 103, High Court of the Republic of Singapore, Selvan J.

NO.

1965—cont.

1776. Rules of the Supreme Court 1965—*cont.*

ord. 88, rule 5, amended: rules 95/2206, rule 45.

ord. 91,

rule 1, substituted: rules 95/2206, rule 5.

rule 3, amended: rules 95/2206, rule 5.

rule 5, amended: rules 95/2206, rule 5.

rule 5A, inserted: rules 95/2206, rule 5.

rule 6, amended: rules 95/2206, rule 5.

ord. 94,

rule 2(2)(b), see *Estate of Kinglsey* v. *Secretary of State for Transport*[1994] C.O.D. 358, D.C.

rule 12(2)(c), see *Wenman* v. *Secretary of State for the Environment* [1994] EGCS 100, Mr David Keene, Q.C.

ord. 102, rule 3, amended: rules 95/2206, rule 46.

ord. 104, rule 4, amended: rules 95/2206, rule 47.

rule 11, substituted: rules 95/2206, rule 48.

ord. 114,

rule 1, amended: rules 95/2206, rule 51.

rule 4, see *Research Corp.'s Supplementary Protection Certificate* [1994] R.P.C. 387, Patents Office.

ord. 115,

rule 1, amended: rules 95/2206, rule 17.

rule 2A, inserted: rules 95/2206, rule 18.

rule 2B, inserted: rules 95/2206, rule 18.

rule 3, amended: rules 95/2206, rule 19.

rule 5, amended: rules 95/2206, rule 20.

rule 6, amended: rules 95/2206, rule 21.

rule 7, amended: rules 95/2206, rule 22.

rule 8, amended: rules 95/2206, rule 23.

rule 9, amended: rules 95/2206, rule 24.

rule 10, amended: rules 95/2206, rule 26.

rule 11, amended: rules 95/2206 rule 27.

rule 11A, inserted: rules 95/2206, rule 28.

rule 12, amended: rules 95/2206, rule 29.

NO.

1965—cont.

1776. Rules of the Supreme Court 1965—*cont.*
ord. 115—*cont*
rule 13, amended: rules 95/2206, rule 30.
rule 14, amended: rules 95/2206, rule 31.
rule 15, amended: rules 95/2206, rule 32.
rule 16A, inserted: rules 95/2206, rule 25.
rule 21, amended: rules 95/2206, rule 33.
rule 23, amended: rules 95/2206, rule 34.

1839. Registration of Births, Still-births, Deaths and Marriages (Prescription of Forms) (Scotland) Regulations 1965.
reg. 16, substituted: regs. 94/3151, reg. 3.
Sch. 16, Form, substituted: regs. 94/3151, reg. 4.
Sch. 23, Form, substituted: regs. 94/3151, reg. 5.
Sch. 24, Form, substituted: regs. 94/3151, reg. 6.

1995. Industrial and Provident Societies Regulations 1965.
Sch. 2, substituted: regs. 95/713, reg. 2.

2013. Patents Etc. (Malawi) (Convention) Order 1965.
revoked: ord. 94/3219, art. 3 (designs), ord. 94/3220, art. 3 (patents).

1966

80. Patents Etc. (Algeria) (Convention) Order 1966.
revoked: ord. 94/3219, art. 3 (designs), ord. 94/3220, art. 3 (patents).

81. Patents Etc. (Cyprus) (Convention) Order 1966.
revoked: ord. 94/3219, art. 3 (designs), ord. 94/3220, art. 3 (patents).

97. Police (Special Constables) (Scotland) Regulations 1966.
reg. 4, amended: regs. 94/3039, reg. 2.
reg. 13, amended: regs. 94/3039, reg. 2.

183. London Trunk Roads (40 M.P.H. Speed Limit) (Amendment) Order 1966.
revoked: ord. 95/296, art. 5.

270. National Insurance (Republic of Ireland) Order 1966.
modified: ord. 95/767, art. 2.

396. Patents Etc. (Bulgaria) (Convention) Order 1966.
revoked: ord. 94/3219, art. 3 (designs), ord. 94/3220, art. 3 (patents).

NO.

1966—cont.

791. Food Hygiene (Markets, Stalls and Delivery Vehicles) Regulations 1966.
reg. 2, amended: regs. 94/3082, reg. 24.
reg. 2, referred: regs. 95/539, reg. 26, regs. 95/540, reg. 27.
reg. 23, amended to: regs. 95/539, reg. 13, regs. 95/540, reg. 14.

1455. Barbados Independence Order 1966.
s. 11, see *King (Gladwyn Ophelia)* v. *Att.-Gen. of Barbados* [1994] 1 W.L.R. 1560, P.C.
s. 16, see *King (Gladwyn Ophelia)* v. *Att.-Gen. of Barbados* [1994] 1 W.L.R. 1560, P.C.
s. 48, see *King (Gladwyn Ophelia)* v. *Att.-Gen. of Barbados* [1994] 1 W.L.R. 1560, P.C.
Sched., see *King (Gladwyn Ophelia)* v. *Att.-Gen. of Barbados* [1994] 1 W.L.R. 1560, P.C.

1967

81. Milk and Dairies (Channel Islands and South Devon Milk) (Scotland) Regulations 1967.
revoked: regs. 95/1372, reg. 23.

158. Patents Etc. (Dahomey) (Convention) Order 1967.
revoked: ord. 94/3219, art. 3 (designs), ord. 94/3220, art. 3 (patents).

395. Veterinary Surgeons and Veterinary Practitioners Registration Regulations 1967.
reg. 16, amended: regs. 95/207, reg. 2.
reg. 20, amended: regs. 95/207, reg. 3.
reg. 23, amended: regs. 95/207, reg. 4.

481. Patents Etc. (Argentina and Uruguay) (Convention) Order 1967.
revoked: ord. 94/3219, art. 3 (designs), ord. 94/3220, art. 3 (patents).

599. Veterinary Surgeons (Examination of Commonwealth and Foreign Candidates) Regulations 1967.
reg. 9, amended: ord. 95/2396, Sch., para. 2.
reg. 10, amended: ord. 95/2396, Sch., para. 2.

720. Compulsory Purchase by Ministers (Inquiries Procedure) Rules 1967.
revoked: rules 94/3264, rule 21.

805. Carriage by Air (Isle of Man) Order 1967.
revoked: ord. 95/1297, art. 2.

1021. Police (Discipline) (Scotland) Regulations 1967.
reg. 2, amended: regs. 95/647, reg. 2.
reg. 3, amended: regs. 95/647, reg. 2.
reg. 4, amended: regs. 95/647, reg. 2.
reg. 5, amended: regs. 95/647, reg. 2.
reg. 6, amended: regs. 95/647, reg. 2.

NO.

1967—cont.

1021. Police (Discipline) (Scotland) Regulations 1967—*cont.*
reg. 7, amended: regs. 95/647, reg. 2.
reg. 8, amended: regs. 95/647, reg. 2.
reg. 9, amended: regs. 95/647, reg. 2.
reg. 9A, amended: regs. 95/647, reg. 2.
reg. 10, amended: regs. 95/647, reg. 2.
reg. 11A, amended: regs. 95/647, reg. 2.
reg. 19, amended: regs. 95/647, reg. 2.
reg. 20, amended: regs. 95/647, reg. 2.
reg. 21, amended: regs. 95/647, reg. 2.
Sch. 3, amended: regs. 95/647, reg. 2.

1310. Industrial and Provident Societies Regulations 1967.
reg. 5, amended: regs. 95/713, reg. 3.

1492. Patents Etc. (Togo) (Convention) Order 1967.
revoked: ord. 94/3219, art. 3 (designs), ord. 94/3220, art. 3 (patents).

1681. Patents Etc. (Bahamas) (Convention) Order 1967.
revoked: ord. 94/3219, art. 3 (designs), ord. 94/3220, art. 3 (patents).

1682. Patents Etc. (Malta) (Convention) Order 1967.
revoked: ord. 94/3219, art. 3 (designs), ord. 94/3220, art. 3 (patents).

1699. Local Review Committee (Scotland) Rules 1967.
rule 8, revoked: rules 95/1272, rule 2.

1769. Pipe-line (Inquiries Procedure) Rules 1967.
revoked: rules 95/1239, rule 20.

1960. Veterinary Surgeons (Practice by Students) Regulations Order of Council 1967.
revoked: ord. 95/2397, art. 2.

1968

208. Police Cadets (Scotland) Regulations 1968.
Sch. 1, amended: regs. 95/1057, reg. 2.
Sch. 2, amended: regs. 95/1057, reg. 3.

272. Trunk Roads (40 M.P.H. Speed Limit) (No. 2) Order 1968.
art. 1, revoked: ord. 95/296, art. 4.
Sch. 1, revoked: ord. 95/296, art. 4.
Sch. 2, amended: ord. 95/296, art. 4.

1389. Patent Rules 1968.
referred to: rules 95/2164, rule 2.

1655. National Insurance and Industrial Injuries (Republic of Ireland) Order 1968.
modified: ord. 95/767, art. 2.

1792. Trunk Roads (40 M.P.H. Speed Limit) (Amendment) Order 1968.
revoked: ord. 95/296, art. 5.

2049. Registration of Births, Deaths and Marriages Regulations 1968.
amended: regs. 95/744, reg. 3.

NO.

1969

384. Family Allowances, National Insurance and Industrial Injuries (Switzerland) Order 1969.
modified: ord. 95/767, art. 2.

594. Civil Aviation Act (Isle of Man) Order 1969.
revoked: ord. 95/1297, art. 2.

597. Tokyo Convention Act 1967 (Isle of Man) Order 1969.
revoked: ord. 95/1297, art. 2.

793. National Insurance (Modification of Local Government Superannuation Schemes) Regulations 1969.
referred to: regs. 95/1019, reg. K18.

865. Patents Etc. (Laos) (Convention) Order 1969.
revoked: ord. 94/3219, art. 3 (designs), ord. 94/3220, art. 3 (patents).

1023. Plant Breeders' Rights (Herbaceous Perennials) Scheme 1969.
revoked: scheme 95/526, art. 2.

1970

72. Isles of Scilly Sea Fisheries District Order 1970.
art. 3, amended: ord. 95/1472, art. 2.

240. Sheep Scab Order (Northern Ireland) 1970.
art. 3, amended: regs. 94/3142, reg. 21.

951. Civil Aviation (Isle of Man) Order 1970.
revoked: ord. 95/1297, art. 2.

1172. Food Hygiene (General) Regulations 1970.
reg. 3, amended: regs. 94/3082, reg. 24.
reg. 3, amended: regs. 95/539, reg. 26, regs. 95/539, reg. 27.

1711. Weights and Measures (Amendment) Regulations 1970.
revoked in remaining pts.: regs. 95/735, reg. 1.

1971

92. Act of Sederunt (Social Work) (Sheriff Court Procedure) Rules 1971.
rule 8, see *P.* v. *Kennedy*, 1995 S.L.T. 476.
rule 8(1), see *P.* v. *Kennedy* (I.H.) 1995 S.C.L.R. 1.
rule 14(2), see *M.* v. *Kennedy*, 1995 S.L.T. 123.

218. Lands Tribunal for Scotland Rules 1971.
Sch. 2, substituted: rules 95/308, rule 2.

450. Road Vehicles (Registration and Licensing) Regulations 1971.
amended by 1994 No. 3296.

729. Farm and Garden Chemicals Regulations 1971.
rèferred to: regs. 95/887, reg. 27.

NO.

1971—cont.

1117. The Employers' Liability (Compulsory Insurance) General Regulations 1971.
amended by 1994 No. 3301.

1158. Registration of Births, Still-births, Deaths and Marriages (Prescription of Forms) (Scotland) Amendment Regulations 1971.
reg. 7, revoked: regs. 94/3151, reg. 7.
Sch. 5, revoked: regs. 94/3151, reg. 7.

1253. Indictment Rules 1971.
rule 9, see *R.* v. *C.* [1994] Crim.L.R. 590, C.A.

1267. Medicines (Surgical Materials) Order 1971.
art. 3, amended: ord. 94/3119, art. 3.
art. 4, inserted: ord. 94/3119, art. 3.

1326. Medicines (Importation of Medicinal Products for Re-exportation) Order 1971.
art. 4, inserted: regs. 94/3142, reg. 21.

1450. Medicines (Exemption from Licences) (Special and Transitional Cases) Order 1971.
art. 2, applied: regs. 95/2364, Sch. 1, Pt. II, regs. 95/1116, reg. 11, Sch. 1.

1742. National Insurance (Republic of Ireland) Order 1971.
modified: ord. 95/767, art. 2.

1745. Hijacking Act 1971 (Isle of Man) Order 1971.
revoked: ord. 95/1297, art. 2.

1972

223. Civil Aviation (Air Travel Organisers' Licensing) Regulations 1972.
revoked: regs. 95/1054, reg. 2.

451. Civil Aviation Act 1971 (Isle of Man) Order 1972.
revoked: ord. 95/1297, art. 2.

702. Offshore Installations (Registration) Regulations 1972.
revoked: regs. 95/738, reg. 23.

703. Offshore Installations (Managers) Regulations 1972.
revoked: regs. 95/738, reg. 23.

765. Premium Savings Bonds Regulations 1972.
reg. 6, revoked: regs. 95/1002, reg. 2.

917. Highly Flammable Liquids and Liquefied Petroleum Gases Regulations 1972.
amended by 1994 No. 3247.

963. Employer's Liability (Defective Equipment and Compulsory Insurance) (Northern Ireland) Order 1972 (N.I. 6).
art. 5(2); regs. 95/50.
art. 10(1); regs. 95/50.

971. Hovercraft (Application of Enactments) Order 1972.
art. 7, revoked: ord. 95/1299, art. 2.
art. 8, amended: ord. 95/1299, art. 2.

NO.

1972—cont.

972. Patents Etc. (Jordan) (Convention) Order 1972.
revoked: ord. 94/3219, art. 3 (designs), ord. 94/3220, art. 3 (patents).

1073. Superannuation (Northern Ireland) Order 1972.
art. 12, applied: regs. 95/365, reg. R7.

1148. Value Added Tax (Supplied by Retailers) Regulations 1972.
see *Customs and Excise Commissioners* v. *Next*, *The Independent*, March 6, 1995, Judge J.
reg. 2(1), see *Primback* v. *Customs and Excise Commissioners* [1994] S.T.C. 957, May J.

1265. Health and Personal Social Services (Northern Ireland) Order 1972 (N.I. 14).
art. 16, applied: regs. 94/3044, Sch. 5, para. 1.
art. 50, amended: 1995, c. 51, Sch., para. 30.
art. 56; regs. 94/500.
art. 98; regs. 95/16, regs. 95/83; regs. 95/135.
art. 106; regs. 94/500, regs. 95/16, regs. 95/83; regs. 95/135.
art. 107(6); regs. 94/500.
Sch. 15; regs. 95/16, regs. 95/83; regs. 95/135.

1268. Mortgaging of Aircraft Order 1972.
referred to: ord. 95/1268, art. 2.

1542. Offshore Installations (Logbooks and Registration of Death) Regulations 1972.
revoked: regs. 95/738, reg. 23.
reg. 1, amended: regs. 95/738, reg. 23.
regs. 2–7, revoked: regs. 95/738, reg. 23.
reg. 12, amended: regs. 95/738, reg. 23.

1587. National Insurance and Industrial Injuries (Jamaica) Order 1972.
modified: ord. 95/767, art. 2.

2076. Medicines (Data Sheet) Regulations 1972.
reg. 1, amended: regs. 94/3142, reg. 21.
reg. 2, amended: regs. 94/3142, reg. 21.
reg. 4, amended: regs. 94/3142, reg. 21.
Sch. 3, amended: regs. 94/3142, reg. 21.

1973

313. Local Government Superannuation (Miscellaneous Provisions) Regulations 1973.
referred to: regs. 95/1019, Sch. A1.

490. Road Vehicles (Registration and Licensing) Regulations (Northern Ireland) 1973.
amended by 1994 No. 3297.

NO.

1973—cont.

773. Patents Etc. (Federal Republic of Germany and German Democratic Republic) (Convention) Order 1973.
revoked: ord. 94/3219, art. 3 (designs), ord. 94/3220, art. 3 (patents).

861. Stanswood Bay Oyster Fishery Order 1973.
art. 3, amended: ord. 95/1257, art. 2.
art. 5, revoked: ord. 95/1257, art. 2.
art. 5A, revoked: ord. 95/1257, art. 2.
art. 6, amended: ord. 95/1257, art. 2.

1260. Local Government (Retirement of Chief Officers) Regulations 1973.
applied: regs. 95/1019, reg. L15.

1762. Protection of Aircraft Act 1973 (Isle of Man) Order 1973.
revoked: ord. 95/1297, art. 2.

1822. Medicines (Pharmacies) (Applications for Registration and Fees) Regulations 1973.
reg. 3, amended: regs. 94/2936, reg. 2.

1842. Offshore Installations (Inspectors and Casualties) Regulations 1973.
revoked: regs. 95/738, reg. 23.

1996. Local Government Superannuation (Miscellaneous Provisions) (No. 2) Regulations 1973.
referred to: regs. 95/1019, Sch. A1.

1974

73. Water Authorities (Retirement of Chief Officers) Regulations 1974.
applied: regs. 95/1019, regs. L15.

289. Offshore Installations (Construction and Survey) Regulations 1974.
applied: regs. 95/743, reg. 2.

348. Montrose Harbour Revision Order 1974.
art. 2, see *Piggins & Rix* v. *Montrose Port Authority*, 1995 S.L.T. 418.
art. 21, see *Piggins & Rix* v. *Montrose Port Authority*, 1995 S.L.T. 418.

468. National Health Service (Financial Provisions) (Scotland) Regulations 1974.
applied: ord. 95/574, art. 5.

506. National Health Service (General Medical and Pharmaceutical Services) (Scotland) Regulations 1974.
revoked: regs. 95/414, reg. 13.
applied: regs. 94/3130, reg. 2.
reg. 20, amended: regs. 94/3130, reg. 11.
reg. 31, applied: regs. 95/365, reg. R1.
Sch. 1, Pt. I, amended: regs. 94/3130, reg. 13, regs. 95/165, reg. 2.
Sch. 1, Pt. IC, amended: regs. 95/165, reg. 2.

520. Local Government Superannuation Regulations 1974.
applied: regs. 95/1019, Sch. A1.

NO.

1974—cont.

549. National Health Service (Professions Supplementary to Medicine) (Scotland) Regulations 1974.
applied: ord. 95/574, art. 5.

896. Lloyd's Underwriters (Tax) Regulations 1974.
revoked: regs. 95/351, reg. 17.

1286. Land Charges Rules 1974.
rule 16, amended: rules 95/1355, rule 3.
rule 19, amended: rules 95/1355, rule 4.
rule 19A, inserted: rules 95/1355, rule 5.

1326. Weights and Measures (Amendment) Regulations 1974.
revoked: regs. 95/735, reg. 1.

1330. Lloyd's Underwriters (Tax) (No. 2) Regulations 1974.
revoked: regs. 95/351, reg. 17.

1367. Toys (Safety) Regulations 1974.
applied: regs. 95/204, reg. 1.

1491. National Health Service (Vehicles) (Scotland) Order 1974.
applied: ord. 95/574, art. 5.

1547. National Health Service (Injury Benefits) Regulations 1974.
revoked: regs. 95/866, reg. 24.

1565. Valuation (Combination of Councils) (Scotland) (No. 2) Order 1974.
referred to: ord. 95/1340, art. 11.

1681. Protection of Eyes Regulations 1974.
reg. 5, see *Gerrard* v. *Staffordshire Potteries* [1995] I.C.R. 502, C.A.
Sch. 1, para. 27, see *Gerrard* v. *Staffordshire Potteries* [1995] I.C.R. 502, C.A.

1802. Civil Aviation (Air Travel Organisers' Licensing) (Amendment) Regulations 1974.
revoked: regs. 95/1054, reg. 2.

2010. Social Security (Benefit) (Married Women and Widows Special Provisions) Regulations 1974.
reg. 3, amended: regs. 95/829, reg. 2.

2054. National Insurance (Non-participation Transitional Provisions) Regulations 1974.
reg. 9, referred to: regs. 95/1019, reg. D19.

2143. Juries (Northern Ireland) Order 1974.
Sch. 2, amended: 1995, c. 35, Sch. 2.

2146. Patents Etc. (Zaire) (Convention) Order 1974.
revoked: ord. 94/3219, art. 3 (designs), ord. 94/3220, art. 3 (patents).

1975

203. Movement and Sale of Pigs Order 1975.
revoked by 1995 No. 11.

299. Lands Tribunal Rules 1975.
rule 48, see *Regalbourne* v. *East Lindsey District Council* [1994] R.A. 1, C.A.

NO.

1975—cont.

330. Fishing Vessels (Safety Provisions) Rules 1975.
applied: regs. 95/1576, reg. 2.
applied: Scheme 95/1609, para. 3.

346. Movement and Sale of Pigs (Amendment) Order 1975.
revoked by 1995 No. 11.

415. Family Allowances, National Insurance and Industrial Injuries (Spain) Order 1975.
modified: ord. 95/767, art. 2.

494. Social Security (Airmen's Benefits) Regulations 1975.
reg. 2, amended: regs. 95/829, reg. 3.

529. Social Security (Mariners' Benefits) Regulations 1975.
reg. 4, amended: regs. 95/829, reg. 4.
reg. 5, amended: regs. 95/829, reg. 4.
reg. 6, amended: regs. 95/829, reg. 4.

533. Medicines (Dental Filling Substances) Order 1975.
art. 2, amended: ord. 94/3119, art. 4.
art. 3, inserted: ord. 94/3119, art. 4.

536. Trade Unions and Employers' Associations (Amalgamations, etc.) Regulations 1975.
reg. 11, amended: regs. 95/483, regs. 2, 3.
reg. 12, amended: regs. 95/483, reg. 4.

555. Social Security (Hospital In-Patients) Regulations 1975.
Sch. 1, amended: regs. 95/829, reg. 5.
Sch. 2, amended: regs. 95/829, reg. 5.

556. Social Security (Credits) Regulations 1975.
reg. 2, amended: regs. 95/829, reg. 6.
reg. 7C, inserted: regs. 95/2558, reg. 2.
reg. 8, amended: regs. 95/829, reg. 6.
reg. 9, amended: regs. 95/829, reg. 6.

563. Social Security Benefit (Persons Abroad) Regulations 1975.
reg. 2, amended: regs. 95/829, reg. 7.

632. Northern Police (Amalgamation) Order 1975.
referred to: ord. 95/2641, Sch., para. 2.

633. South-Eastern Police (Amalgamation) Order 1975.
referred to: ord. 95/2640, Sch., para. 2.

696. National Health Service (General Medical and Pharmaceutical Services) (Scotland) Amendment Regulations 1975.
revoked: regs. 95/414, reg. 13.

762. Medicines (Exemption from Licences) (Wholesale Dealing in Confectionary) Order 1975.
reg. 1, amended: regs. 94/3144, reg. 11.

1024. Transit of Animals (Road and Rail) Order 1975.
amended by 1994 No. 3249;
amended by 1995 No. 11.

NO.

1975—cont.

1049. Civil Aviation (Air Travel Organisers' Licensing) (Second Amendment) Regulations 1975.
revoked: regs. 95/1054, reg. 2.

1220. Valuation (Local Panels and Appeal Committees Model Scheme) (Scotland) Order 1975.
applied: regs. 95/572, reg. 2.

1289. Offshore Installations (Application of Employers' Liability (Compulsory Insurance) Act 1969) Regulations 1972.
revoked: regs. 95/738, reg. 23.

1473. Medicines (Committee on Dental and Surgical Materials) Order 1975.
revoked: ord. 94/3120, art. 2.

1503. Social Security Pensions (Northern Ireland) Order 1975 (N.I. 15).
art. 69(1)(2)(5)(5ZA); ord. 95/39.

1566. Trunk Road (Eastern Avenue, Ilford) (Prescribed Route) Order 1975.
revoked: ord. 95/2215, art. 2.

1918. Borough of Luton (Electoral Arrangements) Order 1975.
applied: ord. 95/1776, art. 9.

2000. Medicines (Child Safety) Regulations 1975.
reg. 2, amended: regs. 94/3144, reg. 11.

2103. Borough of Hartlepool (Electoral Arrangements) Order 1975.
art. 9, substituted: ord. 95/187, art. 13.

2195. Patents Etc. (Iraq) (Convention) Order 1975.
revoked: ord. 94/3219, art. 3 (designs), ord. 94/3220, art. 3 (patents).

2220. Merchant Shipping (Crew Accommodation) (Fishing Vessels) Regulations 1975.
applied: regs. 95/1802, reg. 8.

2234. Goods Vehicles (International Road Haulage Permits) Regulations 1975.
revoked: regs. 95/1290, reg. 2.

1976

137. Act of Sederunt (Rules of Court Amendment) 1976.
reg. 32, amended: regs. 95/137, reg. 2.
reg. 33, amended: regs. 95/137, reg. 2.
reg. 34, amended: regs. 95/137, reg. 2.
reg. 36, amended: regs. 95/137, reg. 2.
Sch. 3, substituted: regs. 95/137, reg. 2.

142. Occupational Pension Schemes (Equal Access to Membership) Regulations 1976.
reg. 4, revoked: regs. 95/1215, reg. 2.
reg. 5A, inserted: regs. 95/1215, reg. 3.
reg. 10, amended: regs. 95/1215, reg. 4.
reg. 12, amended: regs. 95/1215, reg. 5.
reg. 13, amended: regs. 95/1215, reg. 6.

226. Treatment of Offenders (Northern Ireland) Order 1976.
applied: 1995, c. 46, s. 244.
Pt. II, applied: 1995, c. 47, s. 1.

NO.

1976—cont.

284. Borough of Milton Keynes (Electoral Arrangements) Order 1976.
revoked: ord. 95/1769, art. 11.

476. Act of Sederunt (Summary Cause Rules, Sheriff Court) 1976.
rule 13, see *Thomson* v. *Proctor (Sh. Ct.)*, 1995 S.C.L.R. 648.
rule 18(7), see *ESCO Computers & Systems Maintenance* v. *Morris Amusements (Sh. Ct.)*, 1995 S.C.L.R. 551.
rule 18(9), see *Edinburgh District Council, City of* v. *Sinclair* (Sh. Ct.), 1995 S.C.L.R. 194.
rule 19, see *Thomson* v. *Proctor (Sh. Ct.)*, 1995 S.C.L.R. 648.
rule 20, see *ESCO Computers & Systems Maintenance* v. *Morris Amusements (Sh. Ct.)*, 1995 S.C.L.R. 551.
rule 28(1), see *ESCO Computers & Systems Maintenance* v. *Morris Amusements (Sh. Ct.)* 1995 S.C.L.R. 551.
rule 69, see *Main* v. *Reid (Sh.Ct.)*, 1994 S.C.L.R. 948.
rule 91(2), see *Main* v. *Reid (Sh.Ct.)*, 1994 S.C.L.R. 948.
Form V3, see *Main* v. *Reid (Sh.Ct.)*, 1994 S.C.L.R. 948.

598. Occupational Pension Schemes (Friendly Societies) Regulations 1976.
revoked by 1995 No. 35.

615. Social Security (Medical Evidence) Regulations 1976.
reg. 1, amended: regs. 94/2975, reg. 2.
reg. 2, amended: regs. 94/2975, reg. 2, regs. 95/987, reg. 4.
reg. 5, amended: regs. 94/2975, reg. 2.
Sch. 1B, inserted: regs. 94/2975, reg. 3.
Sch. 1B, Pt. I, amended: regs. 95/987, reg. 4.

626. Approved Probation Hostel and Home and Bail Hostel Rules 1976.
revoked: rules 95/302, rule 3.

721. Highways (Inquiries Procedure) Rules 1976.
revoked: rules 94/3263, rule 30.

733. National Health Service (General Medical and Pharmaceutical Services) (Scotland) Amendment Regulations 1976.
revoked: regs. 95/414, reg. 13.

796. Price Marking (Pre-packed Milk in Vending Machines) Order 1976.
art. 1, amended: ord. 94/1853, art. 2.
art. 2, amended: ord. 94/1853, art. 2.

832. Borough of Darlington (Electoral Arrangements) Order 1976.
applied: ord. 95/1772, art. 9.

875. Milk Bottles (Labelling and Cap Colour) (Scotland) Order 1976.
revoked: regs. 95/1372, reg. 23.

NO.

1976—cont.

968. Medicines (Specified Articles and Substances) Order 1976.
art. 2, amended: ord. 94/3119, art. 5.
art. 3, inserted: ord. 94/3119, art. 5.

1019. Offshore Installations (Operational Safety, Health and Welfare) Regulations 1972.
reg. 1, amended: regs. 95/738, reg. 23.
reg. 2, amended: regs. 95/743, reg. 25.
reg. 3, amended: regs. 95/738, reg. 23.
reg. 4, amended: regs. 95/743, reg. 25.
reg. 5, amended: regs. 95/738, reg. 23.
regs. 7–9, revoked: regs. 95/738, reg. 23.
reg. 16, revoked: regs. 95/738, reg. 23.
reg. 17, amended: regs. 95/738, reg. 23.
reg. 18, amended: regs. 95/743, reg. 25.
regs. 18–26, revoked: regs. 95/738, reg. 23.
reg. 30, revoked: regs. 95/738, reg. 23.
reg. 32, amended: regs. 95/738, reg. 23.
reg. 34, amended: regs. 95/738, reg. 23.
Sch. 2, revoked: regs. 95/738, reg. 23.

1073. Police (Scotland) Regulations 1976.
reg. 1, amended: regs. 95/596, reg. 2.
reg. 2, substituted: regs. 95/596, reg. 3.
reg. 5, amended: regs. 95/596, reg. 4.
reg. 7, substituted: regs. 95/596, reg. 5.
reg. 8, substituted: regs. 95/596, reg. 6.
reg. 8A, inserted: regs. 95/596, reg. 7.
reg. 8B, inserted: regs. 95/596, reg. 7.
reg. 21B, amended: regs. 95/2131, reg. 2.
reg. 22, amended: regs. 95/596, reg. 8.
reg. 23, amended: regs. 95/596, reg. 9.
reg. 23A, amended: regs. 95/2131, reg. 3.
reg. 30, amended: regs. 95/137, reg. 2.
reg. 37, amended: regs. 95/596, reg. 10.
reg. 47, amended: regs. 95/2131, reg. 4, regs. 95/596, reg. 11.
Sch. 3, para. 1, amended: regs. 95/2131, reg. 5.
Sch. 3, para. 2, amended: regs. 95/596, reg. 12.
Sch. 3, para. 3, amended: regs. 95/596, reg. 12.
Sch. 3, para. 5, amended: regs. 95/596, reg. 12.
Sch. 3, paras. 11, 12, inserted: regs. 95/2131, reg. 5.
Sch. 9, para. 3, amended: regs. 95/2131, reg. 6.

1168. Veterinary Surgeons (Examination of Commonwealth and Foreign Candidates) (Amendment) Regulations Order of Council 1976.
revoked: ord. 95/2396, art. 2.

1409. Social Security (Invalid Care Allowance) Regulations 1976.
reg. 14, amended: regs. 95/829, reg. 8.
Sch. 1, substituted: regs. 95/829, reg. 8.

NO.

1976—cont.

1542. Offshore Installations (Emergency Procedures) Regulations 1976.
revoked: regs. 95/743, reg. 25.

1574. National Health Service (General Medical and Pharmaceutical Services) (Scotland) Amendment (No. 2) Regulations 1976.
revoked: regs. 95/414, reg. 13.

1726. Medicines (Labelling) Regulations 1976.
reg. 1, amended: regs. 94/3144, reg. 11.
reg. 3A, inserted: regs. 94/3142, reg. 21.

1785. Patents Etc. (Ghana, Libya and Mauritius) (Convention) Order 1976.
revoked: ord. 94/3219, art. 3 (designs), ord. 94/3220, art. 3 (patents).

1820. City of Stoke-on-Trent (Electoral Arrangements) Order 1976.
art. 9, substituted: ord. 95/1779, art. 10.

1883. Drinking Milk Regulations 1976.
reg. 5A, inserted: regs. 95/1086, reg. 24.

1888. Drinking Milk (Scotland) Regulations 1976.
reg. 5A, inserted: regs. 95/1372, reg. 24.

1897. Restrictive Practices Court Rules 1976.
rule 3(1), see *Mackie & Dewar* v. *Director General of Fair Trading (R.P.C.)*, 1995 S.L.T. 1028.
rule 3(3), see *Mackie & Dewar* v. *Director General of Fair Trading (R.P.C.)* 1995 S.L.T. 1028.
rule 5(1), see *Mackie & Dewar* v. *Director General of Fair Trading (R.P.C.)*, 1995 S.L.T. 1028.
rule 6(1), see *Mackie & Dewar* v. *Director General of Fair Trading (R.P.C.)*, 1995 S.L.T. 1028.

1919. Double Taxation (Taxes on Income) (Spain) Order 1976.
art. 6, amended: ord. 95/765, art. 2.

1968. City of York (Electoral Arrangements) Order 1976.
referred to: ord. 95/610, art. 6.

1987. Teachers' Superannuation Regulations 1976.
applied: regs. 95/1019, Sch. D6.

2012. National Saving Stock Register Regulations 1976.
amended by 1994 No. 3277.

2152. Double Taxation Relief (Taxes on Income) (Republic of Ireland) Order 1976.
art. 17A, inserted: ord. 95/764, art. 2.

2169. City of Southampton (Electoral Arrangements) Order 1976.
art. 9, substituted: ord. 95/1775, art. 10.

2186. Milk and Dairies (Milk Bottle Caps) (Colour) Regulations 1976.
revoked: regs. 95/1086, reg. 23.

NO.

1977

171. Milk and Dairies (General) (Amendment) Regulations 1977.
revoked: regs. 95/1086, reg. 23.

217. Royal and other Parks and Gardens Regulations 1977.
referred to: regs. 95/993, reg. 9.

289. Town and Country Planning General Development Order 1977.
art. 5, see *Handoll* v. *Warner Goodman Streat (a Firm)*, *The Times*, December 26, 1994, C.A.

320. Overseas Service (Pensions Supplement) Regulations 1977.
revoked: regs. 95/238, reg. 25.

343. Social Security Benefit (Dependency) Regulations 1977.
reg. 8, see *Social Security Decision No. R(P) 1/93.*
reg. 8(2)(6), see *Social Security Decision No. R(IS) 6/94.*
reg. 15, applied: regs. 95/310, reg. 25.

359. Medicines (Prohibition of Importation and Possession of Veterinary Drugs) Order (Northern Ireland) 1977.
art. 3, amended: regs. 94/3142, reg. 21.

486. Offshore Installations (Emergency Procedures) Regulations 1977.
revoked: regs. 95/743, reg. 25.

655. Medicines (Leaflets) Regulations 1977.
reg. 1, amended: regs. 94/3144, reg. 11.

927. Fruit Juices and Fruit Nectars Regulations 1977.
reg. 2, amended: regs. 95/236, reg. 3.

956. Social Security Benefit (Persons Residing Together) Regulations 1977.
reg. 2, amended: regs. 95/829, reg. 10.

985. Local Land Charges Rules 1977.
rule 11, amended: rules 95/260, rule 2.
rule 13, amended: rules 95/260, rule 2.
rule 16, inserted: rules 95/260, rule 3.

1026. Fruit Juices and Fruit Nectars (Scotland) Regulations 1977.
reg. 2, amended: regs. 95/236, reg. 3.

1038. Medicines (Manufacturers' Undertakings for Imported Products) Regulations 1977.
reg. 2, amended: regs. 94/3144, reg. 11.

1341. Local Government Superannuation (City of London) Regulations 1977.
applied: regs. 95/1019, reg. M3.

1443. Scholarship and Other Benefits Regulations 1977.
referred to: regs. 95/1915, reg. 4.

1633. Patents Etc. (Burundi) (Convention) Order 1977.
revoked: ord. 94/3219, art. 3 (designs), ord. 94/3220, art. 3 (patents).

1634. Patents Etc. (Hong Kong) (Convention) Order 1977.
revoked: ord. 94/3219, art. 3 (designs), ord. 94/3220, art. 3 (patents).

NO.

1977—cont.

1675. Overseas Service (Pensions Supplement) (Amendment) Regulations 1977.
revoked: regs. 95/238, reg. 25.

2008. Police (Scotland) Amendment (No. 2) Regulations 1977.
reg. 7, revoked: regs. 95/137, reg. 5.
reg. 8, revoked: regs. 95/137, reg. 5.
Sch., revoked: regs. 95/137, reg. 5.

2138. National Health Service (Superannuation) (War Service, etc.) (Scotland) Regulations 1977.
reg. 3, applied: regs. 95/365, reg. C.2.

2157. The Rates (Northern Ireland) Order 1977 (N.I. 28).
art. 2(2); ord. 95/55.
art. 7(1); ord. 95/55.
art. 27(4); ord. 95/55.
art. 39A; ord. 95/58.
art. 45(1); ord. 95/57.

2158. Supplementary Benefits, etc. (Consequential Provisions) (Northern Ireland) Order 1977.
art. 2, amended: ord. 95/756, art. 15.

2161. Patents Etc. (Bangladesh) (Convention) Order 1977.
revoked: ord. 94/3219, art. 3 (designs), ord. 94/3220, art. 3 (patents).

1978

32. Diseases of Animals (Approved Disinfectants) Order 1978.
applied: ord. 94/3141, art. 3.
art. 2, amended: ord. 94/3141, art. 15.
art. 6, amended: ord. 94/2965, art. 2.
Sch. 1, substituted: ord. 94/2965, art. 2.
Sch. 2, substituted: ord. 94/2965, art. 2.

40. Medicines (Fluted Bottles) Regulations 1978.
reg. 1, amended: regs. 94/3142, reg. 21.
reg. 3, amended: regs. 94/3144, reg. 11.
reg. 3, amended: regs. 94/3142, reg. 21.

187. Patents Etc. (Republic of Korea) (Convention) Order 1978.
revoked: ord. 94/3219, art. 3 (designs), ord. 94/3220, art. 3 (patents).

216. Patent Rules 1978.
rule 124, applied: rules 95/2164, Sch.

393. Social Security (Graduated Retirement Benefit) (No. 2) Regulations 1978.
reg. 2, substituted: regs. 95/2606, reg. 2.
reg. 3, amended: regs. 95/829, reg. 11.
sch. 1, amended: regs. 95/829, reg. 11.

436. Fire Services (Appointments and Promotion) Regulations 1978.
Sch. 1, Pt. II, amended: regs. 95/2109, reg. 2.
Sch. 2, Pt. II, amended: regs. 95/2109, reg. 2.

NO.

1978—cont.

529. Social Security (Widow's and Widower's Invalidity Pensions) Regulations 1976.
reg. 1, amended: regs. 95/829, reg. 9.
reg. 2, revoked: regs. 95/829, reg. 9.
reg. 3, amended: regs. 95/829, reg. 9.
reg. 4, amended: regs. 95/829, reg. 9.

611. Offshore Installations (Emergency Procedures) Regulations 1978.
revoked: regs. 95/743, reg. 25.

639. Sheffield Assay Office Order 1978.
referred to: 1995 c. v, s. 2.

753. Borough of Hove (Electoral Arrangements) Order 1978.
referred to: ord. 95/1770, art. 11.

795. Merchant Shipping (Crew Accommodation) Regulations 1978.
applied: regs. 95/1802, reg. 8.

1039. Health and Safety at Work (Northern Ireland) Order 1978 (N.I. 9).
applied: regs. 94/3076, Sch. 6.
art. 2, referred to: regs. 94/3260, reg. 2.
art. 2(5); regs. 95/51.
art. 17(1)–(6); regs. 95/51.
art. 17(1)(2); regs. 95/26.
art. 17(1)(2)(4)–(6); regs. 95/3.
art. 17(1)(2)(5); ord. 94/478.
art. 23, referred to: regs. 94/3260, reg. 2.
art. 24, referred to: regs. 94/3260, reg. 2.
art. 26, referred to: regs. 95/3260, reg. 2.
art. 43(2); ord. 94/478.
art. 55(2); regs. 95/3; regs. 95/51.
Sch. 3, para. 1(1)–(3); regs. 95/3, regs. 95/26.
Sch. 3, para. 1(1)(2); regs. 95/51.
Sch. 3, para. 2(1); regs. 95/51.
Sch. 3, para. 5(1); regs. 95/51.
Sch. 3, para. 6; ord. 94/478.
Sch. 3, para. 7; regs. 95/51.
Sch. 3, para. 7(1); ord. 94/478.
Sch. 3, para. 8; regs. 95/51.
Sch. 3, para. 10; regs. 95/51.
Sch. 3, para. 11; regs. 95/3.
Sch. 3, para. 12(1)(3); regs. 95/51.
Sch. 3, para. 13; regs. 95/51
Sch. 3, para. 14(1); regs. 95/51.
Sch. 3, para. 15; regs. 95/3, regs. 95/51.
Sch. 3, para. 19; regs. 95/3.

1096. State Award Regulations 1978.
reg. 7, applied: regs. 94/3044, reg. 12.

1170. Police (Scotland) Amendment (No. 2) Regulations 1978.
reg. 4, revoked: regs. 95/137, reg. 5.
reg. 7, revoked: regs. 95/137, reg. 5.
Append., revoked: regs. 95/137, reg. 5.

1408. Double Taxation Relief (Taxes on Income) (Switzerland) Order 1978.
amended by 1994 No. 3215.

1613. City of Derby (Electoral Arrangements) Order 1978.
art. 9, substituted: ord. 95/1773, art. 9.
Sch. 2, substituted: ord. 95/1773, art. 9.

NO.

1978—cont.

1682. Justices of the Peace Act 1949 (Compensation) Regulations 1978.
reg. 3, substituted: regs. 95/41, reg. 2.

1684. Public Service Vehicles (Lost Property) Regulations 1978.
reg. 3, amended: regs. 95/185, reg. 2.
reg. 7, amended: regs. 95/185, reg. 2.
reg. 8, substituted: regs. 95/185, reg. 2.
reg. 9, substituted: regs. 95/185, reg. 2.

1698. Social Security Benefit (Computation of Benefits) Regulations 1978.
reg. 1, amended: regs. 95/829, reg. 12.
reg. 3, amended: regs. 95/829, reg. 12.
reg. 5, amended: regs. 95/829, reg. 12.
reg. 7, amended: regs. 95/829, reg. 12.

1761. Local Authorities (Goods and Services) (Public Bodies) (Scotland) Order 1978.
applied: ord. 95/789, art. 2.

1762. National Health Service (General Medical and Pharmaceutical Services) (Scotland) Amendment Regulations 1978.
revoked: regs. 95/414, reg. 13.

1907. Health and Personal Social Services (Northern Ireland) Order 1978 (N.I. 26).
art. 8, applied: regs. 94/3130, reg. 5.
art. 8, regs. 94/499.

1979

5. Civil Aviation (Air Travel Organisers' Licensing) (Third Amendment) Regulations 1979.
revoked: regs. 95/1054, reg. 2.

591. Social Security (Contributions) Regulations 1979.
amended: regs. 95/714, reg. 2.
reg. 7, amended: regs. 95/714, reg. 2.
reg. 18, amended: regs. 95/1003, reg. 2.
reg. 23, amended: regs. 95/829, reg. 13.
reg. 28, amended: regs. 95/829, reg. 13.
reg. 38, amended: regs. 95/829, reg. 13.
reg. 39, amended: regs. 95/829, reg. 13.
reg. 98, amended: regs. 95/514, reg. 2.
reg. 115, amended: regs. 95/714, reg. 2.
reg. 123D, amended: regs. 95/714, reg. 2.
Sch. 1A, para. 9C, inserted: regs. 95/1003, reg. 3.
para. 19, inserted: regs. 95/1003, reg. 3.

597. Social Security (Overlapping Benefits) Regulations 1979.
reg. 3, revoked: regs. 95/829, reg. 14.
reg. 4, amended: regs. 95/829, reg. 14.
reg. 10, amended: regs. 95/829, reg. 14.
reg. 14, amended: regs. 95/829, reg. 14.
Sch. 1, amended: regs. 95/829, reg. 14.

642. Social Security (Widow's Benefit and Retirement Pensions) Regulations 1979.
amended by 1995 No. 74.

NO.

1979—cont.

785. Local Government (Compensation for Premature Retirement) (Scotland) Regulations 1979.
reg. 5, amended: regs. 95/340, reg. 13.
reg. 14, amended: regs. 94/3068, reg. 9.
Sch. 1, amended: regs. 95/750, reg. 3.

911. Social Security (Portugal) Order 1979.
modified: ord. 95/767, art. 2.

929. Air Navigation (Isle of Man) Order 1979.
revoked: ord. 95/1296, art. 2.

937. Industrial and Provident Societies (Credit Unions) Regulations 1979.
Sch. 2, substituted: regs. 95/712, reg. 2.

1088. Motor Vehicles (Designation of Approval Marks) Regulations 1979.
referred to: regs. 95/925, reg. 3.

1113. City of Kingston upon Hull (Electoral Arrangements) Order 1979.
art. 9, substituted: ord. 95/600, art. 6.

1170. Police (Scotland) Amendment Regulations 1979.
revoked: regs. 95/137, reg. 5.

1263. Police (Scotland) Amendment (No. 2) Regulations 1979.
reg. 4, revoked: regs. 95/137, reg. 5.
Sch., revoked: regs. 95/137, reg. 5.

1277. Overseas Service (Pensions Supplement) (Amendment) Regulations 1979.
revoked: regs. 95/238, reg. 25.

1347. Borough of Poole (Electoral Arrangements) Order 1979.
applied: ord. 95/1771, art. 10.

1494. City of Portsmouth (Electoral Arrangements) Order 1979.
art. 9, substituted: ord. 95/1775, art. 9.

1535. Medicines (Committee on Dental and Surgical Materials) Amendment Order 1979.
revoked: ord. 94/3120, art. 2.

1567. Milk and Dairies (General) (Amendment) Regulations 1977.
revoked: regs. 95/1086, reg. 23.

1644. National Health Service (Vocational Training) Regulations 1979.
applied: regs. 94/3130, regs. 2, 5.
reg. 8, amended: regs. 94/3130, reg. 10.

1813. Borough of Bournemouth (Electoral Arrangements) Order 1979.
applied: ord. 95/1771, art. 9.

1980

14. Importation of Animal Products and Poultry Products Order 1980.
amended: reg. 94/3144, reg. 11.
art. 2, amended: ord. 94/2920, art. 2.
art. 3, amended: ord. 94/2920, art. 2.
Sch., amended: regs. 94/3142, reg. 21.
Sch., substituted: ord. 94/2920, art. 2.

NO.

1980—cont.

30. National Health Service (Vocational Training) (Scotland) Regulations 1980.
applied: regs. 94/3130, reg. 2, 5, reg. 95/416, Sch. 5.
reg. 4, applied: regs. 95/416, reg. 9.
reg. 8, amended: regs. 94/3130, reg. 10.

51. Consumer Credit (Total Charge for Credit) Regulations 1980.
applied: regs. 94/3045, reg. 7.

79. Enzootic Bovine Leukosis Order 1980.
art. 5A, inserted: ord. 95/13, art. 2.
art. 5B, inserted: ord. 95/13, art. 2.
art. 6, amended: ord. 95/13, art. 2.

188. Civil Aviation Act 1971 (Isle of Man) (Amendment) Order 1980.
revoked: ord. 95/1297, art. 2.

196. Borough of Brighton (Electoral Arrangements) Order 1980.
referred to: ord. 95/1770, art. 11.

297. City of Bristol (Electoral Arrangements) Order 1980.
art. 9, substituted: ord. 95/493, art. 8.

319. Plant Breeders' Rights (Vegetables) (Including Field Beans and Field Peas) (Variation) Scheme 1980.
para. 6, amended: Scheme 95/530, art. 3.
Sch. 2, amended: Scheme 95/530, art. 4.
Sch. 3, amended: Scheme 95/530, art. 5.

362. National Health Service (Superannuation) Regulations 1980.
revoked: regs. 95/300, reg. V2.
referred to: regs. 95/866, reg. 2.

397. County Courts (Northern Ireland) Order 1980 (N.I. 3).
applied: ord. 95/1038, art. 117; regs. 95/1054, reg. 11.
art. 3(1); ord. 94/471; ord. 95/5.
art. 28, amended: 1995, c. 35, Sch. 2.
art. 46; ord. 94/472, rules 95/48.

534. Merchant Shipping (Navigational Warnings) Regulations 1980.
referred to: ord. 95/1299, art. 2.

538. Merchant Shipping (Life-Saving Appliances) Regulations 1980.
Sch. 15, Pt. III, applied: ord. 95/1038, Sch. 4.

564. Maintenance Orders (Northern Ireland Consequential Amendments) Order 1980.
art. 3, amended: ord. 95/756, art. 15.

765. Motorcycles (Sound Level Measurement Certificates) Regulations 1980.
referred: regs. 95/925, reg. 3.

999. Veterinary Surgeons (Examination of Commonwealth and Foreign Candidates) (Amendment) Regulations Order of Council 1980.
revoked: ord. 95/2396, art. 2.

NO.

1980—cont.

1050. Police (Scotland) Amendment Regulations 1980.
reg. 9, revoked: regs. 95/137, reg. 5.
reg. 12, revoked: regs. 95/137, reg. 5.

1177. National Health Service (Superannuation) (Scotland) Regulations 1980.
revoked: regs. 95/365, reg. V2.

1212. Importation of Embryos, Ova and Semen Order 1980.
art. 2, amended: ord. 94/2920, art. 3.

1248. Control of Lead at Work Regulations 1980.
applied: regs. 94/3246, reg. 5.

1254. Teachers (Compensation for Premature Retirement) (Scotland) Regulations 1980.
reg. 5, amended: regs. 95/840, reg. 13.

1413. Land Registration (Scotland) Rules 1980.
Sch. A, substituted: rules 95/248, rule 2.

1759. Offshore Installations (Well Control) Regulations 1980.
reg. 1, amended: regs. 95/738, reg. 23.
reg. 3, amended: regs. 95/738, reg. 23.

1923. Medicines (Sale or Supply) (Miscellaneous Provisions) Regulations 1980.
reg. 5, amended: regs. 94/3142, reg. 21.
reg. 5, amended: regs. 94/3144, reg. 11.

1924. Medicines (Pharmacy and General Sale—Exemption) Order 1980.
art. 5, amended: regs. 94/3142, reg. 21.
Sch. 1, amended: regs. 94/3144, reg. 11.
Sch. 1, Pt. I, amended: regs. 94/3142, reg. 21.

1934. Importation of Animal Products and Poultry Products (Amendment) Order 1980.
revoked: ord. 94/2920, art. 4.

1961. Double Taxation Relief (Taxes on Income) (Netherlands) Order 1980.
art. 10(3), see *Steeple* v. *European Vinyls Corp. (Holdings) BV* [1995] STC 31, Lightman J.

2053. Employment Appeal Tribunal Rules 1980.
rules 25, 26, see *Bass Leisure* v. *Thomas* [1994] IRLR 104, E.A.T.

1981

56. National Health Service (General Medical and Pharmaceutical Services) (Scotland) Amendment Regulations 1981.
revoked: regs. 95/414, reg. 13.

67. Police (Scotland) Amendment Regulations 1981.
reg. 7, revoked: regs. 95/137, reg. 5.
reg. 9, revoked: regs. 95/137, reg. 5.
Sch., revoked: regs. 95/137, reg. 5.

NO.

1981—cont.

154. Road Traffic (Northern Ireland) Order 1981 (N.I. 1).
art. 31A(1); regs. 95/38.
art. 31D(1); regs. 95/38.
art. 218(1); regs. 95/38.

167. County of Humberside (Electoral Arrangements) Order 1981.
referred to: ord. 95/600, art. 2.

171. Value Added Tax (Special Provisions) Order 1981.
art. 9, see *Thorn EMI* v. *Customs and Excise Commissioners*, *The Times*, May 13, 1995, C.A.

228. Legal Aid, Advice and Assistance (Northern Ireland) Order 1981 (N.I. 8).
art. 3(2); regs. 95/75.
art. 7(2); regs. 95/76.
art. 7(3); regs. 95/75.
art. 9(2); regs. 95/77.
art. 12(2); regs. 95/77.
art. 22; regs. 95/75; regs. 95/76; regs. 95/77.
art. 27; regs. 95/75; regs. 95/76; regs. 95/77.

231. Weights and Measures (Northern Ireland) Order 1981.
applied: regs. 94/3076, Sch. 6.

257. Public Service Vehicles (Conditions of Fitness, Equipment, Use and Certification) Regulations 1981.
reg. 35, amended: regs. 95/305, reg. 3.
Sch. 4, amended: regs. 95/305, reg. 4.

314. Civil Aviation (Air Travel Organisers' Licensing) (Fourth Amendment) Regulations 1981.
revoked: regs. 95/1054, reg. 2.

399. Diving Operations at Work Regulations 1981.
reg. 2, amended: regs. 95/738, reg. 23.
reg. 4, amended: regs. 95/738, reg. 23.

467. Transfer of Undertakings (Protection of Employment) Regulations 1981.
reg. 10(2), see *South Durham Health Authority* v. *Unison* [1995] IRLR 407, E.A.T.
reg. 11(8), see *South Durham Health Authority* v. *Unison* [1995] IRLR 407, E.A.T.

552. Magistrates' Courts Rules 1981.
amended: rules 95/585 (L.3), rule 2; regs. 94/3154.
rule 84A, inserted: rules 95/585, rule 2.
rule 93B, inserted: rules 95/585, rule 2.
rule 104B, inserted: rules 94/3154, rule 2.

553. Magistrates' Courts (Forms) Rules 1981.
amended: rules 95/585 (L.3), rule 3.
Sch. 2, amended: rules 95/585, rule 3.
Sch. 2, Form 27, amended: rules 95/1909, rule 2.
Sch. 2, Form 28, amended: rules 95/1909, rule 2.

NO.

1981—cont.

572. Merchant Shipping (Cargo Ship Construction and Survey) Regulations 1981.
regs. 71–78, revoked: regs. 95/1210, reg. 1.

605. Social Security (Austria) Order 1981.
modified: ord. 95/767, art. 2.

741. Value Added Tax (Special Provisions) Order 1981.
art. 12A, see *Co-operative Wholesale Society* v. *Customs and Excise Commissioners* [1994] V.A.T.T.R. 228, Manchester Tribunal.

804. Town and Country Planning (Determination of Appeals by Appointed Persons) (Prescribed Classes) Regulations 1981.
reg. 4, amended: regs. 95/2259, reg. 2.

859. Traffic Signs Regulations and General Directions 1981.
reg. 34, see *D.P.P.* v. *Harris (Nigel)* [1995] RTR 100, D.C.

880. Capital Transfer Tax (Delivery of Accounts) Regulations 1981.
reg. 3, amended: regs. 95/1461, reg. 2.

881. Capital Transfer Tax (Delivery of Accounts) (Scotland) Regulations 1981.
reg. 3, amended: regs. 95/1459, reg. 2.

965. National Health Service (General Medical and Pharmaceutical Services) (Scotland) Amendment (No. 2) Regulations 1981.
revoked: regs. 95/414, reg. 13.

988. Veterinary Surgeons (Practice by Students) Regulations Order of Council 1981.
Sch., amended: ord. 95/2397, Sch.

1011. Health and Safety (Dangerous Pathogens) Regulations 1981.
revoked: regs. 94/3246, reg. 18.
reg. 2, amended: regs. 94/3142, reg. 21.
reg. 2, amended: regs. 94/3144, reg. 11.

1051. Export of Animals (Protection) Order 1981.
amended by 1994 No. 3249.

1077. Merchant Shipping (Tankers) (EEC Requirements) Regulations 1981.
revoked: regs. 95/2498, reg. 2.

1086. Education (Schools and Further Education) Regulations 1981.
regs. 11, 12, revoked: regs. 95/2089, reg. 4.

1113. Wireless Telegraphy (Isle of Man) Order 1981.
art. 2, amended: ord. 95/268, art. 2.
Sch., para. 1, revoked: ord. 95/268, art. 2.
Sch., para. 3, revoked: ord. 95/268, art. 2.

1115. Diseases of Animals (Northern Ireland) Order 1981 (N.I. 22).
art. 2(3); ord. 95/43, ord. 95/44.
art. 5(1); ord. 95/43.
art. 16(2); ord. 95/44.

NO.

1981—cont.

1115. Diseases of Animals (Northern Ireland) Order 1981 (N.I. 22)—*cont.*
art. 19(e)(f)(k); ord. 95/43.
art. 32; ord. 95/43.
art. 44; ord. 95/43.
art. 60(1); ord. 95/43.

1205. National Health Service (Superannuation) Amendment Regulations 1981.
revoked: regs. 95/300, reg. V2.

1238. Importation of Animal Products and Poultry Products (Amendment) Order 1981.
revoked: ord. 94/2920, art. 4.

1373. Road Traffic Acts 1960 and 1972, Road Traffic Regulation Act 1967 and Transport Act 1968 (Metrication) Regulations 1984.
reg. 4, amended: 1995, c. 23, Sch. 8, Pt. II.
Sch., Pt. IIIA, revoked: 1995, c. 23, Sch. 8, Pt. II.

1441. Inheritance Tax (Delivery of Accounts) (Northern Ireland) Regulations 1981.
reg. 3, amended: regs. 95/1460, reg. 2.

1455. Brucellosis (England and Wales) Order 1981.
art. 8A, inserted: ord. 94/2762, art. 2.

1675. Magistrates' Courts (Northern Ireland) Order 1981 (N.I. 26).
art. 11(2); ord. 94/470; ord. 95/5.
art. 96, applied: 1995, c. 43, s. 14; 1995, c. 46, ss. 215, 252.
art. 114, applied: ord. 95/907, art. 4, ord. 95/908, art. 5.
art. 140, applied: 1995, c. 35, s. 30.
art. 154, applied: ord. 95/907, art. 4, ord. 95/908, art. 5.
art. 158A, inserted: 1995, c. 35, s. 27.

1680. National Health Service (Superannuation) (Scotland) Amendment Regulations 1981.
revoked: regs. 95/365, reg. V2.

1687. County Court Rules 1981.
ord. 1,
rule 9, see *Maple* v. *Gribble Booth and Taylor*, May 26, 1995; H.H.J. MacIntosh; Exeter County Ct.
ord. 6,
rule 1(5), see *Hogg* v. *Stockton Plant*, June 12, 1995, H.H.J. Cartlidge, Sunderland County Ct.
ord. 7,
rule 1, see *Maple* v. *Gribble Booth and Taylor*, May 26, 1995; H.H.J. MacIntosh; Exter County Ct.
ord. 8,
rule 2(1), see *Unilever* v. *Chefaro Proprietaries* [1994] F.S.R. 135, C.A.
rule 2(1)(d)(i), see *Agrafax Public Relations* v. *United Scottish Society*, *The Times*, May 22, 1995, C.A.

NO.

1981—cont.

1687. County Court Rules 1981—*cont.*
ord. 9,
rule 2, see *McDermott* v. *Sharp*, May 24, 1995, District Judge Simons, Trowbridge County Ct.
rule 2(6), see *Varsani* v. *Davy*, October 17, 1995, H.H.J. Lowe, Willesden County Ct.
rule 3(6), see *Simpson* v. *Wilson-Lim*, September 11, 1995, H.H.J. Wiggs, Poole County Ct.
rule 10, see *George* v. *Carney*, April 25, 1995; H.H.J. Tibber; Edmonton County Ct.; *Hayes* v. *Colyer*, June 12, 1995, H.H.J. McKinney, Bournemouth County Ct.; *Lovell* v. *Porter (CCRTI 94/0754/F; CCRTI 94/1461/F; CCRTI 94/1531/F)*, May 26, 1995, C.A.; *McDermott* v. *Sharp*, May 24, 1995, District Judge Simons, Trowbridge County Ct.; *Moloney* v. *Coleman*, November 29, 1994; District Judge Somerville; Reading County Ct.; *U.S. Leasing* v. *McKenna Corporation and Peter McKenna*, April 25, 1995; Langley J.; Central London County Ct.; *Webster* v. *Ellison Circlips*, *The Independent*, June 21, 1995, C.A.
rule 12, see *Unilever* v. *Chefaro Proprietaries* [1994] F.S.R. 135, C.A.
ord. 11,
rule 2(3)(a), see *Hughes (Michael David)* v. *Jones (Stephen)* December 2, 1994; District Judge Burgess; Reading County Ct.
rule 3(5), see *Medisure Marketing and Management* v. *Woolven*, November 9, 1994; C.A.; *Talter and Talter* v. *Singh*, February 10, 1995, H.H.J. Wilcox, Birmingham County Ct.
rule 5, see *Hughes* v. *Vose*, August 11, 1995, District Judge Richardson, Birkenhead County Ct.; *Wald* v. *Jones*, July 10, 1995, Deputy District Judge Kirkham, Hull County Ct.
ord. 13,
rule 3(2), see *Schwarz* v. *Gray and Gray*, November 18, 1994; H.H.J. Marr-Johnson; Clerkenwell County Ct.
rule 4, see *Kelliher* v. *E.H. Savill Engineering* [1994] P.I.Q.R. P387, C.A.; *Maple* v. *Gribble Booth and Taylor*, May 26, 1995; H.H.J. MacIntosh; Exeter County Ct.
rule 5(2), see *Thompson (Deborah Anne)* v. *Dixon (Graham)* (CCRTI 94/0685/F), February 2, 1995, C.A.

NO.

1981—cont.

1687. County Court Rules 1981—*cont.*

ord. 13—*cont.*

rule 6, see *Burris* v. *Azadani, The Times*, August 9, 1995, C.A.; *Joyce* v. *Liverpool City Council*; *Wyne* v. *Same*, *The Times*, May 2, 1995, C.A.

ord. 14,

rule 8(1), see *FDR* v. *Holloway* [1995] IRLR 400, E.A.T.

ord. 15,

rule 5, see *Langley* v. *Langley* [1994] 1 F.L.R. 383, C.A.

rule 11(1), see *Jones* v. *Swift Structures*, April 19, 1995, D.D.J. Perry; Romford County Ct.

ord. 17,

rule 2(b), see *Kirkham* v. *Cooper (t/a Carpet and Curtains Centre)*, April 20, 1995, H.H.J. Bush, Leeds County Ct.

rule 11, see *Bailey* v. *J. Dixon (Doncaster)*, November 8, 1994, Leeds County Ct.; *Cassandro* v. *Nembhard*, February 13, 1995; H.H.J. Burford; Aldershot and Farnham County Ct. sitting at Southampton; *Daw* v. *Tilcon*, November 23, 1994; H.H.J. Grenfell; Bradford County Ct.; *Evans* v. *Bristol & West Building Society*, June 14, 1995, H.H.J. Bradbury, Ipswich County Ct.; *Grist (C.)* v. *S.T.C. and the Forestry Commission*, February 16, 1995; District Judge A.T. North; Pontypridd County Ct.; *Gumbley* v. *Barmby*, March 8, 1995, H.H.J. Tetlow, Manchester County Ct.; *Hawkes* v. *Treasures & River Wyatt (LTA 94/5930/F; LTA 94/5931/F)*, October 20, 1994, C.A.; *Hill* v. *Garcia*, July 13, 1995, H.H.J. Harrison Hall, Coventry County Ct.; *Hogg* v. *Stockton Plant*, June 12, 1995, H.H.J. Cartlidge, Sunderland County Ct.; *Hoskins* v. *Wiggins Teape (U.K.)* [1994] P.I.Q.R. P377, C.A.; *McDermott* v. *Sharp*, May 24, 1995, District Judge Simons, Trowbridge County Ct.; *McIntosh and Partners* v. *Dudley*, February 8, 1995; H.H.J. Slot; Guildford County Ct.; *Maple* v. *Gribble Booth and Taylor*, May 26, 1995; H.H.J. MacIntosh; Exeter County Ct.; *Michael Peter Turner* v. *CI Stroud*; February 15, 1995; H.H.J. Wilson-Melor, Q.C.; Oxford County Ct.; *Morley* v. *Jewson Ltd*, January 31, 1995; H.H.J. Quentin Edwards Q.C., Central London County Ct.; *Rawlins (Gillian Mary)* v. *Walsall Health Authority*, February 27, 1995; District Judge Hearne; Walsall County Ct.; *Taylor* v. *Remploy*, January 18, 1995; Norman Francis sitting as a Deputy County Court Judge; Cardiff County Ct.; *Trethowans (Builders)* v. *Osman*, December 20, 1994; District Judge White; Truro County Ct.; *Vallely (John Gerrard)* v. *British Railways Board (LTA 94/5697/F)*, December 19, 1994, C.A.; *Williams and Williams* v. *Parker*, November 1, 1994; H.H.J. Owen, Manchester County Ct.

rule 11(1)(a), see *Kirkham* v. *Cooper (t/a Carpet and Curtains Centre)*, April 20, 1995, H.H.J. Bush, Leeds County Ct.

rule 11(1)(b), see *Trethowans (Builders)* v. *Osman*, December 20, 1994; District Judge D. White; Truro County Ct.

rule 11(1)(o), see *Simpson* v. *Wilson-Lim*, September 11, 1995, H.H.J. Wiggs, Poole County Ct.

rule 11(1A)(3)(d)(9), see *Gleed* v. *Milton Keynes Borough Council*, September 5, 1994; H.H.J. Byrt, Q.C.; Central London County Ct.

rule 11(3)(d), see *Blackman* v. *Myson Group plc*, November 2, 1994; H.H.J. Sumner; Wandsworth County Ct.

rule 11(4)(9), see *Smith* v. *Walker Wheels*, November 1, 1994; H.H.J. Stephenson; Newcastle-upon-Tyne County Ct.

rule 11(8), see *Great Yarmouth Ceilings* v. *Grint Drylining (Freethorpe)*, May 24, 1995, H.H.J. Barham, Norwich County Ct.

rule 11(9), see *Bangar (t/a BSB Builders)* v. *Singh and Kaur*, June 21, 1995, H.H.J. O'Rorke, Nottingham C.C.; *Bourne and Bourne* v. *Currie*, April 10, 1995, H.H.J. O'Brien, Brentwood County Ct.; *Holden* v. *Aber Building Supplies*, July 20, 1995, District Judge R.A. Hoffman, Wrexham County Ct.; *Jointlink* v. *St. Crispins*, September 26, 1995, District Judge Hawthorne, Thanet County Ct.; *McGuire and McGuire* v. *Lambeth London Borough Council*, February 13, 1995; H.H.J. Collins; Wandsworth County Ct.; *Priestly & Priestly* v. *Weyman*, June 22, 1995, H.H.J. Morgan, Barnet County Ct.; *Steniford-Crook* v. *Gardiner*, July 24, 1994; District

NO.

1981—cont.

1687. County Court Rules 1981—*cont.*
ord. 17—*cont*
Judge Meredith; Torquay County Ct.; *Watts* v. *Hastings*, March 16, 1995, District Judge Trent, Barnet County Ct.
rule 11(10), see *Maple* v. *Gribble Booth & Taylor*; May 26, 1995, H.H.J. MacIntosh, Exeter County Ct.
rule 11(11)(a), see *Herring* v. *Churwell Metals*, June 26, 1995, H.H.J. Marr-Johnson, Clerkenwell County Ct.; *Varsani* v. *Davy*, October 17, 1995, H.H.J. Lowe, Willesden County Ct.
ord. 18,
rule 2, see *Barker* v. *Rye*, September 20, 1995, H.H.J. Hamilton, Derby County Ct.
ord. 19,
see *Joyce* v. *Liverpool City Council* [1995] 3 All E.R. 110, C.A.
rule 2(iv)(a), see *Brooke* v. *British Aerospace*, June 1, 1995, Deputy District Judge Furness, Leeds County Ct.
rule 3, see *Afzal* v. *Ford Motor Co.* [1994] 4 All E.R. 720, C.A.; *Duffus and Duffus* v. *Chief Constable of Derbyshire*, March 14, 1995, H.H.J. Styler, Derby County Ct.; *Joyce* v. *Liverpool City Council*; *Wynne* v. *Same*, *The Times*, May 2, 1995, C.A.
rule 3(1), see *Schwarz* v. *Gray and Gray*, November 18, 1994; H.H.J. Marr-Johnson; Clerkenwell County Ct.
rule 4, see *Afzal* v. *Ford Motor Co.* [1994] 4 All E.R. 720, C.A.; *Wald* v. *Jones*, July 10, 1995, Deputy District Judge Kirkham, Hull County Ct.
rule 4(2)(c), see *Fronda* v. *Jackson*, January 24, 1995; H.H.J. Goodman; Croydon County Ct.; *Schwarz* v. *Gray and Gray*, November 18, 1994; H.H.J. Marr-Johnson; Clerkenwell County Ct.; *Wright* v. *Ryder*, March 24, 1995; D.D.J. Healey; Bodmin County Ct.
rule 9(2)(b), see *Frail* v. *L.D.V.*, September 1, 1995, District Judge Singleton, Birmingham County Ct.
rule 14(2), see *Streetscene* v. *C. Mcadams*, August 15, 1995, Deputy District Judge Taylor, Sheffield County Ct.
ord. 20,
rule 12, see *A. and B. (Minors) (No. 2), Re* [1995] 1 F.L.R. 351, Wall J.

NO.

1981—cont.

1687. County Court Rules 1981—*cont.*
ord. 20—*cont.*
rule 12A, see *Taylor* v. *Remploy*, January 18, 1995; Norman Francis sitting as a Deputy Court Judge; Cardiff County Ct.
ord. 24,
amended: rules 95/1582, rule 2.
ord. 25,
amended: rules 95/969, rule 2.
ord. 26,
rule 5, see *Hackney London Borough Council* v. *White*, *The Times*, May 17, 1995, C.A.
rule 17, see *Hammersmith and Fulham London Borough* v. *Hill* (1994) 27 H.L.R. 368, C.A.
ord. 29,
rule 1(3), see *Langley* v. *Langley* [1994] 1 F.L.R. 383, C.A.
ord. 37,
see *National Provincial Building Society* v. *Ahmed (CCRTF 94/1635/E)*, May 5, 1995, C.A.
rule 2, see *Barclays Bank* v. *Curtis (Janice Maureen) (94/5689/F)*, October 27, 1994, C.A.
rule 5, see *Kelliher* v. *E.H. Savill Engineering* [1994] P.I.Q.R. P387, C.A.; *McDermott* v. *Sharp*, May 24, 1995, District Judge Simons, Trowbridge County Ct.
ord. 38,
see *Children Act 1989 (Taxation of Costs), Re* [1994] 2 F.L.R. 934, Cazalet J.
rule 19, see *Fronda* v. *Jackson*, January 24, 1995; H.H.J. Goodman; Croydon County Ct.; *McLeod (Sally)* v. *Wolsey Hall Oxford and Middlesex University and Common Professional Examination Board (L.T.A. 94/569/F)*, February 1, 1995, C.A.
rule 24(4), see *NSP Catalogue Holdings PLC* v. *Truebell Marketing plc and Compare Ltd*, November 15, 1994, H.H.J. Hallgarten Q.C., Central London County Court.
ord. 50,
rule 5, see *Barclays Bank* v. *Curtis (Janice Maureen) (94/5689/F)*, October 27, 1994, C.A.
ord. 59,
rule 1(b), see *Molava* v. *Rahim*, April 10, 1995, C.A.

1694. Motor Vehicles (Tests) Regulations 1981.
reg. 9, amended: regs. 95/2438, reg. 3.
reg. 10, amended: regs. 95/2438, reg. 4.
reg. 12, amended: regs. 95/2438, reg. 7.
reg. 13, amended: regs. 95/2438, reg. 5.
reg. 14, amended: regs. 95/2438, reg. 7.
reg. 15, amended: regs. 95/2438, reg. 7.

NO.

1981—cont.

1694. Motor Vehicles (Tests) Regulations 1981—*cont.*
reg. 16, amended: regs. 95/2438, reg. 7.
reg. 17, amended: regs. 95/2438, reg. 7.
reg. 18, amended: regs. 95/2438, reg. 7.
reg. 20, amended: regs. 95/2438, regs. 6, 7.
reg. 23, amended: regs. 95/2438, reg. 7.

1741. Value Added Tax (Special Provisions) Order 1981.
art. 9(1), see *Thorn EMI* v. *Customs and Excise Commissioners* [1995] STC 674, C.A.
art. 12(1), see *Customs and Excise Commissioners* v. *Padglade* [1995] S.T.C. 602, Schiemann J.

1785. National Health Service (Compensation for Premature Retirement) (Scotland) Regulations 1981.
reg. 4, applied: regs. 95/365, reg. D2.
reg. 5, applied: regs. 95/365, reg. R6.
reg. 6, applied: regs. 95/365, reg. D2.
reg. 7, applied: regs. 95/365, reg. D2.

1787. Strathclyde Regional Council (Loch Poit Na. H–I) (Amendment) Water Order 1981.
revoked: ord. 94/3308, art. 4.

1794. Transfer of Undertakings (Protection of Employment) Regulations 1981.
applied: ord. 95/575, art. 3.
applied: regs. 95/1019, reg. K24.
referred to: 1995, c. 37, Sch. 1, para. 9.
referred to: ord. 95/1340, art. 2.
reg. 2(1), see *National Union of Teachers* v. *Governing Body of St. Mary's Church of England (Aided) Junior School* [1995] I.C.R. 317, E.A.T.
reg. 3, see *Kelman* v. *Care Contract Services* [1995] I.C.R. 260, E.A.T.
reg. 3(1)(2), see *Charlton and Charlton* v. *Charlton Thermosystems (Romsey) and Ellis* [1995] IRLR 79, E.A.T.
reg. 5, see *Milligan* v. *Securicor Cleaning* [1995] IRLR 288, E.A.T.; *Stirling District Council* v. *Allan, (I.H.)*, 1995 S.L.T. 1255.
reg. 8, see *Milligan* v. *Securicor Cleaning* [1995] IRLR 288, E.A.T.; *National Union of Teachers* v. *Governing Body of St. Mary's Church of England (Aided) Junior School* [1995] I.C.R. 317, E.A.T.
reg. 8(1), see *Milligan* v. *Seavicar Cleaning*, *The Times*, May 10, 1995, E.A.T.
reg. 10(2), see *South Durham Health Authority* v. *Unison* [1995] I.C.R. 495, E.A.T.

NO.

1981—cont.

1794. Transfer of Undertakings (Protection of Employment) Regulations 1981—*cont.*
reg. 11(8), see *South Durham Health Authority* v. *Unison* [1995] I.C.R. 495, E.A.T.

1837. National Health Service (Determination of Districts) (No. 2) Order 1981.
art. 3, amended: ord. 95/533, art. 2.
Sch. 1, Pt. I, amended: ord. 95/562, art. 2.
Sch. 2, Pt. I, amended: ord. 95/533, art. 2.

1982

135. Calshot Oyster Fishery Order 1982.
art. 3, amended: ord. 95/1258, art. 2.
arts. 4A, 4B, revoked: ord. 95/1258, art. 2.

162. Patents etc. (People's Revolutionary Republic of Guinea) (Convention) Order 1982.
revoked: ord. 94/3219, art. 3 (designs), ord. 94/3220, art. 3 (patents).

207. Warble Fly (Scotland) Order 1982.
art. 2, amended: ord. 95/2042, art. 2, regs. 94/3142, reg. 21.
art. 5, amended: ord. 95/2042, art. 2.
art. 5A, inserted: ord. 95/2042, art. 2.
Sch., amended: regs. 94/3142, reg. 21.

218. Poison Rules 1982.
applied: regs. 95/414, Sch. 1.

234. Warble Fly (England and Wales) Order 1982.
art. 2, amended: regs. 94/3142, reg. 21.
Sch., amended: regs. 94/3142, reg. 21.

288. Health Services Act 1980 (Consequential Amendments) Order 1982.
Sch. 1, para. 20, revoked: regs. 95/866, reg. 24.
Sch. 1, para. 28, revoked: regs. 95/300, reg. V2.

379. District Probate Registries Order 1982.
art. 2, amended: ord. 94/3079, art. 3.
Sch., amended: ord. 94/3079, art. 4.

555. Town and Country Planning (Structure and Local Plans) Regulations 1982.
reg. 21, see *Alfred McAlpine Homes (North)* v. *Secretary of State for the Environment* [1994] N.P.C. 138, C.A.
reg. 22, see *Alfred McAlpine Homes (North)* v. *Secretary of State for the Environment* [1994] N.P.C. 138, C.A.
reg. 29, see *Pelham Homes* v. *Secretary of State for the Environment and Runnymede Borough Council* (1994) 69 P. & C.R. 64, David Widdicombe Q.C., sitting as a deputy judge.

NO.

1982—cont.

555. Town and Country Planning (Structure and Local Plans) Regulations 1982—*cont.*
reg. 31, see *Pelham Homes* v. *Secretary of State for the Environment and Runnymede Borough Council* (1994) 69 P. & C.R. 64, David Widdicombe Q.C., sitting as a deputy judge.

586. County Court (Forms) Rules 1982.
Sch., amended: rules 95/970, rule 2.

686. Overseas Service (Pensions Supplement) (Amendment) Regulations 1982.
revoked: regs. 95/238, reg. 25.

841. Merchant Shipping (Tonnage) Regulations 1982.
applied: regs. 95/1427, reg. 2.

894. Statutory Sick Pay (General) Regulations 1982.
reg. 7, applied: ord. 95/512, art. 2.
reg. 15, amended: regs. 95/829, reg. 15.
reg. 21A, inserted: regs. 95/513, reg. 3.

1000. Petroleum (Production) Regulations 1982.
revoked: regs. 95/1436, reg. 3.

1004. British Citizenship (Designated Service) Order 1982.
Sch., para. 13, amended: ord. 95/552, art. 2.
Sch., paras. 19, 20, 21, 22, inserted: ord. 95/552, art. 2.

1009. Local Government (Compensation for Premature Retirement) Regulations 1982.
applied: regs. 94/3025, reg. 2.
reg. 5, see *Jones* v. *Mid Glamorgan County Council (CCRTF 91/1544/C)* November 17, 1994, C.A.
reg. 14, amended: regs. 94/3025, reg. 17.
reg. 20, amended: regs. 95/817, reg. 2.
Sch. 1, Pt. 2, amended: regs. 95/817, reg. 3.

1109. Crown Court Rules 1982.
amended; regs. 94/3153.
rule 7, see *R.* v. *Stafford Crown Court ex p. Reid*, *The Independent*, March 13, 1995, D.C.
rule 25A, substituted: rules 94/3153, rule 2.
rule 34, inserted: rules 94/3153, rule 3.
rule 35, inserted: rules 94/3153, rule 3.
rule 36, inserted: rules 94/3153, rule 3.

1163. Motorways Traffic (England and Wales) (Amendment) Regulations 1982.
referred to: regs. 95/1094, reg. 2.
reg. 3, applied: regs. 95/2168, reg. 2.
reg. 12, amended: regs. 95/158, reg. 2.

1236. Income Tax (Interest Relief) Regulations 1982.
reg. 3, amended: regs. 95/1213, reg. 3.
reg. 8B, inserted: regs. 95/1213, reg. 4.
reg. 19, amended: regs. 95/1213, reg. 5.

NO.

1982—cont.

1271. Motor Vehicles (Type Approval for Goods Vehicles) (Great Britain) Regulations 1982.
referred to: regs. 95/925, reg. 3.
reg. 4, amended: regs. 95/1323, reg. 3.
reg. 14, amended: regs. 95/1323, reg. 4.
Sch. 1, Pt. I, amended: regs. 95/1322, reg. 5.
Sch. 1B, Pt. I, amended: regs. 95/1323, reg. 6.
Sch. 2, Pt. I, substituted: regs. 95/1323, reg. 8.
Sch. 4, Pt. III, amended: regs. 95/1323, reg. 9.
Sch. 4, Pt. V, inserted: regs, 95/1323, reg. 10.
Sch. 5, Pt. I, amended: regs. 95/1323, reg. 11.

1279. National Health Service (General Medical and Pharmaceutical Services) (Scotland) Amendment Regulations 1982.
revoked: regs. 95/414, reg. 13.

1408. Social Security (General Benefit) Regulations 1982.
reg. 2, amended: regs. 95/829, reg. 16.

1489. Workmen's Compensation (Supplementation) Scheme 1982.
amended: Scheme 95/746, arts. 2, 3.
art. 5, amended: scheme 95/746, art. 2.
Sch. 1, substituted: scheme 95/746, art. 3.

1637. Merchant Shipping (Tankers) (EEC Requirements) (Amendment) Regulations 1982.
revoked: regs. 95/2498, reg. 2.

1671. Public Health (Aircraft) (Isle of Man) Order 1982.
revoked: ord. 95/267, art. 2.

1672. Public Health (Ships) (Isle of Man) Order 1982.
revoked: ord. 95/267, art. 2.

1759. Macclesfield and Vale Royal (Areas) Order 1982.
referred to: ord. 95/562, art. 2.

1765. National Health Service (Superannuation) Amendment Regulations 1982.
revoked: regs. 95/300, reg. V2.

1983

29. Education (Special Educational Needs) Regulations 1983.
See *E. (A Minor)* v. *Dorset County Council*; *Christmas* v. *Hampshire County Council*; *Keating* v. *Bromley London Borough Council* [1994] 3 W.L.R. 853, C.A.
reg. 10 see *R.* v. *Wiltshire County Council, ex p. D.* [1994] 1 F.C.R. 172, Potts J.

NO.

1983—cont.

272. National Health Service (Superannuation) (Scotland) Amendment Regulations 1983.
revoked: regs. 95/365, reg. V2.

344. Aujeszky's Disease Order 1983.
amended by 1995 No. 11.
art. 9, amended: ord. 94/3141, art. 15.
art. 13, amended: ord. 94/3141, art. 15.
Sch., amended: ord. 94/3141, art. 15.

376. Statutory Sick Pay (Compensation of Employers) and Miscellaneous Provisions Regulations 1983.
revoked: ord. 95/512, art. 5.

422. Parliamentary Constituencies (Scotland) Order 1983.
revoked: ord. 95/1037, art. 4.

468. Returning Officers (Parliamentary Constituencies) (England and Wales) Order 1983.
revoked: ord. 95/2061, art. 2.
art. 3, revoked in pt.: ord. 95/1142, art. 2.
art. 4, revoked in pt.: ord. 95/1142, art. 2.
art. 6, revoked in pt.: ord. 95/1142, art. 2.
Sch. 1, Pt. II, revoked: ord. 95/1142, art. 2.
Sch. 2, Pt. II, revoked: ord. 95/1142, art. 2.
Sch. 3, Pt. II, revoked: ord. 95/1142, art. 2.

506. Redundant Mineworkers and Concessionary Coal (Payments Scheme) Order 1983.
art. 1, amended: regs. 95/829, reg. 24.
art. 9, amended: regs. 95/829, reg. 24.

684. Gas (Meters) Regulations 1983.
reg. 4, amended: regs. 95/1251, reg. 3.

686. Personal Injuries (Civilians) Scheme 1983.
referred to: rules 94/3046, rule 86.
art. 18, amended: ord 95/445, art. 2.
art. 25A, amended: ord. 95/445, art. 3.
art. 76A, amended: ord. 95/445, art. 4.
art. 76B, amended: ord. 95/445, art. 5.
Sch. 3, substituted: ord. 95/445, art. 6.
Sch. 4, substituted: ord. 95/445, art. 6.

713. Civil Courts Order 1983.
Sch. 1, amended: ord. 95/1897, art. 3.
Sch. 3, amended: ord. 95/1897, art. 4.

873. Nurses, Midwives and Health Visitors Rules 1983.
rule 2, amended: rules 95/967, rule 2.
rule 6, amended: rules 95/967, rule 2.
rule 9, substituted: rules 95/967, rule 2.
rule 10, substituted: rules 95/967, rule 2.

883. Naval, Military and Air Forces etc. (Disablement and Death) Service Pensions Order 1983.
art. 18, amended: ord. 95/766, art. 2.
art. 26A, amended: ord. 95/766, art. 3.
art. 29, amended: ord. 95/766, art. 4.

NO.

1983—cont.

883. Naval, Military and Air Forces etc. (Disablement and Death) Service Pensions Order 1983—*cont.*
art. 67A, amended: ord. 95/766, art. 5.
art. 67B, amended: ord. 95/766, art. 6.
Sch. 1, amended: ord. 95/766, art. 7.
Sch. 2, amended: ord. 95/766, art. 7.

938. Milk Labelling (Scotland) Regulations 1983.
referred to: regs. 95/1372, Sch. 10, Pt. I.

941. Fowl Pest Orders (Amendment) Order 1983.
revoked: ord. 94/3141, art. 15.

943. Health and Safety (Emissions into the Atmosphere) Regulations 1983.
Sch. 1, referred to: regs. 95/2258, reg. 4.

973. Education (Fees and Awards) Regulations 1983.
revoked: regs. 94/3042, reg. 17.

1088. Value Added Tax (Horses and Ponies) Order 1983.
revoked: ord. 95/1268, art. 3.

1160. Redundancy Payments (Local Government) (Modification) Order 1983.
art. 1, amended: ord. 95/1157, art. 2.
art. 4, amended: ord. 95/1157, art. 2.
Sch. 1, amended: ord. 95/1157, art. 2.

1212. Medicines (Products Other Than Veterinary Drugs) (Prescription Only) Order 1983.
art. 1, amended: ord. 94/3050, art. 2.
art. 3, amended: ord. 95/1384, art. 2; ord. 94/3016, art. 2.
art. 4, amended: ord. 95/1384, art. 3; ord. 94/3016, art. 3.
Sch. 1, Pt. I, amended: ord. 95/1384, art. 4; ord. 94/3016, art. 4.
Sch. 1, Pt. III, amended: ord. 94/3016, art. 5.
Sch. 1, Pt. IV, amended: ord. 94/3016, art. 6.
Sch. 1A, inserted: ord. 94/3050, art. 4.

1215. Education (Fees and Awards) (Scotland) Regulations 1983.
reg. 4, amended: regs. 95/1271, reg. 2.

1398. Merchant Shipping (Prevention of Oil Pollution) Regulations 1983.
applied: regs. 95/2498, reg. 9.

1455. Control of Noise (Appeals) (Scotland) Regulations 1983.
reg. 4(2), see *Meri Mate* v. *City of Dundee District Council (Sh.Ct.)*, 1994 S.C.L.R. 960.

1508. Milk-based Drinks (Hygiene and Heat Treatment) Regulations 1983.
revoked: regs. 93/1086, reg. 23.

1509. Milk and Dairies (Heat Treatment of Cream) Regulations 1983.
revoked: regs. 95/1086, reg. 23.

1514. Milk-based Drinks (Scotland) Regulations 1983.
revoked: regs. 95/1372, reg. 23.

NO.

1983—cont.

1515. Cream (Heat Treatment) (Scotland) Regulations 1983.
revoked: regs. 95/1372, reg. 23.

1598. Social Security (Unemployment, Sickness and Invalidity Benefit) Regulations 1983.
reg. 1, amended: regs. 95/829, reg. 17.
reg. 2, amended: regs. 95/829, reg. 17.
reg. 3, revoked: regs. 95/829, reg. 17.
reg. 4, amended: regs. 95/829, reg. 17.
reg. 5, amended: regs. 95/829, reg. 17.
reg. 6A, amended: regs. 95/829, reg. 17.
reg. 7, amended: regs. 95/1742, reg. 2; regs. 95/829, reg. 17.
regs. 7A, 8, 8A, revoked: regs. 95/829, reg. 17.
reg. 13, amended: regs. 95/829, reg. 17.
reg. 15, revoked: regs. 95/829, reg. 17.
reg. 17, revoked: regs. 95/829, reg. 17.
reg. 20, amended: regs. 95/829, reg. 17.
regs. 29, 30, 31, 32, revoked: regs. 95/829, reg. 17.
Pt. IV, substituted: regs. 95/829, reg. 17.

1698. Social Security (Cyprus) Order 1983.
modified: ord. 95/767, art. 2.

1709. Patents Etc. (Republic of Mali) (Convention) Order 1983.
revoked: ord. 94/3219, art. 3 (designs), ord. 94/3220, art. 3 (patents).

1727. Medicines (Leaflets for Veterinary Drugs) Regulations 1983.
revoked: regs. 94/3142, reg. 20.

1761. Accounts and Audit (Amendment) Regulations 1983.
reg. 7, amended: regs. 94/3018, reg. 2.
reg. 15A, inserted: regs. 94/3018, reg. 2.
Sch., inserted: regs. 94/3018, reg. 2.

1811. Insurance Companies (Accounts and Statements) Regulations 1983.
reg. 3, amended: regs. 94/3133, reg. 18.
Sch. 1, amended: regs. 94/3133, regs. 19, 20.
Sch. 6, para. 9, amended: regs. 94/3133, reg. 21.

1894. Social Security (New Zealand) Order 1983.
modified: ord. 95/767, art. 2.

1950. Foot-and-Mouth Disease Order 1983.
applied: regs. 95/1086, reg. 9; regs. 95/1372, reg. 9.

1984

125. Social Security (Finland) Order 1984.
modified: ord. 95/767, art. 2.

132. Civil Aviation Act 1980 (Isle of Man) Order 1984.
revoked: ord. 95/1297, art. 2.

NO.

1984—cont.

176. Goods Vehicles (Operators' Licences, Qualifications and Fees) Regulations 1984.
applied: 1995, c. 23, s. 46.
reg. 3, amended: regs. 95/1488, reg. 3.
regs. 4–9, revoked: 1995, c. 23, Sch. 8, Pt. II.
reg. 23A, revoked: 1995, c. 23, Sch. 8, Pt. II.
reg. 32, applied: 1995 c. 23, s. 26, Sch. 2, para. 5.
reg. 33, amended: 1995, c. 23, Sch. 8, Pt. II.
reg. 34A, revoked: 1995, c. 23, Sch. 8, Pt. II.
reg. 35, amended: regs. 95/1488, regs. 4, 5.
Sch. 5, Pt. I, amended: regs. 95/1488, reg. 6.
Sch. 6, revoked: 1995, c. 23, Sch. 8, Pt. II.

177. Road Traffic Acts 1960 and 1972, Road Traffic Regulation Act 1967 and Transport Act 1968 (Metrication) (Amendment) Regulations 1984.
revoked: 1995, c. 23, Sch. 8, Pt. II.

248. Gaming Clubs (Hours and Charges) Regulations 1984.
reg. 5, amended: regs. 95/927, reg. 2.

252. High Court of Justiciary Fees Order 1984.
art. 3, substituted: ord. 94/3266, art. 2.

256. Court of Session etc. Fees Order 1984.
Sch., substituted: ord. 94/3265, art. 2.

265. Adoption Rules 1984.
See *L. v. L. (Minors) (Separate Representation)* [1994] 1 FLR 156, C.A.
rule 4(4), see *P. (Adoption) (Natural Father's Rights), Re* [1994] 1 F.L.R. 771, Ewbank J.
rule 15, see *C. (Minor) (Adoption: Parties), Re, The Times*, June 1, 1995, C.A.
rule 53(2), see *D. (Minors) (Adoption Reports: Confidentiality), Re* [1995] 1 W.L.R. 356, C.A.
Sched. 2, see *P. (Adoption) (Natural Father's Rights), Re* [1994] 1 F.L.R. 771, Ewbank J.

354. Social Security (Israel) Order 1984.
modified: ord. 95/767, art. 2.

367. Patents Etc. (Republic of Rwanda) (Convention) Order 1984.
revoked: ord. 94/3219, art. 3 (designs), ord. 94/3220, art. 3 (patents).

380. Occupational Pension Schemes (Contracting-out) Regulations 1984.
amended by 1995 No. 35.
reg. 24, applied: regs. 95/1019, reg. L20.

457. Redundant Mineworkers and Concessionary Coal (Payments Scheme) Order 1983.
art. 1, amended: regs. 95/829, reg. 24.
art. 9, amended: regs. 95/829, reg. 24.

NO.

1984—cont.

470. Gaming Clubs (Hours and Charges) (Scotland) Regulations 1984.
reg. 5, amended: regs. 95/1022, reg. 2.

552. Coroners Rules 1984.
rule 20, see *R.* v. *H.M. Coroner for the Southern District of Greater London, ex p. Driscoll* [1994] C.O.D. 91, D.C.
rule 36, see *R.* v. *Inner West London Coroner, ex p. Dallaglio* [1994] 4 All E.R. 139, C.A.

981. Motor Vehicles (Type Approval) (Great Britain) Regulations 1984.
referred to: regs. 95/925, reg. 3.
reg. 4, amended: regs. 95/1322, reg. 3.
Sch. 1, Pt. I, amended: regs. 95/1322, reg. 4.
Sch. 1B, Pt. I, amended: regs. 95/1322, reg. 5.

1072. Veterinary Surgeons (Examination of Commonwealth and Foreign Candidates) (Amendment) Regulations Order of Council 1984.
revoked: ord. 95/2396, art. 2.

1115. Fishing Vessels (Certification of Deck Officers and Engineer Officers) Regulations 1984.
referred to: regs. 95/1427, reg. 3.
reg. 1, amended: regs. 95/1428, reg. 3.
reg. 1A, inserted: regs. 95/1428, reg. 4.
reg. 5, amended: regs. 95/1428, reg. 5.
reg. 6A, inserted: regs. 95/1428, reg. 6.
reg. 7A, inserted: regs. 95/1428, reg. 7.
reg. 8, amended: regs. 95/1428, reg. 8.
reg. 9, amended: regs. 95/1428, reg. 9.
reg. 10, amended: regs. 95/1428, reg. 10.
reg. 11, amended: regs. 95/1428, reg. 11.

1159. Industrial Training (Northern Ireland) Order 1984.
art. 30, applied: regs. 95/639, Sch. 4.

1201. Education (Fees and Awards) (Amendment) Regulations 1984.
revoked: regs. 94/3042, reg. 17.

1216. Merchant Shipping (Passenger Ship Construction and Survey) Regulations 1984.
applied: regs. 95/1210, reg. 1; regs. 95/1427, reg. 2.
applied: regs. 95/157, reg. 1.
regs. 81–84, revoked: regs. 95/1210, reg. 1.

1217. Merchant Shipping (Cargo Ship Construction and Survey) Regulations 1984.
regs. 56–62, revoked: regs. 95/1210, reg. 1.

1233. Motor Vehicles Tyres (Safety) Regulations 1984.
revoked: regs. 94/3117, reg. 1.

1286. Areas of Archaeological Importance (Notification of Operations) (Exemption) Order 1984.
Sch., applied: regs. 95/418, reg. 7.

NO.

1984—cont.

1305. Food Labelling Regulations 1984.
reg. 2, amended: regs. 95/1086, reg. 24.
reg. 3, amended: regs. 95/1086, reg. 24.
reg. 24, amended: regs. 95/1086, reg. 24.
reg. 31B, inserted: regs. 95/1086, reg. 24.
regs. 33, amended: regs. 95/1086, reg. 24.
reg. 35, amended: regs. 95/1086, reg. 24.
para. 7, amended: regs. 94/3144, reg. 11.

1310. Slaughter of Pigs (Anaesthesia) (Amendment) Regulations 1984.
revoked: regs. 95/731, reg. 28.

1506. Valuation Appeal Committee Procedure (Scotland) Regulations 1984.
revoked: regs. 95/572, reg. 20.

1519. Food Labelling (Scotland) Regulations 1984.
referred to: regs. 95/1372, Sch. 10, Pt. I.

1694. Patents Etc. (Democratic Republic of the Sudan) (Convention) Order 1984.
revoked: ord. 94/3219, art. 3 (designs), ord. 94/3220, art. 3 (patents).

1696. Social Security (Savings for Existing Beneficiaries) Regulations 1984.
reg. 2, applied: regs. 95/310, reg. 25.

1698. Social Security (Dependency) Amendment Regulations 1984.
reg. 3, applied: regs. 95/310, reg. 25.

1817. Social Security (United States of America) Order 1984.
modified: ord. 95/767, art. 2.

1902. Control of Industrial Major Accident Hazards Regulations 1984.
amended by 1994 No. 3247.

2024. Hill Livestock (Compensatory Allowances) Regulations 1984.
referred to: regs. 95/904, reg. 2; regs. 95/1159, reg. 2.
applied: regs. 95/891, reg. 2.

2035. Court of Protection Rules 1984.
revoked: rules 94/3046, rule 95.

2041. Immigration Appeals (Procedure) Rules 1984.
rule 4(7), see *Adeniyi (Samuel Dele)* v. *Secretary of State for the Home Department* [1995] Imm.A.R. 101, C.A.
rule 6, see *Sogunle* v. *Secretary of State for the Home Department* [1994] Imm.A.R. 554, I.A.T.
rule 6(1), (6)(a), see *Adeniyi (Samuel Dele)* v. *Secretary of State for the Home Department* [1995] Imm.A.R. 101, C.A.
rule 13(1), see *R.* v. *Immigration Appeal Tribunal, ex p. Flores (Ruiz Pablo)* [1995] Imm.A.R. 85.

NO.

1984—cont.

2041. Immigration Appeals (Procedure) Rules 1984—*cont.*
rule 18, see *Assah* v. *Immigration Appeal Tribunal* [1994] Imm.A.R. 519, C.A.
rule 23, see *R.* v. *Secretary of State for the Home Department, ex p. Shamamba* [1994] Imm.A.R. 502, Popplewell J.
rule 26(1), see *R.* v. *Immigration Appeal Tribunal, ex p. Flores (Ruiz Pablo)* [1995] Imm.A.R. 85.
rule 31(2), see *R.* v. *Immigration Appeal Tribunal, ex p. Flores (Ruiz Pablo)* [1995] Imm.A.R. 85.
rule 34, see *Kayanga (Christine Resty)* v. *Secretary of State for the Home Department* [1995] Imm.A.R. 123, C.A.; *R.* v. *Secretary of State for the Home Department, ex p. Mubiru* [1994] Imm.A.R. 516, Brooke J.
rule 34(2), see *Hassan* v. *Secretary of State for the Home Department* [1994] Imm.A.R. 482, C.A.
rule 34(3), see *R.* v. *Secretary of State for the Home Department, ex p. Baira* [1994] Imm.A.R. 487, Popplewell J.
rule 35, see *Kalunga* v. *Secretary of State for the Home Department* [1994] Imm.A.R. 585, C.A.
rule 44, see *Kayanga (Christine Resty)* v. *Secretary of State for the Home Department* [1995] Imm.A.R. 123, C.A.
rule 44(1), see *R.* v. *Immigration Appeal Tribunal, ex p. Flores (Ruiz Pablo)* [1995] Imm.A.R. 85.
rule 44(1)(c), see *Adeniyi (Samuel Dele)* v. *Secretary of State for the Home Department* [1995] Imm.A.R. 101, C.A.
rule 44(1)(e), see *Hassan* v. *Secretary of State for the Home Department* [1994] Imm.A.R. 482, C.A.

2056. Slaughter of Poultry (Humane Conditions) Regulations 1984.
revoked: regs. 95/731, reg. 28.

1985

16. Industrial Tribunals (Rules of Procedure) Regulations 1985.
rule 3(1), see *London Branch of the Nigerian Universities Commission* v. *Bastians* [1995] I.C.R. 358, E.A.T.
rule 3(2), see *Charlton and Charlton* v. *Charlton Thermosystems (Romsey) and Ellis* [1995] IRLR 79, E.A.T.
rule 13(1), see *Charlton and Charlton* v. *Charlton Thermosystems (Romsey) and Ellis* [1995] IRLR 79, E.A.T.

NO.

1985—cont.

16. Industrial Tribunals (Rules of Procedure) Regulations 1985—*cont.*
Sch. 1, see *Charlton and Charlton* v. *Charlton Thermosystems (Romsey) and Ellis* [1995] IRLR 79, E.A.T.; *London Branch of the Nigerian Universities Commission* v. *Bastians* [1995] I.C.R. 358, E.A.T.

39. Family Practitioners Committees (Consequential Modifications) Order 1985.
art. 16, revoked: regs. 95/866, reg. 24.
art. 19, revoked: regs. 95/300, reg. V2.

67. Food (Revision of Penalties) Regulations 1985.
Sch., Pt. I, amended: regs. 95/1086, reg. 23.

68. Milk and Dairies (Revision of Penalties) Regulations 1985.
reg. 2, amended: regs. 95/1086, reg. 23.
Sch., amended: regs. 95/1086, reg. 23.

71. Natural Mineral Waters Regulations 1985.
applied: regs. 95/1763, reg. 2.
reg. 3, amended: regs. 94/3142, reg. 21; regs. 94/3144, reg. 11.

173. Patents Etc. (The People's Republic of China) (Convention) Order 1985.
revoked: ord. 94/3219, art. 3 (designs), ord. 94/3220, art. 3 (patents).

211. Merchant Shipping (Cargo Ship Safety Equipment Survey) (Amendment) Regulations 1985.
revoked: regs. 95/1210, reg. 1.

267. Local Authorities Accounts (Scotland) Regulations 1985.
applied: ord. 95/789, art. 2.

296. National Health Service (General Medical and Pharmaceutical Services) (Scotland) Amendment Regulations 1985.
revoked: regs. 95/414, reg. 13.

358. Occupation Pensions Scheme (Transfer Values) Regulations (Northern Ireland) 1985.
reg. 4, applied: regs. 95/637, reg. 8.

373. Public Trustee (Fees) Order 1985.
art. 29A, substituted: ord. 95/1425, art. 2.

454. Local Elections (Northern Ireland) Order 1985.
Sch. 2, amended: regs. 95/1948, reg. 5.

456. Patents Etc. (Barbados) (Convention) Order 1985.
revoked: ord. 94/3219, art. 3 (designs), ord. 94/3219, art. 3 (patents).

457. Patents Etc. (Mongolian People's Republic) (Convention) Order 1985.
revoked: ord. 94/3219, art. 3 (designs), ord. 94/3220, art. 3 (patents).

NO.

1985—cont.

518. Police (Discipline) Regulations 1985.
reg. 16, amended: regs. 95/1475, reg. 2.

534. National Health Service (General Medical and Pharmaceutical Services) (Scotland) Amendment (No. 2) Regulations 1985.
revoked: regs. 95/414, reg. 13.

573. Merchant Shipping (Cargo Ship Safety Equipment Survey) Regulations 1985.
revoked: regs. 95/1210, reg. 1.

641. Gaming Act (Variation of Monetary Limits) (Scotland) Order 1985.
revoked: ord. 95/2360, art. 4.

693. Value Added Tax (General) Regulations 1985.
reg. 23(1)(a), see *Customs and Excise Commissioners* v. *British Telecom* [1995] S.T.C. 239, Dyson J.

705. Act of Sederunt (Consumer Credit Act 1974) 1985.
para. 2, amended: Act 95/1877, para. 2.
para. 5A, inserted: Act 95/1877, para. 2.
para. 5B, inserted: Act 95/1877, para. 2.

782. Unfair Dismissal (Variation of Qualifying Period) Order 1985.
see *R.* v. *Secretary of State for Employment, ex p. Seymour-Smith and Perez* [1995] IRLR 464, C.A.

804. National Health Service (General Medical and Pharmaceutical Services) (Scotland) Amendment (No. 3) Regulations 1985.
revoked: regs. 95/414, reg. 13.

854. Companies (Forms) Regulations 1985.
Sch. 2, amended: regs. 95/736, reg. 4.

886. Value Added Tax (General) Regulations 1985.
reg. 2, amended: reg. 95/152, reg. 3.
reg. 11, see *Sargent* v. *Customs and Excise Commissioners*, *The Times*, February 23, 1995, C.A.
reg. 12(1), see *Kohanzad* v. *Customs and Excise Commissioners* [1994] S.T.C. 967, Schiemann J.
reg. 23(1)(a), see *Customs and Excise Commissioners* v. *British Telecom*, *The Times*, January 30, 1995, Dyson J.
reg. 26, see *Metropolitan Borough of Wirral* v. *Customs and Excise Commissioners* [1995] S.T.C. 597, Potts J.
reg. 30, amended: regs. 95/1069, reg. 3.

NO.

1985—cont.

886. Value Added Tax (General) Regulations 1985—*cont.*
reg. 30, see *Customs and Excise Commissioners* v. *Deutsche Ruck U.K. Reinsurance Co.* [1995] S.T.C. 495, Auld J.; *Customs and Excise Commissioners* v. *University of Wales College, Cardiff* [1995] S.T.C. 611, Carnwath J.
reg. 31, amended: regs. 94/3015, reg. 3.
reg. 32, substituted: regs. 94/3015, reg. 4.
reg. 33A, amended: regs. 94/3015, reg. 5.
reg. 36A, amended: regs. 94/3015, reg. 6.
reg. 38, amended: regs. 95/152, reg. 4, regs. 95/913, reg. 3.
reg. 47, revoked: regs. 95/913, reg. 4.
reg. 57A, amended: regs. 95/1280, reg. 3.
reg. 57B, amended: regs. 95/1280, reg. 4.
reg. 57D, amended: regs. 95/152, reg. 5.
reg. 57DA, inserted: regs. 95/152, reg. 6.
reg. 58ZA, inserted: regs. 95/1069, reg. 4.
reg. 58(1)(c), see *Bjellica* v. *Customs and Excise Commissioners* [1995] S.T.C. 329, C.A.
reg. 62(1), see *Kohanzad* v. *Customs and Excise Commissioners* [1994] S.T.C. 967, Schiemann J.

960. Films Co-Production Agreements Order 1985.
amended by 1994 No. 3222.

1064. Safety of Sports Grounds (Rugby Football Grounds) (Designation) Order 1995.
Sch., amended: ord. 95/1990, art. 3.

1066. Building (Approved Inspectors etc.) Regulations 1985.
reg. 6, amended: regs. 95/1387, reg. 3.
reg. 8, amended: regs. 95/1387, reg. 4.
reg. 9, amended: regs. 95/1387, reg. 5.
reg. 10, amended: regs. 95/1387, reg. 6.
reg. 10A, inserted: regs. 95/1387, reg. 7.
reg. 11, amended: regs. 95/1387, reg. 11.
reg. 13, amended: regs. 95/1387, reg. 8.
reg. 16, amended: regs. 95/1387, regs. 9, 11.
reg. 17, amended: regs. 95/1387, reg. 10.
reg. 29, amended: regs. 95/1387, reg. 12.
Sch. 2, amended: regs. 95/1387, reg. 13.
Sch. 5, para. 6, revoked: regs. 95/1387, reg. 13.

1068. Food (Revision of Penalties and Mode of Trial) (Scotland) Regulations 1985.
Sch. 1, amended: regs. 95/1372, reg. 23.

NO.

1985—cont.

1071. International Carriage of Perishable Foodstuffs Regulations 1985.
Sch., Pt. III, amended: regs. 95/1716, reg. 2.

1090. Plant Breeders' Rights (Herbaceous Perennials) (Variation) Scheme 1985.
revoked: Scheme 95/526, art. 2.

1190. Social Security (Dependency) Amendment Regulations 1985.
reg. 3, applied: regs. 95/310, reg. 25.

1202. Social Security (Iceland) Order 1985.
modified: ord. 95/767, art. 2.

1205. Credit Unions (Northern Ireland) Order 1985 (N.I. 12).
art. 33(1); regs. 95/31.

1219. Education (Fees and Awards) (Amendment) Regulations 1985.
revoked: regs. 94/3042, reg. 17.

1222. Cream (Heat Treatment) (Scotland) Amendment Regulations 1985.
revoked: regs. 95/1372, reg. 23.

1306. Merchant Shipping (Certification of Deck Officers) Regulations 1985.
referred to: regs. 95/1427, reg. 3.
reg. 2, amended: regs. 95/1429, reg. 3.
reg. 2A, inserted: regs. 95/1429, reg. 4.
reg. 4, amended: regs. 95/1429, reg. 5.
reg. 4A, inserted: regs. 95/1429, reg. 6.
reg 5, amended: regs. 95/1429, reg. 7.
reg. 6, amended: regs. 95/1429, reg. 8.
reg. 10, amended: regs. 95/1429, reg. 9.
reg. 11, amended: regs. 95/1429, reg. 10.
reg. 18, amended: regs. 95/1429, reg. 11.
reg. 19, amended: regs. 95/1429, reg. 12.

1542. Warble Fly (England and Wales) (Infected Areas) Order 1985.
art. 2, amended: regs. 94/3142, reg. 21.

1625. National Health Service (General Medical and Pharmaceutical Services) (Scotland) Amendment (No. 4) Regulations 1985.
revoked: regs. 95/414, reg. 13.

1626. National Health Service (Injury Benefits) Amendment Regulations 1985.
revoked: regs. 95/866, reg. 24.

1713. National Health Service (General Medical and Pharmaceutical Services) (Scotland) Amendment (No. 5) Regulations 1985.
revoked: regs. 95/414, reg. 13.

1861. Artificial Insemination of Cattle (Animal Health) (England and Wales) Regulations 1985.
reg. 2, amended: regs. 95/2549, reg. 2.
reg. 14, amended: regs. 95/2549, reg. 2.
reg. 18, substituted: regs. 95/2549, reg. 2.
reg. 21, amended: regs. 95/2549, reg. 2.
reg. 24, amended: regs. 95/2549, reg. 2.
Sch., inserted: regs. 95/2549, reg. 2.

1884. Waste Regulation and Disposal (Authorities) Order 1985.
applied: regs. 95/1019, Sch. C1.

NO.

1985—cont.

1922. Local Government Superannuation (Overseas Employment) Regulations 1985.
reg. 3, applied: regs. 95/1019, reg. K28.
reg. 3, amended: regs. 95/1019, Sch. M6.

1929. Occupational Pension Schemes (Discharge of Liability) Regulations 1985.
amended by 1995 No. 35.

1931. Occupational Pensions Scheme (Transfer Values) Regulations 1985.
reg. 4, applied: regs. 95/1019, reg. K5; regs. 95/637, reg. 8.

1939. Air Navigation (Dangerous Goods) Regulations 1985.
revoked: regs. 94/3187, reg. 2.

2023. Reporting of Injuries, Diseases and Dangerous Occurrences Regulations 1985.
applied: regs. 94/3140, reg. 19.

2066. Misuse of Drugs Regulations 1985.
applied: regs. 95/414, Sch. 1.
Sch. 1, para. 1, amended: regs. 95/2048, reg. 2.
Sch. 2, para. 1, amended: regs. 95/2048, reg. 2.
Sch. 4, para. 1, amended: regs. 95/2048, reg. 2.

1986

24. Local Government Superannuation Regulations 1986.
applied: regs. 95/1019, Sch. A1.
amended by 1994 No. 3221.
revoked, except Pts. K, L: regs. 95/1019 Sch. M5.
reg. B1, amended: regs. 95/900, reg. 2.
reg. B9, inserted: regs. 95/900, reg. 2.
reg. C2, amended: regs. 95/900, reg. 3
reg. C3, amended: regs. 95/901, reg. 2.
reg. C3A, amended: regs. 95/901, reg. 2.
reg. C7A, amended: regs. 95/900, reg. 3.
reg. C8A, amended: regs. 95/900, reg. 3.
reg. C16, substituted: regs. 95/900, reg. 3.
reg. E2, amended: regs. 95/901, reg. 3.
reg. E3, amended: regs. 95/901, reg. 3.
reg. E11, amended: regs. 95/900, reg. 4.
reg. E22, amended: regs. 95/900, reg. 4.
reg. E29, amended: regs. 95/900, reg. 4.
reg. E33A, inserted: regs. 95/963, reg. 2.
reg. J2, amended: regs. 94/3026, reg. 2.
reg. J13, amended: regs. 94/3026, reg. 3, regs. 95/963, reg. 3.
reg. J13A, revoked: regs. 94/3026, reg. 4.
reg. J14, amended: regs. 95/963, reg. 3. substituted: regs. 94/3026, reg. 5.

NO.

1986—cont.

24. Local Government Superannuation Regulations 1986—*cont.*

reg. J14A, inserted: regs. 94/3026, reg. 6.

reg. J14B, inserted : regs. 94/3026, reg. 6.

reg. K1, amended: regs. 95/1497, reg. 3.

regs. K2–K4, substituted: regs. 95/1497, reg. 2.

reg. L2, amended: regs. 95/1019, Sch. M6.

reg. L5, amended: regs. 95/1019, Sch. M6.

Sch. 1, amended: regs. 95/900, reg. 5.

Sch. 6A, para. 2, amended: regs. 95/900, reg. 6.

Sch. 6A, para. 4, amended: regs. 95/963, reg. 5.

Sch. 6A, para. 6, amended: regs. 95/963, reg. 5.

Sch. 6A, para. 6A, inserted: regs. 95/963, reg. 5.

Sch. 6A, para. 6B, inserted: regs. 95/963, reg. 5.

Sch. 6A, para. 9, amended: regs. 95/900, reg. 6.

Sch. 7, amended: regs. 95/900, reg. 7.

Sch. 15, amended: regs. 95/900, reg. 8.

Sch. 16, amended: regs. 94/3026, reg. 7.

Sch. 18, revoked: regs. 94/3026, reg. 8.

103. Licensed Betting Offices Regulations 1986.

reg. 4, amended: regs. 95/578, reg. 3.

reg. 5, amended: regs. 95/578, reg. 4.

reg. 7, amended: regs. 95/578, reg. 5.

120. Licensed Betting Offices (Scotland) Regulations 1986.

reg. 4, amended: regs. 95/802, reg. 3.

reg. 5, amended: regs. 95/802, reg. 4.

reg. 7, amended: regs. 95/802, reg. 5.

127. Court of Protection (Enduring Powers of Attorney) Rules 1986.

revoked: rules 94/3047, rule 29.

144. Merchant Shipping (Medical Stores) Regulations 1986.

revoked: regs. 95/1802, reg. 1.

reg. 6, amended: regs. 94/3144, reg. 11.

178. Local Authorities' Traffic Orders (Exemptions for Disabled Persons) (England and Wales) Regulations 1986.

reg. 2, applied: regs. 95/1692, reg. 2; regs. 95/1693, reg. 2; regs. 95/1694, reg. 2; regs. 95/1695, reg. 2; regs. 95/1696, reg. 2; regs. 95/1697, reg. 2; regs. 95/1698, reg. 2; regs. 95/1699, reg. 2; regs. 95/1700, reg. 2; 95/1701, reg. 2; regs. 95/1702, reg. 2; regs. 95/1703, reg. 2; ord. 95/335, art. 2, ord. 95/336, art. 2, ord 95/337, art. 2, ord 95/339, art. 2; ord. 95/2245, art. 2; ord. 95/2246, art. 2.

NO.

1986—cont.

183. Removal and Disposal of Vehicles Regulations 1986.

see *Carey* v. *Chief Constable of Avon and Somerset*, *The Times*, April 7, 1995, C.A.

228. Medicines (Veterinary Drugs) (Exemption from Licences) (Importation) Order 1986.

art. 3A, inserted: regs. 93/3142, reg. 21.

art. 4, amended: regs. 94/3142, reg. 21.

237. Borough of Thamesdown (Electoral Arrangements) Order 1986.

art. 6, substituted: ord. 95/1774, art. 9.

303. National Health Service (General Medical and Pharmaceutical Services) (Scotland) Amendment Regulations 1986.

revoked: regs. 95/414, reg. 13.

380. Local Government Superannuation (Miscellaneous Provisions) Regulations 1986.

reg. 3, revoked: regs. 95/1019 Sch. M5.

reg. 4, applied: regs. 95/1019, Sch. B3.

reg. 4, amended: regs. 95/1019, Sch. M6.

regs. 5–14, revoked: regs. 95/1019 Sch. M5.

regs. 17–21, revoked: regs. 95/1019 Sch. M5.

401. Hartlepools Water (Consolidation, etc.) Order 1986.

Whole Order (except s.39(2) and Sch. 4, Part III) revoked: Order 95/79, Sch. 2.

416. Misuse of Drugs (Licence Fees) Regulations 1986.

reg. 3, amended: regs. 95/506, reg. 2.

590. Value Added Tax Tribunals Rules 1986.

rule 4, see *Cumhur Akar* v. *Customs and Excise Commissioners* [1994] VATTR 176, London Tribunal.

rule 6(1), see *Cadman* v. *Customs and Excise Commissioners* [1994] VATTR 296, Manchester Tribunal.

rule 23(2), see *Cumhur Akar* v. *Customs and Excise Commissioners* [1994] VATTR 176, London Tribunal.

rule 26(2), see *Cumhur Akar* v. *Customs and Excise Commissioners* [1994] VATTR 176, London Tribunal.

rule 29, see *Broadway Video (Wholesale)* v. *Customs and Excise Commissioners* [1994] VATTR 271, London Tribunal; *Customs and Excise Commissioners* v. *VAZ. Portcullis (VAT Consultancy), Intervening* [1995] S.T.C. 14, Macpherson of Cluny J.

NO.

1986—cont.

594. Education and Libraries (Northern Ireland) Order 1986 (N.I. 3).
referred to: regs. 95/2016, reg. 19.
art. 50, applied: regs. 95/2018, Sch. 1, para. 8.
art. 50(1)(2); regs. 95/1.
art. 134(1); regs. 95/1.

595. Mental Health (Northern Ireland) Order 1986.
Sch. 5, Pt. I, revoked in pt.: 1995, c. 35, Sch. 3.

625. Redundant Mineworkers and Concessionary Coal (Payments Scheme) Order 1986.
art. 1, amended: regs. 95/829, reg. 24.
art. 9, amended: regs. 95/829, reg. 24.

666. Goods Vehicles (Operators' Licences, Qualifications and Fees) (Amendment) Regulations 1986.
reg. 3, revoked: 1995, c. 23, Sch. 8, Pt. II.
reg. 8, revoked: 1995, c. 23, Sch. 8, Pt. II.
reg. 10, revoked: 1995, c. 23, Sch. 8, Pt. II.

720. Milk-based Drinks (Hygiene and Heat Treatment) (Amendment) Regulations 1986.
revoked: regs. 95/1086, reg. 23.

721. Milk and Dairies (Heat Treatment of Cream) (Amendment) Regulations 1986.
revoked: regs. 95/1086, reg. 23.

758. The Child Resistant Packaging (Safety) Regulations 1986.
revoked by 1994 No. 3247.

789. Cream (Heat Treatment) (Scotland) Amendment Regulations 1986.
revoked: regs. 95/1372, reg. 23.

790. Milk-Based Drinks (Scotland) Amendment Regulations 1986.
revoked: regs. 95/1372, reg. 23.

925. National Health Service (General Medical and Pharmaceutical Services) (Scotland) Amendment (No. 2) Regulations 1986.
revoked: regs. 95/414, reg. 13.

965. National Health Service (General Ophthalmic Services) (Scotland) Regulations 1986.
reg. 2, amended: regs. 95/704, reg. 2.
reg. 14, amended: regs. 95/704, reg. 3.

975. National Health Service (General Ophthalmic Services) Regulations 1986.
reg. 2, amended: regs. 95/558, reg. 2.
reg. 13, amended: regs. 95/558, reg. 3.

1030. The Public Service Vehicles (Traffic Regulation Conditions) Regulations 1986.
amended by 1994 No. 3272.

NO.

1986—cont.

1032. Companies (Northern Ireland) Order 1986.
applied: ord. 95/1536, arts. 2, 4.
art. 603B, referred to: ord. 95/1433, art. 3.
art. 603C, referred to: ord. 95/1433, art. 3.
Sch. 9A, amended: 1995 c. 29, s. 3.

1078. Road Vehicles (Construction and Use) Regulations 1986.
amended by 1994 No. 3270.
reg. 4, amended: regs. 95/1201, reg. 5.
reg. 9, amended: regs. 95/1201, reg. 3.
reg. 15, amended: regs. 95/551, reg. 3.
reg. 16, amended: regs. 95/551, reg. 4.
reg. 17, amended: regs. 95/551, reg. 5.
reg. 18, amended: regs. 95/551, reg. 6.
reg. 21, revoked: regs. 95/1201, reg. 4.
reg. 25, amended: regs. 95/551, reg. 7.
reg. 45, amended: regs. 95/1201, reg. 4.
reg. 58, revoked: regs. 95/1201, reg. 4.
reg. 59, amended: regs. 95/1201, reg. 5.
reg. 61, amended: regs. 95/2210, reg. 3.
reg. 86A, inserted: regs. 95/551, reg. 8.
reg. 103, see *Carey* v. *Chief Constable of Avon and Somerset*, *The Times*, April 7, 1995, C.A.
Sch. 2, amended: regs. 95/551, reg. 9.
Sch. 2, Table 1, amended: regs. 95/2210, reg. 5.
Sch. 3, amended: regs. 95/551, reg. 10.
Sch. 7B, inserted: regs. 95/2210, reg. 4.

1081. Representation of the People Regulations 1986.
reg. 30, amended: regs. 95/1948, reg. 5.
reg. 50, amended: regs. 95/1948, reg. 5.
reg. 97, referred to: ord. 95/546, art. 5.
Sch. 2, Form A, amended: regs. 95/1948, reg. 5.
Sch. 2, Form D, amended: regs. 95/1948, reg. 5.

1082. Units of Measurement Regulations 1986.
reg. 2, amended: regs. 94/2867, reg. 3.
reg. 7, substituted: regs. 94/2867, reg. 3.
reg. 8, amended: regs. 94/2867, reg. 4.
reg. 10, revoked: regs. 94/2867, reg. 3.
reg. 11, amended: regs. 94/2867, reg. 4.
regs. 12, 13, 14, inserted: regs. 94/2867, reg. 4.
Sch. 3, heading, amended: regs. 94/2867, reg. 4.
Sch. 3, Pt. IV, inserted: regs. 94/2867, reg. 4.
Schs. 3A, 3B, inserted: regs. 94/2867, reg. 3.

1091. Representation of the People (Northern Ireland) Regulations 1986.
reg. 30, amended: regs. 95/1948, reg. 5.
reg. 50, amended: regs. 95/1948, reg. 5.
Sch. 2, Form A, amended: regs. 95/1948, reg. 5.

NO.

1986—cont.

1111. Representation of the People (Scotland) Regulations 1986.
applied: ord. 94/3255, art. 8.
reg. 29, amended: regs. 95/1948, reg. 5.
reg. 48, amended: regs. 95/1948, reg. 5.
Sch. 2, Form A, amended: regs. 95/1948, reg. 5.
Sch. 2, Form B, amended: regs. 95/1948, reg. 5.

1159. Child Abduction and Custody (Parties to Conventions) Order 1986.
Sch. 2, substituted: ord. 95/1295, art. 2; ord. 95/264, art. 2.

1296. Safety of Sports Grounds (Designation) Order 1986.
Sch. 1, amended: ord. 95/1990, art. 4.

1319. Trade Marks and Service Marks Rules 1986.
rules 49–52, see *St. Trudo Trade Mark* [1995] F.S.R. 345, Ferris J.
rule 82, see *St. Trudo Trade Mark* [1995] F.S.R. 345, Ferris J.
rule 83, see *St. Trudo Trade Mark* [1995] F.S.R. 345, Ferris J.

1323. Fireworks (Safety) Regulations 1986.
revoked: regs. 95/415, reg. 2.

1335. Costs in Criminal Cases (General) Regulations 1986.
reg. 20, see *R.* v. *Davies (Myles Reece) (94/2987/W3)* February 14, 1995, C.A.

1390. General Medical Council (Constitution of Fitness to Practice Committees) Rules 1986.
rule 11, amended: rules 94/3171, rule 2.

1427. Vehicle Licences (Duration of First Licences and Rate of Duty) Order 1986.
revoked: ord. 94/3095, art. 2.

1428. Vehicle Licences (Duration of First Licences and Rate of Duty) Order 1986.
art. 1A, revoked: ord. 94/3095, art. 3.

1442. Registration of Marriages Regulations 1986.
amended: regs. 95/744, reg. 2.
reg. 4, amended: regs. 95/744, reg. 3.

1507. National Health Service (General Medical and Pharmaceutical Services) (Scotland) Amendment (No. 3) Regulations 1986.
revoked: regs. 95/414, reg. 13.

1510. Control of Pesticides Regulations 1986.
applied: regs. 95/887, reg. 2.
reg. 3, amended: regs. 94/3142, reg. 21.

1668. Public Service Vehicles (Operators' Licences) Regulations 1986.
amended: regs. 95/689, reg. 2.
reg. 5, substituted: regs. 95/689, reg. 2.

1671. Public Service Vehicles (Registration of Local Services) Regulations 1986.
reg. 9, amended: regs. 94/3271, reg. 2.

NO.

1986—cont.

1685. Weights and Measures (Local and Working Standard Weights and Testing Equipment) Regulations 1986.
applied: regs. 95/735, reg. 2.

1713. Combined Probation Areas Order 1986.
amended: ord. 95/747, art. 2.
Sch. 2, applied: ord. 95/2552, art. 2; ord. 95/2553, art. 2; ord. 95/2554, art. 2; ord. 95/2555, art. 2.
Sch. 2, amended: ord. 95/1749, art. 2; ord 95/747, art. 2; ord. 94/3313, art. 2, ord. 94/3314, art. 2, ord. 94/3315, art. 2.

1755. Infectious Diseases of Poultry Order 1986.
revoked: ord. 94/3141, art. 15.

1925. Insolvency Rules 1986.
referred to: regs. 95/1386, reg. 2.
amended: rules 95/586, rule 3.
rule 1.17, see *Cranley Mansions, Re*; *Saigol* v. *Goldstein* [1994] EGCS 95, Ferris J.
rule 1.17(3), see *Cranley Mansions*; *Saigol* v. *Goldstein* [1994] BCC 576, Ferris J.
rule 2.2, see *Practice Note (Ch.D.) (Administration Order Applications: Content of Independent Reports)* [1994] BCC 35.
rule 4, amended: rules 95/586, rule 2.
rule 4.90, see *Bank of Credit and Commerce Intl. SA (No. 3)* [1994] BCC 462, Rattee J.; *Bank of Credit and Commerce International (No. 8), Re* [1994] 3 W.L.R. 911, Rattee J.
rule 5.17, see *Bradley-Hole (A Bankrupt), Re* [1995] 1 W.L.R. 1097, Rimer J.; *Calor Gas* v. *Piercy* [1994] BCC 69, H.H.J. Paul Baker, Q.C.
rule 5.18, see *Bradley-Hole (A Bankrupt), Re* [1995] 1 W.L.R. 1097, Rimer J.; *Calor Gas* v. *Piercy* [1994] BCC 69, H.H.J. Paul Baker, Q.C.
rule 6, amended: rules 95/586, rule 2.
rule 6.5, see *Debtor, A (Nos. 49 and 50 of 1992), Re* [1994] 3 W.L.R. 847, C.A.
rule 7.28, see Application Pursuant to rule 7.28 of the Insolvency Rules 1986, *Re* [1994] BCC 369, Millett J.
rule 9.5 see *Arrows (No. 4) Re*; *sub nom. Hamilton* v. *Naviede and Director of the Serious Fraud Office* [1994] 3 W.L.R. 656, H.L.
rule 12(10), see *Company (No. 003932 of 1995), Re, The Times*, July 25, 1995, Knox J.
rule 13.12, see *Tottenham Hotspur* v. *Edenote* [1995] 1 BCLC 65, Rattee J.
Pt. 4, Ch. 12, see *W. & A. Glaser, Re* [1994] BCC 199, Harman J.
Pt. 6, Ch. 8, see *Wisepark, Re* [1994] BCC 221, Evans-Lombe J.

NO.

1986—cont.

1932. Merchant Shipping (Liability of Shipowners and Others) (Rate of Interest) Order 1986.
revoked: ord. 94/3049, reg. 2.

1935. Merchant Shipping (Certification of Marine Engineer Officers and Licensing of Marine Engineer Operators) Regulations 1986.
referred to: regs. 95/1427, reg. 3.
reg. 2, amended: regs. 95/1429, reg. 14.
reg. 2A, inserted: regs. 95/1429, reg. 15.
reg. 4, amended: regs. 95/1429, reg. 16
reg. 5A, inserted: regs. 95/1429, reg. 17.
reg. 6, amended: regs. 95/1429, reg. 18.
reg. 7, amended: regs. 95/1429, reg. 19.
reg. 9, amended: regs. 95/1429, reg. 20.
reg. 10, amended: regs. 95/1429, reg. 21.
reg. 18, amended: regs. 95/1429, reg. 22.
reg. 20, amended: regs. 95/1429, reg. 23.
reg. 21, amended: regs. 95/1429, reg. 24.

1960. Statutory Maternity Pay (General) Regulations 1986.
reg. 21A, amended: regs. 95/829, reg. 18.
reg. 25A, amended: regs. 95/829, reg. 18.

1994. Insolvency Regulations 1986.
regs. 8, 26, 27, see *W. & A. Glaser, Re*, [1994] BCC 199, Harman J.

2049. Weights and Measures (Packaged Goods) Regulations 1986.
referred to: regs. 95/735, reg. 3.
Sch. 3, Pt. I, amended: regs. 94/1852, reg. 2.
Sch. 4, Pt. II, amended: regs. 94/1852, reg. 2.

2090. Sea Fishing (Enforcement of Community Conservation Measures) Order 1986.
art. 3(1)(b), see *Gnewuch* v. *Adam*, 1995 S.C.C.R. 400.

2129. Air Navigation (Dangerous Goods) (Amendment) Regulations 1986.
revoked: regs. 94/3187, reg. 2.

2209. European Parliamentary Elections Regulations 1986.
reg. 5, amended: regs. 95/1948, reg. 5.
Sch. 1, amended: regs. 95/1948, reg. 5.

2213. Scottish Local Elections Rules 1986.
applied: ord 94/3255, art. 8.
rule 4, amended: regs. 95/1948, reg. 5.
Sch. 2, amended: regs. 95/1948, reg. 5.

2214. Local Elections (Principal Areas) Rules 1986.
rule 4, referred to: ord. 95/546, art. 5; amended: regs. 95/1948, reg. 5.
Sch. 2, referred to: ord. 95/546, art. 5; ord. 95/830, art. 4; amended: regs. 95/1948, reg. 5.
Sch. 3, referred to: ord. 95/546, art. 5.
Sch. 4, referred to: ord. 95/546, art. 5.

NO.

1986—cont.

2215. Local Elections (Parishes and Communities) Rules 1986.
rule 4, referred to: ord. 95/546, art. 5; amended: regs. 95/1948, reg. 5.
Sch. 2, referred to: ord. 95/830, art. 5; amended: regs. 95/1948, reg. 5.
Sch. 3, referred to: ord. 95/546, art. 5.
Sch. 4, referred to: ord. 95/546, art. 5.

2218. Social Security (Adjudication) Regulations 1986.
reg. 65; amended: regs. 95/829, reg. 19.

2230. Misuse of Drugs Act 1971 (Modification) Order 1986.
art. 2, amended: ord. 95/1966, art. 3.

2250. European Parliamentary Elections (Northern Ireland) Regulations 1986.
reg. 5, amended: regs. 95/1948, reg. 5.

2257. Environmentally Sensitive Areas (Cambrian Mountains) Designation Order 1986.
art. 2, amended: ord. 95/243, art. 3.
art. 4, substituted: ord. 95/243, art. 3.
art. 4A, inserted: ord. 95/243, art. 3.
art. 6, substituted: ord. 95/243, art. 3.
Sch. 1, substituted: ord. 95/243, art. 3.
Sch. 2, substituted: ord 95/243, art. 3.
Sch. 3, substituted: ord. 95/243, art. 3.
Sch. 4, substituted: ord. 95/243, art. 3.

2291. Children's Hearing (Scotland) Rules 1986.
s.9(3), see *Kennedy* v. *M.(I.H.)*, 1995 S.C.L.R. 88.
s.24, see *Kennedy* v. *M.(I.H.)*, 1995 S.C.L.R. 88.
Form 10A, see *Kennedy* v. *M.(I.H.)*, 1995 S.C.L.R. 88.

2310. National Health Service (General Medical and Pharmaceutical Services) (Scotland) Amendment (No. 4) Regulations 1986.
revoked: regs. 95/414, reg. 13.

2330. Misuse of Drugs (Amendment) Regulations 1986.
reg. 2, amended: regs. 95/2048, reg. 3.

2331. Misuse of Drugs (Designation) Order 1986.
Sch., Pt. I, amended: ord. 95/2047, art. 2.

1987

2. National Health Service (Food Premises) (Scotland) Regulations 1987.
applied: ord. 95/574, art. 5.

37. Dangerous Substances in Harbour Areas Regulations 1987.
amended by 1994 No. 3247.

133. Authorised Officers (Meat Inspection) Regulations 1987.
Sch., para. 3, applied: regs. 95/539, reg. 8.

NO.

1987—cont.

233. Movement and Sale of Pigs (Amendment) Order 1987.
revoked by 1995 No. 11

293. Local Government Superannuation (Miscellaneous Provisions) Regulations 1987.
reg. 2, applied: regs. 95/1019, Sch. B3.
reg. 2, amended: regs. 95/1019, Sch. M6.
reg. 3, amended: regs 95/1019, Sch. M6.
regs. 4–15, revoked: regs. 95/1019 Sch. M5.

299. Prosecution of Offences (Custody Time-limits) Regulations 1987.
amended: regs. 95/555, reg. 2.
reg. 2, amended: regs. 95/555, reg. 2.
reg. 5, see *R.* v. *Maidstone Crown Court, ex p. Clark* [1995] 1 W.L.R. 831, D.C.
reg. 6, amended: regs. 95/555, reg. 2.
reg. 8, amended: regs. 95/555, reg. 2.
See *R.* v. *Central Criminal Court, ex p. Behbehani* [1994] Crim.L.R. 352, D.C.

307. Criminal Legal Aid (Scotland) Regulations 1987.
reg. 4, amended: regs. 95/2320, reg. 3.
reg. 13, amended: regs. 95/2320, reg. 4.

381. Civil Legal Aid (Scotland) Regulations 1987.
reg. 11A, inserted: reg. 95/1065, reg. 3.
reg. 40, amended: regs. 95/1065, reg. 4.

382. Advice and Assistance (Scotland) Regulations 1987.
reg. 6A, inserted: regs. 95/1066, reg. 3.
Sch. 2, amended: regs. 95/1066, reg. 4.

385. National Health Service (General Medical and Pharmaceutical Services) (Scotland) Amendment Regulations 1987.
revoked: regs. 95/414, reg. 13.

386. National Health Service (General Medical and Pharmaceutical Services) (Scotland) Amendment (No. 2) Regulations 1987.
revoked: regs. 95/414, reg. 13.

408. Merchant Shipping (Seamen's Documents) Regulations 1987.
Sch. 3, amended: regs. 95/1900, reg. 2.

460. Audit (Northern Ireland) Order 1987.
art. 4A, applied: regs. 95/635, reg. 3.

469. Parliamentary Constituencies (Scotland) (Miscellaneous Changes) Order 1987.
revoked: ord. 95/1037, art. 4.

470. Merchant Shipping (Prevention and Control of Pollution) Order 1987.
art. 3, applied: regs. 95/2498.

481. Social Fund Maternity and Funeral Expenses (General) Regulations 1987.
reg. 3, amended: regs. 95/1229, reg. 2.
reg. 7, amended: regs. 95/1229, reg. 3.

NO.

1987—cont.

481. Social Fund Maternity and Funeral Expenses (General) Regulations 1987—*cont.*
reg. 8, amended: regs. 95/1229, reg. 4.
reg. 9, amended: regs. 95/1229, reg. 4.

491. Social Security (Payments on Account, Overpayments and Recovery) Regulations 1987.
reg. 8(2), see *Social Security Decision No. R(IS) 14/94.*

551. Merchant Shipping (Control of Pollution by Noxious Liquid Substances in Bulk) Regulations 1987.
applied: regs. 95/2498, reg. 9.

561. Local Elections (Communities) (Welsh Forms) Order 1987.
Sch., Pt. I, amended: ord. 95/830, art. 6.

562. Local Elections (Principal Areas) (Welsh Forms) Order 1987.
art. 2, referred to: ord. 95/546, art. 5.
art. 4, referred to: ord. 95/546, art. 5.
Sch., Pt. I, amended: ord. 95/830, art. 6.

578. Housing Benefit (General) Regulations 1987.
reg. 61(2), see *R.* v. *Maidstone Borough Council, ex p. Bunce* (1994) 27 H.L.R. 375, Brooke J.
reg. 69(8), see *R.* v. *Maidstone Borough Council, ex p. Bunce* (1994) 27 H.L.R. 375, Brooke J.

586. Merchant Shipping (Reporting of Pollution Incidents) Regulations 1987.
revoked by 1994 No. 3245.

666. Food and Environment Protection Act 1985 (Isle of Man) Order 1987.
revoked: ord. 94/3205, art. 2.

701. Town and Country Planning (Appeals) (Written Representations Procedure) Regulations 1987.
reg. 9, see *Geha* v. *Secretary of State for the Environment* (1993) (1994) 68 P. & C.R. 139, C.A.

710. Agricultural Holdings (Arbitration on Notices) Order 1987.
art. 10A, see *Robinson* v. *Moody* [1994] 37 EG 154, C.A.

764. Town and Country Planning (Use Classes) Order 1987.
See *Kalra* v. *Secretary of State for the Environment* [1994] NPC 111, [1994] 2 PLR 99, David Widdicombe, Q.C.
art. 3, amended: ord. 95/297, art. 2.
Sch., Pt. B, amended: ord. 95/297, art. 2.

806. Value Added Tax (Tour Operators) Order 1987.
art. 7, see *Whittle RA, DL and GA (t/a Go Whittle)* v. *Customs and Excise Commissioners* [1994] VATTR 202, Manchester Tribunal.

NO.

1987—cont.

841. Goods Vehicles (Operators' Licences, Qualifications and Fees) (Amendment) Regulations 1987.
reg. 5, revoked: 1995, c. 23, Sch. 8, Pt. II.

851. Police Regulations 1987.
revoked: regs. 95/215, reg. 70.

926. European Communities (Designation) (No. 2) Order 1987.
revoked in pt.: ord. 95/751, art. 3.

1101. Money Purchase Contracted-out Schemes Regulations 1987.
amended by 1995 No. 35.

1110. Personal Pension Schemes (Disclosure of Information) Regulations 1987.
amended by 1995 No. 35.

1117. Personal and Occupational Pension Schemes (Protected Rights) Regulations 1987.
amended by 1995 No. 35.

1229. Section 19 Minibus (Designated Bodies) Order 1987.
Sch., amended: ord. 95/1540, arts. 4, 5, 6, 7.

1364. Education (Fees and Awards) (Amendment) Regulations 1987.
revoked: regs. 94/3042, reg. 17.

1378. Motor Vehicles (Driving Licences) Regulations 1987.
reg. 19, amended: regs. 95/1200, reg. 3.
reg. 19A, amended: regs. 95/1200, reg. 4.
Sch. 3, amended: regs. 95/2076, reg. 2.

1382. National Health Service (General Medical and Pharmaceutical Services) (Scotland) Amendment (No. 3) Regulations 1987.
revoked: regs. 95/414, reg. 13.

1513. Occupational Pension Schemes (Maximum Rate Lump Sum) Regulations 1987.
applied: regs. 95/639, reg. 4.5.

1521. Counterfeit Goods (Consequential Provisions) Regulations 1987.
revoked: regs. 95/1447, reg. 5.

1523. Materials and Articles in Contact with Food Regulations 1987.
subject to: regs. 95/1372, Sch. 9, para. 1.

1529. Local Government Reorganisation (Pensions etc.) (Greater Manchester and Merseyside) Order 1987.
art. 5, amended: regs. 95/1019, Sch. M6.

1532. Town and Country Planning (Simplified Planning Zones) (Scotland) Regulations 1987.
referred to: regs. 95/2043, reg. 2.
revoked: regs. 95/2043, reg. 23.

1538. Weights and Measures (Quantity Marking and Abbreviation of Units) Regulations 1987.
reg. 2, amended: regs. 94/1852, reg. 2.
reg. 6, substituted: regs. 94/1852, reg. 2.

NO.

1987—cont.

1538. Weights and Measures (Quantity Marking and Abbreviation of Units) Regulations 1987—*cont.*
reg. 7, amended: regs. 94/1852, reg. 2.
reg. 7, revoked: regs. 94/1852, reg. 2.
reg. 8, substituted: regs. 94/1852, reg. 2.
reg. 11, substituted: regs. 94/1852, reg. 2.
Sch. 2, amended: regs. 94/1852, reg. 2.

1579. Local Government Reorganisation (Pensions etc.) (Greater Manchester and Merseyside) Order 1987.
art. 5, amended: regs. 95/1019 Sch. M5.

1597. Hartlepools Water (Red Barns Borehole) Order 1987.
revoked: ord. 95/79, Sch. 2.

1680. Consumer Protection Act 1987 (Commencement No. 1) Order 1987.
art. 6, applied: regs. 95/415.

1753. Police (Amendment) Regulations 1987.
revoked: regs. 95/215, reg. 70.

1806. Value Added Tax (Tour Operators) Order 1987.
art. 10, revoked: ord. 95/1495, art. 2.

1830. Social Security (Austria) Order 1987.
modified: ord. 95/767, art. 2.

1831. Social Security (Portugal) Order 1987.
modified: ord. 95/767, art. 2.

1850. Local Government Superannuation (Scotland) Regulations 1987.
applied: ord. 95/2636, Sch., para. 11; ord. 95/2639, Sch., para. 11; ord. 95/2640, Sch., para. 12; ord. 95/2641, Sch., para. 12; ord. 95/2642, Sch., para. 12; ord. 95/2643, Sch., para. 12; regs. 95/1019, reg. K27.
reg. C1, amended: regs. 95/750, reg. 4.
reg. E2, amended: regs. 95/750, reg. 4.
reg. E24, amended: regs. 95/750, reg. 4.
reg. P6, amended: regs. 95/214, reg. 2.
Sch. 3, Pt. I, amended: regs. 95/750, reg. 4.

1967. Income Support (General) Regulations 1987.
see *Bate (Anne Marie)* v. *Chief Adjudication Officer (93/0820/B)*, November 30, 1995, C.A.
referred to: regs. 95/2352, reg. 2.
amended: regs. 95/625, reg. 5.
reg. 2, amended: regs. 95/516, reg. 17, regs. 95/2303, reg. 6.
reg. 3, amended: regs. 94/3061, reg. 2, regs. 95/516, reg. 18.
reg. 4, amended: regs. 95/482, reg. 5.
reg. 5, amended: regs. 95/516, reg. 19.
reg. 5(2)(b)(i), see *Social Security Decision No. R(IS) 15/94.*
reg. 6, amended: regs. 95/516, reg. 20.
reg. 8, amended: regs. 95/482, reg. 6.
reg. 9, amended: regs. 95/482, reg. 7.
reg. 11, amended: regs. 95/482, reg. 8.
reg. 13, amended: regs. 94/3061, reg. 2.
reg. 13(2), see *Social Security Decision No. R(IS) 9/94.*

NO.

1987—cont.

1967. Income Support (General) Regulations 1987—*cont.*
reg. 17(1)(e), see *Secretary of State for Social Security* v. *McSherry*, 1995 S.L.T. 371.
reg. 21, amended: regs. 95/516, reg. 21.
reg. 22, amended: regs. 95/487, reg. 9.
reg. 31, amended: regs. 95/482, reg. 10.
reg. 32, amended: regs. 95/482, reg. 11.
reg. 38, amended: regs. 95/2303, reg. 6.
reg. 42, amended: regs. 95/516, reg. 22, regs. 95/2303, reg. 6.
reg. 49, Sched. 10, para. 26, see *Social Security Decision No. R(IS) 20/93.*
reg. 49(a), see *Chief Adjudication Officer* v. *Palfrey*, *The Times*, February 17, 1995, C.A.
reg. 51, amended: regs. 95/2303, reg. 6, see *Social Security Decision No. R(IS) 13/93.*
reg. 52, amended: regs. 95/2303, reg. 6, see *Chief Adjudication Officer* v. *Palfrey*, *The Times*, February 17, 1995, C.A.
reg. 61, amended: regs. 95/1742, reg. 2.
reg. 62, amended: regs. 95/1742, reg. 3.
reg. 72, amended: regs. 95/516, reg. 23.
reg. 73, amended: regs. 95/482, reg. 12.
reg. 75, amended: regs. 95/482, reg. 13.
Sch. 1, para. 5, substituted: regs. 95/482, reg. 14; amended: regs. 95/2303, reg. 6.
Sch. 1, para. 7, substituted: regs. 95/482, reg. 15.
Sch. 2, para. 12, amended: regs. 95/482, regs. 16, 17, regs. 95/516, reg. 24, regs. 95/2303, reg. 6.
Sch. 3, see *R.* v. *Social Fund Inspector, ex p. Tuckwood (CO 3807–94)*, April 27, 1995, Popplewell J.
Sch. 3, para. 1, see *Secretary of State for Social Security* v. *McSherry*, 1995, S.L.T. 371.
Sch. 3, para. 4, amended: regs. 95/516, reg. 25, regs. 95/625, reg. 5.
Sch. 3, para. 5A, amended: regs. 95/516, reg. 25.
Sch. 3, para. 7, amended: regs. 95/1045, reg. 62; regs. 95/516, reg. 25.
Sch. 3, para. 7B, amended: regs. 95/516, reg. 25.
Sch. 3, para. 12, amended: regs. 95/2287, reg. 2.
Sch. 7, para. 13A, amended: regs. 95/516, reg. 26.
Sch. 7, para. 19, amended: regs. 95/516, reg. 26.
Sch. 9, para. 2, amended: regs. 95/516, reg. 27.
Sch. 9, para. 9, amended: regs. 95/2303, reg. 6.
Sch. 9, para. 14, revoked: regs. 95/2303, reg. 6.

NO.

1987—cont.

1967. Income Support (General) Regulations 1987—*cont.*
Sch. 9, para. 15A, amended: regs. 95/516, reg. 27.
Sch. 9, para. 18, substituted: regs. 95/516, reg. 27.
Sch. 9, para. 19, amended: regs. 95/516, reg. 27.
Sch. 9, para. 53, amended: regs. 95/2303, reg. 6.
Sch. 10, para. 5, substituted: regs. 95/2303, reg. 6.
Sch. 10, para. 23A, inserted: regs. 95/2303, reg. 6.
Sch. 10, para. 24, amended: regs. 95/2303, reg. 6.

1968. Social Security (Claims and Payments) Regulations 1987.
amended by 1994 No. 3196.
reg. 2, amended: regs. 95/2303, reg. 10.
reg. 7, amended: regs. 95/2303, reg. 10.
reg. 9, applied: regs. 95/310, reg. 6.
reg. 19, applied: regs. 95/310, reg. 5.
reg. 32, amended: regs. 95/2303, reg. 10.
Sch. 1, Pt. I, applied: regs. 95/310, reg. 6.
Sch. 4, para. 2, applied: regs. 95/310, reg. 5.
Sch. 9A, para. 7, amended: regs. 94/2944, reg. 2.

1971. Housing Benefit (General) Regulations 1987.
applied: ord. 95/1954, art. 1.
amended: regs. 95/626, regs. 2–9.
amended: regs. 95/625, reg. 2.
referred to: ord. 95/872, art. 2.
reg. 2, amended: regs. 95/560, reg. 2, regs. 95/626, reg. 2; regs. 95/2303, reg. 5.
reg. 3, amended: regs. 95/560, reg. 3; regs. 94/3061, reg. 4.
reg. 3(4), see *Thamesdown Borough Council* v. *Goonery (James) (CCRT193/1/1771F)*, February 13, 1995, C.A.
reg. 4, amended: regs. 95/560, reg. 4.
reg. 5, amended: regs. 95/560, reg. 5, regs. 95/625, reg. 2; regs. 95/2303, reg. 5.
reg. 6, see *R.* v. *Poole Borough Council, ex p. Ross (CO–3127–93)*, May 5, 1995, Sedley J.
reg. 7, applied: regs. 95/1643, reg. 5.
reg. 7, see *R.* v. *Poole Borough Council, ex p. Ross (CO–3127–93)*, May 5, 1995, Sedley J.; *R.* v. *Sheffield Housing Benefits Review Board, ex p. Smith*, *The Times*, December 28, 1994, Blackburne J.; *Thamesdown Borough Council* v. *Goonery (James) (CCRT193/1/1771F)*, February 13, 1995, C.A.

NO.

1987—cont.

1971. Housing Benefit (General) Regulations 1987—*cont.*

reg. 7(1)(a)(ii), see *R.* v. *Sheffield City Council Housing Benefit Review Board, ex p. Smith* (1995) 93 L.G.R. 139, Blackburne J.

reg. 7(1)(b), see *R.* v. *Solihull Metropolitan Borough Council Housing Benefits Review Board, ex p. L. Simpson* [1995] 1 F.L.R. 140, C.A.

reg. 10, applied: regs. 95/1643, regs. 2, 6.

reg. 10, see *R.* v. *Poole Borough Council, ex p. Ross (CO–3127–93)*, May 5, 1995, Sedley J.

reg. 10(1), see *R.* v. *East Yorkshire Borough of Beverley Housing Benefits Review Board, ex p.* Hare, *The Times*, February 28, 1995, Schiemann J.

reg. 11, amended: regs. 95/626, reg. 3, regs. 95/2303, reg. 5; see *R.* v. *Manchester City Council, ex p. Harcup* (1993) 26 H.L.R. 402, D.C.

reg. 11(2)(c), see *R.* v. *East Yorkshire Borough of Beverley Housing Benefits Review Board, ex p. Hare, The Times*, February 28, 1995, Schiemann J.

reg. 12A, amended: regs. 95/560, reg. 6; applied: regs. 95/1643, reg. 2.

reg. 13, amended: regs. 94/3061, reg. 4.

reg. 21A, amended: regs. 95/560, reg. 7, regs. 95/626, reg. 4.

reg. 31, amended: regs. 95/2303, reg. 5.

reg. 35, amended: regs. 95/560, reg. 8, regs. 95/626, reg. 5; regs. 95/2303, reg. 5.

reg. 43, amended: regs. 95/2303, reg. 5.

reg. 44, amended: regs. 95/2303, reg. 5.

reg. 46, amended: regs. 95/1742, reg. 2.

reg. 48A, amended: regs. 95/626, reg. 6.

reg. 51, amended: regs. 95/1742, reg. 4, regs. 95/626, reg. 7.

reg. 53, amended: regs. 95/1742, reg. 3.

reg. 67, amended: regs. 95/560, reg. 9.

reg. 68, amended: regs. 95/511, reg. 2.

regs. 71–87, see *R.* v. *Stoke City Council, ex p. Highgate Projects* [1994] C.O.D. 414, D.C.

reg. 73, amended: regs. 95/2303, reg. 5.

reg. 83, see *R.* v. *Manchester City Council, ex p. Harcup* (1993) 26 H.L.R. 402, D.C.; *R.* v. *Solihull Metropolitan Borough Council Housing Benefit Review Board, ex p. Simpson* (1994) 92 L.G.R. 719, C.A.

reg. 83(4), (5), see *R.* v. *Solihull Metropolitan Borough Council Housing Benefits Review Board, ex p. L. Simpson* [1995] 1 F.L.R. 140, C.A.

NO.

1987—cont.

1971. Housing Benefit (General) Regulations 1987—*cont.*

reg. 94, see *R.* v. *Stoke City Council, ex p. Highgate Projects* [1994] C.O.D. 414, D.C.

reg. 95, amended: regs. 95/560, reg. 10, regs. 95/2303, reg. 5.

Sch. 1, see *R.* v. *North Cornwall District Council, ex p. Singer; Same* v. *Same, ex p. Barrett; Same* v. *Same, ex p. Bateman* (1994) 26 H.L.R. 360, D.C.

Sch. 1, para. 1(f), see *R.* v. *North Cornwall District Council, ex p. Bateman (QBCOF/0119/D, QBCOF/0110/D and QBCOF/0112/D)*, November 8, 1994, C.A.

Sch. 1A, para. 2, amended: regs. 95/560, reg. 11.

Sch. 2, para. 12, amended: regs. 95/560, reg. 12, regs. 95/626, reg. 8; regs. 95/2303, reg. 5.

Sch. 4, para. 2, amended: regs. 95/560, reg. 13.

Sch. 4, para. 12, revoked: regs. 95/2303, reg. 5.

Sch. 4, para. 52, amended: regs. 95/2303, reg. 5.

Sch. 4, para. 56, inserted: regs. 95/626, reg. 9.

Sch. 4, para. 57, inserted: regs. 95/1339, reg. 9.

Sch. 4, para. 58, inserted: regs. 95/1339, reg. 9.

Sch. 5, para. 6, substituted: regs. 95/2303, reg. 5.

Sch. 5, para. 30A, inserted: regs. 95/2303, reg. 5.

Sch. 5, para. 31, amended: regs. 95/2303, reg. 5.

1973. Family Credit (General) Regulations 1987.

reg. 2, amended: regs. 95/516, reg. 10, regs. 95/2303, reg. 4.

reg. 4, amended: regs. 95/516, reg. 11.

reg. 4A, inserted: regs. 95/1339, reg. 6.

reg. 13A, amended: regs. 95/516, reg. 12.

reg. 22, amended: regs. 95/2303, reg. 4.

reg. 26, amended: regs. 95/516, reg. 13, regs. 95/2303, reg. 4.

reg. 34, amended: regs. 95/2303, reg. 4.

reg. 35, amended: regs. 95/2303, reg. 4.

reg. 37, amended: regs. 95/1742, reg. 2.

reg. 38, amended: regs. 95/1742, reg. 3.

reg. 46, amended: regs. 95/516, reg. 14, regs. 95/1339, reg. 7.

Sch. 2, para. 2, amended: regs. 95/516, reg. 15.

Sch. 2, para. 12, substituted: regs. 95/2303, reg. 4.

Sch. 2, para. 18, substituted: regs. 95/516, reg. 15.

Sch. 2, para. 19, amended: regs. 95/516, reg. 15.

NO.

1987—cont.

1973. Family Credit (General) Regulations 1987—*cont.*
Sch. 2, para. 51, amended: regs. 95/2303, reg. 4.
Sch. 2, para. 55, inserted: regs. 95/516, reg. 15.
Sch. 3, para. 5, substituted: regs. 95/2303, reg. 4.
Sch. 3, para. 24A, inserted: regs. 95/2303, reg. 4.
Sch. 3, para. 48, inserted: regs. 95/516, reg. 16.
Sch. 4, para. 1A, inserted: regs. 95/1339, reg. 8.

1975. Building Societies (Limited Credit Facilities) Order 1987.
art. 4, substituted: ord. 95/1006, art. 6.

2023. Insolvent Companies (Disqualification of Unfit Directors) Proceedings Rules 1987.
rules 4, 6 see *Rex Williams Leisure (In Administration), Re* [1994] 3 W.L.R. 745, C.A.

2026. Environmentally Sensitive Areas (Cambrian Mountains—Extension) Designation Order 1987.
art. 2, amended: ord. 95/242, art. 2.
art. 4A, inserted: ord. 95/242, art. 2.
art. 6, amended: ord. 95/242, art. 2.
Sch. 1, para. 1, amended: ord. 95/242, art. 2.
Sch. 1A, inserted: ord. 95/242, art. 2.
Sch. 4, para. 11, inserted: ord. 95/242, art. 2.

2027. Environmentally Sensitive Areas (Lleyn Peninsula) Designation Order 1987.
art. 2, amended: ord. 95/242, art. 3.
art. 4A, inserted: ord 95/242, art. 3.
art. 6, amended: ord 95/242, art. 3.
Sch. 1A, inserted: ord. 95/242, art. 3.
Sch. 4, para. 11, inserted: ord. 95/242, art. 3.

2049. Consumer Protection (Northern Ireland) Order 1987.
applied: rep. 94/3076, Sch. 6.

2089. Registration of Births and Deaths (Welsh Language) Regulations 1987.
reg. 9, revoked: regs. 95/818, reg. 3.
Sch. 2, amended: regs. 95/818, reg. 2.

2097. Counterfeit Goods (Customs) Regulations 1987.
revoked: regs. 95/1430, reg. 9.

2110. Local Government Reorganisation (Pensions etc.) (South Yorkshire) Order 1987.
art. 6, amended: regs. 95/1019 Sch. M5; regs. 95/1019, Sch. M6.

2115. Control of Asbestos at Work Regulations 1987.
amended by 1994 No. 3247.

NO.

1987—cont.

2115. Control of Asbestos at Work Regulations 1987—*cont.*
applied: regs. 94/3246, reg. 5.
see *Barclays Bank* v. *Fairclough Building, The Times*, February 15, 1995, C.A.; *Barclays Bank* v. *Fairclough Building (QBENF 93/0813/B)*, January 26, 1994, C.A.

2132. Friendly Societies (Long Term Insurance Business) Regulations 1987.
referred to: regs. 95/710, reg. 3.

2174. General Medical Council Health Committee (Procedure) Rules 1987.
rule 8(3), see *Phillips, ex p., The Times*, November 16, 1994, C.A.

2218. National Health Service (Superannuation) Amendment Regulations 1987.
revoked: regs. 95/300, reg. V2.

2237. Fresh Meat Export (Hygiene and Inspection) Regulations 1987.
reg. 4, applied: regs. 95/539, reg. 13.

1988

1. Appropriation (Northern Ireland) Order 1988.
revoked: ord. 95/1969, art. 6.

11. Appropriation (No. 2) (Northern Ireland) Order 1988.
revoked: ord. 95/1969, art. 6.

35. Social Fund (Recovery by Deductions from Benefits) Regulations 1988.
reg. 3, amended: regs. 95/829, reg. 20.

93. Department of Trade and Industry (Fees) Order 1988.
art. 2, amended: ord. 95/1294, art. 2.
art. 8, applied: regs. 95/244, regs. 95/1331, preamble.
art. 10, inserted: ord. 95/1294, art. 2.
Sch. 1, Pt. VII, inserted: ord. 95/1294, art. 2.

110. Act of Adjournal (Consolidation) 1988.
rule 164(1), see *Lamant, Petr*, 1995 S.L.T. 566.
rule 164(2), see *McGettigan, Petr.*, 1995 S.C.C.R. 480.
Sch., amended: Act 95/1875, para. 2.

120. Capacity Serving Measures (Intoxicating Liquor) Regulations 1988.
referred to: regs. 95/735, reg. 3.

128. Measuring Equipment (Liquid Fuel and Lubricants) Regulations 1988.
revoked: regs. 95/1014, reg. 1.

137. Personal Pension Schemes (Appropriate Schemes) Regulations 1988.
amended by 1995 No. 35.

NO.

1988—cont.

316. Financial Services Act 1986 (Investment Advertisements) (Exemptions) Order 1988.
revoked: regs. 95/1266, reg. 19.

332. Local Authorities (Publicity Account) (Exemption) (Scotland) Order 1988.
applied: ord. 95/789, art. 2.

361. Construction Plant and Equipment (Harmonisation of Noise Emission Standards) Regulations 1988.
reg. 2, amended: regs. 95/2357, reg. 2.
reg. 5, amended: regs. 95/2357, reg. 2.

466. Local Government (Superannuation and Compensation) (Amendment) Regulations 1988.
reg. 3, amended: regs. 95/1019 Sch. M5.
regs. 4–8, revoked: regs. 95/1019 Sch. M5.
Sch., revoked: regs. 95/1019 Sch. M5.

536. Welfare Food Regulations 1988.
reg. 5, amended: regs. 95/1143, reg. 2.
Sch. 1, amended: regs. 95/1143, reg. 3.

546. National Health Service (Travelling Expenses and Remission of Charges) (Scotland) Amendment Regulations 1988.
reg. 2, amended: regs. 95/700, reg. 2.
reg. 4, amended: regs. 95/700, reg. 3.
reg. 6, amended: regs. 95/700, reg. 4.
reg. 7, amended: regs. 95/700, reg. 5.
Sch. 1, para. 2, amended: regs. 95/2381, reg. 2.
Sch. 1, para. 4, substituted: regs. 95/2381, reg. 2.
Sch. 1, Pt. II, amended: regs. 95/700, regs. 6.

551. National Health Service (Travelling Expenses and Remission of Charges) Regulations 1988.
amended: regs. 95/642, regs. 2–6.
reg. 2, amended: regs. 95/642, reg. 2.
reg. 4, amended: regs. 95/642, reg. 3.
reg. 6, amended: regs. 95/642, reg. 4.
reg. 7, amended: regs. 95/642, reg. 5.
Sch. 1, para. 2, amended: regs. 95/2352, reg. 2.
Sch. 1, para. 4, substituted: regs. 95/2352, reg. 2.
Sch. 1, Pt. II, amended: regs. 95/642, reg. 6.

590. Social Security (Sweden) Order 1988.
modified: ord. 95/767, art. 2.

640. Profit-Related Pay (Shortfall Recovery) Regulations 1988.
remaining pts. revoked: regs. 95/917, reg. 9.

643. Department of Transport (Fees) Order 1988.
applied: regs. 95/1488.

645. Banking Act 1987 (Advertisements) Regulations 1988.
reg. 6, revoked: regs. 95/1442, reg. 52.

NO.

1988—cont.

662. Housing Benefit (Supply of Information) Regulations 1988.
amended: regs. 95/626, reg. 10.
reg. 2, amended: regs. 95/626, reg. 10.
reg. 3, amended: regs. 95/626, reg. 10.

664. Social Security (Payments on Account, Overpayments and Recovery) Regulations 1988.
reg. 1, amended: regs. 95/829, reg. 21.
reg. 15, amended: regs. 95/829, reg. 21.
reg. 16, amended: regs. 95/829, reg. 21.

668. Pneumoconiosis etc. (Workers' Compensation) (Payment of Claims) Regulations 1988.
reg. 5, amended: regs. 95/1514, reg. 3.
reg. 6, amended: regs. 95/1514, reg. 3.
reg. 8, amended: regs. 95/1514, reg. 3.
regs. 95/1514, reg. 3. Sch., substituted.

716. Financial Services Act 1986 (Investment Advertisements) (Exemptions) (No. 2) Order 1988.
revoked: ord. 95/1536, art. 16.

727. Police (Amendment) Regulations 1988.
revoked: regs. 95/215, reg. 70.

809. Excise Warehousing (Etc.) Regulations 1988.
reg. 6, revoked: regs. 95/1046, reg. 15.
reg. 11, amended: regs. 95/1046, reg. 15.
reg. 16, amended: regs. 95/1046, reg. 15.

876. Weighing Equipment (Non-automatic Weighing Machines) Regulations 1988.
reg. 4, amended: regs. 95/428, reg. 2.
reg. 34A, inserted: regs. 95/428, reg. 2.
reg. 35, amended: regs. 95/428, reg. 2.
reg. 37, amended: regs. 95/428, reg. 2.

944. Town and Country Planning (Inquiries Procedure) Rules 1988
see *Coal Contractors* v. *Secretary of State for the Environment and Northumberland County Council* (1994) 68 P. & C.R. 285, Mr David Keene, Q.C. sitting as a deputy judge.

1009. Medicines (Labelling of Medicinal Products for Incorporation in Animal Feeding Stuffs and Medicated Animal Feeding Stuffs) Regulations 1988.
reg. 2, amended: regs. 94/3142, reg. 21.
reg. 9, amended: regs. 94/3142, reg. 21.
Sch. 2, amended: regs. 94/3142, reg. 21.
Sch. 3, amended: regs. 94/3142, reg. 21.

1024. Stanswood Bay Oyster Fishery Order 1988.
art. 1, amended: ord. 95/1257, art. 3.
art. 2, amended: ord. 95/1257, art. 3.
art. 4, revoked: ord. 95/1257, art. 3.
art. 6, revoked: ord. 95/1257, art. 3.

NO.

1988—cont.

1040. Gloucester Harbour Revision Order 1988.
arts. 3, 4(1), (2), (4), revoked: ord. 94/3162, art. 31(2).
art. 9, revoked: ord. 94/3162, art. 31(1).

1042. Education Authority Bursaries (Scotland) Regulations 1988.
revoked: regs. 95/1739, reg. 6.

1057. Electricity Supply Regulations 1988.
reg. 3, amended: regs. 94/3021, reg. 3.
reg. 30, amended: regs. 94/3021, regs. 4, 5, 6.

1073. National Health Service (General Medical and Pharmaceutical Services) (Scotland) Amendment Regulations 1988.
regs. 1, 2, revoked: regs. 95/414, reg. 13.

1116. Merchant Shipping (Medical Stores) (Amendment) Regulations 1988.
revoked: regs. 95/1802, reg. 1.

1141. Building Societies (Commercial Assets and Services) Order 1988.
Sch. 1, Pt. III, amended: ord. 95/1006, art. 6.

1143. Land Registration (Scotland) Amendment Rules 1988.
revoked: rules 95/248, rule 3.

1145. Leeds Development Corporation (Area and Constitution) Order 1988.
art. 3, revoked: ord. 95/916, art. 2.

1175. Church of England (Legal Aid) Rules 1988.
revoked: rules 95/2034, rule 2.

1199. Town and Country Planning (Assessment of Environmental Effects) Regulations 1988.
referred to: regs. 95/2258, reg. 2.
reg. 2, applied: regs. 95/419, reg. 1.
Sch. 1, applied: regs. 95/417, reg. 2; regs. 95/419, reg. 14.
Sch. 2, applied: regs. 95/417, regs. 2; regs. 95/419, reg. 14.
Sch. 3, para. 3, applied: regs. 95/2258, reg. 9.

1200. Police and Criminal Evidence Act 1984 (Codes of Practice) Order 1988.
revoked: ord. 95/450, reg. 4.

1213. Petroleum (Production) (Seaward Areas) Regulations 1988.
reg. 5, amended: regs. 95/1435, reg. 4.
reg. 6, revoked: regs. 95/1435, reg. 5.
reg. 7, substituted: regs. 95/1435, reg. 6.
Sch. 3, Pt. IV(B), amended: regs. 95/1435, reg. 7.
Sch. 4, amended: regs. 95/1435, reg. 8.
Sch. 5, amended: regs. 95/1435, reg. 9.

1217. Land Drainage Improvement Works (Assessment of Environmental Effects) Regulations 1988.
applied: regs. 95/418, reg. 3.

NO.

1988—cont.

1221. Environmental Assessment (Scotland) Regulations 1988.
Schs. 1, 2, applied: regs. 95/2043, regs. 20, 21; ord. 95/2044, art. 2.

1265. Housing (Right to Buy) (Prescribed Forms) (Welsh Forms) Regulations 1988.
revoked: regs. 94/2932, reg. 1.

1328. Matrimonial Causes (Costs) Rules 1988.
rule 10, see *Children Act 1989 (Taxation of Costs), Re* [1994] 2 F.L.R. 934, Cazalet J.
Sch. 1, para. 1(2)(4)(a), see *Children Act 1989 (Taxation of Costs), Re* [1994] 2 F.L.R. 934, Cazalet J.
Sch. 2, see *Children Act 1989 (Taxation of Costs), Re* [1994] 2 F.L.R. 934, Cazalet J.

1347. Income Tax (Interest Relief) (Housing Associations) Regulations 1988.
reg. 3, amended: regs. 95/1212, reg. 3.
reg. 4, substituted: regs. 95/1212, reg. 4.
reg. 5, substituted: regs. 95/1212, reg. 5.
regs. 5A–5D, inserted: regs. 95/1212, reg. 5.

1371. Local Government Act 1988 (Defined Activities) (Competition) (England) Regulations 1988.
reg. 5, referred to: regs. 95/1973, reg. 3.

1373. Local Government Act 1988 (Defined Activities) (Specified Periods) (England) Regulations 1988.
disapplied: regs. 95/2484, reg. 4.

1391. Education (Fees and Awards) (Amendment) Regulations 1988.
revoked: regs. 94/3042, reg. 17.

1413. Local Government Act 1988 (Defined Activities) (Competition) (Scotland) Regulations 1988.
reg. 3, amended: regs. 95/1972, reg. 2.
reg. 5, amended: regs. 95/1972, reg. 2.
reg. 5A, inserted: regs. 95/1802, reg. 2.

1420. Judicial Pensions (Requisite Benefits) Order 1988.
art. 2, amended: ord. 95/2647, art. 9.
art. 12, amended: ord. 95/2647, art. 9.

1422. Young Offender Institution Rules 1988.
amended by 1994 No. 3194.
rule 4, substituted: rules 95/984, rule 2.
rule 53, amended: rules 95/984, rule 2.
rule 60, amended: rules 95/984, rule 2.

1423. Education Authority Bursaries (Scotland) Amendment Regulations 1988.
revoked: regs. 95/1739, reg. 6.

1454. National Health Service (General Medical and Pharmaceutical Services) (Scotland) Amendment (No. 2) Regulations 1988.
revoked: regs. 95/414, reg. 13.

NO.

1988—cont.

1468. Local Government Act 1988 (Defined Activities) (Competition) (Wales) Regulations 1988.
reg. 5, referred to: regs. 95/1973, reg. 3.

1478. Goods Vehicle (Plating and Testing) Regulations 1988.
see *D.P.P.* v. *Derbyshire* [1994] RTR 351, D.C.

1547. Merchant Shipping (Medical Stores) (Fishing Vessels) Regulations 1988.
revoked: regs. 95/1802, reg. 1.

1551. Leeds Development Corporation (Planning Functions) Order 1988.
revoked: ord. 95/389, art. 2.

1586. Electro-medical Equipment (EEC Requirements) Regulations 1988.
reg. 2, amended: regs. 94/3017, reg. 27.
reg. 3, substituted: regs. 94/3017, reg. 27.

1592. Hartlepools Water (Leechmire Borehole) Order 1988.
revoked: ord. 95/79, Sch. 2.

1652. Teachers' Superannuation (Consolidation) Regulations 1988.
applied: regs. 95/1019, Sch. D6.
reg. B1, substituted: regs. 95/2004, reg. 3.
reg. B2, revoked: regs. 95/2004, reg. 4.
reg. B4, amended: regs. 95/2004, reg. 5.
reg. C8, referred to: regs. 94/2924, reg. 7.
reg. C8A, referred to: regs. 94/2924, reg. 7.
reg. C13, referred to: regs. 94/2924, reg. 15.
reg. E14, amended: regs. 95/2004, reg. 6.
reg. F1, referred to: regs. 94/2924, reg. 11.
reg. H3, amended: regs. 95/2004, reg. 7.
Sch. 1, amended: regs. 95/2004, reg. 8.
Pt. E, referred to: regs. 94/2924, reg. 7.

1657. Control of Substances Hazardous to Health Regulations 1988.
revoked: regs. 94/3246, reg. 18.

1684. Alcoholic Liquors Duties (Beer-based Beverages) Order 1988.
revoked: ord. 94/2904, art. 2.

1715. Central Institutions (Scotland) Regulations 1988.
revoked in pt.: ord. 95/471, art. 47, ord. 95/2216, art. 24.

1724. Social Fund Cold Weather Payment (General) Regulations 1988.
reg. 3, amended: regs. 95/2620, reg. 2.
Sch., amended: regs. 95/2620, reg. 3.

1771. Trade Descriptions (Places of Production) (Marking) Order 1988.
art. 1, amended: regs. 94/3142, reg. 21.
art. 1, amended: regs. 94/3144, reg. 11.

1803. Importation of Milk Regulations 1988.
revoked: regs. 95/1086, reg. 23.

NO.

1988—cont.

1812. Town and Country Planning (Applications) Regulations 1988.
applied: regs. 95/419, reg. 1.

1813. Town and Country Planning General Development Order 1988.
revoked: ord. 95/418, art. 9, ord. 95/419, art. 28.
art. 1, amended: ord. 95/298, art. 3.
art. 3, amended: ord. 95/298, art. 2.
Sch. 2, Pt. 3, amended: ord. 95/298, art. 3.
Sch. 2, Pt. 6, amended: ord. 94/298, art. 4.
Sch. 2, Pt. 32, inserted: ord. 95/298, art. 5.
Class A, Sch. 2, Pt. 6, see *Maidstone District Council* v. *O'Neill* (ref: T/APP/C/93/U2335/630325) (1994) 9 P.A.D. 747.

1814. Importation of Milk (Scotland) Regulations 1988.
revoked: regs. 95/1372, reg. 23.

1821. Police (Amendment) (No. 2) Regulations 1988.
revoked: regs. 95/215, reg. 70.

1856. Patents, Designs and Marks (Guinea-Bissau and Malaysia) (Convention and Relevant Countries) Order 1988.
revoked: ord. 94/3219, art. 3 (designs), ord. 94/3220, art. 3 (patents).

1915. Local Government Act 1988 (Competition) (Defined Activities) Order 1988.
art. 3, applied: regs. 95/1973, reg. 2.

1956. National Health Service (Superannuation) (Scotland) Amendment Regulations 1988.
revoked: regs. 95/365, reg. V2.

1976. Act of Sederunt (Small Claim Rules) 1988.
rule 12(4), see *Calto* v. *Lindsay & Kirk (Sh. Ct.)*, 1995 S.C.L.R. 541.
rule 13(5), see *Calto* v. *Lindsay & Kirk (Sh. Ct.)*, 1995 S.C.L.R. 541.
rule 13(6), see *Calto* v. *Lindsay & Kirk (Sh. Ct.)*, 1995 S.C.L.R. 541.

1992. Parliamentary Constituencies (Scotland) (Miscellaneous Changes) Order 1988.
revoked: ord. 95/1037, art. 4.

2013. Act of Sederunt (Proceedings in the Sheriff Court under the Debtors (Scotland) Act 1987) 1988.
rule 68, amended: Act 95/1876, rule 2; Act 94/3086, para. 2.

2039. Weights and Measures (Intoxicating Liquors) Order 1988.
art. 1, amended: ord. 94/2868, art. 2.
art. 5, amended: ord. 94/2868, art. 2.

2040. Weights and Measures (Miscellaneous Foods) Order 1988.
art. 4, amended: ord. 94/2868, art. 2.

NO.

1988—cont.

2040. Weights and Measures (Miscellaneous Foods) Order 1988—*cont.*
art. 11, amended: ord. 94/2868, art. 2.
Sch. 1, amended: ord. 94/2868, art. 2.

2133. Air Navigation (Dangerous Goods) (Second Amendment) Regulations 1988.
revoked: regs. 94/3187, reg. 2.

2151. Civil Aviation (Joint Financing) Regulations 1988.
revoked: regs. 94/3055, reg. 3.

2162. Police (Amendment) (No. 3) Regulations 1988.
revoked: regs. 95/215, reg. 70.

2190. Milk and Dairies (Semi-skimmed and Skimmed Milk) (Heat Treatment) (Scotland) Regulations 1988.
revoked: regs. 95/1372, reg. 23.

2191. Milk (Special Designations) (Scotland) Order 1988.
revoked: regs. 95/1372, reg. 23.

2206. Milk and Dairies (Semi-skimmed and Skimmed Milk) (Heat Treatment and Labelling) Regulations 1988.
revoked: regs. 95/1086, reg. 23.

2255. General Medical Council Preliminary Proceedings Committee and Professional Conduct Committee (Procedure) Rules 1988.
rule 17, amended: rules 94/3298, rule 2.

2256. Church of England Pensions Regulations 1988.
applied: regs. 95/1019, Sch. B5.

2259. National Health Service (General Medical and Pharmaceutical Services) (Scotland) Amendment (No. 3) Regulations 1988.
revoked: regs. 95/414, reg. 13.

2264. Zoonoses Order 1988.
applied: ord. 95/1928.

2290. Advice and Assistance (Assistance by Way of Representation) (Scotland) Regulations 1988.
reg. 3, amended: regs. 95/1219, reg. 3.

1989

1. Appropriation (Northern Ireland) Order 1989.
revoked: ord. 95/1969, art. 6.

8. Appropriation (Northern Ireland) (No. 2) Order 1989.
revoked: ord. 95/1969, art. 6.

9. Appropriation (Northern Ireland) (No. 3) Order 1989.
revoked: ord. 95/1969, art. 6.

17. Appropriation (Northern Ireland) (No. 4) Order 1989.
revoked: ord. 95/1969, art. 6.

NO.

1989—cont.

32. Personal Community Charge (Students) Regulations 1989.
regs. 2, 3, 6, see *South Norfolk District Council* v. *Norfolk Valuation and Community Charge Tribunal and Emerson*; *Birmingham City Council* v. *Birmingham Valuation and Community Charge Tribunal and Adamson* [1994] RVR 64, Lathan J.

128. Farm and Conservation Grant Scheme 1989.
para. 3, amended: ord. 95/890, para. 3.
para. 5, amended: ord. 95/890, para. 4.
Sch. 1, para. 1, amended: scheme 94/3002, art. 4.
Sch. 1, para. 9C, inserted: ord. 95/890, para. 5.
Sch. 1, para. 9D, inserted: ord. 95/890, para. 5.

285. Zoonoses Order 1989.
applied: regs. 95/540, reg. 16.

326. National Health Service (Charges for Drugs and Appliances) (Scotland) Regulations 1989.
applied: regs. 95/416, Sch. 1.
reg. 3, amended: regs. 95/699, reg. 2.
reg. 7, applied: regs. 95/414, reg. 3.
reg. 8, amended: regs. 95/699, regs. 2, 3.
Schs. 1, 2, 3, substituted: regs. 95/699, regs. 2.

338. Civil Legal Aid (Assessment of Resources) Regulations 1989.
reg. 4, amended: regs. 95/797, reg. 2.
reg. 7, see *R.* v. *Legal Aid Assessment Officer, ex p. Rose* [1994] C.O.D. 244, D.C.
Sch. 3, para. 14B, see *R.* v. *Legal Aid Board, ex p. Clark* (1994) 6 Admin. L.R. 153, Macpherson J.

339. Civil Legal Aid (General) Regulations 1989.
reg. 4, revoked: regs. 95/948, reg. 3.
reg. 50, see *North and North* v. *Ratcliffe*, November 4, 1994, District Judge Butler; Burton-Upon-Trent County Ct. [*Ex rel. David Evans, Barrister*].
reg. 66, see *B. and H. (Minors) (Costs: Legal Aid), Re* [1994] 1 F.L.R. 327, Ward J.
reg. 67, see *B. and H. (Minors) (Costs: Legal Aid), Re* [1994] 1 F.L.R. 327, Ward J.
reg. 107(3)(b), see *Children Act 1989 (Taxation of Costs), Re* [1994] 2 F.L.R. 934, Cazalet J.
reg. 124, see *Barker* v. *Rye*, September 20, 1995, H.H.J. Hamilton, Derby County Ct.
reg. 140, see *Lewis* v. *Lewis*, February 21, 1995; H.H.J. Wilson sitting as a deputy judge.
reg. 142, see *Lewis* v. *Lewis*, February 21, 1995; H.H.J. Wilson sitting as a deputy judge.

NO.

1989—cont.

340. Legal Advice and Assistance Regulations 1989.
reg. 4, amended: regs. 95/949, reg. 4.
reg. 11, amended: regs. 95/795, reg. 3.
reg. 30, amended: regs. 95/949, reg. 5.
Sch. 6, substituted: regs. 95/949, reg. 6.

341. Legal Advice and Assistance (Duty Solicitor) (Remuneration) Regulations 1989.
reg. 2, amended: regs. 95/951, reg. 4.
reg. 5, amended: regs. 95/951, reg. 5.

342. Legal Advice and Assistance at Police Stations (Remuneration) Regulations 1989.
reg. 2, amended: regs. 94/3303, reg. 2.
reg. 5, amended: regs. 94/3303, reg. 3.
Sch., substituted: regs. 95/950, reg. 3.

343. Legal Aid in Criminal and Care Proceedings (Costs) Regulations 1989.
applied: regs. 95/948, reg. 3.
see *R.* v. *Supreme Court Taxing Office, ex p. John Singh & Co*, *The Times*, May 3, 1995, Latham J.
reg. 5, see *R.* v. *Liverpool Justices, ex p. R.M. Broudie & Co.* [1994] C.O.D. 436, D.C.
reg. 6, amended: regs. 95/952, reg. 4.
reg. 9, amended: regs. 95/952, reg. 4.
reg. 40, see *R.* v. *Liverpool Justices, ex p. R.M. Broudie & Co.* [1994] C.O.D. 436, D.C.
Sch. 1, para. 1, substituted: regs. 95/952, reg. 5.
Sch. 1, para. 3(b), see *R.* v. *Legal Aid Board, ex p. R.M. Broudie & Co.* [1994] C.O.D. 435, D.C.
Sch. 1, Pt. I, amended: regs. 95/952, reg. 6.
Sch. 1, Pt. II, amended: regs. 95/952, reg. 7.
Sch. 1, Pt. III, amended: regs. 95/952, reg. 8.

344. Legal Aid in Criminal and Care Proceedings (General) Regulations 1989.
amended: regs. 95/542, regs. 4, 5, 6, 7, 8, 9, 10 and 11.
reg. 3, amended: regs. 95/542, reg. 4.
reg. 4, amended: regs. 95/542, reg. 5.
reg. 8, substituted: regs. 95/542, reg. 6.
reg. 11(3), see *R.* v. *Highbury Corner Magistrates' Court, ex p. Sonn & Co.*, *The Times*, May 23, 1995, D.C.
reg. 12, amended: regs. 95/542, reg. 7.
reg. 17, amended: regs. 95/542, reg. 8.
reg. 19, amended: regs. 95/542, reg. 9.
reg. 23, amended: regs. 95/542, reg. 10.
reg. 23(1), see *R.* v. *Highbury Corner Magistrates' Court, ex p. Sonn & Co.*, *The Times*, May 23, 1995, D.C.
reg. 44(7), see *R.* v. *Highbury Corner Magistrates' Court, ex p. Sonn & Co.*, *The Times*, May 23, 1995, D.C.
Sch. 2, amended: regs. 95/542, reg. 11.
Sch. 4, amended: regs. 95/796, reg. 2.

NO.

1989—cont.

363. National Health Service (Dental Charges) (Scotland) Regulations 1989.
reg. 4, amended: regs. 95/703, reg. 2.

371. Local Government Superannuation (Amendment) Regulations 1988.
regs. 2–13, revoked: regs. 95/1019 Sch. M5.
regs. 15–27, revoked: regs. 95/1019 Sch. M5.
reg. 29, revoked: regs. 95/1019 Sch. M5.

372. Local Government (Superannuation and Compensation) Regulations 1989.
regs. 2–8, amended: regs. 95/1019 Sch. M5.

380. Dairy Produce Quotas Regulations 1989.
See *W.E. & R.A. Holdcroft* v. *Staffordshire County Council* [1994] 28 EG 131, C.A.
reg. 9, see *Holdcroft* v. *Staffordshire County Council* [1994] EGCS 56, C.A.

392. National Health Service (Optical Charges and Payments) (Scotland) Regulations 1989.
reg. 1, amended: regs. 95/2369, reg. 2; regs. 95/1, reg. 2, regs. 95/705, reg. 2.
reg. 4, amended: regs. 95/705, reg. 3.
reg. 8, amended: regs. 95/705, reg. 4.
reg. 9, amended: regs. 95/705, reg. 5.
reg. 10, amended: regs. 95/705, reg. 6.
reg. 11, amended: regs. 95/705, reg. 7.
reg. 17, amended: regs. 95/705, reg. 8.
reg. 20, amended: regs. 95/705, reg. 9.
Sch. 1, amended: regs. 95/705, reg. 10.
Sch. 2, substituted: regs. 95/705, reg. 10.
Sch. 3, para. 1, amended: regs. 95/705, reg. 10.
Sch. 3, para. 2, amended: regs. 95/705, reg. 10.

394. National Health Service (Dental Charges) Regulations 1989.
reg. 4, amended: regs. 95/444, reg. 2.

396. National Health Service (Optical Charges and Payments) Regulations 1989.
amended; regs. 95/34.
amended: regs. 95/691, regs. 2–10.
reg. 1, amended: regs. 95/691, reg. 2, regs. 95/2307, reg. 2.
reg. 4, amended: regs. 95/691, reg. 3.
reg. 8, amended: regs. 95/691, reg. 4.
reg. 9, amended: regs. 95/691, reg. 5.
reg. 10, amended: regs. 95/691, reg. 6.
reg. 11, amended: regs. 95/691, reg. 7.
reg. 17, amended: regs. 95/691, reg. 8.
reg. 20, amended: regs. 95/691, reg. 9.
Sch. 1, amended: regs. 95/691, reg. 10.
Sch. 3, substituted: regs. 95/691, reg. 10.

NO.

1989—cont.

419. National Health Service (Charges for Drugs and Appliances) Regulations 1989.
see *R.* v. *Secretary of State for the Health Department, ex p. Richardson (C–137/94), The Times*, October 27, 1995, ECJ.
amended: regs. 95/643, regs. 2, 3.
reg. 6, amended: regs. 95/2737, reg. 2.
reg. 8, amended: regs. 95/643, reg. 3.

428. European Parliamentary Elections (Welsh Forms) Order 1989.
Sch. 2, amended: ord. 95/830, art. 6.

429. Representation of the People (Welsh Forms) Order 1989.
Sch. 1, amended: art. 95/830, art. 6.
Sch. 2, amended: art. 95/830, art. 6.

438. Community Charges (Administration and Enforcement) Regulations 1989.
applied: regs. 95/247, reg. 4.
amended by 1995 No. 21.
reg. 4(3), see *R.* v. *Preston Justices, ex p. McCosh, The Times*, January 30, 1995, Turner J.
reg. 6, applied: regs. 95/247, reg. 5.
reg. 7, applied. regs. 95/247, reg. 6.
reg. 29, applied: regs. 95/247, regs. 7, 8. 10, 13.
reg. 29, see *R.* v. *Erewash Borough Council and Ilkestone Justices, ex p. Smedburg and Smedburg* [1994] RVR 60, Auld J.
reg. 31, applied: regs. 95/247, reg. 8.
reg. 32, applied: regs. 95/247, regs. 8, 9.
reg. 34, applied: regs. 95/247, reg. 9.
reg. 35, applied: regs. 95/247, reg. 9.
reg. 36, applied: regs. 95/247, reg. 9.
reg. 39, applied: regs. 95/247, regs. 10, 11, 12.
reg. 39, see *Curtis* v. *Gault & Co. and Mid Devon District Council*, March 10, 1995; H.H.J. McKintosh; Exeter County Ct.
reg. 40, applied: regs. 95/247, reg. 11.
reg. 40, see *R.* v. *Oldbury Justices, ex p. Smith* [1995] 35 RVR 7, Turner J.
reg. 41, applied: regs. 95/247, reg. 12.
reg. 41, see *Harrogate Borough Council* v. *Barker, The Times*, June 2, 1995, Harrison J.; *R.* v. *Oldbury Justices, ex p. Smith* [1995] 35 RVR 7, Turner J.; *R.* v. *South Tyneside Justices, ex p. Martin, The Independent*, September 20, 1995, Sedley J.; *R.* v. *Stoke on Trent Justices, ex p. Booth (CO/774/94)*, March 23, 1995, Owen J.; *R.* v. *Erewash Borough Council and Ilkestone Justices, ex p. Smedburg and Smedburg* [1994] RVR 60, Auld J.

NO.

1989—cont.

438. Community Charges (Administration and Enforcement) Regulations 1989—*cont.*
reg. 42, see *R.* v. *Erewash Borough Council and Ilkestone Justices, ex p. Smedburg and Smedburg* [1994] RVR 60, Auld J.; *R.* v. *Oldbury Justices, ex p. Smith* [1995] 35 RVR 7, Turner J.
reg. 44, applied: regs. 95/247, reg. 14.
reg. 44, see *Preston Borough Council* v. *Riley* [1995] RA 227, C.A.
reg. 45, applied: regs. 95/247, reg. 14.
reg. 47, applied: 95/247, reg. 15.

439. Valuation and Community Charge Tribunals Regulations 1989.
referred to: regs. 95/624, reg. 2.
amended: regs. 95/624, regs. 3–7.
reg. 4, amended: regs. 95/363, reg. 3.
reg. 5, amended: regs. 95/363, reg. 4.
reg. 6, amended: regs. 95/363, reg. 5.
reg. 7, amended: regs. 95/363, reg. 6.
reg. 8, amended: regs. 95/363, reg. 7.
reg. 16, amended: regs. 95/363, reg. 8.
reg. 32, see *Codner* v. *Wiltshire Valuation and Community Charge Tribunal,* (1994) 34 R.V.R. 169, Laws J.
reg. 32(2), see *Regalbourne* v. *East Lindsey District Council* [1994] R.A. 1, C.A.
reg. 35, amended: regs. 95/363, reg. 8.

441. Valuation for Rating (Plant and Machinery) Regulations 1989.
referred to: 1995, c. 45, Sch. 5, para. 31.

533. Preservatives in Food Regulations 1989.
applied: regs. 95/540, reg. 2.

550. Legal Advice and Assistance (Scope) Regulations 1989.
applied: regs. 95/1987, reg. 2.
reg. 7, amended: regs. 95/1987, reg. 3.

581. Preservatives in Food (Scotland) Regulations 1989.
applied: regs. 95/540, reg. 2.

603. Town and Country Planning General Development (Amendment) Order 1988.
revoked: ord. 95/418, art. 9, ord. 95/419, art. 28.

635. Electricity at Work Regulations 1989.
see *Geotechnics* v. *Robbins (Inspector of Factories) (CO 470/95)*, May 2, 1995, Curtis J.

684. Medicines (Fixing of Fees Relating to Medicinal Products for Human Use) Order 1989.
Sch. 1, para. 4, substituted: ord. 95/871, art. 2.
Sch. 1, para. 9A, inserted: ord. 95/871, art. 2.
Sch. 1, para. 10, amended: ord. 95/871, art. 2.

NO.

1989—cont.

728. Low Voltage Electrical Equipment (Safety) Regulations 1989.
revoked: regs. 94/3260, reg. 2.
applied: regs. 94/3076, Sch. 6.

730. Building Societies (Money Transmission Services) Order 1989.
applied: ord. 95/1006, art. 3.

804. National Health Service (Superannuation) Amendment Regulations 1989.
revoked: regs. 95/300, reg. V2.

807. National Health Service (Superannuation) (Scotland) Amendment Regulations 1989.
revoked: regs. 95/365, reg. V2.

840. Health and Safety at Work etc. Act 1974 (Application outside Great Britain) Order 1989.
art. 4, applied: regs. 94/3246, reg. 15.
art. 5, applied: regs. 94/3246, reg. 15.
art. 7, applied: regs. 94/3246, reg. 15.

854. Firearms Rules 1989.
Sch. 1, Pt. II, amended: rules 94/3022, rule 2.

869. Consumer Credit (Exempt Agreements) Order 1989.
Sch. 1, Pt. III, amended: ord. 95/1250, art. 2.

879. Movement of Animals (Records) (Amendment) Order 1989.
amended by 1995 No. 11.

889. Firearms (Scotland) Rules 1989.
Sch. 1, Pt. II, amended: rules 94/3198, rule. 2.

895. Police (Amendment) Regulations 1989.
revoked: regs. 95/215, reg. 70.

900. Birmingham Assay Office Order 1989.
referred to: 1995, c. vi, s. 2.

907. Education (National Curriculum) (Attainment Targets and Programmes of Study in English) Order 1989.
revoked: ord. 95/51, art. 2.

946. Teachers' Superannuation (Additional Voluntary Contributions) Regulations 1989.
revoked: regs. 94/2924, reg. 20.

971. Offshore Installations (Safety Representatives and Safety Committees) Regulations 1989.
reg. 2, amended: regs. 95/738, reg. 23.
reg. 3, substituted: regs. 95/738, reg. 23.
reg. 11, amended: regs. 95/738, reg. 23.
reg. 13, amended: regs. 95/738, reg. 23.
reg. 17, amended: regs. 95/738, reg. 23.
reg. 19, amended: regs. 95/738, reg. 23.
reg. 20, amended: regs. 95/738, reg. 23.
reg. 22, amended: regs. 95/738, reg. 23.
reg. 23, substituted: regs. 95/738, reg. 23, amended: regs. 95/743, reg. 24.
reg. 24, amended: regs. 95/738, reg. 23.
reg. 25, amended: regs. 95/738, reg. 23.

NO.

1989—cont.

971. Offshore Installations (Safety Representatives and Safety Committees) Regulations 1989—*cont.*
reg. 27, substituted: regs. 95/738, reg. 23.
reg. 28, amended: regs. 95/738, reg. 23.

978. Offshore Installations (Included Apparatus or Works) Regulations 1989.
revoked: regs. 95/738, reg. 23.

1029. Offshore Installations (Emergency Pipe-line Valve) Regulations 1989.
reg. 2, amended: regs. 95/738, reg. 23.

1056. Non-Domestic Rating (Collection and Enforcement) (Local Lists) Regulations 1989.
reg. 3, see *Hackney London Borough Council* v. *Mott and Fairman* [1994] RA 381, Auld J.
reg. 4, see *Hackney London Borough Council* v. *Mott and Fairman* [1994] RA 381, Auld J.
reg. 12, see *Hackney London Borough Council* v. *Mott and Fairman* [1994] RA 381, Auld J.
see *R.* v. *Basildon Justices ex p. Holding and Barnes* [1994] RA 157, Schiemann J.
reg. 14, see *R.* v. *Basildon Justices, ex p. Holding and Barnes* [1994] RA 157, Schiemann J.
reg. 15, see *R.* v. *Basildon Justices, ex p. Holding and Barnes* [1994] RA 157, Schiemann J.
reg. 16, see *Trull* v. *Restormel Borough Council* [1994] 34 RVR 122, Latham J.
reg. 17, see *Trull* v. *Restormel Borough Council* [1994] 34 RVR 122, Latham J.
reg. 23, see *Hackney London Borough Council* v. *Mott and Fairman* [1994] RA 381, Auld J.

1058. Non-Domestic Rating (Collection and Enforcement) (Local Lists) Regulations 1989.
applied: regs. 95/212, regs. 4, 5, 6.
see *R.* v. *Basildon Justices, ex p. Holding and Barnes* [1994] C.O.D. 378, Schiemann J.
reg. 12, applied: regs. 95/212, reg. 7.
reg. 14, applied: regs. 95/212, reg. 8.
reg. 16(2), (3), (7), see *R.* v. *Highbury Corner Magistrates' Court, ex p. Uchendu* [1994] R.A. 51, Laws J.
reg. 21, applied: regs. 95/212, reg. 10.

1059. Non-Domestic Rating (Discretionary Relief) Regulations 1989.
applied: regs. 95/212, reg. 11.

1105. Registered Designs Rules 1989.
referred to: rules 95/2165, rule 2.

NO.

1989—cont.

1111. Dock Work (Compensation Payments Scheme) Regulations 1989.
reg. 3, see *Baxter* v. *Limb* [1994] IRLR 572, C.A.

1113. Education Authority Bursaries (Scotland) Amendment Regulations 1989.
revoked: regs. 95/1739, reg. 6.

1133. Education (Assisted Places) (Scotland) Regulations 1989.
revoked: regs. 95/1713, reg. 31.

1134. St. Mary's Music School (Aided Places) Regulations 1989.
applied: regs. 95/1712, reg. 6.
revoked: regs. 95/1712, reg. 17.

1235. Education (Assisted Places) Regulations 1989.
revoked: regs. 95/2016, reg. 24.

1236. Education (Grants) (Music and Ballet Schools) Regulations 1989.
applied: regs. 95/1713, reg. 13.
revoked: regs. 95/2018, reg. 16.
reg. 4, applied: regs. 95/2018, reg. 16.

1237. Education (Assisted Places) (Incidental Expenses) Regulations 1989.
revoked: regs. 95/2017, reg. 16.

1275. Toys (Safety) Regulations 1989.
revoked: regs. 95/204, reg. 1.
See *Balding* v. *Lew Ways*, *The Times*, March 9, 1995, D.C.

1287. Education (Grant-maintained Schools) (Finance) Regulations 1989.
applied: regs. 95/936, reg. 3.

1297. Taxes (Interest Rate) Regulations 1989.
reg. 5, amended: regs. 95/2436, reg. 2.

1299. Income Tax (Stock Lending) Regulations 1989.
reg. 2, amended: regs. 95/1283, reg. 3.
reg. 6, amended: regs. 95/1283, reg. 4.

1303. Copyright, Designs and Patents Act 1988 (Commencement No. 4) Order 1989.
Sch. 2, para. 4, amended: regs. 94/3140, reg. 24.

1341. Police and Criminal Evidence (Northern Ireland) Order 1989.
art. 26, applied: regs. 95/271, reg. 11.
art. 81, amended: 1995, c. 35, Sch. 2.
art. 81A, amended: 1995, c. 35, Sch. 2.

1388. Local Government (Direct Labour Organisations) (Competition) Regulations 1989.
reg. 9, amended: regs. 95/1377, reg. 2.

1462. Local Government Superannuation (Water) Regulations 1989.
reg. 2, amended: regs. 95/1019 Sch. M5.
regs. 4–13, revoked: regs. 95/1019 Sch. M5.
Sch., revoked: regs. 95/1019 Sch. M5.

NO.

1989—cont.

1490. Civil Legal Aid (Scotland) (Fees) Regulations 1989.
Sch. 1, amended: regs. 95/1044, reg. 3.
Sch. 2, amended: regs. 95/1044, reg. 4.
Sch. 3, amended: regs. 95/1044, reg. 5.
Sch. 5, amended: regs. 95/1044, reg. 6.

1590. Town and Country Planning General Development (Amendment) (No. 2) Order 1989.
revoked: ord. 95/418, art. 9, ord. 95/419, art. 28.

1624. Local Government Superannuation (Valuation and Community Charge Tribunals) Regulations 1989.
revoked: regs. 95/1019 Sch. M5.

1671. Offshore Installations and Pipeline Works (First-Aid) Regulations 1989.
reg. 2, amended: regs. 95/738, reg. 23.

1690. Social Security Benefit (Dependency and Computation of Earnings) Amendment Regulations 1989.
reg. 4, applied: regs. 95/310, reg. 25.

1745. Police (Amendment) (No. 2) Regulations 1989.
revoked: regs. 95/215, reg. 70.

1749. National Health Service (Superannuation) (Scotland) Amendment (No. 2) Regulations 1989.
revoked: regs. 95/365, reg. V2.

1815. London Government Reorganisation (Pensions etc.) Regulations 1989.
art. 7, amended: regs. 95/1019 Sch. M5; regs. 95/1019 Sch. M6.

1883. National Health Service (General Medical and Pharmaceutical Services) (Scotland) Amendment Regulations 1989.
revoked: regs. 95/414, reg. 13.

1903. Health and Safety (Enforcing Authority) Regulations 1989.
amended by 1994 No. 3247.
reg. 2, applied: regs. 94/3140, reg. 3.
reg. 3, referred to: regs. 94/3140, reg. 22.

1938. Sale of Marks Regulations 1989.
Sch. 1, para. 1, amended: regs. 94/2977, reg. 3.
Sch. 1, para. 2, amended: regs. 94/2977, reg. 3.
Sch. 1, para. 3, amended: regs. 94/2977, reg. 3.
Sch. 1, para. 3A, inserted: regs. 94/2977, reg. 3.
Sch. 1, para. 4, amended: regs. 94/2977, reg. 3.
Sch. 1, para. 6, amended: regs. 94/2977, reg. 3.
Sch. 1, para. 8, amended: regs. 94/2977, reg. 3.
Sch. 1, para. 10, amended: regs. 94/2977, reg. 3.
Sch. 2, para. 1, amended: regs. 94/2977, reg. 4.

NO.

1989—cont.

1938. Sale of Marks Regulations 1989—*cont.*
Sch. 2, para. 3, substituted: regs. 94/2977, reg. 4.
Sch. 2, para. 5, amended: regs. 94/2977, reg. 4.
Sch. 2, para. 6, amended: regs. 94/2977, reg. 4.
Sch. 2, para. 7, substituted: regs. 94/2977, reg. 4.
Sch. 2, para. 8, amended: regs. 94/2977, reg. 4.
Sch. 2, para. 9, amended: regs. 94/2977, reg. 4.
Sch. 2, para. 11, amended: regs. 94/2977, reg. 4.
Sch. 2, para. 14, substituted: regs. 94/2977, reg. 4.

1990. National Health Service (General Medical and Pharmaceutical Services) (Scotland) Amendment (No. 2) Regulations 1989.
revoked: regs. 95/414, reg. 13.

2002. Social Security (Philippines) Order 1989.
modified: ord. 95/767, art. 2.

2004. Air Navigation Order 1989.
revoked: ord. 95/1038, art. 2.
applied: regs. 95/1093.
applied: regs. 94/3011, reg. 3.
applied: regs. 94/3055, reg. 2.
applied: regs. 95/497, reg. 2.
art. 47, applied: regs. 94/3187.
art. 106, applied: regs. 94/3187.
art. 106, applied: ord. 95/418, art. 1.

2053. The Movement of Animals (Records) (Amendment) (No. 2) Order 1989.
amended by 1995 No. 11.
amended by 1995 No. 12.

2061. Bovine Offal (Prohibition) Regulations 1989.
revoked: regs. 95/1955, reg. 2.
reg. 2, amended: regs. 95/613, reg. 2, regs. 95/614, reg. 16, applied: regs. 95/614, reg. 5.
reg. 9, amended: regs. 95/613, reg. 2, regs. 95/614, reg. 16.
reg. 12, amended: regs. 95/613, reg. 2.
reg. 15, amended: regs. 95/613, reg. 2.
reg. 16, inserted: regs. 95/613, reg. 2.

2190. Gaming Act (Variation of Monetary Limits) (No. 2) Order 1989.
applied: ord. 95/2288, art. 3.
revoked: ord. 95/2288, art. 4.

2206. Town and Country Planning (Leeds Urban Development Area) Special Development Order 1989.
revoked: ord. 95/389, art. 2.

2221. Civil Aviation (Joint Financing) (Amendment) Regulations 1989.
revoked: regs. 94/3055, reg. 3.

2249. Gaming Act (Variation of Monetary Limits) (Scotland) (No. 2) Order 1989.
revoked: ord. 95/2360, art. 4.

NO.

1989—cont.

2261. Non-Domestic Rating (Unoccupied Property) Regulations 1989.
reg. 2, amended: regs. 95/549, reg. 2; see *Barnet London Borough Council* v. *London Transport Property, The Times*, May 11, 1995, Harrison J.

2263. Central Rating Lists Regulations 1989.
referred to: 1995, c. 45, Sch. 5, para. 31.
revoked: regs. 94/3121, reg. 8.
reg. 2, amended (retrosp.): regs. 94/3121, regs. 3, 4.

2303. Non-Domestic Rating (Miscellaneous Provisions) (No. 2) Regulations 1989.
reg. 2, amended: regs. 94/3122, reg. 2.
reg. 5, amended: regs. 94/3122, reg. 3.

2325. Medicines (Exemptions from Licences) (Intermediate Medicated Feeding Stuffs) Order 1989.
art. 3, inserted: regs. 94/3142, reg. 21.

2382. Milk and Dairies (Semi-skimmed and Skimmed Milk) (Heat Treatment and Labelling) (Amendment) Regulations 1988.
revoked: regs. 95/1086, reg. 23.

2383. Milk (Special Designation) Regulations 1989.
revoked: regs. 95/1086, reg. 23.

2385. Valuation Roll and Valuation Notice (Scotland) Order 1989.
Sch., amended: ord. 95/573, art. 2.

2386. Valuation Timetable (Scotland) Order 1989.
revoked: ord. 95/164, art. 4.

2405. Insolvency (Northern Ireland) Order 1989.
art. 242, applied: regs. 95/201, reg. 14.
Sch. 9, para. 42, revoked: regs. 95/1442, reg. 52.
Sch. 9, para. 43, revoked in pt.: regs. 95/1442, reg. 52.
Sch. 9, para. 50, revoked in pt.: regs. 95/1442, reg. 52.
Sch. 9, para. 51, revoked: regs. 95/1442, reg. 52.

2426. (L. 19) County Court (Amendment No. 4) Rules 1989.
rule 13, see *Walters* v. *Newton*, February 2, 1994; H.H.J. Irvine; Oxford County Ct.
rule 14, see *Walters* v. *Newton*, February 2, 1994; H.H.J. Irvine; Oxford County Ct.

2471. British Gas plc (Rateable Values) Order 1989.
revoked: ord. 94/3283, art. 4.

2472. British Waterways Board (Rateable Values) Order 1989.
revoked: ord. 94/3281, art. 2.

2473. Docks and Harbours (Rateable Values) Order 1989.
art. 2, amended: ord. 94/3280, art. 2.
art. 3, amended: ord. 94/3280, art. 2.
art. 4, amended: ord. 94/3280, art. 2.

NO.

1989—cont.

2474. Electricity Generators (Rateable Values) Order 1989.
revoked: ord. 94/3282, reg. 4.

2475. Electricity Supply Industry (Rateable Values) Order 1989.
revoked: ord. 94/3282, reg. 4.

2477. Railways (Rateable Values) Order 1989.
revoked: ord. 94/3284, art. 4.

2478. Telecommunications Industry (Rateable Values) Order 1989.
revoked: ord. 94/3281, art. 2.

2479. Water Undertakers (Rateable Values) Order 1989.
revoked: ord. 94/3285, art. 4.

1990

4. Appropriation (Northern Ireland) Order 1990.
revoked: ord. 95/1969, art. 6.

9. Appropriation (Northern Ireland) (No. 2) Order 1990.
revoked: ord. 95/1969, art. 6.

13. Electrical Equipment for Explosive Atmospheres (Certification) Regulations 1990.
reg. 2, amended: regs. 95/1186, reg. 2.
reg. 12, substituted: regs. 95/1186, reg. 2.

27. Financial Services Act 1986 (Investment Advertisements) (Exemptions) Order 1990.
revoked: regs. 95/1266, reg. 19.

105. Non-Domestic Rating (Collection and Enforcement) (Miscellaneous Provisions) Regulations 1990.
reg. 3, see *Ford* v. *Burnley Borough Council, The Times*, March 6, 1995, Pill J.

112. Bovine Offal (Prohibition) (Scotland) Regulations 1990.
revoked: regs. 95/1955, reg. 2.
reg. 2, amended: regs. 95/537, reg. 2.
reg. 2, amended: regs. 95/614, reg. 16.
reg. 6, amended: regs. 95/537, reg. 2.
reg. 11, amended: regs. 95/537, reg. 2.
reg. 12, amended: regs. 95/537, reg. 2.
reg. 17, amended: regs. 95/537, reg. 2.
reg. 24, amended: regs. 95/537, reg. 2.
reg. 26, amended: regs. 95/537, reg. 2.
reg. 27, amended: regs. 95/537, reg. 2.
reg. 32, amended: regs. 95/537, reg. 2.
reg. 34, revoked: regs. 95/537, reg. 2.

193. Electricity (Class Exemptions from the Requirement for a Licence) Order 1990.
revoked: ord. 95/909, art. 6.

322. Social Security (Recoupment) Regulations 1990.
reg. 2, amended: regs. 95/829, reg. 22.

NO.

1990—cont.

364. Merchant Shipping (Light Dues) Regulations 1990.
Sch., Pt. I, amended: regs. 95/525, reg. 2.

380. Act of Sederunt (Copyright, Designs and Patents) 1990.
para. 1, amended: Act 94/3066, para. 2.
para. 2, amended: Act 94/3066, para. 2.
para. 3, amended: Act 94/3066, para. 2.

382. National Health Service (Superannuation) (Scotland) Amendment Regulations 1990.
revoked: regs. 95/365, reg. V2.

396. Rent Officers (Additional Functions) (Scotland) Order 1990.
referred to: ord. 95/872, art. 2.
art. 2, amended: ord. 94/3108, art. 2.
art. 5, amended: ord. 95/2361, art. 2.
art. 8, referred to: regs. 95/1643, reg. 7.
Sch. 1, para. 2A, amended: ord. 94/3108, art. 2.
Sch. 1, para. 6A, inserted: ord. 95/2361, art. 2.
Sch. 1, para. 7, amended: ord. 95/2361, art. 2.

401. Police (Amendment) Regulations 1990.
revoked: regs. 95/215, reg. 70.

423. Education (National Curriculum) (Attainment Targets and Programmes of Study in English) (No. 2) Order 1989.
revoked: ord. 95/51, art. 2.

424. Education (National Curriculum) (Attainment Targets and Programmes of Study in Technology) Order 1990.
revoked: ord. 95/56, art. 2.

426. Local Authorities (Capital Finance) (Approved Investments) Regulations 1990.
reg. 1, amended: regs. 95/1982, reg. 12.
reg. 3, amended: regs. 95/1982, reg. 12.
Sch., para. 29, inserted: regs. 95/850, reg. 13.
Sch., Pt. II, amended: ord. 95/1041, art. 3.

428. Rent Officers (Additional Functions) Order 1990.
referred to: ord. 95/872, art. 2.
art. 2, amended: ord. 94/3040, art. 2.
art. 5, amended: ord. 95/2365, art. 2.
Sch. 1, para. 2A, amended: ord. 94/3040, art. 2.
Sch. 1, para. 6A, inserted: ord. 95/2365, art. 2.
Sch. 1, para. 7, amended: ord. 95/2365, art. 2.

432. Local Authorities (Capital Finance) Regulations 1990.
applied: ord. 95/1041, art. 3.
reg. 2, amended: regs. 95/850, reg. 3.

NO.

1990—cont.

432. Local Authorities (Capital Finance) Regulations 1990—*cont.*
reg. 3, amended: regs. 95/1982, reg. 3.
reg. 4A, inserted: regs. 95/1982, reg. 4.
reg. 7, amended: regs. 95/850, reg. 4.
reg. 8, amended: regs. 95/1982, reg. 5, regs. 95/850, reg. 5.
reg. 9B, amended: regs. 95/850, reg. 10.
reg. 10, applied and amended: regs. 95/798, reg. 13.
reg. 12, applied and amended: regs. 95/798, reg. 13.
reg. 13, applied and amended: regs. 95/798, reg. 13.
reg. 13, amended: regs. 95/1982, reg. 6.
reg. 14, amended: regs. 95/1982, reg. 7, regs. 95/850, reg. 6.
reg. 19D, inserted: regs. 95/1526, reg. 2.
reg. 20, amended: regs. 95/850, reg. 7, regs. 95/1526, reg. 3.
reg. 21, amended: regs. 95/850, reg. 7.
reg. 26, amended: regs. 95/1982, reg. 8, regs. 95/850, reg. 9.
reg. 26A, amended: regs. 95/1982, reg. 9.
reg. 27, amended: regs. 95/850, reg. 11.
Sch. 3, Pt. II, amended: regs. 95/1982, reg. 10, regs. 95/850, reg. 21.
Sch. 4, Pt. II, amended: regs. 95/850, reg. 12.
Sch. 5, para. 6, amended: regs. 95/1982, reg. 11.

457. Town and Country Planning General Development (Amendment) Order 1990.
revoked: ord. 95/418, art. 9.

473. Civil Legal Aid (Scotland) (Fees) Amendment Regulations 1990.
reg. 2, revoked: regs. 95/1044, reg. 7.

502. Central Rating Lists (Amendment) Regulations 1990.
revoked: regs. 94/3121, reg. 8.

503. Local Government Superannuation (Funds etc.) Regulations 1990.
revoked: regs. 95/1019 Sch. M5.

505. Valuation for Rating (Decapitalisation Rate) (Scotland) Regulations 1990.
reg. 3, amended: regs. 94/3256, reg. 5.

545. Community Charge (Deduction from Income Support) (No. 2) Regulations 1990.
reg. 2, see *R.* v. *Newcastle Under Lyme Justices, ex p. Massey* [1993] C.O.D. 464, D.C.

549. Education (Grant-maintained Schools) (Finance) Regulations 1990.
applied: regs. 95/587, reg. 3.
applied: regs. 95/936, reg. 3.

NO.

1990—cont.

563. Town and Country Planning (Fees for Applications and Deemed Applications) (Scotland) Regulations 1990.
reg. 11, amended: regs. 94/3269, reg. 4.
reg. 11A, amended: regs. 94/3269, reg. 2.
reg. 12, amended: regs. 94/3269, reg. 2.
Sch., para. 4, amended: regs. 94/3269, reg. 3.
Sch., para. 6, amended: regs. 94/3269, reg. 3.
Sch., para. 7, amended: regs. 94/3269, reg. 3.
Sch., para. 10, amended: regs. 94/3269, reg. 3.
Sch., para. 16, amended: regs. 94/3269, reg. 3.

566. Medicines (Exemption from Licences) (Wholesale Dealing) Order 1990.
art. 1, amended: regs. 94/3142, reg. 21; regs. 94/3144, reg. 11.
art. 2, amended: ord. 94/3142, reg. 21; regs. 94/3144, reg. 11.

572. Companies (Forms) (Amendment) Regulations 1990.
Sch. 2, amended: regs. 95/736, reg. 4.

582. Non-Domestic Rating (Alteration of Lists and Appeals) Regulations 1990.
reg. 4, see *Hackney London Borough Council* v. *Mott and Fairman* [1994] RA 381, Auld J.
reg. 8, see *Hackney London Borough Council* v. *Mott and Fairman* [1994] RA 381, Auld J.
reg. 9, see *Hackney London Borough Council* v. *Mott and Fairman* [1994] RA 381, Auld J.
reg. 16, see *Hackney London Borough Council* v. *Mott and Fairman* [1994] RA 381, Auld J.

618. Plant Breeders' Rights (Fees) (Amendment) Regulations 1990.
Sch., Pt. II, amended: Scheme 95/606, art. 3.

720. Passenger Transport Executives (Capital Finance) Order 1990.
art. 1, amended: ord. 95/1431, art. 2.
art. 2, amended: ord. 95/1431, art. 2.
art. 5, amended: ord. 95/1431, art. 2.

751. Value Added Tax (Tour Operators) (Amendment) Order 1990.
art. 4, revoked: ord. 95/1495, art. 3.

763. Local Government (Promotion of Economic Development) Regulations 1990.
reg. 2, amended: regs. 95/556, reg. 2.

804. Gas and Electricity Industry's (Rateable Values) (Amendment) Order 1990.
revoked: ord. 94/3282, art. 4.

NO.

1990—cont.

817. Docks and Harbours (Rateable Values) (Scotland) Order 1990.
art. 2, amended: ord. 95/375, art. 2.
art. 4, amended: ord. 95/375, art. 3.
art. 7, amended: ord. 95/375, art. 4.
art. 8, amended: ord. 95/375, art. 4.

851. Local Government Officers (Political Restrictions) Regulations 1990.
applied: ord. 95/789, art. 2.

855. British Waterways Board (Rateable Values) (Scotland) Order 1990.
revoked: ord. 95/374, art. 2.

864. Court of Protection (Enduring Powers of Attorney) (Amendment) Rules 1990.
revoked: rules 94/3047, rule 29.

879. Copyright (Certification of Licensing Scheme for Educational Recording of Broadcasts and Cable Programmes) (Educational Recording Agency Limited) Order 1990.
amended by 1995 No. 12.

883. National Health Service (General Medical and Pharmaceutical Services) (Scotland) Amendment Regulations 1990.
revoked: regs. 95/414, reg. 13.

932. Local Elections (Principal Areas) (Declaration of Acceptance of Office) Order 1990.
referred to: ord. 95/546, art. 5.

1013. Nitrate Sensitive Areas (Designation) Order 1990.
revoked: regs. 95/1708, reg. 3.

1017. Police (Discipline) (Senior Officers) (Scotland) Regulations 1990.
reg. 2, amended: regs. 95/647, reg. 3.
reg. 13, amended: regs. 95/647, reg. 2.

1020. Public Service Vehicles (Conduct of Drivers, Inspectors, Conductors and Passengers) Regulations 1990.
reg. 6, amended: regs. 95/186, reg. 2.

1082. Education (National Curriculum) (Attainment Targets and Programmes of Study in Welsh) Order 1990.
revoked: ord. 95/69, art. 7.

1116. Gloucester Harbour Revision Order (Amendment) Order 1990.
revoked: ord. 94/3162, art. 31(2).

1127. Police (Amendment) (No. 2) Regulations 1990.
revoked: regs. 95/215, reg. 70.

1179. Spirit Drinks Regulations 1990.
reg. 2, amended: regs. 95/732, reg. 2.
reg. 3, amended: regs. 95/732, reg. 2.
reg. 4, revoked: regs. 95/732, reg. 2.
reg. 5, amended: regs. 95/732, reg. 2.
Sch., substituted: regs. 95/732, reg. 2.

1187. Nitrate Sensitive Areas (Designation) (Amendment) Order 1990.
revoked: regs. 95/1708, reg. 3.

NO.

1990—cont.

1199. Drug Trafficking Offences Act 1986 (Designated Countries and Territories) Order 1990.
see *Londono, Re, The Times*, July 11, 1995, C.A.

1240. Slaughter of Animals (Humane Conditions) (Scotland) Regulations 1990.
referred to: regs. 95/539, reg. 2.
revoked: regs. 95/731, reg. 28.

1242. Slaughter of Animals (Humane Conditions) Regulations 1990.
referred to: regs. 95/539, reg. 2.
revoked: regs. 95/731, reg. 28.

1243. Slaughter of Poultry (Humane Conditions) (Amendment) Regulations 1990.
revoked: regs. 95/731, reg. 28.

1345. St. Mary's Music School (Aided Places) Amendment Regulations 1990.
revoked: regs. 95/1712, reg. 17.

1346. Education (Assisted Places) (Scotland) Amendment Regulations 1990.
revoked: regs. 95/1713, reg. 31.

1347. Education Authority Bursaries (Scotland) (Amendment) Regulations 1990.
revoked: regs. 95/1739, reg. 6.

1438. Church of England (Legal Aid) Rules 1990.
revoked: rules 95/2034, rule 2.

1447. Local Government (Politically Restricted Posts) (No. 2) Regulations 1990.
applied: ord. 95/789, art. 2.

1452. Portsmouth (Camber Dock and Flathouse Wharf) Harbour Revision Order 1990.
extended: ord. 95/1063, art. 20.

1507. European Convention on Extradition Order 1990.
art. 5, amended: ord. 95/1962, art. 2.
Sch. 2, Pt. 1, amended: ord. 95/1962, art. 2.
Sch. 3, Pt. 1B, inserted: ord. 95/1962, art. 2.
Sch. 4, amended: ord. 94/3203, art. 2.
Sch. 5, Pt. 4, inserted: ord. 95/1962, art. 2.

1541. Life Assurance (Apportionment of Receipts of Participating Funds) (Applicable Percentage) Order 1990.
art. 5, amended: ord. 95/1211, art. 2.

1546. Education (Assisted Places) (Amendment) Regulations 1990.
revoked: regs. 95/2016, reg. 24.

1547. Education (Assisted Places) (Incidental Expenses) (Amendment) Regulations 1990.
revoked: regs. 95/2017, reg. 16.

NO.

1990—cont.

1548. Education (Grants) (Music and Ballet Schools) (Amendment) Regulations 1990.
revoked: regs. 95/2018, reg. 16.

1564. Local Government Act 1988 (Defined Activities) (Competition) (England) Regulations 1990.
disapplied: regs. 95/2484, reg. 4.

1566. Central Rating Lists (Amendment) (No. 2) Regulations 1990.
revoked: regs. 94/3121, reg. 8.

1573. Police (Amendment) (No. 3) Regulations 1990.
revoked: regs. 95/215, reg. 70.

1584. Milk and Dairies and Milk (Special Designation) (Charges) Regulations 1990.
revoked: regs. 95/1086, reg. 23.

1594. Plant Breeders' Rights (Miscellaneous Ornamental Plants) Scheme 1990.
revoked: Scheme 95/527, art. 2.

1709. Local Government Superannuation (Amendment) Regulations 1990.
revoked: regs. 95/1019 Sch. M5.

1736. Child Resistant Packaging (Safety) (Amendment) Regulations 1990.
revoked by 1994 No. 3247.

1756. National Health Service (District Health Authorities) Order 1990.
referred to: ord. 95/533, art. 1.
art. 2, amended: ord. 95/534, art. 4, ord. 95/563, art. 4.
art. 3, amended: ord. 95/534, art. 4, ord. 95/563, art. 4.
Sch. 2, amended: ord. 95/534, art. 4.

1764. (L. 17) County Court (Amendment No. 3) Rules 1990.
rule 14, see *Walters* v. *Newton*, February 2, 1994; H.H.J. Irvine; Oxford County Ct.
rule 17, see *Walters* v. *Newton*, February 2, 1994; H.H.J. Irvine; Oxford County Ct.

1766. Companies (Forms Amendment No. 2 and Company's Type and Principal Business Activities) Regulations 1990.
Sch. 2, amended: regs. 95/736, reg. 4.

1782. Local Government (Direct Labour Organisations) (Competition) (Scotland) Regulations 1990.
revoked: regs. 95/677, reg. 10.

1849. Goods Vehicles (Operators' Licences, Qualifications and Fees) (Amendment) Regulations 1990.
reg. 2, amended: 1995, c. 23, Sch. 8, Pt. II.
reg. 4, revoked: 1995, c. 23, Sch. 8, Pt. II.
regs. 6, 7, revoked: 1995, c. 23, Sch. 8, Pt. II.

1867. Bovine Animals (Identification, Marking and Breeding Records) Order 1990.
revoked by 1995 No. 12.

NO.

1990—cont.

1868. Movement of Animals (Records) (Amendment) Order 1990.
amended by 1995 No. 11.
amended by 1995 No. 12.

2032. Town and Country Planning General Development (Amendment) (No. 2) Order 1990.
revoked: ord. 95/418, art. 9.

2035. Overhead Lines (Exemption) Regulations 1990.
reg. 2, applied: regs. 95/418, reg. 3.

2101. Retirement Benefits Schemes (Continuation of Rights of Members of Approved Schemes) Regulations 1990.
reg. 5, applied: regs. 95/1019, Sch. C5.

2154. Air Navigation (Amendment) Order 1990.
revoked: ord. 95/1038, art. 2.

2202. Edinburgh College of Art (Amendment) Order 1990.
revoked: ord. 95/471, art. 46.

2231. Income Tax (Building Societies) (Dividends and Interest) Regulations 1990.
reg. 4, amended: regs. 95/1184, reg. 2.

2244. Local Authority Social Services (Complaints Procedure) Order 1990.
see *R.* v. *Avon County Council ex p. M.* [1994] 2 F.L.R. 1006, Henry J.

2277. Occupational and Personal Pension Schemes (Levy) Regulations 1990.
revoked: regs. 95/524, reg. 7.

2278. Register of Occupational and Personal Pension Schemes Regulations 1990.
applied: regs. 95/524, reg. 1.

2298. Parliamentary Constituencies (Scotland) (Miscellaneous Charges) Order 1990.
revoked: ord. 95/1037, art. 4.

2361. Tax-exempt Special Savings Account Regulations 1990.
reg. 2, amended: regs. 95/1929, reg. 3.
reg. 3, amended: regs. 95/1929, reg. 4.
reg. 6, amended: regs. 95/1929, reg. 5.
reg. 7, amended: regs. 95/1929, reg. 6.
reg. 7A, inserted: regs. 95/1929, reg. 7.
reg. 7B, inserted: regs. 95/1929, reg. 7.
reg. 12, amended: regs. 95/1929, reg. 8.
reg. 13, amended: regs. 95/1929, reg. 9.
reg. 14, substituted: regs. 95/1929, reg. 14.

2392. Cream (Heat Treatment) (Scotland) Amendment Regulations 1990.
revoked: regs. 95/1372, reg. 23.

2403. Broadgreen Hospital National Health Service Trust (Establishment) Order 1990.
revoked: ord. 95/477, art. 2.

2419. Homewood National Health Service Trust (Establishment) Order 1990.
revoked: ord. 95/792, art. 2.

NO.

1990—cont.

2421. Leeds General Infirmary and Associated Hospitals National Health Service Trust (Establishment) Order 1990.
revoked: ord. 95/801, art. 2.

2437. Royal Liverpool University Hospital National Health Service Trust (Establishment) Order 1990.
revoked: ord. 95/479, art. 2.

2448. St. James's University Hospital National Health Service Trust (Establishment) Order 1990.
revoked: ord. 95/480, art. 2.

2463. Food Safety (Sampling and Qualifications) Regulations 1990.
Sch. 1, amended: regs. 95/1086, reg. 23, regs. 95/1372, reg. 23.
Sch. 3, amended: regs. 95/1086, reg. 23.

2468. Local Government Act 1988 (Defined Activities) (Specified Periods) (Inner London) Regulations 1990.
disapplied: regs. 95/2484, reg. 4.

2480. Local Government Superannuation (Investments) Regulations 1990.
revoked: regs. 95/1019 Sch. M5.

2486. Food Safety Act 1990 (Consequential Modifications) (England and Wales) Order 1990.
regs. 11–13, revoked: regs. 95/1086, reg. 23.
reg. 16, amended: regs. 95/1086, reg. 23.
Sch. 1, amended: regs. 95/1955, reg. 2.
Sch. 1, Pt. I, amended: regs. 95/1086, reg. 23.
Sch. 4, amended: regs. 95/1955, reg. 2.
Sch. 4, Pt. II, amended: regs. 95/1086, reg. 23.
Sch. 5, amended: regs. 95/1955, reg. 2, regs. 95/1086, reg. 23.
Sch. 10, amended: regs. 95/1955, reg. 2.

2491. Milk and Dairies (Semi-skimmed and Skimmed Milk) (Heat Treatment and Labelling) (Amendment) Regulations 1990.
revoked: regs. 95/1086, reg. 23.

2492. Milk (Special Designation) (Amendment) Regulations 1990.
revoked: regs. 95/1086, reg. 23.

2494. Fresh Meat and Poultry Meat (Hygiene, Inspection and Examination for Residues) (Charges) Regulations 1990.
revoked: regs. 95/361, reg. 15.

2507. Milk and Dairies (Scotland) Regulations 1990.
revoked in pt.: regs. 95/1372, reg. 23.
referred to: regs. 95/1372, reg. 14.
reg. 2, amended: regs. 95/1372, reg. 24.
reg. 10, amended: regs. 95/1372, reg. 24.
reg. 18, amended: regs. 95/1372, reg. 24.
reg. 19, amended: regs. 95/1372, reg. 24.

NO.

1990—cont.

2509. National Health Service (General Medical and Pharmaceutical Services) (Scotland) Amendment (No. 2) Regulations 1990.
revoked: regs. 95/414, reg. 13.

2512. Radioactive Substances (Hospitals) Exemptions Order 1990.
art. 2, amended: ord. 95/2395, art. 2.
art. 3, amended: ord. 95/2395, art. 2.
art. 4, amended: ord. 95/2395, art. 2.
art. 5, amended: ord. 95/2395, art. 2.
Sch. 2, para. 5, amended: ord. 95/2395, art. 2.
Sch. 2, para. 6, amended: ord. 95/2395, art. 2.

2514. Civil Aviation (Joint Financing) (Second Amendment) Regulations 1990.
revoked: regs. 94/3055, reg. 3.

2524. Lloyd's Underwriters (Schedule 19A of the Income and Corporation Taxes Act 1988) Regulations 1990.
revoked: regs. 95/351, reg. 17.

2531. Air Navigation (Dangerous Goods) (Third Amendment) Regulations 1990.
revoked: regs. 94/3187, reg. 2.

2580. Police and Criminal Evidence Act 1984 (Codes of Practice) (No. 2) Order 1990.
revoked: ord. 95/450, art. 4.

2595. Merchant Shipping (Prevention and Control of Pollution) Order 1990.
art. 3, applied: regs. 95/2498.

2605. Merchant Shipping (Dangerous Goods and Marine Pollutants) Regulations 1990.
amended by 1994 No. 3245.

2612. Motor Vehicles (Driving Licences) (Large Goods and Passenger-carrying Vehicles) Regulations 1990.
reg. 21, amended: regs. 95/1162, reg. 2.
reg. 27, amended: regs. 95/2075, reg. 2; referred to: regs. 95/2076, reg. 2.

2619. Police (Amendment) (No. 4) Regulations 1990.
revoked: regs. 95/215, reg. 70.

2625. Food Safety Act 1990 (Consequential Modifications) (Scotland) Order 1990.
art. 12, revoked: regs. 95/1955, reg. 2.
Pt. VI, revoked: regs. 95/1372, reg. 23.
Sch. 1, amended: regs. 95/1955, reg. 2.
Sch. 1, Pt. I, amended: regs. 95/1372, reg. 23.
Sch. 3, amended: regs. 95/1955, reg. 2.
Sch. 3, Pt. I, amended: regs. 95/1372, reg. 23.
Sch. 4, amended: regs. 95/1955, reg. 2, regs. 95/1372, reg. 23.
Sch. 5, amended: regs. 95/1372, reg. 23.
Sch. 8, amended: regs. 95/1955, reg. 2, regs. 95/1372, reg. 23.

NO.

1990—cont.

2626. Weights and Measures (Local and Working Standard Capacity Measures and Testing Equipment) Regulations 1990.
referred to: regs. 95/735, reg. 9.
reg. 2, amended: regs. 95/735, reg. 19.
reg. 18A, inserted: regs. 95/735, reg. 9.
Sch. 2, amended: regs. 95/735, reg. 9.

2628. Welfare of Animals at Markets Order 1990.
amended by 1995 No. 12.

2634. Plant Breeders' Rights (Miscellaneous Ornamental Plants) (Variation) Scheme 1990.
revoked: Scheme 95/527, art. 2.

2640. Goods Vehicles (Operators' Licences, Qualifications and Fees) (Amendment) (No. 2) Regulations 1990.
reg. 4, revoked: 1995, c. 23, Sch. 8, Pt. II.

3240. Environmental Information Regulations 1990.
reg. 3, applied: regs. 94/3076, Sch. 6.

1991

3. Apple Orchard Grubbing Up Regulations 1991.
reg. 2, amended: regs. 95/40, reg. 2.

4. Appropriation (Northern Ireland) Order 1991.
revoked: ord. 95/1969, art. 6.

5. Food Protection (Emergency Prohibitions) (Radioactivity in Sheep) (Wales) Order 1991.
revoked in pt.: ord. 95/46, art. 1.

6. Food Protection (Emergency Prohibitions) (Radioactivity in Sheep) (England) Order 1991.
revoked in pt.: ord. 95/39, art. 2.

15. Appropriation (Northern Ireland) (No. 2) Order 1991.
revoked: ord. 95/1969, art. 6.

20. Food Protection (Emergency Prohibitions) (Radioactivity in Sheep) Order 1991.
amended by 1995 No. 48.

122. Land Registration (Open Register) Rules 1991.
rule 1, amended: rules 95/1354, rule 5.
rule 4B, inserted: rules 95/1354, rule 6.
rule 13, amended: rules 95/1354, rule 7.

152. Returning Officers (Parliamentary Constituencies) (England and Wales) (Amendment) Order 1991.
revoked: ord. 95/2061, art. 2.

167. Occupational Pension Schemes (Preservation of Benefit) Regulations 1991.
amended by 1995 No. 35.

185. Rates and Precepts (Final Adjustments) Order 1991.
amended by 1994 No. 3223.

NO.

1991—cont.

194. Health and Personal Social Services (Northern Ireland) Order 1991.
art. 8, amended: 1995, c. 17, Sch. 1, para. 121.
art. 9, amended: 1995, c. 17, Sch. 1, para. 121.
Sch. 3, para. 19, amended: 1995, c. 17, Sch. 1, para. 121.

243. Local Government (Direct Labour Organisations) (Competition) (Scotland) Amendment Regulations 1991.
revoked: regs. 95/677, reg. 10.

278. Valuation for Rating (Farmer Enterprise Zones) Regulations 1991.
revoked: regs. 95/213, reg. 3.

351. Local Authorities (Members' Allowances) Regulations 1991.
applied: ord. 95/1042, art. 4.
amended by 1994 No. 3124.
reg. 9, amended: regs. 95/553, reg. 2.
reg. 9, applied: ord. 95/570, art. 2.
reg. 10, amended: regs. 95/553, reg. 3.
regs. 11, 12, revoked: regs. 95/553, reg. 4.
reg. 17, amended: regs. 95/553, regs. 4, 5.
reg. 18, amended: regs. 95/553, reg. 5.
reg. 26A, inserted: regs. 95/553, reg. 6.
Sch., revoked: regs. 95/553, reg. 4.

353. Education (Grant-maintained Schools) (Finance) Regulations 1991.
applied: regs. 95/936, reg. 3.

397. Local Authorities Etc. (Allowances) (Scotland) Regulations 1991.
revoked: regs. 95/912, reg. 30.
reg. 2, amended: regs. 95/912, reg. 29.
reg. 8, amended: regs. 95/912, reg. 29.
reg. 13, amended: regs. 95/701, reg. 2.
reg. 19, amended: regs. 95/701, reg. 2.
reg. 22, amended: regs. 95/701, reg. 2.
reg. 24, amended: regs. 95/701, reg. 2.
reg. 26, amended: regs. 95/912, reg. 29.
reg. 27, amended: regs. 95/912, reg. 29.
Sch. 2, substituted: regs. 95/701, reg. 2.

436. Wireless Telegraphy (Television Licence Fees) Regulations 1991.
amended: regs. 95/655, reg. 2.
Sch. 2, amended: regs. 95/655, reg. 2.
Sch. 3, amended: regs. 95/655, reg. 2.

439. Local Government Reorganisation (Capital Money) (Greater London) Order 1991.
art. 4, amended: ord. 95/1974, art. 2.
Sch., substituted: ord. 95/1974, art. 2.

470. Civil Aviation (Navigation Services Charges) Regulations 1991.
revoked: regs. 95/497, reg. 3.

533. Rent Officers (Additional Functions) (Scotland) Amendment Order 1991.
revoked: regs. 95/1643, reg. 7.

NO.

1991—cont.

537. National Health Service (Remuneration and Conditions of Service) (Scotland) Regulations 1991.
applied: ord. 95/574, art. 5.

542. Wireless Telegraphy (Licence Charges) Regulations 1991.
revoked: regs. 95/1331, reg. 2.
reg. 3, amended: regs. 95/244, reg. 3.
reg. 8, amended: regs. 95/244, reg. 4.
reg. 9, substituted: regs. 95/244, reg. 5.
Sch., amended: regs. 95/244, reg. 6.

565. Civil Legal Aid (Scotland) (Fees) Amendment Regulations 1991.
reg. 3, revoked: regs. 95/1044, reg. 7.
reg. 5, amended: regs. 95/1044, reg. 7.
reg. 6, revoked: regs. 95/1044, reg. 7.

572. National Health Service (General Medical and Pharmaceutical Services) (Scotland) Amendment Regulations 1991.
revoked: regs. 95/414, reg. 13.

584. National Health Service Superannuation, Premature Retirement and Injury Benefits (Amendment) Regulations 1991.
regs. 2–7, revoked: regs. 95/300, reg. V2.
regs. 11–15, revoked: regs. 95/866, reg. 24.

587. Housing Benefit and Community Charge Benefit (Subsidy) Order 1991.
referred to: ord. 95/872, art. 1.

679. Offshore Installations (Amendment) Regulations 1991.
regs. 2–4, revoked: regs. 95/738, reg. 23.

681. Education (National Curriculum) (Attainment Targets and Programmes of Study in History) (England) Order 1991.
revoked: ord. 95/54, art. 2.

723. Non-Domestic Rating (Alteration of Central Lists) (Amendment) Regulations 1991.
reg. 3, revoked: regs. 94/3121, reg. 8.

724. High Court and County Courts Jurisdiction Order 1991.
art. 7, amended: ord. 95/205, art. 4.
art. 8, amended: ord. 95/205, art. 5.

751. Education (National Curriculum) (Attainment Targets and Programmes of Study in Geography) (Wales) Order 1991.
revoked: ord. 95/72, art. 2.

752. Education (National Curriculum) (Attainment Targets and Programmes of Study in History) (Wales) Order 1991.
revoked: ord. 95/73, art. 2.

762. Food Safety (Northern Ireland) Order 1991.
art. 2, applied: regs. 95/615, reg. 2.

NO.

1991—cont.

767. Social Security (Norway) Order 1991.
modified: ord. 95/767, art. 2.

809. Health Boards (Membership and Procedure) (No. 2) Regulations 1991.
applied: ord. 95/574, art. 5.
reg. 7, applied: regs. 95/414, Sch. 4.

824. European Communities (Recognition of Professional Qualifications) Regulations 1991.
Sch. 1, Pt. I, amended: regs. 95/1429, reg. 25.

830. Education (Fees and Awards) (Amendment) Regulations 1991.
revoked: regs. 94/3042, reg. 17.

834. Education (Fees and Awards, Allowances and Bursaries) Amendment Regulations 1991.
reg. 4, revoked: regs. 95/1739, reg. 6.

837. Legal Aid in Contempt Proceedings (Remuneration) Regulations 1991.
revoked: regs. 95/948, reg. 1.

890. Arrangements for Placement of Children (General) Regulations 1991.
reg. 13, amended: regs. 95/2015, reg. 3.

893. Placement of Children with Parents etc. Regulations 1991.
see *T. (a Minor) (Care or Supervision Order), Re* [1994] 1 F.L.R. 103, C.A.
reg. 13, amended: regs. 95/2015, reg. 4.

894. Representations Procedure (Children) Regulations 1991.
see *R.* v. *Barnet London Borough Council, ex p. B.* [1994] 1 F.L.R. 592, Auld J.
regs. 4(1), 6(1), 8, 9, see *R.* v. *Brent London Borough, ex p. S.* [1994] 1 F.L.R. 203, C.A.

895. Review of Children's Cases Regulations 1991.
See *R.* v. *Brent London Borough, ex p. S.* [1994] 1 F.L.R. 203, C.A.
reg. 11, substituted: regs. 95/2015, reg. 5.

910. Foster Placement (Children) Regulations 1991.
reg. 9, substituted: regs. 95/2015, reg. 2.
reg. 10, amended: regs. 95/2015, reg. 2.
reg. 16, amended: regs. 95/2015, reg. 2.

914. Scottish Nuclear Limited (Rateable Values) (Scotland) (No. 2) Order 1991.
art. 3, see *Scottish Nuclear* v. *Assessor for Lothian Region (L.V.A.C.)*, 1995 S.L.T. 1026.

915. Caravan Sites and Pitches (Rateable Values) (Scotland) Order 1991.
revoked: ord. 95/374, art. 2.

959. Electricity Supply Industry (Rateable Values) (Amendment) Order 1991.
revoked: ord. 94/3282, art. 4.

981. Petroleum (Production) (Landward Areas) Regulations 1991.
revoked: regs. 95/1436, reg. 3.

NO.

1991—cont.

1115. Children (Assembly of Hearsay Evidence) Order 1991.
see *S.* v. *Merton London Borough* [1994] 1 F.C.R. 186, Ward J.

1126. (L. 10) County Court (Amendment No. 2) Rules 1991.
r. 23, see *Walters* v. *Newton*, February 2, 1994; H.H.J. Irvine; Oxford County Ct.
r. 24, see *Walters* v. *Newton*, February 2, 1994; H.H.J. Irvine; Oxford County Ct.

1158. Act of Sederunt (Rules of the Court of Session Amendment No. 4) (Shorthand Writers' Fees) 1991.
revoked: Act 94/1443, para. 3.

1168. Diseases of Animals (Fees for the Testing of Disinfectants) Order 1991.
Sch., amended: ord. 94/3141, art. 5.

1169. Local Elections (Principal Areas) (Declaration of Acceptance of Office) (Welsh Forms) Order 1990.
art. 2, referred to: ord. 95/546, art. 5.

1176. Broadcasting (Restrictions on the Holding of Licences) Order 1991.
art. 11, amended: ord. 95/1924, art. 3.
art. 11(5), see *R.* v. *Radio Authority, ex p. Guardian Media Group; R.* v. *Radio Authority, ex p. Trans World Communications* [1995] 1 W.L.R. 334, Schiemann J.
art. 12, amended: ord. 95/1924, art. 3.
art. 12(4), see *R.* v. *Radio Authority, ex p. Guardian Media Group; R.* v. *Radio Authority, ex p. Trans World Communications* [1995] 1 W.L.R. 334, Schiemann J.

1183. Act of Sederunt (Rules of the Court of Session Amendment No. 5) (Prevention of Terrorism) 1991.
revoked: Act 94/1443, para. 3.

1184. (L. 12) County Courts (Interest on Judgments Debts) Order 1991.
see *Evans (Lyndon)* v. *Gwent County Council*, April 8, 1994; H.H.J. Pitchford; Gwent County Ct. [*Ex rel. Robin Thompson and Partners, Solicitors*].

1203. Local Government Superannuation (Reserve Forces) Regulations 1991.
revoked: regs. 95/1019 Sch. M5.

1211. Matrimonial and Family Proceedings Act 1984 (Commencement No. 5) Order 1991.
see *Children Act 1989 (Taxation of Costs), Re* [1994] 2 FLR 934, Cazalet J.

1222. County Court Remedies Regulations 1991.
reg. 3, amended: regs. 95/206, reg. 2.

NO.

1991—cont.

1247. Family Proceedings Rules 1991.
amended by 1994 No. 3155.
rule 1.3, see *S.* v. *Merton London Borough* [1994] 1 F.C.R. 186, Ward J.
rules 1.3, 2.57, 9.2, 9.2A, 9.5, see *L.* v. *L. (Minors) (Separate Representation)* [1994] 1 FLR 156, C.A.
rule 2.12, see *Lawlor* v. *Lawlor* [1995] 1 F.C.R. 412, C.A.
rule 2.36, see *Marya* v. *Marya, The Times*, July 25, 1995, C.A.
rule 2.58(3), see *Baker* v. *Baker (95/0103/F)*, April 11, 1995, C.A.
rule 4, amended: rules 94/3155, rules 4–22.
rule 4A, amended: rules 94/3155, rule 23.
rules 4.10–4.11, see *CE (Section 37 Direction), Re* [1995] 1 FLR 26, Wall J.
rule 4.11, see *M. (Minors) (Care Proceedings: Child's Wishes), Re* [1994] 1 FLR 749, Wall J; *T. (A Minor) (Guardian Ad Litem: Case Record) Re* [1994] 1 FLR 632, C.A.; *T. and E. (Proceedings: Conflicting Interests), Re* [1995] 1 FLR 581, Wall J.
rule 4.12, see *M. (Minors) (Care Proceedings: Child's Wishes), Re* [1994] 1 FLR 749, Wall J.
rule 4.14, see *A. and B. (Minors) (No. 2), Re* [1995] 1 FLR 351, Wall J; *W. (A Minor) (Interim Care Order), Re* [1994] 2 FLR 892, C.A.
rule 4.15, see *A. and B. (Minors) (No. 2), Re* [1995] 1 FLR 351, Wall J.
rule 4.16, see *W. (A Minor) (Interim Care Order), Re* [1994] 2 FLR 892, C.A.
rules 4.22, see *P.* v. *P. (Periodical Payments: Appeals)* [1995] 1 FLR 563, Bracewell J.; *S.* v. *Merton London Borough* [1994] 1 F.C.R. 186, Ward J.
rule 4.22(3)(a), see *B.* v. *McL (Leave to Appeal)* [1994] Fam. Law 182, Wilson J.
rule 4.3, see *S.C. (A Minor) (Leave to Seek Residence Order), Re* [1994] 1 FLR 96, Booth J.
rule 6, amended: rules 94/3155, rule 25.
rule 6.3, see *D.* v. *D. (Child Abduction: Non-convention Country)* [1994] 1 FLR 137, C.A.
rule 6.5, see *M. (A Minor) (Child Abduction), Re* [1994] 1 FLR 391, C.A.
rule 6.11, see *H.* v. *H. (Child Abduction: Stay of Domestic Proceedings)* [1994] 1 FLR 530, Thorpe J.
rule 8(1), see *Marya* v. *Marya, The Times*, July 25, 1995, C.A.

NO.

1991—cont.

1247. Family Proceedings Rules 1991—*cont.*
rule 8.2, see *P.* v. *P. (Periodical Payments: Appeals)* [1995] 1 FLR 563, Bracewell J.; *S.* v. *Merton London Borough* [1994] 1 F.C.R. 186, Ward J.
rule 9.2A, see *CE (Section 37 Direction), Re* [1995] 1 FLR 26, Wall J.; *W. (A Minor) (Contact), Re* [1994] 1 FLR 843, Wall J.
rule 9.5, see *CE (Section 37 Direction), Re* [1995] 1 FLR 26, Wall J.
rule 10, amended: rules 94/3155, rule 26.
Appendix 1, amended: rules 94/3155, rule 27.

1259. Companies (Forms) (No. 2) Regulations 1991.
Sch. 2, amended: regs. 95/736, reg. 4.

1328. (L. 14) County Court (Amendment No. 3) Rules 1991.
rule 19, see *Walters* v. *Newton*, February 2, 1994; H.H.J. Irvine; Oxford County Ct.

1341. Merchant Shipping (Radio and Radio-Navigational Equipment Survey) Regulations 1991.
revoked: regs. 95/1210, reg. 1.

1382. Price Marking Order 1991.
art. 5, amended: ord. 94/1853, art. 2.
art. 6, amended: ord. 94/1853, art. 2.
art. 7, substituted and revoked: ord. 94/1853, art. 2.
art. 12, amended: ord. 94/1853, art. 2.
art. 15, revoked: ord. 94/1853, art. 2.
Sch. 1, Pt. I, amended: ord. 94/1853, art. 2.
Sch. 2, Pt. I, amended: ord. 94/1853, art. 2.
Sch. 2, Pt. II, amended: ord. 94/1853, art. 2.
Sch. 2, Pt. III, amended: ord. 94/1853, art. 2.
Sch. 4, Pt. I, amended: ord. 94/1853, art. 2.
Sch. 4, Pt. II, substituted: ord. 94/1853, art. 2.
Sch. 5, inserted: ord. 94/1853, art. 2.

1392. Medicines (Veterinary Drugs) (Prescription Only) Order 1991.
art. 1, amended: regs. 94/3142, reg. 21.
art. 3, amended: regs. 94/3142, reg. 21.
art. 4, amended: regs. 94/3142, reg. 21.
Sch. 1, amended: regs. 94/3142, reg. 21.
Sch. 3, Pt. I, amended: regs. 94/3142, reg. 21.

1395. Family Proceedings Courts (Children Act 1989) Rules 1991.
amended by 1994 No. 3156.
rules 1(2), 21(6), see *C. (a Minor) (Contribution Notice), Re* [1994] 1 FLR 111, Ward J.

NO.

1991—cont.

1395. Family Proceedings Courts (Children Act 1989) Rules 1991—*cont.*
rule 3, see *O. (Minors) (Leave to Seek Residence Order), Re* [1994] 1 FLR 172, Ewbank J.
rule 4, see *C.* v. *Humberside County Council* [1994] 2 FLR 759, Bracewell J.
rule 7, see *F.* v. *Cambridgeshire County Council* [1995] 1 FLR 516, Stuart-White J.
rule 11, see *M. (Minors) (Care Proceedings: Child's Wishes), Re* [1994] 1 FLR 749, Wall J.
rule 12, see *M. (Minors) (Care Proceedings: Child's Wishes), Re* [1994] 1 FLR 749, Wall J.
rule 14, see *A. and B. (Minors) (No. 2), Re* [1995] 1 FLR 351, Wall J.
rule 14(1)(d), see *W. (A Minor) (Contact), Re* [1994] 1 FLR 843, Wall J.
rule 15, see *A. and B. (Minors) (No. 2), Re* [1995] 1 FLR 351, Wall J.
rule 17, see *S.* v. *Merton London Borough* [1994] 1 F.C.R. 186, Ward J.
rule 21, see *S.* v. *Merton London Borough* [1994] 1 F.C.R. 186, Ward J.
rule 21(5)(6), see *D. (Contact: Interim Order), Re* [1995] 1 FLR 495, Wall J.
rule 21(5),(6),(7), see *W. (A Minor) (Contact), Re* [1994] 1 FLR 843, Wall J.
rule 22, see *M. (Local Authority's Costs), Re* [1995] 1 FLR 533, Cazalet J.
rule 22(1), see *Sutton London Borough Council* v. *Davis (No. 2)* [1994] 1 W.L.R. 1317, Wilson J.
rule 28, see *R. (Minors) (Care Proceedings: Care Plan), Re* [1994] 2 F.C.R. 136, Wall J.

1408. Broadcasting (Independent Productions) Order 1991.
art. 3, amended: ord. 95/1925, art. 2, ord. 95/1925, art. 2.

1428. Statutory Sick Pay (Small Employers' Relief) Regulations 1991.
revoked: regs. 95/512, reg. 5.

1474. Medicines (Products for Human Use—Fees) Regulations 1991.
revoked: regs. 95/1116, reg. 22.

1476. Food Safety (Exports) Regulations 1991.
Sch. 1, amended: regs. 95/1086, reg. 23.

1478. Parental Responsibility Agreement Regulations 1991.
amended by 1994 No. 3157.

1494. St. Mary's Music School (Aided Places) Amendment Regulations 1991.
revoked: regs. 95/1712, reg. 17.

NO.

1991—cont.

1495. Education (Assisted Places) (Scotland) Amendment Regulations 1991.
revoked: regs. 95/1713, reg. 31.

1505. Children (Secure Accommodation) Regulations 1991.
reg. 3, amended: regs. 95/1398, reg. 3.
reg. 4, amended: regs. 95/1398, reg. 3.
reg. 6, see *A.E.* v. *Staffordshire County Council* [1995] 2 F.C.R. 84, Kirkwood J.; *C. (Secure Accommodation: Bail), Re* [1994] 2 F.L.R. 922, Hollis J.
reg. 9, amended: regs. 95/1398, regs. 3, 4.
reg. 10, see *C.* v. *Humberside County Council* [1994] 2 F.L.R. 759, Bracewell J.
reg. 11, see *C.* v. *Humberside County Council* [1994] 2 F.L.R. 759, Bracewell J.
reg. 12, see *C.* v. *Humberside County Council* [1994] 2 F.L.R. 759, Bracewell J.
reg. 13, see *C.* v. *Humberside County Council* [1994] 2 F.L.R. 759, Bracewell J.
reg. 14, amended: regs. 95/1398, reg. 3.
reg. 15, amended: regs. 95/1398, reg. 3.
reg. 16, amended: regs. 95/1398, regs. 3, 5.
reg. 17, amended: regs. 95/1398, reg. 3.
reg. 18, revoked: regs. 95/1398, reg. 6.

1506. Children's Homes Regulations 1991.
reg. 2, amended: regs. 94/3142, reg. 21; regs. 94/3144, reg. 11.

1536. Town and Country Planning General Development (Amendment) Order 1991.
revoked: ord. 95/418, art. 9.

1594. Leeds General Infirmary and Associated Hospitals National Health Service Trust (Change of Name) Order 1991.
revoked: ord. 95/801, art. 2.

1620. Construction Products Regulations 1991.
reg. 2, amended: regs. 94/3051, reg. 4.
reg. 4, substituted: regs. 94/3051, reg. 5.
reg. 5, amended: regs. 94/3051, reg. 6.
reg. 7A, inserted: regs. 94/3051, reg. 7.
Sch. 1, substituted: regs. 94/3051, reg. 8.

1621. Act of Sederunt (Rules of the Court of Session Amendment No. 7) (Patent Rules) 1991.
revoked: Act 94/1443, para. 3.

1630. Farm and Conservation Grant Regulations 1991.
Sch. 1, para. 1, amended: regs. 94/3003, reg. 3.

1676. Slaughter of Poultry (Licences and Specified Qualifications) Regulations 1991.
revoked: regs. 95/731, reg. 28.

NO.

1991—cont.

1677. Children (Allocation of Proceedings) Order 1991.
amended by 1994 No. 3138.
art. 12, see *G. (Adoption: Illegal Placement), Re* [1995] 1 F.L.R. 403, C.A.

1683. Education (National Curriculum) (Attainment Targets and Programmes of Study in Welsh) (Amendment) Order 1991.
revoked: ord. 95/69, art. 7.

1688. Education (National Curriculum) (Attainment Targets and Programmes of Study in History) (Wales) (Amendment) Order 1991.
revoked: ord. 95/73, art. 2.

1726. Air Navigation (Second Amendment) Order 1991.
revoked: ord. 95/1038, art. 2.

1767. Education (Assisted Places) (Amendment) Regulations 1991.
revoked: regs. 95/2016, reg. 24.

1830. Education (Assisted Places) (Incidental Expenses) (Amendment) Regulations 1991.
revoked: regs. 95/2017, reg. 16.

1831. Education (Grants) (Music and Ballet Schools) (Amendment) Regulations 1991.
applied: regs. 95/2018, reg. 16.
revoked: regs. 95/2018, reg. 16.

1832. Family Proceedings (Costs) Rules 1991.
rule 2(2), see *Children Act 1989 (Taxation of Costs), Re* [1994] 2 F.L.R. 934, Cazalet J.

1839. Education (Fees and Awards) (Amendment) (No. 2) Regulations 1991.
revoked: regs. 94/3042, reg. 17.

1877. County Court Appeals Order 1991.
see *Molava* v. *Rahim*, April 10, 1995, C.A.

1882. (L. 28) County Court (Amendment No. 4) Rules 1991.
rule 7, see *Walters* v. *Newton*, February 2, 1994; H.H.J. Irvine, Oxford County Ct.

1915. Act of Sederunt (Rules of the Court of Session Amendment No. 8) (Discharge of Judicial Factors) 1991.
revoked: Act 94/1443, para. 3.

1923. Magistrates' Courts (Detention and Forfeiture of Drug Trafficking Cash) Rules 1991.
amended by 1994 No. 3154.
rules 9A, inserted: rules 94/3154, rule 2.

1997. Companies Act 1989 (Eligibility for Appointment as Company Auditor) (Consequential Amendments) Regulations 1991.
Sch., para. 21, amended: regs 95/1163, reg. 4.

NO.

1991—cont.

2032. Children (Prescribed Orders—Northern Ireland, Guernsey and Isle of Man) Regulations 1991.
reg. 8, amended: ord. 95/756, art. 15.

2037. Fresh Meat (Hygiene and Inspection) Regulations 1992.
amended: regs. 95/361, reg. 15, Sch. 3.
reg. 27, amended: regs. 95/361, reg. 15.

2038. Legal Aid in Family Proceedings (Remuneration) Regulations 1991.
regs. 3(1),(2),(4)(c)(7), see *Children Act 1989 (Taxation of Costs), Re* [1994] 2 F.L.R. 934, Cazalet J.
Sch. 1, see *Children Act 1989 (Taxation of Costs), Re* [1994] 2 F.L.R. 934, Cazalet J.; *H. (A Minor): Taxation of Counsel's Costs), Re, The Independent*, August 14, 1995, Cazalet J.
Sch. 2, see *Children Act 1989 (Taxation of Costs), Re* [1994] 2 F.L.R. 934, Cazalet J.

2051. Guardians Ad Litem and Reporting Officers (Panels) Regulations 1991.
see *W. (A Minor) (Contact), Re* [1994] 1 F.L.R. 843, Wall J.

2150. Local Government (Assistants for Political Groups) (Remuneration) Order 1991.
revoked: ord. 95/2456, art. 3.

2197. Fertilisers Regulations 1991.
reg. 3A, inserted: regs. 95/16, reg. 3.
reg. 4, amended: regs. 95/16, reg. 3.
Sch. 1, amended: regs. 95/16, reg. 4.

2213. Act of Sederunt (Rules of the Court of Session Amendment No. 9) (International Commercial Arbitration) 1991.
revoked: Act 94/1443, para. 3.

2239. Goods Vehicles (Operators' Licences, Qualifications and Fees) (Amendment) (No. 2) Regulations 1991.
reg. 4, revoked: 1995, c. 23, Sch. 8, Pt. II.
reg. 7, revoked: 1995, c. 23, Sch. 8, Pt. II.

2241. National Health Service (General Medical and Pharmaceutical Services) (Scotland) Amendment (No. 2) Regulations 1991.
revoked: regs. 95/414, reg. 13.

2246. Bovine Spongiform Encephalopathy Order 1991.
art. 4, amended: ord. 95/1928, art. 27.
art. 9, revoked: ord. 95/1928, art. 27.
art. 12, amended: ord. 95/1928, art. 27.
art. 14, revoked: ord. 95/1928, art. 27.
art. 15, amended: ord. 95/1928, art. 27.
art. 16, amended: ord. 95/1928, art. 27.
art. 17, amended: ord. 95/1928, art. 27.

2268. Town and Country Planning General Development (Amendment) (No. 2) Order 1991.
revoked: ord. 95/418, art. 9.

NO.

1991—cont.

2415. Weybourne Community National Health Service Trust (Establishment) Order 1991.
revoked: ord. 95/481, art. 2.

2431. Control of Substances Hazardous to Health (Amendment) Regulations 1991.
revoked: regs. 94/3246, reg. 18.

2437. Rules of the Air Regulations 1991.
rule 39, applied: ord. 95/1038, arts. 76, 118.

2471. Local Government Superannuation (Interchange) Regulations 1991.
revoked: regs. 95/1019 Sch. M5.

2483. Act of Sederunt (Rules of the Court of Session Amendment No. 10) (Miscellaneous) 1991.
revoked: Act 94/1443, para. 3.

2484. Police (Amendment) Regulations 1991.
revoked: regs. 95/215, reg. 70.

2522. Local Government Superannuation (Miscellaneous Provisions) Regulations 1991.
revoked: regs. 95/1019 Sch. M5.

2562. Education (National Curriculum) (Attainment Targets and Programmes of Study in Geography) (England) (No. 2) Order 1991.
revoked: ord. 95/55, art. 2.

2563. Education (National Curriculum) (Attainment Targets and Programmes of Study in Modern Foreign Languages) Order 1991.
revoked: ord. 95/57, art. 2.

2566. Insurance Brokers Registration Council (Registration and Enrolment) (Amendment) Rules Approval Order 1991.
revoked: ord. 94/3069, art. 3.

2580. Building Societies (Liquid Asset) Regulations 1991.
Sch., Pt. II, amended: regs. 95/550, reg. 2.
Sch., Pt. III, amended: regs. 95/550, reg. 2.

2608. Education (National Curriculum) (Attainment Targets and Programmes of Study in Geography) (Wales) (Amendment) Order 1991.
revoked: ord. 95/72, art. 2.

2644. Child Support Act 1991 (Commencement No. 3 and Transitional Provisions) Order 1992.
see *B. v. M. (Child Support: Revocation of Order)* [1994] 1 F.L.R. 342, H.H.J. Bryant.

2650. Police (Amendment) (No. 2) Regulations 1991.
revoked: regs. 95/215, reg. 70.

NO.

1991—cont.

2652. Act of Sederunt (Rules of the Court of Session Amendment No. 11) (Applications under the Access to Health Records Act 1990) 1991.
revoked: Act 94/1443, para. 3.

2679. Public Supply Contracts Regulations 1991.
revoked: regs. 95/201, reg. 30.

2680. Public Works Contracts Regulations 1991.
applied: ord. 95/789, art. 2.
reg. 2, amended: regs. 95/201, reg. 31.
reg. 4, amended: regs. 95/201, reg. 31.
reg. 6, amended: regs. 95/201, reg. 31.
reg. 8, amended: regs. 95/201, reg. 31.
reg. 12, amended: regs. 95/201, reg. 31.
reg. 13, amended: regs. 95/201, reg. 31.
reg. 14, amended: regs. 95/201, reg. 31.
reg. 15, amended: regs. 95/201, reg. 31.
reg. 18, amended: regs. 95/201, reg. 31.
reg. 31, amended: regs. 95/201, reg. 31.

2749. Simple Pressure Vessels (Safety) Regulations 1991.
reg. 2, amended: regs. 94/3098, reg. 3, 4, 6.
reg. 3, amended: regs. 94/3098, reg. 6.
reg. 4, amended: regs. 94/3098, regs. 4, 6.
reg. 5, substituted: regs. 94/3098, reg. 4.
reg. 6, amended: regs. 94/3098, reg. 6.
reg. 11, amended: regs. 94/3098, reg. 4.
reg. 12, substituted: regs. 94/3098, reg. 4.
reg. 14, amended: regs. 94/3098, reg. 4.
reg. 18, revoked: regs. 94/3098, reg. 4.
reg. 19, substituted: regs. 94/3098, reg. 4.
reg. 20, amended: regs. 94/3098, reg. 4.
reg. 24, amended: regs. 94/3098, reg. 6.
Sch. 2, substituted: regs. 94/3098, reg. 4.
Sch. 5, para. 1, amended: regs. 94/3098, reg. 6.
Sch. 5, para. 2, amended: regs. 94/3098, reg. 6.

2768. Building Regulations 1991.
reg. 5, amended: regs. 95/1356, reg. 2.
reg. 6, amended: regs. 95/1356, reg. 2.

2778. Education (London Residuary Body) (Property Transfer) (No. 4) Order 1991.
art. 4, amended: ord. 94/3078, art. 2.

2792. Civil Aviation (Joint Financing) (Third Amendment) Regulations 1991.
revoked: regs. 94/3055, reg. 3.

2794. Town and Country Planning Development Plan Regulations 1991.
reg. 16(4), see *Ravebuild* v. *Secretary of State for the Environment (CO/2675/94)*, November 21, 1994, Jeremy Sullivan, Q.C.

NO.

1991—cont.

2805. Town and Country Planning General Development (Amendment) (No. 3) Order 1991.
revoked: ord. 95/418, art. 9, ord. 95/419, art. 28.

2825. Food Premises (Registration) Regulations 1991.
reg. 3, amended: regs. 95/1086, reg. 24, regs. 95/1372, reg. 24, regs. 94/3082, reg. 24, regs. 95/539, regs. 25, 26, regs. 95/540, reg. 27.

2843. Animals, Meat and Meat Products (Examination for Residues and Maximum Residue Limits) Regulations 1991.
amended: regs. 95/361, reg. 15, sch. 3.
referred to: regs. 95/361, reg. 2.
reg. 2, amended: regs. 94/3142, reg. 21.
reg. 24, amended: regs. 95/361, reg. 15.

2869. Police (Amendment) (No. 3) Regulations 1991.
revoked: regs. 95/215, reg. 70.

2887. Disability Working Allowance (General) Regulations 1991.
reg. 2, amended: regs. 95/516, reg. 2, regs. 95/2303, reg. 3.
reg. 6, amended: regs. 95/516, reg. 3.
reg. 6A, inserted: regs. 95/1339, reg. 3.
reg. 7, amended: regs. 95/516, reg. 4.
reg. 7A, inserted: regs. 95/482, reg. 2.
reg. 7B, inserted: regs. 95/482, reg. 2.
reg. 15A, amended: regs. 95/516, reg. 5.
reg. 25, amended: regs. 95/2303, reg. 3.
reg. 29, amended: regs. 95/516, reg. 6, regs. 95/2303, reg. 3.
reg. 37, amended: regs. 95/2303, reg. 3.
reg. 39, amended: regs. 95/2303, reg. 3.
reg. 41, amended: regs. 95/1742, reg. 2.
reg. 42, amended: regs. 95/1742, reg. 3.
reg. 51, amended: regs. 95/482, reg. 3, regs. 95/516, reg. 7, regs. 95/1339, reg. 4.
Sch. 1, para. 6, amended: regs. 95/2303, reg. 3.
Sch. 3, para. 2, amended: regs. 95/516, reg. 8.
Sch. 3, para. 11A, inserted: regs. 95/2303, reg. 3.
Sch. 3, para. 18, substituted: regs. 95/516, reg. 8.
Sch. 3, para. 19, amended: regs. 95/516, reg. 8.
Sch. 3, para. 53, inserted: regs. 95/516, reg. 8.
Sch. 4, para. 5, substituted: regs. 95/2303, reg. 3.
Sch. 4, para. 24A, inserted: regs. 95/2303, reg. 3.
Sch. 4, para. 47, inserted: regs. 95/516, reg. 9.
Sch. 5, para. 2A, inserted: regs. 95/1339, reg. 5.
Sch. 5, para. 4, amended: regs. 95/482, reg. 4.

NO.

1991—cont.

2896. Education (National Curriculum) (Attainment Targets and Programmes of Study in Mathematics) Order 1991.
revoked: ord. 95/52, art. 2.

2897. Education (National Curriculum) (Attainment Targets and Programmes of Study in Science) Order 1991.
revoked: ord. 95/53, art. 2.

2924. Non-Domestic Rating (Appropriate Fraction and Rateable Values) Order 1991.
art. 3, amended: ord. 94/3281, art. 2, ord. 94/3285, art. 4.

1992

3. Merchant Shipping (Radio Installations) Regulations 1992.
reg. 47, revoked: regs. 95/1210, reg. 1.

4. Appropriation (Northern Ireland) Order 1992.
revoked: ord. 95/1969, art. 6.

12. Appropriation (Northern Ireland) (No. 2) Order 1992.
revoked: ord. 95/1969, art. 6.

33. Medicines (Veterinary Drugs) (Pharmacy and Merchants' List) Order 1992.
art. 2, amended: regs. 94/3142, reg. 21.
art. 3, amended: regs. 94/3142, reg. 21.
art. 6, amended: regs. 94/3142, reg. 21.
art. 9, amended: regs. 94/3142, reg. 21.
art. 11, amended: regs. 94/3142, reg. 21.
art. 16, amended: ord. 94/3169, art. 3.
Schs. 1–5, substituted: ord. 94/3169, art. 4.
Sch. 1, amended: regs. 94/3142, reg. 21.
Sch. 2, amended: regs. 94/3142, reg. 21.
Sch. 3, amended: regs. 94/3142, reg. 21.
Sch. 4, amended: regs. 94/3142, reg. 21.

39. Animal, Meat and Meat Products (Examination for Residues and Maximum Residue Limits) Regulations (Northern Ireland) 1992.
reg. 2, amended: regs. 94/3142, reg. 21.

88. Act of Sederunt (Rules of the Court of Session Amendment) (Optional Procedure and Miscellaneous) 1992.
revoked: Act 94/1443, para. 3.

158. Bovine Offal (Prohibition) (Scotland) Amendment Regulations 1992.
revoked: regs. 95/1955, reg. 2.

172. Local Government Superannuation (Amendment) Regulations 1992.
regs. 2–11, revoked: regs. 95/1019 Sch. M5.
regs. 14–22, revoked: regs. 95/1019 Sch. M5.
regs. 24–43, revoked: regs. 95/1019 Sch. M5.

NO.

1992—cont.

191. National Health Service (General Medical and Pharmaceutical Services) (Scotland) Amendment (No. 2) Regulations 1992.
revoked: regs. 95/414, reg. 13.

223. Town and Country Planning (General Permitted Development) (Scotland) Order 1992.
art. 3, amended: ord. 94/3294, art. 3.
Sch. 1, Pt. I, amended: ord. 94/3294, art. 4.
Sch. 1, Pt. 6, amended: ord. 94/3294, art. 5.
Sch. 1, Pt. 7, amended: ord. 94/3294, art. 6.
Sch. 1, Pt. 13, amended: ord. 94/3294, art. 7.
Sch. 1, Pt. 14, amended: ord. 94/3294, art. 8.
Sch. 1, Pt. 23, inserted: ord. 94/3294, art. 9.
Sch. 1, Pt. 24, inserted: ord. 94/3294, art. 10.
Sch. 2, para. (4), substituted: ord. 94/3294, art. 11.

224. Town and Country Planning (General Development Procedure) (Scotland) Order 1992.
art. 2, amended: ord. 94/3293, art. 2.
art. 3, amended: ord. 94/3293, art. 6.
art. 4, amended: ord. 94/3293, art. 6.
art. 5, amended: ord. 94/3293, art. 6.
art. 8, substituted: ord. 94/3293, art. 3.
art. 9, amended: ord. 94/3293, art. 6.
art. 12, amended: ord. 94/3293, art. 6.
art. 14, amended: ord. 94/3293, art. 4.
art. 15, amended: ord. 94/3293, art. 5.
art. 15, applied: regs. 95/2043, reg. 3.
art. 16, amended: ord. 94/3293, art. 6.
art. 21, amended: ord. 94/3293, art. 6.
art. 23, amended: ord. 94/3293, art. 6.
art. 25, substituted: ord. 94/3293, art. 6.
Sch. 1, substituted: ord. 94/3293, art. 6.
Sch. 2, para. 9, amended: ord. 94/3293, art. 6.
Sch. 3, amended: ord. 94/3293, art. 6.
Sch. 10, amended: ord. 94/3293, art. 6.

231. Electricity (Northern Ireland) Order 1992.
referred to: ord. 95/2356, art. 2.

274. Financial Services Act 1986 (Investment Advertisements) (Exemptions) Order 1992.
revoked: regs. 95/1266, reg. 19.

275. Police (Amendment) Regulations 1992.
revoked: regs. 95/215, reg. 70.

280. Teachers' Superannuation (Scotland) Regulations 1992.
referred to: regs. 95/365, reg. B2.

NO.

1992—cont.

306. Bovine Offal (Prohibition) (Amendment) Regulations 1992.
revoked: regs. 95/1955, reg. 2.

362. Wireless Telegraphy (Licence Charges) (Amendment) Regulations 1992.
revoked: regs. 95/1331, reg. 2.

372. Civil Legal Aid (Scotland) (Fees) Amendment Regulations 1992.
remaining pts., revoked: regs. 95/1044, reg. 7.

410. Gaming Act (Variation of Fees) (Scotland) Order 1992.
revoked: ord. 95/571, art. 3.

425. Amusements with Prizes (Variation of Monetary Limits) Order 1992.
revoked: ord. 95/928, art. 3.

434. National Health Service (Service Committees and Tribunal) (Scotland) Regulations 1992.
reg. 3, amended: regs. 94/3038, reg. 2.
reg. 8, amended: regs. 94/3038, reg. 3.
reg. 8, applied: regs. 95/416, reg. 36.
reg. 11, amended: regs. 94/3038, reg. 4.
reg. 12, amended: regs. 94/3038, reg. 5.
Sch. 1, para. 4, amended: regs. 94/3038, reg. 6.
Sch. 1, para. 20, amended: regs. 94/3038, reg. 6.
Pt. II, applied: regs. 95/414, Sch. 1; regs. 94/416, Sch. 1.

462. Environmental Protection (Waste Recycling Payments) Regulations 1992.
Sch., substituted: regs. 95/476, reg. 2.

475. Civil Aviation (Navigation Service Charges) (Amendment) Regulations 1992.
revoked: regs. 95/497, reg. 3.

483. Home Energy Efficiency Grants Regulations 1992.
amended by 1995 No. 49.

505. Local Authorities Etc. (Allowances) (Scotland) Amendment Regulations 1992.
revoked: regs. 95/912, reg. 30.

510. Retention of Registration Marks Regulations 1992.
reg. 2, amended: regs. 94/2976, reg. 2.
reg. 3, amended: regs. 94/2976, reg. 2.
reg. 4, amended: regs. 94/2976, reg. 2.
reg. 6A, inserted: regs. 94/2976, reg. 2.
reg. 7, amended: regs. 94/2976, reg. 2.
reg. 10, amended: regs. 94/2976, reg. 2.
reg. 12, amended: regs. 94/2976, reg. 2.
reg. 14, amended: regs. 94/2976, reg. 2.

528. Industrial Relations (Northern Ireland) Order 1992.
art. 91, applied: regs. 95/639, Sch. 4.

NO.

1992—cont.

548. Council Tax (Discount Disregards) Order 1992.
art. 3, amended: ord. 95/619, art. 2.
Sch. 1, para. 4, amended: ord. 95/619,art. 3.
Sch. 2, para. 1, amended: ord. 95/619, art. 4.

549. Council Tax (Chargeable Dwellings) Order 1992.
art. 2, see *Rodd* v. *Ritchings (CO/606/1994; CO/648/1994; CO/858/1994; CO/1396/1994)*, June 14, 1995, Ognall J., *The Times*, June 21, 1995, Ognall J.; *Williams* v. *Bristol District Valuation Officer and Avon Valuation Tribunal* [1995] RA 189, Collins J.
art. 3, see *Rodd* v. *Ritchings (CO/606/1994; CO/648/1994; CO/858/1994; CO/1396/1994)*, June 14, 1995, Ognall J., *The Times*, June 21, 1995, Ognall J.

550. Council Tax (Situation and Valuation of Dwellings) Regulations 1992.
reg. 7, see *Williams* v. *Bristol District Valuation Officer and Avon Valuation Tribunal* [1995] RA 189, Collins J.

551. Council Tax (Liability for Owners) Regulations 1992.
amended: regs. 95/620, regs. 2, 3.
reg. 2, amended: regs. 95/620, reg. 2.
reg. 3, amended: regs. 95/620, reg. 3.

552. Council Tax (Additional Provisions for Discount Disregards) Regulations 1992.
amended: regs. 95/620, reg. 4.
reg. 3, applied: ord. 95/619, art. 5; amended regs. 95/620, reg. 4.

553. Council Tax (Contents of Valuation Lists) Regulations 1992.
reg. 2, see *Williams* v. *Bristol District Valuation Officer and Avon Valuation Tribunal* [1995] RA 189, Collins J.

554. Council Tax (Reductions for Disabilities) Regulations 1992.
applied: regs. 95/209, reg. 5.

555. Education (Grant-maintained Schools) (Finance) Regulations 1992.
applied: regs. 95/936, reg. 3.

558. Council Tax (Exempt Dwellings) Order 1992.
art. 3, amended: ord. 95/619, arts. 5, 6.

575. Gaming Act (Variation of Monetary Limits) Order 1985.
revoked: ord. 95/2288, art. 4.

587. Education (London Residuary Body) (Property Transfer) Order 1992.
amended: ord. 95/627, arts. 2–4.
art. 4, amended: ord. 95/1202, art. 2, ord. 95/627, arts. 2, 3, 4, ord. 94/3105, arts. 3, 4, 5, 6.

NO.

1992—cont.

588. Controlled Waste Regulations 1992.
reg. 3, amended: regs. 95/288, reg. 2.
reg. 7, amended: regs. 95/288, reg. 2.
reg. 9, amended: regs. 95/288, reg. 2.

595. Legal Aid in Contempt Proceedings (Remuneration) (Amendment) Regulations 1992.
revoked: regs. 95/948, reg. 1.

597. Education (National Curriculum) (Attainment Targets and Programmes of Study in Music) (England) Order 1992.
revoked: ord. 95/59, art. 2.

598. Education (National Curriculum) (Attainment Targets and Programmes of Study in Art) (England) Order 1992.
revoked: ord. 95/58, art. 2.

603. Education (National Curriculum) (Attainment Targets and Programmes of Study in Physical Education) Order 1992.
revoked: ord. 95/60, art. 2.

609. Town and Country Planning General Development (Amendment) Order 1991.
revoked: ord. 95/418, art. 9.

613. Council Tax (Administration and Enforcement) Regulations 1992.
amended by 1995 No. 22.
referred to: regs. 95/247, reg. 17.
reg. 4, applied: regs. 95/247, reg. 18.
reg. 34, applied: regs. 95/247, regs. 20, 23, 26.
reg. 37, applied: regs. 95/247, reg. 22.
reg. 39, applied: regs. 95/247, reg. 22.
reg. 40, applied: regs. 95/247, reg. 22.
reg. 41, applied: regs. 95/247, reg. 22.
reg. 45, applied: regs. 95/247, regs. 23, 24, 25.
reg. 46, applied: regs. 95/247, reg. 24.
reg. 50, applied: regs. 95/247, regs. 26, 27.
reg. 51, applied: regs. 95/247, reg. 27.
reg. 53, applied: regs. 95/247, reg. 28.

616. Patents (Fees) Rules 1992.
revoked: rules 95/2164, rule 1.

617. Registered Designs (Fees) Rules 1992.
revoked: rules 95/2165, rule 1.

618. Local Authorities (Members' Interests) Regulations 1992.
reg. 6, amended: regs. 95/789, art. 2.

635. National Health Service (General Medical Services) Regulations 1992.
amended by 1995 No. 80.
applied: regs. 94/3130, reg. 2.
reg. 25, amended: regs. 94/3130, reg. 11.
Sch. 2, para. 22, amended: regs. 94/3130, reg. 12.
Sch. 2, para. 22A, inserted: regs. 94/3130, reg. 12.

NO.

1992—cont.

658. Town and Country Planning General Development (Amendment) (No. 2) Order 1991.
revoked: ord. 95/418, art. 9, ord. 95/419, art. 28.

660. National Health Service (Appellate and Other Functions) Regulations 1992.
revoked: regs. 95/622, reg. 15.
referred to: ord. 95/621, art. 6.

662. National Health Service (Pharmaceutical Services) Regulations 1992.
amended: regs. 95/644, regs. 2–8.
reg. 16, amended: regs. 95/644, reg. 2.
reg. 16A, amended: regs. 95/644, reg. 3.
reg. 18, amended: regs. 95/644, reg. 4.
reg. 20, referred to: ord. 95/652, art. 3.
reg. 22, amended: regs. 95/644, reg. 5.
reg. 24, amended: regs. 95/644, reg. 6.
Sch. 2, Pt. II, amended: regs. 95/644, reg. 7.
Sch. 2, Pt. III, amended: regs. 95/644, reg. 8.

666. Town and Country Planning (Control of Advertisements) Regulations 1992.
reg. 6, see *Berridge v. Vision Posters* (1995) 159 J.P. 218, D.C.
Sch. 3, Class 5, see *Berridge* v. *Vision Posters* (1995) 159 J.P. 218, D.C.

698. Valuation for Rating (Former Enterprise Zones) (Amendment) Regulations 1992.
revoked: regs. 95/213, reg. 3.

712. Telecommunication Meters (Approval Fees) (British Approvals Board for Telecommunications) Order 1992.
art. 4, amended: ord. 94/3163, art. 3, 4.

727. Criminal Justice Act 1991 (Suspension of Prison Custody Officer Certificate) Regulations 1992.
reg. 3, amended: regs. 94/3193, reg. 2.

739. Housing Benefit and Community Charge Benefit (Subsidy) Order 1992.
referred to: ord. 95/872, art. 1.

749. Amusements with Prizes (Variation of Monetary Limits) (Scotland) Order 1992.
revoked: ord. 95/1021, art. 3.

756. Medicines (Products for Human Use—Fees) Amendment Regulations 1992.
revoked: regs. 95/1116, reg. 22.

757. Education (National Curriculum) (Attainment Targets and Programmes of Study in Art) (Wales) Order 1992.
revoked: ord. 95/71, art. 2.

758. Education (National Curriculum) (Attainment Targets and Programmes of Study in Music) (Wales) Order 1992.
revoked: ord. 95/70, art. 2.

NO.

1992—cont.

810. Local Government (Miscellaneous Provisions) (Northern Ireland) Order 1992 (N.I. 6).
art. 28(4); ord. 95/45.

812. Social Security (Barbados) Order 1992.
modified: ord. 95/767, art. 2.

813. Financial Services Act 1986 (Investment Advertisements) (Exemptions) (No. 2) Order 1992.
revoked: ord. 95/1536, art. 16.

894. Act of Sederunt (Rules of the Court of Session Amendment No. 2) (Solicitors' Fees) 1992.
revoked: Act 94/1443, para. 3.

1203. Council Water Charge (Scotland) Regulations 1992.
art. 4, amended: ord. 95/599, art. 2.
Sch. 11, para. 11, applied: regs. 95/597.

1208. Milk (Special Designation) Regulations (Amendment) Order 1992.
revoked: regs. 95/1086, reg. 23.

1227. Legal Aid in Contempt of Court Proceedings (Scotland) Regulations 1992.
reg. 4, amended: regs. 95/2319, reg. 3.

1270. Education (Mandatory Awards) Regulations 1992.
see *R.* v. *London Borough of Bexley, ex p. Jones* [1994] C.O.D. 393, Leggatt L.J.

1278. Police (Amendment) (No. 2) Regulations 1992.
revoked: regs. 95/215, reg. 70.

1280. Town and Country Planning General Development (Amendment) (No. 3) Order 1991.
revoked: ord. 95/418, art. 9.

1302. Serbia and Montenegro (United Nations Sanctions) Order 1992.
see *R.* v. *Searle*, *The Times*, February 27, 1995, C.A.

1303. Serbia and Montenegro (United Nations Sanctions) (Dependent Territories) Order 1992.
applied: ord. 95/1032, art. 3.

1312. Social Security (Australia) Order 1992.
modified: ord. 95/767, art. 2.

1329. Council Tax (Valuation of Dwellings) (Scotland) Regulations 1992.
reg. 3(1), see *Highland Region and Western Isles (Assessor for)* v. *Campbell (I.H.)*, 1995 S.L.T. 1290.

1330. Council Tax (Contents of Valuation Lists) (Scotland) Regulations 1992.
reg. 2, amended: regs. 94/3170, reg. 5.

1332. Council Tax (Administration and Enforcement) (Scotland) Regulations 1992.
Sch. 2, para. 2, amended: regs. 94/3170, reg. 6.
Sch. 2, para. 5, amended: regs. 94/3170, reg. 6.
Sch. 2, para. 8, amended: regs. 94/3170, reg. 6.

NO.

1992—cont.

1333. Council Tax (Exempt Dwellings) (Scotland) Order 1992.
Sch., para. 11, amended: ord. 95/598, art. 2.
Sch., para. 12, amended: ord. 95/598, art. 2.
Sch., para. 24, inserted: ord. 95/598, art. 2.

1335. Council Tax (Reductions for Disabilities) (Scotland) Regulations 1992.
varied: regs. 94/3170, reg. 4.

1370. Motor Vehicles (Off Road Events) Regulations 1992.
revoked: regs. 95/1371, reg. 2.

1372. London Priority Route Order 1992.
Sch., amended: ord. 95/1130, art. 2.

1409. Council Tax (Discounts) (Scotland) Regulations 1992.
Sch., para. 5, inserted: regs. 95/597, reg. 2.

1422. Act of Sederunt (Rules of the Court of Session Amendment No. 4) (Solicitors, Notaries Public, Qualified Conveyances and Executry Practitioners) 1992.
revoked: Act 94/1443, para. 3.

1433. Act of Sederunt (Rules of the Court of Session Amendment No. 3) (Taxation of Accounts) 1992.
revoked: Act 94/1443, para. 3.

1493. Town and Country Planning General Development (Amendment) (No. 4) Order 1991.
revoked: ord. 95/418, art. 9, ord. 95/419, art. 28.

1507. Food Safety (Fishery Products) (Derogations) Regulations 1992.
applied: regs. 95/1763, reg. 3.
reg. 2, amended: regs. 95/1763, reg. 9.
Sch., amended: regs. 95/1763, reg. 9.

1508. Food Safety (Live Bivalve Molluscs) (Derogations) Regulations 1992.
applied: regs. 95/1763, reg. 3.
reg. 2, amended: regs. 95/1763, reg. 9.
Sch., amended: regs. 95/1763, reg. 9.

1520. Medicines (Medicated Feeding Stuffs) (No. 2) Regulations 1992.
applied: regs. 95/1086, reg. 2, regs. 95/1372, reg. 2.
reg. 2, amended: regs. 94/3142, reg. 21.
reg. 3, amended: regs. 95/799, reg. 2.
reg. 4, amended: regs. 94/3142, reg. 21.
reg. 6, amended: regs. 94/3142, reg. 21.
Sch. 2, amended: regs. 94/3142, reg. 21.
Sch. 3, substituted: regs. 95/799, reg. 2.

1523. Motor Vehicles (Off Road Events) (Amendment) Regulations 1992.
revoked: regs. 95/1371, reg. 2.

1533. Act of Sederunt (Rules of the Court of Session Amendment No. 5) (Public Trusts) 1992.
revoked: Act 94/1443, para. 3.

NO.

1992—cont.

1563. Town and Country Planning General Development (Amendment) (No. 5) Order 1991.
revoked: ord. 95/418, art. 9, ord. 95/419, art. 28.

1579. Non-Automatic Weighing Instruments (EEC Requirements) Regulations 1992.
referred to: ord. 95/1011, art. 2.
reg. 9, amended: regs. 95/428, reg. 3.
reg. 28, amended: regs. 95/428, reg. 4.

1582. Merchant Shipping (Signals of Distress) Rules 1992.
referred to: ord. 95/1299, art. 2.

1589. Education (Assisted Places) (Scotland) Amendment Regulations 1992.
revoked: regs. 95/1713, reg. 31.

1590. St. Mary's Music School (Aided Places) Amendment Regulations 1992.
revoked: regs. 95/1712, reg. 17.

1661. Education (Assisted Places) (Incidental Expenses) (Amendment) Regulations 1992.
revoked: regs. 95/2017, reg. 16.

1662. Education (Grants) (Music and Ballet Schools) (Amendment) Regulations 1992.
revoked: regs. 95/2018, reg. 16.

1698. Education (National Curriculum) (Attainment Targets and Programmes of Study in Welsh) (Amendment) Order 1992.
revoked: ord. 95/69, art. 7.

1725. Housing (Northern Ireland) Order 1992.
Pt. II, applied: ord. 95/280, art. 2.

1796. Oil Related and Petrochemical Plants (Rateable Values) (Scotland) Order 1992.
revoked: ord. 95/374, art. 2.

1798. Education (Assisted Places) (Amendment) Regulations 1992.
revoked: regs. 95/2016, reg. 24.

1812. Child Support (Information, Evidence and Disclosure) Regulations 1992.
reg. 2, amended: regs. 95/1045, reg. 22.
reg. 3, amended: regs. 95/1045, reg. 23.
reg. 9A, inserted: regs. 95/1045, reg. 24.

1813. Child Support (Maintenance Assessment Procedure) Regulations 1992.
reg. 8, amended: regs. 95/1045, reg. 28.
reg. 9, amended: regs. 95/1045, reg. 29.
reg. 10, amended: regs. 95/1045, reg. 30.
reg. 11, amended: regs. 95/1045, reg. 31.
reg. 13, amended: regs. 95/1045, reg. 32.
reg. 14, amended: regs. 95/1045, reg. 33.
reg. 17, amended: regs. 95/1045, reg. 34.
reg. 19, amended: regs. 95/1045, reg. 35.
reg. 30, amended: regs. 95/1045, reg. 36.

NO.

1992—cont.

1813. Child Support (Maintenance Assessment Procedure) Regulations 1992—*cont.*
reg. 31, amended: regs. 95/1045, reg. 37.
reg. 36, amended: regs. 95/1045, reg. 38.
reg. 40, amended: regs. 95/1045, reg. 39.
reg. 42, amended: regs. 95/1045, reg. 40.

1814. Council Tax Benefit (General) Regulations 1992.
amended: regs. 95/625, regs. 3, 4, 11–18.
varied: regs. 94/3170, reg. 4.
reg. 2, amended: regs. 95/560, reg. 14, reg. 2, amended: regs. 95/625, reg. 3, reg. 11; regs. 95/2303, reg. 2.
reg. 3, amended: regs. 94/3061, reg. 3.
reg. 3, amended: regs. 95/560, reg. 15.
reg. 4, amended: regs. 95/560, reg. 16.
reg. 4B, inserted: regs. 95/560, reg. 17.
reg. 4C, amended: regs. 95/625, reg. 4; regs. 95/2303, reg. 2.
reg. 13A, amended: regs. 95/560, reg. 18, regs. 95/626, reg. 12.
reg. 14, amended: regs. 94/3061, reg. 3.
reg. 22, amended: regs. 95/2303, reg. 2.
reg. 26, amended: regs. 95/560, reg. 19, reg. 26, amended: regs. 95/626, reg. 13, regs. 95/2303, reg. 2.
reg. 34, amended: regs. 95/2303, reg. 2.
reg. 36, amended: regs. 95/2303, reg. 2.
reg. 38, amended: regs. 95/1742, reg. 2.
reg. 40, amended: regs. 95/626, reg. 14.
reg. 42, amended: regs. 95/1742, reg. 3.
reg. 58, amended: regs. 95/560, reg. 20.
reg. 59, amended: regs. 95/511, reg. 3.
reg. 63, amended: regs. 95/2303, reg. 2.
reg. 71, applied: regs. 95/209, reg. 9.
reg. 72, applied: regs. 95/209, reg. 9.
reg. 80, amended: regs. 95/560, reg. 21.
reg. 92, amended: regs. 95/626, reg. 15.
reg. 93, amended: regs. 95/626, reg. 16.
Sch. 1, para. 13, amended: regs. 95/560, reg. 22, regs. 95/626, reg. 17; regs. 95/2303, reg. 2.
Sch. 4, para. 2, amended: regs. 95/560, reg. 23.
Sch. 4, para. 12, revoked: regs. 95/2303, reg. 2.
Sch. 4, para. 51, amended: regs. 95/2303, reg. 2.
Sch. 4, para. 55, inserted: regs. 95/626, reg. 18.
Sch. 4, para. 56, inserted: regs. 95/1339, reg. 2.
Sch. 4, para. 57, inserted: regs. 95/1339, reg. 2.
Sch. 5, para. 6, substituted: regs. 95/2303, reg. 2.
Sch. 5, para. 27, amended: regs. 95/2303, reg. 2.
Sch. 5, para. 30A, inserted: regs. 95/2303, reg. 2.
Sch. 5, para. 31, amended: regs. 95/2303, reg. 2.

NO.

1992—cont.

1815. Child Support (Maintenance Assessment and Special Cases) Regulations 1992.
reg. 1, amended: regs. 95/1045, reg. 41.
reg. 2, amended: regs. 95/1045, reg. 42.
reg. 6, amended: regs. 95/1045, reg. 43.
reg. 9, amended: regs. 95/1045, reg. 44.
reg. 10, amended: regs. 95/1045, reg. 45.
reg. 11, amended: regs. 95/1045, reg. 46.
reg. 12, amended: regs. 95/1045, reg. 47.
reg. 15, amended: regs. 95/1045, reg. 48.
reg. 16, amended: regs. 95/1045, reg. 49.
reg. 17, revoked: regs. 95/1045, reg. 50.
reg. 22, amended: regs. 95/1045, reg. 51.
reg. 25, amended: regs. 95/1045, reg. 52.
reg. 26, amended: regs. 95/1045, reg. 53.
Sch. 1, para. 1, amended: regs. 95/1045, reg. 54.
Sch. 1, para. 2, amended: regs. 95/1045, reg. 54.
Sch. 1, para. 3, amended: regs. 95/1045, reg. 54.
Sch. 1, para. 5, amended: regs. 95/1045, reg. 54.
Sch. 1, para. 20, amended: regs. 95/1045, reg. 54.
Sch. 1, para. 23, amended: regs. 95/1045, reg. 54.
Sch. 2, para. 24, amended: regs. 95/1045, reg. 55.
Sch. 2, para. 27, amended: regs. 95/1045, reg. 55.
Sch. 3, para. 1, amended: regs. 95/1045, reg. 56.
Sch. 3, para. 2, amended: regs. 95/1045, reg. 56.
Sch. 3, para. 2A, inserted: regs. 95/1045, reg. 56.
Sch. 3, para. 3, amended: regs. 95/1045, reg. 56.
Sch. 3A, inserted: regs. 95/1045, reg. 57.
Sch. 3B, inserted: regs. 95/1045, reg. 57.
Sch. 4, amended: regs. 95/1045, reg. 58.
Sch. 5, para. 2, substituted: regs. 95/1045, reg. 59.
Sch. 5, para. 3, amended: regs. 95/1045, reg. 59.
Sch. 5, para. 3A, inserted: regs. 95/1045, reg. 59.

1816. Child Support (Arrears, Interest and Adjustment of Maintenance Assessment) Regulations 1992.
reg. 4, amended: regs. 95/1045, reg. 7.
reg. 10, substituted: regs. 95/1045, reg. 8.
reg. 11, amended: regs. 95/1045, reg. 9.
reg. 12, substituted: regs. 95/1045, reg. 10.
reg. 13, amended: regs. 95/1045, reg. 11.

1878. Act of Sederunt (Fees of Witnesses and Shorthand Writers in the Sheriff Court) 1992.
Sch. 2, amended: Act 95/1024, rule 2.

NO.

1992—cont.

1898. Act of Sederunt (Rules of the Court of Session Amendment No. 8) (Fees of Solicitors in Speculative Actions) 1992.
revoked: Act 94/1443, para. 3.

1899. Court of Protection (Amendment) Rules 1992.
revoked: rules 94/3046, rule 95.

1905. Act of Sederunt (Rules of the Court of Session Amendment No. 6) (Shorthand Writers' Fees) 1992.
revoked: Act 94/1443, para. 3.

1906. Act of Sederunt (Rules of the Court of Session Amendment No. 7) (Witnesses' Fees) 1992.
revoked: Act 94/1443, para. 3.

1919. Environmentally Sensitive Areas (Loch Lomond) Designation Order 1992.
art. 4A, inserted: ord. 94/3067, art. 2.
art. 5, amended: ord. 94/3067, art. 2.
art. 7A, inserted: ord. 94/3067, art. 2.
Annex, inserted: ord. 94/3067, art. 2.

1920. Environmentally Sensitive Areas (Breadalbane) Designation Order 1992.
art. 4A, inserted: ord. 94/3067, art. 2.
art. 5, amended: ord. 94/3067, art. 2.
art. 7A, inserted: ord. 94/3067, art. 2.
Annex, inserted: ord. 94/3067, art. 2.

1940. Plant Breeders' Rights (Miscellaneous Ornamental Plants) (Variation) Scheme 1992.
revoked: Scheme 95/527, art. 2.

1974. Salmon (Definition of Methods of Net Fishing and Constrcution of Nets) (Scotland) Regulations 1992.
Pt. II, applied: ord. 95/2193, art. 3; ord. 95/2194, art. 3.

1989. Child Support (Collection and Enforcement) Regulations 1992.
reg. 4, amended: regs. 95/1045, reg. 12.
reg. 5, amended: regs. 95/1045, reg. 13.
reg. 8, amended: regs. 95/1045, reg. 14.
reg. 9, amended: regs. 95/1045, reg. 15.
reg. 10, amended: regs. 95/1045, reg. 16.
reg. 11, amended: regs. 95/1045, reg. 17.
reg. 17, substituted: regs. 95/1045, reg. 18.
reg. 20, amended: regs. 95/1045, reg. 19.

2037. Fresh Meat (Hygiene and Inspection) Regulations 1992.
revoked: regs. 95/539, reg. 25.

2051. Management of Health and Safety at Work Regulations 1992.
reg. 3, applied: regs. 95/2038, reg. 7.
reg. 9, applied: regs. 94/3140, reg. 16.

2242. Local Government (Promotion of Economic Development) Regulations 1992.
revoked: regs. 95/556, reg. 2.

NO.

1992—cont.

2289. Act of Sederunt (Rules of the Court of Session Amendment No. 9) (Miscellaneous) 1992.
revoked: Act 94/1443, para. 3.

2318. Banking Coordination (Second Council Directive) Regulations 1992.
reg. 9, amended: regs. 95/1442, reg. 50.
Sch. 8, paras. 13–16, revoked: regs. 95/1442, reg. 52.

2319. Goods Vehicles' (Operators' Licences, Qualifications and Fees) (Amendment) Regulations 1992.
reg. 4, revoked: 1995, c. 23, Sch. 8, Pt. II.

2326. Insurance Companies (Pensions Business) (Transitional Provisions) Regulations 1992.
reg. 4, amended: regs. 94/3036, reg. 2.

2353. Fresh Meat and Poultry Meat (Hygiene, Inspection and Examinations for Residues) (Charges) (Amendment) Regulations 1992.
revoked: regs. 95/361, reg. 15, Sch. 3.

2361. Education (Publication of Draft Proposals and Orders) (Further Education Corporations) Regulations 1992.
reg. 7, applied: ord. 94/2979.

2372. Electromagnetic Compatibility Regulations 1992.
reg. 3, amended: regs. 94/3080, regs. 3, 4, 7.
reg. 8, substituted: regs. 94/3080, reg. 7.
reg. 11, amended: regs. 94/3080, reg. 7.
reg. 22, substituted: regs. 94/3080, reg. 6.
reg. 23, amended: regs. 94/3080, reg. 7.
reg. 27, substituted: regs. 94/3080, reg. 6.
reg. 30, amended: regs. 94/3080, reg. 4.
reg. 33, substituted: regs. 94/3080, reg. 4.
reg. 36, amended: regs. 94/3080, reg. 7.
reg. 39, amended: regs. 94/3080, reg. 7.
reg. 77A, inserted: regs. 94/3080, reg. 4.
reg. 85, substituted: regs. 94/3080, reg. 4.
reg. 94, amended: regs. 94/3080, reg. 4.
reg. 95, amended: regs. 94/3080, reg. 4.
Sch. 4, substituted: regs. 94/3038, reg. 4.

2382. Control of Substances Hazardous to Health (Amendment) Regulations 1992.
revoked: regs. 94/3246, reg. 18.

2383. United Kingdom Ecolabelling Board Regulations 1992.
applied: regs. 94/3076, Sch. 6.

2401. National Health Service (General Medical and Pharmaceutical Services) (Scotland) Amendment (No. 2) Regulations 1992.
revoked: regs. 95/414, reg. 13.

NO.

1992—cont.

2423. Telecommunications Terminal Equipment Regulations 1992.
amended throughout: regs. 94/3129, reg. 7. applied: regs. 94/3129, reg. 10.
reg. 2, amended: regs. 95/144, reg. 3, reg. 94/3129, reg. 4.
reg. 3, amended: regs. 95/144, reg. 3.
amended for certain purposes; regs. 94/3129, reg. 10, regs. 94/3129, reg. 3, reg. 7.
reg. 4, amended: regs. 94/3129, reg. 4.
reg. 5(1), amended for certain purposes; regs. 94/3129, reg. 10.
reg. 8, substituted for certain purposes; regs. 94/3129, reg. 10.
reg. 9, substituted for certain purposes; regs. 94/3129, reg. 10.
reg. 10, amended for certain purposes; regs. 94/3129, reg. 10.
reg. 10, substituted: regs. 94/3129, reg. 7.
reg. 12, amended for certain purposes; regs. 94/3129, reg. 10.
reg. 51, amended: regs. 94/3129, reg. 6.
reg. 53, amended: regs. 94/3129, reg. 6.
reg. 65A, added: regs. 94/3129, reg. 7.
reg. 73, substituted: regs. 94/3129, reg. 7.
reg. 73, amended: regs. 95/144, reg. 3.
Sch. 2, substituted: regs. 94/3129, regs. 5, 7.
Sch. 3, substituted: regs. 94/3129, reg. 7.
Sch. 4, substituted: regs 94/3129, reg. 7.
Sch. 5, amended for certain purposes: regs. 94/3129, reg. 10.
Pt. IVA, inserted for certain purposes; regs. 94/3129, Sched.

2428. Local Authorities (Funds) (England) Regulations 1992.
reg. 4, applied: regs. 94/3115, reg. 2.
reg. 5, applied: regs. 94/3115, reg. 2.
reg. 6, applied: regs. 94/3115, reg. 2.
reg. 11, applied: regs. 94/3115, reg. 2.

2450. Town and Country Planning General Development (Amendment) (No. 6) Order 1991.
revoked: ord. 95/418, art. 9, ord. 95/419, art. 28.

2484. Fosse Health, Leicestershire Community National Health Service Trust (Establishment) Order 1992.
revoked: ord. 95/478, art. 2.

2498. Calderdale Healthcare National Health Service Trust (Establishment) Amendment Order 1992.
art. 3, amended: ord. 95/1469, art. 2.

2499. Royal Hull Hospital's National Health Service Trust (Establishment) Order 1992.
art. 4, amended; 1995 No. 91, art. 2.

2522. East Surrey Hospital and Community Healthcare National Health Service Trust (Establishment) Order 1992.
art. 2, amended: ord. 95/968, art. 2.

NO.

1992—cont.

2545. Durham County Ambulance Service National Health Service Trust (Establishment) Order 1992.
art. 4, amended: ord. 95/1311, art. 2.

2546. Cumbria Ambulance Service National Health Service Trust (Establishment) Order 1992.
art. 4, amended; 1995 No. 92, art. 2.

2554. Princess Royal Hospital National Health Service Trust (Establishment) Order 1992.
art. 4, amended; 1995 No. 88, art. 2.

2561. Wolverley National Health Service Trust (Establishment) Order 1992.
revoked: ord. 95/846, art. 2.

2641. Child Support Appeal Tribunals (Procedure) Regulations 1992.
reg. 2, amended: regs. 95/1045, reg. 2.
reg. 3, amended: regs. 95/1045, reg. 3.
reg. 3A, inserted: regs. 95/1045, reg. 4.
reg. 6, amended: regs. 95/1045, reg. 5.
reg. 11, amended: regs. 95/1045, reg. 6.

2644. Child Support Act 1991 (Commencement No. 3 and Transitional Provisions) Order 1992.
Sch. Pt. I, revoked: 1995 c. 34, s. 18.

2645. Child Support (Maintenance Arrangements and Jurisdiction) Regulations 1992.
reg. 1, amended: regs. 95/1045, reg. 25.
reg. 2, substituted: regs. 95/1045, reg. 26.
reg. 3, amended: regs. 95/1045, reg. 27.

2647. Gaming Act (Variation of Monetary Limits) (No. 4) Order 1992.
applied: ord. 95/2288, art. 3.
revoked: ord. 95/2288, art. 4.

2672. Patents, Designs and Marks (Chile, Gambia, Hong Kong, Italy, Japan, Lesotho and Swaziland) (Convention and Relevant Countries) Order 1992.
revoked: ord. 94/3219, art. 3 (designs), ord. 94/3220, art. 3 (patents).

2677. Sheep Annual Premium Regulations 1992.
reg. 2, amended: regs. 94/2741, reg. 2.
reg. 3, amended: regs. 94/2741, reg. 2.
reg. 3A, inserted: regs. 94/2741, reg. 2.
reg. 3B, inserted: regs. 94/2741, reg. 2.
reg. 4, amended: regs. 94/2741, reg. 2.
reg. 5, amended: regs. 94/2741, reg. 2.
reg. 7, amended: regs. 94/2741, reg. 2.
reg. 8, revoked: regs. 94/2741, reg. 2.

2683. Town and Country Planning (Crown Land Applications) Regulations 1992.
revoked: regs. 95/1139, reg. 4.

2737. Llandough Hospital National Health Service Trust (Establishment) Order 1992.
art. 2, amended: ord. 95/918, art. 2.

NO.

1992—cont.

2755. Gaming (Small Charges) (Scotland) Order 1992.
art. 2, amended: ord. 95/1750, art. 2.

2790. Statistics of Trade (Customs and Excise) Regulations 1992.
reg. 3, amended: regs. 94/2914, reg. 3.

2885. Offshore Installations (Safety Case) Regulations 1992.
reg. 2, amended: regs. 95/738, reg. 23, applied: regs. 95/743, reg. 2.
reg. 8, amended: regs. 95/743, reg. 24.
reg. 14, amended: regs. 95/738, reg. 23.
Sch. 3, amended: regs. 95/738, reg. 23.

2902. Transport and Works (Applications and Objections Procedure) Rules 1992.
referred to: ord. 95/519, art. 2.
applied: ord. 95/2458, ord. 95/2383.
referred to: ord. 95/1332, preamble.

2903. Levying Bodies (General) Regulations 1992.
reg. 1(2), amended: regs. 94/3223, regs. 5, 6.

2921. Meat Hygiene Appeals Tribunal (Procedure) Regulations 1992.
reg. 1, amended: regs. 95/539, reg. 26, regs. 95/540, reg. 27.
reg. 2, substituted: regs. 95/539, reg. 26, amended: regs. 95/540, reg. 27.

2929. Local Authorities (Funds) (Wales) Regulations 1992.
reg. 2, amended: regs. 94/2964, reg. 2.
reg. 6, amended: regs. 94/2964, reg. 2.

2932. Provision and Use of Work Equipment Regulations 1992.
Sch. 1, para. 1, substituted: regs. 94/3260, reg. 2.
Sch. 1, para. 25, substituted: regs. 94/3098, reg. 7.
Sch. 1, para. 28, substituted: regs. 94/3080, reg. 8.
Sch. 1, para. 29, substituted: regs. 94/2063, reg. 5.
Sch. 1, para. 35, revoked: regs. 94/3080, reg. 8.
Sch. 1, para. 36, inserted: regs. 94/3017, reg. 24.

2933. National Health Service (General Medical and Pharmaceutical Services) (Scotland) Amendment (No. 3) Regulations 1992.
revoked: regs. 95/414, reg. 13.

2966. Personal Protective Equipment at Work Regulations 1992.
applied: regs. 95/743, reg. 18.
reg. 2, applied: regs. 95/743, reg. 2.
Sch. 1, applied: regs. 94/3246, reg. 5.
Sch. 1, substituted: regs. 94/3017, reg. 25.
Sch. 2, Pt. VIII, amended: regs. 94/3246, reg. 18.

NO.

1992—cont.

2977. National Assistance (Assessment of Resources) Regulations 1992.
reg. 2, amended: regs. 95/858, reg. 2.
Sch. 2, para. 3, amended: regs. 95/858, reg. 3.
Sch. 3, para. 27, amended: regs. 95/858, reg. 4.

2985. Street Works (Registers, Notices, Directions and Designations) Regulations 1992.
reg. 3, amended: regs. 95/990, regs. 3–5.
reg. 13, amended: regs. 95/1154, regs. 3, 4, 5.

2996. Local Government Finance (Payments) (English Authorities) Regulations 1992.
see *R.* v. *Secretary of State for Wales, ex p. Gwent County Council* [1994] 34 RVR 214, C.A.

3004. Workplace (Health, Safety and Welfare) Regulations 1992.
reg. 2, applied: regs. 95/2038, reg. 8.

3022. Gaming Act (Variation of Monetary Limits) (Scotland) (No. 3) Order 1992.
revoked: ord. 95/2360, art. 4.

3039. Civil Aviation (Joint Financing) (Fourth Amendment) Regulations 1992.
revoked: regs. 94/3055, reg. 3.

3041. Social Security (Dependency) Amendment Regulations 1992.
reg. 4, applied: regs. 95/310, reg. 25.

3046. National Health Service (Superannuation, Premature Retirement and Injury Benefits) (Scotland) Amendment Regulations 1990.
reg. 2, amended: regs. 95/365, reg. V2.
regs. 3–13, revoked: regs. 95/365, reg. V2.

3061. Non-Domestic Rating Contributions (Scotland) Regulations 1992.
reg. 4, amended: regs. 94/3146, reg. 3.
reg. 9, amended: regs. 94/3146, reg. 4.
Sch. 1, para. 2, amended: regs. 94/3061, reg. 5.
Sch. 1, para. 3, amended: regs. 94/3146, reg. 5.
Sch. 1, para. 4, amended: regs. 94/3146, reg. 5.
Sch. 2, para. 1, amended: regs. 94/3146, reg. 6.
Sch. 2, para. 2, amended: regs. 94/3146, reg. 6.
Sch. 2, para. 3, amended: regs. 94/3146, reg. 6.
Sch. 2, para. 4, amended: regs. 94/3146, reg. 6.
Sch. 2, para. 5, amended: regs. 94/3146, reg. 6.
Sch. 3, para. 3, amended: regs. 94/3146, reg. 7.

NO.

1992—cont.

3073. Supply of Machinery (Safety) Regulations 1992.
reg. 2, amended: regs. 94/2063, reg. 4.
reg. 3, amended: regs. 94/2063, reg. 4.
reg. 6, amended: regs. 94/2063, reg. 4.
reg. 7, amended: regs. 94/2063, reg. 4.
reg. 7A, inserted: regs. 94/2063, reg. 4.
reg. 8, amended: regs. 94/2063, reg. 4.
reg. 8A, inserted: regs. 94/2063, reg. 4.
reg. 9, inserted: regs. 94/2063, reg. 4.
reg. 11, substituted: regs. 94/2063, reg. 4.
reg. 17, substituted: regs. 94/2063, reg. 4.
reg. 21, amended: regs. 94/2063, reg. 4.
reg. 22, amended: regs. 94/2063, reg. 4.
reg. 25, amended: regs. 94/2063, reg. 4.
reg. 26, amended: regs. 94/2063, reg. 4.
reg. 28, substituted: regs. 94/2063, reg. 4.
reg. 29, amended: regs. 94/2063, reg. 4.
reg. 30, amended: regs. 94/2063, reg. 4.
Sch. 2A, inserted: regs. 94/2063, reg. 4.
Sch. 3, amended: regs. 94/2063, reg. 4.
Sch. 4, substituted and amended: regs. 94/2063, reg. 4.
Sch. 5, substituted: regs. 94/2063, reg. 4.

3076. Gaming (Bingo) Act (Variation of Monetary Limit) Order 1992.
revoked; 1995 No. 122, art. 2.

3077. Goods Vehicles (Community Authorisation) Regulations 1992.
reg. 13, revoked: regs. 95/1290, reg. 3.
reg. 14, revoked: 1995, c. 23, Sch. 8, Pt. II.

3082. Non-Domestic Rating Contributions (England) Regulations 1992.
amended by 1994 No. 3139.
Sch. 1, Pt. I, applied: regs. 94/3054, reg. 4.

3083. Local Government Superannuation (Remuneration) Regulations 1992.
revoked: regs. 95/1019 Sch. M5.

3087. Motor Vehicles Tyres (Safety) (Amendment) Regulations 1992.
revoked: regs. 94/3117, reg. 1.

3091. Patents (Supplementary Protection Certificate for Medicinal Products) Regulations 1992.
reg. 5, see *Research Corp.'s Supplementary Protection Certificate* [1994] R.P.C. 387, Patents Office.

3094. Child Support Fees Regulations 1992.
reg. 3, amended: regs. 95/1045, reg. 20.
reg. 4, amended: regs. 95/1045, reg. 21.

3107. Motor Vehicles (EC Type Approval) Regulations 1992.
referred to: regs. 95/925, reg. 3.
Sch. 1, amended: regs. 95/2328, reg. 2.

3122. Value Added Tax (Cars) Order 1992.
art. 2, amended: ord. 95/1269, art. 3.
art. 4, amended: ord. 95/1667, art. 3, ord. 95/1269, art. 4.

NO.

1992—cont.

3122. Value Added Tax (Cars) Order 1992—*cont.*
art. 4A, inserted: ord. 95/1667, art. 4.
art. 5, amended: ord. 95/1269, art. 5.
art. 5, substituted: ord. 95/1667, art. 5.
art. 6, amended: ord. 95/1667, art. 6.
art. 6A, inserted: ord. 95/1667, art. 7.
art. 7, amended: ord. 95/1269, art. 6.
art. 8, amended: ord. 95/1667, art. 8.
art. 8, substituted: ord. 95/1269, art. 7.

3129. Value Added Tax (Special Provisions) Order 1992.
revoked: ord. 95/1268. art. 3.
art. 8, amended: ord. 95/957, art. 3.
art. 9, revoked: ord. 95/957, art. 4.

3136. Milk and Dairies (Standardisation and Importation) (Scotland) Regulations 1992.
reg. 2, revoked: regs. 95/1372, reg. 23.
regs. 5, 6, revoked: regs. 95/1372, reg. 23.

3140. Education (National Curriculum) (Attainment Targets and Programmes of Study in Welsh) (Amendment) (No. 2) Order 1992.
revoked: ord. 95/69, art. 7.

3143. Milk and Dairies (Standardisation and Importation) Regualtions 1992.
reg. 3, revoked: regs. 95/1086, reg. 23.
regs. 5, 6, revoked: regs. 95/1086, reg. 23.

3145. Plastic Materials and Articles in Contact with Food Regulations 1992.
reg. 5, amended: regs. 95/360, reg. 2.
reg. 6, amended: regs. 95/360, reg. 2.
reg. 13, inserted: regs. 95/360, reg. 2.
Sch. 1, amended: regs. 95/360, reg. 2.
Sch. 2, amended: regs. 95/360, reg. 2.

3146. Active Implant Medical Devices Regulations 1992.
reg. 7, applied: regs. 95/2487, reg. 4.
reg. 8, applied: regs. 95/2487, reg. 2.

3151. Excise Goods (Drawback) Regulations 1992.
revoked: regs. 95/1046, reg. 2.

3155. Excise Duties (Personal Reliefs) Order 1992.
Sch., see *Customs and Excise Commissioners* v. *Carrier*, *The Times*, December 7, 1994, D.C.

3162. Patents (Supplementary Protection Certificate for Medicinal Products) Rules 1992.
rule 5, see *Research Corp.'s Supplementary Protection Certificate* [1994] R.P.C. 667, Aldous J.
rule 9, see *Research Corp.'s Supplementary Protection Certificate* [1994] R.P.C. 387, Patents Office.

3163. Food Safety (Fishery Products) Regulations 1992.
applied: regs. 95/1763, reg. 3.
reg. 2, amended: regs. 95/1763, reg. 9.

NO.

1992—cont.

3164. Food Safety (Live Bivalve Molluscs and Other Shellfish) Regulations 1992.
applied: regs. 95/1763, reg. 3.
reg. 2, amended: regs. 95/1763, reg. 9.

3165. Food Safety (Fishery Products on Fishing Vessels) Regulations 1992.
applied: regs. 95/1763, reg. 3.
Sch., Pt. I, amended: regs. 95/1763, reg. 9.

3218. Banking Co-ordination (Second Council Directive) Regulations 1992.
applied: regs. 95/1019, regs. L6, L8.
reg. 2, amended: regs. 95/1217, reg. 2.

3222. Value Added Tax (Input Tax) Order 1992.
art. 2, amended: ord. 95/281, art. 3, ord. 95/1267, art. 3.
art. 4, amended: ord. 95/281, art. 4; substituted: ord. 95/1267, art. 4.
art. 5, amended: ord. 95/281, art. 5.
art. 6, substituted: ord. 95/281, art. 6.
art. 7, amended: ord. 95/281, art. 7.
art. 7, referred to: ord. 95/1667, arts. 7, 8.

3230. Transport and Works (Description of Works Interfering with Navigation) Order 1992.
art. 2, applied: ord. 95/519.

3238. Non-Domestic Rating Contributions (Wales) Regulations 1992.
reg. 8, amended: regs. 94/3125, reg. 2.
reg. 9, amended: regs. 94/3125, reg. 2.
Sch. 1, para. 4, amended: regs. 94/3125, reg. 3.
Sch. 2, para. 2, amended: regs. 94/3125, reg. 3.
Sch. 2, para. 8, amended: regs. 94/3125, reg. 3.
Sch. 2, Pt. II, amended: regs. 94/3125, reg. 3.
Sch. 4, substituted: regs. 94/3125, reg. 3.

3239. Billing Authorities (Anticipation of Precepts) Regulations 1992.
Transitional provision applicable generally to 1992 regs.: regs. 94/3223, reg. 4.
reg. 2, amended: regs. 95/235, reg. 2.
reg. 3, revoked: regs. 95/235, reg. 1.

3240. Environmental Information Regulations 1992.
regs. 2, 4, see *R.* v. *British Coal Corp. ex p. Ibstock* [1994] NPC 133, Harrison J.

3279. Utilities Supplies and Works Contracts Regulations 1992.
reg. 33, amended: regs. 95/201, reg. 30.

3280. Genetically Modified Organisms (Deliberate Release) Regulations 1992.
reg. 2, amended: regs. 95/304, regs. 3, 4, 6.

NO.

1992—cont.

3280. Genetically Modified Organisms (Deliberate Release) Regulations 1992—*cont.*
reg. 5, amended: regs. 95/304, reg. 4.
reg. 6, amended: regs. 95/304, regs. 3, 4.
reg. 8, amended: regs. 95/304, regs. 4, 5.
reg. 10, amended: regs. 95/304, reg. 6.
reg. 11, amended: regs. 95/304, reg. 3.
reg. 17, amended: regs. 95/304, reg. 7.
reg. 18, amended: regs. 95/304, reg. 7.
Sch. 1, substituted: regs. 95/304, reg. 3.

3288. Package Travel, Package Holidays and Package Tours Regulations 1992.
referred to: regs. 94/3248, reg. 3.

3300. Fish Health Regulations 1992.
reg. 14, amended: regs. 95/886, reg. 2.
Sch. 2, substituted: regs. 95/886, reg. 2.
Sch. 7, Pt. I, amended: regs. 95/886, reg. 2.

3303. Animal By-Products Order 1992.
applied: regs. 95/614, reg. 2.

3304. Welfare of Animals during Transport Order 1992.
revoked: ord. 94/3249, art. 18(1).

1993

9. Rail Crossing Extinguishment and Diversion Orders 1993.
reg. 2, amended: regs. 95/451, reg. 2.
Sch. 4, amended: regs. 95/451, reg. 2.

10. Town and Country Planning (Public Path Orders) Regulations 1993.
Sch. 2, amended: regs. 95/451, reg. 3.

11. Public Path Orders Regulations 1993.
reg. 2, amended: regs. 95/451, reg. 4.
Sch. 1, substituted: regs. 95/451, reg. 4.

12. Wildlife and Countryside (Definitive Maps and Statements) Regulations 1993.
Sch. 6, amended: regs. 95/451, reg. 5.

29. West Midlands Ambulance Service National Health Service Trust (Establishment) Order 1993.
Sch., see *R.* v. *Wiltshire County Council, ex p. D.* [1994] 1 F.C.R. 172, Potts J.

82. Environmentally Sensitive Areas (North Kent Marshes) Designation Order 1993.
art. 6, amended: ord. 95/199, art. 4.
Sch. 2, amended: ord. 95/198, art. 5.

83. Environmentally Sensitive Areas (Lake District) Designation Order 1993.
art. 2, amended: ord. 95/195, art. 4.
art. 6, amended: ord. 95/960, art. 2, ord. 95/195, art. 5.
Sch. 3, revoked: ord. 95/195, art. 6.
Sch. 5, para. 3, revoked: ord. 95/195, art. 6.

NO.

1993—cont.

84. Environmentally Sensitive Areas (Avon Valley) Designation Order 1993.
art. 6, amended: ord. 95/197, art. 4.

85. Environmentally Sensitive Areas (Lake District) Designation Order 1993.
art. 2, amended: ord. 95/193, art. 4.
art. 6, amended: ord. 95/193, art. 5.
Sch. 3, revoked: ord. 95/193, art. 6.
Sch. 5, para. 4, revoked: ord. 95/193, art. 6.

86. Environmentally Sensitive Areas (South Wessex Downs) Designation Order 1993.
art. 6, amended: ord. 95/196, art. 4.
Sch. 3, para. 4, amended: ord. 95/196, art. 5.

87. Environmentally Sensitive Areas (South West Peak) Designation Order 1993.
art. 2, amended: ord. 95/192, art. 4.
art. 6, amended: ord. 95/192, art. 5.
Sch. 3, revoked: ord. 95/192, art. 6.
Sch. 5, para. 2, revoked: ord. 95/192, art. 6.

90. Connel–Ballachulish Trunk Road (A828) (Creagan Bridge Diversion) Order 1993.
Sch. 1, referred to: regs. 95/1476, Sch. 2.

123. Teddington Memorial National Health Service Trust (Establishment) Order 1993.
art. 4, amended: ord. 95/99, art. 2.
art. 7, amended: ord. 95/99, art. 2.

143. Food Protection (Emergency Prohibitions) (Oil and Chemical Pollution of Fish) (No. 2) Order 1993.
revoked in pt.: ord. 95/292, art. 2.

166. Central Rating Lists (Amendment) Regulations 1993.
revoked: regs. 94/3121, reg. 8.

175. Council Tax (Transitional Reduction Scheme) (England) Regulations 1993.
reg. 6, applied: regs. 95/209, reg. 5.

179. Air Navigation (Dangerous Goods) (Fourth Amendment) Regulations 1993.
revoked: regs. 94/3187, reg. 2.

191. Council Tax and Non-Domestic Rating (Demand Notices) (England) Regulations 1993.
reg. 1(2), amended: regs. 95/23, reg. 3.
reg. 1(3), amended: regs. 95/23, reg. 4.
reg. 6, amended: regs. 95/23, reg. 5.
Sch. 2, Pt. I, amended: regs. 95/121, regs. 2, 3.
Sch. 3, amended: regs. 95/23, regs. 6 and 7.
Sch. 3, Pt. I, amended: regs. 95/121, reg. 3.

NO.

1993—cont.

202. Local Authorities (Standing Orders) Regulations 1993.
applied in pt.: ord. 95/1042, art. 4.
applied: regs. 95/520, reg. 7.

231. Air Navigation (Third Amendment) Order 1993.
revoked: ord. 95/1038, art. 2.

234. Non-Domestic Rates (Levying) (Scotland) Regulations 1993.
reg. 4, applied: regs. 95/548, reg. 12.

252. Non-Domestic Rating (Demand Notices) (Wales) Regulations 1993.
reg. 2, amended: regs. 95/284, reg. 2.
Sch. 1, para. 5, amended: regs. 95/284, reg. 2.
Sch. 2, Pt. I, amended: regs. 95/284, reg. 2.
Sch. 2, Pt. II, amended: regs. 95/284, reg. 2.

255. Council Tax (Demand Notices) (Wales) Regulations 1993.
reg. 2, amended: regs. 95/160, reg. 2.
Sch. 2, Pt. I, amended: regs. 95/160, reg. 2.

277. Council Tax (Transitional Reduction Scheme) (Scotland) Regulations 1993.
varied: regs. 94/3170, reg. 4.

290. Council Tax (Alteration of Lists and Appeals) Regulations 1993.
amended: regs. 95/624, regs. 8–16.
reg. 17, amended: regs. 95/363, reg. 8.
reg. 23, see *Williams* v. *Bristol District Valuation Officer and Avon Valuation Tribunal* [1995] RA 189, Collins J.
reg. 32, see *Williams* v. *Bristol District Valuation Officer and Avon Valuation Tribunal* [1995] RA 189, Collins J.

291. Non-Domestic Rating (Alteration of Lists and Appeals) Regulations 1993.
referred to: regs. 95/623, reg. 2.
amended: regs. 95/623, regs. 3–13.
reg. 2, amended: regs. 95/609, reg. 19.
reg. 4, amended: regs. 95/609, reg. 3.
reg. 4A, inserted: regs. 95/609, reg. 4.
reg. 4B, inserted: regs. 95/609, reg. 4.
reg. 5, amended: regs. 95/609, reg. 3.
reg. 5, revoked: regs. 95/609, reg. 5.
reg. 5A, inserted: regs. 95/609, reg. 5.
reg. 7, amended: regs. 95/609, reg. 6.
reg. 9, substituted: regs. 95/609, reg. 7.
reg. 10, amended: regs. 95/609, reg. 8.
reg. 11, amended: regs. 95/609, reg. 9.
reg. 12, amended: regs. 95/609, reg. 10.
reg. 14, amended: regs. 95/609, reg. 11.
reg. 18, amended: regs. 95/609, reg. 12.
reg. 19, amended: regs. 95/609, reg. 13.
reg. 23, amended: regs. 95/609, reg. 14.
reg. 24, amended: regs. 95/609, reg. 15.
reg. 25, substituted: regs. 95/609, reg. 16.

NO.

1993—cont.

291. Non-Domestic Rating (Alteration of Lists and Appeals) Regulations 1993—*cont.*
reg. 27, amended: regs. 95/609, reg. 17.
reg. 28, amended: regs. 95/609, reg. 18.
reg. 32, amended: regs. 95/363, reg. 8.
reg. 34, amended: regs. 95/609, reg. 19.
reg. 38, amended: regs. 95/609, reg. 19.
reg. 40, amended: regs. 95/609, reg. 19.
reg. 44, amended: regs. 95/609, regs. 19, 20, 21.
reg. 47, amended: regs. 95/609, reg. 19.

313. Police (Amendment) Regulations 1993.
revoked: regs. 95/215, reg. 70.

366. Local Government Superannuation (Remuneration) Regulations 1993.
revoked: regs. 95/1019 Sch. M5.

380. Defence Research Agency Trading Fund Order 1993.
amended: ord. 95/650, arts. 2–4.

426. High Court of Justiciary Fees Amendment Order 1993.
revoked: ord. 94/3266, art. 3.

427. Court of Session etc. Fees Amendment Order 1993.
revoked: ord. 94/3265, art. 3.

439. Council Tax (Alteration of Lists and Appeals) Regulations 1993.
referred to: regs. 95/624, reg. 2.

455. Environmentally Sensitive Areas (Breckland) Designation Order 1993.
art. 2, amended: ord. 95/198, art. 4.
art. 6, amended: ord. 95/198, art. 5.

456. Environmentally Sensitive Areas (Clun) Designation Order 1993.
art. 2, amended: ord. 95/190, art. 4.
art. 6, amended: ord. 95/190, art. 5.
Sch. 6, revoked: ord. 95/190, art. 6.
Sch. 8, para. 1, revoked: ord. 95/190, art. 6.

457. Environmentally Sensitive Areas (North Peak) Designation Order 1993.
art. 2, amended: ord. 95/189, art. 4.
art. 6, amended: ord. 95/189, art. 5.
Sch. 3, revoked: ord. 95/189, art. 6.
Sch. 4, para. 5, revoked: ord. 95/189, art. 6.

458. Environmentally Sensitive Areas (Suffolk River Valleys) Designation Order 1993.
art. 6, amended: ord. 95/194, art. 4.

459. Environmentally Sensitive Areas (Test Valley) Designation Order 1993.
art. 6, amended: ord. 95/191, art. 4.
Sch. 3, para. 4, amended: ord. 95/191, art. 5.

NO.

1993—cont.

488. National Health Service (Fund Holding Practices) (Scotland) Regulations 1993.
reg. 18, applied: regs. 95/416, Sch. 1.

499. Civil Aviation (Navigation Service Charges) (Second Amendment) Regulations 1993.
revoked: regs. 95/497, reg. 3.

503. Bovine Animals (Identification, Marking and Breeding Records) (Amendment) Order 1993.
revoked: ord. 95/12, Sch. 1.

517. Common Agricultural Policy (Wine) Regulations 1993.
referred to: regs. 95/615, reg. 2.

521. National Health Service (General Medical and Pharmaceutical Services) (Scotland) Amendment Regulations 1993.
revoked: regs. 95/414, reg. 13.

543. Educational (Teachers) Regulations 1993.
amended: regs. 95/602, regs. 2–5.
reg. 3, amended: regs. 95/587, reg. 2.
reg. 3A, inserted: regs. 95/587, reg. 3.
Sch. 2, Pts. II, III, substituted: regs. 95/587, reg. 4.
Sch. 3, substituted: regs. 95/587, reg. 4.
para. 2, applied: regs. 94/3044, reg. 12.

547. Friendly Societies (General Charge and Fees) Regulations 1993.
revoked: regs. 95/709, reg. 7.

559. Further and Higher Education Act 1992 (Consequential Amendments) Regulations 1993.
reg. 5, revoked: regs. 94/3042, reg. 17.

567. National Health Service (Fund-holding Practices) Regulations 1993.
amended by regs. 95/693, regs. 2–17.
reg. 1, amended: regs. 95/693, reg. 2.
reg. 2, amended: regs. 95/693, reg. 3.
reg. 3, amended: regs. 95/693, reg. 4.
reg. 4, amended: regs. 95/693, reg. 5.
reg. 5, amended: regs. 95/693, reg. 6.
reg. 8, amended: regs. 95/693, reg. 7.
reg. 10, amended: regs. 95/693, reg. 8.
reg. 10A, inserted: regs. 95/693, reg. 9.
reg. 13, amended: regs. 95/693, reg. 10.
reg. 20, amended: regs. 95/693, reg. 11.
reg. 22A, inserted: regs. 95/693, reg. 12.
reg. 23, amended: regs. 95/693, reg. 13.
reg. 24, amended: regs. 95/693, reg. 14.
reg. 25, amended: regs. 95/693, reg. 15.
Sch. 1, para. 1, substituted: regs. 95/693, reg. 16.
Sch. 1, para. 3, revoked: regs. 95/693, reg. 16.
Sch. 3, para. 1, substituted: regs. 95/693, reg. 17.
Sch. 3, para. 2, revoked: regs. 95/693, reg. 17.
Sch. 3, para. 5, amended: regs. 95/693, reg. 17.

NO.

1993—cont.

567. National Health Service (Fund-holding Practices) Regulations 1993—*cont.*
Sch. 3, para. 10A, inserted: regs. 95/693, reg. 17.
Sch. 3, para. 12, amended: regs. 95/693, reg. 17.

568. Education (Grant-maintained Schools) (Finance) Regulations 1993.
applied: regs. 95/936, reg. 3.

569. Education (Grants) (Travellers and Displaced Persons) Regulations 1993.
reg. 3, amended: regs. 95/543, regs. 3–5.
reg. 5, substituted: regs. 95/543, reg. 6.

572. National Health Service (District Health Authorities) Order 1993.
applied: ord. 95/562, art. 1.

607. Air Navigation (Fourth Amendment) Order 1993.
revoked: ord. 95/1038, art. 2.

609. Further Education (Attribution of Surpluses and Deficits) Regulations 1993.
amended: regs. 95/1453, reg. 4.

644. Local Authorities Etc. (Scotland) (Amendment) Regulations 1993.
revoked: regs. 95/912, reg. 30.

646. Rent Officers (Additional Functions) (Scotland) Amendment Order 1993.
revoked: regs. 95/1643, reg. 7.

720. Police (Common Police Services) (Scotland) Order 1993.
revoked: ord. 95/706, art. 2.

743. Income Tax (Sub-contractors in the Construction Industry) Regulations 1993.
reg. 9, amended: regs. 95/217, reg. 2.
reg. 13, amended: regs. 95/448, reg. 2.

744. Income Tax (Employments) Regulations 1993.
referred to: regs. 95/917, reg. 2.
reg. 39, amended: regs. 95/1322, reg. 3.
reg. 41, amended: regs. 95/216, reg. 2.
reg. 42, amended: regs. 95/447, reg. 3.
reg. 46, substituted: regs. 95/1284, reg. 4.
reg. 46AA, inserted: regs. 95/1322, reg. 4.
reg. 46AB, inserted: regs. 95/1322, reg. 4.
reg. 48, amended: regs. 95/447, reg. 4.
reg. 49, amended: regs. 95/447, reg. 5.
reg. 54, amended: regs. 95/1223, reg. 2.
reg. 55, amended: regs. 95/447, reg. 6.
reg. 81, amended: regs. 95/853, reg. 4.
reg. 87, amended: regs. 95/853, reg. 5.
reg. 101, amended: regs. 95/447, reg. 7.
Chap. IV, inserted: regs. 95/853, reg. 6.

745. Health and Safety (Miscellaneous Modifications) Regulations 1993.
reg. 3, revoked: regs. 94/3246, reg. 18.

NO.

1993—cont.

752. Bingo Duty (Exemptions) Order 1993.
revoked: ord. 94/2967, art. 2.

768. Registered Establishments (Fees) (Scotland) Order 1993.
revoked: ord. 95/749, art. 5.

770. Act of Sederunt (Rules of the Court of Session Amendment) (Interest in Decrees and Extracts) 1993.
revoked: Act 94/1443, para. 3.

772. Water Undertakers (Rateable Values) (Amendment) Order 1993.
revoked: ord. 94/3285, art. 4.

798. Measuring Instruments (EEC Requirements) (Fees) Regulations 1993.
Sch. 2, para. 1, amended: regs. 95/1376, reg. 2.
Sch. 3, para. 1, amended: regs. 95/1376, reg. 2.
Sch. 4, substituted: regs. 95/1376, reg. 2.
Sch. 5, para. 1, amended: regs. 95/1376, reg. 2.
Sch. 6, para. 1, amended: regs. 95/1376, reg. 2.

848. Local Government (Direct Service Organisations) (Competition) Regulations 1993.
reg. 1, amended: regs. 95/1336, reg. 3.
reg. 2, amended: regs. 95/1336, reg. 4.
reg. 3, applied: ord. 95/678, art. 8; amended, regs. 95/1336, reg. 5.
reg. 4, amended: regs. 95/1336, reg. 6.
reg. 5, amended: regs. 95/1336, reg. 7.
reg. 12, amended: regs. 95/1336, reg. 8.
reg. 14A, inserted: regs. 95/1336, reg. 9.
Sch., para. 3, amended: regs. 95/1336, reg. 10.

873. Oil Related and Petrochemical Plants (Rateable Values) (Scotland) Order 1993.
revoked: ord. 95/374, art. 2.

891. A1 Trunk Road (Islington) Red Route Traffic Order 1993.
art. 2, amended: ord. 94/3006, art. 3.
art. 4, amended: ord. 94/3006, art. 4.
art. 7, amended: ord. 94/3006, art. 5.
Sch. 2, para. 1, amended: ord. 94/3006, art. 6.
Sch. 2, para. 3, revoked: ord. 95/1165, art. 3.
Sch. 2, para. 6, substituted: ord. 95/1165, art. 4.
Sch. 2, para. 6A, inserted: ord. 95/1165, art. 5.
Sch. 2, para. 7, revoked: ord. 95/1165, art. 6.
Sch. 2, paras. 7A–C, inserted: ord. 95/1165, art. 7.
Sch. 3, para. 3, substituted: ord. 95/1165, art. 8.
Sch. 3, para. 4, revoked: ord. 95/1165, art. 9.

NO.

1993—cont.

891. A1 Trunk Road (Islington) Red Route Traffic Order 1993—*cont.*
Sch. 3, para. 5, substituted: ord. 95/1165, art. 10.
Sch. 3, paras. 6A, 6B, inserted: ord. 95/1165, art. 11.
Sch. 3, para. 26A, inserted: ord. 94/3006, art. 7.
Sch. 3, para. 32A, inserted: ord. 95/1165, art. 12.
Sch. 3, para. 42, revoked: ord. 95/1165, art. 13.
Sch. 4, para. 26, amended: ord. 94/3005, art. 8.
Sch. 4, para. 40, substituted: ord. 95/1165, art. 14.
Sch. 4, para. 41, substituted: ord. 95/1165, art. 14.
Sch. 4, para. 42, substituted: ord. 95/1165, art. 14.
Sch. 4, paras. 43, 44, revoked: ord. 95/1165, art. 15.

895. A1 Trunk Road (Islington) (Bus Lanes) Red Route Traffic Order 1993.
art. 2, amended: ord. 94/3007, art. 3.
art. 6, amended: ord. 94/3007, art. 4.
Sch., Pt. II, amended: ord. 94/3007, art. 5.

896. A1 Trunk Road (Haringey) Red Route Traffic Order 1993.
art. 2, amended: ord. 94/3004, art. 3.
art. 4, amended: ord. 94/3004, art. 4.
art. 7, amended: ord. 94/3004, art. 5.
Sch. 4, para. 8, substituted: ord. 94/3004, art. 6.

897. A1 Trunk Road (Haringey) (Bus Lanes) Red Route Traffic Order 1994.
art. 2, amended: ord. 94/3005, art. 3.
art. 6, amended: ord. 94/3005, art. 4.

899. Act of Sederunt (Rules of the Court of Session Amendment) (Register of Insolvencies) 1993.
revoked: Act 94/1443, para. 3.

900. Act of Sederunt (Rules of the Court of Session Amendment No. 2) (Fees of Solicitors) 1993.
revoked: Act 94/1443, para. 3.

935. Housing Benefit and Community Charge Benefit (Subsidy) Order 1993.
referred to: ord. 95/872, art. 1.

967. Gaming Act (Variation of Monetary Limits) Order 1993.
revoked: ord. 95/926, art. 5.

985. Building Societies (Designation of Qualifying Bodies) Order 1993.
Sch. 1, Pt. II, amended: ord. 95/1188, art. 4.

987. Retention of Registration Marks Regulations 1993.
reg. 2, amended: regs. 94/2976, reg. 3.
reg. 3, amended: regs. 94/2976, reg. 3.

NO.

1993—cont.

987. Retention of Registration Marks Regulations 1993—*cont.*
reg. 4, amended: regs. 94/2976, reg. 3.
reg. 4A, inserted: regs. 94/2976, reg. 3.
reg. 5, amended: regs. 94/2976, reg. 3.
reg. 7, amended: regs. 94/2976, reg. 3.
reg. 8, substituted: regs. 94/2976, reg. 3.
reg. 9, amended: regs. 94/2976, reg. 3.
reg. 10, amended: regs. 94/2976, reg. 3.
reg. 11, amended: regs. 94/2976, reg. 3.
reg. 12, amended: regs. 94/2976, reg. 3.
reg. 15, amended: regs. 94/2976, reg. 3.

994. National Health Service (Appointment of Consultants) (Scotland) Regulations 1993.
applied: ord. 95/574, art. 5.

996. Environmentally Sensitive Areas (Central Southern Uplands) Designation Order 1993.
art. 4A, inserted: ord. 94/3067, art. 2.
art. 5, amended: ord. 94/3067, art. 2.
art. 7A, inserted: ord. 94/3067, art. 2.
Annex, inserted: ord. 94/3067, art. 2.

997. Environmentally Sensitive Areas (Western Southern Uplands) Designation Order 1993.
art. 4A, inserted: ord. 94/3067, art. 2.
art. 5, amended: ord. 94/3067, art. 2.
art. 7A, inserted: ord. 94/3067, art. 2.
Annex, inserted: ord. 94/3067, art. 2.

1037. Gaming Act (Variation of Monetary Limits) (Scotland) Order 1993.
revoked: ord. 95/1020, art. 5.

1161. Asylum Appeals (Procedure) Rules 1993.
rule 13, see *R.* v. *Secretary of State for the Home Department, ex p. Seidu* [1994] Imm.A.R. 577, Schiemann J.
rule 26, see *Kalunga* v. *Secretary of State for the Home Department* [1994] Imm.A.R. 585, C.A.
rule 30, see *R.* v. *Secretary of State for the Home Department, ex p. Seidu* [1994] Imm.A.R. 577, Schiemann J.

1176. Civil Aviation (Navigation Service Charges) (Third Amendment) Regulations 1993.
revoked: regs. 95/497, reg. 3.

1189. Export of Goods (Control) (Croatian and Bosnian Territories) Order 1993.
revoked: ord. 94/2972, art. 2.

1193. Electricity (Standards of Performance) Regulations 1993.
Schs. 2–4, substituted: regs. 95/687, reg. 2.
Schs. 6–14, substituted: regs. 95/687, reg. 3.

1194. Diseases of Animals (Approved Disinfectants) (Amendment) Order 1993.
revoked: ord. 94/2965, art. 3.

1195. Serbia and Montenegro (United Nations Sanctions) (Dependent Territories) Order 1993.
applied: ord. 95/1032, art. 3.

NO.

1993—cont.

1198. Police (Amendment) (No. 2) Regulations 1993.
revoked: regs. 95/215, reg. 70.

1210. Environmentally Sensitive Areas (Ynys Mon) Designation Order 1993.
art. 2, amended: ord. 95/242, art. 4.
art. 4A, inserted: ord. 95/242, art. 4.
art. 6, amended: ord. 95/242, art. 4.
Sch. 1A, inserted: ord. 95/242, art. 4.
Sch. 4, para. 9, inserted: ord. 95/242, art. 4.

1211. Environmentally Sensitive Areas (Radnor) Designation Order 1993.
art. 2, amended: ord. 95/242, art. 5.
art. 4A, inserted: ord. 95/242, art. 5.
art. 6, amended: ord. 95/242, art. 5.
Sch. 1A, inserted: ord. 95/242, art. 5.
Sch. 4, para. 9, inserted: ord. 95/242, art. 5.

1212. Cod (Irish Sea) (Prohibition of Fishing) Order 1993.
art. 2, substituted: ord. 94/3050, art. 3.

1227. Medicines (Veterinary Drugs) (Renewal Applications for Licences and Animal Test Certificates) Regulations 1993.
revoked: regs. 94/3143, reg. 5.

1257. Designs (Convention Countries) Order 1993.
revoked: ord. 94/3219, art. 3.

1258. Patents and Marks (Convention and Relevant Countries) Order 1993.
revoked: ord. 94/3220, art. 3.

1282. Treatment of Spruce Bark Order 1993.
Sch. substituted: ord. 94/3093, art. 2.

1283. Plant Health (Forestry) (Great Britain) Order 1993.
art. 2, amended: ord. 94/3094, art. 3.
art. 4, substituted: ord. 94/3094, art. 4.
art. 8, amended: ord. 94/3094, art. 5.
art. 8A, inserted: ord. 94/3094, art. 6.
art. 11, substituted: ord. 94/3094, art. 7.
art. 21, amended: ord. 94/3094, art. 8.
art. 30, amended: ord. 94/3094, art. 9.
Sch. 4, Pt. B, substituted: ord. 94/3094, art. 10.
Sch. 4, Pt. C, substituted: ord. 94/3094, art. 10.
Sch. 5, Pt. B, amended: ord. 94/3094, art. 11.
Sch. 6, substituted: ord. 94/3094, art. 12.
Sch. 7, amended: ord. 94/3094, art. 13.
Sch. 8, para. 2, substituted: ord. 94/3094, art. 14.
Sch. 8, para. 6, amended: ord. 94/3094, art. 14.

1312. Eastwood and East Kilbride Districts (Busby) Amendment Order 1993.
see *East Kilbride District Council* v. *Secretary of State for Scotland (O.H.)*, 1995 S.L.T. 1238.

NO.

1993—cont.

1320. Plant Health (Great Britain) Order 1993.
art. 2, amended: ord. 95/1358, art. 3.
art. 3, amended: ord. 95/1358, arts. 4, 5.
art. 5, amended: ord. 95/1358, art. 6.
art. 12, amended: ord. 95/1358, art. 7.
art. 18, amended: ord. 95/1358, art. 8.
art. 22, amended: ord. 95/1358, art. 9.
Sch. 1, amended: ord. 95/1358, art. 10.
Sch. 2, amended: ord. 95/1358, art. 11.
Sch. 3, amended: ord. 95/1358, arts. 12, 13.
Sch. 4, amended: ord. 95/1358, art. 14.
Sch. 5, amended: ord. 95/1358, art. 15.
Sch. 8, amended: ord. 95/1358, art. 16.
Sch. 13, substituted: ord. 95/1358, art. 17.
Sch. 16, amended: ord. 95/1358, art. 18.

1321. Health and Safety (Fees) Regulations 1993.
reg. 2, revoked: regs. 95/743, reg. 25.

1325. Fishing Vessels (Safety Improvements) (Grants) Scheme 1993.
para. 6, amended: Scheme 95/1609, para. 19.

1357. Act of Sederunt (Rules of the Court of Session Amendment No. 3) (Shorthand Writers' Fees) 1993.
revoked: Act 94/1443, para. 3.

1359. Farmed Game Meat (Hygiene and Inspection) (Charges) Regulations 1993.
revoked: regs. 95/361, reg. 15, Sch. 3.
revoked: regs. 95/361, reg. 15.

1360. Fresh Meat and Poultry Meat (Hygiene, Inspection and Examinations for Residues) (Charges) (Amendment) Regulations 1993.
revoked: regs. 95/361, reg. 15, Sch. 3.

1367. Local Government Superannuation (Local Commissioners) Regulations 1993.
revoked: regs. 95/1019 Sch. M5.

1441. Suckler Cow Premium Regulations 1993.
reg. 2, amended: regs. 95/1440, reg. 2.
reg. 3, amended: regs. 95/1440, reg. 2.
reg. 3A, substituted: regs. 95/1440, reg. 2.
reg. 3B, inserted: regs. 95/1440, reg. 2.
reg. 4, amended: regs. 95/15, reg. 2.

1520. Egg Products Regulations 1993.
applied: regs. 95/1763, reg. 3.
reg. 2, amended: regs. 95/1763, reg. 9.
Sch. 8, Pt. I, amended: regs. 95/1763, reg. 9.

1546. Child Resistant Packaging (Safety) (Amendment) Regulations 1993.
revoked: regs. 94/3247, reg. 19(1).

1547. Toys (Safety) (Amendment) Regulations 1993.
revoked: regs. 95/204, reg. 1.

1577. Family Law (Northern Ireland Consequential Amendments) Order 1993.
art. 2, amended: ord. 95/756, art. 15.

NO.

1993—cont.

1591. Wireless Telegraphy (Short Range Devices) (Exemption) Regulations 1993.
reg. 15, substituted: regs. 95/1081, reg. 3.

1622. Air Navigation (General) Regulations 1993.
reg. 4, amended: regs. 95/1093, reg. 2.

1624. Charities (Exemption from Accounting Requirements) (Scotland) Regulations 1993.
reg. 2, amended: regs. 95/645, reg. 3.
Sch., amended: regs. 95/645, reg. 4.

1626. Sheep Annual Premium and Suckler Cow Premium Quotas Regulations 1993.
reg. 2, amended: regs. 94/2894, reg. 2.
reg. 5, amended: regs. 94/2894, reg. 2.
reg. 7, amended: regs. 94/2894, reg. 2.
reg. 10, amended: regs. 94/2894, reg. 2.
reg. 14, amended: regs. 94/2894, reg. 2.
Sch. 2, Pt. II, amended: regs. 94/2894, reg. 2.
Sch. 3, para. 9, amended: regs. 94/2894, reg. 2.

1655. Asylum and Immigration Appeals Act (Commencement and Transitional Provisions) Order 1993.
para. 3(a), see *R.* v. *Secretary of State for the Home Department, ex p. Kazmi (Syed Majid)* [1995] Imm.A.R. 74, Dyson J.

1658. Extraction Solvents in Food Regulations 1993.
reg. 4, amended: regs. 95/1440, reg. 2.
Sch. 1, amended: regs. 95/1440, reg. 2.
Sch. 3, amended: regs. 95/1440, reg. 2.

1659. Education (Assisted Places) (Scotland) Amendment Regulations 1993.
revoked: regs. 95/1713, reg. 31.

1660. St. Mary's Music School (Aided Places) Amendment Regulations 1993.
revoked: regs. 95/1712, reg. 17.

1661. Asylum Appeals (Procedure) Rules 1993.
rule 6(1), see *Kayanga (Christine Resty)* v. *Secretary of State for the Home Department* [1995] Imm.A.R. 123, C.A.
rules 13(1), (2), see *R.* v. *Immigration Appeal Tribunal, ex p. Flores (Ruiz Pablo)* [1995] Imm.A.R. 85
rule 22(3), see *Kayanga (Christine Resty)* v. *Secretary of State for the Home Department* [1995] Imm.A.R. 123, C.A.
rule 36, see *Kayanga (Christine Resty)* v. *Secretary of State for the Home Department* [1995] Imm.A.R. 123, C.A.

NO.

1993—cont.

1678. Immigration (Transit Visa) Order 1993.
Sch., substituted: ord. 95/2621, art. 2.

1734. Beef Special Premium Regulations 1993.
reg. 2, amended: regs. 94/3131, reg. 2.
reg. 3, amended: regs. 95/14, reg. 2.
reg. 9A, inserted: regs. 94/3131, reg. 2.
reg. 9B, inserted: regs. 94/3131, reg. 2.
reg. 10, amended: regs. 95/14, reg. 2.

1746. Chemicals (Hazard Information and Packaging) Regulations 1993.
revoked by 1994 No. 3247.
reg. 4, applied: regs. 94/3246, reg. 2.
reg. 7, applied: regs. 94/3140, reg. 2.
reg. 21, amended: regs. 94/3246, reg. 18.

1810. Local Government Superannuation (National Rivers Authority) Regulations 1993.
applied: regs. 95/1019, reg. L19.
revoked: regs. 95/1019 Sch. M5.

1814. Local Government Superannuation (Part-time Employees) Regulations 1993.
revoked: regs. 95/1019 Sch. M5.

1840. Church of England (Legal Aid) Rules 1993.
revoked: rules 95/2034, rule 2.

1848. Local Government Superannuation (Investments) Regulations 1993.
revoked: regs. 95/1019 Sch. M5.

1897. Management and Administration of Safety and Health at Mines Regulations 1993.
see *R.* v. *Secretary of State for Employment, ex p. National Association of Colliery Overmen, Deputies and Shotfirers* [1994] C.O.D. 218, D.C.

1933. Money Laundering Regulations 1993.
reg. 2, applied: regs. 95/1442, reg. 40.

1936. Education (Assisted Places) (Amendment) Regulations 1993.
revoked: regs. 95/2016, reg. 24.

1937. Education (Assisted Places) (Incidental Expenses) (Amendment) Regulations 1993.
revoked: regs. 95/2017, reg. 16.

1938. Education (Grants) (Music and Ballet Schools) (Amendment) Regulations 1992.
revoked: regs. 95/2018, reg. 16.

1957. Double Taxation Relief (Taxes on Income) (General) (Manufactured Overseas Dividends) Regulations 1993.
reg. 3, amended: regs. 95/1551, regs. 3, 4.

1965. Civil Aviation (Route Charges for Navigation Services) Regulations 1993.
revoked: regs. 94/3071, reg. 2.

NO.

1993—cont.

1983. Education (National Curriculum) (Assessment Arrangements for the Core Subjects) (Key Stage 1) Order 1993.
revoked: ord. 95/2071, art. 2.
reg. 5, applied: regs. 95/605, reg. 2.
reg. 6A, applied: regs. 95/605, reg. 2.

1993. Education (Further Education Institutions Information) (England) Regulations 1993.
revoked: regs. 95/2065, reg. 9.

2001. Value Added Tax (Payments on Account) Order 1993.
art. 4, amended: ord. 95/291, arts. 3, 4.
art. 5, substituted: ord. 95/291, art. 5.
art. 6, amended: ord. 95/291, art. 6.
art. 11, amended: ord. 95/291, arts, 7, 8, 9.
art. 16, amended: ord. 95/291, arts. 10, 11, 12.

2004. Income Tax (Manufactured Overseas Dividends) Regulations 1993.
reg. 2, amended: regs. 95/1324, reg. 3.
reg. 2A, inserted: regs. 95/1324, reg. 4.
reg. 9, amended: regs. 95/1324, reg. 5.
reg. 10, amended: regs. 95/1324, reg. 6.

2005. Cereal Seeds Regulations 1993.
reg. 3, amended: regs. 95/1482, reg. 2.
Sch. 4, Pt. I, amended: regs. 95/1482, reg. 2.

2008. Vegetable Seeds Regulations 1993.
applied: regs. 95/2652, reg. 5.

2047. Police (Amendment) (No. 3) Regulations 1993.
revoked: regs. 95/215, reg. 70.

2190. Education (National Curriculum) (Assessment Arrangements for English, Welsh, Mathematics and Science) (Key Stage 1) (Wales) Order 1993.
revoked: ord. 95/2207, art. 2.
applied: regs. 95/501, reg. 2.

2218. National Health Service (District Health Authorities) (No. 2) Order 1993.
applied: ord. 95/562, art. 1.

2226. Transcripts of Criminal Proceedings (Scotland) Order 1993.
art. 4, amended: ord. 95/1751, art. 2.
art. 5, amended: ord. 95/1751, art. 2.

2242. Valuation Timetable (Scotland) Amendment (No. 3) Order 1993.
revoked: ord. 95/164, art. 4.

2276. Income Tax (Employments) (Amendment) Regulations 1993.
reg. 14, revoked: regs. 95/917, reg. 9.

2345. Environmentally Sensitive Areas (Cairngorms Straths) Designation Order 1993.
art. 4A, inserted: ord. 94/3067, art. 2.
art. 5, amended: ord. 94/3067, art. 2.
art. 7A, inserted: ord. 94/3067, art. 2.
Annex, inserted: ord. 94/3067, art. 2.

NO.

1993—cont.

2360. Clinical Thermometers (EEC Requirements) Regulations 1993.
reg. 5, amended: regs. 94/3017, reg. 26.
reg. 6, amended: regs. 94/3017, reg. 26.
reg. 7, amended: regs. 94/3017, reg. 26.

2398. Medicines (Veterinary Medicinal Products) (Applications for Product Licences) Regulations 1993.
revoked: regs. 94/3142, reg. 20.

2449. National Health Service (General Medical and Pharmaceutical Services) (Scotland) Amendment (No. 2) Regulations 1993.
revoked: regs. 95/414, reg. 13.

2527. Police (Amendment) (No. 4) Regulations 1993.
revoked: regs. 95/215, reg. 70.

2531. Local Government Superannuation (Maternity Absence) Regulations 1993.
revoked: regs. 95/1019 Sch. M5.

2538. Medicines (Applications for Grant of Product Licences—Products for Human Use) Regulations 1993.
reg. 1, amended: regs. 94/3144, reg. 11.

2555. Kent Ambulance National Health Service Trust (Establishment) Order 1993.
art. 4, amended: ord. 95/2697, art. 2.

2571. Robert Jones and Agnes Hunt Orthopaedic and District Hospital National Health Service Trust (Establishment) Order 1993.
art. 4, amended: ord. 95/996, art. 2.

2631. Hill Livestock (Compensatory Allowances) Regulations 1993.
referred to: regs. 95/904, reg. 2, regs. 95/1159, reg. 2.
applied: regs. 95/891, reg. 2.

2665. Agriculture (Northern Ireland) Order 1993 (N.I. 10).
art. 17(2)(3)(6); regs. 95/25.
art. 26(1)–(3); ord. 95/27.

2670. Air Navigation (Fifth Amendment) Order 1993.
revoked: ord. 95/1038, art. 2.

2687. Industrial Tribunals (Constitution and Rules of Procedure) Regulations 1993.
reg. 4(1), see *FDR* v. *Holloway* [1995] IRLR 400, E.A.T.
reg. 4(1)(a), see *British Aerospace* v. *Green* [1995] IRLR 433, C.A.
reg. 13(1), see *FDR* v. *Holloway* [1995] IRLR 400, E.A.T.
reg. 14 see *R.* v. *Southampton Industrial Tribunal, ex p. INS News Group*, *The Times*, April 22, 1995, Brook J.

2688. Industrial Tribunals (Constitution and Rules of Procedure) (Scotland) Regulations 1993.
applied: regs. 95/1717, reg. 2.

NO.

1993—cont.

2706. Building Societies (Designation of Qualifying Bodies) (No. 3) Order 1993.
Sch., Pt. I, amended: ord. 95/1188, art. 4.

2761. Northern Ireland (Emergency Provisions) Act 1991 (Codes of Practice) (No. 1) Order 1993.
revoked: ord. 95/1896, art. 3.

2767. Environmentally Sensitive Areas (Central Borders) Designation Order 1993.
art. 4A, inserted: ord. 94/3067, art. 2.
art. 5, amended: ord. 94/3067, art. 2.
art. 7A, inserted: ord. 94/3067, art. 2.
Annex, inserted: ord. 94/3067, art. 2.

2768. Environmentally Sensitive Areas (Stewartry) Designation Order 1993.
art. 4A, inserted: ord. 94/3067, art. 2.
art. 5, amended: ord. 94/3067, art. 2.
art. 7A, inserted: ord. 94/3067, art. 2.
Annex, inserted: ord. 94/3067, art. 2.

2776. Plant Breeders' Rights (Trees, Shrubs and Woody Climbers) Scheme 1993.
para. 1, amended: Scheme 95/528, art. 2.
Sch., amended: Scheme 95/528, art. 3.

2778. Plant Breeders' Rights (Miscellaneous Ornamental Plants) (Variation) Scheme 1993.
revoked: Scheme 95/527, art. 2.

2780. Plant Breeders' Rights (Herbaceous Perennials) (Variation) Scheme 1993.
revoked: Scheme 95/526, art. 2.

2783. Local Government Superannuation (South Yorkshire Transport Limited) Regulations 1993.
reg. 1, amended: regs. 95/1019, Sch. M6.
reg. 2, amended: regs. 95/1019, Sch. M6.
reg. 4, revoked: regs. 95/1019 Sch. M5.
reg. 5, amended: regs. 95/1019, Sch. M6.

2798. Sex Discrimination and Equal Pay (Remedies) Regulations 1993.
reg. 3(1), see *Harvey* v. *Institute of Motor Industry* [1995] IRLR 416, E.A.T.
regs. 3(1), 5, 6, 7(1)(3), see *Ministry of Defence* v. *Cannock* [1994] IRLR 589, E.A.T.

2833. Building Societies (Aggregation) Rules 1993.
rule 7, amended: rules 95/1187, rule 2.

2854. Employment Appeal Tribunal Rules 1993.
rule 34(1), see *South Durham Health Authority* v. *Unison* [1995] IRLR 407, E.A.T.

NO.

1993—cont.

2877. Motor Vehicles Tyres (Safety) (Amendment) Regulations 1993.
revoked: regs. 94/3117, reg. 1.

2902. Medicines (Pharmacies) (Applications for Registration and Fees) Amendment Regulations 1993.
revoked: regs. 94/2936, reg. 3.

2914. Education (Mandatory Awards) (No. 2) Regulations 1993.
revoked: regs. 94/3044, reg. 6.
reg. 2, amended: regs. 94/3043, reg. 3.
reg. 5, amended: regs. 94/3043, reg. 4.
reg. 11, amended: regs. 94/3043, reg. 5.
reg. 13, amended: regs. 94/3043, reg. 6.
reg. 17, amended: regs. 94/3043, reg. 7.
Sch. 2, para. 2, applied: regs. 94/3045, reg. 6.
Sch. 3, para. 1, amended: regs. 94/3043, reg. 8, regs. 95/1240, reg. 2.

2915. Education (Student Loans) (No. 2) Regulations 1993.
revoked: regs. 94/3045, reg. 2.

2929. Law Hospital National Health Service Trust (Establishment) Order 1993.
art. 3, substituted: ord. 95/741, art. 2.

2932. Royal Infirmary of Edinburgh National Health Service Trust (Establishment) Order 1993.
art. 3, substituted: ord. 95/742, art. 2.

2951. Value Added Tax (Cars) (Amendment) Order 1993.
revoked: ord. 95/1667, art. 9.

2957. Sheriff Court Fees Amendment (No. 2) Order 1993.
Sched., Pt. V, para. 3, see *D.T.Z. Debenham Thorpe* v. *I. Henderson Transport Services*, 1995 S.L.T. 553; *Mellor* v. *Towle (Sh.Ct.)* 1994 S.C.L.R. 953.

2975. Civil Aviation (Joint Financing) (Fifth Amendment) Regulations 1993.
revoked: regs. 94/3055, reg. 3.

3015. Statistics of Trade (Customs and Excise) (Amendment No. 2) Regulations 1993.
revoked: regs. 94/2914, reg. 2.

3016. Retirement Benefits Schemes (Restriction on Discretion to Approve) (Additional Voluntary Contributions) Regulations 1993.
reg. 5, applied: regs. 95/1019, Schs. C4, C10.

3030. Local Government Superannuation (Educational Institutions) Regulations 1993.
revoked: regs. 95/1019 Sch. M5.

3036. Sheep Annual Premium and Suckler Cow Premium Quotas Regulations 1993.
see *R.* v. *Ministry of Agriculture, Fisheries and Food, ex p. National Union of Farmers, The Independent*, September 25, 1995 (C.S.), Macpherson J.

NO.

1993—cont.

3043. Local Government Superannuation (Membership) Regulations 1993.
revoked: regs. 95/1019 Sch. M5.

3050. Notification of New Substances Regulations 1993.
regs. 2(1), 4(d), 6(7), 18(3)(h), amended: regs. 94/3247, reg. 19(8).

3080. Act of Sederunt (Fees to Solicitors in the Sheriff Court) (Amendment and Further Provisions) 1993.
Sch. 1, amended: Act 95/1395, rules 2, 3.

3086. Diseases of Animals (Approved Disinfectants) (Amendment) (No. 2) Order 1993.
revoked: ord. 94/2965, art. 3.

3098. Civil Aviation (Route Charges for Navigation Services) (Second Amendment) Regulations 1993.
revoked: regs. 94/3071, reg. 2.

3103. Education (Schools Conducted by Education Associations) Regulations 1993.
reg. 1(2), amended: ord. 95/61, reg. 2.
reg. 4A, substituted: ord. 95/61, reg. 2.
Sch. 3, amended: ord. 95/61, reg. 2.

3116. Registration of Births, Deaths and Marriages (Fees) Order 1993.
revoked: ord. 94/3257, art. 4.

3135. Severn Bridges Tolls Order 1993.
revoked: ord. 94/3158, art. 3.

3136. Environmentally Sensitive Areas (Argyll Islands) Designation Order 1993.
art. 4A, inserted: ord. 94/3067, art. 2.
art. 5, amended: ord. 94/3067, art. 2.
art. 7A, inserted: ord. 94/3067, art. 2.
Annex, inserted: ord. 94/3067, art. 2.

3144. Child Abduction and Custody (Parties to Conventions) Order 1993.
Sch., substituted: ord. 95/1031, art. 3.
Sch. replaced: ord. 94/3201, art. 3.

3149. Environmentally Sensitive Areas (Machais of the Uists and Benbecula, Barra and Vatersay) Designation Order 1993.
art. 4A, inserted: ord. 94/3067, art. 2.
art. 5, amended: ord. 94/3067, art. 2.
art. 7A, inserted: ord. 94/3067, art. 2.
Annex, inserted: ord. 94/3067, art. 2.

3150. Environmentally Sensitive Areas (Shetland Islands) Designation Order 1993.
art. 4A, inserted: ord. 94/3067, art. 2.
art. 5, amended: ord. 94/3067, art. 2.
art. 7A, inserted: ord. 94/3067, art. 2.
Annex, inserted: ord. 94/3067, art. 2.

3153. Registration of Births, Deaths, Marriages and Divorces (Fees) (Scotland) Regulations 1993.
reg. 3A, inserted: regs. 95/646, reg. 3.

NO.

1993—cont.

3166. Ministerial and Other Salaries Order 1993.
revoked: ord. 94/3206, art. 1(3).

3182. Education (Individual Pupil's Achievements) (Information) Regulations 1993.
reg. 3, amended: regs. 95/924, reg. 2.
reg. 4, amended: regs. 95/924, reg. 3.
reg. 5, amended: regs. 95/924, reg. 4.
reg. 6, amended: regs. 95/924, reg. 5.
reg. 7, amended: regs. 95/924, reg. 6.
reg. 8, amended: regs. 95/924, reg. 7.
Sch. 1, para. 1, substituted: regs. 95/924, reg. 8.
Sch. 1, para. 1A, inserted: regs. 95/924, reg. 8.
Sch. 2, para. 1, amended: regs. 95/924, reg. 9.
Sch. 2, para. 1A, inserted: regs. 95/924, reg. 9.
Sch. 2A, inserted: regs. 95/924, reg. 10.
Sch. 3, substituted: regs. 95/924, reg. 11.

3183. Education (European Economic Area) (Amendment) Regulations 1993.
revoked: regs. 94/3044, reg. 6.
reg. 5, revoked: regs. 94/3042, reg. 17.

3184. Education (European Economic Area) (Scotland) Regulations 1993.
reg. 2, revoked: regs. 95/1739, reg. 6.

3197. Education (Distribution by Schools of Information about Further Education Institutions) (England) Regulations 1993.
revoked: regs. 95/2065, reg. 9.

3198. Nitrate Sensitive Areas (Designation) (Amendment) Order 1993.
revoked: regs. 95/1708, reg. 3.

3211. Town and Country Planning (Fees for Applications and Deemed Applications) (Scotland) Amendment Regulations 1993.
regs. 2, 3, revoked: regs. 94/3269, reg. 5.

3228. Public Services Contracts Regulations 1993.
applied: regs. 95/789, art. 2.
reg. 2, amended: regs. 95/201, reg. 31.
reg. 4, amended: regs. 95/201, reg. 31.
reg. 6, amended: regs. 95/201, reg. 31.
reg. 8, amended: regs. 95/201, reg. 31.
reg. 12, amended: regs. 95/201, reg. 31.
reg. 13, amended: regs. 95/201, reg. 31.
reg. 14, amended: regs. 95/201, reg. 31.
reg. 15, amended: regs. 95/201, reg. 31.
reg. 16, amended: regs. 95/201, reg. 31.
reg. 18, amended: regs. 95/201, reg. 31.
reg. 20, amended: regs. 95/201, reg. 31.
reg. 23, amended: regs. 95/201, reg. 31.
reg. 33, revoked: regs. 95/201, reg. 31.

3236. Council Tax (Transitional Reduction Scheme) (Scotland) (No. 2) Regulations 1993.
varied. regs. 94/3170, reg. 4.

NO.

1993—cont.

3247. Animals and Animal Products (Import and Export) Regulations 1993.
reg. 12, amended: regs. 95/540, reg. 27.

3250. Specified Animal Pathogens Order 1993.
art. 5, amended: regs. 94/3142, reg. 21; regs. 94/3144, reg. 11.

1994

64. Non-Domestic Rates (Scotland) Order 1994.
Sch., applied: regs. 95/548, reg. 11.

105. Medicines (Homoeopathic Medicinal Products for Human Use) Regulations 1994.
reg. 5, amended: regs. 95/541, reg. 2.
reg. 14, amended: regs. 95/541, reg. 3.

117. Companies (Welsh Language Forms and Documents) Regulations 1994.
reg. 4, amended: regs. 95/734, reg. 6.
Sch., amended: regs. 95/734, reg. 5.

134. A23 Trunk Road (Brighton Road, Croydon) (Prohibition of Right Turn and U-Turn) Order 1994.
Arts. 2 and 3 amended: ord. 95/17, art. 5.

144. Free Zone (Humberside) Designation Order 1994.
art. 2, amended: ord. 95/1067, art. 2.

181. East Surrey Learning Disability and Mental Health Service National Health Service Trust (Establishment) Order 1994.
art. 1, amended: ord. 95/2379, art. 2.
art. 2, amended: ord. 95/2379, art. 2.

183. Bexley Community Health National Health Service Trust (Establishment) Order 1994.
art. 1, amended: ord. 95/1235, art. 2.
art. 2, amended: ord. 95/1235, art. 2.

199. Aujeszky's Disease Scheme Order (Northern Ireland) 1994.
Sch., para. 2, amended: regs. 94/3142, reg. 21.
Sch., para. 8, amended: regs. 94/3142, reg. 21.

201. Lyon Court and Office Fees (Variation) Order 1994.
revoked: ord. 95/132, art. 4.

222. Education (Teachers) (Amendment) Regulations 1994.
amended: regs. 95/602, reg. 6.
reg. 4, revoked: regs. 95/587, reg. 6.

227. Child Support (Miscellaneous Amendments and Transitional Provisions) Regulations 1994.
reg. 7, amended: regs. 95/1045, reg. 60.
reg. 11, amended: regs. 95/1045, reg. 61.

228. Legal Aid in Civil Proceedings (Remuneration) Regulations 1994.
see *Practice Direction (Sup.Ct.: Taxing Office (No. 3 of 1994)) (Legal Aid Taxations)* [1994] 1 W.L.R. 1047.

NO.

1994—cont.

229. Civil Legal Aid (General) (Amendment) Regulations 1994.
see *Practice Direction (Sup.Ct.: Taxing Office (No. 3 of 1994) (Legal Aid Taxations)* [1994] 1 W.L.R. 1047.

230. Legal Aid in Family Proceedings (Remuneration) (Amendment) Regulations 1994.
see *Practice Direction (Sup.Ct.: Taxing Office (No. 3 of 1994) (Legal Aid Taxations)* [1994] 1 W.L.R. 1047.

238. Environmentally Sensitive Areas (Clwydian Range) Designation Order 1994.
art. 2, amended: ord. 95/242, art. 6.
art. 4A, inserted: ord. 95/242, art. 6.
art. 6, amended: ord. 95/242, art. 6.
Sch. 1A, inserted: ord. 95/242, art. 6.
Sch. 4, para. 9, inserted: ord. 95/242, art. 6.

239. Environmentally Sensitive Areas (Preseli) Designation Order 1994.
art. 2, amended: ord. 95/242, art. 7.
art. 4A, inserted: ord. 95/242, art. 7.
art. 6, amended: ord. 95/242, art. 7.
Sch. 1A, inserted: ord. 95/242, art. 7.
Sch. 4, para. 9, inserted: ord. 95/242, art. 7.

277. Education (Financial Delegation to Schools) (Mandatory Exceptions) Regulations 1994.
revoked in pt. (England): regs. 95/178, reg. 2.

305. Veterinary Surgeons and Veterinary Practitioners (Registration) (Amendment) Regulations 1994.
regs. 2, 3, 4, revoked: regs. 95/207, reg. 5.

323. Education (School Financial Statements) (Prescribed Particulars etc.) Regulations 1994.
revoked (in England): regs. 95/208, reg. 1.
reg. 5, amended: regs. 95/532, reg. 2.

391. Act of Sederunt (Fees of Messenger-at-Arms) 1994.
Sch. 1, substituted: Act 94/3268, para. 2.

392. Act of Sederunt (Fees of Sheriff Officers) 1994.
Sch. 1, substituted: Act 94/3267, para. 2.

426. Airports (Northern Ireland) Order 1994.
art. 27, applied: ord. 95/2294.

430. Housing Support Grant (Scotland) Order 1994.
art. 2, amended: ord. 95/469, art. 2.
art. 3, amended: ord. 95/469, art. 2.

NO.

1994—cont.

432. Hyde Park and The Regent's Park (Vehicle Parking) Regulations 1994.
revoked: regs. 95/993, reg. 10.

468. Acquisition of Land (Rate of Interest after Entry) Regulations 1994.
revoked: regs. 95/2262, reg. 3.

497. Lands Tribunal for Scotland (Amendment) (Fees) Rules 1994.
revoked: rules 95/308, rule 3.

498. Scottish Land Court (Fees) Order 1994.
revoked: ord. 95/307, art. 4.

503. Civil Aviation (Navigation Service Charges) (Fourth Amendment) Regulations 1994.
revoked: regs. 95/497, reg. 3.

523. Housing Benefit and Community Charge Benefit (Subsidy) Order 1994.
referred: ord. 95/872, art. 1.

528. Local Government Finance (Scotland) Order 1994.
art. 4, revoked: ord. 95/391, art. 6.
Sch. 3, revoked: ord. 95/391, art. 6.

529. Revenue Support Grant (Scotland) Order 1994.
revoked: ord. 95/392, art. 5.

530. National Health Service (Dental Charges) Amendment Regulations 1994.
revoked: regs. 95/444, reg. 3.

546. Certification Officer (Amendment of Fees) Regulations 1994.
revoked: regs. 95/483, reg. 8.

579. Housing Benefit (Permitted Totals) Order 1994.
revoked: ord. 95/1954, art. 5.

582. Rent Officers (Additional Functions) (Scotland) Amendment Order 1994.
revoked: regs. 95/1643, reg. 7.

610. Education (Grant-maintained Schools) (Finance) (Wales) Regulations 1994.
revoked: regs. 95/587, reg. 3.
revoked: regs. 95/587, reg. 3(1).

612. Education (Grants for Education Support and Training) Regulations 1994.
revoked (in Wales): regs. 95/501, reg. 11.
revoked (as respects England): regs. 95/605, reg. 12.

615. Local Authorities (Members' Allowances) (Amendment) Regulations 1994.
revoked: regs. 95/553, reg. 7.

630. Local Authorities Etc. (Scotland) Amendment Regulations 1994.
revoked: regs. 95/912, reg. 30.
reg. 2, revoked: regs. 95/701, reg. 3.

643. Insurance (Fees) Regulations 1994.
revoked: ord. 95/679, art. 2.

NO.

1994—cont.

646. Education (National Curriculum) (Assessment Arrangements for English, Welsh, Mathematics and Science (Key Stage 1) (Wales) (Amendment) Order 1994.
revoked: ord. 95/2207, art. 2.

650. Education (Payment for Special Educational Needs Supplies) Regulations 1994.
reg. 2, amended: regs. 95/629, reg. 2.

653. Education (Grant-maintained Special Schools) Regulations 1994.
Pt. 2, applied: regs. 95/936, reg. 2.

656. Building Societies (General Charge and Fees) Regulations 1994.
revoked: regs. 95/711, reg. 11.

657. Friendly Societies (General Charge and Fees) (Amendment) Regulations 1994.
revoked: regs. 95/709, reg. 7.

658. Industrial and Provident Societies (Credit Unions) (Amendment of Fees) Regulations 1994.
revoked: regs. 95/712, reg. 3.

659. Wireless Telegraphy (Licence Charges) (Amendment) Regulations 1994.
revoked: regs. 95/1331, reg. 2.

660. Industrial and Provident Societies (Amendment of Fees) Regulations 1994.
revoked: regs. 95/713, reg. 4.

669. Carriage of Dangerous Goods by Road and Rail (Classification, Packaging and Labelling) Regulations 1994.
regs. 2(1), 11(5), 14, amended: regs. 94/3247, reg. 19(10).

672. Dairy Produce Quotas Regulations 1994.
reg. 6, amended: regs. 95/254, reg. 3.
reg. 13, amended: regs. 94/2919, reg. 3.
reg. 15, amended: regs. 94/2919, reg. 4.

674. Common Agricultural Policy (Wine) Regulations 1994.
revoked: regs. 95/615, reg. 2.

676. Seeds (National Lists of Varieties) (Fees) Regulations 1994.
reg. 3, amended: regs. 95/607, reg. 2.

678. Town and Country Planning General Development (Amendment) Order 1994.
revoked: ord. 95/418, art. 9, ord. 95/419, art. 28.

682. National Health Service (Regional and District Health Authorities) (Miscellaneous Amendments) Regulations 1994.
amended: regs. 95/622, reg. 15.
reg. 1, amended: regs. 95/622, reg. 15.
reg. 2, revoked: regs. 95/622, reg. 15.

NO.

1994—cont.

693. Housing Renovation etc. Grants (Prescribed Forms and Particulars) (Welsh Forms and Particulars) Regulations 1994.
Sch. 1, amended: regs. 95/857, reg. 2.

696. Medicines (Products for Human Use—Fees) Amendment Regulations 1994.
revoked: regs. 95/1116, reg. 22.

743. Drinking Water in Containers Regulations 1994.
applied: regs. 95/1763, reg. 2.
reg. 3, amended: regs. 94/3144, reg. 11.

781. Housing Benefit and Council Tax Benefit (Subsidy) Regulations 1994.
reg. 1, amended: regs. 95/874, reg. 2.
Sch., para. 7, revoked: regs. 95/874, reg. 3.
Sch., para. 13, substituted: regs. 95/874, reg. 3.
Sch., para. 16, amended: regs. 95/874, reg. 3.
Sch., para. 20, substituted: regs. 95/874, reg. 3.
Sch., para. 21, substituted: regs. 95/874, reg. 3.

826. National Assistance (Sums for Personal Requirements) Regulations 1994.
revoked: regs. 95/443, reg. 3.

834. Non-Domestic Rating (Railways) and Central Rating Lists (Amendment) Regulations 1994.
revoked: regs. 94/3123, reg. 6.

867. Local Government Changes for England Regulations 1992.
applied: ord. 95/1770, art. 16, regs. 94/3167, reg. 2.
referred to: ord. 95/600, art. 2.
amended: regs. 95/590, reg. 2.
applied: ord. 95/600, art. 16, ord. 95/610, art. 15; regs. 95/798, reg. 2.
reg. 2, amended: regs. 95/1748, reg. 2.
reg. 4, substituted: regs. 95/1748, reg. 2.
reg. 27, applied: ord. 95/1779, art. 2.
Sch., para. 2, applied: ord. 95/1770, art. 12.

884. National Health Service (General Medical and Pharmaceutical Services) (Scotland) Amendment Regulations 1994.
revoked: regs. 95/414, reg. 13.

903. Telecommunications Industry (Rateable Values) (Amendment) Order 1994.
revoked: ord. 94/3281, art. 2.

911. Football Grounds (Rateable Values) (Scotland) Order 1994.
revoked: ord. 95/374, art. 2.

912. Mines and Quarries (Rateable Values) (Scotland) Order 1994.
revoked: ord. 95/366, art. 8.

NO.

1994—cont.

913. Industrial and Freight Transport (Rateable Values) (Scotland) Order 1994.
revoked: ord. 95/374, art. 2.

938. Education (Grant-maintained Schools) (Finance) Regulations 1994.
revoked: regs. 95/936, reg. 3.

944. Racing Pigeons (Vaccination) Order 1994.
revoked: ord. 94/3141, art. 15.

948. Local Government Superannuation (Greater Manchester Buses Limited) Regulations 1994.
reg. 2, amended: regs. 95/1019, Sch. M6.
reg. 4, amended: regs. 95/1019, Sch. M6.

950. Foreign Companies (Execution of Documents) Regulations 1994.
reg. 2, amended: regs. 95/1729, reg. 3.
reg. 3, amended: regs. 95/1729, reg. 4.
reg. 6, revoked: regs. 95/1729, reg. 5.

956. Gaming Act (Variation of Monetary Limits) Order 1994.
revoked: ord. 95/926, art. 5.

957. Gaming Act (Variation of Monetary Limits) (No. 2) Order 1994.
revoked: ord. 95/926, art. 5.

958. Gaming Clubs (Hours and Charges) (Amendment) Regulations 1994.
revoked: regs. 95/927, reg. 3.

959. Education (Individual Pupils' Achievements) (Information) (Wales) Regulations 1994.
reg. 2, amended: regs. 95/522, reg. 2.
reg. 3, amended: regs. 95/522, reg. 3.
reg. 7, amended: regs. 95/522, reg. 4.
Sch. 1, para. 1, amended: regs. 95/522, reg. 5.
Sch. 1, para. 1A, inserted: regs. 95/522, reg. 2.
Sch. 2, para. 1, amended: regs. 95/522, reg. 6.
Sch. 2, para. 1A, inserted: regs. 95/522, reg. 6.
Sch. 3, substituted: regs. 95/522, reg. 7.

963. Local Government Superannuation (Greater Manchester Buses North Limited) Regulations 1994.
reg. 2, amended: regs. 95/1019, Sch. M6.

997. Advice and Assistance (Financial Conditions) (Scotland) Regulations 1994.
revoked: regs. 95/1220, reg. 6.

998. Civil Legal Aid (Financial Conditions) (Scotland) Regulations 1994.
revoked: regs. 95/1220, reg. 5.

999. Railways (Rateable Values) (Amendment) Order 1994.
revoked: ord. 94/3284, art. 4.

NO.

1994—cont.

1001. Criminal Legal Aid (Scotland) (Prescribed Proceedings) Regulations 1994.
reg. 3, amended: regs. 95/1222, reg. 3.

1015. Civil Legal Aid (Scotland) (Fees) Amendment Regulations 1994.
reg. 6, revoked: regs. 95/1044, reg. 7.

1029. Poultry Meat, Farmed Game Bird Meat and Rabbit Meat (Hygiene and Inspection) Regulations 1994.
amended: regs. 95/361, reg. 15, Sch. 3.
revoked: regs. 95/540, reg. 26.
reg. 27, amended: regs. 95/361, reg. 15.

1042. Gaming Clubs (Hours and Charges) (Scotland) Amendment Regulations 1994.
revoked: regs. 95/1022, reg. 3.

1043. Gaming Act (Variation of Monetary Limits) (Scotland) Order 1994.
revoked: ord. 95/1020, art. 5.

1047. Education (Special Educational Needs) Regulations 1994.
reg. 3, amended: regs. 95/1673, reg. 2.
reg. 7, amended: regs. 95/1673, reg. 2.
reg. 21, amended: regs. 95/1673, reg. 2.

1056. Waste Management Licensing Regulations 1994.
reg. 1, amended: regs. 95/288, reg. 3.
reg. 12, substituted: regs. 95/288, reg. 3.
reg. 16, amended: regs. 95/288, reg. 3.
reg. 17, amended: regs. 95/288, reg. 3.
reg. 18, amended: regs. 95/288, reg. 3.
Sch. 3, para. 5, amended: regs. 95/288, reg. 3.
para. 40, amended: regs. 95/288, reg. 3.
para. 41, amended: regs. 95/288, reg. 3.
para. 42, amended: regs. 95/288, reg. 3.
para. 43, amended: regs. 95/1950, reg. 2, regs. 95/288, reg. 3.
para. 44, inserted: regs. 95/288, reg. 3.
para. 45, inserted: regs. 95/288, reg. 3.
Sch. 4, Pt. I, amended: regs. 95/288, reg. 3.
Sch. 5, Pt. I, amended: regs. 95/288, reg. 3.

1065. European Convention on Cinematographic Co-production Order 1994.
Sch. amended: ord. 95/2730, art. 2; ord. 94/3218, art. 2; regs. 95/1298, reg. 2; ord. 95/1963, art. 2.

1070. Electricity (Class Exemptions from the Requirement for a Licence) (Amendment) Order 1994.
revoked: ord. 95/909, art. 6.

NO.

1994—cont.

1084. Education (Special Schools Conducted by Education Associations) Regulations 1994.
reg. 4, substituted: ord. 95/61, reg. 3.
Sch. 1, amended: ord. 95/61, reg. 3.

1096. Environmental Protection Act 1990 (Commencement No. 15) Order 1994.
art. 3, amended: ord. 94/3234, art. 2.

1098. Ministry of Defence Police (Police Committee) Regulations 1988.
revoked: regs. 95/939, reg. 2.

1139. Act of Sederunt (Rules of the Court of Session Amendment No. 1) (Fees of Solicitors) 1994.
revoked: Act 94/1443, para. 3.

1140. Act of Sederunt (Rules of the Court of Session Amendment No. 2) (Shorthand Writers' Fees) 1994.
revoked: Act 94/1443, para. 3.

1191. Export of Goods (Control) Order 1994.
art. 1, amended: regs. 95/271, reg. 13.
art. 3, amended: regs. 95/271, reg. 13.

1210. Isle of Wight (Structural Change) Order 1994.
referred to: ord. 95/289, art. 1.

1265. Motor Vehicles (Type Approval and Approval Marks) (Fees) Regulations 1994.
revoked: regs. 95/925, reg. 2.

1308. Police (Amendment) Regulations 1994.
revoked: regs. 95/215, reg. 70.

1312. Social Security (Cyprus) Order 1994.
modified: ord. 95/767, art. 2.

1421. Education (School Information) (England) Regulations 1994.
reg. 3, amended: regs. 95/2480, reg. 2.
reg. 9, amended: regs. 95/2480, reg. 3.
Sch. 2, para. 6, amended: regs. 95/2480, reg. 4.
Sch. 2, para. 10, amended: regs. 95/2480, reg. 4.
Sch. 2, para. 11, amended: regs. 95/2480, reg. 4.
Sch. 2, para. 15, amended: regs. 95/2480, reg. 4.
Sch. 2, para. 15A, inserted: regs. 95/2480, reg. 4.
Sch. 2, para. 16, amended: regs. 95/2480, reg. 4.
Sch. 2, para. 16A, inserted: regs. 95/2480, reg. 4.
Sch. 2, para. 18, amended: regs. 95/2480, reg. 4.
Sch. 2, para. 19, amended: regs. 95/2480, reg. 4.
Sch. 2, para. 21, amended: regs. 95/2480, reg. 4.

NO.

1994—cont.

1443. Rules of Court of Session 1994.
rule 2.1, see *Mains* v. *Uniroyal Englebert Tyres (No. 2) (I.H.)*, 1995 S.L.T. 1127.
rule 2.1(1), see *Wilson* v. *Lothian Regional Council (O.H.)*, 1995 S.L.T. 991.
rule 2.1(2), see *Wilson* v. *Lothian Regional Council (O.H.)*, 1995 S.L.T. 991.
rule 4.16(7), see *Martinez* v. *Grampian Health Board (I.H.)*, 1995 S.L.T. 1261.
rule 24.1(1), see *Wilson* v. *Lothian Regional Council (O.H.)*, 1995 S.L.T. 991.
rule 24.1(2), see *Wilson* v. *Lothian Regional Council (O.H.)*, 1995 S.L.T. 991.
rule 40.2, see *Frost* v. *Bulman*, 1995 S.C.L.R. 579.
rule 42, amended: Act 95/1396, rule 2, Act 95/1023, rule 2.
rule 42.13(3), see *Mains* v. *Uniroyal Englebert Tyres (No. 2) (I.H.)*, 1995 S.L.T. 1127.
rule 43.9, see *Stone* v. *Mountford (O.H.)*, 1995 S.L.T. 1279.
rule 43.9(5), see *Walker* v. *Dunn (O.H.)*, 1995 S.C.L.R. 588.
Form 13.2–A, see *Wilson* v. *Lothian Regional Council*, 1995 S.L.T. 991.
Form 13.2–B, see *Wilson* v. *Lothian Regional Council*, 1995 S.L.T. 991.

1468. Civil Aviation (Route Charges for Navigation Services) (Third Amendment) Regulations 1994.
revoked: regs. 94/3071, reg. 2.

1497. Road Traffic (Special Parking Area) (Royal Borough of Kingston upon Thames) Order 1994.
amended: ord. 95/617, arts. 3 and 4.
art. 4, applied: ord. 95/1333, art. 3.
art. 5, applied: ord. 95/1333, art. 3.
Sch., para. 10, substituted: ord. 95/617, art. 4.

1507. Road Traffic (Special Parking Area) (London Borough of Sutton) Order 1994.
art. 3, amended: ord. 95/618, art. 3.
amended: ord. 95/618, art. 3.

1508. Road Traffic (Special Parking Areas) (London Borough of Lambeth) Order 1994.
art. 2, amended: ord. 95/679, art. 3.
art. 3, substituted: ord. 95/679, art. 3.
Sch. 1, substituted: ord. 95/679, art. 3.
Schs., 2, 3, revoked: ord. 95/679, art. 3.

1509. Road Traffic (Special Parking Area) (London Borough of Redbridge) Order 1994.
amended: ord. 95/616, art. 3.
art. 4, applied: ord. 95/1334, art. 3, ord: 95/1335, art. 3.
art. 5, applied: ord. 95/1334, art. 3, ord. 95/1335, art. 3.

NO.

1994—cont.

1510. Road Traffic (Special Parking Area) (London Borough of Merton) Order 1994.
art. 2, amended: ord. 95/680, art. 3.
art. 3, amended: ord. 95/680, art. 3.
Sch. 1, substituted: ord. 95/680, art. 3.
Sch. 2, revoked: ord. 95/680, art. 3.

1516. Insurance Companies Regulations 1994.
reg. 2, amended: regs. 94/3133, reg. 2.
reg. 27, amended: regs. 94/3133, reg. 4.
reg. 31, amended: regs. 94/3133, reg. 3.
reg. 34, amended: regs. 94/3133, reg. 5.
reg. 43, amended: regs. 94/1516, reg. 6.
reg. 44, amended: regs. 94/3133, reg. 7.
reg. 46, amended: regs. 94/3133, reg. 8.
reg. 48, amended: regs. 94/3133, reg. 9.
reg. 53, amended: regs. 94/3133, reg. 10.
reg. 55, amended: regs. 94/3133, reg. 11.
reg. 57, amended: regs. 94/3133, reg. 12.
reg. 71, amended: regs. 94/3133, reg. 13.
reg. 80, amended: regs. 94/3133, reg. 14.
Sch. 6, para. 4, amended: regs. 94/3133, reg. 5.
Sch. 6, para. 7, amended: regs. 94/3133, reg. 5.
Sch. 6, para. 10, amended: regs. 94/3133, reg. 5.
Sch. 10, para. 5, amended: regs. 94/3133, reg. 15.
Sch. 10, para. 14, amended: regs. 94/3133, reg. 15.
Sch. 10, para. 16, amended: regs. 94/3133, reg. 15.
Sch. 12, para. 6, amended: regs. 94/3133, reg. 16.
Sch. 16, amended: regs. 94/3133, reg. 17.

1519. Traffic Signs Regulations and General Directions 1994.
reg. 4, applied: regs. 95/1692, reg. 8; regs. 95/1693, reg. 8; regs. 95/1694, reg. 8; regs. 95/1695, reg. 8; regs. 95/1696, reg. 8; regs. 95/1697, reg. 8; regs. 95/1698, reg. 8; regs. 95/1699, reg. 8; regs. 95/1700, reg. 8; regs. 95/1701, reg. 8; regs. 95/1702, reg. 8; regs. 95/1703, reg. 8; ord. 95/124, art. 8, ord. 95/125, art. 3, ord. 95/126, art. 8, ord. 95/2245, art. 8; ord. 95/2246, art. 8.
reg. 5, applied: regs. 95/1094, reg. 2.
Sch. 2, applied: regs. 95/2168, reg. 3.

1554. Medicines (Fees Relating to Medicinal Products for Animal Use) Regulations 1994.
revoked: regs. 95/2364, reg. 20.
applied: regs. 94/3142, reg. 15.
reg. 15, applied: regs. 95/2364, reg. 2

1606. Education (Mandatory Awards) (Amendment) Regulations 1994.
revoked: regs. 94/3044, reg. 6.

NO.

1994—cont.

1662. European Parliamentary (United Kingdom Representatives) Revisions (Consolidation and Amendment) Order 1994.
art. 14, referred to: ord. 75/739, art. 7.
Sch. 1, applied: ord. 95/739, art. 3.

1673. Education (School Teachers' Pay and Conditions) (No. 2) Order 1994.
revoked: ord. 95/1743, art. 1.
Document, para. 4 amended: ord. 95/1015, art. 3.

1679. Sea Fishing (Enforcement of Community Quota Measures) Order 1994.
revoked: ord. 95/908, art. 14.

1683. Electricity (Class Exemptions from the Requirement for a Licence) (Amendment) (No. 2) Order 1994.
revoked: ord. 95/909, art. 6.

1696. Insurance Companies (Third Insurance Directives) Regulations 1994.
reg. 69, amended: regs. 94/3132, reg. 12.
reg. 70, amended: regs. 94/3132, reg. 12.
reg. 71, disapplied: regs. 95/679, art. 3.
reg. 71, substituted: regs. 94/3132, reg. 12.

1729. Nitrate Sensitive Areas Regulations 1994.
reg. 2, amended: regs. 95/1708, reg. 2.
reg. 5, amended: regs. 95/2095, reg. 2; substituted: regs. 95/1708, reg. 2.
reg. 7, amended: regs. 95/1708, reg. 2, regs. 95/2095, reg. 2.
reg. 8, amended: regs. 95/2095, reg. 2.
reg. 9, amended: regs. 95/1708, reg. 2.
reg. 12, amended: regs. 95/1708, reg. 2; regs. 95/2095, reg. 2.
reg. 17, inserted: regs. 95/1708, reg. 2.
Sch. 1, amended: regs. 95/1708, reg. 2.
Sch. 4, amended: regs. 95/1708, reg. 2.
Sch. 4, para. 3, amended: regs. 95/2095, reg. 2.
Sch. 6, amended: regs. 95/1708, reg. 2.
Sch. 6, para. 6B, inserted: regs. 95/2095, reg. 2.

1743. Education (National Curriculum) (Attainment Targets and Programmes of Study in History) (Wales) (Amendment) Order 1994.
revoked: ord. 95/73, art. 2.

1744. Education (National Curriculum) (Attainment Targets and Programmes of Study in Geography) (Wales) (Amendment) Order 1994.
revoked: ord. 95/72, art. 2.

1801. Income Related Benefits Schemes (Miscellaneous) (No. 3) 1994.
see *R.* v. *Secretary of State for Social Services, ex p. Sarwar, The Independent*, April 12, 1995, D.C.

NO.

1994—cont.

1803. Chinnor and Princes Risborough Railway Order 1994.
referred to: ord. 95/2458, art. 1.

1826. St. Mary's Music School (Aided Places) Amendment Regulations 1994.
revoked: regs. 95/1712, reg. 17.

1827. Education (Assisted Places) (Scotland) Amendment Regulations.
revoked: regs. 95/1713, reg. 31.

1882. Statutory Maternity Pay (Compensation of Employers) and Miscellaneous Amendment Regulations 1994.
reg. 3, amended: regs. 95/566, reg. 2.

1889. Child Abduction and Custody (Parties to Conventions) (Amendment) (No. 4) Order 1994.
revoked: ord. 94/3201, art. 2.

1895. Immigration (European Economic Area) Order 1994.
para. 2(2), see *R.* v. *Immigration Appeal Tribunal, ex p. Cheung (Wai Kwan)* [1995] Imm.A.R. 104, Popplewell J.

1896. Litter (Northern Ireland) Order 1994 (N.I. 10).
art. 2(5); ord. 95/18.
art. 6(5); regs. 95/17.
art. 14(1)(2); ord. 95/42.

1898.
art. 6; regs. 95/35.
art. 9; regs. 95/35.
art. 14(1); regs. 95/35.

1909. Local Government Superannuation (Investments) Regulations 1994.
revoked: regs. 95/1019 Sch. M5.

1932. Medicines (Advertising) Regulations 1994.
reg. 2, referred to: regs. 95/2321, reg. 2; applied: regs. 95/2321, reg. 2; amended: regs. 94/3144, reg. 11.
reg. 3, amended: regs. 94/3144, reg. 11.
reg. 4, amended: regs. 94/3144, reg. 11.
reg. 9, amended: regs. 94/3144, reg. 11.
reg. 12, amended: regs. 94/3144, reg. 11.
Sch. 2, para. 1, amended: regs. 94/3144, reg. 11.
Sch. 2, para. 2, amended: regs. 94/3144, reg. 11.
Sch. 2, para. 5, amended: regs. 94/3144, reg. 11.

1935. Companies Act 1985 (Audit Exemption) Regulations 1994.
reg. 6, amended: regs. 94/2879, reg. 2.

1936. (L.9) County Court Fees (Amendment) Order 1994.
see *Gumbley* v. *Barmby*, March 8, 1995, H.H.J. Tetlow, Manchester County Ct.

1987. Stonebridge Housing Action Trust (Area and Constitution) Order 1994.
referred to: ord. 95/2248, art. 3.

NO.

1994—cont.

2004. Welfare Food Amendment Regulations 1994.
reg. 4, revoked: regs. 95/1143, reg. 4.

2009. Ecclesiastical Judges and Legal Officers (Fees) Order 1994.
revoked: ord. 95/1961, art. 2.

2010. Legal Officers (Annual Fees) Order 1994.
revoked: ord. 95/1959, art. 3.

2011. Parochial Fees Order 1994.
revoked: ord. 95/1960, art. 4.

2016. Education (Bursaries for Teacher Training) Regulations 1994.
amended: regs. 95/603, reg. 2.
reg. 1, amended: regs. 95/603, reg. 2.

2030. Local Authorities (Recognised Bodies for Heritable Securities Indemnities) (Scotland) Order 1994.
art. 2, amended: ord. 94/3253, art. 2.

2031. Dartford–Thurrock Crossing Regulations 1994.
reg. 4, amended: regs. 95/2060, reg. 2.
reg. 5, amended: regs. 95/2060, reg. 3.
reg. 11, amended: regs. 95/2060, reg. 4.

2033. Dartford–Thurrock Crossing Tolls Order 1994.
revoked: ord. 95/2059, art. 3.

2034. Education (Assisted Places) (Amendment) Regulations 1994.
revoked: regs. 95/2016, reg. 24.

2035. Education (Assisted Places) (Incidental Expenses) (Amendment) Regulations 1994.
revoked: regs. 95/2017, reg. 16.

2036. Education (Grants) (Music and Ballet Schools) (Amendment) Regulations 1994.
revoked: regs. 95/2018, reg. 16.

2068. Alcan Aluminium UK Ltd. (Rateable Values) (Scotland) order 1994.
revoked: ord. 95/372, art. 9.

2069. British Gas plc (Rateable Values) (Scotland) Order 1994.
revoked: ord. 95/368, art. 10.

2070. Railways (Rateable Values) (Scotland) Order 1994.
revoked: ord. 95/929, art. 10.

2071. British Telecommunications plc (Rateable Values) (Scotland) Order 1994.
revoked: ord. 95/374, art. 2.

2072. Electricity Generators (Rateable Values) (Scotland) Order 1994.
revoked: ord. 95/371, art. 10.

2073. Glasgow Underground (Rateable Values) (Scotland) Order 1994.
revoked: ord. 95/374, art. 2.

2074. Lochaber Power Company (Rateable Values) (Scotland) Order 1994.
revoked: ord. 95/372, art. 9.

2075. Mercury Communications Ltd. (Rateable Values) (Scotland) Order 1994.
revoked: ord. 95/374, art. 2.

NO.

1994—cont.

2076. Scottish Hydro-Electric plc (Rateable Values) (Scotland) Order 1994.
revoked: ord. 95/369, art. 11.

2077. Scottish Nuclear Limited (Rateable Values) (Scotland) Order 1994.
revoked: ord. 95/369, art. 11.

2078. Scottish Power plc (Rateable Values) (Scotland) Order 1994.
revoked: ord. 95/369, art. 11.

2079. Water Undertakings (Rateable Values) (Scotland) Order 1994.
revoked: ord. 95/367, art. 9.

2080. Caledonian MacBrayne Ltd (Rateable Values) (Scotland) Order 1994.
revoked: ord. 95/375, art. 5.

2081. Forth Ports plc (Rateable Values) (Scotland) Order 1994.
revoked: ord. 95/375, art. 5.

2095. Police (Scotland) Amendment Regulations 1994.
reg. 5, amended: regs. 95/2131, reg. 7.
reg. 6, revoked: regs. 95/137, reg. 5.
reg. 7, revoked: regs. 95/137, reg. 5.
Sch. 1, revoked: regs. 95/137, reg. 5.

2096. Police Cadets (Scotland) Amendment Regulations 1994.
revoked: regs. 95/1057, reg. 4.

2099. Education (National Curriculum) (Assessment Arrangements for the Core Subjects (Key Stage 1) (Amendment) Order 1994.
revoked: ord. 95/2071, art. 2.

2100. Education (National Curriculum) (Assessment Arrangements for the Core Subjects) (Key Stage 2) (England) Order 1994.
applied: regs. 95/605, reg. 2.

2101. Education (National Curriculum) (Assessment Arrangements for the Core Subjects) (Key Stage 3) (England) Order 1994.
applied: regs. 95/605, reg. 2.

2103. Education (Pupil Referral Units) (Application of Enactments) Regulations 1994.
amended: regs. 95/602, reg. 6.
Sch. 1, Pt. II, amended: regs. 95/587, reg. 6.
Sch. 2, para. 4, amended: regs. 95/587, reg. 6.

2111. Education (Grant-maintained Special Schools) (Finance) Regulations 1994.
revoked: regs. 95/936, reg. 3.

2157. Medicines (Veterinary Medicinal Products) (Applications for Product Licences) (Amendment) Regulations 1994.
revoked: regs. 94/3142, reg. 20.

2195. Police (Amendment) (No. 2) Regulations 1994.
revoked: regs. 95/215, reg. 70.

NO.

1994—cont.

2226. Education (National Curriculum) (Assessment Arrangements for English, Welsh, Mathematics and Science (Key Stage 1) (Wales) (Amendment) Order 1994.
revoked: ord. 95/2207, art. 2.

2227. Education (National Curriculum) (Assessment Arrangements for English, Welsh, Mathematics and Science) (Key Stage 2) (Wales) Order 1994.
revoked: ord. 95/2208, art. 2.
applied: regs. 95/501, reg. 2.

2228. Education (National Curriculum) (Assessment Arrangements for English, Welsh, Mathematics and Science) (Key Stage 3) (Wales) Order 1994.
revoked: ord. 95/2209, art. 2.
applied: regs. 95/501, reg. 2.

2246. Education (Grants for Education Support and Training) (Amendment) Regulations 1994.
revoked (as respects England): regs. 95/605, reg. 12.
revoked: regs. 95/501, reg. 11.

2297. Local Government Act 1988 (Competition) (Housing Management) (England) Regulations 1994.
Sch., Pt. II, referred to: ord. 95/1182, art. 1.

2328. General Product Safety Regulations 1994.
reg. 1, amended: regs. 94/3144, reg. 11.
reg. 11, amended: regs. 94/3142, reg. 21.

2331. Police (Amendment) (No. 3) Regulations 1994.
revoked: regs. 95/215, reg. 70.

2353. Public Record Office (Fees) Regulations 1994.
revoked: regs. 95/991, reg. 3.

2388. Railway Pensions (Substitution) Order 1994.
Sch. 1, para. 4, amended: ord. 95/430, Sch. 3.
Sch. 1, para. 5, revoked: ord. 95/430, Sch. 3.
Sch. 1, para. 6, amended: ord. 95/430, Sch. 3.
Sch. 2, para. 1, amended: ord. 95/430, Sch. 3.
Sch. 2, para. 2, amended: ord. 95/430, Sch. 3.
Sch. 2, para. 3, amended: ord. 95/430, Sch. 3.
Sch. 2, para. 4, amended: ord. 95/430, Sch. 3.
Sch. 2, para. 5, amended: ord. 95/430, Sch. 3.
Sch. 2, para. 6, amended: ord. 95/430, Sch. 3.

NO.

1994—cont.

2388. Railway Pensions (Substitution) Order 1994—*cont.*
Sch. 2, para. 7, amended: ord. 95/430, Sch. 3.
Sch. 2, para. 8, amended: ord. 95/430, Sch. 3.
Sch. 2, para. 9, amended: ord. 95/430, Sch. 3.
Sch. 2, para. 10, substituted: ord. 95/430, Sch. 3.
Sch. 2, para. 11, amended: ord. 95/430, Sch. 3.

2483. Act of Sederunt (Registration Appeal Court) 1994.
revoked: Act 95/1596, para. 2.

2524. Salmon (Fish Passes and Screens) (Scotland) Regulations 1994.
applied: ord. 95/2193, art. 3; ord. 95/2194, art. 3.

2544. Bovine Offal (Prohibition) (Scotland) Amendment Regulations 1994.
revoked: regs. 95/1955, reg. 2.

2595. Town and Country Planning General Development (Amendment) (No. 2) Order 1994.
revoked: ord. 95/418, art. 9, ord. 95/419, art. 28.

2624. National Health Service (General Medical and Pharmaceutical Services) (Scotland) Amendment (No. 2) Regulations 1994.
revoked: regs. 95/414, reg. 13.

2628. Bovine Offal (Prohibition) (Amendment) Regulations 1994.
revoked: regs. 95/1955, reg. 2.

2674. Former Yugoslavia (United Nations Sanctions) (Dependent Territories) Order 1993.
applied: ord. 95/1032, art. 3.

2716. Conservation (Natural Habitats, Etc.) Regulations 1994.
reg. 10, applied: regs. 95/2043, reg. 2.
regs. 60–63, applied: regs. 95/418, reg. 3.

2740. Hill Livestock (Compensatory Allowances) Regulations 1994.
referred to: regs. 95/904, reg. 2, regs. 95/1159, reg. 2.
applied: regs. 95/891, reg. 2.
reg. 2, amended: regs. 95/100, reg. 2.
reg. 3, amended: regs. 95/100, reg. 2.
reg. 11, amended: regs. 95/100, reg. 2.

2767. Parental Orders (Human Fertilisation and Embryology) Regulations 1994.
reg. 2, applied: regs. 94/2981.
Sch. 1, para. 6, applied: regs. 94/2981.
Sch. 1, para. 8, applied: regs. 94/2981.

2792. Child Abduction and Custody (Parties to Conventions) (Amendment) (No. 5) Order 1994.
revoked: ord. 95/264, art. 1.

2793. Consular Fees Order 1994.
Sch. amended: ord. 94/3202, art. 2.

NO.

1994—cont.

2802. Social Security (Jersey and Guernsey) Order 1979.
modified: ord. 95/767, art. 2.

2811. Magistrates' Courts Committees (Constitution) Regulations 1994.
applied: ord. 95/2372, art. 5; ord. 95/2373, art. 5; ord. 95/2375, art. 5.

2825. Local Government Changes for England (Finance) Regulations 1994.
referred to: regs. 95/623, reg. 2, regs. 95/624, reg. 2.
applied: ord. 95/187, art. 9.
applied: ord. 95/493, art. 17.
applied: ord. 95/600, art. 15.

2844. Dangerous Substances and Preparations (Safety) (Consolidation) Regulations 1994.
reg. 3(2), amended: regs. 94/3247, reg. 19(11).

2852. Medicines (Standard Provisions for Manufacturer's Licences for Veterinary Medicinal Products) Regulations 1994.
reg. 2, amended: regs. 94/3142, reg. 21.
reg. 6, amended: regs. 94/3142, reg. 21.
applied: regs. 94/3167, reg. 2.

2877. Merger Reference (Thomas Cook Group Limited and Barclays Bank plc) Order 1994.
revoked: ord. 94/2953, art. 3.

2924. Teachers' Superannuation (Additional Voluntary Contributions) Regulations 1994.
reg. 2, amended: regs. 95/2004, reg. 10.

2945. Social Security (Incapacity Benefit—Increases for Dependants) Regulations 1994.
reg. 13, applied: regs. 95/310, reg. 24.
Pt. I, applied: regs. 95/310, reg. 15.
Pt. III, applied: regs. 95/310, reg. 15.
Pt. V, inserted: regs. 95/829, reg. 23.

2973. Industry Wide Coal Staff Superannuation Scheme Regulations 1994.
applied: regs. 94/3070, reg. 2.

2974. Industry Wide Mineworkers' Pension Scheme Regulations 1994.
applied: regs. 94/3070, reg. 2.

2986. Medicines (Veterinary Medicinal Products) (Veterinary Surgeons from Other EEA States) Regulations 1994.
reg. 3, amended: regs. 94/3142, reg. 21.

2987. Medicines (Restrictions on the Administration of Veterinary Medicinal Products) Regulations 1994.
reg. 2, amended: regs. 94/3142, reg. 21.
reg. 3, amended: regs. 94/3142, reg. 21.
reg. 5, amended: regs. 94/3142, reg. 21.

2993. Police (Amendment) (No. 4) Regulations 1994.
revoked: regs. 95/215, reg. 70.

NO.

1994—cont.

3017. Medical Devices Regulations 1994.
reg. 16, applied: regs. 95/2487, reg. 4.
reg. 17, applied: regs. 95/2487, reg. 2.

3025. Local Government (Compensation for Redundancy) Regulations 1994.
reg. 9, applied: regs. 95/1019, reg. D6.

3026. Local Government Superannuation (Amendment) Regulations 1994.
regs. 2–9, revoked: regs. 95/1019 Sch. M5.
reg. 9, amended: regs. 95/963, reg. 3.
reg. 10, amended: regs. 95/1019, Sch. M6, regs. 95/1019 Sch. M5.

3042. Education (Fees and Awards) Regulations 1994.
reg. 4, amended: regs. 95/1290, reg. 2.

3043. Education (Mandatory Awards) (Amendment) (No. 2) Regulations 1994.
revoked: regs. 94/3044, reg. 6.

3044. Education (Mandatory Awards) Regulations 1994.
applied: regs. 94/3045, reg. 6.
Sch. 2, para. 16, amended: regs. 95/1240, reg. 3.
Sch. 3, para. 1, amended: regs. 95/1240, reg. 3.

3068. Local Government (Compensation for Redundancy) (Scotland) Regulations 1994.
applied: regs. 95/840, reg. 2.
reg. 3, amended: regs. 95/340, reg. 14.

3071. Civil Aviation (Route Charges for Navigation Services) Regulations 1994.
reg. 9, amended: regs. 95/1004, reg. 2.

3082. Meat Products (Hygiene) Regulations 1994.
applied: regs. 94/1763, reg. 3.
reg. 2, amended: regs. 95/1763, reg. 9, regs. 95/539, reg. 26.
Sch. 2, Pt. VIII, amended: regs. 95/1763, reg. 9.

3108. Rent Officers (Additional Functions) (Scotland) Amendment No. 2 Order 1994.
revoked: regs. 95/1643, reg. 7.

3121. Central Rating Lists Regulations 1994.
referred to: 1995, c. 45, Sch. 5, para. 31.
regs. 3, 4, revoked: regs. 94/3121, reg. 8.
Sch., Pt. III, applied: 1995, c. 45, Sch. 5, para. 12.

3129. Telecommunications Terminal Equipment (Amendment and Extension) Regulations 1994.
reg. 3, amended: regs. 95/144, reg. 4.
reg. 8, amended: regs. 95/144, reg. 4.
reg. 10, amended: regs. 95/144, reg. 4.
Sch., amended: regs. 95/144, reg. 4.

NO.

1994—cont.

3130. Vocational Training for General Medical Practice (European Requirements) Regulations 1994.
reg. 11, amended: regs. 95/414, reg. 13.
reg. 5, applied: regs. 95/414, Sch. 1.
reg. 13, revoked: regs. 95/414, reg. 13.

3132. Insurance Companies (Amendment) Regulations 1994.
reg. 15, disapplied: regs. 95/679, art. 3.

3137. Agricultural Processing and Marketing Grant Regulations 1994.
revoked: regs. 95/362, reg. 9.

3142. Marketing Authorisations for Veterinary Medical Products Regulations 1994.
referred to: regs. 95/1086, reg. 2.
applied: regs. 95/1086, Sch. 1, Pt. IV, regs. 95/1372, reg. 2.

3144. Medicines for Human Use (Marketing Authorisations Etc.) Regulations 1994.
applied: regs. 95/1116, reg. 2.
applied: regs. 95/449, reg. 1.

3148. Education (European Community Enlargement) (Scotland) Regulations 1994.
reg. 2, revoked: regs. 95/1739, reg. 6.

3164. Local Government Act 1988 (Competition) (Legal Services) (England) Regulations 1994.
reg. 3, amended: regs. 95/2546, reg. 3.

3165. Local Government Act 1988 (Defined Activities) (Competition) (Supervision of Parking, Management of Vehicles and Security Work) (England) Regulations 1994.
reg. 2, amended: regs. 95/2546, reg. 4; regs. 95/1326, reg. 5.

3166. Local Government Act 1994 (Competition) (Construction and Property Services) (England) Regulations 1994.
reg. 3, amended: regs. 95/2546, reg. 5.

3167. Local Government Charges for England (Direct Labour and Service Organisations) Regulations 1994.
reg. 2, amended: regs. 95/1326, reg. 2.
reg. 12, amended: regs. 95/1326, reg. 4.
reg. 14, amended: regs. 95/1326, regs. 3, 4.
reg. 14A, inserted: regs. 95/1326, reg. 4.

3200. Non-Domestic Rating (Unoccupied Property) (Scotland) Regulations 1994.
Sch., Pt. I, amended: regs. 95/518, reg. 2.

3201. Child Abduction and Custody (Parties to Conventions) (Amendment) (No. 6) Order 1994.
revoked: ord. 95/1031, art. 2.

NO.

1994—cont.

3226. Exchange Gains and Losses (Transitional Provisions) Regulations 1994.
applied: regs. 95/408, reg. 1.
reg. 17, amended: regs. 95/408, reg. 2.

3227. Exchange Gains and Losses (Alternative Method of Calculation of Gain or Loss) Regulations 1994.
applied: regs. 94/3226, reg. 2.
reg. 2, applied: regs. 94/3231, reg. 4.
Sch., para. 1, applied: regs. 94/3231.

3228. Exchange Gains and Losses (Deferral of Gains and Losses) Regulations 1994.
applied: regs. 94/3226, reg. 2.

3230. Local Currency Elections Regulations 1994.
applied: regs. 94/3227, reg. 4.

3245. Merchant Shipping (Reporting Requirements for Ships Carrying Dangerous or Polluting Goods) Regulations 1984.
revoked: regs. 95/2498, reg. 2.

3246. Control of Substances Hazardous to Health Regulations 1994.
reg. 2(1), amended: regs. 94/3247, reg. 19(12).

3247. Chemicals (Hazard Information and Packaging for Supply) Regulations 1994.
referred to: regs. 95/887, reg. 27.

3249. Welfare of Animals During Transport Order 1994.
art. 1, amended: ord. 95/131, art. 2.
art. 7, amended: ord. 95/131, art. 2.
art. 8, amended: ord. 95/131, art. 2.
art. 15, amended: ord. 95/131, art. 2.

3255. Local Government (Transitional Election Arrangements) (Scotland) Order 1994.
art. 2A, inserted: regs. 95/1948, reg. 5.

3259. Electricity (Non-Fossil Fuel Sources) (England and Wales) Order 1994.
Sch. 1, amended: ord. 95/68, art. 3.

3262. Police and Magistrates' Courts Act 1994 (Commencement No. 5 and Transitional Provisions) Order 1994.
art. 4, amended: ord. 95/246, art. 2.
art. 11, amended: ord. 95/246, art. 2.
art. 11, amended: ord. 95/899, art. 2.

3279. Non-Domestic Rating (Chargeable Amounts) Regulations 1994.
reg. 1, amended: regs. 95/961, reg. 2.
reg. 30, amended: regs. 95/961, reg. 2.
reg. 34, amended: regs. 95/961, reg. 2.
Sch. 3, para. 4, amended: regs. 95/961, reg. 2.
Sch. 3, para. 5, amended: regs. 95/961, reg. 2.
Sch. 3, para. 8, amended: regs. 95/961, reg. 2.
Sch. 3, para. 9, amended: regs. 95/961, reg. 2.

NO.

1994—cont.

3282. Electricity Supply Industry (Rateable Values) Order 1994.
art. 7, amended: ord. 95/962, art. 2.
art. 8, substituted: ord. 95/962, art. 3.
art. 8A, inserted: ord. 95/962, art. 2.
art. 8B, inserted: ord. 95/962, art. 3.

3283. British Gas plc (Rateable Values) Order 1994.
referred to: 1995, c. 45, Sch. 5, para. 12.

1995

164. Valuation Timetable (Scotland) Order 1995.
Sch., amended: ord. 95/2455, art. 2

165. National Health Service (General Medical and Pharmaceutical Services) (Scotland) Amendment Regulations 1994.
revoked: regs. 95/414, reg. 13.

201. Public Supply Contracts Regulations 1995.
applied: regs. 95/789, art. 2.

215. Police Regulations 1995.
amended: regs. 95/547, regs. 2–15.
reg. 6, amended: regs. 95/547, reg. 2.
reg. 7, amended: regs. 95/547, reg. 3.
reg. 8, amended: regs. 95/547, reg. 4.
reg. 13, substituted: regs. 95/547, reg. 5.
reg. 13A, inserted: regs. 95/547, reg. 6.
reg. 13B, inserted: regs. 95/547, reg. 6.
reg. 14, amended: regs. 95/547, reg. 7.
reg. 16, amended: regs. 95/547, reg. 8.
reg. 26, amended: regs. 95/547, reg. 9.
reg. 28, amended: regs. 95/547, reg. 10.
reg. 29, amended: regs. 95/547, reg. 11.
reg. 39, amended: regs. 95/547, reg. 12.
reg. 47, amended: regs. 95/547, reg. 13.
Sch. 1, para. 2, amended: regs. 95/547, reg. 14.
Sch. 1, para. 6, amended: regs. 95/547, reg. 14.
Sch. 6, para. 1, amended: regs. 95/547, reg. 15.
Sch. 6, para. 2, amended: regs. 95/547, reg. 15.

239. Non-Domestic Rating (Telecommunications and Canals) (Scotland) Order 1995.
applied: regs. 95/548, reg. 6.
art. 3, applied: regs. 95/548, reg. 16.

244. Wireless Telegraph (Licence Charges) (Amendment) Regulations 1995.
revoked: regs. 95/1331, reg. 2.

263. Health and Safety at Work etc. Act 1974 (Application outside Great Britain) Order 1995.
applied; regs. 95/743, reg. 2; regs. 95/738, reg. 2.

NO.

1995—cont.

271. Dual-Use and Related Goods (Export Control) (Suspension) Regulations 1995.
referred to: regs. 95/1151, reg. 3.
reg. 1, amended: regs. 95/441, reg. 2, regs. 95/1424, reg. 2.
reg. 3, amended: regs. 95/1424, regs. 2, 3.
reg. 5, revoked: regs. 95/1424, reg. 2.
reg. 10, amended: regs. 95/1424, reg. 2.
reg. 11, amended: regs. 95/1424, reg. 4.
reg. 13, substituted: regs. 95/1424, reg. 5.
reg. 14, substituted: regs. 95/1424, reg. 5.
Sch. 3, amended: regs. 95/1424, reg. 6.

288. Waste Management Licensing (Amendment etc.) Regulations 1995.
reg. 4, amended: regs. 95/1950, reg. 3, regs. 95/1959, reg. 3.

298. Town and Country Planning General Development (Amendment) Order 1991.
revoked: ord. 95/418, art. 9, ord. 95/419, art. 28.

300. National Health Service Pension Scheme Regulations 1995.
referred to: regs. 95/866, reg. 2.

310. Social Security (Incapacity Benefit) (Transitional) Regulations 1995.
reg. 13, amended: regs. 95/987, reg. 3.
reg. 17A, inserted: regs. 95/987, reg. 3.
reg. 18, amended: regs. 95/987, reg. 3.
reg. 20, amended: regs. 95/987, reg. 3.
reg. 22, amended: regs. 95/987, reg. 3.
reg. 25, amended: regs. 95/987, reg. 3.
reg. 28A, inserted: regs. 95/987, reg. 3.
reg. 31, amended: regs. 95/987, reg. 3.

311. Social Security (Incapacity for Work) (General) Regulations 1995.
reg. 6, amended: regs. 95/987, reg. 2.
reg. 10, amended: regs. 95/987, reg. 2.
reg. 16, amended: regs. 95/987, reg. 2.
reg. 17, amended: regs. 95/987, reg. 2.
reg. 17A, inserted: regs. 95/987, reg. 2.
reg. 18, amended: regs. 95/987, reg. 2.
reg. 20, substituted: regs. 95/987, reg. 2.
reg. 22, amended: regs. 95/987, reg. 2.
reg. 28, amended: regs. 95/987, reg. 2.

351. Lloyd's Underwriters (Tax) Regulations 1995.
regs. 5–8, applied: regs. 95/352, reg. 5.

353. Lloyd's Underwriters (Special Reserve Funds) Regulations 1995.
reg. 5, amended: regs. 95/1185, reg. 3.
reg. 7, substituted: regs. 95/1185, reg. 4.
reg. 7A, inserted: regs. 95/1185, reg. 4.
reg. 8, amended: regs. 95/1185, reg. 5.

NO.

1995—cont.

361. Meat (Hygiene, Inspection and Examination for Residues) (Charges) Regulations 1995.
Sch. 2, para. (a), amended: regs. 95/539, reg. 26.
Sch. 2, para. (b), amended: regs. 95/540, reg. 27.

369. Electricity Generation Lands (Rateable Values) (Scotland) Order 1995.
art. 3, applied: regs. 95/548, reg. 13.

370. Electricity Transmission Lands (Rateable Values) (Scotland) Order 1995.
art. 3, applied: regs. 95/548, reg. 13.

371. Electricity Generators (Rateable Values) (Scotland) Order 1995.
art. 3, applied: ord. 95/369, art. 3.

372. Electricity Generators (Aluminium) (Rateable Values) (Scotland) Order 1995.
art. 3, applied: ord. 95/371, art. 3.
art. 3, applied: regs. 95/548, reg. 15.

373. Electricity Distribution Lands (Rateable Values) (Scotland) Order 1995.
art. 3, applied: regs. 95/548, reg. 13.

402. Local Government Changes for England (Property Transfer and Transitional Payments) Regulations 1995.
applied: regs. 95/798, regs. 2, 3, 9.
reg. 4, amended: regs. 95/1748, reg. 3.

407. National Health Service Trusts (Originating Capital Debt) Order 1995.
amended: ord. 95/791, art. 2.
Sch., amended: ord. 95/791, art. 2.

414. National Health Service (Pharmaceutical Services) (Scotland) Regulations 1994.
reg. 7, applied: regs. 95/416, reg. 2.

416. National Health Service (General Medical Services) (Scotland) Regulations 1995.
reg. 34, referred to: ord. 95/652, art. 3.
Sch. 10, applied: regs. 95/414, reg. 2.
Sch. 11, para. 31, applied: regs. 95/414, reg. 2.

417. Town and Country Planning (Environmental Assessment and Permitted Development) Regulations 1995.
referred to: regs. 95/2258, reg. 2.
reg. 3, applied: regs. 95/418, reg. 3.

418. Town and Country Planning (General Permitted Development) Order 1995.
Sch. 2, applied: regs. 95/417, reg. 2.

419. Town and Country Planning (General Development Procedure) Order 1995.
art. 10, referred to: regs. 95/2258, reg. 4.

441. Dual-Use and Related Goods (Export Control) (Suspension) Regulations 1995.
reg. 3, revoked: regs. 95/1151, reg. 2.

NO.

1995—cont.

482. Disability Working Allowance and Income Support (General) Amendment Regulations 1995.
reg. 19, amended: regs. 95/2303, reg. 8.

537. Bovine Offal (Prohibition) (Scotland) Amendment Regulations 1995.
revoked: regs. 95/1955, reg. 2.

539. Fresh Meat (Hygiene and Inspection) Regulations 1995.
applied: ord. 95/1928, art. 25, regs. 95/1763, reg. 3, regs. 95/614, regs. 2, 6.
reg. 2, amended: regs. 95/1763, reg. 9.
Sch. 1, para. 1, amended: regs. 95/1763, reg. 9.
Sch. 5, Pt. I, amended: regs. 95/1763, reg. 9.
Sch. 6, Pt. II, amended: regs. 95/1763, reg. 9.
Sch. 6, Pt. III, amended: regs. 95/1763, reg. 9.

540. Poultry Meat, Farmed Game Bird Meat and Rabbit Meat (Hygiene and Inspection) Regulations 1995.
applied: regs. 95/1763, reg. 3; regs. 95/614, reg. 2.
reg. 2, amended: regs. 95/1763, reg. 9.
Sch. 1, para. 6, amended: regs. 95/1763, reg. 9.
Sch. 1, para. 7, amended: regs. 95/1763, reg. 9.
Sch. 5, para. 6, amended: regs. 95/1763, reg. 9.
Sch. 5, para. 7, amended: regs. 95/1763, reg. 9.

546. Local Government (Wales) Act 1994 (Commencement No. 3) Order 1995.
art. 8, amended: ord. 95/851, art. 2.

551. Road Vehicles (Construction and Use) (Amendments) Regulations 1995.
reg. 3, amended: regs. 95/737, reg. 2.

562. National Health Service (Determination of Districts) Order 1995.
applied: ord. 95/563, art. 3.

563. National Health Service (District Health Authorities) Order 1995.
Sch. 2, applied: ord. 95/562, art. 1.

588. Electricity (Class Exemptions from the Requirements for a Licence) Order 1995.
revoked: ord. 95/909, art. 6.

613. Bovine Offal (Prohibition) (Amendment) Regulations 1995.
revoked: regs. 95/1955, reg. 2.

614. Animal By-Products (Identification) Regulations 1995.
reg. 2, amended: regs. 95/1955, reg. 3.
reg. 5, amended: regs. 95/1955, reg. 2.

626. Housing Benefit and Council Tax Benefit (Miscellaneous Amendments) (No. 2) Regulations 1995.
reg. 19, amended: regs. 95/2303, reg. 9.

NO.

1995—cont.

627. Education (London Residuary Body) (Property Transfer) (Modification and Amendment) Order 1995.
art. 2, revoked: ord. 95/1202, art. 3.

634. Judicial Pensions (Preservation of Benefits) Order 1995.
revoked in pt.: ord. 95/2647, art. 10.

636. Judicial Pensions (Transfer Between Judicial Pension Schemes) Regulations 1995.
applied: ord. 95/2647, art. 6.

639. Judicial Pensions (Additional Voluntary Contributions) Regulations 1995.
Pt. IV, referred to: ord. 95/634, art. 5, regs. 95/636, reg. 7.
applied: regs. 95/637, reg. 8.

701. Local Authorities Etc. (Scotland) Amendment Regulations 1995.
revoked: regs. 95/912, reg. 30.

720. European Parliamentary (United Kingdom Representatives) Pensions (Additional Voluntary Contributions Scheme) Order 1995.
revoked: ord. 95/739, art. 1.

738. Offshore Installations (Construction and Survey) Regulations 1995.
applied: regs. 95/743, reg. 2.

755. Children (Northern Ireland) Order 1995.
art. 1, applied: ord. 95/756, art. 1.

798. Local Government Changes for England (Capital Finance) Regulations 1995.
reg. 7, amended: regs. 95/1748, reg. 4.
reg. 15, amended: regs. 95/1748, reg. 4.
reg. 16, amended: regs. 95/1748, reg. 4.

828. Local Government Act 1988 (Defined Activities) (Exemption) (Sports and Leisure Management, Catering and Maintenance of Ground) Order 1995.
art. 2, amended: ord. 95/1707, art. 5.

845. Royal Orthopaedic Hospital National Health Service Trust (Establishment) Order 1995.
art. 4, amended: ord. 95/1709, art. 2.

887. Plant Protection Products Regulations 1995.
referred to: regs. 95/888, reg. 2.

901. Local Government Superannuation (Equality and Maternity Allowance) Regulations 1995.
regs. 2–3, revoked: regs. 95/1019 Sch. M5.
reg. 4, amended: regs. 95/1019 Sch. M6.
reg. 5, amended: regs. 95/1019 Sch. M6.

907. Third Country Fishing (Enforcement) Order 1995.
art. 1, amended: ord. 95/2437, art. 3.
art. 6, amended: ord. 95/2437, art. 4.
Sch. 1, para. 1, amended: ord. 95/2437, art. 5.
Sch. 1, para. 2, amended: ord. 95/2437, art. 5.

NO.

1995—cont.

912. Local Authorities Etc. (Allowances) (Scotland) Regulations 1995.
reg. 29, revoked: regs. 95/912, reg. 30.
Sch. 5, revoked: regs. 95/912, reg. 30.

936. Education (Grant-maintained and Grant-maintained Special Schools) (Finance) Regulations 1995.
reg. 11, amended: regs. 95/1554, reg. 2.
Sch. 4, Pt. V, amended: regs. 95/1554, reg. 2.
Sch. 5, substituted: regs. 95/1554, reg. 2.

957. Value Added Tax (Special Provisions) (Amendment) Order 1995.
revoked: ord. 95/1268, art. 3.

963. Local Government Superannuation (Miscellaneous Provisions) Regulations 1995.
revoked: regs. 95/1019 Sch. M5.

1015. Education (School Teachers' Pay and Conditions) Order 1995.
revoked: ord. 95/1743, art. 1.

1019. Local Government Pension Scheme Regulations 1995.
reg. A1, amended: regs. 95/1985, reg. 7.
Sch. C1, amended: regs. 95/1985, reg. 7.
Sch. C1, Pt. II, amended: regs. 95/1985, reg. 7.
reg. C2, amended: regs. 95/1985, reg. 7; regs. 95/2249, reg. 2.
Sch. D1, para. 11, inserted: regs. 95/2249, reg. 2.

1036. Parliamentary Constituencies (Wales) Order 1995.
referred to: ord. 95/1142, art. 1.

1086. Dairy Products (Hygiene) Regulations 1995.
applied: regs. 95/1763, reg. 3.
reg. 2, amended: regs. 95/1763, reg. 9.
reg. 16, referred to: regs. 95/1122, reg. 3.

1268. Value Added Tax (Special Provisions) Order 1995.
art. 4, amended: ord. 95/1385, art. 2.

1372. Dairy Products (Hygiene) (Scotland) Regulations 1995.
applied: regs. 95/1763, reg. 3.
reg. 2, amended: regs. 95/1763, reg. 9.

1388. Food Protection (Emergency Prohibitions) (Paralytic Shellfish Poisoning) Order 1995.
revoked in pt.: ord. 95/1630, art. 2.

1567. Offshore Installations (Safety Zones) (No. 2) Order 1995.
revoked: ord. 98/1575, art. 2.

1576. Fisheries and Aquaculture Structures (Grants) Regulations 1995.
referred to: Scheme 95/1609, para. 3.

1613. Social Security (Income Support and Claims and Payments) Amendment Regulations 1995.
referred to: regs. 95/2287, reg. 1; regs. 95/2352, reg. 2.

NO.

1995—cont.

1626. Parliamentary Constituencies (England) Order 1995.
referred to: ord. 95/2061, art. 1.

1642. Rent Officers (Additional Functions) Order 1995.
art. 5, amended: ord. 95/2365, art. 3.
Sch. 1, Pt. 3, amended: ord. 95/2365, art. 3.

1643. Rent Officers (Additional Functions) (Scotland) Order 1995.
art. 5, amended: ord. 95/2361, art. 3.
art. 7, amended: ord. 95/2361, art. 3.
Sch. 1, para. 8, amended: ord. 95/2361, art. 3.

1712. St. Mary's Music School (Aided Places) Regulations 1995.
applied: regs. 95/1713, reg. 13.

1713. Education (Assisted Places) (Scotland) Regulations 1995.
reg. 2, applied: regs. 95/1712, Sch. 1, para. 15.

1737. Food Protection (Emergency Prohibitions) (Paralytic Shellfish Poisoning) (No. 6) Order 1995.
revoked: ord. 95/2046, art. 2.

1879. Aberdeen and Grampian Tourist Board Scheme Order 1995.
art. 3, amended: ord. 95/2211, art. 2.
Sch., para. 3, amended: ord. 93/2211, art. 3.
Sch., para. 4, amended: ord. 95/2211, art. 4.
Sch., para. 5, amended: ord. 95/2211, art. 2.
Sch., para. 6, amended: ord. 95/2211, art. 6.

1880. Angus and City of Dundee Tourist Board Scheme Order 1995.
art. 3, amended: ord. 95/2212, art. 2.
Sch., para. 3, amended: ord. 95/2212, art. 3.
Sch., para. 4, amended: ord. 95/2212, art. 4.
Sch., para. 5, amended: ord. 95/2212, art. 5.
Sch., para. 6, amended: ord. 95/2212, art. 6.

1881. Argyll, the Isles, Loch Lomond, Sterling and Trossachs Tourist Board Scheme Order 1995.
art. 3, amended: ord. 95/2213, art. 2.
Sch., para. 3, amended: ord. 95/2213, art. 3.
Sch., para. 4, amended: ord. 95/2213, art. 4.
Sch., para. 5, amended: ord. 95/2213, art. 5.
Sch., para. 6, amended: ord. 95/2213, art. 6.

1882. Ayrshire and Arran Tourist Board Scheme 1995.
para. 4, amended: ord. 95/2232, art. 2.
para. 5, amended: ord. 95/2232, art. 3.
para. 6, amended: ord. 95/2232, art. 4.

NO.

1995—cont.

1883. Dumfries and Galloway Tourist Board Scheme 1995.
para. 4, amended: ord. 95/2233, art. 2.
para. 5, amended: ord. 95/2233, art. 3.
para. 6, amended: ord. 95/2233, art. 6.

1884. Edinburgh and Lothians Tourist Board Scheme 1995.
para. 4, amended: ord. 95/2234, art. 2.
para. 5, amended: ord. 95/2234, art. 3.
para. 6, amended: ord. 95/2234, art. 4.

1885. Greater Glasgow and Clyde Valley Tourist Board Scheme 1995.
para. 4, amended: ord. 95/2235, art. 2.
para. 5, amended: ord. 95/2235, art. 3.
para. 6, amended: ord. 95/2235, art. 4.

1889. Perthshire Tourist Board Scheme 1995.
para. 4, amended: ord. 95/2239, art. 2.
para. 5, amended: ord. 95/2239, art. 3.
para. 6, amended: ord. 95/2239, art. 4.

1890. Scottish Borders Tourist Board Scheme Order 1995.
art. 3, amended: ord. 95/2214, art. 2.
Sch., para. 3, amended: ord. 95/2214. art. 3.
Sch., para. 4, amended: ord. 95/2214, art. 4.
Sch., para. 5, amended: ord. 95/2214, art. 5.

NO.

1995—cont.

1890. Scottish Borders Tourist Board Scheme Order 1995—*cont.*
Sch., para. 6, amended: ord. 95/2214, art. 6.

1891. Shetland Tourist Board Scheme 1995.
para. 4, amended: ord. 95/2240, art. 2.
para. 5, amended: ord. 95/2240, art. 3.
para. 6, amended: ord. 95/2240, art. 4.

1892. Western Isles Tourist Board Scheme 1995.
para. 4, amended: ord. 95/2241, art. 2.
para. 5, amended: ord. 95/2241, art. 3.
para. 6, amended: ord. 95/2241, art. 4.

2016. Education (Assisted Places) Regulations 1995.
reg. 2, applied: regs. 95/2017, reg. 2.

2072. Education (National Curriculum) (Assessment Arrangements for the Core Subjects) (Key Stage 2) Order 1995.
applied: ord. 95/2071, art. 7.

2093. Patent Rules 1995.
referred to: rules 95/2164, rule 2.

2096. Rural Development Grants (Agriculture) Regulations 1995.
revoked: regs. 95/2202, reg. 13.

2287. Income Support (General) Amendment and Transitional Regulations 1995.
referred to: regs. 95/2352, reg. 2.

INDEX

This is the third part of the Current Law Statutes Index 1995 and is up to date to December 1, 1995. References, *e.g.* 12/2, are to the Statutes of 1995, Chapter 12, section 2.

INDEX

INDEX

INDEX

INDEX

INDEX